LAROUSSE

GASTRONOMIQUE

LAROUSSE
GASTRONOMIQUE

With the assistance of the Gastronomic Committee
President Joël Robuchon

Clarkson Potter/Publishers
New York

Published by Clarkson Potter/Publishers, New York
Member of the Crown Publishing Group.

Random House, Inc. New York, Toronto, London,
Sydney, Auckland
www.randomhouse.com

Clarkson N. Potter is a trademark and Potter and
colophon are registered trademarks of
Random House, Inc.

First published in Great Britain in 2001
by Hamlyn, a division of Octopus Publishing
Group Ltd

English edition copyright © 2001
Octopus Publishing Group Ltd

Original French edition copyright
© Larousse-Bordas/HER-2000

Printed in Italy

Library of Congress Cataloging-in-Publication Data
is available upon request.

ISBN 0-609-60971-8

10 9 8 7 6 5 4 3 2 1

GASTRONOMIC COMMITTEE

PRESIDENT
Joël Robuchon

MEMBERS OF THE COMMITTEE

Michel Creignou
Journalist

Jean Delaveyne
Chef, founder of Restaurant Le Camélia, Bougival

Éric Frachon
Honorary president, Evian Water SA

Michel Guérard
Chef, Restaurant Les Prés d'Eugénie, Eugénie-les-Bains

Pierre Hermé
Confectioner, Paris

Robert Linxe
Founder, The House of Chocolate, Paris and New York

Élisabeth de Meurville
Journalist

Georges Pouvel
Professor of cookery; consultant on cookery techniques

Jean-François Revel
Writer

Pierre Troisgros
Chef, Restaurant Pierre Troisgros, Roanne

Alain Weill
Art expert; member of the National Council of Gastronomy

CONTRIBUTORS

Marie-Paule Bernardin
Archivist

Geneviève Beullac
Editor

Jean Billault
Member of the College of Butchery

Christophe Bligny
Paris College of Catering

Thierry Borghèse
Chief Inspector of Consumer Affairs

Francis Boucher
Confectioner

Pascal Champagne
Barman, Hotel Lutetia;
Member, French Association of Barmen

Frédéric Chesneau
Project manager

Marcel Cottenceau
Former technical director, College of Butchery

Robert Courtine
President, Marco-Polo Prize

Philippe Dardonville
Secretary-general, National Union of Producers
of Fruit Juice

Bertrand Debatte
Officer of the Bakery, Auchamps

Jean Dehillerin
President and managing director, E. Dehillerin SA
(manufacturers of kitchen equipment)

Gilbert Delos
Writer and journalist

Christian Flacelière
Journalist

Jean-Louis Flandrin
Professor emeritus, University of Paris VII; Director
of studies, E.H.E.S.S. (College of Social Sciences)

Dr André Fourel
Economist

Dominique Franceschi
Journalist

Dr Jacques Fricker
Nutritionist

Jean-Pierre Gabriel
Journalist

Thierry Gaudillère
Editor, Bourgogne Aujourd'hui (Burgundy Today)

Ismène Giachetti
Director of research, C.N.R.S. (National Centre for
Scientific Research)

Sylvie Girard
Cookery writer

Catherine Goavec-Bouvard
Agribusiness consultant

Jo Goldenberg
Restaurateur

Catherine Gomy
Agribusiness certification officer,
French Association of Standardization

Bruno Goussault
Scientific director, C.R.E.A.
(Centre of Food and Nutrition Studies)

Jacques Guinberteau
Mycologist; Director of studies, I.N.R.A.
(National Institute of Agriculture)

Joseph Hossenlopp
Director of research, Cemagref (Institute of Research
for Agricultural and Environmental Engineering)

Françoise Kayler
Food critic

Jacques Lacoursière
Writer

Josette Le Reun-Gaudicheau
Teacher (specializing in seafood)

Paul Maindiaux
Development officer, Ministry of Agriculture

Laurent Mairet
Oenologist

Jukka Mannerkorpi
Cookery editor

Pascal Orain
Manager, Bertie's Restaurant

Philippe Pilliot
Secretary-general, Federation of French Grocers;
Editor, Le Nouvel Épicier (The New Grocer)

Jean-Claude Ribaut
Cookery correspondent, Le Monde

Isabelle Richard
Bachelor of Arts

Michel Rigo
Deputy head,
National Federation of Fruit Brandies

Françoise Sabban
Master of ceremonies, E.H.E.S.S.
(College of Social Sciences)

Jacques Sallé
Journalist

Jean-Louis Taillebaud
Chef, Ritz-Escoffier (French School of
Gastronomy); Ritz Hotel, Place Vendôme, Paris

Claude Vifian
Chef and professor, College of the Hotel Industry,
Lausanne

Leda Vigliardi Paravia
Writer and journalist

Jean-Marc Wolff
College of the Hotel Industry, Paris

Rémy Yverneau
Secretary-general,
National Federation of Makers of Cream Cheese

ACKNOWLEDGEMENTS

FRENCH EDITION

Editorial Director
Patrice Maubourguet

Production Director
Laure Flavigny

Design Director
Frédérique Longuépée

Assistant to the Design Director
Laurence Lebot

Art Director
Anne-Marie Moyse-Jaubert

Assistant to the Art Director
Marie-Annick Réveillon

Maps
René Oizon

ENGLISH EDITION

Editorial Manager
Jane Birch

Project Manager
Bridget Jones

Design Managers
Tokiko Morishima
Bryan Dunn

Senior Production Controller
Ian Paton

Translation
Rosetta International

Contributors, copyeditors and proofreaders
Pepita Aris
Anne Crane
Lydia Darbyshire
Judith Hannam
Barbara Horn
Alison Leach
Jo Lethaby

Wine consultants
Christine Austin
Sue Crabtree

Cheese and oil consultant
Judy Ridgway

Indexer
Hilary Bird

Typesetting and page make-up
Dorchester Typesetting Group Ltd

USEFUL INFORMATION

The diversity of information available on any food topic is often covered by several different entries. To avoid excessive cross-referencing throughout the text, a general index of key topics and a separate index of recipes are included.

*Asterisks have been used where reference is made to measured quantities of specific recipes or mixtures: the asterisks highlight the alphabetical entry where the recipe, technique or method can be found.

♦ This symbol indicates an illustrated recipe.

WEIGHTS AND MEASURES

Metric, imperial and American measures are used in this book. As a general rule, it is advisable to follow only one set of measures and not to mix metric, imperial and/or cup quantities from any one recipe.

Spoon Measures

Spoon measures refer to standard measuring utensils. Serving spoons and table cutlery are not suitable for measuring as they are not standard in capacity.

¼ teaspoon = 1.5 ml
½ teaspoon = 2.5 ml
1 teaspoon = 5 ml
1 tablespoon = 15 ml

OVEN TEMPERATURES

The following are the standard settings for domestic ovens; however, they vary widely and the manufacturer's instructions should be consulted. Individual ovens also perform differently and experience of using a particular appliance is invaluable for adjusting temperatures and cooking times to give best results. Those working with commercial cooking appliances will be accustomed to using the higher temperatures attained. Many chefs' recipes refer to glazing or cooking in a hot oven for a short period: as a rule, the hottest setting of a domestic appliance should be used as the equivalent. Temperatures and timings refer to a preheated oven.

If using a fan-assisted oven, follow the manufacturer's instructions for adjusting the time and the temperature.

Oven temperatures

Centigrade	Fahrenheit	Gas mark
110°C	225°F	gas ¼
120°C	250°F	gas ½
140°C	275°F	gas 1
150°C	300°F	gas 2
160°C	325°F	gas 3
180°C	350°F	gas 4
190°C	375°F	gas 5
200°C	400°F	gas 6
220°C	425°F	gas 7
230°C	450°F	gas 8
240°C	475°F	gas 9

PREFACE

This new edition of *Larousse Gastronomique* builds on the work that was begun by Prosper Montagné in 1938 and has been updated regularly ever since. It is the ultimate reference work for chefs and cooks, for lovers of good food and all those associated with the business of cooking and eating.

The history and culture of gastronomy is at its heart, an integral part of its art and a source of inspiration; it also acts as a prompt for change. In a world of international values and multicultural influences, today's cooks still owe their fundamental skills in large part to those who played a major role in the development of classic cooking. The history of gastronomy is the story of those who took part in its evolution and were responsible for establishing what is, in effect, one of the cornerstones of civilization. Gastronomy reflects society, and studying its past provides a glimpse of the history of society itself.

Gastronomy is not static. Like music and the visual arts, it has never ceased to evolve. We should always be ready to reassess the past in the light of current knowledge and to consider new trends in the context of dishes enjoyed by previous generations. Would we appreciate the dishes that were cooked in the Middle Ages or serve the elaborate feasts that were prepared by our ancestors? Cooking reflects the customs of its age and present-day habits and preferences as well as those of the immediate past.

This edition of *Larousse Gastronomique* bears witness to the revolution in the availability of food and the art and science of cooking that has taken place over the last thirty years. Not only does this book acknowledge our debt to the past, but it recognizes the modern approach and welcomes changes that are on the horizon. It eschews the outdated and rigid notions that inhibit creativity, while accepting that authenticity and an uncompromising approach to quality are the foundations of a reference work. At the same time, it illustrates that gastronomy is a multilayered subject and one that repays closer study with new sources of inspiration and pleasure.

For the work of updating, a French committee, under the chairmanship of Joël Robuchon, brought together chefs, writers and lovers of good food, all dedicated to the quest for authenticity. During its many meetings, the committee scrutinized the additions to the French edition, taking into account modern trends in cooking. From the finished work, new entries and recipes were selected and translated for the English edition, while existing information was checked and revised. The outcome of the deliberations of the committee combined with the revision of the English text has resulted in a unique work of broad appeal. This book will be of value not only to those who are interested in culinary history and those who enjoy cooking for its own sake, but also to everyone with professional associations with food and its preparation.

The entries in this edition of *Larousse Gastronomique* highlight the diversity of the world of food and cooking. They describe produce, ingredients, techniques and methods, traditions and, where appropriate, innovations. Whether your interest is in the great traditions of French cuisine or in the wide spectrum of food as the international subject it has become, you will find definitions and facts supported by practical information and recipes. This collection of over 3000 recipes takes an overview of cooking past and present, and provides an unrivalled platform from which to create and explore our culinary future.

As you open this book to enter the world of gastronomy and share in the excitement of discovery, we hope that this new edition of *Larousse Gastronomique*, with its thorough and painstaking research, makes eating and cooking an ever more pleasurable experience.

A

ABAISSE A term used in French cookery for a sheet of rolled-out pastry. Hence, *abaisser* means to roll out thin, as for a pastry base. The term *abaisse* is also used for a biscuit (cookie) or a slice of sponge cake on which a filling such as jam or cream is to be spread.

ABALONE See *ormer*.

ABATTOIR An establishment where livestock are slaughtered for their edible products (meat and offal) and their by-products (leather, bristles, horsehair, horns).

Until 1950, slaughtering was often carried out in France by butchers themselves on their own premises. But since 1972, for reasons of hygiene, it has had to be done in a public abattoir. EU regulations have further reduced the number of abattoirs throughout Europe and imposed strict controls. From the gastronomic point of view it is rather less desirable: less than a century ago, beef cattle from Normandy, Limousin or the Nevers region would make their way slowly on foot for a distance of 200 to 400 km (125 to 250 miles) before being slaughtered in the big towns, and this made their meat firmer and more tasty.

Rules govern the intake of live animals, and also the inspections of the viscera (internal organs) and the carcass. If all the inspections are satisfactory the carcass is branded as conforming to legal requirements, either national or for exchanges between EU countries.

Present-day abattoirs are becoming increasingly better equipped, incorporating cutting and sometimes packing departments, deep-freeze units or workshops for processing and cooking the meat, particularly pork. Scientific research is constantly leading to improvements in this field, notably in matters of hygiene and preservation by rapid refrigeration.

■ **Slaughtering in former times** In the past the relationship between people and their livestock was much more intimate. 'The meat of Greek animals is god-given. . . . For the Greeks, matters relating to butchery, religion and cooking were all mixed up in what they called *thusia* and what we call sacrifice. . . . The moment when the sacrifice begins, after the procession, the moment when the blood spurts out, belongs to the gods. . . . The altar and the earth receive it all, then with a special implement and vessel it is collected and spread over the altar. . . . The principal ritual act is the extraction of the noble viscera, essentially the liver; then comes the cutting up of the animal, horizontally, according to a strict procedure. According to the nature of the parts, they are grilled (particularly the viscera, whose perfume is offered to the gods), cooked on a spit, or boiled (the manner of cooking preferred by the Greeks, particularly as fresh meat, already naturally tough and more so when cut in this way, is difficult to eat when roasted). The portions of meat are placed on the table as an offering to the gods, and afterwards they are at the priest's disposal. . . . The priest also receives that part which, at the start, contained the whole animal: the skin. . . . In taking their fill of the edible parts men recognized, at the same time as they replenished their energy, the inferiority of their mortal state. . . . In the language of Homer, to express the idea of the slaughter of livestock, there are no verbs other than those relating to offering up sacrifices to the gods.' (*La Cuisine du sacrifice en pays grec*, by M. Détienne & J.-P. Vernant, published by Gallimard.)

Even today, in some Greek villages, the public killing of livestock is practised as part of popular Orthodox rites, followed by the distribution and consumption of the meat, boiled in large cauldrons with vegetables and herbs. This is called *kourbani*.

ABLUTIONS AT THE TABLE The custom of rinsing the fingers in the course of a meal. The origin of the word (from Church Latin *ablutio*) is a reminder that ablution was originally a ritual practice; the person offering up a sacrifice had to purify his hands before officiating at the ceremony. Table ablutions were customary in ancient Greece and Rome, when food was taken by hand directly from the plate, as is still the practice today in the East. In Europe, since the introduction of forks, the ewer – a basin used for washing the hands – is no longer needed, and finger bowls appear on the table only with such foods as asparagus, artichokes and sea food. Linked to the practice of ablutions is that of the mouth rinse, still current at the beginning of the 19th century. In the Far East it is customary to offer to each guest, on changing from one course to another, a damp perfumed towel.

ABONDANCE An Alpine cheese from Savoie (and an AOC one) made from unpasteurized cow's milk (minimum 45% fat content). It is moulded when half-cooked and the crust is rubbed with salt. Made since the 16th century, Abondance takes its name from the valley where it originated and the local breed of dairy cows. It is round, 8–9 cm (3–3½ in) thick, weighing 7–12 kg (15–26 lb), with a colour varying from ochre to brown. The taste is subtle and nutty, with great fruitiness. The best cheese is made from the milk of Alpine herds.

ABOUKIR A French dessert made of a sponge cake cooked in a charlotte mould, then cut horizontally in slices which are sandwiched with chestnut cream. The cake is iced with coffee fondant icing and decorated with chopped pistachio nuts.

Aboukir almonds are glazed petits fours made with green or pink almond paste, into each of which a blanched almond is pressed. They are glazed by holding them on a skewer and dipping them into caramel or briskly boiled sugar.

ABRICOT-PAYS A fruit from the West Indies, the size of a small melon. Its only resemblance to the apricot is the colour of its flesh, which is, however, firmer than apricot flesh. After removing the thick skin and the harder white parts, the pulp is used to make jams, sorbets and fruit juices.

ABSINTHE A famous, or infamous liqueur, absinthe takes its name from an aromatic plant (see *Artemisia*), which contains an alkaloid used since ancient times as a tonic. Wormwood is the principal one of 14 herbs which are macerated in grape spirit, but hyssop and mint are also included. It is famous for its green colour, and was called the *fée verte* ('green muse') in France (although the Swiss make a blue one).

The liqueur absinthe was first made commercially by H.L. Pernod in 1797. Absinthe may be served with water (as pastis are). However, a big part of the old absinthe ritual was first to balance a sugar lump on a special flat, pierced spoon over the glass and pour the spirit over it. The liqueur was hugely popular in France from the middle of the 19th century, and was taken up by the avant-garde poets and painters. Its use spread to London and Louisiana.

Absinthe contains a powerful drug, which has serious effects on the nervous system, and its manufacture and sale were prohibited by law in France on 16 March 1915 and subsequently across Europe. However, it was never banned totally and has crept back in the 21st century as a specialist drink. Pernod and the various forms of pastis are now flavoured with aniseed.

In his *Grand Dictionnaire de cuisine*, Alexandre Dumas relates the following anecdote:

'De Musset's fatal passion for absinthe, which incidentally perhaps gave his poetry its bitter flavour, caused the Académie to make a modest pun. De Musset was, in fact, missing many of the sittings of this august body, aware that he was in no state to attend.

'One day one of the distinguished forty members said to another: "Really, do you not think that Alfred de Musset absents himself rather too often?"

'"You mean that he absinthes himself rather too often." '

ACCOLADE, EN In France this describes the presentation on the same plate of two similar kinds of food, leaning against each other, usually poultry and game birds. In former times meat and fish might also have been served in this manner.

ACCOMMODER A French term meaning to prepare a dish, including the preceding operations as well as the seasoning and cooking.

ACETABULUM In Roman times, a vessel for storing vinegar (*acetum* in Latin). The word also indicated a measure equivalent to 275 ml (9 fl oz). The Romans used wine vinegar, plain or strongly seasoned with pepper, but in non vine-growing regions they made vinegar from fruit (figs, pears or peaches).

ACETOMEL A syrupy mixture of honey and vinegar used in sweet-and-sour preserved fruits (such as grapes or quartered pears or quinces). The name comes from two Latin words, *acetum* (vinegar) and *mel* (honey).

ACHAR An Indian term for a pickle. Relished throughout the Indian subcontinent, in Réunion Island, Indonesia and the West Indies and brought to Europe by the English in the 18th century, achar is made from a mixture of fruit and vegetables which are chopped and steeped in a spicy sauce, often oil-based and frequently flavoured with saffron. Exotic achars may be made from palm hearts, limes, dates, rose petals, ginger and bamboo sprouts, but onions, pumpkins, cauliflower and capers can be used in the same way. Some achars are very sharp-flavoured and piquant; others are milder and even sweet.

RECIPE

vegetable achar with lemon

Cut thin-rinded lemons into quarters and remove the seeds. Cut some carrots, sweet (bell) peppers and seeded cucumbers into strips about 4 cm (1½ in) long, and cut some thin green beans and cabbage leaves into small pieces. Separate a cauliflower into tiny florets. Steep the lemons and the vegetables separately in coarse salt. After 12 hours, wash the lemons and soak them in cold water for 24 hours, changing the water several times, then boil them in water until the quarters have become soft. Drain and dry them. When the vegetables have been steeping for 36 hours, drain and dry them too. Finely mince or grate some onion and fresh root ginger (or use a blender). Add cayenne pepper, vinegar and powdered saffron, then some best-quality olive oil. Place the lemon quarters and vegetables in a jar and cover with the aromatized oil. Seal and store in a cool place.

ACHARD, FRANZ KARL German chemist (born Berlin, 1753; died Kunern, Silesia, 1821), whose French forebears had emigrated after the revocation of the Edict of Nantes. Carrying out research into a product designed to replace cane sugar, he succeeded in 1796 in perfecting the first industrial process for the extraction of beet sugar. This invention was disregarded by the Institut de France as being of no value, but received the support of the Prussian King Frederick William III, who provided Achard with funds in 1802 for the establishment of a sugar factory in Silesia. This eventually ended in failure as production was too costly, and Achard died in poverty.

ACID The term denotes a taste sensation (it is one of the four fundamental flavours – see *taste, flavour*) as well as a chemical function. Any substance is acid which, in a water solution, can give off hydrogen ions. The degree of acidity is defined by the hydrogen potential (pH), the scale of which varies from 0 (very acid) to 14 (very alkaline), 7 being the pH value of pure water, which is neutral.

Mineral acids, which are generally 'strong' (such as sulphuric acid), may be distinguished from the 'weak' organic acids, such as citric and malic acid in fruit, phosphoric acid in cheese, meat and fish, and tartaric acid in wine. In addition to organic acids, foods contain other assimilable acids: ascorbic acid, amino acids and fatty acids.

■ **Culinary applications** Acid foods and those to which acid (such as acetic acid or vinegar) is added are more easily preserved, for many micro-organisms do not develop when the pH value is low. Also the vitamin C content is better preserved in an acid environment.

A weak acid, such as lemon juice, prevents artichoke hearts, avocados, sliced apples, bananas, chicory (endive) and peeled potatoes from going black through oxidation.

Acids help proteins to coagulate, which is why vinegar or lemon juice is used in a court-bouillon and in the cooking liquor of a blanquette or of poached eggs.

Acidification is a sign of deterioration. When the lactose in milk becomes lactic acid, the milk is said to have gone sour. Sour cream, however, is sometimes used in cooking; it can be made by adding a few drops of lemon juice to fresh cream.

ACIDULATE To turn a liquid or a dish slightly acid, tart or piquant by adding a little lemon juice, vinegar or the juice of unripe fruit. Acidulate also means to make sour cream by adding a few drops of lemon juice to fresh cream.

ACRA Also known as akra. A savoury fritter made by mixing a spiced pureé of vegetables or fish with fritter batter. Acras, which are popular in the Caribbean, are served very hot as a starter, or with punch as cocktail snacks. Acras are also known as *marinades* and *bonbons à l'huile*, as well as 'stamp and go' in Jamaica and *surullitos* in Puerto Rico. They are most often made with salt cod, but alevin (baby salmon), mackerel and crayfish are also used, as well as breadfruit, aubergines (eggplants), palm hearts, Caribbean cabbage, pumpkin and other vegetables.

RECIPE

salt-cod acras

Place about 500 g (18 oz) salt cod in cold water for 24 hours to remove the salt, changing the water several times. Make a fritter batter with 200 g (7 oz, 1¾ cups) plain (all-purpose) flour, a pinch of salt and enough water to obtain a thick batter, then leave it to stand for 1 hour. Place the desalted cod with a little cold water and a bay leaf in a saucepan; cook gently for 10 minutes. Drain and flake the fish, then mix it with 4 teaspoons olive oil, salt and cayenne pepper. Finely chop 2 shallots and 4–5 chives, then add these to the cod. Stir the cod mixture into the batter. Stiffly whisk 2–3 egg whites and fold gently into the mixture. Drop spoonfuls of the mixture into hot oil and deep-fry until crisp and golden, turning once. Drain and serve hot.

ACROAMA A spectacle which livened up a banquet in Roman times: acrobats, flute players and dancers, mimes and parodies, even combats between men or animals. Of Greek origin, the name meant 'that to which one listens'. The acroama tradition continued in different forms, through the medieval story-tellers, jugglers and mountebanks, to become a musical entertainment or accompaniment.

ADVOCAAT A liqueur made with beaten egg yolks, sugar and spirit, served both before and after meals. The best-known brands are made in the Netherlands. It is sometimes used in mixes, especially the snowball (with fizzy lemonade).

AFRICA See *Black Africa, North Africa, South Africa.*

AFRICAINE, À L' The French term is used to describe an accompaniment of olive-shaped potato pieces, which are browned in butter, and two other vegetables – cucumber, aubergine (eggplant) or courgette (zucchini) – which are sliced and either sautéed in oil or steamed. This accompaniment is served with large joints of roast mutton, which may be flavoured with powdered rosebuds (as in Tunisia) or with a combination of herbs and spices, including thyme, bay, cumin, cloves or coriander (cilantro). The sauce for dishes served *à l'africaine* is a rich demi-glace flavoured with tomato.

AGAPE A meal that the early Christians took together. The word comes from the Greek *agape*, meaning love, and was originally used to describe a frugal meal. After the Mass the faithful would come together to share a light meal of bread and wine, the aim of which was to recall the ideals of sharing and charity preached by the Christians.

AGAR-AGAR A viscous substance, also known as Bengal isinglass and Japanese or Ceylon moss, agar-agar is an extract of seaweed from the Indian and Pacific Oceans. It is the vegetarian gelling agent – and produces a firmer jelly which does not melt as readily as gelatine. It is principally used in the food industry, in desserts, ice creams, sauces and canned soup. It comes either in the form of small transparent crumpled strips of various colours, or in loaves or powdered form. When dissolved in water over a low heat, its gum blends with the water; on cooling, it sets to a jelly. Called *Kanten* in Japan, it is added to soups.

AGARIC *psalliote* Any of a genus of field and woodland mushrooms with a white cap, pink then brownish gills, and a stalk bearing a single or a double ring. According to the species, the flesh may be tinted with pink, reddish-brown, brown or yellow. The group includes many edible mushrooms (see *mushroom*) with a delicate flavour and smell, often of aniseed.

AGAVE The Latin and popular name of a family of large plants with enormous spiked fleshy leaves, originating from Mexico, of which Magvey is one type. The fermented sap is used in several Latin American countries to make fermented drinks, such as pulque, mescal and tequila.

AGEING *Vieillissement* The process of keeping a wine with the intention of improving its qualities of taste and bouquet. Most wines spend a period of time in tank after fermentation, but the ageing process usually refers to a period spent in wooden casks, often oak, which allows a gentle form of oxidation to take place, as well as interaction between the wine and wood. Bottle ageing is also an important phase in the maturation of many fine wines, such as traditional red wines of Bordeaux, top-quality Sauternes, vintage port and fine wines from around the world, particularly those made from the Cabernet Sauvignon grape. Wines such as Sherry, Madeira and Vin Doux Naturel are aged in the presence of air to promote controlled oxidation which is an important part of their flavour development.

AGEING OF MEAT The slow change that takes place in meat when it is left for a period of time and reaches a state in which it is suitable for consumption or further processing. After the animal is killed, the flesh is still warm and it passes through a stage known in France as *pantelante* (twitching). Then rigor mortis sets in. In the next stage, *rassise*, the flesh becomes more tender and flavoursome as the sinews are less taut and the muscles relax. The speed and intensity with which meat ages is influenced both by the quality of the meat (which is affected by the animal's diet) and the ambient temperature. See *hanging*.

AGNÈS SOREL A French garnish consisting of cooked button mushrooms, breast of chicken and pickled ox (beef) tongue, cut according to the dish being garnished (omelette, fried or braised veal, or suprême of chicken). In Agnès Sorel soup the garnish is cut into thin strips and added to the thickened soup.

Mistress of the French King Charles VII, Agnès Sorel was a celebrated cook who gave her name to several dishes. 'To attract and keep the attentions of Charles VII, she engaged the best chefs of the time. She had no hesitation in making personal appearances in the kitchens. Two of her creations will go down to posterity: woodcock salmis and her little timbales.' (Christian Guy, *Une Histoire de la cuisine française*, published by Les Productions de Paris.)

RECIPES

Agnès Sorel tartlets
Fill tartlet cases with a layer of creamed chicken purée, containing chopped truffles if desired. Surround with a border of small rounds of cold cooked chicken breast and pickled ox (beef) tongue. On each tartlet place a mushroom cap which has been cooked in a white court-bouillon. Warm through in a preheated oven at 160°C (325°F, gas 3) for 10 minutes. Pour cream sauce over the mushrooms before serving.

Agnès Sorel timbales

Butter a dozen dariole moulds. Put a very thin layer of chopped truffles in half of them and in the other half a similar layer of chopped cooked pickled ox (beef) tongue. Prepare 500 g (18 oz) chicken mousseline (see *forcemeat*) and flavour it with a few spoonfuls of soubise* purée; the mixture should be thick. Cover the base and sides of the moulds with the chicken mousseline. Fill the centre with a salpicon of chicken and truffles, bound with a little reduced Madeira sauce, then cover the tops of the moulds with a final layer of chicken mousseline. Place the moulds in a shallow pan and cook in a bain marie for 12–15 minutes. When ready to serve, turn out of the moulds and arrange on a dish; serve with Madeira sauce separately.

AGRAZ A sorbet made from almonds, verjuice and sugar, popular in North Africa and Spain (its name is the Spanish for verjuice). Agraz, which has an acid flavour, is served in large sorbet glasses and may be sprinkled with kirsch.

AGUARDIENTE An alcoholic spirit from a Spanish-speaking country. In vine-growing regions (like Argentina, Chile and Spain) it is made from grape must, and so is the equivalent of the French marc or the Italian grappa. Spanish ones range from the crudest local Galician spirit to the sophisticated range of anis spirits, sold under brand or regional names. Like grappa they may also be fruit-flavoured (see *anisette*). Aguardiente may also be made from distilled sugar-cane molasses called *caña* in the Mediterranean and Central America.

AÏDA A French way of serving flatfish fillets (brill or turbot). It is distinguished from preparations *à la florentine* by the addition of paprika to the Mornay sauce and the spinach.

AÏGO BOULIDO Provençal name for a soup made from boiled water (hence its name, which may also be spelled *bouido* or *bullido*) and garlic. It is one of the oldest culinary traditions of this region, where they have the saying *l'aïgo boulido suavo lo vito* (garlic soup saves one's life).

RECIPES

aïgo boulido

Bring 1 litre (1¾ pints, 4⅓ cups) water to the boil. Season with ½ teaspoon salt and 6 crushed garlic cloves. Boil for about 10 minutes, then add a small sprig of sage, preferably fresh, one quarter of a bay leaf and a small sprig of thyme. Remove at once from the heat and leave to infuse for several minutes; remove the herbs. Blend 1 egg yolk with a little of the cooled soup, then stir it back into the soup to thicken it. Pour the soup over slices of bread which have been sprinkled with olive oil.

aïgo boulido with poached eggs

Poach some eggs in aïgo boulido stock. Place a slice of bread in each hot soup plate and top this with a poached egg. Ladle the soup over and sprinkle with chopped parsley to serve.

If preferred, 2 chopped and seeded tomatoes, a small sprig of fennel, a pinch of saffron, a piece of dried orange zest and 4 sliced cooked potatoes may be added to the basic aïgo boulido stock. In this case serve the poached eggs separately on the potatoes and pour the flavoured soup over the slices of bread sprinkled with chopped parsley.

AIGUEBELLE A plant-flavoured liqueur made at the Aiguebelle monastery near Montélimar, France.

AIGUILLETTE The French name for a long narrow fillet, taken from either side of the breastbone of poultry (mainly duck) and game birds. This separates easily from the underside of the breast meat and is a popular chef's item for small dishes. An aiguillette can also be a thin strip of any meat. In France the tip of a rump of beef is called *aiguillette baronne*.

RECIPE

jellied beef aiguillettes

Put 1 calf's foot and some veal bones in a saucepan, cover with cold water and bring to the boil. Drain, then cool them and wipe dry. Slice 575 g (1¼ lb) new carrots and 1 large onion, quarter 2 tomatoes and peel 2 small garlic cloves.

Heat 2 tablespoons oil in a flameproof casserole and brown 1.25 kg (2¾ lb) slivers of beef aiguillettes which, if possible, have been larded by the butcher. Add the sliced carrot and onion, the calf's foot and the veal bones; continue to cook until the onions are coloured. Remove any excess oil with a small ladle, then add the tomato quarters, a bouquet garni, a small piece of orange zest, a pinch of salt, pepper (a few turns of the pepper mill), a dash of cayenne pepper, 250 ml (8 fl oz, 1 cup) dry white wine and 500 ml (17 fl oz, 2 cups) water. Cover and slowly bring to the boil, then place the casserole in a preheated oven at 180°C (350°F, gas 4). Cook for about 2½ hours or until the meat is tender, stirring the meat from time to time.

In a large uncovered pan, simmer 30 small peeled button onions with 25 g (1 oz, 2 tablespoons) butter, 2 teaspoons caster (superfine) sugar, a pinch of salt and just enough water to cover them. Cook until the onions are tender and the liquid has evaporated. Toss the onions in the caramel which has formed. Drain the aiguillettes (reserving the cooking liquid) and arrange them in a deep dish or terrine with the sliced carrots and the small onions. Set aside until cold, then refrigerate.

Remove the bones from the calf's foot and cut the flesh into cubes. Strain the cooking liquid back into a saucepan, add the calf's foot cubes and boil for about 10 minutes, then strain. Dissolve 15 g (½ oz, 2 envelopes) powdered gelatine in the minimum of water, then add the strained cooking liquid and 100 ml (4 fl oz, ½ cup) Madeira; check seasoning, then leave to cool until syrupy. Coat the aiguillettes with the setting liquid, then refrigerate until set and ready to serve.

AILLADE A feature of the cuisine of southern France, which varies according to the region where it is made. In Provence, it is either a vinaigrette sauce with garlic or a slice of bread rubbed with garlic, soaked in olive oil and grilled (broiled) (*pain à l'aillade*). In Languedoc, the aillade from the Toulouse area is a variation on aïoli mayonnaise made with blanched and ground walnuts, while in the region of Albi aillade is another name for aïoli.

RECIPE

aillade sauce
Peel 4 garlic cloves, crush or finely chop them and place in a basin with salt and pepper. Gradually blend in 2 tablespoons olive oil, stirring well. Mix in 2–3 teaspoons vinegar, a few sprigs of chopped parsley and, if desired, 2 teaspoons chopped shallots and chives.

AILLÉE A French condiment of the consistency of mustard, made with breadcrumbs, ground almonds and garlic, mixed with stock. The origin of aillée is uncertain, but it is likely that it originated in Paris, where in the 13th century no fewer than nine merchants are known to have dealt in it.

AÏOLI Also known as *ailloli*. A Provençal emulsion sauce of garlic and olive oil, best known in its mayonnaise form with egg yolks. The Provençal name comes from *ail* (garlic) and *oli* (dialect for oil). The Spanish *alioli* of raw garlic pounded with oil was first recorded by Pliny in the first century AD in Tarragona (on the east coast); it too is now made with added yolks. Léon Daudet maintained that the use of garlic in the food of Mediterranean peoples went back to the beginnings of cooking, and he considered the culinary use of garlic had achieved its peak of perfection in aïoli. Frédéric Mistral, who in 1891 founded a journal entitled *L'Aïoli*, wrote: 'Aïoli epitomizes the heat, the power, and the joy of the Provençal sun, but it has another virtue – it drives away flies.'

Aïoli is served with cold poached fish, *bourride* (fish soup), hard-boiled eggs, salad, snails or cold meats. But when a Provençal talks of a *grand aïoli*, which is eaten only two or three times a year, he means a sumptuous dish which, as well as the sauce, includes poached salt cod, boiled beef and mutton, stewed vegetables – carrots, celery, green beans, beetroot (beet), cauliflower and chick peas – and, as a garnish, snails and hard-boiled eggs.

RECIPES

aïoli
Peel 4 large garlic cloves (split them in two and remove the germ if necessary). Pound the garlic with 1 egg yolk in a mortar or blender. Add salt and pepper and, while pounding or blending, very gradually add 250 ml (8 fl oz, 1 cup) olive oil, as for a mayonnaise. The sauce is ready when it is thick and creamy. The bulk of the sauce is sometimes increased by adding 2 teaspoons mashed boiled potato.

aïoli without eggs
Cook a whole head of garlic, unpeeled, in a hot oven for about 30 minutes. Peel the cloves and mash to a purée. Add salt and pepper and thicken like a mayonnaise working in 150 ml (¼ pint, ⅔ cup) olive oil and 150 ml (¼ pint, ⅔ cup) groundnut (peanut) oil.

cod aïoli
Cook 575 g (1¼ lb) small potatoes in their skins in salted water. Keep a little of the cooking water and thicken it with 100 g (4 oz, ½ cup) aïoli (made with egg yolks). Coat the potatoes with the aïoli sauce and sprinkle with chopped parsley. Poach 1 kg (2¼ lb) soaked and drained salt cod in a mixture of water and milk. Arrange the cod on plates and put the potatoes on top.

AISY CENDRE A soft cheese from Burgundy made with unpasteurized cow's milk (minimum 45% fat content), with a washed crust. Made in farms in the Montbard region of the Côte d'Or, it is a round cheese 10 cm (4 in) in diameter and from 3–6 cm (1¼–2½ in) thick, weighing 250–500 g (9–18 oz). It is matured beneath a layer of ashes of vine shoots, from which it acquires its name and its powerful earthy flavour.

ALBACORE In cuisine, canned white tuna, and also the two fish from which it comes, of the family *Scombroidae*. In French-speaking countries *albacore* refers to the yellow-finned tuna, the most gaily coloured of the tunas, a fish that can reach 2 metres (6 ft) long and a weight of 200 kg (440 lb). It is fished in the tropical waters of the Atlantic, and off the African and Japanese coasts. Its slightly-pink flesh provides the greater part of the white tuna that is canned. In Japan it is cooked as *shibi*.

In Britain, America and Australia albacore is *Thunmus alalunga* (*germon* in French). From this comes the canned white tuna of the highest quality. Known as the long-fin (sometimes the white) tuna, it is half the size of the other – it rarely reaches 1 metre (3 ft). It swims in the warm waters of the world and is an eminent sporting fish. The flesh can be fried, poached or braised, but raw is highly prized in Japan for *sushi* and *sashimi*.

ALBERT An English sauce dedicated to Prince Albert of Saxe-Coburg-Gotha, husband and consort of Queen Victoria. It is made from a white consommé seasoned with grated horseradish, thickened with breadcrumbs and enriched with cream and egg yolks. Mustard thinned with vinegar or lemon juice is added to give a final piquant touch. This hot sauce accompanies joints of braised beef.

The name Albert is also given to a method of serving sole, dedicated to Albert Blazer, maître d'hôtel at Maxim's between the World Wars.

ALBIGEOISE, À L' This garnish, named for the town of Albi, consists of stuffed tomatoes and potato croquettes; it accompanies joints of meat.

The term is also applied to methods of preparing dishes using products from south-western France.

RECIPE

shoulder of lamb à l'albigeoise
Bone the shoulder and fill the bone cavity with a stuffing of half sausagemeat and half chopped pig's liver, seasoned with garlic, chopped parsley, salt and pepper. Roll the shoulder as for a ballotine and tie to secure. Weigh the stuffed joint. Brown the rolled shoulder in very hot fat, then place it in a roasting dish; surround with quartered potatoes (or whole small new potatoes) and 12 blanched garlic cloves, season with salt and pepper and sprinkle with a little melted fat. Cook the lamb in a preheated oven at about 200°C (400°F, gas 6), allowing 20 minutes per 450 g (1 lb), plus 20 minutes more. Sprinkle with chopped parsley to serve.

This dish is traditionally cooked and served in an ovenproof earthenware dish.

ALBUFERA, À LA D' The name given to several *haute cuisine* dishes (notably chicken and duck) dedicated by Carême to Napoleon's Marshal Suchet, Duc d'Albufera (the name of the lake at Valencia, near which he won a victory over the English).

RECIPES

Albufera sauce
Prepare a suprême sauce using 500 ml (17 fl oz, 2 cups) thick rich chicken velouté sauce, 400 ml (14 fl oz, 1¾ cups) white chicken stock, 400 ml (14 fl oz, 1¾ cups) crème fraîche and 50 g (2 oz, ¼ cup) butter. While the sauce is cooking, sweat 150 g (5 oz) sliced sweet (bell) peppers in 50 g (2 oz, ¼ cup) butter. Allow to cool, then purée the peppers in a blender. Work in 150 g (5 oz, ⅔ cup) butter and press through a sieve. Reduce the suprême sauce to 500 ml (17 fl oz, 2 cups), then add 3 tablespoons veal stock and 2 teaspoons of the pepper butter. Rub through a fine sieve. Serve the sauce hot.

chicken à la d'Albufera
Half-cook some rice in a white stock and add a salpicon of truffles and foie gras. Stuff a chicken with this mixture and poach in the white stock. Arrange it on a serving dish, surrounded with an Albufera garnish – pickled ox (beef) tongue, sliced and sautéed calves' sweetbreads and mushrooms. Coat with Albufera sauce.

ducklings à la d'Albufera
Dress and truss 2 young ducklings. Cut 12 pieces of smoked Bayonne ham into heart shapes. Put into a saucepan 50 g (2 oz, ¼ cup) best butter, the pieces of ham, then the ducklings, a bouquet garni, an onion stuck with 2 cloves and half a glass of Málaga (or another Muscat) wine. Cover the contents of the saucepan with a circle of buttered paper. In a restaurant this is cooked by placing the pan on a *paillasse* (brick hearth with charcoal fire), with flames above and below but not too fierce, so that the ducklings cook without frying. At home cook in a preheated oven at 200°C (400°F, gas 6). After 20 minutes, turn the ducklings and remove the onion and the bouquet. After a further 20 minutes, strain them, untruss and place on a serving dish. They should be well browned. Garnish with thin slices of ham. Skim off the fat from the juices in the pan and add 2 tablespoons financière* sauce with the fat removed. Add 2 punnets of lightly fried very small mushrooms and coat them with the sauce.

sirloin à la d'Albufera
aloyau à la d'Albufera (from Carême's recipe) Braise a sirloin joint. Make some turtle sauce, add a little butter and some of the beef juice, then stir in a plateful of sliced and sautéed calves' sweetbreads, a plateful of sliced pickled ox (beef) tongue and some mushrooms. Spoon some of this ragoût round the beef and then cook to reheat. Garnish the dish with slices of young rabbit fillet *à la d'Orly* (egged, crumbed and deep-fried) and 10 skewers laid on the beef, each assembled as follows: first a fine double cockscomb, a slice of young rabbit *à la d'Orly*, a cockscomb, a large glazed truffle, a cockscomb, and finally a glazed black truffle. Serve more ragoût in two sauceboats.

ALCARRAZA A porous earthenware vessel used for cooling drinks. The name is Spanish and derives from the Arabic *al karaz* (pitcher). It was introduced into France in the 18th century. The *alcarraza* is suspended, preferably in the shade, in a draughty place. Liquid oozes out through the porous surface of the vessel and evaporates, thus lowering the temperature and cooling the contents of the pitcher.

ALCAZAR A French gâteau made with a base of enriched shortcrust pastry covered with a layer of apricot marmalade and topped with a kirsch-flavoured almond meringue mixture. The gâteau is decorated with apricot marmalade and a lattice of almond paste. It keeps well for two or three days.

RECIPE

alcazar gâteau
Line a flan tin (pie pan) with 250 g (9 oz) *pâte sucrée* (see *pastry*). Prick the base and spread with 2 tablespoons apricot marmalade or jam. Whisk 4 egg whites and 125 g (4½ oz, ½ cup) caster (superfine) sugar over heat to a stiff meringue, then fold in 50 g

(2 oz, ½ cup) ground almonds, 50 g (2 oz, ½ cup) plain (all-purpose) flour and 2 tablespoons melted butter mixed with 1 tablespoon kirsch. Pour this mixture into the prepared flan case and cook in a preheated oven at 200°C (400°F, gas 6) until the top has browned. Turn the gâteau out of the tin and cool it on a wire tray.

Using a piping bag with a fluted nozzle, pipe softened almond paste into a lozenge-shaped lattice over the top of the gâteau and then as a border around the edge. Replace it in the oven to brown the almond paste. Over a low heat reduce 200 g (7 oz, ¾ cup) apricot marmalade or jam and fill each of the lozenge shapes, then place half a pistachio nut in the centre of each one. If desired, the border may also be glazed with apricot jam and coated with chopped roasted pistachio nuts.

ALCOHOL The common name for ethanol. The word was first used by alchemists who derived it from the Arabic *al kohl*, which came to mean any product that represented concentration or the essence of any raw material. From that it came to be known as the product of distillation. In the Middle Ages alcohol was considered an elixir of life (*acqua vitae*, from which it acquired the name *eau-de-vie*) and was mostly reserved for therapeutic use. It came to be used as a drink towards the end of the 15th century, when it was infused with all kinds of herbs and plants. Finally, the invention of the rectification process and the continuous still transformed it into a product for the mass market.

Ethanol is produced by the action of yeast on sugars during the fermentation process. These sugars are the naturally occurring sugars in fruit such as grapes, pears, apples and berries or are obtained from starch sources such as cereals, potatoes and sugar beet, modified by the action of malting enzymes into fermentable sugars.

The source of the fermentable sugar gives each product its own character – grapes ferment into wine, pears into perry, apples into cider and cereals into beer. Distillation of these liquors creates another range of drinks such as brandy, eaux-de-vie, marc and whisky. Vegetable substrates usually pass from fermentation to distillation into products such as vodka and gin. In some parts of the world fermentable sugars are provided by plants such as sugar cane, agape and palm, which in turn produce rum, tequila and various alcoholic liquors.

The alcoholic content of a wine or spirit is now usually measured as the percentage by volume of pure ethanol in the liquor, measured at 20°C (68°F). This has largely replaced the Gay-Lussac scale. Alcohol has antiseptic properties and nutritional value, but it becomes toxic when there is more than a certain amount in the blood.

Alcoholic drinks may be drunk on their own or with soft drinks. They are also widely used in cooking. For example wine, beer and spirits can all be used in savoury and sweet recipes.

AL DENTE An Italian expression (meaning literally 'to the tooth') indicating the correct degree of cooking for pasta, which must be removed from the heat and drained while it is still firm enough to bite into. The expression may also be applied to certain vegetables, such as green beans, which are served while still retaining their crunchiness.

ALEMBIC Apparatus used in distillation. The name derives from the Arabic *al'inbiq* (distilling vessel).

The traditional alembic, made of copper, comprises a boiler (called a cucurbit) in which the mixture to be distilled is heated, a cap where the vapours collect, and a bent pipe that carries the vapours to the serpentine, a spiral coil passing through a cold bath, where they condense. This type of alembic, known as *charentais, discontinu*, or *à repasse* (because the alcohol passes through it twice), is used for distilling most of the great eaux-de-vie or alcoholic spirits, but alembics of the continuous distillation type are also used – for Armagnac, for example – and double-towered alembics, in which the alcohol does not have to pass through twice, are used in industry.

ALEXANDRA The name given to several French dishes (chicken consommé, Parmentier soup with vegetables, fillets of sole, sautéed chicken, potroast quail, noisette cutlets and tournedos steak), served with a sauce and garnished with a thin slice of truffle and with asparagus tips (if the sauce is white) or quartered artichoke hearts (if it is brown).

Alexandra is also the name of a cocktail based on *crème de cacao* (chocolate liqueur).

RECIPE

sautéed chicken Alexandra
Joint a chicken and sauté the joints in butter until cooked. Remove and keep them hot. Add 100 ml (4 fl oz, ½ cup) white stock to the sauté pan and cook briskly to reduce it, then add 1½ tablespoons soubise* purée, moisten with 100 ml (4 fl oz, ½ cup) white stock and reduce again. Finally stir in 2 tablespoons double (heavy) cream and 40 g (1½ oz, 3 tablespoons) butter, then strain the sauce. Arrange the chicken in a dish, coat with the sauce and garnish with buttered asparagus tips.

ALGAE Simple plants which constitute the flora of the seas, lakes and coasts. According to their pigmentation, algae are classified as green (including ulva or sea lettuce, chlorella, chondrus), brown (including fucus and laminaria), red (porphyra) or blue-green (primitive organisms resembling bacteria). Some of them are edible.

Ancient Britons, the Irish, the river-dwellers in Chad and the Mexican Indians all appear to have been very early collectors of algae, with which they made bread and a type of pancake. In the Far East algae have always had particular gastronomic value. Their present-day role in the food industry worldwide on account of their gum content (see *agar-agar, emulsifier, gelling agent*) makes growing them big business.

Algae are quite widely used in Celtic cookery in Europe, the most common being porphyra, rhodymenia and chondrus. (See *carrageen, laver, sloke.*) *Chondrus* is used as a gelling agent for desserts on both sides of the Atlantic. In Japan six kinds of algae are commonly eaten, constituting 10% of total food production. These algae are either taken from the sea or cultivated along the coasts. *Nori*, known as laver in the west, is dried and compressed into violet-coloured leaves, then used for wrapping balls of rice or fish. It is also used in powdered form as an iodized condiment. Dried *kombu* (kelp) is used to season stocks (principally dashi), rice and vegetables. It is also cut into strips and made into little 'nests' which are fried and served with vegetables. *Wakame* (used for miso soup) and *hijiki* are used to make soups and to colour various dishes.

ALGÉRIENNE, À L'
This French garnish consists of sweet potato, either as croquettes or sautéed, and chopped tomatoes seasoned with garlic. It is served with large or small pieces of meat (paupiettes) as well as sautéed chicken. Sweet potato purée is used for the soup *crème algérienne*.

ALHAGI
The Latin name of a small Mediterranean shrub also called camel's thorn. It has edible seeds that, in intense heat, exude a sugary substance which can be shaken from the bush. This may be the manna (from the Hebrew *mânhu*, 'what is it?') mentioned in the Bible.

ALI-BAB
One of the dishes named in honour of Henri Babinsky (born Paris, 1855; died Paris, 1931), whose pseudonym it was. A professional engineer from the École des Mines, he published *Gastronomie pratique* under this name in 1907. During his travels throughout the world prospecting for gold and diamonds, he collected many recipes and cooked for his travelling companions. His book was republished several times with various additions, including an interesting study on treatment for obesity among gourmands (1923). This well-documented and humorous work is still of great interest historically and gastronomically, though of limited practical use.

RECIPE

ali-bab salad
Turn some peeled shrimps in mayonnaise, arrange them in a mound in the centre of a serving dish or salad bowl and sprinkle with chopped fresh herbs. Surround with the following: courgette (zucchini) matchsticks, blanched in salted water; sweet potato, cut into small balls and boiled; hard-boiled (hard-cooked) egg cut into quarters; small tomatoes, peeled, seeded and quartered. Sprinkle the salad with vinaigrette and serve garnished with nasturtium flowers.

ALICA
Semolina made by the ancient Romans from a variety of semi-hard wheat known as *zea*, which was crushed in a wooden mortar. After sifting, it was divided into three categories according to its fineness, and whitened by the addition of crushed chalk. Alica was used to prepare gruels, cakes and a special bread with raisins known as Picenum bread.

ALIGOT
A dish from the Auvergne region of France, made from potatoes, garlic and Cantal cheese. The cheese used must not be fully ripe; fresh Tomme cheese may be used instead, the best being Tomme de Planèze. The most difficult part of the preparation is mixing the cheese with the cooked potatoes, either as a purée or simply mashed with a fork.

A sweet aligot may be made by pouring a generous helping of rum over the *aligot* in a gratin dish, and setting light to it.

RECIPE

aligot
Smoothly mash 1 kg (2¼ lb) soft fondant potatoes (cooked very slowly in butter in a covered pan), add 1–2 crushed garlic cloves, 1 tablespoon bacon fat and sufficient milk to make a purée. Turn the purée into a bain marie, add 575 g (1¼ lb) thinly sliced fresh Laguiole cheese and stir vigorously with a wooden spoon until the cheese is evenly blended into the potato. The aligot is cooked when a smooth flowing elastic purée is formed.

ALIGOTÉ
A white grape with high acidity, grown in Burgundy and in parts of Eastern Europe. Dry and assertive, it is the traditional base for the aperitif Kir or *vin blanc cassis*.

ALIZE PÂQUAUDE
Also known as Alise Pâcaude. A traditional Easter griddle cake from the Vendée region of France, also called *gache vendéenne*. It is made with bread dough enriched with butter and eggs, sweetened and flavoured with orange-flower water, and can weigh up to 2 kg (4½ lb). The cake is supposed to be made on Easter Saturday, and the dough is left to rise for only 2 hours. The name means 'badly risen'.

ALLEMANDE
A white sauce, described as 'German' to differentiate it from the brown espagnole 'Spanish' sauce, although both these basic sauces are of French origin. Made with veal or poultry stock, allemande sauce accompanies offal, poached chicken, vegetables and eggs; made with a fish or mushroom fumet, it is served with fish.

RECIPES

allemande sauce
(from Carême's recipe) Prepare some velouté; pour half of it into a saucepan with an equal quantity of good chicken consommé containing some mushroom

skins and stalks but no salt. Place the pan on a high heat and stir with a wooden spoon until it boils. Then cover the pan and simmer gently for about an hour to reduce the sauce; skim off the fat and return it to a high heat, stirring with the wooden spoon so that it does not stick to the pan. When the sauce is thoroughly reduced and well thickened, it should leave a fairly thick covering on the surface of the spoon. When poured, it should make a coating similar to that of redcurrant jelly at its final stage of cooking.

Remove the saucepan from the heat and make a liaison of 4 egg yolks mixed with 2 tablespoons cream. Put this through a sieve and add a knob of unsalted butter, the size of a small egg, cut up into small pieces. Pour this a little at a time into the velouté, taking care to stir with the wooden spoon to thicken as the liaison blends in. When completely thickened, place the allemande on a moderate heat, stirring all the time, and as soon as it has begun to bubble slightly, remove from the heat and add a dash of grated nutmeg. When well blended, press through a sieve.

allemande sauce based on fish stock

This sauce is prepared in the same way as that based on meat stock except that the meat stock used in the preparation is replaced with a rich fish stock. This sauce may also be flavoured with a concentrated mushroom stock.

allemande sauce based on meat stock

Using a wooden spatula, mix together 2 or 3 egg yolks (according to size) and 400 ml (14 fl oz, 1¾ cups) white meat stock in a heavy-based saucepan over a low heat. Then stir in 500 ml (17 fl oz, 2 cups) velouté. Bring to the boil, whisking constantly to prevent the sauce from sticking, and reduce until it coats the spatula. Check seasoning. Cut 50 g (2 oz, ¼ cup) butter into small pieces and mix into the sauce. Place in a bain marie, topping up the water from time to time. This sauce may be flavoured with a fumet of truffle or mushrooms.

ALLEMANDE, À L'
This French description is applied to a dish served with a white allemande sauce (see above). Alternatively it describes a method of preparing marinated game inspired by German cuisine: haunch or saddle of venison, saddle of hare or rabbit roasted with the vegetables from the marinade. A sauce to serve with the game is prepared by deglazing with the marinade.

RECIPE

calves' brains à l'allemande
Poach the brains in a court-bouillon, drain them and cut each into 4 slices. Coat these with flour and cook gently in butter. Arrange the slices on top of croûtons fried in butter and coat with allemande sauce.

ALLONGER
The French term for extending a sauce, for example adding a liquid (water, stock, wine or bouillon) to a sauce that is too thick or reduced too much. The sauce is thus made thinner, but its flavour is less concentrated.

ALLSPICE
A spice, also known as Jamaican pepper and (in France) as *poivre giroflée*, that is ground from the unripe berries of *Pimenta officinalis*, a tree which grows in the Caribbean, Honduras and Mexico. Allspice has a strong odour of nutmeg, cinnamon and cloves, which is why it is sometimes mistaken for a mixture of different spices. It is used to season sausages, salt beef and pork, pickles, sauces, soused herrings, stuffings and even Christmas cake.

ALLUMETTE
A small pastry strip (the French means 'match') cut from a long rectangle of puff pastry. They are topped with a savoury spread, garnished and baked. If this savoury is to be served hot, the spread, whether made from one item (cheese, anchovies or shrimps) or a mixture, may be sandwiched between two layers of pastry. Iced allumettes are small individual pastries. According to Lacam, a pastrycook called Planta, who came from Dinard but was of Swiss origin, created these when using up some leftover icing (frosting).

Allumette potatoes are very thin matchstick-shaped fried potatoes.

RECIPES

allumette potatoes
Cut some potatoes into small matchsticks 5 mm (¼ in) thick, using a variety that does not disintegrate in cooking. Wash and dry them, then plunge into very hot fat and cook without letting them change colour. Drain, then plunge them back into the hot fat and cook until just golden. Drain and serve.

iced sweet allumettes
Roll out some puff pastry to a thickness of 3 mm (⅛ in), and cut it into strips 8 cm (3 in) wide. Spread with a thin layer of royal icing (frosting). Cut the strips into 2.5–3 cm (1–1¼ in) lengths and place them on a baking sheet. Bake in a preheated oven at 180°C (350°F, gas 4) until the icing turns cream-coloured (about 10 minutes).

savoury allumettes
Roll out some puff pastry to about 5 mm (¼ in) thickness, and divide it into strips 8 cm (3 in) wide. Spread these with the chosen well-chilled filling, and top, if desired, with a pastry strip or a selected garnish. Cut the bands into rectangles 2–3 cm (¾–1¼ in) wide, and place them on a baking sheet. Bake in a preheated oven at about 200°C (400°F, gas 6) for 12–15 minutes. Serve very hot.

Savoury allumettes can be prepared with the following fillings.

• *with anchovies* Anchovy butter filling, garnished with anchovy fillets (may also be served cold).
• *à l'andalouse* Chicken filling with paprika and a salpicon of lean ham and onions cooked slowly in butter.
• *à la chalonnaise* Chicken filling with cockscombs and kidneys and diced mushrooms.
• *à la chavette* Fish filling with crayfish butter, garnished with crayfish tails and truffles.
• *à l'écarlate* Veal filling with a salpicon of pickled tongue.
• *à l'écossaise* Smoked haddock purée bound with béchamel sauce.
• *à la florentine* Spinach gently cooked in butter, mixed with béchamel sauce and grated Gruyère; dust allumettes with Parmesan cheese before baking.
• *à la toscane* When giving the last 3 folds to puff pastry, sprinkle with very finely grated cheese. Dust allumettes with Parmesan cheese before baking.

ALMOND The fruit of the almond tree. (In France the term is more loosely used for the almond kernel and is extended to the kernels within the stones – pits – of such fruits as the apricot and peach.) The outer layer of the almond is oval, green and velvety to the touch; it encloses a thick-shelled nut containing one or two seeds. Originating in Asia and known by the Romans as 'Greek nuts', it was exploited by the Arabs for a range of culinary possibilities. Almonds were widely used in the Middle Ages to make soups, as well as sweet desserts (see *blancmange*).

There are two varieties of almond, both rich in sugar, albumen and oil: the edible sweet almond and the bitter almond, which has a very strong taste and is poisonous in large amounts, containing hydrocyanic acid. California supplies half the world crop of almonds, followed by Spain and Sicily. The so-called Jordan almond (long, flat and slender – and the best 'cocktail' almond) is in fact from Spain, the name being a corruption of *jardín* (a garden). French almonds grow in Provence and Corsica.

Fresh almonds appear early in the year. They are opened with a nutcracker and eaten for dessert. But almonds are mainly used dried and are served salted with aperitifs.

Dried bitter almonds are used in small quantities to flavour cakes, pastries and confectionery and to make an essence. Dried sweet almonds – whole, flaked (slivered), ground or made into paste or cream – are used in making cakes, biscuits (cookies), sweets and various sweetmeats. Celebrated among these are the sugar-coated drageés and various forms of nougat. They also flavour drinks like orgeat and Amaretto di Sarrano, and make a fine-quality oil, used in baking.

In cooking, almonds may also accompany certain fish, in particular trout, or meat such as chicken or pigeon. They are used as ingredients in such preparations as couscous, rice dishes, stuffings, pounded sauces with garlic, and compound butters.

RECIPES

blanched almonds
Put some dried almonds into a strainer and plunge into a saucepan of boiling water, then take the pan off the heat. As soon as their skin gives under the finger, drain some of the almonds, peel them straight away and plunge them into cold water. Do the same with the rest of the almonds, a few at a time. Drain and blot them, then dry them in a sieve over a very low heat; they must not go yellow. Store in a box or well-sealed jar, away from the light.

chopped almonds
Whole blanched almonds may be chopped by hand or in a blender. Flaked (slivered) almonds are thinly sliced lengthways by hand.

salted almonds
Heat some sweet blanched almonds in the oven until they turn slightly yellow, turning them once. Then fry them until golden in butter in a sauté pan, with a pinch of saffron, cayenne pepper and ginger. Drain on a cloth. To store, when cold, coat with a clear solution of gum arabic and dust with fine salt.

toasted almonds
Spread flaked (slivered) almonds on a baking sheet and dry them in the oven, without any fat, until lightly brown.

ALMOND MILK A liquid preparation based on ground almonds. In the Middle Ages almond milk was a soup made with crushed almonds, blanched onions, wine and spices, heated with water until it thickened. The soup was served hot, either as a main dish or as a course between savoury dishes. Later on, almond milk became almost synonymous with blancmange, a cold dessert made from ground almonds and sugar, which are stirred into hot milk and then strained, setting to a jelly when cooled. This dish, which is not as popular as it once was, is now set with gelatine and is used as a base for cold desserts or sundaes, finished off with fruit and ice cream.

The French term *lait d'amande* is also used in classic pâtisserie for a round cake made from a paste of almonds, sugar and eggs. When cooked, it is coated with an apricot glaze, topped with a thin layer of almond paste, glazed again, iced (frosted) and then decorated with chopped roasted almonds.

RECIPE

almond milk jelly
Soak 3 leaves of gelatine in a little water. (¾ oz, 1½ envelopes of dissolved powdered gelatine may alternatively be added to the hot milk). Blanch 250 g (9 oz, scant 2 cups) sweet almonds and 15 g (½ oz, 1 tablespoon) bitter almonds in 500 ml (17 fl oz, 2 cups) water for 2 minutes – or use all sweet nuts.

Alsace

The abundance and variety of the natural resources of this region have made it an area of great gastronomic importance for several centuries. Its fish and game are plentiful and well flavoured. The breeding of livestock, particularly pigs, and poultry provides meats which are deservedly famous, as are the products of the vineyards, orchards and kitchen gardens. The gastronomic reputation of Alsace also owes much to the talent of its chefs, who have harmoniously blended the culinary traditions of eastern France, and its taste for pork products and pastries, with German influence (beer, flour and cherry soups) and Jewish influence too, particularly in the use of spices and the preparation of fish. Goose fat, lard and the bouquet of the local wines give Alsatian cuisine its own characteristic flavour. Strasbourg and Colmar are the two poles of this gastronomic tradition, but it

The façade of this house in Colmar is typical of the architecture of Alsace. Flowers and old signs add to the picturesque impression.

remains a major concern even in the smallest village, where the room (*Stube*) in which the dishes are prepared and eaten symbolizes family intimacy and the warmth of the home.

■ **Meat, poultry and game** To give credit where it is due, it was the Benedictine monks of past centuries who encouraged the breeding of pigs, whose quality now makes Alsatian charcuterie worthy of repute. Pork products are largely responsible for the renown of sauerkraut, which, cooked with Riesling and seasoned with a glass of kirsch, is the Alsatian dish par excellence. Also well known are *Schifela* (shoulder of smoked pork), saveloy, Strasbourg sausages, *Kälerei* (pork cheese), ham (salted, smoked, in pâté) and stuffed piglet *à la peau de goret*.

Another star attraction is the goose – a dish for special occasions either served in salmis or braised with potatoes – and the celebrated terrines and pâtés de foie gras with truffles rival those of south-western France for their fine quality. Other poultry dishes enhance Alsatian cuisine: turkey with chestnuts, chicken with Riesling, chicken with morel mushrooms and fricassee of

chicken with cream. Red meat forms the basis of pies, stews and ragoûts, as typified by *baekenofe*.

Game provides some classic dishes, notably haunch of venison with pears and jugged hare with noodles. Among freshwater fish dishes are carp *à la juive* and fish stew of the River Ill region, and there are numerous local ways of serving trout, pike-perch, pike and eel. Crayfish, which are becoming increasingly rare, are traditionally cooked *cardinalisées* in a flan, or with Alsace wine. Frogs are used in stews, soups and sauces.

■ **Vegetables** The main vegetable is, of course, the cabbage, which is the basis of sauerkraut and is also served in salads. Equally good are red cabbage with chestnuts and kohlrabi with cream.

The cabbage's place of honour can be challenged only by the onion, which is eaten in tarts (*zewelewai*) or in bread dough (*flammenküche*). Hop shoots with cream should also be mentioned and, of course, the potato, which is one of the principal ingredients of everyday cooking, and is also used to make knepfles, noques and pflutters. Fresh noodles, such as spätzle, are often served as a garnish.

Fruit is harvested by hand in the vineyards of the grands crus.

■ **Fruit** Alsatian fruit, which is full of flavour, is used to make white eaux-de-vie which are justly famous (kirsch, Quetsche, Mirabelle and Framboise). Fruits are used in tarts and provide colourful decoration on Alsatian pâtisserie, flavoured with aniseed, cinnamon, lemon and almonds. In this field, the best-known speciality is kugelhopf. Not to be forgotten are such sweetmeats as cherries in kirsch, crystallized (candied) mirabelle plums, macaroons and gingerbread.

WINE Vines were probably first introduced into Alsace by the Romans and wine-making has continued through the centuries despite periods when wars have virtually devastated the

This old carving on a barrel is displayed in the Unterlinden museum in Colmar.

countryside. The Thirty Years War in the 17th century was possibly the period of greatest destruction, but subsequent invasions, particularly during the French Revolution and World War I and II have all made an impact on vineyard plantings, trade and markets. At the end of the 19th century the vineyards were affected by oidium (powdery mildew) and phylloxera, which resulted in the better quality hillside vineyards being abandoned while flatter plains were replanted with low-quality vines. Since being restored to France after World War II, an overall plan of improvement in all aspects of vineyard management and winemaking has given new life to the land and resulted in exceptional quality wines. In 1962 the wines of Alsace were granted their own *appellation d'origine contrôlée* and in 1972 a law was

passed making it obligatory for all Alsace wines to be bottled in the region of production.

Despite being the northernmost vine-growing area of France, Alsace benefits from special climatic conditions. The Alsace plain was formed by a series of subsidences, revealing different layers of rock where faults occurred. This explains the great diversity of the rocks and resultant soils: yellow granite, pink sandstone, chalky clay soil, loess, sand, gravel and marl. It is in this area that the vines are situated. Planted on the lower foothills of the Vosges mountains and on the plain, facing the Rhine but sheltered from the cold north-east winds, the vineyards extend over 100 km (60 miles) from Thann, west of Mulhouse, to Marlenheim, west of Strasbourg, in a narrow strip 1–5 km (½–3¼ miles) wide. They are protected from the Atlantic winds by the natural barrier of the Vosges and benefit from a semicontinental climate, sunny and dry. Spring frosts, hail and dull summers do some damage, although many of the vineyards, planted at an altitude varying from 200 to 450 m (650 to 1475 ft), face south, south-east and east and enjoy microclimates that are quite exceptional in the Rhine valley. This great variety of microclimates and the unusual character of the soil types explain why generalizations about the wines are difficult to make.

The grapes used for Alsace ▶

◀ wines are Riesling, Gewurztraminer, Muscat, Pinot Gris (traditionally known as Tokay Pinot Gris), Pinot Blanc, Pinot Noir and Sylvaner. While most wines are bottled as 100% single varietal, blends of these varieties are known as Edelzwicker. While the appellation covers the whole of the region, 50 individual vineyard sites have been selected as *grand cru* according to strict criteria of geology and microclimate. The maximum permitted yield for these sites is lower than for non-*grand cru* wines and only four grape varieties are permitted – Riesling, Muscat, Pinot Gris or Gewurztraminer. Individual *grand cru* vineyard names are often specified on the label.

In an outstanding vintage, some grapes are allowed to become very ripe and produce *Vendange Tardive* (late-picked) wines. These wines may be produced only from the four selected varieties (Riesling, Muscat, Pinot Gris and Gewurztraminer). If the grapes are exceptionally ripe, often affected by Botrytis or Noble Rot, the wine is known as *Sélection des Grains Nobles* (from individually selected grapes). Both categories are very special wines, always produced in tiny quantities and the finest wines of Alsace.

In addition, an increasing amount of sparkling wine known as *Crémant d'Alsace* is produced in this region. This is made using the traditional, bottle-fermentation method.

Still Alsace wines are bottled in tall green bottles known as *flûtes*. Many Alsace wines are enjoyable while young, and finer examples are capable of ageing and developing for some years. As with all quality white wines, the fragrance is enhanced by not overchilling them.

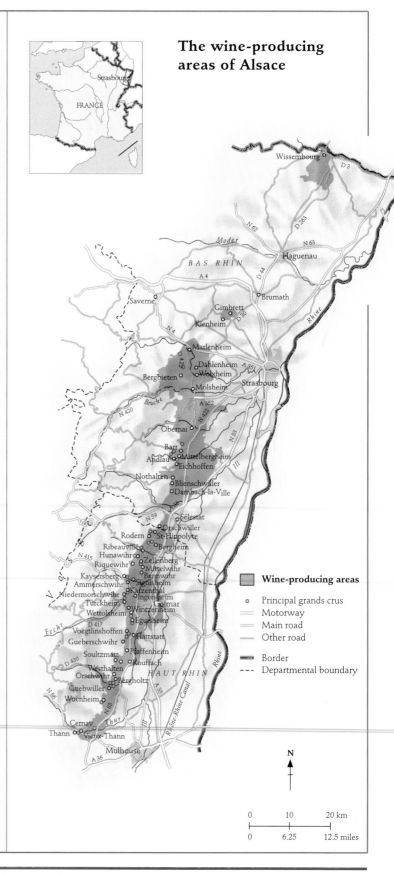

The wine-producing areas of Alsace

Wine-producing areas

○ Principal grands crus
Motorway
Main road
Other road
Border
--- Departmental boundary

N

| 0 | 10 | 20 km |
| 0 | 6.25 | 12.5 miles |

Drain and skin the almonds and pound them thoroughly in a mortar, adding a few drops of iced water to prevent the nuts turning into oil. When the paste is completely smooth, strain the gelatine liquid into the almond paste (reserving the leaves) and stir. Stretch some muslin (cheesecloth) over a bowl and pour the mixture on to the cloth. Twist and squeeze the muslin to obtain 500 ml (17 fl oz, 2 cups) almond milk. Pour the milk into a saucepan. Crush the leaves of gelatine and add to the almond milk, together with 200 g (7 oz, 1 cup) caster (superfine) sugar. Bring slowly to the boil, stirring continuously. Then strain through a fine sieve. Spoon into individual dishes or into a ring mould. Chill until set.

ALMOND PASTE A confectionery preparation consisting of ground sweet almonds mixed with their own weight of icing (confectioner's) sugar and a little glucose syrup. Almond paste was traditionally prepared by adding the ground almonds to a sugar syrup, then crushing the mixture.

Coloured and flavoured, almond paste is sold in slabs or as individual sweets in the form of vegetables, fruits and animals (see *marzipan*). It is also used to fill sweets (candies), chocolates and dried fruits (such as dates and prunes) served as petits fours.

Almond paste is used extensively in pâtisserie, particularly for decorating or covering cakes. Granulated almond paste – in which half the icing sugar is replaced with caster (superfine) sugar, and egg yolk often replaces the glucose syrup – is used for coating cakes and petits fours.

RECIPE

almond paste
Grind 250 g (9 oz, 2 cups) blanched sweet almonds in a blender, in small quantities, as they turn oily if too many are worked together. Cook 500 g (18 oz, 3 cups) caster (superfine) sugar, 50 g (2 oz, 1/3 cup) glucose and 150 ml (1/4 pint, 2/3 cup) water to the 'small ball' stage (see *sugar*). Remove the saucepan from the heat, add the ground almonds and stir briskly with a wooden spoon until the mixture becomes granular. Leave to cool completely, then knead the paste by hand in small quantities until it is soft and easy to work.

ALOXE-CORTON A commune of the Côte de Beaune in eastern France which produces some of the greatest Burgundy wines: both red and white are equally good, which is rare. Its reputation is centred on two *grands crus*, both situated on the hill of Corton, which overlap slightly into two neighbouring communes, Ladoix-Serrigny and Pernand-Vergelesses. The hill of Corton is planted with vineyards on three sides and includes the *grands crus*, Corton for red wines and Corton-Charlemagne for whites. Red wines are made only from the Pinot Noir grape and those from Corton may be described as such or may annex the name of their specific vineyard, such as Bressandes and Renardes. Each vineyard pro-

duces wine with its own particular characteristics; overall, the red wines of Corton are of exceptional quality – dense and tannic when young, maturing to fine wines with excellent aromas and fine palates.

Corton-Charlemagne is the largest white *grand cru* appellation in Burgundy. The wines, made only from Chardonnay grapes, are refined, concentrated and capable of long ageing.

Of a total vineyard area of 265 hectares (655 acres), over half is *grand cru*. The remainder is given the communal appellation Aloxe-Corton and produces notable, but not exceptional, red and white wines.

ALSACE See *page 12*.

ALSACIENNE, À L' This French description is given to dishes garnished with sauerkraut, ham, salted bacon and/or Strasbourg sausages. This garnish goes with roast or braised pork, fried pheasant, braised duck and goose. *A l'alsacienne* is also used to describe *timbales* (pies and terrines containing foie gras), as well as fruit tarts covered with an egg mixture.

RECIPES

fried eggs à l'alsacienne
Fry some eggs in goose fat, then arrange them on a bed of braised sauerkraut, alternating them with half-slices of ham. Surround with a border of demi-glace sauce.

pheasant à l'alsacienne
Truss the pheasant and cook it (unbarded) in butter in a flameproof casserole, turning until it is lightly brown, about 25 minutes. Braise some sauerkraut and bacon rashers (slices) in goose fat and put the sauerkraut in the casserole, placing the pheasant on top of it. Cover and cook in a preheated oven at 190°C (375°F, gas 5) for about another 25 minutes, or until the pheasant is tender. Cut the pheasant into portions. Slice some heated saveloys and cut up the hot bacon. Make a bed of sauerkraut on a hot serving dish, and garnish with the pieces of pheasant, bacon and saveloy.

soft-boiled or poached eggs à l'alsacienne
Cook the eggs. Put a layer of braised sauerkraut on a dish and place the boiled or poached eggs on it, alternating them with large strips of bacon which have been cooked in their own fat. Coat with a demi-glace sauce.

AMANDINE An almond-based fancy pastry, of which there are several French kinds. It may be a tart or individual tartlets made with enriched shortcrust pastry, filled with a mixture of whole eggs, sugar, ground almonds, flour and melted butter, flavoured with rum and sprinkled with flaked (slivered) almonds. After cooking, the top is glazed with apricot jam and decorated with crystallized (candied) whiteheart cherries.

A classic variation is to make a sponge cake with sugar, egg yolks, vanilla, ground almonds, flour, stiffly whisked egg whites and butter. The mixture is poured into a savarin (ring) mould and, after cooking, is iced with white fondant (frosting).

The flavour of an amandine cake may be enhanced with lemon peel or bitter-almond essence.

Tartelettes amandines are small almond cakes, attributed to the pastrycook-poet Ragueneau, whose recipe Edmond Rostand gives in verse in *Cyrano de Bergerac*.

AMANITA A genus of mushrooms including some edible as well as many poisonous, indeed deadly, species; the latter include *A. phalloides* (death cap), *A. verna* and *A. virosa* (destroying angel). The most sought-after edible species is *A. caesarea*, the Italian *oronge* (see Caesar's mushroom). Two other species are regarded as delicacies, both eaten cooked. *Amanita rubescens* is called 'the blusher' because its reddish-brown cap turns purplish-red in contact with the air. *Amanita vaginata* is France's common *grisette*, named for its delicate grey cap, which is ribbed around the edges. Common under beech trees, it is one of the best wild fungi.

AMARANTH Plants of the *Amaranthus* family have a wide variety of food use. One was used to make a red food dye from the purple flower (the name comes from the Greek and means 'unfading'). This was synthesized to make the food dye E123, which was banned everywhere by the late 1970s.

A relative of spinach (and of similar flavour), varieties are eaten in India, Africa (where they may be called 'bush greens') and South-east Asia. There are two sorts of 'Chinese spinach', eaten fresh or salt-pickled. The better, and very early, one has red stems and is known as 'red in snow'.

AMARETTO DI SARANNO An Italian liqueur flavoured with apricot kernels, almonds and aromatic extracts. It may be used to flavour fruit salads and whipped cream.

AMBASSADEUR Also known as ambassadrice. A dish involving very elaborate preparation, typical of classic cuisine on a grand scale. For large joints, ambassadeur or ambassadrice garnish includes artichoke hearts stuffed with duxelles, and duchess potatoes piped into rosettes and browned in the oven. The dish is accompanied by grated horseradish served separately. Ambassadeur soup is made with fresh peas.

RECIPES

ambassadeur soup
To 1.5 litres (2¾ pints, 6½ cups) Saint-Germain* soup, add 3 tablespoons shredded sorrel or a mixture of sorrel and lettuce softened in butter, together with 1½ tablespoons rice cooked in consommé, and finally some sprigs of chervil.

boiled or poached eggs ambassadrice
Bind a mixture of chopped truffles and foie gras with a well reduced demi-glace sauce flavoured with sherry. Fill puff pastry tartlet cases with this mixture and arrange the eggs on top. In the centre place a bunch of asparagus tips. Coat with suprême sauce.

chicken ambassadrice
Use a velouté sauce to bind a mixture of chopped lamb's sweetbreads, truffles and mushrooms; stuff a good-sized chicken with this mixture. Cook the chicken until tender in a flameproof casserole with a purée of vegetables cooked in meat stock. Arrange the fowl on a round dish and surround it with tartlets filled with sautéed chicken livers (formerly cockscombs and kidneys would have been added). Place a thin slice of truffle on each tartlet. Deglaze the casserole with Madeira and veal stock, and coat the fowl with this sauce.

chicken croûtes ambassadrices
Fill some small croûtes with chicken purée. Top each with a thin slice of truffle and 1 teaspoon vegetable mirepoix*.

eggs en cocotte ambassadrice
Butter some ramekin dishes and spread the bottoms with a layer of foie gras purée sprinkled with chopped truffle. Break an egg into each ramekin and cook in a bain marie. Coat with suprême sauce flavoured with sherry and garnish with hot asparagus tips.

suprêmes of chicken ambassadeur
Sauté the suprêmes in butter. Fry some croûtons in butter and cover them with the suprêmes, each garnished with a thin slice of truffle. Surround the croûtons with mushrooms cooked in cream and with buttered asparagus. Coat lightly with suprême sauce.

AMBERGRIS A waxy substance of greyish colour, giving off a strong musky scent, which is secreted in the intestine of the sperm whale and collected from the surface of tropical seas, where it floats. The Chinese were the first to use it as a spice. Throughout the Middle Ages it was used in ragoûts, pies, custards and jams. Richelieu was particularly fond of ambergris pastilles, and hot ambergris chocolate was a very popular drink in the 18th century, supposedly having aphrodisiac and restorative qualities. Today ambergris is almost entirely used in perfumery.

AMBRE A French cake with almond-flavoured crème mousseline and chocolate crème mousseline enriched with caramelized walnuts. The mousselines are arranged alternately on a chocolate sponge and the top is covered with a marbled icing (frosting) decorated with chocolate cones. Square or rectangular, depending on its size, *ambre* ('amber') has become a classic since it was created in 1986 by the French pastry chef Lucien Peltier.

AMBROSIA In Greek mythology, ambrosia was the food of the gods and gave them immortality. Ancient authors are rather vague as to the nature of ambrosia, implying only that it was solid (while nectar, on the other hand, was liquid). This mysterious substance is described by the poet Ibycus as 'nine times sweeter than honey'.

The name ambrosia was also given to an aperitif liqueur with a sweet taste, for which *Larousse ménager* gives the following recipe:

'Macerate for one month in 10 litres (17 pints, 10½ quarts) old eau-de-vie, 80 g (3 oz) coriander, 20 g (¾ oz) cloves and 20 g (¾ oz) aniseed. Decant and filter it, then add 5 litres (8½ pints, 5½ quarts) white wine and finally a syrup made with 5 kg (11 lb) sugar in 6 litres (10 pints, 6½ quarts) water.'

AMERICA See *United States of America.*

AMÉRICAINE, À L' This description is given to a classic French dish of shellfish, particularly lobster, created by Pierre Fraisse, a French chef known as Peters who settled in Paris about 1860 after having worked in America.

The term is also applied to fish garnishes containing thin slices of lobster tail and américaine sauce, as well as to dishes consisting of egg and grilled (broiled) poultry or meat – chicken, steak, kidneys – garnished with tomatoes and bacon.

■ **À l'américaine or à l'armoricaine?** The description *à l'américaine* applied to lobster has given rise to much controversy, and continues to do so, many claiming that *à l'armoricaine* is the only valid name. Armorica is an old name for Brittany and a French regional origin has been claimed for the best French lobster dish. But the region is scarcely associated with tomatoes, essential to the dish. Curnonsky received the following letter from a Monsieur Garrique, a restaurateur, on this subject:

'I think I can tell you the exact name given to this dish by its inventor.

'As you quite rightly say, lobster *à l'américaine* was created in France and, of course, by a Frenchman, Peters, born in Sète and whose real name was Fraisse.

'I knew Peters about 1900, when at about 78 or 80 years of age he was living quietly with his wife in the Rue Germain-Pilon. One evening when he felt in a confiding mood, he talked to me about this famous lobster. On returning to Paris from America where he had been a chef in Chicago, he founded the Peters restaurant; if I remember correctly, this was a little before 1860.

'Now one evening when dinner was long over, eight or ten customers turned up almost at closing time and insisted that Peters serve them dinner, on the pretext that they had only one hour to spare.

'Peters, who was kindness itself, agreed to return to his kitchens, not without wondering anxiously what he was going to be able to serve to them. "While they are eating the soup and the hors-d'oeuvre," he said to himself, "I've got time to prepare a fish dish!" But there was no fish. There were only some live lobsters, reserved for the following morning . . . but there was not enough time to cook them in a court-bouillon.

'It was then that Peters, in a flash of inspiration, threw into a pan some butter, tomatoes, crushed garlic, shallot . . . then some white wine, a little oil and finally a good helping of brandy . . . When it was all boiling, Peters said to himself: "There is only one way to cook the lobster quickly – that is to cut it into pieces and throw them into the sauce!"

'This he did, and the result was marvellous. His enthusiastic customers asked the great restaurateur what this exquisite dish was and what he called it. And Peters, still under the influence of his recent stay in America, said without thinking, "Lobster *à l'américaine!*"

'Peters himself gave me the recipe and it is the one I always use. As far as the history of the creation of this famous dish is concerned, I believe it to be completely authentic, as Peters was the soul of frankness, honesty and goodness.'

RECIPES

boiled or poached eggs à l'américaine
Fry some croûtons and top them with boiled or poached eggs and slices of lobster *à l'américaine*. Cover with the américaine sauce in which the lobster was cooked (not all the sauce produced will be required for this dish).

fried eggs à l'américaine
Fry the eggs and garnish with slices of bacon and grilled (broiled) tomato halves.

scrambled eggs à l'américaine
Add cubes of smoked bacon fried in butter to some beaten eggs. Mix them together and cook. Arrange them in a mound and garnish with slices of grilled (broiled) bacon and small grilled tomato halves.

additional recipe See *lobster*.

AMIRAL, À L' The term used to describe a French garnish for such superior fish dishes (good enough for an admiral) as poached sole, fillets of sole, stuffed turbot or braised salmon. It contains some of the following ingredients: fried oysters and mussels, crayfish tails or whole crayfish, mushroom caps and truffle slices. The dish is coated with Nantua sauce.

RECIPE

consommé à l'amiral
Lightly thicken a fish consommé with arrowroot and garnish with small pike quenelles in crayfish butter, poached oyster halves, julienne of truffles cooked in Madeira and sprigs of chervil.

AMOURETTE French for the delicately flavoured spinal bone marrow of beef, mutton or veal. Amourettes may be prepared and dressed like calve's brains; they can be cut into small pieces and used in fillings for croûtes, timbales, tarts and vol-au-vent or used as an ingredient for salads.

RECIPES

preparation
Clean the amourettes in cold water, remove the membranes, poach for a few minutes in a court-bouillon and allow them to cool.

amourettes au gratin
Butter a gratin dish and cover the base with mushroom duxelles. Arrange the cold cooked amourettes on the mushroom layer and sprinkle with a little lemon juice. Cover with duxelles sauce and scatter with golden breadcrumbs. Pour melted butter over and brown in the oven or under the grill (broiler).

amourette fritters
Marinate the amourettes in a mixture of olive oil and lemon juice seasoned with chopped parsley, salt and pepper for about 30 minutes. Drain, coat with fritter batter and cook them in boiling hot oil until crisp and golden. Drain, then salt the fritters and serve them piping hot on a napkin, garnished with fried parsley. Serve with a well-seasoned tomato sauce.

AMPHICLES A probably fictional chef of ancient Greece, noted for his opposition to very complicated dishes and the excessive use of spices. For him, a hare had to be served rare, roasted on a spit and barely seasoned with fennel. He would cook red mullet in a fig leaf and lark in a vine leaf, among cinders. A defender of natural foods and opposed to the disguising of natural flavours, Amphicles can still serve as an example. He is probably an invention of the Abbé Barthélemy (author, in 1788, of *Voyage du jeune Anacharsis en Grèce au IV siècle de l'ère vulgaire*), included and embellished by Prosper Montagné in his dictionary.

AMPHITRYON A person who entertains guests at his table. According to mythology, Zeus, wishing to seduce the mortal Alcmene, took on the appearance of her husband, Amphitryon, and gave her a son, Heracles. In Molière's comedy inspired by this fable, the servant Sosie, embarrassed at having to serve two masters and deciding finally for the one who guarantees him board and lodging, says: 'The real Amphitryon is the host who provides dinner.'

But to provide dinner is not sufficient; one has to know the art of how to do it. Grimod de La Reynière was one of the first to indicate in his *Manuel des amphitryons* (1808) the rules of correct behaviour at the table. According to him, tact is necessary, as well as generosity, organization, a good chef and the appreciation of good food. More recently, Auguste Michel, in the *Manuel des amphitryons au début du X° siècle*, and Maurice des Ombiaux, in *L'Amphitryon d'aujourd'hui* (1936), have brought these rules into accord with modern tastes. Although the term is hardly used nowadays, one rule, decreed by Brillat-Savarin, remains unchanged: 'To invite someone to be our guest is to undertake responsibility for his happiness all the time that he is under our roof.'

AMPHORA A Greek or Roman two-handled jar (the Greek word means 'carried from both sides') that was used to store oil and wine. Some amphorae (*psykters*) had double walls between which iced water was poured to keep the contents of the jar cool. The *stamnos*, sometimes compared to a cooking pot, was also used for storing wine. It had a fairly narrow mouth with small horizontal handles, and was very popular in the 5th century BC.

Amphorae used for transporting wine were closed with clay corks and sealed with pitch or plaster. A label indicating the vineyard, the year, the capacity of the jar and sometimes its maker's name, was either tied to the jar or engraved on it.

AMPHOUX, MADAME 19th-century French distiller. She owned a distillery in Martinique (Caribbean) and the liqueurs des Îles (made from vanilla, tea, cocoa and coffee) were named after her. These liqueurs were very fashionable at the time of the Consulate and the Empire. Balzac refers to them several times, notably in *La Vieille Fille*: 'Finally, Mademoiselle sacrificed three bottles of the celebrated liqueurs of Madame Amphoux, the most illustrious of overseas distillers, a name dear to lovers of liqueurs'; and, further on: 'Bless my soul, there is nothing but liqueurs of Madame Amphoux, which are only brought out on high days and holidays.'

AMUNATEGUI, FRANCIS French author of gastronomic articles and books (born Santiago, Chile, 1898; died Paris, 1972) who abandoned his career as an engineer in 1947 in order to write. He was responsible for one of the earliest series of articles dedicated to restaurants, which came into their own again after the Occupation. These appeared in the periodical *Aux écoutes*. He published *L'Art desmets* (1959), *Le Plaisir des mets* (1964) and *Gastronomiquement vôtre* (1971). He was a member of the 'Academy of the Psychologists of Taste' and founded the A.A.A.A.A., which extols the virtues of andouillettes. His style blends humour and historical and literary references with an acute observation for everything connected with regional cuisine.

ANCHOVY A small sea fish, maximum length 20 cm (8 in), with a greenish-blue back and silvery sides. The anchovy is very abundant in the Mediterranean, the Black Sea, and the Atlantic and Pacific Oceans. It lives in tightly packed shoals and is fished for the canning industry. When sold fresh – which is rare – it may be fried, while the usual Italian and Spanish method is to marinate the split-open raw fish.

Anchovies are sold layered with salt, as whole fish in oil, in jars or cans as fillets (or rolled round a caper) in oil, and in piquant sauce. These must be stored in the refrigerator once opened. Salted anchovies may be sold whole, and need filleting, skinning and washing under water. In Asia, salted, then sun-dried, they are the principal fermented fish product. Anchovies also constitute such traditional seasonings as ready-cooked anchovy butter, bottled English anchovy sauce and the spread gentleman's relish.

In ancient times, anchovies were used to make a condiment (*garum*). There has always been a European trade in anchovies, which were transported in special small casks called *barrots*. They are a characteristic feature of the cuisines of southern Europe. In Italy they are used in sauces like that of *bagna cauda*, in pasta sauces like the tomato, garlic and caper *alla putanesca*, and for *pizza* toppings in the south. 'Jansson's Temptation', an extremely popular Swedish dish, is a gratin of anchovies and potatoes. See also *kilka, sprat*.

RECIPES

anchovy fillets à la portugaise
Cut desalted anchovy fillets into thin strips. Place a layer of tomato sauce cooked in oil in the base of an hors d'oeuvre dish and arrange the anchovy fillets on top in a crisscross pattern. Garnish with capers, chopped parsley and lemon slices with the skin and pith removed. Moisten with a little olive oil before serving.

anchovy fillets à la silésienne
Poach some fresh soft herring roe in stock and then either rub through a fine sieve or purée in a blender. For 300 g (11 oz) roe, add 2–3 chopped shallots and a few sprigs of parsley (chopped). Place the mixture in an hors d'oeuvre dish and arrange a lattice of pickled anchovy fillets over the top. Make a salad with diced potatoes, dessert (eating) apples and beetroot (beet) moistened with a well-seasoned vinaigrette, and arrange it around the purée. Sprinkle with chopped parsley.

anchovy fillets à la suédoise
Cut desalted anchovy fillets into thin strips. Arrange them on a layer of diced dessert (eating) apples and beetroot (beet) seasoned with vinaigrette. Garnish with parsley sprigs and with the yolks and whites of hard-boiled (hard-cooked) eggs, chopped separately. Moisten with more vinaigrette.

anchovy fillets with hard-boiled eggs
Cut desalted anchovy fillets into thin strips and arrange them in an hors d'oeuvre dish. Garnish with small black Nice olives, hard-boiled (hard-cooked) egg whites and yolks (chopped separately), capers and chopped parsley. Moisten with a little olive oil.

anchovy purée
Add 2 tablespoons desalted anchovies to 150 ml (¼ pint, ⅔ cup) well-reduced béchamel sauce and mix in a blender. Then rub the mixture through a sieve. Stir in some heated butter just before serving. Anchovy purée may be used in fritters, vol-au-vent and rissoles.

cold anchovy croustades
Flatten some well-wiped anchovy fillets previously desalted in milk. Spread them with anchovy butter containing chopped tarragon and roll them up into paupiettes. Put a layer of puréed tuna fish with mayonnaise in the base of some very small puff pastry cases and then place an anchovy paupiette on top of each. Pipe a rosette of anchovy butter on each paupiette and sprinkle with fresh chopped parsley.

cold anchovy sauce
Thoroughly desalt 6–8 anchovy fillets by soaking them in milk. Drain, wipe and purée them in a blender with 1 tablespoon capers, 100 ml (4 fl oz, ½ cup) oil, the juice of half a lemon and salt and pepper. Serve as a dip with an assortment of raw vegetables – small artichokes, cauliflower florets, small sticks of carrot and seeded cucumber, thin slices of green or red sweet (bell) peppers, small quarters of fennel or raw mushrooms – or with fish poached in a court-bouillon, either hot or cold.

fried anchovies
Take fresh anchovies, remove the heads and gut (clean) by pressing with the thumb. Wipe, but do not wash the fish as their flesh is very fragile. Dip them in milk, then drain, and roll each one in flour. Plunge them, a few at a time, into very hot fat, then drain, dust with fine salt and arrange them in a pyramid on a napkin. Garnish with fried parsley and quarters of lemon.

fried eggs with anchovies
Fry some slices of very stale round sandwich bread in butter. Cover each of these croûtons with a fried egg and 2 desalted anchovy fillets arranged in the form of a cross. The fillets may be moistened with noisette butter.

freezing anchovies
After preparing and cleaning, arrange fresh anchovies in layers separated by plastic sheets and place inside large plastic bags. Then seal each bag, place in a freezer box and put into a freezer. When the fish are frozen, remove the bags from the boxes and place in a second bag to prevent the strong smell of the fish from escaping. Then label the bags and replace in the freezer for storage.

hard-boiled eggs stuffed with anchovies
Reduce some desalted anchovy fillets to a purée in a mortar or blender. Halve some hard-boiled

(hard-cooked) eggs and remove the yolks. Mix the yolks with the anchovy purée and a little mayonnaise; replace in the egg cases. Dip some anchovy fillets in oil and roll each around a stoned (pitted) black olive. Place one on each egg case.

hot anchovy sauce

Add 2 tablespoons anchovy butter to 200 ml (7 fl oz, ¾ cup) béchamel sauce. Check the seasoning. This sauce can be served with any fish poached in a court-bouillon.

hot anchovy toast

Fry some stale breadcrumbs in butter. Toast some sliced sandwich bread and cut it into rectangles. Garnish the toast with desalted anchovy fillets, sprinkle with the fried breadcrumbs and brown in the oven or under the grill (broiler) for a few minutes.

marinated anchovies

Prepare 500 g (18 oz) fresh anchovies as in the recipe for fried anchovies. Lay them on a plate, dust with salt and leave for 2 hours. Pat the anchovies dry, then fry in very hot oil just long enough to stiffen them. Drain and place them in a dish. Prepare a marinade as follows. Add 5–6 tablespoons fresh oil to the oil in which the anchovies were cooked. Fry a medium onion and a carrot (both finely sliced) with 3 unpeeled garlic cloves and add 100 ml (4 fl oz, ½ cup) vinegar and an equal quantity of water. Season with salt and add a sprig of thyme, half a bay leaf, a few parsley stalks and a few crushed peppercorns. Boil for 10 minutes and pour the hot marinade over the anchovies. Leave to marinate for 24 hours. Serve on an hors d'oeuvre dish garnished with slices of lemon.

soft-boiled or poached eggs with anchovies

Take some small warm bread or pastry cases and place either a soft-boiled or a poached egg in each. Coat with anchovy sauce. Place a desalted anchovy fillet rolled into a ring on each egg.

other recipes See *barquette, brioche (filled savoury brioches), butter (flavoured butters), canapé, dartois, fritter, mayonnaise, olive, omelettes (cooked with their flavouring), pannequet, purée, tournedos.*

ANCHOYADE
Also known as *anchoïade*. A Provençal dish consisting of a purée of anchovies mixed with crushed garlic and olive oil, and sometimes a few drops of vinegar. It is usually served with raw vegetables and may also be spread on slices of bread and heated in the oven. At Draguignan, *anchoyade à la dracenoise* is an anchovy purée mixed with onions and chopped hard-boiled (hard-cooked) eggs. The mixture is spread in a thick layer on slices of home-baked bread, moistened generously with olive oil and browned in a hot oven.

ANCIENNE, À L'
The description *à l'ancienne* is given to certain fricassées (chicken or lamb) or white stews (turkey, veal or lamb) in which the garnish includes small sliced onions and button mushrooms (see *bonne femme*). This term, widely used in bourgeois cookery, may also be applied to braised dishes (sweetbreads, beef or fowl) and to pastry cases (pie shells) baked blind and filled with ragoûts of cockscombs and kidneys or quenelles of truffles and mushrooms.

See *béatilles, feuilleton, talmouse.*

RECIPES

scrambled eggs à l'ancienne
Toss some diced mushrooms and truffles in butter. Add them to some scrambled eggs and place the mixture in a flan case (pie shell) which has been baked blind. Garnish with chicken kidneys in a sherry-flavoured velouté sauce with cream. Surround with fried cockscombs and sherry-flavoured suprême sauce.

soft-boiled or poached eggs à l'ancienne
Arrange the eggs on a bed of rice that has been cooked in meat stock. Coat them with velouté sauce and place between each egg 1 tablespoon julienne of truffles bound with a highly reduced Madeira sauce.

ANCIENT GREECE
The Homeric heroes apparently feasted on shoulder of mutton or roasted chine of pork, flavoured with oregano and cumin, and on olives, figs, walnuts, goat's cheese and cakes made with flour and honey. Vegetables, which were difficult to grow in the dry soil, are rarely mentioned. Nevertheless, they formed the basic diet of the common people, mainly in the form of cabbage and lentil purées. The ancient Greeks, in a country surrounded by sea teeming with fish, were very fond of seafood and fish. Salted tuna, eels, red mullet, sole, turbot, octopus, sea bream, porgy, torpedo fish and conger eels are often mentioned in the texts. Game was also abundant: apart from pheasants, partridges and wood pigeons, the ancient Greeks also hunted jackdaws, owls, flamingos and even seagulls. Ground game included roebucks, wild boars, hares, foxes, white-breasted martens, moles and even cats! The ancient Greeks originally drank hydromel, but from 2000 BC onwards this was superseded by heavy strong wines, always drunk with water (sometimes even sea water).

■ **The earliest cooks** In Homer's time, cooks as such did not exist. Female slaves ground the corn and prepared the food. According to the *Iliad* and the *Odyssey*, the host himself, however exalted, prepared and cooked the meals with the help of friends when he received distinguished guests. Later, the baker (*mageiros*) cooked as well as baked for his masters. In time he became *archimageiros* (chef de cuisine) and was given assistants. Great houses had a hierarchy of slaves, under a steward, the *eleatros*.

Each slave had definite duties. The *opsonomos* or *agorastes* (from *agora* or market place) bought the food, while the *opsartytes* looked after the fires, did rough jobs and prepared food for the household slaves. A woman, the *demiourga*, made sweetmeats and other delicacies. Women had free access to the kitchen. Other slaves prepared meals or served at table: the *trapezopoios* laid the table and washed the dishes; the *oinophoros* had charge of the wine; the *oinochoikos*, a young slave, filled the wine cups of the guests.

In the 4th century BC, Athenian cooks were often slaves. They played an important role in the life of the city and ruled as masters over all the other slaves in the household. A special law permitted the cook who invented a new dish the privilege of making it and selling it to the public.

Many Greek cooks became famous. Cadmos was cook to the king of Sidon in Phoenicia, and, according to legend, introduced writing into Greece. As a result of the burning of the library in Alexandria, only a few fragments and the authors' names remain from Greek literature of gastronomy.

■ **Hippocrates and dietetics** Even though there were few refined gourmets, the ancient Greeks, especially the Spartans and the Athenians, were discriminating in their eating habits, unlike the Boeotians, the Thessalians and the Macedonians. Epicurus recommended 'simple dishes that satisfy us as much as sumptuous feasts'. In *The Republic*, Plato defines, through Socrates, the diet of the model citizen: bread, olives, cheese, vegetables and fruit. Both Hippocrates (5th century BC) and later Galen (2nd century AD) studied the effects of food both on the sick and those in good health.

In *De la gastronomie française*, R. Dumay acknowledges that the ancient Greeks made four major contributions to cookery. First, they established the market (*agora*), where the master of the house himself often went to choose the food for his household. Secondly, they knew how to appreciate both their cooks and culinary art in general – in the town of Sybaris, in Magna Graecia, famous for its refined way of life, chefs were awarded patents to protect their recipes. Thirdly, they cultivated a simplicity in their cooking, using few basic ingredients, preferring roasts and grills to dishes with sauces and including herbs to bring out the authentic flavour of the food. Finally, they left us a legacy of various recipes that have been handed down through the generations – black pudding (blood sausage), fried scampi (jumbo shrimp), turbot with herbs, thrushes with honey and grilled (broiled) frogs' legs.

ANCIENT ROME The ancient Romans were pioneers of gastronomy, adding to their own culinary habits those of the Greeks and the peoples of Asia Minor and eagerly adopting new methods and ingredients. The traditional picture of orgies where great quantities of rare foods were served, drowned in spiced sauces and cooked in the most lavish fashion, is false. If the works of Petronius, Juvenal and Martial are full of detailed accounts of sumptuous banquets, it is because these were the exception: flamingos' tongues, camels' heels, dormice stuffed with chestnuts, wild boar stuffed with thrushes and other extravagant fancies were far from being everyday fare.

True, Maecenas was the first to mention mule flesh, which epicureans considered less tasty than wild ass, and Elagabalus feasted on elephant trunk and roast camel. To amuse the Emperor Aurelian, the actor Faron is said to have swallowed a ewe, a sucking pig and a wild boar, with a hundred small loaves and as many bottles of wine. Petronius, in the *Satyricon*, paints an evocative portrait of Trimalcion. Nevertheless, true Latin cooking had its origins in a humble and frugal tradition. Stockrearing and agriculture were carried out in the Tiber valley, but it was due to the trade in salt, a commodity produced by evaporation at the river mouth, that commercial links were established with the Greek and Etruscan colonies.

From the earliest times, the staple food of the Romans was *pulmentum*, a porridge of millet, barley or chick pea flour, sometimes diluted with milk. As the art of bread-making developed, the first bakers appeared in Rome. Other basic foods were: ewe's-milk cheese, boiled mutton, cabbage, cardoons and broad (fava) beans. Fruit was important in the Roman diet: apples were no longer a scarce commodity, as they had been in ancient Greece, but imported apricots from Armenia and peaches from Persia were very expensive. Lucullus is credited with introducing the cherry tree; figs grew in abundance and dates were imported from Africa. Melon growing developed in the region round Cantalupo (which gave its name to the cantaloupe melon).

It was after the defeat of Antiochus III the Great (189 BC) that the Romans, advancing into Asia Minor, gradually discovered the refinement of the Greek courts in the Hellenized East. The best-known fact about the General Lucullus is that he adopted their lifestyle. According to Livy: 'The army returning from Asia brought foreign luxury to Rome. It became a lengthy and costly business to prepare a meal. Cooks, who used to be regarded as slaves, began to demand high wages. That which had been toil became art.'

In order to meet the tastes and needs of her citizens, Rome began to develop a more complex system of food production and distribution, operating chiefly through large warehouses and markets. The most famous of these was that of Trajan, where Romans could buy corn from Egypt, olive oil from Spain, spices from Asia, hams from Gaul, numerous varieties of fish, which were often farmed (Moray eels, sea bass, monkfish, plaice and turbot), and various types of shellfish, including whelks, sea urchins and especially oysters, which Sergius Orata believed were the first to be reared in oyster beds. It was the Romans who invented the process of force-feeding geese with figs, to enlarge their livers.

Wealthy Romans ate large quantities of meat, preferring pork to mutton. They enjoyed, for example, pork stuffed with oysters and small birds, roasted on one side, then spread with a paste of oats, wine and oil and poached in boiling water on the other side. Apicius, author of many recipes, mentioned, among other things, fresh ham painted with honey and cooked in a pastry case with figs and bay leaves. Poultry was much esteemed: capons, Numidian fowl (guinea fowl), domestic pigeons, wild duck (of which only the brain and breast were eaten) and roast goose. In Marguerite Yourcenar's book *Memoirs of Hadrian*, the emperor reflects: 'It was in Rome, during the long official repasts, that I began to think of the relatively recent origins of our riches and of this nation of thrifty farmers and frugal soldiers, who formerly ate garlic and barley, now suddenly enabled by our conquests to revel in the cooking of Asia, devouring this complicated food with the greed of starving peasants.'

Several modern Italian recipes go back to the days of ancient Rome, such as gnocchi and ricotta cheese tart. Another very common cake made with cheese was *libum* (or *savillun*), flavoured with honey and poppy seeds.

Roman cooking was characterized by the use of quite highly spiced sauces, including *garum* based on fermented fish. Particularly popular was a sweet-and-sour condiment for which Apicius gave the recipe: pepper, mint, pine nuts, raisins, grated carrot, honey, vinegar, oil, wine and musk. As sugar was not available, the Romans sweetened their food with either honey or grape syrup. They made a variety of different cheeses, most of them from ewe's milk. Great wine lovers, they preferred to drink their wines young and diluted with water. Several types of wine were produced, which were sold quite cheaply: straw wine (*passum*); honeyed wine (*mulsum*); vinegar diluted with water (*posca*), which was a thirst-quenching drink favoured by soldiers on campaign; imitation wines (flavoured with wormwood, roses and violets); and fruit wines.

The most highly prized wines, however, were the *grands crus* from the Campania region: Capua, Pompeii, Naples, Vesuvius and Cumae. The most famous of these, the red and white Falernian wines, were aged over a long period. These high-quality wines were stored in amphorae and were usually filtered at table before serving, to improve their clarity.

Wine was a common offering to the gods and its use in religious ceremonies gave rise to great wine festivals. A law of Romulus forbade women to drink wine, though apparently this prohibition applied only to fermented wines.

ANDALOUSE, À L' A French garnish usually served with large joints of meat, particularly beef and saddle of lamb. Inspired by Andalucía in southern Spain, it includes sweet (bell) peppers (stuffed or sautéed), tomatoes in some form, rice (pilaf or risotto with peppers), fried aubergine (eggplant) slices and sometimes chorizo. It may also be served either in a consommé or with sole fillets.

RECIPES

andalouse salad
Boil some rice in salted water, drain it well and mix with a well-seasoned vinaigrette containing chopped onion, parsley and a touch of crushed garlic. Place the rice in a mound in a salad bowl surrounded by thin strips of peeled green and red sweet (bell) peppers and tomato quarters, arranged so that the colours alternate around the dish. Sprinkle with chopped chervil.

andalouse sauce
Reduce 300 ml (½ pint, 1¼ cups) velouté sauce by one-third and add 2 tablespoons tomato purée (paste). Mix and reduce further. Add a crushed garlic clove and salt and pepper. Wash and chop a small bunch of parsley. Blanch a green sweet (bell) pepper and half a red (bell) pepper in boiling water, then peel and cool. Remove the seeds and dice the flesh (2 tablespoons altogether). Add the diced peppers to the reduced velouté and the chopped parsley.

beefsteaks à l'andalouse
Soften 50 g (2 oz) chopped onion and a chopped garlic clove in butter. Add salt and pepper. Mix with 400 g (14 oz, 2 cups) minced (ground) beef and form into 4 rounds. Coat these with flour and fry in oil. Sauté 4 large tomato halves in oil and place a cooked hamburger on each. Arrange them on a plate with a rice pilaf in the centre. Deglaze the cooking juices of the steaks with 2–3 tablespoons sherry. Reduce, add some butter, and pour the sauce over the steaks.

fried eggs à l'andalouse
Grill (broil) some small tomatoes, sweat some green and red (bell) peppers and fry some onion slices and eggs in oil. Arrange the eggs around the edge of a round plate and place the garnishes in the centre. The tomatoes may be replaced with slices of aubergine (eggplant).

additional recipe See *squid*.

ANDOUILLE A type of French sausage made from the stomach and intestines of the pig to which may be added other parts of the animal (neck, breast, head or heart), the whole enclosed in a black skin. Rabelais, in *Pantagruel*, names andouille as one of the favourite dishes of his contemporaries: it features in 'the war of the *Andoyles* against *Quaresmeprenant*'. Various sausages, bearing the name of the region where their recipes originated, are now called andouilles, but there are only two authentic varieties – those of Vire and those of Guémené. Andouille is cut into thin slices and eaten cold in hors d'oeuvres.

Guémené andouille, which is protected by a trademark, has the appearance of concentric circles when sliced, as the intestines are placed one inside another, according to their size, during preparation. The andouille is then tied up, dried, smoked and, lastly, either cooked in a bouillon or steamed.

The 'genuine Vire andouille' (with guaranteed method and area of production) includes both intestines and stomach, cleaned, washed, cut up and salted, then enclosed in a skin. The andouille is smoked over beech wood for two months, which allows the natural black colour of the coating to develop. It is then tied and cooked, either in water or in an aromatized court-bouillon. It measures 25–30 cm (10–12 in) in length and 4–6 cm (1½–2½ in) in diameter.

The 'Vire andouille' (without guarantee) is made all over France by similar methods, using the same ingredients as for the genuine Vire andouille with the addition of the neck and the breast, which make it more fatty. The locally made *andouilles de pays* also contain pig's heart and pig's head without the skin removed. The andouille of Val-d'Ajol and that of Aire-sur-la-Lys should also be mentioned. The andouille of Jargeau, made from shoulder and breast without any intestines, is not sold ready-cooked. Andouilles made from pork rind are a speciality of south-western France.

ANDOUILLETTE

A type of sausage made from pork intestines (*chaudins*), often with the addition of pork stomach and calf's mesentery, precooked in stock or milk and packed into a skin. Andouillettes, which are sold in 10–15 cm (4–6 in) lengths and are sometimes coated with breadcrumbs, aspic jelly or lard, are eaten either grilled (broiled) or fried. Several regions are known for their production of andouillettes. The Troyes andouillette, made solely from pork, has a greasy consistency and is prepared from the intestines and belly of pork, cut into fairly wide strips. The andouillette from Cambrai is usually made from veal only. The Lyonnais andouillette is made from calf's mesentery with, sometimes, a bit of pork belly, while the Provençal andouillette consists of a mixture of thin slices of pork intestines and neck, plus the rind. The drier andouillette from Rouen is made from pig's bowels without the belly and calf's mesentery. The andouillette is traditionally served with mustard and garnished with fried potatoes, red beans, lentils and a purée of celery, apples or red cabbage. In Strasbourg it is served on a bed of sauerkraut.

The Association Amicale des Amateurs d'Authentiques Andouillettes (A.A.A.A.A.), a gastronomic society founded by F. Amunategui, upholds the tradition, and Charles Monselet dedicated a sonnet to the andouillette.

RECIPES

andouillettes à la lyonnaise
Lightly prick the andouillettes. Soften some onion slices in butter without browning. Fry the andouil-lettes in a pan with a little lard, and add the softened onion 5 minutes before the end of the cooking time. Just before serving, pour some vinegar into the pan (1 tablespoon per 2 portions of andouillette), heat and serve the andouillettes very hot with the juices from the pan. Sprinkle with chopped parsley.

andouillettes à la tourangelle
Lightly slit 6 andouillettes, pour some Armagnac over them and let them steep for 24 hours. Slice 500 g (18 oz, 5–6 cups) button mushrooms and sprinkle them with lemon juice. Butter a cooking dish, place the mushrooms in it, add salt and pepper and arrange the andouillettes on top. Pour a glass of dry Vouvray wine over the food and cook in a preheated oven at 180°C (350°F, gas 4) for 40 minutes, turning the andouillettes several times and basting them. Add a little more wine or boiling water if needed.

grilled andouillette
Prick the andouillette and grill (broil) it slowly, preferably over charcoal, so that it warms right through.

ANGELICA

An aromatic umbelliferous plant growing in the cold north from Scandinavia to central Russia, which was introduced into France by the Vikings and cultivated by the monks. Its young green stalks are candied in sugar and used in cakes, gingerbreads, puddings and soufflés. It is a speciality of the town of Niort, and Austin de Croze has described lyrically what he considers to be the best way to enjoy it: 'Have a dozen choice brioches, kept hot, a fruit dish filled with sticks of candied angelica, a bottle of angelica liqueur, a carafe of iced water and a box of Egyptian cigarettes. Light a cigarette, take a draught of iced water, crunch a piece of Niort angelica with a mouthful of very hot brioche, inhale, draw in and distil a few drops of angelica liqueur in the mouth, then start again. Then you only need the room to be sprayed with a light fresh perfume, such as verbena or citronella, to know what blissful enjoyment a discreet sybaritism can give.'

Liqueur manufacturers also use the crushed stems and roots of angelica in the production of Melissa cordial, Chartreuse, Vespétro and gin.

RECIPES

angelica liqueur
Put 1 kg (2¼ lb) young angelica stalks, cut into small pieces, and 1 litre (1¾ pints, 4⅓ cups) brandy in a bottling jar. Macerate for a month. See that the jar is hermetically sealed. Expose it to the sun whenever possible.

Add 575–800 g (1¼–1¾ lb) lump sugar dissolved in a very little water. Press the whole through a silk or fine muslin (cheesecloth) sieve. Leave to stand for a few hours, then pour the liqueur through filter paper. Bottle, cork and seal.

candied angelica

Cut some young angelica stems into 15–20 cm (6–8 in) lengths. Soak them for 3–4 hours in cold water, then plunge into boiling water until the pulp softens. Drain, cool and peel carefully to remove all the stringy parts. Macerate the stems for 24 hours in a syrup of 1 cup sugar to 1 cup water. Drain. Boil the syrup to 102°C (215°F) and pour it over the pieces of angelica. Repeat this operation once a day for three days. On the fourth day cook the syrup until it reaches the 'pearl' stage, 105°C (221°F). Add the angelica and boil for a few moments. Remove the pan from the heat, cool and drain the angelica in a sieve. When the angelica pieces are dry, lay them out on a slab, dust with caster (superfine) sugar and dry in a slow oven. Store in hermetically sealed containers.

ANGELOT The original name of several cheeses made in Normandy, including Pont-l'Évêque, Livarot and of course Neufchâtel. Guillaume de Lorris mentioned it in *Le Roman de la Rose (The Romance of the Rose)*, 1230-35. The name refers to the region of Auge, where the cheeses are made.

ANGEL SHARK *ange de mer* A fish of the shark family (*Squatinidae*) that resembles a skate with its wing-shaped pectoral fins. It is cooked in the same way as skate. There are several species, which are widespread in temperate European coastal regions and in tropical seas. The average size of the angel shark varies from 90 cm (3 ft) to 1.2 m (4 ft), but some specimens may reach 2 m (6½ ft) and weigh more than 60 kg (132 lb). Its skin is wrinkled, its back greenish-brown flecked with grey and its underside a creamy-white colour. The flesh is quite tasty, but is not considered to be as palatable as that of the skate.

ANGLAISE, À L' This description, given to vegetables, meat and fish prepared in a variety of straightforward ways, reflects the French view of English cooking. Various dishes from the British gastronomic repertory are named *à l'anglaise*, including sauces, desserts, pies and egg dishes. *Crème anglaise* is a basic preparation of classic cuisine: see *custard*.

For example, vegetables *à l'anglaise* are cooked in water and served plain with chopped parsley, knobs of butter, melted butter or a herb sauce. Meat and poultry *à l'anglaise* are poached, boiled or cooked in a white stock. According to the dish, vegetables are cooked at the same time or separately, either boiled or steamed.

Fish or pieces of meat which are coated in breadcrumbs before being sautéed or fried are also described as *à l'anglaise*. Fish grilled *à l'anglaise* (cut into steaks if they are large or slit if they are small) are brushed with oil or melted butter (and coated with flour if they have a delicate flesh); they must be cooked over a low heat. They are served with melted butter or maître d'hotel butter and, if desired, with steamed or boiled potatoes or with other boiled vegetables, such as spinach or the white part of leeks.

RECIPES

eggs au plat à l'anglaise
Grill a rasher (slice) of bacon and put it on a small buttered plate. Break 2 eggs on top and cook in the oven until set.

panure anglaise
A coating for various foods (croquettes, vegetables, fish fillets and escalopes) that are to be fried or sautéed *à l'anglaise*. It is made of eggs beaten with a few drops of oil, salt and ground pepper. A little water can be added if necessary. It is applied after coating with flour and before dipping in breadcrumbs.

sauce à l'anglaise
(from Carême's recipe) Chop 4 hard-boiled (hardcooked) egg yolks very finely and mix them in a saucepan with some fairly thick velouté of the kind used as a sauce for an entrée. Then add a dash of pepper, some grated nutmeg, the juice of a lemon and a little anchovy butter.

ANGOSTURA BITTERS A brownish-red bitters made with various herbs (its exact formula is a secret). It has tonic and fever-reducing properties as it includes quinine and it was created at Angostura, Venezuela (renamed Ciudad Bolívar in 1846) by a surgeon of Bolívar's army to combat the effects of the tropical climate. Angostura is now made in Trinidad and is used mainly for flavouring cocktails and 'pink gins', the cocktail associated with the British Royal Navy. It may also be used successfully in salads and desserts.

ANIMELLES Animal testicles used for meat, especially those of the ram, the lamb, and bull calves. *Animelles* were formerly very popular in the East, in Mediterranean countries, and in France under Louis XV. They are still popular in Italy and in Spain as 'white kidneys' (fried *criadillas*). They are either prepared in the same way as kidneys or served with a vinaigrette.

RECIPES

preparation
Plunge the animelles into boiling water for about 2 minutes, cool under cold water and immediately skin them. Soak them in cold water for about 10 hours to remove impurities, then drain and press between 2 plates.

animelles à la crème
Cut the animelles into thin slices, season with salt and pepper and partly cook them in butter for 6–7 minutes. Then moisten with a few tablespoons cream sauce and slowly finish cooking. Add a little butter at the last moment and check the seasoning. Blanched or sautéed sliced mushrooms may also be added.

Anjou

The cuisine of this region of the Loire Valley, which is well balanced and subtly blended, includes recipes dating from the Middle Ages and the Renaissance, particularly for river fish and sweet dishes.

The Loire fish are prepared in traditional ways, such as pike in white butter sauce (a recipe also claimed by Nantes), stuffed shad with sorrel, grilled salmon, perch with prunes, *bouilleture* and other fish stews, braised fish and eel pie.

■ **High-quality meat, poultry and charcuterie** The meat of the region is excellent, particularly Le Mans beef, and tasty specialities are made from veal, such as rump of veal *à l'angevine* served with onion purée, matelote of veal with red wine and stuffed breast of veal. Lamb's pluck is cooked in white wine. The tender plump poultry is used to make excellent fricassees, such as Taillevent's *cominée de gélines*.

The art of charcuterie is especially well developed with such dishes as *rillettes* and *rillons*, as well as white puddings and *gogues*. Sausages and andouillettes are also renowned.

■ **Fruit and vegetables** The region is also noted for its vegetables: green cabbages (*piochons*) and cauliflowers are used to make fricassées. *Chouées* (boiled cabbage sprinkled with melted butter), stuffed artichokes, and *nouzillards* (chestnuts cooked in milk) are popular vegetable dishes.

The orchards of the region provide excellent fruit: Belle-Angevine pears, often cooked in red wine; dessert and cider apples; plums and mirabelles, used in pies; and strawberries, served with cream.

■ **Cheese** Cheeses are often served with salad and walnut oil; specialities include the small local goat's-milk cheeses, as well as *chouze* from Saumur and *entrammes* (a forerunner of Port-Salut). Crémets make a delicate dessert.

A tributary of the Sarthe, the Loire river winds its way peacefully through Anjou. Its banks are lined with châteaux, such as this one at Durtal.

■ **Sweet specialities** These include *bottereaux*, *bijane* (cold bread and wine soup) or soup *à la pie*, *millière* (maize and rice porridge), and *fouée* (a pancake made from dough covered with fresh butter), all of which date back to much earlier times, as do the *fouaces* appreciated by Rabelais and *guillaret* (a sweet pastry). Biscuits (cookies) are very varied and include *sablés*, *croquets*, the aniseed biscuits of Angers, almond and hazelnut balls, and macaroons.

WINE Wines have been made in the region of Angers, capital of Anjou, for centuries, and as Henry II of England was the Count of Anjou, they certainly would have been familiar to the English court in medieval times. They are mentioned in an edict of King John and, among the French kings, Philip Augustus, Louis XI and François I are known to have enjoyed them. The River Loire provided a means of exporting them, as well as transporting them to other regions within France. The Anjou climate is influenced by the proximity of the Atlantic; it is usually mild in winter, with hot summers and long warm autumns – almost ideal for wine-making, although there can be dangers from spring frosts and sudden hailstorms. Soils are very varied, including shale, sandstone, clay, chalk, sand and gravel. The vines tend to be planted on the slopes alongside the river and its

tributaries, the vineyards ideally sited so that they face south and southwest.

A huge range of wines are made throughout the region: dry to medium-sweet and very sweet still whites, reds, rosés and sparkling wines. There are numerous AOCs for the various areas within the region. The main grape for white wines is Chenin Blanc (here often called Pineau de la Loire), but increasing amounts of Sauvignon Blanc and Chardonnay are also used. The red wines come from the Cabernet Franc and some of the rosés are also made from this, although there are other red varieties planted, including the Gamay and Groslot. Most export markets feature the rosés, which vary from dry to sweetish, and the straightforward white wines. The reds have been helped in popularity by the creation of the appellation *Anjou-Villages* which is used for the red wines of 46 villages made only from Cabernet Franc and Cabernet Sauvignon grapes. These have much better ageing potential than straightforward Anjou Rouge. Sweet wines are made in the Anjou region under the appellation *Anjou-Coteaux de la Loire*, but most botrytis-affected sweet wines have their own appellations such as *Bonnezeaux* and *Coteaux du Loire*.

The sparkling wines, many of them made around Saumur, are made as white and sometimes rosé wines using the traditional method.

fried animelles

Skin 3 fresh animelles and cut each into 8 similar pieces. Put them into a terrine dish with salt, pepper, 2 tablespoons each tarragon vinegar and olive oil, a little thyme, half a bay leaf, a sliced onion and a few sprigs of parsley. Cover the dish. Drain them after an hour and replace in the terrine with all the ingredients and the juice of half a lemon. Just before serving, drain the animelles on a cloth and press lightly. Coat them with flour and fry them until lightly browned. Arrange in a pyramid on a napkin and garnish with fried parsley.

ANISE An aromatic umbelliferous plant originating in the Near East, known to the ancient Egyptians and Romans, and taken to India. The seeds (aniseed) are used particularly in Germany and Central Europe for flavouring bread such as *Knackebrot*, biscuits (cookies), and especially for gingerbread. Aniseed is also used in confectionery – sugar-coated for comfits and Flavigny dragées. In southern Europe the oil anethole flavours many spirits.

The seeds are stronger and less subtle than those of dill, but are used with fish in Tuscany, while the chopped leaves may be used to season pickled vegetables, salads and fish soups in the south of France.

RECIPES

aniseed biscuits

Whisk together 500 g (18 oz, 2¼ cups) caster (superfine) sugar and 12 eggs in a copper basin, as for an ordinary sponge cake.

When pale and light-textured, add 500 g (18 oz, 4½ cups) plain (all-purpose) flour, 200 g (7 oz, ¾ cup) cornflour (cornstarch) and 50 g (2 oz, ¼ cup) aniseed. Mix well. Drop tablespoons of the mixture on to a wetted baking sheet. Place in a warm place to dry. When the biscuits (cookies) begin to rise slightly, bake in a preheated oven at 160°C (325°F, gas 3) for about 15 minutes.

aniseed liqueur

Put 25 g (1 oz) crushed aniseeds, ¼ teaspoon cinnamon and 1½ tablespoons coriander (cilantro) into 1 litre (1¾ pints, 4⅓ cups) spirits. Infuse for a month. Add 500 g (18 oz, 2¼ cups) sugar dissolved in a little water. Filter and bottle.

ANISETTE The flavour of the many liqueurs known as anisette or anise varies according to which seeds are used – aniseed or star anise. These liqueurs are very popular as digestives. Well known in France are the anisettes of Bordeaux (especially that of Marie Brizard) while *pacharán* is Spain's most popular liqueur, flavoured also with sloes and drunk 'on the rocks' Anise has long been the favourite flavouring of Mediterranean aperitifs – pastis, ouzo and arak. They are drunk either diluted with water or with water as an accompaniment.

ANJOU See *page 25.*

ANNA The name of a French potato dish created by Adolphe Dugléré to accompany roast meat and poultry. It was dedicated to Anna Deslions, a woman of fashion at the time of the Second Empire. The dish is cooked in a special round two-handled casserole with an interlocking lid. The potatoes are sliced and covered during cooking. When the potatoes are cut into strips rather than rounds, the dish is called Annette potatoes.

RECIPE

pommes Anna

Peel 1 kg (2¼ lb) potatoes and cut into thin even round slices. Wash, wipe and season with salt and pepper. Slightly brown 75 g (3 oz, 6 tablespoons) butter in a special casserole (or in a sauté pan) and arrange the potatoes in circular layers, making sure that they are evenly coated with butter, then compress them into a cake with a wooden spatula. Cover and cook in a hot oven for 25 minutes. Quickly turn the whole cake over on to a flat dish and slide it back into the casserole to brown the other side.

ANNATTO *rocou* A food colouring extracted from the red wax coating around the seeds of the annatto tree of Central America. In the west it is used to give an orange, yellow or red colour to items of charcuterie, various cheeses (Edam, Mimolette, Cheshire and Cheddar), dried, salted, and smoked fish (notoriously haddock), and also to sweets and butter. Annatto is widely used in Latin American cooking. The seeds are fried in oil which then imparts a distinct flavour as well as colour to food. Spanish traders took annatto to China, where it is now used to colour roast pork.

ANTELOPE A ruminant mammal belonging to the cattle family, found chiefly in Africa and Asia. There are more than a hundred species of antelope, varying in size from that of a lamb to that of a horse. Their habits are similar to those of the European deer, but their meat is firmer and sometimes has a very strong flavour. According to the culinary traditions of the aboriginal populations who eat antelope, the meat may be roasted, braised or boiled, although it is sometimes necessary to marinate it first or ripen it in the sun. The highly regarded meat of the gazelle (a small antelope) is prepared in the same way as venison.

ANTIBOISE, À L' This description is given to various Provençal dishes that are specialities of Antibes. They include eggs cooked in the oven with browned *nonnats* (tiny Mediterranean fish), crushed garlic and chopped parsley; a gratin of scrambled eggs in layers alternating with sautéed courgettes (zucchini) and a fondue of tomatoes in oil; oven-grilled tomatoes garnished with anchovy fillets, pieces of tuna and breadcrumbs crushed with garlic; and cold stuffed tomatoes.

ANTILLAISE, À L' This French description referring to the Antilles in the Caribbean, is applied to numerous ways of preparing fish, shellfish and poultry, generally served accompanied either with rice coated with a thick sauce of small vegetables and tomato or with pineapple or banana. Desserts *à l'antillaise* are made by combining exotic fruits with rum or vanilla. All dishes *à la créole* are very similar.

ANTILLES CUCUMBER A variety of cucumber that is common in the West Indies; they are oval in shape and prickly like a horse chestnut. Known as *anguries* in French, they are eaten in salads or pickled in vinegar, like gherkins.

ANTIPASTO An Italian term for cold hors d'oeuvres. The name is derived from the Italian word *pasto* (meal), with the Latin prefix *ante* (before). An antipasto might consist of Parma ham with fresh figs, or a Piedmontese cheese fondue (raw vegetables accompanied by condiments and a melted cheese sauce), but is more usually a colourful assortment of starters served either as cocktail snacks with the aperitif or at the beginning of a meal instead of pasta. Typical antipasti, which may be served with warm, crusty bread or *grissini* (bread sticks), include marinated vegetables and fish, seafood with lemon, olives, cooked pork products, mushroom salad or artichoke hearts arranged in hors d'oeuvre dishes.

ANVERSOISE, À L' The French description is given to a garnish, in the style of Antwerp (Belgium), composed essentially of young hop shoots cooked slowly in butter or cream. Primarily a garnish for eggs (soft-boiled, poached or *sur le plat*), it may sometimes be used with potatoes (boiled or browned) or with roast contre-filet and veal paupiettes.

Hop shoots may also be served in tartlets or on artichoke hearts.

RECIPES

lamb cutlets with hop shoots
Sauté some lamb cutlets in butter. Arrange them in a ring on a round dish, alternating with triangular croûtons which have been fried in butter. Garnish the centre of the dish with hop shoots in a cream sauce. Deglaze the cooking juices in the sauté pan with a little dry white wine and pour over the cutlets.

veal sweetbreads with hop shoots
Braise the sweetbreads in white stock. Strain and reduce the cooking juices to make a sauce. Coat the sweetbreads with the sauce and serve surrounded with hop shoots in cream sauce and small potatoes browned in butter.

AOC See *appellation d'origine*.

APERITIF Since time immemorial, certain plants have been known to have the property of restoring, or 'opening' (from Latin *aperire* 'to open'), the appetite. Aperitive drinks were made from such plants, but these were more therapeutic than gastronomic and were not drunk before meals. The Romans had a liking for wine with honey, and in the Middle Ages people believed in the benefits of wines mixed with herbs or spices. Then hippocras (an old English spiced wine), vermouths, bitters and sweet wines came into being. The word aperitif has been in use as a noun only since the late 19th century, and it was not until the 20th century that the habit of taking an aperitif before a meal became a generally accepted custom. Aperitifs include drinks based on wine (such as vermouth) and certain spirits and the less sweet liqueurs (such as anise and bitters).

The custom of having an aperitif follows fashions, and indeed rituals, which vary according to the country, the surroundings and the circumstances. It is better to avoid very strong alcoholic drinks that may spoil the palate. *Larousse ménager* (1926) recommended: 'A bowl of bouillon with the fat skimmed off taken half an hour before a meal is an excellent apéritif. It stimulates the salivary and stomach secretions and promotes the production of pepsin in the gastric juice.' Some people would prefer a glass of champagne.

APICIUS The name of three Romans famous for their taste for good living. The first, a contemporary of Sulla (2nd–1st century BC), is known only for his gluttony. The third Apicius, who lived in the 2nd century AD, deserves mention for having discovered a way of keeping oysters fresh, even at the end of a long journey. The most famous is Marcus Gavius Apicius, born about AD 25, who is reputed to have compiled a recipe book, *De re coquinaria libri decem* ('Cuisine in Ten Books'), which was used as a reference work for several centuries. Regarded by some as a refined connoisseur, by others as a libertine, he was known for his extravagance and expensive tastes. He is credited with inventing a process for force-feeding sows with dried figs in order to fatten their livers, as well as devising recipes for flamingo or nightingale tongues, camel's heels, sow's udder and a large number of cakes and sauces. Athenaeus relates that Apicius chartered a ship to go and check if the Libyan squillas (scampi or jumbo shrimp) were as large as they were reputed to be. Disappointed, he did not even set foot on land. He spent all his fortune on sumptuous banquets until the day when, calculating how much money he had left, he decided to poison himself rather than turn to a more modest way of living.

APLATIR The French term for beating and thus flattening a small piece of meat (entrecôte, escalope) or fish with the flat part of a meat mallet. As this process breaks down muscle fibres, the flesh becomes more tender and easier to cook.

APOTHEKA A storeroom in which the ancient Greeks kept wine. (The Roman equivalent is a *fumarium.*) The wine was placed near the chimney shafts and developed a very good flavour. As the effects of the heat made it more concentrated until it acquired the consistency of honey, it had to be diluted before serving.

APPAREIL The French term for the mixture of different ingredients necessary to prepare a dish for cooking. The word *masse* is also used. Appareils are particularly common in cake and pastry-making.

APPELLATION D'ORIGINE This, according to French law, is the 'name of a country, region or locality used to designate a product which originates there, the quality and characteristics of which are due to the geographical situation, including natural and human factors'. Its use, which is strictly regulated, concerns wines, spirits, certain cheeses and such local products as Le Puy lentils and Bresse poultry. It is a system that has been adopted for wine and foods by the EC itself and many nations within it.

Present legislation in France concerning *appellations d'origine* has been inherited from laws that were in force up to the French Revolution (1792). At the beginning of the 20th century the quality of French wines had deteriorated as the vineyards, decimated by phylloxera in the previous century, had been replanted with inferior varieties. Series of laws passed in 1905 and 1909 were designed to protect the consumer. In 1919, under pressure from the vine-growers' lobby, further legislation ensured the protection of both the producer, who agreed to abide by precise regulations, and the consumer. The relevant law dates from 6 May 1919 and was modified by that of 6 July 1966.

To maintain the quality of French wines, an Order in Council of 1935 created an organization that united the wine professionals with the representatives of other interested bodies: this was the Institut National des Appellations d'Origine (INAO). It controls the production of wine at all stages. The organization has legal powers and has codified quality wines to determine their precise origin.

Four categories of *appellation d'origine* exist in France.
• AOC *(Appellation d'Origine Contrôlée)*. This is reserved for the greatest wines. AOC lays down strict rules concerning not only the place of production, but also the varieties of vines, the yield per hectare, and the cultivation and vinification methods. Today there are more than 250 AOCs, constituting the aristocracy of French viticulture.
• VDQS *(vins délimités de qualité supérieure)* A regional designation which effectively acts as a testing ground for smaller wine regions, most of which are eventually promoted to full AC status.
• VINS DE PAYS Country wines.
• VINS DE TABLE Basic French wine.

APPENZELL A Swiss cheese with a golden-brown rind made from unpasteurized cow's milk (45% fat content). This compressed cooked cheese has holes and is very firm without being hard or brittle. It must be full-flavoured and tangy, but never pungent. Originating from the canton of Appenzell, the cheese is manufactured in the form of a round weighing 6–8 kg (13–18 lb). It is of good quality from summer to winter. Appenzell is eaten at the end of a meal and can replace Gruyère cheese in cooking. It is used in the preparation of the Swiss speciality *chäshappen* – spirals of pastry (made with melted cheese, milk, flour, yeast and eggs) piped through a piping (pastry) bag into a pan and fried. They are drained and served very hot with a salad.

APPERT, NICOLAS French inventor and father of the canning industry (born Châlons-sur-Marne, 1749; died Massy, 1841). He learned the art of cooking from his father, who was an hotelier. He worked at first in the service of the Duke of Deux-Ponts and was *officier de bouche* to the Princess of Forbach. In 1780 he established himself in business as a confectioner in the Rue des Lombards in Paris. The Directory government offered a prize of 12,000 francs for the discovery of a process to preserve the food destined for the Army. Appert perfected a sterilization method which was named after him – *appertisation*. In 1804 he built a factory at Massy (on land where peas and beans had been cultivated) and started up the production of bottled preserved foods. In 1810 the government officially recognized his discovery and awarded him the prize. In the same year, Appert published *L'Art de conserver pendant plusieurs années toutes les substances animales et végétales*, which generously made his process available to all. Moreover, his work was republished in 1811 and 1813 under the title *Livre de tous les ménages*. The fall of the Empire ruined him, but in 1822 (by which time others had become rich on his discovery) the state recognized his invention by granting him a small income. In the premises which were then allowed him, he pursued his experiments on the clarification of wines, the purification of bone gelatine and preservation in cans, but he subsequently died in poverty.

APPETITE Psychologists define under the term 'natural appetite' the tendencies which instinctively cause us to satisfy the needs of the body.

In physiology appetite is defined as something rather different from hunger. Hunger in reality is nothing more than the need to eat, whereas appetite is the lure of pleasure experienced while eating.

The sensation of hunger, which usually develops at regular mealtimes, sometimes disappears if it is not satisfied at the usual hour. The appetite is stimulated by the sight and smell of food; bitter substances frequently awaken lost appetite by releasing digestive secretions.

In certain psychiatric conditions, appetite can degenerate into a craving for offensive and nonedible substances. The opposite of appetite is anorexia, which means distaste for food.

In France spring onions (scallions), chives and the small onions used for seasoning are known generally as *appétits*, as they all stimulate the appetite.

APPLE The fruit of the apple tree, the most widely cultivated fruit tree in the world, which originated in Asia Minor and was growing wild in Europe by prehistoric times. Known throughout the ancient world, the apple was cultivated early in many varieties and features in many ancient recipes. In his *Traité du sidre* (1588) Julien Le Paulmier lists several dozen varieties. Olivier de Serres refers to the *pomme appie* (today known as *pomme d'api*: small, red and sweet), named after Claudius Appius, who brought it to Rome from the Peloponnese; he also mentions the Court-Pendu, the Reinette, the Rambure (from Rambures in the Somme region), the Grillot, the Rougelet and the Curetin.

Several different types of apple are of food use. They can be grouped as apples for cider, crab apples (close to wild apples and used for gelling) and dessert apples. They are grown in temperate climates from the Asturias in Spain, through the Ukraine, to China (where production equals that of the US); and from Tasmania (once called Apple Island), to South Africa and South America. Some 15,000 varieties are known, almost half of them American, with about 2,000 each in Britain and China. In the past, orchard art consisted in cultivating different species to produce a continuing supply of fresh apples throughout the autumn and winter. Now differing seasons round the world, and cold storage with a whiff of carbon dioxide, ensure a year-round supply of a few reliable types. The American Delicious apple, in its varieties, accounts for half the apples in commerce. Nevertheless, the apple remains a totem fruit in many countries, with powerful regional movements to preserve the loved, old varieties.

The apple is the most popular fruit in the US, Britian, Germany and France. France is known for its exports of Golden Delicious, but it continues to grow many traditional varieties, such as Reine des Reinettes, Grise du Mans, Belle de Boskoop and rarer ones like the scented Calville Blanche d'Hivers (described as the most delicious of all, and dating to the 15th century in Normandy).

'American as apple pie' expresses the US dedication to the first fruit to be planted on the continent. Carried westward after Independence by the legendary Johnny Appleseed (John Chapman; died 1845), apples are turned into desserts like apple grunt, cobbler and pandowdy. Golden Delicious, first raised in West Virginia, has become the leading apple of warmer countries, but there are thousands of local varieties, and loved old ones, like Corland (1898), Rome Beauty (1848) and Newton Pippin (1759).

Britain grows a wide diversity of seasonal fruit and claims some of the finest flavours. Favourites are the aromatic, crisp Cox's Orange Pippin (1825), with a

long heritage from pippins; the densely sweet Worcester Pearmain, going back to the 13th century pearmains, and the brown-skinned Egremont Russet, praised by Edward Bunyard in *The Anatomy of Dessert* (1929) as one of 'the richest late autumn fruits'. An English speciality is the 'cooking' apple, typically the late-summer Bramley Seedling that disintegrates to a fluff (in contrast to dessert apples, which hold a shape when cooked).

Particular apples are associated with different countries. Notable among them is Granny Smith, found fruiting in a Sydney backyard in the 1860s by Mrs Ann Smith, and an Australian export by the 1930s; Canada's juicy white-fleshed purplish McIntosh; pink-flushed Gravenstein (possibly German) with savoury, juicy flesh, and important in northern areas like Scandinavia, Canada and Russia; and the greenish Japanese honey-flavoured Crispin (renamed from Mutsu), much used in pies.

Apples are best as dessert fruit from October to April. They should be firm, without blemishes or wrinkles, and red- and yellow-skinned varieties should not be too green. Picked when ripe, apples can be stored in a ventilated room (stalk down, away from damp, heat and draughts) or in cold store. They can also be sliced into thin rings and dried, while cooked apple freezes well.

The apple can be preserved in the form of jellies (or jam); in syrup, as apple paste or the American apple butter; and as apple sugar. English specialities are apple cheese and apple chutney. The high pectin in apple seeds and peel are helpful in jelling other foods, while the juice obtained from crushing fresh apples helps to make jellies from watery fruits, because it does not alter their flavour. Apple juice is a popular drink, special varieties of apple are used for cider, while apple brandies, American apple jack and, notably, Calvados are produced by distilling.

Stewed apple can be flavoured with cinnamon, vanilla, cloves or lemon juice, and is excellent with fresh cream. Desserts are legion and include fritters, turnovers, charlottes, puddings, compotes and mousses. Each country has its favourites; well-known are the Normandy apple tart with its wheel of slices, the British top-crusted pie (sometimes accompanied by cheese) and the Austrian apple-and-raisin strudel.

In savoury dishes, the apple is traditionally associated with black pudding (blood sausage), grilled (broiled) chitterlings and roast pork (especially as apple sauce), but is also used with poultry (roast chicken, goose, duck and turkey) and with grilled herring or mackerel instead of gooseberries (as an unsweetened compote or in quarters fried in butter) and with red cabbage or braised chestnuts. The French joke has it that they are *pommes en l'air* (apples in the air) as opposed to *pommes de terre* (potatoes, literally earth apples). Apple goes well with dishes cooked in cider. It is also used for salads, especially with celery, lamb's lettuce (corn salad) walnuts, raisins and beetroot (beet) together with a mustard vinaigrette or a rémoulade sauce.

RECIPES

apple charlotte with brown sugar

Peel, core and quarter 4 Belle de Boskoop or Granny Smith apples. Remove the crusts from 10 slices of white bread and fry in 65 g (2½ oz, ¼ cup) butter. Drain and use to line the bottom and the sides of a charlotte mould. Melt about 75 g (3 oz, ⅓ cup) butter in a frying pan, add 200 g (7 oz, 1¼ cups) soft brown sugar, then the apple quarters, and cook for 10 minutes, stirring from time to time. Flame with 1½ tablespoons warmed Calvados. Heap this mixture in the lined mould and bake in a preheated oven at 200°C (400°F, gas 6) for 30 minutes. Cool under a press, then turn out and serve with custard cream.

apple conserve

marmelade de pommes Peel and core some apples, cut into quarters and weigh. For 500 g (18 oz) apples, allow 300 g (11 oz, 1⅓ cups) sugar. Put the apples and sugar in a preserving pan with 2 tablespoons water. Cook gently until the apples crush under a spoon. Rub them through a strainer over a bowl. Put the purée back into the pan, bring to the boil, stirring continuously, and cook until the purée reaches a temperature of 106°C (223°F). Pot in the usual way.

apple crown à la normande

Peel and core some dessert apples, and poach in a vanilla-flavoured syrup. Leave to cool in the syrup, then drain. Prepare an egg custard (see *custard*) flavoured with Calvados, and cook in a plain ring mould in a bain marie. Leave to cool, then turn out on to a serving dish. Arrange the drained apple halves in the centre in a dome. Decorate with very thick Chantilly cream using a piping (pastry) bag with a fluted nozzle. Serve with an apricot sauce flavoured with Calvados.

apple crumble

Into a food processor put 150 g (5 oz, 1¼ cups) plain (all-purpose) flour, add 150 g (5 oz, ⅔ cup) butter cut into pieces, and 150 g (5 oz, ⅔ cup) caster (superfine) sugar. Process until the mixture looks like breadcrumbs. Peel and core 1.5 kg (3¼ lb) apples. Cut into quarters, arrange in an ovenproof dish and cover with the crumble mixture. Cook for 35 minutes in a preheated oven at 200°C (400°F, gas 6). Serve with custard or thick crème fraîche.

apple flan grimaldi

Peel and core 4 dessert (eating) apples and cut into quarters. Cook in a vanilla-flavoured syrup. Make a pastry dough with 250 g (9 oz, 2¼ cups) plain (all-purpose) flour, 125 g (4½ oz, ½ cup) butter, 1 egg yolk, a pinch of salt and 2 tablespoons water. Roll into a ball and leave in a cool place for 1 hour. Roll it out, line a 22 cm (9 in) flan ring, and bake blind.

Prepare some rice in milk (see *rice*) using 150 g (5 oz, ¾ cup) round-grain rice. When it is cold, mix in 100 g (4 oz, ½ cup) chopped crystallized (candied) fruit, 100 g (4 oz, ½ cup) chopped candied orange peel, a small liqueur glass of Curaçao and 50 g (2 oz, ¼ cup) butter. Fill the flan case with this mixture, level it off, then arrange the drained apple quarters on top. Sprinkle with crushed macaroons and caster (superfine) sugar and glaze in a preheated oven at 240°C (475°F, gas 9).

apple gratiné

Make 1 litre (1¾ pints, 4⅓ cups) syrup per 1 kg (2¼ lb) apples, using 500 g (18 oz, 2¼ cups) sugar per 1 litre (1¾ pints, 4⅓ cups) water. Peel some firm dessert (eating) apples, cut them in half and poach gently in the syrup, making sure that they do not disintegrate. Drain and leave to cool. Prepare an apple conserve (see recipe above) and use it to line a buttered ovenproof dish, then arrange the apple halves on top. Mix some fine breadcrumbs with half as much ground almonds. Scatter liberally over the apples, sprinkle with melted butter and brown in a preheated oven at 220°C (425°F, gas 7).

The syrup in which the apples have been cooked can be strained and used to cook apples or other fruit.

apple jelly

Wash 3 kg (6½ lb) apples (Granny Smiths or Cox's), cut into quarters or eighths without peeling or coring, and sprinkle lemon juice over the cut surfaces. Place in a preserving pan with 3 litres (5 pints, 13 cups) water. Bring quickly to the boil, then cook for about 30 minutes (the apples must disintegrate). Place a strainer over a large container and pour the contents of the pan into it. Allow the juice to drain away on its own, without pressing, so as not to cloud it. Measure the juice obtained and then pour it back into the pan, adding the same weight of granulated sugar and the juice of 2–3 lemons. Bring quickly to the boil, then boil uncovered, reducing the heat slightly when the syrup begins to froth. Continue cooking until setting point is reached; the temperature should then be 105°C (220°F). Pot and seal in the usual way.

apples flamed with calvados

pommes flambées au calvados Peel some apples, core them and arrange in a buttered ovenproof dish. Sprinkle with sugar and melted butter and cook in a preheated oven at 220°C (425°F, gas 7) until just tender. Arrange the apples in a silver timbale or flameproof dish and heat it. Sprinkle with warmed Calvados and set alight.

apple soufflés ♦

Cut 8 large dessert apples in half, core them and then scoop out half the pulp without piercing the skin. Cook the pulp for 5 minutes with 2 tablespoons water, without stirring, in a covered saucepan. Then add 300 g (11 oz, 1⅓ cups) caster (superfine) sugar and continue cooking, stirring to obtain a very smooth purée. Sprinkle the inside of

A SELECTION OF APPLES

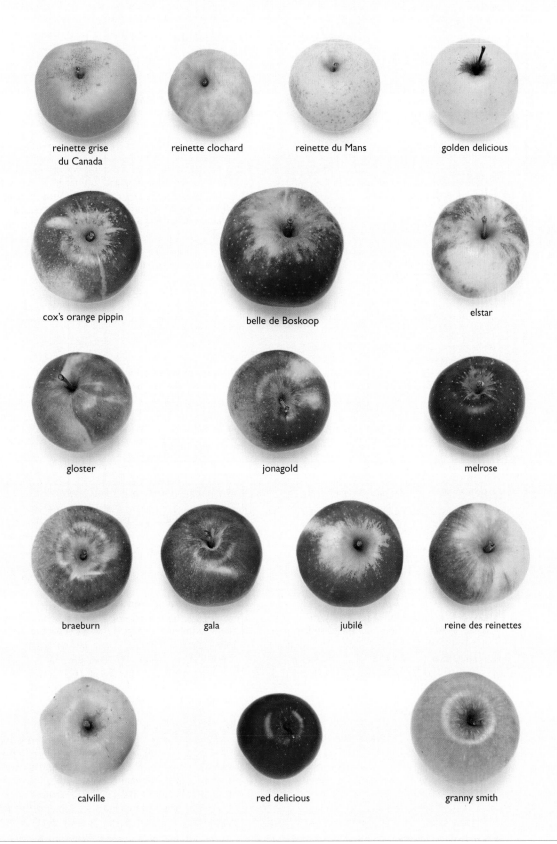

reinette grise
du Canada

reinette clochard

reinette du Mans

golden delicious

cox's orange pippin

belle de Boskoop

elstar

gloster

jonagold

melrose

braeburn

gala

jubilé

reine des reinettes

calville

red delicious

granny smith

Apple varieties

variety	size	skin	flesh
Belle de Boskoop	large; irregular and asymmetrical	rough and matt, yellowish-green	firm and sharp
Braeburn	medium	yellow well streaked with red	firm and crisp, juicy, acidic and slightly sweet
Calville	large	lemon yellow and shiny	very fine, tender, sweet, juicy, slightly acid
Cox's Orange Pippin	small and round	yellowish-green tinged with red	crisp, juicy, aromatic, sweet, some acidity
Egremont Russet	medium	matt, reddish-brown	tender, very sweet, slightly acid
Elstar	medium to large	golden yellow well streaked with red to orange	juicy, slightly sweet and acidic
Gala	small to medium	smooth, red-streaked skin can be quite thick	sweet, tender with slight acidity
Gloster	large	dark red over yellow-green	sweet, juicy and delicately flavoured, crunchy
Golden Delicious	medium	pale green or yellow, depending on degree of ripeness	yellowish-white, sweet, juicy and soft, little flavour
Granny Smith	medium	bright green and waxy	firm and very juicy, acid, crisp
Jonagold	large to very large	red streaked over yellow-green	crisp, juicy with a sweet and acidic flavour
Jubilé	large	bright red, slightly tinged with yellow, fine skin	crisp and juicy
Laxton's Superb	medium	green tinged with red	firm, crisp, sweet, juicy, some acidity
Melrose	large	thick skinned, dark red over yellow-green	sweet, acidic and refreshing
Red Delicious	medium to large	dark red	sweet or very sweet, sometimes with a hint of acidity
Reine des Reinettes	medium to large	golden yellow, streaked with red	yellow, firm and fine, crisp, juicy and sweet
Reinette Clochard	small to medium	yellow skin, tinged with green	delicate flavour
Reinette du Mans	small to medium	yellow	very sweet
Reinette Grise du Canada	medium to very large	thick, brown-grey skin	slightly grainy, with a sweet, slightly acidic flavour
Starking Delicious	medium to large; elongated and thick-skinned	red-brown	yellowish, extremely mellow, fine and juicy
Worcester Pearmain	medium	clear red	white and crisp, sweet and juicy

Apple soufflés, see page 30.

the fruit halves with 100 ml (4 fl oz, ½ cup) brandy and add 100 ml (4 fl oz, ½ cup) brandy to the apple purée. Stiffly whisk 5 egg whites and fold them into the apple purée. Arrange the apple halves in a well-buttered ovenproof dish, use a spoon or piping bag to fill them with apple purée and sprinkle with 50 g (2 oz, ⅓ cup) icing (confectioner's) sugar. Cook in a preheated oven at 230°C (450°F, gas 8) for 10–12 minutes until browned. Serve immediately. The pommes soufflés may be served on a caramel sauce, made by adding single (light) cream to caramel, or a caramel dessert sauce based on a custard, flavoured with light caramel. Diced red, yellow and green apple make an attractive decoration.

apples with honey and salted butter

Peel, halve and core 8 dessert (eating) apples. Pour 250 g (9 oz, ¾ cup) liquid acacia honey into a flameproof baking dish, spreading it evenly. Place this dish over a brisk heat until the honey has browned. Remove from the heat and arrange the apple halves in the dish with their curved sides underneath and a small knob of salted butter in each. Cook in a preheated oven at 240°C (475°F, gas 9) for 10 minutes. Serve immediately.

baked apples

pommes bonne femme Make a light circular incision round the middle of some firm cooking apples. Core them and then place them in a large buttered ovenproof dish. Fill the hollow in each apple with butter mixed with caster (superfine) sugar. Pour a few tablespoons of water into the dish. Cook in a preheated oven at 220°C (425°F, gas 7) until the apples are just tender, about 30 minutes. Serve the apples in the dish in which they were cooked.

buttered apples

Core and peel some apples and place them for 2 minutes in boiling water with some lemon juice added to it (or squeeze the lemon juice over the apples). Drain, arrange in a buttered ovenproof dish, sprinkle with caster (superfine) sugar and moisten with a few drops of water. Cover and cook in a preheated oven at 220°C (425°F, gas 7) until tender. Place each apple on a round slice of bread fried in butter. Add a few tablespoons of sugar or golden (corn) syrup and some butter to the cooking juices and pour over the apples.

le jeu de pommes

Make a fine pastry by combining in a processor 200 g (7 oz, 1¾ cups) plain (all-purpose) flour, 150 g (5 oz, ⅔ cup) rather firm butter, a pinch of salt, 1 teaspoon sugar and a little olive oil. Incorporate 100 ml (4 fl oz, ½ cup) water and work together briefly (the particles of butter should still be visible). Remove the dough and roll it out finely; cut out 16 circles about 12 cm (5 in) in diameter using a pastry (cookie) cutter. Place them on non-stick baking sheets, cover them with very thin slices of apple, brush with 50 g (2 oz, ¼ cup) melted but-

ter and sprinkle lightly with caster (superfine) sugar. Bake in a preheated oven at 220°C (425°F, gas 7) for 15 minutes.

Turn each tartlet over on the baking sheet using a spatula and dust the reverse side with icing (confectioner's) sugar. Put the tartlets under the grill (broiler). As it caramelizes, the sugar forms a glossy crackly film. Leave to cool for 15 minutes. Take 4 dessert plates and place 4 tartlets on top of each other on each plate (apples upwards). Just before serving, cover each *jeu de pommes* with 1 tablespoon warmed acacia honey and sprinkle with a little Calvados and a few drops of lemon juice. This dessert may be accompanied by a lemon sorbet.

other recipes See *charlotte, compote, crêpe, fritter, fruit paste, kirsch, pudding, sauce, tart, turnover.*

APPLE-CORER A small kitchen gadget consisting of a tubular steel gouge attached to a handle, used for taking the cores out of apples. Apples are cored before being baked in the oven or sliced into rings to be made into fritters. In France an apple-corer was formerly known as a *colonne*.

APPLE SUGAR *sucre de pomme* A confectionery speciality of the city of Rouen, where it was created towards the middle of the 16th century.

Apple sugar was formerly prepared by mixing one part of concentrated juice of cooked dessert apples to three parts of sugar syrup cooked to the hard crack stage (see *sugar*). This mixture was used to form little sticks, tablets or pastilles, which were coated with a layer of sugar. This recipe has been improved by adding a little glucose initially, then adding some natural apple essence and a little lemon juice to obtain a perfectly transparent apple sugar, which keeps well without softening.

It is sold in traditional 10 cm (4 in) sticks in a grey, gold and white wrapper, decorated with the famous clock tower of Rouen; this design was created in 1865.

APPRÊT The French word to describe all the culinary processes involved in the preparation of a dish.

APRICOT A round yellow-orange fruit with velvety skin, having tender, sweet and fragrant flesh and very little juice. The smooth stone (pit), which comes away easily, contains an edible kernel (*almond* in French) which is used to flavour apricot jam. The name is derived from the Latin *praecoquus*, meaning precocious or early-ripening.

The apricot tree grew wild in China several thousand years ago. It was later grown in India, then in Persia and Armenia, from where it gets its Latin name, *Prunus armeniaca*. It was probably introduced into Europe after the conquest by Alexander the Great. The ancient Greeks called the apricot the 'golden egg of the Sun'. Introduced to Sicily and Spain by the Moors, it was not cultivated in France until the 17th century. Apricots are now cultivated in the warmer temperate regions of the world, in China, parts of the former USSR, the Mediterranean, North America, South Africa and Australasia. Popular brands in Britain are Moorpark, and Blenheim in California. Also noteworthy is the Kecskemé apricot of Hungary; intensely flavoured and fragrant, this ugly pock-marked fruit is used to make brandy.

■ **Uses** The apricot should be bought properly ripe, since once picked it stops ripening and might either be hard and bitter or become soft and floury. Apricots usually do not travel well and may therefore be canned (plain or in syrup, whole or in halves). They are also made into fruit juices, used to flavour brandies and to make alcoholic spirit like the Hungarian *barack pálinka*.

The apricot is delicious eaten fresh. Its skin may be removed, if required, by dipping it in boiling water. The apricot is one of the fruits most widely used in sweet dishes (hot and cold desserts, cakes and pastries, fruit salads and ices) and in preserves (candied fruits, jams and conserves).

■ **Dried apricots** Dried apricots are produced in Iran, California and Australia: fairly large, pale and a little dull-looking. Turkish dried apricots are renowned and are dark orange with a muscatel flavour. Hunza in Kashmir is known for fine marble-sized apricots. These need 24-hour soaking (but no cooking). Dried apricots have a much higher calorific value than the fresh fruit and are sold ready-to-eat. Others must be rehydrated by immersing them in tepid water for two hours. They are used in much the same way as fresh apricots in desserts, particularly stewed in winter. Amardine, dried and pressed apricots, is a ready source of sugar to break the Ramadan fast in the Middle East and makes some famous sweetmeats. Dried apricots are prized for the intense flavour they bring to desserts. They are also good in some meat ragoûts.

Apricots can be dried at home, by splitting them to remove the stones (pits), leaving them in halves if they are large, and either placing them in a very cool oven or leaving them in the sun on a wooden rack until they become dark red. After drying, the apricots should be flattened with the fingers to give them a regular shape.

RECIPES

apricot marmalade
Slowly cook 1 kg (2¼ lb) stoned (pitted) apricots in 100 ml (4 fl oz, ½ cup) water for 15–20 minutes until soft, stirring frequently to prevent sticking. Purée the fruit in a blender, then press it through a sieve to make a smooth thick purée. Return the purée to the pan, add 575 g (1¼ lb, 2½ cups) sugar and cook slowly, stirring until the sugar has dissolved, then increase the heat and continue cooking. To determine whether the marmalade is cooked, drop a little on to a plate. If it remains in a blob without spreading out, the marmalade is cooked. Pot as for jam.

A SELECTION OF APRICOTS

bergeron

jumbocot

rouge du Roussillon

orangé de Provence

apricots à l'ancienne

Poach large apricot halves in a vanilla-flavoured syrup. Drain them and arrange on a layer of sponge cake which has been soaked with rum and coated with sweet apple purée. Sprinkle the apricots with chopped almonds and sugar, spoon over a little melted butter and bake in a preheated oven at 220°C (425°F, gas 7) until brown on top. Serve with a sauce made of apricot jam diluted with a little hot water, sieved and then flavoured with rum.

apricots Colbert

Poach apricot halves in a sugar syrup until barely tender, then pat dry. Fill each half with thick cold rice pudding; sandwich the halves together and coat with egg and breadcrumbs. Deep-fry the coated apricots, drain and serve with an apricot sauce flavoured with kirsch.

apricots Condé

Poach apricot halves in a sugar syrup and arrange around a thick ring of cold rice pudding. Decorate with glacé (candied) cherries and angelica. Insert split blanched almonds between the apricots. Heat the apricot ring in a preheated oven at 160°C (325°F, gas 3) and serve with a kirsch-flavoured apricot sauce.

apricots flambé

Allow 4–6 poached and drained apricot halves per person; while still hot place in individual dishes. Spoon 2–3 tablespoons of the hot poaching syrup over each portion, warm a scant tablespoon kirsch for each portion and set alight.

apricots preserved au naturel

Wipe the apricots and cut in half to remove the stones (pits), then replace the halves together and pack tightly into preserving jars, without adding water or sugar. Screw on the lids (loosen bands a quarter turn), then immerse the jars in a large saucepan of lukewarm water. Bring the water up to 90°C (194°F) and maintain at this temperature for 15–20 minutes. Remove the jars, seal, dry and store when cold.

apricots preserved in syrup

Choose slightly under-ripe fruit. Prick them and put in a basin. Cover with a very heavy syrup. Soak in the syrup for 3 hours. While the fruit is soaking prepare a 26° syrup (see *sugar*) with lump sugar. Clarify the syrup with egg white – one white for 2 litres (3½ pints, 9 cups) syrup. Strain the syrup through a straining bag or cloth. Leave to cool. Drain the apricots. Put them into wide-mouthed jars and cover with the boiling clarified syrup so that it reaches at least 3 cm (1¼ in) above the level of the fruit. Fix on the tops and screw bands tightly, then give the bands one half-turn to loosen them. Place a wire rack in the bottom of a large preserving pan and arrange the bottles on it so they do not touch. Fill the pan with cold water, making sure it covers the jars. Boil rapidly for a full 10 minutes. Remove the bottles, wipe and seal them. Keep in a cool place, away from the light.

Halved apricots can also be used for this recipe. Put in a basin and soak in a very heavy syrup. Crack half the number of stones (pits), peel the kernels and put into the preserving jars with the apricots.

apricot water ice

Cook some stoned (pitted) apricots with a little water until soft. Drain and press the fruit through a sieve (or purée in a blender), adding sufficient cooking juice to make a purée of pouring consistency. Prepare a sugar syrup by heating 225 g (8 oz, 1 cup) sugar with 600 ml (1 pint, 2½ cups) water. Stir from time to time until the sugar has completely dissolved. This yields 750 ml (1¼ pints, 3¼ cups) syrup. Combine equal quantities of apricot purée and sugar syrup, and flavour to taste with lemon juice – 1 lemon to each 600 ml (1 pint, 2½ cups) mixture. Either pour the cooked mixture into a prepared ice-cream maker, or freeze until slushy in a freezer, then beat thoroughly before refreezing until firm.

preserved apricots or apricot comfits in eau-de-vie

Choose very small firm apricots of uniform size. Put them, a few at a time, in a copper pan full of cold water, so that they are completely covered. Place the pan over a low flame. As soon as the

Apricot varieties

variety	appearance	quality and uses
Bergeron	large, firm and elongated	fragrant, good for preserving
Canino	large and fairly soft	medium quality
Early Colomer	small	travels well
Jumbocot	large and firm, orange	acidic, good for cooking
Luizet	large and elongated	fragrant but fragile
Polonais or Orangé de Provence	large and firm, light pinkish-orange	rather tart, best in syrup or jams
Rouge du Roussillon	medium-sized and firm, golden red speckled with black	excellent eaten fresh or preserved
Rouget de Sernhac	medium-sized, highly coloured	fragrant

apricots rise to the surface, take them out of the water with a perforated spoon and feel them to see if they are thoroughly softened; this is the blanching operation. Soak them in cold water for an hour, drain and put them in syrup, which should be brought up to 25° (see *sugar*).

Leave them in the syrup at this degree for 4 days, then drain and put them into preserving jars. Fill with the following mixture: the syrup in which the fruit was candied, 1 litre (1¾ pints, 4⅓ cups); neutral tasteless alcohol of 90°, 1 litre (1¾ pints, 4⅓ cups). Add a piece of vanilla pod (bean) or 1 teaspoon vanilla essence, or 100 ml (4 fl oz, ½ cup) rum or kirsch per 2 litres (3½ pints, 9 cups) liquid. Mix well. When the jars have been filled, seal them with their special tops or with cork lids.

Keep in a cool place, protected both from heat and humidity for one month before use.

other recipes See *Bourdaloue; jams, jellies and marmalades; sauce.*

APRICOTING *abricoter* The process of spreading a thin layer of sieved apricot jam over the surface of a sweet or a cake, in order to give it a glossy appearance. If a cake is to be covered with fondant icing (frosting), this is made easier by apricoting the cake beforehand.

APRIL FOOL *poisson d'avril* A practical joke that is played on an unsuspecting victim on 1 April, April Fools' Day or All Fools' Day. In France, it is traditional to eat chocolate, marzipan or sugar fish, and in Alsace cakes are moulded into the shape of fish.

Apparently, the origin of April fool goes back to the 16th century, at which time the new year started on 1 April in France. In 1564, Charles IX issued a decree that fixed the beginning of the year at 1 January instead of 1 April. This innovation was not very popular, and on 1 April 1565, both as a protest and as a joke, people started sending one another worthless presents as mock New Year's gifts. As the sun happened to be in the constellation of Pisces on this date, the gifts became sweetmeats in the shape of fish (*poisson d'avril*).

AQUAVIT Also known as akvavit. A grain-based spirit often flavoured with cumin, aniseed or fennel, which has been manufactured in Scandinavia since the 15th century. Its name comes from the Latin *aquavitae* (water of life). It has a high alcoholic content and should be served really cold: ideally the bottle should be chilled in the freezer. Aquavit may also be distilled from potatoes. (See *schnapps*.)

ARAIGNÉE The name given in French to the muscle in an ox that lines the socket of its hock bone. The membrane that covers it is streaked with veins like a spider's web (hence the name, which means 'spider'). As a highly prized piece of meat that is rarely for sale, the araignée is best eaten grilled (broiled) because of its succulence.

ARAK A strong alcoholic spirit, usually flavoured with aniseed and popular in Eastern countries. Its name comes from the Arabic *araq* (juice, sap). Arak is distilled from dates in Egypt and the Middle East; grapes and seeds in Greece, where it is called *raki*; palm sap in India; and sugar-cane juice in Java.

ARBELLOT DE VACQUEUR, SIMON French journalist, novelist and historian (born Limoges, 1897; died St Sulpice d'Excideuil, 1965). A member of the academy of gastronomes, he was one of the last witnesses of the Belle Époque. As well as *J'ai vu mourir le Boulevard* and *Un gastronome se penche sur son passé*, he wrote *Tel plat, tel vin* (1963) on the selection of the correct wines for the correct dishes, and in 1965 published the biography of his master and friend Curnonsky.

He wrote a large number of articles, particularly in *Cuisine et Vins de France*, in which he described the Parisian appreciation of good food in all walks of life. For example, of the modest Laveur guesthouse he wrote: 'A good smell of vegetable soup, the memory of tripe, the scent of a jam omelette comes back at once to my nostrils and keeps running through my mind, evoking the good eating experiences of our studious youth which, in some aspects, are well worthy of those of today.' On the other hand, at a sumptuous dinner at Larue, 'We heard one evening, under the eye of the imperturbable Paul, a foreign lady ask for a milk chocolate drink to accompany a fillet of sole Cubat, the chef's speciality. Sacrilege! Just as well that Marcel Proust and Boni de Castellane were not here to see that.'

ARBOIS An AOC wine from Franche-Comté, in the Jura. Two famous men have contributed to the fame of the wines of this district – the gourmet Brillat-Savarin and the great scientist Louis Pasteur. The latter did much of his work in the region and it was because of the curious nature of certain of the Jura wines – those that form a 'veil' on the surface while they are in cask – that he worked out his theories about the action of bacteria.

The three main districts are Arbois, Château-Chalon and l'Étoile; although until very recently the wines were seldom seen outside their locality, even within France, some of them are beginning to feature on export lists. As well as red, white and rosé wines, sparkling wines are produced. The grapes used for white wines are Savagnin, Melon d'Arbois (Chardonnay) and Pinot Blanc; for the reds the varieties are Poulsard, Trousseau, and Gros Noirien (Pinot Noir). Two very curious wines of the Côtes du Jura are the *vin de paille* (straw wine) and the *vin jaune* (yellow wine).

ARBOLADE Also known as arboulastre. In the cuisine of former times, either a sweetened cream custard made with eggs, or a sweet or savoury omelette. The arboulastre mentioned in the *Ménagier de Paris* (1393) is a thick omelette made with a mixture of chopped herbs (such as wild celery, tansy, sage, beet, spinach, lettuce and mint) and sprinkled with grated cheese. La Varenne's recipe for arbolade (1651) is a sweet dessert.

RECIPE

arbolade
(from La Varenne's recipe) Melt a little butter and add some cream, egg yolks, pear juice, sugar and a pinch of salt. Cook this mixture lightly, sweeten with flower water and serve.

ARBUTUS BERRY
The fruit of the strawberry tree or shrub called madrono in Spanish and in America. It grows in the forests of North America, Ireland and southern Europe and is cultivated in the south of France. The rather tart red berries have a stippled surface and are pulpy inside, but do not have the flavour of strawberries. They are used to make a fruit wine, spirits and a liqueur, as well as jellies and jams. The city of Madrid was formerly surrounded by forests and has a strawberry tree and a bear on its coat of arms.

ARCHESTRATUS
Greek poet and gastronome of the 4th century BC, who came from Gela, in Sicily. He wrote a long poem entitled *Gastronomy* (also known under the names of *Gastrology*, *Deipnology* or *Hedypathy*). Only a few fragments, quoted by Athenaeus, remain: they are presented as a body of advice for the aesthete, the gourmet and the gastronome. A great traveller, the author shares his discoveries with the reader, presenting such dishes as dog's or sow's abdomen cooked in oil and sprinkled with cumin, and dispensing his advice on where to obtain the best products, such as wild boar from Lucania or sturgeon from Rhodes. Above all, he reveals his tastes, particularly with regard to fish; his recipes include conger eel boiled in brine and wrapped in herbs and eels cooked in beet leaves.

ARCHIDUC
The name given to French dishes inspired by Austro-Hungarian cuisine at the time of the Belle Époque. Eggs, sole and poultry are cooked with onion and paprika and coated with hongroise sauce. The pan juices are deglazed with either a fumet of fish or a demi-glace sauce, whichever is appropriate, and flavoured with brandy, whisky, Madeira or port.

RECIPES

oeufs sur le plat archiduc
Soften some sliced onions seasoned with paprika in a little butter in a small dish. Break the eggs and cook them on top of the onions. Garnish if desired with a salpicon of truffles heated in butter, or surround with a border of suprême sauce with paprika.

poulet sauté archiduc
Joint a chicken and sauté the pieces in butter. When half-cooked, add 2 tablespoons chopped onions softened in butter and ¼ teaspoon paprika.

Drain the chicken pieces and keep hot. Deglaze the juices in the pan with 100 ml (4 fl oz, ½ cup) dry white wine and heat to reduce. Add 150 ml (¼ pint, ⅔ cup) double (heavy) cream and reduce further. Finally, add a trickle of lemon juice and 50 g (2 oz, ¼ cup) butter. Strain the sauce (if desired) and use it to coat the chicken pieces. Sliced cucumber, steamed in butter, may be served at the same time.

ARDENNAISE, À L'
The term, meaning in the style of the French Ardennes, is given to several dishes of game, either birds (such as thrush) or animals (such as pickled hare or boar), in which juniper is used (in the form of spirits or berries).

ARGENTEUIL
The French name given to dishes with a sauce or garnish containing either asparagus tips or asparagus purée. The Argenteuil area of the Val-d'Oise has been famous for the cultivation of asparagus since the 17th century – there is even a society, the Compagnons de l'asperge d'Argenteuil. The description may also be applied generally to 'white' dishes, such as poached or soft-boiled eggs, sole or fillets of sole, and poached fowl.

RECIPES

salad argenteuil
Cook some potatoes in their skins, dice them and dress with tarragon mayonnaise. Pile into a salad bowl and garnish with white asparagus tips seasoned with oil and lemon. Make a border with shredded lettuce and quartered hard-boiled (hard-cooked) eggs.

scrambled eggs argenteuil
Scramble some eggs and garnish with asparagus tips that have been parboiled in salted water and then slowly cooked in butter. Serve with triangular croûtons fried in butter and a cream sauce.

soft-boiled (or poached) eggs argenteuil
Arrange the cooked eggs on croûtons fried in butter. Coat with a white asparagus purée and garnish with asparagus tips which have been slowly cooked in butter.

ARGENTINA
See *opposite*.

ARIÉGEOISE, À L'
This description is given to typical dishes of the cuisine of south-western France, particularly chicken and boned breast of mutton, which are served with stuffed cabbage and potatoes. The chicken is poached in a broth (which is served first, as a soup) and then served with stuffed green cabbage leaves, pickled pork and potatoes.

RECIPE

stuffed breast of mutton à l'ariégeoise
Make a cavity in a breast of mutton, season with salt and pepper, and fill with a fairly firm stuffing

ARGENTINA

There are few traces of the Spanish occupation in the culinary tradition of this country. Since the country's economy is largely based on cattle breeding, Argentinians eat a large amount of meat. Gastronomic differences therefore lie mainly in the preparation of the meat, particularly beef, prepared as large quarters which are roasted (*asados*) or grilled (*churrascos*), accompanied by red kidney beans, rice, sweetcorn or fresh pasta, an inheritance from Italian settlers.

Besides these very straightforward dishes, there is also a more elaborate cusine, such as a stew garnished with pumpkin and corn on the cob; *matambre* ('hunger stopper'), a dish of salt beef stuffed with vegetables and hard-boiled (hard-cooked) eggs, roasted and boiled, served cold as a starter; and *carbonara criolla*, a ragoût simmered in a pumpkin skin.

Argentina also produces many cheeses which are much appreciated locally, such as *tafi* (a hard cheese like the French Cantal), and the speciality famous throughout South America, *dulche de leche* (sweetened, flavoured concentrated milk).

WINE Argentina's wine industry was created by Jesuit missionaries in 1557, near Santiago del Estero. Today winegrowing has become so important that Argentina is the largest wine-producing country in South America, and the fifth largest producer in the world. The quality of Argentinian wine, in particular the reds, has greatly improved in recent years.

Of Argentina's production, 70% comes from the state of Mendoza at the foot of the Andes mountains, where the melting snows provide water for controlled irrigation. Together with the region of San Juan, slightly to the north, this central area to the west accounts for 91% of Argentina's production. Wine grape plantings are dominated by Bonarda, a light, fruity red variety, and Torront's, a dry white aromatic grape, but increased plantings of Malbec, Cabernet Sauvignon, Merlot, Syrah and a range of Italian grape varieties (such as Tempranillo, Sangiovese and Barbera) are now responsible for much of the red wine sent for export. Chenin Blanc, Ugni Blanc and Chardonnay are the important white grapes after Torrontés.

Much of the new impetus for quality wine production has been generated by flying winemakers from France, Australia and California. Foreign investment, particularly in the sparkling wine industry by major Champagne houses, such as Möet and Chandon, Mumm and Piper-Heidsieck have contributed to the rate of change.

---

made with breadcrumbs soaked in stock and squeezed, fat and lean unsmoked bacon, chopped parsley and garlic, bound together with eggs and well seasoned. Sew up the opening in the breast. Put the meat in a buttered braising pan, lined with fresh pork rinds and sliced onions and carrots. Add a bouquet garni, cover and cook gently for 15 minutes. Moisten with 150 ml (¼ pint, ⅔ cup) dry white wine and reduce. Add 3 teaspoons tomato purée (paste) and 300 ml (½ pint, 1¼ cups) thickened brown gravy. Keep covered and cook in the oven for a further 45–60 minutes. Drain the mutton breast and arrange it on a long dish. Surround with a garnish consisting of balls of stuffed cabbage and potatoes cooked in stock and butter. Strain the cooking juices, skim off the fat, reduce and pour over the meat.

ARLEQUIN In popular 19th-century French parlance, an assortment of leftover food from restaurants or large houses that was made to look palatable and resold at low prices either in certain markets or in cheap restaurants. Today in France they would be called *rogatons* (leftovers). In *Paris à table* (1846) Eugène Briffault recalls, 'all the remains that are thrown out which take on the lively name of *arlequin*, this *olla podrida* (pot pourri) of the Paris Bohemians.' The sellers were called 'jewellers', because of the care they took with the presentation of these disparate remnants, as colourful as Harlequin's coat.

ARLÉSIENNE, À L' The term, meaning in the style of Arles, is given to dishes with a garnish of aubergines (eggplants) fried in oil, sautéed tomatoes, and onion rings dredged in flour and fried. The garnish accompanies sole, tournedos steaks (filet mignons) or noisettes of lamb.

RECIPE

escargots à l'arlésienne
Take some medium-sized snails, stand them in tepid water to remove the impurities and then blanch with a handful of salt. Remove them from their shells and drain. Put a little diced bacon into a saucepan, sprinkle with flour, moisten with dry white wine and add the snails, together with some garlic and plenty of herbs. Bring to the boil and cook gently for about 10 minutes. When the snails are cooked, drain and replace in their shells. Make a sauce with a glass of Madeira, a pinch of cayenne pepper and the juice of a lemon. Pour the sauce over the snails and sprinkle with chopped parsley.

other recipes See *egg (scrambled eggs), salad.*

ARMAGNAC Brandy made from wine from a region in Gascony almost entirely in the department of Gers. It has an *appellation d'origine contrôlée*.

The main production zone is Bas-Armagnac (in the west, around Gabarret, La Bastide-d'Armagnac, Cazaubon, Eauze and Nogaro, up to

Villeneuve-de-Marsan and Aire-sur-l'Adour), which produces very fine Armagnac with a particular bouquet. The Ténarèze region completes the Bas-Armagnac region to the east (around Nérac, Condom, Vic-Fezensac and Aignan) and produces strongly scented and supple brandies. Haut-Armagnac, which extends to the east and south, around Mirande, Auch and Lectoure, produces less of the total production.

Armagnac's name (and presumably the spirit itself) has been recorded as early as 1411, but since 1909 certain controls have defined its area and how it should be made and labelled. The main grapes used are: Piquepoul, St Émilion, Colombard, Jurançon, Blanquette, Mauzac and Clairette Meslier. A special type of still is used to handle the white wines and this is now done by a continuous process, although the Armagnac still is quite different from the continuous still (Coffey or patent still) used in making other spirits. Some of the stills were, until the mid-20th century, travelling stills, going around the country making the brandy for the wine growers. These still exist, but the big firms mostly carry out their own distilling in their headquarters or buy from growers who distill.

Armagnac is matured in oak and the age of the spirit, when bottled, can be: three star or XXX (three years old); VO (from five to ten years); or VSOP (up to 15 years). 'Hors d'Age' means that the brandy is at least 25 years old, although, like Cognac, it will not improve indefinitely in wood. Sometimes bottled in a flagon-shaped bottle known as a *basquaise*, Armagnac may also be put into tall bottles. It should be served in a small tulip or flattish goblet-type glass, able to be cupped in the hand when it is drunk neat as a liqueur, although the more ordinary Armagnacs are useful in mixed drinks. Armagnac is different from Cognac but – a common delusion – it is not weaker in any way, nor is it, quality for quality, cheaper.

ARMENONVILLE A garnish that bears the name of a Parisian restaurant in the Bois de Boulogne. The basic ingredients are either *Anna* or casseroled potatoes, together with morel mushrooms in cream sauce. It is served with noisettes of lamb, tournedos steaks (filet mignons), sautéed or casseroled chicken and soft-boiled or poached eggs. These are coated with demi-glace sauce flavoured with either Cognac or Madeira. The name is also given to a dish of sole or sole fillets.

RECIPE

sole armenonville
Prepare a pancake of Anna potatoes. Skin and prepare 2 good sole and poach them in a very shallow dish in fish stock. Make a white wine sauce and stir in the cooking juices from the sole. Cut some cep mushrooms into thin strips, cook them gently in butter in a covered pan and add them to the sauce. Arrange the Anna potatoes on the serving dish, place the sole on top, coat with sauce and serve immediately.

In the traditional recipe, the sole is served surrounded by a border of duchesse potatoes enriched with truffles.

ARMORICAINE, À L' The description *à l'armoricaine* is given to dishes with a sauce of prawns and shrimps which are cooked *à l'américaine*. These days it is acknowledged that *armoricaine* is a corruption of *américaine*, itself a Parisian dish. Moreover, the incorporation of garlic, tomatoes and oil in the sauce and the fact that it was created by a chef of southern French origins, proves that the recipe has nothing to do with Brittany (Armorica is the ancient name for Brittany).

AROMA The distinctive smell of a food that is produced by a complex mixture of volatile compounds. A product is aromatized by introducing into it an aroma, natural or otherwise, that gives it a flavour or reinforces one that it has already.

Natural aromas or flavours are extracted from plants, such as mint, vanilla or the zest of citrus fruits. Certain processes, such as smoking or maceration in alcohol, also give a natural flavour.

To keep costs down, and to maintain the quality and keeping properties of its products, the food industry has increasingly used artificial and synthetic flavourings. Artificial flavourings have chemical formulae identical to those of natural flavours, such as vanillin or menthol, while synthetic flavourings have chemical formulae that do not exist in nature. For example, amyl acetate, which smells of bananas, is used in liqueurs and processed cheeses; diacetyl is used in margarine; and the valerianates are widely used in preserves because of their fruity smell.

In France flavourings are not regarded as additives and their use is not governed by the same set of regulations. On the other hand, it is obligatory to include the word '*fantaisie*' (imitation) on labels for aromatized alcohols and syrups, and the words 'natural flavour', 'reinforced natural flavour' or 'artificial flavour' on other food labels, depending on the circumstances. However, the actual nature of the flavouring remains a secret of the manufacturer.

The name *arômes* is given to Lyonnais cheeses, such as Rigotte and Pélardon, which are refined in grape marc or white wine to give them a piquant flavour.

AROMATIC Any fragrant plant that is used as a condiment or for flavouring. Various parts of the plant may be used: the leaves (basil, marjoram, mint, chervil and tarragon), the flower buds (caper and nasturtium), the seeds (dill, aniseed, caraway, coriander and mustard), the fruits (juniper and pimiento), the roots (horseradish), the stems (angelica, savory and wild thyme) or the bulbs (garlic and onion). Certain vegetables, such as carrots, celery, parsnips and leeks, are also used in cooking as aromatics.

Although they have no nutritional value, aromatics constitute an indispensable item in cooking. They may be added directly to the preparation during cooking, to achieve a suitable blending of flavours and aromas (particularly for dishes that are boiled or braised for a long time), or are used indirectly in vinegars and oils, mustards, condiments, stuffings, court-bouillons, marinades, fumets and macerations. They are also widely used to make alcoholic and nonalcoholic drinks and in the preserving industries.

Aromatics may be used fresh or they may be preserved by refrigeration, freezing or drying; dried aromatics, whole or crushed, should be stored in opaque well-sealed pots.

Aromatics are distinguished from spices in that the latter are of exotic origin; for example, pepper, nutmeg, saffron, vanilla and betel. A spice is necessarily aromatic but it may also be very pungent, while the aromatic is used essentially for its fragrance. To spice means 'to give taste to', while to aromatize means 'to perfume'. In ancient times, substances such as benzoin, myrrh and rosewater were frequently used in cooking. In the Middle Ages, simples and herbs, both medicinal and culinary, played an essential role. Later, oriental spices competed with them, but different regions continued the local practice of aromatic cooking using indigenous plants, such as garlic, anise, basil, oregano and thyme in the Mediterranean countries, dill and fennel in Scandinavia, and artemisia, juniper and cumin in the the East. In France, the situation is summarized by Raymond Dumay: 'We have only one condiment, in three shapes: garlic in Marseilles, shallots in Bordeaux and onions in Dunkirk; these are the three pillars of our national cuisine.'

RECIPE

aromatic sauce
Cover and infuse for 20 minutes a mixture consisting of 250 ml (8 fl oz, 1 cup) boiling consommé, a pinch each of chopped chives, savory, marjoram, sage and basil, a chopped shallot, 4 peppercorns and a little grated nutmeg. Strain the infusion and then add it to a white roux made with 25 g (1 oz, 2 tablespoons) butter and an equal amount of flour. Cook for 10 minutes. Add a trickle of lemon juice and a teaspoon each of chopped chervil and chopped tarragon. This sauce can be served with poached fish.

ARQUEBUSE A herby liqueur that was originally supposed to possess therapeutic qualities in cases of gunshot wounds. The recipe for *eau d'arquebuse* or *d'arquebusade* was recorded in the 19th century by a Marist monk from the Hermitage Abbey (Loire) and includes agrimony and gentian. Today it is used as a digestive and 'pick-me-up' – it is said to be the French answer to Fernet Branca!

ARRACACIA ROOT *pomme de terre-céleri* The starchy long rhizome (underground stem) of the arracacia, also known as the celery potato, native to Colombia. It can be ground to produce flour or cooked like the yam or the sweet potato.

ARROWROOT The starch extracted from the rhizomes (underground stems) of several tropical plants. It is so called because of the therapeutic qualities attributed to it by American Indians in the treatment of arrow wounds. A fine white powder, it is useful in the kitchen as a last-minute thickener of sauces. Arrowroot should be blended to a smooth, thin paste with a little cold liquid before being added to hot liquid. Unlike cornflour (cornstarch), which gives a cloudy sauce, arrowroot clears when it boils. It reaches optimum thickness at boiling point and should be removed from the heat immediately as further cooking makes the arrowroot thin down slightly. Being clear and requiring brief cooking, arrowroot is the ideal thickener for fruit glazes, sauces and syrups. Traditionally it is also used in soups and to prepare gruels for invalids and desserts.

RECIPES

arrowroot glaze
To make a thick set cold glaze for fruit, thicken fruit juice or a light fruit syrup as for Thin fruit sauce, below, but using 5 teaspoons arrowroot to 300 ml (½ pint, 1¼ cups) liquid. Use while hot or warm.

thin fruit sauce
To thicken a fruit juice sauce to a thin pouring consistency, use 1 tablespoon arrowroot for every 300 ml (½ pint, 1¼ cups) liquid. Slake the arrowroot with a little cold water or juice. Stir in a little of the hot sauce, then pour the arrowroot mixture into the main batch of sauce. Bring to the boil, stirring continuously, and remove from the heat. Serve at once or cover the surface of the sauce with cling film (plastic wrap) to prevent a skin from forming and leave to cool.

ARTAGNAN, À LA D' The name of the fourth musketeer is given to a garnish consisting of cep mushrooms *à la béarnaise* (his province), small stuffed tomatoes and croquette potatoes. It is served with poultry and meat joints.

ARTEMISIA *armoise* A genus of aromatic plants with a scent of camphor growing throughout Europe and Asia. Wormwood (*A. absintium*) has been used as a vermifuge (hence the name) for thousands of years. It has also been used as a febrifuge (to abate fever). One of the principal herbs in absinthe, it also gives its name to vermouth, via the German *Wermut*. It is aromatic, but very bitter. Indeed, a flavouring for spirits (and perhaps a tonic) is one of the principal uses for herbs of this family, an Alpine variety being used for the Swiss *génépi*. The leaves of some varieties are used as a fresh condiment to flavour fatty meats and fish, such as pork and eel, and may also be an ingredient in certain marinades. Artemisia is mainly used in Germany, the Balkans and Italy.

ARTICHOKE, GLOBE A perennial vegetable related to the thistle, whose edible immature flower head is formed of a fleshy base (*fond*) and heart surrounded by scaly leaves or bracts. The base is eaten after the inedible hairy central core (choke) has been removed. The bases of the leaves cradle a small portion of tender flesh that is also edible. Each leaf is dipped in a little sauce or dressing and the tender edible part nibbled off before the rest of the leaf is discarded.

The heart is the central clump of close-packed, tender and completely edible leaves from young vegetables in which the choke has not formed. Very young vegetables are entirely edible, with the minimum of trimming necessary to remove a few outer leaves. At this stage the small artichokes may be sliced, quartered or cooked whole, in fritters or braised. Very young artichokes are also eaten raw.

Originating from Sicily and still very widely used in Italian cooking, the artichoke was first regarded in France mainly as a remedy for various ailments. At the beginning of the 18th century, Louis Lemery said in his *Treatise on Food:* 'Artichokes suit elderly people at all times, and those of a phlegmatic and melancholy disposition.' It was also reputed to be an aphrodisiac and women were often forbidden to eat it. Catherine de'Medici, who was fond of artichokes, encouraged their cultivation in France.

Artichokes are grown in many parts of Europe, while California is the major region in the US. In France they are grown in Brittany, producing the large round heavy Camus with a large heart; around Paris, known for the large green Paris or Laon (with more spiky leaves); and in Provence, where the violet artichokes of spring and autumn may be eaten raw, or braised and eaten whole.

■ **Selecting and cooking** Artichokes are best in the summer. Choose one that is firm and heavy, with stiff tightly packed leaves (these may be brilliant green, blue-green or violet-coloured, according to the variety). Because the artichoke is a flower bud, open leaves indicate that it is overripe and will therefore be hard and have too large a choke. When it has been kept for a long time after picking, the tops of the scales go black. Uncooked artichokes may be kept fresh for 1–3 days if their stalks are put into water, like a bunch of flowers. Placing them in the salad compartment of the refrigerator is the practical alternative. After cooking, they will keep for 24 hours in the refrigerator.

Artichokes are an essential item in the Italian diet. Young small *carciofi* (such as the *chioggi* or Venice violet, and the Tuscan violet) are eaten raw, dipped in olive oil or are cooked whole and preserved in oil, to serve as an antipasto. Big globulose artichokes are grown in Rome, and the city boasts recipes such as *carciofi alla giudea* (fried whole in oil).

Large artichokes, cooked in water or steamed, are served whole, either hot or cold with the central choke removed, and accompanied by a sauce or vinaigrette (sometimes a second sauce within the leaves). They are eaten by pulling off the leaves,

dipping the base in the sauce, eating this and discarding the leaves. Finally the base or bottom (*fond*) is eaten. When young and tender, artichokes can be served au gratin, sliced for an omelette filling and even fried. The bottoms may be topped with a stuffing, cooked *à la barigoule*, used as a garnish for hot or cold dishes, or served in a salad. Only the small violet ones can be eaten raw with salt.

Artichoke bottoms and hearts may be sold ready-prepared in Italy and are available canned (the bottom sometimes with a fringe of leaf) or frozen. The whole artichoke, or the heart only, may be preserved in brine. A mixture of water, olive oil, lemon, thyme, bay leaf and coriander (cilantro), is often used for small artichokes.

RECIPES

artichoke hearts: preparation
Break off the stalk of the artichoke by bending it until it comes away from the base; the stringy parts will come away with the stalk. Using a very sharp knife, cut the base flat and then remove the tough outer leaves. Neatly trim the outside of the artichoke, then cut off the top and remove the choke. Rub with lemon to prevent it going black, even if it is to be used immediately.

artichokes à la cévenole
Blanch the artichokes and gently cook them in butter. Garnish with chestnut purée flavoured with soubise purée. Sprinkle with grated Parmesan cheese and melted butter and brown in the oven or under the grill (broiler).

artichokes à la duxelles
Blanch the artichokes and cook in butter, then stuff with mushroom duxelles.

artichokes à la niçoise
Blanch the artichokes and sauté in olive oil. Garnish with thick tomato sauce, sprinkle with white breadcrumbs and olive oil, and brown in the oven or under the grill (broiler).

artichokes à la portugaise
Gently cook the prepared artichokes in oil with chopped onion. Add 2 peeled seeded chopped tomatoes, a little grated garlic and some chopped parsley. Cover and cook over a very low heat. Garnish with a well-reduced tomato sauce and sprinkle with chopped parsley.

artichokes aux fines herbes
Lightly blanch the artichokes, then sauté them (either whole or sliced) in butter. Arrange in a vegetable dish and sprinkle with chopped chervil and parsley. If the artichokes are very tender, the raw hearts may be sliced, rubbed with lemon and sautéed in butter.

Examples of the types of globe artichoke – there are many green or purple, large and small varieties.

GLOBE ARTICHOKES

Italian romanesco

camus

small purple
artichokes – *poivrades*

purple artichokes from
Provence – *violets de
Provence*

macau

Spanish green
artichokes – *blancs d'Espagne*

Turning an artichoke bottom

This is a preparation method for raw artichokes. Have a bowl of acidulated water ready to hold the prepared vegetables as they discolour quickly once cut. Cook the artichokes promptly following preparation.

1 *Snap or cut off the stalk and remove all the large outer leaves. Then pare the outside off the artichoke bottom. Rub the artichoke with a cut lemon.*

2 *Remove the slightly loose, fairly large leaves covering the small clump of tender leaves on top of the choke.*

3 *Carefully cut away the small clump of tender leaves, sliding the knife over the top of the choke and leaving it in place on the bottom. (The tender clump of leaves can be replaced when the choke has been discarded, to be cooked with the artichoke bottom.)*

4 *Pull or scoop out the inedible hairy choke, taking care to remove it completely. Use a small teaspoon to scrape the bottom clean.*

artichokes cooked in butter or à la crème

Prepare and trim the hearts. Rub with lemon and blanch for 10 minutes in boiling salted water with a few drops of lemon juice. Drain, arrange in a well-buttered sauté pan and season with salt and pepper. Sprinkle with melted butter and cook, covered, for about 20 minutes. The hearts may then be served *à la crème* by covering them with hot crème fraîche that has been reduced by half. They may be cut into slices if they are too large.

artichokes soubise

Blanch the artichokes and steam them in butter. Garnish with soubise purée. Sprinkle with Parmesan cheese and brown in the oven or under the grill (broiler).

artichoke mirepoix

Prepare 12 small young artichokes. Place 200 ml (7 fl oz, ¾ cup) fondue of vegetable mirepoix with some butter in a sauté pan and add 2 tablespoons finely diced lean ham. Arrange the artichokes in the sauté pan and cover. Cook very gently for 5 minutes, then moisten with 4 tablespoons dry white wine and reduce. Add 100 ml (4 fl oz, ½ cup) veal gravy, cover again and cook for 35 minutes. Arrange in a vegetable dish, pour the mirepoix over and sprinkle with chopped parsley.

artichoke ragoût

Prepare 2 kg (4½ lb) small artichokes. Heat some oil in a large flameproof casserole and toss the artichokes in it. Brown them, stirring constantly, for 5 minutes. Add sufficient water to cover, season with salt and pepper and, without covering the casserole, simmer very gently for 15 minutes. Sauté 2 kg (4½ lb) small new potatoes in a little oil. Blanch 150 g (5 oz) lean diced bacon and add to the potatoes. Cook for 5 minutes to brown. Drain and add to the artichokes, cover and complete the cooking without stirring (about 20 minutes).

artichokes à la bretonne

These are boiled artichokes accompanied by a white sauce prepared from the cooking liquid enriched with crème fraîche; butter is added to the sauce just before serving.

artichokes à la lyonnaise

(from Paul Bocuse's recipe) Choose medium-sized artichokes with long spread-out leaves, either the green or the violet variety. Break off the stalks, cut the artichokes into four, cut the leaves down to two-thirds their length and remove the choke. Plunge them into a saucepan of boiling water, half-cook them and then drain. Heat a mixture of equal parts of oil and butter in a flameproof pan and soften a chopped onion in it. Add the artichokes, season with salt and pepper and cook over a moderate heat until the vegetables begin to brown. Add 1 tablespoon flour and about 300 ml (½ pint, 1¼ cups) stock. When the artichokes are cooked, arrange them on a dish and keep them hot. Add a little more stock to the pan and reduce. Add some chopped parsley and then stir in a good-sized piece of unsalted butter and the juice of half a lemon. Pour the sauce over the artichokes and serve.

boiled artichokes

Using scissors or a very sharp knife, trim off the top third of the outer leaves of the artichokes and wash the heads in plenty of water. Break off the stalk level with the leaves (do not cut it); the stringy parts will come away with the stalk. Tie up each artichoke with string so that the head retains its shape during cooking and plunge the vegetables into acidulated boiling salted water. Keep the water boiling vigorously. The cooking time (average 30 minutes) depends on the size and freshness of the artichokes. (Allow 10–12 minutes after the steam begins to escape when using a pressure cooker.) The artichokes are cooked when the outside leaves come away when pulled upwards. Drain the artichokes by placing them upside down in a colander, remove the string and serve immediately. If they are to be eaten cold, put them under the cold tap as soon as they are cooked and then drain them; do not untie them until the last moment. To serve, take out and discard the centre leaves which hide the choke and remove the choke with a small spoon.

Artichokes may be eaten hot with melted butter, a white sauce (prepared with the cooking water enriched with fresh cream), a cream sauce (or simply cream flavoured with lemon and heated), a hollandaise sauce or a mousseline sauce. Cold artichokes may be served with mayonnaise, mustard sauce, soy sauce, tartare sauce, or vinaigrette and flavoured, if desired, with chopped parsley or chervil.

braised stuffed artichokes

Cut and prepare large artichokes as in the previous recipe. Blanch for 5 minutes in boiling water, cool under the tap, drain and remove the small central leaves and the choke. Season with salt and pepper. Fill the artichokes with a meat stuffing (made, for example, with 4 parts sausagemeat to 1 part onion softened in butter, and some chopped parsley). Wrap them in thin slices of fat bacon and tie them. Butter a sauté dish and line the base with bacon rashers (slices), and sliced onions and carrots. Place the artichokes on top, season with salt and pepper, and add a bouquet garni. Cover and begin cooking over a low heat. Moisten with a small quantity of dry white wine, and reduce. Add a few tablespoons of veal stock, cover and cook in a preheated oven at 180°C (350°F, gas 4) for about an hour, basting frequently. Drain the artichokes, untie them and remove the bacon rashers. Arrange the artichokes on a round dish. Strain and skim fat from the cooking liquor, add some demi-glace or any other reduced sauce, and use to coat the artichokes.

casseroled artichokes

Choose small Italian or violet Provençal artichokes, and trim the leaves to two-thirds of their length. Blanch the artichokes in boiling water, drain, remove the centre leaves and choke, and fill them with a stuffing made from breadcrumbs, chopped garlic, capers, parsley and salt and pepper. Arrange the artichokes close together in a casserole, moisten with a generous quantity of olive oil and season with salt and pepper. Cook in a preheated oven at 180°C (350°F, gas 4), uncovered, for about 50 minutes, basting from time to time. To serve, arrange the artichokes on a dish and pour the cooking juices over them.

young whole, trimmed artichokes

These may be braised without stuffing, devilled, cooked *à la lyonnaise* or *à la mirepoix*, or used in any of the recipes for artichokes.

other recipes See *barigoule, Clamart, Crécy, florentine, piémontaise.*

ARTOIS, D' In classic cuisine, the name of the future Charles X of France (reigned 1824–30) is given to a haricot (navy) bean soup and a garnish for roast baron of lamb made with small potato croustades filled with young garden peas and accompanied by Madeira sauce.

RECIPE

potage d'artois

To 1.5 litres (2¾ pints, 6½ cups) haricot (navy) bean soup, add 4 tablespoons finely shredded vegetables softened in butter. Sprinkle the soup with 1 tablespoon chopped chervil.

ARTUSI, PELLEGRINO Italian banker, man of letters and gastronome (born in Formimpopoli 1820, died Florence 1921). Author of *La scienza in cucina e l'arte di mangiar bene* ('Science in cooking and the art of eating well'). This work, first published in 1891, enjoyed an unprecedented success in Italy, with 14 different editions. With its 790 recipes, 'Artusi' is still the great classic of Italian cuisine and it is also a great pleasure to read. His original style combines technical accuracy, literary imagination, hygienic education and ethnographic or historical observations.

ASAFOETIDA A milky resin extracted from the tap root of an oriental umbelliferous plant widely cultivated in the Middle East. It is dried and crushed and sold as powder in Iran, India and Afghanistan, where it is commonly used as a condiment. The first impression of this spice is of its foul smell and powerful unpleasant flavour if sampled raw. The Germans call it *Teufelsdreck*, or devil's dung. When it is cooked in minute quantities, its smell diminishes and it gives a slightly onion-garlic flavour to food. It is a valued seasoning in many Indian vegetable and pulse dishes. It was popular with the Romans (see *silphium*), but was later used mainly as a medicine to treat flatulence.

ASH A tree of the genus *Fraxinus*, which grows in temperate climates. The leaves of the European ash (*F. excelsior*) are used for a fermented drink called *frénette*, or to make a type of tea. The very young green keys can be preserved in vinegar and used instead of capers.

RECIPE

frénette cordial
Boil 50 g (2 oz) ash leaves with the thinly sliced zest of 10 oranges in 2 litres (3½ pints, 9 cups) water for 30 minutes. Strain through a fine cloth. Dissolve 3 kg (6½ lb) sugar in the strained infusion and add 50 g (2 oz) citric acid. Pour into a barrel with a capacity of about 50 litres (11 gallons, 14 US gallons). Dissolve 25 g (1 oz, 2 cakes) fresh (compressed) yeast in 2 tablespoons cold caramel and pour the mixture into the barrel. Fill with water, leave to ferment for 8 days, bottle and cork.

ASIAGO An Italian DOP cheese made from unpasteurized cow's milk. It has a supple but sliceable texture with numerous small holes. The flavour is slightly nutty, with lemon tones which take on a more tangy nature as the cheese matures. It was first manufactured from ewe's milk in the village of Asiago in the province of Vicenza. The cheese comes in rounds weighing 7–10 kg (16–22 lb). According to its maturing time (one, two or six months), it is eaten fresh, medium or mature respectively. (Mature cheeses are graded as *vecchio*, nine months, and *stravecchio*, two years.)

Asiago Pressato is a much more common and commercial type of Asiago. Made from pasteurized cow's milk, it is pressed to speed up the ripening process and then matured for a very short time. The texture is rather rubbery and the flavour is very mild.

ASPARAGUS A perennial plant with an underground stem (crown) that produces edible shoots, with a nascent bud of different colours, which are regarded as a delicacy. It is a native of central and southern Europe, North Africa and central and West Asia. Known to the Egyptians and the Romans, it was not cultivated in France until the time of Louis XIV: the Sun King had a great liking for this vegetable and received supplies from La Quintinie from December onwards. In about 1875, the Orleans district became the favourite area for growing asparagus – thanks to Charles Depezay, a cavalryman who took grafts from plants near Argenteuil during the siege of Paris, and afterwards dedicated himself to growing asparagus.

■ **Types** Three varieties of asparagus are grown in continental Europe, the season starting in March. Holland and Belgium (in Brabant in the south and around Limburg) favour white asparagus, earthed up as it grows, with a yellowish tip. Fat and white is the favourite in Alsace and southern Germany, and in Spain, where huge quantities are canned in the Ebro valley. White, but lavender-tipped, asparagus, allowed to colour naturally, has rather more flavour. It grows in Italy round Bassano (in the Veneto) and, in France round Argenteuil, in Aquitaine, the Charentes and the Loire. All-green asparagus (which extends the European season until June) has the best flavour of all. It is harvested when the stalks are about 15 cm (6 in) long, and is the favourite in California (the US is the largest commercial producer) and Britain, where the Vale of Evesham is celebrated. 'Sparrow grass' is a local name there, and 'sprue', for the thinner stalks. In France green asparagus is grown on the Rhône (Lauris) – thanks to the efforts of the chef Auguste Escoffier.

Several types of wild asparagus grow in Europe, from Britain to Poland and Turkey, and in California and Australia. The one from a thorny bush is best. These feature in regional dishes; for example, Italian asparagus tips with Parmesan cheese. Wild asparagus tends to be bitter.

■ **Selecting, cooking and serving** Fresh asparagus stems should be firm and uniformly coloured. The cut ends of the shoots should be white. They may be kept for a maximum of three days if the ends are wrapped in a damp cloth or in an airtight polythene bag or container. Store in the refrigerator. Allow a bunch per person when serving the vegetable as a starter – usually 250 g (9 oz). Asparagus is always cooked in water or steamed before further use. The French serve it hot and plain with butter. The Italians also eat it cold with vinaigrette. It can also be served in a hot or cold sauce, in a salad, in a tart, au gratin, as a purée, in velouté sauce, as an omelette filling or with scrambled eggs. Canned white asparagus or green tips may be used.

A variety of kitchen equipment is associated with asparagus. There is a special tall steamer that keeps the tips out of the water and handsome dishes with draining racks, or with hollows for sauces, plus various scoops and tongs. The tips may be eaten with a fork and the rest of the stem with the fingers, or the whole vegetable may be eaten with the fingers. A finger bowl may be provided.

TYPES OF ASPARAGUS

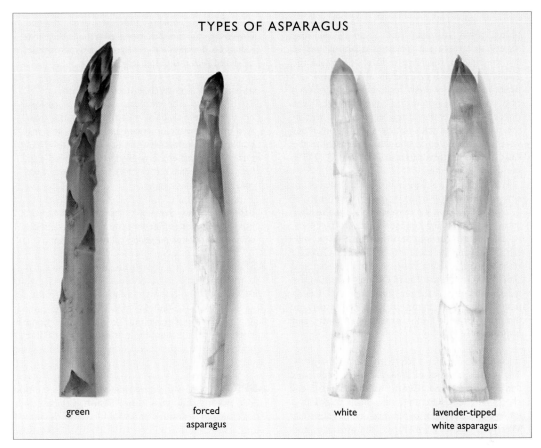

green   forced
asparagus   white   lavender-tipped
white asparagus

RECIPES

preparation

Lay the asparagus stalks flat on a chopping board and cut them all to the same length. Peel them, working from the tip to the base, and clean the tips with a pointed knife if necessary. Wash the asparagus in plenty of water but do not soak. Drain and tie into bunches or small bundles.

cooking in water

Plunge the bundles of asparagus into boiling salted water – 1½ teaspoons salt to 1 litre (1¾ pints, 4⅓ cups) – water. Allow 20–30 minutes cooking depending on the thickness of the stems. Remove the asparagus from the water as soon as it is tender, and drain either on a plate covered with a napkin or on a draining rack. There are special cylindrical pans for cooking asparagus. The stalks are held upright in a basket and enough water is added to cover the stems but not the tips. The lid is replaced during cooking. The tips are more tender if they are cooked in the steam.

At the end of the season, asparagus becomes a little bitter. Blanch for 5 minutes and drain it, then complete cooking in fresh water.

asparagus served hot

Serve with clarified melted butter (flavoured with lemon if desired), noisette butter or any of the fol-lowing sauces: Chantilly, cream, hollandaise, maltaise or mousseline.

asparagus served warm

The accompanying sauce may be mayonnaise, mustard sauce, tartare sauce, or a plain or seasoned vinaigrette. It is better served just warm than cold.

asparagus au gratin

Cook the asparagus in salted water, drain and arrange on an ovenproof dish, staggering the layers in order to expose the tips and hide the stalks. Coat the tips with Mornay sauce. Place a strip of greaseproof (wax) paper over the uncoated parts. Sprinkle with grated Parmesan cheese, drizzle over melted butter and brown in the oven or under the grill (broiler). Remove the greaseproof paper just before serving.

asparagus mousse with orange butter ♦

Cook 200 g (7 oz) trimmed green asparagus spears in well-salted boiling water. Cool down quickly in a bowl of iced water, drain and dry on a cloth. Place in a blender with 2 whole eggs, 1 egg yolk, 50 g (2 oz) uncooked white chicken meat and 2 tablespoons crème fraîche. Add 7 tablespoons pouring cream, 2 tablespoons truffle juice, salt and pepper. Purée in a blender until the mixture is smooth.

Butter 4 stainless steel rings 6 cm (2½ in) in diameter and 4 cm (1½ in) high. Place on a roasting tin (pan) which will act as a bain marie. Cook 100 g (4 oz) green asparagus tips, 5 cm (2 in) long. (Check that there are sufficient asparagus tips to line the sides of the rings; reduce or increase the quantity as necessary.) Carefully arrange them vertically at regular intervals around the edge of each ring, with the flat side turned inwards. Next fill the rings to the top with the asparagus mousse so that the asparagus tips stick out by 1 cm (½ in). Pour water into the tin up to one-third the height of the rings. Cook in a preheated oven at 110°C (225°F, gas ¼) for 20 minutes.

In a small sauté pan, reduce the juice of an orange with the blanched, finely shredded zest of ½ orange. (Reserve the remaining blanched zest for garnishing.) Whisking continually, add 100 g (4 oz, ¼ cup) butter cut into small pieces. Season with salt and pepper. Put aside in a warm place. Carefully transfer each stainless steel ring to a serving dish, slide a thin knife blade round the ring to loosen the mousse and remove the ring slowly upwards. Gently pour the orange butter around the asparagus mousse. Garnish with orange segments and blanched zest.

asparagus ragoût with young garden peas
Take equal quantities of shelled young garden peas and peeled asparagus. Cut the asparagus into 2 cm (¾ in) lengths. Sauté some new small onions in a casserole with butter, oil, or preferably, goose fat. When they have browned, add the asparagus and peas, cover, and sweat for 5 minutes. Add salt, pepper, a little sugar and enough poultry stock to just cover. Cover the casserole and cook over a low heat for 15 minutes. Arrange the ragoût in a vegetable dish and serve.

asparagus tart
Cover a pastry case (pie shell), baked blind, with a layer of creamed chicken purée. Garnish with asparagus tips that have been gently cooked in butter. Coat with cream sauce or suprême sauce. Sprinkle with fried breadcrumbs and brown in the oven.

asparagus tips: cooking
Break or cut off the tips of a suitable variety of green asparagus, discarding the stalks where they start to become hard. Tie up these tips, about 10 cm (4 in) long, in bundles of 10 or 12. Peel the lower parts of the asparagus stems and cut into small pieces. Cook them in boiling salted water for 4 minutes, then add the bundles of asparagus tips. Cook them, uncovered, for 7–8 minutes, then drain the bundles and the pieces. Dip the bundles of tips in cold water. The asparagus pieces, together with the cooking water, may be used for soup or a garnish. White asparagus should be cut into tips 5–6 cm (2–2½ in) long.

asparagus tips for cold garnishes
Asparagus tips used for garnishes or cold salads should be dipped in cold water as soon as they have finished cooking and then well drained. Depending on the dish being garnished, they may either be dressed with vinaigrette or mayonnaise, or glazed with meat aspic jelly.

asparagus tips with butter or cream
The tips should be well drained and, if necessary, dried for a few seconds over heat or in the oven. Add melted butter or cream and arrange in a vegetable dish. Alternatively, the tips may be used as a garnish for poached, scrambled, or soft-boiled eggs, fish dishes, small meat joints, veal sweetbreads, roasting chicken or game.

other recipes See *aspic, buisson, cream soup, flamande, omelette (filled omelettes: Argenteuil), polonaise, royale, salpicon (vegetable salpicons), soup.*

ASPARTAME A very strong artificial sweetener, 180 to 200 times sweeter than saccharose (sugar) with a very low calorie content. It is the artificial sweetener with a flavour most closely resembing sugar. Its harmlessness and its lack of aftertaste means that it is an ingredient of thousands of dietary products; on the other hand it is not so stable when heated.

ASPIC A way of presenting cold cooked food (meat, poultry, foie gras, fish, shellfish, vegetables or even fruit), by setting it in a moulded and decorated aspic jelly. Many authors believe that this name comes from the asp, a serpent whose icy coldness recalls that of the jelly, but it is more probably derived from the Greek word *aspis*, which means buckler or shield. It was, in fact, in this form that the first moulds were made; others were made in the shape of a coiled snake, doubtless to justify the name aspic. Today, aspics are made in plain moulds, charlotte moulds, savarin (ring) moulds or in individual ramekins or darioles; aspic moulds may also be fluted or decorated. The type of aspic used (made from meat, poultry or fish, or pectin-based for fruits) varies according to the nature of the principal ingredient (poultry slices, sole fillets, medallions of foie gras, sliced fresh vegetables or fruit segments). It is flavoured with port, Madeira, Marsala or sherry.

RECIPES

preparation of aspic moulds and dishes
Place the selected mould in the refrigerator until it is very cold. Prepare some aspic jelly. Pour into the mould some jelly (which has cooled but not set), turning it so that it coats the base and sides. Replace the mould in the refrigerator so that the aspic just sets but is not too firm, and then place the items used for garnishing on the base and around the sides. The garnish (which should be

Asparagus mousse with orange butter, see page 47.

chosen according to the principal item to go in the aspic), should be cut up into small pieces; for example, slices of truffle, rounds of hard-boiled (hard-cooked) egg, slices of lean ham or tongue, tarragon leaves or smoked salmon may be used. When adding these items, the appearance of the jelly when it is turned out of the mould must be considered. Replace the mould in the refrigerator to allow the garnish to set firmly. Then carefully fill the mould with the prepared filling and press it down into the jelly. The preparation may be placed in layers alternating with layers of jelly, in which case, the jelly should be allowed to set before the subsequent layer of prepared food is laid on top. Alternatively, the mould can be filled with the prepared food then filled with jelly. Replace the filled mould in the refrigerator until the moment of serving. Unmould the firmly set aspic by plunging the mould for a few seconds into boiling water. Turn it upside down on to a cold plate and replace in the refrigerator for a few moments before serving.

asparagus aspic

Coat the base and sides of ramekins with aspic jelly. Cut asparagus tips to the height of the ramekins and arrange them so that they stand upright around the edge, closely pressed together. Fill the centre with a purée of foie gras. Cover with aspic and leave in the refrigerator for several hours before serving.

aspic of ham and veal (or chicken)

Prepare an aspic jelly flavoured with herbs, and coat the mould with it. Garnish the mould with some diced cooked ham and some casseroled veal (or chicken) cut into even-sized slices. Fill the centre with a layer of ham mousse, then a layer of Russian salad, finishing with a layer of aspic jelly. Place in the refrigerator to set. Unmould before serving.

crab aspic (or aspic of shrimps, lobster or langouste)

Prepare a fish fumet with 500 g (18 oz) white fish bones and trimmings, 300 ml (½ pint, 1¼ cups) dry white wine, an onion stuck with 2 cloves, a bouquet garni, a small bunch of herbs and 5 or 6 peppercorns. Do not add salt. Add 1 litre (1¾ pints, 4⅓ cups) water, cover, bring to the boil and cook gently for 30 minutes. Hardboil (hardcook) 2 eggs, cool them under running water, and shell them. Strain the fish fumet through a sieve and allow it to cool. Use a small amount of the fumet to dissolve 45 g (1½ oz, 6 envelopes) powdered gelatine. Whisk 3 egg whites and add the remainder of the fumet, whisking constantly. Add the dissolved gelatine and mix in. Bring the mixture to the boil, still whisking constantly. Check the seasoning, take off the heat and leave to settle for 10 minutes. Strain the fumet through a sieve or fine cloth and set aside to cool.

Slice the hard-boiled eggs and 3 small tomatoes. Wash and dry a few tarragon leaves. Coat the mould with the jelly and arrange the slices of tomato and egg and the tarragon leaves over it. Pour a little more jelly over them and leave to set in the refrigerator.

For an aspic of lobster or langouste, cut the tail into sections and remove the shell from the claws and feet. For crab aspic, shell the claws and feet and take out the flesh from the body. For shrimp aspic, use the shrimps shelled but whole. Place the shellfish or shrimps in the mould and finish with shrimp mousse, heaping it up a little. Pour in the rest of the jelly and leave in the refrigerator for 5 or 6 hours.

Unmould and serve on a plate garnished with asparagus tips or lettuce leaves.

fish aspic

This is prepared as for crab aspic, but replacing the shellfish by fillets or slices of fish, and the shrimp mousse with fish mousse. The mousse may alternatively be replaced by Russian salad.

foie gras aspic

Prepare an aspic jelly flavoured with herbs, and use it to coat the mould. Arrange slices of foie gras and thick slices of truffle in the mould. Fill the mould with half-set aspic and allow to set completely in the coldest part of the refrigerator. Unmould just before serving.

smoked salmon aspic

Prepare an aspic jelly flavoured with herbs, and use it to coat the mould. Place some Russian salad on slices of smoked salmon and roll them up. Arrange in the mould, alternating a layer of salmon rolls with a layer of salmon mousse, and finishing with the aspic jelly. Place in the refrigerator to set. Unmould before serving.

ASPIC JELLY A clear savoury jelly prepared from basic white or brown stocks (fish, poultry, game or meat). They are produced naturally when the stock is prepared with items rich in gelatine such as veal knuckle, calf's foot, bacon hock and rind, poultry bones and some fish trimmings. Gelatine is added when the ingredients used for the stock are not rich in gelatinous substances to ensure a good set. Leaf or powdered gelatine is soaked in cold water, then dissolved in the stock before it is clarified. Clarification ensures that an aspic is sparkling clear. Aspic jelly powder is readily available for fish or poultry; it is simply dissolved in water and left to cool.

Fish, poultry, meat, eggs or vegetables can be set in aspic, then turned out to make a savoury mould. Aspic is also used to glaze cold preparations (suprêmes of chicken, quails, steaks or fillets of fish). As a garnish, aspic is used to line containers for chilled terrines or savoury mousses, so that they are coated in an attractive glistening jelly when turned out. Garnishes are usually set in the aspic. Aspic is also poured over the top of such cold dishes that are served in their containers. Set aspic can be diced or chopped and used to garnish cold foods.

Depending on their use, aspic jellies can be coloured (with caramel or edible carmine to obtain an amber tint) and flavoured with a wine or spirit, such as port, Madeira, sherry or brandy.

RECIPES

fish aspic
Prepare a strong fumet. Put 1 kg (2¼ lb) white fish trimmings (bones and heads of brill, hake, whiting, sole or turbot), 2 onions, 150 g (5 oz) mushroom parings, 2 shredded carrots, a large bouquet garni, salt, pepper, 7 tablespoons dry white wine (or red wine when cooking salmon, salmon trout or carp) and 2 litres (3½ pints, 9 cups) cold water in a large saucepan. Bring to the boil and then simmer for 30 minutes. Dissolve 45–75 g (1½–3 oz, 6–12 envelopes) gelatine, depending on the degree of firmness required for the aspic in a little water. Chop up 2 whiting fillets. Mix the dissolved gelatine with the whiting flesh and 2 or 3 egg whites. Strain the fish fumet, pressing the liquid out of the ingredients, and pour it back into the clean saucepan. Add the whiting mixture and bring to the boil, stirring continuously. When it boils, stop stirring and simmer for 30 minutes. Gently strain through a fine cloth and flavour the aspic with champagne or sherry.

meat aspic
Brown 1 kg (2¼ lb) leg of beef and 500 g (18 oz) knuckle of veal, cut into pieces, 1 calf's foot, 500 g (18 oz) veal bones, and 250 g (9 oz) bacon rind, trimmed of fat, in a preheated oven at 200°C (400°F, gas 6). Peel and shred 2 onions, 4 carrots and 1 leek. Place all these ingredients in a stockpot together with a large bouquet garni, 1 tablespoon salt and pepper. Add 3 litres (5 pints, 13 cups) water and bring to the boil. Skim, then add a ladleful of very cold water and simmer for 5 hours. Carefully strain the liquid through a strainer lined with muslin (cheesecloth), let it cool completely and put it in the refrigerator so that the fat which solidifies on the surface can be removed easily. Clarify the stock with 200 g (7 oz) lean beef, 2 egg whites and a small bouquet of chervil and tarragon.

The aspic can be flavoured with Madeira, port, sherry or with any other liquor. If this is done, the flavouring is added just before straining the aspic. White aspic is obtained in a similar fashion, but the meat and bones are not browned. Game aspic is obtained by adding to meat aspic 1.25 kg (2¾ lb) game carcasses and trimmings, which have been previously browned in the oven, and several juniper berries.

Chicken aspic is obtained by adding to meat aspic either a whole chicken or 1.5 kg (3¼ lb) chicken carcasses and giblets, both browned in the oven.

ASSIETTE ANGLAISE
An assortment of cold meats arranged on a plate or dish – the French idea of simple English cooking. It may consist of cooked ham, roast beef, tongue or galantine, garnished with gherkins (sweet dill pickles) and jelly and served with mustard and condiments. The term *assiette froide* (cold plate) is also used. The Italian *affettato* is a selection of pork sausages only.

ASTI
A town in Piedmont, Italy, south of Turin, and centre of an important wine region, in particular well-known for production of a sparkling Moscato-based wine which used to be known as Asti Spumante but is now renamed Asti. It is made by a unique variation on the Charmat (cuve close) method. Asti is light, grapey and relatively low in alcohol at around 9%. Moscato d'Asti is less effervescent and even lower in alcohol at around 5.5%.

ATHENAEUS
Greek writer and grammarian, born at Naucratis, Lower Egypt, in the 3rd century AD. His compilation *Deipnosophistai* ('Authorities on Banquets') is a mine of information about the daily and cultural life of ancient Greece. There are numerous references to chefs and their recipes, discoveries, cooking utensils and special dishes.

ATHÉNIENNE, À L'
The description given in France to dishes thought to be of Greek origin (such as poultry, lamb or kebabs) that are cooked with olive oil and lightly fried onion. They are usually garnished with aubergines (eggplants) – fried, sautéed or stuffed – sweet (bell) peppers (sautéed or stuffed) and rice pilaf *à la grecque*.

ATTELET
A small ornamental skewer with a decorative head in the shape of a hare, boar or fish. The word comes from the Latin *hasta* (a rod or staff), and these skewers were used for garnishing hot or cold dishes served in the grand style, sometimes being threaded with kidneys, sweetbreads and other small items of food. *Le Nouveau Cuisinier royal et bourgeois* (1714) recommends a *plat du milieu* (a dish served between the main courses and the dessert) consisting of 'a piece of beef garnished with small pâtés and hâtelettes of sweetbreads.'

Attelets were never used during cooking, as the soldering on the decorative motifs would melt.

Today this form of garnish is hardly ever seen, as modern cooks tend to avoid any garnish that is not actually edible.

ATTEREAU
A hot hors d'oeuvre consisting of various raw or cooked ingredients that are threaded on to a skewer, dipped in a reduced sauce, coated with breadcrumbs and fried. The skewer used, also called an *attereau*, is made of wood or metal. The word comes from the Latin *hasta* (spear).

The principal ingredient of an *attereau* is usually offal, either cut in pieces or sliced, but it can also be made with seafood or vegetables. The supplementaries like mushrooms, tongue or ham, may be used and the sauce for coating is varied. An *attereau* may also be a hot dessert, in which case it is made with fruit and pastry, dipped in a fried custard mixture (see *custard*), coated with breadcrumbs and then fried.

The name *attereau* is also given to a Burgundian speciality consisting of minced (ground) liver and neck of pork, wrapped in a caul. Shaped like large balls, they are baked side by side in an earthenware dish and are eaten cold.

RECIPES

Savoury Attereaux
attereaux à la niçoise
Assemble the attereaux with large stoned (pitted) olives, mushrooms, pieces of tuna fish (marinated in olive oil and lemon) and anchovy fillets. Make a Villeroi sauce and add to it 1 tablespoon reduced tomato sauce and chopped tarragon. Coat the attereaux with sauce, then with breadcrumbs, and fry.

attereaux of chicken livers à la mirepoix
Sauté some chicken livers in butter, drain and allow to cool. Dice some cooked ham and clean some small button mushrooms. Assemble the attereaux with these 3 ingredients, threading the mushrooms on lengthways. Roll them in a mirepoix and coat them with breadcrumbs. Plunge them into very hot fat, drain and season with salt and pepper. Serve with fried parsley.

attereaux of mussels
Prepare the mussels *à la marinière* and remove them from their shells. Drain them and roll them in mustard. Thread them on skewers alternating with small button mushrooms. Coat with breadcrumbs and complete as for attereaux of oysters.

attereaux of oysters
Poach and drain several large oysters. Cut some mushrooms into thick slices and sauté them in butter. Assemble the attereaux by alternating the oysters with the mushrooms. Dip them in Villeroi sauce made with a fish fumet, coat them with breadcrumbs and plunge them into very hot fat. Serve with fried parsley and lemon halves.

Sweet Attereaux
attereaux of pineapple
Peel a fresh pineapple and cut into cubes. Thread the cubes on to skewers, dip them into a *crème frite* mixture (see *custard*), coat with breadcrumbs and plunge them into the frying fat.

ATTRIAU A type of sausage in the form of a flattened ball, made with a mixture of minced (ground) pork liver, veal, onion and herbs and cooked in a frying pan (skillet). This rustic dish is found in several French provinces.

AUBERGINE (EGGPLANT) An elongated or rounded vegetable (which is, in botanical terms, a fruit) with a firm shiny skin covering pale, creamy white or greenish flesh. Aubergines are familiar as a purple vegetable, though early European versions were white, the shape and size of eggs (with white flesh), hence the American name.

Originating in India and known very early in China, they were brought by the Arabs to Sicily in the 11th century. The French name comes from the Catalan *berenjena*, which has the same Arab derivation as the Indian *brinjal*. They reached north Italy by the 15th century, but were not grown north of the Loire until the time of the French Revolution. Requiring warmth and abundant irrigation, they are now cultivated in the US, West Indies, Israel and Africa.

Colours and sizes vary enormously, from the small cylindrical 7.5 cm (3 in) Japanese ones, to the huge black Enorma, grown in the US. Northern Italy favours a long one, while the Italian south boasts pink ones and several striped varieties, like the Listada de Gandia. Oriental and Indian aubergines are generally slimmer and not so bitter. Check the weight at time of purchase: the aubergine should feel heavy.

The aubergine has a delicate flavour and is used as a vegetable in numerous Eastern and Mediterranean dishes. Typical is the Italian *melanzane parmigiana*, layered with tomato sauce, mozzarella and grated Parmesan cheese. For popular dishes with tomatoes, courgettes (zucchini), garlic and olives, see *imam bayildi, moussaka, ratatouille, tian*. It is delicious as an accompaniment to mutton and white meats. It may be eaten hot, either as a main dish (stuffed or in a soufflé) or as a garnish (sautéed, in fritters crumbed and fried, or puréed), or cold (in the form of a purée or as a salad ingredient). See *baba ghannouj, caponata*.

RECIPES

preparation of aubergines
Formerly, it was the custom to peel aubergines (eggplants), but this is no longer done except for so-called 'white' dishes. Traditionally, the slightly bitter taste of the vegetable was minimized by sprinkling the sliced or cut up flesh with salt and leaving it for 30 minutes to draw out bitter juices. The aubergine was then rinsed and dried before cooking. This process of degorging is no longer necessary as commercially cultivated aubergines are not as bitter as they used to be.

Aubergines may be stuffed in two ways depending on their size and shape. They may be cut in half lengthways and the flesh scooped out of each half. Alternatively, the top may be removed and the aubergine hollowed out inside. Use a sharp knife to remove the flesh, leaving a thickness of 5 mm (¼ in) around the edge, and scoop out the remainder of the flesh from the base with a grapefruit knife. Sprinkle the empty case and the flesh with lemon juice to prevent discoloration.

aubergine caviar
Cook 3 big, heavy, whole aubergines (eggplants), in a preheated oven at about 200°C (400°F, gas 6) for

A SELECTION OF AUBERGINES

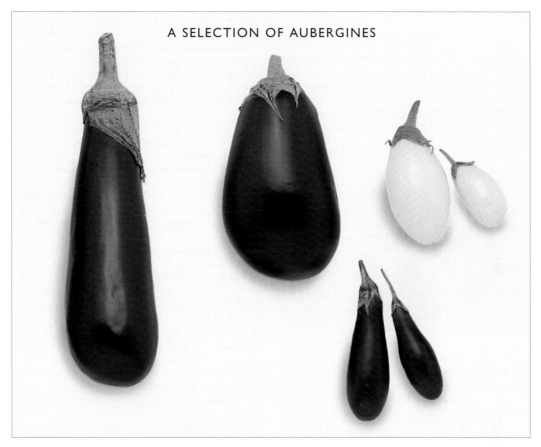

Aubergines may be purple or white, or of different shades of streaked purple-white, and of various sizes, from bite-sized examples to long and slim, or plump, rounded vegetables.

15–20 minutes until tender. Hard boil (hard cook) 4 eggs, cool under a cold tap and shell them. Peel and seed 2 tomatoes and chop the flesh. Peel and finely chop an onion. Cut the aubergines in half, remove the flesh and chop it up with a knife. Mix the tomatoes, aubergine flesh and onion in a salad bowl. Season with salt and pepper and slowly work in 1 small glass olive oil, stirring as for mayonnaise. Alternatively, purée the mixture in a blender. Place in the refrigerator until ready to serve. Garnish with quarters of hard-boiled eggs and tomato slices.

aubergines au gratin à la toulousaine or à la languedocienne

Cut the aubergines (eggplants) into thick slices and sauté in olive oil in a frying pan. Fry some tomato halves in oil in a separate pan. Arrange the tomatoes and aubergines in alternate layers in a gratin dish and sprinkle generously with breadcrumbs mixed with chopped garlic and parsley. Pour on a little oil and brown in the oven or under the grill (broiler).

aubergine soufflés

Cook the aubergine (eggplant) shells and flesh for stuffing as described in the 'caviar' recipe above.

Press the flesh through a sieve or purée in a blender and add an equal quantity of reduced béchamel sauce. Bind with egg yolks and season with salt, pepper and grated nutmeg. At the last moment, fold in very stiffly whisked egg whites. Fill the aubergine cases with the mixture and arrange them in a gratin dish. Sprinkle with Parmesan cheese, if desired, and cook in a preheated oven at 200°C (400°F, gas 6) for about 10 minutes.

For aubergine soufflés *à la hongroise*, add 2 tablespoons chopped onion softened in butter to the filling and season with paprika.

sautéed aubergines

Cut the aubergines (eggplants) into 2 cm (¾ in) cubes and coat with flour. Sauté the slices in olive oil in a frying pan. Arrange in a vegetable dish and sprinkle with chopped parsley.

stuffed aubergines

Prepare 6 small aubergines (eggplants) for stuffing as described in the 'caviar' recipe above. Sprinkle each hollow shell with salt and a tablespoon olive oil and arrange in an ovenproof dish. Cook them in a preheated oven at 220°C (425°F, gas 7) for 15 minutes. Place all the diced flesh in another dish, cover and cook it in the oven at the same time. Meanwhile, stone (pit) and finely chop 100 g (4 oz) large black olives and put them in a large bowl. Heat 1 tablespoon olive oil in a frying pan,

Making pancake aumônière

A variety of savoury or sweet fillings can be used, including fish or seafood, poultry, meat or vegetables coated in a little sauce. Poached or stewed fruit can be used for sweet aumônière; fresh berries are also suitable, especially when combined with a little crème patissiere. An example of the method is included in the entry for morel, where a savoury filling of lobster and morels is used.

1 *Lightly cook the pancakes. Prepare small pancakes – about 15 cm (6 in) in diameter – for sweet fillings or when making savoury purses for a first course; use slightly larger pancakes for enclosing a larger amount of filling, for example for a savoury main course. Place the filling on the middle of the pancake and fold it up neatly over the top.*

2 *Shape the pancake into a neat, evenly gathered purse around the filling.*

3 *Secure the pancake by tying a blade of blanched chive around each one.*

add 6 anchovy fillets and mash them to obtain an oily purée. Pour this purée into the bowl of olives and add the cooked crushed aubergine flesh together with a crushed garlic clove and some thyme. Season with salt and pepper and mix well. Fill the aubergine shells with the mixture and flatten with a fork. Heat thoroughly in a hot oven.

stuffed aubergines à l'italienne
Cook aubergine (eggplant) shells and flesh as in the previous recipe and place them on an oiled dish. Mix the chopped flesh with an equal quantity of risotto seasoned with chopped parsley and garlic. Fill the aubergine shells with this mixture and sprinkle breadcrumbs over the top. Sprinkle with olive oil and brown in the oven or under the grill.

other recipes See *catalane, cumin, escalope, fritter, gratin languedocien, omelette (cooked with their flavouring), rougail, salpicon (vegetable salpicons).*

AUMALE, À LA D' This French description is given to a dish of fattened pullet that is stuffed and braised. It was created by the head chef of Henri d'Orléans, the fourth son of Louis-Philippe. The particularly elaborate garnish consists of croustades garnished with trimmed cucumber pieces cooked in butter and with scooped-out onion halves, filled with a salpicon of tongue and foie gras bound with a Madeira sauce.

Scrambled eggs *à la d'Aumale* include crushed tomatoes and diced sautéed kidneys with Madeira.

AUMÔNIÈRE, EN The French name refers to the traditional shape of the almoner's purse. It is given to an original apricot dessert: the apricots, whose stones (pits) are replaced with lumps of sugar, are encased in triangles of shortcrust pastry (basic pie dough) sealed at the edges. These tarts are cooked in the oven, decorated with chopped grilled (broiled) almonds and served with a hot apricot sauce.

The term is also used for filled pancakes or crêpes, gathered up into a purse shape around a savoury or sweet filling. The pancake aumônière are heated and browned in the oven before being served, usually with a sauce.

AURORE The French name means 'dawn', given to a velouté sauce flavoured with tomato purée (paste) and also to some dishes containing tomato purée. The name is also applied to dishes of egg and chicken coated with the sauce.

RECIPES

sauce aurore
The traditional sauce is made by adding 500 ml (17 fl oz, 2 cups) very thick puréed tomato sauce to 200 ml (7 fl oz, ¾ cup) velouté* sauce. Finish with 50 g (2 oz, ¼ cup) butter and put the sauce through a sieve.

Today, however, sauce aurore is a light béchamel sauce flavoured with tomato purée (paste) and butter.

soft-boiled or poached eggs aurore
Arrange the boiled or poached eggs on croûtons fried in butter and coat with sauce aurore. Sprinkle with chopped hard-boiled (hard-cooked) egg yolks. Surround with a border of tomato sauce.

stuffed hard-boiled eggs aurore
Hard boil (hard cook) some eggs and cut in half. Mash most of the yolks with an equal volume of sauce aurore containing chopped herbs. Fill the egg whites with the mixture. Put a layer of sauce aurore in a gratin dish and arrange the egg halves on it. Cover with grated Parmesan or Gruyère cheese. Sprinkle a little melted butter over the cheese and brown in a preheated oven at 240°C (475°F, gas 9). Remove from the oven and sprinkle with the remaining chopped egg yolks.

AUSLESE A category of German or Austrian wines made with late-harvested grapes, which in the best years are affected by noble rot. Depending on the concentration of sugar, these wines may be dry (*trocken*) or sweeter (*halbtrocken, süss*).

AUSONIUS Roman poet (born at Burdigala [Bordeaux] *c*. AD 310; died *c*. AD 395), who was tutor to Gratian, a son of Emperor Valentinian I. Ausonius was made a consul in 379 and retired in 383 to the region around present-day Saint-Émilion. He wrote: 'Happy are the inhabitants of Bordeaux, for whom living and drinking are one and the same!' His name survives in the red Bordeaux wine, Château-Ausone. He left a work concerning the breeding of oysters.

AUSTRALIA See *page 56*.

AUSTRIA See *page 58*.

AUTOCLAVE A hermetically sealed vessel designed for sterilizing food products. The food is immersed in water that is heated under pressure so that the temperature rises to 120–180°C (250–350°F). No bacteria can survive in temperatures of 120°C (250°F) or above. The apparatus is provided with an adjustable safety valve.

The principle of the autoclave, derived directly from the Papin marmite (invented by Denis Papin), enabled Nicolas Appert to perfect his method of food preservation. The preserving industry still uses autoclaves. See *pressure cooker*.

AUTRICHIENNE, À L' The French name, homage to Austria, is given to various dishes seasoned with paprika. Sometimes lightly fried onion, fennel or soured (sour) cream may be included.

AUVERGNATE, À L' This French name is given to numerous dishes made with products of the Auvergne: pickled pork, bacon and ham (used in stews, stuffed cabbage and lentil and potato dishes), and also cheeses, such as blue cheese (for soup) and Cantal (for aligot and truffade).

AUVERGNE See *page 59*.

AUXEY-DURESSES A village in Burgundy, close to Meursault, producing red and white wines. Many are labelled as Côte de Beaune Villages.

AVGOLEMONO A simple Greek sauce, or soup, of egg yolks and fresh lemon juice beaten together, with a suitable hot liquid then added. Once made, it must be placed in a bain marie, or it will curdle.

AVICE, JEAN French pastrycook at the beginning of the 19th century. A chef in the best pâtisserie of the time – Bailly, in the Rue Vivienne, Paris, he was also appointed purveyor to Talleyrand. He trained the young Carême who, when he became famous, paid tribute to 'the illustrious Avice, master of choux pastry'. Avice is considered by some to be the creator of the *madeleine*.

AVOCADO A pear-shaped or round fruit from a tropical tree originating in Central America. The name comes from the Mexican *ahuacatl*, which means 'testicle'. Its skin, which may be grained or smooth and shiny, is dark green or purplish-brown in colour. It has pale-green flesh surrounding a large hard round stone (pit), which comes away easily. The flesh has a buttery consistency and a slight flavour of hazelnuts. A fruit like no other, it is ripe when it gives under the pressure of the finger. It has the virtue of ripening off the tree so it can be retarded in the refrigerator, or ripened at room temperature. Occasionally, miniature 'cocktail' avocados are seen, without the stone (pit).

The Spanish discovered the avocado tree and sent saplings to several tropical countries. The fruit's popularity was slow to spread, only being cultivated in the US at the end of the 19th century. It did not reach French recipe books until the 1950s and it was the huge investment by Israel in the fruit after World War II that established its popularity in Europe. It is now cultivated in America, Israel, Australia, the West Indies and many areas of Europe with Mediterranean climates, in many varieties. Popular American ones are Fuerte, large and green (which reflects the West Indian type) and Hass, wrinkled and dark-skinned (like Guatamalan avocadoes). The latter explains one of the earlier names of 'alligator pear'.

Avocados discolour on exposure to the air, so are either prepared at the last minute or need acidulating. They are commonly served halved with a sauce or a stuffing such as seafood. Sliced, they are popular in salads, and may also make mousses and even ice cream.

The fruit is popular in Mexico in such dishes as guacamole (crushed avocado with chilli and garlic),

AUSTRALIA

To the unknown continent of Australia in 1788 the first British immigrants brought their food traditions. The swagman, cooking potatoes in his 'billy' can; and the meat pie 'floater' served in tomato sauce (a national dish); tea drinking and cakes like Anzacs (coconut, rolled oats and golden syrup) and Lamingtons (cubes of sponge, chocolate and coconut-coated) are part of this.

The new Australians reared livestock of exceptionally high quality, particularly sheep and lamb. Breakfasting on steak with a fried egg, and feasting on meat three times a day, are traditions of the outback, along with beer (now a big export) and the 'barbie' (barbecue). But they were slow to explore indigenous food. The kangaroo is venison-like when correctly cooked (rare); eventually it was made into pasties, stews and soup. (Eating it is now banned, except in South Australia.)

With Chinese immigration in the 1890s came the demand for and growth of vegetables, and new species were planted like the choko (custard marrow). Temperate fruits had been grown since the 1920s and tropical ones followed. Australia adopted the passion fruit and the meringue pavlova became the national dessert. The macadamia nut is the only indigenous fruit to be exported.

■ **Contemporary food and cooking** Excellent fish, like the barramundi, King George whiting and snapper, shellfish like yabbies (crayfish) and bugs (see *slipper lobster*), the best being the Moreton bay and Balmain bugs, are the basis of Australia's 'new' cuisine and fish are air-freighted to the big cities.

Despite the continent's size, however, there is no regional cuisine, except perhaps in the Barossa Valley which maintains a German food and wine culture. Passable city restaurants date only from the 1900s. The changes of the last decades of the 20th century came partly because good food usually associates with good wine-growing, but more from a changing ethnic population, including Italians and Greeks, and the big influx from Asia. City food is becoming 'Pacific rim', like that of California.

WINE Australian wine-growing dates from 1788, when the first vines were planted in the place now known as Sydney, and by the late 19th century Australian wines were winning medals at major European exhibitions. More recently, Australian wine production was dominated by fortified wines, known as 'port' and 'sherry', but technical advances in viticulture and vinification have seen a transformation of the industry. With a range of reliable red, white and sparkling wines, Australia is at the forefront of quality wine production.

Most Australian wine production is concentrated in the south-eastern corner of the Continent, spread between the states of South Australia, Victoria and New South Wales, although there are also significant plantings in Western Australia.

● SOUTH AUSTRALIA This state produces around 50% of Australia's wine, much of it from the irrigated Riverland area, but there are a number of high quality districts. The Barossa is famed for its Shiraz (Syrah) made from old vines; Clare and Eden Valley make excellent Rieslings; and Coonawarra is building its reputation on Cabernet Sauvignon.

● VICTORIA The River Murray forms the northern boundary of this state and much bulk wine comes from irrigated vineyards in surrounding areas. The Yarra and Mornington Peninsula in the south of the State are known as quality wine areas where Pinot Noir and Chardonnay excel.

● NEW SOUTH WALES This state owes its viticultural heritage to its proximity to Sydney, but it has established a fine reputation for wines from the Hunter Valley. As well as Shiraz and Chardonnay, Semillon is particularly fine. New areas, such as Orange, are now being planted. Inland, the area known as Griffith or Murrumbidgee Irrigation Area (M.I.A.) is a producer of bulk wine.

● TASMANIA Contributing just a minimal amount to Australia's production, Tasmania offers cool climate conditions for Pinot Noir and grapes for sparkling wine.

● WESTERN AUSTRALIA Margaret River is the leading fine wine area in this state, producing refined Cabernet Sauvignon and Chardonnay wines.

---

which may be served with tortillas and bread rolls. In Martinique, it is the basis of *féroce* (avocado mixed with chopped salt cod). It is used throughout South America for garnishing hot or iced soups and ragoûts. In Africa, avocado leaves are used to make the sparkling and slightly alcoholic drink known as *babine*.

RECIPES

avocado salad archestrate
Cut the heart of a head of celery into thin strips. Dice 3 cooked artichoke hearts and 3 peeled and seeded tomatoes. Halve 4 avocados and carefully remove the flesh, keeping each half intact. Slice the flesh and sprinkle with lemon juice. Season the avocado and vegetables with vinaigrette, arrange in a salad bowl and sprinkle with chopped herbs.

avocado salad with crab
Cut 3–4 avocados in half and scoop out the flesh with a small spoon. Mix the flesh with crumbled crab meat, diced tomato flesh, slices of hard-boiled (hard-cooked) egg, pepper and a little tomato purée or ketchup. Sprinkle with chopped herbs and serve cold.

The wine-producing regions of Australia

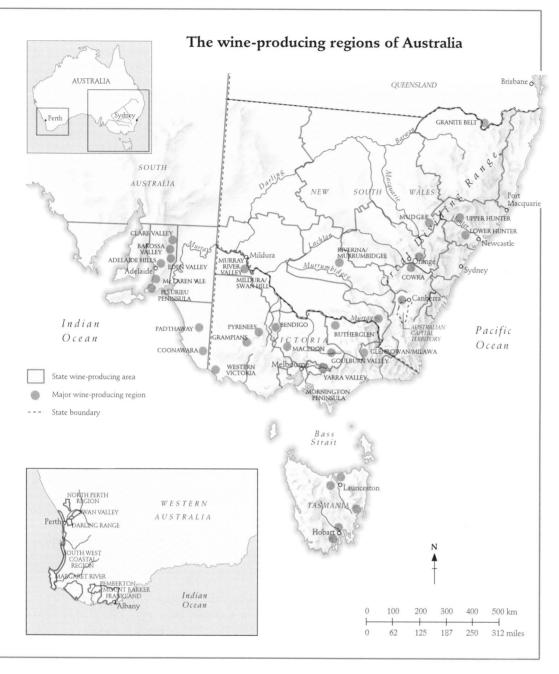

AUSTRALIA

Perth

Sydney

SOUTH AUSTRALIA

QUEENSLAND

Brisbane

GRANITE BELT

NEW SOUTH WALES

Port Macquarie

MUDGEE

UPPER HUNTER

LOWER HUNTER

Newcastle

CLARE VALLEY

BAROSSA VALLEY

ADELAIDE HILLS

EDEN VALLEY

Adelaide

McLAREN VALE

FLEURIEU PENINSULA

Mildura

MURRAY RIVER VALLEY

MILDURA/ SWAN HILL

RIVERINA/ MURRUMBIDGEE

Orange

COWRA

Sydney

Canberra

AUSTRALIAN CAPITAL TERRITORY

Indian Ocean

Pacific Ocean

PADTHAWAY

PYRENEES

GRAMPIANS

BENDIGO

RUTHERGLEN

VICTORIA

MACEDON

GLENROWAN/MILAWA

COONAWARRA

GOULBURN VALLEY

WESTERN VICTORIA

Melbourne

YARRA VALLEY

MORNINGTON PENINSULA

☐ State wine-producing area

⬤ Major wine-producing region

- - - State boundary

Bass Strait

Launceston

TASMANIA

Hobart

NORTH PERTH REGION

SWAN VALLEY

Perth

DARLING RANGE

WESTERN AUSTRALIA

SOUTH WEST COASTAL REGION

MARGARET RIVER

PEMBERTON MOUNT BARKER FRANKLAND

Albany

Indian Ocean

N

| 0 | 100 | 200 | 300 | 400 | 500 km |
| 0 | 62 | 125 | 187 | 250 | 312 miles |

avocado salad with cucumber

Assemble equal quantities of avocado (halved, stoned, peeled, diced and sprinkled with lemon juice) and halved, seeded and sliced cucumber. Dress with vinaigrette, strongly flavoured with mustard, and sprinkle with chopped herbs.

avocado sauce

Blend together avocado flesh with lemon juice in the following proportions: 2 tablespoons lemon juice to a medium-sized avocado. Mix with an equal volume of whipping cream. Serve very cold with hot or cold meat or poultry, with quarters of lemon.

avocados stuffed with crab

Prepare a mayonnaise and season it with mustard and cayenne pepper. Crumble some crab meat (fresh, canned or frozen). Halve the avocados and scoop out the flesh in large pieces, then cut it into even-sized cubes. Sprinkle the flesh and the insides of the avocado shells with lemon juice and season them with salt and pepper to taste. Mix the mayonnaise with the crab meat and carefully add the chopped avocado flesh. Pile the filling into the shells. If you like, the avocados can be garnished with mayonnaise coloured with a little tomato

AUSTRIA

Austria is at the heart of Europe, so its cuisine reflects the different nationalities who have shaped its history – the Germans, the Hungarians and the Italians. This is why it includes not only cabbage, ragoûts and charcuterie, but also cream cheeses with poppy seeds and a taste for onion and paprika (goulash is an Austrian dish as well as being a Hungarian speciality). Gastronomy holds a place of honour in Vienna, where the splendours of the Empire survive in such bastions of tradition as the Hotel Sacher, the Demel pâtisserie and the old cafés (Hewelka, Landtmann), as well as the Naschmarkt, the oldest of the Viennese markets.

The river resources have inspired some classic fish dishes, such as trout *au bleu*, stuffed pike and fried carp, which is traditionally eaten at Christmas, and also crayfish with fennel. *Tafelspitz* (very well-hung boiled meat) is the pride of Austrian cooks. There are several variations and it is served with salads and compotes. However, the dish that is best known abroad is the Wiener Schnitzel (escalope of veal), which can also be made with beef or pork. Poultry has always featured in Austrian cuisine, particularly chicken. It may be roasted, coated with breadcrumbs and fried in lard (shortening), or prepared with soured (sour) cream, paprika or cabbage.

■ **Regional specialities** Small traditional restaurants (*Gasthof* or *Heuriger*) serve the best wines with regional dishes such as roast hare, goose with red cabbage, pork quenelles, stuffed crêpes (*Palatschinken*), Carinthian ravioli (*Nudin*), beef with onions and cumin (*Zwiebel-fleisch*) and Styrian spiced ragoûts, followed by salads dressed with pumpkin-seed oil. Soups and ragoûts are popular everywhere. The classic ones are made with potatoes and mushrooms and served with bread or liver knödel. The Tyrol is famous for its charcuterie, and sauerkraut, bacon quenelles and calves' liver with onions are also popular. *Nockerln* is the Austrian version of Italian gnocchi, and the same word is also used for a sweet soufflé from Salzburg.

■ **Famous pâtisserie** Above all, Austria is a country renowned for its pâtisserie, which is served, like coffee, with lashings of whipped cream (*Schlagobers*). As well as the three great classics – sachertorte, strudel, and linzertorte – other specialities are dried fruit and poppy-seed cream puffs, meringues, crystallized (candied) fruit, cream cheese or cherry tarts, *Kaiserschmarrn* (a thick very sweet pancake), *krapfen* (fritters), *Zwetschenknödel* (stoned, or pitted, prunes coated in pastry and fried) and *Tascherln* and *Buchteln* (Swiss or jelly rolls or cakes filled with jam).

WINE Despite a very long history of growing grapes and making wine, the Austrian wine industry suffered an almost fatal blow in 1985, when a small number of producers were caught adding a banned substance to their wines in order to boost its apparent quality. This led to a complete overhaul of the Austrian wine legislation, making it one of the most exacting in Europe.

Grapes are grown in the eastern part of the country, with the Lower Austria, Burgenland and Styria being the most important. The climate is essentially continental with harsh winters and hot dry summers, capable of ripening grapes to high sugar levels. While grape varieties and styles of wine are in some cases close to those of Germany, many Austrian wines are unique.

Grüner Veltliner is Austria's most planted white grape variety, accounting for around 36% of vineyard area. It makes refreshing wines for drinking while young. Zweigelt and Blaufränkisch are the major red varieties. Sweet wines from around Neusiedlersee rank among the finest in the world.

---

purée (paste) piping it with a star (fluted) nozzle. Dust with paprika.

avocados stuffed with shrimps
These are prepared as for the previous recipe, using large pink shelled shrimps instead of crab meat. The dish will be enhanced by marinating the shrimps in lemon juice and herbs.

Californian avocado salad
Peel 2 grapefruit, removing all the pith, then cut the segments from between the membranes. Place the fruit segments in a salad bowl. Halve 3 avocados, remove the flesh, dice it and sprinkle with lemon juice. Add to the salad bowl together with 150–200 g (5–7 oz) shelled shrimps. Sprinkle with 2 tablespoons gin or brandy and add 3–5 table-spoons mayonnaise with a little ketchup and cayenne pepper. Garnish with slices of lemon.

cornmeal pancakes with avocados
Make a pancake batter with 250 g (9 oz, 2 cups) cornmeal, 3 whole eggs, salt, pepper, 2–3 table-spoons oil or melted butter and 500 ml (17 fl oz, 2 cups) warm milk, or a mixture of milk and water. Beat the ingredients together until smooth and set the batter aside. Purée the flesh of 3 avocados in a blender, adding cayenne, salt, pepper and 3 table-spoons olive oil. Cover with cling film (plastic wrap) and put in a cool place. Add some chopped tar-ragon to the oatmeal batter and make the pan-cakes, then allow them to cool. Spread them with avocado purée, roll up and hold them together with cocktail sticks (toothpicks). Serve cold, with a tomato salad sprinkled with snipped chives.

grilled avocado with mozzarella
Mix 4 finely chopped spring onions (salad onions) with 100 g (4 oz) finely diced mozzarella cheese

Auvergne

The Auvergne, including the picturesque Velay region, is farming country with a good simple cuisine, described by Curnonsky as *droite en goût* (with unadulterated flavours). The copious food of the region, generally considered to be fortifying rather than refined, is not however limited to the traditional potée, a cabbage soup common to many provinces. Delicate dishes of the Auvergne include *mourtayrol, cousinat,* Cantal soup and *soupe au farci* (a stew containing a cabbage stuffed with sausagemeat). The freshwater fish are excellent: carp, pike, tench, eel and perch are prepared in tasty matelotes (fish stews), while trout may be eaten *à la meunière, au bleu* or *au lard* (with bacon). Salmon is found upstream as far as Brioude, where it is made into a delicious pie.

The pork of the Auvergne is renowned, and the charcuterie consists of dried and smoked hams, dried sausages, large country sausages, black puddings (blood sausages), *fritons* (crisp pork pieces) and *fricandeaux.* Stock breeding results in the production of excellent meats, notably beef from Salers; veal, used to make *falette*; and the sheep of Vassivières and Chaudes-Aigues, to which the famous gigot *brayaude* owes its reputation. Even though the poultry of the region does not have a national

reputation, turkey with chestnuts is a delectable dish, as is the coq au vin cooked with Chanturgues, a local red wine. The high-quality game is used in such dishes as braised partridge with lentils and hare *à l'auvergnate.*

■ **The regional produce** The land of the Auvergne is fertile. The vegetables are magnificent and the orchards of the Limagne provide very good fresh fruit – apricots, peaches, apples, pears and cherries – a large proportion of which is made into crystallized (candied) fruit by the local industries. Auvergne walnuts and chestnuts, appropriately used in cooking, are particularly tasty.

Varied and abundant mushrooms are found in the meadows, forests and undergrowth. They feature in some classic dishes of the gastronomy of the Auvergne – *cul de veau aux mousserons* (rump of veal with St George's mushrooms) *crépinette de foie aux cèpes, aux*

In this northern range of mountains in the Auvergne, the old volcanoes known as puys contain the many fresh water springs that are renowned for their purity.

bolets or *aux oronges* (a special flat sausage of liver with ceps, boletus or Caesar's mushrooms), and *omelette aux girolles* (chanterelle omelette). In addition, many kinds of meat and poultry are served with morels, either in gravy or cream sauce.

Some other well-known specialities include omelette *brayaude, aligot, friand* de Saint-Flour, meat pie, *truffade, pounti,* and potatoes with bacon. The famous local cheeses – Cantal, Saint-Nectaire, Savaron, Bleu, Gaperon, Murol and Fourme d'Ambert – are best eaten with the local wines. The excellent pâtisserie includes *fouace* du Cantal, the crisp petits fours of Mauriac, Murat pastry horns and *picoussel* of Mur-de-Barrez.

---

and the grated rind (zest) from 1 lemon. Peel, seed and dice 2 tomatoes. Halve and stone 2 firm but ripe avocados, then arrange them in a fireproof tin (pan) or dish, supporting them with crumpled foil. Sprinkle with lemon juice and trickle with olive oil. Grill (broil) until hot and lightly browned. Divide the tomatoes between the avocados, sprinkle with seasoning, then top with the mozzarella mixture. Continue grilling until golden brown and bubbling. Serve at once.

guacamole

Finely chop ¼ small onion and mix with 2 peeled, seeded and diced tomatoes, 1 seeded and finely chopped green chilli, 1 finely chopped large garlic clove, the juice of ½ lime and a little grated zest from about a quarter of the lime. Mash the flesh from 2 large ripe avocados in a mixing bowl, then add the vegetable mixture and gradually beat in 2 table-spoons olive oil. Stir in 2–3 tablespoons chopped fresh coriander (cilantro) and seasoning to taste.

AYRAN Turkish yogurt drink, made by diluting yogurt with water and ice. The drink may be flavoured with mint. Refreshing yogurt drinks are prepared throughout the Balkan countries and the Middle East. *Airan, eyran, ajran* or *dhalle* are all names for similar drinks. Lassi is the Indian version.

The icy, diluted yogurt is the perfect complement for spicy dishes and it is a cooling choice in hot climates. Flavouring ingredients may be added, for example salt, rosewater, lemon, cucumber or spices such as cardamoms, ginger or even chillies.

AYU Japanese river fish, known as sweetfish in English. The ayu is caught from June through to the end of summer, and it is considered a delicacy for its excellent, slightly sweet, flavour. The fish is small, growing to about 30 cm (12 in) but caught at 13–15 cm (5–6 in).Traditionally, trained cormorants are used to catch the fish. Working at night, the cormorant handlers train their leashed birds to dive into the water and catch the fish, then they retrieve the fish from the birds' grasp. Line and rod fishing methods are mainly used now. Salt grilling – *shioyaki* – is a popular method of cooking freshly caught ayu. The fish are rubbed with salt and allowed to stand for 30 minutes. A dipping sauce of seasoned dashi (stock) and vinegar may be served with the fish.

AZAROLE A large red or orange hip from the tree *Crataegus azarolus*, related to the hawthorn. It is grown in southern France, Spain and the US, though at its best in Italy. The fruit needs a ripening period after picking, when it becomes fragrant and sugary, so can be eaten raw. It is used for confectionery and jelly, especially in northern Italy, and is fermented for a drink.

AZUKI BEAN Also known as aduki bean. A tiny, dull-red bean very squat in shape and sweetish in flavour. It is a native of Japan, India and South East Asia and keeps for many years. After soy, it is the most-used bean in Japanese cookery, mixed with rice, or red bean paste and used in many desserts and cakes, both as an ingredient in the main mixture and as a filling when made into a sweetened paste. In Japanese tradition, eating azuki beans was thought to bring good luck.

B

BABA A cake made from leavened dough that contains raisins and is steeped, after baking, in rum or kirsch syrup. Typically it is served either as individual small cakes baked in dariole moulds or individual ring moulds but may be a large cake, often decorated with angelica and glacé (candied) cherries.

The origin of this cake is attributed to the greediness of the Polish king Stanislas Leszcsynski, who was exiled in Lorraine. He found the traditional *kouglof* (see *kugelhopf*) too dry and improved it by adding rum. As a dedicated reader of *The Thousand and One Nights*, he is said to have named this creation after his favourite hero, Ali Baba. This recipe was a great success at the court of Nancy, where it was usually served with a sauce of sweet Málaga wine. Carême writes, however: 'It was well known that the true Polish baba should be made with rye flour and Hungarian wine.'

Sthorer, a pastrycook who attended the court of the Polish king, perfected the recipe using a brioche steeped in alcohol; he made it the speciality of his house in the Rue Montorgueil in Paris and called it 'baba'. Around 1850, several renowned pastrycooks, taking their inspiration from the baba, created the *fribourg* in Bordeaux, the *brillat-savarin* (later known as the savarin) in Paris, and the *gorenflot*.

RECIPE

rum babas ♦
Soak 100 g (4 oz, ¾ cup) raisins in 300 ml (½ pint, 1¼ cups) rum and soften 100 g (4 oz, ½ cup) butter at room temperature.

Mix 25 g (1 oz, 2 cakes) fresh (compressed) yeast or 2 teaspoons dried yeast with 2 tablespoons warm water. Make a well in 250 g (9 oz, 2¼ cups) sifted strong plain (bread) flour and add 2 tablespoons sugar, a generous pinch of salt, 2 whole eggs and the yeast mixture. Mix with a wooden spatula until the ingredients are combined, then add another egg. Work this in, and then add a further egg and work that in. Finally add the softened butter and work the dough until it is elastic before adding the drained raisins. Reserve the rum from the raisins for soaking the babas.

Melt 50 g (2 oz, ¼ cup) butter over a low heat and use to brush the insides of 16 dariole moulds or individual ring moulds. Divide the dough equally among the moulds. Leave in a warm place until the dough has risen to fill the moulds. Bake in a preheated oven at about 200°C (400°F, gas 6) for 15–20 minutes. Turn the babas out immediately on to a rack and allow to cool completely.

Prepare a syrup using 1 litre (1¾ pints, 4⅓ cups) water and 500 g (18 oz, 2¼ cups) sugar. Dip each baba in the boiling syrup and leave submerged until no more air bubbles are released. Drain and place on a wire rack resting over a dish. When the babas have cooled slightly, soak them in the reserved rum, adding extra rum as necessary to soak the babas generously. As the rum syrup collects in the dish repeatedly spoon it back over the babas to ensure they are very moist.

Serve the babas topped or filled with whipped cream and fresh fruit, such as raspberries. Crème anglaise may be served with the babas: streak the sauce with a little chocolate sauce and add a few rum-soaked raisins for decoration.

BABA GHANNOUJ A mezze or vegetable side dish eaten throughout the Middle East. The smoky flesh of grilled (broiled) aubergine (eggplant) is puréed with garlic, salt, lemon juice and good olive oil (sometimes tahini) to make a paste known as 'poor man's caviar'. Widely eaten in the West, the dish started the whole tradition of vegetable 'caviars', while this name is an inspired translation of 'spoiled old daddy', which is its Lebanese meaning.

BABACO A fruit related to the papaya, originating in the highlands of Ecuador, it is grown in temperate climates in New Zealand, Britain and America. Also known as chamburo. Resembling an elongated, fluted melon with a star-shaped cross-section when cut, the babaco can measure up to 30 cm (12 in) but it is usually smaller. The whole greenish-to-yellow fruit is edible for it has a soft skin and no pips. The babaco is juicy but low in sugar, so not especially sweet and it can be used in the same way as cucumber in salads and savoury dishes as well as in sweet dishes when sweetened.

BACCHUS In Roman mythology, the god of vines and wine, the counterpart of the Greek god Dionysus. His functions were many: he represented Nature (symbolized by the rod he carried, which was wrapped in ivy and vine leaves, with a pine cone at one end); he was the father of viticulture, since he had taught man to cultivate the vine and make wine; and he was the incarnation of fertility and became the god of procreation, often symbolized by a goat or a bull. Bacchus is usually accompanied by a cortege of satyrs, sirens and bacchantes. Dionysus, in whose honour mysteries were celebrated, inspired the birth of Greek dramatic poetry, whereas Bacchus has essentially remained part of the sensual and carnal world of drunkenness and the pleasure of drinking (hence 'bacchic').

BACON Lean cured sides of pork, generally sold as thin slices, 'rashers' in Britain, which are eaten fried or grilled (broiled), especially with eggs (see *breakfast*), principally in the British Isles and Canada. The cured side of pig, smoked in one piece, keeps almost indefinitely. In Britain it has been a traditional cottage food for centuries. Large-scale bacon curing dates to the 1770s in Wiltshire, still a bacon centre. Cures may be dry (in salt), like the classic Wiltshire cure, or wet (in brine) of which Danish exports are the leading example. Since the introduction of refrigeration the amount of salt used has dropped considerably, though regional tastes (and cures) persist and the Irish and the Scots like their bacon salty. Bacon remains a gourmet product in the English-breakfast world, with differing cures and types of smoking on offer, for example over apple wood.

Sides are cut to give slices consisting of lean back meat and a fatty streaky belly end. Sold with or without the cured skin (rind), which may be retained for cooking. As well as slices, in Britain larger steaks (thick slices) or joints are prepared, the latter for boiling or roasting. The traditional pigs, bred for bacon, were the Gloucester Old Spot,

Blacks, Saddleback and Tamworth; now the white Danish Landrace is the prominent breed.

The Italian *pancetta* is belly with a slightly sweeter cure than the English type. It is best known in its rolled form, which is flavoured with cloves and pepper, and sliced for use. Some is smoked. German *Speck*, Spanish *tocino* and Polish *slonina* are streaky fatty products, sold as slabs with rind, so they may be used for barding. Many pan dishes are started with a fried mixture of onions and bacon, called *soffritto* in Italy. In France lard has the same uses, called *poitrine fumé* if it is smoked. French *bacon* is cured loin, dried, steamed and smoked; either could go into *quiche lorraine*. Strips, or lardons, of fatty bacon are used for larding; cut short, they are fried and used to flavour cooked dishes or salads.

The word derives from the old French *bakko*, meaning ham, itself from the German for pig. In French this became *bacon*, meaning a piece of salt pork or even the whole pig (a *repas baconique* was a festive meal where only pork dishes were served). The word was then adopted by the English and returned to France with its present meaning.

RECIPES

bacon omelette
Cut thick slices of rindless bacon into cubes and fry in butter. Add to the eggs, beat together and make an omelette. It may be served covered with slices of bacon fried in butter.

calves' liver with bacon
Season slices of calves' liver with salt and pepper and then coat in flour, shaking them to remove any excess. Fry and then drain two thin slices of rindless bacon for each slice of liver. Cook the liver for about 10 minutes in the same frying pan, arrange on a plate, and garnish with the bacon and slices of lemon. Keep warm. Make a sauce in the frying pan using the meat juices and lemon juice or vinegar. Pour over the liver and sprinkle with parsley.

BAEKENOFE Also known as *backenoff*. An Alsatian dish comprising a stew of various meats. The origin of this speciality is linked to the traditional way of life in the country. On their way to the fields in the morning, the peasants would leave earthenware pots prepared by their wives (containing meat marinated overnight, onions, potatoes and seasoning added that morning) with the village baker, who would bake (*baeken*) them in his oven (*ofen*) after the batch of bread. The baekenofe was usually prepared on Mondays (washing day) when the housewife was too busy to cook. The baker himself sealed the pots with bread dough.

The baekenofe, which is still prepared in Alsace, requires long slow cooking in the oven to bring out the full flavour. It is often served with a green salad.

Rum babas,
see page 61.

RECIPE

baekenofe

Cut 450 g (1 lb) shoulder of mutton, 450 g (1 lb) shoulder of pork and 450 g (1 lb) beef into large cubes and marinate overnight in 500 ml (17 fl oz, 2 cups) Alsace wine, 1 large finely chopped onion, 1 onion stuck with 2–3 cloves, 2 crushed garlic cloves, a bouquet garni and salt and pepper. The next day, peel and slice 2 kg (4½ lb) potatoes and 225 g (8 oz) onions. Grease a large casserole with lard, then fill with layers of the ingredients, as follows: a layer of potatoes, a layer of meat and a layer of onions. Repeat until all the ingredients have been used, ending with a layer of potatoes. Remove the bouquet garni and the onion stuck with cloves from the marinade and pour the liquid into the casserole. The liquid should just reach the top layer; if necessary, top up with water. Cover and cook in a preheated oven at about 160°C (325°F, gas 3) for 4 hours.

BAGEL A small Jewish roll-with-a-hole, bagels are also identified with the American East Coast from the turn of the 20th century, and with New York in particular, where a breakfast may be bagels, lox (pickled salmon) and cream cheese. Created by a Jewish baker in Vienna in 1683, the dough includes both yeast and egg (and nowadays a choice of other flavourings). The dough is left to rise, then shaped into overlapping rings. Traditionally these are poached briefly in boiling, salted water until they rise to the surface, giving them a characteristically close texture and firm, moist crust which is slightly 'chewy'. They are then glazed with egg and may be sprinkled with poppy or caraway seeds before baking until golden.

BAGNA CAUDA A hot dip (literally a 'hot bath'), this speciality of Piedmont in northern Italy is a festival dish, dating back to the 16th century. The purée is made from olive oil with a little butter, pounded garlic and anchovy fillets, heated for some minutes, then served over a lamp, like a fondue. White truffles may be added in season. It is scooped up with pieces of raw vegetables; for example cabbage strips, celery, fennel, cauliflower and peppers. Cardoons are also traditional for dipping. Red wine goes with bagna cauda which is not eaten at a meal, but as a party snack.

BAGNES A Swiss cheese made from cow's milk (45% fat content); it is a cooked pressed cheese with a slightly rough brushed crust. Firm but springy to the touch, it has a fruity flavour which makes it suitable for the table, but it is most widely known along with Conches, Gomser and Orsières, as a cheese for making raclettes. A product of Valais (particularly the Bagnes valley), it is a flat round cheese, 35–40 cm (14–16 in) in diameter, 7–8 cm (3–4 in) thick, and weighing about 7 kg (16 lb). Some gourmets prefer it slightly more mature (up to six months old instead of the usual three), which makes it quite a strong cheese.

BAGRATION The name given to various dishes inspired by recipes dedicated by Carême to Princess Bagration, whose service he entered on his return from Russia in August 1819. These recipes often include macaroni (to accompany meat soups, salad and stuffed eggs), Russian salad (to accompany crayfish and fillet of sole), creamed chicken, or salpicon of truffles and pickled ox (beef) tongue, but the garnishes have changed and are now more simple than in the original recipes.

RECIPES

Bagration eggs

Butter a number of dariole moulds and line with cooked chopped macaroni mixed with quenelle forcemeat. Break 1 egg into each mould. Cook in a bain marie for 6–8 minutes. Turn out into small pastry cases. Coat with a cream sauce and garnish with a slice of truffle warmed through in butter.

Bagration fish soup

Prepare in the same way as Bagration meat soup, but use 225 g (8 oz) fillet of sole instead of veal. Reduce cooking time to 30 minutes.

Bagration meat soup

Sauté 450 g (1 lb) diced lean veal in butter to seal in the meat juices. Add to 1 litre (1¾ pints, 4⅓ cups) velouté soup* and simmer for 1 hour. Strain the veal, chop it finely, and return to the velouté. Stir in 3 egg yolks mixed with 100 ml (4 fl oz, 7 tablespoons) cream to bind the soup and adjust the seasoning. Stir in about 50 g (2 oz, ¼ cup) butter and hot chopped macaroni. Serve accompanied by grated cheese.

Bagration salad

This dish is composed of equal quantities of blanched artichoke hearts and celeriac (celery root), cut into thin strips, and cold chopped macaroni. The ingredients are bound together with tomato mayonnaise and shaped into a mound, sprinkled with chopped hard-boiled (hard-cooked) egg yolk and chopped parsley, and garnished with a salpicon of truffles and pickled ox (beef) tongue.

Bagration timbales

Butter a number of dariole moulds. Stick small pieces of truffle and pickled tongue to the sides of the moulds. Line with smooth chicken forcemeat. Fill with a mixture of cooked macaroni (chopped and mixed with cream) and salpicon of truffles and pickled ox (beef) tongue. Cook in a bain marie for about 15 minutes. Turn out on to a plate and coat with suprême sauce.

BAHUT A deep cylindrical container with two handles. Of variable size, it has no lid and is made of tin, stainless steel or aluminium (enamelled plate is to be avoided). This catering vessel is designed for storing cooked food, sauces, creams or anything that needs keeping.

BAIN MARIE A water bath for keeping cooked food or dishes, such as sauces and soups, warm or without allowing them to continue cooking. A bain marie is also used for melting ingredients without burning them or for cooking delicate foods and dishes very slowly.

Bain marie was originally a term used in alchemy. It was then referred to as *bain de Marie* (Mary's bath) after Moses's sister, who was known to be an alchemist. It was also considered to refer to the Virgin Mary, the symbol of gentleness, since the term implies the gentleness of this method of cooking.

In the classic catering kitchen a cylindrical bain marie (with a handle and a lid) is used to hold soups, sauces and creams. This is placed in a shallow rectangular bain marie dish, containing warm water, which may be large enough to hold up to ten such containers. Large restaurants and cafeterias have heated vats arranged on these principles.

A special double saucepan (double boiler) is used for cooking individual sauces. This pan is in two parts which slot one inside the other (the lower part contains hot water). In domestic cookery, a gratin dish or baking tin (pan) containing water is often used as a bain marie for cooking delicate ingredients or mixtures, such as pâtés, custards, chicken-liver mousse or baked eggs, either on top of the stove or in the oven. Whichever method is used, the water must not be allowed to boil in case the mixture inside overheats and then curdles, or water in the form of condensation gets into the preparation.

BAISER A French petit four consisting of two small meringues, joined together with thick cream, butter cream or ice cream.

BAKE BLIND Also referred to as blind-bake, this is a method of cooking an empty pastry flan case (pie shell). Pastry cases are part-cooked before adding a liquid or creamy mixture, which would otherwise soak into the pastry base, or completely cooked before filling with fruit or any other filling that does not need to be cooked.

Prepare a short pastry and use to line the flan dish or tin. Prick the base all over, then leave to rest in the refrigerator for at least 1 hour. The pastry case can be covered with cling film (plastic wrap) and chilled for up to 24 hours.

Line the pastry case with greaseproof (waxed) paper and sprinkle with baking beans or dried beans. Bake for 10-15 minutes in a preheated oven at 200°C (400°F, gas 6). Remove the paper and beans and add any filling, then continue baking as required. Alternatively, to cook the pastry case completely, after 15 minutes baking, remove the paper and beans, then return the pastry case to the oven for a further 10 minutes or until the pastry is cooked and lightly browned. Cool before adding a cold filling that does not require cooking.

BAKED ALASKA The novelty of this dessert lies in the contrast between the ice cream inside and the very hot meringue surrounding it. The classic baked Alaska consists of a base of Genoese sponge soaked in liqueur on which is placed a block of vanilla ice cream, the whole thing being masked with plain or Italian meringue. This is cooked in a hot oven for a very short time so that the meringue is coloured but the ice cream is not melted. It is served immediately, sometimes flamed.

The original recipe is said to have been perfected, or rather brought back into fashion, at the Hôtel de Paris in Monte Carlo, by the chef Jean Giroix. An American doctor, and investor, honoured as Count Rumford, is credited with the invention of this dessert, which is based on the principle that beaten egg white is a poor conductor of heat. However, according to Baron Brisse, in his cookery column in *La Liberté* (6 June 1866), a chef to a Chinese delegation visiting Paris introduced this dessert to the French:

'During the stay of the Chinese delegation in Paris, the chefs of the Celestial Empire exchanged courtesies and recipes with the chefs at the Grand Hotel. The French dessert chef was delighted at this opportunity: his Chinese colleague taught him the art of cooking vanilla and ginger ices in the oven. This is how the delicate operation is performed: very firm ice cream is enveloped in an extremely light pastry crust and baked in the oven. The crust insulates the interior and is cooked before the ice cream can melt. Gourmands can then enjoy the twofold pleasure of biting into a crisp crust and at the same time refreshing the palate with the flavoured ice cream.'

RECIPE

baked Alaska

First prepare some vanilla ice cream: make a custard using 7–8 egg yolks, 200 g (7 oz, 1 cup) caster (superfine) sugar, 750 ml (1¼ pints, 3 cups) single (light) cream and a vanilla pod (bean) or 1 teaspoon vanilla sugar. Freeze in an ice-cream churn. When the ice cream is fairly hard, pack it into a square cake tin (pan) and leave it in the freezer for 1 hour.

Meanwhile, make a sponge by beating 125 g (4 oz, ½ cup) caster sugar with 4 egg yolks until the mixture turns thick and white. Sprinkle with 150 g (5 oz, 1¼ cups) sifted plain (all-purpose) flour, then add 40 g (1½ oz, 3 tablespoons) melted butter and fold in 4 egg whites whisked to stiff peaks with a pinch of salt. Pour the batter into a greased square cake tin and bake in a preheated oven at 200°C (400°F, gas 6) for 35 minutes. Turn the sponge out and leave it to cool.

Immediately before serving make a meringue mixture whisking 4 egg whites, a pinch of salt and 6 tablespoons caster sugar and put the mixture into a large piping (pastry) bag. Split the sponge in two through the middle and trim the edges neatly, if necessary, then arrange the pieces side by side on a baking sheet. Sprinkle with 3 tablespoons sugar flavoured with Cointreau or Grand Marnier. Unmould the ice cream and place on the sponge. Mask the sponge and ice cream entirely with half of the meringue, smoothing it with a metal spatula. Use the rest of the meringue to decorate the top with swirls. Dredge with icing (confectioner's) sugar and place in a preheated oven at 250°C (475°F, gas 9) until the meringue is coloured. Serve immediately.

Baked Alaska can be flamed when it is taken out of the oven, using the same liqueur that was used to flavour the sponge.

BAKERY The place where bread is manufactured and sold. The application of industry to the production of bread, the ability to distribute it, once made, very widely and quickly, and the knowledge of how to produce and package loaves that do not become stale immediately were all made possible during the 20th century. The latter part of the century, however, was marked by a movement back towards better-quality bread and more diversity of choice. Many industrial countries elected consciously for smaller, and more local, bakeries. While the uses of industry were obvious – bread available in supermarkets and grocers' shops – customers wanted more choice. In France, bread was baked at home until after World War I, and bread-making is still carried out largely in small-scale establishments. French history provides an example of the organization of this envied food over the years.

■ **History of baking** Well-organized bakeries were depicted on the frescoes of ancient Egyptian tombs. These establishments produced mainly unleavened griddle cakes but also, for the upper classes, bread leavened with brewer's yeast. Herodotus reported that the Greeks learned the secret of leavened bread from the Egyptians.

In 168 BC, following the victorious campaign against Perseus, King of Macedonia, the bakers who travelled with the Greek army were taken as slaves by the Romans. They were known as *pistores* (grinders) because they ground the corn with a mortar. Even today many Italian bakers have Greek names. In AD 100, the emperor Trajan created a bakers' guild that was granted many privileges. In this way, he completed the measures taken by his predecessors to ensure that Rome was supplied with food, thus avoiding insurrection. Bread was distributed free to the poorest citizens, numbering about 300,000 to 400,000 people. In the reign of Augustus, there were 326 bakers in Rome catering for a million inhabitants. This led eventually to the nationalization of the bakers, who were paid directly by the state and were not allowed to sell their businesses. The brick ovens that were found in the bakeries among the ruins of Pompeii had flat beds and vaulted roofs and were very similar to those used in rural France today.

After the Roman conquest and under Roman law, the Gallic bakers were united into organizations, and in this way the oldest food profession was created. As early as the beginning of the Middle Ages, feudal lords raised taxes by making their serfs grind their corn in the baronial mill and bake the dough in the communal oven.

In the 12th century the guild of bakers was established in France: they were known as *tameliers* (sifters) because they had to sift the flour that was delivered to them. There were 62 of them at the time and Philip Augustus granted them the monopoly on the manufacture of bread within the boundaries of Paris. According to the *Livre des métiers* of Étienne Boileau (c. 1268), the *tamelier* bought his entitlement from the king (the Grand Baker). He served an apprenticeship of four years and had to complete various formalities. The master baker had a junior, or first boy, at his command. The guild also provided insurance against illness; every day, the baker delivered one or two loaves to a hospital, and in return was guaranteed free priority hospitalization. The baker who supplied free bread to the executioner placed the bread that was intended for him upside down so that the other customers could be sure that the executioner's hand would not touch any other loaves. This gave rise to the superstition that it is unlucky to place bread upside down. The word *boulanger*, which eventually replaced the word *tamelier*, comes from the Picardy word *boulenc*, meaning 'one who makes round bread'. The quality, weight and price of bread were precisely fixed by royal decree. Any loaves below the prescribed weight were confiscated and distributed to the poor. The *Grand Panetier* judged the bakers' misdemeanours.

■ **Bakery reforms in France** Philip the Fair reformed baking legislation so that any fines meted out became proportional to the misdemeanour. He also reduced the bakers' privileges and authorized private individuals to buy grain. In 1366 Charles V introduced regulations concerning the places and times for the sale of bread, as well as the price, which varied according to the type of flour used. Charles VII introduced further regulations and imposed limits on the places and times wheat and flour could be bought. In the meantime, it became more and more usual to make bread at home.

The 17th century saw many changes in the Parisian bakery trade. Bread manufacture was improved, flour (without bran) was delivered in larger quantities, the use of brewer's yeast was prohibited, and the number of markets increased. In 1635 Richelieu introduced the following measures: 'Bakers of bread rolls and pastrycooks will not buy grain before eleven o'clock in winter and noon in summer; bakers of large loaves will not buy grain before two o'clock. This will enable the people of the town to obtain their supply first. Bakers shall put a distinctive trademark on their loaves, and keep weights and scales in their shops, under penalty of having their licences removed.' Bakers were also obliged to sell their own bread, and not through a third party.

Towards 1710, markets were established in Paris for the sale of bread and they were frequented by 500–600 bakers from Paris and the suburbs. A further thousand came from the surrounding area because the bread they produced was famous – from Gonesse, Corbeil, Chilly and Saint-Germain-en-Laye. In 1724 there were 1524 bakers, most of whom sold their bread in the Great Hall in the Place Maubert, at the Marché Neuf de la Cité in the Rue Saint-Honoré, and at the market of Marais-du-Temple. Marie de Medici brought in Italian bakers who introduced new products. Gradually, the Parisians became more and more partial to light white bread made with pure wheat flour.

■ **From the French Revolution** During the 18th century methods of wheat cultivation and production made real progress, and the spectre of famine was gradually eradicated. But the farsighted royal administration accumulated large quantities of grain. When a shortage of food occurred in 1773, the people accused the farmers and merchants of signing a 'pact of famine' in order to speculate on grain. In reality, these preventative purchases were to be resold at the normal price.

In 1774 Turgot decided that there should be free trade in grain throughout France. Unfortunately, this decision was premature and in the following year there was rioting and pillaging of grain stores. This was called the 'war of famine'.

The day after the storming of the Bastille, the continuing shortage of food exasperated the people: the bakers asked for sentries to protect them and prevent their shops from being ransacked. Paris did not have enough bread and, to cries of 'Let's get the baker, the baker's wife and the baker's assistant', the people, led by the market women, took the road to Versailles. On 2 March 1791 the Constitution did away with guild wardenships and masterships, and bakery supposedly became 'free' but was still subject to the regulations of the public authorities. Bakery products continued to evolve: in 1840, Viennese products became popular and many Austrian bakers came to Paris.

■ **Modern times** Bread continues to be an essential part of the daily diet in France, as in most European countries. Though there is now the convenience of being able to buy bread elsewhere, the bakery is a part of small-town life. In France, however, the craze for the Parisian baguette has resulted in the disappearance of many regional breads, while some regional bakeries have now become merely bread shops.

In former times, the village baker's oven was often the only one locally, and certain slow-cooked dishes, such as meat stews, including Boston baked beans in Puritan America, and even roasts and pastries, were taken by the villagers to the baker, to be cooked in the residual oven heat after the bread had been removed. In some Mediterraniean countries peppers are still baked this way and sold by bread shops, but the social function of a communal village oven has passed away now that domestic ovens are commonplace. Commercial bakeries have been in operation in France since 1959, but in the latter part of the 20th century only accounted for about 10% of the total production. Most – and this is typical throughout continental Europe – bread-making continues to be carried on in numerous small-scale bakeries.

■ **Bakery equipment** From antiquity to the beginning of the 20th century the baker's equipment changed very slowly. Roman frescoes show a kneading machine driven by animals and it is known that the workers of this period wore hygienic masks. The mechanical kneader used in modern bakeries dates from 1920. Ovens, formerly heated by burning wood and then coal, are now heated by gas, electricity or oil. Since the original Roman vault-shaped cooking chamber, the bread oven has seen the introduction of the rotating disc and stacking in layers. The most commonly used oven nowadays rotates internally and contains a vertical trolley which can be removed when the bread is cooked.

There have been many improvements. High-speed kneading machines oxygenate and whiten the bread. Refrigerated fermentation chambers (instead of incubators) mean that the baker can prepare the bread the previous evening because the fermentation process takes longer. However, the high proportion of yeast required does not improve the quality. Deep-freezing is very commonly practised in the United States.

In addition to various types of bread, many local bakers also make pastries and sell confectionery.

BAKING POWDER A raising (leavening) agent invented in America and introduced to Europe in the 1840s, it consists of 2 parts bicarbonate of soda and 1 part cream of tartar mixed with a flour or starch. Several types are distinguished in America. Fast-action baking powder works immediately in the cold dough, another type only on the dough going into the oven. Baking powder is commonly used in domestic baking, particularly for cakes and scones (biscuits).

BAKING SHEET A tray, with only a very slightly raised edge, on which all kinds of unmoulded pastries, biscuits (cookies), small cakes and tarts are placed to be baked in the oven. It can be lined with greaseproof (waxed) paper or greased and coated with flour if required.

BAKING TIN (PAN) A wide flat cooking utensil that comes in various sizes and depths. The roasting tin (pan), made of aluminium or tinned copper plate, is usually rectangular with two handles and shallow vertical sides; it may be fitted with a grid so that the meat or poultry does not rest in its own cooking juices.

BAKLAVA A sweet pastry widely eaten in the Middle East consisting of several very thin layers of filo pastry filled with chopped toasted almonds, pistachios and walnuts mixed with sugar and then cut into lozenges (diamonds) before baking. When they are taken out of the oven, a honey or sugar syrup flavoured with rose water and lemon juice is poured over the baklavas.

RECIPE

baklavas with pistachio nuts

In a food processor mix 575 g (1¼ lb, 5 cups) plain (all-purpose) flour, 25 g (1 oz) salt and enough water to obtain a firm, elastic dough. Make 12 balls of equal size. Flatten the first ball with the hand. Sprinkle a pinch of cornflour (cornstarch) over it to prevent it from sticking. Place a second ball on top. Flatten this with the hand and sprinkle a pinch of cornflour over it. Repeat with the other 10 balls. This results in a pastry consisting of 12 layers. Gradually flatten this pastry with a rolling pin, taking care not to crush or tear it, stretching it gently along the edges in order to obtain a circle of about 30 cm (12 in) in diameter. Cover the pastry with a cloth and allow to rest for 1 hour.

Then remove the first layer of the pastry, turn it over and sprinkle it with a pinch of cornflour. Repeat with the other layers, so that both sides of each layer are coated with cornflour, and pile them on top of each other again. Sprinle cornflour on a marble surface and place the stack of pastry on top, then stretch it out gently with the hands into a circle 50 cm (20 in) in diameter and 3–4 cm (1¼–1½ in) thick. Because the top stretches more than the bottom, turn the stack of pastry over and repeat the stretching operation. Roll out carefully with a very long rolling pin into a circle about 80 cm (32 in) in diameter. Place the rolling pin in the middle of the pastry and roll 6 layers around it, one by one, sprinkling each with cornflour, then roll them on the table. Repeat the operation with a second rolling pin and the 6 remaining layers. Finally, bring the 12 layers together; by now they will have become extremely thin.

Chop shelled pistachio nuts. Place the pastry over an ovenproof dish 70 cm (28 in) in diameter. The edges will overhang by about 20 cm (8 in); cut out the circle of pastry and set aside. Cut the rest into 4–6 lozenge (diamond) shapes. Divide in two (6 layers). Decorate with the chopped pistachio nuts and cover with the other half (6 layers). Cover the lozenges with the circle of pastry and carefully seal the edges. Melt 1.5 kg (3¼ lb, 6½ cups) butter and pour slowly on to the pastry. Allow to rest for 30 minutes.

Bake in a preheated oven at 180°C (350°F, gas 4) for 20–30 minutes. Take the baklavas out of the oven and allow to cool. Mix 7 parts of sugar, 2 parts of water and 2 tablespoons orange flower water and cook gently for 5 minutes. Pour the hot syrup over the baklavas and leave them to cool.

BALKAN STATES See *opposite page..*

BALLON A round French bread roll, made from *fleur* (French white flour), with a crisp, crumbly crust. It must be eaten very fresh.

BALLOTINE A hot or cold dish based on meat, poultry, game birds or fish in aspic. The flesh is boned, stuffed, rolled and tied up with string, usually wrapped in muslin (cheesecloth) – sometimes in the skin – then braised or poached (see *galantine*).

RECIPES

ballotine of chicken in aspic

Bone a 2.5 kg (5½ lb) chicken as in the recipe for braised ballotine of chicken. Dice the flesh from the chicken together with 150 g (5 oz) cooked ham, 150 g (5 oz) pickled tongue and 150 g (5 oz) bacon. Combine this meat with 225 g (8 oz) sausagemeat, 225 g (8 oz) lean minced (ground) veal, 2 eggs, 7 tablespoons Cognac, 150 g (5 oz) chopped truffles or pistachios, a generous pinch of mixed spice and salt and pepper. Knead the mixture well with wet hands. Shape the stuffing into an oblong, place on the boned chicken and shape the ballotine by drawing the skin all round the stuffing. Rinse and squeeze out a piece of muslin (cheesecloth) and roll up the ballotine tightly in it. Tie with string at both ends, slightly compressing the ballotine, then tie in the middle and between the middle and each end.

Prepare a jelly (aspic) stock using 2 calf's feet, 300 g (11 oz) pork rind, 800 g (1¾ lb) knuckle of veal, 2 carrots, 1 onion, 2 leeks (white part only), a bouquet garni, about 3.5 litres (6 pints, 3½ quarts) chicken stock (or water), and 400 ml (14 fl oz, 1¾ cups) Madeira, adding the chicken carcass and giblets (except the liver) and other giblets if desired. Simmer the ballotine gently in the prepared stock for 1¾ hours. Remove from the stock and allow to cool. Unwrap. Rinse the muslin in warm water, squeeze out thoroughly, and wrap up the ballotine again. Tie up and allow to cool for 12 hours under a weight. Clarify the stock, adding gelatine if necessary, and coat the cold ballotine with the half-set aspic, then chill and serve when completely cold.

ballotine of chicken in chaud-froid sauce

Prepare the ballotine as for ballotine of chicken in aspic, but coat with chaud-froid sauce instead of aspic.

ballotine of duck

Bone a 2.5 kg (5½ lb) duck, remove all the flesh and dice the breast meat. Draw the sinews from the rest of the meat and finely chop with an equal weight of unsmoked fatty bacon, half this weight of lean veal, and 75 g (3 oz, 1½ cups) fresh breadcrumbs soaked in milk. Combine these ingredients in a food processor with 4 egg yolks. Season with salt, pepper and allspice. Add to this stuffing 150 g (5 oz) fresh foie gras, cut into large cubes and

BALKAN STATES

The countries of central Europe, bordered by Austria, Russia, Italy, Greece and Turkey, have a characteristic national gastronomy, in which soups and stews, cooked meats, ewe's- and cow's-milk cheeses and strong liqueurs predominate. (Hungary, where the cuisine has a character of its own, is an exception.)

■ **Bulgaria** The long domination by the Turks left in its wake a taste for mezze, halva and raki. Yogurt, characteristic of this region, is widely used in such stews as *ghivetch* (meat and vegetables simmered with spices and topped with eggs and yogurt) and with raw vegetable salads such as *tarator* (cucumber with yogurt and pounded nuts). The staple dish is *tchorba*, a soup made with chicken, lamb offal or tripe (variety meats), but dried salted meat (*pastirma*), *kebabcha* (sausage kebabs), and flaky pastry filled with cheese or vegetables are also highly appreciated. *Sirene* is a famous ewe's-milk cheese. As well as good red or white wines, *slivovica* (plum brandy) is drunk in Bulgaria.

■ **Romania** The Black Sea and the Danube delta provide a plentiful supply of fish (one of which is sturgeon – hence caviar). But the staple dish is a soup (*ciorba*) made from fish, chicken or veal. Hors d'oeuvres are very important, particularly aubergine (eggplant) purée with olive oil and lemon, and *mititei* (small grilled sausages). Carp, crayfish and pike are prepared in the Austrian style (stuffed or fried), but stuffed braised cabbage leaves or vine leaves are cooked in the same way as they are in Greece. Rumania produces several ewe's-milk cheeses (such as *brandza* and *kaskaval* or *katshkawalj*), some mild and matured with milk, others piquant and matured in pine bark; its cow's-milk cheeses are sometimes eaten with corn broth (*mamaliga*) and prepared in as many different ways as the Italian polenta. Turkish domination left its mark in sweet pastries and rose-petal jam.

■ **The Czech Republic** Pilsen beer, cooked meats (black puddings and sausages) and Prague ham, together with foie gras, are the best-known ambassadors of Czech gastronomy. The influence of Russian and Polish cuisine is also apparent – calves' lights (lungs) soup, fillets of carp with mushrooms – but the national dish is *hovasy maso* (boiled beef served with very spicy sauces). Poultry (particularly goose) and game are served with *brambory* (potatoes) and sauerkraut. They are followed by pastries inspired by Austrian cookery. The Czechs are very fond of plum dumplings, sweet omelettes and *livances* (pancakes with jam).

■ **Serbia, Croatia and Montenegro** There are many culinary traditions in these neighbouring lands, but the common factor is once again a thick soup (*corba*) made with vegetables and meat or fish. Pig's trotters (feet) in aspic and Dalmatian smoked ham are traditional hors d'oeuvres, often served in the Italian way. In Croatia, where the Austrian influence is again strong, schnitzels are eaten and also plenty of fish and shellfish. Paprika is produced close to the Hungarian border and is used to season sauces for stews and onion fondues served with meatballs and kebabs. In Bosnia and Montenegro, the Turkish and Greek influence is evident in pilaf, stuffed cabbage leaves, moussaka (prepared with chicken or veal), and Oriental pastries. There are several famous cheeses, and the wines (Marastina and Ljutomer and red Blatina), plum (see *slivovitz*) or juniper brandies, and the famous cherry Zara Maraschino are also worthy of note.

WINE Vines have been grown in this part of Europe for centuries.

■ **Bulgaria** During the Ottoman Empire grape production was limited to table grapes for religious reasons. The present wine industry was established in the 20th century. The most important stages were between 1907 and 1985, when there were new plantings and a general programme of winery improvements was set in place. This resulted in a wave of good-quality, low-cost exports in an attempt to gain foreign currency. Between 1985 and 1989 a period of vine-pulling took place to reduce production by over 50%. The revolution in 1989 lost Bulgaria its established markets but at the beginning of the 21st century Bulgaria is poised to make good quality wines.

Grapes grow in all areas of Bulgaria. The most recognized areas for quality vine-growing are Russe and Suhindol in the north, Schumen in the eastern region, and Sakar in the southern region. Grape varieties reflect the mixed cultures of Eastern Europe and international influence. So Cabernet Sauvignon, Merlot and Chardonnay are grown extensively, but Mavrud, Melnik and Rkatsiteli are also represented. Bulgaria has its own quality grading system. '*Controliran*' indicates that the grapes for a wine have come from a specific vinyard site of particular note. Country wines are the equivalent of *vins de pays*.

■ **Romania** Romania produces a wide range of wines full of character. Wine-growing dates back to several centuries BC, to the time of the Thracians. Today Romania is among the top ten wine producers in the world. The grape varieties cultivated are Babeasca and Kadarka for reds, and Feteasca Alba, Feteasca Regala, Mustoasa and Tamiñoasa for whites, as well as some Burgundy and Bordeaux varieties.

The wines are classed in several categories: ordinary wines of superior quality, wines of superior quality with *appellation d'origine* (VOS), wines of superior quality with *appellation d'origine* and degrees of quality (VSOC), and finally sparkling wines and liqueurs.

Filling and shaping ballotine

When preparing a ballotine of poultry or a game bird, avoid cutting or puncturing the skin when boning the bird, especially when preparing game, such as pheasant, with areas of fine, thin skin. Here the ballotine of duck is prepared, keeping the foie gras and breast fillets separate from the main batch of stuffing.

1 *Lay the boned duck on the prepared muslin (cheesecloth) and arrange a layer of the stuffing (about two-thirds) down the middle. Top with strips of foie gras.*

2 *Mix the diced breast meat with the remaining stuffing and arrange on top of the foie gras.*

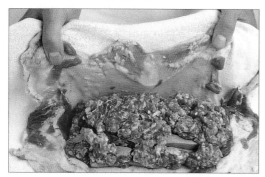

3 *Using the muslin to lift the duck, fold the sides and ends over the stuffing to enclose it completely and neatly in a long roll.*

4 *Fold the muslin tightly around the ballotine and shape it into a firm, even roll.*

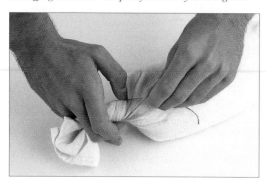

5 *Twist the ends of the muslin to wrap the ballotine tightly, then tie them with string.*

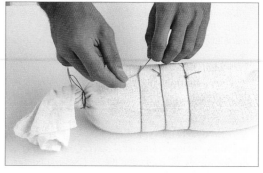

6 *When both ends are secure, tie the middle of the ballotine to keep it in shape and the muslin in place during cooking.*

quickly fried in butter, 1 truffle and the diced breast meat. Add 2 tablespoons Cognac and mix well.

Wet and squeeze out a piece of muslin (cheese-cloth) and spread out on the table. Place the duck skin, opened flat, on the muslin and spread evenly with the stuffing. Roll into the ballotine shape. Tie at both ends and in the middle.

Boil the ballotine immersed in a rich stock for 2–3 hours, arrange on a serving dish, and garnish

as desired (châtelaine, chipolata, forestière, Godard, Lucullus, braised chestnuts, or lettuce and other vegetables braised or cooked in butter. Baste the ballotine with a few spoonfuls of reduced sieved pan juices. Serve the remainder of this liquid separately.

To serve the ballotine cold, increase the foie gras to at least 200 g (7 oz). Once the cooked ballotine has been unwrapped, rewrap it very tightly in the same muslin, rinsed and wrung out, and allow to cool between two plates under a weight. Refrigerate overnight, then glaze with aspic jelly made from the well-reduced stock and chill to set before serving.

ballotine of guinea fowl Jeanne d'Albret

Bone 2 raw guinea fowl without damaging the skin and reserve the breasts whole. Make a forcemeat with the flesh of the thighs and their trimmings, 300 g (11 oz) lean Bayonne ham, 300 g (11 oz) fat bacon and 200 g (7 oz) mushrooms. Use a food processor to reduce these ingredients to a paste or mince (grind) them finely, then bind together with 2 raw eggs. Press through a sieve. Spread a piece of muslin (cheesecloth) on the table, place on it two strips of uncured fat bacon, and spread the skin of the guinea fowls over these. Spread with half of the forcemeat. Slice the breasts into thin strips and arrange half of them on the forcemeat; add a slice of foie gras and two truffles on either side, lengthways. Make two more layers with the rest of the sliced breasts and the remaining forcemeat.

Roll into a ballotine in a muslin cloth and tie it up at both ends and in the middle. Place in a braising pan with a good white stock and a crushed calf's foot, the bones and carcasses of the guinea fowls, a carrot, a small bouquet garni, the white part of a leek and 100 g (4 oz) of bacon rind or pork rind. Cook for 1½ hours.

The following day, strain the stock through a cloth and clarify it using 2–3 eggs to obtain a full-flavoured aspic jelly. Turn out the ballotine on to a long dish and glaze with the half-set aspic. Make a crown with a piece of truffle and some chopped aspic and garnish the ballotine with cubes of aspic jelly and truffles.

ballotine of lamb in aspic

Make a stuffing of a salpicon of pickled tongue, ham and stoned (pitted) black olives. Spread this mixture on a boned flattened shoulder of lamb, roll it up, wrap it in muslin (cheesecloth) and tie with string. Cook the lamb in a casserole on a bed of vegetables with bacon and stock for about 1¾ hours, as in the recipe for braised ballotine of lamb. Drain and unwrap the ballotine (straining and reserving the liquor), squeeze out the muslin and use it to wrap up the ballotine again. Tie at both ends and in the middle and allow to cool for 12 hours under a weight. Unwrap and place in a dish. Warm the liquor and pour it over the ballotine, adding more warmed jellied stock, if necessary, to cover. Chill for at least 24 hours until firmly set before serving.

ballotine of pork

Prepare a boned shoulder of pork in the same way as for braised ballotine of lamb.

ballotine of veal

Prepare using boned shoulder or breast of veal, in the same way as for ballotine of lamb.

braised ballotine of chicken

Cut off the feet and pinions (wing tips) of a chicken. To bone, cut through the middle of the back from the neck to the tail and then, using a small sharp knife, working one side of the backbone at a time, gently ease the flesh away from the bone, taking care not to pierce the skin. Then carefully remove the bones from the legs and wings. Spread the chicken out flat on the table. Remove the breast meat and as much as possible of the legs and wings and cut it into cubes.

Prepare a stuffing from finely minced (ground) pork and veal – about 225 g (8 oz) of each – mixed with 100 g (4 oz) cooked ham, 2 eggs, 7 tablespoons Cognac, a generous pinch of allspice, and salt and pepper. Continue as for braised ballotine of lamb.

The same method can be used to make hot or cold ballotines of turkey or pigeon, adding foie gras and truffles, if required, in proportions corresponding to the size of the bird.

braised ballotine of lamb

Ask the butcher to bone a shoulder of lamb. To prepare the stuffing, first finely chop 3 onions, and cook in 20 g (¾ oz, 1½ tablespoons) butter until soft. Mince together a bunch of parsley and 2 garlic cloves. Combine this mixture with the onions, 450 g (1 lb) sausagemeat and salt and pepper and work together by hand or in a food processor. Open out the boned shoulder, spread with the stuffing, then roll up and tie with string.

Dice 100 g (4 oz) carrots, 3 onions, 1 celery stick and 100 g (4 oz) bacon. Melt 25 g (1 oz, 2 tablespoons) butter in a large flameproof casserole and brown the stuffed lamb. Remove and set aside. Cook the vegetable mixture in the butter remaining in the pan until soft. Add a small sprig of thyme, then replace the vegetables. Add 200 ml (7 fl oz, ¾ cup) dry white wine, 200 ml (7 fl oz, ¾ cup) stock or meat juices, a bouquet garni, salt and pepper. Bring to the boil and cook, uncovered, for 5 minutes. Turn the shoulder over in the vegetables, cover the casserole and continue cooking in a preheated oven at 200°C (400°F, gas 6) for 1½ hours. Remove the bouquet garni. Untie the ballotine and serve very hot, either on its own or with spinach, mixed vegetables, noodles, pilaf or risotto.

cold ballotine of eel

Prepare and cook the ballotine as for hot ballotine of eel. Drain and unwrap, squeeze out the muslin (cheesecloth), and wrap the ballotine up again in the same cloth; tie up with string and cool for 12 hours under a weight. In the meantime, make a fish aspic using the stock in which the ballotine was cooked. Unwrap the eel and place in a dish, coat with aspic and chill until firmly set.

hot ballotine of eel

Skin a large eel weighing at least 900 g (2 lb), cut off the head and tail, open out and remove the backbone. Flatten the eel and season with salt and pepper. Spread with forcemeat for fish and reshape the eel, taking care to ensure that it is the same thickness all the way along. Wrap it in muslin (cheesecloth), tie it up with string and place on a grid in a fish kettle. Prepare enough fish court-bouillon to cover the eel in its pan. Allow to cool, then pour over the eel. Cover and poach very gently for about 20 minutes. Drain the ballotine, unwrap it and put it in an ovenproof dish. Strain the stock and reduce by boiling until syrupy. Coat the fish with the stock and put in the oven for a few minutes. Serve very hot.

hot ballotine of eel bourguignonne

Add chopped parsley to godiveau Lyonnais (pike forcemeat) or a forcemeat made from whiting. Use to stuff an eel which has been prepared according to the previous recipe. Poach in a court-bouillon of red wine; drain and keep warm. Prepare a bourguignonne sauce with the cooking stock and pour over the eel. This dish can be garnished with small fried croûtons.

small ballotines of chicken

Bone and stuff legs of chicken and cook until tender in the same way as for ballotine of chicken in aspic.

BALTHAZAR This word is used to describe both a magnificent feast and, since 1800, a large bottle of champagne. In both cases it refers to an episode in the Old Testament in which Balthazar, the last king of Babylon, offers a sumptuous banquet to a thousand of his dignitaries. During the banquet he has the wine served in sacred vases which his father, Nebuchadnezzar, stole from the Temple in Jerusalem. That same night the sacrilege is punished by the hand of God. The word Balthazar has an ironic meaning when applied to a banquet. However, it still remains the technical name for a bottle of champagne containing the equivalent of 16 ordinary bottles. The next size up, containing 20 bottles, is known as a Nebuchadnezzar.

BALZAC, HONORÉ DE French author (born Tours, 1799; died Paris, 1850). During his creative periods Balzac, the author of *La Comédie Humaine*, shut himself away, drinking too much coffee and eating only eggs and fruit. When he re-emerged, he displayed a gargantuan appetite. At the Véry restaurant, he was seen to devour 'a hundred Ostend oysters, twelve cutlets of salt-meadow mutton, a duck with turnips, two partridges and a Normandy sole', followed by desserts, fruit, coffee and liqueurs.

Balzac has created a number of gourmets in his novels, such as Cousin Pons, who loved *escargots au gratin* and *boeuf miroton*, Père Rouget (from *La Rabouilleuse)*, who considered that an omelette was more delicate when the whites and the yolks were beaten separately, and the Vidame de Pamiers (from *Le Cabinet des antiques*), who decreed that for a din-

ner party to be successful no more than six guests must be present.

The author often used famous restaurants of the Paris of the 1830s as his setting and described their specialities in his books: turbot with oysters from the Rocher de Cancale, cutlets Soubise from the Café de Paris, cod in garlic from the Frères Provençaux and grilled meats from the Café Anglais, where Rastignac gave a princely welcome to Delphine de Nucingen. However, provincial cooking was often more highly esteemed by Balzac because dishes were 'more studied and better thought out'. Angevin potted meat (*Le Lys dans la vallée*), cling peach jam (*Eugénie Grandet*) and Isoudun marzipan (*La Rabouilleuse*) were considered worthy of his praise.

Balzac also edited a collection of gastronomic texts (*Le Gastronome français ou l'Art de bien vivre*, 1828), for which he wrote an unsigned preface, and published the *Physiologie gastronomique* in 1830. He also published a study of contemporary stimulants (1838) and wrote a treatise on the same subject as an appendix to the new edition (1839) of the *Physiologie du goût* by Brillat-Savarin.

BAMBOCHE, EN The French term applied to a preparation of fried cod, sometimes served with fried eggs. The word is derived from the Italian *bamboccio*, meaning 'jumping jack', perhaps fancifully referring to the way the pieces of cod jump around in the hot fat.

RECIPES

fried eggs bamboche

Bind together a mixture of hot cooked vegetables with cream and arrange in a ring on a serving dish. Fill the centre with strips of fried cod. Arrange fried eggs on the ring of vegetables.

salt cod en bamboche

Soak the fish to remove the salt and cut into thick slices the size of fillets of sole. Moisten with milk, dust with flour and plunge into boiling fat. Drain, pat dry and arrange on a bed of assorted vegetables mixed with butter or cream.

BAMBOO A plant several metres tall, common throughout tropical Asia, whose young, tender and slightly crunchy shoots are served as a vegetable. The Japanese also enjoy bamboo seeds, which have a slightly floury texture, and in Vietnam and China food is steamed in bamboo leaves. In Cambodia, the bamboo canes themselves are used for cooking minced (ground) meat in.

Bamboo shoots used for cooking are ivory white in colour, spring from the base of the plant and are cut when conical in shape, averaging 7 cm (2½ in) in diameter at the base and 10 cm (4 in) in length. When fresh, the fine needle-sharp hairs which cover them must be removed before use. In Europe they are usually found dried or canned in water, brine or vinegar (under their Japanese name of *takenoko* or their Chinese name of *sun ki*). Once opened, keep preserved bamboo shoots in the refrigerator in a closed container filled with water.

Popular throughout China and the whole of tropical Asia, bamboo shoots cut into strips or sticks are an ingredient of many dishes, including soups, stews and braised dishes, and stir fries. In China the shoots are salted, dried in the sun and macerated in sweet wine with star anise and rose petals to make a seasoning. In Japan bamboo shoots are the basic spring-time vegetable added to *sukiyaki*. They are used in family stews and in the delicate dishes of the tea ceremony all year round.

Strips of mature fine bamboo are used in the Far East for making lattice mats, on which to cook food or to roll sushi, and also for Chinese steamers, which are set over a wok.

RECIPE

chicken with bamboo shoots
Place a chicken in a large pan and cover with water. Bring to the boil. Immediately remove and drain the chicken. Cool the stock by standing the container in cold water. Skim the stock, replace the chicken and bring back to the boil. Add 5–6 shiitake mushrooms, 1–2 scented Chinese mushrooms, 100 ml (4 fl oz, 7 tablespoons) soy sauce, 3 tablespoons sugar, salt and pepper, and continue cooking. After 1 hour, drain 225 g (8 oz) preserved bamboo shoots, rinse in a colander with cold water, then cut into thick sticks, add to the pan and simmer gently until the chicken is cooked – about 20 minutes for a tender bird or 1 hour for a boiling fowl.

Drain the chicken, remove the skin and cut all the meat into thin strips. Arrange the chicken on a serving dish and surround with the mushrooms and bamboo shoots. Just before serving, trim 3–4 spring onions (scallions) and fry quickly in oil. Add 2 tablespoons soy sauce and use to garnish the dish. The stock, highly seasoned with pepper and with fine rice stick vermicelli added, can be served at the end of the meal.

BANANA The fruit of the banana tree, a long-leaved plant originating in India and cultivated in tropical regions (West Indies, Africa and South America). Each plant bears clusters of 50–200 fruits with sweet, white, floury and fleshy pulp.

There are two major kinds of banana: fruit bananas, which are eaten cooked or raw, and plantain bananas, which are cooked as vegetables.
■ **Fruit bananas** According to an Indian legend, where Paradise is on the island of Sri Lanka, the banana was the forbidden fruit and Adam and Eve, banished from the Garden of Eden, covered their bodies with banana leaves. Because Europeans first called bananas figs, this explains the ancient names of 'Adam's fig' and 'Paradise banana'. Still rare in the Renaissance, bananas, introduced to France by the Portuguese, became common from the 18th century onwards.

Indigenous varieties bear a short roundish fruit with a purplish red skin and highly scented flesh. Bananas cultivated for export in South America (*poyo, gros Michel,* Cavendish, *grande naine*) are long with brown-stained yellow skin. They are harvested green, shipped in banana boats at a temperature of about 13°C (55°F), and stored in a humid environment where they ripen at a temperature between 16.5°C (61.5°F) and 20°C (68°F). There are also sweet dwarf Canary bananas, 'lady fingers' from Thailand and 'apple' bananas from East Africa and Malaysia.

Cooking bananas brings out their full flavour and, when combined with sugar, butter or alcohol, they make a delicious, if heavy, dessert.

Bananas also contain pectins, which contribute to the smoothness of the flesh, and malic acid, which makes them refreshing when eaten raw. Well protected by their thick skin, they are transported unripe so continue to ripen after purchase. (They should not, however, be put in the refrigerator because they turn black at very low temperatures.) The skin is generally removed, as are the white threads which cling to the flesh. Bananas make many sweet dishes – poached, sautéed, flambéed, fritters, fruit salads, sweet omelettes, ice cream, flans and purées.

Dried bananas are black in colour and sweet with a good flavour. Slices of unripe fruit are made into banana chips.

In South America and the Far East, curled banana leaves are used to steam or wrap food such as rice or minced (ground) meat.
■ **Plantain** With its green skin and fairly firm pink flesh, the plantain is the staple food of East Africa – and accounts for roughly half of banana production. The plantain is usually flatter and longer than the fruit banana and contains more starch and less sugar. They are firmer in texture and have a slightly 'dry' flavour. Cooking time varies according to the variety and state of maturity, but they are baked, boiled (in salted water for 15–45 minutes), fried, mashed or used in stews. Plantains are served as an accompaniment to many West Indian, South American or African dishes.

RECIPES

Savoury Banana Recipe
bananas with bacon
Peel the required number of bananas. Wrap a rasher (slice) of rindless smoked or unsmoked bacon around each banana as it is peeled and secure with wooden cocktail sticks (toothpicks). Cook the bacon-wrapped bananas under a hot grill (broiler) until the bacon is browned. Turn and cook the second side. Serve at once. Alternatively, the bananas can be fried in a little olive oil.

Chunks of bananas can be wrapped in short lengths of bacon and threaded on metal skewers, then grilled on both sides until golden.

Serve with cooked rice tossed with raisins, a

pinch of cayenne, a few roasted peanuts and a little grated fresh root ginger.

Bananas fried in a little unsalted butter are delicious with grilled bacon for breakfast or a light lunch – serve with warm crusty bread or on warm waffles or lightly toasted English muffins.

Sweet Banana Recipes

baked bananas

Bake unpeeled bananas in a preheated oven at 220°C (425°F, gas 7) for 10–20 minutes. Peel off a third of the skin lengthways to form a boat shape and serve with melted butter and caster (superfine) sugar or with redcurrant jelly.

banana ice cream

Peel firm, ripe bananas and purée in a food processor or blender with lemon juice (use 1 lemon for 6 bananas). Mix with an equal volume of sugar syrup. Flavour with rum and freeze in the usual way.

bananas à la créole au gratin

Select firm bananas and peel off a wide strip of skin from each. Remove the flesh in one piece, without crushing and sprinkle with lemon juice. Blanch the skins for 2 minutes in boiling water, cool by dipping in cold water and pat dry. Slice the flesh and soak for 30 minutes in lemon juice, sugar and rum. Put a layer of cooked rice pudding mixed with finely chopped crystallized (candied) fruit into each skin. Arrange the banana slices vertically on top and cover with finely crushed macaroons. Coat with melted butter and place under a hot grill (broiler).

They can be served with a rum-flavoured apricot sauce.

bananas flambé

Peel some firm bananas and cook in butter or a vanilla-flavoured sugar syrup, without allowing them to become soft. Drain. Warm some rum, Calvados, Armagnac or Cognac and pour over the bananas. Set alight and serve immediately.

bananas in butter

Peel some just-ripe bananas and arrange in a buttered ovenproof dish. Pour some melted butter over and dust with sugar. Bake in a preheated oven at about 200°C (400°F, gas 6) for 15 minutes.

banana soufflés

Select some firm ripe bananas. Peel off a strip of skin and remove the flesh. Sprinkle the flesh with lemon juice, mash and mix with a very little confectioner's custard (pastry cream). Fold in whisked egg whites to prepare a soufflé mixture. Fill the skins with the soufflé mixture. Smooth the surface. Bake in a preheated oven at about 200°C (400°F, gas 6) for 8–9 minutes. Serve immediately.

grilled bananas

Peel some bananas, brush with melted butter and grill (broil) gently for 15 minutes. Arrange the bananas in a dish, dust with caster (superfine) sugar and coat with sour cream, soft (whipped) cream cheese or a dessert sauce.

BANANA SPLIT An ice-cream dish created in the United States, the main ingredient of which is a banana split in two lengthways. This is topped with three balls of ice cream (of the same or different flavours: vanilla, chocolate and strawberry), coated with chocolate sauce and decorated with whipped cream and glacé (candied) maraschino cherries. The melted chocolate may be replaced by strawberry sauce. An alternative decoration is sliced almonds or chopped walnuts, with a meringue shell on either side.

BAN DES VENDANGES In medieval times, the proclamation of the date when the picking of grapes for the wine harvest could begin depended on the condition of the grapes and certain local traditions; for example, the 'Hundred days after the flowering of the lilies' in Burgundy or the flowering of the vine anywhere else. The Ban des Vendanges might be subject to the control of the overlord or vineyard owner – in feudal times there were equally strict dates when pruning, sowing and so on might start – and prevented anyone from making wine from grapes not fully ripe. Even today the earliest date for harvest is arrived at by discussion between the growers and the wine authorities of each region. Some wine fraternities still proclaim the Ban des Vendanges, holding reunions and ceremonies, such as that of the Jurade de Saint-Émilion, second oldest of all the wine orders, when the vintage is announced from the top of the Tour du Roi.

BANDOL An AOC wine produced in the wine-growing region of Bandol, a small Provençal port between Toulon and La Ciotat. The vines are cultivated in terraces (Provençal: *restanques*) on arid sandy limestone soil. The varieties grown for red and rosé wines are mostly Mourvèdre (50% minimum), Cinsault and Grenache. Other varieties cannot exceed 20% of the entire crop. The main varieties grown for white wine are: Clairette, Ugni Blanc and Bourboulenc. A subsidiary variety is Sauvignon, which does not exceed 40% of the crop.

Red wines of this region are rare but it is to these that Bandol owes its reputation. Clean, solid, generous and harmonious, they have a good dark-red colour. They are a little rough when young, but mellow during the compulsory 18-month (at least) aging period and become remarkably velvety thanks to the Mourvèdre grape. The white and rosé wines are fresh and versatile with a pleasant bouquet and are best drunk fairly young.

BANON A French cheese bearing the name of a village in Haute Provence. Made from cow's, goat's, or ewe's milk (45% fat content), it has a soft texture, a natural crust and is a squat round shape, 7–8 cm (3 in) in diameter and 3 cm (1¼ in) thick. It is presented wrapped in chestnut leaves steeped in brandy and tied up with raffia. With its sweet or nutty flavour, Banon is very good from May to November. It is sometimes scented with sprigs of savory and is then known as 'Banon au pèbre d'aï', *pèbre d'aï* being the Provençal name for savory.

BANQUET

BANQUET An ostentatious or formal meal for a large number of guests, either for a festival or to mark the occasion of a political or social event. In view of the large amount of food to be prepared and served, banquets are rarely of great gastronomic quality, but their purpose is to unite people rather than to feed them lavishly. The word, which dates from the 14th century, comes from the Italian *banchetto*, meaning a small bench on which the guests used to sit.

■ **Sacred right and civic function** Since the earliest times the idea of the communal meal has been associated with a magical rite. Every man had to gain the favour of the mysterious forces of nature to be lucky in the chase; by eating the animal he had killed with his companions, he regenerated his mental and physical strength. Greek sacrifices were also followed by a banquet: the meat was roasted, distributed amongst the participants and eaten close to the altar. This was one of the rare occasions on which citizens ate meat (especially beef). In this way, the banquet was a very important act of communion, as it was for the early Christians in their love feasts (see *agape*). There were also banquets in ancient Greece where the main purpose was conversation, philosophical debate, games and song. Plato describes one of these in *The Banquet*.

The Greeks also held civic banquets to commemorate the Elders. These ceremonial 'city meals' took place within the Prytaneum and were attended by chosen citizens dressed in white and wearing a crown of flowers. They even became obligatory in Sparta. This tradition was revived during the French Revolution with 'Lacedaemonian Tables' for the nation 'to hold its great banquet' in the hope of seeing rich and poor united in joyful public reunions 'drinking toasts to the sound of all the bells'. But these convivial meals were short-lived.

■ **Private and public celebrations** With the Romans, the banquet became an occasion for ostentatious luxury with great attention to the setting, regardless of whether the occasion was public or private. From the time of Charlemagne, custom required that vassals offered a banquet to their lords at least once a year. Pomp and circumstance were the order of the day. Table settings, ever richer, were part of the sumptuous ostentation. Banquets were organized whenever an occasion brought the people and their sovereign together. In February 1548 Swiss ambassadors visiting Fontainebleau for the baptism of Claude, seventh child of Henry II and Catherine de Medici, were invited to an 'historical' banquet. As this was during Lent, fish was served instead of meat and included lamprey, turtle, trout, char, anchovy, herring, snails, frog pâté, carp and eels. In 1571 the City of Paris celebrated the arrival of Elizabeth of Austria in the capital with a lavish banquet which included whale on the menu.

■ **Power and politics** Banquets inevitably became more numerous when used as the tool of political ambition. When Louis XIV entertained hundreds of courtesans at Versailles, he sought to demonstrate his power by the splendour of the reception. Talleyrand, who used culinary art in the service of diplomacy, said to Louis XVIII: 'Sire, I have greater need of cooking pots than of instructions.'

The banquet was also an instrument of internal politics. Under Louis-Philippe, minister Guizot removed the right to hold public meetings for political purposes, so voters met at banquets where they discussed politics under the guidance of famous men such as Lamartine and Ledru-Rollin. Guizot eventually prohibited these banquets, but he was too late. It is reported that the King declared confidently that 'the Parisians will never trade a throne for a banquet'.

■ **The biggest banquet in the world** On 14 July 1889 Gambetta assembled all the mayors of France at the Palace of Industry in Paris to celebrate the centenary of the storming of the Bastille. Eleven years later, the idea was repeated by Émile Loubet for the famous 'mayors' banquet' on 22 September 1900. The menu included fillet of beef Bellevue, Rouen duck loaf, chicken from Bresse and ballotine of pheasant. This menu was designed to revive the republican spirit in the city officials: 22,295 mayors were entertained in the Tuileries Gardens in tents specially erected for the occasion and served by waiters from Porel and Chabot, who covered the 7 kilometres (4 miles) of tables on bicycles.

Nowadays banquets are less extravagant. Although still fashionable for heads of state, they hardly ever take place otherwise, except for associations, corporations and fellowships in banqueting halls rented out by restaurants equipped to provide this kind of service. Social events now tend to be celebrated at luncheons, cocktail parties and garden parties.

BANQUIÈRE A rich French garnish (hence the name, which means banker) composed of quenelles of chicken, mushrooms and slivers of truffle, served as an accompaniment to poultry and calves' sweetbreads and used as a filling for pies and vol-au-vent with banquière sauce. The same garnish (without mushrooms) also accompanies tournedos (filet mignons) or sautéed noisettes of lamb arranged on croûtons and coated with the pan juices mixed with Madeira and stock.

RECIPE

banquière sauce
3 tablespoons Madeira to 200 ml (7 fl oz, ¾ cup) suprême* sauce. Sieve, then add 2 tablespoons chopped truffle or truffle peelings.

BANYULS A high-class French *vin doux naturel* that rivals port. Its name comes from one of the four communes of Roussillon where it is produced (Banyuls, Cerbère, Collioure and Port-Vendres). The vineyards, where the grape traditionally grown is the Grenache noir, are situated on the steep dry hillsides where the work of the vine growers is particularly hard. Little arable soil is available and this is washed away each year by torrential rain and must be brought back to the tops of the slopes. This happens in spite of the terraces which have been built on the hillsides in an attempt to control the run-off effect and to protect the vines from the icy blast of the north wind.

The grapes are picked when extremely ripe. After partial fermentation, alcohol is added to stop the action of the yeast (a process known as mutage). The wine is aged in barrels or large glass jars. The AOC 'Banyuls' requires that the mutage takes place before the end of the year in which the grapes are harvested and that the wine remains in the cellars until 1 September of the following year. The *Banyuls grand cru* (vintage Banyuls) must be aged in wooden barrels for at least 30 months before sale. It is classed as *sec* or *brut* (dry) when it contains less than 54 g (about 2 oz) natural sugar per 1 litre (1¾ pints, 4⅓ cups). The name *rancio* is given to the vintage when particular ageing conditions have given it a mature taste.

BAR A retail outlet for drinks, which are generally consumed standing up (or sitting on a bar stool) in front of a counter which may be fitted with a copper or wooden bar as a foot rest (hence the name). The word appeared in the French language in 1837 and also applies to the counter itself.

The tradition of the American bar began in Paris in about 1910 and developed between the wars with the fashion for cocktails. Some bars frequented by celebrities became famous. This fashion has been in decline in France since the 1950s but the neighbourhood bar flourishes in the USA.

Some French restaurants, such as the Coupole or the Closeric des Lilas, and some hotels, such as the Crillon or the George V, have bars reserved for their own customers, and these are sometimes used as a background for political, society or artistic events. Other establishments, opening in the evening and sometimes all night, often with musical entertainment, are simply bars where only alcoholic beverages are consumed. Among the famous bars of Paris are Fouquet's, a meeting place for the world of cinema, the Bar Romain, a favourite haunt of show-business artistes, and the Pont-Royal, a focal point of literary life.

In France, as elsewhere, by far the majority are café-bars or *bars-cafés-tabacs*, which are open all day and serve snacks, as well as alcoholic and non-alcoholic drinks.

BARACK PÁLINKA An unsweetened apricot brandy produced in Hungary from a distillation of fresh apricots, the best of which come from the orchards of Kecskemet. Barack Pálinka from Austria

and Hungary are often sold in long-necked bottles known as *fütyülös*.

BARBADINE African name for the giant granadilla, related to passion fruit.

BARBARESCO A red Italian wine from Piedmont made from the Nebbiolo grape. It comes from the communes of Barbaresco and Neive and is characterized by its fine fruity flavour.

BARBECUE An open-air cooking apparatus or outdoor grill, usually charcoal burning, for grilling or spit-roasting meat or fish and, by extension, a social occasion, much favoured in America and Australia.

Charcoal cookery is the most ancient of cooking methods, still the common way of cooking in Mediterranean and tropical climates, while roasting an animal on a fire has been a way of feasting in all places and in all eras. In America the outdoor grill is associated with the push westward and opening up the new continent. In its modern form, outdoor cookery has become a leisure activity, characterized by tongs and the apron and, sometimes, expensive cooking equipment, and is distinct from day-to-day cookery.

The word probably comes from the Haitian *barbacoa*, meaning grill, but some attribute its origin to the French *de la barbe à la queue* (from the beard to the tail), referring to the method of impaling the animal on the roasting spit. There may even be a connection with the French *barbaque*, which comes from the Romanian *berbec*, meaning roast mutton. In Japan the *hibachi* or table barbecue is a small cast-iron hearth, equipped with a grid. Traditionally, each guest grills his or her own kebabs or other items, which have been cut up in advance. Hibachi grills are now popular outdoor alternatives to large barbecues, used in the same way.

■ **Equipment** Types of barbecue vary according to the site. The most basic consist of a hearth containing charcoal and a grid (rack). The most complex are complete garden cookers with a spit (often electric), removable hood, oven and dripping pan. Camping barbecues are made to fold away and are equipped with a wind break.

A hearth barbecue is made either of cast iron (they do not lose their shape but are heavy and breakable) or steel plate (this must be fairly thick), which sometimes tips to a vertical position. The rectangular or circular grid is made of steel and the height is adjustable.

The most commonly used fuel is wood charcoal, specially prepared from carbon-purified sticks, which greatly prolong the intense heat of the charcoal. When wood is used, its type affects both the speed of cooking and the flavour the smoke gives to the food. Very hard wood gives intense heat and in Europe vine prunings have always been used, in America mesquite. The US also favours hickory and oak. A classic addition to the fire in France, to flavour fish, is fennel stalks.

Some barbecues operate with lava stones heated by butane gas or even solar energy. There are various accessories which may come in handy: poker, tongs, bellows, oven gloves, long-handled spoon and fork, and a variety of racks for enclosing fish and meat and enabling them to be turned neatly.

■ **Cooking methods** Almost anything can be grilled or roasted on a barbecue, with the exception of thin veal and delicate fish. Corn cobs, peppers, tomatoes and large mushrooms can be cooked directly on the grid, brushed with oil or melted butter and other vegetables (such as potatoes) can be enclosed in foil, or be chopped and cooked inside sealed foil parcels. Cooking begins when the charcoal has reached the glowing ember stage.

Some meats have a better flavour if they have been marinated. Barbecued food can be served with any of the sauces which traditionally accompany grills and fondue bourguignonne (pepper, béarnaise or tartare).

• SPIT-ROAST MEAT Distribute the weight of the meat to be cooked evenly along the length of the spit. If chicken is being cooked, hold the limbs in place with small wooden skewers so that they do not become charred. Initially place the meat close to the embers so that the heat causes a crust to form, sealing in the juices, and then move it further away so that the meat will cook slowly right through.

• GRILLED FISH OR MEAT Since they are either enclosed in a folding grill rack or cooked directly on the grid, each item must be brushed with oil all over so that it does not stick to the hot metal. Large fish should be gutted (cleaned) and washed, but not scaled (so that the flesh remains tender). Remove the scales and skin together before serving. Split a small chicken in two, remove the giblets, flatten and season. Scampi (jumbo shrimp) and oysters (in their shells) can be placed directly on the grid without further preparation.

• KEBABS Brush each piece of food with oil before putting the kebabs on the grill. Wrap fragile pieces (such as shellfish and liver) in a thin slice of lean bacon.

BARBEL *barbeau* A freshwater fish related to carp with a brown back, yellowish sides and white abdomen, named for the beardlike projections from its lower jaw. It is found in many rivers in Europe, Asia and Africa. In France the common river barbel is about 50 cm (20 in) long, weighing up to 2 kg (4½ lb), while the southern barbel is smaller. Its flesh is bland and full of bones. In the Loire and Burgundy regions it is served poached or braised and flavoured with red wine and herbs. Young barbel are either fried or grilled (broiled).

BARBERA An Italian grape which has given its name to a red wine produced in large quantities in Piedmont. Barbera is a full-bodied dark wine, often drunk when young.

BARBERRY A prickly European shrub, also found in America, that favours dry soil and sunny spots. In

October it produces tart, bright-red very slim berries in bunches. They are rich in tartaric and malic acids, which are used to make jellies and syrups, and also for flavouring rice pilaf in Iran. Cooked and dried, they can be made into a fine powder, which was formerly used as a seasoning. The unripe green berries can be preserved in vinegar, like capers.

BARD Thin slices of pork or bacon fat which are placed around meat, some game birds and poultry, and even some fish before roasting, to prevent them from drying out in the heat of the oven. Barding is not advised for some very tender meats as the strong flavour of the bard might overshadow the taste of the meat. Bards are also used as a lining for pâtés cooked in pastry or terrines.

In order to bard a roast, the meat is covered with strips of bard held in place with string. To bard terrines and pâtés, the inside of the pie crust or mould is lined with bards.

The bards are generally removed before serving, but it is usual to serve partridge, other game and pâtés still barded.

BARDATTE A Breton speciality from the region of Nantes, which used to be prepared at harvest time and eaten cold by the peasants in the fields. It consists of a cabbage stuffed with rabbit or hare meat flavoured with herbs, which is wrapped in a thick wide slice of bacon (*barde*, hence its name), put in an earthenware dish, moistened with stock and baked slowly in the oven.

BARIGOULE, À LA The French term used to describe a particular method of preparing stuffed braised artichokes. *Barigoule* is the Provençal name for the milk-cap mushroom, once solely used in the recipe. Originally, the country recipe consisted of cooking the artichokes like mushrooms, that is, cut off flat at the base, sprinkled with oil and grilled (broiled). Provençal cooks subsequently developed a stuffing of ham and mushrooms for the artichokes.

RECIPE

artichokes à la barigoule
Prepare the artichokes for stuffing. Clean and chop 75 g (3 oz, 1 cup) mushrooms for each artichoke. Mince (grind) 50 g (2 oz) fat bacon and the same quantity of ham. Mix these ingredients together with chopped parsley, salt and pepper. Fill the artichokes with the mixture, bard, tie up with string, and braise in white wine to which a little olive oil has been added. Thicken the cooking liquor with a very small amount of softened butter.

BARLEY The earliest known cereal to be cultivated, used formerly for bread and, still, for beer. Barley is the staple grain of northern lands, where it is too cold for wheat, and has been grown in the Near East since 8000 BC. High in starch, it produces a low-gluten flour and consequently a heavy, flat, nourishing loaf (but one that keeps well). Until the 16th century it supplied Europe's main bread. Its flat loaves were used as plates, which were then eaten. Something of this tradition continues in the ever-popular Scandinavian flat breads, and its Scottish use for griddle cakes like bannocks (and for porridge).

It is also used for drinks, like barley water (with lemon juice), gives its name to orgeat and makes barley beer. The grain's main modern use is as a basic ingredient in malting and beer brewing (the best varieties for brewing are those with a double row of seeds).

Pearl barley is the hulled and milled grain, pot barley is unhulled; both are used chiefly in soups, broths and stews, such as oxtail soup, *cholent* and Scotch broth. Pearl barley can be boiled and served as an alternative to rice.

RECIPES

consommé with pearl barley
Wash 100 g (4 oz, ½ cup) pearl barley in warm water and add it, with 1 celery stick to 2.5 litres (4¼ pints, 11 cups) clarified beef stock. Simmer for 2 hours, then remove the celery and serve the soup in cups.

cream of barley soup
Wash 300 g (11 oz, 1½ cups) pearl barley and soak it for 1 hour in warm water. Add the barley and 1 sliced celery stick to 1 litre (1¾ pints, 4⅓ cups) clear white stock and simmer for 2½ hours. Rub the soup through a fine sieve and dilute with a few tablespoons of stock or milk. Heat the soup through again and add 200 ml (7 fl oz, ¾ cup) double (heavy) cream.

BARLEY BEER *cervoise* An alcoholic drink that the Gauls made from fermented barley, oats, rye or sometimes wheat, flavoured with various spices. It was an earlier form of beer, which appeared with the introduction of hops in the 14th century. The French word possibly derives from the Gallic *cerevisia*, a combination of Cerès, Roman goddess of harvests, and the Latin *vis* (strength). Barley beer was originally matured in pottery jars and later in casks. Throughout the Middle Ages, because of privileges granted by Charlemagne, monks were the major producers. In 1268 the *Livre des métiers* laid down regulations for the *cervoisier* (barley-beer maker): 'No one may brew barley beer from anything except water and grain, either barley, wheat and rye mixture, or *dragie* (barley residue).' The maker was forbidden to add to it 'berries, spiced honey-sweetened wine or resin'. In present-day Iberian languages, *cerveza* and *cerveja* are words for beer.

BARLEY SUGAR A traditional sweet (candy) of cooked sugar in both France and Britain, made originally from a mixture of hot sugar syrup and a decoction of barley to colour it.

Back in fashion under the French Second Empire because Napoleon III enjoyed it, barley sugar became a speciality of the spa towns of France (Evian, Plombières, Cauterets and Vichy, in particular). It has been made in the form of small cylindrical sticks (from a ribbon of drawn sugar rolled by hand, then wrapped in coloured cellophane), twisted sticks and flat tablets, cut out on an oiled baking sheet. Modern forms are made of cooked sugar without barley, with various flavourings, shaped into a round stick or cut out by a pressing machine.

Two specialities are worth mentioning: Tours barley sugar, flavoured with apple or cherry; and Moret barley sugar, amber-coloured, in the shape of a heart marked with a cross. The latter was created in 1638 by the nuns of the convent of Moretsur-Loing (Seine-et-Marne) and its recipe remains a secret: lost under the Revolution, it was preserved by one of the nuns and later sold to a lay confectioner of the town.

The Nancy bergamot, the Vosges *granit*, and the honey-flavoured pastille of Saint-Benoît-sur-Loire (in the shape of a little monk) are also barley sugar.

RECIPE

old-fashioned barley sugar
Gently cook 250 g (9 oz, 1¼ cups) hulled barley in 5 litres (8½ pints, 5½ quarts) water for 5 hours. Strain this liquid (which resembles white jelly) and return it to the pan. Add 1 kg (2¼ lb, 4 cups) warmed sugar, stir until dissolved over a gentle heat, then boil the mixture just to the hard crack stage (see *sugar*) and pour it over an oiled marble slab. As soon as the barley sugar begins to cool, cut it into long strips and twist them.

BARNACLE, GOOSE *pouce-pied* A crustacean which lives on sea-washed rocks, fixed at the foot and standing about 5 cm (2 in) high. It is difficult to harvest and therefore very expensive. The outside is blackish and mottled and, fancifully, a group look like a gaggle of geese with upstretched necks because the tips are whitish, like parted beaks. Found on the stormiest parts of Europe's Atlantic coast, and in Canada, it is a speciality in Galicia. The Spanish name is *percebe*.

Cooked briefly in court-bouillon or boiling water, it is eaten with or without vinaigrette after peeling, or squeezing out the soft orange cylindrical inside.

BAROLO An Italian red wine from the hills of Piedmont around the village of Barolo. It is a wine with a fairly high alcoholic content made from the Nebbiolo grape, which is improved by being aged in the barrel before bottling. Dark in colour with a flavour giving hints of raspberries, truffles and chocolate, Barolo is a powerful but smooth wine with a burnt aftertaste.

BARON The cut of mutton or lamb that includes the saddle (loins) and both hind legs. The term was applied originally to beef, but since a baron of beef is so big, it is hardly ever cooked as such. Baron of lamb is oven- or spit-roast, and is served with vegetables such as braised chicory (endive), green beans, flageolets and potatoes, and moistened with the meat juices. It is one of the most spectacular roasts of French cuisine.

The noble title given to this cut has an historical origin. Henry VIII of England was presented with a spit-roast double sirloin and was so impressed by this magnificent joint that he dubbed it Sir Loin, Baron of Beef. The corresponding cut of mutton was subsequently given the same name.

In 1952 the Académie Française attempted to impose the name *bas-rond* but, because of the protests, it was decided that the French would keep to the original English name.

RECIPE

baron of lamb à la périgourdine
Cook and shell 1 kg (2¼ lb) chestnuts. Cover the baron with a light even coat of butter and season with salt and pepper. Roast in a preheated oven at 200°C (400°F, gas 6) for 18–20 minutes per 450 g (1 lb). While the meat is cooking, fry some small tomatoes (preferably in goose fat) and keep warm. Repeat the process with the chestnuts. Arrange the baron on a warm plate surrounded with alternating tomatoes and chestnuts. Deglaze the dripping with boiling water and reduce until richly flavoured. Serve the meat juice in a sauce boat. The baron can also be served with potatoes lightly fried and enriched with truffle peelings.

BARQUETTE A small boat-shaped tart made of short-crust pastry (basic pie dough) or puff pastry, baked blind and then filled with various sweet or savoury ingredients. Sometimes the pastry boats are filled before they are baked. Savoury barquettes are served hot or cold as hors d'oeuvre or entrées. Sweet barquettes, filled with fruit or cream, are served cold.

RECIPES

Savoury Barquettes
anchovy barquettes
Remove salt from the anchovy fillets by soaking them in a little milk. Dice some mushrooms and onions, fry in butter, and bind with a little béchamel sauce. Dice the anchovy fillets and add to the béchamel mixture. Fill cooked barquette cases with this mixture, sprinkle with fried breadcrumbs, and bake for a few minutes in a preheated oven at 240°C (475°F, gas 9).

avocado and prawn barquettes
Mix some mashed avocado to which some lemon juice has been added with an equal volume of mayonnaise. Season with salt and pepper and add a little cayenne. Fill the cooked barquettes with this mixture and garnish with shelled prawns (shrimp).

barquettes à l'américaine
Fill cooked barquette cases with a salpicon of shellfish *à l'américaine*. Sprinkle with fried breadcrumbs and bake in a preheated oven at 230°C (450°F, gas 8) until the filling is hot and the crumbs are crisp.

cheese barquettes
Finely chop some mushrooms and sauté them. Prepare a béchamel sauce and add some grated Gruyère cheese, then the sautéed mushrooms. Fill the cooked barquettes with the mixture, sprinkle with white breadcrumbs and melted butter, then brown under the grill (broiler).

mushroom barquettes
Prepare some scrambled eggs and a mushroom duxelles. Spread a layer of scrambled eggs and a layer of mushrooms in each cooked barquette. Fry some breadcrumbs and sprinkle over the barquettes. Bake for a few minutes in a preheated oven at 200°C (400°F, gas 6) just to warm the barquettes through.

scrambled egg and asparagus barquettes
Prepare some scrambled eggs and asparagus tips. Fill the cooked barquettes with scrambled eggs. Garnish with asparagus tips, sprinkle with melted butter and warm through in the oven.

soft-roe barquettes
Poach some soft roe (carp, herring or mackerel) in court-bouillon. Finely chop and sauté some mushrooms. Prepare a small quantity of béchamel sauce. Fill the bottom of each cooked barquette with mushrooms. Place one piece of roe in each barquette. Coat with béchamel sauce, sprinkle with grated Gruyère cheese and brown under the grill (broiler).

other recipes See *Bagration, Beauharnais, bouquetière, normande.*

Sweet Barquettes
apricot barquettes
For about 15 barquettes, prepare pastry using 225 g (8 oz, 2 cups) sifted flour, 1 teaspoon salt, 1 tablespoon sugar, 1 egg yolk, 100 g (4 oz, ½ cup) butter, and about 7 tablespoons water. Roll out the pastry to a thickness of 3 mm (⅛ in). Cut with a fluted oval pastry (cookie) cutter. Line the moulds with the pastry, prick the bottom of each one, and sprinkle with a little icing (confectioner's) sugar. Remove the stones (pits) from the apricots and cut each one into four. Lay the apricot quarters lengthways in the pastry boats, skin-side down. Bake in a preheated oven at 200°C (400°F, gas 6) for about 20 minutes. Turn out and allow to cool on a wire rack. Coat each barquette with sieved apricot jam and decorate with 2 blanched almonds. Puff pastry can also be used. Alternatively, the pastry boats may be baked blind, filled with crème au beurre and topped with apricots cooked in syrup.

chestnut barquettes

Bake some pastry barquette cases blind and then fill them with chestnut cream. They can be decorated with piped whipped cream and a sugar violet. Alternatively, shape the cream into a dome with two sides and ice (frost) one side with coffee icing (frosting) and the other with chocolate icing and top with piped crème au beurre.

BARRACUDA A tropical fish of the *Sphyrenidae* family. There are several species, all with an elongated body, a long, wide head and a pointed muzzle. The small barracuda, seldom longer than 1 metre (3 ft 3 in), has a golden band along its side, and is sometimes called 'false pike' (*faux brochet*). It is fished off the coast of Africa and sold fresh in French markets. The Pacific barracuda is a sporting fish, weighing up to 5.5 kg (12 lb), and prized for cooking in California. Easy to cook, either grill (broil) or eat as carpaccio, thinly sliced and raw.

The great barracuda, common in the Western Atlantic and the Caribbean islands, is not recommended, as it may cause ciguatera poisoning.

BARRAMUNDI The giant perch of the *Lates* family of northern Australia, named by the aboriginals. This is the best eating fish in Australia. Golden brown, up to 1.5 m (5 ft) long and prized as a game fish, the barramundi ranges from the Philippines to the Persian Gulf.

BARREL Probably developed by the Celts for transporting many types of goods, the wine barrel has an important influence on wine styles. Barrels are made in many sizes, from a standard Bordelaise at 225 litres (49 UK gallons, 61 US gallons) to traditional large Italian or German casks which may contain 10 or 20 times more. Wood is shaped into staves and held in a cylindrical shape by iron hoops – nails are not used in the construction of a barrel. Oak, from forests in France, Eastern Europe or America, is most favoured although other woods, such as chestnut, may be used for large casks.

BARSAC A sweet wine from Bordeaux, Barsac is the largest of the five communes in Sauternes and may call its wine either AOC Barsac or AOC Sauternes. Made from botrytis-affected Semillon and Sauvignon grapes, Barsac wines are often slightly less sweet and more fruity than Sauternes.

BASELLA A tropical climbing plant, also known as vine spinach, Ceylon spinach or Malabar spinach. Ceylon spinach is used for the red-leaved variety while Malabar spinach refers to the green-leaved plant. The stem, which can grow as high as 2 m (7 ft), bears leaves which are harvested as the plant grows and are eaten like spinach. Thought to be native to India, basella is grown in China, South-east Asia and Africa. In the West Indies, basella is prepared like *brèdes*.

BASIL An aromatic herb, both the main types originated in India; its name is derived from Greek *basilikos*, meaning royal, for only the sovereign (*basileus*) was allowed to cut it. (It is still important in the cooking of Thailand, Laos and Vietnam, in salads and curries.)

Sweet basil is now widely grown as a herb with many cultivars. Common basil has large soft leaves 3 cm (1¼ in) long, but there are ruffled, lettuce-leaved and purple varieties, with lemon and cinnamon among their smells. Basil is a warm-weather annual, one reason why it is grown in pots inside windows; another is that it keeps away flies. In France it is associated with Provence, but the strongest association is with Liguria in northern Italy, and Genoa, where it is ground with Parmesan to make the famous pesto sauce. The leaves have a strong flavour of lemon and jasmine. Basil has an affinity with tomatoes, and is used in salads, stuffings, sauces and omelettes as well as soups (see *pistou*) and pasta dishes.

BASIN Originally, a basin in France was a wide deep circular container made of copper or tin, which was used to collect the water poured over the hands during table ablutions. These gradually became richly worked gold pieces used more as ornaments on side-boards and dressers. From the 17th century onwards pottery basins were used in France either for ablutions or, more commonly, for serving meat or fruit. Some reached such dimensions that it required two men to carry them. They disappeared as serving dishes in the 18th century and were replaced by smaller bowls or dishes.

BASQUAISE, À LA The French term used to describe several recipes (particularly for omelettes and sautéed chicken) using tomatoes, sweet peppers, garlic and often Bayonne ham associated with the French Basque country. A basquaise garnish, for large cuts of meat, consists of Bayonne ham with cep mushrooms and Anna potatoes.

RECIPES

consommé à la basquaise

Cook 4 tablespoons rice and 3 tablespoons diced red pepper cut into strips in 1.5 litres (2¾ pints, 6½ cups) clear beef or chicken broth. Add 2 tablespoons diced tomatoes 5 minutes before the rice is cooked. Sprinkle with chopped chervil before serving.

sautéed squid à la basquaise

Wash and dry 500 g (18 oz) ready-cleaned white squid and cut it into strips. Seed and chop 4–5 red and green peppers, finely chop 4 onions, and peel and finely chop 500 g (18 oz) fresh tomatoes. Fry the peppers in oil, then add the onions, the squid and 1–2 crushed garlic cloves. After cooking for 15 minutes, add the tomatoes and a bouquet garni and season with salt and pepper. Half-cover and cook gently for 10 minutes. Sprinkle with chopped parsley before serving.

stuffed potatoes à la basquaise

Prepare a tomato sauce flavoured with garlic. Dice some red and green peppers and fry in oil. Hollow out some large peeled potatoes, place in boiling water for 5 minutes and wipe dry. Dice some Bayonne ham and moisten it with the tomato sauce, adding the peppers. Fill the potatoes with the mixture. Oil a dish, arrange the potatoes in it and season them with salt and pepper. Sprinkle with oil or melted goose fat. Cover the dish and bake in a preheated oven at about 180°C (350°F, gas 4) for 30–40 minutes. When the potatoes are cooked, sprinkle with breadcrumbs and melted fat and brown under the grill (broiler).

BASS *bar* A fish of the family *percichthyidae*, the sea bass is caught principally in the Mediterranean. Also known as sea perch (because of its similarity to the perch) and – around the Provençal coast – as *loup* (wolf), and *lubina* in Spanish, because of its reputed ferocity, it is a voracious predator, 35–80 cm (14–32 in) in length. It is also relatively rare and, therefore, expensive. Valued since Roman times, the sea bass has fine, compact and delicate flesh with few bones. It is served poached, grilled (broiled), braised, stuffed or flambéed. Normally fillets are only prepared from very large fish which are difficult to cook whole. Once the skin has been removed, these fillets can be cooked simply by frying in a little butter or olive oil.

The striped bass (*bar tacheté*) has an olive green back and is distinguished from the sea bass by its many horizontal black stripes; it is normally up to 60 cm (24 in) long. It lives off the Atlantic coast from the Bay of Biscay to Senegal, off the Gulf of St Lawrence to the Gulf of Mexico, and has successfully been introduced to the Pacific as a sporting fish. It is an inshore fish, preferring calm muddy water. In France it is caught only off the Vendée, where it is baked covered with sea salt.

The black sea bass ranges north from Florida, and is a common catch off Cape Cod. It is another excellent fish for frying and baking. The speckled bass, which is smaller and has less flavour, is fished off the coasts of Morocco.

RECIPES

preparation of bass

Clean the fish through the gills and through a small incision at the base of the stomach in order to grasp the end of the gut. If the bass is to be braised, fried or grilled (broiled), remove the scales, working from the tail to the head. Do not remove the scales if it is to be poached because the scales help to hold the fragile flesh intact. Wash and dry the fish. When grilling, make a few shallow incisions with a sharp knife in the fleshy part of the back.

bass à la livournaise

Scale and clean 4 bass each weighing 250–300 g (9–11 oz). Season with salt and pepper. Butter or oil an ovenproof dish. Spread 200 ml (7 fl oz, ¾ cup) well-seasoned tomato* sauce over the bottom and arrange the bass on top. Sprinkle with breadcrumbs and melted butter or olive oil and bake in a preheated oven at about 230°C (450°F, gas 8) for about 15 minutes. Sprinkle with chopped parsley before serving.

bass à la portugaise

Scale and clean 2 bass each weighing about 400 g (14 oz). Make incisions in the back and season with salt and pepper. Butter an ovenproof dish, arrange the bass in the dish, and moisten with a mixture of equal proportions of dry white wine and fish stock. Bake in a preheated oven at 230°C (450°F, gas 8) for about 15 minutes, basting the fish two or three times during cooking. Drain the fish. Pour the liquor into a small pan, reduce and add butter. Cover the bottom of the cooking dish with tomato sauce, arrange the bass on top and cover with the remaining sauce. Glaze in a preheated oven at 240°C (475°F, gas 9) and serve sprinkled with chopped parsley.

bass braised in red Graves wine

Fillet a 1.5 kg (3¼ lb) sea bass. Season with salt and pepper and fry both sides quickly in butter in a frying pan. Drain. In the same butter, fry 100 g (4 oz) thinly sliced mushrooms and 100 g (4 oz) small white onions. Put the fillets back on top of the mushrooms and onions. Add ½ bottle red Graves and a little fish stock. Cover with buttered greaseproof (waxed) paper and simmer for 5 minutes over a low heat. Drain the fillets on paper towels, remove the skin and place them in an ovenproof dish. Drain the garnish and arrange it around the fish. Reduce the cooking juices and thicken with butter; just before serving, stir in a little hollandaise sauce, strain and pour over the fillets. Brown under the grill (broiler) and garnish with croûtons fried in butter.

braised bass

Select a bass weighing 1.25 kg (2¾ lb). Peel and finely chop 2–3 carrots, 2 onions and 1 shallot. Melt 25 g (1 oz, 1 tablespoon) butter in a frying pan, add the chopped vegetables and cook until they begin to change colour. Chop a small bunch of parsley and mix with 1 tablespoon butter, salt and pepper. Stuff the fish with the parsley butter. Spread the partly cooked vegetables in a large buttered ovenproof dish and gently place the fish on top of the vegetables. Add a bouquet garni and 300 ml (½ pint, 1¼ cups) dry white wine. Melt 25 g (1 oz, 1 tablespoon) butter and pour over the bass, then cover the dish. Bake in a preheated oven at about 220°C (425°F, gas 7) for about 25 minutes. Drain the fish, arrange on a serving dish and keep warm. Discard the bouquet garni, sieve the pan juices and reduce. If desired, beat in butter to thicken the sauce. Skin the bass and cover in sauce. The braised bass may be served on a bed of mushroom duxelles or sorrel fondue, or surrounded by slices of aubergine (eggplant) lightly fried in oil.

cold poached bass

Prepare as for hot poached bass and allow the fish to cool in the poaching liquor. Drain, arrange on a napkin and remove the skin. Garnish with lemon halves, artichoke hearts and small tomatoes stuffed with chopped vegetables. Serve with mayonnaise, vinaigrette or any other sauce suitable for cold fish.

cream of ginger bass

Prepare the cream of ginger: soften 4 chopped shallots in butter, add 100 ml (4 fl oz, 7 tablespoons) dry white wine and 200 ml (7 fl oz, ¾ cup) fish fumet, and reduce. Add 325 ml (11 fl oz, 18 cups) double (heavy) cream and a pinch of salt. Reduce by half, until you have the required consistency. Add 1 tablespoon grated fresh root ginger and allow to simmer for 2 minutes. Strain through muslin (cheesecloth) or a fine strainer. Thicken the sauce with 75 g (3 oz, 6 tablespoons) butter (cut into small knobs), beating with a whisk.

Prepare 400 g (14 oz) well-washed spinach without stalks and braise in butter. Take 4 escalopes (scallops) of sea bass, each weighing 175 g (6 oz), and season with ground white pepper and salt. Fry quickly in oil. Drain them on paper towels so as to remove all traces of cooking oil. Make a bed of spinach in the middle of each plate and arrange the sea bass on top. Pour the cream of ginger over them and garnish with sprigs of chervil.

crowns of bass with red peppers

Fillet and clean a 1 kg (2¼ lb) sea bass. Cut the flesh into strips and plait (braid) 3 strips together. Repeat with the remaining strips. Season with salt. Shape the plaits into crowns and keep chilled.

Grill (broil) 2 red peppers until their skins are blistered and blackened. Cool slightly, then peel, halve and seed them. Cut out 4 strips and 5 small petal shapes. Purée the rest and reduce the purée over a gentle heat. Cook some broccoli in boiling salted water, drain, reserve a little for the crown centres and purée the remainder.

Brown 2 chopped shallots in butter, then add some white wine and reduce by half. Add 500 ml (17 fl oz, 2 cups) single (light) cream and heat through. Divide this mixture in two: stir the pepper purée into one half, and the broccoli purée into the other. Check the seasoning and keep warm.

Fry the crowns of sea bass in butter. Spoon the sauces on to the plates. Arrange the sea bass crowns on top and garnish with the pepper strips and petals. Spoon the reserved broccoli into the centres. Serve the rest of the sauce separately.

fillets of bass with lettuce ♦

(from a recipe by Roger Vergé) Clean and scale a 1.4 kg (3 lb) bass. Remove and skin the fillets.

Divide each fillet into two pieces, season with salt and pepper, and dust with flour. Melt a knob of butter and a dash of olive oil in a frying pan. Fry the fillets for 1 minute on each side, then put to one side. Plunge the outer leaves of 2 or 3 lettuces into 2 litres (3½ pints, 9 cups) boiling salted water and transfer immediately to a colander. Rinse in cold water and drain. Split the leaves in two vertically and flatten slightly. Then dry them on a towel and wrap the fillets up in them.

Butter a gratin dish, sprinkle with finely chopped shallots and arrange flattened lettuce hearts on top, followed by the fillets wrapped in lettuce leaves. Pour over 3 tablespoons dry white wine and the same amount of vermouth. Bake in a preheated oven at about 180°C (350°F, gas 4) for 12 minutes. Drain the fillets and the lettuce hearts and arrange on a warm serving dish.

Strain the cooking liquor into a pan and reduce to about 175 ml (6 fl oz, ¾ cup) over a fierce heat. In a bowl mix together 3 tablespoons cream and 1 egg yolk and add to the pan. Whisk the mixture. Remove from the heat and heat in 50 g (2 oz, ¼ cup) cubed butter. Season with salt and pepper. Use to coat the fillets and serve. A little diced, peeled and seeded ripe tomato may be added as a garnish, if required.

fried bass

Clean and scale bass weighing not more than 400 g (14 oz) each. Make incisions along the back, dip in milk and coat in flour. Deep-fry in fat or oil. Drain, pat dry and dust with fine salt. Arrange on a serving dish and garnish with lemon halves. Steaks of a larger bass can be prepared in the same way.

grilled bass

Scale and clean a bass weighing not more than 1 kg (2¼ lb). Make a few small incisions in the back and brush with seasoned olive oil. Cook gently, preferably using a folding double grill (broiler) grid to enclose the bass so it can be turned during cooking without breaking. In the south of France, small bass are cooked on charcoal, on top of sprigs of dry fennel, which flavour the fish. Serve with anchovy or garlic butter or one of the special sauces for grilled fish, such as béarnaise or rémoulade.

hot poached bass

Clean and wash the bass without removing the scales and place in a fish kettle. Cover with cold salted water and heat gently until simmering. As soon as the liquid is about to boil, reduce the heat and poach the fish in barely simmering water. Drain the bass, arrange on a dish covered with a napkin (or on a rack) and garnish with fresh parsley. In a separate dish serve melted butter, hollandaise sauce, or any other sauce suitable for poached fish. Serve with boiled or mashed potatoes, spinach, fennel or broccoli.

additional recipe See *Dugléré*.

Fillets of bass with lettuce.

BASSELIN, OLIVIER 15th-century French poet from Vire, in Normandy. A fuller by trade, he found his inspiration in the bottle. His lively satirical poetry, known as *vaudevire* after his birthplace, is the origin of many table songs. Basselin's *vaudevires* were published at the end of the 17th century. *Vaudevire* gave its name to the type of musical entertainment known as vaudeville.

BASTE The term for lightly moistening food cooking in the oven, on a rotisserie or under a grill (broiler) by spooning over melted fat or the cooking juices from the dish itself. This operation is repeated several times and stops the surface of the food from getting too dry. A dish cooked au gratin may be basted with melted butter to facilitate browning.

BASTELLA In Corsican cookery, a turnover stuffed with vegetables and meat. Bastelle are called *inarbittate* when they are made with Swiss chard or spinach; *inzuchatte* when made with marrow (squash) or pumpkin, and *incivulate* when they are made with onions. The ingredients are blanched and drained, then finely chopped and mixed with pork or veal. Bastelle should properly be made with bread dough, but puff pastry is now more commonly used.

BA-TA-CLAN A French cake made from fresh almonds, ground using a pestle and mortar, to which the following ingredients are added: eggs (one at a time), sugar, rum and flour. The cake is cooked in a flat or fluted mould and coated with vanilla-flavoured fondant icing (frosting). Its name derives from the Parisian café-concert famous at the end of the 19th century, but the recipe is attributed to Lacam, a 19th-century pastry chef who wrote treatises on pâtisserie.

BÂTARDE A hot French sauce, also known as butter sauce, served with vegetables and boiled fish.

RECIPE

sauce bâtarde
Prepare a sauce using 25 g (1 oz, 2 tablespoons) melted butter, 25 g (1 oz, ¼ cup) plain (all-purpose) flour and 250 ml (8 fl oz, 1 cup) boiling salted water. Beat in 1 egg mixed with 1 tablespoon very cold water and 1 tablespoon lemon juice and then, over a very low heat, add 100 g (4 oz, ½ cup) butter, cut into small pieces. Season with salt and pepper and sieve or strain if necessary.

BÂTELIÈRE, À LA The French term describes a fish dish garnished with poached button mushrooms, small glazed onions, fried eggs and prawns (shrimp). The name also applies to a preparation of fillets of sole arranged as small boats (hence the name) on a salpicon of prawns and mussels in a white wine and herb sauce. Mackerel *à la bâtelière* is simply grilled (broiled) and served with a separate green sauce.

BÂTON Also known as *bâtonnet*. A French petit four in the form of a small stick made of puff pastry or almond paste. They are served with desserts and buffets.

Vegetables may be cut *en bâtonnets* (in thin sticks) for cooking.

RECIPES

almond bâtonnets
Pound 225 g (8 oz, 1⅔ cups) blanched almonds with 225 g (8 oz, 1 cup) caster (superfine) sugar, or combine in a blender. Bind to a thick paste with 2–3 egg whites and then add 7 tablespoons white rum. Roll out thinly on a floured marble slab or work surface. Cut into strips 8 cm (3½ in) wide and cut these into sticks 2 cm (¾ in) wide. Lightly beat 2 egg whites. Dip the sticks in the egg whites, then in sugar. Arrange on a buttered and floured baking sheet and bake in a preheated oven at about 170°C (325°F, gas 3) until the sugar crisps.

bâtons with vanilla icing
In a processor combine 225 g (8 oz, 1⅔ cups) ground almonds and 225 g (8 oz, 1 cup) caster (superfine) sugar to a firm paste with 2–3 egg whites. Flavour with 2 teaspoons natural vanilla essence (extract). Roll out the paste to a thickness of 1 cm (½ in). Cover with vanilla-flavoured royal icing (frosting). Cut into strips 2 cm (¾ in) wide by 10 cm (4 in) long. Place the sticks on a buttered and floured baking sheet and bake in a preheated oven at about 160°C (325°F, gas 3) for about 10 minutes or until the icing turns white.

chocolate bâtonnets
Proceed as for almond bâtonnets, but use a paste made from 225 g (8 oz, 1⅔ cups) blanched almonds, 225 g (8 oz, 1 cup) caster (superfine) sugar, 200 g (7 oz, 1½ cups) cocoa powder (unsweetened cocoa), 2 tablespoons vanilla-flavoured sugar and 3 egg whites.

iced bâtons
Roll puff pastry out to a thickness of about 3 mm (⅛ in). Cut into strips 8 cm (3 in) wide and coat with royal icing (frosting). Cut across these strips to make sticks 4 cm (1¾ in) wide. Place on a buttered baking sheet and bake in a preheated oven at about 200°C (400°F, gas 6) for about 5 minutes until the pastry puffs up and the icing turns white.

BÂTONNAGE A French term for lees stirring or stirring the wine in a barrel with a stick so as to disturb the fine lees deposited on the bottom. This allows better development of the wine by controlling its contact with oxygen and with the wood. The practice was developed in making the best white wines, particulary Chardonnays.

BATTER A term based on the texture of a mixture. A liquid, varying in thickness from a thin pouring consistency to an elastic mixture which is too soft to hold its shape but not thin enough to pour easily and evenly. A wide variety of ingredients may be used, from the classic, basic batter made with flour, eggs and milk to a mixture of ground rice and pulses used to make Indian pancakes known as *dosa*.

■ **Types of batter** Batters may be unleavened or include raising agents. Fine French crêpes are made from a thin batter of flour, eggs and milk without raising agent, and the batter is allowed to stand before cooking so that air bubbles disperse, preventing the crêpe from bubbling. (The standing time also allows the flour to absorb liquid, so that a little extra may be added to make a thin batter for fine-textured pancakes.)

The same type of batter can be baked to make Yorkshire pudding or a variety of sweet puddings, including clafoutis, a cherry batter pudding. A slightly thicker version may be used to coat ingredients before deep-frying.

Leavened batters are used for making waffles and for coating. A raising agent may be added to the batter or a thick batter may be prepared, then stiffly whisked egg whites may be folded in; both raising agent and egg whites are used for waffle batter. The egg whites soften the batter and make it puff up during cooking. This type of mixture is also used to make Polish-style apple pancakes by stirring the fruit into the batter, then flattening small portions on a hot pan. Thick batter containing raising agent is also used to make small, thick and light British pancakes, known as drop scones or Scotch pancakes.

Some enriched breads are made from a mixture resembling batter rather than dough. The yeast mixture for Italian panettone is too soft to be kneaded but usually too stiff to be beaten with a spoon, so the palm of the hand is used to beat it with a slapping motion until it becomes smooth and elastic. Small Greek doughnuts, *loukoumades*, served in honey syrup, may be made from a thick, yeasted batter rather than being shaped from a dough (some recipes use a dough).

The ingredients for many cakes are mixed to a thick, pouring batter, rather than a mixture with a firmer, dropping consistency. Those made by the melted method, such as gingerbread and parkin, and American muffins, are made from batters. American cornbread is also made from a thick cornmeal batter.

Generally, it is important that the dry and liquid ingredients are thoroughly combined and beaten until smooth. (There are exceptions to this, notably the batter used for Japanese tempura, where whisked egg whites are very lightly folded through the flour mixture, leaving the ingredients partly mixed.) Achieving the right balance of ingredients and texture for the particular batter is also important: a coating batter that is too thin will not coat and one that is too thick will be stodgy when cooked. The correct proportion of flour, eggs and liquid are important for making thin, fine pancakes – if there is too little egg and flour, the pancakes will not set and too much flour will make the pancakes stodgy.

RECIPES

basic batter
This is a simple, British-style batter used for thin pancakes or baked puddings, such as Yorkshire pudding. Sift 100 g (4 oz, 1 cup) plain (all-purpose) flour into a bowl with a pinch of salt. Make a well in the middle and add 2 beaten eggs. Gradually beat in 300 ml (½ pint, 1¼ cups) milk and 1 tablespoon oil or melted butter, working in the flour and milk a little at a time. Beat until smooth. Leave to stand for 30 minutes, then stir in 2 tablespoons water.

coating batter
This batter is suitable for coating food before deep-frying. Sift 200 g (7 oz, 1¾ cups) plain (all-purpose) flour into a bowl. Add 2 teaspoons baking powder, 2 tablespoons groundnut (peanut) oil, a pinch of salt and 250 ml (8 fl oz, 1 cup) warm water. Mix the ingredients thoroughly and beat until smooth, then leave the batter to rest in a cool place for at least 1 hour. Just before using, fold in 2 stiffly whisked egg whites.

BAUDELAIRE, CHARLES French poet (born Paris, 1821; died Paris, 1867). Baudelaire, who loved to play chess at the Café de la Régence and the brasserie in the Rue des Martyrs with his artist and poet friends, sang 'the profound joys of wine' in verse and prose (*Wine and Hashish*, 1851; 'The Soul of Wine', a poem in *Flowers of Evil*, 1857). Although his usual restaurant was Dinochau, he dreamed of a more exotic cuisine rich in truffles and spices, 'pimiento, English powders, saffron, musk and incense' (*Fanfario*, 1847), which was supposed to combine 'the violence of prussic acid with the volatile lightness of ether'.

BAUMÉ SCALE An old scale of measurement for the density or specific gravity of sugary liquids, evaluated using a saccharometer. It has been replaced in the measurement of cane and beet sugars by the Brix scale. However, the Baumé scale is still used in the corn-refining industry for measuring the density of sugar syrups derived from cornstarch.

BAUMKUCHEN A celebrated Austrian festival cake, hollow inside and usually conical because it is cooked on a spit. It has also been adopted for family celebrations in Luxembourg. It is made with a sponge batter, often flavoured with cardamom and other spices, grated lemon zest, vanilla and rum. This liquid batter is poured layer by layer on to a roller, which is rotating in front of open heating elements. The layers remain visible after cooking, giving the cake the appearance of a cut tree trunk, from which it gets its name (literally, 'tree cake'). Baumkuchen must remain soft and it is served set upright and decorated. It may be as much as 1 metre (3 ft 3 in) high.

BAVARIAN CREAM *bavarois* A cold dessert made from an egg custard stiffened with gelatine, mixed with whipped cream and sometimes fruit purée or other flavours, then set in a mould.

It is not known whether there is a connection between this dessert and Bavaria, where many French chefs used their talents at the court of the Wittelsbach princes. Carême gives various recipes under the name of *fromage bavarois* (Bavarian cheese). Many cookery books confuse Bavarian cream with a similar dish, the *moscovite*, which was perhaps invented by a French chef in the service of a great Russian family.

RECIPES

Bavarian cream

Soak 15–20 g (½–¾ oz, 2–3 envelopes) gelatine in 3 tablespoons cold water. Heat 600 ml (1 pint, 2½ cups) milk with a vanilla pod (bean). Work together 8 egg yolks, 100 g (4 oz, ½ cup) caster (superfine) sugar and a pinch of salt. When the mixture is smooth, strain in the milk, stir well, then add the gelatine and mix. Stir continuously over a gentle heat until the mixture coats the back of a spoon. The mixture must not boil. Pour into a bowl and allow to cool, then refrigerate until the custard is cold and just beginning to thicken.

Chill 350 ml (12 fl oz, 1½ cups) double (heavy) cream and 75 ml (3 fl oz, ⅓ cup) milk in the refrigerator. Then whip together. As soon as it begins to thicken, add 50 g (2 oz, ¼ cup) caster sugar. Fold the cream into the cooled mixture. Brush the inside of a Bavarian cream (or soufflé or savarin) mould with oil, preferably almond oil. Fill to the brim with the Bavarian cream mixture. Cover with lightly oiled paper and refrigerate until firmly set. To loosen the cream, dip the bottom of the mould in hot water, place a serving dish on top of the mould and quickly turn them over together.
- *Coffee Bavarian cream* Add 2 tablespoons instant coffee to the milk instead of the vanilla pod.
- *Chocolate Bavarian cream* Add 100 g (4 oz, 4 squares) melted plain (bittersweet) chocolate to the milk.
- *Lemon or orange Bavarian cream* Add the juice of 2 lemons or oranges.
- *Bavarian cream liqueur* Add about 2 teaspoons liqueur or more depending on its particular strength of flavour.

Bavarian cream à la normande

Line the base of a suitable mould with a thick layer of the basic Bavarian cream flavoured with Calvados. Leave to set. Prepare an apple purée and stir in sufficient dissolved gelatine to set it. Allow 15 g (½ oz, 2 envelopes) gelatine for 300 ml (½ pint, 1¼ cups) purée. Whip 150 ml (¼ pint, ⅔ cup) double (heavy) cream with 2 tablespoons icing (confectioner's) sugar until thick. Mix the whipped cream with the apple purée, spoon into the mould and top with a layer of the basic Bavarian cream.

Bavarian cream au parfait amour

(from a recipe by Carême) Finely shred the zest of half a lemon and place in a bowl. Add 475 ml (16 fl oz, 2 cups) boiling milk, 6 cloves and 100 g (4 oz, ½ cup) caster (superfine) sugar, stir well, then leave to infuse for 1 hour. Strain the mixture and add 15–20 g (½–¾ oz, 2–3 envelopes) gelatine dissolved in 6 tablespoons hot water and sufficient cochineal or red food colouring to give a pink colour. Chill the bowl and as soon as the mixture begins to set, stir in 125 g (4½ oz, ½ cup) soft cream cheese. Turn into a dish and refrigerate until firmly set.

bavarois aux fruits

Soak 25 g (1 oz, 4 envelopes) gelatine in 5 tablespoons cold water. Warm 500 ml (17 fl oz, 2 cups) heavy sugar syrup (see sugar), add the gelatine and stir to dissolve. Cool slightly, then add the juice of 3 lemons and 500 ml (17 fl oz, 2 cups) thick fruit purée (apricot, pineapple, blackcurrant, strawberry, raspberry) and refrigerate until on the point of setting. Whip 450 ml (¾ pint, 2 cups) double (heavy) cream with 50 g (2 oz, ¼ cup) caster (superfine) sugar until softly thick and gently fold into the half-set fruit jelly. Turn the mixture into an oiled mould and refrigerate until firmly set, then turn out. It may be served with a fruit sauce (preferably matching the fruit used in the cream).

striped chocolate and vanilla Bavarian cream

Creams of different colours and flavours placed in alternating layers in the mould. Striped Bavarian cream can also be made directly in crystal or glass bowls: preparation is quicker and the cream more delicate because the amount of gelatine used can be significantly reduced as the bavarois will not be turned out.

Soak 15–20 g (½–¾ oz, 2–3 envelopes) gelatine in 3 tablespoons cold water. Heat 500 ml (17 fl oz, 2 cups) milk with a vanilla pod (bean). Put 225 g (8 oz, 1 cup) caster (superfine) sugar, a pinch of salt and 8 egg yolks in a saucepan and stir together. Add the vanilla-flavoured milk (without the vanilla pod) and the dissolved gelatine and mix. Warm this cream over a gentle heat, stirring constantly. As soon as it coats the back of a spoon, remove from the heat. Strain or sieve and then divide into two portions. Melt 50 g (2 oz, 2 squares) plain (bittersweet) chocolate and add to half the Bavarian cream mixture.

Complete each half of the cream separately and add to each, as soon as they start to thicken, half the prepared whipped-cream mixture made from 350 ml (12 fl oz, 1½ cups) chilled double (heavy) cream and 60 ml (2 fl oz, ¼ cup) cold milk. Brush the inside of a mould with oil. Fill with alternate layers of the two creams, taking care not to pour in the next layer before the previous one has set. Chill until completely set, then turn out.

All kinds of flavourings and combinations may be

used, such as vanilla and strawberry, vanilla and coffee, chocolate and coffee, pistachio and strawberry and vanilla with praline.

other recipes See *cévenole, créole.*

BAY A Mediterranean evergreen tree, *Laurus nobilis*, also known as bay laurel or true laurel, that is widely cultivated in temperate regions for ornament and for its glossy aromatic leaves, which have a slightly bitter smell. The English name derives from the French *baie*, meaning 'berry' and the tree has conspicuous black fruit, which yield an oil.

Bay leaves are among the most commonly used culinary herbs: a leaf is always incorporated in a bouquet garni and court-bouillon. Bay leaves may be used fresh or dried when the flavour is stronger. The leaves are used to pack dried fruit, like figs, and to line a grill for barbecuing fish. They are indispensable to season stocks, ragoûts, stews, pâtés and terrines.

In ancient times bay leaves were used to make the laurel wreaths with which poets and victorious soldiers were crowned and the tree gives its botanical name to the poet laureate.

The cherry laurel, *Prunus laurocerusus*, is *cerisier* in France, where it has long been associated with custards, but it should be shunned because the leaves contain prussic acid.

BAZINE A leavened semolina cooked in boiling water with oil. In Arab countries, this boiled springy dough constitutes the traditional morning meal during Ramadan, served before sunrise. Bazine is served with butter, honey and lemon juice. This basic preparation is also part of everyday cooking, served in fish soup or with raisins and small pieces of fried meat. It can also be cooked unleavened in chicken stock and served with scrambled eggs or shaped into balls to be cooked in stock.

BEANS, DRIED The dried matured seeds of legumes or fresh beans, these are known as pulses. They are an important source of protein for poorer communities and in vegetarian diets. Being the most important source of nutrition after cereals, there is a vast range of dried beans, including many regional varieties. Different names are applied to similar beans or the same name is sometimes used for related types.

The Old World had brown broad (fava) beans (with the closely related ful medames), a bean sent back by Alexander the Great from Mesopotamia (probably the horse bean), the Indian lablab bean, and black-eyed beans and pigeon peas in Africa. It is a nice irony of history that these latter two were carried back to America (where so many others originated), with black slaves and they are now identified with the cooking of the Caribbean and the American Deep South.

Columbus introduced kidney beans, butter (lima) beans and the scarlet runner bean (all belonging to the *Phaseolus* family) to Europe from South America in the first decade of the 16th century. They were quickly adopted, for they were easier to cook and had greater palatability. In their new localities, however, the podded beans were given the old names. The Spanish *haba*, or fava, is no longer the broad bean (*Vicia faba*).

Spain seized joyfully on the new products. It boasts some of the best varieties, and is a country of bean fanciers, with hundreds of regional varieties in all colours and sizes from *arrancini* ('rice sized') up to monsters the size of two thumbnails like *judiones*. Kidney beans were so enthusiastically adopted in Florence in Italy under the patronage of Alessandro Medici (murdered 1537), the first duke, that the Tuscans became known as *mangie-fagioli*, 'the bean eaters'.

Piero Valeriano described haricot beans as 'these multicoloured red and white seeds, resembling precious stones that might have been lodged in the earth'. Catherine de' Medici probably brought beans in her entourage to France, when she married the future Henri II. First cultivated on the banks of the Loire, *les haricots* spread rapidly to other French regions, and over the centuries different varieties were cultivated. Beans, *frijoles*, are particularly important in Latin America (where all kidney-shaped beans originated) as valuable protein in a region that lacked the European sources of cattle, sheep, goats and pigs until the 16th century. They have remained on the menu for rich and poor. In Mexico, for example, small bowls of beans are served after the main course and before dessert. *Frijoles refritos* or refried beans (cooked beans, pan-fried to serve) is a well-known Latin American dish.

■ **Bean types** The following are the main varieties of beans eaten dried. See also *broad bean (fava bean), ful medames, mung beans, pigeon (gunga) peas, soya beans* and *bean sprouts.*

• BLACK BEANS The shiny smooth *frijoles negros*, or turtle beans, are black-skinned kidney beans, white inside. They are identified with the cooking of Africa, the West Indies and Latin America (and Tolosa in Spain), particularly Venezuela, where they make *caviar criollo*, and Brazil, where the national dish, *feijoada completa*, is black bean stew, complete with sausages and ham hocks. Black bean soup is a common Latin American dish.

• BLACK-EYED PEAS (BEANS) Small creamy beans with a black spot, they are more easily digested than other pulses. There are two almost indistinguishable strains, one from China, also eaten in India and Africa, and the other from Latin America. Of the several varieties, one is the cow pea (named for its use as a forage plant). Now much cultivated in California, they are an ingredient in traditional dishes of the southern states of America, cooked with ham hocks and collard greens or, in Hoppin' John, with spiced rice. The purée is used for fritters in Central America.

• BORLOTTI BEANS These attractive Italian, longish beans range from pale creamy pink to beige with brown speckles (which disappear on cooking). In France they are called *rose-cocos*. Pleasantly moist, with a creamy consistency and slightly sweet when cooked, they are Italy's most popular bean. Used in salads, they also give their pink colour to the Tuscan oil-and-bean soup *frantoiana*.

• BUTTER BEANS Flat and white, these are a type of lima bean. The so-called 'true' lima bean was introduced to East Africa in the 18th century, which now exports the Madagascar (or calico), a large flat bean about 2 cm (¾ in), mainly to Britain. The Italian *bianco de spagna* is this type. America prefers a smaller-sized dried bean (called the *siéva* or Carolina bean), and also exports these beans. Butter beans cook comparatively quickly, and become mushy when overcooked. They may be cooked with onions and tomatoes, Mediterranean style, or made into a purée. They are also used in salads and for *fabada* outside Spain.

• CANNELLINI BEANS Small white kidney beans originally from Argentina, these have been adopted by Italy (which also grows a smaller version called *toscanelli*). Cannellini are used for Florence's *fagioli all' uccelletto*, stewed with tomato, garlic, sage and olive oil, and both types are good sautéed or in salads like *tonno e fagioli* (with canned tuna).

• FLAGEOLETS Gourmet kidney beans, perhaps the finest of all pulses, they are harvested when very young and small (August and September in France), pale green or white. The flageolet is so named because the French decided it resembled a flute. Flageolets were produced by chance in 1872 by Gabriel Chevrier who lived near Arpajon in Brittany. (Flageolets are therefore also known as *chevriers* in France.)

In France they are grown in the Arpajon region and central France, and are the classic accompaniment to leg of lamb and blade of pork.

• 'GREEK' BEANS This is the common description in the Middle East of a type of dried broad bean that has no brown skin. They are large, flat, almost round and pale – similar to a butter bean (the usual substitute), but without the kidney shape. In Greece *fassólia gigántes* are stewed with vegetables, including tomato, the local oregano, oil and perhaps honey, and served hot or cold with a little lemon juice. The beans purée splendidly, so old dishes like the Italian *macco* or *maccu* are of interest to modern cooks.

• LARGE WHITE KIDNEY BEANS The Spanish *fabes de la granja*, vast, flat and buttery in texture, is a prince among kidney beans, but is little exported. Even in its own country it commands a price higher than lamb; it is the Spanish bean for *fabada*. The *judiones* from the west of Spain are probably the biggest of all beans, challenged by the *garrafones* of Valencia. Large white French beans include the *soisson* and the *lingots* of northern France and the Vendée, which keep for a long time. *Cocos* are grown in Brittany, the Vendée (where they are also called *mogetes*) and south-eastern France, and often used for cassoulet and ragoûts.

• PINTO BEANS A smaller kidney bean than borlotti, pink and speckled, pintos are identified with the American south-west, and are eaten in Latin America too.

• RED KIDNEY BEANS Not much eaten in France, but popular in northern Spain, these shiny kidney beans are at home in the US and Canada, north-east Spain and Latin America. Traditionally cooked with bacon and onion, these are favoured in the West Indies and for spicy dishes like chilli con carne.

• SMALL WHITE HARICOT (NAVY) BEANS The seeds of the haricot (French bean), these are used in France for cassoulet (a south-western name is *mounjetos*). There are several similar ones in Spain that have DO (legally protected) names, for example the *alubias* of León and the *judias* of El Barco de Avila.

The navy bean is a strain specially bred in the US for the canning industry, the navy connection dating from 1875, when the beans were canned with molasses to feed the fleet. Mr H.J. Heinz, of Pittsburgh, Pennsylvania, entered on the scene in 1895 with a canned brand, beans in tomato sauce. The first printed recipe for Boston baked beans appeared in Mrs Putnam's *Receipt Book* in 1856.

The Great Northern bean is another American white bean, about twice the size of the navy bean.

■ **Cooking dried beans** Dried beans are usually soaked before cooking, as this reduces the cooking time. Soaking also allows the skins to rehydrate and the beans to plump up, preventing both from separating during boiling. Overnight soaking in plenty of cold water is best, though soaking in boiling water will reduce the time. Beans should not be left in warm water or in a warm room and they should not be soaked for more than 24 hours, as they may ferment and produce poisonous substances. For this reason always use fresh water for cooking. Boil beans rapidly to destroy natural toxins, then reduce the heat to keep the water just boiling. Cook for 45 minutes to 1½ hours, or longer for soya beans to become tender. A bouquet garni, 1 onion studded with 2 cloves, 1 garlic clove and 1 diced carrot can be added during cooking. Do not add salt, as this will prevent the beans from becoming tender or will even harden part-cooked beans. Season beans when they are thoroughly tender. The old way was to include a pinch of bicarbonate of soda (baking soda) in the cooking water to speed cooking, but this is not advised now, for nutritional reasons.

The repertoire of bean dishes includes stews, salads, bean creams and desserts.

RECIPES

haricot bean salad
Cook the beans, allow them to cool and then drain. Add a chopped mild onion to the beans, mix with a well-flavoured vinaigrette, and sprinkle with chopped herbs (parsley, chervil and chives).

haricot beans with onions
Cook and drain the beans. Cook some sliced onions gently in butter – allow 200 g (7 oz) onions

for each 1 kg (2¼ lb) cooked beans. Add the beans, cover the pan, simmer for 6 minutes and serve sprinkled with chopped parsley.

haricots à la crème

Cook the beans, drain them and warm them gently in a saucepan until nearly all the moisture has evaporated. Cover with fresh cream, warm through again, add some chopped savory; serve very hot.

An alternative method is to butter a gratin dish, pour in the cooked beans mixed with cream, sprinkle the dish with white breadcrumbs and melted butter, and brown in a very hot oven or under the grill (broiler).

haricot beans in tomato sauce

Cook the beans with 500 g (18 oz) lean bacon in one piece for each 1 kg (2¼ lb) beans. When the beans are cooked, drain them and mix with 300 ml (½ pint, 1¼ cups) tomato* sauce. Drain the bacon, dice it and add it to the beans. Simmer for about 10 minutes and serve very hot. This dish can also be browned in the oven.

red kidney beans with red wine and bacon

Cook the beans adding bacon (as above), a bouquet garni, onion studded with cloves, garlic and carrot. Use a mixture of half water and half red wine. Part-drain them, leaving enough cooking liquor to lightly coat the beans, and put them into a sauté pan. Cut the bacon into dice, fry it in butter and add it to the beans. Finally, thicken with a knob of beurre manié.

BEANS, FRESH A vegetable of which there are many varieties. They can be divided into two main groups: those with edible pods (green beans) and those of which only the seeds are eaten. The former group includes the French bean (*haricot vert*), called string bean in the United States, and the runner bean. The latter group is described in *beans, dried*.

■ **French (string) beans** The colour varies in different varieties from pale green or yellow to dark green, sometimes spotted with purple. Grown at first for their seeds, it was not until the end of the 18th century, in Italy, that the whole pods began to be eaten. In France they were still rare and expensive throughout the 19th century. These can be further divided into dwarf beans and snap beans. They may be podded, and the seeds sold fresh. Fresh podded beans (the seeds) do not absorb the flavour of a sauce in the same way as dried ones.

Dwarf French beans (*haricots filets* or *haricots aiguilles*) have long thin green pods which are picked while still young, before they become stringy and tough. There are many varieties for commercial cultivation or growing at home, varying from very fine beans to dark green or green and purple types.

Snap beans are either green or yellow (*haricots beurre*, called *butirro* in Italy), and large and plump without being stringy. When harvested young, they are used in the same way as dwarf French beans.

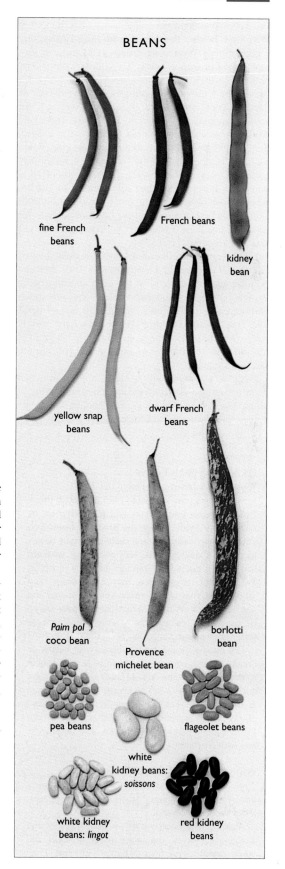

BEANS

fine French beans

French beans

kidney bean

yellow snap beans

dwarf French beans

Paim pol coco bean

Provence michelet bean

borlotti bean

pea beans

white kidney beans: *soissons*

flageolet beans

white kidney beans: *lingot*

red kidney beans

The yellow variety is generally juicier than the green.

■ **Runner beans, flat beans and long beans** The scarlet runner bean, originating in Mexico, is not much liked in France; nor is it a popular commercial crop, since their long pods – up to 30 cm (12 in) – have to be hand-picked, though they have plenty of flavour. They are green, rough-surfaced and are eaten complete with their flecked seeds (normally pink). As they become tough (with a scaly inside), they should be picked at about half this size, when slightly unripe, and the strings scrupulously removed. Available in the US, their consumption is limited in Europe, but they are popular in Britain, where most households in the middle of the 20th century owned a small square kitchen gadget for thinly slicing these beans on the diagonal: the best way to cook them.

Flat beans (sometimes sold as 'stringless' beans) are similar in size and appearance. They became popular towards the end of the 20th century, being exported by Spain and East Africa. They are paler and smoother than runner beans, and are snapped into lengths for cooking. Both these are simply called 'beans from Spain' in France. The flat bean is the Spanish *ferrula*, a classic ingredient of the Valencian paella.

Long beans, originating in Africa, are the principal bean of Southeast Asia. They are eaten immature, at about 38 cm (15 in) but will grow longer, hence the names 'yard-long' or 'yard' beans.

RECIPES

cooking French beans

Top and tail (stem and head) the beans, remove strings (if necessary on either side), and wash them. Cut long beans into shorter lengths if required, or slice runner beans. Plunge the prepared beans into salted boiling water and boil rapidly, without covering them. Cooking times vary with size; whereas fine young beans are tender and still crisp in 3–5 minutes, large beans may need more than 10 minutes. They should retain some crispness and not be soft. Drain them immediately. If they are to be used cold, refresh them under running cold water after draining and then drain them again.

The cooked beans can be mixed with butter or cream, puréed, cooked as a gratin or served cold in a salad. In Italy the are served with garlic and anchovies (*à la genovese*) or cream and Parmesan (*à la milanese*). In France, however, they are used chiefly as an ingredient of dishes typical of the French countryside (*à la lyonnaise*, *à la bérichonne*, and with charcuterie).

cooking podded fresh haricot beans

Cook in boiling salted water with a bouquet garni and vegetables to flavour (such as carrots, turnips, leeks and diced celery).

Alternatively, cook either 1 sliced onion and 1 sliced carrot or the white parts of leeks and some sliced celery sticks in butter until soft. Then add sufficient water to amply cover the beans when they are put in, together with a bouquet garni and a 300 g (11 oz) blanched and drained piece of lean green bacon. Cook for 30 minutes, add the beans, and simmer until they and the bacon are cooked (the time required will depend on the freshness and tenderness of the beans).

French beans à la lyonnaise

Cook the beans in boiling salted water and drain them well. For every 800 g (1¾ lb) beans, prepare 225 g (8 oz) sliced onions and cook gently in butter in a sauté pan until golden brown. Add the beans, season with salt and pepper, and sauté until the beans are slightly browned. Add 1 tablespoon vinegar and mix well. Turn into a dish and sprinkle with chopped parsley.

French beans in tomato sauce

Boil the beans in salted water until they are three-quarters cooked, and drain thoroughly. Cook them gently in butter for about 5 minutes, add a few tablespoons of concentrated tomato sauce and simmer. Turn into a dish and sprinkle with chopped parsley or basil.

French bean salad

Cook the beans just long enough for them to remain slightly crisp. Drain them and dry off any remaining water. Cut them in two and leave them to cool. Add a few chopped spring onions (scallions) and some well-flavoured vinaigrette. Mix and sprinkle with chopped parsley. Alternatively, the beans can be tossed in olive oil, sprinkled with pine kernels, and arranged in a lattice with long strips of marinated red peppers.

French beans sautéed à la provençale

Cook the beans in the usual way and drain them thoroughly. Heat some olive oil in a large saucepan and brown the beans lightly. At the last moment add some chopped garlic and parsley; use 1 garlic clove and a small bunch of parsley for every 800 g (1¾ lb) beans.

French beans with cream

Boil the beans in salted water until they are three-quarters cooked, Drain. Cover with single (light) cream and simmer until the cream is reduced by half. Add salt and pepper and transfer to a serving dish. A sprinkling of chopped parsley can also be added.

This dish can be prepared *à la normande*: for every 450 g (1 lb) beans, add 1 egg yolk and 40 g (1½ oz, 3 tablespoons) butter after removing the pan from the heat.

mixed green beans

Take equal quantities of French beans and flageolets and cook them separately. Drain well and mix together. Blend in some butter or cream and sprinkle with chopped *fines herbes*.

purée of French beans

Half-cook the beans. Drain them thoroughly and then cook gently in butter for 7–8 minutes, allowing 50 g (2 oz, ¼ cup) butter for every 800 g (1¾ lb) beans. Purée the beans in an electric blender or rub them through a fine sieve. (A quarter of its volume of mashed potato can be added to the bean purée.) To serve, warm through and add more butter.

purée of fresh podded haricot beans

Cook the fresh white beans using the basic method above. Drain them, then rub through a sieve to remove the skins. Pour this purée into a saucepan and warm gently, stirring with a wooden spoon until the mixture is smooth. If it seems to be too thick, add a few tablespoons of boiling cream or milk. Just before serving, blend in 50–100 g (2–4 oz, ¼–½ cup) butter for each 1 kg (2¼ lb, 4½ cups) purée.

BEAN SPROUTS Most beans and lentils can be sprouted, to produce a fresh shoot 2–5 cm (1–2 in) long. The Chinese sprout beans (though Indians prefer lentils) and they are an important part of vegetarian diets. Alfalfa yields the finest threads, but green mung and yellow soy are the common choice. Soy shoots should be blanched, as they can be slightly poisonous, but other shoots can be eaten raw – though they are normally stir-fried. Other seeds can also be sprouted, for example fenugreek and triticale (wheat crossed with rye), which is quick to sprout because it has no husk, and will yield eight times the original weight.

BEAR A large quadruped, once common in Europe but now very rare, even in mountainous areas. In Canada and Russia the bear is still hunted as a game animal. The Gauls enjoyed it stewed, and in North America the fat was valued for cooking. At the beginning of the 19th century a few Parisian restaurateurs, encouraged by Alexandre Dumas, brought bear back into fashion. Chevet created the speciality of 'bear ham'. The best parts of this animal are its paws. Urbain Dubois suggested a recipe for bear paws marinated and braised with bacon, then grilled (broiled) and served with a highly seasoned sauce. In China bear's palm is listed among the 'eight treasures' of traditional cuisine.

BÉARN The cuisine of Béarn in France's southwest is rich and wholesome with southern touches, rather reminiscent of that of the Basque country. The unrivalled specialities of Gascony, the land of Henri IV, are the *poule au pot* (boiled chicken) and *garbure*, a thick, nourishing soup which is accompanied by *trébucs* (pieces of preserved goose or pork) to make a unique dish. There is an endless variety of soups, such as the *cousinat* or *cousinette*, containing subtly spiced chard and carrots, and *ouillat*, a kind of onion soup. Game and fish play an important part in local gastronomy while lamb and beef are famous

for their very special flavour. Leg of lamb and daubes made with beef from the Ossau or Barèges regions; conserves, hams, saucissons and andouilles (chitterlings made into sausages) from Oloron; and pâté de foie gras from Orthez are all much appreciated by gourmets.

Meals are rounded off with hearty desserts such as *broye* (a kind of porridge made from maize flour), *millas* (the same, fried as a cake), *pastis* (an orange blossom flavoured yeast cake), *galettes aux pruneaux* (prune pastry) and puff pastries made with goose fat. The dishes are washed down with the strong regional wines, among the best known being Jurançon, Pacherenc du Vic-Bihl and Madiran.

■ **Wine** The vineyards of the region situated in the eastern part of the Pyrénées-Atlantiques department overflow into the departments of Hautes-Pyrénées (six communes) and Gers (three communes). Since 1975, the three traditional appellations (Jurançon and Pacherene-du-Vic-Bihl representing white wines and Madiran representing red) have been joined by the Béarn AOC. This appellation, which previously applied to VDQS wines, now covers very pleasant dry white wines and particularly reds and rosés with a low alcoholic content, popular with both tourists and locals.

BÉARNAISE A classic hot creamy French sauce made from egg yolks and reduced vinegar, whisked together over a low heat and mixed with butter. It is usually served with grilled (broiled) meat or fish. Sauces derived from it (arlésienne, Choron, Foyot, paloise, tyrolienne and Valois) are béarnaise flavoured with additional ingredients. A béarnaise sauce which has curdled can be saved by gradually beating in a tablespoon of hot water (if the sauce is cold) or cold water (if the sauce is hot).

The association between the name of this sauce and the birthplace of Henri IV has probably arisen because it was first made by Collinet in the 1830s in a restaurant in Saint-Germain-en-Laye called the Pavillon Henri IV. But a similar recipe appears in *La Cuisine des villes et des campagnes* published in 1818.

Some recipes are called *à la béarnaise* even when they are not accompanied by this sauce. These are dishes directly inspired by the cuisine of Béarn, such as daube, poule au pot, and game confits with cep mushrooms.

RECIPE

béarnaise sauce

Put 1 tablespoon chopped shallots, 2 tablespoons chopped chervil and tarragon, a sprig of thyme, a piece of bay leaf, 2½ tablespoons vinegar, and a little salt and pepper in a pan. Reduce by two-thirds, then allow to cool slightly. Mix 2 egg yolks with 1 tablespoon water, add to the pan and whisk over a very low heat. As soon as the egg yolks have thickened, add 125 g (4½ oz, ½ cup) butter in small pieces, a little at a time, whisking continuously.

Preparing béarnaise sauce

Béarnaise sauce is a liaison of egg yolks and butter, prepared on a reduction of herbs in a little vinegar. Do not overheat or overcook the sauce as it will curdle. Here the reduction is cooled sufficiently for the egg yolks to be whisked straight into it and clarified melted butter is added a little at a time. Alternatively, the egg yolks can be combined with a little cold water before adding to the reduction and the butter can be added in small knobs.

1 *Following the recipe, reduce the herbs, vinegar and seasoning, then leave to cool until lukewarm before whisking in the egg yolks off the heat.*

2 *Place the pan in a bain marie or over a very low heat and cook gently, whisking lightly, until thickened.*

3 *Gradually whisk in the butter, either in small knobs or trickling it in a little at a time when using melted clarified butter. Add a little lemon juice and adjust the seasoning. Strain the sauce or remove the herb sprigs before adding chopped chervil and tarragon.*

Adjust the seasoning, adding a dash of cayenne pepper if desired, and a little lemon juice. Add 1 tablespoon each of chopped chervil and tarragon and mix. The sauce can be kept in a warm bain marie until required, but it must not be reheated once it has cooled.

BEAT To work a substance or mixture energetically to modify its consistency, appearance or colour. The operation is performed in many ways according to the nature of the ingredients, the utensils used and the purpose. A variety of mixtures are beaten, usually with a wooden spoon, to incorporate air. To give volume to a yeasted dough, it is beaten with the hands either in a bowl, on a worktop or in a food processor. When eggs are to be used as a binding agent, they are lightly beaten with a fork.

BÉATILLES An old French term for various small ingredients (such as cockscombs and kidneys, lamb's sweetbreads, diced foie gras and mushrooms) bound with cream sauce and used as a filling for vol-au-vent cases or savoury tarts.

BÉATRIX The French name given to a garnish of spring vegetables for large cuts of meat, which includes fresh steamed morel mushrooms, small glazed carrots, sautéed artichoke hearts (quartered) and fried or boiled new potatoes.

It is also the name of a mixed salad of chicken breasts with potatoes and asparagus tips dressed with a light mayonnaise flavoured with mustard; a slice of truffle is the final touch.

BEAUCAIRE The French name given to various recipes, including a mixed salad, soup and chitterlings (intestines), associated with Provençal cuisine.

The Beaucaire fairs were celebrated by the poet Mistral, who wrote of merchants who 'ate celery hearts in the open air'. Celery still figures in the traditional Christmas supper salad which inspired a mixed salad: thin strips of celery and celeriac (celery root) with chicory, ham and sharp apples, with beetroot (red beet) and potatoes arranged around the edge. The ingredients of Beaucaire soup are cabbage, leek and celery (sweated in butter and mixed with white chicken stock flavoured with basil and marjoram). It is garnished with pearl barley and diced chicken liver and served with grated cheese. Eel Beaucaire is boned, stuffed with a fish mixture, placed on a bed of shallots, onions and mushrooms, and braised in a mixture of white wine and Cognac.

RECIPE

boeuf à la mode de Beaucaire

This is the traditional dish of the Beaucaire fair. It is delicious but takes a long time to prepare. Take 1.2 kg (2½ lb) thin slices of beef cut from the thigh or shoulder blade allowing about 200 g (7 oz) per person. Bard the meat with fat which has been rolled in salt and pepper and moisten with brandy.

Then marinate for 24 hours in 4 tablespoons vinegar to which a chopped onion, a bouquet garni, 4 tablespoons brandy and 4–5 teaspoons olive oil have been added.

Cover the bottom of an earthenware cooking pot with 225 g (8 oz) bacon, cut in thick rashers (slices). Chop 4 onions and 2 garlic cloves and place on top of the bacon. Place the slices of beef on this bed, season with salt and pepper, and then pour the marinade over the meat. Cover and cook in a preheated oven at 120°C (250°F, gas ½) for 2 hours. Then slowly (so as not to overcool the contents) add 1 litre (1¾ pints, 4⅓ cups) red wine, a bouquet garni, 1 tablespoon capers and an onion stuck with 3 cloves. Cover and cook gently for a further 2 hours.

Just before serving, thicken the sauce with a generous 1 tablespoon flour and add 3 pounded anchovy fillets. When the dish is ready, pour 3 tablespoons olive oil over and serve.

BEAUFORT A French AOP cheese from the Haute Savoie made from unpasteurized cow's milk (at least 48% fat content). It is cooked and then pressed until it is firm and ivory-coloured with a natural brushed crust. It is a round cheese without holes (but occasionally with a few 'threads' – thin horizontal splits), and it has a concave base (these characteristics differentiate it from other Gruyères). It can weigh up to 50 kg (110 lb) with a diameter of 40 cm (16 in) and a height of 20 cm (8 in), but some rounds are smaller. Made from the milk of cows from the mountain pastures of Maurienne, Beaufortin and Tarentaise, it has a fine fruity flavour.

The best cheeses are labelled Beaufort d'Alpage. They are made high in the mountain chalets from the late summer milk. After maturing for 5–6 months, these cheeses reach the shops in March or April. The dairy Beaufort produced in cooperative cheese dairies is not entitled to the *appellation contrôlée*. It is finer than Emmental and is used for gratins and fondues.

BEAUHARNAIS A French garnish usually served with small grilled (broiled) or fried cuts of meat, made of stuffed mushrooms and sautéed or steamed artichoke quarters. Beauharnais also describes a recipe for soft-boiled (soft-cooked) eggs on a bed of artichoke hearts. It is thought that these recipes were dedicated to Countess Fanny de Beauharnais, cousin by marriage of Empress Josephine, who had a reputation for being a gourmet. Sweet Beauharnais recipes (based on bananas and rum) reflect the Creole origins of Napoleon's first wife.

RECIPES

Savoury Preparations

Beauharnais sauce
Mix together 200 ml (7 fl oz, ¾ cup) béarnaise* sauce and 25 g (1 oz, 2 tablespoons) tarragon-flavoured butter. This sauce is served with grilled (broiled) and fried meat and grilled fish.

soft-boiled or poached eggs à la Beauharnais
Sweat some artichoke hearts in butter and garnish with Beauharnais sauce. Place a soft-boiled (soft-cooked) or poached egg on each artichoke heart and coat with a reduced demi-glace sauce to which butter has been added.

other recipes See *chaud-froid (white chaud-froid sauce), medallion, noisette, trout.*

Sweet Preparations

Beauharnais bananas
Peel 6 bananas and arrange in a buttered ovenproof dish. Sprinkle with sugar and 4 tablespoons white rum. Bake in a preheated oven at 200°C (400°F, gas 6) for 5–8 minutes. Pour some double (heavy) cream over, sprinkle with crushed macaroons and a little melted butter, then glaze in a preheated oven at 240°C (475°F, gas 9). Serve in the baking dish.

Beauharnais barquettes
Bake some pastry barquette cases blind. Peel some bananas, mash the flesh and add lemon juice and a little white rum. Fill the barquettes with the mixture and bake in a preheated oven at 240°C (475°F, gas 9) for 7–8 minutes, then sprinkle with a little stale, finely crumbled brioche and melted butter. Bake for a further 5 minutes in a very hot oven.

BEAUJOLAIS One of the best-known red wines in the world, made from the Gamay grape (full name Gamay Noir à Jus Blanc). Although the region may be said to be a continuation of the Burgundy vineyard, Beaujolais is, in fact, more correctly a Lyonnais wine, because the vineyards are in that department, with the exception of one section which is actually in Burgundy. These days, however, Beaujolais is usually considered separately from Burgundy. The writer Léon Daudet said that three rivers flow through Lyon: the Rhône, the Saône and the Beaujolais! Until fairly recently the locals were the main consumers of this lip-smacking wine, often served in 450 ml (¾ pint, 2 cup) 'pots' in the bistrots. However, during World War II many Parisian writers, including the author of *Clochemerle*, came to live in the Beaujolais, discovered the local tipple, and publicized it with gusto. Much additional publicity has been gained by the announcement of when the 'Nouveau', or first consignments of the young Beaujolais, are released. It is carried literally all over the world and has inspired many other wine countries to publicize their own 'Nouveaux' within weeks of it being vintaged.

There are ten 'growths' (*crus*) of Beaujolais and, within them, a few estate wines, although the majority are sold under their regional names plus the name of the shipper. These growths are: Brouilly, Côte de Brouilly, Chénas, Chiroubles, Fleurie, Juliénas, Saint-Amour, Morgon, Moulin-à-Vent and Regnié. Each has its own AOC. In addition to straight 'Beaujolais', there are 'Beaujolais-Villages' wines from a number of communes (parishes) entitled to this AOC. Most Beaujolais is at its delectable best when fairly young, although the wines of both Morgon and Moulin-à-Vent can age agreeably for a few years. Traditionally, young Beaujolais is served cool – at cellar temperature.

In addition to the region's red wine, some white and rosé, Beaujolais are also made.

BEAUJOLAIS-VILLAGES Wine from 39 communes from the northern part of Beaujolais may be called Beaujolais-Villages. This accounts for around a quarter of the total production. It has more body and more alcohol than Beaujolais.

BEAUNE This town, 'capital of Burgundy', is situated at the southern end of the Côte de Nuits; the Côte de Beaune encircles and extends to the south. Both red and white wines are produced; there are a number of AOCs, many of them world-famous names, and also many specific vineyards of repute. It is generally true to say that, although the red wines of the Côtes de Beaune can be very good indeed, the region is chiefly famous for its white wines, of which the Meursaults, Puligny, the various Montrachet wines and the exceptional Corton Charlemagne can be magnificent. The wines of the southern sections below the Côte de Beaune are becoming extremely popular too.

Beaune itself is one of the most attractive of wine towns. In the centre, the Hôtel Dieu is part of the Hospices de Beaune. Established in the 15th century by the Chancellor of Burgundy, Nicolas Rolin, and his wife Guigone de Salins, this charitable organization runs the Hospice de la Charité, which is an old people's home, and a modern hospital.

Since the middle of the 19th century, wines from the vineyards belonging to the Hospices de Beaune have been publicly auctioned every November, on the second Sunday of the month (in very poor years they are sold privately). For the occasion, many other tastings and ceremonies take place in or near Beaune, including the 'Trois Glorieuses' (the Saturday banquet at Clos de Vougeot, the post-sale dinner in the Bastion de Beaune and, on the Monday, the 'Paulée' luncheon at Meursault). The occasion provides the first indication of the character of the year's vintage.

BEAUVILLIERS A rich nourishing French cake made of crushed almonds and sugar mixed with butter, eggs and a lot of flour (wheat flour and rice flour). After cooking it is wrapped in foil to ensure that it keeps well. It is the oldest form of 'travelling' cake. It was invented at the beginning of the 19th century by a M. Mounier, a pastrycook in Paris, who named it after the great cook, to whom he had been apprenticed.

BEAUVILLIERS, ANTOINE French cook (born Paris, 1754; died Paris, 1817). In 1782 he founded the Grande Taverne de Londres in the Rue de Riche-

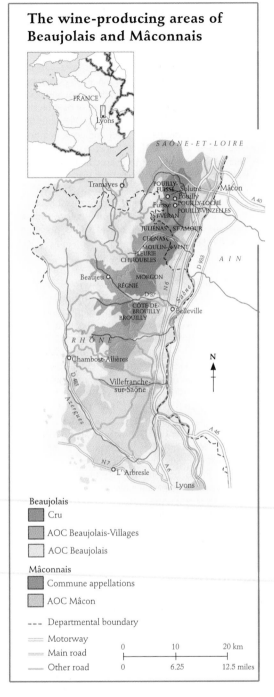

The wine-producing areas of Beaujolais and Mâconnais

Beaujolais
- Cru
- AOC Beaujolais-Villages
- AOC Beaujolais

Mâconnais
- Commune appellations
- AOC Mâcon

--- Departmental boundary
=== Motorway
=== Main road
— Other road

| 0 | 10 | 20 km |
| 0 | 6.25 | 12.5 miles |

lieu, which was the first real restaurant in Paris. His success was so great that, on the eve of the French Revolution, Beauvilliers opened another restaurant in his own name in the Galerie de Valois du Palais-Royal. Brillat Savarin wrote that 'he was the first to have an elegant salon, well turned-out waiters, a carefully chosen cellar and superb cuisine'. Beauvilliers' renown, despite a brief eclipse in the Reign of Terror (1793), was maintained under the Empire and the Restoration and the doors of his establishment did not close until 1825.

Having been the chef of the Count of Provence, Beauvilliers received his clients wearing his sword, in the uniform of an *officier de bouche de réserve*. In 1814 he wrote *L'Art de cuisiner*, in which he treats cooking, food management and service as an exact science. He collaborated with Carême in writing *La Cuisine ordinaire*.

The surname of this famous restaurateur is used, among other things, for a garnish for large braised cuts of meat made from salsify sautéed in butter, small seeded tomatoes stuffed with a purée of brains and grilled (broiled), and spinach kromeskies. The accompanying sauce is made from the cooking juices.

BEAVER An aquatic rodent native to North America, but also found in Savoy in France, Scandinavia and Germany, hunted for its meat as well as its fur. Despite its distinctly gamey taste, the medieval church classed it with water fowl, and permitted its consumption during Lent. The meat was made into pâté and preserves. Nowadays it is a protected species.

It should not be confused with the South American coypu, which was introduced into Europe in the 20th century for fur ranching. Several French producers have promoted its meat for quality pâtés.

BÉCHAMEIL, LOUIS DE French financier (born 1630; died 1703). Farmer-general and steward of the house of the Duke of Orleans, Louis de Béchameil, Marquis of Nointel, became major domo to Louis XIV. Saint-Simon reported that he was rich, a gourmet, an informed art lover and a handsome man, but it is very unlikely that he created the sauce which bears his name, abbreviated to béchamel. This sauce is probably an improvement of an older recipe by one of the King's cooks, who dedicated his discovery to the King's major domo, which made the jealous old Duke of Escars say: 'That fellow Béchameil has all the luck! I was serving breast of chicken *à la crème* more than 20 years before he was born, but I have never had the chance of giving my name to even the most modest sauce.'

BÉCHAMEL A white sauce made by combining hot flavoured or seasoned milk with a roux. (The original béchamel sauce, which owes its name to the Marquis of Béchameil, was prepared by adding large quantities of fresh cream to a thick velouté.)

One of the basic sauces, the classic recipe calls for milk flavoured by heating it with a bay leaf, a slice of onion and a blade of mace or some nutmeg. Celery, carrot, ham and/or mushroom peelings may even be added. This is then left for about 30 minutes to infuse. The Italian *balsamella* (sometimes infused with garlic, bay leaf and/or onion) is now a white sauce with nutmeg. Béchamel commonly refers to a white sauce with simple seasoning.

Béchamel is widely used, particularly for egg, vegetable and gratin dishes, and for filled scallop shells. It can be used as a basis for other sauces, made by adding different ingredients.

RECIPE

béchamel sauce
Gently heat 500 ml (17 fl oz, 2 cups) milk with 1 bay leaf, a thick slice of onion and 1 blade of mace. Remove from the heat just as the milk boils, cover the pan and set aside for at least 30 minutes. Strain the milk and discard the flavouring ingredients. Melt 40 g (1½ oz, 3 tablespoons) butter over a low heat in a heavy based saucepan. Add 40 g (1½ oz, 6 tablespoons) flour and stir briskly until the mixture is smoothly blended, without allowing it to change colour. Gradually stir in the milk and bring to the boil, beating well to prevent any lumps forming. Season with salt and pepper and (according to the use for which the sauce is destined) a little grated nutmeg. Simmer the sauce gently for 3–5 minutes, stirring from time to time.

BEECHNUT *faine* The small triangular brown nut of the beech tree. Beechnuts grow in twos or threes in a hairy brownish capsule and are gathered in October. They have a high oil content and a similar flavour to the hazelnut. They can be eaten raw but have a slightly bitter taste; it is best to grill (broil) or roast them. The oil extracted from them is considered to be second only to olive oil in quality. It keeps well and is excellent for frying and salad dressings.

BEEF The meat of all the large domestic cattle, including heifer, cow, ox, bullock and bull.

Our prehistoric ancestors hunted the wild ox for food and domestic cattle are descended from it. Cattle have been domesticated for more than 40 centuries. In the Middle Ages 'noble' dishes were prepared using the better cuts of beef, from the upper and rear parts of the animal. In 1756 the Duc de Richelieu chose the menu for a famous meal that was given for his illustrious prisoners during the Hanoverian War. The 12 dishes of the first course and the 10 dishes of the second course were all of beef.

The quality and the yield (the weight of edible meat in relation to the weight of the live animal) vary according to the breed of cattle. Beef cattle are specially bred for meat production. The most popular breeds in France are the Charolais and Limousin. Scotland produces the Aberdeen Angus, England the Hereford, the Belgians have *blanc-bleu* and the Japanese their Wadakin. Sometimes whole regions are known for their beef, like the Val di Chiana in Italy and Texas in the USA. The proportion of muscle is high with relatively little fat. Young males may be castrated (steers) to accelerate the fattening process. But uncastrated males grow more rapidly and can therefore be slaughtered young, but their meat is sometimes criticized for its lack of flavour. Young bullocks are also a source of meat (under 24 months they are termed *bouvillons* in France). Heifers that are not required for breeding are also slaughtered to provide meat which is very tender and full of flavour.

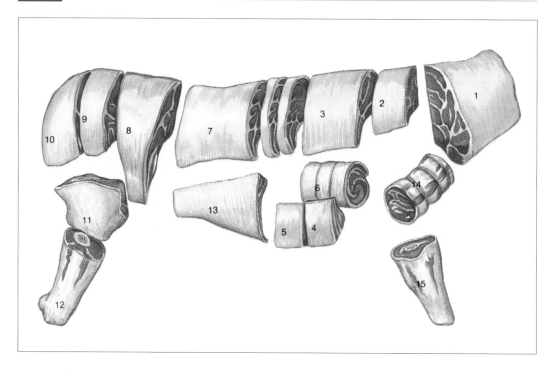

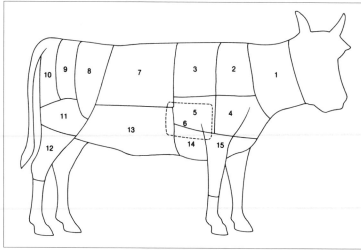

British cuts of beef

*1 neck and clod; 2 chuck and
blade; 3 fore rib; 4 thick rib;
5 thin rib; 6 rolled ribs; 7 sirloin;
8 rump; 9 silverside; 10 topside;
11 thick flank; 12 leg; 13 flank;
14 brisket; 15 shin*

The problem of BSE (bovine spongiform encephalitis), commonly known as 'mad cow disease' precipitated a major review of cattle rearing and slaughtering in the late 20th century in Britain.

All continents, and almost all countries, enjoy beef, the notable exception being southern India. And some countries like Argentina, Australia and, to a certain extent, North America, eat a great deal of it. Britain once known – and mocked by the French – for its huge consumption of *roshif*, had changed its habit by the close of the 20th century. The main exporting countries are South America, Australia and New Zealand, the principal importers being the United States and Japan.

■ **Choosing beef** Good-quality beef is bright red and shiny in appearance and firm and springy to the touch with a sweet light scent. It has a network of white or slightly yellowish fat; when a lot of fat is present in the muscle, the meat is described as marbled. In order to be tender and palatable, beef must be matured after slaughtering, for a period varying from a few days to a week (see *ageing of meat*).

• TRADITIONAL CUTS The method by which the meat is butchered varies, with portions being removed and prepared differently according to country and even region. The diagrams and lists provided in this section illustrate classic beef cuts from Britain, France and America. There are many more cuts available in supermarkets, with the emphasis on boneless portions that require minimum preparation and provide maximum flexibility in choice of cooking method. Ultimately, the choice of cut depends on the cooking method and type of dish. Many consider the best beef cut to be

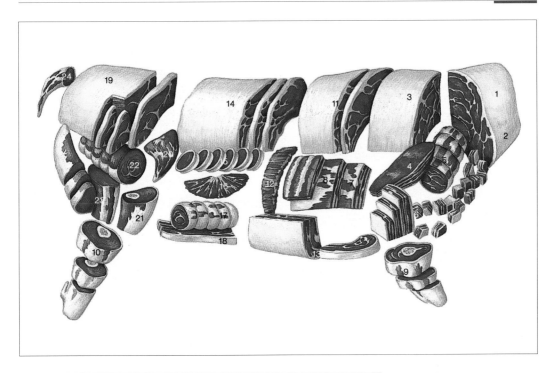

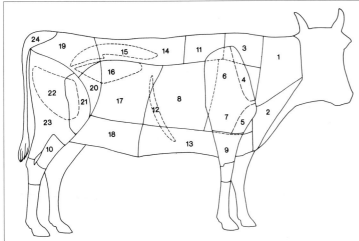

French cuts of beef

1, 2 collier (neck); 3 basses-côtes; 4 jumeau for grilling (broiling) or frying; 5 jumeau for stewing; 6 macreuse; 7 plat de côtes découvert (uncovered rib); 8 plat de côtes couvert (covered rib); 9 gîte de devant; 10 gîte de derrière; 11 entrecôte; 12 hampe; 13 poitrine; 14 faux-filet; 15 filet; 16 bavette for grilling or frying; 17 bavette for stewing; 18 flanchet; 19 romsteck (rump steak); 20 aiguillette baronne; 21 rond de tranche basse; 22 tranche; 23 gîte à la noix; 24 queue (tail)

sirloin, while the great classics are tournedos (filet mignons), chateaubriand, fillet (tenderloin) *en croute*, and rib. The hindquarter provides the so-called 'noble' cuts, which can be cooked quickly, while the forequarter gives mostly slow-cooking and boiling pieces.

Beef cuisine is as varied as the countries that enjoy it. But certain methods are common to many of them. Beef may be boiled (the Austrian-Hungarian *Tafelspitz*), pot roasted (like the German *Sauerbrauten* marinated in buttermilk, wine and vinegar) or baked inside pastry (like British beef Wellington). Strips may be quick-fried (like Japanese *teriyaki*) and subsequently sauced (like beef Stroganov), or stuffed in medieval fashion, like beef olives. It can be casseroled slowly, like the Flemish *carbonnade*, go into pies and puddings or be pickled (Irish spiced brisket). Beef is eaten raw (*carpaccio* and

steak tartare) and twice-cooked in dishes using leftovers from a roast joint, such as rissoles. It is even made into an old-fashioned invalid drink (beef tea).

• MINCE (GROUND) BEEF This may be bought ready minced, prepared as required or prepared in larger batches and deep frozen. It is usually made from less tender cuts, such as stewing beef (hind shank or neck) or silverside (bottom round). The meat is trimmed of excess fat. If prepared from a superior beef cut, it will be so labelled. Mince is used to make hamburgers and *bitokses* and is made into spiced meatballs, such as *fricadelle* and *kofta*.

• OFFAL (VARIETY MEATS) Edible offal includes heart, liver, kidneys and brains, while the word 'ox' identifies the lesser types in English. Only tongue (smoked or pickled), ox tail, bone marrow and tripe are highly regarded in gastronomic circles.

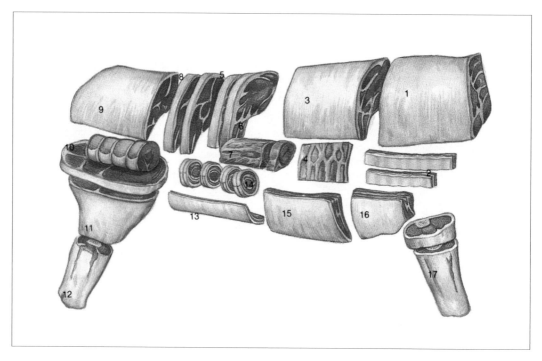

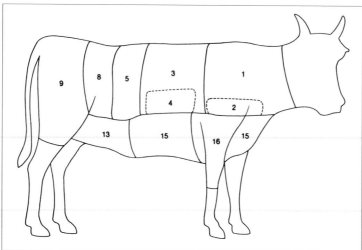

American cuts of beef
1 chuck; 2 flanken-style ribs;
3 rib; 4 back ribs; 5 short loin;
6 Porterhouse steak; 7 tenderloin;
8 sirloin; 9 round; 10 boneless
rump roast; 11 round steak;
12 hind shank; 13 flank; 14 flank
steak rolls; 15 short plate;
16 brisket; 17 fore shank

• BEEF PRODUCTS The simplest types of dried beef are jerky (from the Spanish *charqui*, dried), which the American colonists inherited from the Indians, and the South African biltong (often dried and smoked). Pastrami, originally a wind-dried meat from Armenia (see also *pastirma*), is spiced brisket of beef, a Jewish speciality, while smoked beef goes into *cholent*. Sophisticated air-dried meats include the Italian *bresaola* and rather similar Swiss *Bündnerfleisch* from the Jura mountains.

Corned beef is the American name for salt beef. (In Britain, corned beef is a type of canned meat.) Suet is processed beef fat for reuse; it has its own role in steak and kidney pudding and a host of dumplings.

■ **Roast beef** Cuts of beef for roasting are generally taken from the hindquarter and include fillet, sirloin,

rump, topside and rib; the prime roasts are fillet, sirloin and rolled rib.

In France the meat is usually barded and tied up by the butcher: it will taste fresher cut and prepared on demand. In Britain the cooked roast is served pink and very tender inside, browned outside with lightly crisped fat. The traditional accompaniments are horseradish sauce and Yorkshire pudding. In France it is cooked with the inside a little bloody, the rest of the meat pink, and the outside rather browner.

• ROASTING TIMES Take the beef out of the refrigerator at least 1 hour before cooking. The meat will be more tender if it is cooked steadily in a moderately hot oven, rather than rapidly in a hot oven. Put the meat in a preheated oven at 230ºC (450ºF, gas 8) for about 15 minutes, then reduce the temperature to

200°C (400°F, gas 6) and cook for 15–20 minutes per 450 g (1 lb) for a medium roast (a little longer if the joint is thick). A very tender prime roast can be cooked rapidly in a hot oven, allowing 12–15 minutes per 450 g (1 lb).

Before slicing the beef, cover it with foil and leave it to rest for 10 minutes in a warm place so that the juices are distributed throughout the meat and do not run too much when the joint is cut.

• MAKING GRAVY Put the roasting tin (pan) on top of the stove over a low heat. If they are not already well browned, brown the juices lightly without burning them, pour off some of the fat, then deglaze the pan with a little light brown veal stock or water. Continue adding stock and stirring to remove all cooking residue from the roasting tin. Make double the volume of gravy finally required, then reduce it by half. Adjust the seasoning, strain and keep hot.

• ACCOMPANIMENTS There is a wide choice of accompaniments – served French style the following may be offered: dauphine potatoes, artichoke hearts filled with mushrooms, braised lettuce, sautéed tomatoes, potato croquettes, stuffed mushrooms. Garnishes are du Barry, bouquetière, forestière and Richelieu. Alternatively, roast potatoes, roast parsnips, Yorkshire pudding, mustard or horseradish sauce, glazed carrots, buttered spinach and/or other lightly cooked vegetables may be served.

RECIPES

beef Brandenburg

Cut 1 kg (2¼ lb) top ribs of beef (chuck steak) into large dice and season. Heat 40 g (1½ oz, 1½ tablespoons) lard in a heavy based saucepan and brown the meat lightly on all sides. Remove the meat, and fry 800 g (1¾ lb) thinly sliced onions until soft but not brown. Add a bay leaf, 2 crushed cloves, and 600 ml (1 pint, 2½ cups) cold water. Bring to the boil, return the meat to the pan and leave to simmer, covered, for 1½ hours. Drain the meat and keep it warm in a covered serving dish. Blend 2 slices crumbled stale gingerbread, 1 tablespoon drained capers, the juice and zest of a lemon, and some ground pepper with the cooking liquor. Simmer, uncovered, for 5 minutes. Pour the sauce over the meat and serve piping hot with a celery purée.

beef on a string

Place 2 kg (4½ lb) veal bones in a roasting tin (pan) with 2 large onions, unpeeled and cut in half, and 1 large glass of water; sprinkle a little caster (superfine) sugar on top. Brown in a hot oven. Then put all the ingredients in a large flameproof casserole with 6 litres (10 pints, 6½ quarts) water. Carefully deglaze the juices in the roasting tin and pour into the casserole with 4 large, peeled carrots, the green tops of 8 leeks, 1 head garlic, peeled and crushed, the stalks of 1 bunch of parsley, 1 sprig thyme, 2 bay leaves, 4 cloves, 10 peppercorns, 2 sprigs tarragon, 1 celery stick and 4 tomatoes (or a small can of tomato purée).

Cook, skimming frequently, until only 2 litres (3½ pints, 9 cups) of stock remain. Drain the vegetables and bones thoroughly, then filter the stock. Put the bouillon back on the heat, skim, degrease, season with salt and add a bunch of 8 small turnips, 8 small carrots with their leaves, the whites of the 8 leeks, 1 small cauliflower and 8 small new potatoes and cook, making sure that the vegetables, except for the potatoes, remain crunchy. Put aside in a warm place. Poach 4 marrow bones in the stock over a low heat so that they do not lose their content and put aside. Skim and degrease the stock one final time. Put a 800 g (1¾ lb) unbarded, loosely tied, seamless piece of beef (in France cut lengthways from rump steak, more conveniently a trimmed beef fillet), in the stock, and cook for 10 minutes. Allow to rest for 10 minutes so that the heat distributes itself evenly inside while the vegetables and marrow bones are reheated. Then slice the rare meat into very thin slices and garnish with the vegetables, surrounding it with marrow bones. Pour some boiling stock over the meat and sprinkle with finely chopped flat-leaved parsley.

boeuf à la mode

Cut about 250 g (9 oz) fat bacon into thick strips and marinate for 5–6 hours in 100 ml (4 fl oz, 7 tablespoons) Cognac. Use the strips to lard a piece of rump weighing about 2 kg (4½ lb). Season with salt and pepper and marinate for 5–6 hours (turning the meat several times) in the Cognac used to marinate the bacon mixed with at least 1 litre (1¾ pints, 4⅓ cups) good red wine, 100 ml (4 fl oz, 7 tablespoons) olive oil, 250 g (9 oz, 2¼ cups) chopped onions, 1 kg (2¼ lb) sliced carrots, 2–3 garlic cloves, a bouquet garni and a few peppercorns.

Blanch a boned calf's foot and some bacon rind from which some of the fat has been removed. Drain the meat and dry it, and then drain the other ingredients of the marinade. Brown the meat on all sides in olive oil, then place in a large casserole. Add the drained ingredients of the marinade followed by the bacon rinds and the calf's foot. Moisten with the marinade and about 750 ml (1¼ pints, 3¼ cups) stock and season with salt.

Place the covered casserole in a preheated oven at 200°C (400°F, gas 6) and cook for about 2½ hours, until tender. When the beef is cooked, slice it evenly and serve surrounded with the carrots and the diced meat of the calf's foot. Strain the braising stock over the meat. Small glazed onions may be added to garnish.

boeuf bourguignon

Cut 1 kg (2¼ lb) braising steak (rump) into cubes and coat with flour. Cut 150 g (5 oz) belly pork into thin strips and fry in a flameproof casserole or heavy based saucepan. Add the steak, a chopped shallot and 2 sliced onions and continue to fry. If desired, add a small glass of brandy and set alight. Add 500 ml (17 fl oz, 2 cups) red wine and a generous glass of stock. Season with salt and pepper and add a bouquet garni and a crushed clove of garlic. Cover and simmer gently for at least 2 hours. A dozen small onions lightly fried in butter may be added 20 minutes before cooking ends. Just before serving, bind the sauce with 1 tablespoon beurre manié.

boiled beef

For 6 servings, place about 800 g (1¾ lb) beef or veal bones in a large saucepan with 2.5 litres (4¼ pints, 11 cups) water, and bring to the boil. Skim the surface of the liquid and remove the foam deposited on the sides of the pan. Boil for about an hour, then remove bones. Add 1.25–2 kg (2¾–4½ lb) beef, depending on the cut and the proportion of bone to meat: silverside (bottom round), cheek, shoulder, chuck, flank or oxtail may be used. Bring back to the boil and skim. Then add the following vegetables: 6 carrots, 3 medium turnips, 6 small leeks (tied together), 2 celery sticks (cut into short lengths and tied together), a piece of parsnip, 2 onions (one stuck with 2 cloves), a good bouquet garni and, if desired, 1–2 garlic cloves. Season with salt and pepper, cover to bring back to the boil, and simmer for about 3 hours. Drain the meat, cut into even-sized pieces, and serve surrounded with the drained vegetables. Serve with coarse salt, pickled onions, gherkins and mustard.

If a marrow bone is available, wrap this in muslin (cheesecloth) and add it to the pan not more than 15 minutes before serving. The bone may be served with the dish or the marrow can be removed and spread on toasted croûtons. To make the dish look more attractive, select vegetables of a similar size, cut the leeks and celery to the same length and form into neat bunches, and serve the onions slightly browned.

braised beef à l'ancienne

Trim and tie a piece of rump and braise until almost cooked, but still slightly firm. Drain and untie the meat and place it either under a press or on a plate under a weight until cool. Trim the sides of the cooled meat. Cut away the central portion, leaving a thickness of about 2 cm (¾ in) of meat on the sides and bottom. Brush with beaten egg and cover with a mixture of soft breadcrumbs and grated Parmesan cheese (3 parts breadcrumbs to 1 part cheese). Ensure that the breadcrumb mixture covers the meat completely. Place the hollow meat case on a plate, sprinkle with melted butter and brown in the oven.

Meanwhile, slice the remaining portion of meat very thinly. Place the slices in a sauté dish, add some thin slices of tongue and some sliced mushrooms, which have been gently fried in butter, and moisten with a few tablespoons of the reduced, strained, braising stock (from which the fat has been removed). Add 2½ tablespoons Madeira and simmer without boiling. To serve, place the hollow piece of beef on a large serving dish and arrange the sautéed meat slices inside it. Serve any extra sauce in a sauceboat.

braised beef à la bourgeoise

Marinate a rump cut of beef in white wine and then braise it with a calf's foot. Half way through the cooking, remove the meat to a casserole, adding some sliced carrots and small glazed onions. Complete the cooking in the casserole.

braised beef à la bourguignonne

Lard the meat and marinate in brandy. Then braise in red wine.

braised beef à la créole

Cut 1 kg (2¼ lb) braising steak (top round or rump) into cubes and thread a large piece of larding bacon into each cube. Marinate in a mixture of spices (especially cayenne) and Cognac for 5–6 hours. Heat some lard and oil in a heavy frying pan, then add 3 large sliced onions and the drained pieces of beef. Sauté together for several minutes, then turn into a casserole. Add 2 tablespoons tomato purée (paste), 1 crushed garlic clove, a sprig of thyme, a small bunch of parsley and a pinch of saffron powder. Season with salt and pepper, cover and cook very gently in a low oven for 3 hours. During the cooking period, add a few tablespoons of either boiling water or, even better, stock. Adjust the seasoning.

braised beef à la gardiane

Ask the butcher to lard and tie a piece of topside (beef round) weighing about 1.25 kg (2¾ lb). Peel and slice 800g (1¾ lb) onions. Heat some olive oil in a flameproof casserole and brown the meat in the oil. Add the sliced onions, 5–6 peeled garlic cloves, 2 cloves, a pinch of nutmeg and the same amount of basil, bay, rosemary, savory and thyme. Cover and cook very gently for at least 2½ hours. Serve the meat sliced and coated with the cooking liquor.

braised beef à la mode

Prepare in the same way as braised beef *à la bourgeoise*, but marinate the meat in red wine instead of white wine.

braised rib of beef

The cooking method is the same as for braised rump of beef. Ask the butcher to cut a large rib weighing 2–3 kg (4½–6½ lb).

braised rump of beef

Cut 200 g (7 oz) fat pork or bacon into larding strips. Season with spices, soak in Cognac and use them to lard a piece of beef (cut from the rump) weighing 3 kg (6½ lb). Season the meat with salt, pepper and spices, and tie into a neat shape with string. Marinate for 5 hours in either red or white wine with thyme, bay, parsley and 2 crushed garlic cloves. Blanch, cool and tie 2 boned calf's feet. Peel and slice 2 large onions and 2 carrots and heat gently in butter. Crush into small pieces a mixture of 1.5 kg (3¼ lb) beef bones and veal knuckle bones together with the bones from the calf's feet. Brown in the oven. Place the browned bones and the vegetables in a flameproof casserole or a braising pan. Add the beef, a bouquet garni and the marinade. Cover and simmer gently until the liquid has almost completely reduced. Add 3 tablespoons tomato purée (paste) and enough veal bouillon to cover the meat. Place the covered casserole in a preheated oven at 180°C (350°F, gas 4) and cook for about 4 hours until tender. To serve, drain the meat, untie it and glaze in the oven, basting it with the strained cooking liquor. Arrange the meat on a large serving dish and surround with the chosen garnish. Keep warm. Remove the fat from the braising pan, reduce the cooking liquid and pour over the meat.

oven-roast rib of beef

Place the rib in a roasting tin (pan), brush with butter or dripping, and roast uncovered in a preheated oven at 240°C (450°F, gas 9) for 15–18 minutes per 450 g (1 lb) plus 15 minutes. To ensure that it is cooked through completely, treat as for spit-roast rib of beef.

poached rump of beef

Lard the meat or not, as preferred. Tie the meat into a neat shape with string and cook in a large pan using the same method as for a pot-au-feu and the same vegetables. Bring to the boil, skim and season. Simmer gently for 4–5 hours, but do not cover the pan completely. To serve, drain and untie the meat and place it on a large serving dish with the garnish. Serve with the strained cooking liquor, grated horseradish and coarse salt. Cooked in this way, rump provides both a soup and a main course. To provide additional flavour to the soup, add small pieces of fleshy beef bones to the cooking liquid.

pressed beef

Take 3 kg (6½ lb) lightly larded brisket. Prick with a large larding needle and soak the meat in brine for 8–10 days, depending on the season (brine penetrates the meat more quickly in summer). The brine used is the same as that in the recipe for pickled ox tongue. The meat must be completely submerged and it is advisable to use a weighted board to achieve this. Just before cooking, wash the meat in cold water. If more than one mould is used, then cut the meat into pieces to fit them. Cook in water until tender with some carrots, cut into pieces. Place the meat in square moulds, each covered with a small weighted board. When the meat is quite cold, turn it out of the moulds and coat with several layers of meat aspic, coloured reddish brown by adding caramel and red food colouring. This provides the meat with a strong protective coating that retards deterioration. To serve, cut into very thin slices and garnish with fresh parsley.

salt (corned) beef

This method is mostly used for preparing brisket, but may also be used for flank and chuck. The meat is soaked in brine for 6–8 days in summer and 8–10 days in winter. It is then rinsed to desalt, and cooked in water for 30 minutes per 1 kg (2¼ lb). Salt beef is served hot with vegetables that are traditionally associated with it, such as braised red or green cabbage and sauerkraut. It is also used for pot roasting.

spit-roast rib of beef

Trim the boned rib and tie firmly to hold in shape, covering the exposed meat with thin rashers (slices) of fat bacon. Pierce evenly on to a spit and brush with butter or oil. Cook rapidly at first and then at a moderate heat, allowing 15–18 minutes per 1 kg (2¼ lb). Remove from the spit, untie, trim, season with salt and serve with the desired garnish. To ensure the meat is cooked through, remove from the spit just before completely cooked, wrap in foil and leave in a hot oven that has been turned off or in a very low oven for 30 minutes.

BEEFSTEAK MUSHROOM *langue-de-boeuf*

The common name for *Fistulina hepatica*, a mushroom that grows on oak and horse chestnut trees in the form of a red fleshy mass with a sticky surface. The thick flesh, which exudes an acidic reddish juice, can be sliced and fried like liver or eaten raw with a green salad. It is cut into thin strips, soaked in salted water, then drained and dressed with chives and a vinaigrette.

BEEF TEA

A highly nutritious concentrated meat juice used chiefly in the past as food for invalids. Lean beef is cut into small dice, placed in a hermetically sealed container without any water, and cooked in a bain marie.

BEER

An alcoholic beverage obtained by the fermentation of extracts of malted cereals, principally barley, and flavoured with hops. Most countries allow a percentage of maize and rice, but in Germany this practice is forbidden and beers are made solely from barley, malt, hops, yeast and water. British beer varies from 100% malt to 70% malt plus 30% unmalted cereals, together with sugar, hops, yeast and water.

Beer is both the most widespread and the oldest alcoholic drink in the world. The first traces of 'liquid bread' based on fermented cereals were found in Mesopotamia. The Mesopotamians and the Egyptians were the greatest beer drinkers of the ancient world and drank their beer warm. It was made from barley bread crumbled in water and fermented in date juice flavoured with cumin, myrtle, ginger and honey.

The Gauls, Celts and Saxons produced beer which, like earlier fermented drinks, did not contain hops with ingredients such as sorb-apples. Hops were introduced for making beer in the 13th century by Bavarian monks.

■ **Manufacture** The brewer's basic raw material is a cereal rich in starch; the latter does not ferment naturally in the presence of yeast (whereas the sugar contained in apples or grapes can be directly fermented to produce cider and wine). The cereal must therefore be 'processed' in order to obtain a fermentable extract (known to brewers as 'wort'). For the cereal barley, this is usually done by first malting the raw grain and then extracting the soluble sugars with hot water using the natural enzymes of the malt.

• MALTING The grain is soaked, allowed to start germinating, then dried under control in a kiln.

• BREWING The malt is ground, then mixed with hot water. Malt enzymes release soluble sugars from the starch, the solution being run off from the insoluble husk. The resulting wort is heated to boiling point and hop flowers are added to give the beer its bitter flavour and hop bouquet. Yeast is added when the liquid is cold.

There are two major types of beer according to the type of yeast used. Traditionally, lager yeast is used at lower temperatures than ale yeast, therefore the fermentation period is longer.

• LAGER FERMENTATION Typically seven days at a temperature of 7–12°C (45–54°F), giving a lightly flavoured product whose character is mainly determined by the hops and the malt used. Lager beers dominate the world beer market.

• ALE FERMENTATION Typically three days at a temperature of 18–25°C (64–77°F), giving more fruity beers in which the flavour is more directly influenced by the fermentation process. In continental Europe these are 'special' beers, Belgian Trappist beers and brown beers, whereas in Britain they are the very popular ales. In very dark beers, such as stouts, the use of roasted cereals contributes significantly to the flavour as well as to the colour.

After fermentation the beer is placed in a cool cellar, where it is allowed to mature. The maturation period can vary from a few days to several months, depending on the nature and strength of the beer. Finally, it is clarified before being bottled, canned or racked into barrels. Clarification is commonly done by a combination of settling and filtration. In Britain, however, settled beer is traditionally racked directly into casks, final clarification being achieved by addition of 'finings' directly into the cask followed by a period of 'stillage'.

■ **Colour and content** The colour is not related to the length of fermentation, degree of processing or alcoholic strength, but to the degree to which the malt is heated during kilning. The heating produces caramel, which is extracted from the malt and eventually colours the beer brown. Highly kilned malt gives English stout, Belgian Chimay and Munich basses their particular flavours. Pale beers (porter and ale, Czech Pilsner and German Dortmund) are distinguished by their bitter flavour.

■ **Beer around the world** Beer is the drink of the people. Industrially produced beer for mass consumption, with the emphasis on quenching thirst rather than flavour, is the mainstream in many countries, including France.

The countries that show most interest in beer-making as an art are Germany, the Czech Republic and Belgium. But from the late 1970s there has been a renaissance of interest in beer, reflected in the 'real ale' campaign in Britain.

Germany (with its Munich Beer Festival in October and its custom of drinking beer all the year round and at every opportunity), has as many breweries as the rest of Europe put together, while Bavaria has the world's largest hop industry. The beer is unpasteurized (swift consumption is guaranteed), which means it is bottled not canned – they are the experts in bottle-conditioning the beer, which usually tastes rather bitter. Its production is very widespread but the most famous German beers come from Bremen, Cologne, Dortmund and Munich (Spaten, Kapuziner and Löwenbräu). Also worthy of mention are Berliner Weisse, a 'white' beer from Berlin which is drunk with raspberry syrup or lemon, and 'smoked' Bamberg beer.

Belgium is the country of origin of the legendary Gambrinus, who is said to have invented brewing and Belgian beers are noteworthy for their originality: Gueuze, which is strongly flavoured and similar to Mort Subite (considered to be one of the best), Krick (red beer with cherries), Roddenbach (amber-coloured, with a sharp flavour) and Chimay and Jumet brewed in abbeys (see *lambic*). Cooking with beer is especially popular here.

Czech Pilsner is pale, hoppy beer with a flowery bouquet and dryness of palate that is imitated by 'pils' or 'pilsener' types of beer all over the world. It is labelled pilsner Urquell (original source of Pils) when exported. It is a land of breweries, making the full range (including the Czech Budweis).

Traditional pubs, selling cask-conditioned beer, are at the heart of British beer drinking, and pub ownership by the breweries influences sales. The last decades of the 20th century saw new smaller breweries appearing. Among English beers, brown and pale Whitbread are typical, the latter being suitable as an apéritif. Pale ale is refreshing as well as being good for cooking. Scottish Gordon is prepared only at Christmas, whereas the dark and sweet Scotch ale is drunk all year round. Irish Guinness is a famous strong beer – very dark, dry and bitter.

France makes some 'de luxe' beers, not generally drunk with meals, include Champigneulles, Kanterbräu, Mutzig and Meuse, corresponding to the two main brewing regions of France: the north and Alsace. 'Special' French beers are finer (such as Kronenbourg and Ancre Old Lager).

Danish and Dutch beers are light yet quite bitter (for example, Carlsberg and Heineken).

Russia is a large beer consumer, while Australia both consumes a great deal of cold beer from 'tinnies' and 'stubbies' (cans and polystyrene cooling tubes) and exports it. The US makes the world's biggest selling brand in Budweiser (transplanting the name in 1856 to St Louis, Missouri). American beer is also made from other grains than barley: corn is widespread as an adjunct. However the last quarter of the 20th century saw many micro-breweries appear, while a city like Milwaukee has numerous breweries, beer festivals and a critical public. In the United States beers are very light, delicately flavoured with just a hint of bitterness. They are drunk very cold.

India and the Far East have also turned to beer drinking. The Tiger beer of Singapore is known abroad; Japan has Kirin, the biggest brewer outside the US, while San Miguel is another big brewer in the Philippines.

■ **Consumption** There are three characteristic features of any beer: its bitterness (which should never reach acridity), produced by hops and tannin; its clarity, proving that it has been well produced and properly clarified; and finally its head, which must be well-formed and stable.

Beer is served with meals and as a refreshment. It is also used in the preparation of drinks and various cooked dishes (soups, fish – particularly carp – stews and carbonnades), to which it adds smoothness and a slight bitterness. It can also accompany some cheeses successfully (such as Gouda and Maroilles) and is used instead of yeast in the preparation of pancakes and fritters.

Lager should be served at 7–9°C (45–48°F); dark beer is consumed at room temperature. Bottles should be stored upright; once open, beer goes flat very quickly.

Balloon glasses and tumblers are suitable for normal beers. Very frothy beers are best served in tulip or tall beer glasses. In Germany stone tankards are used as they keep the beer cool. Pewter tankards are favoured by connoisseurs of English beer.

Beer is poured by directing the flow to the bottom of the glass to form a layer of froth, then along the side of the glass to prevent too much froth being formed, and finally righting the glass to produce the head.

RECIPES

beer soup
Pour 2 litres (3½ pints, 9 cups) chicken stock into a saucepan with 300 ml (½ pint, 1¼ cups) German beer and 250 g (9 oz) stale bread with the crust removed. Season with salt and pepper, cover and cook very gently for 30 minutes. Purée in a blender and then add a little grated nutmeg and 100 ml (4 fl oz, 7 tablespoons) single (light) cream. Check the seasoning and serve scalding hot.

carp cooked in beer
Prepare a carp weighing about 2 kg (4½ lb) and carefully remove the roe. Season with salt and pepper inside and out. Chop 150 g (5 oz) onions and fry them gently in butter in a covered pan until transparent. Dice 25 g (1 oz) gingerbread and finely chop 50 g (2 oz) celery. Butter an ovenproof dish. Place the onions, gingerbread and celery in the bot-

tom and arrange the carp on top, adding a bouquet garni and sufficient Munich-type German beer to almost cover the fish. Cook in a preheated oven at about 170°C (325°F, gas 3) for 30 minutes. In the meantime, poach the roe in a little stock, then drain and slice thinly. Remove the carp from the oven, arrange on a serving dish with the slices of roe and keep warm. Reduce the cooking stock by one-third, strain and add butter. Serve in a sauce-boat with the carp.

chicken cooked in beer
Cut a 1.25 kg (2¾ lb) chicken into pieces and brown in butter on all sides in a flameproof casserole. Add 2 chopped shallots and cook until brown. Pour 3 tablespoons gin on to the chicken pieces and set alight. Then add 400 ml (14 fl oz, 1¾ cups) Alsatian beer, 3 tablespoons crème fraîche, a bouquet garni, salt and a little cayenne. Cover and allow to simmer. Chop 225 g (8 oz) cleaned mushrooms and add to the casserole. Cook for about 45 minutes, then drain the chicken pieces, arrange on the serving dish and keep warm. Remove the bouquet garni from the casserole, add 3 tablespoons crème fraîche and reduce by half. Mix an egg yolk with a little of the sauce, add to the casserole and stir well. Pour the sauce over the chicken pieces, sprinkle with chopped parsley and serve very hot with steamed new potatoes.

BEET, BEETROOT Beet includes any of several varieties of a plant with a fleshy root. Some are cultivated for the sugar industry and distilling (sugar beet), others for fodder (mangel wurzel). The beetroot (beet), with its fine dark red flesh, is used as a vegetable and as a food colouring. Beetroot was eaten in antiquity and was described in 1600 by Olivier de Serres, who was a self-appointed publicist of newly imported products in France, as 'a very red, rather fat root with leaves like Swiss chard, all of which is good to eat'. Nowadays, the leaves are rarely eaten, but they can nevertheless be prepared like spinach and are commonly used in soups in eastern Europe (see also *chard*, in the same family).

Beetroot can be eaten raw (grated), but is usually cooked and served cold (as an hors d'oeuvre or in salads). It is occasionally served hot in traditional dishes, particularly with game or in soups, and is more widely used in contemporary recipes, both hot and cold, including mixed vegetables dishes and risottos. Beetroot is especially characteristic of Flemish and Slav cuisine (see *borsch, botvinya*).

The long-rooted varieties (*rouge noir des vertus* and *rouge crapaudine*, which are both of good quality) have more flavour and are sweeter than the round varieties (red globe and dark red Egyptian), but the latter are more widely cultivated. They are harvested in Europe from the end of June to the first frosts. The roots are stored in silos or cellars and are mostly marketed in autumn and winter. Often sold cooked, they can also be bought raw for cooking at home (baked in the oven or boiled in salted water).

This takes at least 2 hours. Very small beetroots are also preserved in vinegar (especially in Germany, where they are served with boiled meat) and are used for making pickles.

RECIPES

beetroot à la lyonnaise
Parboil some beetroot (beet) in salted water, peel and slice. Cook until tender in butter with thinly sliced onions. Add a little thickened brown stock or bouillon to which 10 g (⅓ oz, 1 teaspoon) of softened butter has been added. Heat through and serve.

beetroot salad à l'alsacienne
Peel some baked beetroot (beet) and slice or dice. Make a vinaigrette dressing with mustard and add some finely chopped shallots and herbs. Pour over the beetroot and marinate for 1 hour. Just before serving, garnish with slices of saveloy.

braised beetroot with cream
Parboil some beetroot (beet) in salted water, peel and slice. Cook in a little butter in a covered pan until tender. Remove the beetroot and keep hot. Boil some cream, add to the cooking liquor and reduce to half its volume, seasoning with salt and pepper. Remove from the heat and stir in 25 g (1 oz, 1 tablespoon) butter. Pour this sauce over the beetroot slices.

cold beetroot soup
Wash thoroughly 1 kg (2¼ lb) small raw beetroots (beets), cook gently in salted water, then add the juice of 1 lemon and allow to cool. Cook 3–4 egg whites in a small flat-bottomed dish in a bain marie. Wash and chop a few spring onions (scallions), including the stems. Peel the cold beetroot and slice into thin strips. Add with the diced egg whites, 2 diced Russian gherkins and the chopped onions to the liquid in which the beetroot was cooked, together with a generous pinch of sugar and 150–200 ml (5–7 fl oz, ⅔–¾ cup) crème fraîche. Stir well and place in the refrigerator. Just before serving, sprinkle chopped parsley over the soup.

Scandinavian beetroot salad
Peel some baked beetroot (beet) and cut into cubes. Peel and slice some onions and separate the rings. Hard boil (hard cook) some eggs and cut into quarters. Cut some sweet smoked or unsmoked herring (a speciality of Scandinavia) into pieces. Sprinkle the beetroot with highly seasoned vinaigrette and place in a salad bowl. Garnish with the herrings, hard-boiled eggs and onions, and sprinkle with chopped parsley.

BEIGLI An item of Hungarian pâtisserie, made from a light brioche dough rolled around a filling of almonds, walnuts or poppy seeds. It is made particularly for the festivals of Christmas and Easter.

BELGIUM See *page 106*.

BELLE-HÉLÈNE In about 1865 several chefs from the restaurants of the Grands Boulevards of Paris started to use the title of this famous operetta by Offenbach to name several different recipes.

Grilled tournedos (broiled filet mignons) Belle-Hélène are garnished with crisp potato straws, sprigs of watercress, and artichoke hearts filled with béarnaise sauce. Sautéed chicken suprêmes Belle-Hélène are arranged on croquettes of asparagus tips crowned with a slice of truffle (deglaze the sauté pan for a sauce to pour over this dish). Large cuts of meat Belle-Hélène are surrounded with chopped tomatoes, fresh green peas with butter, glazed carrots and potato croquettes.

Belle-Hélène is also the name of a cold dessert consisting of fruit (usually pears) poached in syrup, cooled, drained, served on vanilla ice cream, and coated with hot chocolate sauce (the latter may be served separately in a sauceboat if desired).

BELLET An AOC wine from Nice, which comes from the hillsides above the Var valley. The small vineyard produces delicate red wines, light rosés and definite whites with a fresh bouquet. The reds and rosés are made from Folle and Braquet grapes and the whites are made principally from the Rolle, Roussanne, Clairette and Chardonnay, but other varieties can be included in the wines.

BELLEVUE, EN The French term applied to cold preparations of shellfish, fish or poultry glazed with aspic jelly. For lobster, the flesh is cut into medallions, which are garnished, glazed and arranged in the shell. For small birds (the woodcock, quail and thrush), the animal is boned, stuffed, poached in game stock, cooled, coated in a brown chaud-froid sauce, garnished and glazed with aspic. The name would appear to come from the Château de Belleville, owned by Madame de Pompadour, who used to prepare attractive dishes to stimulate the appetite of Louis XV.

RECIPE

glazed salmon en bellevue
Prepare and poach the salmon whole in a concentrated fish stock. Allow to cool completely in the cooking liquor, then drain. Remove the skin from both sides and dry the fish gently with paper towels. Clarify the stock to make an aspic jelly and glaze the salmon with several coats, allowing each coat to set in the refrigerator before applying the next. Coat the bottom of the serving dish with a thin layer of aspic and lay the glazed salmon on top. Garnish with diced or cut shapes of aspic and keep in a cool place until ready to serve. (Salmon steaks and fillets can be prepared in the same way.)

BEL PAESE One of Italy's best known cheeses, enjoyed world wide and manufactured in Lombardy since 1906. Made from cow's milk (45% fat content), it is creamy and mild, an uncooked pressed cheese, creamy yellow in colour, with a washed crust; it is usually wrapped in foil in small rounds, 20 cm (8 in) in diameter. Meaning 'beautiful country' it was named by its creator, Egidio Galbane, after a children's book, whose author's portrait (along with a map of Italy, appears on the wrapping in Europe).

BENEDICT, EGGS Served on an English muffin, a poached egg laid on a slice of ham sautéed in butter, coated with hollandaise sauce and garnished with a slice of truffle. This American dish, attributed to several hotels, but closely associated with Brennan's restaurant in New Orleans, may be loosely based on a benedictine dish of poached egg on top of puréed salt cod. Early versions lay the egg on anchovy-smeared toast.

BENEDICTINE An amber-coloured herby French liqueur used primarily as a digestive. Dom Bernardo Vincelli, an Italian Benedictine monk from the old Abbey of Fécamp, is credited with first producing it. The recipe was discovered in 1863 by a local merchant, Alexandre Le Grand, in some family archives. He perfected the formula and began selling the liqueur, which was immediately successful. As a homage to the monks, he called it Benedictine and printed D.O.M. (*Deo Optimo Maximo*, 'To God, most good, most great'), the motto of the Benedictines, on the bottle.

Benedictine is based on 27 different plants and spices, which are incorporated in what is still a secret formula at the distillery at Fécamp in Normandy. 'B and B' (Benedictine and Brandy) is a compounded version of the liqueur.

BÉNÉDICTINE, À LA The French term applied to several dishes using either a purée of salt cod and potato, or salt cod pounded with garlic, oil and cream. Cod is traditionally eaten during Lent, hence the allusion to the Benedictine monks. Many of these dishes can be enriched with truffles.

RECIPES

bouchées à la bénédictine
Add diced truffle to a purée of salt cod with oil and cream. Use to fill small cooked puff pastry bouchée cases. Garnish each bouchée with a slice of truffle. Heat through in a hot oven.

salt cod à la bénédictine
Soak 1 kg (2¼ lb) salt cod in cold water to completely remove the salt. Poach the fish very gently in water without allowing it to boil. Boil 450 g (1 lb) potatoes in water. Drain the cod, remove the skin and bones, and dry in the oven for a few minutes. Drain the potatoes. Pound the cod with the potatoes in a mortar, then gradually work in 200 ml (7 fl oz, ¾ cup) olive oil and 300 ml (½ pint, 1¼ cups) milk. (A blender or food processor may

be used, but for no longer than strictly necessary, otherwise the starch in the potatoes will agglutinate.) Spread the mixture in a buttered gratin dish and smooth the surface. Sprinkle with melted butter and brown in the oven.

soft-boiled or poached eggs à la bénédictine
Add white or black truffles to salt cod à *la bénédictine*. Prepare soft-boiled (soft-cooked) or poached eggs. Shape the purée in a dome, arrange a circle of eggs around the dome and cover with a cream sauce.

BERCHOUX, JOSEPH French solicitor (born Saint-Symphorien-de-Lay, 1768; died Marcigny, 1839). His name survives as the author of a long poem in four cantos entitled *Gastronomie ou l'Homme des champs à table*, published in 1801. This lively composition was very popular in the Directory period, following the Reign of Terror, during which the French rediscovered the joys of good food. In the first canto, 'Histoire de la cuisine des Anciens', Berchoux describes, in brisk alexandrine verse, such subjects as the death of Vatel and Spartan gruel. In the following cantos, 'Le Premier Service', 'Le Second Service' and 'Le Dessert', he sings the praises of good simple cooking. His philosophy is summed up in the following lines: 'A poem was never worth as much as a dinner' and 'Nothing must disturb an honest man while he dines.' It was he who introduced the word *gastronomie* to the French language.

RECIPE

salmon trout Berchoux
Stuff a 2 kg (4½ lb) salmon trout with a creamy pike forcemeat with chopped truffles. Place the trout in a buttered ovenproof dish on a bed consisting of a chopped carrot, a medium-sized chopped onion (lightly fried in butter), a good handful of mushroom trimmings and a bouquet garni. Add fish stock with white wine until it comes halfway up the trout. Season with salt and pepper, cover, place in a preheated oven at 180°C (350°F, gas 4), and cook for about 40 minutes, basting frequently until the fish is just cooked. Remove the central portion of skin and the dark parts of the flesh. Strain the cooking liquor, pour a few tablespoons of this liquor over the trout and glaze slightly in the oven.

Prepare the garnish: 8 small pastry barquettes filled with soft carp roe and coated with normande sauce; 8 small croquettes made of diced lobster, mushrooms, and truffles bound with a thin velouté sauce; and 8 very small artichoke hearts, partly cooked in white stock, sweated in butter, filled with a salpicon of truffles bound with cream, sprinkled with Parmesan, and browned in the oven. Add 300 ml (½ pint, 1¼ cups) velouté* fish sauce to the remaining cooking liquor and reduce over a high heat, gradually adding 300 ml (½ pint, 1¼ cups) double (heavy) cream to the sauce. Add butter and

BELGIUM

France's northern neighbour, with the EC capital at Brussels. Well-known Belgian specialities include a portion of chips (french fries) with mussels and a tankard of *gueuze* (a beer), bread and butter with coffee, and cold meats (particularly pork) with a glass of gin. The Liège Christmas table is famous and includes black and white puddings (blood sausages), pressed pig's head, and pig's ears and trotters (feet). As early as the Roman Empire, the famous Ardennes ham was sold in the markets of Lugdunum (Lyon)

■ **Local specialities and classic dishes** Belgian cuisine has many local culinary treats. The following is an example of a typical Walloon festival menu: pea and smoked ham soup, followed by a casserole of St George's mushrooms in their own juice, saddle (both loins) of hare with mountain cranberries surrounded with crunchy *cwènes di gattes* (small Ardennes potatoes shaped like goat's horns), thrushes simmered with sage and juniper berries, a creamy runny Herve cheese and, finally, a *rombosse* (apple cooked in a square of pastry) or a *doreye* (rice tart,

sometimes filled with macaroons), served with coffee.

In addition to these regional, local and even family specialities, Belgian cuisine also has its own great classics, such as *hotch-potch*, *waterzooi* and *vogel zonder kop* (literally 'birds without heads' – rolled beef 'olives'). Potatoes and chicory (*witloof* – endive) dominate the vegetables, which also include asparagus, young hop shoots and Brussels sprouts. Fish are particularly important, especially eel (*au vert* – in a green sauce with nettle, mint, tarragon and chervil – also in pies and fish stews, and braised), whiting cooked in buttered paper or white wine and herring in any shape or form.

■ **International influences** The vicissitudes of history have left their mark on Belgian cuisine; for example, both fish *escabèche* and goose *à l'instar de Visé* (casseroled, then cut into pieces coated with breadcrumbs and roasted, served with garlic and cream sauce) are recipes inspired by Spanish cookery dating back to the 16th century. The country still divides into a Flemish community looking north, and the French-speaking Walloons.

Moreover, trade has always been an essential activity in this

country. In the 13th century, Norwegian butter, Portuguese grapes and honey, English cheese, and Moroccan cumin and sugar were imported into Damme. The Flemish brought back *couques*, said to be inspired from a Gallo-Roman recipe from Lyon.

■ **Belgian beer** The other major ingredient of Belgian cuisine is beer (*chimay, gueuze, orval, trappistes* and *kriek*). This national drink (sometimes competing with French wine) is used in the preparation of several culinary specialities, including carbonade, rabbit with prunes, *choesels*, kebabs with *gueuze* and Orval flan (with leeks and ham). Beer is often served with the fragrant cheeses: Herve, Boulettes de Charleroi or Potkese (made of spiced curds).

■ **Sweet success** Belgian cakes and pastries are rich and abundant, including Namur and Brussels waffles, Verviers brioches with sugar candy, *cramiques* with raisins, *spéculos*, Ghent *moques*, almond bread and gingerbread and the famous *flamiche* from Dinant, oozing with melted butter. And, of course, the renowned chocolates.

See also *anversoise, brabançonne, bruxelloise, liégeoise*.

then strain or sieve. Use to coat the bottom of the dish and serve the rest in a sauceboat.

This traditional recipe can be modified by simplifying the garnishes.

BERCY A district of Paris, which for a long time had the largest wine market in Europe and which has given its name to several cooked dishes based on a wine sauce. These dishes were originally prepared in small restaurants but from 1820 onwards spread into the surrounding area. These restaurants served fried fish, fish stews and grills, very often prepared with wine and shallots or served with shallot butter (for instance, the famous entrecôte Bercy). Eggs Bercy is also typical of this style of cuisine.

RECIPES

Bercy butter or shallot butter for meat
Poach 500 g (18 oz) diced beef marrow in salted water and drain. Cook 1 tablespoon chopped shal-

lots in 1 tablespoon butter in a saucepan without browning. Add 200 ml (7 fl oz, ¾ cup) dry white wine and heat gently. Soften 200 g (7 oz, ¾ cup) butter and add to the pan, together with the marrow, 1 tablespoon chopped parsley, the juice of half a lemon, salt and a generous pinch of milled pepper. This butter is poured on top of grilled (broiled) meat or fish and may also be served separately in a sauceboat.

Bercy sauce or shallot sauce for fish
Cook 1 tablespoon chopped shallots gently in 1 tablespoon butter without browning in a saucepan. Add 100 ml (4 fl oz, 7 tablespoons) white wine and 100 ml (4 fl oz, 7 tablespoons) fish stock. Reduce to half the volume. Add 200 ml (7 fl oz, ¾ cup) thin velouté* sauce and boil vigorously for a few moments. Chop a small bunch of parsley. Remove the pan from the heat and add 50 g (2 oz,

This Brussels shop offers an irresistible array of biscuits and gingerbreads.

¼ cup) softened butter; finally, add the chopped parsley, salt and pepper. This sauce is a suitable accompaniment to poached fish.

brill à la Bercy
Prepare a brill weighing about 800 g (1¾ lb), making an incision along the middle of the dark side of the fish and gently loosening the fillets. Season with salt and pepper inside and out. Butter a flameproof dish, sprinkle with chopped shallots and parsley and lay the brill on top. Add 7 tablespoons dry white wine and the same quantity of fish stock. Dot with 50 g (2 oz, ¼ cup) butter. Start cooking on top of the stove, then transfer to a preheated oven at 180°C (350°F, gas 4) and cook for 15 minutes, basting frequently. Then place the dish under the grill (broiler) to glaze the fish. Finally sprinkle with a dash of lemon juice and chopped parsley. The fish stock may be replaced by dry white wine diluted with the juice of half a lemon and water.

calves' liver à la Bercy
Toss some slices of calves' liver in seasoned flour and grill (broil). Serve with Bercy butter.

calves' kidneys à la Bercy
Cut cleaned calves' kidneys crossways into slices 1 cm (½ in) thick and brush with melted butter. Season with salt and pepper and dip in white breadcrumbs. Grill (broil) quickly and serve with Bercy butter.

eggs à la Bercy
Grill (broil) or fry some chipolata sausages. Arrange scrambled (or fried) eggs in a pie dish. Garnish with the chipolatas and surround with a ribbon of tomato sauce.

entrecôte Bercy
Grill (broil) a steak and garnish with Bercy butter.

grilled red mullet à la Bercy
Clean and remove the scales from some red mullet, making a shallow slit along the back of each one. Season with salt and pepper, brush with oil and grill (broil) gently. Arrange on a serving dish and top with half-melted Bercy butter. The fish may be marinated in a little olive oil with salt, pepper and chopped parsley before cooking.

sole Bercy
Butter an ovenproof dish and sprinkle with chopped shallots and parsley. Place the prepared sole in the dish, add 2 tablespoons dry white wine and a dash of lemon juice and dot with 15 g (½ oz, 1 tablespoon) butter. Cook in a preheated oven at 220°C (425°F, gas 7) for 15 minutes basting the fish several times in order to glaze it.

BERGAMOT A small yellow sour citrus fruit similar to the orange, mostly cultivated in Calabria (Italy). The rind contains an essential oil used in perfumery (the basis for eau-de-cologne), confectionery and Earl Grey tea. The zest is used in pâtisserie.

Bergamot is also the French name of a small, square, honey-coloured barley sugar, flavoured with natural bergamot essence, which has been a speciality of the town of Nancy since 1850. There is also a variety of pear called bergamot: it is almost round with a yellowish skin and very sweet, fragrant, juicy flesh.

A family of herbs native to North America and related to mint is also known as bergamot. One of them was used by the American Indians to make Oswego tea, and any of them can flavour iced drinks. The flavour is similar to that of the citrus fruit.

BERGERAC Wine from the Dordogne area of south-western France. This wine-growing region, situated in the district of Bergerac, has been famous since the Middle Ages for the quality of its white wines. Now its red wines are equally important while the rosé wines are appreciated locally.

Bergerac blanc, which may be a crisp white wine or a full-bodied slightly sweet one, is made from the Sauvignon, Sémillon and Muscadelle grapes. The red wines are made from the Bordeaux grapes Cabernet-Sauvignon, Cabernet Franc, Malbec and Merlot. The reds from the left-bank vineyards of the Dordogne are more full-bodied than those on the right, where the wines are more supple. All are subject to controls, for the AOC 'Bergerac' and 'Côte de Bergerac'.

BERLINGOT A pyramid-shaped French boiled sweet, usually flavoured with peppermint, with alternating clear and opaque stripes (called a 'humbug' in Britain). Some authorities say that it was created in the Middle Ages, but its present formula was perfected under Louis XVI by a certain Madame Couet, who handed it down to her descendants. In 1851, at Carpentras, Gustave Esseyric revived the recipe using peppermint cultivated in Vaucluse. This peppermint gives a particular flavour to the *berlingots* which are produced in this town, using sugar syrups left over from the preparation of crystallized (candied) fruit. Nantes (since 1780), Saint-Quentin and Caen are also famous for their *berlingots*. Although most are flavoured with peppermint, fruit-flavoured mixtures are also used (see also *bêtise*).

Berlingots are manufactured by wrapping a sausage shape of boiled, flavoured and coloured sugar in bands of transparent sugar alternating with bands of beaten sugar. The sausage is then stretched and shaped in a *berlingotière* (a rotating machine with four blades) or a ring press.

Some say the name is derived from the Italian *berlingozzo* (a very sweet cake), others that it comes from the Provençal *berlingan* (knucklebone). By extension, the word is also used (in France) for a pyramid-shaped cardboard container for milk.

BERNIS, PIERRE DE French diplomat (born Saint-Marcel-d'Ardèche, 1715; died Rome, 1794). A protégé of Madame de Pompadour, he was elected to the Académie Française at the age of 29 for his elegant verse; he then became a cardinal and ambassador, first to Venice, then to Rome at the Holy See. In all these posts, he proved himself to be a remarkable ambassador of French cuisine and his table was known as 'the best inn in France'. Chefs have given his name to various egg dishes using asparagus.

RECIPE

cold eggs Bernis
Coat poached eggs in white chaud-froid sauce and garnish with truffles. Line a dish with chicken mousse. Arrange the eggs on the mousse, separated by bunches of green asparagus tips. Coat with a light covering of half-set aspic.

BERNY A French method of preparing croquette potatoes, which are coated in chopped almonds, then fried. A *berny* garnish consists of small tarts filled with lentil purée and served with game.

BERRICHONNE, À LA The adjective for regional dishes from Berry. Large joints of meat garnished *à la berrichonne* are served with braised green cabbage (stuffed or plain), poached chestnuts, small glazed onions and slices of lean bacon; the meat juice is slightly thickened. Chicken fricassee *à la berrichonne* is served with new carrots; potatoes *à la berrichonne* are cooked with onions and fat bacon.

RECIPES

chicken fricassée à la berrichonne
Scrape some new carrots and fry in butter with a small onion, then drain. Using the same butter, brown a chicken cut up into portions. Add 250 ml (8 fl oz, 1 cup) boiling water or clear chicken stock, then the carrots, a bouquet garni, salt and pepper. Cover and cook gently for 30 minutes. Drain the chicken and keep warm. Mix together 2 egg yolks, a pinch of salt, 2 tablespoons cream and 1 tablespoon vinegar and add to the cooking liquor; heat but do not allow to boil. Roll the chicken pieces in the sauce and serve very hot.

potatoes à la berrichonne
Chop 2 onions. Cut 100 g (4 oz) streaky bacon into small strips. Brown the onions and bacon in a flameproof casserole, then add 1 kg (2¼ lb) very small potatoes and brown slightly. Pour in just enough stock to cover, add a bouquet garni, salt and pepper, then cover and cook gently for 20–25 minutes (test the potatoes with a fork to check they are cooked). Serve sprinkled with chopped parsley.

BERRY The gastronomy of this old French province (now called Limousin) in the Loire valley is influenced by pig, poultry and sheep farming. This is well illustrated in its typical meat dishes: seven-hour braised leg of lamb, *saupiquet*, *sagourne*, Easter pâté made from pork and hard-boiled (hard-cooked) eggs, *sanguette*, black roast turkey, and chicken *en barbouille* (a red wine sauce thickened with blood). Cuisine *à la berrichonne* is typified by the tasty, sometimes rustic, simplicity of its slow-cooked dishes. Soups and stews (with *fritons* known as *grignaudes*) play an important role, together with the accompanying vegetables, *tartoufes* (potatoes) and pumpkin (also used in a cake). Chestnuts and field mushrooms have inspired recipes for carp (steamed), lamprey and salmon (braised).

One of the characteristics of this wine-growing region, which produces AOC wines (such as Reuilly, Chateaumeillant, Sancerre, Quincy and Menetou-Salon) and rosé wines, is the use of wine in cooking: eggs in red wine, and meat and fish stews cooked with wine. Cheeses are made mostly from goat's milk (Valençay, Pouligny, Chavignol, Levroux, Sellessur-Cher). Fruit and nut trees are grown – cherry (for kirsch), pear, walnut and hazelnut – and fruit is used in sweet desserts (see *sanciay*) and fritters. *Lichouneries* (confectionery shops) sell *forestines* from Bourges (with hazelnuts), marzipan, barley sugar and *croquets*.

BERRY Any small fleshy stoneless (pitless) fruit containing one or more seeds. Berries occur singly, in bunches (such as grape and redcurrant) or in clusters (elderberry). Wild berries may be eaten raw or cooked.

BERYX Fish of the *Berycidae* family, reddish-orange in colour and with delicious flesh. The long beryx is about 35 cm (14 in) in length, while the longer common beryx has a thicker body and grows up to 40 cm (16 in) long. They are fished 600 metres (1,970 ft) deep in the North Atlantic from Ireland to Norway, and are sold under the name of 'pink bream', usually as fillets.

BÊTISE A mint-flavoured boiled sweet (candy) manufactured in France since 1850. Although the Afchain company of Cambrai has long claimed to be sole inventor of *bêtises*, their exact origin is not known. Legend has it that a clumsy apprentice poured the ingredients (sugar, glucose and mint) carelessly, but perhaps it was a flash of genius on the part of a confectioner who had the idea of blowing air into the sugar. The microscopic air bubbles incorporated into the hot boiled sugar make the sweet light and opaque. *Bêtises* remain a speciality of Cambrai but are imitated by the *sottises* made in Valenciennes.

BEURRE BLANC A classic French sauce made with reduced vinegar and shallots to which butter is added, called white butter sauce in English. It is the standard accompaniment to pike and shad. The Nantes region and Anjou both claim to be its birthplace. It is said that a chef from Nantes called

Making beurre blanc

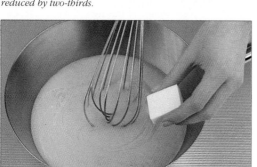

1 *Boil the shallots, wine vinegar and fish stock until reduced by two-thirds.*

2 *Remove the pan from the heat and whisk in all but 1 or 2 pieces of the butter.*

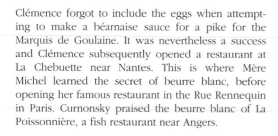

3 *Add the last of the butter and tilt the pan or stir the sauce occasionally until the butter has melted and the sauce is no longer foamy from whisking.*

4 *When the butter has melted, give the sauce a brief vigorous whisk in a large movement to mix it in evenly without making the sauce frothy.*

Clémence forgot to include the eggs when attempting to make a béarnaise sauce for a pike for the Marquis de Goulaine. It was nevertheless a success and Clémence subsequently opened a restaurant at La Chebuette near Nantes. This is where Mère Michel learned the secret of beurre blanc, before opening her famous restaurant in the Rue Rennequin in Paris. Curnonsky praised the beurre blanc of La Poissonnière, a fish restaurant near Angers.

RECIPE

beurre blanc
Put 5–6 chopped shallots in a saucepan with 250 ml (8 fl oz, 1 cup) wine vinegar, 325 ml (11 fl oz, 1⅓ cups) fish stock and ground pepper; reduce by two-thirds. Cut 225 g (8 oz, 1 cup) very cold butter (preferably slightly salted) into small pieces. Remove the pan from the heat and add all but one piece of the butter all at once, beating briskly with a whisk until smooth. Finally, add the last piece of butter and mix it in gently, stirring and turning the pan so that the sauce is not frothy. Season with salt and pepper. Pour the sauce into a warmed sauceboat and place in a lukewarm bain marie until required for serving.

The emulsion can be stabilized by adding 1 tablespoon double (heavy) cream – this is Nantes butter (*beurre nantais*).

BEURRE MANIÉ A mixture of butter and flour used as a thickening for soups, sauces, stews and other liquors towards the end of the cooking time. Equal quantities of butter and flour are used to make the paste. Soften the butter, then work in the flour with a fork or by creaming the mixture until the paste is smooth. Add small knobs to the simmering liquid, whisking or stirring vigorously, and allow each knob to melt before adding another. Bring to the boil, still whisking or stirring, and simmer for at least 3 minutes to cook the flour. Large quantities of beurre manié can be made in a food processor and frozen in small lumps, ready for whisking straight from the freezer into boiling liquid.

BHAJI A spicy Indian vegetable fritter consisting of one or more vegetables, such as onion, potato, aubergine (eggplant) and/or cauliflower, in a chickpea flour batter.

BIARROTE, À LA A French garnish for small cuts of meat, which are arranged on a base of potato galettes (prepared as for duchess potatoes) and surrounded by a ring of grilled (broiled) cep mushrooms. This name refers to the resort of Biarritz (on the mountainous Basque coast), where several new restaurants were opened as a result of visits by the emperor Napoleon III and the empress

Eugénie. It is also applied to a recipe for sautéed chicken in white wine, which may also be garnished with ceps.

RECIPE

sautéed chicken à la biarrote
Cut a 1.4 kg (3 lb) chicken into pieces and sauté until brown on all sides and cooked through. Deglaze with 100 ml (4 fl oz, 7 tablespoons) dry or medium white wine. Reduce the liquid, then add 100 ml (4 fl oz, 7 tablespoons) tomato sauce* and a small crushed garlic clove. Using a separate pan, sauté 100 g (4 oz, 2 cups) ceps, 100 g (4 oz, ⅔ cup) diced potatoes and 1 diced aubergine (eggplant) in olive oil. Fry a thinly sliced onion, separating the rings. Arrange the chicken in a heated serving dish, coat with the sauce and arrange the garnish in bouquets around it.

BIB *tacaud* A coastal fish (family *Gadidae*), similar to cod (but less good), commonly found in the English Channel and the Bay of Biscay. Shaped like an elongated triangle, with a copper-coloured back and silvery sides and belly, it measures 20–30 cm (8–12 in) and weighs about 200 g (7 oz). It has a short barbel on the lower jaw, long thin pelvic fins, and two abdominal fins connected by a membrane. The flesh, although lean, is rather tasteless and full of bones and deteriorates rapidly. Bib must therefore be prepared and eaten as soon as it is caught. It is cooked like cod (but is mostly used for fish meal).

BICARBONATE OF SODA (BAKING SODA)
An alkaline powder used in medicine as an antacid. In former times bicarbonate of soda was used to soften water for cooking vegetables, such as dried beans, and to preserve the colour of green vegetables. This has been rejected, as it results in the destruction of vitamins.

Bicarbonate of soda is one of the main ingredients of raising (leavening) agents: it improves the action of baking powder in many commercial preparations such as cake mixes and processed flour. It is used as a raising agent in some non-yeast breads, such as soda bread, and certain cakes. Combined with cream of tartar, it is the traditional raising agent for British scones.

BIERWURST A large, cured, coarse German pork and beef sausage, flavoured with garlic, and sliced as an accompaniment to beer, hence its name. It is always eaten cold and has a peppery taste. *Bierschinkenwurst* includes small chunks of ham.

BIGNON, LOUIS French restaurateur (born Hérisson, 1816; died Macau, 1906). He began his career in Paris as a waiter at the Café d'Orsay, then moved to the Café au Foy, which he acquired and passed on to his brother in 1847. He then took over the management of the Café Riche, redecorated the restaurant, and made it one of the best in Paris. His

activities also extended into viticulture and agriculture. He was a founder member of the Société des Agriculteurs de France and during the World Fairs from 1862 to 1880 he won the highest prizes for various agricultural products, wines and foods. He became a knight of the order of the Légion d'honneur in 1868 and an officer in 1878, and was the first restaurant owner to wear the rosette of the Légion d'honneur.

BIGOS The Polish national dish, also called 'hunter's stew', made of sauerkraut and meat simmered for a long time. Traditionally it was stored in wooden casks or stoneware pots, taken travelling (and hunting) and reheated many times, which improved the flavour. Large Polish boiling sausage is also cut up and added to the stew, which often includes wild mushrooms. Traditionally *bigos* preceded the soup course. It may be prepared with just one type of meat or with any mixture of duck, boiled beef, ham, mutton, pickled pork or even venison, and there are many variations.

RECIPE

bigos
Rinse 4 kg (9 lb) sauerkraut and drain it well. Peel, core and dice 4 dessert apples, sprinkling the pieces with lemon juice, and add to the sauerkraut with 2 large chopped onions. Melt 4 tablespoons lard in a flameproof casserole and cover with a fairly thick layer of sauerkraut, then add a layer of diced meat. Continue filling the pot with alternate layers of meat and sauerkraut, finishing with sauerkraut and adding a little lard every now and then. Pour in enough stock to cover the sauerkraut. Cover the pot and cook in a preheated oven at 180°C (350°F, gas 4) for 2–3 hours. Make a white roux and add some of the cooking liquor. Pour this sauce over the *bigos* and cook for a further 30 minutes.

BILBERRY *myrtille* A low, heathland shrub of the genus *Vaccinium* native to northern regions of Europe, America and Asia. Related to the blueberry, it is also known as whortleberry. Its small purplish-blue berries have a slightly acid flavour, but they can be eaten uncooked, with sugar and cream. However, bilberries are usually used for making tarts, ices and sorbets, as well as compotes, jams, jellies, syrups and liqueurs. They freeze well.

RECIPES

bilberry flan
Make some shortcrust pastry (basic pie dough) with 200 g (7 oz, 1¾ cups) plain (all-purpose) flour, 100 g (4 oz, ½ cup) butter cut into pieces, a pinch of salt, 1 tablespoon caster (superfine) sugar and 3 tablespoons cold water (see *short pastry*). Form into a ball and leave it to stand for 2 hours.

Wash and dry 300 g (11 oz, 2¾ cups) fresh bilberries (or use frozen fruit). Prepare a syrup with

100 g (4 oz, ½ cup) sugar and 250 ml (8 fl oz, 1 cup) water. Simmer for 5 minutes, then add the bilberries and leave to soak for 5 minutes. Return to a gentle heat and cook for 8 minutes, until all the syrup is absorbed.

Roll out the pastry and line a buttered 23 cm (9 in) flan tin (pie pan). Line with greaseproof (wax) paper, sprinkle with baking beans and bake blind in a preheated oven at 200°C (400°F, gas 6) for 12 minutes. Remove the paper and beans, and continue cooking for a further 6–7 minutes until the flan base is golden. Leave until lukewarm before unmoulding.

Fill the cold pastry case with the bilberries, smoothing the top. Warm together 2 tablespoons apricot purée and 1 teaspoon water, sieve and coat the bilberries with the glaze. Leave until cold.

Prepare a Chantilly cream by whipping 7 tablespoons double (heavy) cream with 1 tablespoon chilled milk, 1 teaspoon vanilla sugar and 1 tablespoon icing (confectioner's) sugar. Using a piping (pastry) bag fitted with a fluted nozzle, pipe the cream on top of the tart and decorate with a few sugared violets, if wished.

bilberry jam
Stalk and wash the berries briefly, then dry and weigh them. Put them into a preserving pan with 100 ml (4 fl oz, ½ cup) water per 1 kg (2¼ lb) berries. Bring to the boil, skim and simmer for about 10 minutes. Then add a weight of sugar equal to the weight of the fruit. Bring back to the boil, skim again, then leave to cook for about 15 minutes, stirring regularly. Pot and seal in the usual way.

BILLY BY A French mussel soup, also called *bilibi*, said to have been created by Barthe, the chef of Maxim's, for a regular customer called Billy, who adored mussels. Billy by is made of mussels cooked in white wine with onions, parsley, celery and fish stock. The soup is served hot or ice-cold with double (heavy) cream, the mussels and grated Parmesan cheese being served separately. Other sources claim that billy by was invented in Normandy, after the Normandy landings, when a farewell dinner was given to an American officer called Bill. So it was called 'Billy, bye bye', which degenerated to 'billy by'.

BIRDS Many varieties of wild and domesticated birds are used in cookery. The consumption of small wild birds has declined as protection orders become more stringent everywhere. However, a wide variety of birds for the pot is still plentiful in Spain. In France all birds smaller than the thrush are protected, except for larks, ortolans and sparrows in some regions. In times past, however, bird-catchers supplied the gourmand with many small birds: tits, warblers, curlews, jays, sandpipers, robins, wagtails and sparrows (whose delicate meat was reserved for the sick and convalescent). As a general rule, the only birds to escape the slaughter were nightingales and wrens. The rook was much sought after for soup or, in England, for pies. The wild birds most esteemed were whole roast heron, scoter-duck and plover roasted with hot pepper, roast partridge and turtle-doves served with cinnamon or ginger sauce and turtle-dove pâté.

The rearing and consumption of domestic poultry, on the other hand, continues to expand. Quail-rearing has to some extent filled the gap left by the banning of other wild birds.

BIRDSEYE, CLARENCE American businessman and inventor, father of the frozen food industry (born New York, 1886; died New York, 1956). During a journey to Labrador in 1920 he observed that fish caught by the Eskimos and exposed to the air froze rapidly and thus remained edible for several months. On his return to the United States, Birdseye succeeded in perfecting a mechanical process for ultra-rapid freezing. In 1924 he formed a company to produce and distribute these frozen products, but the economic crisis forced him to sell his process and name to a food company. The name of this pioneer of cold storage, split into 'Bird's Eye', became an international trade name for deep-frozen food.

BIRD'S-FOOT TREFOIL A common leguminous plant of North America and Europe, known in France as *lotier, mélilot, trèfle de cheval* or *mirlirot*, according to the species. When dried, the leaves, flowers and stems impart a very pleasant smell and can be used to flavour marinades. In some areas it is used to flavour rabbit, which is stuffed with the leaves and flowers after it has been cleaned. In Switzerland *mélilot* is used to make herbal tea. Some cheeses (notably the German cow's-milk cheese Schabzieger and curd cheeses) are flavoured with the yellow flowers of bird's-foot trefoil.

BIRDS' NESTS Nests built by the salangane, a type of Chinese swallow, in the Philippines and New Guinea and used in traditional Chinese cookery to make bird's-nest soup. Just before the breeding season, the birds feed on gelatinous seaweed, which makes their salivary glands secrete a thick whitish glutinous saliva with which they construct their nests. After being soaked in water the nests become transparent and gelatinous, giving the soup its characteristic odour and sticky texture. The nests may also be used in stews and as an ingredient in certain garnishes. The first European travellers to discover them, at the beginning of the 17th century, believed that they consisted of a mixture of lime and sea foam, or else the sap of trees. It was the French naturalist Buffon who established their true composition, after hearing an eye-witness account of the nests from the explorer Poivre.

BIREWECK An Alsatian cake, also called *pain de fruits* ('fruit loaf'). It is made from leavened dough flavoured with kirsch and mixed with fresh, dried and crystallized (candied) fruit. Usually shaped into small balls, it can also be made in one large piece and sold in slices.

RECIPE

bireweck

Cook 500 g (18 oz) pears, 250 g (9 oz) apples, 250 g (9 oz) peaches, 250 g (9 oz) dried figs and 250 g (9 oz) prunes in a little water, but do not allow them to become pulpy. Mix 1 kg (2¼ lb, 9 cups) sifted plain (all-purpose) flour and 25 g (1 oz, 4 packets) easy-blend dried yeast with enough hand-hot cooking water from the fruit to form a soft dough. Leave to rise until doubled in size. Meanwhile, finely dice 100 g (4 oz, ⅔ cup) candied citron and 50 g (2 oz, ⅓ cup) angelica. When the dough has risen, mix in the diced candied fruit, 250 g (9 oz, 1½ cups) sultanas (golden raisins), 125 g (4½ oz, ¾ cup) hazelnuts, 125 g (4½ oz, ¾ cup) almonds, 125 g (4½ oz, 1 cup) walnuts, 50 g (2 oz) blanched strips of orange zest, 125 g (4½ oz, ¾ cup) stoned (pitted) dates, and the drained cooked fruit. Add 200 ml (7 fl oz, ¾ cup) kirsch and mix well. Divide the dough into 200 g (7 oz) portions (about 28). Shape into rolls and smooth the surface with water. Place on a greased baking sheet, cover loosely and leave to rise until doubled in size. Bake in a preheated oven at 160°C (325°F, gas 3) for about 1¾ hours.

BIRIANI A North Indian rice dish of Persian origin. Lamb or mutton were the original meats, but chicken or fish may be used. Channa dal may be added and in the West prawns (shrimps) are popular. Basmati rice, spiced with saffron, turmeric and black cardamom, and often enriched with raisins and almonds, is layered with the spiced cooked meat mixture. Then the biriani is cooked in a tightly covered pot to which ghee or milk may be added. When served for special occasions, birianis may be finished with a garnish of edible silver leaf.

BISCÔME A type of gingerbread traditionally eaten in Lucerne, Switzerland, on the feast of Saint Nicholas, celebrated on 6 December. At the culmination of the festival a large procession sets off across the city, led by two heralds who are followed by Saint Nicholas, laden with an enormous basket of *biscômes*, and a number of bogeymen charged with punishing children who have not been well behaved during the year.

BISCOTTE PARISIENNE A light French biscuit (cookie) cooked once in the oven (unlike the true *biscotte* or rusk, which is cooked twice). It is made from almonds, egg yolks, whisked egg whites and cornflour (cornstarch), flavoured with kirsch and piped on to a buttered baking sheet.

BISCUIT (COOKIE) A small, dry, flat cake, traditionally with good keeping qualities, eaten as a snack or accompaniment to a drink, and sweet or savoury.

Sweet biscuits are eaten as an accompaniment to coffee, tea or milk – and mid-morning wine in Italy – and partner desserts or ice cream. They are used to make desserts – charlottes, in particular – and macaroon crumbs are often added to custards or creams. There is also a long European tradition of crumbling biscuits into soups and sauces as a thickener.

Savoury biscuits, or crackers, make snacks with alcoholic drinks or are served with cheese.

In Britain biscuits are historically plainer and less expensive than on the European continent, where they have associations with entertaining, Christmas and present-giving. Biscuit consumption is high in Britain, the US, Ireland and Belgium. In France biscuits are simply regarded as one aspect of petits fours, with their own wide repertoire. Although biscuits have become a convenient supermarket item, regional specialities continue to be produced in many countries, while they remain a popular item with the home baker.

■ **History** Their English and French name comes from the Latin *bis* meaning twice and *coctus* meaning cooked, for biscuits should in theory be cooked twice, which gives them a long storage life. The French Reims biscuit was originally a flat cake that was put back in the oven after being removed from its tin (pan). This made it drier and harder but improved its keeping qualities.

This very hard, barely risen biscuit was for centuries the staple food of soldiers and sailors. Roman legions were familiar with it and Pliny claimed that 'Parthian bread' would keep for centuries. In his account of the Crusades, the Lord of Joinville talks of 'bread called "bequis" because it is cooked twice'. Soldiers' biscuits or army biscuits were known under Louis XIV as 'stone bread' (*pain de pierre*). In 1894 French army biscuits were replaced by war bread made of starch, sugar, water, nitrogenous matter, ash and cellulose, but the name 'army biscuit' stuck. It did not disappear until soldiers on campaign were supplied with proper bread.

'Animalized' biscuits were also made. These were flat cakes containing meat juices and thought to be very nourishing. Vitamin biscuits appeared during World War II and these were distributed in schools in France. The cereal bar (with or without dried fruit) is the modern successor.

Biscuits were also a staple item in explorers' provisions. In his record of his adventures in the New World, Chateaubriand wrote: 'Reduced to a solitary existence, I dined on ship's biscuits, a little sugar and lemon.' 'Travellers' biscuits', in the 19th century, were hard pastries or cakes wrapped in foil, which kept well (see *beauvilliers*).

■ **Biscuit manufacture** The industrial manufacture of biscuits (cookies and crackers) began in Britain. The Carr establishment, founded in Carlisle in 1815, was the first factory that specialized in the production of biscuits, and was soon followed by MacFarlane in Edinburgh and Huntley and Palmers in Reading. These manufacturers exported their specialities all over the world, often sponsored by famous names. For example, the Albert was a small savoury biscuit bearing the name of the Prince Consort. It was not until 1840 that Jean-Honoré Olibet, a baker's son from Bordeaux, founded the first French biscuit factory. Soon other industrialists followed suit. In 1882 the Lefèvre-Utile factory invented the *petit-beurre* ('butter biscuit').

Biscuit-making is an active branch of the food industry. The ingredients used include varying proportions of flour, vegetable fats (shortening) or butter, sugar (usually sucrose, but sometimes glucose or maltose), starch, milk, eggs and baking powder. Permitted additives, such as antioxidants, colouring agents, emulsifiers and flavourings, must be listed on the packaging. Flavourings include coffee, vanilla, chocolate, coconut, aniseed, cinnamon and ginger. Liqueurs, jam, dried or crystallized (candied) fruit and nuts may also be incorporated. Production is automatic at all stages, which include kneading, shaping, baking, cooling, sorting and packing.

Sweet or savoury, biscuits are classified, in France, by the consistency of the dough.

• HARD OR SEMI-HARD DOUGH Used for *petits-beurres*, tea biscuits (filled or plain), shortbread, griddle cakes and various crackers and aperitif biscuits that may be seasoned with salt and other flavourings (cumin, cheese or paprika). These biscuits, which are the most widely consumed, contain about 70% flour and are made without eggs.

• SOFT DOUGH Used to make either crisp or soft biscuits, such as cigarettes, *tuiles*, *palets*, *langues-de-chat*, *palmiers*, sponge fingers, *nonettes*, *madeleines*, macaroons, *rochers*, some petits fours, *congolais* and *croquignoles*. These biscuits are made with a high proportion of egg white.

• BATTER Used to make wafer biscuits (dry, iced or filled). These biscuits have a high liquid content (water or milk) and small amounts of fat and flour.

■ **The cookie jar** The American term evokes the comfort of the sweet, ready snack, which is a feature particularly of German and American kitchens. The word 'cookie' comes from the Dutch *koek* (cooked), and the repertoire is enormous.

Sugar and butter are predominant tastes, and also make a very short biscuit: Scottish shortbread, the French Nantes *petit-beurre* and Normandy *sablé* (sandy), and the plain maria (British by invention, but hugely popular in Spain).

Spiced biscuits are a feature of Germany and Central Europe. The German *Lebkuchen* and *Pfeffernüsse* are part of the *bunte Teller* ('good biscuit' display), a feature of Christmas Eve, with 15 or more varieties and shapes, including chocolate kisses (small balls decorated with a nut), wasps' nests (almond and chocolate macaroons), vanilla crescents and cinnamon stars. This group may also include the white, south German aniseed *Springerle*, which is shaped with a carved wooden mould or an embossed rolling pin.

Nuts are a favourite in southern Europe; flaked almonds often decorate the *tuile*; the French also make almond sticks (like *croquets* and the Alsatian *schenkeles*). The popular macaroon is known as an *amaretto* in Italy, though this name is applied in other countries to a tissue-wrapped delicacy; ratafias (flavoured with bitter almonds) are the miniature version. The Italian *cantuccini*, sliced and then baked once more, hark back to earlier biscuit history. Other nuts also go in a host of biscuits, for example pine nuts in the Catalan *piñones*.

Among chocolate biscuits, two sandwiches stand out: the British bourbon, a neat rectangle with a cream filling and the round, all-American Oreo (used to make Mississippi mud pie). Other notables are the luscious Italian florentine, a combination of flaked almonds, candied peel and cherry, backed by fork-raked chocolate; the jaffa cake, where chocolate covers a sponge drop topped with orange jelly; and the American chocolate-chip cookie, which continues to conquer Europe.

Some countries have their own associations, like that of Britain with golden (light corn) syrup (imported from the US from 1885) combined with oats for flapjacks, and the lacy, rolled 'brandy' snaps, from which brandy quickly disappeared. Coconut is used in Australia for anzacs (named after the Australian and New Zealand Army Corps, which fought at Gallipoli in 1915). America has also contributed molasses, apple sauce and peanut butter cookies, and the concept of an icebox or refrigerator cookie (where dough waits to be sliced and baked in an instant).

■ **Savoury biscuits** Dry descendants of the original ship's biscuit, both British water biscuits (thin and dry, with slight brown bubbles over the surface) and cream crackers, favoured since the late 19th century, are eaten with cheese and, sometimes, other spreads. Bath Olivers are the most recherché of these, while other popular choices are the digestive (a mildly sweet wheatmeal biscuit), wheat wafers, Scandinavian rye crispbreads, rice cakes and Scottish oat cakes.

Flavoured crackers have been taken up in the US, salty (or with chilli), to stimulate the appetite, like the salted German pretzel (traditionally eaten alongside beer), and a range that includes cheese straws, tortilla chips and small shapes flavoured with cheese, onion or bacon bits.

RECIPE

galettes bretonnes

In a bowl, mix 1 egg yolk and 3 eggs with 600 g (1 lb 5 oz, 2⅔ cups) sugar and 1 teaspoon ground cinnamon. Mix in 750 g (1 lb 10 oz, 3¼ cups) softened slightly salted Breton butter until the mixture is smooth. Add a little brown rum, vanilla essence (extract) and essential oil of bergamot. Sift 1 kg (2¼ lb, 9 cups) plain (all-purpose) flour, add a generous pinch of baking powder and work into the butter mixture. Turn out the resulting dough on to a cloth dusted with flour. Fold the cloth over and knead the dough inside the cloth for 3 minutes, adding flour to the cloth occasionally to prevent the dough from sticking. Leave the dough wrapped in the cloth overnight in a cool place but not in the refrigerator. (Too cold an environment hardens the butter.)

The following day, divide the dough into 5 lumps, each about 500 g (18 oz), flatten them into shallow pie dishes, glaze with beaten egg and a little milk and decorate by scoring with a fork. Bake in a pre-heated oven at 220°C (425°F, gas 7) for about 20 minutes, until deep golden brown. Take care not to allow the galettes to burn.

rolled brandy snaps
Melt 100 g (4 oz, ½ cup) butter with 100 g (4 oz, ½ cup) sugar. Stir in 100 g (4 oz, ¼ cup) golden (light corn) syrup, 100 g (4 oz, 1 cup) plain (all-purpose) flour and 1 teaspoon ground ginger. Mix well. Ladle the mixture in small heaps, very well spaced, on to a baking sheet. Place in a preheated oven at 180°C (350°F, gas 4) and bake for 7–8 minutes. Take the biscuits (cookies) out of the oven and wrap each one round a wooden spoon handle, pressing them together where they join so that they do not unroll.

BISE, MARIUS French restaurateur (born Annecy, 1894; died Talloires, 1969). In 1902 his father, formerly maître d'hôtel on the boats on Lake Annecy, bought a small restaurant on the lakeside. It was known at that time as the Petit Chalet and specialized in fried lake fish dishes using pollan and char. One day the artist Paul Cézanne offered to pay for a meal with one of his paintings. He was refused! Marius succeeded his father shortly after World War I, having completed his studies as maître d'hôtel in several major Paris restaurants. He made his wife Marguerite, who was a remarkable cook, responsible for food from the ovens. In 1928 the extended Petit Chalet was renamed Petite Auberge and became known as l'Auberge du Père Bise. A gratin of crayfish tails and braised chicken in tarragon cream are two of the creations of Mère Marguerite Bise, who died in 1965.

BISHOP An ancient punch made with wine, citrus fruit and spices, served either hot or iced. In his *Dictionnaire de cuisine*, Alexandre Dumas says that this drink was called 'bishop' (German *Bischof*) when made with red Bordeaux (because of its purple colour), 'cardinal' when made with red Rhine wine, and 'pope' when made with Tokay (white). Originating in the Rhineland, it came to France through Alsace, where hot spiced wines are popular, The classic English bishop is made by heating claret with orange and lemon peel, cinnamon and cloves. It is still a popular winter drink. There are many other traditional British recipes for punches of this sort, named after church officials: prebendary, beadle and churchwarden.

RECIPES

iced bishop
Pour a bottle of champagne and 500 ml (17 fl oz, 2 cups) strained lime-blossom tea into a large bowl. Add an orange and half a lemon, thinly sliced. Add sufficient sugar syrup (density 1.2850) to obtain a mixture with a density of 1.1425. Leave in a cool place to macerate for 1 hour. Strain, then freeze to a slushy consistency. Just before serving, add 4 small liqueur glasses brandy. Serve in punch glasses.

Rhine wine bishop
Dissolve 250 g (9 oz, 1 cup) sugar in 300 ml (½ pint, 1¼ cups) water over a low heat with the zest of an orange and a lemon, 2 cloves and a cinnamon stick. Simmer for 5 minutes. Add a bottle of Rhine wine and heat until a fine white froth begins to appear on the surface. Strain and serve in a jug (pitcher) or in a large punch bowl. This drink is sometimes flavoured with a little Madeira, sherry or Marsala.

BISON A wild ox or buffalo formerly widely distributed over the plains of North America and also in Europe, and still in reserves in Poland. It was the symbol of prosperity and plenty for the American Indians, who used its meat, fat, hide and horns. It was systematically hunted from the end of the 19th century onwards and now reconstituted herds live either on reserves or on ranches, where they are bred for the meat trade. Bison flesh is juicy with a pronounced flavour and is eaten mostly in the American West and Canada. (A cross between the bison and the cow has produced beefalo, whose meat is popular in some areas.) Bison is most commonly eaten either smoked (especially the tongue) or marinated. The hump is considered to be a delicacy. A typical Canadian dish is bison in brine, desalted, boiled for several hours, and then served with cabbage, carrots, potatoes, cream and seasoning. Bison meat may also be minced (ground) for making meat balls or smoked, powdered, mixed with fat and used either to make soups or to spread on bread.

These methods of preparation are mostly inspired by ancient Indian recipes such as the Cheyenne recipe described by C. Lévi-Strauss in *The Origin of Table Manners:* 'They placed thin slices of hard meat carefully on a bed of charcoal, first on one side, then the other. They beat them to break them into small pieces which they mixed with melted bison fat and marrow. Then they pressed it into leather bags, taking care that no air was left inside. When the bags were sewn up, the women flattened them by jumping on them to blend the ingredients. Then they put them to dry in the sun.' See also *buffalo*.

The Polish bison (remnant of the European/Russian herd) is of interest chiefly because its chosen fodder, bison grass, is a major flavouring of vodka, notably the Polish zubrowka.

BISQUE A seasoned shellfish purée flavoured with white wine, Cognac and double (heavy) cream, used as the basis of a soup. The flesh of the main ingredient (crayfish, lobster or crab) is diced as for a salpicon and used as a garnish. The shells are also used to make the initial purée.

The word 'bisque' has been in use for centuries

and suggests a connection with the Spanish province of Vizcaya, which lends its name to the Bay of Biscay. Bisque was originally used to describe a highly spiced dish of boiled meat or game. Subsequently, bisques were made using pigeons or quails and garnished with crayfish or cheese croûtes. It was not until the 17th century that crayfish became the principal ingredient of this dish, which soon after was also prepared with other types of shellfish. The word is now used imprecisely for several pink puréed soups.

RECIPES

crayfish bisque

Prepare 5–6 tablespoons mirepoix* cooked in 40 g (1½ oz, 3 tablespoons) butter until soft. Allow 1.25 litres (2¼ pints, 5½ cups) consommé or fish stock. Cook 75 g (3 oz, ⅓ cup) short-grain rice in 500 ml (17 fl oz, 2 cups) of the consommé until soft. Dress and wash 18 good-sized crayfish. Add the crayfish to the mirepoix together with salt, freshly ground pepper and a bouquet garni, and sauté the crayfish until the shells turn red. Heat 3 tablespoons Cognac in a small ladle, pour on to the crayfish and set alight, stirring well.

Add 7 tablespoons dry white wine and reduce by two-thirds. Add 150 ml (¼ pint, ⅔ cup) consommé and cook gently for 10 minutes.

Shell the crayfish when cold. Finely dice the tail meat and reserve for the garnish. Pound the shells, then process with the cooked rice and the cooking liquor. Press as much as possible through a fine sieve. Place the resulting purée in a saucepan with the remaining consommé and boil for 5–6 minutes. Just before serving, cool the bisque slightly, then add a dash of cayenne pepper and 150 ml (¼ pint, ⅔ cup) crème fraîche, followed by 65 g (2½ oz, 5 tablespoons) butter cut up into very small pieces. Add the diced tail meat and serve piping hot.

lobster bisque

Prepare in the same way as crayfish bisque, but replace the crayfish with an equal weight of small lobsters cut into pieces and sautéed in the mirepoix. If desired, it can be prepared using only the meat from the thorax, legs and claws (the meat should be finely diced). The tails can then be used for medallions.

BISTRO A bar or small restaurant, also known as a bistrot. The origin of this familiar word is obscure. It first appeared in the French language in 1884, and perhaps comes from the Russian word *bistro* (quick), which the Cossacks used to get quick service at a bar during the Russian occupation of Paris in 1815. There also appears to be a relationship with the word *bistreau*, which in the dialects of western France describes a cow-herd and, by extension, a jolly fellow – an apt description of an innkeeper. The most likely origin is doubtless an abbreviation of the word *bistrouille*. Modern French bistros are of modest appearance and frequently offer local dishes, cold meats and cheese with their wine.

BISTROUILLE Also known as *bistouille*, the term used in northern France for a mixture of coffee and brandy. It is derived from *bis* (twice) and *touiller* (to mix), and may be used to describe cheap brandy.

BITOKE A French dish made with minced (ground) lean beef moulded into a flat, oval or round shape. It was introduced into French cuisine by Russian émigrés in the 1920s. In Russian cookery, minced meat is often used for meatballs (*bitki*) and croquettes.

RECIPE

bitoke

To make a single *bitoke*, finely mince (grind) 125 g (4½ oz, ½ cup) lean beef and add 25 g (1 oz, 2 tablespoons) butter, salt, pepper and a little grated nutmeg. Shape the mixture into a flattened ball, coat in flour and sauté in clarified butter. Add 1 tablespoon cream and 1 teaspoon lemon juice to the cooking liquor to make a sauce. Coat the *bitoke* with the sauce and garnish with fried onion. Serve with sauté potatoes. Alternatively, the minced beef may also be coated with egg and breadcrumbs before cooking.

BITTER Having a sharp or acid flavour. Certain bitter plants are used in cooking: they include chicory (endive), bay, ginger, rhubarb, orange and bitter almond. Others, whose bitterness is brought out by infusion or distillation, are used essentially in drinks: wormwood, camomile, centaury, gentian, hops and cinchona.

BITTER ORANGE See *Seville orange*.

BITTERS An aromatic alcoholic or non-alcoholic drink with a bitter flavour. The very aromatic types are usually drunk alone or with soda; the others, such as peach or orange bitters, are used for flavouring mixed drinks. Many bitters come from Italy (for example, Campari and Fernet-Branca). They are usually wine-based, and common flavourings are gentian and orange rind. Bitters may be served as aperitifs, digestives or pick-me-ups and in various cocktails. French bitters include Amer Picòn, Selestat, Toni-Kola, Arquebuse and Suze.

BLACK AFRICA See *page 118*.

BLACKBERRY The fruit of a prickly European shrub, with related species elsewhere. The blackberry is black, firm and ripens in September. Traditionally a wild fruit with some domestic cultivation, blackberries are now cultivated at a commercial level. In North America the dewberry is a similar, smaller fruit which ripens earlier than the blackberry.

It is used to make jam, compote, jelly, tarts, pies, iced desserts, syrup, liqueur and ratafia. It is also used in confectionery (for fruit jellies).

RECIPES

blackberry jam
Wash and weigh the blackberries, put them in a deep bowl with 175 ml (6 fl oz, ¾ cup) water per 1 kg (2¼ lb) fruit, and leave to soak for at least 12 hours. Pour the fruit and water into a preserving pan, add lemon juice, using 1 lemon per 1 kg (2¼ lb) fruit, bring to the boil and cook gently for 10 minutes. Then add 900 g (2 lb, 4 cups) sugar per 1 kg (2¼ lb) fruit, bring back to the boil, skim and cook for 15 minutes, stirring from time to time. Pot and seal in the usual way.

blackberry syrup
Wash and weigh the blackberries, put them in a deep bowl with 175 ml (6 fl oz, ¾ cup) water per 1 kg (2¼ lb) fruit, and leave to soak for at least 12 hours. Then crush the fruit in a food processor and pour the fruit and juice into a jelly bag or muslin (cheesecloth) bag. Squeeze over a bowl and measure the juice. Pour it into a preserving pan and add 400 g (14 oz, 1¾ cups) sugar per 600 ml (1 pint, 2½ cups) juice. Stir until dissolved (without heating), then pour it into bottles to within 2 cm (¾ in) from the top. Seal and store in a cool place.

blackberry tartlets
Put into a food processor 200 g (7 oz, 1¾ cups) plain (all-purpose) flour, 5 tablespoons sugar and 1 egg, and work to a coarse dough. Add 100 g (4 oz, ½ cup) softened butter cut into small pieces and work quickly until smooth. Form into a ball and leave it to stand for 2 hours.

Roll out the dough and use to line 6 buttered tartlet tins (moulds). Prick the bottom with a fork, sprinkle with caster (superfine) sugar and fill with 800 g (1¾ lb) washed blackberries, packing them closely together. Sprinkle with sugar again. Bake the tartlets in a preheated oven at 200°C (400°F, gas 6) for about 30 minutes. Remove from the oven, leave until lukewarm, then unmould them on to a wire rack. Serve warm or cold accompanied by crème fraîche, or decorated with piped Chantilly cream. A tart is prepared in the same manner.

BLACKBIRD *merle* A bird of the thrush family ranging from northern to southern Europe. The female has a brown plumage and the male is black; both have yellow beaks. Its flesh has a fine texture and its taste varies depending on the diet of the bird, which itself depends on the region in which it lives and the season of the year. The flavour is usually slightly bitter but is at its most fragrant in the autumn. Blackbirds are cooked in the same way as thrushes, although they are less delicate. Corsican blackbirds are used to make a delicious pâté.

BLACKCURRANT A shrub native to northern Europe but now widely cultivated for its black juicy berries, which are sour and aromatic. The medicinal properties of both the fruit and leaves were known by the 14th century. The French *cassis* comes either from *casse*, the husk of the blackcurrant, or from *cassia* (senna), known for its purgative qualities. In France its cultivation really began in the Côte d'Or following the perfection of blackcurrant liqueur (*cassis*). The first bushes were established in the park of the château at Montmuzard near Dijon in 1750.

Blackcurrants are grown especially in Burgundy but also in Orléanais and Haute Savoie, as well as in Germany, Belgium and Holland. They are harvested at the end of June or the beginning of July. The variety Noir de Bourgogne, with dense clusters of small berries, is exceptionally tasty and aromatic; varieties with larger less dense fruit tend to be more watery.

The fruit is used to make jellies, jams, syrups and liqueur. Frozen or concentrated into a purée, the berries can also be used in the preparation of sorbets, Bavarian cream, charlottes, soufflés and tarts. Dried blackcurrants are sometimes sold commercially; they can be used instead of raisins in cake-making.

RECIPES

blackcurrant jelly (1)
Wash, dry and stalk some blackcurrants. Weigh them, place in a saucepan and add 150 ml (¼ pint, ⅔ cup) water per 1 kg (2¼ lb) fruit. Heat until the berries burst (if a perfectly clear jelly is required), then place the fruit in a cloth and wring to extract the juice. (If a thicker jelly is preferred, rub the contents of the saucepan through a sieve or mouli.) Measure the liquid obtained, then, for every 1 litre (1¾ pints, 4⅓ cups) fruit juice, put 850 g (1 lb 14 oz, 3¾ cups) preserving sugar into a saucepan together with the juice of a lemon and 175 ml (6 fl oz, ¾ cup) water. Heat to a temperature of 109°C (228°F), then add the blackcurrant juice. Stir thoroughly over a high heat until the jelly coats the back of the spoon. Skim and pour the boiling jelly into sterilized jars. Allow to cool completely. Cover, label and store in a cool place.

blackcurrant jelly (2)
Prepare a blackcurrant jelly as described in the previous recipe but using 1 kg (2¼ lb, 4½ cups) sugar per 1 kg (2¼ lb) of fruit. Cook the sugar in the same way, then take the saucepan off the heat, add the juice and stir thoroughly. Then pour the jelly into sterilized jars, leave to cool and proceed as in the previous recipe.

blackcurrant sorbet
Place 250 g (9 oz, 1¼ cups) sugar and 400 ml (14 fl oz, 1¾ cups) water in a saucepan. Heat to dissolve the sugar. (The density should be 1.14; if it is less than this, add a little more sugar.) Warm the syrup, then add 350 ml (12 fl oz, 1½ cups)

BLACK AFRICA

The cuisine of the countries of Black Africa is little known in Europe, since it calls for ingredients difficult to obtain elsewhere. These include the meats of buffalo, zebra, camel, snake and monkey as well as that of elephant, hippopotamus and lion, which are now protected species. Among the fish, there are *tiof*, a near relative of the bass, *capitaine* and the freshwater fish *manvi*. Plant foods include monkey bread, *n'dole* leaves, cassava, *fonio*, shea nuts and sorghum.

African cooking is more varied in the west of the continent than in the east, except in Ethiopia (where it is very sophisticated: a characteristic dish is a rich and elaborately prepared meat sauce known as *went*). It has generally retained a rustic character – most cooking takes place over a wood fire using a boiling pot in which everything cooks together. In Madagascar and Réunion Island there is a notable Indian influence.

■ **Unusual flavours** The most common African dishes are ragoût and *canari* – a dish cooked without water in an earthenware vessel; both are seasoned with a vast assortment of condiments. As well as traditional spices like pepper, ginger, garlic (*thoum*), chilli (*pili pili*) and nutmeg, Africans use *atokiko* (mango stones or pits), tamarind, *tô* (millet paste), *lalo* (powdered baobab leaves) and *soumbala* (dried and crushed fruit rind), as well as dried larvae and locusts. Peanuts, palm oil and coconut also add their distinctive flavours to meat and fish dishes. Cassava is the basic starchy food, and sorghum the most extensively used cereal.

Salads and raw vegetables are unknown in African menus, but there is a great variety of soups: *nkui*, based on okra, husks, and maize (corn) dumplings, in Cameroon; *pepe supi* (in which meat is mixed with fish) in Guinea; 'churching' soup (made from chicken and tripe) in Mali; and *caidou* (made from fish and rice) in Senegal. Many countries have a single traditional dish that is regarded as the national dish: *zegeni* (mutton with pimiento paste and vegetables, served with unleavened biscuits) from Eritrea; *cosidou* (a kind of stew similar to Portuguese *cocido*) from Benin; *dou lou* (shin and foot of beef with okra) from Chad; *vary amin* (stew made of zebra, with chow-chow, tomatoes and ginger) from Madagascar; *yassa* from Senegal; *mafé* (beef with peanuts and millet) from West Africa; *kourkouri* (pork stew) from Burkina Faso; *bosaka* (cockerel fried in palm oil) from the Ivory Coast; and *massale* (curried kid) from Réunion Island.

Couscous is made throughout Africa, but based on millet rather than wheat, like *bassi salte* from Senegal; it is also made with maize in Cameroon, and with whole wheat in Chad. Vegetable accompaniments vary according to local resources: green cabbage and unroasted peanuts in Mali; dates, raisins and artichoke hearts in Niger; pumpkin and aubergines (eggplants) in Burkina Faso.

The basic dish which distinguishes African cooking relies on the association of a starchy food (cassava, yam, sweet potato, taro or plantain) or a cereal (rice, *fonio*, sorghum or millet), reduced to a paste or gruel, and a substantial ragoût sauce, combining vegetables (spinach, palm seeds, tomatoes, okra), meat and/or fish, pistachios, peanuts and green mangoes. According to its country of origin, this dish is called *foutou* (or *foufou*), *placali*, *gari* or *aitiou*, based on maize.

Gourds and tuberous roots, particularly yams in West Africa, are the main African vegetables, with 'green leaves' of pumpkin, aubergine (eggplant) or beans and all varieties of banana, which are eaten as a paste, croquettes, sautéed (as in *dop* in Cameroon) or fried.

■ **A wide variety of resources** While African cooking is closely related to local resources – ragoût of viper in Cameroon, crocodile tail in Burkina Faso, monkey kebabs in Casamance (Senegal), camel with yams in Mali – it includes dishes less unusual to European and North American palates. Chicken, in particular, is prepared in many ways – for example, with coconut, ginger, unripe bananas and/or peanuts – while beef and pork are usually braised or cooked in a stew, and mutton is grilled (broiled).

On the coasts the supply of fish provides variety in the menu, particularly in Benin (*ago glain* – ragoût of crab with rice), Senegal (*tiê bou diéné*), and in Guinea and Togo (sea perch with ginger, stuffed mullet). Giant oysters and crayfish are eaten fried. Tuna fish *achar* is a typical dish of Réunion Island, and cod, in salad or cooked in breadcrumbs, is a speciality of Guinea.

■ **Desserts and drinks** Although goat's milk curds are eaten, Africa produces practically no cheese, except henna cheese (in Mali, Niger and Benin), which is used in sauces. There is a great variety of fruits. Avocados and custard apples are made into compotes and custards. Fruit accompanies rice and semolina puddings, while bananas make delicious fritters, and pancakes are made from sweet potato, which is also used with coconut to make cakes.

Drinks, too, are made from fruits – coconut or custard-apple milk, banana juice and pineapple cider. A great deal of alcohol is consumed: *mengrokom* – a spirit made with maize and cassava – in Gabon, millet beer in Togo, palm spirits and wine, and *babine*, a drink fermented from avocado leaves. Finally, there are many extracts which make refreshing drinks and also have some medicinal properties: infusion of *kinkeliba*, lemon-and-ginger water, and honey and lime drinks.

A Cameroonian woman sells cabbages, chillies, maize (corn) and okra (protected from the sun by ferns).

blackcurrant juice and the juice of half a lemon. Mix well and pour the mixture into an ice-cream machine or freeze, beating at intervals. 'Real' sorbet is made by adding a quarter of the volume of Italian meringue to the ingredients.

blackcurrant syrup

Crush the blackcurrants, put into a muslin (cheesecloth) bag and leave to drain; do not press. The pulp is very rich in pectin, which turns the syrup into jelly. Measure the juice and allow 800 g (1¾ lb, 3½ cups) sugar per 500 ml (17 fl oz, 2 cups) juice. Put the sugar and juice into a saucepan and heat, stirring well until the sugar has completely dissolved. When the temperature reaches 103°C (217°F), skim and pour into sterilized bottles. Label and store in a cool dry place.

frozen blackcurrant charlotte

Line the base and sides of a charlotte mould with sponge fingers dipped in blackcurrant syrup and cut to fit the mould. Fill the mould with alternate layers of blackcurrant ice cream and sponge fingers soaked in the syrup. Finish with a layer of fingers. Weight the top, then place in the freezer. Turn out the frozen charlotte just before serving. It can be served with custard or decorated with Chantilly cream and blackcurrants cooked in a sugar syrup.

BLACK FOREST GÂTEAU
A chocolate cake, *Schwarzwälder Kirschtorte*, made in Bavaria during the summer. The fame of this rich gâteau has risen since the early years of the 20th century. It consists of dark chocolate sponge layered with sweetened whipped cream and sour black Schmidt cherries. The cherries are lightly cooked and macerated in kirsch, and this liquor is used to moisten the cake before it is layered.

RECIPES

Black Forest gâteau ♦
Whisk 250 g (9 oz, 1 generous cup) caster (superfine) sugar with 6 eggs until pale, very thick and creamy. Then gently fold in 100 g (4 oz, 1 cup) plain (all-purpose) flour sifted with 50 g (2 oz, ½ cup) cocoa, and 150 g (5 oz, ⅔ cup) melted butter. Butter and flour 3 round 23 cm (9 in) cake tins (pans) and pour in the cake mixture. Bake in a preheated oven at 180°C (350°F, gas 4) for about 25 minutes. Turn the cakes out of the tins and allow to cool.

Make a syrup with 200 g (7 oz, ¾ cup) caster sugar and 350 ml (12 fl oz, 1½ cups) water. Flavour with kirsch. Grate 200–250 g (7–9 oz, 7–9 squares) bitter (semisweet) chocolate into thick shavings and put in the refrigerator. Soak the cooled layers of cake in the syrup.

Make some Chantilly cream by whipping together 750 ml (1¼ pints, 3¼ cups) chilled double (heavy) cream, 200 ml (7 fl oz, ¾ cup) very cold milk, 75 g (3 oz, ⅔ cup) icing (confectioner's) sugar and 2 teaspoons vanilla sugar. Cover each layer of cake with a quarter of the cream and a dozen brandy-flavoured cherries. Cover the sides of the cake with the remaining cream. Decorate the whole cake with chocolate shavings. Serve chilled.

BLACK PUDDING (BLOOD SAUSAGE)
boudin noir A savoury sausage made across Europe and Russia consisting largely of seasoned pig's blood and fat contained in a length of intestine, which forms the skin. It may be sold whole, cut from a length or in presealed pieces. Ox, calves' or sheep's blood can also be used, but this results in a coarser pudding. In France the fat consists partly of *chons*, which are granular fragments (cracklings) obtained from melting down pig's fat. One of the oldest known cooked meats, black pudding is said to have been invented by Aphtonite, a cook of ancient Greece. Some are eaten fresh, others are semi-preserved by drying or smoking.

With few exceptions, blood sausages are cooked to serve (and often poached, then fried). In France they are traditionally fried or grilled (broiled) and served with apples or mashed potato, in Germany with hot potato salad. In Spain they commonly flavour pulses; but in Britain and Ireland bacon and potatoes are favourite accompaniments.

■ **French boudins noirs** There are as many types of *boudin noir* as there are pork butchers. Although the *boudin de Paris* traditionally contains equal quantities of blood, fat and cooked onions, the proportions can vary widely; butchers may use a range of different seasonings and add fruit or vegetables, aromatic herbs, milk, cream, semolina and crustless bread. In Lyon, they add raw onions, sometimes marinated in brandy and herbs; in Nancy, they add milk. The Auvergne boudin contains milk together with a pig's head cooked with its crackling. Strasbourg smoked boudin contains cooked pork rind and bread soaked in milk. Poitou boudin is prepared without fat but with cooked spinach, cream, semolina and eggs. Various regional boudins contain fruit, including apples (Normandy), prunes (Brittany), raisins (Flanders) or chestnuts (Auvergne). Alsace has two local specialities that are similar to black pudding: *Zungenwurst*, or tongue sausage, which in addition to the basic ingredients includes pieces of ox or pig's tongue, wrapped in bacon, and arranged geometrically in an ox intestine; and *Schwarzwurst*, or smoked black sausage, which is made from a paste of pig's blood, pork rind, ears, boned head and trotters, fat trimmings and onions, with diced pork fat and enclosed in ox intestine. See also *gogues*.

■ **Blood sausages worldwide** Italy makes fresh *sanguinaccio* – in Lecce made with pig's brains and blood – and there are many German varieties of *Blutwurst* (some including calf's or pig's lung and bacon). Belgium has the Brussels *bloedpens* and a *boudin noir* (cousin to a French one) that contains eggs, butter and cream.

Black Forest gâteau.

In Spain there are *butifarras* on the east coast and the Balearics and *morcillas* in the north and south. In the north these may be flavoured with aniseed, cloves and other spices, and are plumped with either onions or rice. Both the Burgos and Aragon *morcillas* contain rice with pine nuts. The Asturian *morcilla* is smoked and wrinkled, swelling up in the pot (see *fabada*). Most southern *morcillas* are in loops; again onions and rice are the common fillers. *Morcilla dulce* (a sweet one), highly spiced with creamy fat (like fruit cake), is eaten as a tapa. It is a taste shared in Sicily, where raisins, almond pieces and candied pumpkin may be included – and in Scandinavia where they may contain raisins.

British black puddings are different in using cereals (oatmeal or barley) to absorb the blood, and traditionally are horseshoe-shaped. They remain popular in Scotland and the English Midlands and north (and interest London chefs). The best are the short, fat ones made in Bury in Lancashire, flavoured with marjoram, thyme, mint, penny royal and celery seed. Irish drisheen is made with pig's blood in Cork (sometimes with liver), and sheep's blood in Kerry. (Others use goose or turkey blood.) The finest sausages include cream and breadcrumbs, with pepper and mace; tansy is a traditional herb.

RECIPES

boudin noir

Add 1 tablespoon wine vinegar to 1 litre (1¾ pints, 4⅓ cups) pig's blood to prevent it coagulating. Chop 400 g (14 oz) onions and gently cook them in 100 g (4 oz, ½ cup) lard without browning. Dice 800 g–1 kg (1¾–2¼ lb) fresh pork fat and soften in a pan very gently without frying, until it becomes translucent. Add the onions and a bouquet garni and cook for about 20 minutes. Remove from the heat and, stirring constantly, add the blood, 2–3 teaspoons salt, 175 ml (6 fl oz, ¾ cup) white wine, ½ teaspoon freshly ground pepper and ½ teaspoon allspice. Sieve to remove remaining lumps of fat at this stage, if required, then add 200 ml (7 fl oz, ¾ cup) crème fraîche.

Turn some clean pig's intestines inside out, wash and dry them, rub with lemon juice, and turn right side out. Knot the end of one of the pieces of intestine and, using a funnel, fill the intestine with the mixture, pushing it with the hand towards the knotted end. When the sausage is about 10 cm (4 in) long, twist the intestine several times to seal it. Repeat for the other sausages.

Plunge in boiling water and poach for about 20 minutes without boiling. As the puddings rise to the surface, prick them with a pin to release the air, which would otherwise burst them. Drain them and leave to cool under a cloth.

boudin noir à la normande

Chop about 800 g (1¾ lb) dessert (eating) apples for 1 kg (2¼ lb) sausage, sprinkle with lemon juice (if desired) and fry in butter in a large pan. Poach the black pudding, slice into portions and fry in butter in a separate pan. Add the slices to the apple and fry together for a few seconds. Serve piping hot.

boudin noir bearnais

Gently cook 1 kg (2¼ lb) minced (ground) pig's throat, or fatty pork, for 30 minutes in the bottom of a large stock pot or heavy based saucepan. Peel 1 kg (2¼ lb) onions and 250 g (9 oz) garlic and add to the meat, together with 5 tablespoons chopped thyme and a bunch of chopped parsley. Simmer for 1½ hours. In a large saucepan, boil half a pig's head seasoned with coarse salt, with 1 kg (2¼ lb) leeks, 500 g (18 oz) onions stuck with cloves, 4 red sweet (bell) peppers and 500 g (18 oz) carrots. When the head is cooked, bone it, chop the meat and vegetables, discarding the cloves from the onions, and add to the stock pot. Adjust the seasoning and add some allspice. Add 5 litres (8½ pints, 5½ quarts) blood. Stir well. Put in containers, cover and sterilize in a pan of boiling water for 2 hours. Serve sliced cold or grilled (broiled).

BLADDER

BLADDER A membranous bag in animals in which urine is stored; after slaughter it has various uses in cooking and charcuterie. Pig's bladder is used to enclose poultry (chicken or duck) for poaching in stock. It must be soaked in water with coarse salt and vinegar to remove impurities, then carefully rinsed and dried before inserting the bird. The poultry is then presented at table *en vessie* or *en chemise*. If the dish is to be served cold, it is left to cool in the intact bladder. This cooking method, in which the bird is effectively sealed, concentrates the flavours of the forcemeat and the aromatic cooking liquid inside the bladder.

In former times dried pig's bladders were used as containers for tallow and melted lard. Sometimes they were filled with air and used as shop signs for *charcutiers* (suppliers of cooked meat).

RECIPE

chicken en vessie Marius Vettard

Singe and carefully clean a roasting chicken weighing 1.7–1.8 kg (3¾–4 lb). Leave it to soak in iced water for 4 hours to ensure that the flesh remains white. Meanwhile, soak a pig's bladder.

Prepare a forcemeat with the chicken liver, 150 g (5 oz) fresh truffles, and 250 g (9 oz) foie gras, using an egg to bind it. Season the forcemeat with salt and pepper and add about 150 ml (¼ pint, ⅔ cup) champagne. Stuff the chicken with the forcemeat and truss it.

Insert the chicken into the well-rinsed and dried bladder in such a way that the opening of the bladder is along the back of the chicken. Add 2 generous pinches of coarse salt, a pinch of pepper and a glass each of Madeira and good-quality champagne. Sew up with fine string pulled tightly and prick it about 10 times all around to stop it from bursting. Then poach in a good consommé for 1½ hours. Serve the chicken in the bladder with shaped potatoes, carrots, turnips and the white part of some leeks (or with rice pilaf). Open the bladder at the last moment, slitting it along the seam. A light Burgundy is a good accompaniment to this dish.

BLAFF In West Indian Creole cuisine a fish or shellfish dish in a sauce. The selected ingredients, usually sea-urchin eggs (*chadrons*) or firm-fleshed fish (even shark), are first marinated in lime juice with hot chilli pepper and garlic. They are then simmered in stock flavoured with onion, thyme, parsley and cloves. The name of this dish is onomatopoeic, derived from the noise the fish makes as it is plunged in boiling water. Blaff may also be cooked in white wine. The dish is served with rice and red kidney beans.

BLAGNY An AOC wine from the Côte de Beaune. The vineyards of the hamlet of Blagny extend to the parishes of Meursault and Puligny-Montrachet. The elegant white wines are similar to Meursault and are sold as 'Meursault Premier Cru' or 'Meursault-Blagny'. Only the reds, made from the Pinot Noir grape and somewhat similar to the Volnay wines, carry the Blagny AOC.

BLANC, À A French term used to describe a stage of cooking when food is cooked or partially cooked but not coloured, for example by gently frying onions without allowing them to colour.

Cuire à blanc is also the French term for baking a pastry flan case (pie shell) blind.

BLANC, AU The French description of food (especially poultry and veal) in either a *blanc de cuisson* or a white stock.

RECIPE

chicken au blanc
Poach a boiling chicken in white stock for 1¼–1¾ hours, depending on its size and tenderness. The legs and wings should come away in the hand without using a knife. Reduce a bowlful of the cooking liquor and add an equal volume of allemande sauce. Coat the chicken with the sauce and serve piping hot with rice and carrots cooked in stock.

BLANC DE BLANCS White wine made solely from white grapes. Until recently, this term was used mainly in reference to champagne made from the Chardonnay grape. Today the term is often applied to other wines made only from white grapes and is used in many countries both for still and sparkling wines.

BLANC DE CUISSON The French term for a liquor used for cooking white offal and certain vegetables. It is used both to aid whitening and to prevent discoloration of the food. A simple *blanc* is made by blending a little flour with water, then adding more water, with lemon juice or vinegar to acidulate it. Butter is another possible addition, to float on the surface and insulate the vegetables (or other ingredients) from the air. See also *court-bouillon*.

RECIPE

blanc for offal and meat
This stock is used for cooking certain types of offal, such as sheep's tongue and trotters, calf's head and cockscombs and kidneys.

Blend together 25 g (1 oz, ¼ cup) flour and 4 tablespoons water. Add a further 1 litre (1¾ pints, 4⅓ cups) water, mix and strain. Season with 1 teaspoon salt. Add the juice of half a lemon, 2–3 tablespoons chopped raw calf's or ox kidney fat, 1 quartered carrot, a bouquet garni and 1 onion stuck with a clove. Place the ingredients to be cooked in the stock when it is boiling.

BLANC DE NOIRS White wine made from black grapes, the juice being run off before the skin pigments can tint it. The term is used in Champagne for wines made exclusively from Pinot Noir and Pinot Meunier grapes. Wines such as white Zinfandel, which are pale pink in colour, may also be described as Blanc de Noirs.

BLANCHING This term is used for several different operations.
• PAR-BOILING Lightly cooking raw ingredients for varying amounts of time in boiling water with or without salt or vinegar. The ingredients are then refreshed in cold water and drained or simply drained and then cooked normally. Blanching may be carried out for several reasons: to make firmer, to purify, to remove excess salt, to remove bitterness, or to reduce the volume of certain vegetables. In some cases, the ingredients are placed in cold water and brought to the boil: potatoes (before frying); diced bacon (to be browned or sautéed); previously soaked white offal (prior to cooking); poultry; meat and bones (when they are to be cooked in water); and rice (to remove starch and to facilitate cooking, especially in milk). In other cases, the ingredients are plunged directly into boiling water: for example, cabbage and lettuce (before braising). Blanching is equivalent to complete cooking with such vegetables as spinach, very young French (green) beans and fresh peas.
• PART-FRYING Preliminary frying of certain potato preparations such as chips (French fries), so that they partially cook without changing colour. They become crisp and golden when fried for a second time at a higher temperature, just before serving.
• SOAKING BRIEFLY Covering fruit, vegetables or nuts with boiling water for a few seconds to facilitate removal of the skin. Tomatoes, peaches, almonds and pistachios are treated in this way; the skin can then be removed easily without damaging the inside.
• BEATING EGG YOLKS This usage is not common. It refers to the vigorous beating of a mixture of egg yolks and caster (superfine) sugar until the volume increases and it becomes light and fluffy. This method is used particularly for making custard and some sponge cake mixtures.

Blanching tomatoes

Blanching is used to loosen the skin on tomatoes and other fruit, such as peaches, so that they can be peeled easily.

1 *Remove the tough stalk end and core from the tomatoes. Cut a shallow cross in each tomato, on the rounded side opposite the stalk.*

2 *Bring a pan of water to the boil. Turn off the heat and immediately lower the tomatoes into the water. Alternatively, place the tomatoes in a bowl and pour freshly boiled water over them. Leave to stand for 30–60 seconds until the skins loosen and begin to peel back from the slits.*

3 *Drain and peel the tomatoes.*

BLANCMANGE In classic cuisine a much-prized jellied almond cream. One of the oldest desserts, it was said by Grimod de La Reynière to have originated in Languedoc. In the Middle Ages blancmange was both a white meat jelly made of pounded capon or veal and a dessert made from honey and almonds. Although the modern word is used to embrace milk jellies, often based on cornflour (cornstarch), traditional blancmange is made with sweet almonds and a few bitter almonds that are pounded, pressed, sweetened and mixed with a flavouring and gelling agent. The latter was originally grated stag's horn, subsequently replaced by beef or mutton juice, isinglass and finally gelatine. This dessert was often regarded as difficult to make because it had to be white and perfectly smooth.

RECIPES

traditional almond blancmange

Blanch 450 g (1 lb, 3 cups) sweet almonds and about 20 bitter almonds. Leave them to soak in a bowl of cold water, which renders them singularly white. Drain in a sieve and rub in a napkin to remove the skins. Pound in a mortar, moistening them, little by little, with 1½ tablespoons water at a time, to prevent them turning into oil. When they are pounded into a fine paste, put into a bowl and dilute with 1.15 litres (2 pints, 5 cups) filtered water, added a little at a time. Spread a clean napkin over a dish, pour the almond mixture into it and, with two people twisting the napkin, press out all the almond milk. Add to the milk 350 g (12 oz, 1½ cups) sugar and rub through a fine sieve. Strain the liquid through a napkin once again and add 25 g (1 oz plus 4 grains) clarified isinglass a little warmer than tepid – or use 25 g (1 oz, 4 envelopes) gelatine dissolved in warm water. Blend with the blancmange. Pour into a mould and place in a container with crushed ice.

• *Variations* To make rum blancmange, add ½ glass rum to the mixture described above. To make a Maraschino blancmange, add ½ glass Maraschino.

To serve this dessert in small pots, prepare two-thirds of the quantity given in the recipe; you will, however, need less gelling agent, as when the blancmange is served in small pots it should be more delicate than when it is to be turned out.

Blancmanges can be flavoured with lemon, vanilla, coffee, chocolate, pistachio nuts, hazelnuts and strawberries. Whipped cream can also be incorporated.

modern almond blancmange

Blanch and skin 450 g (1 lb, 3 cups) sweet almonds and 20 bitter almonds (or use all sweet almonds). In a blender purée the almonds with 1 litre (1¾ pints, 4⅓ cups) hot water; when the liquid is milky and the almonds are very fine, strain the mixture through muslin (cheesecloth). Sprinkle 25 g (1 oz, 4 envelopes) gelatine over 5 tablespoons almond milk and leave to swell. Heat the remaining almond milk with 100 g (4 oz, ½ cup) sugar, stirring frequently. When the sugar has dissolved and the liquid is almost boiling, stir into the gelatine, and continue stirring until the gelatine has melted. Pour the almond blancmange into a 1.15 litre (2 pint, 5 cup) mould, leave until cold, then refrigerate until firmly set.

BLANQUETTE The French term for ragoût of white meat (veal, lamb or poultry) cooked in white stock or water with aromatic flavourings. Theoretically, the sauce is obtained by making a roux and adding cream and egg yolks. However, the roux is more often than not omitted. Blanquette had a very important place in historical cuisine and became a classic of bourgeois cookery. Blanquettes are also made with fish (monkfish) and vegetables (chard and celery).

RECIPES

preparation of blanquette
Cut the meat or fish into about 5 cm (2 in) cubes. Seal by frying the cubes in butter without browning. Cover with white stock or bouillon, season, quickly bring to the boil and skim. Add 2 onions (one stuck with a clove), 2 medium-sized carrots cut into quarters and a bouquet garni. Simmer gently (15 minutes for monkfish, 45 minutes for poultry, 1¼ hours for veal). Drain the pieces of meat or fish and place in a sauté pan with small onions and mushrooms that have been cooked *au blanc*, in a thin white sauce. Heat gently and, just before serving, bind the sauce with cream and egg yolks and flavour with a little lemon juice. Place in a deep serving dish, sprinkle with parsley and garnish with heart-shaped croûtons fried in butter.

Blanquette is usually served with rice *à la créole* but may also be served with celeriac (celery root), halved celery hearts, carrots, braised parsnips or leeks, cucumber (cut into chunks and blanched for 3 minutes in boiling salted water), braised lettuce or lettuce hearts.

blanquette of lamb à l'ancienne
This is prepared with shoulder, breast and best end (rib chops) of lamb. The stock for 1.8 kg (4 lb) lamb is made with 2 carrots cut into quarters, 2 medium onions (one stuck with a clove) and a vegetable bouquet garni consisting of 2 celery sticks and 2 small leeks (white part only). The garnish is made with 200 g (7 oz) baby onions, 200 g (7 oz) mushrooms (preferably wild) and 8 croûtons fried in butter. To bind the sauce, use 50 g (2 oz, ¼ cup) butter and 50 g (2 oz, ½ cup) plain (all-purpose) flour for the roux, then 3 egg yolks, 150 ml (¼ pint, ⅔ cup) double (heavy) cream, the juice of half a lemon, and a pinch of grated nutmeg.

blanquette of lamb with beans and lamb's feet
Cut the meat from a shoulder of lamb into large cubes. Cover with iced water and keep for 12 hours in the refrigerator, changing the water once or twice. Soak 350 g (12 oz, 2 cups) dried white haricot (navy) beans for about 12 hours in cold water with an onion stuck with a clove, 4–5 whole carrots, a leek and a bouquet garni.

Rub 3 lamb's feet with lemon juice, blanch for 10 minutes in boiling water, refresh with cold water and trim. Make a paste of 1 tablespoon flour, lemon juice and water in a pan. Add the feet, together with 2 carrots, an onion, a bouquet garni and some peppercorns, and simmer for about 2 hours. When the feet are cooked, drain, skin and dice the flesh.

Cook the beans with the flavouring ingredients for about 1½ hours, skimming frequently at first, and add salt after 15 minutes.

Drain the pieces of lamb shoulder. Start cooking them in cold water and add a lamb stock (bouillon) cube, 2 carrots, an onion, a bouquet garni, peppercorns and a little salt. Simmer for about 1½ hours. When cooked, drain the pieces of lamb and arrange them in a large dish. Reduce the cooking liquor to 1 litre (1¾ pints, 4⅓ cups). In a separate pan, mix together 300 ml (½ pint, 1¼ cups) double (heavy) cream, 3 tablespoons Dijon mustard and 4 egg yolks. Pour the sieved reduced cooking liquor on to the mixture and heat gently, stirring constantly. Season with salt and pepper. As soon as the mixture approaches boiling, strain it over the pieces of lamb. Drain the beans and mix them and the diced feet with the blanquette.

blanquette of monkfish
Cut 1.5 kg (3¼ lb) monkfish into 5 cm (2 in) cubes and seal in 40 g (1½ oz, 3 tablespoons) butter without browning. Complete the cooking as in the basic blanquette recipe using 150 g (5 oz, 1 cup) diced carrots, 2 medium onions (one stuck with 2 cloves), 2 leeks, 225 g (8 oz) baby onions and 225 g (8 oz) very small button mushrooms (optional). To bind the sauce, use 2–3 egg yolks, 150 ml (¼ pint, ⅔ cup) double (heavy) cream and the juice of 1 lemon.

blanquette of veal
This may be prepared with shoulder, breast or flank, either on or off the bone. For 1.5 kg (3¼ lb) meat use the same ingredients as for blanquette of lamb *à l'ancienne*. Seal the pieces of veal in butter without allowing them to brown and cook in bouillon.

BLANQUETTE DE LIMOUX A sparkling white AOC wine produced in the department of Aude near the town of Limoux (near Carcassonne). It is made mainly from the Mauzac grape, which used to be called Blanquette because the undersides of the leaves are covered in white down. Increasing amounts of Chardonnay and some Chenin Blanc are also used. The wine is made sparkling by the traditional method. Blanquette Méthode Ancestrale is a sweeter version, made without disgorgement of the sediment. The region also produces still white wines under the Limoux appellation.

BLAYE A fortified town on the right bank of the Gironde, opposite the Médoc. Wine has been produced in this area for longer than in the Médoc, although now its importance is reduced. The most important wines are red, made from Merlot and Cabernet Sauvignon grapes under the Premières

Côtes de Blaye appellation. Some whites are also made from Ugni Blanc and Sauvignon Blanc grapes, sold under the names Côtes de Blaye, Blaye or Blayais.

BLEAK *ablette* A small elongated fish (*Alburnus alburnus*), abundant in European lakes and quiet waterways. Its scales, which are thin and silvery, come away easily. The flesh of the pond bleak is of poor quality, but that of the river variety is fairly good, although full of little bones. The bleak, which is about 15 cm (6 in) long, is invariably served fried. In Sweden the roe of the bleak is a popular type of 'caviar'.

BLENDER An electric device used to liquidize, crush or mix foods. It is used in the preparation of sauces, soups, fruit and vegetable purées, fine force-meats, mousses and mousselines.

There are two kinds of blender: the hand-held type and the goblet type. The former consists of a motor unit with a handle and a column fitted with a blade which turns at about 10,000 r.p.m. It can be operated either in the receptacle used for cooking or preparing the food or in a tall narrow container, useful for making mayonnaise. Sometimes it is equipped with a slower blade, which can be used to mash potatoes and purée chestnuts (otherwise the excessive rotary speed of the mixer would release the starch, making the purée sticky and viscous).

In the goblet type the motor unit serves as a base and the blade turns in the goblet. The goblet has a limited capacity, so only relatively small quantities can be processed at a time. It is particularly useful for puréeing soups and sauces, and is used when a finer texture is needed than that obtained in a food processor. For thicker mixtures, when a blender would need to be stopped and the mixture scraped down on to the blades, a food processor does a better job.

BLENDING *assemblage* The practice of combining several wines of different grape varieties or vintages. In the vineyards of northern Europe where the hours of sunshine are often inadequate, a fruity varietal, usually from a single grape variety, is often used to enhance another wine with its bouquet.

Further south, varieties are sometimes mixed to achieve a better balance between the degree of alcohol, acidity and tannins in the case of red wines; so, for instance, in the Bordeaux one combines Cabernet Sauvignon for its structure, Merlot for its roundness, and Cabernet Franc for its fruit. Wines of different years are also mixed to obtain the best possible result.

BLEU, AU The French term applied to a method of cooking fish (trout, carp or pike) by plunging it either alive or extremely fresh into a court-bouillon containing vinegar, salt and herbs. A trout, for example, is skinned, cleaned, sprinkled with vinegar (which makes the slimy liquid covering its body turn blue) and immediately plunged into boiling court-bouillon.

BLEWIT *bluet* A mushroom family (*Tricholoma*) found in Europe and America, named for the purplish colouring of the cap and stems. The wood blewit is one of the few wild mushrooms traditionally eaten in Britain. Its small creamy-topped caps, about 3–10 cm (1¼–4 in), appear on forest floors (especially under spruce) in rings in late September. It smells of fresh meal or new potatoes, and it has no surface skin, so that it cannot be dried. In Britain blewits are cooked with sage and onions (like tripe). Two further varieties are canned in France.

BLINI A small thick savoury pancake made with a yeast batter that contains both wheat and buckwheat flours, further lightened with whisked egg whites before cooking. Of Russian origin (where *blin* is the singular, *blini* the plural), the batter in the pan forms vertical holes (like crumpets) as the leavening works. Traditionally blinis are made in a pan of 15 cm (6 in) diameter, of which a household would own a set. They are folded round the filling by the eaters, or sold as street food, for example at Maslenitsa, the 'butter festival' like Shrove Tuesday that precedes Lent. As blinis have become popular in Europe and America, the tendency is to make smaller ones, which are then topped. They are served with soured (sour) cream and melted butter as an accompaniment to hors d'oeuvres, caviar, salt herring or smoked fish.

Other batters can be used: rice with a mixture of wheat flour and rice flour; chopped hard-boiled (hard-cooked) eggs can be added to the basic mixture; semolina and milk can be used instead of buckwheat and water; and puréed carrots can be worked into the batter.

In Jewish cuisine a blintz is a small pancake made of a similar batter but with added egg, rolled around a savoury or sweet filling. The batter may be made from other ingredients.

RECIPE

blinis à la française
Blend 20 g (¾ oz, 1½ cakes) fresh (compressed) yeast or 1 teaspoon dried yeast with 50 g (2 oz, ½ cup) sifted strong plain (bread) flour with 500 ml (17 fl oz, 2 cups) warmed milk and leave to rise for 20 minutes in a warm place. Then mix in 250 g (9 oz, 2¼ cups) sifted strong plain flour, 4 egg yolks, 300 ml (½ pint, 1¼ cups) warm milk and a generous pinch of salt. Mix the ingredients well. Leave the batter to rest for a minimum of 1 hour. At the last moment, add 4 stiffly whisked egg whites and 100 ml (4 fl oz, 7 tablespoons) whipped cream. Make small thick pancakes by frying quantities of the batter in butter in a small frying pan, turning them over after a few minutes.

BLONDIR A French culinary term meaning to lightly brown food by frying gently in fat. Onions and shallots may be cooked like this and the term is also applied to flour, which is lightly browned in melted butter to make a white roux.

BLOOD The vital fluid of vertebrates. Pig's blood, an ingredient of black pudding (blood sausage), is that most frequently used in cookery. Fresh blood is either a symbol of vigour, or, for Jews, something to be shunned as unhygienic. It is a tapa in Spain, solidified and cut into squares, and it is considered a fortifying food, especially in cold countries, hence the ancient Swedish *swartsoppa* (black soup), made with goose blood; also the Polish *czernina* (or *tchernina*), eaten with rice, noodles or fried croûtons, to which fresh poultry, game or pig's blood is added before it is thickened with a purée of chicken livers. There are also various French regional dishes using blood.

To use, blood must be stirred with vinegar, salt or alcohol without delay, to prevent deterioration and clotting. Thickening with blood is widely used in traditional European cookery, for *civets* and, in France, dishes described as *en barbouille*. When poultry or game blood is not available, fresh pig's blood can be used instead.

Duck *au sang* is very popular in the cookery of Rouen. A gamey taste is induced by smothering the duck (without blood loss) rather than shooting it. The *à la presse* method of presenting it also means the bloody juices from the partially roast, crushed duck enrich the final sauce.

The French expression *cuit à la goutte de sang* ('cooked to the drop of blood') is applied to young game or poultry which is just cooked; similarly, the term *saignant* (rare; literally, bleeding) corresponds to a specific degree of cooking for grilled (broiled) or roast meat.

BLOOD SAUSAGE See *black pudding*.

BLUEBERRY Fruit of three species of shrub of the *Vaccinium* genus, related to bilberry, and one of the only seven native northern American foods to be cultivated on a large scale. The lowbush blueberry, called *bluets* or *perles bleues* in Quebec, is smaller, sweeter and very flavourful (and still sold as 'wild blueberry'). The fruit of the highbush, cultivated in the northern United States since the 1920s (and now in Australasia), is considerably larger than the bilberry, especially the aromatic Dixie. Blueberries should not be stored in the refrigerator. They make excellent tarts, pies, upside-down desserts, sauce for ice cream and blueberry muffins.

BLUE CHEESE Most distinguished, and with the longest traditions, are the French ewe's-milk Roquefort, English Blue Stilton and Italian Gorgonzola. But several European countries, and America, make blue cheeses from cow's, ewe's and goat's milk (whole or semi-skimmed), using a penicillin fungus, either the Roquefort or Gorgonzola strain, to induce veining. Flavours range from forceful to delicate, textures from hard and crumbly to creamy, while rinds vary from hard to the white Camembert-style flor.

Many soft blue-veined cow's-milk cheeses are produced in France, mostly in the Auvergne, Savoy and Jura. If the cheese is made from other milk, the label must specify 'Bleu de Chèvre' (blue goat's milk cheese) or 'Bleu de Brebis' (blue ewe's-milk cheese).

In France, the name 'Bleu' also applies to white cheeses in which only the crust turns blue and is covered with a natural pale blue down, such as Olivet Bleu and Vendôme Bleu. The most important of the blue-veined cheeses are produced in Auvergne, Bresse, the Causses, Corsica (from ewe's milk), upper Jura, Lagneuille, Landes, Quercy, Sainte-Foy, Sassenage and Thiézac.

■ **Making blue-veined cheese** The precise methods by which blue cheeses are made vary according to type and regional techniques. The curds are cut into cubes, drained and moulded. During coagulation or, more frequently, during moulding, spores of the fungus *Penicillium glaucum* are added. For some cheeses the fungus may be added earlier in the process, for example to the milk at the beginning of production. This fungus gives the blue veining. The moulded curds are then salted and finely perforated to encourage the growth of the spores, and finally matured for varying periods in damp cellars. The best seasons for blue cheese are summer and autumn.

A good blue cheese is ivory- or cream-coloured, firm and springy and rather fatty, with evenly distributed light or dark green-blue veins. The naturally formed crust may be rough or smooth. Blue cheeses are sometimes wrapped in foil.

■ **French blue cheeses**

• Bleu d'Auvergne AOP (Cantal, Puy-de-Dôme, Haute-Loire) A cylindrical cheese, varying in size, with a firm fatty paste (45% fat content), a strong smell and a slightly piquant flavour.

• Bleu de Bresse (Ain) A small cylindrical cheese with a soft smooth paste (50% fat content), a fine smooth blue crust and a medium to strong flavour.

• Bleu des Causses AOC (Rouergue) This cylindrical cheese, formerly made with cow's milk mixed with ewe's milk, has a firm fatty paste (45% fat content), a strong smell and a distinct bouquet.

• Bleu de Corse The name reserved for Corsican white ewe's-milk cheeses that are not taken to Roquefort for maturing and are not, therefore, as superb as the famous cheese matured in the cellars of Aveyron. Cylindrical in shape, it has a fine paste (45% fat content), a good piquant flavour and a strong smell.

• Bleu de Haut Jura AOC (Ain and Jura: Bleus de Gex and Septmoncel) Made from unpasteurized cow's milk. A flat wheel shape with a slightly convex base, the cheese is springy to the touch with heavy veining (45% fat content), slightly bitter and having a full flavour.

• BLEU DE LOUDES Also known as Bleu de Velay. This cylindrical cheese has a firm paste (25–33% fat content) and full flavour; it hardens and becomes brittle.

• BLEU DU QUERCY (Aquitaine) This cylindrical cheese has a firm full paste (45% fat content) and a mild flavour.

• BLEU DE SASSENAGE (Dauphiné) Quoted in 1600 by Olivier de Serres and described in Diderot's *Encyclopaedia*. This cylindrical cheese has a springy odourless paste (45% fat content), a fine light-coloured crust and a pronounced, slightly bitter flavour.

See also *fourme*.

■ **Blue cheese worldwide** Because the penicillin fungus needs a cool temperature to multiply, blue cheese is a northern phenomenon or a mountain product.

Italy, well-known for Gorgonzola, makes a lighter version in Dolcelatte, which is smooth, mild and delicate (the name means 'sweet milk'). Castelmagno is a similar blue-veined cow's-milk cheese, named after a village near Dronero (Piedmont), while the rare Montecenisio (cow's or goat's milk) is produced on the Italian–French border. In the mountains of the Asturias, Spain produces Cabrales and the associated Picos and Gamonedo.

Britain is unusual in that the best-known blue cheeses, blue Stilton (see *Stilton*), blue Cheshire, Shropshire blue and blue Wensleydale are hard. Blue Cheshire and blue Wensleydale are blue-veined versions of white cheeses. Blue Cheshire at one time was a randomly occurring blue version (called Green Fade) of Britain's oldest cheese, made in Shropshire and Cheshire. Subsequently, production became more orderly, with *Pencillium roquefortii* added to the cow's milk before renneting. Only the red Cheshire cheese is blued, to produce a rich cheese (combining Cheshire saltiness with the mould flavour), with a 48% fat content, 22 kg (48 lb) in size. Blue Shropshire is even brighter orange in colour, with vigorous deep blue veining. Blue Wensleydale is a white (barely a hint of cream), close-textured cheese, lighter and more acid than many blues, and with a delicate flavour. As in the Cheshire cheese, the penicillin is added directly to the cow's milk, to make a 48% fat-content cheese, 2.5 kg (5½ lb) in size. Blue Vinney (also called Dorset blue) is a skimmed-milk cheese, very mouldy, with a crumbly texture and thick rind. Other blues are Lanark blue, from Scotland, a ewe's-milk cheese, similar in many ways to Roquefort, with a herbaceous flavour and a tangy finish; and the ewe's-milk Beenleigh blue from Devon. Beenleigh is made from unpasteurized ewe's-milk and it has a fruity but mellow flavour; available September to February. Ireland has a notable blue in Cashel from Tipperary. Made from cow's milk, the young cheese is fresh and crumbly but after 12 weeks or so it takes on a much stronger character.

The Danes have created successful cheeses on French and German models. Danablu (simply 'Danish blue' abroad) is an early 20th-century substitute for Roquefort made from cow's-milk; with a 50–60% fat content, it is 3 kg (6½ lb) in size and very sharp and salty. Blå Castello is a modern, small cow's-milk cheese, 70% fat content, with sharply defined dark blue veins and a downy white surface mould. It is mild and similar to Bavarian blue. Mycella is another Danish cheese, with a slightly creamy texture and greenish-blue veins in bands, in a creamy-yellow paste. Norway has a unique, old cheese in Gamelost, while Finland's cow's-milk Aura and the Swedish cow's-milk Adelost are both modelled on Roquefort.

The German Edelpilzkïse is literally 'glorious mould cheese'. With very dark blue, vertical veins in a pale ivory paste, 45% fat content and 2–5 kg (4–11 lb) in size, it may be round or loaf-shaped. The modern Bavarian blue, with a pale-cream paste with blue splodges (rather than veins), has a 70% fat content because additional cream is added to the cow's milk. The rind is white, with flor of the Camembert type, and the cheese weighs 1 kg (2¼ lb). Other blues worth mentioning are the Czech Niva, and the Israeli Galil, a strongish ewe's-milk cheese, green-veined, in the Roquefort style.

Australia makes a Gorgonzola-style cheese, while America has the renowned Maytag Blue Cheese from Iowa.

■ **Serving blue cheese** Blue cheeses are served at the end of a meal, preferably alone or as the last course, so that their often distinct flavour can be savoured with full-bodied aromatic red wines (for strong cheeses) or with more fruity red wines (for more mellow cheeses). In France they may also be served with sweet dessert wines, such as Sauternes. They are often used for canapés (sometimes mixed with butter or chopped nuts, or with celery) and may also be used in the preparation of mixed salads, regional soups and fondues. They are used to enliven such meat dishes as hamburgers and beef olives or as a sauce for game, and are often used in soufflés and quiches. Avoid refrigeration.

BOARD Traditionally a wooden slab, usually 4–6 cm (1½–2½ in) thick (usually beech), rectangular, round or oval in shape. Various types of plastic boards are now used. Being dishwasher-safe and non-absorbent, plastic boards are often more hygenic than wooden ones. Toughened glass and laminated boards are available for lighter use. The kitchen board is used for slicing, chopping or cutting up meat, fish, vegetables and bread. Boards designed specially for carving meat or poultry have a wide groove around the perimeter for catching the juice. Bread boards are sometimes made of horizontal laths fitted to a frame with a tray beneath to prevent crumbs from scattering. Pastry boards, used for kneading and rolling out pastry dough, must be smooth and big enough to hold the rolled-out dough.

Boards are also used for pressing – fitting into the tops of tins (pans) or terrines – and occasionally for cooking. An oiled board, put into a cold oven with a fish upon it, the heat then raised, is used for 'planked' fish (see *shad*).

BOCKWURST A generic German name for all sausages that are very finely ground. These include frankfurters, the larger *weiners* and *knackwurst*, similar dumpy links of pork with beef, flavoured with garlic and cumin. They are poached or fried.

BOCUSE, PAUL French cook (born Collonges-au-Mont-d'Or, 1926). He comes from a line of restaurateurs and cooks established on the banks of the Saône since 1765. Michel Bocuse opened a café in an old Collonges mill which was taken over by his son Philibert. Philibert's son Nicolas bought the nearby Hôtel de l'Abbaye and ran it with his three sons, Jean-Noël, Nicolas and Georges. Georges bought the Hôtel-restaurant du Pont, also in Collonges.

Georges's son, Paul, was first apprenticed to Fernand Point and then to Lucas-Carton and Lapérousse in Paris. He began working in 1942 in a restaurant in Lyon and in 1959 saved the small family restaurant in Collonges from ruin and made it into a gastronomic Mecca. Attached to the tradition and cuisine of Lyon, he renewed the great classics without entering into the excesses of nouvelle cuisine. His family nickname was *primat des gueules* ('primate of the palate'). With his forceful personality, he became the ambassador of French gastronomy throughout the world, giving conferences and cookery classes, especially in Japan. He published *La Cuisine du marché* in 1980 and *Bocuse dans votre cuisine* in 1982. His creations include black truffle soup, lobster Meursault and a chocolate gâteau that is a speciality.

BOHÉMIENNE, À LA Various dishes have been named after Balfe's successful comic opera, *La Bohémienne* (1869). These include a soft-boiled (soft cooked) egg dish, a salpicon and a sauce served with cold dishes, which uses a cold béchamel base to bind an emulsion of egg yolks and oil flavoured with tarragon vinegar.

The ingredients of sautéed chicken *à la bohémienne* – garlic, fennel, red or green (bell) peppers and tomato – are similar to those of a Provençal dish called *boumanie*, which is a kind of ratatouille. The dish is served with plain rice. Rice with crushed tomato and fried onion rings are also ingredients in noisette of lamb *à la bohémienne*.

RECIPES

salpicon à la bohémienne
Dice some foie gras and truffles. Reduce some Madeira sauce, add a little essence of truffle and use the sauce to bind the salpicon of foie gras and truffles. Diced onions cooked in butter and seasoned with paprika may also be added. This salpicon may be used as a filling for vol-au-vents, small flans, poached eggs and tartlets.

sautéed chicken à la bohémienne
Season a medium-sized chicken with paprika and sauté in a flameproof casserole or large heavy saucepan until brown. Cover and continue cooking very slowly either on top of the stove or in a preheated oven at 180°C (350°F, gas 4). Cut 4 red or green (bell) peppers into thick strips. Peel 2 tomatoes and slice thickly. Finely dice an onion and then blanch it. Prepare 1 tablespoon chopped fennel. Add all these ingredients, together with a pinch of crushed garlic, to the pan when the chicken is half-cooked (after about 20 minutes). At the end of the cooking time, when the chicken is tender, deglaze the casserole with 100 ml (4 fl oz, 7 tablespoons) white wine. Add 60 ml (2 fl oz, ¼ cup) thickened veal stock or well-reduced bouillon. Finally, add a dash of lemon juice. Pour the sauce over the chicken and serve with saffron rice.

BOIL To bring a liquid (such as water or stock) to boiling point and maintain it at that temperature, thereby cooking ingredients that are placed in it. Boiling occurs at a fixed temperature, which for water is 100°C (212°F). If a recipe contains an instruction to 'boil rapidly', this means that the ingredients should be agitated to prevent them from sticking to each other or to the bottom of the pan. In most cases, it is sufficient for the liquid to simmer. Liquids are also boiled to reduce them.

Oil and other fats used for frying have boiling points of up to 200°C (400°F). The boiling point of sugar syrup varies according to the concentration, which increases as the water evaporates.

BOILED BEEF See *beef*.

BOLETUS The Latin name of a wild mushroom family easily recognized by the spore-bearing tubes (rather than gills) on the undersurface of its cap. They are prized in most European countries, as far as Russia, but also grow in North America and most other parts of the world. There are various edible species (and some poisonous ones), one of the best known being the cep, *Boletus edulis*.

BOLIVIA The country where the potato originated (with Peru), Bolivia boasts some three hundred varieties. *Chuños*, potatoes which have been frozen, then dried, are a favourite potato product – they are very light and are soaked before being cooked. Besides a fondness for chillies, spicy soups and fried food, Bolivia has another interesting speciality: the *conejo estirado*, a rabbit which is stretched as much as possible, making its flesh extremely tender and delicate.

BOLLITO MISTO A celebrated Italian stew originating in Piedmont. The name of the dish literally means 'boiled mixed' and its composition can vary according to region, availability of ingredients and family traditions. As a general rule, it contains rump of beef, knuckle of veal and chicken (stuffed or plain), often with a pork sausage or a *zampone* (stuffed pig's foot). Some recipes also include pig's trotters, ox tongue or rolled head of veal. The meat is cooked in stock with onions, carrots and celery. The accompanying vegetables, such as carrots, turnips and celeriac (celery root), are then cooked in a little of the strained stock. It is customary to serve *bollito misto* with gherkins, capers, small pickled onions, green salad and Cremona mustard – a sweet-and-sour fruit mustard similar to chutney.

RECIPE

bollito misto
Put 500 g (18 oz) flank of beef, 500 g (18 oz) oxtail and 500 g (18 oz) blade-bone of beef (or silverside) in a braising pan and fill with water. Bring to the boil, skimming often. Add 2 onions, 3 celery sticks, 3 peeled garlic cloves, 5 sprigs flat-leaved parsley, 1 sprig rosemary, 10 peppercorns and a little sea salt. Cover and cook for 1½ hours. Remove the pieces of meat gradually as and when they become tender. Meanwhile cook 1 split calf's head and 1 split calf's foot in water flavoured with 1 onion and 1 celery stick. In another braising pan, cook 1 calf's tongue, skin it very carefully and set aside. Prick a *cotechino* (Italian sausage) and cook it in a little stock. Arrange the meats on a serving dish and serve very hot, accompanied by the traditional sauces (green, pink and *pearà* – see *sauce*), spring onions (scallions), Verona mustard (a type of mustard with apple purée) and Cremona mustard (made from several kinds of fruit, cooked in a very hot mustard syrup).

BOLOGNAISE, À LA
The French term for several dishes inspired by Italian cookery, especially that of Bologna, that are served with a thick sauce based on beef and vegetables, particularly tomato, popularly associated with pasta. In Italy this becomes *alla bolognese* and the sauce is known as *ragù* (a corruption of the French word *ragoût*). It is richer than the French-style sauce, as it contains chopped ham, various vegetables, beef, lean pork, chicken livers and white wine.

RECIPES

bolognese sauce
Chop 4 celery sticks and 5 large onions. Add 4 sage leaves and 2 sprigs rosemary to a traditional bouquet garni. Coarsely chop 500 g (18 oz) braising steak (chuck or blade beef or flank). Peel and crush about 10 large tomatoes and 4–5 garlic cloves. Heat 5 tablespoons olive oil in a heavy-based saucepan. Brown the meat and then the onion, celery and garlic in the olive oil. Add the tomatoes and cook for about 10 minutes. Lastly, add the bouquet garni, 350 ml (12 fl oz, 1½ cups) beef stock, 250 ml (8 fl oz, 1 cup) red wine, salt and pepper. Cover and cook very gently for at least 2 hours, adding a little water from time to time. Adjust the seasoning.

Bolognese sauce may be prepared in large quantities. The length of the cooking time means that it can be kept for several days in the refrigerator, and several months in the freezer. It is served with spaghetti and macaroni, and in gratin dishes and lasagne.

timbale of pasta with bolognese sauce
Cook and drain some short pasta (such as macaroni). Add some mushrooms lightly fried in butter with chopped garlic, shallots and parsley, some diced ham (turned in hot butter to avoid drying out) and (optional) a little grated white truffle. Pack these ingredients firmly into a timbale mould, then turn out. Coat the timbale with a light bolognese sauce and reheat it in the oven. Serve with grated Parmesan cheese, or sprinkle with grated Parmesan and a little melted butter and brown in the oven before serving.

BOMBE GLACÉE
A frozen dessert made from a bombe mixture, often enriched with various ingredients, and frozen in a mould. The dessert was named after the spherical mould in which it used to be made. Nowadays, cylindrical moulds with rounded tops are used.

Traditionally, bombe moulds are filled with two different mixtures. The bottom and sides of the mould are lined with a layer of plain ice cream, a fruit ice or a sorbet; the inside is filled with the chosen bombe mixture. The mould is then hermetically sealed, clamped and frozen. To serve, the bombe is turned out on to a folded napkin placed on the serving dish. The bombe may be decorated in a number of ways depending on its ingredients: crystallized (candied) fruit or violets, marrons glacés, pistachios, fruit macerated in liqueur or whipped cream.

RECIPES

lining the mould with ice cream
Chill the mould in the refrigerator for about 20 minutes. At the same time soften the ice cream or water ice chosen to line the mould. Spread it roughly on the bottom and sides of the mould with a plastic or stainless steel spatula. Place the mould in the freezer for about 15 minutes to harden and then smooth the ice with the spatula. Replace the mould in the freezer for a further hour before filling with the bombe mixture, unless the mixture is a parfait, in which case pour it down the sides of the lined mould until filled and place in the freezer for 5–6 hours.

bombe mixture
In traditional cuisine, the mixture is made with 32 egg yolks per 1 litre (1¾ pints, 4⅓ cups) syrup (density: 1.285, see *sugar*). Pour the syrup and egg yolks into a saucepan and place the pan in a bain marie over a moderate heat. Whisk vigorously until the mixture is thick and creamy, then press it through a very fine sieve. Whisk again, away from the heat, until completely cold: by this stage it

Lining a bombe mould

1 *Soften the ice cream, if necessary, to a stiff spreading consistency and spread it around the base and sides of the chilled mould, working it back and forth slightly to remove any air bubbles. Ensure that the layer is evenly thick and build it up around the top edge.*

2 *Return the lined mould to the freezer, if necessary, to firm up the top edge of the ice cream. Use a palette knife to trim and level off the top of the ice cream.*

should be light, fluffy and white. Finally add an equal volume of whipped cream and the chosen flavouring.

Bombes are often made with a far lighter mixture. For example, a 1 litre (1¾ pint, 4⅓ cup) bombe Hawaii can be made using 500 ml (17 fl oz, 2 cups) pineapple sorbet to line the mould and 500 ml (17 fl oz, 2 cups) kirsch parfait made with 2 egg yolks, about 60 ml (2 fl oz, ¼ cup) syrup (density: 1.2407) and about 250 ml (8 fl oz, 1 cup) whipped cream mixed with 1½ teaspoons kirsch.

bombe Aïda
Line the mould with tangerine ice cream and fill with vanilla bombe mixture flavoured with kirsch.

bombe Alhambra
Line the mould with vanilla ice cream and fill with strawberry bombe mixture (a combination of strawberry purée, Italian meringue and whipped cream). Turn out the bombe and surround with large strawberries macerated in kirsch.

bombe archiduc
Line the mould with strawberry ice cream and fill with praline bombe mixture.

bombe chateaubriand
Line the mould with apricot ice cream and fill with vanilla bombe mixture mixed with crystallized (candied) apricots macerated in kirsch.

bombe diplomate
Line the mould with vanilla ice cream and fill with maraschino bombe mixture mixed with diced crystallized (candied) fruit macerated in maraschino.

bombe Doria
Line the mould with pistachio ice cream and fill with vanilla bombe mixture mixed with pieces of marrons glacés macerated in rum.

bombe duchesse
Line the mould with pineapple ice cream and fill with pear bombe mixture.

bombe Grimaldi
Line the mould with vanilla ice cream and fill with kümmel-flavoured bombe mixture. Decorate with crystallized (candied) violets and halved pistachio nuts.

bombe Monselet
Line the mould with tangerine ice cream and fill with port-flavoured bombe mixture mixed with chopped crystallized (candied) orange peel that has been macerated in brandy.

BONDON DE NEUFCHÂTEL A Normandy cheese made from cow's milk (45% fat content), soft with a red-tinged crust. Originating from the most important market town in the Bray region, it is cylindrical in shape, 4–6 cm (1½–2½ in) in diameter and 6–8 cm (2½–3 in) high, with a fruity yet salty flavour.

BONE The solid element in the carcass of a vertebrate animal. Bones are made of cartilage impregnated with calcium salts. When cooked in a boiling liquid they yield gelatine, essential for the smoothness and palatability of certain cooking stocks; veal bones are particularly valuable for this purpose. Crushed bones, which may be browned in the oven, are usually cooked with aromatic vegetables and herbs to make stock for sauces.

Some bones, particularly those from beef and veal, contain marrow. The pot-au-feu may include thick slices of shin (shank) bone (fore or hind leg) complete with marrow. Osso bucco, a traditional Italian dish, is prepared with slices of unboned veal knuckle.

Meat cooked on the bone is generally preferred to that off the bone: the surface remains sealed in a natural way, while the bone is a good conductor of heat. Rib of beef on the bone is a prime cut; it can be grilled (broiled) as it is or butchered to make the famous T-bone steak of American barbecues. York ham cooked on the bone should also be mentioned – it is delicious. Lamb chops and cutlets (rib lamb chops), and rack of lamb (from which the latter are cut) all may need some little preparation. For example, trimming the fat towards the end of the bone (and between them, too, in the case of rack), and shortening the bone itself. To serve, the bone tip can be garnished with a paper collar or frill.

BONE MARROW A soft fatty substance in the cavities of long bones. In cooking, beef marrow is usually used and it is an important feature in the Italian osso bucco, a stew of veal shin cooked on the bone. Slices of gently poached beef marrow are served with grilled (broiled) or roast beef. Marrow is also used as a filling for artichoke hearts, cardoons, omelettes, bouchées and croûtes and it may be included in salpicons, garnishes and soups, while the marrow from one bone will flavour a risotto. It is often used to prepare sauces for grilled meat or fish. A marrow bone is a favourite in the French stockpot and often cooked with boiled rolled beef. The bone is then served with the meat and the marrow may be extracted with a teaspoon. Bone marrow may also be bought in jelly form. *Amourette* is the French name for spinal marrow.

RECIPES

bone-marrow canapés
Wrap some fresh or frozen bone marrow in a small piece of muslin (cheesecloth), plunge it into boiling salted beef stock and poach gently without boiling (about 5 minutes for fresh marrow and 7–8 minutes for frozen marrow). Lightly toast some small slices of bread. Unwrap the marrow, drain it carefully and cut half of it into small dice and the other half into rounds. Garnish each canapé with diced marrow and place a round of marrow on top. Season with salt and pepper, sprinkle with finely chopped parsley and serve immediately, as marrow loses its creamy texture very quickly.

bone-marrow sauce
Put 3 finely chopped shallots in a saucepan. Add 350 ml (12 fl oz, 1½ cups) white wine, season with salt and pepper and reduce by half. Stir in 2 tablespoons thickened veal stock or well-reduced meat sauce. Poach 75 g (3 oz) bone marrow and cut into small dice. Remove the sauce from the heat and whisk in 100 g (4 oz, ½ cup) butter cut into tiny pieces, then add 1 tablespoon lemon juice and the diced bone marrow. Sprinkle with chopped parsley.

BONING The removal of bones from meat, poultry, fish or game. Boning raw meat or poultry is carried out with a special boning knife and requires skill to avoid damaging the meat.

The same term is used for the removal of the backbone of a fish that is subsequently stuffed and reshaped before cooking.

BONITO Any of several marine migratory fishes (family *Scombridae*) that are related to, but smaller than, the tuna and live in shoals in warm seas.

The Atlantic bonito (*pélamide*), with a steely blue back with slanting dark blue stripes, ranges as far north as Cape Cod, and is fished in the Mediterranean. The light-coloured flesh is oily and prepared in the same way as tuna, being popular in northern Spain. It is often canned.

Two other varieties range the Pacific ocean. The dark, dried flesh of the Oriental bonito plays a major role in Japanese cuisine. Sold in blocks called *katsuobushi*, or shaved to make tissue-thin, buff-coloured bonito flakes, it is the major flavouring of all *dashi* (stock) and broths, and is used for sauces, often teamed with *kombu* (kelp). A version with rosy-pink threads is also used for garnishing (particularly with bean curd).

BONNE FEMME The French term, meaning 'good wife', applied to dishes that are prepared in a simple, family or rustic manner, similar to dishes cooked *à la ménagère* and *à la paysanne*. Such dishes are often served in the container in which they are cooked (a pan, casserole or even a plate).

RECIPES

brill bonne femme
Prepare and clean a brill. Butter a dish and sprinkle with chopped shallot and parsley. Add 250 g (9 oz, 3 cups) chopped button mushrooms. Place the brill in the dish and add 7 tablespoons dry white wine and the same quantity of fish stock. Dot with very small knobs of butter. Cook in a preheated oven at 220°C (425°F, gas 7) for 15–20 minutes, basting the brill two or three times. Towards the end of cooking, cover with foil to prevent the fish from drying out. The same method may be used for sole and whiting.

chicken bonne femme
Trim a chicken weighing 1.8–2 kg (4–4½ lb), season with salt and pepper, then truss. Brown the chicken slowly on all sides in butter in a flameproof casserole or heavy based saucepan. Blanch 100 g (4 oz, ⅔ cup) finely diced unsmoked streaky (slab) bacon. Add the diced bacon and 20 small onions to the casserole. Cover and cook gently for 15 minutes. Add 500 g (18 oz) potato balls or small new potatoes and continue cooking slowly, basting the chicken from time to time, until tender. Garnish with the cooked vegetables and serve.

green beans bonne femme
Partially cook 1 kg (2¼ lb) green beans in salted water. Blanch 250 g (9 oz, 1½ cups) diced unsmoked streaky (slab) bacon. Brown the blanched bacon in a frying pan, then add the drained beans and 150 ml (¼ pint, ⅔ cup) rich meat stock. Adjust the seasoning, cover and cook until the beans are tender. Dot with butter and sprinkle with chopped parsley before serving.

vegetable soup bonne femme
Cook 100 g (4 oz) finely sliced leeks (white part only) in butter. Add 1.5 litres (2¾ pints, 6½ cups) white consommé or chicken broth and 250 g (9 oz) sliced potatoes. Season with salt and simmer until the potatoes are soft. Just before serving add 50 g (2 oz, ¼ cup) butter and some chervil. Serve with thin slices of French bread that have been dried in the oven.

BONNEFONS, NICOLAS DE A 17th-century French writer who was a valet in the court of Louis XIV. He published a work in 1654 (which was reprinted several times until 1741) called *Les Délices de la campagne*. This book marks a turning point in the history of French culinary art which, at that time, was still influenced by the precepts of the Middle Ages, with its emphasis on decoration and excessive use of spices, which detracted from the nature of the food.

The work was divided into three parts: 'Drinks, bread and wine' (this section was dedicated to the ladies of Paris); 'Vegetables, fruit, eggs and milk' (dedicated to the Capuchin monks famous for their skill as gardeners); and 'Meat, poultry and fish' (with a foreword for head waiters and, as a supplement, instructions for feasts). Bonnefons recommended cleanliness in the preparation of dishes, diversity of menus and, above all, simplicity: 'Let a cabbage soup be entirely cabbage ... and may what I say about soup be a law applied to everything that is eaten.' He quoted recipes of the era, such as a special health soup (with four meats) and *poupelin* (a rich pastry cake). He also advocated the use of some well-matched flavours, such as mackerel with green fennel.

BONNEFOY A Parisian restaurant of the 1850s that is still associated with a type of bordelaise sauce, served with certain fish and fillets of fish prepared *à la meunière*. The sauce contains shallots reduced in white wine but not strained.

BONNES-MARES A *grand cru* vineyard of just 13 hectares (32 acres) in the Burgundy village of Chambolle-Musigny. It overlaps slightly into the neighbouring village of Morey-St Denis. It produces exceptional quality wines which age well and after a few years attain a remarkable smoothness and fine bouquet.

BONNEZEAUX A sweet AOC white wine, produced in Anjou from the Chenin Blanc (or Pineau de la Loire) grape in a very small wine-growing region on a steep hillside on the right bank of the Layon (a tributary of the Loire). This aromatic Coteaux-du-Layon, which ages extremely well, rivals the best sweet wines of south-western France.

BONTEMPS A sauce made with cider and mustard, served with grilled (broiled) meat and poultry.

RECIPE

bontemps sauce
Cook 1 tablespoon chopped onion in butter in a saucepan. Add salt, a pinch of paprika and 200 ml (7 fl oz, ¾ cup) cider. Reduce by two-thirds. Add 200 ml (7 fl oz, ¾ cup) meat-based velouté* and bring to the boil. Remove from the heat and add 40 g (1½ oz, 3 tablespoons) butter and 1 generous tablespoon white mustard. Sieve before serving.

BOOPS *bogue* A spindle-shaped fish (family *Sparidae*) abundant in the Mediterranean and the Bay of Biscay. It is 20–30 cm (8–12 in) long with spines along its back. It is mostly used in fish soups.

BORAGE A herbaceous perennial plant of the Mediterranean and central and northern Europe with five-petalled blue flowers and a peaked central black boss. It is used in cooking and in herbal remedies. The herb tea made from borage is used as a diaphoretic (it causes sweating), its name being derived from the Arabic *abamu 'amaraq*, meaning literally 'father of sweat'.

La Quintinie describes borage as a soup vegetable but the stems are hairy and it is tedious to wash. The young leaves can be used to flavour salads or sweet fritters and the larger leaves to fill pies or pasta. They have a slight flavour of cucumber. The Germans use borage leaves in stews and stock and the Spanish eat them with potatoes and oil. There are Oriental recipes in which they are stuffed like vine leaves. The flowers are often used to garnish gin drinks; they make fritters or may be crystallized (candied) to decorate pastries.

BORD-DE-PLAT A small chef's utensil used to protect the border of a dish on which sauce is being served.

BORDELAIS AND THE LANDES See *page 134*.

BORDELAISE, À LA The name given to a wide range of dishes (eggs, fish, shellfish, kidneys and steak) which use such ingredients as bone marrow, shallots and – significantly – wine (white for fish and white meat and red for red meat). This is the adjective of Bordeaux, a principal wine region.

RECIPES

bordelaise sauce
(From a recipe by Carême) Place in a saucepan 2 garlic cloves, a pinch of tarragon, the seeded flesh of a lemon, a small bay leaf, 2 cloves, a glass of Sauternes and 2 teaspoons Provençal olive oil. Simmer gently. Skim off all the fat from the mixture and mix in enough espagnole sauce to provide sauce for an entrée and 3–4 tablespoons light veal stock. Reduce the mixture by boiling down and add half a glass of Sauternes while still simmering. Strain the

Bordelais and The Landes

Situated in the south-west of France, Bordelais and neighbouring Landes share some culinary traditions and celebrate their own specialities. The city of Bordeaux is a centre for the wine trade and traditionally dominates the gastronomy of the region, rivalling Lyon for cuisine and Burgundy for wine. Bordelais is probably better known internationally for its wine than for its food. Indeed, wine is used to the full locally, both in the preparation of food and as an accompaniment to dishes.

■ **Rich natural resources** The cooking benefits from the range of locally sourced ingredients as well as wines. The proximity of the sea provides many specialities, notably Arachon oysters, but also mussels, shrimps, sardines, gilt-head bream (*daurade*) and bonito from the Landes coast. Traditionally, small soles were

The cannele – *literally fluted – is a little cake typical of the pâtisserie of the Bordelais. The crisp crust encloses a soft, vanilla-flavoured centre.*

curiously named 'lawyers' tongues'. The strange, eel-like lamprey is enjoyed here, cooked *à la bordelaise*, with vegetables and a little ham in red wine; the sauce is enriched with the blood of the lamprey just before serving. Trout is outstanding among the freshwater fish – the Landes has developed as one of the important French areas for trout farming.

Local goose and duck provide fine fillets of breast meat, foie gras and cooking fat, and they are used to make excellent confits. The lamb of Pauillac and the beef of Hazas and Chaslosse are highly regarded. Landes is known for its excellent hams and charcuterie.

The forests of the Landes shelter an abundance of ceps that are widely appreciated for simple or complex dishes and the pine trees yield a generous harvest of pine nuts.

■ **Inspired culinary combinations** While it is hardly surprising that ceps, ham and the use of goose fat are typical of dishes prepared *à la landaise*, many traditional dishes from these regions reflect innovation in the use of local foods. For example, local oysters could be served with little crepinettes (a type of flat sausage or faggot) or even with pâté, and walnut leaves may

provide a bed on which to serve grilled (broiled) shad or stuffed fish. Shallots are used to flavour many recipes – with fish and seafood, snails, meat, poultry or grame. Snails *à la Caudéran* (a suburb of Bordeaux), simmered in white wine flavoured with shallots, garlic and a little ham, are traditonally eaten during Lent.

Tourin is another speciality – a veritable institution during harvest time. This garlic-flavoured onion soup enriched with egg yolks is poured over slices of day-old good country bread. Traditionally, when all the bread was eaten a glass of red wine was poured into the bowl to enrich the last of the liquor.

■ **Sweet finesse** Bordeaux may not be renowned for its cheese but the pâtisserie of this entire region is prepared with great finesse. There are macaroons from St Émilion or dacquoise – a layered almond meringue gâteau filled with crème au beurre – from Landes. The bordelais *tourtillon* is a classic Twelfth-Night cake, made with crowns of rich yeasted dough decorated with citron peel.

BORDEAUX WINE Already known in the Gallo-Roman period and praised by Roman writers, Bordeaux wines became popular in England during the period 1154–1453, when the province of Aquitaine belonged to the English. Since then they have found new admirers and have been world-famous since the 19th century.

The vine-growing area lies on both sides of the Gironde in the department of the same name. It includes several wine regions, whose names are familiar to lovers of good wine: Médoc on the left bank of the Gironde; Graves and Sauternes on the left bank of the Garonne; Entre-Deux-Mers between the rivers Garonne and Dordogne; and St Émilion, Pomerol, Fronsac, Bourg and Blaye, on the right bank of the Dordogne and the Gironde. This vast vine-growing area extends mainly over stony undulations and the banks of rivulets that seem ill-suited to vine-growing. But it

produces a huge range of wines, distinguished by their overall regions, their specific areas and their parishes. Each is subject to controls relating to area and quality.

• GENERAL APPELLATIONS 'Bordeaux' and 'Bordeaux Supérieur' are good everyday red or white wines which do not have their individual appellations or are declassified wines whose owners did not consider a particular vintage good enough for marketing under the estate's name. There are also Bordeaux rosé wines, some sparkling Bordeaux (usually white, produced by the champagne method) and 'Bordeaux clairet', which is not a rosé, but a light red wine fermented for a short period. It should be drunk young.

• REGIONAL APPELLATIONS These correspond to the main areas of production: Médoc and Haut-Médoc (red); Graves (red and white); the Entre-Deux-Mers (white) and so on. Each of these is governed by the regulations controlling the regional AOC.

• COMMUNE OR PARISH APPELLATIONS These are the AOCs within the generic areas, also governed by the AOCs, but being

somewhat stricter: thus, Sauternes, Barsac (white) and, in the Médoc, Pauillac, Margaux, St Estèphe, St Julien, and the subdivided categories of St Émilion and others.

• CLASSIFIED GROWTHS The most famous classification is that of 1855, drawn up by the brokers of Bordeaux for the Paris Exhibition, although there had been earlier classifications of the better-known wines. The 1855 classification was based on the prices that the wines of certain estates were likely to fetch at the Paris Exhibition in that

The Château d'Yquem, dating back to the Renaissance and modified in the 18th century, is the home of the most prestigious premier grand cru Sauternes wine.

year; consequently, some estates that were undergoing a bad period, or that had been subdivided, were either not categorized or were placed in a lower category than would now be thought appropriate in terms of quality. The 1855 classification ▶

Pruning vines in Médoc.

◄includes many of the famous growths of the Médoc and one red Graves (Haut Brion). Since then, the main regions of Bordeaux have been classified (with the exception of Pomerol), in some instances the outstanding estate wine being described as *grand cru*, above *premier cru*. The *crus*

bourgeois have likewise been arranged in classified categories. Attempts to recategorize the Médoc estates have failed. While it is true to say that the term 'classified growth' in this context conveys the significance of a wine with a pedigree and reputation, it is misleading to suppose that the

five categories of the 1855 classification refer to absolute quality: some wines in the fifth, fourth, third and second growth sections might nowadays be rated higher, although the first growths (Lafite, Latour, Margaux, Haut Brion and, since 1973, Mouton) are usually outstanding.

The wine-producing areas of Bordeaux

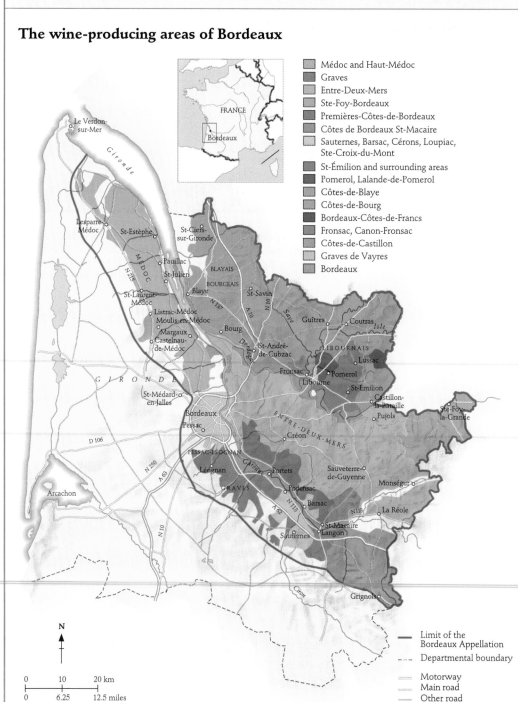

Médoc and Haut-Médoc

Graves

Entre-Deux-Mers

Ste-Foy-Bordeaux

Premières-Côtes-de-Bordeaux

Côtes de Bordeaux St-Macaire

Sauternes, Barsac, Cérons, Loupiac, Ste-Croix-du-Mont

St-Émilion and surrounding areas

Pomerol, Lalande-de-Pomerol

Côtes-de-Blaye

Côtes-de-Bourg

Bordeaux-Côtes-de-Francs

Fronsac, Canon-Fronsac

Côtes-de-Castillon

Graves de Vayres

Bordeaux

Limit of the Bordeaux Appellation

Departmental boundary

Motorway

Main road

Other road

0   10   20 km

0   6.25   12.5 miles

sauce when it is the right consistency. Just before serving add a little butter and the juice of half a lemon.

bordelaise sauce for grilled meat (1)

Boil down by two-thirds 200 ml (7 fl oz, ¾ cup) red wine with 1 tablespoon chopped shallot, a sprig of thyme, a piece of bay leaf and a pinch of salt. Pour in 200 ml (7 fl oz, ¾ cup) demi-glace* sauce. Boil down by one-third, then remove from the heat, add 25 g (1 oz, 2 tablespoons) butter and strain. Add 25 g (1 oz) beef marrow cut in dice, poached and drained, and 1 teaspoon chopped parsley.

Grilled (broiled) meats served with bordelaise sauce are usually garnished with slices of poached, drained beef marrow.

bordelaise sauce for grilled meat (2)

Prepare some concentrated red wine as in the preceding recipe, but boil it down only by half. Thicken with 40 g (1½ oz, 3 tablespoons) beurre manié. Boil for a few moments. Add meat glaze or meat extract equal in bulk to a walnut. Finish as in the preceding recipe.

calf's liver à la bordelaise

Quickly fry slices of Bayonne ham in butter. Season slices of calf's liver with salt and pepper, coat with flour and fry in butter. Arrange on the serving dish, alternating with slices of the ham. Coat with bordelaise sauce.

fillets of sole à la bordelaise

Prepare some button mushrooms and baby (pearl) onions and cook in butter. Butter a small fish kettle or flameproof casserole and sprinkle the bottom with finely chopped onions and carrots. Season the fillets of sole with salt and pepper and arrange in the fish kettle. Add a bouquet garni and 175–350 ml (6–12 fl oz, ¾–1½ cups) white Bordeaux wine, according to the size of the container. Poach the fillets for 6–7 minutes, then drain, retaining the liquor. Arrange the fillets on the serving dish surrounded by the mushrooms and baby onions; cover and keep warm. Add 2 tablespoons demi-glace* or fish stock to the cooking liquor and reduce by half. Add a knob of butter, sieve and pour over the fillets.

sautéed calf's kidney à la bordelaise

Poach 2 tablespoons diced beef marrow in salt water, drain and keep warm. Trim the calf's kidney, slice thinly, season with salt and pepper, and fry briskly in very hot butter, turning the pieces over as they cook. Drain, retaining the juice, and keep the kidney warm. Deglaze the frying pan with 100 ml (4 fl oz, ½ cup) white wine; add 1 tablespoon finely chopped shallots and boil off the liquid. Then add 250 ml (8 fl oz, 1 cup) veal stock and the juice from the kidney, and reduce by half. Thicken with a little arrowroot and adjust the seasoning. Replace the kidney in the sauce, add the beef marrow and stir. Arrange in a mound and sprinkle with chopped parsley.

tournedos (filet mignons) à la bordelaise

Poach some slices of bone marrow in salt water, drain and keep warm. Grill the steaks, over very hot charcoal (if possible use dry vine prunings). Place a slice of bone marrow on each steak and sprinkle with chopped parsley. Serve with bordelaise sauce.

BORDER A mixture that is shaped, moulded or cut to form a border or ring around the edge of a dish, either for decorative effect or to hold other ingredients in the centre. Special round, plain or ridged moulds or savarin moulds are usually used to shape the border. The ingredients of the ring depend on whether the dish is hot or cold, sweet or savoury.

- For HOT DISHES Rice, semolina, quenelle mixture, duchess potatoes.
- For COLD DISHES Hard-boiled (hard-cooked) eggs, aspic jelly (cut into triangles, crescents or cubes), sliced tomatoes, oranges or lemons.
- For DESSERTS Moulded creams, creamed rice, semolina.

RECIPES

Savoury Rings

egg ring à la princesse

Prepare in the same way as egg ring Brillat-Savarin, but flavour the eggs with diced truffle and asparagus tips. The latter may be replaced by crayfish tails, shelled prawns (shrimp), shellfish or mushrooms.

egg ring Brillat-Savarin

Prepare a veal forcemeat ring as in the recipe for veal forcemeat ring with calves' marrow or brains; turn the hot ring out on to an ovenproof dish. Meanwhile, prepare some scrambled eggs and add either some Parmesan cheese or diced truffle (or truffle peelings). Pour the scrambled eggs into the centre of the ring, sprinkle the eggs and the ring with grated Parmesan and melted butter and brown rapidly in a preheated oven.

fish forcemeat ring with medallions of lobster à l'américaine

Prepare a whiting forcemeat. Butter a ring or savarin mould and press the forcemeat into it. Poach gently in a preheated oven at 180°C (350°F, gas 4) in a bain marie for 25 minutes or until the fish is cooked, then cover and leave for 30 minutes in the oven with the door open (this helps the mould to relax and to set well). Turn the hot fish ring out on to a warm plate and fill the centre with medallions of lobster à l'américaine.

fish forcemeat ring with shellfish ragoût

Prepare the fish forcemeat ring mould as in the previous recipe. Cook shellfish (for example, mussels à la marinière, oysters, clams or scallops poached in white wine) and remove the shells. Cook some langoustines (jumbo shrimp) in court-bouillon and shell the tails. Fry some mushrooms in butter. Bind all these ingredients with a well-seasoned white sauce made from fish stock or with a shrimp sauce. Turn the ring out of the mould and fill the centre with the shellfish ragoût. Garnish the ring with slices of truffle or add truffle peelings to the sauce.

rice ring with various garnishes
Butter a ring or savarin mould and fill with pilaf rice, risotto or rice cooked in consommé and bound with egg. Cover the mould and cook in a preheated oven at 160°C (325°F, gas 3) for about 10 minutes, then turn the ring out on to a serving dish. The filling can be a ragoût of shellfish, poultry or offal, medallions of lobster à l'américaine, crayfish à la bordelaise or curried fillets of fish.

ring of calves' brains à la piémontaise
Prepare slices of calves' brains à la poulette and add some chopped mushrooms which have been cooked in butter. Butter a ring or savarin mould, fill with risotto, and press in lightly. Heat through in a preheated oven at 180°C (350°F, gas 4). Turn the ring out on to a warmed plate and arrange the mixture of brains and mushrooms in the centre. Garnish with slices of white truffle, if desired.

ring of sole à la normande
Prepare a forcemeat of creamed fish. Generously butter a ring or savarin mould and fill with the forcemeat. Poach in a bain marie in a preheated oven at 180°C (350°F, gas 4) for about 25 minutes. Let it stand for 30 minutes in the oven with the door open. Turn the ring out on to a serving dish. Fill the centre of the ring with a shellfish ragoût mixed with normande sauce, then add some fried smelts. Poach some folded fillets of sole in white wine and arrange on top of the ring. Also poach some oysters and place one on each fillet. Garnish with sliced truffle. Warm the dish through and garnish round the edges with shrimps cooked in court-bouillon.

veal forcemeat ring with calves' marrow or brains
Prepare a veal forcemeat. Generously butter a ring or savarin mould and press the forcemeat into it. Poach gently in a bain marie in a preheated oven at 180°C (350°F, gas 4) for about 25 minutes, then cover and leave for about 30 minutes in the oven with the door open to set properly. Meanwhile, prepare some calves' marrow or calves' brains à la poulette and, separately, some lightly fried mushrooms cooked au blanc. Turn the veal ring out on to a heated serving dish. Pour the marrow or brains à la poulette into the centre of the ring and sprinkle with chopped parsley. Garnish the ring with the mushrooms and cover with more poulette sauce.

Sweet Rings
rice ring à la créole
Butter a ring or savarin mould. Fill with thick rice pudding, press down, heat through in the oven, then turn out on to a serving dish. Poach 16 half slices of pineapple in vanilla-flavoured syrup and fill the centre of the ring with them. Decorate with cherries and angelica. Serve either slightly warmed, or very cold, with apricot sauce flavoured with rum.

rice ring à la montmorency
Prepare a rice ring as in the previous recipe. Separately prepare some confectioner's custard (pastry cream) flavoured with kirsch (see custard), and also some stoned (pitted) cherries poached in syrup. Fill the centre of the ring with alternate layers of confectioner's custard and cherries. Sprinkle with crushed macaroons and melted butter and place in a preheated oven at 240°C (475°F, gas 9) for a few minutes. Serve with cherry sauce flavoured with kirsch.

semolina ring with fruit
Butter a ring or savarin mould and fill with a stiff, cooked dessert semolina mixed with a salpicon of crystallized (candied) fruit. Place in a preheated oven at 160°C (325°F, gas 3) for a few minutes, until set. Turn the ring out on to a serving dish. Fill the centre with whole, halved or cubed fruit, poached in vanilla-flavoured syrup. Heat again for a few minutes in the oven. Just before serving, sprinkle the ring with a very hot fruit sauce flavoured with rum or kirsch.

BÖREK A cheese fritter in Turkey, where it is a national appetizer, and a rich fried or baked Middle Eastern pastry, generally savoury but sometimes sweet, also widely eaten in the Balkans.

Its preparation was well described in the magazine Le Pot-au-Feu (1 January 1900): 'The true Turkish method consists of wrapping cigar-shaped pieces of katschkawalj cheese in thin sheets of pasta dough and frying them in oil.' This description remains valid, and böreks are made with a very thick béchamel sauce mixed with katschkawalj, a ewe's-milk cheese common throughout the East (this may be replaced by diced or grated Gruyère or Emmental). When cold, the mixture is shaped into thin rolls, which are then wrapped in pasta dough (or puff pastry), rolled out to a thickness of 2 mm (⅛ in) and cut with a pastry (cookie) cutter into oval shapes about 10 × 5 cm (4 × 2 in). The fritters are sealed with beaten egg and deep-fried for 8–10 minutes; when cooked, they rise to the surface. The dough can also be shaped into rectangles or circles and made into turnovers, which may be coated with breadcrumbs before frying.

BORSCH Also known as borscht. A beetroot (beet) soup, eaten hot or cold, popular in the Ukraine, Russia and Poland, and also an Ashkenazi Jewish dish. The essential character and colour come from the root, but the soup may include chicken or beef with other vegetables including mushrooms, which supply the stock in meatless versions. In the Ukraine the broth is served with *piroshki*. The chilled version is fashionable abroad, see also *botvinya*, *chlodnik*.

Borsch is traditionally served with *smetana* – soured (sour) cream – and diced meat as required, but it is customary to eat only the beetroot, mushrooms and white kidney beans with the soup, reserving the meat cooked in the stock for another purpose. There is a fish borsch, also made with beetroot, and a green borsch made with sorrel, spinach and either loin of pork or oxtail.

Borsch was one of the first Russian dishes to become popular in France, with the arrival of Russian émigrés in the 1920s. There are many varieties of this very popular dish, some richer than others. The recipe given by Carême, who had the opportunity of preparing it for the court of St Petersburg, is one of the most elaborate.

RECIPE

Ukrainian borsch

Fry 2 chopped onions and 200 g (7 oz) raw sliced beetroot (beet) in lard, cover and continue to cook gently. Bring I kg (2 lb) stewing (chuck) steak to the boil in 2.5 litres (4¼ pints, 11 cups) water, then skim. Add 500 g (18 oz) shredded white cabbage, 3 carrots, a bunch of parsley, small trimmed celery sticks, and the beetroot and onion. Season with salt. Cook 4 ripe tomatoes in a little water, sieve and add them to the soup. Cook for 2 hours, then add a few potatoes, cut into quarters. Prepare a roux with lard and flour, mix with a little stock and pour it into the borsch with 2 tablespoons chopped fennel. Boil for a further 15 minutes and serve.

This Ukrainian borsch is served with a bowl of fresh cream, garlic cloves (which should be eaten between spoonfuls of soup), buckwheat kasha with bacon, and *piroshki*, little dumplings filled with meat, rice and cabbage.

BOTARGO Also known as *boutargue* or *poutargue* in French. The pressed, then salted and dried female roe of the grey mullet, called *batrakh* in the Middle East. The entire egg sack of the fish is treated whole. In Greece the roe is lightly smoked and may be sold from barrels in markets; known as *avgotaraho*, it is a winter and Lent speciality, preserved from summer-caught fish. Roes are also sold singly, looking like longish, rather flat, red sausages. Sardinian roes are covered in beeswax for protection. The method of preserving the roes seems to have been invented by the Phoenicians, but it may be Jewish in origin.

Known as 'white' caviar, *botargo* is the forerunner in Europe of caviar and it is mentioned more than once in Samuel Pepys' *Diaries*. It is very salty and must be rinsed. In France and Greece it is eaten sliced very thinly, with a drizzle of lemon juice and/or oil, sometimes on toast. In Greece it is more commonly grated and made into taramasalata. In Italy *bottarga* makes an excellent pasta sauce and swordfish roe is also used. In Sicily and Sardinia the bluefin tuna gives a deep golden-brown, slightly metallic-tasting roe, weighing 2–5 kg (4½–11 lb) and looking like square-sectioned sausages. Seabass roe is also used.

In France grey mullet were specially bred in Lake Bere for their roes and *poutargue* became a speciality of Martigues, in Provence.

North Africa is a main source of supply. In California roe from the striped or black mullet is served on crackers. It is also salted and dried for export to Japan, where it is known as *karasumi*.

BOTERMELK A Belgian dessert, known in northern France as *lait battu* ('milk whip'). It consists of milk boiled very gently for 1½ hours with pearl barley (or rice, semolina, tapioca or very fine vermicelli) and brown sugar. The mixture, which is sometimes bound with potato starch, is then mixed with molasses or honey; raisins or other dried fruits soaked in warm water are then added.

BOTHEREL, MARIE, VICOMTE DE French politician, financier and originator of the modern restaurant car (born La Chapelle-du-Lou, 1790; died Dinan, 1859). In 1839 he had the idea of installing mobile kitchens on buses operating in the Parisian suburbs. In order to keep his bus-restaurants stocked with hot and cold food, he built vast and expensive kitchens, featuring such modern equipment as a steam machine that kept colossal pots permanently boiling. All Paris admired the venture, but the enterprise was doomed to failure and the Vicomte has passed into obscurity.

BOTTEREAUX Geometrically shaped French fritters (square, round or triangular) made from raised (leavened) dough that has been flavoured with brandy or liqueur. They are traditionally made during mid-Lent in the Charentes and Anjou regions and can be eaten hot or cold.

RECIPE

bottereaux

Stir together 20 g (¾ oz, 1½ cakes) fresh (compressed) yeast and 100 ml (4 fl oz, 7 tablespoons) slightly warm milk. Put in a food processor 400 g (14 oz, 3½ cups) strong plain (bread) flour, a pinch of salt, 3 tablespoons caster (superfine) sugar and 2 tablespoons rum. Add the yeast mixture and process thoroughly to form a dough. Roll out to a thickness of 5 mm (¼ in). Distribute 125 g (4½ oz, ½ cup) butter cut into small pieces evenly over the surface. Fold the dough in two and roll out evenly, then work the dough again to incorporate the butter. Roll into a ball, flatten and roll into a ball again. Leave to rise for 3 hours. Roll out the dough very thinly, about 3 mm (4 in) and cut out the shapes with a pastry (cookie) cutter. Fry them in very hot oil, then drain on paper towels before dusting with icing (confectioner's) sugar.

BOTTLE A narrow-necked vessel for holding and storing liquids. It is a way of packaging and of marketing the contents.

A successful design also advertises the contents. For many years in France claret was known for its high-shouldered bottle, while Burgundy bottles had sloping shoulders: these now have become universal bottle types, adopted by purveyors only for their suitability. The champagne bottle (both its wide profile and the gold foil top) is another French example, born of the technical requirements for thicker glass and a securer cork to hold a sparkling wine. Bottles with successful marketing images are the round Portuguese Mateus Rosé bottle, the Paul Masson carafe, the Gallo pot-bellied flask – and the Coca-Cola bottle, grippable round its waist (launched in 1916), at one time the world's most universally recognized symbol.

In the ancient world wine was stored and transported in amphorae; it could undergo an unpleasant change if exposed to air. The cask, supposedly invented by the Gauls, was a considerable improvement. Small quantities of wine were transported in goatskins, known as *boutiaux* or *boutilles* (from the Low Latin *butticula*, a small cask) and, probably, the origin of the word 'bottle'.

In the Middle Ages wine was served at table either in tin vessels or pots – long-term storage in glass bottles did not become widespread until the 18th century. An etching, dated 1750 and showing wine bottles with driven-home corks (instead of mere bungs or stoppers), makes it possible to date their appearance. The first French glassworks to specialize in making wine bottles was set up in Bordeaux in 1723 by an Irishman.

On labels the phrase '*mise en bouteilles au château*' or '*au domaine de la production*' signifies that the wine has been bottled at the place where it has been made. Certain wines (such as those of Alsace) must be bottled in the region of production.

Bottles were individually hand-blown until about the middle of the 19th century, so that their shape and size varied according to the region. At first bottles were dumpy, like flagons, but they gradually became cylindrical and more refined. Before 1850 they had a more slender shape (the Burgundy type). In 1866 the shape and size of Bordeaux, Burgundy and Mâcon bottles was legally defined.

Quantities in wine bottles vary. The standard wine bottle (even champagne) now holds 75 cl (and earlier quantities, prevalent until the mid-20th century, for champagne and Alsatian, Moselle and Rhine wines have been abandoned). Half bottles are universally 37.5 cl. Bordeaux makes some larger sizes: the double (4 bottles) holds 3 litres, the jeroboam (6.67 bottles) holds 5 litres and the impériale (8 bottles) is 6 litres. Burgundy boasts a 2-bottle magnum at 1.5 litres.

■ **Serving wine** Current practice is to serve wine from its original bottle, placed directly on the table or on a coaster. The practice of laying the bottle on its side in a basket is only for very old wines, which may have a sediment. They should be drawn from the wine bin in a recumbent position hours before decanting. If they are not to be decanted, they should stand upright for some hours.

BOTTLING AND CANNING FOOD A method of preserving food by hermetically sealing it in jars, bottles or cans and then heating it to temperatures above 100°C (212°F), preferably 110–115°C (230–239°F), which destroys all the micro-organisms and enzymes liable to cause spoilage. The original process was invented by Nicolas Appert and is still referred to as *appertisation* in France. This form of sterilization is now an industrial process.

Thorough sterilization necessitates heating the foodstuff for long enough to destroy the micro-organisms but not so as to impair its eating qualities. For example, milk is heated to very high temperatures – 135°C (275°F) – for a very short time – 4 minutes. UHT (ultra-heat-treated) milk is heated to 140°C (284°F) for 1–3 seconds, normally by steam injection, and then cooled and further processed in sterile containers to eliminate the 'cooked' taste.

Before home freezing was popular, domestic sterilization techniques were used for bottling fruit and vegetables. Canning was also used by the home cook. Although these methods are sometimes used, for food safety reasons they are no longer practical everyday methods for home preservation. Special pans, jars, cans and sealing equipment are necessary and reliable recipes essential for good, safe results.

BOTTOM CUTS Cuts of meat from the lower part of the animal (when it is in a standing position). The term is not derogatory but applies to second- and third-category meats (for braising and boiling) which are not considered as fine as fillet (sirloin) and other top cuts, which are to be grilled (broiled) or roasted. The bottom cuts include shin, brisket, flank, skirt and leg of beef; knuckle and shin, breast and flank of veal; knuckle and breast of lamb and pork. Slow-cooking dishes (braised, stewed, *navarin*) are smoother and tastier when prepared with the bottom cuts, as these include a certain amount of fat and cartilage. The bottom cuts are the most economical and also represent 50% of the edible meat of a beef carcass.

BOTVINYA A cold sweet-and-sour Russian soup made from beetroot (beet) leaves, spinach and sorrel. It is garnished with either cucumber or small pieces of fish.

RECIPE

botvinya
Wash and tear up 400 g (14 oz) spinach, 250 g (9 oz) beetroot (beet) leaves and 200 g (7 oz) sorrel. Cook gently in melted butter until soft, then purée in a blender. Transfer the purée to a soup tureen and stir in 250 ml (8 fl oz, 1 cup) dry white wine, 1 litre (1¾ pints, 4⅓ cups) stock, 1½ teaspoons salt, 2 teaspoons sugar, 100 g (4 oz) diced

cucumber, a chopped shallot and 1 tablespoon each of chopped chervil and tarragon, and chill. Before serving add about 10 ice cubes, mix again and serve very cold.

BOUCAN Originally, boucan was meat smoke-dried by the Caribbean Indians. Now it is a classic form of Caribbean barbecue, consisting of a stuffed sheep cooked in a trench heated with charcoal, then covered with hot sand and embers.

BOUCHE DU ROI The French name for the combined royal kitchen staff at the French court before the Revolution (1789). The oldest order defining their duties dates from 1281, when there were ten people responsible for the bread pantry and for cupbearing, 32 for cooking and four for fruit (see *cupbearer, écuyer tranchant, serdeau*). A hundred years later, the number had more than tripled and under Louis XIV there were over 500. Managed by the highest officials, it became a very hierarchical structure with numerous lower officials. The goblet office included the pantry and the cupbearers, and was closely allied to the cuisine office. There followed the three offices of common pantry, common cup-bearing and common cuisine. There were also the fruiterer's office and the quartermaster's office (which provided wood porters and tradesmen like carpenters). The eighth office was that of the tradesmen's kitchen.

The king's kitchen was the most important office, with a team of four chefs, four roasters, four soup-makers, four pastrycooks, three kitchen boys, ten equerries, keepers of the table service (who looked after the gold and silver table services) and washers (for washing-up and laundry). There were also chair carriers and table carriers. As the king moved around, he was accompanied by warners, who gave the cooks timely notice of when the king wished to eat. When the king went hunting, a wine runner followed, carrying a light snack with him on his horse. A more substantial meal would be brought by carriage.

All *bouche du roi* offices, which carried the right to wear a sword, were expensive honours to buy and gave little return. They were held by high noblemen; the grand master of the *bouche du roi* was the Prince of Condé. Towards the end of Louis XIV's reign, however, some of the rich bourgeoisie acquired these positions, which gave them the honour of *bouche à la cour*. The *bouche* was abolished by the Revolution but Napoleon re-established some offices, particularly that of *écuyer tranchant* (slicing equerry). The system was finally abolished in 1830.

BOUCHÉE, SAVOURY A small round puff pastry case with any savoury filling is a *bouchée salée* in France. Bouchées are served hot. A salpicon of one or more ingredients, with or without sauce, is added just before serving. The first small bouchées (*bouchées à la reine*) were probably invented by Marie Leszczyinska, Queen of Louis XV. It is safe to assume that the queen at least made them fashion-

able, as she did other dishes and delicacies – historians agree on the subject of her appetite!

Making bouchées without lids

1 *When brushing the pastry circles with beaten egg, take care not to brush any egg around the outside cut edges of the pastry as this will set during baking and prevent the bouchées from rising evenly.*

2 *Lay the rings of pastry neatly on top. Brush the tops of the rings with a little beaten egg, again taking care not to brush any around the cut edges.*

RECIPES

making traditional bouchées with lids
Dust the working surface with flour and roll out some puff pastry to a thickness of about 5 mm (¼ in). Using a round, crinkle-edged pastry (cookie) cutter, 7.5–10 cm (3–4 in) in diameter, cut out circles of pastry and place them on a damp baking sheet, turning them over as you do so. Use a 7.5–10 cm (3–4 in) ring cutter to stamp out rings of pastry. Brush the edge of the pastry bases with beaten egg and place the rings on top. Chill the cases for about 30 minutes. Bake in a preheated oven at 220°C (425°F, gas 7) for 12–15 minutes. Using the point of a knife, cut out a cirlce of pastry from inside each bouchée, lift it out and set aside to use as a lid. If necessary remove any soft pastry inside the case. The bouchées are now ready to be filled.

bouchées à la julienne
Cook a julienne of vegetables (carrots, parsnips, leeks, celery or fennel) in butter. Bind with cream and spoon into the cases.

bouchées à l'américaine

Prepare the bouchée cases as above and fill with a salpicon of lobster, crayfish or monkfish *à l'américaine*.

bouchées à la périgourdine

Make some very small cases, about 4 cm (1½ in) in diameter. Prepare a salpicon of truffle and foie gras and bind with Madeira sauce. Spoon into the cases.

bouchées à la reine

Prepare and bake some bouchée cases. Prepare a salpicon *à la reine* for the filling as follows. Dice some chicken breasts poached in stock; also, dice some truffle and poach in white wine. Cut some trimmed button mushrooms into four; sprinkle with lemon juice and cook very gently in butter so they retain their original colour. Prepare a white sauce with the stock from the chicken, add some cream, and, if desired, some egg yolk. For 500 ml (17 fl oz, 2 cups) stock, use 40 g (1½ oz, 3 tablespoons) butter, 40 g (1½ oz, ⅓ cup) plain (all-purpose) flour, 100 ml (4 fl oz, 7 tablespoons) double (heavy) cream, and 1 egg yolk. Using this sauce, bind the chicken, truffles and mushrooms together.

Heat the bouchée cases in a preheated oven at 180°C (350°F, gas 4) for 5 minutes. Fill them with the hot mixture and replace the lids. If the truffles are omitted from the filling, equal quantities of chicken breast and mushrooms should be used. A salpicon of calves' sweetbreads, quenelles and brains braised in white sauce may be added to the filling.

bouchées with bone marrow

Prepare some very small cases, 4 cm (1½ in) in diameter. Poach some beef marrow in court-bouillon, drain and cut into small cubes. Season with plenty of pepper, bind with Madeira sauce, then spoon into the cases.

bouchées with crayfish in Nantua sauce

Fill the cases with a ragoût of crayfish tails in Nantua sauce.

bouchées with mushrooms

Make smaller cases using a 6 cm (2½ in) diameter pastry (cookie) cutter. Fill with morel (or button) mushrooms in cream or in a cream sauce.

bouchées with prawns

Fill the cases with a ragoût of prawn (shrimp) tails in prawn sauce.

BOUCHÉE, SWEET A petit four made from sponge-cake shapes with some type of filling is a *bouchée sucrée* in France. The small cakes are hollowed out, filled with confectioner's custard (pastry cream) or jam, then sandwiched together and coated in coloured fondant icing (frosting). For example, a filling of confectioner's custard flavoured with coffee or chocolate could be used with fondant icing of the same flavour. Alternatively, a raspberry jam filling could be used with pink fondant icing. Other combinations include green confectioner's custard flavoured with kirsch plus green fondant icing decorated with pistachios, and vanilla-flavoured confectioner's custard paired with white fondant icing.

RECIPE

apricot bouchées

Place 250 g (9 oz, 1 cup) caster (superfine) sugar and 8 eggs in a bowl and whisk together over a pan of hot water. When the mixture is thick and fluffy, fold in alternately 200 g (7 oz, 1¾ cups) sifted plain (all-purpose) flour and 200 g (7 oz, ¾ cup) melted butter to which a small glass of rum has been added. Three-quarters fill some small round moulds with the mixture and bake in a preheated oven at 180°C (350°F, gas 4) for about 20 minutes. Turn out on to a rack and allow to cool. Cut in two, spread the bottom half with apricot jam flavoured with rum and sandwich the two halves together. Reduce some apricot jam, flavour with rum and brush it on the top and sides of the bouchées. Decorate with blanched toasted almonds and a glacé (candied) cherry.

BOUCHÈRE, À LA The French name (meaning 'the butcher's wife's way') given to various dishes that feature a garnish of bone marrow. Examples are: chopped cabbage consommé, served with slices of poached bone marrow; soft-boiled (soft-cooked) or poached eggs *à la bouchère*; and omelette filled with diced poached bone marrow, surrounded with a ring of demi-glace and garnished on top with slices of bone marrow.

The name is also given to veal chops that are marinated in oil with salt, pepper and chopped parsley, then grilled (broiled) for about 15 minutes and served garnished with parsley and vegetables in season.

BOUCHON A type of small bistro in Lyon where two of the gastronomic traditions of the city are maintained: the lavish *mâchon* and the *pot* – a 45 cl bottle for tasting Beaujolais. The word literally means a bung and comes from the Old French *bousche*, a bottle stopper made of hay, straw or leaves. The insignia of taverns used to be a bunch of greenery or a bundle of straw.

BOUDIN See *black pudding*.

BOUDIN ANTILLAIS A Caribbean sausage, also called *boudin cochon*, that is grilled (broiled), fried in lard or simply heated in very hot (not boiling) water. It is often eaten as an appetizer to accompany punch. The filling is fairly liquid and can be sucked out from one end of the skin.

RECIPE

boudin antillais

For 6–8 sausages, add 2 tablespoons vinegar to 1.5 litres (2¾ pints, 6½ cups) fresh pig's blood; this prevents the blood from coagulating. Moisten 250 g (9 oz, 2½ cups) stale white breadcrumbs (without crusts) with 120 ml (4½ fl oz, ½ cup) milk. Turn some clean pig's intestines inside out, wash and dry them, rub with lemon juice, and turn right side out. Finely chop 250 g (9 oz) onions and brown gently for 7–8 minutes in 100 g (4 oz, ½ cup) lard (shortening). In a food processor purée the breadcrumbs and blood, adding the drained onions. Then add 5 large garlic cloves, finely chopped, a small chilli pepper, about 20 chopped chives or the same quantity of spring onions (scallions), salt to season and 1 tablespoon flour. Work together well and adjust the seasoning. The mixture must be highly flavoured.

Knot the end of one of the pieces of intestine and, using a funnel, fill the intestine with the mixture, pushing it with the hand towards the knotted end. When the sausage is about 10 cm (4 in) long, twist the intestine several times to seal it. Repeat for the other sausages.

Place them together in boiling water seasoned with chives, bay leaves, peppers and sandalwood and allow to barely simmer for about 15 minutes, or until no more fat comes out when they are pricked. Drain the sausages and allow to cool completely.

BOUDIN BLANC A white-meat sausage made throughout Europe, and in Britain, wherever black pudding (blood sausage) is made, and associated with the Christmas period in France.

The filling is a fine white-meat paste (poultry, veal, pork or rabbit), to which has been added pork or veal fat. Sometimes cream, milk, eggs, flour (or crustless breadcrumbs) and spices are used, even fish. The filling is stuffed into intestine casings and poached, fried gently, baked in the oven or cooked in buttered paper.

In France the traditional Christmas *boudin blanc* dates from the Middle Ages: after leaving Midnight Mass, the faithful would eat a milky gruel to warm themselves up. The pork butchers had the idea of binding it with eggs and adding minced (ground) meat. There are many types of *boudin blanc*, some of which contain truffles (see *bougnette, coudenou*). The *boudin à la Richelieu* is based on chicken forcemeat and a salpicon *à la reine* and is cooked in small individual moulds. Le Havre *boudin blanc* is the only one sold all year round. It contains no meat, only pork fat, milk, eggs, crustless bread and rice flour. Avranches *boudin blanc* contains chicken breasts, calves' sweetbreads, fish fillets and fresh cream. Le Mans *boudin blanc* combines hard back pork fat and lean pork (neck or leg) with eggs, onions, milk and spices.

Spain is another country where white puddings are important, particularly the *buttifara blanca* in Catalonia and the Balearics, containing very finely chopped lean pork (also with tripe and pine nuts). The Catalan *bisbe blanc* is spherical, stuffed into tripe intestines and tied with string.

White puddings are traditional in Ireland, shaped like a horseshoe and made of toasted oatmeal with flaked lard, seasoned with cloves, salt and black pepper. Eaten fresh, they are sliced and fried for breakfast. The West Country of Britain also makes oatmeal and pork sausages.

RECIPES

boudin à la Richelieu
Butter some small ovenproof moulds, smooth-edged and oval in shape. Line the bottom and side of each with a finely ground chicken forcemeat. Now add a mixture similar to that used to fill bouchées *à la reine* but cut up more finely. Finally, cover with more forcemeat and smooth the surface using a knife blade dipped in cold water. Place the moulds in a bain marie and cook in a preheated oven at 180°C (350°F, gas 4) for about 25 minutes. Turn the puddings out of the moulds and allow to cool. Arrange them in a circle on a serving plate with fried parsley in the centre. Serve with Périgueux sauce or suprême sauce to which has been added diced truffle or truffle peelings.

boudin blanc
Skin and bone a chicken and finely mince (grind) the flesh together with 250 g (9 oz) York ham. To 150 g (5 oz, 2½ cups) fresh breadcrumbs add just enough milk to moisten them. Cook over a gentle heat, stirring, to thicken, then leave to cool.

Prepare a duxelles using 400 g (14 oz, 4 cups) button mushrooms, the juice of half a lemon and 4 finely chopped shallots. Thoroughly mix the bread mixture, the minced chicken and ham and the duxelles with 2 egg yolks, 100 g (4 oz, 1 cup) ground almonds, 200 ml (7 fl oz, ¾ cup) double (heavy) cream, a glass of Madeira or sherry, a large pinch of paprika, salt, pepper, a dash of cayenne, 2 tablespoons chopped parsley, a generous pinch of powdered thyme and (if desired) a few truffle peelings. Whisk 2 egg whites until stiff and add to the mixture. Prepare and fill the intestines as for *boudin antillais*. Poach in the same way, then cool.

boudin blanc with prunes
Soak some prunes in a little lukewarm water or weak tea, then remove the stones (pits). Prick some *boudins blancs* with a fork, arrange in an ovenproof dish and surround with the prunes. Sprinkle with melted butter and cook in a preheated oven at 240°C (475°F, gas 9) until golden brown.

grilled boudin blanc
Prick some *boudins blancs* with a fork, roll each one in oiled greaseproof (wax) paper, and grill (broil) gently. Remove the paper and serve hot with mashed potatoes, apple sauce or celery purée.

BOUGNETTE A charcuterie speciality of southwestern France. The *bougnette de Castres* is a flat sausage made from chopped belly of pork combined with a mixture of bread and eggs, fried or baked in fat and eaten cold. *Bougnette* from Albi is larger.

In the Cévennes, *bougnette* is a kind of fritter, while in Auvergne it is a type of coarse pancake.

BOUGON A goat's milk cheese (46% fat content), soft with a red-tinged crust. Made exclusively by the cooperative of La Mothe-Bougon in Poitou, Bourgon is a boxed round cheese, 11 cm (4½ in) in diameter and 2.5 cm (1 in) thick, weighing 250 g (9 oz). Its pronounced flavour is at its finest from May to September, the period when goat's milk is of the best quality.

BOUGRAS A vegetable soup from Périgord, prepared with the water used for cooking black pudding (blood sausage). It was traditionally prepared at carnival time, when the pig was killed.

BOUILLABAISSE A dish comprising fish boiled with herbs, which is traditionally associated with the Provence region, especially Marseille, although it has long been enjoyed further afield. The word is a contraction of two verbs, *bouillir* (to boil) and *abaisser* (to reduce), and in fact bouillabaisse is more a method of rapid cooking than an actual recipe; there are as many 'authentic' bouillabaisses as there are ways of combining fish.

Bouillabaisse was originally cooked on the beach by fishermen, who used a large cauldron over a wood fire to cook the fish that was least suitable for market, such as *rascasse* (scorpion fish or rockfish) – essential for an authentic bouillabaisse and hardly ever eaten otherwise. Shellfish are added, including squill fish, mussels and small crabs (lobster is a city dweller's refinement). The dish is flavoured with olive oil, spices, including pepper and saffron, and dried orange zest.

In 1895 J.-B. Reboul listed in *La Cuisinière provençale* 40 types of fish suitable for bouillabaisse (including mackerel and sardines, which other experts reject as too oily). In fact, bouillabaisse should be prepared using rockfish, ideally caught with rod and line just before cooking. Species of the northern Mediterranean coast give even more authenticity to the dish and include sea bass, moray eel, rainbow wrasse, bonito and wrasse.

The fish and its soup are served separately, with the soup traditionally poured on to slices of dried (not fried or toasted) home-made bread; in Marseille, a special bread called *marette* is used. But bouillabaisse can also be served with croûtons rubbed with garlic and *rouille* sauce.

In 1980 the restaurateurs of Marseille signed a bouillabaisse charter designed to protect and defend the authentic recipe, but this has since been contested by other 'specialists'.

Provençal cuisine offers several variations on the bouillabaisse soup. At Martigues, where it is usual to serve the soup with potatoes (cooked separately), there is also a black bouillabaisse, containing cuttlefish and their ink. Sardine and cod bouillabaisses are also characteristic of the region, as are *bourride* and *revesset* (both Provençal fish soups). White wine is sometimes added to the liquid.

Other French coastal regions have their own local methods of preparing fish soups: *bouillinada* from Roussillon, *cotriade* from Brittany, *chaudrée* from Charentes (which gave rise to the American chowder), *marmite* from Dieppe, Flemish *waterzooi* and *ttoro*, of the Basque region.

RECIPES

bouillabaisse ♦
For 8–10 servings, use about 3 kg (6½ lb) fish and shellfish. Place the following ingredients in a large deep flameproof casserole: 300 g (11 oz, 2¾ cups) chopped onions or 100 g (4 oz, 1 cup) leeks and 200 g (7 oz, 1¾ cups) onions, 2 large sliced carrots, and 3 large skinned and finely chopped tomatoes, 3–4 tablespoons crushed garlic, 1 sprig fennel, a small bunch of parsley, 1 sprig thyme, a bay leaf and a piece of dried orange rind. Add the prepared shellfish, then the firm-fleshed fish cut into uniform pieces with heads, bones and skin removed, as necessary. Moisten with 200 ml (7 fl oz, ¾ cup) olive oil and season with salt and freshly ground pepper. Add a generous pinch of powdered saffron and leave to marinate, covered and in a cool place, for a few hours.

Add sufficient water (or fish stock prepared with the heads and trimmings of the fish) to cover the fish. Cover and boil rapidly for 7–8 minutes. Then add the prepared soft-fleshed fish and continue to boil rapidly for a further 7 minutes. Remove the fish and shellfish and place in a large round dish. Line a soup tureen with dry bread and strain the soup on to it. Sprinkle the soup and the fish with coarsely chopped parsley and serve both at the same time.

Caribbean bouillabaisse
Heat some olive oil in a large saucepan and gently cook 1 large chopped onion, some quartered tomatoes, 1 large crushed garlic clove, and 1 small crushed chilli pepper; add some thyme, grated nutmeg, salt and pepper. Finally add some prepared West Indian fish (such as devil fish and bonito), a small lobster (or a large lobster tail) and 3 crabs. Cover, bring to the boil, and cook for about 20 minutes for fresh; for frozen fish, continue cooking for 15 minutes after they have thawed. Five minutes before cooking is complete, add a little curry powder and 2 generous pinches powdered saffron.

Marseille bouillabaisse
Scale, clean and remove the head of 2 kg (4½ lb) of several kinds of whole fish (conger eel, sea bream, red gurnard, monkfish, whiting, scorpion fish, John

Bouillabaisse.

Dory). Cut into pieces. Fry 1 onion, 1 garlic clove, 2 leeks and 3 celery sticks, all peeled and finely chopped, in 7 tablespoons of oil until golden. Add the fish heads and trimmings. Cover with water, bring to the boil and simmer for 20 minutes. Strain the mixture through a sieve and press to obtain as much of the cooking juices as possible. Crush 3 peeled tomatoes. Peel and chop 1 onion, 2 garlic cloves and 1 fennel bulb and fry in oil in a saucepan until golden. Add the stock, tomatoes and bouquet garni. Add the scorpion fish, red gurnard, monkfish, conger eel, sea bream, 10 little crabs (*étrilles brossées*) and a few strands of saffron. Cook over a high heat. Then add the John Dory and whiting. Cook for another 5–6 minutes. Moisten a slice of bread with the stock and squeeze it. Pound it with 3 garlic cloves and 1 chopped red chilli. Add 1 egg yolk, then 250 ml (8 fl oz, 1 cup) olive oil while whisking this *rouille* like a mayonnaise. Cut a baguette into slices and toast lightly or brown in the oven. Arrange the fish and trimmings on a large dish, pour the bouillon into a soup tureen, and serve with the *rouille* and croûtons.

salt cod bouillabaisse
Completely desalt 800 g (1¾ lb) fillets of salt cod, changing the water several times, then cut them into square pieces. In some oil, gently fry 100 g (4 oz, 1 cup) chopped onions and 50 g (2 oz, ½ cup) chopped leeks, without allowing them to change colour. When these vegetables are soft, add 2 peeled, seeded, and finely chopped tomatoes and 1 crushed garlic clove. Cook rapidly for 5 minutes, then add 6 tablespoons white wine, 500 ml (17 fl oz, 2 cups) water or fish stock and a generous pinch of saffron. Bring to the boil and place the drained cod in the cooking liquor; cover and continue to boil rapidly for about 25 minutes. Just before serving add 1 tablespoon chopped parsley. Serve the bouillabaisse in a deep dish with slices of dried bread. Alternatively, the stock may be served separately from the fish, garnished with slices of French bread.

sardine bouillabaisse
Fry 1 chopped onion and 2 chopped leeks (white part only) in olive oil. Add 1 large peeled, seeded and chopped tomato, 2 large crushed garlic cloves, a bay leaf, a fennel stick, and a small piece of dried orange peel. Add 750 ml (1¼ pints, 3¼ cups) water. Season with salt, pepper and a generous pinch of powdered saffron. Add 6 potatoes, sliced fairly thickly. Cover and simmer for 25 minutes. Meanwhile, clean some fresh sardines and remove the scales under the cold tap; wash them and wipe dry. When the potatoes are almost cooked, lay the sardines on top and cook for 7–8 minutes. Pour the liquid on to slices of stale French bread arranged in a soup tureen; place the sardines and potatoes in another dish. Sprinkle both soup and fish with chopped parsley.

BOUILLETURE Also known as *bouilliture*. An eel stew thickened with beurre manié and garnished with mushrooms, baby onions, and prunes; it is served with toast and sometimes quartered hard-boiled (hard-cooked) eggs. In Anjou, *bouilleture* is prepared with red wine; white wine is used in Poitou.

RECIPE

angevin bouilleture
For 1 kg (2¼ lb) eel, allow 750 ml (1¼ pints, 3¼ cups) red wine, 10 medium-sized shallots, 40 g (1½ oz, 3 tablespoons) butter, 1 glass brandy, 250 g (9 oz) sautéed button or wild mushrooms, 150 g (5 oz) glazed small onions, 250 g (9 oz) prunes, 2 tablespoons flour, a bouquet garni, salt and pepper.

Skin the eel and cut into thick slices. Peel and chop the shallots and soften in butter in a flameproof casserole. Add the slices of eel, brown them, then flame with the brandy. Season with salt and pepper; add the red wine, the bouquet garni and the prunes. Cook for 20 minutes, then remove and drain. Prepare some beurre manié, add it to the casserole and boil for 2 minutes, stirring constantly. Pour the sauce containing the prunes over the eel and garnish with the sautéed mushrooms and the glazed onions.

BOUILLEUR DE CRU In France a landowner, vine grower, fruit producer or owner of any other product that can be distilled (such as perry or cider) who is allowed to carry out the distillation for himself or herself. The expression is much used in the Cognac region, where the large establishments may buy in brandy already distilled by a *bouilleur de cru* if they do not carry out the distillation process themselves. There are also some individual *bouilleurs ambulants*, who, as the term implies, travel around with some kind of portable still (*alambic*) and either operate this for anyone who hires them, or rent it out.

In the past such people were kept busy, but large-scale distilling is now done at centrally placed establishments, while improved methods of transport enable the product for distillation to be brought to the distillery without loss of time.

The more modest procedures of distillation can be – and sometimes are – carried out in a very small space, so that an individual type of spirit may be produced. The systems of taxation and controls, however, have complicated what was at one time quite a common way of life, and though the person entitled to be a *bouilleur de cru* may still proudly continue to practise, the occupation has now altered and is not followed by as many people as in former times.

BOUILLON (RESTAURANT) A type of cheap restaurant that was opened in France at the end of the 19th century (see *Duval*), serving meals at one set price. Originally its main dish was boiled beef (*bouilli*) served with its stock but this ample and economical menu was later complemented by other dishes. In Paris, several chains of such restaurants were opened, including the Boulant and Chartier *bouillons*. One of these is still running, complete with its 1900 decor, sawdust on the floor, Thonet furniture and a menu written with purple ink.

BOUILLON (STOCK) The plain unclarified broth obtained from boiling meat or vegetables. It is used instead of water or white stock for cooking certain dishes and for making soups and sauces. 'Bouillon is the soul and quintessence of sauces', said F. Marin in 1739. The food industry has now developed solid or liquid extracts that can be mixed with water to obtain an instant meat or chicken stock.

In French cookery, the term *bouillon* applies principally to the liquid part of a pot-au-feu.

RECIPES

giblet bouillon
Put the giblets from 2 chickens in a pan with 2 litres (3½ pints, 9 cups) cold water and bring to the boil. Chop 4 carrots, 2 turnips, 3 leeks (white part only), 2 celery sticks and a small piece of parsnip. Skim the liquid, then add the vegetables together with an onion stuck with cloves, a bouquet garni, salt and pepper. Simmer gently until completely cooked (about 1½ hours). Just before serving, bone the giblets and return the meat to the bouillon, adding the juice of half a lemon and some chopped parsley. Adjust the seasoning.

If desired, this can be prepared in the Greek way by cooking 2 handfuls of rice in the stock and thickening with a beaten egg yolk or, preferably, a whole beaten egg.

herb broth
Use 40 g (1½ oz) fresh sorrel leaves, 20 g (¾ oz) lettuce leaves, 10 g (¼ oz) fresh chervil leaves, ½ teaspoon sea salt, 5 g (¼ oz, 1 teaspoon) butter and 1 litre (1¾ pints, 4⅓ cups) water. Wash the vegetables and cook them in the water. Then add the salt and butter. Strain.

Beetroot (beet) or spinach leaves may be added to the stock if desired and, just before serving, parsley and lemon juice can be included.

quick stocks
Home cooks no longer have stockpots bubbling away permanently on a corner of the stove. However, stock is still the basis of many recipes, so here are a few simple and quick recipes. Depending on the purpose of these stocks, a little thyme or parsley and salt and pepper may be added. Stock can be kept for 2–3 days in the refrigerator or frozen for longer storage. Good-quality stock is also available from supermarkets, usually sold chilled, rather than in cube or powder form.
• *Quick beef stock* Coarsely chop 100–150 g (4–5 oz) beef, a small carrot, a white leek, a small celery stick, a medium onion and a clove. Place all the ingredients in 1.5 litres (2¾ pints, 6½ cups) water and simmer gently for 20 minutes. Strain.
• *Quick veal stock* Use the same method as for quick beef stock but use lean veal (haunch or shoulder) instead of beef.
• *Quick chicken stock* Use the same method as for quick beef stock but with 400–500 g (14–18 oz) chicken wings instead of the beef.

vegetable bouillon
Use vegetables that are generally included in a stockpot – carrots, onions, leeks, celery, garlic cloves, tomatoes and turnips are typical. Potatoes and parsnips tend to make the stock cloudy; strongly flavoured vegetables give the stock a distinctive flavour – for example, broccoli, cauliflowers, swede (rutabaga) or fennel. Chop them, cook gently in butter, then pour boiling water over them to cover. A bouquet garni, salt and pepper (optional) are added and the broth is simmered until the vegetables are cooked. Alternatively, simply add all the ingredients to boiling water and simmer until cooked, either conventionally or using a pressure cooker. In both cases, the broth must be strained before it can be served.

BOUKHA Also known as *boukhra*. A Tunisian spirit made from figs and drunk as a digestive throughout North Africa. The figs most commonly used are Hordas figs from Turkey.

BOULANGER The owner of a Parisian café in the Rue des Poulies (now Rue du Louvre) who, in 1765, became the first restaurateur of the capital. (Before that time guests obtained their meals from inns, hostelries and caterers.) Since he did not belong to the guild of caterers who sold sauces, cooked dishes and stews, Boulanger was entitled to offer his clients only drinks and 'restorative broths'. One day in 1765 he served sheep's feet in white sauce and won his case against the caterers because Parliament had decreed that sheep's feet were not a stew. His success assured, Boulanger now added poultry *au gros sel* to his menu. Diderot said that at the Boulanger establishment 'one was well but expensively fed'. Grimod de La Reynière spoke of the 'first restaurateur of Paris, called Champ-d'Oiseau, established in the Rue des Poulies in 1770'; this may have been a nickname for Boulanger or an early competitor. A certain Roze de Chantoiseau set up in the same street, but his business foundered a few years later.

Boulanger is known only by this name (which means baker); some authorities claim that he was a baker whose real name has been lost.

BOULANGÈRE, À LA Oven-baked dishes, usually lamb but sometimes fish, such as cod (originally cooked in the baker's oven, hence the term), garnished with potatoes and chopped onions, and sometimes topped with butter. At one time using the public oven was a common practice in Europe and America (see *bakery*), before domestic ovens became universal.

RECIPES

cod à la boulangère

Season a piece of cod with salt and pepper and put it in an ovenproof dish. Thinly slice some potatoes and onions and arrange these around the fish, seasoning and adding a pinch of thyme and a pinch of crumbled bay leaf. Sprinkle with melted butter. Cook in a preheated oven at 190°C (375°F, gas 5) for 40 minutes. Cover the dish as soon as the fish turns golden, to prevent it from drying out. Sprinkle with chopped parsley and serve, piping hot.

herring à la boulangère

Clean 6 good herrings, preferably some with soft roes, and season with salt. Butter an ovenproof dish and place the herrings in it. Slice 400–500 g (14–18 oz) potatoes and 150 g (5 oz) onions and arrange around the herrings. Add salt, pepper, a pinch of thyme and a crumbled bay leaf. Sprinkle with about 40 g (1½ oz, 3 tablespoons) melted butter and cook in a preheated oven at 200°C (400°F, gas 6) for 30 minutes, basting from time to time. Cover the dish with foil if the potatoes begin to dry out in the final stages of cooking.

loin of lamb (or pork) à la boulangère

Prepare and roast the meat as for a leg of lamb, allowing 22–25 minutes per 1 kg (2¼ lb). Add sliced potatoes and onions 30 minutes before cooking is complete.

roast leg of lamb à la boulangère

Season a 2.5 kg (5½ lb) leg of lamb with salt, pepper and garlic, and rub with butter. Roast in a preheated oven at 220°C (425°F, gas 7) for 40 minutes. Slice 675–800 g (1½–1¾ lb) potatoes and 300 g (11 oz) onions. Arrange them round the joint, baste with the meat juices and about 50 g (2 oz, ¼ cup) melted butter, and season with salt and pepper. Reduce the oven temperature to 200°C (400°F, gas 6) and cook for a further 40–50 minutes, basting four or five times. Finally, cover the dish with foil and leave it in the open oven for a good 15 minutes for the meat to relax.

shoulder of lamb à la boulangère

Bone a shoulder of lamb (or ask the butcher to do it for you) and season the inside with salt and pepper. Roll and tie the meat, then season the outside with salt and pepper. Complete the preparation and roast as for leg of lamb, allowing 25–30 minutes per 1 kg (2¼ lb). Add the garnish of potatoes and onions 30 minutes before cooking is complete.

BOULE DE BÂLE A small, short, stocky sausage, made in Basle (Switzerland), consisting of a fine mixture of pork meat and pork fat forced into a straight synthetic skin. After being lightly hot-smoked, the sausage is heated to 70–75°C (158–167°F) and then quickly cooled. It is eaten cold with bread and mustard, in a salad, grilled (broiled), or in pastry.

BOULE-DE-NEIGE A small French cake, shaped like a ball, which is completely covered with whipped cream. It is made of layers of Genoese sponge spread with butter cream. The name means 'snowball'.

The same name is also used for a petit four the size of a large marble. It consists of either two small meringues sandwiched together with a cream or miniature cakes made of a rum baba dough (without raisins) filled with kirsch cream and decorated with white fondant icing (frosting).

Boule-de-neige is also the French name for a moulded round ice-cream dessert (see *snowball*).

BOULETTE Minced (ground), chopped or puréed meat or fish shaped into a ball (hence the French name) before cooking. *Boulettes* are usually coated with breadcrumbs and then deep-fried, but they may also be sautéed or poached. They are often made to use up leftover meat or fish and may be served with tomato sauce or brown sauce. See *fricadelle, kofta, knödel*.

BOULETTE D'AVESNES A French cow's-milk cheese (50% fat content), made by mixing Maroilles cheese with parsley, tarragon and spices. Its reddish crust is washed in beer. A speciality of Thiéraches, Boulette d'Avesnes is shaped by hand into a cone, 8 cm (3½ in) in diameter and about 10 cm (4 in) high. It has a very strong piquant flavour.

BOULETTE DE CAMBRAI A French cow's-milk cheese with a soft smooth paste (45% fat content) flavoured with parsley, tarragon, chives and salt. It is shaped into a small ball, 6–8 cm (2½–3½ in) in diameter. It is not matured and has a milder flavour than the Boulette d'Avesnes. Caffut cheeses, also from the Cambrai region, have a stronger flavour and are made from either spoiled or old cheese mixed with herbs. They are not entitled to the 'Boulette' appellation. A similar type of aromatic, often strong-smelling, cheese is made in Belgium, especially in Charleroi and Romedenne. It is used to make cheese and leek flans.

BOUQUET The aroma produced by the evaporation of the volatile products evident in wine. It is one of the main elements – together with colour, fruitiness and vinosity – that may enable the origin of a wine and, for the experienced, also its area and vintage to be identified.

Aromas are frequently described in terms of fruits, honey, nuts, spices or wood, depending on the age and style of each wine. Aeration, which consists of uncorking a bottle in advance, perhaps decanting it into a carafe, and gently turning the wine in the glass while warming the glass in the cupped hand, allows the bouquet to develop.

BOUQUET GARNI A selection of aromatic plants used to flavour a sauce or stock. They are usually tied together in a small bundle to prevent them from dispersing in the liquid and are removed before serving. A bouquet garni generally consists of 2–3 sprigs parsley, 1 sprig thyme, and 1–2 dried bay leaves, but its composition may vary according to local resources. Sage and rosemary go into the Italian *mazzetto* and celery, leek and savory can be added or a strip of orange zest. In Provence rosemary is always included. In old French cookery, bouquets garnis contained cloves as well as herbs, and the whole bundle was wrapped in a thin slice of bacon. A bouquet garni may also be enclosed in a small muslin (cheesecloth) bag.

BOUQUETIÈRE, À LA A French garnish composed of vegetables that are arranged in bouquets of different colours around large meat roasts, fried chicken or tournedos (filet mignon) steaks. The term is also used for a macédoine of vegetables bound with béchamel sauce.

RECIPES

barquettes à la bouquetière
Bind a macédoine of vegetables with béchamel sauce and use the mixture to fill barquette pastry cases. Place a small bouquet of asparagus tips on top of each barquette, sprinkle with melted butter and heat through.

bouchées à la bouquetière
Bind a macédoine of vegetables with béchamel sauce. Gently heat some small bouchée cases in the oven and fill with the hot mixture. Garnish with chopped parsley and replace the lids on the bouchées.

roast rib of beef à la bouquetière
Prepare a *bouquetière* garnish by cooking some small carrots, pod-shaped pieces of turnip, small green beans, artichoke hearts and small cauliflower florets in salted water. Drain the vegetables and warm them in clarified butter. Cook some peas and use them to stuff the artichoke hearts. Fry some small new potatoes in butter. Season a thick (two-bone) slice of rib of beef with salt and pepper, brush with melted butter. Roast in a preheated oven at 240°C (475°F, gas 9) for about 16–18 minutes per 1 kg (2¼ lb) or until cooked as required. Drain the fat and place the meat on a serving dish surrounded by the vegetables arranged in bouquets. Deglaze the dish in which the meat was cooked with a mixture of Madeira and stock. Reduce and pour the meat juices over the rib of beef.

BOURBON An American whiskey named after Bourbon county in Kentucky. Bourbon is usually distilled from maize (corn), and malted rye and barley are added in varying quantities. It is aged for at least two years in charred wooden barrels. 'Straight' bourbon has not been blended; 'blended straight' bourbon is a mixture of several bourbons and 'blended' bourbon is a mixture of straight bourbon and neutral alcohol. The higher the proportion of maize, the more full-bodied the bourbon will be. Drunk mostly in the south and west of the United States, bourbon varies in flavour according to the maker and has its own distinctive and individual taste. It is drunk straight, with water or in a mix.

BOURBONNAIS The ancient French province of Bourbonnais includes the department of Allier and part of Puy-de-Dôme, Cher and Creuse. Its rustic cuisine is similar in many ways to that of its neighbours – Auvergne, Berry and Nivernais.

The natives of Bourbonnais are said to be hearty eaters and consume a wide variety of vegetable dishes. These include thick soups made with potatoes, celeriac (celery root), cabbages and sometimes chestnuts; these become stews with the addition of smoked sausages and bacon. Other substantial dishes are enjoyed – *truffiats*, *pompes aux grattons*, meat pies and *sanciaux*, also popular in other provinces of central France.

High-quality meat and poultry are produced here and the region has its own specialities, such as *oyonnade* and *fricassin*. The towns, especially Vichy, are famous for such vegetable dishes as Vichy carrots, vichyssoise soup and carp *à la Vichy* (stuffed with mushrooms). In the area around Saint-Pourçain, wine is used in many recipes, such as *paupiettes bourbonnais* (beef olives), *matelotes* and dishes *en meurette*. Many desserts are prepared with the choice fruit from the countryside: prune tarts, *millias* with black cherries, *flaugnardes*, *tartibas* (pancakes) with grapes, *picanchâgnes* with pears and other fruit pies.

BOURDALOUE A French dessert created by a pastrycook of the Belle Époque whose establishment was in the Rue Bourdaloue in Paris. It consists of halved William (Bartlett) pears that are poached and then immersed in vanilla-flavoured frangipane cream. They are then covered with crushed macaroons and glazed in the oven. A tart bearing the same name is filled with this dessert.

Bourdaloue is also the name of a similar dessert made with semolina or pudding rice and other poached fruits (apricots, peaches and pineapple). *Bombe bourdaloue* is flavoured with anisette.

RECIPES

apricots bourdaloue
Poach 16 apricot halves in a light vanilla-flavoured syrup. Drain and wipe with paper towels. Two-thirds fill a flameproof dish with cooked dessert semolina. Arrange the apricot halves on top. Cover with a thin layer of semolina and top with 2 crushed macaroons and 1 tablespoon sugar. Place in a very hot oven for a short time to glaze the top. Serve with apricot sauce. Pudding (short-grain) rice may be used instead of semolina and peaches or bananas instead of apricots.

bombe bourdaloue
Line a mould with vanilla ice cream. Fill with an anisette-flavoured bombe mixture and freeze the ice cream until set. Turn out and decorate with candied violets.

BOURDELOT A baked apple or a pear enclosed in pastry from Normandy. The core is removed (the fruit may also be peeled) and the centre of the fruit is filled with caster (superfine) sugar moistened with 1 teaspoon Calvados and topped with a knob of butter. The fruit is then placed on a square of shortcrust pastry (basic pie dough) or puff pastry that is large enough to wrap around it. The corners of the pastry square are folded and pressed together and glazed with egg yolk. *Bourdelots* are baked in the oven and may be eaten hot or cold. See *douillon, talibur*.

BOURG A small town surrounded by vineyards of the Côtes de Bourg, situated on the right bank of the river Dordogne, close to its confluence with the Garonne. Most wine is good quality drinking red, made from Merlot grapes although a small amount of white is made from Ugni Blanc and Colombard.

BOURGEOISE, À LA The French term used for dishes typical of family meals, without a set recipe, particularly those made with braised meat – chuck, silverside (bottom round), knuckle of veal, leg of mutton and calf's liver. Such dishes normally include a garnish of carrots, small onions and pieces of bacon, which are usually arranged in bouquets around the meat.

RECIPES

calf's liver à la bourgeoise
Mix together in a shallow dish 4–5 tablespoons brandy and 2 tablespoons oil, then add some chopped parsley, salt, pepper and (optional) a small amount of cayenne pepper. Marinate some pieces of bacon fat in this mixture for at least 30 minutes and then use to lard a piece of calf's liver. Tie the liver and braise it in a mixture of red wine and stock. Sauté some mushrooms in butter and glaze some small onions. When the liver is cooked, remove it to a serving dish with the mushrooms and onions, and keep warm. Skim the fat from the cooking liquid, strain and reduce to make a thick smooth sauce. Pour it over the liver and serve.

chicken à la bourgeoise
Season a chicken with salt and pepper and cook in butter in a covered dish in a preheated oven at 180°C (350°F, gas 4) for 30 minutes. Then add 100 g (4 oz, ⅔ cup) diced fat bacon that has been lightly fried and 20 small carrots fried in butter. Cook for about another 35 minutes, basting the chicken with its own juice from time to time. Place the chicken and the garnish in a dish and keep warm. Deglaze the cooking pot with 7 tablespoons each of white wine and stock. Then strain the sauce and reduce it by about one third, adding about 20 glazed small onions, cooked in butter. Pour the sauce over the chicken and sprinkle with chopped parsley.

other recipes See *giblets, tendron, tongue*.

BOURGUEIL Red or rosé wines from the Indre-et-Loire region of Touraine, made from the Cabernet Franc grape (known in the locality as 'Breton') and up to 25% Cabernet Sauvignon. Rabelais celebrated them and put his legendary Abbey de Thélème in the region. The soils are partly sand, partly clay, producing light and fragrant wines; those from the flat sections make good drinking when young, while those from the slopes tend to be more full-bodied and benefit from moderate to long-term maturation. Crisp and delicate, Bourgueil wines somewhat resemble those of their neighbour, Chinon, although Bourgueil tends to smell of raspberries, Chinon of violets. St Nicholas de Bourgueil, in the west of the region, produces light, fragrant, elegant wines.

BOURGUIGNONNE, À LA The French name for several dishes cooked with red wine (poached eggs, meat, fish and sautéed chicken), the most famous of which is *boeuf bourguignon* (see *beef*). They are usually garnished with small onions, button mushrooms and pieces of fat bacon. The term also applies to preparations inspired by the regional cuisine of Burgundy.

RECIPES

bourguignonne sauce for fish
Prepare a fish stock using 1 litre (1¾ pints, 4⅓ cups) red wine, the bones and trimmings of the fish to be used in the finished dish, a medium-sized chopped onion, a small bouquet garni, a handful of mushroom peelings, salt and pepper. Strain, reduce to half its volume and thicken with some beurre manié according to taste.

bourguignonne sauce for meat and poultry
Cut 75 g (3 oz) bacon into small strips, blanch, drain and cook in butter until golden brown. Finely chop some onions and mushrooms, mix together and cook 4–5 tablespoons of the mixture in butter, together with 2 generous tablespoons mirepoix*. Stir in the diced bacon and transfer the mixture to the pan in which the chicken or meat has been cooked. Stir well and cook until golden brown. Add 2 tablespoons flour and stir well. Then add 500 ml (17 fl oz, 2 cups) red wine, 200 ml (7 fl oz, ¾ cup) stock, a bouquet garni, salt and pepper. Reduce by two-thirds. When ready to use, sieve the sauce and thicken with 50 g (2 oz, ¼ cup) beurre manié.

chicken à la bourguignonne
For a chicken weighing about 2 kg (4½ lb), use 100 g (4 oz) bacon, cut into larding strips and then blanched. Peel 20 small onions, and clean and slice

20 mushrooms. Put the cleaned and trussed chicken in a hot flameproof casserole and gently colour the outside in 25 g (1 oz, 2 tablespoons) butter. Remove the chicken and fry the bacon, onions and mushrooms in the same casserole. Remove and add 2 tablespoons mirepoix*, stirring well. Deglaze the casserole with 400 ml (14 fl oz, 1¾ cups) red wine and an equal quantity of chicken stock, boil down by half and add a bouquet garni. Return the chicken to the casserole, bring to the boil, then cover and cook gently for 20 minutes. Add the prepared garnish of bacon, mushrooms and onions, together with salt and pepper. Bring to the boil, cover and simmer gently for a further 45 minutes, or until cooked.

Drain the chicken and its garnish and remove the bouquet garni. Add 1 tablespoon beurre manié to the juices in the casserole, stirring well for 2 minutes, adjust the seasoning and pour the sauce over the chicken.

other recipes See *ballotine, beef, entrecôte, giblets, goose, liver (calf's liver), snail, trout.*

BOURGUIGNOTTE, À LA
In *L'Art de la cuisine française au XIXᵉ siècle* Carême gives a recipe for a sauce for freshwater fish that he calls *à la bourguignotte*:

'Prepare a medium-sized eel, cut it into pieces and place the pieces in a saucepan together with 2 chopped onions, 225 g (8 oz, 2½ cups) chopped mushrooms, 2 garlic cloves, a pinch of ground pepper, 2 shallots, a bouquet garni, a pinch of allspice, 4 rinsed anchovies and ½ bottle Volnay wine. Simmer, allowing the sauce to reduce a little, then press it through a sieve. Return the sauce to the pan and add 275 ml (9 fl oz, 1 cup) reduced espagnole sauce* and 225 g (8 oz, 2½ cups) fried mushrooms, together with their cooking liquor. Boil the mixture rapidly to reduce and add 1 glass of Volnay. When the sauce is sufficiently reduced, place it in a bain marie to keep it warm. Just before serving, add some crayfish butter, about 30 crayfish tails and the same number of white button mushrooms.'

BOURRICHE
A long wicker French basket used for transporting shellfish, especially oysters. The baskets were once used to transport game and fish. The word is also used to describe the contents of the basket.

BOURRIDE
A Provençal fish soup. After cooking, the liquid is strained and bound with aïoli (garlic mayonnaise). The authentic *bourride* from Sète is made with monkfish, but elsewhere whiting, sea perch, grey mullet and red mullet are sometimes mixed together.

RECIPE

bourride
Cut 1 kg (2¼ lb) monkfish into pieces and boil rapidly for 20 minutes in a mixture of 1 litre (1¾ pints, 4⅓ cups) water and an equal amount of white wine, together with the sliced white part of 1 leek, 2 chopped onions, 2 chopped carrots, 2 chopped garlic cloves, a little dried orange peel, salt, and pepper. When the fish is cooked, place each piece on a slice of stale bread and sprinkle with a little saffron. Strain the stock, reduce by half, remove from the heat and blend in some very thick aïoli. Pour the sauce over the fish.

BOURRIOL
A fairly thick French pancake made from a leavened batter of potato purée, wheat flour and buckwheat flour mixed with milk. It is a speciality of Auvergne.

BOUTEFAS
A large sausage from the Vaud region of Switzerland, much appreciated in the French-speaking part of Switzerland, made from pork meat and fat coarsely chopped and stuffed into a skin. *Boutefas* is gently poached for a long time and eaten as an accompaniment to sauerkraut and winter vegetables.

BOUTON-DE-CULOTTE
A French goat's-milk cheese that is classified as a soft paste cheese (40–45% fat content), but is eaten when it is very dry and brittle. Shaped like a truncated cone, with a greyish-brown crust, it has a strong piquant flavour. The cheese is made in the Mâcon area and is also called Chèvroton de Mâcon, Mâconnet or Rougeret. It is often served at Beaujolais wine-tastings.

BOUZOURATE
A refreshing Arab drink made from dried melon seeds. These are grilled (broiled), ground, soaked in water and squeezed through fine cloth bags. The liquid is then sweetened and served very cold. It may also be used to make sorbets and water ices.

BOUZY
A commune of Montagne de Reims, France, which has given its name to the appellation of a light, delicate red wine with a bouquet of fruit (see *Champagne*).

BOWL
A hemispherical container with little or no handle. A wide selection is used for kitchen utensils or tableware, for preparing, cooking or serving food. There is a strong European tradition for breakfast bowls. Traditionally these hold more than coffee cups and are used in France for holding coffee and for dunking breakfast breads. A small bowl with handles, called a *bolée*, is traditional for drinking cider in Normandy and Brittany. The British breakfast bowl is deep enough to hold breakfast cereal and milk. Similar bowls are popular for desserts.

Small crystal, porcelain or metal bowls are used as individual finger bowls. A punch bowl is a very large container made of glass, crystal or silver plate with a large ladle (and possibly matching cups) used for serving punch, sangria or hot wine.

Bowls used as kitchen utensils may be wide and shallow or deep and varying in size from those small enough to hold a tiny amount of chopped flavouring ingredients to others large enough to mix generous quantities of ingredients for cakes or doughs. Some are designed to ease common kitchen tasks. These include a pastry bowl with a flat side, so that the bowl may be tipped comfortably over for hand-working the contents; or a bowl with a lip (facing across from a handle) for pouring. The classic British pudding basin is tapering in shape with a narrow base, widening and having a fairly deep external rim around the top. The rim allows string to be tied under it to keep a cloth or foil covering securely in place.

BRABANÇONNE, À LA A French garnish made with typical produce from Brabant: Brussels sprouts, chicory (endive) and hops. These are served with large roast joints of lamb or mutton (such as baron, rack or leg) and also with tournedos (filet mignon) and sautéed noisettes. The vegetables are arranged in barquettes, coated with Mornay sauce and glazed. They are served either with small round croquette potatoes that have been lightly browned in butter or with creamed potatoes.

BRAGANZA *bragance* A French garnish named after the fourth and last Portuguese dynasty, made of croquette potatoes and small braised tomatoes filled with béarnaise sauce. It is used as a garnish for tournedos (filet mignon) or noisettes of lamb.

Braganza is also a dessert made with Genoese sponge cake. The cake is cut into two rounds and soaked in a syrup flavoured with orange liqueur. The rounds are sandwiched together with a layer of custard cream, to which has been added orange liqueur, chopped candied orange peel and butter. The cake is then completely covered with the same cream and decorated with candied orange peel.

BRAIN This is a type of meat grouped with offal (variety meats), the internal organs of the animal. The best are lamb's brain, weighing about 100 g (4 oz), and sheep's brain, weighing about 150 g (5 oz). Both are barely tinged with pink. Calf's brain, weighing 250–300 g (9–11 oz), has a similar flavour but is deeper in colour. Ox brain, weighing 500–675 g (18–24 oz), is firmer and veined with red. Pig's brain is rarely used. Calf or ox brains, although less choice, are also less expensive; they are used as a filling for pies and timbales and also in meat loaves and gratins.

RECIPES

preparation of brains
Wash the brains in cold running water, then remove the membranes and blood vessels that surround them. Soak them in cold water for 1 hour and wash them again. The brains may then be blanched in salted water, cooked gently in a court-bouillon, or cut into thin slices and cooked directly in butter or oil.

brains with noisette butter
Cook the prepared brains in a court-bouillon — about 10 minutes for lamb's or sheep's brain and about 15 minutes for calf's brain. Cut calf's brain into even slices; leave smaller brains whole or divide them into two.

Melt some butter in a shallow frying pan until it turns golden; then add some lemon juice or vinegar and some capers. Reheat the sliced or whole brains in this butter and serve with the butter, sprinkled with chopped parsley.

calf's brain in tomato baskets
Cook a prepared calf's brain in well-flavoured court-bouillon. Drain and press under a light weight until cool, then cut into thin slices. Marinate in olive oil containing a pinch of chopped garlic, lemon juice, salt and pepper. Choose 3 large well-shaped tomatoes, remove their stalks, wash and wipe them. Make several vertical cuts stretching two-thirds of the way up the sides and slip a slice of brain into each slit. Serve with anchoyade.

calves' brains in red wine
Prepare 24 glazed small onions and 24 mushroom caps and sauté them in butter. Prepare 750 ml (1¼ pints, 3¼ cups) court-bouillon with red wine and cook 2 prepared calves' brains in the court-bouillon. Remove, drain and cut into thin slices. Arrange these escalopes with the onions and mushrooms on a serving dish. Cover with foil and keep hot in the oven. Meanwhile, reduce the cooking liquid by half, then thicken it with 1 tablespoon beurre manié. Coat the brain and its garnishes with this sauce. Garnish with small triangular croûtons fried in butter or oil.

crumbed and fried calf's brain
Prepare and cook a calf's brain in court-bouillon for about 10 minutes. Drain and rinse in cold water, wipe the brain and press it lightly until cold. Cut into thin slices and marinate these for 30 minutes in 1 tablespoon cooking oil, lemon juice, chopped parsley, salt and pepper. Coat the slices with egg and breadcrumbs, fry them and arrange on a serving dish with some fried parsley. Serve with a well-seasoned tomato sauce.

sautéed brain à la provençale
Cook either a prepared lamb's brain (whole) or a calf's brain (cut into even slices) in court-bouillon. Remove, drain, dust with flour and sauté in olive oil. Sprinkle with chopped basil, garnish with black olives and serve with a sauce of tomatoes *à la provençale*.

other recipes See *allemande, border, crépinette, forcemeat, meunière, poulette, salpicon (meat, poultry, game, offal and egg)*.

BRAISING A moist cooking method using a little liquid that barely simmers at a low temperature on the top of the stove or in the oven.

When cooking was carried out directly on the hearth, braising meant cooking slowly in hot embers. The cooking container had a lid with a rim on which embers could be placed, so that heat came from both above and below.

In modern cookery, braising is used for semi-tough cuts of meat, large poultry and also for some vegetables, such as cabbage, chicory (endive), artichokes and lettuce.

As well as being long and slow, and therefore useful for rendering tough or firm foods tender, braising is a delicate method of cooking certain firm-fleshed fish, such as monkfish, carp and salmon.

■ **Braising techniques** Braising joints or birds are often barded and marinated before cooking. Then they are browned in a little hot fat and arranged on a bed of lightly cooked vegetables, such as onions, carrots and celery. Liquid is added to cover the vegetables and come a short way up the joint or bird. The dish or pan is tightly covered to retain the moisture from the evaporating liquid. With long, slow cooking, the meat becomes tender and a full-flavoured sauce is obtained.

When the food to be braised contains a lot of water (particularly vegetables), it cooks mainly in its own juice and the minimum extra liquid is added.

The cooking liquid is chosen according to the type of food that is to be braised: it may be a strained marinade, white wine (for fish or poultry), red wine (for red meat), or meat or fish stock. Sometimes a few chopped tomatoes alone provide sufficient moisture for braising. However, the liquid added at the beginning may not be sufficient to maintain the level of humidity required for long cooking (some joints of meat require a cooking time of 5–6 hours). In this case, liquid must be added during cooking: it must be at the same temperature and should be added gradually and in small quantities to maintain a concentrated flavour.

When the cooking is finished, the juice is strained, excess fat is removed and the liquor reduced if necessary. The sauce may be intensified by adding wine or spirits and boiling, or enriched with cream. Beurre manié may be added to thicken sauces in the final stages.

BRAISING PAN *braisière* An oval or rectangular two-handled cooking pan with a well-fitting lid. Braising pans are used in catering for the long, slow cooking or braising of meat and vegetables. One type of braising pan has a hollow lid that is filled with water during braising. Cast-iron casseroles are suitable for braising, or earthenware dishes are used, some types placed directly into the embers of a fire. Embers are also placed on top of the lid to ensure simultaneous cooking above and below.

The word *braisière*, in restaurant terminology, is also used for a brown stock made with veal and beef bones, carrots, onions and garlic, simmered for a long time in water with added herbs. The fat is removed and the stock is strained. This stock is used in the preparation of the classic brown sauces.

BRAN The husk or outer layers of cereal grains, separated from the grain in the milling process – for example, when preparing white flour and white rice. The germ or embryo (the part of the grain that grows) is removed with the bran during milling. The germ is a rich source of nutrients and the bran provides valuable fibre.

Bran is now added to many proprietary breakfast cereals and can be bought separately to sprinkle on at home. It can also be added to soups, stews, pastry and cakes during preparation. (Wheat germ is also available as a product in its own right.)

BRANCAS A French garnish for small joints of red meat, white meat and poultry, consisting of Anna potatoes and chiffonade of lettuce with cream. It was probably dedicated to Louis, a member of the Brancas family (originally from Italy). A friend of Voltaire, Louis Brancas also gave his name to a brill dish and to a consommé.

RECIPES

brill à la Brancas
Clean a brill weighing about 800 g (1¾ lb) and cut it into even-sized pieces. Finely shred 2 large onions, the white part of 2 leeks and half a head of celery. Braise the vegetables for 10 minutes with 25 g (1 oz, 2 tablespoons) butter and a pinch of salt. Then add 125 g (4½ oz, 1½ cups) mushrooms, also finely shredded, and braise for a further 6–7 minutes.

Butter an ovenproof dish and season lightly with salt and pepper. Spread half the shredded vegetables in the dish. Arrange the pieces of brill in the dish so that they form the shape of the original fish, season with salt and pepper, and cover with the remaining vegetables. Add a little lemon juice, 200 ml (7 fl oz, ¾ cup) white wine and a bouquet garni. Dot with butter. Bring to the boil on top of the stove, then cook in a preheated oven at 200°C (400°F, gas 6) for about 15 minutes, basting once or twice, until the fish is tender.

Serve the cooked fish surrounded with tomato fondue, made by gently simmering 4 peeled and chopped tomatoes in butter for 30 minutes with 1 tablespoon chopped onion. Season the tomato fondue with salt, pepper and a little chopped parsley before spooning it around the fish.

This method of cooking, derived from brill à la Dugléré, can be used for other flatfish and also for whiting and slices of hake.

consommé Brancas
For 1 litre (1¾ pints, 4⅓ cups) consommé of beef or poultry, prepare a garnish using 2 tablespoons each of finely shredded lettuce and sorrel, finely shredded vegetables softened in butter and vermicelli poached in the consommé. Sprinkle with sprigs of chervil just before serving.

BRANDADE A purée of salt cod, olive oil and milk, which is a speciality of Languedoc and

Provence. It does not include garlic, but in Marseille and Toulon crushed garlic is added to the dish, and even the croûtons used as a garnish are rubbed with garlic. A similar preparation is made in many Mediterranean countries where dried cod is enjoyed, usually with oil and garlic. One of the best known is the Venetian *baccalà mantecato* (stockfish with oil). However, most recipes include, even in France, a potato purée, although this is not the true brandade. Some French chefs have enriched the preparation further by adding truffles or even crayfish ragoût *à la Nantua*.

The word is derived from the Provençal verb *brandar*, meaning to stir. Adolphe Thiers was known to be passionately fond of brandade and his historian friend Mignet sent him pots of it from Nîmes, which he ate alone in his library. Alphonse Daudet founded the Dîners de la Brandade in a café in the Place de l'Odéon in Paris: the meal cost 6 francs and included 'a brandade and two speeches'.

RECIPES

brandade sauce à la provençale
This sauce is not made with salt cod, but it is served with poached salt cod. Put 2 tablespoons thin allemande sauce*, 3 egg yolks, a pinch of grated nutmeg, a pinch of fine pepper, a pinch of crushed garlic, the juice of a large lemon and a pinch of salt into a saucepan. Stir continuously over a low heat until the sauce is smooth and velvety. Remove the pan from the heat and add (a tablespoon at a time) about 250 ml (8 fl oz, 1 cup) good Aix olive oil. Just before serving, add the juice of a lemon and 1 tablespoon chopped blanched chervil.

Nîmes brandade
Desalt 1 kg (2¼ lb) salt cod, changing the water several times. Cut the fish into pieces and poach it very gently in water for 8 minutes. Drain, then remove the bones and skin. Heat 200 ml (7 fl oz, ¾ cup) olive oil in a thick flat-based saucepan until it begins to smoke. Add the cod, then crush and work the mixture with a wooden spoon, while heating gently. When it forms a fine paste, remove the pan from the heat. Continue to work the bran-dade and, while stirring continuously, gradually add 400–500 ml (14–17 fl oz, 1¾–2 cups) olive oil, alternating with 250 ml (8 fl oz, 1 cup) boiled milk or double (heavy) cream. Season with salt and white pepper. The result should be a smooth white paste with the consistency of potato purée. Pile the brandade into a dish and garnish with triangles of crustless bread fried in oil. It can also be put in the oven to brown, just before serving.

other recipes See *bénédictine, croque monsieur*.

BRANDY A spirit distilled from wine, the best known being Cognac and Armagnac. (The English word, originally 'brandwine', is derived from the Dutch *brandewijn* – 'burnt' or distilled wine.) The word is also used to denote a spirit distilled from certain fruits, such as kirsch, framboise or Mirabelle, and it is used more loosely to signify a liqueur made from fruits and berries, such as cherry brandy or apricot brandy. It is also a general term applied to distillates from the 'debris' of wine, such as marc and the Italian grappa, and also to spirits distilled from cider, such as applejack, the American version of Calvados.

BRASSERIE Originally a brewery, a brasserie is a café or restaurant where beer, cider and other drinks are served. The distinction of all brasseries is that they serve a limited menu at any time of day and often until fairly late at night. A *brasserie alsacienne* (selling beer and sauerkraut dishes) is common in many French cities.

In countries where a lot of beer is consumed, there was at first little to distinguish the brasseries from inns. They had the same wooden benches and wooden tables, like the traditional brasseries found in Bavaria – in Munich, one of the oldest (opened in 1589) is still in operation. In Paris, however, the refugees who came from Alsace-Lorraine, after the war of 1870, started a new fashion for brasseries. They became elegant places, and were as ornately decorated as the great cafés of the capital.

From 1870 to 1940, the brasseries of Paris were frequented by writers, artists, journalists and politicians: customers could argue, drink, play chess, write and eat – all at the same table. Among the establishments that have now disappeared are the Brasserie Pousset, once the rendezvous of journalists and artists (a tradition continued by Lipp at Saint-Germain-des-Prés), the Brasserie Steinbach, which was situated in the Latin Quarter (and is now the Balzar), and the brasserie in the Rue des Martyrs, frequented by Nadar, Baudelaire, Courbet and Manet. Those that have retained the turn-of-the-century decor and atmosphere are Bofinger at the Bastille and Flo in the Passage des Petites-Ecuries. Renewed interest in beer towards the end of the 20th century encouraged several brasseries to specialize in French and foreign beers. Some 'Belgian bars' or 'academies of beer' offer up to 300 different brands, mostly served with cold meats, cheese or even mussels.

BRATWURST A fine German uncured sausage with a coarse filling of pork and pork fat, sometimes with veal. There are many regional variations in size and seasoning, usually named for the town of origin. Bratwurst can be grilled (broiled) or boiled and are often served with sauerkraut.

BRAWN Also known as head cheese, this is a charcuterie product of meat from a pig's head (excluding the brain), set in aspic from the reduced cooking liquor. Brawn is well flavoured with seasoning ingredients and/or herbs, and set in a mould, which may be as simple as a small bowl or basin. The brawn is cut into slices and eaten as a first course or with bread and salad for a light meal. In French, brawn is also known as *pâté de tête* and *fromage de cochon*.

Hure is a type of brawn made with boar's or pig's head. *Hure à la parisienne* consists of the tongue and the skin set in aspic in a mould. In Alsace there are three variations: *hure rouge* is a kind of brawn made from the head and packed into a large red skin from the animal's gut; *hure blanche* combines the head, cured forehock, and skin; and *hure de Francfort* is a smaller version.

BRAZIL See *page 156*.

BRAZIL NUT A large nut with a very hard, brown, three-sided shell from one of the tallest forest trees, exported by Brazil and Paraguay. The white kernel can be eaten as a dessert nut or used in cooking.

BREAD A basic food made from a flour-and-water dough, normally with yeast, which is baked in the oven. When yeast is used as the raising agent, it gives bread its characteristic texture. No other food is so redolent of myth, tradition and rite as bread. Central to meals until almost the end of the second millennium (more so than meat), it is indeed the 'staff of life'. The breaking of the bread is central to the Christian sacrament and 'our daily bread' is a euphemism for food (and, in modern times, also for money). The custom of signing loaves with a cross before baking, or making the sign of the cross before cutting bread, continues in parts of Europe where religion strongly influences everyday customs, such as southern Italy.

The communal bread oven was a focal point for many communities as domestic ovens were not universal until the 19th century – or, in southern Europe, until the 20th century (see *boulangère, à la*). The supply of bread – or lack of it – has long been of concern to governments, ever since its link with civil unrest during Roman times, when the people were promised 'bread and circuses'.

■ **History** Bread-making dates back to at least 9000 BC. The first breads were cooked on heated bakestones, and many of this type still survive. The invention of leavened bread (around 5000 BC) is attributed to the Egyptians, who made bread from millet and barley. They may have discovered fermentation by chance, when a piece of dough had become sour. At the time of the Exodus, the Hebrews did not take with them any leaven, hence the tradition of unleavened bread to commemorate the crossing of the Red Sea (see *matzo*).

The Greeks cooked loaves made of rye or oats, or sometimes wheat, on a grid or in a kind of oven. The Romans often flavoured their bread with the seeds of poppy, fennel or cumin, or with parsley and they cooked it in household ovens made of brick and earth. The use of bread spread throughout the Roman empire. Rotary hand querns, for producing a fine-milled flour, appeared in Spain and spread during the 1st century AD. The Gauls kneaded barley beer into flour to make dough and obtained a well-risen bread of good quality.

It was in the Middle Ages that the bakery trade began to develop; from this time, bread became very varied and many different kinds were produced. These included hall bread, for distinguished guests; hulled bread (made from bran), intended for servants; wholemeal bread, with a well-cooked crust, kept for making breadcrumbs; and trencher bread, used as plates for meat (subsequently given to the poor or to dogs). Soft or queen's bread was enriched with milk and egg yolk; German wheat bread had a very light-coloured crumb; chapter bread was flat and very hard; fine, white Gonesse and Melun loaves were supplied for a long time to the best bakeries of Paris; and variegated bread was made of alternate layers of brown and white bread.

In the 17th century a new method of fermentation was developed, using milk, salt and beer barm, to manufacture finer loaves made in long moulds: Gentilly, Segovia, bread *à l'esprit*, bread *à la maréchale* and horned bread. For a long time, the quality of bread depended on the flour used and therefore on its colour: white bread for the rich, black bread for the poor. The principal government concern was to prevent adulteration of flour, and therefore bread.

In 1840 the Viennese oven was introduced to France by a man called Zang, secretary of the Austrian embassy in Paris. Introducing moisture into the oven using high-pressure steam jets caused the bread to expand rapidly, giving the maximum surface area and a thin golden crust when baked. The bakery used Viennese methods, kneading wheat flour with milk (a Vienna loaf in Britain is a milk loaf), and it started a tradition of fine pâtisserie, known in France as *viennoiserie*. More conspicuously, it produced the long loaves, pandering to the Parisian taste for the maximum crisp crust, that have become the classic French loaves.

Oven temperatures and times affect both the crumb and the thickness and quality of the bread crust. Humid conditions, with very slow baking, also help very heavy flours, such as used in the German *Kastenbrot* breads, to rise. Manipulating all these factors, as well as the careful choice of ingredients, is part of the baker's art, developed over generations and throughout the world. It gives a huge spectrum of choice.

■ **Yeasted breads** Strong plain (bread) flour is the basis for most yeast doughs. It differs from ordinary flour in that it has a high gluten content. Gluten is a protein found in some grain, particularly wheat. The gluten content varies considerably according to the type of wheat and its area of cultivation – for example, wheat from northern countries, like Canada, contains more gluten than wheat from southern countries. Wheat with a high gluten content is referred to as hard wheat (as opposed to soft wheat with a low gluten, content). Rye and barley do not contain as much gluten, and flours made from these grains are often mixed with a proportion of wheat flour for making bread dough.

BRAZIL

Strongly influenced by the Portuguese, the cuisine of Brazil is one of the most varied and sophisticated in South America. The Indians contributed manioc flour, cocoa, sweet potato and groundnuts (peanuts), while the black population brought yam, banana, coconut and palm oil (*dende*). The national dish is *feijoada*, a stew made from black beans and lightly salted meats. It is traditionally preceded by a *batida*, a whisked cocktail consisting of cane sugar brandy and lime.

Fish and seafood are enjoyed in the north-east of the country, particularly *fritada de mariscos* or seafood fritters including mussels, oysters and chunks of crab dipped in batter and fried. Large prawns (jumbo shrimp) are also popular – cooked with coconut in *vatapa*, made into fish-balls or fried with red kidney beans; they are also added to *xinxin de galinha*, a fricassée of chicken with groundnuts and manioc. A wide range of tropical fruit is eaten throughout the country, but the pâtisserie and sweet dishes of this region are justly celebrated. Delicacies, such as flavoured custards, coconut cakes, pastries

with prunes, and egg yolks whisked with sugar, take colourful names, including angel cheeks, young girl's saliva and mother-in-law's eye.

In central Brazil, as in Argentina, the typical dish is *churrasco* (grilled meat), while fromage frais sweetened with guava jam is eaten at any time of the day.

In the south, the food is richer. Typical dishes include offal (variety meats) and tripe cooked in a stew; chicken stuffed with fruit; and, most important, a purée of black beans, manioc and bacon which is the staple food of the region.

Gluten is important because it gives the dough elasticity. When combined with water or similar liquid and kneaded, the gluten becomes tough and stretchy. The dough becomes elastic and springy, in which state it traps the gas produced by fermenting yeast and rises, developing the characteristic light texture full of tiny holes. Yeast dough made with low-gluten or soft flour of the type used for general cooking, is not sufficiently elastic to trap gas from fermenting yeast well and thus expand or rise; it is also likely to collapse during baking.

Traditionally, dough is kneaded by pushing and folding for about 10 minutes to develop the gluten. Then it is left to rise, 'knocked back' (this British term means 'to punch down'), shaped and left to rise a second time. The second rising is known as proving. Warmth is important for the yeast to ferment and the dough to rise quickly; however, at a low temperature, such as in the refrigerator, bread will still rise over many hours. Breads made with wholemeal flour, added bran or non-wheat flours tend not to rise as much as white bread and the process is slower. Added ingredients, such as butter, eggs, sugar and milk, reduce the elasticity of the dough and retard rising.

■ **Sourdough breads** Historically French *pain de campagne* (country bread) and many of the older types of bread are made with natural leaven or sourdough rather than yeast. In a warm place, flour and water will ferment over a period to produce a starter dough which can be used as a raising agent for a larger batch of dough. In a regular baking sequence, a little dough is kept back from each batch to start the next. Sourdough breads are not as light as yeasted breads, they have a closer texture and may have a characteristically tangy flavour.

French sourdough breads, called *pain au levain*, are characterized by their thick crust, spongy crumb and sour-sweet flavour. One famous modern sourdough is that prepared in San Francisco, where local

bacilli or yeasts come from the Bay area to give the bread a characteristic taste.

■ **Making bread commercially** Bread-making comprises three main operations, largely mechanical: kneading, fermentation and baking. See also *bakery*.

• KNEADING This combines the water, yeast or leaven, and flour, with a little salt to improve the final taste, into a homogeneous mixture. In the past, kneading was done entirely by hand. Modern bakeries use mechanical kneading, and ingredients are added to the dough to shorten the process of kneading and rising. However, the results obtained by traditional methods are often preferred and premium breads are made to such standards.

• FERMENTATION This occurs at a favourable temperature when a raising agent is mixed into the flour-and-water dough. In endogenous fermentation (the sourdough method) a little of the leaven is reserved from one day's dough and added to the next batch. In exogenous fermentation, the raising agent is industrial yeast.

The prime purpose of fermentation is to make the bread lighter; it also gives the bread its characteristic texture, appearance and smell. Traditional slow fermentation with leaven gives bread a slight acidity. The yeasts ferment with sugars in the damp hot dough to produce alcohol and carbon dioxide, which forms gaseous bubbles that raise (prove) the dough.

The first stage of fermentation takes place in the kneading trough. The dough is subsequently weighed and shaped into loaves and again left to rise until it has doubled its volume, called proving. The surface may then be scarified (scratched or cut) and the bread is ready to be baked.

• BAKING On a large commercial scale baking is as technically advanced as the mixing, kneading and fermenting. Vast ovens with rotating baking racks

Bright melons and yellow and green bananas adorn a Brazilian doorway.

process a high volume of loaves at controlled temperature levels. Traditional cooking using a wood fire is still preferred by some. This may be in an oven adjacent to the heat but, classically, in a domed brick oven, where the fire is allowed to die down and the bread is cooked by the heat retained in the walls.

The loaves are put in the oven as quickly as possible, with the aid of a wooden shovel with a very long handle. When cooked and a good colour, they are taken out of the oven and placed in the cooling-off room, ventilated but without draughts, to cool to room temperature. The bread loses its humidity before being put on the shop shelves or packaged.

■ **Daily bread** In many countries, bread is present on the table at every meal and remains there to be consumed with all the courses, to accompany almost all dishes, including a dessert of fruit and cheese. Concern about bread quality during two World Wars raised the quality of bread in industrialized countries. The traditional baker's targets of whiteness and lightness, which were automatically equated with wholesomeness, have been balanced by concern for retaining the food value of the grain. The message about the benefits of wholemeal bread was preached in America by the Rev. Sylvester Graham, a 19th-century Massachusetts clergyman. In 1840 he produced a wholemeal flour from various grains and his name is now synonymous in the US with wholemeal bread, called *pain intégrale* or *pain complet* in France and *Schotbrot* in Germany.

A good bread must have a crisp crust, an attractive golden colour and a soft crumb. Growing stale too quickly is a sign of bad quality, as are tastelessness and insipidity.

Most bread should be served fresh but not hot from the baker's oven. Rye bread, however, should be slightly stale, and large farmhouse loaves are best left until the day after they have been baked. Slice loaves just before serving. The slices should not be too thin, in order to retain all the flavour of the bread, and in many countries there is a tradition of breaking bread. Baguettes and other long loaves should be cut in small diagonal sections.

■ **Types of bread** Made from wheat, rice, maize (corn) or rye, Western-style bread is usually baked in the oven, but in Africa and Asia, some breads are fried, baked in earthenware vessels or steamed.

• FLATBREADS Bakestone and griddle breads predate leavened bread. Examples of breads still cooked by this method include traditional Indian breads cooked on a cast-iron griddle called a *tava*: the wheat chapati, flat, soft and 15–20 cm (6–8 in) across, is typical. *Paratha* is a speckled, flaky, layered bread, enriched with ghee. Puris are deep-fried breads which puff up during cooking. The Mexican corn tortilla, cooked on a griddle, is made from maize (corn) or wheat flour. In Europe unleavened flat breads include the Jewish matzo and northern crisp-breads, such as the Swedish rye *knäckerbröd* with a central hole (made for storing on a pole for a long period).

Yeasted flat pocket breads, such as *khobz Arabi* (Arab bread), are well-known outside the Middle East as white or wholemeal pitta. *Lavash* (or *mark-ouk*) is the most widely eaten and also the most ancient Middle-Eastern bread. Thin, brittle and somewhat crisp, in 60 cm (2 ft) rounds, it is classically cooked in a *saj* (a dome-covered fire) with wood chippings and camel dung. The Punjabi naan is a white-flour, yeasted flat bread enriched with a little ghee – its tear-shape comes from being slapped on the side of a tandoor oven and baked partly hanging vertically.

• WHITE BREAD is traditional in Europe. The classic white loaf is the round, firm-crumbed French *pain de campagne*. The 2 kg (4½ lb) *pain poilâne* (from the Parisian baker, Lionel Poilâne), thick-crusted, made with organic flour and sourdough, hand-shaped and wood-baked, marks a conscious return to this tradition in the last decades of the 20th century. Similar European breads include the *hogaza* of Castilian Spain.

The French 'stick', or Parisian baguette, dates only from the 19th century, and it is a very individual yeast bread, because it uses soft wheat flour instead of the usual strong flour made from hard wheat. It became so fashionable in the French provinces in the 20th century that many traditional French breads began to be forgotten.

Traditional British breads are frequently distinguished by their shape (rather than their crumb): the tin loaf (with a high-domed crust along its long, fairly narrow shape); the bloomer (an oval loaf slashed at intervals); the coburg (round with a cross-cut top); and the cottage loaf (a smaller head on a round loaf). The Greak *daktyla* (white or wholemeal) is another interesting shape, made of overlapping sections that pull into portions, and with a thick crust sprinkled generously with sesame seeds.

The sandwich loaf, is a wider, square tin-shaped, bread. This has been used as the 'model' on which inferior-quality pre-sliced white loaves are manufactured, but the traditional sandwich loaf has an even, thin crust and good-quality crumb which gives good thin slices. Called *pain de mie* in France, it is baked in a closed tin (pan).

• ROLLS AND SMALL BREAD The Swiss, with the reputation of being Europe's best bakers, have contributed several rolls to the restaurant table, known by their shapes, among them the St Gall, *quatrefoil*, *cornetti* and the rounded kaiser roll (also called the Parisian). The kaiser has five sections like a star, the points of which are flipped over to the centre and pressed down with the thumb. Bread sticks are another example of a small bread, particularly Italian *grissini*, Greek sesame-coated bread sticks and the salted German *Salzstange*, which has the same function as a pretzel, to stimulate thirst.

Slashed oval rolls include the French and Belgian *pistolet*, and the more elaborate American Parker House roll (from America's first commercial hotel, in Boston, and dating to 1855). Made from an oval creased along the centre, brushed with melted butter

and with its edges pressed, this pod-shape features plenty of extra crust. The long frankfurter bun was invented in St Louis in the 1880s. The Jewish bagel, a poached and baked ring-shaped roll, grew in size when it reached America. British rolls include round, soft baps, and finger-shaped bridge rolls, named for providing a base for snacks at a bridge (the card game) party or social function.

In Germany, bread rolls are called *Kleingebäck* (small baked goods) and there are about 1,200 shapes to choose from. Slightly richer breakfast rolls are popular, a taste echoed across Europe and America, with France's *pain au lait*, and the exceptional Majorcan *ensaimada*, a snail's curl of flaky pastry sold across half Spain.

• OIL-RICH BREADS The best-established olive-oil bread is the tasty sourdough *pan pugliese*, a soft white Italian bread with a deep crust. The modern ciabatta and ancient foccacia breads are both enjoyed in other countries. Flat loaves enriched with oil are also made in North Africa.

• WHOLEMEAL BREADS These have returned to popularity in recent decades thanks to their fibre content which is important in a healthy diet. Among proprietary loaves are the Grant loaf, pioneered by British health reformer Doris Grant in the late 1960s, a type of wholemeal loaf needing only one rising in the tin (pan); the Vogel loaf, from Dr Alfred Vogel in

French Farmhouse bread, hand made by traditional methods at Saint-Brice-en-Coglès in the Ille-et-Vilaine area.

Switzerland; and the branded Hovis (which includes concentrated wheat germ). Granary flour is another branded product used to make Granary bread. It is a brown flour with malted grains of wheat added to give a particularly nutty taste and texture.

• NON-WHEAT BREADS Different forms of millet are staples in Asia and Africa. European breads have been made in the past from grains like spelt and barley, while maslin (a mixture of rye and wheat) was used from medieval times until well into the 18th century. The change-over to wheat happened both because the grain tastes good and because it performs well. But the alternatives remain popular, particularly in northern Europe, Russia and Central Europe.

Cornmeal breads are usually American and identified with the southern states. Cornmeal does not contain gluten, so these breads rely on alternative raising agents to yeast; examples include corn pone, hoe cakes, Johnny cake (pioneers' bread) and salt risin' and anadama breads. Many are also egg-and-spoon breads or batters baked in a greased pan. Boston brown bread is made with cornmeal and rye, with bicarbonate of soda (baking soda) as the raising agent and flavoured with molasses. It used to be baked in a tall coffee can. Cornmeal breads are rarer in Europe, but there are examples, including the Portuguese *broa* and the Spanish *borona* of Galicia, wrapped in leaves and baked overnight in embers.

• GERMAN DARK LOAVES are invariably based on sourdoughs which are considerably more sour than French sourdough. They are baked very slowly (for about 20 hours) in an enclosed tin, hence the name *Kastenbrot* (box bread), in a special steam oven, which produces the characteristic dark and chewy texture. Pumpernickel is best known, but others are *Schwarzbrot* (black bread); *Vollknombrot* (wholemeal); and *Roggenbrot*, meaning rye, although the bread is often lightened with wheat – *Landbrot* is the lightest, with a sturdy texture like a *pain de campagne*. There are many more – too numerous to list.

• NON-YEAST BREADS Baking powder can be used instead of yeast to make breads with a lighter, more cakelike texture. Bicarbonate of soda (baking soda) combined with an acid, such as cream of tartar, sour milk or buttermilk, is a traditional raising agent. Irish soda bread, raised with bicarbonate of soda and buttermilk, has a tradition back to the 1840s. This type of bread is quick to make and, unlike yeast breads, does not require strong (bread) flour. Americans eat muffins (or breakfast 'biscuits') in a variety of flavours such as raisin, blueberry or bacon; these are a form of non-yeasted bread.

• SWEET BREADS AND TEABREADS There are many types, including the Welsh bara brith, a speckled, spiced fruit loaf; the Scots Selkirk bannock; and Irish barm brack (barm being the yeast drawn off fermented malt). Malt bread is sweetened with malt extract and it may contain sultanas (golden raisins). All these are eaten sliced and buttered. The Belgian *cramique*, Alsacian *bireweck* and Swiss *bimbrot* all contain fruit – the latter has dried pears and prunes.

• HOLIDAY BREADS OR ENRICHED BREADS These exist in most countries. Notable ones include the Kugelhopf of Alsace, Germany and Austria; the plaited Jewish challah; and the Italian panettone. Christmas breads include Genoa's *pandolce*, a shallow dome stuffed with crystallized (candied) pumpkin, citron and muscat grapes; and the Verona *pandoro* which is an iced (frosted) golden star. The Greek Easter bread is *tsoureki*, made from a butter-enriched dough, flavoured with caraway or lemon and with a dyed egg nestling in its centre.

RECIPES

white bread

Blend 15 g (½ oz, 1 cake) fresh (compressed) yeast with a little warm water taken from 400 ml (14 fl oz, 1¾ cups). Add more of the water to thin the paste to a milky consistency, then cover and leave in a warm place until frothy. Alternatively, dissolve 1 teaspoon sugar in the warm water, then sprinkle on 2 teaspoons standard (regular) dried yeast. Leave in a warm place for 10 minutes until dissolved and frothy.

Mix 675 g (1½ lb, 6 cups) strong white (bread) flour and 2 teaspoons salt and rub in 15 g (½ oz, 1 tablespoon) butter. Add the yeast liquid to the dry ingredients and mix to form a firm dough, adding a little extra flour if it is too sticky. Turn the dough on to a lightly floured surface and knead until smooth and elastic. Shape the dough into a ball, place inside a large oiled plastic bag, and leave to rise in a warm place until doubled in size. Remove from the plastic bag, then knock back (punch down). Shape into loaves or rolls. Cover with a cloth and leave to rise until doubled in size.

Bake in a preheated oven at 200°C (400°F, gas 6) for about 40 minutes for a large loaf, 30–35 minutes for small loaves, or 15–20 minutes for rolls.

• *Using dried yeast* Always follow the packet instructions, as products vary. As a guide, standard (regular) dried yeast should be sprinkled over lukewarm water to which a little sugar has been added. Cover and leave, without stirring, until the yeast granules have absorbed the water, dissolved and become frothy. Then stir well.

Easy-blend dried (active dry) yeast should be added to the flour and other dry ingredients before any liquid is added. The liquid should be slightly hotter than normal – hand-hot, rather than lukewarm – and the dough should then be mixed and kneaded as usual.

Fast-action easy-blend dried (quick-rising dry) yeast should be mixed with the dry ingredients and the water and dough prepared as for easy-blend dried yeast. After kneading, the dough should be shaped and proved – this yeast requires one rising, not two.

wholemeal bread

Blend 25 g (1 oz, 2 cakes) fresh (compressed) yeast with a little warm water taken from 400 ml (14 fl oz, 1¾ cups). Add more of the water to thin the paste to a milky consistency, then cover and leave in a warm place until frothy. Alternatively, dissolve 1 teaspoon sugar in the warm water and sprinkle on 3 teaspoons standard (regular) dried yeast. Leave in a warm place for 10 minutes or until dissolved and frothy.

Mix together 675 g (1½ lb, 6 cups) strong plain (bread) wholemeal flour and 2 teaspoons salt. Rub in 15 g (½ oz, 1 tablespoon) butter. Add the yeast liquid and mix to form a firm dough, adding a little extra flour if it is too sticky. Knead thoroughly until smooth and elastic. Shape the dough into a ball and place inside a large oiled plastic bag and leave to rise until doubled in size. Knock back (punch down) and shape into loaves or rolls. Cover with a cloth and leave to rise once more.

Bake in a preheated oven at 200°C (400°F, gas 6) for about 40 minutes for a large loaf, 30–35 minutes for small loaves, or 15–20 minutes for rolls.

bacon bread

Grill (broil) 300 g (11 oz) smoked bacon, then chop it. Prepare a basic bread dough using 500 g (18 oz,

4½ cups) strong (bread) wholemeal flour with 300 ml (½ pint, 1¼ cups) water and 15 g (½ oz, 1 cake) fresh (compressed) yeast, kneading until smooth and elastic. Work in the bacon and leave the dough to rise until doubled in volume. Shape the dough into an oblong and place it in a 1 kg (2¼ lb) earthenware dish. Cover and leave to rise until doubled in volume. Bake in a preheated oven at 200–220°C (400–425°F, gas 6–7) for about 25 minutes. Turn out and leave to cool on a wire rack.

milk rolls

Place 500 g (18 oz, 4½ cups) sifted strong plain (bread) flour on the worktop (work surface) and make a well in the centre. Add a generous pinch of salt, 20 g (¾ oz, 1½ tablespoons) caster (superfine) sugar and 125 g (4½ oz, ½ cup) softened butter. Mix the ingredients, then moisten with 250 ml (8 fl oz, 1 cup) tepid milk. Work together, then add 200 g (7 oz) white bread dough. Combine them, then form into a ball, cover it with a cloth and leave to rise, sheltered from draughts, for 12 hours. Then divide the dough into about 20 balls of about 50 g (2 oz). Make a cross-shaped cut on the top, glaze them with egg and bake in a preheated oven at 200–220°C (400–425°F, gas 6–7) for about 25 minutes. This type of Vienna bread is served at breakfast or tea.

pains aux raisins

Soak 100 g (4 oz, ¾ cup) currants in warm water to cover for at least 1 hour. Mix 15 g (½ oz, 1 cake) fresh (compressed) yeast with 3 tablespoons milk and 3 tablespoons strong plain (bread) flour. Sprinkle with 3 tablespoons flour and leave to rise in a warm place for about 30 minutes.

Put 300 g (11 oz, 2¾ cups) strong plain (bread) flour in an earthenware bowl, add the yeast mixture, then add 2 tablespoons caster (superfine) sugar, 3 eggs and 1 teaspoon salt. Knead for 5 minutes, slapping the dough flat on the worktop (work surface) to make it elastic. Sprinkle with 3 tablespoons milk and mix well. Soften 150 g (5 oz, ⅔ cup) butter and blend it with the dough. Drain the currants and work them into the dough. Knead for a few minutes, then cover and leave to stand for 1 hour in a warm place, or until doubled in volume.

Shape the dough into long thin rolls, coil each roll into a spiral and place on a baking sheet. Cover loosely and leave to rise until doubled in volume. Glaze with beaten egg and sprinkle with sugar. Bake in a preheated oven at 200°C (400°F, gas 6) for about 20 minutes, or until well browned and cooked through. Serve lukewarm or cold.

BREADCRUMBS Fresh breadcrumbs (*panure* in French) are made from fresh bread and are soft and large-crumbed. Dried breadcrumbs (*chapelure* in French) are finer, made from bread that has been dried in the oven or is slightly stale, or by drying fresh breadcrumbs and crushing them. Browned breadcrumbs are dried crumbs that are lightly toasted. (Alternatively, the bread may be baked until browned before it is crumbed.) Breadcrumbs are used in cooking for coating food or as a topping for dishes. They are also used for binding mixtures or thickening soups or sauces.

• COATING WITH BREADCRUMBS Breadcrumbs are used to coat delicate foods before frying, typically fish or seafood, chicken breast fillets, croquettes or fritters. Dry white crumbs do not absorb as much fat as fresh crumbs; they produce a fine, crisp coating and turn golden on cooking. The food is first dusted with flour, then dipped in beaten egg and finally coated with breadcrumbs. This gives a secure coating, ideal for soft mixtures which may melt during frying. Less delicate items can be moistened with melted butter or milk before a fine layer of crumbs is pressed on – this is useful when baking or grilling (broiling) the food. Dishes coated with fresh breadcrumbs must be cooked slowly so that the crumbs do not brown before the foods are properly cooked.

BREADFRUIT A tree 15–20 m (50–65 ft) high that grows in the Sunda Islands, Polynesia and India, and was introduced to the West Indies by Captain Bligh of the *Bounty*. Its egg-shaped fruits have a thick greenish warty skin, weigh from 300 g–3 kg (11 oz–6½ lb) and form a staple part of the diet in the tropics. The white flesh has a texture like bread and its flavour is similar to that of the globe artichoke. When peeled and the seeds removed, the breadfruit is cooked in salted water. In Tahiti these fruits are the subject of legend and religious rites: they may be roasted, cooked in water or simmered in a stew (as in the West Indies, where they are also made into *acras* – savoury fritters). The large seeds are also edible and have an artichoke flavour.

BREAD SAUCE An English sauce made with breadcrumbs and seasoned milk. It traditionally accompanies roast game and poultry.

RECIPE

bread sauce

Place 300 ml (½ pint, 1¼ cups) milk, a bay leaf and a small onion stuck with 2–3 cloves in a saucepan and bring to the boil. Set aside to infuse for 15 minutes. Remove the onion and bay leaf, add 5–6 tablespoons fresh white breadcrumbs, then stir over a low heat until boiling. Gradually beat in 25 g (1 oz, 2 tablespoons) butter, away from heat, and season to taste with salt and pepper before serving hot. The sauce may be thinned down with a little cream if desired.

BREAD STICKS See *grissini*.

BREAKFAST The first meal of the day, which literally breaks the fast of the night. Two quite different breakfast traditions can be traced – the first hot drink (and pick-me-up) of the day, and the first meal of the day, which is much more substantial. In

France this is the *petit déjeuner*, milky coffee with bread in some form, now commonly called the 'continental' breakfast, and often bought in a café, on the way to work. In hot climates this is often the only time milk is consumed by adults. Other simple foods that are popular for breakfast include fresh fruit and yogurt.

The British breakfast has fried eggs and bacon at its foundation, perhaps with fried bread, grilled (broiled) tomatoes and/or mushrooms. Kippers (grilled or poached) and various egg dishes are also traditional. Other favourites are grilled kidneys and the rice, smoked fish and egg dish known as kedgeree. A traditional full breakfast includes a first course of cereals, muesli or fruit such as a half grapefruit or prunes, and it ends with toast with marmalade, the whole accompanied by coffee or tea. There are regional variations, such as fried cakes of laver bread with bacon in Wales and black pudding (blood sausage) with bacon and eggs in Lancashire and Ireland.

Lighter alternatives include poached eggs with haddock; eggs on toast; boiled eggs; or savouries such as grilled mushrooms on toast. In fact, on an everyday basis, most people have a far lighter breakfast, such as cereal with milk, fruit or toast. A cooked British breakfast is very much a weekend or holiday meal.

America has its own breakfast tradition, with freshly-squeezed orange juice, eggs, bacon, ham or excellent peppery pork 'breakfast' sausages as well as toast and jam. Waffles, pancakes and muffins also feature for breakfast. Brunch is a substantial alternative to breakfast, served later in the morning and combining lunch with the first meal of the day.

Before the arrival of coffee in Europe, the first drink of the day was soup, and this continued well into the 19th century. Vichyssoise was created when Louis Diat remembered the breakfast leek soup of his childhood. The Basque *zurraputuna* (salt cod soup) in Spain is in this tradition, as is the sweetened *gramatka* of Poland, made with beer. The British seem to have preferred beer with bread on the side. A pleasant Italian variation – albeit a more modern one – is coffee with bread and lemon sorbet.

The workman's second breakfast (perhaps bread, cheese and sausage), at about 10.30 a.m., is well-recognized in all Mediterranean countries – for those who dine at 2 or 3 p.m. In Germany this is the *Zweites Frühstück* (second breakfast), at which *Frühstückskäse* (breakfast cheese) is eaten.

In the late 18th century the English bread-and-beer breakfast was joined by cold meat and cheese to become a full-blown meal, with ham, ox (beef) tongue and omelettes served in Victorian times. Prime Minister Gladstone gave political breakfasts where considerable quantities of food were eaten.

■ **Cereal breakfasts** Porridge made from oats is a traditional Scottish breakfast dish, but quick breakfast cereals are comparatively modern. In a clinic in Battle Creek, Michigan, Dr John Kellogg came up with cornflakes, made from maize (corn). Dr Max Bircher-Benner invented muesli at his clinic in Zurich, combining fruit, nuts and soaked oats. He recommended the beneficial effects of raw food.

Granola is a variation on muesli in which oats, and sometimes wheat and rye, is combined with various nuts, seeds, dried fruits, honey or brown sugar and oil and baked. The mixture is then allowed to cool, and is eaten as a cold cereal.

BREAM *brème* A freshwater fish of the family *Cyprinidae* found across Europe in pools and slow rivers and in the Baltic. It is 30–60 cm (12–24 in) long, has a greenish-brown back and its sides and belly are grey with shiny gold spots. Bream was often used in medieval recipes. Although its flesh is soft, somewhat tasteless and full of bones, it is used for *matelotes* (fish stews) in France and braised dishes, in the same way as carp. Only the large river bream are used: before being cooked they are soaked in fresh water to eliminate the taste of silt, for they rest and feed at the bottom of rivers.

RECIPE

grape harvest bream

Clean a I kg (2¼ lb) bream and season the inside with salt and pepper. Butter an ovenproof dish and sprinkle the bottom with chopped shallots; add 2 thyme sprigs and a bay leaf cut into four and lay the bream on top. Moisten with white wine (about 250 ml, 8 fl oz, I cup). Cook in a preheated oven at 230°C (450°F, gas 8) for about 20 minutes, basting the fish 3 or 4 times. Meanwhile, peel some large grapes, removing the seeds, and chop some parsley. When the bream is cooked, drain and keep warm. Strain the cooking liquor into a saucepan, add 7 tablespoons double (heavy) cream and reduce by a quarter. Adjust the seasoning. Add I teaspoon beurre manié and I teaspoon lemon juice (optional). Heat the grapes in the sauce, then pour the sauce over the bream. Sprinkle with chopped parsley.

BREAM, RAY'S A fish of the *Bramidae* family, known in France as *grande castagnole*, and *castagnola* on the Mediterranean coast. It has a very jagged black fin and is oval in shape, with a grey-brown-black body – hence the French name's allusion to a chestnut. It is also called *hirondelle de mer*, 'sea swallow' – perhaps because it has a way of appearing and disappearing. It is fished off the French and Spanish Atlantic coasts and is also found in the Indian and Pacific Oceans. The excellent flesh is faintly pinkish and in long strands.

BREAST A cut of meat consisting of the muscle of the chest. In beef this cut is known as brisket and is boiled, pot-roasted, salted or used for minced (ground) meat.

Breast of mutton or lamb is slow-roasted whole, boned and stuffed. It can also be marinated or cooked in stock and then cut into pieces for frying, grilling (broiling) or baking in a barbecue sauce, or for stews or soups.

Breast of veal – a fairly lean cut – may be sautéed (for veal Marengo or blanquette) or braised (boned and stuffed).

Fresh breast of pork (known as belly) is used in ragoûts or can be grilled or baked. When soaked in brine, it is known as salt or pickled pork (see *salting*). When cured (salted and sometimes smoked too) belly pork becomes streaky bacon used for rashers (slices) and lardons (see *aiguillettes*).

Breast of chicken comprises the two pieces of white meat attached to the breastbone. When served with truffles, chaud-froid or with a sauce, it is known as the *suprême*. Breast of chicken may be diced or chopped and used in the preparation of mixed salads or as a garnish for consommé.

RECIPES

braised breast of veal à l'alsacienne
Open a breast of veal and remove the bones without piercing the flesh. Make a forcemeat by mixing 500 g (18 oz, 2¼ cups) fine sausagemeat, 250 g (9 oz, 2¼ cups) dry breadcrumbs (soaked in milk and well drained), a bunch of chopped parsley, 1 crushed garlic clove, 125 g (4½ oz, 1 cup) chopped onions and 125 g (4½ oz, 1½ cups) sliced mushrooms fried gently in butter, salt, pepper and a little grated nutmeg or mixed spice. Stir the mixture well until it is smooth. Stuff the veal with this forcemeat and sew up. Cook as for braised stuffed breast of veal, but only for 1 hour.

Prepare some sauerkraut *à l'alsacienne*. Add the stuffed partly cooked breast of veal 30 minutes before the sauerkraut has finished cooking. Remove the string from the veal and serve piping hot with the meat cut in slices.

braised stuffed breast of veal
Open a breast of veal and remove the bones without piercing the flesh. Season inside and out with salt and pepper. Prepare the forcemeat as follows: soak 400 g (14 oz, 3½ cups) dry breadcrumbs in milk and squeeze, then mix with 2 chopped garlic cloves, a chopped bunch of parsley, 250 g (9 oz) mushroom duxelles*, 2 egg yolks, 100 g (4 oz, ⅔ cup) chopped onions and 2 chopped shallots fried gently in butter, salt, pepper and a little cayenne pepper. Stuff the breast and sew up the opening.

Line the bottom and halfway up the sides of a lightly buttered casserole with pork rind from which most of the fat has been removed. Finely dice a carrot, the white part of 1 leek, 3 celery sticks and 1 onion. Sweat them together in 25 g (1 oz, 2 tablespoons) butter in a covered pan for about 10 minutes and then spread them over the rind in the casserole. Brown the stuffed breast on both sides in 25 g (1 oz, 2 tablespoons) butter and place it in the casserole. Add half a boned calf's foot and 2 tablespoons tomato purée (paste) diluted with 200 ml (7 fl oz, ¾ cup) dry white wine and an equal quantity of stock.

Cover the casserole and bring to the boil. Then cook in a preheated oven at 200°C (400°F, gas 6) for 1¾ hours. Drain the meat. Skim the fat from the cooking stock, strain it, then reduce by one-third. Pour it over the meat. Braised spinach in butter or braised artichoke hearts may be served as a garnish.

stuffed breasts of lamb
Open 2 breasts of lamb or mutton and remove all the rib bones without piercing the meat. Rub the flesh with garlic, and season both the inside and outside with salt and pepper. Prepare a forcemeat by mixing 300 g (11 oz, 2¾ cups) dry breadcrumbs (soaked in milk and well strained) with 2 beaten eggs, 150 g (5 oz, ⅔ cup) finely diced ham, 150 g (5 oz, 1⅔ cups) diced mushrooms, some chopped parsley and garlic, and salt and pepper. Spread the stuffing on one piece of meat and cover with the second one, with the skin sides outwards. Sew up all round the edge.

Line a lightly buttered casserole with pork rind from which the fat has been removed, then add 2 sliced onions and 2 sliced carrots. Place the meat in the casserole, add a bouquet garni, cover and cook gently on the top of the stove for about 20 minutes. Add 200 ml (7 fl oz, ¾ cup) dry white wine and boil down to reduce. Then add 100 ml (4 fl oz, 7 tablespoons) tomato* sauce seasoned with garlic and diluted with 200 ml (7 fl oz, ¾ cup) stock. Cover and cook in a preheated oven at 220°C (425°F, gas 7) for about 45 minutes.

When the meat is cooked, remove the string, slice and arrange on the serving dish. Keep warm. Skim the fat from the cooking liquid, reduce if necessary to blend and thicken it, and pour over the meat. Serve piping hot.

BRÉBANT-VACHETTE A Parisian restaurant in the Boulevard Poissonnière, which was famous during the Second Empire. It was established in 1780 and was known successively as the Café des Grands Hommes, the Café Mathon and the Café Allez as it changed owners. Vachette (the father of the author Eugène Chavette) transformed it and then sold it to Paul Brébant, a restaurateur and art lover, who sometimes accepted a drawing as payment. It was in this great brasserie that the '*dîners du Boeuf Nature*' took place, involving Zola, Daudet, Flaubert and others of the Naturalist school. The Bixio dinners also took place here, where financiers and industrialists rubbed shoulders with writers (Daudet, Dumas, Mérimée, Sainte-Beuve and Sardou among them). Finally, it was the venue for the Magny dinners, presided over by Sainte-Beuve.

BRÈDES The name given in some of the old French colonies of the West Indies to a dish made from the leaves of various plants cooked with bacon and spices and served with rice *à la créole*. The most commonly used leaves are those of white or green cabbage, watercress and lettuce, although spinach, manioc leaves and pumpkin shoots are used as well. A variation of this dish, *bred*, is a mixture of pounded cassava leaves boiled with fish and coconut.

RECIPE

watercress brèdes
Put some oil or lard in a cast-iron casserole and fry 150 g (5 oz, ⅔ cup) diced bacon and a chopped onion in the fat until brown. Crush 2 garlic cloves with some salt and a peeled, seeded, crushed tomato. Add them to the casserole. When the mixture is quite hot, add 275 ml (9 fl oz, 1 cup) water. Slightly reduce the liquid and add a bunch of washed watercress. Cook for about 30 minutes. Serve with a separate dish of rice *à la créole*.

Use the same recipe to make lettuce brèdes, but soak the leaves in cold water beforehand. Blanch spinach leaves before making brèdes.

BRÉHAN A French garnish for large cuts of meat, consisting of artichoke hearts filled with broad (fava) bean purée, cauliflower florets, hollandaise sauce and potatoes with parsley.

BRESAOLA Salted and then air-dried meat, eaten raw, and unusual in that it is one of the rare preserved meats made from beef (the fillet or tenderloin), rather than pork. It is a speciality of Valtellina in Lombardy, and is ready to eat after about three months, when it is a very dark red, as an hors d'oeuvre. Sliced very thinly, it is dressed at the last moment with a few drops of olive oil, lemon juice and black pepper.

BRÉSOLLES An old French meat dish, consisting of alternating layers of meat and forcemeat. The forcemeat is made with lean ham, onions, chives, mushrooms and a little garlic, seasoned with salt, pepper and nutmeg, and moistened with a dash of olive oil. A layer of forcemeat on the bottom of a buttered earthenware casserole is covered with thin slices of veal, beef or mutton, then the layers are alternated to fill the casserole. The casserole is covered and baked, then turned out and served with Madeira sauce and braised chestnuts.

Controversy surrounds the origin of this recipe, which is traditionally attributed to the head cook of the Marquis de Brésolles: in 1742 Menon gave a variation under the name of *brézolles* (strips of veal with shallots) and Austin de Croze describes *brésolles* as a dish from Agen (round slices of veal with bordelaise sauce). The word could be derived from the verb *braiser* (to braise) or from the Italian *braciola* (a slice of meat).

BRESSANE, À LA A French term applied to several dishes in which Bresse poultry is an important ingredient, including chicken stuffed with foie gras and mushrooms (sometimes with slices of truffle slipped under the skin) and then braised or fried; a flan or cake prepared with light-coloured Bresse chicken livers; and puff pastries and mixed salads.

RECIPE

Bresse chicken salad
Season some whole lettuce leaves with vinaigrette and use to line the bottom and sides of a salad bowl. Hard-boil (hard-cook) some eggs, shell them and cut into quarters. Cook and drain some asparagus tips. Finely chop the white meat of a chicken cooked in stock and season with vinaigrette. Cut some red and green sweet (bell) peppers into very thin strips. Place all these ingredients on the lettuce leaves. Arrange a mayonnaise and colour with a little sieved and well-reduced tomato sauce. Pipe a garnish of tomato mayonnaise on the salad and sprinkle with chopped parsley. Serve the remaining mayonnaise in a sauceboat (in the traditional recipe the top of the salad is garnished with slices of truffle).

BRESTOSIS A cake with a firm consistency and which keeps well, once a speciality of the town of Brest in Brittany. It is made from Genoese sponge, to which are added blanched ground almonds, lemon essence (extract) and orange liqueur. The mixture may be poured into small brioche moulds and baked gently until golden brown. The cold cakes, wrapped in foil, will keep for several days. The mixture can also be cooked in a round cake mould. The cake is then split into two halves, filled with apricot jam, covered with apricot glaze and decorated all over with sliced toasted or raw almonds.

BRETON A table decoration, created in Paris around 1850 by the pastrycook Dubusc, made of almond biscuits (cookies) of various sizes, glazed with fondant icing (frosting) of different colours, decorated and arranged in a pyramid. It was mostly used to decorate large sideboards and side tables.

Breton is also the name of a large round fairly thick cake, rich in slightly salted butter and egg yolks. The surface is glazed with egg yolk and crisscrossed. The same mixture can also be used to make individual round or boat-shaped cakes.

BRETONNE, À LA The term given to dishes associated with the produce of Brittany in north-west France. Primarily these are dishes with haricot (white) beans (famous there), served with mutton or shoulder or leg of lamb. Breton sauce, used to coat simply cooked eggs or fish, is a combination of leek, celery and mushrooms with cream.

RECIPES

Breton sauce
Cut the white part of 1 leek, ¼ celery heart and 1 onion into thin strips. Soften gently in a covered pan with 1 tablespoon butter and a pinch of salt for about 15 minutes. Add 2 tablespoons thinly sliced mushrooms and 175 ml (6 fl oz, ¾ cup) dry white wine. Reduce until dry. Add 150 ml (¼ pint, ⅔ cup)

thin velouté* sauce and boil vigorously for 1 minute. Adjust the seasoning and stir in 1 tablespoon double (heavy) cream and 50 g (2 oz, ¼ cup) butter. Serve at once. If the sauce is to be served with braised fish, cook the sliced vegetables with the fish, adding 175 ml (6 fl oz, ¾ cup) fish stock or white wine and finishing with cream and butter.

eggs with Breton sauce

Fry the eggs or bake them in butter in small individual dishes and surround with a ring of Breton sauce. Alternatively, line small buttered dishes with puréed haricot (white) beans, break an egg into each dish, bake in a preheated oven at 200°C (400°F, gas 6) for 6–8 minutes and surround with a ring of Breton sauce.

sauce à la bretonne

(from Carême's recipe) Cut 6 large onions into rings and brown in clarified butter. Drain and add 2 ladles each of consommé and thickened espagnole* sauce. Add a little sugar, a little white pepper, then a little butter and a little chicken stock. Finally, press this sauce through a fine sieve.

other recipes See *artichoke, crab.*

BRICK A cow's-milk cheese (45% fat content) which originated in Wisconsin in the United States. John Jossi wanted to make a cheese like Limburg but with a firmer texture, so he pressed the cheese between two bricks to obtain the required result. Hence the name Brick. It has a natural reddish rind and a firm but supple texture with numerous small holes. The flavour is fairly pungent, but not nearly as strong as Limburg. Sold in blocks 25 × 12.5 × 7 cm (10 × 5 × 3 in), it is used mainly for sandwiches, canapés and cheeseburgers.

BRICQUEBEC A French cow's-milk cheese (45% fat content), moulded uncooked and with a washed crust. Made by the monks of the Abbey of Bricque-bec in the region of Cotentin, it is a flat disc 22 cm (8½ in) in diameter and 4 cm (1½ in) thick. Bricque-bec has a sweetish taste with a fine bouquet and is excellent all the year round.

BRIE A cow's-milk cheese (45% fat content), originating in the Île-de-France, which has a soft texture and a crust that is springy to the touch, covered in white down and tinted with red. It is made in the shape of a disc of variable diameter, often placed on a straw mat; since it is drained on an inclined surface, the finished cheese is sometimes of uneven thickness. The thinnest part is the most matured. The body of the cheese is light yellow, flaxen or golden in colour, with a delicate flavour and a bouquet of varying strength depending on whether the Brie is farmhouse (now rare) or dairy. Brie is served towards the end of a meal, but it is also suitable for use in vol-au-vent, croquettes and canapés.

Brie appears to have been in existence in the time of Charlemagne, who is said to have eaten it at the priory of Rueil-en-Brie. Philip Augustus offered it to the ladies of his court, and Charles of Orleans sang a madrigal about it. The poet Saint-Amant compared it to gold: 'Fromage, que tu vaux d'écus!' ('Cheese, you are worth your weight in gold!').

Condé the Great served it to celebrate the victory of Rocroi, and bouchées *à la reine*, inspired by Marie Leszczynska, were originally made with Brie. In 1793 it was said that Brie, 'loved by rich and poor, preached equality before it was suspected to be possible'. Talleyrand, an informed diplomat and gastronome, had it proclaimed king of cheeses during a dinner organized during the Congress of Vienna. (He thus had his revenge on Metternich, who had managed to have Sachertorte recognized as the king of cakes.) Of the 52 different cheeses offered to the guests, it was a Brie from the farm of Estourville at Villeroy which was voted the best.

Brie was also once used to make a pie pastry (and brioches, according to Alexandre Dumas, who thus explained the etymology of the brioche, which was based on Brie). Eugène Sue quotes Brie in *The Seven Deadly Sins*.

Brie enjoys the same prestige today, even though it is usually dairy-manufactured. There are four types: Meaux, Melun, Montereau and Coulommiers.

• BRIE DE MEAUX AOP The most famous and the most widespread, 26 or 35 cm (10 or 14 in) in diameter and 2.5 or 3 cm (1 or 1¼ in) thick; it is matured for one month. The best come from the valleys of Grand Morin and Petit Morin; good from May to October, it goes well with Burgundy.

• BRIE DE MELUN AOP Moulded by hand with a ladle, like Meaux Brie; 27–28 cm (11 in) in diameter and 3 cm (1¼ in) thick, it is sold either matured for two months, or fresh and very white, with a very pronounced taste and smell of milk, or fresh and dusted with powdered wood charcoal (it is then described as blue). Matured, it is good from June to October and goes well with Bordeaux.

• BRIE DE MONTEREAU Its fat content can be as little as 40%; 18 cm (7 in) in diameter and 2.5 cm (1 in) thick, the best is from Ville-Saint-Jacques. It is good from May to October.

• BRIE DE COULOMMIERS Measuring 25 cm (10 in) in diameter and 3 cm (1¼ in) thick, this cheese is matured for one month. The best is from Coulommiers itself; good from October to April, it goes well with Burgundy or Côte-du-Rhône.

BRIK 'A large triangle of very flaky pastry containing a soft-boiled (soft-cooked) egg surrounded by succulent minced (ground) meat; one can imagine nothing better.' This is how André Gide described this Tunisian speciality in his *Journal* in 1943. It is a very fine pastry shaped in a semi-circle around a filling of spiced vegetables or mutton with onions and mint. A small hole is made in the filling and an egg is broken into the hole. The pastry is then folded to enclose everything and the brik fried in oil. It is usually served with slices of lemon.

The success of this appetizer lies entirely in the fineness of the pastry, which is called *malsouqa* in Tunisia (and *wasqa* in Morocco). A dough of elastic consistency is obtained by boiling semolina in water; it is then prepared and cooked using a very delicate technique. The palm of the hand is dipped in cold water, then in the semolina, which is spread out on a griddle with circular movements; almost immediately it stiffens and the fine sheet of *malsouqa* is lifted with a knife (care must be taken not to make any holes in it) and laid on a dry cloth. It takes considerable dexterity and patience to make briks by hand, but commercially manufactured sheets of brik pastry can be obtained.

RECIPE

brik with egg

Spread out a sheet of brik pastry on a worktop (work surface), or use 2 layers of buttered filo (phyllo). Break an egg on to it, then season with salt and pepper and add a pinch each of chopped parsley and coriander (cilantro). Fold the pastry in two diagonally, then fold over both edges and finally the tip so that the egg is well sealed. Fry immediately till golden, basting with spoonfuls of oil so that the pastry puffs up. Drain the brik on paper towels and serve piping hot.

BRILL *barbue* A marine flatfish of the family *Bothidae* similar to the turbot, with the same fine white nutritious flesh. Brill is less expensive than turbot, in spite of the considerable waste involved in its preparation. However, it is becoming scarcer in the sandy bed of the eastern Atlantic from which it is fished. It is 30–75 cm (12–30 in) long and weighs 1–2 kg (2¼–4½ lb), sometimes 3 kg (6½ lb). The top of the body is smooth, grey or beige in colour, with small pearly markings. The underside is creamy white.

Brill can be prepared in many ways, particularly with red or white wine, champagne or cider. It can also be grilled (broiled) whole or baked. It can be served cold with various sauces. When poached, it can be garnished with prawns (shrimp), mussels, oysters or crayfish. The famous chef Dugléré gave his name to a recipe for brill, which he created at the Café Anglais in Paris.

RECIPES

preparation of brill

Clean the fish by making a transverse incision underneath the head, on the dark side. Remove the scales. Trim all round the fish, slightly shortening the tail, and wash. If the brill is to be cooked whole, braised or poached, make a longitudinal incision along the centre of the dark side. Slightly loosen the fillets and break the backbone in two or three places. If prepared in this way, the brill does not lose its shape during cooking.

To fillet the fish, lay the cleaned, scaled and washed brill on the table, dark side down. Make an incision along the centre from top to tail, then slide the knife blade underneath the flesh and, keeping it flat against the bone, gently ease away the fillets and lift them, detaching them at the head (by cutting round the head) and the tail. Turn the fish over and repeat for the other side. Lay the fillets on the table, skin side down. Holding the fillet by the tail end, slide the blade of a filleting knife between the skin and the flesh with one quick movement.

braised brill

Season the brill and put it in a shallow pan on a bed of sliced carrots and onions which have been lightly fried in butter. Add concentrated fish stock, thyme, parsley and a bay leaf. Bring to simmering point, cover and cook in a preheated oven at 160°C (325°F, gas 3) for 25 minutes for a 1.5 kg (3¼ lb) fish, basting frequently.

Drain the brill and remove the backbone. This is most easily done by placing the fish, dark side up, on a well-buttered long plate or dish. Remove the fillets with a very sharp knife, take out the bone and replace the fillets. Reheat briefly.

Choose your garnish and matching sauce from the list below before cooking the fish. Make the sauce using the well-reduced and strained cooking liquor. Braised brill moistened with red wine fish stock reduced to the consistency of a fumet can be served with the following garnishes: bourguignonne, Chambertin or mâconnaise. Brill braised in white wine can be served with one of the garnishes used for fish cooked in white wine, especially those recommended for sole.

brill chérubin

Prepare and cook as for braised brill. Arrange the fish on a long dish and surround with small mounds of very thick tomato sauce, alternated (if desired), with diced truffles. Fry thin strips of red (bell) pepper in butter. Strain the cooking stock, reduce until syrupy, then add it to a hollandaise sauce with the strips of pepper. Coat the brill with the sauce and glaze rapidly in a preheated oven at 230°C (450°F, gas 8).

brill stuffed with salmon

Clean a brill weighing about 2 kg (4½ lb) and slit it lengthways down the middle on the dark side. Remove the central bone through this opening, taking care not to tear the white skin. Season the brill and stuff it with a cream forcemeat made of salmon and truffles. Lay the fish in a buttered flameproof dish, season, moisten with 400 ml (14 fl oz, 1¾ cups) white wine fish fumet, cover and bring gently to simmering point. Poach gently in a preheated oven at 180°C (350°F, gas 4) for about 30 minutes. When the brill is cooked, drain, then blot with paper towels and transfer carefully to a serving dish. Keep warm. Boil down the juices, add to normande sauce and pour over the fish. The following garnishes are suitable: amiral, cancalaise, cardinal, champenoise, diplomate, Nantua, Polignac or Victoria.

fillets of brill with mushroom duxelles

Prepare about 400 g (14 oz, 3½ cups) mushroom duxelles*, bind with tomato sauce and spread in the bottom of a serving dish. Keep warm. Season the fillets with salt and pepper, coat with flour and fry in a mixture of butter and oil. Arrange the cooked fish on the mushroom duxelles and coat with the hot butter left in the pan after frying the fish. Sprinkle with chopped parsley and garnish with slices of lemon.

poached brill

Place the cleaned brill in a fish kettle or large saucepan. Cover with cold fish stock and poach gently for about 10 minutes after reaching simmering point, until just tender. Drain and remove the dark skin. Prepared in this way, it can be served with various sauces – prawn (shrimp), Mornay or Nantua – or garnished with spinach, *à la portugaise, à la provençale, à la russe* or with lobster escalopes (scallops) *à l'américaine.* It can also be served au gratin in the same way as sole.

other recipes See *Bercy, bonne femme, Brancas, cardinal, créole, dieppoise, fermière, florentine, provençale, Véron.*

BRILLAT-SAVARIN

A cow's-milk cheese from Normandy named after the French author who said that 'a meal without cheese is like a beautiful woman with only one eye'.

The cheese was invented early in the 20th century by Androuet, the famous Parisian master cheesemaker. It has a soft triple-cream paste (75% fat content), a white downy crust and a mild flavour, and it smells of cream. Brillat-Savarin is disc-shaped, 13.5 cm (5½ in) in diameter and 3.5 cm (1½ in) thick. It is a more refined version of another cheese from Bray, called Excelsior.

BRILLAT-SAVARIN, JEAN-ANTHELME

French magistrate and gastronome (born Belley, 1755; died Saint-Denis, 1826). The eldest of eight children, Jean-Anthelme Brillat spent all his youth in Bugey, where he became interested in cooking; his mother, whose Christian name was Aurore, was an accomplished cordon bleu cook (see *oreiller de la Belle Aurore*). An aunt, called Savarin, left him her fortune on condition that he took her name.

After studying law at Dijon, followed by elementary chemistry and medicine, Brillat-Savarin joined the bar at Belley. In 1789 the young solicitor, elected deputy to the National Assembly, came to the notice of the Forum, in particular because of a speech against the abolition of the death penalty. Returning to his own region, he was elected president of the civil court at Ain, then mayor and commander of the National Guard. The fall of the Girondins forced him into exile because the Revolutionary tribunal accused him of moderatism and issued a summons against him. He said that the day before his departure for Switzerland he had a memorable dinner at an inn in the Jura, where he enjoyed a 'fricassee of chicken liberally garnished with truffles', served with a 'sweet and generous' white wine.

■ **Exile and return** Brillat-Savarin went to Switzerland, then Holland, where he embarked for the United States. He stayed there for three years, living on the proceeds of French lessons and as a violinist with the orchestra of the John Street Theater in New York. There he discovered roast turkey and Welsh rarebit, taught the art of scrambling eggs to a French chef in Boston (who subsequently sent him, by way of thanks, venison haunches from Canada), and enjoyed pot-roast goose, corned beef and punch. In 1797 he obtained permission to return to France, but he had lost all his possessions, in particular a vineyard. After a few temporary jobs, he was appointed counsellor to the Supreme Court of Appeal and kept this post until his death.

He remained a bachelor and spent his leisure time drafting various treatises on economics and history and an essay on the duel. He was interested in archaeology, astronomy, chemistry and, of course, gastronomy, appreciating good restaurants, especially Grand Véfour, Véry, Beauvilliers and Tortoni. He entertained frequently at home in the Rue de Richelieu in Paris and cooked some specialities himself, including tuna omelette, stuffed pheasant garnished with oranges, and fillet of beef with truffles. Having survived so many regimes, from the Empire to the Restoration, he died after catching cold at a mass celebrated in memory of Louis XVI in the basilica of Saint-Denis. On 8 December 1825, two months before his death, the book which was to make him famous had appeared in the bookshops: *Physiologie du goût ou Méditations de gastronomie transcendante, ouvrage théorique, historique et à l'ordre du jour, dédié aux gastronomes parisiens par un professeur, membre de plusieurs sociétés littéraires et savantes.*

■ **The professor of gastronomy** The work was immediately successful and aroused the enthusiasm of Balzac but the envy of others, such as Carême and the Marquis de Cussy, and even the contempt of Baudelaire. Grimod de La Reynière had led the way in gastronomic literature, but it was Brillat-Savarin's ambition to make the culinary art a true science, calling on chemistry, physics, medicine and anatomy, which made the text somewhat pedantic. His didactic spirit led him to treat his subject as an exact science, tracing cause from effect. But Brillat-Savarin was also a storyteller with numerous anecdotes and a defender of greed, with an elegant humorous style. His *Physiologie* remains a pleasant read, instructive in spite of certain omissions (such as the absence of a chapter on wine).

• STORYTELLER AND EPICURE In spite of his sometimes excessive 'theorems' and some doubtful aphorisms, Brillat-Savarin's work has been constantly reissued. It came at the right time for the education of a well-informed and prosperous bourgeoisie, who respected the past and admired progress and who wanted to live well. As the author himself said,

'Greed is a passionate, reasoned and habitual preference for those objects which flatter taste.'

The best pages of the *Physiologie* contain Brillat-Savarin's observations on certain foods and preparations: the pot-au-feu and broth, poultry and game (with his personal memories of hunting in the New World), truffles, sugar, coffee and chocolate. His 'Théorie de la friture' combines anecdote with culinary accuracy. His 'Histoire philosophique de la cuisine' is both erudite and humorous and covers the period from the discovery of fire to the end of the age of Louis XVI; it ends with a description of the restaurants of Paris in the years 1810–1820. In his 'Variétés' there are still more tasty morsels to be found, such as the priest's omelette, which was 'round, large-bellied, and cooked to a turn' and for which he gives the recipe. He expresses his indignation at the fingerbowl practice, finding it 'useless, indecent and disgusting; he imparts the secret of an improvised way of steaming turbot 'on a bed of pungent herbs; he describes the Chevalier of Albignac demonstrating French salad before a British audience; and, after giving the recipe for Swiss fondue, he ends with a selection of gastronomic poems. As a postscript, the professor gives the reader the addresses of his favourite suppliers (the grocery shop of Madame Chevet at the Palais-Royal, the pastrycook Achard and his neighbour the baker).

■ **A ubiquitous surname** The name of the author of the *Physiologie du goût* has been given to a variety of preparations and to a garnish made of a salpicon of foie gras and truffles. This may be placed in small tarts or in shells of duchess potatoes to be served with game or noisettes of lamb, or it may be used as a filling for an omelette. Another Brillat-Savarin garnish is based on asparagus tips served with soft-boiled (soft-cooked) eggs.

RECIPES

boned partridge Brillat-Savarin
Open out the partridge and remove as much bone as possible. Flatten the partridge and season with salt and pepper. Seal by frying rapidly in butter. Cover both sides with a forcemeat of foie gras and truffle. Wrap the partridge in a piece of pig's caul, coat with breadcrumbs, and grill (broil) gently. Place on a bed of lentil purée. It can be served with a well-reduced Madeira sauce, containing game stock.

croûtes Brillat-Savarin
Bake some small savoury pastry cases (pie shells) blind. Fill with a salpicon of calves' or lambs' sweetbreads and sautéed mushrooms and, as in the original, some cockscombs and kidneys, all bound with a reduced demi-glace or Madeira sauce.

flan Brillat-Savarin
Make a flan case (pie shell) of fine savoury pastry and bake blind. While still warm, fill with very creamy scrambled eggs with truffles. Heat some sliced truffles in clarified butter, season with salt

and pepper, and arrange on the eggs. Sprinkle with grated Parmesan cheese and melted butter. Brown well.

oeufs en cocotte Brillat-Savarin
Butter some ramekin dishes and fill with small cooked pasta shapes sautéed in butter. Break an egg into each ramekin dish and bake in a bain marie. Heat some asparagus tips in butter and use to garnish the eggs. Add a ring of well-reduced Madeira sauce.

timbale Brillat-Savarin
Bake some brioche dough in a charlotte mould. Scoop out the middle, leaving a thickness of 1 cm (½ in) lining the bottom and sides. Prepare a confectioner's custard (pastry cream) containing crushed macaroons, then cook some pear quarters in vanilla-flavoured syrup. Heat some apricot purée mixed with kirsch and brush it around the inside of the brioche case. Warm this through gently in the oven. Fill the timbale with alternate layers of confectioner's custard and pears, finishing with a layer of pears. Decorate with crystallized (candied) fruit and warm it in the oven once more. This timbale may be served with apricot sauce.

BRIMONT A name given in classic French cookery to certain decorative dishes, probably originally dedicated by a chef to his master.

RECIPES

brimont salad
Cook and peel some potatoes and prepare cooked artichoke hearts. Dice both vegetables coarsely and mix with mayonnaise flavoured with sherry. Arrange in a dome in the centre of a serving dish and surround with clusters of stoned (pitted) black olives, crayfish tails and quartered hard-boiled (hard-cooked) eggs, all seasoned with olive oil and sherry vinegar. Garnish the salad with a few slices of truffle. The crayfish tails may be replaced by large peeled prawns (shrimp).

soft-boiled (or poached) eggs brimont
Add some Madeira or cream to a chicken velouté and reduce. Fill a cooked, shallow puff pastry pie crust (shell) with creamed mushrooms. Arrange the eggs in a ring on top. Fill the centre with small chicken croquettes. Coat with reduced velouté sauce and garnish each egg with a slice of truffle.

BRINDAMOUR A sheep's-milk cheese from Corsica (45% fat content), which is soft and has a crust sprinkled with thyme and savory. Brindamour is a large square with rounded corners, weighing 600–800 g (1¼–1¾ lb). Also known as *fleur du maquis* ('flower of the maquis'), it has a sweet, scented flavour.

BRINE A salt solution used to preserve meat, fish or vegetables. Brine sometimes also contains saltpetre, sugar and flavourings. Small items can be pickled in brine on a domestic scale, but large items come within the sphere of industrial salting.

The pink colour of ham is due to the saltpetre in the brine. In charcuterie brine is often injected into the meat before immersion. Cooked hams were traditionally treated either with old brine, brought to the required concentration by the addition of salt and nitrate, or with fresh brine mixed with the remains of the old brine, which provided some nitrate-reducing bacteria and some ready-made nitrite. Fresh brines containing selected bacteria strains are usually used for modern curing. Unfortunately, this change has led to faster salting, which, with the addition of polyphosphates, does not improve the flavour of ham.

BRINZEN Also known as Bryndza. A Hungarian ewe's-milk cheese in the shape of a cylinder weighing 5, 10, 20 or 30 kg (11, 22, 44 or 66 lb). Left to ferment in brine and milk during the winter, it is eaten in spring and has a strong piquant flavour. Brinzen is similar to the Romanian *brandza* (which is milder, stored in salt water, and cut into cubes) and the Russian *brynza*.

BRIOCHE A soft loaf or roll made from a yeast dough enriched with butter and eggs.

The word 'brioche' first appeared in 1404, and for a long time its etymology was the subject of controversy. Some maintained that it originated in Brie, and Alexandre Dumas claimed that the dough was originally kneaded with cheese from Brie. It is now considered that brioche is derived from the verb *brier*, an old Norman form of the verb *broyer* meaning 'to pound' (this is found in *pain brie*, a speciality of Normandy). This explanation is all the more likely since the brioches from Gournay and Gisors in Normandy have always been highly regarded.

The dough is a mixture of flour, yeast, water or milk, a little sugar, eggs and butter. The substitution of baker's yeast (dating from the 18th century) for brewer's yeast made it lighter. Brioche dough can be moulded in many ways. The traditional *brioche à tête*, or Parisian brioche, is made with a smaller ball on top, like a head. Brioches are also moulded into hexagonal shapes with marked-out sections: these are Nanterre brioches (or brioche loaves). The *brioche mousseline* is tall and cylindrical and is the most delicate. A traditional variation consists of adding raisins to the brioche dough.

The brioche, often in the shape of a ring, is one of the most widespread regional pastries, eaten by all sections of society. When the revolutionary crowd marched on Versailles, protesting that they had no bread, Queen Marie Antionette in ignorance replied, 'Let them eat brioche'. Varieties worthy of mention are the *brioche coulante (fallue)* from Normandy; brioche with pralines from Saint-Genix; the Twelfth-Night cake (*tourtillon*) from Bordeaux; *gâtais de la mariée* from Vendée, which can measure up to 1.3 m (over 4 ft) in diameter; brioche stuffed with hazel-

nuts, raisins and dried pears from the Vosges; and brioche with cream cheese or Gruyère from Gannat. Not to be forgotten are *fouaces, pompes, couques* and *cramiques, koeckbotteram* from Dunkirk; *campanili* from Corsica; and *pastis* from Béarn – all of which are rustic brioches with various flavourings.

Brioche is served as a dessert or with tea, but it also has many culinary uses. Ordinary brioche dough is suitable for koulibiac and fillet of beef en croûte; *brioche mousseline* accompanies foie gras, sausage and *cervelas* (saveloy) from Lyons. Small individual brioches are used as cases for various sweet or savoury sauced mixtures served as hot main dishes or as desserts.

RECIPES

classic brioche dough

Soften 225 g (8 oz, 1 cup) butter at room temperature. Crumble 7 g (¼ oz, ½ cake) fresh (compressed) yeast and stir in 1 tablespoon warm water. In a separate container stir 1 tablespoon sugar and a pinch of salt into 2 tablespoons cold milk. Sift 250 g (9 oz, 2¼ cups) strong plain (bread) flour, make a well in the centre, and add the yeast mixture and 1 lightly beaten egg. After working in a little flour, add the sugar and salt mixture, and another lightly beaten egg. Continue to work the dough until it becomes smooth and elastic. It should stretch easily. Mix a third of the dough with the softened butter, then add the second and finally the remaining third of the dough to the mixture.

Put the dough in a 2 litre (3½ pint, 9 cup) container, cover with a cloth, and leave to rise in a warm place until it has doubled in volume. Then separate the dough into 3 pieces, knead lightly and leave to rise again. Leave to rest for a few hours in a cool place: the dough is now ready to be shaped and baked.

• *Standard brioche dough* This is prepared in exactly the same way, but the quantity of butter is reduced to 175 g (6 oz, ¾ cup).

• *Pâte levée pour tartes* This yeasted brioche dough is used for tarts and flans. Prepare as for brioche dough, but use 250 g (9 oz, 2¼ cups) plain (all-purpose) flour, 7 g (¼ oz, ½ cake) fresh (compressed) yeast, ½ teaspoon salt, 2 teaspoons caster (superfine) sugar, 2 eggs, 100 g (4 oz, ½ cup) butter and 6 tablespoons milk.

brioche bordelaise

Lightly flour the worktop (work surface). Place 300 g (11 oz) brioche dough (classic or standard) on the floured surface and flatten with the hand to make a thick disc. Finely chop 65 g (2½ oz, ½ cup) crystallized (candied) fruit and distribute it evenly over the surface of the dough. Bring the edges of the dough to the centre to form a ball. Place the ball of dough on a buttered baking sheet and leave it to rest for 10 minutes. Push both thumbs into the centre of the ball and pull the dough gently into the shape of a ring. When the hole is about 10 cm

(4 in) in diameter, leave to rest for about 1½ hours.

Brush the ring with beaten egg. Crush 12 sugar lumps with a rolling pin. Using scissors dipped in water, cut 5 mm (¼ in) deep sloping notches into the surface of the ring. Bake in a preheated oven at 200°C (400°F, gas 6) for at least 30 minutes, then take the brioche out of the oven and decorate with whole crystallized (candied) fruits and crushed sugar.

brioche mousseline

Cut 2 pieces of foil twice the height of a cylindrical 1 litre (1¾ pint, 4⅓ cup) mould. Line the mould with the double thickness of foil shaped into a cylinder. Butter the bottom of the mould and the full height of the foil. Place a 300 g (11 oz) ball of fine brioche dough in the mould and leave to rise at room temperature until it comes to 1 cm (½ in) below the top of the mould.

Brush the surface of the brioche with a beaten egg and make 2–4 cross-shaped incisions in the top of the dough using a pair of wetted scissors. Bake in a preheated oven at 200°C (400°F, gas 6) for about 30 minutes. Turn out of the mould while still warm.

fruit brioche ♦

Toss prepared and diced seasonal fruit (such as peaches and pears, plums and apricots, or plums and pears) in the juice of 1 lemon. Sprinkle with a little sugar and pour a little fruit liqueur or suitable spirit over and mix well. Cover and set aside to macerate. Prepare frangipane cream and leave to cool.

Line a large or the required number of individual round moulds or tins (pans) with brioche dough. Spread with frangipane cream, leaving a border around the edge. Drain the fruit (reserve the soaking liquor to flavour a fruit coulis to accompany the brioche) and arrange it in a layer on top of the frangipane cream. Cover with brioche dough, pressing the edges together to seal in the filling, then leave to rise in a warm place for about 1 hour, until doubled in size.

Brush the brioche or brioches with beaten egg and bake until golden. A large brioche will take about 30 minutes in a preheated oven at 200°C (400°F, gas 6); individual brioches will take about 15 minutes in a preheated oven at 220°C (425°F, gas 7). Dust with icing (confectioner's) sugar and serve hot, decorated with pieces of fresh fruit. Fruit coulis goes well with the brioche – prepare it using the same type of fruit as in the filling and flavour the coulis with the reserved soaking liquor.

Parisian brioche (brioche à tête)

Lightly flour the hands and the worktop (work surface), then divide 275 g (10 oz) brioche dough into 2 balls, 225 g (8 oz) for the body of the brioche and the remaining 50 g (2 oz) for the head. Roll the large ball by hand until it is perfectly round. Butter a 500 ml (17 fl oz, 2 cup) brioche mould and place the larger ball inside it. Roll the small ball of dough into a pear shape. Make a hole in the top of the

large ball and insert the pointed end of the small ball; press down with the fingertips. Allow to double in volume at room temperature, for about 1½ hours.

Make some small incisions in the large ball, from the edges towards the head, using wet scissors. Brush the brioche with beaten egg and bake in a preheated oven at 200°C (400°F, gas 6) for 30 minutes. Turn out of the mould while still warm.

• *Individual Parisian brioches* These are made in the same way as the large brioches, using small brioche moulds. Bake in a preheated oven at 225°C (425°F, gas 7), but allow only 15 minutes for cooking.

rolled brioche with raisins

Soak 75 g (3 oz, ½ cup) raisins in 4 tablespoons rum. Butter a 20 cm (8 in) Genoese mould (a sponge cake mould with sides sloping outwards towards the top) and line it with 150 g (5 oz) flattened brioche dough. Cover with a thin layer of confectioner's custard (pastry cream). Lightly flour the worktop (work surface). Place 165 g (5½ oz) dough on the floured surface and roll out to a rectangle 20 × 12 cm (8 × 5 in). Cover this rectangle with confectioner's custard, then spread with the drained raisins. Roll the rectangle into a sausage 20 cm (8 in) long and cut into 6 equal portions. Lay these portions flat in the lined mould and leave to rise for 2 hours in a warm place.

Brush over the entire surface of the brioche with beaten egg. Bake for about 30 minutes in a preheated oven at 200°C (400°F, gas 6). If the brioche colours too quickly, protect it with a sheet of foil. Take the cooked brioche out of the oven, sprinkle with vanilla or rum syrup, then turn out of the mould while still warm. When the brioche is cold, brush with syrup made from 65 g (2½ oz, ½ cup) icing (confectioners') sugar mixed with 2 tablespoons hot water.

Filled Savoury Brioches
brioches with anchovies

Using standard brioche dough without sugar, prepare some very small (cocktail size) Parisian brioches in tiny fluted moulds. When cooked, allow to cool completely, wrap in foil and place in the refrigerator for 1 hour. Then remove the heads of the brioches and carefully scoop out the insides of the brioche bases, using the bread taken out to make very fine breadcrumbs. Add these to the same volume of softened anchovy butter. Fill the brioches with this mixture and put the heads back on. Put in a cool place until required for serving. The mixture of breadcrumbs and anchovy butter can be lightened by adding a little whipped cream.

brioches with cheese

Prepare the brioches as for brioches with anchovies (but make them a little bigger). Fill with a thick

Fruit brioche.

Mornay sauce mixed with diced York or Bayonne ham. Reheat in the oven.

brioches with foie gras

Prepare the brioches as for brioches with anchovies. Fill with a mousse of foie gras mixed with softened butter. Put in a cool place until ready to serve.

brioches with mushrooms

Prepare the brioches as for brioches with anchovies (but make them a little bigger). Fill with mushroom duxelles mixed with a little béchamel sauce. Heat in the oven.

Filled Sweet Brioches

brioche with raspberries

Make a large brioche mousseline and allow to cool completely. Slice off the top and scoop out the inside, leaving a thickness of about 1 cm (½ in) at the bottom and sides. Add some kirsch to melted butter and sprinkle this mixture over the inside of the brioche; fill with a mixture of raspberries and whipped cream. (Wild strawberries may be used instead of raspberries.)

Alternatively, the brioche may be filled with confectioner's custard (pastry cream) lightened with whipped cream and mixed with stoned (pitted) cherries, poached in syrup and drained.

Caribbean brioche

Hollow out a large brioche mousseline in the same way as for brioche with raspberries. Cut the brioche removed from the inside into cubes and brown these in butter. Reduce the syrup from a can of pineapple by three-quarters and flavour with rum. Cut the pineapple into large dice. Cut some firm ripe bananas into thin slices and heat these with the pineapple dice in butter; place the fruit in the reduced syrup. Add the cubes of brioche, mix together, and fill the brioche with the mixture. Replace the top and heat in the oven.

BRISSE, BARON LÉON French journalist (born Gémenos, 1813; died Fontenay-aux-Roses, 1876). Having begun his career in the Water and Forestry department, which he was obliged to leave after a scandal, he turned to journalism and specialized in gastronomic articles. It was his idea to print a different menu every day in the newspaper *La Liberté*. These recipes were put together in 1868 in a collection called *Les trois cents soixante-six menus du Baron Brisse*. He also published *Recettes à l'usage des ménages bourgeois et des petits ménages* (1868), *La Petite Cuisine du Baron Brisse* (1870) and *La Cuisine en Carême* (1873). He was often reproached for not being able to cook and his recipes are sometimes whimsical and even extraordinary, such as 'scoter duck with chocolate', a burlesque way of preparing a kind of duck with tough oily flesh. But he also gives a recipe for terrine of foie gras and *garbure* (cabbage and bacon soup). The 'paper gastrophile' as he was nicknamed by his colleagues, this

enormous and truculent individual died at an inn in Fontenay-aux-Roses, where he had taken up lodgings. For several years his friends, including Monselet and Gouffé, observed the anniversary of his death by meeting at the inn, where the landlord, Gigout, symbolically laid Baron Brisse's place.

His name has been given to a garnish for large joints of meat, consisting of onions with chicken forcemeat and stuffed olive tartlets.

BRISTOL A garnish served with large roasts of meat (beef or lamb), noisettes of lamb and tournedos. Consisting of small risotto croquettes, flageolet beans cooked in butter and château potatoes, it probably takes its name from the Parisian hotel of the same name.

BRITTANY See *opposite page*.

BRIX SCALE A scale of measurement for the density or specific gravity of syrups made with cane or beet sugar, evaluated using a saccharometer. It replaced the Baumé scale in 1962.

BROAD BEAN (FAVA BEAN) An annual leguminous plant cultivated for its flat seeds, used as food for man and animals since the Bronze Age, possibly of Near East origin. It was known in ancient Egypt (see *ful medames*), but the Greeks had religious reservations about eating it – it brought bad luck. Named from the Latin *Vicia faba*, it was the European staple for centuries. It is the original bean in the Twelfth-Night cake, which made it a 'good luck' bean. They are cultivated across the world, including China.

Broad beans are easily distinguished from kidney beans because they lie across the pod, so the contact point is on the end. There are several varieties, the pale green one being common; the Windsor bean, with four beans to the pod, is the largest. Tiny fresh beans are eaten raw at the meal's end in Italy, accompanied by Pecorino cheese. Cook fresh, podded beans in simmering salted water – savory is the classic herb flavouring. Larger beans are best skinned, to reveal their bright green interiors. In America favas are combined with sweetcorn, to make succotash, but the classic European preparation is a purée (good with pork) because traditionally it was pressed through a sieve to remove the skins. *Favá*, the Greek salad with yogurt and lemon juice, is one example.

Dried beans are more nutritious than fresh ones because they are allowed to grow to full size before being harvested. Broad beans contain a chemical substance to which some people, particularly in the Mediterranean and Iran, are allergic. The allergy, known as favism, is inherited and it leads to destruction of red blood cells, resulting in severe anaemia.

Dried broad beans were the original bean used in the famous dried bean dishes cassoulet and *fabada* (though both are made with different beans in contemporary recipes). The dried bean, dark and

Brittany

The cuisine of France's extreme north-western province benefits from being well supplied with prime products of land and sea. Livestock rearing provides good meat, particularly sheep grazed on the salt meadows. The most popular specialities are buckwheat and bacon soup, the substantial *potée bretonne* (shoulder of lamb boiled with duck, sausage and vegetables), *pâte de Bécherel* (garlic pie), chitterling sausages (hot or cold), potted pork from Vallet, *boudin blanc* from Rennes, *courraye* or *pâté de courres* (galantine of offal), poached eggs *à la bretonne* and a range of buckwheat savoury pancakes, garnished with eggs, cheese, various cold meats or fried sardines, which constitute a complete meal in themselves.

The list of shellfish is impressive, including razor fish, scallops, clams and oysters. Sea urchins, prawns and shrimps are used for specific regional dishes, but there are more varied recipes for crabs and lobsters – *à la vinaigrette, à la mayonnaise*, grilled (broiled), *au naturel, à l'armoricaine* and *à la morlaisienne*. Scallops are prepared *à la nantaise, à la nage* or cooked with cream; monkfish is cooked with cider; cod is prepared *à la bretonne*; tuna is

fried; sardines are grilled (broiled); shad is stuffed; eel is cooked *à la ploërmelaise*, marinated and grilled (broiled); pike is cooked *au beurre blanc*; and lamprey is prepared *à la matelote. Cotriade* and conger eel soup are the delight of all fish lovers.

Meat specialities include *côte au farci, casse*, leg of lamb *à la bretonne, potée bretonne*, Nantes bacon (belly of pork braised with rind, offal, herbs and white wine) and rabbit with nutmeg. Poultry dishes include duck with peas, *bardatte* and grilled Janze chicken. These dishes are served with choice early vegetables and cooked vegetable dishes: cauliflower (stuffed, or served in its own cooking liquor or butter,

This trawler, returning to the harbour of Guilvinec, in Finistère, is laden with freshly caught fish to be sold at auction.

or *à la crème*), artichokes, potato cakes and beans *à la bretonne* are all washed down with excellent cider.

Among the desserts are the famous Breton crêpes made from wheat flour and eaten hot, spread with butter or jam, or with melted chocolate, lemon juice or liqueur. Pastries include *crêpes dentelle* (very thin pancakes), *bigoudens*, Mam'Goz fritters, *craquelins, far kouing aman* (a rich yeast cake), Breton cake and *maingaux* (a whipped cream dessert) from Rennes.

---

wrinkled, needs very long slow cooking. It survives in southern Italy and in traditional European dishes, but the leathery skin is best removed after cooking. However the 'Greek' bean is a much better white derivative, without the heavy skin (see *beans, dried*). This butter bean and the dried lima are often the cook's alternative for the original dried fava bean.

RECIPES

broad beans with savory
Shell, skin and cook some broad beans in salted boiling water with a bunch of savory. Drain them well and heat in a shallow frying pan for a few moments until thoroughly dry. Add a generous knob of butter and a little cream. Mix gently over a low heat for a few seconds, taking care to ensure that the beans do not break.

purée of fresh broad beans
Shell and skin 500 g (18 oz) fresh broad beans and simmer in a covered pan with 7 tablespoons water, 50 g (2 oz, ¼ cup) butter, a sprig of savory, a pinch of salt and 1 teaspoon sugar. Pureé in a blender. Add some consommé to the purée if liked.

BROCCIO Also known as Brocciu or Brucciu. A cheese from Corsica made of ewe's milk, or sometimes goat's milk, with an oily texture (45% fat content). It is generally eaten fresh, from the end of autumn to the beginning of spring, but it can also be matured (*demi-sec*). It is used in the preparation of many local dishes and pastries, including *imbrucciata, fiadone*, stuffed pancakes, omelettes, sardines, artichokes and courgettes (zucchini). Traditionally drained in small cane moulds, Broccio (a corruption

BROCCOLI

romanesco

calabrese

the US in the early 20th century by Italian immigrants, and is now cultivated in California.

Sprouting broccoli (usually purple-budded, but also white) became popular in northern Europe in the 18th century. This has a number of loose terminal heads, about 15 cm (6 in) long, but also smaller heads in the axils of the leaves lower down the plant. It overwinters, to provide an early spring vegetable. Known in America since the 18th century, the heads are steamed or poached, while the stalks are sometimes eaten like asparagus.

Romanesco is the autumn broccoli with the large yellowish-green heads divided into conspicuous little peaked groups.

RECIPES

broccoli, potato and bacon pot with soup
Soak a piece of unsmoked streaky bacon about 500 g (18 oz) in cold water, then place in a large saucepan with 2 litres (3½ pints, 9 cups) cold water; simmer for about 1½ hours. Add 1 kg (2¼ lb) prepared broccoli, 2 crushed garlic cloves, with a little salt. Add 575 g (1¼ lb) quartered potatoes and boil for 15 minutes.

Drain the broccoli, chop coarsely and heat with 40 g (1½ oz, 3 tablespoons) butter. Cut the bacon into slices and brown in 25 g (1 oz, 2 tablespoons) butter. Drain the potatoes and slice. Layer the broccoli, then the potatoes and finally the slices of bacon in a heated dish. Sprinkle with the butter used for cooking.

Add 25 g (1 oz, 2 tablespoons) butter to the water in which the bacon and vegetables were cooked. Pour this stock into a soup tureen over thin slices of wholemeal bread dried in the oven. Sprinkle with chopped parsley and serve the soup before the hotpot.

broccoli à la crème
Prepare 1 kg (2¼ lb) broccoli, then blanch it in 2 litres (3½ pints, 9 cups) boiling salted water for about 30 seconds. Drain the broccoli and chop very coarsely. Lightly brown 50 g (2 oz, ¼ cup) butter in a frying pan and add 150–200 ml (5–7 fl oz, ⅔–¾ cup) double (heavy) cream. When the cream is coloured, add the broccoli. Season with pepper and again with salt if necessary. Simmer for about 10 minutes. Serve the broccoli very hot with roast or sautéed meat or with certain types of fish, such as bass, cod or hake.

of *brousse*, meaning 'brush') is eaten within 48 hours. Otherwise it is salted and left to dry; when hard it is wrapped in dry asphodel leaves and stored in a cool place. When it is used to flavour a dish, it must be desalted for some time in cold water.

BROCCOLI A vegetable of the brassica family cultivated for its fleshy heads of flower buds. There are several varieties, including small-headed purple sprouting and large-headed calabrese.

Originating in Italy (the name is derived from the Italian *broccolo*, meaning cabbage sprout), this vegetable was popular in Roman times. It was introduced to France by Catherine de' Medici. Calabrese (the Italian name) has substantial dark green flower heads (occasionally purple or bluish). It is cooked like cauliflower. In Italy it remains one of the most popular new season vegetables, being cooked with olive oil, white wine and garlic. It was introduced to

BROCHETTE A large slightly flattened skewer, usually made of stainless steel, on which pieces of meat, fish and vegetables are threaded for cooking under a grill (broiler) or over charcoal. If the ingredients are to be fried, the skewer is made of wood. There are single brochettes, with a ring or handle, and double brochettes (with two needles). Electric rotating grills may be equipped with vertical brochettes and some rôtisseries are fitted with brochette drums.

The preparation cooked in this way is also called a brochette. The traditional ingredients are kidneys or pieces of calves' sweetbreads, scallops, large cubes of beef or mutton (sometimes marinated), possibly small birds, alternating with sliced mushrooms, lean bacon, quartered tomatoes, pieces of onion and sweet (bell) pepper. Most brochettes have more flavour – and are more tender – if their ingredients are marinated in oil, chopped herbs, sometimes garlic and brandy, salt, pepper and various spices. (Since the ingredients of kebabs are small, 30 minutes' marinating is quite sufficient.) The ingredients are then threaded on to the skewer and cooked. Brochettes are served as a hot hors d'oeuvre or as a main dish with a garnish of rice or ratatouille. (See *attelet, attereau, kebab, shashlyk.*)

RECIPES

Brochettes of Fish and Seafood

eel brochettes
Skin and clean a large eel, cut off the head and the tail. Wash, wipe dry and then cut the body into 8 portions. Marinate for 30 minutes in the same mixture as for seafood brochettes. Cut some streaky bacon into thick strips and marinate with the eel. Then, without draining them, thread the pieces of eel on to skewers with the bacon. Grill (broil) under a high heat for about 15 minutes, basting with a little flavoured oil. Serve these brochettes with green mayonnaise, tartare sauce, rémoulade sauce or hot shallot sauce.

monkfish brochettes
Cut the flesh of a monkfish (taken from the tail, which is less expensive than the middle of the fish) into 2.5 cm (1 in) cubes and marinate with halved slices of aubergine (eggplant) for 30 minutes in the same mixture as for seafood brochettes (see below). Thread the skewers, alternating monkfish and aubergine, and grill (broil) under a medium heat for 16–18 minutes.

mussel brochettes
Place some large cleaned mussels in their shells (discard any open shells) in a pan with some finely chopped shallots, chopped parsley, a good pinch of thyme, ground pepper and a little dry white wine. Cook over a high heat until the mussels opened, then take them out of their shells. (Discard any unopened shells.) Stir a little cold water into some white mustard powder and spread on a plate. Roll the mussels in the mustard, then in breadcrumbs and thread on to the skewers. Leave for 1 hour. Just before cooking, sprinkle with a little melted butter; grill (broil) under a medium heat for about 10 minutes.

seafood brochettes
Prepare a marinade using olive oil, plenty of lemon juice, finely chopped herbs and garlic, fresh crumbled thyme, salt and pepper. Marinate an assortment of seafood for 30 minutes: oysters poached for 1 minute in their liquor, mussels opened by heating in the oven, raw scallops, lobster tails, large peeled prawns (shrimp) and scampi. Thread on to skewers without draining, alternating with very small mushrooms (pierced through the bottom of the cap) and fresh blanched cubed bacon (optional). Grill (broil) under a high heat.

Brochettes of Meat

brochettes of marinated fillet of beef
Prepare a marinade using 150 ml (¼ pint, ⅔ cup) olive oil, salt, pepper and chopped herbs. Cut up 500 g (18 oz) fillet of beef into 2.5 cm (1 in) cubes and cut 150–200 g (5–7 oz) smoked belly pork or bacon into strips; marinate these for 30 minutes. Remove the seeds from a green (bell) pepper and cut the flesh into 2.5 cm (1 in) squares. Cut off the stalks from 8 large button mushrooms, sprinkle with lemon juice and sauté briskly in oil with the pieces of pepper; drain as soon as the pepper is slightly softened. Thread the ingredients on to skewers, adding 2 whole baby onions to each skewer, one at each end of the other ingredients. Grill (broil) under a very high heat for 7–8 minutes.

lamb brochettes
Cut some well-trimmed fillet or leg of lamb into pieces 5 mm (¼ in) thick. Thread the pieces of meat on to skewers, alternating with blanched bacon strips and sliced wild mushrooms (optional) tossed in butter. Season with salt and pepper. Brush the brochettes with melted butter, roll in white breadcrumbs, sprinkle again with butter, then grill (broil) under a high heat.

pork brochettes with prunes
Remove the stones (pits) from the prunes. Wrap each prune in a short piece of smoked streaky bacon. Cut some pork loin into cubes. Marinate these ingredients for 30 minutes in a mixture of groundnut (peanut) oil, salt and pepper with a little grated nutmeg and cayenne pepper. Drain the pork and the bacon-wrapped prunes, thread on to skewers and grill (broil) under a medium heat for about 10 minutes.

Brochettes of Offal (Variety Meats)

calf's liver brochettes
Prepare the liver and some (bell) peppers as for lamb's liver brochettes, but add some large quartered onions to the marinade. Soften some chopped shallots in a little butter; add a little chopped garlic, then some wine vinegar. Assemble the brochettes and grill (broil) under a very high heat. Bring the flavoured vinegar to the boil and pour over the piping hot brochettes.

kidney brochettes
Skin some lambs' kidneys, then cut in half and remove the white core. The kidneys may then be brushed with oil, seasoned with salt and pepper

and threaded on to skewers to be grilled (broiled) under a very high heat. Alternatively, the kidneys may be seasoned with salt and pepper, brushed with melted butter, rolled in white breadcrumbs, and threaded on to the skewers, alternating with blanched strips of bacon. The whole is sprinkled with melted butter and grilled under a high heat. Serve the kidneys with maître d'hôtel butter.

Sliced calves' or lambs' sweetbreads, small pieces of beef or lamb, and chicken livers can also be prepared in this way.

lamb's liver brochettes

Cut the lamb's liver into 2.5 cm (1 in) cubes. Seed some red and green (bell) peppers and cut the flesh into 2.5 cm (1 in) squares. After marinating, thread these ingredients on to skewers, placing a cube of liver between a square of red pepper and a square of green pepper. Grill (broil) under a high heat.

BRODETTO An Italian soup containing a large assortment of fish and shellfish. It is possibly the Mediterranean's oldest fish soup, and certainly older than bouillabaisse, with which it shares a large number of ingredients. There are many regional variations. The Venetian version contains no tomato, the one made in the Marches contains saffron, while in the Abruzzi the latter is replaced by chilli.

BROILER See *grill*.

BROILING See *grilling*.

BROTH See *bouillon*.

BROU DE NOIX A liqueur made from green walnut husks. The soft shells are hollowed out, ground, flavoured with cinnamon and nutmeg, and macerated in alcohol. Sugar syrup is added and the mixture is then filtered. This traditional liqueur from Dauphiné, Quercy and central France is served as a digestive. Similar walnut liqueurs are made elsewhere in Europe.

BROUET In modern France 'brouet' is a pejorative term applied to any coarse and weak soup or stew. Originally it referred to the national dish of the Spartans, in particular under the tyranny of Lycurgus. 'Black *brouet*' was a sort of liquid stew made of fat, meat, blood and vinegar. It was served at communal civic meals which all citizens aged between seven and 60 years were required to attend. It is said that Denys the Ancient brought a Spartan cook to Syracuse and ordered him to prepare a *brouet* according to the rules. When he indignantly rejected it, his cook pointed out to him that the essential seasoning was missing; this was hunger, fatigue and thirst.

The word *brouet* was commonly used (without a pejorative meaning) in French cooking in the Middle Ages for a soup (*brouet* of oysters or fish), a stew (*brouet* of pullets) or a sauce (white *brouet* with

almonds, eggs and ground meat). The *Ménagier de Paris* gives a recipe for *brouet* from Germany, a very popular soup at the time. From it was derived *brouet d'accouchée*, a broth made from eggs, milk and sugar which used to be given to women in labour and newly married women the day after their wedding.

BROUFADO A Provençal speciality made with marinated beef cooked in a casserole with herbs, gherkins (sweet dill pickles) or capers, and fillets of anchovy. Mistral describes this dish as a 'fried meat with pepper sauce', but it is more of a stew or casserole, and is probably an old seaman's recipe.

RECIPE

broufado

Cut 900 g (2 lb) stewing beef into 5 cm (2 in) cubes. Marinate in a cool place for 24 hours in a mixture of 5 tablespoons red wine vinegar, 3 tablespoons olive oil, a large bouquet garni, a large sliced onion and some pepper. Desalt 6 anchovies. Drain the meat and heat in a flameproof casserole with 2 tablespoons olive oil. Add a large chopped onion, then the marinade and 175 ml (6 fl oz, ¾ cup) red or white wine. Bring to the boil, then cover and cook in a preheated oven at 200°C (400°F, gas 6) for 2 hours. Add a few small pickled onions and 3–4 sliced gherkins (sweet dill pickles). Cook for a further 15 minutes. Wash the desalted anchovies, remove the fillets and cut them into small pieces, mix with 2 teaspoons beurre manié and add to the casserole. Stir the broufado well for 2 minutes and serve piping hot with jacket potatoes.

BROUILLY A distinguished Beaujolais *cru*. The vineyards around the Montagne de Brouilly produce a very fruity wine, which must be drunk young. Côte-de-Brouilly, from the slopes of the mountain, owes its quite remarkable qualities to the soil and aspect. A little more full-bodied than Brouilly, it is one of the best Beaujolais wines and its bouquet is refined by a few years' maturation.

BROULAÏ A Caribbean fish stew cooked with sweet cassava roots or potatoes. The vegetables are browned in oil in a stewing pan, then removed and replaced by pieces of firm-fleshed fish, tomato purée (paste), onion and chilli pepper. Water is added and the mixture brought to the boil, then the vegetables are put back in the pan with a bay leaf. When the fish and vegetables are cooked, they are taken out of the pan and rice is cooked in the stock. The rice and stew are served together.

BROUSSE A French curd cheese (45% fat content) made in Provence from autumn to the beginning of spring; ewe's milk is used for Brousse du Rove (the most famous), and goat's or ewe's milk for Brousse de la Vésubie. White, mild, and creamy, unmatured and without crust, Brousse (from the Provençal *brousso*, meaning curds) is made from curds drained on muslin (cheesecloth), first into an earthenware dish with holes in to separate the buttermilk, then into cylindrical tin moulds with smaller holes. The paste must not be too dry.

Brousse is served with sugar and double (heavy) cream, with fruit (fresh or stewed), or with vinaigrette, herbs, garlic and chopped onions.

BROWN To cook meat or poultry in hot fat or oil until it takes on a golden-brown colour. The term is also applied to chopped or sliced onion which is first sweated, then cooked until dark.

BROWNIE A very sweet, moist sponge cake bar or square, much loved in America, made with dark chocolate and named for its colour. Originally a cookie, the present form, with a high sugar and butter content, which gives it a crisp outside and a fudgy inside, has been known at least since the *Boston Cooking School Cook Book*, by Fannie Merritt Farmer, was first published in 1896. Baked in a cake tin (pan), and then cut, there are many forms. Chopped walnuts are a popular addition.

BROYE Also known as *broyé*. In Béarn, *broye* is a broth of maize flour (cornmeal). Simin Palay gives a recipe in *La Cuisine du pays* which differs by using white or browned flour.

In Poitou, *broyé* is a large biscuit made of a shortbread-type dough.

RECIPES

broye béarnaise

When white (not roasted) maize flour (cornmeal) is used, *broye* is prepared like an ordinary gruel. Vegetable stock or plain salted water is boiled and flour is added little by little until the consistency is fairly firm. When the gruel is cooked, and it must be stirred constantly during cooking, it is served with a greased ladle so that the gruel does not stick to the utensil. If the flour is first roasted to brown it, a well is made in the centre of the flour in an earthenware container, the stock or water is added and mixed well, and the mixture is then cooked. The cold *broye* can be sliced and fried in very hot fat until well coloured.

broyé poitevin

Place 250 g (9 oz, 1 cup) caster (superfine) sugar and a pinch of salt in an earthenware dish; make a well and drop 1 whole egg and 250 g (9 oz, 1 cup) butter, cut into pieces, into the centre. Knead by hand to mix thoroughly. Add 500 g (18 oz, 4 cups) plain (all-purpose) flour, a spoonful at a time, then 1 tablespoon rum or brandy and knead until the dough no longer sticks to the fingers (it should be fairly soft). Butter a pie dish 25 cm (10 in) in diameter and spread the dough in the dish, smoothing it with the palm of the hand. Brush the surface with 1 egg yolk mixed with 2 teaspoons black coffee.

Draw a crisscross pattern or geometric designs with a fork. Bake in a preheated oven at 180°C (350°F, gas 4) for 30 minutes. Allow to cool before turning out of the mould dish; as the cake is very crumbly.

BRÛLÉ The French term means 'burnt'. Crème brûlée, in which the sugar topping is caramelized with a red-hot iron, under the grill (broiler) or with a blow-torch, is one of the most famous desserts. In common French kitchen use, however, brûlée usually identifies a disaster.

In France dough is said to be brûlée when flour and fat have been mixed too slowly and the mixture has become oily (the same thing happens to brioche dough when the room is too hot).

When egg yolks are left with caster (superfine) sugar without beating, small bright yellow particles appear and are difficult to mix into creams and doughs: the yolks are said to be *brûlés*.

BRÛLOT Alcohol that is flamed before being drunk (or poured into a drink) or before being added to food (as in an omelette *flambée*). *Brûlot* is a familiar term in France for a sugar lump soaked in alcohol, held in a spoon over a cup of coffee, and flamed before being dropped into the coffee.

'Café brûlot' is a typical drink of Louisiana. It is made by heating rum with sugar, cinnamon, an orange stuck with cloves, and lemon zest. When the sugar has dissolved, scalding coffee is poured on to the mixture and the resulting liquid is filtered and served in hot cups.

BRUNCH A meal originating in America, being a combination of breakfast and lunch. This type of meal is commonly eaten on Sundays, when people gather round the table in a relaxed atmosphere between 10 a.m. and 2 p.m. The menu combines traditional British breakfast items with those of a cold meal: cereals, bacon and fried or scrambled eggs, salads of fruit and green vegetables, pancakes with jam or maple syrup, fruit juice, tea and coffee. Pies and cold meats may also be served. There is often a fruit loaf (called a 'coffee cake'), corn bread or French toast (slices of bread dipped in beaten egg, then fried and sprinkled with sugar).

BRUNOISE This French term is applied both to a method of cutting vegetables into minute dice and to the resulting diced vegetables (either a single type or a mixture). Often braised in butter, *brunoise* is used as a garnish for soups, sauces and stuffings and also serves as a flavouring (for preparing crayfish or *osso bucco*, for example).

Brunoise is generally used as soon as it is ready, but it can be kept briefly under a damp cloth.

RECIPES

brunoise-stuffed pancakes

Stew a *brunoise* of vegetables in butter. Bind with a little light béchamel sauce. Make some pancakes (see *pannequet*) and fill with the mixture; roll up, cut into thick slices, coat in breadcrumbs and fry.

consommé à la brunoise

For 4 servings, finely dice 200 g (7 oz) carrots, 100 g (4 oz) new parsnips, 100 g (4 oz) leeks (white part only), 25 g (1 oz) onions and 75 g (3 oz) well-trimmed celery sticks. Braise gently in 25 g (1 oz, 2 tablespoons) butter, then add 750 ml (1¼ pints, 3¼ cups) consommé and cook for 15 minutes. Just before serving, adjust seasoning and add 150 g (5 oz) each cooked green peas and green beans (cut into short lengths).

BRUSCHETTA A slice of bread, grilled (broiled) on both sides and eaten warm with olive oil and, frequently, a savoury garnish. Of Italian origin, bruschetta was a way of checking the quality of the new season's olive oil. Best made with ciabatta or an open-textured, light bread, and excellent plain, rubbed with garlic, it has become both a barbecue item – for example, topped with baked (bell) peppers – and a canapé base to accompany drinks.

BRUSSELS SPROUT A vegetable that is widely cultivated for its green buds, which resemble tiny cabbages, 2–4 cm (¾–1½ in) in diameter, and grow in the leaf axils along a stem up to 1 m (3 ft) high. Although now cultivated mainly in northern Europe, the Belgians consider that Brussels sprouts were imported into their country from Italy by the Roman legions. Brussels sprouts are an overwinter vegetable. They also freeze very well.

Brussels sprouts should be very green and compact, without yellow leaves; the best are usually found after the first frosts. They are prepared by removing the stump and one or two leaves around it, then washed in water to which vinegar has been added. Cooked in boiling water (preferably after blanching), they are generally served with meat (in butter, cream or white sauce), but are also used for gratins and purées. They can also be braised and mixed with thin strips of bacon and chestnuts. They may be served raw, very finely sliced in a salad.

Sprouts are essential for bruxelloise and brabançonne garnishes.

RECIPES

Brussels sprouts au gratin

Prepare some buttered Brussels sprouts. Butter a gratin dish, tip the sprouts into it, sprinkle with grated cheese and melted butter, and brown for about 10 minutes in a very hot oven.

Brussels sprouts mornay

Heap some buttered Brussels sprouts in a buttered gratin dish, coat generously with Mornay sauce, sprinkle with grated cheese and melted butter, and brown for about 10 minutes in a very hot oven.

Brussels sprout purée

Purée some well-cooked buttered Brussels sprouts in a food processor. Then pour into a saucepan and heat, stirring to lose some moisture. Add a quarter of its volume of potato purée and double (heavy) cream, using about 100 ml (4 fl oz, 7 tablespoons) cream for 1 litre (1¾ pints, 4⅓ cups) purée. Season with salt and pepper and serve very hot, preferably with roasted or braised white meat.

Brussels sprouts with butter or cream

Plunge the sprouts into boiling salted water and cook them quickly, uncovered. When they are still slightly firm, remove and drain. Melt some butter in a shallow frying pan, using about 25 g (1 oz, 2 tablespoons) for 800 g (1¾ lb) sprouts, and brown the sprouts. Adjust the seasoning, cover and simmer until the sprouts are completely cooked.

If desired, the sprouts may be coated with double (heavy) cream, using 100 ml (4 fl oz, 7 tablespoons) for 800 g (1¾ lb) vegetables, before they are covered to finish cooking.

sautéed Brussels sprouts

Cook some sprouts in boiling water until tender, then drain thoroughly. Melt some butter in a frying pan and toss the sprouts lightly in it. Transfer them to a vegetable dish and sprinkle with chopped parsley.

They may also be served with noisette butter (moistened first with lemon juice), *à l'indienne* (accompanied by a curry sauce and boiled rice), *à la milanaise* (sprinkled with grated Parmesan, then moistened with noisette butter), or *à la polonaise*, like cauliflower.

BRUXELLOISE, À LA A French garnish of stewed Brussels sprouts, braised chicory (endive) and château potatoes, served with small joints of meat, either sautéed or roasted. Egg dishes *à la bruxelloise* are garnished with Brussels sprouts or chicory.

RECIPE

eggs à la bruxelloise

Bake some small pastry cases (pie shells) blind. Gently cook some thinly sliced chicory (endive) in butter, bind with a little béchamel sauce and put into the pastry cases. Place a soft-boiled (soft-cooked) or poached egg in each case and coat with piping hot cream sauce.

B'STILLA Also known as *bisteeya* and *bestilla*. The celebratory pigeon pie of Morocco, and Fez in particular, eaten as a first course using the fingers of one hand. It is also distinguished by its layers of extremely thin *warqa* pastry (described in *brik*), the fact that it is made with butter, and its size, which may be 50 cm (20 in) across. The name is related to the Spanish *pastilla* (little pie), and the *pastel murciana* is similar, though it is certainly of Moorish origin. *Briouts* are small pastry envelopes stuffed with similar fillings.

The pastry layers are arranged in a buttered round mould, interleaved with layers of filling. Besides pigeon (unboned), the pie may include chicken, hard-boiled (hard-cooked) eggs and almonds with sugar. The filling is highly spiced with cinnamon, saffron, ginger, fresh coriander (cilantro) and parsley, and garlic, mint or harissa may be added. Other versions may include mutton or beef and spinach. The pastry layers are folded over and the top glazed. Traditionally, it is cooked on glowing charcoal and turned out on to a dish of the same size to cook the second side. Alternatively, it is gently fried until golden brown on both sides, while versions with filo (phyllo) as a substitute may be baked, well moistened with butter, without turning. The *b'stilla* is served dusted with sugar and cinnamon.

Dessert versions are also made, filled with rice and almond milk, custard or vermicelli cooked in milk with sugar and cinnamon.

BUCHTELN A plum dessert, much appreciated in Austria. *Buchteln* consists of squares of yeast dough, folded over plum jam, white cheese or chopped nuts, left to rise in the warm, then baked and served hot with prune jam or custard.

BUCKET A roughly cylindrical container with a handle, originally used for carrying water. The champagne bucket, which is made of stainless steel or silver-plated metal, is used for keeping a bottle of champagne, dry white wine, rosé, Asti or sparkling wine cool in iced water. The ice bucket, which is smaller, is used to store or serve ice cubes for drinks. Modern ones are insulated, with double walls and a lid, to prevent the ice cubes from melting.

BUCKWHEAT A cereal plant originating in the Orient and cultivated in Europe since the end of the 14th century. The name is derived from the Middle Dutch *boecweite*, from *boeke* (beech) and *weite* (wheat), probably because the seeds resemble beechnuts. The name 'Saracen corn' in France and Italy probably comes from the dark colour of the grain. In France it is also called *blé noir, beaucuit* or *bucail*.

Buckwheat flour is grey with black flecks. It is unsuitable for making bread, but is used in Russia for blinis and in France for traditional buckwheat pancakes (galettes; see *crêpe*), porridge and *fars*. When husked, crushed and cooked, buckwheat forms the basis of the Russian dish kasha. In Japan, buckwheat flour is used for making soba noodles, which are eaten in soup, or served cold on ice with dipping sauces. Nowadays some pasta is made with buckwheat too.

Until the end of the 19th century buckwheat was one of the staple foods of Brittany and Normandy, and also of north-eastern Europe and Russia, but its cultivation has diminished considerably. In southern Normandy buckwheat porridge was formerly a very common meal; the flour was soaked either in curdled skimmed milk or in plain water and then stirred in a pan over the heat. Then the pan was placed on a trivet and a hollow was made in the centre of the porridge and filled with melted butter. 'Everyone took a spoonful of the porridge, and then dipped it into the butter before eating it. When the meal was over, the leftover porridge was either put aside in a large dish, to be eaten with sweetened warm milk, or taken to the fields to be eaten later as a light meal. Thin slices of porridge, known as *soles de guéret*, were fricasséed and browned in sizzling butter.' (Jean Séguin, *Vieux Mangers, vieux parlers Bas-Normands*, Librairie Guénégaud.)

BUFFALO Members of the ox family, including a ferocious wild one in Africa and a domesticated one in India, important for both food and its labour. The buffalo was first imported to Italy, Hungary and the Balkans by the Romans. (The American buffalo, or bison, is a much larger animal.)

The meat of the young water buffalo, especially the female, is tender and tastes very similar to beef. Buffalo milk contains 40% fat (like cow's milk). In India, it is used to make surati, a cheese matured in earthenware vases which are also used to transport it. In Italy, provolone (a round cheese with a springy curd and mild paste) was originally made from buffalo milk. However, it is best known as the milk from which top-quality mozzarella is made; it must be eaten a few days after manufacture. Buriello is an Italian cheese with a light paste and a ball of buffalo butter in the middle. The milk is also used in Eygypt to make dumyāti, a cheese eaten fresh or brine-packed, aged and dark.

BUFFET A buffet in a restaurant is a large (tiered) table, often set near the entrance, on which dishes of meats, poultry, fish, cold desserts and pastries are arranged in a decorative manner. It is, in fact, a show of choice edibles.

At a reception (such as for a ball or wedding) the food is dispensed from a buffet or the guests come to the table to be served with sandwiches, cold meats, pastries and various drinks. It is an idea copied, for its ease of serving, for larger domestic parties.

In France buffet restaurants (*buffets de gare*) were established in the principal railway stations. The speed of transport has considerably reduced their importance, especially when buffet cars provide food and refreshments on trains. However, there are still some celebrated buffets, such as those at Lille, Épernay, Avignon, Valenciennes and Colmar. In Paris the buffet (the Train bleu) at the Gare de Lyon is classed as an historic monument for its architecture and paintings; the quality of its cuisine attracts a larger clientele than just travellers.

BUGLOSS A herbaceous plant common in Europe. Its name, derived from the Greek *buglossa* (meaning 'ox tongue'), comes from its fleshy, bristly, slightly rough leaves. Similar to borage, it has the same uses and its flowers are also used to prepare a refreshing drink.

BUGNE A large fritter from France's Lyonnais region, traditionally eaten on feast days, especially Shrove Tuesday. In the Middle Ages fritter-makers sold *bugnes* in the open air, from Arles to Dijon. They have become a speciality of Lyon, as common during the *vogues* (fairs) as waffles are in other regions. *Bugne* dough was originally made from flour, water, yeast and orange flowers. When the consumption of dairy products until Ash Wednesday became permitted by the Church, the dough was enriched with milk, butter and eggs, and *bugnes* became true pastries. They are cut with a pastry wheel into ribbons which are then knotted. *Bugnes* are better hot than cold. The *beugnon* is a smaller version, from central France.

RECIPE

bugnes

Put in a food processor 250 g (9 oz, 2¼ cups) plain (all-purpose) flour, 50 g (2 oz, ¼ cup) softened butter, 2 tablespoons caster (superfine) sugar, a large pinch of salt, 2 large beaten eggs and 1½ tablespoons rum, brandy or orange-flower water. Process thoroughly, then shape into a ball and allow to rest for 5–6 hours in a cool place. Roll the dough out to a thickness of 5 mm (¼ in). Cut the dough into strips about 10 cm (4 in) long and 4 cm (1½ in) wide. Make a slit in the middle 5 cm (2 in) long. Thread one end of the dough through the slit; this makes a kind of knot. Fry the *bugnes* in hot oil, turning once. Drain, place on paper towels, and sprinkle with icing (confectioner's) sugar.

BUISSON Traditionally a method in France of arranging food, especially crayfish and asparagus, pressed together in a pyramid. The term is also used for fried smelts and *goujonnettes* of sole arranged in a dome with a garnish of fried parsley.

RECIPES

buisson of asparagus in pastry

(from a recipe by Carême) Cook some very thick white asparagus tips in salted water, keeping them slightly firm. Drain and wipe dry. One by one, coat them in a little mayonnaise stiffened with gelatine. Bake a thin pastry case (pie shell) blind and half-fill with a salad of green asparagus tips and very fine slices of truffle. Arrange the white asparagus tips on top in a pyramid.

buisson of crayfish

Boil the crayfish in plenty of water, then drain them. Roll a napkin into a cone shape, tucking in the bottom to make it flat and thus keep it stable, and place it on a round serving plate. Truss the crayfish by tucking the ends of the 2 claws over the top of the tail. Arrange the crayfish along the napkin, tails in the air, wedging them against each other. The top of the dish can be garnished with a sprig of parsley.

BULGUR Also known as boulghour, bulghur or burghul. The Turkish and Persian names for a treated wholewheat grain product, including the wheat germ. It is made by cooking the wheat, then drying and cracking it. It is then cooked in twice its volume of boiling water for about 10 minutes, until the liquid is absorbed. It is often used in vegetarian cooking – to make soups and gruels with pulses and flavourings, to stuff vegetables (in place of rice), or served as a salad garnished with raw vegetables in vinaigrette (like *tabbouleh*, a Middle Eastern salad).

BULLHEAD *chabot* A fish of the *Cottidae* family. Although it is also called sea scorpion or sea devil, it is a freshwater or coastal fish, common in Britain and found in Russia and the Balkans. It is distinguished by its large head and fan-shaped fins; the fins and the gill cover are spiny. It can be eaten fried or in soup.

BULL'S BLOOD The best-known Hungarian red table wine, from vineyards around the town of Eger. It is made from the Kadarka, Merlot and Pinot Noir grapes.

BUN A small, round yeast roll, usually sweet. The name comes from the French *bugne* (swelling), which defines them beautifully. In Britain, buns are made from an enriched dough and may have dried fruit added. They may be glazed or iced.

There are many traditional regional or seasonal specialities. Bath buns are made from a rich egg dough with small lumps of sugar (originally caraway comfits) on top. Chelsea buns are dough spirals filled with fruit and baked in a tin (pan), giving them a square shape. Cornish splits are large plain buns filled with clotted cream and jam. Hot cross buns are made from a spiced fruited dough and have a cross of lighter dough or icing on top or are cut in the shape of a cross on top. Eaten on Good Friday, the tradition was to keep one bun for a full year, and throw it away when the new batch was made.

Many countries bake similar goods and the distinction between a roll and a bun can be difficult to define. Buns are generally eaten alone as a snack or for breakfast, or with tea or coffee. In America the term is more loosely applied to bread rolls such as the large flat rolls in which hamburgers and hot dogs are sandwiched. In Chinese cooking, the bun can be savoury – the steamed, white and fluffy buns filled with a full-flavoured savoury pork mixture are good examples – or sweet.

RECIPE

buns

Crumble 25 g (1 oz, 2 cakes) fresh (compressed) yeast into a bowl, then gradually stir in 250 ml (8 fl oz, 1 cup) lukewarm milk. Cover and leave at room temperature until frothy. Mix 675 g (1½ lb, 6 cups) strong plain (bread) flour with 1 teaspoon salt and the grated zest of 1 lemon. Rub in 125 g (4½ oz,

½ cup) butter, then stir in 125 g (4½ oz, ¾ cup) raisins. Make a well in the dry ingredients. Add 500 ml (17 fl oz, 2 cups) lukewarm milk, 1 beaten egg and the yeast mixture. Gradually mix the dry ingredients into the liquid to make a dough. Knead for about 10 minutes, until smooth and elastic.

Place the dough in a bowl, cover with a cloth and leave in a warm place until doubled in volume (about 5 hours). Then divide the dough into balls about the size of a tangerine. Place them on a greased large baking sheet, brush them with butter, cover with tented foil and allow to rise for a further 5 hours or until 2½ times their original size.

Bake the buns in a preheated oven at 200°C (400°F, gas 6) for 20 minutes. Meanwhile, heat 250 ml (8 fl oz, 1 cup) milk with 1 tablespoon sugar and bring to the boil. A few minutes before they are cooked, brush the buns with the syrup and return them to the oven. Cool on a wire rack.

BURBOT *lotte de rivière* A freshwater fish of the *Gadidae* family found across central Europe to Siberia and across the whole of North America, with a yellowish, elongated cylindrical body, speckled with brown and covered in a slimy substance. The burbot, also called eel pout, can grow to a length of 1 m (3 ft), and in France is particularly abundant in the lakes of Savoy. Once caught, it is skinned and then prepared like eel or lamprey. Its oily, white and almost boneless flesh is very popular (hence the reference to *lotte* – monkfish), but in France it is eaten primarily for its enormous liver. There is a French proverb: *'Pour un foie de lotte, une femme vendrait sa cotte'* (A woman would sell her soul for a burbot's liver). It is made into pâté or fried like calf's liver.

BURDOCK A large herbaceous plant common in uncultivated land. In cooking, the fleshy roots are prepared like salsify or asparagus. The young stalks and leaves, which have a refreshing and slightly bitter flavour, are used in soups or are eaten braised, especially in the south of France and Italy. The larger leaves are used in some areas for wrapping butter or soft cheeses. Burdock grows wild in Europe and America and is only eaten locally, but in Japan it is cultivated as a vegetable.

BURGHUL See *bulgur*.

BURGOS From the province of the same name in Spain, this is the best-known of Spain's fresh cheeses. Made from a variety of milks, but most famously from ewe's milk, it is sold in plastic pots with a little whey, still marked from the draining basket. There are many similar ones, such as that from Ronda. It is often eaten with honey and nuts for dessert.

BURGUNDY See *page 182*.

BUSTARD A migratory bird, Europe's largest game bird, is now rare, but was formerly highly prized.

The great bustard, with a 1.5 m (5 ft) wingspan, was once found on the Belgian plains and was bred in Britain; the little bustard, or field duck, is much smaller and is fully protected. The bustard was roasted in the same way as a goose or a duck. In the Middle Ages it was considered to be more tender and less stringy than goose, while under the Ancien Régime it was described as 'a fine ceremonial roast dish'.

BUTCHER'S BLOCK A solid block of wood with a flat top used as a base for chopping meat with a cleaver. It is cut across the grain of wood to give it more strength when used. Butcher's blocks were formerly set on three wooden feet.

BUTCHER'S SHOP A shop for selling meat, especially lamb and beef. Horse and donkey flesh tends to be sold by specialist butchers in France, as is the meat from the bull ring in Spain and hallal meat (butchered according to Muslim law). Pork, although sold in butchers' shops, is mostly retailed through delicatessens or specialist pork butchers in both France and Italy.

In ancient Rome the butcher's profession was regulated, carried privileges and was specialized according to the various types of meat. The Roman legions were accompanied by butchers, who were responsible for buying beasts to feed both their own troops and the occupied countries.

■ **History in France** Inspired by the Roman master butchers, a tradition of hereditary butchers was well established throughout the ancient province of Gaul, now France, by the Middle Ages. In 1096 the first butcher's shop in Paris began trading (on the present Place du Châtelet). Under King Philippe II (Augustus), there were about 18 shops and butchers obtained a permit from the king granting them the right to own their stalls in perpetuity. Thus was formed the rich and powerful butchers' guild, which, dominated for a long time by a few families, wielded considerable political power. Charles VI tried to limit the power of the butchers, who had taken the side of the Bourguignons against the Armagnacs, and in 1416 the guild was dissolved, its privileges revoked and its shops destroyed. But it re-formed a few years later. Philip the Bold had authorized the butchers to sell fish as well as meat, but they later lost this right and also had to abandon the pork trade to pork butchers. Statutes recorded in 1589 laid down the rights and obligations of butchers until 1789. These obliged them to own scales and sell meat by weight, not by guesswork, as had previously been the practice.

Until abattoirs were set up under Napoleon I, the Grande-Boucherie quarter, around the Châtelet, remained a dreadful place: 'Blood flows in the streets and congeals under the feet,' wrote Mercier in 1783. In his *Dictionnaire des rues de Paris*, Hillairet mentions the Rue de la Triperie ('Tripe Street'), previously known as Rue de l'Araigne ('Spider Street') after the four-pronged hook from which meat was

Burgundy

Thanks to a carefully maintained tradition from the lavish period of the Dukes of Burgundy, this region considers itself to be the centre of French cuisine. The former duchy of Burgundy covered a large area corresponding to Côte-d'Or, Saône-et-Loire, Yonne and parts of Ain, Nievre and Aube. Burgundy has a reputation not only for its wine but also for its prestigious cuisine, which is more aristocratic than provincial.

■ **Culinary excellence in Dijon** Dijon, the former capital of the duchy, could, on its own, sustain the reputation of the province on account of its famous products. Dijon mustard, a sizeable commercial business by the mid-14th century, is made from verjuice (from Burgundy grapes) mixed with mustard seeds. No preparation *à la dijonnaise* would be complete without it.

Another famous product, the Dijon blackcurrant liqueur cassis, is considered to be one of the best in the world. Dijon gingerbread was introduced into the province by the Dukes of

A variety of wonderful mustard pots has been created for the famous Dijon mustard. These examples are from the house of Maille.

Burgundy, whose cooks imitated and perfected the recipes for cakes made in Flanders. Although mustard, cassis and gingerbread are the best-known specialities of Dijon, there are many other prestigious dishes – ham with parsley, salmon with Chablis, and game, fish and crayfish prepared in various ways. The excellence of Dijon cuisine has made it a centre for the world of gastronomy conferences.

■ **Dishes enlivened with wine** Burgundy cuisine owes its liveliness to red or white wine, while spices, condiments, onions, garlic and shallots add a certain piquancy to dishes which already have a strong flavour and colour. The quality of the country produce also contributes to this sophisticated cuisine, with the famous Charolais cattle, chicken from Bresse, fish from the Saône, ham and game from Morvan,

The Château of Rully is in the Côte Chalonnais, which produces several premier cru wines with the Rully, Mercurey or Montagny appelations.

crayfish and frogs from Dombes, and vegetables from the Auxonne area. All dishes *à la bourguignonne* or *à la meurette* include a sauce made with red wine and a garnish of mushrooms, small onions and pieces of fat bacon. The sauce and the garnish may be used with meat, poultry, game, eggs or fish. Famous recipes include boeuf bourguignon, coq au vin, chicken in Chambertin, hare in Pommard, ham fried in wine, pork chops sautéed in white wine, and chitterlings cooked in red wine. These few recipes prove – if proof were needed – that the bouquet of Burgundy wines is indispensable to the cuisine of the region.

■ **A far-reaching reputation** The reputation of many other gastronomic specialities has travelled beyond the limits of the province. Although *potée bourguignonne* is similar to stews from other regions of France, snails simmered in garlic and butter or sometimes cooked *en meurette* remain a speciality of Burgundy. *Pochouse*, a tasty soup made with freshwater fish, is another famous dish, said to have been invented by an innkeeper of Chalon-sur-Saône in the 16th century. Other specialities include *gougère*, with its strong smell of cheese, and *ferchuse* or pig's fry, traditionally eaten at meals to ▶

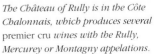

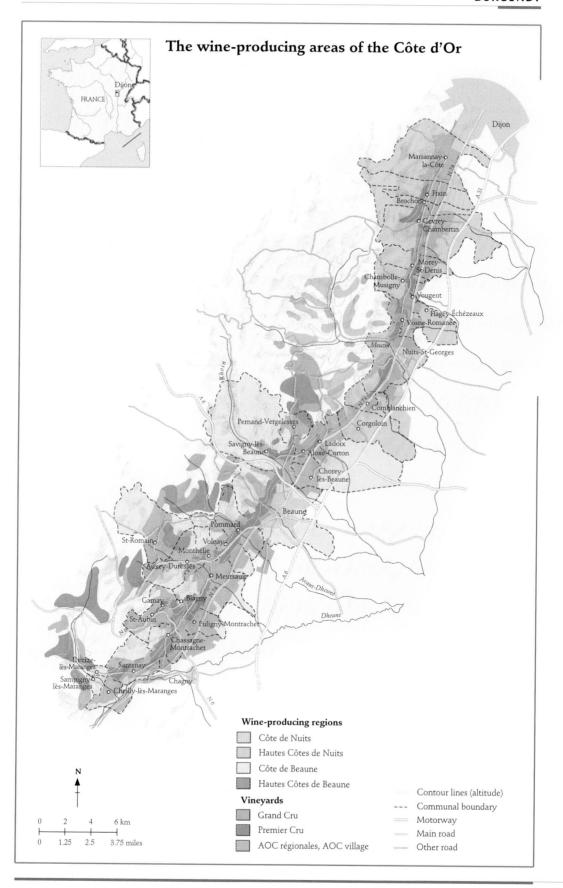

The wine-producing areas of the Côte d'Or

FRANCE
Dijon

Dijon

Marsannay-
la-Côte

Fixin
Brochon
Gevrey-
Chambertin

Morey-
St-Denis
Chambolle-
Musigny
Vougeot
Flagey-Échézeaux
Vosne-Romanée

Meuzin

Nuits-St-Georges

Rhoin

Comblanchien

Pernand-Vergelesses
Corgoloin

Savigny-lès-
Beaune
Ladoix
Aloxe-Corton
Chorey-
lès-Beaune

Beaune

Pommard
St-Romain
Volnay
Monthélie
Auxey-Duresses
Meursault
Avant-Dheune

Gamay
Blagny
Dheune
St-Aubin
Puligny-Montrachet
Chassagne-
Montrachet
Dezize-
lès-Maranges
Santenay
Sampigny-
lès-Maranges
Chagny
Cheilly-lès-Maranges

Wine-producing regions

- Côte de Nuits
- Hautes Côtes de Nuits
- Côte de Beaune
- Hautes Côtes de Beaune

Vineyards

- Grand Cru
- Premier Cru
- AOC régionales, AOC village

Contour lines (altitude)
Communal boundary
Motorway
Main road
Other road

N

| 0 | 2 | 4 | 6 km |
| 0 | 1.25 | 2.5 | 3.75 miles |

◀ celebrate the wine harvest. Pork products, such as sausages, pâtés and puddings, are specialities that each town and village prepares in its own way.

■ **Excellent cheeses** As well as being a great wine region, Burgundy also produces excellent cheeses: goat's-milk cheeses stored in grape marc, Saône-et-Loire cream cheeses, Saint-Florentin and Soumaintrain, and Époisses, with its orange crust washed in white wine. These strong cheeses, which have a powerful aroma and are often flavoured with marc, thyme, bay or tarragon, are a perfect complement to the produce of the Burgundy vineyards.

■ **Desserts and confections** The desserts of the region are comparable to those of the neighbouring provinces and include *bugnes*, *flamusses*, pumpkin pies, *rigodons* and *corniottes* (triangular cream-cheese pastries). The towns of Burgundy also produce delicious confectionery, usually based on fruit.

WINE Although wine was already being made in Burgundy in the Gallo-Roman era, it was the monks of the Middle Ages who were responsible for achieving its quality and renown. Beaune wines, which first introduced Burgundy vineyards to the world, did not begin to be appreciated outside the region until the 13th century, and the first large establishments of shippers who distributed and publicized the reputation of Burgundy throughout the world date only from the 18th century.

The Burgundy vineyard area extends over four departments – Yonne, Côte d'Or, Saône-et-Loire and Rhône – and is made up of six sub-regions: Chablis (near Auxerre), then, going north to south to the right of the River Saône, the Côte de Nuits, the Côte de Beaune, the Côte Chalonnaise, the Mâconnais and the Beaujolais. All produce magnificent wines, mainly from two grapes: Pinot

The cellars of the Bernard Bachelet domain at Dezize-lès-Maranges.

Noir for the reds, and Chardonnay for the quality whites; Gamay is used for red Beaujolais and Aligoté for some whites. Bourgogne Passe-Tout-Grains is made from a minimum one-third Pinot Noir, with Gamay making up the balance.

Compartmentalized in the extreme, the area produces a large number of wines, each of which has its own qualities and originality. There are 113 *appellations contrôlées* of various categories and thousands of single sites (*climats*) – more than 800 for the Côte de Beaune alone. Each *appellation d'origine contrôlée* (AOC) applied to Burgundy will stipulate, among other details, how much wine may be made in a delimited area (usually expressed in hectolitres per hectare) and also the minimum alcoholic content of the finished wine. The appellation system in Burgundy is complicated, but is arranged in a pyramid of hierarchy. At the base are 22 regional appellations which will always have Bourgogne in their name, such as Bourgogne Rouge or Bourgogne Hautes Côtes de Nuits, plus district appellations, such as Mâcon. At the next level are village appellations, such as Volnay or Meursault. In many cases a village will have attached the name of its most famous vineyard to the village name, hence Gevrey-Chambertin and Puligny-Montrachet. These are

often the best value wines from the Côte d'Or. Some specific vineyards within these villages are rated as *premiers crus* (561 vineyards) and some are ranked as *grands crus* (30 vineyards). *Premiers crus* are allowed to use the name of the vineyards on the label, *grands crus* use only that name.

Attempts have been made to categorize the Côte d'Or wines: those labelled *premier cru* will give the name of the specific vineyard. *Deuxième cru* wines tend to be sold with the village name only. The *grands crus* may be labelled solely with the name of their respective great vineyards without that of their villages.

Since a vineyard in Burgundy may be divided between several owners, it is important to differentiate between their wines, so the name of the producer is just as important as the name of the vineyard. The quality of any wine is ultimately the responsibility of the grower, winemaker, *négociant* and merchant.

Crémant de Bourgogne may be a white or a rosé sparkling wine. Bourgogne Passe-Tout-Grains is a red wine produced by 'passing', or making the wine from the two Burgundy grapes (Pinot Noir and Gamay), of which at least one-third must be Pinot Noir.

hung in the open air; Rue Pierre-à-Poisson ('Fish Stone Street'), which alludes to the butchers' right to sell fish; Rue de la Tuerie ('Slaughterhouse Street'); Rue de l'Écorcherie ('Knacker's Yard Street'); and the Vallée de la Misère ('Vale of Tears'), the site of an open-air market that sold poultry, game, lamb and goat, as well as butter, eggs and milk (in the former Paris food market – Les Halles – the Vallée was the poultry and game section).

The traditions of the butchers' guild persisted until the Revolution. The feast day of their patron saint, St Nicholas, was celebrated on 6 December. Butchers were traditionally close to the religious authorities (in the early 20th century butchers' shops were closed on Fridays). Those aspiring to the title of master butcher had to give a candle and an egg cake to the head of the guild and four pieces of meat to his wife. Another important ceremony for Parisian butchers was the Fat Beef Procession, held at carnival time, just before Lent. A magnificent ox, decorated with ribbons and given a name that was often inspired by popular contemporary literature (for example, Monte Cristo or Wandering Jew), was paraded with great pomp through the streets of the capital. The tradition was maintained until the Second Empire.

Napoleon reorganized the profession by limiting the number of butchers' shops in Paris, but this measure was rescinded in 1863.

■ **Modern meat retailing** With the growth of large supermarkets, meat retailing has changed. Traditional butchers still occupy independent shops, but there are far fewer of them, particularly in large towns and cities. The whole process of slaughtering and butchering is subject to national and international legislation, as is the business of food handling and retailing. Many of the remaining butchers' shops are high-quality, specialist outlets (particularly in cities) focusing on specially reared meat or premium products. They offer expertise, advice and variety that is often unavailable from supermarket meat counters.

In supermarkets, meat may be prepacked or there may be a meat counter where butchers provide specialist service. Depending on the particular outlet, its facilities and the experience of the staff, the meat counter can be far inferior to traditional or specialist shops. The range available from meat counters in supermarkets is usually comparatively limited. The better supermarkets prepare meat to order, but often availability is limited by central supplies and some cuts are simply not offered.

BUTIFARRA
A black pudding (blood sausage) of eastern Spain (Catalonia and the Levante), made of pig's blood and pieces of fat, sometimes with meat. There are many types – the Catalan sausage is *botifarra*. *Bisbe* (meaning 'bishop') is another large, black sausage. Many contain rice – typically in the Valencia area, though the region also has a highly spiced meat version. Butifarras are sliced and fried, then added to casseroles. *Boutifar* is the North African version, containing blood, fat and meat, about 8–10 cm (3½–4 in) in diameter, and is eaten cold.

White butifarras (see *boudin blanc*), often made with lean pork and stuffed into tripe skins, are popular in Catalonia and the Balearic islands.

BUTTER
A fatty substance obtained from churned cream, containing at least 80% fat, 2% milk solids and not more than 16% water. Butter hardens at low temperatures, becomes soft in a warm environment and melts when heated. The colour varies from creamy white to golden yellow.

■ **The history of butter** Butter was known in ancient times and was introduced to the Greeks by the Scythians. Herodotus, quoted by Montesquieu, spoke of the Scythians who 'poked out the eyes of their slaves so that nothing would distract them from churning their milk'. The Greeks and Romans, however, used it mainly as a remedy (particularly for healing wounds) and relied almost entirely on oil for cooking purposes.

Butter was produced by the Gauls, but it was the Normans, using knowledge acquired from the Danes, who firmly established its reputation. By the Middle Ages, the small-scale local production of butter had become widespread. Large pats of butter, sometimes wrapped in leaves of sorrel or herbs, were sold in French markets and stored in earthenware pots covered with salt water. Colouring (with marigold flowers) was prohibited, as was selling butter on a fish stall. Butter was not supposed to be eaten during Lent (but a dispensation could be obtained by making a contribution to the 'butter chest').

In Europe, butter is made from cow's milk, but in Africa and Asia the milk of the buffalo, camel, goat, ewe, mare and donkey is used to manufacture butters with very strong flavours. In Britain a few small independent producers make nanny butter (from goat's milk).

■ **Alternatives to butter** There are many alternatives to butter, both for cooking and as spreads. Margarine is the long-standing substitute for use in baking and there are many brands for table use. Low-fat spreads and reduced-fat butters are spreadable products with a high moisture content, aimed at people who want to reduce either their calorie intake or consumption of animal fats. Some of these products are not suitable for cooking.

■ **Butter-making** The milk is skimmed and the cream is used for making butter. The cream is pasteurized and transferred to an ageing or maturation tank. The cream is then churned so that globules of fat form and the buttermilk is separated. The cream is cooled and ripened at a low temperature to produce sweet cream butter, the traditional British butter. Alternatively, the cream is ripened at a higher temperature with the addition of a culture of lactic bacteria. This produces a butter with more flavour, known as lactic butter, the type traditionally preferred in France, Denmark, the Netherlands and Germany. The butter is then washed and blended or worked to give the right water content and characteristic texture. During this stage the butter may be salted and permitted colouring ingredients may be added. Finally, the butter is weighed and packaged.

■ **Types of butter** There are two main types of butter produced by the different ripening or ageing processes described above. Sweet cream butter is the traditional British type and lactic butter is the classic French butter. Sweet cream butter is usually salted or lightly salted. Lactic butter may be lightly salted or unsalted.

Butter keeps well in the refrigerator, with the salted type having a longer shelf life than unsalted butter. Butter also freezes well, but in this case the unsalted type has a longer storage life. Butter should always be stored in a covered container or sealed packet, as it readily absorbs aromas given off by other foods and these taint its flavour. Butter left in warm, light conditions becomes rancid, especially the unsalted type, so it should be covered and replaced in the refrigerator after use.

In addition to these key types, and the choice of unsalted, lightly salted or salted, there are many regional variations in butter. Milk varies according to the breed of cow from which it is obtained, the diet on which the cows are reared or the pastures where they graze; this in turn influences the flavour of the butter. Some areas, such as Normandy, in France, are renowned for making high-quality butter; distinct or subtle differences are quite evident between major regional brands, while less-common local butters are available from small producers.

■ **Cooking with butter** Butter has numerous uses in cooking and unsalted butter is often preferred as it is less likely to burn when frying and it enriches food without adding too much salt, which is particularly important for baking, when salted butter can spoil the flavour of sweet pastries, cakes and biscuits (cookies).

As a cooking medium, butter can be used to sweat, sauté or fry foods and to moisten them before and during grilling (broiling), roasting or baking. Clarified butter (or ghee) is butter from which the water content has been evaporated and the milk solids separated, leaving a clear yellow fat which can be heated to a high temperature without burning. This is ideal for frying or other cooking. When ordinary butter is used, it should be heated gently and slowly to avoid burning.

A little oil is often added to butter for cooking, contributing a good flavour and reducing the risk of burning. This is also a good compromise for those who enjoy the flavour but want to avoid consuming large quantities of animal fats.

For making pastries, biscuits, cakes and enriching doughs, butter gives a superior flavour to margarine. When beaten with sugar, it becomes light and creamy. Combined with flour and water, butter flavours and shortens doughs, producing a crumbly texture. When butter is incorporated by being rolled between layers of flour and water dough, it produces fine, crisp layers that separate as trapped air expands during baking, giving a light result This technique is used for making puff pastry and croissants.

Butter is also a key ingredient in a variety of sauces and it can be added to soups and casseroles to enrich the cooking liquor. Plain or flavoured butter can be served with food to moisten and enhance plain ingredients; for example, it is the classic dressing for vegetables, grilled (broiled) fish, meats or poultry. In the same way as other fats, butter complements starchy foods, making them more palatable.

Butter also has a variety of uses in desserts and sweet dishes, for example to make British buttercream when beaten with icing (confectioner's) sugar or French *crème au beurre* and other custards enriched with softened butter. Butter is also a valuable flavouring for confectionery, such as toffee.

• FLAVOURED BUTTERS Various herbs and other ingredients can be added to salted or unsalted butter to produce different colours and flavours. They are sometimes referred to as compound butters or *beurres composés*. They may be served cold with freshly grilled (broiled) meat, fish or boiled vegetables. Flavoured butters are added to sauces or the other dishes. They are also spread on canapés or between slices of bread to be heated and served hot.

Butters that are prepared hot can be flavoured with crushed crustacean shells (lobster for cardinal butter, crayfish for Nantua butter). Most flavoured butters are prepared cold. Raw additions (such as garlic, shallot, tarragon or horseradish) are rubbed through a sieve, crushed, chopped, finely grated or puréed. Other ingredients are cooked in liquid until well reduced (for example, blanched shallots are reduced with white wine).

To accompany grilled meat or fish, a flavoured butter of a creamy consistency is served separately. Alternatively, it may be shaped into a small cylinder, wrapped in greaseproof (wax) paper or foil, and hardened in the refrigerator. It is then unwrapped and cut into slices 1 cm (½ in) thick, to top the meat or fish. (These slices may also be stored with water and ice cubes to retain their appearance.)

RECIPES

Flavoured Butters
preparation of flavoured butter
Whatever the ingredients, the butter must first be creamed, using a spoon or (for large quantities) an electric mixer. The following recipes give ingredients to flavour 225 g (8 oz, I cup) butter.

almond butter
Blanch 100 g (4 oz, I cup) sweet almonds and reduce to a paste in a blender with I tablespoon cold water. Add to the softened butter and press through a sieve. Very fresh ground almonds can also be used. This butter is used in the preparation of petits fours and cakes. Make walnut butter the same way.

anchovy butter
Soak 100 g (4 oz) canned or bottled salted anchovies to remove the salt. Purée the fillets in a blender, season and, if liked, add a dash of lemon

juice. Work into the softened butter. This butter is used for vol-au-vents, canapés and hors d'oeuvres and to accompany grilled (broiled) meat and fish or cold white meat.

Sardine butter is prepared the same way, using the filleted and skinned canned fish.

caviar butter

Blend 100 g (4 oz) pressed caviar, work into the softened butter and then press through a sieve. This butter is used to garnish canapés or various cold hors d'oeuvres and to flavour some fish sauces.

crab or prawn butter

Blend 225 g (8 oz) shelled prawns (shrimp) or crabmeat (cooked in court-bouillon and with all cartilage removed). Work into the softened butter. This butter is used to garnish canapés, cold fish or hors d'oeuvres, and to complete fish and shellfish sauces.

crayfish butter

Pound in a mortar (or crush in a processor) 250 g (9 oz) chopped and cooked crayfish shells and trimmings. Add to the softened butter in a bain marie. Melt the butter mixture slowly but thoroughly. Place some muslin (cheesecloth) over a bowl containing iced water. Pour the melted butter on to the cloth and wring so that the butter goes into the bowl. Place in the freezer or refrigerator to set the butter quickly. As soon as the butter has set, remove from the bowl and blot it dry. Crayfish butter is used for preparing canapés, soups, stuffings, shellfish dishes and sauces.

garlic butter with cooked garlic

Peel 8 large garlic cloves and plunge in boiling salted water. Boil for 7–8 minutes, dry and purée. Work into the softened butter. Garlic butter is used to complete some sauces, and adds the final touch to garnishes for cold hors d'oeuvres.

garlic butter with raw garlic

Crush 2–4 garlic cloves and add to the softened butter. Mix well. A little finely chopped parsley and grated lemon zest can be added to complement the raw garlic.

green butter

Wring 1 kg (2¼ lb) raw crushed spinach in muslin (cheesecloth) until all the juice is extracted. Pour this juice into a dish and cook in a bain marie until separated, then filter through another cloth. Scrape off the green deposit left on this cloth and work it into the softened butter. This butter is used to garnish hors d'oeuvres and cold dishes.

hazelnut butter

Lightly grill (broil) some hazelnuts, then make and use like almond butter.

horseradish butter

Grate 100 g (4 oz) horseradish. Work it into the softened butter in a blender, then sieve. It is used in the same way as garlic butter.

hôtelier butter

In a blender, purée an equal quantity of chopped parsley, lemon juice and mushroom duxelles. Work into the softened butter. This butter is served with fish and grilled (broiled) meat.

lemon butter

Blanch the zest of a lemon, chop as finely as possible, and work it into the softened butter in a blender, with a dash of lemon juice, salt and pepper. This butter is used to garnish cold hors d'oeuvres.

lobster butter

This is prepared in the same way as prawn butter using the meat and eggs of the lobster cooked in court-bouillon. It is used for the same purposes.

maître d'hotel butter

Work 2 tablespoons finely chopped parsley, 1–2 dashes lemon juice and a pinch of salt into the softened butter. This butter is served with grilled (broiled) fish, fish fried in an egg-and-breadcrumb coating, and various steamed or boiled vegetables.

Montpellier butter

Blanch 10 g (½ oz, ½ cup) each parsley leaves, chervil leaves, cress leaves, spinach and 1 shallot in salted water. Rinse in cold water and drain thoroughly. Blend with a gherkin (sweet dill pickle), a small garlic clove and a hard-boiled (hard-cooked) egg. Work in the softened butter and season with salt and pepper. Montpellier butter is served with large cold fish. It is sometimes softened by adding a very fresh raw egg yolk and 4 tablespoons olive oil.

mustard butter

Add 2 tablespoons tarragon mustard to the softened butter and season with salt and pepper. A hard-boiled (hard-cooked) egg yolk, some chopped herbs and a dash of lemon juice may also be added. Use like anchovy butter.

pepper butter

Remove the seeds from a large green or red (bell) pepper, dice and cook very gently in butter until it is soft enough to be puréed. Work the puréed pepper into the softened butter, season with salt and pepper, add a pinch of cayenne pepper and press through a sieve. Pepper butter is used to finish some sauces or garnish hors d'oeuvres.

red butter

Prepare with the crushed shells of various shellfish, in the same way as crayfish butter. The uses are the same.

Roquefort butter

Purée 150 g (5 oz) Roquefort cheese with 1 tablespoon Cognac or white brandy and 2 teaspoons white mustard (optional). Work into the softened butter. This butter is used to garnish canapés, vol-au-vent and puff pastries, or served with raw vegetables.

shallot butter
Peel 150 g (5 oz) shallots and chop finely. Blanch for 2–3 minutes in boiling water, blot and purée in a blender. Work into 150 g (5 oz, ⅔ cup) softened butter. Season with salt and pepper. This butter is served mainly with grilled (broiled) fish and meat.

tarragon butter
This is prepared in the same way as watercress butter and is used to finish sauces or garnish cold hors d'oeuvres.

watercress butter
Blanch 150 g (5 oz) watercress leaves, soak in cold water and blot. Purée, then work into the finely softened butter, season with salt and pepper. Watercress butter is used principally for canapés and sandwiches.

Plain Butters and Butter Sauces
beurre noir
This recipe for black butter is a very old one, dating from the 16th century. Cook some butter in a frying pan until dark brown in colour. Add capers and chopped parsley, together with a little vinegar, which is warmed through in the same pan.

Black butter was formerly an essential accompaniment to skate poached in stock.

clarified butter
Melt some butter gently in a heavy based saucepan; do not stir. Continue to heat gently until the butter ceases spitting – this indicates that the water content has evaporated. There should be a small amount of white residue in the bottom of the pan. Carefully pour the butter into another container so that the whitish sediment stays in the pan. Clarified butter is used particularly for frying and for emulsified sauces.

creamed butter
Cream the butter in a warm earthenware container, carefully adding lemon juice and a little cold water. Serve with fish in court-bouillon and Vichy carrots.

landais butter
Roll small balls of butter in breadcrumbs until thickly and evenly coated, then cook under a hot grill (broiler) to form a golden crust, turning and sprinkling with melted butter. Serve with grilled (broiled) meat and fish.

melted butter
Melt the butter very gently in a heavy based saucepan with lemon juice, salt and white pepper. This butter is used with poached fish or steamed or boiled vegetables.

noisette butter
Gently heat some butter in a frying pan until it is golden and gives off a nutty smell. Serve scalding hot with lambs' or calves' sweetbreads, fish roe, vegetables (boiled and well drained), eggs or skate poached in stock. Noisette butter is known as meunière butter when lemon juice is added.

BUTTER DISH A container for keeping butter or serving it at the table. For storage it must have a lid, since fresh butter is particularly delicate and readily absorbs smells. For setting on the table, the appearance of the dish and its size must be the main guide. Flavoured butters are usually served in a sauceboat or a small dish.

Formerly, butter had to be stored either submerged in salted water or in a glass container placed in a double porous earthenware bell into which water was poured daily. Refrigerators made such methods obsolete.

BUTTERMILK A slightly sour whitish liquid obtained after churning cream to separate the butterfat. Buttermilk is slightly acidic with a tangy flavour. Buttermilk was once recommended for feeding children and was used for making soups. Traditionally, buttermilk is used in combination with bicarbonate of soda (baking soda) to act as a raising agent (its acidity is important in this context) for scones and breads, such as soda bread, and thick pancakes, such as drop scones. It is still a popular drink in Scandinavian countries. The supermarket product is often skimmed milk thickened with a culture.

BUVETTE Under the Ancien Régime in France, a *buvette* was a small bar set up within the precincts of the courts of law, where judges and lawyers could take light refreshments between sessions. The word has retained this meaning in the case of the Buvette de l'Assemblée nationale. Nowadays a *buvette* is a small bar in a railway station, theatre or public garden. It can also serve ice creams, sandwiches or sweets. In a spa, the *buvette* is the place where people drink the waters.

BUZET Red AOC wines from a small vine-growing area situated east of Agen in south-western France. The reds are from Bordeaux grapes – Cabernet Sauvignon, Cabernet Franc, Merlot and Malbec. They are usually matured in wood, thanks to the efforts of the Buzet-sur-Baise cooperative. Up to the end of the last century the region was large, but the vineyard was completely destroyed by phylloxera and has only recently been rehabilitated. A small amount of white wine is made from Semillon, Sauvignon Blanc and Muscadelle grapes: these are best enjoyed when fresh and young.

BYZANTINE, À LA A French side dish for meat, particularly beef, consisting of potato shells browned in the oven, garnished with cauliflower *à la crème*, and lettuce halves stuffed with mushroom duxelles and braised in the oven on a bed of herbs. Also called *à la bisontine*, meaning 'from Besançon'.

CABARDÈS French red and rosé wines produced in the region of the Aude, to the north of Carcassonne, by 2,200 hectares (5,400 acres) of vineyard next to those of the Minervois. The varieties of vine from which these wines are made include Grenache Noir, Cinsault, Carignan, Syrah, Cabernet Sauvignon and Merlot. Now upgraded to AC status, these are promising wines with a pleasing bouquet and good ageing potential. Drink with grilled (broiled) dishes, roast pork, kidneys and calf's liver.

CABARET (establishment) The modern cabaret, a nightclub or restaurant with a floor show, has little in common with the original French cabaret, which until the end of the 19th century was a modest bar serving mainly wine.

Before the 17th century, there was a clear distinction in France between the taverne and the cabaret. Originally, the novelty of the cabaret consisted of selling wine *à l'assiette*, serving it on a table at which the customer could sit and possibly have something to eat. If the cabaret proprietor did not have permission to do this, the wine was sold *au pot* (by the jug).

Henri IV reorganized the wine retailers as follows: (1) wine merchants selling wine by the jug did so without having a *taverne* – an opening was made in the outer grille of the shop, through which the purchaser would pass his jug; (2) tavern-keepers sold drinks in a place arranged for this purpose; (3) proprietors of cabarets served not only drinks, but also food – they had permission to provide *nappe et assiette* (tablecloth and plate) service. Both tavern-keepers and proprietors of cabarets employed criers to go through the streets announcing the price of the wine sold in their premises.

In the 13th century, among the first cabarets were the Trois Mailletz, frequented by scholars from the Sorbonne who were extremely rowdy, according to the priests of Saint-Séverin, and the Pomme de Pin. In the course of the following centuries, the best-known cabarets were the Sabot (Saint-Marcel district), where Ronsard was a frequent customer, and the Écu d'Argent (near the Place Maubert), where Ménage was said to have set up residence. The Épée de Bois and the Mouton Blanc (in the Rue de la Verrerie) were the meeting places of La Fontaine, Boileau and Racine (who wrote *Les Plaideurs* there). Cabarets thus became fashionable in the 17th century and were frequented, in particular, by writers and artists, who later patronized the cafés, restaurants and brasseries. In the 19th century, low-class cabarets again attracted the Romantics. Some of them were squalid hovels, like those described by Eugène Sue in *Les Mystères de Paris*. It was at the gate of one such cabaret – the Chat Blanc – that the body of Gérard de Nerval was found hanging.

The etymology of the word has given rise to various interpretations. Possible roots are the Hebrew word *cabar* (to meet), the Celtic words *cab* (head) and *aret* (ram – an animal sacrificed to Bacchus), the Latin *cabare* (to dig, to make a cellar), the Arabic *khamarat* (a place where drinks are sold), and, more recently, the Dutch *cabret*, itself derived from the old Picardy word *cambrette*, meaning 'little room'.

CABASSOL A stew made from sheep's heads simmered in white wine. It is a speciality of Albi in Languedoc (in this region *cabassol* means 'head'). At Réquista (Aveyron) there is a Cabassol Club, where it is customary to eat the stew on Shrove Tuesday. The tongue, brains, cheeks and ears are considered to be delicacies. At Lodève near Hérault, *cabassol* is made with lamb's feet, heads and mesentery (intestinal membranes), cooked with ham and knuckle of veal. It is served with vinaigrette and a purée of lamb's brains. Sometimes, it is eaten with stockpot vegetables and herbs. In Rouergue, *cabassol* is simply a lamb stock.

CABBAGE A widely cultivated vegetable of the family *Cruciferae*. Wild cabbage, from which all the cultivated varieties are derived, is a perennial with broad thick curly leaves, growing in coastal regions of western Europe. Known for over 4,000 years in Europe, it was at first valued for its medicinal properties, but later was used as food, particularly as a basis for soups. Through cultivation and selection, white, green and red varieties of cabbage were produced, as well as many other brassicas – including Brussels sprouts, cauliflower and broccoli.

The different varieties of full-hearted cabbage are distinguished by their colour (white, green or red), their shape (rounded for winter cabbages, pointed for spring cabbages), the texture of their leaves (crinkly in Savoy cabbages, or smooth) and whether they are soft- or hard-hearted. Ideally, cabbage should have crisp shiny leaves and, where applicable, a dense heart. Cabbage is included in numerous garnishes (*à la flamande, à l'auvergnate, à la berichonne, à la strasbourgeoise*) and can be prepared in many ways. It is used as a base for soups, stews and stuffings. White and red cabbage predominate in the cookery of eastern and northern Europe, while green cabbage is more popular in the west and south.

RECIPES

Green or White Cabbage
braised cabbage
Prepare a cabbage: blanch, drain, cool in cold water and drain once again. Separate the leaves and discard the large ribs. Scrape and dice a carrot. Line a flameproof casserole with bacon rashers (slices) stripped of half their fat and add the diced carrot, then the cabbage, forming a heap. Add salt, pepper, a little grated nutmeg, an onion stuck with a clove and a bouquet garni. Two-thirds cover the cabbage with stock and put a very thin strip of bacon on top. Cover and bring to the boil over a ring. Then place the casserole in a preheated oven at 180°C (350°F, gas 4) and cook for about 1½ hours.

green cabbage salad
Remove any withered outer leaves, cut the cabbage into four and blanch for about 12 minutes in boiling salted water. Drain, cool and wipe. Cut the quarters into a julienne and season with a well-spiced vinaigrette. Sprinkle with chopped herbs or finely shredded spring onions (scallions).

paupiettes of cabbage
Blanch a whole cabbage for 7–8 minutes in boiling salted water, then drain and cool it. Pull off the large outer leaves, removing the tougher ribs. Chop the leaves from the central heart and to them add an equal volume of forcemeat. Make paupiettes by rolling this mixture in the large leaves, using 1 tablespoon per leaf; tie them up with kitchen thread. Braise as for stuffed cabbage, but reduce the cooking time to 1¼ hours. These paupiettes form a perfect garnish for braised meat.

stuffed cabbage
Blanch a whole cabbage in salted boiling water for 7–8 minutes. Cool it in cold water, drain and remove the stump (core). Moisten a piece of fine cloth or muslin (cheesecloth), wring it out and lay it on the working surface. On top of the cloth, lay four lengths of kitchen thread to form a star shape. Place the cabbage in the centre of the crossed threads and open out the larger leaves one by one. Remove the central heart, chop and mix with an equal volume of fine well-seasoned pork forcemeat. Fill the centre of the cabbage with the mixture, then fold back the large leaves to recreate the original shape. On top, place two very thin strips of fat bacon in a cross and secure them by knotting the threads over them. Wrap the cabbage in the cloth and tie it up.

Line a flameproof casserole with 100 g (4 oz) bacon, 150 g (5 oz, 1 cup) diced carrots and 150 g (5 oz, 1 cup) finely diced onion. Put the cabbage on top and barely cover it with rich stock. Cover, bring to the boil, then cook in a preheated oven at 200°C (400°F, gas 6) for 1½ hours. Drain the cabbage, unwrap it and remove the strips of fat bacon. (Alternatively, the cabbage may be prepared and cooked in a net, and without the strips of bacon.) Serve the cabbage in a deep dish, keeping it hot, and coat with the cooking juices, reduced by half.

Red Cabbage
pickled red cabbage
Prepare the cabbage: cut it into quarters, remove and discard the large ribs, then cut it into strips. Place in a large basin, sprinkle with a generous tablespoon of fine salt and mix. Cover and leave for at least 48 hours in a cool place, turning over several times. Drain the cabbage and arrange it in layers in an earthenware jar, inserting between each layer 4–5 peppercorns, 3 small pieces of bay leaf and half a garlic clove, chopped. Boil enough red wine vinegar to cover the cabbage, leave to cool, then cover the cabbage with it. Seal the jar and leave to marinate for at least 36 hours. It can be served in various hors d'oeuvre or as a condiment with cold beef or pork.

red cabbage à la flamande
Remove any withered leaves, slice off the stump (core) at the base of the leaves and cut the cabbage into four, then into thin strips. Wash and dry. Melt 40 g (1½ oz, 3 tablespoons) butter in a saucepan, add the cabbage, sprinkle with salt and pepper, moisten with 1 tablespoon vinegar, then cover and

CABBAGE FAMILY

Chinese leaves

soft-hearted,
smooth-leafed cabbage

pak choi

white cabbage

red cabbage

firm-hearted, crinkly-leafed Savoy cabbage

cauliflower

cook over a gentle heat. Meanwhile, peel 3 or 4 tart apples, cut them into quarters, remove the core and slice them finely. Add them to the cabbage after I hour of cooking, sprinkle with I tablespoon brown sugar, replace the lid and cook for a further 20 minutes. Serve to accompany boiled pork or boiled or braised beef.

red cabbage à la limousine

Prepare the cabbage and cut it into thin strips. Melt 4 tablespoons lard (shortening) in a saucepan. Add the cabbage and about 20 large peeled sweet chestnuts. Add sufficient stock to barely cover the vegetables. Season with salt and pepper, cover the pan and leave to cook gently for about I½ hours. Serve to accompany roast pork or pork chops.

red cabbage salad

Select a very fresh and tender red cabbage (break off a large leaf to test it), remove the large outer leaves, cut the cabbage into four and remove the white centre. Slice the quarters into fine strips, about 5 mm (¼ in) wide, blanch them for 5 minutes in boiling water, then cool and wipe them. Place in a salad bowl, sprinkle with 200 ml (7 fl oz, ¾ cup) boiling red wine vinegar, mix, cover and leave to marinate for 5–6 hours. Drain the cabbage and season it with salt, pepper and oil. Unblanched red cabbage can be used for a very crisp salad: shred the wedges finely. Add 2 tablespoons of soft brown sugar with the vinegar if liked.

other recipes See *confit, sausage, sou-fassum*.

CABÉCOU A small soft French cheese (45% fat content) from Quercy and Rouergue, made from a mixture of goat's milk, ewe's milk and cow's milk. (The literal meaning of the word is 'little goat'.) It is a fairly firm ivory-white cheese with a fine bluish crust and a nutty flavour. The main varieties of Cabécou are Cahors, Gramat, Entraygues, Livernon, Rocamadour and Gourdon, all in season from April to November. Some of the cheeses are wrapped in vine leaves and stored in a jar with vinegar. They are eaten when they turn pink. In Quercy, the cheese is soaked in plum brandy.

CABERNET FRANC The eighth most important red grape variety in France, grown particularly in Bordeaux and the Loire, but also grown extensively in Italy, California and Argentina. Depending on the region, it is known as *Bouchet* (in Bordeaux), *Bouchy* (in the Pyrenees) and *Breton* (in the Loire Valley). Its loose, medium-sized bunches have small black berries with a thin skin which ripen a week earlier than Cabernet Sauvignon.

The Cabernet Franc is used in making most of the AOC red wines of Bordeaux (particularly St-Emilion), where it is often blended with Cabernet Sauvignon, Merlot and Malbec.

Used on its own in the Loire Valley (Chinon, Bourgeuil, Saint-Nicolas-de-Bourgeuil, Saumur-

Champigny), it produces wines with bouquets of strawberries and violets, which should be drunk fairly young.

CABERNET SAUVIGNON The noblest of French red grape varieties and now grown extensively around the world. It has small, tightly packed bunches of grapes which are dark and thick-skinned, with a high ratio of pips to juice.

The vine buds and the fruit ripens late, which can be a problem in marginal climates. It is used as a major variety in many Bordeaux blends to provide colour and structure along with a bouquet and flavour reminiscent of blackcurrants. It is planted extensively in Chile, California and Australia where the grapes ripen fully to give softer berry flavours. Many New World winemakers prefer not to blend Cabernet Sauvignon with other varieties.

CABESSAL, EN A method of preparing stuffed hare, which is tied up with string so that it forms a round and can be cooked in a circular dish. It is then said to be *en cabessal*. The method originated in the regions of Limousin and Périgord. A *cabessal* (or *chabessal*) is also a French dialect word for the twisted cloth that women wore on their heads to carry a pitcher of water.

RECIPE

hare en cabessal

Skin and gut a hare, reserving the liver and blood. Pound the liver with a garlic clove, then add the blood and I tablespoon vinegar. On the day before cooking, place the hare in a marinade of red wine, oil, carrots, thinly sliced onions and shallots, thyme, a bay leaf, a clove, salt and pepper. Prepare a stuffing with 500 g (18 oz) fillet of veal, 250 g (9 oz) raw ham, 250 g (9 oz) fresh pork, 2 garlic cloves and 2 shallots. Chop the ingredients finely, season with salt and pepper, and bind with an egg. Remove the hare from the marinade, wipe and stuff.

Sew up the opening in the belly. Bard the hare all over with larding bacon, then tie it with string so that it forms a round. Place it in a round dish with a little goose or pork grease, some pieces of larding bacon and a few small onions. Add a small glass of brandy and a bottle of good-quality red or white wine, then a roux made with flour and goose fat. Cover the dish and cook in a preheated oven at 150°C (300°F, gas 2) for 4 or 5 hours. When three-quarters cooked, add the pounded liver and blood. Check the seasoning. When cooking is complete, the sauce should be substantially reduced.

When serving, remove the string, the larding bacon and the bones (which should come away easily from the flesh). Serve with croûtons of bread fried in goose fat, which may be rubbed with garlic if desired.

CABINET PARTICULIER A private room placed at the disposal of customers by certain de luxe restaurants. They were very fashionable in Paris under the Second Empire and during the Belle Époque in such establishments as the Café Anglais, the Café de Prunier and the Café de Lapérouse.

CABOULOT A small French suburban or country café, or a small modest restaurant that permits dancing. The term appeared in 1852, being a Franche-Comté word meaning 'hut' or 'small room'. It is described as a popular meeting place in a song by Francis Carco.

CABRALES This DOP handmade blue cheese (45–48% fat content) from the Picos de Europa mountain region of northern Spain is made from a mixture of unpasteurized goat's, ewe's or cow's milk. Commercial versions use pasteurized milk. Produced in 18–20 cm (7–8 in) diameter wheels weighing around 2.5–4.5 kg (5–9 lb), the cheese is wrapped in green foil instead of the original leaves. The best cheeses are available in the spring. The paste has intense purple veining with a robust flavour and salty tang. Serve as part of a cheeseboard or mix with chopped black olives to spread on toast. The Spanish also use this cheese in sauces to serve with steak or vegetables.

CACIOCAVALLO An Italian DOP cheese made from cow's milk (44% fat content) and often smoked. It is a spun-curd or *pasta pilata* cheese with a compact, straw-coloured paste and a pale, fine, oily crust. It is moulded into the shape of a narrow gourd with a smaller swelling on top and weighs 3–4 kg (6½–9 lb). Its name, a combination of the Italian words *cacio* (cheese) and *cavallo* (horse), could come from the fact that the ripening cheeses are tied together in pairs with wisps of straw and hung on sticks (*à cheval*, that is mounted) to dry. Another possibility is that it was named after the seal of the kingdom of Naples, which depicted a galloping horse and was imprinted on the cheese in the 14th century. It is also possible that it was so named because Caciocavallo was originally made with mare's milk. Today, the best Caciocavallo still comes from southern Italy. It is usually eaten at the end of a meal. If it is matured for a long period, it becomes very hard and is then grated before it is used.

CADILLAC A sweet white wine area, situated in the Bordeaux region, across the Garonne River from the Sauternes vineyard. The wines are made from the Sémillon, Sauvignon Blanc and Muscadelle vines, the grapes being picked when ripe or overripe. Formerly, Cadillac was included in the Premières Côtes de Bordeaux AOC, but now it is produced in 21 parishes (communes), including Langoiran and Gabarnac. Usually drunk as a dessert wine, it may also be enjoyed with foie gras or as an apéritif.

CADRAN BLEU A former café-restaurant in Paris, in the Boulevard du Temple. Having opened in 1773 as a small café, it was damaged during the storming of the Bastille and was subsequently used as a meeting place for the leaders of the uprising of 10 August 1792. It became a very popular restaurant under the Consulate (1799–1804) and the Empire, specializing in weddings and banquets ('with its room, seating a hundred people, but poorly heated and lighted', according to Monsieur de Jouy in 1813). The establishment also provided private rooms of dubious repute: 'The house had not one upright window or storey,' wrote Balzac in *Le Cousin Pons*. Around 1840, the Cadran Bleu had declined as a fashionable place. A battery of artillery shook the building in the Revolution of 1848, and in 1860 it was demolished.

CAERPHILLY Shaped like a small millstone weighing around 3.5 kg (8 lb), this semi-hard pressed cow's milk cheese was traditionally made in Wales, but it is now produced in both England and Wales. The best cheeses are farm-made from unpasteurized milk. They are lightly pressed and brined for 24 hours before being rubbed with rice flour. The flavour is delicate but subtle, with a lightly salty quality.

CAESAR'S MUSHROOM Edible wild mushroom with an orange-yellow cap, known as the royal agaric or the 'king of mushrooms' because of the fineness of its fresh and its scent. Found in southern France, Caesar's mushroom likes warmth and even survives a certain amount of dryness. It grows spontaneously in woods, particularly in open oak groves with a good aspect, and also in coppices and plantations of sweet chestnut trees, from summer to autumn. When harvested in its juvenile stage, it is important not to confuse it with the white agaric (*amanite blanche*), which is fatal, or the fly agaric, which is highly toxic.

RECIPE

hazelnut and Caesar's mushroom soup
Clean, peel and finely dice 675 g (1½ lb) Caesar's mushrooms, then wash and shred 6 round lettuces. Season the lettuce with salt and pepper and 1½ tablespoons caster (superfine) sugar. Heat 75 g (3 oz, 6 tablespoons) butter in a saucepan until it begins to turn brown, then put in the lettuce and the mushrooms; cook over a low heat, with the pan covered, for 30 minutes. Add a knuckle of veal, 1 litre (1¾ pints, 4⅓ cups) milk and 6 tablespoons rice which has been boiled for 1 minute. Salt lightly and mix in 1 tablespoon fairy-ring mushrooms (*Marasmius oreades*) or wood blewits (*Lepista nuda*) in dried or powdered form. Cook over a moderate heat for 2 hours.

Take out the knuckle and rub the soup through a fine sieve. Return it to a low heat. Pound a handful of shelled and skinned hazelnuts and mix them with 75 g (3 oz, 6 tablespoons) butter. Press this paste through a fine sieve into a hot soup tureen; add 3 egg yolks and 120 ml (4½ fl oz, ½ cup) double (heavy) cream. Pour on the soup, beating vigorously.

CAFÉ A place selling drinks (particularly coffee, beer, wine, apéritifs and fruit juices) and also snacks (sandwiches and salads). Originally, only coffee was served in these establishments.

The first café in the world was opened in Constantinople in 1550. In 1672, an Armenian called Pascal set up a little stall selling cups of coffee at the Saint-Germain fair in Paris. His success was only fleeting and he left to try his luck in other European countries. For some time, the fashion of selling coffee to be drunk at home continued in Paris. The French gradually, however, discovered the social aspects of drinking coffee in a public place, combined with the delights of conversation. Until then, there had only been premises selling wine, such as the cabarets and tavernes. The cafés, or *maisons de café*, began to open: they sold brandy, sweetened wines and liqueurs, as well as coffee. In 1696 the lemonade and brandy vendors' guild was formed.

■ **Palais-Royal, Grands Boulevards, Left Bank and bougnats** The first café (in the modern sense) was the Café Procope, opened in 1696 by an Italian. Cafés soon became a new way of life: people read the news there, played chess or cards, exchanged ideas, talked politics and smoked. The hero of Montesquieu's *Lettres persanes* said: 'If I were the king of this country, I would close the cafés, because the people who frequent those places become tediously overheated in the brain when they go there.' The 'club' cafés boasted a clientele of artists, officers and writers. In the 17th century, and more especially the 18th century, the cafés became the meeting places of men of letters and literary critics: La Fontaine, Crébillon, Fontenelle and the Encyclopedists were the habitués. The cafés of the Palais-Royal galleries – the 'porticoes of the Revolution' – included the Foy, Régence, Mille Colonnes, Aveugles and Caveau; they became highly fashionable meeting places for discussing politics and listening to the best orators.

After the revolutionary turmoil, rustic cafés, cafés with performers, and pleasure gardens, such as the Tivoli and Frascati, opened. However, the return of the Bourbons put the political cafés (for example, the Lemblin) back into fashion. Here, in front of the bourgeoisie, dandies vied for the limelight with journalists. The Romantics deserted the Palais-Royal and literary life took refuge in the salons, where tea was the main drink.

Soon, when the Grands Boulevards became the focus of attention in the capital, it was the ice-cream sellers and the restaurateurs who drew the crowds with establishments such as the Café Riche, the Café de Paris and the Tortoni, but nevertheless the café survived. It often took the form of a club or society. On the terraces of the fashionable cafés and in the first *cafés-concerts* (cafés with performers) – supervised by the 'garçon de café' clad in his black jacket and long white apron – artists and singers, writers, dandies, *grisettes* (French working girls) and young celebrities could be found. Such establishments included the Café des Variétés and the Divan Lepeletier. The cafés of the Left Bank also began to become important. These were the domain of writers, poets and intellectuals, while the newly emerging brasseries constituted serious competition for the café-restaurants. In the early 1900s, the Montmartre cafés served many artists. Later on, Montparnasse stole the limelight with the Closerie des Lilas, and the Parisian tradition of café life survived after the war in the Café de Flore and at the Deux Magots.

After the arrival of the *bougnats* (wine and coal merchants) in the 19th century, the corner cafés owned by the *bougnats* became firmly established; here the '*petit noir*' (cup of black coffee), the '*ballon de rouge*' (glass of red wine) and pastis are consumed at the bar and card games are played. (Note that in France, *café* or *vin de café* is a light red wine served in cafés at the bar.)

■ **Cafés in Europe** In England, coffee was at first regarded as a panacea against alcoholism, and the coffee houses were all the more successful as the turmoil in the political parties at the end of the 17th century created a need for public meeting places. Also, English literature was then going through its 'French' period.

In Germany, cafés were set up in Hamburg, Berlin and especially Leipzig, a town of printers that was frequented by writers and wits (J.S. Bach even composed a Coffee Cantata). At the beginning of the 18th century, the right to sell coffee was restricted to four 'distillers', but the fashion for drinking coffee became so widespread that the law was flouted and coffee beans were illegally roasted. Bootlegging was organized and ersatz versions of coffee appeared. In Berlin, cafés assumed the singing tradition of cabarets. However, in Germany, most coffee was drunk at home, with plenty of cakes. It was, moreover, more of a woman's drink, as men usually preferred beer.

In Vienna, the café became firmly established in 1683, when the invading Turks abandoned 500 sacks of coffee. This was given to Kolschitzky, the hero of the victory over the invaders, and it was he who turned Turkish coffee into Viennese coffee. It was filtered, flavoured with honey, enriched with cream and usually served with croissants. The Viennese had always considered the café to be a natural extension of their homes and offices. They spent many hours there – in the morning to read the news, in the afternoon to discuss business and in the evening to talk, receive guests and play billiards. It was in Vienna that the café-concert was born. The great Viennese cafés that perpetuate the tradition, with their hangings, soft lights and wooden panelling, are the Landtmann, the Hewelka (with a literary and artistic tradition) and the Sacher, a veritable national institution. The same grand scale is seen in the *salon de thé* (tea room), an important meeting place for political and literary notables in Lisbon and Budapest.

Italian cafés existed before the first ones opened in France – especially in Venice, where the coffee shop (celebrated by Goldoni) was part of daily life. However, the most famous ones date from the 18th century: the Greco opened in Rome in 1760, and the Florian, which opened in Venice in 1720, held public concerts under the arcade of Saint Mark's Square; its elegant rooms were frequented by such figures as Mme de Staël, George Sand, Alfred de Musset and Marcel Proust.

CAFÉ ANGLAIS An establishment set up in the Boulevard des Italiens in Paris in 1802. It was named in honour of the Peace of Amiens, which had just been signed and which, everybody hoped, would mark the start of a long period of peace with England. English breakfast was served there (see *Café Hardy*). At first, it was frequented by coachmen and servants, but in 1822 its new owner, Paul Chevreuil, made it into a fashionable restaurant, famous for its roast and grilled (broiled) dishes. According to Véron, this was 'the place in Paris where one dines best'. However, it was with the arrival of Adolphe Dugléré that the Café Anglais acquired a great gastronomic reputation; it was here that this great chef created potage Germany, poulard *à la d'Albufera*, sole Dugléré and Anna potatoes. At that time, the clientele of the Café Anglais came from the world of finance and the smart Parisian set. The Grand Seize (one of its private rooms where the King of Prussia, Emperor Nicolas II and Bismarck had supper) was immortalized in Offenbach's *La Vie parisienne*. The house was demolished in 1913, but its cellar, and the wood panelling of the Grand Seize, were purchased by André Terrail, the owner of the Tour d'Argent, who married the daughter of the last owner of the Café Anglais.

Before the Revolution, another Café Anglais existed in Paris, at the Quai Conti. Its habitués used to meet there to read the English newspapers.

CAFÉ AU LAIT Coffee made with milk. It is usually drunk at breakfast in France. The fashion originated in Vienna and goes back to the end of the 17th century in France: café au lait was the favourite drink of Marie-Antoinette.

Opinions have always been divided about the benefits of this drink, which is said to be indigestible and rather unrefined. Madame de Sevigné, however, wrote in 1680: 'We have a fancy to skim the good milk and mix it with sugar and good coffee. It is marvellous, and will greatly console me for Lent. Du Bois, my doctor, approved it for the chest and for chills.' In those days it was called *lait cafeté*, or *café laité*, and was recommended for its nutritional properties. It rapidly became popular and Sebastian Mercier remarked, in his *Tableaux de Paris*: 'Café au lait has become the eternal breakfast of workers on building sites. They say that in most cases, it keeps them going until evening.' However, Balzac, in his *Nouvelle Théorie du déjeuner*, was intransigent: 'To offer café au lait is not a mistake, it is ludicrous. Only porters now drink such a vulgar mixture. The drink saddens the soul . . . and weakens the nervous system.' For many years in the countryside of northern and eastern France, the evening meal consisted of a bowl of café au lait with bread and cheese.

CAFÉ DE FOY An establishment set up in Paris in 1725, under the arcade of the Montpensier gallery at the Palais-Royal. Famous for its ice creams and sorbets, it was the legendary place where Camille Desmoulins harangued the crowd on 13 July 1789. The following day he stormed the Bastille. The Jacobins and Muscadins alternately made it their headquarters, on each occasion purifying the premises by burning gin. It was fashionable until 1820, after which it declined, and Grimod de La Reynière deplored its 'smoked wood panels, dim gothic chandeliers, cups without handles and cracked glasses'. The freehold was put up for sale in 1863, but no purchaser was found.

CAFÉ DE LA PAIX This Parisian café, which was decorated by Garnier, opened in 1862 on the ground floor of the Grand Hôtel, Boulevard des Capucines. It was frequented mainly by foreigners staying in the Grand Hôtel. In the belle époque (the Edwardian era), the smart set came to eat an English breakfast (see *Café Hardy*) or to have supper after the opera, savouring the specialities of the chefs, Nignon and then Escoffier. Massenet, Zola, Maupassant, and later Truman, Leclerc, Callas and Chagall were among the habitués of the Café de la Paix, an international meeting place for artists and high society.

CAFÉ DE MADRID An establishment in the Boulevard Montmartre in Paris, which suddenly became fashionable in 1861, when the owner of the Café des Variétés, situated opposite, refused to subscribe to the newspaper *Le Boulevard*, which one of his customers had just set up. To support the founder of the paper, some of the customers deserted the Café des Variétés for the Café de Madrid, where the opponents of the imperial regime were already meeting. Gambetta, Henri de Rochefort, Baudelaire, Villiers de l'Isle-Adam, Monselet, and future members of the Commune frequented it assiduously; Alphonse Allais was also an habitué of the Madrid.

CAFÉ DE PARIS An establishment that opened in Paris in 1822 in the Boulevard des Italiens. Regarded as the 'temple of elegance', it was frequented by dandies, fashionable ladies and such celebrities as Musset, Balzac, Dumas, Gautier and Véron. Successive managers brought with them a spectacular cuisine: Belle Alliance pheasant stuffed with truffles and rock partridges *sur piédestal*. The owner (the Marchioness of Hertford) specified in the lease that the café must always close its doors at 10 pm. It ran successfully for 20 years, but then declined and finally disappeared in 1856.

Another Café de Paris, just as splendid, smart and expensive as the first one, was in business in the capital from 1878 to 1953, in the Avenue de l'Opéra. Opened by Auguste Joliveau, it was frequented by the Goncourts and their friends and the Prince of Wales, the future Edward VII. Léopold Mourier managed it from 1897 to 1923, engaging famous chefs (such as Tony Girod) whose creations marked a milestone in culinary history, with such dishes as snipe *à la Diane*.

CAFÉ DES AVEUGLES An establishment that opened during the Revolution, at the Palais-Royal in Paris, in the basement of the Lemblin. It was frequented at first by the *sans-culottes*. A notice announced: 'Here you will be honoured by the title of "citizen" and can use the familiar form of address, and smoke.' An orchestra composed of five blind people, including one woman, inspired boisterous evenings, and it was claimed that blind musicians were employed so that they could not see the scenes of debauchery taking place before them. The Café des Aveugles (literally, café of the blind) closed down in 1867.

CAFÉ DES VARIÉTÉS An establishment that opened in 1807 in Paris, in the Boulevard Montmartre. It began modestly, in a one-storey building backing on to the Passage des Panoramas, but was extended in 1831. The natural meeting place of actors from the Théâtre des Variétés, it remained open late at night, attracting such famous customers as Villiers de l'Isle-Adam, Daudet, Murger, Baudelaire and Banville, who would come and enjoy the onion soup. Its decline began in the 1860s.

CAFÉ D'ORSAY Set up in Paris at the beginning of the 19th century, on the corner of the Quai d'Orsay (now the Quai Anatole-France) and the Rue du Bac, this establishment was the meeting place of officers from a barracks then occupying the site of the Palais d'Orsay. Musset and Barbey d'Aurevilly were also customers. The café then became the headquarters of the members of the central committee of the Commune. It had a particularly high reputation in 1875 and was later frequented by the editors of *L'Officiel*.

CAFÉ DU CAVEAU An establishment that was opened in Paris in 1784 by Cuisinier, in the Beaujolais gallery at the Palais-Royal. It was frequented by artists and musicians, including Boieldieu, Méhul, Talma, David, Chénier and Redouté, and it was here that supporters of Puccini and admirers of Gluck confronted one another. Coffee with cream and hot chocolate were served. In a small columned temple called La Rotonde, built in front of the café's arcade in 1802, it was possible to see the table at which Bonaparte had eaten. The Café du Caveau (not to be confused with the Caveau) was in business until about 1885.

CAFÉ HARDY This was opened in 1799 in the Boulevard des Italiens, in Paris. It became famous after 1804, when Mme Hardy started serving English breakfasts. Customers selected their meat from a buffet, then a head waiter would skewer it on a fork and have it grilled (broiled) on a silver grill in a white marble fireplace. The gourmets of the capital ate there, paying very high prices for kidneys, cutlets, andouillettes with truffles and poultry joints *en papillote*. This caused Cambacérès to say: 'You have to be very rich to go to Hardy, and very hardy to go to Riche' (another famous café in the same boulevard). The establishment declined in about 1836, and the building was demolished. Four years later, a new restaurant (La Maison Dorée) opened on the same site.

CAFÉ LIÉGEOIS An iced dessert, made of coffee mixed with fresh cream. Alternatively, it may be made with coffee ice cream, served in a large glass, with a tablespoon of very strong coffee and topped with Chantilly cream. The origin of this dessert is actually Viennese. *Café viennoise* was popular all over Europe, but the Germanic associations of its name caused it to be changed during World War I.

CAFÉ NAPOLITAIN Situated in Paris at No. 1, Boulevard des Capucines, this establishment (originally called the Café de la Ville de Naples) was famous from 1870 to 1910 for its selection of ice creams and sorbets. Its elegant terrace was frequented by fashionable Parisians, with such personalities as Courteline, Catulle Mendès, Barbey d'Aurevilly, Lucien Guitry, Jean Lorrian and Laurent Tailhade among the clientele.

CAFETERIA A self-service restaurant. The ready-prepared hot and cold dishes are displayed on the counters or placed in automatic dispensers. In the latter, the choice is reduced to such food as sandwiches, pizzas, quiches, and cakes and pastries. The food may be eaten sitting down or standing. Hot and cold drinks may also be supplied, often in automatic vending machines. The word appeared in France in the 1950s, and came from Spain. In France, 'coffee-shops' are similar establishments that may be supplemented by table service.

CAFETIÈRE A utensil for making or serving coffee. The word cafetière appeared in 1685, when coffee-drinking began in France, and the use of the cafetière became widespread in the reign of Louis XV; it was later provided with a heating plate and a spirit lamp. Flaubert recalls this antique device in *Madame Bovary*: 'Madame Homais reappeared, bearing one of those unsteady machines that have to be heated with spirit of wine, for Homais liked to make his coffee at the table, having, besides, roasted it himself, ground it himself and compounded it himself.'

For a long time only two models of coffee maker were known in France: the infuser, in which the coffee was held in a filter, and the Dubelloy cafetière, in which the coffee was filtered. The latter, which appeared after 1850 and is known as *cafetière de grandmère*, was a wide pot, made of fire clay. Another method of making coffee became widespread in the period between the World Wars – the Cona. It consists of two interconnecting toughened glass vessels placed one on top of the other and heated either with a spirit lamp or with an electric or gas heater.

During the 1950s Italian coffee makers began to be widely used in many coffee bars and restaurants. These aluminium or stainless steel coffee makers are placed directly over heat. Water is heated up in the base until it boils, then it is forced up under pressure, through a metal filter basket filled with ground coffee.

At about this time coffee makers using filters (either filter paper or filter pistons) began to be used for very finely ground coffee. Electric coffee makers use this method; they work by heating water in a container and passing it through a filter full of coffee into a glass jug which stands on a thermostatically controlled hotplate, keeping the coffee hot for a limited period of time. Espresso coffee makers make stronger coffee using finely ground coffee; they work under pressure using the same principle as that for the Italian coffee makers.

The traditional coffee pot, which is often part of a coffee service, may be made of porcelain, earthenware, silver, silver gilt or stainless steel. It is used for making coffee using the 'jug method', the simplest and quickest way of making coffee. Allow 1 tablespoon medium-ground coffee per person, and scald the pot before adding the coffee. Although this method is still used occasionally, electric coffee makers have gained in popularity.

CAFÉ TURC
A Parisian establishment opened in 1780 in the Boulevard du Temple and decorated entirely in the Turkish style. There were summerhouses, arbours and bowers that were lit up every night in the gardens alongside the boulevard, and a well-known orchestra played quadrilles. The Café Turc was still fashionable under Louis-Philippe, but did not survive the changes in the boulevard. It became a restaurant for weddings and banquets.

CAFFEINE
An alkaloid present in coffee (1–2%), tea (1.5–3%) and cola nuts (2–3%), with stimulating, tonic and diuretic properties. When taken in excessive amounts, caffeine can become toxic. The quantity of caffeine contained in a cup of coffee varies according to the origin of the beans. Robusta beans contain two and a half times more caffeine than arabica beans. Indian and Sri Lankan (Ceylon) teas are normally richer in caffeine than China teas. Decaffeinated coffees and teas have become popular.

CAGHUSE
Also known as *caqhuse*. A speciality from Picardy, made with a piece of pork knuckle, liberally covered with finely sliced onions and butter. It is cooked in the oven and served cold. The caghuse is traditionally made in an earthenware dish, greased with lard (shortening).

CAHORS
A red wine from south-western France. It was awarded the *appellation d'origine contrôlée* in 1976. After the fall of the Roman Empire, the Cahors region produced a red wine that was very famous in the Middle Ages. The Hundred Years' War and the protectionism practised by the citizens of Bordeaux curtailed the selling of Cahors wines, which had to be transported by boatmen down the Rivers Lot and Garonne to the Gironde region and the port of Bordeaux, from where they might be shipped to England and northern Europe.

The region of Cahors is situated to the east of Bordeaux and to the north of Toulouse, not far from the Bergerac vineyard. It is a limestone plateau (Les Causses) through which the River Lot flows. The vineyard extends over the reddish stony soil, along the banks of the Lot, between Cahors and Soturac. It is made up of small plots scattered over 50 km (31 miles) and is exposed to the south and southeast. The main vine variety is the Malbec (or Cot), which the Cahors vine-growers call Auxerrois. Other varieties are Merlot and Tannat. Cahors wine is so dark and tannic that it should traditionally be kept for three to five years in cask and five to ten years in bottle before being drunk. The young wine is inclined to be harsh and unrewarding, but later it becomes fine, full of fragrance, well balanced and dark red. Modern versions are becoming less tannic and they mature earlier. It is an elegant accompaniment to many spiced dishes, meats with sauce and game.

CAILLEBOTTE
In Poitou and Anjou, a dish made with curdled milk and served cold with fresh cream and sugar. The word comes from *cailler* (to curdle) and *botter* (to coagulate on a rush mat). In other regions, the name is given to a cream cheese made from cow's milk (in Aunis and Saintonge) or from goat's milk (in Saintonge and Poitou). When *caillebotte* is drained in a woven rush basket, it is called *jonchée*. The traditional preparation of Poitou *caillebotte* involves adding a pinch of cardoon flower to curdle the milk. Le Varenne's *Le Confiturier français* (1664) contained a recipe for this dish.

RECIPE

poitou caillebottes
Infuse a pinch of cardoon flower in a very small amount of water for 5–6 hours. Pour the liquid into 1 litre (1¾ pints, 4⅓ cups) fresh milk and leave until it coagulates. Using a knife, cut the resulting solid mass into squares and heat gently until it boils. The curds are cooked when the pieces separate and float in the whey. After chilling, remove the whey and replace it with fresh milk. Top with fresh cream and sweeten to taste.

CAILLETTE
A small flat sausage made of minced pork and green vegetables. It is cooked in the oven and may be eaten hot or cold. *Caillettes* are said to have originated in the Ardèche, but they are prepared in the whole of south-eastern France. The seasoning and secondary ingredients vary from region to region, and even from village to village: truffles

are used in Pierrelatte, spinach in Soyans, greens in Chabeuil (where a *caillette*-tasting society, the Confrérie des Chevaliers du Taste-Caillette, was established in 1967), pig's liver and beet in Valence and pig's liver *à la pugétoise* in Puget-Théniers. *Caillettes* are similar to a type of sausage made in Cornwall, which is served with mustard and mashed potato.

RECIPES

Ardèche caillettes

Blanch 250 g (9 oz, 3 cups) beet leaves, an equal quantity of spinach and a large handful of dandelion leaves, nettles and poppy leaves. Drain and chop finely. Also chop 250 g (9 oz, 1 firmly packed cup) pig's liver, an equal quantity of lights (lungs) and a little fat bacon and mix together. Brown a chopped onion in some lard (shortening) and add the meat, vegetables and a garlic clove; season with salt and pepper. Cook for 5 minutes, stirring continuously. Remove from the heat, divide the mixture into 8 pieces and roll each into a ball. Wrap each ball in pig's caul and pack them close together in an earthenware dish. Put a strip of fat bacon on each *caillette* and cook in a preheated oven at 200°C (400°F, gas 6) for 30–40 minutes. Cool the *caillettes* and store in earthenware pots, covered with lard. They may be served hot, browned in lard, or cold with a dandelion salad.

provençale caillettes

Use only beet leaves, spinach and fine sausagemeat. Make a mixture consisting of half meat and half vegetables, season with salt and pepper, and add some chopped garlic. Divide the mixture into balls about the size of a tangerine, wrap them in caul fat, and flatten them slightly. Bake in a preheated oven at 200°C (400°F, gas 6) for about 40 minutes. Serve the *caillettes* either very hot, with a well-seasoned tomato sauce, or completely chilled with a salad.

CAILLIER A wooden drinking vessel used in the Middle Ages and until the end of the 16th century. The largest of these vessels were used as containers for wine and the bowl-shaped lids were used as drinking cups.

CAISSES Also known as *caissettes*. Cases used in cookery, pastry-making and confectionery. Savoury preparations *en caisse* (in cases) or *en caissette* (in small cases) are served as hot hors d'oeuvre or small entrées. They are generally filled with salpicons, ragoûts or the various fillings used for barquettes, patties, pies or tartlets. The cases are served in small round or oval receptacles made of ovenproof china, tempered glass, metal, plastic or light aluminium (frequently used for caterers' preparations). Petits fours, certain sweetmeats (bouchées) and cakes (such as individual babas) are placed in *caissettes* made of pleated paper. 'Caisses de Wassy' are famous sweetmeats from Champagne made of meringue with almonds, apparently created because Mary Stuart stayed in the town.

The term *caisse* is also used in France to denote various tins (pans) and similar kitchen utensils.

CAJUN COOKERY Cajun cooking was introduced to Louisiana by the Acadians, descendants of 17th-century French settlers in Nova Scotia (then known as Acadia), who were driven out in the mid-18th century by the British. They fled to New Orleans, taking with them their French-influenced cooking style. Cajun evolved from *Cagian*, the Indian interpretation of Acadian.

Cajun cooking is often grouped with Creole cooking (see *Creole cookery*) and the two styles overlap in the use of ingredients and seasonings. Cajun cooking is referred to as more country style than Creole, with its full-bodied, spicy and rich approach. With the same local ingredients, it is hardly surprising that onions, peppers and celery provide the same base for many savoury dishes, often seasoned and thickened with filé powder. Shared recipes include gumbo and jambalaya.

Features of Cajun cooking include the traditional use of pork fat and a dark roux, cooked to a rich brown as a starting point for many stews. Etouffée combines freshwater crayfish with onions, peppers and tomatoes; crayfish are just as likely to feature in a bisque or jambalaya. The same stew may be prepared with chicken instead of crayfish, with the chicken fried to a deep rich brown in the first stages. Dirty rice is a Cajun dish of rice cooked with chicken giblets – taking its name from the colour given by the liver and other giblets; the flavour is good and rich.

The idea of browning ingredients seasoned with dry spices until they are virtually black is associated with contemporary Cajun cooking. A mixture of dry spices is rubbed on ingredients before grilling or pan-frying them in a heavy dry pan until almost black and the spices smoke. This method is particularly good for oily fish and rich or fatty meats.

CAKES AND GÂTEAUX Although both terms can be used for savoury preparations (meat cakes or vegetable gâteaux) their main use is for sweet baked goods. Cakes can be large or small, plain or fancy, light or rich. Gâteau is generally used for fancy, but light, preparations, often with fresh decoration, such as fresh fruit or whipped cream. Whereas a cake may remain fresh for several days after baking or even improve with keeping, a gâteau usually includes fresh decoration or ingredients that do not keep well, such as fresh fruit or whipped cream. In France, the word 'gâteau' designates various pâtisserie items based on puff pastry, shortcrust pastry (basic pie dough), sweet pastry, pâte sablée, choux pastry, Genoese and whisked sponges and meringue. To these may be added various additional ingredients, such as ground almonds, almond paste, chocolate, fruit (fresh, preserved or dried), fondant or water icing (frosting), pastry and butter creams, liqueurs and fresh cream.

The word 'gâteau' is derived from the Old French *wastel*, meaning 'food'. The first gâteaux were simply flat round cakes made with flour and water, but over the centuries these were enriched with honey, eggs, spices, butter, cream and milk. From the very earliest times, a large number of French provinces have produced cakes for which they are noted. Thus Artois had *gâteaux razis*, and Bourbonnais the ancient *tartes de fromage broyé, de crème et de moyeux d'oeulz*. Hearth cakes are still made in Normandy, Picardy, Poitou and in some provinces of the south of France. They are called variously *fouaces, fouaches, fouées* or *fouyasses*, according to the district.

Until the 17th century it was usual at Whitsuntide in Paris to throw down *nieules* and *oublies* (wafers), local Parisian confections, on the heads of the worshippers gathered under the vaulted roofs of the Cathedral of Notre-Dame. At the same time blazing wicks were showered on the congregation.

Among the many pastries which were in high favour from the 12th to the 15th centuries in Paris and other cities were: *échaudés*, of which two variants, the *flageols* and the *gobets*, were especially prized by the people of Paris; and darioles, small tartlets covered with narrow strips of pastry. Two kinds of darioles were made, one filled with cream cheese, the other with frangipane cream. *Talemouses*, which are known today as *talmouses* (cheese turnovers), were also much appreciated.

Casse-museau is a hard dry pastry still made today; *ratons, petits choux* and *gâteaux feuilletés* are mentioned in a charter by Robert, Bishop of Amiens in 1311, which proves that puff pastry was known in France before the 17th century, when, some writers claim, the process of making puff pastry was invented.

In the following centuries, pastrycooks, organized into guilds, produced not only the pastries listed above, but also brioches, spice cakes, waffles of various kinds, marzipan biscuits, tarts and flans decorated in various ways, *pâtes royales* (a kind of meringue), almond cakes, dough cakes, cracknels and *flamiches*. Then came grand architectural creations (*pièces montées*), often more decorative than delectable. In the 18th and 19th centuries, cakes became masterpieces of refinement and ingenuity, especially where pastrycooks were in the service of a prince or a large house.

■ **Traditional cakes** Many cakes have a ceremonial or symbolic significance, linked to a religious feast – such as Christmas, Easter, Epiphany (Twelfth-Night cake) and Candlemas. In addition, cakes have always featured prominently in family celebrations (for baptisms, birthdays and weddings). Formerly, *tourteaux fromagés* were served in Poitou at wedding breakfasts. In Brittany, the bride and groom were given the *gâteau de la demande*. In the country, cakes were provided for social evenings and gatherings, market days and threshing days.

A number of foreign cakes are also well-known in France (strudel, fruit cake, baklava, vatrushki, linzertorte and panettone). On this subject, Jean-Paul Sartre gives a surprising example of culinary anthropomorphism: 'Cakes are human, they are like faces. Spanish cakes are ascetic with a swaggering appearance, they crumble into dust under the tooth. Greek cakes are greasy like little oil lamps: when you press them, the oil oozes out. German cakes are bulky and soft like shaving cream; they are made so that obese easily tempted men can eat them indulgently, without worrying what they taste like but simply to fill their mouths with sweetness. But those Italian cakes had a cruel perfection: really small and flawless, scarcely bigger than petits fours, they gleamed. Their harsh and gaudy colours took away any desire to eat them; instead, you felt like placing them on the sideboard like pieces of painted porcelain.'

RECIPES

fruit cake

Soften 125 g (4½ oz, ½ cup) butter at room temperature. Cream it with 125 g (4½ oz, ½ cup) caster (superfine) sugar and a pinch of salt until pale and soft. Add 3 eggs, one at a time. Mix 175 g (6 oz, 1½ cups) plain (all-purpose) flour with 1 teaspoon baking powder. Wash and dry 250 g (9 oz, 1½ cups) currants or mixed dried fruit and add them to the flour. Mix well and stir into the mixture of butter, sugar and eggs. Refrigerate the mixture for 30 minutes.

Butter a loaf tin (pan) about 23 cm (9 in) long, line it with buttered greaseproof (wax) paper and fill with the cake mixture. Bake in a preheated oven at 240°C (475°F, gas 9) for about 12 minutes, then reduce the temperature to 180°C (350°F, gas 4) and bake for 45 minutes. Check that the cake is sufficiently cooked by piercing with the point of a knife, which should come out clean. Allow the cake to become lukewarm before removing from the tin. Cool on a rack.

gâteau Alexandra

Gently melt 100 g (4 oz, 4 squares) sweetened chocolate in a bowl over a pan of hot water. Whisk 3 egg yolks, 1 whole egg and 125 g (4½ oz, ⅔ cup) caster (superfine) sugar in a basin until the mixture is almost white and is very thick. Blend in 75 g (3 oz, ¾ cup) ground almonds, then the melted chocolate, 3 tablespoons plain (all-purpose) flour, and 75 g (3 oz, ⅔ cup) cornflour (cornstarch). Whisk 3 egg whites with a pinch of salt until stiff, then gently blend them into the chocolate mixture together with 75 g (3 oz, ⅓ cup) melted butter.

Grease and flour an 18 cm (7 in) square cake tin (pan) and pour in the mixture. Bake in a preheated oven at 180°C (350°F, gas 4) for 50 minutes. When cool, cover the cake with 200 g (7 oz, ⅔ cup) apricot jam, then refrigerate for about 10 minutes.

Meanwhile, melt 75 g (3 oz, 3 squares) chocolate with 2 tablespoons water and, in another saucepan, very gently warm through 200 g (7 oz, 1 cup) fondant*. Add the melted chocolate to the fondant: the mixture must be liquid enough to be spread easily. Cover the cake with this chocolate fondant, then store in a cool place until ready to serve.

gâteau flamand

Make a smooth pastry dough by mixing 175 g (6 oz, 1½ cups) sifted plain (all-purpose) flour, 65 g (2½ oz, 5 tablespoons) butter, 50 g (2 oz, ¼ cup) sugar, 1 egg and a pinch of salt. Roll it out to a thickness of 3 mm (⅛ in) and use to line a buttered manqué mould or sandwich tin (layer cake pan) 20 cm (8 in) in diameter. Place it in the refrigerator.

For the filling, mix together 125 g (4½ oz, ⅔ cup) caster (superfine) sugar, 1 teaspoon vanilla sugar and 100 g (4 oz, 1 cup) ground almonds. Whisk in 3 egg yolks, one by one, then add 3 tablespoons kirsch and continue to whisk the mixture until it turns white. Then add 25 g (1 oz, ¼ cup) cornflour (cornstarch). Whisk 3 egg whites until very stiff and blend them into the mixture together with 40 g (1½ oz, 3 tablespoons) melted butter.

Pour the filling into the lined mould and bake in a preheated oven at 200°C (400°F, gas 6) for about 45 minutes. Then remove from the oven and allow to cool for at least 15 minutes before taking out of the mould. Melt 200 g (7 oz, 1 cup) fondant* very slowly in a saucepan. Blend in 3 tablespoons kirsch and spread the fondant over the cake. Decorate with glacé (candied) cherries and sticks of angelica.

gâteau le parisien

Pare the zest from a lemon, blanch it for 1 minute, cool, dry and cut into short very fine julienne strips. Whisk 3 egg yolks with 100 g (4 oz, ½ cup) caster (superfine) sugar until the mixture is almost white. Pour in 25 g (1 oz, ¼ cup) plain (all-purpose) flour, 40 g (1½ oz, ⅓ cup) cornflour (cornstarch), 1 teaspoon vanilla sugar and the zest, then carefully fold in the 3 egg whites, whisked with a pinch of salt until very stiff. Pour this mixture into a buttered fairly deep 23 cm (9 in) sandwich tin (layer cake pan) or manqué mould and bake in a preheated oven at 200°C (400°F, gas 6) for 40 minutes.

During this time, make a frangipane* cream with 3 egg yolks, 75 g (3 oz, 6 tablespoons) caster sugar, 25 g (1 oz, ¼ cup) cornflour, 400 ml (14 fl oz, 1¾ cups) milk, 1 teaspoon vanilla sugar and 125 g (4½ oz, 1 cup) ground almonds. Blend in 125 g (4½ oz, ½ cup) chopped crystallized (candied) fruits.

When the cake is cooked, leave it to cool. Make some Italian meringue with 3 egg whites, 2 tablespoons icing (confectioner's) sugar, and 175 g (6 oz, ¾ cup) caster sugar. Cut the cooled cake into 3 equal rounds. Cover each layer with the frangipane cream and crystallized fruit mixture and re-form the cake. Spread some meringue on the top, then fill a fluted piping bag with the rest of the meringue and decorate all round the cake with regular motifs. Sprinkle the meringue with icing sugar and put in a preheated oven at 180°C (350°F, gas 4). Take out the cake as soon as the meringue turns brown. Leave to cool completely.

honey and cherry cake

Soften 100 g (4 oz, ½ cup) butter at room temperature, divide into small pieces, and then cream with 100 g (4 oz, ½ cup) caster (superfine) sugar, a large pinch of salt and 2 tablespoons liquid honey. Mix in 1 teaspoon baking powder, 200 g (7 oz, 1¾ cups) plain (all-purpose) flour and 3 eggs, added one at a time. Flavour with 2 tablespoons rum. Halve 125 g (4½ oz, ½ cup) glacé (candied) cherries and add them to the cake mixture. Pour immediately into a buttered loaf tin (pan) and bake in a preheated oven at 190°C (375°F, gas 5) for about 45 minutes. If the cake is browning too quickly, cover it with a piece of foil. Turn the cooked cake out of the tin when lukewarm and leave to cool on a rack. Decorate with glacé cherries and pieces of angelica.

marble cake

Melt 175 g (6 oz, ¾ cup) butter very slowly, without letting it become hot. Whisk in 200 g (7 oz, ¾ cup) caster (superfine) sugar and then 3 egg yolks. Sift 175 g (6 oz, 1½ cups) plain (all-purpose) flour and 1 teaspoon baking powder and stir into the egg mixture. Whisk 3 egg whites with a pinch of salt until stiff and fold them into the mixture. Divide the mixture in half. Fold 25 g (1 oz, ¼ cup) cocoa into one portion. Pour the two mixtures into a greased 20 cm (8 in) cake tin (pan) in alternate thin layers. Bake in a preheated oven at 180°C (350°F, gas 4) for 1–1¼ hours.

strawberry gâteau

Wash, hull and dry 1 kg (2¼ lb) large strawberries. Bring 150 g (5 oz, ⅔ cup) granulated sugar and 5½ tablespoons water to the boil, add 2 tablespoons of kirsch and 2 tablespoons wild strawberry liqueur. Place an 18 × 23 cm (7 × 9 in) rectangle of sponge cake on a baking sheet lined with greaseproof (wax) paper. Soak it with one-third of the syrup. Whip 500 g (18 oz, 2¼ cups) butter cream* to make it lighter and, using a wooden spatula, incorporate 100 g (4 oz, ½ cup) of confectioner's custard* (pastry cream). Spread one-third of this mixture on the sponge cake. Arrange the strawberries on top, very close together and pointing upwards, pressing them well into the cream. Pour 2 tablespoons kirsch on top and sprinkle on 25 g (1 oz, 2 tablespoons) caster (superfine) sugar. Level the top of the strawberries using a serrated knife and cover with the remaining butter cream mixture, smoothing the top and sides with the spatula. Cover with another rectangle of sponge cake the same size and pour the remaining syrup over it. Coat the gâteau with a thin layer of pistachio-flavoured almond paste (75 g, 3 oz, ⅓ cup). Leave the strawberry gâteau for at least 8 hours in the refrigerator. Before serving, tidy the edges with a knife dipped in hot water. Decorate with strawberries sliced into a fan shape and coated with 100 g (4 oz, ⅓ cup) of apricot glaze, applied with a pastry brush.

CALABASH The fruit of various plants of the gourd family. The sweet calabash is a creeping shrub from America and Africa. Its soft delicate flesh may be eaten raw in a salad, baked in the oven, boiled, stewed with bacon and herbs (in Martinique) or curried with beef (in Sri Lanka). In Japan, the flesh of some calabashes is dried, cut into thin strips and used as a garnish for soups. When dried, the fruit becomes hard and woody. These gourds are hollowed out and used as kitchen utensils, drinking vessels and other articles.

In South America a liquid extracted from the pulp is used to make a syrup.

CALAMARI See *squid*.

CALCIUM A mineral that is essential for the development and functioning of the human body and is an important constituent of the bones and teeth. The principal sources of calcium are milk, yogurt and cheese. Calcium is also found in fish in which bones are eaten, green leafy vegetables and a variety of other foods.

CALDEIRADA A thick Portuguese soup made from molluscs and fish with white wine, poured over slices of bread glazed with olive oil.

RECIPE

caldeirada

Mix together I finely chopped onion, ¼ chopped pepper, 2 small tomatoes, peeled, seeded and crushed, ½ teaspoon crushed garlic, salt and black pepper from the mill. Place 12 clams in a heavy-based casserole with 60 ml (2 fl oz, ¼ cup) olive oil. Cover with half the mixture of vegetables, then add 400 g (14 oz) white fish, skinned, filleted and cut into pieces, and 300 g (11 oz) squid, cleaned and cut into strips. Cover with the remaining vegetables and add 200 ml (7 fl oz, ¾ cup) white wine. Bring to the boil, then cover and simmer for 20 minutes. Heat 60 ml (2 fl oz, ¼ cup) olive oil in a frying pan and fry 4 slices of sandwich bread on both sides until golden. Drain on paper towels. Put I slice of bread on each plate. Pour a ladle of stock over each slice, then arrange the fish, clams and squid on top. Sprinkle generously with finely chopped parsley.

CALDO VERDE A Portuguese national dish consisting of a soup made with olive oil, potatoes and dark green Portuguese curly cabbage. It is garnished with slices of garlic sausage and served with maize (corn) bread and red wine. The cabbage has a very strong flavour and is cut into very thin strips.

CALIFORNIAN WINE Despite California's long history of winemaking, its influence did not become important until the latter part of the 20th century. California's grasp of modern winemaking in the 1970s was the driving force in opening up the New World of wine. A small cluster of wines from the Napa Valley, produced by pioneers such as Robert Mondavi, Joe Heitz and Warren Winiarski, were the first to prove that quality winemaking was not necessarily confined to the classic regions of Europe.

Vine-growing was introduced to Mexico by Cortés in the early 16th century and slowly spread to the north via the Spanish missions. It was not until the second half of the 19th century, when California ceased to be Mexican and became one of the States of the Union, that modern vine-growing really began. The credit for this goes to a few pioneers, including the great Hungarian nobleman, Agoston Haraszthy, considered to be the 'father' of Californian vine-growing. They imported a large number of European vines to replace that of the Mission – a variety of grape formerly introduced by the Jesuits, which has a very high yield but produces only mediocre wines.

Phylloxera in the late 1800s followed by prohibition had a severe effect on the industry. In the late 1980s the resources of California's wine industry were tested again when a second wave of Phylloxera swept through the State. Many growers used this as an opportunity to replant with greater consideration to variety, density, training and soil type.

Three-quarters of California's grape growing is concentrated in the Central Valley – between Sacramento in the north and Bakersfield in the south. This hot, dry, irrigated area is the source of much of California's inexpensive, 'jug wine' made from a range of grapes, including French Colombard, Chenin Blanc and Zinfandel.

In contrast with the Central Valley, the Napa Valley, north of San Francisco, is renowned for its quality rather than quantity. This narrow, flat, 30 km (18 mile) long valley has a unique climate, heavily influenced by a natural fog bank extending from the San Francisco Bay which lowers temperatures. This is the heartland of California's top-quality producers, many of whom make wines which can challenge the best from around the world. Cabernet Sauvignon does particularly well here, as do Syrah and Chardonnay. Sonoma Valley to the west of Napa and Mendocino to the north are less famous but also capable of making good wines. Los Carneros to the south produces some excellent Pinot Noir and this is the centre of California's quality sparkling wine industry, some of which is owned by outposts of French champagne houses. South of San Francisco, the Santa Cruz Mountains, Monterey and Santa Barbara all produce quality wines for international and local markets.

After a fairly erratic development, involving trial and error, the European vine finally became adapted to growth in the varied soils and climates of California. Two major vine-growing areas can be distinguished: the relatively cold north coast, which produces table wines, some of which are excellent, and the much warmer inland valleys, producing mainly sweet wines and dessert wines, which are high in alcohol but in general of rather indifferent quality.

■ **Table wines** The Californian wineries are outstandingly well equipped and planned. They make, in general, three main types of wine. The inexpensive red, white and rosé 'jug wines' are often from table grapes (such as Thompson Seedless) and tend to be somewhat mediocre. Some of the better-quality wines bear European names, often those of classic grape varieties, but the use of classic regional names is declining and it must be said that such wines bear scant relation to their French counterparts. The 'varietal wines' bear the names of the grape or grapes from which they are made, although regulations do not yet insist on a 100% use of these varieties, which is something often stressed on labels by top producers. Such wines can equal in quality many European fine wines.

■ **Sweet and sparkling wines** The apéritif and sweet wines are, in general, versions of European classics – sherry, port, Tokay, and so on, few of them attaining more than ordinary quality. The sparkling wines, however, made by the champagne process, can be really good, notably the dry ones.

CALISSON A diamond-shaped sweetmeat from Provence produced on a small scale. Calissons are actually a centuries-old speciality of Aix-en-Provence. In the 17th century they were distributed among the congregation during religious ceremonies held in memory of the plague of 1630. Later, they were traditionally eaten at Easter. The Provençal word *calissoun* (or *canissoun*), which comes from the Latin *canna* (a reed), is used for the wire stand on which confectioners display crystallized (candied) fruit and calissons.

Calissons are made of 40% blanched almonds and 60% crystallized fruit (melon with a little orange) mixed with orange-flower water and syrup. The mixture is placed on a base of unleavened bread and coated with royal icing. Calissons should be bought when very fresh and soft and kept only for a short time. They must be protected from the air as they dry quickly.

CALVADOS Brandy made by distilling cider. Cider distillation is a very old tradition in Normandy – it was mentioned in 1553 in the diary of Gilles de Gouberville, a gentleman of the Cotentin. The best Calvados is made with cider that is over a year old.

Distilling may be carried out throughout the year, but it is usually from March to April and August to September. Traditional stills with a double distillation are used for the *appellation contrôlée* Calvados, which is made in the Auge region, comprising part of the department of Calvados and several communes of the Orne and Eure. The *appellation réglementée* Calvados are made by a single distillation process.

Calvados is a harsh rough brandy, 72° alcohol per volume, which must mature for a time in oak casks. It may be sold only after a year's ageing. It is usually categorized as follows: 'Trois étoiles' or 'Trois Pommes' Calvados are aged for two years in wood; 'Vieux' or 'Réserve' are aged for three years; 'VO' (Very Old) or 'Vieille Réserve' for four years; 'VSOP'

for five years; 'Extra', 'Napoléon', 'Hors d'Âge' or 'Âge Inconnu' for more than five years.

Since the middle of the 20th century, Calvados has been subject to strict controls and, in export markets, has become one of the most sought-after French spirits. (It is not, however, the same as the American spirit applejack.) Old Calvados is to be enjoyed as a digestive, in a tulip glass. The Normans and Bretons have popularized the custom of *café-calva*: the brandy is either served in a small glass at the same time as the coffee, or else is poured into the empty coffee cup while this is still warm. (See *Trou normand*.)

Like most spirits, Calvados may be used in cooking and pastry-making, particularly in dishes that are Norman specialities, such as chicken or leg of mutton with cream and Calvados, apple desserts, omelettes and *crêpes flambées*.

CAMACHO'S WEDDING An episode in *Don Quixote* in which the hero and Sancho Panza attend the wedding feast of a wealthy farmer, Camacho. The enormous number of dishes served at this repast has become proverbial and the expression *noces de Camache* is used to describe a particularly sumptuous feast costing an inordinate amount of money. 'The first thing that met Sancho's eyes was a whole ox spitted on the trunk of an elm and, in the hearth over which it was to roast, there was a fair mountain of wood burning. Six earthen pots were arranged around this blaze ... Whole sheep disappeared within them as if they were pigeons. Innumerable skinned hares and fully plucked chickens, hanging on the trees, were soon to be swallowed up in these pots. Birds and game too, of all kinds, were also hanging from the branches so that they were kept cool in the air ... There were piles of white loaves, like heaps of wheat in barns. Cheeses, built up like bricks, formed walls and two cauldrons of oil, bigger than dyer's vats, were used for frying pastries, which were lifted out with two sturdy shovels and then plunged into another cauldron of honey standing nearby.'

CAMBACÉRÈS, JEAN-JACQUES RÉGIS DE French jurist, politician and gastronome (born Montpellier, 1754; died Paris, 1824). During a particularly turbulent period in French history (from the French Revolution to the Restoration), Cambacérès adroitly advanced his career in the public sphere. He proved equally skilful in gastronomy. His table was reputed to be the most sumptuous and lavish in Paris, equalling that of Talleyrand, and the dinners that he gave at his house in Rue Saint-Dominique were celebrated. Cambacérès chose the dishes himself and knew all the gastronomic skills, so that he was regarded as a supreme arbiter of taste. But he was accused of stinginess and gluttony by the famous chef, Carême, probably in an effort to blacken the name of the man that rivalled Carême's employer Talleyrand, who also practised 'table politics'. During the Congress of Lunéville, when Bonaparte ordered

CAMBODIA

Cambodian cuisine is mainly based on local produce; the population relies for its food on rice-growing, market gardening, fruit-growing and fishing.

■ **Vegetables and fish** Meals are based on soups, such as *kâko*, a vegetable soup with meat, fish or chicken, or on salads such as *nhoam*, a salad with chicken, seasoned with fish-based sauce, lemon juice, mint and chilli pepper, or a salad of green mangoes with dried or salt fish. Fish is also eaten fresh or sautéed with vegetables. Smoked fish is used to make *prahoc*, a salty, strong-smelling sauce which is prepared and then kept from year to year.

■ **Puddings** Cambodians usually eat only fruit: mangoes, bananas, papayas, oranges, lychees or longans. Pastries are made with eggs, sugar and coconut milk. The most popular are called *yeup, vôy, kroap-khnor* and *san-khyas*. Some are made with sticky rice (*ansâm-chrouak, tréap-bay*) or with seaweed jelly (*chahuoy-ktiset*). Orange juice is popular.

---

that postal services should carry nothing but despatches and food parcels were banned, Cambacérès pleaded: 'How can one make friends without exquisite dishes! It is mainly through the table that one governs!' The First Consul decided in his favour.

More often than not, Cambacérès was accompanied by the Marquis d'Aigrefeuille, his faithful taster and table companion, to whom Grimod de La Reynière dedicated his first *Almanach des gourmands*, an anecdotal guide to Paris. Cambacérès also presided over Grimod's 'Jury of Tasters' from 1805 onwards. A hearty eater and generous host, who entertained distinguished guests on behalf of Napoleon, he died of apoplexy at the age of 70, after Louis XVIII granted him permission to return from exile.

Three very elaborate dishes were named after him: a cream soup of chicken, pigeon and crayfish, garnished with quenelles made with the same meats; a timbale of macaroni and foie gras; and salmon trout with crayfish and truffles.

CAMBODIA See *above*.

CAMBRIDGE SAUCE An emulsified sauce found in traditional English cooking that is made from anchovies, egg yolks and mustard. It is served as an accompaniment to cold meats.

RECIPE

Cambridge sauce
Thoroughly desalt 6 anchovies, then remove the bones. Blend together 3 hard-boiled (hard-cooked) egg yolks, the anchovy flesh, 1 teaspoon capers and a small bunch of tarragon and chervil. Add 1 teaspoon English mustard to the mixture and season with pepper. Thicken with groundnut (peanut) oil or sunflower oil, as for mayonnaise, then add 1 tablespoon vinegar. Adjust the seasoning. Add chopped chives and parsley.

CAMEL A ruminant mammal of Asia and Africa, which possesses either one hump (dromedary) or two. Camel meat, mostly from young animals, whose tender flesh is similar to veal, is consumed in several countries of North Africa and the Middle East. The thigh joint of the dromedary is cooked chopped, as meatballs, or whole in a marinade. In Mongolia, the fat from the hump is used to make a widely used butter. The heart and other offal are also eaten. Considered unclean in the Bible, the camel was highly esteemed in Imperial Rome, where its grilled feet were a choice dish. In Paris, during the 1870 siege, it appeared on the Christmas Eve menu at the Voisin restaurant. Camel's milk is a nutritious and well-balanced food for humans.

CAMELINE A cold condiment for pâtés, roasts and fish, used in medieval times. It was made of grilled bread soaked in wine, drained, squeezed and ground with spices (cinnamon, ginger, pepper, cloves and nutmeg), then diluted with vinegar. After sieving, the sauce was kept in a pot, ready for use. Taillevent criticized lazy people 'who, rather than make a pepper sauce to accompany stuffed young pig, are content to eat it with cameline'. A special version, served with fried fish, was called *aux camelins* (bread, cinnamon and garlic cloves ground with vinegar and fish liver).

CAMEMBERT A soft cheese (45–50% fat content) made from cow's milk, pale yellow in colour with a white furry skin speckled with brown flecks. Each cheese measures about 11 cm (4½ in) in diameter and is 3–4 cm (1¼–1½ in) thick.

There is a story that this cheese was invented at the time of the French Revolution in the Auge region of Normandy. A certain Marie Harel, who had hidden a recalcitrant priest from Brie, developed a new cheese by combining the method used in Normandy with that used in Brie. Marie Harel disclosed her secret to her daughter, who set herself up in the village of Camembert near Vimoutiers (Orne) to sell the cheeses. While passing through the region for the opening of the Paris-Granville line, Napoleon III tasted the cheese and found it delicious. On learning that it came from Camembert, the Emperor named it after the village. However, Camembert cheese is recorded in parish records as having been around as early as 1681. Whatever its origins, the name was never registered and a judgment of 1926 stipulated that Camembert could not have an *appellation d'origine*. This is why Camembert is now mass-produced throughout France and even in other countries.

Towards the end of the 19th century, a certain M. Ridel invented the cylindrical wooden box that enabled the cheese to be transported. The white mould with which Camembert is covered today was selected in 1910. (Originally, Camembert was covered with blue mould and wrapped in straw.)

■**Manufacture** Real farmhouse Camembert cheeses are rare today, but dairy cheeses are manufactured on both a small and large scale. It takes 4 litres (7 pints, 4 quarts) milk to make a Camembert. The best cheeses, made from raw milk curdled with rennet, are moulded with a ladle, then drained, salted, turned over, removed from the mould and left to mature for about a month in a dry cellar so that the skin forms naturally. The cheese should be wrapped in transparent parchment paper, thereby showing the slightly bulging skin with its uneven coating of fur and orange streaks. The aroma should be delicate and full-flavoured. Since August 1983, the AOP Camembert de Normandie has been reserved for cheeses manufactured in the five departments of Normandy, which are produced in this way and are sold in thin wooden boxes. The village of Camembert is not in these regions and no cheese is actually made there.

Mass-produced Camemberts are made from pasteurized skimmed milk to which pasteurized cream is added. They are of uniform quality and keep longer than traditionally made cheeses, but the taste is never as good. They are drained faster and moulded mechanically. *Demi-Camemberts* (half-Camemberts) and Camembert portions are also found.

CAMERANI, BARTHÉLEMY-ANDRÉ

Italian comedian and gastronome (born Ferrara, c. 1735; died Paris, 1816). Working mainly in France, he became administrator of the Favart and Feydeau theatres. But above all, Camerani was famous for his gourmandise, being a member of Grimod de La Reynière's 'Jury of Tasters' and giving his name to a soup which he invented and which was served around 1810 in the Café Anglais, when he was working at the Opéra-Comique.

In classic French cuisine, the name of Camerani is also applied to a garnish for poached chicken and calves' sweetbreads, consisting of small tartlets filled with a purée of foie gras (topped with slices of truffle and pickled ox tongue cut into the shape of cockscombs) and macaroni *à l'Pitalienne*, all bound together with suprême sauce.

RECIPE

Camerani soup

Slowly cook in butter 200 g (7 oz, 1½ cups) finely shredded mixed vegetables, including a small turnip. Add 2 chicken livers, peeled and diced very finely, season with salt and pepper, and brown over a brisk heat. Meanwhile, cook 125 g (4½ oz) Naples macaroni in fast-boiling salted water. Drain, bind together with butter and season. In a serving dish, buttered and sprinkled with grated Parmesan,

arrange alternate layers of the macaroni and the chicken liver mixture, also sprinkled with Parmesan. Heat gently for a few minutes before serving.

CANADA See *page 206*.

CANAPÉ

A slice of bread cut into various shapes and garnished. Cold canapés are served at buffets or lunches or with cocktails or apéritifs; hot canapés are served as entrées or used as foundations for various dishes. When served with game birds, canapés are generally fried in butter and spread with *à gratin* forcemeat, a purée made of the internal organs of the bird (cooked undrawn) or foie gras.

RECIPES

preparation of canapés

Unlike sandwiches, which consist of 2 slices of bread with a filling in the middle, canapés are made with a single slice of bread; they may be rectangular, round or triangular in shape and the bread can also be lightly toasted. Cold canapés are usually made from white bread (slightly stale, so that it does not crumble, and with the crust removed) or rye bread; hot canapés are made from white or wholemeal bread. Cold canapés should be served as soon as possible after preparation so they do not dry out. They may be stored in a cool place covered with a cloth (a damp cloth if kept in a hot or dry place).

There is a wide variety of garnishes for canapés, including all the garnishes indicated for croûtes as well as various flavoured butters, spinach mixed with béchamel sauce and Parmesan (*à la florentine*), ham, scrambled eggs with cheese, and sardines (fresh sardine fillets or purée of sardines in oil with hard-boiled – hard-cooked – egg and English mustard).

Cold Canapés

canapés à la bayonnaise

Spread some slices of bread with parsley butter and garnish with very thin slices of Bayonne ham cut to the exact size of the bread. Glaze with aspic.

canapés à la bordelaise

Spread some slices of bread with shallot butter. Garnish with a salpicon of cooked cep mushrooms and lean ham surrounded by a thin border of paprika butter.

canapés with anchovies

Spread some Montpellier butter on lightly toasted rectangular slices of bread cut to the same length as the anchovies. Garnish each canapé with 2 anchovy fillets separated by cooked egg white and egg yolk (chopped separately) and chopped parsley.

canapés with asparagus

Spread some thickened mayonnaise on rectangular slices of bread. Arrange very small asparagus tips on each canapé and 'tie' each bunch with a thin strip of green or red sweet pepper.

canapés with caviar

Spread fresh butter on some round slices of bread and garnish with caviar. Sprinkle each with a little lemon juice and a pinch of chopped chives. Very thick soured (sour) cream may be used instead of butter if desired.

canapés with shrimps, lobster or langouste

Spread shrimp (or lobster) butter on some round slices of bread. Garnish each canapé with a rosette of shrimp tails (or a medallion of lobster or langouste tail) and a border of chopped parsley or shrimp butter.

canapés with smoked eel

Spread some round slices of bread with mustard butter or horseradish butter. Garnish each slice with 2 or 3 thin slices of smoked eel arranged in a rosette. Surround with a double border of hard-boiled (hard-cooked) egg yolk and chopped chives. Sprinkle with a little lemon juice.

canapés with smoked salmon

Butter some slices of bread and garnish with slices of smoked salmon cut to the exact size of the bread. Garnish each canapé with half a slice of fluted lemon.

canapés with watercress

Spread watercress butter on some round or rectangular slices of bread. Garnish each canapé with a centre of blanched watercress leaves and a border of chopped hard-boiled (hard-cooked) egg (yolk and white together).

Danish canapés

Spread horseradish butter on some rectangular slices of black rye bread. Garnish with strips of smoked salmon or smoked herring, filling the spaces with salmon roe or peeled rounds of lemon cut in half and fluted.

harlequin canapés

Spread some flavoured butter or thickened mayonnaise on slices of bread cut into various shapes. Garnish with various chopped items: pickled ox (beef) tongue, ham, truffles, yolks and whites of hard-boiled (hard-cooked) eggs, parsley. Surround the canapés with a thin border of butter.

herring canapés à la hollandaise

Spread some slices of bread with a purée of herring soft roe. Garnish each canapé with strips of smoked herring fillet, arranged to form a lattice, sprinkle with a little lemon juice and fill the lattice spaces with chopped hard-boiled (hard-cooked) egg yolk.

Hot Canapés
canapés with cheese

Butter some slices of bread. Top with a thick layer of Gruyère cheese (or Comté, Beaufort, Cheddar, Appenzell), either grated or cut into very thin strips. Brown in a hot oven. The canapés may be served with seasoned tomato sauce. Alternatively, grated Gruyère can be added to a well-reduced béchamel sauce, seasoned with cayenne, and spread over the slices of bread, which are then sprinkled with grated Gruyère or small cubes of Gruyère and browned in a preheated oven at 230°C (450°F, gas 8).

canapés with crab

Finely crumble the crab meat (fresh or canned), removing all the cartilage, and flavour with a little lemon juice. Add an equal amount of béchamel sauce seasoned with nutmeg or saffron. Butter some lightly toasted slices of white bread and spread them with the crab mixture. Sprinkle with fresh breadcrumbs and melted butter and brown in a preheated oven at 230°C (450°F, gas 8). Garnish with half a round of fluted lemon.

canapés with mushrooms

Prepare a dry well-browned duxelles of mushrooms and add béchamel sauce (1 part to 3 parts duxelles). Spread this on lightly toasted slices of bread and sprinkle with fresh breadcrumbs and a little melted butter. Brown in a preheated oven at 230°C (450°F, gas 8).

CANCALAISE, À LA A term describing several fish dishes using oysters from the Bay of Cancale, in Brittany. Whiting, sole or brill *à la cancalaise* are stuffed with poached oysters and prawn tails and coated with Normandy sauce or white wine sauce.

Fish consommé *à la cancalaise* with tapioca is garnished with poached oysters. Sometimes sole fillets cut into small strips (*en julienne*) or small quenelles of pike are added.

RECIPES

fillets of sole à la cancalaise

Fillet the soles and poach some oysters, allowing 2 per fillet. Fold the fillets and poach them in a full-bodied fish fumet to which the poaching water from the oysters has been added. Drain the fillets, retaining the juices, and arrange them on a dish in the form of a turban. Garnish the centre of the dish with peeled prawns (shelled shrimp) and arrange 2 oysters on each fillet. Coat with a white wine sauce to which the reduced cooking juices have been added.

ragoût à la cancalaise

Remove the beards from some oysters and poach in their own liquid or a well-seasoned fish fumet. Add some peeled prawns (shelled shrimp) and bind all the ingredients together with normande sauce. This ragoût is used for filling pies, tarts and vols-au-vent. It can also accompany whole fish or fish fillets, such as whiting, sole or brill.

CANADA

Four-fifths of the country consist of stretches of water and forests, rich in ground game (large cervids, such as deer, and small mammals) and game birds (geese, duck and partridge). However, the state forbids the sale of these delicious foods which are reserved for private consumption. In spite of the richness of its natural resources, Canadian cuisine is not very different from that of the United States, the ethnic origins and living conditions in the two countries being very similar.

■ **Regional specialities** In the west, British Columbia is bounded by the Pacific Ocean. Vancouver's Chinese quarter is the second largest in North America, after San Francisco. However, British traditions continue to flourish – for instance, the traditional high tea is still served. Sophisticated cuisine here is based on seafood and the orchards of the Okanagan valley. Sourdough bread dates back to the time of the gold rush.

In the prairie provinces, Central European Jewish, Scandinavian, Icelandic and Mennonite culinary traditions are all found, but the most predominant cuisine is Ukrainian (*borsht, pirojki* and conserve of rose petals). A local wild berry, the saskatoon, is used in the pie of the same name. Honey from the Peace River in the north has a worldwide reputation, and wild rice is delicious with game bird dishes.

The main traditions of Ontario are British (steak and kidney pie, Yorkshire pudding and trifle), German (a wide range of cooked meats, and carrot cake) as well as Mennonite (shoofly pie, with spicy molasses and crumb filling). The province has also been influenced by the cuisine of more recent immigrants from Hungary and Italy. There are two original regional dishes: spiced beef (pickled and braised meat which is then pressed before being served cold in thin slices) and

fillets of pork stuffed with fruit.

The Atlantic provinces draw on the resources of the sea. Cod is prepared very simply, fresh or salted, often served with potatoes and salted herbs, and without sauce. The tongue and cheek of the fish are considered gourmet dishes. Herring, mackerel, sparling, plaice and halibut are prepared in the same way.

The cuisine of Acadia (the French-speaking part of Canada) has long been self-sufficient. It has evolved in an original manner while retaining the memory of its French connection with dishes such as *fricots, pots-en-pots,* and *râpures* (oysters opened over heat and stuffed with butter, herbs and garlic). Based on potatoes, fish and shellfish, some of the traditional dishes have great subtlety, such as washed Indian corn and *poutine à trou,* a kind of stuffed pastry.

In the province of Quebec, the cooking happily combines Anglo-Saxon traditions and old recipes from Normandy. The local regional cuisine is high in calories, having long been dominated by meat and game pâtés (*tourtières* and *cipâtes),* which are baked in pastry cases, meat-based stews (*ragoût de pattes*) and vegetable-based dishes (beans with bacon, pea soup). But over several decades, this cuisine has gradually become increasingly refined, to such an extent that Montreal and Quebec have become peaks of gastronomy in North America.

Drawing its inspiration from classic French cuisine and *nouvelle cuisine,* ingredients such as apples and maple syrup are skilfully used to prepare sophisticated dishes such as *canard du lac Brome* or roast smoked ham. The crosiers of young ferns picked in early spring and served with caribou or with salmon from the Gaspé Peninsula in the St Lawrence River will delight lovers of unusual food. Immigrants from Greece, Italy, Lebanon and Vietnam have brought their own regional dishes with them, thus adding to the

cosmopolitan variety of Quebec cuisine.

WINE Canadian wine has progressed enormously. The industry used to be based on American grapes which gave an odd, foxy taste to the wine but many of these have been replaced by Vitis Vinifera vines. The main vineyard areas are concentrated in British Columbia in the west and Ontario in the east.

In British Columbia, vineyards are concentrated in the Okanagan Valley, a dry, desert-like area which has high daytime temperatures and very cool nights. Irrigation is necessary here for the Riesling, Auxerrois, Chardonnay, Pinot Noir and Merlot vines planted. Thousands of miles to the east, vineyards in Ontario are mainly planted in the Niagara Peninsular where temperatures are moderated by Lakes Erie and Ontario. About 7,000 ha (18,000 acres) of vineyard are planted to a variety of grapes, including Chardonnay, Gewürztraminer, Riesling, Cabernet Franc, Pinot Noir and Merlot grapes. Many hybrid varieties are also grown, including Maréchal Foch, Baco Noir, Seyval Blanc and Vidal. Eiswein, made from frozen grapes, is a particular speciality of Canadian wines and is often made from Vidal or Riesling grapes.

Canada is famous for its maple trees and the syrup produced from their sap. 'Sugaring' or 'sapping' is the process of boring holes into the trees and draining the sap into collecting buckets; the sap is then boiled to form maple syrup. The new season syrup is first sampled locally as a type of sticky toffee: it is boiled down further and swirled on to containers of compacted snow where it sets instantly. Wooden sticks are used to scoop up the maple candy.

CANCOILLOTTE A speciality of the Franche-Comté region based on *metton*, a skimmed cow's-milk cheese. *Metton* takes the form of hard hazelnut-sized grains with a strong smell and has a long ripening process. The cheese is mixed in a bain marie with salted water and fresh butter to form a pale-yellow homogeneous paste, with a strong flavour. It is sweetened with white wine and eaten warm.

CANDIED FRUIT See *crystallized fruit*.

CANDIES See *sweets*.

CANDISSOIRE A flat rectangular cooking utensil with raised edges and a removable wire grid forming the base. The *candissoire* is used to hold such items as crystallized (candied) fruits or fresh petits fours after glazing with melted sugar. It is also used for draining small pastries soaked with alcohol, especially individual babas.

CANDLEMAS The Christian festival held on 2 February to celebrate the Presentation of Christ at the Temple and the Purification of the Virgin Mary. The word comes from the Latin *festa candelarum* (feast of the candles) because many candles are lit in churches on that day. The origin of Candlemas is the ancient Roman festival of fertility, Lupercalia, dedicated to the god Pan. Pope Gelasius I abolished it in 492 and replaced it with processions holding lighted candles to symbolize the light of the divine Spirit. The festival also coincided with the resumption of work in the fields after the rigours of winter. This is probably why Candlemas is the occasion when flour-based dishes, such as pancakes and fritters, are made. Pancakes were considered to be a symbol of the sun because of their round shape and golden colour. To use the wheat from the previous harvest was also a means of attracting a blessing upon the future harvest.

The tradition of making pancakes is a very old one. It was mentioned in *Le Ménagier de Paris* (1393), and there are various superstitions attached to it. In Burgundy, you must toss one on to the top of the cupboard to avoid being short of money during the year! While pancakes are being made, shame on the clumsy one who drops it while turning it! At the Candlemas of 1812, prior to his departure for the Russian campaign, Napoleon made some crêpes *à la Malmaison*. It is said that four out of the five he made were successful, thus forecasting his victory in four battles. The fifth spoilt pancake worried him, and on the day of the Moscow fire, he said to Marshal Ney: 'It is the fifth pancake!'

CANDYFLOSS A confection, known as cotton candy in the United States, made from coloured sugar syrup (usually white or pink), cooked and spun using a special machine into spidery threads which are rolled around a stick like wool on a distaff. The earliest machine, operated by a crank shaft, appeared in France at the Paris Exposition of 1900. Today, high-speed electric machines are used.

CANDY SUGAR Refined crystallized sugar. The Arabic word *qandi* means 'cane sugar', but candy sugar can be made from sugar beet or sugar cane. It was used therapeutically from the 12th century onwards and was often flavoured with rose, violet, lemon or redcurrant.

Candy sugar takes the form of large crystals, which are obtained by slowly cooling a concentrated sugar syrup so that it crystallizes around threads stretched out in the tank. Brown candy sugar is obtained from a brown syrup.

Candy sugar dissolves very slowly and is preferred to ordinary sugar for preparing fruits in brandy and domestic liqueurs, since it allows time for the flavour of the fruits to emerge. It is also used in making champagne.

CANELLING The technique of making V-shaped grooves over the surface of a vegetable or a fruit for decoration, using a canelle knife. The vegetable or fruit is often sliced after the canelle grooves have been cut, to make decorative borders to the slices.

Using a canelle knife

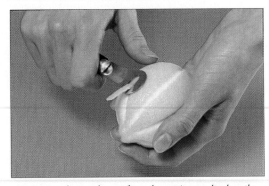

Cut grooves down a lemon for a decorative result when the fruit is sliced. Press firmly to cut narrow but fairly thick strips of peel which can be used to flavour dishes or they can be simmered in water until tender and used as a garnish.

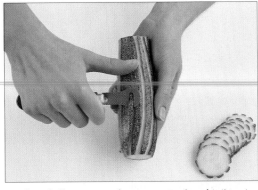

Cut fine, shallow grooves along courgettes (zucchini) to give decorative slices. Carrots can also be cut in this way.

CANESTRATO Traditionally made in central and southern Italy from ewe's milk or a mixture of cow's and ewe's milk, this semi-hard cheese takes it name from the baskets in which it ripens and the imprint they leave on the rind. The ewe's milk cheeses may also be known as Pecorino Canestrato or Pecorino Siciliana.

CANETTE A traditional French beer bottle characterized by having a porcelain bung with a rubber washer, which is attached with a metal clamp. This bung has been largely replaced with a seal. The word *canette* originated in Picardy and originally meant an elongated jug. It is also used to hold sparkling lemonade.

CANNA A vigorous tropical plant with a thick fleshy underground stem, which is eaten as a vegetable. Some varieties produce an edible starch, used particularly in Australia, where it is known as 'Queensland arrowroot'.

CANNELLONI A type of pasta dish originating in Italy. The word derives from *canna* (reed) and literally means 'big tubes'. Pasta squares are simmered in water and a knob of savoury filling is placed in the centre of each. They are then rolled up into cylinders to form the cannelloni, usually covered with tomato sauce and cooked au gratin. Alternatively, cannelloni can be bought in the form of dried tubes, ready for filling.

RECIPES

cannelloni à la béchamel

Chop 2 large onions and soften them in 25 g (1 oz, 2 tablespoons) butter. Chop 3 slices of ham and about 250 g (9 oz) cooked chicken; add these to the onions and adjust the seasoning. Make a béchamel sauce with 50 g (2 oz, ¼ cup) butter, 50 g (2 oz, ½ cup) plain (all-purpose) flour, 500 ml (17 fl oz, 2 cups) milk, salt, pepper and grated nutmeg. Add 75 g (3 oz, ¾ cup) grated cheese and the chopped meat and onion. Fill fresh pasta rectangles with this mixture, then roll them up. Alternatively, use bought cannelloni tubes cooked according to the packet instructions. Butter an ovenproof gratin dish and arrange the cannelloni in it. Cover with the remaining béchamel sauce. Sprinkle with 50 g (2 oz, ½ cup) grated cheese and a few knobs of butter. Brown in a preheated oven at 240°C (475°F, gas 9) or under a hot grill (broiler).

cannelloni à la florentine

Hard-boil (hard-cook) 2 eggs and remove the shells. Boil some spinach and drain it. Make a very smooth béchamel sauce. Roughly chop the spinach and heat it gently in butter, allowing 25 g (1 oz, 2 tablespoons) butter to 1 kg (2¼ lb) spinach. Finely chop the hard-boiled eggs and add to the spinach. Also add 2 raw egg yolks mixed with 100 ml (4 fl oz, 7 tablespoons) double (heavy) cream, 40 g (1½ oz, ⅓ cup) grated Parmesan cheese, salt, pepper and grated nutmeg.

Gently reheat the mixture without boiling, then leave to cool. Fill fresh pasta rectangles with this mixture and roll them up. Alternatively, use bought cannelloni tubes cooked according to the packet instructions. Arrange in a buttered ovenproof dish, cover with the béchamel sauce and sprinkle with grated Parmesan cheese and a few knobs of butter. Cook in a preheated oven at 240°C (475°F, gas 9) or under a hot grill (broiler) until the surface is brown and crusty.

meat cannelloni

Fill fresh pasta rectangles with a meaty bolognese sauce. Roll them up and arrange in a buttered ovenproof dish. Alternatively, use bought cannelloni tubes cooked according to the packet instructions. Cover with tomato sauce, sprinkle with grated cheese, and place in a preheated oven at 240°C (475°F, gas 9) or under a hot grill (broiler) until the surface is well browned.

seafood cannelloni

Fill fresh pasta rectangles with a stuffing of crab meat or chopped peeled prawns (shelled shrimp) bound with a well-seasoned béchamel sauce. Roll up the cannelloni and arrange in a buttered ovenproof dish. Alternatively, use bought cannelloni tubes cooked according to the packet instructions. Cover with normande sauce, sprinkle with a few knobs of butter and cook in a preheated oven at 240°C (475°F, gas 9) or under a grill (broiler) until the surface is well browned.

CANOLE A dry biscuit that is a speciality of Rochechouart (Haute-Vienne region). It originated in 1371, during the Hundred Years' War. The town, which had been under siege by the English, was relieved by du Guesclin. The inhabitants duly pillaged the enemy camp and found wheat and fresh eggs, with which they made these biscuits, mockingly named after the captain of the English troops, Sir Robert Canolles (or Knolles).

CANON-FRONSAC AOC red wines from Fronsac, east of Bordeaux and near Libourne. The vineyards are on limestone slopes overlooking the Dordogne. Canon-Fronsac is part of Fronsac. The wines are full-bodied, well-balanced and deep in tone; they usually benefit from 3–5 years' bottle age.

CANOTIÈRE, À LA A name usually given to poached freshwater fish covered with bâtarde sauce. It is also given to a carp dish in which the carp is stuffed with a fish mousse, baked in a white wine stock, then arranged on a gratin dish with sliced shallots and mushrooms and lemon juice, and sprinkled with breadcrumbs. The sauce, which is made with the reduced cooking juices, is thickened with butter. The dish is garnished with crayfish cooked in court-bouillon, and with *fleurons* (crescents of puff pastry). The same stuffing and garnish are used for *matelote à la canotière*.

RECIPE

matelote à la canotière ♦

Butter a frying pan and make a bed of 150 g (5 oz, 1 cup) sliced onions and 4 crushed garlic cloves. Add 1.5 kg (3¼ lb) freshwater fish (carp, eel) cut into equal-sized pieces, a large bouquet garni and 1 litre (1¾ pints, 4⅓ cups) dry white wine. Bring to the boil. Add 100 ml (4 fl oz, 7 tablespoons) brandy and flame. Cover and gently simmer for about 25 minutes. Drain the fish pieces, placing them in another frying pan, and retain the stock. To the fish add 125 g (4½ oz, 1½ cups) cooked button mushrooms and 125 g (4½ oz, ¾ cup) small glazed onions. Reduce the fish stock by two-thirds and bind with beurre manié – for a litre (1¾ pints, 4⅓ cups) of stock, bind with 50 g (2 oz, ½ cup) plain (all-purpose) flour kneaded with 50 g (2 oz, ¼ cup) butter; finally, add a further 150 g (5 oz, ⅔ cup) butter. Pour the sauce over the fish and simmer gently. Serve the *matelote* plain, with rice, or garnished with gudgeons fried in breadcrumbs, or whitebait, and crayfish cooked in a court-bouillon.

CANTAL A high-fat (45% fat content) cow's-milk cheese from the Auvergne region of France. It is ivory in colour with a naturally darker crust, a flexible finely granulated texture and a sweet nutty flavour; riper cheeses are a little firmer and more highly flavoured. It is also called Fourme du Cantal or Fourme de Salers (where the cows produce a rich full-flavoured milk). An AOP label means that the production region is strictly defined as the department of Cantal and the arrondissements of Tulle, Ussel, Brioude, Clermont-Ferrand and Issoire. Cantal is considered the ancestor of French cheeses: Pliny the Elder mentioned it, as did Grégoire de Tours. The similarity of its manufacture to that of British Cheddar suggests that the Romans may have introduced the technique to the Bretons across the English Channel.

Cantal comes in the form of a cylinder, 35–40 cm (14–16 in) high and the same in diameter, weighing 35–45 kg (77–100 lb). Dairy Cantal is produced all the year round, whereas farm Cantal comes from the shepherds' huts of the Cantal. Connoisseurs prefer it when it has matured for three months: the thick crust sinks into the cheese, forming brown marks, and it has a fairly sharp taste. A smaller Cantal is also produced, called a *cantalet* or *cantalon*, weighing 4–10 kg (9–22 lb). An intermediate *petit cantal* weighs 20–22 kg (44–48 lb). Cantal is often served after a meal, with wine and fruit; it is also widely used in gratins, croûtes, soups and soufflés, as well as in typically regional dishes (such as aligot, gâtis, patranque and truffade).

CANTHARUS A bell-shaped drinking vessel used by the Greeks and Romans. Made of ceramic, bronze or silver, it stood on a single foot and had two vertical handles that rose above the rim.

CANTONNAISE, À LA The French term for a garnished rice dish inspired by Cantonese cuisine. For Cantonese fried rice, the grains must be well separated from each other after cooking. The rice is cooked plain, then left to rest for a few hours in the refrigerator; it should be fluffed up from time to time to aerate it. For the garnish, some lard (shortening) is heated in a frying pan, together with salt, smoked bacon (or ham, or even lacquered pork) cut up into small pieces, chopped celery sticks and prawns (shrimp). After a few minutes, the rice is added; when this is hot, some eggs are broken into the pan. The mixture is stirred until the eggs are just set.

The dish can also include crab meat, shellfish, bamboo shoots or peas. The traditional Chinese seasoning is soy sauce and rice alcohol.

CAPACITY Also referred to as content. The volume of a vessel, which determines the quantity of a substance it can hold. In practice, the term capacity is used for bottles and cans of liquid and content for other receptacles. There is always a difference between the nominal content of a receptacle (the capacity) and the actual content (volume or net weight contained).

CAPE GOOSEBERRY The fruit of a bush originating in Peru, which grows wild in hedgerows and thickets in the warm coastal regions of the Atlantic and Mediterranean. Also called physalis, Chinese lantern, strawberry tomato, love-in-a-cage and winter cherry, the Cape gooseberry is yellow or red, the size of a small cherry, and is enclosed in a papery brown calyx. It has a tart flavour and is used to make syrups, jams and apéritifs, as well as in fruit salads, sorbets and ice creams. It also makes an excellent accompaniment to some savoury foods, particularly fish or rich meats.

RECIPES

Cape gooseberry compote

Dissolve 500 g (18 oz, 2¼ cups) lump or granulated sugar in 200 ml (7 fl oz, ¾ cup) water. Strip the fruits from their calyces and drop them into the boiling syrup. Cook for 5 minutes, then drain and put them into a compote dish. Add the rind of a lemon to the syrup, reduce this by a quarter and pour it over the fruit. The rind should not be cooked with the fruit as it would affect its flavour.

Cape gooseberry jam

Gently heat 800 g (1¾ lb, 3½ cups) lump or granulated sugar with 800 g (1¾ lb) cape gooseberries. Stir from time to time until the sugar is dissolved, then bring to the boil. Boil the jam until the setting point is reached, then pour into jars immediately.

Matelote à la canotière

CAPER The flower bud of a shrub which is native to eastern Asia but widespread in hot regions. Capers are used as a condiment, either pickled in vinegar or preserved in brine or in dry, coarse salt. Salted capers are rinsed before use. When pickled, they are sour but still full of flavour. The Romans used them to season fish sauces. Capers are also used to flavour rice and meatballs (lamb and veal) and garnish pizzas; they go well with mustard and horseradish (see *Gribiche, Ravigote*). The flower buds of nasturtium, buttercup, marigold and broom are sometimes used as substitutes for capers.

RECIPE

caper sauces
To accompany boiled fish, add 2 tablespoons pickled capers, well drained, to 250 ml (8 fl oz, 1 cup) hollandaise* sauce or butter sauce*.

To accompany English-style boiled mutton, prepare melted butter sauce, adding the mutton cooking juices to the roux, followed by well-drained capers and a little anchovy essence (extract) or a purée of desalted anchovies.

CAPERCAILLIE The largest species of grouse. The adult male is the size of a turkey and can weigh up to 8 kg (18 lb). The hunting of female and young capercaillies is forbidden. The bird lives in coniferous hilly woodlands, feeding on conifer shoots, which gives its flesh a pronounced flavour of resin. It is rare in France, being found in the mountains of the Ardennes, Vosges and Pyrenees. The black grouse is often preferred for cookery: its delicate flesh is whiter than that of the pheasant, but it is prepared in the same way.

CAPILOTADE A ragoût, originally from classic French cookery, made of cooked meat leftovers (poultry, beef or veal) that are stewed until they disintegrate. The word comes from the Spanish *capirotada*, which was a brown sauce made with garlic, eggs and herbs, used to cover the cut pieces of meat. The expression *en capilotade* (meaning in small pieces) is used in cookery, particularly for poultry dishes.

RECIPE

chicken en capilotade
Take a chicken (boiled, braised, poached or roasted) and remove the bones. Cut the meat into small pieces and place in a well-reduced cold sauce (chasseur, Italian, Portuguese or Provençal). Cover and leave to simmer gently until the meat forms a hash. Then pour into a deep dish.

Alternatively, the chicken and sauce can be poured into a gratin dish, sprinkled with breadcrumbs and knobs of butter, then cooked in a preheated oven at 240°C (475°F, gas 9) or under a hot grill (broiler) until the surface is well browned. Serve with rice *à la créole*.

CAPITAINE Sea fish related to the sea bass, sometimes called *grand pourceau* ('big swine'), living off the coast of West Africa, where it enters the estuaries and swims up the rivers. About 50 cm (20 in) long, it has a pinky-white flesh with a very delicate flavour which it preserves well and does not lose in cooking. It may be steamed, grilled (broiled) on one side like salmon, cooked *en papillote* or chopped up with tartare sauce, herbs and lemon. In Senegal, it often forms part of *tié bou diéné*.

RECIPE

capitaine in banana leaves ♦
Wash 4 medium-sized banana leaves, remove the central rib, then scald briefly to soften them. Lay them out flat and place 1 capitaine fillet on each one. Plunge 2 tomatoes in boiling water for a few seconds, then remove the skin and seeds, and roughly chop the flesh. Halve and thinly slice 1 onion, then cook it briefly in a little olive oil until slightly softened but not cooked. Allow long enough to take the raw edge off the flavour of the onion. Season the pieces of fish with salt and pepper. Arrange the tomatoes and onion on top. Fold the banana leaves over and secure with cocktail sticks (toothpicks). Steam for 30 minutes. Sautéed or steamed okra go well with the steamed fish.

CAPLIN Either of two species of marine fish, up to 15 cm (6 in) long. One is a Mediterranean species; the other is common in the English Channel and the Bay of Biscay. They have a fairly thickset body, brownish-yellow on the back, silver-grey on the sides and white on the belly. The large head has large bulbous eyes and a barb under the chin. The two species are distinguished by the spacing of the caudal fins. The caplin, whose delicate flesh flakes easily, is used especially in fish soups.

CAPON A young cock that has been castrated and fattened. The meat is remarkably tender and this method of rearing poultry is a very ancient one. It was a speciality of the French city of Le Mans, but gradually disappeared because of the cost and the length of time involved. In the 1980s, it was taken up again in Bresse and Landes. Hormonal castration of cockerels has been banned since 1959. Capon is prepared in the same way as chicken.

The abundance and great delicacy of the flesh of a capon is due to the accumulation of fat, which is stored in successive layers in the muscles. A capon may weigh as much as 6 kg (13 lb).

Capons from Landes are fed on maize (corn) and are yellow, whereas those from Bresse are white. They are suitable for serving on festive occasions when there are plenty of guests.

Capitaine in banana leaves.

RECIPE

roasted poached capon with pumpkin gratin ◆

Season the body cavity of a 3–3.5 kg (6½–8 lb) capon. Place 1 peeled onion and a large bunch each of tarragon and parsley in the cavity, then truss the capon securely. Place in a large pan and pour in enough chicken stock to cover. Heat gently until simmering, then cover and simmer gently for 30 minutes. Drain the capon well and transfer it to a roasting tin (pan).

Dot the capon with 50 g (2 oz, ¼ cup) butter and roast it in a preheated oven at 240°C (475°F, gas 9) for 30 minutes. Reduce the temperature to 220°C (425°F, gas 7) and cook for a further 30 minutes. Baste the bird well, then add 2 diced carrots, 1 chopped onion, the chopped green part of 1 leek, 1 diced celery stick, 1 crushed garlic clove and 1 bouquet garni to the container. Turn the vegetables in the juices and cook for a further ½–1 hour, basting frequently, until the capon is cooked. Cover the top loosely with foil, if necessary to prevent the capon from becoming too brown.

Meanwhile, peel and seed a 3 kg (6½ lb) pumpkin and cut it into wedges. Cook the pumpkin in boiling salted water with 1 bouquet garni and 3 peeled garlic cloves for 12 minutes, or until tender. Drain the pumpkin thoroughly.

Press the garlic cloves over the bottom of a large gratin dish. Coarsely mash the pumpkin with a fork, adding salt to taste, a little grated nutmeg and a pinch of cayenne pepper. Spread the pumpkin out evenly in the dish. Pour 400 ml (14 fl oz, 1¾ cups) double (heavy) cream over the pumpkin and sprinkle with 90 g (3½ oz, 1 cup) grated Gruyère cheese. Place the pumpkin gratin in the oven with the capon for the final 15–20 minutes cooking, until it is golden and bubbling.

Transfer the capon to a serving platter. Skim off and reserve excess fat, then add 100 ml (4 fl oz, 7 tablespoons) dry white wine to the vegetables remaining in the roasting tin. Boil until well reduced and nearly dry. Pour in 250 ml (8 fl oz, 1 cup) chicken stock and bring to the boil, then boil for a few minutes, scraping all the cooking juices into the liquor. Strain through a fine sieve and return to the pan. Bring to the boil and boil until reduced slightly and full flavoured. Whisk in a knob of butter and a little of the reserved cooking fat. Serve this sauce with the carved capon and the pumpkin gratin.

CAPONATA A Sicilian speciality made of aubergines (eggplants), celery and tomatoes, sliced and fried in olive oil and flavoured with capers, olives and anchovy fillets. This dish is served as a cold hors d'oeuvre.

RECIPE

caponata

Peel 4 aubergines (eggplants), cut into large dice and sprinkle with salt. When they have lost some of their water, wash and wipe them and fry in oil. Cut the following ingredients into very small pieces: 100 g (4 oz, ¾ cup) olives, a head of celery scalded in salted water, 4 desalted anchovies and 50 g (2 oz, 3 tablespoons) capers. Slice an onion and brown in oil. Heat up 200 ml (7 fl oz, ¾ cup) tomato passata (purée) with 50 g (2 oz, ¼ cup) sugar until it is well reduced and darker in colour. Then add 3 tablespoons vinegar and leave to simmer for a few minutes. Season with salt and pepper, add some chopped parsley, then mix the sauce with the aubergines and other ingredients. Allow to cool thoroughly. Arrange in the shape of a dome in a vegetable dish.

CAPSICUM The botanical name for the species of plants bearing peppers. *Capsicum annuum* includes the mild peppers, simply referred to as peppers, and sometimes known as capsicums, sweet or bell peppers, pimiento or pimento. *Capsicum frutescens* produces hot peppers or chilli peppers, known as chillies, and *Capsicum chinense* also yields hot chillies, including the Scotch bonnet and Habañero varieties. Belonging to the same family as the tomato and aubergine (eggplant), they were discovered by Christopher Columbus in America and described by botanists at the beginning of the 16th century; they soon spread through Europe and the rest of the world. Capsicums are sold fresh, dried or ground. See *Pepper* and *Chilli*.

CAPUCIN A small savoury tartlet, filled with Gruyère choux pastry and served as a hot entrée.

RECIPE

capucins

Make a rich shortcrust pastry (basic pie dough) using 200 g (7 oz, 1¾ cups) plain (all-purpose) flour, 100 g (4 oz, ½ cup) well-softened butter, a large pinch of salt and 2 or 3 tablespoons very cold water. Use this pastry to line 8 tartlet tins (pans). Also make some choux pastry using 250 ml (8 fl oz, 1 cup) water, 50 g (2 oz, ¼ cup) butter, a large pinch of salt and 125 g (4½ oz, 1 heaped cup) plain flour. Then, away from the heat and one at a time, add 3 whole eggs and 75 g (3 oz, ¾ cup) grated Gruyère cheese. Place a ball of the Gruyère choux pastry in each tartlet and bake in a preheated oven at 190°C (375°F, gas 5). Serve hot.

CAQUELON An earthenware dish with a glazed interior, used in southern France to cook dishes that require simmering. Originally it was placed in hot ashes. When used on a cooker (stove), a diffusing device must be placed between the *caquelon* and the gas flame or hotplate. It is customary to rub the inside with a garlic clove the first time it is used, so that it does not crack. In south-western France, it is called a *toupin*.

Roasted poached capon with pumpkin gratin.

CARAFE A glass or crystal vessel with a wide base and narrow neck, which can sometimes be sealed with a glass stopper. It is used to serve water and wine at the table. Liqueurs and spirits may also be kept in carafes or stoppered *carafons* (small carafes). In the 19th century, a *carafon* was a metal bucket in which bottles were cooled.

Carafe wines are light, fresh, young and inexpensive open ones, which restaurants serve in carafes, half or quarter carafes, or jugs. In the UK the contents of a carafe used in a catering establishment must be stated.

CARAMBOLA Also known as star fruit. The fruit of a tree that is grown in the West Indies, Indonesia and Brazil. Golden-yellow and elongated, with projecting ribs, the carambola is sliced and eaten fresh, either with cream and sugar for dessert, or with vinaigrette like avocados. The fruit is star-shaped in cross section and the flesh is juicy and acidic.

CARAMEL Melted sugar that has been browned by heating. The word comes from the Latin *cannamella* (sugar cane). Heated above 150°C (300°F), sugar syrup changes colour, gradually losing its sweetness and giving off an increasingly strong 'burnt' odour. Eventually it becomes inedible. The end product is determined by temperature, depending on what the caramel is to be used for.

Caramel is also used commercially as a colouring agent, particularly for liqueurs and alcohols, as well as for certain ready-made sauces.

■ **Preparing caramel** Caramel can be prepared either by heating sugar in a dry pan (or with a little water) until it melts and then boiling until it caramelizes or by dissolving the sugar in water to make a heavy syrup, then boiling until the syrup is reduced and caramelized. Dissolving the sugar first is an easier and practical method for less-experienced cooks.

Heat the sugar and water gently at first, stirring occasionally, until the sugar has dissolved completely. When stirring, try not to splash the syrup around the sides of the pan as it may form crystals and encourage the rest of the syrup to crystallize before it cooks to a caramel. Bring to a full boil and stop stirring. Stirring will encourage the syrup to form crystals.

Continue boiling until the syrup turns a pale golden colour. If there are any signs of white crystals forming around the inside of the pan at any stage during cooking, use a pastry brush to trickle a little cold water down the side of the pan to dissolve them. Continue boiling until the caramel is as dark as required – this may be a light golden colour, a medium or dark rich brown. Take care when making a dark caramel as cooking it for a few seconds too long will make it too bitter or burnt.

Pour the caramel out of the pan immediately into a heatproof dish or container. Alternatively, for pouring caramel, carefully add a little hot water to the pan. To coat a dish, protect your hands with an ovenglove or folded tea towel (dish cloth) and tilt

Making caramel

1 *Dissolve the sugar without boiling, stirring occasionally. Brush the inside of the pan with cold water to remove any sugar crystals that are splashed up or form, both in the early stages and throughout the boiling process.*

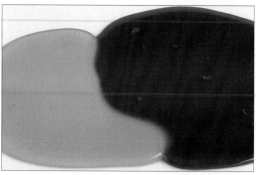

2 *Boil the syrup rapidly without stirring until the caramel reaches the required strength: this is a light caramel.*

3 *The strength of darkness of the caramel depends on its use. Light caramel is mild and useful for decorative purposes. The darker the caramel, the stronger the flavour. Medium caramel gives baked custard a rich flavour; dark caramel can be used to flavour creams and sauces or to coat nuts.*

the dish until the caramel coats it completely inside.

When dipping ingredients, such as choux buns or fruit, in the caramel, submerge the base of the pan in cold water to arrest the cooking process and to prevent the caramel from overcooking from the heat of the pan.

• VERY PALE CARAMEL Almost white and used to glaze petits fours and sugar-coated fruits. Stop heating as soon as the syrup starts to turn yellow at the edges of the pan. A teaspoon of vinegar will help it stay liquid for longer.

• PALE CARAMEL Used to caramelize choux pastry, coat citrus fruits and bind meringues and other items. Make only small quantities at a time since, once hardened, it changes colour if reheated.

• MEDIUM CARAMEL Mahogany in colour and used to coat moulds, make nougatine, and flavour puddings, creams, compotes and ice creams. Never make the caramel directly in the cake mould.

• SLAKED CARAMEL A small quantity of cold water is carefully added when the caramel has turned a mahogany colour, in order to stop the cooking process. Some of the syrup solidifies immediately. Used for flavouring, it is put back on a low heat and melted while stirring.

• BROWN CARAMEL Amber-red and used to colour consommés, sauces and stews.

• DRY CARAMEL Cooked without water, but with a few drops of lemon juice. Used in a few recipes, including nougatine and caramel ice cream.

• LIQUID CARAMEL Sold ready for use, in bottles or sachets, to flavour desserts, yogurts and ice creams, or to caramelize moulds or cover desserts.

RECIPES

caramel sauce

(from a recipe by Carême) Melt some caster (superfine) sugar without adding any water, and leave it to colour gradually over a gentle heat (this takes about 15 minutes). When it has turned amber-red, add 175 ml (6 fl oz, ¾ cup) water, turn up the heat to high and boil for a few minutes. The result should be a beautiful amber-red caramel.

coating caramel

Place 200 g (7 oz, generous ¾ cup) granulated sugar and 4 tablespoons water in a heavy based saucepan. Dissolve the sugar over a low heat. Add about 1 teaspoon lemon juice. When the liquid is boiling, stop stirring. When the mixture begins to change colour, shake the pan to obtain a uniformly coloured caramel; do not continue to stir as the caramel will stick to the spoon in a mass. When the caramel is a golden colour, add 1 tablespoon hot water and shake the pan to mix. Add the same quantity of water again and stir. The mixture should still be very liquid. It will harden as it cools.

CARAMELIZE To turn sugar into caramel by gently heating it, an operation that requires care and precision. Alternatively, it can mean coating a mould with caramel, flavouring a pudding or similar preparation with caramel, glazing sugar-coated fruits and choux pastry with caramel, or colouring the top of a cake or biscuit by powdering it with sugar and

Making a caramel sugar cage

1 *Pour the liquid caramel on to an oiled ladle and use a fork to pull it into threads.*

2 *Drag the threads of caramel to make a fairly close trellis.*

3 *Trim off the ends of the threads overhanging the edge of the ladle (kitchen scissors are useful for this) and lift the cage carefully, sliding it off the ladle and taking care not to crush the caramel.*

putting it under the grill (broiler). Certain vegetables, such as small onions, carrots or turnips, are 'glazed' – or lightly caramelized – by being heated with some sugar and a small quantity of water or butter in a saucepan.

RECIPE

caramelizing a mould

Place 100 g (4 oz, ½ cup) granulated sugar, 1 teaspoon lemon juice and 1 tablespoon water in a small thick saucepan. Heat until the mixture turns a pale caramel colour at 160°C (325°F). Pour the caramel into the mould and tilt the mould in all directions to distribute the caramel over the bottom and sides. Continue to tilt until the caramel no longer flows.

CARAMELS Sweets (candies), often square-shaped, made from a mixture of sugar, cooked glucose syrup and dairy products (milk, butter or cream), plus vegetable fats and flavourings. There are various types – hard and soft caramels, fudge, *hopje* and toffee – depending on the composition, degree of cooking, shape and flavour. The French town of Isigny, famous for its milk, also makes famous caramels.

• HARD CARAMELS These are made using glucose syrup, sugar, water and milk. Fats and flavourings are also added. After homogenization, the mixture is heated until it reaches the required degree of hardness, then cooled, cut up and (if required) wrapped. Hard caramel is also made into lollipops. Although cocoa, coffee or vanilla can be used as flavouring, it is essentially milk, more or less caramelized, that gives it its flavour.

• SOFT CARAMELS The glucose syrup is dissolved in an emulsion of milk and fats, then cooked and flavoured with vanilla, cocoa, coffee or hazelnuts. Cutting is done after cooling.

Making caramel at home requires special equipment, particularly a wooden frame in which the caramel sets.

RECIPES

hard chocolate caramels

Mix 250 g (9 oz, generous 1 cup) granulated sugar, 100 ml (4 fl oz, 7 tablespoons) double (heavy) cream, 50 g (2 oz, 2 tablespoons) honey or glucose and 50 g (2 oz, ½ cup) cocoa in a thick saucepan. Heat while stirring continuously with a wooden spoon, until the mixture reaches a temperature of 142°C (288°F). Oil a marble or other heat-resistant surface and a caramel frame, pour the caramel into the middle of the frame and leave to harden, but do not allow to cool completely. Remove the frame and pass a flexible metal spatula under the sheet of caramel to detach it from the surface. Cut the caramel into 2 cm (¾ in) squares.

hard coffee caramels

Mix 250 g (9 oz, generous 1 cup) granulated sugar with 100 ml (4 fl oz, 7 tablespoons) double (heavy) cream, 1 tablespoon coffee extract and 12 drops of lemon juice in a thick saucepan. Heat while stirring continuously with a wooden spoon, until the mixture reaches a temperature of 142°C (288°F). Oil a marble or other heat-resistant surface and a caramel frame, and proceed as for chocolate caramels.

soft butter caramels

Place 250 g (9 oz, generous 1 cup) granulated sugar, 100 ml (4 fl oz, 7 tablespoons) milk, and 3 tablespoons honey or liquid glucose in a thick

saucepan. Add a vanilla pod (bean) split into two and bring to the boil while stirring continuously with a wooden spoon. Add 150 g (5 oz, ⅔ cup) butter in small quantities and lower the heat. Continue to cook while stirring, until the temperature reaches 120°C (248°F). Oil a marble or other heat-resistant surface and 4 caramel rules or an 18 cm (7 in) tart ring. Remove the vanilla pod from the saucepan and pour the caramel into the ring or between the rules, on top of the prepared surface. Leave to cool completely for 2–3 hours before cutting up the caramel with a large knife.

soft cream caramels

Put 250 g (9 oz, generous 1 cup) granulated sugar, 250 ml (8 fl oz, 1 cup) double (heavy) cream, 1 tablespoon coffee extract and 3 tablespoons honey or liquid glucose into a thick saucepan. Stir over a high heat with a wooden spoon, then reduce the heat and allow the cooking to continue at a simmer, still stirring, until the temperature reaches 120°C (248°F). Continue as for soft butter caramels. The coffee can be replaced with 75 g (3 oz, ¾ cup) cocoa or 150 g (5 oz, 1¼ cups) crushed hazelnuts or pistachio nuts, moistened with boiling milk and pressed through a sieve.

CARAWAY An aromatic plant, common in central and northern Europe, that is grown mainly for its brown oblong seeds. When dried, these are used as a spice, particularly in eastern Europe, to flavour sauerkraut and stews and to accompany certain cheeses (Gouda and Munster). In Hungary and Germany, where caraway is very popular, it is used to flavour bread and cakes. In Britain, it is added to cooked potatoes and baked in cakes and biscuits (Shakespeare's Shallow invites Falstaff to partake of 'a last year's pippin of mine own graffing, with a dish of caraways'). In France, it is used to flavour Vosges dragées. Caraway is also widely used in making liqueurs, such as Kümmel, Vespétro, schnapps and aquavit. Caraway was used in prehistoric times (the seeds have been found at ancient sites) and was appreciated by the Romans, who ate the root like a vegetable.

CARBONADE A Flemish speciality made of slices of beef that are browned and then cooked with onions and beer. The word comes from the Italian *carbonata* (charcoal-grilled). The name *carbonade* (or *carbonnade*) is also given to grilled (broiled) pork loin, as well as to certain beef stews with red wine prepared in the south of France.

RECIPE

carbonade à la flamande

Slice 250 g (9 oz, 1½ cups) onions. Cut 800 g (1¾ lb) beef flank or chuck steak into pieces or thin slices, and brown over a high heat in a frying pan in 40 g (1½ oz, 3 tablespoons) lard. Drain. Fry the onions until golden in the same fat. Arrange the meat and onions in a flameproof casserole in alternate layers, seasoning each layer with salt and pepper. Add a bouquet garni. Deglaze the frying pan with 600 ml (1 pint, 2½ cups) beer and 3 tablespoons of beef stock (fresh or made with concentrate). Make a brown roux with 25 g (1 oz, 2 tablespoons) butter and 25 g (1 oz, ¼ cup) plain (all-purpose) flour, and add the beer mixture, then ½ teaspoon brown sugar. Adjust the seasoning. Pour the mixture into the casserole, cover and leave to cook very gently for 2½ hours. Serve in the casserole.

CARCASS An animal after slaughter and processing at the abattoir. The ratio between the weight of the carcass and the weight of the live animal represents the killing-out percentage and reflects the animal's meat yield. Large cattle, calves and sheep are bled after slaughter, then skinned and eviscerated; the feet and head are cut off. Pigs, on the other hand, are not skinned, and the carcass includes the head and feet. For large cattle, the carcass is cut into four quarters: fast-cooking parts are at the back, slow-cooking parts at the front. The 'fifth quarter' comprises the offal and byproducts. The carcasses are hung from large pegs, called *chevilles* in French, which is why butchers' wholesale suppliers are called *chevillards*.

CARDAMOM Also known as cardamon. An aromatic plant from the Malabar region of south-western India, whose capsules contain seeds that are dried and used as a spice. Cardamom is used much more in the East than in Europe, except for Scandinavian countries, where it is used to spice mulled wines, stewed fruit, cakes, flans and some charcuterie products. White cardamoms, occasionally found in some Indian stores and used in some sweet recipes, are bleached green cardamoms. Green cardamoms are the most widely used. The small, papery, pale green and conical pods cover chambers containing tiny black seeds. Their flavour is refreshing, with citrus and eucalyptus qualities; it is light but distinctive and invasive.

Brown cardamoms are large, hairy and brown-black in colour. They are used in Indian cooking in some savoury dishes, to which they are added whole and removed after cooking. Their flavour is less 'clean', not as fresh and not as distinct. Cardamom is widely used in Indian cooking, both savoury and sweet. It is also chewed as a breath freshener. In Arab countries its spicy flavour is appreciated with coffee.

CARDINAL A fish dish that is garnished with lobster escalopes (or sometimes slices of truffle) or coated with a white sauce containing lobster stock. The name refers to the colour of the lobster after cooking, just as the French verb *cardinaliser* is used to describe shellfish cooked in stock – their shells become red, like a cardinal's robes.

Cardinal is also the name of iced desserts containing red fruit (such as bombe cardinal) or fruit desserts.

The fruit can either be cold (raw or poached), sometimes arranged on vanilla ice cream and coated with a strawberry or raspberry sauce, or hot (poached) and coated with the reduced cooking juice plus cassis (blackcurrant liqueur), as in pears cardinal.

RECIPES

bombe cardinal
Line a conical ice mould with strawberry or raspberry ice cream and fill the inside with vanilla mousse mixture flavoured with praline.

brill cardinal
Prepare the fish, season with salt and pepper, then stuff with pike forcemeat to which lobster butter has been added. Poach the brill in white wine, drain and arrange on the serving dish. Garnish with thin medallions of lobster, cover with cardinal sauce and sprinkle with lobster coral.

cardinal eggs in moulds
Butter some dariole moulds, sprinkle the bottom and sides with lobster coral, break an egg into each mould and cook in a bain marie. Fill some baked tartlet cases with salpicon cardinal and invert each mould into a tartlet. Cover with cardinal sauce.

cardinal sauce
Heat 200 ml (7 fl oz, ¾ cup) cream sauce* and 100 ml (4 fl oz, 7 tablespoons) fish stock and reduce by half. Add 100 ml (4 fl oz, 7 tablespoons) cream and bring to the boil. Remove from the heat and add 50 g (2 oz, 4 tablespoons) lobster butter*. Season with a little cayenne and strain through a conical strainer. Garnish with a spoonful of chopped truffles, unless the recipe already contains them.

salpicon cardinal
Chop some lobster meat, truffles and mushrooms, and bind with cardinal sauce.

strawberries cardinal
Arrange some chilled strawberries in glass goblets. Cover with fresh raspberry purée and sprinkle with fresh almond flakes.

other recipes See *croûte, lobster.*

CARDOON A southern European plant, related to the globe artichoke, whose leafstalk is eaten as a vegetable. Cardoons are available at the end of autumn and in winter; in the south of France they were formerly traditionally eaten with Christmas dinner. In Tours, they are cooked au gratin.

When purchased, the stalks must be firm, creamy-white in colour, wide and plump. They are sold with the leafy part and top of the root, which means they can be kept for a few days in cold salted water. The stalks are especially good fried or with bone marrow; they can also be served cold, with vinaigrette.

They are usually used to garnish white or red meats (with the meat juice, butter or béchamel sauce).

RECIPES

cooking cardoons
Clean the base of the cardoon, cutting off the hard stems. Remove the tender stalks, one by one, and cut into 7.5 cm (3 in) slices; sprinkle with lemon juice. Cut the heart into four and plunge the stalks and heart into boiling water. Bring back to the boil, cover and leave to simmer very gently until tender.

buttered cardoons
Braise some blanched cardoons in butter for 20 minutes. Arrange in a vegetable dish and sprinkle with roughly chopped mint or parsley.

cardoon purée
Prepare some buttered cardoons and reduce to a purée by pressing through a sieve or using a blender. If desired, a third of its volume of potato purée or a few tablespoons of thick béchamel sauce may be added. Add butter to serve.

cardoon salad
Cut some cooked cardoons into thick matchsticks. Add some well-seasoned vinaigrette and sprinkle with chervil and roughly chopped parsley.

cardoons in béchamel sauce
Drain the blanched cardoons and arrange on a flameproof dish. Add butter, cover and leave to simmer for 15 minutes. Now add some béchamel sauce and simmer for another 5 minutes. Serve in a vegetable dish.

cardoons Mornay
Drain the cooked cardoons and arrange on a buttered gratin dish. Cover with Mornay sauce and sprinkle with grated Parmesan cheese and melted butter. Brown in a preheated oven at 240°C (475°F, gas 9).

cardoons with herbs
Braise some blanched cardoons in butter. Add several tablespoons of fines herbes sauce and simmer for 10 minutes.

fried cardoons
Drain the cooked cardoons and marinate for 30 minutes in a mixture of olive oil, lemon juice and chopped parsley. Then dip the cardoons in batter and deep-fry in hot oil. Drain and season with salt.

additional recipe See *lyonnaise*.

CARÊME, MARIE-ANTOINE (known as Antonin)
French chef and pastrycook (born Paris, 1783; died Paris, 1833). Born into a large and very poor family, the young Carême was put out on the street at the age of ten, to be taken in by the owner of a low-class restaurant at the Maine gate, where he learned the rudiments of cookery. At 16, he became an apprentice to Bailly of the Rue Vivienne, one of the best pastrycooks in Paris. Amazed by Carême's abilities and willingness to learn, Bailly encouraged him, in particular by allowing him to study in the print-room of the National Library. Here Carême copied architectural drawings, on which he based his pâtisserie creations; these were greatly admired by Bailly's customers, including the First Consul himself. Carême met Jean Avice, an excellent practitioner of cuisine, who also advised and encouraged him. Then the young man's talents became noticed by Talleyrand, who was a customer at Bailly's, and he offered to take Carême into his service.

■ **Carême's genius** For 12 years Carême managed the Talleyrand kitchens. The culinary and artistic talents of his chef enabled Talleyrand to wield gastronomy effectively as a diplomatic tool. Carême also served the Prince Regent of England, the future King George IV, and was then sent to the court of Tsar Alexander I; he was responsible for introducing some classic Russian dishes into French cuisine, including borsch and koulibiac. Carême numbered among his other employers the Viennese Court, the British Embassy, Princess Bagration and Lord Steward. He spent his last years with Baron de Rothschild and died at 50, 'burnt out by the flame of his genius and the charcoal of the roasting-spit' (Laurent Tailhade), but having realized his dream: 'To publish a complete book on the state of my profession in our times.'

The works written by Carême include *Le Pâtissier pittoresque* (1815), *Le Maître d'hôtel français* (1822), *Le Pâtissier royal parisien* (1825), and, above all, *L'Art de la cuisine au XIXe siècle* (1833). This last work was published in five volumes; the last two were written by his follower, Plumerey. Written in majestic style, Carême's books invite the reader to the table of the emperors, kings and princes for whom their author worked. Alexander I said to Talleyrand: 'What we did not know was that he taught us to eat.'

■ **Carême's contribution** A theoretician as well as a practitioner, a tireless worker as well as an artistic genius, Carême nonetheless had a keen sense of what was fashionable and entertaining. He understood that the new aristocracy, born under the Consulat, needed luxury and ceremony. So he prepared both spectacular and refined recipes, including chartreuses, desserts on pedestals, elaborate garnishes and embellishments, new decorative trimmings and novel assemblies.

A recognized founder of French *grande cuisine*, Carême placed it at the forefront of national prestige. His work as theoretician, sauce chef, pastrycook, designer and creator of recipes raised him to the pinnacle of his profession. Some of his formulae are still famous, especially his sauces.

Carême was proud of his unique art: sensitive to decoration and struck on elegance, he always had a sense of posterity. He wanted to create a school of cookery that would gather together the most famous chefs, in order to 'set the standard for beauty in classical and modern cookery, and attest to the distant future that the French chefs of the 19th century were the most famous in the world'.

In parallel with his strictly culinary or literary activities, Carême was also concerned with details of equipment. He redesigned certain kitchen utensils, changed the shape of saucepans to pour sugar, designed moulds and even concerned himself with details of clothing, such as the shape of the hat. The vol-au-vent and large meringues are attributed to him. Although an incomparable pastrycook, he was also famous for sauces and soups (there are 186 French ones and 103 foreign ones in *L'Art de la cuisine*). Yet on reading some of his recipes, one may wonder if he was concerned more with ceremony than gastronomy. In fact, Carême used money, political power and social connections to enhance his reputation; indeed, he considered that only the great people in the world could appreciate him. Certainly, his name lives on in the recipes he created and the dishes named in his honour.

RECIPES

eggs in moulds Carême
Butter some dariole moulds; sprinkle the bottom and sides with truffles and pickled ox (beef) tongue cut up into small squares. Break an egg into each mould and cook in a bain marie. Remove the eggs from the moulds and place on some artichoke hearts. Garnish with a ragoût of lamb's sweetbreads, truffles and mushrooms. Add some cream to a Madeira sauce and cover the eggs with the mixture. Place a round of pickled ox tongue, cut out in a saw-tooth pattern, on each one.

soft-boiled or poached eggs Carême
Braise some artichoke hearts in butter and arrange the eggs, either soft-boiled (soft-cooked) or poached, on them. Garnish as in the previous recipe.

CARIBBEAN See *page 222.*

CARIBBEAN CABBAGE The edible root of an arum, which is cultivated in the West Indies as a vegetable. It is prepared like turnip: scraped, washed, cut into slices and cooked in boiling water. The Caribbean cabbage and the closely related Asheen cabbage are ingredients in West Indian stews (the leaves are also used) and accompany colombos and curries. The grated root is used in the preparation of acras. The root is also a source of starch and even of a drink (*laodgi*, typical of Jamaica).

CARIBOU Canadian name for reindeer, which is generally held to be the most highly flavoured of game animals. Its commercial production is permitted and regulated, and carried out by the Inuit people, who maintain their ancestral rights to hunt it. The animal is butchered and cooked in the same way as beef. It is often served rare with a pepper sauce, accompanied by a pear cooked in red wine or by winter vegetables, such as grated celeriac or beetroot (red beet).

Caribou is also the name of a Quebec apéritif, made of sweet red wine with added alcohol.

CARIGNAN, À LA A traditional *haute cuisine* dish made with lamb cutlets and fillet (sirloin) steak, sautéed, then arranged on Anna potatoes (shaped into little tarts) and served with a sauce made by deglazing the pan with port and tomato-flavoured veal stock. The garnish consists of buttered asparagus tips and eggs moulded in a duchesse mixture, breaded, fried, scooped out and filled with foie gras purée.

The same name is used for a cold dessert in which a pear, peach or apple is poached, hollowed out and filled with chocolate ice cream, then arranged on a Genoese sponge base and covered with vanilla fondant.

CARMÉLITE, À LA A cold dish consisting of chicken suprêmes, covered with chaud-froid sauce, garnished with slices of truffle and dressed with a mousseline of crayfish and crayfish tails.

The name, because of its association with the Carmelite nuns' white habit and black veil, is also used for an egg dish, in which soft-boiled (soft-cooked) or poached eggs are arranged in a flan crust, garnished with creamed mussels and covered with white wine sauce.

CARMEN Any of various dishes, including consommé, eggs or fillets of sole, that contain tomato or pimiento and, generally, a highly seasoned garnish or flavouring *à l'espagnole*.

Carmen salad consists of boiled rice, diced white chicken, strips of red sweet pepper and peas, all flavoured with a mustard and chopped tarragon vinaigrette.

RECIPE

eggs sur le plat Carmen
Cook some eggs *sur le plat*, then cut round the whites with a circular pastry (cookie) cutter. Fry in oil some round slices of stale bread with the crusts removed. Cover each slice of bread with a slice of ham of the same size and place an egg on top. Cover with well-seasoned and reduced tomato sauce.

CARMINE A natural red food colouring, also called cochineal or carminic acid (E120). It is used especially in confectionery and pâtisserie – jams, jellies, filled biscuits (cookies), fruit pastes, ice creams, instant desserts and preserved red fruits. Carmine is also used to colour delicatessen meats and cured meat products, preserved shrimps and dried fish, syrups, liqueurs and apéritifs, and flavoured cheeses and milks.

CARIBBEAN

The Caribbean cuisine owes much to South American Indian influences, with contributions from European explorers and settlers from France (Guadeloupe and Martinique), Spain and Britain, and America (Haiti, Cuba, Jamaica and Puerto Rico).

The introduction of a vast population of slaves from Africa influenced the cooking of the islands. Both their ingredients and the methods the slaves used to make the most of the inferior rations on which they had to survive, contributed colourful African characteristics to the cooking styles. When the use of African slaves was eventually abandoned, Indian and Chinese workers were brought in and they too contributed to the cooking of these islands.

■ **Colourful, eclectic cooking** The cuisine that emerged is characterized by sweet-and-savoury mixtures, fried dishes and highly spiced ragoûts. The abundance of tropical fruit and vegetables, coconut, sugar cane and spices along with the varied seafood provide a cornucopia of ingredients. Spicy chillies and bright tomatoes often feature. There is also a contrast in styles, inherited from the sophistication of the planters and the hearty simplicity of their workers. Seafood, meats and tropical vegetables are prepared by traditional methods, using recipes that require slow cooking and the expert use of spices.

The Caribbeans are proud of their culinary secrets; they make it a point of honour, for example, to use the *lélé*, a three-branched stick that replaces the wooden spoon and the blender, without which they would be unable to prepare broths such as *calalou* (a thick spiced purée of herbs with bacon and sweet potato leaves, sorrel, okra, cucumber, Caribbean cabbage, *mousambe,* and *siguine*) or *soupe des habitants*, made with beef, sweet potatoes, pumpkin, celery, purslane and green beans. There are also soups made with *cribiches* or *ouassous* (large crayfish also made into kebabs), *tourlourous* (land crabs), *pisquettes* or *tiritis* (small fish and alevins, also used in omelettes and ragoûts), or tripe; these are always mixed with vegetables and a variety of herbs and spices, including pimiento, garlic, onion, cloves, thyme and bay.

A Caribbean meal may begin with crudités of raw vegetables and fruit, such as bamboo shoots, palm cabbage, palm-hearts, breadfruit and papaw in vinaigrette, served with the famous acras and accompanied by *féroce* (spiced avocado purée, with salt cod). Other starters include stuffed avocados, the highly seasoned Creole pudding, and omelettes made with shellfish, *pisquettes* or pineapple.

■ **Fish and seafood** Fish and seafood are a traditional speciality, usually simmered in a marinade of lime and pimiento seasoned with spices. Such dishes include *blaff*, made with devilfish, bonito, *coulirous* (mackerel), or *chadrous* (sea urchins' eggs); *touffé*, made from shark that is first marinated, then braised and served coated with tomato sauce; *broulai* (fish sautéed with cassava, tomatoes and onions); and turtle colombo. Salt cod is widely used, cooked in such dishes as *macadam* (browned in a roux, then simmered in sauce) or *chiquetaille* (flaked over rice and tomatoes). Fish (fried, marinated or stuffed), spiny lobsters, crabs (stuffed or cooked in a stew), and molluscs (*lambis*) are traditionally served, as are meats, with rice and red beans. Among the most exotic recipes are smoked fish with mangoes, bass with ginger, and *sopito*, a kind of bouillabaisse made with coconut milk.

■ **Meat and vegetables** Meat dishes are prepared using the same variety and richness of spices. In the French Antilles, curry and calumba are used with beef, chicken and mutton. Specialities are *pâté en pot* (sheep's belly, head, feet, breast and liver cooked with vegetables) and pork *vindaye* (cooked coated with a thick paste of ginger, garlic, onion, saffron and pimiento). Ham with rum and pineapple, pork braised with maize and chicken with coconut milk and bananas complete the range. Vegetables are prepared in traditional ways – *giraumonade* (pumpkin purée), *mange-mêle* (vegetables with bacon), and calabash stew with peanut bread and shrimps. In Jamaica, curried young goat is served with unripe bananas and saffron rice. In Puerto Rico, the South American influence can be seen in *pasteles* (stuffed and steamed plantain leaves), *piononos* (stuffed fried banana slices), and *asapao*, a chicken ragoût that is served as a soup. In Curaçao, a noteworthy dish is *stoba*, a goat ragoût seasoned with cumin, capers and olives, cooked with cucumbers and lemon.

■ **Desserts** Besides the classic tropical fruits, the sapodilla plum should be mentioned, as well as the custard apple and cinnamon apple. Fruit salads, compotes, jellies and jams, flans and blancmanges (flavoured with coconut, vanilla and cinnamon), soufflés and very sweet fritters – all flavoured with rum – are the most popular desserts.

CARNIVAL A programme of popular festivities and masquerades that traditionally took place in the days preceding Shrove Tuesday and Ash Wednesday, the start of Lent. The word comes from the Italian *carnevale* (Shrove Tuesday), which derives from *carne levare* (leaving out meat), a reference to the Lenten fast immediately following the carnival period, during which the Church forbade the consumption of meat and cakes.

The carnival theoretically extended from Twelfth Night to Ash Wednesday, but it used to reach a climax at the Shrove Tuesday meal, traditionally marked by an abundance of all types of meat (hence the custom of a procession with the fatted ox). In the Champagne region, this last rich meal had to include pigs' trotters (feet), and in Ardèche, pigs' ears. The cocks that had lost that day's fight were eaten in the Marne region, while in Touraine the special dish was a leg of goat. Other traditional Shrove Tuesday dishes included a stuffed rabbit (in Limousin), a huge vol-au-vent containing chicken in salsify sauce (Quercy) and the famous aïoli (garlic mayonnaise) of Provence.

Carnival originated in the Roman feasts of the calends (first day) of March, which celebrated the awakening of nature. On this occasion, the rules were broken and disguises worn. Straw dolls were burned amidst shouting and chanting. (The word *carnaval* in folk tradition still means a grotesque mannequin that is solemnly burned or buried on Ash Wednesday.) Hence, in the French countryside, magical rites are combined with feasting. In particular, the stock from the stockpot was sprinkled around the houses of the Morvan region to ward off snakes, around the hen houses to ward off foxes in Angoumois, or on the manure heap to make it bigger, in Limousin.

The large attendance at these festivities meant there was a need for fairly cheap cakes, quickly prepared using a blazing fire, hence the tradition of pancakes and also waffles and fritters: *crespets des Landes, merveilles* and *bottereaux*, Sainte-Menehould *faverolles* and Sologne *beugnons*. Also worthy of mention are Belfort *séchu* (dried apples or pears with slices of bacon) and the cheese soup in Isère. In Nivernais, the Shrove Tuesday meal consisted of: pasta bouillon, boiled beef with vegetables, *coq au sang* (or with white sauce), roast goose or turkey, garlic and nut-oil salad, white cheese with cream and plum tart with flamed marc brandy.

CAROB The bean from the carob tree, which is native to the Mediterranean region but is cultivated in other warm climates. Up to 30 cm (12 in) long, the carob bean has a nutritious refreshing pulp, as rich in sugar as molasses. It contains hard reddish seeds, which in the Kabylia region of North Africa are crushed and used to make pancakes. In the food industry, carob meal (E410) is widely used as a gelling agent (for jams) and as a texturing agent.

CAROLINE A savoury miniature éclair, baked in the oven, then filled with a cheese or ham mixture, or with caviar, salmon mousse or foie gras. *Carolines*, also known as Karoly éclairs, are served hot or cold as buffet snacks. They can also be made to the size of an ordinary éclair and served as an hors d'oeuvre or as a hot entrée.

RECIPES

carolines à la hollandaise

Prepare a sugarless choux paste. Using a piping bag, squeeze out some small éclairs, about 4 cm (1½ in)

long, on to a baking sheet. Brush with beaten egg, bake in a preheated oven at 220°C (425°F, gas 7) for 10 minutes. Reduce the temperature to 180°C (350°F, gas 4) and continue to cook for a further 10 minutes. Allow to cool. To make enough filling for 12 carolines, desalt 4 herring fillets, trim and wipe them. Pound the fillets, or put them into a blender, together with 2 hard-boiled (hard-cooked) egg yolks and 75 g (3 oz, 6 tablespoons) butter. Add 1 teaspoon chives and 1 teaspoon chopped parsley. Gently split the éclairs along the side and put the filling into this opening with a piping bag. Brush the carolines with melted butter and immediately sprinkle with a little hard-boiled egg yolk and chopped parsley. Cool before serving.

carolines à la mousse de foie gras

Make some small éclairs as for carolines à la hollandaise. Prepare some duck (or goose) foie gras mousse and add an equal quantity of butter and (optional) a little Cognac. Pipe the filling into the split éclairs. Chill before serving.

carolines Joinville

Make some small éclairs as for carolines à la hollandaise. To fill 12 carolines, prepare a thick béchamel sauce using 25 g (1 oz, 2 tablespoons) butter, 25 g (1 oz, ¼ cup) plain (all-purpose) flour, and 200 ml (7 fl oz, ¾ cup) milk. Heat 75–100 g (3–4 oz, about ½ cup) peeled (shelled) shrimps in some butter, flame them with marc brandy and add to the béchamel sauce. Season with salt and pepper and leave to cool. Finally, pipe the filling into the split éclairs and brush the éclairs with melted butter. Cool before serving.

CARP A freshwater fish, found in sluggish rivers and also reared commercially on fish farms. Up to 1 m (39 in) long, the carp's thick body is covered with thick scales and is brownish on the back, golden yellow on the sides and whitish on the belly. Its small toothless mouth has four minute barbs. Improved yields have been obtained by crossbreeding, which has produced the leather carp that has scales only in mid-body and at the base of the fins, and the mirror carp, which is the finest variety, with scales only at the base of the fins. When buying carp, choose a plump one that is carrying eggs, or milt. With spawning taking place between April and June, carp are 'empty' at this time. If a live carp is chosen, the fishmonger should kill and gut it, removing the gall bladder, which is at the base of the throat and is difficult to extract. It is advisable to soak the gutted and scaled fish in a bowl of vinegar and water (which should be replenished as necessary) in order to remove its 'muddy' taste.

The carp can be roasted, stuffed (especially *à la juive*), grilled (broiled), cooked in court-bouillon or stewed in white wine or beer. Small fish can also be fried. Carp has been eaten since the Middle Ages, and used to be the dish of kings. They were usually cooked in wine with a lot of spices. The tongue was considered a delicacy. Carp is also the fish most prized by the Chinese; the lips are considered the finest part. Deep-frozen Asiatic carp are sold in France; their flesh is regarded as firmer and tastier than French carp.

RECIPES

carp à la chinoise

Clean and gut a carp weighing about 1.5 kg (3¼ lb) and cut it into sections. Finely chop 2 large onions and fry in oil until slightly brown. Add 2 tablespoons vinegar, 1 tablespoon sugar, 1 tablespoon freshly grated root ginger (or 1 teaspoon ground ginger), 1–2 tablespoons rice alcohol (or marc brandy), salt, pepper and a glass of water. Stir, cover and leave to cook for about 10 minutes. Fry the carp pieces in oil for 10 minutes, then add the sauce and leave to cook for another 4–5 minutes. Some strips of cucumber may be added to the carp along with the sauce, if desired.

carp à l'alsacienne

Choose a carp weighing at least 1.5 kg (3¼ lb) and clean and gut it. Fill it with a fish cream forcemeat, place in a buttered ovenproof dish and add a mixture of court-bouillon and white wine so that it half-fills the dish (one-third court-bouillon to two-thirds white wine). Cook for 30–40 minutes in a preheated oven at 220°C (425°F, gas 7) protecting with buttered greaseproof (wax) paper if necessary. Drain, retaining the liquid, and arrange the fish on a bed of sauerkraut, surround it with small boiled potatoes and keep hot. Reduce the cooking liquid, bind with a little beurre manié and cover the fish with it.

fried carp

Select a small carp, weighing about 400 g (14 oz). Clean, gut, wash and wipe the fish. Immerse it in milk, then in flour, and then deep-fry in hot oil. When cooked, remove, drain and add salt. Garnish with fried parsley and lemon quarters.

stuffed carp à l'ancienne

(from a recipe by Carême provided by Plumerey) Take a large carp that is carrying eggs (milt), remove the scales and bones, and lift off the flesh, taking care to leave the backbone intact, complete with head and tail. To the carp flesh, add the meat from a small eel, as well as desalted anchovies, and make a fairly firm quenelle forcemeat in the usual way, but without adding any sauce. Scald the roes, cut into several pieces, sauté in butter with a little lemon juice, add some truffles and mushrooms and bind with a few spoonfuls of thick allemande sauce.

Take a tin tray that is as long as the carp and butter it thickly. Spread a layer of stuffing on it, about 2.5 cm (1 in) thick, making it into the shape of the carp. On this, place the carp backbone with head and tail still attached. Cover the backbone with a little stuffing and cover this with the roe ragoût; then add another layer of stuffing, 2.5 cm (1 in) thick, still in the shape of the carp. Smooth with a knife dipped in hot water.

Butter a baking sheet large enough to hold the carp and sprinkle breadcrumbs on the butter. Carefully heat the tin tray so that the butter melts and slide the carp on to the baking sheet without damaging the shape. Brush with beaten egg, coat the top with breadcrumbs, press the breadcrumbs down firmly and cover with clarified butter. Then, with the tip of a small spoon, press in a pattern of scales, starting at the head.

Cook the carp in a preheated oven at 200°C (400°F, gas 6) for 45 minutes, basting frequently with clarified butter during cooking so that it turns a golden colour. When it is cooked, transfer it carefully from the baking sheet to the serving dish with a long fish slice. Work some fish essence into a financière sauce and serve in a sauceboat to accompany it.

other recipes See *beer, chambord, juive.*

CARPACCIO An Italian antipasto (appetizer) consisting of very thin slices of raw beef served cold with a creamy vinaigrette sauce made with olive oil. This dish, named in honour of the Renaissance Venetian painter, originates from Harry's Bar in Venice (not connected with the famous American bar in Paris).

RECIPE

carpaccio

Remove the fat, nerves and gristle from a piece of very tender sirloin weighing 1.25 kg (2¾ lb) so as to obtain a neat cylinder. Put in the freezer. When it has hardened sufficiently, cut into very thin slices using a very sharp knife. Arrange these slices on plates, season lightly with salt and put back in the refrigerator for at least 15 minutes. Mix 200 ml (7 fl oz, ¾ cup) mayonnaise with 1 or 2 teaspoons of Worcestershire sauce and 1 teaspoon of lemon juice. Season with salt and white pepper. Pour a little of this sauce over the slices of meat, making a few decorative motifs with it.

CARPET SHELL (CLAM) *palourde* A bivalve mollusc, 3–5 cm (1¼–2 in) long, that is more plentiful on the Atlantic coast and in the English Channel than in the Mediterranean. Its thin shell, convex in the centre, is pale yellow to dark grey marked with brown spots and two series of very fine streaks, one radiating, the other concentric, forming a lattice. Carpet shells are eaten raw in a seafood platter or stuffed, like mussels.

Three very closely related species of false carpet shells (or clams) are distinguished by the colour of the inside of the valves (gold or pink instead of pale grey) and by the fineness of the radiating streaks, only visible with a magnifying glass. They are less delicate than the true carpet shells.

CARRAGEEN Also known as carragheen. A red seaweed, known as Irish moss, of the group that also produce agar-agar, so much used in the food processing industry as a gelling agent. Its fan-shaped fronds grow on the low water-line on the rocks of the American and European northern Atlantic shore (up as far as Scandinavia), but it is particularly associated with Ireland. In late summer it is picked, washed and dried for about ten days in the sun, when it turns silvery white. It is named after the Irish village of Carragheen. The classic Irish dish in which it is used is milk jelly.

CARRÉ DE L'EST A soft high-fat (45% fat content) cheese made from pasteurized cow's milk and originating from Champagne and Lorraine, where it is now mass-produced. Sold in boxes 7.5–10 cm (3–4 in) square and 2.5–3 cm (1–1¼ in) deep, Carré de l'Est is a mild cheese with a white downy crust.

The term 'Carré' is also applied to Normandy cheeses, related to Bondard, from the Pays de Bray or the Pays d'Auge.

CARRÉ, FERDINAND French engineer (born Moislains, Somme, 1824; died Pommeuse, Seine-et-Marne, 1900), who pioneered methods of refrigeration. One of Carré's machines was installed in 1859 at the Velten brewery in Marseille. In 1862 at the Universal London Exhibition, he exhibited an ice machine with an output of 200 kg (440 lb) per hour. In 1877, after setting up a business exporting machines to Germany, England and the United States, he repeated Tellier's experiment: he equipped the ship *Paraguay* with refrigerated holds and loaded it with 80 tons of meat destined for Buenos Aires. On the return voyage, with Argentine meat on board, Carré's refrigerator ship ran aground on the coast of Senegal. In spite of a two-month delay, the meat arrived at Le Havre in perfect condition and a great banquet was held to celebrate the event.

CARROT A vegetable grown widely for its orange-red edible root. It is one of the most popular and versatile of vegetables.

Although the ancients recognized that carrot is good for the eyesight, they did not cultivate it as a vegetable. Until the Renaissance era, carrots had a yellowish tough root, very woody in the centre, and, like other root crops, it never appeared among high-class foodstuffs. Little by little, the carrot was improved and cultivated varieties were sold in the markets. Its orange colour dates from the middle of the 19th century.

■ **Carrots throughout the year** The first new carrots may be round or slightly elongated and sold in bunches. Traditional early carrots include Grelots – tender, sweet and full of flavour – or the Bellot variety. Nantaise carrots are another classic variety – long with a crisp texture.

Long or semi-long main crop carrots are used freshly dug or stored for winter use. They are not as sweet, light and crisp as the new and early varieties, but they have a full flavour and crunchy, firm texture. If the carrots are old, split them in half and hollow them, discarding the yellow core.

■ **Cooking** To retain the maximum nutritional value, carrots should not be scraped or peeled, but brushed under running water, because the vitamins are concentrated in the skin. However, because of the risk of pesticide residues, it is advisable to peel or scrape them.

Carrots are widely used in savoury dishes worldwide. Along with onions, carrots are an essential flavouring ingredient for stocks, soups, casseroles and sauces; they are also used in a standard mirepoix of vegetables as a base for roasting poultry and meat. Carrots flavour fish and seafood dishes, from lightly steamed shellfish to baked chunky fillets, steaks and whole fish. They are also used to flavour dishes or mixed vegetables, pulses and grains.

Carrots are also a valuable ingredient in their own right. They make delicious soup. As a vegetable accompaniment, they can be cut in a variety of ways – across into thick or fine slices; lengthways into wedges, fingers or julienne strips; or they can be cut into chunks or dice. Baby carrots are usually cooked whole. They can be boiled, steamed, stir-fried or glazed by cooking with the minimum of water and a little butter. The latter method is excellent for fine fingers or julienne to accompany fish, poultry or meat main dishes. They can be cooked on their own or in combination with other vegetables. Tarragon goes very well with carrots as does orange.

Used raw, they may be coarsely or finely grated, or pared into ribbons for use in salads. Dressed with a little vinaigrette and tossed with chopped parsley, chervil or tarragon, they make an excellent salad. They are an ingredient in the classic coleslaw. Carrot sticks are popular crudités.

The sweet flavour of carrots is appreciated in sweet cookery. They are the main ingredient for carrot halva – a fabulous Indian dessert of grated carrot simmered in milk and sugar, flavoured with a little cardamom and enriched with nuts and raisins. They are used in cookies and the popular American-style carrot cake. Carrots also feature in preserves, including an Indian syrup-based preserve. Carrots were used very successfully to make a sweet preserve resembling marmalade when oranges were scarce in the 1940's.

Carrot juice is also a popular drink, both bought and freshly extracted.

RECIPES

carrot flan
Bake a pastry flan case blind and fill with a lightly sweetened carrot purée. Cover with slices of glazed carrot, pour over the cooking juices from the carrots, and place in a preheated oven at 240°C (475°F, gas 9) for a few minutes.

carrot purée
Cook 500 g (18 oz) sliced new carrots in salted water to which 1 teaspoon granulated sugar and

CARROTS

round baby carrots

new carrots

long, medium and short main crop carrots

I tablespoon butter has been added. When the carrots are cooked, drain and make into a purée by pressing them through a fine sieve or using a blender. Heat the purée, adding a few spoonfuls of the carrots' cooking liquid if it is too thick. At the last moment, add 50 g (2 oz, ¼ cup) fresh butter. Mix well and arrange on a vegetable dish. Carrot purée can also be made using the carrots from a pot-au-feu.

carrot purée with cream
Heat 4 tablespoons double (heavy) cream and add to some carrot purée.

carrots with cream
Cut some old carrots into segments and hollow out the centres. Cook in salted water, and before they become soft, drain, cover with boiling cream and reduce by two-thirds. Arrange in a vegetable dish and serve very hot.

carrots with raisins
Cut some new carrots into slices and fry in melted butter. Lightly sprinkle with flour, then add just enough water to cover them and I tablespoon brandy. Cover. Halfway through cooking (after about 15 minutes), add a handful of raisins. Finish cooking with the lid on over a gentle heat.

glazed carrots
Clean some new, preferably fat, carrots, leaving medium-sized ones whole, but cutting large ones into halves or quarters. Place in a frying pan large enough to hold them all without overlapping. Cover with cold water. For every 500 ml (17 fl oz, 2 cups) water add 25 g (1 oz, 2 tablespoons) sugar, 50 g (2 oz, ¼ cup) butter and ½ teaspoon salt. (When old carrots are used, hollow out the centres, scald them and drain, then cook with sugar and butter.) Bring to the boil over a high heat. When the water is boiling briskly, lower the heat, cover the pan and leave to simmer until the liquid has almost completely evaporated. The carrots should now be cooked. Shake the pan so that the carrots are coated with the syrupy liquid.

Glazed carrots may be served with béchamel sauce (add a few spoonfuls of the sauce at the last moment), butter, cream (cover with boiling cream and reduce by two-thirds), herbs (sprinkle with chopped parsley or chervil) or meat juices (add a few spoonfuls of roast veal or poultry cooking juices).

grated carrots with currants
Steep some dried currants in barely tepid lemon juice, then add them to grated raw carrots mixed with well-seasoned olive oil vinaigrette.

other recipes See *forestière, loaf, royale, soufflé, Vichy.*

CARROT CAKE A cake typical of North America, consisting of a sponge made of flour, eggs, sugar and oil, in which puréed or grated carrots are incorporated. Alternatively, a creamed butter and sugar mixture may be used as a base. Thick and moist, carrot cake is coated with a vanilla icing (frosting), and it may be served with nuts and raisins.

CARVING The action of slicing or cutting up meat, poultry, game or fish into sections, either for serving or for further preparation.

The art of carving was formerly held in great esteem and attended by a certain amount of ceremony (see *Écuyer tranchant*). In ancient times, specialist carvers gave courses in cutting up and carving, using wooden 'chickens' with pieces that could be fitted together again. Noblemen in the Middle Ages liked to show off their skill, and Joinville recounts with pride that he carved one day at the King of Navarre's table. In the 17th century, young gentlemen were trained in the carving of meat and thus learned how to distinguish the best joints: 'the wing of birds who scratch at the earth with their feet; the leg of birds who live in the air; the white meat of large roast poultry; the skin and the ears of a suckling pig; the saddle and the legs of hares and rabbits'. Large fish, such as salmon or pike, were cut in two, and the front portion, considered the most delicate, was placed at the head of the table, where the honoured guest sat.

Modern carvers, particularly in the catering trade, must combine culinary competence with a knowledge of anatomy, manual dexterity and a certain panache. Each joint of meat or species of poultry requires a particular carving technique. As a general rule, meat is carved perpendicularly to the direction of the muscle fibres; the slices should be as large as possible and of even thickness. The introduction of service *à la russe* (Russian style), in which meat is presented already cut up, has caused the disappearance from many tables of an operation that was formerly done with pride by the master of the house.

CARVING KNIFE A knife with a very long – 18–35 cm (7–14 in) – flexible blade and a sharp point. It is used for thinly slicing bacon and roast meat, hot or cold.

CASANOVA DE SEINGALT, GIOVANNI GIACOMO Italian adventurer (born Venice, 1725; died Dux, Bohemia, 1798). Famous for his romantic and chivalrous exploits, Casanova was an attentive observer of contemporary gastronomic etiquette. This, and his own culinary tastes, occupy an important place in his *Mémoires*: he invented a special vinegar to season hard-boiled (hard-cooked) eggs and anchovies; he advocated Chambertin as an accompaniment to Roquefort cheese; and he claimed that forcemeat of *béatilles* and very frothy chocolate worked as an effective restorative. Between adventures, he would often make a detour to taste famous pâtés, the rare Hermitage Blanc of the Côtes-du-Rhône, Grenoble's liqueur, Genoese cep mushrooms and Leipzig's skewered larks. Truffles, oysters, champagne and Maraschino owe their reputation as aphrodisiacs largely to him. The Prince of Ligne said of him: 'At 73, no longer a god in the garden or a satyr in the forest, he is a wolf at table.'

CASHEW APPLE A fleshy pear-shaped swelling that is part of the fruit of the cashew tree; the cashew nut hangs below this swelling. The cashew apple is picked when ripe and usually eaten with sugar because it is slightly tart. In Brazil, where it is widely used, it is made into jams, jellies, compotes and beverages, and fermented to produce a dessert wine and a vinegar.

CASHEW NUT The fruit of the cashew tree, originally from South America but widely cultivated in India and other tropical countries since the 16th century. The nut contains a smooth creamy-white kidney-shaped kernel with a mild, slightly sweet flavour and tender texture. In Europe it is usually eaten dried, roasted and salted as an appetizer and in salads. In Indian cooking it is used in a variety of dishes, including lamb curry, beef stew, rice with prawns, vegetable dishes, stuffings for chicken, and cakes and biscuits (cookies).

CASK *tonneau* Wine casks come in a wide range of different sizes, some of which have special regional names, such as the Bordeaux *barrique*. The word *tonneau*, however, comes from *tonne*, a very large cask formerly used, especially in the port of Bordeaux, to store wine and then ship it, the mighty cask being rolled from the quayside into the hold of a ship in the wine fleet. According to how many *tonnes* the hold could take, the capacity of the vessel began to be given in terms of tonnage, a system still in use today. The *tonne* itself is no longer used, but the English word 'tun' perpetuates its association with a gigantic wooden container, such as is still used for cider and beer.

CASSATA An iced dessert of Italian origin, made of bombe paste set in a rectangular mould and lined with fruit ice cream. The name means 'little case', due to its brick shape, although triangular cassatas can be found. A cassata can also be an ice cream shaped like a brick, consisting of several ice creams of different flavours with a filling of Chantilly cream.

On the other hand, Sicilian cassata, also in the shape of a brick, is a cake. It is made with slices of Genoa cake (a type of light fruit cake) steeped in Maraschino or Curaçao and covered with a mixture of Ricotta cheese, flaked chocolate, crystallized (candied) fruits and sugar syrup; the whole is finally coated with a thick layer of chocolate. This Christmas and Easter cake is also traditionally eaten at weddings.

RECIPE

strawberry cassata
Prepare 500 ml (17 fl oz, 2 cups) strawberry ice cream (see *Ices and ice creams*), the same quantity of vanilla* ice cream, and 400 ml (14 fl oz, 1¾ cups)

whipped cream mixed with crystallized (candied) fruits steeped in brandy or a liqueur. Spread the vanilla ice cream in a rectangular mould, cover with the whipped cream and fruits, and place in the freezer until the cream just hardens. Cover with the strawberry ice cream, press down firmly, smooth the surface and leave to set.

CASSAVA See *manioc*.

CASSE-MUSEAU A very hard biscuit (cookie) that keeps well; it was formerly very common in France, but is now made only in certain areas. The name, meaning 'jaw breaker', comes from its hardness and from the custom of tossing biscuits at the face during certain popular festivals, such as the Rogation Procession held in Poitiers. In Corsica they are known as *sciappa denti* (tooth-breaker). The casse-museau is usually made of a mixture of coarsely chopped almonds and curd cheese, which is rolled into a sausage shape, cooked, then cut into slices and returned to the oven; this double baking produces the very hard consistency.

CASSEROLE A cooking utensil, made of metal or other ovenproof material, which is fitted with a lid and designed for long, slow cooking in the oven. Many are decorative enough to use as serving dishes. The name is also given to the food cooked in a casserole.

In classic French cookery, a casserole is a dish generally made with cooked rice moulded into the shape of a casserole or timbale; it can also be made in a duchess potato mould. Rarely made nowadays, these dishes can have various fillings, including mousses, fat or lean minced (ground) meat, game purée, calves' or lamb's sweetbreads and escalopes of truffled foie gras. Casseroles can also be garnished *à la Sagan*, *à la vénitienne*, *à la bouquetière*, *à la régence* and *à la Nantua*. If the contents are cold, they can be glazed with aspic jelly.

RECIPE

rice casserole à l'ancienne
(from a recipe by Carême) Wash about 1 kg (2¼ lb) long-grain rice in several changes of warm water, then place it in a large saucepan. Cover with cold water and heat; after it has boiled for several seconds, drain, then moisten the rice with about two to three times its own volume of beef stock and thicken with fat skimmings from a chicken broth. Return the pan to the heat. As soon as the rice boils, take it off the heat and remove the scum from the surface. Now simmer gently, stirring after about 1 hour and again after a further 20–25 minutes. The rice should now be soft. (Further stock may be added during cooking in order to keep the rice moist.) Remove from the heat, stir for several minutes with a spatula and allow to cool.

When the rice is only just warm, work it with a wooden spoon until the grains have all burst and the rice is a smooth paste, adding a little stock if necessary. Pile the rice into a baking tin (pan), forming a casserole shape about 13 cm (5 in) high; smooth it well. Garnish with slices of carrot. Now coat the surface of the rice casserole with a little clarified butter and cook in a preheated oven at 160°C (325°F, gas 3) for about 1½ hours. During cooking, it will turn bright yellow. When cooked, carefully remove the garnished top crust and remove from the inside all the rice that does not adhere to the crust, even if this means that the crust is very thin. Mix a large spoonful of rice taken from the interior with a little sauce (béchamel, espagnole or any other suitable sauce, depending on the filling to be used), and glaze the crust with this mixture after putting the filling in the case.

If good stock or fat are unavailable, the rice can be moistened with water, butter and salt. This will make the rice much whiter.

Carême also gave a recipe for small individual rice casseroles (*casserolettes*). They are placed on a baking sheet in a hot oven and cooked until evenly coloured.

CASSIS AOC wines from a vineyard close to the small Provençal port of Cassis, between Marseille and La Ciotat. This vineyard, famous since the 15th century, is known especially for its dry white wine. The vines, planted on the chalky cliffs overlooking the sea, include such varieties as Clairette, Marsanne, Sauvignon Blanc and Ugni Blanc. The sunny southerly aspect is sheltered by the hills, which protect the vines from the Mistral. They are also protected from excessive heat by the proximity of the sea. Cassis also produces a little red and rosé wine from Grenache, Mourvèdre, Carignan, Cinsault and other varieties of grape. But the white wines remain the most attractive and are enjoyed particularly for their fruitiness, freshness and delicacy. They are among the best white wines of Provence and are a delightful complement to bouillabaisse.

CASSIS A liqueur of pronounced flavour made by macerating blackcurrants in spirit and sweetening the resulting liquid. There are several categories: 14° for most ordinary and culinary purposes; 15° for 'crème de cassis'; 20° for 'double crème' or 'super-cassis'; and there are even versions of 25°. Cassis is a speciality of Dijon and the Côte d'Or; it was first made commercially in 1841 by one Claude Joly. The popularity of Kir has stimulated production. This drink, a Burgundy apéritif consisting of a spoonful of cassis liqueur topped up with dry white wine, has acquired the name of the late Canon Kir, Mayor of Dijon and a Resistance hero. 'Kir royale' is made with sparkling wine.

RECIPE

cassis

For every litre (1¾ pints, 4⅓ cups) of eau de vie, take 12 small washed leaves from the tip of a blackcurrant branch and place them in a bowl together with 1 clove and a good pinch of crumbled stick cinnamon. Wash and dry the blackcurrants and weigh them. Crush them roughly and put them in the bowl, allowing 1 kg (2¼ lb, 9 cups) blackcurrants per 1 litre (1¾ pints, 4⅓ cups) eau de vie. Now add 800 g (1¾ lb, 3 cups) granulated sugar per kg (2¼ lb, 9 cups) of blackcurrants and mix all the ingredients thoroughly. Pour into jars, seal and store, preferably in a warm sunny place, for about 1 month. Then pour the contents through a cloth secured over a large bowl and extract all the liquid. Filter and bottle. If the liqueur is too strong, some sugar dissolved in cold water can be added – about 500 g (18 oz, 2¼ cups) sugar per 500 ml (17 fl oz, 2 cups) water.

CASSOLETTE A small container with lugs or a short handle, made of heatproof porcelain, tempered glass or metal, which is used to prepare and serve hot entrées or certain hors d'oeuvre and cold puddings. The word can also apply to a variety of dishes that are served in *cassolettes*. Savoury *cassolettes* may consist of salpicons and ragoûts of all sorts, including sweetbreads, chopped chicken, mushrooms and fish mousses, bound with a white or brown sauce; sweet *cassolettes*, which are sometimes served in nougat cups instead of the *cassolette* itself, can include flavoured creams, custards and poached fruit.

CASSONADE Raw crystallized sugar extracted directly from the juice of the sugar cane. The small irregular crystals have a light-brown colour and a slight taste of rum, caused by the residues of gum and wax. When further refined, cassonade makes white cane sugar.

Cassonade is used to make chutneys and features in certain recipes from northern Europe, including civet of hare, Flemish red cabbage and black pudding (blood sausage), and in some southern European ones, such as Pézenas mutton pie. In cake-making it gives a special flavour to tarts and yeast cakes.

Until the 16th century cassonade was called *casson* and took the form of an irregular loaf of crumbly sugar.

RECIPES

Belgian cassonade tart

Make some pastry using 250 g (9 oz, 2¼ cups) plain (all-purpose) flour, 125 g (4½ oz, ½ cup) butter, a pinch of salt, and 4 tablespoons cold water. Roll into a ball and leave to rest for 3–4 hours. Then use it to line a tart tin (pan) and bake blind in a preheated oven at 200°C (400°F, gas 6). Grind 150–200 g (5–7 oz, 1¼–1¾ cups) almonds in a blender and mix with 3 egg yolks, 200 ml (7 fl oz, ¾ cup) double (heavy) cream, and 300 g (11 oz, 1⅔ cups) cassonade (raw brown sugar). Beat 3 egg whites until they form stiff peaks and add to the mixture. Pour into the tart case and bake for about 40 minutes.

French cassonade tart

Mix together 125 g (4½ oz, ½ cup) melted butter, 2 egg yolks and a pinch of salt. Sprinkle in 250 g (9 oz, 2¼ cups) sifted self-raising flour and add sufficient water to give a smooth firm dough – about 3½ tablespoons. Roll the dough into a ball, wrap it in a cloth and leave to rest for 1 hour. Butter a baking sheet and roll out the pastry into a circle. Pinch around the rim and, with the tip of a knife, lightly trace lozenge shapes on the top. Sprinkle evenly with 150 g (5 oz, ¾ cup) cassonade (raw brown sugar) and divide 50 g (2 oz, 4 tablespoons) butter into small balls and place these on top of the sugar. Place in a preheated oven at 200°C (400°F, gas 6) and bake for about 35–40 minutes.

CASSOULET A dish, originally from Languedoc, which consists of haricot (navy) beans cooked in a stewpot with pork rinds and seasonings. A garnish of meats, which varies from region to region, and a gratin topping are added in the final stages. The word comes from *cassole*, the name of the glazed earthenware cooking pot traditionally used.

The haricot beans (known as *mounjetos*) are the essential ingredient, giving cassoulet its creaminess and flavour – originally, fresh broad (fava) beans were used; haricots come from Spain and were not used in France until the 19th century. *Cassoulet* is divided into three types according to the meats used. Prosper Montagné called them the 'Trinity', the 'Father' being the *cassoulet* from Castelnaudary, the 'Son' the *cassoulet* from Carcassone and the 'Holy Ghost' that from Toulouse. The first, which is undoubtedly the oldest, contains pork (loin, ham, leg, sausages and fresh rinds) with perhaps a piece of preserved goose. In Carcassone, leg of mutton and, during the shooting season, partridge are used. The same ingredients are used in Toulouse as in Castelnaudary but in smaller quantities, the difference being made up with fresh lard, Toulouse sausage, mutton and duck or goose. Other variations exist, including Montauban (with Pamiers beans garnished with sausages and garlic sausage) and Comminges (with pork rinds and mutton). There is also a fish *cassoulet*, made with salt cod (which replaces the duck or goose).

Whatever the ingredients, the États Généraux de la Gastronomie française of 1966 decreed the following proportions for *cassoulet*: at least 30% pork (which can include sausage and Toulouse sausage), mutton or preserved goose; 70% haricot beans and stock, fresh pork rinds, herbs and flavourings.

The preparation of *cassoulet* requires that the beans and the meat are cooked at the same time (pork and mutton are cooked separately) while braising the rinds and cooking the sausages. A final coating of breadcrumbs is essential for a fine golden crust. Purists insist on certain refinements, such as rubbing the cooking pot with a garlic clove and, above all, breaking the gratin crust several times (seven times in Castelnaudary and eight times in Toulouse).

Now far removed from the mutton and bean stew made by the Romans and Spaniards, *cassoulet* has become a classic dish. In 1909, at a journalists' lunch, President Fallières, a native of Lot-et-Garonne, had a *cassoulet* made to his own instructions, which he then ordered to be put on the menu at the Élysée Palace once a week. But this dish remains a subject of controversy, especially regarding the addition of mutton; this is considered by some a sacrilege (except in the Toulouse version, according to Clos-Jouve) and by others, such as Prosper Montagné and James de Coquet, as indispensable. Curnonsky, however, would accept only the inclusion of poached sausages, a small piece of shoulder of lamb, goose in tomato sauce and garlic sausage.

The *Guide gourmand de la France* (Hachette) by Gault and Millau describes the preparation of the Toulouse *cassoulet*: 'We give this recipe for the *cassoulet de Toulouse*, as set out by the famous local cook and eminent gastronomic writer from the south-west, Louis Cazals. Soak the white haricot beans (known as *cocos*) for 12 hours. Boil them in salted water for a good hour, then drain. Return them to the cooker (stove), this time into boiling water, and add the bacon rinds, which have first been blanched and rolled up, the carrots, cut into rounds, and some garlic cloves. Add a sausage and leave the ingredients to cook together. Meanwhile, lightly brown a goose quarter with good-quality goose fat and two crushed garlic cloves, plus two peeled seeded tomatoes. Add the goose to the haricot beans and leave to cook for a further 2 hours. Do not forget a bouquet garni. Put the sausage (cut into slices) and the haricot beans into a stewpot or earthenware casserole, add the fresh sausage and cook in a slow oven. Allow a crust to form, which you then break eight times during the cooking. Serve in the cooking pot. To conclude, it is said that the Toulouse cassoulet is the most complete (or least simple) of all the regional *cassoulets*. It is, of course, subject to minor variations. The dish is generally accompanied by a Corbières wine (which is found more and more often on the wine lists of Toulouse) or, better still, by a hearty old Villaudric.'

The syndicat d'initiative (tourist office) of Castelnaudary, which proclaims its city to be 'the world capital of *cassoulet*', provides the following recipe: 'Here we give the ingredients for the *true* dish as it is still prepared by local families in Castelnaudary. First of all is the choice of bean, preferably the *lingot*. Secondly the meat – hock of pork, pork ribs, pork rinds, local sausage and preserved goose liver from Lauragais. Place the beans in a pot (preferably earthenware), cover them with cold water and blanch them by bringing to the boil for 5 to 10 minutes. Drain off this water and cover the beans with fresh warm water. Garnish by adding a good helping of pork rinds cut into reasonably large pieces and add some hash made from a large piece of salted fat, a small piece of slightly rancid fat and a generous quantity of garlic. Add some salt and leave to simmer for about 2 hours, preferably on the hearth. The beans should be well cooked but remain firm. In a large pan melt the fat off the preserved goose, then remove the goose and fry the meat in the fat. (If preserved goose is not available, goose or pork fat can be used.) When these preparations have been completed, place the ingredients in a *cassole* (never use any other type of utensil, for example, enamel or glass) as follows: first a layer of beans, rinds and juice; then a layer of meat, which is then covered by the remaining beans. Pepper the surface generously. Separately cook a fresh sausage in a frying pan or in the oven until it is lightly browned. Then coil the sausage on the surface of the *cassoulet*, press down lightly and sprinkle the whole surface with the boiling hot fat from the sausage. Put the *cassole* into the oven and leave to cook until a brown uniform crust forms on top. Break the crust and allow it to reform several times, as desired. Check the *cassoulet* from time to time and if it appears to be dry, sprinkle with warm water, but be careful not to drown it. Allow to cook for 3 to 4 hours. Serve very hot in its cooking pot. Make it the day before to serve at lunchtime, or early in the morning for the evening meal.

Important note – Never use smoked fat, smoked meat, Strasbourg sausages or mutton.

RECIPES

cassoulet (1)

(from a recipe given by a gourmet from Castelnaudary) Use a glazed earthenware pot, known as a *toupin*, to cook white haricot (navy) beans – those from Pamiers and Cazères are best – with seasoning, plus the usual meat, vegetables, garlic and herbs. When the beans are well cooked but still whole, put them in a special cooking pot (of Issel earthenware), the sides of which have been lined with fresh bacon rinds (these are cooked with the beans). Add the pork hock, fat, sausage and a leg of preserved goose. Sprinkle the top with coarse breadcrumbs and then with goose fat. Place in a baker's oven (ideally fuelled by mountain gorse) and cook gently for several hours. When a beautiful golden crust has formed, break it with a wooden spoon; repeat this essential operation two or three times. Then you will have a fine cassoulet that can be served with either a fine red Aquitaine wine or an old Minervois wine.

cassoulet (2) ◆

(from a recipe by Prosper Montagné) For 8 people, soak 1 litre (1¾ pints, 4⅓ cups) white haricot (navy) beans in cold water for a few hours (but do not allow them to ferment). Drain, then add to them 300 g (11 oz) pork fat, 200 g (7 oz) fresh pork rind tied in a bundle, a carrot, an onion studded with cloves and a bouquet garni containing 3 garlic cloves. Season carefully, using very little salt as the fat contains salt. Add enough water to allow the beans to 'swim' well. Simmer gently so that the beans remain intact but are well cooked.

Place some dripping or goose fat in a separate pan and brown 800 g (1¾ lb) pork sparerib or bladebone and 500 g (18 oz) boned shoulder of mutton, well seasoned with salt and pepper. When the meats are well browned, put them in a large frying pan containing 200 g (7 oz, 1¾ cups) cooked chopped onion, a bouquet garni and 2 crushed garlic cloves. Cover and cook. Moisten from time to time with good meat juice or stock from the stockpot. If desired, add some spoonfuls of tomato purée or 3 peeled, seeded and crushed tomatoes.

When the beans are almost cooked, remove the vegetables and bouquet garni and add the pork, mutton and onions, together with some garlic sausage, a leg of preserved goose or duck, and, if desired, a piece of home-made sausage. Simmer gently for a further hour. Remove all the meat from the beans and drain. Cut the mutton, pork and goose (or duck) into equal pieces and cut the rind into rectangles, the sausage into slices (removing the skin) and the fresh sausage into small rings.

Line a large earthenware dish or individual dishes with the rind, then add a layer of beans, a layer of the various meats (moistened with their sauce) and another layer of beans, seasoning each layer with freshly ground pepper. On top of the final layer place the pieces of fat, the remaining rind and some sliced sausage. Sprinkle with white breadcrumbs and melted goose fat. Cook gently in the oven (preferably a baker's oven) for about 1½ hours. Serve in the cooking dish.

CASTIGLIONE, À LA A preparation in which small pieces of meat are fried, arranged on slices of aubergine (eggplant) fried in butter, topped with slices of poached bone marrow and garnished with large mushroom caps stuffed with risotto and gratin mixtures. Sole or fish fillets (plaice, whiting) *à la castiglione* are glazed with white wine and garnished with mushrooms, lobster pieces and steamed potatoes.

CASTILLANE, À LA A term used for tournedos (filets mignons) or noisettes of lamb, topped with crushed tomatoes thickened in olive oil (these are sometimes placed in tartlets and arranged beside the meat) and served with croquette potatoes and fried onion rings. The sauce is based on veal and tomato. This preparation is used only for lamb or mutton, which is a famous product of the Castile region of Spain.

CATALANE, À LA A term used to describe garnishes inspired by Spanish cooking (Catalonia, in particular, is famous for its seafood and garlic). Chicken, lamb or veal sautéed *à la catalane* is garnished with tomato quarters fried in butter, chestnuts poached in consommé, chipolatas and stoned (pitted) blanched olives. Large pieces of meat are garnished with diced aubergines (eggplants) fried in oil and rice pilaf. Grilled tournedos and noisettes of lamb are arranged on a bed of artichoke hearts and surrounded by grilled tomatoes.

RECIPES

fried eggs à la catalane

Cook separately some seeded tomato halves and aubergine (eggplant) slices in olive oil. Add salt, pepper, a little crushed garlic and some chopped parsley. Cover a serving dish with the vegetables. Fry the eggs in the same pan and slide on to the vegetables.

sausages à la catalane

In a frying pan, fry 1 kg (2¼ lb) thick sausages in dripping until they are golden, then drain and remove them. Add 2 tablespoons flour to the pan and stir until it is coloured, then add 1 teaspoon tomato purée (paste), 120 ml (4½ fl oz, ½ cup) white wine, and 120 ml (4½ fl oz, ½ cup) stock. Stir well, cook for 10 minutes, then sieve. Blanch 24 peeled garlic cloves. Return the sausages to the frying pan, add the garlic, a bouquet garni and a piece of dried orange peel. Pour the sieved sauce on to the sausages, cover and cook gently for 30 minutes. Fresh breadcrumbs may be used instead of flour, if desired.

stuffed aubergines à la catalane

Cut 2 good-sized aubergines (eggplants) in half lengthways to form boat shapes. Leaving a 1 cm (½ in) rim around the top, scoop out the flesh without damaging the skin. Chop the flesh together with 2 hard-boiled (hard-cooked) eggs, 2 crushed garlic cloves and some parsley. In olive oil, lightly cook 2 large chopped onions per aubergine, add it to the egg and aubergine mixture, and fill the aubergine boats. Arrange in an oiled ovenproof dish, sprinkle with fresh breadcrumbs and oil, and cook in a preheated oven at 220°C (425°F, gas 7–8).

CATERER One who prepares meals to order for private individuals or dishes to be taken away.

Under the Ancien Régime, *traiteurs* formed a corporation, specializing in weddings, feasts and banquets. They also had the right to hire out cutlery, crockery and table linen. The profession of *traiteur* was at that time considered more honourable than that of innkeeper or *rôtisseur*. The *traiteur* was the predecessor of the restaurateur, the difference being that customers were not able to eat on his premises. In addition, as Brillat-Savarin said at the end of the 18th century, *traiteurs* 'could only sell whole joints; and anyone wishing to entertain friends had to order in advance, so that those who had not the good fortune to be invited to some wealthy house left the great city without discovering the delights of Parisian cuisine'. Restaurants were not yet in existence and respectable people did not frequent inns. However, following the success of restaurants towards the end of the 19th century, the term *traiteur* acquired a rather derogatory meaning and was applied to restaurants of the lowest class and wine merchants who provided meals.

The modern caterer specializes in banquets, cocktail parties and lunches, served either in the clients' homes or in hired rooms. These services can be provided by pastrycooks, confectioners, restaurateurs and delicatessen owners.

The kitchen of the pastrycook who provides a catering service is very different from that of the restaurateur, firstly because the transport and reheating of dishes require special methods and secondly because he has to cater sometimes for several thousand and sometimes for a mere dozen. The dishes provided typically include croustades, bouchées, timbales, vol-au-vent, pâtés, galantines and ballotines, chauds-froids, dishes in aspic, canapés and, of course, set pieces for special occasions and a variety of desserts, ice creams and petits fours. Restaurants providing a catering service often offer dishes from their menu which can be easily transported, such as cassoulet, sauerkraut, confit and civet.

CATFISH An American freshwater fish that inhabits calm waters and is found principally in the Mississippi basin. It is 30–35 cm (12–14 in) long with scaleless, sticky, blackish skin, a massive head with eight whisker-like barbels around the mouth and a second fatty dorsal fin. Despite its ugly appearance, the flesh is excellent and practically boneless. It can be prepared in the same way as trout or perch.

The European catfish (*Silurus glanis*) is a very large freshwater fish of central European origin, which is found in the Danube, some Swiss lakes and sometimes in the River Doubs in France. Growing up to 4 m (13 ft) long and weighing as much as 200 kg (440 lb), it has a massive six-barbed head, a small dorsal fin close to the head and a very long anal fin which extends over more than half the abdomen. Its flesh, which is firm and white but rather fatty, resembles that of the eel.

CAUCHOISE, À LA Describing dishes of the Caux region in France, especially saddle of hare or rabbit, marinated in white wine with herbs, cooked in the oven, then sprinkled with the reduced marinade and coated in a sauce made by binding the reduced juices with fresh thick cream and mustard. Serve garnished with Reinette apples fried in butter.

Sole *à la cauchoise* is braised in cider in the oven, then coated with a sauce made from the cooking juices and butter. It is garnished with shrimps (famous in the Caux region) cooked in a courtbouillon to which fried mussels, poached oysters and mushrooms have been added.

Cauchoise salad combines potato slices, slender celery sticks and slivers of cooked ham. It is seasoned with a sauce made of fresh cream, cider vinegar and chervil.

Cassoulet (2), see page 231.

RECIPE

tarte cauchoise

Prepare some short-crust pastry (basic pie dough). Roll into a ball and leave to rest in a cool place for at least I hour. Line a flan tin (tart pan) and bake blind. Soften 800 g (1¾ lb, 5 cups) finely chopped onion in butter. Beat I whole egg, mix in 200 ml (7 fl oz, ¾ cup) double (heavy) cream, then add salt, pepper and a little grated nutmeg. Allow to thicken on a gentle heat, without boiling, then add the onions. Fill the flan case with chicken leftovers or finely chopped veal or ham and cover them with the onion mixture. Dot with flecks of butter and cook in a preheated oven at 200°C (400°F, gas 6) for 15–20 minutes.

CAUL Also known as caul fat. A thin membrane veined with fat that encloses the stomach of animals, particularly that of the pig. In charcuterie, the caul is soaked to soften it and make it easier to handle; it is used, for example, to wrap around the sausagemeat when making crépinettes. Numerous other culinary preparations use caul to hold together the ingredients during cooking: stuffed cabbage leaves, larded calf's liver, fricandeau, foie gras, pâtés and terrines.

CAULDRON A large deep vessel made of cast iron or copper, with a detachable handle. It was formerly used for cooking thick soups and stews in the hearth, hanging from a chimney-hook. Varying in shape according to different regions (curved sides, with or without feet), it is used today mainly for decoration.

CAULIFLOWER Described by Arab botanists and known to the Romans, the cauliflower originally came from Cyprus and was introduced to France from Italy in the middle of the 16th century. Having been served to Louis XIV, the cauliflower was cultivated extensively, particularly in Brittany. The edible part is the flower head, popularly known as the 'heart' or 'head'; it is white, compact and hard with many compressed flower buds. The trimmed cauliflower may weigh 1–2.5 kg (2¼–5½ lb). Very small cauliflowers can also be found, each providing a single portion. These are firm and white, but do not have the flavour of the large cauliflowers.

The heart is surrounded by crisp bluish-green leaves, whose condition is a good guide to the freshness of the heart. The heart should be compact, white, firm and undamaged, with no green shoots between the florets. The leaves should be very crisp; do not buy a cauliflower without leaves – it is probably old. Cauliflowers are sold individually, not by weight, and only about half is usable. Allow about 200 g (7 oz) per person if served cooked and 100 g (4 oz) if served raw.

■ **Cooking cauliflowers** Cauliflower is the most easily digested member of the cabbage family and can be cooked either whole or as florets. It often gives off a strong smell during cooking. It can be blanched in fast-boiling unsalted water, then cooked in a white stock; a crust of stale bread can be added to absorb some of the smell. Lemon juice may be added after cooking to keep the cauliflower white. It can be eaten raw, in a vegetable fondue, cooked in water (for soup, purée or cold salad), in a soufflé, au gratin, *à la hollandaise, à la polonaise,* and also lightly braised, sautéed or fried after blanching. It is included in pickles and is a feature of all Du Barry preparations. The leaf ribs and the stump (core) may be used to prepare soups or vegetable loaves.

RECIPES

cauliflower au gratin

Divide the heart into florets and cook them in salted water or steam. Remove, drain and toss them in butter. Transfer to a buttered gratin dish, coat with Mornay sauce, sprinkle with grated Gruyère cheese and melted butter, and brown for about 10 minutes in a preheated oven at 230°C (450°F, gas 8). The Gruyère may be replaced by Parmesan, which may be sprinkled in the dish before adding the cauliflower.

sautéed cauliflower

Divide the heart into florets and steam them until they are still slightly firm and do not disintegrate. Heat some butter in a frying pan or sauté pan and lightly brown the florets. Arrange them in a vegetable dish and moisten with the cooking butter. Cauliflower may also be sautéed in olive oil with chopped garlic.

additional recipe See *du Barry.*

CAVEAU A literary, epicurean and gastronomic society founded in Paris in 1729 by Piron, Collé, Gallet and Crébillon the Younger, during a dinner at Landelles' famous restaurant, Le Caveau, in the Rue Buci. Boucher, Rameau and Maurepas were also members. The rule of the society was strict: any member who lacked decorum during the discussions had to drink water. The society was dissolved in 1757 after internal disputes, but was restarted some years later at the Palais-Royal on the initiative of General Pelletier. It lasted until 1796 and was patronized by the performers of the Vaudeville theatre, who published nine volumes of songs entitled *Les Dîners du Vaudeville.* A new Caveau, founded by Armand Gouffé, was named the Caveau Moderne – Ségur the Older, Désaugiers, Cadet-Gassicourt, Grimod de La Reynière and Béranger were members. For several years the society published *Le Journal des gourmands et des belles,* and it held dinners at the Rocher de Cancale until 1817. The last Caveau was reformed in 1834 but did not last long and never achieved the success of its predecessor.

CAVIAR Sturgeon's eggs that have been salted and allowed to mature. The word comes from the Italian *caviale,* itself derived from the Turkish *kâwyâr.* It appears as early as 1532 in Rabelais' *Pantagruel,* in which caviar is described as the choice hors d'oeuvre; Colbert organized the production of caviar in the Gironde using the sturgeons passing through the estuary. But the caviar we know today is Russian. It was introduced to France in the 1920s following the exile of Russian princes; during the Universal Exhibition of 1925 the Petrossian Brothers learnt, through their Russian friends, that caviar was known to very few French people. Charles Ritz formally launched caviar by putting it permanently on the menu at his hotel.

The sturgeon lives in the sea, but returns in winter to estuaries throughout temperate regions of Asia to lay its eggs. Today the Caspian Sea provides 98% of the world's caviar. The sturgeon was still common in the Gironde at the beginning of the 20th century, but it became so rare that fishing for it is prohibited.

The former Soviet Union was for a long time the sole producer of caviar. But since 1953, factories on Iran's Caspian coast have produced 180 tonnes annually; Russia produces 1,800 tonnes every year.

The eggs constitute about 10% of the female's body weight. After they have been removed, they are washed, drained, put into brine, drained again and finally packed into tins (cans). There are two sorts: caviar in grains and pressed caviar. The name 'red caviar' is sometimes used incorrectly for salmon eggs.

■ **Types of caviar** Sold fresh or sometimes pasteurized, there are three types, differentiated by size, colour and species of sturgeon.

• BELUGA The most expensive and produced by the largest species, which can weigh up to 800 kg (1,760 lb). The eggs are more or less dark grey, firm, heavy and well separated. These are the biggest but most fragile eggs, and if they burst the caviar becomes oily.

• OSSETRA Characterized by smaller more even grains, which are golden yellow to brown and quite oily; considered by many as the best.

• SEVRUGA Produced by small sturgeons, which are the most prolific and give very small light- to dark-grey eggs. This is the cheapest type.

■ **Pressed caviar** This is made from the ripest eggs, taken towards the end of the fishing season, which are then compressed. About 5 kg (11 lb) fresh caviar are needed to make 1 kg (2¼ lb) pressed caviar. It has a strong and rather oily taste and is sometimes considered too salty, although it is appreciated by Russian connoisseurs.

Caviar is a semi-conserve and perishable; it should be kept between –2°C and +4°C (28–39°F). As an hors d'oeuvre, allow 50 g (2 oz, 3½ tablespoons) per person. It should be served cold but not frozen, preferably on crushed ice; take the tin (can) out of the refrigerator an hour before serving. Blinis and soured (sour) cream or lightly buttered toast make an ideal accompaniment. Never use lemon, which affects the taste.

RECIPES

raw scallops with caviar
Open and trim the scallops. In an earthenware dish, mix 2 tablespoons pure olive oil and 3 tablespoons groundnut (peanut) oil. Slice the raw white and coral meat into rings. Dip each ring in the oil mixture, wipe off the excess oil and put them on a plate, allowing 2 scallops per serving. Season each plate with 3 pinches of salt and 3 turns of the pepper mill. With the tip of a coffeespoon handle, place 5–6 grains of caviar on each ring and surround the caviar grains with slices of coral meat. Serve with hot buttered toast.

smoked salmon frivolities with caviar
Cut six 18 × 7.5 cm (7 × 3 in) rectangles from 6 very fine, large slices of smoked salmon and set aside. Place the leftovers in a blender and add 25 g (1 oz, 2 tablespoons) unsalted butter, at room temperature. Purée the contents briefly until smooth. Gently heat 60 ml (2 fl oz, ¼ cup) prawn stock over a low flame. Add 1½ sheets of leaf gelatine or 1¼ teaspoons (½ envelope) powdered gelatine, previously softened or sponged in cold water, to the stock and stir until dissolved. Pour this mixture into the blender, then add 1 drop of Worcestershire sauce and 2 drops of Tabasco. Pulse the blender just 2 or 3 times. Whip 120 ml (4½ fl oz, ½ cup) chilled double (heavy) cream in a cold mixing bowl until it forms stiff peaks on the whisk. Add one-third of the salmon purée and stir carefully until thoroughly combined, then stir in the rest of the purée.

Place pieces of cling film (plastic wrap), slightly larger than the rectangles of salmon, on the work surface. Lay the pieces of salmon on the cling film and spread 2 tablespoons of the mousse lengthways along the centre of each. Using the cling film, roll up the salmon slices from their long sides into cigar shapes. Twist the ends of the cling film to keep the salmon rolls in shape. Chill for at least 2 hours, but not more than 24 hours.

Remove the cling film from the rolls and cut them in half. Arrange in a V-shape on very cold plates and garnish with a ribbon of caviar along the line where the edges meet. Garnish with slices of lemon and serve.

CAVOUR The name given to two garnishes inspired by Piedmontese cooking and named after the Italian statesman. One is used with veal escalopes (scallops) or veal sweetbreads, which are fried, drained and arranged on polenta biscuits. They are then surrounded with grilled (broiled) mushrooms and garnished with puréed chicken livers and slices of truffle.

The other Cavour garnish, for large pieces of meat, consists of croquettes of semolina and ravioli.

CELERIAC A variety of celery grown for its fleshy swollen stem base, which can weigh 800 g–1 kg (1¾–2¼ lb). Celeriac has a rough surface and thick skin. It is sold without the leaves, looking like a heavy white ball. Select vegetables that have as even a surface as possible to avoid waste when peeling. The celeriac should not be cracked. Celeriac is treated like the majority of root vegetables in that it is peeled and (usually) cut up before cooking. It can be used raw – grated, shredded or cut into sticks. Its pale flesh discolours with prolonged exposure to air, so it should be tossed with lemon juice or a suitable dressing. Celeriac is milder than celery and it has a 'firm' rather than crisp texture. Coarsely grated or shredded, it goes well with creamy dressings.

Celeriac can be cooked in a variety of dishes. Plain boiled celeriac can be mashed with butter or puréed with cream; it goes well with potatoes, mashed to a smooth and fluffy texture. It can be braised and served coated with sauce or used in soups and casseroles. Fine strips of celeriac are suitable for stir-frying.

Celery salt, which is extracted from dried pulverized celeriac, is used as a condiment for tomato juice, vegetable moulds and salad sauces. It is also used in salt-free diets.

RECIPES

preparation of celeriac

Peel like a potato, rinse and sprinkle with lemon juice. To eat cooked, cut into pieces and blanch for 5 minutes in boiling salted water. To serve as a vegetable, it may be braised, cooked in its juices or prepared as a julienne and braised. It can also be prepared as a purée (like cardoons) and as a cream soup. Steamed in slices, it retains all its flavour.

celeriac croquettes

Peel a celeriac root, cut it into pieces and blanch. Then cook in salted water for about 30 minutes. Add the same weight of peeled potatoes and leave until cooked. Drain the vegetables and dry, either in the oven or in a saucepan. Pass them through a vegetable mill and mix the resulting purée with egg yolks – 4 per 1 kg (2¼ lb) of purée – and chopped parsley. Divide the paste obtained into little balls, flatten them out and coat in batter. Plunge the croquettes into boiling oil or fat and leave to turn golden, then remove and drain on paper towels. Serve with roast beef, veal, pork, leg of lamb or leg of venison.

celeriac en rémoulade

Peel a large celeriac root, grate it coarsely and blanch for 2 minutes in boiling salted water. Drain and refresh with cold water. Dry thoroughly. Add rémoulade sauce and, if desired, sprinkle with chopped parsley.

celeriac julienne

Peel a celeriac root and cut into thick strips. Blanch for 3 minutes in boiling salted water, then refresh in cold water and drain. Put the strips into a pan with a knob of butter and a little sugar, to taste. Cover and sweat for about 15 minutes. Adjust the seasoning and sprinkle with finely chopped herbs. Use to garnish roast meats, fried meats and braised fish, such as cod.

stuffed celeriac à la paysanne

Cut some small celeriac roots in half and blanch them. Scoop out the pulp, leaving a lining at least 1 cm (½ in) thick. Dice the pulp and add an equal volume of both carrots and onions softened in butter. Season with salt and pepper. Fill the half celeriacs with this mixture and place on a buttered ovenproof dish. Sprinkle with grated Gruyère cheese and small knobs of butter. Pour 3 tablespoons stock into the dish and cook in a preheated oven at 220°C (425°F, gas 7) until browned.

other recipes See *ragoût, salpicon, soup.*

CELERY
A vegetable grown for its roots, stems, leaves and seeds, all of which can be used. Wild celery, from which cultivated strains have been developed, was used both gastronomically, for soups and fish dishes, and therapeutically, as smelling salts. For a long time, both popular opinion and gastronomic writers considered celery to be an aphrodisiac.

Several varieties of cultivated celery are grown for their white fleshy sticks, which are easily broken when fresh. Canned celery hearts and slices, preserved in natural juice, are used as a garnish; celery is also very suitable for freezing. It can be kept fresh for several days if the bottoms of the sticks are stood in cold salted water; it becomes limp if simply put in the refrigerator. The sticks are eaten raw, in mixed salads or cooked.

The leaves, fresh or dried, can serve as a garnish for salads, soups, sauces and stock and may be used in braised dishes. The seeds are used as a seasoning, having a taste similar to fennel. Celery salt is prepared from celeriac.

RECIPES

preparation of celery

Remove the hard outer stems and the green leafy branches. Trim the base to a point and cut the sticks to a length of about 20 cm (8 in). For eating raw, detach the sticks from one another, wash them and remove the stringy fibres. For cooking, wash the trimmed celery in cold water, splaying out the stems. Remove the stringy outer sticks, rinse the rest, then blanch in boiling salted water for 10 minutes. Drain, salt the insides and tie the sticks in bunches. Braised celery hearts can accompany fatty meats, roasts and chicken. Celery can also be cooked in béchamel sauce, au gratin, in meat juice or gravy, or with bone marrow. Celery purée is used in soups and in a sauce for boiled or braised poultry.

braised celery

Drain some blanched celery sticks on a cloth. Tie them in bunches of two or three, and place them in a buttered flameproof casserole lined with bacon rinds or chopped bacon, chopped onions and sliced carrots. Add sufficient stock to cover the vegetables and seasoning to taste. Bring to the boil over the heat, then cover and transfer to a pre-heated oven at 180°C (350°F, gas 4) to cook for 1½ hours.

Celery can be prepared *au maigre* by omitting the bacon rinds and replacing the stock with water.

celery in butter
Blanch and drain the sticks and place them in a well-buttered pan. Add salt and pepper. Moisten with several spoonfuls of white stock or water, cover and cook for about 45 minutes.

celery sauce
Trim and slice the tender sticks and hearts from two bunches of celery. Place in a saucepan with a bouquet garni and an onion studded with cloves. Add sufficient stock just to cover the contents, cover and heat until simmering. Simmer until the celery is tender. Purée the celery with its cooking juices and return it to the rinsed pan. Add 200 ml (7 fl oz, ¾ cup) cream sauce*, and reduce until the required consistency is achieved. Adjust the seasoning and sprinkle with very finely chopped parsley. This sauce can accompany boiled or braised poultry.

celery with béchamel sauce
Braise the celery and arrange in a buttered dish. Sweat for 10 minutes. Cover with béchamel sauce and simmer for a few minutes.

celery with cream
Blanch the celery and cut each stick in half lengthways. Arrange in a buttered flameproof casserole and season with salt and pepper. Cover with light stock and bring to the boil. Cover the casserole and transfer to a preheated oven at 180°C (350°F, gas 4) to cook for about 1 hour.

Drain the celery and bend the pieces in half, arranging them in a vegetable dish. To make the sauce, skim any butter off the cooking liquid, reduce, and add 3 tablespoons béchamel* sauce. Moisten with 200 ml (7 fl oz, ¾ cup) double (heavy) cream and reduce by half. Add 1 tablespoon butter, mix, sieve and pour the sauce over the celery.

other recipes See *milanaise, royale.*

CÉLESTINE A chicken dish named by the chef at the Cercle restaurant in Lyon in honour of the owner of the restaurant. A young chicken is fried with mushrooms and peeled tomatoes, flamed with Cognac, moistened with white wine and served with powdered garlic and chopped parsley. This recipe was given by its creator to Lucien Tendret, who made it famous.

The name is also used for a chicken soup thickened with tapioca and garnished with strips of pancake seasoned with fines herbes, poached chicken breast and a coating of chervil (a brunoise of truffles can replace the fines herbes in the pancakes). Certain ingredients of this soup are found in omelette *à la Célestine.*

CELERY AND CELERIAC

white-stemmed celery

green-stemmed celery

celeriac

RECIPE

omelette à la Célestine
Prepare two small flat omelettes. Place one on a round plate, garnish with chicken breast and cover with a thick cream sauce containing chopped parsley. Place the second omelette on top and sprinkle with melted butter.

CENDRÉ One of various cow's-milk cheeses produced in Burgundy (Aisy Cendré, which contains 45% fat) or in Orléanais and Champagne (the Cendrés of Argonne, Riceys and Rocroi, which contain 30% fat). Soft-centred and yellow in colour, Cendrés are fairly firm to the touch and disc-shaped. They are matured in wooden boxes or pots lined with the ashes and have a fairly strong flavour.

CENDRE, SOUS LA A rustic method of cooking, meaning literally 'under the ashes', which requires an open hearth or a wood fire. It is used mainly for cooking potatoes and truffles. It is also possible to cook poultry or an animal with a protective coat, such as a hedgehog, in this way.
• POTATOES SOUS LA CENDRE Preferably choose some fine Fontenay potatoes; wash and dry them. Slide them under the hot coals (with the fire extinguished) and leave without disturbing for 35–40 minutes. Dust them off and serve with semi-salted butter. They can be cooked wrapped in foil if the fire is still glowing and there are few ashes.

• TRUFFLES SOUS LA CENDRE Brush the truffles carefully in cold water, wash and wipe them. Dip them in Cognac or Armagnac, then wrap them singly in pieces of buttered foil or greaseproof (wax) paper. If the embers are very hot, the truffles are placed in an earthenware pie dish with a lid, which is slipped under the embers. If the fire is almost out, the wrapped truffles may be placed directly under the cinders. Cooking takes 35–45 minutes.

CENTREPIECE An item of gold plate or porcelain that is placed in the centre of the table as a decoration for a large formal dinner. The centrepiece is usually in the form of a long tray lined with mirror, on which candelabra, baskets of fruit or vases of flowers are displayed.

The use of centrepieces goes back to the Middle Ages, but it was in the 17th, 18th and 19th centuries that this type of table decoration had its heyday.

CEP *cèpe* An edible boletus mushroom with a large bulbous stalk that resembles a tree trunk; known as porcini in Italian and particularly popular as a dried fungi. There are over 20 edible varieties, which may be recognized by their swollen stalks and the distinctive tubes (the 'choke' or 'beard') that line the inner surface of the cap.

Two varieties are highly valued in gastronomy: the Bordeaux cep (whitish to dark brown cap; swollen stalk; becomes cylindrical when the mushroom is old), traditionally known as the 'penny bun' in England, and the bronzed cep (very dark-coloured; bulging stalk) which is particularly delicious and flavoursome in mid-September. These varieties are grown in south-western France, Sologne and Alsace and are sold between July and October. The pine cep (mahogany-brown) and the reticulated cep (yellow-ochre) are also very highly esteemed.

Ceps are always better when young; then it is sufficient to wipe them gently with a damp cloth. The bases of the stalks are removed when they are too ripe or maggoty. In wet weather, the 'choke' of certain ceps becomes slimy and must be removed, as it would spoil any dish.

The finest ceps may be eaten raw in salad, cut into thin slices, but they are especially delicious cooked, particularly in an omelette, in a velouté or as a garnish (for confit, stew or river fish). They may be preserved by drying or in oil.

Many French regions have cep specialities. In Auvergne, Châtaigneraie ceps are eaten stuffed. In Aquitaine, they are prepared *en cocotte*, stuffed or cooked in embers. In Poitou and south-western France, they are grilled (broiled) in walnut oil. Bordeaux ceps, always cooked in oil (rather than butter), are dressed with garlic or parsley. Auch is famous for its ceps in white wine. In Gascony, they are eaten *à la viande* (studded with garlic and accompanied by raw ham), grilled, in a stew or with salmis. Brantôme is one of the most important producing centres in France; several hundred tonnes of ceps are sent to Bordeaux and Paris each year.

The culinary value of ceps has been appreciated only since the 18th century. Their popularity can be traced to the court of Stanislas Leszczýnski in Lorraine, hence the adjective *polonais* (Polish) applied to the Bordeaux cep.

RECIPES

baked ceps
Wipe 4 perfect cep caps. Make a cross-shaped cut on top of each and place in an ovenproof dish or roasting tin (pan). Season lightly with salt and pepper and add a drop of olive oil. Put in a preheated oven at 240°C (475°F, gas 9) for 5 minutes. Turn the ceps, season again and bake for a further 3 minutes. Arrange the ceps with their undersides facing upwards and garnish each with a very thin slice of lightly cooked foie gras or diced, lightly grilled Parma ham. Serve with a red chicory salad, in a dressing of sherry vinegar and olive oil.

ceps à la bordelaise
Trim the ceps; cut them into thin slices if they are very large, halve them if of medium size, or leave them whole if they are small. Put them in a shallow frying pan with oil and lemon juice, leave to cook slowly with the lid on for 5 minutes, then drain. Heat some oil in another frying pan, place the ceps in it and sprinkle with salt and pepper. Lightly brown them, then drain. Sprinkle with chopped parsley and serve very hot.

In Paris, ceps *à la bordelaise* are lightly fried and served with chopped shallots, fried bread and chopped parsley.

ceps à la hongroise
Trim and wash 500 g (18 oz) ceps. Cut them into thin slices if they are large; leave them whole if they are small. Cook them slowly in butter with 2 tablespoons chopped onion, salt, pepper and 1 teaspoon paprika. Then add sufficient crème fraîche to cover the contents of the pan and reduce. Finally, sprinkle with chopped parsley if desired.

ceps à la mode béarnaise
Trim and wash some large ceps and put them in the oven to release the excess juices. Stud them with garlic, sprinkle with salt and pepper, coat with oil and grill (broil) them. Chop and mix some breadcrumbs, garlic and parsley and brown this mixture in a frying pan with oil. Scatter the grilled ceps on top and serve immediately.

ceps à la provençale
Prepare as for ceps *à la bordelaise*, but use olive oil and fry for longer. When cooked, sprinkle with chopped garlic as well as parsley.

ceps au gratin
Trim the ceps, separating the caps from the stalks; season with salt and pepper, then coat with melted butter or oil. Arrange the caps in a buttered or

oiled gratin dish with their tops downwards. Chop the stalks and add 1 chopped shallot for every 200 g (7 oz, 2 cups) stalks, together with some parsley; brown in oil and season with salt and pepper. Finally add 1 tablespoon fresh breadcrumbs for every 200 g (7 oz, 2 cups) stalks and mix all the ingredients together. Fill the caps with this mixture, sprinkle with some more fresh breadcrumbs, moisten with oil or melted butter, and brown in a preheated oven at 240°C (475°F, gas 9) or under a hot grill (broiler).

ceps en terrine

Trim and wash 800 g (1¾ lb) ceps and separate the caps from the stalks. Chop the stalks together with 3–4 garlic cloves, 3–4 shallots and a small bunch of parsley and brown everything in a shallow frying pan in 3 tablespoons olive oil. Add salt and pepper. Place the caps in a separate covered frying pan with 2 tablespoons olive oil and some salt, and heat gently until they have discharged their juices. Drain them. Line the bottom and sides of an ovenproof earthenware dish with very thin rashers (slices) of smoked belly bacon. In it, place a layer of the caps, then the chopped mixture, then a second layer of caps. Cover with more smoked rashers, put the lid on the dish, place in a preheated oven at 200°C (400°F, gas 6) and leave to cook for just under an hour.

grilled ceps

Thoroughly clean and trim some fresh ceps. Lightly slit the caps and marinate the ceps for at least 30 minutes in a mixture of olive oil, lemon juice, chopped garlic, chopped parsley, a pinch of cayenne, salt and pepper. Drain the ceps and grill (broil) them. Sprinkle with chopped parsley and serve very hot. Alternatively, the ceps, moistened with melted butter or simply washed and wiped, may be sprinkled with salt and pepper, quickly grilled and basted with oil or melted butter at the time of serving.

marinated ceps

Trim and wash 800 g (1¾ lb) ceps and cut into thin slices. Plunge them into boiling oil for 2 minutes, then cool them under cold water and wipe off the excess. For the marinade, heat a mixture of 200 ml (7 fl oz, ¾ cup) olive oil, 3 tablespoons wine vinegar, 1 tablespoon chopped fennel, 2 teaspoons lemon peel, a bay leaf cut into four, 2 small sprigs of thyme, salt and freshly ground pepper. Bring this mixture to the boil and leave to boil for 5 minutes. Place the ceps in an earthenware dish and cover with the boiling marinade, strained through a sieve. Add 2 large garlic cloves and 1 tablespoon chopped parsley. Stir, then leave in a cool place for at least 24 hours before serving.

other recipes See *chicken, egg (scrambled eggs), omelette (omelettes cooked with their flavouring), sauté.*

CÉPAGE The French word meaning variety of vine, or 'varietal'. The grape vine, *Vitis vinifera*, has existed since before records were kept. There are thousands of varieties, but in France only about 50 types are in use. The Institut National des Appellations d'Origine specifies the *cépages* for each AOC wine and others subject to regional controls. Some wines, such as red Bordeaux (claret), are made from several grape varieties in conjunction; others are made from a single variety – red Burgundy and Beaujolais, Muscadet, Sancerre, and so on. In Alsace the wines are named after the single grape varieties that are used to make them – Sylvaner, Riesling, Gewürztraminer, and others. It should be noted that in some regions a variety may have a local name or nickname; for example, the Chenin Blanc may be known as the Pineau de la Loire, and the Sauvignon is the Blanc Fumé of Pouilly-sur-Loire.

CEREAL Any of several grasses cultivated widely for their seeds (grain), which provide a staple food for humans and their livestock. Different cereals are grown in different regions of the globe: wheat and barley in temperate parts of Europe and Asia; rye and oats in northern and eastern Europe; rice in the wetter warm-temperate and subtropical parts of Asia; maize (corn) on the American continent; and millet and sorghum in Africa. Cereals in their simplest forms remain the basic foodstuff in many countries, especially the poorest ones, but industrialized countries have tended to favour more elaborate processed foods. Types of refined cereals that are easy to prepare and quick to cook have replaced crude grains. Products such as pastas, pastries, breads and breakfast cereals are popular. However, there is a renewed interest in natural foods, including unprocessed cereals.

Their dietary role as important sources of unrefined carbohydrate and fibre is valued and they are also appreciated for their texture, flavour and versatility.

• WHOLE CEREALS The husks have to be removed from some grains, such as rice, barley and oats, as they are too hard for human consumption. Wheat and rye can be milled with their husks. Refined cereals have less flavour and are less nutritious than whole cereals.

• FLAKES Grains of wheat, oats or maize (corn) that have been crushed, steam-cooked, crushed again and grilled.

• PUFFED GRAINS Grains of maize (corn) or rice that have been subjected to a vacuum, thus causing them to swell up; they are sometimes coated with sugar.

• PRETREATED GRAINS Grains that have been cooked slowly in their husks before refining; this operation concentrates the nutrients in the centre of the grain.

• PRECOOKED GRAINS Grains (whole or portions of grains) partially steam-cooked and then dried; this reduces the cooking time.

CERISE SUR LE GÂTEAU A milk chocolate gâteau, created in 1993 by Pierre Hermé (a French pastry chef born in 1961), who was responsible for the composition, and Yann Pennor, who designed it. The round gâteau consists of a *biscuit dacquoise* (crushed almond sponge mixed with butter cream) on which rests a layer of almond-flavoured puff pastry and chocolate cream filling separated by thin leaves of milk chocolate. The top consists of crème Chantilly flavoured with chocolate. This assembly is then cut into equal parts; six of these parts are piled up on top of each other and put in a milk chocolate shell, decorated with golden threads and topped with a crystallized (candied) cherry. The gâteau is presented in a specially made case, which gives the illusion that it is a large slice of cake lying on its side.

CERVELAS The French name for a type of saveloy.

CERVELLE DE CANUT A speciality of Lyons, traditionally served in taverns as a mid-morning snack. It consists of fairly soft curd cheese known as *claqueret*, which is well beaten, seasoned with salt and pepper and blended with shallot chopped with herbs, crème fraîche, white wine and a little oil.

CÉVENOLE, À LA A term describing one of many sweet or savoury dishes that contain chestnuts, a speciality of the Ardèche region of France. Used in purées, stews, whole or poached, chestnuts can accompany a range of roast and braised meats, including loin of pork, mutton, calves' sweetbreads, fillet of beef and game. Marrons glacés are used in a variety of hot, cold and iced sweets.

RECIPES

ragoût à la cévenole
The garnish for this ragoût consists of braised chestnuts, small glazed onions and very coarsely diced lean bacon, blanched and lightly fried. The pan juices from the braised meat of the ragoût are used to bind the garnish.

Sweet Dishes
Bavarian cream à la cévenole
Make a Bavarian cream mixture and add an equal volume of puréed marrons glacés flavoured with kirsch. Brush a round mould with sweet almond oil and heap the mixture into it. Set in the refrigerator, then turn out on to the serving dish. Decorate with piped Chantilly cream and halved marrons glacés.

choux à la cévenole
Prepare some sweet choux buns. Mix together equal volumes of chestnut cream and whipped cream sweetened with vanilla-flavoured sugar and fill the choux with it.

coupe glacé à la cévenole
Prepare separately 500 ml (17 fl oz, 2 cups) vanilla* ice cream and 300 ml (½ pint, 1¼ cups) Chantilly* cream. Add 1 liqueur glass of kirsch to 250 g (9 oz, 1¼ cups) marron-glacé fragments and divide equally between 4 sundae glasses. Cover each with

a layer of the vanilla ice cream and smooth the surface. Use a piping bag with a fluted nozzle to decorate with the Chantilly cream, then arrange some marrons glacés and sugar violets on top.

crêpes à la cévenole
Prepare some sweet pancakes. Spread them out on the worktop and cover each with a thin layer of marron-glacé purée flavoured with rum. Fold the pancakes over, arrange them in an ovenproof serving dish, dust with sugar and glaze in the oven. Serve very hot.

CEVICHE Also known as *cebiche*. A dish, characteristic of Peruvian cookery, that is based on raw fish marinated in lemon juice and is served with sweet limes, raw onion rings, tomatoes and boiled sweetcorn.

CHABICHOU A small goat's-milk cheese from Poitou, which contains 45% butterfat and has a soft centre and a natural crust. Usually in the shape of a truncated cone, but sometimes cylindrical, it weighs about 100 g (4 oz) and is sold unwrapped when farm-produced, wrapped in paper from a dairy. It may be eaten fresh. When ripened, it is firm without being hard, with a fairly pronounced flavour and a strong goatlike smell. It is at its best in the summer.

CHABLIS White Burgundy of worldwide repute. Situated between Tonnerre and Auxerre and crossed by the small unnavigable River Serein, the Chablis vineyard acquired fame because of the high quality of its white wines. Monks played a great part in the history of the vineyard. The first monks, in 867, were those of the abbey of Saint-Martin-de-Tours; the Cistercians of Pontigny arrived three centuries later. Since then, the sale of Chablis wines has been increasing all the time, in spite of the ravages of wars, vine phylloxera (in 1893) and, above all, frosts, which almost completely destroyed the vineyard in 1957 and did much damage in 1985. The name 'Chablis' has acquired common usage in the United States and Australia as a generic term to describe any dry white wine of unspecified origin. Within the European Union, its use is protected to refer only to the wines of the specific Chablis region.

Chablis, situated in the north of Burgundy, is nearer to certain vineyards of the Loire (Pouilly and Sancerre) than to Beaune. The vines are grown on hillsides in poor, shallow, chalky soil. The Chardonnay vine, which is called *beaunois* (of Beaune) in the region, is today the only one authorized for the production of AOC Chablis. The work of the grower, already arduous on such a barren soil, is often ruined by May frosts, as the vineyard is particularly exposed.

Chablis is a very dry white wine that can keep well. Pale yellow in colour with glints of green, it is at the same time powerful and delicate. There are, in order of merit, four categories – Chablis *grand cru*, Chablis *premier cru*, Chablis, and *petit Chablis* – originating from different soils and grown under conditions of varying exposure.

• Seven Chablis *grands crus* are officially recognized: Vaudésir, Les Clos, Grenouilles, Les Preuses, Bougros, Valmur and Blanchots.
• Chablis *premiers crus*, of which there are about 40, come from neighbouring parishes situated on the banks of the River Serein. Some well-known names are Montmains, Vaillons, Beugnons, Monte-de-Tonnerre and Fourchaume.
• Chablis and *petit Chablis* come from within the delimited AOC region.

CHAFING DISH A small item of portable kitchen equipment consisting of a pan fitted over a source of heat, usually a spirit lamp, but sometimes a butane gas burner or an electric element. Made of copper, stainless steel or silver plate, it is used to cook dishes at table, such as fondues (when it forms part of the fondue set) or flambé dishes.

It can also serve as a hotplate, for keeping cooked dishes warm.

CHAI This term, meaning 'wine store', is mostly used in the Bordeaux region, where underground cellars cannot be excavated, to designate the place where the wines mature, in vat or cask. The *maître de chai* decides when to draw off the wine and bottle it.

CHAKCHOUKA A traditional Arabian and North African dish comprising a ragoût of potatoes and onions, cooked in oil and seasoned with chilli peppers, harissa, and tomato sauce, over which eggs are broken; when the eggs are cooked, the dish is sprinkled with dried mint. The potatoes may be replaced by green peas, beans, a mixture of sweet peppers and tomatoes or courgettes (zucchini) and aubergines (eggplants). Chakchouka is often garnished with grilled merguez or slices of dried meat.

CHALEUTH A dessert of Jewish cuisine, made from a mixture of breadcrumbs, finely sliced apples, eggs and sugar, flavoured with rum, raisins and cinnamon. The dish is baked in an oiled casserole and served warm. It is also prepared by cooking sliced apples with sugar and cinnamon, again in a casserole but between two pastry crusts, the top being sprinkled with small pieces of fat.

CHALLAH Jewish loaf, pronounced 'Hallah' (the spelling that may be used in Arab countries). Made from white bread dough enriched with eggs, and sometimes flavoured with saffron, the loaf is plaited and glazed with egg, then sprinkled with poppy or seasame seeds. Challah is served on the sabbath and for festivals.

CHALONNAISE, À LA A classic garnish, now rarely used, intended to accompany poultry and calves' sweetbreads. Named after the town of Chalon-sur-Saône in France, it consists of cockscombs and kidneys, mushrooms and thin slices of truffle in a suprême sauce.

CHAMBARAND An unpasteurized soft cow's-milk cheese (45% fat) from Dauphiné, lightly pressed and with a natural washed crust. Created by the Trappists of the Abbey of Chambarand, it is a small round, 8 cm (3½ in) in diameter, weighing 165 g (5½ oz). Smooth and light ochre in colour, it has a mild, creamy flavour.

CHAMBERTIN A famous red Burgundy vineyard in the Côte-de-Nuits which, together with Chambertin Clos de Bèze, make up a 28 hectare (70 acre) vineyard. The names derive from the plot (*clos*) at Gevrey, given in about AD 630 to the monks of the Abbey of Bèze. The owner of the adjacent field, a man called Bertin, copied the monks' successful methods. The Pinot Noir is grown on a chalky soil that also includes ferruginous marls. There are a number of *grands crus* sites that may put their names before that of Chambertin – Charmes, Latricières, Mazis, Griottes, Ruchottes and Chapelle. They are all magnificent wines and should be served with respect and in the context of fine food.

RECIPES

Chambertin sauce
Peel and dice 2 carrots and 2 onions. Soften them with 20 g (¾ oz, 1½ tablespoons) butter in a shallow frying pan. Add a bouquet garni, 100 g (4 oz, 1¼ cups) chopped mushrooms (including stalks and peelings), half a chopped garlic clove, 250 g (9 oz) trimmings from white fish, salt and pepper. Moisten with 500 ml (17 fl oz, 2 cups) Chambertin and cook for at least 20 minutes in a covered pan. Remove the lid and reduce by a third. Pass through a conical strainer and bind with 1 tablespoon beurre manié.

fillets of sole with Chambertin
Season some fillets of sole with salt and pepper and fold them in two. Butter an ovenproof casserole and line the bottom with finely diced carrots, chopped onions, fresh crumbled thyme and a crushed bay leaf. Add some chopped mushroom stalks; the caps will serve for the garnish. Arrange the fillets in the dish, dab them with knobs of butter and barely cover them with Chambertin. Cover with the lid and bake in a preheated oven at 240°C (475°F, gas 9). Remove and drain the fillets, then arrange them in the serving dish; keep hot. Reduce the cooking liquid by one-third, pass through a conical strainer and bind the strained liquor with 1 tablespoon beurre manié. Coat the fillets with this sauce and garnish with sautéed mushroom caps and small glazed onions.

other recipes See *duck, salmon (cold dishes)*.

CHAMBOLLE-MUSIGNY A parish in the Côte-de-Nuits in Burgundy, famous for the Musigny and Bonnes Mares *grands crus* vineyards among others. These cover about 24 hectares (59 acres). Other well-known wines originating here, and combining their names with that of the parish, include *premiers crus* Les Amoureuses, Les Charmes, Les Combettes and Les Grands Murs. A very small quantity of white Chambolle-Musigny is made but is seldom found outside the region.

CHAMBORD A classic method of preparing large fish, such as carp, salmon or sole, which are to be cooked whole. Requiring high-quality produce and meticulous preparation, the fish is stuffed and braised in red wine and garnished with a mixture of quenelles of fish forcemeat, fillets of sole, sautéed soft roes, mushroom caps, truffles shaped like olives and crayfish cooked in a court-bouillon.

RECIPES

carp Chambord
Select a carp weighing 2–3 kg (4½–6½ lb), trim it, stuff it with a cream fish forcemeat and sew it up. Remove a thin strip of skin from the back on either side of the backbone and lard the bare area with small pieces of fat bacon. Butter a baking dish and line it generously with a brunoise of carrot, turnip, leek, celery and onion mixed with mushroom peelings and softened in butter. Add a bouquet garni. Two-thirds cover the carp with a mixture of fish stock and red wine, and cook in a preheated oven at 220°C (425°F, gas 7), basting from time to time. While the carp is cooking, slice some mushroom caps and cook them in a white court-bouillon. Remove the cooked carp, drain and arrange on the serving dish, keeping it hot. Prepare a little brown roux, add it to the pan juices from the carp along with 2 tablespoons tomato purée (paste) and cook for at least 30 minutes. Pass through a conical strainer. Return the carp to the oven until it is glazed, then coat it with the sauce and surround it with a Chambord garnish, including the mushroom caps.

Chambord sauce
Prepare a genevoise sauce with the braising stock of the fish that is being cooked: dilute it with red wine and coat the fish with it.

CHAMBRER A French term meaning to bring a wine to the temperature of the room where it will be drunk. White, rosé and sparkling wines are most enjoyable served at 5–10°C (41–50°F), but reds should be served at 15–18°C (59–64°F). The bottle should take a room temperature gradually and never be plunged into hot water or put near a fire. Not only will this shock the wine but currents will be created within it and churn up any sediment.

CHAMOIS A wild mammal, resembling a deer, that is considered one of the finest venisons. The flesh is tender and has a distinctive flavour without being too strong, especially in animals under three years old. It is hunted in the mountainous regions where it lives, such as the southern Alps and the Pyrenees, where it is called *izard* (wild goat). It is prepared in the same way as venison; old animals must be marinated.

CHAMPAGNE A sparkling wine produced in the delimited Champagne region of France. The wine of the Champagne region was formerly a still wine, though always with a certain vivacity. It was in the 17th century that a Benedictine monk, Dom Pierre Pérignon, perfected the means of sealing the sparkle in the bottle, thanks to the rediscovery of the use of cork as a stopper. The gas in champagne is the result of secondary fermentation.

All wines tend to 'work' in the spring, and there is a secondary fermentation producing carbon dioxide gas, which, in the ordinary way, is given off when the wine is in the cask or vat. If the wine is in a bottle, however, the gas remains in it, and the bottle and the stopper must resist the pressure in the wine.

Situated north-east of Paris, the champagne wine-growing region is the most northerly in France, extending over the departments of Marne, Aube and Aisne. The main production areas are the Montagne de Reims, the Marne Valley and the Côte-des-Blancs. Just three grape varieties are permitted: Pinot Noir, Pinot Meunier and Chardonnay. If the black grape skins are not left long enough in the must to tint it, a wholly white wine will result. The key feature of champagne production is that it is a blended wine – wines from separate areas of the region are fermented into *vins clair*. Then they are blended together and in some cases as many as 50–200 different elements are assessed and blended to achieve the required style. Many champagnes also use a proportion of *vins de reserve* from previous vintages. Before the wine is bottled, it is blended with a little sugar and selected yeasts to initiate a secondary fermentation in the bottle.

The *prise de mousse* (development of the sparkle) takes about three months. The bottles remain in the cellar and are rotated and shaken, so that the deposit slides down on to the cork. Then, when required, they are 'disgorged' – the first cork and the deposit are removed and, before the final cork goes in, any sweetening is added. The vogue for very dry champagnes is comparatively recent, being drunk as apéritifs and with certain first courses. The sweeter champagnes are agreeable at the end of a meal.

Champagnes should be served chilled but not iced. Care should be taken when opening, as the force behind the cork is great – never point a bottle at anyone and never let go of the cork once the muzzle of wire is removed. Tulip glasses or goblets are correct – coupes tend to flatten the wine. Vintage champagne is usually considered to be at its best 5–10 years from its vintage. (Most champagne, however, is non-vintage.) It is stored like any fine wine. If it becomes very old, it loses its freshness and sparkle and turns a deeper golden. Highly esteemed by Madame de Pompadour 'whom it left full of beauty after drinking it', champagne has, since the 18th century, been the supreme wine for celebrations, in France and throughout the world.

RECIPES

chicken in aspic with champagne

Select a chicken weighing about 1.8 kg (4 lb) and season it with salt and pepper, inside and out. Brown it in butter in a flameproof casserole. Add finely diced vegetables, including carrot, turnip, leek, celery, onion, mushroom stalks and a bouquet garni. Cover the pan and place in a preheated oven at 220°C (425°F, gas 7) for 45 minutes, turning the chicken over so that it cooks on all sides.

Remove the lid, add half a bottle of champagne, stir and check the seasoning. Then leave the chicken to finish cooking without the lid.

Prepare some liquid aspic jelly using aspic crystals and the rest of the champagne. Strain the juice in which the chicken was cooked and add it to the jelly.

Leave the bird to cool completely, then cut it up and arrange the pieces in the serving dish. Coat them twice with the syrupy jelly, leaving it to set in the refrigerator between coats.

salmon with champagne

Cut some fairly thick salmon steaks. Butter a baking dish and line the bottom with chopped shallots and a few diced vegetables. Arrange the salmon steaks in it and half-cover them with a mixture of equal parts of fish stock and champagne. Cook in a preheated oven at 220°C (425°F, gas 7), then remove the salmon steaks, drain and keep hot. Strain the pan juice and add some cream, using 100 ml (4 fl oz, 7 tablespoons) per 250 ml (8 fl oz, 1 cup) juice, and reduce by half. Adjust the seasoning. Add a generous lump of butter cut into small pieces and beat energetically. Coat the steaks with this sauce.

Fillets of sole may be prepared in the same way.

truffles with champagne

Take 1.4 kg (3 lb) large well-rounded truffles, ideally ones that are of a good black colour. Rinse them in two or three lots of water. When they are well drained, place them in a saucepan lined with slices of bacon and cover with more bacon.

Coarsely dice 450 g (1 lb) desalted ham, and also the same quantity of fillets of veal and fresh pork. Cook in butter in a saucepan, adding finely sliced carrots and onions, sprigs of parsley, a few pieces of thyme, bay leaf, basil, half a garlic clove and 2 cloves; season with a little salt, white pepper, grated nutmeg and a dash of spices. When these ingredients begin to colour slightly, pour on 2 bottles of champagne (Ay is best); bring to the boil; skim and leave to simmer on a low heat without reducing. Then press through a sieve and pour it over the truffles.

Start cooking the truffles 1 hour before serving. Leave to boil gently for 45 minutes, then remove from the heat and keep very hot, without boiling. Just before serving, drain them and arrange them on a napkin folded on a silver dish; cover to keep them piping hot.

CHAMPAGNE AND ARDENNES See *page 244.*

CHAMPEAUX A Parisian restaurant founded in 1800 in the Place de la Bourse by a man called Champeaux. It was a favourite haunt of stockbrokers and businessmen, who appreciated its substantial food and speedy service. It also possessed a winter garden. In 1903, the first Goncourt Prize was awarded at Champeaux's restaurant: the members of the Académie sometimes met there after leaving the Grand Hotel and before going to Drouant's house. The restaurant closed in about 1908.

CHAMPIGNY A rectangular tart consisting of a puff pastry case filled with apricot jam.

CHAMPVALLON A dish of mutton cutlets baked between a layer of onions and a layer of potatoes. This classic preparation dates from the reign of Louis XIV in the 18th century; it was invented by one of his mistresses, who supplanted the Marquise de Maintenon for a time by indulging the gluttony of the king. (The Marquise de Maintenon herself invented lamb chops *en papillotes.*)

RECIPE

mutton cutlets champvallon

Peel 800 g (1¾ lb) potatoes and cut them into round slices. Peel and chop 125 g (4½ oz, ¾ cup) onions and 1 garlic clove. Brown 6 trimmed mutton cutlets (rib chops) in 20 g (¾ oz, 1½ tablespoons) butter, drain them and then soften the onions in the same butter with the lid on the pan. Place the onions in a buttered dish and arrange the chops on top. Sprinkle a little thyme, salt and pepper over the chops. Cover with 100 ml (4 fl oz, 7 tablespoons) stock and a further 20 g (¾ oz, 1½ tablespoons) melted butter. Place in a preheated oven at 240°C (475°F, gas 9) and cook for 20–25 minutes. Then arrange the potatoes over the chops, season with salt and pepper, and add the same amount of stock and melted butter as before. Return to the oven and cook for about 25 minutes.

CHANFAINA A West Indian dish made with slices of fried lamb's liver arranged in an earthenware dish and covered with quarters of tomato fried in oil, crushed garlic and thinly sliced (bell) peppers.

In Spain, *chanfaina* (or *xanfaina*) is a typical Catalonian sauce made with onions, peppers, small pieces of various fresh vegetables cooked in very hot oil, fresh mint, parsley, cumin and pepper. The sauce is served with poultry, white meat or lobster escalopes.

CHANOINESSE, À LA Describes various dishes that evoke the important role occupied by cookery in certain religious orders of canonesses during the Ancien Régime. Chicken *à la chanoinesse* is poached chicken served with tartlets filled with crayfish tails in a suprême sauce made with crayfish

Champagne and Ardennes

After the second fermentation, the remueur – here in a Taittinger cellar – regularly rotates the bottles of champagne so that the yeast deposits settle on the cork.

Famous throughout the world for its wines, the French region of Champagne is not, however, noted for outstanding gastronomy. This paradox can be partly explained by the numerous political and social upheavals experienced by the province in the course of time. But the underlying causes are of a sociological nature: as one of the economic and military crossroads of western Europe, Champagne has been exposed to numerous influences. These conditions, unfavourable for the development of any great local traditions, could explain the modesty of the region's cuisine.

The adjective *champenois* as used in gastronomy must not be confused with the region; it is customarily used to describe any dish from any region that is cooked in champagne or in a still wine from the Champagne region.

■ **Rustic cooking** The true culinary specialities of Champagne are staunchly rustic. Stews formerly made with pickled pork and cabbage are now more likely to include bacon, smoked ham, sausages, cabbage and other vegetables. Fish stews are prepared from young pike, bream, eels and small carp with a still white wine; pike may also be cooked in a blanquette, with white sauce, or stuffed with ham. Vine snails are classically stuffed with garlic. There is a good choice of meat loaves, pâtés and terrines of chicken, hare, goose or pigeon.

Hams are cooked in pastry or with boudin blanc. Rabbit may be used to make quenelles while poultry may be stuffed or stewed. There are puffy gougères and cheese fritters to sample with wine.

In fact, the originality of Champagne cooking depends on a method of preparation called *à la Sainte-Menehould*, which is applied to pigs' trotters and a great variety of other offal dishes. The traditional accompaniment to such dishes is a type of pease pudding.

■ **From Ardennes** Fish is plentiful: trout and pike, dotted with pieces of diced bacon, carrots and gherkins (sweet dill pickles), in sauce, baked; eels (stewed); and small mixed fried fish.

In Ardennes, game reigns supreme: roebuck and wild boar (in roasts, pies, tarts and terrines); hare (jugged, in pies and terrines); and thrushes (roasted in sage leaves or stuffed with sage, or *en terrine* with juniper). Rabbit is often stuffed (with cooked ham). Fresh ham is served moulded or in paupiettes, rolled around chicory (endive). Red cabbage is cooked with apples; potatoes are cooked in the frying pan.

■ **Sweet specialities** Apart from *gâteau champenois*, made with crushed pink Reims biscuits, raisins, crystallized (candied) fruit, and champagne marc, and the soft

The church of Ville-Dommange overlooks the vineyard of Montagne de Reims, which is mainly planted with Pinot Noir.

Ardennes gâteau, desserts are fairly conventional. There is, on the other hand, a wide variety of biscuits (cookies) and confectionery, including Reims biscuits, croquettes, small meringue cases, galettes, madeleines, nonnettes and gingerbread. Jam made from small black plums (*norbertes*) is a speciality of the Ardennes.

■ **Cheese** The best-known cheeses come from the Île-de-France: Brie, Coulommiers, Chaource and Cendré.

WINE The region is, of course, famous for its sparkling wine (on which there is a separate entry). In addition to the various types of sparkling wine, the Champagne region produces a small amount of still wine now with the AOC Coteaux Champenois. They can be red (that of Bouzy is famous), still white and rosé (the Rosé de Riceys is well known).

The wine-producing areas of Champagne

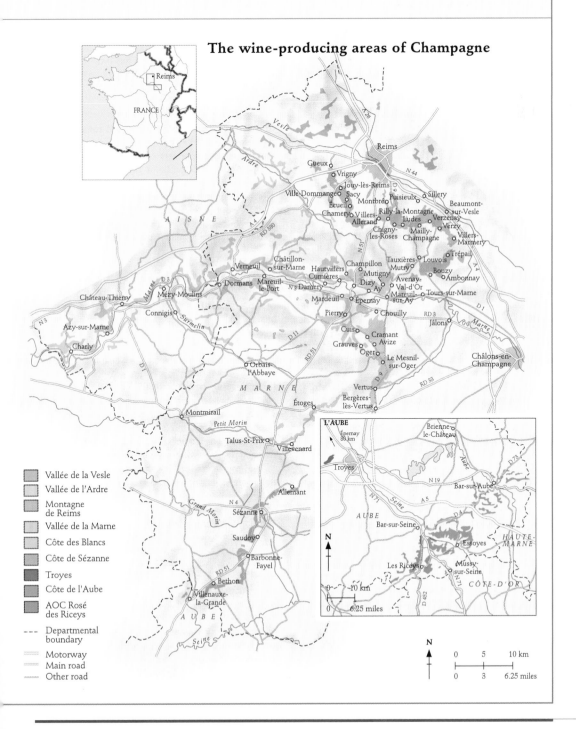

Vallée de la Vesle
Vallée de l'Ardre
Montagne de Reims
Vallée de la Marne
Côte des Blancs
Côte de Sézanne
Troyes
Côte de l'Aube
AOC Rosé des Riceys
- - - Departmental boundary
Motorway
Main road
Other road

stock. A cream soup or velouté *à la chanoinesse* also contains crayfish stock. The name is also given to calves' sweetbreads and soft-boiled (soft-cooked) or poached eggs garnished with truffles and small carrots cooked in cream and coated with a sauce made from sherry-flavoured veal stock.

CHANTECLER Name given to various lobster and langouste dishes. The crustacean is cut in half lengthways, lightly sprinkled with curry powder and then sautéed in butter. The flesh is then sliced into escalopes and put back in the shell. This is placed on a bed of rice, coated with a curry-flavoured Nantua sauce, accompanied with mushrooms, prawns (shrimps) and cockscombs, and browned under the grill (broiler).

The name also describes a way of serving noisettes and tournedos, which are coated with a port sauce and garnished with a julienne of truffles, accompanied by lamb's kidneys dotted with cockscombs and served with asparagus tip tartlets.

CHANTERELLE Known as *girolle* in French, this funnel-shaped mushroom is picked between June and October in hardwood and coniferous forests. It has thick swollen gills extending over the stalk. The fragile chanterelle is very delicate and tasty, orange-yellow in colour, with a delicate yellow or pale yellow-white stalk. It has a slight apricot-like aroma and some believe they detect an apricot-like hint in its flavour. Several varieties are used, including the cockscomb chanterelle, which has a thicker and shorter stalk; its flavour is inferior.

Chanterelles should be cooked gently as they harden if cooked too quickly. Sautéed, they are used as a filling for omelettes and scrambled eggs, or to accompany rabbit or veal. They can also be eaten raw after being marinated in a herb-flavoured vinaigrette. It is important to clean them carefully – young chanterelles, which are usually quite clean, are simply brushed; others are washed quickly under the tap, then drained on paper towels.

RECIPE

salad of chanterelles with endive
Wash and drain 1 large endive (chicory) and 250 g (9 oz) chanterelles. Season the chanterelles with salt and pepper and sauté in butter for 2 minutes. Add 2 chopped shallots and 4 tablespoons chopped flat-leaf parsley and cook for 1 minute. Make a vinaigrette with 2 tablespoons wine vinegar, 6 tablespoons olive oil, 2 tablespoons groundnut (peanut) oil, 1 tablespoon walnut oil, salt and pepper. Toss half the dressing with the endive and the remainder with the warm chanterelles. Arrange the endive on plates and place the chanterelles on top. Sprinkle with chopped chives, parsley and chervil.

CHANTILLY Chantilly cream is fresh cream beaten to the consistency of a mousse, sweetened and flavoured with vanilla or other flavours. It is used as an ingredient of, or an accompaniment to, various desserts, including meringues, sundaes, Bavarian creams, charlottes and custards. Preparations *à la Chantilly*, for example chicken *à la Chantilly*, are made using whipped cream.

The name is also given to cold emulsified sauces (such as mayonnaise) and hot sauces (such as hollandaise) to which whipped cream is added; these sauces are also called mousselines.

Although the name is derived from the château of Chantilly, whose cuisine enjoyed a fine reputation under the supervision of Vatel in the mid-17th century, none of the preparations named after it was created there; they in fact date only from the 19th century.

RECIPES

Chantilly cream
Chill some double (heavy) cream and some milk in the refrigerator. Mix the well-chilled cream with a third of its volume of very cold milk and whisk until frothy. Add 65–75 g (2½–3 oz, 5–6 tablespoons) caster (superfine) sugar to each 500 ml (17 fl oz, 2 cups) cream, flavour with vanilla extract or vanilla-flavoured sugar and continue to whip until the cream remains in the coils of the whisk. Return to the refrigerator immediately until ready to use.

Chantilly sauce
Dilute 200 ml (7 fl oz, ¾ cup) very thick suprême* sauce with 100 ml (4 fl oz, 7 tablespoons) whipped cream. Use hot to coat a chicken or poached white offal.

charlotte à la Chantilly
Line the bottom and sides of a charlotte mould with 18–22 sponge fingers (ladyfingers). Prepare some Chantilly cream with 500 ml (17 fl oz, 2 cups) double (heavy) cream gently blended with about 3 tablespoons mixed crystallized (candied) fruit. Fill the mould with the mixture and place in the refrigerator until time to serve. Turn out on to a serving dish and decorate with crystallized fruits.

The crystallized fruits may be replaced with strawberries or raspberries.

chicken à la Chantilly
Make a stuffing with some boiled rice, truffle peelings and diced foie gras. Stuff the chicken, sew up the aperture and brown the bird in a flameproof casserole with some butter. Take care not to overcook. Season with pepper, cover the pan and cook for about 1 hour. Cook some truffles slowly in port and sauté some slices of foie gras in butter. When the chicken is cooked, drain it and arrange on a serving dish, surrounded by the truffles and foie gras. Keep it hot. Add some chicken velouté to the pan juice; reduce by half and add several tablespoons of whipped cream. Coat the chicken with the sauce.

additional recipe See *peach.*

CHAOURCE A French cheese made in the Champagne region from cow's milk (50% fat content). It is a very white, soft creamy cheese with a whitened crust and a milky fruity flavour. It is named after the chief town of the canton of Aube and enjoys AOP status. It is cylindrical in shape, 11 cm (4½ in) in diameter and 7.5 cm (3 in) high, and weighs about 500 g (18 oz). The 'petit Chaource', weighing 275 g (10 oz), measures 9 cm (3½ in) by 5 cm (2 in). The cheese is in season in summer and autumn and is sold wrapped in a band of paper. It used to be wrapped in lettuce leaves to protect it during transport.

CHAPATI An unleavened, flat, circular bread made from wholewheat flour that is served throughout India and Pakistan. The dough is rolled out into very thin rounds and then cooked without fat or oil on a *tava* (griddle).

CHAPON A crust of bread rubbed with garlic. *Chapons* are cut from a long thin French loaf (a *ficelle*) and left to harden for 24 hours. They are rubbed with a garlic clove (which is itself sometimes called a *chapon*) and sprinkled with a little olive oil and vinegar. They are usually prepared half an hour in advance so that they have enough time to become well-impregnated. In the south of France, and especially in Languedoc, bread treated in this way is used to garnish a green salad, especially one made with endive (chicory).

The word *chapon* (meaning literally a capon) came to be used in this sense to describe the large piece of bread served with a thin soup when one could not afford to serve a real capon.

In Normandy, a crust of bread dipped in boiled milk is called a *chapon*.

CHAPTALIZATION The process of adding sugar to the must to enable the wine yeasts to do their work and raise the alcoholic content in the finished wine. It is subject to strict controls, but, correctly performed, is helpful to wines in some northerly vineyards, such as Burgundy. If carried to excess; it unbalances the wine.

CHAR *omble chevalier* Also spelt charr or known as Arctic char. A fish related to the salmon, found in the North Atlantic as far south as northern Newfoundland, Iceland and northern Norway. Freshwater (or land-locked) fish are found in the cold lakes of the Alps, particularly Lac Léman, and in Lake Windermere in England. The Arctic char is a large deep-bodied fish with a very wide mouth, a grey-green back dotted with round pale spots and an orange belly. It can weigh up to 8 kg (18 lb) and it has an excellent flavour. The freshwater fish vary in colour, and there are several related species.

The lake trout, also known as the speckled or brook trout, imported from Canada to Europe at the end of the 19th century, is related to, but smaller than, the char. Grey-green all over, with lighter stripes on its back and sides, it has a very delicate flavour and is now widely farmed.

CHARBONNÉE A term used to describe food cooked over a charcoal grill. In Berry, the term also describes pork civet thickened with blood. In the Île-de-France, it is used for a slow-cooking beef stew made with red wine, onions, carrots and spices. This is also thickened with pig's blood towards the end of the cooking period.

CHARCUTERIE Products based on pork meat or offal. The word also designates the shop where such products are sold and also the group of tradesmen who sell it. Charcuterie, or pork butchery, is particularly well developed in regions and countries where rearing pigs has been a longstanding tradition, such as the Auvergne, Alsace, Italy and Germany.

The Roman *porcella* law fixed the manner of rearing, feeding, slaughtering and preparing pork, and the Romans were probably the instigators of pork butchery as a trade. It was not until 1475 that, in France, an edict of the provostship of Paris granted to '*maîtres chayrcutiers-saucissiers-boudiniers*' the right to sell cooked and prepared pork flesh (and also fish during Lent). In 1476, these tradesmen formed a special category, distinct from the roasters (or *oyers*, with whom they had been confused until then), but they still formed part of the corporation of butchers. It was not until 1513 that the *chaircuitiers* (from *chair*, 'flesh' and *cuit*, 'cooked') had the right to lay in a supply of pork meat directly, without being obliged to go to the butchers.

The numerous preparations of charcuterie include cured meats, fresh and smoked sausages, pâtés, *andouilles*, *andouillettes*, black puddings (blood sausage), boudins blancs, sausagemeat, hams, galantines, *pâtés en croûte*, ready-cooked dishes and forcemeats. For a long time, these remained regional specialities, dominated by the processes of salting and smoking. At the end of the 19th century, charcuterie began to appear on gala menus, partly thanks to a pork butcher named Louis-François Drone. He was born in 1825 in Sarthe and became established in Paris under the Second Empire, which imposed new methods in this field. Nicknamed 'the Carême of charcuterie', he published a monumental *Traité de la charcuterie ancienne et moderne*. On 9 December 1893, a menu entirely of charcuterie was published in *Le Figaro*, signed by Gustave Carlin, the great Parisian chef and author of *La Cuisine moderne* (1887). It consisted of cold hors d'oeuvre: mortadella, large sausages from Arles and Lyons, foie gras; hot hors d'oeuvre: Clamecy *andouillettes*, Richelieu croquettes stuffed with meat and Tonnerre black pudding; entrées: pork pies, loin of pork in pepper sauce, pigs' trotters *à la Périgueux* and ham in aspic with pistachios; roasts: sucking pig stuffed *à l'anglaise*, jellied brawn and lettuce in a green salad with grilled strips of larding bacon; entremets: spinach with roast-pork gravy, stuffed artichokes *à la barigoule* and soufflé fritters.

In 1963, L'Association des Chevaliers de Sainte-Antoine was founded to study and promote the gastronomy of pork and charcuterie.

CHARCUTIÈRE, À LA Describing charcuterie preparations, such as *côte charcutière* (sautéed pork chop), roast loin of pork, *crépinettes* and *kromeskies*, which are served with a charcutière sauce. This sauce is a Robert sauce containing thin strips of gherkins (sweet dill pickles). Eggs *à la charcutière* are prepared with poached or soft-boiled (soft-cooked) eggs arranged on sautéed *crépinettes* and coated with reduced charcutière sauce.

RECIPES

charcutière sauce

Soften 3 tablespoons peeled chopped onions by frying gently in a covered pan, in 1 tablespoon lard (shortening). Sprinkle with 1 tablespoon white dried breadcrumbs until lightly coloured. Add 3 tablespoons white wine and 3 tablespoons stock and boil for 3–4 minutes. Stir in 2 tablespoons finely diced gherkins (sweet dill pickles) and then 1 tablespoon mustard. Adjust the seasoning before serving.

fried eggs à la charcutière

Grill (broil) some *crépinettes*. Fry several eggs in lard (shortening) and arrange them in a circle on a plate. Place the *crépinettes* in the centre and garnish with fried parsley. Serve with a charcutière sauce.

additional recipe See *potato*.

CHARD The succulent leaves and stalks of a variety of beet, *Beta vulgaris cicla*. The name is also given to the edible inner leaves of the cardoon. Chard is used as a vegetable, especially in Provence and the Rhône Valley. Cooked in water or in a thin white sauce, it is served with the cooking juices or a well-seasoned white sauce, to enhance its rather neutral taste.

CHARDONNAY One of the finest white grape varieties, orginally from Burgundy, which is known by other names according to the region in which it is grown: Melon Blanc in Jura, Roussot in Yonne, Noirien Blanc in Côte d'Or, Épinette in Marne, and Weiss Klevner, Weiss Edler and Weiss Silber in Alsace. It has compact bunches with amber yellow grapes and sweet juice. From it, the greatest white Burgundies are made, yellow gold such as Montrachet, Meursault, Corton-Charlemagne, Chablis and Pouilly-Fuissé, and also the excellent champagnes of Épernay's Côte-des-Blancs.

CHARENTE The ancient provinces of Angoumois, Aunis and Saintonge, which today form the Charente, pride themselves on their simple and straightforward cooking – described as 'peasant' by Curnonsky. Its charm is due mainly to the high quality of the products in the region. The sea provides shellfish, crustaceans and fish, which are prepared in various ways: oysters (often eaten with grilled sausages) from Marennes, La Tremblade and Château-d'Oléron; mussels served in soup, *en éclade*, or *en mouclade*; scallops *aux fines herbes*; razor clams stuffed with breadcrumbs, garlic and parsley (like snails); clams from Oléron and La Rochelle; cockles (*sourdons*); stewed *lavgnons* (cockle-like molluscs); fried cuttlefish (*casserons*) and *raiteaux* (small rays); prawns (*chevrettes*) or shrimps (*boucs*); hake in soup; sole and sardines from Royan; grey mullet and bass, roast eel and fried elvers. All kinds of freshwater fish are also cooked, although the River Touvre, which flows through Angoulême, is no longer, as it was in the time of Clément Marot, 'paved with trout and bordered by eels and crayfish'.

High-quality cattle and salt-meadow sheep are bred in the region. Typical dishes include Charente casserole, boned and rolled leg of veal, calf's head *saintongeaise*, Angoulême tripe and *gigorit*. Charcuterie includes choice products such as rillettes, large and small sausages, saveloys and brawn, white and black puddings, terrines and pâtés (foie gras garnished with truffles at Barbezieux or Angoulême, partridges at Ruffec, larks at Excideuil). Game is plentiful and dishes such as jugged hare with redcurrant jelly and *salmis d'oiseaux de mer* (a stew made with sea birds) are specialities. Chicken recipes are varied and include chicken pie with salsify, *sanguette* and chicken *à l'anglaise*.

The vegetables of the region are excellent. Peas from Aunis have a reputation for being tender and sweet – they are canned at Bordeaux and La Roche-sur-Yon. Broad (fava) beans have as fine a flavour as haricot beans and red beans (*mojhettes*). Cabbages are often cooked *en farée*. Mushrooms, both cultivated and wild, are considered to be excellent, as are nectarines from Saintonge, apples from Saint-Porchain and white grapes from the various vineyards.

The region also produces a butter, which is comparable to the best Normandy types, and is used to cook much of this produce, especially when cooking in a casserole. It goes well with radishes (*rifauts*), raw beans dipped in salt and braised garlic. Cheeses are important products and include Oléron made with goat's milk, Ruffec made with cow's milk, Jonchée (a soft white cheese made in a rush basket) and also caillebotte (curds).

Among the sweet preparations worth mentioning are *merveilles*, *cruchade* with jam, cheesecake, chocolate tartlets flavoured with Cognac, *gâteau d'assemblé*, Taillebourg brioches, *raisiné* (a jam), Pons sponge fingers (ladyfingers), frangipane tart, crystallized (candied) fruits and angelica liqueur.

The red wines of the region are fairly ordinary but the whites are used for producing Cognac, for which the region is so well known.

CHARLOTTE Two kinds of dessert, one hot and the other cold or iced, are known by this name.

The original charlotte (which appeared at the end of the 18th century, perhaps in honour of Queen Charlotte, the wife of George III of England) is inspired by English desserts. It is made from a thick fruit purée flavoured with lemon and cinnamon, poured into a round mould with a slightly flared rim, lined with slices of buttered bread. The dish is baked in the oven, then turned out of the mould and served warm with a cold custard cream. The classic example is apple charlotte, but other fruits may be used.

Carême invented charlotte russe. This is a chilled uncooked dish consisting of vanilla Bavarian cream (or chocolate mousse, coffee mousse, a bombe mixture or Chantilly cream) poured into a charlotte mould lined with sponge fingers (ladyfingers). The latter can be soaked in liqueur or coffee beforehand. The preparation is allowed to cool and then turned out of the mould. Carême named his creation *charlotte à la parisienne*, but this name was changed during the Second Empire, when Russian dishes became very fashionable.

Savoury charlottes may also be made, using vegetables or fish; they are cooked in an unlined charlotte mould.

RECIPES

Cold Charlottes
preparing cold charlottes
For 20–22 sponge fingers (ladyfingers), prepare a syrup with 200 g (7 oz, generous ¾ cup) granulated sugar and 175 ml (6 fl oz, ¾ cup) water. Flavour the syrup (by adding 2 tablespoons of rum, for example). Line the bottom of a charlotte mould with sponge fingers that have been cut into a point and then steeped in the syrup. Line the sides of the mould with sponge fingers that have been cut to the height of the mould and soaked in syrup. Place them tightly together (cut-side down). Place the chosen filling in the mould and cover with the remainder of the sponge fingers, also dipped in the syrup. Smooth the mixture down well and place in the refrigerator until ready to serve (or in the freezer if it is an iced charlotte). Turn out the charlotte and decorate it just before serving.

Strips of bread (cut in the same way) may be used instead of sponge fingers.

basic filling for cold charlottes
Dissolve 15 g (½ oz, 2 envelopes) powdered gelatine in 2 tablespoons hot water over a pan of simmering water. Prepare 500 ml (17 fl oz, 2 cups) custard*, mix in the dissolved gelatine and stir continuously with a wooden spoon until the mixture is almost completely cool. Prepare a Chantilly cream by whipping 250 ml (8 fl oz, 1 cup) double (heavy) cream diluted with slightly less than 100 ml (4 fl oz, 7 tablespoons) milk and 5 drops of vanilla extract or 1 teaspoon vanilla-flavoured sugar. Blend the Chantilly cream with the custard. Add the other ingredients to this preparation according to the recipe.

charlotte à la valentin
Cook 1 kg (2¼ lb, 3 cups) raspberry jam until it is almost caramelized. Cover a round sheet (the detachable bottom of a flan ring, for example) with sponge fingers (ladyfingers) and spread with a layer of jam; build up the cake with alternate layers of sponge fingers and jam. Trim the shape with a very sharp knife so that it forms a round cake. Pour the remaining jam over the cake and spread it evenly over the whole surface with a metal spatula. Leave to cool thoroughly and then place the cake on a sheet of gold embossed paper.

Make a meringue with 4 egg whites and 250 g (9 oz, generous 1 cup) caster (superfine) sugar. Decorate the cake with it. Sprinkle with 100 g (4 oz, 1 cup) flaked almonds. Place in a preheated oven at 230°C (450°F, gas 8) to colour it, then chill it until ready to serve.

charlotte majestic
Butter a charlotte mould. Decorate the bottom with crystallized (candied) fruits and then line the mould with sponge fingers (ladyfingers). Prepare a Bavarian cream of the desired flavour and pour into the mould. Cover with sponge fingers and place in the refrigerator. To turn out, quickly dip the mould in hot water.

chocolate charlotte
Break 250 g (9 oz, 9 squares) bitter (semisweet) chocolate into pieces and melt them very gently in a bain marie to obtain a smooth paste. Remove from the heat and add 4 egg yolks one by one, mixing well. Then add 2 tablespoons double (heavy) cream. Beat 6 egg whites into very stiff peaks and add 150 g (5 oz, ⅔ cup) caster (superfine) sugar. Blend the chocolate carefully into this mixture. Line a charlotte mould with sponge fingers (ladyfingers) – 300 g (11 oz) are required. Fill with the chocolate mixture. Place in the refrigerator for at least 4 hours. Turn out the charlotte and serve it with custard cream.

pear charlotte
Peel 1 kg (2¼ lb) Williams pears and poach them in a syrup prepared with 250 ml (8 fl oz, 1 cup) water and 500 g (18 oz, generous 2 cups) granulated sugar. Cut them into medium-sized slices and set aside in the syrup.

Soften 8 sheets leaf gelatine or sponge 20 g (¾ oz, 3 envelopes) powdered gelatine in cold water. Then drain and dissolve the leaf gelatine in a little water or dissolve the sponged gelatine. Prepare a custard with 500 ml (17 fl oz, 2 cups) milk, 250 g (9 oz, generous 1 cup) caster (superfine) sugar, 8 egg yolks, and 1 vanilla pod (bean). Remove from the heat and add the gelatine. When the custard is completely cold, blend in 120 ml (4½ fl oz, ½ cup) juice extracted from Williams pears and 750 ml (1¼ pints, 3¼ cups) Chantilly* cream.

Line a charlotte mould with sponge fingers (ladyfingers) and then fill it with alternate layers of cream and drained slices of pear. Place in the refrigerator for at least 4 hours or until set. Prepare a raspberry sauce by puréeing 300 g (11 oz, 2 cups) fruit, 125 g (4½ oz, 1 cup) icing (confectioner's) sugar and the juice of a lemon. Invert the charlotte and serve it with the sauce.

raspberry charlotte

Make a syrup with 300 g (11 oz, 1⅓ cups) granulated sugar and 250 ml (8 fl oz, 1 cup) water. Add 500 g (18 oz, 3¼ cups) raspberries and cook for 30 minutes. Dissolve 15 g (½ oz, 2 envelopes) powdered gelatine in 2 tablespoons hot water over a pan of simmering water and mix with the raspberries. Allow to cool. Soak some sponge fingers (ladyfingers) in kirsch and use them to line a charlotte mould. Whip 250 ml (8 fl oz, 1 cup) double (heavy) cream and mix it with the raspberries. Fill the lined mould with the mixture and leave to set in the refrigerator for at least 3 hours. Serve with custard.

spiced gingerbread fruit charlotte ♦

Heat 200 ml (7 fl oz, ¾ cup) milk. Pour 50 g (2 oz, 3 tablespoons) clear honey into a saucepan and dilute with milk. Add 2 tablespoons very finely chopped candied orange peel and the same of candied lemon peel, with 1 teaspoon powdered cinnamon, 1 powdered clove and a pinch of grated nutmeg. Allow to infuse off the heat.

Beat 4 egg yolks and 25 g (1 oz, 2 tablespoons) caster (superfine) sugar until the mixture has thickened and doubled in volume. Stir this mixture into the flavoured milk and cook gently over a low heat, stirring all the time without boiling until the mixture thickens. Remove from the heat.

Roast 40 g (1½ oz, ¼ cup) chopped almonds and hazelnuts under the grill (broiler) until golden. Soak and dissolve 3 sheets of leaf gelatine or 7 g (¼ oz, 1 envelope) powdered gelatine in a little cold water. Stir the dissolved gelatine into the candied fruit custard. Add 250 ml (9 fl oz, 1 cup) very cold whipped cream, then the almonds and nuts. Flavour with 2 teaspoons kirsch. Put in the refrigerator.

Mix 250 ml (8 fl oz, 1 cup) sugar syrup and 4 teaspoons kirsch. Dip 12 slices of gingerbread in this syrup and line the bottom and sides of a charlotte mould with them, overlapping them slightly. Fill with the cooled cream, smooth the top and cover with gingerbread. Leave in the refrigerator for at least 6 hours.

Soak mixed dried fruits (prunes, apricots, figs and raisins) and fresh raisins in warm Gewürztraminer and place in a dish. Unmould the charlotte on a dish, sprinkle with crushed praline and serve with the dried fruit.

• *Individual charlottes* Instead of making a large charlotte, ramekins or individual soufflé dishes can be used to make individual charlottes. Line the bases only – not the sides of the dishes – and top the mixture with gingerbread. Chill any leftover cream, then scoop it into neat ovals (as for quenelles) and serve with the charlottes. The charlottes may be served on plates flooded with crème anglaise, feathered with chocolate custard, and the dried fruit can be spooned into tuile or brandy snap cups.

strawberry charlotte

First prepare some sponge fingers (ladyfingers): beat together 6 egg yolks and 150 g (5 oz, ⅔ cup) caster (superfine) sugar until pale and creamy; whisk 7 egg whites until they form stiff peaks. Combine a quarter of the beaten egg whites with the yolk-sugar mixture, then add the rest of the egg whites together with 150 g (5 oz, 1¼ cups) plain (all-purpose) flour. Butter and flour 4 baking sheets. Mark a 23 cm (9 in) diameter circle on 3 of the sheets; pipe the mixture through a piping bag in a circular pattern within the circles on these sheets. Pipe the remaining mixture in diagonal lines to cover the fourth sheet. Bake in a preheated oven at 240°C (475°F, gas 9) for 10–12 minutes.

Now prepare a strawberry Bavarian cream. Reduce 1 kg (2¼ lb, 8 cups) strawberries to a purée and press through a sieve. Heat 450 ml (¾ pint, 2 cups) of this purée with 25 g (1 oz, 2 tablespoons) sugar until it boils. Soak and dissolve 3 sheets leaf gelatine or 7 g (¼ oz, 1 envelope) powdered gelatine in a little cold water and add to the strawberry pulp. Set aside to cool. When the mixture is cold, mix in 450 ml (¾ pint, 2 cups) whipped cream.

Line the sides of a 23 cm (9 in) deep round cake tin (pan) with strips cut from the diagonally piped sponge mixture. Place a sponge round in the base. Fill with the Bavarian cream (inserting the second round of sponge in the centre). Cover with the last sponge and refrigerate for 4 hours. Unmould the charlotte and dust with icing (confectioner's) sugar. Prepare a sauce by mixing the remaining strawberry purée with the juice of half a lemon and 125 g (4½ oz, ½ cup) caster sugar. Dip a large strawberry in this sauce and place in the centre of the charlotte; serve the rest of the sauce in a sauceboat.

Hot Charlottes

apple and rice charlotte

Butter a charlotte mould. Line the bottom and sides with a layer of cold milky rice pudding to which an egg yolk and a stiffly whisked egg white have been added. Fill the mould with a well-reduced apple purée. Cover with a layer of rice pudding and place the mould in a bain marie. Bring to the boil on top of the cooker (stove) and then place the bain marie in a preheated oven at 220°C (425°F, gas 7) and cook for 40 minutes. Turn out on to a serving dish and coat with a hot blackcurrant sauce.

apple charlotte (1)

Peel and core 3 kg (6½ lb) apples and cut into quarters. Slice them thinly and place in a shallow frying pan with 800 g (1¾ lb, 3½ cups) caster (superfine) sugar and 150 g (5 oz, ⅔ cup) butter. Place the pan over a brisk heat, stir the ingredients quickly with a wooden spatula, add a vanilla pod (bean) and reduce to a thick purée.

Spiced gingerbread fruit charlotte.

Butter a cold charlotte mould and dust it lightly with caster sugar. Slice a loaf of bread. Remove the crusts and cut the slices into 8 heart-shaped pieces and 16 very thin strips, 4 cm (1½ in) wide and the exact height of the mould. Dip the pieces in 100 g (4 oz, ½ cup) melted butter. Place the 8 hearts in a rosette in the bottom of the mould and arrange the 16 strips around the sides of the mould, so that they overlap. To make it easier to unmould, brush the strips lining the inside with beaten egg: this coating will stiffen the lining during cooking.

Mix the well-reduced apple purée with 200 ml (7 fl oz, ¾ cup) thick sweetened apricot purée and pour into the mould. Cook in a preheated oven at 220°C (425°F, gas 7) for 25–30 minutes. Leave to stand for a short time before turning out; serve hot.

apple charlotte (2)

Line the mould with sponge fingers (ladyfingers) as for a cold charlotte. Peel and slice about 12 apples. Melt 1 tablespoon butter in a shallow frying pan, add the apples, 250 g (9 oz, generous 1 cup) caster (superfine) sugar, 1 vanilla pod (bean) and a little grated lemon rind. Cover and leave to cook for 5 minutes. Remove the lid from the pan and cook for a further 10 minutes, stirring from time to time. Then add 4 tablespoons apricot jam. Remove the vanilla pod and pour the purée into the lined mould. Cover with pieces of sponge finger. Place in a preheated oven at 190°C (375°F, gas 5) and bake for 30–40 minutes. Take the charlotte out of the oven, leave it to stand for about 15 minutes and then turn it out of the mould. Coat it with a hot apricot sauce.

two-fruit charlotte

Cut thin slices of stale bread into strips and trim them to a suitable length to line a charlotte mould. Butter the mould and line the bottom and sides with the strips of bread. Mix some apple purée with some apricot purée and reduce – 100 ml (4 fl oz, 7 tablespoons) of the mixture are required. Peel some apples, cut them into pieces and sprinkle with a little lemon juice, sugar and vanilla-flavoured sugar. Fill the mould with alternate layers of purée and pieces of raw apple. Cover with breadcrumbs and press down firmly. Cook in a preheated oven at 200°C (400°F, gas 6) for about 40 minutes.

Iced Charlottes
iced charlotte with chestnuts

Line a charlotte mould with sponge fingers (ladyfingers). Prepare a syrup with 175 g (6 oz, ¾ cup) granulated sugar, 1 tablespoon lemon juice and 3 tablespoons water. Cook for 3–4 minutes. Gradually add the syrup to 500 g (18 oz, 2 cups) chestnut purée (fresh or canned). Prepare 1 litre (1¾ pints, 4⅓ cups) custard*, using 9 or 10 egg yolks. Put half on one side. Flavour the other half with rum and add it to the chestnut purée. Pour a little of this mixture into the mould, cover with a

layer of sponge fingers soaked in the syrup, then fill the mould with the remainder. Cover with more sponge fingers. Place in the freezer for 30 minutes. Turn out and serve with the remaining custard.

vanilla ice cream charlotte

Line a charlotte mould with sponge fingers (ladyfingers). When ready to serve, fill the inside of the mould with vanilla ice cream, vanilla-flavoured bombe mixture, or plombières ice cream.

Savoury Charlottes
red mullet charlotte

Wash 1 kg (2¼ lb) aubergines (eggplants), dry them and cut each in half. Make cuts on the flesh, sprinkle with salt and leave for 1 hour so that the juice seeps out. During this time, skin and gut (clean) six 150 g (5 oz) red mullet. Retain the livers and remove the fillets. Drain the aubergines and wipe them. Brush them with olive oil and bake them in a preheated oven at 220°C (425°F, gas 7). When the pulp is completely soft, remove it with a spoon and reduce it to purée. Add the juice of a lemon and then stir it over a very gentle heat, adding 150 g (5 oz, ⅔ cup) butter, salt, pepper and a garlic clove. Chop the mullet livers and add them gradually. Season the mullet fillets and fry them in olive oil. Drain them and use to line a buttered charlotte mould. Pour the filling into the mould and press down lightly with a plate. Place in the refrigerator for 2 hours. Serve with a tomato sauce.

vegetable charlotte

Trim 1 kg (2¼ lb) very fine green asparagus. Cook it in a generous quantity of salted water and then drain. Set aside 6 asparagus tips and pass the remainder through a fine sieve or a blender. Pour the resulting purée into a small saucepan and dry it out over a very gentle heat.

Plunge 12 small tomatoes into boiling water, peel them and remove the seeds. Soften them over a gentle heat and add salt and pepper. Peel 12 small onions, brown them in butter, add some stock and cook them until they are very tender. Make a zabaglione with 1 egg yolk, omitting the sugar.

Beat 2 eggs in a bowl with some salt and pepper. Add the tomatoes, asparagus purée, onions and half the zabaglione. Stir gently with a wooden spoon until thoroughly mixed. Warm 100 ml (4 fl oz, 7 tablespoons) double (heavy) cream in the oven, whisk it slightly, and then add it to the vegetable mixture.

Pour the preparation into a buttered charlotte mould. Place it in a preheated oven at about 160°C (325°F, gas 3) and cook for just under an hour. Heat the 6 asparagus tips in a bain marie. Turn out the cooked charlotte on to a serving dish and surround with a rosette of asparagus tips. Coat with the remaining zabaglione.

CHARMOULA In Arab cooking, a thick sweet-and-sour sauce prepared with a highly spiced hot ragoût of onions (containing *ramas al-hamanout*, bay leaf and dried rose buds), vinegar, honey and raisins, and sometimes carrots, celery and shredded shallots. It may be served cold or hot with grilled meat, especially camel and game. It is also used to coat fish preparations, such as bonito, tuna and sea bream. The fish are marinated, drained, coated with flour and fried. They keep for several days in this sauce.

CHAROLAIS A soft goat's-milk cheese (45% fat) from Burgundy with a bluish natural crust. Weighing about 200 g (7 oz), the Charolais has the characteristic shape of handmade goat's cheeses of the district, a cylinder 5 cm (2 in) in diameter and 8 cm (3½ in) long. It has a nutty flavour, more or less pronounced according to its maturity, and it is at its best from April to December. The Charolais is recognized as a particularly good goat's cheese.

CHAROLAIS One of the best French breeds of beef cattle. The name is often used in restaurant menus as a synonym for beef. An example is *pavé de charolais*.

CHAROLAISE A piece of very bony beef from the region of the elbow, which is used for making a pot-au-feu.

CHARTRES, À LA A method of cooking various egg and meat dishes in tarragon. Lamb chops are braised with tarragon and coated with tarragon-flavoured gravy. Fillet steak (sirloin) and noisettes are coated with a tarragon-based sauce and then sautéed. They are served with blanched tarragon leaves. The garnishes may vary and could consist of château potatoes, potato fondantes, stuffed mushrooms, braised lettuce and pea purée.

Eggs *à la Chartres* are either hard-boiled (hard-cooked), coated with a tarragon-flavoured chaud-froid sauce and covered with tarragon leaves and aspic, or soft-boiled (or cooked in a mould) and served on slices of toast with a tarragon-flavoured sauce and tarragon leaves.

CHARTREUSE A herb liqueur made according to a very ancient recipe by the Carthusian monks at Voiron, near Grenoble.

The original recipe was probably created by Carthusians established at Vauvert (near Paris), who are thought to have sent it to the monastery of Grande-Chartreuse, near Grenoble, in 1735. Here the apothecary, Jérôme Maubec, may have used it to make a medicinal herb elixir. In 1789, the monks were dispersed and the formula for the elixir seemed doomed to disappear. However, by chance, in the time of the First Empire, a copy of the formula reached the Ministry for the Interior. It was intended for the archives, but as no-one understood the document, it was sent back to the now reconstituted monastery at Grande Chartreuse. In 1835, the monks resumed the production of both the elixir and a green liqueur. In 1838, officers visiting the monastery discovered the liqueur and decided to encourage its distribution. Today, the Carthusians prepare a 71% elixir, a 55% green Chartreuse and a 40% sweeter yellow Chartreuse (created in 1840). During their second exile in Spain (1903–29), they continued to manufacture their liqueur at Tarragona and sold it under this name.

The composition of Chartreuse is a secret, but it is known that it is prepared from various plants and herbs, including balm, hyssop, angelica leaves, cinnamon bark, mace and saffron. A computer link between the monastery and distillery means that the monks visit only occasionally. Only three monks know the recipe and they are allowed to speak to each other just once a week.

CHARTREUSE A preparation of vegetables (particularly braised cabbage) and meat or game, moulded into a dome and formed of layers of alternating colours. It is cooked in a bain marie, turned out and served hot. Carême considered the chartreuse to be the 'queen of entrées'.

In former times, a *chartreuse* consisted solely of vegetables, and its name evoked the vegetarian diet of the Carthusian monks. Today, the term is usually used to denote a dish of partridge with cabbage.

Chartreuses may also be made with fish (such as tuna); lettuce is used instead of cabbage and it is seasoned with sorrel, which provides a slightly acid taste. Braised cabbage (with other vegetables) is still used to make chartreuse of eggs.

RECIPES

chartreuse à la parisienne en surprise (from a recipe by Carême) Cook 8 truffles in champagne. When they are cold, pare and cut them in the direction of the greatest length. Peel (shell) 100 crayfish tails – these can be replaced by carrots prepared in the same way as for a chartreuse of partridge – and begin to form a crown on the bottom of a buttered mould. Trim the truffles and place them on the crayfish tails. Add chicken fillets previously stiffened with butter and trimmed. Set on top of this border a crown of crayfish tails to form a parallel with the crayfish border underneath.

Chop the trimmings of the truffles very finely and scatter them on the bottom of the mould. Cover these with a 2.5 cm (1 in) thick layer of quenelle mixture made with chicken instead of veal. Cover the border too. Fill the middle with a blanquette of chicken, veal or lamb sweetbreads, slices of game fillets or with a ragoût *à la financière* or *à la Toulouse*. The mould should not be quite filled.

Form a layer of forcemeat 13 cm (5 in) in diameter and 1 cm (½ in) thick on a round of buttered paper. Place this on top of the filling (stuffing-side down). To remove the paper, put on it, for a second only, a hot lid which melts the butter. Secure the forcemeat lid to the forcemeat surround with the point of a knife.

Cover the top of the chartreuse with a circle of buttered paper and put it in a bain marie for 1½ hours.

To garnish, place a ring of small white mushrooms on the chartreuse, and in the centre put a rosette of 8 filets mignons à la Conti (fowl or game, according to the nature of the basic ragoût) in the form of a crescent, topped by a mushroom.

chartreuse of eggs in a mould

Prepare and braise some cabbage. Dice some carrots and turnips, and cut some French beans into small even slices. Cook the vegetables in salted water: they must be just firm. Also cook some peas. Drain the vegetables and toss them in melted butter. Use them to line some buttered dariole moulds. Break an egg into each mould, season and place the moulds in a bain marie. Cook until the eggs set. Cover the serving dish with the braised cabbage and unmould the eggs on the top.

chartreuse of partridge

Braise some cabbage in goose dripping, together with an old partridge (the latter provides more flavour). Cut some turnips and carrots into very thin 1 cm (½ in) squares. Prepare a veal quenelle forcemeat and use it to line a small round casserole. Then cover the bottom and sides with the carrot and turnip squares to form a decorative chequered pattern. Place enough of the well-drained cabbage in the pan so that it comes a third of the way up the side. Put a piece of slightly salted bacon (which has been poached for at least 2 hours) on top of the cabbage. Roast one or two partridges to seal them. Cut them into pieces and arrange them on top of the bacon. Cover with the remaining cabbage. Cover the pan and cook in a bain marie in a preheated oven at 180°C (350°F, gas 4) for 30–40 minutes. Remove from the oven. Cool for a short time and turn out on to the serving dish.

CHASSAGNE-MONTRACHET
Red and white wines of the Côte-de-Beaune, in Burgundy. In the 18th century, the commune of Chassagne (which is present-day Chassagne-Montrachet) was noted for its red wines. Today, it is famous for its whites, which – like all fine white Burgundy – are made from Chardonnay grapes. They are dry elegant subtle wines, with a rich bouquet and lingering taste. They acquire full maturity after 4–6 years. The *appellation* covers three *grands crus* – a part of Montrachet, a part of Bâtard-Montrachet and the whole of the small vineyard Criots-Bâtard-Montrachet, plus 51 *premiers crus*, the most famous of which are the Boudriotte, Clos-Saint-Jean, Grande Ruchottes, Caillerets and Abbaye-de-Morgeot. The red wines, made from the Pinot Noir grape, are more full-bodied and robust than the other Côtes-de-Nuits. They stand maturation (five years or more) quite well.

CHASSE-MARÉE
A fish cart. In the 18th century, the carts were used to bring fish and especially oysters to Paris as quickly as possible from the coasts of Normandy and Picardy. The fish carts were given priority at the coaching inns and no-one was permitted either to stop them on the way or to seize their horses. A special fund was provided to replace exhausted horses or to repay the cost of any fish that might be spoiled despite the speed of the journey. The oysters brought by these carts were known as *huîtres de chasse*, whereas those conveyed by boats coming up the Seine, and sold at a lower price, were called *huîtres de rivière*.

CHASSEUR
Any of various sautéed dishes (such as chicken, kidneys, medallions, escalopes and veal chops) that are served with a sauce made from mushrooms, shallots, tomatoes and white wine.

This sauce, with the addition of sautéed chicken livers, is also suitable for poached or shirred eggs, and may also be used as an omelette filling.

In classic French cookery, *chasseur* describes various preparations which include game purée (including soup, bouchées and eggs *en cocotte*).

RECIPES

chasseur sauce

Sauté 150 g (5 oz, 1⅓ cups) finely chopped mushrooms (mousserons if possible) and 2 chopped shallots in butter. Add 100 ml (4 fl oz, 7 tablespoons) white wine and reduce by half. Then add 150 ml (5 fl oz, ⅔ cup) stock and 2 tablespoons reduced tomato sauce and reduce by a further third. Add 1 teaspoon beurre manié (or arrowroot) and boil for 2 minutes. Finally add 25 g (1 oz, 2 tablespoons) butter and 1 tablespoon chopped herbs (tarragon, chervil and parsley).

omelette chasseur

Fill an omelette with sautéed chicken livers and mushrooms. Sprinkle with chopped parsley and surround with a ribbon of chasseur sauce.

salpicon chasseur

Sauté equal amounts of diced chicken livers and mushrooms in butter. Bind with a well-reduced chasseur sauce. This salpicon may be used as a garnish for fried or scrambled eggs.

sautéed chicken chasseur

Sauté a chicken in a mixture of oil and butter. Season, cover and cook for about 35 minutes. Add 150 g (5 oz, 1⅓ cups) thinly sliced raw mushrooms and cook for about 10 minutes more. Drain the chicken and keep it hot. Brown 1 or 2 chopped shallots in the pan juices and add 100 ml (4 fl oz, 7 tablespoons) white wine and 1 tablespoon well-reduced tomato* sauce. Reduce by a half and then add 1 tablespoon marc and 1 tablespoon chopped tarragon. Bring to the boil and coat the chicken with the sauce. Sprinkle with parsley and serve very hot.

shirred eggs chasseur
Garnish some shirred eggs with sautéed chicken livers and mushrooms. Sprinkle with chopped parsley and a ribbon of chasseur sauce.

tournedos chasseur
Sauté some tournedos steaks (filets mignons) in butter and then drain them. Use the butter in which they were cooked to prepare a chasseur sauce, and coat the steaks with it.

other recipes See *consommé (hot), giblets, mutton, noisette, potato, sauté, tendron.*

CHASSEUR Also known as *saucisson du chasseur.* A small sausage, weighing less than 250 g (9 oz) consisting of equal amounts of lean belly of pork and a fine paste of beef and pork. The chasseur is quickly dried and cold-smoked. It is golden in colour and is suitable for snacks and cold meals.

CHÂTEAU An estate or plantation, especially in the Bordeaux region, that produces wine. There are in some cases grand country houses (châteaux) attached to the estates, but in others there are not. A château wine is one that is produced from such an estate in the Bordeaux region; its label bears the name of its château, such as Château Ausone or Château Cheval-Blanc. This form of appellation is also used in other regions of France quite properly, although in Burgundy it is used only rarely as vineyards tend to belong to several proprietors.

CHÂTEAU AUSONE A red Bordeaux, one of 13 *premiers grands crus classés* of St-Émilion, officially re-classified in 1996 and, with Château Cheval-Blanc, rated as class A. Tradition has it that the vineyard occupies the site of the villa where the poet Ausonius lived in the 4th century. This generous and elegant wine matures in cellars hollowed out centuries ago in the soft stone below St-Émilion. The exceptional quality of the great vintages justifies the prices fetched by this wine.

CHATEAUBRIAND A slice of very tender fillet steak about 3 cm (1¼ in) thick. It is grilled (broiled) or fried and often served with a sauce (traditionally béarnaise).

This French version of English beef-steak was probably dedicated to the Vicomte de Chateaubriand (1768–1848) by his chef, Montmireil: at that time, the steak was cut from the sirloin and served with a reduced sauce made from white wine and shallots moistened with demi-glace and mixed with butter, tarragon and lemon juice. An alternative spelling is *chateaubriant* and some maintain that the term refers to the quality of the cattle bred around the town of Chateaubriand in the Loire-Atlantique.

Pellaprat, probably wrongly, specifies: 'The dish was created at the Champeaux restaurant; it was shortly after publication of Chateaubriand's book *L'Itinéraire de Paris à Jérusalem* (1811) that this grilled steak, comprising a thick slice from the heart of a beef fillet, made its first appearance; its cooking is a delicate process on account of the thickness, for if it is sealed too much, a hard shell is formed on either side and the centre remains uncooked; it must be cooked more slowly than a piece of ordinary thickness.'

RECIPES

grilled Chateaubriand
Brush the chateaubriand with oil, sprinkle with pepper and grill (broil) under a brisk heat. Sprinkle with salt and serve very hot. A vertical grill is perfect for cooking chateaubriand to a turn: sealed on the outside, underdone inside.

sautéed Chateaubriand
Sauté the chateaubriand briskly in butter: the outside must be sealed, the inside underdone. It may then be served like tournedos chasseur, or else drained, kept hot and surrounded with boiled vegetables mixed with the butter in which the meat was cooked. Alternatively, the cooking butter may be removed and the chateaubriand served with a pat of maître d'hôtel or marchand de vin butter.

CHÂTEAU-CHALON The best known of the yellow Jura wines, named after a small town in the region where it is produced, it is sold in a special 62 cl bottle called a *clavelin*. Golden amber in colour, Château-Chalon is produced from the Savagnin grape and is aged in cask for six to ten years before being bottled. It may then keep remarkably well for decades.

CHÂTEAU CHEVAL-BLANC A red Bordeaux, one of the 13 *grands crus* of St-Émilion. The vineyard is situated at the edge of the region of St-Émilion, next to the Pomerol vineyard. The 35 hectares (86 acres) of the estate consist of various types of soil. This accounts for the unusual *encépagement* of 66% Cabernet Franc, 33% Merlot and 1% Malbec. Its proximity to Pomerol makes it deeper in colour and more concentrated than most St-Émilions. Badly affected by the frosts of 1956, production was greatly reduced for many years. Today, however, Château Cheval-Blanc is on a par with the finest growth of Médoc. It combines delicacy and power and is one of the most celebrated wines of the world.

CHÂTEAU D'YQUEM A white Bordeaux, from the region of Sauternes, considered by many to be the best sweet white wine in the world. At the time of the classification of 1855, it was the only one of all the Bordeaux wines, red or white, entitled to the designation *grand premier cru*. The grapes are mainly Sémillon and Sauvignon Blanc and they are gathered, often individually, when the fungus *Botrytis cinerea* – the noble rot – has worked on the grapes. The yield is so small that each vine will produce only one glass of wine each vintage. This wine has to be perfect: in less than perfect years it is declassified and may be sold as just Sauternes. Golden and of incomparably smooth delicacy, it may benefit from ageing in wood, when it can retain all its qualities for more than a century.

CHÂTEAU GRILLET A white wine of the Rhône valley. The vineyard surrounds a 13th-century château and is the second smallest (2.5 hectares, 6¼ acres) to have its own AOC. It is planted with the Viognier Doré, a vine that does not begin to yield adequately for seven or eight years. Delicate, somewhat resembling both Hermitage Blanc and Condrieu, Château Grillet is a wine with an outstanding bouquet, dry yet at the same time mellow, well-balanced and fragrant. Because of the minute size of the vineyard, only small quantities are made.

CHÂTEAU HAUT-BRION Haut-Brion is the only Graves that was designated *premier cru* in the 1855 classification of Bordeaux. The estate at Pessac, in the suburbs of Bordeaux, is one of the oldest estates of Bordeaux (the records go back to the beginning of the 16th century). The vineyard is planted with Cabernet Sauvignon, Cabernet Franc, Merlot and Malbec vines. Its aspect, its soil and its position encourage early ripening of the grapes. Tannic and succulent, the wine, like many Graves, can acquire a full-bodied character with age, plus a bouquet of a rare delicacy, lingering flavour and velvety power. A small quantity of white wine, fine and dry, is also made from the Sauvignon and Sémillon grapes.

CHÂTEAU LAFITE One of the four first growths of the Médoc in the 1855 classification of Bordeaux. The vineyard is situated on a small hill, not far from Pauillac. It is planted with Cabernet Sauvignon, Cabernet Franc, Merlot and Petit Verdot vines. The large proportion of Merlot (15%) is one of the reasons for the special character. Impeccably made, Château Lafite is the traditional claret. An aristocratic wine, it has a delicate bouquet and possesses smoothness, charm and power.

CHÂTEAU LATOUR One of the first four classified first growths of Médoc according to the 1855 classification of Bordeaux. It was already highly esteemed in the time of Montaigne, who speaks of it in his *Essais*. This great wine, with its incomparable bouquet, is named after a medieval fortress of which only a tower remains, restored under Louis XIII. The estate is situated on the upper region of Pauillac, which is particularly arid and stony, and is planted mainly with Cabernet Sauvignon, plus Merlot, Cabernet Franc and Petit Verdot. The vines are allowed to produce up to an advanced age, which adds to the quality although to the detriment of the yield. The production of the wine is slow, both as regards fermentation and maturation. Considered by many wine-lovers as possibly the best balanced

Bordeaux, Château Latour will keep for a long time, in a good vintage. Included in the AOC Pauillac, Château Latour, designated with first growth status in the 1855 classification, should not be confused with the very many 'Latour' or 'La Tour' estate wines found in the Bordeaux region, of which there are nearly 80.

CHÂTEAU MARGAUX The first growth of the 1855 classification of Bordeaux. Château Margaux was already famous in the 15th century, when it was called 'Margou' or 'Margouse'. Today, its fame is justified. The 78 hectares (192 acres) of vines are planted on gravelly soil, which gives the wine delicacy and finesse. They produce red wine from Cabernet Sauvignon, Merlot, Cabernet Franc and Petit Verdot grapes. A small amount of Pavillon Blanc de Château Margaux is made from Sauvignon Blanc grapes planted on 12 hectares (30 acres) of a separate vineyard. Changes in recent years at the estate have brought about a marked improvement in the wine. Wines bearing the generic parish name 'Margaux' should not be confused with the important wine of Château Margaux.

CHÂTEAU MOUTON-ROTHSCHILD A great Pauillac wine, which, after many years of campaigning by its owner, Baron Philippe de Rothschild, was rated as a first growth in 1973. (The price had, for a long while, been equal to that of other first growths.) It is an important assertive wine, based very much on the Cabernet Sauvignon. The estate is now run by the late Baron Philippe's daughter, Baroness Philippine, who annually commissions a well-known artist to design a label and these are now themselves the subject of exhibitions.

CHÂTEAUNEUF-DU-PAPE A large and famous vineyard area at the southern end of the Rhône Valley. There are a number of quite well-known estates making this wine, of which 97% is red. The vineyard, on the left bank of the river, owes its name to the residence of the popes, when they lived in Avignon in the 14th century during the period when the papacy abandoned Rome. Burned down during the later Wars of Religion, the château has been no more than a ruin since 1552, and it was not until the 19th century that it gave its name to the wine, formerly called 'wine of Avignon'. Planted with a dozen or so different permitted varieties of vine, including Grenache, Syrah and Mourvedre, the region often suffers from drought. The hot sun is reflected from the huge stones that cover part of the ground, holding the heat, resulting in a powerful wine with a pronounced bouquet. Strict production controls make it one of the best Rhône wines, having a minimum alcohol content of 12.5° but often higher.

CHÂTEAU PÉTRUS An outstanding red wine from a small 11.5 hectare (28 acre) estate in Pomerol, in the Bordeaux region. It often equals or exceeds the prices at auction of the first growths of the Médoc. Made from Merlot, Malbec and Cabernet grapes, it has a complex truffle-scented bouquet, full-bodied, generous, yet with great delicacy. Pétrus can, according to its vintage, have a long life.

CHÂTEAU POTATOES

A dish consisting of potatoes cut or pared into neat oval, olive shapes (or left whole if they are quite small and new), blanched and sautéed in butter, with little strips of streaky bacon if desired, until they are well browned. They form the traditional garnish for grilled chateaubriand steak with béarnaise sauce and they are found in numerous garnishes (*maraîchère, Orloff, Richelieu*).

RECIPE

château potatoes

Scrub some fairly small new potatoes, wash and wipe. Heat some butter in a shallow frying pan, add the potatoes and cook gently with the lid on. Add salt and pepper and serve with roast meat or with braised meat or fish.

CHÂTELAINE, À LA

A method of garnishing simple dishes. For egg dishes, the châtelaine garnish includes chestnuts; for meat, artichoke hearts. For large joints of meat, the artichoke hearts are filled with Soubise chestnut purée, cooked au gratin, and accompanied by braised lettuce and noisette potatoes. Small pieces of meat are sautéed, a sauce is made from the pan juice and a court-bouillon, and the meat is simply drained and served with noisette potatoes.

Alternatively, the artichoke hearts may be cut into quarters, sautéed in butter and accompanied by small skinned tomatoes, braised celery hearts and château potatoes.

RECIPES

omelette à la châtelaine

Add 150 g (5 oz, ⅔ cup) finely sliced onions, softened in butter, to 500 g (18 oz, 3 cups) braised and coarsely crumbled chestnuts. Fill an omelette with this mixture and surround it with a thin line of cream sauce.

soft-boiled or poached eggs à la châtelaine

Prepare some shortcrust pastry tartlets and bake blind. Prepare some chestnut purée and add a quarter of its volume of Soubise purée. Season well. Fill the bottom of the tartlets with this mixture, place 1 soft-boiled (soft-cooked) or poached egg in each of them and coat with a chicken velouté sauce. Serve very hot.

CHATOUILLARD

A method of preparing potatoes by cutting them into long strips with a special utensil and frying them like soufflé potatoes. Rarely served in restaurants, the dish owes its name, according to

Prosper Montagné, to the nickname given to an old chef skilled in roasting and frying.

RECIPE

chatouillard potatoes

Pare some potatoes in a spiral to obtain strips 3 mm (⅛ in) thick; wash, wipe and plunge into frying oil heated to only 160°C (325°F). Gradually increase the temperature until the strips rise to the surface – at about 170°C (338°F). Drain them and leave them to cool slightly. Just before serving, plunge them into the frying oil heated to 180°C (350°F); they must swell up. Drain on paper towels before serving.

CHAUCHAT

A preparation of fish (sole, brill or whiting), either whole or in fillets, which are poached and coated with a béchamel sauce made from the cooking liquid bound with egg yolks and thickened with butter; the garnish is a simple border of rounds of boiled potatoes.

CHAUD-FROID

A dish that is prepared as a hot dish but served cold. Chauds-froids are pieces of meat, poultry, fish or game, coated with brown or white sauce, then glazed with aspic. Typically, they form part of a cold buffet, but are also served as an entrée.

Since the time of Carême, the presentation of chauds-froids has been simplified by eliminating the decorated stands or pyramid arrangements, but they remain very decorative dishes. The pieces of poultry or game, coated with chaud-froid sauce, are garnished with fine slices of truffle, rounds of hard-boiled (hard-cooked) egg white or tongue coated with brown aspic, before being glazed with a very clear jelly that contains little gelatine and is therefore purer.

Philéas Gilbert asserts that chaud-froid was created in 1759 at the Château de Montmorency and was named by the marshal of Luxembourg (which casts doubts upon the existence of a certain Chaufroix, vegetable cook of the royal kitchens under Louis XV, to whom some people attribute the dish). 'One evening, the marshal of Luxembourg had invited a large number of illustrious guests to his château. Occupying a place of honour on the menu was a fricassee of chicken in white sauce. When it was time to sit down at table, a messenger arrived: the marshal was summoned without delay to the king's Council. The marshal gave orders that his absence should not delay the serving of the food, and he left. Returning late, and desiring only one dish, he was served with the cold chicken fricassee, congealed in the ivory-coloured sauce. He found this food succulent and a few days later expressed a wish to have it served again. Presented under the name of *refroidi* (cooled), this term displeased the marshal, who insisted on the name of chaud-froid.'

■ **Chaud-froid sauce** The sauce is prepared to a coating consistency and aspic or gelatine is added. Béchamel sauce forms the base for many white chaud-froid coatings, but a variety of well-flavoured sauces may be used, typically velouté sauce. White sauces may be enriched with cream, butter or egg yolks. Aspic or full-flavoured stock and gelatine are added to complement the food to be coated.

RECIPES

brown chaud-froid sauce for fish and game

Mix 500 ml (17 fl oz, 2 cups) demi-glace* and 500 ml (17 fl oz, 2 cups) greatly reduced and clarified fish or game fumet (it must have the consistency of wobbly jelly). Gradually pour the hot mixture over 16 egg yolks and add 200 g (7 oz, ¾ cup) butter, whisking all the time.

brown chaud-froid sauce for meat

To make 500 ml (17 fl oz, 2 cups) sauce, put 350 ml (12 fl oz, 1½ cups) demi-glace* glaze and 200 ml (7 fl oz, ¾ cup) light brown gelatinous stock into a heavy-based sauté pan. Reduce by a good third over a high heat, stirring with a spatula and gradually adding 400 ml (14 fl oz, 1¾ cups) aspic*. Test the consistency by pouring a little sauce on to a chilled surface: if it is not thick enough, add several tablespoons of aspic and reduce again. Remove from the heat, add 2 tablespoons Madeira or any other dessert wine; strain through muslin (cheesecloth). Stir the sauce until completely cooled.

The following variations may be used for this brown chaud-froid sauce:

• *game chaud-froid* Prepare a game fumet with the carcasses and trimmings of the game used; replace the light brown stock with 100 ml (4 fl oz, 7 tablespoons) game fumet and flavour the sauce with Madeira or any other dessert wine.

• *à la niçoise* Add 3–4 anchovy fillets, completely desalted, reduced to a purée and pressed through a sieve, then strain the sauce and add 1 tablespoon coarsely shredded tarragon leaves.

• *à l'orange* For ducks and ducklings. Prepare a duck fumet with the carcasses and giblets of the poultry and use it in place of the light brown stock; reduce the chaud-froid sauce more than usual so that adding orange juice does not make it too weak; blend the juice of 1 orange with the sauce, strain through muslin (cheesecloth), add 2 tablespoons orange zest cut into fine strips, blanched, cooled and drained.

chaud-froid of chicken with tarragon ♦

Take a chicken of about 2.5 kg (5½ lb) with its own giblets. Place the giblets and 500 g (18 oz) chicken wings in a saucepan, cover with cold water, and bring to the boil; drain and rinse in cold water. Peel 3 onions, 2 carrots and 1 turnip. Place in a saucepan with the white part of 1 leek. 3 cloves, a large bouquet garni, the giblets and chicken wings. Cover with plenty of water (about 3.5 litres, 6 pints, 3½ quarts), add salt and pepper, and cook quite gently (without a lid in order to reduce the stock) until the flesh falls off the giblets and chicken wings. Season the whole chicken inside with salt and pepper, and add 3 or 4 sprigs of tarragon. Truss the bird, place it in the stock; cover the pan and leave to cook very gently for about 1½ hours. When the chicken is cooked, leave it to cool in the stock, then drain it on a rack. Strain the stock, discarding the giblets and wings and skim off excess fat. Return it to the pan and add a bunch of tarragon, then boil until reduced to about 1 litre (1¾ pints, 4⅓ cups).

To prepare the chaud-froid sauce, soften 5 leaves of gelatine in 120 ml (4½ fl oz, ½ cup) cold water. Then dissolve the gelatine in the water. Make a very pale roux with 125 g (4½ oz, ½ cup) butter and 100 g (4 oz, 1 cup) plain (all-purpose) flour, leave it to cool, then gradually add the boiling stock, stir briskly over the heat; leave to simmer gently for 10 minutes, then add a small glass of brandy and the same of port, 400 ml (14 fl oz, 1¾ cups) double (heavy) cream, spoonful by spoonful. Finally stir in the dissolved gelatine. Leave this chaud-froid sauce to cool, stirring to prevent a skin from forming.

Skin the chicken and cut it into pieces, then put them into the refrigerator. When chilled, coat the pieces of chicken with several layers of chaud-froid sauce, putting them in the refrigerator between each application of sauce. To collect the sauce which drains away, arrange the chicken on a rack over a tray or piece of foil. Dilute the sauce with a little cold stock for the last two applications. Garnish the pieces of chicken with tarragon leaves and other fresh herbs.

chaud-froid of duckling

Cook a fine duckling weighing about 1.8 kg (4 lb) in a preheated oven at 230°C (450°F, gas 8), keeping it slightly underdone (40–45 minutes). Remove the skin, detach the legs and cut the fillets into long thin slices. Prepare a white sauce or fumet from the carcass and the skin (and possibly some of the giblets), and use it to make an orange-flavoured chaud-froid sauce. Coat the duck slices with the sauce, following the same method as for the chaud-froid of chicken.

chaud-froid of salmon

Poach some slices or steaks of salmon, simmering very gently in a plentiful and well-seasoned fish stock: this is later used for making the chaud-froid sauce.

When the slices are cooked (they must still be slightly firm), leave them to cool in the stock, then drain them on a rack. Prepare the chaud-froid sauce with the strained stock, keeping it fluid, and coat the slices of salmon with it in three successive applications. After the last, garnish with round slices of truffle or black (ripe) olives and small decorative shapes cut from a green pepper. Glaze with very light aspic.

Chaud-froid of chicken with tarragon.

tomato chaud-froid sauce

Add 350 ml (12 fl oz, 1½ cups) aspic* to 500 ml (17 fl oz, 2 cups) puréed tomatoes; reduce by a third. Strain through muslin (cheesecloth) and stir until completely cooled.

white chaud-froid sauce for poultry

Soak a knuckle of veal in cold water, drain and place it in a braising pan with 1.5 kg (3¼ lb) chicken and turkey carcasses, 3 litres (5 pints, 13 cups) cold water, 3–4 onions cut into quarters, 1 onion stuck with 4 cloves, 3–4 white parts of leek, 3–4 celery sticks sliced and cut into sections, a large bouquet garni and some ground pepper. Do not add salt: the broth must reduce a great deal. Cover, bring to the boil, then half uncover and skim; leave to simmer gently for about 3 hours, occasionally skimming off the surface fat. Strain and leave to cool: the broth will change into jelly.

Bring the jellied broth back to the boil. For every 1 litre (1¾ pints, 4⅓ cups) broth, add 100 ml (4 fl oz, 7 tablespoons) double (heavy) cream, one after the other, 16 egg yolks blended one at a time into the cream-jelly mixture and, as it cools, 300 g (11 oz, 1⅓ cups) fresh butter. Leave the sauce to cool, but for coating meat and poultry do not allow it to set.

white chaud-froid sauce for white offal, eggs and poultry

To make 500 ml (17 fl oz, 2 cups) sauce, place 350 ml (12 fl oz, 1½ cups) velouté* and 100 ml (4 fl oz, 7 tablespoons) mushroom* fumet in a thick-bottomed sauté dish. Reduce over a full heat, stirring continuously with a spatula, and gradually add 400 ml (14 fl oz, 1¾ cups) aspic* and 150 ml (5 fl oz, ⅔ cup) double (heavy) cream. Reduce until the white sauce coats the spatula well. Ensure a good consistency by cooling a small quantity of sauce on ice: if it is not sufficiently firm, add a few spoonfuls of aspic to it and reduce again. Strain through a sieve or muslin (cheesecloth) and stir until completely cooled.

According to the dish being prepared, this white chaud-froid sauce can be varied with any of the following ingredients:
• à l'andalouse Flavour with sherry and with 2 tablespoons orange peel cut into fine strips, blanched, cooled and drained.
• à l'aurore Add 3 tablespoons thick tomato purée (paste).
• à la banquière Add 3 tablespoons Madeira and finely chopped truffles.
• Beauharnais Colour with 2 tablespoons purée made from tarragon and chervil, which have been blanched, cooled, drained and pressed through a fine sieve or puréed in a blender.
• à l'écossaise Flavour with Madeira and add 2 tablespoons very finely diced carrot, the white parts of a leek and a celery stick cooked in white stock, 1 tablespoon tongue coated with brown aspic and 2 tablespoons finely sliced truffle.
• à la nantua For fish and shellfish. Add 2 tablespoons crayfish purée and, after straining, 1 tablespoon finely diced truffle.
• à la royale Add 2 tablespoons truffle purée diluted with 1 tablespoon sherry.

CHAUDIN The large intestine of a pig, used as a skin in charcuterie, particularly for chitterlings.

CHAUDRÉE A French fish soup of the Vendée and Saintonge coast, which is made with small skates, soles, small cuttlefish (casserons), and sometimes sections of eel and gurnets. The fish are cooked in Muscadet with butter, thyme, bay leaf and a little garlic, the hard varieties (such as conger eels) being placed in the saucepan first. Some recipes include potatoes. Fouras chaudrée, in which the stock is poured over bread and the fish served separately, is a famous bouillabaisse of the Atlantic coast. Caudière and caudrée are similar soups from the northern coastal regions of France.

RECIPES

chaudrée gaspésienne
Cut 125 g (4½ oz) salt pork into slices. Fry lightly in a saucepan over a low heat until golden . Arrange 200 g (7 oz) dried cod's tongue, 200 g (7 oz) dried cod's cheek, 250 g (9 oz) diced potatoes and 125 g (4½ oz) chopped onions in successive layers on top of the salt pork. Season with salt and pepper, cover with water and simmer for 45 minutes. Serve very hot.

chaudrée saintongeaise
Sweat 100 g (4 oz) peeled, chopped garlic, flat-leaf parsley and finely chopped tarragon in 50 g (2 oz, ¼ cup) butter. Season with pepper. Add 500 ml (17 fl oz, 2 cups) white wine, 500 ml (17 fl oz, 2 cups) fish fumet (concentrated fish stock) and a bouquet garni. Simmer for 1 hour. Fry the following in olive oil in a large sauté pan until golden, adding them one after the other, in this order: 200 g (7 oz) conger eel cut into pieces, 200 g (7 oz) small skate, 200 g (7 oz) sole or céteaux, 200 g (7 oz) brill or plaice, 200 g (7 oz) casserons (small cuttlefish) and 200 g (7 oz) live langoustines. Cook in the fish stock for 3–4 minutes each. Then put in a preheated oven at 160°C (325°F, gas 3) for 10 minutes. Thicken the cooking juices with 200 g (7 oz), ¾ cup) butter. Serve with small croûtons roasted in the oven and lightly buttered with garlic butter.

CHAUDUMER Also known as chaudumé or chaudumel. A medieval recipe similar to fish stew, chaudumer (the name is probably derived from chaudron, a cauldron) consists of sections of eel and pike, first grilled (broiled), then cooked in a wine and verjuice sauce flavoured with ginger and saffron, and finally thickened with pike livers.

CHAUSSON AUX PRUNEAUX A Viennese pastry made from sweet pastry filled with prune cream. Crunchy, this *chausson* is similar to a sandwiched biscuit (cookie). Halfway between a biscuit and a Viennese pastry, it is very common in all regions where prunes are produced.

CHAUSSON NAPOLITAIN A Viennese pastry richly stuffed with preserved fruits or almond paste mixed with confectioner's custard (pastry cream) enriched with little cubes of preserved fruit (*crème napolitaine*). There are a large number of variations, all made on the same principle, and usually based on brioche dough.

CHAYOTE See *custard marrow*.

CHEDDAR An English cow's-milk cheese (containing 45% butterfat), cylindrical in shape, with a compressed paste and a natural oily rind, wrapped in cloth. Firm to the touch, with a nutty flavour, and white or creamy yellow in colour, it originates from Cheddar in Somerset. It is mass-produced in all English-speaking countries (often coloured red), and when it appeared towards the end of the 16th century it spread to the British colonies. In the United States, it is sold under the names of Daisy Longhorn, Flat or Twin; often it is simply known as 'American'. In Canada it is called Store of Bulk or Black Diamond, and in Australia it is often known as Coon.

The production of Cheddar is characterized by the cheddaring process. After the rennet is added, the curds are cut to the size of peas and gently heated. When the whey is drawn off, the curds are cut into large blocks which are then manhandled and stacked on top of each other so that more whey is drained off. The curd is milled again, salted and packed into moulds. In factory production, the cheddaring is done in a cheddar tower and the process is practically continuous. Farmhouse Cheddar is not as common but is much better in texture and flavour than the factory variety. It has a wonderful piquant and nutty flavour which increases and mellows with time.

A giant 500 kg (1,100 lb) Cheddar was offered to Queen Victoria on the occasion of her marriage, but it normally weighs 27–35 kg (60–77 lb) and has a diameter and height of 35–40 cm (14–16 in). Commercially, it is sold in the form of 6.25 kg (14 lb) blocks.

Cheddar is a popular cheese for many uses, for example in sandwiches or savoury snacks, both hot and cold. It melts well, so is a favourite for grilling, typically on toast or in savouries such as Welsh rarebit. Cheddar is also widely used in cooking.

CHEEK Either side of the lower jaw of an animal, including the muscles. Sold as part of the whole head, the cheeks are regarded as offal; when sold separately, however, this cut (particularly in the case of beef) is very good boiled or braised.

The cheek of certain fish, especially the monkfish, is regarded as a delicacy.

braised ox cheek
The day before they are required, clean 2–4 ox cheeks, removing all the gristle and fat. Cut the meat into large pieces and put them into an earthenware bowl; leave overnight in a marinade consisting of salt and pepper, 3 tablespoons olive oil, 175 ml (6 fl oz, ¾ cup) white wine, thyme and bay leaves. Cut 4 carrots into small cubes. Cut 300 g (11 oz) salted belly pork (salt pork) into strips, blanch for 3 minutes, then refresh them. Blanch 300 g (11 oz, 2 cups) stoned (pitted) green olives for 3 minutes in boiling water. Melt 50 g (2 oz, ¼ cup) butter in a flameproof casserole and brown the drained meat, the strips of pork, the carrots and the olives. Pour in the warm marinade, then add a bottle of white wine, 4 crushed garlic cloves and 6 onions, peeled and quartered. Bring to the boil and cook for about 15 minutes, then cover the casserole and cook for a further 3 hours over a very low heat or in a preheated oven at 150°C (300°F, gas 2).

CHEESE A dairy product made from coagulated milk, cream, skimmed milk or a mixture of any of these, drained in a mould (or *forma* in Latin, hence its French name, *fromage*). A distinction is made between soft fresh cheeses (including cream and curd cheeses), fermented cheeses (which are more numerous and varied) and processed cheese.

■ **The history of cheese** Cheese-making goes back to the earliest livestock farmers: letting the milk curdle, then beating it with branches, pressing it on stones, drying it in the sun and sprinkling it with salt, was an excellent way of converting surplus milk into a form that could be stored.

In ancient Greece, a number of pastries were based on goat's- or ewe's-milk cheese; when dried, this served as a long-lasting food for soldiers and sailors. The Romans were masters of the art of cheese manufacture; they preferred it fairly dry and, very often, smoked, according to a treatise on agronomy written by Columellus. This dates from the 1st century AD, when cheese presses were first used for pressing the curd. Roman cookery used *moretum*, a condiment made from cheese, garlic and herbs; it also featured a 'cheese stew' based on cheese, salted fish, brains, chicken livers, hard-boiled (hardcooked) eggs and herbs, a recipe which later reappeared in the works of Taillevent as 'cheese and egg gruel'. It was not until the time of Charlemagne and the chronicles of Eginhard (770–840) that cheese was again mentioned in writing. The famous emperor discovered blue cheeses – the ancestors of Roquefort – while on a journey into the heart of his territory, and a stop at the priory of Rueil-en-Brie enabled him to sample the delights of Brie, which was given to him as a tithe.

Over the centuries, the development of various manufacturing techniques has led to a great diversity of cheeses and the emergence of the major regional characteristics of French cheeses: soft curd in the west and north, goat's-milk cheeses around Tours and Poitou, blue cheese from the central region, cooked cheeses in the Alps. The monastic orders in particular played an important role in perfecting manufacturing processes, as the names of the cheeses indicate – Munster, Trappistes, Saint-Paulin, Saint-Nectaire, Tête-de-Moine.

Cheese is a highly nutritious food enjoyed at all levels of society. Always a basic foodstuff of the peasants, it was 'ennobled' by Charles d'Orléans, who started the custom of offering it as a New Year's gift to the ladies of his court. It was also used in cookery and some recipes from the Middle Ages have survived, such as arboulastre, talmouses, dari-oles, ramekins and a number of regional specialities, including tourteau, aligot, truffade, cheese flans and various soups. At the end of the 15th century, Charles VIII returned from his campaigns in Italy with moulds for cooked curd cheeses, thus introducing a new manufacturing method. From the Renaissance onwards, there are many written accounts on the art of cheese-making. The most popular varieties of the time were the cream cheeses of Blois, Clamart and Montreuil, the angelots of Normandy, Auvergne cheeses and Brie. Dutch and Swiss products were also sold in French markets.

In the 17th century, cheese was used a great deal in cookery, particularly in sauces and pastry-making. During the Revolution, difficulties of supply diminished the popularity of cheese, but it recovered from the time of the Empire onwards, and Cheshire, Maroilles from Hainaut, Normandy Neufchâtel, Swiss Gruyère, Roquefort and Italian Parmesan were all popular; Brie was hailed as the 'king of cheeses' during a dinner at the Congress of Vienna (1814–15). In the 20th century, pasteurization and industrialization tended to replace traditional manufacturing methods: some new products, mostly very rich, creamy and generally very mild in taste, made their appearance, while genuine farm-produced cheeses had become increasingly rare until recently.

■ **Manufacture** The hundreds of varieties of cheese can be distinguished firstly by the type of milk used: cow's, goat's, or ewe's (sometimes mixed), or even mare's and buffalo's; also, the milk can be whole, skimmed or enriched. In addition, the characteristics of the manufacturing methods give rise to several classes of cheeses. There are four stages in the basic process:

• ACIDIFICATION OF THE MILK This is sometimes performed by lactic yeasts.

• COAGULATION OR CURDLING The casein (milk protein) coagulates following the addition of rennet or, more rarely, by natural lactic fermentation of the micro-organisms in the milk. The milk then separates into the solid curds and liquid whey.

• CUTTING AND DRAINING THE CURDS After being separated from the whey, the curds can either be made into fresh cheese or processed further, in which case the curds are stirred, kneaded or cut; in some cases they are cooked. They are then put into moulds (sometimes a bacteria culture is added) and left to drain, an operation which is promoted by salting (either on the surface or by immersion in brine).

• RIPENING This allows the cheese to develop its characteristic texture, colour and flavour. The cheese is left for varying lengths of time in a damp or dry atmosphere, often in special places (cellars, caves or drying rooms).

■ **The classification of cheeses**

• FRESH CHEESES Unripened, coagulated by the action of micro-organisms in the milk without the addition of rennet, drained slowly, usually having a high water content, sometimes salted (demi-sel) or beaten with cream (Petit-Suisse).

• SOFT CHEESES WITH DOWNY RIND Obtained by mixed curdling (i.e. rennet and natural fermentation), not kneaded, drained spontaneously, shaped, coated with a bacteria culture, then ripened. Examples: Camembert, Brie, Chaource, Neufchâtel and Saint-Marcellin.

• SOFT CHEESES WITH WASHED RIND Made by mixed curdling and cut to accelerate draining; the surface is washed in salted water during ripening. Examples: Livarot, Munster, Feta, Caboc (Scottish), Époisses, Langres and Pont l'Évêque.

• VEINED CHEESES Cut after curdling, sometimes stirred, then cultured with bacteria at the time of shaping to give green or blue veins. Examples: blue cheeses, Fourmes, Stilton, Blue Cheshire and Gorgonzola.

• PRESSED CHEESES Curdled by rennet and draining accelerated by cutting, stirring and pressing. Examples: Cantal, Reblochon, Saint-Nectaire, Tommes and Cheddar. Some, particularly Dutch cheeses such as Edam, have an inedible wax rind.

• PRESSED AND COOKED CHEESES Manufactured as above, but heated for more than 1 hour during the cutting and stirring stages. Examples: Comté, Beaufort, Gruyère and Emmental.

• GOAT'S-MILK CHEESES These may be soft or hard, depending on their age and have a downy rind (sometimes coated in ashes), except in fresh cheeses and some veined cheeses, such as Bleu des Aravis.

• EWE'S-MILK CHEESES These can be fresh cheeses (Larzac and Broccio), soft cheeses (Venaco), veined cheeses (Roquefort) or pressed cheeses (Pecorino).

• MIXED-MILK CHEESES From goat's and cow's milk, or ewe's and cow's milk, these may be fresh or soft; including some veined cheeses and Chevrotons.

• SHAPED-CURD CHEESES mainly Italian (Mozzarella, Provolone – only the immature ones, Caciocavallo); after cutting, the curds are mixed with whey, heated, kneaded or stretched to obtain an elastic, slightly rubbery consistency, then shaped; they are eaten fresh, dried or smoked.

• PROCESSED CHEESE Obtained by cooking several cheeses; often flavoured.

■ **Protected designation of origin** In 1993, European Union legislation came into force to provide a simpler system for the protection of food names on a geographical or traditional recipe basis. Under the system, a named food registered at European level will be given protection against imitation throughout the European Union. The new Protection of Designated Origin (PDO) for cheese replaces systems such as the French *Appellation d'Origine Controlee* (AOC or AC) and the Italian *Denominazione di Origine Controllata* (DOC). The new titles are as follows.

France *Appellation d'Origine Protégé* (AOP)
Italy *Denominazione di Origine Protetta* (DOP)
Spain *Denominacion de Origen* (DO)

■ **Choosing cheese** Farmhouse cheeses, made by craftsmen according to traditional methods, are always preferable to dairy cheeses, which are mass-produced in factories. Among the latter, cheeses manufactured from untreated milk are better than those made from pasteurized milk. Seasonal variations in quality and availability must also be considered, besides, of course, compatibility with the meal. American law does not allow the importation of cheese made from unpasteurized milk unless it has been matured for at least 60 days. This means that AOP cheeses, such as Brie de Melun, Epoisse and Langres, cannot be sold.

Ideally, cheeses should be stored in a cool room, larder or cellar; they may be kept in the bottom of the refrigerator in an airtight wrapping to prevent them from drying out. Cheeses should be taken out about one hour before they are to be eaten. Soft cheeses that are not ripe through to the 'heart' will improve if left for a few days in a cool place. Blue cheeses should be slightly damp, and there is an old tradition that Gruyère should be kept in an airtight box with a lump of sugar.

Formerly, cheese was frequently served instead of dessert. In the 19th century, it was considered to have a 'masculine' taste and was served in the smoking room along with the liqueurs and brandy. Nowadays, besides its role in cookery, cheese is regarded as an extension of the meal. In France it is served after the salad and before the dessert, while in Britain and the United States it is usually eaten after the dessert. The cheeses may be served with butter, a controversial subject in France, as is the question of whether the rind should be eaten or not: experts are divided on both these points. In general, at least three types of cheese should be offered: a cooked cheese, a veined cheese and a soft cheese with either a downy or a washed rind. Enthusiasts, however, like to have a choice of five or six cheeses: one goat's-milk cheese, one with a pressed curd, one hard cheese, one veined, one soft cheese with a downy rind and one soft cheese with a washed rind. Sometimes a single cheese that has been carefully chosen and ripened is served; for example, a farmhouse Camembert, Vacherin, Brie or Munster. Cutting the cheese is governed by certain rules of etiquette: they demand a special knife with a two-pronged blade for both cutting and picking up the desired piece, since cheese should never be touched with a fork.

■ **Cheeses throughout the year**

• GOOD ALL YEAR ROUND Bel Paese, industrially made blue cheese, Brillat-Savarin, Caciocavallo, Camembert, Cantal, Carré de l'Est, Chabichou, Cheddar, Cheshire, Comté, Coulommiers, Crème de Gruyère, Derby, Edam, Edelpilz, Emmental, Excelsior, Feta, Fontainebleau, Fourme, Gammelost, Gérardmer, Gjetöst, Gloucester, Gorgonzola, Gouda, Lancashire, Leyde, Limburger, Liptauer, Manchego, Mimolette, Mozzarella, Munster, Murol, Mysöst, Nantais, Neufchâtel, Parmesan, Pecorino, Port-Salut, Provolone, Reblochon, Ricotta, Saint-Nectaire, Saint-Paulin, Sbrinz, Scamorze, Schabzieger, Sovietski, Stracchino, Tilsitt, Tomme.

• BEST BETWEEN MID-APRIL AND MID-NOVEMBER Bagnes, Banon (goat's milk), blue farmhouse cheeses, Bondard, Bossons macérés, Boulette, Broccio, Cabécou, Cachat, Cendré, Chevrotin, Coeur-de-Bray, Crottin de Chavignol, Dauphin, Époisses, Fontina, Herve, Labouille, Laguiole, Livarot, Maroilles, Mont-d'Or, Niolo, Pavé d'Auge, Pélardon, veined cheeses, Picodon, Poivre-d'Âne, Pouligny-Saint-Pierre, Pourly, Rigotte, Roquefort, Sainte-Maure, Saint-Marcellin, Selles-sur-Cher.

• BEST BETWEEN MID-NOVEMBER AND MID-APRIL Appenzell, Asiago, Baguette de Thiérache, Banon (ewe's milk), Beaufort, Bouton-de-Culotte, Brie, Brousse, Feuille de Dreux, Fribourg, Gaperon, Géromé, Gris de Lille, Gruyère, Katschkawalj, Olivet, Pithiviers, Pont-l'Evêque, Rollot, Saint-Florentin, Soumaintrain, Stilton, Vacherin, Vendôme.

■ **Wine to accompany cheese** Wine remains the best accompaniment to cheese. As a general rule, light red wines are mostly served with soft cheeses that have downy rinds and with goat's-milk cheese and pressed cheeses; more robust wines are best with soft cheeses that have washed rinds and with veined cheeses. Goat's-milk cheeses can also be served with dry fruity white wines, while cooked and processed cheeses go well with a rosé, blue cheeses and Roquefort with a smooth white, and Comté is delicious with a yellow Jura wine. Beer and cider are particularly suitable for drinking with some cheeses. Finally, in order to get the best out of a cheese, it is wise to have a choice of bread or biscuits; for example, farmhouse and rye bread, or some crackers and crispbread.

■ **Cheese in cookery** Many cheeses can be used in cookery, as a basic ingredient or to add flavour. They can either be used raw (in mixed salads, canapés, pastry and on bread) or, more often, cooked (for soufflés, omelettes, sauces, pancakes, puff pastries, pizzas and soups). There is a large variety of dishes based on cheese: *flamiche*, fondue, *keshy yena*, Welsh rarebit, *raclette*, *gougère*, *croque-monsieur*, croûtes, *patranque*, *goyère*, *truffade*, *imbrucciata*, *aligot*. Fresh soft cheese is used more in pâtisserie.

■ **Fresh soft cheeses** These are unripened cheeses that are made solely by natural lactic fermentation; they are drained slowly and have a water content of 60–82%. They are called *fromage frais* or *fromage* *blanc* in France or Quark in Germany and varieties made with cow's milk, sold in pots, are marketed under these names and as 'soft cheese' in Britain. Many are low-fat cheeses (less than 20% fat), but some contain up to 70% fat; they can either be smooth, with added cream (cream cheese), or have the appearance of curdled milk (curd and cottage cheeses). Variously flavoured, they can be eaten as a dessert – alone, with fruit or with a compote. They can also top baked potatoes and various cooked vegetables. Slightly salted cheeses (demi-sel) can also be bought, as well as such specialities as Petit-Suisse and Coeur à la Crème. Regional French cheeses, with a fat content of 40–75% or over, are sometimes eaten with sugar or various flavourings; they include Boursin, Caillebotte, Cervelle de Canut, Crémet, Fontainebleau, Gournay Frais and Jonchée. In northern France and Alsace, fresh soft cheese is mixed with horseradish, herbs and other flavourings; this speciality is also found in Hungary, where Liptó (a cheese made from ewe's and cow's milk) may be flavoured with mustard, spices, herbs or capers. These flavoured cheeses are often served with boiled potatoes.

Ewe's milk can also be used to make fresh soft cheeses, such as Broccio from Corsica, Brousse from Provence, Cachat and Tomme Fraîche. Goat's milk is used for Claquebitou from the Burgundy region, Lusignan and Sableau from Poitou. The Mediterranean and Balkan countries have several fresh soft cheeses made from ewe's and goat's milk, including Greek Feta, Rumanian Braidza and Italian Ricotta (made from whey), which are used mainly in cookery.

Russian pâtisserie uses soft cheese in such dishes as *paskha* (Easter cakes), *vatroushki* (patties made with cottage cheese) and *cyrniki* (cheese fritters). It is also found in some Turkish preparations, such as *böreks* and stuffed aubergines (eggplants). In traditional French cookery, fresh soft cheese can sometimes partly replace cream to make a dish less rich; it is also used in salad dressings and stuffings for vegetables and fish. But, above all, it makes variously flavoured desserts and is used in pâtisserie for pies, galettes, soufflés and ice creams.

■ **Processed cheese** This typically contains a variety of ingredients, combined together and melted by heat. A processed cheese spread, which may be based, for example, on Gruyère, Emmental, Cheddar or Cheshire, contains – in addition – milk, cream, butter, casein and various flavourings (ham, paprika, pepper, walnuts, raisins). A processed cheese contains at least 50% dry matter and at least 40% fat. A cheese spread contains less dry matter. In France, when the cheese makes up at least 25% of the product, it can be called 'Crème de . . .' followed by the name of the cheese.

Processed cheeses are sold in portions wrapped in foil (triangles or cubes) or in very thin slices; they are used on bread and for canapés, appetizers, *croques-monsieur* and for gratins.

■ **Vegetarian cheese** This is usually a hard cheese that has the same ingredients as normal cheese, but uses microbial enzymes to clot the milk, instead of animal-derived rennet.

■ **Strong cheese** (*fromage fort*) This is made from one or more types of cheese (usually dry and matured) which are ground or coarsely grated and steeped in a mixture of oil, wine, spirits, stock and flavourings in a sealed earthenware pot. After a few weeks, this gives it a very strong flavour. Strong cheeses are mostly home-made and are a speciality of Beaujolais and the Lyon area, but they can also be found in Provence and northern France. They are eaten with bread and on toast. Special mention should be made of the strong cheeses from Mont Ventoux (based on Cachat, with salt and pepper and garnished with onion), from Beaujolais (Bouton-de-Culotte, dry Gruyère, oil, butter and marc brandy) and from the Lyon area (dry goat's-milk Tomme, Saint-Marcellin, brandy, stock, thyme and tarragon). Similar to strong cheeses are Pétafine from Dauphiné and Fremgeye from Lorraine (salted and peppered fresh cheese, left to ferment in a sealed pot), which is identical to the Belgian Pottekees.

CHEESECAKE A cake made from soft cheese. Creamy and dense, baked cheesecake consists of a base made from flour, butter and sugar. This is covered with a mixture of soft cheese, eggs and sugar, with lemon zest and/or dried fruit. The cheesecake is baked, cooled and served lightly chilled. There are many examples of baked cheesecakes from Scandinavia, Russia, Europe and the USA. Eastern European countries, in particular, make traditional rich, baked cheesecakes.

Traditional chilled cheesecakes include *pashka*, a moulded cheese mixture prepared for Easter, and Italian ricotta desserts. Chilled set cheesecakes on a biscuit base are the modern version: they may be rich and dense, or light. They are often served with fresh fruit or fruit coulis.

CHEESECLOTH See *muslin*.

CHEESE STRAW A small stick of pastry, flavoured with strong cheese, such as Parmesan or mature Cheddar, served as a snack or garnish, with apéritifs, consommés, fish or cheese.

CHEF A person who prepares food as an occupation in a restaurant, private house or hotel. Today's top chefs are often media personalities, authors and demonstrators; those who are not famous are not necessarily less talented and their roles may be equally diverse, including those of business executive, public relations and promotions manager.

Chefs have occupied an important role in society from the 5th century BC onwards and in the Middle Ages, with the creation of guilds, they constituted a hierarchical community. In France, in the reign of Henri IV, the guilds split up into several separate branches: *rôtisseurs* were responsible for *la grosse viande* (the main cuts of meat), *pâtissiers* dealt with poultry, pies and tarts, and *vinaigriers* made the sauces. The *traiteurs* (caterers) included the master chefs, the cooks and the *porte-chapes* (the *chape* was a convex cover to keep dishes hot), and they had the privilege of organizing weddings and feasts, collations and various meals at home. These *chefs cuisiniers* (head cooks), as they were now called, served a period of apprenticeship, at the end of which they had to create a masterpiece of meat or fish.

High-ranking chefs were revered, and some of them, like Taillevent, were raised to the nobility. The most famous of all was undoubtedly Carême. Under the Ancien Régime, a distinction was made between the *officier de cuisine*, who was the actual cook, and the *officier de bouche*, who was in fact the butler (Vatel held this office). From the 18th century onwards, chefs wore a large white hat to distinguish them from their assistants (hence their nickname of of *gros bonnet*, 'big hat'). It seems that the hat first made its appearance in the 1820s. At the time when massive joints were served in England, the cook who supervised their preparation on the spit wore a black cap to facilitate carrying the roast to the table on a silver platter on his head. This form of headgear is retained at the Mansion House, official residence of the Lord Mayor of London, at Simpson's restaurant in the Strand and at a single coaching inn in Devon. In these three establishments alone the chief cook holds the title 'Master Cook', not chef.

The patron saints of male and female cooks are Fortunat (bishop of Poitiers and a famous 7th-century poet) and Radegonde (who founded a monastery of which Fortunat became the chaplain). Radegonde was an excellent cook, as testified by this letter from Fortunat, thanking her for a meal that she had prepared for him: 'Next a superb piece of meat was brought, arranged in the shape of a mountain and flanked by high hills, the spaces between which were filled with a garden of various stews that included the most delicious products of earth and water . . . A black earthenware jar provided me with milk of the utmost whiteness: it was quite sure to please me.'

CHEILLY-LÈS-MARANGES
One of the most southern villages of the Côte d'Or, producing strong-flavoured wine which may be blended with Côte-de-Beaune-Villages or sold as AOC Maranges.

CHEMISE, EN
Denoting a dish in which the main ingredient is wrapped or retains its natural covering. Pigeons *en chemise* are wrapped in a slice of ham and cooked in a casserole (with spices and stock, diluted halfway through cooking with a little wine vinegar). Duckling *en chemise* is stuffed, wrapped in a napkin and poached in a brown stock; it is served with orange quarters and a rouennaise sauce. Garlic cloves *en chemise* are added whole, unpeeled, to a stew or a roast (they are removed before serving, but the pulp may be squeezed into the cooking juice). Potatoes *en chemise* are boiled in their skins. Truffles *en chemise* are baked in the oven, wrapped in buttered greaseproof (wax) paper.

RECIPE

quails en chemise
Clean some pork intestine. Stuff the quails with *à gratin* forcemeat, then truss, sprinkle with salt and pepper, and wrap each one separately in a small piece of intestine. Tie up each end. Plunge the quails into boiling clear stock and poach for about 20 minutes. Drain, reduce the stock and coat the quails with it. Instead of stock, a well-seasoned and well-reduced clarified chicken consommé may be used.

CHEMISER
A French culinary term meaning to coat or line the sides or bottom of a mould, either with something to prevent the food from adhering to the container and enable it to be turned out easily, or with different ingredients which form an integral part of the dish. In the case of an aspic, a thin film of jelly is spread on the bottom and against the inner sides of the mould. For caramelized desserts, caramel is used. For bombe ices, the inside of the mould is first coated with cream or ice cream. The bottom and sides of a charlotte mould are coated with sponge fingers, rolled-out Genoese sponge or slices of bread with the crusts removed. Some moulds are lined with buttered greaseproof (wax) paper.

CHÉNAS
One of the ten Beaujolais *crus* (growths). Most of the vineyard is in the Moulin-à-Vent region and therefore many of its wines are sold under this more famous name. Those made in the north of the parish, lighter in weight than Moulin-à-Vent, are sold as Chénas.

CHENIN BLANC
A grape variety originally from Anjou, which is also known as Plant d'Anjou, Blanc d'Anjou, Plan de Brézé, Pinet d'Anjou, Pinot de la Loire, Pinot d'Anjou and Pinot de Savennières. Chenin Blanc has fairly compact bunches of grapes with crisp grapes of average size, golden yellow, with dense flesh and sweet juice. This makes soft wines such as Coteaux-du-Layon, Coteaux-de-Saumur, Bonnezeaux and Quarts de Chaume, but also dry, severe wines such as Coteaux de la Loire and Savennières, while in Touraine it forms the basis of sparkling wines. This variety has been successfully introduced in other wine-growing regions around the world.

CHÈRE
In modern French, this word designates the food served during a meal: *bonne chère* means savoury and plentiful food. Formerly, however, the word was used mainly in the expressions *faire bonne chère à* (someone) and *faire chère lie*, meaning to welcome someone in a friendly manner; *faire chère lie* now means to offer someone a good meal.

CHERRY
A small round stone fruit with a skin varying from pale yellow to dark red and a pulp that can be firm or tender, sweet or sour, according to the variety. In Europe cherry trees cultivated for their

fruits are mostly derived from two species: these originated from Asia Minor and were first cultivated in the Middle Ages.

The wild sweet cherry tree was known by the Egyptians, Greeks and Romans; its fruit is rather acid (though full of flavour) and is used mainly to make jams, syrups and liqueurs. It has given rise to both the hard crisp bigarreaus and the soft sweet cherries known as *guignes* in France and geans in England. These are popular dessert fruit and are also used in tarts and for preserves (jams, liqueurs and syrups).

The bitter cherry was apparently brought to Rome by Lucullus after the campaigns against Mithridates; modern varieties, which are derived from it, produce the amarelle and morello cherries which are used for preserves in syrup or brandy, crystallized (candied) fruits and jams. The sourish 'English' cherries are used mainly as fruits in brandy.

Cherries are frequently used in pâtisserie and in other types of cooking. Fresh and thoroughly washed, they are used in compotes, fruit salads and ice-cream sundaes, as well as tarts, flans, soufflés and Black Forest gâteau. Glacé (candied) cherries are popular in cakes and for decoration. In confectionery, cherry liqueur (particularly that made from morello cherries) is used to fill chocolates. Cherries are used to make soup in Alsace; in Germany they are employed in the preparation of sweet-and-sour dishes and pickles. They are also used as a condiment and as an accompaniment, particularly for game and duck (see *Montmorency*).

Of the cherry-based liqueurs and alcoholic drinks, the most noteworthy are the English cherry brandy, Guignolet from Anjou, Maraschino from Italy and kirsch from Alsace; a 'cherry wine' is made with fermented cherry juice and the Belgian *kriek lambick* is flavoured with cherry.

Cherries can be frozen freshly picked with their stalks removed and stoned (pitted) if required. They are available ready frozen, canned or dried. Dried cherries can be used in baking, desserts or in savoury dishes; they are also good in salads.

RECIPES

Savoury Dishes
cherry soup
Butter some slices of bread, dust them with flour and fry in butter on both sides until golden. Heat some stoned (pitted) cherries (preserved *au naturel*) in a mixture of equal parts of red wine and water. Season with a little salt, pepper and sugar and pour the soup over the slices of bread arranged in each bowl.

In Alsace, this soup is traditionally made on Christmas Eve.

hare with cherries
Choose a hare weighing between 1.5 and 2 kg (3½–4½ lb) and cut into pieces. Brown the pieces in olive oil in a flameproof casserole until they are golden, then remove. In the same oil, brown a large onion and a shallot, both chopped, and a finely diced carrot. Sprinkle in 1 tablespoon flour and stir until it turns golden brown, then replace the pieces of hare. Moisten with ½ bottle of red Burgundy and add a bouquet garni, a crushed garlic clove, a clove, salt and pepper. Cover and leave to cook gently for 1 hour.

Remove the stalks and stones (pits) from 1 kg (2¼ lb) cherries, cook them with 250 g (9 oz, generous 1 cup) sugar and a little water, then remove and drain. Caramelize the syrup slightly, then add 100 ml (4 fl oz, 7 tablespoons) wine vinegar, bring to the boil and reduce to obtain a syrupy mixture. Roll the cherries in this syrup. Arrange the pieces of hare in the serving dish, coat with the strained cooking stock and distribute the cherries around the dish.

Cherry varieties

variety	characteristics
bigarreaus	
Bing	large, deep red, sweet with a full flavour.
Black	large, purple, and shiny; crisp, juicy, and fragrant.
Early Burlat	large, dark red, and shiny; firm, full of flavour and sweet.
Hedelfingen Giant	large, black, and shiny; crisp and moderately fragrant; withstands transport and keeps well in a cool place.
Napoleon	fairly large, pale yellow, tinged with light red; firm, fragrant, and slightly sour.
Pigeon's heart	fairly large, bright red striped with dark red; firm, little flavour.
Reverchon	large and round, glossy dark purple; firm and sweet.
William	large and pointed, bright purple; quite firm, fairly juicy, sweet, and fragrant.
geans	
Early Basle (or Ceret)	fairly small, blackish-purple; soft, juicy, sour, travels badly.
Early Rivers	medium-sized, dark purple; sweet, fragrant, and juicy; very small stone.
English cherry	small, bright orange-red; soft translucent flesh.
Montmorency	medium-sized, very sour.
Morello	small, dark red; fairly firm sharp flesh.

quails with cherries

Remove the stalks and stones (pits) from 1 kg (2¼ lb) morello cherries, then place them in a saucepan with 250 g (9 oz, generous 1 cup) sugar and 100 ml (4 fl oz, 7 tablespoons) water and leave them to cook for 8–10 minutes. Add 3 tablespoons redcurrant jelly and cook for a further 5 minutes. Roast some quails. When they are cooked, add the cherries and a little syrup to the roasting pan and reheat. Serve the quails surrounded by the cherries.

Alternatively, canned cherries in syrup may be used and the syrup thickened with a little arrowroot.

additional recipe See *roebuck*.

Sweet Dishes
cherries flambéed à la bourguignonne

Remove the stalks and stones (pits) from some cherries and cook them with sugar and water, using 350 g (12 oz, 1½ cups) sugar and 3 tablespoons water per 1 kg (2¼ lb) cherries. Cook gently for 8–10 minutes, then add 2–3 tablespoons redcurrant jelly and reduce for about 5 minutes. Pour into a flambé pan, sprinkle with Burgundy marc, heated in a small saucepan or a ladle, and flame the cherries just before serving.

cherries in brandy

Sterilize storage jars to hold the cherries. Dissolve some preserving sugar in brandy, allowing 350 g (12 oz, 1½ cups) sugar to 1 litre (1¾ pints, 4⅓ cups) brandy. Choose sound Morello or Montmorency cherries, cut off half of each stalk and pierce each cherry opposite the stalk with a needle. Arrange the cherries in jars, cover them completely with the sweetened brandy, seal well and store in a cool place away from the light. Wait 3 months before serving.

cherries in vinegar à l'allemande

Remove the stalks and stones (pits) from some cherries; wash and wipe them. Sterilize some storage jars and arrange the cherries in them. Prepare an aromatic vinegar using 1 litre (1¾ pints, 4⅓ cups) vinegar, 200 g (7 oz, 1⅓ cups) light brown sugar, 3 cloves, a piece of stick cinnamon, and a pinch of grated nutmeg. Bring the ingredients to the boil, then leave to cool. Fill the jars so that the cherries are completely covered with the vinegar. Seal and store well away from light for at least 2 months.

cherry-filled soufflé fritters

Remove the stalks and stones (pits) from some cherries and cook them in syrup. Remove and drain the cherries and reduce the syrup until it coats a wooden spatula. Flavour it with kirsch. Return the cherries to the syrup and coat them thoroughly. Prepare some fritter batter; dip the cherries in the batter and fry. Arrange the fritters in a bowl or compote dish and dust them with icing (confectioner's) sugar.

cherry jam

Remove the stones (pits) from the cherries and weigh them. Use 1 kg (2¼ lb, 4½ cups) sugar and 100 ml (4 fl oz, 7 tablespoons) water per 1 kg (2¼ lb) fruit. Boil the water and sugar for 10 minutes, add the cherries and cook until the fruit is transparent. Pour into jars, cover and seal.

cherry syrup

Reduce some stoned (pitted) cherries to a purée in a blender. Strain the purée through a very fine sieve and leave the juice to ferment at room temperature for at least 24 hours. Decant and filter the juice. Add 1.5 kg (3¼ lb, 6½ cups) sugar per 1 litre (1¾ pints, 4⅓ cups) of cherry juice and leave to dissolve. Then transfer to a saucepan, bring to the boil and strain. Store in bottles with airtight seals and keep in a cool place away from light.

cherry water ice

Reduce some stoned (pitted) cherries to a purée in a blender. Add a sugar syrup flavoured with kirsch, using 200 ml (7 fl oz, ¾ cup) water and 400 g (14 oz, 1¾ cups) sugar to 1 litre (1¾ pints, 4⅓ cups) purée and thoroughly mix everything together. Set in an ice cream freezer, then turn out and serve with a cherry sauce.

Danish cherry flan

Remove the stones (pits) from some bigarreau cherries and macerate the fruit with sugar and a pinch of cinnamon.

Line a flan dish with shortcrust pastry (basic pie dough) and fill with the stoned cherries. Mix 125 g (4½ oz, ½ cup) butter, 125 g (4½ oz, ½ cup) caster (superfine) sugar, 125 g (4½ oz, 1 cup) ground almonds, 2 whole beaten eggs and the juice from the cherries. Cover the cherries with this mixture and bake in a preheated oven at 220°C (425°F, gas 7) for 35–40 minutes. Leave to cool, then cover with redcurrant jelly and a white rum-flavoured icing (frosting).

jubilee cherries

These are prepared in the same way as flambéed cherries, but the syrup is thickened with a little arrowroot and the fruit is arranged in individual ramekins and coated with syrup. Just before serving, pour 1 tablespoon kirsch into each ramekin and flame.

other recipes See *clafoutis, compote, Condé, fruit juice, liqueur, sauce, soufflé (fruit soufflé), tart*.

CHERRY BRANDY A liqueur obtained by macerating a purée of cherries and their crushed kernels in brandy. This liqueur, which may have first been made in England, is usually sweet, slightly syrupy and ruby red in colour. (Most liqueur establishments now make a cherry brandy.) Its inventor in England was Thomas Grant, a distiller in Kent, a county famous for morello cherries. Depending on the whereabouts of the establishment, different varieties of cherry are used.

CHERRY, WINTER See *Cape gooseberry*.

CHERVIL

An aromatic umbelliferous plant, originating from central Asia but now common throughout Europe, that is used as a herb. Chervil has a delicate flavour that goes well in mild soups, omelettes, sauces (béarnaise, gribiche, vinaigrette) and fish. It loses its flavour with prolonged heating, so it should be added at the end of cooking. Chervil keeps well when frozen.

In addition to common chervil and curly chervil (which is especially decorative), there is the delicate but rare bulbous chervil: its tuberous roots, aromatic and with a high starch content, are eaten like Jerusalem artichokes.

RECIPES

chervil-leaf butter sauce

(from a recipe by Carême) In a saucepan, boil a generous ladleful of butter sauce, adding to it a little salt, pepper, grated nutmeg, the juice of half a lemon, a large knob of butter and 1 tablespoon small blanched chervil leaves.

chervil soup

Wash and chop a large bunch of chervil. Soften it in a covered shallow frying pan with 25 g (1 oz, 2 tablespoons) butter for 5–6 minutes, then add 1 litre (1¾ pints, 4⅓ cups) thin white sauce* made with chicken stock. Leave to cook gently for about 10 minutes, then purée in a blender. Add 200 ml (7 fl oz, ¾ cup) double (heavy) cream and reduce by boiling briskly for 5 minutes. Pour into a soup tureen and sprinkle with chervil leaves ready for serving.

CHERVIS

A plant originating from China, widely cultivated in the past for its floury sweet roots. Olivier de Serres praised this vegetable, which was prepared like salsify; however, because of its low yield it was abandoned in favour of salsify.

CHESHIRE

An English cow's-milk cheese (containing 45% butterfat), with a compressed uncooked paste and a natural oily rind. Cylindrical in shape and 35–40 cm (14–16 in) high, it weighs 22–40 kg (49–88 lb). Granular in appearance, it is firm and oily to the touch, with a mild flavour which is more pronounced when it has been matured for a long time (up to two years); its particular taste is due to the deposits of salt in the pastures where the cows graze. It originates from Cheshire, where it appeared in the reign of Elizabeth I. There are three varieties: red (the best known), white and blue (fairly rare).

CHESTER

The name given in France and Belgium to Cheshire and Cheddar cheeses, and also to similar

French cheeses that are mass-produced by the Cheddar-making process (introduced in Castres after World War II). These cow's-milk cheeses (containing 45% butterfat) are used mostly for croûtes and canapés.

CHESTNUT

The fruit of the sweet chestnut tree, which is edible when cooked. The spiky husk generally contains three separate chestnuts, but improved cultivated varieties (called *marrons* in France) contain a single large nut.

Chestnuts were very popular in the days of the Roman empire and today are a basic food in Sardinia, Corsica, the Massif Central and in parts of northern Italy. The main production areas in France are the Ardèche, the Dordogne, Lozère and Corsica; chestnuts are also imported from Spain and Italy.

Chestnuts are energy-rich and highly nutritious. They contain a high proportion of starch, together with potassium and vitamins B and C. Fresh chestnuts, available in the winter months, should be heavy, hard and shiny brown.

Whole chestnuts can be roasted in their shells, then peeled and eaten as they are. Alternatively, they may be peeled and preserved, frozen or puréed, with or without sugar added. Whole chestnuts are cooked and preserved in sugar and, known by their French name of marrons glacés; they are eaten as a sweetmeat. Chestnuts are also used to manufacture chestnut flour. Peeled chestnuts can be boiled, grilled (broiled), braised or cooked in butter or milk for use as a garnish or vegetable. They make a good accompaniment to Brussels sprouts and are served with many winter dishes, particularly poultry and game. Puréed chestnuts are also used as a garnish, and are an ingredient of various stuffings. Chestnuts are also used for making sweet desserts and play an important role in the pâtisserie and confectionery industries.

In France, chestnuts are used in various regional recipes, such as chestnut *estouffade*, Ardèches salad and Corsican *brilloli* (a chestnut polenta) and *castagnacci* (a chestnut cake). In the Cévennes and south-western France, they are used for making soups, gruels and jams. In Valais, *brisolée* is a dish of chestnuts roasted with cheese.

RECIPES

peeling fresh chestnuts

Slit the shells of the chestnuts on the domed face with a sharp knife. Put them in a baking tin (pan) with a little water and roast in a preheated oven at 240°C (475°F, gas 9) for about 8 minutes. Peel them while they are still hot.

After slitting the shells, the chestnuts may alternatively be deep-fried for 2–3 minutes in very hot oil, cooked for 5 minutes in boiling water or placed beneath very hot embers.

Some authorities recommend that chestnuts should be shelled when they are raw and then boiled in slightly salted water for about 20 minutes. The inner skin can then be easily removed and the chestnuts are ready to eat or otherwise use.

Savoury Chestnut Dishes

boiled chestnuts

Place some peeled chestnuts in a saucepan and cover with cold water. Season with salt and pepper and add some chopped celery. Bring to the boil and simmer gently for 35–45 minutes. Drain the chestnuts well and serve with butter.

braised chestnuts

Peel some chestnuts and spread them evenly over the bottom of a large greased casserole. Place a bouquet garni and a celery stick in the centre, season with salt and pepper and add enough stock to just cover them. Cover the casserole and cook in a preheated oven at 220°C (425°F, gas 7) for about 45 minutes (do not stir the chestnuts during cooking in case they break). Serve with braised or roast meat.

chestnut purée

Boil some peeled chestnuts, drain them, press them through a sieve and place the purée in a saucepan. Add 150 ml (¼ pint, ⅔ cup) double (heavy) cream per 1 kg (2¼ lb) chestnuts and reheat, stirring constantly. Then add 50 g (2 oz, ¼ cup) butter and adjust the seasoning. If the purée is too thick, add a little of the strained cooking liquid.

Chestnut purée can be used to make soup or a savoury soufflé.

roast chestnuts

Using a sharp pointed knife, cut a circular incision around the chestnuts through the husk and the inner skin. Roast in a pan over hot embers, shaking them often.

They can also be roasted in a very hot oven. In this case, add a little water to the pan.

stewed chestnuts

Peel the chestnuts and place them in a buttered sauté pan. Cover them either with clear white stock or with water. Add a pinch of salt, 1 teaspoon caster (superfine) sugar and a chopped celery stick. Bring to the boil, cover and cook gently for about 45 minutes.

Sweet Chestnut Dishes

chestnut charlotte

Mix 200 g (7 oz, ⅔ cup) chestnut purée (see recipe above) with 125 g (4½ oz, ⅓ cup) chestnut preserve (see recipe below) and add 2 tablespoons pure malt whisky. Soak 15 g (½ oz, 2 envelopes) gelatine in sufficient cold water to swell, blend with 3 tablespoons double (heavy) cream and then add the chestnut mixture. Mix 150 g (5 fl oz, ⅔ cup) double cream with 2 tablespoons vanilla sugar, beat well and add the chestnut mixture a little at a time.

Soak 18 sponge fingers (ladyfingers) in a mixture of 2 tablespoons whisky and an equal quantity of syrup and use them to line the bottom and sides of a charlotte mould. Pour the chestnut mixture into the mould and leave to set for at least 6 hours in the refrigerator.

chestnut cream

Make some chestnut preserve (see recipe below) and put into sundae dishes. Decorate with Chantilly cream piped through a fluted nozzle and top each with a crystallized (candied) violet. The amount of sugar in the preserve may be reduced by a quarter if desired.

chestnut preserve

Peel 2 kg (4½ lb) chestnuts, cover them with cold water in a saucepan, bring to the boil and cook for 40 minutes. Drain and press them through a sieve. Weigh the resulting purée and add an equal quantity of granulated sugar. Put the sweetened purée in a preserving pan with 100 ml (4 fl oz, 7 tablespoons) water per 1 kg (2¼ lb) sweetened chestnut purée and 2 vanilla pods (beans). Heat the mixture fairly gently, stirring continuously. The preserve is ready when it comes away from the bottom of the pan when stirred. Remove from the heat, take out the vanilla pods and put into jars.

chestnut soufflé Mont-Bry

Boil 100 ml (4 fl oz, 7 tablespoons) milk with 40 g (1½ oz, 3 tablespoons) caster (superfine) sugar and a pinch of salt. Blend 25 g (1 oz, ¼ cup) plain (all-purpose) flour with a small quantity of cold milk in a pan. Add the sweetened milk and cook for 2–3 minutes, stirring constantly. Remove from the heat and blend in 4 egg yolks and 15 g (½ oz, 1 tablespoon) butter, followed by 4 tablespoons sweetened vanilla-flavoured chestnut purée and a few pieces of marron glacé. Whisk 5 egg whites until very stiff and fold carefully into the mixture. Put the mixture into a buttered soufflé dish and bake in a preheated oven at 200°C (400°F, gas 6) for 35 minutes.

other recipes See *barquette, cévenole, charlotte (iced charlottes), compote, croquette, mont-blanc, Nesselrode.*

CHESTNUT CREAM A sweetened chestnut purée with an oily consistency, used in confectionery and pâtisserie. It is a processed product, with good keeping qualities, that has become a speciality of the Ardèche region of France: since 1882, a Privas firm has manufactured a chestnut cream made from a purée of sweet chestnuts, fragments of marrons glacés, sugar and glucose; it is often flavoured with vanilla. Chestnut cream is used for making iced desserts (Bavarian cream, ices, vacherins), sometimes finished off with marrons glacés; it also serves as a filling for pastries and sweets (*gâteau roulé*, barquettes, meringues, and pancakes). It may be served chilled with Chantilly cream and plain biscuits (cookies). It must not be confused with unsweetened chestnut purée, which accompanies game and is used in forcemeats.

CHEVAL, À Describing small pieces of grilled (broiled) beef (steak, hamburger or entrecôte) with one or two fried eggs on top. Angels on horseback (*anges à cheval*) are grilled (broiled) oysters placed on a rasher (slice) of bacon on toast.

RECIPE

steak à cheval
Season a steak with salt and pepper and sauté in butter. Arrange it on a plate, place a fried egg on top and sprinkle with the cooking butter.

CHEVALER A French culinary term meaning to arrange the components of a dish (slices, cutlets) so that they partly overlap. On a long dish, the items are set out in a line or in a staggered arrangement; on a round dish, they are placed so as to form a crown.

CHEVALIÈRE, À LA Describes two elaborately garnished preparations, one of sole and the other of eggs. The fillets of sole are poached, arranged on a fish forcemeat with crayfish trunks, surrounded by oysters, poached mushrooms and crayfish tails bound with américaine sauce, then garnished with thin slices of truffle. The eggs are served with the garnish in a flan case.

RECIPE

eggs à la chevalière
Bake a flan case blind. Arrange some soft-boiled (soft-cooked) or poached eggs around the edge and fill the centre with a ragoût of mushrooms, cockscombs and kidneys bound with velouté sauce. Coat the eggs with suprême sauce. Dip some cockscombs in egg and breadcrumbs and fry them. Place a fried cockscomb between each egg and a thin slice of truffle on top of each egg.

CHEVERNY An AOC wine from the Loire valley. The *appellation* covers 23 communes of Loir-et-Cher, situated south of Blois and Chambord, not far from the famous 17th-century château, to the border of Sologne. The siliceous soil yields a relatively small quantity of dry white wines, fruity reds and fresh rosés, which are particularly appreciated in the region. Grape varieties include Gamay, Pinot Noir and Cabernet Franc for reds and Sauvignon Blanc, Chardonnay and Chenin Blanc for whites. Wines made from local grape variety Romorantin are given the AOC Cour-Cheverny.

CHEVET, GERMAIN CHARLES Parisian caterer and food retailer (died Paris, 1832). A descendant of the rosegrower de Bagnolet, he set up a shop in the Palais-Royal and founded a dynasty of caterers famous under the Empire and until the end of the 19th century. His shop was frequented by Grimod de La Reynière, Balzac, Rossini and Brillat-Savarin, and won him international fame; he supplied venison, foie gras, fish, pâtés and shellfish. His son Joseph took over in 1832, and later the trade was carried on by the founder's grandsons. Henriette Felicité Corcellet, daughter of another celebrated Parisian caterer, married into the family in 1844.

CHEVREUIL, EN Denoting meat prepared and served like venison: tournedos and noisettes of lamb are placed in a marinade, then drained, sautéed in butter and served with a poivrade sauce and a chestnut purée, as for roebuck. Also prepared *en chevreuil* are filets mignons of beef (larded, marinated and sautéed), and horse joints or legs of mutton (trimmed, larded, marinated and roasted, served with a sauce for game).

RECIPES

filets mignons of beef en chevreuil
Cut the filets mignons into triangles, flatten them slightly and lard with fat bacon. Marinate them for between 36 hours (in summer) and 3 days (in winter), turning them frequently in the marinade. Drain, wipe and sauté briskly in oil or clarified butter. They may be served with a purée (of celeriac, lentils, chestnuts or onions) and a sauce (for example chasseur, hongroise, poivrade or romaine).

leg of mutton en chevreuil
Bone a fine leg of mutton and lard it with thin strips of bacon. Prepare a marinade as described in the following recipe and marinate the mutton for between 36 hours (in summer) and 3 days (in winter), turning it over several times. Wipe, then roast in a preheated oven at 200°C (400°F, gas 6). Serve with a roebuck or poivrade sauce.

marinade for meats en chevreuil
Coarsely chop 75 g (3 oz) onions, 75 g (3 oz) carrots, 2 fine shallots, 3–4 celery sticks (stripped of their strings), and 1 garlic clove. Brown these vegetables slightly in oil, adding ½ teaspoon chopped parsley, a little crumbled thyme, 1 clove, a piece of bay leaf and some ground pepper. Moisten with 750 ml (1¼ pints, 3¼ cups) white wine and 175 ml (6 fl oz, ¾ cup) white wine vinegar, and cook gently for 30 minutes. Leave to cool completely before pouring over the meat, which has been seasoned with salt and pepper.

additional recipe See *horse*.

CHEVREUSE The name given to various preparations in classic French cookery. The Chevreuse garnish for noisettes of lamb or tournedos of beef consists of noisette potatoes and artichoke hearts garnished with a duxelles of mushrooms topped with a thin slice of truffle glazed with butter. The pieces of meat are coated with a sauce made with the pan juice flavoured with Madeira and a demi-glace. Velouté Chevreuse is a thick cream of chicken soup flavoured with chervil leaves. Omelette Chevreuse is filled with a mixture of chopped chervil softened in butter and blanched chervil. Eggs Chevreuse are baked in the oven (*au miroir*), sprinkled with grated cheese and bordered with a fairly firm purée of French beans. The presence of market-garden produce in the recipes explains the name, as the Chevreuse valley has been famous for its vegetables since the 18th century.

CHIANTI An Italian DOCG red wine from Tuscany, produced in the hills between Florence and Siena. There are seven zones of Chianti, including Chianti Classico and Chianti Rufina. Of these, Chianti Classico is the most important as the heartland of quality and innovation; it can be identified by the black rooster on the Consorzio's seal on each bottle.

Chianti has suffered from a poor reputation in the past, mainly because the original legislation allowed the addition of white grapes to the blend. Many top estates dropped out of the DOC system to classify their top wines as *Vini da Tavola*, which became known as Supertuscan wines. This legislative anomaly has now been corrected and a new initiative in terms of clonal selection, fermentation and ageing has seen the quality and price of Chianti rise substantially. The main grape used in Chianti is Sangiovese, but up to 10% of a non-traditional grape variety, usually Cabernet Sauvignon, is permitted. This has helped some of the Supertuscan wines return to DOCG classification instead of remaining as *Vini da Tavola*.

CHIBOUST A 19th-century pastrycook, who in 1846 created the Saint-Honoré, a cake named in honour of the Paris district in which he worked, and also in honour of Saint-Honoré, the patron saint of bakers and pastrycooks.

Chiboust cream, which traditionally accompanies the Saint-Honoré, is a confectioner's custard (pastry cream), usually flavoured with vanilla, and blended when still warm with stiffly whisked egg whites. Pastrycooks often use Chantilly cream instead, as it is quicker to make.

RECIPE

Chiboust cream

Soak 4 leaves of gelatine in cold water, then dissolve over hot water. Boil 500 ml (17 fl oz, 2 cups) milk with half a vanilla pod (bean). Beat 4 egg yolks with 125 g (4½ oz, ½ cup) caster (superfine) sugar until the mixture lightens in colour. Add 75 g (3 oz, ¾ cup) plain (all-purpose) flour and mix well. Gradually pour in the boiling milk, whisking continuously. Pour the mixture into a saucepan, add the dissolved gelatine and heat gently, stirring continuously. Remove from the heat as soon as it begins to boil. Add a pinch of salt to the 4 egg whites and beat into stiff peaks. Reheat the cream until it starts to simmer and pour it immediately over the egg whites. Mix with a spatula, lifting the whole mixture, but taking care not to beat it, so that a smooth cream is obtained.

CHICHA A highly alcoholic Latin American drink obtained from the fermentation of maize flour (cornmeal). In Peru, it is prepared on a small scale with grains of maize (corn) that the women chew, spit out and then ferment with pieces of meat. The name derives from the expression *de chicha y nabo* (of little value) and the spirit is consumed by the rural and working classes. It is also mass-produced from maize that is fermented with molasses and then distilled.

CHICKEN A domestic fowl reared (raised) for both its meat and its eggs. It is one of the most popular types of meat, being used in recipes the whole world over, from paella to chop suey, from jambalaya to *brathendl*, from chicken pie to *waterzootje*, from curry to pilaf.

The popularity of chicken is reflected in the wide choice of products available, but until the middle of the 20th century chicken was regarded as a luxury poultry. Intensive rearing methods changed its status, making it plentiful and inexpensive. Birds reared by these methods yield meat that is quite different from that of traditional farmed poultry. Meat from intensively reared chicken lacks flavour and its texture is soft and grainy, due to lack of exercise and the young age at which the birds are slaughtered. By comparison, traditional chicken meat has a firm texture and good flavour.

■ **Choice of chicken** Chicken is classified according to rearing methods and diet, age and weight. Various standards and grades are applied, and the butcher, supermarket or other retailer should be able to provide full information or details of relevant organizations that can answer specific queries on rearing methods. The majority of chicken, whole or sold prepared in cuts, is intensively reared and young; any product originating from a different background will be clearly marked as such. The best chicken is organic, free-range, reared to old-fashioned standards on a traditional grain diet, which allows for slow growth and gives a bird both a good flavour and texture. The following are some of the terms for different types of chicken.

• POUSSIN Young chicken weighing about 350–450 g (12–16 oz) and providing 1 portion. The meat has a very light flavour and is often marinated or well seasoned before cooking. Poussin can be grilled, fried or roasted.

• SPRING CHICKEN This is a young bird, older and larger than a poussin, but suitable for similar cooking methods and usually providing 2 portions. Spring chicken is not as common as poussin and the latter is often used instead.

• CHICKEN Most chickens weigh about 1.4–1.8 kg (3–4 lb), though larger birds can weigh up to 2.75 kg (6 lb). The larger chickens are older and have slightly more flavour, but they are still young, tender birds.

• BOILING FOWL The French *poule*, this is a mature hen with tough flesh and a good, full flavour. Boiling fowl are excellent for stocks, broths or long-cooked casseroles. They are not readily available in supermarkets, but some butchers can obtain them.

• CAPON A castrated young cock, larger and with more flavour than a chicken. In Britain the rearing of capons is illegal, but imported birds are available from specialist poulterers.

• FREE-RANGE AND ORGANIC CHICKENS Birds raised by methods other than intensive battery farming. Various terms are applied, relating to different rearing conditions, including housing and diet. These birds are slightiy older, yielding meat with a better texture and more flavour.

• CORN-FED CHICKEN This refers to the diet rather than the rearing method. The birds are fed on a diet of corn (maize) or rich in corn. Yellow-skinned corn-fed chicken takes on the colour from the artificial colour in the feed and this seeps out of the skin during cooking – this is especially noticeable when frying corn-fed chicken. The flavour and texture of the chicken is not necessarily any better than that of ordinary chicken.

• BRESSE CHICKEN An example of a particular breed of French bird, known as *poulet de Bresse* in France, raised by traditional standards and sold as a premium quality product. Similar identification and labelling schemes are used for other classic breeds of other regions or countries, raised to similar high standards.

• CUTS OF CHICKEN As well as whole birds (usually without giblets), chicken is available jointed into quarters (with leg or wing joints), part-boned breasts, drumsticks, wings and thighs (on or off the bone). Boneless chicken breasts or breast fillets, traditionally referred to as supremes, are popular; diced chicken, strips of boneless chicken and minced chicken are also available ready prepared.

■ **Drawing a chicken** Cut through the skin down the length of the neck and remove the trachea (windpipe) and the oesophagus (gullet), pulling out the crop at the same time; leave the neck as it is or sever it at the base, without cutting through the skin. Make an incision at the tail end and pull out the intestines, gizzard, liver, heart and lungs. Remove the gall bladder from the liver immediately. Split the gizzard on the rounded side and remove the grain sac. Singe the chicken to remove all the remaining down. Clean the giblets and replace in the cavity if not to be used straight away. Cut off the pinions (wing tips), bend back the rest of the bottom joint and tuck the ends underneath the bird to form a neat shape. Cut off the feet at the joint with the drumstick. Fold back the neck (if it is still on) under one wing, or else fold back the skin of the neck over the breast. Truss the chicken.

■ **Cooking methods for chicken** Most chicken is tender and versatile – suitable for cooking by all methods, including roasting, sautéing, shallow or deep-frying, grilling (broiling), poaching and casseroling. Boiling fowl require long and moist cooking by boiling, stewing or lengthy poaching.

If the chicken is to be roasted, a larger, slightly fatty bird is best, as the fat prevents the flesh from drying out. It may be stuffed or sprinkled with a little thyme or tarragon.

Poussin, part-boned breast joints, boneless breasts and diced chicken or chicken strips are good choices for sautéing, frying or stir-frying. Breadcrumb-coated portions (boneless breast or larger joints on the bone) can be deep-fried, but it is important to cook large joints at a comparatively low temperature so that they cook through without over-browning. The same cuts are suitable for grilling: cutting deep slashes into thick areas of meat helps to ensure they cook through. Spatchcock chicken is also suitable for grilling.

A chicken for casseroling should be plump and firm, but not too fatty. Similarly, when poaching a chicken, it is best to choose a plump older bird that is not too fatty. Chicken joints, such as drumsticks, thighs or quarters, are suitable for casseroling and poaching; boneless breasts are also ideal for brief braising or poaching.

There is a great variety of recipes for chicken, from the very simple to the very elaborate, including chicken chaud-froid, ballotine or hash. It can be made into croquettes, sausages, cutlets, fritters, pâtés and mousses. Chicken can be used in sauces for pasta, pie fillings, rice dishes such as Italian risotto or Indian biriani, and the cold cooked meat is ideal for salads, sandwich fillings and savouries.

RECIPES

chicken à blanc
Joint a raw chicken: cut into four if it is small; separate the wings, legs and breast if it is larger (the thigh bones can be removed if desired). Sprinkle the pieces with salt and pepper. Heat 40 g (1½ oz, 3 tablespoons) butter in a sauté pan or flameproof casserole and cook the pieces gently until firm but not coloured (first the thighs, which take longer to cook, then the wings and breast, which are more tender). Then cover and cook gently for about 40 minutes. Remove the pieces in the same order that they went in. Pour off the cooking fat; deglaze the pan with white stock, wine, cream, mushroom stock or other suitable liquid.

chicken à brun
Follow the recipe for chicken *à blanc*, but fry the chicken pieces over a brisk heat until brown all over. Cover and finish cooking, removing the wings and breast first, as these cook more quickly. Pour off the cooking fat, then add the sauce or required garnish and return the pieces of chicken to the pan. Reheat, but do not allow to boil.

chicken à la minute
Sauté a chicken *à brun* and arrange it in a serving dish. Pour over the very hot butter in which it was cooked and a little lemon juice. Sprinkle generously with chopped parsley.

Jointing a chicken

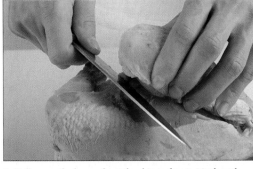

1 *Put the chicken on its side with the breast towards you. Holding the chicken firmly, cut the skin all the way along the backbone.*

2 *Pull away the leg and cut the skin to free it. Mark each quarter of the chicken and free the small nugget of meat, known as the oyster, from under the back of the carcass. Cut and remove any tendons, then remove the leg portion. Do the same with the other leg.*

3 *Keep the wings attached to the breast. Cut the bones along the rib cage, starting from the point of the wishbone. Remove the entire section in one piece, then cut off the wings.*

4 *Trim off the small bones, any small sections of bone and pieces of torn skin. Neaten the portions by cutting off the skin and meat from the end of each drumstick bone.*

chicken à l'ancienne

Sauté a chicken *à blanc*. Deglaze the pan with 100 ml (4 fl oz, 7 tablespoons) white stock or mushroom stock, reduce by two-thirds, then add 150 ml (¼ pint, ⅔ cup) chicken velouté sauce. Boil for 5 minutes, then add 150 ml (2 oz, 4 tablespoons) butter cut up into small pieces; whisk and allow it to melt before straining the sauce. Add 2 tablespoons chopped truffle and 3 tablespoons of port. Arrange the chicken in the serving dish with the sauce poured over.

chicken à la niçoise

Sauté a chicken *à brun* in oil alone; drain it and keep warm. Deglaze the pan with 100 ml (4 fl oz, 7 tablespoons) white wine and 150 ml (¼ pint, ⅔ cup) tomato sauce*. Add 1 crushed garlic clove and reduce. Put the chicken back in the sauce and reheat without boiling, then arrange it in a serving dish, surrounded with artichoke quarters cooked in butter, braised courgettes (zucchini) and stoned black olives (pitted ripe olives). Pour the sauce over and sprinkle with chopped herbs.

chicken à la piémontaise

Stuff a large roasting chicken with risotto mixed with 100 g (4 oz, 1 cup) diced white truffles. Roast it in butter in a flameproof casserole, then drain it and place it on a warm serving dish. Deglaze the casserole with white wine and thicken the sauce with a little beurre manié; serve this in a sauceboat. Serve the chicken with risotto sprinkled with Parmesan cheese.

chicken à la polonaise

Sauté chicken pieces in butter in a flameproof casserole for about 20 minutes. When cooked, pour over the juice of a lemon and cover with about 25 g (1 oz, ½ cup) fresh breadcrumbs mixed with 125 g (4½ oz, ½ cup) noisette* butter. Serve very hot with red cabbage, braised chestnuts or braised celeriac (celery root).

chicken à la portugaise

Cook a large roasting chicken in butter in a flameproof casserole in the oven until it is three-quarters cooked. While it is cooking, peel and seed 8 tomatoes, chop the flesh and cook in butter with 1 tablespoon chopped onion. Add this to the chicken and finish cooking, only half-covering the casserole.

Place the chicken in a serving dish and keep warm. Deglaze the casserole with a little white wine, reduce, season with salt and pepper to taste and pour this sauce over the chicken. Sprinkle with chopped parsley and serve at once.

chicken à l'italienne

Sauté a chicken *à brun* in equal quantities of oil and butter. Deglaze the pan with 150 ml (¼ pint, ⅔ cup) white wine and reduce; add 150 ml (¼ pint, ⅔ cup) sauce italienne*. Pour this sauce over the chicken and sprinkle with chopped parsley.

chicken annette

Sauté a chicken *à brun* and prepare a base of Annette potatoes. Arrange the drained chicken pieces on top of this and keep warm. Deglaze the cooking pan with 100 ml (4 fl oz, 7 tablespoons) white wine; add 1 chopped shallot, reduce, moisten with 150 ml (¼ pint, ⅔ cup) chicken stock, reduce a little more, then thicken with 1 tablespoon beurre manié. Add a squeeze of lemon juice and some chopped parsley, chervil and tarragon. Pour this sauce over the chicken.

chicken boivin

Sauté a chicken *à brun*; halfway through, add some small new onions softened in butter, blanched artichoke quarters and some tiny new potatoes. Finish cooking, then arrange the drained chicken and its garnish in a serving dish. Deglaze the cooking pan with some pot-au-feu broth, some meat glaze and a little lemon juice. Whisk in some butter. Pour this sauce over the chicken.

chicken casserole

Clean a chicken weighing 1.8 kg (4 lb) and truss it. Heat 50 g (2 oz, ¼ cup) butter in a flameproof casserole and brown the chicken on all sides (if a poulard is not used, cover the chicken breast with strips of fat bacon to keep it moist). Sprinkle with salt and pepper and cover the casserole; place in a preheated oven at 230°C (450°F, gas 8) and cook for about 1 hour. Serve the chicken with its own gravy, accompanied by glazed small (pearl) onions or carrots.

chicken clos-jouve

Joint a large Bresse chicken into 6 pieces and bone them. Prepare and cook a concentrated stock with the crushed chicken bones, the green part of 1 leek, 1 onion, 1 calf's foot (partially boned) and some thyme and bay leaf. Strain, deglaze with port, then moisten with stock and white wine until the ingredients are just covered; cook for 1½ hours until the stock resembles a rich demi-glace.

Prepare a forcemeat with the white parts of 3 leeks (shredded), 125 g (4½ oz, 1¼ cups) horn of plenty (or cultivated) mushrooms browned in butter, the liver of the chicken and 150 g (5 oz, ⅔ cup) foie gras (both diced), 100 ml (4 fl oz, 7 tablespoons) double (heavy) cream and 1 egg yolk. Season the forcemeat with salt and pepper and use it to stuff the boned chicken pieces. Tie them up (not too tightly), brown in butter in a flameproof casserole, then reduce the heat, cover the pan and cook

gently – turning once – until cooked through (about 35 minutes). Remove the chicken and arrange on a serving dish; keep warm. Add the demi-glace to the casserole, heat through, adjust the seasoning and pour over the pieces of chicken.

chicken cooked in beer

Cut a 1.25 kg (2¾ lb) chicken into pieces and fry them in butter in a casserole until golden. Add 2 peeled, chopped shallots and fry lightly. Add 60 ml (2 fl oz, ¼ cup) Dutch gin and flambé it. Now add 400 ml (14 fl oz, 1¾ cups) beer, 60 ml (2 fl oz, ¼ cup) crème fraîche, 1 bouquet garni, salt and a little cayenne pepper. Cover and simmer. Clean and finely slice 250 g (9 oz) mushrooms and add the contents of the casserole. After 45 minutes of cooking, take the chicken pieces out of the casserole, drain and arrange on a serving dish. Put aside in a warm place. Remove the bouquet garni, add 60 ml (2 fl oz, ¼ cup) crème fraîche and reduce by half. Mix a little of the sauce with an egg yolk and stir, then pour back into the casserole and beat vigorously. Pour the sauce over the chicken and sprinkle with finely chopped parsley.

chicken dauphinoise

Insert some slivers of truffle beneath the skin of a good large Bresse chicken. Sprinkle with salt and pepper inside, then stuff with its own liver and 100 g (4 oz, ½ cup) foie gras, both diced, mixed with a little chopped truffle. Truss the bird and put it in a pork bladder, sprinkle again with a little salt and pepper, add 3 tablespoons brandy and the same quantity of Madeira, then seal the bladder.

Make some stock with the giblets, pour it into a flameproof casserole, add the chicken in the bladder and bring to the boil. Cook gently for 45 minutes. Remove the chicken from the pan, being careful not to pierce the bladder, untie it and drain the cooking liquid into a bowl. Remove the forcemeat from the chicken and press it through a sieve. Cut the chicken into joints and arrange on a warm dish. Thicken the cooking liquid with the sieved forcemeat and serve separately in a sauceboat.

chicken in a salt crust

In a bowl mix together 1 kg (2¼ lb, 9 cups) plain (all-purpose) flour, the same weight of coarse sea salt and 100 ml (4 fl oz, 7 tablespoons) cold water. Knead this dough and roll it out on a pastry board. Sprinkle the inside of a chicken with salt and pepper and insert a sprig of rosemary, a bay leaf, its own liver and the livers of 2 other chickens. Place the chicken on the dough, wrap it up and seal it, place on a baking sheet and cook in a preheated oven at 160°C (325°F, gas 3) for 1½ hours. Break off the hard salty crust and discard; remove the chicken and carve. Serve with a salad dressed with walnut oil.

chicken Maryland

Cut the raw chicken into joints and dip the pieces into cold milk. Drain them, coat with flour and fry in butter until golden. Continue cooking over a very low heat, turning once, until cooked through. Meanwhile, place the carcass and giblets in a saucepan with garlic, onion, a little stock and some milk. Bring to the boil and simmer for a few minutes, then strain the liquid and pour over the fried chicken pieces. Garnish with fried bacon rashers (slices) and serve with corn fritters or grilled (broiled) corn-on-the-cob.

chicken mireille

Heat 65 g (2½ oz, 5 tablespoons) butter in a sauté pan and gently cook a large Bresse chicken, cut into 8 pieces, until the meat turns white. As soon as the pieces are firm, but not coloured, add 500 ml (17 fl oz, 2 cups) dry white wine and reduce until almost all the liquid has evaporated. Add 1 kg (2¼ lb) fresh morels, carefully cleaned, washed and patted dry, then 1 litre (1¾ pints, 4⅓ cups) double (heavy) cream; cook gently for 35 minutes.

Remove the pieces of chicken and the morels and arrange on a hot serving dish. Reduce the cooking liquid to 500 ml (17 fl oz, 2 cups). Thicken it with 1 egg yolk, whisking over the heat but not allowing it to boil. Pour this sauce over the chicken.

chicken petit-duc

Cook some morels and truffle slivers in butter. Sauté a chicken *à brun*, then drain it and keep warm in a serving dish. Deglaze the pan in which the chicken was cooked with 3 tablespoons Madeira, reduce and then moisten with 150 ml (¼ pint, ⅔ cup) demi-glace* sauce. Garnish the chicken with the morels and truffles and pour the sauce over.

chicken rosière

Stuff a large roasting chicken with panada forcemeat made with cream, truss and bard it, then cook in white stock, like chicken with tarragon. Prepare separately some slices of calves' sweetbreads cooked in white stock, and a mushroom purée. Untie the chicken, remove the barding fat, cut into joints and arrange in a round dish, surrounded by the calves' sweetbreads and the forcemeat, cut into slices. Pour over all this a sauce made from the cooking liquid, strained and reduced. Serve the mushroom purée separately.

chicken with artichokes

Sauté a chicken *à brun*, adding some artichoke quarters (blanched in salted water) halfway through the cooking period. Drain the chicken and its garnish, arrange in a serving dish and keep warm. Deglaze the cooking pan with white wine and stock; reduce, thicken with a little beurre manié and pour this sauce over the chicken and artichokes. Sprinkle with chopped parsley.

chicken with basil

Sauté the chicken *à brun*. Drain it and arrange on a warm dish. Deglaze the cooking pan with 200 ml (7 fl oz, ¾ cup) dry white wine. Add 1 tablespoon chopped fresh basil and whisk in 50 g (2 oz, 4 tablespoons) butter. Pour this sauce over the chicken.

chicken with ceps

Sauté a chicken *à brun* in equal quantities of butter and oil. Three-quarters of the way through the cooking time, add 300 g (11 oz, 4 cups) ceps or other mushrooms, sliced and sautéed in oil, then 2 chopped shallots. Finish cooking. Arrange the drained chicken and mushrooms in a serving dish. Deglaze the casserole with 100 ml (4 fl oz, 7 tablespoons) white wine; reduce, then pour it over the chicken and mushrooms. Sprinkle with chopped parsley. A small crushed garlic clove can be added to the sauce.

chicken with cream

Sauté a chicken *à blanc*; drain it, arrange on a serving dish and keep warm. Pour off the cooking fat from the pan, add 150 ml (¼ pint, ⅔ cup) dry cider and reduce until all the liquid has evaporated. Then mix in 200 ml (7 fl oz, ¾ cup) double (heavy) cream and reduce just enough to make the sauce very smooth; adjust the seasoning. Pour the sauce over the chicken and sprinkle with chopped parsley. The chicken can be flamed in Calvados, or the cider can be replaced with white wine.

chicken with oysters

Sauté a chicken *à blanc*. Poach 12 oysters in their own liquid. Drain the cooked chicken and keep warm in a serving dish. Deglaze the cooking pan with 100 ml (4 fl oz, 7 tablespoons) white wine and the liquid from the oysters; reduce by half and add 100 ml (4 fl oz, 7 tablespoons) chicken velouté* sauce. Add a squeeze of lemon juice, then 40 g (1½ oz, 3 tablespoons) butter, whisking all the time. Arrange the oysters around the chicken and pour the sauce over.

chicken with plantains

Sauté a chicken *à brun* in a flameproof casserole; when golden, add 1 large chopped onion, 5 peeled tomatoes and 250 g (9 oz) streaky bacon cut into pieces. Cook for 1 hour, occasionally adding a little cold water to prevent the fat from blackening; season with salt and pepper. While the chicken is cooking, cut 12 plantains in half and boil them in a saucepan of water for 30 minutes. Drain them and place in the casserole with the chicken; simmer for a further 15 minutes. Serve very hot.

chicken with rice à la bourbon

Fry a large roasting chicken with a little lard (shortening) in a flameproof casserole, until just golden. Add 1 finely chopped onion, 2 whole carrots, 1 tablespoon tomato purée (paste) and a bouquet garni. Season with salt and pepper, half-cover with stock and cook gently for 1¼–1½ hours, according to the size of the bird.

Blanch 250 g (9 oz, 1¼ cups) rice for 5 minutes, then drain and cool. Add twice its volume of stock to the rice and cook until soft, but do not allow the grains to disintegrate (about 18 minutes). Pack into a greased ring mould and unmould on to a round serving dish. Cut the chicken into pieces and arrange in the middle. Strain the chicken cooking liquid and pour it over the chicken.

chicken with rice and suprême sauce

Truss a large chicken as for roasting and cook it in white stock, like chicken with tarragon, but for only 40 minutes. Blanch 250 g (9 oz, 1¼ cups) rice for 5 minutes, drain it, rinse it and drain once more. Drain the half-cooked chicken, strain the stock, then return the chicken to the casserole; add the drained rice and the stock – it should come to about 3 cm (1¼ in) above the rice. Add 25 g (1 oz, 2 tablespoons) butter and continue cooking gently for 20 minutes. With the rest of the stock, make a suprême sauce. Place the chicken on a warm dish, pour over a little of the sauce and surround with rice. Serve the remaining sauce separately in a sauceboat.

chicken with tarragon

Clean a large roasting chicken and put a bunch of tender tarragon sprigs inside it. Truss as for roasting, rub lightly with half a lemon and bard the breast and back with thin slices of rindless bacon. Place in a flameproof casserole and just cover with white stock, adding a small bunch of tarragon. Cover, bring quickly to the boil, then cook gently for about 1 hour (when pricked, the juice which comes out of the chicken should be clear). Drain the chicken, untie it and remove the barding fat and the tarragon from inside. Garnish with blanched tarragon leaves and put it in a warm place on a serving dish.

Thicken the cooking liquid with a little arrowroot or beurre manié; strain it and add 2 tablespoons chopped fresh tarragon. Pour a little of this sauce over the chicken and serve the remainder in a sauceboat.

Alternatively, the casserole can be deglazed with a glass of white wine and a little thickened and strained veal stock to which a handful of chopped tarragon leaves has been added.

chicken with tarragon in aspic

Cook a large roasting chicken in white stock as in the recipe for chicken with tarragon. Drain it, untruss it and pat dry; leave it to cool, then place it in the refrigerator.

Skim the fat off the cooking liquid and strain it, then heat it, adding 20 g (¾ oz, 3 envelopes) powdered gelatine completely dissolved in cold water. In a saucepan, whisk together 100 g (4 oz, ¾ cup) lean minced (ground) beef, 1 egg white and a handful of tarragon leaves, roughly chopped. Add the cooking liquid, whisking all the time, and bring to the boil. Simmer gently for 30 minutes, then strain the liquid, add 100 ml (4 fl oz, 7 tablespoons) Madeira and leave to cool.

When the aspic is nearly set, coat the chicken with several layers, placing it in the refrigerator after each application. Garnish the chicken with blanched tarragon leaves, arranged in a decorative pattern, before the last application of aspic. Finally, place the chicken on a serving dish surrounded with any remaining set aspic cut into cubes.

chicken with vinegar

Peel and dice 2 carrots, 1 turnip, the cleaned white parts of 2 leeks and 1 celery stick; stud 1 large onion with 2 cloves. Brown the giblets of the chicken, plus those of 2 others, in a little butter. Place all these giblets into a pan with 1 litre (1¾ pints, 4⅓ cups) cold water and bring to the boil; then add all the vegetables, a bouquet garni, 4 shallots, 2 peeled crushed garlic cloves, 175 ml (6 fl oz, ¾ cup) dry white wine, some salt, pepper and a small pinch of cayenne pepper. Simmer gently for 45–60 minutes.

Heat 40 g (1½ oz, 3 tablespoons) butter in a flameproof casserole and cook the chicken, cut into 6 pieces, for about 10 minutes until golden brown; cover and simmer for another 35 minutes.

Reduce the liquid in which the giblets were cooked by half, then strain it and add 175 ml (6 fl oz, ¾ cup) white wine vinegar; reduce again by one-third. Purée the chicken liver. When the chicken is cooked, pour the vinegar sauce into the casserole, stir well and cook together for 5 minutes; thicken with 1 tablespoon beurre manié. Dilute the liver purée with 1 tablespoon vinegar and blend into the sauce, away from the heat. Serve very hot.

roast chicken

Clean a chicken, weigh it and calculate the cooking time, allowing 15 minutes per 450 g (1 lb), plus 15 minutes. Sprinkle with salt and pepper inside and outside, truss it, then brush lightly with clarified butter. Place it on its breast in a roasting tin (pan) and cook in a preheated oven at 200°C (400°F, gas 6) for half the cooking time. Then turn it on to its back to finish cooking. Baste it from time to time with its own juice. Transfer the chicken to a platter, deglaze the roasting dish with a little boiling water and serve the chicken and its gravy separately.

sautéed chicken with tarragon

Sauté a chicken à brun, then drain it and keep warm in a serving dish. Deglaze the cooking pan with 150 ml (¼ pint, ⅔ cup) white wine; add 1 chopped shallot, reduce, then add 150 ml (¼ pint, ⅔ cup) thickened gravy (or chicken or veal stock thickened with a little arrowroot). Finally, add 1 tablespoon lemon juice and 2 tablespoons tarragon leaves, blanched and chopped. Pour this sauce over the chicken.

This dish can also be prepared in the same way as sautéed chicken with cream, replacing the parsley with tarragon. Another variation is to replace the tarragon with a mixture of parsley and chervil (unblanched) and blanched tarragon, all chopped.

steamed stuffed chicken with ragoût of broccoli ◆

Peel 100 g (4 oz) carrots and 100 g (4 oz) turnips. Chop very finely and cook in boiling water. At the same time, cook separately 100 g (4 oz) unpeeled courgettes (zucchini) in boiling water, making sure they remain firm. Drain thoroughly and dice.

Braise 500 g (18 oz) calves' sweetbreads until brown and cut into small dice. Strain the braising juices and reduce to a quarter of their original quantity. Pour 100 ml (4 fl oz, 7 tablespoons) of the reduced juices on to the sweetbreads, finely chopped carrots, turnips and courgettes.

Using a wide kitchen knife, flatten 4 chicken fillets between 2 pieces of cling film (plastic wrap). Sprinkle a little pepper on top, then put a small amount of sweetbread mixture in the centre. Roll individually into small cylinders and wrap in cling film. Steam for 20 minutes.

Cook 575 g (1¼ lb) broccoli for a few minutes in boiling salted water. Fry 1 finely chopped onion and 150 g (5 oz, ⅔ cup) lardons of smoked streaky bacon in 20 g (¾ oz, 1½ tablespoons) butter, until golden, then add the broccoli. Season with salt and pepper and keep warm. Unwrap the chicken fillets and cut them in half. Put 2 half chicken fillets on each plate and pour over the braising juice. Arrange the broccoli and the smoked bacon around the fillets.

stuffed chicken à la mode de sorges

Fill the inside of a chicken with a forcemeat made up of its liver chopped and mixed with stale breadcrumbs, chopped bacon, parsley, chives, shallots, garlic, salt, pepper, mustard and the bird's blood (if available), all bound together with an egg yolk. Truss it as for roasting.

Brown all over in goose fat, then place it in a flameproof casserole and cover with boiling water; season with salt and pepper. Bring to the boil, skim, then add 3 carrots and 2 turnips (peeled), the white part of 3 leeks tied together in a bundle, 1 celery heart, 1 onion stuck with a clove and a few leaves of Swiss chard tied in a bundle. Simmer very gently for about 1¼ hours. Drain the chicken, untruss it and place it on a dish, surrounded with the vegetables, cutting the carrots and turnips into pieces.

Prepare some Sorges sauce to be served separately: make a highly seasoned vinaigrette, add chopped parsley, chives and shallots, then bind with the yolks of 2 eggs boiled for 3 minutes. Continue cooking the egg whites for 2 minutes in the chicken stock, dice them and add to the sauce. As they do in Périgord, serve the strained chicken cooking stock first as a soup, either poured over slices of toast or garnished with large boiled vermicelli.

truffled chicken à la périgourdine

Wash and peel 1 kg (2¼ lb) truffles, reserving the outer skins and trim to the size and shape of pigeon's eggs; chop the trimmings finely. Melt 250 g (9 oz) chicken fat and the same quantity of unsmoked bacon over a low heat and strain through a sieve, pressing down well to extract as much flavour as possible. Pour this fat into a saucepan containing the truffles, the truffle trimmings, some salt, pepper and mixed spices, half a bay leaf, a small sprig of thyme and a little grated nutmeg. Simmer, covered, for 15 minutes, then remove from the heat and leave to cool.

Stuff a large roasting chicken with this mixture, making sure the openings are well sewn up and completely closed. Place the chicken in a terrine and cover it with the reserved outer skins of the truffles; leave the chicken like this for 3 or 4 days in a cool place. On the last day, remove the truffle skins and cook them in butter with an onion and a carrot (both chopped) and some sprigs of parsley. Secure the chicken on a spit; cover with strips of unsmoked bacon and, on top of this, the vegetable mixture. Wrap securely in a double thickness of oiled greaseproof (wax) paper and spit-roast for 1½ hours. Five minutes before serving, unwrap the chicken and allow it to brown. Take it off the spit, untruss it and serve with Périgueux sauce.

Spring Chicken

devilled spring chicken

Prepare the spring chicken *en crapaudine*. Sprinkle with salt and pepper, brush lightly with clarified butter on both sides and half-roast it in a preheated oven at 240°C (475°F, gas 9). Mix 2 tablespoons mustard with a little cayenne and brush this over the chicken. Coat generously with fresh breadcrumbs and sprinkle with a little clarified butter. Finish cooking under the grill (broiler), on both sides. Serve with gherkins (sweet dill pickles), lemon halves and a devilled sauce.

fried spring chicken

Cut a spring chicken into 6 pieces (2 wings, 2 legs and 2 pieces of breast). Mix 2 tablespoons oil with 1 tablespoon lemon juice, some salt and pepper, a little cayenne, 1 finely chopped garlic clove, 1 tablespoon very finely chopped parsley, and, if liked, ½ teaspoon ground ginger. Marinate the chicken pieces in this mixture for 30 minutes. Drain them, coat in breadcrumbs, then deep-fry in very hot oil (180°C, 350°F). When they are golden (13–15 minutes), drain on paper towels, sprinkle with fine salt and serve with lemon quarters.

spring chickens à la sicilienne

Boil some pasta shapes in salted water. Drain, reheat for a few minutes in very hot butter, then mix with a purée of pistachio nuts. Sprinkle with salt and pepper and leave to cool. Stuff the chickens with this mixture and truss them, then spit-roast, basting frequently. Three-quarters of the way through cooking, sprinkle with fresh breadcrumbs and allow to colour. Serve the cooking juices as a gravy separately.

other recipes See *piémontaise, viennoise.*

CHICK PEA A bushy leguminous plant cultivated in southern Europe for its rounded edible pealike seeds, which are enclosed in pods. The English name is derived from the French *chiche*, from the Latin *cicer*. Cicero is said to have been so nicknamed because of the pea-shaped wart on the end of his nose. The plant originated in the Mediterranean basin and the seeds may be sold dried or precooked in cans.

Dried chick peas should always be soaked before cooking. Canned chick peas are cooked and need draining, then rinsing. Used in purées, soups and stews, they feature in numerous dishes in the south of France and also in Spain and the Middle East: *olla podrida*, *puchero*, *hummus* and *cocido*. They are a traditional ingredient in sauces served with couscous and are used in various preparations with dried beans and even in salads. Chick peas and chick pea flour (*besan*) are also popular in Indian cooking.

RECIPES

chick peas à la catalane
Soak 500 g (18 oz, 3 cups) chick peas in cold water for at least 12 hours, changing the water several times. Drain them and place in a pan with a carrot, an onion, 2 celery sticks and the white part of a leek, all thinly sliced. Add a piece of smoked bacon weighing about 250 g (9 oz) and a bouquet garni and cover with 2 litres (3½ pints, 9 cups) cold water. Bring to the boil, skim, add salt and pepper, reduce the heat and add 3–4 tablespoons oil.

Simmer gently for 2–3 hours, depending on the quality of the chick peas. Then add a piece of strong *chorizo* and cook for a further 30 minutes. Remove the bouquet garni, the bacon and the *chorizo* and drain the chick peas. Then put the chick peas into a saucepan together with 200 ml (7 fl oz, ¾ cup) tomato* sauce spiced with garlic. Cut the *chorizo* into slices, slice the bacon and add them to the chick peas. Simmer for 15 minutes, pour into a deep dish and serve piping hot.

ragoût of mutton with chick peas
Soak some chick peas in cold water for at least 12 hours, changing the water several times. Then place in a large pan of cold water allowing 2 litres (3½ pints, 9 cups) for every 500 g (18 oz, 3 cups) chick peas. Bring to the boil, skim, add some salt and simmer gently for about 2½ hours. Drain.

Prepare a mutton ragoût *à la bonne femme*, but add the chick peas (instead of potatoes) with the bacon. Cook for a further 30 minutes.

CHICORY (ENDIVE) A winter vegetable with tightly bunched leaves that form a firm elongated heart. In about 1850, a peasant from the Brussels suburbs observed that wild chicory roots cultivated in warmth and shade grew elongated shoots with yellowish edible leaves. Later, a Belgian botanist called Brézier improved the technique of etiolation to produce the modern chicory. It first appeared at Les Halles in Paris in October 1879.

The nomenclature of this vegetable is rather confusing: it is called chicory in England and endive or Belgian endive in the United States (in England, endive is a curly-leaved salad plant called chicory in America). For the sake of clarity, the English nomenclature is used in this article.

The reason for the confusion is that chicory and endive are closely related, belonging to the Compositae family of plants. *Cichorium intybus* produces the young shoots harvested as chicory; *Cichorium endivia* is the frizzy endive. There are many varieties of both vegetables, including red-leaved radicchios, available as tight chicory-like buds or as slightly larger, leafy rosettes. Leafy, green rosettes of chicory are also harvested.

Chicory is grown in northern France, Belgium (where it is called *chicon* or *witloof* and cooked au gratin, virtually a national dish) and the Netherlands, and is available from October to May. Carefully cleaned and packed, and kept in the dark to prevent it from turning green, the chicory should be firm, shiny, swollen and unblemished.

■ **Chicory for coffee** Certain varieties of chicory in the north of France and in Belgium with large smooth roots are used as a substitute for coffee. These roots are dried, cut, roasted and then ground to make an infusion. Chicory is produced commercially in the form of grounds, a soluble powder or as a liquid extract. It gives a bitter and very dark-coloured drink, which is often blended with breakfast coffee. Chicory has been used as a substitute for coffee since 1769, first in Italy and then in Germany. It does not have the aroma or stimulating properties of coffee.

■ **Trimming and preparation** Remove any damaged leaves, rinse the chicory quickly in water, dry and wipe. Avoid soaking it in water, because this makes it bitter. Hollow out a small cone about 2.5 cm (1 in) high from the base using a knife: this is where the bitterness is concentrated. Never scald or blanch chicory.

Chicory can be served raw in salads – with vinaigrette and often with hard-boiled (hard-cooked) eggs and any of the various ingredients used in winter salads, including beetroot (red beets), apples, nuts, cheese and orange or grapefruit quarters. For cooked dishes, chicory heads are braised and drained; they can then be coated with béchamel sauce, sprinkled with noisette butter, served with gravy or with plain butter and herbs, topped with grated cheese and browned, or made into a purée. They can be served as an accompaniment to roasts and poultry. They can also be braised, made into a *chiffonade* or prepared as fritters (especially when served with fish). As a main dish, chicory is braised, rolled in slices of ham and coated with a port and raisin sauce, or stuffed (with a fatty or lean stuffing) and browned on top.

Steamed stuffed chicken with ragoût of broccoli, see page 277.

RECIPES

braised chicory

Trim and wash 1 kg (2¼ lb) chicory and place in a flameproof casserole with 25 g (1 oz, 2 tablespoons) butter, a pinch of salt, the juice of a quarter of a lemon, and 3 tablespoons water. Bring quickly to the boil without a lid, then leave to boil over a medium heat for 35 minutes.

The chicory can also be braised by cooking very gently in 50 g (2 oz, 4 tablespoons) butter, with a pinch of salt and a few drops of lemon juice, but without water, for 45 minutes.

chicory à la Mornay

Braise some chicory heads, drain them, and add 300 ml (½ pint, 1¼ cups) Mornay* sauce to the cooking juices. Coat an ovenproof dish with this sauce and put the chicory in the dish. Cover with more sauce, sprinkle with grated cheese and then lightly with melted butter, and brown in a preheated oven at 240°C (475°F, gas 9).

chicory au gratin

Braise some chicory heads and drain them thoroughly. Arrange them in a gratin dish that has been buttered and sprinkled with grated cheese (Comté, Gruyère, Parmesan or even dried Edam). Sprinkle the chicory with more grated cheese and melted butter, then brown in a preheated oven at 240°C (475°F, gas 9).

chicory fritots

Braise some chicory heads, keeping them fairly firm, then drain thoroughly and leave to cool. Cut them into quarters and steep for 1 hour in olive oil containing some lemon juice and pepper. Drain, dip in batter and deep-fry in very hot oil (180°C, 350°F). When the fritters have turned golden, remove, sprinkle with fine salt and serve with fried parsley.

chicory purée

Braise some chicory until very soft, then rub through a sieve or use a blender to obtain a purée. Butter or cream can be added (reduce the cream a little first), as can white sauce – use 300 ml (½ pint, 1¼ cups) sauce per 1 kg (2¼ lb) purée. The purée can be browned in a hot oven if desired.

chicory salad à la flamande

Wash and wipe some fresh chicory. Separate the leaves and divide them in half, trimming if necessary. Wipe thoroughly. Sprinkle lightly with lemon juice to prevent discoloration. Add some diced cooked beetroot (red beet) and garnish with peeled orange quarters. Season with a mustard vinaigrette and sprinkle with chopped hard-boiled (hard-cooked) egg yolk and chopped chives.

chicory with ham

Braise some chicory heads. Prepare some very thick white sauce (enough for 2–4 tablespoons per head) and add 50 g (2 oz, ½ cup) grated Gruyère cheese per 250 ml (8 fl oz, 1 cup) sauce. Drain the chicory heads, wrap each in a slice of Paris ham and arrange side by side in a buttered gratin dish. Cover with the hot white sauce, sprinkle with grated Gruyère cheese and dot with butter. Brown in a preheated oven at 240°C (475°F, gas 9).

chicory with noisette butter

Braise some chicory heads, drain them and put them in a serving dish. Add 20 g (¾ oz, 1½ tablespoons) butter to the cooking juices and reduce until they turn brown. Sprinkle the chicory with the noisette butter.

scallop and chicory cassolettes

Cut 1 kg (2¼ lb) chicory into 1 cm (½ in) segments, wash, drain and sprinkle with lemon juice. Season with salt and sugar, add 2 tablespoons groundnut (peanut) oil and fry for 7–8 minutes in butter without covering the pan. Shell and trim some scallops, put them in a frying pan, season with salt, pepper and a little cayenne, and brown (3–4 minutes), keeping them fairly soft. Arrange them in *cassolettes* on top of the chicory. Reduce 3 tablespoons port by two-thirds, add the juice of a lemon and 50 g (2 oz, 4 tablespoons) butter cut into pieces, then whisk into an emulsion. Add a little lemon zest, pour over the scallops and serve.

other recipes See *chiffonnade, cream soup*.

CHIFFONNADE A preparation of sorrel, chicory (endive), lettuce or other leaves, cut into even shreds or strips. Cutting *en chiffonnade* is the term for shredding green leaves. The leaves may be cut very finely or into wider strips, as required for the recipe. A chiffonnade may be softened in butter, moistened with stock, milk or cream and used as a garnish for soup. Lettuce chiffonnade may be used to garnish cold hors d'oeuvre.

RECIPES

chiffonnade of chicory with cream

Wash and dry the chicory (endive) and remove the small bitter cone situated at the root. Cut the leaves into thin strips 1 cm (½ in) wide. Melt some butter in a shallow frying pan and add the chicory – use 40–50 g (1½–2 oz, 3–4 tablespoons) butter for each 1 kg (2¼ lb) chicory. Stir and add ½ teaspoon sugar, 2 tablespoons lemon juice, and salt and pepper. Cover the pan and cook gently for 30–35 minutes. Stir in 100–150 ml (4–5 fl oz, ½–⅔ cup) double (heavy) cream and heat quickly. Serve very hot.

chiffonnade of cooked lettuce

Prepare in the same way as *chiffonnade* of raw lettuce. Melt some butter in a shallow frying pan and add the lettuce *chiffonnade* and some salt – use 40 g (1½ oz, 3 tablespoons) butter per 500 g (18 oz)

CHICORY AND ENDIVE

green chicory

endive or curly endive

red Treviso

endive or curly endive –
frisée

sugarloaf

chicory

scarole

radicchio

lettuce leaves. Cook gently without a lid until all the vegetable juice from the lettuce has evaporated. Then add 2 tablespoons double (heavy) cream and reheat.

chiffonnade of raw lettuce

Wash and dry some lettuce leaves, discarding the coarser leaves. Roll up several leaves and cut each roll into very thin strips. Toss in vinaigrette if it is to be used as a garnish for meat, fish or cold shellfish. It may also be mixed with green walnuts, a julienne of ham, meat or cold chicken and Emmental cheese, and then sprinkled with vinaigrette and chopped herbs.

CHILE See *opposite page.*

CHILL To cool an item of food, a drink or a dish quickly. Ice cream (or a similar iced mixture) is chilled by surrounding it with crushed ice or by placing it in the freezer so that it sets. Jellies, cold mousses and terrines are chilled in the coldest part of the refrigerator prior to serving. When preparing some foods, such as certain forcemeats, the ingredients should be chilled when mixed by placing them in a bowl over crushed ice.

Champagne is chilled by placing the bottle in a bucket of crushed ice and water (never in the refrigerator). A cocktail is chilled by shaking it with ice in a cocktail shaker or pouring the mixture over crushed ice.

CHILLI Related to the pepper (sweet or bell pepper), this is a hot fruit of the capsicum family, generally referred to as a spice but, depending on type, also used as a vegetable. Native to South America, there is now a vast array of different chillies, ranging from mild varieties to extremely fiery examples, and a large number of types are found in Mexico and the West Indies. Some traditional West Indian varieties have colourful names, for example *zozio* pepper, meaning parrot's tongue, Chinese lantern pepper and 'seven courts-bouillons pepper'.

Portuguese and Spanish explorers introduced chilli peppers to Asia; they were then taken to the Middle East, Africa and Europe. Harissa, a chilli sauce used in North African cooking, is known particularly as a seasoning for couscous. Pickled chillies are often served whole in the Middle East. Several kinds of chillies are used in Indian cooking, fresh or dried as chilli powder, and India is one of the world's foremost chilli producers. Sichuan cuisine, in China, makes use of small hot chillies; many Indonesian and Thai dishes are also spiced with small, hot chillies.

In Europe, the cooking of Spain and Portugal includes mild and hot chillies; dried chillies feature in Italian dishes and fresh chillies are used in some regional Italian specialities.

Chilli products include dried chillies, whole or crushed in flakes; chilli powder, of which there are different types; chilli sauces; chilli paste; and chilli oil (oil infused with chillies).

■ **Mild and sweet to fiercely hot** One of the best-known scales for grading the heat of chillies is the Scoville heat scale, devised in the United States of America early in the last century and based on taste tests for detecting capsaicin, the substance that gives the chillies their hot flavour. The score ranges from 0 units for sweet peppers to 120,000 units or more for some of the very fiery African chillies. In terms of buying chillies for home use, most stores indicate whether they are mild, hot or very hot; it is a good idea to remember that some of the very small chillies are extremely hot. Small and dark green are usually good indicators of a hot flavour. There are, of course, also large and/or red varieties with a powerful flavour.

Individual taste also varies and those who are used to eating chillies do not notice the heat, so they require more for an intense flavour. Those who do not eat chillies often should take care when making authentic dishes from areas where chillies are widely used, such as Mexico and India, as the amount suggested may be far too hot for the uninitiated palate. Try chillies and their products sparingly at first until acquainted with their flavour.

■ **Types of chillies** Chillies range in colour from pale creamy-white through green, yellow, orange, red to black. They may be tiny or large and long, similar to long sweet peppers. As for all ingredients, as their international popularity has grown and their use become more varied, many plants have been crossed to provide a broader range. The following examples give some indication of the choice, but there are literally hundreds used in cooking around the world.

• Anaheim Green through to red, mild to hot, these American chillies were first cultivated in California.
• Ancho Heart-shaped and mild to fairly hot, this is a large dried Mexican chilli with a dark red-brown colour. Known as *poblano* when fresh.
• Banana or sweet banana Pale yellow and long, these may be mild or they may be hot, when they are known as hot Hungarian wax or Hungarian wax.
• Bird chilli No more than 2 cm (¾ in) long and very hot. Sold dried and ground in cayenne pepper. Used in Indian cooking and known as *usimulagu*.
• Bonnet or Scotch bonnet Small and rounded, with a slightly folded or squashed, bonnet-like appearance, these may be green, yellow, orange or red. They are extremely hot.
• Cayenne Long, thin and slightly wrinkled hot chilli with a sharp flavour. Dried cayenne are ground and used for the spice of the same name.
• Cherry Plump, rounded and mild or hot, they may be green through to red.
• Chipotle Conical, dark red in colour and hot dried Mexican chilli.
• Choricero A mild, sweet bell-shaped chilli used in Spanish cooking and essential in chorizo sausages. Threaded in large bunches and hung out to dry in the autumn sun.
• Fresno Fairly hot green or red Mexican chillies.
• Guindilla Small hot chilli used in Spanish

CHILE

Chilean cuisine is essentially
based on meat, especially lamb,
which is usually served grilled
(broiled). But it also uses fish and
seafood, which is abundant along
its coast: conger eel soup is a
famous speciality of the country.
Its dishes are all highly seasoned
with spices and onions. Stews
(*chupes*) contain a mixture of
tripe, vegetables or dried meat,
and *empanadas* (pies filled
with meat or fish) are just
as varied.

WINE Strongly influenced by
French wine-making, Chile
produces some of the best wines
in South America. The first
vineyards were planted at the end
of the 18th century. Today they
stretch over some 120,000
hectares (300,000 acres), along
2,000 kilometres (1,250 miles) of
the Pacific coast, between the 30th
and 40th parallel. The soil is fertile
and varied, with excellent
exposure to the sun and no spring
frosts. The melting snow from the
Andes provides the necessary
irrigation, thus compensating for
the low rainfall. Chilean wine-
growing is concentrated in two
main regions.

■ **Central region** The north
central region produces wines
with a high alcohol content which
are often used for making spirits,
while the central valley is mainly
planted with classic grape
varieties such as Cabernet
Sauvignon, Cabernet Franc,
Merlot, Chardonnay, Sauvignon
Blanc and Riesling. Vinification
techniques there are similar to
those of Bordeaux. In the south
central region the pais variety is
grown, producing slightly coarse
wines, while the southernmost
region makes acceptable wine
when conditions are good.

■ **Secano** The central region of
Secano grows the pais variety and
produces good quality wines. The
southern part of Secano produces
40% of all Chilean wine, and it is
particularly interesting for its
vineyards of white grape varieties
such as Sauvignon Blanc, Riesling
and Muscat which do well and
produce good wines, although in
very limited quantities.

Good wines are often named
after the noble varieties from
which they were made. Some
carry the appellations 'Sauternes',
'Chablis', 'Borgona' (Burgundy) or
even 'Rhine', and these may be of
excellent quality.

cooking, particularly the dishes of the north-west of
the country.
• HABAÑERO Extremely hot (said to be the hottest),
ranging from green through to orange, these are
related to, but not the same as, the bonnet or Scotch
bonnet.
• HONTAKA Hot Japanese chilli, small, red and wrinkled.
• JALAPEÑO From green through to red and mild to
fairly hot, these Mexican chillies are used fresh, pickled or smoked.
• MALAGUETA Very hot small green or red chilli.
• ÑORA Sweet chilli used in Spanish cooking, particularly in the rice dishes of the east coast. About the
size and shape of a golf ball, this is known as
romesco in Catalonia, where it is used to make
romesco sauce, with garlic and hazelnuts.
• PEPERONCINO Italian chilli used fresh and frequently in the regional cooking of Abruzzi and Basil-
icata in a wide variety of dishes, as well as to season
sausages and salami. Also pickled.
• PIMIENTO Mild or through to hot, green, yellow or
red.
• POBLANO Mexican large fresh green chilli, usually
mild and suitable for stuffing. Known as *ancho*
when dried.
• SERRANO Small, very hot green chillies, widely
used in Mexican cooking.
• TABASCO The hot chilli grown in the USA and used
to make the chilli sauce of the same name.
• THAI Known as *prik*, the common chillies used in
Thai cooking are the small very hot green or red
variety. Also known as bird's eye chillies.
• TOGARASHI Japanese red chilli available dried
whole or ground. Used in pickles.

■ **Preparing chillies** Chillies may be used whole
(then removed from the dish before serving for a
mild flavour) or cut up. Large mild chillies can be
stuffed or prepared in other ways as a vegetable.
The seeds inside chillies are extremely hot and
should be removed unless a fiery result is required.
Capsaicin is the alkaloid substance that give chillies
their hot flavour; it is also a severe irritant which
can burn the skin, particularly delicate areas around
the eyes and nails or any cuts. Capsaicin is
particularly concentrated in the white fibrous core
and pith, and the seeds. When rinsed under
running water, hot chillies give off a peppery gas.
Always wash your hands thoroughly after
preparing chillies and avoid touching your eyes;
alternatively, use disposable plastic gloves to prepare chillies.

CHILLI CON CARNE A Mexican dish that is
popular throughout the United States: it was a
typical dish in the cookery of the pioneers of Texas.
The name means literally 'chilli peppers with meat',
and the authentic dish is a ragoût of minced
(ground) or cubed beef cooked with thinly sliced
onions and seasoned with chilli peppers, powdered
cumin and other spices. Red kidney beans are
sometimes added during the cooking, although
purists object to them.

CHILLI POWDER A hot spice prepared from
ground dried red chillies and varying in intensity.
The type of chillies are not usually specified and the
spice is usually hot; some products are labelled as
hot chilli powder, indicating that they are extremely
hot. Some types of chilli powder include other

spices or ingredients; for example, chilli powder or seasoning used for chilli con carne may be flavoured with cumin, garlic and oregano.

CHIMAY, À LA The name of various preparations dedicated to the Princess of Chimay (formerly Madame Tallien), who was a regular guest at the sumptuous dinners given by the Vicomte de Barras under the Directory. Chicken à la Chimay is a dish of lightly braised chicken stuffed with buttered noodles and forcemeat, coated with gravy and served with noodles and bunches of asparagus tips. Hard-boiled (hard-cooked) or soft-boiled (soft-cooked) eggs à la Chimay are prepared with mushrooms and cooked au gratin.

RECIPE

hard-boiled eggs à la Chimay
Cut some hard-boiled (hard-cooked) eggs in half lengthways and remove the yolks. Pound the yolks in a mortar with an equal amount of very dry mushroom duxelles. Fill the whites with the mixture and arrange them in a buttered ovenproof dish. Coat with Mornay sauce and sprinkle with grated Gruyère cheese. Moisten with melted butter and bake for a few minutes in a preheated oven at 240°C (475°F, gas 9).

CHINA See *opposite page*.

CHINESE ARTICHOKE A plant cultivated for its edible tubers. Originating in Japan, this delicate vegetable was brought to France by the agronomist Pailleux and first cultivated in 1882 at Crosne (Essonne). Chinese artichokes taste similar to Jerusalem artichokes; once cleaned and blanched, they may be fried, cooked slowly in butter or prepared like Jerusalem artichokes. The Chinese artichoke was a very popular exotic vegetable between 1890 and 1920, but since then its popularity has declined, despite its delicate flavour, because it dries out quickly and takes a long time to peel.

RECIPE

preparation of Chinese artichokes
Instead of peeling with a vegetable peeler, place the Chinese artichokes in a strong linen cloth with a handful of sea salt and shake them vigorously. Wash them and remove all the remaining skin. Alternatively, they may be scrubbed and cooked in their skins. Blanch slightly in salted water, then cook them slowly in butter in a pan with the lid on, without letting them colour. Prepared in this way, Chinese artichokes may be served as a vegetable or as a garnish for roasts. They may also be dressed with cream, herbs or gravy.

CHINESE CABBAGE Of the numerous varieties of Chinese cabbage, two are readily available in most supermarkets: pak choi (bok choy) and *pe-tsai*.

Examples of these are shown in the illustration of vegetables in the cabbage family accompanying the entry on *Cabbage*. (In specialist Oriental stores; there are also preserved cabbage products, including cabbage that is salted, preserved in vinegar or sweetened.)

Pak choi does not form a heart; its white and fleshy leaf stalks somewhat resemble celery sticks and it has bright green leaves. The elongated leaves have smooth edges and are 20–50 cm (8–20 in) long. Pak choi is stir-fried or added to soups and casseroles.

The popular Chinese cabbage or Chinese leaves, known as *pe-tsai*, resembles a large cos (romaine) lettuce; the heart reaches 40–50 cm (16–20 in) and its irregularly serrated leaves extend to the base of their stalks. It is eaten raw and finely shredded in salads, poached or stir-fried.

In Chinese cookery, stir-fried or braised cabbage is often part of composite dishes of fish and shellfish, poultry or meat. The cabbage may also be used in mixed vegetable dishes or in vegetarian dishes (for example, with tofu). The leaves may be filled, folded into bundles or rolled and steamed. They are sometimes used as scoops for eating finely cut, full-flavoured cooked mixtures, such as minced (ground) poultry, pigeon or meat.

RECIPES

Chinese cabbage à la pékinoise
Remove the outer leaves from a Chinese cabbage and slice the heart into 10 cm (4 in) strips. Cut some very thin slices of ham to the same length and finely slice 5 or 6 spring onions (scallions) and their stems. Heat 2 tablespoons oil in a shallow frying pan, add the cabbage and brown for 2–3 minutes. Arrange the pieces of cabbage in a steaming basket, add the sliced onion and a little fine salt, and steam for 30 minutes. Then insert the slices of ham between the pieces of cabbage and steam for a further 4–5 minutes. Serve the cabbage and ham together.

Sichuan-style Chinese cabbage
Clean a Chinese cabbage and cut it into pieces about 3 cm (1¼ in) long. Wash, blanch, cool and drain. Heat 3 tablespoons oil in a frying pan. Chop a large garlic clove and lightly brown it in the oil. Add the cabbage, a little Sichuan pepper and some salt; stir well and leave to cook for 1 minute. Then add 1 teaspoon marc brandy and 1 teaspoon caster (superfine) sugar and stir well for 1 minute. Adjust the seasoning and serve very hot.

CHINOIS A conical strainer with a handle. There are various models: the chinois with a metallic mesh is used for straining broths, sauces, fine creams, syrups and jellies, which need to be very smooth; the perforated tinplate chinois is used to strain thick sauces, which are pressed through with a pestle to remove the lumps.

CHINA

In China, nutrition and cookery have been subjects for discussion and reflection by philosophers, writers and emperors throughout the centuries. Traditionally, there is no dividing line between philosophy, religion and food, and the types of dishes and rituals associated with meals are full of symbolism. For example, traditionally braised turtle signifies long life, while a ragoût of stag with mushrooms means a favourable result and success in an undertaking.

Food satisfies two fundamental purposes and this is appreciated in Chinese cooking. First, it is essential for life; secondly, it is a source of pleasure. On a basic level, simple foods, such as rice or noodles, provide sustenance; rich dishes and feasts are enjoyable. An important feature of Chinese cookery is the quest for harmony, which is achieved through contrasts. A crisp dish is followed by a creamy preparation and a spicy course is served with a sweet garnish. Soups provide a palate-clearing or balancing break between courses during grand meals; rice may be served to settle the stomach after a rich feast. The originality and subtlety of this cuisine is sometimes expressed by balancing four basic flavours (sour, salt, bitter and sweet) in the same dish. For example, thinly sliced pork with scrambled eggs and lily flowers is served with black mushrooms, a plum sauce and small salted pancakes.

■ **Philosophy and excellence**
Because of its paramount importance for centuries, classic Chinese cuisine became more complicated in the struggle for perfection. (Lao Tseu compared the art of governing the Chinese Empire to that of frying a small fish.) The preoccupation with the broader implications of diet has always played an equal part alongside the quest for flavour. Ingredients may be valued for their aphrodisiac properties in some dishes; for example, sharks' fins, swallows' nests, tigers' bones and hundred-year-old eggs. The traditional repertoire of Chinese recipes, which originates from the great Mandarin tradition, includes foods considered to be beneficial for their medicinal or even magical properties. Examples include bears' palms, carps' lips, rhinoceroses' armpits or frogs' stomachs, valued not only for their flavour, aroma and colour, but also for their contribution to general well-being. The medicinal benefits of dishes containing these ingredients were thought to be enhanced by magical properties.

■ **Practical principles** Basic meals consisting of a high proportion of starchy food with a modest accompaniment for flavour are the norm, particularly in poor communities. Cooking methods have historically been conditioned by the acute lack of fuel in China. Cooks invented dishes that were cooked on embers in 10–15 minutes by cutting all items of food into small pieces. This also enabled the food to be easily impregnated by the seasonings. For many dishes ingredients may be cut into cubes, thin strips, dice, small sticks or slanting slices. This preparation is also important to facilitate eating the food with chopsticks – these, along with spoons, being the only table implements.

Cutting is also decorative – spring onion (scallion) curls or feathers, tomato petals and turnips or carrots shaped into stars. Even with simple dishes, cooks spend more time perfecting the mixtures than cooking them; the art of obtaining the correct proportions is fundamentally important.

One of the most frequently used methods of cooking is stir-frying, which retains all the natural succulence and flavour of ingredients, such as crisp vegetables and tender beef. Stir-frying is not the only method. There are many soups, cooked over a brisk heat using full-flavoured stocks; these are often very clear. Steaming and braising are also important techniques, particularly for fish and vegetables. In practice, many Chinese dishes rely on a combination of cooking methods – food may be stir-fried, then braised or deep-fried before being simmered in a sauce; similarly, ingredients braised in the first stages may be finished by brief stir-frying when the liquid has evaporated.

Finally, the artistic presentation of the dish is important, for the dish must appeal to the guest by appearance and aroma, and sometimes through texture or even the sound it makes. For example, a colourful soup with tender ingredients and soft textures may be garnished with crisp, fried rice cakes that may be heard to crackle.

■ **Regional cooking styles**
Traditionally, China was a country with distinctly regional cuisines. Cultural changes, an opening up of the country to the West and increased affluence in some communities may have reduced the marked differences, but local dishes and styles remain an important feature.

Rice is the staple food in south China, the main rice-growing area; wheat is the staple in the north, where noodles and steamed buns or breads are the basic food. Corn (maize) and millet are common in the north, providing sustenance for the poorer communities instead of wheat products.

Beijing, formerly Peking and the old capital of China, is considered to be the original high-table of the cuisine and a source of fine dishes produced by talented chefs recruited to the emperor's court. Famous specialities include the celebrated Peking duck and firepot or hotpot meals introduced to Peking by early visiting Mongolians. The firepot, a type of table-top charcoal burner with a ring-shaped cooking pot surrounding a central chimney, is used to simmer broth in which diners cook prepared ingredients – a type of fondue, referred to as *fondue chinois* in French, for ▶

cooking in stock rather than in oil. Sweet and sour flavours and delicate, subtly seasoned dishes also feature.

Cantonese cooking, in the south, is characterized by diversity. When the Ming dynasty was overthrown, many chefs escaped from Peking to Canton. En route, they acquired the taste for the cooking of other regions, eventually bringing a cornucopia of flavours and rich cooking styles to Cantonese cuisine. On the coast and with a climate in which tropical fruit flourishes, this area traditionally benefits from a wealth of ingredients.

To the east, Shanghai has long had a cosmopolitan reputation and Western influences are evident in the style of cooking. Further down the east coast, Fukien is famous for producing high-quality soy sauce, an important flavouring ingredient. Dried fish and mushrooms are also typical ingredients.

Sichuan, in the west, has a hot, tropical climate and spicy food is popular, seasoned with Sichuan pepper and hot chillies. Smoked foods and pickles are also regional features. Yunnan, in the south-west is famous for its ham.

■ **Great variety in ingredients** Many foods used throughout China are familiar in Western shops and the variety of regional specialities is too vast to cover. Fish and seafood, poultry and meat are all familiar. Wind-dried duck – split and flattened – and spicy, slightly sweet wind-dried sausages are typical of preserved ingredients. Hen and duck eggs are eaten throughout China and they are preserved to be sold as salted eggs or thousand-year eggs (preserved for about ten weeks). There is a great variety of noodles, rice sticks and vermicelli made from flours from rice and other grains as well as wheat.

Vegetables are always selected according to their texture and their taste. They may be steamed, braised or stir-fried. Many have long been familiar to Western cooks (carrots, peppers, cucumber and spring onions), but others are comparatively new (bean sprouts, Chinese mustard greens, pak choi and Chinese cabbage) and some are only usually available canned, rather than fresh, in Western supermarkets (bamboo shoots, water chestnuts and lotus roots.) As well as ordinary mushrooms, shiitake or black mushrooms are used fresh or dried, as are scented or straw-mushrooms. Soya beans are used in various ways: to make delicate bean curd or tofu, or a variety of full-flavoured seasoning pastes and ingredients, including soy sauce, hoisin sauce and fermented black beans.

Among the many other flavouring ingredients, some of the best known include sesame seeds (and their oil, usually toasted), lotus seeds and red dates. Dried seafood include shrimps, squid, shark's fin and jellyfish (dried into small flat cakes that are finely sliced or shredded). Oyster sauce is a dark, rich and salty seasoning.

Chinese five-spice powder (anise seed, fennel, clove, cinnamon and Sichuan pepper), star anise, ginger, Sichuan pepper, coriander and tangerine peel are typical seasonings.

There is a sufficient variety of fresh fruits to make light desserts, including lychees, longans, mangoes and papayas. They may be served plain, in heavy syrups or in fruit salads.

Drinks include tea, soya milk and syrup of sesame or ginseng seeds. Rice wine, commonly known as yellow wine, is served warm and used in cooking. The best known liqueur is *mei kuei lu* (rose dew), distilled from sorghum blended with rose petals. It is drunk during meals, between courses.

■ **Settings, menus and manners**
The simple place setting comprises a bowl, sometimes with a plate, chopsticks and a spoon. For a festive occasion, a wine glass, a tea cup and a second bowl are added. Table napkins are not used; instead, small hot damp towels are handed around towards the end of the meal. The place of honour, which is allotted to the oldest guest, faces south and is opposite the entrance door of the dining room. Traditionally, women sat on one side of the table and men on the other.

Everyday meals are centred on rice or noodles (or other filling, starchy food). Prepared simply but with care, plenty is provided to satisfy the appetite. Dishes of vegetables and other well-seasoned accompaniments are served in modest amounts. Fish, poultry or meat are presented in small quantities. At a family meal all the dishes are placed on the table simultaneously. It is easy to choose and mix, nothing is wasted. A guest may be invited at the last minute, but the meal retains its intimate character. When a special meal is prepared, for example to entertain or as a dinner party, more dishes may be served as separate courses.

The courses of a traditional Chinese meal are presented in a different order from those of a European meal: first cold dishes, then hot dishes, then a light soup and finally, perhaps, a dessert. For a ceremonial meal, a thick soup is served and a large festive dish, such as Peking duck, is also provided. This is followed by a light broth and then sweetmeats. In total, the festive meal may include a succession of courses numbering between 12 and 20. On such occasions, rice and starchy food do not feature largely, but rice may be served at the end.

On a street in the ancient city of Fozhou, capital of Fujian province, aromatic dishes and tempting dim sum are cooked in stacks of bamboo steamers ready to be savoured by diners sitting at small tables in the open air.

CHINOIS CONFIT The French name for a small bitter Chinese orange, macerated in several syrups of increasing concentration, then drained and crystallized (candied). The tree that produces this fruit is native to China, but grows wild in Sicily. The chinois is usually green, as it is picked before it is ripe, when it is considered to be at its best for crystallization.

CHINON A mainly red AOC wine of the Loire. The area extends over the left bank and to the banks of the Vienne, its tributary, around the ruins of the castle where Joan of Arc came to find the Dauphin (later Charles VII) and encouraged him to 'kick the English out of France'. Later, Rabelais, whose family had a vineyard at the foot of the citadel, sang the praises of the wine of Chinon. He called it 'this good Breton wine that does not grow in Brittany', because Chinon is made from the Cabernet Franc grape, known locally as the 'Breton'.

Fuller styles of Chinon with potential for long-term ageing are produced mainly on the tuffeau limestone slopes of Cravant-les-Coteaux, while lighter wines are produced from vines grown on the sandy, gravelly soils near the river.

CHINONAISE, À LA In classic French cookery, a garnish for large joints of meat comprising potatoes sprinkled with chopped parsley and small balls of cabbage stuffed with sausagemeat and braised.

In the region of Chinon, hare and lamprey, lightly browned in walnut oil, are also described as *à la chinonaise*.

CHIPOLATA A small fresh sausage, about 2 cm (¾ in) in diameter, made with medium or coarsely chopped sausagemeat enclosed in a natural casing (sheep's intestine) or a synthetic one. Chipolatas are eaten fried or grilled (broiled). The name comes from the Italian word *cipolla* (onion), and was originally applied to a stew made with onions and small sausages.

CHIPOLATA, À LA A garnish for game, braised poultry, meat or eggs consisting of braised chestnuts, glazed small (pearl) onions, glazed carrots, sautéed mushrooms, blanched and lightly fried strips of bacon and fried chipolatas. The garnish may be bound with reduced Madeira sauce.

In classic French cookery, the term describes a pudding based on pig's kidney, forcemeat and small sausages.

RECIPE

pudding à la chipolata
Stone (pit) 12 Agen prunes and steep for 1 hour in red wine. Brown a thinly sliced pig's kidney and a chopped shallot in some butter in a pan. Drain and flame with rum. Make a forcemeat with 200 g (7 oz) lean pork and an equal quantity of finely chopped veal. Flavour with mixed spice and salt. Cook

4 tablespoons large macaroni until al dente. Grease and flour a fine cloth. Mix the kidney, macaroni, forcemeat and prunes with 16 chipolatas and tie the mixture very tightly in the cloth. Poach for 1 hour in either a chicken broth or a very concentrated stock. Untie the pudding and serve hot with a charcutière sauce.

CHIPS (FRENCH FRIES) Fingers of potatoes, deep-fried until crisp and golden outside, tender inside. Chips are thicker than French fries, which are cut in thin sticks. American potato chips are called crisps in Britain.

Good chips are cooked in very hot, high-quality oil or fat, drained when tender and very lightly browned, then fried very briefly a second time. This makes the chips crisp and slightly puffy. See *Pont-neuf potatoes*.

CHIQUE A large bonbon made of cooked sugar filled with almonds and flavoured with mint, aniseed or lemon. *Chiques* from Montluçon and Allauch (Bouches-du-Rhône) are famous.

CHIQUETER A French culinary term meaning to indent the edges of vol-au-vent cases, pies and cheese straws with a small knife. This helps them to swell during cooking and is decorative.

CHIROUBLES One of the Beaujolais regional wines – smooth, light and fruity, this is possibly the one that is the most enjoyable when drunk young and cool.

CHIVES An alliaceous plant, related to the spring onion (scallion), that produces small elongated bulbs and clumps of tubular green leaves. The leaves are chopped and used for seasoning salads and omelettes.

CHIVRY A flavoured butter containing herbs that may be used with cold hors d'oeuvre. It is also used to flavour chivry sauces. The chivry sauce served with fish is made with a fish stock, while the sauce served with poached chicken or soft-boiled (soft-cooked) or poached eggs is prepared with a chicken velouté.

RECIPES

chicken à la chivry
Poach a chicken in a white stock. Slowly cook some green asparagus tips in butter and prepare some green peas *à la française*. Cook some artichoke hearts in a court-bouillon and use half of them to garnish the asparagus tips and the other half to garnish the peas. Arrange the vegetables around the chicken and coat with chivry sauce.

chivry butter
To prepare about 250 g (9 oz, 1 cup) butter, use 150 g (5 oz, 2 cups) mixed parsley, tarragon,

chervil, chives and, if possible, burnet, and 2 tablespoons chopped shallot. Blanch the mixture for 3 minutes in boiling water, drain, cool immediately in cold water and wipe dry. Chop very finely (or pound in a mortar), add 200 g (7 oz, ¾ cup) butter, season with salt and pepper and press through a fine sieve.

chivry sauce for eggs and poultry

Put 100 ml (4 fl oz, 7 tablespoons) dry white wine, 1 teaspoon finely chopped shallot and 1 tablespoon chopped chervil and tarragon in a small saucepan. Reduce by half. Add 300 ml (½ pint, 1¼ cups) chicken velouté and reduce by a third. Finally add 2 tablespoons chivry butter and press through a fine sieve.

soft-boiled or poached eggs à la chivry

Fry some round croûtons and place a soft-boiled (soft-cooked) or poached egg on each. Garnish with asparagus tips that have been slowly cooked in butter and coat with chivry sauce.

CHLODNIK An iced soup of Polish origin, common to several Slavonic countries. The word literally means refreshment. The soup is made with sorrel, beetroot (red beet) leaves and cucumber purée. It is sometimes thickened with wheat semolina, flavoured with fennel and tarragon, and garnished with various ingredients, such as slices of hard-boiled (hard-cooked) eggs, crayfish and fresh diced cucumber.

CHOCOLATE Essentially a mixture of cocoa and sugar, to which milk, honey, dried fruits or other products may be added.

The first French chocolate factory was situated in Bayonne, where a guild of chocolate-makers had existed since 1761. The city exported chocolate to Spain and Paris, and its trade calendar of 1822 quotes more than 20 prestigious firms. (Cocoa also provided a nutritious food for the fishermen of Saint-Pierre-et-Miquelon.)

In 1778 the first hydraulic machine for crushing and mixing the chocolate paste appeared in France, and in 1819 Pelletier built the first factory to use steam. It was at about this time that the famous family businesses were set up in Europe: Van Houten in the Netherlands (1815) – C.J. Van Houten discovered a 'method of solubilization' in 1828 (now known as 'dutching' in English); Menier in France (1824); Cadbury and Rowntree in England; and Suchard, Nestlé, Lindt and Kohler in Switzerland. Docteur Peter, a Swiss, was responsible for the invention of milk chocolate in 1818. After 1850, the chocolate industry was developed throughout the world.

Chocolate is not only used in confectionery but is also an essential ingredient of numerous cakes, pastries and desserts.

Soon after its introduction into France, the medical profession considered chocolate to be a panacea for fevers and chest or stomach illnesses. Cocoa was registered in the Codex in 1758 and the confectioners of the 18th and 19th centuries gladly became apothecaries: chocolate was believed to have medicinal properties and various types of medicinal chocolates were sold by Debauve (a former pharmacist of Louis XVI) and others of his profession. These included purgatives, cough mixtures, aids to digestion, aids to put on weight, antispasmodics (with orange blossom), anti-inflammatories (with milk of almonds), tonics and carminatives. The expression 'health chocolate', for the mixture containing only sugar and cocoa, remained common until the beginning of the 20th century.

■ **Chocolate products** Apart from the wide variety of confectionery and chocolate snack products, there are also preparations intended for use in cooking.
• Cocoa powder This is normally unsweetened. It is strongly flavoured and widely used in cooking, particularly in baking, as well as for flavouring drinks.
• Drinking chocolate This is a mixture of sugar and cocoa. Its main use is for flavouring drinks. It is used in some baking recipes, but its sugar content makes it unsuitable as a direct substitute for cocoa powder; its flavour is also milder.
• Chocolate-flavoured cake coverings These are inexpensive products with a low cocoa butter content and containing a high proportion of vegetable fat. They are manufactured to melt easily and successfully, but they have an inferior flavour and are not recommended for use in good-quality recipes.

■ **Types of chocolate**
• Chocolate couverture This is high-quality plain or bitter chocolate for use in cooking and preparing confectionery. It has a high cocoa butter content and is suitable for use in gâteaux, mousses and chocolate icing (frosting) or sauces.
• Plain or bitter dessert chocolate (semisweet or bittersweet) This is dark in colour and lightly sweetened. There are many types of different quality, some less sweet and more bitter than others.
• Milk chocolate This is sweeter and has milk solids added. Again, the types and quality vary.
• White chocolate This is available in varying qualities. It is made from sweetened pale cocoa butter.

■ **The quality of chocolate** The quality of chocolate depends both on the quality of the raw materials and on the care taken at the different stages of manufacture: roasting and crushing the cocoa beans and mixing the cocoa paste or 'mass' with sugar and possibly milk.

A good chocolate is shiny brown, breaks cleanly and is free of lumps, tiny burst bubbles and white specks. It melts on the tongue like butter, has a true flavour of chocolate rather than of cocoa and is neither greasy nor sticky.

The cocoa butter content and price are indicators of quality. Inferior chocolate may contain a small proportion of cocoa butter and other vegetable fats.

For cakes and desserts, it is best to choose a dessert chocolate with a high cocoa content; the flavour may be intensified by adding unsweetened cocoa. For coating, decoration, icing (frosting) or making fondants, chocolate couverture is used.

■ **Tempering chocolate** The different fats in cocoa butter melt at different temperatures. To achieve a smooth, glossy result, some types of chocolate with a high cocoa butter content have to be tempered before use. This involves heating and cooling to specific temperatures, then working the chocolate with a palette knife or spatula to ensure that the fats are thoroughly combined. Chocolate couverture has to be tempered before use.

■ **Classic chocolate dishes** The basis of chocolate cakes is often a sponge cake mixture, a Genoese cake mixture or a meringue. *Sachertorte, Doboschtorte* (made with caramel and chocolate) and Black Forest gâteau bear witness to the quality of chocolate pâtisserie in Germany and Austria. Italy is renowned for the traditional New Year's Eve cake, the *pan pepato* of Ferrara – a brioche flavoured with cocoa, sweetened with honey, enriched with almonds and lemon zest, coated with chocolate and decorated with sweets (candies) – and Sicilian cassata. In France, the great classics are the Queen of Sheba (a sponge cake filled and coated with chocolate), the Yule log, the *dacquoise*, marble cake, *pavés* and the various desserts that are decorated with chocolate vermicelli or grated chocolate. Chocolate can also be added to confectioner's custards (pastry creams) and it may be mixed with butter (see *Ganache*) and used as a filling, for example in éclairs and choux. It may also be used in the sauce that coats profiteroles, Belle-Hélène fruits, puddings, brioches or iced desserts.

Chocolate is a basic flavouring for ices, ice-cream desserts and cooked custards. It is also used in various charlottes, soufflés and mousses.

When making biscuits (cookies), it may be used as a filling or a coating and in Viennese baking it is used to make small chocolate-flavoured loaves.

Chocolate is used extensively in confectionery for making a great variety of bouchées, truffles, chocolates and Easter eggs.

The use of chocolate in savoury cookery is less well known. Chocolate was commonly used by the Aztecs and one of the great dishes of Mexican cookery is still *mole poblano de guajolote* (a turkey stew with unsweetened chocolate, flavoured with chilli peppers and sesame). In 1869, Baron Brisse suggested cooking scoter (a type of sea duck) with chocolate. In Spain, two dishes use bitter chocolate in a sauce: calves' tongue and langouste, specialities of Aragon. Finally, in Sicily, there is a popular recipe for jugged hare with chocolate.

RECIPES

Bacchus ♦
Two days in advance, prepare some macerated raisins: wash 75 g (3 oz, ⅔ cup) Californian raisins or sultanas (golden raisins) in lukewarm water, changing the water several times. Soak for 4 minutes, then drain and place in a non-stick saucepan.

Making chocolate caraque or cigarettes

Use a confectioner's spatula with a fine-edged blade to spread the melted chocolate in a thin layer on marble and leave until just cool and set. Scrape off rolls of chocolate by holding the spatula at an acute angle. Alternatively, a palette knife can be used by holding either side of the blade to keep it steady and at the right angle for scraping the chocolate into curls.

Making chocolate shavings

Use a confectioner's spatula with a fine-edged blade to spread the melted chocolate in a thin layer on marble and leave until just cool and set. Score the chocolate into regular diamond shapes. Use a knife, holding it firmly at an acute angle, to scrape off shavings of chocolate.

Cook gently, stirring, until the raisins are hot. Add a small liqueur glass of rum and flambé while rotating the saucepan. When the raisins have coloured slightly, remove from the heat, then transfer to a dish. Cover and leave to macerate for 2 days.

Make two meringue bases using 6 egg whites and 100 g (4 oz, ¾ cup) icing (confectioner's) sugar, whisked into a soft meringue. Fold in 100 g (4 oz, 1 cup) ground almonds and bake the mixture in a Swiss roll tin (jelly roll pan). Leave to cool in the tin. Make a chocolate sponge cake base and a whipped chocolate ganache. Prepare a syrup with equal quantities of water and granulated sugar flavoured with a little rum.

Saturate the chocolate sponge with this syrup. Add two-thirds of the raisins to the ganache. Assemble the cake, starting with a layer of the

Bacchus.

almond base, then add a layer of ganache with raisins, chocolate sponge, another layer of ganache and, finally a second layer of the almond base. Decorate the top with a few raisins. Glaze the whole cake with pouring (unwhipped) ganache. Place in the refrigerator until set. Serve with crème anglaise and any remaining macerated raisins.

chocolate cake

Separate 3 eggs. Add 125 g (4½ oz, ½ cup) caster (superfine) sugar to the yolks and beat until the mixture is pale, thick and foamy.

Break 150 g (5 oz, 5 squares) bitter (bittersweet) chocolate into small pieces in a saucepan. Heat it gently with 4 tablespoons milk in a bain marie with the lid on.

Blend 125 g (4½ oz, ½ cup) softened butter with the chocolate, stir until it has melted and become smooth and then pour the chocolate mixture into a warm mixing bowl. Immediately add the egg yolk mixture and stir briskly. In a clean bowl, whisk the egg whites until stiff. Add 125 g (4½ oz, 1 cup) plain (all-purpose) flour to the chocolate mixture and stir until combined. Then quickly fold in the whisked egg whites.

Pour the mixture into a buttered manqué mould and bake in a preheated oven at 190°C (375°F, gas 5) for about 45 minutes.

Meanwhile, prepare a caramel with 2 tablespoons sugar, 1 tablespoon water and 1 tablespoon vinegar. Roll 10 walnuts in the caramel and set aside on an oiled plate.

When the cake is cooked, leave it to cool in its mould and prepare a chocolate icing (frosting). Turn out the cold cake on to a rack over a dish. Pour the icing over the cake and spread it over the top and sides with a palette knife. Decorate with the walnuts.

chocolate Genoese sponge

Melt 65 g (2½ oz, 5 tablespoons) butter in a bain marie and use part of it to butter a Genoese mould.

In a heatproof bowl, mix 75 g (3 oz, 6 tablespoons) caster (superfine) sugar with an equal quantity of cocoa and 4 eggs. Place over a saucepan of hot, not boiling, water or in a bain marie, and whisk until the mixture is greatly increased in volume and thick. Remove from the heat or bain marie and continue to whisk until completely cool (the mixture should run off the whisk in a ribbon).

Fold in 125 g (4½ oz, 1 cup) plain (all-purpose) flour and the remaining melted butter. Pour into the mould and cook in a preheated oven at 180°C (350°F, gas 4) for 25 minutes.

Turn the cake out on to a rack and leave it to cool. Cut the cake horizontally in half. Sandwich the layers of cake together with chocolate butter cream or whipped cream. The outside may be spread with cream and coated with toasted chopped almonds.

chocolate ice cream

Beat 8 egg yolks and 200 g (7 oz, ¾ cup) caster (superfine) sugar together until pale and thick. Melt 250 g (9 oz, 1½ cups) grated bitter (bittersweet) chocolate in a covered pan with 200 ml (7 fl oz, ¾ cup) water. Add 1 litre (1¾ pints, 4⅓ cups) boiling milk to the chocolate and stir well until the mixture is completely smooth. Pour the boiling chocolate mixture over the egg yolk mixture and cook over a very gentle heat until the custard coats the spoon. Immediately dip the saucepan in cold water to prevent further cooking and continue to beat until the cream is lukewarm. Stir it occasionally until it is completely cold. Complete the ice cream in the usual way.

For a richer ice cream, replace 200 ml (7 fl oz, ¾ cup) of the milk with the same volume of double (heavy) cream, and use 10 egg yolks instead of 8.

chocolate icing

Sift 100 g (4 oz, 1 cup) icing (confectioner's) sugar. Melt 125 g (4½ oz) bitter (bittersweet) chocolate in a bain marie, working it with a wooden spoon. Add the sifted icing sugar, then 65 g (2½ oz, 5 tablespoons) softened butter cut in small pieces. Continue to stir until the mixture is completely melted and remove from the heat. Gradually stir in 100 ml (4 fl oz, 7 tablespoons) cold water. Use the icing (frosting) when slightly warm.

chocolate sauce

Melt 100 g (4 oz) bitter (bittersweet) chocolate in a bain marie with 100 ml (4 fl oz, 7 tablespoons) milk and 20 g (¾ oz, 1½ tablespoons) butter. When the mixture is completely smooth, add 40 g (1½ oz, 3 tablespoons) caster (superfine) sugar and 1 tablespoon double (heavy) cream. Stir until smooth, then remove at once from the heat.

other recipes See *bâton, caramels, charlotte, chocolate truffle, creams, custard, marquise, mousse, parfait, pudding, sachertorte, soufflé (dessert soufflés), sponge cake.*

CHOCOLATE (beverage) A hot or cold drink made by mixing chocolate or cocoa in water or milk, or a mixture of both.

It was in the form of a drink that chocolate was discovered in Mexico and then introduced into Europe by the Spanish. The Aztecs prepared a highly spiced beverage (*xocoatl*) with cocoa beans that were roasted, pounded in a mortar and mixed and flavoured with pepper, chillis, vanilla, annatto (to dye it red) and sometimes honey and dried flowers. The emperor Montezuma had *xocoatl* of different colours served in gold cups at the end of meals. The people also consumed large quantities of chocolate in the form of a thick paste, often thickened with cornflour (cornstarch).

The Jesuits were the first to improve this exotic product in order to make a profit from it. Chocolate, at this time, was always prepared with water, but it was very sweet and flavoured with vanilla, strengthened with ambergris and musk. Soon, chocolate became fashionable among Spanish high society.

In 1615, Ann of Austria introduced this novelty to the French court and her maids of honour circulated the recipes. Even under Louis XIV, who had little sympathy for his queen's liking for this drink, chocolate was still regarded as a curiosity. It was in England that it became customary to prepare it with milk and even to add Madeira and beaten eggs. The Church did not consider that chocolate broke the fast (although doctors thought it more nourishing than beef and mutton) and the days of Lent became agreeably sweetened! Society ladies had the drink served in church during the sermons. The Marquise de Sévigné wrote: 'The day before yesterday, I took some chocolate to digest my dinner in order to sup well, and I took some yesterday evening so as to nourish myself well and be able to fast until the evening: that is why I find it pleasant, because it acts according to the purpose.'

■ **A rapid rise in popularity** In about 1670, Paris had only one chocolate merchant, but in 1705 an edict allowed café owners to sell it by the cup, like coffee. It was not until the time of the Regency, under Louis XV, that chocolate became fashionable in high society. To be admitted to the 'Regent's chocolate' was a special honour. The Marquise de Sévigné then retracted her previous statements and wrote: 'All those who spoke well of it to me now speak badly. It is cursed, accused of all the ills that one has, it is the cause of vapours and palpitations.' Nevertheless, chocolate had become part of the way of life. It was served at collations (light meals), at breakfast and with the afternoon snack.

It was in Austria, Spain and France, the countries where most chocolate was drunk, that chocolate powder began to be retailed during the 19th century. Balzac did not think highly of it: 'Who knows whether the abuse of chocolate has not had something to do with the debasement of the Spanish nation, which, at the time of the discovery of chocolate, was about to recreate the Roman Empire.' But Brillat-Savarin rose to its defence: 'Chocolate is one of the most powerful restoratives. Let any man who has spent working a considerable portion of the time that should be spent sleeping, let any man of wit who feels himself temporarily become stupid, let any man who finds the air damp, the time long, and the atmosphere difficult to tolerate, let any man who is tormented by an obsession that prevents him from thinking clearly, let all those men dose themselves with a good half-litre of amber-coloured chocolate . . . and they will see a miracle.'

Today, thanks to instant products, chocolate may be quickly prepared. However, true hot chocolate needs to be prepared the previous day in order to be full of flavour and frothy. As Brillat-Savarin had already recommended, on the advice of a mother superior: 'When you wish to take some good chocolate, make it the evening before in an earthenware coffeepot and leave it. The night rest concentrates it and gives it a smoothness that improves it.'

RECIPES

foamy chocolate
For 1 litre (1¾ pints, 4⅓ cups) milk, allow 200–250 g (7–9 oz, 7–9 squares) chocolate and 1 tablespoon vanilla-flavoured sugar or a pinch of powdered cinnamon. Break the chocolate into small pieces in a saucepan and heat gently. When the chocolate begins to soften, add the chosen flavouring together with a small cup of boiling milk. Beat the chocolate thoroughly with a whisk. Then gradually pour in the remaining milk. Warm over a gentle heat, whisking all the time to make the chocolate foamy. For a richer drink, 100 ml (4 fl oz, 7 tablespoons) single (light) cream may be added. The vanilla or cinnamon may be replaced by 1 tablespoon instant coffee.

iced chocolate
Prepare a foamy chocolate as in the recipe above, but reduce the quantity of chocolate to 125–150 g (4½–5 oz, 4½–5 squares) and add 2–3 tablespoons caster (superfine) sugar. Allow the chocolate to cool completely and then put it in a blender, adding crushed ice. Serve immediately.

Viennese chocolate
Melt 200 g (7 oz, 7 squares) chocolate in a bain marie with a cup of milk. Stir, while letting it come to the boil slowly (about 10 minutes). Heat 750 ml (1¼ pints, 3¼ cups) milk with 1 tablespoon sugar. Pour it into a saucepan and whisk for 5 minutes. Make a Chantilly cream by whisking 5 tablespoons double (heavy) cream with 2 tablespoons icing (confectioner's) sugar and flavour with vanilla. Pour the chocolate into cups and top each with a dome of Chantilly cream.

CHOCOLATE POT A tall vessel for serving hot chocolate. It is often shaped like a truncated cone or like a jug, with a spout and a horizontal wooden handle. The chocolate pot has a lid pierced with a hole for a beater to pass through to make the chocolate foam. The pot may be made of silver-plated metal, solid silver, porcelain or earthenware. The first models, which came from Spain with Maria-Theresa of Austria, appeared in France in the reign of Louis XIV.

CHOCOLATES Confectionery made from chocolate or covered in chocolate. There are many different types of filled chocolate; the filling may consist of coloured and flavoured fondant cream, praline, almond paste, soft caramel, nougat, liqueur or liqueur-soaked fruit. The chocolate coating is very liquid when hot and rich in cocoa butter. In the case of liqueurs, these are first poured into starch moulds to crystallize; the liqueur sweets are then removed from the starch and carefully brushed before being coated. Fruit, such as cherries in brandy, are first dipped in fondant and then coated in chocolate; after about two weeks, the moisture from the cherry causes the fondant layer to liquefy, producing a cherry liqueur.

The coating for moulded chocolates is poured into moulds, which are immediately turned over, thereby emptying most of the chocolate and leaving only a thin film, which forms the outside of the chocolate. The filling is then poured into the mould and allowed to set. Finally, the chocolates are sealed with chocolate coating, which becomes the base.

French regional specialities include *bouchons de champagne, cabaches de Châlons* (chocolate pralines iced with pistachio-flavoured sugar), *chardons des Alpes* (white chocolate balls filled with liqueur), *granits de Sémur-en-Auxois* (toasted almond clusters dipped in orange-flavoured white chocolate), *guignes de Bordeaux* (cherries in brandy, coated in chocolate, with the stalk sticking out), *joyaux de Bourgogne* (white chocolate shells tinted green or pink and filled with almond paste), *mojettes de Poitou* (small bean-shaped chocolates), *quernoux d'Angers* (nougatine dipped in white chocolate that has been tinted blue and shaped like small roofing slates) and *muscadines à la nantais* (truffles stuffed with grapes).

CHOCOLATE TRUFFLE Confectionery made of chocolate, melted with butter or cream, sugar and sometimes eggs. The truffles are flavoured with brandy, rum, whisky, vanilla, cinnamon or coffee and shaped into balls, which are coated with chocolate or rolled in cocoa.

Chocolate truffles, which keep only for a short time, are traditionally given at Christmas in France. They are a good accompaniment to coffee. *Muscadines* are long truffles, dipped in chocolate, then sprinkled with icing (confectioner's) sugar. Chambéry truffles, or *truffettes*, a speciality of the town, are made of praline mixed with chocolate, fondant icing (frosting) and butter, then coated with cocoa and sugar or rolled in grated chocolate.

RECIPES

chocolate truffles with butter
To make 20 truffles, melt in a bain marie 250 g (9 oz, 9 squares) bitter (bittersweet) chocolate with 1 tablespoon milk. When the mixture is very smooth, add 100 g (4 oz, ½ cup) butter cut into small pieces and mix well. Blend in 2 egg yolks, then 3 tablespoons double (heavy) cream and 125 g (4½ oz, 1 cup) icing (confectioner's) sugar. Leave in the refrigerator for 24 hours. Shape the truffles rapidly, spooning out the paste with a teaspoon and rolling it into walnut-sized balls on a marble surface with the palm of the hand. Drop them one by one into a bowl containing 50 g (2 oz, ½ cup) unsweetened cocoa, twisting the bowl to coat the truffles with cocoa. Store in a cool place.

chocolate truffles with cream
Melt 300 g (11 oz, 11 squares) bitter (bittersweet) chocolate and 75 g (3 oz, ¾ cup) pure cocoa with 120 ml (4½ fl oz, ½ cup) strong coffee in a bain marie. Mix well. Heat 250 ml (8 fl oz, 1 cup) double (heavy) cream and, as soon as it starts to boil, mix with the chocolate paste. Remove from the heat and leave for a few hours in a cool place. Pipe into small balls on foil, leave in a cool place for 1½ hours, then roll in pure cocoa.

truffles in paprika
Melt 150 g (5 oz, 5 squares) bitter (bittersweet) chocolate. Add 175 ml (6 fl oz, ¾ cups) boiling whipping cream and mix well. Leave to cool. Finely chop 40 g (1½ oz, 3 tablespoons) prunes in Armagnac and incorporate into the paste. Shape into small balls and roll in a mixture of half unsweetened cocoa, half mild paprika. Store in a cold place.

CHOESELS A speciality of Belgian cookery consisting of a ragoût made with various kinds of meat and offal (variety meats), especially beef pancreas, simmered with onions and beer.

RECIPE

choesels à la bruxelloise
Clean and blanch a choice calf's sweetbread, cool it under a press and cut it into thin slices. Cut an oxtail into pieces. Clean a heifer's kidney and cut it into pieces. Peel and finely slice 100 g (4 oz, 1¼ cups) onions. Heat 100 g (4 oz, ½ cup) clarified beef dripping in a frying pan, add the pieces of oxtail and sweetbread, and brown gently for 45 minutes. Then add 1 kg (2¼ lb) breast of veal cut into even-sized pieces, together with the thinly sliced onions. Brown again, still stirring, for 30 minutes. Add the pieces of kidney. When they have stiffened, add 300 ml (½ pint, 1¼ cups) lambic (Belgian beer), a bouquet garni, salt and a pinch of cayenne. Cook very gently for 30 minutes. Finally, add a bottle of lambic and 500 ml (17 fl oz, 2 cups) mushroom stock to the choesels.

CHOISEUL A preparation of poached sole or fillets of sole coated with a white wine sauce containing a julienne of blanched truffles.

CHOISY Any of various preparations containing lettuce. The Choisy garnish for meat (tournedos steak, veal chops or rib of veal) combines château potatoes with braised lettuce. Choisy omelette is filled with a creamed lettuce *chiffonnade* and surrounded by a thin border of cream sauce. Sole Choisy is poached, coated with white wine sauce and garnished with a julienne of lettuce and mushrooms. Potage Choisy is a cream of lettuce soup.

CHOLENT A Jewish stew containing beans and kosher beef or chicken, traditionally prepared in a sealed pot and cooked in ashes. The name is derived from the Hebrew word for 'warm'. (See *dafina*.)

CHOP The technique of cutting food into very small pieces, using either a knife or a hand chopper or food processor. The resulting food is cut into small pieces, fairly even in size (but not as precisely as dicing) and the texture varies from very coarse to very fine, depending on requirements. The French term *hachage* can also describe food that has been chopped, although the more common French word is *hachis* (see *Hash*).

CHOP Also known as a cutlet. A small cut of meat comprising a rib bone and the meat attached to it. The animals whose meat is sold by butchers normally have 13 pairs of ribs, commonly called 'ribs' for beef, 'chops' or 'cutlets' in veal and lamb, 'chops' in pork and 'cutlets' or 'noisettes' in stag or venison.

■ **Beef** The rib with the bone in is a prime cut, for roasting in the oven or grilling (broiling). It is marbled and full of flavour and can be of various thicknesses. The back ribs, which are cut into slices entrecôte style, are somewhat firmer in texture; when boned, they can be roasted in the same way as boned middle rib, whose flavour is very fine.

■ **Mutton and lamb** Best end of neck cutlets (rib chops), cut from the loin with a long bone (which is often decorated with a paper frill when serving), have lean flesh which forms a central 'nut' surrounded by fat. The middle neck cutlets are more fatty, with meat which extends along the bone. Loin chops (both loins) do not have the long bone and the 'nut' is joined to a band of meat with strips of fat in it, rolled up on itself.

What the French call 'mutton chops' are very thick cutlets cut from mutton fillet; a skewer is stuck through them before grilling, to keep the round part in place.

What the French call 'lamb chops' are lamb cutlets cut across the best end (ribs) and comprising two cutlets joined together at the bone, but cut less thick than a single one. They are also known as '*lunettes d'agneau*' ('lambs' spectacles') or, in England, as butterfly chops, and are grilled (broiled).

■ **Pork** Loin chops from the hind loin have lean and fairly dry meat. When cut from the foreloin, they are more fleshy, wider and more tender. When taken from the spare rib (shoulder), they are more fatty. Chinese spare ribs come from the belly and are often barbecued. In wild boar, both mature and young, the cutlets can be eaten marinated and fried (escalopes can also be cut from them).

■ **Veal** Prime and best end of neck cutlets (ribs) are lean and tender in the centre, more fatty at the edge, and can be fried or grilled (broiled). Middle neck cutlets (shoulder chops), which are firmer and more sinewy, are better fried. Loin chops are fairly wide; they are often stuffed and sometimes coated in breadcrumbs. The 'Parisian' chop is a slice from the breast.

CHOPE A large cylindrical goblet with a handle, used for drinking beer. (The word comes from the German *schoppen*.) It appeared in France in about 1845, at the time when the great Paris brasseries were set up. The *chope* is made of stoneware, pottery, thick glass or sometimes pewter and may be fitted with a hinged lid.

CHOPSTICKS Chopsticks are used as cooking and eating utensils in the Far East. They can be made of bamboo, lacquered wood, plastic, china or ebony and often bear simple designs or elaborate decoration. Chinese chopsticks are sometimes slightly larger than Japanese chopsticks, and the latter are tapered to pointed ends.

In the same way as etiquette is applied to the use of knives and forks, there are correct and polite methods of handling chopsticks. They must not be sucked (since they are considered to be an extension of the fingers) and the tips should be at the same level; the ends, however, must never be stood on the table in order to bring them together. According to Chinese etiquette, they must be held in the middle. If they are held too high, it is considered a sign of arrogance; too low means lack of elegance. In Japan, however, the higher they are held, the better. Etiquette also dictates the ways in which chopsticks should be laid on the table and set aside during, or at the end of, a meal.

Chopsticks used in food preparation and cooking are larger and longer. Especially long ones are used for rearranging and mixing food during cooking; for example, when stir-frying.

CHOP SUEY A popular Chinese-style dish invented at the end of the 19th century in the United States by immigrant Chinese cooks for their American customers. It consists of a mixture of Oriental vegetables, particularly bean sprouts, sometimes accompanied by seafood or meat (such as chicken or pork).

RECIPE

chop suey
Prepare a julienne of young vegetables in season, such as carrot, turnip, leek, onion, peppers and courgettes (zucchini). Place them in a shallow frying pan with some oil – 2 tablespoons for 500 g (18 oz, 4½ cups) vegetables. Stir well, and cook for 4–5 minutes, stirring frequently. During the cooking time, cut some spring onions (scallions) into small sticks. Pick over and rinse some bean sprouts and drain. Chop finely 1 small garlic clove and dice some peeled and seeded tomatoes. Add the bean sprouts to the pan, mix well and stir-fry for 1 minute. Finally add the tomato, onion, garlic, pepper and 2 tablespoons soy sauce to 500 g (18 oz, 4¼ cups) vegetables with a little salt if necessary. Mix and serve hot. This mixture may also be seasoned with 1 teaspoon sesame oil.

CHORBA A thick Arabic soup, made from pieces of lamb's tail and lamb cutlets sautéed in oil with onions and tomatoes, to which courgettes (zucchini), garlic, thyme and bay leaves are added. This is covered with water, finished off with whole haricot (navy) beans or chick peas, and seasoned with red pepper, black pepper and saffron. Before the soup is served, macaroni or vermicelli and dried fruit is added. Similar dishes are found in the cooking of the Balkans, with the Yugoslav *corba* and the Romanian or Bulgarian *ciorba*.

CHORIZO Spanish sausage flavoured with red peppers, available as two main types, The cooking variety is Spain's main pork sausage and it may be smoked or plain, varying according to local recipes, but red in appearance and yielding bright-coloured juices flavoured with garlic during cooking. Sausages tied with red string are hotter than those with ordinary string.

The second type of chorizo is the cured sausage. Longer and larger than the cooking sausage, this *'para tapear'* is sliced and eaten as a tapa, served uncooked on bread.

CHORON A French cook from Caen who became *chef de cuisine* of the famous Voisin restaurant. He invented a hot emulsified sauce to serve with grilled (broiled) fish, tournedos steaks and soft-boiled or poached eggs, and also a garnish for sautéed meat consisting of noisette potatoes with artichoke hearts filled with either green peas or asparagus tips in butter. During the siege of 1870, Choron served several dishes at Voisin based on elephant – including elephant's trunk in chasseur sauce and elephant bourguignon.

RECIPE

Choron sauce
Dilute 200 ml (7 fl oz, ¾ cup) béarnaise* sauce with 2 tablespoons tepid tomato purée which has been well reduced and sieved. It is essential to use a very concentrated purée.

CHOU A small sweet or savoury bun, made from choux paste, eaten cold, often filled with a cream or garnish. In pâtisserie, choux are often used to make *croquembouches* or are filled or iced to make profiteroles. Savoury choux, filled with savoury mixtures, such as shellfish, vegetables, cream cheese and foie gras, are served as hors d'oeuvre.

CHOULEND A kind of Jewish ragoût made with braised beef. Since the rules of the Sabbath forbid fires being lit from sunset on Friday until sunset on Saturday, dishes are placed in the oven on Friday evening and allowed to simmer until midday on Saturday. The prolonged slow cooking gives these dishes a remarkable flavour.

CHOUQUETTE A small unfilled chou bun sprinkled with a little granulated sugar. Made from ordinary choux paste, *chouquettes* are sold at baker's and confectioner's shops.

CHOUX PASTE Although it is often referred to as choux pastry, choux is completely different from other types of pastry, such as shortcrust, flaky, puff, filo and so on. The mixture is based on a paste of flour and water, enriched with butter, then lightened with egg and by thorough beating. When cooked, the paste rises to form a crisp shell with a thin moist lining of cooked paste and a hollow centre. The paste can be baked to make small or large buns (*chou* in French), fingers (for éclairs) or rings (large or small). It can also be deep-fried.

The first stage in making the paste is to heat the liquid (water or water and milk) and butter until the butter melts. This should be done slowly at first, without allowing the liquid to boil (it the liquid boils too soon before the fat melts, it will reduce). When the butter has melted, bring the mixture to the boil as quickly as possible. Add the sifted plain (all-purpose) flour immediately and all at once, and remove the pan from the heat. Stir the mixture until it forms a smooth thick paste that comes away from the side of the pan in a soft ball. If the mixture is too thin, cook it briefly until thickened. Do not beat the paste at this stage or the fat will separate out slightly, making it oily. Leave the paste to cool slightly, then gradually mix in beaten eggs and beat until the mixture is smooth and glossy.

Flavouring ingredients, such as grated cheese, herbs, spring onions, a little sugar or vanilla, can be added to the paste. To make fritters or beignets, chopped or diced ingredients, such as vegetables or fruit, can be added.

Use a piping bag or spoon to shape the paste. Bake the paste at a high temperature first, so that it rises well, then reduce the temperature to allow the shell to cook. When cooked, the choux paste should be browned and crisp outside, hollow and moist inside. To prevent the cooked paste from softening, slit it as soon as it is removed from the oven to allow steam to escape.

Uncooked choux paste freezes well. Shape and open freeze the mixture, then pack the pieces in polythene bags when firm. Cook from frozen, allowing slightly longer. Unfilled cooked paste also freezes well, but it tends to soften, so should be placed in a hot oven for 1–2 minutes to crisp up before any filling is added.

RECIPES

choux paste
To make about 40 small buns, 20 larger buns or éclairs, measure 250 ml (8 fl oz, 1 cup) water or milk and water (in equal proportions) into a saucepan. Add a large pinch of salt and 65 g (2½ oz, 5 tablespoons) butter cut into small pieces. Add 2 teaspoons caster (superfine) sugar for sweet choux. Heat gently until the butter melts, then bring to the boil. As soon as the mixture begins to boil, take the pan off the heat, add 125 g (4½ oz, 1 cup) plain (all-

purpose) flour all at once and mix quickly. Return the saucepan to the heat and cook the paste until it thickens, stirring: it takes about 1 minute for the paste to leave the sides of the saucepan. Do not overcook the mixture or beat it vigorously as this will make it greasy or oily. Remove from the heat and cool slightly. Beat in 2 eggs, then 2 more eggs, one after the other, continuing to beat hard until a smooth glossy paste is obtained. Use as required.

making choux buns or fingers

Transfer the pastry to a piping bag fitted with a plain nozzle, 1 cm (½ in) in diameter, and pipe small balls, 4–5 cm (1½–2 in) in diameter, on to a lightly oiled baking sheet, spacing them out so they do not stick to each other as they swell during cooking. Alternatively, pipe the paste into larger buns or fingers to make éclairs.

Bake choux pastries in a preheated oven at 220°C (425°F, gas 7) for 10 minutes. Reduce the temperature to 180°C (350°F, gas 4) and continue to cook, allowing a further 10 minutes for small buns or up to 25 minutes for large puffs. Transfer cooked choux pastries to a wire rack to cool and split them immediately to allow steam to escape, so that they stay crisp outside, but slightly moist on the inside.

Savoury Choux
cheese puffs

Prepare a béchamel sauce using 25 g (1 oz, 2 tablespoons) butter, 25 g (1 oz, ¼ cup) plain (all-purpose) flour and 300 ml (½ pint, 1¼ cups) milk. Add 75 g (3 oz, ¾ cup) grated Gruyère or Cheddar cheese, or 50 g (2 oz, ½ cup) Parmesan, a little grated nutmeg, salt and pepper. Leave to cool until lukewarm. Fill the split choux buns or fingers with this mixture. Cover with foil and reheat gently in a preheated oven at 160°C (325°F, gas 3). As an alternative, the quantity of cheese may be reduced by half and 75 g (3 oz, ¾ cup) finely diced ham added.

choux à la nantua

Fill some small cooled choux buns or fingers with cold crayfish mousse. Keep them cool. They can be served with a hot Nantua sauce if desired.

green vegetable puffs

Fill some small cooled choux buns or fingers with a thick purée of green peas, French beans and asparagus tips, bound with cream.

Sweet Choux
almond choux fritters

To make about 20 fritters, use 500 g (18 oz) choux paste and 100 g (4 oz, 1 cup) shredded almonds. Scatter the almonds over a baking sheet and bake in a preheated oven at 220°C (425°F, gas 7) until golden. Mix these almonds with the choux paste. In a deep pan, heat some oil to 175°C (345°F). Drop teaspoonfuls of paste into the oil to make the fritters, which turn over by themselves in the oil when they are cooked (about 6 minutes). Cook them in

batches of 10. Drain the fritters on paper towels and serve them hot, sprinkled with plenty of icing (confectioner's) sugar. They may be accompanied with a fruit sauce, such as apricot, cherry or raspberry.

apple cream puffs

Fill some choux with a well-blended mixture of thick apple purée and a third of its weight of confectioner's custard flavoured with Calvados. Dust the choux generously with icing (confectioner's) sugar.

Chantilly cream puffs

These are made to resemble swans. Prepare some choux paste, using the quantities in the basic recipe, and place it in a piping bag fitted with a plain 1.5 cm (⅝ in) diameter nozzle. On to a lightly oiled baking sheet, pipe 10 oval-shaped buns, each about the size of a soupspoon. Now replace the nozzle with one 4–5 mm (about ¼ in) in diameter and pipe 10 'S' shapes, 5–6 cm (2–2½ in) long on to the sheet. Cook the 'S' shapes, which will be the swans' necks, following the basic recipe, allowing about 15 minutes for the 'S' shapes once the temperature is reduced and 20–25 minutes for the buns.

During this time, prepare the Chantilly cream, using 400 ml (14 fl oz, 1¾ cups) very cold double (heavy) cream, 100 ml (4 fl oz, 7 tablespoons) very cold milk, 40 g (1½ oz, 3 tablespoons) caster (superfine) sugar and 1 tablespoon vanilla sugar. Place the cream, milk and vanilla sugar in a chilled bowl and begin to whip. When the cream starts to thicken, add the caster sugar while continuing to whip. Place the cream in cool place.

Split and cool the buns. Then cut the top off each bun and cut the tops in half lengthways; they will form the swans' wings. Fit the piping bag with a large-diameter fluted nozzle, fill the bag with the Chantilly cream and fill the buns with it, forming a dome on each. Place a 'neck' at one end of each bun and stick the 'wings' into the cream on either side. Dust generously with icing (confectioner's) sugar.

cherry cream puffs

Prepare some confectioner's custard, flavour it with kirsch and add some stoned (pitted) well-drained cherries in syrup. Separately prepare some white fondant icing (frosting) flavoured with kirsch. Fill and decorate the choux as for coffee cream puffs.

Chiboust coffee cream puffs

Prepare enough choux paste for 12 puffs. Using a piping bag, pipe the paste into balls on a buttered baking sheet and sprinkle with shredded almonds. Cook them, leave to cool, then fill with Chiboust cream flavoured with coffee. Cool before serving so that the cream becomes firm.

chocolate cream puffs

Prepare some confectioner's custard and flavour it with melted chocolate. Separately prepare some chocolate fondant icing (frosting) using 200 g (7 oz, ¾ cup) fondant* icing and 50 g (2 oz, ½ cup) cocoa blended with 2 tablespoons water. Fill and decorate the choux as in the recipe for coffee choux.

coffee cream puffs

Fill some cooked choux with confectioner's custard flavoured with coffee essence (strong black coffee). Prepare 200 g (7 oz, ¾ cup) fondant* icing (frosting), flavour it with coffee essence (or instant coffee made up with 2 tablespoons of water) and heat until it is runny. Ice the tops of the puffs with the fondant and leave to cool completely.

pastry cream puffs

Prepare 12 choux and fill them with confectioner's custard made using 250 ml (8 fl oz, 1 cup) milk, 3 egg yolks, 50 g (2 oz, ¼ cup) caster (superfine) sugar, 100 g (4 oz, 1 cup) plain (all-purpose) flour. Flavour the custard to taste. The filled puffs may be dusted with icing (confectioner's) sugar or iced with fondant and, if desired, decorated with crystallized (candied) fruits.

pastry cream puffs with grapes

Prepare some confectioner's custard, flavour it slightly with marc brandy and add some fresh grapes with the skins and seeds removed. Fill some choux with the custard and sprinkle them generously with icing (confectioner's) sugar.

other recipes See *cévenole, éclair, Paris-Brest, pets-de-nonne, profiterole, Saint-Honoré, salammbô.*

CHRISTMAS The feast of the Nativity of Christ, some of whose customs and celebrations are taken from the pagan festival of the same date, which it officially replaced in AD 336.

Prominent among the festivities is the distribution of gifts, a custom often associated with one of the great figures of popular myth – St Martin in Belgium, Germany and the Netherlands; St Nicholas in the north and east of France; and Father Christmas. An ancient custom in many regions of France is for godparents to give their godchildren a cake in the shape of a puppet, a swaddled infant or perhaps just a spindle. In Ardèche this cake is known as *Père Janvier*. In northern France it is called *cougnou* (*cugnot* or *cougnat; kerstbroden* in Flemish) and consists of a brioche cake decorated with raisins and sprinkled with icing (confectioner's) sugar. In Berry the cake is called *naulet.*

The custom of the village children going from house to house on Christmas Eve is a very ancient one. Good wishes and Christmas carols brought their reward, traditionally food – bacon, eggs, flour, sweets (candies), dried fruit and cakes. In Burgundy the *cornette*, a cornet-shaped wafer made from cornmeal, has given its name to the annual round of visits. In Touraine, children are given the *guillauneu*, a long cake split at both ends, specially made for the event.

■ **The Christmas meal** The main celebration of Christmas centres on a special meal, although what is eaten varies from country to country. In France, the traditional Christmas meal was the *réveillon*, a supper eaten on Christmas morning, immediately on returning from Midnight Mass. The word comes from *réveiller*, meaning to begin a new watch (*veillée*) after Midnight Mass. The length of the three low masses and the time taken to walk to church and back used to justify a substantial meal eaten in the early hours of Christmas morning.

Virtually throughout France, roast turkey with chestnuts has become the classic Christmas dish. In former times, different regions of France had their own specialities: a *daube* (beef in red wine) in Armagnac, sauerkraut and goose liver in Alsace, *aligot* in Auvergne, black pudding (blood sausage) in Nivernais and goose in south-western France. In the southeast, a large supper was eaten before Mass, consisting of cauliflower and salt cod with raïto, or perhaps snails, grey mullet with olives or omelette with artichokes and fresh pasta. It always ended with the so-called 'thirteen Christmas desserts', recalling the 13 participants at the Last Supper; a fruit pastry known as *pompe à l'huile*, raisins, quince paste, marzipan sweets, nougat, *fouace* (a rich cake), crystallized (candied) citrons, walnuts and hazelnuts, winter pears, Brignoles plums, dried figs, almonds and dates.

All over the Christian world, the traditional dishes of Christmas are handed down from generation to generation. E. de Pomiane mentions that 'the Russians eat *koutia*, wheat grain cooked with dried fruit. The Poles break a Host and eat foods containing poppy seeds. The French gorge themselves on onion soup, grilled black pudding (blood sausage) and truffled turkey. Every year the English eat Christmas pudding.' In Italy, *pan pepato*, originally from Ferrara, appears mainly on New Year's Eve, although it is also a traditional dessert during the week preceding Christmas. In Rome, the festivities begin during the night of Christmas Eve with a grand procession: here the main item of food is eels, together with a stuffed roast capon. In Bologna, home of fresh pasta, Christmas begins with tortellini stuffed with minced (ground) pork, turkey, sausage, cheese and nutmeg. For sweetmeats, there may be *nocciata*, made with walnuts and honey and cut into triangles, cassata flavoured with Ricotta cheese and chocolate, and *torrone*, made with almonds.

In Germany, carp is the traditional Christmas dish, and in some regions carp are still fattened for Christmas from August onwards. However, the main dish today is more likely to be goose, turkey, venison, wild boar, a roast or even veal schnitzel. Some traditional foods are always eaten, particularly apples, walnuts and almonds (the first being the symbol of the Tree of Knowledge, and the nuts, with their shells, representing life's difficulties).

In Sweden, a centuries-old tradition at Christmas was marinated ling (a fish related to cod), served in a white sauce with butter, potatoes, mustard and black pepper. This has been replaced by a new favourite dish, roast goose stuffed with apples and prunes and garnished with red cabbage, caramelized potatoes and cranberry sauce; dessert may be rice porridge or rice with almonds covered with cherry compote. In Norway, large roast pork chops are served with sauerkraut flavoured with cumin, while the Finns cook a ham in a rye-flour pastry case. All Scandinavian countries celebrate Christmas with a sumptuous smorgasbord.

In most European countries a special cake is eaten at Christmas: in England, it is the Christmas cake; in Germany, the *stollen* containing crystallized (candied) fruit; and in France, the *bûche de noël*. In Alsace, the seasonal cakes are *bireweck* containing nuts and dried and crystallized fruit, served with compotes, and *lebkuchen* (gingerbread), traditionally eaten before Midnight Mass; in Brittany the traditional cake is star-shaped.

CHRISTMAS CAKE A fruit cake traditionally eaten in Britain over the Christmas period. Rich in dried fruits, almonds, spices and usually alcohol. After baking, the top and sides are spread with apricot jam, covered with a thin layer of almond paste, then coated with icing (frosting) and decorated. Glacé (candied) cherries and sprigs of holly can provide a simple seasonal finishing touch.

CHRISTMAS PUDDING A British steamed fruit pudding traditionally served at Christmas and also known as plum pudding. Containing suet, breadcrumbs, flour and a high proportion of dried fruit, it is boiled or steamed for several hours and served flambéed with rum or brandy. It improves with keeping and can be stored for up to a year.

This pudding has a long recorded history. It was first made as a Christmas Eve dish of frumenty, with hulled wheat and milk. By the early medieval period, it was made with meat broth thickened with oatmeal and flavoured with eggs, currants, dried plums and spices such as mace and ginger; it had become plum porridge. Elizabethans changed the oats to breadcrumbs and added suet, ale or wine. The big change came with the invention of the floured cloth for boiling puddings. By 1675 it became a round cannonball shape, and remained so for 250 years. The Victorians replaced the dried plums with raisins, currants and peel. Basin puddings were introduced well into the 20th century.

Charles Dickens, in *A Christmas Carol*, alluded to this distinctive pudding, to which the English remain greatly attached: 'Oh! All that steam! The pudding had just been taken out of the cauldron. Oh! That smell! The same as the one which prevailed on washing day! It is that of the cloth which wraps the pudding. Now, one would imagine oneself in a restaurant and in a confectioner's at the same time, with a laundry next door. Thirty seconds later, Mrs Cratchit entered, her face crimson, but smiling proudly, with the pudding resembling a cannon ball, all speckled, very firm, sprinkled with brandy in flames and decorated with a sprig of holly stuck in the centre. Oh! The marvellous pudding!'

Christmas pudding
Finely chop 500 g (18 oz, 3½ cups) suet. Wash and dry 500 g (18 oz, 3 cups) seedless raisins, the same amount of sultanas (golden raisins), and 250 g (9 oz, 1½ cups) currants. Finely chop 250 g (9 oz, 1½ cups) candied peel – or 125 g (4½ oz, ¾ cup) orange peel and 125 g (4½ oz, ½ cup) glacé (candied) cherries, 125 g (4½ oz, 1 cup) blanched almonds and the zest of 2 lemons. Mix all the ingredients together with 500 g (18 oz, 9 cups) fresh breadcrumbs, 125 g (4½ oz, 1 cup) plain (all-purpose) flour, 1 tablespoon mixed spice, the same amount of cinnamon, half a nutmeg (grated) and a pinch of salt. Add 300 ml (½ pint, 1¼ cups) milk and, one by one, 7 or 8 beaten eggs. Next, add 300 ml (½ pint, 1¼ cups) rum (or brandy) and the juice of 2 lemons. Mix everything together thoroughly to obtain a smooth paste.

Wrap the mixture in floured cloths, shaping the portions into balls, or spoon into a greased pudding basin (heatproof mould). Steam or boil.

Keep the pudding in its cloth or basin for at least 3 weeks, in a cool place. Before serving, steam the pudding for 2 hours, then turn it out, sprinkle it with rum or brandy and serve it flambéed, decorated with a sprig of holly.

CHRISTMAS YULE LOG A log-shaped cake, traditionally prepared for the Christmas festivities. It is usually made of rectangular slices of Genoese sponge, spread with butter cream and placed one on top of the other, and then shaped into a log; it is coated with chocolate butter cream, applied with a piping bag to simulate bark. The cake is decorated with holly leaves made from almond paste, meringue mushrooms and small figures. A Swiss roll (jelly roll) may be used instead of sliced Genoese cake. There are also ice cream logs, some made entirely of different flavoured ice creams and some with the inside made of parfait or a bombe mixture.

This cake is a fairly recent creation (after 1870) of the Parisian pastrycooks, inspired by the real logs which used to be burned in the hearth throughout Christmas Eve. Before then, the cakes of the season were generally brioches or fruit loaves.

chestnut log
Line 2 shallow square cake tins (pans) measuring about 23 cm (9 in) square with squares of greaseproof (wax) paper. Prepare a Genoese cake mixture using 125 g (4½ oz, 1 cup) plain (all-purpose) flour, 4 eggs and 125 g (4½ oz, ½ cup) caster (superfine) sugar. Spread the mixture in the buttered lined tins with a moistened metal spatula, leaving a gap of 2 cm (¾ in) between the mixture and the top of the tin. Put straight into a preheated oven at about 180°C (350°F, gas 4) and bake for

25–30 minutes. Take the tins out of the oven, turn over on to a cloth and immediately remove the paper from the bottom of the cakes. Cover with another cloth and allow to cool.

Prepare 200 ml (7 fl oz, ¾ cup) sugar syrup by boiling 100 g (4 oz, ½ cup) granulated sugar with 100 ml (4 fl oz, 7 tablespoons) water and flavour it with rum or vanilla. To prepare the chestnut mixture, soften 225 g (8 oz, 1 cup) butter with a spatula and add 450 g (1 lb, 2 cups) chestnut* cream and, if desired, 2 tablespoons rum. Beat the mixture for 6–8 minutes until light and fluffy, then divide into 2 portions. Soak the 2 squares of cake in the cooled sugar syrup and spread each with half the chestnut mixture. Place the 2 squares of cake facing each other and roll the first one up tightly, then wrap the second one over the first. Cut both ends off diagonally and stick these to the top of the log to represent knots in the wood. Place the cake in the refrigerator for 1 hour. Soften the remaining cream again and cover the entire log with it. Mark with the prongs of a fork to imitate the bark. Decorate with 8 marrons glacés, put back in the refrigerator and dust with icing (confectioner's) sugar just before serving.

chocolate log

Prepare Genoese cakes as for the chestnut log. To prepare the syrup, boil 100ml (4 fl oz, 7 tablespoons) water and 100 g (4 oz, ½ cup) granulated sugar in a small saucepan, allow to cool, then add 2 tablespoons rum. Finally, prepare a chocolate-flavoured butter cream (see *custard*) using 400 g (14 oz, 1¾ cups) butter. Using a pastry brush, cover the 2 cakes with rum syrup; coat with three-quarters of the cream and roll up as for the chestnut log. Completely cover the log with the remaining cream and make uneven furrows along it with a fork. Decorate with small sugar or meringue shapes and store in a cool place until required for serving (the butter cream may also be flavoured with coffee or vanilla).

CHRYSANTHEMUM The petals are used in Japan, China and Vietnam for adding to salads. Their taste is similar to that of cress.

CHTCHI Also known as *tschy* or *stschy*. A thick Russian soup, based on braised sauerkraut cooked in a thickened stock, to which are added pieces of blanched brisket of beef, poached duck or chicken, salted bacon and smoked sausages. *Chtchi* is served in a soup tureen with *smetana* (soured cream) and fennel or chopped parsley. *Chtchi* is also prepared with green vegetables (spinach, sorrel, nettle).

CHUB A freshwater fish, 30–50 cm (12–20 in) long, with a greenish-brown back and silvery belly. Several species are known: the common chub has a big round head, others have angular heads. All have quite soft flesh but are full of bones; they are therefore kept for fish stews (except for the smallest ones, which are sometimes eaten fried).

CHUCK A lean boneless cut of beef from the shoulder, also known as blade. This traditional cut for casseroles and stews is gelatinous and best braised slowly in dishes such as carbonade, daube or beef *à la mode*. The name *macreuse* is used for a type of wild duck whose flesh could formerly be eaten during Lent.

CHUFA Also known as tiger nut or earth almond, this is a small vegetable tuber from a plant in the sedge family. The outside is brown and slightly wrinkled; the flesh white and crisp, with a slightly sweet, nutty flavour. It can be eaten raw or cooked.

CHUMP END (LOIN) A joint of lamb, mutton or venison lying between the leg (*gigot*) and loin. It may be tied up, boned and stuffed before roasting or cut into succulent chops for grilling (broiling).

The French equivalent, *selle*, means 'saddle', but it should not be confused with the English saddle of meat, which consists of the two joined loins. The two legs, chump end and saddle together, make an elegant banqueting dish called a baron.

The chump end is a prime piece of meat, which inspired Monselet to write:

'Sors du mouton qui te recèle,
Selle,
Et sur un coulis béarnais
Nais!'

This is a witty little command to the chump end to emerge from the animal, to be eaten with béarnaise sauce!

RECIPES

chump end of lamb Belle Otéro

Bone a chump end of lamb weighing 2.25 kg (5 lb). Make a stock with 250 g (9 oz, 1½ cups) finely diced trimmings browned in butter with the bones, a carrot and a medium-sized onion (cut up into small pieces), and season with salt and pepper. After browning, add 100 ml (4 fl oz, 7 tablespoons) white wine. Reduce, then add 300 ml (½ pint, 1¼ cups) stock; simmer for 1 hour, then pass through a fine strainer.

Prepare the forcemeat. Finely dice an onion, a celery stick and a carrot, and cook gently in a knob of butter. Add 100 g (4 oz) whole truffles, and then 100 ml (4 fl oz, 7 tablespoons) port and 200 ml (7 fl oz, ¾ cup) strong chicken stock. Season with salt and freshly ground pepper. Cook for 15 minutes. Take the truffles out and reduce the liquid. Prepare a duxelles with 500 g (18 oz, 6 cups) button mushrooms (cleaned and finely chopped, then wrung out in a cloth to extract all their juice) cooked for 10 minutes in butter with 4 chopped shallots, salt, pepper and nutmeg. To the duxelles, add 50 g (2 oz, ⅓ cup) cooked diced truffles and 65 g (2½ oz) foie gras cut into matchsticks. Bind with a little of the truffle cooking liquid and season with salt and pepper.

Stuff the lamb with this forcemeat, then arrange the remaining truffles on top, together with another 65 g (2½ oz) foie gras matchsticks. Roll and tie up the meat, wrap it in barding, then tie it up again. Roast for 50 minutes in a preheated oven at 220°C (425°F, gas 7). Serve the meat juices mixed with the truffle juices in a sauceboat. Untie the string, remove the barding and garnish the meat with bunches of buttered asparagus tips or braised artichoke hearts. Médoc would complement this dish.

chump end of lamb Callas

Bone a chump end of lamb weighing about 2.75 kg (6 lb), trim the excess fat and season with salt and pepper. Prepare a mushroom julienne, cook it in butter and leave it to cool. Also prepare a julienne of fresh truffles. Put the truffle julienne down the centre of the meat with the mushroom julienne on each side. Roll and tie up the joint. Roast in a preheated oven at 220°C (425°F, gas 7), allowing 12 minutes per 450 g (1 lb). Deglaze the roasting pan with a little veal stock and sherry. Serve with buttered asparagus tips.

CHUNK A regular-shaped piece obtained by cutting up an elongated foodstuff or preparation, such as a celery stick or a croquette mixture. The French word *tronçon* also refers to a short wide piece cut from the middle of a large flatfish such as turbot or brill.

CHURN The apparatus used for agitating cream to make butter. The traditional churn is a teak barrel which rotates about a horizontal axis. The plungers fixed to the walls assist the churning process. Modern commercial churns are made of stainless steel and the churning process is continuous. They are equipped with beaters and mixers which give the butter the required consistency and are maintained at a constant temperature of 10–13°C (50–55°F). The speed of rotation varies from 25 to 50 rpm.

Small plastic household churns of 3 litre (5 pint, 13 cup) capacity with stainless steel beaters are also available. They should only be half filled to allow the mechanical action to take place, as the weight of the cream falls from one end to the other.

CHURROS Long, thin Spanish fritters, rolled or wound round on themselves, prepared with a batter made of cornflour (cornstarch), water with salt, and fried in boiling oil. *Churros* are eaten with sugar for breakfast.

CHUTNEY A savoury preserve made of fruits or vegetables (or of a mixture of the two) cooked in vinegar with sugar and spices until it has the consistency of jam. Chutney is served as a condiment or relish. Considered as typically Indian, chutney – from the Hindustani *chatni* (strong spices) – is in fact a British speciality dating from the colonial era

(like pickles). Chutneys, sold in jars under various trade names, may contain exotic fruits (mango, coconut, pineapple, tamarind pulp), as well as tomatoes, onions and familiar vegetables. Some chutneys are reduced to a pulp; others retain recognizable pieces of their ingredients; all are characterized by a syrupy and sometimes highly spiced juice which coats the ingredients.

As well as cooked chutneys, fresh chutneys, made from raw ingredients, may be prepared. Indian cooking includes many fresh chutneys of finely cut vegetables mixed with chopped fresh herbs and/or spices. These are not preserves, but are prepared specifically as an appetizer or to accompany particular dishes.

RECIPES

apple and mango chutney
Peel and finely slice 1.5 kg (3¼ lb) cooking apples. Bring 1 litre (1¾ pints, 4⅓ cups) white vinegar to the boil, put the apples in it and cook for 5 minutes. Add 500 g (18 oz, 3¼ cups) brown sugar, 25 g (1 oz, ¼ cup) finely sliced chillies, 200 g (7 oz, 1¼ cups) seedless raisins, 200 g (7 oz, 1¼ cups) sultanas (golden raisins), 100 g (4 oz, ½ cup) sorted and washed currants, 500 g (18 oz, 2¾ cups) candied lemon peel cut into large dice and 2 crushed garlic cloves. Season with 25 g (1 oz, 1½ tablespoons) salt, 125 g (4½ oz, ½ cup) mustard seeds and 2 tablespoons ground ginger. Finally, add 500 g (18 oz) well-drained canned mangoes. Cook for about 25 minutes. Scald some jars and pour the hot chutney into them; cover and seal.

fruit chutney
Cut ¼ red (bell) pepper into 3 mm (⅛ in) dice, having first removed the membranes and seeds. Peel 1 pear, 1 Granny Smith apple and 1 pineapple and cut into 5 mm (¼ in) dice. Peel 25 g (1 oz) of fresh root ginger and chop very finely. Put 2 tablespoons rice vinegar and 2 tablespoons soft brown sugar in a saucepan and bring to the boil. Add the diced pepper and fruits, ginger, 1 tablespoon currants and 5 cumin seeds. Bring to the boil and cook over a brisk heat for 15 minutes. Remove from the heat and put in a jar. It will keep a few days in the refrigerator.

pineapple chutney
To 1 litre (1¾ pints, 4⅓ cups) white vinegar, add 500 g (18 oz, 3¼ cups) moist brown sugar, 2 tablespoons mustard seeds, 5 cloves, 1 cinnamon stick and 1 teaspoon ground ginger. Boil for 15 minutes, then add the drained contents of 2 large cans of pineapple pieces and 250 g (9 oz, 1½ cups) of both sultanas (golden raisins) and raisins. Leave to cook gently without a lid until the mixture has the consistency of jam. Scald some bottling jars, preferably ones with a rubber ring and a metal clip (which is removed when the chutney has cooled), and pour the hot chutney into them.

Spanish-onion chutney

Peel and slice 2 kg (4½ lb) Spanish onions or large mild onions. Tip them into a large saucepan along with 675 g (1½ lb, 3½ cups) brown sugar, 400 g (14 oz, 2½ cups) raisins or sultanas (golden raisins), 400 ml (14 fl oz, 1¾ cups) dry white wine, 400 ml (14 fl oz, 1¾ cups) white wine vinegar, 2 garlic cloves, 300 g (11 oz) crystallized (candied) ginger cut into pieces, a pinch of curry powder and 5 cloves. Boil for 1¾–2 hours, leave to cool completely, then put in jars.

CIDER A drink produced by the natural fermentation of apple juice (pears are sometimes mixed with the apples). The word comes from the Greek *sikera* (intoxicating drink) and the production of cider certainly dates from antiquity. In France regulations were introduced under Charlemagne, and in the 12th century cider-making became established in Normandy and Brittany, where the climate is very favourable for growing apples. Here, cider completely supplanted barley beer.

Calvados, Manche, Orne, Ille-et-Vilaine and Mayenne remain the most important areas of production. The ciders of Dinan and Fouesnant are equally famous. Britain also produces and consumes a great range of ciders, generally pale in colour with a higher alcohol content than in France, where processes such as sweetening and reconstitution with apple concentrate are prohibited. In the United States the term cider refers to pressed apple juice which is used to make sweet cider, hard cider, vinegar and applejack.

Several hundred varieties of apple are used for the manufacture of cider (including Bedan, Duret, Bisquet, Fréquin and Saint-Martin); some are sweet, but most are rather bitter or even sour. The cidermaker's skill lies in blending different varieties to obtain an agreeable and well-balanced cider. The apples are gathered when ripe, then left in a heap for several days before being crushed and pressed. Fermentation, which occurs naturally without the addition of yeasts or sugar, takes about a month. According to its style and quality and the intended market, it may then be filtered to clarify it, and pasteurized to make it keep longer. Both still and sparkling ciders are produced. Its thirst-quenching tang and fruity flavour make cider a refreshing drink.

The use of cider in cooking is a characteristic of Brittany and Normandy, particularly in recipes for fish (*matelote*, sole, brill), chicken, rabbit and tripe. In Brittany, 'one sits by the fire in the evenings eating chestnuts and drinking sweet cider', as Théodore Botrel sang in *La Paludicie*. The 'bowl' or cup of cider traditional in Brittany is an excellent accompaniment to the region's pancakes.

RECIPES

chicken with cider

Peel, quarter and core 500 g (18 oz) sour apples; cut half of them into thin slices. Season the inside of a large chicken with salt and pepper, stuff it with the apple slices and sew up the opening. Baste the chicken with melted butter and brown in a flameproof casserole for about 20 minutes. Meanwhile, chop up 3 shallots and brown them lightly in butter. When the chicken is golden brown, surround it with the remaining apples and add a little crumbled thyme, 2 crushed cloves, salt, freshly ground pepper, the shallots and ½ bottle of cider, already heated. Bring to the boil, partly cover and cook for about 40 minutes. Remove the chicken and keep it hot. Add 200 ml (7 fl oz, ¾ cup) double (heavy) cream to the casserole and reduce by a third. Cut the chicken into portions and serve coated with the sauce.

cider fruit cup

Peel some fresh fruit, sprinkling with lemon juice those that tend to turn brown. Apples, pears, oranges, pineapples and bananas can be used; or cherries, strawberries, apricots, melon and pears; or melon, peaches, plums and grapes. Leave the smaller fruit whole and cut the others into thin slices. Add 2 tablespoons Calvados for every 1 litre (1¾ pints, 4⅓ cups) of sweet cider, then add sugar to taste and mix. Sprinkle the fruit generously with the cider and place in the refrigerator for at least 1 hour before serving.

fillets of fish in cider

Prepare a fish stock, but replace the white wine and half the water with rough cider. Poach the fish fillets in this stock, then drain and arrange on the serving dish, keeping them hot. Strain the cooking liquid and reduce by half. To it, add the same volume of double (heavy) cream and reduce a little more. Coat the fillets with the sauce and glaze in a preheated oven at 240°C (475°F, gas 9).

knuckle of veal braised in cider

Melt 25 g (1 oz, 2 tablespoons) butter in a large saucepan and in it lightly brown a knuckle of veal weighing about 1.7 kg (3¾ lb), having cut 3 cm (1¼ in) off the end. Peel and chop 6 shallots, add three-quarters of them to the pan, leave to colour and flame with Calvados. Then pour into the saucepan ½ bottle of dry sparkling cider add salt and pepper, cover and cook for 2½ hours over a gentle heat. Turn the knuckle over once or twice during cooking.

Meanwhile, peel about 30 small white (pearl) onions and cook them gently in a covered saucepan with 50 g (2 oz, ¼ cup) butter until they are soft. Add salt and pepper. Peel and core 3 dessert (eating) apples and cut them into slices, about 3 mm (⅛ in) thick. Brown lightly in a frying pan with 25 g (1 oz, 2 tablespoons) butter. Keep them hot.

When the knuckle is nearly ready, sauté 200 g (7 oz) fresh chanterelle mushrooms in butter, along with the remaining chopped shallots; cover. The knuckle is cooked when the flesh comes away from the bone by itself. Remove the pieces of skin and the gelatine that surround the meat, cut the meat into pieces and arrange in a warmed serving dish.

Lightly brown the apple slices under the grill (broiler). Wash, wipe and chop some parsley. Mix 1 egg yolk with 1 tablespoon double (heavy) cream, add it to the veal cooking liquor, then strain everything. Beat this sauce with a whisk and adjust the seasoning. Arrange the onions and mushrooms around the knuckle. Coat the knuckle with the sauce, putting a little on the garnish too. Sprinkle with chopped parsley and serve the well-browned apple slices separately.

wild rabbit with farm cider

Remove the bones from a baron (saddle and legs) of young rabbit weighing about 1.5 kg (3¼ lb). Prepare a *brunoise* of carrots, celeriac, celery sticks and leeks (green parts). Blanch the vegetables separately, then cool and bind together using 3 egg yolks. Sprinkle with salt and pepper. Prepare 200 ml (7 fl oz, ¾ cup) rabbit stock using the bones, 1 carrot, 1 onion, a bouquet garni, 250 ml (8 fl oz, 1 cup) farm cider, 250 ml (8 fl oz, 1 cup) water, salt, and pepper.

Spread the baron of rabbit out on its back, season with salt and pepper, and stuff it with the *brunoise*. Pull the sides of the legs and belly together over the *brunoise* and tie up with string. Lay the rabbit in an ovenproof earthenware dish or casserole containing a bed of diced vegetables (2 carrots, 2 red onions and 2 shallots) mixed with diced dessert (eating) apple. Roast it with butter in a preheated oven at 240°C (475°F, gas 9) for 15–20 minutes so that it remains pink. Keep it hot, covered with a sheet of foil.

Boil 1 litre (1¾ pints, 4⅓ cups) milk and allow to cool. Peel and slice 1 kg (2¼ lb) potatoes. Shred half a green cabbage, blanch and cool. Butter an ovenproof, preferably earthenware, dish and arrange in it a layer of the potatoes, sprinkled with salt and pepper, then a layer of the cabbage, a layer of Emmental cheese, and so on, finishing with a layer of potatoes and Emmental. To the cooled milk, add 4 well-beaten eggs and a few knobs of butter and pour over the potatoes. Cook in a preheated oven at 200–220°C (400–425°F, gas 6–7) for 45 minutes. Keep hot.

For the sauce to accompany the rabbit, add 500 ml (17 fl oz, 2 cups) farm cider to the pan juices and reduce by two-thirds; add a small glass of demi-glace, the rabbit stock and 250 ml (8 fl oz, 1 cup) double (heavy) cream. Cook over a gentle heat for 5 minutes. Chop some chives and chervil and sprinkle over the sauce.

Surround the rabbit with cress and serve it with the sauce and the potato cake.

CIGARETTE A cylindrical biscuit (cookie), also called *cigarette russe*, prepared with *langues-de-chat* mixture. After baking, the discs are rolled into a cylinder shape around a wooden stick while they are still lukewarm and malleable.

RECIPES

cigarettes russes

Butter a baking sheet. Melt 100 g (4 oz, ½ cup) butter in a bain marie. Whisk 4 egg whites into very stiff peaks, adding a pinch of salt. In a mixing bowl, blend 90 g (3½ oz, 1 cup less 2 tablespoons) plain (all-purpose) flour, 165 g (5½ oz, ¾ cup less 1 tablespoon) caster (superfine) sugar, 1 tablespoon vanilla-flavoured sugar and the melted butter. Carefully add the egg whites. Spread this mixture on the baking sheet, making very thin discs about 7.5 cm (3 in) in diameter; bake only 3 or 4 at a time. Place them in a preheated oven at 180°C (350°F, gas 4) and cook for 10 minutes or until the biscuits turn golden. Loosen them and roll each around the handle of a wooden spoon while still hot. Leave them to cool completely.

lemon cigarettes

Prepare as in the previous recipe, but before baking add to the mixture some finely chopped candied lemon peel; use 100 g (4 oz, ⅔ cup) peel for the quantities given in the recipe. Once the cigarettes have cooled, fill both ends with lemon-flavoured butter cream (see *creams*) using a piping bag.

CINCHONA A tree originating in Peru and cultivated chiefly in Indonesia for its bark, which is rich in quinine. Cinchona bark is also used in the manufacture of apéritifs and alcoholic drinks.

CINGHALAISE, À LA Describes preparations of cold fish or white meats accompanied by cinghalaise, or Ceylon-style, sauce, a kind of vinaigrette to which a salpicon of vegetables in oil and herbs is added. Only the presence of the curry powder is evocative of Sri Lanka (Ceylon).

RECIPE

cinghalaise sauce

Peel a courgette (zucchini) and cook it in water until it is just slightly firm. Finely dice equal quantities of green and red sweet peppers, tomato pulp, cucumber and the cooked courgette. To this salpicon, add some sieved hard-boiled (hard-cooked) egg yolk, curry powder, salt, pepper, lemon juice, oil and chopped parsley and chives.

CINNAMON A spice obtained from the bark of several tropical trees. The bark is removed, dried and rolled up to make a tube, light fawn or dark grey in colour, depending on the species. The most popular varieties of cinnamon are from Sri Lanka and China. Cinnamon imparts a sweet penetrating aroma and has a mild warm and spicy flavour. It is also commonly found in the form of a powder and sometimes as an oil or an extract. It is one of the oldest spices, mentioned in Sanskrit texts and the Bible and used by the ancients to flavour wine. In the Middle Ages it was widely used in stews, soups, custards and poultry fricassées. In France it is mainly used in compotes and desserts, and to flavour mulled wine. In eastern Europe its uses are much more numerous, in pâtisserie, soups and meats. In Indian and Asian cooking it is widely used in savoury dishes as well as for sweet recipes.

RECIPE

mulled wine with cinnamon and cloves
Wash a small orange and stick 2 cloves into it. Leave to macerate for 24 hours in I litre (1¾ pints, 4⅓ cups) red wine. Remove the orange, pour the wine into a pan, sweeten to taste and add I cinnamon stick. Bring to the boil, then remove from the heat and allow the cinnamon to infuse according to taste. Remove the cinnamon and reheat the wine.

CIOPPINO A dish from San Francisco consisting of a stew of white fish, large prawns (shrimp), clams and mussels, with a garlic, tomato and white-wine base.

CÎTEAUX An uncooked pressed cow's-milk cheese (45% fat) from Burgundy with a washed crust. Made by the Cistercian monks of the Abbey of Cîteaux, Côte d'Or, it is a disc-shaped cheese 18 cm (7 in) in diameter and 4 cm (1¾ in) thick, weighing about 1 kg (2¼ lb). Cîteaux is similar to Saint-Paulin, but its taste is more fruity.

CITRON A citrus fruit originally from China (not Persia, as was formerly believed) and similar to the lemon. It has been used since the 16th century or before. In France the citron tree is cultivated particularly in Corsica and on the Côte d'Azur. The fruit is larger than the lemon and slightly pear-shaped, with a thick glossy skin. It is rarely eaten raw and gives little juice, which can be used like lemon juice. Although employed in jams and marmalades, the citron is used mainly for its peel, which is candied as an ingredient for cake-making and for biscuits and puddings. In Corsica it is also used to make a liqueur, Cédratine, and to fill sweets (candies).

CITRONNER A French culinary term meaning to flavour or sprinkle a dish with lemon juice. The term also means to rub the surface of certain vegetables (artichoke hearts, celeriac, mushrooms) with a cut lemon, or to sprinkle them with lemon juice, to prevent discoloration.

CITRUS FRUITS Fruits of the genus *Citrus*, including the orange, Seville (bitter) orange, bergamot, grapefruit, pomelo (shaddock), tangerine, clementine, lemon, lime, citron and sweet lime, as well as hybrids of this genus (citrange) and related genera (kumquat). Originally from Asia, citrus fruits – whose French name, *agrumes*, comes from the Latin *acrumen* (bitter flavour) – gradually spread throughout the world, particularly to Mediterranean countries (Israel, Spain, Italy) and to the United States (Florida, California).

These fruits, which are rich in vitamin C, have an acid flavour to varying degrees. They are widely consumed either as fresh fruit or in cakes, pastries and preserves, such as crystallized (candied) fruit (particularly citron and bergamot), jams and sweets (candies). They are also used in distilling (Curaçao) and in some recipes are combined with meat (pork) and poultry (duck). The most important role of citrus fruits, however, is in the fruit juice industry (natural or concentrated). Several by-products play an important part in the food industry: aromatic essential oils, extracted from the skin; pectin, which comes from the white part of the rind; and oils made from some pips. (*Agrume*, in the singular, is the French name for the Ente plum, from which Agen prunes are made.)

CIVET A game stew typically made from wild rabbit, hare, venison or young wild boar, prepared with red wine and thickened with the animal's blood or pig's blood; this gives it its oily texture and distinctive colouring. Small onions and pieces of larding bacon are generally included. The name is derived from *cive* (spring onion or scallion), which was formerly used to flavour all stews, particularly hare.

Certain seafood and fish dishes served in sauce are also called *civet*; at Dinard, abalones *en civet* are cooked in red wine with onions and strips of larding bacon. In French provincial areas, *civets* are also prepared from goose giblets or squirrel; in southwestern France, squirrel is cooked in a roux moistened with red wine, with onions and orange zest.

RECIPES

civet of hare or jugged hare (basic preparation)
Skin and gut (clean) the hare. Carefully collect the blood and put to one side along with the liver, having removed the gall-bladder; add I tablespoon vinegar. Detach the thighs and forelegs and chop each thigh in half, splintering the bones as little as possible; cut the saddle into 4 pieces. Place all the pieces in a deep dish and season with salt, pepper, thyme and powdered bay leaf. Add a large finely sliced onion, 3–4 tablespoons oil and at least I tablespoon Cognac. After marinating for 24 hours, the hare is ready to be cooked *à la flamande*, *à la française* or *à la lyonnaise*.

civet of hare ◆
Prepare a hare as described above and marinate overnight in red wine containing 3 onions (halved), a sliced carrot and a sprig of thyme.

The following morning, drain the hare in a colander. Heat 250 ml (8 fl oz, I cup) oil and 40 g (1½ oz, 3 tablespoons) butter in a frying pan and lightly brown the pieces of hare on each side, as well as the onions and carrots from the marinade.

Civet of hare.

Then place the pieces in a saucepan and sprinkle with flour. Moisten with the wine from the marinade, a trickle of Cognac and 1 tablespoon tomato purée (paste); add 2 garlic cloves crushed in their skins, a bouquet garni, a quarter of a bay leaf (crushed), salt and pepper. Mix well and leave to simmer for 2 hours.

Separately, cook 20 small onions in a little water to which 1 teaspoon caster (superfine) sugar has been added. Cut 250 g (9 oz) small mushrooms into quarters (or leave tiny button mushrooms whole) and brown them in some butter. Dice 150 g (5 oz) smoked bacon, blanch it, then cook it gently in a frying pan.

When the hare is cooked, arrange the pieces in a dish and keep hot. Chop up the hare's liver and mix it with the blood. Add it to the cooking liquor and bring to the boil. Pass through a fine strainer to form a sauce. Add the garnish of onions, mushrooms and pieces of bacon. Adjust the seasoning, pour the sauce over the hare and serve accompanied by fresh noodles.

civet of hare à la flamande
Marinate a hare as described in the basic preparation of civet of hare. Drain the pieces of marinated hare, brown them in about 40 g (1½ oz, 3 tablespoons) butter in a flameproof casserole, dust them with 2 tablespoons flour and again lightly brown them, turning them with a wooden spoon. Press the liver through a sieve along with the blood and add to it 1 litre (1¾ pints, 4⅓ cups) red wine; then add 200 ml (7 fl oz, ¾ cup) wine vinegar. Pour this mixture into the casserole; add some salt, pepper, 25 g (1 oz, 3 tablespoons) moist brown sugar and a large bouquet garni. Cover and cook for 15 minutes.

During this time, peel and finely slice 500 g (18 oz) onions and brown them in some butter. Add them to the casserole after the 15 minutes have elapsed and leave to finish cooking gently with the lid on. Cooking time depends on the age of the animal; the tip of a knife should pass easily into the flesh when it is cooked.

Remove the cooked hare, drain and place the pieces in a sauté dish. Strain the cooking liquid to remove the onions, pour it into the sauté dish, cover and simmer for 5 minutes. Fry some croûtons in butter and spread them with redcurrant jelly. Serve the civet in a deep dish, garnished with the croûtons. If desired, the ends of the croûtons can be dipped in the sauce and then in chopped parsley.

civet of hare à la française
Marinate a hare as described in the basic preparation of civet of hare. Cut 200 g (7 oz) streaky bacon into strips, blanch them in boiling water for about 5 minutes, drain, then colour slightly in a shallow frying pan containing 40 g (1½ oz, 3 tablespoons) butter.

Remove and drain the bacon and in the same butter brown 2 large onions cut into quarters; sprinkle with 2 tablespoons flour and, using a wooden spoon, turn until golden brown. Add the drained pieces of hare to this roux and continue to stir (the pieces of hare may be sealed in butter beforehand, if desired). Cover with red wine and add a bouquet garni and a crushed garlic clove, cover and cook gently for 45 minutes.

Meanwhile, prepare 24 mushroom caps and brown them in some butter. When the hare is cooked, remove and drain the pieces and place them in a casserole. Add the strips of bacon and the mushrooms. Add the marinade to the cooking juices in the frying pan, mix well, then pour it over the hare. Cover and cook in a preheated oven at 200°C (400°F, gas 6) for about 1 hour, depending on the age of the hare.

Prepare 24 glazed onions; fry in butter some croûtons cut into triangles. Five minutes before the hare has finished cooking, thinly slice the liver and add it to the casserole; thicken the blood by mixing in 2–3 tablespoons double (heavy) cream to form a sauce. Serve the civet in a deep dish, garnished with the glazed onions and fried croûtons.

civet of hare à la lyonnaise
This is prepared as for civet of hare à la française except that the mushrooms are replaced by chestnuts, which are cooked in consommé and caramelized in their cooking liquid when it has been well reduced.

civet of saddle of hare with fresh pasta
Peel and dice 3 carrots and 1 onion; peel and chop 2 shallots; peel and crush 2 garlic cloves. Coarsely chop 2 foreparts of hare, brown the pieces in a pan containing 20 g (¾ oz, 1½ tablespoons) butter, add the diced onion and carrot, and brown for about 10 minutes. Then add 100 ml (4 fl oz, 7 tablespoons) wine vinegar, 500 ml (17 fl oz, 2 cups) red wine, the garlic and the shallots. Lightly season with salt and pepper and bring to the boil. Add a bouquet garni and simmer gently for 2 hours, skimming from time to time.

Take out the vegetables and process in a blender. Pour the remaining cooking liquid through a strainer, pressing well to extract all the juices; add the blended vegetables to the strained pan juice, return to the heat and simmer for 30 minutes. Strain again, leave to cool and place in the refrigerator; after about 6 hours, the fat will have collected on the surface and can be skimmed off. Then return to the heat and reduce for a further 5 minutes; away from the heat add a small glass of hare's blood while stirring with a hand whisk. Then add 50 g (2 oz, ¼ cup) butter, plus salt and pepper. At the last moment, finish the sauce with 1 teaspoon cranberries.

Season 2 saddles of hare with salt and pepper; heat some oil in a frying pan and cook the saddles over a brisk heat, turning them over. Cut the hare into thin slices and serve coated with the sauce and accompanied with fresh pasta.

CLAFOUTIS A dessert from the Limousin region of France, consisting of black cherries arranged in a buttered dish and covered with fairly thick batter. It is served lukewarm, dusted with sugar. As a rule, the cherries are not stoned (pitted), but simply washed and stalked, since the kernels add their flavour to the batter during cooking. The Académie française, which had defined clafoutis as a 'sort of fruit flan', were faced with protests from the inhabitants of Limoges and changed their definition to a 'cake with black cherries'. Nevertheless, there are numerous variations using red cherries or other fruits. The word comes from the provincial dialect word *clafir* (to fill).

RECIPE

clafoutis
Remove the stalks from 500 g (18 oz) washed black cherries, dust them with 50 g (2 oz, ¼ cup) caster (superfine) sugar and leave for at least 30 minutes. Butter a baking tin (pan) and fill it with the cherries. Put 125 g (4½ oz, 1 cup) plain (all-purpose) flour in a mixing bowl and add a pinch of salt, 50 g (2 oz, ¼ cup) caster sugar and 3 well-beaten eggs; mix well; then add 300 ml (½ pint, 1¼ cups) milk and mix thoroughly again. Pour the mixture over the cherries and bake in a preheated oven at 180°C (350°F, gas 4) for 35–40 minutes. When it is lukewarm dust with icing (confectioner's) sugar.

CLAIRET A light-coloured French wine, deeper in tone than pink, but not a vibrant red, which is a speciality of the Bordeaux region. In the past, it might have been made by mixing red and white wine – illegal for rosé wines today (with the exception of champagne).

The word derives from the colour of the wines of Bordeaux, which in the Middle Ages, when the English Crown owned the entire region of the Gironde, were lighter in tone (*plus clair*) than the wines of the hinterland that were shipped through the port of Bordeaux. This is why the English term for red Bordeaux is still claret – in spite of attempts within the EC to impose the use of 'red Bordeaux', it had to be agreed that centuries of use of the word claret entitled the UK to retain the expression.

CLAIRETTE A white wine grape, grown mainly in the Midi. Because of its 'grapey' flavour it has often been used with the Muscat. It is found in many wines of the south of France, including some with AOC. Clairette de Die, made in the Drôme, is a sparkling wine made using no more than 30% Clairette grapes, fermented according to the *méthode dioise*, a two-part fermentation process followed by decantation and rebottling. Crémant de Die is made from 100% Clairette grapes fermented using the traditional method.

The Clairettes of Bellegarde and of Languedoc are full-bodied, dry, still white wines, of a definite yellow colour. The former are at least 11.5°, the latter about 13°.

CLAM Name given to a vast number of related shellfish, all bivalve molluscs. They include the venus shells (*verenidae*) which cover over 500 types. The hinged shells are marked with fine circular striations and they may also have ribs radiating from the hinged area outwards. Clams are gathered from sandy and muddy estuaries, particularly on the east coast of the United States, but also in the French region of Charente. They are eaten raw or cooked like oysters or *à la commodore*.

Clams are cooked by a variety of methods, depending on their size and texture. Small clams are tender and cook quickly, but very large, giant clams are cut up and simmered or stewed until tender. Small shellfish can be steamed, fried or grilled (broiled); medium-sized examples can be braised or stuffed and baked.

Clam chowder is a soup made from vegetables, onions and clams garnished with strips of larding bacon; it originated in New England. A clambake is a picnic, originally along the east coast of the United States, at which clams and other shellfish are cooked on heated stones under a layer of seaweed.

■ **Types of clam** The following examples, themselves including different species, give some indication of the variety of shellfish covered by this term.

• CARPET-SHELL CLAM A medium-sized clam with a white, yellow or light brown shell. Known as *palourde* in French, this may be eaten raw or cooked, depending on size and species. They are popular in Spain and Portugal.

• QUAHOG OR HARD-SHELL CLAM Also known as lord, littleneck, baby or Manila clam, depending on size. These tough-shelled American clams vary in colour, from brown and white to yellow or sand coloured. Some have red markings. They also vary in size from 3–13 cm (1¼–5 in). It is rarely found in the Mediterranean but is abundant in the Atlantic and English Channel coasts, living in the sand on the seashores. Some are known in France as *rigadelle* or *coque rayee*: the small clams can be eaten raw (preferably without lemon juice, so as not to hide its subtle flavour) or cooked; larger shellfish are cooked, with the largest being used in chowders.

• SOFT-SHELL OR LONG-NECK CLAM Also known as sand gaper, steamer or Empire clam, this can grow up to about 15 cm (6 in). The shell is not literally soft, but it is fine and brittle, and breaks easily. The oval shell gapes slightly, allowing sand in, therefore these clams are usually kept in fresh water with oatmeal or cornmeal added for 1–2 days to rid them of their gritty content before they are prepared – a process known as purging and used to clean shellfish of unwanted grit and sand before cooking. These clams are used for clambakes or chowders; they may also be battered and fried.

• SURF OR BAR CLAM Also known as hen clam, this is a large pale-shelled clam which grows up to 20 cm (8 in). They are popular in America, particularly for chowders.

• SMOOTH OR BROWN VENUS SHELL Medium-sized clam growing from 7.5–13 cm (3–5 in). The fairly smooth brown shell has a distinct sheen, hence its French name, *verni*, meaning varnished.

• WARTY VENUS Also known as baby clam and *praire* in France, this is a small to medium brown-shelled clam. The concentric grooves in the shell are crossed by spines radiating down its length, creating irregular wart-like bumps.

RECIPE

clam soup
Dice 100 g (4 oz) salted bacon, 1 medium-sized onion, 2 celery sticks, 1 red pepper and 1 green pepper. Blanch the bacon for 3 minutes in boiling water, then cool it, wipe it and soften it in a pan containing some butter, without colouring it. Then add the vegetables, sprinkle on 1 tablespoon flour and cook for 2 minutes, stirring all the time. Sprinkle with 1.5 litres (2¾ pints, 6½ cups) stock and bring to the boil.

Open 36 clams near a heated oven, retaining the liquid. Prepare the clams; chop up the trimmings and put them in a saucepan with the clam liquor plus 200 ml (7 fl oz, ¾ cup) water. Cook for 15 minutes, strain and add this stock to the soup. Return the soup to the boil, add the clams, bring to the boil again, cover, then turn off the heat. Boil 300 ml (½ pint, 1¼ cups) double (heavy) cream and add it to the soup along with 1 tablespoon chopped parsley and 100 g (4 oz, ½ cup) butter. Heat and serve with crushed or whole crackers.

CLAMART Any of various dishes that include green peas, either whole or in a purée. It is named after a district of the Hauts-de-Seine that used to be famous for its pea crops. Clamart soup is a purée of fresh green peas in consommé, served with fried croûtons; poached eggs Clamart are served on canapés spread with purée; scrambled eggs Clamart are served with the peas left whole. The name is also given to puff-pastry patties filled with creamed purée, to chicken *en cocotte*, to a sauté and to sweetbreads served with fresh green peas or a Clamart garnish.

The true Clamart garnish, for small items of sautéed red meat, comprises tartlets or artichoke bottoms filled with green peas in butter; for larger pieces, château potatoes are added.

RECIPE

artichokes Clamart
Clean a lettuce and cut it into long thin shreds. Wash 12 small young globe artichokes; break off the stalks and cut away the large leaves. Butter a flameproof casserole and arrange the artichokes in it. Add 500 ml (17 fl oz, 2 cups) shelled fresh green peas, the lettuce, some salt, 1 teaspoon caster (superfine) sugar and 3 tablespoons water. Cover and cook very gently. Serve in the cooking dish, adding 1 tablespoon butter at the last minute.

other recipes See *lamb, sauté*.

CLAQUEBITOU An unpasteurized goat's-milk cheese from Burgundy, not aged, creamy, and flavoured with garlic, parsley and chopped herbs. Of varying shape and weight, Claquebitou is strong-smelling and has a fragrant taste which is much appreciated as a *goutaillon* ('snack' in the dialect of Burgundy).

CLARENCE Name of various fish and shellfish dishes whose only common feature is a curry-flavoured Mornay or Newburg sauce.

Salmon cutlets Clarence are prepared by lining a mould with salmon escalopes and filling it with salmon or lobster mousse. This is then poached, removed from the mould, arranged on a base of the same mousse and garnished with mushrooms and shrimps. The sauce is served separately. Fillets of sole are poached and arranged on a rosette of duchesse potatoes, coated with sauce and garnished with slices of truffle.

The word also describes a bombe of pineapple ice cream filled with a violet bombe mixture.

CLAREQUET In old French cookery, a transparent jelly prepared with verjuice and apples or gooseberries. The fruits were reduced to a purée, mixed with their weight in sugar, then put in glass moulds, called *clarequet* moulds; these were placed in a drying oven to set the jelly, so ensuring that it would keep.

CLARET See *clairet*.

CLARIFICATION The process of rendering a turbid or cloudy substance clear. Clarification is applied mainly to liquids, especially stocks and jellies, but the term is also used for sugar, butter and eggs (clarified egg white contains no trace of yolk).

■ **Clarification of stock** Poultry or other stock can be served like soup, garnished in different ways, without having been clarified – this is white consommé, which can also be used in sauces, stews or braised dishes. Clarified stock is used for fine soups, such as consommé, and for savoury jellies, such as aspic. Clarification of beef stock involves using chopped lean beef, egg white and an aromatic vegetable *brunoise*. When the broth boils, the egg whites coagulate, trapping the particles that were making the liquid cloudy. The consequent loss in flavour is restored by the lean beef and the vegetables.

Fish, poultry or game stocks are clarified by simmering with egg white, with or without the main ingredients. For charcuterie items with a jelly base, the egg whites are often replaced by blood.

■ **Clarification of wine** This is achieved by various processes, including filtration and fining – the addition of a suitable agent (egg white, blood, albumen, bentonite) to the wine in cask or vat. The fining agent will attract any particles in suspension in the young wine. Filtration usually takes place prior to bottling.

■ **Clarification of beer and cider** Before it is put in barrels or bottles, beer is filtered (under pressure so that the carbon dioxide gas does not escape).

Cider is cleared by coagulating the pectin with enzymes as soon as it comes out of the press; it is then siphoned off and drawn into casks.

■ **Clarification of syrups, liqueurs and non-alcoholic drinks** Syrups and fruit and vegetable juices are filtered through paper or muslin.

Fermented fruit drinks are clarified with egg white whisked to a fluffy consistency, then filtered.

Liqueurs and creams are filtered through cotton; fining with egg white is also sometimes necessary.

RECIPE

clarification of beef stock

In a deep heavy-based saucepan, put 800 g (1¾ lb) finely chopped lean meat and 100 g (4 oz, 1 cup) very finely diced vegetables. Add the white from a very fresh egg and mix well. Gradually add 2.5 litres (4¼ pints, 11 cups) tepid stock. Whisk while heating until it boils. Reduce the heat and simmer very gently for 1½ hours. Strain the stock through a muslin-lined (cheesecloth-lined) sieve.

CLAVARIA *clavaire* Any mushroom of a genus containing many species. Usually found in woodland, they are generally whitish or yellow and shaped like a club, lacking a distinct cap, hence their name, from the Latin *clava* (a club). Nearly all are edible, but they are not great delicacies. After removing the tip of the stalks, clavaria may be cooked au gratin, sautéed with garlic or preserved in vinegar.

CLEAN To remove the viscera from fish, poultry or game before cooking.

Sea fish, usually sold partly cleaned, must be trimmed and scaled and the grey skin should be removed. Large round fish, such as hake, are cleaned through an incision made in the belly. Smaller fish, such as whiting or trout, are cleaned by removing the viscera through the gill covers, thus avoiding opening the belly (unless they are to be stuffed). Large flatfish such as turbot are cleaned on the dark side, while smaller flatfish, like sole, are cleaned by removing the grey skin and then making an incision on the right side. In most cases, the gills are removed. After cleaning, the fish are carefully washed.

Poultry is often sold with the intestines already removed. Drawing, which takes place after singeing and trimming, is carried out by first loosening the skin around the neck to remove the digestive and respiratory tracts, fat, glands and crop. Then the index finger should be inserted through the neck to loosen the lungs. Finally, the anal orifice should be enlarged slightly and the gizzard, liver, heart and lungs pulled through together, taking care not to damage the gall bladder. If the intestines have not previously been removed from the birds, they are taken out at this point. The bird is then ready to be trussed or jointed.

CLEMENTINE A hybrid of the tangerine and Seville (bitter) orange, produced in 1902 in Algeria

Clarifying butter

1 *Heat the butter gently until it has stopped bubbling and sizzling. By this stage, the water content has evaporated and a sediment forms in the base of the pan. Use a straining spoon to skim off any scum that forms on the surface.*

2 *Pour or ladle the butter from the pan, leaving the sediment behind. The last of the butter can be strained through muslin (cheesecloth) if there is a significant amount left with the sediment.*

by Père Clément. Small, orange-coloured and spherical, the clementine has a firm skin, which adheres to the juicy pulp.

Clementines, which are more acid and less aromatic than tangerines, come principally from Spain, Morocco, Italy or Algeria.

The Corsican clementine has orange-red skin, is highly scented and contains no seeds. It is usually sold with its leaves.

The Spanish clementine comes in several varieties, including the choice smaller fruit and the larger Nules and Oroval varieties.

The Monréal clementine, from Spain or Algeria, is fairly rare. It appears from mid-October.

Clementines may also be crystallized (candied) or preserved in brandy. The juice is used for sorbets and drinks. It is used in pâtisserie and confectionery in the same way as the orange. A liqueur is made from it and in England it is used with vinegar and spices to make pickles.

CLERMONT Any of several dishes containing chestnuts or cabbage, characteristic products of the Auvergne, of which Clermont-Ferrand is the capital.

Clermont garnish for large pieces of red meat combines *paupiettes* of green cabbage with lightly fried potatoes; a sauce is made from the pan juices of the meat, plus the liquid in which the *paupiettes* of cabbage were cooked; with braised meat, the braising base or a demi-glace sauce is used.

Clermont garnish for small sautéed pieces of meat comprises fried artichoke quarters and onions stuffed with chestnut purée and braised; the whole is coated with a Madeira déglaçage. Bavarian cream *à la Clermont* is a cold dessert made with rum and chestnut purée.

CLIMAT In Burgundy, each of the different parcels of land that comprise a *vignoble* – a wine-growing region. Each *climat* is defined by its geographic and microclimatic conditions.

CLITOCYBE Any mushroom belonging to a genus containing numerous species, some of which are edible. Clitocybes are characterized by having gills that extend along the stalk and a drooping cap with a depression in the centre; the name comes from the Greek *klitos* (sloping) and *kubê* (head). The best for eating are the funnel-shaped clitocybe (pale-buff or yellow-ochre cap), the nebulous or *petit-gris* clitocybe (grey-brown), the geotropic or *tête-de-moine* clitocybe (yellow-ochre) and the sweet-smelling clitocybe (green). All must be picked when young and consumed fresh, with the stalks discarded. Their aniseed, bitter almond or mint flavour is sometimes fairly strong, so they are used in small quantities to flavour a dish of more insipid mushrooms. They must be cooked thoroughly.

RECIPE

omelette with green clitocybes
Choose 18 caps of aniseed-flavoured green clitocybes and clean them thoroughly. Brown the 6 choicest ones whole in butter with 1½ teaspoons chopped onions. Cook in a covered pan for 10 minutes over a gentle heat. Season with salt and pepper and keep warm. Cut the remaining 12 caps into thin strips and cook in butter for 5 minutes over a moderate heat. Remove and drain in a fine sieve.

Beat 8 fresh eggs lightly as for an omelette, add salt and a little curry powder, and blend in 8 knobs of butter, then the drained julienne of mushrooms. Cook the omelette in very hot olive oil, constantly moving the frying pan over a brisk heat and lifting up the edges. Serve garnished with the 6 whole caps and accompanied with a green salad dressed in walnut oil containing ½ teaspoon anisette.

CLITOPILE PETITE-PRUNE A greyish-white edible mushroom, also called *meunier* or *mousseron*. Its tender flesh has a delicate smell of fresh flour and cooks rapidly. It is used to flavour blander mushrooms and, when dehydrated, serves as a condiment.

CLOCHE A convex dish-cover made of stainless steel or silver-plated metal with a knob or a handle. The cloche is used mainly in restaurants to keep food hot. Some restaurants, which provide 'plate service', use individual cloches for their dishes. It was formerly widely used in Britain, where hot breakfast or dinner dishes were traditionally placed on the sideboard.

The cheese cloche, hemispherical and made of glass or wire gauze, protects cheeses from the air and from flies; it generally rests on a round wooden or marble tray.

CLOD Butcher's term for a neck muscle of beef. The clod is soft and gelatinous and can be braised, cooked *à la mode*, in a *carbonade* and in a *pot-au-feu*.

CLOS-DE-VOUGEOT A classified *grand cru* of the Côte-de-Nuits and one of the most famous wine-growing regions of Burgundy. The vineyard, created by Cistercian monks in the 12th century, is a true *clos* (i.e. it is enclosed by walls). But it is subdivided between over 60 owners, each with individual methods of viticulture, wine-making and marketing. The soil of the 50-hectare (124-acre) site is not uniform: the ground is drier at the top of the slope than at the bottom. The Clos-de-Vouget (or Clos-Vougeot) wines cannot therefore be all the same. They are, however, usually magnificent reds of substance, but delicate, well-balanced and with a lingering taste and a strong aroma. In the centre of the vineyard stands the original establishment constructed by the monks in the 16th century to house the press. This has been altered and enlarged many times since then and today is owned by the Confrérie des Chevaliers du Tastevin, who hold their 'chapters' or ceremonies there.

CLOS-DES-MORILLONS A Parisian wine made from vines planted in terraces in the Square Georges-Brassens in the 15th arrondissement, where the enormous abattoirs of the Rue des Morillons used to stand. The grape harvest is enough to make about 600 bottles, and it is a very pleasant occasion for all who live in the vicinity and for many curious visitors.

CLOSE, JEAN-JOSEPH French cook (born Dieuze, Moselle, 1757; died Strasbourg, 1828). He did not invent foie gras, as the legend claims, neither was he responsible for its truffle garnish, but he did have the idea of wrapping goose livers in a thin veal forcemeat and covering them with a pastry crust. This pie was named *à la Contades* because in about 1782 Close was in the service of the Maréchal de Contades, governor of Alsace. It was sent as a gift to the king from the Maréchal, who was rewarded with an estate in Picardy. It is said the cook received a gratuity of 20 pistoles. When his master left Strasbourg in 1788, Close married the widow of a pastrycook of the city and opened a shop in order to sell his *pâtés à la Contades*, thus creating the first production centre of Alsatian foie gras.

CLOVE The sun-dried flower bud of the clove tree, used since ancient times as a spice. Brown and hard, cloves are about 1 cm (½ in) long, with a head 4 mm (⅙ in) in diameter.

Introduced into Europe in about the 4th century, cloves were for a long time in as much demand as pepper. The Chinese used them well before the Christian era for their medicinal and culinary properties. Cloves originated in the Moluccas, where the Dutch for many years held the monopoly of their cultivation, but they were introduced into Réunion in the 17th century and then into the West Indies. In the Middle Ages, great use was made of cloves for their alleged medicinal properties: oranges studded with cloves were supposed to guard against the plague, and in Naples clove pastilles were made as aphrodisiacs.

Cloves traditionally act as a preservative of meat and meat products. The great cooks of the 18th century continued to use recipes inherited from the Renaissance. Cloves are used in a wide variety of savoury and sweet cooking. Onions studded with a few cloves are used in sauces and braised and boiled meat dishes. Cloves are popular in rich meat and game recipes. They feature widely in marinades, chutneys, relishes and pickles. They are a popular flavouring for rice in Indian cooking and dishes of other countries. They are used in spice mixes for both Indian and Chinese dishes.

In sweet cookery, cloves are used with fresh and dried fruit, and preserved fruits in brandy or other liquor. They have an affinity with apples.

COAT To cover an item with a batter, sauce or other preparation in order to protect it during cooking or improve its appearance or taste. Food is dipped in batter or coated in egg and breadcrumbs to protect it during deep-frying (in particular, fish and seafood or vegetable and offal fritters).

Traditionally, before refrigerators and freezers were common, a coating of fat was applied to prevent air from entering and spoiling pots of cooked food. A layer of clarified butter or other set fat is the classic topping for pâtés and terrines. Confits should always be completely coated with fat for better preservation. A layer of olive oil (or other oil) on the surface of some preserves serves the same purpose.

In pâtisserie, petits fours, cakes, sweets (candies) and chocolates can be coated with chocolate, icing (frosting) or glazed sugar. Individual ice creams can be coated with chocolate or praline.

In the food industry, many foodstuffs are coated with a neutral substance to improve presentation and extend shelf-life (especially delicatessen sausages). 'Coated' coffee has been treated to make the beans black and shiny.

COCHON AU PÈRE DOUILLET A dish of suckling pig popular in an earlier age. Pierre de Lune, the official in charge of the catering in the household of the Prince of Rohan, gave the recipe in *Le Cuisinier* (1654): 'Cut the pig into pieces. Blanch

Coating with egg and breadcrumbs

Egg and breadcrumbs make a fine coating for light foods or they can be applied thickly in several layers on heavier or more substantial items. A double or treble layer can be applied to foods that require extra protection, such as chicken Kiev, which needs a thick coating to keep the chicken in shape and retain the butter filling during cooking. The breadcrumbs should be dry, fine and white. The food should be prepared and dusted with seasoned flour. Once it is coated, the food should be chilled, if possible, before cooking to set the coating.

1 *Use one or two forks to turn the pieces of floured food in beaten egg. A spoon and fork can be used for turning and lifting larger items.*

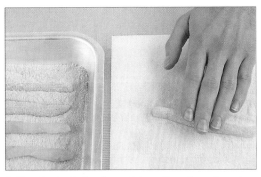

2 *Transfer the food to the container of breadcrumbs and sprinkle some crumbs on top. Then pat on the crumbs or roll the food in crumbs to ensure that it is evenly coated.*

the pieces and interlard with pork fat cut partly from the outer layer and partly from the belly. Put them in a cloth and season with salt, pepper, whole cloves, nutmeg, bay leaves, limes and spring onions. Cook in a pot with stock and a little white wine. Make sure that the finished dish is highly seasoned. Leave to stand until lukewarm. Serve with slices of lemon.'

Menon, in *La Cuisinière bourgeoise* (1742), gives a more elaborate version of *cochon par quartiers au Père Douillet*: the animal is cooked in bouillon, allowed to get cold in its jelly and served reshaped on a large dish, garnished with crayfish. There is also a recipe using sweetbreads, in a sauce flavoured with pomegranate seeds and verjuice.

The name of the dish is attributed to Madame de

Maintenon, who named it after her confessor. Although Pierre de Lune does not explicitly call his recipe *au Père Douillet*, this name appears in *L'Art de bien traiter* (1674) in the recipe for *cochon de lait au perdouillet*.

COCHONNAILLE A synonym for charcuterie, sometimes used ironically, suggesting the idea of abundance. The traditional French country buffets and village feasts featured vast assortments of sausages, galantines, hams, pâtés and other charcuterie.

COCIDO A Spanish *pot-au-feu* (from the verb *cocer*, to cook). The ordinary cocido originated in Castile, but numerous regional varieties exist. The cocido of Madrid consists of three dishes served in turn from a pot that has simmered for a long time: firstly the stock, strained, enriched with vermicelli and traditionally served with white wine; next a dish of chick peas and boiled vegetables – potatoes, carrots and cabbage – which are added to the cocido in the final stages of cooking and become impregnated with the juices from the meats; and finally a dish of meats comprising pieces of beef, chorizo, pickled pork, loin of pork, chicken and little meat balls – sometimes marrow bones, black pudding (blood sausage) and fresh bacon are added. The vegetables and meats are served with red wine and accompanied by sauces (tomato, cumin and mint) and each dish is eaten with crusty bread.

In Castile, the three dishes are called *sota, caballo* and *rey* (the knave, queen and king of playing cards) – cocido is 'ennobled' as it progresses!

Lavish or simple (it may be only a dish of chick peas with a piece of bacon), easy to make and nourishing (the only precaution is to soak the chick peas overnight beforehand), cocido is a staple dish throughout Spain and Portugal. The three major variants are Catalan cocido (dried beans and sometimes rice, local sausages, *boutifar*, oxtail), in which the three dishes are served together; Andalusian cocido (lighter and fragrant, with chilli peppers, mint, saffron and green beans); and Galician cocido (which always contains pork, turnips with their tops, bacon and several varieties of dried beans).

COCKAIGNE A mythical land of plenty, where men live happily without working and there is an abundance of everything. The myth, which is found in Germany and in Italy, is particularly deeply rooted in Flemish tradition and dates back to a time when the spectre of famine often became reality. In the legend, the lucky man arrives at the land of plenty by travelling through a tunnel cut into a mountain of buckwheat flour; there he discovers a roasted pig walking about with a carving knife in its belly, a table covered with pies and tarts, hedges made of sausages and other marvels, while roast pigeons drop into his mouth. A famous painting of 1567 by Pieter Brueghel (the elder) depicts three men of different classes in the Cockaigne setting, probably based on a comic story about the mythical place.

By extension, *cocagne* used to refer to a table generously provided and richly loaded. In 17th-century Naples, the *cocagne* (or *cuccagna*) was a traditional feast, when a heap of victuals was arranged as a sign of rejoicing and reconciliation.

COCK-A-LEEKIE A Scottish speciality, whose name means literally 'cock and leek'. It is a substantial soup, based on chicken and leeks, with barley and prunes. A more refined version is based on chicken consommé, leek and chicken.

RECIPE

cock-a-leekie
Prepare a chicken consommé. Cut the white parts of some leeks into fine strips; 200 g (7 oz) are required for 1 litre (1¾ pints, 4⅓ cups) consommé. Cook this julienne slowly in 20 g (¾ oz, 1½ tablespoons) butter for 15 minutes. Cut into strips the white chicken flesh that was used to prepare the consommé and add the leek and chicken juliennes to the consommé.

COCKLE A bivalve mollusc, 3–4 cm (1¼–1½ in) long, which is found near or on the sea-bed. The two equal shells have 26 clearly marked ribs and enclose a knob of flesh and a tiny coral. Sold by volume, cockles may be eaten raw, but are generally cooked, like mussels. Since they retain sand inside the shell, they should be left to clear in salt water for 12 hours or so before they are consumed. The cockles of Picardy, called *hénons*, are highly regarded.

COCKSCOMB A fleshy red outgrowth on the top of the head of a cock. For use in cookery it needs to be fairly large, but nowadays most breeds of domestic fowl have small combs and in any case are usually slaughtered when young. Today cockscombs are used in recipes as a garnish for barquettes and croustades. They were frequently used in traditional French cookery (often with cock's kidneys) in numerous garnishes, including ambassadeur, chalonnaise, financière, gauloise, Godard and Régence.

Pickled ox (beef) tongue and fine slices of truffle are sometimes cut into the shape of cockscombs for garnish.

RECIPES

preparation of cockscombs
Prick the combs lightly with a needle and put them under cold running water, pressing them with the fingers to dispel the blood. Cover with cold water and cook until the water reaches a temperature of 40–45°C (104–113°F), when the skin of the combs begins to detach itself. Drain the combs and rub them one by one in a cloth sprinkled with fine salt.

Remove the outer skin; put the combs in cold water and, when they are white, plunge them into a boiling white court-bouillon. Cook for 35 minutes.

cockscombs en attereaux à la Villeroi

Cook the cockscombs as described above, drain and dry them, then cover with Villeroi sauce. Leave to cool on a grid. Cover the combs with egg, sprinkle with breadcrumbs and fry in clarified butter.

salpicon of cockscombs

Cook the cockscombs in the manner described above and dice them. Heat them for a few minutes in Madeira or any other dessert wine. Add a few tablespoons of chicken velouté, white sauce or a very reduced Madeira sauce.

COCKTAIL A mixed drink made according to a variety of recipes and containing liqueurs, spirits, syrup, spices, and so on, the end product being pleasing to both eye and palate. The origin of the word is somewhat obscure: it may refer to the shades of colour in a cock's tail, but it is more likely to derive from American racecourse slang, dating from the early part of the 19th century.

Drinking cocktails became particularly fashionable between the two World Wars, a time when famous bars were opened in all the capitals of Europe. Barmen, expert in the art of making cocktails, christened their creations with names that have become classics – Manhattan, gin fizz and Bloody Mary. A competent barman should have a wide repertoire of cocktails, ranging from the world's most famous – the dry martini – to the more complicated sours, smashes, fizzes, crustas, sangarees, flips, shrubs and drinks that may be created for topical events. Cocktails that are based on spirits without much dilution are usually served in a small stemmed glass. Longer drinks, such as juleps, Pimm's and recipes incorporating soda or sparkling wine, may be served in tall glasses, large goblets or tumblers.

There is a fine distinction between those cocktails that are stirred and those that are shaken, subsequently to be poured through crushed ice; the garnish also varies, and includes lemon zest, olive and cherry. Touches such as frosting the edges of glasses (by dampening them and then turning them in sugar) or serving any 'frappé' with straws are all part of the barman's expertise.

Non-alcoholic cocktails using fruit or vegetable juices or even flavoured milk are very popular.

The word cocktail is also used in cookery to describe various cold hors d'oeuvre, such as prawn cocktail or lobster cocktail. A macédoine of fruit may also be called fruit cocktail.

COCKTAIL SNACK Known in France as *amuse-gueule,* this is a small bite-sized savoury item that is served with apéritifs. Depending on the occasion, cocktail snacks may comprise an extensive or limited range of hot or cold hors d'oeuvre. Examples include plain or stuffed olives, salted nuts, savoury biscuits (crackers) flavoured with cheese, paprika or ham, potato crisps (chips), small hot cocktail sausages, cubes of hard cheese on small sticks, canapés, miniature pizzas or quiches, savoury *allumettes* and shredded raw vegetables.

COCO The plumlike fruit of a tropical tree cultivated in the West Indies and Central America, which is also known as icaco plum. The skin is yellow, white, red or purplish, depending on the variety. The white flesh is soft with a rather sour taste and the kernel is edible. The fruit is also known as the handle plum or the cotton plum and may be eaten raw or used as a preserve.

COCOA A powder made from cocoa (cacao) beans, which are the seeds of the cacao, a tropical tree 4–12 m (13–39 ft) high. Each fruit (pod) contains 25–40 beans, rounded or flattened in shape and grey, purplish or bluish in colour depending on the variety. The beans are extracted from the ripe pods and heaped up into mounds so that they ferment. This process destroys the germ and helps to develop their flavour. They are then sorted, washed, dried and roasted.

The word cocoa is derived from the Aztec word *cacahuatl.* According to legend, the cacao tree was the most beautiful tree in the paradise of the Aztecs and they attributed many virtues to it. It was thought to appease hunger and thirst, give universal knowledge and cure sickness. In 1502, Christopher Columbus was offered, as a sign of welcome, weapons, fabrics and sacks of brown cocoa beans, the latter, in Aztec society, serving as currency as well as food. In 1519, Cortés discovered the New World civilization and the first cargo of cocoa reached Spain in 1524. It was not until the 17th century that cocoa, or chocolate, became a fashionable drink, and it was not until the 19th century that chocolate bars were first manufactured.

There are several varieties of cocoa. The finest and most aromatic one comes from Venezuela and is known as Caracas cacao. Brazilian cocoa, known as Maranhào cacao, has a pleasant bitter taste, like the cocoas of Ecuador and the West Indies. The latter two varieties are used to flavour weaker cocoas, with which they are mixed. The African cocoas, which give a high yield but are poor in quality, are used mainly for commercial products. Cocoa beans are also produced in Sri Lanka and Java.

The raw material of all cocoa- or chocolate-based products is cocoa paste (chocolate liquor). This bitter oily substance is made by crushing the cocoa beans after they have been fermented, roasted and shelled. The fat content of cocoa paste amounts to 45–60%, according to the quality of the beans. Crushing is very important, as it determines the fineness and smoothness of the paste.

Cocoa butter is the natural fatty material in cocoa beans. It is a relatively firm product, yellowish-white in colour and is pressed from the paste in variable proportions when manufacturing cocoa powder. Extra cocoa butter is sometimes added in the manufacture of block chocolate, to make it liquid enough to coat sweets (candies) and cakes.

Cocoa powder is obtained by grinding cocoa

cake, which is cocoa paste with most of the fat removed. Cocoa powder contains between 8 and 20% fat, depending on how much cocoa butter has been extracted from the cocoa cake.

COCONUT The fruit of the coconut palm, a tall tree probably originating in Melanesia, but now widely cultivated throughout the tropics. The coconut has a very hard woody shell and is enclosed in a thick fibrous husk. The shell is lined with a firm white pulp and the hollow centre contains a sweet milky-white liquid which makes a refreshing drink. The pulp is rich in fat which is, unlike other vegetable oils, high in saturated fat.

Used as food in south-east Asia and Polynesia from the earliest times, the coconut was 'discovered' by the explorer Marco Polo, who described 'the Pharaoh's nut' as a fruit full of flavour, sweet as sugar and white as milk, providing at the same time both food and drink. A Portuguese doctor who made a detailed study of the coconut in the 16th century wrote: 'This fruit is called *coquo* because it has three pores on its surface, giving it the appearance of a human head.' The first specimen to arrive in Paris was presented to the Académie Française by Charles Perrault in 1674.

In western countries coconut is most commonly used in desiccated (shredded) form, for biscuits (cookies), cakes and confectionery, as well as for jam and ices. However in Indian, Indonesian, African and South American cooking, the pulp is used fresh (grated and sieved) or dried (grated and mixed with water) in condiments, to season raw vegetables and fish, and as an ingredient in chicken, beef or shellfish stews. Coconut milk, much used in Indian cooking, gives a distinctive taste and smoothness to curries, sauces and rice. In Polynesia it is used in soups, jams and fish marinades. In Brazil and Venezuela the richer coconut cream is poured over desserts and pastries, while in Vietnam and the Philippines, pork, beef and poultry are marinated in it.

A coconut can be opened either by cracking the shell with a hammer or by first piercing the two ends so that the liquid runs out and then heating it in the oven until it cracks; the pulp can then be extracted quite easily. The dried pulp (copra) is refined and deodorized to produce coconut butter, used as a cooking fat.

RECIPES

coconut cake
Prepare a syrup using 200 g (7 oz, ¾ cup) caster (superfine) sugar and 200 ml (7 fl oz, ¾ cup) water. Whisk 4 egg yolks in a bowl over hot (but not boiling) water, then slowly pour in the sugar syrup, whisking constantly. When the yolks have almost doubled in volume, remove the bowl from the hot water and whisk until the mixture is cold. Make 250 ml (8 fl oz, 1 cup) fresh Chantilly* cream, adding 1 teaspoon vanilla sugar and 2 tablespoons

rum. Blend well, then add the egg-yolk mixture and 300 g (11 oz, 4 cups) fresh or desiccated (shredded) grated coconut. Pour into a deep sandwich tin (layer cake pan) and put in the freezer until the mixture is firm to the touch. Then remove the cake from the tin, cover with grated coconut and keep in the refrigerator until required.

coconut preserve
Open some coconuts, extract the pulp and grate it. Prepare a syrup using 1 kg (2¼ lb) granulated sugar to 1 litre (1¾ pints, 4⅓ cups) water and flavour it with either vanilla extract or 1 teaspoon vanilla sugar. Mix together equal quantities of the grated pulp and the syrup and cook very gently until the jam becomes transparent. Pot as for jam.

coconut pyramids
Open a coconut, extract the pulp and grate it. Add 75 g (3 oz, ¾ cup) ground almonds, 150 g (5 oz, ⅔ cup) sugar, 2 teaspoons vanilla sugar (or a few drops of vanilla extract) and 2 or 3 egg whites, depending on their size. Mix well together, then add another 3 egg whites, whisked to stiff peaks with a pinch of salt. Divide this mixture into portions about the size of tangerines, shape them into pyramids and arrange them on a buttered or oiled baking sheet. Bake in a preheated oven at 180°C (350°F, gas 4) for about 12 minutes.

COCOTTE A round or oval cooking pan with two handles and a well-fitting lid, used for slow-cooking dishes such as daubes, braised dishes and casseroled meat. The pan is also used for various preparations described as *en cocotte* or *à la bonne femme*.

The origin of the cocotte goes back to the beginning of the 19th century. At first it was made of black cast iron, which is a good conductor of heat but tends to break and rust. Modern cocottes (or *coquelles*) are usually made of enamel, aluminium (which is lighter), stainless steel (which is unbreakable but not such a good conductor of heat), copper (for small pans), tempered glass (ovenproof, but not able to withstand direct heat), or glazed ceramic (a good conductor of heat, easy to clean and without the drawbacks of tempered glass).

Dishes *en cocotte* or *en casserole* almost always need to be fried lightly over a brisk heat before they are left to simmer. It is therefore necessary that the material from which the cocotte is made will be able to withstand differences in temperature and it is also important that the food does not stick. In order to ensure a more gentle heat, the bases of some cocottes are grooved, but these cannot be used on the hotplates of an electric cooker (stove), when a flat-based pan must be used. Some cocottes have a lid designed to hold cold water. This is poured into it during the cooking period and causes internal condensation, thus preventing the food from drying out.

COD A large fish, up to 1.8 m (6 ft) long, with an elongated powerful body, very pronounced fins and a large head. It has a heavy whisker-like barbel on its lower jaw. Its colour varies from greyish-green to brown and it has dark spots on the back and sides and a whitish belly. Cod is found in the cold seas of the North Atlantic – 0–10°C (32–50°F). The female is very fertile and can lay up to 5 million eggs. The eggs, known as roe, can be sold freshly boiled or smoked.

Fresh cod has a white flaky delicate flesh that can be prepared in many different ways. Small and medium-sized fish, weighing 1–3 kg (2¼–6½ lb), are sold whole, although there is a large amount of waste. They can be roasted in the oven (which concentrates the flavour), braised in white wine like brill or poached in a flavoured court-bouillon. They are served hot or cold with a sauce. Large cod, which are more generally used, are cut into fillets, slices or pieces. The skinned fillets are good value and can be prepared in many different ways. Slices have little waste (only the backbone, skin and part of the fin); they are prepared *à l'anglaise* or *à la meunière*. The cod's delicate flesh requires careful cooking because of the whitish liquid that seeps from it. Prolonged cooking harms both the flavour and the presentation. Cod pieces are especially suited to cooking in the oven or in a court-bouillon, usually in white wine. Cod is rarely grilled (broiled), because of the flaky texture of its flesh. The tail yields a nicely presented piece of flesh for roasting or braising, whereas the part near the head, which has a very fine flavour, has a less elegant appearance and needs to be tied up with string before cooking.

Cod is also used to make croquettes, fish cakes, gratins, coquille dishes (served in scallop shells) and mousses. Cod may be frozen whole, in fillets or in the form of croquettes or fingers, covered with breadcrumbs and ready for frying. Cod is rich in mineral salts and is not a fatty fish; it is available practically all the year round.

In France, cod that has been salted and dried is sold under the name of *morue*. For recipes for cod preserved in this way, see *salt cod*.

RECIPES

braised cod à la flamande
Season slices of cod with salt and pepper. Butter an ovenproof dish and sprinkle with chopped shallots and parsley. Arrange the cod in the dish and just cover with dry white wine. Place a slice of peeled lemon on each piece of cod. Bring to the boil, then cook in a preheated oven at 220°C (425°F, gas 7) for about 15 minutes. Remove the fish and drain. Arrange the slices on the serving dish and keep warm. Reduce the juices by boiling, then add some pieces of butter, stir and pour the sauce over the cod. Sprinkle with roughly chopped parsley.

cod braised in cream
Cut 800 g (1¾ lb) cod fillets into 5 cm (2 in) squares. Season with salt and pepper. Cook 150 g (5 oz, ⅔ cup) chopped onions in melted butter in a pan and then add the cod. Fry the pieces on all sides until firm. Add 200 ml (7 fl oz, ¾ cup) dry white wine and reduce by three-quarters. Add 200 ml (7 fl oz, ¾ cup) double (heavy) cream, cover the pan and simmer slowly until the fish is nearly cooked. Remove the lid and reduce the cream over a high heat.

cod in aspic
Prepare a fish aspic. Make a ratatouille with 3 tomatoes, 1 aubergine (eggplant), 2 courgettes (zucchini), 1 onion, 2 garlic cloves, 3 tablespoons olive oil, some thyme, bay leaves and basil. Dissolve 15 g (½ oz, 2 envelopes) gelatine in 4 tablespoons hot water over a pan of simmering water and add to the ratatouille. Lightly oil 4 ramekins and half fill them with the ratatouille. Set aside to cool and then place in the refrigerator. In the meantime, place the cod fillets in an ovenproof dish, add butter and white wine, and cook in a preheated oven at 220°C (425°F, gas 7). Arrange a piece of fillet in each ramekin, and cover with the fish aspic. Refrigerate until it is time to serve, remove from the moulds and serve chilled.

cod with herbs
Coarsely chop ½ bunch flat-leaf parsley, ½ bunch of fresh coriander (cilantro) and ½ bunch of fresh mint. Finely chop 2 white onions. Mix together. Prepare the sauce with 80 ml (3 fl oz, ⅓ cup) lemon juice, 60 ml (2 fl oz, 1¼ cup) groundnut (peanut) oil, 4 teaspoons soy sauce, salt and pepper. Peel the tomatoes, cut into quarters, remove the seeds and cut into diamond shapes. Arrange them round the 4 plates and in the centre of each plate put 25 g (1 oz) spinach shoots. Steam 4 fillets of cod, 200 g (7 oz) each. Pour the sauce over the herb mixture. Place the fish on the spinach and pour the herb sauce over it.

cold poached cod
Poach the fish as in the recipe below for hot poached cod until nearly cooked. Leave to finish cooking as it cools in the salt water. Drain the cooled fish, wipe and arrange on a napkin. Garnish with either fresh parsley or lettuce hearts and quarters of hard-boiled (hard-cooked) eggs. Serve with a suitable cold sauce, such as *gribiche*, mayonnaise, *ravigote*, *rémoulade*, tartare, sauce vert, vinaigrette or Vincent.

fillets of cod with cucumber
Remove both ends of a good firm cucumber and cut it into 3 segments. Peel and cut each segment lengthways into slices, avoiding the seeds. Cut the slices into very thin strips resembling matchsticks and soak in cold water for 10 hours. Chop 2 shallots. Peel and dice a tomato. Prepare about 325 ml (11 fl oz, 1⅓ cups) concentrated stock using white fishbones. Butter a long ovenproof dish and cover the base with the shallots. Season 4 cod fillets, each weighing about 175 g (6 oz), with salt and pepper and arrange them in the dish. Add 200 ml (7 fl oz,

¾ cup) dry white wine followed by the warm stock. Cover with buttered greaseproof (wax) paper. Bring to the boil and poach very gently for 6 minutes. Remove the cod fillets and keep warm. Reduce the cooking liquid by three-quarters in a small pan. Adjust the seasoning and add some lemon juice. Add 500 ml (17 fl oz, 2 cups) double (heavy) cream and reduce by boiling. Drain the cucumber matchsticks and cook them with the diced tomato in a pan of salted water for 1 minute. Drain and add them to the sauce. Coat the fillets with the sauce, with the tomato and cucumber on top, and simmer for 1 minute. Serve with a little roughly chopped parsley.

grilled cod

Season some cod steaks with salt and pepper. Coat lightly with flour or oil and sprinkle with melted butter. Alternatively, the cod steaks can be marinated in a mixture of olive oil, garlic, chopped parsley and lemon juice for 30 minutes. Cook under a moderate grill (broiler). Garnish the cod with slices of peeled lemon and fresh parsley. Serve with maître d'hôtel butter or one of the sauces recommended for grilled fish.

hot poached cod

Place a piece of cod, either whole or cut up into chunks, in a pan of salted water – allow 1 tablespoon salt per 1 litre (1¾ pints, 4⅓ cups) of water. Bring to the boil, then lower the heat and poach gently with the lid on, taking care not to boil, until the flesh flakes easily. Drain the fish, arrange on a napkin and garnish with fresh parsley. Serve with a sauce suitable for poached fish, such as anchovy, butter, caper, prawn, herb, hollandaise, lobster or *ravigote*.

pimientos del piquillo stuffed with cod

Soak 300 g (11 oz) salt cod in cold water for 24 hours to remove the salt. Peel 2 onions and slice very finely; peel and cut up 3 garlic cloves. Sweat for 30 minutes in a small saucepan in 4 teaspoons olive oil. Flake the cod, making sure that no bones are left behind. Cook for 1 minute with the onion and garlic. Remove from the heat and add 75 g (3 oz, 1½ cups) breadcrumbs. Check and adjust the seasoning. Put to one side. Stuff 12 *pimientos del piquillo* with this mixture. Cook 3 more peppers in 150 ml (¼ pint, ⅔ cup) light whipping cream for 5 minutes. Blend and strain this coulis through a conical strainer. Season with salt and add a pinch of sugar. Beat 1 egg with 3 tablespoons cold milk. Coat the peppers with flour and dip them in the egg. Fry them on both sides in 5½ tablespoons olive oil over a moderate heat until golden. Coat the serving dish with some of the pepper coulis (serve the rest in a sauceboat). Arrange the stuffed pimientos on the coulis and garnish with a sprig of parsley. Serve piping hot.

roast cod

Trim a cod weighing 1.5–1.8 kg (3¼–4 lb). Season with salt and pepper, sprinkle with oil and lemon juice, and leave to steep for 30 minutes. Drain the cod, place it on a spit and brush with melted butter. Then roast before a brisk fire, basting frequently with melted butter or oil, for 30–40 minutes. Arrange on a serving dish and keep hot. Deglaze the cooking residue in the pan with dry white wine, reduce and spoon the juice over the fish. The fish may also be roasted in the oven, provided that it is placed on a wire rack so that it does not lie in the cooking juices.

sautéed cod à la crème

Season some cod steaks with salt and pepper, and fry in hot butter until golden. Add sufficient double (heavy) cream to the pan to reach halfway up the steaks. Finish cooking with the pan covered until the fish flakes easily. Drain the fish, arrange on a serving dish and keep hot. Reduce the cream in the pan and add 2 teaspoons to every 4 slices of fish. Pour the sauce over the cod and serve.

other recipes See *boulangère, dieppoise*.

COEUR DE NEUFCHÂTEL
A soft cow's-milk cheese (45% fat) from Normandy with a red-tinged crust, white and downy. Coeur de Neufchâtel is a smooth, heart-shaped cheese with an astringent, fruity flavour, weighing 165–300 g (5½–11 oz).

COFFEE
The coffee tree, native to the Sudan and Ethiopia, but now widely cultivated, bears small red berries that contain the seeds (the coffee beans). The word coffee comes from the Italian *caffè*, which is derived from the Turkish *kahve* and the Arabic *qahwah*. The Arabic word originally designated any stimulating drink.

■ **From Turkey to the tropics** The invention of the drink itself and the discovery of its properties is the subject of many stories and legends. One version attributes its discovery to a goatherd, who noticed that his goats became agitated when they chewed the leaves of certain bushes. Another story is that a dervish, mullah or hermit used coffee to stay awake at night in order to pray. Some people attribute its discovery to the famous Arabic doctor, Avicenna. Whichever story is true, coffee was being drunk in Aden as early as 1420. The custom passed on to Syria and then in 1550 to Constantinople. Italian ambassadors in Turkey called it 'black water extracted from seeds called *cavee*'. The first Westerners to import coffee were the Venetians in 1615. It was introduced to France in 1644 by a French traveller called La Royne, but in fact it was Soliman Aga, the ambassador of the Turkish government to Louis XIV, who, in 1669, made it popular. Initially, it was considered to be an exotic and rather therapeutic product. The 'new flavour', as it was called, became a fashionable drink at court and among the nobility. The invention of the coffee mill in 1687 greatly contributed to the widespread use of coffee and coincided with the publication of *Le Bon Usage du thé, du caffé, et du chocolat pour la préservation et pour la guérison des maladies*.

In 1690, a coffee plantation was established at the Jardin des Plantes, but the coffee tree remains an essentially tropical plant. Its cultivation spread throughout Africa, South America and the West Indies. The price fluctuations of this colonial commodity together with such political vicissitudes as the Continental System (Napoleon's plan in 1806 to blockade Britain by excluding her ships from ports on the mainland of Europe) caused various substitutes for coffee to appear, such as acorns, barley, maize, rye, butcher's broom, dried beans, dried peas, but especially chicory.

Nowadays, two species of coffee tree provide 95% of world production. They are *Coffea arabica* and *Coffea robusta*. Arabica coffees, having beans that are elongated, oval and flat, are mild and aromatic and generally considered to be the best. They come mainly from Brazil, but also from Ethiopia and the Yemen (Mocha beans). They are also grown in Mexico and Costa Rica, but although this coffee is full of flavour, the quality is not as good. However, the arabica coffee from Colombia has a good, slightly acid flavour and is highly rated by connoisseurs. Robusta coffee beans are smaller and have an irregular convex shape. The beans contain two and a half times more caffeine than arabica coffee beans and yield a more full-bodied and bitter drink. They are grown in the Ivory Coast, Angola and Zaïre. More full-bodied arabica coffees can be obtained by mixing them with other varieties, such as canephora, liberica and excelsa.

■ **Harvesting to grinding** The fruits of the coffee tree are treated to remove the pulp, and the yellowish-grey beans are hulled, graded and bagged. In this form the beans are known as green coffee, which keeps for a long time provided that it is protected from damp. It may then be sold and exported.

Roasting the coffee beans releases various complex volatile constituents, which are responsible for the characteristic flavour and aroma of coffee. The beans are continuously stirred during the roasting process. At 200°C (392°F), they are light brown and have doubled in volume. At 250°C (482°F), they are noticeably darker. Well-roasted coffee should be fairly dark reddish-brown, but never black or shiny. Insufficient roasting produces a harsh, colourless, tasteless infusion, whereas excessive roasting yields a very black, bitter and astringent brew. Until the end of the 19th century, green coffee was still roasted at home in special coffee burners. (Alexandre Dumas tells how Napoleon, coming upon a priest in the middle of roasting his coffee during the period of the Continental System, heard him reply: 'I am doing the same as Your Majesty, I'm burning colonial produce!'). Nowadays, the food industry makes more or less standardized flavours according to prevailing tastes: very lightly roasted coffee for North Americans; slightly more heavily roasted coffee for the French and the Italians; fairly dark coffee for the Dutch; and 'burnt' coffee for countries in the Middle East. After roasting, coffee does not retain its aroma

for long and becomes stale in the open air: it should therefore be stored in a sealed jar in a cool place.

The final operation is grinding. The fineness of the grounds depends on which method is used to brew the coffee. Ideally, grinding should be done just before the coffee is made, as ground coffee loses its aroma very quickly.

The stimulating effect that coffee has on the body is due to the alkaloid called caffeine. In his *Treatise on Modern Stimulants*, Balzac remarked: 'Coffee sets the blood in motion, so that the driving force springs from it. This stimulation speeds up digestion, takes away the desire for sleep and enables one to exercise one's mental faculties for a little longer.'

The 19th-century *Larousse* states that coffee 'is particularly indicated for men of letters, soldiers, sailors, all workers who have to stay in hot surroundings and lastly, to all inhabitants of a country where cretinism is rife'.

■ **Different types of coffee** Coffee sold and labelled as an arabica variety must contain only that particular variety: Mocha, Manilla or Bourbon (for a choice aromatic coffee) Colombia or Menado (for a very mild coffee) or Haiti (for a full-bodied coffee). If sold without such a label, it will be either a robusta (if cheap) or a mixture of arabica and robusta (if more expensive). Coffee lovers of the 19th century recommended the following as best: 'a Mocha coffee, mixed with Bourbon coffee and Martinique coffee'. Nowadays, so-called superior coffee is sold with a guarantee that there are no more than 10% of faults in the beans. It must also be labelled with the date of roasting. Coated coffee (for industrialized packaging) is very black and shiny because of the addition of glucose, gum arabic or vegetable oil after roasting. It keeps longer, and has a full-bodied flavour, but is slightly syrupy.

After roasting, coffee is sold either in the form of coffee beans or as ground coffee. It should preferably be ground as needed in a coffee mill, which preserves the flavour as much as possible. Ground coffee is often vacuum-packed, but must be consumed quickly once the packet has been opened. Since the 1930s, decaffeinated coffee has been produced. Instant coffee is a great commercial success. Either spray-dried or freeze-dried (which denatures it less), with or without caffeine, it is instantly soluble in hot water.

Lastly, there is liquid coffee essence (extract), which is widely used as a flavouring in desserts, cakes and confectionery.

■ **Coffee-drinking** At the end of the 17th century, it was the custom in French high society to serve coffee after a meal. By about 1860, coffee-drinking in France was firmly established at all social levels. Also at this time, coffee became an integral part of military rations. The French slang term *jus* was widely used for black coffee by the end of the 19th century, and indicates how popular it had become. It is served in a variety of ways, depending on the country or region. In Greece, Turkey and the Arab countries, it is highly concentrated, often sweetened,

Arabic mocha coffee beans.

and served with a glass of cold water. In Switzerland, Germany and Holland it is served with a chocolate, while in Belgium and Britain it may be served with biscuits (cookies). In northern France it is very often served with a small jug of cream. Coffee after a meal is traditionally served with liqueurs. Finally, there are many regions of France (especially Normandy and Lorraine) where coffee is served with a 'dash' of alcohol.

• FILTER COFFEE The popular method of making coffee is to pour boiling water on to ground coffee (which is less finely ground than that used to make Turkish coffee), held between two perforated discs that act as a filter. This procedure is known technically as *lixiviation*. A disposable paper filter supported in a cone over a jug may be used instead of the metal filters. Automatic filter machines heat the water and pass it through the coffee.

Filter coffee must never be boiled and certainly not reheated. (In the 19th century, however, the taste of boiled coffee was highly appreciated in the French provinces.) Purists recommend the use of bottled still water rather than tap water, as any chlorine in tap water ruins the flavour. One tablespoon of coffee per person is generally advised. A porcelain or earthenware coffee pot is preferable to one made of metal, as the latter spoils the flavour. The water must be just below boiling point when it is

poured over the coffee. Cups should be filled three-quarters full.

• ITALIAN COFFEE Espresso is a black Italian-style coffee. It is also very popular in Austria, where it is usually known as *moka*, even if it is not made from Mocha coffee beans. It is made in a special pressurized apparatus by forcing steam from boiling water through the ground coffee.

The Italians also make cappuccino, so-called because of its pale brown colour, reminiscent of the robes of the Capuchin monks. This consists of strong coffee to which frothy cream or milk is added. It is sometimes served with a pinch of powdered chocolate on the top. This type of coffee is the same as the Austrian *kapuziner*. White coffee (coffee with milk) was in fact introduced by the Viennese. True Austrian white coffee is made by putting a spoonful of either whipped cream or fresh double (heavy) cream on to the surface of the hot coffee, without stirring.

• TURKISH COFFEE The Turkish method of making coffee consists of adding ground coffee (which has been reduced to an extremely fine powder) into boiling water, together with an almost equal quantity of sugar. The mixture is then heated until it is on the point of boiling; this operation is repeated three times. A special small conical pan with a wide base is used for the process. Before serving, a few drops of cold water are poured into the saucepan to settle the grounds. The piping hot coffee is served either in cups or in small glasses. Turkish coffee is commonly drunk in Mediterranean countries and the Middle East.

• ARABIC COFFEE In Arab countries, two Madagascan cardamom seeds are often added.

• GREEK COFFEE In Greece, coffee is made by a similar method to that used in Turkey. It may be very strong and sweet, moderately strong with only a little added sugar, or tepid and sugarless; sweetened coffee may be reboiled several times.

• SOUTH AMERICAN COFFEE In South America, where coffee-growing was introduced in 1720, the best varieties are exported, but large quantities of *tinto* (strong, black, very sweet coffee) are consumed there. In Argentina and Mexico, people also drink a type of coffee that has been roasted with sugar and has a pronounced caramel flavour. In the West Indies, coffee is flavoured with vanilla, cinnamon or ginger.

RECIPES

Arabic coffee
Put 50 g (2 oz, ⅓ cup) very finely ground arabica coffee and 100 g (4 oz, ½ cup) granulated sugar into a coffee pot that has a wide bottom and a narrow neck. Boil 500 ml (17 fl oz, 2 cups) water in a small saucepan and pour it into the coffee pot all at once. Heat the coffee pot until the coffee boils, stirring continuously. Remove the pot from the heat and then replace it. Repeat this procedure twice more. When the coffee boils for the third time, tap the bottom of the coffee pot sharply on a flat surface. The coffee grounds will then begin to sink towards the bottom. Pour the coffee into cups, adding 1 teaspoon hot water to each cup. The grounds will then settle completely.

coffee essence
Pour some boiling water over ground coffee placed in a filter, using 450 g (1 lb, 5 cups) coffee per 1 litre (1¾ pints, 4⅓ cups) water. Collect the coffee and pour it through the filter 3 more times. The colour may be intensified by adding a little caramel.

coffee ice cream
Blend together 6 eggs, 200 g (7 oz, ¾ cup) caster (superfine) sugar and 3 tablespoons instant coffee to make a custard. Whip 200 ml (7 fl oz, ¾ cup) cold double (heavy) cream with a quarter of its volume of very cold milk and 1 tablespoon vanilla sugar. Fold the whipped cream gently into the cold custard and leave it to freeze in an ice-cream maker. The ice cream can be decorated with sugar coffee beans or coffee sugar crystals.

coffee syrup
Finely grind 500 g (18 oz, 5½ cups) coffee, and pour 1.5 litres (2¾ pints, 6½ cups) boiling water very slowly over it. Add the hot coffee to 2.5 kg (5½ lb, 11 cups) granulated sugar in a pan and dissolve over a very low heat to prevent it from boiling. Remove the syrup from the heat just before it reaches boiling point.

coffee with burgundy marc
Put some very hot coffee into a hot coffee pot. Add sugar, according to taste, and stir. Add a liqueur glass of Burgundy marc for each 500 ml (17 fl oz, 2 cups) coffee and stir again. Foam will form on the top of the coffee. Put 1 teaspoon crushed ice into each cup followed by the very hot coffee.

iced coffee
Use 300 g (11 oz, 3½ cups) freshly ground coffee and 750 ml (1¼ pints, 3¼ cups) boiling water. Pour into a bowl with 575 g (1¼ lb, 2½ cups) granulated sugar. Dissolve the sugar and chill the infusion. Add to the coffee 1 litre (1¾ pints, 4⅓ cups) vanilla-flavoured cold boiled milk and 500 ml (17 fl oz, 2 cups) single (light) cream. Serve chilled.

other recipes See *creams, custard, Genoese sponge, soufflé (dessert soufflés).*

COGNAC A world-famous brandy distilled from wine, made in the delimited region around Cognac in the Charente region of France. Distillation of the local wine began in the 17th century, when the market for both wine and salt, especially to the Dutch and Hanseatic League export markets, suffered a decline and was also at a disadvantage because of the popularity of Bordeaux wines. Distillation not only disposed of the surplus crop, but brandy as such was easier to transport.

History attributes the invention of Cognac to a certain Chevalier de la Croix-Marrons, who is said to have been the first to have had the idea of heating wine to 'capture its soul'. He then put the distilled wine through the still once more. This distillation, at first considered to be a last resort in times of glut, came into general use. The brandy from the Cognac region soon gained an exceptional reputation for quality. The name 'Cognac' was not applied to the brandy itself until 1783.

Today, Cognac is made exclusively by the distillation of white wine from selected grapes, mainly Ugni Blanc. The wine is made and distilled within the delimited area, which spreads over two departments. Brandies distilled elsewhere have neither the same taste nor the same quality.

Six main areas within the region have been defined. The Grande Champagne region (around Cognac and Segonazac) produces the finest, most delicate and most fragrant brandies. Petite Champagne, which surrounds the Grande Champagne region from the south-west to the east, produces less subtle brandies that mature more rapidly. The brandies of the Borderies (a series of hills to the north of Grande Champagne) are rounder and softer. Encircling these three areas are the Fins Bois, the Bons Bois and the Bois Ordinaires, which produce brandies of a lesser quality. They are used mainly for blending with other brandies and are rarely sold commercially under their regional names. 'Fine Champagne' Cognac is a blend of the first two types, which must have at least 50% Grande Champagne in it.

■ **Manufacture** Cognac results from a double distillation in what is known as the Charentais alembic. The wine is heated for the first time to give an alcoholic content (*brouillis*) of about 30°. This is distilled a second time giving *la bonne chauffe*. The 'heads' and 'tails' of the process are removed from what is known as the 'heart' or 'flower of the vine', to be redistilled; it is a matter of great skill to 'cut' these out, once the still is running and the brandy coming across. It takes 9 litres (15 pints, 9½ quarts) of white wine to make 1 litre (1¾ pints, 4⅓ cups) of the resulting clear spirit, which has a distinctive smell but is rough and not agreeable in flavour. It now has an alcoholic content of 70° and must mature. The maturing is carried out in casks made of oak from the forests of Limousin and Tronçais, seasoned out of doors. Cognac acquires much of its character from the cask. Up to five years old, it is pale yellow with a slight vanilla taste; aged between five and ten years, the colour deepens and the flavour becomes more pronounced; up to 30 years, there is a slight drop in the alcohol content. It takes around 50 years for the alcohol content to begin to decline to around 40°. Brandies of different ages and styles go into the great commercial blends. Their content can be reduced by breaking them down with distilled water. Maturing Cognac is expensive – the quantity of spirit evaporated (known traditionally as the 'angels' share') is equivalent to more than 20 million bottles each year from the whole region.

Each season's brandy is given the number 0 on the 31 March following the vintage and it cannot be sold commercially until it has been numbered 2 (two years later). This is often known as 'Three Star'. There are other categories, such as 'VO', 'VSOP' and 'Réserve', corresponding to five years' maturing, and 'Napoléon', 'Extra' and 'Vieille Réserve', which are seven years old or more. In fact, the different qualities sold are the result of blending spirits both of different ages and from different areas – old brandies (10, 20, 30 years old or more) can be blended with younger ones, the age given to the overall blend always being categorized as that of the youngest Cognac in the blend.

■ **Drinking Cognac** When Cognac is drunk by itself, as an after-dinner liqueur, it should be served in a small balloon glass, which can be held in the hand, the only means of slightly warming the spirit and releasing the bouquet. (The heating of the glass is anathema to anyone who appreciates fine brandy of any kind!) Some people, however, prefer to drink Cognac quite cool.

Depending on the quality of the Cognac, it may be served alone, diluted with water or soda, or sometimes in mixes. Cognac (or brandy) and ginger ale is enjoyed in Britain; in the United States Cognac is an ingredient in many cocktails; in Canada iced Vichy water is often added; and in the Far East Cognac may be drunk straight, throughout an entire meal. It should be noted that the stars system as used on the labels of Cognac can be applied to other brandies, but does not, however, indicate equivalent quality.

The incomparable bouquet of Cognac is also utilized in cookery. It is used in various sauces, flamed preparations and marinades, and in such dishes as rabbit casserole, fricassée of chicken, pancakes and *zabaglione*, not to mention fruit preserves and chocolates.

COLA NUT Also known as kola nut. The seeds of the cola tree of Africa and South America. Rich in caffeine, they are chewed for their stimulating effects. The caffeine content is similar to that of coffee, but its tonic effect is less harsh and more prolonged.

In the United States and Europe, cola nuts are used to make biscuits (cookies) and, more importantly, in the manufacture of non-alcoholic fizzy cola drinks. These drinks are made with natural fruit extracts and also contain caffeine and preservatives. They are drunk chilled and are sometimes flavoured with lemon. Colas are an ingredient in certain cocktails, particularly those containing whisky or rum. The oldest and best-known is Coca-Cola, which was created in Atlanta in the United States in 1886.

COLBERT The name given to a method of preparing fish, especially sole, in which the fish is filleted and dipped in egg and breadcrumbs before frying. It is served with a flavoured butter, such as maître d'hôtel butter or Colbert butter. Colbert butter is also served with grilled (broiled) meat, other grilled fish, fried oysters and soft-boiled eggs. Colbert sauce is used as an accompaniment to vegetables as well as grilled meat and fish. Finally, the name Colbert is also given to a chicken consommé (containing diced vegetables and garnished with very small poached eggs), to an egg dish and to a dessert made with apricots.

All these preparations are probably dedicated to Jean-Baptiste Colbert, a minister of Louis XIV, who employed Audiger as the head of his household.

RECIPES

Colbert butter

Add 1 tablespoon chopped tarragon and 1 tablespoon meat glaze to 200 g (7 oz, ¾ cup) maître* d'hôtel butter.

Colbert sauce

Blend 2 tablespoons meat glaze with 1 tablespoon water in a saucepan and bring to the boil. Remove from the heat and incorporate 125 g (4½ oz, ½ cup) softened butter. Season and add a generous pinch each of grated nutmeg and cayenne. Stir continuously while adding the juice of half a lemon, 1 tablespoon chopped parsley and 1 tablespoon Madeira.

fried oysters Colbert

Shell the oysters and poach them in their own liquid. Drain them, remove the beards and allow to cool. Dip each oyster in milk and coat with flour. Deep-fry in oil and arrange on a napkin. Garnish with lemon quarters and fried parsley. Serve with Colbert butter.

soft-boiled or poached eggs Colbert
Bind a macédoine of vegetables with béchamel sauce. Use the mixture as a filling for croustades and top each one with an egg. Garnish with Colbert butter.

sole Colbert
Remove the dark skin from the sole and slit the flesh on either side of the backbone. Raise the fillets and break the backbone in 2 or 3 places so that it may be easily removed after cooking. Dip in milk and coat in egg and breadcrumbs. Fry the sole, drain it and remove the backbone. Fill the cavity with Colbert butter. Serve on a long dish and garnish with fried parsley.

COLBY This popular American hard pressed cow's-milk cheese (45% fat) is dyed a deep orange-yellow colour as for American Cheddar, but it is softer and more open, with a lacy texture and a mild flavour. Colby cheeses made in an elongated shape are known as Longhorn.

COLCANNON A very popular Irish dish made from mashed potatoes and green cabbage, mixed with butter or milk and strongly flavoured with chopped chives, parsley and pepper.

COLÈRE, EN A method of preparing whole fried whiting, in which the fish is served with its tail between its teeth. It is garnished with fried parsley and quarters of lemon. A tomato sauce is served separately.

COLIFICHET A term borrowed from women's fashion (where it referred to a small fancy ornament fixed on to a head-dress) that describes small ornamental items in pâtisserie. They were used to decorate the table and buffets and were called *colifichets* to distinguish them from the main dishes. *Colifichets* are rarely seen nowadays, except at culinary exhibitions, wedding receptions and christenings. Carême said: 'I compare a pastrycook who makes good *colifichets* to a distinguished fashion designer, endowed with perfect taste, who can make charming things with very little material. In the same way, out of almost insignificant scraps of pastry, we have to create pleasing and graceful things that also tempt the appetite.'

COLIN The name given to hake in Paris markets. It is also used commercially to denote other white-fleshed sea fish, such as cod and haddock.

COLLAGE The French term for 'fining' – separating particles in suspension in young wine. This is done by adding a fining agent; according to the region and the wine, this may be egg white, albumen, gelatine or bentonite. The fining agent is mixed with the wine in cask or vat and attracts the particles to itself, so that the wine may then be racked off. (See also *Clarification*.)

COLLATION Originally, a light meal eaten by Roman Catholics on fasting days. The word comes from the Latin word *collatio*, meaning 'coming together'. It marked a devotional meeting of monks that was followed by a light repast. A collation may also be used to mean a quick meal usually eaten outside normal mealtimes.

COLLE The French term for gelatine that has been softened in water ready to dissolve in certain savoury or sweet preparations that require thickening. The word is also applied to melted aspic added to some cold sauces.

COLLER The French word for adding dissolved gelatine to give body to a preparation. Gelatine is added to consommés, to aspic jellies to clarify them, to fruit jellies, to Bavarian creams and to mayonnaise. The word can also be used when slices of truffle, hard-boiled (hard-cooked) egg white, leek or carrot are stuck together with a small amount of jelly and used to garnish certain cold dishes.

COLLIOURE A red wine from the Roussillon. The *appellation contrôlée* refers only to the table wine, the *vin doux naturel* (produced in the same region) being known as Banyuls. They are named after the towns of Collioure and Banyuls-sur-Mer, both nearby on the Mediterranean coast, close to the Spanish border. Collioure table wine, made mainly from the Mourvèdre, Syrah and Grenache Noir grapes, is dry, robust and full-bodied, about 12°–15°. It matures in wood and cannot be bottled and sold until the July after its vintage.

COLLYBIA The generic name of numerous species of mushrooms with gills, usually of medium size, sometimes very small, with a soft texture, and liable to become putrid. Only the 'velvet-foot' (*patte de velours*), today called *flammuline à pied velouté*, is of any culinary interest in the West, and only for its cap. It has long been known, cultivated and eaten in the Far East.

COLOMBIAN COOKING Colombian cuisine is generous and nourishing. Colombians have hearty appetites, eating scrambled eggs with tomatoes and onions for breakfast, and *tamales* and *empanadas* throughout the day. Meals are often built around 'complete' stews such as *ajiaco*, which includes meat or poultry, maize (corn), potatoes and avocado, seasoned with peppers, or *sancocho*, with meat or fish served with manioc and green bananas. Maize cakes, *arepas*, are eaten instead of bread. Coconuts are very common and are used both in savoury and sweet dishes. Tropical fruit such as papayas and passion fruit mingle with strawberries and oranges in the markets. See *South America*.

COLOMBINE A croquette consisting of a moulded outer layer of semolina mixed with Parmesan cheese, filled with a salpicon, a purée or any filling used for vol-au-vent or barquettes. Coated with breadcrumbs and fried, *colombines* are served as a hot hors d'oeuvre.

COLOMBO A mixture of spices that are often used in the French West Indies. It was imported by Ceylonese (now Sri Lankan) coolies who had come to work in the Caribbean and was named after Colombo, the capital city of Sri Lanka. Colombo powder is a mild variation on curry powder and contains garlic, coriander, 'Indian wood' (Jamaican chilli), saffron, curcuma, dried mango pulp and cinnamon.

The term colombo is also used for any West Indian dish that is seasoned with colombo powder. Locally, turtle, agouti and even iguana flesh is used, but the most common colombos are based on chicken, crab, pork or firm-fleshed fish. They are served with rice *à la créole* and red kidney beans. Yams, breadfruit, aubergines (eggplants) and pieces of custard marrow (chayote) are sometimes added to the stew.

Colombo is also the name of an African climbing plant whose root is used to make tonic and apéritif drinks.

COLOURING AGENTS Additives used in confectionery, cake-making, dairy products and drinks. Their function is essentially a psychological one – to give the products a more appetizing appearance, which can often mislead the consumer about the composition of the products.

The use of colouring agents in food is not a new innovation. In the Middle Ages, butter was coloured with marigold flowers, and even at that time their use was subject to certain regulations. Saffron, spinach and caramel have been used as colouring agents for many centuries.

Some colouring agents are natural or manufactured according to a natural formula; others are synthetic. The former are almost all of vegetable origin, except for cochineal and carmine, which are obtained from insects. The red azo dyes form the most important group of synthetic colouring agents. All additives have to be stated in lists of ingredients on packaging.

■ **Colouring food during cooking** The colour of a dish may be intensified or changed during cooking by adding vegetable colouring matter, such as spinach juice, beetroot (red beet) juice, caramel, tomato purée (paste) or crustacean shells. Meat is coloured by sealing it in very hot fat, which has the effect of browning the surface. The same effect is achieved by placing it under a hot grill (broiler) before cooking.

COLRAVE Name used in some parts of French-speaking Switzerland to describe the firm cabbage known as *chou pommé*. There are flat, round and convex varieties, greenish-white, dark green and violet-blue in colour.

COLTSFOOT A plant with yellow flowers, the dried leaves of which are smoked, like eucalyptus, to soothe coughs. They are also used to make tisanes and, in Canada, as an aromatic, especially with fish.

COMINÉE In ancient times, a culinary term for dishes that contained cumin. This spice was widely used in the Middle Ages for seasoning soups, poultry dishes and fish dishes. Taillevent's *Viandier* gives recipes for *cominée d'amandes* (a sort of poultry soup made with verjuice and flavoured with shelled almonds, ginger and cumin), *cominée de gélines* (of chickens) and *cominée d'esturgeon* (sturgeon cut into pieces and boiled with cumin and almonds).

RECIPE

cominée de gélines
(from an ancient recipe) Boil some chickens in wine and water. Skim off the fat and remove the chickens. Beat some egg yolks, mix them with the cooking liquid from the chickens and add cumin. Replace the chickens.

COMMODORE A term used to describe a very elaborate garnish for poached fish, in which fish quenelles, crayfish tail croquettes and mussels *à la Villeroi* are mixed together in a crayfish bisque.

Consommé commodore is made with a fish stock thickened with arrowroot and garnished with pieces of poached clam and diced tomatoes cooked in the stock.

COMPOTE A preparation of fresh or dried fruit, cooked either whole or in pieces in a sugar syrup. It does not keep for as long as jam.

Fresh fruit should be cooked by poaching it in syrup over a gentle heat, or else by fast boiling. A compote can be made with several different kinds of fruit. The fruit should be arranged in a fruit bowl or dish and served as a dessert. It may be served either slightly warm or chilled, accompanied by whipped cream or sprinkled with cinnamon, vanilla sugar or biscuit (cookie) crumbs. Fresh fruit compotes may be used to prepare rather more elaborate desserts, such as sundaes and mousses. This kind of fruit purée can also be used as an ingredient in turnovers, tarts and charlottes.

Before cooking, dried fruit should be soaked for varying lengths of time in cold or warm water, to which some kind of alcohol (such as kirsch, rum or Frontignan) or tea may be added.

Whether the fruit is fresh or dried, the cooking syrup (or the compote itself) can be flavoured with various ingredients, such as vanilla, lemon or orange peel, cinnamon powder (or cinnamon sticks in the case of syrup), cloves, ground almonds, grated coconut, crystallized (candied) fruit or raisins.

The term compote is also used for certain dishes containing game, such as pigeons, partridges or rabbit, that have been cooked in a roux for a fairly long time over a gentle heat. The game is usually cooked with small (pearl) onions and bacon; at the end of the cooking time, the flesh has disintegrated completely. Onions and peppers may also be reduced to a compote.

Recipes

apple compote

Prepare a syrup as for apricot compote (recipe below). Peel the apples, cut them into quarters, remove the pips (seeds) and cover them with lemon juice. Boil the syrup, add the apples and remove as soon as they are tender. Serve either warm or cold.

apricot compote

Halve the apricots, remove the stones (pits) and extract and blanch the kernels. Cook the fruit for about 20 minutes in syrup: use 350 g (12 oz, 1½ cups) granulated sugar to 600 ml (1 pint, 2½ cups) water. Arrange the apricot halves in a fruit bowl with half a kernel on each; pour the syrup over.

baked apricot compote

Place some apricot halves in an ovenproof dish. Sprinkle them with sugar and bake in a preheated oven at 180°C (350°F, gas 4) for about 20 minutes. Serve in a fruit dish.

baked cherry compote

Stone (pit) the cherries, place them in a deep dish and sprinkle with caster (superfine) sugar to taste. Leave for 3–4 hours so that the juice runs out, then cover and cook in a preheated oven at 180°C (350°F, gas 4) for about 20 minutes.

bilberry compote

Dissolve 500 g (18 oz, 2¼ cups) caster (superfine) sugar in 200 ml (7 fl oz, ¾ cup) water. Add a little grated lemon zest, and boil for 5 minutes. Clean 1 kg (2¼ lb, 5 cups) bilberries (huckleberries), add them to the syrup and boil for 8–10 minutes. Drain the bilberries using a slotted spoon and place them in a bowl. Reduce the syrup by one-third and pour it over the bilberries. Serve well chilled. When prepared by this method, the bilberries can be used to make a tart.

cherry compote

For each 1 kg (2¼ lb, 4½ cups) stoned (pitted) cherries, use 300 g (11 oz, 1½ cups) caster (superfine) sugar and 5 tablespoons water to make a sugar syrup. Cook until it has reached the 'large ball' stage. Add the cherries and cook with the lid on for 8 minutes over a low heat. Drain the cherries and place in a bowl. Mix 2 tablespoons kirsch with the syrup and pour over the cherries. Cool before serving.

chestnut compote

Slit the shells of the chestnuts, plunge them into boiling water for 5 minutes and peel them while they are still hot. Cook them gently in a vanilla-flavoured syrup (using proportions of sugar and water as for apricot compote) for about 45 minutes. Pour the chestnuts and syrup into a bowl, cool and refrigerate before serving.

compote du vieux vigneron

Peel 1 kg (2¼ lb) fairly sour apples. Cut them into quarters, remove the pips (seeds) and place them in a heavy based saucepan together with 150 g (5 oz, ⅔ cup) sugar. Cover and stew the apples over a very gentle heat until they disintegrate. Prepare a syrup with 575 g (1¼ lb, 2½ cups) granulated sugar and 750 ml (1¼ pints, 3¼ pints) red wine. Peel 800 g (1¾ lb) pears and an equal quantity of peaches. Cut the pears into quarters and remove the pips. Cut the peaches in half and stone (pit) them. Add the peaches and pears to the boiling syrup together with 2 or 3 cloves and ½ teaspoon powdered cinnamon. Cook for 15–18 minutes.

Add 50 g (2 oz, ¼ cup) butter to the hot apples, mix well and pour into a bowl. When the peaches and pears are cooked, drain them and arrange them on top of the stewed apples. Add 250 g (9 oz) grapes to the boiling syrup, leave for 3 minutes and then drain. Use them to decorate the other fruit. Remove the cloves from the syrup and reduce it until it thickens. Pour it over the compote and allow it to cool completely.

If no grapes are available, soak some raisins in a little weak tea. When they have swollen, use as for fresh grapes.

fig compote using dried figs

Soak the figs in cold water until they swell. Prepare a syrup with half red wine and half water, using 350 g (12 oz, 1½ cups) granulated sugar to 600 ml (1 pint, 2½ cups) liquid; flavour it with finely grated lemon zest. Bring the syrup to the boil, add the figs and cook very gently for 20–30 minutes.

fig compote using fresh figs

Peel some white or black figs. Put them in boiling vanilla-flavoured syrup, made with 350 g (12 oz, 1½ cups) granulated sugar to 600 ml (1 pint, 2½ cups) water, and poach for a few minutes only. Drain, reduce the syrup and pour it over the figs.

four-fruit compote

Use equal quantities of apples, quinces and oranges, together with a few large grapes. Prepare a syrup as for apricot compote. Peel the apples and quinces, remove the pips (seeds), slice thickly and sprinkle with lemon juice. Plunge the slices of quince in the boiling syrup; 15 minutes later, add the apples. Meanwhile, peel and slice the oranges, removing the pith, and add them to the other fruit 20 minutes after the beginning of the cooking time. Continue to cook for another 10 minutes. Peel and, if possible, remove the pips from the grapes. Add them to the syrup as soon as the pan has been removed from the heat. Allow to cool and chill in the refrigerator.

peach compote

Prepare a vanilla-flavoured syrup using proportions of sugar and water as for apricot compote. Plunge the peaches for about 30 seconds in boiling water and cool them under cold running water. It should then be easy to peel them. Either leave them whole or cut them in half and remove the stones (pits). Poach them in boiling syrup for 13 minutes if cut in half, or 18 minutes if they are whole.

pear and apple caramel compote

Cook the apples and pears separately, as described in the individual recipes. Drain them and arrange them in layers in a fruit bowl. Place the bowl in the refrigerator. Mix the two lots of syrup together and reduce until it begins to turn pale gold in colour. Pour this boiling syrup over the cold fruit and set aside to cool. Do not refrigerate.

pear compote

Peel the pears, cut them into quarters and remove the seeds. (If the pears are small, leave them whole.) Cook them in boiling vanilla-flavoured syrup (prepared as for apricot compote) until they become translucent. Remove and place in a bowl. Reduce the syrup and pour it over the pears. Cool before serving. Some pear brandy may be added to the cold syrup if desired.

pineapple compote

Remove the skin and core of a pineapple. Slice the fruit and cook in some vanilla-flavoured syrup for about 15–20 minutes. Arrange the pineapple slices in a dish, reduce the syrup and pour it over the pineapple. Cool completely, and keep in the refrigerator until ready to serve.

plum compote

Stone (pit) the plums carefully without splitting them in two. Poach them in boiling syrup (prepared as for apricot compote) for 10–12 minutes. Serve well chilled, with or without cream.

This recipe can also be prepared using mirabelle plums.

quince compote

Peel the quinces, cut them into quarters and remove the seeds. Cut each quarter into two and blanch the pieces. Cool them under cold running water and pat dry. Cook until tender in a vanilla-flavoured syrup made with 350 g (12 oz, 1½ cups) granulated sugar to 600 ml (1 pint, 2½ cups) water. Arrange in a dish and pour the syrup over.

raspberry compote

This is prepared in the same way as strawberry compote, but the syrup should not be flavoured with orange.

redcurrant compote

Pull the fruit very carefully from the stalks with a fork and place in a saucepan. Cover with boiling syrup, prepared as for apricot compote, bring back to the boil, then pour both the fruit and the syrup into a dish. Cool, then place in the refrigerator. (Raw strawberries or raspberries can be added if desired.)

rhubarb compote

Use only fresh sticks and carefully remove the strings. Cut the sticks into pieces 6–7.5 cm (2½–3 in) long. Blanch them in boiling water for 3 minutes, drain and cool. Place them in a preserving pan and cover with a syrup made as for apricot compote. Cover and cook without stirring. Serve either warm or cold. This compote can be used as a filling for tarts.

strawberry compote

Wash, hull, dry, but do not cook the strawberries. Arrange them in a dish and pour boiling syrup (prepared as for apricot compote) over them. The syrup may be flavoured with orange or other flavourings.

COMPOTER A French term meaning to cook a dish very gently so that the ingredients are reduced to a sort of compote or purée (see *Capilotade*). Onions and rabbit pieces may be cooked in this way.

COMPOTIER A large dish (made of porcelain, crystal, glass or earthenware) on a raised base. It is used for serving compotes, cream desserts or other sweet dishes. Earthenware or glass *compotiers* may also be used for arrangements of fresh fruit.

COMTÉ A cheese made with cow's milk (minimum 45% fat content), which is cooked and pressed. It is ivory-coloured or pale yellow and has a natural brushed rind, varying from golden yellow to brown. It is matured for three to six months. The cheese comes from the Franche-Comté region of France and is also known as Comté Gruyère. Traditionally, it should have small 'eyes' or holes, a fruity flavour and a strong (but never pungent) bouquet.

Its manufacture is governed by AOP status. The name is followed by a clear indication of the department or district in which it has been made. The departments include the Doubs, the Jura and the Haute-Saône, together with the area around Belfort, and the districts of Belley, Bourg-en-Bresse, Gex, Nantua, Beaune, Dijon, Langres, Chalon-sur-Saône, Louhans, Épinal and Neufchâteau. The origin and also the month of its manufacture is marked on a piece of green casein attached to the cheese.

The cheese has a straight or slightly convex rind and measures 40–70 cm (16–28 in) in diameter and 9–13 cm (3½–5 in) in height. Comté is a very ancient cheese and the first dairy to make it is recorded as far back as the 13th century. It is served as part of a cheeseboard and is widely used in cooking. It may be grated or sliced and used for a wide variety of dishes, including toppings, soufflés, mixed salads, canapés, fondues and fritters.

COMUS The ancient Roman god of drinking and revelry. He was invoked during nocturnal feasts that were accompanied by music and dancing. Comus was represented as a young man crowned with flowers, holding a flaming torch in his right hand.

CONCASSER The French term for chopping or pounding a substance, either coarsely or finely. For example, when skinned seeded tomato flesh is finely chopped, it is known as tomato *concassée*. The term may also be applied to tender herbs, such as parsley, chervil or tarragon that have been chopped on a flat board with a few rapid strokes of a knife. Meat, poultry, game and fish bones can be 'concasséed' with a cleaver or chopper when preparing a stock or flavouring. The term may also be used for the crushed ice used to line a serving dish for chilled melon and caviar.

CONCENTRATE A substance in which the water content has been reduced by evaporation or some other process. In cookery, the method is used for meat, poultry or fish glazes. These are stocks that have been cooked slowly over a long period. The juices are concentrated and form a syrupy substance used to enhance the flavour of certain sauces.

Tomato purée (paste), a concentrate that can be home-made or bought, is made by reducing the liquid extracted from tomatoes and filtering it to remove the skins and seeds. It is widely used in the preparation of sauces and stews. Fruit juices are industrially processed to obtain concentrates, which, when diluted with water, give reconstituted drinks.

Evaporated and condensed milks are prepared in a vacuum and are sold in cans. Condensed milk is sweetened, evaporated milk is not, but both keep for a long period. They are particularly useful in the preparation of iced desserts and are much used in the industrial preparation of confectionery, cakes and pastries.

CONCORDE A garnish for large joints of meat, consisting of creamed potatoes, trimmed and glazed new carrots and peas in butter.

CONDÉ Name given to various methods of preparing food which were dedicated to the French general, Condé the Great (1621–86) and his descendants by family chefs. Also sometimes referred to as *à la Condé*.

Savoury dishes are characterized by the presence of a purée of red kidney beans.

Condés, or Condé cakes, are small cakes made of puff pastry covered with a layer of royal icing with almonds (Condé icing).

The terms are also applied to cold desserts based on rice and poached fruit; classically, the fruit should be apricots in syrup, arranged in a crown around a 'cake' of rice coated with an apricot and kirsch sauce and decorated with cherries and crystallized (candied) fruit. This basic recipe has many variations, using slices of pineapple, peaches or strawberries,

but always including rice cooked in milk and a fruit sauce.

RECIPES

Savoury Dishes
Condé soup
Cook some red kidney beans with a very little salt until they can be reduced to a fine purée. Add sufficient chicken stock to obtain a liquid soup. Thicken with fresh butter and serve very hot, with or without small croûtons fried in butter or oil.

shirred eggs Condé
Grease an individual egg dish; pipe a border of puréed red kidney beans round the edge. Gently fry 2 slices of bacon in butter and lay them on the dish. Break 2 eggs on top and cook in a preheated oven at 180°C (350°F, gas 4).

Sweet Dishes
cherries Condé
Stone (pit) the cherries and poach them in syrup. Fill an ovenproof dish with rice cooked in milk, smooth over the top and decorate with some of the drained cherries, candied angelica cut into diamond shapes, and shelled almonds. Purée the rest of the cherries and add enough of the syrup to obtain a very liquid sauce; reduce this sauce until it becomes syrupy. Reheat the decorated rice in the oven. Serve with the cherry sauce.

Condé cakes
Roll out some puff pastry to a thickness of about 5 mm (¼ in). Cut out strips 7.5–10 cm (3–4 in) wide and cut these into rectangles 4 cm (1½ in) wide. Coat the top of the rectangles with Condé icing and then sprinkle with icing (confectioner's) sugar. Place the cakes on a baking sheet and cook in a preheated oven at 200°C (400°F, gas 6) until they are just golden. They may be split while still warm and filled with a little sieved strawberry jam.

Condé icing
Chop 250 g (9 oz, 1½ cups) shelled almonds finely in a blender, without reducing them to a paste. Mix 350 g (12 oz, 2 cups) icing (confectioner's) sugar, 1 tablespoon vanilla sugar and the chopped almonds in an earthenware dish. Beat 2 egg whites and a small pinch of salt with a fork until fluffy but not stiff, and add them little by little to the sugar – the mixture should be liquid enough to spread easily over the cakes, without overflowing while cooking.

strawberries Condé
Bind some rice cooked in milk, flavoured with sugar and vanilla, with egg yolk, and fill a ring mould. Cook in a bain marie for 30 minutes in a preheated oven at 200°C (400°F, gas 6), then leave to cool and turn out of the mould on to a serving dish. Wash some large strawberries, drain, hull and divide into 2 equal quantities. Sprinkle half with sugar and

brandy and leave in a cool place to macerate for at least 1 hour. Press through a sieve the other half of the strawberries, together with some raspberries (a quarter of the weight of strawberries); add some lemon juice – 1 tablespoon per 500 g (18 oz) strawberries – and just enough caster (superfine) sugar for the purée not to taste sour. Drain the whole strawberries and arrange in the middle of the rice, serving the fruit purée at the same time.

CONDIMENTS

Food substances used to heighten the natural flavour of foods, to stimulate the appetite, to aid digestion or else to preserve certain products (the word comes from the Latin *condire*, to preserve). The term condiment is used today to include spices, seasonings, sauces, fruit and various cooked or uncooked preparations. Strictly speaking, however, a seasoning is a substance added to food while it is being prepared, whereas a condiment, chosen to harmonize with the taste of the food, can be either an accompaniment (mustard, pickled fruit, ketchup or gherkins), or an ingredient (truffles, dried fruit, alcohol, herbs or spices), or a preserving agent (vinegar, salt, oil or sugar).

The custom of adding condiments to food is as ancient as cookery itself. Originally, it was a means of preserving (in very spicy sauces such as the Roman *garum*, or in the saltpetre and verjuice of the Middle Ages). Most condiments are of vegetable origin: herbs, spices, dried or crystallized (candied) fruit, and aromatic vegetables; some, such as the Vietnamese *nuoc-mâm*, are based on dried and pounded fish or shellfish.

Condiments are used either raw and untreated (onion, fresh herbs, cress) or else after some form of preparation (sweet-and-sour sauces, purées, mustards, capers, chutneys). Customary use varies from one country to another; in Britain and the United States large quantities of bottled sauces and condiments are used to accompany salads, cold meat and charcuterie, whereas in Oriental and northern countries sweet-and-sour sauce is a basic ingredient of many condiments. Mention should also be made of products such as cocoa, sometimes used as a condiment in Mexico. Finally, the term can also include natural colourings (caramel, beetroot juice, spinach green), as well as essences and extracts (anchovy, aniseed, almond), wines and spirits, some flowers and even cheese (Parmesan, Gruyère, Mozzarella and blue cheeses).

CONDRIEU

An AOC white wine from the Rhône Valley, which is produced in such small quantities that until recently it was practically unknown outside the region. Only one type of vine (the Viognier) is used. Condrieu is an unusual wine, firm in style with a distinctive bouquet. It should be drunk young, 2–4 years old.

CONFECTIONER'S CUSTARD (PASTRY CREAM) See *custard*.

CONFECTIONERY

Food products based on sugar. The French term can be applied not only to sweets (candies), but also to the confectioner's shop and to the techniques of the craftsman or the whole industry.

Numerous raw materials are used in the manufacture of confectionery products: sugar, glucose syrup and invert sugar, honey, milk (whole or skimmed, fresh, concentrated or powdered), animal and vegetable fats, fruit (fresh, preserved, frozen or in pulp), cocoa, dried fruit, gum arabic, pectin, starches, gelatine, liquorice juice, certain acids, natural or synthetic aromatic products and permitted colourings.

The large majority of confectionery products are bought on impulse and purchases are spread out over the year. Some kinds are eaten mostly on special occasions (Easter and Christmas). In France this is particularly true of sugared almonds, marrons glacés, bonbons and crystallized (candied) fruit, which are sold in fancy wrappings and are most often bought as presents. Packaging has always been particularly important for confectionery.

■ **Development of French confectionery** The confectioner's art is very old. Its evolution has followed the ingredients available; before sugar was introduced, honey was used to coat grains and fruits and to make the type of sweets (candies) still eaten in the Middle East. The introduction of cane sugar into Europe by the Crusaders allowed confectionery to develop. Like the chemists, the confectioners of Paris were members of the grocers' guild, whose charters date from 1311. Until the end of the 17th century, the chemists and confectioners quarrelled over the right to make and sell sugar products, but the confectioners with their growing specialization obtained the definitive right to produce sweets for everyday consumption, so that they were no longer available only for the rich. The first important producer was the house of Oudard in the Rue des Lombards, Paris, who was praised by Grimod de La Reynière. The extraction of sugar from sugar beet gave the profession a boost; mechanization was also coming in.

At the end of the 19th century, confectionery comprised plain and iced biscuits (cookies), chocolate, cooked sugar sweets (candies), shaped fruit jellies, sugar-coated nuts and ices. In France there are still about 300 small family firms where the cooking is done on an open fire; there are also large industrial firms which are entirely mechanized. As a general rule, these manufacturers do not make the same type of product: boiled sweets (hard candies), toffees, sugar-coated sweets and chewing gums are produced by the large firms, while fruit jellies, marzipan and marrons glacés are made by small firms or craftsmen. Certain regional specialities are still made, such as the sugar-coated almonds of Verdun, nougat from Montélimar and fruit jellies from the Auvergne.

CONFIRE

A French culinary term for preparing certain foods in particular ways in order to preserve them, either by cooking them slowly in their own fat (confits of pork, goose and duck), by coating them with sugar syrup (confectionery) or by bottling them in alcohol (cherries and prunes in brandy), in vinegar (capers, gherkins and pickles) or in a sweet-and-sour preparation (chutneys).

CONFIT A piece of pork, goose, duck or turkey cooked in its own fat and stored in a pot, covered in the same fat to preserve it. The confit is one of the oldest forms of preserving food and is a speciality of south-western France. Simin Palay, in *Cuisine du pays*, describes this speciality from the Basque and Béarn regions: 'Lean pork or a quarter of fowl is rubbed with salt, soaked in brine, then drained and dried and cooked slowly in fat with flavourings and seasonings; finally, it is put into a pot and stored in a cool dry place. Confit of goose or duck, fattened on maize (corn), is often prepared with a mixture of pork and poultry fats. If the pot is made of tin plate, the confit must always be well covered by fat.'

The long life of confit, the fact that it can be eaten hot or cold, and its delicate flavour have won it a high place in the gastronomy of the Gers, Périgord and Landes regions. It is used in the preparation of *garbure* and cassoulet, but it is above all eaten as a meat dish, accompanied by a variety of vegetables: cep mushrooms (*à la basquaise*), fried potatoes (*à la béarnaise* or *à la sarladaise*), fresh peas and Bayonne ham (*à la landaise*), a sorrel fondue (*à la périgourdine*) or white beans, cabbage or lentils. When eaten cold, with the fat removed, it is often accompanied by a dandelion, endive (chicory) or white cabbage salad.

Neighbouring regions have their own confit specialities, such as confit of mallard served with new potatoes in Saintonge, confit of duck or truffled turkey in Brantôme and confit of young turkey in Bordeaux.

The leg (thigh) is considered the most succulent part of preserved poultry and the wing the tenderest. The weight of meat, without the fat, must represent at least 55% of the total weight of a pot of preserved poultry.

Goose is most commonly used for making confit as its meat is often too tough to roast. A special container known as a *grésale* (stoneware pot) is used to marinate the meat in brine with a clove, thyme, pepper, a bay leaf and garlic. Traditionally, it is cooked the day after a pig is slaughtered, when pâtés, terrines and pork dishes are prepared; a deep copper cauldron is the most suitable utensil for this. To check that the legs and wings (which are surrounded by fat) are cooked, a knitting needle is inserted: if it comes out without a trace of blood, the meat is cooked. The confit is stored in stoneware pots (called *toupins*), which are preferable to glass jars as no light can get in. Either goose fat or dripping is used to make a hermetic final seal.

Other meats can be prepared as confits, especially chicken, guinea fowl, rabbit, woodcock (in the Gers region) and veal.

RECIPES

confit of goose
Clean the inside of a fat goose thoroughly and remove the bones, keeping the carcass whole. Cut into quarters. Place in a container and season very liberally with coarse salt, then leave in a cold place for 24 hours to allow the salt to penetrate thoroughly into the flesh. Cook in a large copper cauldron with 2 kg (4½ lb) goose fat for 2 hours. Make sure the fat simmers while cooking, but do not allow it to boil. While the fat is still hot, strain it into a stoneware pot and place the pieces of goose in the fat so they are completely covered. Leave to cool and then cover the pot. To obtain an authentic *confit*, store in a cellar for 5–6 months. For *confit* of duck, follow the same method.

confit of goose à la béarnaise
Heat a quarter of preserved goose in its own fat and keep hot in a serving dish. Peel and slice some potatoes and fry them in the *confit* fat. Chop some parsley and garlic together, add to the potatoes and reheat. Surround the *confit* with the potatoes and serve very hot.

confit of goose à la landaise
Peel 6 small onions and dice 75 g (3 oz, ½ cup) Bayonne ham. Heat 1 tablespoon goose fat in an earthenware casserole and cook the onions and ham for 5 minutes, then add 1 litre (1¾ pints, 4⅓ cups) freshly shelled peas. Sprinkle with 1 tablespoon flour and stir for a few moments with a wooden spoon. Moisten with 150 ml (¼ pint, ⅔ cup) water; add pepper and ½ teaspoon sugar (salt is not needed because the ham is already salty). Add a bouquet garni with chervil, cover and leave to cook for about 30 minutes. Then add a quarter of preserved goose and leave until cooked, the total cooking time depending on the tenderness of the peas.

confit of goose à la sarladaise
Prepare as for *confit* of goose *à la béarnaise*, but add slices of truffle when the potatoes are cooked.

confit of goose with green cabbage
Braise potato quarters with green cabbage arranged on top. Press a piece of preserved goose, with a little of its fat, into the cabbage layer and reheat. Arrange the *confit* on a dish surrounded by the potatoes and cabbage.

CONFRÉRIES Also known as orders and brotherhoods. In the Middle Ages in France, many of those involved with wine formed associations devoted to preserving local traditions and upholding the quality of their particular wines, in addition to acting as benevolent societies to assist members and their families in need. They exercised considerable control over the production and marketing of wines and spirits, but at the time of the French Revolution many ceased their operations, both because of the civic disturbance and because, in many regions, the great estates and vineyards changed hands. But records and certain traditions were not quite lost. In Alsace, for example, where the Confrérie Saint-Étienne was founded in the 14th century, the *ban* (proclamation of the vintage) announced to growers that they could start picking their grapes.

Since the 1930s, however, many *confréries* have been revived and those that had managed to keep going have progressively engaged in many activities, most of them now of a promotional rather than restrictive type. In some regions in France, where wine-growing has become more structured and the wines are enormously improved, there are a number of recently formed similar organizations. All of them usually have a set of rules and an annual list of fixtures, such as chapters at which new members are admitted by the organizing council, banquets and festivals, especially at the times of the flowering of the vine in the spring, the vintage and on the feast day of any of the numerous saints associated with wine. In many instances, would-be members have to submit themselves to a preliminary test and the insignia they wear denotes their rank within the fraternity – apprentice, fellow, master or some similar honorary title.

Although the best-known *confréries* are those concerned with wine, there are many others associated with other commodities, such as those of the cheese makers, that are similar to the medieval guilds and livery companies of the City of London.

■ **Wine orders** Often originating many centuries ago, possibly as dining clubs, wine orders evolved as corporations administering the business of the wines of their particular locality. Few regions of France today are without some organization of this sort, from the Ordre des Coteaux in Champagne, founded as an aristocratic 'Bacchic society' (really a version of a drinking club) in the 17th century, to the humbler groupings of regions such as those of the Auvergne or Jura. Both the highly reputed Sacavins d'Anjou (1905) and the Chevaliers du Tastevin are examples that are widely known. The latter was re-established in 1934 at a gala dinner at Nuits-Saint-Georges and subsequently acquired the great building of Clos-de-Vougeot. Here their ceremonies, 'oiled' by wine and song and followed by lengthy banquets, have done much to promote Burgundy throughout the world, including Britain and the United States (where there are branches of the Tastevins).

• BORDEAUX In order to combat the economic problems of 1949, the wine trade of the Médoc decided to found both an Academy of Bordeaux wines and a wine order, following the example of the successful Chevaliers du Tastevin; this was approved and supported by the leading wine personalities of the area. The wine order, the Commanderie du Bontemps de Médoc et des Graves, takes its name from the little wooden bowl (*bontemps*) used for whisking the egg whites for fining the wines. The order was inaugu-

rated by well-known personalities from the worlds of art and literature as well as businessmen, civic dignitaries and the heads of the university, wearing the claret-coloured velvet robes and medieval toque head-dresses topped by a piece of pleated white silk – to represent the egg whites. (Those officers belonging to the Graves wear golden velvet robes.) There are annual reunions and celebrations, notably at the flowering of the vine in June and the Ban des Vendanges at vintage time in September. The Bontemps have been followed by other regions within the Gironde, such as the Commandeurs du Bontemps de Sainte-Croix-du-Mont (1963) and the Commandeurs du Bontemps de Sauternes et de Barsac (1959). Many of these orders have chosen a name historically associated with the region: for example, the Jurade de Saint-Émilion (1948) took their name from the charter given to the local council by King John of England in 1199; the *jurade* was equivalent to the town council – there was one in Bordeaux. The Compagnons de Loupiac (1971) like to associate themselves with the Roman poet Ausonius, who is said to have had a villa in the region. The Hôpitaliers de Pomerol (1968) have taken as their emblem the Maltese Cross, in honour of the Knights Hospitallers of St John of Jerusalem (the St John's Ambulance Brigade is their descendant in Britain), some of whom were landowners and wine-makers in the region. The Gentilhommes de Fronsac associate themselves with the famous – one might almost say notorious – Duc de Richelieu, marshal of France and governor of the old province of Guyenne. These and other *confréries* are represented at the Grand Conseil de Bordeaux, which co-ordinates their activities.

• BURGUNDY The part played by the wine orders in the economic and social life of the various regions is both recognized and approved. In Burgundy, the Chevaliers du Tastevin organize many functions throughout the year, notably the great banquet at Clos-de-Vougeot on the Saturday before the annual sale of the Hospices de Beaune wines in November. They also arrange processions throughout the region to celebrate the Feast of St Vincent, patron of winegrowers, on 22 January. The Confrérie Saint-Vincent de Mâcon, representing the wines both of Mâcon and Pouilly-Fuissé, have chosen the same saint who, local legend says, was able to offer the very first *vin nouveau* to the Father Almighty! The Piliers Chablisiens (1952), so-called because Chablis is the 'golden gate' to Burgundy, hold their jollifications in a real cellar; at the end of November they celebrate 'Saint Cochon', a survival of the medieval period when pigs were killed and preserved in various ways for winter. The Master of the Piliers is known as the 'Grand Architrave' – typical Burgundian humour. The Confrères des Trois-Ceps (1965), an offshoot of the Piliers, celebrate the 'Sauvignon Festival' on 11 November – indicating that Chardonnay is not the only white grape of the area!

• LOIRE It is not surprising that there are plenty of Bacchic brotherhoods in the Loire, especially around Chinon, birthplace of François Rabelais. Although many of the wines he wrote about have disappeared, there are plenty more. Since 1937 the Chevaliers de la Chantepleure de Vouvray have gathered every mid-June and mid-September in various places, in and out of doors, sometimes in cellars hollowed from the limestone cliffs of the Loire banks, to sample Vouvray. There are many orders associating themselves with Rabelais: the Entonneurs Rabelaisiens (1962) who meet at Chinon (the word *entonnoir* means a funnel, signifying the copious draughts of wine under consideration); the Compagnons de Grandgousier at Onzain (1958); and the Fins Gouziers d'Anjou, who wear black velvet hats in the style of Henri III. The Confrérie des Tire-Douzils (1953) in Marigny-Brizay in Poitou and the Fripe-Douzils (1952) of Ingrandes-de-Touraine in the Bourgueil region have chosen as their emblem the little wooden peg inserted into a barrel to draw out the wine for tasting. The Chevaliers de Sancerre (1964) and the Baillis de Pouilly (1949) aim to promote the wines of Sancerre and Pouilly-sur-Loire; the Chevaliers Bretvins at Nantes vow to drink Muscadet and Gros Plant, while at Angers the Sacavins d'Anjou quaff the wines of their region. The majority of the Loire wine orders have fine robes for their officers: the Commandeurs des Grands Vins d'Amboise (1967) wear plumed hats and red robes with sleeves slashed open to reveal their yellow undersleeves (the colours representing both red and white wine). The Compagnons d'Honneur des Sorciers et Birettes (1951), concerned with Bué and the Sancerre area, have a reunion on the first Sunday in August, when they wear white capes with red and green facings and wizards' masks.

• THE SOUTH-WEST AND THE MEDITERRANEAN There are plenty of wine orders maintaining the names and traditions of the past in other parts of France. Some of the better known include the Viguiers Royaux du Jurançon (1953), who wear a Béarn beret and a ruffled collar in the style of Henri IV, the Chevaliers du Tursan (1963), the Confrères du Vin de Cahors (1966) and the Consuls de la Vinée de Bergerac (1954). There are also the fraternities of the spirit producers: the Mousquetaires d'Armagnac (1952), the Principauté de Franc-Pineau (1950) and the Confrérie des Alambics Charentais (1946), who wear green coats and toque-style headgear. All organize festivities in France and abroad to promote Cognac, Armagnac and Pineau des Charentes.

As the wines of the Mediterranean coast and hinterland are possibly the most ancient of France, the Latin name is retained in the names of some of the wine orders: the Consuls de Septimanie (1970) are associated with this classical poet; they celebrate the Narbonne vineyards in August. The name of the Échansons du Vidauban (1970), who wear an apron and a red scarf, comes from the Latin *vitis albanus* (white vine). The Ordre Illustre des Chevaliers de Méduse (1951) of Arcs-sur-Argens, holding its annual chapter in September, wear azure blue capes lined with purple. The Échansons des Papes (1967) of Châteauneuf-du-Pape chose a bronze key (the sign

of St Peter) as their emblem; the Commandeurs de Tavel wear a red cape with a black velvet collar when they celebrate the rosé wine of the Gard. In southeastern France and near the Spanish frontier, in the Roussillon and Corbières border regions, there are the Senhores de la Vinhas (1971) in Lézignan-Corbières, sumptuously attired in purple coats with gold facings, and the Seigneurs de Commande Majeure de Roussillon (1964), wearing a caped Catalan costume in honour of King Peter of Aragon.

■ **Gastronomic confréries** These societies, whose aim is to publicize the quality and fame of French cooking, are as varied and numerous as the wine lodges. They are often created to promote a regional product – cheese, charcuterie and other specialities, and the members may be professional cooks, food-producers or simply gourmets.

The *confréries* today no longer spend 18 hours enjoying three successive meals lasting from Saturday evening to Sunday lunchtime, as did the famous Club des Grands Estomacs during the Second Empire. Today's gourmets often meet friends or members of the same profession to enjoy a good meal. The famous Club des Cent, which was founded in 1912 at the time of the birth of the motorcar, was the inspiration of the journalist Louis Forest and had a gastronomic and sporting aim. The rules allowed the admission only of 'gourmets who have travelled forty thousand kilometres for a fine meal'. The great Académie des Gastronomes was founded in 1928 by Curnonsky, along with Édouard de Pomiane, Maeterlinck, Paul Reboux and the Marquis de Polignac, and was directly inspired by the Académie Française: each of its 40 members had to write an eulogy to an ancestor. Also founded in 1928, the Compagnie des Gentilhommes de Gueule organize a monthly dinner for their president, who is a well-read scholar. The Académie des Psychologues du Goût, established in 1922, are a sort of gastronomic Jockey Club whose members include ambassadors and other well-known personalities. The Académie du Malt Whisky, founded in 1970, awards two prizes each year.

• DIPLOMAS AND MEDALS Some of these associations are more directly involved in cookery and award diplomas and medals. Among the first was Joseph Favre's Académie de Cuisine (1883), which was the first school of cookery. It served as a model for the Académie Granet at Bourg-en-Bresse, the Académie des Chroniqueurs de Table, the Maîtres Cuisiniers de France (1949), the Poulardiers de Bresse and the Club Prosper-Montagné (1948): all share the same aims and work to promote the quality of cookery throughout France. The Chaîne des Rôtisseurs, founded in 1950 and allied with the Ordre Mondial des Gourmets, favour the use of the spit which 'by its neat and straightforward operation is the symbol of true French cookery'.

The old French tradition of characuterie has given rise to many *confréries* in every province. Remembering Rabelais' famous battle of the *andouilles*, two or three *confréries* dispute the science of making *andouilles*; the learned and distinguished gourmands of the Confrérie des Taste-Andouilles du Val d'Ajol (1965) have founded an interesting *andouille* museum. The Confrérie du Goûte-Andouille de Jargeau (1970) is a more recent group, while the Association Amicale des Amateurs d'Authentiques Andouillettes is one of the most exclusive clubs as it has only five members, who have awarded diplomas to characutiers and restaurateurs since 1960. In charcuterie western France is represented by the Confrérie du Goûte-Boudin de Mortagne-au-Perche (1963), the Confrérie des Chevaliers des Rillettes Sarthoises (1968) and the Confrérie de Gastronomie Normande la Tripière d'Or (1952); in Paris the Chevaliers de Saint Antoine (1963), wearing a white jacket and blue cape lined with black silk, hold all the secrets of charcuterie. The Confrérie du Jambon de Bayonne was founded in 1962 in the Basque country.

There is also a great variety of societies concerned with cheese: the Chevaliers de Taste-Fromage (1954) wear a green costume braided with gold and the Chevaliers de Faste-Fromage have violet costumes. In Carvagna (Italy) the Guilde des Maîtres Fromagers et Compagnons de Saint Uguzon holds chapter on 12 July, in robes bordered with fur, in memory of the saint, a Lombard shepherd who was persecuted to death – pilgrimages to his birthplace are organized.

The numerous culinary specialities of France have given birth to almost as many associations: the Confrérie du Cassoulet de Castelnaudary (1970), the Ordre de Collier de l'Escargot de Bourgogne (1956), the Ordre du Taste-Quiche (1969), the Confrérie des Chevaliers de la Pochouse (1949), the Confrérie des Taste Cancoillotte de Franche-Comté (1970), the Ordre des Fines Goules du Poitou (1972) and the Compagnie de la Madeleine de Commercy (1963). Oysters are adored by the Galants de Verts-Marennes (1957) and vegetables by the Tastos Mounjetos du Comminges, the Mangeux d'Esparges de Sologne and the Compagnons de l'Asperge d'Argenteuil. Whether great public bodies or simply gatherings of friends, these *confréries* continue to develop and there appears to be no lack of progress in conviviality.

CONGER EEL A common fish in the English Channel and the Atlantic. It is called *sili mor* in Brittany, *orratza* in Gascony; it is also found in the Mediterranean, where it is known as *fiela* or *fela*. Its body is long and smooth and its skin is of a brownish-grey colour without visible scales. It is a carnivore and has large jaws and strong teeth. Normally it measures 0.5–1.5 m (1½–5 ft) and weighs 5–15 kg (11–33 lb) but it can reach 3 m (10 ft) and 50 kg (110 lb). The conger can be found on the market all the year round, either whole (gutted and without the head), in pieces or sliced. The flesh, which is firm but rather tasteless, is particularly suitable for soups and *matelotes* (chaudrée, cotriade). Slices cut between the middle of the body and the head (having less bones than the tail) can be roasted.

CONGOLAIS A small biscuit (cookie) or sweet (candy) made of Italian meringue with grated coconut. It is also known as 'coconut rock'.

CONSOMMÉ Meat, poultry or fish broth served hot or cold as a soup course, generally at dinner, at the beginning of the meal. Consommé may be used as a rich stock and the basis for other, more complicated, soups or dishes. Other ingredients may be added to clear consommé as a garnish. Thinly sliced meat, vermicelli, tapioca, mixed vegetables, bone marrow, poached eggs, grated cheese, croûtons, little quenelles or ravioli are typical examples. True consommé is clarified both by careful preparation, without stirring or boiling rapidly, and by boiling with egg whites before straining. Alternatively, egg whites can be added in the first stage of preparation to give a clear soup without two separate cooking stages. Double consommé is a reduced, full-flavoured clarified broth which may be garnished in many different ways depending on the base from which it is made. Beef and chicken are the most common bases; game or fish and seafood may be used. Consommés may be thickened with arrowroot or with egg yolks and cream to make a richer soup. Cold consommés are normally placed in the refrigerator 1–2 hours before serving. They may be lightly jellied from ingredients used to flavour the broth (poultry or meat bones) or additional gelatine can be added and the consommé served diced, as a type of savoury jelly.

RECIPES

Basic Consommés
simple beef consommé
Cut up 2 kg (4½ lb) lean beef and 1.5 kg (3¼ lb) shin of beef (beef shank) (with bone) and put them into a big stockpot. (To extract the maximum amount of flavour from the bones, ask the butcher to break them into chunks.) Add 7 litres (12 pints, 7½ quarts) cold water. Bring to the boil and carefully remove the scum that forms on the surface. Season with coarse salt (it is better to adjust seasoning at the end than to add too much at the beginning). Add 3 or 4 large carrots, 400 g (14 oz) turnips, 100 g (4 oz) parsnips, 350 g (12 oz) leeks tied in a bundle, 2 celery sticks, sliced, a medium-sized onion with 2 cloves stuck in it, a garlic clove, a sprig of thyme and half a bay leaf. Simmer very slowly so that boiling is hardly perceptible, for 4 hours. Remove the meat and very carefully strain the stock. Remove surplus fat carefully.

clear beef consommé
For 3 litres (5 pints, 13 cups) stock, use 800 g (1¾ lb) lean beef, chopped and trimmed, 100 g (4 oz) carrots, 100 g (4 oz) leeks and 2 egg whites. Clean the vegetables and cut into small dice. Put them into a pan with the chopped beef and the egg whites. Add the stock cold, or at most, tepid. Heat gently, stirring constantly, until the stock is just boiling. Then reduce the heat, if necessary, to prevent

the stock from boiling, and simmer slowly for 1½ hours. Remove surplus fat and strain the consommé through a damp cloth.

simple chicken consommé

Proceed as for simple beef consommé, but replace the lean beef by a small chicken and 3 or 4 giblets browned in the oven, and the shin of beef (beef shank) by 800 g (1¾ lb) veal knuckle. For clarification, proceed as for clear beef consommé, using 4 or 5 chopped chicken giblets instead of the chopped beef. The chicken may then be used for croquettes or patties.

simple fish consommé

For 5 litres (8½ pints, 5½ quarts) consommé use 1.5 kg (3¼ lb) pike, 575 g (1¼ lb) white fish bones, 1 kg (2¼ lb) turbot heads, 300 g (11 oz) onions, 200 g (7 oz) leeks, 75 g (3 oz, 1 cup) parsley sprigs, 25 g (1 oz) celery, a sprig of thyme, a bay leaf, 2 tablespoons salt and 600 ml (1 pint, 2½ cups) white wine.

Proceed as for simple beef consommé, but chop the onions and leeks finely and boil slowly for 45 minutes only. Strain the stock through a sieve. To clarify the consommé, use 1.5 kg (3¼ lb) whiting or chopped pike, 150 g (5 oz) leeks, 50 g (2 oz, ¾ cup) parsley sprigs, and 4 egg whites. Proceed as for clear beef consommé, but cook very slowly and only for about 30 minutes; finally strain the consommé.

simple game consommé

For 5 litres (8½ pints, 5½ quarts) consommé, use the following: 2 kg (4½ lb) shoulder or neck of venison, 1 kg (2¼ lb) forequarter of hare or the equivalent of rabbit, an old pheasant and an old partridge (these proportions may be modified according to availability), 300 g (11 oz) carrots, 300 g (11 oz) leeks, 300 g (11 oz) onions, 150 g (5 oz) celery, 50 g (2 oz, ¾ cup) parsley sprigs, 2 garlic cloves, 2 thyme sprigs, a bay leaf, 50 g (2 oz, ⅓ cup) juniper berries, 3 cloves and salt.

Clean the game, then brown it in a lightly greased pan in a prehetaed oven at about 240°C (475°F, gas 9). Put the game (including the meat juices) into the stockpot, add 6 litres (10 pints, 6½ quarts) cold water and bring to the boil. Meanwhile prepare and chop the vegetables, and brown them in the pan. Tie the juniper berries and the cloves in a muslin (cheesecloth) bag. When the stock has come to the boil, add the vegetables and herbs and return to the boil. Simmer gently for 3½ hours. Remove surplus fat and strain the stock. It is now ready to serve as a soup or to be clarified in the same way as beef stock.

The game used in this consommé can be boned, made into a purée or salpicon, and used for various garnishes.

Cold Consommés

These recipes will make about 1.5 litres (2¾ pints, 6½ cups) consommé.

celery-flavoured consommé

Use beef or chicken consommé. Finely chop the inner sticks of a head of celery and add to the other ingredients when clarifying the consommé.

consommé with wine

Use beef consommé. Strain the consommé and when nearly cold add 150 ml (¼ pint, ⅔ cup) Madeira, Marsala, port or sherry.

tarragon-flavoured consommé

Use chicken consommé. Add 20 g (¾ oz, ¼ cup) fresh tarragon leaves to the consommé after it has been clarified and before straining, and leave to infuse.

truffle-flavoured consommé

Use beef or chicken consommé. Add 40 g (1½ oz, ⅓ cup) fresh truffle peelings to the consommé 5 minutes before it has finished clarifying, and pour 1 tablespoon port or sherry into each soup dish.

Hot Consommés with Garnishes

consommé à la parisienne

Use chicken consommé. Garnish the consommé with shredded vegetables lightly cooked in butter, rounds of plain *royales* and chervil leaves.

consommé à l'impériale

Use chicken consommé. Poach some very small cockscombs and cock's kidneys in stock. Cook 1½ tablespoons rice in the consommé, adding 1–2 tablespoons garden peas cooked in water, the cockscombs and kidneys, and finely shredded savoury pancakes.

consommé à l'infante

Use chicken consommé. Fill 20 small profiteroles with a purée of foie gras mixed with a thick chicken velouté. Thicken the consommé with arrowroot and serve with the profiteroles.

consommé au diablotins

Use chicken consommé. Prepare a number of very small *diablotins*. Lightly thicken the consommé with tapioca and garnish with the *diablotins*.

consommé Bizet

Use chicken consommé. Make some very small chicken quenelles mixed with chopped tarragon leaves and poach them in the consommé. Clarify the consommé and thicken it lightly with tapioca. Garnish with quenelles and sprinkle with chervil leaves. Serve immediately with very small profiteroles filled with a *brunoise* of vegetables, which have been braised in butter.

consommé Brillat-Savarin ♦

Use chicken consommé. Thicken the consommé with cornflour (cornstarch) or leave it thin, as preferred. Garnish with 1½ tablespoons finely shredded breast of poached chicken,

1½ tablespoons savoury pancakes cut up into very small diamond shapes, and 1½ tablespoons mixed finely shredded lettuce and sorrel. Sprinkle with chervil leaves.

consommé chasseur
Use game consommé. Cook 2 tablespoons finely shredded mushrooms in 3 tablespoons Madeira. Thicken the consommé slightly with tapioca. Add the mushrooms and sprinkle with chervil leaves. Small profiteroles filled with game purée may be served at the same time.

consommé Colbert
Use chicken consommé. Garnish the consommé with 3 tablespoons finely shredded vegetables cooked in butter and poach 1 egg in the consommé for each person. Sprinkle with chervil leaves.

consommé croûte au pot
Use beef consommé. Dry some hollowed-out bread crusts in the oven. Sprinkle each one with a little stockpot fat and brown lightly or garnish with chopped stockpot vegetables. Serve with the consommé.

consommé Dalayrac
Use chicken consommé. Thicken the consommé with tapioca. Garnish with shredded breast of chicken, mushrooms cooked in a court-bouillon and truffles.

consommé Florette
Use beef consommé. Cook 150 g (5 oz, ¾ cup) shredded leek lightly in butter, moisten with consommé and reduce. Cook 1½ tablespoons rice in consommé and add the leek. Serve with double (heavy) cream and grated Parmesan cheese.

consommé Léopold
Use beef consommé. Lightly cook 2 tablespoons shredded sorrel in butter. Cook 4 teaspoons semolina in the consommé, then add the sorrel and some chervil leaves.

consommé Leverrier
Use chicken consommé. Thicken the consommé with tapioca and garnish with *royales* cut into star shapes and chervil leaves.

consommé Monte-Carlo
Use beef consommé. Cut some very thin slices of bread into circles; butter, sprinkle with Parmesan and toast lightly. Serve with the consommé.

consommé Pépita
Use chicken consommé. Prepare a tomato *royale* and cut it into dice. Peel a green sweet pepper, chop it finely and cook in a little consommé. Season 4 teaspoons tomato purée (paste) with paprika and add it to the consommé, along with the *royale* and the pepper. (The *royale* may be omitted.)

consommé Princess Alice
Use beef consommé. Separately cook shredded artichoke hearts (enough for 2 tablespoons) and finely shredded lettuce (enough for 1 heaped tablespoon) in butter. Cook 2 tablespoons fine vermicelli in the consommé, add the artichoke and lettuce garnishes, and finally some chervil leaves.

consommé princesse
Use chicken consommé. Cook 15 green asparagus tips in butter. Prepare 15 small chicken forcemeat quenelles and poach them in stock. Add them to the consommé with the asparagus tips and some chervil leaves.

consommé with chicken pinions
Use chicken consommé. Poach in a simple consommé 4 chicken pinions and 2 necks cut into 3–4 sections and tied in a muslin (cheesecloth) bag. When they are cooked, clarify the stock, cut the meat up into even pieces and add it to the clarified consommé.

consommé with profiteroles
Use beef, chicken or game consommé. Prepare 20 small profiteroles filled with a purée of meat, game, vegetables or chicken. Thicken the consommé with tapioca and sprinkle with chervil leaves. Place the profiteroles in an hors d'oeuvre dish and serve with the consommé.

consommé with rice
Use beef, fish or game consommé. Cook 65–75 g (2½–3 oz, ½ cup) rice in simple beef consommé. Add it to the consommé chosen for a base and cook for about 20 minutes. Serve with grated cheese.

other recipes See *amiral, brancas, brunoise, julienne, madrilène, nesselrode, oxtail, reine, royale, Saint-Hubert, tapioca.*

CONSTANTIA A wine from one of the oldest wine estates in South Africa, planted towards the end of the 17th century in the vicinity of Cape Town. It became very popular in Britain in the 19th century and also in France, where it was known as 'Vin de Constance' – a full-bodied sweet dessert wine, based on the Muscat Blanc à Petits Grains grape. Today, however, fine table wines are made on the property, which has been rehabilitated by the government.

CONTI The name given, in classic French cookery, to dressings made from lentils. For meat which is roasted, fried or braised, the garnish consists of a lentil purée cooked with streaky bacon cut into strips. Another Conti garnish consists of croquettes

Consommé Brillat-Savarin, see page 331.

of lentil purée accompanied by potato rissoles. For eggs *sur le plat à la Conti*, the lentil purée should be piped along the edge of the dish. For Conti soup, the purée is diluted with stock and fresh butter and croûtons are added.

It is possible that these dressings were originally dedicated to the Prince of Conti, who employed in his kitchen two of the three famous 'Provençal brothers', Barthélemy and Simon.

CONTISER A term for the process of encrusting chicken fillets, or those of game or fish (chiefly sole), with truffles or other ingredients cut in the shape of little cockscombs. These are soaked in egg white so as to make them adhere properly and set at regular intervals into cuts made in the fillets.

CONTRE-FILET See *faux-filet.*

CONVERSATION A small pastry with an almond filling. According to the *Dictionnaire de l'Académie des gastronomes*, they were created at the end of the 18th century, taking their name from the title of a popular work, *Les Conversations d'Émilie*, by Mme d'Épinay (1774). They consist of covered puff pastry tartlets filled with a rum-flavoured frangipane or with almond cream and topped by a layer of royal icing (frosting). The tartlets are decorated with thin bands of pastry crisscrossed over the top.

RECIPE

conversations
Break 3 eggs, separating the yolks from the whites. Work 150 g (5 oz, ⅔ cup) butter into a paste with a wooden spatula, adding 150 g (5 oz, ⅔ cup) caster (superfine) sugar, then the 3 yolks one by one. Mix well, then add 175 g (6 oz, 1½ cups) ground almonds, 50 g (2 oz, ½ cup) cornflour (cornstarch) and 1 teaspoon vanilla-flavoured sugar. Beat thoroughly to obtain a well blended mixture.

Cut 400 g (14 oz) puff pastry into 3 portions, 2 of them equal, the third smaller. Roll out the 2 equal portions into sheets and use one of them to line 8 greased tartlet moulds. Fill each tartlet with the almond cream and moisten the edges of the pastry with water. Then place the moulds close together and cover them with the second sheet of pastry. Pass the rolling pin over this, cutting the pastry off on the rims of the moulds.

Whisk 2 of the egg whites until stiff, adding 200 g (7 oz, 1¼ cups) icing (confectioner's) sugar. Spread this icing (frosting) over the tartlets. Roll out the remaining pastry, cut it into thin strips and inter-twine these in diamond shapes on the icing. Leave for 15 minutes before cooking in a preheated oven at 190°C (375°F, gas 5) for 30 minutes. Allow them to cool before serving.

CONVIVIALITY The satisfaction felt by people enjoying a meal together. In *L'Amphitryon d'aujour-d'hui* (1936), Maurice des Ombiaux wrote: 'The spirit of sociability, of cordiality, of conviviality, lies at the heart of all gastronomy.'

Among all traditions the communal partaking of nourishment has been of socially fundamental importance. Hence the symbols of welcome, especially in Russian civilization and in the civilizations of the Middle East: a stranger is welcomed by the sharing of bread and salt, or by the offer of a drink of tea. A meal shared creates mutual rights and obligations: the host protects his guest, but the guest respects the rules of whoever receives him and should not betray the confidence of his host.

In feudal society, the knight about to be honoured had the right to carve the peacock or the pheasant; it was the custom for one partaker of the feast to have a morsel of his choosing carried to another by a page. In all societies, every circumstance in life from birth to death, every event of a social or religious nature, is celebrated by a meal, the distribution of cakes or confectionery, or by some sort of special food. Meals taken together for some special occasion even today proceed in accordance with protocol and good manners.

COOKER (STOVE) A cooking appliance operating by gas, electricity, oil or solid fuel. Gas and electric cookers are the most popular today, and have largely replaced the more traditional cooking range that was fired by coal or wood. Most cookers consist of a hob (stove top) with several burners and an oven. There is sometimes a separate compartment for grilling (broiling) food situated either at eye level, just above the oven, or inside the oven. Cookers do not always include oven and hob – these may be housed separately in two appliances, using different fuels, such as a gas hob and electric oven.

In Britain the words 'cooker' and 'range' remained synonymous for a considerable period of time. Édouard de Pomiane called the gas cooker a range in 1934 when he wrote an article describing its merits: 'The gas range has a much greater heating surface than your enormous coal-burning cooker. On the front, you have two burners, but both burners provide equal amounts of heat, while on an average coal-burning cooker, there is one very good source of heat and another on which it is impossible to boil a saucepan of water! The gas range is one of the most important discoveries made by the inventive genius of man.' Shortly afterwards, electricity began to be used more frequently, first for special boiling rings and then for complete cookers. Gas and electricity from then on were the two greatest sources of power for cookers, but certain models, especially those used in the country, are still designed to operate with wood, coal or other domestic fuel.

Ranges in traditional solid-fuel style, with two or more ovens and extensive cooking space on top, are available fuelled by oil, gas or electricity. In the same way as traditional solid-fuel ranges, these appliances can also provide a supply of hot water, as well as heat a room. Contemporary domestic cooking appliances provide a high degree of temperature control, both for hob-top cooking, in the oven and under the grill. From this simple standard, the choice broadens to include a wide variety of sophisticated options.

COOKERY BOOKS The oldest cookery book in the world was undoubtedly that of Archestratus (4th century BC), but unfortunately it has not survived. A few centuries later, however, Apicius and Athenaeus produced works that were for many centuries considered to be the main authorities on culinary matters. The first medieval cookery book was written in French (rather than Latin) and dates from the early 14th century. Two of its most striking aspects are that the recipes require large quantities of spices and that it contains a wealth of recipes for fish and game. But the first real cookery books, giving details of the different ways of preparing food, cooking techniques and recipes, were Taillevent's *Viandier* (c. 1380) and the anonymous *Ménagier de Paris* (1392–94). These two books which were the authoritative works until virtually the 17th century, are full of recipes for spicy sauces, stews, soups, tarts, pâtés, roast meat, and flans. A treatise by the Italian humanist Platina in 1474 brought the art of good cooking back into fashion.

Apart from the interest in literary history, books on food and cooking provide an overview of evolving culinary fashions and food philosophy. Taking French publications as examples, the first important changes came with the Italian cooks who arrived in France with Catherine de Medici. Their influence was seen in the introduction of new sweet dishes, jams and crystallized (candied) fruit. *Le Bastiment de recettes*, published in Venice and translated in Lyon in the same year (1541), was a manual for making fruit preserves. It inspired the Frenchman Jehan Bonfons to write *La Manière de faire toutes confitures* (1550) and Nostradamus to produce his *Opuscule à tous nécessaire qui désirent avoir connaissance de plusieurs exquises receptes* (1555). During the Renaissance and the period up to the beginning of the 17th century, the royal physicians contributed to culinary literature. Jacques Pons' *Le Traité des melons* (1583) and Joseph du Chesne's *Le Pourtrait de santé* (1606) recommended certain fruit remedies, preferred game to domestic animals and laid down set times for meals, and *Le Trésor de santé* (J.A. Huguetan, 1607) contained a wealth of vegetable and herb recipes. Books on agriculture also had an influence on the cuisine of that period, especially *Le Théâtre d'agriculture* (1600) by Olivier de Serres and *La Maison rustique*, published at the end of the 17th century.

An important turning point came in the 17th century with the publication of La Varenne's *Cuisinier français*, which was a proper recipe book. La Varenne also wrote one of the first books about pâtisserie. Another great cook, Pierre de Lune, produced a treatise on cookery (*Le Cuisinier*, 1656), while servants' duties at table and in the house were set down in *L'Ecole des officiers de bouche* (1662). New food products brought new books, including

Traités nouveaux et curieux du café, du thé, et du chocolat (1685), by Philippe Sylvestre Dufour, and French cookery became both more sophisticated and simpler, as seen in *L'Art de bien traiter* (1674), signed 'L.S.R.', one of the most remarkable collections of recipes of its time. Two important contributions to culinary literature date from the end of the 17th century: Massialot's *Le Cuisinier royal et bourgeois* (he had already published *Nouvelles Instructions pour les confitures*) and Audiger's *La Maison réglée* (1692).

The 18th century brought with it a boom in the publication of cookery books, most notable of which were: *L'Abstinence de la viande rendue aisée* (1700), by Doctor B. Linand, which claimed that Lenten fasts did no harm to the body and which also provided many vegetarian recipes; *Le Traité des aliments* (1702) by Louis Lemery, a great advocate of vegetarian food, famous for the lessons in chemistry and natural science that he gave in the Jardin du Roi; *Le Cuisinier moderne* (1735; first published in English as *The Modern Cook* in 1733) by La Chapelle, the creator of a sophisticated and methodical way of cooking and the only man acknowledged by Carême to be his superior; *Le Festin joyeux* (1738) by J. Lebai, in which cookery is perceived as a challenge of orchestration; *Les Dons de Comus ou les Délices de la table* (1739) by Marin, who came down on the side of 'modern' cookery in this, the first complete manual on the theory of the culinary arts; *Le Cuisinier gascon* (1740), published anonymously by the Prince des Dombes, which brought together some rather strange-sounding dishes (chicken in bat, wooden-leg soup, veal in donkey's dung). Menon's works mark the return of the great classic tome: *La Cuisinière bourgeoise* (1746) and *Les Soupers de la Cour* (1755), among others, are massive volumes (400 pages on poultry in the latter, and countless recipes using truffles, sweetbreads and foie gras, as well as some amazing pâtisserie recipes). Sweets and desserts were also in their heyday, as shown by *Le Cannaméliste français* (Gilliers, 1751) and *L'Art de bien faire les glaces d'office* (Emery, 1768).

The democratic wind of the Revolution even extended to the kitchens. A Parisian bookseller, Madame Mérigot, wrote and published *La Cuisinière républicaine* (1794), a collection of basic and inexpensive recipes (potato was a popular ingredient). The following year saw the appearance of *Le Petit Cuisinier économe* by Jannet, another bookseller, who published his *Le Manuel de la friandise ou les Talents de ma cuisinière Isabeau mis en lumière*, inspired by the works of Menon, in 1796.

The great renaissance in French cuisine did not come until the first decades of the 19th century, with such chefs as Viard, with his *Cuisinier impérial* (1810), and, of course, Carême, whose writings on all kinds of cookery were seminal – *Le Pâtissier royal parisien* (1815), *Le Cuisinier parisien* (1828) and *L'Art de la cuisine française au XIXe siècle* (finished by Plumerey, 1843–44). The 19th century also saw restaurateurs putting pen to paper, including

Beauvilliers with his *L'Art du cuisinier* (1814), and their more discerning customers were not to be left out: Grimod de La Reynière (*Almanach des gourmands*, 1803–12), Brillat-Savarin (*La Physiologie du goût*, 1825), the Marquis de Cussy (*L'Art culinaire*, 1835), Colnet (*L'Art de dîner en ville*, 1810), Cadet de Gassicourt (*Les Dîners de Manant-Ville*, 1809) and Berchoux (*La Gastronomie*, 1801). Gastronomy and the art of cooking had become a literary genre, with Alexandre Dumas *père* as its foremost exponent (*Le Grand Dictionnaire de cuisine*, 1873); it was even the province of journalists, with Monselet's *Almanach des gourmands* (1863–70) and *La Cuisinière poétique* and Baron Brisse's 366 menus which appeared in *La Liberté*.

But the great chefs continued to publish theoretical and practical books which are accurate guides to the way that cooking in that era was practised and taught. Among these are Urbain Dubois' *La Cuisine classique* (1856), Jules Gouffé's *Livre de cuisine* (1867) and works by Garlin.

With the dawn of the 20th century, cookery books began to become very diversified. Great French chefs such as Montagné, Nignon, Escoffier, Guillot, Denis Oliver, Paul Bocuse and Chapel contributed publications. Technological advances brought colour illustrations and new media into the business of importing information. Television provides cooks and presenters with opportunities for showing precisely how to approach ingredients and techniques. More so than ever before, programme-makers, traditional and electronic publishers are not only in a position to chart culinary history but also to influence trends at the broadest level. Television and computing brings information and ideas into the home at the flick of a switch or twitch of a mouse.

COOKIE The American term for a sweet biscuit. Cookies are flavoured with various ingredients such as chocolate chips, ginger, walnuts or pecan nuts.

COOKING The process of heating food so as to render it safe and palatable. While some foods have to be cooked before eating, others are usually consumed raw and many may be eaten either raw or cooked, depending on the result required. The reasons for cooking are not always purely aesthetic, but they may be for food safety. Cooking can destroy natural toxins that make some raw foods poisonous – dried kidney beans and other beans are a good example. Cooking also makes food digestible.

The effect of cooking depends on the method used, the type of food and additional ingredients. Complex chemical changes take place during preparation and cooking to alter the appearance, texture, flavour and aroma of food.

Food may become tender or firm on cooking. Solid fats melt, oils become more fluid and foods with a high fat content, such as cheese, soften and may become runny. Other types of food soften – vegetables and fruit become tender, then soft and they may break down; rice and grains (and their products) absorb liquid to swell and become soft. The texture of protein foods, such as fish, poultry and meat, changes from soft to firm during cooking; eggs are gradually set from a liquid to solid texture. As meat becomes firm, rather than soft and 'flabby', the connective tissue in tough cuts slowly softens and breaks down to give a result that is firm, but tender, rather than chewy.

As the food changes it may absorb flavours of other ingredients or release flavour. Substances contained in the food often separate out or are released and they may be important for the success of some methods. For example, fat is visibly rendered from some meat and it often helps to keep the food moist. Pectin, a gel-like substance in some fruit, is released during cooking; when sugar is boiled with the cooked fruit and pectin-rich juices, the mixture forms a gel when cool – this is vital for the success of jams and jellies.

■ **Cooking methods** Cooking can be broadly divided into moist or dry methods. For example, boiling, simmering, braising, stewing, poaching and steaming are moist methods; frying, grilling (broiling), roasting and baking are dry methods. Traditional methods rely on transmitting heat to the food from an outside source by physical conduction of heat from the source, as when placing food in a hot pan and when the heat travels through the food itself. The food may be heated by convection, as when boiling, or by circulating hot air around the food, as when baking; or by radiation, as when exposing food to a radiant heat source, such as a grill (broiler). In practice, heat travels by more than one method and through the food during cooking. Microwave cooking relies on a process of generating heat within the food itself; as foods contain moisture, the internal heat makes the water content evaporate and creates a cooking environment similar to high-speed steaming from the inside out. Therefore in broad terms, microwave cooking is a moist method – it does not produce results associated with dry techniques, such as grilling, roasting or baking.

The choice of method depends on the type of food and result required. Food does not brown, become crisp or form a crust when cooked by moist methods, but all of these are possible when dry methods are used. These fundamental differences are reflected in flavour, appearance and texture.

■ **Moist methods** These can produce two extremes of flavour, depending on the technique used. Comparatively short steaming, boiling, simmering and poaching allow the clear, simple flavour of an ingredient to prevail; by contrast, long, slow braising and stewing can produce a deep, intense result.

Moist methods are ideal for delicate foods that require brief cooking, for example as when poaching eggs or fish; they are necessary for softening grains and hard dry ingredients that soften when they absorb liquid; and they are essential for giving tender results with tough meats.

The amount of liquid used varies – a large quantity is used for some boiling; the minimum amount is used to create a moist environment when sweating ingredients. Moist and dry methods are combined in pot-roasting, where a little liquid is used in a tightly closed pot in the oven.

■ **Dry methods** These can be fierce and ideal for tender foods that cook quickly. Fish, poultry and tender meat can be roasted, grilled or fried. Although they are dry methods, oil or other fat may be added to prevent the food from drying out and to encourage browning or give a crisp result. Dry methods are not suitable for tough foods or ingredients that require moisture to become soft.

The fat used and the process of browning makes a marked difference to the flavour of the food. The 'raw' or natural flavours are changed. These methods are often used as a first stage for moist methods, for example to soften onions or brown meat or vegetables before making a soup, sauce or casserole.

Whereas roasting is a process of cooking food uncovered at comparatively high heat, basting with fat, baking can be at a low, medium or high temperature. Baking is associated with breads, cakes and pastries, where the heat is used to make food rise, set and form a crust; but it is also used when ingredients such as meat or vegetables are cooked at a slower pace than roasting, possibly covered or part-covered.

COOKING BALL
A perforated metal utensil of variable size consisting of two halves that open, either to enclose food that needs to be cooked in boiling water, or to immerse dried plants for infusion.

• THE TEA EGG is a round or oval utensil, the size of an egg, made of aluminium or stainless steel and perforated with small holes. It is filled with tea or any other plant for infusion and plunged into boiling water in a teapot. It prevents the dispersion of the tea leaves and makes it easier to clean the teapot. A spoon version also exists for making tea directly in the cup.

• THE RICE BALL is an aluminium spherical utensil with a diameter of about 15 cm (6 in) and with slightly larger holes than the tea egg. It should never be more than half-filled, as rice swells during cooking. It is primarily used for cooking rice in the stock remaining after a chicken has been cooked. It is then used as a garnish. Rice balls are also used to enclose aromatic ingredients used to flavour a dish, at the same time preventing their dispersal through the liquid.

• THE VEGETABLE BALL is an oval wire basket in two halves joined by a hook. It enables the vegetables to be removed from the liquid in which they were cooked without having to strain the liquid.

COOLER
A deep cylindrical or oval receptacle made of glass, china or metal. Bottles are plunged into the iced or salted water in the container to keep cool. The cooler can also be set on the table to serve certain foods which must be eaten very cold, such as caviar; it sometimes has a double bottom, which contains crushed ice.

Coolers have been in use since the Middle Ages;

in the 17th and 18th centuries they formed part of the table setting. Glasses, particularly champagne glasses, could be cooled in china receptacles with sloping deeply channelled sides in which the glasses were placed upside down.

COPPA
Italian or Corsican charcuterie, a type of salami, made by deboning and trimming loin or collar of pork, curing and marinating it with garlic and red wine. It is then rolled out and tied in gut or sausage skin. *Coppa*, or *coppa crudo* as it is sometimes known to distinguish it from the similar product mentioned below (made from all the scraps left over from the pig's carcass), has a fine flavour. It is served raw, cut in thin slices as for prosciutto or Parma ham. It can also be used as bacon. The word means 'nape of the neck' in Italian and in fact it is the part of the loin near the neck that is used.

There is another type of *coppa* made from the remnants of the pig carcass, highly seasoned and cooked, and quite different from *coppa crudo*.

COPPER
A reddish metal used in the manufacture of many cooking utensils. It is an excellent conductor of heat and cooking pans with a copper base distribute heat evenly. Copper heats up and cools down rapidly and therefore enables greater control to be exercised in certain cooking methods (such as simmering). Although uncoated copper was popular for cooking utensils, especially in professional kitchens, the uncoated metal reacts with food and liquids, particularly acidic ingredients, and corrodes quickly, forming an oxide coating that is toxic when eaten in significant amounts or regularly.

To avoid all direct contact with food, copper pans are coated inside, the older or cheaper ones with a layer of tin, which has to be renewed regularly. Good-quality pans combine copper with a coating of stainless steel. Copper bowls with a round bottom are traditional containers in which to whisk egg whites as the reaction between the metal and the whites strengthens them, giving a better volume and more stable whisked whites. Since only a small amount of copper is transferred to the whites and they are not eaten often, these bowls are still used in some kitchens. Copper preserving pans, once popular for boiling acidic fruit and giving a sparkling result, should never be used.

COPRA
The dried kernel of the coconut, from which an oil is extracted. This oil, called coconut oil or copra oil, is then refined and used in the manufacture of margarine.

COQ
The French word for a cock and now used as a synonym for chicken in certain dishes. In traditional stock farming, cocks which were good breeders were kept as long as they could fulfil their function. They would be several years old before they were killed and therefore needed long and slow braising in a casserole (*coq au vin*). Nowadays, coq au vin is usually made with a chicken or hen.

The combs and the kidneys of the cock serve as a garnish, rare now; but frequently used in the elaborate cuisine of former days.

RECIPES

coq au vin
(from an old recipe) Cut up a chicken of about 1.8 kg (4 lb) into 6 pieces. Gently fry 90 g (3½ oz, ⅔ cup) diced lean bacon and about 20 small onions (pearl onions) in 40 g (1½ oz, 3 tablespoons) butter in an earthenware or cast iron pot. When these are lightly browned, add the chicken pieces, 1 finely chopped garlic clove, a bouquet garni and about 20 morels or other mushrooms. Sauté, covered, over a brisk heat until golden. Remove the lid and skim off the fat. Pour a little good brandy over the chicken, set light to it, then pour on 500 ml (17 fl oz, 2 cups) old Auvergne wine (a Chambertin or a Mâcon). After cooking over a brisk heat for about 1¼ hours, take out the chicken, thicken the sauce with beurre manié, and pour it over the chicken.

coq en pâte
Despite its name, this dish is usually prepared with a fine roasting chicken (*poularde*). When the chicken has been dressed and singed, remove the breastbone and stuff it copiously with a mixture of foie gras and large pieces of truffle (seasoned with salt and spices, and moistened with a little Cognac) and a small quantity of fine forcemeat. Truss the chicken, tucking the legs into the sides. Brown on all sides in butter – about 20 g, (¾ oz, 1½ tablespoons). Cover the chicken with a *matignon** of braising vegetables – about 300 g (11 oz, 2 cups) – and wrap it in a pig's caul soaked in cold water and wiped dry.

Make some lining pastry using 500 g (18 oz, 4½ cups) plain (all-purpose) flour, 300 g (11 oz, 1⅓ cups) butter, 1 egg, 100 ml (4 fl oz, 7 tablespoons) water and 1½ teaspoons salt. Place the chicken on an oval sheet of pastry and cover it with a similar sheet. Pinch the edges together. (Nowadays, the chicken is usually put in an oval terrine which exactly contains it and then simply covered with chosen short pastry.) Brush the pastry with egg and cut several slits in the top to allow steam to escape.

Cook in a preheated oven at 190°C (375°F, gas 5) for about 1½ hours, protecting the top of the pastry with foil once it is browned. *Coq en pâte* is traditionally accompanied by a Périgueux sauce served separately.

country-style coq au vin ♦
Cut 1 cockerel into pieces and season well. Peel 12 small pickling or pearl onions. Scald 125 g (4½ oz) lean bacon rashers (slices). Melt 50 g (2 oz, ¼ cup) butter and 1 tablespoon oil in a casserole. Add the bacon and onions and fry until golden. Remove and drain thoroughly. Brown the pieces of cockerel in the fat in the casserole, turning them over several times. Return the bacon and onions to the casserole. Heat 1 tablespoon Cognac, pour into the casserole and ignite. Pour in 750 ml (1¼ pints, 3¼ cups) red wine, 1 bouquet garni and 2 crushed garlic gloves. Bring slowly to the boil, cover and simmer for 1 hour.

Thinly slice 200 g (7 oz) button mushrooms. Fry in 25 g (1 oz, 2 tablespoons) butter and add to the casserole. Continue cooking for another 20–25 minutes. A few minutes before serving, cream 50 g (2 oz, ¼ cup) butter with 1 tablespoon flour. Gradually stir in a little cooking liquid from the casserole, then pour this mixture slowly into the casserole. Cook, stirring, for 5 minutes, then add 3 tablespoons of cockerel blood and allow to thicken, without boiling, for 5 minutes, stirring constantly. Serve with steamed potatoes or fresh pasta.

Mme Maigret's coq au vin
Prepare and finely slice a carrot, a leek and an onion. Cut up a chicken of about 2 kg (4½ lb) into pieces. Put the vegetables, a bouquet of parsley and the chicken legs into a pot. Pour over 300 ml (½ pint, 1¼ cups) water and cook gently for 30 minutes to obtain a chicken stock.

Meanwhile cut 2 carrots in round slices and chop 4 shallots and 2 garlic cloves. In another pot brown the remaining chicken pieces in 2 tablespoons lard (shortening) over a brisk heat. Take these out and put in the carrot slices and the chopped shallots and garlic. Reduce the heat and lightly brown for 10 minutes. Put the chicken pieces back into the pot. Sprinkle with 1 tablespoon flour and stir.

Pour over the chicken stock – there should be about 100 ml (4 fl oz, 7 tablespoons) after reduction with the same quantity of Riesling. Season with salt and pepper, a little grated nutmeg and dried thyme. Cook for about 1½ hours (depending on the age of the chicken). Take out the chicken pieces and place them on a warm dish. Thicken the sauce away from the heat with an egg yolk thinned with 100 ml (4 fl oz, 7 tablespoons) single (light) cream. Finally, add the juice of a lemon and 2 teaspoons sloe brandy. Pour the sauce over the dish and serve.

other recipes See *beer, cider*.

COQUE A cake made in the south-west of France for the Easter celebrations. Shaped like a crown, it is made with brioche dough and crystallized (candied) fruit. The Limoux *coque* is flavoured with citron; in the Aveyron it is flavoured with citron, orange-flower water or rum. Very large *coques* were formerly made for the Feast of the Boatmen of the Tarn at Whitsun (the seventh Sunday after Easter), when the priest would bless the waters of the river (this tradition disappeared during the 1960s).

Country-style coq au vin.

COQUE, À LA The French term for describing the familiar method of cooking a soft-boiled (soft-cooked) egg, by immersing the whole egg for 3–4 minutes in boiling water and eating it from the shell. This expression is also applied to any food which is poached without peeling (peaches, for instance) or indeed to any which is eaten directly from its skin, such as avocados or artichokes.

RECIPE

avocado à la coque
Cut an avocado in half just before serving and remove the stone (pit). Pour into the centre a vinaigrette flavoured with chopped shallots, a mayonnaise to which a little lemon juice and tomato ketchup have been added or a tomato sauce with a dash of Worcestershire sauce.

COQUELET A young cock weighing 450–575 g (1–1¼ lb). Its meat, which has scarcely had time to mature, is rather tasteless. It may be roasted, grilled (broiled) or fried in breadcrumbs, and requires a sauce with a strong flavour (lemon, green pepper). Young cocks should not be cut into pieces; they are generally cut in two, lengthways.

RECIPE

coquelets en crapaudine à l'américaine
Split and flatten 2 young cocks as spatchcocks. Chop 2–3 garlic cloves and some parsley. Add salt, 3 tablespoons oil, a good quantity of pepper, 2 teaspoons ground ginger and a pinch of cayenne. Cover the cocks inside and outside with this mixture, then marinate them for 1 hour. Grill (broil) briskly and serve them with a green salad or mixed salad.

COQUES À PETITS FOURS Shell shapes made with ground almonds and a meringue mixture, joined together in pairs with a stiff fruit *marmelade* or other filling and glazed with fondant icing (frosting). These petits fours can alternatively be filled with flavoured French butter cream or chestnut cream.

COQUILLE À RÔTIR An old cooking utensil resembling a round box, made of cast iron or thick terracotta. This was filled with charcoal and used to roast meat and chicken on the spit, making it the ancestor of the modern spitroaster. It was still in use in many households at the end of the 19th century.

CORBIÈRES A large Languedoc vineyard of 14,000 hectares (34,500 acres) extending from Narbonne nearly to Carcassonne and as far as the northern regions of Roussillon. Its wines were elevated to AOC status in 1985; consequently production almost halved and quality improved. The main grape varieties are Carignan and Grenache although Syrah and Mourvèdre are also planted. The bulk of the production is red, although a little rosé and an even smaller quantity of white wine is also made. The hot hill-sides are conducive to full-bodied fruity wines, which sometimes develop a pronounced herby bouquet with some bottle age. A characteristic of red Corbières wines is that they are agreeable to drink when lightly chilled.

CORCELLET A famous Parisian seller of gourmet foods, who moved into the Beaujolais galleries, at the Palais-Royal, during the Empire. In his *Itinéraire gourmand*, Grimod de La Reynière enthusiastically praised his shop: 'One should be happy to know that it is hither that Strasbourg goose pâté de foie, Toulouse duck liver, Pithiviers larks, chickens and plovers from Chartres, Périgueux partridges, etc., are inclined to make their way when they arrive in Paris. Here they find themselves in familiar country with Nérac terrines, mortadellas from Lyons, sausages from Arles, little tongues from Troyes, the galantines of M. Prévost and other succulent compatriots.'

M. Corcellet left the Palais-Royal for the Avenue de l'Opéra at the end of the 19th century. His shop was still in business at the turn of the century, after several changes of management, on the Avenue Victor Hugo.

CORDÉE A French term: pastry is described as *cordée* when too much water has been used in the mixing, making it hard and tough. A purée is said to be *cordée* when the potatoes are pressed through a sieve with a rotary movement, which makes them sticky. (The potatoes should be pressed through the sieve vertically.)

CORDIAL A beverage, often sweet, which is generally alcoholic and aromatic. It is supposed to have a tonic effect, as the etymology of cordial suggests (from the Latin *cor*, heart). In France, the word has fallen into disuse, being used only for the names of certain so-called 'household' preparations (various squashes, creams and liqueurs), but in English-speaking countries it is occasionally used as a synonym for liqueur or brandy, to designate spirits with particular strength as well as a distinctive flavour.

CORDON BLEU This was originally a wide blue ribbon worn by members of the highest order of knighthood, L'Ordre des Chevaliers du Saint-Esprit, instituted by Henri III of France in 1578. By extension, the term has since been applied to food prepared to a very high standard and to outstanding cooks. The analogy no doubt arose from the similarity between the sash worn by the knights and the ribbons (generally blue) of a cook's apron. In *Paris à table* (1846), the words of Eugène Briffault have lost none of their force: 'Those who underestimate the feminine sex where culinary matters are concerned forget their high level of achievement which has earned them the accolade of cordon-bleu. It is impossible to bring more skill and delicacy, more taste and intelligence to the choice and preparation of dishes than women have brought.'

CORIANDER (CILANTRO) An aromatic umbelliferous plant used both for its dried seeds, either whole or ground and its leaves. The Hebrews flavoured their cakes with coriander seeds and the Romans made use of them for preserving meat. Charlemagne encouraged cultivation of the plant. In the 18th century, the seeds, covered with sugar, were chewed. However, coriander has played only a modest role in France (except in making such liqueurs as Izarra and Chartreuse) compared with the place it occupies elsewhere (in soups, with vegetables, in marinades and pastries). In Germany, coriander seeds are used for seasoning cabbage and in marinades for game. Their most classic uses are for the preparation of vegetables *à la grecque* and of pickles in vinegar.

Coriander leaves, sometimes known as Arab parsley or Chinese parsley in France and as cilantro in the United States, can be used like parsley: the leaves feature especially in the cuisine of China, South-east Asia, South America and Mexico.

CORKSCREW
An implement used to open a bottle sealed by a cork. The standard corkscrew has a spiral thread, which can be flat or rounded and is usually nickel-plated. The rounded stem is preferable because there is less risk of the cork crumbling. The spiral must be 6–8 cm (2¼–3½ in) long so that the cork, which is quite long in a good bottle, is pierced all the way through. Its tip must be sharp and designed in such a way that it is not centred in the spiral.

There are numerous models of corkscrew, some fitted with a casing to protect the neck of the bottle, others with a lever or even with a gearing-down system to limit the strain, but also to avoid moving the bottle too much. Some corkscrews are also fitted with a bottle opener and a blade for cutting the seal.

Another system operates with two blades of unequal length, which are inserted between the neck and the cork, and this obviates the need to pierce the cork. There is also a device which pierces the cork and injects gas underneath. This has the effect of effortlessly forcing out the cork. It is only recommended for a crumbly cork which is in danger of breaking.

CORN
See *maize*.

CORNAS
A northern Rhône AOC red wine, from the Vivarais side of the river valley. The Syrah is the basic grape. The Romans probably laid down the original vineyard when they came up the Rhône from the south and began to settle around here and in the foothills of the Massif Central. Emperor Charlemagne is said to have esteemed the full robust wine and, with some bottle age, it can develop very pleasantly. Revival of interest in the area has resulted in more vineyards being planted and much improved quality.

CORNED BEEF
Cured beef, of American origin, which may be sold in cans. Pieces of beef are cooked, preserved with salt or brine, and then canned with beef fat and jelly. From the end of the 19th century military slang gave the name 'bully beef' to the preserved beef distributed by the army. During World War I, the corned beef salvaged from American stocks was known as bully beef. It can be eaten cold with salad, or heated up and served with an onion sauce; in the United States it is mostly eaten in a hash or sandwiches.

CORNELIAN CHERRY
The edible fruit of a species of cornel, a shrub which grows in undergrowth and hedges in central and southern Europe. Cornelian cherries are picked in September, when they are red, fleshy, oval, about the same size as olives, and taste sharp and slightly oily. They can be eaten when very ripe on their own, made into jelly or preserved in sugar or honey; if they are picked when barely ripe, they can be preserved in brine.

CORNET
A cone-shaped pastry. The cornets used as ice-cream cones are made from wafer biscuit. Filled cornets (often known as cream horns) are usually made from puff pastry, cooked while rolled around cornet moulds, and then filled with confectioner's custard (pastry cream), Chiboust cream or Chantilly cream and decorated with chopped crystallized (candied) fruit. Murat cornets (a speciality of the Auvergne) are made from the mixture used for *langues de chats*, filled with sweetened whipped cream and sometimes decorated with candied violets.

The word is also used for a slice of ham or salmon rolled up, filled with a cold preparation and served as an hors d'oeuvre.

RECIPES

ham cornets with foie gras mousse
Roll up some small but fairly thick slices of ham into cornets. Fill them with foie gras mousse (using a piping bag). Arrange on a bed of lettuce or on a dish garnished with cubes of port-flavoured aspic jelly.

smoked salmon cornets with fish roe
Roll up some small slices of smoked salmon into cornets. Fill them with fish roe (caviar, salmon or lumpfish). Arrange them on a bed of shredded lettuce dressed with vinaigrette. Garnish with fluted lemon halves. The base of the cornet can be filled with a little cream mixed with a few drops of lemon juice and grated horseradish, or else this cream can be served in a sauceboat at the same time as the cornets, with hot blinis.

CORNISH PASTY
A pastry turnover traditionally made with short pastry but often made using puff pastry. Filled with a mixture of diced beef, onions, potatoes and other root vegetables. Originally from the county of Cornwall in England, they were lunchtime snacks for miners. The twisted pastry at the ends of the turnover acted as 'handles' for the men to hold, then discard when they were blackened by dirty fingers. Traditionally, large pasties were

CORSICA

A Mediterranean island, which is a French department. Corsican cookery is not well known internationally. The diversity of the natural resources of the island, which often do not travel well, give considerable individuality and refinement to Corsican cuisine. As well as typically Mediterranean products, such as olives, citrus fruits, tomatoes, aubergines (eggplants), it uses chestnuts (in *brilloi*, fritters, pancakes and cakes) and also fairly rare berries, such as those of the *arbutus*. Corsican dishes are not highly spiced; they make use of the herbs of the *maquis* (rosemary and thyme) and those of the garden (basil and mint), which are seldom used in Provençal cookery.

■ **Smoked meats** This originality can also be found in the traditional technique of the *fucone*: the fire lit on a clay slab heats the family room while its smoke, filtering through the laths of the ceiling to the loft, adds its flavour to the various products made from the pig killed in the autumn. The fame of Corsican charcuterie rests on the quality of its smoked specialities, such as *figatelli*, *coppa* and *lonzo*. Pickled pork (*petit salé*) is also used in some wonderful ragoûts with broad (fava) beans and red kidney beans. However, other meats are also worthy of the attention of the gastronome; roast kid, blackbirds fed on myrtle and *arbutus*, woodcock in salmis and mutton stew (*stufatu*).

■ **Fish** There is an even wider range of fish specialities in an island well provided with rivers and streams. They include the bouillabaisse (*ziminu*) from Corte, dried cod, eel in red wine (*tiano*), and fried trout. As in Provence, anchovies appear in many dishes, including *anchoyade*. The shellfish have a reputation for freshness.

■ **Flavours of Corsica** The Corsicans know how to enhance their cooking with spiced tomato purée or mushrooms, which are numerous and diverse in the countryside. Above all, Broccio brings excellent flavour to a wide variety of dishes. Thanks to this cheese, which is made from the whey of ewe's milk, some Italian specialities (such as lasagne and cannelloni) take on a special character when cooked Corsican style. The vegetables are also full of that 'freshly picked' flavour. They may be stuffed or used in fritters: courgettes (zucchini), aubergines (eggplants), artichokes, onions and leeks are all popular. Polenta, another dish that is popular in Italy, is here generally made from chestnut flour, which contributes its own bitter, smoky taste. The local tarts made with vegetables, herbs and Broccio have the same fabulous strength of flavour and there is no equivalent recipe on the mainland.

■ **Desserts** Corsican housewives are skilled at making desserts, in which Broccio is again a prime ingredient – without it, neither the fritters (*fritelles*) nor the custard creams (*fiadone*) would have their delicacy. Honey, pine kernels, bitter almonds and aniseed are also included in various specialities. Mention should also be made of Corsican crystallized (candied) citrus fruit, tomatoes and figs; wild fruit conserves; ratafias made from cherry, fig; and sorb apple, and myrtle liqueurs.

WINE The vin de pays name for certain wines of Corsica is 'Île de Beauté' and, although the terrain is well suited to vine cultivation, the wines were for many years neither well known nor well reputed outside their homeland. More recently, however, the vineyards have been expanding and the wines are mostly being made by producers well acquainted with modern technology, so that the overall standard of Corsican wines is much improved and certain of them have an AOC, notably those of Patrimonio. The fine wine region is the Cap Corse peninsula, homeland of the island's world-famous apéritif of the same name, but other wine areas include Bastia, Ajaccio, Calvi Caro, Sartène, Bonifacio and Santa Lucia di Tallano. The Corsican grapes tend to be of Italian origin: Sciaccarello, Nielluccio, Barbarosso (for the reds); Vermentino, Riminese, Rossola Bianca (for the whites); but in recent years some of the classic varieties, including Carignan, Cinsault and Syrah, have been successfully introduced on the island.

Napoleon is said always to have

The bay of Porto-Vecchio is typical of Corsica's wild beauty. The rugged rocks of hard, red porphyry descend dramatically to the deep-blue sea from mountains covered with maquis, the dense shrub that grows abundantly in these coastal regions.

had a bottle of Patrimonio on his table, and generations of tourists have appreciated the red, white and rosé wines. As might be expected from this sunny island, these are full-bodied and aromatic (Corsica is often referred to as 'the scented isle'), the rosé in particular being very charming and distinctive.

The smoking house is important for the preparation of Corsican charcuterie, which includes specialities such as figatelli *(the long thin sausages) and* coppa.

made with a savoury filling one side and sweet the other. In modern times, Cornish pasties are smaller and lighter, and served as a hot snack.

CORN SALAD See *lamb's lettuce*.

CORSÉ The French term used to describe strong black coffee. It is also used to describe a wine with a high alcoholic strength, of definite character, whose taste fills the mouth: the English equivalent is 'full-bodied' or 'robust'.

CORSICA See *opposite page*.

CORTINARIUS A genus of mushrooms of which there are very many species, most of them inedible and some highly poisonous and known to have caused fatalities. The mountain *cortinarius*, a species which is fairly rare in France, is deadly Among the edible types there is the oddly named remarkable (or Berkeley) *cortinarius*, which has a brown cap marked with white and violet. This mushroom is fleshy, has a pleasant fragrance and is well suited to stuffed preparations.

CORTON-CHARLEMAGNE An AOC white *grand cru* wine, from the parish of Aloxe-Corton but partly shared with Pernand-Vergelesses in the Côte de Beaune. It is a very great white Burgundy, but the vineyard, which is smallish anyway, suffers from being on steep slopes, so that there is a risk of the topsoil being brought down in heavy rain. Corton-Charlemagne is a noble and powerful fine wine, comparable in breeding to Meursault, although less soft. It needs ten years maturing to be at its best.

This section of the Corton hillside, thought to have been the personal property of Emperor Charlemagne, was ceded to the Abbey of St Andochre in 775.

COSTIÈRES-DE-NÎMES Formerly known as Costières-du-Gard and attributed AC status in 1986, these wines are the produce of the right bank of the Rhône, to the south of Nîmes. The wines are similar in style to those of Côtes-du-Rhône.

COTEAU The word means hillock and is often used to indicate the small undulations in the ground, as differentiated from the more definite slopes or foothills (*côtes*). The name was applied sarcastically in the 17th century to those who today would be dubbed wine snobs – gourmets who boasted that they could not only pick out blind the finest wines, but could actually distinguish the particular slope or the very vineyard from which a wine came. These self-styled connoisseurs came to be known as members of the 'Ordre des Coteaux'.

The original joke is said to have been made by the then Bishop of Le Mans, who had invited the Marquis de Saint-Évremond to dinner. (It was this gentleman who, exiled to England, introduced Charles II and his court to the pleasures of champagne, which he used to order to be sent to London from his friends' vineyards, including those owned by the Comte d'Olonne and the Marquis de Bois-Dauphin.) 'These gentlemen,' commented the Bishop, 'carry everything to extremes in an attempt at refinement. They disdain to drink unless the wine comes from one of the vineyards (*coteaux*) of Ai (Ay), Hautvillier (Hautvillers) or Avenay.' Saint-Évremond passed on this remark and soon the three friends became known as 'Les Trois Coteaux'. There is today an Ordre des Coteaux, for celebrating and promoting the wines of the Champagne region.

COTEAUX-CHAMPENOIS Still wines, with their own AOC. They may be red, white or rosé and are produced within the delimited Champagne area. Formerly they were referred to as 'champagne nature'.

COTEAUX-D'AIX-EN-PROVENCE Red and rosé AOC wines from a large appellation around Aix-en-Provence. Several estates have been replanted with Grenache, Cinsault and Mourvèdre grape varieties. A very small amount of white wine is also produced.

COTEAUX-D'ANCIENS VDQS wines from the area around Ancenis in the lower part of the Loire.

The Cabernet Franc and Gamay grapes are used for the reds and rosés, Chenin Blanc or Pinot Gris for the whites. They are lightweight, pleasant and fruity.

COTEAUX-DE-L'AUBANCE An Anjou white wine, with its own AOC, from the banks of the Aubance, a small tributary of the Loire. The Chenin Blanc is used: if the 'noble rot' (*Botrytis cinerea*) develops on the overripe grapes, sweetish wines can be made. Dry wines are known as Anjou Blanc. Some rosé is also made, from the Cabernet Franc, with the AOC 'Cabernet d'Anjou'.

COTEAUX-DE-PIERREVERT VDQS red, white, and rosé wines from Provence, coming from some of the highest vineyards in France near the confluence of the Rivers Verdon and Durance. These light-bodied fairly fruity wines with lively acidity are usually most enjoyable when drunk young.

COTEAUX-DU-GIENNOIS AC wines produced around Gien, in the upper Loire region. Gamay is used for the reds, Sauvignon Blanc for the whites. As production is small, the majority are drunk in the locality.

COTEAUX-DU-LANGUEDOC A large appellation which covers over 7,700 hectares (19,000 acres) through the Hérault department, from Narbonne to Nîmes. The quality of wines from this region have improved enormously in recent years. Carignan and Cinsault grape varieties have diminished while Syrah, Grenache and Mourvèdre have increased. Whites are made from Grenache Blanc, Clairette and Picpoul. Many individual appellations within Coteaux-du-Languedoc have built up good reputations. Faugères and St Chinian have their own AOCs while La Clape, Montpeyroux, Pic St Coup and Quatorze (among others) are allowed to add their names to the overall AOC.

COTEAUX-DU-LAYON White wines from Anjou, with their own AOC. They are made from the Chenin Blanc grape, locally known as the Pineau de la Loire. They are usually sweet and those produced from grapes affected by the 'noble rot' (*Botrytis cinerea*) can be extremely luscious and may have an alcohol content of up to 15° in certain years. Among the famous wines of the region are those of Quarts-de-Chaume and Bonnezeaux.

COTEAUX-DU-LOIR An *appellation contrôlée* covering red, rosé and white wines of Touraine, which should not be confused with the Coteaux-de-la-Loire, which are white wines from Anjou. The red and rosé Coteaux-du-Loir are made mainly from Gamay and Cabernet Franc, which is rapidly superseding the old Pineau d'Aunis. The whites are made from the Chenin Blanc, known locally as Pineau de la Loire. They are fine and fruity, varying in dryness according to the vintage.

COTEAUX-DU-TRICASTIN AOC red, rosé and a small amount of white wines from the Rhône Valley. The vineyard area is in the Drôme and near to the region covered by the AOC 'Côtes-du-Rhône'. The same grape varieties are used and the wines are somewhat similar, notably the well-constituted reds, in which some drinkers detect an aroma and flavour of truffles.

COTEAUX-DU-VENDÔMOIS VDQS wines from the small area alongside the River Loir, west of Vendôme. The rosé, made from the Pineau d'Aunis grape, is dry and fruity, with an unusual fragrance. The red, made from the Gamay Noir and the Pineau d'Aunis, is a 'cosy' type of wine, slightly akin to those of the Coteaux-du-Loir. The dry white, made from the Chenin Blanc and Chardonnay, is popular locally.

CÔTE CHALONNAISE One of the most beautiful wine regions of Burgundy, in the natural extension of the Côte d'Or (see *Burgundy*).

COTECHINO A fresh Italian sausage, made with pork and lightly seasoned with spices, including nutmeg. *Cotechino* is boiled and sliced or used in stews.

CÔTE-DE-BEAUNE The southern part of the escarpment which forms the Côte d'Or, around Beaune itself and running from Ladoix in the north to Santenay in the south. The vines are Pinot Noir (for the reds) and Chardonnay (for the whites). The red wines may not often be as outstanding in quality and style as those of the neighbouring Côte-de-Nuits, but they are generally very good. It is the dry whites that are superb – the best of Burgundy. The AOC 'Côte-de-Beaune-Villages' is used for the wines from two or more of the parishes along the slopes.

CÔTE-DE-BROUILLY Perhaps the least known wine from Beaujolais, made from vines grown on hillsides situated on the southern flank of Mount Brouilly (see *Beaujolais*).

CÔTE-DE-NUITS The Burgundy region stretching from Nuits-Saint-Georges up to the outskirts of Dijon in the Côte-d'Or. Here, nearly all the wines are red, made from the Pinot Noir, and many of them are world-famous. Each one, from the different specific sites, will possess an individual character, due to the portions into which the vineyards are divided, so that the owner of even a small plot can endow the wine he makes with its own special style. The majority are certainly wines for keeping, possessing a most beautiful character and outstanding bouquet. The AOC 'Côte-de-Nuits-Villages' applies to wines (mostly red) coming from the parishes at the northern and southern extremes of the region; they are usually not quite as good as those bearing specific parish names, but are higher in overall quality than the wines that are merely categorized by the AOC 'Bourgogne'.

CÔTE-ROANNAISE VDQS red and rosé wines from vineyards on the banks of the upper Loire, near Roanne. The grape is Gamay-Saint-Romain à Jus Blanc. The wines are light and fresh in style and are drunk young.

CÔTE-RÔTIE Red wines from the right bank of the Rhône, opposite Vienne. The steep slopes have been terraced and are, as the name suggests, very sunny. Côte-Rôtie (AOC) is, together with Châteauneuf-du-Pape, the best-known of the Rhône wines. Syrah is the only red grape variety allowed, with a small amount of Viognier added to improve the aroma of the wine. The result is a rich, concentrated wine with a flavour evocative of raspberries.

CÔTES-D'AUVERGNE Red, rosé and white VDQS wines from an area around Clermont-Ferrand but considered as part of the Loire region. The vineyard produces light pleasant wines with definite fragrance and character. They are drunk young and are liked locally. The white wines are made from the Chardonnay grape and the reds and rosés from the Pinot Noir and the Gamay Noir à Jus Blanc.

CÔTES-DE-BLAYE White wines made mainly from Ugui Blanc and Sauvignon Blanc grapes from Blaye, or the right bank of the Gironde, facing the Médoc. Reds from this area are known as Premières Côtes-de-Blaye, made mainly from Merlot and Cabernet Sauvignon.

CÔTES-DE-DURAS AOC red and white wines from the Lot-et-Garonne region in south-western France, between the Bordeaux and Bergerac areas. The reds are made from the grape varieties used for Bordeaux – Cabernet Sauvignon, Cabernet Franc, Merlot and Malbec. The whites are also made from grapes grown in Bordeaux – Sémillon, Sauvignon Blanc, Muscadelle and some Mauzac. Both red and dry white wines are agreeable. Some whites are slightly sweet.

CÔTES-DE-LA-MALEPÈRE AOC (upgraded from VDQS) red and rosé Languedoc wines, from vineyards near Carcassonne.

CÔTES-DE-PROVENCE Red, white and especially rosé wines, harvested between Nice and Marseilles. In 1977 they were given an *appellation d'origine contrôlée*. The three main wine-growing regions are the coast between La Ciotat and Saint-Tropez, the north of the Maures massif, and the valley of the Argens, near Fréjus. The wines produced include full reds, dry assertive whites and fruity rosés with a pronounced bouquet. They are considered to be the perfect accompaniment to the cuisine of the south. The rosés come mainly from the Grenache, Cinsault, Mourvèdre and Carignan grapes. They are drunk chilled and usually while young.

CÔTES-DE-TOUL A VDQS wine from Lorraine, now made in fairly small quantities from vineyards around Toul. The French description is a *vin gris* (grey wine), as the wine is a pale pinkish colour, made from Gamay, Pinot Meunier and Pinot Noir grapes.

CÔTES-DU-FOREZ VDQS red and rosé wines from the top of the Loire, the vineyards being on the foot-hills of the Forez Mountains.

CÔTES-DU-FRONTONNAIS Red and rosé AOC wines from southwestern France, produced in the Tarn-et-Garonne and the Haute-Garonne, to the south of Montauban. The main grape is the Négrette and the *appellation* may be followed by the suffixes 'Fronton' or 'Villaudric'.

CÔTES-DU-JURA An AOC used for various wines from the rocky spurs of the Jura, covering a dozen districts in the Apremont region. The AOC covers dry whites, made from the Savagnin grape, yellow wines (see *Vin de jaune*) and straw wines (see *Vin de paille*). There are also some fruity rosés, made from both black and white grapes; good full-bodied reds; and fully sparkling wines. Formerly mostly drunk locally, many are now exported.

CÔTES-DU-LUBERON AOC red, white and rosé wines from Haute-Provence. Pleasantly fruity, they are beginning to be widely known, thanks to improvements in vine growing and wine making.

CÔTES-DU-MARMANDAIS AOC red and white wines from south-western France, the vineyards extending along both banks of the Garonne and really being a continuation of the Entre-Deux-Mers.

CÔTES-DU-RHÔNE This name may be used to describe red, rosé and white AOC wines, from the section of the Rhône valley between Lyon and Avignon. In fact it is mainly used for the wines which come from the flatter vineyards of the southern Rhône. In the north, the river banks are steep and the granite slopes, exposed to the strong sun of the Midi, are admirably suited to vines. About 20 different permitted grape varieties produce varied wines. The most famous are sold under their own appellations: Côte-Rôtie, Château-Grillet, Hermitage, Crozes-Hermitage, Clairette-de-Die, Châteauneuf-du-Pape, Tavel and many more. Wines bearing the AOC 'Côtes-du-Rhône' are appealing, on account of their immediate attractiveness, redolent and evocative of their warm homeland. The best have the name of their parish added – including Côtes-du-Rhône-Cairanne, Côtes-du-Rhône-Chusclan and so on. However, the Côtes-du-Rhône-Villages are a step up in quality and come from a number of specific villages.

CÔTES-DU-RHÔNE-VILLAGES AOC red, rosé and white wines, produced in the regions of Gard, Vaucluse and in particular Drôme (see *Rhône*).

CÔTES-DU-ROUSSILLON Red, rosé and white AOC wines from the Pyrénées-Orientales department, covering the same regions as Rivesaltes. The *appellation* covers the robust dark reds, produced mainly from the Carignan and the Grenache noir, also the fruity rosés and the crisp whites. The AOC 'Côtes-du-Roussillon-Villages' applies to reds of superior quality from 25 parishes specified in the *appellation*.

CÔTES-DU-VENTOUX AOC wines from the Rhône Valley and the sunny slopes of Mont Ventoux. They are mainly red wines with a beautiful ruby-red colour and, in smaller quantities, elegant fruity rosés. White wines are produced in very small quantities.

CÔTES-DU-VIVARAIS VDQS wines from the Ardèche region, on the right bank of the Rhône. They can be very pleasant and appeal in style and value to today's drinker.

COTIGNAC A pink sweetmeat, popular in France, made from a sweetened quince paste. It is sold in small round boxes made of thin wood and its pink colour is due to the natural oxidation of the fruit while it is drying out. It can be home-made, although the most famous *cotignac* is the one made industrially at Orléans. It is said that *cotignac* was made in France in the time of Joan of Arc, and her effigy is used to decorate the boxes, but there is no evidence of its existence before the time of Louis XI.

Quince paste has its origins in antiquity and ancient recipes indicate that it was formerly made with honey. Greek legend recounts how the nymphs offered it to Jupiter when he was a child. This has given rise to the popular 19th-century tradition that to eat *cotignac* from Orléans benefited the minds of unborn children – a good pretext for satisfying the craving of pregnant women for sweet things!

RECIPE

cotignac
Wash and peel some quinces; remove the seeds and tie them in a small piece of muslin (cheesecloth). Cut the quinces into quarters and place them in a pan with a small amount of water – about 5 tablespoons per 1 kg (2¼ lb) fruit – together with the seeds in a muslin bag. Cook over a very low heat until the quinces are soft and squeeze the bag of seeds to obtain the maximum flavour. Remove the seeds and reduce the pulp to a purée.

Weigh the purée and pour it into a basin with 400 g (14 oz, 1¾ cups) sugar to each 500 g (18 oz, 2¼ cups) purée. Reduce the purée, stirring continuously with a wooden spoon, until a small ball of the mixture is able to retain its shape. Spread the paste evenly on an oiled baking sheet and leave to dry out, preferably in a very cool oven. Cut the paste into squares and coat with caster (superfine) sugar. Pack into boxes, separating the layer with greaseproof (wax) paper, and store in a dry place.

Cotignac can also be made with the leftover pulp when the fruit is used to prepare a jelly.

CÔTOYER The French term for turning a joint while it is roasting so that the entire surface is exposed to the heat source.

COTRIADE A fish soup from the coast of Brittany, prepared with butter or lard (shortening), onions and potatoes. The word is said to have been derived from *cotret*, one of the pieces of wood on which the cauldron rested when the fish was cooked over a wood fire. Another possibility is that it is derived from the French word *coterie*, an old name for the ship's crew, who were given certain fish as food. Thus, a *cotriade* would have been made with the more common types of fish, the more rare or expensive ones, such as turbot or sole, being reserved for sale.

RECIPE

cotriade
The fish should be selected from the following: sardines, mackerel, sea bream (porgy), angler, hake, conger eel, gurnard and horse mackerel (saurel). (For a more delicate dish, do not allow the proportion of oily fish, such as sardines and mackerel, to exceed a quarter of the total weight.) 1 or 2 large fish heads may also be included.

Cut 3 good-sized onions into quarters and cook in a large pan with 25 g (1 oz, 2 tablespoons) butter or lard (shortening) until they are pale golden. Add 3 litres (5 pints, 13 cups) water and 6 peeled sliced potatoes. Flavour with thyme, bay leaf and other herbs. Bring to the boil and cook for about 15 minutes, then add 1.5 kg (3¼ lb) cleaned pieces of fish. Cook for a further 10 minutes. Pour the stock from the resulting soup on to some slices of bread and serve the fish and potatoes separately, with a sauceboat of vinaigrette.

COTTAGE CHEESE A fresh cow's-milk cheese (4–8% fat content). Cottage cheese has a soft, more or less granular consistency and an acid taste.

COUCOULELLI Small diamond-shaped cakes from Corsica and the area around Nice, made with flour, olive oil and white wine, blended together.

COUDENOU A *boudin blanc* (white pudding or sausage) made with equal quantities of pork rind and a paste made with egg and breadcrumbs. The mixture is stuffed into ox (beef) intestines and poached in water. The dish is a speciality of Mazamet in south-western France.

COULEMELLE French name for *parasol mushroom*.

COULER The French term for pouring an aspic jelly into a cold cooked meat pie through a hole in the top of the pastry. A piece of card rolled into a tube can be used to make the operation easier. The warm jelly fills the spaces beneath the crust that form when the pie is cooked. When the jelly sets, it improves the consistency of the filling and makes it easier to cut the pie into slices.

COULIS A liquid purée of cooked seasoned vegetables or shellfish (see *bisque*). It may be used to enhance the flavour of a sauce, it may itself be used as a sauce, or it may be used as an ingredient in soup. Fruit coulis are sauces made with raw or cooked fruit. Red fruit (redcurrants, strawberries or raspberries), yellow fruit (apricots or mirabelle plums), berries (blackberries or bilberries) or exotic fruit (kiwi fruit) may be used; the sauces are served as an accompaniment to hot or cold desserts, including ice creams.

In the past, sauces of any kind were called coulis and were prepared in advance using a type of funnel known as a *couloir* (hence the name).

RECIPES

fresh fruit coulis
Prepare 1 kg (2¼ lb) fresh fruit (apricots, strawberries, peaches, redcurrants or any other suitable fruit in season). Chop into pieces where necessary, and purée in a blender with some caster (superfine) sugar – use 575–800 g (1¼–1¾ lb, 2½–3½ cups) – depending on the acidity of the fruit). Add the sugar a little at a time while blending.

raspberry coulis
Sort, clean and wipe 1 kg (2¼ lb) raspberries. Reduce to a purée in a blender together with about 500 g (18 oz, 2¼ cups) caster (superfine) sugar.

tomato coulis
Choose firm ripe tomatoes. Cover them with boiling water and allow to stand for about 30 seconds, then peel them. Halve the tomatoes and remove their seeds. Sprinkle the cut surfaces of the tomatoes with salt and turn them over so that the juice drains away. Then purée in a blender with a little lemon juice and 1 teaspoon caster (superfine) sugar for each 1 kg (2¼ lb) tomatoes used. After blending, reduce the resulting purée further by boiling it for a few minutes (this is not always necessary). Press through a sieve, season with salt and pepper, and cool.

COULOMMIERS A French cow's-milk cheese (40–50% fat content) with a soft paste and a whitish rind. It is similar to Coulommiers Brie, but smaller – 13 cm (5 in) – in diameter and often contains more fat. When it is wrapped in fern leaves, it is called *fougeru*.

COUNTRY WINES Beverages, usually of fairly low alcoholic strength, made from fruits, flowers or even roots or vegetables. They are not widely produced commercially, but they are made extensively at home. The ingredients are crushed and allowed to ferment naturally in their own juice, which often has water and sugar added to it to facilitate fermentation and storage. Home wine-making is an excellent way of using up a glut of garden produce and is quite a popular hobby.

Of course these 'wines' are no substitute for commercial wines made from grapes according to officially defined procedures, although such beverages make very enjoyable drinks.

RECIPES

blackcurrant wine
Select ripe sound blackcurrants, crush them by hand and allow to stand for 24 hours. Press through a sieve or coarse cloth; measure and reserve the juice. Add to the fruit residue a volume of water equal to that of the measured juice and macerate for 12 hours. Press through the sieve again, then mix the two lots of juice. Measure the volume of the mixture, and add to it 50 g (2 oz, ¼ cup) granulated sugar per 1 litre (1¾ pints, 4⅓ cups) juice. Pour into a small cask and leave to ferment.

At the end of about 4 weeks, cork up the cask, leaving a very small opening. A week later, uncork the cask to allow any carbon dioxide to escape; repeat this operation from time to time until no more gas remains in the cask. (Alternatively, pour into a demijohn fitted with an airlock and leave in a warm place until fermentation ceases.) Bung the cask (or demijohn) and draw off at the end of 6 months.

Cherry wine is made in the same way.

orange wine
Peel some good-quality sweet oranges and press them in a fruit press to extract the maximum amount of juice (or use a juice extractor). Add 1 kg (2¼ lb, 4½ cups) granulated sugar per 4 litres (7 pints, 4 quarts) juice, mix in, and put into bottles. Cork, wire as for bottles of cider and leave to ferment for 6 months before drinking.

COUP A French term for three customs at table during the Ancien Régime. The *coup d'avant* was a glass of vermouth, generally served in the drawing room while the guests were waiting to go to the table. The *coup d'après* was a glass of wine drunk after the soup, and the *coup du milieu* was a small glass of spirit that was drunk after the roast meat (see also *Trou normand*). Between 1850 and 1900, this was often replaced by either a rum sorbet or a glass of sherry.

These are extracts from *L'Almanach des gourmands*, by Grimod de La Reynière:

'A few years ago, the *coup du milieu* was introduced to Paris, having been popular for a considerable time in Bordeaux and other maritime towns.

'It is drunk immediately after the roast meat and consists of a small glass of a bitter liqueur or spirit, often both, which aids digestion. Normally an extract of Swiss absinthe is served, or failing that, Jamaican rum, or else simply very old Cognac.

'There are two ways of serving the *coup du milieu*: either the host pours it into small crystal glasses especially designed for this purpose and passes them to each guest, starting on his right; or else a young blonde girl, aged between 15 and 19, wearing no ornament on her head and with her arms bare to above the elbow, serves each guest. She holds a glass tray in her right hand and the bottle in her left and goes around the table serving each guest in succession. They must not take any liberties with this new kind of Hebe, who should be a virgin if possible (though 19-year-old virgins are extremely rare in Paris).

'However the *coup du milieu* is served, no pretext can be used to dispense with drinking it.

'Whether all the guests have arrived or not, five minutes before the meal is due to start, the host will appear in the drawing room (unless he is already there). After greeting the guests collectively or individually, the *coup d'avant* will be served (if this is a custom of the house). It consists, as is well known, of a glass of vermouth. The host will then invite his guests to follow him into the dining room.'

COUPAGE In wine and spirit making, the process of blending the components in order to achieve a balanced and harmonious product. The skill of the maker is required to ensure that all the components – including grapes, vineyards and vintages – contribute satisfactorily to the whole.

In Champagne and Bordeaux the similar process of *assemblage* involves the blending of the contents of various vatings or casks made at vintage time, which, the following spring, are blended together according to the judgment of the maker in order to attain the required uniformity and consistency of the wine.

COUP DE FEU The French term describing the browning, charring or other changes that result from the sudden exposure of a piece of meat to too high a temperature during roasting. It also describes a cake mixture that has been overbaked in too intense a heat. This can be prevented by covering the cooking dish with buttered greaseproof (wax) paper.

In catering (food service), the expression is used colloquially to describe the hurried last-minute preparations that have to be carried out in a restaurant to serve the food to perfection.

COUPE A rounded receptacle of varying size. Individual coupes are cups or goblets of glass, stainless steel or silver plate, often on a stem, in which ice cream, fruit salads or similar desserts are served. These desserts themselves are also known as coupes. They may be simple or elaborate, coated with syrup or chocolate sauce, and decorated with whipped cream, crystallized (candied) fruit, biscuits or wafers. Coupes made with ice cream (*coupes glacées*) are known as sundaes in Britain and the United States.

The champagne coupe is a stemmed glass goblet that is wider than it is high. Large coupes, with or without a stem, are used for arranging fresh fruit, fruit salads and desserts.

RECIPES

apricot coupes
Soak some diced fresh or canned apricots and some apricot halves in brandy. Divide the diced fruit among some sundae dishes (2 tablespoons per dish). Cover with a layer of apricot water ice, smooth out the surface and top with an apricot half and some fresh split almonds. Sprinkle with a few drops of brandy or kirsch.

coupes à la cévenole
Prepare 500 ml (17 fl oz, 2 cups) vanilla ice cream, as described in the recipe below. Macerate 300 g (11 oz, 1⅓ cups) split marrons glacés in 200 ml (7 fl oz, ¾ cup) rum for 1 hour. Chill 6 sundae dishes in the refrigerator. Fifteen minutes before serving, divide the marrons glacés among the sundae dishes and cover with vanilla ice cream. Decorate the dishes with whipped cream using a piping bag. Each dish can be topped with crystallized (candied) violets.

coupes malmaison
Prepare 500 ml (17 fl oz, 2 cups) vanilla ice cream, as described in the recipe below. Remove the seeds from 400 g (14 oz) Muscat grapes, plunge them into a saucepan of boiling water and then immediately into cold water, then drain and peel them. Boil together 3 tablespoons water with 150 g (5 oz, ⅔ cup) caster (superfine) sugar until the sugar just caramelizes. Divide the ice cream among 4 sundae dishes, cover with the grapes and top with the caramel.

Hawaiian cream coupes
Prepare 500 ml (17 fl oz, 2 cups) almond* milk and keep it in a cool place. Wash, pat dry and hull 300 g (11 oz, 2½ cups) strawberries, cutting large ones in half. Peel and dice the flesh of a fresh pineapple. Line some sundae dishes with the strawberries and diced pineapple and completely cover with the almond milk. Top with a layer of raspberry coulis* – about 100 g (4 oz, ½ cup). Decorate each dish with piped rosettes of whipped cream.

Jamaican coupes
Prepare 500 ml (17 fl oz, 2 cups) coffee* ice cream, having added 1 tablespoon coffee extract to the boiling milk. Chill 6 sundae dishes in the refrigerator. Clean 165 g (5½ oz, 1 cup) currants and macerate them in 100 ml (4 fl oz, 7 tablespoons) rum for 1 hour. Peel a pineapple and cut the flesh into

small dice. Divide the diced pineapple among the sundae dishes and cover with coffee ice cream. Sprinkle the drained currants over the top.

pear and caramel-cream coupes

Prepare 250 g (9 oz, 1¼ cups) caramel cream (see *creams*) and keep in a cool place. Divide 500 ml (17 fl oz, 2 cups) almond* milk among 8 sundae dishes and place in the refrigerator. Divide 16 diced canned pear halves among the dishes, cover with caramel cream and put into a cool place. A few moments before serving, decorate with piped rosettes of whipped cream.

pineapple coupes

Cut some fresh or canned pineapple into dice and diamond shapes and macerate them for 1 hour in white rum. Place 2 tablespoons diced pineapple in each dish, cover with vanilla ice cream (see recipe below) and smooth out the surface. Decorate each dish with the pineapple diamonds and sprinkle with a few drops of the white rum.

vanilla ice cream for coupes

For about 500 ml (17 fl oz, 2 cups) ice cream, use 4 egg yolks, 250 ml (8 fl oz, 1 cup) milk, 1 vanilla pod (bean), 125 g (4½ oz, ½ cup) caster (superfine) sugar, and 2 tablespoons double (heavy) cream. Split the vanilla pod in two, add it to the milk, and bring to the boil. Work the egg yolks into the sugar with a wooden spoon. When the mixture lightens in colour, add the boiling milk, little by little, whisking constantly. (Remove the vanilla pod from the milk beforehand.) Heat the mixture, add the cream and continue to heat until the mixture is thick enough to coat the wooden spoon. Strain the mixture into a bowl and allow to cool, stirring continuously. Pour into an ice-cream churn and operate this until the ice cream is frozen.

COUPOLE A restaurant, bar and brasserie situated on the Boulevard du Montparnasse in Paris. It opened in 1927, and was frequented by such customers as the painters of 'La Ruche', the musicians of the group 'Les Six', political exiles such as Lenin and Trotsky and various foreign poets and artists who were at that time unknown in France (Foujita, Hemingway, Picasso and Eisenstein). These faithful habitués, nicknamed the 'Montparnos', also met at Le Dôme and Le Sélect (which opened in 1923). People also came to La Coupole to listen to jazz in the bar and Louis Armstrong composed several pieces there. In the 1930s, La Coupole was considered to be a mecca for artistic, talented and creative people, and it continues to be patronized by the world of show business, the arts and literature.

COUQUE A Flemish cake, also known as *couke* and *koucke*, that is served at breakfast or with tea. It is eaten warm, split in half and buttered. *Couques* are made from a brioche mixture with currants, a gingerbread mixture (a speciality of Verviers) or from puff pastry topped with icing (frosting). The *couques* from Dinant in Belgium are famous. The name is derived from the Dutch word *koek* (cake).

COURBINE A fish with a slight resemblance to bass, commonly found in the Mediterranean and the Bay of Biscay. It is usually about 1 m (3 ft) long, but may measure up to 2 m (6½ ft). The courbine can be cooked like bass, but its flesh does not have such a delicate taste.

COURCHAMPS, MAURICE COUSIN, COMTE DE French writer and gastronome (born Pierre Marie Jean Cousin – or Cousen – de Courchamps, Saint-Servan-Saint-Malo, 1783; died Paris, 1849). An eccentric man of letters, he published anonymously, in 1839, his *Néophysiologie du goût ou Dictionnaire général de la cuisine française ancienne et moderne*, which is full of anecdotes, portraits of diners, culinary secrets and peremptory judgments on what a true gourmet should eat and drink.

He also wrote an apocryphal autobiography, in which he described himself as Irish, a nobleman and an ex-diplomat. On the other hand, his enemies claimed that he was a former servant who had made his way by means of intrigue and developing the art of parasitism to perfection, obtaining the patronage of hostesses anxious to acquire his latest recipes and tips for entertaining. He published a new edition of his dictionary in 1853, dedicating it to 'the author of the *Souvenirs de la marquise de Créquy*', who was none other than himself!

COURGETTE (ZUCCHINI) A variety of marrow (summer squash) usually eaten when young and immature. It has a fine, shiny outer skin, which is edible, and firm flesh with a delicate taste. For a long time it was used primarily in Mediterranean countries, but it is now widely popular and available throughout the year.

Courgettes vary in size from baby vegetables with their flowers still intact and small, firm and fine-textured examples, to large, slightly woolly produce. As well as the usual long, green-skinned vegetables, there are yellow courgettes and round courgettes.

■ **Preparing and cooking** The peel may be left on or the courgettes may be very finely peeled, leaving a bright green layer covering the creamy white flesh. They may be thickly or thinly sliced; or cut into wedges, sticks or fine julienne. Courgettes can be steamed, braised, sweated in a little butter, fried, deep-fried or cooked as fritters. They are equally delicious baked, stuffed, coated in sauce or cooked au gratin.

Courgettes are also good raw – cut into fingers or wedges to be served with crudités or used in salads. Coarsely grated courgette may be tossed with a little vinaigrette and chopped fresh herbs or pared ribbons of courgette go well in green salads.

Courgette flowers are a delicacy when deep-fried in a light batter and served with lemon juice. They may be stuffed and fried as fritters or steamed.

RECIPES

preparation of courgettes

Remove the stalks from the courgettes and wipe them. Depending on the recipe, courgettes may or may not be peeled (it is essential to peel them for purées, but optional for fritters). Strips of peel may be removed from the courgettes to make them look decorative – in a ratatouille, for example.

courgette flowers with truffles

Chop 500 g (18 oz) button mushrooms and sprinkle them with the juice of ½ lemon. Melt 25 g (1 oz, 2 tablespoons) butter in a frying pan and add 1 tablespoon chopped shallots. As soon as the butter begins to sizzle, add the mushrooms, season with salt, stir and cook for 3–4 minutes. Drain in a fine colander over a small saucepan and reserve the liquid. Return the mushrooms to the pan and dry over a high heat, then reduce the heat to the minimum setting or turn it off. Pour 5 tablespoons single (light) cream into a mixing bowl, add 2 egg yolks and stir the mixture with a whisk. Add to the mushrooms, stirring with the whisk, and cook very gently for 2 minutes. Do not overheat or boil the mixture as it will curdle. Check the seasoning and allow to cool.

Drain 6 black truffles (each 15 g, ½ oz) and add their juice to that of the mushrooms. Taking great care not to damage them, wipe clean 6 courgette (zucchini) flowers without washing them. Open up the petals and put 2 teaspoons of the mushroom mixture inside each flower. Put 1 truffle in the middle of each flower and close up the petals again. Place the flowers in the top part of a couscous pan or steamer and cover with foil. Trim and wash 500 g (18 oz) tender spinach or mâche, and set aside.

Reduce the mushroom juice until only 3 tablespoons remains. Whisk in 250 g (9 oz, 1 cup) butter cut into small pieces. Season with salt and pepper and transfer to a bain marie.

Steam the flowers for 15 minutes. Arrange the uncooked spinach or mâche on a dish and place the courgette flowers on it. Pour the butter sauce over the courgette flowers. Sprinkle with chervil and serve.

courgette purée

Peel and slice the courgettes, place them in a saucepan and just cover them with water. Add some salt and 3–4 garlic cloves and cook them, covered, for about 15 minutes. If the resulting purée is very watery, dry it carefully on the heat without allowing it to stick to the bottom of the pan. Add some butter. Pour the purée into a vegetable dish and sprinkle with chopped herbs, or spread it in a greased gratin dish, top with grated Gruyère cheese and butter, and brown in the oven.

courgettes à la créole

Peel the courgettes and remove the seeds. Dice the flesh and cook in a little lard (shortening) until golden brown. Add salt, cover, and cook them over a very gentle heat, stirring from time to time. When completely softened (after 20–25 minutes), mash them with a fork, and continue to cook, stirring continuously until the pulp has become golden brown. Adjust the seasoning.

courgette salad

Peel the courgettes and cut the flesh into fine strips. Toss with a little well-seasoned vinaigrette and sprinkle with a mixture of chopped chervil and tarragon. Serve at once.

courgette salad with lime

Lightly peel and coarsely grate the courgettes. Toss with a little lime juice and the grated zest of ½–1 lime. Add a generous sprinkling of snipped chives and a little chopped fresh coriander leaves (cilantro). Season to taste, toss well and serve at once.

courgettes à la niçoise

Partially peel the courgettes, slice them thinly and sauté them in oil with an equal quantity of peeled tomatoes. Add some parsley and garlic, and season with salt and pepper.

courgettes à la provençale

Do not peel the courgettes. Cut them into long thick slices, sprinkle them with salt and leave for 15 minutes. Then pat them dry, coat them with flour and sauté them in oil in a frying pan. Brush a gratin dish with oil, cover the bottom with rice cooked in meat stock, then add some of the courgette slices. Sauté some slices of tomato and onion in oil and add chopped parsley and garlic. Place the onion and tomato slices in the gratin dish on the courgettes and cover with the remaining courgettes. Sprinkle with grated cheese and brown in a preheated oven at 230°C (450°F, gas 8).

glazed courgettes

Cut the courgettes into small uniform olive-shaped pieces. Blanch them lightly in salted water and drain them. Place them in a sauté pan with 2 tablespoons butter, a pinch of salt and a small amount of sugar. Cover with cold water, bring to the boil and cook, covered, over a low heat until the liquid has almost completely evaporated. Sauté the courgettes in this reduced sauce.

Glazed courgettes may be used as a garnish for poached fish or roast, fried or sautéed white meats.

sautéed courgettes

Slice the courgettes and toss them with a little flour. Season with salt and sauté in oil or butter. Sprinkle with freshly ground black pepper and a squeeze of lemon juice. Serve immediately.

stuffed courgettes

Cut the courgettes in half lengthways and hollow them out. Prepare the following stuffing: cook

COURGETTES

There are many types varying in shape, colour and size according to whether they are young or well developed.

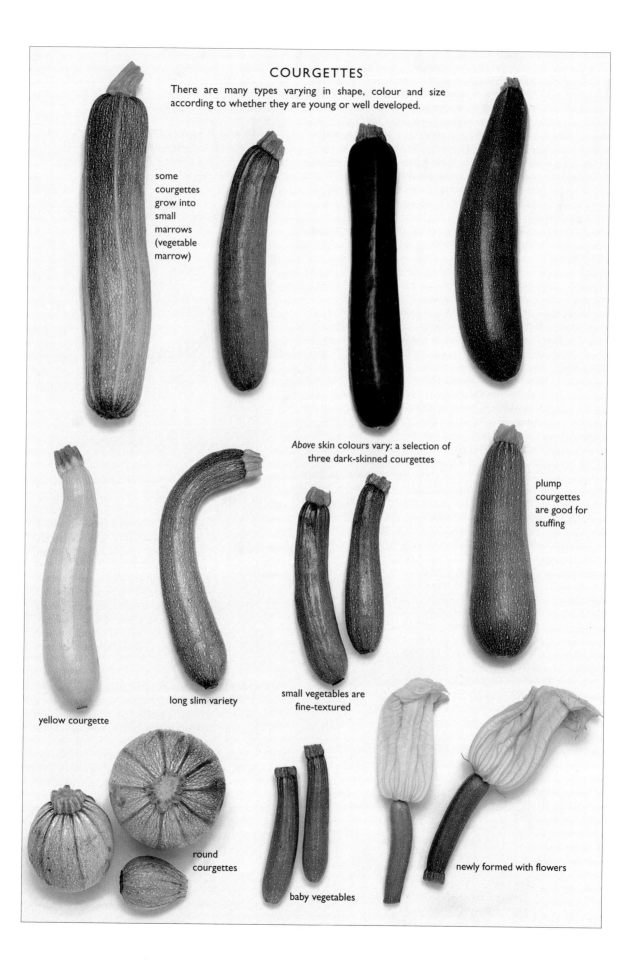

some courgettes grow into small marrows (vegetable marrow)

Above skin colours vary: a selection of three dark-skinned courgettes

plump courgettes are good for stuffing

yellow courgette

long slim variety

small vegetables are fine-textured

round courgettes

baby vegetables

newly formed with flowers

some rice and drain. Mix with minced (ground) lamb, chopped onion and fennel softened in butter, crushed garlic and seasoning.

Fill the courgette halves with the stuffing and place them close together in a greased ovenproof dish. Cover and cook in a preheated oven at 180°C (350°F, gas 4) for about 1 hour or until the filling is cooked and the courgettes are tender. Uncover for the final 20 minutes. Serve coated with tomato sauce.

other recipes See *escalope, mentonnaise, omelette (flat omelettes), ratatouille.*

COURT-BOUILLON

A spiced aromatic liquor or stock used mainly for cooking fish and shellfish, but also for preparing white offal (variety meats) and certain white meats (such as chicken and veal). Wine and vinegar may sometimes be added to the court-bouillon, which is usually prepared in advance and allowed to cool. Food cooked in the liquid absorbs the flavour of the ingredients. Freeze-dried court-bouillon is available in France; it is easy to use and time-saving, as it is simply diluted with water.

■ **Cooking in court-bouillon** Depending on the size of the item to be cooked, either a fish kettle or a large saucepan can be used. Large fish should be wrapped in a cloth (and tied to the grid if a fish kettle is used). The cooled court-bouillon is poured into the receptacle first. (If the court-bouillon is boiling hot, the liquid makes the flesh shrink and delays the cooking time.) The liquid is brought to the boil and the heat is then reduced so that the fish simmers. Cook for 25 minutes for fish 5 cm (2 in) thick and 1 hour for fish 13 cm (5 in) thick. When cooked, the flesh should be firm but supple.

If there is not enough court-bouillon, the fish should be covered with either a cloth or some celery leaves, to prevent the surface from drying out. Cold water should never be added.

When cooked, fish that are to be served hot are drained, arranged on a dish and served with sauce (separately) and, traditionally, steamed potatoes, although other vegetables can be served. When served cold, the fish should be allowed to cool in the cooking liquid. The skin may then be removed. However, the court-bouillon should not be discarded as it can be strained and used in a soup or white sauce. It can be kept in a sterilized jar in a refrigerator and used over again for a number of cooking sessions. In this way, its flavour is progressively enriched.

RECIPES

court-bouillon eau de sel

This is the easiest kind of court-bouillon to prepare as it consists only of salted boiling water – use 15 g (½ oz, 1 tablespoon) coarse sea salt per 1 litre (1¾ pints, 4⅓ cups) water. It is not usually flavoured, but a little thyme and a bay leaf may be added if desired.

court-bouillon with milk

Add 1 finely shredded onion, a sprig of thyme, salt and pepper to equal quantities of milk and water (the court-bouillon should cover the food that is to be cooked). It is used principally for cooking flatfish, such as brill or turbot, or smoked or salted fish, such as smoked haddock or salt cod (in the latter case, do not add salt).

court-bouillon with wine

For every 2.5 litres (4¼ pints, 11 cups) water, add 500 ml (17 fl oz, 2 cups) dry white wine, 50 g (2 oz, ⅓ cup) grated carrot, 50 g (2 oz, ⅓ cup) grated onion, a sprig of thyme, a piece of bay leaf, 25 g (1 oz, 2 tablespoons) coarse salt and possibly a small celery stick, chopped, and a sprig of parsley (although these have a strong flavour). Add 2 teaspoons peppercorns 10 minutes before the end of the cooking time.

The wine should be chosen for its fruity flavour. The amount of wine can be increased if the amount of water is reduced by the same quantity. Red wine may also be used, especially if the court-bouillon is to be used to make an aspic jelly, which will then have a pale pink colour. Court-bouillons with white wine are used for cooking shellfish and fish of all types. Court-bouillons with red wine are used for cooking lean white-fleshed fish such as bass, which are served cold.

lemon or vinegar court-bouillon

For every 3 litres (5 pints, 13 cups) water, allow 250 g (9 oz, 1¼ cups) sliced carrots, 150 g (5 oz) onions (quartered, and, if desired, studded with a clove), 1 sprig thyme, a bay leaf, 1–2 parsley sprigs, 25 g (1 oz, 2 tablespoons) coarse sea salt, either the juice of 2 lemons or 200 ml (7 fl oz, ¾ cup) vinegar, and finally 2 teaspoons peppercorns (added 10 minutes before the end of the cooking period).

This court-bouillon can be used when the natural colour of the fish is to be preserved, for example, when cooking salmon or salmon trout, and also when cooking shellfish, as it makes the shell turn bright red.

COUSCOUS

A traditional North African ingredient made with hard wheat semolina and sometimes with barley or, in Tunisia, with green wheat. It was discovered by the French during the reign of Charles X during the conquest of Algeria. There is still some doubt about the original meaning of the word, which is derived from the Arabic *kouskous.* Some experts believe that the word was originally used for the food in a bird's beak used to feed its young. Léon Isnard, who considers that it is the Gallic form of *rac keskes* ('to pound until small'), maintains that it is derived phonetically from the words *koskos, keuscass, koskosou* and *kouskous,* used in different parts of North Africa for a cooking pot in which semolina is steamed. Made of earthenware or alpha glass, the pot, which is pierced with holes, sits on top of another similar pot containing water or stock.

Other experts believe that the sound of the word describes the noise made by the steam as it passes through the holes in the pot.

■ **A spicy stew** Couscous (in Arabic: *t'âam*) is also the name for the national dish of Algeria, Morocco and Tunisia. It is served in Algeria after the *méchoui* (the barbecued food) and in Morocco after the *tajines*. The couscous is served with a spicy stew of poultry or meat with vegetables, or of vegetables and pulses on their own. The couscous grains are scooped into small balls with the fingers and quickly put in the mouth.

In Algeria, couscous is served with chick peas, broad (fava) beans and a wide variety of other vegetables, including artichokes, courgettes (zucchini), potatoes, aubergines (eggplants), chard, fennel and peas, and sometimes meat. *Mesfouf*, a couscous made with fresh broad beans and raisins, is served at dawn during the month of Ramadan. It is eaten while drinking whey (*leben*) or curdled milk (*raïb*).

Saharan couscous is served without vegetables or stock. In Tunisia, chick peas are the essential ingredient for couscous which can be made with rabbit, partridge or mutton. The most traditional recipe is for couscous made with fish (such as sea bream or grouper), but there is also a type of couscous in which the meat, fish and vegetables are replaced by raisins, almonds, pistachios, dates and walnuts, which are mixed with fresh milk and sprinkled with sugar.

In Morocco couscous is served with chicken and (usually) two stocks – one to moisten the semolina, the other (seasoned with red pepper) to spice it. The numerous ingredients – turnips, courgettes (zucchini), raisins, chick peas and onions – are cooked for a very long time until they are reduced to a sort of mash. Another Moroccan recipe is for sweet couscous flavoured with cinnamon.

Whatever the variations in each country, there are two rules that must be observed in the preparation of an authentic couscous. Firstly, the grain must be of the right quality and consistency, which depends on the art of rolling the grain by hand and cooking the semolina correctly. Secondly, the vegetables and spices used to prepare the stock must be chosen to give the meat and the couscous its full flavour.

■ **Ready prepared couscous** There are many brands of prepared couscous that are simple to cook and of excellent quality. These include instant couscous, prepared simply by soaking in the minimum of boiling water, and part-cooked types that are ready after brief soaking and steaming, but do not involve the skilful rolling. The latter give very good results. Follow packet instructions closely for prepared products.

RECIPES

preparing traditional couscous

In country villages, where couscous is simply a dish of semolina flavoured with rancid butter (*smen*) and served with whey, the women prepare the grain in the traditional way by skilfully rolling it by hand. Hard-wheat semolina and flour are placed in a wooden dish (*kesra*) or in an earthenware dish, together with a small amount of cold salted water. By rolling the semolina, the flour progressively binds itself around each grain. The grain is then sieved, which enables the particles to be sorted according to their size.

cooking traditional couscous

The grain is steamed in a couscous pan. Fill the pot two-thirds with water or stock and bring it quickly to the boil. Then fit the *keskès* (steamer) containing the semolina on to the pot. Tie a damp cloth around the part where the *keskès* and the pot meet so that no steam escapes. After about 30 minutes, remove the semolina from the couscous pan, put it in a large round dish with a raised edge, coat the grains with oil and break up the lumps with the hands. Put the couscous back in the *keskès* to steam it and repeat the operation twice more, without forgetting to work the grain between each steaming. After the third steaming, arrange small knobs of butter on the semolina and serve.

During the second and third steaming, vegetables or meat are added to the pot and raisins are mixed with the grain.

couscous with fish

(Tunisian recipe) Steam some whiting fillets in the *keskès* (for 10 minutes). Flake them, and mix them with a purée of onions, some finely chopped garlic, paprika, harissa, chopped parsley, salt and pepper, 1 egg and some stale bread that has been soaked in cold water. Form the mixture into balls and brown them in a frying pan.

Steam 1.5 kg (3¼ lb, 9 cups) semolina. Scale, trim and gut 4 sea breams or 1 grouper weighing in total about 1.5 kg (3¼ lb). Marinate the fish in a mixture of 3 tablespoons olive oil, 2 teaspoons each of fennel seeds and ground caraway, a pinch of cayenne and 1 teaspoon paprika for 30 minutes.

Meanwhile, brown 3 grated onions, 3 chopped courgettes (zucchini), 4 chopped carrots and 2 artichoke hearts (cut into quarters) in olive oil. Then cover with 1.5 litres (2¾ pints, 6½ cups) water and add 225 g (8 oz, 1¼ cups) each soaked chick peas and fresh broad (fava) beans, a pinch of cayenne, 3 peeled and roughly chopped tomatoes, 2 cloves, 1 small cinnamon stick, 1 teaspoon caraway seeds and, if desired, some harissa mixed with water. Bring the vegetables to the boil and then reduce the heat.

Grill the fish 15 minutes before serving. Pile the prepared couscous on to a dish and garnish it with the fish and the fish balls. Serve the vegetables and stock separately.

Some people prefer to cook the fish in the stock with the vegetables. In this case a cabbage, 6 medium-sized potatoes and 4 red or green (bell) peppers (cut in half) may be added.

couscous with meat

Steam 1.5 kg (3¼ lb, 9 cups) couscous once only. Pour away the water in the pot. Use the meat from a 1.8 kg (4 lb) chicken and a small shoulder of mutton. Cut the meat into pieces and place it in the couscous pot with 8 pieces of neck of mutton and 5 tablespoons olive oil. Brown the meat in the oil and add 4 onions, cut in half. Make sure that the onions brown without burning. Add 8 halved carrots, 4 chopped leeks, 1 chopped fennel bulb, 6 roughly chopped tomatoes, a little tomato purée (paste) thinned with water, 4 crushed garlic cloves, a bouquet garni and a small pinch of coarse salt. Cover the ingredients with cold water and then add 225 g (8 oz, 1⅓ cups) chick peas (previously soaked for 24 hours). Put the lid on the pot and bring to the boil. Cook for 20–25 minutes.

Add 4 turnips (cut into quarters), 4 large chopped courgettes (zucchini), and 4 small trimmed and quartered globe artichokes. Place the *keskès* containing the couscous on top of the pot and continue cooking for about 30 minutes.

Meanwhile, prepare some meatballs by mixing 450 g (1 lb, 4 cups) minced (ground) mutton with a small bunch of parsley, 2 chopped garlic cloves, 2 chopped onions, 4 slices of bread (crumbled, moistened with milk and squeezed out), 1 teaspoon harissa, salt and pepper. Work the mixture well and divide it into 8 small balls. Roll each ball in flour and brown them in a frying pan with olive oil over a brisk heat.

When the grain is cooked, turn it into a large dish, add butter, and garnish with the pieces of meat, *merguez* fried in oil and the meatballs. Serve with the vegetables and the stock.

couscous with vegetables

The preparation is almost the same as for couscous with meat. All the vegetables are placed in the pot when the grain is being cooked. Use chick peas (soaked for 24 hours), broad (fava) beans (preferably fresh), grated onions, chopped turnips, chopped carrots and sliced tomatoes, all seasoned with salt. Just before serving, enhance the flavour by seasoning with black pepper or mixed spices (*qâlat daqqâa,* or *râs al-hânout*) according to taste. Add small knobs of butter (rancid, if preferred). A wider range of vegetables can be used, such as cabbage, artichokes, potatoes, beet, chard, courgettes (zucchini) and peas.

COUSCOUS PAN
A *couscoussier* in French, consisting of two parts, one on top of the other. The lower part consists of a curved pot with handles for the vegetable or meat stock or stew, or plain water. The upper receptacle is a type of steamer called the *keskès,* in which the semolina or other ingredients are steamed. Its base is pierced with small holes. The couscous pan has a lid that is also perforated to allow the steam to escape.

Formerly in North Africa, a couscous pan was either a simple earthenware utensil pierced with holes or it was made of interlaced grasses. The semolina was placed inside and the receptacle was then placed on top of an ordinary cooking pot filled with water or stock.

COUSINAT
In the Auvergne, a soup made with chestnuts, celeriac, onions and the white parts of leeks. It is traditionally finished with fresh cream and Salers butter.

On the Basque coast, *cousinat* is a ragoût consisting of Bayonne ham cooked in lard (shortening), with beans, *poivrade* artichokes, carrots and pieces of pumpkin.

COUSINETTE
A soup from Béarn made with spinach, sorrel, lettuce and other finely chopped green vegetables. When served, it is poured into bowls containing thin slices of bread.

RECIPE

cousinette
Wash 150 g (5 oz, 1 cup) spinach leaves, 150 g (5 oz, 1 cup) Swiss chard leaves, 150 g (5 oz, 1 cup) lettuce leaves, 50 g (2 oz, ½ cup) sorrel leaves and a small handful of wild mallow leaves. Shred all the leaves finely to make a very fine *chiffonnade* and brown them gently in 50 g (2 oz, ¼ cup) butter or goose fat. Cover and braise gently for 10 minutes. Add 1.5 litres (2¾ pints, 6½ cups) water or preferably chicken stock and, if desired, 250 g (9 oz, 1¼ cups) finely sliced potatoes. Continue cooking for about 30 minutes. Just before serving, adjust the seasoning and add a knob of fresh butter. Pour the soup on to thin slices of bread that have been dried in the oven.

COUVE
A cake from the Dauphiné region in southeastern France. Made in Crest, originally for the Palm Sunday feast but nowadays all the year round, it is a sort of *galette* (French Twelfth-Night cake) flavoured with vanilla and lemon and cut in the shape of a broody hen. The cake is glazed with egg, pricked so that it does not swell and baked in the oven. It is generally served with Clairette de Die, a sparkling white wine.

COVER
The set of table implements (plate, glass, cutlery) that mark a place at table. In a more restricted sense, it can mean simply the knife, fork and spoon, or even just the spoon and fork.

Until the 15th century, it was customary to serve 'under cover' (*à couvert*), that is, to cover the courses and dishes with a large white napkin to show the guests that all precautions had been taken to avoid poisoning. Hence the expression *mettre le couvert* (to lay the table – literally 'to put on the cover'). Since the word also meant the diner's place at the table, it began to be applied to the meal itself: *avoir son couvert mis chez quelqu'un* (to have one's place set at someone's house) means to have breakfast or dinner there regularly.

Under the Ancien Régime, a distinction was made between *le grand couvert,* the large setting or banquet reserved for the king alone or the royal family; *le petit couvert,* the small setting or ordinary meal, which the king ate with his intimate friends;

and *le très petit couvert*, the very small setting which, although a very intimate meal, nevertheless consisted of three courses. Modern table conventions, with their tendency towards simplification, were introduced during the 18th and 19th centuries.

Table setting is classically based on precise rules governing such aspects as the folding of napkins, the number of glasses (up to five glasses of various capacities were used in the 19th century) and the position of the fork (on the left, prongs against the tablecloth in France), the knife (on the right, blade facing inwards) and soupspoon if required (on the outer right, convex side upwards in France). Knife rests, which imply that the setting is not changed between courses, are fast disappearing and the rules for table settings are becoming much less formal.

Since silver-plated metal came into general use, tableware designs have often merely reproduced previous styles. The early 20th century saw the beginning of a modern style, influenced by such people as Jean Puiforcat who, after World War I, created a style in which shape took precedence over decoration. German, and later Scandinavian, silversmiths have led the development of European designs, emphasizing the functional aspects and the beauty of the materials, which include wood, steel and Plexiglas. However, Louis XIV shells, Louis XV festoons, Louis XVI pearls and 18th-century fillets still adorn many items of French household tableware, whether silver-plated or stainless steel. The standard setting is often supplemented with special implements, depending on the dish being served, such as snail tongs, a leg-of-mutton sleeve, fish knife and fork, and grapefruit spoon.

COVERING FOOD

Covering food influences the cooking process, encouraging moisture and heat retention and in some cases speeding up the cooking. Covering reduces or prevents food from browning, becoming crisp and forming a skin when baking, roasting or grilling (broiling).

■ **Boiling, simmering, poaching and steaming** When heating food in liquid, covering the pan helps to retain heat and reduce the time taken, for example when bringing liquid to the boil. Covering or part-covering a pan is a useful method of fine-tuning the speed at which food cooks as the additional heat retention will encourage slightly faster cooking, for example encouraging liquid to simmer steadily rather than barely bubble. When boiling food steadily or rapidly, covering may cause the liquid to froth up and boil over, as when boiling pasta, but part-covering can keep cooking water boiling without frothing over, particularly when cooking root vegetables, such as swede or potatoes. When poaching or cooking food very gently in liquid, particularly fish or chicken, covering the pan will retain sufficient heat to keep the liquid bubbling very gently, just below a steady simmer; this can be difficult to achieve solely by adjusting the temperature setting. Also, when a small amount of liquid is

used and the food is partly submerged, covering the pan prevents the surface of the ingredients from drying.

Steamers have to be covered in order to retain the steam, but some ingredients are steamed in a covered pan. For example, one method of cooking rice combines steaming with boiling: once the water boils rapidly, the rice is stirred once, the pan covered tightly and the heat reduced to the very minimum to encourage evaporation without continued simmering. The rice cooks by absorbing the water and the condensing steam.

■ **Sweating and frying** Sweating uses the minimum of fat to prevent ingredients such as vegetables from sticking to the pan. The pan is covered to retain moisture evaporating as the ingredients give up their juices. This liquid condenses and the ingredients sweat in their own juices. If the pan is uncovered, the moisture evaporates, the ingredients become dry and may burn.

In general, when frying at high temperatures, food is not covered. Moisture evaporating and condensing to fall back into the pan spits as it comes in contact with the hot fat. This is important when carrying out some deep-frying and shallow frying at a high temperature. However, there are occasions when covering can assist shallow frying; for example, when frying eggs, covering the pan helps to set the whites by combining moist and dry cooking methods. Similarly, items such as chicken breast fillets may be browned on both sides in a little fat, then the pan may be covered to encourage even cooking.

■ **Roasting and grilling** Covering retains heat and moisture in the first stages of roasting to prevent food from drying out or cooking too quickly near the surface; covering part-way through the cooking time prevents overbrowning. The cover is removed towards the end of cooking to encourage browning and crisping. When grilling, foil may be used to cover food for part of the time to prevent burning.

■ **Baking** A wide variety of dishes are covered during baking to retain moisture, prevent surface drying and encourage even cooking. Pâtés, terrines, casseroles, stews, baked fish, poultry or vegetable dishes, braised and baked fruit are all good examples. The food may be uncovered towards the end of cooking. Custards may be covered during baking by laying greased greaseproof (wax) paper directly on the mixture to prevent a skin from forming. Foods can be wrapped completely in foil or greaseproof paper (*en papillotte*) to retain moisture, flavour and aroma.

■ **Covering food during storage** Covering or wrapping food during storage prevents it from drying out, discolouring and being tainted with (or tainting other ingredients) odours. Some foods readily absorb aromas which taint their flavour – butter, milk and cream will quickly take on the flavour of strong ingredients if both are left uncovered in the refrigerator. Covering food before placing it in the refrigerator also prevents cross contamination by micro-organisms from uncooked to cooked foods. Food should always be covered when it is set aside on the worksurface during preparation or placed on the dining table before a meal to prevent contamination from air-borne micro-organisms and insects. Food should always be well wrapped before freezing. Covering also helps to prevent or reduce rancidity promoted by exposure to air.

COW The female of the domestic cattle from the time of its first calving (before this it is called a heifer). The cow is generally bred for producing milk and calves, but in France a good proportion of 'beef' comes from milch cows which are no longer needed for milk. Such cows are fattened up for the butcher at an early age, giving meat which is often more tender and has more flavour than that from a bullock.

COZIDO A type of Portuguese and Spanish stew consisting of *chorizo* sausage, cabbage, carrots, chick peas, white haricot beans, pig's ears, and a piece of charcuterie similar to a black pudding (chopped meat and breadcrumbs soaked in milk) or white pudding (chopped meat with plenty of animal fat). With the addition of vermicelli, the cooking liquid is eaten as soup.

CRAB One of a large group of crustaceans characterized by a wide flat body protected by a hard shell (carapace). Crabs are decapods, having five pairs of legs; these vary in size according to the species, but the first pair (pincers) are generally much larger and equipped with strong claws.

In general, crab may not be as highly rated as lobster but its white meat is fine and delicate while the brown meat found in the body, and including the liver and roe, is rich and full flavoured. When buying live crab, look for a plump and heavy creature. Male crabs have larger claws and provide more meat than females. To determine the sex, check the tail or abdomen which is curled under the crab: the female has a wide rounded tail flap while the male has a narrow, more pointed tail. Crab is usually sold cooked and often dressed. When buying whole cooked crab, shake the shell and reject it if it contains water.

Crabmeat is available frozen or canned. Canned Russian chatka crab from the cold waters of the Kamchatka peninsula is a world-class delicacy; when referred to as 'extra' this indicates that the can contains 100% claw meat. Canned crab claws from other species are also available. By way of complete contrast, crab sticks are a manufactured fish product that bear no resemblance to crab and they are to be avoided.

■ **Types of crab** There are hundreds of types and species, including freshwater and land crabs, many available only locally.

• BLUE CRAB Also known as the Atlantic blue crab, this is a swimming crab. (The swimming crabs differ from the common crab in that their fifth pair of legs is developed to form paddles and their bodies are lighter, so they are good swimmers.) The blue crab is popular in America for its good quality meat and also as a soft shell crab (see below).

• COMMON CRAB OR EDIBLE CRAB Known as *tourteau* in France. These are usually about 20 cm (8 in) across but there are species measuring up to 30 cm (12 in) and weighing up to 6 kg (13 lb). The shell is brown or red-brown in colour with well-developed front claws that contain plump nuggets of firm white meat.

• DUNGENESS CRAB Also known as California crab or market crab, this is popular on the west coast of America. Similar in size to the common crab, but brown in colour, turning red when cooked.

• FRESHWATER CRABS Found in Mediterranean and Balkan rivers and lakes, as well as in the tropics and South America. These are usually appreciated locally, as for example the Italian freshwater crab which is preferred as a soft shell crab.

• HERMIT CRABS There are many different types of hermit crabs. They are not true crabs in the sense of having a body under the large shell, but they do have the legs, claws and upper part of the body protected by shell. The elongated tail is not covered by a shell. The creature lives in a discarded shell or other suitable crevice, concealing the tail end and protecting the opening to its home with its armoured claws. The tail meat is considered a delicacy.

• JONAH CRAB Very similar to the rock crab, with the same colouring, but slightly larger and providing more, slightly better, meat.

• LAND CRABS These tropical crabs live on land but return to the sea to breed. Land crabs are popular in Caribbean cooking.

• MITTEN CRAB Also known as Chinese mitten crab or Shanghai crab, so named for the mitten-like covering at the ends of the male's claws; they are popular in China. These crabs can survive in both fresh water and sea water.

• ROCK CRAB Also known as common rock crab, this has a pale yellow shell with brown, red-brown or purple spots.

• SNOW CRAB Also known as queen or tanner crab, this is a type of spider crab. It has long legs and large claws that yield excellent meat. Popular in Japan, also America and Canada.

• SOFT SHELL CRABS Soft shell crabs are not a separate species, but they are crabs that have moulted or shed their shells. Crabs shed their shells in order to grow. Just before they shed their shells, they are known as peelers or comers; they are known as peelers, shedders or busters while shedding their shells, then as soft crabs immediately after shedding them. After moulting the new shell begins to form as a paper shell, hardening to a buckram or buckler, by which time the shell is too firm for the crab to be classed as a soft shell. The new shell is formed in about 24 hours, so the crabs are caught and retained until they are at the soft shell stage.

• SPIDER CRAB OR SPINY CRAB A rough-shelled, rounded and domed crab with fine claws. Known as *araignée de mer* in French and prized in French cooking.

• STONE CRAB OR SOUTHERN STONE CRAB Prized in America for their heavy claws with black-edged pincers, yielding excellent meat. (There are many species of stone crab with heavy, thick shells and large pincers, ranging from giant crabs in Tasmania to Italian stone crabs that are appreciated locally for their small quantity of high-quality meat.)

■ **Preparing crab** To kill a live crab, stab it several times with a sharp metal skewer into the underside directly behind the eyes or centrally under the tail flap. If in doubt about the humane method, consult a fishmonger.

Cook the crab by boiling it in salted water for 20–30 minutes, then drain and rinse under cold water. When cool, remove the claws and legs. Turn the shell over and push the body out by applying pressure behind the tail flap, upwards and outwards. The pale, short finger-like gills (known as dead men's fingers) should be discarded. The stomach sac and related parts attached to the shell should be discarded too, but the soft brown meat in the shell is edible.

Use a skewer to pick out meat from the body before discarding it. Crack the legs and claws and poke out all the meat.

Crab can be eaten cold with mayonnaise; in Saint-Malo it is served shelled, with mayonnaise and quartered hard-boiled (hard-cooked) eggs. Traditionally, crabs are served with special tongs and eaten using thin forks with two prongs; finger bowls should be provided.

Dressed crab refers to shelled cooked cooked crab, seasoned and replaced in the washed and dried shell with the white meat arranged neatly on the brown meat.

Crabmeat can be used in a variety of hot and cold dishes. Whole soft shell crabs can be fried or grilled (broiled). Crab claws in their shells or shelled can be cooked in spicy sauces or a ragoût.

RECIPES

crab à la bretonne

Plunge a live crab into boiling lemon or vinegar court-bouillon. Cook for 8–10 minutes, then drain and cool. Remove the legs and claws and take out the contents of the shell. Clean the shell thoroughly. Cut the meat from the shell in two, put it back in the clean shell and arrange the legs and claws around. Garnish with parsley or lettuce leaves and serve with a mayonnaise.

crab feuilletés ♦

Prepare 500 g (1 lb 2 oz) puff pastry. Wash and scrub 2 crabs; plunge them into boiling water for 2 minutes and then drain them. Pull off the claws and the legs, crack the shells and cut the bodies in two. Remove the 'dead man's fingers' and discard. Chop 1 carrot, 1 onion, 1 shallot, white part of ½ leek and 1 celery stick.

Heat 40 g (1½ oz, 3 tablespoons) butter in a saucepan, add the pieces of crab, then the chopped vegetables and cook, stirring frequently, until the crab shell turns red. Add 3 tablespoons heated Cognac and flame. Then add 1 bottle dry white wine, 1 generous tablespoon tomato purée (paste), a piece of dried orange peel, salt, pepper, a dash of cayenne pepper, 1 crushed garlic clove and a small bunch of parsley. Bring just to the boil, cover the pan and cook for 10 minutes. Remove the crab and cook the sauce, uncovered, for a further 10 minutes. Shell the pieces of crab to remove the meat. Purée the sauce in a blender and rub it through a sieve, then mix half of it with the crab meat. Allow to cool completely.

Roll out the pastry to a thickness of 5 mm (¼ in). Cut it into rectangles measuring about 13 × 8 cm (5 × 3 in), and score their tops in criss-cross patterns with the tip of a knife. Glaze with beaten egg and cook in a preheated oven at 230°C (450°F, gas 8) for about 20 minutes. When the feuilletés are cooked, slice off their tops. Place the bases on serving plates and top with the crab mixture. Replace the pastry tops and serve with the remaining sauce.

crab salad

Clean and cook 2 large crabs. Wash, scald and cool 500 g (18 oz, 4½ cups) bean sprouts and dry them. Mix 4 tablespoons mayonnaise, 1 tablespoon ketchup or very concentrated sieved tomato purée and at least 1 tablespoon brandy. Mix the crabmeat, the bean sprouts and the sauce and serve on a bed of lettuce leaves. Sprinkle with chopped herbs.

crabs in broth

Chop a large onion. Peel and roughly chop 4 tomatoes. Peel and crush 2 large garlic cloves. Plunge 2 crabs in salted boiling water, cook for 3 minutes, then remove the claws and legs and take out the contents of the shell. Crush the empty shell and the intact legs and brown them in 25 g (1 oz, 2 tablespoons) fat or 2 tablespoons oil together with the onion. Add the tomatoes, a large pinch of ground ginger, a pinch of saffron, a pinch of cayenne, the garlic and a sprig of thyme. Moisten with plenty of stock (fish, meat or chicken), cover and simmer very gently for about 2 hours.

Strain through a sieve, pressing well to obtain a fairly thick sauce. Adjust the seasoning. Crush the claws and remove the flesh, cut the flesh from the shell in four, then brown all the flesh together in fat or oil in a sauté pan. Pour the sauce over the top, bring back to the boil and cook for 5–6 minutes. Serve in a soup tureen, accompanied with rice *à la créole*.

stuffed crabs à la martiniquaise

Clean 4 medium-sized *tourteau* crabs and cook them in court-bouillon. Add about a cup of milk to a bowl of dry breadcrumbs. Trim and finely chop 3 good slices of ham and, separately, 5–6 shallots. Brown the shallots in oil or butter. Chop together a small bunch of parsley and 3–4 garlic cloves, add them to the shallots and stir. Crumble the crabmeat and add it to the pan together with a good pinch of cayenne, the breadcrumbs (softened but well squeezed) and the chopped ham. Thoroughly stir the whole mixture and reheat.

Adjust the seasoning so that the forcemeat is highly spiced. Mix 2 egg yolks with 2 tablespoons white rum, bind the forcemeat with this mixture and use to fill the shells. Sprinkle with white breadcrumbs, pour on some melted butter and bake in a preheated oven at 180°C (350°F, gas 4).

stuffed crabs au gratin

Wash and brush some crabs. Plunge them in courtbouillon with lemon. Bring back to the boil, cook for about 10 minutes, then drain and leave to cool. Detach the claws and legs and remove their meat. Take out all the meat and creamy parts from the shells, discarding any gristle. Crumble or dice the meat finely. Wash and dry the shells.

Mix the creamy parts with a few spoonfuls of Mornay sauce (the quantity depends on the size of the crabs) and spread this mixture over the bottom of each shell. Then fill with diced or crumbled crabmeat and top with Mornay sauce. Finally, sprinkle with grated cheese, pour on some melted butter, and bake in a preheated oven at 240°C (475°F, gas 9) until the surface is brown.

other recipes *aspic, avocado, cucumber, feuilleté, loaf, soufflé.*

CRACKED WHEAT See *bulgur.*

CRACKER
A light crisp savoury biscuit of British origin. The manufacturing method gives it a flaky crumbly texture. In Anglo-Saxon countries, crackers are served mainly with cheese. In France, they are usually flavoured and accompany aperitifs.

CRACKLING
The crisply cooked pork fat and rind covering a roast joint. Before cooking the rind is scored so that the crackling can be removed easily in small sections. Commercially produced crackling is sold as snacks (unpleasantly termed pork scratchings in Britain) or used in various ways, for example to flavour omelettes, spinach, purées and soups. Cracklings are also used in black pudding (blood sausage) and to flavour savoury breads.

CRAMIQUE
In Belgium and northern France, brioche bread with currants or raisins in it. It is served warm with butter.

CRANBERRY
The red berry of any of several related shrubs of the genus *Vaccinium*. Cranberry sauce is a traditional accompaniment to roast turkey and is always served at Thanksgiving dinners in the United States.

The mountain cranberry is found in heath and woodland in cold mountainous regions. Also known as lingonberry and cowberry, it is eaten mainly in the United States, Scandinavia and Germany. The mountain cranberry has a very tart flavour and is rich in vitamin C and pectin. Its juice is reputed to have medicinal qualities. The berries are used to make compotes and sweet jellies, as well as sauces and condiments to accompany savoury dishes. The traditional roast goose of the Danish Christmas dinner is served with red cabbage and stewed cranberries. Plain cranberries may also accompany game and boiled meat and are used to make iced mousse (*kissel*) and puddings.

RECIPES

cranberry compote

Combine 500 g (18 oz, 2¼ cups) caster (superfine) sugar, the grated zest of half a lemon and 200 ml (7 fl oz, ¾ cup) water in a saucepan; slowly bring to the boil, then boil for 5 minutes. Add 1 kg (2¼ lb) washed and stalked cranberries and cook over a high heat for 10 minutes. Remove the fruit from the liquid with a perforated spoon and place in a fruit dish. Reduce the syrup by one-third if the compote is to be eaten straight away, or by half if it is to be kept for a few days in the refrigerator. Pour the syrup over the fruit and allow to cool for 1 hour. Serve with vanilla-flavoured meringues.

cranberry jam

Clean and stalk 2 kg (4½ lb) berries. Place in a large preserving pan with 500 ml (17 fl oz, 2¼ cups) water and bring to the boil. Reduce the heat, stir and cover the pan, then cook gently until the berries are completely tender. Add 1.5 kg (3¼ lb) preserving or granulated sugar and heat gently, stirring, until the sugar dissolves. Bring to a full boil and boil hard until setting point is reached. Remove the pan from the heat and pot the jam immediately.

cranberry jelly

Clean and stalk 2 kg (4½ lb) cranberries and 1 kg (2¼ lb) redcurrants. Place in a large pan and add enough water to come halfway up the fruit. Cover and cook until completely soft. Strain the fruit through a jelly bag overnight – do not press or squeeze the fruit or the jelly will be cloudy. Pour the juice into a pan with 3 kg (6½ lb) lump (cube) or granulated sugar and stir until the sugar dissolves. Bring to a full boil, skim, then boil hard until setting point is reached. Remove the pan from the heat and pot the jelly immediately.

cranberry sauce

Cook 250 g (9 oz, 2 cups) cranberries with 250 ml (8 fl oz, 1 cup) water until the fruit is tender. Add 175 g (6 oz, ¾ cup) sugar, stir until it dissolves, then bring to the boil and remove from the heat. Leave to cool before serving. (For a smooth sauce, press the cooked fruit through a sieve before adding the sugar.)

Crab feuilletés, see page 357.

CRANE A large migratory long-legged wading bird, formerly a prized game bird, but no longer used for food as it is a protected species. The Romans cherished this bird and fattened it specially to give it a richer flavour. From the Middle Ages until the 18th century cranes were highly regarded as food, although the flesh is tough: they were served reconstituted and decorated with their feathers.

Lémery, in his *Traité des aliments* (1702), sets great store by them: 'The younger they are, the more tender, delicate, easy to digest and tastier they are.' But Liger, in *La Nouvelle Maison rustique* (1749), comments: 'They have a tough skin that needs to be hung.'

CRAPAUDINE, EN The French term for preparing a small chicken or pigeon as a spatchcock. The split and flattened bird looks like a toad – hence the name, from *crapaud*, a toad. The spatchcocked birds are often coated with breadcrumbs and grilled (broiled). The flavour is retained, since the juices are concentrated and the flesh does not dry out. Lemon slices, bunches of cress and maître d'hôtel butter, devilled sauce or sauce Robert are typical accompaniments. See *spatchcock*.

RECIPE

chicken à la lyonnaise en crapaudine

Spatchcock a chicken by splitting and flattening it. Season with salt and pepper and coat with mustard. Leave for 30 minutes, then roll it in fresh breadcrumbs. Sprinkle with melted butter and grill (broil) gently until cooked through. Serve with a mustard and cream sauce.

CRAPIAU A large savoury pancake, also known as *grapiau*, from the Morvan region of France, which is cooked in melted bacon fat. *Crapiau* batter is sometimes made more substantial with grated potato. In Nevers, sweet *crapiaux* are made from batter containing finely sliced apples steeped in brandy.

CRAQUELIN A small light crunchy cake or biscuit (cookie). It can be a dry petit four (a speciality of Saint-Malo, Binic, Vendée and Beaume-les-Dames), a sort of *échaudé* (in Cotentin) or a cake of unrisen unsweetened dough made into various shapes. *Craquelins* formerly resembled three-cornered hats or eggs. The word, known as early as 1265, derives from the Dutch *crakeline*.

RECIPE

craquelins as petits fours

Knead 250 g (9 oz, 2¼ cups) plain (all-purpose) flour with 125 g (4½ oz, ½ cup) butter, 2 egg yolks, 3 tablespoons cold milk, 25 g (1 oz, 2 tablespoons) caster (superfine) sugar and a generous pinch of salt. Leave the dough to rest for 2 hours, then roll it out to a thickness of 1.5 cm (⅝ in). Cut it into 5 cm (2 in) squares, arrange the squares on a baking sheet, glaze them with egg and bake in a preheated oven 240°C (475°F, gas 9) until golden brown. Sprinkle with vanilla-flavoured sugar when cooked.

CRAQUELOT A young herring, lightly smoked (traditionally in walnut leaves), eaten in northern France from October to December, usually two or three days following its preparation. In Dunkirk it is served grilled (broiled) with fresh butter after being soaked in milk.

CRATER A large vessel in which the Greeks mixed water with wine during meals (wine was rarely drunk undiluted as it was very thick). Craters were made of pottery or bronze and varied in size and shape. Big-bellied craters with *colonnettes* had small vertical double handles; *volute* craters, such as the famous example found at Vix in the Côte-d'Or, had a more slender shape with vertical handles ending in scrolls; the chalice crater is so called because of the shape of the belly, at the base of which are the two handles. A pitcher with a trefoil-shaped mouth, the *oenochoé*, or an elongated version, the *olpé*, was used to draw wine from the crater in order to fill a cup (*kylix, cantharus*) or a goblet (*skyphos*). Each guest could also serve himself with a *cotyle*, a drinking and drawing vessel, or with a *kyathos*, which had a long handle and was also used as a measure for determining the proportions of the mixture.

CRAWFISH Salt water crayfish. See *langouste*.

CRAYFISH A freshwater crustacean resembling a small lobster, the species found in Europe growing to 15–20 cm (6–8 in) long.

During the late 19th and 20th centuries, crayfish became rare in Europe as a result of overfishing, pollution and disease. However, stocks have returned to some areas and crayfish are also farmed. Different species fished in France include the red-clawed crayfish found particularly in the Auvergne; the smaller white-clawed variety; a mountain-stream variety; and the comparatively newly introduced American species.

The American crayfish native to California is known as the signal crayfish for its blue-green stripes on the pincers. Being more resilient than the original European species, this crayfish is now stocked in Sweden and Germany. The Madagascar crayfish is one of the largest species and the Murray River crayfish (or Murray lobster) of Australia is the second largest type, growing to 50 cm (20 in) long. The Marron is another species native to Australia and subject to farming in order to protect the natural stocks.

■ **Cooking crayfish** When preparing live crayfish, add them in small batches to a large pan of vigorously boiling stock or court-bouillon. The liquid must be boiling rapidly and there should be plenty of it to kill the crayfish speedily. Boil for about 3–4 minutes, then use a draining spoon to remove them from the pan. If the crayfish are to be served plain boiled, without further cooking, they should be boiled for 5–6 minutes.

Most of the flesh of a crayfish is in its tail (about one-fifth of its total weight), although the claws, when crushed in a nutcracker, also yield a little meat. The shell is pounded to make bisques (thick soups) and savoury butters. Before the preparation of any crayfish dish, the bitter-tasting gut must be removed. The 17th-century writer Nicolas de Bonnefons described the task: 'They have to be cleaned by removing the gut, which is attached to the media lamina at the end of the tail. After giving it half a turn, pull it, and the gut comes out at the end.' This task is not necessary if the crayfish are kept without food for two days and hung up in a net in a cool place.

Crayfish have been eaten in France since the Middle Ages. They took their place in haute cuisine in the 17th and 18th centuries, in recipes such as pigeon with crayfish, crayfish *cardinalisées* (plunged in boiling court-bouillon) or crayfish pudding. However, it was in the 19th century that they became really fashionable. In the days of the Second Empire and the Belle Époque they became more and more rare and expensive. Crayfish bisque and a *buisson* of crayfish were then the great classics (a *buisson*, which literally means a bush, was a special tiered dish on which cooked crayfish were mounted).

Crayfish remain the major ingredient in some of the most famous recipes of the gastronomic provinces: Jura, Alsace, Bordelais, and Lyonnais, in particular, offer gratins, soufflés, turnovers, rissoles, pies, mousses, moulds, veloutés and dishes *à la nage*. When they are served whole, cooked in stock, crayfish may be picked up in the fingers in order to shell them easily. When served as an accompaniment to other dishes, they are trussed (the ends of the claws are tucked into the base of the abdomen before cooking).

RECIPES

crayfish à la bordelaise

Prepare a finely diced mirepoix of vegetables. Toss 24 crayfish in melted butter and season with salt, pepper and a little cayenne. Pour brandy over the crayfish and set alight, then just cover with dry white wine. Add the vegetable mirepoix and cook together for a maximum of 10 minutes. Drain the crayfish and arrange them in a deep dish. Keep hot. Bind the cooking stock with 2 egg yolks, then beat in 40 g (1½ oz, 3 tablespoons) butter. Adjust the seasoning to give the sauce a good strong flavour. Cover the crayfish with this sauce and serve at once, piping hot.

crayfish mousse

Cook 36 crayfish as in the recipe above for crayfish *à la bordelaise*. Drain the crayfish and shell the tails. Pound the shells in a mortar with the mirepoix, adding 50 g (2 oz, ¼ cup) cold meatless velouté* and 100 ml (4 fl oz, ½ cup) melted aspic jelly*.

Press this mixture through a sieve and add 400 ml (14 fl oz, 1¾ cups) partly whipped cream and the crayfish tails, diced. Line a charlotte mould with white paper and fill with the mixture. Leave in the refrigerator for 6 hours, then turn out of the mould and garnish with truffle slices.

crayfish sauce

(from Carême's recipe) Wash 50 medium-sized crayfish. Cook them with half a bottle of champagne, a sliced onion, a bouquet garni, a pinch of coarsely ground pepper and a little salt. When the crayfish have cooled, drain them and strain the cooking liquor through a silk strainer. Boil down by half, then add 2 tablespoons white sauce. Reduce again to the desired consistency and add half a glass of champagne. After reducing again, strain the sauce through a sieve. Just before serving, add a little glaze and best butter, then the shelled crayfish tails. Add to the sauce crayfish butter made with the pounded crayfish shells.

crayfish tails au gratin à la façon de maître la planche

Make a ragoût of crayfish tails thickened with highly seasoned crayfish purée, using crayfish cooked in a mirepoix, as for crayfish *à la bordelaise* (see above). Put this ragoût in a buttered gratin dish, alternating with layers of fresh truffles which have been cut in thick slices, seasoned and quickly tossed in butter. Sprinkle with finely grated cheese and brown in a preheated oven at 190°C (375°F, gas 5) standing the dish in a pan of warm water to prevent the sauce from curdling.

crayfish timbale à l'ancienne

Prepare crayfish tail ragoût *à la Nantua*. Line a shallow pie dish with fine lining pastry. Line with a thin layer of fine pike forcemeat. Mix coarsely diced truffles, tossed in butter and left to cool, with the ragoût; fill the pie with this. Cover the ragoût with a layer of pike forcemeat. Cover the pie with pastry and seal. Garnish with puff pastry motifs. Make a small hole in the pastry lid to allow the steam to escape. Brush with egg. Bake in a preheated oven at 180°C, (350°F, gas 4) for 45–60 minutes. When the pie is ready, pour into it a few tablespoons of thin Nantua sauce.

grilled crayfish with garlic butter

Prepare some garlic butter by mixing 100 g (4 oz, ½ cup) softened butter with 1 crushed garlic clove, 1 finely chopped shallot and 2 teaspoons chopped herbs (tarragon, chives and parsley). Gut the crayfish and fry them on their fronts in a little olive oil for a few minutes only (until they turn red). Turn them over, grease with a little garlic butter and finish cooking in a preheated oven at 190°C (375°F, gas 5) for 3 or 4 minutes.

other recipes See *bisque, buisson, butter (flavoured butters), egg (scrambled eggs), marinière, nage, nantua, soup.*

CREAM A dairy product consisting of the part of milk, rich in fat, which has been separated by skimming or otherwise. Often an increase in the thickness of cream denotes an increase in fat content, but this is not always true as the viscosity of cream can be controlled by manufacturing processes, giving a variation in the thickness of creams of the same fat content. For example, double (heavy) cream is available in either pouring or 'spooning' consistencies.

Originally the cream was separated from the milk by gravity. When milk is left to stand in a vessel, fat globules cluster or aggregate and, being lighter than the rest of the milk, float to form a layer of cream. This can be skimmed off by hand.

Manufacturers use centrifugal force to separate the cream. In Britain regulations control the composition and descriptions of cream on the basis of milk-fat content. The label must bear a description, and the fat content of the cream should comply with the requirement for that description.

The following are common types of cream available in the UK with the legal minimum milk fat content by weight. In the United States the milk fat content of the different types of cream varies slightly from those given below.

- CLOTTED CREAM With a 55% fat content. This is produced by scalding, cooking and skimming milk or cream. The traditional farmhouse method of making clotted cream is to pour milk into shallow pans and leave undisturbed for 12–24 hours for the cream to rise. The pans are then heated or scalded to about 82ºC (180ºF) and held at this temperature for about an hour. The surface cream develops a rich yellow wrinkled crust. The pans are then cooled slowly and the cream crust skimmed off. The heating of the cream improves its keeping qualities by destroying bacteria which may cause souring.

Clotted cream is produced commercially, mainly in Devon, Cornwall and Somerset, by heating pans of 55% cream in water jackets. Commercial clotted cream tends to be smoother than farmhouse cream, but has the same distinctive scalded flavour. Clotted cream is traditionally served with scones, fruit and fruit pies.

- DOUBLE (HEAVY) CREAM With a 48% fat content. This is sometimes homogenized; it may be pasteurized. It can be used as a rich pouring cream, for whipping or floating.
- WHIPPING CREAM With a 35% fat content. This is not usually homogenized, but may be pasteurized. Whipping cream will double its volume when whipped. It is lighter in texture and less likely to curdle through overwhipping.
- WHIPPED CREAM With a 35% fat content. This is sold pasteurized and mainly in frozen form, although some is sold chilled. Commercially whipped cream may have a fairly high sugar content.
- SINGLE (LIGHT) CREAM With an 18% fat content. This is normally homogenized to prevent separation during storage. It may be pasteurized. Single cream is widely used as an accompainiment for desserts and in cooking, savoury and sweet.

- HALF CREAM With a 12% fat content. This is homogenized to prevent separation; it may also be pasteurized. It is sometimes known as 'coffee cream' or 'top of the milk'.
- SOURED CREAM With an 18% fat content. This is pasteurized, homogenized single cream soured by the addition of a culture of bacteria which convert the natural sugar, lactose, into lactic acid to give a piquant refreshing flavour.
- UHT CREAM This is subjected to ultra-heat treatment, which destroys any viable micro-organisms and their spores that may be present in the cream. There is a slight change in the flavour. The treated cream is homogenized, poured into sterile containers, and sealed. Double, whipping and single cream can all be preserved by UHT.
- FROZEN CREAM Single, whipping or double cream is pasteurized, cooked and commercially frozen either by blast freezing for about 45 minutes or by passing the cream, sandwiched between two belts, through a zone where it is frozen to –18ºC (0ºF) in 2–4 minutes. It is usually sold in chips (pats) or stick form to make it easy to select the amount needed.
- AEROSOL CREAM Ultra-heat treated and packed in aerosol containers. Nitrus oxide is used as a propellant to release the whipped cream and aid aeration. There is a volume increase of 400%. This type of product is usually slightly sweetened. It is a popular topping in many fast-food-type catering establishments, but the whipped cream starts to collapse soon after it has been squirted out.

See also *crème fraîche*.

CREAM SOUP A thickened, smooth soup enriched with milk and/or cream. Traditionally, cream soups are based on a roux of fat and flour with stock and milk added. This is used to cook the main ingredients for the soup until tender. The soup is then puréed or pressed through a sieve and enriched with cream before serving. Alternatively, a white sauce may be used or the soup can be thickened with flour, rice flour or cornflour (cornstarch). Root vegetables, such as potatoes or celeriac, may be puréed with liquid to thicken the soup. Breadcrumbs also give a creamy consistency. The basic ingredients can be fish or shellfish, poultry, vegetables or grains. Bright herbs, such as parsley, chives or chervil, bring colours to pale cream soups (for example chicken soup) and crisp garnishes, such as croûtons, provide contrasting texture.

RECIPES

traditional basic cream soups

Shred and blanch the chosen vegetable, then cook it in butter in a covered pan, using 40–50 g (1½–2 oz, 3–4 tablespoons) butter per 500 g (18 oz) vegetables. Prepare 750 ml (1¼ pints, 3¼ cups) white sauce by adding 900 ml (1½ pints, 1 quart) milk to a white roux of 25 g (1 oz, 2 tablespoons) butter and 40 g (1½ oz, 6 tablespoons) plain (all-purpose) flour. Mix this sauce with the lightly cooked vegetables and simmer gently for 12–18 minutes depending on the vegetable used. Purée in a food processor or blender, then press through a sieve if necessary. Dilute with a few tablespoons of white consommé (or milk if the soup is to be meatless). Heat and adjust the seasoning. Add 200 ml (7 fl oz, ¾ cup) single (light) cream and stir while heating.

cream-enriched puréed soups

Cook 1 large finely chopped onion and 1 large thinly sliced leek in 50 g (2 oz, 4 tablespoons) butter until soft without browning. Dice 1 large potato and add to the onion, stirring to coat the pieces in butter. Pour in 600 ml (1 pint, 2½ cups) chicken or vegetable stock and bring to the boil. Cover and simmer for 5 minutes. Add the prepared chosen vegetable, such as 450 g (1 lb) broccoli florets or spinach; 2 bunches of watercress; 225 g (8 oz) sliced carrots; or 225 g (8 oz) sliced button mushrooms, and continue to simmer, covered, until the potato is completely tender.

Purée the ingredients with their cooking liquid, then return the purée to the rinsed-out saucepan. Reheat until just simmering, then add 300 ml (½ pint, 1¼ cups) single (light) cream and seasoning to taste. Reheat gently without boiling. Taste for seasoning before serving.

This method can also be used for mixed vegetables, such as peeled and seeded fresh tomatoes with red peppers, or lettuce, spinach and watercress, or for seafood or poultry soups. For seafood soups, use good fish stock and white fish, prawns or crab; add half the fish or seafood when the potatoes are tender and cook for about 5 minutes, until the fish is just cooked. Simmer the remaining fish or seafood in the puréed soup until just cooked before adding the cream. For poultry soup, use excellent poultry stock and purée half the prepared boneless meat with the soup, then reheat the remainder with the soup before stirring in the cream.

enriching with cream and egg yolks

To enrich a soup in the final stages, just before serving, beat 2 egg yolks with 150 ml (¼ pint, ⅔ cup) single (light) cream until smooth. Stir in a ladleful of the hot soup. Reduce the heat under the soup to ensure that it is not boiling, then stir in the egg yolk and cream mixture. Cook gently for 1–2 minutes, stirring, but do not allow the soup to boil or the egg and cream will curdle.

cream of asparagus soup

Following the recipe for traditional basic cream soups, blanch 400 g (14 oz) asparagus tips and cook them in butter in a covered pan. Add 750 ml (1¼ pints, 3¼ cups) white sauce and purée in a food processor or blender. Do not cook the asparagus and béchamel together, but reheat and season the soup before serving.

cream of beetroot soup

Cook 200 g (7 oz) beetroot (beet) in a preheated oven at 180°C (350°F, gas 4). Finely shred 50 g

(2 oz) of the cooked beetroot and set it aside. Purée the remainder in a food processor or blender. Press through a sieve into a large saucepan and sprinkle with lemon juice. Following the recipe for traditional basic cream soups, add 500 ml (17 fl oz, 2 cups) white sauce, and the same amount of consommé*. Cook for 10 minutes. Add 100 ml (4 fl oz, 7 tablespoons) single (light) cream and heat without boiling. Add the reserved beetroot and adjust the seasoning before serving.

cream of celery soup

Chop 2 celery hearts. Following the recipe for traditional basic cream soups, cook the celery in 50 g (2 oz, 4 tablespoons) butter until tender. Finish as in the basic recipe, simmering the soup for 12 minutes.

cream of chicken soup

Put a small tender chicken into a saucepan containing 1 litre (1¾ pints, 4⅓ cups) white consommé*, bring to the boil and skim. Add a bouquet garni supplemented with the white parts of 2 leeks and 1 celery stick. Simmer very gently with the lid on until the meat comes away from the bones. Drain the chicken, retaining the stock, and remove the skin and bones.

Keep the breast fillets and reduce the remaining meat to a purée using a food processor. Press through a sieve. Shred the breast fillets finely and keep them hot in a little consommé. Add 750 ml (1¼ pints, 3¼ cups) béchamel* sauce to the chicken purée and bring to the boil. Add a few spoonfuls of the chicken stock and whisk. Adjust the seasoning and sieve again. Add 100 ml (4 fl oz, 7 tablespoons) single (light) cream and whisk while heating. Add the finely shredded breast fillets just before serving.

cream of leek soup

Shred 500 g (18 oz) leeks. Following the recipe for traditional basic cream soups, cook the leeks in butter in a covered pan until tender. Finish as in the basic recipe.

cream of mushroom soup

Clean 675 g (1½ lb) mushrooms, putting 100 g (4 oz) aside. Cook the remaining mushrooms in butter in a covered pan and make the soup following the recipe for traditional basic cream soups. Finely shred the reserved mushrooms and sprinkle them with lemon juice. Add them to the soup just before serving.

cream of shrimp soup

Prepare 100 ml (4 fl oz, 7 tablespoons) vegetable mirepoix* and cook it gently in about 25 g (1 oz, 2 tablespoons) butter. Add 350 g (12 oz, about 2 cups) unpeeled raw shrimps and sauté them. Season with salt and pepper. Moisten with 3 tablespoons white wine and 1 tablespoon brandy that has been ignited. Cook for about 5 minutes. Reserve 12 shrimps for the garnish and purée the rest in a blender or food processor. Sieve and add 750 ml (1¼ pints, 3¼ cups) white* sauce and finish as described in the method for traditional basic cream soups. Peel the reserved shrimps and garnish the soup with them just before serving.

Cream of prawn, crayfish, lobster, langouste or scampi soups can be made in the same way; peel these larger shellfish before cooking them.

cream of watercress soup

Clean 500 g (18 oz) watercress and remove the large stems. Clean, blanch and chop the watercress, cook it in butter in a covered pan, then follow the method for traditional basic cream soups.

du Barry cream soup

Steam a small fresh cauliflower until it breaks up easily. Put it through the food processor, then add 750 ml (1¼ pints, 3¼ cups) white* sauce and follow the method for traditional basic cream soups.

additional recipe See *barley*.

CREAMS Sweet preparations with the consistency of cream. The term for a wide variety of desserts and dessert toppings or accompaniments, creams may be based on custards or sweet sauces, enriched with cream or lightened with whipped cream. Whipped desserts, such as zabaglione or syllabub, are classed as creams.

Alternatively, creams may be prepared from set mixtures, for example with gelatine or melted chocolate. Bavarian cream is an example of a custard mixture lightened with whipped cream, usually with an additional setting agent, such as gelatine or melted chocolate.

A cooked sauce, thickened with flour or arrowroot, may form the base for a cream as can a fruit purée. Fruit fools, purées of cooked fruit lightened and enriched with custard and/or whipped cream, are also included in this category.

Although traditionally enriched with milk or cream, yogurt or fromage frais may be used for contemporary, lighter results. Similarly, creamy mixtures resembling dairy creams can be prepared from bean curd or by grinding and puréeing plain nuts (neither roasted nor seasoned) with a little fruit juice, typically apple juice.

RECIPES

almond cream

Beat 2–3 whole eggs as for an omelette and put them aside. Beat 150 g (5 oz, 1 cup) blanched or ground almonds with the same weight each of sugar and of butter until pale and creamy. When the mixture is thoroughly blended, beat in the eggs one by one.

caramel cream for decorating desserts

Cook 200 g (7 oz, ¾ cup) caster (superfine) sugar in 100 ml (4 fl oz, 7 tablespoons) water to obtain a golden caramel. Pour 250 ml (8 fl oz, 1 cup) double (heavy) cream into a large deep basin, sprinkle it

with the caramel, and whisk. Then transfer the mixture to a saucepan and cook over a gentle heat. Meanwhile work 225 g (8 oz, 1 cup) butter with a spatula in the deep basin until soft. Test a drop of the caramel cream in a bowl of cold water: if it forms a firm ball, the cream is cooked. Then pour it over the butter, whipping briskly. Set aside in a cool place until until used.

lemon cream

For 8 people, use 2 lemons, 5 eggs, 125 g (4½ oz, ½ cup) butter and 200 g (7 oz, 1½ cups) icing (confectioner's) sugar. Grate the rind from one of the lemons. Then squeeze both lemons and strain the juice. Whisk the eggs with a fork. Melt the butter over a very gentle heat, add the sugar and lemon juice and bring to the boil. Sprinkle the whisked eggs with this mixture, whisking quickly to obtain a very smooth cream. Return to the saucepan, add the grated lemon zest and bring to the boil over a gentle heat, whisking all the time. Pour the lemon cream into a bowl and leave to cool before placing it in the refrigerator.

set custard (with gelatine)

Prepare a crème anglaise (see *custard*). When it is cooked, add 7–15 g (¼–½ oz, 1–2 envelopes) powdered gelatine softened in cold water and drained. Strain into the custard and stir until completely cool. This custard is used in the preparation of Bavarian cream and charlotte russe.

French Butter Creams

French butter cream or *crème au beurre* may be used to sandwich and coat layered cakes or gâteaux. It can be piped and used for decoration.

crème au beurre (with syrup)

Boil 125 g (4½ oz, ¼ cup) caster (superfine) sugar in 500 ml (17 fl oz, 2 cups) water for 10 minutes to a temperature of 120°C (248°F). Meanwhile, beat 4 egg yolks in a small bowl. Gradually pour on the boiling syrup, whisking for 3 minutes. Continue to whisk until the mixture is lukewarm. Then whisk in 125 g (4½ oz, ½ cup) butter cut into small pieces and whisk for a further 5 minutes.

crème au beurre (with custard)

Prepare the recipe for crème anglaise (see *custard*). Bring 225 g (8 oz, 1 cup) butter to room temperature, then cut it into small pieces. Blend the butter with the custard cream, working with a whisk, and flavour as desired (with coffee, chocolate, liqueur, praline, lemon zest or orange zest).

crème au beurre (with sugar)

Beat together 250 g (9 oz, 1 cup) caster (superfine) sugar and 6 egg yolks. Then blend in a few drops of vanilla extract and 100 ml (4 fl oz, 7 tablespoons) double (heavy) cream until the mixture is quite smooth. In a separate bowl, work 225 g (8 oz, 1 cup) butter into a soft paste using a wooden spatula. Place the first basin in a bain marie and whisk the mixture until it becomes white and foamy. Remove it from the bain marie and continue to whip until completely cool. Then gradually blend this mixture with the creamed butter.

chocolate crème au beurre

Follow the recipe for crème au beurre (with custard), but dissolve plain (unsweetened) chocolate in the milk, using 100 g (4 oz, 4 squares) chocolate to 500 ml (17 fl oz, 2 cups) milk. For crème au beurre made with sugar syrup, dissolve the chocolate in a bain marie and incorporate in the finished crème au beurre.

coffee crème au beurre

Add coffee essence (extract) or instant coffee to the milk used when making a custard base. To flavour cream made with sugar syrup, blend the coffee essence or instant coffee with cream, using 1 teaspoon coffee essence to 300 ml (½ pint, 1¼ cups) double (heavy) cream; the mixture should become homogeneous when heated.

praline crème au beurre

Blend some finely crushed praline into the prepared cream, using 50 g (2 oz, ½ cup) praline for 300 ml (11 fl oz, 1⅓ cups) cream.

other recipes See *Chantilly, chestnut, Chiboust, frangipane, ganache, plombières, Saint-Honoré.*

CRÉCY Any of various dishes that contain carrots. Purée Crecy is a carrot purée used as a base for a soup and as a garnish for various dishes, including poached eggs, omelette and fillets of sole. In consommé Crécy, the carrots are shredded into a *brunoise*, while for tournedos Crécy they are turned and glazed.

It is not known whether the name derives from the produce of Crécy-la-Chapelle (Seine-et-Marne) or Crécy-en-Ponthieu in Somme.

RECIPES

artichokes Crécy

Prepare 12 very small fresh artichokes and put them in a generously buttered sauté pan. Turn 800 g (1¾ lb) small new carrots and add them to the sauté pan. Season with salt and a pinch of sugar. Moisten with 4 tablespoons water, cover, and cook slowly for about 40 minutes. Add 1 tablespoon unsalted butter just before serving.

Crécy soup

Scrape 500 g (18 oz) very tender carrots, slice thinly and cook them with 50 g (2 oz, ¼ cup) butter in a covered pan. Add 1 tablespoon shredded onion, a pinch of salt and ½ teaspoon sugar. When the vegetables are soft, add 1 litre (1¾ pints, 4⅓ cups) beef or chicken consommé*, bring to the boil and add 100 g (4 oz, ½ cup) rice. Cook slowly

with the lid on for about 20 minutes, then put it through a blender and strain. Add a few more spoonfuls of consommé, heat and add 25 g (1 oz, 2 tablespoons) butter. Adjust the seasoning. Serve with small croûtons fried in butter.

eggs sur le plat Crécy

Butter a gratin dish and spread 1 tablespoon carrot purée on it. Break 2 eggs into the dish, bake in a preheated oven at 180°C (350°F, gas 4), then surround with a border of cream sauce.

fillets of sole Crécy

Wash, clean and fold up the fillets of sole. Poach them in a fish fumet for 5 minutes, drain them and arrange on a long dish. Strain the stock, reduce and add 2 tablespoons béchamel* sauce and the same amount of carrot purée. Mix well and heat. Coat the fillets with this sauce and garnish them with very small glazed new carrots.

CRÉMANT This term was used to describe champagne wines with less atmospheric pressure than fully sparkling champagne, but it is now reserved for the finest French sparkling wines made by the traditional method. The principal sources of Crémant are Alsace, Die, Bourgogne, Loire, Limoux and Bordeaux.

CRÈME A sweet liqueur with a syrupy consistency. Crèmes are obtained by soaking various substances in brandy or a spirit containing sugar syrup: fruits (pineapple, bananas, blackcurrants, strawberries, tangerines, sloes, raspberries), various plant parts (vanilla, mint, cocoa, tea, coffee) or flowers (violet, rose). These liqueurs were very fashionable in the 19th century and often had exotic names, such as *crème de Barbade* and *crème créole*. Crèmes are usually drunk as a digestant in small glasses. They are also included in cocktails and sometimes served as an apéritif with ice and water.

The French word *crème* is also used in a culinary context for cream soups, for dairy cream (see *crème fraîche*) and for a wide variety of sweet preparations (see *creams*).

CRÈME BRÛLÉE A dessert consisting of a rich custard of egg yolks, sugar and cream, often flavoured, which is set by cooking in the oven. The chilled custard is covered with brown sugar and caramelized under a very hot grill (broiler) or with a blowtorch. See *custard*.

CRÈME CATALANE A Spanish cooked cream, similar to confectioner's custard (pastry cream) but thicker as a result of slightly different proportions of ingredients, and flavoured with lemon zest and cinnamon. Traditionally served in flat-bottomed stoneware ramekins, the top is often caramelized.

CRÈME FRAÎCHE Cream to which a lactic bacteria culture has been added, which thickens the cream and gives it a slightly sharp but not sour flavour.

Crème fraîche is a traditional ingredient in French cooking. In Normandy, where it is sometimes combined with Calvados, it is used with sole, leg of mutton, chicken and mussels. Crème fraîche is also used in cooking north of the Loire (fricassée of rabbit or poultry in Anjou), in Lorraine and Alsace (soups, vegetable flans), in the traditional stockpot of Dieppe, for hare à la crème in the Bourbonnais, and for chicken with morels in Franche-Comté. More generally, crème fraîche enlivens vegetables (green beans, mushrooms, cauliflower), is sometimes used as a salad dressing (for lettuce hearts, cucumber), adds a finishing touch to soups and *blanquettes*, and, above all, is an essential ingredient in numerous sauces (*bonne femme, breton, normande, poulette, princesse, rémoulade, suprême*). Finally, crème fraîche is used in pâtisserie, as an ingredient, filling or decoration, and in confectionery, for caramels. It is also added to certain drinks (coffee, cocktails).

Crème fleurette (12–15% fat) is light and semi-liquid and must be consumed within 48 hours (unless it is UHT). It is used for preparing Chantilly cream and for accompanying fromage frais, pastries, fruits or coffee.

CRÉMER A French culinary term meaning to add fresh cream to a preparation (such as a soup or sauce) in order to bind it and obtain a smooth consistency and a softer taste. Eggs *en cocotte* are covered with fresh cream before cooking.

CRÉMET A dessert made with cow's-milk fromage frais, stiffly whisked egg whites and whipped cream. *Crémets* are a speciality of Angers and Saumur. When the mixture is quite firm, it is placed in small perforated moulds, each lined with a piece of muslin (cheesecloth), and left to drain in a cool place. This delicate and light dessert is served with fresh cream and sugar.

CRÉOLE, À LA The name given to numerous sweet and savoury preparations inspired by West Indian cookery. In particular, the term refers to a method of preparing rice by cooking it in plenty of water, draining it and then drying it in the oven in a buttered dish. It is finished with tomatoes, sweet peppers and onions, and served with various meats, poultry, fish and shellfish. Sweet dishes à la créole contain rum, pineapple, vanilla or banana.

RECIPES

Savoury Dishes
calves' liver à la créole
Cut some fat bacon into very small strips and marinate them in a mixture of oil, lime juice, salt and pepper. Use them to lard some slices of calves' liver and then marinate the liver for 20 minutes in the same mixture. Drain them, coat them with flour and cook them in a frying pan in some lard (shortening). Remove the slices of liver from the pan and keep them warm in a buttered dish. For every 6 slices of liver, flavour the juices in the frying pan with 2 tablespoons chopped onion and 1 tablespoon chopped parsley. Brown the onion and parsley and then add 1 tablespoon white breadcrumbs, salt, pepper and 1 tablespoon tomato purée (paste) diluted with 3–4 tablespoons white wine. Heat the sauce, stirring continuously, and adjust the seasoning. Coat the liver with the sauce.

chicken à la créole
Cut a chicken of about 1.5 kg (3¼ lb) into 8 pieces and season with salt and pepper. Heat 3 tablespoons oil in a sauté pan and brown the chicken pieces. Cover and cook gently for 20–30 minutes. Then add a small glass of rum, flame the chicken pieces and keep them hot on a serving dish. Skim the fat off the cooking juices and add 4 slices of canned pineapple (cut into pieces) to the sauté pan, together with 3–4 tablespoons of the pineapple syrup. Then add 2 tablespoons lime juice and a dash of cayenne. Reduce the sauce and adjust the seasoning. Coat the chicken pieces with sauce and garnish them with pineapple.

fillets of brill à la créole
Remove the fillets from a brill, clean them and season with salt, pepper and a pinch of cayenne. Coat them in flour and cook them in oil in a frying pan. When they are cooked, sprinkle them with lemon juice and arrange them on a warmed serving dish. In the same pan fry a mixture of chopped garlic and parsley (1 tablespoon for 6 fillets) and pour this over the fillets, together with some oil flavoured with chilli peppers. Brown some halves of tomato in oil and stuff them with rice pilaf. Garnish the fillets with the stuffed tomatoes and with diced sweet peppers that have been slowly cooked in oil.

other recipes See *beef, curry, okra, paupiette, rice, salt cod.*

Sweet Dishes
Bavarian cream à la créole
Grease a mould with sweet almond oil and fill it with alternating layers of rum-flavoured and pineapple-flavoured basic Bavarian cream, separating the layers with finely chopped bananas soaked in rum. Place in the refrigerator for about 3 hours. Then turn it out on to a dish and decorate with Chantilly cream. Sprinkle with chopped pistachio nuts.

iced pineapple à la créole
Slice the top off a pineapple and keep it in a cool place, wrapping the leaves so that they do not wilt. Carefully scoop out the flesh of the pineapple and discard the core. Make a pineapple water ice with the pulp. Soak some finely chopped crystallized (candied) fruit in a little rum. When the pineapple ice is frozen, fill the pineapple by placing the

crystallized fruits between two layers of pineapple ice. Replace the top of the pineapple and keep it in the freezer until ready to serve. Serve on a bed of crushed ice.

other recipes See *banana, border, pannequet, persimmon.*

CREOLE COOKERY
In the broadest sense, the term Creole is used to describe a cuisine that has evolved from two or more distinctly different styles of cookery. 'A mixture of Caribbean, African and Hindu recipes, in which there is a blend of subtlety and violence, embellished by the scent of herbs, spices and peppers' (Albert Veille). There are, in fact, as many types of Creole cookery as there are African culinary traditions. They have been introduced gradually into the cuisine of various tropical countries, such as Brazil and former French, British, Spanish and Dutch colonies.

In practice, the term is used for the cooking of Louisiana – the Creole cuisine born of French, Spanish and African influences. The name evolved from *Criollo*, the name given by the Spanish governors of New Orleans to those of European descent. This is a sophisticated, colourful cooking style which is well-balanced and subtle. Sometimes referred to as city cooking, the influence of French cooking is evident in dishes enriched with butter or cream. While a simple crab soup rich in the use of butter and cream, spiced with pepper, mace and Worcestershire sauce is a good example of the elegant and subtly spicy characteristics to be found, bright and bold dishes are typical. Onions, peppers and celery are the basis for many savoury dishes, often combining a variety of ingredients. Crab, freshwater crayfish, pork and salt pork feature, with herbs, spices, garlic, tomatoes and okra. Rice is important and red beans are used. Filé powder, made from ground sassafras leaves, is used for seasoning and thickening.

Jambalaya is one of the famous dishes of Creole cooking. Possibly originating from the Spanish paella and the French *jambon*, or ham, this rice dish varies widely according to the cook and may include seafood, chicken, meat, peppers, tomatoes and onions. Gumbo is another speciality which varies in its content. A stew of seafood, poultry and/or sausages and meat with vegetables, including tomatoes and okra, it is thickened with filé powder in addition to the okra. Gumbo z'herbes is famous as the traditional Good Friday stew, containing at least seven (and sometimes more than a dozen) types of greens and/or herbs.

Cajun cooking is the other famous cooking style of the area. Although there is great overlap between Cajun and Creole cooking, Cajun cooking is simpler, more rural and less urban. See *Cajun cooking.*

CRÊPE
A pancake, made by cooking a thin batter sparingly in a very thin layer in a frying or special crêpe pan. The word comes from the Latin *crispus*, meaning curly or wavy.

Crêpe batter is prepared in advance and allowed to stand so that the flour swells and any air beaten in during preparation has time to dissipate. After standing a little extra liquid may by added if the batter has become slightly too thick. Standing and thinning ensures that the batter does not rise and that the crêpes are fine and even. Wheat or buckwheat flour may be used (if the latter, they are often called *galettes*) and either milk or water to mix. If beer is used to mix the batter, it rises slightly. The number of eggs used depends on the individual recipe, but the batter must always have a pouring consistency. Some recipes require the addition of sugar. The crêpes may be fried in oil or butter.

Pancakes are traditionally served on Candlemas and Shrove Tuesday, to celebrate renewal, family life and hopes for good fortune and happiness in the future. It is customary in France to touch the handle of the frying pan and make a wish while the pancake is turned, holding a coin in the hand. In French rural society, crêpes were also considered to be a symbol of allegiance: farmers offered them to their landowner. Pancakes are popular, not only throughout France but also in other countries, including Germany, the United States and Austria. In the United States they are soaked in butter, coated with maple syrup or filled with blueberries, cranberries or applesauce. Some regional French crêpes are the *tantimolles* of Champagne, the *landimolles* of Picardy, the *chialades* of Argonne, the *sanciaux* of Limousin and Berry and the *crespets* of Béarn.

In western France, particularly in Brittany, crêpes are prepared throughout the year and served with salted butter. *Crêpes dentelles* (lace pancakes), a speciality of Quimper, are crisp biscuits made of small thin tongue shapes of batter, baked and then rolled up. In central France, the Auvergne, Lorraine and the Lyonnais district, the batter is often enriched (or even replaced) by finely sliced or puréed potatoes in such dishes as *bourriols, criques* and *matafans.*

Crêpes, a speciality of Agen (particularly on the occasion of the Fête des Félibres), were extolled by Anatole France in *Le Temps.* He wrote, 'Sprinkled with sugar and eaten hot, they form an exquisite dish. They have a golden hue and are tempting to eat. Thin and transparent like muslin, their edges are trimmed to resemble fine lace. They are so light that after a good dinner, a man from Agen is still willing to sample three or four dozen of them! Crêpes form an integral part of every family celebration. Served with white wine, they take pride of place on all joyful occasions.'

In traditional cookery, crêpes are served as a hot hors d'oeuvre, filled with a fairly thick mixture based on a béchamel or velouté sauce with mushrooms, ham, Gruyère cheese or seafood. They may also be cut into fine strips and used to garnish soup. More often, however, crêpes are prepared as sweet dishes. They may be served plain and dusted with sugar, or filled with jam, cream (sometimes mixed with a salpicon of fruits), honey, melted chocolate or chestnut cream. They may be served warm, or flamed, or even layered on top of one another to form a cake.

RECIPES

Savoury Crêpes

savoury crêpe batter

Mix 500 g (18 oz, 4½ cups) plain (all-purpose) flour with 5–6 beaten eggs and a large pinch of salt. Then gradually add 1 litre (1¾ pints, 4⅓ cups) milk or, for lighter pancakes, 500 ml (17 fl oz, 2 cups) milk and 500 ml (17 fl oz, 2 cups) water. The batter may also be made with equal quantities of beer and milk, or the milk may be replaced by white consommé. Finally, add 3 tablespoons oil, either one with little taste, such as groundnut (peanut) oil or sunflower oil or, if the recipe requires it, use olive oil; 25 g (1 oz, 2 tablespoons) melted butter may also be added. Leave the batter to stand for 2 hours. Just before making the crêpes, dilute the batter with a little water (100–200 ml, 4–7 fl oz, ½–¾ cup).

buckwheat crêpes or galettes

Mix 250 g (9 oz, 2¼ cups) buckwheat flour and 250 g (9 oz, 2¼ cups) plain (all-purpose) flour (or use all buckwheat flour) in a bowl with 5–6 beaten eggs and a large pinch of salt. Add, a little at a time, 500 ml (17 fl oz, 2 cups) milk and 750 ml (1¼ pints, 3¼ cups) water and then 3–4 tablespoons oil. Leave the batter to stand for 2 hours at room temperature. Just before making the crêpes, thin the batter with 100 ml (4 fl oz, 7 tablespoons) water as necessary.

egg and cheese crêpes

Prepare some buckwheat crêpes as described above. After turning each crêpe over in the pan to cook the other side, break an egg on top. As soon as the white is set, season lightly, sprinkle with grated cheese and fold each crêpe into a square. Serve immediately, very hot.

ham crêpes

Prepare 12 savoury crêpes. Prepare separately a béchamel sauce with 40 g (1½ oz, 3 tablespoons) butter, 40 g (1½ oz, 6 tablespoons) plain (all-purpose) flour, 500 ml (17 fl oz, 2 cups) milk, nutmeg, salt and pepper. Add 150 g (5 oz, ⅔ cup) diced Paris or York ham and 50 g (2 oz, ½ cup) grated cheese to the sauce. Cool and fill each crêpe with one-twelfth of this mixture. Roll up the crêpes and arrange them in a buttered ovenproof dish. Sprinkle with 50 g (2 oz, ½ cup) grated cheese and 25 g (1 oz, 2 tablespoons) melted butter and brown in a preheated oven at 230°C (450°F, gas 8).

mushroom crêpes

Prepare some savoury crêpe batter as above and leave it to stand. Meanwhile, prepare a duxelles with 500 g (18 oz, 6 cups) mushrooms, 1 or 2 shallots, a small garlic clove 20 g (¾ oz, 1½ tablespoons) butter, salt and pepper, and 300 ml (½ pint, 1¼ cups) béchamel* sauce.

Make 12 crêpes, cooking each one as follows: melt a knob of butter in a frying pan and pour a small quantity of batter into the pan, tilting it in all directions to spread a thin film of batter. Cook over a moderate heat until the crêpe slides when the pan is shaken. Then turn the crêpe over and cook the other side for about 2 minutes. Place a tablespoon of the mixed béchamel sauce and duxelles on each crêpe and roll it up. Arrange the crêpes close together on a lightly buttered ovenproof dish and sprinkle them with 50 g (2 oz, ½ cup) grated cheese. Top with 25 g (1 oz, 2 tablespoons) melted butter and either brown them under the grill (broiler) or reheat them in a preheated oven at 230°C (450°F, gas 8). Serve very hot.

The béchamel sauce may be replaced by 6 tablespoons double (heavy) cream.

onion crêpes

Prepare some buckwheat crêpes, fill each one with 1 tablespoon onion purée, roll it up and finish as for mushroom crêpes.

Roquefort-cheese crêpes

Make 12 savoury crêpes. Mix about 12 tablespoons béchamel* sauce with 4 tablespoons Roquefort cheese that has been pounded into a paste. Season with pepper and a little nutmeg. Fill each crêpe with a heaped tablespoon of the mixture, roll them up and place in a lightly buttered ovenproof dish. Sprinkle with grated cheese and brown them in a preheated oven at 230°C (450°F, gas 8).

Brie, blue cheese or Gruyère cheese may be used instead of Roquefort cheese.

spinach crêpes au gratin

Prepare savoury crêpes and creamed spinach. Put about 1 tablespoon spinach on each crêpe and roll it up. Finish as for mushroom crêpes.

Sweet Crêpes

sweet crêpe batter

Mix 500 g (18 oz, 4½ cups) plain (all-purpose) flour with 1 tablespoon vanilla-flavoured sugar (or a few drops of vanilla extract), 5–6 beaten eggs and a small pinch of salt. Gradually stir in 750 ml (1¼ pints, 3¼ cups) milk and 250 ml (8 fl oz, 1 cup) water. Flavour with a small glass of rum, Cognac, Calvados or Grand Marnier, depending on the recipe. Finally, add 40 g (1½ oz, 3 tablespoons) melted butter or a mixture of 25 g (1 oz, 2 tablespoons) melted butter and 2 tablespoons oil. Leave the batter to stand for 2 hours. Just before making the crêpes, dilute the batter with a little water or milk – 100–200 ml (4–7 fl oz, ½–¾ cup).

It was formerly the custom to add 2–3 tablespoons caster (superfine) sugar to the batter, in addition to the vanilla-flavoured sugar. Today, the crêpes are usually sprinkled with sugar when cooked, according to individual tastes.

almond crêpes

Prepare some crêpe batter and leave it to stand. Meanwhile, make some confectioner's custard (see *custard*), adding 75 g (3 oz, ¾ cup) ground almonds to each 600 ml (1 pint, 2½ cups) custard. Cook the pancakes and fill them with the almond cream. Roll them up, arrange them in an ovenproof dish, dust with caster (superfine) sugar, and brown them quickly in a preheated oven at 230°C (450°F, gas 8).

apple and walnut crêpes
Make some sweet crêpes. Lightly brown some thin slices of apple in butter and sprinkle them with sugar. Cover a quarter of each crêpe with the apple slices and a few peeled moist walnuts. Fold the crêpes in four and sprinkle with sugar. The crêpes may be flamed with Calvados or with another fruit liqueur.

Chartreuse crêpes
Prepare a crêpe batter in the usual way. Fifteen minutes before making the crêpes, prepare the filling. Beat 50 g (2 oz, ¼ cup) butter to a soft paste and add 50 g (2 oz, ¼ cup) caster (superfine) sugar, 3 crushed meringues and 3 tablespoons green Chartreuse. Add 6 crushed macaroons, the grated zest of an orange and 3 tablespoons Cognac to the batter and mix well. Thin the batter with 100 ml (4 fl oz, 7 tablespoons) water and cook the crêpes. Spread each one with the filling and fold in four. Dust with icing (confectioner's) sugar and serve very hot.

cherry crêpes
Prepare a crêpe batter with 250 g (9 oz, 2¼ cups) plain (all-purpose) flour, 75 g (3 oz, 6 tablespoons) caster (superfine) sugar, a pinch of salt, 3 beaten eggs and 1 egg yolk, gradually adding 500 ml (17 fl oz, 2 cups) milk. Leave to stand for 2 hours at room temperature. Remove the stalks and stones (pits) from 400 g (14 oz, 1⅔ cups) fresh cherries – or use 300 g (11 oz, 1¼ cups) cherries preserved in syrup. Cut them in two, mix them with the batter and allow to stand for 2 hours.

Cook the crêpes and keep them hot on a plate over a saucepan of boiling water. Coat each crêpe with a thin layer of orange marmalade – about 200 g (7 oz, ⅔ cup) is required. Roll up the crêpes and arrange them on an ovenproof dish. Sprinkle with caster sugar and glaze in the oven.

crêpes à la cévenole
Prepare some sweet crêpes and coat each one with a thin layer of rum-flavoured chestnut cream. Roll up the crêpes and arrange them in a buttered ovenproof dish. Dust generously with caster (superfine) sugar and grill (broil) to caramelize the sugar. Serve with Chantilly cream if desired.

crêpes à la condé
Prepare a crêpe batter with 250 g (9 oz, 2¼ cups) plain (all-purpose) flour, 3 eggs, 500 ml (17 fl oz, 2 cups) milk, 2 teaspoons dried yeast and 2 tablespoons oil. Let it stand for 2 hours at room temperature. Soak 50 g (2 oz, ⅓ cup) chopped crystallized (candied) fruits in 100 ml (4 fl oz, 7 tablespoons) rum.

Boil 2 litres (3½ pints, 9 cups) water in a saucepan, add 100 g (4 oz, ⅔ cup) short-grain rice, boil for a few seconds and then rinse the rice in cold water. Set aside to drain. Boil 400 ml (14 fl oz, 1¾ cups) milk with a vanilla pod (bean). Remove the pod and add to the milk 75 g (3 oz, 6 tablespoons) caster (superfine) sugar, 25 g (1 oz, 2 tablespoons) butter, a generous pinch of salt and the rice. Bring to the boil, stir and pour the mixture into an ovenproof dish. Cover with a sheet of foil and cook in a preheated oven at 200°C (400°F, gas 6) for 20 minutes.

Cook the crêpes and keep them hot on a plate over a saucepan of boiling water. Remove the rice from the oven, stir and allow it to cool for 5 minutes. Add 3 egg yolks one by one, followed by the crystallized fruits and the rum. Mix well. Fill the crêpes with the rice mixture, roll them up and arrange them in an ovenproof dish. Sprinkle them with caster sugar and brown lightly for a few minutes in a preheated oven at 230°C (450°F, gas 8).

crêpes à la russe
Heat 600 ml (1 pint, 2½ cups) milk until lukewarm. Mix a little of the milk with 15 g (2 oz) fresh yeast or 7 g (¼ oz) dried yeast and add to the remaining milk together with 20 g (¾ oz, 1½ tablespoons) caster (superfine) sugar, 200 ml (7 fl oz, ¾ cup) single (light) cream and a large pinch of salt. Blend 400 g (14 oz, 3½ cups) plain (all-purpose) flour with the milk mixture in a deep bowl. Allow the mixture to rise in a warm place for 1 hour. Whisk 2 egg whites into stiff peaks and blend them carefully with the batter using a metal spoon. Cook the crêpes (which swell as they start to brown). Roll them up when they are cooked, arrange them on a warmed serving dish and sprinkle them generously with fine caster sugar. Serve them hot.

crêpes mylène
Prepare a crêpe batter by mixing 200 g (7 oz, 1¾ cups) plain (all-purpose) flour, 2 whole eggs, 200 ml (7 fl oz, ¾ cup) beer, 2 tablespoons oil, a pinch of salt, the grated zest of a lemon and about 200 ml (7 fl oz, ¾ cup) water to thin the batter. Leave to stand for 1 hour at room temperature.

Twenty minutes before cooking the crêpes, make a sauce as follows: put a large knob of butter in a frying pan with 200 g (7 oz, ¾ cup) caster (superfine) sugar, the juice of 2 oranges and 1 lemon, and a small glass of Cognac. Cook over a gentle heat, stirring continuously to obtain a smooth sauce. Keep it warm. Cut 3 peeled pears into fine slices, cook them for a few minutes in boiling syrup and drain them. Toast 100 g (4 oz, 1 cup) flaked (slivered) almonds in a preheated oven at 230°C (450°F, gas 8), stirring them from time to time.

Cook the crêpes and keep them hot on a plate over a saucepan of boiling water. Fill each crêpe with some slices of pear, roll them up and place them in the frying pan with the sauce. Heat for 2 minutes, then pour over a small glass of mirabelle plum brandy and flame over a brisk heat, gently shaking the frying pan. Arrange the crêpes in a warmed serving dish and serve sprinkled with the roasted almonds.

crêpes normandes

Prepare a crêpe batter with 250 g (9 oz, 2¼ cups) plain (all-purpose) flour, 3 eggs, 300 ml (½ pint, 1¼ cups) milk, 200 ml (7 fl oz, ¾ cup) water, a pinch of salt, 1 tablespoon single (light) cream, 2 tablespoons Calvados and 1 tablespoon melted butter. Leave to stand for 2 hours at room temperature. Peel and slice 2 dessert (eating) apples and toss them in 40 g (1½ oz, 3 tablespoons) butter in a frying pan until they brown lightly. (The apples may be soaked in a little Calvados before they are cooked.) Cool and add them to the crêpe batter. Make the crêpes and pile them up on a serving dish. Sprinkle with caster sugar and serve very hot with fresh cream.

gâteau de crêpes

Make a dozen sweet crêpes. Prepare a Chantilly cream with 200 ml (7 fl oz, ¾ cup) double (heavy) cream, 500 ml (17 fl oz, 2 cups) milk, 1 tablespoon vanilla-flavoured sugar (or a few drops of vanilla extract), and 25 g (1 oz, 2 tablespoons) caster (superfine) sugar. Lay a crêpe on the serving dish and spread with strawberry jam. Cover with a second crêpe and spread with Chantilly cream. Continue in this way, alternating the layers of jam and cream. Finish with a crêpe. Sprinkle with icing (confectioner's) sugar and trace a pattern of diamond shapes for decoration. Serve immediately.

jam crêpes

Make some sweet crêpes and keep them hot. Sieve some apricot, plum or peach jam and heat it, possibly adding some rum or a fruit liqueur. Spread the crêpes with jam, roll them up, sprinkle them with caster (superfine) sugar and serve immediately. The crêpes may also be placed for a few moments under the grill (broiler) to caramelize the sugar.

lemon crêpes

Add the grated zest of a lemon to 500 ml (17 fl oz, 2 cups) milk. Bring to the boil and leave to cool. Make a crêpe batter with the lemon-flavoured milk, 250 g (9 oz, 2¼ cups) plain (all-purpose) flour, 3 eggs, and a pinch of salt. Strain and let it stand for at least 1 hour at room temperature. Add 25 g (1 oz, 2 tablespoons) butter to the batter and thin with 100 ml (4 fl oz, 7 tablespoons) water. Make the crêpes and keep them hot on a plate over a saucepan of boiling water. Fold the crêpes in four, arrange them on a buttered serving dish and dust generously with caster (superfine) sugar.

additional recipe See *Suzette*.

CRÊPE PAN A shallow flat-bottomed frying pan for cooking crêpes. Cast-iron pans, used mainly for buckwheat crêpes (or *galettes*), are also called *tuiles*, *galettières* or *galetoires*. There are also electric nonstick pans for use at table, with either a flat or a convex hotplate. When using the flat pan, the batter is poured on to it and then spread out with a scraper.

CRÊPERIE A restaurant or shop specializing in serving various sweet and savoury crêpes. Crêperies were originally established in Brittany, but are now found throughout France and in many other countries. Cider is the traditional Breton drink to serve with crêpes and sometimes there are other Breton specialities on the menu, such as grilled sardines.

CRÉPINETTE A small flat sausage, generally made of sausagemeat mixed with chopped parsley and wrapped in caul (*crépine*). *Crépinettes* may also be made with lamb, veal or poultry, prepared with a salpicon of meat and mushrooms, sometimes garnished with truffles and bound with white or brown stock. This mixture is enclosed in fine forcemeat and the whole is wrapped in caul. *Crépinettes* are brushed with melted butter (and sometimes coated with white breadcrumbs) and may be grilled (broiled), sautéed or cooked in the oven. They are served with a potato purée, lentils or boulangère potatoes. They can be served with a strongly seasoned sauce or, if they are truffled, with a Périgueux sauce.

Cinderella pork *crépinettes* (*pieds de Cendrillon*) are made of fine truffled pork forcemeat. A salpicon of pig's feet is mixed with diced truffles and mushrooms, bound with concentrated veal stock and placed in the middle of each *crépinette*. Traditionally cooked in wood-ash, wrapped in pieces of buttered paper, today they are wrapped in caul or in paperthin pieces of pastry before being cooked in the oven.

Crépinettes may be used to stuff game and poultry with rather dry flesh, such as rabbit or guinea fowl. In the Gironde, *crépinettes* are fried and served with oysters from the Arcachon basin and white wine.

RECIPES

calves' brain crépinettes

Soak a pig's caul in cold water for a few hours. Clean 2 calves' brains in cold water to which vinegar has been added. Then gently simmer the brains in 1 litre (1¾ pints, 4⅓ cups) well-seasoned courtbouillon for about 10 minutes. Drain, wipe them thoroughly and allow to cool. Fry 400 g (14 oz, 4½ cups) chopped mushrooms, 1 chopped shallot, 1 chopped garlic clove and some chopped parsley in a tablespoon of oil in a frying pan. Season with salt and pepper.

Wipe the caul, stretch it gently so as not to tear it, and cut it into 5 pieces. Cut each brain into 5 slices. Lay each slice in the middle of a piece of caul, cover with mushrooms and place a second slice of brain on top. Wrap in the caul. Roll the crépinettes in 40 g (1½ oz, 3 tablespoons) melted butter, then in some fresh white breadcrumbs, and fry lightly in butter until they turn brown. Serve very hot with a vegetable purée.

chicken crépinettes

Prepare a forcemeat of 3 parts minced (ground) chicken and 1 part fat bacon. Shape into small sausages, wrap them in caul and cook them as for pork crépinettes.

pork crépinettes

Prepare some small flat sausages using either fine pork forcemeat or sausagemeat flavoured with chopped herbs and Cognac (a few diced truffles may also be added to the mixture). Divide the forcemeat into portions of about 100 g (4 oz, ½ cup) and wrap each one in a rectangular piece of previously soaked and dried pig's caul. Coat each crépinette in egg and breadcrumbs, brush with melted butter and grill (broil) under a moderate heat. (The crépinettes may be grilled or fried without a coating of breadcrumbs.) The classic garnish is a purée of potatoes or of haricot (navy) beans, but they may also be served with buttered green vegetables.

pork crépinettes Sainte-Menehould

Prepare some pork crépinettes with a salpicon of pig's feet mixed with diced truffles, bound with a very reduced demi-glace and sandwiched between 2 layers of fine well-seasoned pork forcemeat. Dip in egg and coat with breadcrumbs and fry in butter over a gentle heat.

rabbit crépinettes

Use a 1.5 kg (3¼ lb) rabbit. Bone the saddle and legs and season with salt and pepper. Cut the saddle into 3 pieces. Soak a pig's caul. Clean and chop 1 or 2 shallots, 250 g (9 oz, 3 cups) mushrooms, a small sprig of parsley and 400 g (14 oz) smoked belly of pork (salt pork). Add some pepper, a pinch of thyme, some powdered bay leaf, and 1 tablespoon Cognac or marc (it is not necessary to add salt as the belly is salted). Mix the ingredients well and adjust the seasoning if necessary after browning a knob of the forcemeat in a frying pan and tasting it.

Fill the inside of each piece of rabbit with one-fifth of the forcemeat. Wipe the caul, stretch it gently and cut it into five. Roll each piece of stuffed rabbit in a piece of caul and place them in a lightly buttered gratin dish. Brush with a little melted butter and cook in a preheated oven at 230°C (450°F, gas 8) until the crépinettes are golden-brown. Turn them over to brown the other side and then reduce the temperature to 180°C (350°F, gas 4). Cook for a further 30 minutes. A little chicken stock flavoured with mustard may be poured into the cooking dish after the crépinettes have browned and they can be served coated with the resulting pan juices.

CRÉPY A white wine from Haute Savoie, coming from slopes alongside Lake Geneva and made from the Chasselas grape. The wines are light-bodied and some are slightly sparkling (*pétillant*).

CRESS Any of various plants of the mustard family which are cultivated for their sharp-tasting leaves, which can be eaten raw or cooked.
- ALÉNOIS CRESS A type of cress that grows abundantly in the region of Orléans (*alénois* is a corrupt form of *orléanais*). The young plants are sold in bunches throughout the year and are easily recognized by their small leaves arranged in a rosette. The leaves have a piquant flavour and are used as a condiment in salads and sauces, as a garnish for canapés and sandwiches, and sometimes for garnishing grilled (broiled) dishes.
- GARDEN CRESS This is available from July to March. It has shiny leaves and a strong flavour and is used raw in salads or cooked in soups and purées.
- MEADOW CRESS This plant grows wild in damp places and its leaves resemble those of watercress, except that they are firmer.
- WATERCRESS This is the most popular type of cress and is available all the year, but is at its best from April to October. It grows in running water and is widely cultivated. It has a distinctive peppery taste and is delicious eaten raw, but it can also be cooked in soups and forcemeats.

Cress is believed to be native to the Middle East but is naturalized and widely cultivated in Europe. In the 14th century, it was used mainly for medicinal purposes, but gradually began to be used in soups. It was not until about 1810 that methods of cultivating the cress in cress beds were introduced in France from Germany. The district of Senlis specialized in growing cress and it soon found a niche in gastronomy – in about 1850, the Café Riche included cress purée on its menu.

Today, cress is produced in France mainly in Oise, Essonne and Seine-Maritime. When cress is to be eaten raw, it should be picked over carefully, the thicker stems and yellowing leaves removed, and the rest washed and drained carefully. It should not be left to soak in water. Wild cress should not be eaten as it can transmit parasites.

RECIPE

watercress purée

Cook some watercress in butter for about 5 minutes, until wilted. Purée in a blender or food processor. Add one-third of its volume of either potato purée or a purée of split peas. Add some fresh butter or cream and finish with a little finely chopped raw cress.

other recipes See *brèdes*, butter (*flavoured butters*), *canapé*, cream soup, *mayonnaise*.

CRESSONNIÈRE, À LA A name given to preparations that contain watercress. Potage *à la cressonnière* is a cream of watercress and potato soup thickened with egg yolks and cream and garnished with blanched watercress leaves. Salad *à la cressonnière* is a mixture of potatoes and watercress topped with chopped hard-boiled (hard-cooked) eggs and chopped parsley.

RECIPES

baked eggs à la cressonnière

Edge a buttered ovenproof dish with a border of very thick watercress purée. Break 2 eggs in the centre, pour a little fresh cream around the yolks and bake in a preheated oven at 180°C (350°F, gas 4) until the eggs have set.

hard-boiled eggs à la cressonnière

Cover a serving dish with a layer of watercress purée. Top with hard-boiled (hard-cooked) eggs coated with watercress sauce. Cold soft-boiled (soft-cooked) eggs may also be arranged on a bed of cress and coated with watercress sauce.

poached eggs à la cressonnière

Coat a buttered dish with a layer of watercress purée. Arrange some soft-boiled (soft-cooked) or poached eggs on the purée and coat with cream sauce.

watercress sauce

Remove the leaves from some watercress. Wash, drain and dry them, chop finely and blend them with a mixture of chopped hard-boiled (hard-cooked) eggs, salt, pepper, oil and vinegar.

CRETONNÉE OF PEAS

A very old recipe in which a purée of stewed green peas, which has been browned in lard (shortening), is mixed with breadcrumbs soaked in milk containing saffron and ginger and some cooked chicken. To finish, the mixture is bound with egg yolks and served garnished with thinly sliced breast of chicken.

CREVER, FAIRE

A French culinary term meaning to remove part of the starch from rice by boiling the grains in salted water for several minutes. This operation reduces the cooking time required for rice pudding. (The literal meaning of the word – to burst – has sometimes given people the mistaken idea that the rice has to be cooked to the point of bursting.)

CRIQUE

A small pancake from the Viverais made with grated raw potato and eggs. In the Auvergne, *criquettes* are potato cakes.

CRISPBREAD

A small thin crisp biscuit (cracker) made from wholemeal (whole-grain) rye flour (or, less often, from wheat flour). It is sometimes flavoured with sesame seed, linseed or cumin. It was originally made by Swedish peasants and was intended to be stored for long periods. Today it is manufactured on a large scale, especially in Scandinavia, Germany (where it is called *Knäckebrot*) and

Britain. Exported all over the world, it is buttered and eaten with cheese and smoked fish. It is also recommended for low-caloric diets.

CRISPS (POTATO CHIPS)

Thin round slices of fried salted potato that are mass-produced and sold in bags. Crisps are served in France and Britain with apéritifs or with grills and roasts. This method of preparing fried potatoes is a very old one: it used to be called *pommes en liards* (the *liard* once being a small coin of some European countries). In the United States they are known as potato chips.

RECIPE

potato crisps

Wash and peel some large firm potatoes. Cut them into very thin round slices (preferably with a mandolin cutter or in a food processor) and immediately place them in cold water. Leave to soak for 10 minutes and then dry them thoroughly. Plunge the slices once only into frying oil at 185°C (365°F). Drain on paper towels and sprinkle with salt.

CROCKERY

All the items and accessories made of earthenware or china needed for service at the table or use in the kitchen: plates, cups, saucers, bowls, dishes, egg cups and so on.

CROCODILE

A reptile with strong-smelling flesh, highly appreciated in Africa and South America. The legs and the tail of young crocodiles are used: the firm white meat is seasoned and either stewed in palm oil or roasted. Some have compared crocodile meat to that of lobster: but it is more suitably linked by comparrison to pork or chicken for colour and texture. The meat is firm and quite dry, breaking up like tender long-stewed pork (or firm tuna). It is similar to alligator, with a full flavour. Crocodile tripe is considered to be a delicacy in Ethiopia, and the eggs apparently make excellent omelettes. Only the yolks are used, as the whites do not contain any albumen and therefore do not coagulate. Crocodile is farmed for consumption.

CROISSANT

A crescent-shaped roll generally made with a leavened dough.

This delicious pastry originated in Budapest in 1686, when the Turks were besieging the city. To reach the centre of the town, they dug underground passages. Bakers, working during the night, heard the noise made by the Turks and gave the alarm. The assailants were repulsed and the bakers who had saved the city were granted the privilege of making a special pastry in the form of a crescent in memory of the emblem on the Ottoman flag.

Bakers usually sell two sorts of croissants: those made with butter and 'the others', which no law obliges them to declare are 'made with margarine'. Croissants may be served at breakfast or tea, or filled with ham, cheese, mushrooms or chicken.

A very popular speciality in Lorraine is the

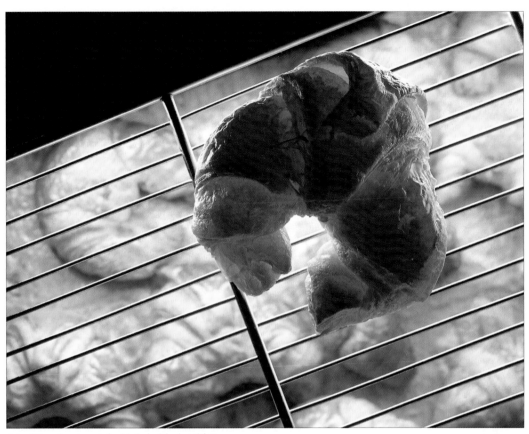

A traditional croissant, freshly baked for breakfast.

croissant alsacien, filled with dried fruit and coated with egg white or sugar. The term 'croissant' is also used for a semicircular petit four made with almond paste and topped with pine nuts or flaked almonds.

RECIPES

Parisian croissants
Blend 25 g (1 oz) fresh yeast (2 cakes compressed yeast) or 15 g (½ oz) dried yeast (3 teaspoons active dry yeast) with 250 ml (8 fl oz, 1 cup) luke-warm milk. Put 500 g (18 oz, 4½ cups) plain (all-purpose) flour into a mixing bowl and add 65 g (2½ oz, ⅓ cup) caster (superfine) sugar and 7 g (¼ oz, 1½ teaspoons) salt. Make a well in the flour mixture and pour the mixture of milk and yeast into the centre. Mix quickly with the fingertips and, as soon as the liquid is completely absorbed by the flour, cover the dough with a cloth and leave it to stand for 30–60 minutes, depending on the room temperature.

Roll out the dough into a rectangle and dot with butter. Fold into three and repeat rolling, dotting with butter and folding twice more using 250 g (9 oz, 1 cup) softened butter. Allow the dough to stand for 30 minutes.

Then roll it out to a rectangle about 45 × 15 cm (18 × 6 in) and cut it into triangles. Roll up the triangles, starting at the base and working towards the top. Place the croissants on a baking sheet, curving them into crescents. Allow them to rise further in a draught-free place for 15–45 minutes, depending on the room temperature. Brush with beaten egg yolk and bake in a preheated oven at 220°C (425°F, gas 7) for about 10 minutes.

Viennese croissants
Blend 15 g (½ oz) fresh yeast (1 cake compressed yeast) or 7 g (¼ oz) dried yeast (1½ teaspoons active dry yeast) with 1 tablespoon tepid water. Dissolve 25g (1 oz, 2 tablespoons) caster (superfine) sugar and a pinch of salt in 1 tablespoon milk. Heat 25 g (1 oz, 2 tablespoons) butter with a mixture of 5 tablespoons water and 5 tablespoons milk. Put 250 g (9 oz, 2¼ cups) plain (all-purpose) flour into a large bowl, make a well, and add the sugar/salt/milk mixture followed by the mixture of butter, water and milk. Finally add the diluted yeast. Mix all these ingredients together thoroughly to obtain a smooth paste. Leave the dough in a warm place for 1 hour so that it doubles in volume.

Spread out the dough on a floured dish and cool in the refrigerator for 30 minutes. Then roll out the dough into a thin rectangle on a floured surface. Cut 75 g (3 oz, 6 tablespoons) butter into small pieces and distribute them over two-thirds of the rectangle. Fold it into three, starting with the unbuttered third. Roll the dough out a second time, cover and replace in the refrigerator for 1 hour. Repeat the operation again using a further 75 g (3 oz, 6 tablespoons) butter and finish by rolling out the dough into a square of about 20 cm (8 in). Cover and refrigerate again for a further 30 minutes.

Then roll it out into a very thin rectangle measuring 30 × 60 cm (12 × 24 in). Cut the rectangle into two lengthways, and cut each half into 6 triangles. Roll up each triangle from base to top. Arrange the croissants on a buttered baking sheet, allowing plenty of space between them. Leave them to stand for 1 hour. Brush the croissants with beaten egg and bake for 3 minutes in a preheated oven at 240°C (475°F, gas 9). Lower the temperature to 200°C (400°F, gas 6) and bake for about a further 12 minutes. Watch them carefully during the last few minutes to ensure they do not overcook.

Savoury Croissants
cheese croissants
Split some baked croissants on one side. Butter the inside and fill with thin slices of Gruyère or Emmental cheese. Sprinkle with pepper and heat through in a preheated oven at 240°C (475°F, gas 9). Serve immediately. The butter and cheese may be replaced by a well-reduced béchamel sauce containing cheese.

shrimp croissants
Use 6 croissants baked without sugar. Make 200 ml (7 fl oz, ¾ cup) well-reduced prawn sauce (see *shrimps and prawns*). Split the croissants on one side and fill them generously with the sauce. Heat through in a preheated oven at 240°C (475°F, gas 9) and serve very hot.

Sweet Croissants
small almond croissants
Pound together in a mortar 300 g (11 oz, 2¾ cups) whole shelled almonds and 150 g (5 oz, ⅔ cup) vanilla-flavoured sugar, gradually moistening with sufficient egg white to obtain a paste that can be rolled in the hand. Add 2 tablespoons flour to the paste and divide it into pieces about the size of a walnut. Roll each piece with the hands into the shape of a cigar with slightly pointed ends (flour your palms if necessary). Dip each 'cigar' in beaten egg, roll in some flaked (slivered) almonds and shape into small croissants. Arrange them on sheets of greaseproof (wax) paper on baking sheets. Glaze with egg yolk and cook for about 12 minutes in a preheated oven at 200°C (400°F, gas 6) until they are golden brown. As soon as they are cooked, brush them with sweetened milk.

Viennese jam croissants
Prepare 500 g (18 oz) dough as for Viennese croissants. Roll it out into a rectangle measuring 30 × 60 cm (12 × 24 in). Cut it lengthways into 2 strips and cut each strip into 6 triangles using a fluted pastry (cookie) cutter. Place 1 tablespoon sieved strawberry, raspberry or apricot jam at the base of each triangle and shape the croissants by rolling them up from the base to the top. Place the croissants on a buttered baking sheet, leaving plenty of space between them, and brush with beaten egg. Cook in a preheated oven at 200°C (400°F, gas 6) for 18–20 minutes. When cooked, dust them with icing (confectioner's) sugar.

CROQUANTE A large item of pâtisserie formerly used as a table decoration. It was made of interlaced strips of cooked almond paste, placed on a pastry base and iced with green or pink sugar; the whole preparation was decorated with hollowed-out rounds of puff pastry, garnished with glacé (candied) cherries. *Croquantes* were also made of iced (frosted) brandy snaps, built up like a *croquembouche*.

A *croquante* is also a small dry crunchy petit four. Saint-Geniez croquanets are made of a mixture of almonds and hazelnuts. Parisian *croquantes* are sweets (candies) made of worked sugar.

CROQUE AU SEL, À LA Describes vegetables served raw with salt as the only seasoning, but sometimes accompanied by unsalted butter. New young artichokes, radishes and beans can be served in this way, provided that they are very fresh. Roger Lamazur and other gourmets maintain that this is the best way of eating fresh truffles.

CROQUEMBOUCHE A decorative cone-shaped preparation built up of small items of pâtisserie or confectionery and glazed with a caramel syrup to make it crisp. The *croquembouche* is usually placed on a base of nougat. It is built around a conical mould, also called a *croquembouche*, which is removed through the base when the small pieces are securely fixed to each other by the solidified caramel. It is traditionally served in France at buffets, weddings and first-communion meals.

The traditional *croquembouche* is made of little chou buns, sometimes filled with some kind of cream and dipped in sugar cooked to the crack stage. *Croquembouches* are also made with crystallized (candied) or sugar-coated fruits, brandy snaps, marzipan sweets (almond paste candies), meringue, or nougat. They can be decorated with sugar-coated almonds, sugar flowers or spun caramel.

RECIPE

chestnut croquembouche
(from Carême's recipe) Take 60 choice roasted chestnuts, peel them carefully and remove any traces of burning. Glaze by dipping them in sugar cooked to the crack stage (see *Sugar*), one by one, and place them on a smooth round mould, 18 cm (7 in) in diameter and 13 cm (5 in) deep. This *croquembouche* must be assembled at the last minute before serving, because the moisture in the chestnuts tends to soften the sugar and make it lose both its consistency and its gloss.

CROQUE-MONSIEUR A hot sandwich, made of two slices of buttered bread with the crusts removed, filled with thin slices of Gruyère cheese and a slice of lean ham. The croque-monsieur is lightly browned on both sides, either in butter in a frying pan or under the grill (broiler). The top may be coated with a Gruyère béchamel sauce and cooked au gratin. There are several possible variations on the basic recipe: the ham can be replaced by white chicken meat, the Gruyère cheese by Gouda, and a slice of tomato or even pineapple can be added. If the croque-monsieur is served with an egg on top, it is then called a *croque-madame*.

The first croque-monsieur was served in 1910 in a Parisian café on the Boulevard des Capucines. It is still a popular dish in cafés and snack bars, and is also served as an entrée or a hot hors d'oeuvre.

RECIPE

croque-monsieur à la brandade
Lightly coat with oil 2 slices of bread from which the crusts have been removed. Spread brandade of salt cod on one of the slices, cover with slices of tomato, then place the second slice of bread on top. Brown on a grid in a preheated oven at 240°C (475°F, gas 9) or under a grill (broiler).

CROQUET A dry petit four in the shape of a small stick, generally made of almonds, sugar and egg white. Croquets are very often regional specialities. The best-known are the croquets of Berry, Sologne, and Périgord, the golden croquets of Sens, the lace-like croquets of Nivernais, the croquets of Bar-sur-Aube and Bordeaux (made with unskinned almonds), and the croquets of Vinsobres and Valence (made with whole almonds).

RECIPES

almond croquets
Soften 50 g (2 oz, ¼ cup) butter with a palette knife (spatula); coarsely chop 75 g (3 oz, ¾ cup) unskinned almonds. In a basin, mix 200 g (7 oz, 1¾ cups) plain (all-purpose) flour with ½ teaspoon baking powder, 75 g (3 oz, ⅓ cup) caster (superfine) sugar, 1 egg and the butter; add the chopped almonds and knead the paste to make it smooth. Shape the paste into a sausage 20 cm (8 in) long and flatten it with the hand into a rectangle 10 cm (4 in) wide. Place on a buttered baking sheet and leave to stand for 15 minutes.

Prepare a caramel with 1 tablespoon sugar and the same amount of water, leave until lukewarm, then add 1 egg and beat all together with a fork. Brush the rectangle with this mixture and use a fork to score the surface. Cook in a preheated oven at 200°C (400°F, gas 6) for 10 minutes, remove from the oven and immediately cut into rectangles about 2 × 5cm (¾ × 2 in).

Bar-sur-Aube croquets
Mix together in a basin 500 g (18 oz, 2¼ cups) caster (superfine) sugar and 250 g (9 oz, 2 cups) ground almonds, then work in 8 egg whites, one by one. Carefully blend in 275 g (10 oz, 2½ cups) plain (all-purpose) flour and 1 teaspoon vanilla sugar. Turn this paste out on to the worktop, cut it into small tongue shapes and place these on an oiled baking sheet. Bake in a preheated oven at 180°C (350°F, gas 4). When ready, cool the croquets on a marble slab and store them in a dry place, in a jar or airtight tin.

Bordeaux croquets
Finely pound 300 g (11 oz, 2¾ cups) skinned almonds in a mortar with 150 g (5 oz, 1⅓ cups) unskinned almonds, 300 g (11 oz, 1⅓ cups) sugar, 125 g (4½ oz, ½ cup) butter, 2 eggs, the grated zest of a lemon or an orange, 3 teaspoons dried (active dry) yeast and a pinch of salt. Chop this mixture coarsely with a knife, then roll it up into a large sausage shape, slightly flattened at the edges. Place on a buttered baking sheet, glaze with egg yolk and score the surface. Bake in a preheated oven at 180°C (350°F, gas 4) for 15 minutes. Cut up into even-sized slices.

CROQUETTE A small savoury or sweet preparation. Savoury croquettes, made with a salpicon of fish, meat, poultry, ham, mushroom or calves' sweetbreads, are served hot as an hors d'oeuvre or as a garnish (especially potato croquettes); sweet croquettes are made with rice, chestnuts or semolina.

The basic mixture is bound with a fairly thick sauce: white, suprême, velouté, curry, tomato or cheese béchamel for savoury croquettes; confectioner's custard (pastry cream) for sweet croquettes. Croquettes are shaped into corks, sticks, balls or rectangles. They are usually coated with breadcrumbs, plunged into very hot oil and fried until they are crisp and golden. They are arranged in the shape of a pyramid, turban or crown on a dish lined with a doily or napkin, and savoury croquettes are sprinkled with fried parsley. Croquettes are always served with a sauce related to the main ingredient of the mixture (salt cod croquettes with tomato sauce, chicken croquettes with Périgueux or Villeroi sauce, game croquettes with chasseur sauce; custard cream or fruit coulis for sweet croquettes). The most common are fish croquettes (made with salt cod, for example, and all the preparations frozen in 'sticks') and croquette potatoes, served with sautéed or grilled meat.

Sweet croquettes may also be made with very thick confectioner's custard, cut into diamond shapes or rectangles, which are coated with breadcrumbs and fried (fried custard; see *custard*).

RECIPES

Savoury Croquettes
preparation of croquette mixture
Mix 500 g (18 oz, 4½ cups) of the main ingredient of the croquettes (cooked poultry, game, veal,

lamb, offal), minced (ground) or cut into very small dice, with 250 g (9 oz, 3 cups) cooked diced mushrooms – and possibly 75 g (3 oz, 1 cup) diced truffles). Moisten with 100 ml (4 fl oz, 7 table-spoons) Madeira, place in a covered pan, and heat gently. Then add 400 ml (14 fl oz, 1¾ cups) well reduced velouté* sauce, thickened with 3 egg yolks. Stir the mixture well, over the heat, then spread evenly on a buttered baking sheet and dab the surface with butter to prevent it from forming a crust. Leave to cool completely before making the croquettes.

Divide the cold mixture into portions of 50–75 g (2–3 oz). Roll these out on a floured flat surface and shape them into corks, balls, eggs or rectangles. Dip them in a mixture of egg and oil beaten together and then cover them completely with fine breadcrumbs.

Place the croquettes in a frying basket, plunge into oil heated to 175–180°C (347–356°F), and deep-fry until they are crisp and golden. Drain on paper towels and arrange on a napkin in a pyramid or turban shape. Garnish with parsley and serve with an appropriate sauce.

• *Variations* When the croquette mixture is made with various meats, poultry or game, a salpicon of cooked lean ham or tongue is often added to it. When it is made with fish or shellfish, traditionally the only additional items it contains are truffles and mushrooms. Croquette mixtures may also be made by replacing the velouté sauce with reduced demi-glace sauce.

When the croquettes are served as a small entrée, they are often accompanied by a garnish of fresh vegetables coated in butter or a purée of veg-etables. The croquettes themselves, if they are made very small, may be used as a garnish for large roasts, joints, poultry, game or fish.

beef croquettes

Cut some boiled beef and some lean ham into very small dice. Make a well-reduced béchamel sauce with 50 g (2 oz, ¼ cup) butter, 50 g (2 oz, ½ cup) plain (all-purpose) flour, 500 ml (17 fl oz, 2 cups) milk, grated nutmeg, and salt and pepper; beat in 1 egg yolk. Bind the salpicon with the sauce and leave to cool. Finish according to the basic method and serve with a well-seasoned tomato sauce.

The béchamel may be replaced by rice, using two-thirds salpicon to one-third rice cooked in meat stock.

cheese croquettes (1)

Make a béchamel sauce with 50 g (2 oz, ¼ cup) butter, 50 g (2 oz, ½ cup) plain (all-purpose) flour, 400 ml (14 fl oz, 1¾ cups) milk, a little grated nut-meg, salt and pepper. Add to the boiling béchamel 100 ml (4 fl oz, 7 tablespoons) double (heavy) cream and 125 g (4½ oz, 1 cup) grated cheese (Gruyère, Emmental or Edam). Stir until the cheese is melted and adjust the seasoning. Leave to cool. Finish the preparation as in the basic recipe.

cheese croquettes (2)

Beat together 3 whole eggs and 2 yolks. Boil 500 ml (17 fl oz, 2 cups) milk. Pour into a saucepan 50 g (2 oz, ½ cup) sifted flour and 50 g (2 oz, ⅓ cup) rice flour. Add the beaten eggs and mix well. Dilute with the boiled milk and season with salt and pepper, grated nutmeg and a dash of cayenne. Bring to the boil and cook for 5 minutes, stirring all the time. Add 125 g (4½ oz, 1 cup) grated cheese (Gruyère, Emmental or Edam) and stir until melted. Leave to cool and finish the preparation as in the basic recipe.

Viennese croquettes

Make a salpicon of equal quantities of lamb's sweet-breads poached in court-bouillon, lean ham, mush-rooms, which have been cooked slowly in butter, and chopped onions softened in butter; add just enough velouté sauce, reduced and seasoned with paprika, to bind everything together well. Finish the croquettes according to the basic method, moulding them into disc shapes. Serve with round slices of fried onion and a paprika-flavoured tomato sauce.

mussel croquettes

Prepare a salpicon of mussels *à la marinière* and thinly sliced mushrooms which have been cooked slowly in butter. Add half of its volume of well-reduced béchamel sauce to which some filtered juice from the mussels has been added. Finish the croquettes according to the basic method. Serve with a white wine sauce.

potato croquettes

Peel and quarter 1.5 kg (3¼ lb) floury potatoes and cook in salted boiling water until they are quite ten-der (at least 20 minutes). Drain the potatoes and dry them out over a low heat. Press through a sieve or blend them to a purée, add about 50 g (2 oz, ¼ cup) butter and gradually work in 4 beaten egg yolks with a fork. Spread the purée in a buttered dish and leave to cool completely.

Work the purée into a ball, using floured hands, then roll the ball into a long narrow cylinder; cut it into sections about 6 cm (2½ in) long. Round these sections slightly. Roll them in flour, coat with a mix-ture of 2 eggs lightly beaten with 1 tablespoon oil, and cover with breadcrumbs. Deep-fry the croquettes in oil heated to 180°C (356°F) for about 3 minutes, until they turn golden. Drain on paper towels and serve very hot with roast or grilled (broiled) meat.

rice croquettes

Mix together 500 g (18 oz, 3 cups) rice cooked *au gras* with 125 g (4½ oz, 1 cup) grated Parmesan cheese. Bind with a beaten egg and check the sea-soning. Mould into cork shapes and finish according to the basic method. Serve with a well-seasoned tomato sauce.

rice croquettes à l'ancienne

(from Carême's recipe) Cook 175 g (6 oz, ⅔ cup) short-grain rice in good stock. Mix it with

1 tablespoon thick velouté sauce, 2 tablespoons grated Parmesan cheese and a little nutmeg. Divide into 10 portions, make hollows in each and fill them with a salpicon of game or fowl combined with reduced velouté sauce. Close up the balls, roll in finely grated Parmesan, and finally in the palm of the hand to make the croquettes completely round. Dip in egg and coat with breadcrumbs mixed with finely grated Parmesan cheese, and deep-fry. Garnish with fried parsley.

salt-cod croquettes

Soak some salt cod in water to desalt it. Poach in water, then crumble it very finely. Add one-third of its volume of duchess potatoes and just enough béchamel sauce to bind the mixture well. Finish the croquettes according to the basic method, moulding them into ball shapes. Serve with a well-seasoned or garlic-flavoured tomato sauce.

other recipes See *celeriac, montrouge, mushroom, spinach.*

Sweet Croquettes

apricot croquettes

Cook 500 g (18 oz) apricots in syrup, drain, dry and cut into large dice. Add 400 ml (14 fl oz, 1¾ cups) very thick confectioner's custard (see *custard*). Flavour the mixture with rum and leave to cool completely. Divide into portions of 50–65 g (2–2½ oz). Mould each portion into a small ball, flatten slightly and roll in flour, beaten egg and fresh breadcrumbs. Deep-fry in oil heated to 175–180°C (347–356°F) and serve with hot apricot sauce.

chestnut croquettes

Dip some chestnuts in boiling water and peel them. Cook them in a light syrup – 500 g (18 oz, 2¼ cups) granulated sugar per 1 litre (1¾ pints, 4⅓ cups) water flavoured with vanilla. Press the chestnuts through a sieve to obtain a purée and thicken it with egg yolks and butter – 5 egg yolks and 50 g (2 oz, 4 tablespoons) butter per 500 g (18 oz, 2¼ cups) purée. Spread the mixture on a buttered baking sheet and leave to cool completely. Cut into rectangles of about 50 g (2 oz), cover with egg and breadcrumbs and deep-fry in oil heated to 180°C (356°F). Serve the croquettes very hot with a fruit sauce flavoured with Cognac or Armagnac.

Instead of chestnuts, 500 g (18 oz, 4½ cups) sieved marrons glacés may be used, blended with 400 ml (14 fl oz, 1¾ cups) confectioner's custard (see *custard*) flavoured with rum, Cognac or Armagnac.

rice croquettes

Prepare some rice in milk using 125 g (4½ oz, ⅔ cup) rice; after cooking, add 5–6 egg yolks (or 3 whole eggs beaten as for an omelette). Leave to cool completely, then divide into portions of about 50 g (2 oz). Mould them into cork shapes, coat with egg and breadcrumbs, and deep-fry in oil heated to 180°C (356°F) until golden. Drain on paper towels. Serve with a hot fruit sauce flavoured with Grand Marnier.

CROQUIGNOLE A very small light crisp cake, served with tea, creams or ices. It is made from a mixture of sugar (or royal icing), flour and egg white and the top is covered with vanilla-flavoured icing (frosting) or a light syrup. The best-known *croquignoles*, made since the 16th century, are those of Paris and Navarrenx (in the Pyrenees).

The word seems to come from *croquer* (to crunch) and from *nieule* (a kind of wafer). It also means a flick of the finger, which presumably derives from the ancient custom of people throwing small cakes at each other at certain festivals.

CROTTIN DE CHAVIGNOL A French goat's-milk cheese made in Sancerre. Containing at least 45% butter-fat, it has a soft centre and a natural crust, mottled with white, blue or brown mould. Crottin can be eaten when it has ripened for three months until dry, when it is crumbly, with a piquant flavour, and gives off a fairly strong smell; it is also eaten fresh, when it is milder and white. Originally, only very mature cheeses, with a strong smell and almost black colour, were entitled to be called Crottin. Crottin comes in the form of a small flattened ball, weighing about 50 g (2 oz). A distinction is made between farm Crottin, which is enjoyed with a full-bodied wine, and dairy Crottin, slightly more insipid and rarely matured, which may be used for soufflés and salads. In Berry, Crottin was traditionally prepared by placing it under the grill (broiler) for a few minutes, sometimes coated with breadcrumbs, and then serving it hot accompanied by a green salad of endives or dandelions.

RECIPE

roasted crottins de Chavignol on a salad with walnuts of Corrèze

Arrange 6 well-matured Crottins de Chavignol on a baking sheet and put them in a preheated oven at 240°C (475°F, gas 9): they must lose their first fat. Fry 6 slices of *pain de campagne* in butter until golden. Place the little cheeses on top and serve with a green salad including 65 g (2½ oz, ½ cup) chopped green walnuts (or use pickled walnuts), seasoned with vinaigrette.

CROUPION The rear end of the body of birds, consisting of the last two dorsal vertebrae and bearing the tail feathers. Called the parson's nose in Britain, it is a very tasty part, particularly from chickens and turkeys.

In ducks and geese, the sebaceous glands situated on either side of the parson's nose must be removed before cooking as they can give the meat an unpleasant taste.

CROUSTADE A preparation consisting of a case of lining pastry, puff pastry, hollowed-out bread, duchess potato mixture, semolina or rice, which is fried or heated in the oven and filled with a salpicon, ragoût, vegetables or a purée, bound with a suitable reduced sauce. Croustades, which were originally made in the south of France, are eaten as hot hors d'oeuvre, but they are also used in certain garnishes for large-scale cookery (filled with kidneys, vegetables or crayfish tails).

RECIPES

bread croustades

Cut some thick stale bread into slices 5–6 cm (2–2½ in) thick, remove the crusts and trim to the desired shape. On the top, make a circular incision with the tip of a knife to a depth of 4–5 cm (1½–2 in) to mark the lid. Deep-fry the croustades in oil heated to 175–180°C (347–256°F) until they are golden. Drain. Take off the lid and remove all the crumb from the inside. Line the croustades with a thin layer of forcemeat (according to the filling). Leave for 5–6 minutes at the front of a hot oven with the door open. Fill with the chosen mixture. All the fillings recommended for timbales and vol-au-vent are suitable for bread croustades. These croustades may also be made using round bread rolls.

duchess potato croustades

Spread the duchess potato mixture in a 4–5 cm (1½–2 in) thick layer on an oiled baking sheet and leave to cool completely. Use a smooth round cutter to cut into shapes 7.5 cm (3 in) in diameter. Coat these croustades with egg and breadcrumbs. To mark the lid, make a circular incision in the top 1 cm (½ in) from the edge and 3–4 cm (1¼–1½ in) deep. Deep-fry in oil heated to 180°C (356°F) until golden. Drain and dry on paper towels. Remove the lid and hollow out the inside, leaving only a base and a wall, about 1 cm (½ in) thick. Fill the croustades according to the instructions given in the recipe.

puff pastry croustades

Sprinkle the worktop with flour and roll out puff pastry to a thickness of about 1–2 cm (½–¾ in). Using a pastry (cookie) cutter, cut rounds 7.5–10 cm (3–4 in) in diameter. With a smaller cutter, make a circle centred on the first, with a diameter 2 cm (¾ in) smaller, taking care not to cut right through the pastry: this smaller circle will form the lid of the croustades. Glaze with egg yolk and place in a preheated oven at 230°C, (450°F, gas 8). As soon as the crust has risen well and turned golden, take the croustades out of the oven. Leave until lukewarm, then take off the lid and, with a spoon, remove the soft white paste which is inside. Leave the croustades to cool completely.

Alternatively, roll the pastry to a thickness of only 5 mm (¼ in) and cut half of it into circles 7.5–10 cm (3–4 in) in diameter, and the rest into rings of the same external diameter and 1 cm (½ in) wide. Brush the base of the rings with beaten egg and place them on the circles; glaze the whole with beaten egg and cook.

rice or semolina croustades

Cook some rice or semolina au gras. Bind with egg yolks – 5 yolks per 500 g (18 oz, 3 cups) rice or semolina. Spread out in a layer 4–5 cm (1½–2 in) thick and leave to cool completely. Finish as for duchess potato croustades.

Fillings
croustades à la grecque

Fill some rice croustades with a fondue of tomatoes à la grecque. Garnish each with 3 onion rings, coated in batter and deep-fried.

croustades à la marinière

Prepare some mussels à la marinière. Strain the juice and mix with fresh cream to make a thick velouté sauce. Fill croustades made of puff pastry with the mussels. Coat with the sauce and serve very hot.

quail croustades à la périgueux

Prepare and cook some stuffed quails. Cover the bottom of each bread croustade with Périgueux sauce. Place a quail on it and coat with more sauce. Garnish with a slice of truffle and serve very hot.

other recipes See *anchovy, langouste, liver, Montrouge*.

CROÛTE A pastry case or slice of bread used to hold a savoury or sweet preparation. Pastry croûtes (puff or shortcrust) are cooked blind and then filled; they include timbales, vol-au-vent and bouchées.

Croûtes served as hot hors d'oeuvre are round or square slices of bread from which the crusts have been removed, fried in butter until they are a golden colour and topped with various preparations (ham, mushrooms, anchovies or seafood); they are sometimes coated with a little thick sauce and cooked au gratin (see *Welsh rarebit*).

Croûtes served as hot desserts are stale slices of savarin, brioche or milk bread, dried in the oven and spread with poached or crystallized (candied) fruits moistened with syrup, sprinkled with shredded almonds or coated with jam, and often arranged in a border or crown shape.

RECIPES

Savoury Croûtes
preparation

Cut some round pieces of bread, 4–5 cm (1½–2 in) in diameter and 2 cm (¾ in) thick, from a stale loaf. Use a round cutter with a diameter smaller than that of the croûtes to press lightly on each croûte to mark the lid. Fry the croûtes in butter or oil. When they are golden, drain and remove the central circles for lids, then hollow out. Fill according to the recipe instructions. Instead of frying the croûtes, they can be brushed with butter and browned in a preheated oven at 220°C (425°F, gas 7).

croûtes à la diable

Fill some croûtes with a salpicon of York ham and mushrooms which have been cooked slowly in butter, bound with well-reduced demi-glace and seasoned with a pinch of cayenne. Sprinkle the top of the croûtes with breadcrumbs fried in butter, and brown in a preheated oven at 220°C (425°F, gas 7).

croûtes à la livonienne

Prepare some croûtes. Reduce to a purée some cooked soft herring roes, add to the purée an equal volume of béchamel sauce and coat the croûtes with the mixture. Place on each croûte a spoonful of a salpicon of kipper fillets and dessert apples, flavoured with lemon. Sprinkle with fine breadcrumbs, which have been fried in butter, and brown in a preheated oven at 220°C (425°F, gas 7).

croûtes à la nantua

Prepare some croûtes cut into rectangles. Cover with a layer of béchamel sauce to which crayfish butter has been added. Add some shelled crayfish tails and coat with cream sauce flavoured with crayfish butter. Sprinkle with grated Parmesan, moisten with melted butter and brown quickly in a preheated oven at 220°C (425°F, gas 7).

croûtes cardinal

Prepare some croûtes. Bind a salpicon of lobster and truffle with a béchamel sauce to which lobster butter has been added. Fill the croûtes with this mixture. Sprinkle with breadcrumbs and brown in a preheated oven at 220°C (425°F, gas 7). Just before serving, garnish each croûte with a small (hot) scallop of lobster and a fine slice of truffle.

mushroom croûtes

Prepare some croûtes and fill them with mushrooms (preferably field mushrooms) à la crème. Sprinkle with breadcrumbs and brown in a preheated oven at 220°C (425°F, gas 7) or under the grill (broiler). Serve hot.

seafood croûtes

Cut some slices of bread and remove the crusts. Lightly fry them in butter and then coat them with a cheese béchamel sauce. Place on these slices various types of shellfish (oysters, mussels, clams), cooked in white wine as for a marinière, and coat them with a sauce prepared with their cooking stock. Sprinkle with fresh breadcrumbs, moisten with melted butter, and brown quickly in a preheated oven at 220°C (425°F, gas 7). Peeled prawns (shelled shrimp) may be added to the shellfish.

other recipes See ambassadeur, Brillat-Savarin, du Barry, rouennaise*.

Sweet Croûtes

banana croûtes à la maltaise

Proceed as for turban of croûtes à la Beauvilliers but replace the semolina mixture with a thick confectioner's custard flavoured with orange zest and mixed with split almonds.

crown of croûtes à la Montmorency

Cut stale brioches into slices 1 cm (½ in) thick. Arrange these slices on a baking sheet, dust them with sugar and glaze them in a preheated oven at 230°C (450°F, gas 8). Cover each slice with a thin layer of frangipane cream flavoured with cherry brandy, then arrange them in a crown on a round dish, placing them very close to one another. Fill the centre of this crown with a dome of stoned (pitted) cherries, cooked in a vanilla-flavoured syrup and drained well. Decorate the border of the crown with more cherries. If liked, coat with redcurrant sauce laced with cherry brandy and serve more of this sauce separately.

crown of croûtes with pears

Cut a brioche or a stale savarin into 4 slices, dust with sugar and glaze in a preheated oven at 230°C (450°F, gas 8). Peel and core 3 apples and 2 pears and cut into thin slices. Put them in a saucepan with the juice of half a lemon, 500 ml (17 fl oz, 2 cups) red wine, 150 g (5 oz, ⅔ cup) caster (superfine) sugar, 1 clove and a large pinch of cinnamon. Cook quickly for 15 minutes, then drain the fruits.

Peel 4 pears, leaving them whole, and place them, stalks upwards, in the saucepan containing the cooking syrup. Add some water so that the liquid comes halfway up the fruit. Bring to the boil, then simmer gently for 12 minutes. Remove the clove and leave to cool.

Arrange the croûtes in a crown on a large round dish. Fill the centre with the thin slices of apple and pear, and place the whole pears on top of the croûtes. Warm in a preheated oven at 220°C (425°F, gas 7) and serve with Chantilly cream.

fruit croûtes

Cut a stale savarin into slices 1 cm (½ in) thick. Place these slices on a baking sheet, dust them with fine sugar and glaze them in a preheated oven at 230°C (450°F, gas 8). Reassemble the savarin on a large round dish, alternating the croûtes with slices of canned pineapple. Place around this crown, alternately, quarters of pears and apples, cooked in vanilla-flavoured syrup and well drained. Fill the inside of the crown with a salpicon of various fruits cooked in syrup and drained. Decorate the top with glacé (candied) cherries, angelica lozenges, quarters of crystallized (candied) apricots, small golden and green preserved oranges and halved almonds. Warm the crown in a preheated oven at 150°C (300°F, gas 2).

When ready to serve, coat it with apricot sauce flavoured with rum or kirsch, and serve more of this sauce separately. Croûtes containing other types of fruit cooked in syrup (apricot, peach, pear, plum, nectarine) are prepared in the same way.

turban of croûtes à la Beauvilliers

Cut from a stale brioche 12 rectangular slices, 6 cm (2½ in) long and slightly wider than a banana. Arrange these slices on a baking sheet, dust with caster (superfine) sugar and glaze in a preheated oven at 230°C (450°F, gas 8). Peel 6 bananas and cut them in half lengthways. Lay these banana halves on a buttered baking sheet, sprinkle them with caster sugar and cook them for 5 minutes in the preheated oven at 230°C (450°F, gas 8).

Make a turban shape on a round ovenproof dish, alternating the bananas and the slices of brioche. Cook some semolina in sweetened vanilla-flavoured milk, bind with egg yolks, and add a salpicon of crystallized (candied) fruit, macerated in a fruit liqueur. Fill the centre of the turban with this mixture. Sprinkle the whole preparation with finely crumbled macaroons, moisten with melted butter and brown in the preheated oven. Just before serving, surround the turban with a thin ribbon of apricot sauce flavoured with rum or with a fruit liqueur.

CROÛTES FOR SOUP
Thick slices of French bread (*flûte*) which have been partly hollowed out or cut in two lengthways and dried in the oven. Croûtes are served with all kinds of soups, usually separately, either plain, garnished or filled.

Croûtes *à l'ancienne* are stuffed with stockpot vegetables (chopped or sieved) and cooked au gratin. Croûtes *au pot* are moistened with the stockpot fat and browned in the oven. The name *consommé croûte au pot* is sometimes given to the stockpot broth garnished with vegetables cut into small pieces, grated Gruyère cheese and round slices of *flûte*, hollowed out and grilled (broiled) or baked. (Served separately, these are also called *croûtes en dentelle*.) Diablotins are croûtes covered with reduced béchamel sauce, sprinkled with grated cheese and a pinch of cayenne, then cooked au gratin. Plain croûtes (lightly browned and sometimes rubbed with garlic) are usually called croûtons.

In the Middle Ages, the thin slices of bread soaked in stock, wine or milk, which were served with gruels or liquid stews, were called *soupes*. Later, the name croûte was given to lightly browned slices of bread served after the soup: these were coated with purée, garnished with crayfish or asparagus tips, and moistened with partridge gravy or cooked au gratin using Parmesan cheese.

RECIPES

croûtes for consommé

Divide a French loaf (*flûte* or *ficelle*) into slices 5 cm (2 in) long. Cut each slice in half lengthways and remove the soft part. Dry out the croûtes in a cool oven and arrange them in a dish. Alternatively, the slices can be brushed with melted butter or olive oil and baked in the oven until golden. Serve separately with the broth from a pot-au-feu or a consommé.

stuffed croûtes à l'ancienne

Cut a French loaf (*flûte*) into slices 4 cm (1½ in) long. Remove three-quarters of the soft part and dry the crusts in a cool oven. Fill them with vegetables from the stockpot, which have been chopped or pressed through a sieve. Arrange them in a dish, sprinkle with grated cheese, moisten with melted butter and brown them in a preheated oven at 230°C (450°F, gas 8) or under the grill (broiler). These croûtes may also be prepared with very small round rolls, hollowed out, dried, filled and cooked au gratin.

additional recipe See *diablotin*.

CROÛTON
A small piece of bread which is toasted, lightly browned in butter, fried in oil or simply dried in the oven. Diced croûtons are used to garnish certain preparations (soups, green salads, scrambled eggs, omelettes, buttered spinach) and are included in composite garnishes (such as *grenobloise*). Cut into hearts, diamonds, crescents, triangles, circles or stars, they are used as a complementary garnish for dishes in sauces (salmis, blanquettes, matelotes, sautés) or purées and to decorate the border of the serving dish. Croûtons spread with à gratin forcemeat are used as a base for some types of game and poultry (see *Canapé*). Large croûton supports are used to raise large hot or cold items for buffets so that added garnishes do not mask the food. They are not intended to be eaten.

The name croûton is also given to small decorative aspic shapes used to garnish cold dishes.

RECIPES

croûton omelette

Beat some eggs for an omelette, add some small diced croûtons which have been fried in butter and cook the omelette. Serve the omelette with a ribbon of well-reduced spiced tomato sauce poured around it and sprinkle with chopped herbs.

croûtons flavoured with thyme

Peel the cloves of half a head of garlic and remove the green part from each clove. Place in a blender with 100 g (4 oz, ½ cup) slightly salted butter, ½ teaspoon flat-leaf parsley, ½ teaspoon powdered thyme, ½ teaspoon thyme leaves, ½ teaspoon oregano, ½ teaspoon marjoram, 1 small can anchovies with the oil, and ½ teaspoon freshly ground pepper. Cut a stale *baguette* into diagonal slices, coat generously with this mixture, and put under the grill (broiler) until crusty yet soft.

CROWN
A method of arranging certain sweet or savoury dishes in the form of a ring (using a ring mould), a border (for rice) or a crown (lamb cutlets arranged back to back). The centre of the arrangement is usually decorated or garnished. The terms 'turban' or 'border' are also used.

Brioches and bread *en couronne* are shaped in the form of a crown or ring.

CROZE, AUSTIN DE French writer (born Lyon, 1866; died Lyon, 1937), a specialist in folklore and gastronomy. Originator of the Journées Régionales du Salon d'Automne in 1923 and 1924, he contributed to the collection and distribution of local recipes and regional products. His principal work, *Les Plats régionaux de France* (1928), which lists 1400 specialities, constitutes a traditional heritage which is accepted as an authority. He also wrote a *Psychologie de la table* and was the original creator of the Association des Gastronomes Régionalistes.

CROZES-HERMITAGE Red and white AOC wines of the Rhône Valley from vineyards adjacent to those producing Hermitage.

CROZETS Quenelles made from a mixture of flour (wheat or buckwheat), potato purée, eggs, water and walnut oil: a speciality of the Dauphiné. *Crozets* (or *crousets* as they are also known) are poached, drained, then arranged in layers in a gratin dish, with crumbled blue cheese and grated Gruyère cheese between layers, sprinkled with melted lard (shortening) and cooked in the oven until golden. *Crozets* are often the traditional dish served on Christmas Eve.

CRU The French word meaning 'a growth', which is widely used in wine-growing. In the Bordeaux area, a *cru classé* is a term reserved for vineyards which have been given a classification recognized by INAO (Institute National des Appellations d'origine), usually according to the classification of 1855 when wines were appraised according to the prices they were likely to fetch at the Paris Exhibition, rather than exclusively on their quality. Categories include the *premiers crus* (first growths), *grands crus* (great growths) and *crus exceptionnels* (exceptional growths). Subsequent categorization has been attempted in certain areas, including Côtes-de-Provence in 1955, but it should be remembered that each region's labelling laws are likely to be autonomous.

CRUCHADE A gruel made from cornflour (cornstarch) with milk or water, traditional in south-west France. In the Béarn, the gruel is cooled, then cut into even-sized pieces which are then fried. The Saintonge *cruchade* is a thin round cake made from maize (corn), fried and served with jam. *Cruchades* in the Landes region are small savoury or sweet biscuits (crackers or cookies) which can be fried.

CRUDITÉS Raw vegetables or fruits served as an hors d'oeuvre, generally thinly sliced, grated or cut into little sticks and accompanied by cold sauces. Crudités include carrots, celeriac, cucumber, sweet peppers, red cabbage, celery, fennel, fresh broad (fava) beans, cauliflower (in very small florets), tomatoes, mushrooms, radishes, small artichokes, quarters of grapefruit, orange and apple, round slices of banana sprinkled with lemon, slices of avocado and,

although it is cooked, beetroot (red beet). The various items are often presented as an assortment, with several sauces. A plate of crudités may also include a hard-boiled (hard-cooked) egg in mayonnaise.

RECIPE

basket of crudités
Choose some very fresh raw vegetables: little carrots, celery sticks, radish, cucumber, sweet peppers, very small artichokes known as *poivrades*, cauliflower, mushrooms, fennel.

Scrape the carrots and radishes, leaving the small green leaves on the radishes. Thoroughly remove the strings from the celery sticks, cut them into sections of about 10 cm (4 in) and split the heart into four. Peel the pepper (optional), cut open, take out the white membrane and seeds, and cut the flesh into thin strips. Peel the cucumber and cut into sticks. Pull the cauliflower apart into small florets. Wipe and slice the mushrooms. Clean the fennel bulb and cut it into thick slices. Just before serving, break the stalks of the artichokes, cut them in four, remove the chokes and sprinkle the cut part with lemon juice.

Line a wickerwork basket with a napkin and arrange the vegetables in it, in bunches. If it is not to be served immediately, cover it with a cloth and put it in a cool place. Serve accompanied by a mayonnaise with herbs, a tarragon vinaigrette, an anchovy sauce and a cream cheese sauce.

CRUET STAND A table set consisting of a base holding containers for oil and vinegar, a salt cellar, a pepper pot and a mustard pot. It may be made of glass, porcelain or metal.

CRUMBLE A popular simple dessert consisting of a fruit base, such as apple, and crumble topping. This is a quick and easy alternative to making a fruit pie. The topping is made by rubbing fat into flour as when making short crust pastry, then sweetening it with sugar. The crumbly topping is sprinkled over the fruit in a deep baking dish – there should be a thick layer of topping, about half the depth (or slightly more) of the fruit. The dessert is cooked in the oven until the fruit is tender and the crumble is golden and crisp on top.

The proportions for the crumble topping are half fat to flour, with butter and plain (all-purpose) flour used. Brown sugar may be used instead of white and a variety of ingredients may be added to vary the flavour and/or texture of the mixture. For example, rolled oats, chopped nuts, grated orange or lemon rind or spices may be added.

A sauce or accompaniment is usually offered with fruit crumble – typically custard or cream, but fromage frais, yogurt or vanilla ice cream are all options.

Savoury crumbles are made by omitting the sugar and adding grated cheese and herbs to the crumble topping. The topping may be used to cover fish, poultry or meat in a sauce, or braised vegetables.

CRUMB TRAY A small dustpan equipped with a soft-bristled brush, used for brushing the crumbs off the tablecloth, usually before the dessert is brought in (the bread basket and the salt cellar should be removed at this point) and sometimes between other courses. There is an automatic model, consisting of a case containing a brush, which picks up the crumbs as it is rolled over the table.

CRUMPET A small spongy yeast cake with holes on the top surface, cooked on a griddle in a special ring about 7.5 cm (3 in) in diameter. In England, crumpets are usually served at tea-time, toasted and spread with plenty of butter.

RECIPE

crumpets

In a bowl, mix 2 tablespoons tepid water, 25 g (1 oz) fresh yeast (2 cakes compressed yeast) and ½ teaspoon sugar until completely dissolved. Leave the bowl in a warm place until the mixture has doubled in volume. Put 150 g (5 oz, 1¼ cups) plain (all-purpose) flour and a pinch of salt in a large mixing bowl. Make a well and pour 100 ml (4 fl oz, 7 tablespoons) milk into the middle. Add 1 whole egg. Stir the batter with a spoon, add 1 tablespoon butter and the yeast mixture, and continue to mix until a really smooth batter is obtained. Cover the bowl with a napkin and put it in a warm place, sheltered from draughts, for 1 hour or until the batter has doubled in volume.

Clarify 50 g (2 oz, ¼ cup) butter and use to grease the bottom of a large heavy griddle or frying pan and also the insides of some 7.5 cm (3 in) rings. Place 3 or 4 rings on the griddle over a moderate heat. Drop 1 tablespoon batter into each ring: it spreads immediately and fills the ring. When the crumpets begin to bubble, turn them over with a palette knife (spatula), then lightly brown the other side for 1–2 minutes. Place the crumpets on a dish and cover them with foil. Butter the rings and the griddle again and continue making crumpets until the batter is used up. Toast before serving.

CRUSTACEANS See *shellfish*.

CRYSTALLIZED (CANDIED) FRUIT Whole fruit or pieces of fruit preserved in sugar syrup. By putting the fruit into increasingly concentrated syrup solutions, the syrup gradually replaces the water in the fruit. The concentration of the syrup depends on the type, size and origin of the fruit. It is heated to precise temperatures, so that it neither crystallizes nor caramelizes. The impregnation must be progressive so that the fruit flesh does not break or shrivel up.

The method is described by Olivier de Serres in his *Théâtre d'agriculture* (1600). But the reputation of the crystallized fruits of Apt was established as long ago as the 14th century, their manufacture having begun at the start of the Avignon papacy (1309). In the Middle Ages, crystallized fruits, then known as *épices de chambre*, were very popular, especially plums, apricots, pistachios, pine nuts and filberts.

In theory, any fruit can be crystallized, but the process works better for some than others in practice. Besides whole fruit or fruit slices, it is also possible to use angelica stems, the peel of citrus fruits (citron, orange, lemon) and even certain flowers (particularly violets).

The fruit is picked before it is fully ripe so that is has plenty of flavour but will not disintegrate. Then it is blanched (except strawberries and apricots), cooled and drained. The sugaring process starts with a light syrup, which is then made more and more concentrated; the syrup is heated in a copper pan. Between each step, the fruit rests in its syrup in an earthenware terrine. The duration of the process varies from a few soakings for bigarreau cherries to a dozen or so for large fruit, which takes a month or two. This traditional method is always used for apricots, strawberries, plums, pears, figs, pineapples and small green oranges; less fragile fruit (such as melon and bigarreau cherries), citrus peel and angelica are crystallized continuously in batteries of vats, taking, on average, six days to complete.

Crystallized fruit may be sold plain or glazed with sugar, either loose or in packaged assortments. Glazing improves the appearance of the fruit, makes it less sticky and better to handle, and prolongs its shelf life (up to six months away from heat). The glazing process involves coating the fruit with a concentrated syrup just when it has started to crystallize; it is then cooled and drained. Some fruit is reconstituted; for example, large crystallized strawberries can be hollowed out and filled with smaller crystallized strawberries, and stoned (pitted) apricots are filled with crystallized apricot pulp.

In the 19th century, the Auvergne was the leading area for crystallizing fruit; nowadays it has been overshadowed by the south of France. Apt, a traditional Mecca for lovers of these delicacies, exports to the whole world. Dauphiné and Provence are also noted for crystallized fruit, while Clermont-Ferrand remains the specialist town for the glazed varieties. Privas is the capital for marrons glacés.

Although widely known as confectionery items, crystallized fruits are also used in baking, for certain cakes (fruit cakes, brioches) and for ice creams. When diced, they are used to decorate desserts and puddings (cherries, angelica and citron in particular). In Britain, candied peel is an ingredient of mincemeat, for mince pies.

CUCHAULE A Swiss bread originating from Fribourg, prepared with *fleur* (superfine white) flour, butter and milk, lightly sweetened and with saffron. The top is marked with a chequer pattern and gilded with egg. Cuchaule is spread with butter and Bénichon mustard and eaten for breakfast or with white wine drunk as an aperitif.

CUCUMBER The fruit of an annual climbing plant of the gourd family, which is generally eaten raw but it is also good cooked.

Originating in the foothills of the Himalayas, where it once grew wild, the cucumber has been cultivated in India for more than 3000 years. It was introduced into Egypt and carefully cultivated by the Hebrews in Galilee. Pliny recounts that the Romans and Greeks were very fond of cucumber. In France, cucumber was eaten during the reign of Charlemagne, but it was La Quintinie who organized its cultivation under glass, so that it could be served at Louis XIV's table as early as April. It is long and cylindrical in shape, with firm, watery, pale green flesh, which is crisp, cool and slightly bitter to the taste; its fine green skin is shiny and usually smooth.

■ **Varieties** There are several varieties of cucumber, classified in two types – those grown exclusively in greenhouses, known as Dutch, and those cultivated either in the open or under glass frames, known as ridge; they differ more in size, shape and shade of green than in taste.

Cucumber should be bought very fresh and firm, never wrinkled. It is often peeled, since its skin can be quite bitter. When served raw, it is sometimes salted and drained to extract excess water and intensify the flavour of the vegetable. Salting does make the flesh soft but careful salting and draining prevents the liquor from the cucumber diluting the flavour of any seasoning or dressing – tarragon dressing, cream or yogurt, for example.

Cucumber can also be eaten cooked, either baked in the oven, sautéed in butter or else cooked au gratin. Served in its own juice or in a sauce, it can accompany meat or fish. It can also be stuffed, either raw or cooked. Cucumber is just as popular in northern and eastern European cookery (sweet-and-sour cucumber, cold Russian soups) as in Mediterranean countries (minted cucumber, gazpacho, cucumber *à la grecque*, mixed salads).

RECIPES

preparation of cucumbers
For hot dishes, peel the cucumbers, split in half lengthways and remove the seeds; cut the flesh into even-sized chunks and then again into segments; plunge into boiling water for 2 minutes to blanch them, then drain.

For cold dishes, peel the cucumbers, split in half lengthways and remove the seeds; they can then either be kept intact for stuffing, cut into segments or else simply cut into semicircular slices or quarters; the flesh can also be cut into circular slices without splitting lengthways.

Cold Dishes
cold cucumber soup
Cut a large cucumber into small pieces. Peel 12 small new onions and cut into quarters. Chop these vegetables in a food processor and put them into a blender with the same quantity of cottage cheese and some salt and pepper: the resultant purée should be well seasoned. Place in the refrigerator

CUCUMBERS AND GHERKINS

large ridge cucumber

smooth-skinned Dutch cucumber

medium ridge cucumber

gherkins

small gherkins

until ready to serve. Then dilute the purée with iced water to obtain the consistency of a fairly thick soup and sprinkle with chopped chives or parsley.

cucumber salad

Cut the cucumbers into semicircular slices. Add a well-seasoned vinaigrette generously flavoured with herbs (parsley, chervil, chives) or coarsely chopped fresh mint leaves. This salad can be served as an hors d'oeuvre or to accompany cold white meat or fish.

cucumber stuffed with crab

Split in half and hollow out 3 medium-sized cucumbers of regular shape. Sprinkle with fine salt and leave to sweat for about 1 hour. Mash 250 g (9 oz, 1 cup) crabmeat (fresh or canned) and dice some fennel finely (enough for 3 tablespoons). Also dice very finely 150 g (5 oz) cooked ham heel (rind). Make some mayonnaise with 1 egg yolk, 2 teaspoons mustard and 250 ml (8 fl oz, 1 cup) oil; add salt, pepper and 1 tablespoon each of wine vinegar and tomato ketchup. Mix together the mayonnaise, crabmeat, fennel and ham. Adjust the seasoning. Drain the cucumber halves thoroughly and fill with the stuffing. Keep in a cool place; when ready to serve, sprinkle the cucumbers with chopped herbs and arrange on lettuce leaves.

Instead of mayonnaise, double (heavy) cream flavoured with tomato ketchup, lemon juice and cayenne can be used, and shelled prawns (peeled shrimp) can be substituted for the crabmeat.

stuffed cucumber à la russe

Finely slice a cucumber and cut each slice into quarters. Cut 3 other cucumbers into boat shapes. Mash the contents of a can of tuna or salmon, roughly chop 6 small (pearl) onions and mix together the fish, onions, and quartered cucumber slices with 300 g (11 oz, 1⅓ cups) cottage cheese (well drained). Season with salt and pepper. Fill the cucumber boats with this mixture and put in a cool place. When ready to serve, sprinkle with 1 sieved hard-boiled (hard-cooked) egg and chopped herbs.

Hot Dishes
buttered cucumber

Place blanched segments of cucumber in a sauté pan with some butter – allow 50 g (2 oz, ¼ cup) per 1 kg (2¼ lb) of cucumber; add salt, pepper, and 2 tablespoons water. Begin by boiling fast, then cover and simmer very gently for about 30 minutes. Just before serving, add a fresh piece of butter, stir, pour into a vegetable dish and sprinkle with chopped herbs. Buttered cucumber can be served with poultry and white fish.

cucumbers with cream

Cut the cucumber flesh into segments and blanch. Grease a sauté pan, add the pieces of cucumber with some salt and pepper, cover and cook very gently for about 10 minutes; then add some heated double (heavy) cream – allow 200 ml (7 fl oz, ¾ cup) per 1 kg (2¼ lb) of cucumber flesh – and continue cooking uncovered. The cucumber can also, after salting and draining, be cooked au gratin or served with Mornay sauce.

stuffed cucumber

Peel 2 medium even-shaped cucumbers, split them in half lengthways and remove the seeds and a little of the flesh. Prepare an à gratin forcemeat. Grease a gratin dish or, better still, line it with pieces of pork rind with the fat removed. Cover with a layer of finely chopped carrots and onions and sprinkle with a little chopped parsley. Fill the cucumber halves with the stuffing and arrange them in the dish. Add beef or chicken stock until it comes two-thirds of the way up the cucumber boats.

Bring to boiling point on the hob (stove top), then transfer to a preheated oven at 220°C (425°F, gas 7) and cook for 35 minutes. Cover with foil as soon as the top of the stuffing starts to dry out. Arrange the cucumbers on a serving dish and keep warm. Reduce the cooking liquid to 200 ml (7 fl oz, ¾ cup), thicken with beurre manié, pour over the cucumber and serve very hot.

CUISINE CLASSIQUE All the cookery techniques of traditional French cuisine which every chef should know and master. These are codified in the *Guide culinaire* by Auguste Escoffier, the result of important research in the course of which the complex cuisines of Antonin Carême, Jules Gouffé and Urbain François Dubois were simplified and refined. *Cuisine classique* also includes the inheritance of traditional regional recipes. Many chefs of the present have drawn heavily on this melting pot to create some of the greatest contemporary dishes.

CUISSE-DAMES A small rectangular Swiss fritter, flavoured with kirsch. In the French-speaking part of Switzerland, the rolls of batter are fried in hot oil, which makes them blow up and split open lengthways. In Ajoie, *cuisses-dames* are known as *pieds-de-biche* ('doe's feet').

CUL-DE-POULE A hemispherical basin with a rolled rim. It lacks a handle, but is fitted with a small ring to hang it up when not in use. It is used mainly for whisking egg whites or for holding mixtures which are cooked over a pan of hot water. Traditionally, the *cul-de-poule* was made of untinned copper, but it is now usually made of stainless steel.

CULINARY EXHIBITIONS Until 1914, there were two rival exhibitions in Paris, dating back to the beginning of the century: the Salon Culinaire and the Exposition Internationale d'Alimentation et d'Hygiène. Consisting mainly of demonstrations of very elaborate and decorative dishes, this type of exhibition is rarely held today. However, the food industry still organizes shows to demonstrate new materials, products and services.

CULTIVATEUR A clear soup made with vegetables and salted belly of pork (salt pork). It is the 'restaurant' version of the classic vegetable and bacon soup. It is served with diced lean bacon, which may be placed on thin slices of bread.

RECIPE

potage cultivateur
Cut 2–3 small carrots and 1 small turnip into large dice; prepare 6 tablespoons diced leeks (white part only) and 2 tablespoons diced onions. Season with salt and a pinch of sugar. Cook the prepared vegetables together in 50 g (2 oz, ¼ cup) butter in a covered pan. Moisten with 1.5 litres (2¾ pints, 6½ cups) white consommé* and cook for 1¼ hours. About 25 minutes before serving, add 150 g (5 oz, ¾ cup) sliced potatoes and 75 g (3 oz, ½ cup) well-blanched diced bacon.

The potatoes can be replaced by rice.

CUMBERLAND SAUCE A traditional English sweet-sour sauce that is usually served cold with venison, braised ham, mutton, or roast or braised duckling. It is made with port, orange and lemon juice and zest, and redcurrant jelly.

RECIPE

Cumberland sauce
Remove the zest from an orange and a lemon and cut into fine strips; cook 1 generous tablespoon of the zest very gently in 200 ml (7 fl oz, ¾ cup) port for about 20 minutes. Remove the zest and add to the port 2 tablespoons redcurrant jelly, then a pinch of cinnamon and a pinch of cayenne. Mix, bring to the boil, add the juice of the orange and lemon, then strain. Mix in the cooked strips of zest.

CUMIN An aromatic plant with small, elongated spindle-shaped seeds that are used as a spice, either whole or ground. They have a piquant and slightly bitter taste combined with a warmth that is evident in their aroma. There are biblical references to its use in soup and bread, and the Romans used it to flavour sauces and grilled (broiled) fish and to preserve meat. It was often included in the recipes of the Middle Ages (see *Cominée*). Cumin is widely used in cooking. It is a classic flavouring for bread (especially in eastern Europe) and is also used in certain preparations of cold meat and cheeses, such as Munster cheese. Cumin seeds are popular for rice dishes and ground cumin is essential in many Indian dishes.

CUP A drinking receptacle in various shapes, sizes and materials and provided with a handle.

Cups are made of porcelain, faïence, earthenware, glass, plastic or even metal. In former times, cups were made without a handle, or with two handles, or even with a lid, and they were not always accompanied by a saucer. In the 15th century, cups were used for both hot and cold drinks. Peasants drank from plain or engraved wooden cups. Before the French Revolution, the wine provided in cabarets was served in cups made of heavy faïence. Decorative cups, usually made of hard stone mounted in gold or silver, were embellished with precious stones. From the 18th century onwards, faïence and porcelain services became very widespread, but individual cups were also made, such as the *trembleuse* (the base being placed on a saucer with a slightly larger centre) and the *tasse à moustaches*, with an inner lip that enabled men to drink from it without wetting their moustaches.

There are four traditional sizes of cup: breakfast cups, tea cups, coffee cups and mocha cups. There are also cups for drinking chocolate, broth and tisanes. The consommé cup is shallow and wide and has two handles. It is generally placed on a small matching plate.

In the United States a cup is an official measure of capacity equal to 250 ml (8 fl oz).

CUP A mixed drink usually with one ingredient used as a base and often prepared for several servings. Cups may be made by macerating fruit (such as peeled citrus fruits, cherries, pears, peaches or bananas) in liqueurs, spirits, wine or sometimes cider, beer, champagne or sparkling wines. Cups were enormously popular in the 19th century and, more recently, for parties. Some cups may be ideal as thirst quenchers when based on wine diluted with fruit juice or lemonade. Pimms is perhaps the best-known commerical cup. See also *Bishop, Mulled wine, Sangria*.

RECIPES

cider cup
Mix together 1 glass of Calvados, 1 glass of Maraschino, 1 glass of Curaçao and 1 litre (1¾ pints, 4⅓ cups) sweet cider. Add some ice cubes, slices of peeled orange and chilled soda water. Stir gently and decorate with thin slices of fruit.

peach cup
Slice 500 g (18 oz) stoned (pitted) ripe peaches, add 150 g (5 oz, ⅔ cup) caster (superfine) sugar and 500 ml (17 fl oz, 2 cups) apple juice and leave to macerate for 1 hour. Then add 1 litre (1¾ pints, 4⅓ cups) dry white wine and 3 tablespoons Curaçao and place in the refrigerator. Add 500 ml (17 fl oz, 2 cups) chilled soda water just before serving.

Saint James's cup
Dissolve 200 g (7 oz, ¾ cup) caster (superfine) sugar in 250 ml (8 fl oz, 1 cup) water. Add 500 ml (17 fl oz, 2 cups) Cognac, an equal quantity of rum, 1 glass of Curaçao, 1 litre (1¾ pints, 4⅓ cups) very strong cold tea and some crushed ice. Mix with 1 bottle of dry sparkling cider just before serving.

Sauternes cup

Mix together I glass of Curaçao, I glass of Cognac, about 12 cherries in brandy, I bottle of Sauternes and a little chilled soda water. Add a few slices of lemon, cucumber peel and ice cubes.

CUPBEARER An officer in charge of serving drinks to kings and princes under the French Ancien Régime. The position of cupbearer, which was instituted in France during Carolingian times, can be traced back to the Byzantine court. This was one of the most prestigious and lucrative posts concerned with serving the royal food and drink, but in practice the cupbearer himself only fulfilled this function at coronations.

The *grand échanson* ('grand cupbearer') was a high-ranking officer of the court, who had the privilege of adding two silver-gilt flagons stamped with the king's arms to his own heraldic arms. The *échansonnerie de l'hostel du roi* was the staff of cupbearers, which varied in numbers depending on the epoch. In 1285, besides the grand cupbearer, there were four ordinary cupbearers, two butlers (to receive the wine), two cellar-men (in charge of the cellars and barrels), two bottle-men (to prepare the drinks), a potter and a clerk (for the accounts). Under the reign of Louis XIV, there were 12 *chefs par quartier* (head officers), four assistants, four butlers (for receiving the wine and looking after the cellars and the plate), one cellar master, four wine runners and two leaders of the horse, who went with the king on his hunting expeditions (loaded with all his requirements), as well as a number of underlings.

CURAÇAO A liqueur based on sweet or bitter oranges (originally it was made from the dried peel of the bitter oranges from the island of Curaçao, off the north coast of Venezuela). It is now made by many liqueur houses and often sold as 'triple sec'; it may be colourless, yellow or orange (or even blue). Curaçao is used in various cocktails and also for culinary purposes, notably for flavouring cakes, pastries, soufflés, and above all, for making crêpes Suzette. The best-known form of this popular liqueur is the one evolved by Cointreau, one of the top-selling liqueurs of the world.

RECIPE

Curaçao

(domestic recipe) Macerate 250 g (9 oz, 1½ cups) dried orange peel and the grated rind of 2 Seville (bitter) oranges in 3 litres (5 pints, 13 cups) alcohol in a large hermetically sealed jar for I month. Make a syrup with 1.25 litres (2¼ pints, 5½ cups) water and 2.5 kg (5½ lb, 11 cups) granulated sugar. Strain the maceration, mix with the syrup, bottle and leave to mature. If liked, the liqueur may be coloured with a little caramel.

CURD Milk coagulated either by the action of rennet or by natural fermentation. Curdling is the first stage in the manufacture of cheese. In the French countryside, naturally curdled milk has always been a standard dessert, sometimes forming an essential part of the dinner. It may be eaten sweetened or mixed with fruit, or savoury and seasoned with herbs. The savoury dish is usually accompanied by boiled potatoes, particularly in Brittany where it is called *lait cuit* (cooked milk) or *marri*, and in Lorraine where it is called *matton* or *brocq*. In Corsica, it is the custom to give a young bride on the threshold of her new home a bowl of goat's milk curdled with the stomach (*caillette*) of a suckling kid.

CURNONSKY (born Maurice Edmond Sailland) French writer, journalist and gastronome (born Angers, 1872; died Paris, 1956). After secondary-school education, he went on to study literature at the Sorbonne. The attractions of journalism speedily enticed him away from a university career, and in 1892 he began to frequent newspaper offices and literary circles. He made friends wherever he went.

On the advice of one of these friends, Alphonse Allais, the young Sailland decided to choose a pseudonym. It was the period of Franco-Russian entente. 'Why not Sky?' someone suggested. He replied, translating this suggestion into Latin, 'Cur non Sky?' The pseudonym had been found.

Simon Arbellot, his biographer, gives the following description of the life and career of this unrivalled prince-elect of gastronomes.

'Tracing Curnonsky's life through the early part of the century means reliving all the gay ostentation of the boulevard and breathing again the perfumed air of what is called *la belle époque*. He was to be found wherever imagination triumphed over conformity. P.J. Toulet and Jean de Tinan were friends of his; Willy invited him into his circle and Curnonsky was later to become one of his favourite collaborators. Everyone knew that the old master humorist, author of so many licentious novels, had the knack of surrounding himself with young intellectuals who had fun ghosting for him. *Un petit vieux bien propre* is attributed to Curnonsky; Toulet is supposed to have written a part of *Maugis en ménage*; and the two together wrote a great many now-forgotten works signed "Willy", the titles of which have a strong *fin de siècle* savour: *Le Bréviaire des courtisanes, Le Métier d'amant, Jeu de prince*.

'Curnonsky was to be found wherever there was a meeting of minds. Léon Daudet, in his *Souvenirs*, gives us a picture of him as a regular visitor to Weber's, joining in the debates of Forain, Maxime Dethomas, Adrien Hébrard, Maurice de Fleury; while the slight and vaguely disturbing shadow of Marcel Proust hovered in the background. He was also to be found at Maxim's conversing with Feydeau and Maurice Bertrand. He used to join Paul Fort occasionally in the evenings at the Closerie des Lilas, but secretly he preferred the poetry of George Fourest and Raoul Ponchon to symbolism.

'One day he yielded to the temptations of travel and distant horizons. On his return he wrote the account of the African expeditions of the duc de Montpensier. He was to become a skilful "biographer" of this hunting prince. He moved on to China where the cuisine of the country left an indelible imprint on his mind; he proclaimed it to be the best of the world.

'This somewhat bohemian way of life was, nonetheless, marked by a considerable literary output. Novels, short stories, an anthology and collections of anecdotes made the name of Curnonsky a familiar one in the press and in the publishing world. For Dranem he wrote *Une Riche Nature*, for Charles Barret, *Un Homme qui a bien tourné*.

'Writing was his passion. And his masters? First and foremost was La Bruyère, whose advice he loved to repeat to his young friends: "If you wish to say it is raining, then *say* it is raining." Then Anatole France (the Anatole France of *Jacques Tournebroche* rather than of *M. Bergeret*), for the clarity of his old-fashioned methodical style: "I have heard Curnonsky cry out in indignation at the sight of a solecism." Language was no mere form of words to him.

'Then came the gastronomic period, together with princedom and public acclaim. Fifty or so academies and clubs fought for his presidency and solicited his presence at their feasts. "Cur" had always loved his food. The Anjou wine and the *rillauds* of his childhood had trained his appetite, and while the Rue Jacob period – so discreetly touched on by Madame Colette – seems to have been somewhat disappointing in this respect, the Maxim and Weber era followed closely on its heels. Later, with the collaboration of an epicure and great amphitryon, Marcel Rouff, Curnonsky undertook what amounted to a tourist crusade. It was to this cause that he began to devote all his time. *La France gastronomique* (32 volumes, interrupted at the 28th by the death of his collaborator) is a monument of erudition and a tribute to the richness of our soil. There are also dozens of cookery books, each one no less a literary than a gastronomic delight.

'A public referendum in May 1927 crowned him Prince of Gastronomes, and there was no respite for him after that. He went from *disnées* to light snacks, inaugurations and enthronements, *tastevins* and barbecues without a break. Wherever he went there was a table laid ready for him, the finest wines placed at his disposal.

'On 23 March 1928 he founded the Academy of Gastronomes, modelled on the Académie française, with 40 seats and with symbolic titles ranging from Epicure to Talleyrand. His friends joined him – Maeterlinck in Vergilius Maro's seat, Marcel Rouff in that of Honoré de Balzac. For himself he chose the seat of Brillat-Savarin, in whose honour he gave an address.

'Curnonsky enjoyed a sprightly old age. Honoured and fêted wherever he went, he had the satisfaction of seeing his young disciples carrying on his good work and realizing the idea that was so close to his heart, that of linking the route to the good restaurant to the interests of tourism. He died as the result of an accident in 1956.'

CURRANTS See *dried vine fruits*.

CURRY The idea of curry as a dish flavoured with curry powder was a British invention or, more appropriately, a misrepresentation of spiced Indian dishes. Originating from *kari*, meaning sauce and used to describe the spicy Indian sauces served with rice or other foods. Curry does not exist in traditional Indian cooking as a particular dish seasoned with a set mixture of spices. However, the name has been adopted by some Indian restaurants, often to describe a range of inferior dishes prepared by simmering different ingredients in a standard sauce. The sauce is often varied by increasing the quantity of chilli powder to produce mild, medium or hot curries.

In Europe the mixtures were prepared to fixed formulas during the era of the East India Company and sold by the Dutch and British; the first were published at the beginning of the 18th century. Beauvilliers proposed one in 1814. In 1889, at the Universal Paris Exhibition, the composition of curry powder was set by decree: 34 g (1.2 oz) tamarind; 44 g (1.5 oz) onion; 20 g (0.7 oz) coriander: 5 g (0.17 oz) chilli pepper; 3 g (0.1 oz) turmeric; 2 g (0.08 oz) cumin; 3 g (0.1 oz) fenugreek; 2 g (0.08 oz) pepper; 2 g (0.08 oz) mustard.

A typical contemporary curry powder may include, for example, turmeric, coriander, cumin, pepper, cloves, cardamom, ginger, nutmeg, tamarind and chilli pepper. It may be further seasoned with fennel, caraway, ajowan seeds, dried basil, mustard seeds and cinnamon.

In India the spices in *kari* vary according to the individual cook, the region, caste and customs, as well, of course, as the main ingredient or dish which it is intended to complement. Even though a cook may use a favourite mixture, traditionally it would be freshly prepared for each dish. In practice, mixtures such as garam masala (a combination of spices roasted and ground together ready for flavouring dishes during or at the end of cooking), may be made in larger quantities and stored in an airtight container.

■ **Well-balanced flavour** The seasoning of the dish does not begin and end with a mixture of ground spices: fresh spices, such as ginger or chillies, and whole spices, typically cardamoms, are often vital. Onions and garlic frequently feature and bay leaves, fenugreek leaves or curry leaves may be used. The ultimate flavour of the sauce or dish is also the result of careful preparation – roasting the spices, frying the flavouring ingredients and adding spices at different stages during cooking. Many dishes are finished with a final dressing of spices cooked in butter or ghee or sprinkled with ground roasted spices. The important point that early curry recipes or spice mixtures missed is that a hot flavour is not necessarily a prerequisite. Warm flavours from mild spices, such as cinnamon, cloves and cardamom, and the refreshing eucalyptus-citrus tones of cardamoms are often important. Finally, rarely are such dishes dominated by a single overpowering flavour; even fiery dishes laden with chillies should be carefully balanced so that the flavour of the main ingredients and any other spices are clearly in evidence.

■ **International curries** Although the typical European interpretation of a curry based on an inferior, lurid yellow curry powder may have tainted the image of dishes taking the name, in practice a wide variety of good-quality international dishes have evolved. Curries feature in the cooking of many countries where Indian spice mixtures are used in combination with local ingredients and cooking styles. African and Southeast Asian curries are well known, especially those of Thailand, Malaysia and Indonesia. Rich in the use of coconut milk, lime and dried shrimps or shrimp paste, there are many delicious Oriental seafood curries and spiced noodle dishes.

■ **Curry products** Commercial curry powders, pastes and sauces have improved and they are often associated with particular regional Indian origins or styles of cooking. Superior brands and carefully blended spices are available and these, along with high-quality pastes or sauces, can be useful for seasoning savouries and dishes that are not intended to be authentic. However, inferior products still exist and cheap hot and bright yellow curry powders must be avoided.

■ **Preparing curries or spiced dishes** Paying attention to technique is as important as the careful use of spices. Roasting spices before grinding them enhances their flavour and is recommended when they are to be added during the later stages of cooking or directly to a sauce. When roasting spices, take care not to overcook them or allow them to become too hot and burn as this will make them bitter. They are aromatic and just changing colour when ready.

When whole or ground unroasted spices are used, they should be cooked gently in a little butter, ghee or oil before the liquid is added. Spices are often cooked with onions, ginger and other ingredients fried in the first stages of cooking. Cooked spices and flavouring ingredients can be puréed to a paste and used as a marinade.

Marinating allows the spices to penetrate the main ingredients before cooking. The spices may be mixed with an oil or yogurt paste or they may be roasted and used as a dry rub. This is also a good method of helping to achieve tender results, especially when using citrus fruit juice and yogurt.

Long gentle cooking allows time for the spices to mingle and for the flavour of the dish to mature. Some spiced dishes benefit from being cooked in advance, cooled, chilled and thoroughly reheated before serving (particularly meat curries).

Warm spices may be added at the end of cooking, particularly cumin, coriander, cinnamon or nutmeg. These can be roasted and ground or whole (or crushed) spices can be cooked in a little butter and trickled over the dish – this method is often used for *dal* or dishes of cooked pulses.

RECIPES

curry powder

This is a useful general spice mixture and enough for seasoning 600–900 ml (1–1½ pints, 2½–3¾ cups) sauce or a dish to yield 4–6 portions, depending on the ingredients. Place 1 cinnamon stick, 4 cloves, 4 green cardamoms, 2 tablespoons cumin seeds and 4 tablespoons coriander seeds in a small saucepan. Roast the spices gently, shaking the pan frequently, until they are just aromatic. Remove from the pan and cool, then grind to a powder in a spice grinder or pestle and mortar. Mix in 2 teaspoons ground fenugreek, ½ teaspoon ground turmeric and ½ teaspoon chilli powder.

chicken curry

Draw, singe and clean a medium-sized chicken, then cut it into quarters and divide each quarter into 3–4 pieces (make sure the chicken bones are cut cleanly, without splintering). In a flameproof casserole containing lard (shortening) or butter, cook 2 medium onions, 100 g (4 oz, ¾ cup) ham and 2 peeled dessert (eating) apples, all chopped and seasoned with crushed garlic, thyme, bay leaf, cinnamon, cardamom and powdered mace. Then add the chicken pieces and cook until they are firm, stirring them in the mixture without letting them get too coloured.

Add the prepared curry powder (above). Add 2 tomatoes, peeled, crushed and seeded, and mix well. Moisten with 250 ml (8 fl oz, 1 cup) coconut milk (or almond milk). Simmer with the lid on for about 35 minutes. Ten minutes before serving, add 150 ml (¼ pint, ⅔ cup) double (heavy) cream and the juice of 1 lemon. Continue to reduce the sauce until the desired consistency is achieved.

Arrange the chicken pieces in a dish and serve with rice prepared as follows: boil 250 g (9 oz, 1½ cups) rice for 15 minutes in salted water, stirring often; drain and wash several times in cold water. Empty on to a metal plate, wrap in a towel and dry in a preheated oven at 110°C (225°F, gas ¼) for 15 minutes.

Chicken curry can also be made using the recipe for lamb curry.

lamb curry

Mix 1 tablespoon freshly grated root ginger (or 1 teaspoon ground ginger), a pinch of saffron, 3 tablespoons oil, a large pinch of cayenne, salt and pepper. In this mixture, roll 1.5 kg (3¼ lb) neck or shoulder of lamb cut up into pieces, and leave to marinate for 1 hour. Peel and crush 3 large tomatoes. Brown the pieces of meat in a large saucepan containing 25 g (1 oz, 2 tablespoons) lard (shortening), then remove from the pan.

In the same fat, fry 4 large sliced onions until golden, then add the crushed tomatoes, the prepared curry powder (above), 3 finely chopped garlic cloves and a bouquet garni. Leave to brown for 5 minutes. Peel and grate an acid apple, add to the pan and stir for 2–3 minutes. Replace the meat in the pan, stir, add a small cup of coconut milk or semi-skimmed milk, cover and leave to finish cooking gently for about 40 minutes. Adjust the seasoning.

Serve this curry very hot with boiled rice, cashew nuts, raisins, and pineapple and banana dice flavoured with lemon juice, all in separate dishes.

monkfish curry à la créole

Cut about 1 kg (2¼ lb) monkfish into pieces, fry in oil until golden, then drain. In the same oil, fry 100 g (4 oz, ¾ cup) finely chopped onion until golden, then add 2 or 3 peeled crushed tomatoes, a pinch of saffron, 1 tablespoon freshly grated root ginger (or 1 teaspoon ground ginger), 2 finely chopped garlic cloves, a bouquet garni, a piece of orange peel and 2 teaspoons of the prepared curry powder (above). Stir over a medium heat for 5–6 minutes, then add 250 ml (8 fl oz, 1 cup) hot water, cayenne, salt and pepper. Cover and leave to cook very gently for 30 minutes. Remove the bouquet garni and orange peel and serve with rice à la créole.

CUSSY, LOUIS, MARQUIS DE One of the wittiest gastronomes of the early 19th century (born Coutances, 1766; died Paris, 1837). He held the post of prefect of the palace under Napoleon I. If his great friend Grimod de La Reynière is to be believed, Cussy invented 366 different ways of preparing chicken – a different dish for each day, even in a leap year.

In 1843 he published *Les Classiques de la table*, in which he devoted many pages to the history of gastronomy. He also wrote several articles. As principal steward of the emperor's household, he looked after the wardrobe, the furniture and the provisions of the court. When Louis XVIII succeeded Napoleon, it is said that at first he refused to have anything to do with Cussy, but that later, learning that he was the creator of strawberries à la Cussy, he gave him a post of responsibility.

Chefs have dedicated several recipes to him, including a garnish for meat or poultry consisting of artichoke hearts filled with mushroom purée, cooked au gratin, topped with cocks' kidneys and fine slices of truffle, and coated with a port or Madeira sauce.

RECIPES

potatoes à la Cussy

Cut off both ends of big yellow potatoes, and cut them with a special cutter (called a *colonne*) into cork-shaped chunks, about 2.5 cm (1 in) in diameter. Cut them into slices 5 mm (¼ in) thick. Dry on a cloth to absorb all water. Put them into a big pan with 225 g (8 oz, 1 cup) hot clarified butter and cook gently so that they colour without sticking to the pan or drying up. In the meantime, slice 6–8 truffles, toss them in butter with 1 tablespoon Madeira and a walnut-sized piece of chicken aspic.

When the potatoes are cooked and have acquired a fine golden colour, remove them from the heat and add the truffles and the juice of half a lemon and serve piping hot.

salpicon à la Cussy

Prepare a salpicon of braised calves' sweetbreads, truffles and mushrooms which have been cooked slowly in butter. Bind with concentrated Madeira sauce.

turnovers à la Cussy

Fill circles of puff pastry with a forcemeat of creamed whiting or other white fish to which anchovy fillets (cut into small strips) and chopped truffles have been added. Fold the pastry over into turnovers. Place on a buttered baking sheet, brush with beaten egg, and bake in a preheated oven at 230°C (450°F, gas 8) until golden brown.

CUSTARD A hot or cold mixture, set or thickened with eggs or egg yolks. The term primarily refers to sweet mixtures of milk or cream with eggs. There are several basic types of sweet custard and numerous variations on them; they also form the base for a wide range of desserts. There are two main types: pouring custards or custard sauces and baked or set custards.

• CRÈME ANGLAISE This is the basic custard sauce or pouring custard served hot or cold as an accompaniment for desserts. It may also be used as the base for a variety of desserts, such as set creams. This consists of milk flavoured with vanilla and lightly sweetened, thickened with egg yolks.

• CUSTARD SAUCE Some custard sauces are thickened with a combination of whole eggs and egg yolks. Flavoured with vanilla and sweetened with sugar, custard sauce is usually used to describe a richer, slightly more 'eggy' and sweeter sauce than the classic crème anglaise.

• SIMPLE OR QUICK CUSTARD SAUCE Thickened with a small amount of cornflour (cornstarch) in addition to egg yolks, this is more stable and less likely to curdle. The proportion of cornflour should be kept small to avoid a gloopy result.

• CRÈME PÂTISSIÈRE OR CONFECTIONER'S CUSTARD This is a thick sauce used as the basis for a cream or other dessert, or as a filling for pastries. Plain (all-purpose) flour and egg yolks are used with milk to make a thick sauce. The sauce may be made with part cream and part milk. When used as a filling for gâteaux or pastries, crème pâtissière is allowed to cool, then beaten or whisked until smooth; it may be lightened and enriched by folding in whipped cream or whisked egg whites.

• SABAYON This is a light, whisked custard with a mousse-like texture, made by whisking egg yolks and white wine over a bain marie until very light and thickened. Sabayon may be served as a sauce or used as the base for a dessert. The Italian equivalent is zabaglione.

• BAKED CUSTARD This is a combination of milk, or

cream and milk, with egg yolks or whole eggs (or a mixture of both), baked until set. The proportion of egg to milk determines whether the custard is lightly set or firm; egg yolks give a softer, richer and more creamy result than whole eggs. Single (light) or double (heavy) cream may be used instead of, or as well as, milk. Crème caramel is a good example of a typical light custard made with milk or single cream and a mixture of whole eggs and egg yolks. Crème brûlée is a rich custard made with double cream and all egg yolks.

■ **Custard desserts** Any of the custard sauces, including a sabayon, may be used as the base for frozen desserts, including ice creams or parfaits. They are often used as a base for chilled set creams, mousses or soufflés.

Many cooked desserts, hot or cold, rely on a baked custard. British bread and butter pudding is a good example – the layers of buttered bread are soaked in a custard mixture before baking. More sophisticated desserts are made on the same principle, for example with sponge cake, enriched with alcohol. Baked custard fillings are also used for tarts.

Baked custards also feature in unusual puddings, such as fried custard, made by coating and frying chilled set custard, and delicately spiced Indian desserts prepared from sweet cake or bread soaked in saffron custard and baked. Bread soaked in custard and fried is also a classic peasant pudding.

■ **Savoury custards** The same principle is also used for certain savoury mixtures. The typical filling for quiche is a good example, where cream and eggs are set on a base of savoury ingredients. Light fish custards or vegetable custards may be steamed or baked in individual dishes. Oriental cooking also includes savoury custards, based on eggs but without the cream or milk (dairy produce is not used), flavoured with finely cut savoury ingredients. A savoury dish of bread soaked in custard and baked, especially flavoured with cheese, makes a classic family supper; similarly, slices of bread soaked in beaten eggs and milk can be fried and served as a savoury snack.

■ **Making custards** Custards rely on lightly set egg for success: overheating the mixture or cooking it for too long will make the egg set completely and it will separate from the liquid, becoming curdled. Gently heating, usually over a bain marie or pan of hot (not boiling) water on the hob (stove top) or in a bain marie in the oven, is essential to avoid curdling. The perfect, smooth, baked custard is strained and allowed to stand, then cooked gently for just the right length of time: any slight bubbles or open texture indicate overcooking or too high a temperature.

For best results, the liquid should be heated and allowed to cool until warm or hand hot before it is added to the eggs. The eggs should be well beaten and the custard mixture strained through a fine sieve.

Crème pâtissière is boiled because the flour prevents the egg yolks from curdling. A little cornflour (cornstarch) can be added to custards to help stabilize them and reduce the risk of curdling.

■ **Custard products** Custard powder, invented by Alfred Bird in Birmingham, England in 1837, is a cornflour (cornstarch) product with dried egg, colouring and flavouring. It does not resemble egg custard. Various products are produced based on this type of flavoured cornflour mixture.

RECIPES

Confectioner's Custard (Pastry Cream)
confectioner's custard (1)

In a thick-based saucepan, place 50 g (2 oz, ½ cup) plain (all-purpose) flour, 175 g (6 oz, ¾ cup) caster (superfine) sugar, a pinch of salt, 15 g (½ oz, 1 tablespoon) unsalted butter and 4 whole eggs. Work this mixture with a whisk. Infuse a vanilla pod (bean) in 500 ml (17 fl oz, 2 cups) milk, bring to the boil and add it to the mixture. Stir well, place the saucepan over the heat and boil for a few minutes, stirring all the time to prevent the custard from sticking to the bottom. Remove the vanilla pod, pour the custard into an earthenware dish and allow to cool, stirring from time to time.

confectioner's custard (2)

Split a vanilla pod (bean), boil it in 500 ml (17 fl oz, 2 cups) milk, then remove it. Beat 3 egg yolks with 75 g (3 oz, 6 tablespoons) caster (superfine) sugar; when the mixture has turned white, add 40 g (1½ oz, ⅓ cup) cornflour (cornstarch). Then gradually add the boiling vanilla-flavoured milk, whisking all the time. Put the mixture in a saucepan over a gentle heat and boil for 1 minute, whisking vigorously. Pour the custard into a deep bowl and leave to cool.

chocolate confectioner's custard

Use 75–100 g (3–4 oz, 3–4 squares) cooking chocolate for 500 ml (17 fl oz, 2 cups) confectioner's custard. Cut the chocolate into small pieces, add them to the hot custard and stir with a wooden spoon until they have melted completely.

coffee confectioner's custard

Stir 1 teaspoon coffee essence (coffee extract) or 1 tablespoon instant coffee into every 500 ml (17 oz, 2 cups) hot confectioner's custard.

Crème Anglaise
crème anglaise ◆

Blend 250 g (9 oz, 1 cup) caster (superfine) sugar, a pinch of salt and 8 egg yolks in a pan using a whisk. Boil 500 ml (17 fl oz, 2 cups) milk flavoured with vanilla or the zest of either a lemon or an orange. When the sugar-egg yolk mixture forms ribbons, gradually add the warm (not boiling) milk. Mix well, keeping the pan on the heat and stirring continuously until the first signs of boiling. At this point the yolks are sufficiently cooked and the custard should cling to the spoon. Press the hot custard through a fine sieve or a silk strainer. Keep it hot in a bain marie if it is to accompany a hot

Making crème anglaise

Dip a spatula in the crème anglaise and then wipe your finger across the spatula. When cooked, the crème anglaise holds the finger mark.

dessert; otherwise pour it into a basin, stir until it is completely cool and keep it in a cool place.

A simpler and lighter version of this can be made by reducing the number of egg yolks to 5–6 and adding ½ teaspoon arrowroot, starch or cornflour (cornstarch) when mixing the eggs and sugar. This gives a slightly thicker consistency and helps to prevent the custard from curdling if allowed to overheat.

caramel-flavoured custard
Add caramel to the boiling milk used for preparing the custard.

custard cream with liqueur
When the custard is completely cold add 1 tablespoon liqueur (Curaçao, kirsch, Maraschino or rum, for example).

custard flavoured with coffee or tea
Add coffee essence (extract) or instant coffee to the milk used for preparing the custard. Alternatively, tea can be infused in the milk, which is then strained.

orange or lemon custard
For the quantities in the basic recipe, add the finely grated zest of 1 orange or lemon to the milk and infuse for 1 hour before making the custard. If required, shred the pared zest of 1 fruit very finely, boil until tender, and add to the warm custard.

Baked Custards
chocolate custard
Melt 100 g (4 oz, 4 squares) cooking (unsweetened) chocolate in a bain marie with 1 tablespoon milk; when the mixture is quite smooth, add 500 ml (17 fl oz, 2 cups) milk, bring to the boil, then remove from the heat. Whisk 6 eggs with 100 g (4 oz, ½ cup) caster (superfine) sugar until pale and thick. Gradually add the chocolate-flavoured milk, whisking it all the time. Strain the custard into 6 ramekins and cook in a bain marie in a preheated oven at 190°C (375°F, gas 5) for 25–30 minutes.

Take the moulds out of the bain marie, leave to cool and chill well.

crème brûlée
Slit open a vanilla pod (bean) lengthways and remove all the little seeds using a knife. Place them in a bowl with 3 egg yolks and 50 g (2 oz, ¼ cup) caster (superfine) sugar and mix well with a whisk. Gradually whisk in 300 ml (½ pint, 1¼ cups) single (light) or double (heavy) cream and 60 ml (2 fl oz, ¼ cup) milk. Strain through a chinois. Pour this mixture into small ramekins and place in a bain marie. Cook for 30 minutes in a preheated oven at 190°C (375°F, gas 5). Allow to cool completely and place in the refrigerator for at least 1 hour.

Sprinkle 100 g (4 oz, ⅔ cup) soft brown sugar on top to cover the custards completely. Place under a very hot grill (broiler) until the sugar has caramelized. Refrigerate before serving.

crème caramel ♦
Boil 500 ml (17 fl oz, 2 cups) milk with a vanilla pod (bean) split in two. In a mixing bowl, blend 2 whole eggs, 4 egg yolks and 125 g (4½ oz, ½ cup) caster (superfine) sugar; gradually add the boiling milk (having removed the vanilla pod), whisking it quickly. Pour the resulting custard into a caramel-coated mould, place the mould in a bain marie and cook in a preheated oven at 190°C (375°F, gas 5) for about 40 minutes or until the custard is lightly set. Then take the mould out of the bain marie and allow it to cool completely. Turn out on to a dish and cool before serving.

Fried Custard
fried custard fritters
Boil 500 ml (17 fl oz, 2 cups) milk with 1 tablespoon vanilla-flavoured sugar. In a mixing bowl, beat 5 egg yolks with 100 g (4 oz, ½ cup) caster (superfine) sugar until the mixture is white. Beat in 75 g (3 oz, ¾ cup) plain (all-purpose) flour and gradually add the boiling milk, whisking it well. Pour the mixture into a saucepan, boil over a gentle heat for 3 minutes, stirring all the time, then remove from the heat and leave to cool until lukewarm. Spread the custard evenly over a buttered baking sheet to a thickness of 1.5 cm (⅝ in) and leave it to cool completely. Cut it into rectangles, diamonds or circles, dip these in batter and plunge them into hot oil at a temperature of 170–180°C (338–356°F). Drain and dust with icing (confectioner's) sugar.

fried custard with crystallized fruits
Macerate 100 g (4 oz, ⅔ cup) diced crystallized (candied) fruits in 100 ml (4 fl oz, 7 tablespoons) Grand Marnier. Prepare some custard for frying as in the previous recipe and blend the fruit with it. Lightly oil a baking sheet and pour the custard on to it to form an even layer, 2 cm (¾ in) thick; leave to cool before putting in the refrigerator for

2–3 hours. Then cut the custard into diamond shapes and coat with beaten egg and breadcrumbs. Fry in hot oil at a temperature of 175–180°C (347–350°F) until lightly browned, then drain on paper towels. Dust with icing (confectioner's) sugar and serve very hot.

CUSTARD APPLE The fruit of a tree that originated in Peru and is cultivated in many tropical countries. Similar fruits produced by related species include the soursop (or bullock's heart) and the cinnamon apple. The custard apple is grown in the Near East, Central America and the south of Spain. It is the size of an orange, with a rough green skin, which turns blackish-brown when the fruit is properly ripe. The flesh is white and juicy and has a sweet-sour flavour with a rose-like scent. The chilled fruit is cut in half, the black seeds are removed and it is usually eaten with a small spoon. It can also be used in sorbets and fruit salads.

CUSTARD MARROW A species of climbing gourd which is eaten as a vegetable; it is called *chayote* in France, *christophine* or *brionne* in the West Indies and *chouchoute* in Madagascar and Polynesia. Originating from Mexico, where its young shoots are eaten like asparagus, the custard marrow is cultivated in tropical countries and in North Africa. It resembles a green or white pear, sometimes with a fairly rough skin and several spines, and is as big as two fists, with deep longitudinal ribs. Its firm homogeneous white flesh is crisp. It does not have a very pronounced flavour; it has a high water content.

The custard marrow keeps for a long time. Before completely ripe, it may be consumed raw in salads, peeled, cored and finely sliced. It is especially common in Caribbean cookery. Not fully ripe until it starts to germinate, the gourd is peeled and puréed for making *acras* and very fine gratins. It is an essential ingredient in *mange-mêle* (ratatouille with streaky bacon and coconut milk) and accompanies spiced dishes such as kid colombo or pork curry (it is then diced for sautéing or braising). It may also be made into a soufflé.

RECIPES

custard marrows à la martiniquaise
Press some boiled custard marrows in a cloth to extract the maximum amount of water and mix this pulp with bread soaked in milk. Brown some peeled and finely sliced spring onions (scallions) in butter, then blend with the mixture of bread and custard marrow. Season and spread out in a gratin dish, smoothing the top. Moisten with olive oil, sprinkle with fresh breadcrumbs and reheat in the oven.

custard marrows au blanc
Divide the custard marrows into quarters and cut into large lozenge shapes. Cook in a blanc, keeping them slightly firm, or blanch for 5 minutes in salted water. Drain, dry and arrange them flat in a shallow frying pan in which 3 tablespoons white consommé* or water have been heated. Cover and cook very gently. When cooked, arrange in a serving dish and pour over the buttery pan juice; alternatively, serve with béchamel sauce, cream, au gratin, in a salad, with a well-seasoned vinaigrette, with Mornay sauce or with tomato sauce.

custard marrows braised in gravy
Divide the custard marrows into quarters and cut into lozenge shapes; blanch for 5 minutes in salted water and drain. Cover a shallow frying pan with bacon rinds, carrots and onions peeled and cut into rings, and arrange the custard marrows on top. Season with salt and pepper and cover with stock made from clarified bouillon. Cook quite gently, first covered, then uncovered. When the liquid is three-quarters reduced, add some meat juice and leave to simmer for a few minutes. Drain the custard marrows and keep them hot in the serving dish. Strain the pan juice, add butter and pour it over the custard marrows. Sprinkle with chopped parsley.

CUTLET A shaped cutlet (*côtelette composée*) consists of boned minced (ground) meat, poultry or fish that is bound with a sauce and shaped into a cutlet. It may then be dipped in egg and breadcrumbs, and fried in butter. Egg cutlets are made in a similar way. Hard-boiled (hard-cooked) eggs are chopped, bound with a reduced béchamel sauce containing raw egg yolks, coated with breadcrumbs and fried. Mushrooms, ham or pickled tongue can be added. Shaped cutlets are served as a hot starter. (See also *chop*.)

RECIPE

shaped cutlets
Chop cooked poultry, game or meat into small dice or reduce to a very dry paste. Slowly and gradually add a thick béchamel sauce (with or without tomato purée), a thick Mornay sauce or an allemande sauce. The resulting mixture must have an even consistency. Add some chopped herbs (parsley, tarragon, mint). Roll out the mixture evenly on a greased surface and allow it to cool completely. Divide the mixture into portions weighing about 75 g (3 oz). Shape each portion into a cutlet, dip in beaten egg with a little added oil and coat with fresh breadcrumbs. Fry the cutlets in clarified butter. Serve garnished with vegetables and quarters of lemon.

other recipes See *egg (hard-boiled eggs)*, *pojarski*, *salmon*.

Crème caramel, see page 391.

CYPRUS

The country's reputation for hospitality remains as true today as it was in the past when gods shared their meals with men. Cypriot cuisine combines Greek and Turkish traditions. Garlic, spices and herbs are much used in all Cypriot dishes.

■ **Starters** The traditional *meze* (an assortment of appetizing items) is popular because it is a symbol of conviviality and friendliness.

Mezedhes are hors d'oeuvre or other foods cut into small pieces. They are numerous and varied and may be very simple, such as smoked ham, smoked sausage (*kipriaka loukanica*), olives, eggs and beans, or they may consist of salads (such as *melintzanosalata* with aubergine (eggplant), or be much more elaborate, such as *koupes* (spiced minced meat wrapped in a paste of ground corn). Pilaf is another speciality made with rice, often served with lentils or spinach; the rice can also be replaced by ground corn.

■ **Meat and fish** Meat – beef, lamb, veal and especially pork – is usually served grilled (broiled) on a skewer or in a stew, such as the beef stew *vodhino casarolas*. Minced (ground) meat is added to the stuffing of any of the Mediterranean vegetables, or it may be used to prepare dishes like *moussaka* or *kaloyirka* (pasta with minced meat).

As in all Mediterranean countries, fish and seafood are very popular: cod, swordfish, octopus and squid are cooked in the oven, grilled, or served with a sauce (*octaphodhi stifado*, octopus with onions, or *kamamaria yiemista*, stuffed squid).

■ **Fruits and desserts** The many fruits grown on the island are used to produce a variety of syrups and liqueurs, including a mandarin orange liqueur.

Pastries are often made with syrup and honey in the proper Eastern tradition (*lokmades, pishies*).

WINE The Egyptians, the Greeks and the Romans all appreciated the wines of Cyprus, and in the Middle Ages Cypriot wines were introduced to the whole of Western Europe by the crusaders. The most famous of these is Commandaria, whose name evokes the Templars; it is a dessert wine made from a blend of overripe red and white grapes and it has been produced for over eight centuries.

The commonest grape variety is Mavro, which produces powerful reds, much appreciated by the locals, and also rosés. Excellent dry white wines are produced from the Xynisteri grape variety, such as Aphrodite and Arsinoë. Cyprus also produces many excellent dessert wines, similar to sherry, which are mainly exported.

CUTTLEFISH A mollusc related to the squid, which is about 30 cm (12 in) long and lives on weedy coastal sea beds. Its body resembles a greyish oval bag with a mauve sheen and it has a fairly large head with ten irregular tentacles, two of which are very long. The 'bag' is almost completely surrounded with fins and encloses a hard part – the cuttlebone. The cuttlefish has several regional French nicknames – *margate, sépia, supion*. Like the squid, the cuttlefish has an ink sac, which means that it can be cooked in its ink as it is in Spain (*en su tinta*). Cuttlefish are cooked like squid, but the flesh is quite tough and has to be beaten vigorously. The Romans were very fond of it and it is still eaten in Italy, Spain and south-western France, especially stuffed or *à l'américaine*.

CUVÉE The contents of a wine vat (*cuve*), and hence a blending of various vats or casks into a harmonious whole. The term is used particularly in Champagne, where the ingredients of the *cuvée* come from different wines of different vineyard plots, different grapes, and, for the non-vintage wines, of different years.

Terms associated with this word include *tête de cuvée* and *première cuvée*, but the legality of their use depends on the region's laws.

CYRNIKI Also known as *cierniki*. Dumplings made with cottage cheese, served as a hot hors d'oeuvre with soured (sour) cream. Alternatively, they may be poached and served with melted butter or cooked in timbales with grated cheese and butter. *Cyrniki* are of Polish origin, but also form part of the repertoire of Russian cuisine. The cheese is mixed with eggs and flour (seasoned with salt and pepper) until it forms a soft dough. Small triangles or discs, about 2 cm (¾ in) thick, are cut out of this dough, floured, and then lightly browned in butter in a frying pan.

DAB *limande* Any of several related flatfish found in the North Sea, the English Channel and the Atlantic, north of the Bay of Biscay. There are several varieties of dab. The true (or European) dab is lozenge-shaped; its upper surface is brownish with orange-yellow spots. The false dab (or red dab) is a rather elongated oval in shape, brownish-grey on the upper surface and light sandy grey underneath. The lemon dab (or lemon sole) is rounder and has a superior flavour; it is reddish-brown with darker spots, and the gills are bordered with an orange line. The American dab is similar to the European species. Dabs are 20–35 cm (8–14 in) long and weigh 175–250 g (6–9 oz). However, 40% of their body weight is lost during cleaning and filleting. They are sold either whole or filleted, and are usually grilled (broiled) or baked.

DACQUOISE A traditional gâteau of southwestern France, also called *Palois* (the Dacquois are the inhabitants of Dax, the Palois those of Pau). It consists of two or three layers of meringue mixed with almonds (or almonds and hazelnuts). This base, a variant of *succès*, is light and crisp and should be stored as for meringue. The layers are sandwiched together with whipped cream or French butter cream, variously flavoured. Fresh fruit may be added to the filling, particularly strawberries. The top is usually dusted with icing (confectioner's) sugar.

RECIPE

coffee dacquoise
Whisk 8 egg whites with a pinch of salt until they form stiff peaks. Then gradually add 200 g (7 oz, 1 cup) caster (superfine) sugar and 2 teaspoons vanilla sugar, whisking continuously, and continue whisking until the meringue is firm and shiny. Gently fold in 150 g (5 oz, 1¼ cups) ground almonds and 75 g (3 oz, ¾ cup) chopped blanched hazelnuts. Butter three 20 cm (8 in) flan (pie) rings, place them on buttered baking sheets and divide the mixture between them. Cook in a preheated oven at 180°C (350°F, gas 4) for about 20 minutes. When the meringue rounds are cooked, turn them out and allow to cool.

Prepare a coffee crème au beurre (see *creams*) for the filling using 250 g (9 oz, 1 cup) sugar cooked with 100 ml (4 fl oz, 7 tablespoons) water, 8 egg yolks, 250 g (9 oz, 1 cup) butter and 1 tablespoon coffee essence (extract). Toast 100 g (4 oz, 1 cup) flaked almonds. Place the coffee cream in a piping (pastry) bag fitted with a fluted nozzle and sandwich the meringue rounds with thick layers of piped cream. Sprinkle the top with toasted almonds and dust with icing (confectioner's) sugar.

DAFINA The Sephardi version of Cholent. This Arab ragoût of beef cooked with chick peas, potatoes and whole eggs cooked in their shells, layered with spices, can be traced back as far as the 2nd century AD, when it was cooked in pots sealed with a flour-and-water paste (lute) and taken to the public bakehouse for cooking. The word *dafina*, used in English, is taken from Moroccan Arabic (*adafina* in Spanish, *tfina* in French and Arabic).

DAIKON Also known as dai-co, mooli, Japanese radish or Satsuma radish. A type of white-skinned radish, widely cultivated as a vegetable in the Far East, for use raw, in cooked dishes or as a garnish. Its large fleshy root can grow up to 1 m (3 ft) in length and weigh several kilograms. As well as being added to soups and braised dishes, finely grated or shredded white radish is a popular salad ingredient and it is used to make fresh relishes. It is also pickled in salt.

DAIQUIRI A rum cocktail named after a small village on the Cuban coast near Santiago, where, in the 19th century, the Americans supposedly landed after defeating the Spanish. Generally served in a frosted glass, fresh fruit, such as strawberries, may be added and the cocktail may be diluted with mineral water.

RECIPE

daiquiri
To frost a glass, dip the rim in water and then in sugar. Into a cocktail shaker put 1 measure of cane sugar syrup, 2 of lemon juice, 3 of white rum and 1 tablespoon crushed ice. Shake for several seconds, then pour into the glass.

DAL Also dhal and various other spellings. A Hindi word meaning 'leguminous' and applied to split pulses (as opposed to whole pulses, known as gram). Vegetarian dishes are important in Indian, Pakistani and Sinhalese cooking, and dal are a good source of vegetarian protein. The term is also applied to dishes of the cooked split pulses prepared to thin or thick soup-like consistency.

There are many types of dal, the names of which are subject to regional variations and different spellings. Common types include *channa dal*, prepared from Indian chick peas; *moong dal* or *mung dal* are hulled split mung beans; *masoor dal* are lentils; *toor dal* are pigeon peas; *urid dal* are prepared from small round black beans; and *dhuli urd* is a superior dal prepared from the same small black beans but washed until white.

For dal, the dish, the split pulses are cooked in water, often until reduced to a purée. Spices and other flavouring ingredients, such as onion, garlic or ginger, may be added. Before serving, the dal may be garnished with a flavouring mixture, including ingredients such as whole seeds, fresh or dried spices, garlic and/or onions cooked in oil or ghee. Herbs, such as curry leaves, fenugreek leaves or fresh coriander (cilantro) may also be added. Dal are also used to make kofta (little savoury balls) or they may be soaked and ground to a batter to make light pancakes or fritters known as *dosas* (often with rice). Dal are added to some vegetable or meat dishes to thicken them.

DAME BLANCHE Any of various desserts in which white or pale colours predominate. The name applies particularly to vanilla ice cream used as a bombe filling or served with whipped cream and a chocolate sauce to provide contrast; fruit in syrup or alcohol may also be added. Other kinds of *dame blanche* include a sponge cake filled with cream and crystallized (candied) fruits and completely covered

with Italian meringue, a lemon *île flottante* and an almond ice cream.

RECIPES

coupes dame blanche
Prepare some Chantilly cream by mixing 200 g (7 oz) double (heavy) cream with 2 tablespoons milk, 25 g (1 oz, 2 tablespoons) caster (superfine) sugar, a little vanilla sugar or essence (extract) to taste and a crushed ice cube; whip until the cream forms peaks. Chill. Melt 200 g (7 oz, 7 squares) dark chocolate in a bain marie with 2 tablespoons milk. Add 25 g (1 oz, 2 tablespoons) butter and mix well; then add 3 tablespoons single (light) cream. Keep the sauce hot in the bain marie.

Take 6 individual sundae glasses and put 2 scoops of vanilla ice cream into each. Using a piping (pastry) bag fitted with a fluted nozzle, pipe a dome of Chantilly cream into each glass. Serve the hot chocolate sauce separately in a sauceboat (gravy boat).

peaches dame blanche
Macerate 4 slices pineapple in 1 tablespoon each of kirsch and Maraschino. Make a syrup using 250 ml (8 fl oz, 1 cup) water, 250 g (9 oz, 1 cup) caster (superfine) sugar and half a vanilla pod (bean), split in two. Peel 2 large peaches and poach gently in the syrup for about 10 minutes, turning them frequently, then remove from the heat.

Prepare some Chantilly cream by whipping 150 ml (¼ pint, ⅔ cup) double (heavy) cream with 1 tablespoon milk, 1 tablespoon caster (superfine) sugar and a little vanilla sugar or essence (extract) to taste; chill. Drain the peaches, halve them and remove the stones (pits). Divide 500 ml (17 fl oz, 2 cups) vanilla ice cream between 4 sundae glasses, add a slice of pineapple and a peach half to each, and decorate with a 'turban' of Chantilly cream using a piping (pastry) bag fitted with a fluted nozzle. Serve immediately.

DAME-JEANNE The French name for a large glass or earthenware vessel holding up to 50 litres (11 gallons, 13 US gallons) liquid. Usually encased in basketwork, it was traditionally used to transport wines and spirits. In the Bordeaux region its capacity is about 2.5 litres (4¼ pints, 11 cups) – between a magnum and a double magnum. The close link between this region and England explains how *dame-Jeanne* was corrupted to 'demijohn' in English.

DAMIER A gâteau made of rum-flavoured Genoese sponge cake filled with butter cream and covered with praline. The sides are coated with flaked almonds and the top is decorated in a chequerboard pattern.

RECIPE

damier
Make a Genoese* sponge cake using 40 g (1½ oz, 3 tablespoons) butter, 3 egg yolks, 90 g (3½ oz,

7 tablespoons) caster (superfine) sugar, 90 g (3½ oz, 1 cup) plain (all-purpose) flour and a pinch of salt. Allow the cake to rest in the tin (pan) for 24 hours.

Prepare a syrup by boiling 300 g (11 oz, 1⅓ cups) caster sugar in 300 ml (½ pint, 1¼ cups) water, allow to cool and then add 3 tablespoons rum.

Prepare a butter cream (see *creams*) using 3 egg yolks, 150 g (5 oz, ⅔ cup) butter, 125 g (4½ oz, ½ cup) caster (superfine) sugar, 2 tablespoons water and 50 g (2 oz, ¼ cup) ground praline. Gently melt 250 g (9 oz, 9 squares) dark chocolate in a bowl over hot water. Prepare some royal icing* (frosting) using 1 egg white and 75 g (3 oz, ½ cup) icing (confectioner's) sugar. Toast some flaked almonds and coarsely chop them.

Cut the sponge into two equal rounds and sprinkle the rum syrup over them. Spread half the butter cream over one of the rounds with a palette knife (spatula). Cover with the second round and decorate this with the remaining butter cream. Sprinkle the sides of the gâteau with flaked almonds. Using a piping (pastry) bag, pipe the royal icing over the butter cream to form a chequerboard pattern of 3 cm (1¼ in) squares. Fill alternate squares with royal icing and the rest with the melted chocolate.

DAMPFNUDELN A sweet dessert, made in Germany and Alsace, consisting of rounds of leavened dough baked in the oven and served either with compote, fruits in syrup, jam or vanilla cream, and dusted with sugar and cinnamon. Alternatively, it may be filled with a compote of apricots in rum and folded like a small turnover.

Originally, *dampfnudeln* was a savoury dish (the name means 'steamed noodles'), usually accompanied by green salad.

RECIPE

dampfnudeln
Prepare a starter dough by creaming 15 g (½ oz, 1 cake) fresh (compressed) yeast in 200 ml (7 fl oz, 1 cup) warm milk until dissolved (alternatively, sprinkle 1½ teaspoons dried (active dry) yeast over the milk and stir until dissolved) and leave in a warm place until frothy. Then mix into 125 g (4½ oz, 1 cup) strong plain (bread) flour. Leave this starter in a warm place until doubled in volume.

Now gradually work into the dough 100 g (4 oz, ½ cup) melted butter, a pinch of salt, the grated zest of 1 lemon, 5 egg yolks, 100 g (4 oz, ½ cup) caster (superfine) sugar and 375 g (13 oz, 3¼ cups) strong plain flour. Roll out with a rolling pin and leave to rest for 5 minutes. Cut the dough into rounds and leave to rise in a warm place for 1 hour. Brush with melted butter, dust with icing (confectioner's) sugar and bake in a preheated oven at 180°C (350°F, gas 4), for about 15 minutes until lightly browned.

DAMSON Oval stone fruit similar to plum, but smaller, with blue-black skin and sharp, full-flavoured flesh. Related to the bullace, a small round plum either black (black bullaces) or pale yellow-green (known as white bullaces). Originating from Eastern Europe and West Asia, the damson is named after Damascus, from where it was taken to Europe. Known as a hedgerow fruit, damsons are also cultivated.

Neither damsons nor bullaces are eaten raw, but are used in cooking. The tart, fruity flavour of damsons makes excellent preserves, particularly fruit butters and cheeses. These thick purées have a high sugar content and the cheese boils down to give a slicing consistency when cold.

DANDELION A perennial flowering plant that grows wild in Europe. *Pissenlit* in French, the English name is derived from the alternative French name *dent-de-lion* (literally 'lion's tooth', referring to its serrated leaves); *pissenlit* is a reference to its supposed diuretic properties!

Dandelion leaves are usually eaten raw in salads, but may be cooked like spinach. Wild dandelion leaves should be picked before the plant has flowered (January–March), when they are small and sweet. In France cultivated varieties of dandelion are available from October to March; they have longer, more tender leaves but sometimes lack flavour. In salads, dandelions are traditionally accompanied by diced bacon and garlic-flavoured croûtons (as in *salade du groin d'âne*, literally 'donkey's snout salad', typical of Lyon), hard-boiled (hard-cooked) eggs or walnuts.

RECIPE

dandelion and bacon salad
Thoroughly wash and dry 250 g (9 oz) dandelion leaves. Dice 150 g (5 oz, ¾ cup) green or smoked streaky (slab) bacon and brown gently in a frying pan. In a salad bowl prepare some vinaigrette using 1 tablespoon white wine, 2 tablespoons oil, salt and pepper. Add the dandelion leaves and toss thoroughly. Pour 1 tablespoon white wine vinegar over the diced bacon and stir with a wooden spoon, scraping the bottom of the frying pan. Pour the contents of the frying pan into the salad bowl. Quartered hard-boiled (hard-cooked) eggs may be added to the bowl before adding the bacon if wished.

DANICHEFF The name is used for three quite separate dishes: a salad, an iced dessert and a gâteau. The salad is a mixed one consisting of a julienne of cooked artichoke hearts, raw mushrooms, blanched celeriac, asparagus tips and thin slices of potato. The salad is dressed with mayonnaise and garnished with hard-boiled (hard-cooked) eggs, truffles (either sliced or in a julienne) and crayfish tails.

The name *danicheff* is also given to a gâteau and a praline parfait ice with coffee and rum. The origin of the name is unknown, but it seems to date from the beginning of the 20th century.

RECIPE

danicheff gâteau

Prepare a Genoese* sponge using 4 egg yolks, 50 g (2 oz, ¼ cup) butter, 125 g (4½ oz, ½ cup) caster (superfine) sugar and 125 g (4½ oz, 1 cup) plain (all-purpose) flour; leave the cake to rest for 24 hours.

Boil 300 g (11 oz, 1¼ cups) caster sugar with 300 ml (½ pint, 1¼ cups) water in a saucepan, then allow to cool and add 2½ tablespoons kirsch. Prepare some confectioner's custard (see *cream*) using 250 ml (8 fl oz, 1 cup) milk, 2 egg yolks, 50 g (2 oz, ¼ cup) caster sugar, and 1–1½ tablespoons cornflour (cornstarch). Also make an Italian meringue* using 4 egg whites, 200 g (7 oz, 1 cup) caster sugar, and 3 tablespoons water.

Cut the sponge cake into two equal rounds and spoon the sugar syrup over them. Place one of the rounds on a baking sheet and thickly spread with the confectioner's custard. Dice a large can of pineapple rings, sprinkle with kirsch, place them on top of the confectioner's custard and cover with about 100 g (4 oz, ⅓ cup) apricot jam. Place the other round of sponge cake on top and completely coat the surface of the gâteau, including the sides, with the Italian meringue paste, spreading it with a palette knife (spatula). Sprinkle with about 200 g (7 oz, 2 cups) flaked almonds and dust with icing (confectioner's) sugar. Brown in a preheated oven at 200°C (400°F, gas 6) for about 5 minutes. Allow to cool before transferring to a serving dish.

DANISH BLUE A Danish cow's-milk cheese, blue with a whitish rind, containing about 45% fat. It has a strong and slightly piquant flavour and is sold, wrapped in foil, in rounds 20 cm (8 in) in diameter, 10–12 cm (4–5 in) thick, and weighing 2.5–3 kg (5½–6½ lb).

DANISH PASTRY A sweet pastry, made from a rich yeasted dough rolled and folded with butter as for puff pastry. The pastry is cut and shaped to enclose a sweet filling. Shapes include combs (*kammar*) and pinwheels (*spandauers*). An almond paste or marzipan mixture is one of the classic fillings but various ingredients are used, such as dried or fresh fruit, nuts, jams or conserves. The pastries are glazed or iced when cooked.

Often referred to simply as 'Danish', these pastries are popular with coffee or tea. In Denmark they are called *weinerbrod* (Vienna bread); in Vienna they are known as *kopenhagener*. Danish pastries are included in Viennoiserie but not all Viennoiserie are Danish pastries. The Danish dough and shapes of pastry differ from the Viennese dough, which is not as light and crisp due to a different proving or rising method.

DANZIG GOLDWASSER A liqueur made from spirits in which citrus fruit zest, herbs and mace have been steeped. It is filtered and sweetened, and then tiny particles of gold or silver leaf are added.

Of Polish origin, it was especially popular in the 19th century and it is the classic flavouring for soufflé Rothschild.

DÃO A large wine region in the north of Portugal where the best vineyards are in the hillsides 200–500 m (660–1640 ft) high, with a very granitic soil. Traditionally, the red wines were lean and very tannic, but with modern winemaking techniques and a change in the minimum ageing laws, younger, fruit-driven wines of excellent quality are being produced.

DARBLAY A Parmentier (potato) soup mixed with a julienne of vegetables, thickened with egg yolks and cream, and garnished with chervil.

RECIPE

potage julienne Darblay

Prepare 1 litre (1¾ pints, 4⅓ cups) puréed potatoes and dilute with about 500 ml (17 fl oz, 2 cups) consommé. Add 4 tablespoons julienne of vegetables which have been gently cooked in butter. Mix 3 egg yolks with 100 ml (4 fl oz, 7 tablespoons) double (heavy) cream and use this liaison to thicken the soup. Before serving, blend in about 50 g (2 oz, ¼ cup) butter and garnish the soup with chervil.

DARIOLE A small deep round mould with sloping sides, or the preparation cooked in such a mould. Dariole moulds are used to make small pastries, cheese flans, individual babas, set custards or flans, small cakes, rice puddings and vegetable pasties. They are sometimes referred to as castle tins or moulds.

The original dariole, mentioned by Rabelais, was a small puff pastry case filled with frangipane; its name is derived from an old Provençal word *daurar* (to brown, turn golden), referring to its crust. It is still traditional fare in Reims, on the feast of St Rémy, and also in Beauvais, where the frangipane is flavoured with kirsch and dusted with sugar.

Dariole moulds are used to bake British madeleines, small cakes coated with jam and desiccated coconut, and topped with glacé (candied) cherries.

RECIPES

almond darioles

Lightly butter 6 dariole moulds and line them with puff pastry. Prepare some frangipane* cream using 75 g (3 oz, 6 tablespoons) caster (superfine) sugar, 75 g (3 oz, ¾ cup) plain (all-purpose) flour, 1 whole egg, 3 egg yolks, 500 ml (17 fl oz, 2 cups) milk, 6 crushed macaroons, 1 tablespoon ground almonds and 25 g (1 oz, 2 tablespoons) butter. Allow to cool completely, then fill the pastry-lined moulds with this mixture. Bake in a preheated oven at 220°C (425°F, gas 7) for about 30 minutes. Remove the pastries from the moulds and dust with icing (confectioner's) sugar. Alternatively, the moulds may be filled simply with frangipane cream, without the puff pastry.

cheese darioles

Butter 6 dariole moulds. Bring 500 ml (17 fl oz, 2 cups) milk to the boil. In a mixing bowl, beat 2 whole eggs and 4 egg yolks; add 65 g (2½ oz, ½ cup) grated cheese, salt and pepper. Use a whisk to blend in the boiled milk. Fill the buttered moulds with this mixture, place them in a bain marie and bring the water to the boil; then transfer to a pre-heated oven at 220°C (425°F, gas 7) and cook for about 20 minutes. Remove the firm custards from the moulds on to a serving dish. Coat with a sauce made from very hot fondue of tomatoes to which mushroom duxelles or a light béchamel sauce has been added. Alternatively, serve with a good tomato sauce. Serve immediately.

DARNE A thick transverse slice of a large raw fish, such as hake, salmon or tuna. The word comes from the Breton *dam* (meaning 'piece'). A *dalle*, on the other hand, is a thin slice or escalope (scallop) of fish. Both *darnes* and *dalles* may be poached, braised or grilled (broiled); *dalles* may also be sautéed.

DARPHIN A flat potato cake made of grated or julienne potato, cooked first in a frying pan, then in the oven, until it is brown on both sides but soft in the centre. Named after the chef who created the recipe, this dish is served with Madeira or Périgueux sauce to accompany fillet of beef and fried tournedos steaks (*filets mignons*). It may also be called *paillasson de pommes de terre* ('potato doormat').

RECIPE

Darphin potatoes

Peel 1 kg (2¼ lb) potatoes, rinse and soak in cold water for 1 hour; grate or cut into thin matchsticks and remove excess moisture with a cloth. Pour 250 ml (8 fl oz, 1 cup) oil into a flan tin (pie pan) or dish and heat in a preheated oven at 240°C (475°F, gas 9). Melt 50 g (2 oz) butter in a frying pan, add half the potatoes and sauté them for 5 minutes. Then transfer them to the flan tin and press down. Repeat with the remaining potatoes. Sprinkle with a little extra oil and cook in the oven for about 20 minutes. Turn out the potato cake and serve very hot.

DARTOIS A hot pastry or hors d'oeuvre comprising two strips of puff pastry enclosing a savoury or sweet filling. It is said to have been named after the vaudeville artist François-Victor Dartois, who was very well known in France in the 19th century.

The fillings for savoury Dartois (also called *sausselis*) are the same as for *allumettes*: anchovies, sardines, crayfish, chicken and truffled foie gras are most often used. Sweet Dartois are filled with confectioner's custard (pastry cream) which is sometimes flavoured with crystallized (candied) fruits, frangipane, jam or fruit purées. Frangipane Dartois is also called *gâteau à la Manon*, in honour of the composer Massenet, who was very fond of it.

RECIPES

Savoury Dartois

anchovy Dartois

Prepare some puff pastry and a fish forcemeat. Roll and cut the pastry into two rectangular strips of equal size and thickness. Add some anchovy butter to the forcemeat and spread one of the strips with it, leaving a border of 1 cm (½ in) all round the edge. Drain the oil from some anchovy fillets and arrange on top. Cover with more fish forcemeat, then place the second pastry strip on top and seal the edges. Cook in a preheated oven at 220°C (425°F, gas 7) for 20–25 minutes.

seafood Dartois

Prepare 400 g (14 oz) puff pastry. Poach 8 scampi in a court-bouillon for 5 minutes. Prepare 8 scallops and poach in a small casserole for 6–7 minutes with 100 ml (4 fl oz, 7 tablespoons) white wine, 150 ml (¼ pint, ⅔ cup) single (light) cream, 1 good-sized shallot (chopped), salt and pepper. Drain the scampi, shell the tails and cut into sections. Drain the scallops, reserving the liquor, and dice. Add 50 g (2 oz, ⅓ cup) shelled shrimps and gently heat all the seafood ingredients together in butter. Add some Calvados or marc brandy and set it alight. Pour the reserved cooking juices from the scallops over the mixture and thicken with 1 tablespoon beurre manié. Adjust the seasoning, allow to cool completely and proceed as for anchovy Dartois, but using the seafood filling instead.

Sweet Dartois

apricot jam Dartois

Prepare 500 g (1 lb 2 oz) puff pastry and chill for 1 hour. Then divide the pastry in half and roll each half into a rectangle 15 cm (6 in) wide, 25 cm (10 in) long and about 3 mm (⅛ in) thick.

Place one of the rectangles on a baking sheet and cover with about 400 g (14 oz, 1¼ cups) apricot jam. Cover with the second rectangle of pastry and bake in a preheated oven at 220°C (425°F, gas 7) for about 15 minutes. Dust with icing (confectioner's) sugar and return to the oven to caramelize for 5 minutes. Serve warm.

frangipane Dartois

Prepare 500 g (1 lb 2 oz) puff pastry and chill for 1 hour. To make the frangipane, soften 100 g (4 oz, ½ cup) butter with a wooden spatula. Blend 2 egg yolks in a mixing bowl with 125 g (4½ oz, 1 cup) ground almonds, 125 g (4½ oz, ½ cup) caster (superfine) sugar, a little vanilla essence (extract) and the softened butter. Cut the pastry into two rectangles 25 cm (10 in) long and 15 cm (6 in) wide. Complete as for apricot jam Dartois.

raspberry and apple Dartois

Prepare 500 g (1 lb 2 oz) puff pastry and chill for 1 hour. Peel 575 g (1¼ lb) cooking apples, cut into quarters, core and slice finely, then toss in

2 tablespoons lemon juice. Put the apples into a saucepan with 125 g (4½ oz, ½ cup) caster (superfine) sugar, 40 g (1½ oz, 3 tablespoons) butter and half a vanilla pod (bean) cut in two. Add 1 tablespoon water and cook over a low heat, stirring from time to time. When the apples are reduced to a purée, remove the vanilla pod and allow to cool.

Roll out the pastry to a rectangle, 3 mm (⅛ in) thick, and cut it into twelve 10 cm (4 in) squares. Mix the stewed apples with 2 tablespoons raspberry jam and place a generous spoonful of the filling in the centre of six of the pastry squares. Moisten the edges of each square with water and cover with one of the remaining squares. Pinch the edges to seal the pastry. Complete as for apricot jam Dartois.

DARTOIS Also *à la d'Artois*, the name of various preparations, all dedicated to the Comte d'Artois, future Charles X of France. The Dartois garnish for large pieces of meat consists of glazed carrots and turnips, braised celery hearts and lightly fried potatoes (*pommes de terre rissolées*) arranged in bouquets around the meat. Dartois soup is a purée of white beans with the addition of a light julienne of vegetables. In baron of lamb Dartois, the joint is surrounded by potato cases (shells) filled with petits pois and served with Madeira sauce.

DASHI The Japanese name for stock. Stocks used in Japanese cookery are very light, made by soaking dried konbu seaweed and/or other ingredients in water. Dried cured bonito flakes (*katsuobushi*) may be used with the konbu. Niboshi, small dried fish, may be used instead of bonito flakes, depending on the type of dashi required. The ingredients may be soaked more than once; the first stock, known as ichiban dashi, has the best flavour and it is used for fine or light soups and dishes. Niban dashi is the stock resulting from the second soaking and this is used in soups or dishes with stronger or a wider variety of ingredients.

Dried bonito flakes and other ingredients for dashi are sold in sachets for adding to a stated quantity of water. Instant dashi powders or other types of convenience dashi are available.

DATE The fruit of the date palm. Brown and fleshy, about 4 cm (1½ in) long, and growing in clusters, the date is rich in sugar. The Greeks, who called it *daktulos* (finger) because of its shape, used it in sauces for fish or meat and included it in various cakes and pastries.

Thought to have originated in the Persian Gulf, the date palm was the 'tree of life' for the Chaldeans, who ate both the fruit and buds, drank the sap, used its fibres for weaving and its nuts as fuel. Dates may be soft, with light tender flesh ideal for eating fresh; semi-dried, with a good flavour and moderately sweet, ideal for selling as the popular dried date. Hard dates are very sweet, high-fibre fruit known as

camel or bread dates. Dates are now cultivated throughout North Africa and Arabia, and in Pakistan, the USA (California) and Australia. Only a few of the many varieties are exported, notably *deglet noor* (meaning 'date of the light'), native to Tunisia, but also grown in Algeria and the USA. This is golden brown, with a mild flavour and a light flesh which is slightly transparent. It is also known as *deglet nour* or *ennour*, or muscat date. Others include the *halawi* (also *hallawi* or *halawy*), a pale coloured date which is very sweet, and the *khaleseh*, which has orange-brown skin and is very fragrant. The *Khadrawi* date is similar to the *halawi*, but it is not too sweet; known as *chadrawi* in Israel, this variety is grown particularly in southern Iraq. *Medjool* or *medjul* dates are red, full flavoured, and fleshy; they are grown in Egypt and California.

Dates are used fresh – they are frozen for export to prevent them from over-ripening, then thawed for sale as 'fresh' produce. Semi-dried dates are whole, tender and succulent with a good flavour balancing their sweetness. Dried dates are firm, sticky and very sweet; they are available pressed into blocks or chopped and rolled in sugar as well as whole.

The sap of the date palm produces a 'wine', greyish and sweet, which ferments rapidly to become sparkling. This refreshing drink is also consumed in India, where dates are used to make spiced sauces, confectionery and cakes. Thibarine is a rich, sweet Tunisian date liqueur. In Iraq, date juice serves as a condiment for soups and salads.

Dates are eaten as sweetmeats, often stuffed or iced (frosted). North African cuisine makes varied use of them, notably in *tajines* (ragoûts), sweet couscous and curry-flavoured dishes, and even for stuffing fish (shad). Dates are also used in baking, fritters, nougats and jam, and are crystallized (candied).

RECIPES

date fritters
Remove the stones (pits) from some dates and fill each one with very thick confectioner's custard (pastry cream) flavoured with kirsch or rum. Coat the dates in batter and deep-fry them, then drain and dust with icing (confectioner's) sugar.

date nougat
Remove the stones (pits) from 1 kg (2¼ lb) dates. Toast 250 g (9 oz, 2 cups) blanched almonds in a frying pan, without fat. Prepare a syrup by boiling 250 g (9 oz, 1 cup) caster (superfine) sugar with 4 tablespoons water until the temperature reaches 110°C (230°F). Remove from the heat, stir in 250 g (9 oz, ¾ cup) honey, then quickly mix in the dates, almonds, 2 pinches of white pepper, 1 teaspoon ground ginger and the same quantity of tahini (sesame paste) or ground sesame seeds. Form the mixture into a sausage shape and slice into rounds. Store in an airtight container.

stuffed dates

Prepare some almond paste as follows: heat 150 g (5 oz, ⅔ cup) caster (superfine) sugar in a heavy-based saucepan with 500 ml (17 fl oz, 2 cups) water and 1 tablespoon liquid glucose. When the temperature reaches 'soft ball', 115°C (240°F), remove from the heat and add 75 g (3 oz, ¾ cup) ground almonds. Stir with a wooden spatula to obtain a granular texture. Allow to cool.

Remove the stones (pits) from about 30 dates, without separating the two halves. When the paste is cold, knead it in small quantities until supple and then form it into a large ball. Hollow this out, and pour into the hollow a good tablespoon of kirsch and 3 drops green food colouring. Knead the paste again to spread the colour evenly. With the palm of the hand, roll the paste into a long sausage, cut into slices, and roll each slice into an olive shape; use one to fill each date. Serve the stuffed dates in individual paper petit four cases. They may also be sprinkled with crystallized sugar.

DAUBE A method of braising meat (beef, mutton, turkey, goose, pheasant, rabbit, pork, chicken), certain vegetables (boletus mushrooms, palm hearts), and some fish (tuna). Meat cooked *en daube* is braised in red-wine stock well seasoned with herbs; the name is thought to come from the Spanish *dobar* (to braise). The word daube alone generally means a joint of beef braised in wine, a popular dish in several southern provinces of France where it is served hot or cold.

RECIPES

daube of beef à la béarnaise

Cut 2 kg (4½ lb) top rump or chuck beef into 5 cm (2 in) cubes. Lard each cube crossways with a small piece of pork streaky (slab) bacon rolled in chopped parsley and garlic seasoned with crushed thyme and bay leaf. Marinate these beef cubes for at least 2 hours in 1 bottle red wine and 4 tablespoons brandy with 1 large sliced onion, 2 sliced carrots and a bouquet garni of parsley, thyme and bay leaves. Drain, reserving the marinade, pat the cubes of meat dry and roll them in flour. Brown the meat and vegetables separately.

Line the bottom of a flameproof casserole with slices of Bayonne ham, then add alternate layers of the meat cubes and vegetables. Add the bouquet garni, 2–3 crushed garlic cloves to the reserved marinade and a few spoonfuls of stock; then boil for 30 minutes. Strain and pour over the meat. Cover the casserole and seal on the lid with a flour-and-water paste. Bring to the boil on the hob (stove top), then cook in a preheated oven at 120°C (250°F, gas ½) for 4–5 hours.

Serve the daube from the casserole after skimming off some of the fat. In Béarn this daube is served with a cornmeal (maize) porridge, which is eaten cold and sliced as an alternative to bread.

daube of beef à la provençale

Cut 1.5 kg (3¼ lb) lean chuck or silverside (bottom round) into 6 cm (2½ in) cubes. Lard each cube crossways with a piece of fat bacon rolled in chopped parsley and garlic. Put the meat into an earthenware dish or casserole with a calf's foot, if available, and cover with 600 ml (1 pint, 2½ cups) white wine mixed with 2 tablespoons olive oil, 1 tablespoon brandy, salt and pepper. Marinate for 24 hours; reserve the marinade. Mix together 150 g (5 oz, 1⅔ cups) mushrooms, 75 g (3 oz, ⅔ cup) chopped raw onion, 2 crushed tomatoes, 150 g (5 oz, 1 cup) diced and blanched thick streaky (slab) bacon and 100 g (4 oz, 1 cup) black olives.

Remove the fat from some bacon rinds, blanch, wipe and use the rinds to line the bottom of an earthenware casserole just large enough to contain the meat and its garnishes. Add 2 sliced carrots, then add alternating layers of meat cubes and the vegetable and bacon mixture. In the centre of the meat place a large bouquet garni consisting of parsley stalks, thyme, a bay leaf and a small piece of dried orange peel. Add the white wine mixture from the marinade plus an equal volume of beef stock so that it just covers the meat.

Cover the casserole, seal the lid with a flour-and-water paste, and cook in a preheated oven at 120°C (250°F, gas ½) for 6 hours. Remove the bouquet garni, allow to cool, then skim off the fat. Serve the daube cold in slices, like a terrine, or hot (reheated in the oven).

other recipes See *goose, tuna, turkey*.

DAUBIÈRE A braising pot of stoneware, earthenware or galvanized copper, used for making daubes and other braised dishes which require a long slow cooking time. Like the *braisière* (braising pan), it was originally designed for cooking over charcoal; the *daubière* has a lid with a raised edge for holding burning charcoal or boiling water.

DAUDET, LÉON French writer and journalist (born Paris, 1867; died Saint-Rémy-de-Provence, 1942). Founder, with Charles Maurras, of *L'Action française*, Daudet was an unashamed polemicist and one of the greatest gastronomes of his time. In *Paris vécu*, he evokes Parisian life through its restaurants and its chefs, from the best known to the humblest. At the pension Laveur, he invented *kaulback* (which he said was dedicated to a Bulgarian general), comprising white haricot beans, sautéed potatoes and eggs *sur le plat*. He was a regular customer at La Grille, a bistro where journalists from *L'Humanité* and *L'Action française* rubbed shoulders over the beef hash and pickled pork. But he also patronized the Tour d'Argent, where, with his friend Babinsky, he discussed such topics as the merits of an endive (chicory) salad, 'lightly crushed in absinthe', to accompany foie gras; his description of Frédéric cutting up *canard au sang* (duck cooked in its blood) is famous in gastronomic circles. At Weber's house, he described Marcel Proust, 'a doe-eyed young gentleman muffled up in an enormous overcoat', being served with grapes or pears.

A founder member of the Académie Goncourt, he organized the lunch at which the first Prix Goncourt was awarded. For this first lunch at the Grand Hotel and for subsequent ones at Champeaux, the Café de Paris and Drouant, Daudet compiled the menus until his death. He sang the praises of Provençal and Lyonnaise cooking, as well as that of Beaujolais, the 'third river of Lyon'.

His famous judgments on his contemporaries reflect the acerbity of a committed journalist and his love of the good life: the eloquence of Jaurès was 'full like a Gruyère of which each hole is a metaphor'; Renan was 'gracious with lust and sauce'; Briand started to 'wriggle like shellfish sprinkled with lemon'; as for Clemenceau, he was 'as appetizing as a cabbage soup in which the spoon of eloquence would stand up'.

Persuaded that 'the best therapy for all ills is good food', he waxed lyrical when he met a chef who fully satisfied him, such as Madame Génot, his favourite restaurateur of the Rue de la Banque, who was 'to gastronomy what Beethoven is to music, Baudelaire to poetry, and Rembrandt to painting'.

Daudet's second wife was Marthe Allard, his cousin, who was responsible, under the pseudonym of Pampille, for the gastronomic column in *L'Action française* and edited *Les Bons Plats de France* (1924).

DAUMONT, À LA

Designating an opulent garnish dating from the time of the Restoration (and no doubt dedicated to the Duc d'Aumont), designed principally for large braised fish, such as shad, salmon or turbot. It comprises fish quenelles, slices of truffle, crayfish tails *à la Nantua* (in shells or barquettes), button mushrooms and soft roe, all coated with fresh breadcrumbs and sautéed in butter. The dish is served with a normande sauce finished with crayfish butter.

Today, the name is given to simpler fish dishes, as well as to a dish of soft-boiled (soft-cooked) or poached eggs with crayfish and mushrooms.

RECIPES

poached eggs à la Daumont
Cook some large mushroom caps in butter, drain and top each one with a spoonful of a salpicon of crayfish tails *à la Nantua*. Arrange a poached egg on each mushroom cap, coat with Nantua sauce and garnish with a slice of truffle.

sole fillets à la Daumont
Prepare about 150 ml (¼ pint, ⅔ cup) salpicon of crayfish tails *à la Nantua*. Fillet 2 large sole. Prepare 400 g (14 oz, 2 cups) fine whiting forcemeat and add 50 g (2 oz, ¼ cup) crayfish butter. Spread the sole fillets with the stuffing and fold them over. Place them in a buttered gratin dish, add sufficient fish fumet to just cover them and poach gently.

Gently cook 8 large mushroom caps in butter, drain and top each with the crayfish salpicon. Drain the sole fillets and place one on each mushroom. Coat with normande sauce and serve very hot.

DAUPHIN

A soft cow's-milk cheese from Hainaut in France, with a brown rind and containing at least 50% fat. Excellent from September to May, Dauphin cheese is made from the same type of curds as Maroilles cheese but is highly seasoned with parsley, tarragon, pepper and cloves. It can be shaped like a croissant, heart, shield or rod.

Created in the reign of Louis XIV, it owes its name to a royal edict that exempted carters from Maroilles from the penny tithe payable to the Dauphin, which was levied at Cambrai on each waggon coming from Hainaut in Belgium.

DAUPHINÉ See *opposite page*.

DAUPHINE, À LA

A method of preparing vegetables, such as celeriac (celery root) or aubergines (eggplants), in the same way as dauphine potatoes. If the purée obtained is too watery – as can happen with courgettes (zucchini) – it is dried off in the oven.

The name is also given to joints of meat or game garnished with dauphine potatoes.

DAUPHINE POTATOES

Potatoes reduced to a purée, added to choux paste, shaped into balls and fried in very hot fat. They are used to accompany grilled (broiled) or roast meat or game. The mixture may be enriched with grated cheese or Bayonne ham, especially for croquettes (see *lorette*).

RECIPE

dauphine potatoes
Peel 1 kg (2¼ lb) floury potatoes, cut into quarters and cook in salted water until very soft. Drain thoroughly and mash to a purée. Prepare some choux* paste using 500 ml (17 fl oz, 2 cups) water, 125 g (4½ oz, ½ cup) butter, 250 g (9 oz, 2¼ cups) plain (all-purpose) flour, 7 eggs, a pinch of grated nutmeg, salt and pepper. Mix the dough with an equal volume of the potato purée. Heat some cooking oil to about 175°C (347°F) and drop the mixture into it a spoonful at a time. When the potato balls are puffed up and golden, drain on paper towels, dust with fine salt and serve very hot.

DAUPHINOISE, À LA

A method of preparing potatoes that is a speciality of the 'country of the four mountains' (Lans-en-Vercor, Villard-de-Lans, Autrans and Sassenage). The potatoes are cut into *taillons* (round slices) and arranged with single (light) cream in a gratin dish which has been rubbed with garlic and buttered. However, *gratin dauphinois* is often made by pouring a mixture of eggs, milk and cream over the potato slices and sprinkling the dish with grated cheese. *Gratin savoyard*, from the neighbour-

Dauphiné

A region of France that extends from Savoy to Provence. Its geographical diversity gives rise to a wide range of produce, including fish (trout and crayfish), beef and lamb, game (hare and game birds), chestnuts, walnuts, almonds, olives, mushrooms (boletus, morels and truffles), peaches, plums and grapes. The region's cheeses include

Beauchastel, set in the mountains and surrounded by orchards, is one of the charming little villages not far from the road running alongside the Rhône.

In the Vivarais, chestnuts are turned over at regular intervals as part of the drying process. For a long time chestnuts were a staple food of the region.

Sassenage blue, Sérac and fresh or dried Tomme from Saint-Marcellin. The cuisine retains its rustic style. Beef and veal daubes are very popular. Small game birds are cooked *à la dauphinoise*, with juniper berries, in pâtés, and in salmis. The young guinea fowl, chickens and poussin may be roasted or sautéed with garlic; smaller cuts and portions may be cooked with white wine and morels.

■ **Famous gratins** The abundance and quality of the Dauphiné's milk have made cream a feature of the region's traditional cuisine. Cream is used in Dauphinoise soup, Vercors salmon trout, and the famous gratins: *gratin dauphinois*, based on potatoes, is the best-known, but gratins may also be made of macaroni, minced (ground) meat, pumpkin, beets, cardoons, ceps and crayfish tails.

■ **Pâtisserie** The local pastry speciality is a tart called *pogne*, which has a thick-edged crust and is filled with fruit – plums, peaches or pumpkin – according to the season. In the Drôme area, the *pogne* is a large brioche; those from Romans are renowned. Grenoble is famous for its walnut gâteau. Noted among its sweetmeats are the *pruneaux fleuris* (a type of prune) of Sahune, the honey *touron* from Gap and Montélimar's nougat.

WINE Of the local wines, white or red Hermitage and sparkling Clairette de Die are well known. Finally, the liqueurs of Grenoble and Voiron, and above all the green or yellow Chartreuse, are world-famous.

ing region, is made without milk, cream or eggs; instead it consists of alternating layers of potato and grated Beaufort cheese with knobs of butter, all covered with bouillon.

DÉBARRASSER A French word meaning literally 'to clear away', used in cuisine to describe the transfer of food from the cooking vessel to a place, such as a cupboard or a marble slab, where it can be cooled or kept for later use.

In catering, *débarrasser une mise en place* is to remove from the vicinity of the oven (stove) or work station the utensils that were employed in preparing a dish or meal.

DECANT To transfer a liquid from one vessel to another after allowing suspended impurities to settle. In French, *décanter* is used in a variety of contexts: melted butter is decanted after skimming, as is deep-frying fat and stock after use. The same word is even used for extracting meat from the stock or sauce in which it has been cooked; the cooking liquid is then strained, thickened if necessary, and used to make a sauce in which the meat is given a final simmer.

Wine is decanted by transferring it carefully into a carafe so that any deposit that has formed in the bottle during maturation is left behind. Decanting wine also permits oxygenation, which is often beneficial. In practice, only old red wines are habitually decanted; the bitter tannin and solid pigments they contain must remain in the bottle. Fully matured wines should be decanted just prior to serving – they can be so fragile that exposure to the air may cause deterioration. Young concentrated wines with pronounced tannins may also benefit from decanting as this gives the flavour an opportunity to 'open up'.

DECOCTION The extraction of the constituents of a food by boiling it in water for varying lengths of time. In this way meat or vegetable bouillons, court-bouillons and aromatic extracts are made. This procedure should not be confused with infusion, in which boiling water is poured over the substance but the boiling is not continued.

DÉCOUPOIR A small, slightly conical cutter, of stainless steel or galvanized iron, that cuts decorative slices in the form of a star, trefoil, heart, diamond, spade or leaf, from soft foods such as truffles, tomatoes and jelly. It should not be confused with a pastry (cookie) cutter, used in pâtisserie.

DÉCUIRE A French term meaning to lower the cooking temperature of sugar syrup or jam by adding to it gradually, while stirring, sufficient cold water to give it the correct consistency.

DEEP-FRYING A method of frying food by submerging it completely in fat. Common as a commercial means of cooking fast food, it is also a good method of preparing fine ingredients when carried out by a skilled cook. Savoury and sweet items can be deep-fried, from plain ingredients to delicate croquettes and fritters, light doughnuts, crisp pastries and exotic batters. Carried out in deep pans in the Western kitchen or in the curved base of the Oriental wok, this is an international method.

The wok may be traditional for deep-frying a few small items in a comparatively small amount of oil, but when cooking large items, such as fish fillets, or a large batch of food cut in small pieces, a deep pan is essential to prevent the fat from boiling over. The pan should be no more than a third filled with cold fat as this level rises when ingredients are added and the fat bubbles up and spits.

Deep-frying is carried out at a high temperature so that the food is sealed, becomes crisp and browns quickly. If the fat is not hot enough, some is absorbed by the food and the result is greasy. Also, at too low a temperature the outside does not become crisp or it takes too long to do so, forming a thick, often hard and greasy, crust.

■ **Choice of fat** Using the right type of fat is essential for good results and safe cooking. Fats melt, boil and burn at different temperatures. When overheated, fats begin to decompose or break down and produce smoke – this is called the smoking point. The flavour of the fat is also spoilt, becoming acrid or rancid and tainting food cooked in it. When greatly overheated some fats will spontaneously ignite. Repeated heating and cooling of the fat makes it break down and smoke more easily; similarly, overcooked debris from deep-fried food also encourages the fat to break down. Not only are overheated fats undesirable for culinary use but they are not suitable for a healthy diet and should not be consumed regularly.

Animal fats, such as lard or meat dripping, are tra-ditional fats for deep-frying because they can be heated to a high temperature without burning. Many vegetable oils are also suitable and they are both more convenient and versatile as they do not taint the food in the same way as some meat dripping. Vegetable oils are also more appropriate for balanced eating.

Groundnut (peanut), soya, corn, sunflower and grapeseed oils are suitable for deep-frying. Palm oil is suitable, but it is high in saturated fat and blended vegetable oils often contain a high proportion of palm oil. Olive oil breaks down and burns easily; although some foods are deep-fried in olive oil, it is not generally considered suitable for this.

■ **Food for deep-frying** Tender foods that cook quickly are suitable. The pieces should be small or thin so that they cook through before becoming too brown outside. Fish, chicken, small pieces of tender meat, vegetables, fruit, eggs and cheese can all be deep-fried. The method is also used for prepared mixtures, such as croquettes, rissoles, pastries and fritters.

Chicken and meat should be cut into fingers (goujons), thin slices (escalopes/scallops) or small cubes (as for Chinese-style sweet-and-sour pork) to ensure they are cooked through. Slightly larger portions of chicken, such as breast fillets, quarters or drumsticks, require the temperature to be regulated carefully to ensure that they cook right through.

Eggs set and become crisp when deep-fried. Beaten eggs are an important ingredient for setting coatings in place. Whole eggs can be deep-fried from raw – they should be cracked into a cup and slid into the hot fat. Their high water content causes much spitting as it evaporates, then they rapidly set outside and puff up into crisp balls, with the yolks remaining soft in the centre. They should only ever be deep-fried individually as they cook in seconds and require close attention.

■ **Coatings for deep-frying** Delicate foods or items that soften easily during cooking are coated before all types of frying. This is particularly important for deep-frying. The coating should cook quickly to form a crust, preventing the food from absorbing fat and protecting the surface from overcooking. Delicate fish, light vegetables and fruit all have to be coated before deep-frying otherwise they overcook, disintegrate or fall apart.

The coating should also be strong enough to contain certain ingredients or mixtures, for example the coating on deep-fried cheese prevents the cheese from running and disintegrating. Similarly, when making light croquettes bound in a sauce, the coating sets quickly to retain the mixture, which is then soft and fluid when the croquettes are cut open.

• FLOUR This is a simple coating for foods that are resilient and require the minimum of protection. It is used mainly for pan frying or shallow frying, which is not as harsh a method as deep-frying, but it can be used for some deep-fried ingredients. Season the flour and then roll the prepared food it in. The food should be moist or slightly damp to encourage the flour to stick and it should be added to the hot fat immediately it is coated. Sometimes the food is moistened with milk before being floured.

• EGG AND BREADCRUMBS This is a firmer coating, affording more protection. Dry white breadcrumbs are usually the best as they make a fine, crisp coating that turns golden brown during cooking. Ready browned breadcrumbs tend to become too brown. Soft white breadcrumbs can be used for some foods, but they tend to be slightly greasy as they absorb more fat. The food should be dusted with flour, then dipped in beaten egg and, finally, coated in crumbs. The coating can be repeated when a thick layer is required, for example, when preparing croquettes from a well-chilled light sauce which is likely to run quickly. Similarly, when making chicken Kiev, where the fillets of chicken are folded around a pat of garlic butter that melts during cooking, the coating must be thick and even to retain the garlic butter. Chilling food after coating in egg and breadcrumbs helps to set the coating and keep it in place during cooking.

• BATTER A batter is a liquid coating that sets quickly and becomes brown and crisp when deep-fried. The batter may well rise during cooking, to give a puffy coating. Flour, eggs and water or milk are typical ingredients, but a variety of mixtures can be used, including light beer or sparkling mineral water, to lighten the batter. A fairly thick flour-and-water, mixture may be lightened with stiffly whisked egg white to give a batter with good coating properties, becoming light, puffed and crisp during cooking. The food is usually dusted in flour before being dipped in batter and added straight to the hot fat. The thickness of the batter depends on the type of food: fine foods that cook very quickly are coated in fine light batter; a thicker batter may be used for firmer foods.

• PASTRIES Choux paste can be deep-fried very successfully, either as the main mixture for making fritters or as a batter-type coating. Puff pastry can also be deep-fried – it rises well to become crisp and golden outside. It should be rolled fairly thinly and used to enclose simple ingredients that cook quickly. Filo pastry is often used for deep-fried items, such as small pastries with savoury fillings of fish, vegetables or cheese.

■ **Temperatures for deep-frying** These vary according to the food, ranging between 140–180°C (275–350°F). Use a thermometer to check the temperature when heating the fat and during cooking to maintain the temperature as the ingredients are added, also to prevent overheating during cooking. Another method of checking whether the fat is hot is to add a small cube of day-old bread to the fat: the fat should bubble and the bread should rise to the surface, becoming brown in about 30 seconds.

• 140–160°C (275–325°F) is suitable for large items or foods that require time to become tender or cook through; examples include chicken and potato wedges.

• 160–175°C (325–347°F) is the most popular temperature, suitable for foods that cook quickly; for example those coated in breadcrumbs and batters.

• 180°C (350°F) is a high temperature for small items, such as whitebait or fish goujons, that cook very quickly. This is also used for the second stage when double-frying ingredients; for example to crisp and puff potato chips (French fries).

■ **Successful frying** Deep-frying is an excellent cooking method, but one that suffers from poor implementation, particularly as a means of cooking inferior fast foods.

The food must be well prepared, cut evenly so that it cooks at the same rate throughout or across a batch cooked together. An appropriate coating should be used. Foods that are not coated (such as potatoes) should be thoroughly dried before being added to the hot fat otherwise they spit and the splashing fat can be dangerous.

The choice of fat and temperature control is important. The fat should be heated to the right temperature before cooking and the food should be added in modest batches that do not lower the temperature too much. A thermometer should be used for checking the temperature throughout cooking to prevent the fat from overheating.

The cooked food should be thoroughly drained in a frying basket or using a draining spoon, then on paper towels before serving immediately.

The fat should be cooled and strained after use. If it has overheated slightly, it should be discarded. Fat for deep-frying should not be used repeatedly: twice is usually enough, depending on the food and temperature.

DEEP FREEZING, COMMERCIAL A method of preserving food. For commercial preservation the food is subjected to rapid and intense freezing as low as –50°C (–58°F) so that the temperature at the centre of the food is lower than –18°C (0°F) but the degree of crystallization is not such as to cause moisture loss at the time of defrosting. Packaging precedes or immediately follows deep-freezing. After this the temperature must be kept consistently low until the product is used (–18°C, 0°F).

It is very important to maintain the low temperature of deep-frozen products, and worth checking that they are best quality before buying them. Check the temperature of the freezer compartments (which should always have a thermometer); ensure the packaging is not torn or damaged; the products may be covered by a very thin layer of frost (caused by the freezing of the surrounding air), but they should not have trails of ice; chopped vegetables and individually frozen small products must sound like pebbles rattling in the packet. Display cabinets should not be overfilled to the top, since products above a certain level are no longer cool enough.

The foods should be taken home in insulated bags as quickly as possible, and stored in a freezer or in the 4-star compartment of a fridge-freezer; if these are not available, they may be stored for 24 hours only in a refrigerator or for 3 days in the ice-making compartment.

The rule which applies to the use of deep-frozen

foods is never to refreeze a thawed product. Many frozen products are suitable for cooking directly from frozen: check the manufacturer's instructions carefully for cooking methods, times and temperatures. Other items have to be thawed before they can be cooked, either for best results or for reasons of food safety. Fish and meat are often better when thawed before cooking than when cooked from frozen; larger portions of poultry and whole birds usually have to be thawed completely before cooking to ensure that they cook through completely. For example, although a frozen chicken may be simmered for several hours to make stock, with every confidence that it will be completely cooked throughout, to roast a bird from frozen would mean that the outside was overcooked before the meat in the thickest areas had properly thawed and cooked.

■ **Thawing frozen food** Follow the manufacturer's instructions for prepared products. As a general rule, when thawing plain ingredients, remove them from their wrapping and place in a clean, deep container to catch any drips. Cover the dish tightly and leave it in a cool room or the refrigerator, depending on the room temperature, size of the food and likely thawing time. When poultry or meat requires lengthy thawing, the drips or liquid that seeps from it should be drained off regularly.

To thaw baked goods, such as bread, unwrap and place them on a wire rack, then cover with a clean tea towel or paper towels. Leaving these, or pastries, in their freezer bags can make them soggy. Refresh the texture of cooked breads or pastries by heating them briefly in a hot oven.

■ **Freezing food** Home freezers are now highly efficient, designed to reach low temperatures for freezing fresh food. The better appliances are well insulated and designed for the minimum of loss of cold air when opened; with integral thermometers and alarms.

In the early days of home freezing, the recommended preparation of fruit and vegetables was daunting. Research into the deterioration of food during freezing indicates that if the food is frozen rapidly to a low temperature, properly packed and the low temperature maintained during storage, reduction in quality is minimal. The technique of blanching vegetables before freezing does not significantly improve the quality of the produce.

Make sure that the freezer is on the fast-freeze setting well in advance. Use good-quality freezer bags to prevent freezer burn and seal them well. Add food in modest batches that will freeze quickly. Always prepare the produce ready for cooking and toss ingredients that discolour (such as apples) in lemon juice. Open-freeze the produce or pack it in quantities that will be used in one go. Always label the produce well, especially prepared dishes as it is almost impossible to identify them.

Cooking food first can be the best solution, providing dishes in advance for everyday meals, especially by making large batches. Soups and sauces for pasta are practical and take up minimum freezer space. Meat casseroles, burgers or patties, croquettes, pasta bakes, filled pastries ready for baking and filled pancakes are a few examples. Stewed fruit, compotes or purées have many excellent uses and they take up less space than bulky packages of apples, gooseberries or rhubarb and other fruit that falls and become watery when thawed if frozen raw.

It makes sense to freeze items used frequently and in quantity, such as breads, and others that are ideal as a special treat, such as cakes. The freezer is also ideal for storing prepared ingredients ready for cooking or emergency supplies: stock; butter (plain or flavoured); bay leaves; chopped fresh herbs; ground roasted spices; prepared chillies; prepared fresh root ginger; fresh yeast (keeps well for up to 1 year); whipped double (heavy) cream; breadcrumbs; grated cheese for cooking; and knobs of beurre manie (it keeps for 2 months). See *freezing*.

■ **Quality** As a preserving method, freezing is excellent for retaining nutrients as well as taste. Good-quality purchased frozen vegetables are processed so quickly after harvesting that they have a better vitamin content than the slightly stale examples sometimes found on the supermarket shelves. Similarly, using the freezer for storing home-cooked dishes is a good way of having high-quality convenience foods. Batch cooking many savoury dishes and simple sweet mixtures, cakes or pastries requires barely more effort than making a standard portion – the batches do not have to be enormous to be practical, just a double or treble portion will provide two or three meals instead of one.

DEER Ruminants of temperate regions, including red deer (*cerf* in French), roe deer (*chevreuil* in French), fallow deer (*daim* in French) and the white-tail deer of North America. Other related species include reindeer, antelope, elk, moose and caribou, all providing a source of meat, but they are not as important as the four main types. The meat is known as venison and its quality varies according to the type of deer, its age, sex and habitat. Traditionally game animals, deer are now farmed as demand for venison has increased.

Deer have been valued for their meat since prehistoric times and there is evidence of attempts to capture them in ancient Egypt. In the Middle Ages, deer were the most highly prized game animals, reserved exclusively for the nobility in vast parks where they provided hunting sport as well as meat for rich tables.

They inspired some highly decorative culinary displays, in which the beast was virtually reconstructed lying on gigantic dishes. Deer meat was also used to lard poultry. Both stag and hind were eaten roasted, stewed or jugged; deer-knuckle soup was a famous dish. In the 16th century, stag's antlers, cut into sections and fried, were considered fit for a king, as were the *menus droits* (comprising the tongue, muzzle and ears). Stag's horn was commonly sold by grocers: when ground, it was used to prepare jellies and sweets.

Deer retained its status as a luxury food until the latter part of the 20th century, when 'farming' increased availability. More a method of controlling and encouraging the growth of herds than of domesticating and applying contemporary rearing methods, deer farming has produced meat that is in demand for its healthy properties compared to intensively reared animals. In common with other game, deer hunting is subject to strict controls and seasons.

DEGLAZE To boil a small quantity of wine, stock or other liquid with the cooking juices and sediment left in the pan after roasting or sautéing in order to make a sauce or gravy. The sediment may be cooked first, so that excess juices evaporate and the concentrated sediment caramelizes, and excess fat should be skimmed off. A small quantity of liquid is poured into the pan over a medium to high heat and the mixture is boiled, stirring continuously to dissolve all the pan juices. The liquor is boiled and reduced until the right consistency is achieved. This may be quite syrup-like in texture. Cooking is vital to ensure a mellow, rich flavour, evaporating alcohol and making the liquor less acidic. Deglazing is sometimes preceded by flaming the contents of the pan after sprinkling with spirits. When the liquid is well reduced, it may be seasoned and served. Alternatively, further liquid, such as stock, may be added and the sauce thickened. Rich sauces can be prepared by adding cream to the deglazing liquor or by whisking in knobs of butter. Finally, the seasoning is adjusted and the sauce may be strained or sieved before being served.

DÉGORGER A French term meaning to soak meat, poultry, fish or offal in cold water (with or without vinegar) to eliminate impurities and blood, particularly for 'white' dishes, or to dispel the 'muddy' taste of river fish.

The term is also used for the process of sprinkling certain vegetables, particularly cucumber and cabbage, with salt to draw out excess water. The same method can be used to draw out bitter juices, traditionally a method for preparing aubergines (but modern cultivars are no longer bitter, so the process is not necessary for most commercial varieties). It also applies to the preparation of snails.

DÉGRAISSER A French culinary term meaning to remove excess fat from an ingredient, dish or cooking vessel. Fat is removed from raw or cooked meat using a small butcher's knife; for hot bouillons, gravies or sauces, a small ladle or spoon is used to skim off the fat; and for cold liquids, where the fat has solidified, a skimming ladle should be used, or the liquid may be strained. Fat can be completely removed from hot clarified consommé by putting paper towels on the surface. It is necessary to remove excess fat from a cooking vessel before deglazing it.

DÉJEUNER The French word for lunch, the midday meal, as opposed to *petit déjeuner* (breakfast) and *dîner*

(dinner). But according to its etymology (from the Latin *disjejunare*, later *disjunare*, to break one's fast), the word originally meant the first meal of the day, comprising essentially bread, soup and even wine (before coffee, tea and chocolate appeared on the scene).

The introduction of the midday *déjeuner* dates from the French Revolution. Until that time, the midday meal was called *dîner*. But because the sessions of the constituent Assembly began at midday and finished about 6 p.m. dinner had to be eaten at the end of the afternoon. The deputies, being unable to go without food from breakfast until dinner, acquired the habit of eating at about 11 a.m., a second breakfast that was more substantial than the first. A certain Madame Hardy, who in 1804 ran a café on the Boulevards near the Théâtre des Italiens, invented the *déjeuner à la fourchette* (fork lunch), offering her customers cutlets, kidneys, sausages and other grills served on a sideboard. The development of cabarets and cafés, then the birth of restaurants, turned *déjeuner* into an important social occasion.

Nowadays in France, lunch is eaten generally at about 12.30 p.m. It is often a quick and light meal, although in professional circles it has become more substantial as the 'business lunch'. Certain events, such as the awarding of literary prizes, often take place at a special lunch (see *Drouant*). But even today, the Sunday lunch remains a symbol of family life, not so far removed from the type of lunch served in the 1850s, mentioned by Marguerite Yourcenar: 'Every Sunday, Reine presides over a meal to which all the family are invited. The tablecloth laid for this ceremony, hardly less sacred than High Mass, is resplendent with silverware and the soft gleam of old porcelain. Poultry *quenelles* are served at midday; the dessert and sweetmeats at about five o'clock. Between the sorbet and the saddle of lamb, it is understood that the guests have the right to take a turn about the garden or even, with a slight apology for taking pleasure in such a rustic amusement, a game of bowls.' (*Archives du Nord*, Gallimard.)

DELESSERT, BENJAMIN French industrialist and financier (born Lyon, 1773; died Paris, 1847). Having founded a sugar refinery in 1801 in the district of Passy in Paris, in 1812 he perfected the process of sugar extraction from sugar beet (see *Marggraf, Achard*). Napoleon visited the factory and saw the potential of this discovery, which could make it unnecessary to import cane sugar from the West Indies. He granted large funds to Delessert, earmarked a great deal of land in the north for sugar beet cultivation and, on Delessert's advice, opened one of the first 'sugar schools' at Douai. Meanwhile, Delessert plunged into political life and became one of the founders of savings banks in France.

DELICATESSEN A shop, or department in a store or supermarket, selling high-quality, luxury food and/or specialist products. The word, meaning delicacies, originated in Germany in the 18th century. Foods may be specific to one country, in which case regional specialities rarely available in general grocery departments are usually an important feature. International food specialities are more common, with canned, dried and preserved products, including unusual herbs and spices, complemented by cheeses, cooked meats, pâtés and other prepared items. A range of excellent marinated foods, salads, pastries and sauces or dips frequently feature in contemporary delicatessens. High-quality breads and cakes are often sold. Fine wines, liqueurs and spirits, as well as confectionery, may be on offer.

With the growth in popularity of delicatessen foods and a wide range of such outlets now open, it is important to distinguish between those selling a range of prepared and slightly unusual foods and others providing true quality. Those running and working in a good establishment (or department) will have detailed knowledge of the products they sell, the suppliers and other foods of the same type. They will usually advise on the preparation, serving and accompaniments for their products. Many superior delicatessens offer a hamper service or prepare culinary gifts to order.

DÉLICE OR DÉLICIEUX Fancy names given to various desserts, gâteaux and sweetmeats.

RECIPES

apple délicieux

Prepare and bake 675 g (1½ lb) apples on a baking sheet in a preheated oven at 190°C (375°F, gas 5). Reduce the pulp to a purée and allow to cool. Beat 5 egg yolks with 100 g (4 oz, ½ cup) caster (superfine) sugar until the mixture becomes light and foamy. Whisk the 5 whites stiffly and fold a little at a time into the egg–sugar mixture alternately with the apple purée and 65 g (2½ oz, ⅔ cup) dried white breadcrumbs. Empty the mixture into a buttered and floured soufflé dish and cook in a preheated oven at 190°C (375°F, gas 5) for 40–45 minutes. Dust with sugar and serve very hot.

délicieux surprise

Gently melt 125 g (4½ oz, 4½ squares) dark chocolate in a bowl over hot water. Add 1 tablespoon single (light) cream, 20 g (¾ oz, 1½ tablespoons) butter, 1 tablespoon milk and the grated zest of an orange. Keep the sauce hot over the hot water. Cut a large brioche mousseline into 6 thick slices, put them in a dish and sprinkle with 100 ml (4 fl oz, 7 tablespoons) rum. Peel 3 pears, remove the seeds, slice and place on the brioche slices. Whip 150 ml (¼ pint, ⅔ cup) double (heavy) cream with 1 tablespoon very cold milk and slowly add 50 g (2 oz, ¼ cup) caster (superfine) sugar. Cover the brioche and pears with a dome of the whipped cream and pour over the hot chocolate sauce. Serve immediately.

lemon délice

Melt 100 g (4 oz, ½ cup) butter in a bain marie. Measure 250 g (9 oz, 2¼ cups) self-raising flour into a mixing bowl, then add the melted butter,

4 eggs, 200 g (7 oz, 1 cup) caster (superfine) sugar, the grated zest and juice of a lemon, and 100 g (4 oz, ¾ cup) crystallized (candied) fruits cut into very small dice. Mix until evenly blended, then turn the mixture into a 25 cm (10 in) round loose-bottomed cake tin (pan) and cook for 40 minutes in a preheated oven at 190°C (375°F, gas 5).

Meanwhile, prepare a French butter cream (see *creams*) using 125 g (4½ oz, ½ cup) caster sugar cooked to the thread stage (see *sugar*) in 3 tablespoons water, 4 egg yolks, 125 g (4½ oz, ½ cup) butter and the grated zest and juice of a lemon.

When the cake is cooked, turn out on to a wire rack, allow to cool and cut into three rounds. Cover two of the rounds with a thick layer of the lemon butter cream and sandwich together. Dust generously with icing (confectioner's) sugar and keep in a cool place (not the refrigerator) until ready to serve. (The layers may be sprinkled with lemon sugar syrup if liked.)

nut délices

Combine 125 g (4½ oz, 1 cup) plain (all-purpose) flour with 50 g (2 oz, ¼ cup) softened butter, 1 egg yolk, 1 tablespoon water, 3 tablespoons caster (superfine) sugar and a pinch of salt. When the dough is smooth, roll it into a ball and chill.

Cream 65 g (2½ oz, 5 tablespoons) butter; add 65 g (2½ oz, ⅓ cup) caster sugar and 1 egg, then 65 g (2½ oz, ½ cup) ground almonds, and finally 25 g (1 oz, ¼ cup) fecula (potato flour); mix well. Roll out the chilled dough to a thickness of 3 mm (⅛ in). Cut out 8 discs and line tartlet moulds with them. Prick the bottoms and cover with the almond cream. Cook in a preheated oven at 190°C (375°F, gas 5) for 15 minutes.

Meanwhile, prepare a French butter cream (see *creams*) using 125 g (4½ oz, ½ cup) sugar cooked to the thread stage (see *sugar*) in 3 tablespoons water, 4 egg yolks, 125 g (4½ oz, ½ cup) butter and 1 teaspoon coffee essence. Chop 100 g (4 oz, 1 cup) fresh walnuts and mix with the cream. Allow the tartlets to cool, then turn out and top each with a dome of the walnut cream. Put in a cold place for 30 minutes.

Warm 250 g (9 oz) fondant icing (frosting) to about 32°C (90°F), flavour it with a few drops of coffee essence and add just enough water to make it spread easily. Dip the top of each tartlet into the fondant, smoothing it evenly over the cream with a palette knife (spatula). Place a fresh walnut on each *délice* and store in a cool place.

strawberry délices ◆

Work together in a mixing bowl 125 g (4½ oz, 1 cup) plain (all-purpose) flour with 1 egg, 50 g (2 oz, ¼ cup) caster (superfine) sugar, a pinch of salt, 1 tablespoon water and 50 g (2 oz, ¼ cup) butter cut into small pieces. When the mixture is a smooth dough, put it in the refrigerator to chill.

Strawberry délices.

Meanwhile, wash and hull 175 g (6 oz, 1 cup) strawberries and macerate in 50 g (2 oz, ⅓ cup) icing (confectioner's) sugar for 1 hour.

Roll out the dough to a thickness of 3 mm (⅛ in), cut out 6 rounds and use them to line 6 buttered tartlet moulds; prick the bottom of each one with a fork and bake blind for about 10 minutes in a preheated oven at 190°C (375°F, gas 5). Remove the paper and baking beans and cook for a further 3–5 minutes, until the pastry is cooked. Cool on a wire rack.

Sieve the macerated strawberries and gradually beat the purée into 125 g (4½ oz, ½ cup) unsalted butter. Fill the tartlet cases with this mixture and top with 175 g (6 oz, 1 cup) strawberries. Decorate with sprigs of mint and serve with a sweetened redcurrant coulis.

DELTEIL, JOSEPH French writer (born Villar-en-Val, 1894; died Grabels, 1978). Having figured in Parisian literary circles, Delteil retired in 1930 to Languedoc, to a house whose facade bears the motto of Confucius: 'Live humbly'. Of Delteil's work, *La Cuisine paléolithique* (Robert Morel, 1964) features a selection of recipes for *cuisine naturelle* using unprocessed foods, such as bean soup, cassoulet, snails, grilled (broiled) beef, *poule au pot* and dandelion salad, as well as such aphorisms as 'Eat with the fingers, drink with the nose' and 'Food responds to our soul's dream as to our stomach's appetite'. It also offers some judicious advice: 'Don't prick the roast, it will bleed'; 'Ham: 40 days in salt, 40 days hanging, in 40 days eaten'; and a quick guide to cooking times: 'Pork at walking pace, beef at a trot, game at a gallop'.

DEMI-DEUIL Meaning literally 'half-mourning', this term describes dishes containing both black and white ingredients. In classic cuisine, the 'white' foods (poached poultry and eggs, sweetbreads in white stock, potato salad, shellfish) are *contisés* (encrusted) with slices or strips of truffle and coated with suprême sauce.

Chicken demi-deuil is one of the most renowned dishes of Lyonnais cuisine, particularly the version given by Mère Fillioux: the chicken is stuffed with truffle, poached, garnished with slices of truffle between skin and flesh, served with the vegetable ingredients of the cooking stock and coated with the strained cooking juices.

RECIPES

chicken demi-deuil
Poach a chicken in white stock, place on a serving dish and keep hot. Prepare 8 tartlets or croustades and fill them with a salpicon of calves' or lambs' sweetbreads braised in white stock, and mushrooms gently cooked in butter – all mixed with suprême sauce. Garnish each tartlet with a slice of truffle heated in Madeira. Arrange the tartlets around the chicken and coat it with suprême sauce.

demi-deuil salad
Boil 675 g (1½ lb) potatoes until tender. Drain, cool, peel and slice the cooked potatoes. Cut 75–100 g (3–4 oz) truffles into thin strips. Make a sauce using 3 tablespoons single (light) cream, 1 teaspoon mustard, salt and pepper.

In a large salad bowl make a bed of lettuce seasoned with a little vinaigrette. Place the potatoes mixed with the sauce on it, then sprinkle with the strips of truffle.

eggs demi-deuil
Prepare some individual puff pastry croustades. Fill each one with mushrooms in cream sauce and top with a soft-boiled (soft-cooked) or poached egg. Coat with suprême sauce and garnish with a slice of truffle.

DEMIDOF A chicken dish dedicated to Prince Anatole Demidof, the husband of Napoleon's niece, Princess Mathilde. Demidof was one of the celebrated *bons viveurs* of the Second Empire and an habitué of the Maison Dorée, where this recipe was created. The name is also given to a dish of sautéed chicken.

RECIPES

chicken Demidof
Stuff a large chicken with a mixture comprising one-third *quenelle* stuffing and two-thirds *à gratin* forcemeat. Prepare a very thick matignon* vegetable fondue using 125 g (4½ oz) carrots, 50 g (2 oz) celery, 25 g (1 oz) sliced onion, half a bay leaf, a sprig of thyme, a pinch of salt and a pinch of sugar. Soften the vegetables in butter, moisten with 100 ml (4 fl oz, 7 tablespoons) Madeira and reduce until almost dry.

Brown the chicken in a preheated oven at 220°C (425°F, gas 7). Cover it with the vegetables, then wrap it in a pig's caul or bard it with streaky (slab) bacon or pork fat. Tie it up and braise it in a covered casserole, adding a small quantity of chicken stock, at 180°C (350°F, gas 4) for about 2 hours, or until the chicken is cooked through. Add more hot stock to the casserole occasionally to prevent it from drying up. Uncover the casserole to brown the chicken for the final 15–20 minutes cooking time.

Arrange the chicken on a serving dish and surround with artichoke hearts cooked in butter and topped with the vegetable fondue. Garnish each artichoke heart with an onion ring (covered in batter and deep-fried) and a slice of truffle. Deglaze the cooking vessel used for the chicken with Madeira and pour over the chicken.

sautéed chicken Demidof
Remove the giblets from a chicken and cut off the breast, wings and legs. Brown the remaining carcass and giblets in oil, dust with flour and brown again. Moisten with 150 ml (¼ pint, ⅔ cup) dry white

wine and bouillon and cook gently for 30 minutes. Strain and reserve this cooking liquid.

Cut 2 carrots, 1 turnip, 2 celery sticks and 1 onion into thin julienne strips. Flour the chicken portions and brown them in a saucepan. Add the vegetable julienne and the strained cooking liquid, cover and cook gently for 30 minutes. Add a slice of smoked ham and a diced truffle. Cook for a further 15 minutes, then deglaze with Madeira and demi-glace sauce.

DEMI-GLACE A rich brown sauce made by boiling and skimming espagnole sauce and adding white stock or *estouffade*. It usually has the addition of Madeira, sherry or a similar wine.

RECIPE

demi-glace
Boil down to reduce by two-thirds a mixture of 500 ml (17 fl oz, 2 cups) espagnole sauce and 750 ml (1¼ pints, 3¼ cups) clear brown stock. Remove from the heat, add 3 tablespoons Madeira and strain. A handful of sliced mushroom stalks may be added during cooking.

DEMI-SEL A soft French cheese made from pasteurized cow's milk. It has a mild flavour and contains 40–45% fat and less than 2% added salt. It is sold in small squares wrapped in foil and is used as a cheese spread. It may be flavoured with herbs, paprika or pepper. Demi-sel was first made at the end of the 19th century and is a speciality of Normandy.

DÉNERVER A French culinary term meaning to remove tendons and membranes from raw meat, poultry or game. It promotes even cooking and tender results, and improves presentation.

DENIS Born Lahana Denis. French chef and restaurateur (born Bordeaux, 1909; died Paris, 1981). He opened the restaurant Chez Denis in Paris and devoted himself to perfecting inventive and luxurious dishes. A cultured man, motivated by his love of cooking, he replied to certain chefs who criticized him for not having worked his way up through the profession: 'I have eaten my way through six inheritances in the great restaurants, so I know what good cuisine is all about.' He persuaded himself that the gourmets of his time were, like him, capable of spending fortunes on such dishes as suprêmes of Bresse chicken, chaud-froids of ortolan *au chambertin* and fresh truffles *à la serviette*, and on bottles of Château-Latour 1945. Consequently, he was ruined and forced to close his restaurant.

He published *La Cuisine de Denis* (Laffont, 1975), in which fundamental techniques, various tricks of the trade and basic recipes are presented with simplicity, precision and good sense. His recipe for scallops, is as follows: 'Sauté the scallops quickly in clarified butter, without browning. Moisten with fumet (use about 1 tablespoon for 6 scallops). Add a few drops of absinthe or, failing this, of Pernod, some pieces of very cold butter [about 65 g (2½ oz, 5 tablespoons) for 6 scallops], herbs, salt and pepper. Keep moving the sauté pan back and forth over a high heat. When the cooking liquor boils, pour the entire contents of the pan on to the serving dish.'

DENMARK See *page 412*.

DENSITY The mass of a substance per unit of volume; in practice, the weight of something divided by its volume. Density has units of grams per cubic centimetre.

The term density is sometimes used loosely (especially in cookery) to mean *relative density*, which is the mass of a given volume of substance divided by the mass of an equal volume of water; ideally the water should be at 4°C (39.2°F) but this is unimportant in cookery. Relative density is also called *specific gravity*. It is used in winemaking, brewing, cider-making, the fats industry (oil, margarine) and the dairy industry (fat content of milk). Sugar concentration – important in making sweets, jams and other preserves – is now also expressed by relative density (rather than by degrees Baumé). Relative density can be measured by a hydrometer – an instrument which floats in the liquid, the relative density being read directly from its graduated stem.

DENTEX *denté, denti* A Mediterranean fish of the *Sparidae* family with long, sharp, sometimes hooked teeth and powerful jaws. The young fish are silvery grey and the adults are reddish-brown. Related to but much larger than the sea bream, up to 90 cm (36 in) long, it has firm, rather tasty flesh and is cooked in the same way as sea bream.

DENTS-DE-LOUP Triangular croûtons used for garnish, arranged as a border around the edge of a dish with the points to the outside (hence the name, which means wolves' teeth). The *dents-de-loup* used to garnish hot dishes are triangles either cut from sandwich bread and fried in oil or butter or made from puff pastry and baked. Cold dishes are garnished with *dents-de-loup* cut out of strips of aspic.

The name is also used for certain kinds of crisp biscuits (cookies). One variety, a speciality of Alsace, is a long pointed biscuit flavoured with lemon and brandy. Another kind is crescent-shaped and flavoured with cumin or aniseed.

DERBY An English cheese made with cow's milk, containing about 45% fat. It is a firm pressed mild cheese which resembles Cheddar, but is slightly flakier and more moist. The cheese is traditionally wheel-shaped, 38 cm (15 in) in diameter, 12 cm (5 in) high, and weighing about 14 kg (31 lb). Sage Derby is marbled with green and is made by adding chopped sage leaves to the curd for additional colouring and flavouring. It was traditional to make this speciality at Christmas and at harvest time.

DENMARK

Danish cuisine is nourishing and always generous in its helpings; traditionally it uses a lot of cream and butter. The principal classic ingredients are herring, pork and potato.

■ **Fish and meat** In Denmark it is said that there are over 60 ways of preparing herring: marinated, preserved in vinegar, in spicy sauce, fried . . . the list goes on. It is always present on the famous 'Scandinavian platters' which also include salmon, eel and fish roe, served with creamed horseradish. Meat is stewed, roasted or minced (ground). Popular dishes include loin of pork stuffed with prunes and apples, roast pork with crackling, and *hakkerbøf*, minced beef steak with onions and brown sauce.

Poultry dishes, such as chicken stuffed with parsley, roast goose and duck, are still reserved for special occasions. The vegetables that accompany these dishes may be caramelized potatoes, braised cabbage or boiled kale served with cream.

■ **Buffet** A Danish lunch is usually organized around a cold buffet (*kolt bord*) with national specialities such as *frikadeller* (meatballs with onions, bound with egg), slices of liver pâté, prawn salad, cucumber salad, scrambled eggs with bacon or smoked eel, brain fritters and roast pork. All these dishes are invariably served with buttered slices of wholemeal or rye bread (*smørrebrød*), which each person then covers with whatever they like. One of the most famous open sandwiches is a slice of rye bread with liver pâté, a slice of bacon, a slice of tomato, a layer of jelly, and grated horseradish on top; this has been named after Hans Christian Andersen no less.

Throughout Scandinavia, the Christmas festivities start on 13 December, the feast of St Lucia, providing the perfect opportunity for friends and family to get together and enjoy roast goose or duck stuffed with apples and prunes, and rice pudding with whipped cream with an almond hidden in it, like the coin in a Christmas pudding.

■ **Desserts** Red fruits and apples play a major part in Scandinavian puddings, such as cherry tarts and *rødgrød* (stewed red berries served with cream). There are some very popular pastries, such as the large puff pastry turnovers with a variety of fillings, or the traditional *kransekager*, a huge tiered cake made from rings of almond paste, decorated with crystallized (candied) fruits and icing (frosting). The Danes are also fond of home-made dry biscuits (cookies) such as the Christmas speciality *brunekager* (with spices, almonds and brown sugar), gingerbread and shortbread made with butter.

Commercially, Sage Derby is now produced using dried sage and spinach juice.

DERBY, À LA A method of preparing chicken, created in the early 1900s by Giroix when he was chef at the Hôtel de Paris in Monte Carlo. It was dedicated to a member of a distinguished British family with a predilection for French cuisine. Chicken *à la Derby* is stuffed with truffled rice and foie gras; truffles cooked in port and slices of sautéed foie gras provide the garnish, and the chicken is coated with the cooking juices deglazed with port.

Derby soup is a cream of onion and curried rice soup, garnished with poached rice, *quenelles* of foie gras and chopped truffle.

DÉROBER A French culinary term meaning to remove the skins of shelled broad (fava) beans. It also means to remove the skins of blanched tomatoes or almonds and unpeeled boiled potatoes.

DERVAL A garnish for beef tournedos and noisettes of lamb, made with artichoke quarters sautéed in butter.

DESALTING The removal of salt from certain foods that have been preserved in brine. Desalting is carried out by soaking the food in cold still or running water so that the salt dissolves gradually and forms a deposit on the bottom of the vessel. Salt cod needs to be soaked the day before it is required,

changing the water several times. Traditional salted ham or gammon must be soaked for several hours before cooking. Lardons cut from streaky (slab) bacon may be desalted by blanching. As a general rule, the salt used for preservation should not be used for seasoning – it is better to desalt too much and season again later.

Drained canned or bottled anchovies may be desalted by soaking briefly in milk. Dry salted anchovies (sold packed in salt) are soaked in water.

DÉSAUGIERS, MARC ANTOINE French song writer and poet (born Fréjus, 1772; died Paris, 1827). The author of numerous drinking songs, he was secretary of Caveau Moderne, a gastronomic and somewhat bacchanalian literary society. His philosophy may be summed up in this verse which he wrote in the form of an epitaph:

'Je veux que la mort me frappe
Au milieu d'un grand repas,
Qu'on m'enterre sous la nappe
Entre quatre large plats,
Et que sur ma tombe on mette
Cette courte inscription:
"Ci-gît le premier poète
Mort d'une indigestion".'

At a traditional Danish smoke house, the salmon is checked regularly by hand for perfect results.

(I pray that death may strike me
In the middle of a large meal.
I wish to be buried under the tablecloth
Between four large dishes.
And I desire that this short inscription
Should be engraved on my tombstone:
'Here lies the first poet
Ever to die of indigestion'.)

DESCAR A garnish for large joints of meat consisting of potato croquettes and artichoke hearts cooked gently in butter and stuffed with diced breast of chicken. The garnish was created in honour of the Duc des Cars, the head of the royal household in the reign of Louis XVIII of France. He was a celebrated gourmet who, unfortunately, died of indigestion!

DES ESSARTS (born Denis Déchanet) French actor (born Langres, 1737; died Barèges, 1793). He practised as a lawyer before throwing in his lot with the theatre. He specialized in playing financiers and peasants, roles in which he was well served by an extraordinary stoutness, due to an insatiable appetite and a legendary gluttony. His contemporaries bore witness to his joviality and his proven lyricism for anything concerning good living, as shown in his aphorisms ('Good cuisine fattens a clear conscience'), or his culinary judgments, such as the one on the leg of lamb which, according to him, should be 'mortified (hung) as a liar caught in the act, golden as a young German girl, and bloody as a Caribbean'. He died of apoplexy in a spa where he was taking the waters.

DESSERT The last course of a meal. The word comes from *desservir* (to remove that which has been served) and consequently means everything offered to guests after the previous dishes and corresponding serving utensils have been cleared away.

In former times at great banquets, dessert, which was the fifth course of the meal, was often presented in magnificent style. Large set pieces fashioned in pastry, described often and in great detail by Carême, whose accounts are accompanied by splendid illustrations, were placed on the table at the beginning of the meal. These owed more to architecture than to the art of cooking, and had a purely decorative function. Just before the sweet course, a multitude of desserts were elegantly arranged on the table with the set pieces, for every ceremonial table was laid in accordance with a detailed plan. The dishes had to harmonize with gold plate, crystal, magnificent baskets of fruit and the tall candelabra: a dazzling spectacle. It was not until about 1850 that the word 'dessert' took on its present meaning.

In ancient times, meals generally ended with fresh or dried fruit, milk or cheese dishes, or honey. In France in the Middle Ages, the main sweet dishes, often served between meat courses, consisted of jellies, flans, blancmanges, tarts, compotes, *nieules* (flat round cakes), *fouaces* (fancy pastry), *échaudés* (poached pastry), waffles and various other small cakes. The dessert proper consisted of the *issue*, a glass of hippocras served with *oublies* (wafers), followed by *boutehors* (dragées with spice and crystallized fruit).

In the 17th century, desserts had become more elaborate and were decorated with flowers. They included marzipan, nougat, pyramids of fruit, dry and liquid preserves, biscuits (cookies), creams, sugar sweets (candies), sweet almonds in sugar and orange-flower water, green walnuts, pistachios and marrons glacés. At the end of the century, ice creams made their appearance, and at the same time pâtisserie became extremely diversified, with different basic mixtures, such as puff pastry, sponge, choux pastry and meringue.

In the 20th century, dessert in France evolved to include cheese and fresh fruit as well as sweet dishes. However, the term is usually taken to mean the sweet course of the meal, whether it is served before or after the cheese course. The contemporary dessert may include one of a wider range of dishes, from elaborate gâteaux and pastries to simple fruit salads. It is still usual to serve two or three sweet dishes at a dinner party, especially when one may be a light fruit recipe and another a rich concoction, but the dessert course is no longer the wildly extravagant affair it once was. Instead of elaborate centrepieces, individual presentation is a popular alternative, born of restaurant-style food trends.

■ **Pudding or dessert** Whereas dessert has long been regarded as a special or superior sweet course, pudding was traditionally the homely, everyday alternative. Although this is still true to some extent, pudding tends to refer to traditional, hot or hearty sweets while dessert is cool or lighter, or more elaborate. Very simple, everyday sweet dishes may be referred to as a 'sweet'.

■ **Regional and foreign specialities** Apart from the creations of the Parisian master pastrycooks, the desserts of the provinces provide a good example of the diversity of French cuisine: *kouing-aman* from Brittany, *poirat* from Berry, *bourdelot* from Normandy, *eierkückas* from Alsace, *crémets* from Angers, *pogne* from Romans, *pithiviers* and *flaugnarde* from the Auvergne, *clafoutis* from Limousin, in addition to brioches, waffles, pancakes and various fritters, not forgetting the 'thirteen desserts' from Provence, traditionally served at Christmas.

In Great Britain, Germany, Austria and Belgium, where good-quality butter, cream, milk, eggs and chocolate are also abundant, there is a wide selection of desserts and pâtisserie. In the Mediterranean countries, the Far East and South America, sweetmeats and fruits clearly predominate. In eastern Europe, cooked fruits, brioches and spiced biscuits (cookies) are served at the end of the meal, while in China and Japan, dessert does not exist! Ice creams and pies are particularly popular in the United States, together with fruit and pancakes.

■ **The choice of a suitable dessert** When choosing a dessert, the previous courses must be considered to ensure a well-balanced menu. The choice depends largely on the content of the main course, whether or not a cheese course is provided and also on the season of the year.

In terms of dishes already served, the dessert does not have to be in the same style – it is quite acceptable to include foods of different countries and cooking styles in one meal. It is important that they complement each other in all aspects. Sympathetic flavours are vital – light, cooling, yet slightly exotic, mixtures go well after full-bodied spicy main courses. When fruit features largely in the savoury courses, a change is welcome in the dessert. To avoid clashing styles, it is best to moderate distinctly different types of dishes, playing down their characteristics to encourage contrasts, rather than clashes.

A light dessert is suitable for rounding off a substantial, rich or fairly heavy meal. When planning a rich, filling or elaborate dessert, the main course should be light and not over-filling in order that the finalé of the meal will be enjoyed. Texture is important: crisp foods are good following moist courses; to serve a soup first, followed by a casserole and then a creamy dessert would be a mistake.

Finally, colour and appearance are important: these dishes must look attractive. The dessert should bring a meal to a glorious end, not allow it to die a sad death. Where more than one dessert is served, they should contrast with and complement each other as well as the rest of the meal. Many restaurants offer a *grand dessert* display or a sweet trolley, bearing a whole range of desserts from which the diner may choose. This type of display of desserts originated in Italy, where it was introduced to encourage the young women and girls to stay at table during family gatherings.

DESSERTE

DESSERTE The French term for the food that is left over after a meal. In some instances, it may be used as a basis for another meal. The simplest type of *desserte* consists of slices of various cold meats with gherkins or pickles. *Desserte* may be used to prepare certain cold dishes, such as mixed or meat salads, canapés and mousses, or hot dishes, such as shepherd's pie, various stuffings, croquettes, bouchées, pilaf and risotto. Under the Ancien Régime, the members of the royal household in charge of food did a brisk trade in *desserte* with outside caterers and restaurateurs. In certain French restaurants, such food (apart from a few items) belongs to the waiters.

A *desserte* is also a small sideboard on which the dishes are stacked after their removal from the table.

DÉTAILLER A French term meaning to cut up various items of food into dice, rounds, slices or cubes. Vegetables cut up in this way can be used for preparing a julienne, brunoise, mirepoix or macédoine. The *détail* of meat includes all the joints cut up by the butcher, especially the pieces cut into a special shape or thickness – escalopes (scallops), medallions, noisettes and *grenadins*.

DÉTENDRE A French culinary term meaning to soften a paste or a mixture by adding an appropriate substance, such as beaten eggs, milk or stock.

DÉTREMPE The French culinary term for a paste made with flour and water in the first stage of making pastry, before the addition of butter, eggs and milk. It is best to let the *détrempe* rest in a cool place for about 10 minutes before adding the remaining ingredients. (A *détrempe* is rarely used on its own, except as a luting paste.)

To *détremper* a paste or dough is to allow the flour to absorb all the necessary water, kneading it with the fingertips without working it too much.

DEVILLED In French, *à la diable*. The name given to dishes with a piquant or hot marinade, spice mixture or sauce, usually based on mustard. Worcestershire sauce, cayenne pepper and paprika are other typical seasonings. They may be combined with the food – for example, devilled crab is seasoned and may be finished by grilling (broiling) – or used in an accompanying sauce. Marinades are popular, particularly for chicken and meat, or a dry rub may be used to import a typical devilled flavour. Grilling is the usual cooking method, but pan frying, roasting or baking are also used.

Foods may be dipped in egg and coated with breadcrumbs before cooking, and served with a piquant devilled sauce. These dishes are very popular in traditional English cookery. Devilled chicken or pigeon, for example, is prepared by slitting the bird open along its back, spreading it out flat, seasoning it and then grilling it. It is served with a devilled sauce.

The essential characteristic of any devilled food is the piquancy and slight heat of flavour, distinguishing it from a more complex spiced mixture or very fiery flavour.

RECIPES

devilled beef
Cut some cold boiled beef into fairly thick slices. Coat each slice with mustard, sprinkle with oil or melted butter, coat with fresh breadcrumbs and grill (broil) under a low heat until each side is golden brown. Serve with devilled sauce.

devilled herrings
Scale, wash and dry the herrings, then slit them along the back and sides. Season and coat with mustard, sprinkle with fresh white breadcrumbs and oil, and cook slowly under the grill (broiler). Serve with mustard sauce, ravigote sauce or devilled sauce.

devilled meat dishes
In England, this is a way of using pieces of leftover poultry or game or the remains of a joint to make a tasty meal. Mix together the following: 1 tablespoon English mustard, 1 tablespoon mustard with

herbs, 2 tablespoons olive oil, 1 egg yolks, 1 tea-spoon each of Worcestershire sauce, salt and anchovy paste, and a pinch of cayenne pepper. Curry powder or paste, tomato purée (paste) or a concentrated onion purée may be added if desired. Coat the meat with this mixture and grill (broil) under a medium heat until brown. Serve piping hot with a good gravy.

devilled oysters

Poach, drain and remove the beards of the oysters. Thread the oysters on small kebab skewers, coat with melted butter seasoned with a little cayenne pepper and dip them in fresh white breadcrumbs. Grill (broil) under a low heat and serve with devilled sauce.

devilled sauce (1)

(English recipe) Add 1 tablespoon chopped shallots to 150 ml (¼ pint, ⅔ cup) red wine vinegar and reduce by half. Then add 250 ml (8 fl oz, 1 cup) espagnole sauce and 2 tablespoons tomato purée (paste). Cook for 5 minutes. Just before serving, add 1 tablespoon Worcestershire sauce, 1 table-spoon Harvey sauce or spiced vinegar, and a dash of cayenne pepper. Strain the sauce. This sauce is generally served with grilled (broiled) meat.

devilled sauce (2)

Mix 150 ml (¼ pint, ⅔ cup) dry white wine with 1 tablespoon vinegar, then add 1 tablespoon finely chopped shallots, a sprig of thyme, a small piece of bay leaf and a generous pinch of pepper. Reduce the sauce by two-thirds, then add 200 ml (7 fl oz, ¾ cup) demi-glace* and boil for 2–3 minutes. Strain through a sieve. Just before serving, add 1 teaspoon chopped parsley and check the seasoning, adding a little cayenne pepper if liked. Alternatively, omit straining the sauce and add 1 tablespoon butter or beurre manié.

devilled tongue

Cut braised or poached cold ox (beef) or calf's tongue crossways into fairly thick slices or cut sheeps' tongues in half lengthways. Spread with mustard, dip in melted butter and fresh bread-crumbs and grill (broil) gently until both sides are brown. Serve with devilled sauce.

other recipes See *croûte, ear.*

DIABLE A cooking pot consisting of two porous earthenware pans, one of which fits over the other as a lid. It is designed for cooking certain vegetables, such as potatoes, beetroot, chestnuts and onions, without adding water. Each pan has a flat base; halfway through cooking, the diable is turned upside down. The diable from Charentes resembles a small round casserole, with a handle and a tightly fitting lid.

The diable is never washed, because the drier it is, the more tender are the vegetables. Sometimes the inner surfaces are rubbed with a clove of garlic. It

was originally meant to be used when cooking on hot charcoal, but may also be used in an ordinary oven. If placed directly on an electric hotplate or a gas ring, it is advisable to start off the cooking very slowly over a gentle heat; otherwise, a heat diffuser should be placed under the base.

DIABLE, À LA See *devilled.*

DIABLOTIN A very thin, small round slice of bread (sometimes first coated with reduced béchamel sauce) sprinkled with grated cheese and browned in the oven. *Diablotins* are usually served with soup, particularly consommé. If a full-flavoured cheese is used, such as Roquefort, they can be served as cocktail snacks.

Formerly the name *diablotin* was used for a small fritter made of a deep-fried thick sauce. It is also the name of a small spoon used to measure spices for cocktails.

RECIPES

cheese diablotins

Cut a *ficelle* (long thin French loaf) into slices 5 mm (¼ in) thick. Butter them and coat with grated cheese (Comté, Emmental or Beaufort, which melt, or Parmesan, which doesn't). A thin slice of Gruyère or Edam may be used instead. Brown the slices quickly and serve with soup.

diablotins with walnuts and Roquefort cheese

Cut a long French loaf into slices about 5 mm (¼ in) thick. Mix some butter with an equal quantity of Roquefort cheese and add some coarsely chopped green walnuts, allowing 1 tablespoon per 75 g (3 oz, ⅓ cup) of the mixture. Spread the mixture on the slices of bread and quickly heat in a preheated oven at 240°C (475°F, gas 9).

DIABOLO A refreshing non-alcoholic drink made with lemonade and fruit syrup. The most common *diabolos* are those made with mint and grenadine.

DIANE, À LA The description *à la Diane* is given to certain game dishes that are dedicated to the god-dess Diana (the huntress). Joints of venison *à la Diane* are sautéed and coated with sauce Diane (a highly peppered sauce with cream and truffles). They are served with chestnut purée and croûtons spread with game forcemeat. The name may also be given to a game purée, used to garnish either soft-boiled (soft-cooked) eggs on croûtes with salmis sauce or mushroom barquettes with sauce chasseur. This purée can also form the basis of a cream soup, flavoured with port. Quails *à la Diane* are simmered in stock and tomato-flavoured demi-glace, then gar-nished with *quenelles* and braised lettuce.

DIEPPOISE, À LA A method of preparing fish named after the port of Dieppe, which is famous for the excellence of the sole fished in its waters. Sole, whiting or brill *à la dieppoise* are cooked in white wine, garnished with mussels, shrimps and often mushrooms, and masked with a white wine sauce made with the cooking stock of the fish and mussels. This method is also suitable for cooking pike and even artichokes. Dieppoise garnish consists of mussels, prawns (shrimp) and mushrooms cooked in white wine and is used for bouchées, barquettes, salads and a velouté sauce.

Mackerel and herrings marinated in white wine are considered to be a speciality of Dieppe; they are also called *à la dieppoise*. (See also *marmite dieppoise*.)

RECIPES

brill à la dieppoise
Prepare 500 ml (17 fl oz, 2 cups) fish fumet. Clean 1 kg (2¼ lb) mussels and cook them *à la marinière*, reserving the cooking stock. Make a white roux with 25 g (1 oz, 2 tablespoons) butter and 25 g (1 oz, ¼ cup) plain (all-purpose) flour and gradually add the fish fumet together with 100 ml (4 fl oz, 7 tablespoons) strained cooking stock from the mussels. Add 1 tablespoon coarsely chopped mushrooms and a bouquet garni. Check the seasoning and boil gently for 20–25 minutes to reduce. Shell the mussels and keep them hot in the remainder of their cooking stock, taking care not to boil them.

Season a brill weighing about 800 g (1¾ lb) with salt and place in a buttered flameproof dish. Pour over 150 ml (¼ pint, ⅔ cup) white wine. Bring to the boil, uncovered, then cook in a preheated oven at 220°C (425°F, gas 7) for 15–18 minutes, basting the fish frequently. Mix 2 egg yolks with a little of the partially cooled mushroom sauce. Add 50 g (2 oz, ⅓ cup) peeled prawns (shelled shrimp) and the cooking liquor from the fish to the remaining mushroom sauce. Mix well, heat, add the hot drained mussels then the egg-yolk mixture and coat the brill with this sauce. This recipe may also be used for fresh cod.

scallops au gratin à la dieppoise
Poach the white flesh of 16 scallops very gently for 4 minutes in 500 ml (17 fl oz, 2 cups) fish fumet mixed with 200 ml (7 fl oz, ¾ cup) dry white wine. Cook 1 kg (2¼ lb) small mussels *à la marinière*. Prepare a sauce from a roux, the mussel cooking liquor and the fish fumet as described in the previous recipe. Add 1 tablespoon chopped mushroom stalks and a bouquet garni to the sauce; check the seasoning and cook gently for 20–25 minutes.

Keep the scallops hot in a covered, lightly buttered gratin dish over a saucepan of hot water. Shell the mussels and keep hot in the rest of their cooking liquor, without boiling. Add 75 g (3 oz, ½ cup) peeled prawns (shelled shrimp). When the sauce is cooked, strain it and add the strained mussels and prawns. Dilute 1 egg yolk with a little of the sauce and whisk it in. Coat the scallops with

the sauce, scatter with very fine fresh breadcrumbs, sprinkle with melted butter and brown quickly in a preheated oven at 220°C (425°F, gas 7) or under the grill (broiler).

additional recipe See *smelt.*

DIETETICS The study of everything concerned with diet and all that relates to the therapeutic use of food. The importance of having a sensible balanced diet to maintain good health has been amply proved. The science of dietetics is particularly relevant in the planning of diets for those with special needs, such as diabetics.

DIETICIAN A specialist in the study and regulation of food intake and food preparation (dietetics), who has had scientific and paramedical training. Dieticians may work in hospitals, supervising and dealing with all aspects of the patient's diet; in various educational establishments or with health authorities, advising on and supervising the formulation of menus and various dietary aspects of health; and also in the food industry. A dietician may also be called upon to carry out investigations, to give private consultations and to prepare information for the mass media.

DIGESTIVE The French *digestif*, a liqueur or spirit that may be taken after a meal, more for the pleasure of drinking it than for any digestive action. Digestives are served plain or with ice.

DIJONNAISE, À LA The description *à la dijonnaise* is given to various dishes prepared with a speciality of Dijon, particularly mustard (for savoury dishes) or blackcurrants (for sweet dishes). Dijonnaise sauce is a mustard-flavoured, mayonnaise-type sauce served with cold meats.

RECIPES

dijonnaise sauce
Pound together 4 hard-boiled (hard-cooked) egg yolks and 4 tablespoons Dijon mustard. Season with salt and pepper. Work in 500 ml (17 fl oz, up to 2 cups) oil and lemon juice, as in a mayonnaise.

sweet omelette à la dijonnaise
Beat 8 eggs together, then add 5–6 finely crushed macaroons, 2 tablespoons single (light) or double (heavy) cream, and 1 tablespoon caster (superfine) sugar. Make 2 flat omelettes. Mix about 300 ml (½ pint, 1¼ cups) thick confectioner's custard (pastry cream) with 1 tablespoon ground almonds and 2 tablespoons blackcurrant jelly. Cover one of the omelettes with the mixture and place the second omelette on top. Cover completely with a meringue made with 3 or 4 egg whites. Dust with 1 tablespoon icing (confectioner's) sugar and glaze in a preheated oven at 240°C (475°C, gas 9). Serve surrounded with a border of blackcurrant jelly.

DILL An aromatic umbelliferous plant originating in the East and introduced into Europe in ancient times. It is commonly called false anise or bastard fennel but in fact it has an excellent and distinct, yet delicate flavour of its own. The French name *aneth* comes from the Greek *anethon* (fennel), and in Roman times it was the symbol of vitality.

Dill leaves are used as a culinary herb and the seeds are used as a spice in cooking in North Africa (in the preparation of meat), the former Soviet Union and particularly in Scandinavia, where they are used in the preparation of salmon and crayfish. Dill has a particular affinity with fish and seafood, eggs, creamy dishes and delicate vegetables. It is also used to make an aromatic vinegar and as a flavouring for various pickles, including gherkins.

DIM SUM A Cantonese speciality, consisting of a collection of steamed and deep-fried snacks, usually served from mid-morning right through the afternoon. Traditionally served in tea houses dim sum are now offered in many restaurants during the day. Some restaurants specialize in these snacks. Dim sum includes a wide variety of dishes, such as spring rolls, steamed dumplings filled with meat or shrimp, steamed pork wrapped in noodle dough and fluffy white wheat buns stuffed with sweet roasted meat. Small portions of spicy spareribs, battered seafood or steamed wind-dried specialities may be offered.

The dim sum may be ordered in one go or a few at a time until diners are satisfied. Steamed foods are served straight from the bamboo steamers, brought to tables stacked and covered to keep their contents hot.

DINNER The main meal of the day. This is normally eaten in the evening or in the middle of the day (instead of luncheon). In France before the Revolution, dinner was eaten in the morning or at midday. It is generally thought that the French word *dîner* is derived from the Latin *disjunare* (to break the fast), as is *déjeuner*, the French word for lunch. This is because the word was originally used for the morning meal that was eaten after Mass, first at 7 a.m. and later at 9 or 10 a.m. It consisted of bacon, eggs and fish and was one of the two main meals of the day, the other being supper (taken at about 5 p.m.). However, other theories concerning its origin have also been put forward: *dîner* might have been derived from *decim hora* (the tenth hour, 10 o'clock), or from the words of the blessing *dignare dominum*, or even from the Greek word *deipnon* (the meal eaten after sunset).

The hour for eating dinner became progressively later when the daily rite of Mass was observed less strictly and, in time, the habit of serving a light meal on rising developed. This meal, the *déjeuner*, later became the *petit déjeuner* (breakfast). Dinner was at midday in the reigns of Louis XIII and Louis XIV, and Furetière describes the meal thus: 'Midday is the normal time for dinner. When one wants to go and see people, it is advisable to do so between eleven o'clock and midday, certainly not later, for then one would be preventing them from taking their meal.'

In the 18th century, dinner was moved on to 2 p.m., but supper often remained the principal meal of the day. Finally, at the time of the Revolution, dinner was eaten at the end of the afternoon, lunch was taken at midday, and supper was served (in the towns) when there was a soirée. In the country, there was less change and supper continued to be the main meal for a considerable period of time.

Today, dinner usually takes place at about 7 p.m., earlier in Scandinavian countries, later in Mediterranean countries. It may be a formal occasion for receiving guests. Alexandre Dumas defined dinner as the 'principal act of the day that can only be carried out in a worthy manner by people of wit and humour; for it is not sufficient just to eat at dinner. One has to talk with a calm and discreet gaiety. The conversation must sparkle like the rubies in the *entremets* wines, it must be delightfully suave with the sweetmeats of the dessert, and become very profound with the coffee.' According to the chef Denis, the composition of a formal dinner must be varied and abundant, and hot dishes must alternate with cold ones. For a big occasion, he recommends: consommé, followed by a cold entrée, a large hot entrée, a sorbet, a hot roast, a cold roast, vegetables, sweet dessert, pâtisserie and fruit. This prescription is now simplified to consommé, fish served in a sauce, roast meat and garnish, and pâtisserie. Some gastronomes advise against serving cheese at dinner.

In family households the main meal of the day varies according to the working patterns of the adults and whether they have children. Whether the evening meal consists of dinner or supper is very much a matter of lifestyle. Where both adults work, dinner is likely to be an evening meal and lunch a light snack. Children at home may well be served a main meal in the middle of the day, and the whole family may have dinner at this time on a Sunday. Although few people live close enough to their place of work and have someone at home to prepare dinner during the day, in retired households the main meal may be eaten instead of lunch. It is also worth remembering that the major social changes of the 20th century greatly influenced eating patterns. Meals are no longer subject to rigid definition, eating patterns vary between weekdays and weekends, and individual or family choices dominate.

DIOT A small vegetable and pork sausage made in Savoy. *Diots* may be dried like *saucissons*; fresh *diots* are browned in lard (shortening) with sliced onions, then gently simmered in a little white wine.

DIPLOMATE, À LA The description *à la diplomate* is given to dishes that include truffles and lobster, thus evoking the idea of luxury and refinement. Diplomat sauce, also called riche sauce, is made with lobster butter, truffles and lobster flesh and accompanies delicate fish, such as John Dory (St Peter's fish), sole and turbot.

RECIPES

diplomat omelette

Prepare a salpicon with 2 tablespoons diced lobster flesh cooked in court-bouillon and 1 tablespoon diced truffles. Mix 3 tablespoons béchamel* sauce (or thick cream sauce) with 1 tablespoon lobster butter flavoured with brandy. Add the salpicon. Make 2 flat omelettes (each containing 3 eggs). Cover one of the omelettes with the lobster and truffle mixture and place the second omelette on top. Mix 200 ml (7 fl oz, ¾ cup) thin béchamel sauce, 3 tablespoons double (heavy) cream and 40 g (1½ oz, ⅓ cup) mixed grated Gruyère and Parmesan cheese. Add 1 tablespoon lobster butter. Cover the top of the second omelette with this sauce, sprinkle lightly with grated cheese, then with a little melted butter, and brown quickly either in a preheated oven at 240°C (465°F, gas 9) or under the grill (broiler).

diplomat sauce

Add 2 tablespoons truffle parings or chopped mushroom stalks to 200 ml (7 fl oz, ¾ cup) fish fumet and reduce by half. Make 75 g (3 oz) white roux and add 750 ml (1¼ pints, 3¼ cups) fish stock (use the cooking liquid of the fish specified in the recipe). Strain the reduced fumet and add it, together with 200 ml (7 fl oz, ¾ cup) double (heavy) cream, to the sauce. Reduce again by half. Add 50 g (2 oz, ¼ cup) lobster butter, 4 tablespoons double cream, 1 tablespoon brandy and a pinch of cayenne pepper. Strain. If the sauce is served separately, add to it 1 tablespoon diced lobster flesh (cooked in a court-bouillon) and 1 tablespoon diced truffles.

sole diplomat

Remove the skin from a good-sized sole, slit its flesh along the backbone and free the top fillets, working outwards from the centre. Cut the backbone at the head and tail and remove it completely. Prepare 125 g (4½ oz, ½ cup) whiting forcemeat à la crème, adding 1 tablespoon diced truffles. Insert the forcemeat underneath the top fillets. Gently poach the sole in a fish fumet but do not cover. Drain, remove the small lateral bones, arrange on the serving dish and surround with diced lobster flesh. Keep hot. Use the cooking liquid to make some diplomat sauce and coat the fish with it.

DIPLOMAT PUDDING A cold dessert prepared in a mould by one of two different methods. The more common version consists of sponge fingers (ladyfingers) soaked in syrup flavoured with rum or kirsch, layered with crystallized (candied) fruits, apricot jam and a cooked egg custard or a Bavarian cream. After chilling and setting, the pudding is unmoulded and coated with fruit sauce or custard cream.

In the second version, the sponge fingers are replaced by layers of brioche. The pudding is soaked with a custard mixture and baked in a bain marie. It is then chilled and unmoulded.

Individual diplomats are barquettes filled with a cream containing crystallized fruits, glazed with apricot jam, covered with fondant icing (frosting) and decorated with a crystallized cherry.

Bombe diplomate is made with ice cream and crystallized fruits (see *bombe glacée*).

RECIPES

baked diplomat pudding ♦

Coarsely chop 100 g (4 oz) crystallized (candied) fruits. Put in a bowl with 75 g (3 oz, ½ cup) raisins and add 100 ml (4 fl oz, 7 tablespoons) rum. Leave to macerate for 1 hour. Slice a loaf of brioche. Remove the crusts, butter and lightly toast the slices until golden. Butter a 1.5 litre (2¾ pint, 6½ cups) charlotte mould and sprinkle with icing (confectioner's) sugar. Line the bottom with brioche slices and cover with a layer of the drained macerated fruit, reserving the rum. Fill the mould in this way with alternate layers of bread and fruit.

Beat 200 g (7 oz, 1 cup) caster (superfine) sugar, 100 ml (4 fl oz, 7 tablespoons) milk and 1 teaspoon vanilla sugar with 6 eggs and the rum in which the fruit was macerated. Gradually pour this mixture into the mould, allowing the brioche to soak up the liquid. Cook for 1 hour in a bain marie in a preheated oven at 150°C (300°F, gas 2), making sure the liquid in the bain marie does not come to the boil. Allow to cool completely. Remove from the mould and serve with crystallized fruit.

diplomat pudding

Make a syrup with 100 ml (4 fl oz, 7 tablespoons) water and 100 g (4 oz, ½ cup) caster (superfine) sugar. Bring to the boil and add 50 g (2 oz, ⅓ cup) sultanas (golden raisins). Leave for a few minutes, drain and reserve the syrup. Dice 50 g (2 oz, ⅓ cup) crystallized (candied) fruits and soak in 3 tablespoons rum.

Make a Bavarian cream: soak 15 g (½ oz, 1 tablespoon) gelatine in 3 tablespoons cold water. Boil 500 ml (17 fl oz, 2 cups) milk with half a vanilla pod (bean). Beat 4 large egg yolks with 125 g (4½ oz, ½ cup) caster sugar until the mixture is light and creamy, then add the boiling milk a little at a time, stirring with a wooden spatula. Pour the mixture into a saucepan and cook over a low heat, stirring continuously, until the custard cream is just thick enough to coat the spoon. Stir the gelatine into the custard cream, then press through a sieve. Leave to cool. Whip 200 ml (7 fl oz, ¾ cup) double (heavy) cream until stiff with 1 tablespoon very cold milk and fold into the cold custard.

Strain the rum from the crystallized fruit and add it to the reserved syrup. Use the rum-flavoured syrup to soak 200 g (7 oz) sponge fingers (ladyfingers). Put some of the crystallized fruit in the bottom of a greased mould, cover with a layer of the Bavarian cream, and then with a layer of sponge fingers sprinkled with sultanas and crystallized fruit. Coat with a little apricot jam. Continue to fill the mould with layers of Bavarian cream, sponge fingers, sultanas, crystallized fruits and apricot jam. Chill for at least 2 hours.

Heat some apricot jam until melted and add to it 3 tablespoons rum. Unmould the diplomat pudding on to a dish and coat it with the apricot sauce or, if preferred, with a little thin custard.

diplomat pudding with prunes

Place 200 g (7 oz, 1¼ cups) dried prunes in a small bowl and add just enough weak tea to cover them. Cover and leave to soak for 24 hours. Place the tea and the prunes in a saucepan, add 4 tablespoons caster (superfine) sugar, bring to the boil and cook gently for 15 minutes. Put 2 egg yolks in another saucepan together with 3 tablespoons caster sugar, 1 tablespoon vanilla sugar and 1 tablespoon cornflour (cornstarch). Slowly add 250 ml (8 fl oz, 1 cup) cold milk and stir over a low heat until the mixture boils and the custard thickens. Set aside to cool.

Drain and stone (pit) the prunes, reserve the cooking liquid and add to it 1 liqueur glass of rum or kirsch. Soak 28 sponge fingers (ladyfingers) in this syrup. Cover the bottom of a greased charlotte mould with some of the soaked sponge fingers, ensuring that the rounded surface of each finger is in contact with the mould. Place successive layers of custard cream, prunes and sponge fingers in the mould, finishing with sponge fingers. Chill thoroughly and turn the pudding out just before serving. Serve with a thin rum- or kirsch-flavoured custard cream.

individual diplomats with crystallized fruit

Make a short* pastry with 125 g (4½ oz, 1 cup) plain (all-purpose) flour, a pinch of salt, 3 table-spoons caster (superfine) sugar, 1 egg yolk and 75 g (3 oz, 6 tablespoons) softened butter. Roll the dough into a ball; wrap and chill.

Mix 75 g (3 oz, 6 tablespoons) softened butter with 75 g (3 oz, 6 tablespoons) caster sugar, 1 egg and 75 g (3 oz, ¾ cup) ground almonds. Roll 50 g (2 oz, ⅓ cup) sultanas (golden raisins) and 50 g (2 oz, ¼ cup) diced crystallized (candied) fruits in 3 tablespoons plain flour. Stir the fruit into the almond mixture, then add 3 tablespoons light rum and mix well.

Roll out the pastry until it is about 3 mm (⅛ in) thick, then cut out about 10 oval shapes with a pas-try (cookie) cutter. Butter some barquette moulds and line them with the pastry shapes, leaving an excess of about 3 mm (⅛ in) around the edges. Fill with the fruit–almond mixture and bake in a pre-heated oven at 200°C (400°F, gas 6) for 30 minutes. Remove the moulds from the oven and cool. Turn the barquettes out of the moulds and glaze with apricot jam that has been melted over a low heat.

Heat 100 g (4 oz) fondant icing (frosting) very gently so that it melts, and use to coat the diplomats. Decorate each diplomat with a glacé (candied) cherry and keep in a cool place.

additional recipe See *bombe glacée.*

DIPPING PIN A small confectionery utensil consisting of a stainless steel rod with a wooden handle and a spiral, a ring, or a two- or three-pronged fork at the end. The pin (or ring) is used for plunging a sweet in sugar fondant or melted chocolate to coat it, or for dipping a petit four or a sugar-coated fruit in boiling sugar to glaze it.

DISTILLATION The process of boiling a liquid and cooling and collecting the vapour, so as to separate components of the liquid mixture. It is the basic process used in making strong alcoholic spirits, either from wine or from other fermented material such as grain or potatoes. It depends on the fact that different substances boil at different temperatures; alcohol, in particular, boils more easily than water, so the vapour from, for instance, boiling wine will contain more alcohol than the original wine. Distillation, then, is a method of increasing the alcohol content – over and above that possible by normal fermentation. The distilled liquor also contains other substances from the original mixture, to give flavour. In many distillation processes, a second distillation (or rectification) is used. This is sometimes followed by the addition of aromatic substances – for example, Cognac is matured in oak barrels; gin is flavoured with juniper berries. Usually, the process is carried out in an alembic – a large copper vessel with a long neck in which the vapour condenses and from which the distillate drips. (The word 'distillation' comes from the Latin *distillare* – to fall drop by drop.)

DIVAN-LE PELETIER A brasserie situated in the Rue Le Peletier in Paris, founded in 1837 and called the Café du Divan. At that time, the Opéra was situated nearby in the same street and so the café was frequented by writers and actors. Balzac and Gavarni rubbed shoulders with Alfred de Musset (who went there to drink beer laced with absinthe), Meissonier, Daumier and Henri Monnier. Besides the beer, the clientele enjoyed the brasserie's sweet liqueurs, which were sold under such picturesque names as 'Parfait Amour', 'Crinoline', 'Alma', 'Sebastopol', 'Ligue Impériale' and 'Le Retour de Banni'. The establishment closed in 1859.

DODINE A dish of boned, stuffed and braised poultry (particularly duck) or meat, similar to a bal-lotine. In medieval cookery the term dodine was used for a classic sauce for which Taillevent gives three recipes: white dodine (milk boiled with ginger, egg yolks and sugar), red dodine (toast soaked in red wine, pressed through a sieve and boiled with fried onions, bacon, cinnamon, nutmeg, cloves, sugar and salt), and verjuice dodine (egg yolks, ver-juice, crushed chicken livers, ginger, parsley and bouillon). These sauces were placed under roasting poultry, so that the fat and meat juices ran into the

Baked diplomat pudding, see page 419.

sauce and were thus blended in. Dodines were used to accompany duck, teal, plover and capons. The dish was served with roast potatoes.

Nowadays, the names 'duck *à la dodine*' or 'guinea fowl *en dodine*' are still given to certain haute cuisine dishes in which the bird is roasted and carved, the legs and sliced breast meat are set aside, and the carcass is browned with carrots and onions (or mushrooms), wine, spices and the cooking juices. The sauce is then sieved and the uncooked chopped liver of the bird is added, together with fresh cream. The sauce is poured over the joints before serving. Dodine of duck is a well-known speciality in Aquitaine, Burgundy (served with Chambertin wine), the Morvan and Touraine.

RECIPE

dodine of duck

Bone a duck without damaging the skin, keeping the breast meat intact as far as possible. Remove all the flesh from the skin. Cut the breast meat into thin slices (*aiguillettes*) and marinate them for 24 hours in 2 tablespoons brandy, a pinch of ground fennel seeds, salt and pepper. Chop the remaining flesh and mix it with 250 g (9 oz, 1 cup) chopped fat bacon, 250 g (9 oz, 1 cup) chopped lean pork, 250 g (9 oz, 1 cup) chopped veal, 250 g (9 oz, 3 cups) chopped button mushrooms, 50 g (2 oz, ½ cups) ground almonds and a chopped small bunch of parsley. Work 2 tablespoons truffle parings (or diced truffles), 1 egg, salt and pepper into the mixture. Cook a knob of the mixture in a sauté pan and taste it, then adjust the seasoning if necessary.

Spread out the skin of the duck and cover it with half of the stuffing. Arrange the slices of breast on top and cover with the remaining stuffing. Fold the skin towards the centre at the neck and the tail, roll and tie up the dodine. Either wipe a soaked pig's caul and tie it around the dodine or tie the dodine in shape with string. Pork fat or streaky (slab) bacon may be used to bard the dodine. Braise the dodine in a little white wine in a preheated oven at 180°C (350°F, gas 4), basting it several times. Cook for 1½–1¾ hours, until the juices that run out when it is pricked are clear.

If the dodine is to be served hot, cut the thread and remove any parts of the caul that have not melted. Skim the fat from the cooking juices and add 2 tablespoons port and a few tablespoons of stock. Reduce by half. Cut the dodine into slices, garnish with watercress and serve with the sauce.

If the dodine is to be served cold, allow it to cool completely before cutting the thread. Serve with a green or mixed salad.

DOGFISH Fish of the *Scyliorhinidae* family, called dogfish because its small round fins at four corners make it look like a dog running underwater. Appreciated in Mediterranean countries as a cheaper alternative to swordfish, the larger spotted dogfish is known as *cazón* in Spain. Called huss in Australia and Britain, where until the late 1970s it was known as rock salmon (the term was outlawed as misrepresentative). The large spotted dogfish, up to 120 cm (48 in) long, is also known as nurse-hound; the lesser-spotted, up to 75 cm (30 in), and regarded as better tasting, is also known as rough hound.

DOLICHOS A genus of pulses of which several varieties are cultivated in warm and tropical regions. The most common is the mongette dolicho, which is widely cultivated in China and Louisiana (United States) and is also grown in the south of France (where it is known as *bannette*) and in Italy. It is similar to a haricot (navy) bean, but the seeds are smaller. The young pods may be cooked and eaten like French (green) beans. The asparagus bean has very long pods – up to 1 metre (3 feet) – and its beans vary in colour. The lablab dolicho (or bonavist bean) is cultivated in Africa and the West Indies.

DOLMA A stuffed vine leaf. A popular Turkish and Greek dish, the main form of which comprises a vine leaf stuffed with cooked rice and/or minced (ground) lamb, rolled into a cylinder and braised in a little stock with olive oil and lemon juice added. Dolmas (or dolmades) are served warm or cold as hors d'oeuvres. They may also be made with cabbage or fig leaves, or even with the leaves of the hazel tree. In Turkey, they are traditionally cooked in sheep-tail fat.

RECIPE

yalanci dolmas

Choose large sound vine leaves. Blanch for a maximum of 2 minutes, cool under running water and wipe dry. For about 50 dolmas, half-cook 125 g (4½ oz, ⅔ cup) long-grain or pilaf rice in meat stock. Peel and coarsely chop 400 g (14 oz) onions and cook gently in olive oil until soft but not brown. Mince (grind) 250 g (9 oz, 1 cup) mutton or lamb and gently brown it. Finally chop 1 tablespoon mint. Mix all these ingredients together. Place a small ball of stuffing on each vine leaf, fold up the tip and base of the leaf, roll into a cylinder and tie with kitchen thread.

Oil a sauté pan and place the dolmas in it, packing them closely together. Sprinkle with 4 tablespoons olive oil, the juice of 2 lemons and about 175 ml (6 fl oz, ¾ cup) stock flavoured with 1 tablespoon coriander (cilantro) seeds. Cover and simmer gently for about 30 minutes. Allow the dolmas to cool completely before removing the thread.

DOMYOJI AGE A Japanese dish of prawns (shrimp) coated with dried rice and deep-fried, served with sliced green (bell) pepper, aubergine (eggplant) and lemon. It is a classic example of the type of dish that combines contrasting textures, colours and flavours, much favoured in Japanese cookery.

DONKEY A mammal used essentially as a draught or pack animal; its meat is only a subsidiary edible product. In some Oriental countries young donkey meat is very popular, as it was in France at the time of the Renaissance. Nowadays, the meat of large donkeys (the Poitou breed) is put into the same class as horsemeat. In the south of France, where donkeys are smaller, their meat, which is firmer and has a stronger flavour, is used mainly in such products as the Arles sausage. Asses' milk, which has a composition similar to human milk, was used for a long time to feed nursing babies; it was also considered to have restorative properties. In the Balkans it is made into cream cheese.

This is what Alexandre Dumas says of the donkey in his *Grand Dictionnaire de cuisine*: 'Tastes change. We have recently seen the horse on the verge of replacing the ox, which would be quite just, since the ox had replaced the donkey. Maecenas was the first in Roman times to make use of the flesh of the domestic donkey ... Monsieur Isouard of Malta reports that, as a result of the blockade of the island of Malta by the English and the Neapolitans, the inhabitants were reduced to eating all the horses, dogs, cats, donkeys and rats: "This circumstance", he says, "led to the discovery that donkey meat was very good; so much so, in fact, that gourmands in the city of Valetta preferred it to the best beef and even veal ... Particularly boiled, roast, or braised, its flavour is exquisite. The meat is blackish and the fat verging on yellow. However, the donkey must only be three or four years old and must be fat." '

DORIA The name of various classic dishes, probably dedicated to a member of the famous Genoese Doria family who was an habitué of the Café Anglais in Paris in the 19th century. These dishes evoke the image of Italy, either by combining the colours of the Italian flag (green, white and red) or by including Piedmontese white truffles.

RECIPES

bombe Doria
Coat a bombe mould with pistachio ice cream. Macerate some pieces of marrons glacés in Curaçao, then add them to a vanilla-flavoured bombe mixture. Fill the mould with this mixture and place in the refrigerator to set.

Doria salad
Dress shredded celeriac (celery root) with rémoulade sauce and pile it in a deep salad bowl. Cover with thin slices of white truffle. Surround with a border of cooked green asparagus tips and thin strips of cooked beetroot (red beet) that has been seasoned with vinaigrette. Sprinkle with sieved hard-boiled (hard-cooked) egg yolk and chopped parsley.

sautéed chicken Doria
Brown a small chicken in 1 tablespoon oil and 25 g (1 oz, 2 tablespoons) butter in a flameproof casserole. Add salt and pepper, cover the casserole and continue cooking over a low heat for 30 minutes. Brown 675 g (1½ lb, 6 cups) peeled chopped cucumber in butter in a separate pan and add to the chicken. Cook for a further 20 minutes. Finish cooking the chicken, uncovered, in a preheated oven at 220°C (425°F, gas 7) for a further 20–30 minutes, or until brown and tender. Remove the chicken, drain and carve. Arrange the slices on the serving dish surrounded by the cucumber. Keep hot. Make a sauce by deglazing the casserole with the juice of a lemon and pour it over the chicken and cucumber.

DORMOUSE A small rodent that nests in the branches of trees and feeds on nuts, berries and seeds. In ancient times it was considered to be a delicacy, but is no longer eaten. The Romans were so fond of dormice that they bred them in special containers made of mud with holes through which the animals were fed with chestnuts, acorns and nuts. When the dormice had been fattened up, they were either stewed or roasted and then coated with a sauce made from honey and poppyseeds. As late as the 17th century, it was still possible to find dormouse pie in France.

DOSA Indian pancake made from a batter of rice and/or dal. The uncooked rice and dal are washed, soaked and ground or processed to a purée with enough water to make a batter. The batter may be flavoured with chillies, ginger or other ingredients before being cooked on a greased griddle. The pancakes may be thick or thin, served plain or with a filling. Dosas are usually grouped with Indian breads and served as snacks, for example for breakfast, or instead of bread to scoop up a main dish.

DOUGH The name given to a moistened mixture of ingredients that is firm enough to handle. A dough is usually brought together with the fingers or hand into a ball or solid lump and it may be kneaded until smooth. The consistency of the dough depends on type, ranging from dry and crumbly or firm to soft and sticky. A dough is never soft enough to be beaten (when it would be a mixture or batter).

Wheat flour and water are basic dough ingredients but other cereals and liquids may be used. Salt is often added for flavour and sugar for sweetening. Fat (lard, butter, shortening or oil) and eggs enrich dough. Milk or other liquids may be used instead of water to bind the ingredients. Raising agents, such as yeast or baking powder, may be used to make the dough rise during baking.

■ **Types of dough** Yeasted bread dough is the most common mixture to take the name. Made from flour, salt and water, with yeast as a raising agent, this type of dough may have a small proportion of fat added. This type of dough has a comparatively high moisture content and is kneaded until smooth and elastic. Flour with a high protein content is used as it becomes stretchy when kneaded, which is important for trapping the gas produced by the fermenting yeast to make the dough rise. Although the dough is smooth and easy to handle, if it is allowed to rest for too long in the hand, it tends to become sticky. (Dusting with flour prevents this.)

Doughs made with self-raising flour or using baking powder or similar raising agents are softer in texture. They may include more liquid or fat and are kneaded briefly or pressed into shape. Examples include Irish soda bread and British scones.

The mixture for pastry is also referred to as dough. These vary according to the type of pastry, but a typical short pastry has a high proportion of fat with a small amount of water. Plain (all-purpose) flour is used without a raising agent. The result is a firm, crumbly dough. It should not be sticky from the moisture content but may be so from the fat it contains. When cooked, the dough is very light and crumbly (short), with a slight crispness to its texture. The more fat used, the shorter (more crumbly) the result; when slightly more water is used, the dough will become crisp but too much water and heavy handling will result in a tough, heavy and close, not crumbly, texture.

Biscuit (cookie) doughs are similar to pastry, but usually richer with more fat or added egg, plus flavouring ingredients.

Pasta dough differs from yeast and pastry dough. A typical Italian pasta dough is moistened with eggs, a little oil and sometimes with a little water to give a firm, not short or soft dough. It does not contain a raising agent and, although more stretchy than a short pastry dough, it is not elastic in the same way as yeast dough.

Examples of other mixtures usually referred to as dough during preparation include almond paste or marzipan and sugarpaste or roll-out icing.

DOUGHNUT

DOUGHNUT A traditional pâtisserie of Quebec prepared from leavened dough (flour, eggs, milk and butter), often made in the shape of a ring, and deep-fried. It is eaten hot or at room temperature, plain or sprinkled with caster (superfine) sugar. The *soufflet* doughnut or *croquignole* is made from choux pastry. The French term *beigne* also describes the doughnut topped with sugar icing (frosting), made commercially, which is a fast-food item in North America.

RECIPE

doughnuts
Mix 15 g (½ oz, 1 cake) fresh (compressed) yeast with 150 ml (¼ pint, ⅔ cup) warm milk. (Alternatively, use 1½ teaspoons dried yeast.) Put 500 g (18 oz, 4½ cups) strong white (bread) flour, 100–125 g (4–4½ oz, ½ cup) caster (superfine) sugar, a generous pinch of salt and ½ teaspoon grated nutmeg into a large bowl. Make a well in the centre and mix a beaten egg with the dry ingredients as thoroughly as possible. Add 2 more eggs, one at a time. Work 65 g (2½ oz, 5 tablespoons) melted butter into the mixture, then add the warm yeast mixture. Knead the dough until it becomes elastic. Leave to rise until doubled in size.

Roll out the dough on a floured surface to a thickness of about 1 cm (½ in) and cut it into rounds with a pastry (cookie) cutter 6 cm (2½ in) in diameter. Fry the doughnuts in hot fat – at least 185°C (365°F) – until they swell up and become golden brown. Drain on paper towels, dust with caster (superfine) sugar and serve very hot with maple syrup or a cranberry compote.

DOUGH TROUGH A large wooden trough used in the past for kneading dough or for keeping bread. A regional name for this trough is *la maie*.

DOUILLON A speciality of Normandy, consisting of an apple or pear wrapped in a pastry case and baked in the oven. See also *bourdelot*.

RECIPE

douillons
Mix 500 g (18 oz, 4½ cups) plain (all-purpose) flour, 350 g (12 oz, 1½ cups) softened butter, 2 eggs, 3 tablespoons milk, 1½ tablespoons caster (superfine) sugar and 1 teaspoon salt to make a smooth dough. Roll it into a ball and place in the refrigerator while cooking the pears.

Peel 8 small pears, remove the cores and place a knob of butter in the centre of each. Cook in a preheated oven at 190°C (375°F, gas 5) for 10 minutes. Remove and allow them to get completely cold. (Do not turn the oven off.)

Roll out the pastry to a thickness of about 3 mm (⅛ in) and cut it into 8 squares of equal size. Place a well-drained pear in the centre of each square and fold the corners upwards, stretching the pastry a little. Seal the sides and the top by pinching with damp fingers. Draw lines on the pastry with the point of a knife. Glaze the *douillons* with an egg yolk beaten in 2 tablespoons milk and bake in the oven for 25–30 minutes. Serve hot, warm, or cold, with crème fraîche.

DOUM PALM An African palm tree with edible fruits. Palm wine is made from the sap of this tree. Alexandre Dumas writes in his *Grand Dictionnaire de cuisine*: 'The doum palm produces a refreshing fruit, in which I was able to detect the taste of gingerbread. A lady in Cairo . . . once offered me a cool sorbet of doum fruit.'

DOURO River with its source in Spain, where it crosses several wine regions, before continuing its course through Portugal, where the demarcated Douro valley is the birthplace of port wine and is gaining a reputation for excellent table wines. Port is produced in the three regions of Cima (Higher) Cargo, Baixo (Lower) Cargo and the Upper Douro.

DOVE *tourterelle* A bird similar and related to the pigeon, but smaller. There are several varieties, including the rock dove and ring dove (see *pigeon*), the turtledove, the collared dove, the palm dove, and the rufous turtledove. The latter four species are hunted in France, though they are of minor gastronomic interest. Plump young doves were formerly considered to make a delicious meal. In the 16th century, doves, together with curlews, wood pigeons, squabs and egrets, were more highly prized by some than beef, veal and pork. In Arab cookery, doves cooked in a cocotte with artichoke hearts, nutmeg and raisins are a choice dish.

DRAGÉE An item of confectionery consisting of an almond with a hard coating of sugar. The coating may be white or coloured, and hazelnuts, pistachio nuts, nougat, almond paste, chocolate or liqueur may also be used as centres for these sweets (candies).

Honey-coated almonds were popular sweetmeats with the ancient Greeks and Romans, and the name 'dragée' is derived from the Greek word for these sweets (*tragemata*). The dragée was mentioned for the first time in 1220, in the archives of the town of Verdun. At that time, the apothecaries (with whom confectioners were still confused) coated certain spices – aniseed, coriander and fennel – with honey. These *épices de chambre* were considered to be medicinal spices, eaten to sweeten the breath or as an aid to digestion. When cane sugar was introduced into Europe, dragées as we now know them appeared – sugar-coated almonds, pumpkin seeds or cucumber seeds. In 1660, Colbert noted that Verdun was the centre of trade in dragées, and it remains famous for their production to the present day. Dragées are traditionally given at christenings, first communions and weddings. The *obus de Verdun* is a chocolate novelty fitted with a fuse which, when lighted, explodes to release dragées and small party novelties.

Before 1850, dragées were hand-made by craftsmen. The almonds were suspended in rotating vats of sugar syrup so that they would be evenly coated. In that year, however, the first mechanical turbine was invented, and the process is now carried out mechanically by spraying sugar syrup on to the kernels under pressure and drying them in warm air.

■ **The range of dragées** The sugar-coating process is the same for every type of filling. The most popular varieties of almonds are the flat Italian *avolas* and the slightly rounded Spanish *planetas*. The almonds are put into the turbine, dipped three times in a mixture of gum arabic and sugar, dried and coated with a concentrated sugar syrup. They are then blanched in a sugar syrup with added starch, smoothed and coloured if required.

Chocolate, nougat, fondant icing (frosting), almond paste or liqueur fillings are moulded before being coated with sugar. Specialities include *olives de Provence*, different types of *cailloux* and *galets*, and *anis de Flavigny*. *Perles d'argent* are made by coating a sugar centre with a gelatine-based solution, then with pure silver.

Soft dragées (also called *dragées à froid* or *dragées Julienne*) are shaped like beans or peas and their centres consist of clear or opaque boiled sugar coated with a dilute glucose solution and then with icing (confectioner's) sugar.

DRAGON FRUIT See *pitahaya*.

DRAIN To pour a liquid off a solid with the primary intention of saving the solid. For example, water is drained from raw foodstuffs that have been washed or from foods that have been cooked or blanched in water. A colander or sieve is used for the purpose; if the cooking liquid is required the colander should be placed over a bowl. Alternatively, a pan may be covered with a lid, leaving a small gap for the liquid to be poured off – this is a useful method for potatoes.

Small items can be lifted from cooking water (or fat) on a draining spoon and held over the pan until excess liquid has dripped off. Spinach can be squeezed with the hands or excess water can be pressed out with the back of a spoon. Bread soaked in milk (used to make a stuffing) can also be squeezed by hand. Foods that have been deep-fried are also drained to remove the excess oil or fat.

DRAMBUIE A Scotch whisky-based liqueur, which can be drunk at any time. Its formula is the property of the Mackinnon family, who keep it a secret. The origin of the name apparently comes from the Gaelic expression *an dram buidheach* ('the liqueur that satisfies'). Drambuie, little known in continental Europe, is popular in the United States.

DRESSER A French culinary term with several different meanings. In cooking, it means to arrange attractively on the serving dish all the items that comprise a particular preparation, including the principal ingredient, the garnish, the sauce and any decorations. In pâtisserie, *dresser* means to roll out pastry for lining a mould or flan tin (pie pan), or to force dough through a piping (pastry) bag.

In restaurants, *dressage* takes place as soon as the dishes are *à point* (ready to be served). Garnishes must always be kept in perfect condition for use. For example, sprigs of parsley and bunches of watercress are kept in fresh water; maître d'hôtel butter is kept cold in water with ice cubes; mushrooms are sprinkled with lemon juice; and flavoured butters are shaped into rolls, wrapped in foil and stored in the refrigerator.

The items used in *dressage* include serving dishes, radish dishes, hors-d'oeuvre dishes (divided into sections), sundae glasses, timbale dishes, copper platters for serving game, vegetable dishes, sauceboats (gravy boats), salad dishes, soup tureens, terrine dishes, fruit dishes and toast racks. *Fonds de plat* and *bords de plat* were used at one time. The former were either round or oval pieces of wood that were placed on the bottom of a plate to form a raised base for cold dishes. They were usually covered with silver paper. *Bords de plat* were wide-rimmed decorative dishes made of solid silver or silver plate on which the garnishes were arranged around the principal item.

Certain dishes require a particular style of *dressage*; for example, oysters and other seafood are served on a large plate covered with crushed ice, mounted on a support. Other dishes need to be placed on a plate-warmer. Certain items call for specific utensils, such as special plates and tongs for snails or asparagus cradles.

■ **Methods of dressage** The items of food may be presented in various ways. Game and poultry are often served on slices of fried bread. Potatoes are often used in various ways for *dressage* – borders, duchess potatoes, nests of potato straws, little piles of noisette potatoes. Artichoke hearts, tomatoes and mushrooms are also used in this way.

The plates and dishes for *dressage* must be kept at the correct temperature for the food they are to hold (for example, sundae glasses must be ice-cold).

The present tendency in French restaurants is for *service à l'assiette*, in which the individual portion is placed directly on the plate, coated with sauce and garnished with vegetables.

DRESSING FISH, POULTRY AND GAME
The preparation of fish, poultry and game birds for cooking.
• DRESSING FISH The fish must be successively trimmed, scaled, gutted (cleaned) and washed (some of this may be carried out by the fishmonger). The dressing will vary depending on the type of fish (flat, round, small or large) and on the way it is to be served. For example, if a whole sole is to be served, only the black skin is removed, whereas a sole fillet is not trimmed, but the skin is removed completely.
• DRESSING POULTRY AND GAME BIRDS The bird must first be plucked, carefully picked over and singed. Poultry is then drawn, usually trussed, and often larded, but the preparation will vary according to the type of bird. Feathered game is not always completely gutted; trussing or tying, and sometimes larding, complete the dressing. All the above operations apply to birds that are to be cooked whole. When they are to be cut into portions, the giblets, white meat and breasts are removed, and it is therefore only necessary to pluck, singe and draw the bird.

DRIED VINE FRUITS
Currants, sultanas (golden raisins) and raisins. These dried fruits are all produced by exposing ripe grapes to hot dry air so that the moisture is drawn out. This leaves the flesh and skin so concentrated that the activities of enzymes and the growth of moulds and bacteria are inhibited. It takes 1.8 kg (4 lb) grapes to produce 450 g (1 lb) currants, sultanas or raisins.

For all types of dried vine fruit, the grapes are dried naturally in the sun or artificially by hot air. The dried fruit is sorted and graded, the seeds and stalks are removed, and the fruit is then usually spin-washed, dried and a light coating of preservative applied before it is finally packed.
• CURRANTS Produced mainly in Greece, the quality varies with the type of grape used and the soil conditions. Traditionally, the finest are Vostizza but excellent fruit is produced in the Zante Gulf and Patras regions. The grapes are gathered in August and September and generally sun-dried. Currants are also grown in Australia, California and South Africa, but the limited production is usually for domestic consumption.
• SULTANAS (GOLDEN RAISINS) These come from grapes that are green when fresh but darken in colour when dried. Light-coloured fruit is generally obtained by drying in the shade, and darker fruit by sun-drying. In both cases drying is natural, using the hot dry harvest weather. Many countries in the northern hemisphere produce sultanas – Greece, France, Turkey, Iran, Afghanistan, China, the United States and Mexico. In the southern hemisphere the producers are Australia, South Africa and Chile.
• SEEDLESS RAISINS Produced in the United States, Mexico and South Africa, they are obtained from the Thompson sultana grape and are green when harvested. They are sun-dried, the action of the sun caramelizing the sugars and causing the fruit to darken to a purplish-brown colour. A red raisin grape is produced in Afghanistan; after drying, it is essentially of the same appearance as the other.
• STONED (PITTED) RAISINS These come from large red grapes that are generally used as wine and table grapes, although some are sun-dried. To extract the seeds, the fruit is steamed to soften it, then put through special machinery that squeezes the seeds out. The skin is then sealed by a light coating to prevent the fruit from sugaring. Australia, South Africa and Spain are the main producers.

Dried vine fruits are widely used in all areas of cookery. They are used in savoury or sweet recipes, raw or cooked, including salads, casseroles and stuffings for meat or poultry. They are added to rice dishes and cooked with some vegetables. Dried vine fruits are also essential in many chutneys and pickles.

In sweet cookery, they contribute sweetness and a rich flavour to compotes, sauces, salads and baked desserts or puddings. In baking they are essential for a wide variety of cakes and pastries; and they bring character to many sweet breads.

RECIPE

raisin tart
Soak 500 g (18 oz, 3 cups) raisins in brandy. Beat 8 whole eggs lightly, then whip them together with 1 litre (1¾ pints, 4⅓ cups) double (heavy) cream, 350 g (12 oz, 1½ cups) caster (superfine) sugar and 2 teaspoons vanilla sugar or a few drops of vanilla essence (extract). Line a flan tin (pie pan) at least 28 cm (11 in) in diameter with 450 g (1 lb) puff pastry. Pour the cream into the pastry case, add the raisins and bake in a preheated oven at 220°C (425°F, gas 7) for at least 30 minutes.

additional recipe See *carrot*.

DRINK
The simplest and most natural drink, and the only one essential for the survival of all living organisms, is water. The average consumption of liquid in a temperate climate is 1 litre (1¾ pints, 4⅓ cups) per day, but needs to vary according to the

climate and the diet. For example, meat and salted, spiced or sweetened dishes all increase the thirst. Human kind has used its intelligence to vary the flavour of drinks, which may be sweet, aromatic, fermented or spirit-based.

Water-based drinks, which may be still or sparkling, hot or cold, include lemonades, sodas and syrups, broths, infusions, tea, coffee, chocolate and chicory. Drinks of vegetable origin may or may not be alcoholic; for example, fruit and vegetable juices, wine, cider, beer and perry. Such drinks can be transformed by distillation into brandy, liqueurs and spirits. These different liquids have given rise to countless variations – cocktails, liqueurs, apéritifs, punches and grogs. Milk from animals is really a liquid food, but may also be used to prepare drinks such as milk shakes and kefir.

Drinking habits vary considerably depending on the customs of a country and the latitude. As a general rule, Orientals and Russians do not drink with their meals, but take tea at the end of a meal. Tea is the most widely consumed drink in the world after water.

In France, mineral water, beer and wine are the drinks that traditionally accompany meals. Family and social life also offer numerous other occasions to consume drinks for pleasure.

■ **Drinking establishments** These considerably predate restaurants; they include pubs and taverns, bars, milk bars and tea rooms. Such establishments may even vary from region to region in the same country; in France, for example, there are the *bouchons* of Lyon, the *estaminets* of the north and the *guinguettes* (pleasure gardens) and bistros of Paris.

The code of drinking establishments classifies drinks into five groups: non-alcoholic drinks (water, fruit juice, lemonade); fermented non-distilled drinks (wine, beer, cider); wine-based apéritifs and red fruit liqueurs; rums and spirits obtained by distillation; and all other alcoholic drinks.

In former times, most drinks were either produced in the home or by local makers – home-made beers and liqueurs, orgeat, mulled wine. Today, drinks are produced commercially and the market has grown considerably, particularly for the sale of fruit juices. Drinks are sold in various packagings (bottles and cans) and in a variety of forms (concentrated, powdered, frozen).

DRIPPING PAN A metal pan to catch juices or melted fat from a roasting joint, poultry or any meat or when grilling (broiling) food. The French word, *lèchefrite*, has been used since the end of the 12th century; before this the pan was called a *belle-bouche*. In former times these receptacles were made of wrought iron and were fitted with a long handle, so that they could be slipped under meat being roasted in huge fireplaces. They were also made of silver.

DROIT DE BANVIN The monopoly on the sale of new wine reserved by the landlords on their own land during a set period (generally 40 days before the opening of the selling season). In some areas this feudal right, dating back to the time of Charlemagne, began at Easter and ended at Whitsun, seven weeks later.

DROUANT A restaurant opened in Paris in 1880 by an Alsatian, Charles Drouant, on the corner of Place Gaillon and Rue Saint-Augustin. Specializing in seafood, it attracted a clientele of writers and journalists, such as Jean Ajalbert, Léon Daudet, Octave Mirbeau and the Rosny brothers. Drouant expanded his business and his fame spread, thanks to his cellar (particularly white vintages). In October 1914 the restaurant really found a place in literary history, when the Académie Goncourt decided to hold its lunches there. There were numerous gourmets among the Goncourt academicians, particularly Léon Daudet, who introduced the serving of *blanc de blancs*. Edmond de Goncourt's will stipulated that the meal must cost 20 francs per person, and the academicians still pay that modest sum. Here are a few menus for Goncourt lunches, which are traditionally served in the Louis XVI salon on the second floor, at a round table with a damask tablecloth.
• 1933 (prizewinner: André Malraux for *La Condition humaine*): oysters, pike boulangère, roast turkey with thinly sliced roast potatoes, cep mushrooms *à la bordelaise*, cheeses, praline ice and fruit.
• 1954 (prizewinner: Simone de Beauvoir for *Les Mandarins*): oysters, grilled turbot, Bresse chicken with champagne, cheeses, liqueur soufflé and fruit.
• 1981 (prizewinner: Lucien Bodard for *Anne-Marie*): beluga caviar, foie gras in port aspic, lobster Drouant, haunch of venison Saint-Hubert, chestnut cream, cheeses, iced hazelnut soufflé with *mignardises* (small biscuits or cakes).

DRUMSTICK The lower leg of a fowl or game bird, consisting of the bone, meat and a thin layer of fat, giving it the shape of a pestle (hence the French name *pilon*, which means pestle). It is fleshier and juicier than the white meat, but inferior to the thigh.

DRYING One of the oldest methods of preserving food. Drying slows down the proliferation and activity of the bacteria that cause spoilage and decay, but it considerably alters the appearance of food, due to the loss of its water. Since prehistoric times, cereals, nuts and fruit have been dried in the sun before being stored. The American Indians used to dry buffalo meat in the same way to make pemmican. Pastrami and various salted meats are dried quite heavily, and may subsequently be smoked. The process of drying in the open air and wind is applied to fish (generally salted fish) in Scandinavia, Senegal and India. The drying of fruit and vegetables has been widely practised since time immemorial – in Greece (for grapes), in Turkey (for apricots), in Iran and Spain (for tomatoes), in Hungary (for peppers), and in most other countries for pears, sliced apples, plums, whole cherries and grapes. Vegetables are usually dried flat on trestles in the sun, the drying often being completed in the oven.

With the success of freezing and its characteristics for retaining the food value of ingredients, drying is no longer an essential means of preserving food for times when it may be out of season or expensive. However, it is an important method of preparing specific ingredients such as dried beans and pulses, and dried fruit, as well as a wide variety of specialist food products, many of which were originally dried for local (and domestic) preservation. Sun-dried tomatoes and peppers are good examples, available seasoned or reconstituted in a marinade. Drying is still the method used to preserve wild mushrooms.

Drying is often supplemented (or preceded) by smoking, salting, fumigation (dried vegetables) or spraying with sulphur dioxide (dried fruit).

■ **Modern commercial drying** In industry, the selection of the drying process depends mainly on the texture and size of the foodstuff, but factors such as ease of transport and convenience in use must also be considered. For modern industrial methods of drying, which eliminate a very large proportion of water, the term dehydration is used. Dehydration is carried out in the food industry for several reasons: to preserve the product for a considerable period of time; to reduce the weight and usually the volume of the product, thus making it easier to transport and store; and to reduce the preparation time (as with instant coffee and dried soups).

The concentration of a product involves partial dehydration by evaporation, filtration or centrifugation. Certain products (such as milk, soups, meat extracts, vegetable concentrates and fruit juices) retain between a third and half of their natural water content and always remain in a liquid form.

Desiccation, or dehydration in the true sense of the word, is achieved by different processes.

• Drying on trays Solid foods are cut into small pieces and constantly moved forward in an oven or tunnel through which a current of hot dry air is directed in the opposite direction. The moisture is gradually absorbed.

• Drying on drums Soft foods (purées, baby foods, soups) are spread in a thin layer on the outside wall of a rotating drum that is heated from the inside. Special knives scrape off the dry film, which is subsequently reduced to a powder or to flakes.

• Atomization Liquids (such as milk or coffee) are atomized to form a fine spray. The tiny particles in the vapour are dehydrated with a current of hot air and collected in powder form.

Products subjected to desiccation contain no more than, on average, 6% of their original water content, and will keep for very long periods in hermetically sealed containers. See also *freeze-drying*.

Recipes

drying apples and pears
Peel and core some cooking apples. Cut them into slices 1 cm (½ in) thick and put into water containing lemon juice or 2 teaspoons citric acid per 1 litre (1¾ pints, 4⅓ cups) water. Drain and place flat, without overlapping, on a wooden trestle in the sun. Leave the fruit (bringing it in at night) for 2–3 days; if necessary finish off the drying in the oven on its coolest setting. The apple rings should be flexible but must contain no more water.

Pears (sound ones only) may be dried whole and unpeeled in the sun. Finish off in the oven as for apples. When cooled, dried pears may be flattened between boards.

In countries where the weather is not so clement, the fruit may be dried in the oven or suspended from the ceiling, threaded on string.

drying herbs
Gather the herbs just before they flower (avoid picking them after it has been raining). Wash, then shake off the water. Roll up small-leaved herbs (thyme, rosemary and savory) in muslin (cheesecloth) loosely, without squashing them together, then hang them up in a warm place. Herbs with large leaves (bay, mint, sage, parsley and basil) can be dried in bunches, tied together by the stalks and hung upside down. Alternatively, the leaves may be removed and wrapped in muslin. When the herbs are dried, leave them whole or crush them with a rolling pin. Keep them in sealed jars in a dark dry place. Drying in a microwave gives perfect results.

drying vegetables
Using a needle, thread some young sound French (green) beans on to thick thread. Ensure that they are not too tightly packed together, tying a knot occasionally to separate them. Dip in boiling salted water – use 2 teaspoons salt per 1 litre (1¾ pints, 4⅓ cups) water – drain them, and hang them in a fairly shady place for 3–4 days, bringing them inside at night (or suspend from the ceiling).

Mushrooms can be dried in the same way, once the earthy part of the stalk has been cut off. Small green chilli peppers, which become dark red when dried, can be threaded through the stalk, as can baby onions, garlic bulbs and shallots. Store green beans, peppers and mushrooms out of the light in sealed jars. Rehydrate before use by soaking for 12 hours in tepid water.

DRYING OFF Eliminating excess water from cooked food by heating it over a low heat. It is necessary to dry off potatoes before mashing with milk and butter. The excess moisture absorbed by vegetables during cooking may be evaporated by tossing them rapidly in a sauté pan before coating with butter.

In France, the term *dessécher* is used particularly for the initial cooking of choux paste. The mixture of water, butter and flour is worked vigorously over a high heat with a wooden spatula until the paste detaches itself from the walls of the pan and forms a ball. Thus, excess water evaporates before the eggs are added and the choux is baked.

Drying off is not synonymous with reducing, which refers only to the process of boiling down certain liquids so that they are reduced in volume.

DU BARRY The name given to several dishes that contain cauliflower. A Du Barry garnish for joints of meat consists of château potatoes and small florets of blanched cauliflower coated with Mornay sauce, sprinkled with grated cheese, browned under the grill and arranged *à la serviette*. These dishes were dedicated to the Comtesse du Barry, the favourite of Louis XV.

RECIPES

croûtes Du Barry
Prepare some individual croûtes and top with cauliflower florets cooked gently in butter. Coat with Mornay sauce, sprinkle with grated cheese and brown in a preheated oven at 240°C (475°F, gas 9).

Du Barry salad
Steam some very small white cauliflower florets for about 4 minutes in a pressure cooker or about 12 minutes in an ordinary saucepan. Drain and cool completely, and heap them in a salad bowl. Garnish with radishes and small sprigs of watercress. Pour some well-seasoned vinaigrette with added lemon over the salad and sprinkle with chopped herbs. Toss the salad just before serving.

Du Barry soup
Cook a cauliflower in salted water, then press it through a sieve (or purée in a blender). Mix with it a quarter of its weight of potato purée, then add enough consommé or milk to obtain a creamy consistency. Finally, add some single (light) cream – about 150 ml (¼ pint, ⅔ cup) for 5 portions. Adjust the seasoning, and sprinkle with chopped parsley. Butter may also be added.

other recipes See *lamb, omelette (flat omelettes)*.

DUBLEY A garnish for large joints of meat, consisting of grilled (broiled) mushrooms and duchess potato croustades surrounded by a border of mushroom purée.

DUBOIS, URBAIN FRANÇOIS French chef (born Trets, 1818; died Nice, 1901). Dubois began his career in Paris with Tortoni, then moved to the Rocher de Cancale, and later to the Café Anglais. Most of his life, however, was spent abroad. In Russia he was chef to Prince Orloff, and in Germany he was joint chef of Wilhelm I with Émile Bernard, who had been in the service of Napoleon III.

Dubois produced a large collection of written work, but is remembered mainly for *La Cuisine classique* (1856), written in collaboration with Émile Bernard. His other publications include *La Cuisine de tous les pays* (1868), *La Cuisine artistique* (1870), *L'École des cuisinières* (1876), *La Nouvelle Cuisine bourgeoise pour la ville et pour la campagne* (1878), *Le Grand Livre des pâtissiers et des confiseurs* (a major work for pastrycooks and confectioners; 1883), *La Cuisine d'aujourd'hui* (1889) and *La Pâtisserie d'aujourd'hui* (1894).

DUCHESSE A sweet or savoury preparation of choux pastry that may be served as an entrée, a garnish or a dessert (like profiteroles). Savoury duchesses are filled with a mousse or a salpicon. Duchesses for dessert are filled with vanilla-flavoured confectioner's custard (pastry cream) or whipped cream, dusted with icing (confectioner's) sugar, and scattered with chopped pistachio nuts, flaked almonds or dusted with cocoa.

Duchesses are also petits fours consisting of meringue shells or circles of langue-de-chat biscuit (cookie) mixture, stuck together in pairs with flavoured butter cream.

Duchesse is also the name of a variety of winter pear, and of certain desserts that include pears.

RECIPE

duchesse petits fours
Grease 3 baking sheets and dust with flour. Mix together 100 g (4 oz, 1 cup) ground almonds, 100 g (4 oz, ½ cup) caster (superfine) sugar, and 40 g (1½ oz, 6 tablespoons) plain (all-purpose) flour. Whisk 6 egg whites until very stiff and fold into the mixture with a metal spoon. Melt 40 g (1½ oz, 3 tablespoons) butter and add to the mixture. Put the mixture into a piping (pastry) bag and pipe small rounds on to the baking sheets. Cook in a preheated oven at 190°C (375°F, gas 5) for 7–8 minutes, remove from the oven and carefully lift off the rounds of meringue with a palette knife (spatula). Mix 200 g (7 oz, 1 cup) ground praline with 225 g (8 oz, 1 cup) crème au beurre (see *creams*) and use to sandwich the duchesses together. Store in a cool place.

DUCHESSE, À LA The description *à la duchesse* is given in French cuisine to various dishes garnished, surrounded or served with duchess potatoes. In pâtisserie, the name applies to certain preparations containing almonds.

RECIPES

amandines à la duchesse
Make a dough with 150 g (5 oz, 1¼ cups) plain (all-purpose) flour, 75 g (3 oz, 6 tablespoons) softened butter, 3 tablespoons caster (superfine) sugar, a pinch of salt, 1 egg yolk and 4 teaspoons water. Roll it into a ball and place in the refrigerator. Beat 100 g (4 oz, ½ cup) butter until soft and mix into it 100 g (4 oz, ½ cup) caster sugar. Add 2 eggs, one at a time, and beat the mixture. Stir in 100 g (4 oz, 1 cup) ground almonds, then 50 g (2 oz, ½ cup) cornflour (cornstarch), and mix well. Add 100 ml (4 fl oz, 7 tablespoons) kirsch.

Roll out the chilled dough to a thickness of about 3 mm (⅛ in) and cut out 8 rounds with a pastry (cookie) cutter. Use these to line 8 buttered tartlet moulds and prick the bottom of each one with a fork. Put a few cooked redcurrants into each of the tartlets and cover with the almond mixture. Bake in a preheated oven at 200°C (400°F, gas 6) for 20 minutes. Allow the amandines to cool completely before turning them out of the moulds. Warm 100 g (4 oz, ⅓ cup) redcurrant jelly and use to glaze the amandines. Decorate the tops with redcurrants and keep in a cool place.

peaches à la duchesse

Make a dough with 150 g (5 oz, 1¼ cups) plain (all-purpose) flour, a pinch of salt, 3 tablespoons caster (superfine) sugar, 75 g (3 oz, 6 tablespoons) softened butter, 1 tablespoon water and 1 egg yolk. Roll into a ball and place in the refrigerator. Dice 8 slices canned pineapple and macerate them in kirsch. Put 50 g (2 oz, ½ cup) flaked almonds on to a baking sheet, moisten with water, dust with sugar and bake in a preheated oven at 200°C (400°F, gas 6) until golden brown, turning often.

Roll out the chilled dough to a thickness of about 3 mm (⅛ in) and cut out 8 circles with a pastry (cookie) cutter. Use to line 8 tartlet moulds, prick the bottom of each one with a fork, place a piece of greaseproof (wax) paper in each and fill with baking beans. Cook for 5 minutes in the oven, remove the paper and baking beans, and cook for a further 7 minutes. Cool and then turn out of the moulds.

Prepare a zabaglione by whisking 100 g (4 oz, ½ cup) caster sugar and 3 egg yolks in a bain marie until the mixture is warm and frothy. Add 3 tablespoons of both kirsch and Maraschino, whisking until the mixture has thickened. Soften 500 ml (17 fl oz, 2 cups) vanilla ice cream by crushing it with a wooden spatula. Add the diced pineapple. Place some of the ice-cream mixture in the bottom of each tartlet, put a canned peach half on each, and coat with the zabaglione. Sprinkle with flaked almonds and chill briefly.

The peaches may be replaced by pears.

poached eggs à la duchesse

Spread some cold duchess potato mixture on a buttered dish and cut out circles about 7 cm (2¾ in) in diameter. Bake in a preheated oven at 220°C (425°F, gas 7) until golden brown and arrange a poached egg on each. Coat with béchamel sauce, Mornay sauce, tomato sauce, cream sauce or any other suitable sauce.

DUCHESS POTATOES Potatoes puréed with butter and egg yolk, piped into decorative shapes and baked. Duchess potatoes are served with roast meat or they may be used as a garnish. The mixture is also used to make croquettes, Berny potatoes (mixed with chopped truffles, coated with flaked almonds, shaped into rounds and fried) and Saint-Florentin potatoes (mixed with chopped ham, coated with fine uncooked vermicelli, shaped into small corks and fried).

duchess potato mixture

Cut 500 g (18 oz) peeled potatoes into thick slices or quarters. Boil them briskly in salted water. Drain, put in a warm oven for a few moments to evaporate excess moisture, and press through a sieve. Put the purée into a saucepan and dry off for a few moments on the hob (stovetop), turning with a wooden spoon. Add 50 g (2 oz, ¼ cup) butter and season with salt, pepper and a little grated nutmeg. Mix in 1 egg and 2 yolks.

This mixture is easier to pipe while hot: it may be piped for borders or into swirls on a greased baking sheet to be served as duchess potatoes proper. Brush the cooled swirls of potato with beaten egg and brown them in a hot oven.

Alternatively, spread the purée on a buttered baking sheet, leave until cold and shape as indicated in the recipe.

fried duchess potatoes

Heat some oil for deep-frying to about 180°C (350°F). Put some cooled duchess potato mixture in a piping (pastry) bag with a plain nozzle about 2 cm (¾ in) in diameter and pipe the mixture into the hot oil, cutting it off into about 4 cm (1½ in) lengths. Cook until golden brown, drain on paper towels and serve very hot.

Instead of piping the mixture, it may be spread out on a buttered baking sheet, cooled and cut into even-sized rectangles. These can be rolled into cylinders and then deep-fried.

additional recipe See *croustade*.

DUCK A web-footed bird that was domesticated in China over 2000 years ago. In France, the most common breeds are the Nantes duck and the Barbary duck. The mulard duck, produced by crossing these two breeds, is reared mainly in south-western France for the production of foie gras since the 1970s and is highly esteemed by gourmets. Whatever the breed, duck should be consumed within three days of killing.

• AYLESBURY British breed originally from the town of the same name, this is a white duck with light, tender flesh.

• BARBARY DUCK French breed. Raised in the wild; firmer and leaner flesh with a slightly musky flavour.

• GRESSINGHAM A British wild-domestic crossbreed between the mallard and a domestic duck.

• LONG ISLAND Descending from the Peking duck, this is the popular American duck.

• NANTES DUCK (or Challans duck – after the name of the marshland where it is raised in a semi-wild state). Smaller but fatter, with fine, delicately flavoured flesh.

• NORFOLK British duck from the county of the same name, a primary area for rearing poultry.

• PEKING DUCK A small white duck crossed with the Aylesbury in Britain and the bird from which the Long Island duck has developed in America.

Originally bred only in the Imperial Palace in China before being taken to America. Very fine, with delicate flesh.

• ROUEN DUCK The excellent Rouen duck, in particular the Duclair (named after a village in Normandy), is mainly sold locally. Very fine flesh, tinged with red, with a special flavour due to the fact that the bird is smothered, not bled, so that the blood remains in the muscles.

Modern breeding methods have made duck leaner and more widely available in large supermarkets, as whole birds or in portions and prepared breast fillets. In French cookery, the term *canard* applies to birds two to four months old. *Caneton* (duckling) is used for younger birds and in grande cuisine. The female duck (*cane*) is smaller but plumper than the drake; it is preferred for roasts because its meat is finer and tastier. A female duckling is called a *canette*.

Duck's eggs, which have a greenish-white shell and weigh 75–125 g (3–4½ oz), are very popular in the Far East. However, because they often carry salmonella bacteria, duck's eggs should only be eaten cooked.

■ **Cooking methods** Very tender birds: roast on a spit; tender birds: roast in the oven (for both these methods, the cooked meat should be pale pink); less tender birds: braise or roast (stuffed), and garnish with onions, turnips, olives and acid fruits; very large birds: use for pâtés; ballotines and cassoulets.

Choose for preference a fairly young bird with a flexible beak; the pinion flesh as well as the skin should be supple and the breast plump. When a duckling is killed too young, the breastbone is still soft and the flesh is not developed sufficiently. The current tendency in restaurants is to use ducklings, although some preparations can only be successfully made with more mature birds. The cold dishes using duck are the same as those made with roasting chicken.

■ **Pressed duck** Created at the beginning of the 19th century by a restaurateur from Rouen called Méchenet, the recipe for pressed duck owed much of its immediate success to the Duke of Chartres, who commended it highly in Paris. When the renowned cook Frédéric took over the restaurant La Tour d'Argent, he began numbering all the pressed ducks that he served, intending to make the dish the speciality of his restaurant. By the end of 1996, a million had been served; No. 328 was served to Edward VII, then Prince of Wales, in 1890; No. 33,642 was provided for Theodore Roosevelt and No. 253,652 for Charlie Chaplin.

Léon Daudet, in *Paris vécu*, describes the cook at work: 'You ought to have seen Frédéric with his monocle, his greying whiskers, his calm demeanour, carving his plump quack-quack, trussed and already flamed, throwing it into the pan, preparing the sauce, salting and peppering like Claude Monet's paintings, with the seriousness of a judge and the precision of a mathematician, and opening up, with a sure hand, in advance, every perspective of taste.'

Pressed duck is prepared in front of the customer. Thin slices of breast (*aiguillettes*) are cut from the bird and placed in a dish of well-reduced red wine standing on a hotplate. The rest of the duck, except for the legs, which are served grilled (broiled), is pressed in a special screw press. The juice obtained is flavoured with Cognac, thickened with butter and poured over the *aiguillettes*, which finish cooking in the sauce.

■ **Wild duck** There are many breeds of wild duck. The most common species include the mallard (*colvert*), also the largest and with exquisite flesh. The male has green and grey plumage with a touch of brown and white. The female is brown. Practically sedentary from October to March, the mallard migrates south only in very cold weather. Teal (*sarcelle*) is another popular duck of which there are several types.

Other wild ducks that are well known in gastronomy include the shoveler duck (*souchet*), which has a spatulate beak, the gadwall (*chipeau*), which is grey and white with a brown border on the wings (in eastern France), the baldpate (*siffleur*), which is a smaller, coastal species, and the pintail (*pilet*), which is less highly regarded. The sheldrake (*tadorne*) and the merganser (*harle*) are now protected species.

Generally speaking, only the legs and fillets of wild ducks are eaten (this is why one bird is required for every two servings). These game birds are not hung, but used fresh: young tender birds are roasted on a spit or in the oven; older birds are prepared as a salmis or fricassee. Dishes made using domestic duck are also applicable to wild duck.

The shooting of wild duck is subject to regulation in the same way as other game. In Britain, mallard and teal are in season from September to January, and best in November and December.

RECIPES

Amiens duck pâté

• *Preparing the pastry* Spread 500 g (1 lb 2 oz, 4½ cups) plain (all-purpose) flour out on a board or work surface, make a well in the centre and put in 1 teaspoon table salt. Break an egg into the well and mix with the salt, then add 1 tablespoon olive oil. Soften 125 g (4½ oz, ½ cup) lard (shortening) by kneading if necessary, then mix it with the liquid part in the centre of the flour. Then blend the flour and lard, without moistening at all. When the pastry is well blended, spread it out and sprinkle with about 1½ tablespoons cold water. Roll the pastry together into one lump and leave to rest in a cool place for at least 2 hours before use. (This pastry has the advantage of rising very little during cooking.)

• *Preparing the duck* To make this pâté, use only young ducklings, which can be cooked very quickly. Pluck, draw and singe the bird, carefully removing any innards that may remain. Cut off the wing tips just below the first joint from the shoulder. Cut off the feet at the joint. Season the inside and outside with spiced salt. Cut up a side of streaky (slab) bacon and fry over a low heat in a little cooking fat. Remove it and brown the duck in the fat over a low heat, turning it so that it browns all over. Drain the duck on a dish and leave to cool before making the pâté.

• *Preparing the forcemeat* À gratin forcemeat is always used for this pâté. The ingredients may vary, depending on what is available, and may include veal or poultry liver, in addition to the liver from the duck. Melt 150 g (5 oz, 2/3 cup) finely chopped fat over a low heat and use it to brown 500 g (1 lb 2 oz) veal or poultry liver, which has been suitably trimmed and coarsely diced. When the liver is well browned, add 1 chopped onion and 2 chopped shallots, and season with 1 tablespoon spiced salt, some chopped thyme and bay leaves. Cover and leave for a few minutes on a low heat. Remove and allow to cool, then pound the mixture in a mortar and pass through a fine sieve.

• *Making the pâté* Divide the pastry into two equal portions and roll one half into an oval about 1 cm (1/2 in) thick so it is a little longer and wider than the duck. Place this pastry in the centre of a metal baking sheet or ovenproof pie dish that has been lightly moistened with a little cold water. Next, spread a quarter of the forcemeat in the middle of the pastry and lay the duck, on its back, on top; season the duck with more spiced salt and a little cayenne pepper. Completely cover the duck with the remaining forcemeat. Roll out the remaining pastry in an oval shape and place over the duck, sealing it well at the edges. Crimp up the sides, garnish the top with some pieces of pastry cut into fancy shapes and make an opening in the centre for the steam to escape. Finally, glaze the pastry with beaten egg. Bake the pâté in a preheated oven at 220°C (425°F, gas 7) for 1 1/4–1 1/2 hours, depending on the size.

braised duck

Singe and truss a duck weighing about 2 kg (4 1/2 lb). Put it into an ovenproof braising pan lined with fresh bacon rind and containing a carrot and a medium-sized onion cut into rounds and tossed in butter. Add a bouquet garni, season and cook, covered, for 15 minutes, browning the duck on all sides. Moisten with 100 ml (4 fl oz, 7 tablespoons) white wine, reduce and add 300 ml (1/2 pint, 1 1/4 cups) chicken stock. Boil, then transfer to a preheated oven at 220°C (425°F, gas 7) and cook, covered, for about 1 hour. Drain the duck, untruss it, arrange on a serving dish and surround with fresh garden peas. Sprinkle with a few spoonfuls of the braising juices, reduced and strained, and serve the remainder in a sauceboat (gravy boat).

The same method is used for duck *à l'alsacienne*, which is surrounded with braised sauerkraut and a garnish of streaky (slab) bacon and Strasbourg sausages; duck *à la chipolata*, which is garnished with braised chestnuts, small glazed onions, lean

rashers (slices) of blanched bacon and chipolata sausages cooked in butter; and duck with olives, which uses green olives, stoned (pitted) and blanched.

braised Rouen duck

Rouen duck may be braised, although this is an unusual way of cooking it. It may be prepared *à la bigarade* (see *Seville orange*), with cherries – use stoned (pitted) morello cherries and dilute the pan juices with Madeira; with champagne – dilute the pan juices with 300 ml (1/2 pint, 1 1/4 cups) dry champagne and, if liked, a few tablespoons of thickened veal stock; or *au chambertin* – finish off the cooking with 125 g (4 1/2 oz) blanched and fried larding bacon and mushroom caps tossed in butter.

cold duck pâté

This is made using a boned duck, stuffed with *à gratin* forcemeat to which foie gras and truffles have been added, either *en pantin* (see *pâté pantin*), like cold lark pâté, or in a mould, like cold timbale of woodcock.

duck à l'agenaise

Singe a duck weighing about 2 kg (4 1/2 lb). Season the inside with salt and pepper, stuff with a dozen or so stoned (pitted) prunes soaked in Armagnac and sew up. Brown the duck in a pan containing 25 g (1 oz, 2 tablespoons) butter, sprinkle with a glass of Armagnac and set alight. Cover the pan and cook for about 40 minutes. Meanwhile, poach the grated zest of half an orange for 5 minutes in half a bottle of Bordeaux wine, together with 2 cloves, a little grated nutmeg, 5 or 6 crushed peppercorns, a sprig of thyme and a bay leaf. In a saucepan, brown 100 g (4 oz, 1/2 cup) very small lardons of smoked bacon, 2 tablespoons diced carrot, 1 tablespoon diced celery and a large chopped onion, adding a knob of butter if required. Sprinkle with 1 tablespoon flour, then add the orange-flavoured wine, having strained it. Season with salt and pepper, stir well and cook slowly for 20 minutes. Drain the duck and keep it hot. Pour the wine sauce into the juices from the duck and add a small glass of Armagnac and about 20 stoned (pitted) prunes. Reheat the sauce. Garnish the duck with prunes and cover with the sauce.

duck à l'orange Lasserre

Prepare a Nantes duck weighing about 2 kg (4 1/2 lb), brown it in butter, then cook gently for 45 minutes. Sprinkle with 100 ml (4 fl oz, 7 tablespoons) Grand Marnier and leave to cook for a further 5 minutes. Remove the duck from the pan and keep hot. Strain the liquor and pour it into a saucepan, adding 1 tablespoon each vinegar and caster (superfine) sugar, the juice of 3 oranges and 100 ml (4 fl oz, 7 tablespoons) each of mandarin and apricot liqueur to make the sauce. Peel 6 oranges down to the flesh, cut them into slices, removing all fibres and seeds, and place them in a frying pan with a few spoonfuls of the sauce. Heat without boiling. Now carve the duck, arrange it on a hot dish and surround with slices of orange. Cover with some of the sauce and serve the remainder in a sauceboat (gravy boat).

duck suprêmes with truffles

This is made with the breast fillets (suprêmes) of a Rouen duck. Roast the duck in a preheated oven at 200°C (400°F, gas 6) for about 30 minutes, so it is still slightly pink. Cut the fillets into large slices and arrange them in a timbale mould together with thick slices of truffle which have been tossed in butter. Keep hot. Roughly chop the remaining carcass and trimmings, moisten with Madeira, port or sherry, and reduce. Add a few tablespoons of reduced demi-glace and boil for a few seconds, then strain. Return to the boil, then add 1 tablespoon flamed brandy and 2 tablespoons butter. Pour the sauce over the fillets.

duck with crystallized turnips and cider

Make a stock with the roast giblets from a 2 kg (4½ lb) duck, 1 sliced onion and 1 sliced carrot. Add 1 litre (1¾ pints, 4⅓ cups) cider, 1 apple and 2 large turnips, peeled and cut into pieces. When the liquid has reduced to half its original volume, add 1 litre (1¾ pints, 4⅓ cups) clear stock and cook gently for 20 minutes. Pour the liquid through a strainer. Roast the duck in a preheated oven at 200°C (400°F, gas 6), lying on each leg for 10 minutes and on its back for 5 minutes. Remove from the oven and allow to rest. In a sauté pan, heat 50 g (2 oz, ¼ cup) butter, add a pinch of sugar and 24 small turnips and fry until golden. Put the duck in a cast-iron casserole with the turnips and stock and simmer for 10 minutes. Thicken the sauce with 50 g (2 oz, ¼ cup) butter and add 1 bunch of coriander (cilantro), chopped, and a dash of cider.

duck with peas

Cut 200 g (7 oz) larding bacon into large dice, and blanch. Brown these, together with 12 small onions, in butter in a casserole. Remove the onions and diced bacon from the pan and replace with a trussed Nantes duck. Brown the duck on all sides and then drain, retaining the juices. Dilute the pan juices with 100 ml (4 fl oz, 7 tablespoons) dry white wine and 250 ml (8 fl oz, 1 cup) veal or chicken stock and put the duck into this liquor. Add 1 litre (1¾ pints, 4⅓ cups) shelled fresh garden peas, the onions, the bacon, and a bouquet garni. Season and add 2 teaspoons sugar. Simmer gently with the lid on for 35–40 minutes. Drain the duck and arrange on a serving dish, surrounding it with the peas. Reduce the pan juices and pour over the duck. Arrange a lettuce, shredded into a chiffonnade or cut into quarters, on the peas. Alternatively, cook the duck in the same way but leave it slightly underdone. Add 1 litre (1¾ pints, 4⅓ cups) fresh garden peas cooked à la française and simmer gently for a few minutes.

jellied fillets of Rouen duck à l'orange ♦

Cook a 2 kg (4½ lb) duck for about 35 minutes in a preheated oven at 240°C (475°F, gas 9) so that it remains slightly pink. Remove the legs and cut the breast fillets diagonally into slices, leaving them attached at the base. Coat the breast fillets with a brown chaud-froid sauce à l'orange. Glaze with a aspic and chill.

Prepare a mousse using the flesh off the legs, adding diced truffles. Fill tiny dome-shaped moulds (or a parfait mould) with the mousse and place in the refrigerator to set.

From a loaf, cut croûtons to the size of the moulds and butter them, then toast or fry until crisp and golden. Cool. Turn the set mousses out on to the croûtons. Arrange the fillets of duck on plates, taking care to keep the tops of the slices neatly closed together. Pour a few spoonfuls of half-set aspic on to the plates and arrange some orange segments as a garnish. Garnish the duck fillets with shreds of pared orange zest and add a mousse-topped croûton to each plate. Chill before serving.

mallard with green peppercorns

Select a mallard duck weighing about 1.4 kg (3 lb). Season the inside and outside with salt and pepper and place in a roasting pan. Sprinkle with 2 tablespoons oil and cook for 30 minutes in a preheated oven at 200°C (400°F, gas 6). Then cover the dish with foil to keep the duck hot. Peel 2 good-sized Granny Smith apples, cut them into halves, and remove the seeds and cores. Cook in a preheated oven at 180°C (350°F, gas 4) for about 10 minutes. For the sauce, pour 5 tablespoons white wine and 1 tablespoon Armagnac into a saucepan, and reduce by about two-thirds. Add the juice from a can of green peppercorns and 4 tablespoons stock (duck or other poultry). Reduce again for 2–3 minutes. Add 200 ml (7 fl oz, ¾ cup) single (light) cream, lightly season with salt and cook until the sauce achieves a uniform consistency. Check the seasoning and at the last moment add 4 teaspoons port and 1½ tablespoons green peppercorns. Cut off the breast fillets of the duck and arrange on a serving dish. Cover with the sauce and garnish with the apple, cut into quarters.

roast duck

Season the duck with salt and pepper both inside and out, truss and roast in the oven or on a spit. A duckling weighing about 1.25 kg (2¾ lb) should be cooked in a preheated oven at 220°C (425°F, gas 7) for 35 minutes, or for 40–45 minutes on a spit.

roast duck with peaches

Roast the duck. Meanwhile, peel some medium-sized peaches and poach them whole in a light syrup. When the duck is roasted, drain it and keep it hot. Dilute the pan juices with a little peach syrup and reduce to the consistency of a sauce. Add the peaches to the sauce to flavour them, heat them through and arrange them around the duck. Serve the sauce in a sauceboat (gravy boat).

roast duck with maple syrup

Peel 2 Williams (Bartlett) pears, cut in half lengthways and remove the cores. In a frying pan, combine 50 g (2 oz, ¼ cup) caster (superfine) sugar with 250 ml (8 fl oz, 1 cup) dry white wine and the juice of 2 lemons and 2 oranges. Bring to the boil. Add the pears, 250 ml (8 fl oz, 1 cup) pure maple syrup and a pinch of ground allspice. Simmer until the pears have softened, then remove them from the liquor and put aside in a warm place. Reserve the maple syrup liquor.

Meanwhile, wash 2 ducks. Prick the skin of the breasts with a fork and season. Place in an ovenproof dish and roast in a preheated oven at 200°C (400°F, gas 6) for 15 minutes. Peel and chop 2 carrots, 2 onions, 3 celery sticks, 1 salsify and 2 garlic cloves. Add to the ducks with 2 cloves, 2 bay leaves and 1 bunch of thyme, chopped. Reduce the oven temperature to 150°C (300°F, gas 2). Skim the excess fat from the dish and baste the ducks every 10 minutes with the reserved maple syrup mixture. As soon as the vegetables begin to turn slightly brown, pour in 500 ml (17 fl oz, 2 cups) chicken stock. Continue the cooking process (1½ hours in all), basting regularly with the juices in the dish. When the ducks are cooked, remove them from the dish and put aside in a warm place. Remove as much fat as possible from the liquid in the dish, leaving the duck juices. Put the vegetables and juice in a smaller saucepan and heat. Add 1 tablespoon tomato purée (paste) and cook for 2–3 minutes. Add a further 500 ml (17 fl oz, 2 cups) chicken stock and any remaining maple syrup mixture. Simmer for 15 minutes and strain. Bone the ducks. Place the pieces of duck on a serving dish and garnish with slices of pears, arranged in a fan shape. Pour the cooking juices over the pieces of duck.

Rouen duck en chemise

Remove the breastbone from a Rouen duck. Prepare a stuffing by frying 1 heaped tablespoon chopped onion with 125 g (4½ oz, ⅔ cup) diced bacon, without browning the onion. Add an entire duck's liver and 2 or 3 additional duck or chicken livers cut into thin fillets, salt and pepper, a pinch of allspice and some chopped parsley. Cook all the ingredients in butter, cool, and blend in a food processor. Stuff the duck with this mixture, truss and roast in a preheated oven at 240°C (475°F, gas 9) for 8–12 minutes. Leave to cool.

To follow the traditional method, place the duck, head downwards, in a large pork bladder that has been soaked in cold water. Tie the opening with string and poach in clear braising stock for 45 minutes. Arrange the duck, still in the bladder, on a serving dish.

Alternatively, the duck can be cooked wrapped in a piece of muslin (cheesecloth) or a white table napkin with both ends tied, like a galantine. It is then served unwrapped, surrounded with orange quarters. Serve rouennaise sauce separately.

Rouen duck in port

Cook a trussed Rouen duck in butter for 30–40 minutes, so that the flesh remains slightly pink. Drain the duck and arrange it on a long dish. Prepare the sauce as follows: dilute the pan juices with 250 ml (8 fl oz, 1 cup) port, add 250 ml (8 fl oz, 1 cup) thickened brown veal stock, boil for a few moments, add some butter and strain. Pour a few spoonfuls of the sauce over the duck and serve the rest separately in a sauceboat (gravy boat). The port can be replaced by Banyuls, Frontignan, Madeira, sweet sherry or any other dessert wine.

Rouen duck (or duckling) soufflé

This very stylish dish is made with 2 birds, the larger to be served and the smaller to make the forcemeat. Roast a trussed Rouen duck in a preheated oven at 200°C (400°F, gas 6) for 10–15 minutes; the meat should still be very rare. Remove the breast fillets, which should be kept for the final garnish, and remove the breastbone, so that the carcass forms a hollow case. Season the inside with salt, pepper and spices, and sprinkle with a spoonful of brandy. Fill the carcass with a forcemeat made from the raw meat of the smaller duck, boned and prepared as for mousseline forcemeat, 150 g (5 oz) raw foie gras and the livers of the 2 ducks used. Stuff the carcass so it is re-formed into its original shape. Cover the duck with buttered greaseproof (wax) paper and tie it so that it will hold the forcemeat during cooking. Place the stuffed duck on a baking sheet, coat with melted butter and roast in a preheated oven at 150°C (300°F, gas 2) for 30–35 minutes. Remove the greaseproof paper and arrange the duck on a serving dish.

Make some tartlet cases from short pastry (basic pie dough), bake blind, heap with a salpicon of truffles and mushrooms bound with concentrated Madeira sauce, and cover each with a slice of duck breast fillet and a thick slice of truffle heated in butter. Arrange the tartlets around the duck. Serve with rouennaise sauce or Périgueux sauce.

Instead of being used to fill the tartlets, the duck fillets can be cut into thin slices and embedded in the mousseline forcemeat in the duck carcass.

The same filling can be used to make Rouen duck mousses and mousselines. The former are made in large charlotte moulds and the latter in small individual moulds. They are poached in a bain marie in the oven. The forcemeat can also be used for duck soufflé en timbale: put it in buttered soufflé timbale moulds and bake as for other soufflés.

Jellied fillets of Rouen duck à l'orange, see page 433.

wild duck à la tyrolienne

Stew some cooking apples, adding a little cinnamon and mace, to form a hot apple purée. Stuff a wild duck with this purée, tie securely and place the duck on a spit for roasting. Boil 2 tablespoons red wine vinegar together with a small knob of butter (about the size of a walnut), ½ teaspoon caster (superfine) sugar and a few grains of coarsely ground pepper. Baste the duck constantly with this preparation while it is cooking on the spit, placing a small pan beneath to catch the juices. Cooking should take about 30–35 minutes. When finished, take the duck off the spit, untruss and arrange on a dish. Strain the collected juices into a saucepan and heat, adding 1½ teaspoons redcurrant jelly. Finally pour this sauce over the duck.

wild duck à la Walter Scott

Draw, singe and truss a wild duck. Cook in a pre-heated oven at 220°C (425°F, gas 7). Meanwhile, fry the duck's liver in butter, mash and mix it with 20 g (¾ oz) foie gras. Fry 2 croûtons in clarified butter and spread them with the liver paste. Core 2 apples, stud each with 4 cloves and cook as for apples bonne femme. Dilute some Dundee marmalade with 2 tablespoons whisky and heat gently. When the duck is cooked, arrange it on a serving dish. Remove the cloves from the apples and place the latter on the croûtons, then pour the marmalade into the holes in the apples. Arrange the croûtons around the duck. Serve the juice in a sauceboat (gravy boat), without skimming off the fat.

wild duck au Chambertin

Roast the duck for 18–20 minutes in a preheated oven at 240°C (475°F, gas 9) or fry over a brisk heat, so that the flesh stays slightly pink. Arrange on a serving dish and cover with Chambertin sauce to which the pan juices have been added. Garnish with mushrooms and, if liked, with strips of truffle.

DUGLÉRÉ, ADOLPHE French chef (born Bordeaux, 1805; died Paris, 1884). A pupil of Carême, he became head of the kitchens of the Rothschild family and later managed the restaurant Les Frères Provençaux. In 1866 he became head chef at the Café Anglais, with which his name is always associated. He is described as 'a taciturn artist who revelled in contemplative isolation', and his culinary creations made the Café Anglais one of the most famous restaurants in Paris during the Second Empire. His creations included potage Germiny, Anna potatoes, sole and sea bream *à la Dugléré* and soufflé *à l'anglaise*. It was Dugléré who drew up the menu for the historic dinner of the 'Three Emperors'. Among the illustrious guests who attended were Alexander II (the Russian emperor), his son (the future Alexander III), Wilhelm I of Prussia (the German emperor) and Bismarck. The dinner, it is said, cost 400 francs a head!

7 June 1867
Menu for the dinner
arranged by Adolphe Dugléré,
The 'Mozart of cuisine'

SOUPS
Impératrice and Fontanges
HORS D'OEUVRE
Soufflés à la reine
REMOVES
Fillets of sole à la vénitienne
Escalopes of turbot au gratin
Saddle of mutton with Breton purée
ENTRÉES
Chicken à la portugaise
Hot quail pâté
Lobster à la parisienne
Champagne sorbets
ROASTS
Duckling à la rouennaise
Canapés of ortolan
ENTREMETS
Aubergines à l'espagnole
Asparagus spears
Cassolettes princesse
DESSERTS
Bombes glacées
WINES
Retour de l'Inde Madeira, sherry,
Château-d'Yquem 1847,
Château-Margaux 1847, Château-Lafite 1847,
Château-Latour 1848,
Chambertin 1846, Champagne Roederer

RECIPES

bass à la Dugléré

Butter a shallow flameproof dish. Peel and chop 1 large onion, 1–2 shallots, a small bunch of parsley, a garlic clove and, if liked (it is not traditional), 150 g (5 oz, 1⅔ cups) button mushrooms. Skin, seed and chop 4 tomatoes. Spread all these ingredients on the bottom of the dish, then add a sprig of thyme and half a bay leaf. Scale a 1 kg (2¼ lb) bass and cut into sections. Arrange these sections in the dish, dot with knobs of butter, moisten with 200 ml (7 fl oz, ¾ cup) dry white wine and cover with foil. Bring to the boil, then transfer to a preheated oven at 220°C (425°F, gas 7) and cook for 12–15 minutes. Drain the pieces of bass and arrange on a serving dish in the original shape of the fish.

Remove the thyme and bay leaf from the oven dish and add 2 tablespoons velouté made with fish stock. Reduce by one-third, then add 50 g (2 oz, ¼ cup) butter. (The velouté and butter may be replaced by 1 tablespoon beurre manié.) Pour the sauce over the fish and sprinkle with chopped parsley.

Sea bream and brill may be prepared and served in the same way.

sole à la Dugléré

Skin and clean a sole weighing about 500 g (18 oz) and prepare the ingredients as for bass *à la Dugléré*, but halving the quantities. Cook in the same way, but reduce the cooking time in the oven to 7 minutes. Drain the sole and keep it hot. Reduce the cooking liquid and thicken it with butter and velouté sauce made with fish stock.

DUMAINE, ALEXANDRE French chef (born Digoin, 1895; died Digoin, 1974). At the age of 12 he became an apprentice at a hotel in Paray-le-Monial, and gradually worked his way up in the profession, eventually becoming *grande toque* (head chef) in such famous establishments as the Carlton (in Vichy, then in Cannes), the Café de Paris and the Hotel Louvois in Paris, and the Oasis Hotel at Biskra. In 1932 he opened a restaurant at Saulieu, which, with the help of his wife, Jeanne, became a gastronomic shrine. The Hôtel de la Côte-d'Or was, with Point at Vienne and Pic at Valence, one of the three outstanding centres of provincial cuisine in France from 1930 to 1950. After retiring in 1964, Dumaine collaborated with Henry Clos-Jouve in producing *Ma cuisine*, a book of recipes and various reminiscences, from which the following recipes for braised beef and a coffee and chocolate gâteau are taken.

RECIPES

braised beef
Brown a joint of beef in a large pan. Remove the joint and brown a large mirepoix of carrots and onions in the fat from the meat. Brown some small pieces of bone from a loin of veal and some chicken bones in butter. Put into a braising pan with the skimmed mirepoix, the joint of beef, a blanched pig's foot and some crushed tomatoes. Season with salt and pepper, add 250 ml (8 fl oz, 1 cup) white wine and boil gently until all the liquid has evaporated. Then add a bouquet garni and sufficient red wine and stock (1 part wine to 2 parts stock) to cover three-quarters of the beef. Cover and cook gently for 3 hours, turning the meat occasionally.

gâteau 'le prélat'
Prepare 1 litre (1¾ pints, 4⅓ cups) strong, lightly sweetened coffee, flavoured with white rum. Allow to cool. Beat together 2 whole eggs and 6 egg yolks, add 300 g (11 oz, 1½ cups) sugar boiled to the thread stage and whisk until cold. Blend in 300 g (11 oz, 2 cups) melted bitter (semisweet) chocolate pieces, some grated orange zest and 750 ml (1¼ pints, 3¼ cups) lightly whipped double (heavy) cream. Mix well.

Cover the bottom of a buttered rectangular mould with sponge fingers (ladyfingers) soaked in a little of the cold coffee. Cover with some of the chocolate mixture. Top with another layer of soaked sponge fingers and continue layering until the mould is full, finishing with a layer of sponge fingers. Place in the refrigerator for 24 hours before turning out of the mould. Melt 450 g (1 lb) dark chocolate and mix with 150 g (5 oz, ⅔ cup) butter and 2 tablespoons light oil. Coat the gâteau with this mixture.

DUMAS, ALEXANDRE French author (born Villers-Cotterêts, 1802; died Dieppe, 1870). In 1869 Dumas, best known as the author of *The Three Musketeers* and other historical romances, accepted an assignment from a young publisher, Alphonse Lemerre, to write a *Grand Dictionnaire de cuisine*. To find the peace and quiet necessary to compile such a monumental work (1152 pages), Dumas retired to Roscoff (Finisterre) with his cook Marie. The work was completed in March 1870, a few weeks before his death, and was published in 1872. It is not considered to be a very reliable work from a strictly culinary point of view, in spite of the friendly collaboration of Joseph Vuillemot, a pupil of Carême, who published a revised and abridged version in 1882. But in spite of its errors, its gaps and its trenchant opinions, the work is written in an alert and amusing style and is full of anecdotes.

Dumas was a great habitué of Parisian restaurants: he had his own private room at the Maison Dorée, and attended the 'Bixio dinners' at Brébant-Vachette, the Rocher de Cancale, the Jockey Club where his protégé Jules Gouffé presided, and the Restaurant de France in the Place de la Madeleine. Here his friend Vuillemot gave a famous dinner in his honour which included lobster *à la Porthos*', 'fillet of beef Monte-Cristo', 'salad *à la Dumas*' and *gorenflot* (rum-soaked sponge cake).

Dumas made it a point of honour to dress the salad himself: 'I place in a salad bowl one hard-boiled egg yolk for every two persons. I pound it in oil to make a paste. I then add chervil, crushed thyme, crushed anchovies, chopped gherkins, the chopped whites of the hard-boiled eggs, salt and pepper. I mix it all with a good vinegar, then I put the salad into the salad bowl. Then I call a servant and ask him to toss the salad. When he has finished, I scatter a pinch of paprika over it. It remains only to be served.' Another famous Dumas salad was made with truffles 'peeled with a silver knife' and seasoned, according to the mood of the host, with champagne, a liqueur or almond milk.

DUMPLING A ball of dough, originally savoury and served as an accompaniment to meat or as a dessert. Sweet versions are also prepared.

A simple, satisfying food, dumplings were boiled and served to extend small amounts of meat. Originally made by shaping small portions from a batch of bread dough before specific mixtures were developed using flour, cereals, pulses, stale bread, potatoes or cheese, sometimes with raising agent added or enriched with fat in the form of suet, were developed. Local ingredients and methods are used across Europe to make a variety of large or small dumplings, plain or flavoured with herbs, vegetables, spices or other ingredients.

Germany (particularly Bavaria) and Austria in particular are known for excellent examples, along with Czechoslovakia, Poland and Hungary. Fresh or dry bread; mashed or grated raw potatoes; soft cheese; or semolina are just as likely to be used as flour and the dumplings may be bite-sized or large enough for slicing into portions. The tradition in Czechoslovakian kitchens was to shape the bread-based dumpling mixture into a long, thick sausage on clean napkins and suspend it over simmering water or broth. Instead of a knife, the dumpling was traditionally sliced with string, rather like cutting through a cheese with a wire. Spinach, herbs, caraway or bacon may be added for flavour and the dough enriched with butter or eggs. Finely chopped liver flavours *leberknodel* served Austrian-style in light broth or as a main dish in Germany.

Dumplings are closely related to pasta. Italian gnocchi are good examples of small dumplings usually grouped with pasta and the *spatzle* of Germany and Austria, made from batter simmered until set in finger noodles, also hover between the two descriptions. Polish plain or filled dumplings are also very similar to gnocchi or filled pasta.

In Britain dumplings were originally made with either a bread or suet dough and served with boiled beef and carrots and pease pudding. Suet dough became more widely used, with regional variations on the basic dough developing. Some doughs were unleavened, others used local cereals such as oats. As well as being served with boiled meat, dumplings are traditional with soups and stews. Sweet versions are also prepared, no longer as simple accompaniments but as dishes in their own right. An apple dumpling (an apple encased in pastry) is made with suet crust and boiled or with shortcrust pastry and baked. Large fruit dumplings are not the only sweet option – they may be yeasted and cooked in milk; filled with small whole fruit (plums or cherries) or jam and simmered in water.

In the United States, dumplings can accompany roast and boiled meat dishes. Made with flour, baking powder, egg and milk, they are shaped into walnut-sized balls and simmered very gently in vegetable soups, stews and beef and poultry consommés. They may also contain cornmeal, potato purée, grated cheese or breadcrumbs. Sweet-pastry dumplings sometimes made with a yeast dough are poached in fruit juice and served with compotes, fruit purées, melted butter or cream. They are sometimes stuffed with fruit.

The name dumpling is also used for Oriental specialities, such as the small filled dumplings of Chinese cookery, related more closely to pasta than to European-style dumplings (see *dim sum*).

DUNAND The surname of two Swiss cooks, father and son, also spelt Dunan and Dunant. The father was in charge of the kitchens of the Prince of Condé. His son inherited the post and, in 1793, followed the prince into exile. He returned to France 12 years later and entered the service of Napoleon I. Chicken Marengo is attributed to him even though the French victory over the Austrians took place in 1800, and Dunand remained in the service of the Prince of Condé until 1805! On the other hand, it is known that Napoleon greatly enjoyed his *crépinettes*.

On the fall of the Empire, Dunand went into the service of the Duc de Berry, but resumed his post with the emperor during the Hundred Days.

DUNDEE CAKE A Scottish fruit cake. This is a light cake, not as dark as the classic British Christmas or wedding cake, but rich with butter and still containing sufficient dried fruit to keep well for 2–3 months. Flavoured with ground almonds and candied peel, the cake's defining feature is a slightly domed top studded with neat concentric circles of whole blanched almonds. The almonds are arranged on the uncooked cake to become a rich golden brown when baked. Dundee cake is thought to have originated in the 19th century, in the city of the same name, where it was made by Keiller, the company known for orange marmalade. The leftover orange peel from the marmalade was used up in the cakes, the manufacture of which provided work when seasonal Seville oranges were not available and marmalade was out of production. The commercial cakes were glazed with an orange syrup while still warm. Later versions of the cake were sold in decorative tins and were popular alternatives to Christmas cake.

RECIPE

Dundee cake

Cream 225 g (8 oz, 1 cup) butter with 225 g (8 oz, 1¼ cups) caster (superfine) sugar and the grated zest of 1 orange until pale and soft. Sift 225 g (8 oz, 2 cups) self-raising flour with 100 g (4 oz, 1 cup) plain (all-purpose) flour. Beat 4 eggs with 1–2 drops oil of bitter almonds. Stir the eggs into the butter mixture, adding the occasional spoonful of the sifted flours to prevent the mixture from curdling. Mix 225 g (8 oz, 1½ cups) each of raisins and sultanas (white raisins) with 100 g (4 oz, ¾ cup) chopped mixed candied orange, lemon and citrus peel. Add 100 g (4 oz, 1 cup) chopped blanched almonds, 100 g (4 oz, 1 cup) ground almonds and a spoonful of the measured flours, then mix well. Fold the remaining flour into the cake mixture, then stir in the fruit and almond mixture.

Line and grease a 20 cm (8 in) round deep cake tin (pan) and turn the mixture into it. Spread the mixture out evenly. Cover the top with whole blanched almonds, starting with a circle around the edge and working in towards the middle. Press the nuts lightly into the mixture, placing them close together as they separate slightly when the cake rises during baking. Bake in a preheated oven at 160°C (325°F, gas 3) for about 4 hours. Cover the top of the cake loosely with foil, if necessary, to prevent the nuts from becoming too dark. Insert a clean metal skewer into the middle of the cake to check if it is cooked: if the skewer is clean the cake is cooked; if it has sticky mixture on it, the cake is not ready, continue baking for 15 minutes before testing again.

Leave the cake to cool in the tin (pan) for 30 minutes, then turn it out on to a wire rack and leave to cool completely. Wrap the cake in grease-proof (wax) paper and place in an airtight container, then leave to mature for 2–4 weeks before serving.

DUNDEE MARMALADE British preserve made from bitter Seville oranges by Keiller, a company in Dundee, Scotland. Mrs Keiller first created the sharp-sweet preserve in 1797. Her son set up the company and sold the preserve in its characteristic white pots. By the mid to late 19th century the company was making 1.5 million jars of marmalade annually.

DURAND A Parisian restaurant that was situated in the Place de la Madeleine. In the 1860s, according to A. Luchet, it was considered to be 'the third wonder in the art of good living' (after the Café Riche and the Café Hardy). It was frequented by writers and politicians, notably Boulanger, Anatole France and Émile Zola (who wrote *J'accuse* there). The chef Voiron created Mornay sauce in this restaurant.

DURAND, CHARLES French chef (born Alès, 1766; died Nîmes, 1854). Called 'the Carême of Provençal cooking', he was chef to the bishops of Alès, Nîmes and Montpellier before opening restaurants in Alès (1790) and Nîmes (1800). Above all, he was responsible for popularizing French regional cuisine at a time when it was practically unknown elsewhere. *Le Cuisinier Durand* (1803) is a collection of authentic Provençal recipes that enabled *brandade* (a dish of salt cod) and other specialities of the south to be enjoyed in Paris.

DURIAN A tree that is widely cultivated in Southeast Asia, especially in Vietnam and the Philippines, for its fruit. Durian fruits are round or oval, up to 20 cm (8 in) in diameter and weighing up to 5 kg (11 lb), with a hard greenish rind covered with large thorns. The flesh is whitish or coffee-coloured with a creamy texture and a strong, unpleasant and distinctive smell that becomes nauseating when the fruit is overripe. The flesh contains large seeds that are edible when cooked (baked or roasted, when they may be eaten with rice).

The fruit is ready to eat when the skin begins to crack and is usually eaten raw either as an hors d'oeuvre or as a dessert. Its flavour is complex and contradictory to those unfamiliar with it: a mixture of sweet, fruity characteristics with 'savoury' tones, almost cheese-like but sometimes compared to garlic or cooked onion because of the aftertaste. It may also be eaten as a compote with sugar and fresh cream, and in Java it is made into a fruit jelly with coconut milk. Durian is also used to flavour confectionery, such as little boiled sweets (candies) in which its flavour is evident, but less intense. The large shiny seeds may be prepared in the same way as chestnuts.

DUROC A dish dedicated to General Duroc, a soldier at the time of the Empire. It consists of small joints of meat or sautéed poultry garnished with new potatoes browned in butter, covered with crushed tomatoes and coated with chasseur sauce.

DURUM WHEAT A type of hard wheat with a high gluten content, valued particularly for making semolina and pasta.

DUSE A garnish named in honour of the great Italian actress, Eleonora Duse. It consists of fresh green beans cooked in butter, with seeded steamed tomatoes and Parmentier potatoes. It accompanies large joints of meat. The name is also given to poached stuffed fillets of sole arranged in a ring with rice, coated with Mornay sauce and glazed. The centre is filled with a salpicon of shrimps bound with a white wine sauce and sprinkled with chopped truffles.

DUTCH CHEESES The best-known Dutch cheeses are Edam and Gouda. Cheeses made in the Netherlands always carry a government control stamp which gives the name of the cheese, the fat content in the dry matter, the country of origin (expressed as Holland) the number indicating where, on what date, and from which curd batch the cheese was made, and the code of the relevant government control station. They are made only from pasteurized milk.

DUTCH OVEN A large, heavy cooking pot with a close-fitting lid, authentically made of cast iron and hung over an open fire. Thought to be of 16th century Pennsylvania Dutch origin, the pot was used for stewing and braising; however, other types of dishes, such as breads, were also cooked in it. The term has also been applied to a variety of other utensils used for cooking over an open fire, including a type of plate or rack fitted to the front of a fire grate and on which to stand cooking pans or dishes. In modern terms, it is sometimes used for glazed pots for cooking in the oven or on top of the stove.

DUVAL, PIERRE-LOUIS French butcher (born Montlhéry, 1811; died Paris, 1870). He supplied the Tuileries kitchens and owned several retail butcher's shops in Paris. In 1860 he had the idea of creating a number of small restaurants serving a single dish – boiled beef and consommé – at a fixed price. The first 'bouillon', in the Rue de Montesquieu, was soon followed by a dozen others.

His son Alexandre successfully developed the chain of restaurants and made an immense fortune. A well-known figure of Parisian life, nicknamed 'Godefroi de Bouillon' by humorists of the time, he composed a *Marche des petites bonnes* in honour of his waitresses, who all wore a coif of white tulle and, for the first time, replaced the traditional *garçons* in restaurants.

DUXELLES A basic preparation of chopped mushrooms, onions and shallots sautéed in butter.

Preparing duxelles

The ingredients must be cut very finely and evenly. The onion, shallot and mushrooms are all finely chopped. Cutting the mushrooms into fine strips, then cutting across to chop them, ensures that all the pieces are even.

Duxelles is used as a stuffing or garnish, as a complementary ingredient of a sauce, and in the preparation of various dishes called *à la duxelles*. The derivation of the word is disputed: some claim that duxelles was created at Uzel, a small town in the Côtes-du-Nord, while others attribute it to La Varenne, chef of the Marquis d'Uxelles.

RECIPES

preparation

Clean and trim 250 g (9 oz, 3 cups) button mushrooms and chop them finely, together with 1 onion and 1 large shallot. Melt a large knob of butter in a frying pan, add the chopped vegetables, salt and pepper and a little grated nutmeg (unless the duxelles is to accompany fish). Cook over a brisk heat until the vegetables are brown and the water from the mushrooms has evaporated. If the duxelles is for use as a garnish, add 1 tablespoon cream.

duxelles sauce

Prepare 4 tablespoons mushroom duxelles. Add 100 ml (4 fl oz, 7 tablespoons) white wine and reduce until almost completely dry. Add 150 ml (¼ pint, ⅔ cup) demi-glace* sauce and 100 ml (4 fl oz, 7 tablespoons) sieved tomato* sauce. Boil for 2–3 minutes, pour into a sauceboat (gravy boat), and sprinkle with chopped parsley.

Alternatively, the duxelles may be moistened with 150 ml (¼ pint, ⅔ cup) consommé and 100 ml (4 fl oz, 7 tablespoons) sieved tomato sauce and thickened with 1 tablespoon beurre manié.

eggs en cocotte à la duxelles

Prepare 4 tablespoons mushroom duxelles. Butter 6 ramekin dishes and divide the duxelles between them. Break an egg into each ramekin, then add to each a spoonful of single (light) cream, salt and pepper. Cover with foil and cook the eggs in a bain marie on the hob (stovetop) for about 4 minutes, timing from when the water in the bain marie begins to boil.

omelette à la duxelles

Prepare 4 tablespoons mushroom duxelles with cream added. Make an omelette with 8 eggs and fill it with the duxelles. Stud the omelette with small fried croûtons and serve with duxelles sauce.

sautéed veal chops à la duxelles

Prepare 4 tablespoons mushroom duxelles. Sauté 4 veal chops in butter. When the chops are almost cooked, add the duxelles to the pan and complete the cooking over a low heat. Drain the chops and arrange on a serving dish; keep hot. Add 100 ml (4 fl oz, 7 tablespoons) double (heavy) cream and half a glass of white wine or 2 tablespoons Madeira to the duxelles in the pan and reduce until the mixture thickens. Coat the chops with this sauce and serve very hot.

E

EAR A piece of offal, usually from pigs or calves, used in cooking or in the preparation of brawn (head cheese) and various other forms of charcuterie. It can be boiled, fried, sautéed, braised, stuffed, made into a gratin, or grilled (broiled), and is an ingredient of great number of tasty recipes.

RECIPES

Calves' Ears
calves' ears braised à la mirepoix
Clean the insides of 4 calves' ears thoroughly and blanch them for 8 minutes; refresh them, then drain, scrape and dry them. Put into a casserole and cover with 200 ml (7 fl oz, ¾ cup) vegetable mirepoix*; add a bouquet garni, salt, pepper and 100 ml (4 fl oz, 7 tablespoons) white wine. Reduce the liquid completely, then pour in 300 ml (½ pint, 1¼ cups) brown veal stock, cover the dish, and cook in a preheated oven at 180°C (350°F, gas 4) for 1½ hours. Drain the ears. Remove the skin which covers the inside and the outside of the thin part of the ears; pull this part down and trim it. Arrange the ears in a round serving dish, possibly on slices of bread fried in butter. Skim the fat from the braising liquid and sprinkle over the ears.

stuffed calves' ears du Bugey
Blanch, refresh, then carefully clean 1 calf's ear per guest. Rub the ears with lemon and sew each one into the shape of a cornet. Put them into a pan with 1.5 litres (2¾ pints, 6½ cups) well-flavoured beef stock, 1 litre (1¾ pints, 4⅓ cups) dry white wine, a bouquet garni, 1 sliced onion, 2 sliced celery sticks and 2 sliced carrots. Add plenty of salt and pepper and cook gently for about 2½ hours. Drain the ears and put them aside, covered with a damp cloth.

Dice 1 calf's sweetbread that has been braised in white wine, 1 chicken wing and 1 fresh truffle. Fry 100 g (4 oz, 1⅓ cups) coarsely chopped wild mushrooms in butter; add salt and pepper. When they are half-cooked, add the truffle, the sweetbread and the chicken meat; continue to cook over a low heat. Add 200 ml (7 fl oz, ¾ cup) slightly soured cream, then take the pan off the heat and add 2 egg yolks. Blend everything well and leave to cool.

Spoon the cold mixture into the ear 'cornets'. Dip the ears in flour, then beaten egg, then breadcrumbs, and fry in butter, without allowing them to brown. Drain, arrange on a serving dish and sprinkle with fried curly parsley.

Pigs' Ears
boiled pigs' ears
Singe 4 pigs' ears and clean the insides thoroughly; cook them in boiling salted water, using 1 teaspoon salt per 1 litre (1¾ pints, 4⅓ cups) water with 2 carrots, 1 onion studded with 2 cloves, and a bouquet garni. Simmer for about 50 minutes, then drain.

Boiled pigs' ears can be used in several ways. They can be chopped, dipped in batter and deep-fried; or spread with butter, dipped in fresh breadcrumbs and grilled (broiled), to be served with mustard or horseradish sauce and mashed potatoes or purée of celeriac (celery root). Pigs' ears *à la lyonnaise* are cut into large strips and sautéed in butter with sliced onion. They can also be served cold with vinaigrette, or browned in the oven with a white sauce.

braised pigs' ears
Singe 4 pigs' ears and clean the insides thoroughly. Blanch them for 5 minutes in boiling water, drain

them and cut them in half lengthways. Grease a flameproof casserole, cover the bottom with pieces of pork rind, add I sliced onion and I sliced carrot, and arrange the pieces of ear on top in a flat layer; put a bouquet garni in the middle.

Cover the casserole and cook over a medium heat for 10 minutes, then add 200 ml (7 fl oz, ¾ cup) white wine and reduce until syrupy. Add 400 ml (14 fl oz, 1¾ cups) thickened veal juices or stock and cook, covered, in a preheated oven at 180°C (350°F, gas 4) for 50 minutes. Drain the ears and arrange them on a serving dish. Garnish with braised celery hearts or steamed cauliflower. Pour over the strained and reduced braising liquid.

stuffed and fried pigs' ears
Braise the ears whole. Meanwhile, make a chicken forcemeat and some Villeroi sauce. Allow the ears to cool, then slit them and stuff with the chicken forcemeat. Dip them into the Villeroi sauce and leave for 30 minutes. Roll the ears in egg, then breadcrumbs, and fry them in very hot oil. Drain, arrange on the serving dish and serve with tomato sauce.

EASTER The major Christian festival, which celebrates the resurrection of Jesus Christ. It was associated in the early days of Christianity with the Jewish feast of Passover, commemorating the passing over or sparing of the Israelites in Egypt, when God smote the firstborn of the Egyptians (the French word for Easter is derived from the Greek *Paskha* and the Hebrew *Pesah*, meaning 'passage'). Passover is celebrated for a week at the beginning of spring (from the 14th to the 21st of the month of Nisan), during which no alcohol or leavened food is consumed; the feast begins with a formal meal of a roasted lamb, sacrificed according to the kosher method.

Easter Day, fixed at the Council of Nicaea in AD 325 to fall on the first Sunday after the first full moon following the spring equinox, can occur between 22 March and 22 April. It corresponds to the height of the period of the renewal of life after winter and, as Easter also follows the abstinence of Lent, numerous culinary traditions mark this festival.

In all countries, eggs are the symbol of Easter. In France, the custom of offering painted or decorated hard-boiled (hard-cooked) eggs goes back to the 15th century, when it was particularly common in Alsace. The paschal omelette, sometimes made with eggs laid on Good Friday, is usually enriched with bacon or sausage to emphasize the end of the period of abstinence.

The omelette is traditionally followed by a dish of meat, generally roebuck or lamb but also pork (grilled sucking pig at Metz, ham sprinkled with chopped parsley in the Côte-d'Or). In Charente, Poitou, Touraine, Berry and Bresse, the Easter Sunday menu includes a pie filled with a mixture of chopped meats and hard-boiled eggs. Little noodles in vinaigrette (*totelots*) are typical in Lorraine, fritters in Roussillon, and large thick pancakes (*pachades*) in Auvergne. A variety of special cakes and pastries are prepared for Easter: *pognes* and *pompes* in Provence, Savoy and the area around Lyon; *alise pacaude* in the Vendée; *cavagnats* in Menton (shaped like baskets and containing eggs dyed red); *cacavelli* (crowns topped with eggs) in Corsica; *alléluias* in Castelnaudary; *pagnottes* in Forez; gingerbreads in the shape of horses in Touraine; darioles in Reims; *flônes* in the Aveyron region; and *soupe dorée* in Savoy (called *soupe rousse* in the Creuse), which is a kind of French toast (*pain perdu*).

Russian cookery includes several traditional cakes for Easter Day, such as *kulich* and *pashka*. In Germany the Easter cake is the *Ostertorte*, a type of sponge cake filled with a mocha-flavoured butter cream and decorated with chocolate eggs.

The British simnel cake is now traditional at Easter although originally it was a cake made to celebrate Mothering Sunday.

EAU-DE-VIE A French term meaning 'water of life', from the Latin *aqua vitae*. It is nowadays generally applied to brandy (not necessarily Cognac or Armagnac) and also to the *alcools blancs* (white alcohols) – spirits distilled from fruits or herbs and kept in glass (not wood) without any sweetening. The various marcs are known as *eaux-de-vie-de-vin*, as they are distilled from wine. Distillates from other basics, such as Scotch whisky, vodka, gin, Schnapps and so on, are not strictly speaking eaux-de-vie, although the Gaelic for Scotch whisky – *usque béatha* – means 'water of life'.

ÉCAILLER A French culinary term meaning to open shellfish. An *écailler* is the person employed to open the oysters in a restaurant having its own oyster bed. Écaillers are also traders specializing in the sale of shellfish and seafoods.

The verb *écailler* also means to scale fish.

ÉCARLATE, À L' The French term describing traditional pickled pork or beef, especially ox (beef) tongue. Saltpetre (potassium nitrate) was used with salt to pickle meat; it coloured the meat bright red, hence the name, meaning 'scarlet'. This was further enhanced by rubbing red food colouring (liquid carmine) over the cured meat before it was hung in storage. The traditional recipe is given below: saltpetre is not used in modern commercial curing and is not readily available. Meat can be pickled at home without saltpetre or using nitrites available to the food industry, but it does not have the traditional keeping qualities. The method should be used for the flavour it yields rather than as a means of long-term preservation.

Pickled tongue is served hot with vegetables or cold as an hors d'oeuvre. It is also an ingredient of dishes described as *à l'écarlate*, which are served with some kind of red sauce, such as tomato, and it is often used as a garnish (cut into cockscombs).

Beef can also be pickled, cooked, pressed and used in the same way.

Fromage à l'écarlate, a speciality of classical cookery, is a type of butter made with crayfish (and therefore reddish): a recipe is given by the chef Menon in *La Science du maître d'hôtel cuisinier* (1749).

RECIPES

traditional pickled ox tongue

Soak a trimmed ox (beef) tongue in cold water for 24 hours, then drain and wipe it. Prick it lightly all over, rubbing the surface with salt mixed with saltpetre. Put the tongue in a stoneware container. Prepare a brine by adding 2.25 kg (5 lb, 6¼ cups) coarse salt, 150 g (5 oz) saltpetre, 300 g (11 oz, 1¾ cups) brown sugar, a sprig of thyme, a bay leaf, 12 juniper berries and 12 peppercorns to 5 litres (9 pints, 5½ quarts) water. Boil for a few minutes, then leave it to become cold. Cover the tongue with this brine, place a wooden board with a weight on top over it, and leave it to steep in a cool place for 6 days in summer, or 8 days in winter.

Drain the tongue and soak it for a few hours in fresh water to draw out the salt, then cook in water without any seasonings or condiments for 2½–3 hours, depending on its size. Drain the tongue, then strip the skin off completely while still hot. Cover it with buttered paper to prevent blackening and leave it to cool. Wrap the tongue in very thin pieces of fat bacon, tie it up and wrap in muslin (cheesecloth), tying it at each end. Poach the tongue in a large quantity of simmering water for about 10 minutes. Drain immediately, remove the muslin and brush the tongue with red food colouring. Hang it up and leave to cool. Prepared in this way, the tongue will keep for several weeks in a cool dry place.

canapés à l'écarlate

Cut some thin slices of bread into rounds or rectangles, and spread them with a little softened butter mixed with paprika, cayenne pepper and a little Worcestershire sauce. Place a slice of pickled tongue on each round and garnish with a thin line of the same butter.

ÉCHAUDÉ A small light crisp biscuit (cracker), very popular in France up to the 19th century. It was made from a mixture of water and flour (to which an egg and some butter was added), poached in boiling water (hence its name, which means 'scalded'), and then drained and dried in the oven. Formerly, during Lent, the egg was omitted and the butter replaced with oil.

Échaudés are mentioned for the first time in a charter dated 1202, under the name of *panes qui discuntur eschaudati* ('bread known as scalded'). In the 13th century they were scalloped; later they were round, triangular or heart-shaped. They used to be sold in the street, like wafers. In his *Grand Dictionnaire de cuisine*, Alexandre Dumas describes them as 'a sort of unsweetened cake which is made for the birds and for children rather than for adults'. The Parisian pastrycook Favart, who brought them back into fashion at the beginning of the 18th century, in the Rue de la Verrerie, was thought for a long time to have invented them.

The échaudé remains a traditional biscuit in several provinces, particularly in Aveyron (aniseed-flavoured) and in the west of France (along with the *craquelins*). It can also be made with a raising (leavening) agent.

ÉCHÉZEAUX A region in the Côte-de-Nuits, Burgundy, where 11 vineyards entitled to the AOC make fine red wine, labelled according to their specifications: one of them is a *grand cru*, the highest rating in Burgundy. Very few of the wines are sold just as 'Échézeaux', as many Vosne-Romanée people have difficulty pronouncing the name!

ÉCLADE Also known as *églade*. A traditional dish prepared from mussels, which is typical of Saintonge on the Atlantic coast of France, particularly of La Tremblade. The mussels are scraped and cleaned and then arranged on the *fumée*, a thick plank of hard olive wood, which is sometimes covered with a layer of clay so that the mussels will stay in place. The plank and mussels are then covered with a layer of dry pine needles, which are set alight. When the needles have been reduced to ashes, the mussels are ready. They are eaten very hot and plain, with country bread and butter.

ÉCLAIR A small, log-shaped bun of choux pastry, filled with cream and coated with chocolate fondant icing (frosting). The paste is piped on to a baking sheet and cooked until crisp and hollow.

After baking, the éclair is split lengthways and filled with whipped cream or confectioner's custard (pastry cream), plain or flavoured with coffee or chocolate. The top is iced with chocolate fondant icing or melted chocolate. Éclairs can also be filled with chestnut purée or a filling made from fruits preserved in syrup.

RECIPES

chocolate éclairs

Prepare some choux* paste with 125 g (4½ oz, 1 cup) plain (all-purpose) flour, 65 g (2½ oz, 5 tablespoons) butter, a large pinch of salt, 250 ml (8 fl oz, 1 cup) water and 4 eggs. Using a piping (pastry) bag with a smooth nozzle, 2 cm (¾ in) in diameter, pipe thick fingers of dough, 6–7.5 cm (2½–3 in) long, on to a baking sheet, well spaced apart so that they will be able to rise without sticking together. Beat an egg yolk with a little milk and use to glaze the éclairs. Bake the éclairs in a preheated oven at 190°C (375°F, gas 5) until pale golden in colour. This will take 20 minutes at the most. The inside must still be soft. Leave the éclairs to cool completely, then split them down one side.

ECUADOR

Ecuadorian cuisine is very similar to that of Peru. The national dish *par excellence* is *ceviche* – raw fish, marinated in lemon, lime or, more unusually, Seville orange juice – available from 'restaurants' in all the markets. Ecuadorians are also very fond of *tamales*, maize (corn) cakes, pasties and thick, colourful soups, served with delicious rolls. The numerous varieties of banana are used in many recipes, both savoury and sweet, as are haricot (navy) beans, rice, maize and potatoes. Chilli-hot sauces are extremely popular. On All Saints' Day (1 November), innumerable little decorated sweet pastries are baked to be eaten by families beside the graves of their loved ones.

Make a confectioner's custard (see *custard*) with 50 g (2 oz, ½ cup) plain flour, 1 whole egg, 2 egg yolks and 50 g (2 oz, ¼ cup) caster (superfine) sugar. Add 1 tablespoon cocoa (unsweetened cocoa) to the cream mixture. Leave to cool completely, then put into a piping bag and use to fill the éclairs. Heat 200 g (7 oz, 1 cup) fondant icing* (frosting) over a low heat, add 50 g (2 oz, 2 squares) melted dark chocolate, and mix well. Coat the top of the éclairs and leave to cool.

coffee éclairs

Use the same process as for chocolate éclairs, but flavour the cream filling with 2 teaspoons instant coffee dissolved in 250 ml (8 fl oz, 1 cup) milk brought to the boil with 40 g (1½ oz, 3 tablespoons) unsalted butter. Add coffee essence (extract), drop by drop to taste, to the icing (frosting).

ÉCOLE DE SALERNE A collection of the health precepts of an Italian school of medicine that was highly regarded in the Middle Ages as a dietetic and therapeutic recipe manual. Translated from Latin into French in about 1500, and edited and enlarged several times, these precepts were rewritten in the form of little verses, easy to remember; for example:

Fennel seeds when soaked in wine
Revitalize a heart that love makes pine,
And reawaken the old man's flame;
The salutary usage of the seed, you know,
From liver and lung doth banish pain,
And quells the wind that in the gut doth blow.

ÉCOSSAISE, À L' A French term primarily used to describe a soup inspired by Scottish cookery (Scotch broth). This is a clear soup made with diced boiled mutton, pearl barley and a vegetable mixture. This mixture is also used to make écossaise sauce, served with white offal (variety meat), eggs or poached fish and poultry. The name is also used for various dishes, particularly egg dishes containing salmon.

RECIPES

écossaise sauce

Gently braise in butter 4 tablespoons vegetable brunoise* and some French (green) beans cut up into very small dice. Prepare 200 ml (7 fl oz, ¾ cup) cream sauce and put through a strainer. Add the vegetable mixture.

soft-boiled (or poached) eggs à l'écossaise

Prepare 4 tablespoons salmon purée by mixing some finely crumbled poached salmon with the same quantity of thick white sauce*. Heat up this purée and use it to fill 4 warmed puff pastry croustades. Arrange a soft-boiled (soft-cooked) or poached egg in each case, and cover with shrimp sauce. Each egg may be garnished with a slice of truffle.

ÉCOT A French term meaning each diner's share in a meal paid for communally. The word, which comes from the Old French *skot* ('contribution'), is hardly used at all now, except in the expression *payer son écot* (to pay one's share).

ECUADOR See *above*.

ÉCUELLE A small, round rimless bowl for individual portions of food. Wooden, earthenware or tin *écuelles* are among the most ancient of table utensils. In the Middle Ages, one bowl was sometimes used by two people. Nowadays, *écuelles* are usually made of earthenware or pottery, and are generally only used to serve thick vegetable soups or rustic dishes.

ÉCUYER TRANCHANT An officer in charge of cutting the meats and serving at the king's table under the Ancien Régime. The post was sometimes shared, the *écuyer tranchant* doing the cutting and the *grand écuyer tranchant* the serving (known as the *premier tranchant* when he officiated for the queen). The *écuyer tranchant* was a nobleman, who had the right to display representations of a knife and fork with fleur-de-lis on the handles under his heraldic arms. The post itself gradually became honorary, but remained highly lucrative owing to the privileges attached to it.

In the 15th century, Olivier de La Marche reported that the *écuyer tranchant* had to 'keep his knives clean' at his own expense. These knives were luxury utensils bearing his lord's emblem or coat of arms, and at this time there were three of them. The largest one, which had a wide blade with two cutting edges, served not only for cutting, but also for presenting morsels to the diners; the second knife was for carving roasts and poultry; and the third one, which was smaller and known as the *parepain*, was for cutting the slices of bread used as trenchers for the meat.

EDAM A Dutch cow's-milk cheese, containing 30–40% fat, in the shape of a large ball with a yellow or red waxed coating. The semi-hard pressed cheese is firm but elastic, free of holes, and light yellow to yellow ochre in colour, depending on its degree of maturity. Edam is described as 'young' after two or three months in a dry cellar, when it has a sweet nutty flavour; after six months it is 'semi-matured', with a stronger flavour; at the end of a year's maturing it is described as 'matured' and has a slight bite. Edam is also known in mainland Europe as *tête de mort* or *tête de Maure* (dead man's head or Moor's head), *Manbollen* and *Katzenkopf*, due to its characteristic head-like shape. Measuring about 13 cm (5 in) in diameter, it weighs between 1.5 and 1.7 kg (3¼–3¾ lb). A 'baby' Edam is also available, weighing 1 kg (2¼ lb), and a triple Edam, weighing 6.5 kg (14½ lb).

Edam is made all over the Netherlands, and even in France and Belgium, but authentic Edam, from the small port in the northern Netherlands, is protected by a label of origin. It is usually served after a meal, often with pale ale, but it is also used a good deal in cookery. Young or semi-matured cheese is suitable for sandwiches, pastries, canapés, croque-monsieurs and mixed salads; matured cheese is used in gratins, soufflés and tarts. Lastly, it is used in a traditional dish called *keshy yena* from Curaçao, the main island in the Netherlands Antilles.

RECIPE

keshy yena
Using a young Edam, cut a round slice from the top and hollow out the inside of the cheese with a knife, leaving the walls 1 cm (½ in) thick. Cut the hollowed-out cheese into small cubes, mix with a cooked ragoût made of diced or chopped pork or beef, then add some stoned (pitted) olives, tomatoes cut into small segments and sliced onions. Fill the Edam ball with this mixture; replace the round slice at the top and hold it in place with cocktail sticks (toothpicks). Bake in a preheated oven at 160°C (325°F, gas 3) for 1 hour.

EDELPILZ A German cow's-milk cheese with a 55% fat content. A blue-veined pale-yellow cheese with a natural crust, it has a sweet flavour with a slight tang. Made in the Bavarian Alps, Edelpilz is sold in a round, a loaf, or individual portions, wrapped in silver paper. Its name means literally 'noble mushroom'.

EDELZWICKER A white Alsace wine made from a blend of certain permitted 'noble' grapes. A pleasant drink, it goes well with various Alsatian recipes.

EDWARD VII While still the Prince of Wales, the future king of England was a notable personality in fashionable Paris at the end of the 19th century. He was an habitué of the great restaurants (Voisin, Café Hardy, Paillard) and sumptuous dishes were dedicated to him. For example, *turbot prince de Galles* was a dish of poached turbot garnished with oysters and fried mussels and coated with a champagne sauce seasoned with curry spices and enriched with crayfish butter.

When he became king, he continued to receive the honours of haute cuisine. *Barbue Edouard VII* is brill poached in white wine, garnished with duchess potato rosettes and served with an oyster mousseline sauce. *Poularde Edouard VII* is chicken stuffed with foie gras, rice and truffles, coated with a curry sauce containing diced red (bell) pepper, and served with cucumbers in cream. In *oeufs Edouard VII*, soft-boiled (soft-cooked) or poached eggs are arranged, with slices of pickled tongue, on a truffle risotto and garnished with slices of truffle. *Edouard VII* itself is a small boat-shaped cake filled with rhubarb and topped with green icing (frosting).

EEL A snakelike fish with a smooth slippery skin. Eels mature in fresh water where they are fished, and migrate to the Sargasso Sea to breed. The larvae (*leptocephali*) are carried by the ocean currents over a period of two or three years to the coasts of Europe. When they enter the estuaries, they are transparent and have grown to a length of 6–9 cm (2½–3½ in). These are the glass-eels or elvers, which make a popular fried dish in Nantes, La Rochelle, Bordeaux and the Basque country. Those larvae that survive grow larger and the skin becomes pigmented. The 'yellow' eel has a brown back, becoming greenish, with a yellowish underbelly that later becomes silvery white. It is at this time, when it starts to travel back to the Sargasso Sea, that the eel, now described as 'silvered' or 'descending', is most prized. The male measures about 50 cm (20 in) and the female 1 m (40 in). Eels are sold alive. They are killed and skinned at the last moment as the flesh deteriorates rapidly, and the raw blood is poisonous if it enters a cut – for example, on one's finger. Eels are very fatty fish, but tasty.

Eels were popular with the Romans and widely eaten during the Middle Ages. Taillevent's *Viandier* gives a whole range of recipes for preparing eel dishes: in broth, in galantine, in tarts or pâtés, as Lent flan, with garlic or mustard, roasted, salted, 'dusted with spices', or as a roulade. Today, eels appear in numerous French regional recipes (*catigot, matelote, bouilleture, au vert, à la flamande*). However, classic haute cuisine dishes (ballotine, pâté), or even more simple ones (*à la tartare, à la poulette*), are less often prepared than they used to be.

Jellied eels are famous in Britain, served cold in the jellied stock in which they were cooked; eel pie and eel broth are also traditional dishes. Smoked eel is a popular dish in Scandinavia and in northern Germany. The skin should be shiny and almost black, and it is served as an hors d'oeuvre, with rye bread and lemon.

Eels are particularly popular in Japan, especially opened and skewered, then grilled as *kabayaki*. Eel is also served on rice or cooked in *nabemono* style as part of a one-pot meal prepared at the table. Eel is farmed in Japan (as well as other countries, including Italy, to a lesser extent).

RECIPES

preparation

To kill an eel, seize it with a cloth and bang its head violently against a hard surface. To skin it, put a noose around the base of the head and hang it up. Slit the skin in a circle just beneath the noose. Pull away a small portion of the skin, turn it back, take hold of it with a cloth, and pull it down hard. Clean the eel by making a small incision in its belly. Cut off and discard the head and the end of the tail. Wash and wipe dry. Alternatively, when the eel has been killed, it can be cut into sections and grilled (broiled) for a short time. The skin will puff up and can then be removed. This method has the advantage of removing excess fat from the eel, particularly if it is large.

devilled eel

Cook an eel weighing about 800 g (1¾ lb) in a court-bouillon of white wine and let it cool in the liquor. Drain and wipe the eel, then smear it with mustard, brush with melted butter, and grill (broil) slowly. Arrange the eel on a round dish and garnish with gherkins (sweet dill pickles) if desired. Serve with a devilled sauce.

eel à la bonne femme

Soften 4 large tablespoons chopped onion in butter and place in a sauté pan. Put slices of a medium-sized eel weighing about 800 g (1¾ lb) on top of the onion layer. Add salt and pepper, a bouquet garni and 300 ml (½ pint, 1¼ cups) white wine. Cover and poach slowly for 25 minutes. Drain the slices of eel and arrange them on croûtons of sandwich bread fried in butter. Garnish with large diced potatoes sautéed in butter. Coat the eel with the liquor from the pan, after reducing it by half and thickening it with 1 tablespoon beurre manié.

eel à la provençale

Cook 2 tablespoons chopped onion gently in a large pan with a little oil. Cut a medium-sized eel into even-sized slices, add to the pan, and cook until they have stiffened. Season with salt and pepper, and add 4 peeled, seeded chopped tomatoes, a bouquet garni and a crushed garlic clove. Moisten with 100 ml (4 fl oz, 7 tablespoons) dry white wine, cover the pan, and cook slowly for 25–30 minutes. About 10 minutes before serving, add 12 black olives. Arrange on a dish and sprinkle with parsley.

eel au vert

Skin and prepare 1.5 kg (3¼ lb) small eels and cut each one into 4 sections. Cook the sections in a sauté pan in 150 g (5 oz, ⅔ cup) butter until they have stiffened. Add 100 g (4 oz, 1½ cups) each of chopped spinach and sorrel leaves, reduce the heat, and continue cooking until the vegetables are soft. Add 325 ml (11 fl oz, 1⅓ cups) dry white wine, a bouquet garni, 2 tablespoons chopped parsley and 1 tablespoon each of chopped sage and tarragon. Season well and simmer for 10 minutes. Brown 6 slices of stale sandwich bread in butter. When the eels are cooked, add 2 or 3 egg yolks mixed with 2 tablespoons lemon juice to the sauté pan and thicken the mixture without letting it boil. Place the sections of eel on the slices of fried bread and coat with the sauce. Eels *au vert* may also be served cold without the bread.

eel brochettes à l'anglaise

Cut a boned eel into even-sized pieces and marinate them for an hour in a mixture of oil, lemon juice, pepper, salt and chopped parsley. Drain the eel pieces, roll in flour and coat with fresh breadcrumbs. Thread the eel on to skewers, separating the pieces with slices of fat bacon. Grill (broil) under a low heat until the flesh separates easily from the bone. Arrange on a long dish, garnished with parsley and surrounded with half-slices of lemon. Serve with tartare sauce.

eel pie

Bone an eel, cut the fillets into 5–6 cm (2–2½ in) slices and blanch them in salted water. Drain and cool the eel slices. Hard-boil (hard-cook) and slice some eggs. Season the fish and eggs with salt, pepper and grated nutmeg, and sprinkle them with chopped parsley. Layer the eel and egg slices in a deep, preferably oval, dish. Add sufficient white wine to just cover the fish and dot with small knobs of butter. Cover with a layer of puff pastry, making a hole for the steam to escape. Brush with beaten egg and score the top. Bake in a preheated oven at 200°C (400°F, gas 6) for 30 minutes, then reduce the temperature to 180°C (350°C, gas 4) and cook for a further 1 hour. Just before serving, pour a few tablespoons of demi-glace sauce (made with fish stock) into the hole at the top of the pie. The pie may also be eaten cold.

eel pie aux fines herbes (à la ménagère)

Bone an eel and cut the fillets into slices. Flatten each slice and season with salt, pepper and spices to taste. Arrange in a deep dish and moisten with a few tablespoons of dry white wine, a little Cognac and a few drops of oil. Leave to marinate for 2 hours in a cool place. Drain and wipe the slices, and reserve the marinade. Cook the fish briskly until stiff in butter in a sauté pan, then sprinkle generously with chopped parsley and shallots. Take the pan off the heat and pour the marinade over the fish. Leave until completely cold.

Line a shallow oval pie dish with shortcrust pastry (basic pie dough) and spread the base and sides with a layer of pike forcemeat containing chopped parsley. Fill the pie with alternating layers of the flattened eel slices and the pike forcemeat. Moisten each layer with a little of the marinade. Finish with a 2 cm (¾ in) layer of forcemeat and sprinkle with melted butter. Cover with a layer of pastry (dough) and trim the top with leaves cut from the pastry trimmings. Make a hole in the top for the steam to escape and brush the pastry with beaten egg. Bake in a preheated oven at 180°C (350°F, gas 4) for 1¾–2 hours.

Remove the pie from the dish and place it on a long serving dish. Pour a few tablespoons of demi-glace sauce, made with fish stock, through the hole in the top of the pie. Anchovy fillets may also be included with the eel slices, or some anchovy butter or dry duxelles may be added to the pike forcemeat. If the pie is served cold, pour enough fish jelly into the hole in the top of the pie to fill the gaps left by the cooking process. Leave for 12 hours until completely cold.

roulade of eel à l'angevine

Prepare a 1.5 kg (3¼ lb) eel as for a ballotine, and stuff with a pike forcemeat to which a salpicon of mushrooms and truffles has been added. Reshape the eel and wrap it in thin slices of bacon. Tie it up in the form of a ring. Slice a large onion and a carrot and soften in butter in a sauté pan. Spread the vegetables evenly in the pan and place the eel on top, with a large bouquet garni, a leek and a sprig of savory in the centre. Add just enough medium dry white wine, such as Anjou, to cover the eel. Bring to the boil, skim, then cover and simmer slowly for 35 minutes. Prepare 24 small mushroom caps, keeping the stalks, and toss in butter. Drain the eel (reserving the liquor), remove the bacon slices, and put into another sauté pan with the mushrooms. Keep hot.

To prepare the sauce, strain the cooking liquor and make a white roux with 50 g (2 oz, ¼ cup) butter and 50 g (2 oz, ½ cup) plain (all-purpose) flour. Moisten with the strained juices and add the mushroom stalks. Reduce the sauce over a high heat and add 350 ml (12 fl oz, 1½ cups) single (light) cream. When the sauce has reached the correct consistency, take it off the boil and add 100 g (4 oz, ½ cup) crayfish butter*. Coat the rolled-up eel with the sauce.

other recipes See *ballotine, bastion, bouilleture, brochette, canapé, fricassee, matelote, Orly.*

EFFILER A French culinary term meaning to prepare green beans for cooking by breaking off the ends with the fingers, as close as possible to the tip, and removing the strings, if any.

When applied to almonds and pistachio nuts, *effiler* means to cut into thin slices lengthways, either with a knife or with a special instrument. The word is also used for slicing chicken or duck breasts.

Some chefs use the term *effilocher*, particularly for cutting leeks into fine shreds.

EGG The round or oval reproductive body laid by the female of many animals, containing the develop-ing embryo and its food reserves and protected by a shell or skin. Although the eggs of many birds, fish and even reptiles can be used as food, the word 'egg' unqualified applies exclusively to hen's eggs. All other types of egg offered for sale must be labelled appropriately – quail's eggs, duck eggs, plover's eggs. There are also exotic rarities such as crocodile or ostrich eggs.

The average weight of a hen's egg is 50 g (2 oz). The shell makes up about 12% of the total weight of the egg and is made of a calcareous porous substance which is pervious to air, water and smells. It is lined with a delicate pellucid membrane which separates itself from the shell at the larger end of the egg to form the air chamber. The size of this chamber is in inverse proportion to the freshness of the egg – the fresher the egg, the smaller the chamber.

The albumen, or white of the egg, is a thick viscous transparent liquid containing half the 14% protein content of the egg; it also has a high percentage of water and some mineral substances. Albumen is soluble in cold water, congeals at 70°C (158°F), and remains from then on insoluble. It forms about 58% of the total weight of the egg.

The yolk of the egg (30% of the total weight) is an opaque soft substance which congeals in heat. The yolk is composed of albumins, fats containing vitamins, lecithins, nucleins, chlorestins and mineral substances including a ferruginous pigment called *haematogen*, which gives it its colour. It contains the germ (visible in a fertilized egg – this does not mean the egg is inedible), the remaining proteins, and all the fats (especially lecithin), together with iron, sulphur and vitamins A, B, D and E.

■ **Varieties and qualities** Contrary to popular opinion, a brown egg is neither better nor more 'natural' than a white one; it is, in fact, usually smaller and less well-filled. However, it is easier to examine for freshness against a bright light because the shell is thinner and less opaque. The colour of the yolk (deep or pale yellow) has no bearing on the quality of the egg, and any blood spots that may be found in the white or the yolk have no significance.

Fresh eggs should be used within 1 month and stored unwashed, with the pointed end down, in their box in the refrigerator. Washing an egg makes the shell permeable to smells. A raw egg yolk will keep for 24 hours and a raw egg white from 6 to 12 hours. A dessert containing raw eggs, such as a mousse, should be eaten within 24 hours. Fresh eggs can be frozen if they are broken into a bowl, beaten, and poured into suitable containers.

■ **Freshness of eggs** A fresh egg is heavy and should feel well-filled. An egg loses a tiny fraction of its weight every day by evaporation of water through the porous shell. It is easy to test the freshness of an egg by plunging it into salted water containing 125 g (4½ oz, ⅓ cup) salt per 1 litre (1¾ pints, 4⅓ cups) water. An egg up to 3 days old will sink at once to the bottom; an egg 3–6 days old will float halfway up the water; if it is bad, it floats horizontally on top of the water. Another method is to break an egg on to a plate. If the yolk is compact and positioned in the centre, the egg is fresh. If the egg is 1 week old, the yolk is not in the centre, and in an egg that is 2–3 weeks old, the yolk has a tendency to spread. The freshness of an egg can also be tested by holding it up to the light – a very small air chamber indicates a very fresh egg.

■ **Uses** Eggs are among the most versatile ingredients used in cooking. They are of prime importance in many branches of the food industry, especially those concerned with making pasta, ices, biscuits (cookies) and cakes. In the kitchen they have innumerable uses, such as liaisons, egg and breadcrumb coatings, glazing pastry, preparing emulsified sauces and forcemeats. They are an ingredient in many basic doughs and batters.

Eggs can be cooked in a great variety of ways and served with all sorts of garnishes. According to James de Coquet, 'There is not a celebrity, a marshal, a composer, or an opera singer who has not given his name to a method of preparing eggs.' Simple cooking methods include poaching, boiling, frying and baking; eggs can be scrambled or made into omelettes. They can be served plain or with an incredible array of garnishing ingredients, sauces or other accompaniments.

The nutritive value and versatility of eggs ensured that they became part of the human diet all over the world from the earliest times; they were frequently associated with rites and traditions. Enormous numbers of eggs were eaten in the Middle Ages and, as in ancient Rome, the diner crushed the shell in his plate to prevent evil spirits from hiding there. Eggs were forbidden during Lent because of their 'richness', and it was traditional in France to search for and collect eggs on Maundy Thursday and Good Friday and have them blessed on Easter Saturday ready for their prolific consumption over Eastertide. The French word for the yolk at that time was *moyeu*, meaning centre or hub, and some people believe that the word 'mayonnaise' is derived from it. The French word for the white was *aubun* (now *blanc*).

RECIPES

Eggs en Cocotte
Break the eggs into small buttered cocottes or ramekins and cook in a bain marie in a preheated oven at 200°C (400°F, gas 6) for 6–8 minutes.

eggs en cocotte à la tartare
Mix some minced (ground) raw beef with chopped chives, salt and pepper. Put a layer of the mixture into some buttered ramekins and break the eggs on top. Pour a ribbon of double (heavy) cream around the yolks. Cook in a bain marie as above.

eggs en cocotte bachaumont
Butter some ramekin dishes and put some vegetable mirepoix that has been softened in butter in the bottom of each. Break 1 or 2 eggs into each ramekin and cook in a bain marie in a preheated oven. When cooked, season with salt and pepper and garnish with 1 tablespoon diced mushrooms, which have been sautéed in butter and bound with concentrated veal stock.

eggs en cocotte bérangère
Put a thin layer of quenelle forcemeat made with truffled chicken into the bottom of some buttered ramekin dishes. Break 1 or 2 eggs into each dish and cook in a bain marie in a preheated oven. When cooked, garnish with 1 tablespoon ragoût of cockscombs and kidneys with suprême sauce.

eggs en cocotte Jeannette
Put a layer of chicken quenelle forcemeat into each ramekin. Break the eggs on top and cook in a bain marie in a preheated oven. Garnish with buttered asparagus tips and surround with velouté sauce.

eggs en cocotte with cream
Pour 1 tablespoon boiling double (heavy) cream into each ramekin. Break 1 egg on top and place a knob of butter on the yolk. Cook in a bain marie in a preheated oven. When cooked, add salt and pepper. The eggs may also be sprinkled with a little grated Parmesan cheese and moistened with melted butter before cooking.

eggs en cocotte with tarragon
Cook the eggs in a bain marie in a preheated oven and pour some reduced tarragon-flavoured veal gravy around each yolk. Garnish with blanched drained tarragon leaves arranged in the form of a star. If wished, chopped tarragon can be sprinkled in the bottom of the buttered ramekins and the veal gravy can be replaced with reduced tarragon-flavoured cream.

other recipes See *ambassadeur, Brillat-Savarin, duxelles, périgourdine, rouennaise.*

Eggs in a Mould
This dish from the *grande cuisine* is rarely made nowadays but is very simple to prepare. Break the eggs into buttered dariole moulds and sprinkle with some type of chopped flavouring (parsley, ham, truffle). Cook in a bain marie in a preheated oven at 200°C (400°F, gas 6) and turn out on to a croustade, fried bread or an artichoke heart. Coat with sauce and serve.

eggs in a mould Bizet
Butter the dariole moulds and line them with a mixture of minced (ground) pickled tongue and diced truffle. Break the eggs into the moulds and cook them in a bain marie in a preheated oven. Unmould them on to braised artichoke hearts. Cover with Périgueux sauce and garnish with a slice of truffle.

other recipes See *Bagration, cardinal, Carême, chartreuse, Polignac.*

Eggs sur le Plat or Shirred Eggs

Eggs *sur le plat* are cooked in individual dishes in a preheated oven at 160°C (325°F, gas 3). The size of the cooking dish is important as the yolks do not cook as well when the whites have too much room to spread out. Some cooks recommend separating the whites from the yolks, cooking the whites first until they begin to set, and then placing a yolk in the centre of each white. It is advisable to put salt on the white only as it will show up as white specks on the yolk.

eggs au miroir

Eggs *au miroir* are also baked in the oven but at a far higher temperature, so that the yolks when cooked are shiny. Melt a knob of butter in a small flameproof egg dish. When it begins to sizzle, break 2 eggs on to a plate and slide them into the dish. Sprinkle with a pinch of salt and top with soft butter. Cook in a preheated oven at 240°C (475°F, gas 9) until the white has set. Serve very hot while the yolks are still shiny. Alternatively, the eggs can be cooked on the hob (stove top), basting them constantly with the hot butter in the cooking dish.

eggs sur le plat à la chaville

Cook a salpicon of mushrooms in butter and put a tablespoon into individual egg dishes. Break the eggs on top and cook them in a preheated oven. Garnish with 1 tablespoon tomato sauce flavoured with chopped tarragon.

eggs sur le plat à l'agenaise

Line some individual egg dishes with 1 tablespoon chopped onion that has been sautéed in goose fat. Break an egg into each dish and cook in a preheated oven. When they are cooked, add a little chopped garlic and parsley. Garnish with coarsely chopped sautéed aubergines (eggplants). Alternatively, the eggs can be cooked in a single large dish.

eggs sur le plat à l'antiboise

Roll 4 spoonfuls of whitebait in flour and sauté them in olive oil. When they are brown, add 1 tablespoon finely diced Gruyère cheese and a little crushed garlic to the pan. Break 4 eggs into the same pan and cook them in a preheated oven. Serve sprinkled with chopped parsley.

eggs sur le plat à l'orientale

Soften some chopped onions in butter and spread 1 tablespoon on the bottom of individual egg dishes. Break the eggs into the dishes and cook in a preheated oven.

To serve, garnish with a ragoût of sweet (bell) peppers *à l'orientale* and saffron-flavoured rice *au gras*. Pour tomato sauce round the eggs.

eggs sur le plat archduke

Soften some chopped onion in butter, season with paprika, and use it to line individual dishes. Break the eggs on top and cook in a preheated oven. Garnish with cooked diced truffles. Surround with suprême sauce seasoned with a little paprika.

eggs sur le plat Jockey Club

Cook the eggs in a large buttered dish. Trim them with a pastry (cookie) cutter, leaving only a narrow border of white around each yolk. Toast some slices of bread and spread them with puréed foie gras. Place an egg on each slice and arrange them in a circle on a round dish. Fill the centre of the dish with sliced calves' kidneys sautéed in Madeira. Top each egg with a slice of truffle.

eggs sur le plat Louis Oliver

Cook a slice (about 40 g, 1½ oz) of fresh foie gras in a little butter in a large egg dish until heated through. Season with salt and a pinch of cayenne pepper. Add a little more butter and, when very hot, break 2 eggs into the dish, one on either side of the foie gras. Coat the latter with a little very hot chicken velouté sauce and cook for 2 minutes over a high heat. Surround the eggs with Périgueux sauce and serve immediately.

eggs sur le plat Montrouge

Butter individual egg dishes and pipe a border of mushroom duxelles in each. Break the eggs into the dishes, surround the yolks with a ribbon of double (heavy) cream and bake in a preheated oven.

eggs sur le plat with bacon

Heat a little butter in a frying pan and lightly fry some thin rashers (slices) of bacon. Break the eggs on to the bacon and cook, basting them with the fat that runs from the bacon. Alternatively, line small individual dishes with thin strips of lightly browned bacon. Break an egg into each dish, pour bacon fat over them and bake in a preheated oven.

other recipes See *anglaise, archiduc, Bercy, bretonne, Carmen, chasseur, chipolata, Condé, Crécy, écarlate, lorraine, maraîchère, Meyerbeer, Parmentier, Rothomago.*

Fried Eggs

Break each egg into a cup, season with salt and pour into a frying pan containing hot oil, butter, goose fat or lard. Immediately draw the white neatly around the yolk and baste with hot fat until the white is set. Drain well. To deep-fry, add the egg to hot fat and fold the white over the yolk. Turn after cooking for a few seconds. As soon as it is lightly browned, remove and drain. The white should be crisp and the yolk soft.

fried eggs à la bayonnaise

Deep-fry some small round slices of bread, then place a slice of fried Bayonne ham cut to the same shape on each one. Fry the eggs in oil and place one on each slice of bread. Garnish with sautéed mushrooms (preferably ceps).

fried eggs à la Catalane

Fry halved, seeded tomatoes and aubergine (eggplant), cut into rounds, separately in olive oil. Add salt and pepper, a little crushed garlic and chopped parsley. Spread the vegetables over a dish. Fry the eggs and slide them on to the vegetables.

other recipes See *alsacienne, américaine, anchovy, andalouse, bamboche, charcutière, ménagère, provençale.*

Hard-boiled Eggs

Cook the eggs in their shells in boiling water for 10–12 minutes, then plunge them into cold water for 7–8 minutes to cool them before shelling. The white and the yolk should be completely set. The eggs must not be allowed to boil for longer because the white becomes rubbery and the yolk crumbles.

hard-boiled egg cutlets

Dice the whites and yolks of 4 hard-boiled (hardcooked) eggs and blend them with 4 tablespoons thick béchamel* sauce to which 2 raw egg yolks have been added. Chill thoroughly.

Divide the mixture into 50 g (2 oz) portions and shape them into cutlets. Dip in egg and breadcrumbs and deep-fry at 175°C (347°F) or shallowfry in butter. Arrange them on a dish, and put a paper frill on the narrow end of each cutlet. Sprinkle with fried curly parsley. Serve with tomato sauce and a garnish of green vegetables blended with butter or cream, or with a vegetable macédoine, tomato fondue or risotto.

The recipe may be varied by adding a little diced mushroom, truffle, lean ham or tongue to the egg mixture.

hard-boiled eggs à la macédoine

Cook and shell the eggs. Cut off the larger ends and finely dice them. Remove the yolks carefully without damaging the whites. Make some mayonnaise and blend half of it with a well-drained chilled macédoine of vegetables, using 1 tablespoon mayonnaise to 5 tablespoons macédoine. Colour the remaining mayonnaise with a little tomato purée (paste) and blend with the mashed yolks and the finely diced egg white. Fill the egg whites with this mixture, shaping the top into a dome. Line a dish with the macédoine, smooth the surface and press the eggs into it so that they stand upright. Garnish with the remaining tomato mayonnaise.

hard-boiled eggs Elisabeth

Cut the ends off some hard-boiled (hard-cooked) eggs so that they look like little barrels. Extract the yolks taking care not to break the whites. Press the yolks through a fine sieve and mix with an equal quantity of fairly thick artichoke purée with a little chopped truffle added. Season with salt and pepper. Fill the eggs with this stuffing, rounding the top into a dome shape. Arrange the eggs in a gratin dish, placing each one on an artichoke heart which has been cooked gently in butter. Cover with Mornay sauce, sprinkle with grated cheese and moisten with melted butter. Brown the eggs in a preheated oven at 220°C (425°F, gas 7).

hard-boiled eggs in breadcrumbs

Hard-boil (hard-cook) 8 eggs, cool under cold running water, and shell them. Wash half a bunch of watercress, dry it and arrange on a dish. Grate 150 g (5 oz, 1¼ cups) dry Tomme cheese. Mix half of it with 50 g (2 oz, ½ cup) dried breadcrumbs. Beat 2 eggs lightly and season with salt and pepper. Cut 8 very thin slices from a sandwich loaf and fry them in oil until golden brown. Sprinkle the remaining cheese on to the pieces of fried bread and put them in a preheated oven at 190°C (375°F, gas 5) for 5 minutes. Roll the eggs in the breadcrumbs, dip them in the beaten egg, then once more in the breadcrumbs. Fry them quickly, turning them in the oil. Arrange the pieces of fried bread on the watercress and put an egg on each.

hard-boiled eggs with sorrel

Take a good handful of young sorrel, remove the stalks, wash and dry the leaves, and shred them finely. Cook slowly in a saucepan with 40 g (1½ oz, 3 tablespoons) butter until all the moisture has evaporated. Add 1 tablespoon flour, cook for 5 minutes over a gentle heat, and allow it to cool. Gradually add 400 ml (14 fl oz, 1¾ cups) boiling milk, stirring constantly with a wooden spoon. Add salt and pepper and simmer for 15 minutes. Press the mixture through a fine sieve. Return to the pan and bring to the boil. Remove from the heat and add 2 tablespoons cream. Adjust the seasoning. Hard-boil (hard-cook) 4 eggs, arrange them in a hot dish and pour the sauce over them.

other recipes See *anchovy, aurore, Chimay, salpicon, Soubise, Verdier.*

Poached Eggs

Break the egg into a cup and then slip it quickly into gently boiling water with 1 tablespoon vinegar added per 1 litre (1¾ pints, 4⅓ cups). Cook for 3–5 minutes with the water barely simmering, depending on how firmly set the yolk needs to be. If the egg is very fresh, it will not spread out in the water and the white will coagulate instantly. When cooked, remove with a spoon, refresh in cold water, drain on a cloth and trim. The eggs should be poached one by one so that they do not merge together in the water. They can be kept warm in water at 70°C (158°F).

poached eggs almaviva

Cook 4 artichoke hearts in salted water, drain them and braise them in butter. Spread a knob of foie gras over each and top with a poached egg. Coat them with Mornay sauce and glaze in a preheated oven at 230°C (450°F, gas 8). When the eggs are browned, sprinkle with finely chopped fresh truffles and serve immediately.

poached eggs in aspic

First make a good aspic jelly, flavouring it with a few tarragon leaves.

Poach 2 eggs per person for 3 minutes in barely simmering unsalted water containing 2 tablespoons white wine vinegar. Then chill the eggs in iced water. Arrange some strips of ham, dipped in aspic, and 2 tarragon leaves in the bottom of each ramekin and pour a thin layer of aspic over the top. Drain and trim the poached eggs and place one in each ramekin. Surround each egg with a julienne of cooked ham and fill the dishes with aspic. Leave to set in the refrigerator. Unmould when ready to serve.

Alternatively, place the drained and trimmed eggs in ramekins and surround with a julienne of ham. Coat with aspic. Garnish with chervil, ham and tarragon, and cover with aspic. Leave to set.

poached eggs with braised turnips

Peel 4 large young turnips. Put them into a saucepan with a little stock, 20 g (¾ oz, 1½ tablespoons) butter, salt and pepper. Cover with foil and cook until all the liquid has evaporated. Set the pan aside. Poach 4 eggs and keep them warm. Prepare a sabayon sauce (see *zabaglione*) with 4 egg yolks and cook over a low heat. Off the heat, fold in 175 g (6 oz, ¾ cup) clarified butter. Season with salt and pepper.

Hollow out the turnips, chop the flesh and add it to the sabayon sauce together with some chopped parsley and 100 ml (4 fl oz, 7 tablespoons) single (light) cream. Place an egg in each hollowed-out turnip and coat with the sauce.

other recipes See *Daumont, espagnole.*

Scrambled Eggs

Melt 50 g (2 oz, ¼ cup) butter in a small heavy based saucepan but do not let it boil. Beat 8 eggs together lightly and season with salt and pepper. Pour into the pan and cook over a low heat (a double saucepan can be used), stirring constantly with a wooden spoon. As the eggs begin to set at the edge of the pan, draw them into the centre and ensure that they do not stick to the bottom. Remove from the heat and add 40 g (1½ oz, 3 tablespoons) butter cut into small pieces, or 2 tablespoons double (heavy) cream. Mix well and keep hot in a double saucepan or a bain marie until ready to serve.

scrambled eggs à l'arlésienne

Halve some courgettes (zucchini), remove most of the pulp and cut into dice. Cook the empty cases lightly in olive oil and also sauté the diced flesh in oil. Prepare a concentrated garlic-flavoured tomato fondue. Make the scrambled eggs and add the diced courgettes and the tomato fondue (1 tablespoon per 2 eggs). Fill the courgette shells with the mixture and arrange them in an oiled gratin dish. Sprinkle with grated Parmesan cheese and a little olive oil and brown quickly in a preheated oven at 240°C (475°F, gas 9).

Poaching eggs

1 *Prepare a shallow pan of simmering water with 1 tablespoon vinegar added. Crack a fresh egg into a small container, then slide it into the water.*

2 *Use a spoon to fold the setting white over and around the egg so that it cooks neatly.*

3 *Press the egg gently to check that the white is cooked and the yolk still soft. Drain well, trim off any untidy pieces of egg white and serve at once. Alternatively, transfer to a dish of chilled water if the eggs are to be served cold, then drain and trim.*

scrambled eggs with artichokes

Cook the artichokes in water and remove the leaves and the choke. Slice the artichoke hearts crossways and sauté them in butter. Make the scrambled eggs and add half the artichoke hearts. Arrange the mixture on a dish, garnish the top with the remaining slices of artichoke and fried croûtons, and surround with a ribbon of concentrated veal stock.

scrambled eggs with cep mushrooms

Slice some cep mushrooms, season with salt and pepper, and sauté them in butter or oil with a little garlic. Make the scrambled eggs and add the ceps. Place in a serving dish with a generous tablespoon of fried ceps in the centre. Sprinkle with fried croûtons.

Other varieties of mushroom may be used: chanterelles, blewits, horn of plenty, or cultivated button mushrooms.

scrambled eggs with chicken livers

Make the scrambled eggs and pile them into a heated dish. Garnish with sliced chicken livers, sautéed in butter and blended with demi-glace sauce. Sprinkle with chopped parsley.

scrambled eggs with shrimps

Add some peeled (shelled) shrimps or prawns heated in butter to the scrambled eggs. Arrange them in a heated dish and garnish with peeled shrimps that have either been tossed in butter or blended with shrimp sauce. Surround with croûtons fried in butter and a ribbon of shrimp sauce.

This recipe can be varied by using crayfish tails and Nantua sauce.

scrambled eggs with smoked salmon

Cut some smoked salmon into thin strips, allowing 25 g (1 oz) per 2 eggs. Pile the scrambled eggs into a hot dish or into a warm puff-pastry case. Garnish with the smoked salmon and some croûtons fried in butter.

other recipes See *américaine, ancienne, Argenteuil, barquette, Bercy, Massenet, princesse, reine, romaine, Rossini.*

Soft-boiled Eggs

There are three methods of preparing these: (1) plunge the eggs into boiling water and cook for 3 minutes; (2) plunge them into boiling water, boil for 1 minute, remove the pan from the heat, and leave them to stand for 3 minutes before taking them out of the hot water; (3) put the eggs into a saucepan with cold water, heat and remove the eggs as soon as the water boils. Whichever method is chosen, ensure that the eggs are at room temperature before cooking them. The precise cooking time depends on personal preference – those suggested in these methods give whites that are softly set and runny yolks. Increase the time slightly for firmly set whites and slightly set yolks.

When several eggs are to be boiled at once, they can be cooked together in a special egg-holder.

All the following recipes given for soft-boiled (soft-cooked) eggs can also be used for poached eggs.

soft-boiled eggs Aladdin

Prepare some saffron-flavoured rice *au gras*. Peel and dice some sweet peppers and fry them in oil together with some chopped onion. Spread the rice over the bottom of a hot dish and arrange the peppers in the centre. Place the cooked eggs in a circle round the peppers. Cover with tomato sauce seasoned with a pinch of cayenne pepper.

soft-boiled eggs Amélie

Prepare some cream sauce and some morels cooked in cream. Make some croustades with puff pastry. Prepare a fine mirepoix of vegetables cooked slowly in butter and deglaze the pan with a little Madeira. Reheat the croustades, fill them with the mirepoix, and place a soft-boiled (soft-cooked) egg in each. Coat the eggs with the cream sauce and garnish with the morels.

soft-boiled eggs béranger

Make a shortcrust pastry (basic pie dough) flan case and bake it blind in a preheated oven at 200°C (400°F, gas 6). Line it with a fairly thick onion purée (see *Soubise*). Arrange the cooked eggs on top and coat them with Mornay sauce. Sprinkle with grated cheese and melted butter and brown quickly in a preheated oven.

soft-boiled eggs Berlioz

Make some oval croustades with duchess potato mixture and brown them lightly in a preheated oven. Fill them with a salpicon of truffles and mushrooms blended with a very reduced Madeira sauce and place a cooked egg on each. Coat very lightly with suprême sauce.

Garnish the centre of each croustade with a cockscomb fried *à la Villeroi*, if desired.

soft-boiled eggs bonvalet

Hollow out some rounds of bread and fry them in butter until golden. Place the cooked eggs in the hollows and coat them with velouté sauce. Surround with a ring of very thick, tomato-flavoured béarnaise sauce and garnish each egg with a slice of truffle that has been heated through in butter.

soft-boiled eggs chénier

Make some saffron-flavoured pilaf rice and shape it into small round cakes in individual ramekins. Place a cooked egg on top of each one and surround with slices of fried aubergine (eggplant). Coat with tomato sauce.

EGG CUP A small wooden, metal or china cup designed as a holder for boiled eggs and placed on a saucer or plate. Sets of two, four or six egg cups are often presented together on a tray.

Called *oviers* in France in the Middle Ages, *coquetiers* (or *coquetières*) in the 16th century were little tables with a cover and several cavities where the eggs were placed. These egg stands often incorporated a salt cellar. Today a *coquetière* is an egg-holder used for boiling several eggs at the same time.

EGG CUSTARD The name often given to a baked sweet custard, a dessert made by pouring sweetened hot milk on to beaten eggs lightly sweetened with caster (superfine) sugar. The milk is usually flavoured with vanilla. The custard is cooked in one large dish or individual moulds in a bain marie in the oven. The same, or a similar, mixture may be cooked in a part-baked pastry case (pie shell) to make custard tart.

RECIPE

egg custard

Boil 1 litre (1¾ pints, 4⅓ cups) milk with 125 g (4½ oz, ½ cup) caster (superfine) sugar and a vanilla pod (bean). Beat 4 eggs lightly in a deep bowl. Gradually pour the boiling milk over the eggs, stirring constantly. Strain into an ovenproof dish or into ramekins and cook in a bain marie in a preheated oven at 160°C (325°F, gas 3) for about 40 minutes. Serve cold.

EGGNOG A nourishing drink served either hot or cold. To make it, beat an egg yolk with a tablespoon of sugar. Add a glass of hot milk and lace with rum or brandy.

Prosper Montagné gave a recipe for beer eggnog (*lait de poule à la bière*), a German speciality that they call *Biersuppe*. It is actually more like a substantial soup.

RECIPE

eggnog with beer

Boil 2 litres (3½ pints, 9 cups) pale ale with 500 g (18 oz, 2¼ cups) sugar, a pinch of salt, a little grated lemon zest and a pinch of ground cinnamon. Add 8 egg yolks beaten with 1 tablespoon cold milk, strain, and chill. Soak 125 g (4½ oz, ⅔ cup) each of raisins and currants in 500 ml (17 fl oz, 2 cups) warm water until plump. Drain well and add to the eggnog. Add a bowl of wholemeal (wholewheat) croûtons, just before serving.

EGGPLANT See *aubergine*.

EGG SAUCE A hot English sauce made of diced hard-boiled (hard-cooked) eggs and butter, most often served with poached fish.

Scotch egg sauce is a béchamel sauce containing sieved hard-boiled egg yolks and whites cut into small strips. It is served with similar dishes.

RECIPE

egg sauce

Boil 2 eggs for 10 minutes, then remove their shells and dice them. While still hot, add the diced egg to 125 g (4½ oz, ½ cup) melted butter, season with salt and pepper, and flavour with lemon juice. Sprinkle with chopped parsley.

EGG THREADS Eggs poached in such a way that they form long threads, used to garnish consommé or soup. The raw eggs are lightly beaten and poured through a fine strainer into the boiling consommé.

The fine threads of egg dropping through the strainer set instantly in the boiling liquid. They can be cooked in boiling water, drained, and added to thicker soups, such as vegetable soup, cream of watercress soup or cream of sorrel soup.

EGG TIMER A small gadget consisting of two transparent bulbs linked by a very narrow opening. The upper bulb contains sand or some other powdery material, which runs into the lower bulb in a given length of time. Many egg timers are designed so that the time taken for the sand to run through is 3 minutes, the average cooking time for a soft-boiled (soft-cooked) egg. Some are graded from 3 to 5 minutes to suit varying tastes.

ÉGRUGEOIR A small wooden mortar (usually of boxwood) used for crushing coarse salt and peppercorns. The word *égrugeoir* is also used for a small salt or pepper mill. Salt crushed in an *égrugeoir* keeps the flavour of coarse salt, and freshly crushed pepper also has a better flavour.

EGYPT See *page 454*.

ÉGYPTIENNE, À L' Describing various dishes using rice, aubergines (eggplants) or tomatoes, together or separately. Aubergines *à l'égyptienne* are stuffed with a mixture of chopped aubergine pulp and onions and served with fried tomatoes. A garnish *à l'égyptienne* is made of fried aubergine rounds, rice pilaf and tomato fondue. The term also describes a mixed salad of rice with chicken livers, ham, mushrooms, artichoke hearts, peas, pulped tomatoes and red (bell) peppers. Fried eggs *à l'égyptienne* are served with tomato halves filled with saffron rice, and potage *à l'égyptienne* is a cream of rice soup made with leeks and onions softened in butter, sieved, and then finished with milk.

RECIPE

chicken medallions à l'égyptienne

Remove the breasts from a raw chicken and trim and flatten them into round or oval medallions. Cut some large aubergines (eggplants) into rounds about 1 cm (½ in) thick and sprinkle with lemon juice. Prepare some rice pilaf. Fry the chicken medallions and aubergine rounds separately in olive oil, then arrange them alternately round a serving dish. Fill the centre of the dish with rice pilaf. Deglaze the pan in which the chicken was cooked with white wine, add this juice to a thick and well-seasoned tomato fondue, and serve separately in a sauceboat (gravy boat).

ELDER A common European tree or shrub with aromatic flowers that are prepared as fritters (like mimosa fritters) and used to flavour syrup or cordials, jams, vinegars and wine. Elderflower champagne is a traditionally British non-alcoholic, but sparkling, summertime drink. The young shoots

EGYPT

Cookery at the time of the Pharaohs had certain refinements. Some game dishes were prepared, and asparagus, several types of onions and leeks, and many spices (including turmeric) and fruits were used. Contemporary Egyptian gastronomy has much in common with that of other Middle Eastern and Arab countries.

The staple food is bread made from maize (corn). Brown beans called *ful medames* are used in large quantities; green vegetables include okra (*bamia*) and broad beans. Dried broad beans are also used to make rissoles and a dip flavoured with garlic and herbs. *Molokheya* (or *mouloureija*) soup is regarded by Egyptians as their national dish. It is a thick sweetish soup seasoned with herbs, to which chicken or rabbit, spices and tomato sauce are added. The commonest meat is mutton, which is grilled (broiled), minced (ground) or stewed with eggs and vegetables, and fresh or dried fruit. Beef is not usually eaten, since it is tough. A type of very large prawn (shrimp) is prepared in a pilaff containing (bell) peppers and tomatoes, and mullet roe is also popular. Dried vegetables are used frequently.

Egyptian pâtisserie is typical of the Middle East, with *loukoums* (Turkish delight) and baklavas predominating. Dates are widely consumed in many forms. They are used in pâtisserie, especially to make *menenas*, a dough ball flavoured with almonds and orange-flower water, filled with stoned (pitted) dates, almonds, pistachio nuts and cinnamon, and then baked in the oven. Other fruits include plums, pomegranates, mangoes, bananas, limes and watermelons.

The Egyptians mainly drink water flavoured with orange-flower water or rose water, unfermented sugar cane juice, and a typical red brew called *karkade*, tasting of redcurrants, made with redcurrant blossom from Guinea. They have also tried to revive the famous wines the Pharaohs used to have buried in jars in their tombs. Some interesting wines are produced for export, the best known of which are whites: Cru-des-Ptolémées and Queen Cleopatra. Omar Khayyám is a red wine smelling of dates.

---

contain an edible and delicate core, which is prepared like asparagus. Elderberries are used to make jam, jelly and wine.

RECIPES

elderflower wine with lime blossom
Pour 7 litres (12 pints, 7½ quarts) water over a handful of elderflowers and a handful of lime blossom. Add 250 g (9 oz, 1 cup) caster (superfine) sugar, 2 lemons cut into slices, and 6 tablespoons white wine vinegar; leave to macerate for 3 days. Stir each day. Strain off the liquid and bottle it; secure the corks with string. Leave to stand for 5 days before consuming.

elder shoots
Peel some elder shoots, stripping the woody parts away from the core. Cut the core into sticks about 7.5 cm (3 in) long; tie the sticks into bundles like asparagus and cook them in boiling salted water for 10–15 minutes. Drain them thoroughly and serve them hot, with cream, gravy or melted butter containing chopped hard-boiled (hard-cooked) egg yolk, or cold, with a vinaigrette dressing.

ELECTRICAL APPLIANCES Electrical appliances underwent spectacular development in the kitchen during the 20th century. At the beginning of the 1920s, most household appliances were mechanical, but soon the first electrical ones began to appear. The ancestor of the dishwasher was introduced by 1930, together with waffle irons and electric boiling rings. Ten years later toasters, kettles and refrigerators were readily available.

It was after 1948 that electrical appliances really started to take off in Europe: electric mixers were followed by blenders and automatic toasters. During the 1960s the first fully automatic dishwashers appeared and, during the 1970s, food processors, microwave ovens and domestic freezers.

Small household electrical appliances save time and energy, but to be worthwhile they must be used regularly. Some have reached a high degree of sophistication; others are subject to the fluctuations of fashion.

ELEPHANT A large mammal of which there are two species: the Indian elephant, trained as a beast of burden, and the African elephant, formerly widely hunted as game and a source of ivory. Strict measures are now in force to preserve the species. Reports by travellers and hunters from the 17th century onwards indicate that elephant meat is tough but tasty, provided that it is cooked for more than 15 hours or has been hung for a long time in the open air. The feet and the trunk are of greatest culinary interest: their flesh, which is muscular and gelatinous, resembles ox (beef) tongue.

During the 1870 siege of Paris, the flesh of elephants from the Jardin des Plantes appeared in butchers' shops and restaurants. The menu of the Café Anglais offered braised elephant's feet with ham, garlic, spices and Madeira, and one butcher was selling elephant blood pudding (sausage).

ÉLEVAGE Term used to describe processes which include ullaging, racking, fining and filtration, used for high-quality wines after their fermentation to

A variety of beans and pulses on sale in a souk at Luxor, Egypt.

ensure the best flavour and long life. These processes enable the biological and physio-chemical development of the wine to be controlled and are carried out in tanks, vats or more especially in small oak casks, which allow very slow aeration; they take a varying length of time from a few months in the case of Beaujolais and Muscadet to 1–2 years for Burgundy and Bordeaux, and at least 6 years for *vins jaunes*.

ELF-CUP FUNGUS A cup-shaped fungus of the genus *Peziza*, usually brown or orange in colour. Elf-cups grow wild on the surface of the ground or on dead branches of trees. They are prepared in the same way as morel mushrooms, but are not as good. However, Doctor Ramain, in his *Mycogastronomie*, believes that they are underestimated and recommends the veined hare's (or ass's) ear variety, which loses its smell of chlorine when cooked and has delicate tasty flesh. He also recommends the orange variety, which can be eaten raw with sugar and kirsch.

ELIXIR A solution of aromatic substances in alcohol. In the Middle Ages elixirs were used as potions to which magical properties were sometimes attributed. The word comes from the Arabic *al-iksïr* (essence), from the Greek *ksêron* (dry medicine). Some elixir formulae, most of which are prepared by monks, have lasted for centuries and are still being made today (notably the Grande-Chartreuse plant elixir). Many plant liqueurs bear the name 'elixir' and are sweet and scented to the taste, such as the golden-coloured Anvers elixir, made of plants steeped in wine brandy, and elixir of Garus, made of vanilla and saffron steeped in alcohol, to which is added syrup flavoured with maidenhair fern and orange-flower water.

ELK A large deer living wild in Scandinavia and Siberia (where attempts are being made to tame them); it is also found in North America, where it is known as a moose. Its meat is prepared in the same way as venison, which it resembles. In the Rocky Mountains, minced (ground) moose meat is used to make various dishes, including hamburgers and also pies (with apples and grapes).

EMBALLER A French culinary term meaning to wrap up an article that is to be poached or stewed in stock (a large fish, stuffed cabbage, a ballotine, any dish cooked in a caul). The food is wrapped in a pig's caul or a piece of muslin (cheesecloth) or linen, to hold it together while cooking. In French charcuterie, *emballer* means to fill the moulds with a mixture to be cooked such as pâté and galantines.

EMBOSSER To put a piece of meat or stuffing in a net, skin or mould so as to give it its final form before cooking. The technique allows draining, steaming, drying or smoking to be carried out without too much distortion or loss of weight.

EMILIA-ROMAGNA Northern Italian wine producing area making a range of wines from Lambrusco and Trebbiano di Romagna to quality wines, including Cabernets and Sauvignon Blanc from the Colli Bolognesi, and, in particular, Chardonnay, Pinot Noir and Cabernet Sauvignon from Colli Piacentini.

ÉMINCER A French culinary term meaning to cut vegetables, fruit or meat into thin slices or rounds. This is usually done with a slicing knife on a chopping board (for cucumbers, leeks, mushrooms, pears and apples), but a mandolin can be used for carrots, turnips and potatoes, and a food processor with a slicing disc for potatoes. There is a special instrument for slicing tomatoes thinly and for cutting them into a 'fan', with the slices still joined at the base.

ÉMINCÉS A dish consisting of thin slices of leftover meat (roast, braised or boiled) placed in an ovenproof dish, covered with a sauce, and gently heated in the oven. (An *émincé* is a thin slice of meat.) Émincés are most often made with beef, lamb or mutton, sometimes with game (venison), and less frequently with pork, poultry or veal, as white meats are always drier when reheated.

Beef émincés are prepared with Madeira sauce and mushrooms, bordelaise sauce and slices of bone marrow, or with chasseur, lyonnaise, piquante, Robert, tomato (well-reduced and highly seasoned), or Italian sauce; they are accompanied by sautéed potatoes, green vegetables tossed in butter or cream, braised vegetables, purées, pasta or a risotto. Venison eminces are covered with poivrade, grand veneur or chasseur sauce and served with chestnut purée and redcurrant jelly. The sauces for mutton émincés are mushroom, tomato, paprika or Indian; the accompanying vegetables are rice and courgettes (zucchini). Pork émincés are made with piquante, Robert or charcutière sauce and served with a potato or split pea purée. Veal or poultry émincés are covered with tomato, royal or suprême sauce; the accompanying vegetables are the same as for beef émincés.

By extension, the word émincé is also used for various other dishes made of items sliced thinly before cooking. In veal émincé, for example, thin slices of veal cut from the noix (the fleshy upper part of the leg) are quickly fried and then covered with stock, gravy or sometimes cream; the dish is served with fried mushrooms.

RECIPES

beef émincés with bordelaise sauce
Make some bordelaise sauce. Poach some slices of beef bone marrow in stock. Arrange thin slices of boiled beef on a lightly buttered ovenproof dish and garnish with the hot slices of bone marrow. Generously coat with bordelaise sauce and heat through gently in the oven.

beef émincés with mushrooms

Arrange some thin slices of boiled beef in a long ovenproof dish. Prepare some Madeira sauce. Trim and slice some mushrooms and heat them in butter. Place the mushrooms on the meat and cover generously with hot Madeira sauce; heat through gently in the oven.

veal or chicken émincés à blanc

Lightly butter an ovenproof dish. Cut some poached or boiled veal or chicken into thin slices. These slices can then be treated as for beef émincés with mushrooms, or they can be coated with tomato, Breton, royal or suprême sauce.

other recipes See *italienne, miroton.*

EMMENTAL A Swiss unpasteurized cow's-milk cheese containing 45% fat, named after the Emme valley in the canton of Bern, where it was first made. It is a hard, ivory-coloured cheese with a good many holes and a golden-yellow to brown rind. Emmental is matured for 6–12 months in a cool cellar and marketed in a wheel shape with convex edges, 80–85 cm (31–34 in) in diameter, 22 cm (8¾ in) thick, and weighing 80–100 kg (176–220 lb). The edge of the cheese bears the word 'Switzerland' stamped in red.

The cheese was introduced into Haute-Savoie in the middle of the 19th century by German Swiss immigrants, and a Savoy Emmental, made in the cheese dairies of Savoy, is very similar in appearance and flavour to the Swiss cheese. It is marketed in wheel shapes, 70–100 cm (27½–39 in) in diameter, 13–25 cm (5–10 in) thick, and weighing 60–130 kg (132–286 lb). Swiss and Savoy Emmentals are used for the table.

Another type of French Emmental (also spelt Emmenthal) is produced in the flatter regions of France, such as Franche-Comté and Burgundy. It is matured for 2 months in a warm cellar and resembles Gruyère, with large holes. It is used for cooking (especially grated). A similar cheese is made in the United States, known as American Lace.

RECIPE

croque-Emmental

Place a slice of ham on a slice of Emmental or Gruyère (cut to half the size of the ham slice), fold over and secure with a cocktail stick (toothpick). Coat with flour, then dip in batter and fry in hot oil. Put a fried egg on each croque-Emmental and serve very hot.

EMPANADA A pie or pasty filled with meat or fish, popular all over Spain and in parts of South America. The classic *empanada* comes from Galicia and is made with chicken, onions and peppers. It can also be made with seafood, sardines, eel or lamprey. Formerly made with bread dough, *empanada* is now usually made with flaky pastry and often eaten cold. It is also prepared in the form of small individual pies.

In Chile and Argentina, *empanadas* are small pasties with scalloped edges. They are filled with a mixture of minced (ground) meat, raisins, olives and onions, spiced with pepper, paprika and cumin. They are served as a hot hors d'oeuvre or snack, often with wine.

RECIPE

empanada

Cut 500 g (18 oz) lean beef into small cubes and cook gently in a little oil with 100 g (4 oz, ⅔ cup) chopped onion, ½ seeded and diced sweet (bell) green pepper and leaf pimento (*ignara*), 1 teaspoon ground cumin and 1 crushed garlic clove. When the meat is cooked, add 2 tablespoons raisins, previously soaked, and 1 chopped hard-boiled (hard-cooked) egg. Put a layer of this mixture on a piece of pastry and make little pasties. Bake in a preheated oven at 180°C (350°F, gas 4) for 30 minutes and serve very hot.

EMPEROR FISH Fish of the *Beryciform* family, which lives at great depths in the eastern Atlantic, from Ireland to Spain, and in the Pacific around New Zealand. It is about 60 cm (2 ft) long, and is identified by its red colour and by its dorsal fin being longer than its anal fin. Sold as fillets, its excellent flesh is similar to that of monkfish, and it is cooked in the same way.

EMU Flightless bird of the *Dromiceidae* family, which can be as tall as 1.6–1.8 m (5¼–6 ft). Originally from Australia, the emu is now bred in several countries, including France. It is slaughtered aged about 10–12 months, when it weighs about 40 kg (88 lb). Its flesh is pink and tender with a taste reminiscent of game, and is cooked in the same way. The parts commonly used are fillet, *aiguillettes* of fillet, haunch fillet and leg.

EMULSIFIER A food additive used to preserve the texture of emulsions. Among natural emulsifiers are lecithins, extracted from almonds or other seeds (especially soya beans in chocolate-making) or from egg yolk (in powdered milk). Mono- and diglycerides of fatty acids are used in making margarine and mayonnaise. Gum arabic and gum tragacanth are also often used to stabilize emulsions.

EMULSION A preparation obtained by dispersing one kind of liquid (in the form of tiny droplets) in another liquid, with which it does not mix. An emulsion consisting of a fatty substance, such as oil or butter, dispersed in vinegar, water or lemon juice will only remain smooth and stable if it is bound with an emulsifier, usually egg yolk. This preparation is the basis of emulsified sauces, such as hollandaise, mousseline and their derivatives. Milk is a natural emulsion consisting of globules of cream suspended in a watery solution containing protein (which acts as an emulsifier).

EN-CAS The French term for a light meal, usually cold, eaten between main meals (the word literally means 'in case', of hunger in this context). In the old châteaux, an *en-cas de nuit*, consisting of cheese, fruit and cold meats, was arranged on a pedestal table for the refreshment of travellers returning home late at night. At Versailles, the king's *en-cas de nuit* consisted of three loaves, two bottles of wine and a carafe of water. Wishing to publicize his support for Molière, Louis XIV invited him to share his snack, in order to teach a lesson to the courtiers who refused to allow the famous dramatist to sit at their table.

ENCHAUD A speciality from Périgord consisting of a piece of boned pork fillet (tenderloin) rolled up, tied with string and cooked in the oven in a casserole. It can also be stuffed. Cold enchaud is particularly delicious.

RECIPE

enchaud
Bone a piece of pork fillet (tenderloin) weighing about 1.5 kg (3¼ lb), and keep the bone. Spread out the fillet on the work surface. Season with salt and pepper, sprinkle lightly with crushed thyme and insert small pieces of garlic. Roll up the meat tightly, tie it up with string and keep it cool.

The next day, heat 2 tablespoons lard (shortening) in a flameproof casserole and brown the enchaud on all sides. Add a small glass of warm water, a sprig of thyme and the pork bone. Season with salt and pepper. Cover and seal the lid with a flour and water paste. Cook in a preheated oven at 180°C (350°F, gas 4) for about 2 hours. When the enchaud is cooked, drain it and keep it hot on the serving dish. Remove the bone and the thyme from the casserole and skim as much fat as possible from the cooking juices; add 4 tablespoons stock and reduce. Serve the enchaud with this sauce, accompanied by potatoes sautéed with garlic.

The garlic can be replaced by small sticks of truffle. In this case, the pork is stuffed with about 400 g (14 oz, 1¾ cups) well-seasoned fine forcemeat, to which 1 teaspoon brandy and some truffle peel have been added. Roll up and cook the enchaud as in the previous method and serve cold, with a salad dressed with walnut oil.

ENDAUBAGE A mixture of ingredients used for braising; it can include bacon, sliced carrots, onions, shallots, a bouquet garni, wine, spirits, oil, vinegar, garlic, peppercorns, salt and various flavourings. *Endaubage* formerly described a conserve of stewed meat with lard (shortening), which was stored in barrels and used, in particular, by the navy.

ENDIVE (CHICORY) A plant with leaves that may be eaten raw in salads or cooked as a vegetable. Most varieties have bitter leaves. The variety commonly used is the curly endive. The hearts, known as *gourilos*, may also be eaten.

There is confusion about the names endive and chicory, arising from the fact that the plants are closely related. There are many varieties of both vegetables. In England, endive means the curly-leaved salad plant, generally called chicory in the United States. Chicory in England is what the French and Americans call endive or Belgian endive: the tightly closed shoots or buds. For the sake of clarity, preference is given in this article to the English usage. Examples of endive and chicory are illustrated together in the entry on chicory.

• WILD ENDIVE When young and tender, it is eaten in salads in the spring. It may be found growing on the roadsides. It is usually cut into fine strips (a *chiffonnade*) and has a very bitter flavour. It is an ingredient of *mesclun niçois*. If planted out in a shady place, 'improved' winter varieties of endive are produced, including 'Capucin's beard'. This is tender, white and slightly bitter and is tossed in vinaigrette or cut into small sticks for pickling in vinegar.

• CURLY ENDIVE There are several summer and winter varieties of curly endive. In France it is cultivated in the Paris area and in the west and is eaten mainly in salad. The heart is white or yellow, and the leaves, which are very thin and serrated, are yellow in the centre and greener towards the outside. Curly endive is seasoned with vinaigrette flavoured with shallot, mustard or garlic. It is often served with *chapons* or strips of larding bacon. In the west of France, the vegetable is served with haricot (navy) beans in butter with a walnut oil dressing.

RECIPES

braised endive
Prepare the endive as for endive *au gratin*. Make a white roux, using 40 g (1½ oz, 3 tablespoons) butter and 40 g (1½ oz, 6 tablespoons) plain (all-purpose) flour for every 500 g (18 oz) endive; season with salt, pepper, a little sugar and some grated nutmeg, then add 600 ml (1 pint, 2½ cups) stock. Add the chopped endive and cook briefly on the hob (stove top) in a flameproof casserole. Then cover the casserole and cook in a preheated oven at 180°C (350°F, gas 4) for about 1½ hours. Veal gravy may be added to enhance the flavour.

endive au gratin
Remove the hard or dark green leaves from the heads of curly endive. Cut the remaining leaves at the beginning of the stump and rinse well in water. Drain and blanch for 10 minutes in plenty of boiling salted water. Cool, drain, chop finely and then mix with 4–5 tablespoons béchamel* sauce per 450 g (1 lb) endive. Arrange the endive on a buttered gratin dish and sprinkle with 75 g (3 oz, ¾ cup) grated Gruyère cheese and 2 tablespoons melted butter. Brown in a preheated oven at 240°C (475°F, gas 9).

endive salad with bacon

Cut 250 g (9 oz) smoked bacon for each head of curly endive into very fine strips and brown them in butter in a frying pan. Clean the endive, rinse it and dry it as thoroughly as possible. Season with a well-flavoured vinaigrette and then scatter the sizzling-hot bacon strips over the top. Tiny fried garlic-flavoured croûtons are usually added. Serve immediately.

stewed endive

Prepare the endive as for braising, and place it in a saucepan with 50 g (2 oz, ¼ cup) butter for each 450 g (1 lb) endive. Season, add 500–600 ml (17–20 fl oz, 2–2½ cups) water, cover and cook in a preheated oven at 180°C (350°F, gas 4) for 1½ hours. When cooked, the endive may be tossed in butter, reduced cream or béchamel sauce just before serving.

ENGLAND See *page 460.*

ENTOLOMA The majority of mushrooms in this genus are poisonous, so great care should be taken to select only the edible variety – the buckler entoloma, *Entoloma prunuloides*, a fleshy mushroom with a grey-brown cap and pink gills.

ENTRECÔTE (RIB STEAK) A piece of prime-quality beef, which should be cut from 'between two ribs' (*côtes*) – hence the name. However, it is usually cut from the boned set of ribs. Marbled and tender, entrecôte steak should be grilled (broiled) or fried. Steaks cut from the lower ribs are prepared in the same way but tend to be firmer. Ideally, the steak should be about 2 cm (¾ in) thick, flat and well-trimmed, with just a thin margin of fat, which is cut at intervals to prevent it curling up during cooking.

The following is an interesting account of a method of barbecuing entrecôte over vine shoots.

Letter to gourmets, gourmands, gastronomes, and gluttons . . . (James de Coquet, Simoën, 1977)

'Grilled? Fried? It doesn't matter. The only essential thing is that it should be properly sealed. Season well and brown until it is slightly charred outside but bright red inside. In passing, let us make a recommendation to the profane: do not scorn the end of the entrecôte steak, the crusty part. It is delicious. The entrecôte steak has a penchant for shallots, which is where the famous *entrecôte maître de chai* comes from. This dish is grilled, needless to say, on an open grill or barbecue. But not just any old fuel will do; it must be vine shoots, and not just any old vine shoots! You have to use Cabernet Sauvignon vine shoots, which were put away to dry for this very purpose at least a year ago. Once the first side is done, turn the steak over and slice the shallot over it. Add some melted butter. When the second side of the steak is duly sealed, turn it over quickly and put it in a very hot dish in which a knob of butter is gently melting. Sprinkle with shallot, add a second knob of butter, and place another very hot dish over the top, thus making an oven in which your steak can poach for two or three minutes. Next, take a large knife and . . .'

RECIPES

fried entrecôte

Season the steak with salt and pepper. Melt some butter in a frying pan. When it bubbles, add the steak and brown both sides over a high heat. Then drain, arrange on the serving dish, and garnish with a knob of butter (plain butter, maître d'hôtel butter or marchand de vin butter). Alternatively, serve with a red wine sauce or sprinkle with the cooking butter plus a few drops of lemon juice and some chopped parsley.

fried entrecôte à la bourguignonne

Fry a 400–500 g (14–18 oz) steak in butter, drain and keep hot on the serving dish. Pour 100 ml (4 fl oz, 7 tablespoons) each of red wine and demi-glace into the frying pan and heat until reduced, then coat the steak with this sauce.

The demi-glace can be replaced by the same amount of well-reduced consommé bound with 1 teaspoon beurre manié.

fried entrecôte à la fermière

Prepare about 450 g (1 lb) vegetable fondue. Fry a 450 g (1 lb) steak in butter, place in a serving dish and keep hot. Surround with the vegetable fondue. Deglaze the pan with 100 ml (4 fl oz, 7 tablespoons) white wine and the same amount of beef consommé*, reduce and bind with 1 teaspoon beurre manié. Pour this sauce over the steak.

fried entrecôte à la hongroise

Season a 450 g (1 lb) steak, then fry it in butter. When it is three-quarters cooked, add 1 tablespoon chopped onion. Drain the steak, place it on a serving dish and keep hot. Finish cooking the onions, add a little paprika and adjust the seasoning. Deglaze the frying pan with 100 ml (4 fl oz, 7 tablespoons) white wine and the same amount of velouté*. Reheat and pour over the steak. Serve with boiled potatoes.

fried entrecôte à la lyonnaise

Thinly slice 2 large onions and fry them gently in butter. Fry a 450 g (1 lb) steak in butter; when three-quarters cooked, add the onions. When cooked, drain the steak and onion, place in a serving dish and keep hot. Deglaze the frying pan with 2 tablespoons vinegar and 100 ml (4 fl oz, 7 tablespoons) demi-glace. Reduce, stir in 1 tablespoon chopped parsley and pour over the steak. (The demi-glace can be replaced with reduced consommé bound with 1 teaspoon beurre manié.)

fried entrecôte with mushrooms

Fry a 450 g (1 lb) steak in butter. When three-quarters cooked, add 8–10 mushroom caps to the

ENGLAND

While contemporary cooking across Britain reflects its multi-cultural society and the vast array of ingredients and culinary skills imported from around the world, Scotland, England and Wales retain their food heritage. England is a country of tradition, where the cooking is straightforward: roast beef and boiled puddings are typical of its past. The national style has always been to give priority to good ingredients: superb beef, game, salmon, 'native' oysters, Dover sole, field mushrooms and a multiplicity of different apples.

■ **Meat, poultry and game** Traditionally, the British have a reputation for generous meat consumption – roast beef and lamb; beef steaks with oyster sauce; the mixed grill; chops and cutlets. Boiled beef and carrots, beef 'olives' and boiled leg of mutton with caper sauce are part of the tradition, along with very good casseroles, such as Lancashire hot pot (named for the tall brown and white container in which it was cooked) made with lamb chops and, sometimes, kidneys, onion and potato. Boiled suet puddings, such as beef pudding with oysters, gave way to pastry-topped pies, with fillings of steak and pigeon, or beef with kidney in the 19th century. While jellied pork pies, made in Melton Mowbray, were once favourites on traditional pub menus, raised game pies are associated with hunting parties, Christmas and party fare.

Ham and sausages play a vital role, including the long, coiled Cumberland and Oxford veal and pork sausages. Famous hams, boiled and carved cold on the bone, include York and the black Bradenham. There have also been centuries of reliance on bacon in many forms: Quorn bacon roll is made with suet, onions, sage and bacon. Caul-wrapped faggots of pig's fry with sage, onions and crumbs, oxtail casserole and cold,

sliced ox (beef) tongue are old-fashioned regional favourites.

The love of meat explains the great number of dishes made with left-overs (accompanied by boiled vegetables if hot). The wide range of cold meats, including spiced brisket, veal and ham pie and brawn (head cheese), has encouraged the development of interesting accompaniments. Jellies, such as rowan and redcurrant; traditional sauces, including Cumberland sauce made with oranges, port, redcurrant jelly and mustard; pickled walnuts; and numerous chutneys and pickles are prepared to complement meat and poultry dishes. Many chutneys and pickles are highly spiced from the Indian and Asian influence, and date from the 18th century, as do a range of bottled sauces – mushroom ketchup and Worcestershire sauce are typical. Mustard, grown in East Anglia, is another favourite condiment, eaten strong and used to make devilled dishes.

Traditional recipes for poultry include chicken pie and boiled chickens with oysters or parsley sauce. Duck may be stuffed 'with plenty of onion and plenty of sage' and eaten with peas. Geese, popular in the 16th and 17th centuries, have largely given way to turkey, stuffed for Christmas and served with bacon and chipolata sausages. Game birds include red grouse, pheasant and the superior grey-leg partridge, roasted and served with berry sauces, or casseroled. Mallard and teal are prepared *à l'orange* and hare is jugged (casseroled with wine).

■ **Vegetables** Potatoes feature in a vast array of cooked dishes, including soups, pies, purées, fried cakes and stews. They may be boiled and served with butter. Chips should not be forgotten, including game chips – wafer-thin crisps (potato chips) accompanying roast birds – and the proper chips, cut large and traditionally fried in beef fat, then sold wrapped in paper by fish-and-chip shops. New peas; broad (fava) beans; asparagus

from the Vale of Evesham; samphire in June with fish; a fondness for parsley; watercress with grills; and winter vegetables like cabbage and parsnips are other specialities.

■ **Fish and seafood** Fish, once a cheap commodity, suffered a reversal in the latter half of the 20th century. Dover sole has long been famous fried in butter; turbot is traditional with shrimp or lobster coral sauces; mackerel is served with gooseberries; and poached salmon is offered with sorrel. Pike in Isaac Walton's recipe (1653) was stuffed with oysters, anchovy and herbs, while many modern dishes use smoked haddock. Kippers (see *herring*) retain their popularity. Jellied eels, Whitstable oysters, cockles with vinegar, shrimps potted with butter and mace, and dressed crab in its shell are all enjoyed.

■ **Regional cooking** Local dishes and culinary customs are still important. Examples include Hindle wakes from Lancashire, dating back to the 12th century, a chicken stuffed with prunes and herb-flavoured crumbs, cooked with vinegar and glazed with a lemon cream sauce. Toad-in-the-hole is a dish of sausages baked in a batter and angels on horseback are bacon-wrapped oysters grilled, then served on croûtons. Northumberland singin' hinnies are lardy buns with currants, cooked on a griddle, and Richmond maids of honour are tartlets with ground almonds and brandy. Black puddings (blood sausage) are a favourite in Lancashire, and tripe with onions is popular in the north-east. Cornwall is famous for its potato-and-meat pasties and for stargazey pie, made with pilchards; Yorkshire is known for its batter pudding.

■ **Breakfast and teatime** These are meals invented in Britain – the former known for bacon and eggs with field mushrooms, plus toast and marmalade. Tea has become an afternoon interlude for the tired, or a holiday treat, with cucumber sandwiches and scones with strawberry jam in summer or hot buttered teacakes in winter. Sliced cake and Earl Grey tea flavoured with bergamot are also traditional for tea. Sandwiches, another English idea, can also be eaten outside proper meal times. Other additions to the menu include the invention of the savoury to end the meal. The country is also known for a range of cups, hot drinks such as negus (hot port with lemon and nutmeg), grog and nogs (milk, beaten eggs and rum), and hot and cold wine punches.

■ **The sweet tooth** The national need for a 'cuppa' (a cup of tea, perhaps up to five a day) with a snack may account for the variety of buns, crumpets and muffins, and the early invention of manufactured biscuits to supplement the home-made jumbles, fairings, ginger and brandy snaps. Baking, cake-decorating and jam-making are still enjoyed even if they are no longer daily pastimes. The wide variety of cakes include the butter sponge known as a Victoria sandwich and the sponge that once partnered a mid-morning glass of Madeira, duly known as Madeira cake. Saffron, a spice once grown in East Anglia and Devon and Cornwall, is a traditional ingredient in dough-based cakes.

Other cakes are flavoured with ginger (like Grasmere gingerbread) or dried fruit. Caraway seed cake was popular in the 18th century but is less so now. Simnel cake, with a history dating back to the 17th century, was once coloured with saffron and made for Mothering Sunday, but it is now an Easter cake, baked with a marzipan layer.

Fruit is cultivated with great care. Apple orchards supply the tart Bramley cooking apple (which cooks to a full-flavoured fluff) and the famous Cox. Strawberries are synonymous with tennis and Wimbledon. Wild fruit, such as blackberries, are made into pies and preserves, including bramble jelly. Cider is made, particularly in the West Country, as are syrups and liqueurs.

Celebrated desserts include Eton mess (mashed strawberries and cream); baked apples; gooseberry fool; rhubarb pie; fruit crumble; Bakewell tart with a ground almond layer inside pastry; and 'treacle' tart with crumbs and golden (light corn) syrup. Puddings are the most popular desserts, many of them using bread – like summer pudding – or steamed in a bowl, such as cabinet pudding with sponge fingers (ladyfingers), candied fruit and custard. Prince Albert's pudding is steamed sponge with raisins. Suet puddings, made from suet pastry, include spotted dick with raisins and jam rolypoly, both eaten with hot pouring custard. Milk puddings are lighter and are made with rice, semolina or tapioca. Creams include syllabubs, Boodles' orange fool, junkets, possets and trifle.

■ **Cheese and beer** Cheese is eaten occasionally at the end of a meal, after the dessert, accompanied by crackers or plain biscuits, such as Bath Olivers. These biscuits are lightly baked plain, unsweetened crackers. They were invented in the 18th century by William Oliver, a doctor who attended wealthy visitors to the spa town of Bath. Cheese may be served with chunks of bread as a light meal. One of the world's great blues, Stilton, traditionally served whole in a napkin and partnered with port and nuts originated in Leicestershire. England also excels at hard cheeses, including Cheddar and Cheshire, excellent both mild or mature, Sage Derby, Red Leicester and the mellow Double Gloucester. These cheeses cook and toast well. They also go excellently with beer or cider for a 'ploughman's lunch' – a pub speciality of bread, cheese and sweet pickle.

Cask-conditioned beer is sold in pubs in glass mugs: brown or pale ale, bitter ale, which is amber-coloured, strong brown beer, mild, which is a light beer with a hint of hops, and the famous draught stout, black with a good head of foam.

■ **History** The first English cookery book, *Forme of Cury* ('Cooking Methods'), attributed to the cooks of Richard II, is of the same period as *Viandier* by Taillevent. French was the menu language until halfway through the 20th century and kitchen traditions ran in parallel with France, but Britain has had a different focus, away from chef cooking. The public has always shown more interest in the women authors who concentrated on domestic cooking, like Hannah Glasse, *The Art of Cookery Made Plain and Easy* (1747); Eliza Acton, *Modern Cookery for Private Families* (1845); and Mrs (Isabella) Beeton, *Book of Household Management* (1861). Even well-known chefs, such as Escoffier and Alexis Soyer, wrote books for domestic use. The core of culinary tradition remains in home cooking, from country houses to farmhouse fare and lovingly prepared bakes and preserves. Simple family dishes and the Sunday roast have always been prepared with great success in the home kitchen and they are far superior to the majority of average restaurant attempts at mass production of homely meals. Institutions like the Oxbridge colleges and London's gentlemen's clubs, have contributed more to the good reputation of the best British dishes than restaurants.

Boudin (pudding) bacon, *rosbif* and *bifteck* are all French words with English origins. Crème brûlée bridges the gap. Both Carême and later Escoffier worked in London, and specialities they introduced to France include turtle soup, oyster soup, fried whitebait from the Thames estuary, curries in their infinite variety, eel pie, eggs and bacon, plum cake and a whole range of puddings.

A substantial empire bequeathed a habit of adopting imported food. Indian spices and dishes were adopted from the late 18th century on and dishes like kedgeree (rice with smoked fish) and mulligatawny (curried soup) joined the repertoire.

frying pan. Place the steak in a serving dish and keep hot. Finish cooking the mushrooms, then arrange them around the steak. Deglaze the frying pan with 100 ml (4 fl oz, 7 tablespoons) each of white wine and demi-glace, and reduce. Sieve, add 1 tablespoon fresh butter, stir and pour the sauce over the steak.

Instead of demi-glace, the same quantity of well-reduced consommé bound with 1 teaspoon beurre manié can be used.

grilled entrecôte

Lightly brush the steak with oil or melted butter, season with salt and pepper and cook over very hot wood charcoal or grill (broil) in a vertical grill, under the grill (broiler) of the cooker (stove), or over an iron grill. The surface of the steak must be sealed so that the juices will not escape. (Some cooks advise against seasoning with salt before cooking because this draws out the blood.) Serve with château potatoes, bunches of cress and béarnaise sauce (separately), if liked.

grilled entrecôte à la bordelaise

In the authentic recipe, the steak is simply grilled (broiled) over vine-shoot embers, seasoned, then served with a knob of butter. However, in certain gastronomic circles, the steak is grilled, garnished with slices of beef bone marrow poached in stock and sprinkled with chopped parsley. It is served with bordelaise sauce.

other recipes See *Bercy, grand-mère, marchand de vin, ménagère, Mirabeau, vert-pré.*

ENTRE-DEUX-MERS

An AOC white wine from the Bordeaux region. Some red wine is also produced from Merlot and Cabernet Sauvignon grapes and is sold as Bordeaux AOC. The production area is between two rivers, the Garonne and Dordogne, hence a name which means 'between two seas'. White wines sold as Entre-Deux-Mers AOC are dry, crisp and fruity and are made mainly from Sauvignon Blanc, Sémillon, Muscadelle and Ugni Blanc grapes. They provide a good accompaniment to most fish and shellfish dishes, including the oysters that are a speciality of the Gironde region.

ENTRÉE

Today, the entrée is usually the main course of a meal, but in a full French menu it is the third course, following the hors d'oeuvre (or soup) and the fish course and preceding the roast. At a grand dinner, the entrée is either a hot dish in a sauce or a cold dish. Mixed entrées are composite dishes, such as croustades and timbales. When more than one entrée is served, they must be clearly differentiated: distinctions were formerly made between *entrées volantes de boucherie* (meat entrées), *entrées d'abats* (offal entrées) and *entrées diverses* (various entrées).

With the trend towards simplification and reduction in the number of courses, modern menus usu-

ally centre on a main dish, preceded by a starter and followed by a salad, cheese and dessert. In the Middle Ages, entrées included such items as crystallized (candied) melon peel, oyster tarts, *andouillettes*, forcemeats and cheese ramekins. Today (when present) they include fish, shellfish, caviar, foie gras, fish terrine, pasta dishes (such as gnocchi, macaroni, spaghetti and ravioli), quenelles, savoury pastries (such as quiches, patties, timbales, tarts and vol-au-vent), egg dishes (including soufflés), and even vegetable dishes (artichokes and asparagus). In theory, cold charcuterie, fish in marinades or oil, raw vegetables, mixed salads, melon and radishes are considered to be hors d'oeuvre.

ENTREMETS

The sweet course, which in France is always served after the cheese (the word is also used to mean a specific dessert). Formerly, all the dishes served after the roast, including vegetables and sweets, were called entremets (the word literally means 'between dishes'). In the royal households of the Middle Ages, the entremets were a real showpiece, being accompanied by music, juggling and dancing. In restaurants, the word still embraces the vegetable dishes (which in large establishments are the responsibility of the *entremettier*), as well as the *entremets de cuisine* (soufflés, savoury pancakes and fritters, pastries, croquettes and omelettes) and the desserts. The latter are subdivided into three categories.

• HOT ENTREMETS Fritters, pancakes, flamed fruits, sweet omelettes and soufflés.

• COLD ENTREMETS Bavarian creams, blancmanges, charlottes, compotes, pastries, creams, chilled fruits, meringues, puddings, rice or semolina desserts and moulds, often with fruit.

• ICED ENTREMETS Fruit ice creams, sorbets, iced cups, frosted fruits, ice cream, cakes, bombes, mousses, parfaits, soufflés and vacherins.

■ **From the Middle Ages to the 19th century** Taillevent proposed the following as entremets: frumenty, broth, oyster stew, rice pudding, fish jelly, stuffed poultry, almond milk with figs. All these dishes were served throughout the meal, alternating with the roasts and fish dishes, and mixing sweet and savoury. Certain spectacular entremets, such as 'swan in its skin and all its feathers', were purely decorative showpieces, presented with great pomp and musical accompaniment. At the marriage of Charles VII's daughter to the king of Bohemia, an entremet was served consisting of a huge château built on a high strong rock, with damsels at the windows, waving Hungarian banners, and groups of singing children. One of the most theatrical on record must be the 'pheasant's vow', presented in 1454 at the court of Philip the Good: a gigantic pâté was followed by a circus show with trumpet players and an elephant, and a procession of knights and ladies preceding a long gold dish, which held a live pheasant decorated with precious stones.

In 1655, Nicolas de Bonnefons gave as entremets: 'dishes cooked with butter and fat, all types of egg dishes, lamb cooked in its juices in the oven; also sweet dishes, both hot and cold, jellies of all colours and blancmanges, with artichokes, cardoons and celery with pepper in the middle.'

During the reign of Louis XIV and until the 19th century, the entremets continued to be a combination of sweet and savoury dishes. After the entrée, a sweet was sometimes served as an entremet (croquembouche or nougat, for instance) or a ham or a small fowl. After the roast a second entremet would be served: perhaps fruit and green vegetables, jellies and fritters.

Towards the 1850s, the menu of the famous Véry restaurant offered the following under 'entremets': a range of hot vegetable dishes, mushroom pastries, herb omelette, poached eggs with verjuice and Italian macaroni. The 'sweet entremets' comprised small pots of rum jelly, cream meringues, jam omelettes, apricot fritters, cherry tart, apricot charlotte and soufflé omelette with rice.

ÉPÉE DE BOIS

ÉPÉE DE BOIS A Parisian tavern that was situated in the Rue Quincampoix, in a 16th-century house; it was demolished in 1958. In 1658, the tavern became the meeting place of dancing masters and violin masters, who later established the Académie de Danse, which formed the nucleus of the Paris Opéra. In 1719, a financier called Law set up his bank in the same street, and the tavern served as a meeting place for speculators and money-lenders. It is said that the tavern was frequented by Abbé Prévost, who probably wrote a large part of *Manon Lescaut* there.

ÉPERONS BACHIQUES Literally meaning 'drinking spurs', this expression was coined by Rabelais to describe spicy salty dishes, such as *andouilles* and other sausages, which act on the thirst like spurs on a horse. The expression (in the singular) is now little used, except perhaps at reunion dinners of Bacchic societies by guests who wish to evoke the atmosphere of the past.

The expression (in the singular) is also used for a cheese, called 'the drunkard's biscuit' by Grimod de La Reynière and 'Bacchus' cotignac' by Saint-Amand.

ÉPIGRAMME A dish consisting of two cuts of lamb, both cooked dry. These two pieces are a slice of breast and a cutlet or chop, dipped in egg and breadcrumbs and grilled (broiled) or fried.

Philéas Gilbert explains the origins of the term épigramme as follows: 'It was towards the middle of the 18th century. One day a young marquise overheard one of her guests at table remark that when he was dining the previous evening with the Comte de Vaudreuil, he was charmingly received and, furthermore, had had a feast of excellent epigrams. The marquise, though pretty and elegant, was somewhat ignorant of the meaning of words. She later summoned Michelet, her chef. "Michelet," she said to him, "tomorrow, I shall require a dish of épigrammes!"

'The chef withdrew, pondering the problem. He looked up old recipes, but found no reference to anything of the kind. None of his colleagues had ever heard of the dish. But no French master chef is ever at a loss. Since he could discover nothing about the dish, he set about inventing one. Next day, inspiration came and he created a most delicate dish.

'At dinner, the guests fell into ecstasies over the dish put before them and, after complimenting the lady of the house, desired to know its name. The chef was called. With perfect composure he replied, "Épigrammes of lamb *à la Michelet*".

'Everyone laughed. The marquise was triumphant, though she could not understand the amusement of her guests. From that moment, the culinary repertoire of France was enriched by a name still used to this day.

'But whereas this name was originally used for slices of breast of lamb dipped in breadcrumbs, fried in butter, and arranged in a circle round a blanquette of lamb, by the end of the 18th century it had been completely transformed into what it is today, cutlets as well as slices of breast, dipped in egg and breadcrumbs and fried in butter or grilled.'

RECIPE

épigrammes
Braise a breast of lamb, or poach it in a small quantity of light stock. Drain and bone the meat, and cool it in a press. Cut it into equal portions and coat with egg and breadcrumbs. Coat the same number of lamb cutlets with egg and breadcrumbs. The cutlets and breast portions should then be grilled (broiled) or fried in butter and oil, and arranged in a round dish. Garnish the cutlet bones with paper frills, then put a few spoonfuls of reduced and sieved braising stock around the épigrammes. Garnish with glazed vegetables (carrots, turnips and baby onions), mushrooms, tomatoes fried in oil, or aubergine (eggplant) fritters, arranged in the centre of the dish.

ÉPOISSES A soft French AOP unpasteurized cow's-milk cheese named after a village on the Côte-d'Or and made in almost every part of Burgundy. Containing 45% fat, it has an orange washed crust (flavoured first with sage, then with Burgundy marc) and a soft creamy inside that is light- to brownish-yellow (depending on the degree of maturity), with a very strong flavour. Brillat-Savarin considered it the 'king of cheeses', and it was highly appreciated by Napoleon I. Each cheese is flat and round, 10 cm (4 in) in diameter and 3–6 cm (1¼–2½ in) thick, with a slight depression in the middle. It is sometimes sold surrounded with vine leaves, or in a box. It may be flavoured with cloves, fennel and black pepper. Époisses is given the collective regional brand mark 'Bourgogne'. It is eaten fresh in the summer; mature cheeses are very good from June to the end of March, but are best in winter.

ESAU The name of this biblical character, who sold his birthright to his brother Jacob for a mess of pottage, is given to a thickened soup made from lentil purée and white stock or consommé. This also serves as a basis for other soups, such as Conti. Soft-boiled (soft-cooked) or poached eggs Esau are arranged on lentil purée, garnished with heart-shaped croûtons, and coated with concentrated veal stock with butter added. Alternatively, the eggs are arranged in a croustade of crustless bread, fried, hollowed out and filled with lentil purée; the whole is covered with concentrated veal stock with butter added.

ESCABÈCHE A spicy cold marinade intended for preserving cooked foods and originating in Spain. It is used chiefly for small cooked fish (sardines, mackerel, smelt, whiting, red mullet). The fish are headed (hence the name, from *cabeza*, 'head'), then fried or lightly browned; they are then marinated for 24 hours in a cooked and spiced marinade. The fish then keep for up to a week in a refrigerator.

The preparation has spread throughout the Mediterranean region: it is called *scabetche* in North Africa, *escabecio* or *scavece* in Italy, and *escavèche* in Belgium. In Berry a similar preparation of fried gudgeon is called *à la cascamèche*. *Escabèche* is also used for poultry and game birds. In Spain, partridge is fried quickly in oil with garlic, then drained and marinated in its cooking juices with spices, and served cold. In Chile, chicken in *escabèche* is prepared in the same way and served cold with lemon and onions.

RECIPE

fish in escabèche
Gut some small fish (smelt, sand eels, weevers) and remove the heads; clean, wash and wipe the fish. Dip in flour and fry in olive oil until golden. Drain and arrange in an earthenware dish. Slice an onion and a carrot thinly. Heat the oil used for cooking the fish until it begins to smoke, then fry the onion and carrot and 5–6 unpeeled garlic cloves for a few moments. Remove from the heat and add 150 ml (¼ pint, ⅔ cup) red wine vinegar and 150 ml (¼ pint, ⅔ cup) water. Add a bouquet garni containing plenty of thyme and season with salt, pepper, a pinch of cayenne pepper, and a few coriander seeds. Cook for about 15 minutes, then pour the boiling marinade over the fish and leave to marinate for at least 24 hours. Serve as an hors d'oeuvre.

ESCALOPE (SCALLOP) A thin slice of white meat. The word comes from the Old French *escalope* (nutshell), probably because the slice tends to curl up during cooking (it is sometimes snipped on one side to prevent the flesh from shrinking). If taken from the fillet, veal escalopes are usually tender and lean; escalopes from lower down the leg are firmer and more sinewy. Italian *scaloppine* (small escalopes), prepared as saltimbocca or piccata, are cut from the fillet. Turkey escalopes, cut from the breast or wing, may be prepared in the same ways as veal.

Veal escalopes, usually oval in shape, are flattened before being lightly fried or sautéed. Because they tend to be slightly dry and can lack flavour, they are often cooked in sauce with cream or with mushrooms. The classic method of preparing escalopes is to coat them with breadcrumbs (*à la milanaise* or *à la viennoise*). Paupiettes are prepared from escalopes.

An escalope can also be a slice from a fillet of a large fish (particularly salmon) or from lobster flesh.

RECIPES

escalopes à la mandelieu
Flatten some escalopes (scallops), sprinkle them with salt and pepper, and sauté in clarified butter until golden. Then flame in Cognac, using 1 tablespoon Cognac for 4 escalopes. Cover each with a thin slice of Gruyère or Comté cheese and sprinkle with a few dried breadcrumbs. Moisten with melted butter and brown in a preheated oven at 240°C (475°F, gas 9). Prepare 250 g (9 oz, 3 cups) mushrooms and sauté them in the butter in which the escalopes were cooked. Add 2 tablespoons tomato purée (paste) and 250 ml (8 fl oz, 1 cup) reduced consommé; cook for about 5 minutes. Adjust the seasoning and serve this sauce with the escalopes.

escalopes à l'anversoise
Cut some round slices of bread, 1 cm (½ in) thick, and fry them in butter. Lightly fry some very small new potatoes in butter, and prepare some hop shoots in cream. Flatten some round escalopes (scallops), sprinkle with salt and pepper, and sauté them in a frying pan containing clarified butter. Drain and arrange while hot on the fried bread slices. Add to the frying pan a little white wine or beer and some very concentrated consommé. Reduce to a sauce and pour over the escalopes. Serve piping hot with the potatoes and the hop shoots.

escalopes casimir
Slowly cook in butter as many artichoke hearts as there are escalopes (scallops). Stew 4 tablespoons julienne of carrots in butter and, separately, a little julienne of truffles. Cut some escalopes from the fillet, flatten them, season with salt, pepper and paprika, then sauté in clarified butter; halfway through cooking, add 1 tablespoon chopped onion. Arrange the artichoke hearts in the serving dish, place an escalope on each one and garnish with the julienne of carrots. Add some cream to the pan juices from the escalopes and reduce. Coat the escalopes with this sauce and garnish with the julienne of truffles.

escalopes with aubergines and courgettes
Slice, without peeling, 2 medium-sized courgettes (zucchini) and a choice aubergine (eggplant). Sauté them in seasoned olive oil in a frying pan. Cut 4 escalopes (scallops), flatten them, sprinkle with salt and pepper, and sauté in clarified butter. Arrange

them in a serving dish, garnish with the aubergine and courgettes, and keep hot. Add to the pan juices 5 tablespoons white wine and 2–3 tablespoons meat juices; reduce by half. Add a small chopped garlic clove and reduce further. Pour the sauce over the escalopes and sprinkle with chopped parsley.

other recipes See *Brancas, lobster, salmon, sweetbread, viennoise.*

ESCALOPER
A French culinary term meaning to carve thin slices (escalopes) of meat, such as veal or poultry, large fish fillets, lobster or certain vegetables, such as mushroom caps or artichoke hearts.

ESCARGOT AUX RAISINS
Swiss brioche made with a sausage of dough rolled up like a snail, spread with confectioner's custard (pastry cream) and raisins, and sometimes flavoured with kirsch. It is then iced with a white fondant (frosting).

ESCAROLE
A vegetable, also called batavia, similar to curly endive (chicory), but with broader leaves (which are fairly curly and very crisp). It usually has a heart of white leaves edged with yellow.

Escarole is generally eaten raw, in a green salad (often with seasoning flavoured with mustard or shallots), possibly with tomatoes or scalded French (green) beans, or in a winter salad with nuts and raisins. It can also be cooked like spinach.

ESCOFFIER, AUGUSTE
Renowned French chef (born Villeneuve-Loubet, 1846; died Monte-Carlo, 1935). He began his career at the age of 13 with his uncle, who ran a famous restaurant in Nice, then worked in Paris, Nice, Lucerne and Monte-Carlo. In 1890, in association with Ritz and Echenard, two masters of the hotel business, he moved to the Savoy Hotel in London and remained in this illustrious establishment until 1898 when, for personal reasons, he gave up the direction of the Savoy kitchens to take charge of those of the Carlton Hotel, then one of the most famous in Europe.

Escoffier's culinary career was brilliant. He was regarded as the emperor of the world's kitchens, a title conferred upon him by the Emperor William II, who spent some time on the steamer *Imperator* of the Hamburg-America Line. Escoffier had joined the company to take charge of the imperial kitchens. In the course of conversation, the Emperor, congratulating Escoffier, said: 'I am the Emperor of Germany, but you are the Emperor of chefs.'

As a reward for all he had done to enhance the prestige of French cooking throughout the world, Escoffier was made a Chevalier of the Legion of Honour in 1920, and Officer of the Legion in 1928. Escoffier retired in 1921 aged 74, having practised his art for 62 years. In all the history of cookery, there is no other example of such a long professional career. He died in February 1935, nearly 89 years old.

The culinary writings of Escoffier are works of authority. The best-known are *Le Guide culinaire* (1903) and *Le Livre des menus* (1912), both written in collaboration with Philéas Gilbert and Émile Fétu, and *Ma cuisine* (1934). Other works include *Le Riz* (1927), *La Morue* (1929), the magazine *Le Carnet d'Épicure* (1911), and *Les Fleurs en cire* (1910, a new edition of *Le Traité sur l'art de travailler les fleurs en cire*, 1886). Escoffier created numerous recipes in honour of the Australian singer Nellie Melba, most notably peach Melba. His other recipes include chaud-froid Jeannette (in memory of a ship trapped in polar ice), *cuisses de nymphe aurore* (a dish of frog's legs) for the Prince of Wales, as well as Réjane salad and Rachel mignonettes of quail, in homage to two great actresses of the time.

The house where he was born was transformed into a museum of culinary art in 1966, at the suggestion of one of his former cooks, Joseph Donon.

ESCUEDELLA
A Catalan pot-au-feu traditionally made in the Perpignan region. The ingredients include beef and vegetables with eggs, a mixture of chopped meat and pasta and sometimes stuffed turkey. Its full name is *escuedella de Nadal* (literally 'Christmas bowl'), but it is also cooked on many other festive occasions.

ESPAGNOLE, À L'
The name of several preparations inspired by Spanish cuisine. The main ingredients are tomatoes, sweet (bell) peppers, onions and garlic, usually fried in oil. The garnish *à l'espagnole*, used for small sautéed or lightly braised items, consists of tomatoes stuffed with tomato-flavoured rice, braised sweet peppers, small braised onions and Madeira sauce. Mayonnaise *à l'espagnole* contains chopped ham, mustard, a dash of garlic and red pepper.

There are a considerable number of ways to cook eggs *à l'espagnole*. Soft-boiled (soft-cooked) or poached eggs are arranged on cooked tomatoes (stuffed with a salpicon of sweet peppers), coated with tomato sauce and garnished with fried onion rings. Baked eggs are arranged on a bed of finely sliced onions and garnished with tomato sauce, fried diced peppers, halves of tomato and fried onion rings; they are served with a tomato sauce to which a salpicon of sweet peppers has been added. Scrambled eggs are garnished with diced tomatoes and peppers and served with fried onion rings.

RECIPES

calf's liver à l'espagnole
Season slices of calf's liver with salt and pepper. Coat with flour and sauté them in oil. Arrange the liver slices on tomatoes that have been softened in olive oil and seasoned with garlic. Garnish with fried onion rings and fried curly parsley.

poached eggs à l'espagnole
Coat some onion rings in flour and fry them in oil. Prepare a salpicon of slowly cooked sweet (bell) peppers in a tomato sauce flavoured with a dash of cayenne pepper. Cut the ends off some tomatoes

and cook the tomatoes in oil. Garnish each tomato with a little of the salpicon and top with a poached egg. Place the onion rings in the centre of a serving dish, arrange the tomatoes and eggs around them, and coat the eggs with tomato sauce.

ragoût of sweet peppers à l'espagnole
Seed and peel 6 sweet (bell) peppers, and cut them into large strips. Fry 100 g (4 oz, ⅔ cup) finely sliced onions in some olive oil in a shallow frying pan. Add the strips of pepper, some salt, pink pepper, and a large crushed garlic clove. Stir in 1 tablespoon flour and add 300 ml (½ pint, 1¼ cups) beef stock and 2 tablespoons tomato purée (paste). Cook very gently, covered, for 35 minutes. Adjust the seasoning. Serve in a vegetable dish sprinkled with chopped parsley.

soft-boiled eggs à l'espagnole
Coat some soft-boiled (soft-cooked) eggs with meat aspic to which a little tomato purée (paste) has been added. Garnish each egg with a blanched onion ring with a pinch of chopped parsley in the centre. This should stick to the half-set jelly. Spread a mixture of mustard and butter on some round slices of toast and place an egg on each slice. Hollow out some very small tomatoes and marinate them in a mixture of oil, vinegar, salt and pepper. Fill them with diced green (bell) peppers seasoned with vinaigrette and place them around the eggs.

Spanish omelette
Dice some sweet (bell) peppers and cook them slowly in olive oil. Cut some tomato pulp into cubes, add a little garlic and some chopped parsley, and fry briskly in butter. Beat some eggs and add some of the sweet peppers and tomato pulp (1 large tablespoon of each vegetable for 6 eggs). Season with salt and pepper. Make an omelette, roll it up and serve with a highly seasoned tomato sauce.

ESPAGNOLE SAUCE A brown sauce, which is used as a basis for a large number of derivative brown sauces, such as Robert, genevoise, bordelaise, Bercy, Madeira and Périgueux. It is made with a brown stock to which a brown roux and a mirepoix are added, followed by a tomato purée. Cooking takes several hours and the sauce needs to be skimmed, stirred and strained when a particular stage in the cooking is reached. The meat stock may be replaced by a fish stock, depending on the requirements of the particular recipe. Carême's recipe is considered to be the classic method of preparing an espagnole sauce. Nowadays, a shoulder of veal is used instead of a noix, and partridge is not used in the stock.

RECIPES

espagnole sauce (1)
(From Carême's recipe) Put 2 slices of Bayonne ham into a deep saucepan. Place a noix of veal and 2 partridges on top. Add enough stock to cover the veal only. Reduce the liquid rapidly, then lower the heat until the stock is reduced to a coating on the bottom of the pan. Remove it from the heat. Prick the noix of veal with the point of a knife so that its juice mingles with the stock. Put the saucepan back over a low heat for about 20 minutes. Watch the liquid as it gradually turns darker.

To simplify this operation, scrape off a little of the essence with the point of a knife. Roll it between the fingers. If it rolls into a ball, the essence is perfectly reduced. If it is not ready, it will make the fingers stick together.

Remove the saucepan from the heat and set it aside for 15 minutes for the essence to cool. (It will then dissolve more readily.) Fill the saucepan with clear soup or stock and heat very slowly.

Meanwhile prepare a roux: melt 100 g (4 oz, ½ cup) butter and add to it enough flour to give a rather liquid consistency. Put it over a low heat, stirring from time to time so that gradually the whole mixture turns a golden colour. As soon as the stock comes to the boil, skim it, and pour 2 ladles into a roux. When adding the first ladleful of stock, remove the roux from the heat, then replace it and stir in the second ladleful until the mixture is perfectly smooth. Now pour the thickened sauce into the saucepan with the veal noix. Add parsley and spring onions (scallions), ½ bay leaf, a little thyme, 2 chives, and some mushroom trimmings. Leave to simmer, stirring frequently. After 1 hour skim off the fat, then 30 minutes later, skim off the fat again.

Strain through a cloth into a bowl, stirring from time to time with a wooden spoon so that no skin forms on the surface, as easily happens when the sauce is exposed to the air.

espagnole sauce (2)
Make a brown roux with 25 g (1 oz, 2 tablespoons) butter and 25 g (1 oz, ¼ cup) plain (all-purpose) flour. Add 1 tablespoon mirepoix*, 50 g (2 oz, ⅔ cup) chopped mushrooms and 1 kg (2¼ lb) crushed tomatoes. Stir in 2.25 litres (4 pints, 10 cups) brown stock and simmer gently for 3–4 hours, skimming the sauce occasionally. Pass through a very fine sieve, or preferably strain through muslin (cheesecloth), when cold.

ESROM A semi-hard Danish cow's-milk cheese made in flat rectangular shapes and sold wrapped in foil. The pale yellow paste is supple with irregular small holes. The flavour is quite rich and aromatic and the mature cheese is quite spicy. It is served on open sandwiches.

ESSAI The ceremony of tasting the king's food and drink at the French royal courts. The cups used for tasting were also called *essais*.

The fear of poisoning in the Middle Ages gave rise to a complicated ceremonial attending the sovereign's meals. In France, this was minutely regulated by court etiquette, which continued with slight modifications until the Revolution, to be revived under the Empire.

The knife, fork, spoon, salt cellar, spices and napkin were locked in the *cadenas* or nef. The maître d'hôtel rubbed all the cutlery and the dishes with balls of breadcrumbs which he made sure were eaten by the squires of the pantry, who, previously, had subjected the servants who had handed them the dishes to the same ordeal.

For drinks, the ceremonial was equally complicated. When the king called for a drink, the cupbearer made a sign to the wine butler and his assistant. The first of these brought the wine in a flagon, and the king's glass, covered; the second brought a silver jug full of water. The cupbearer took the glass and uncovered it; the wine butler poured in the wine, then the water. The cupbearer poured some of this watered wine into two little silver-gilt cups. He drank from one, the wine butler from the other. Only then did the cupbearer proffer the cup, now covered once more, across the table to the king. He did not uncover it until the very moment that the king was about to drink.

The same ceremonial took place for the queen. By special favour, Louis XIV bestowed the same prerogative upon the dauphine (the wife of the heir to the throne).

ESSENCE (EXTRACT)
A concentrated aromatic liquid used either to enhance the flavour of certain culinary preparations or to flavour certain foods that have little or no flavour of their own. They are plant extracts obtained by distillation or infusion and include lemon oil, rose oil and essence of oranges, cinnamon and vanilla. Natural essences are obtained by three methods: by extracting the essential oil of a fruit or a spice (lemon, bitter almond, orange, rose, cinnamon); by reducing an infusion or a cooking liquid (mushroom, tarragon, chervil, tomato, game carcass, fish trimmings); or by infusing or marinating items in either wine or vinegar (truffles, onions, garlic, anchovy).

Essences sold commercially sometimes contain artificial flavourings and colourings.

ESSENTIAL OIL
An oily substance which has a strong flavour and is extracted from the flowers, fruit, leaves, seeds, resin or roots of certain plants. Essential oils are used principally in the perfume industry and in aromatherapy but they are also used to flavour food. Examples are citrus oils, almond oil and peppermint oil.

ESTAMINET
Until the 18th century in France, an estaminet was a café where people could drink beer and wine, and were permitted to smoke. Today, the term is rare and often pejorative, being used in northern France and Belgium to designate a bistro or, more specifically, the room in a café reserved for smokers. It derives from a word of Germanic origin, meaning 'column' (the ceilings of tavern rooms were supported by wooden columns).

ESTOFINADO
A local name in Provence for salt cod *à la provençale* (it is also called *stoficado, estoficado* and *stocaficado*). The word is a Provençal transcription of 'stockfish' (Norwegian dried salt cod). In Marseille and Saint-Tropez, the dish is a well-seasoned ragoût of salt cod cooked with tomatoes, onions, garlic, olive oil and various spices. (In Nice, it is also prepared with hake.)

Under the name *stoficado*, it is also a speciality of Aveyron, especially at Villefranche-de-Rouergue and Decazeville: the cod is poached and mixed with potatoes. The mixture is then mashed with very hot walnut oil, butter, garlic, parsley, beaten raw eggs and cream.

There have been a number of theories to explain why salt cod has been so popular for such a long time in Provençal cookery. One suggestion is that recipes were brought back from the Netherlands and Scandinavia by southern French soldiers. Another seemingly more probable theory is that salt cod was introduced by northern European merchants travelling to the Italian cities. Its presence in the Rouergue could also be associated with the fact that it was introduced into the area when there was a constant trade in iron ore between the mines of Auvergne and the fishing port of Bordeaux.

RECIPE

estofinado

Soak a stockfish in water for several hours, changing the water frequently to remove the salt. Scrape the skin carefully to remove the scales and cut the flesh into 5 cm (2 in) pieces. Fry 1 or 2 chopped onions lightly in 1 tablespoon oil in a large flameproof earthenware casserole. Then add 3 tomatoes, peeled, seeded and chopped. Cook over a low heat for 4–5 minutes, stirring with a wooden spoon. Add 2–3 garlic cloves, peeled and chopped, a bouquet garni consisting of celery, parsley, basil, bay leaf and thyme, carefully tied together, and a pinch of cayenne pepper. Crushed anchovy or grated nutmeg could also be used to season if wished. Place the pieces of fish in a larger pan and add 100 ml (4 fl oz, 7 tablespoons) white wine, the tomato mixture and enough water to cover the fish. Cook for 30 minutes over a low heat. Cut 4–6 potatoes into thick slices and add to the pan (one potato per person). Add a generous dash of Cognac and 8 olives per person 5 minutes before the end of the cooking time. Remove the bouquet garni and serve.

ESTOUFFADE
A dish whose ingredients are slowly stewed. The word comes from the Italian *stufato* (a daube), and is applied most often to beef in wine sauce, with carrots and small onions.

In traditional cookery, estouffade is also a clear brown stock used to dilute brown sauces and moisten ragoûts and braised dishes.

RECIPE

estouffade of beef

Dice and blanch 300 g (11 oz, 15 slices) lean bacon. Brown the bacon in butter in a flameproof casserole, drain and set aside. Cut 1.5 kg (3¼ lb) beef, half chuck steak, half rib, into cubes of about 100 g (4 oz) and brown in the same pan. Cut 3 onions into quarters, add them to the beef and brown. Season with salt, pepper, thyme, a bay leaf and a crushed garlic clove. Then stir in 2 tablespoons flour and add 1 litre (1¾ pints, 4⅓ cups) red wine with an equal quantity of stock. Add a bouquet garni and bring to the boil. Cover and cook in a preheated oven at 160°C (325°F, gas 3) for 2½–3 hours.

Drain the ragoût in a sieve placed over an earthenware dish. Place the pieces of beef and the strips of bacon in a pan and add 300 g (11 oz, 3½ cups) sautéed sliced mushrooms. Skim the fat from the cooking liquid, strain and reduce. Pour it over the meat and mushrooms and simmer gently, covered, for about 25 minutes. Serve in a deep dish.

ESTOUFFAT A Languedoc dialect word for a dish that is stewed very slowly. In that region it is used mainly for a stew of pork and haricot (navy) beans, flavoured with garlic, onions and tomatoes.

In south-western France the word is also used for various braised dishes (made with game and tripe).

RECIPE

estouffat of haricot beans à l'occitane

Brown a diced carrot and a sliced onion in either goose fat or lard in a pan. Add 1.5 litres (2¾ pints, 6½ cups) water and a bouquet garni, bring to the boil and simmer for about 20 minutes. Add 1.5 litres (2¾ pints, 6½ cups) fresh white haricot (navy) beans and cook until almost tender, then drain. Cut 250 g (9 oz) slightly salted belly bacon into cubes, blanch and brown in goose fat or lard. Add to the pan 150 g (5 oz, ¾ cup) chopped onions, 2 large tomatoes (peeled and crushed) and 1 crushed garlic clove, and cook for a further 10 minutes. Then add the drained beans, cover the pan and gently simmer until cooking is completed.

If liked, 200 g (7 oz) rind from preserved pork may be added to the bean cooking liquid. When cooked, the rind is cut into squares and added to the beans in the serving dish.

EWE A female sheep. The ewes of breeds reared for meat are allowed to breed for 4–6 years and are then fattened up for slaughter. (In the past, ewes were allowed to breed for longer before being slaughtered, but consumers today prefer meat with a milder flavour.) Ewe's meat provides most of the joints sold as mutton.

Ewe's milk contains more fat than cow's milk (8.5% as opposed to 4%). It is used for making cheese that is traditionally manufactured in dry mountainous areas. The most famous is Roquefort, but other regions produce notable cheeses, including Broccio and Niolo from Corsica, Oloron and Laruns from Béarn, and Esbareich and Arnéguy from the Basque region. Cachat and Rocamadour also deserve a mention.

In Spain and Portugal, the best cheeses are made from ewe's milk, for example, Hecho, Villalon and Serra; in Italy, Pecorino and Fiore Sardo are good ewe's-milk cheeses. Liptai is the Hungarian national cheese. In Greece, the Balkans and the Caucasus, Feta and various types of Katschkawalj and Brandza are the most common cheeses. Fresh ewe's-milk cheese is served with sugar or fresh cream. It may also be used for making tarts or as a filling for puff pastry turnovers.

EWER A tall vessel formerly used for serving water at table – for washing the hands at the start and finish of a meal rather than for drinking. It had a base, spout and handle and a tray or bowl beneath it to catch the water poured over the hands. Ewers were made of gold or silver until the 18th century; materials used later included pewter, glazed earthenware and marble.

EXCELSIOR A cow's-milk cheese from Normandy with 72% fat content. The skin is white with brown markings and the ivory-coloured paste is soft, fine and dense in texture, with a mellow, slightly nutty, flavour.

Created in 1890, Excelsior is the oldest of the double- or triple-cream cheeses (along with Fin-de-Siècle, Explorateur, Lucullus and Brillat-Savarin).

EXCELSIOR A garnish for lamb tournedos and noisettes that consists of braised lettuce and *pommes fondantes* (potatoes cut into small pieces and cooked, covered, in butter). The term also refers to a method of preparing sole, which is rolled into paupiettes, poached and arranged in a crown around diced lobster *à la Newburg*. The fish is then coated in normande sauce and garnished with slices of truffle and prawn tails.

EXPLORATEUR Triple-cream (75% fat content) soft cheese from the Île-de-France made from enriched unpasteurized cow's milk. It is a cylinder 8 cm (3¼ in) in diameter and 6 cm (2½ in) tall. Invented after World War II, it has a firm, very creamy texture.

EXTRA An adjective printed on French labels to denote particular features of certain products when they are marketed. In France, 'extra' eggs have a special label with white letters on a red background and this indicates to the customer that they are fresh and have been packed within three days of being laid. They retain this label for seven days. 'Extra' fruit and vegetables have a red label and are of superior quality. An 'extra gras' cheese has a fat content of between 45% and 60% (and is also labelled as 'crème'). An 'extra sec' champagne is fairly dry (really dry champagne is labelled 'brut').

EXTRACT See *essence*.

FABADA The bean stew of the Asturians, in Northern Spain, made with large flat beans that melt in the mouth, salt pork (or salt beef), perhaps also fresh pork, chorizos and the wrinkled, smoked *morcilla*, the local black pudding (blood sausage). It takes its name from the fava (broad bean) but these have long been replaced by the finest large kidney beans in Spain *fabes de la granja*; use butter or dried lima beans outside Spain. One of Spain's three great bean pots, along with *cocido* and *olla podrida*.

FAGGOT British speciality, a type of sausage or meatball, similar to French crepinette. A ball of minced (ground) offal (variety meats) and pork, including kidney and liver, mixed with breadcrumbs, onion and well flavoured with herbs. Traditionally wrapped in caul fat and fried or baked. One popular way of serving faggots is with cooked dried peas (or with mushy peas) and onion gravy.

FAÏENCE A type of white or patterned pottery widely used for tableware. The earthenware is covered with tin glaze (lead glaze made opaque by the addition of tin ashes) so that the colour of the earthenware is completely masked. This pottery takes its name from the Italian town of Faenza.

Very little is known about the origins of faïence pottery, but from the very earliest times a brilliant vitreous lead glaze, coloured by means of metallic oxides, was known to potters. It is to be seen in the hypogeum of Ancient Egypt, on its vases, funeral images and also on the glazed bricks which decorated the walls of Nineveh and Babylon. The ancient mosques of Asia Minor have preserved for us the magnificent craftsmanship of the Persians, who passed on their skill to the Arabs.

From the 13th century there were important centres for the manufacture of faïence in Spain, at Malaga and in Majorca, which gave its name to the Italian *majolica*. Up to the 17th century the most famous factories were in Valencia. But it was mainly through the discovery of tin glaze by Luca della Robbia towards the middle of the 15th century, that the ceramic industry was able to develop, first at Faenza and then in other Italian towns, notably Urbino, Gubbio, Druta, Durante, Venice, Milan and Turin.

In France, in the 16th century, faïence pottery called Henri II faïence was produced, the most important being the very individual pieces made by Bernard Palissy. During the same period Italian potters tried to introduce the faïence industry into France. The Conradi, coming from Savona, settled at Nevers. Early abortive attempts to produce faïence in Rouen were made in the 16th century, but it was not until the 17th century that this city began to produce the beautiful specimens which remain one of the glories of the French faïence industry. These were very fashionable in the 18th century and were copied everywhere, both in France and other countries. Moustiers, from the end of the 17th century, made famous faïence pieces in the style of Tempesta, or copied from Bérain and Bernard Toro. At Strasbourg, in the 18th century, the Hannong family created a style which was quickly adopted by the factories of Lunéville and Niederwiller. In Paris, Saint-Cloud, Meudon, Lille and Marseille, there were also a large number of less important factories.

Outside France, some of the finest work was produced at Delft in Holland, which was, for a long time, the most active centre of the faïence industry in Europe.

Fine pottery, called clay pottery, made its appearance towards the middle of the 18th century, and this industry was most fully developed in England, at Leeds and at Burslem in Staffordshire, where Josiah Wedgwood opened the first of his factories. In France, this type of pottery was made especially at Pont-aux-Choux, Paris, Lunéville and Orléans.

With the advent of porcelain, faïence became less sought-after and less highly prized, but modern manufacturers have given it a new lease of life.

FAIRY-RING MUSHROOM A small mushroom with a pleasant smell that is fairly common in meadows. Its Latin name is *Marasmius oreades* and in France it is known as *marasme d'oréade* or *faux mousseron*. The stalk is tough and should be discarded, but the cap can be dried. The dried caps can be crushed and used as a condiment, or rehydrated by soaking in water and then added to meat dishes, sauces, omelettes and soups.

FAISSELLE A type of basket with perforated sides used for draining cheese. The material from which it is made varies, depending on the type of cheese and the region where it is manufactured. *Faisselles* may be square, cylindrical or heart-shaped and can be made of wood, earthenware, pottery, wicker or plastic. In France the word *faisselle* is also used for a table on which the apple residue is drained after the brewing of cider.

FALAFEL Spicy snack made from a purée of chick peas, rolled into small balls or shaped into patties and then fried in oil. Popular throughout the Middle East, especially in Israel, where they are traditionally eaten in pitta bread. They are sometimes made from other pulses, for example dried broad (fava) beans are used in Egypt where the patties are also known as *ta'amia*.

FALERNO An Italian wine harvested on the sunny slopes of the Massico mountains, in Campania, to the north of Naples. Three styles are produced: Bianco, a dry white made from Falanghina grapes, Rosso, from mainly Aglianico and Piedirosso varieties, and Primitivo.

The Falerno of today is nothing like the highly prized Falernian wine of the ancient Romans, which rivalled the prestigious Greek wines. The poet Horace praised it in verse but deplored its high price – too expensive for him to drink it in the quantities that he would have liked! Pliny the Elder described three types: a light dry white, a fairly sweet yellow, and a dark red – all very highly regarded. He also divulged that Falernian was the only wine that ignited on contact with a flame. The wine was also reputed to keep indefinitely, the Greek physician Galen was of the opinion that it was not good until it had matured for ten years and that it was at its best between 15 and 20 years old. Although it is not known which grape the ancient Falernian was made from, it is supposed to have resembled the present-day Lacrima Christi.

FALETTE A speciality of the Auvergne, particularly Espalion. It is made with breast of mutton browned with carrots and onions and cooked slowly in the oven for a long time, then sliced and served with haricot (navy) beans.

RECIPE

falettes

Bone and season 2 breasts of mutton. Make a stuffing with 300 g (11 oz, 4 cups) chopped Swiss chard leaves, 200 g (7 oz, 2½ cups) spinach, 50 g (2 oz, 1 cup) fresh parsley, 2 garlic cloves and 1 large onion. Mix the ingredients with 100 g (4 oz, 4 slices) crustless bread soaked in milk and 100 g (4 oz, 2 cup) sausagemeat. Season with salt and pepper.

Flatten out the boned breasts on top of some bacon rashers (slices). Spread the stuffing along the length of each breast and roll up, including the bacon, then tie. Brown the falettes in a flameproof casserole with 200 g (7 oz, 1½ cups) sliced onions and 100 g (4 oz, 1 cup) sliced carrots. Deglaze the casserole with some white wine and add a generous quantity of mutton stock. Add ½ garlic clove and a bouquet garni, and cook, covered, in a preheated oven at 180°C (350°F, gas 4) for 2½ hours.

Meanwhile, soak 500 g (1 lb 2 oz, 2½ cups) haricot (navy) beans in cold water for 2 hours. Drain and boil in fresh water for 10 minutes. Drain and cool quickly by rinsing under the cold tap.

Sauté 100 g (4 oz, ¾ cup) sliced onions, 100 g (4 oz, ¾ cup) chopped Auvergne ham and 100 g (4 oz, ¾ cup) chopped tomatoes in a large saucepan until soft. Add the beans, a bouquet garni and enough mutton stock to cover the beans generously. Bring to the boil, reduce the heat and cover the pan. Then simmer gently for about 1½ hours.

Remove the falettes from the casserole and leave to cool briefly; then untie them, remove the bacon and cut them into slices. Strain and reduce the cooking liquid and pour it over the sliced falettes. Serve the beans separately.

FALLOW DEER A small deer of temperate regions. The strong-tasting flesh of adult stags should be marinated in a tannin-rich wine; methods of preparation are as for roebuck. Females and fawns yield meat with a less pronounced flavour and may be roasted.

FANCHONNETTE Also known as *fanchette*. A little tart made with puff pastry filled with confectioner's custard (pastry cream), coated with meringue and decorated with tiny meringue balls. The larger version is known as *gâteau fanchette*.

Fanchonnette and *fanchette* are also the names of certain petits fours. One type consists of a boat-shaped piece of nougat filled with a hazelnut-flavoured confectioner's custard and covered with coffee-flavoured fondant icing (frosting). Another consists of a macaroon base with strawberry-flavoured butter cream and covered with pink fondant icing.

FAR BRETON A flan (tart) with prunes that may be eaten warm or cold. The French word *far* was originally used for a porridge made with durum wheat, ordinary wheat or buckwheat flour, with added salt or sugar and dried fruit. It was a popular dish throughout Brittany. Traditionally, it was cooked in a linen bag, pocket or sleeve, hence its various dialect names: *far sach, far poch* and *far mach.* Slices of the flan may be served as a dessert or as an accompaniment to meat or vegetables.

RECIPE

far breton
Soak 125 g (4½ oz, 1 cup) currants and 400 g (14 oz, 2¾ cups) stoned (pitted) prunes overnight in warm weak tea, then drain them. Make a well in the centre of 250 g (9 oz, 2¼ cups) plain (all-purpose) flour and mix in a large pinch of salt, 2 tablespoons sugar and 4 well-beaten eggs to make a batter. Thin the batter with 400 ml (14 fl oz, 1¾ cups) milk and mix in the currants and prunes. Pour into a buttered tin (pan) and bake in a preheated oven at 200°C (400°F, gas 6) for about 1 hour, until the top is brown. Sprinkle with icing (confectioner's) sugar.

FARCI A speciality of Périgord consisting of forcemeat wrapped in cabbage leaves. It is traditionally cooked inside a boiling fowl in meat or vegetable stock. However, it is now more usually made by wrapping the stuffed cabbage leaves in muslin (cheesecloth) or securing with string and cooking directly in stock.

RECIPES

farci
Crumble 350 g (12 oz, 12 slices) stale crustless bread and soak in fatty stock or in milk. Mix together 350 g (12 oz, 2 cups) fresh chopped ham or bacon, 2 chopped garlic cloves, 2 chopped shallots (or 1 chopped onion) and a bunch of chopped parsley, tarragon or other herbs. If liked, add some chopped chicken liver. Squeeze out the bread and mix it with the chopped ingredients. Season with salt, pepper and a generous pinch of mixed spice and bind with 2 or 3 egg yolks. Mix well until smooth, and keep in a cool place.

Blanch some large cabbage leaves in boiling water for 5 minutes. Cool quickly under cold running water, pat them dry, and arrange them like flower petals on a flat surface. Shape the forcemeat into a ball, place it on the cabbage leaves and fold them over to wrap it up. Secure with string to keep the shape, or wrap the leaves in muslin (cheesecloth), and cook in vegetable or meat stock for about 1¾ hours. Remove the muslin or string. Cut the farci into slices and serve very hot with the stock or with a chicken, depending on the recipe. (Farci can also be served cold.)

small stuffed provençal vegetables
Trim the tops off 6 onions, 6 small aubergines (eggplants), 6 round courgettes (zucchini), 6 sweet (bell) peppers and 6 medium-sized tomatoes to reduce them to three-quarters of their original height, and cut the aubergines and peppers in half. Use a teaspoon to hollow out the vegetables and mix the pulp with the trimmings. Fry the pulp lightly in a little olive oil, then leave to cool. Cut 5 slices of bread into small dice and soak in 100 ml (4 fl oz, 7 tablespoons) milk. Mix with the vegetable pulp and add 400 g (14 oz) sausagemeat, 5 garlic cloves, chopped, 75 g (3 oz, 1¼ cups) finely chopped parsley, 3 tablespoons chopped basil, 3 whole eggs (beaten), 100 g (4 oz, 1 cup) grated Parmesan cheese, salt and pepper. Stir the mixture until smooth with a wooden spatula.

Bring a saucepan of water to the boil and cook the onions lightly, followed by the courgettes, peppers and aubergines, cooked separately. Drain each batch on a cloth or paper towels.

Stuff all the vegetables with sausagemeat mixture and arrange them in a roasting pan (tin), greased with olive oil.

Carefully remove the flowers of 6 courgettes and set aside. Chop the courgettes finely and fry gently in 2 tablespoons olive oil for 5–8 minutes, stirring often. Remove from the heat and add 2 chopped basil leaves, 1 tablespoon finely chopped parsley and 1 finely chopped garlic clove. Leave to cool, then incorporate 1 tablespoon fresh breadcrumbs and half a beaten egg.

Fill the flowers with the sausagemeat mixture, fold over the petals and place the flowers side by side in a second roasting pan (tin). Pour over a mixture of 120 ml (4½ fl oz, ½ cup) boiling water, 1 chicken stock (bouillon) cube and 2 tablespoons olive oil. Cover with foil.

Cook both batches of vegetables in a preheated oven at 200°C (400°F, gas 6) for 15–20 minutes. The stuffed vegetables and courgette flowers may be eaten hot or cold.

FARCIDURE A speciality of Limousin, consisting of poached balls of forcemeat or chopped ingredients. In Guéret, where farcidure (or *farce dure* – literally 'hard stuffing') is particularly famous, the balls are made with buckwheat flour and a mixture of chopped green vegetables, such as sorrel, Swiss chard and cabbage. When made with wheat flour, they are known as *poule sans os* ('boneless chicken'), contain chopped bacon and sorrel, and are deep-fried. If garnished with salt pork, they are boiled in cabbage soup. Farcidure with potatoes is made with a mixture of puréed potatoes, herbs, garlic, onions and rashers (slices) of bacon, to which beaten eggs are sometimes added. The balls are poached and then fried in lard or goose fat.

FARÉE A speciality of Charentes, consisting of cabbage stuffed with bacon or sorrel and served with bacon and crustless bread. It is cooked in the stock from a pot-au-feu or a soup.

FARINACEOUS Containing flour, or a high content of starch. The term is applied particularly to cereals and pulses, such as peas, beans, lentils and broad (fava) beans.

FARINADE A Corsican gruel made from chestnut flour mixed with olive oil. When cooked, it is poured on to a floured cloth so that it forms a ball. It is then sliced and either served on its own, while still hot, or with fresh Broccio or goat's milk. The slices may also be fried in oil.

FARINAGE The French term for any dish or dessert based on flour. Generally, it is used to describe pasta dishes served as a main course, as well as quenelles, *knödel, knepfles, floutes* (quenelles made with mashed potatoes) and gnocchi, which are popular dishes in Italian, Austrian, German and Alsatian cookery. Farinages also include dishes made with cornmeal (maize), such as polenta, *gaudes* and *miques*, and potato flour, such as gruels and panadas, and also semolina puddings. Pastries and crêpes are not included.

FARINETTE A sweet or savoury pancake made with beaten eggs and flour. There are several variations to be found in different parts of the Auvergne, where they are also known as *omelette enfarinée* ('floured omelette'), *pachade* (in Aveyron) and *farinade*.

FAST To avoid eating food or abstain from certain foods. Fasting is associated with religion – Christians abstain from eating certain foods during Lent; Muslims fast during Ramadan. Complete fasting or avoiding certain foods is practised on certain days in religious calendars.

In the Roman Catholic Church fasting meant abstaining from eating meat and fat during Lent and on fast days. Originally only vegetables were allowed to be eaten on fast days with meats and all animal products (butter, fats, milk and eggs) proscribed. Over the years the rules were relaxed, and gradually eggs, then fish and shellfish, were allowed to be eaten on fast days. However, the eating of butter necessitated the payment of extra offerings. When fish was permitted, wild duck and other waterfowl were also included. Brillat-Savarin tells the amusing story of a fasting cleric who enjoyed an omelette with tuna tongues and carp's roe. The last restrictions were removed for Catholics in 1966 with the lifting of Friday fasting, but the tradition of serving fish on that day remains.

In cookery, dishes prepared *au maigre* (sauces, stuffings, salpicons), as opposed to those prepared *au gras*, do not include lard (shortening), bacon, sausagemeat or any other meat-based ingredients, especially pork. Butter, however, can be used.

FAT Lipid substances containing glycerol and fatty acids. Fats are solid at low temperatures; oils, however, are liquid at room temperature, due to their higher content of unsaturated fatty acids, and will solidify in the refrigerator. Fats and oils do not dissolve in or mix with water, but they may be emulsified with water.

There are two types of fats: saturated fats (or saturates) and unsaturated fats (these include monounsaturated fats and polyunsaturated fats). Saturated fats are found in dairy products (butter, milk, cheese) and animal meats and fats (lard, pork fat, suet). They are also found in some vegetable fats, such as coconut oil and palm oil. Unsaturated fats are found in vegetable oils: monounsaturates in olive and peanut oils; polyunsaturates in corn, sunflower, grapeseed, rapeseed (canola) and soya oils. They are also found in oily fish, such as herring and mackerel.

■ **Fat in cooking** Fats are used as a cooking medium for frying and roasting. They are also used to baste food during grilling. Their role is far broader than this, including moistening ingredients and mixtures; forming the base for creamed cakes; giving pastries their inimitable textures; and acting as dressings or sauces. Fats make starches and dry ingredients taste more appealing. They also improve or enhance the flavour of many foods, either raw (for example when butter is eaten with bread) or cooked by giving a crisp finish, for example when frying.

Traditionally, of the animal fats, lard (shortening), obtained from pork fat, is most widely used for cooking in Europe. However, beef suet is also used sometimes, particularly in England. Sheep suet or sheep-tail fat is used especially in Oriental cookery. In France, goose fat, which is highly esteemed by gastronomes, is specific to Gascony, Béarn and Languedoc, being used especially for confits. It is also used in Scandinavian and Jewish cookery. Calf fat is used in certain forcemeats. The use of some fats is limited to particular culinary traditions: *smen* in North Africa and ghee in India, for example.

In French cooking, recipes or dishes are described as *au gras* (literally, 'fat') when they contain meat products, and *au maigre* when they do not contain meat, being based on fish or vegetables. The introduction of vegetable oils has led to a significant reduction in the role of animal fats in cooking.

Vegetable fats are traditionally used for cooking in many African and Eastern countries, usually taking the form of white waxy rectangular blocks. Their melting point is lower than that of animal fats but, like oils, they have high boiling points, which enables them to be used for frying food.

With greater awareness of the roles of different nutrients in the diet, and in particular concern about increased consumption of fat in the Western diet, vegetable oils are often used in place of animal fats in some traditional dishes. This applies particularly to everyday eating and to fats used for cooking, where olive oil and other vegetable oils have grown in popularity among those who traditionally relied on lard or butter. A broader range of fats are used by cooks who once used only butter and meat dripping for cooking, with one or two vegetable oils reserved solely for salad dressings.

FAUBONNE A thick soup made with a purée of white haricot (navy) beans, split peas or peas, mixed with a white stock or a consommé containing finely shredded vegetables (carrots, turnips, leeks, celery) and seasoned with parsley and chervil. Formerly, Faubonne soup was garnished with thin strips of roast or braised pheasant.

FAUCHON, AUGUSTE FÉLIX A famous French grocer (born 1856; died Paris, 1939). He arrived in Paris from Normandy in 1886 and opened a food store in the Place de la Madeleine that dealt exclusively in the best French products, including groceries, poultry, charcuterie, cheese, biscuits (cookies), confectionery, wines and liqueurs. Auguste Fauchon did not stock exotic products, and sent customers requiring such items to his friend Hédiard. Between the two wars, he opened a *salon de thé-pâtisserie* and also started a catering service. After the death of its founder, the store began to stock specialities from all over the world, at the same time maintaining a selection of luxury French products.

FAUGÈRES A spicy, robust red AOC wine produced in the Languedoc region mainly from Carignan, Syrah, Mourvèdre and Grenache. Whites from Marsanne, Viognier, Roussane, Grenache Blanc and Rolle are sold as Coteaux du Languedoc.

FAUX-FILET (TENDERLOIN) Also known as *contre-filet*. Part of the beef sirloin located on either side of the backbone above the loins. It is fattier and less tender than the fillet but has more flavour; when boned and trimmed, it can be roasted or braised. Unlike fillet, it is not essential to bard the meat, unless it is to be braised. Slices of faux-filet can be grilled (broiled) or fried.

RECIPES

faux-filet braised à la bourgeoise
Marinate some lardons of bacon in brandy for about 30 minutes. Season with salt, pepper and ground allspice. Insert the lardons into the faux-filet (tenderloin). Season and marinate the meat for 12 hours in red or white wine flavoured with thyme, bay leaf, chopped parsley and 1 crushed garlic clove. Drain the meat and brown it in either butter or oil. Fry 2 large sliced onions and 2 large diced carrots in butter, and brown a few crushed veal bones in the oven. Place the vegetables in the bottom of a braising pan and lay the faux-filet on top. Add the browned bones, 1 or 2 blanched boned calves' feet, the marinade, 2–3 tablespoons tomato purée (paste) and enough stock to just cover the meat. Then add a bouquet garni and season with salt and pepper. Cover, bring to the boil on the hob (stove top) and then transfer to a preheated oven at 150°C (300°F, gas 2) for about 2½ hours. Add some wedges of carrot and continue

cooking for another hour. Prepare some small glazed onions. When the meat is cooked, drain it, and keep it warm in a deep dish. Skim the fat off the cooking liquid, boil to reduce and add a knob of softened butter. Dice the meat from the calves' feet and arrange it around the meat together with the carrots and small onions. Coat with the cooking liquid.

roast faux-filet
Bone and trim the meat. Bard it on top and underneath, shape into a square and tie. Cook in a preheated oven at 240°C (475°F, gas 9) so that the outside is sealed but the inside remains pink or rare, allowing 10 minutes per 450 g (1 lb). The meat can be untied and debarded to brown the outside thoroughly 5 minutes before the end of the cooking time. Season with salt and pepper.

FAVA BEAN See *broad bean*.

FAVART A sumptuous garnish for poultry or calves' sweetbreads, dedicated to Charles Simon Favart, an 18th-century playwright and director of the Opéra-Comique. It is made of poultry quenelles with tarragon, and small tarts filled with a salpicon of cep mushrooms and cream. The accompanying sauce is a chicken velouté flavoured with crayfish butter.

The name is also given to a preparation of soft-boiled (soft-cooked) or poached eggs, served in little tarts garnished with a salpicon of lamb sweetbreads, truffles and mushrooms in a velouté sauce.

FAVORITE, À LA Describing various preparations created during the last century in honour of a popular Donizetti opera, *La Favorita* (1840). Soup *à la favorite* is a cream soup of asparagus and lettuce garnished with asparagus tips. Asparagus tips also feature in a garnish for small sautéed joints of meat (together with slices of foie gras topped with slivers of truffle, coated with the meat juices deglazed with Madeira and demi-glace) and in a mixed salad. There is another garnish of the same name for large roasting joints, consisting of sautéed quartered artichoke hearts, celery hearts and château potatoes.

RECIPE

salad à la favorite
Arrange in a salad dish, in separate heaps, asparagus tips, shelled crayfish and sliced white truffles. Season with oil, lemon juice, salt and pepper. Sprinkle with chopped celery and herbs.

FAVRE, JOSEPH Swiss-born chef (born Vex, 1849; died Paris, 1903). After his apprenticeship in Switzerland, Favre finished his studies in Paris, with Chevet, then worked in Germany, England and again in Paris, with Bignon. He is best known as a theoretician: his *Dictionnaire universel de cuisine et d'hygiène alimentaire* (1st edition 1889–1891, 2nd edition 1902) contains not only a large number of recipes but also a very interesting history of cookery. In 1877 he founded the journal *La Science culinaire* in Geneva, and in 1893 he founded the first Academy of Cookery.

FÉDORA A garnish for large roasting joints, consisting of barquettes filled with asparagus tips, pieces of glazed carrot and turnip, quarters of orange and braised shelled chestnuts.

FEET AND TROTTERS The feet and trotters of slaughtered animals are classified as white offal (variety meat). Sheep's or lamb's trotters, which can be obtained from the butcher already blanched, must be boned, singed and the little tufts of hair between the cleavage in the hoof removed. They are first cooked in a court-bouillon, and can then be braised, grilled (broiled), fried, prepared *à la poulette* or used for a fricassee or a salad. They are also included in the Provençal speciality *pieds et paquets*, particularly popular around Marseille.

Pig's trotters are also sold blanched and cleaned. A particularly savoury way of cooking them is *à la Sainte-Menehould:* they are parboiled, dipped in egg and breadcrumbs, then grilled (broiled) and served with mustard or Sainte-Menehould sauce. They may also be boned and mixed with forcemeat, often with truffles. Pig's trotters may also be cooked in a flavoured stock, grilled, cooked *en daube* or braised.

Calves' feet are used primarily as a source of gelatine in stock, but they may also be prepared separately after being boned, cleaned, blanched and then cooked in white stock. They can then be fried, curried, prepared *à la poulette*, or dipped in egg and breadcrumbs, grilled and served with devilled or tartare sauce. All the recipes for calf's head can be used for calves' feet.

RECIPES

Calves' Feet
cooking calves' feet
Calves' feet can be bought already blanched and partially boned (the long foot bones only). They are usually cooked in a white court-bouillon for about 2 hours, like a calf's head. They can be served with a curry sauce and rice, for example.

Alternatively, they can be left to cool under a press, brushed with melted butter and coated in breadcrumbs, grilled (broiled) and served with a tartare sauce.

calves' feet à la Custine
Soak 2 pigs' cauls (pieces of caul fat) in cold water. Place the calves' feet in a large pan, cover them with cold water and bring to the boil. Boil for 5 minutes, remove the calves' feet, drain and leave to cool. Add 4 tablespoons flour, 4 tablespoons oil, the juice of 2 lemons, 4 litres (7 pints, 4 quarts) cold water, some salt and the calves' feet. Bring to the boil and simmer gently for about 2 hours (the feet must be very tender).

Mix 4 chopped shallots with 800 g (1¾ lb) chopped button mushrooms; season with salt and pepper and sprinkle with the juice of half a lemon. Cook the resulting duxelles over a brisk heat until the mixture is dry. Add a small glass of Madeira.

Drain the calves' feet, remove the bones and dice the flesh finely. Mix it with the duxelles. Divide the forcemeat into 6 equal portions. Wipe the cauls, spread them out flat on the work surface and cut into 6 equal pieces. Shape the portions of forcemeat into rectangles and wrap each one in a piece of caul. Brown them lightly in hot butter. To serve, sprinkle with the butter in which they have been cooked.

Pigs' Trotters
cooking pigs' trotters
Buy blanched trimmed pigs' trotters (feet). Tie them in pairs and place them in a pan of cold water. Bring to the boil, skim and add carrots, turnips, leeks, celery, an onion studded with cloves and a bouquet garni. Simmer gently for 4 hours. Drain and leave to cool. If they are to be grilled (broiled), place them between 2 thin boards tied with string, while still hot, to press them as they cool.

daube of pigs' trotters
Cut 3 pigs' trotters (feet) in half and place the 6 halves in a stewpan, together with a slightly salted knuckle of veal and 2 slightly salted pigs' tails. Cover with cold water and leave to soak for 3 hours. Drain and rinse the meat, then place in a flameproof casserole. Cover with cold water. Bring to the boil, skim and cook gently for 10 minutes with the lid off. Drain the meat.

Rinse and wipe the pan. Add 3 tablespoons groundnut (peanut) oil and return to the heat. When the oil is hot, add 4 diced carrots, 3 diced onions, and 2 chopped celery sticks. Cook for about 6 minutes until the onions are transparent, stirring occasionally. Then add 3 or 4 crushed garlic cloves, a few chopped sage leaves, 1 tablespoon flour, 1 tablespoon tomato purée (paste) and 4 peeled diced tomatoes. Cook for 2 minutes. Add 3 tablespoons dry white wine, 2 pinches of caster (superfine) sugar and 3 pinches of salt. Bring to the boil. Add a bouquet garni and a pinch of cumin seeds tied in a muslin (cheesecloth) bag. Add the meat, remove from the heat, cover the casserole with a lid and cook in a preheated oven at 140°C (275°F, gas 1) for at least 3 hours.

Arrange the meat on a heated serving dish, cover it with the sauce and vegetables and sprinkle with chopped parsley.

pigs' trotter sausages
Soak a large pig's caul (caul fat) in cold water. Cook the trotters (feet) in stock until really tender and bone them completely. Dice the flesh and mix it with an equal quantity of fine pork forcemeat (diced truffle may be added if wished). Add salt, pepper, a pinch of mixed spice and a dash of Cognac. Divide the mixture into 4 portions of

about 100 g (4 oz). Shape into little flat sausages (*crépinettes*) and top with a slice of truffle if wished. Wipe the caul, spread it out on the work surface and cut it into pieces. Wrap each *crépinette* in a piece of caul, coat with melted butter, roll in fresh breadcrumbs and cook gently under the grill (broiler).

Sheep's Trotters
fricassee of sheep's trotters with pieds-de-mouton mushrooms

Boil 10 trimmed blanched sheep's trotters (feet) gently for 4 hours in a mixture of water, white wine and lemon juice, with an onion studded with cloves, a bouquet garni, 2 garlic cloves, salt, pepper and curry powder. Place 800 g (1¾ lb) sliced mushrooms (use the variety known as *pieds-de-Mouton*, if available) in a strainer and plunge them for 3 minutes in boiling vinegar and water.

Pour 300 ml (½ pint, 1¼ cups) boiling water into a saucepan containing 6 tablespoons chopped parsley and 1 tablespoon chopped fennel. Cover the pan and boil for 45 minutes to reduce by three-quarters. Strain through muslin (cheesecloth) and twist the muslin to squeeze out the maximum quantity of liquid. Lightly brown 50 g (2 oz, ⅓ cup) chopped onions and 2 tablespoons chopped shallots in butter. Add the sheep's trotters, sauté them for 5 minutes, then add 2 tablespoons skimmed stock and a dash of lemon juice. Add 2 tablespoons chopped parsley, 1 tablespoon chives, 1½ tablespoons chopped fennel, salt and curry powder. Mix and cook for 1¼ hours, uncovered, over a gentle heat. Drain the cooked sheep's trotters, bone them completely and slice the flesh. Keep hot.

Make the sauce as follows: prepare a roux with 25 g (1 oz, 2 tablespoons) butter, 25 g (1 oz, ¼ cup) plain (all-purpose) flour, and 300 ml (½ pint, 1¼ cups) boiling salted water. Whisk and incorporate the cooking liquid together with 1 tablespoon double (heavy) cream. Mix the trotters with the mushrooms, arrange them in a vegetable dish and coat them with the sauce.

sheep's trotters à la rouennaise

Blanch the trotters (feet) whole and braise them in a good strong stock until really tender. Drain, then remove all bones.

Fill the boned trotters with sausagemeat mixed with 1 lightly browned chopped onion, chopped parsley and the stock left over from the braising, reduced and strained. Dip the trotters in egg and fresh breadcrumbs and deep-fry in sizzling fat. Alternatively, bake until crisp and golden, turning once. Serve immediately, garnished with fried curly parsley.

additional recipe See *pieds et paquets*.

FEIJOA A fruit native to South America, but now grown mainly in New Zealand. Sometimes called pineapple guava, the fruit, which is 2–8 cm (¾–3¼ in) long, has thin green skin (turning yellow as the fruit ripens) and coarse white flesh containing edible seeds. The feijoa is aromatic and similar in flavour to strawberries with a hint of pineapple. It can be eaten raw when ripe or it can be poached. It can also be used to make sorbets, jams and jellies.

FEIJOADA A Brazilian speciality whose basic ingredient is the black bean (*frijol negro*). It is a complete dish served on special occasions, not dissimilar to cassoulet. A large pot is used to cook slightly salted and previously soaked pork meat, such as shoulder, trotters (feet), rib and tail, and black beans. Flavourings include chopped onions, celery, garlic, (bell) pepper and bay leaf; other meat may be added, such as smoked streaky (slab) bacon, dried beef and cooked sausage.

Feijoada is served as follows: a mixture of meat and beans is poured into the centre of the plate and surrounded by rice *au gras*, green cabbage (thinly sliced and fried) and a few slices of orange (peel and pith removed). A mixture of grilled (broiled) manioc flour, onion and other ingredients, together called *farofa*, is sprinkled over the whole plate. The dish is served with a very spicy sauce, *molho carioca*, made with cayenne pepper, vinegar, the cooking liquid from the beans, chopped tomatoes and onions.

RECIPE

feijoada

Soak 1 kg (2¼ lb) black beans in cold water for 12 hours and, in another container, 1 semi-salted pig's tail and 500 g (1 lb 2 oz) lean, smoked bacon, changing the water in both containers several times. Peel 5 garlic cloves. Drain the beans and put them in a large braising pan. Cover with plenty of water and season with salt. Add 4 garlic cloves and 3 bay leaves. Bring to the boil and simmer gently for 1 hour. Drain the meats and boil for 10 minutes, then set aside. Seed 2 sweet (bell) peppers and cut into strips. Scald 500 g (1 lb 2 oz) tomatoes, peel, seed and crush. Finely chop 1 small bunch parsley and 1 small bunch chives. Heat 3 tablespoons oil in a frying pan. Add 1 chopped onion and fry until golden. Add the peppers, tomatoes, the remaining garlic clove and the parsley. Cook for 20 minutes over a medium heat, stirring all the time. Season to taste. When the beans can be crushed between the fingers, remove a ladleful of them and a ladleful of cooking liquid. Purée the beans and return to the frying pan. Sprinkle with chives and set aside. Slice 6 small fresh sausages, 6 small smoked sausages and 1 chorizo. Place the various meats in the braising pan. Season with salt and paprika. Cook for a further hour, adding the tomato and onion purée halfway through the cooking process. Stir well.

Prepare the farofa. Soak 100 g (4 oz, ⅔ cup) raisins in lukewarm water for 10 minutes. Melt 40 g (1½ oz, 3 tablespoons) butter in a frying pan and fry 1 large chopped onion. Add salt and 100 g (4 oz, 1 cup) manioc flour, then 40 g (1½ oz, 3 tablespoons) butter to

obtain a kind of light, sand-coloured mixture. Add
1 sliced banana, the drained raisins and 50 g (2 oz,
½ cup) grilled (broiled) cashew nuts. Serve with rice
mixed with slices of orange and onion, allowing each
person to sprinkle over more farofa.

FENDANT A Swiss white wine, produced mainly
in the Valais in the upper Rhône valley. It is made
from the Fendant, a local name for the Chasselas
grape, and is a dry, elegant and refreshing wine. Fendant is sometimes slightly sparkling (*pétillant*), which
accentuates its freshness. It is generally sold under
the name of the commune in which it is harvested,
or, more rarely, under the name of a vineyard.

FENNEL An aromatic umbelliferous plant of
Mediterranean origin, which is now widely cultivated. It is a hardy perennial which grows to
1.2–1.5 m (4–5 ft) high. The feathery leaves and
seeds have a slight aniseed flavour and both are
used as a herb and spice in a variety of recipes. The
herb goes particularly well with fish and chicken;
the spice is good with lamb and vegetables, particularly in marinades for wild mushrooms. The leaves
are also used as a garnish.

Florence fennel resembles ordinary fennel as a
plant but it produces a swollen leaf base which is
eaten as a vegetable. Known as a bulb or head of
fennel, the overlapping stem bases are closely
packed around a small tough, central core. Fennel is
similar in texture to celery. The feathery leaves,
which grow to about 60 cm (2 ft), are used as a herb
or as a garnish. The fennel bulb can be used raw in
salads or cooked in a wide variety of dishes.

RECIPES

braised fennel
Trim, halve and core fennel bulbs. Put them in an
ovenproof dish. Sauté 2 diced bacon rashers
(slices), 1 chopped onion and 1 diced carrot in a
little olive oil until slightly softened, then sprinkle
over the fennel. Moisten with a few tablespoons of
chicken stock or dry white wine (or a mixture of
both). Season to taste. Cover and cook in a
preheated oven at 180°C (350°F, gas 4) for about
1 hour or until tender. Turn the fennel halfway
through cooking and add a little extra stock or
wine, if necessary, to keep the vegetables moist.

fennel salad
Hard-boil (hard-cook) 2 eggs and shell them. Boil
100 g (4 oz, ¾ cup) long-grain rice. Leave to cool.
Peel 12 small pickling (baby) onions. Clean 1 large
bulb of fennel and slice it finely. Cut 4 small tomatoes into quarters. Add a little well-seasoned vinaigrette to the rice and put into a salad bowl. Place
all the other ingredients on top of the rice,
together with some black olives. Sprinkle with
chopped herbs and serve with anchovy sauce.

other recipes See *grècque*, *sea bream*.

FENNEL FLOWER See *nigella*.

FENUGREEK An aromatic leguminous Mediterranean plant originating in the Middle East. Belonging to the pea family, it produces long slender
curved pods containing oblong flattened brownish
seeds. The seeds, which have a slightly bitter taste,
are roasted and ground, then used as a flavouring in
curries. Their flavour is distinct and easily recognized as one of the ingredients of curry pastes and
powders. They are very hard – resembling tiny
stones – and can only be ground using a heavy
pestle and mortar or in a special grinder.

In North Africa, the seeds were traditionally used
to fatten women, who regularly consumed a mixture
of fenugreek flour, olive oil and caster (superfine)
sugar. The leaves have a very strong smell and in
Turkey, various Arab countries and India, they are
used either fresh or dried, as a vegetable or herb.

FERCHUSE A culinary speciality of Burgundy,
made from pig's offal (variety meat), traditionally
prepared on the day the pig was killed. (*Ferchuse* is
a corruption of the French word *fressure*, offal.) The
heart, lungs and liver are cut into pieces, browned in
lard with shallots and garlic, then floured and moistened with 2 parts red wine and 1 part stock. The
dish is simmered for 1 hour. A bouquet garni, some
sliced onions and slices of sautéed potato are added
and the dish is cooked for a further 45 minutes.

FERLOUCHE Also known as farlouche. Tart filling
from Quebec. It is made by boiling 300 g (11 oz,
1 cup) molasses, 200 g (7 oz, 1 cup) brown sugar
and 750 ml (1¼ pints, 3¼ cups) water with a pinch
of nutmeg and some orange zest. Off the heat, add
3 tablespoons cornflour (cornstarch) mixed with a
little cold water, then cook over a low heat until
thick, stirring continuously. The hot mixture is
poured into a pre-cooked flan case (pie shell) and
decorated with chopped hazelnuts or raisins.

FERMENTATION The biochemical change brought
about by the action of certain yeasts or bacteria on
certain food substances, particularly carbohydrates.
These micro-organisms are either naturally present in
the food or are added because of the requirements
of a particular process. The type of fermentation
varies depending on the type of food, the nature of
the fermenting agent and the length of time the
process takes, resulting in the formation of acids or
alcohols. For example, alcohol is produced by the
fermentation of natural sweet juices such as grapes
and sugar cane. Vinegar is a dilute solution of acetic
acid produced by the fermentation of various dilute
alcoholic liquids, such as wine or beer. Lactic acid is
produced in the souring of milk by bacteria.

The main foods that are fermented include dough,
milk products (curds, yogurt and cheese), meat (raw
sausage) and alcoholic drinks, such as beer, wine
and cider. Certain cereal preparations are also fermented, especially in India and Africa. Fermented

vegetables include sauerkraut, cucumber and beetroot (in eastern Europe) and mixed, thinly sliced vegetables (in China).

The greatest variety of fermented foods can be found in the Far East. They are based on soya, rice, leguminous plants and even fish (*nuoc-mâm*). In the Middle East, cereals and milk are fermented, and in eastern and northern Europe, vegetables, alcohol, bread and cheese. Fermentation is an excellent method of preservation.

FERMIÈRE, À LA A special method of preparing braised or pot-roasted meat, poultry or fish, using a garnish of vegetables that have been cooked slowly in butter until tender and are sometimes added to the main ingredient while it is being cooked. Vegetables prepared in this way can also be used to garnish omelettes and soups.

RECIPES

brill à la fermière
Thinly slice 2 carrots, 2 onions, the white part of 2 leeks and 3 or 4 celery sticks. Cook them slowly in 25 g (1 oz, 2 tablespoons) butter. Place half the vegetables in a greased ovenproof dish. Clean and season a medium-sized brill and place it on top of the vegetables. Cover with the remaining vegetables and add a few tablespoons of dry white wine or, better still, a concentrated fish stock made with white wine. Top with small knobs of butter and cook in a preheated oven at 220°C (425°F, gas 7), basting frequently. When the brill is cooked, place it on a serving dish and keep warm. Add 2–3 tablespoons cream to the cooking liquid from the fish and reduce by half. Pour the sauce over the brill and allow it to caramelize for a few moments in the oven.

omelette à la fermière
Slice 2 medium carrots, 1 large onion, the white part of 1 large leek and 2 or 3 celery sticks and cook gently in 25 g (1 oz, 2 tablespoons) butter. Season with salt and pepper. Lightly beat 8 eggs, add the vegetables and 1 tablespoon chopped parsley, beat again and adjust the seasoning. Brown 2 tablespoons diced ham in 20 g (¾ oz, 1½ tablespoons) butter in a frying pan. Pour the egg and vegetable mixture into the pan and cook the omelette. Serve very hot with crusty bread.

sautéed chicken à la fermière
Sauté a chicken in some butter until brown. Prepare 200 ml, (7 fl oz, ¾ cup) of the vegetable mixture used for brill *à la fermière*, ensuring that the vegetables remain fairly firm. Add the vegetables 15 minutes before the chicken is cooked. Place all the ingredients in an ovenproof casserole and add 2 tablespoons diced ham. Cover and cook in a preheated oven at 220°C (425°F, gas 7) for about 10 minutes. The cooking liquid can be deglazed at the last moment with 100 ml (4 fl oz, 7 tablespoons) thick gravy or thick veal stock.

soup à la fermière
Finely shred 2 or 3 small carrots, 1 small turnip, 1 leek (white part only), 1 onion and 75 g (3 oz, 1¼ cups) cabbage heart. Season and cook gently in 50 g (2 oz, ¼ cup) butter in a covered pan. Add 750 ml (1¼ pints, 3¼ cups) water in which white beans have been cooked, and 600 ml (1 pint, 2½ cups) white consommé. Cook gently for 1¼ hours. Add 100 ml (4 fl oz, 7 tablespoons) single (light) cream, 4 tablespoons cooked white beans and some chervil leaves.

other recipes See *entrecôte, mutton, pea, pinion, rissole, timbale.*

FERN The young shoots or fronds (also called 'violin scrolls') are harvested in Quebec and New Brunswick in early spring. They are shaken to remove the fine reddish dust covering them, then blanched for a few minutes. The shoots are either eaten cold or reheated in butter and sprinkled with lemon juice. They are a good accompaniment for meat and fish.

FERVAL A garnish for main courses consisting of braised artichoke hearts and potato croquettes filled with finely diced ham.

FESTONNER A French culinary term meaning to arrange decorative items in festoons around the edge of a serving dish. This is a garnish to add on the dish, rather than on the food. Croûtons, slices of aspic and half slices of fluted lemon can be used for this purpose.

FETA The best-known Greek cheese, made from ewe's milk, cow's milk or goat's milk and containing 45% fat. It is made by traditional methods, even though it is now manufactured on an industrial scale. The curdled milk is separated and allowed to drain in a special mould or a cloth bag. It is cut into large slices that are salted and then packed in barrels filled with whey or brine. Feta is often crumbled over the top of mixed salads and may be cut into cubes and served as a snack with olives and farmhouse bread.

FEUILLE D'AUTOMNE Round cake consisting of meringue and chocolate mousse, presented in a container made of fine pleated dark chocolate leaves. Made popular by the pâtissier Gaston Lenôtre, *feuille d'automne* is made of two layers of vanilla-flavoured French meringue and one layer of almond-flavoured meringue, sandwiched with a butter-based chocolate mousse.

FEUILLETÉ A piece of puff pastry cut into the shape of a finger or triangle and filled or garnished with cheese, ham or seafood. Feuilletés are served hot as an entrée.

The name is also given to small sticks of flaky pastry brushed with a little egg yolk and sprinkled with cumin seeds, cheese or paprika. They are served hot or cold as cocktail snacks.

RECIPES

feuilletés of chicken or duck liver ♦

Make the feuilletés with puff pastry and warm them in the oven. Clean the chicken or duck livers. Separate the lobes and cut into very thin escalopes (scallops). Season with salt and pepper and sauté them briskly in butter; then use a draining spoon to remove them and set aside. Sauté a small quantity of finely chopped shallots, fines herbes, and a few tiny button mushrooms or wild mushrooms, thinly sliced if large, in the butter remaining in the pan. Use the draining spoon to remove the mushrooms, then boil the cooking juices until virtually dry. Replace the mushrooms and livers, then add sufficient Madeira sauce to coat all the ingredients. Cook until the livers are heated through. Cut the middle out of the feuilletés, reserving the top as a lid. Fill the feuilletés with this mixture and replace the pastry lids; serve piping hot.

feuilletés with calves' sweetbreads

Prepare some feuilletés as in the previous recipe. Braise some calves' sweetbreads in well-seasoned white stock and use to fill the feuilletés. Serve very hot with cream sauce.

Roquefort feuilletés

Prepare some puff pastry. Mix together 200 g (7 oz) Roquefort cheese, 200 g (7 oz) soft cream cheese, 200 ml (7 fl oz, ¾ cup) double (heavy) cream, some chopped herbs and some pepper. Then add 4 eggs, one by one, beating the mixture continuously. Adjust the seasoning. Roll out the dough into 2 rounds about 3 mm (⅛ in) thick. Line a tart plate with one of the rounds and prick with a fork. Spread it with the cheese filling and cover with the second round. Seal the edges carefully. Bake in a preheated oven at 230°C (450°F, gas 8) for about 35 minutes, protecting the top with a sheet of foil about halfway through cooking if it is browning too quickly. Cut into triangles before serving.

scallop feuilletés

Open, trim and clean 16 scallops. Sauté them over a brisk heat in a sauté pan with 200 g (7 oz, 1 cup) butter and some freshly ground pepper for 3 minutes, turning them once. Put 2 tablespoons finely chopped shallots into a frying pan with 250 ml (8 fl oz, 1 cup) vermouth and boil to reduce to a syrupy consistency. Add 750 ml (1¼ pints, 3¼ cups) single (light) cream, 1 teaspoon mustard, a little ground pepper and 200 g (7 oz, 2¼ cups) diced mushrooms. Reduce over a brisk heat, then add the scallops, together with the liquid from the sauté pan. Reduce again for 2 minutes.

Roll out 400 g (14 oz) puff pastry and cut it into 8 rectangles about 3 mm (⅛ in) thick. Place 4 scallops on each of 4 rectangles together with a little

sauce. Cover with the remaining pieces of pastry. Brush the edges of the pastry with egg yolk and seal each pastry case tightly. Cook in a preheated oven at 230°C (450°F, gas 8) for about 12 minutes. Serve hot, with the remaining sauce.

snail feuilletés

Prepare about 500 g (1 lb 2 oz) puff pastry made with butter and roll it out to a thickness of about 3 mm (⅛ in). Cut out 8 rectangles measuring 14 × 9 cm (5½ × 3½ in). Arrange them on a baking sheet, cover loosely and leave them to stand for 30 minutes.

Prepare the garnish as follows. Finely chop 125 g (4½ oz, 1 cup) shelled pistachios. Cook 96 snails *à la bourguignonne*, but use champagne instead of white wine. Drain the snails, roll in flour and sauté in 4 tablespoons oil and 40 g (1½ oz, 3 tablespoons) butter. Add a dash of cayenne pepper, then a small glass of whisky, and flame, tilting the sauté pan in all directions. Then add 500 ml (17 fl oz, 2 cups) double (heavy) cream and heat to reduce, making sure the cream is oily but not curdled.

Brush the top of the rectangles of pastry with egg and make criss-cross patterns on them with the tip of a knife. Bake them in a preheated oven at 230°C (450°F, gas 8) for about 20 minutes (the feuilletés rise while baking). Add the chopped pistachios to the sauce and heat for 2–3 minutes. When the feuilletés are cooked, split them in two. Arrange the snails and some sauce on the bottom half of each feuilleté, replace the top halves and serve very hot. If any sauce remains, serve it separately.

FEUILLETON Thin slices of veal or pork beaten flat, spread with layers of forcemeat, and laid one on top of the other. The layers are then wrapped in strips of bacon or caul and tied with string. A feuilleton may also be made with a single piece of meat that is cut into parallel slices but not completely through, leaving them attached at one end. Forcemeat is then spread between each adjoining slice and the meat is tied up with string. The feuilleton is stewed or braised and served with a bourgeoise garnish or with braised vegetables, such as celery, chicory (endive) or lettuce.

RECIPES

feuilleton of veal à l'ancienne

For a feuilleton weighing 2 kg (4½ lb), cut 10 thin slices from a noix or sous-noix (loin) of veal and flatten them into rectangles with a mallet. Season with salt, pepper and a pinch of mixed spice. Prepare a fine pork forcemeat and add one-third of its weight of *à gratin* forcemeat and an equal amount of dry duxelles. Bind the forcemeat with egg. Cut a thin slice of pork fat slightly larger than the slices of

Feuilletés of chicken or duck liver.

veal and spread it with a layer of forcemeat. Top with a piece of veal and spread it with some forcemeat. Continue to build up the feuilleton in this way, ending with a layer of forcemeat. Coat the sides of the feuilleton with the remaining forcemeat and cover with a second strip of pork fat that is also larger than the slices of veal. Fold the edges of the bottom slice of pork fat upwards and the edges of the top piece of pork fat downwards so that the feuilleton is covered.

Tie the feuilleton into a neat shape. Put it in a buttered casserole lined with bacon rinds, sliced onions and carrots. Add a bouquet garni. Cover and simmer for 20 minutes. Moisten with 250 ml (8 fl oz, 1 cup) white wine and boil to reduce by half. Add 250 ml (8 fl oz, 1 cup) veal stock and boil to reduce to a concentrated glaze. Moisten with 500 ml (17 fl oz, 2 cups) good stock. Cover and cook in a preheated oven at 190°C (375°F, gas 5) for 1¾ hours, basting frequently. Drain the feuilleton, untie and arrange it on an ovenproof serving dish. Pour over a few tablespoons of braising stock and glaze in the oven, basting frequently.

feuilleton of veal l'Échelle

Season a boned fillet of veal and brown it quickly in very hot butter to seal. Leave it to cool. Cut it into slices lengthways, but do not cut completely through the joint. Prepare a forcemeat with a mixture of dry mushroom duxelles, chopped lean ham, diced truffles, and a vegetable mirepoix, bound with a beaten egg. Spread each of the slices with the forcemeat and reshape the fillet.

Cover the feuilleton with mirepoix and wrap it in a pig's caul (caul fat). Braise the feuilleton for 2–3 hours in butter, very slowly, then place it in an ovenproof dish. Garnish it with lettuce and potatoes that have been braised in butter. Pour over a little of the pan juices and return it to the oven to glaze. Make a sauce with the remainder of the juices in the pan by adding some Madeira and some veal stock.

This feuilleton may be served cold in aspic. In this case, a boned calf's foot is cooked in the stock.

FIADONE Several recipes exist for this Corsican cake, one of which consists of blending stiffly whisked egg whites with a mixture of the egg yolks, sugar, mashed fresh Broccio cheese and lemon zest. The cake is sometimes flavoured with a little brandy.

FIASQUE The French word for a type of Chianti bottle. It is derived from the Italian *fiasco*, meaning flask or straw-covered bottle. The bottle has a long narrow neck and is usually partly wrapped in woven straw.

FICELLE A long thin loaf of French bread (the word literally means 'string').

FICELLES PICARDES Savoury pancakes filled with a slice of ham and chopped creamed mushrooms with cheese. They are rolled up, arranged in an ovenproof dish, covered with cream and grated Gruyère cheese, and then browned in the oven. A speciality of northern France, they are served as a hot entrée.

FIG Pear-shaped or globular fruit that is eaten fresh or dried. Probably originating in Asia Minor and now widespread throughout the Mediterranean region, figs are mentioned in the Old Testament and were highly prized by the Ancients.

■ **Fresh figs** There are three types of fig: the white one (including green figs), the purple and the red. These types are subdivided into a large number of varieties. The best-known varieties of French figs are *buissone, bellone, bourjasotte, célestine, col de dame* and *dauphine violette*. These figs are grown in the Midi, mostly in Var, and exported fresh between June and November. Figs are also grown throughout the Mediterranean basin. Algeria is the principal supplier of dried figs.

Fresh or canned figs are usually eaten in their natural state. They can be served as an hors d'oeuvre with raw ham (Parma ham) in the same way as melon. Figs can also be cooked in various ways. All recipes for apricots are suitable for figs.

A fermented drink is made from figs, and also a spirit which is highly prized by the Arabs. In central Europe roast figs are used to flavour coffee, as chicory is in France.

■ **Dried figs** Very ripe autumn fruit is used. The figs, spread out on trestles, are exposed to the sun. They have to be turned several times during drying and, before they are completely dry, they are slightly flattened. Treated in this way, figs will keep for a very long time. The best dried figs are sold tied up with a piece of raffia and selected for their size and ripeness. They may be eaten plain or stuffed with almonds or walnuts. Dried figs are also sold in blocks. Figs, like prunes, are improved by soaking for 24 hours before use. They are eaten in compotes, cooked in wine, accompanied by milky rice pudding and vanilla cream. They are also used in savoury cooking; for example with pork or rabbit, like prunes, and are particularly delicious with braised pheasant and guinea fowl (soaked in port until swollen, then added to the pan at the end of cooking). A drink is also made from them (see *figuette*).

RECIPES

Savoury Recipes
Corsican anchoiade with figs

Soak 5 anchovy fillets in cold water to remove the salt, then wipe them dry. Pound them with 450 g (1 lb) fresh figs and 1 small garlic clove. Spread this paste on slices of bread moistened with olive oil. Sprinkle with chopped onions and serve.

figs with Cabécou en coffret ◆

Coarsely chop a small bunch of chives. Cook 400 g (14 oz) very fine green beans in salted water,

Figs with Cabécou en coffret.

keeping them al dente. Soak 65 g (2½ oz, ⅓ cup) sultanas (golden raisins) in 60 ml (2 fl oz, ¼ cup) vinaigrette until very soft.

Cut 2 Cabécou goat's cheeses into quarters. Cut 8 figs 1.5 cm (¾ in) from the top, reserving the tops, and remove one-third of the flesh. Fill each fig with one quarter of Cabécou. Using a pastry (cookie) cutter with a fluted edge, cut out 6 cm (2½ in) rounds of very thinly rolled puff pastry and coat with beaten egg. Place a fig on each piece of puff pastry and bake in a preheated oven at 200°C (400°F, gas 6) for 20 minutes. After 15 minutes, replace the tops of the figs.

Toss the green beans with the sultana vinaigrette and add the chives. Arrange 2 figs in puff pastry on each plate and add some of the bean salad. Sprinkle with toasted flaked almonds and serve at once.

fresh figs with Parma ham

Choose some very fresh green or purple figs that are ripe but still slightly firm. Split them into four without completely separating the quarters (these should be held together by the stalk). Gently loosen the skin near the stalk. Roll some very thin slices of Parma or Bayonne ham into cornets, arrange the figs and ham in a dish and serve cold.

lamb cutlets with figs and honey

Wash and wipe 1 kg (2¼ lb) fresh figs, but do not peel. Place them, stalks upwards, in a generously buttered ovenproof dish. Cover with a glass of water, add some pepper and a little ground cinnamon and grated nutmeg, and cook in a preheated oven at 200°C (400°F, gas 6) for 30–35 minutes. About 10 minutes before the end of the cooking time, melt 40 g (1½ oz, 3 tablespoons) butter in a frying pan and fry 4–8 lamb cutlets (depending on their size) for 3–4 minutes per side. Season with salt and pepper and arrange the cutlets in a warmed serving dish. Keep hot. Melt 2 tablespoons honey in a little hot water and add the pan juices from the cutlets to make a sauce. Adjust the seasoning. Arrange the figs around the meat. Coat the cutlets and the figs with honey sauce. Serve immediately.

Sweet Recipes
fig jam

Peel and quarter some large white figs that are just ripe but firm. Prepare a syrup, using 200 g (7 oz, 1 cup) sugar and 4 tablespoons water per 1 kg (2¼ lb) fruit. Add the figs to the boiling syrup and cook until the gelling stage is reached. Pot and cover in the usual way.

fig tart

Prepare 350 g (12 oz) shortcrust pastry (basic pie dough, see *short pastry*) and use it to line a 23 cm (9 in) flan ring. Prick and bake blind. Allow it to cool. Peel and halve some fresh figs and leave for 30 minutes. Mix a little rum with some apricot jam,

sieve the mixture and spread it over the base of the flan. Arrange the drained fig halves on top, coat them with apricot jam and decorate with Chantilly cream.

figs with raspberry mousse

Peel some fresh ripe figs and cut them into quarters. Make a raspberry mousse with 200 ml (7 fl oz, ¾ cup) Chantilly cream for each 250 g (9 oz, 1½ cups) sieved sweetened raspberries. Arrange the fig quarters in a shallow bowl, cover with the mousse and chill for 30 minutes before serving.

roast figs with a coulis of red fruits

Melt 50 g (2 oz, ¼ cup) butter in a frying pan. Add 16 fresh ripe figs and 3 tablespoons icing (confectioner's) sugar. Fry until lightly golden, then cook in a preheated oven at 200°C (400°F, gas 6) for 8–10 minutes. Remove from the oven and, using scissors, cut the figs open to look like flowers. Fill the figs with 200 g (7 oz) fresh raspberries. Pour 300 ml (½ pint, 1¼ cups) strawberry or raspberry coulis on 4 plates and decorate with the figs. Place 1 scoop of vanilla ice cream in the centre of each plate. Serve immediately.

other recipes See *compote, fritter.*

FIGATELLI A Corsican charcuterie product in the form of long thin sausages, smoked and very spicy, made with liver (*fegato*), lean and fat pork, and sometimes heart and kidney. They are flavoured with garlic, bay leaf and white wine and are eaten raw or grilled (broiled).

FIGUETTE A drink made from dried figs and juniper berries soaked in water for a week, using 5 juniper berries per 450 g (1 lb) figs in 5 litres (8½ pints, 5½ quarts) water. The liquid is then strained, bottled and left for 4–5 days before drinking.

FILBERT Fruit of the hazel, a small tree of the *Corylaceae* family, known in the French grocery trade as *noisette franche*. It has a hard shell covered by a foliated envelope. There are several species, the best known coming from Piedmont and Sicily. Filberts (also known as hazelnuts or cobnuts) are eaten fresh or dried. They provide hazelnut oil (not much used) and are used to make the sugared almonds known as *avelines*.

FILET MIGNON Piece of a small section of beef, positioned within the thoracic cage, along the first dorsal vertebrae. When trimmed, the filet mignon makes one or two steaks.

In relation to pork, it corresponds to fillet of beef; it can be roasted or fried, cut into medallions, or cut into small pieces for kebabs.

FILLET The undercut of the sirloin of beef, also used for the same cut in pork, veal and lamb. In Britain the word can also refer to the fleshy part of the buttocks of other animals. Either cut is prime meat, tender and with a delicate flavour.

If it is to be served whole, fillet of beef must be trimmed, larded or barded, and secured with string. It may be roasted in the oven or on a spit, fried or braised, according to the recipe. The fillet may alternatively be cut into steaks and grilled (broiled) – chateaubriands are cut from the middle of the fillet and tournedos from the end. The end of the fillet also provides pieces of meat suitable for kebabs.

In France, fillet of veal is used for *grenadins* and for fillet chops (*côtes-filet*), which are broader than ordinary chops, and fillet of lamb provides fillet cutlets (without knuckle) and mutton chops. Pork fillet (tenderloin) provides particularly tender cuts of meat, especially from the middle or end of the fillet. The boned end of pork fillet provides a slightly dry roast joint, which it is advisable to bard with rashers (slices) of bacon. *Filet de Saxe* (Saxony fillet) is a fillet of smoked salted pork wrapped in a caul. It resembles bacon but is smoother.

• BEEF AND VEAL The filet mignon is a small, choice cut of meat from the end of the fillet. Pork filet mignon is cut from the boned fillet and is particularly tender. It may be lightly braised in a single piece, sliced into two lengthways and stuffed, or cut into pieces for kebabs.

• POULTRY AND GAME BIRDS The fillet is the underside of the breast, or the entire breast, cut off before cooking and prepared in various ways. However, the breasts of poultry and game are more often known as suprêmes. (The fillet of a duck reared for its foie gras is called a *magret*.)

• FISH The fillets are cut lengthways off the backbone. (There are four in a flatfish, and two in a round fish.) They may be removed before cooking and poached, fried, marinated or rolled into *paupiettes*. When a fish is cooked whole, the fillets are removed at the time of serving.

RECIPES

cold fillet of beef à la niçoise
Garnish the cold roasted fillet with small tomatoes that have been marinated in olive oil and stuffed with a salpicon of truffles, small artichoke hearts filled with a salad of green asparagus tips, large olives, anchovies and pieces of aspic jelly.

cold fillet of beef à la russe
Surround the cold fillet with halves of shelled hard-boiled (hard-cooked) eggs stuffed *à la russe* and covered with aspic jelly, artichoke hearts stuffed with vegetables in mayonnaise and chopped aspic.

cold fillet of beef in aspic
Cold roasted fillet either whole, or cut into thin slices, may be covered with aspic jelly. If the piece is big enough to be served whole, place it on a rack and coat with several layers of aspic jelly, which may be flavoured with Madeira, port or sherry. (It must be placed in the refrigerator between each coating.)

Then arrange it on a serving dish and garnish with chopped aspic or with croûtons and watercress. Slices of fillet are either coated separately or placed in a row on the serving dish and coated with aspic. They are garnished in the same way.

Serve with a cold sauce, such as mayonnaise or tartare sauce, and cold vegetable barquettes or a salad.

fillet of beef à la périgourdine
Trim the fillet of beef, stud it with truffles, cover it with bacon rashers (slices), tie it with string and braise in Madeira-flavoured stock. Drain, remove the bacon, glaze in the oven and arrange it on the serving dish. Surround it with small slices of foie gras that have been studded with truffles and sautéed in clarified butter. Reduce the braising stock by half, strain it and pour it over the fillet.

fillet of beef en brioche
Prepare some brioche dough without sugar, using 500 g (1 lb 2 oz, 4½ cups) plain (all-purpose) flour, 20 g (¾ oz) fresh yeast (1½ cakes compressed yeast), 100 ml (4 fl oz, 7 tablespoons) water, 2 teaspoons salt, 6 medium-sized eggs, and 250 g (9 oz, 1 cup) butter. Melt 25 g (1 oz, 2 tablespoons) butter and 3 tablespoons oil in a pan and lightly brown a piece of fillet of beef weighing about 1.5 kg (3¼ lb), tied with string to maintain its shape. Then place the pan, uncovered, in a preheated oven at 240°C (475°F, gas 9) and cook for 10 minutes, basting the meat 2 or 3 times. Drain it, season with salt and pepper and leave to cool completely.

Lower the temperature of the oven to about 220°C (425°F, gas 7). Roll out the brioche dough into a fairly large rectangle. Remove the string from the beef and place it in the centre of the dough lengthways. Brush the meat with beaten egg and fold one of the sides of the dough over it. Brush the other side of the rectangle with beaten egg and wrap the fillet completely in the dough, tucking in the edges. Trim and cut both ends of the dough just beyond the meat and seal the edges with beaten egg. Brush the top with beaten egg. Garnish the top with the remaining pieces of dough. Brush with beaten egg. Place on a floured baking sheet and bake in a preheated oven at 220°C (425°F, gas 7) for about 30 minutes. Fillet of beef *en brioche* is traditionally served with a Périgueux sauce.

fried fillet steaks
Cut the fillet into thick 125–150 g (4–5 oz) steaks. Slightly flatten the steaks, then seal in very hot butter. Season with salt and pepper. Remove the steaks and keep them hot. Make a sauce with the pan juices mixed with a little Madeira; reduce and coat the steaks.

grilled beef fillet steaks
Cut the trimmed fillet into thick steaks, each weighing 125–150 g (4–5 oz). Slightly flatten each steak, sprinkle with pepper, brush with oil, season

with herbes de Provence (or mixed dried herbs) and cook under a hot grill (broiler) or over glowing embers, so that the outside is sealed while the inside remains pink or rare. Top each steak with a pat of maître d'hôtel butter.

grilled filets mignons

Slightly flatten some filets mignons of beef, each weighing about 125–150 g (4–5 oz). Season with salt and pepper, dip in melted butter and coat with fresh breadcrumbs. Moisten them with clarified butter and cook under a low grill (broiler). Serve with maître d'hôtel butter, Choron sauce, lemon butter or tarragon-flavoured tomato sauce mixed with white wine.

roast fillet of beef

Trim the fillet, bard it top and bottom (or brush with melted butter) and tie with string. Cook it in a preheated oven at 240°C (475°F, gas 9), allowing 10–12 minutes per 450 g (1 lb) and basting it several times with the meat juices, to which a very small amount of water has been added. Drain the meat, remove the barding strips and keep it hot on a serving dish. Make a sauce with the pan juices mixed with stock or reduced veal gravy. Reduce and serve with the fillet.

sautéed filets mignons

Slightly flatten some filets mignons of beef, season with salt and pepper and sauté them quickly in very hot clarified butter. Garnish as for tournedos.

spit-roasted fillet of beef

Trim the fillet, put it on the spit, season with salt and pepper and coat with melted butter. Roast, allowing about 10–12 minutes per 450 g (1 lb). Remove from the spit and leave the meat to rest for a few minutes. Cut it into even slices and serve with the reserved meat juices.

other recipes See *chevreuil, matignon*.

FILLETING FISH The process of removing the fillets from a whole fish that has been cleaned, by cutting the flesh off the main backbone. Small bones and some stray larger bones may remain in the fillet, but this essentially a boneless cut. Stray bones should be removed before cooking. A filleting knife, known in France as a *couteau à filets de sole*, has a long, narrow and flexible blade.

FILO PASTRY Also known as phyllo, this is a paper-thin pastry made from flour and water. The pastry is either rolled very thinly or stretched with the hands until paper thin. Similar in style to strudel pastry, it is used several layers thick. The layers are brushed with melted butter or oil so that they adhere but form crisp and flaky layers when baked. Filo pastries can also be fried.

This type of pastry is used throughout the Mediterranean for making a variety of savoury and sweet dishes. In Greece it is used to make feta cheese and spinach pies, known as *spinakopita*, or it is layered with nuts to make baklava, the famous sweet drenched in honey syrup. Baklava is also popular in Turkey, where *yufka* is the same type of pastry, used for savoury pastries called boreks. In North Africa, a similar type of thin pastry, known as *maisouqaa* or *ouarka* (meaning paper), is used to make brik, a fried large semi-circular pasty filled with spicy vegetables with an egg nestling in the filling.

■ **Buying and handling** Filo is available fresh or frozen and ready to use. When exposed to air, the sheets rapidly dry out, becoming crumbly and unusable, so it is important to unwrap only the required number of sheets and to keep the remainder covered with cling film (plastic wrap) or in a polythene bag until they are to be used.

Dampening the pastry reduces it to a sticky paste, so the work surface must be clean and dry. Brushing the pastry with melted butter or oil (or a mixture of both) will stick the layers of pastry together, sealing the folds to keep the filling in place and preventing the pastry from becoming flaky and dry around the edges. When cooked, the fat makes the pastry layers crisp and separate. Although many traditional recipes use generous quantities of melted butter, a light brushing is sufficient to give good results, especially through the middle layers, with more brushed over the outside or to seal folds.

In contemporary cookery, filo is brushed very lightly with oil (olive oil is good with savoury fillings) and used as an alternative to fat-rich short and puff pastries. It makes an excellent casing for fillets of fish, chicken, meat or vegetables. It is also popular for savoury finger snacks, such as little filled parcels and bundles.

FILTER A utensil or a material that is porous or perforated, enabling the separation of solid matter from a liquid by retaining the former and allowing the latter to pass through. In cookery, liquids can be filtered through a clean cloth strainer or a piece of muslin (cheesecloth), a colander or a sieve.

A coffee filter holds ground coffee and near boiling water is poured over it. It can be made of perforated metal, earthenware, porcelain or cloth (*la chaussette*), or a cone of filter paper that is placed in a special cone-shaped holder. *Café-filtre* (or *filtre*) is coffee made this way filtered directly into the cup.

FINANCIER A cake made from a sponge mixture using ground almonds and whisked egg whites. Small financiers are oval or rectangular in shape; they may be used as a base for iced petits fours.

Large cakes made with the same mixture are decorated with shredded almonds and crystallized (candied) fruits. These large financiers may be cooked in cake tins (pans) of decreasing size and then built up in layers to form a large gâteau.

RECIPE

almond financiers

Butter 16 tins (pans), each 10 × 5 cm (4 × 2 in). Put 100 g (4 oz, 1 cup) plain (all-purpose) flour into a mixing bowl. Add 100 g (4 oz, 1 cup) ground almonds, 300 g (11 oz, 1⅓ cups) caster (superfine) sugar, 2–3 tablespoons vanilla sugar and a pinch of salt. Mix everything thoroughly. Add a pinch of salt to 8 egg whites and whisk them into very stiff peaks. Fold them carefully into the cake mixture. Quickly fold in 150 g (5 oz, ⅔ cup) melted unsalted butter. Divide the mixture between the tins and bake in a preheated oven at 200°C (400°F, gas 6) for 15–20 minutes until the financiers are golden brown, then turn them out and cool on a wire rack. They may be coated with kirsch- or chocolate-flavoured fondant icing (frosting).

FINANCIÈRE, À LA A very rich classic garnish for joints of meat, calves' sweetbreads or braised poultry. It may also be used as a filling for croûtes, timbales, bouchées or vol-au-vent. It consists of a ragoût of cockscombs, chicken quenelles, finely sliced mushrooms and shredded truffles flavoured with Madeira, all bound with a sauce containing Madeira and truffle essence. The same ingredients are used to make *attereaux à la financière*, the quenelles being optional. There is also a financière sauce flavoured with Madeira and truffles.

RECIPES

calves' sweetbreads à la financière

Soak the sweetbreads in cold water until they become white. Poach in salted water, drain and trim, removing skin and membranes. Place between 2 cloths in a meat press. Cut some truffles and some cooked tongue coated with aspic into matchstick shapes and use them to stud the sweetbreads. Braise the sweetbreads in a brown stock. Arrange them in croustades of puff pastry and cover with financière garnish.

financière garnish

Prepare some poached chicken quenelles and some cockscombs. Slowly cook some finely sliced mushrooms and shredded truffles in butter. Add a little Madeira. Bind all these ingredients with financière sauce.

financière sauce (1)

(from Carême's recipe) Put some shredded lean ham, a pinch of mignonette (coarsely ground white pepper), a little thyme and bay leaf, some shredded mushrooms and truffles, and 2 glasses of dry Madeira into a saucepan. Simmer and reduce over a gentle heat. Add 2 tablespoons chicken consommé and 2 tablespoons well-beaten espagnole* sauce. Reduce by half, press through a fine sieve, strain, then heat again, stirring in 3 tablespoons Madeira. Reduce to the desired consistency and serve in a sauceboat (gravy boat).

When this sauce is intended for a game entrée, the chicken consommé is replaced by game fumet. Add a little butter just before serving.

financière sauce (2)

(modern recipe) Make 200 ml (7 fl oz, ¾ cup) Madeira* sauce, adding 100 ml (4 fl oz, 7 tablespoons) truffle essence while it is reducing. This sauce is usually used to bind the financière garnish.

stuffed quails à la financière

Prepare some stuffed quails* in cases, coat them with a sauce made with their cooking juices mixed with Madeira, and glaze them in the oven. Arrange on fried croûtons or croustades of puff pastry. Garnish with finely sliced truffles and surround with a financière garnish.

suprêmes of chicken à la financière

Sauté some suprêmes of chicken in clarified butter. Arrange them on fried croûtons or puff pastry croustades. Coat with financière sauce and surround with a financière garnish.

additional recipe See *vol-au-vent*.

FINE The French word for a brandy distilled from wine (as opposed to another alcoholic liquid). It should be distinguished from marc, which is distilled from the grape debris left after pressing.

FINE CHAMPAGNE A category of Cognac coming from the delimited regions of Grande and Petite Champagne and containing not less than 50% Grande Champagne Cognac in the blend (it has nothing to do with the delimited area producing champagne).

FINES HERBES A mixture of chopped aromatic herbs, such as parsley, chervil, tarragon and chives, in various proportions. The mixture is used to flavour sauces, cream cheeses, meat, sautéed vegetables and omelettes. In the past, chopped mushrooms were added, and today celery sticks, fennel, basil, rosemary, thyme and bay leaf may be added.

RECIPES

omelette garnished with fines herbes

Add enough coarsely chopped parsley, chervil, tarragon and chives to the beaten eggs to colour the omelette green – allow 3 tablespoons chopped fines herbes for 8 eggs.

sauce with fines herbes

Make 250 ml (8 fl oz, 1 cup) demi-glace sauce or brown stock and add 2 tablespoons chopped parsley, chervil and tarragon. Reduce, press through a very fine sieve, add a few drops of lemon juice and adjust the seasoning. This sauce is served with poached poultry.

FINLAND

Traditional Finnish cuisine reflects the geographic and historical situation of the country, with one eye to the West and one ear to the East.

■ **Regional specialities** In eastern Finland, as in Alsace, vegetables are fermented (sauerkraut of cabbage and turnips, cucumber and red beets in brine). Karelian stew (*karjalanpaisti*) is made with pork, beef and lamb. The Slav influence is reflected in the Finns' fondness for borsch, blinis, Karelian *pirojkis*, *karjalanpiirrakka* – a small rye pasty filled with mashed potato or rice, served with melted butter and hard-boiled (hard-cooked) eggs – and *vorschmack* minced (ground) lamb, beef and salt herring, seasoned with garlic and onion.

In western and southern Finland, Scandinavian cuisine predominates with an abundance of cold starters. Pastries, dry bread and cardamom-flavoured brioches (*pulla*) are also very popular.

The north is strongly influenced by Lapp cooking traditions. Reindeer meat is salted, dried, smoked or cooked slowly with marrow bones; it is also eaten raw like carpaccio. The classical dish par excellence is *poronkäristys*, thin slices of sautéed reindeer, served with mashed potatoes and sweetened, crushed cranberries.

■ **Where fish is king** Finland is the greatest European reserve of freshwater fish. Because its salt content is so low, the Baltic Sea too has many of the same varieties of freshwater fish that live in the thousands of lakes in the country: eels, lavaret (*siika*), white coreginids (*muikku*), char, perch, trout, pike-perch and salmon, as well as bream, pike and herrings, are smoked, salted and pickled. The nourishing *kalakukko* is rye bread stuffed with coregonids or small perches and bacon, and tartare of perch fillet is very popular. To celebrate the festival marking the end of summer, crayfish cooked in a court-bouillon seasoned with dill make a sophisticated dish, washed down with generous amount of *koskenkorva* (vodka schnapps).

There is also plenty of game, including mallards, elk, grouse and hare.

■ **The pleasure of picking** Picking food in the wild is much enjoyed in Finland. Besides the wild mushrooms that are added to pickles, stews, salads, sauces and soups, all sorts of berries, such as cranberries, bilberries, wild strawberries, cloudberries, arctic blackberries and sorb apples, are eaten as an accompaniment or as desserts (with cream or as a mousse). Some are also turned into mild or strong liqueurs (*lakka*, made from cloudberries). These liqueurs, like the soured milk, thickened to a greater or lesser degree, are drunk with desserts made from rye, malt, molasses and zest of bitter orange, or oat porridge, served with a purée of wild rose hips or raisins, or melted butter.

veal chops with fines herbes

Sauté some veal chops in butter in a frying pan (skillet), drain them and arrange on a hot serving dish. Add some chopped shallots and white wine to the butter and cook for a few minutes to reduce. Then add some chopped parsley, chervil and tarragon, adjust the seasoning, stir and pour the sauce over the chops. Formerly, demi-glace sauce was added to the white wine to make a richer, smoother and creamier sauce.

FINGER BOWL A small individual metal, glass or china bowl filled with warm water, usually perfumed with lemon, and used for rinsing the fingers at the table. It is an essential component of the table setting when serving shrimps or prawns, which need to be shelled with the fingers, or asparagus or artichokes, which are eaten with the fingers. The finger bowl is placed to the left of the dinner plate towards the end of the course and is removed as soon as the course is finished and the guest has rinsed his or her fingertips, an operation which should be carried out rapidly and with the minimum of fuss.

FINISH To complete the preparation of a dish, for example by adjusting the seasoning or the consistency and adding decorations or garnishes. Certain soups are finished by adding herb leaves, fresh butter or cream. A *civet* (rich game stew) is generally finished by thickening it with the blood of the animal used in the recipe. A dish coated with Mornay sauce is finished by browning. A sweet dish is finished by adding a decoration.

FINLAND See *above*.

FISH Aquatic vertebrates with fins (for swimming) and gills (for breathing), which represent an important source of food. At present, more than 30,000 species are known (as many as all other vertebrates put together). Most fish live in the seas and oceans, at varying depths. Freshwater fish are much less numerous. Some fish, such as eels and salmon, are migratory, spending part of their life in the sea and part in fresh water.

Fish are classified into two broad groups, according to their skeletons: cartilaginous fish (sharks, rays, dogfish, skate) and bony fish (the vast majority). Several basic body shapes can be distinguished:
• tapering, adapted to swimming in the open water (herring, cod, salmon, mackerel, carp, pike) – these are the most numerous;

In Helsinki, Finland's main sea port, herrings and also potatoes are sold from the fishing boats.

Buying fresh fish

whole fish	*odour*	fresh and pleasant: sea fish should smell of seaweed; freshwater fish of waterweeds
	body	glossy, with metallic and iridescent colours; firm elastic flesh; shiny close-fitting scales that feel damp to the touch and are covered with a light transparent mucus
	head	bulging eyes, damp bright-red gills
	guts	belly should not be torn, sagging, swollen or taut; when the fish is opened, the guts should be smooth and clean
gutted fish		belly wall quite pale, never dark red or brown; backbone adhering well to the flesh
steaks		section of backbone embedded in the flesh; firm flesh, not dark in colour around the backbone
fish fillets		firm pale flesh

• flatfish compressed vertically, with the eyes on the darker dorsal (upper) surface (skates and rays) – the ventral (lower) surface is white;
• flatfish compressed laterally, with both eyes either on the right side of the head (plaice, flounder, dab, sole) or on the left (turbot, brill), the blind side usually being without pigment;
• elongated and snakelike (eels).

Fish can also be differentiated by colour, the number and shape of the fins, the width of the mouth, the presence or absence of teeth, the thickness of the skin, and any spines, spurs and barbels.

■**Buying fish** There are three main factors to consider when buying fish: its freshness, its availability (depending on the season) and the percentage of waste. The season is less important now than it used to be, because fish caught off the African or northern coasts are sold almost all the year round. However, it is always preferable to eat fish in season: it tastes better and is cheaper.

Freshness is extremely important. Fish is subject to speedy decay by bacterial action and often causes food poisoning if it is not absolutely fresh. It is at its best when first caught, but the speed of modern transport and the excellent methods of preservation mean that fish can be enjoyed far from the fishing grounds without loss of flavour. Fish is refrigerated for transport and sold in melting ice, care being taken that the melting water drains off properly. This practice is sometimes considered to detract from the flavour, but it still remains the only method of transporting fresh fish for long distances from the fishing grounds.

Most methods of preserving fish date back to ancient times; freezing (practised by the Romans), drying (especially for herring and cod), smoking (salmon, haddock, eel) and salting in casks or barrels. Preservation by canning has considerably increased the consumption of tuna, sardines, pilchards and salmon in particular and freezing has enabled many more types of fish to be made available all the year round. The process of freezing freshly caught fish in factory ships has greatly improved the quality of frozen fish. High-quality frozen fish is often superior to 'fresh' fish from some shops where poor handling impairs the quality. When selecting frozen fish, the price and quality are good indicators of the standard to expect. Packing is also important as poor wrapping leads to freezer burn and deterioration in texture, moisture content and flavour.

For culinary purposes, fish can be divided into white fish, including all the cod family (haddock, whiting), the white flatfish (plaice, sole), and the perch family (including bass, red mullet and skate); and oily fish, including sardines, mackerel, herring, and trout, tuna, salmon, moray and lamprey.

■**Preparing fish** This depends on the type of fish, the dish and the cooking method. Large fish are usually sold prepared ready for cooking in the form of cleaned whole fish, fillets, steaks or cutlets. Some smaller fish may be displayed whole and have to be gutted, but the fishmonger will usually do this. Some very small fish are cooked and eaten whole, such as whitebait, and small sardines may be grilled (broiled) whole, then the fish is picked off the carcass as it is eaten.

Fish preparation: proportion of waste

	fish	proportion of waste	made up of
whole	sea bream, hake cod, coley, John Dory	50–60%	large head, large backbone, skin, fins, guts
	plaice, sole, herring, mackerel, sardine, dab	30–40%	average or small head, backbone, skin, fins, guts
headless	monkfish, dogfish, hake, cod, coley	15–25%	backbone, skin, fins
steaks		about 10%	section of backbone, possibly pieces of fin, skin
fillets		nil	

FRESHWATER FISH
See individual entries on each freshwater fish

salmon

pike-perch

carp

rainbow trout

Arctic char

perch

pike

shad

eel

SEA FISH
See individual entries on each sea fish

plaice

red mullet

red gurnard

turbot

Senegal red mullet

brill

Dover sole

pink or rose bream

sea bream

lemon sole

bass

sardine

anchovy

scorpion fish

gilthead bream

John Dory

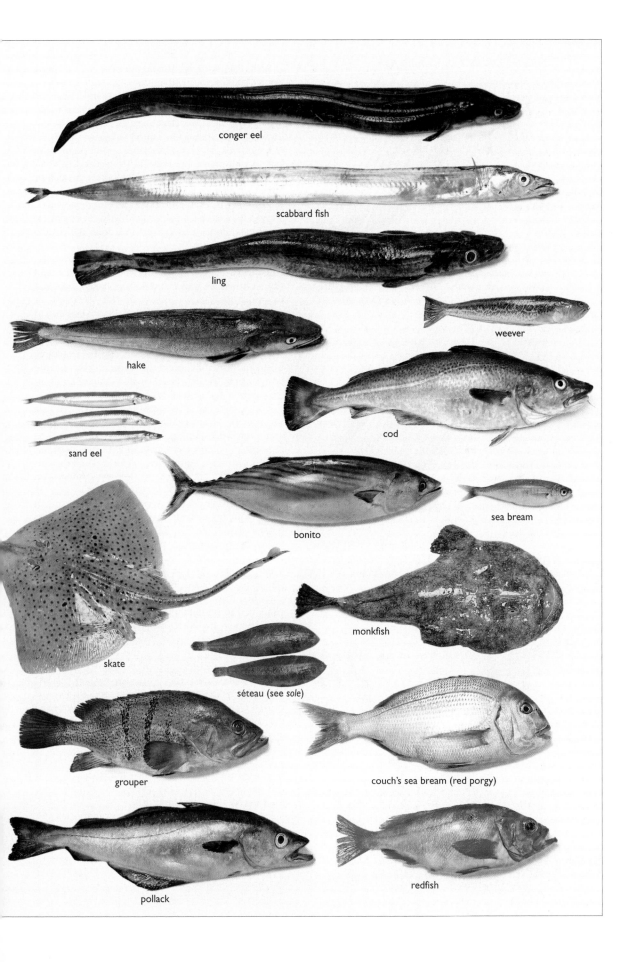

conger eel

scabbard fish

ling

hake

weever

sand eel

cod

bonito

sea bream

skate

monkfish

séteau (see *sole*)

grouper

couch's sea bream (red porgy)

pollack

redfish

Filleting and skinning round fish

1 *Clean the fish and cut off the fins. Cut the flesh around the head behind the gills down as far as the bones. Cut along the back, working from head to tail and slightly above the central bone. Hold the fish firmly by laying one hand flat on top as you cut.*

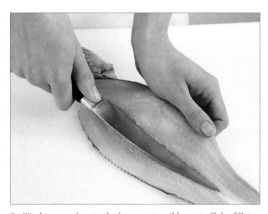

2 *Working as close to the bone as possible, cut off the fillet using long strokes. Lift the fillet away as it is cut free. When the fillet is completely removed, turn the fish over and repeat on the second side. Alternatively, instead of turning the fish over, cut the bones off the lower fillet, sliding the knife under them to free them from the flesh. Cut the fillet free across the head and tail.*

3 *To skin a fish fillet, rub your fingertips with coarse salt and hold the tail firmly in place. Holding the knife at an acute angle, cut between the skin and the flesh using a side-to-side sawing action. Fold back the fillet as it is freed from the skin.*

Scaly fish, such as salmon, are descaled or scaled before cooking by scraping the skin with a knife to remove all the scales. This is a messy task, which is easier when carried out under cold running water. Whole flat fish or fillets may be skinned before cooking; the skin may be cut off cutlets or steaks.

Round fish, such as mackerel or trout, may be boned with or without their heads in place. Alternatively, the fillets can be cut off the bones of small or large fish. Smaller flat fish, such as plaice or sole, are often sold whole and the bones may be removed to leave a pocket in the fish or the fillets can be cut off the bones. Bones may be removed from the middle of cutlets or steaks.

■ **Cooking fish** This requires care, to avoid overcooking, when the flesh becomes very flaky and dry. Fish may be grilled (broiled) or baked, poached in water or stock, cooked in fat, steamed or wrapped in buttered paper or foil, before cooking in the oven. Raw fish, either lightly cured, marinated or with carefully selected condiments, is considered to be a delicacy by some, but it needs to be absolutely fresh and carefully prepared. Such dishes include *ceviche* from Mexico and Ecuador, *gravad lax* from Scandinavia and sashimi from Japan.

Hot or cold fish dishes can be accompanied by a wide variety of sauces, flavoured butters, vegetables, and even fruit. Fish can also be cooked in soups (*chaudrée, bouillabaisse, cotriade*), in pies (*koulibiaca*), in mousses, quenelles, aspics, salads, in scallop shells or gratin dishes, on skewers, curried, as a *matelote*, and in many other ways.

■ **History** In the Middle Ages, river fish were much more common than they are today, but even then coastal fish from the English Channel, especially mackerel and herring, were being sold in Paris. However, the eels of Maine, France, the barbels of Saint-Florentin, the pike of Chalon, the lampreys of Nantes and Bordeaux, the loach of Bar-sur-Seine, the dace of Aisne and the carp of the lakes of Bondy continued to be highly regarded. During the Renaissance period, haddock, anchovies, turbot, skate and whiting were eaten more frequently, but the river continued to supply most of the fish markets. The following is an extract from *Blasons domestiques* (by G. Corrozet, 1539): 'There you can see the eel and the lamprey ... the fresh salmon, the stub-nosed carp, the large pike, the frisky sole, the fat porpoise, the savoury shad, then the sturgeon and the amorous trout, some boiled, the others roasted to sharpen human appetites.'

In the 15th century, salt cod was considered to be worthy of the best tables, while the so-called 'royal fish' (basically dolphin, sturgeon and salmon) were reserved for the king's table.

In France certain fish, especially river species, are now becoming rare (pike, char, shad and dace), while others are less frequently cooked (eel and sturgeon). On the other hand, some are in greater demand than in the past (red mullet, sea bass and sea bream). Concerns about fish stocks and overfishing; the wide variety of 'exotic' species, for

Skinning and filleting Dover sole

1 *The tough skin on Dover sole is usually removed before cooking the fish, whether it is cooked whole or as fillets. Cut the skin across the tail and slide the point of the knife a short way under it to free the end from the flesh. Holding the tail firmly on the surface, pull the skin off at an acute angle. Repeat on the second side.*

2 *To remove two fillets from each side of the fish, use a flexible, fine-bladed filleting knife and cut the flesh along the central bone.*

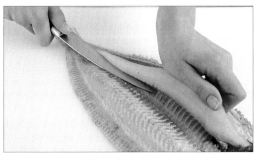

3 *Slide the point of the knife under the flesh, working as close to the bones as possible, to remove the flesh in one piece. Carefully lift the flesh off the bones as it is freed. Turn the fish around and work on the other side, then turn it over and remove the remaining fillets.*

4 *Trim off the rough edges of the fish to give even fillets, with neat edges.*

example from Africa and New Zealand, offered as alternatives to traditionally popular seafood; and fish farming are contemporary issues that influence the availability and promotion of fish.

FISH AND CHIPS Fried battered fish and chips (French fries), widely considered to be Britain's national dish. As such, there is great regional variation – and debate – over the way fish and chips should be prepared. The most popular fish are cod, haddock and plaice, in that order. Haddock is predominantly caught on the east coast of Britain and cod on the west, which reflects local preferences. The cooking fat varies, with the North favouring lard or beef dripping; the Midlands and the South opting for vegetable oil. Certain potato varieties are said to give superior results, with the floury Desirée and Maris Piper being the most popular.

FISH KETTLE A long, deep cooking receptacle with two handles, a grid and a lid. The fish kettle is used to cook whole fish, such as hake, salmon, pike, in a court-bouillon. The removable grid enables the fish to be taken out without breaking it. The wide turbot kettle is specially designed for cooking large flat fish.

FISH SLICE A table utensil, in the form of a silver-plated or stainless steel spatula, for serving fish. It is usually perforated, since fish cooked in a court-bouillon, even if it has been drained, is often still rather watery. The blade is rounded, pointed or has its corners cut off. The French word *truelle* may also be applied to a cake slice.

FITOU A red AOC wine from Languedoc, produced around Corbières, south of Narbonne. The appellation divides into two areas – Fitou Maritime producing supple, lighter wines with less tannin, best drunk young, and Fitou Montagneux where the wines have firmer structure and longer ageing potential. Both styles must be kept for a minimum of nine months before bottling. The main grapes are Carignan, Grenache and Syrah.

FIVE SPICES A mixture of five Chinese spices: star anise, clove, fennel, cinnamon and Sichuan pepper. It is widely used in Chinese cookery. The flavour is strong, particularly of anise, and the spice is used with care, in small amounts.

FIXIN A fine red Burgundy (AOC), from the most northerly of the Côte-de-Nuits vineyards. The finest *climats* or terroir are considered to be Les Arvelets, Les Hervelets, Le Chapitre, La Perrière and Clos Napoléon. Other wines may be sold as Côte de Nuits Villages. Fixin wines are particularly fragrant, capable of long lives and appreciated for their finesse and pedigree.

FLAMANDE, À LA The name given to various preparations derived from the regional cookery of northern France. The *flamande* garnish consists of stuffed braised balls of green cabbage, shaped pieces of glazed carrot and turnip, potatoes *à l'anglaise*, and, sometimes, diced belly of pork (salt pork) and slices of sausage that are cooked with the cabbage. It is also the name of a garnish and a hot-pot which is used especially for large cuts of meat (such as rump of beef) or for braised goose. The entire dish is coated with demi-glace, veal stock or a sauce made with the pan juices from the meat.

Among other preparations described as *à la flamande* are Brussels sprouts (puréed, mixed with an equal quantity of potatoes or used to garnish a consommé) and chicory (endive), either raw in a mixed salad, or cooked in a *chiffonnade* for garnishing an omelette served with cream sauce. *À la flamande* is also a method of preparing asparagus with sieved hard-boiled (hard-cooked) egg yolks.

RECIPES

asparagus à la flamande
Cook some asparagus in salted boiling water. Serve hot with melted butter to which sieved yolks of hard-boiled (hard-cooked) eggs and chopped parsley have been added.

Flemish salad
Cook some peeled potatoes in salted water and blanch some large peeled onions. Cut the potatoes into slices and chop the onions coarsely. Clean some chicory (endive) and cut the leaves lengthways and across. Place all the ingredients in a salad bowl and mix with a fairly well-seasoned vinaigrette. Arrange in a dome and garnish with fillets of salt herring cut into strips. Sprinkle with chopped parsley and chervil.

other recipes See *cabbage, carbonade, civet, cod.*

FLAMBER A French culinary term meaning to pour spirits over food, then ignite it, both to enhance the flavour and for culinary showmanship.

When flaming a savoury dish, the spirit must be warmed and then ignited, preferably with a long taper. As it catches fire, it is poured over the dish. Brandy, rum or whisky are the spirits most commonly used, and the procedure is usually carried out when making a sauce from the pan juices.

In some restaurants, sweet dishes, such as crêpes or sweet omelettes, are flamed with rum or a liqueur at the serving table on special hotplates.

FLAMBÉ TROLLEY A small table on castors, fitted with one or two burners (spirit or butane) and used in restaurants for flaming dishes at table. The flambé trolley often has a bottle rack and a cabinet for cutlery.

FLAMICHE Also known as *flamique*. A type of sweet or savoury tart made in northern France and Flanders (*flamiche* is the Flemish word for cake). Formerly, it was a cake made of bread dough and eaten freshly baked, spread with butter. Nowadays, a *flamiche* contains vegetables or cheese. The vegetables are cooked slowly in butter, then mixed with egg yolks and seasoned. The best-known *flamiche* is made with leeks; in Picardy, where it is known as *flamique à porions*, it is also prepared with pumpkin or onions.

Cheese *flamiches* are usually made with a Maroilles or similar full-flavoured cheese. *Flamiche à l'ancienne* is made with a three-turn puff pastry mixed with semi-matured Maroilles cheese and butter. It is cooked in a very hot oven and is eaten as a hot entrée with beer. Another way of making a *flamiche* is to line a pie plate with bread dough and fill it with slices of Maroilles cheese, alternating with cream seasoned with black pepper and butter. Yet another variation is prepared in Hainaut, where cheese *flamiche* is made as a pie (with a pastry lid). In Dinant the tart tin is lined with shortcrust pastry (basic pie dough) but the covering is a mixture of strong cheese, butter and eggs.

RECIPE

leek flamiche
Make 500 g (1 lb 2 oz) shortcrust pastry (basic pie dough, see *short pastry*). Roll out two-thirds of the dough to line a 28 cm (11 in) pie plate. Cut and thinly slice 1 kg (2¼ lb) leeks (the white parts only) and slowly cook them in butter. Add 3 egg yolks and adjust the seasoning. Spread the mixture over the pastry on the pie plate. Roll out the remaining dough large enough to cover the top of the dish. Dampen and pinch the edges together to seal and mark a criss-cross pattern on the top with the tip of a knife. Glaze with beaten egg. Make a slit in the centre and bake in a preheated oven at 200°C (400°F, gas 6) until the pastry is golden brown.

FLAMMENKÜCHE An Alsatian speciality, whose name means literally 'flame cake'. Traditionally prepared by the baker, it consists of a large rectangle of very thin bread dough with a raised edge; it is filled with finely sliced lightly fried onions mixed with fresh cream and topped with small strips of fried smoked bacon. *Flammenküche* may also be filled with a mixture of cream cheese, cream and egg yolks and topped with onions and strips of bacon. It must be cooked very quickly in a very hot oven.

FLAMRI Also known as flamery. A baked semolina pudding prepared with white wine instead of milk and served cold. It is coated with a purée of sweetened red fruit.

RECIPE

flamri
Place 500 ml (17 fl oz, 2 cups) sweet white wine and 500 ml (17 fl oz, 2 cups) water in a saucepan and bring to the boil. Gradually stir in 250 g (9 oz, 1¼ cups) fine semolina and simmer gently for 25 minutes. Remove from the heat and add 250 g

(9 oz, 1 cup) caster (superfine) sugar, 2 beaten eggs and a generous pinch of salt. Then stir in 6 stiffly whisked egg whites. Pour the mixture into a buttered charlotte mould in a bain marie. Cook in a preheated oven at 200°C (400°F, gas 6) for 30 minutes. Allow to cool, then turn out on to a serving dish and coat with a sauce made from a purée of uncooked red fruit that has been sweetened with sugar.

FLAMUSSE An apple pudding made in the same way as clafoutis. It is a speciality of Burgundy and Nivernais.

RECIPE

apple flamusse
Put 65 g (2½ oz, ⅔ cup) plain (all-purpose) flour in a mixing bowl. Make a well in the centre and add 75 g (3 oz, 6 tablespoons) caster (superfine) sugar, a generous pinch of salt and 3 beaten eggs. Mix with a wooden spoon until smooth. Gradually add 500 ml (17 fl oz, 2 cups) milk and mix well. Peel 3 or 4 dessert (eating) apples and cut them into thin slices. Arrange them on a buttered pie plate so that they overlap. Pour the batter mixture over the top and cook in a preheated oven at 150°C (300°F, gas 2) for 45 minutes. When cooked, turn the flamusse over to serve, and sprinkle the apples generously with caster sugar.

FLAN An open tart filled with fruit, a cream or a savoury mixture. A flan may be served as a hot entrée or as a dessert. The word comes from the Old French *flaon*, from the Latin *flado* (a flat cake).

Flans have been in existence for centuries. They are mentioned in the works of the Latin poet Fortunatus (AD 530–609), and featured in medieval cookery – Taillevent gave numerous recipes for flans.

The word flan is also used in France and Spain for an egg custard, often caramel-flavoured, that is made in a mould, turned out and served cold.

RECIPES

flan case baked blind
Prepare 350 g (12 oz) pastry dough (short or shortcrust, sweet, fine lining or puff) and roll out to a thickness of 3 mm (⅛ in). Grease and flour a 28 cm (11 in) pie plate or flan ring and line it with the pastry, pressing firmly around the edges to ensure that it stays in place and taking care not to stretch the pastry. Leave a thicker edge of pastry at the top so that it does not shrink while it is being baked. Trim off the excess pastry by rolling the rolling pin around the rim of the plate or by trimming with a sharp knife. Prick the bottom with a fork and completely cover the pastry with lightly buttered greaseproof (wax) paper or foil, greased side down. To keep the base of the flan flat, sprinkle the surface of the paper with baking beans or dried peas. Bake in a preheated oven at 200°C (400°F, gas 6)

for about 10 minutes. Remove the paper or foil and baking beans, glaze the crust with beaten egg, and return to the oven for 3–4 minutes, or until the pastry is cooked and dried out. The flan case (pie shell) may then be filled.

Savoury Flans
cheese flan
Bake a flan case (pie shell) blind. Heat 500 ml (17 fl oz, 2 cups) double (heavy) cream with 50 g (2 oz, ¼ cup) butter. Season with salt, pepper and grated nutmeg and add 100 g (4 oz, 1 cup) plain (all-purpose) flour. Whisk over a gentle heat to obtain a fairly smooth cream. Remove from the heat and add 4 egg yolks and 150 g (5 oz, 1¼ cups) grated cheese. Whisk 4 egg whites into very stiff peaks and fold them into the cream mixture. Fill the flan case and bake in a preheated oven at 200°C (400°F, gas 6) for about 30 minutes, or until set and browned.

chicken liver flan chavette
Bake a flan case (pie shell) blind. Thickly slice 500 g (18 oz) trimmed chicken livers. Season and sauté quickly in hot butter. Drain and keep warm. Sauté 200 g (7 oz, 2⅓ cups) sliced mushrooms in the same butter. Season, drain and keep warm with the chicken livers.

Make a sauce by adding 200 ml (7 fl oz, ¾ cup) Madeira to the juices in the pan in which the chicken livers and mushrooms were cooked. Reduce a little. Add 350 ml (12 fl oz, 1½ cups) thin béchamel* sauce and 200 ml (7 fl oz, ¾ cup) single (light) cream and reduce the sauce until it has a creamy consistency. Strain it, then add the chicken livers and mushrooms. Simmer gently without allowing the sauce to boil.

Prepare some very soft scrambled eggs (using 8–10 eggs) and then add 2 tablespoons grated Parmesan cheese and 2 tablespoons butter.

Arrange the chicken livers and mushrooms in the bottom of the prepared flan case. Top with the scrambled egg mixture and sprinkle with grated cheese. Pour some melted butter over the top and brown very quickly in a preheated oven at 240°C (475°F, gas 9) so that the scrambled eggs are not overcooked.

seafood flan
Bake a flan case (pie shell) blind. Prepare a ragoût of shellfish (such as oysters, mussels and cockles). Blend the shellfish with a fairly thick normande sauce and fill the flan case with the mixture. Sprinkle with toasted breadcrumbs and a little melted butter and brown in a preheated oven at 240°C (475°F, gas 9).

Sweet Flan
cherry flan
Line a flan ring with sweetened pastry (*pâte sucrée*) and bake blind. Remove the stalks and stones (stems and pits) from 400 g (14 oz, 2 cups) black cherries (Bing cherries). Boil 300 ml (½ pint,

1¼ cups) milk with a vanilla pod (bean) split in two and then stir in 3 tablespoons double (heavy) cream. Beat 3 eggs with 100 g (4 oz, ½ cup) caster (superfine) sugar in a bowl, add the vanilla-flavoured milk and whisk until the mixture has cooled completely. Place the cherries in the flan case (pie shell) and carefully pour the mixture over. Cook in a preheated oven at 190°C (375°F, gas 5) for 35–40 minutes. Serve either lukewarm or cold, sprinkled with sugar if wished.

FLANDERS The cuisine of this northern province has much in common with that of the neighbouring provinces of Artois and Picardy. The North Sea provides maritime Flanders with an abundance of fish, particularly mackerel and herrings. Crops and vegetables of the interior include wheat, potatoes, endive (chicory), hops and sugar beet. High-quality livestock is also important and includes pigs and sheep, and also dairy and beef cattle, whose meat is highly regarded. With all these resources, the cuisine of Flanders is a rich one – dishes are usually cooked slowly in a covered pan.

The most typical Flemish soups are *soupe verte* (green soup) and beetroot (red beet) soup. Fish specialities include Dunkerque bloaters, *wam* (dried fish), mackerel stuffed with shallots, spring onions (scallions), parsley and butter, cod *à la flamande* (sautéed with shallots and cooked in white wine), red herring salad (with potatoes and beetroot) and eels in beer.

Typical meat dishes include smoked tongues of Valenciennes, baby chitterlings (*andouillettes*) of Cambrai and Armentières, the traditional Flemish hotch-potch, *carbonades*, *potjevfleisch*, rabbit *à la flamande* (with prunes and raisins), *coq à la bière* (in beer) and *poule au blanc* (chicken cooked in white stock).

Vegetables are used to make *flamiches* and also to make such specialities as red cabbage *à la lilloise* (cabbage, apples and onions, simmered for 3 hours, reduced to a purée and cooked briefly in the oven in a soufflé mould).

The best-known cheeses, which all have a strong flavour, are Bergues, Mont-des-Cats, Coeur d'Arras, Boulette d'Avesnes, Dauphin, Vieux-Lille and Maroilles. Omelettes and *flamiches* are made with Maroilles cheese, as is the *goyère* (Maroilles cheese tart) of Valenciennes.

The production of sugar from sugar beet has given rise to a variety of regional pastries and confectionery. The best known are the apple pies of Avesnes, plum tarts, *craquelins* of Roubaix, *carrés* of Lannoy, *galopins* (little oblongs of bread dipped in milk, mixed with eggs, and fried), *couques*, and the *bêtises* (mint humbugs) of Cambrai.

The local drink is beer, and good-quality spirits are distilled from beetroot or cereals, often flavoured with juniper berries.

FLANK The abdominal muscles of beef, which form a second-category joint. Thick flank steaks cut on the perpendicular from the internal muscles are lean, tasty, coarse-grained and slightly tough (they must therefore be hung); they are eaten grilled (broiled) or sautéed. Thin flank is similar but slightly tougher. Cuts taken from the two external muscles give fibrous, rather tough meat, suitable for broths and stews.

RECIPES

flank with shallots
Chop some shallots, allowing 1 level tablespoon chopped shallots for each steak. Fry the steaks quickly in butter, add the chopped shallots to the frying pan (skillet) and brown. Season with salt and pepper. Remove the steaks and deglaze the meat juices with vinegar (1 tablespoon per steak) and a little stock, then reduce. Pour the shallots and juice over the steaks.

grilled flank
Brush some steaks with oil, sprinkle with chopped herbs (fresh thyme and parsley) and grill (broil) quickly for 7–8 minutes. Season with salt and pepper at the end of cooking.

FLAN RING A ring of tin-plate of varying diameter (6–33 cm, 2½–13½ in). Many pastrycooks prefer it to a mould for preparing tarts and flans. When placed directly on the baking sheet, it ensures a better diffusion of heat through the pastry and enables the cooked tart or flan to be easily removed. A loose-bottomed metal flan tin is often used instead, particularly by home cooks.

FLAUGNARDE Also known as flagnarde, flognarde or flougnarde. A flan made in the Auvergne, Limousin and Périgord regions of France. The name is derived from the Old French *fleugne*, meaning soft or downy. The flan resembles clafoutis and is made with apples, pears or prunes, flavoured with cinnamon, vanilla, rum, brandy, orange-flower water or lemon. It resembles a large pancake and is served lukewarm or cold (Curnonsky recommended the latter), generously sprinkled with icing (confectioner's) sugar and sometimes spread with jam.

RECIPE

flaugnarde
Beat 4 eggs with 100 g (4 oz, ½ cup) caster (superfine) sugar in a bowl until the mixture is light and frothy. Gradually add 100 g (4 oz, 1 cup) plain (all-purpose) flour and a pinch of salt. Slowly beat in 1.5 litres (2¾ pints, 6½ cups) milk. Mix well, then flavour with 100 ml (4 fl oz, 7 tablespoons) rum or 4 tablespoons orange-flower water. Peel and core 3 pears, cut them into thin slices and add them to the mixture. Butter an ovenproof dish, pour in the mixture and dot the surface with small pieces of butter. Bake in a preheated oven at 220°C (425°F, gas 7) for 30 minutes. Serve hot or cold.

FLAVOUR The sensation produced when food comes into contact with the taste buds on the tongue. There are four basic tastes – sweet, salty, sour and bitter – which are detected by taste buds on different parts of the tongue. The particular flavour of a dish comes from the combination of several of these tastes: when one predominates, the dish is described is sweet, salty, sour or bitter.

Extreme temperatures (very hot or very cold) temporarily numb the sense of taste. When flavours are mixed, they can mask each other or bring each other out. Salt masks the sweetening power of sugar, but a pinch of salt in a sweet dish (especially in pastries and doughs) makes it seem sweeter. A little sugar added to some savoury foods (peas, tomatoes, sauces) enhances their flavour. A contrasting taste will modify the flavour of foodstuffs; for example, fruit tastes sour after a sweet dish and sweet after cheese or a spiced dish. The skilful cook combines contrasting or similar flavours to produce a harmonious whole, the flavours being enhanced by texture, consistency, colour and temperature.

FLAVOURING A substance added to a preparation to improve its flavour. Before the 18th century, it was customary to use exotic flavourings which are now usually reserved for perfumery, such as essence of rose and other flowers, benzoin, amber and musk. Today, the herbs and spices commonly used for flavouring include thyme, bay, savory, coriander, cinnamon, cumin, aniseed, pepper and ginger. Orange-flower water, almond essence (extract), vanilla and the zest of citrus fruits are used for flavouring cakes, pastries and confectionery.

Wines, fortified wines (Madeira, Frontignan, port and sherry), spirits and brandies are used extensively for flavouring sauces and gravies and for enhancing the taste of game stews, salmis, shellfish *à la bordelaise* or *à l'américaine*, and flamed meat and poultry dishes. A variety of extracts, essences and fumets are also used. Other methods of flavouring include steam-cooking with aromatic plants, smoking with specially scented wood, and macerating with spices.

FLEURIE One of the ten Beaujolais regions distinguished by an AOC. Charming and fruity, the wines are sometimes associated with the 'floweriness' of the place name. They are usually at their best when drunk young.

FLEURISTE, À LA Describing a preparation of small cuts of sautéed meat garnished with château potatoes and tomatoes. The latter are hollowed out, slowly baked and filled with a *jardinière* of vegetables mixed with butter.

FLEURON A small puff-pastry shape used to garnish pie crusts or served with dishes of fish cooked in sauce. *Fleurons* are cut into crescents or other shapes from the leftover pastry trimmings, rolled out very thinly. They are then brushed with beaten egg and baked or fried.

FLICOTEAUX A Parisian restaurant, situated in the Place de la Sorbonne, that was frequented in the 19th century by generations of students, journalists and impoverished writers because of its fixed-price menus. Balzac gave a vivid description of the two long low rooms, each with a narrow table. The tablecloths were changed on Sundays in 'Flicoteaux I' and twice a week in 'Flicoteaux II' in order to compete with other restaurants. He made this comment about the cooking: 'The female ox prevails and potatoes are inevitable. When the whiting and mackerel shoals teem on the Atlantic coasts, they rebound into the restaurant of Flicoteaux.'

FLIP Formerly, a flip was a hot alcoholic drink made with beer, rum and beaten eggs. Today it is usually a cold cocktail made with wine or spirits mixed with beaten eggs, sugar, nutmeg and various flavourings. The best known is the port flip.

FLOATING ISLANDS A cold dessert consisting of a light egg custard topped with egg whites that have been stiffly whisked with sugar, shaped with a tablespoon and poached either in boiling water or in the milk used to make the custard. In the latter case, the dish is more difficult to make successfully and the whites are not as meltingly soft. Floating islands are served drizzled with pale caramel or crushed praline.

Île flottante, in French, was formerly made with slices of stale Savoy sponge-cake or brioche that were moistened with liqueur and sandwiched together with apricot jam containing chopped almonds and raisins. It was served cold with custard cream or a purée of strawberries, raspberries or redcurrants.

RECIPES

floating islands ◆
Boil 750 ml (1¼ pints, 3¼ cups) milk with a vanilla pod (bean) or 1 teaspoon vanilla sugar. Whisk 8 egg whites to stiff peaks with a pinch of salt, then fold in 3 tablespoons caster (superfine) sugar. Using a tablespoon, gently drop portions of the whisked egg whites into the boiling milk. Turn the whites so that they are cooked all over. Remove after 2 minutes and drain on a cloth. Make an egg custard with the same milk, the 8 egg yolks, and 250 g (9 oz, 1 cup) sugar. When completely cold, pour the custard into a deep dish, place the cooked egg whites on top, and chill until ready to serve. Serve drizzled with caramel.

floating island with pink pralines
Make a custard* with 500 ml (17 fl oz, 2 cups) boiled milk, 6 egg yolks, 200 g (7 oz, 1 cup) sugar and half a vanilla pod (bean). Pour it into a serving dish to cool completely. Butter a deep cake tin (pan) that has a slightly smaller diameter than the serving dish. Crush 100 g (4 oz) pink pralines with a rolling pin and sprinkle three-quarters over the

Shaping and poaching floating islands

1 *For best results, shape the meringue by the same method as used when preparing quenelles. Scoop up a portion of meringue on one spoon and gently smooth the top with a second spoon.*

2 *Transfer the meringue from one spoon to another until it is smoothed into a neat oval shape.*

3 *Add the shaped meringues to simmering water or milk and poach gently, turning once. Use a draining spoon to remove the meringues.*

bottom of the mould. Whisk 4 egg whites with a pinch of salt and 8 tablespoons caster (superfine) sugar until very stiff. Fold in the remaining crushed pralines and fill the mould with the mixture. Cook in a bain marie in a preheated oven at 140°C (275°F, gas 1) for 30–40 minutes. Unmould while still hot on to the chilled custard. Decorate with pralines.

FLORENTINE, À LA A method of preparation used mainly for fish, white meat or eggs in which spinach (and usually Mornay sauce) are included. The connection between the city of Florence and spinach is not known and seems strange, as the vegetable is consumed throughout Italy.

In Italy the term *alla fiorentina* is used for dishes that are typically Florentine, such as tripe cooked in chicken stock, garnished with green vegetables and served with Parmesan cheese, or saddle of pork simmered with spices, or omelette with artichoke hearts, or *bistecca alla fiorentina*, a beefsteak that is marinated before being grilled (broiled).

RECIPES

artichoke hearts à la florentine
Slowly cook some artichoke hearts and spinach (separately) in butter. Stuff each artichoke heart with a heaped tablespoon of prepared spinach and coat with Mornay sauce. Sprinkle with grated cheese and brown in a preheated oven at 240°C (475°F, gas 9).

brill à la florentine
Cook some spinach slowly in a little butter. Drain well. Poach some fillets of brill in a little white wine stock. Prepare a Mornay sauce.

Spread out the spinach in a buttered dish and arrange the drained brill fillets on top. Cover with Mornay sauce, sprinkle with grated cheese and a little melted butter, and brown in a preheated oven at 240°C (475°F, gas 9). If a whole brill is used rather than fillets, it should be boned and trimmed before arranging it on the spinach.

fritters à la florentine
Prepare 250 g (9 oz, 1 cup) spinach purée and dry it out gently over the heat, turning it with a wooden spoon. Mix the purée with 200 ml (7 fl oz, ¾ cup) well-reduced béchamel* sauce and blend in 50 g (2 oz, ½ cup) grated Gruyère cheese. Cool the mixture completely and divide it into about 15 portions. Roll each portion in flour, dip into a prepared batter and deep-fry in oil, heated to 180°C (350°F), until golden brown. Drain on paper towels, sprinkle with salt and serve very hot.

soft-boiled or poached eggs à la florentine
Slowly cook some spinach in butter and drain well. Butter some small ramekin or soufflé dishes and place a little spinach in each, making hollows to hold 2 soft-boiled (soft-cooked) or poached eggs. Coat the eggs with Mornay sauce, sprinkle with grated cheese and brown under a hot grill (broiler).

suprêmes of chicken à la florentine
Season some suprêmes of chicken or young turkey with salt and pepper and brush with melted butter. Melt some butter in a pan, add the suprêmes and flavour with a little lemon juice. Cover the pan and

Floating islands, see page 497.

place it in a preheated oven at 220°C (425°F, gas 7). Cook for 12–15 minutes. Cook some spinach in butter and spread it in an ovenproof dish. Arrange the suprêmes on top, coat with Mornay sauce, sprinkle with grated cheese and melted butter, and brown in a preheated oven at 240°C (475°F, gas 9).

other recipes See *cannelloni, kromesky, liver, pannequet, potato, salmon (hot dishes), salt cod.*

FLORIAN

A garnish for large joints of meat made with braised lettuce, small glazed onions, shaped glazed carrots and small potato croquettes.

FLOUNDER

A flatfish that is often found in estuaries, although it is actually a sea fish. The European species, *Platichthys flesus*, has a greenish or brownish mottled skin covered with tiny scales and can be up to 50 cm (20 in) long.

In France, the flounder is sometimes known as *flandre* (or *flondre*) *de rivière* or *de picard*. In former times, it was incorrectly called *fléton*, which means halibut.

In northern Europe, especially in Norway, flounders are preserved by drying and smoking. Recipes for turbot, brill, dab and plaice are suitable for flounders. In American cuisine, the word flounder is used for a larger variety of flatfish than in Europe.

Flounder is the only flat fish caught in any quantity in Australia. There its quality is on a par with plaice.

FLOUR

Finely ground cereal, such as wheat, barley, oats, rye, rice and maize (corn). In Britain, the word 'flour' usually refers to flour produced from wheat. The milling of grain dates back to prehistoric times and over thousands of years this has developed into an important and highly automated industry. There is evidence that wheat or corn was crushed and used as food at least 6000 years ago. The pounding stones used for this purpose have been discovered in archaeological digs throughout Europe.

The Romans were the first to apply rotary motion to milling. This involved grinding the grain between circular stones, one rotating and the other stationary. The domestic quern mills were turned by hand; the larger mills by slaves or donkeys. The milled flour was sifted through a boulting bag of linen or rushes, which separated the white flour from the bran and wheatgerm.

The water wheel came to Britain from Rome. The earliest were laid horizontally in the water; later they were set vertically. Windmills first appeared about 1200 and were widely used until the Industrial Revolution. After this, steel roller mills were introduced from Hungary. These produced finer flours as we know them today and roller milling is still the system used in all large commercial mills.

The wheat grain is composed of three parts: endosperm, germ or embryo, and bran. The object of milling is to separate the endosperm from the bran and germ, because white flour is derived from the endosperm, which generally comprises 85% of the grain (compared with 2% germ and 14% bran). Today wheat is cleaned before milling, foreign matter being removed on the basis of shape, size and density. After this the wheat is moistened and allowed to 'temper', a process that toughens the bran and makes separation more complete.

Wheat grains are initially ground on break (or fluted) rolls that are designed to shear open the grains and release the endosperm. The ground material is then sieved; the bran flakes with endosperm still attached to them are reground by finer break rolls, and large endosperm pieces are sent to purifiers which remove small bran particles using air currents. The purified endosperm pieces (semolina) are then ground on mat-surface rolls (reduction rolls) to produce flour. A number of reduction passages are required to convert the semolina into flour. Flour is removed from the sifters at various stages throughout the milling process. These various machine flours are blended to produce a range of flours to meet bakery specifications. Wheatgerm is removed during the milling of wheat into white flour and is sold separately.

Hard milling wheats mill easily to give high yields of granular free-flowing flour, whereas soft milling wheats produce fine flours of poor sieving and packing qualities.

■ **Flour grades** Flour is milled to different specifications and consistencies, including soft, hard or strong, bread and pasta 00 (Italian grades) and varies from country to country. American flour used to be far finer than its British counterpart, but these days there is little to differentiate them, as roller milling processes have been standardized.

The main types of flour available in Britain are plain (all-purpose), used for general baking and containing 75% of the wheat grain; self-raising (self-rising), which is plain flour with baking powder added; strong or bread flour, used for bread dough; brown flour, which contains 85% of the wheat grain; and wholemeal flour, which is 100% wheat grain. The last two contain more fibre and are less processed and can be used in place of whole flour, where appropriate. Improvers in the form of ascorbic acid (vitamin C) are added to the flour supplied to commercial bakers. This helps to strengthen the gluten, giving better rising properties.

In other parts of the world, flour is made from a variety of cereals and starchy ingredients, including spelt, maize (corn), potatoes and rice. In Italy, pasta is made from 00 flour. Containing 70% of the wheat grain, this flour is milled from the middle part of the wheat's endosperm, giving a much whiter result. Wholewheat pasta flour uses 100% of the grain.

FLOURING

The process of lightly covering an item of food with flour, or sprinkling a mould, cake tin (pan) or work surface with flour. Items of food are often floured before frying or sautéing; the excess flour can be removed by shaking or tapping.

Flouring should not be done too far in advance as the flour should be dry. Foods may also be floured before being coated with egg and breadcrumbs. Finally, items of sautéed meat or poultry may be floured after being browned as a method of thickening a ragoût or casserole (the French word for this process is *singer*).

A work surface or a pastry board is floured before the dough is rolled out to prevent it from sticking. Some baking tins (pans) and sheets need to be floured lightly before mixtures are poured in or before being lined with pastry. The tin or sheet is usually greased beforehand. This makes it easier to turn out the item after cooking or to prevent a mixture from spreading out too much on a baking sheet when cooking begins.

In bakery, *bannetons* (wicker moulds lined with cloth) are dusted with a special rye flour: this process is known as *fleurage*.

FLOUTES Speciality of the Jura consisting of mashed potato, flour, eggs and cream, fried in a pan until golden. Traditionally, *floutes* accompany meat.

FLOWERS Throughout history, flowers have been used in cookery. The Romans used them to flavour certain dishes – the recipes of Apicius include brains with rose petals, sweet marjoram flowers in various hashes, and a sauce with safflower petals – and Roman wines were flavoured with roses or violets. Today flowers are used mostly in Oriental cookery: dried rosebuds are used as a condiment; jam is made from rose petals; salads incorporate chrysanthemum, nasturtium or marigold petals; jasmine and hibiscus flowers flavour poultry and fish dishes; and yellow lilies provide seasoning for sauces and stocks.

In Europe, flowers are used in aromatic drinks, wines and spirits (elderflower wine, hyssop syrup and pink ratafia). Some well-known spices and flavourings are made from flowers and buds, notably cloves, capers, nasturtium flowers in vinegar and orange-flower and rose waters.

Several chefs have invented recipes that include flowers, either as an ingredient or as decoration. Jules Maincave, a great French chef at the beginning of the 20th century, declared that seasonings were 'pitifully limited, whereas the progress of modern chemistry would enable us to use rose, lilac and lily-of-the-valley'. Alexandre Dumas suggested a recipe for herb soup *à la dauphine* containing marigold flowers. Usually flowers are added to soups at the end of cooking. In salads they obviously play a more decorative role, particularly nasturtium, but also red poppy, borage, violet and honeysuckle. They can be arranged in a crown or in bunches, and the colours are used to match or complement the colours of the other ingredients. Vinegar changes the colour of flowers, and if they are to be used in a salad with a vinaigrette dressing, they must be added at the last moment and the salad must not be tossed until it is time to serve. Certain flowers are especially suitable for fritters: mimosa, gourd, elder and jasmine. Pumpkin flowers can be eaten stuffed and are also used to garnish omelettes. Flavoured butters are seasoned with the petals of jasmine, orange, lemon or garlic flowers. Flowering mint is suitable for fish, together with lime and jasmine flowers. The latter may also be used in various forcemeats. Aromatic infusions are also made from flowers and may be drunk or used in certain steamed dishes. Wild violets complement the taste of beef; savory flowers complement veal; sage is used with pork; and mint and thyme with mutton.

Flowers have always been used in confectionery, for example in rose-water jellies, rose jam, crystallized (candied) violets, mimosa, forget-me-nots and primulas, and praline-flavoured orange blossom. These sweet delicacies and decorations were very popular in France at the time of the Second Empire.

FLÛTE A long thin French roll, weighing about 100 g (4 oz), midway between a *baguette* and a *ficelle* in size. Flûtes are usually split in half and grilled (broiled) for croûtes, or served with soups and broths.

In France, a flûte is also a tall thin bottle used traditionally for white Alsace wines.

FLUTE GLASS A glass with a stem and a narrow body, for serving champagne and other sparkling wines. The narrow body (as opposed to a wide one) enables the wine to keep its sparkle, as the gas bubbles are not released so quickly.

FLUTING The technique of making V-shaped grooves over the surface of a purée, cream or mousse, using a spatula. Pieces of pastry are described as fluted when they have been cut out with a serrated pastry (cookie) cutter. A toothed piping nozzle is also described as fluted.

FLYING FISH A small fish, 18–25 cm (7–10 in) long, common in warm and tropical seas. It has a blue back and a silvery belly and its pectoral fins are winglike, enabling it to glide above the surface of the water. It is often fished in the Caribbean islands; its tasty flesh is prepared like mackerel.

FOCCACIA An Italian olive-oil flat bread, of very ancient origin, since it dates to bakestone days. It is a hearth bread, traditionally flung into the oven just after the fire has been raked out, when the temperature is still too high to bake a larger loaf without burning the crust. In northern Italy it plays a similar role to that of pizza in the south – eaten as a snack (frequently as street food) or with cheese or antipasti.

Originating from Genoa (and related to *fougasse* or *fouace* from the south of France) but now made all over Italy, including the south, *foccacia all genovese* is made with plenty of olive oil and salt. It is usually baked (traditionally in large round copper baking tins), but occasionally fried. There are many different regional variations, for example with onions, chard, salt cod or mozzarella.

Schiacciata is the focaccia of Tuscany, often with herbs, and *pan sciocco* (also *pane toscano*) is the unsalted version, traditionally eaten with salty foods.

FOIE GRAS Goose or duck liver that is grossly enlarged by methodically fattening the bird. The force-feeding of geese was done as early as Roman times when figs were used. As soon as the bird was slaughtered, the liver was plunged into a bath of milk and honey, which made it swell as well as flavouring it. Nowadays the birds are fattened with maize (corn); each liver weighs 675–900 g (1½–2 lb) for geese – the record is 2 kg (4½ lb) – and 300–400 g (11–14 oz) for ducks.

Foie gras from Toulouse geese is ivory-white and creamy; from Strasbourg geese, pinker and firmer. It is a highly prized delicacy, yet opinions vary as to its suitability for culinary preparation in comparison with duck foie gras; the latter is also delicate (but slightly darker in colour than goose liver) but melts and breaks down more during cooking and has a slightly more pronounced flavour. André Daguin, a leading chef of Auch, prefers duck foie gras. France also imports foie gras from Austria, the Czech Republic, Hungary, Israel and Luxembourg, as demand exceeds French production.

Charles Gérard, in *L'Ancienne Alsace à table*, wrote: 'The goose is nothing, but man has made of it an instrument for the output of a marvellous product, a kind of living hothouse in which there grows the supreme fruit of gastronomy.' Foie gras is available in four forms in France.

• RAW FOIE GRAS (*foie gras cru*) Increasingly in demand, this is sold during the holiday season at the end of the year. It must be well-lobed, smooth and round, but not too large (so that not all its fat is rendered down in the cooking process), and putty-coloured (if yellowish, it has a tendency to be grainy). Its preparation and cooking must be meticulous, and only worthwhile for fine-quality livers.

• FRESH FOIE GRAS (*foie gras frais*) This can be purchased cooked from delicatessens, usually in pots. It will keep at the most for a week, covered, in the refrigerator.

• SEMI-COOKED PASTEURIZED FOIE GRAS (*foie gras mi-cuit pasteurisé*) Sold in cans, this will keep for three months in the refrigerator once opened. It retains the taste of fresh foie gras quite well, and its manufacture is governed by very strict regulations. The best-quality products must have a perfect consistency, aroma and flavour, and must not exude fat. The labels 'foie gras d'oie entier' (whole goose foie gras), 'foie gras d'oie entier truffé' (whole goose foie gras prepared with truffles), 'foie gras de canard entier' (whole duck foie gras), and 'foie gras de canard entier truffé' (whole duck foie gras prepared with truffles) apply to pure whole livers (formerly labelled 'foie gras au naturel'). Goose or duck 'parfait de foie gras', with or without truffles, is a liver reconstituted from small pieces (formerly labelled 'bloc de foie gras'). 'Pâté de foie d'oie truffé' (goose-liver pâté with truffles) is a whole goose liver coated with forcemeat (formerly called 'parfait de foie d'oie truffé'). The labels 'délice', 'lingot', 'suprême', 'timbale', 'roulade' and 'tombeau' designate products coated with forcemeat or barding, or both (with a minimum of 20% foie gras). When the foie gras is referred to as 'truffé', with no other indication, it contains at least 3% truffles.

• PRESERVED FOIE GRAS (*foie gras de conserve*) Sold in jars, this is the most traditional preparation. Sterilized and preserved in its own fat, it will keep for years in a cool dark dry place and improves like wine.

In addition to the labels for semi-cooked foie gras, there is also the label 'purée de foie d'oie' (goose-liver purée). This contains 50–75% finely pounded goose liver, and the term replaces the former 'mousse'.

■ **Tradition and innovation** Whether from the goose or the duck, foie gras has always been considered a rare delicacy, but the way in which it is served has changed according to culinary fashion. At one time it was served at the end of the meal. The traditional truffle and aspic accompaniments are now thought to be superfluous by some, who prefer to serve it with lightly toasted farmhouse bread (leavened and slightly acid), rather than with plain slices of toast. Nouvelle cuisine set as much store by foie gras as classic cuisine, and sometimes gave it novel accompaniments, such as green leeks, pumpkin or even scallops. However, the classic recipes, both hot and cold, still retain their prestige.

Most dishes described as *à la périgourdine* or *Rossini* are prepared with foie gras.

RECIPES

preparation of raw foie gras

Carefully remove all the tubes and skin from the liver, using the point of a thin-bladed knife. First make an incision in each lobe starting from the larger end, where the main vein is located. Separate it. Still using the knife, pull on the vein. It will come away by itself, showing the rest of the network, which can then be easily removed. Once the lobes are open, season them with ½ teaspoon salt and ¼ teaspoon freshly ground pepper per 450 g (1 lb). Close up each lobe, wrapping it tightly in muslin (cheesecloth), and chill overnight.

The next day, place the liver in a terrine, cover it with goose fat and poach it, allowing 4 minutes per 100 g (4 oz) foie gras when the fat starts to simmer. When it is cooked, cool and drain the liver on a wire rack, then chill for at least 24 hours. Remove the muslin before serving the foie gras cold, possibly with a hot truffle cooked *en papillote*.

The taste of the liver can be enhanced by marinating it for 48 hours in port mixed with 10% Armagnac.

Duck Foie Gras
cold duck or goose foie gras escalopes with grapes and truffles

Prepare the raw liver and cook as described in the basic preparation above. Cut the liver into equal-sized slices. On each of these escalopes (scallops) place I large slice of truffle dipped in aspic jelly and leave to set, then glaze the whole escalope with aspic. Arrange the escalopes in a crown shape in a shallow glass bowl. In the middle of the crown, heap a dome of fresh peeled seeded grapes which have been steeped in a little liqueur brandy. Coat everything lightly with clear port-flavoured aspic. Cover and then chill well before serving.

duck foie gras with white pepper and green leeks

Prepare a foie gras weighing 300–400 g (11–14 oz) as above. Boil some young green leeks in salted water and purée them with a little cream. Put this purée in a small greased cake tin (pan). Season the foie gras with salt and coarsely ground pepper and arrange it on the leek purée. Cover the tin with foil and bake in a preheated oven at 140°C (275°F, gas 1) for 35 minutes. Leave to cool for 45 minutes (the last 15 minutes in the refrigerator).

duck or goose foie gras mousse

Press a cooked foie gras through a fine sieve, and place the purée in a bowl. For each litre (1¾ pints, 4⅓ cups) purée, add 250 ml (8 fl oz, 1 cup) melted aspic* jelly and 400 ml (14 fl oz, 1¾ cups) chicken velouté* sauce. Beat the mixture lightly over ice. Season, then add 400 ml (14 fl oz, 1¾ cups) partly whipped double (heavy) cream. Line a round mould with aspic jelly and garnish with slices of truffle, the thinly sliced whites of hard-boiled (hard-cooked) eggs and tarragon leaves. Then fill with the mousse up to 1.5 cm (¾ in) from the top of the mould. Cover the mousse with a layer of aspic jelly, allow to cool, and then chill.

Turn out the mousse on to a serving dish, or a buttered croûton, and surround it with chopped aspic jelly. The foie gras mousse can also be served in a silver dish or a crystal bowl, at the bottom of which a layer of aspic jelly has been left to set. Smooth the top of the mousse, which should be slightly dome-shaped. Garnish with slices of truffle and glaze lightly with any remaining aspic jelly.

glazed duck foie gras

Season a fine duck foie gras with salt and pepper, then marinate it in port for at least 24 hours. Draw a 2.5 kg (5½ lb) duck through the neck, remove the breastbone and open out the tail end. Put the liver into the duck and truss it up. Brush the duck with oil and cook in a covered casserole in a preheated oven at 200°C (400°F, gas 6) for 1 hour 20 minutes. While the duck is cooking, prick the skin frequently with a fork so that it does not burst. Remove from the casserole and leave to cool. Add the port marinade and some aspic jelly made with the duck's giblets to the pan juices. Glaze the duck with this clarified aspic and chill.

Poach some prunes in water, some cherries in a red-wine jelly, and some apple quarters in butter. Flavour all these fruits with ginger and glaze with the remaining duck aspic. Stuff some stoned (pitted) green olives with foie gras or ham mousse. Peel the segments of a large orange. Arrange the duck in the serving dish with all the fruits, making the orange segments into a rosette.

steamed duck foie gras with Sauternes

Prepare some stock with duck bones, 1 bottle of Sauternes, 2 carrots, 1 turnip, 2 celery sticks, 2 shallots and the white part of a leek (all sliced). Season with salt and pepper. Trim the foie gras and remove the tubes, season with salt and pepper and chill (with the strained stock) for 24 hours. Pour the stock into a steamer, place the foie gras in the steamer basket and cook for about 15 minutes. Cut the foie gras into slices, pour over a little of the stock and serve hot or cold.

Goose Foie Gras
baked foie gras

Prepare a foie gras weighing about 575 g (1¼ lb), season it with coarse salt and keep in a cool place for 24 hours. Wash the liver, wipe it and marinate for 48 hours with ground paprika, spices and Armagnac brandy. Drain the liver, place it in an ovenproof dish and half-fill the dish with melted goose fat. Bake in a preheated oven at 190°C (375°F, gas 5), turning it over while cooking, for about 15 minutes per 450 g (1 lb). To see if it is done, pierce with a skewer: the drop of juice that appears should be only just pink.

foie gras en brioche (hot)

Soak a pig's caul (caul fat) in cold water. Prepare some unsweetened brioche dough. Take a firm foie gras weighing 675–900 g (1½–2 lb) and stud it with truffles which have been seasoned and moistened with brandy. Season the foie gras with spiced salt, moisten it with brandy and leave to marinate for a few hours. Drain the pig's caul, wipe it dry and wrap the foie gras in it. Cook in a preheated oven at 190°C (375°F, gas 5) for 18–20 minutes, then leave to cool.

Line the bottom of a plain greased timbale mould with a fairly thick layer of brioche dough, then add the liver and cover it with another, thinner, layer of dough. Cover the mould with a piece of buttered greaseproof (wax) paper and tie with string to prevent the dough from spilling out when cooking. Leave the dough to rise for 2 hours in a warm place, then bake in a preheated oven at 200°C (400°F, gas 6) for 50–60 minutes. To see if the brioche is done, pierce with a needle, which should come out clean. Turn out the brioche and serve.

foie gras purée

Prepare some thick chicken velouté sauce and double its volume of foie gras, cooked and pressed through a fine sieve. Stir together over heat, then bind with egg yolk. This purée can be used as it is for filling bouchées, barquettes, tartlets or brioches. It can also be mixed with white breadcrumbs to stuff artichoke hearts or mushroom caps, or used plain to garnish cold hors d'oeuvre and eggs.

goose foie gras with sultanas

Prepare a foie gras weighing about 575 g (1¼ lb) in the usual way. Cook in a saucepan over a gentle heat for 5–6 minutes, drain and remove the fat. Fry 1 chopped onion in goose fat, sprinkle with a little flour and add the liver cooking juices, a little white wine, 1 chopped tomato, a bouquet garni and some stock. Cook for 30 minutes, then strain. Put the liver in a heavy-based casserole with this sauce, add some sultanas (golden raisins) that have been soaked in warm Madeira until swollen, and leave to simmer for 20 minutes. Serve with croûtons fried in goose fat and drain well.

potted foie gras with truffles

Remove the tubes from a goose foie gras and divide it in half. Trim the lobes and reserve the trimmings. Stud the liver with pieces of truffle. Season with spiced salt, pour over some brandy and leave to marinate for 5–6 hours. Prepare a forcemeat made of 375 g (13 oz) lean pork meat, 450 g (1 lb) fatty pork, the foie gras trimmings, 150 g (5 oz, 1 cup) diced truffles, 3 tablespoons Madeira and 2 tablespoons spiced salt.

Line the bottom and sides of an oval terrine or ovenproof dish with thin slices of pork fat, then cover the inside with a thin layer of the forcemeat. Place half the remaining foie gras on top of the forcemeat and press down. Cover with another layer of forcemeat, then place the foie gras on top. Finish with the rest of the forcemeat. Cover with a thin slice of pork fat. Press well to flatten the ingredients and place half a bay leaf and a sprig of thyme on top. Cover the terrine, seal the lid with a flour-and-water paste and place in a bain marie. Bring to the boil, then place in a preheated oven at 180°C (350°F, gas 4) and bake for 1¼–1½ hours, depending on the size of the terrine.

Cool, uncover, then leave under a light weight until the next day. Turn out the potted foie gras by standing the dish in hot water for a few seconds. Remove the pork fat and dry the top of the foie gras with a cloth, pressing down a little to firm it. Pour a thin layer of lard (shortening) mixed with goose fat (rendered during cooking) over the bottom of the terrine and leave it to set. Replace the foie gras in the terrine and pour some more lard and goose fat mixture (just warm) over the top. Chill for at least 12 hours and serve in the terrine.

truffled foie gras with Madeira

Trim a foie gras and remove the tubes. Stud with truffle sticks and season with spiced salt. Pour brandy over it and leave to marinate for a few hours. Wrap the foie gras in a pig's caul (caul fat) or

in thin strips of bacon fat and place in a braising pan lined with fresh pork skin, sliced onions and carrots tossed in butter. Cover and simmer for 7–8 minutes. Add 250 ml (8 fl oz, 1 cup) Madeira, port or sherry and simmer for several minutes. Add 200 ml (7 fl oz, ¾ cup) concentrated brown veal stock (containing some dissolved gelatine if the foie gras is to be served cold) and cook in a preheated oven at 190°C (375°F, gas 5) for 45 minutes.

Drain the foie gras, unwrap it and place it on a serving dish. Strain the cooking juices and skim off all the fat. Pour over the foie gras and serve hot.

To serve cold, place the drained and unwrapped foie gras in a terrine just large enough to hold it. Pour over the strained cooking juices and leave to cool for 12 hours (of which at least 2 hours should be in the refrigerator). Remove the layer of solidified fat on the surface of the sauce and serve the foie gras from the terrine.

truffled pâté de foie gras

Prepare 1 kg (2¼ lb) pâté pastry dough, made with butter or lard (shortening), and leave to rest for 12 hours. Prepare 2 firm foies gras in the usual way. Stud the lobes with peeled truffles cut into sticks, seasoned with spiced salt and moistened with brandy. Season the livers well. Soak them in brandy and Madeira for 2 hours. Prepare 1 kg (2¼ lb) pork and foie gras forcemeat.

Line a hinged pâté mould (round or oval) with some of the dough, then spread a layer of forcemeat over the bottom and sides of the mould. Put the foie gras into the mould, pressing it well. Cover with a domed layer of forcemeat. On top of this lay a slice of pork fat, half a bay leaf and a small sprig of thyme. Cover the pâté with a layer of dough and seal the edges. Garnish the top with decorative pastry motifs shaped with pastry (cookie) cutters (lozenges, leaves, crescents) or strips of plaited dough. In the middle put 3 or 4 round pieces of dough shaped with a fluted pastry cutter. Make a hole in the middle of these so the steam can escape during baking. Brush with egg. Bake in a preheated oven at 190–200°C (375–400°F, gas 5–6) until the dough is cooked thoroughly and golden brown.

Cool. When it is lukewarm, pour into it either half-melted lard, if it is to be kept for some time, or Madeira-flavoured aspic if it is to be used at once.

Pâté de foie gras must be made at least 12 hours before using. The mould can be lined with a forcemeat made entirely of foie gras instead of with pork and foie gras forcemeat.

other recipes See *aspic, brioche, forcemeat, Montrouge, Rossini, salpicon, Souvarov.*

FOND See *stock.*

FONDANT Sugar syrup containing glucose, cooked to the 'soft ball' stage, then worked with a spatula until it becomes a thick opaque paste. This is then kneaded by hand until smooth, soft and white. In this state, fondant keeps well in an airtight container. Professional-quality fondant is available from specialist cake decorating suppliers.

Flavoured fondant is used in confectionery, to fill chocolates and sweets (candies). When heated in a bain marie with a little syrup or alcohol, the fondant is used as an icing (frosting) to coat marzipan, fresh or dried fruits and brandied cherries. Diluted in this way and flavoured with chocolate, coffee or lemon, it can also be used to ice (frost) cakes and pastries.

RECIPE

fondant icing
Put the following ingredients in a heavy-based saucepan: 2 kg (4½ lb) lump sugar, 75 g (3 oz, 6 tablespoons) glucose and 120 ml (4½ fl oz, ½ cup) water. Cook over a high heat, skimming regularly. Take the pan off the heat when the sugar reaches the 'soft ball' stage, at about 118°C (245°F), see sugar. Oil a marble slab, pour the sugar mixture over it and allow to cool until just warm. Working with a metal spatula, alternately spread out and scrape up the fondant until the mixture is uniformly smooth and white. Place in a bowl, cover and keep cool. When it is needed, heat the fondant gently in a small saucepan and add a little syrup cooked to the 'short thread' stage – 101.5°C (215°F) and the selected flavouring (coffee liqueur, essence or extract, or melted chocolate). Alternatively, add a few drops of edible food colouring.

FOND DE PÂTISSERIE
A French term meaning a sweet base or shell used for a gâteau or dessert. It may be made of shortcrust pastry (basic pie dough), flan pastry, puff pastry, Genoese sponge, meringue or various biscuit (cookie) mixtures. In the catering trade, the *fonds* are prepared in advance and filled, decorated, mounted into set pieces or iced (frosted) when required.

RECIPES

pearl fond
Whisk 350 g (12 oz) egg whites (10–12 whites, depending on the size) into very stiff peaks with a pinch of salt. Mix together 250 g (9 oz, 2 cups) ground almonds and 250 g (9 oz, 1 cup) caster (superfine) sugar, and carefully fold in the whisked egg whites. Place a hot flan ring on a greased and floured baking sheet and fill with the mixture. Spread evenly with a spoon and dust with icing (confectioner's) sugar. Remove the flan ring and bake the base in a preheated oven at 180°C (350°F, gas 4) until just dried out, crisp and light golden.

walnut or hazelnut fond
Crush 250 g (9 oz, 2 cups) walnuts or unblanched hazelnuts, add 250 g (9 oz, 1 cup) caster (superfine) sugar and mix together. Work into this mixture 450 g (1 lb) egg yolks (12–13 yolks, depending on the size) and 100 g (4 oz, ½ cup) butter softened

with a wooden spatula. Mix in 125 g (4½ oz, 1 cup) potato starch or cornflour (cornstarch) and then carefully fold in 350 g (12 oz) egg whites (10–12 whites), which have been whisked into stiff peaks with a pinch of salt. Spread the mixture on lightly greased and floured baking sheets (it can be used for large gâteaux or small individual cakes) and bake in a preheated oven at 180°C (350°F, gas 4) until light golden brown.

FONDRE
A French culinary term meaning to cook certain vegetables in a covered pan in a little fat but no other liquid apart from their natural moisture. The contents of the pan should be stirred regularly to prevent them from sticking. This method is also used to prepare fondant potatoes.

FONDU CREUSOIS
A Limousin speciality made from cow's-milk cheese melted over a low heat in a saucepan with water and milk. Butter and egg yolks are added with seasoning. This smooth fondu (French for melted) is served with chips (French fries), which are dipped one by one into the pan. Alternatively, it can be poured over potato purée and browned under a hot grill (broiler).

FONDUE
A Swiss speciality consisting of one or more cheeses melted in a special pottery fondue dish with white wine and flavouring. When the mixture becomes creamy, the dish is placed over a spirit lamp on the table to keep it hot. The diners spear pieces of bread on a long two-pronged fork, dip them in the fondue and eat them piping hot.

The fondue recipe which Brillat-Savarin gives in his *Physiologie du goût* is in fact a dish of scrambled eggs with cheese. However, there are several Savoy and Swiss recipes that may be considered authentic. Androuet, in *La Cuisine au fromage*, mentions several. *Fondue comtoise* is made with mature full-flavoured Comté cheese, semi-matured Comté cheese, dry white wine, kirsch and garlic. *Fondue des Mosses* from Vaud is made with Gruyère, Appenzell and Bagnes or Tilsitt, dried boletus mushrooms, dry white wine, garlic and plum brandy. *Swiss Jura fondue* is made with full-flavoured salty Jura Gruyère, dry white wine, kirsch, garlic and nutmeg. *Fondue savoyarde* uses mature salty Beaufort and full-flavoured Beaufort, dry white wine and kirsch. A classic variant is *fondue normande*, made from Camembert, Pont l'Évêque and Livarot (with the rind removed), cream, milk, Calvados and shallots. *Fondue piémontaise* is made with Fontina from the Aosta Valley, butter, milk and egg yolks, to which chopped white truffles are added. This fondue is not served in a fondue dish, but poured into dishes garnished with croûtons. Swiss raclette (melted cheese served with boiled potatoes and pickles) is a rustic variant of fondue.

There are several other dishes derived from, or inspired by, cheese fondue. *Fondue bourguignonne*, like cheese fondue, is prepared on the table in a metal fondue dish placed over a heating device and filled with hot oil. A long-handled fork is used to skewer cubes of beef (fillet steak, sirloin or rump steak) and dip them in the very hot oil until they are cooked. They are then dipped in one of an assortment of flavoured sauces (béarnaise, barbecue, aïoli, mayonnaise, horseradish, tomato) and eaten. Condiments such as gherkins (sweet dill pickles), pickles, chutneys or pickled onions can also be served at the same time, as well as potato crisps (chips).

Chinese fondue is prepared using the same principle as *fondue bourguignonne*. Strips of beef and pork, thin slices of chicken breast or little pieces of fish are cooked in a chicken stock kept simmering in a fondue pot over a special charcoal burner incorporated into it. This traditional Chinese dish was introduced to the Far East by the Mongols in the 14th century and was originally made with mutton. It is accompanied by sliced fresh vegetables arranged in bowls (Chinese cabbage, spinach and onions), a purée of haricot (navy) beans and rice vermicelli. This fondue is also served with soy-, ginger- and sesame oil-based sauces. In Vietnam, where this fondue is served on festive occasions, it is made with beef, prawns and fish, cooked in coconut milk and served with a prawn sauce and sweet and sour condiments. Scallops and strips of prepared squid are sometimes also included.

Chocolate fondue consists of chocolate melted in a bain marie and kept liquid over a spirit lamp on the table. It is used for dipping pieces of cake, biscuits (cookies), pastries and fruit.

■ **Vegetable fondues** The name fondue is also given to a preparation of finely cut vegetables cooked slowly in butter over a very low heat until they are reduced to a pulp. Vegetable fondues made with chicory (endive), fennel, onions, sorrel, carrots, leeks, celery, or celeriac can be used as an ingredient in another dish (as a braising sauce for ragoûts or baked fish) or as an accompaniment. Tomato fondue is most often used in egg dishes, sauces and Mediterranean garnishes (*à la madrilène*, *à la provençale* and *à la portugaise*). It can also be added to certain forcemeats, and when cold can be used to give piquancy to hors d'oeuvre or fish (as can onion fondue). When seasoned with coriander, it is used for preparations *à la grecque*.

RECIPES

fondue à la piémontaise

Cut 575 g (1¼ lb) Fontina cheese into cubes. Place in a fairly shallow container and cover with cold milk. Leave for at least 2 hours. Put the cheese and milk in a saucepan and add 6 egg yolks and 125 g (4½ oz, ½ cup) butter. Cook in a bain marie over a medium heat, stirring continuously, until the mixture melts and acquires a creamy consistency. The ideal cooking point corresponds with the first bubbles of the water in the bain marie. Serve in a soup tureen and garnish the bowls with small triangles of toasted bread or bread fried in butter.

fondue du valais

Rub the bottom of an earthenware fondue dish with garlic. Cut 150–200 g (5–7 oz) good-quality Gruyère cheese per person into very thin slices. (Alternatively, use a mixture of Beaufort, Emmental and Comté.) Put the cheese into the fondue dish and just cover it with dry white wine (in Switzerland Fendant is normally used). Stir over the heat until the cheese has melted, then add a little freshly ground pepper and 1 liqueur glass of kirsch. In Switzerland this fondue is served with Grisons (air-cured) meat or raw ham cut into very thin slices.

Brillat-Savarin's cheese fondue

(From Brillat-Savarin's recipe) Weigh the number of eggs you wish to use, according to the number of diners. Grate a piece of good Gruyère cheese weighing one-third of this and take a piece of butter weighing one-sixth. Break the eggs into a heavy-based saucepan and beat them well, then add the butter and cheese. Put the pan over a moderate heat and stir with a spatula until the mixture is thickened and smooth. Season with a little salt and a generous amount of pepper, which is one of the distinguishing characteristics of this ancient dish. Serve in a warmed dish.

tomato fondue

Peel and chop 100 g (4 oz, ¾ cup) onions. Peel, seed and finely chop 800 g (1¾ lb) tomatoes. Peel and crush 1 garlic clove. Prepare a bouquet garni rich in thyme. Soften the onions in a heavy-based saucepan with 25 g (1 oz, 2 tablespoons) butter, or 15 g (½ oz, 1 tablespoon) butter and 2 tablespoons olive oil, or 3 tablespoons olive oil. Then add the tomatoes, salt and pepper, the garlic and bouquet garni. Cover the pan and cook very gently until the tomatoes are reduced to a pulp. Remove the lid, stir with a wooden spatula and continue cooking, uncovered, until the fondue forms a light paste. Adjust the seasoning, strain through a sieve and add 1 tablespoon chopped parsley or herbs.

FONTAINEBLEAU A soft fresh cow's-milk cheese containing 60–75% fat, originating in Île-de-France. It is not matured or salted, but wrapped in muslin (cheesecloth) and sold in a small waxed cardboard container. It is prepared from a foamy mixture of whipped cream and slowly coagulating curds, which is drained for 30 hours and then smoothed. It is served with sugar and frequently with strawberries or jam; enthusiasts often add fresh cream.

Fontainebleau is also the name of a classic garnish consisting of a macédoine of vegetables cut into very small pieces, cooked with butter, and arranged in barquettes made of duchess potato mixture browned in the oven.

FONTANGES A soup probably dedicated to Mlle de Fontanges, who was a favourite of Louis XIV for a short time. It is made of a purée of fresh peas, topped with beef or chicken consommé, and contains shredded sorrel cooked slowly in butter. Just before serving, it is enriched with an egg yolk mixed with double (heavy) cream and sprinkled with chervil.

FONTENELLE, À LA Describing a preparation of asparagus served with melted butter and soft-boiled (soft-cooked) eggs. The asparagus is dipped first in the melted butter, then in the egg yolk. The name commemorates the greediness of Bernard Le Bovier de Fontenelle (1657–1757), a philosopher and permanent secretary of the French Academy of Sciences. Once, when he invited his friend, the Abbé Terrasson, to dinner, Fontenelle had arranged to have half the asparagus served with butter (which he preferred) and half with vinaigrette (favoured by the Abbé). Approaching the table, the Abbé suddenly dropped dead of apoplexy, and it is said that Fontenelle immediately shouted to his chef, 'Serve them all with butter! All with butter!'

FONTINA An Italian cow's-milk cheese (45% fat content), with a pressed cooked centre and a brushed, sometimes oiled, crust. Elastic to the touch, and with a few small holes, the cheese tastes delicately nutty. It originated in the Aosta Valley in the Alps, where it has been made since the 12th century, and it comes in rounds 40–45 cm (16–18 in) in diameter and 7–10 cm (3–4 in) high. It is made over almost all northern Italy and even in France (under the name of Fontal and made mainly from pasteurized milk). The name Fontina is reserved for the DOP cheese made with unpasteurized milk from the Aosta Valley. Young Fontina is served at the end of a meal or on canapés; it is also used in cooking, particularly in *fondue piémontaise*. When matured, it is grated and used like Parmesan cheese.

FOOD A substance eaten to sustain life; as part of a well-balanced diet, it promotes growth and maintains health. No one food is nutritionally perfect as it does not supply all the nutrients in the right proportions to support health. So, to satisfy nutritional needs and individual tastes, we need to eat, in moderation, a variety of different foods. There are many combinations of foods that supply the right balance of nutrients and energy. A good diet in Mexico, for example, is based on very different foods from an equally nutritious diet in France, Japan or Italy, since the daily diet of a country still reflects its social, religious and family traditions, as well as its agricultural practices. The diet will vary according to the habits and way of life of the individual.

FOOD ADDITIVE A substance added to food during manufacture or processing to help improve its keeping qualities, taste or colour; additives do not necessarily improve the nutritional value of the food.

Under European and American law, each food item must show clearly each food additive on the label or packet under its own E number. Water that has been added to foods (such as ham or bacon) must also be listed clearly on the label. Labelling regulations state that ingredients must be listed in descending order by weight, as a guide to the quantity of additives included.

Without additives many foods would quickly become unsafe to eat and have a very short shelf life. Salt, sugar, spices, vinegar, and such products as caramel or spinach-green have been used for years. The growth of the food industry, however, has considerably enlarged the number of additives and changed their nature and conditions of use. Many food additives are derived from natural sources and are essential and harmless; but many are synthetic and non-essential.

FOOD PROCESSOR Electrically powered item of kitchen equipment that can do many of the time-consuming tasks involved in food preparation. A typical food processor consists of a motor and a bowl in which the accessories operate under a protective lid. The accessories usually include a double-bladed curved knife for chopping, puréeing and producing crumbs; a plastic or blunt blade for beating and mixing; slicing discs; grating discs; a chip (French fry) cutter; and a whisk. The appliance generally has sufficient power to chop, mix, purée, grate or grind food (cooking chocolate, Parmesan cheese, nuts); it may even be able to crush ice. Special attachments are available for mixing dough. Some models also have a juice extractor.

The food processor was designed to do the work of several other appliances, including the blender and mincer, and to some extent the food mixer. In practice, results vary and, although the food processor is the most versatile and useful of appliances, some procedures are slightly less successful than others. For example, soups and sauces are far smoother when puréed in a blender and the texture of processed meat is either finely chopped or ground to a near paste consistency rather then being minced.

FOOD SAFE A type of cage with a wooden frame and wire mesh for storing foodstuffs away from flies and other insects. The food safe was often equipped with a handle and hung in the cellar or in a cool place. Sometimes food was stored in an outside larder with shutters or ventilation grilles, installed in big old houses under the kitchen window, square with the wall. Nowadays both types have been replaced by the refrigerator, but they are still sometimes used for cheeses, which are spoiled if they are kept at too low a temperature.

In France in the Middle Ages and up to the end of the 18th century, the word *garde-manger* was applied to the cool well-aired place where provisions were stored.

FOOD SUBSTITUTE A food product used as a substitute for another, usually because the latter is very rare or expensive but sometimes because of health reasons (artificial sweeteners instead of sugar, for example). During wars or times of shortage substitutes are often devised, such as Guinea pepper (seeds from a plant related to the cardamom) for real pepper and safflower for saffron.

In a book of recipes published in 1941, Prosper Montagné suggested malt extract and concentrated grape juice as acceptable substitutes for sugar in pastries, cakes and confectionery. Some substitutes are for emergency use only, until the genuine article becomes available, like roasted acorns for making coffee; others, such as chicory (for coffee), margarine and beet sugar, have acquired universal acceptance. Certain substitutes have remained acceptable in everyday use, though acknowledged as inferior; for example, slices of gherkins (sweet dill pickles) as substitutes for pistachios in mortadella and lumpfish roe for caviar.

Some novel substitutes appeared at the end of the 19th century: at the time of the Paris Exhibition of 1878, machines were introduced for cutting out mare's udders into the shape of tripe, for twisting ox lights into the shape of *petit-gris* (edible brown snails), for graining cheeses with verdigris using copper needles to sell them as Roquefort, and for making bread with starch or couch-grass powder.

The most famous substitute preparations were cooked by Chavette, chef of the Brébant Restaurant, in order to mystify Monselet, a well-known gastronome. Monselet praised the swallow's-nest soup, brill, chamois cutlets and capercaillie, served with hocks and Tokay wines, which proved to be a purée of noodles and small kidney beans, fresh cod cooked on a fine comb (to simulate the brill's backbone), lamb cutlets marinated in bitters and a young turkey sprinkled with absinthe; the 'Tokay' was Mâcon wine mixed with punch, and the 'Johannisberg' an ordinary Chablis flavoured with thyme essence!

FOOL A chilled dessert of English origin, made of fruit purée strained through a fine sieve, sweetened and chilled (but not frozen). Just before serving, the purée is mixed with twice its volume of whipped cream.

FORCED FRUIT AND VEGETABLES Horticultural products that appear on the market before their normal season. Often expensive and lacking the flavour of fruit and vegetables in season, these forced products are the result of cultivation under glass or shelter of produce normally sensitive to weather conditions, such as peas and asparagus. Improved transport facilities have made forcing less necessary in regions with a poor climate.

FORCEMEAT OR STUFFING A seasoned mixture of raw or cooked ingredients, chopped or minced (ground), used to stuff eggs, fish, poultry, game, meat, vegetables or pasta, such as ravioli and cannelloni. Forcemeats are also the basis for several pâtés, meat pies, terrines, galantines and ballotines, not to mention all the different kinds of sausages. They are also used to make forcemeat balls, quenelles and some borders, and to fill barquettes, vol-au-vent and tartlets. À *gratin* forcemeats are used to garnish croûtes, croûtons and hot canapés.

There are three major categories of forcemeat: those made with vegetables; those made with meat, game or poultry; and those made with fish. In addition, there is a fourth, more minor category of forcemeat, based on egg yolk.

The composition of a forcemeat depends in principle on the food that it is intended to stuff or fill. The basis for a forcemeat is usually minced meat or fish; the additional ingredients, for example, gherkins (sweet dill pickles), herbs, onion, ham, foie gras, crustless bread soaked in milk or egg whites, give it character and consistency. Seasoning is also extremely important. A panada may be added to give it some substance, and most forcemeats made of meat, poultry or game are bound with eggs. The stuffing for a food that is to be boiled needs to be more strongly seasoned than one for food to be roasted. However, in the latter case, the stuffing must contain sufficient fat to prevent the food from drying out, especially in the case of poultry.

RECIPES

preparation
The ingredients for some forcemeats need to be very finely minced or even ground in a mortar or food processor and then forced through a sieve. Fine forcemeats need to be minced (ground) twice. Sometimes only some of the ingredients need to be minced. Add seasoning to taste and about 6 tablespoons brandy per 1 kg (2¼ lb) forcemeat. Allow 1 large egg to bind 450 g (1 lb) forcemeat.

Forcemeats Made with Egg Yolks
cold egg yolk stuffing
Sieve 10 hard-boiled (hard-cooked) egg yolks and place them in a terrine together with 100 g (4 oz, ½ cup) softened butter. Season with salt and white pepper and mix all the ingredients together. This is used as a spread for cold canapés and as a filling for halved hard-boiled egg whites and artichoke hearts.

hot egg yolk stuffing
Add some sieved hard-boiled (hard-cooked) egg yolks to half their weight of hot thick béchamel sauce. Press through a very fine sieve and season with salt and pepper. A teaspoon of dry duxelles and some chopped parsley are usually added as well. This mixture is used to fill halved hard-boiled eggs, vol-au-vent or barquettes, or to stuff vegetables prepared au gratin.

Forcemeats Made with Fish and Shellfish
cream forcemeat
This is a mousseline forcemeat made by replacing the meat with either boned and skinned whiting or pike.

forcemeat for fish mousses and mousselines
Skin and bone 1 kg (2¼ lb) fish (pike, whiting, salmon, sole or turbot) and season with 4 teaspoons salt, a generous pinch of pepper and grated

nutmeg. Pound the fish in a mortar, add 4 lightly whisked egg whites (one by one), transfer to a blender and then press through a fine sieve. Put the resulting purée in a terrine, smooth out with a wooden spatula and chill for at least 2 hours. Then place the terrine in a bowl of crushed ice or ice cubes and incorporate 1.25 litres (2¼ pints, 5½ cups) double (heavy) cream, working it in gently with a spatula. Keep in the refrigerator until needed. This forcemeat can also be used for quenelles and to garnish large braised fish or fillets of sole or turbot.

prawn forcemeat
Cook 125 g (4½ oz, ¾ cup) prawns or shrimps in some salted water. Pound them in a mortar with 100 g (4 oz, ½ cup) butter and then press the mixture through a fine sieve. Add to this mixture half its weight of finely sieved hard-boiled (hard-cooked) egg yolks. Mix together well.

shellfish forcemeat
This is a mousseline forcemeat made with crayfish, lobster or crab meat. Allow 4 egg whites, 1.5 litres (2¾ pints, 6½ cups) double (heavy) cream, 1 tablespoon salt and a generous pinch of white pepper for each 1 kg (2¼ lb) shellfish meat.

smoked herring or sardine forcemeat
Make a white roux with 1 tablespoon butter and 2 tablespoons flour. Add 100 ml (4 fl oz, 7 tablespoons) warm milk and cook for about 10 minutes, stirring continuously with a wooden spoon. Remove from the heat when very thick. Add 1 whole egg and 2 egg yolks. Put either 1 large smoked herring fillet (soaked in a little milk to remove some of the salt if necessary) or 4 medium sardines in a blender and reduce to a purée. Incorporate this into the roux and cook for 3–4 minutes. Press through a sieve. This forcemeat is used as a filling for croustades, *dartois* and small pastry cases.

Forcemeats Made with Meat, Game and Poultry
à gratin forcemeat
Fry 150 g (5 oz, 1 cup) finely chopped unsmoked bacon in a sauté pan until soft. Add 300 g (11 oz) chicken livers, 2 thinly sliced shallots, 50 g (2 oz, ⅔ cup) finely chopped mushrooms, a sprig of thyme and half a bay leaf. Season with a generous pinch of salt, some pepper and a little mixed spice. Sauté quickly over a high heat. Allow to cool completely, then pound in a mortar (or purée in a blender) and press through a fine sieve. Cover with buttered or oiled greaseproof (wax) paper and chill until needed. This forcemeat is spread on croûtons of fried bread that are used as a base for small roast game birds or served with salmis or *civets*.

American stuffing
Cut some smoked belly of pork into very small dice and fry. Add some finely chopped onion and allow to sweat without colouring. Remove from the heat and add fresh breadcrumbs until the fat is completely absorbed. Season with salt and pepper, a little ground sage and the finest thyme. This forcemeat is used for stuffing young cockerels, young pigeons, guinea fowls and poussins.

brain forcemeat
Cook a calf's brain in a court-bouillon. Drain, pat dry and press through a sieve. Add an equal volume of béchamel sauce, or one-third of its volume of either cream or velouté sauce. This forcemeat is used to fill barquettes, vol-au-vent, tartlets or hollowed-out croûtes.

foie gras forcemeat
Finely pound in a mortar (or purée in a blender) 375 g (13 oz) lean pork meat, 450 g (1 lb) unsmoked streaky (slab) bacon and 250 g (9 oz) thinly sliced foie gras. Add 1½ teaspoons spiced salt and 100 ml (4 fl oz, 7 tablespoons) brandy, and press through a sieve. This forcemeat is used for making pâtés and terrines.

forcemeat for poultry
This consists of fine sausagemeat mixed with one-fifth of its weight each of fresh breadcrumbs and finely chopped onion cooked in a little butter until soft, together with chopped parsley. Chill until required.

game forcemeat
Prepare with the appropriate game meat in the same way as poultry forcemeat. To make it richer, add thin slices of fresh foie gras or game liver forcemeat. This forcemeat is used for making pâtés and terrines.

liver forcemeat
Brown 250 g (9 oz, 12 slices) diced unsmoked streaky (slab) bacon in 25 g (1 oz, 2 tablespoons) butter in a sauté pan. Remove and drain. In the same fat, sauté 300 g (11 oz) pig's (pork), calf's, game or chicken liver cut into cubes. Mix 40 g (1½ oz, ¼ cup) finely chopped shallots and 75 g (3 oz, 1 cup) finely chopped cultivated mushrooms together. Replace the bacon in the sauté pan, add the mushrooms and shallots and season with salt, ground white pepper and allspice; then add a sprig of thyme and half a bay leaf. Mix together and sauté for 2 minutes.

Remove the cubes of liver. Deglaze the pan with 150 ml (¼ pint, ⅔ cup) dry white wine, pour the sauce over the cubes of liver and purée all the ingredients in a blender or food processor, together with 65 g (2½ oz, 5 tablespoons) butter and 3 egg yolks, until very smooth. Press the forcemeat through a sieve and store, covered, in the refrigerator. This forcemeat is used for making pâtés, terrines or meat loaves. Minced, cleaned truffle peelings can be added to it if wished. If game liver is used, add an equal amount of rabbit meat and replace the white wine with 100 ml (4 fl oz, 7 tablespoons) Madeira.

mousseline forcemeat

Pound 1 kg (2¼ lb) boned veal, poultry or game in a mortar (or reduce to a purée in a blender). Then press through a fine sieve. Whisk 4 egg whites lightly with a fork and add them to the meat purée a little at a time. Season with 4 teaspoons salt and a generous pinch of ground white pepper. Press through the sieve a second time, place in a terrine, and then chill for 2 hours. Remove the terrine from the refrigerator and place in a bowl of crushed ice. Then work in 1.5 litres (2¾ pints, 6½ cups) double (heavy) cream using a wooden spoon. (It is essential to keep the cream and the pâté as cold as possible to prevent curdling.) This forcemeat is used for fine quenelles, mousses and mousselines.

panada forcemeat with butter

Purée 1 kg (2¼ lb) minced (ground) veal or poultry in a blender with salt, ground white pepper and grated nutmeg. Also blend 450 g (1 lb) panada* with an equal quantity of butter. Add the puréed meat and beat the mixture vigorously. Then add 8 egg yolks, one at a time. Press the forcemeat through a fine sieve, place in a terrine and work with a spatula until smooth. Chill, covered, until required. This forcemeat is used for quenelles, borders and meat loaves, and to stuff poultry and joints of meat.

panada forcemeat with cream

Pound 1 kg (2¼ lb) minced (ground) veal or poultry in a mortar (or reduce to a purée in a blender). Season with 2 teaspoons salt, a generous pinch of white pepper and some grated nutmeg. Add 4 lightly whisked egg whites one at a time, followed by 400 g (14 oz) bread panada*. Beat vigorously until the mixture is very smooth. Press through a fine sieve over a terrine and chill for 1 hour, together with 1.5 litres (2¾ pints, 6½ cups) double (heavy) cream and 2 tablespoons milk. Then place the terrine in a basin of crushed ice or ice cubes. Add one-third of the cream to the forcemeat, working it in vigorously with a spatula. Lightly beat the remaining cream with the milk and then fold it into the forcemeat. Chill until needed. This forcemeat is used for quenelles.

poultry forcemeat

Dice 575 g (1¼ lb) chicken or other poultry meat, 200 g (7 oz) lean veal and 900 g (2 lb) bacon; work together in a blender until smooth. Add 3 eggs, 1 tablespoon salt and 200 ml (7 fl oz, ¾ cup) brandy. Mix well, press through a sieve and chill until required. This forcemeat is used for pâtés and terrines.

veal forcemeat

Pound 1 kg (2¼ lb) lean minced (ground) veal in a mortar (or reduce to a purée in a blender). Season with 1 tablespoon salt, some white pepper and grated nutmeg. Purée 300 g (11 oz) flour panada*; when really soft, add the veal, together with 65 g (2½ oz, 4½ tablespoons) butter, and beat the mixture well. Finally, beating continuously, add 5 whole eggs and 8 yolks, one by one. Then add 1.25 litres (2¼ pints, 5½ cups) thick béchamel* sauce. Press through a fine sieve and work with a spatula to make the forcemeat smooth. Chill until required. This forcemeat is used for borders and large quenelles.

Forcemeats Made with Vegetables

forcemeat for fish

Crumble 250 g (9 oz, 9 slices) crustless bread and soak it in milk. Sauté 75 g (3 oz, ⅔ cup) chopped onions and 150 g (5 oz, 1⅔ cups) chopped button mushrooms in 25 g (1 oz, 2 tablespoons) butter. Add a small handful of chopped parsley and cook for a few minutes. Meanwhile, add 4 tablespoons white wine to 3 chopped shallots in a separate pan and reduce. Add the shallots to the other vegetables and mix. Squeeze out the bread and place in a terrine. Add the vegetable mixture and work together well. Then bind with 2 egg yolks and season with salt and pepper and, if liked, a generous pinch of grated nutmeg and half a garlic clove, chopped.

forcemeat for vegetable terrine

Peel 500 g (1 lb 2 oz) celeriac (celery root) and cut into quarters. Steam, drain and purée in a blender. Dry slightly in a warm oven but do not allow the celeriac to colour. In the bowl of a mixer, combine the celeriac purée with 2 egg yolks, 150 ml (¼ pint, ⅔ cup) single (light) cream and 2 stiffly whisked egg whites. Season to taste with salt, pepper and nutmeg. Other vegetables, in equal quantities, may be added to the stuffing: diced carrots, petits pois, green beans, blanched or cooked in steam. The vegetable terrine can then be cooked in the oven or in a bain marie.

mushroom forcemeat

Sauté 2 peeled and finely chopped shallots and 175 g (6 oz, 2 cups) button mushrooms, also finely chopped, over a high heat in a frying pan, with 40 g (1½ oz, 3 tablespoons) butter and a generous pinch of grated nutmeg. When cooked, allow to cool. Make 100 g (4 oz) bread panada* and purée it in a blender, adding the mushrooms and shallots. Finally, add 3 egg yolks and mix thoroughly (it is not necessary to sieve this forcemeat). It is used to stuff vegetables, poultry, game and fish.

FORESTIÈRE, À LA A method of preparing small cuts of meat or chicken (or even eggs or vegetables), which are garnished with mushrooms (usually chanterelles, morels or ceps) cooked in butter, generally accompanied by potato noisettes or rissoles and blanched browned bacon pieces. It is served with gravy, thickened veal stock or the deglazed pan juices.

RECIPES

carrots à la forestière

Braise some carrots in butter, then add half their volume of mushrooms, also braised in butter. Adjust the seasoning and sprinkle with parsley.

soft-boiled or poached eggs à la forestière

Clean some mushrooms and fry them in butter. Cut some lean bacon into small dice, then scald and brown in butter. Mix the mushrooms and bacon together and spread the mixture over bread croustades. Place a soft-boiled (soft-cooked) or poached egg on top of each one. Add a few drops of lemon juice, pepper, a little cayenne pepper and some chopped parsley to some melted butter and pour it over the eggs.

FORK An implement usually made of metal with two, three or four prongs on the end of a handle, used at the table either for lifting food to the mouth or for serving food. Forks are also used in the kitchen for turning food in cooking.

The fork has very ancient origins and is mentioned in the Old Testament. It was first used as a ritual instrument to grip pieces of meat destined for sacrifices; later it was used in the kitchen. According to the 11th-century Italian scholar Damiani, forks were introduced into Venice by a Byzantine princess and then spread throughout Italy. But it was Henri III of France who first introduced to the French the custom of using a two-pronged fork at the table. Before this time, it had been regarded as a decorative item fashioned in gold or silver; forks were mentioned in 1379 in an inventory of the French king, Charles V. After visiting the court at Venice in 1574, Henri III noted that a two-pronged table fork was being used and he launched this fashion among the nobility. It seemed a very useful implement for putting food into the mouth above the high collars and ruffs that were worn at that time! In 14th-century England, it is recorded that Piers Gaveston, a favourite of Edward II, ate a pear with a fork, but it was not until the 18th century that it became widely used. Louis XIV ate with his fingers and, in the reign of Louis XVI, it was common to eat food from the tip of the knife.

Forks then came to have three prongs, and later four, and their use spread from Italy and Spain into France and England. Nowadays, only a carving fork has two prongs. These may be straight or slightly curved. Table forks are more diversified and are made in many sizes and many metals. They may even be made of wood or plastic. Salad servers consist of a fork and spoon, and carving sets consist of a knife, a fork and often a steel for sharpening the knife. There are table forks, fish forks and fruit forks, diminishing in size down to small pastry forks. Certain forks are modified for a particular use; for example, snail forks, oyster forks, shellfish forks and fondue forks.

Etiquette varies as to the proper way of holding and using a fork. E. Briffault ends his *Paris à table* (1846) with this assessment: 'The two-pronged fork is used in northern Europe. The English are armed with steel tridents with ivory handles – three-pronged forks – but in France, we have the four-pronged fork, the height of civilization.'

FORME D'AMBERT A semi-hard blue cheese from the Auvergne, now factory-produced from pasteurized milk but with a firm ivory paste and a good fruity flavour. The cheese (45% fat content) is shaped into cylinders about 20 cm (8 in) high and 12–15 cm (4–5 in) in diameter. Forme de Montbrison and Forme de Forez are similar cheeses from neighbouring regions. They have AOP status.

FORTIFIED WINE Wine to which a certain quantity of spirit is added in the course of production. Increasing the alcoholic strength has the effect of interrupting the work of the yeasts in the fermentation of the must, so that the grape sugar cannot be converted into alcohol. The resulting wine may be dry or retain a considerable proportion of its natural sugar. Fortified wines include port, sherry and Madeira.

FOUACE Also known as fouasse or fougasse. One of the oldest of French pastries. It was originally a pancake made of fine wheat, unleavened, and cooked under the cinders in the hearth (in Latin *focus*, hence the name *focaccia pasta*, which in turn became *fouace, fouasse* or *fougasse*). Rabelais gave the recipe for it in his *Gargantua*: 'Best-quality flour mixed with best egg yolks and butter, best saffron and spices, and water.' The fouaces from the regions of Chinon and Touraine have had a fine reputation for centuries.

Fouaces are still produced in many areas of France. Nowadays they are usually rustic dough cakes baked in the oven, sometimes salted and flavoured, and usually made for Christmas or Twelfth Night. They used to be very widespread in western and central France (Caen, Vannes, La Flèche and Tours), but are now most common in the south. At Najac, in Rouergue, a 'fouace festival' is held every year. In Languedoc, a *fouace aux grattons* is eaten with Frontignan wine. In Auvergne, the fouace is made with crystallized (candied) fruits. In Provence, where it is called fougasse, sometimes a little orange-flower water is poured on to the pastries and brushed over the top and sides. This is one of the desserts traditionally eaten at Christmas. The *fougassette*, which is made of brioche dough, is a speciality of the Nice area. This small fougasse is shaped like a plaited loaf and flavoured with orange-flower water and saffron. It sometimes contains candied citron.

RECIPE

fouace

Dissolve 15 g (½ oz) fresh yeast (1 cake compressed yeast) in a few tablespoons of warm milk or water. Add 125 g (4½ oz, 1 cup) strong plain (bread) flour and then enough milk or water to make a slightly soft dough. Cover the dough with a damp cloth or greased cling film (plastic wrap) and leave to rise until it has doubled in volume.

Heap 375 g (13 oz, 3¼ cups) strong plain flour on a work surface. Make a well in the centre and add a large pinch of salt, 100 g (4 oz, ½ cup) softened butter, 1 liqueur glass of rum, brandy or orange-flower water, 4 tablespoons sugar (optional) and 4 beaten eggs. Knead this mixture together, adding a little milk or water to obtain a smooth dough. Then add the risen dough and (if wished) a filling of 150–200 g (5–7 oz, 1¼ cups) crystallized (candied) fruits. Work the dough again until it is elastic. Knead it into a ball, cut a cross in the top and leave it to rise, loosely covered (it should double in volume).

Place the fouace on a lightly buttered baking sheet, in a ball, loaf or crown shape, glaze with beaten egg and bake in a preheated oven at 230°C (450°F, gas 8) for about 40 minutes or until golden (the base should sound hollow when tapped).

FOUGASSE See *fouace.*

FOUGERU Soft cow's-milk cheese from Brie (45% fat content) with a reddish crust. Fougeru is a disc about 13 cm (5 in) in diameter and 3–4 cm (1¼–1½ in) thick, weighing 500–600 g (18–21 oz), packed in fern fronds. Its taste is similar to Coulommiers.

FOUQUET'S A restaurant and café on the Champs-Élysées in Paris. Originally (in 1901) it was a small public house for cab drivers, which bore the name of its owner, Louis Fouquet. In 1910 Léopold Mourier, well-known in the Parisian restaurant trade and the tutor of the founder's children, purchased it, anglicized its name to 'Fouquet's' (like Maxim's), redecorated it in the Belle Époque style (which survived until 1961) and set up an English bar and a grill room, where 'the Longchamp racegoers were accustomed to meeting before or after the races, with their grey top hats over their ears, and their binoculars in deerskin cases over their shoulders' (R. Héron de Villefosse). A restaurant was also opened on the first floor. Since World War II, most of Fouquet's regular customers have been actors.

FOUR FRUITS *quatre-fruits* The phrase used in French to designate four red summer fruits – strawberries, cherries, redcurrants and raspberries – which are cooked together to make jams, syrups or compotes. The phrase 'four yellow fruits' (*quatre-fruits jaunes*) is sometimes used to refer to oranges, lemons, Seville (bitter) oranges and citrons. In practice, 'four-fruits' jams and compotes may be made from a combination of any four fruits, fresh or dried.

RECIPE

four-fruits compote
Wash and seed 2 bunches of Muscat grapes. Peel 4 bananas and cut them into thick rounds. Peel and finely dice 4 apples and 4 pears. Put all the fruit into a saucepan with the juice of 1 lemon, a pinch of ground cinnamon, 300 g (11 oz, 1⅔ cups) caster (superfine) sugar, the juice of 2 oranges and 100 ml (4 fl oz, 7 tablespoons) water. Bring to the boil, cook very gently for 30 minutes and then pour into a glass fruit bowl. When the compote is cold, chill until ready to serve. If wished, liquid caramel can be poured over it just before serving.

FOURME Any of various cow's-milk cheeses from central France that usually contain parsley and are used in the same way as blue cheese. The French word *fourme* is derived from the Latin *forma* (a mould); it then became *formage* and later *fromage.*
• FOURME D'AMBERT (45% fat content) This has a special label of origin (an AOC) and comes from the Loire, Puy-de-Dôme, and the district of Saint-Flour. It has a firm paste flavoured with parsley and a dry dark-grey crust mottled with yellow and red. It has a strong flavour and is shaped into tall cylinders, 13 cm (5 in) in diameter and 20 cm (8 in) high. It is usually served cut horizontally. Fourme de Pierre-sur-Haute, Fourme du Forez (named after Monts du Forez) and Fourme de Montbrison are similar cheeses.
• FOURME DU MÉZENC (30–40% fat content) This is also known as Bleu du Velay, Bleu de Loudes or Bleu de Costaros. It is flavoured with parsley and has a natural crust. Like Fourme d'Ambert, it is cylindrical and has a pronounced flavour.

The name 'Fourme' is also used, albeit incorrectly, for Cantal, Salers and Laguiole.

FOURRER The French term meaning to insert a raw or cooked filling into a sweet or savoury item. For example, omelettes and pancakes may be filled with various mixtures before being folded. Choux pastries and sponge cakes can be filled with butter cream, almond cream, confectioner's custard (pastry cream) or a fruit filling. Bread rolls can be filled with various savoury mixtures.

FOUR SPICES A mixture of spices, usually consisting of ground pepper, grated nutmeg, powdered cloves and ground ginger or cinnamon. It is used in stews, *civets*, charcuterie, terrines and game dishes. This spice mixture is also used in Arab cookery. It should not be confused with five spices (*cinq-épices*) or allspice (*toute-épice*).

FOUTOU A traditional African dish based on cassava (manioc root) together with plantains (green bananas) or yams. The cassava and plantains or yams are boiled in water, drained and then pounded into a smooth paste that is shaped into several small rounds or a single large one. *Foutou* is always served with very rich and highly spiced sauces, based on meat and vegetables or on fish. These sauces are actually more like ragoûts, and their composition is very varied. *Foutou* is very common in Africa, particularly in Benin and the Ivory Coast.

FOYOT A Parisian restaurant which was situated on the corner of the Rue de Tournon and the Rue de Vaugirard. It was originally a hotel, and the Emperor Joseph II, brother of Marie Antoinette, once stayed there. In 1768 it was converted into a restaurant, known as the Café Vachette, and in 1848 it was bought by Foyot, the former chef of Louis-Philippe, and renamed.

The proximity of the Palais du Luxembourg meant that the clientele included many senators. The specialities served by Foyot at that time included the famous veal chops Foyot, sheep's trotters (feet) *à la poulette*, pigeons Foyot and Ernestine potatoes. No-one is certain that these dishes were actually invented by Foyot himself, but they certainly made the restaurant very famous. It was while breakfasting at Foyot in 1894 that the poet Laurent Tailhade was seriously injured by an anarchist's bomb.

The restaurant was finally closed in 1938 and the building was demolished.

RECIPES

Foyot sauce
Make 200 ml (7 fl oz, ¾ cup) béarnaise* sauce and strain it. Add 2 tablespoons meat glaze or stock, stirring well. If the sauce is not to be served immediately, keep it warm in a bain marie. (The meat glaze is made by boiling down a concentrated meat stock until it becomes thick and syrupy.)

veal chop Foyot
Make a thick cheese paste with dried breadcrumbs, 25 g (1 oz, ¼ cup) grated Gruyère cheese, and 20 g (¾ oz, 1½ tablespoons) butter. Season and flour a large veal chop, weighing about 250 g (9 oz) and roast it in a preheated oven at 150°C (300°F, gas 2) with 20 g (¾ oz, 1½ tablespoons) butter for 20–30 minutes. When half-cooked, turn it over and cover with the cheese paste. Stuff a small tomato with a mixture of breadcrumbs, parsley and butter and place it in the roasting pan. Finish cooking the chop and baste regularly with the butter. Drain the meat and the tomato and arrange them on a serving dish. Add a peeled and chopped shallot to the cooking juices and deglaze with 4 tablespoons dry white wine and an equal quantity of veal stock. Boil and reduce by half. Add 10 g (1½ teaspoons, ¼ oz) butter and pour the sauce over the veal.

FRAISIER A gâteau consisting of two squares of Genoese sponge moistened with kirsch syrup and sandwiched together with a layer of kirsch-flavoured butter cream and strawberries. The top of the gâteau is covered with a layer of butter cream coloured red with cochineal and decorated with strawberries. When the gâteau is cut, the strawberries can be seen, cut in half.

There are several variations of this gâteau, which is also called *fragaria* or *fraisalia*. The sponge may be made with ground almonds and covered with several layers of kirsch-flavoured strawberry jam. It is then brushed with apricot glaze, covered with pink fondant icing (frosting) and edged with sugar and chopped blanched almonds. The top is decorated with a large strawberry made from red marzipan (almond paste) and leaves made from boiled sugar. Another method is to fill the sponge with a layer of strawberry cream and ice it with a pink fondant icing containing crushed strawberries. Fresh strawberries are then used for the decoration. Finally, it may be filled with strawberry jam, covered with a thin layer of pink almond paste, dusted with icing (confectioner's) sugar and edged with chopped roasted almonds.

FRAMBOISE A spirit made from raspberries, especially in the Alsace region.

FRANÇAISE, À LA Describing a preparation of joints of meat served with asparagus tips, braised lettuce, cauliflower florets coated with hollandaise sauce and small duchess-potato nests filled with diced mixed vegetables. The sauce served with dishes *à la française* is a thin demi-glace – or a clear veal gravy.

Peas *à la française* are prepared with lettuce and onions (see *pea*).

FRANCE For a culinary history, see *French cooking*.

FRANCHE-COMTÉ See *page 515*.

FRANCIACORTA Region in Lombardy producing good quality white, red and sparkling wines. DOCG Franciacorta is applied to sparkling wines produced by the traditional method (see *méthode champenoise*) from Chardonnay, Pinot Noir, Pinot Blanc and Pinot Gris, whilst DOC Terre di Franciacorta refers to the quality still wines.

FRANCILLON A mixed salad consisting of potatoes marinated in a white wine vinaigrette, mussels cooked *à la marinière*, and chopped celery, garnished with sliced truffles. The original recipe was given by Dumas *fils* in his play *Francillon*, first performed at the Comédie-Française on 9 January 1887. The Paris restaurateurs took advantage of the event by putting the new salad on their menus. The restaurant Brébant-Vachette substituted Japanese artichokes for the potatoes, and Francillon salad was renamed 'Japanese salad' (it is often called Japanese salad even when it is made with potatoes).

There follows a passage from the play, in which Annette, a cordon-bleu cook, gives the recipe to Henri, the leading man, who intends to make the salad as a special treat.

Annette

Boil some potatoes in stock, cut them into pieces as for an ordinary salad, and while they are still warm, season them with salt, pepper, very good-quality fruity olive oil, and vinegar . . .

Henri

Tarragon vinegar?

Annette

Orléans vinegar is better, but that's not important. What is important is to add half a glass of white wine, Château-Yquem if possible, and plenty of herbs, chopped very, very small. At the same time cook some very large mussels in stock with a celery stick, drain them thoroughly, and add them to the seasoned potatoes. Mix everything together gently.

Thérèse

Less mussels than potatoes?

Annette

One-third less. One has to become gradually aware of the mussels. They must be neither anticipated nor imposed.

Stanislas

Very well put!

Annette

Thank you, sir. When the salad is finished and stirred . . .

Henri

Gently . . .

Annette

Cover it with rounds of truffle. That puts a finishing touch to it.

Henri

Cooked in champagne.

Annette

That goes without saying. Do all this two hours before dinner so that this salad will be cold when served.

Henri

We could surround the salad bowl with ice.

Annette

No! It mustn't be rushed. It is very delicate, and all the flavours have to combine together slowly for his mother, a great gourmand. In the modern recipe, the truffles are omitted and the vinaigrette is flavoured with Chablis.

A *bombe glacé* coated with coffee ice cream and filled with a champagne-flavoured bombe mixture is known as *bombe Francillon*.

FRANGIPANE A pastry cream used in the preparation of various desserts, sweets, cakes and pancakes. It is made with milk, sugar, flour, eggs and butter, mixed with either crushed macaroons (to give a lighter cream) or with ground almonds. A few drops of bitter almond essence (extract) may be added to intensify the flavour. The name is derived from that of a 16th-century Italian nobleman, the Marquis Muzio Frangipani, living in Paris. He invented a perfume for scenting gloves that was based on bitter almonds. This inspired the pastrycooks of the time to make an almond-flavoured cream which they named frangipane. La Varenne mentions *tourtes de franchipanne* (frangipane tarts) several times in his treatise on pâtisserie.

In classic cookery, frangipane is also the name of a kind of savoury panada made with flour, egg yolks, butter and milk and cooked like a choux pastry. It is used in poultry and fish forcemeat.

RECIPES

frangipane

Combine 75 g (6 oz, 1¼ cups) icing (confectioner's) sugar, 175 g (6 oz, 1½ cups) ground almonds and 2 teaspoons cornflour (cornstarch). In a mixing bowl, soften 125 g (4½ oz, ½ cup) butter without making it foam (which would make the cream rise during the cooking process and then sink again and lose its shape). Add the sugar, almond and cornflour mixture, then 2 eggs one by one, stirring with a wooden spatula. Next add 1 tablespoon brown rum and finally 300 g (11 oz, 1½ cups) confectioner's custard (pastry cream). Cover with cling film (plastic wrap) and place in the refrigerator.

frangipane cream

Boil 750 ml (1¼ pints, 3¼ cups) milk with a vanilla pod (bean) or 1 teaspoon vanilla sugar. Put 100 g (4 oz, 1 cup) plain (all-purpose) flour, 200 g (7 oz, 1 cup) caster (superfine) sugar, 4 beaten eggs and a pinch of salt in a heavy based saucepan and mix together thoroughly. Gradually add the hot milk and cook slowly for about 3 minutes, stirring all the time, until the cream thickens. Pour the cream into a bowl and stir in 75 g (3 oz, ¾ cup) crushed macaroons and 50 g (2 oz, ¼ cup) softened butter. Mix well.

crêpes à la frangipane

Make some crêpes and prepare some frangipane cream, using 500 ml (17 fl oz, 2 cups) milk for the cream and an equal quantity for the crêpe batter. Coat the crêpes with the cream and fold into four. Arrange in a buttered ovenproof dish, dust with icing (confectioner's) sugar and lightly caramelize in a very hot oven or under the grill (broiler). Serve very hot.

FRANGY Appellation white wine from Savoy, entitled to the prefix 'Roussette de Savoie' and made from the Roussette grape. Pleasantly fragrant, it can have a slightly honeyed flavour, although it is essentially a dry wine.

FRANKFURTER A German smoked sausage, originating from the Frankfurt area, made of finely

Franche-Comté

This province comprises the Jura, Doubs and Haute-Saône districts, with mountainous regions, high plateaux and valleys. The area provides a variety of excellent foods.

■ **Freshwater fish** In the rivers, streams and ponds numerous kinds of fish are found in great quantities. The local people cook them in delicious ways, notably in succulent stews. Known for their delicacy are Saulon carp, red mullet, pike from Ognon, Doubs and Dessoubs trout and Breuchin salmon trout, the flesh of which is very well flavoured. In the Breuchin there are also good crayfish.

■ **Meat and dairy produce** The cattle of Franche-Comté and the Jura are famous for their well-flavoured meat and high-quality milk, from which cheese and other dairy products are made.

Cheeses from Franche-Comté include Septmoncel, which some people consider a rival to Roquefort, and Comté cheese, a kind of Gruyère.

The charcuterie of Franche-Comté is excellent and can be bought in Paris and many other large towns. It includes smoked ham, mainly from Luxeuil, different kinds of sausages, including caraway sausage from Montbozon, and stuffed tongue from Besançon.

■ **Culinary specialities** Foremost among the culinary specialities are maize (corn) porridge, *potée franccomtoise*, which is prepared like *potée* from other regions but has Morteau sausage added to it. Soups include the classic frog's-leg soup; a simple soup thickened with bread and enriched with butter; cherry soup; and soups made with fresh vegetables.

The most famous dishes include the fish stews made from fresh-water fish with white or red wine, onions and herbs. Vesoul is known for its pike quenelles; a traditional *pain d'écrevisses* or

Les Bouchoux is a pretty little village typical of the Jura. Perched on a hill, it is surrounded by pastures and large pine forests.

crayfish loaf is also prepared. Meat is braised in wine, cooked very slowly in a covered casserole to preserve all the meat juices. Game is also abundant and jugged hare *à la franccomtoise* is a typical stew.

There are all sorts of savouries, including many ways of using wild mushrooms with meat dishes or eggs, or quite simply in soufflés or served on toast. Cheese is used in fondue or on gratins and in *flamusse* (a cheese tart).

■ **Baking and pâtisserie** *Sèche* is a flat bread made with eggs and sugar. Other specialities include *viques*, milk rolls from Montbéliard; *craquelins* of Baume-les-Dames; almond pastry and biscuits (cookies) of Montbozon; *malakoff* (almond pastry) of Dole; *galette de goumeau* of Saint-Amour; *gaufres* (waffles) *de chanoinesses* of Baume-les-Dames; chestnut cakes; and

gingerbread of Vercel and Dole. In the orchards of Franche-Comté, excellent fruit, particularly stone fruit, is grown. Two notable fruit preserves are the quince paste from Baume-les-Dames and bilberry and whortleberry jam from Melisey.

WINE Franche-Comté (particularly the department of Jura) produces white, red and rosé wines of different qualities as well as *vin jaune* and *vin de paille* (straw wine), which are special-ities of the region. The *vin jaune* is made from the Savagnin white grape. It demands strictly controlled and highly specialized methods of vinification, fermentation and conservation. The best-known *vin jaune* is that of Château-Chalon. *Vin de paille* is so-called because the grapes are sun-dried on straw mats before being pressed.

A cheese press, in Cernans (Jura) used in making Comté cheese. In Franche-Comté, this cheese has been made in co-operatives since the Middle Ages.

minced (ground) pork. Beef or veal may be used with the pork and kosher frankfurters are made with beef without any pork. Frankfurters are sold blanched or fully cooked, readying for reheating, and are available fresh (loose), vacuum-packed or in cans. In Germany they are typically served accompanied by sauerkraut and hot or cold potato salad. Elsewhere, they are often placed in rolls, smeared with mustard or tomato ketchup and served as hot dogs.

FRANKLIN, ALFRED-LOUIS-AUGUSTE French
writer (born Versailles, 1850; died Paris, 1917). He spent most of his working life in the Mazarine library in Paris, becoming successively librarian, chief librarian and, finally, administrator. He published 27 reference books dedicated to *La Vie privée d'autrefois* ('private life in bygone days'): these serious works contain numerous details about the table menus, kitchens and domestic economy of bygone days, subjects too often neglected by historians.

FRASCATI A gaming house-cum-restaurant situated on the corner of the Rue de Richelieu and the Boulevard des Italiens in Paris. It was founded in 1796 by the Neapolitan ice-cream merchant Garchi, who named it after one of the most famous holiday resorts for well-to-do Romans. Its gardens were illuminated at night and during the Directory and the Empire it had the reputation of being the most famous gaming house in Paris. In addition, the clientele could dine, eat ice cream and watch the firework displays. It was also frequented by women of easy virtue. The restaurant was eventually closed after 50 years with the suppression of gaming houses and was subsequently succeeded by the Pâtisserie Frascati.

The name Frascati is used for a garnish for meat dishes and for various desserts. It is also the name of a famous Italian dry white wine.

RECIPE

fillet of beef à la Frascati
Prepare a demi-glace sauce flavoured with port. Sauté some very large mushrooms in butter or bake them in the oven. Cook some very short green asparagus tips in butter and quickly sauté some small slices of foie gras (preferably duck) in butter. Keep all these ingredients hot. Roast a fillet of beef and place it on a serving dish. Fill two-thirds of the mushroom caps with the asparagus tips and the remainder with a salpicon of truffles braised in Madeira. Arrange the mushrooms and the slices of foie gras around the meat. Pour the demi-glace over the top.

FRASCATI Famous white wine produced in Lazio, Italy, almost at the gates of Rome. It has been known and enjoyed since antiquity. Mostly made from the Malvasia di Candia and Trebbiano Toscano grape varieties, the wines of Frascati may be dry, sweet or sparkling. The best of them add the description 'superiore' to the label, so long as the alcohol content is over 11.5%.

FREEZE-DRYING A method of preserving food, known also as cryodesiccation and lyophilization, in which the product is frozen and then dehydrated. The food is treated in three stages: first the product is deep-frozen; next it is subjected to a vacuum, which sublimates the ice trapped in it; and finally the water vapour is removed, leaving the product dry and stable. A solid food that has been processed in this way becomes extremely light because it contains only 1–2% of its original water content; but it retains its volume, cellular structure and shape, allowing rapid and even rehydration. The nutritional qualities remain more or less the same as those of fresh food. As it is a costly process it is only used for quality products. The best results are obtained with liquids and small pieces of food. Coffee is still the principal freeze-dried product, but mushrooms, onions and prawns are also preserved successfully in this way.

FREEZER An electric appliance for freezing food and storing ready frozen food. Either in chest or cupboard form, a freezer is used to store food at a temperature of −18°C (0°F) after it has been frozen at −24°C (−11°F) minimum. The size and type varies widely, from large chest or upright models to a small compartment in combination with a separate refrigerator (a fridge-freezer).

Features include fast-freeze settings; thermometers; alarms to warn of a rise in temperature (for example if the door is accidentally left open); frost-free operation (no need to defrost the appliance); and fan-assisted cooling to allow optimum operation in a warm environment (for example in the average kitchen). Quality of the cabinet and level of insulation (which influences running cost) vary according to the type and cost of the appliance. These are some of the facts to consider; the space available for the appliance and its likely use should also be assessed before purchase.

The icebox in a refrigerator is not a freezer as such but a storage compartment for the preservation of ready frozen foods; it is unsuitable for deep-freezing.

FREEZING Submitting a perishable foodstuff to extreme cold to preserve it. The temperature at the centre of the food must be reduced to between −10°C and −18°C (14°F and 0°F) as quickly as possible.
■ **What to freeze** Almost all foods can be frozen, although some require preliminary preparation: eggs, for example, cannot be frozen in their shells but can be stored when lightly beaten. The main rule is that the food is fresh and of good quality. Prepared ingredients and meals and cooked dishes can be frozen successfully. The possibilities are broad and depend as much on personal preference and eating patterns.
■ **Preparing for food for freezing** Always prepare ingredients as though they are to be cooked – for

example, trim and peel vegetables, if necessary; gut and clean fish; and trim and cut up fruit.

• VEGETABLES For long-term storage, blanching is recommended. Blanch quickly in boiling unsalted water (except for tomatoes and mushrooms), then drain, wipe, plunge into iced water, drain again and dry thoroughly. However, the majority of vegetables keep well without blanching, especially for up to 2 months.

• FRUIT Peel and remove the stones (pits), wipe thoroughly without washing.

• MEAT Remove excess fat and cut into joints or serving-sized pieces.

• POULTRY Pluck, draw, singe, remove fat, stuff with crumpled foil and truss (or cut into pieces).

• FISH Gut (clean), scale, dry, stuff with crumpled foil if whole (or cut into slices), trim and dry.

• SOFT-FAT (SOFT-RIPENED) CHEESES Choose when just ripe and wrap.

• COOKED DISHES Reduce cooking time by 10–20 minutes.

• PASTRY (DOUGH) Wrap portions of pastry or roll out and shape on to foil trays.

■ **Packaging** The package must be impermeable to smells; it should be light and not bulky. Heavy-quality polythene bags are practical as are rigid plastic containers. Foil wrapping and containers are also useful. Some ovenproof glassware is also freezerproof. Food that is inadequately wrapped looses moisture, which forms ice crystals outside it, and becomes dry on the surface; a condition known as freezer burn. Excluding air from packets and wrapping foods closely, then sealing bags with wire ties, helps to prevent surface damage.

■ **Defrosting frozen food** Preliminary defrosting is not necessary for small cuts of meat, fish or vegetables. They should be heated immediately to maximum temperature in boiling water or a preheated oven or under a grill (broiler) so that they are defrosted, sealed and cooked in one. In general, frozen vegetables cook more quickly than the same fresh vegetables (since the former have been blanched before freezing), while frozen meats require longer cooking than fresh meats. Precooked dishes which are placed directly in a saucepan or in the oven in their container always heat very quickly. Defrosting is, however, essential for larger items (whole birds, roasts), shellfish, pastry, pastry dishes and cheeses. This should preferably take place in the refrigerator (2–20 hours according to the type and size of the product). No defrosted food should ever be refrozen.

FRENCH BEAN
Variety of thick, fleshy, stringless green or yellow bean (*haricot beurre*). When picked young, they are known as dwarf French beans (see *bean*). The yellow beans are usually juicer than the green ones.

FRENCH COOKING
Throughout history, bread has always been an important part of the French diet. In ancient Gaul, which was essentially an agri-cultural region, the peasants used to prepare flat cakes of millet, oats, barley and wheat. They were good hunters and ate game, poultry and also pork, the fat of which was used in various culinary preparations. Because of the abundance of herds of wild pigs in the forests, the Gaul perfected the art of preserving meat by salting and smoking and the pork butchers (*lardarii*) of the time had such a high reputation that they even exported their pork to Rome. Meals were washed down with *cervoise* (barley beer), and in the Marseilles region wine was drunk as well. Centuries earlier, the Greeks had introduced vines into the region and Marseilles also imported wine from Italy.

■ **From the Romans to the barbarians** The Romans, with their refined habits and their tradition of great cookery, exerted a profound influence on the Gauls from the 1st century onwards, above all on the wealthy classes: the recipes of Apicius were handed down until the Middle Ages. Whereas their ancestors took their meals seated around the table, the Gallo-Roman noblemen dined on reclining couches and enjoyed, as had the Romans, beans, chick peas, grilled (broiled) snails, oysters, dormice stuffed with walnuts, and jam made from violets and honey. Cooking food in olive oil gained ground, and orchards were developed. It is even recorded that fig trees used to grow in little Lutetia (ancient Paris). However, the most important and influential factor of all was the widespread establishment of vine-growing areas: Italian vine plants were introduced into the Bordeaux region, the Rhône valley, Burgundy and Moselle. Soon, the wine merchants of Gaul invaded the markets of the Empire to the detriment of Roman wines, all the more successfully since the Gauls had discovered that wine could be kept longer if it was stored in casks. Competition became so lively that in AD 92 the emperor Domitian ordered half the vineyards of Gaul to be destroyed.

After the Germanic invasions, Gaul went through a tragic period of food shortage and famines that marked the beginning of the Middle Ages. The Merovingian and, later, the Carolingian nobles imitated the luxurious example set by the Romanized Gauls and feasted on a wide variety of highly spiced game (boar, wild ox, reindeer and even camel), while the masses contented themselves with oatmeal gruels, and the basic dish was a hearty soup made with root vegetables enriched with bacon. Meat was eaten only on special occasions. Agricultural techniques regressed, the economy became autarkic – self sufficient – and until the 8th century, there was a massive slump in trade.

■ **The influence of the church** What remained of the ancient culture had found a refuge in the monasteries. The great religious orders extolled manual labour and vast areas of land were cleared for cultivation. Kilns, workshops and hostelries for pilgrims were also established near the abbeys. The monks undertook the essential responsibility for selecting vine plants, and also supervised the manufacture and maturing of cheeses. Above all, however, the

Church altered the diet of the population by forcing people to abstain on certain days in the year from eating any kind of animal fat or meat which 'kindle lust and passion'; as a result, this encouraged both fishing and the breeding of pike, eels and carp in the fish ponds. Whale blubber, a greatly prized food, was permitted during Lent; furthermore, the increased consumption of fish brought about improved methods of salting and smoking.

Consequently, the attics and cellars of the great Carolingian cities and those of the abbeys were always well stocked, and the banquets were sumptuous. The emperor Charlemagne personally supervised the good management of the imperial estates. Above all, he enjoyed hunting, and the word *gibier* (game) dates from this time. But abundance was still preferred to culinary elegance, and serious food shortages continued. The study of monastic meals reveals impressive rations of leguminous plants rich in proteins: 200 g (7 oz) dried vegetables, 2 kg (4½ lb) bread, 100 g (4 oz) cheese, together with honey, salt and wine. Such a keen appetite can be explained by the struggle against the cold, by fear of food shortages and by the lack of protein and other fortifying foods with a small volume. The population, which had dropped to perhaps 8 million inhabitants, lived mainly as its ancestors had done, but in a world where insecurity and lack of communications often caused shortages, or even famine. The absence of methods of food preservation meant that food frequently went bad: for example, flour infected with ergot caused ergot poisoning.

■ **The openings up of the Mediterranean region** The setting up of the feudal society in the 8th and 9th centuries contributed to the restoration of relative security. The resumption of trade caused new cities to be built and a new class to develop – the middle class or *bourgeois*, a group dominating the poorer citizens, such as journeymen, labourers and unskilled workers. The cities needed regular provisions, which brought about the establishment of fairs and markets.

The taste for fish and poultry predominated, but products became more varied with the gradual expansion of trade in the Mediterranean region and also because of the pilgrimages and the Crusades. Plums from Damascus (damsons), figs from Malta, dates, pomegranates, pistachio nuts, rice, buckwheat and above all spices (cinnamon, ginger, aniseed, cloves and nutmeg) appeared on the tables of the rich together with various seasoned dishes whose freshness sometimes left much to be desired! Soon, condiments became indispensable aids to cooking, and the citizens of Dijon added their contribution in the 12th century by discovering mustard, an adaptation from an old Roman recipe. Also, by the 10th century, the sugar trade was established in the Mediterranean region, centred on Venice.

City dwellers are traditionally eaters of bread and meat and guilds of butchers and bakers were powerful organizations in the cities, where people's fortunes were assessed by the quantities of bread that they bought. Pork was the main type of meat, but joints of mutton and beef formed part of the menus of the rich, and at the same time, *rôtisseurs* (sellers of roast meat) and pie makers multiplied. Cheeses were made in all parts of France and, gradually, wine ousted beer in popularity, except in Flanders and Picardy. Cider, which had been made for several centuries, gained ground in Brittany from the 14th century onwards.

■ **Prestigious meals** Because of his rank, the nobleman was obliged to keep open house in his château: he was responsible for feeding his *maisnie*, which included not only his family but also his equerries and vassals. The menservants set up the table with trestles and planks of oak in the communal rooms. There was no tablecloth and the plates and dishes were very basic, made of baked clay, wood or tin. The cutlery consisted of spoons and knives, and in the 12th century a type of two-pronged fork came into use. As the kitchen was separated from the keep through fear of fires, the servant brought the dish to the table covered with a cloth to keep it warm. The meal consisted of either game or roast pork, poultry of some kind, eggs prepared in various ways, either cheese or curdled milk, and cooked fruits.

These meals were sometimes veritable feasts. The elaborate arrangement of the dishes on the table, following the recipes of Apicius, demonstrated the power, generosity, taste and prestige of the nobleman. The famous 14th-century chef Guillaume Tirel, known as Taillevent, was head cook to Charles V. He was the author of *Le Viandier*, a collection of his recipes and a complete record of the cuisine of that period. The edible game at that time included almost all species of feathered or furred animals, including the cormorant, swan and whale. The royal menus consisted of five dishes, with roasted peacocks and herons, partridges with sugar, young rabbits in spiced sauce, stuffed capons and kids, together with pies, cress, creams, pears, walnuts, honeyed wines and *nulles* (dessert creams).

The discovery of the Americas at the end of the 15th century resulted in the introduction of a new variety of foods, including sweetcorn, guinea fowls, turkeys, tomatoes and potatoes. At the same time, table manners became more refined, individual plates were used and the tables were beautifully decorated with various items of silver.

■ **The splendour of the Renaissance** The Renaissance heralded a new way of life. The marriage of Catherine de' Medici and the future Henri II marked the beginning of the Italian influence on French cuisine, destined to play an important role. It had only very slightly impinged in the reign of François I, a great lover of veal and poultry who, according to Rabelais, had revived the days of feasting and drinking. The middle classes had also acquired an interest in cooking. Whale meat and even donkey were still popular and garlic was widely used as a flavouring, but new foods had also become part of the diet: pasta (such as macaroni and vermicelli), Italian sausages, vegetables (such as artichokes and asparagus) and aromatic herbs (such as basil, sweet marjoram and sage), which had gradually become more popular than the traditional herbs inherited from the Romans, such as cardamom and cumin.

Catherine de' Medici was also responsible for introducing the Florentine art of decorating the table, considered to be the most advanced in Europe. The fine tablecloths, earthenware, glassware and silverware, together with the introduction of the fork (which was welcomed with uncertainty), contributed to the pleasure of meals. At the end of the 16th century, Italian cooks and pastrycooks came to France under the influence of Catherine and Marie de' Medici. At this time, the Italian *maîtres queux* (head chefs) were considered to be the best in the world. They taught the French many recipes that have remained in the French culinary repertoire. Cooks of this era were already aware of their role and social importance.

Banquets were magnificent, and a meal served to Henri II himself included a profusion of lampreys in hippocras sauce, hotpots, ducklings *à la malvoisie*, slices of muraena (an eel-like fish) served with a sauce of egg yolks and herbs, ducks *à la didone*, sturgeon fillets *à la lombarde*, quarters of roebuck, partridges *à la tonelette*, and a whole series of puddings, such as darioles and *échaudes*.

■ **French cooking in the 17th century** The reign of Henri IV is symbolized by the famous *poule au pot*, which the king promised that his subjects would enjoy once a week, as a symbol of modest comfort and an improvement in the condition of the serfs. In fact, the beginning of the 17th century was marked by the contribution of the agronomist Olivier de Serres, who introduced all garden vegetables into cookery, for example, cauliflowers and asparagus. However, the king had a preference for sweet things and so sugared almonds, marzipan (almond paste) and tarts with musk and ambergris became fashionable, together with all kinds of jam. As early as 1555 the Italian café owners had taught the French how to make sorbets, and ice creams followed a century later. Heavily spiced food declined in popularity and a number of cookery books were written, the best-known of which is *Cuisinier français*, by François de la Varenne, which appeared in 1651. It was the first book to fix rules and principles and thus to establish some order in cooking. It included recipes for cakes and also for the first mille-feuilles. In 1691, the *Cuisinier royal et bourgeois* by Massaliot was published. Its instructions were precise and it showed that the cuisine was becoming more varied.

In the reign of Louis XIV, cooking was spectacular rather than fine or delicate, and the festivities of the Prince of Condé at Chantilly, for example, were particularly sumptuous. The famous Vatel was maître d'hôtel of Condé the Great, a very important position! A great number of dishes were served at each meal and there are many descriptions of the meals served at the table of Louis XIV, who ate too heavily for a true gourmet.

The Palatine Princess wrote: 'I have very often seen the king eat four plates of different soups, an entire pheasant, a partridge, a large plateful of salad, mutton cut up in its juice with garlic, two good pieces of ham, a plateful of cakes and fruits and jams.'

However, Louis XIV established the habit of having dishes served separately. Before this time, everything was piled up together in a large pyramid. In his reign, the culinary utensils of the Middle Ages were replaced by a *batterie de cuisine*, which included many new pots and pans in tinplate and wrought iron and, later, the introduction of silver utensils.

Louis XIV had a passion for vegetables, which led La Quintinie to develop gardening: green peas were produced in March and strawberries in April. Oysters and lamb were particularly highly prized, and elaborate dishes were concocted. One sauce became famous: béchamel, named after the financier Louis de Béchameil, who drafted recipes and precepts in verse.

Coffee, tea and chocolate were favoured by the aristocracy, and doctors debated about their advantages and drawbacks. Establishments were set up specializing in these exotic drinks. For example, in 1680 the Café Procope opened in Paris. Here, fruit juices, ices and sorbets, exotic wines, hippocras, orgeat pastes, crystallized (candied) fruits and fruits preserved in brandy were sold. In addition to the coffee houses, taverns, inns and cafés had multiplied in the city and were visited frequently by princes and their courtiers.

■ **French cooking from the Regency to Louis XVI** The Regency and the reign of Louis XV are regarded as the golden age of French cookery. At the same time, the produce of rural France slowly improved both in quality and quantity and there was no further famine. The Age of Enlightenment united the pleasures of the table with those of the mind, and gastronomy, a new word, was the main topic of conversation: the *petits soupers* (little suppers) of the Regent and the choice meals prepared for the king and his great noblemen did more to perfect the culinary art than the showy banquets in the reign of Louis XIV. Great chefs rivalled each other in imaginative cookery. They discovered how to make stocks from meat juices and began to use them to add flavour to sauces. Mahonnaise sauce appeared at the table of the Marshal de Richelieu, the conqueror of Port-Mahon; pâté de foie gras garnished with truffles might have been the idea of Nicolas-François Doyen, chef of the first president of the Parliament of Bordeaux; La Chapelle, the chef of Marie Leszczynska, prepared *bouchées à la reine* (chicken vol-au-vent), and Marin, the butler of the Marshal de Soubise, was the first to glaze meat and deglaze (make a sauce from) the juices. It was in the mansions of rich financiers that the culinary art expanded. Food shops, pastrycooks and confectioners achieved perfection and people also learnt how to recognize foreign specialities, such as caviar, beefsteak, curry and Madeira. At the same time, the concern for maintaining regular food supplies encouraged methods of cultivating and storing grain.

During the first years of the reign of Louis XVI, culinary methods continued to become more refined. More order and logic was established, menus for festive occasions became more elegant, and there were further improvements in all branches of catering. The first restaurant was established during this period and menus of the restaurants at that time provide valuable information about the cuisine of the era. The menus included 12 soups, 24 hors d'oeuvre, 15–20 entrées of beef, 20 entrées of mutton, 30 entrées of fowl or game, 12–20 entrées of veal, 12 dishes of pâtisserie, 24 dishes of fish, 15 roasts, 50 *entremets* and 50 desserts.

Louis XVI is also famous for encouraging Parmentier, the economist and agronomist, in his written works on food. These included several reports on ways of using potatoes, and he finally succeeded in popularizing this once-scorned vegetable.

■ **From the Revolution to the Second Empire** The Revolution caused a distinct slowing-down in the development of French cuisine, but Carême, a young pastrycook already famous for his *pièces montées*, saved it from sinking into obscurity. Furthermore, science contributed to its revival with the discoveries of Appert (food-preserving techniques) and Delessert (sugar extraction from sugar beet). Already the chef Laguipière and the gastronome Cussy showed a taste for the display of the Empire; two tables were particularly famous, that of Cambacérès and that of Talleyrand. At the same time, the fashion for restaurants made accessible to a greater number what had until then been the privilege of an elite. Gastronomic literature, invented by Grimod de La Reynière and illustrated by Brillat-Savarin, played an important part. Louis XVIII himself created recipes. In the reign of Charles X, the French discovered couscous, and trout farming was developed. The kneading machine improved the quality of bread, and after 1840 railways ensured that provisions were fresher. Stock rearing made considerable progress, and the quality of the meat produced superb results. In about 1860, horse meat, less expensive than beef, was widely available for sale; horse butchers multiplied. The invention of the gas cooker was another great milestone, and many more cafés and restaurants were established, particularly on the country side of tollgates near Paris. Meals during the Second Empire reached a peak of excellence. This period was marked by an obsession with good living, particularly among the great writers: Flaubert, the Goncourt brothers, and Sainte-Beuve.

After the Palais Royal, the 'Boulevard' became the centre of famous restaurants. Joseph Favre pursued his career at the Café de la Paix, then at the Café Riche; Dugléré composed succulent menus for the Café Anglais, where he received the king of Prussia (1867) and Czar Alexander II, who had come to hear Offenbach's *La Grande Duchesse de Gérolstein*.

The meals included in turn soups, entrées, roasts and desserts. It is not so much the quantity of dishes which is surprising but the position of the courses: there was no hesitation in serving a pâté as an *entremet* and sweet dishes as an entrée.

■ **The 20th century** At the beginning of the 20th century, French cooking gained supremacy throughout the world. Its chefs reigned supreme in the kitchens of Buckingham Palace, the Winter Palace of St Petersburg and the great international hotels. Paris became the Mecca of gastronomy. The Edwardian era was the age when great books were written about cooking by such authors as Urbain Dubois, Auguste Bernard, Escoffier and Bignon. The Académie Goncourt organized its first dinner in 1903, and Prosper Montagné, the most famous chef of the first half of the century, opened the most luxurious restaurant of this frivolous era. There was also a fashion for local bistrots, run by natives of the Auvergne and Périgord, and also by gastronomic associations. At the end of the 20th century the influence of Curnonsky still prevailed and the great classic dishes of the cuisine of provincial France continued to uphold the reputation of French cookery, with such dishes as pot-au-feu, blanquette, tripe, bouillabaisse, cassoulet, bourguignon and tarte Tatin. French cookery has also been introduced to, and influenced by, other culinary traditions, with the result that exotic and foreign restaurants flourish. The great classics of European cuisine have long been incorporated, but the French are now discovering Chinese, Indian and Scandinavian cookery. See also *nouvelle cuisine*.

FRENCH DRESSING See *vinaigrette*.

FRENCH FAIRS AND MARKETS *foires et marchés* The oldest market in Paris, in the heart of the city, was established at the beginning of the 12th century for the sale of wheat. Not long afterwards Louis le Gros established another market in the place where Les Halles operated right up to 1969, when it moved out to Rungis. The art of selecting the right ingredients and looking for top-quality food is still practised. All over France, markets take place on fixed days, once or twice a week, in the open air or in market buildings. No matter how small the purchase, the customer is keen to obtain the best produce that is available. Careful inspection of the foods on offer is still part of the shopping process.

The great annual fairs used to be held in the church square on the parish saint's day. In Paris, the ham fair, which began on the last Tuesday of Lent, was held in the church square of Notre-Dame before being moved to the Boulevard Richard-Lenoir and then to Pantin. The Lendit fair, established by King Dagobert, was held on the Plaine Saint-Denis for a fortnight in June. The products sold at this fair came from all over France and even from abroad, especially Flanders. The Saint-Germain fair, established by Louis XI in 1482 near the church of Saint-Germain-des-Prés, started on 3 February and lasted until Holy Week: it flourished until 1785 and sold all types of goods in small wooden booths. Plays were also performed and coffee was served for the first time in France by an Armenian called Pascal. The Saint-Laurent fair, the Saint-Ovide fair and the Temple fair were the forerunners of the great annual exhibitions now known as the Salon de l'agriculture (Agricultural Show) and the Foire de Paris (Paris Show). Several other towns in France specializing in certain types of products also hold fairs, including Arpajon (beans) and Excideuil (foies gras).

FRENCH TOAST *pain perdu* A dessert consisting of slices of bread (or brioche or milk bread) soaked in milk, dipped in eggs beaten with sugar, then lightly fried in butter. French toast is served hot and crisp. It was formerly called *pain crotté, pain à la romaine* or *croûtes dorées*. In the south of France, it was traditionally eaten on feast days, particularly at Easter. Originally intended to use up crusts and left-over pieces of bread, French toast today is usually made with milk bread. It may be accompanied by custard, cream, jam or compote.

RECIPE

French toast ♦
Boil 500 ml (17 fl oz, 2 cups) milk with half a vanilla pod (bean) and 100 g (4 oz, ½ cup) caster (superfine) sugar, then leave to cool. Cut 250 g (9 oz) stale brioche into fairly thick slices. Soak them in the cooled milk, without letting them fall apart, then dip them in 2 eggs beaten as for an omelette with a little caster sugar. Heat 100 g (4 oz, ½ cup) butter in a frying pan and fry the slices. When golden on one side, turn them over to cook the other side. Arrange them on a round dish, dust them with caster sugar and decorate with strawberries.

FRENEUSE A soup made with turnips and potatoes in light stock or consommé, thickened with fresh cream. It can be garnished with small turnip balls.

FRIAND A small puff-pastry case filled with sausagemeat, minced (ground) meat, ham or cheese, baked in the oven and served as a hot hors d'oeuvre.

A *friand* is also a small sweet pastry – a barquette often made with an almond paste filling and elaborately decorated.

RECIPE

sausage rolls
Mince (grind) together 2 peeled shallots, 100 g (4 oz) mushrooms, 200 g (7 oz) veal, 200 g (7 oz) smoked pork and a bunch of parsley (a food processor may be used). Add 1 tablespoon cream and season with salt and pepper. Mix together well. Dust the work surface with flour and roll out 500 g (1 lb 2 oz) puff pastry to a thickness of about 3 mm (⅛ in); cut in into 6 rectangles of equal size. Divide the filling into 6 portions and roll into sausage shapes the same length as the width of the pastry rectangles. Put a 'sausage' at one end of each rectangle and roll it up. Score the top with the point of a knife and glaze with beaten egg. Bake in a preheated oven at 220°C (425°F, gas 7) for about 30 minutes.

The filling can also be made with fine sausage-meat mixed with chopped onion, parsley, salt and pepper.

FRIANDISE The French word for a delicacy when referring to pâtisserie or sweetmeats. The word is often used for petits fours or sweets (candies) eaten between meals. It used to mean a treat in the general sense, and the term *friandises de confiseur* (confectioner's treats) was used for chocolates, crystallized (candied) fruits, nougats and fruit jellies, which were also referred to as *mignardises*. Friandises may be served with coffee or tea, or at the end of a meal following the dessert, in which case an assortment of such delicacies may be served.

FRIBOURG The name sometimes used in France for Swiss Gruyère cheese, because the Gruyère Valley, where the best Gruyère cheese is manufactured, is in the district of Fribourg.

FRICADELLE A meatball or burger made of minced (ground) meat or forcemeat. *Fricadelles* may be deep- or shallow-fried or cooked in a ragoût. They are Belgian or German specialities and are sometimes cooked in beer. They are served with a sauce (tomato, paprika or curry), together with fresh pasta, rice or a vegetable purée.

FRICANDEAU A dish made of noix of veal larded with bacon and braised, roasted or fried. It is usually served with spinach, a sorrel fondue, peas or a jardinière of vegetables. It can also be served cold, having been left to cool in the cooking juices.

The name is also applied to slices or fillets of fish, mainly those of sturgeon, tuna or even salmon steak, braised in a fish stock.

Fricandeau is also a special item of charcuterie from southwestern France. It consists of minced pork neck, liver and kidneys flavoured with herbs, shaped into balls, wrapped in caul and cooked in the oven. They are served cold, coated with aspic jelly and lard.

RECIPE

veal fricandeau with sorrel
Lard a slice of noix of veal, about 3–4 cm (1¼–1½ in) thick, with some thin strips of fat bacon that have been marinated for 30 minutes in a mixture of oil, chopped parsley, salt and pepper. Then brush the veal with melted butter or with oil containing crushed veal bones. Sauté 2 diced carrots and 2 sliced onions in butter until golden brown and put them in a braising pan. Place the veal on top of the vegetables with the crushed

bones, a bouquet garni and half a calf's foot that has been boned and blanched. Add enough white or red wine to half-cover the meat; season with salt and pepper. Cover the pan and bring to the boil. Place the pan in a preheated oven at 220°C (425°F, gas 7) and cook, uncovered, for 1 hour. Remove the pan and replace on the top of the cooker.

Mix 1 tablespoon tomato purée (paste) with 500 ml (17 fl oz, 2 cups) stock and add it to the pan so that the veal is now covered. Bring back to the boil, return to the oven and cook for a further 1½ hours. Drain the meat and arrange it on an ovenproof dish. Strain the liquid in the pan, pour some of it over the meat and glaze it in the oven. Serve the fricandeau with a sorrel fondue and the remainder of the sauce in a sauceboat (gravy boat).

FRICASSÉE A preparation of chicken in a white sauce (veal and lamb may also be prepared in this way). Formerly in France, the term denoted various kinds of ragoût of chicken meat, fish or vegetables in white or brown stock. Nowadays, the meat is cut into pieces, an aromatic garnish is added and it is then sautéed over a low heat, without browning. The meat is then coated with flour, some white stock is added and the meat is cooked in the thickened liquid. A fricassée is usually cooked with cream and garnished with small glazed onions and lightly cooked mushrooms. Fricassées are also made with fried fish which is subsequently cooked in a sauce.

In the 17th century, when La Varenne referred to fricassées of calves' liver, calves' feet, chicken, young pigeon, potato and asparagus, this method of cooking was very common and not highly regarded. Subsequently, the word became distorted to *fricot*, which, in popular parlance, designates any simple but popular tasty dish.

RECIPES

eel fricassée
Skin and prepare a large eel weighing about 800 g (1¾ lb) or several small eels totalling the same weight. Cut the eels into pieces about 6 cm (2½ in) long. Season with salt and pepper. Peel 12 small onions – if they are spring onions (scallions), trim them first – and blanch them for 3–4 minutes. Place the eel in a buttered frying pan (skillet), together with the onions and a large bouquet garni. Add a mixture of half dry white wine, half water until the ingredients are just covered. Cover the pan, bring to the boil and simmer for 10 minutes. In the meantime, prepare some small croûtons fried in oil or butter. Then add about 12 thinly sliced mushrooms to the frying pan and cook for a further 7–10 minutes. Drain the pieces of eel, the onions and the mushrooms, place in a dish and keep hot. Strain the cooking juices and reduce by two-thirds. Blend 2 egg yolks with 100 ml (4 fl oz, 7 tablespoons) single (light) cream and thicken carefully. Pour the sauce over the eel pieces, garnish with the fried croûtons and serve immediately.

fricassée of chicken à la berrichonne
Joint a chicken. Brown 350 g (12 oz, 3 cups) new carrots in 50 g (2 oz, ¼ cup) butter in a pan. Drain them, and then brown the chicken pieces in the same butter. Add 250 ml (8 fl oz, 1 cup) chicken stock, the carrots, a bouquet garni and some salt and pepper. Bring to the boil, reduce the heat, cover the pan and cook gently for 45 minutes. Remove the chicken pieces and keep them hot. Mix 2 egg yolks and a pinch of caster (superfine) sugar with 200 ml (7 fl oz, ¾ cup) double (heavy) cream, 1 tablespoon white wine vinegar, and a few drops of the chicken stock. Pour the mixture into the pan and mix thoroughly with the pan juices. Heat without boiling so that the sauce thickens a little. Serve the chicken coated with the sauce and sprinkled with chopped parsley.

fricassée of chicken Cardinal La Balue
Cut a chicken into 8 portions, season and brown in 40–50 g (1½–2 oz, 3–4 tablespoons) butter in a flameproof casserole. Put the casserole in a preheated oven at 220°C (425°F, gas 7) and cook for about 40 minutes. Prepare a stock with 1 sliced carrot, 1 sliced onion, a bouquet garni, 150 ml (¼ pint, ⅔ cup) white wine, 750 ml (1¼ pints, 3¼ cups) water and some salt and pepper. Cook for about 30 minutes. Clean a dozen crayfish, wash them and cook them for 5 minutes in the stock. Drain the crayfish and shell the tails. Pound the shells and press through a fine sieve to make a purée. Mix the purée with 50 g (2 oz, ¼ cup) butter.

Drain the cooked chicken pieces and place them in another casserole, with the thighs at the bottom. Add the crayfish tails, cover and put the casserole in the oven, which should be either turned off or at a very low heat, so that the chicken does not become tough. Pour 500 ml (17 fl oz, 2 cups) double (heavy) cream into the casserole in which the chicken was cooked, heat up and deglaze the pan. Heat for a few minutes to reduce the cream (but do not boil), then add the crayfish butter and whisk. Arrange the chicken pieces on a heated serving dish and coat with sauce. Serve very hot.

fricassée of chicken with Anjou wine
Cut a large chicken into medium-sized portions and season with salt and pepper. Peel 24 button onions and 24 button mushrooms. Brown the chicken portions in butter, then add the onions and mushrooms. Add sufficient white Anjou wine to just cover the chicken, cover the pan and simmer gently for 30–35 minutes.

Add 200 ml (7 fl oz, ¾ cup) double (heavy) cream and adjust the seasoning. Serve very hot, with small steamed new potatoes or a mixture of carrots and glazed turnips. A small turkey can be prepared in the same way.

French toast, see page 521.

fricassée of sea fish with Bellet zabaglione

To serve 6, you will need 800 g (1¾ lb) young tur-bot, 1.5 kg (3¼ lb) John Dory, 4 slices of monkfish, 2 red mullet, 4 scampi and 500 ml (17 fl oz, 2 cups) white Bellet wine or a good Provençal wine. Fillet the turbot and the John Dory. Wash the fillets and season with salt and pepper. Heat 3 tablespoons olive oil and 40 g (1½ oz, 3 tablespoons) butter in a large frying pan. When the mixture foams, add all the fish and the scampi. Add a large chopped shal-lot and cook for a few seconds. Add about 100 ml (4 fl oz, 7 tablespoons) Bellet wine. Remove the red mullet, fillet them and replace in the pan. Add 3 tablespoons concentrated fish stock and finish cooking. Arrange the fish on a dish and keep hot.

Make a zabaglione with 8 egg yolks and 400 ml (14 fl oz, 1¾ cups) white Bellet wine. Season with salt and pepper and add 500 ml (17 fl oz, 2 cups) hot double (heavy) cream. The zabaglione should be hot and foamy, but must not boil. Adjust the seasoning. Coat the fricassée with the zabaglione. Sprinkle with fresh chervil and serve with lightly cooked (al dente) French (green) beans, with a knob of butter on top.

lamb fricassée

Wash and wipe some pieces of lamb (fillet, lean leg or shoulder), fry in butter without browning and season with salt and pepper. Sprinkle with 2 table-spoons flour and stir over the heat. Add some white stock or consommé and a bouquet garni, and bring to the boil. Simmer with the lid on for 45–60 minutes. Fry some mushrooms in butter and glaze some button onions. Remove the pieces of lamb from the pan, replace with the onions and mushrooms, and stir them into the pan juices. Take off the heat and add an egg yolk to thicken. Pour the sauce into a large heated dish, add the lamb and sprinkle with chopped parsley. Serve hot.

minute fricassée of chicken

Joint 2 chickens in the usual way and put them in a saucepan with 175 g (6 oz, ¾ cup) good-quality melted butter. Fry the chicken without browning, add 2 tablespoons flour and season with salt, pepper and grated nutmeg; then add sufficient water to make a lightly thickened sauce. Add 6 blanched but-ton onions and a bouquet garni and cook over a brisk heat, ensuring that the chicken pieces do not burn and the sauce is gradually reduced. After 25 minutes, test one of the thighs to see that it is cooked. Add 250 g (9 oz, 3 cups) button mushrooms and skim the fat off the sauce. Blend in 4 egg yolks to thicken the sauce and add a dash of fresh lemon juice.

FRICHTI A colloquial French name for a light meal or snack cooked at home. The word was probably introduced into the French language in the 1860s by Alsatian soldiers and is derived from the German *Frühstück* (breakfast).

FRITELLE A Corsican fritter made with leavened dough containing egg yolks and oil. It contains a mixture of chopped beet, mint and marjoram leaves, or a slice of Corsican sausage, or a square of Broccio (a fresh cream cheese). Fritelles can also be made with chestnut flour and flavoured with fennel seeds. They are then sweetened with plenty of sugar.

FRITON A charcuterie speciality from southwestern France. Resembling a *rillette*, it is made with the residue of melted pork fat and fatty pork pieces, such as belly, which is mixed with pieces of offal (tongue, heart, kidneys or even head) and cooked in lard (shortening).

The word *fritons* is also used for the crisp residues of goose fat and cubes of pork fat, although the more usual word is *grattons* or *gratterons*.

FRITOT Also known as friteau. A kind of savoury fritter made from small pieces of cooked marinated food that are dipped in a light batter and deep-fried. Fritots are usually made with frogs' legs, shellfish, leftovers of fish, poultry or meat, various types of offal (variety meats), or vegetables. They are usually arranged on a paper napkin, garnished with fried parsley and slices of lemon, and served as a hot hors d'oeuvre, accompanied by a spicy tomato sauce.

RECIPES

fritots of meat or poultry

Bone some poached or braised meat or poultry (or use leftovers), cut into even-sized pieces and mari-nate in a mixture of oil, brandy, chopped parsley, salt and pepper. Finish as for frogs'-leg fritots.

frogs'-leg fritots

Trim the frogs' legs and marinate them for 30 min-utes in a mixture of oil, chopped garlic, chopped parsley, lemon juice, salt and pepper. Then dip them in a light batter and deep-fry until they are golden brown. Drain on paper towels and serve with fried parsley, quarters of lemon and either curry sauce (see *indienne, à l'*) or gribiche sauce. The frogs' legs can also be threaded on to small skewers before being dipped in the batter and fried.

mussel fritots

Prepare the mussels *à la marinière*, remove from their shells, drain and dry. Finish as for oyster fritots.

oyster fritots

Remove the oysters from their shells and poach gently in their own liquor. Drain and dry, then mari-nate as for frogs'-leg fritots, but add a pinch of cayenne pepper to the marinade. Finish as for frogs'-leg fritots and serve with Italian sauce (see *italienne, à l'*).

salmon fritots

Cut some raw salmon into thin slices or large dice and marinate in a mixture of oil, lemon juice, chopped parsley, salt and pepper. Finish as for frogs'-leg fritots and serve with tomato or hollandaise sauce or sauce verte.

sole fritots

Cut some sole fillets in two (or four if large fillets) and prepare as for frogs'-leg fritots. Serve with a flavoured mayonnaise sauce, for example with grated lemon zest and chopped capers.

other recipes See *chicory, liver (chicken liver)*.

FRITTER A preparation consisting of a piece of cooked or raw food coated in batter and fried in deep fat or oil. Other types of fritter can be made using choux paste, yeast dough or waffle batter. Some believe that fritters were of Saracen origin and were brought back by the Crusaders. They are served, according to their ingredients, as an hors d'oeuvre, a main course or a dessert, almost always hot and dusted with fine salt or sugar.

When cooking fritters, plenty of oil must always be used because the fritters drop to the bottom of the pan when they are placed in the oil and then rise to the surface as the heat cooks the batter. Fritters should be turned halfway through cooking. The temperature of the oil is usually moderate but can vary considerably according to the type of batter used, whether the food coated in the batter is raw or cooked, and whether the fritter is sweet or savoury.

The principle of the fritter is simple, but the dishes vary enormously in shape and taste and range from regional specialities to classical dishes.

• FRITTERS MADE WITH BATTER Some foods containing a large amount of water must be coated with batter for making fritters. Raw ingredients are cut small so they cook quickly; ready-cooked ingredients may or may not be marinated. Savoury fritters (made with vegetables, fish or cheese) are served as an hors d'oeuvre, a main course (sometimes with a sauce) or as a cocktail snack, such as prawn (shrimp) fritters.

Sweet fritters are made with fruit or flowers. The best known of the former are apple fritters, but they can also be made with bananas and apricots. Flower fritters were very popular in the Middle Ages, using violets, elderflowers and lilies; today mimosa flowers, elderflowers and marrow (squash) flowers are practically the only ones still used. Sweet fritters can also be prepared with a cold cream sauce, cold rice pudding or semolina cut into squares or rectangles and coated in batter.

• FRITTERS MADE WITH CHOUX PASTE Fritters made using sweet or savoury choux paste are known as soufflé fritters and are usually called beignets (French for fritters); they are served as hors d'oeuvre or desserts. In savoury recipes, the pastry can be flavoured with grated cheese, diced ham and almonds. Sweet choux paste gives a basic sweet fritter.

• FRITTERS MADE WITH YEAST DOUGH These fritters are made of sweet dough rounds, sometimes filled with jam, plunged into boiling oil. When puffed and golden they are removed from the oil and dusted with sugar.

• FRITTERS MADE WITH WAFFLE BATTER Fritters made of waffle batter are moulded in long-handled waffle irons of various shapes (stars, boats, hearts, roses). In France they are mostly used for decoration, but in the USA they are served for breakfast or as a dessert, often with maple syrup.

Fritters are among the most ancient and widespread of regional dishes. Made of special flavoured dough, they are often associated with traditional celebrations: for instance, *bugnes* from Lyons, *merveilles* and *oreillettes* from Montpellier, *beugnons* from Berry, *bignes* from Auvergne, *roussettes* from Strasbourg, *tourtisseaux* from Anjou and *bottereaux* from Nantes.

RECIPES

fritter batter (1)

Sift 250 g (9 oz, 2¼ cups) plain (all-purpose) flour into a bowl. Heat 200 ml (7 fl oz, ¾ cup) water until just lukewarm. Make a well in the flour and add 150 ml (¼ pint, ⅔ cup) beer, the warm water and a generous pinch of salt to the middle of it. Mix, drawing the flour from the sides to the centre of the well. Add 2 tablespoons groundnut (peanut) oil and mix. Leave to rest for 1 hour if possible. When required for use, stiffly beat 2 or 3 egg whites and fold into the batter. Do not stir or beat. For sweet fritters, flavour the batter with Calvados, Cognac or rum. The batter may also be sweetened with 1½ teaspoons sugar and the oil replaced with the same amount of melted butter.

fritter batter (2)

Put 250 g (9 oz, 2¼ cups) sifted plain (all-purpose) flour in a mixing bowl. Make a well in the centre and add 1 teaspoon salt, 2 whole eggs and 300 ml (½ pint, 1¼ cups) groundnut (peanut) oil. Whisk the eggs and oil together, incorporating a little of the flour. Add 250 ml (8 fl oz, 1 cup) beer and, stirring well, gradually incorporate the rest of the flour. Allow to stand for about 1 hour. A few minutes before using the batter, whisk 3 egg whites stiffly and fold into the batter using a wooden spoon or rubber spatula.

Savoury Fritters
anchovy fritters

Soak anchovy fillets in milk to remove all the salt. Mix together with a fork (or in a blender) some hard-boiled (hard-cooked) egg yolk, a little butter and some chopped parsley. Spread the mixture on the anchovy fillets and roll up. Dip in batter, deep-fry in hot oil and serve with fried parsley.

artichoke fritters

Trim some small, young globe artichokes (harvested before their chokes have formed). Blanch for 5 minutes until just tender, then drain and cut each one into four. Sprinkle with plenty of lemon juice and a little oil, season with salt and pepper and leave to marinate for 30 minutes. Drain, dip in batter, deep-fry in hot oil, drain and serve on a napkin. (Brussels sprout fritters are prepared in the same way.)

aubergine fritters

Peel some aubergines (eggplants), slice them and marinate for 1 hour in oil, lemon juice, chopped parsley, salt and pepper. Continue as for anchovy fritters. The same method may be used for broccoli, cardoons, celery, celeriac (celery root), courgettes (zucchini), cauliflower, marrow (squash) flowers, salsify, tomatoes and Jerusalem artichokes.

Bernese fritters

Cut some Gruyère cheese into rounds 6 cm (2½ in) in diameter. Chop some ham and add to a thick béchamel sauce; spread on the Gruyère rounds and sandwich the rounds together in pairs. Dip in batter and continue as for anchovy fritters.

cheese fritters (1)

Cut some Gruyère or Comté cheese into 5 cm (2 in) squares about 4 cm (1½ in) thick. Dip in batter and continue as for anchovy fritters. Serve with highly seasoned tomato sauce.

cheese fritters (2)

Add grated cheese (Gruyère or Parmesan), chopped parsley and pepper to a thick béchamel sauce. Allow to cool completely. Divide into 25 g (1 oz) portions and roll into balls. Dip in batter and continue as for anchovy fritters.

chicken liver fritters

Remove the gall from the chicken livers (if present) and marinate for 30 minutes in oil seasoned with salt, pepper and chopped herbs to taste. Then dry and dip in batter. Continue as for anchovy fritters.

lamb's or calf's brain fritters

Poach the brains in stock. Slice them and marinate in oil, chopped parsley and lemon juice. Dip in batter and continue as for anchovy fritters.

mushroom fritters

Wash some small, fresh, tightly closed button mushrooms. Pat dry and coat with flour. Dip in batter and continue as for anchovy fritters. They can be served with a highly seasoned tomato sauce.

salsify fritters

Cut some cooked salsifies into short lengths. Dry, dip in flour and then in batter. Continue as for anchovy fritters. These fritters make a particularly good accompaniment to roast beef, pork or veal.

scampi fritters

Shell cooked scampi tails (discarding the heads) and marinate for 30 minutes in oil, lemon juice and cayenne pepper. Dip in batter and continue as for anchovy fritters.

soft roe fritters

Poach some soft roes (herring, carp or mackerel, for example) in fish stock, drain and marinate for 30 minutes in oil, lemon juice and cayenne pepper. Dip in batter and continue as for anchovy fritters.

soufflé fritters

Prepare 250 g (9 oz) unsweetened choux paste. Using a spoon, divide the paste into small balls the size of a walnut. Plunge into hot oil until the fritters are puffed and golden. Drain on a cloth and arrange in a heap on a napkin. The following are some alternative recipes for soufflé fritters.

• *with anchovies* Add 2 tablespoons finely chopped anchovy fillets (previously soaked in milk) to the choux paste.

• *à la hongroise* Add 3 tablespoons onions lightly fried in butter and seasoned with paprika to the paste.

• *with cheese* Add 50 g (2 oz, ½ cup) grated cheese (preferably Parmesan) seasoned with a little nutmeg to the paste.

• *à la toscane* Add a little cooked lean ham and a little chopped white truffle to the paste.

other recipes See *acra, florentine, oyster, skate, sweetbread.*

Sweet Fritters
apple fritters

Core the apples with an apple corer, peel and cut into rounds about 3 mm (⅛ in) thick. Sprinkle with lemon juice and macerate for 30 minutes in Cognac or Calvados. Drain, dip in batter and continue as for apricot fritters.

apricot fritters

Stone (pit) some ripe apricots and macerate for 30 minutes in sugar and rum (or kirsch or Cognac). Drain thoroughly, dip in sweetened or unsweetened batter and deep-fry in hot oil. Remove the fritters and drain. Dust with caster (superfine) sugar and arrange on a napkin. Fritters may also be served dusted with icing (confectioner's) sugar and glazed in a hot oven or under a grill (broiler).

banana fritters

Peel some bananas and cut in half lengthways. Macerate for 1 hour in white or dark rum with sugar. Dip in batter and deep-fry in hot oil. Drain and continue as for apricot fritters.

dauphine (or Viennese) fritters

Sift 500 g (1 lb 2 oz, 4½ cups) plain (all-purpose) flour. Set aside three-quarters of the flour, place the remaining quarter in a bowl and make a well in the centre. Put 20 g (⅔ oz) fresh yeast (1½ cakes compressed yeast) in the well and stir with a little warm milk or water. Then add enough warm water so that the mixture can be kneaded into a softish dough. Shape the dough into a ball, make a cross in the top with a knife, cover and leave in a warm place.

Make a well in the remaining flour on the table. Put 4 eggs and 2 tablespoons warm water in the centre of the well and work together to form a dough, pounding it several times. Dissolve 25 g (1 oz, 2 tablespoons) sugar and 15 g (½ oz) salt in a very small quantity of water and add to the dough. Soften 200 g (7 oz, 1 cup) butter and work this into the dough. Then add 2 eggs, one at a time, working the dough continuously. Pound several times, then flatten out on the table and put the yeasted dough in the centre. Mix both doughs together, kneading well. Put in a bowl, cover with a cloth and leave in a warm place to rise for 5–6 hours. Knead the dough again and leave, covered, in a cool place until required.

Divide the dough in half and roll each piece out to a thickness of 5 mm (¼ in). On one half, arrange at regular intervals small blobs of apricot jam, not more than 4 cm (1½ in) in diameter. Moisten the dough around each blob with water and cover with the other piece of dough. Press down well between the jam to stick the dough together and cut with a plain 5 cm (2 in) diameter pastry (cookie) cutter.

Spread a cloth on a plate. Dust with flour and arrange the fritters on the cloth. Allow to rise for 30 minutes and then deep-fry the fritters in oil at 180°C (356°F). When they have puffed and are light golden on one side, turn and cook the other side. Drain the fritters. Arrange on a napkin and dust with icing (confectioner's) sugar.

elderflower fritters with honey

Put 250 g (9 oz, 2¼ cups) plain (all-purpose) flour into a mixing bowl. Make a well in the centre and add 1 teaspoon salt, 4 teaspoons sugar and 4 egg yolks. Very gently incorporate 325 ml (11 fl oz, 1⅓ cups) light beer to make a smooth dough, but without working it. Allow to rest for 1 hour in a cool place. Heat oil in a deep-fryer to 180°C (356°F). Whisk 4 egg whites until stiff and fold into the mixture very carefully. Dip the flowers of 24 racemes of elderflower into the mixture, holding them by the stem. Turn them between the fingers to remove excess dough and fry them head downwards. Drain on paper towels. Sprinkle the fritters with icing (confectioner's) sugar and pour a little acacia honey over them. Serve hot.

fig fritters

Peel and quarter some figs and macerate for 30 minutes in brandy (or liqueur) and sugar. Dip in batter and continue as for apricot fritters.

Nanette fritters

Cut a stale brioche into round slices. Prepare a confectioner's custard (pastry cream) and add to it some chopped crystallized (candied) fruit which has been macerated in kirsch or rum. Spread a little of this mixture on each slice of brioche and sandwich together in pairs. Moisten with a little sugar syrup flavoured with kirsch or rum. Dip in batter and continue as for apricot fritters.

pineapple fritters

Slice a peeled fresh pineapple (or use canned pineapple). Sprinkle the slices with caster (superfine) sugar and kirsch or rum and macerate for 30 minutes. Continue as for apricot fritters.

rice fritters

Prepare a thick rice pudding. Spread in a layer 1.5 cm (½–¾ in) thick and allow to cool completely. Cut into small squares, rectangles or lozenges. Dip in batter and continue as for apricot fritters.

semolina fritters

Add some small raisins soaked in rum to thick semolina pudding and proceed as for rice fritters.

Semolina and rice fritters may also be made of two rounds of the chilled mixture spread with confectioner's custard (pastry cream) and sandwiched tightly together.

other recipes See *bottereaux, bugne, cherry, custard, dampfnudeln date, doughnut, gourd, Mont-Bry.*

FRITTO MISTO An Italian speciality (meaning literally 'fried mixture'), made from an assortment of savoury fritters: sliced chicken, calves' brains or sweetbreads, chicken livers, cauliflower, asparagus tips, artichoke hearts, rice or macaroni croquettes. The ingredients are sometimes marinated, then dipped in a light batter and plunged into very hot deep fat. They are served hot, with lemon quarters, and sometimes accompanied by very small marinated veal escalopes (scallops), coated in breadcrumbs and sautéed in butter. *Fritto misto mare* uses an assortment of seafood and fish.

FRIULI The region is situated in the north of Italy, bordering Austria and Slovenia, and the wines reflect the melange of cultural influences with a wealth of different grape varieties planted. Mainly white wines are produced in a crisp, dry fruity style.

FROG A web-footed amphibian found in damp marshland or alongside ponds and streams. Certain species are edible, but only the leg meat. Frogs' legs were regarded as a tasty dish in the Middle Ages, particularly during Lent. In France two main species are found: the green or common frog, and the rusty or mute frog (so called because the male has no larynx). The green frog has three dark bands on its back and is considered to taste better. The draining of marshlands has considerably reduced its numbers, but it can still be found in the Dombes (hence its fame in Lyonnais gastronomy), in Auvergne, Sologne, Brittany and Alsace. The rusty or mute frog is darker and only approaches the water to mate. It generally inhabits cool places, not necessarily near water. Its flesh is rather less delicate than that of the common frog.

Most of the frogs eaten in France are imported from central Europe and Yugoslavia. They tend to be larger and have more meat than the local species. Frozen frogs' legs, from bullfrogs, are also imported from Cuba or the United States. These are nearly as big as the legs of guinea fowl but they have very little flavour.

The delicate flavour of the meat is enhanced by seasoning, and frogs' legs are often prepared with herbs, garlic and chopped parsley. They are also made into blanquettes, soups, omelettes and mousselines, and can be fried or sautéed. The most highly regarded recipes come from Lyons, Alsace and Poitou. The *Ménagier de Paris* contained recipes for cooking them in soups and in pies.

Frogs' legs are also eaten in Germany and Italy, but they have usually filled the British with disgust. When Escoffier was chef of the Carlton Hotel in London, he managed to have them accepted at the table of the Prince of Wales by calling them *cuisses de nymphes aurore* (legs of the dawn nymphs).

RECIPES

preparation
Skin the frogs by slitting the skin at the neck and pulling it back. Cut the backbone so that the legs are still joined to it and can be cooked in pairs. Cut off the feet. Skewer the legs and soak them in very cold water. Change the water 3 or 4 times over a period of 12 hours, so that the flesh whitens and swells. Dry the legs and cook them according to the recipe. Usually 3 pairs per serving are allowed.

brochettes of frogs' legs
Marinate the frogs' legs for at least 2 hours in a mixture of olive oil, lemon juice, grated garlic, finely chopped parsley and a pinch each of cayenne pepper, powdered bay leaf, salt and pepper. Drain, dry and thread them on to skewers. Fry for 7–10 minutes in the oil in which they were marinated, or grill (broil) them gently for 15–20 minutes. Test with a fork to see if they are cooked. Sprinkle with chopped parsley and serve very hot, garnished with slices of lemon.

fried frogs' legs
Season the prepared frogs' legs with salt and pepper and dip them in flour (or in egg and breadcrumbs). Sauté them in butter or olive oil in a shallow frying pan for 7–10 minutes over a brisk heat. Drain and arrange in a heated serving dish. Sprinkle with chopped parsley and lemon juice. If they were cooked in butter, pour it over them; otherwise use maître d'hôtel butter. Serve with boiled potatoes.

frogs' legs à la lyonnaise
Prepare the frogs' legs and sauté them in butter as for fried frogs' legs. Add 2 tablespoons finely chopped onion to the frying pan and brown the ingredients. (A finely chopped shallot may be added to the onions.) Arrange on a heated serving dish and sprinkle with chopped parsley and vinegar.

frogs' legs à la meunière
Prepare the frogs' legs, season with salt and pepper and dip them in flour. Sauté them in butter for 7–10 minutes over a brisk heat. Place in a timbale dish and sprinkle with chopped parsley. Keep hot. Heat some butter in the sauté pan until it turns brown; add the juice of half a lemon and, if necessary, a little fresh butter. Pour this over the frogs' legs and serve immediately.

frogs' legs with garlic purée and parsley juice
Remove the stalks from 100 g (4 oz, 2 cups) parsley and wash. Cook for 3 minutes in boiling water, leave to cool and then purée in a blender. Poach the cloves of 4 heads of garlic for 2 minutes in boiling water seasoned with salt. Remove the garlic from the water, peel and return to the boiling water to cook for another 7–8 minutes. Repeat 6–7 times until the garlic is soft. Purée the garlic in a blender and put in a casserole with 500 ml (17 fl oz, 2 cups) milk. Season with salt and pepper. Season the frogs' legs with salt and pepper. Heat some olive oil and a knob of butter and fry the frogs' legs for 2–3 minutes until golden. Heat the parsley purée with 100 ml (4 fl oz, 7 tablespoons) water. Drain the frogs' legs on paper towels. Pour the parsley sauce into a warm serving dish. Arrange the garlic purée in the middle and surround with the frogs' legs.

FROMAGE DES PYRENEES Uncooked pressed cow's-milk cheese (50% fat) with a naturally brushed crust, made in Ariège, Béarn and the Basque country. It is drum-shaped, 30 cm (12 in) in diameter and 10 cm (4 in) thick, weighing 3.5–4.5 kg (7¾–10 lb). A supple cheese pricked with little holes, it has a slightly acid taste. Fromage des Pyrenees can also be made from sheep's milk, using the same method.

FROMAGE FRAIS The French term for unripened fresh cheese (see *cheese*). Made from whole or skimmed milk, fromage frais has a thick creamy consistency. Depending on its fat content, it can be rich and creamy or very light and slightly tangy in flavour. It is used in sweet or savoury dishes; in dips and salad dressings; to make coeur a la crème; with fruit or fruit conserves to make simple desserts; or plain as a dessert topping.

FROMAGE GLACÉ A cone-shaped ice cream of the 18th and early 19th centuries. They originally consisted simply of ice cream in various flavours, but later became what we now call bombes. At that time, the name *fromage* (cheese) was used not only for fermented milk products but for all preparations based on milk, cream and sugar, provided they were shaped in a mould: thus, a Bavarian cream was known as a *fromage bavarois*. Grimod de La Reynière stated that it was 'in error that this name is given to all sorts of ice creams made in large quantities in moulds ... Whatever one calls them, however, these fluted iced cheeses are the most beautiful ornamental desserts. They have the advantage over ice creams served in sundae dishes that they keep longer without melting, and they are better than slabs of ice cream because they are softer.'

Among the *fromages glacés* popular during the Second Empire were *fromage à l'italienne* (flavoured with lemon marmalade and orange blossom), *fromage de parmesan* (with cinnamon and cloves, poured into a mould and sprinkled with grated Parmesan) and *fromage à la chantilly* (with whipped cream and citron peel).

FROMENT A French term for various types of wheat – soft, hard and spelt. In cookery, the word *froment* is used in preference to *blé* to avoid any confusion with buckwheat, commonly known as *blé noir* (black wheat). *Fine fleur de froment* (fine wheaten flour) traditionally denotes a superior quality flour used for baking.

FRONSAC Fruity and well-rounded AOC red wine from Libournais. The appellation *canon-fronsac* is limited to the communes of Fronsac and Saint-Michel-de-Fronsac (see *Bordeaux*).

FRONTIGNAN A vin doux naturel (see *vin doux naturel*) made from the Muscat Blanc à Petits Grains grape grown around the town of Frontignan in the Hérault. Very popular at one time as *Frontignac* or *Frontiniac*, it has a minimum alcoholic strength of 15°.

FRONTON AOC red and sometimes rosé, supple, fruity and with little tannin, made from the Négrette grape on a plateau between the Tarn and Garonne rivers.

FROST To shake some ice cubes in an empty glass so that an opaque mist forms on the sides of the glass before a cocktail or a fruit-based spirit is poured in. Alternatively, a glass is frosted by moistening the rim with lemon juice or egg white, then dipping it upside down in caster (superfine) sugar (which may be coloured), chocolate powder or vanilla sugar.

Frosted fruit is whole pieces or clusters of fruit brushed with egg white or lemon juice, then dusted with caster sugar.

FROSTING The American term for icing, used as a noun to describe the mixture applied as a cake covering and filling, and as a verb to describe the process of applying it. Frosting covers soft icings and cake fillings, such as buttercream, chocolate icing, or glacé icing, but not royal icing, which is known by the same name. Outside America, the soft cake covering and filling made by whisking sugar syrup into egg whites is usually called American frosting. The quick version, made by whisking egg whites and sugar over hot water, is seven-minute frosting.

Frosting is also a term for applying a sugar coating to fruit or mint leaves by first brushing them with egg white or water, then sprinkling with caster (superfine) sugar and allowing to set. The rims of drinking glasses are also frosted with sugar for some cocktails. Frosting also describes the way chilled glasses become cloudy when removed from the refrigerator or freezer.

RECIPES

American frosting

Make a sugar syrup using 225 g (8 oz, generous 1 cup) sugar and 5 tablespoons water. Bring to the boil and cook until the syrup reaches 121°C (250°F). Meanwhile, use an electric beater to whisk 2 egg whites and a pinch of cream of tartar until stiff in a heatproof bowl over a saucepan of hot, not boiling, water. Remove the syrup from the heat. Whisking continuously, pour the syrup into the egg whites in a slow, steady steam. Whisk in ½ teaspoon natural vanilla essence (extract). Remove from the heat and cool slightly, then spread the frosting over the cake.

quick frosting

Place 225 g (8 oz, generous 1 cup) caster (superfine) sugar, 3 tablespoons water, 2 egg whites and a pinch of cream of tartar in a heatproof bowl. Using an electric beater, whisk the mixture over a pan of water that is barely simmering, not boiling, for 5 minutes, until the mixture is stiff and white. Do not stop whisking as the mixture will begin to cook on the hot bowl. Remove the bowl from the pan and add ½ teaspoon natural vanilla essence (extract). Whisk for 2 minutes, then use immediately.

FRUIT Botanically speaking, the fruit is the part of the plant that develops from the ovary of the flower and contains the seeds. This definition covers not only the sweet fleshy fruits but also certain vegetables – courgettes (zucchini), aubergines (eggplants), cucumbers – and nuts.

Fruit can be divided into three main groups.
• Fleshy fruits with a high water content (up to 90%). These include citrus fruits, pears, pineapples, apples, peaches, mangoes and strawberries.
• Fleshy fruits with a high sugar content. These include dates and dried fruits.
• Dry fruits with a high fat content and low water content. These include nuts (walnuts, hazelnuts, almonds) and are usually considered in a separate category (see below).

■ **Exotic fruit** The term covers a wide variety of fruit and includes many that are now familiar, such as mango, kiwi, papaya, passion fruit and lychee. Others are still sporadic in availability and not widely used either as dessert fruit or in cooking. These fruit vary widely in appearance, texture,

EXOTIC FRUITS

Ettinger avocado

Hass avocado

pineapple

red banana

banana

apple banana

fresh dates

pomegranate

maracoya

carambola
(star fruit)

mango

custard apple

passion fruit

guava

pitahaya
(dragon fruit)

lychee

kiwano

mangosteen

papaya

pepino

fresh tamarind pods

jujube

tamarillo

ambarella

kiwi fruit

nashi pear

prickly pear

rambutan

Cape gooseberry
(physalis)

flavour and culinary characteristics. Many are characterized by fragrant flesh and a 'scented' flavour – mango, passion fruit and guava are good examples – while others are delicate in flavour but with distinctive texture, such as carambola or star fruit and the crisp nashi pear. The ambarella, and related hog plum and Jamaica plum, are similar in having an aroma that has been compared to that of turpentine. Passion fruit, kiwano and maracoya all contain crunchy edible seeds in a soft juicy pulp; dragon fruit, prickly pear and pomegranate also contain edible seeds. Being comparatively expensive, exotic fruit are not widely used as the main ingredient in set sweet preserves; however, physalis have a good pectin content and they make fragrant, full-flavoured jams and conserves. Exotic fruit are excellent on their own, for flavouring desserts or in fruit salads. The punchy flavour of many of these fruit is also an excellent match for rich savoury foods.

■ **Desserts** Raw fruit for dessert should always be sound and just ripe. Fresh fruit can also be served chilled (pineapple, strawberries), poached in wine (peaches, pears), flamed (bananas), with rice, semolina or soft cheese, in fritters or kebabs, or baked (apples bonne femme, apricot meringue). Fruit is also used for a wide range of mousses, creams, ice creams, sorbets, charlottes, soufflés, jellies, pies and tarts. Finally, diced fruit can be used in omelettes, pancakes and puddings and as a sauce or purée to accompany ice creams and desserts.

■ **Fruit in cookery** Fruit can be used for making jam, marmalade, compotes and jellies, as well as for drinks, either alcoholic (liqueurs, brandies, spirits, wines and cider) or non-alcoholic (fruit juices, syrups). Natural fruit extracts are used in confectionery, baking, dairy products and drinks.

Although fruit is mostly used in sweet preparations, it also goes well with meat, fish, poultry or vegetables. Apart from lemon, the following fruits can be used in cooking: pineapples and bananas with pork and chicken; cranberries and redcurrants with game and turkey; figs with cured ham and partridge; grapefruit with crab and fish; cherries with duck and game; quince with *tajines*; mango with beef; orange with duck and calf's liver; grapes with quail and fish; prunes with rabbit and pork; and apple with black pudding (blood sausage) and red cabbage.

■ **Preserving fruit** Various preservation methods are used for fleshy fruit, depending on the type. Many fruits can be sterilized and then preserved (with or without syrup) in bottles or jars. This method does not alter the vitamin content very much but the mineral content may be affected. Fruits preserved in this way may be used for fruit salads, sundaes and compotes, and in cooked dishes; they are not suitable for jams or ice creams or (except as decoration) for pastries.

Freezing is particularly successful for raspberries, cherries, blueberries and redcurrants, as well as for fruit purées.

Fruits can also be preserved in sugar (see *crystallized fruit*).

• FRUIT IN ALCOHOL Fruit can be preserved in brandy or other alcohol. Examples are morello cherries in marc brandy; bigarreau cherries in Maraschino; prunes and plums in Armagnac; pears in Calvados; grapes in brandy; and tangerines in orange liqueur. They can be used in fruit salads, sundaes and confectionery (sugar-coated and marzipan fruit) and are served after coffee.

• PICKLED FRUIT Small fruits can be bottled in vinegar (spiced with cinnamon, cloves, pepper) and sugar. The fruits most commonly used are cherries (morello cherries or very firm bigarreau cherries), oranges, peaches, grapes, small green melons and green walnuts. Pickled fruits are used to accompany cold and boiled meats, fish and cheese; they are also ingredients of mixed pickles and chutneys.

• DRIED FRUIT Fruit can be dried in the sun or in a very slow oven. Fruits suitable for drying include apples, pears, peaches, dates, apricots, figs and bananas; plums are dried to produce prunes, and grapes to produce raisins, sultanas (golden raisins) and currants (see *dried vine fruits*). Dried fruits retain many of the qualities of fresh fruit, but their energy content is concentrated. They can be eaten on their own as a sweetmeat (see *mendiants*) and are often included in breakfast cereals and health bars. If soaked for a few hours in tea, warm water, fruit juice or alcohol, they can replace fresh fruit in compotes and some desserts; they are also used in baking (fruit cakes, puddings) or flamed (raisins in rum). They can also be used in preparing other dishes (mutton stew with apricots, partridge with figs, various stuffings, rabbit with prunes).

■ **Nuts** These are dry fruits with an edible kernel enclosed in a hard woody shell. Examples are almonds, walnuts, hazelnuts, pistachios, pine nuts, pecans, cashew nuts and peanuts. When roasted and salted, they are eaten as appetizers with apéritifs. They are also used in desserts and confectionery (almond paste, nougat, pralines, flavourings for cream desserts and ice creams), in charcuterie (pistachios), in forcemeats, and in preparing other dishes (almonds with trout, walnuts or pine nuts in mixed salads and sauces).

■ **Sugar-coated and marzipan fruit** Sugar-coated fruits are small fruits (strawberries, blackcurrants, cherries, plums), either fresh or preserved in brandy, which are coated with fondant icing (frosting) or caramel. Marzipan fruits are made from very thick fruit purée or a few drops of edible food colouring mixed with almond paste, moulded into the shape of the fruit.

• CARAMEL-COATED FRUIT The sugar used for the caramel should contain a generous amount of glucose to stop it crystallizing and should be heated to 154°C (310°F), extra-hard crack; the pieces of fruit should be lightly dried with paper towels to remove any excess moisture, placed on a fork or dipping skewer, dipped in the caramel, then placed on an oiled marble slab until cool and set.

• FONDANT-COATED FRUIT Any small fruits preserved in brandy and some fresh fruit, such as strawberries, slices of tangerine, pineapple segments and Cape gooseberries, can be dipped in fondant. Greengages and mirabelle plums are normally blanched and soaked in syrup before being coated. The fondant is flavoured and sometimes coloured: small whole apricots preserved in brandy (the stone is replaced by a ball of almond paste) are coated with pink or white fondant; large blackcurrants are coated with violet fondant flavoured with brandy; cherries in brandy, fresh raspberries and fresh strawberries are all coated with pink fondant. Small green oranges or kumquats are coated with yellow or white fondant, small pears (soaked in brandy flavoured with kirsch and raisins) with orange fondant, and greengages with green fondant flavoured with vanilla or kirsch.

RECIPES

fondant-coated or marquise cherries
Thoroughly drain about 50 cherries (complete with their stalks) preserved in brandy or eau-de-vie. Pat dry, removing any excess liquid. Put 375 g (13 oz) fondant into a small heavy-based saucepan and heat rapidly, adding 4 tablespoons kirsch; mix well with a wooden spatula. When the fondant is liquid, remove from the heat and incorporate 3–4 drops of red food colouring, mixing briskly. Hold each cherry by the stalk and dip it in the fondant; let any excess drip back into the saucepan. Then lay the cherries on a work surface or marble slab sprinkled lightly with icing (confectioner's) sugar to prevent the fruit from sticking. Transfer each cherry to a small paper case.

Alternatively, add colouring to only half the fondant, to give 25 pink and 25 white cherries. (The same method can be used for large blackcurrants preserved in brandy; use pink fondant.)

fruit brochettes en papillotes
Peel some oranges, remove the pith and seeds, and cut the segments into pieces; peel some pears, apples and bananas, cut into cubes or slices and sprinkle with lemon juice; cut some fresh or canned pineapple into cubes. Macerate all these ingredients for 30 minutes with some sugar to taste and a liqueur or spirit (Curaçao, brandy, rum or Grand Marnier), then thread the pieces on to small skewers, mixing the various fruits. Lay each skewer on a piece of lightly buttered foil or greaseproof (wax) paper and dot the fruit with small pieces of butter. Wrap the brochettes in the foil or paper, lay them on the shelf (rack) in a preheated oven at 240°C (474°F, gas 9), and cook for about 15 minutes. Serve the brochettes in their wrapping. To microwave, use buttered greaseproof paper and cook the brochettes for about 3 minutes on full power.

glacé cherries filled with almond paste
Prepare some almond paste with 125 g (4½ oz, 1 cup) ground almonds, 250 g (9 oz, 1 cup) sugar, 4 tablespoons glucose powder, 5 tablespoons water and some kirsch. Split 50 glacé (candied) cherries in half, but without separating the halves completely. Shape the almond paste into small balls and insert one into each cherry. Serve on a tray sprinkled with icing (confectioner's) sugar.

FRUIT GIVRÉ A dessert consisting of a hollowed-out fruit skin filled with ice cream, sorbet or iced soufflé made with the flesh of the fruit. This method is particularly suitable for citrus fruit (such as oranges, lemons or tangerines), pineapple, melon and persimmon.

FRUITIER During the Ancien Régime, the member of the royal household charged with supervising the supply of fruit, as well as tapers and candles.

FRUIT JUICE The liquid extracted from a fruit by pressure or by centrifugal force. Fruit juice is a refreshing drink, often rich in vitamins, which can be drunk plain or diluted with water or soda water (seltzer). Concentrated fruit juices have been developed, either in liquid form or in crystals, which can be diluted to taste. The fruit juices most widely consumed are apple, grape, orange, grapefruit, mango, pineapple and tomato. For fruits that are more fleshy (apricots, mangoes, pears) or more acid (gooseberry, blackcurrant, raspberry) the juices have a larger proportion of added water and sugar.

Fruit juices are used mainly as drinks but they are also used to make ices and sorbets as well as in more general cooking (especially citrus fruits and pineapple). Lemon juice has its special uses. In many diets, natural fruit juices are complemented by vegetable juices, served as non-alcoholic apéritifs (for example, carrot juice, red cabbage juice and spinach juice often mixed together).

RECIPES

fermented cherry juice
Remove the stones (pits) from 1 kg (2¼ lb) red cherries and 100 g (4 oz) black cherries. Press the fruit into a sieve placed over a mixing bowl, crushing them hard; put the crushed pulp in a fruit press to extract all the juice, then add this to the juice in the bowl and leave to ferment at a temperature of 12–15°C (54–59°F), until the juice is no longer cloudy (about 24 hours). Strain through muslin (cheesecloth) or a jelly bag, then add 450 g (1 lb, 2 cups) caster (superfine) sugar to every 600 ml (1 pint, 2½ cups) juice. Stir until dissolved, strain again, bottle and seal.

Raspberry, gooseberry or blackberry fermented juice is prepared in the same way.

fermented quince juice
Proceed as for fermented cherry juice, but grate or finely chop the fruit before crushing it to a pulp.

FRUIT PASTE A confectionery item made with fruit pulp, sugar and pectin. It is prepared in a similar way to jam, but is a much drier mixture. The fruit pulp represents 50% of the finished product (40% for quinces and citrus fruits). In industrially manufactured fruit paste, this pulp usually consists of one-third apricot pulp, one-third apple pulp and one-third pulp of the fruit that gives its name to the paste, usually with a flavouring and sometimes a colouring. The pulp is cooked with sugar, glucose syrup and pectin, then flavoured, coloured and poured into moulds of starch (or on to trays to be cut into shapes later). After 12–24 hours the fruit pastes are turned out, brushed (if they have been moulded in starch) and dried, then rolled in caster (superfine) sugar or icing (confectioner's) sugar. They are stored at a moderate temperature in a slightly humid atmosphere.

Certain French regional specialities have a basis of fruit paste: Vosges 'apricots' (with a filling of kirsch liqueur), Dijon *cassissines* (blackcurrant paste filled with blackcurrant liqueur), Auvergne *guignolettes* (cherry paste filled with a kirsch-soaked cherry) and Dauphiné 'mulberries' (mulberry paste in the shape of a mulberry).

RECIPES

apple paste

Peel and core some good dessert (eating) apples. Put them in a pan with about 750 ml (1¼ pints, 3¼ cups) per 1 kg (2¼ lb) apples and cook, turning them over occasionally with a wooden spoon, until they are soft. Remove the apples and put them in a sieve over a bowl. When they are cold, press them through the sieve and reduce the pulp by half over the heat. Pour the thick pulp into a glazed earthenware dish or a terrine. Make a syrup with the same quantity of sugar, cook it to the 'soft ball' stage, take the pan off the heat and pour in the apple pulp. Stir well over a low heat with the mixture gently bubbling, until the bottom of the pan can be seen. Pour into a mould (as for apricot paste).

apricot paste

Stone (pit) some very ripe apricots, put them in a pan, just cover them with water and bring to the boil. Drain and peel the fruits, then pass them through a vegetable mill. Weigh the pulp obtained. For 1 kg (2¼ lb) pulp, weigh 1.1–1.2 kg (2½–2¾ lb) caster (superfine) sugar. Mix 100 g (4 oz, ½ cup) of this sugar with 60 g (2 oz, ⅓ cup) powdered gelatine. Pour the pulp into a heavy-based saucepan and bring to the boil. Add the sugar–gelatine mixture and bring back to the boil, stirring with a wooden spatula. Pour in half of the remaining sugar and bring back to the boil, then add the rest of the sugar, still stirring. Boil fast for 6–7 minutes.

Lay a sheet of very lightly oiled greaseproof (wax) paper on a marble slab and place on top a rectangular wooden frame, specially for making fruit paste. Pour the paste inside the frame, smooth the surface and leave to cool completely (about 2 hours). Then cut the paste out into squares or rectangles, roll them in caster sugar and store them in an airtight tin, separating the layers with greaseproof paper.

cherry paste

Stalk and stone (pit) the cherries and put them through a vegetable mill. Prepare as for apricot paste but use equal weights of sugar and cherry pulp and 65 g (2½ oz, 2½ tablespoons) powdered gelatine per 1 kg (2¼ lb) pulp.

plum paste

Use ripe plums or greengages and the same procedure as for apricot paste.

quince paste

Peel 1 kg (2¼ lb) quinces, seed and cut into pieces. Put in a saucepan with 150 ml (¼ pint, ⅔ cup) water and cook until the fruit is reduced to a purée. Strain through a vegetable mill using the disc with medium-sized holes. Return the purée to the pan. Add 1.25 kg (2¾ lb) sugar and cook for about 45 minutes, until the mixture comes away from the bottom of the pan. Stir continuously to make sure the mixture does not stick. Pour the mixture into a frame placed on a marble slab coated with granulated sugar. The next day, when the quince paste is very cool, cut into pieces. Dip into granulated sugar and leave to dry.

strawberry paste

Wash and hull the strawberries and put them through a vegetable mill. Use equal weights of sugar and strawberry pulp and 65 g (2½ oz, 2½ tablespoons) gelatine per 1 kg (2¼ lb) pulp. Prepare as for apricot paste but note that the brisk boiling stage should last only 5 minutes.

FRUIT SALAD A dessert consisting of pieces of sliced or chopped fruit or whole small fruit (such as grapes), stoned (pitted) and peeled if necessary, macerated in sugar and often in alcohol (sweet wine or liqueur) and served in a fruit dish. Traditionally a syrup was used to coat the fruit, but fruit salads are often served unsweetened, moistened with fruit juice. The dish is placed on crushed ice or chilled and the fruit salad may be served with cream or ice cream.

The fruit used varies according to the season; sometimes exotic fruits are used, such as lychees, kiwi fruit, mangoes or passion fruit. The fruit can be raw, poached and cooled, or dried, soaked and poached. Canned fruit can also be used (in this case the fruit juice or syrup is used instead of sugar) and crystallized (candied) or dried fruit can be used as decoration.

RECIPES

exotic fruit salad with lime

Peel a very ripe pineapple and dice the flesh. Peel and stone (pit) 3 mangoes; cut the flesh into strips. Peel 3 bananas, slice them and roll (but do not soak) the slices in the juice of a lime. Put all these ingredients in a bowl, sprinkle with 3–4 tablespoons sugar and chill for at least 3 hours before serving.

fruit salad à la maltaise

Macerate an assortment of sliced bananas, stoned (pitted) cherries and cubes of fresh pineapple in a mixture of Curaçao and sugar. Chill. Put a layer of orange-flavoured ice cream in the bottom of a glass fruit bowl; arrange the drained fruit on top. Decorate with whipped cream and peeled orange segments. Alternatively, the ice cream can be omitted and orange juice mixed with Curaçao poured over.

fruit salad à la normande

Peel and core a pineapple and cut the flesh into cubes. Peel and slice some bananas. Peel and core some apples, cut them into cubes and sprinkle with lemon juice. Macerate all the fruit in some Calvados mixed with sugar. Chill. Arrange the fruit in a glass bowl and pour the fruit liquid over it. Cover with single (light) or Chantilly cream.

fruit salad à l'occitanienne

Peel and core some pears, slice thickly and sprinkle with lemon juice. Peel and slice some figs. Peel some large black and white grapes. Arrange the ingredients in layers in a glass bowl, sprinkle with sugar and pour over some Blanquette de Limoux (a sparkling white wine) and a little brandy. Chill for at least 1 hour. Cover with Chantilly cream and decorate with peeled grapes.

fruit salad with gin

Chill 4 shallow glass sundae dishes. Peel 2 pink grapefruit; detach the segments and skin them completely. Peel 2 papayas, remove the seeds and cut the flesh into thin slices. Peel 4 kiwi fruit and slice the flesh. Shell about 20 lychees, removing the stones (pits) if wished, or carefully drain 20 canned lychees.

Remove the dishes from the refrigerator; arrange the grapefruit segments alternately with the slices of papaya, insert slices of kiwi fruit here and there, and arrange the lychees in the centre of each dish. The decoration can be completed with a large raspberry in the middle. Put the filled dishes in the least cold part of the refrigerator.

Squeeze 2 oranges, dissolve 2 tablespoons caster (superfine) sugar in the juice and add 4 tablespoons gin. Just before serving, divide the juice between the dishes. Serve with vanilla-flavoured meringues.

fruit salad with kirsch and Maraschino

Peel 6 peaches, 3 pears and 2 apples and slice thinly; slice 4 bananas and cut 6 apricots into chunks. Mix all the fruit in a bowl; then add 25 g (1 oz) hulled strawberries, 75 g (3 oz) raspberries, and 125 g (4½ oz) seeded white grapes. Sprinkle with 5–6 tablespoons caster (superfine) sugar; pour over 300 ml (½ pint, 1¼ cups) kirsch and 300 ml (½ pint, 1¼ cups) Maraschino. Gently mix the ingredients together. Surround the bowl with crushed ice and leave to macerate for 1 hour. Then pour the contents into a glass fruit bowl, also surrounded by crushed ice. Decorate with about 50 g (2 oz) strawberries, some grapes and 25 blanched and halved almonds.

pear and peach salad with raspberries

Peel 4 pears and 4 peaches, dice the flesh and put in a bowl with the juice of a lemon; sprinkle with 3 tablespoons sugar. Clean 200 g (7 oz, 1½ cups) raspberries, add them to the bowl and chill for at least 3 hours. Just before serving, mix very gently.

salad of Maltese oranges with candied zest

Prepare a syrup with 250 g (9 oz, 1 cup) sugar, 200 ml (7 fl oz, ¾ cup) grenadine syrup, 250 ml (8 fl oz, 1 cup) water and the juice of 1 lemon. Thoroughly wash 3 kg (6½ lb) Maltese oranges. Peel, without removing the white pith from the fruit. Cut the zest into very fine strips. Cook these strips for 1 hour in the syrup which should bubble only lightly. Allow the candied zest to cool in the syrup and set aside in a cool place. Then remove and discard the white pith. Place the orange segments in a salad bowl and pour the syrup on top. Decorate the orange salad with the candied zest and serve immediately.

other recipes See *grapefruit, kiwi fruit, orange.*

FRUIT STONER (PITTER) A special utensil designed to remove the stones (pits) from certain fruits, particularly cherries and olives, without spoiling the flesh. It is a type of pincers with a cup-shaped depression at the end of one arm in which the fruit is held, and a short rod at the end of the other arm that acts as a pusher and inserts itself in the fruit. When the pincers are squeezed together, the stone is pushed out. The stones are removed from olives before stuffing them. A type of cherry stoner with a receptacle for catching the stones is quicker and more efficient to use.

FRUIT STORE On farms or in country houses, a room used for storing fresh fruit, such as apples, pears and quinces after harvesting. The room must be cool and well ventilated with moderate humidity. It is fitted with shelves and grids covered with straw or bracken on which the fruit is laid, ensuring that individual items do not touch. The fruit should be protected from direct sunlight.

FRUMENTY A very old country dish, consisting of a porridge or gruel made from wheat boiled with milk, then sweetened and spiced. Originating in Touraine, it is mentioned as a dessert in *Le Ménagier de Paris* (1383), being made with milk in which almonds have been boiled to give flavour and served either warm and semi-liquid or cold and set.

In the Berry region, frumenty was made with water and served with butter or fresh cream.

FRYING Cooking food in hot fat. Different types of fat may be used, including lard, dripping, butter or oil. Fat can be heated to a far higher temperature than water so this is often a fierce cooking method. The type and amount of fat used depends on the particular method and the result required. The minimum fat can be used to prevent food from sticking to the pan; a shallow layer can be used; or the food can be submerged in fat (see *deep-frying*). When the minimum of fat is used, it may form the base for a sauce or, in the case of butter or olive oil, it may be used to dress the cooked food.

The cooking temperature is important. When fat overheats it burns and develops off-flavours which spoil the food. Not only must the fat be prevented from overheating, but it must be kept hot enough to cook the food quickly and evenly. Food may be fried in small batches rather than all at once, not only because the pan may be too small but also to avoid reducing the temperature of the cooking fat too drastically by adding a large quantity of cold ingredients.

The food is often protected by an outer coating before it is fried. Flour, egg and breadcrumbs or batter are typical. The coating becomes brown and crisp quickly, and helps to prevent the food from absorbing fat; it also retains some moisture in the food and prevents mixtures that are likely to run or disintegrate from falling apart. This is not essential for all foods as some form their own crusts quickly, for example steaks are not coated when cooked in a little fat, and eggs and potatoes quickly form an exterior crust.

The fat is usually heated before the food is added to the pan so that the surface of the food becomes crisp and browns quickly before any juices are released. This produces the characteristic flavour and crisp texture of fried food. If the fat is not hot enough, the fried food will be greasy, especially when deep-frying or cooking in a layer of fat. Pan-frying is an alternative term for shallow frying, usually to describe the method of cooking in the minimum of fat rather than a puddle.

Sautéeing and stir-frying are both methods of frying over high heat, turning or stirring the food constantly. When sautéeing, the food may be moved or tossed by shaking or flipping the pan.

A wide range of foods can be fried, including savoury and sweet items. Fish, poultry, meat and vegetables can all be cooked by this method. Frying is suitable for filo, puff and choux pastries, yeasted doughs and batters. Some sweet biscuits (cookies) are fried. In savoury cooking, frying may be the first stage in the preparation of a dish, especially for onions, garlic and vegetables used to flavour moist dishes. Deep-frying and stir-frying are popular methods for fast-food restaurants and take-away vendors.

When frying is the main cooking method, the high temperature at which the food is cooked produces food with a characteristic full, rich flavour, brown colour and crisp texture. Tart or citrus flavours complement fried foods, so lemon wedges are often served so that their juice can be squeezed over the food.

FRYING PAN (SKILLET) A round or oval shallow pan with a long handle, used for frying or sautéing food. The French word *poêle* comes from the Latin *patella*, meaning a small dish. Meat, fish, vegetables, eggs and various mixtures (croquettes, omelettes, pancakes) may be sautéed or fried. The classic frying pan, made of steel with a matt black finish, is thick and heavy so that it does not buckle and food does not burn. To prevent it from rusting, it must be dried thoroughly after cleaning and lightly oiled using a cloth pad or paper towels.

There is now a wide choice of pans and finishes. Many people prefer lighter pans because they are easier to work with and maintain: pans of glazed aluminium with a ceramic interior are light and good conductors of heat. Stainless steel pans are bad conductors of heat, and must have a copper or aluminium base lining; they also tend to make the food stick. Enamelled cast iron is heavy but can easily be damaged, and only gives moderate results. Aluminium frying pans with a non-stick coating (PTFE) are good conductors of heat, easy to clean and require a minimum of cooking fat, but the non-stick surface is easily scratched and spoilt. The base of such a pan must be strengthened so that it does not buckle. Various non-stick finishes are available, some of very high quality.

The classic frying pan is round, with a slightly raised rim, and is a very versatile utensil, being used for potatoes, omelettes and meat. There are also frying pans designed for a specific use. The trout pan is oval and suitable for cooking fish *à la meunière*. The crêpe pan is round and very shallow so that the pancakes can be turned over easily. The omelette pan is often lined with copper plate and is deeper, enabling the eggs to be cooked evenly throughout; it also has a curved base rim for easily sliding and folding the omelette. The blini pan is similar to the omelette pan but smaller. Chestnuts can be grilled in a special round perforated pan with a very long handle designed for use over hot coals. The chafing dish is an elegant copper pan used especially for flaming food at the table. Finally, there is an electric frying pan with a lid fitted with a safety valve. This can be used for roasting meat or poultry as well as for frying or even for baking.

FUDGE A very soft caramel that melts in the mouth and is not sticky. It originated in the 19th century from an error made during the manufacture of normal toffee, when the sugar recrystallized. It can be flavoured with fruit, nuts, chocolate or coffee, and is cut into squares when cold.

RECIPE

vanilla fudge

Heat 150 g (5 oz) unsweetened condensed milk and 1 vanilla pod (bean) in a large, heavy-based saucepan. Add 400 g (14 oz, 1¾ cups) caster (superfine) sugar, 65 g (2½ oz, 5 tablespoons) butter and 1 teaspoon vinegar. Bring slowly to the boil, stirring all the time. Cover and simmer over a low heat for 2 minutes, then remove the vanilla pod and cook until the mixture starts to form a pliable ball. Place the bottom of the pan in cold water and beat until the mixture thickens, lightens in colour and loses its shine. Pour immediately on to a marble work surface or a greased baking sheet. Smooth over with a rolling-pin and cut the fudge into pieces before it has completely cooled.

FUFU Also called *foufou* or *foutou*, a traditional starchy African savoury pudding or thick porridge. Fufu may be made from vegetables, such as cassava, yam, sweet potato and/or plantain, a flour or meal ground from root vegetables or corn (maize) or rice. The starchy ingredient is cooked in water to make a smooth, thick porridge or mixture as thick as a dough which can be shaped in a dish. Fufu is served as an accompaniment to rich and spicy fish, meat and/or vegetable stews or soups. See *Black Africa*.

FUGU Japanese name for a fish of the *Tetraodontidae* family, also called blowfish or puffer. The species valued in Japan is notorious for its poisonous liver and other innards. The fish has to be prepared with skill to avoid contaminating the edible flesh with poisons from the internal organs. Chefs are specially trained in the preparation of fugu and only those who are qualified are allowed to prepare the fish, which is served in licensed restaurants. The excitement of possibly dicing with death by eating the fish is one of the reasons for its popularity (deaths are occasionally recorded as a result of preparation by unqualified home cooks). Fugu is served as sashimi, cut in fine slices. It is also served, simmered, with tofu and a dipping sauce. The fins are dried, salted and toasted, then used to flavour sake.

There is a related northern swellfish, puffer or blowfish that is not poisonous, found in the North Atlantic.

FULBERT-DUMONTEIL, JEAN CAMILLE French journalist and writer (born Vergt, 1831; died Neuilly-sur-Seine, 1912). He was the author of numerous articles and about 30 books, starting his career with the *Mousquetaire* newspaper (owned by Dumas *père*) and later moving to *Le Figaro*. In 1906 he published a collection of articles on gastronomy entitled *La France gourmande*, which reflect his Belle Époque spirit and love of food. He chose as his coat of arms 'truffles and smiles on a field of roses'. Besides gastronomy, he was passionately interested in zoology and travel, which inspired some flights of lyricism on exotic cookery: 'If I had magic powers, I should like to wave my golden fork over the confined cookery of Europe and enlarge it to infinity; I would like to . . . offer French nationality to the many hardly known but delicious foreign dishes; . . . I would like to put the whole of natural history on the spit, in stews, in fricassées, in court-bouillon, in grills . . .'

FUL MEDAMES Also known as foul medames. The name of the Egyptian national dish, and of the type of bean from which it is made, a bean as old as the Pharaohs. (*Ful* comes from the same root as *fava*.) *Ful* in Egypt also embraces the dried brown broad bean, but the name is specifically identified with a smallish, squat, smooth brown bean, unusual in that the contact point with the pod is on the end (unlike kidney beans, where it is in the middle). In Egypt it is an important source of nutrition in the average diet. It is eaten throughout the Middle East, commonly seasoned with olive oil, garlic and lemon juice, and eaten with *hamine*, eggs and/or bread. Traditionally the beans are long-cooked in a pot buried overnight in the fire ashes (*mudammas* means 'buried'). As such it is Egypt's national breakfast, and an essential mezze.

FUMET A liquid, obtained by reducing a stock or cooking liquid, that is added to a sauce or cooking stock to enhance its flavour or give it extra body. Literally meaning 'aroma', the word *fumet* is used for concentrated mushroom and fish stocks; for meat, poultry and game stocks, the word *fond* is used.
- MUSHROOM FUMET The concentrated cooking liquid obtained by boiling cultivated mushrooms in salted, lemon-flavoured water with butter; it is used to improve the flavour of some sauces and can be kept, in a well-sealed bottle, in the refrigerator or freezer. Truffle fumet can be made by cooking truffle peelings with Madeira and reducing the liquid.
- FISH FUMET Made with fish trimmings and bones, onions, shallots, mushrooms and other flavourings boiled in water and wine (white or red, according to the intended use). It is used for braising or poaching fish and for making sauces to accompany a dish (normande, suprême, white wine).

RECIPES

fish fumet
Crush 2.5 kg (5½ lb) bones and trimmings of white fish (sole, lemon sole, whiting, brill, turbot). Peel and thinly slice 125 g (4½ oz, 1½ cups) onions and shallots; clean and thinly slice 150 g (5 oz, 1⅔ cups) mushrooms or mushroom stalks and trimmings; squeeze the juice from half a lemon; tie 25 g (1 oz) parsley sprigs into a bundle. Put all the ingredients in a saucepan and add a small sprig of thyme, a bay leaf, 1 tablespoon lemon juice and 1 tablespoon coarse sea salt. Moisten with 2.5 litres (4¼ pints, 11 cups) water and 500 ml (17 fl oz, 2 cups) dry white wine (or red for some recipes). Bring to the boil, then skim and boil very gently for 30 minutes. Strain through muslin (cheesecloth) and leave to cool.

mushroom fumet
Bring 500 ml (17 fl oz, 2 cups) water to the boil with 40 g (1½ oz, 3 tablespoons) butter, the juice of half a lemon, and 1 teaspoon salt; add 500 g (1 lb 2 oz) cleaned mushrooms to this mixture and leave

to boil for about 10 minutes. Remove the mushrooms (which can be used as a garnish) and reduce the cooking liquid by half. This fumet will keep in the refrigerator, covered, until required.

FUNGUS, CHINESE The white fungus has a sponge-like texture and is brilliant white in colour. Wood ear (black fungus) is a grey-black curly fungus used in soups or chopped up in spring rolls. It is almost flavourless, but retains its texture after cooking.

FUNNEL A utensil for filling bottles or other containers. Generally conical (oval for brandy), with a long narrow stem, funnels are made of glass, stainless steel, tin plate, enamelled metal or plastic. There is sometimes a tap for controlling the flow. An icing funnel has a wooden stick to control the aperture and is used to pour certain types of confectionery into moulds.

In charcuterie, a type of funnel called an *embossoir*, equipped with a wooden rammer, is used to fill sausage skins.

FUSION COOKING A term used to describe cooking styles making use of techniques, ingredients and seasonings from Asian and Western cuisines for any one dish. Fusion food, the description often applied to the resulting dishes, may consist of European ingredients cut and cooked by a Chinese method, seasoned with Asian or Southeast Asian herbs or spices. Stir-frying and steaming are typical cooking methods; noodles, dim sum wrappers and Chinese pancakes are versatile ingredients; dipping sauces are likely accompaniments; and salads bring together hot and cold, Western and Oriental vegetables or dressings. Fusion cooking reflects the fashion for meals that are light, but satisfying, and full of contrasting flavours and textures. Dishes often have a high proportion of vegetables and a comparatively small amount of fish, meat or poultry, with a small quantity of thin, but full-flavoured sauces and dressings.

FUZZY MELON Also called fuzzy squash or hairy melon, this vegetable is used in Chinese and Asian cooking. This long green squash is covered with short hairs and the peel has to be removed before cooking. The flesh is firm and mild, and it readily takes on the flavour of ingredients with which it is cooked. It is braised with meat or seafood, stir-fried in a variety of Chinese dishes or seasoned with curry spices in Indian dishes.

G

GAILLAC Wine from southwestern France, produced on both banks of the Tarn from some of the oldest vineyards in France.

The appellation Gaillac applies to white, red and rosé wines. White Gaillac can be dry, sweet, sparkling or *perlé* (slightly *pétillant*) and is predominantly made from the Mauzac grape. The spicy, full-bodied red wines are mainly produced from the Duras grape.

GALANGAL A spice from India and the Far East, obtained from rhizomes of two plants in the ginger family, with orange or whitish pulp and a reddish skin. Both resemble ginger in appearance but have a more aromatic and peppery flavour. The more commonly used greater galangal has white flesh, and is used fresh, dried and ground in Indonesian, Malaysian and Thai cooking. The ground form is also known as Laos powder. Lesser galangal is smaller, has reddish skin and orange flesh and a stronger flavour.

GALANTINE A dish made from lean pieces of poultry, game, pork, veal or rabbit, mixed with a forcemeat containing eggs, spices and various other ingredients and pressed into a symmetrical shape. The term is commonly used to described a boned stuffed bird, in which the trimmings and forcemeat are enclosed in the skin and meat. Galantines are cooked in an aspic stock and served cold as an entrée, glazed with aspic (the name comes from the Old French *galantine*, meaning 'jelly').

Galantines are sometimes cooked wrapped in a cloth, which gives them a cylindrical shape; they should then, strictly speaking, be called ballotines. Galantines can also be made with fish; a *soupresse* of fish, which was cooled under a board with a weight on top, was a form of galantine.

RECIPE

galantine of chicken

Cut the wing tips off a 2 kg (4½ lb) chicken. Slit the bird along the back and, with a small, sharp-pointed knife, bone it completely without tearing the flesh. This operation, which at first sight seems awkward, is actually fairly simple: follow the joints of the chicken and work inwards towards the carcass, shaving off the flesh as close to the bone as possible. This separates the carcass from the body of the chicken. Now remove the bones from the legs and wings, still being careful not to tear the skin. Spread out the bird on the table and cut away the breast and the flesh of the thighs and wings, then cut these pieces into squares.

Now prepare the forcemeat: finely mince (grind) 250 g (9 oz, 1 cup) boned loin of pork and 250 g (9 oz, 1 cup) shoulder of veal. Dice 150 g (5 oz, ¾ cup) fat bacon, 150 g (5 oz, ¾ cup) ham, and 150 g (5 oz, ¾ cup) pickled tongue into 1.5 cm (½ in) cubes; mix with the chicken squares, 150 g (5 oz, 1¼ cups) blanched pistachios, the minced meat, 2 beaten eggs, 6 tablespoons brandy, salt, pepper and ½ teaspoon allspice. Wet your hands in order to work this mixture and blend it together. Shape it into a ball, then into a rectangular block.

To prepare the galantine, place the block of forcemeat over the central third of chicken and enclose it by folding over the parts of the chicken skin that project at the sides and ends, stretching it without tearing. Soak a coarse linen cloth in water and wring it out, then spread it flat on the table. Place it so that a flap about 25 cm (10 in) wide hangs over the edge of the table. Place the galantine lengthways on this cloth, about 10 cm (4 in) from the edge of the table and breast upwards. Wrap the galantine in the cloth as tightly as possible. Tie both ends of the cloth securely. Tie the galantine with string in 3 places to keep it in shape.

Prepare an aspic stock with 2 partly boned calf's feet, 500 g (18 oz) fresh pork skin, 2 kg (4½ lb) knuckle of veal, 2 large sliced carrots, a large onion studded with cloves, 2 shredded leeks, a bouquet garni enriched with celery, 5 litres (8½ pints, 5½ quarts) white stock, 400 ml (14 fl oz, 1¾ cups) Madeira (optional), salt and pepper. Cook the stock for 1½ hours, then add the galantine, bring rapidly to the boil and simmer for 2¾–3 hours. Remove the galantine. Let it stand for 15 minutes before unwrapping it. Remove the cloth, rinse in lukewarm water and wring thoroughly. Spread it on the table and carefully wrap the galantine in it as before, taking care to keep the slit part of the chicken underneath. Tie up the galantine. Press it on a slab, covering it with a wooden board with a weight on top. Allow to cool for at least 12 hours; it can be kept for several days if it is stored in a cool place.

The galantine is served garnished with its own clarified aspic jelly.

GALETTE A flat, round cake of variable size. The galette probably dates from the Neolithic era, when thick cereal pastes were cooked by spreading them out on hot stones. In ancient times people made galettes from oats, wheat, rye and even barley, sweetened with honey. Then came the hearth cakes of the Middle Ages and all the regional varieties: the galette of Corrèze, made with walnuts or chestnuts; the galette of Roussillon, made with crystallized (candied) fruits; the marzipan galette of the Nivernais; the curd cheese galette of the Jura; the puff pastry galette of Normandy, filled with jam and fresh cream; the famous galette of Perugia, a delicate yeasted pastry, like brioche, flavoured with lemon rind (zest) and topped with butter and sugar; and, of course, the traditional puff pastry Twelfth Night cake (*galette des Rois* or *gâteau des Rois*).

Galettes are not always sweet. In rural France galettes are traditionally made with potatoes (finely sliced or puréed) or with cereals (maize, millet, oats).

■ **Buckwheat crêpes** In Brittany, Basse-Normandie and the Vendée, galettes are crêpes traditionally made with buckwheat flour. They may be savoury, filled with ham, cheese, an egg, a sausage or grilled (broiled) sardines, or sweet with fruit or a jam filling.

■ **Butter biscuits** The word galette also applies to a small shortbread biscuit (cookie) made with butter, which is a great Breton speciality, and to dry, round, crunchy cakes, sometimes with crimped edges, which are variously flavoured, filled or iced (especially with coffee or chocolate).

RECIPES

galette de plomb
Make a well in 300 g (11 oz, 2¾ cups) sifted plain (all-purpose) flour and add 1 teaspoon caster (superfine) sugar, 2 teaspoons salt dissolved in 1 tablespoon single (light) cream, and 200 g (7 oz, ¾ cup) softened butter cut into small pieces (dot these pieces all over the flour). Mix all the ingredients together with the tips of the fingers. Beat together 1 whole egg and 1 yolk. Add them to the dough and knead towards the centre. If necessary, add another tablespoon of cream. Work the dough into a ball, cover with a cloth and leave to stand for 30 minutes.

Flour the work surface, spread out the dough with the flat of the hand into a rectangle, fold it 3 times upon itself, roll it into a ball again and flatten it into a round shape, 2–3 cm (¾–1¼ in) thick. Place it on a buttered tart dish, trace rosettes on the top with the point of a knife, brush it with beaten egg and bake in a preheated oven at 220°C (425°F, gas 7) for about 30 minutes. Serve lukewarm or cold.

galette fondante
Mix 300 g (11 oz, 2¾ cups) sifted plain (all-purpose) flour with 50 g (2 oz, ¼ cup) softened butter. Add 1 beaten egg and 1 yolk, 6 tablespoons single (light) cream, 20 g (¾ oz, 1½ tablespoons) sugar and a generous pinch of salt. Roll the dough into a ball and leave to stand for 30 minutes. Roll it out and incorporate 200 g (7 oz, ¾ cup) butter, as for puff pastry. Fold and roll the dough a further 4 times, as for puff pastry, allowing it to rest for 10 minutes between the first 2 turns but rolling the final 2 turns without resting. Roll the dough out into a circle and score a lattice pattern on the top with the point of a knife. Brush with beaten egg and bake in a preheated oven at 240°C (475°F, gas 9) until golden brown. Sprinkle the galette with icing (confectioner's) sugar and put it back in the oven for a moment to glaze it.

potato galette
Bake 6 large floury (baking) potatoes in the oven for 45–60 minutes until soft. Cut them open and remove the flesh, then mix 400 g (14 oz, 3¾ cups) of this with 4 egg yolks, added one by one, and 1 teaspoon salt. Soften 150 g (5 oz, ⅔ cup) butter with a spatula and mix it in. Roll the potato dough into a ball and flatten it with the palm of the hand. Shape it into a ball again and repeat the operation twice more. Butter a baking sheet and flatten the dough to form a galette 4 cm (1½ in) thick. Trace a pattern on the top with the point of a knife, brush it with beaten egg, and bake in a preheated oven at 220°C (425°F, gas 7) until golden brown. If the galette is to be served as a dessert, add to the dough 125 g (4½ oz, ½ cup) sugar, orange-flower water and chopped blanched orange and lemon rind (zest).

small orange galettes
Make a well in 250 g (9 oz, 2¼ cups) sifted plain (all-purpose) flour. In the centre place 125 g (4½ oz, ½ cup) sugar, 150 g (5 oz, ⅔ cup) butter, a

pinch of salt, the rind (zest) of 2 oranges rubbed on lumps of sugar and 6 egg yolks. Mix these ingredients together and gradually blend the flour into the mixture. Knead the dough into a ball and allow it to stand for a few hours in a cool place. Roll out the dough to a thickness of about 5 mm (¼ in). Cut it into rounds with a fluted cutter 5–6 cm (2–2½ in) in diameter. Place the galettes on a buttered baking sheet, brush with egg beaten with a pinch of sugar and bake in a preheated oven at 240°C (475°F, gas 9) for about 6 minutes until lightly golden.

Twelfth Night cake

galette des rois Roll out 500 g (18 oz) puff* pastry and cut out 2 circles. Place one on a baking sheet and brush the edge with beaten egg. Mix 100 g (4 oz, ½ cup) softened butter with 100 g (4 oz, ½ cup) sugar, 100 g (4 oz, 1 cup) ground almonds, a few drops of vanilla essence (extract) and 1 tablespoon rum. Mix in 200 g (7 oz) crème pâtissière (see *custard*). Spread the almond mixture on the pastry on the baking sheet, leaving the glazed edge uncovered, and put in a dried bean. Cover with the other circle of pastry and press the edges together, then trim them with a pastry cutter. Brush with beaten egg. Allow to rest for 1 hour in the refrigerator and bake in a preheated oven at 190°C (375°F, gas 5) for 25 minutes.

additional recipe See *crêpe (savoury crêpes).*

GALICIEN A type of sponge cake filled with pistachio-flavoured cream, iced (frosted) green and decorated with finely chopped pistachio nuts. It was apparently created at the old Pâtisserie Frascati in Paris.

RECIPE

galicien

Prepare a round Genoese* sponge cake using 40 g (1½ oz, 3 tablespoons) butter, 3 eggs, 90 g (3½ oz, ½ cup) caster (superfine) sugar, 90 g (3½ oz, scant 1 cup) plain (all-purpose) flour, and a pinch of salt. Slice the cake in half horizontally, then sandwich it back together with a layer of confectioner's custard flavoured with finely chopped pistachio nuts. Spread the cake with apricot jam. Make an icing (frosting) with 3 egg whites, the juice of 1 lemon, 300 g (11 oz, 2¾ cups) icing (confectioner's) sugar, and 3 drops of green colouring. Cover the cake with the icing, decorate with chopped pistachios and keep cool until ready to serve.

GALINGALE A perennial Mediterranean plant that produces scaly brown tubers the size of hazelnuts, the sweet, white, farinaceous pulp of which earned them the French name *amandes de terre* (earth almonds). They may be eaten dry, raw or roasted like chestnuts.

In North Africa the tubers are generally ground and used in forcemeats for poultry, meatballs and spice mixtures.

In Spain the galingale is called *chufa*; grown in the Valencia region, it is used for making a popular drink, *horchata*, which is similar to orgeat. It also yields an oil, which has a lower freezing point than water and which does not turn rancid, and a flour used in confectionery.

GALL BLADDER The organ that stores bile, a greenish, very bitter substance secreted by the liver. When poultry or game birds are drawn, care must be taken not to pierce or break the gall bladder attached to the liver, because the bile is so bitter that it would taint the flesh.

GALLIMAUFRY *galimafrée* In the Middle Ages a dish of finely sliced cooked meat (usually chicken or mutton), fried in lard or goose fat, mixed with finely chopped onions and then moistened with wine and verjuice sauce spiced with ginger. At that time gallimaufry was the feast dish of the people (its name comes from *galer*, to enjoy oneself, and *mafrer*, to eat ravenously). It was only in the 17th century that the word took on the pejorative meaning that it has today: a badly prepared and unappetizing dish.

GAMAY Red grape with white juice, hardy and fertile, mostly grown in Beaujolais, but also in Burgundy, Auvergne, the Loire valley and Savoie-Dauphiné. It is also well established in the United States, Brazil and Austria.

GAME All wild animals and birds that are hunted and those that are or were hunted and now are farmed. The French word comes from the Old French *gibecer* (to hunt), which derives from the Latin *gibbosus* (hunchback). Hunters brought home the game they killed in a bag that they usually carried on their backs. Thus, the hunter's bag was called a *gibecière*, from which it was an obvious step to *gibier* (the contents of the bag).

Hunting was once an important means of providing meat for the table. Today, in industrialized countries, game is only a minor and occasional food, but hunting continues to be enjoyed as a sport.

Game appears on the market only during the open season, when hunting is permitted, unless the animals or birds have been specially bred, as in the case of quails and pheasants, for example. In Britain several birds are protected all year round, including blackbird, bustard, cygnet, heron, lapwing, lark, rail, swan and swift. Other birds and animals, such as crow, beaver and dormouse, are no longer hunted at all, tastes having changed.

■ **Ground and winged game** Game can be divided into two broad categories: ground and winged. Ground game is subdivided into large game (deer, roebuck, wild boar and, in North America, bison) and small game (hare and wild rabbit). The French term *bête fauve* applies specifically to the large herbivorous game (deer of both sexes) as distinct from the *bête noire* (wild boar) and *bête rousse* (fox,

Cooking times for game

	roasted in a preheated oven at 200°C (400°F, gas 6)	casseroled	fried
wild duck	25–30 mins		
pheasant, per 450 g (1 lb)	20–25 mins	30–35 mins	
young partridge	20–30 mins	40 mins	
partridge	20–30 mins	2–2½ hours	
small birds	10–15 mins	15–20 mins	
venison, per 450 g (1 lb)	15–20 mins	1½ hours	noisettes: 2–3 mins each side
young wild boar, per 450 g (1 lb)	12–15 mins	1½–2 hours	cutlets: 3–4 mins each side
hare, per 450 g (1 lb)	15–20 mins	2 hours	
rabbit, per 450 g (1 lb)		45 mins	

badger). Winged game in France includes woodcock, pheasant, hazel grouse, grouse, partridge, partridge poult, rail, wood pigeon, capercaillie and black grouse. Small game birds include lark, garden warbler, thrush, blackbird, ortolan and plover, while water game includes godwit, wild duck, curlew, wild goose, moorhen, teal and lapwing.

■ **Digestibility of game** The way of life and the feeding habits of game are reflected in the texture and flavour of its flesh, which has a strong, fragrant aroma, which becomes stronger with age. The flesh is more compact and almost leathery in old animals, with a strong colour and less fat than other meat.

Before cooking, game meat is generally hung for a certain length of time to allow it to mature, which makes it tender and gives it a stronger flavour (see *hanging*).

The length of time for which the game is left to mature varies according to its age and type: for example, 4 days for a woodcock or a pheasant, 3 for a thrush or a duck, 2 for a hare, and 6–8 days for large game. During the maturing process the flavour and tenderness of the game improves.

Game sold commercially is already matured. When purchasing, it is advisable to choose a young animal or bird that is not 'high'.

■ **Cooking game** The cuts of meat and the culinary methods are the same for large game as for other meat, except that game is often marinated: haunches, saddles and loins are roasted; breasts, shoulders and necks are eaten in ragoûts and civets; noisettes and cutlets are sautéed or grilled (broiled). Winged game is prepared like poultry. Terrines and pâtés can be also made from game. A sweet accompaniment (apples, chestnuts, grapes, red fruits, whortleberries) is sometimes chosen in order to bring out the strong taste of the dark meat, which is often served with highly seasoned sauces (grandveneur, poivrade, Périgueux, Cumberland). Fullbodied wines with a distinct bouquet are usually served with game.

GAMMELÖST A Norwegian semi-soft, yellowish-brown cheese made from cow's or goat's milk. Its rind is brown and becomes darker as it ages. Maturing can take up to 6 months, but Gammelöst, which has a strong, aromatic flavour, can also be eaten after 1 month. It is made in 15 cm (6 in) blocks, either rectangular or cylindrical in shape, depending on whether it is made of goat's or cow's milk.

GANACHE A flavoured cream made with chocolate and fresh cream, sometimes with butter added, used to decorate desserts, to fill cakes or sweets and to make truffles or petits fours. It was created in Paris in about 1850 at the Pâtisserie Siraudin.

RECIPES

ganache

Melt 250 g (9 oz, 9 squares) plain (unsweetened) chocolate over a low heat and add 65–75 g (2½–3 oz, 5–6 tablespoons) unsalted butter. Cool, then fold in whipped cream, either 250 ml (8 fl oz, 1 cup) whipping cream or 200 ml (7 fl oz, ¾ cup) double (heavy) cream whipped with 3 tablespoons milk.

whipped ganache

Bring 100 ml (4 fl oz, ½ cup) double (heavy) cream to the boil. Remove from the heat and add 225 g (8 oz, 8 squares) plain (unsweetened) chocolate, broken into squares. Stir until the chocolate has melted and is thoroughly combined with the cream. Leave until cool, but not set, then whip until pale, thick and light. Alternatively, the cooled, but not whipped, ganache may be stirred and poured over cakes as a chocolate icing (frosting).

GAPERON Also known as Gapron. A cheese from the Auvergne region of France made of skimmed cow's milk or buttermilk (*gape* in the local dialect), shaped like a ball flattened at one end, 9 cm (3½ in) in diameter. The cheese is compressed and flavoured with garlic and pepper, which give it a pronounced flavour, but a strong smell is a sign that it is overripe. The best season for Gaperon is between October and March.

GARAM MASALA A spice mixture used in Indian cookery. The exact mix varies according to the cook's taste and requirements, but mild, warm-flavoured spices are used, typically cardamom, cinnamon, cloves, cumin and black pepper. The whole spices are roasted together before being ground. Because it is roasted, unlike raw spices that are cooked in the first stages of preparation, garam masala is one of the spice mixtures that may be added to dishes in the final stages of cooking or sprinkled over as a final seasoning before serving. The spice mix may be prepared especially for each dish, or a slightly larger quantity can be made and stored in an airtight container.

GARBURE In the Béarn region of France a kind of stew based on vegetable stock, cabbage and *confit d'oie* (preserved goose). However, there are several versions of varying richness, including *briscat* (maize garbure). According to some authors, the word comes from the Spanish *garbías* (ragoût or stew). This etymology is disputed by Simin Palay: 'The root is undoubtedly *garbe* (a sheaf or bunch). And indeed it is a bunch of vegetables which is the very basis of the garbure.'

RECIPE

garbure

(from Simin Palay's recipe) Boil some water in an earthenware pot glazed on the inside (cast-iron or iron pots spoil the delicacy of the flavour). When it is boiling, throw in some potatoes, peeled and cut into thick slices. Add other fresh vegetables in season: haricot (navy) or broad (fava) beans, peas or French (green) beans. Season with salt and pepper. Cayenne may be used in place of white pepper. Flavour with garlic, a sprig of thyme, parsley or fresh marjoram. Leave the stock to cook, making sure that the water is constantly on the boil.

Shred tender green cabbage as finely as possible, cutting across the width of the leaves and removing any tough portions. When the rest of the ingredients are thoroughly cooked, throw the cabbage into the boiling stock. Cover the pot to keep the cabbage leaves green and, 30 minutes before serving, put in a piece of pickled meat, preferably goose (*lou trébuc*); the fat on this will be sufficient. If pickled pork *trébuc* is used, the addition of a little goose fat will enhance the flavour of the stew. Cut stale wholemeal (wholewheat) bread into thin slices and add to the stock and vegetables. The mixture must be thick enough for the ladle to stand up in it when it is set in the centre of the tureen.

It is possible to make a good garbure without *trébuc*, but in that case it is necessary to put a piece of ham bone or a sausage or, at the very least, lean bacon (thin flank) in the cold water. White cabbage may be used instead of green cabbage. For an everyday garbure it is usual to make do with a piece of bacon or ham, or bacon chopped with crushed garlic. According to the time of year, a few slices of swede (rutabaga) or roast chestnuts are added.

If dried beans are used, they have to be cooked in advance and drained after cooking, because their water would destroy the characteristic flavour of the garbure. To thicken the broth, the cooked beans are sometimes crushed and rubbed through a sieve. The meat is served separately from the broth, either by itself or with the vegetables. Some cooks brown the *trébuc* in a pan before putting it in the stock. In this case, some fat must be added, but the fat in which the *trébuc* was browned should not be used.

Simin Palay concludes: 'A good *goudale* is an indispensable complement to every garbure.' (A *goudale* is the broth remaining when the vegetables have been eaten, which is enriched with red or white wine.)

GARDE-MANGER In a classic French kitchen the member of the staff in charge of cold items, hors d'oeuvres, some desserts and all decorative work.

GARFISH *orphie* An elongated sea fish with a long, spear-like snout, which has earned it the nickname of sea-snipe. The garfish has a bluish-green back, a whitish belly and can reach a length of 80 cm (31 in) and a weight of 1.5 kg (3 lb). The flesh has a delicate flavour and is prepared in the same way as conger eel; it can also be fried. Unfortunately, its strong smell and the fact that its bones, green in their natural state, become mauve when cooked are disconcerting to some people.

GARGOTE Originally, a gargote was an inn where it was possible to eat inexpensively. Since the 19th century the word has come to mean any small, cheap, dirty restaurant serving poor quality food, its proprietor being called a *gargotier*. The word appears to come from the Old French *gargate* (throat). R. Dumay, in *Du silex au barbecue*, gives a more amusing etymology: according to him, the word is derived from *cargator*, the cook on board the boats carrying pilgrims to Jerusalem, who were packed together uncomfortably.

GARGOULETTE A porous earthen vessel in which water is cooled by evaporation. The gargoulette usually has a handle and a spout, which makes it possible to drink from it without the vessel touching the drinker's lips.

GARLIC A bulbous plant and, like onions, a member of the *Allium* genus. It probably originated in central Asia and has been known since ancient times for its curative properties. The Greeks and Romans held garlic in high esteem; Hippocrates classified it as a sudorific medicine, stating that garlic was 'hot, laxative and diuretic'. The Crusades helped to make it known in Europe, where it soon took on the role of a panacea, even against the plague and possession by devils. Its culinary use is probably as old as its medicinal use. One of the most widely used medieval sauces was *sauce d'aulx*, in which crushed garlic was mixed either with parsley and sorrel to accompany fish dishes or with vinegar and breadcrumbs to go with grills.

■**Varieties** Garlic is grown and used as a condiment in most parts of the world. The bulb or 'head' of garlic is formed of 12–16 bulblets, commonly called 'cloves', each protected by a parchment-like skin, which is white, violet or reddish according to variety. The most widely used garlic in France, for example, has a white or grey skin and is grown in Provence and southwest France. The smaller variety of garlic cultivated in the Auvergne has a violet- or rose-coloured skin (Billom pink garlic); garlic from the Douai region has a red-brown skin. Garlic from the Charentes is considered to be less pungent, while Spanish garlic, or rocambole, is similar to a shallot. The most widely used garlic in the United States is grown in California.

■**Storing** The bulbs must be thoroughly dry. They can be stored in a cold place (from –0.5 °C to + 1°C, 31–34°F) or at a moderate temperature (18°C, 64°F), either laid out flat or hanging in bunches to improve aeration. If spots appear on them or the cloves become soft, the garlic is no longer usable. In general, white garlic keeps for about 6 months, pink garlic for nearly a year.

■**Use in cooking** Garlic is widely used in all sorts of savoury dishes, both raw and cooked. Raw garlic has a powerful aroma and flavour but this mellows with cooking, becoming quite sweet. (The contrast between raw and cooked onion is similar.) The preparation also influences the flavour: crushed or finely chopped garlic often imparts a stronger flavour than coarsely cut or whole cloves. When garlic is added to a marinade or early in the cooking, its flavour permeates the main ingredients, mingles and, depending on the cooking method, mellows. When it is added during the final stages (for example in a dressing), its flavour can be immediately evident and pronounced.

• Raw garlic may be added as whole peeled, cut or crushed cloves to marinades based on oil, wine, fruit juice or vinegar. It may be crushed and used generously with onions and spices to flavour Indian-style pastes, often with yogurt.

• Oil, vinegar, dressings, dips and Chinese dipping sauces are often flavoured with raw garlic, either crushed, sliced or finely chopped. Aioli is a mayonnaise-style sauce made with raw garlic; pesto is an uncooked sauce of basil, garlic, Parmesan cheese and pine nuts; and tzatziki is a garlic-flavoured dip of cucumber in yogurt.

• Roast meat, particularly lamb, is often flavoured with garlic by inserting slivers of the raw cloves into shallow slits all over the surface of the meat.

• Skinned whole raw cloves may be rubbed on bread (*frottée à l'ail, aillade,* fried *chapons*) or around the sides of a salad bowl or pan.

• Chopped or crushed raw garlic is used to season raw vegetables or to flavour garlic butter.

• Whole heads of garlic may be roasted and served with crusty bread and olive oil: the tender flesh is squeezed from the skin and spread on the bread.

GARLIC

freshly harvested garlic

white garlic

violet-skinned garlic

rose-skinned garlic

Whole cloves can be peeled and roasted with poultry, meat or vegetables.

• Sliced, chopped or crushed garlic is fried in a little oil or butter, on its own or with onions and other flavouring ingredients, in the first stages of cooking many stews, sauces and braised dishes. It is cooked during the first stages of stir-fries or when sautéing ingredients. It may be fried in butter or oil and used as a final dressing on some foods or dishes, for example to finish vegetables, rice or lentils and other pulses.

RECIPES

garlic oil
Blanch and crush garlic cloves, add olive oil and press through a sieve. Alternatively, add grated garlic to olive oil and press through a muslin cloth (cheesecloth). Garlic oil is used to season salads and raw vegetables.

garlic purée
Blanch some garlic cloves, then gently sweat them in butter. Add a few spoonfuls of thick béchamel sauce and either press through a sieve or liquidize in a blender. Garlic purée is used in sauces and stuffings.

garlic stuffing
Crush the yolks of hard-boiled (hard-cooked) eggs in a mortar with an equal quantity of blanched garlic cloves. Add fresh butter (half the volume of

ingredients in the mortar), season with salt and pepper and press through a sieve or crush in a blender. Chopped herbs may also be added. This stuffing is used to garnish cold hors d'oeuvres, to spread on canapés and in various other dressings.

roast garlic

Remove any loose outer layers of papery covering from a large head of garlic and trim off the stalk at the top. Brush with a little oil and wrap in foil. Prepare 1 head for 2 portions. Cook in a preheated oven at 200°C (400°F, gas 6) for 30–40 minutes. Use a sharp knife to slice the head of garlic horizontally in half. Serve with salt, olive oil and warm crusty bread.

GARLIN, GUSTAVE French chef. Born in Tonnerre in 1838, he worked for wealthy private households and said of himself: 'I taught myself in the embassies, in the Senate, in the ministries and in some of the better houses of the Faubourg Saint-Germain.' He is the author of a basic cookery book, published in 1887, *Le Cuisinier moderne, ou les Secrets de l'art culinaire*.

GARNISH A single item or combination of items accompanying a dish. The garnish can be placed around meat, chicken, fish or game, or served separately.

Whether simple or composite, the garnish always blends with the flavour of the basic dish and the sauce (if there is one). The range of garnishes in French cookery is very diverse, although the blending of flavours necessitates the use of certain traditional garnishes (leg of mutton with small kidney beans, poached fish with boiled or steamed potatoes, venison with chestnut purée).

Simple garnishes consist of a single element, usually a vegetable (braised, sautéed, bound with butter, or cooked in cream), rice or pasta.

Composite garnishes are made from several ingredients whose flavours blend both with each other and with the main dish. They consist of ordinary items (such as pieces of bacon, small onions, fresh vegetables, mushrooms prepared in a variety of ways) or more elaborate ingredients (such as cockscombs, crayfish tails, truffles, filled croustades, quenelles, croûtons) depending on the nature of the dish.

The garnish may also be a kind of ragoût, made of a composite salpicon (chicken, calves' sweetbreads, quenelles, mushrooms), blended with brown or white sauce and arranged in small pastry shells.

In all cases, the garnish should be placed around a dish so as to achieve an overall harmony of shapes and colours pleasing to the eye.

Some garnishes were invented by chefs of old (Choron, Foyot, Laguipière); some are dedicated to historical figures (Cavour, Condé, Du Barry, Meyerbeer, Rossini, Talleyrand); some bear the name of the town or region where their main ingredient originates (anversoise, Argenteuil, bordelaise, Clamart, Nantua, Périgueux); while others evoke either the

preparation of which they are part (batelière, commodore, grand veneur) or their own arrangement (bouquetière, jardinière).

GARUM A condiment widely used by the ancient Greeks and Romans, obtained by soaking intestines and pieces of fish in brine with aromatic herbs. (Pissalat from Nice and the Vietnamese *nuoc-mâm* have a similar formula.) According to contemporary writers, the best garum was made in Carthage using mackerel, but it was also made with fry, salmon, sardines and shad, and there were many variants: with wine, vinegar or water, or strongly seasoned with pepper. Garum had a very strong smell and flavour and formed part of most recipes; it was also used as a condiment added at the table.

GASCONY See *page 546*.

GASCONY BUTTER *beurre de gascogne* A mixture of fine melted and seasoned veal fat and puréed blanched garlic cloves. This condiment is badly named since it does not contain butter. It is served with grills, breadcrumbed preparations and boiled vegetables.

GASTRIQUE A reduced mixture of vinegar and sugar used in the preparation of hot sauces accompanying dishes made with fruit (such as duck with orange). Gastrique is prepared by heating the ingredients together (seasoning as necessary) until the liquid has almost entirely evaporated.

GASTRONOME, À LA A term used to describe a dish of pot-roasted stuffed chicken or calves' sweetbreads with small poached truffles, chestnuts and morels in butter, garnished with cockscombs and kidneys. The cooking pot is deglazed with champagne and demi-glace, seasoned with truffle essence and used as a sauce.

The name is also given to a dish of sautéed potatoes accompanied by truffles, attributed to the Marquis of Cussy.

GASTRONOMIC TESTS *éprouvettes gastronomiques* 'Some dishes are of such indisputable excellence that their appearance alone is capable of arousing a level-headed man's degustatory powers. All those who, when presented with such a dish, show neither the rush of desire, nor the radiance of ecstasy, may justly be deemed unworthy of the honours of the sitting, and its related delights.'

This test, described by Brillat-Savarin in Meditation XIII of the *Physiologie du goût*, was intended to identify the true gourmet. However, the test would have to be adapted according to the gourmet's income and social status. Brillat-Savarin, therefore, suggested three series of tests, according to the gourmet's prescribed income (mediocre, comfortable or large). The first was fillet of veal larded with fat bacon and cooked in its own juices, or a dish of garnished sauerkraut, followed by *oeufs à la neige*

Gascony

This French province, which extends from the Landes on the coast to Haute-Garonne and from Gers to Hautes-Pyrénées, enjoys a reputation for good and abundant food, which was recognized by the ancient Romans in their nickname for it: 'the granary of the Gauls'.

■ **Fish and shellfish** There is a wide range of fish: trout from the mountain torrents and the Adour, bonito, carp, gilthead bream, lamprey, elver (young eels), mullet, pike, salmon, sardines, shad and other sea fish on the Landes coast. Shellfish include the oysters Arcachon and Cap Breton.

■ **Poultry and game** Fed on corn (maize), the poultry are one of the glories of the region – especially the geese and ducks. Its game, in addition to the wood pigeons and ortolans of the Landes, includes ducks, larks, thrushes and woodcocks, wild boar in the woods of the Adour and wild goats in the Hautes-Pyrénées.

■ **Fruit and vegetables** A wide variety of fruits (including the grape) and vegetables (the garlic of Beaumont-de-Lomagne is famous for its quality) are grown in Gascony. The cep mushrooms of its woods (*cèpes des Landes*) are much sought after.

Gascony is an attractive agricultural region, where sturdy buildings of honey-coloured stone are surrounded by fields or vineyards. This farm in the vicinity of Cassaigne (Gers) is typical.

■ **Variety and flavour** Gascon cookery, traditionally based on goose fat, pork fat or oil rather than butter, makes good use of garlic, shallots and spices. Highly flavoured, though not to excess, the cookery of this vast region offers a wide variety of dishes. In the Gers, garbure and tourin are prepared; in the Landes, *chaudeau* (hot broth) and bouillon of goose giblets; in Hossegor, fish soup.

The raw hams of the Landes, Dax and Saint-Sever and the sausages of Masseube are well known. The goose and duck foies gras are among the gems of the region, prepared with grapes or made into pâtés and terrines. The flesh of these birds, like pork, is used for making confits (preserves), and their giblets are used in the preparation of *alicot*. Goose intestines, cooked with onions, garlic, blood and wine, make *abignades* (Landes). Pork stewed with haricot beans makes *estouffat*. Other specialities include daubes of beef or goose from Auch and Condom, tripe *à la landaise*, civet of hare in Armagnac, stuffed fowl, leg of lamb *à la gasconnade*, roast lamb from the Landes, wood pigeons, larks or woodcocks cooked in a salmis or roasted, stuffed ortolans (buntings) in Armagnac from Chalosse, matelotes of lampreys and eels, fried elvers and *aillade*. There is also a wide variety of sweets: cruchade, Gascon pastis, *feuillantines* (prune or apple pastries) from the Gers, madeleines from Dax, chocolate from Lourdes, and prunes and fruit in Armagnac.

WINE The local wines are of high quality, the most highly esteemed being Madiran, a full-bodied red country wine. The liqueurs include *eau de noix* (made with walnuts), *eau de coings* (made with quinces) and cassis, but the glory of the province is Armagnac.

Geese roam in semi-freedom on the farms where they are bred until they are four months old, to produce the best foie gras.

(floating islands); the second was leg of salt-meadow lamb *à la provençale* and petits pois, or haunch of venison with chopped gherkin sauce; and the third was a pheasant *à la Sainte-Alliance*, or a seven-pound fowl stuffed with Périgord truffles until quite round.

GASTRONOMY The art of good eating, which Monselet defines as 'the joy of all situations and of all ages'. Derived from the Greek *gastros* (stomach) and *nomos* (law), the word came into general use in France in 1801, the year that *La Gastronomie ou l'Homme des champs à table* by J. Berchoux was published. Two years later, *Le Gastronome à Paris* by Croze Magnan appeared.

In 1835 the Académie Française made the word *gastronomie* official by including it in its dictionary: it therefore rapidly gained currency despite being rather pedantic and unwieldy.

Rabelais introduced the Greek stem word into his play *Pantagruel* through the character of the god Gaster, honoured by gluttons. Various neologisms have been coined from the same model, such as *gastrolâtrie* and *gastromanie*, which designate various degrees of excessive love of eating, and *gastrotechnie*, invented by E. de Pomiane, meaning the science of cooking. But the best verbal invention is attributed to Curnonsky, the founder of the Académie des Gastronomes, who coined the term *gastronomades* to designate tourists who are lovers of regional specialities.

True gastronomes, while appreciating the most refined products of the culinary art, enjoy them in moderation; for their normal fare, they seek out the simplest dishes, which are, however, the most difficult to prepare to perfection. Although they are not themselves practitioners of the culinary art, they know enough of its methods to be able to pass judgement on a dish and to recognize the ingredients of which it is composed. In addition, they are familiar with the history of cooking and food and interested in foreign and exotic dishes.

On the other hand, as J.-F. Revel says in *Un festin en paroles*: 'The gastronome is at the same time inquisitive and timid; he explores faint-heartedly. He spends half his time remembering past satisfactions and the other half sceptically calculating future possibilities.'

Often, however, gastronomy is reduced to following fashion and reflects contemporary social attitudes. In 1925 a well-known journalist, Clément Vautel, wrote a report on 'snobbish gastronomy': 'The curious thing is that snobbish gastronomes look for a traditional classic – even rough and rustic – simplicity. They leave the bourgeois eating swallows' nests in pseudo-Chinese restaurants and go to inns with a Norman décor to enjoy blanquette de veau served unpretentiously by skilled cooks.'

GÂTEAU See *cakes and gâteaux*.

GÂTEAU À LA BROCHE A speciality that is claimed to come from both the Aveyron and the Ariège regions. It is made with a thick, oily paste flavoured with rum or orange-flower water, which is gradually poured over a special rotating spit. The spit rod is a long cone of wood wrapped in oiled paper; the mixture is ladled on to this as it turns slowly in front of a very hot fire. The cake cooks in a series of layers, which are wound in a long, jagged band. When the cake mixture is used up, the cone is carefully withdrawn and the cake is left to cool. It keeps perfectly well for several days.

GÂTE-SAUCE Now synonymous with 'scullion', this term originally designated the *gars de sauce*, the kitchen assistant or cook's boy whose job was to prepare the sauces under the instructions of the sauce chef or head chef.

GÂTIS A speciality of the Rouergue region of France, made of a yeasted dough. It was created in about 1900 in Saint-Affrique by Léonie Cazes. Today the gâtis is made of a ball of brioche dough in the centre of which a mixture of Laguiole and Roquefort or Roquefort and Cantal cheese is inserted; the whole is covered with a slice of Laguiole or Cantal. The brioche is then left to rise, brushed with egg and baked in the oven.

GAUDEBILLAUX An old French dish akin to tripe, which Rabelais describes in *Pantagruel*: 'Gaudebillaux is fatty tripe from coiraux. Coiraux are oxen fattened at the manger and in guimaux meadows. Guimaux meadows are those which have two crops of grass a year.' Rabelais states that this tripe, prepared immediately the ox was slaughtered, did not keep for very long, 'from which it was concluded that people should stuff themselves with it, so as not to waste anything'.

GAUDES A cornmeal porridge that used to be the traditional evening meal in Burgundy, Franche-Comté and Bresse. The word is derived from *gaude*, a plant yielding a yellow dye, which was grown in France in the 19th century. However, some inhabitants of Franche-Comté claim that it comes from the Latin *gaudeamus* (let us rejoice).

Gaudes is served hot in a soup plate or a bowl, and topped up with milk, cream or even wine. Sometimes pieces of larding bacon are added. The thick porridge may also be poured into a large dish, spread out and left to cool. It can then be cut up into pieces, browned in a frying pan in butter and served as a dessert with caster (superfine) sugar, jam or honey.

GAULOISE, À LA The term applied to a number of quite elaborate dishes incorporating cockscombs and kidneys. These include a chicken consommé blended with tapioca and garnished with poached cockscombs and kidneys; soft-boiled (soft-cooked) eggs on croûtons with a salpicon of ham in tomato sauce, garnished with browned kidneys and cockscombs; and a garnish for bouchées or tartlets, made of cockscombs and kidneys with a salpicon of truffles and mushrooms added, thickened with suprême sauce flavoured with Madeira.

However, cockscombs and kidneys are not included in the garnish *à la gauloise* for large braised or poached fish. This consists of barquettes filled with a salpicon of truffles and mushrooms in cream thickened with matelote sauce, and trussed crayfish cooked in court-bouillon.

GAZELLE'S HORN An Oriental crescent-shaped pastry made from two types of paste. One is a mixture of ground almonds, sugar, butter and orange-flower water, which is rolled into small sausage shapes about the size of a finger. The other is a very smooth and elastic dough, which is rolled out to a thickness of 2–3 cm (about 1 in). This dough is cut into 10–12 cm (4–5 in) squares, on each of which is placed an almond-paste sausage, diagonally across. Each square is then rolled into a crescent shape. Gazelles' horns are cooked in a warm oven and sprinkled with icing (confectioner's) sugar.

GAZETIN DU COMESTIBLE A periodical that appeared between January and December 1767, the object of which was to tell its readers how to obtain all the necessary foodstuffs to eat well. Although this forerunner of modern culinary guides ran for only 12 issues, it provides valuable information on the provisioning of Paris in the 18th century and the prices that were charged.

GAZPACHO A Spanish soup, originally a labourers' dish, made with bread and vegetables, including cucumber, tomato, onion and red (bell) pepper. Seasoned with olive oil and garlic and sharpened with vinegar, the soup is served ice cold. It is commonly served with bowls of garnishes, such as chopped black olives, red pepper, hard-boiled (hard-cooked) egg and croûtons rubbed with garlic. Its name, of Arabic origin, means 'soaked bread'. Traditionally prepared in a large clay bowl, which gives it a characteristic taste, gazpacho originally came from Seville but there are numerous variants. In Jerez it is garnished with raw onion rings; in Malaga it is made with veal bouillon and sometimes garnished with grapes and almonds; in Cadiz it is served hot in winter; in Cordoba it is thickened with cream and maize flour (cornmeal); in Segovia it is flavoured with cumin and basil and prepared with a mayonnaise base.

Alice B. Toklas, in her *Cookery Book*, states that a Chilean writer of Catalonian origin, Marta Brunet, describes gazpacho as the meal of the Spanish muleteers, who 'take with them on their travels an earthen dish, garlic, olive oil, tomatoes and cucumbers, as well as some dry bread, which they crumble up. By the side of the road, they crush the garlic between two stones with a little salt, then add some oil. They coat the inside of the dish with this mixture. Then they cut up the cucumbers and tomatoes and place them in the dish in alternate layers with breadcrumbs, finishing with a layer of breadcrumbs

and oil. Having done this, they take a wet cloth, wrap the dish in it and leave it in the sun. The contents are cooked by evaporation and when the cloth is dry, the meal is cooked.'

RECIPES

Seville gazpacho
Put 4 crushed garlic cloves, 1 teaspoon salt, ½ teaspoon ground cayenne and the pulp of 2 crushed medium-sized tomatoes in a bowl. Thoroughly mix these ingredients and add 4 tablespoons olive oil, drop by drop. Then add a Spanish onion cut into slices as thin as tissue paper, a green or red (bell) pepper (cored and diced), a cucumber (peeled, seeded and diced) and 4 tablespoons croûtons. Add 750 ml (1¼ pints, 3¼ cups) water and mix well. Serve chilled.

lobster gazpacho
Peel and slice 100 g (4 oz) cucumber. Wash the white part of 4 leeks and 4 sticks of celery and cut them in julienne strips. Blanch all these vegetables in boiling salted water (5 minutes for the cucumber, 10 minutes for the leeks and celery). Drain, cool under cold water and dry thoroughly. Remove the leaves from a bunch of chervil. Peel, seed and slice 1.5 kg (3¼ lb) tomatoes. Seed and slice 350 g (12 oz) red (bell) peppers. Peel and seed 250 g (9 oz) raw cucumber. Peel and crush 5 garlic cloves. Cook 4 lobsters for 5 minutes in court-bouillon. Shell them, put aside the coral and cut the flesh into slices. Arrange the slices on a large dish.

Liquidize the raw vegetables (tomatoes, peppers, garlic and cucumber) with parsley, salt, pepper and 1 tablespoon vinegar. Put the vegetable purée into a saucepan and bring to the boil to make a bouillon. Separately, bring to the boil 500 ml (17 fl oz, 2 cups) single (light) cream. Mix the vegetable bouillon and cream together, adjust the seasoning and boil the mixture for 2–3 minutes. Take off the heat, blend in the reserved coral and strain. Pour this purée over the lobster slices and leave to cool.

Refrigerate until well chilled before serving. Garnish with the slices of cucumber, the blanched julienne of leeks and celery and the chervil leaves.

GEFILTE FISH A classic Jewish cold fish dish, suitable for the Sabbath, when, according to the strict rules of the religion, cooking is not allowed. Originally a stuffed freshwater fish – pike or carp – with the cooked flesh carefully removed and boned, then combined with matzo meal and seasonings before being stuffed back into the skin and poached. (Gefilte means stuffed in Yiddish.) The modern version differs in that the fish mixture is shaped into small balls or oval cakes, rather than being stuffed back into the skin. The poached fish balls are glazed with a little of the cooking liquor, which sets in the same way as aspic, and are served cold with a beetroot (beet) and horseradish sauce. White sea fish may be used instead of pike or carp.

GELATINE A colourless, odourless substance extracted from the bones and cartilage of animals and from certain algae (agar-agar, alginates). Gelatine can be in the form of powder or translucent leaves. It is soaked in cold water until it swells and is then dissolved either over or with a little boiling water and blended with the mixture for which it is intended. Gelatine is used for making jellies, numerous cold or iced desserts, and for the fining of wines and fruit juices. It is also used in industrial confectionery.

■ **Using gelatine** Leaf gelatine should be soaked in cold water until soft, then drained and dissolved in a measured quantity of hot water, stirring occasionally, until the liquid is clear. Powdered gelatine should be sprinkled evenly over the surface of a small amount of cold water and left, without stirring, until it swells and becomes spongy. Then it should be dissolved over a pan of simmering water until clear.

Adding a small amount of dissolved gelatine to a very cold or chilled liquid or mixture will make it set almost immediately into strings or lumps. Dilute the dissolved gelatine with liquid or a liquid mixture at room temperature before combining it with any chilled mixture or ingredients.

The amount of gelatine to use depends on the set required, which may be soft and slightly creamy or firm enough to support the shape of a moulded mixture. As a guide, 1 sachet powdered gelatine usually contains 7 g (¼ oz), the equivalent of 2¼ teaspoons. This is sufficient to set 600 ml (1 pint, 2½ cups) liquid, giving a soft set. For a firm set – for example to support pieces of fruit in a moulded jelly or terrine – allow 4 teaspoons powdered gelatine to 600 ml (1 pint, 2½ cups). When using leaves, allow 3 leaves to set the equivalent of 7 g (¼ oz) or 2¼ teaspoons powdered gelatine.

GELLING AGENT A food additive used to give a preparation a jelly-like consistency. The main gelling agents are pectins, alginic acid and its derivatives (E400–405), agar-agar, carrageen, starch and carob bean gum, which are used in a variety of products, including flans, ice creams, jams and porridge.

GENDARME A popular French name for pickled herring, referring to the stiffness of the fish when it is dried and smoked.

The name is also given to a small, flat sausage of Swiss origin (called *Landiäger*), which is common in Germany and Austria. Rectangular in shape, it is made of lean beef and pork fat, dried and smoked, and eaten raw or cooked.

GÉNÉPI An alpine species of wormwood, well known for its tonic properties. It is used in the preparation of herb teas and is the main ingredient in a number of plant liqueurs, including the famous *génépi des Alpes*.

GENEVOISE, À LA A term used to describe fish dishes served with genevoise sauce, made of fish fumet, mirepoix and red wine, thickened with butter. Genevoise sauce was originally called *génoise* (Carême's recipe is made with consommé and espagnole sauce), the name being changed to avoid confusion with Genoese sponge cake. Nevertheless, some cookery books still include a 'génoise sauce', made in the same way as genevoise sauce but with white wine. A variant of genevoise sauce, called *gourmet sauce*, includes lobster butter, crayfish tails, quenelles and truffles, and is used to coat slices of eel cooked in court-bouillon.

RECIPES

genevoise sauce

Crush 500 g (18 oz) salmon trimmings. Peel and dice a large carrot and a large onion. Cut 10 parsley sprigs into small pieces. Sauté all these in 15 g (½ oz, 1 tablespoon) butter for 5 minutes over a low heat. Add a sprig of thyme, half a bay leaf, pepper and the fish trimmings. Cook very slowly in a covered saucepan for 15 minutes. Add a bottle of red wine (Chambertin or Côtes-du-Rhône) and a little salt to the pan juice. Boil down slowly for 30–40 minutes. Strain the sauce, then thicken it with 1 tablespoon beurre manié (1 tablespoon anchovy butter may also be stirred in). Adjust the seasoning.

génoise sauce

Pour into a saucepan 250 ml (8 fl oz, 1 cup) red Bordeaux wine. Add 2 tablespoons fines herbes (consisting of mushrooms, truffles, parsley and 2 shallots, all blanched and chopped), a small pinch of *quatre-épices* (a mixture of white peppercorns, nutmeg, cinnamon or ginger and cloves), and a pinch of finely ground pepper. Boil down almost completely, add 2 tablespoons consommé, 250 ml (8 fl oz, 1 cup) espagnole* sauce and 120 ml (4½ fl oz, ½ cup) Bordeaux wine. Boil down to the desired consistency and transfer the sauce to a bain marie. Blend in a little unsalted butter just before serving. (Traditionally, high quality butter from Isigny, Normandy, would be added.)

GENOA CAKE *pain de gênes* A type of rich sponge cake made with ground almonds, not to be confused with Genoese sponge cake. Of varying degrees of lightness, depending on whether or not the beaten egg whites are incorporated separately, Genoa cake is traditionally cooked in a round mould with a fluted edge. It is served plain or with various decorations and fillings.

RECIPE

Genoa cake

Work 125 g (4½ oz, ½ cup) butter into a soft paste with 150 g (5 oz, ⅔ cup) caster (superfine) sugar, then whisk until the mixture becomes white. Blend in 100 g (4 oz, 1 cup) ground almonds, then add 3 eggs, one by one, 40 g (1½ oz, ⅓ cup) cornflour (cornstarch) and a pinch of salt. Work everything well together. Flavour the mixture with 1 tablespoon liqueur (such as Curaçao). Butter a round cake tin (pan), line the bottom with a circle of buttered greaseproof (wax) paper, and pour in the mixture. Bake in a preheated oven at 180°C (350°F, gas 4) for 40 minutes. Turn out immediately on to a wire rack and remove the paper.

GENOESE SPONGE *génoise* A light sponge cake that takes its name from the city of Genoa. Genoese sponge is made of eggs and sugar whisked over heat until thick, then cooled and combined with flour and melted butter. It can be enriched with ground almonds or crystallized (candied) fruits and flavoured with liqueur, the rind (zest) of citrus fruits or vanilla. Genoese sponge (which should not be confused with Genoa cake) differs from ordinary sponge cake in that the eggs are beaten whole, whereas in the latter the yolks and whites are usually beaten separately. Genoese sponge is the basis of many filled cakes. Cut into two or more layers, which may be covered with jam, cream or fruit purée, it is coated, iced (frosted) and decorated as required.

RECIPES

Genoese sponge

Melt 125 g (4½ oz, ½ cup) butter gently without allowing it to become hot. Put 275 g (10 oz, 1⅓ cups) caster (superfine) sugar, 8 beaten eggs, 2 large pinches of salt and 1 teaspoon vanilla sugar into a basin and place it in a tepid bain marie; whisk the mixture until it becomes thick, pale and foamy. Remove from the heat and continue to whisk until it cools down completely. Carefully fold in 250 g (9 oz, 2¼ cups) shifted flour and then trickle in the tepid melted butter at the side of the bowl. Mix in gently until it is evenly blended. Pour this mixture into a large buttered sandwich tin (layer cake pan) and bake in a preheated oven at 200°C (400°F, gas 6) for 10–15 minutes.

apricot Genoese sponge

Bake a Genoese sponge cake. When completely cold, slice it horizontally into 3 layers of equal thickness. Cover each with apricot jam rubbed through a fine sieve, flavoured with a little rum and warmed over a gentle heat. Reassemble the cake. Ice with fondant icing (frosting) and decorate with toasted almonds and crystallized (candied) fruits.

Genoese sponge with coffee filling

Prepare a Genoese sponge cake using half the given quantity and bake it in a large sandwich tin (layer cake pan). Allow it to cool completely. Slice it into 2 layers of equal thickness and cover each layer with coffee butter cream. Reassemble the cake and cover the sides with butter cream. Decorate the top and sides with chopped toasted almonds and pipe a rosette of butter cream on the top.

Genoese sponge with crystallized fruits

Make a Genoese sponge mixture with 125 g (4½ oz, ½ cup) sugar, 4 eggs, a pinch of salt, ½ teaspoon vanilla sugar, 125 g (4½ oz, 1 cup) sifted plain (all-purpose) flour and 100 g (4 oz, ½ cup) butter. Chop up 150 g (5 oz, 1 cup) crystallized (candied) fruits into very small pieces. Roll them in flour, shake in a sieve to remove the excess flour and add to the sponge mix. Pour the mixture into a buttered deep sandwich tin (layer cake pan) or manqué mould and bake in a preheated oven at 200°C (400°F, gas 6) for 25–30 minutes. Make a syrup with 150 g (5 oz, ⅔ cup) sugar and 150 ml (¼ pint, ⅔ cup) water and boil for 4–5 minutes. When cool, add 2½ tablespoons white rum and pour this syrup over the cake while it is still warm.

other recipes See *chocolate, normande.*

GENTIAN A plant from the mountains of Europe, picked especially in the Jura and the Alps. The root is used as a substitute for cinchona. Before the latter was introduced into the Old World (1639), the large yellow gentian (*Gentiana lutea*), the panacea of the mountain dwellers, was prescribed as an infusion or a syrup as a tonic, stimulant and febrifuge. Nowadays it is mainly used for its aperitif and digestive properties. Gentian essence, amber yellow in colour, is an excellent bitter tonic with a strong pungent flavour; it is an ingredient of many aperitifs.

GEORGIA See *opposite page.*

GEORGETTE A name given to various dishes at the end of the 19th century. It was the title of a play by Victorien Sardou, which had a successful run at the Vaudeville Theatre in Paris in 1885. Pommes Georgette, which were served for the first time at the Paillard restaurant near the theatre, are potatoes cooked whole, hollowed out, then stuffed while still hot with a ragoût of crayfish tails *à la Nantua*. Poached or scrambled eggs Georgette are served in potatoes with the same garnish. There is also a Georgette soup: cream of tomato and cream of carrot mixed and blended with *perles du Japon* (tapioca). Finally, crêpes Georgette are sweet pancakes filled with a salpicon of pineapple in rum thickened with apricot jam, sprinkled with sugar and glazed in the oven.

GERBAUDES A traditional festival held at the end of the harvest in the central provinces of France, also called 'Revolle' in Dauphiné and Lyonnais and 'Chien de Moisson' 'Tue-Chien' or 'Chien' in Franche-Comté, Lorraine, Côte-d'Or and Champagne. Elsewhere, there were different festivals to mark the end of other great agricultural events, such as walnut gathering. The common feature of all these festivals was a gargantuan communal meal, accompanied by singing and dancing. Ceremonial dishes were served on these occasions: roast cockerel in Sologne, rabbit *au sang* in Cher and Indre, and tripe in Creuse,

GEORGIA

Bordered by the Black Sea and Turkey to the south, Georgia's cuisine takes advantage of the region's fertile soil and warm, sunny climate, which allows the cultivation of a wide range of fruit and vegetables.

■ **A Mediterranean-style cuisine** The regional dishes are very similar to many of those prepared in other regions around the Mediterranean, such as aubergines (eggplants) cooked in the oven with fried onions and tomatoes (*adjersandal*) and pot-roasted chicken with tomatoes.

Meat, especially mutton and lamb, is cooked on skewers (see *brochettes, shashlyk*) or macerated with spices and garlic, before being dried (see *pastirma*). Meat and meat dishes are traditionally eaten with rice.

The sauces are made with nuts to accompany meat, fish and poultry dishes; with herbs to accompany red kidney beans, which are extremely popular; and with prunes to accompany chicken in aspic.

Other popular specialities are yogurt, *touchouri* (hard cheeses) and *ghomi* (porridge made from maize semolina).

WINE Georgia's winegrowing history dates back to antiquity, the first vines having been planted 7000–5000 BC. Its climate is influenced by the region's proximity to the Black Sea and the Caspian Sea, and it is ideally suited to winegrowing. There are almost a thousand grape varieties in the country, twenty of which are used in the production of wine; the main ones are Chinuri, Gurdzhaani, Murkhranuli, Saperavi, Tasitska, Tsinandali and Tsolikouri.

The two best known winegrowing regions are Khakethia and Imeretia. Winegrowing in Khakethia depends on irrigation, and it produces remarkable wines: fragrant dry whites, aged for three years in oak barrels, and tannin-rich reds with a dark ruby colour, some of which are reminiscent of Burgundies. Imeretia produces red wines (Khvantchkara was Stalin's favourite) and whites, which are named after the grape varieties. There are various sparkling wines made by the classic method.

served with galettes, fritters and *matefaims* (thick pancakes). In Burgundy the meal consisted of char-cuterie meats followed by stuffed mutton with pars-ley, braised shoulder of veal, hot pies, *corniottes au fromage* (triangular cream-cheese pastries) and, varying from village to village, flamusse (sweet fruit omelette), prune galette or brioche. The table was decorated with a sheaf of ears of corn (wheat) tied up with ribbons. The festival expressed people's sat-isfaction at having laid in a sufficient store of food to guard against scarcity in winter.

GERMANY See *page 552.*

GERMINY A soup made with sorrel, which Francis Amunategui called 'a soup fit for the governor of the Bank of France'. Indeed, the soup is attributed to the cook of Charles Gabriel Le Bègue, Count of Germiny and governor of the Bank of France. According to another version, it was created in his honour by the chef of the Café Anglais.

RECIPE

Germiny soup
Wash 300 g (11 oz) sorrel, finely shred into a chiffonnade and soften in butter. Add 1.5 litres (2¾ pints, 6½ cups) beef or chicken consommé. Mix 4–6 egg yolks with 300–500 ml (10–17 fl oz, 1¼–2 cups) single (light) cream. Use this to thicken the soup until the consommé coats the spatula. Do not allow to boil. Add 1 tablespoon chervil leaves and serve with slices of French bread, dried in the oven.

GÉROMÉ A cow's-milk cheese (containing 45–50% fat) made in the Vosges and very similar to Munster.

Its name is that of the town of Gérardmer in local dialect. A soft cheese with a washed reddish rind, it is always ripened. Pliable to the touch, it has a strong smell and a highly seasoned taste; it may be flavoured with caraway seeds. It is marketed in round blocks, 11–20 cm (4½–8 in) in diameter and 2.5–3.5 cm (1–1½ in thick).

GEVREY-CHAMBERTIN Red Burgundy AOC from the Côte de Nuits producing some of Burgundy's best red wine from Pinot Noir grapes. This parish owes its reputation to two top wines, Chambertin and Clos de Bèze, the latter bearing the vineyard name of 'Cham-bertin' before its own. The other great wines in the parish, also of the highest quality, are entitled to put this place name only after their own: Latricières-Chambertin, Mazoyères-Chambertin, Mazis-Chambertin, Charmes-Chambertin, Ruchottes-Chambertin, Griotte-Chambertin and Chapelle-Chambertin. Also of high quality are Gevrey-Chambertin and Gevrey-Cham-bertin-Premier-Cru wines, which are produced mainly in Gevrey-Chambertin but can also come from the vineyards of the adjacent parish of Brochon.

GEWÜRZTRAMINER White Alsace wine made from the spicy (*Gewürz*) Traminer grape and having a very aromatic bouquet. It can make outstanding wines in the special categories of the late pickings in certain years. The Gewürztraminer grape is also grown in Germany, Italy and Austria, and in Califor-nia and some other New World vineyards. The wines are an excellent accompaniment to dishes from Thai-land, China and the Far East.

GHEE Clarified fat, commonly used in Indian cook-ing. An ancient food, it is mentioned in the *Purāna*, a

GERMANY

German cooking is famous for being substantial and served in copious portions; it is less well known for the variety it offers. In cold, damp north Germany, where Dutch, Scandinavian and Polish influences mingle, thick soups, smoked meat and fish are popular. Central Germany is known for the famous 'beer, rye bread and ham' trilogy, but ragoûts, fresh vegetables and Slav pastries are equally appreciated. The cuisine is lighter in the south, particularly in the province of Baden and in the Rhineland, the wine country, where game is predominant. In Bavaria the emphasis is on meats and pâtisserie.

German cooking has an ancient tradition: stuffed roast goose with potatoes and peppered hare are dishes that go back to the time Charlemagne. The princely courts in each state cultivated a taste for haute cuisine, often securing the services of French chefs. There are also time-honoured rustic dishes, such as the popular *Himmel und Erde* (heaven and earth), which is a purée made of potatoes and tart apples, topped with a grilled sausage.

One of the characteristics of German cuisine is its marked emphasis on sweet–savoury combinations, which are evident both in Hamburg's cherry soup and eel soup (with carrots, peas, asparagus, prunes and dried apricots) and in Black Forest saddle of venison, served with apples stuffed with whortleberries.

■ **The land of charcuterie** It is, above all, the products of the pork butcher that have made the gastronomic reputation of the region beyond the Rhine, particularly in Swabia, Westphalia and Bavaria, where the hams are renowned, as they are in Holstein and Saxony. There is an astonishing range of sausages, both hot and cold: sausages for sandwich spreads, made of liver or smoked pork; sausages for grilling, smoked or stuffed with herbs, particularly in Nuremberg; and sausages for poaching, lightly or heavily spiced, including the delicious white *Weisswurst*, made from veal, beef and parsley; the large *Bockwurst*, crunchy and juicy; and, of course, the frankfurter, which is always eaten with a round roll and mustard. There are also the saveloys, brawns (head cheeses) and black puddings (blood sausages). This charcuterie, often served cold, forms the main part of the family dinner.

Other basic foods, such as bread and milk products, are equally varied: quark, a soft, creamy white cheese eaten in great quantities, is mixed with onion, paprika or herbs; hard cheeses contain ham or are smoked; and blue cheeses are eaten with beer. Bread comes in different forms with varying degrees of colour: wholewheat, wheaten or rye bread, flavoured with linseed, sesame or cumin (knackebrot, pumpernickel).

■ **Meat and fish** Meat platters are encountered everywhere, served with the two major condiments of German cuisine – horseradish and onion. Stews and ragoûts are generally well spiced and sometimes cooked with soured (sour) cream; for example, boiled pork knuckle from Berlin, the four-meat ragoût (beef, lamb, pork and veal) of the traditional *Pichelsteiner Fleisch*, and the chine of smoked pork as cooked in Kassel, on a bed of sauerkraut. Also popular are beef paupiettes stuffed with gherkins (sweet dill pickles) in a piquant sauce, meatballs with capers, *Labskaus* and minced (ground) meat as prepared in Berlin or Hamburg (which became the hamburger).

Poultry, particularly chicken, has a prominent place. Birds are spit-roasted by the thousand during the Munich Beer Festival, and in Berlin poultry is cooked in a fricassée with asparagus and mushrooms – a French-inspired dish, imported by the Huguenots. Some places are particularly renowned for their products: Hamburg for its fowls, which are cooked in a ragoût with white wine, mushrooms and oysters or mussels; and its *poussins* (chicks), which are actually tender and tasty spring chickens. Equally famous is the Pomeranian goose, the breasts of which are smoked.

Game provides dishes of a high quality, such as the stuffed pheasant of the Rhine and venison cutlets with mushrooms. Sea fish is predominant in the north, particularly herring, which is prepared in innumerable ways (in a sauce, smoked, marinated, fried, with horseradish, with mustard, with beer or as rollmops), and turbot. Shellfish and oysters are also popular, as are eels, Rhine salmon, pike from the Mosel and trout from the Black Forest, which are cooked *en papillotes*.

■ **Vegetables** Among vegetables, cabbage reigns supreme: white, red or green, it may be served raw or marinated, in salads or as sauerkraut. The potato is equally popular, being prepared with unparalleled ingenuity: as purée, croquette and pancakes, but above all as dumplings, *klösse* and *knödel*, served in a sauce or as a garnish to soup. Some regions are well known for their fresh vegetables: small turnips from Teltow (Berlin), green beans and kidney beans from Westphalia, the Leipzig macédoine (young peas, carrots and asparagus) and asparagus from Brunswick.

■ **Fruit, desserts and baking** The fruit from German orchards, known for their apples and cherries, is often dried or made into a sweet-and-sour conserve. Jellies made from wild berries and the clear eaux-de-vie are excellent.

German pastries, although less distinguished than the Viennese variety, are very popular with the Germans, who eat them at all hours of the day in the *Konditoreien* (tearooms), which are as numerous as the *Bierstuben* (beer bars). There is a vast range of tarts and filled biscuits, as well as Nuremberg gingerbread and marzipan cakes from Lübeck, traditionally eaten at Christmas, and the great classic confections: stollen from Dresden, Black Forest gâteau and *Baumkuchen* from

Berlin (gigantic Christmas cakes in the shape of trees). Almonds, cinnamon, dried fruit, lemon and poppyseeds are popular in homemade pastries.

WINE Wines are mainly produced in the following regions: Ahr, Mittelrhein, Mosel-Saar-Ruwer, Rheingau, Nahe, Rheinhessen, Pfalz/Palatinate, Baden, Franken, Hessische Bergstrasse and Württemberg. The wines are predominantly white, although some light and fruity to full-bodied red wines are produced in the Ahr and Baden regions from Spätburgunder (Pinot Noir), Portugieser and Dornfelder varieties.

In most regions it is the Riesling grape that produces the finest wines. An exception is Franken, where the Sylvaner makes good wines that are very popular in local restaurants. Other substantial plantings are of the Gewürztraminer, Müller-Thurgau, Weisser Burgunder (Pinot Blanc) and Rülander/Grauburgunder (Pinot Gris) varieties, and recently some successful crossings have been achieved, such as Kerner and Scheurebe.

Wines are usually styled dry (trocken), off-dry (halb-trocken) or sweet (süss or lieblich). Sparkling wines known as Sekt are produced either by the traditional (see *méthode champenoise*) or Charmat method. In Württemberg a type of pale rosé called Schillerwein is made, and in Baden one of the local specialities is Weissherbst. The wine quality laws base the quality categories of wine on the ripeness of the grape at the time of picking. Tafelwein is at the basic level, followed by Qualitätswein, which is subdivided into Qualitätswein bestimmter Anbaugebiete (QbA) wines, light fruity wines for everyday drinking, and Qualitätswein mit Prädikat (QmP), which includes the finest wines in Germany. The latter name is divided into six categories, which are, in ascending order of ripeness and with the wines gaining richness and an intensity and concentration of flavour: Kabinett, Spätlese, Auslese, Beerenauslese, Eiswein and Trockenbeerenauslese.

Bottles used for the finer German wines vary somewhat according to the region but, in general, brown glass, flute-shaped bottles are used for Rhine wines and green for those from the Mosel. Flagon-shaped bottles are traditionally used for Sylvaner Franken wines.

A considerable amount of brandy is made in Germany, together with other spirits, which are usually referred to as schnapps.

The wine-producing regions of Germany

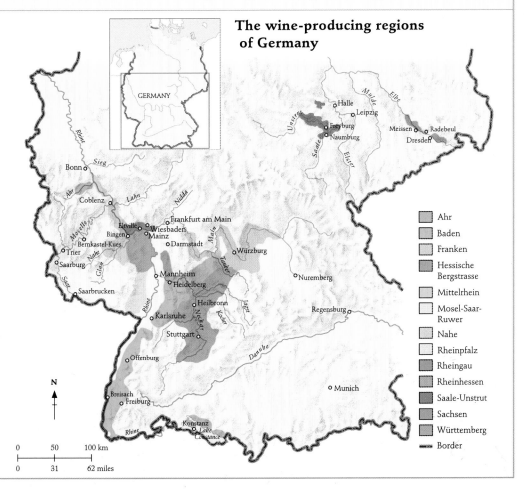

collection of legends, religious precepts and rules for practical living, in which the human body is represented in the form of circles associated with primordial foods: palm sugar, wine, ghee, milk, yogurt and water. The best ghee is made of butter from buffalo's milk (which is twice as rich in fat as cow's milk). It is used as an ingredient in pâtisserie, as a cooking fat and to enrich vegetable purées, rice and dal. Among poorer people ghee is made of seasame oil or mustard. In Nepal it is made of yak's milk.

GHERKIN A variety of cucumber whose small fruits are picked while still unripe, then pickled in vinegar and used as a condiment (the French name *cornichon* means 'little horn'). The tradition of preserving small cucumbers in vinegar is an old one in several countries. In the USA they are known as sweet dill pickles.

In France the plants are grown in open fields, especially in southwestern and central areas, and are harvested from June to September. Traditional varieties include Paris small green, which is prickly and straight, light green, fine and crunchy; picked when 5 cm (2 in) long. Meaux fine is less prickly, longer, darker and more watery; most widely used industrially. Massy green is fairly prickly, long and deep green; particularly suitable for gherkins *à la russe* or sweet-and-sour gherkins.

The fruits are washed, brushed, left to sweat and then plunged into a bath of brine, or they may be placed in wooden vats and sprinkled with salt or rubbed with salt and then immersed in brine. They are then rinsed to get rid of the salt, washed, blanched and covered with spirit vinegar. Finally, they are drained and placed in glass or earthenware jars, where they are steeped in vinegar flavoured according to each manufacturer's particular recipe (with tarragon, pepper, thyme, bay leaves, nasturtium buds or small onions). The best gherkins are pickled in white wine vinegar. Pasteurization has become more common, and this normally produces gherkins that are more crunchy, less salty, less acid and that keep for longer, but with a slight loss in flavour and aroma. Gherkins can be preserved equally well on a domestic scale.

In some countries they are eaten as a vegetable rather than as a condiment. Gherkins *à la russe, à la polonaise* or *à l'allemande* are made according to Russian, Polish or German recipes, respectively. These use large, smooth-skinned gherkins in a sweet-and-sour preparation, only mildly acid and usually not very crunchy. Before being plunged into vinegar, to which sugar is added, they are steeped in brine with herbs, dill and some leaves of oak, blackcurrant or wild cherry.

In France and elsewhere gherkins are used principally as an accompaniment for cold meat and boiled dishes (salt beef, brisket, pastrami and *poule au pot*), pâtés, terrines and other charcuterie, and dishes using aspic. They are an ingredient of some sauces (piquante, charcutière, hachée, ravigote, gribiche, reform) and can be used in mixed salads.

RECIPES

gherkins à la russe

Boil some salted water with caster (superfine) sugar, using 1 tablespoon salt and 1 teaspoon sugar per 1 litre (1¾ pints, 4⅓ cups) water. Allow to cool completely. Wash some large fresh gherkins in warm water and cool them in cold water. Drain and pat dry. Lay them in a jar in layers, separating each layer with a few fragments of fennel sprigs and, if available, a few fresh blackcurrant leaves (taken from the ends of the twigs). Press down well. Fill the jars with salted water (it should completely cover the gherkins) and leave to marinate in a cool place for at least 24 hours before serving.

When preserving these gherkins, they can be sterilized, but they become softer in the process.

gherkins pickled in vinegar (prepared cold)

Prepare and marinate the gherkins with salt as in the previous recipe. Then wash them in vinegared water, wipe them dry one by one and place them in jars. Add peeled white pickling onions, some fragments of bay leaf, sprigs of thyme and tarragon (which have been scalded, cooled and dried), 2–3 cloves, 1–2 small garlic cloves, 1 small chilli, a few black peppercorns and a few coriander seeds. Cover with white vinegar, seal the jars hermetically and store in a cool place. These gherkins can be eaten after 5–6 weeks, but they will improve with time (up to a year).

gherkins pickled in vinegar (prepared hot)

Rub the gherkins with a rough cloth, then place them in a terrine. Add some coarse salt, stir and leave for 24 hours. Remove the gherkins and dry them one by one. Place them in a terrine and cover with boiled white wine vinegar. Marinate for about 12 hours. Strain off the vinegar and add 500 ml (17 fl oz, 2 cups) fresh vinegar to each 3 litres (5 pints, 13 cups) boiled vinegar, bring to the boil and, while still boiling, pour over the gherkins. Repeat the process the next day, then leave to cool completely. Scald some jars with boiling water and let them dry. Lay the gherkins in them in layers, adding seasoning every 2 layers (fragments of bay leaf, sprigs of thyme and tarragon, which have been scalded, cooled and dried, cloves and 1–2 chillies per jar). Cover with vinegar, seal the jars with cork stoppers and store in a cool place.

GIANT GRANADILLO Known as barbadine in Africa, this is a climbing plant originally from South America, introduced to the West Indies in the 19th century. Related to the passion flower, its green ovoid fruits are 20–30 cm (8–12 in) long. When unripe they are used as vegetables in the same way as squashes or vegetable marrow. As they ripen they become yellowish, and their tart, whitish flesh is then used as for passion fruit, for example in the preparation of drinks, jams and sorbets. The bark of the plant is used to make a jelly.

GIBELOTTE A savoury stew of rabbit in white or red wine. The word derives from the Old French *gibelet* (platter of birds), which was prepared in this way. Pieces of rabbit are browned in the fat of blanched and sautéed bacon. They are then floured, put in a cocotte with the bacon, some small onions and a bouquet garni, and moistened with bouillon and wine. Mushrooms are added during cooking, and pounded liver when the rabbit is cooked. In Quebec a *gibelotte* is a ragoût of various vegetables and fish.

GIBLETS The edible inner parts of poultry, including the gizzard, heart, liver and kidneys, plus the external giblets – the head, neck, pinions (wingtips) and feet.

The external giblets of large poultry (chickens, turkeys, geese) can be bought separately in France and are used to make ragoûts, fricassées and pot-au-feu. Giblets are a common ingredient in French home cooking, the internal giblets being used in stuffings, garnishes, terrines, pies and even kebabs or fritters.

■ **Duck and goose giblets** Only the neck, gizzard, liver and heart are used. The feet are not cooked, and the pinions are not separated from the body. *Heart*: simply take it out. *Neck*: cut it off close to the head and the body, then remove the skin. *Liver*: separate it from the entrails, then remove the gall bladder, taking care to cut generously around it in order not to burst the bladder, because the bitter bile would make the liver inedible. *Gizzard*: remove the thick skin with the tip of a sharp knife and use only the two fleshy parts.

■ **Chicken and turkey giblets** These are prepared in the same way, but while the head and feet of the chicken are eaten, only the turkey's pinions, heart, liver, gizzard and neck are used. *Pinions:* separate them from the bird at the first joint and cut them off at the second. *Neck:* slice it off close to the head and body, then remove the skin. *Heart and liver:* prepare these as for duck. *Gizzard:* slit it on the fleshy side without piercing the gravel-sac, which should be thrown away. *Chicken's feet:* cut off the claw-joint, then singe and skin the rest. *Head:* singe the head of a chicken (do not use a turkey's head).

RECIPES

giblets à la bourgeoise

Dice 100 g (4 oz) thick streaky (slab) bacon and blanch for 5 minutes in boiling water. Strain and leave to cool. Prepare 800 g (1¾ lb) turkey or chicken giblets. Peel 100 g (4 oz) small onions, 300 g (11 oz) baby carrots and a garlic clove. Brown the diced bacon in a sauté pan in 25 g (1 oz, 2 tablespoons) butter, lard or goose fat, then strain and remove from the pan. In the same fat cook the onions until golden, strain and remove. Next brown the giblets (except the liver) in the pan, then add the crushed garlic. Stir well, sprinkle on 25 g (1 oz, ¼ cup) flour, and mix in until coloured.

Add 100 ml (4 fl oz, 7 tablespoons) dry white wine and let it reduce for a few minutes. Season lightly and add a bouquet garni, the bacon, onions and carrots, and 1.15 litres (2 pints, 5 cups) water or poultry stock to cover the giblets. Cover and bring to the boil, then reduce heat and simmer for about 30 minutes. Add the liver and stir gently, then continue cooking for about 10 more minutes until the liver is cooked. Place the giblets and vegetables in a shallow dish and pour the sauce over.

giblets à la bourguignonne

Prepare as for giblets à *la bourgeoise* but replace the carrots by 100 g (4 oz, 2 cups) button mushrooms and the white wine by red Burgundy.

other recipes See *bouillon, consommé, pinion.*

GIGONDAS Red or rosé AOC wine from vineyards at the foot of the Dentelles de Montmirail in the Rhône valley. The red wines, produced mainly from Grenache, Syrah, Mourvèdre and Cinsaut grapes, are powerful, spicy and tannic, and the best can be bottle-aged for at least ten years. Rosés, however, are usually drunk young.

GIGOT A French cut of meat corresponding to a leg of mutton or lamb. The name derives from the word for an ancient musical instrument (*gigue*), which had the same shape. The whole gigot (haunch or long leg) consists of the actual leg itself (or *gigot raccourci*, short leg) and the muscles extending from it, which form the French cut *quasi* or *selle de gigot* (chump end – not to be confused with the English saddle). The two pieces can be cut and cooked separately: the chump end, tied up with string, can be a very fine roast, whereas the short leg may be roasted, boiled, pot-roasted, braised or even sliced and grilled (broiled). By steeping a short leg of mutton in a marinade before cooking in the oven, it is transformed into *gigot chasseur*, tasting of venison. The flavour of lamb combines well with garlic, and roast gigot of lamb studded with garlic and garnished with kidney beans is the French traditional dish for family celebrations and special meals. The leg can also be cooked with white wine, bacon and onions with juniper berries, garnished with red cabbage; or with caper sauce, garnished with steamed potatoes and turnips. Other recipes include brochettes *à la turque* (lamb on skewers) and daubes or braised dishes, such as the famous *gigot de sept heures* or *à la cuiller*, which is cooked for a long time over a very gentle heat, so it can be cut with a spoon, and served with the braising liquor strained and boiled down. Gigot of lamb can also be served cold with aïoli, in aspic with a green salad or with a spicy tomato salsa.

Leg of lamb is carved either parallel to the bone (the slices are all equally cooked) or perpendicular to the bone, slightly on the slant (the meat is more tender, but cooking is graduated). Lamb cooked in

Carving a gigot or leg of lamb

1 *Hold the bone. Cut off the gristle and meat around the top end of the bone. Discard the gristle, then cut the meat into small, neat slices.*

2 *Rest the leg on the meaty side and slice the shallow area of meat from the underside parallel with, and down as far as, the bone.*

3 *Make a cut – not too deep – on each side of the bone using a filleting knife. These cuts are made to loosen the meat from the bone so that it can be carved more easily into neat slices.*

4 *Turn the meaty side uppermost. Carve the meat at right angles to the bone. Some professionals prefer to slice the main portion of meat before trimming the underside and loosening the meat from the bone.*

the French style is generally pink in the centre, hence the cooking graduation.

Manche de gigot ('handle' of leg of lamb) is the name given to the knuckle bone, which is traditionally decorated with a paper frill for presentation purposes and to which can be attached the *manche à gigot* (meat-carving tongs), a utensil for keeping the piece of meat steady while it is carved.

By analogy, the word *gigot* is also used for the drumstick and leg of a turkey or a chicken, tied together (and possibly stuffed) for roasting or braising. The term is also applied to monkfish braised with tomato and white wine.

RECIPES

boiled leg of lamb with caper sauce

This classic British dish was traditionally prepared with mutton. The meat must be cooked gently so that it becomes tender and succulent. Season a trimmed leg of lamb, wrap in a buttered and lightly floured muslin cloth (cheesecloth) and tie up with string. Put it into a pan of boiling salted water, together with 2 carrots cut into quarters, 2 onions (one studded with a clove), a bouquet garni and a

garlic clove. Simmer gently but steadily, allowing 30 minutes per 1 kg (15 minutes per 1 lb) or until tender and cooked through. Drain, unwrap and place on a long serving dish.

For the sauce, prepare a roux with 40 g (1½ oz, 3 tablespoons) butter and 40 g (1½ oz, 6 tablespoons) plain (all-purpose) flour. Gradually stir in 300 ml (½ pint, 1¼ cups) milk and 300 ml (½ pint, 1¼ cups) cooking stock from the lamb. Bring to the boil, then simmer for 3 minutes. Stir in 4 tablespoons capers and seasoning to taste. This dish may be accompanied by a purée of turnips or celeriac (celery root), cooked with the leg of mutton, potatoes or white haricot (navy) beans. Broad beans are also a delicious accompaniment.

In Provence leg of lamb is boiled in a reduced stock. The meat is served pink with the pot vegetables and aïoli. In Normandy, near Yvetot, leg of lamb is cooked in a vegetable stock flavoured with a tablespoon of Calvados. It is served with pot vegetables and a white sauce with capers.

Braised leg of lamb with spring onions, see page 558.

braised leg of lamb à la bordelaise

Cook a leg of lamb in a mixture of butter and oil in a covered casserole in a preheated oven at 180°C (350°F, gas 4), allowing 40 minutes per 1 kg or 20 minutes per 1 lb, plus an additional 40 or 20 minutes. When one-third done, add 575 g (1¼ lb) tiny potato balls and 250 g (9 oz) fresh cep or button mushrooms, lightly tossed in oil. Season. When the leg and garnish are cooked, sprinkle with noisette butter in which 4 tablespoons breadcrumbs and 1 tablespoon chopped parsley and garlic have been fried.

braised leg of lamb with spring onions ♦

Calculate the cooking time for a leg of lamb at 40 minutes per 1 kg, 20 minutes per 1 lb, plus an additional 40 or 20 minutes. Cook the lamb in a covered flameproof casserole in a preheated oven at 200°C (400°F, gas 6) for 25 minutes, then drain. Melt some butter in the casserole. Lightly coat 1 kg (2¼ lb) spring onions (scallions) in sugar, then fry them in the butter. Place the leg of lamb on the onions and put the casserole back in the oven. When the onions have softened, add 2 tomatoes, peeled and cut into 8 pieces, and 500 ml (17 fl oz, 2 cups) white wine. Complete the cooking process, turning the leg to make sure it is browned all over and basting it as required with reduced beef stock.

Remove the leg of lamb from the casserole, draining off all the cooking liquor. Drain the spring onions. Cover both and keep hot. Thicken the cooking juices with beurre manié. Carve the lamb. Arrange the spring onions on plates and coat with the sauce. Arrange the lamb on the plates and serve.

Léa's roast leg of lamb

Crush 4 anchovy fillets in 4 tablespoons olive oil mixed with 2 level tablespoons mustard, sage, basil, rosemary and crushed garlic. Rub the meat with this mixture and marinate for 2 hours, turning from time to time. Calculate the cooking time for the lamb at 30–40 minutes per 1 kg, 15–20 minutes per 1 lb, plus an additional 30–40 or 15–20 minutes, according to how well cooked you require the meat to be when served. Drain and roast in a preheated oven at 200°C (400°F, gas 6).

While the meat is cooking, boil down the marinade with some butter, gradually adding half a bottle of champagne. Strain and thicken with softened butter.

roast leg of lamb

Stud the leg near the projecting bones with 2–3 cloves of garlic. Cook it on a spit or in a preheated oven at 220°C (425°F, gas 7), allowing 20–22 minutes per 1 kg (9–10 minutes per 1 lb). Place it on a long serving dish and serve with a sauce made from the cooking juices, kept quite fatty, with slices of lemon and chopped watercress. Roast leg of lamb is accompanied by French (green) beans in butter, white haricot (navy) beans in juice, or vegetables prepared à la jardinière or as a purée.

This is the French method for roasting lamb, and the flesh will be pink. For fully cooked meat, reduce the oven temperature to 190°C (375°F, gas 5) when placing the joint in the oven and allow 45 minutes per 1 kg (20 minutes per 1 lb) and add 20 minutes to the total time.

roast leg of lamb en chevreuil

Completely skin a very fresh leg of lamb and lard with lardons. Then put it in a special marinade; see chevreuil, en. Leave it to steep for some time, depending on the tenderness of the meat and the temperature (2 days in summer, 3–4 days in winter). Dry the leg with a cloth, then roast. Serve a roebuck sauce or a poivrade sauce separately.

roast leg of lamb with 40 cloves of garlic

Desalt some anchovy fillets. Trim a leg of lamb as necessary. Stud it with slivers of garlic (2–3 cloves) and the anchovy fillets cut into fragments. Brush with a mixture of oil, thyme, powdered rosemary and pepper. Roast on a spit or in the oven as for roast leg of lamb, basting occasionally with a little of the herbs and oil. As the meat starts to cook, put 250 g (9 oz) unpeeled garlic cloves into boiling water. After boiling for 5 minutes, drain the garlic and put into a saucepan with 200 ml (7 fl oz, ¾ cup) stock. Simmer for 20 minutes. Add a small cup of this liquor to the meat juices and pour over the meat. While completing the cooking, wash some watercress thoroughly in running water and chop coarsely. Arrange the leg on a serving dish, surrounded by the cloves of garlic and chopped watercress. Serve the juice in a sauceboat.

spit-roast leg of lamb with parsley

Spit-roast a leg of lamb. Before cooking is completed, cover it evenly with a layer of fresh breadcrumbs mixed with chopped parsley and possibly some chopped garlic. Finish cooking the lamb until the surface turns golden brown. Put it on a long serving dish and garnish with chopped watercress and halved lemons. Serve the juice separately.

GIGUE Haunch of roebuck or deer, also called *cuissot* in French. Once the sinews are drawn, a haunch is usually studded with lardons, marinated if necessary, then roasted in a preheated oven at 200°C (400°F, gas 6). Allow 30 minutes per 1 kg, 15–18 minutes per 1 lb. Celery or chestnut purée, mushroom fricassee and red- or whitecurrant jelly are the conventional garnishes.

GILBERT, PHILÉAS French cook (born La Chapelle-sur-Dreuse, 1857; died Couilly-Pont-aux-Dames, 1942). After an apprenticeship as a cook/pastrycook in Sens, he travelled around France, working with Escoffier, Émile Bernard, Ozanne and Montagné. He became a great practitioner, theoretician and scholar. The author of numerous books, including *La Cuisine rétrospective*, *La Cuisine de tous les mois* and *L'Alimentation et la Technique culi-*

naire à travers les âges, he collaborated in the writing of Escoffier's *Guide culinaire*. He also wrote numerous articles in professional magazines and cookery journals, becoming known for raging controversies with his colleagues.

GILLIERS The official chef of King Stanislas Leszczyński. In 1751 he published *Le Cannaméliste français* (*cannaméliste* comes from *cannamelle* or *canne à miel*, an old French term for sugar cane). This is a valuable document both for its history of *friandises* (sweet delicacies) and for its illustrations by Dupuis, engraved by Lotha, which depicted the masterpieces of 18th-century glassware and goldsmiths' work.

GIMBLETTE A small ring biscuit (cookie) in the shape of a crown, a speciality of Albi. The word seems to come from the Italian *ciambella* (a ring-shaped cake similar to an *échaudé*). The dough – made from flour, ground almonds, sugar, egg yolks, yeast and grated citron, orange and lemon rind (zest) – is not the same as that for *échaudés*, but the cooking principle is the same: the biscuits are first immersed in boiling water, then drained, dried and browned in the oven. Fernand Molinier, a pastrycook in Albi and author of *Recherches historiques sur les spécialités gourmandes du Tarn*, thinks that gimblettes were invented by the monks of Nanterre, who entrusted the recipe to the canons of Albi in the 15th century.

RECIPE

orange gimblettes
Grate the rind (zest) of half an orange on a lump of sugar; crush the sugar to a fine powder and mix it with caster (superfine) sugar so that the whole amount measures 175 g (6 oz, ¾ cup). Pound thoroughly 100 g (4 oz, ⅔ cup) fresh almonds. Place 225 g (8 oz, 2 cups) sifted plain (all-purpose) flour in a circle around this mixture, and in the centre put 15 g (½ oz, 1 cake) fresh yeast dissolved in 70 ml (2½ fl oz, ¼ cup) milk. Add 50 g (2 oz, 4 tablespoons) butter, 2 egg yolks, a pinch of salt, the almonds and the orange-flavoured sugar. Knead all these ingredients in the usual way and leave the dough in a warm place for 5–6 hours to allow the yeast to ferment.

Knock back the dough and divide it into 5–6 strips, each the width of a little finger. Cut the strips diagonally into pieces 13 cm (5 in) long. Make these into little rings so that the joins are invisible. Drop the rings into a large saucepan of boiling water. Stir gently with a spatula for a few minutes to prevent the rings from sticking and to bring them to the surface. Drain them and drop them into cool water. When cold, drain again, then toss to dry them.

Dip each ring in a little beaten egg (2 eggs should be used in all) 2–3 times. Leave them to drain for a few minutes. Arrange them carefully on 3 lightly greased baking sheets and bake them in a preheated oven at 200°C (400°F, gas 6) for 20–30 minutes, until they are a good colour.

Little plaited biscuits (cookies) or little rolls about as long as a thumb can also be made this way. These gimblettes may also be flavoured with the rind (zest) of lemon, citron or Seville (bitter) orange, or with aniseed, vanilla or orange-flower water.

GIN Pure alcohol, distilled usually from grain, into which are infused aromatic plant products, particularly oil of juniper. The two basic types are Dutch and British. Dutch gin (genever), directly stemming from medicinal compounds evolved in the Netherlands in the 16th century, is heavily aromatic; it is usually drunk chilled and neat. Dry gin, the universal style, originated in London in the 1870s. Much lighter and more popular than the older genever, it is essentially a versatile mixing spirit – with tonic water, juices and in numerous cocktails. Dry gin is made in many countries, with many premier brands carrying English names. Flavoured gins have declined, but sloe gin is still popular in Britain and the United States. Gin's culinary uses are confined mainly to offal and game dishes.

GINGER A plant of South-east Asian origin that is cultivated in hot countries for its spicy, aromatic rhizomes (underground stems), which are used fresh, preserved in sugar or powdered. Widely appreciated in the Middle Ages, ginger was used as a flavouring and as a sweetmeat. Since the 18th century it has fallen out of use in classic European cookery, except in pâtisserie and confectionery, biscuits (cookies), cakes, pickles and jams, particularly in Britain, Alsace and the Netherlands, and for flavouring drinks. However, it continues to be an important seasoning in eastern cookery – fresh or dried, grated or preserved in sugar, syrup or vinegar. In India and Pakistan it is used to flavour curries, meat, fish in sauce, rice and vegetable purées, and to flavour tea. In China and Japan it is widely used fresh, shredded in court-bouillon, marinades and soups. It is an essential seasoning for fish and whale fillets. It is also eaten pickled between courses. In South-east Asia crystallized (candied) ginger is the most widespread sweetmeat.

RECIPE

ginger cake
Cut 100 g (4 oz, ½ cup) preserved ginger into very small cubes. Soften 100 g (4 oz, ½ cup) butter with a wooden spatula. Vigorously whisk together 3 large eggs, 1 tablespoon rum and 2 tablespoons hot water. When the mixture is thick and foamy, gradually add 175 g (6 oz, ¾ cup) caster (superfine) sugar, continuing to whisk. Sift together 250 g (9 oz, 2 cups) plain (all-purpose) flour and 2 teaspoons baking powder, make a well in the middle and blend in the beaten eggs, the softened butter and the ginger. Mix well and pour into a buttered manqué

mould or deep sandwich tin (layer cake pan) 22 cm (8¾ in) in diameter. Bake in a preheated oven at 220°C (425°F, gas 7) for about 40 minutes.

GINGER ALE Aerated water to which colouring and ginger essence are added, often used to make gin or whisky into a long drink.

GINGER BEER A fizzy soft drink, traditionally widely consumed during summer months in Britain. One traditional method of making home-made ginger beer is from a ginger beer 'plant', by fermenting ground ginger and sugar with yeast in a small amount of liquid for about a week. Sugar is added daily to 'feed' the plant. At the end of this fermentation, the plant is strained and the liquid diluted with lemon juice, water and sugar, then bottled. The bottles have to be stored with their caps loose initially, then, when fermentation has subsided, the caps are tightened and the bottles stored in a cool place. The result is a bubbly, spicy, lemon drink.

GINGERBREAD British gingerbread is a cake flavoured with ginger and treacle (molasses). The French equivalent (*pain d'épice*), whose name means literally 'spice bread', is a cake with a basis of flour, honey and spices (it need not contain ginger). The use of honey as the only sweetening product for breads or cakes goes back to ancient times. Aristophanes mentions *melitunta*, which was made with sesame flour, eggs and fresh cheese, and coated generously with honey after cooking. The Romans prepared *panis mellitus* with German wheat flour, honey, pepper and dried fruit. The Chinese *mikong* (honey bread) is mentioned as part of the rations of the horsemen of Genghis Khan. It is generally believed that gingerbread was introduced to Europe during the time of the Crusades. At Pithiviers, however, it is held that gingerbread was introduced into the city by St Gregory, an Armenian bishop who took refuge there in the 11th century. Whatever the case, it was from that time that the manufacture of gingerbread spread into the Netherlands, Britain, Germany, Belgium, France and Italy.

The guild of *pain d'épiciers*, founded at Reims, was officially recognized by Henri IV in 1596. According to A. Sloïmovici in *Ethnocuisine de la Bourgogne* (1973), *pain d'épice* 'was the monopoly of the city of Reims, and at first manufactured exclusively with rye flour. In Burgundy, however, the *boichet* or *boichée*, made with wheat flour, honey and leaven, had been known since the 14th century, and *gaulderye* bread, made of honey and millet flour, was known in the 15th century.' Reims retained the monopoly until the Revolution, then Dijon, where the local production gave rise to a flourishing trade, took it over.

Gingerbread was formerly regarded primarily as a fairground delicacy. In Paris the Gingerbread Fair, which became the Throne Fair in the 19th century, had been held since the 11th century on the site of the present Saint-Antoine Hospital, where there was then an abbey. The monks sold their own gingerbread cakes there, in the shape of little pigs. Gingerbread was sold in many different shapes (animals, little men, flowers) as well as the large traditional *pavé* or the ball. Belgian *spéculos*, which are made of gingerbread, depict all kinds of popular characters (Harlequin, Columbine, Saint Nicholas).

Today two types of gingerbread are made in France: that of Dijon, made with wheat flour and egg yolks; and *couque*, made with rye flour. The *demi-couque*, or *couque bâtarde*, made with a mixture of flours, is used mainly for the large gingerbread *pavé* loaves. In industrially manufactured products, the honey is totally or partially replaced by other sweetening agents (invert sugar, glucose, grape must) and the spices are often artificial essences. However, it is always prepared according to the traditional method: the flour and sweetening agents are mixed together and matured in a cool, dry place for about a month (formerly for several months). It is then mixed with baking powder and spices, shaped, glazed with milk and eggs, and baked in the oven. Ordinary gingerbread is baked in *pavé* loaves, while fancy gingerbread is cut into hearts and various other shapes.

Although it is eaten mainly at teatime or at festivals (particularly in Belgium and Germany), gingerbread also has some uses in cookery, for thickening sauces, ragoûts and carbonades, especially when beer is used in the recipe.

Gingerbread can easily be made at home. The best results for *pain d'épice* are achieved with a strongly flavoured honey, traditionally buckwheat or heather honey. Wheat flour is generally used (sometimes mixed with rye flour), and flavourings can include orange-flower water, orange or lemon rind (zest), star anise or cinnamon, or a mixture of spices as well as ginger. Orange or apricot marmalade may also be added to the mixture. After baking, the top of the cake may be decorated with pieces of angelica, green walnuts or candied orange peel.

RECIPES

gingerbread

Warm together 100 g (4 oz, ½ cup) margarine or lard (shortening) and 200 g (7 oz, ¾ cup) black treacle or molasses. Add 150 ml (¼ pint, ⅔ cup) milk and allow to cool. Sift 200 g (7 oz, 2 cups) plain (all-purpose) flour, 1 teaspoon mixed spice, 2 teaspoons ground ginger and 1 teaspoon bicarbonate of soda (baking soda) into a bowl. Add the treacle mixture, 50 g (2 oz, ¼ cup) brown sugar and 2 eggs. Beat well. Pour into a 18 cm (7 in) square tin (pan) lined with greaseproof (wax) paper. Bake in a preheated oven at 150°C (300°F, gas 2) for 1¼–1½ hours, until firm to the touch.

pain d'épice

Heat 500 g (18 oz, 1½ cups) honey to boiling point, then skim it. Place in an earthenware bowl 500 g (18 oz, 4½ cups) sifted plain (all-purpose) flour, make a well in the centre, pour the honey into it and mix with a wooden spoon. (Some flours absorb more liquid than others; it may be necessary to add more liquid in order to obtain a firm paste.) Gather the paste into a ball, wrap it in a cloth and let it stand for 1 hour. Then add 2½ teaspoons baking powder and knead the paste thoroughly. Mix in 2 teaspoons aniseed, a generous pinch of cinnamon, the same amount of powdered cloves and ½ teaspoon grated lemon or orange rind (zest).

Alternatively, mix the sifted flour directly with the same weight of liquid honey. Let the paste stand, then knead it hard with 100 g (4 oz, ½ cup) caster (superfine) sugar, 2 teaspoons cream of tartar, 1 teaspoon bicarbonate of soda (baking soda), 50 g (2 oz, ½ cup) skinned and chopped almonds and 65 g (2½ oz, ½ cup) mixed and chopped candied orange and lemon peel.

Pour the mixture into a 23 cm (9 in) square cake tin (pan) or a buttered manqué mould. Bake in a preheated oven at 190°C (375°F, gas 5) for about 30 minutes. As soon as the cake is cooked, quickly brush the top with some milk sweetened to a thick syrup or with sugar cooked to the fine thread stage (see *sugar*) and glaze for a few seconds in a cool oven.

GINGER WINE Water, ginger, yeast, sugar, lemon, raisins, pepper and sometimes alcohol; mixed with whisky to make Whisky Mac.

GINKGO NUT The oval, pale green fruit of the Asian ginkgo tree. The olive-sized kernel is much used in Chinese and Japanese cooking, either roasted or grilled (broiled), as a garnish for fish or poultry or, in the autumn, simply as a dessert nut. A typical dish consists of large prawns (shrimp) mixed with ginkgo nuts, pieces of chicken and mushrooms cooked on hot cooking salt in an earthenware casserole.

GINSENG The root of a plant growing in mountainous regions of Korea and Manchuria. It is considered to be the 'root of life' by the Chinese, who have attributed many therapeutic, magical and aphrodisiac properties to it. Used mainly in a tonic drink, ginseng is also used to make a herbal tea, sweets (candies), pastilles, dyes and ointments. It can also be preserved whole in alcohol or dried and used as seasoning, in the same way as ginger. Its taste is similar to that of fennel.

GIRAUMON A type of gourd cultivated mainly in the West Indies and some tropical countries. There are two varieties: one with a large fruit (3–4 kg, 6½–9 lb), the other with smaller fruit (about 1 kg, 2¼ lb), the latter being preferred, because giraumons do not keep once they are opened. Its firm flesh is sweet and slightly musky. Also called *bonnet turc* (Turkish bonnet) and *citrouille iroquoise* (Iroquois pumpkin), giraumons can be eaten raw like cucumbers, but are usually cooked like pumpkins, espe-

cially in West Indian cookery (in a ratatouille called *giraumonade* and in ragoûts). When green, they are used to make jam, and the leaves are sometimes used like sorrel.

GIRELLA *girelle* A small, brightly coloured Mediterranean rock fish, with spiky rays on its dorsal fin. Its flesh is delicate and tasty but full of bones. Girella is sometimes served fried, but it is used mainly in bouillabaisse.

GIROLLE The French name for the chanterelle.

GÎTE À LA NOIX A French cut of beef from the top of the leg. With the round of beef, which extends from it, it was formerly classified as braising meat but is now used for grilling (broiling) and roasting. The round of beef is lean, tender and tasty. *Gîte à la noix* is also used to make steak tartare and beef on skewers. For roasting, it is larded and tied with string.

GIVRY Red and white AOC wines from the Côte Chalonnaise in southern Burgundy. The reds are made from Pinot Noir, the whites from Chardonnay. The Côte Chalonnaise has a proud history and is said to have been planted with vines since Roman times.

GIZZARD A digestive pouch in birds, consisting of a thick muscle. If the gizzard is not cooked with the bird or if it is not minced in the stuffing, it can be fried or roasted separately (particularly duck or goose gizzard) or prepared in a ragoût of giblets. It is also often preserved. When a chicken is drawn, the gizzard is slit in two to remove the small stones and the thick envelope that surrounds them.

GJETÖST Originally made in Norway from goat's milk whey, this sweet, brown cheese is now factory made from pure goat's milk or a mixture of cow's and goat's milk, which is cooked until caramelized. The designation *Ekte Gjetöst* on the label means that the cheese is made solely from goat's milk – *gjet* means goat in Norwegian. It is moulded in blocks weighing between 200 g (7 oz) and 4 kg (9 lb).

GLACÉ Describing fruits that are crystallized (candied) or in liqueur and petits fours that are coated with a syrup cooked to the 'crack stage' so that they have a hard, shiny layer. The word is also used for fruits and chestnuts (marrons glacés) preserved in syrup.

In France the term is also applied to many iced desserts and drinks, and to cakes and pastries covered with icing (frosting).

GLASSWARE Common soda glass is a transparent or translucent material made from the fusion of silica (sand), sodium carbonate (soda) and calcium carbonate (lime). Crystal glassware is made from flint glass, a very clear glass containing lead oxide, silica, potassium carbonate and potassium nitrate; good quality crystal glass makes a clear ringing sound when struck. Common and crystal glassware may be engraved, coloured or gilded. In spite of its fragility and poor resistance to sudden changes in temperature, glass is widely used for table- and kitchenware, not to mention bottles, because of its transparency and resistance to chemicals.

■ **The history of glass** Egyptian paintings show that the art of glass-blowing was known as far back as the 4th century BC, and glass objects have been in existence for more than 5,000 years. Until the Middle Ages, however, pottery utensils were more common in ordinary households, glassware being rather rare and reserved for luxury use. The glass industry in France dates from the Gallo-Roman era. In the 6th century the glassware of Clotaire I consisted of cone-shaped, stemless goblets, their borders decorated with a fine strip of coloured glass. There were also bottles and white-enamelled dessert cups. But the use of glass in tableware as we know it today did not come until the 14th century. The 16th-century Venetian glass-blowers were the first to obtain a colourless glass, which they named *cristallo*. Shortly afterwards, the glass-makers of Bohemia discovered that clear glass could also be made by adding limestone to the glass paste. However, it was an Englishman, George Ravenscroft, who in 1675 discovered lead crystal. In France the Cristalleries de Baccarat dates, in its present form, from 1816.

The industrial and technical progress made during the 19th and 20th centuries has produced a wide range of drinking glasses. Venetian glasses ornamented with filigree work, heavily patterned Bohemian crystal, coloured and engraved tall wine glasses from the Rhine and wide-mouthed flute glasses from Dutch glassworks have become collectors' items. Coloured glass is not often used for wine glasses, so that the natural colour of the wine may be appreciated. The wine glass should never be completely filled, and it must be wide enough for the aroma of the wine to be appreciated, since part of the pleasure of drinking wine is to sample its bouquet.

■ **Glassware** For a formal meal, three matching glasses are required (in decreasing size) for water, for red wine and for white wine. The set is sometimes completed by a champagne flute. However, it is inadvisable to set out too many glasses, because they can get in the way of the cutlery and the setting is, therefore, often reduced to two glasses, one for water and the other for wine. For an informal meal, the latter may be used for several different wines or be changed in the course of the meal.

Glasses come in a wide range of shapes and sizes. Most wine-producing regions have designed thin-walled glasses of a particular shape to allow the best possible tasting of their wine. Thin-walled balloon glasses are used for Cognac, Armagnac and marc brandy; liqueur glasses are usually short and narrow, made of thicker glass and often without a stem. Beer is served in a tankard or tall glass. 'Short' cocktails are served in a cocktail glass of 80–120 ml (2½–4 fl oz, ¼–½ cup) capacity, while long drinks are served in a tall 300 ml (10 fl oz, 1¼ cups) Collins glass. Large glass goblets may be used for mineral water and fruit cups, medium goblets for wines and for aperitifs with water or a mixer, and small goblets for dry aperitifs, port and short drinks, such as sherry. There are also various specially designed glasses, such as champagne tulips and brandy goblets. A mixing glass may be used instead of a cocktail shaker to prepare cocktails; it has a capacity of 600–700 ml (20 fl oz, 2½ cups).

GLASSWORT A small fleshy plant, also called marsh samphire, with salty sap. It grows in European salt marshes as far north as Norway and also in the Camargue (Mistral calls it *sans-souiro*). It is similar to rock samphire. The plant is harvested in summer for its tender green tips, which can be eaten in a salad, cooked like French (green) beans or pickled and used as a condiment, like gherkins (sweet dill pickles).

GLAZE OR STOCK GLAZE *glace de cuisine* A syrupy substance obtained by boiling down an unthickened stock of meat, poultry, more rarely game, or even fish. Stock glazes are used as an essence to be added to certain sauces in order to enhance their flavour or to baste dishes to be browned in the oven. They are also used as the base for a sauce when adding other ingredients.

Stock glazes may be used to speed up the preparation of soups, coulis and aspics. Ready-made meat glazes, marketed as 'extracts' or 'essences', are available; they are mostly made of beef and vegetable matter. They offer a more limited range of flavours than cooked glazes, but the latter no longer play as important a role in cooking as they used to because they take a long time to prepare, as is demonstrated in this impressive recipe taken from *Secrets de la nature et de l'art concernant les aliments* (1769):

'Take a quarter of a large ox, a whole calf (or a part only, depending on its size), two sheep, two dozen old hens and two old cocks, or a dozen old turkeys, plucked and drawn. After defatting all this meat and scalding and cleaning the calf's and sheep's feet separately, put it all in a large boiler. Add the hot liquor from 12–14 litres of stag's horn gratings, boiled separately, and put through the press. Then pour four buckets of spring water over it all. Put the lid on the boiler, sealing the edge with a flour-and-water paste. Apply a weight of 50–60 pounds. Boil the meat over a low even flame, without skimming it, for 6 hours or more if necessary, until it is sufficiently cooked, when the bones can be easily detached. Remove the largest bones, leaving the boiler over the heat to keep the meat very hot. Take the meat out as quickly as possible, chop it up immediately and then put it in a large press with hot iron plates to extract all the juices. As soon as this operation is completed, add the extracted juices to the hot stock left in the boiler and strain immediately through a large horsehair strainer.'

The word 'glaze' is also used for any substance used to give food a glossy surface (see *glazing*).

RECIPE

meat glaze

glace de viande Remove all the fat from a brown stock. When it is as clear as possible, boil it down by half. Strain through a muslin cloth (cheesecloth), then boil it down again and strain. Continue this process until it will coat the back of a spoon, each time reducing the temperature a little more as the glaze becomes more concentrated. Pour the meat glaze into small containers and keep them in the refrigerator.

A similar method is used with a poultry or game stock to obtain a poultry or game glaze.

By boiling down a fish fumet to a syrupy consistency, then decanting it and straining it through muslin, a light-coloured fish stock is obtained, which is used to enhance the flavour of a fish sauce or to pour over fish before putting it in the oven.

GLAZING The process of creating a glossy surface on food. This may be achieved by several methods, according to the effect required.

Cold food is brushed with such glazes as arrowroot, aspic jelly, stock glazes and sugar syrup.

Desserts, such as fruit tarts and flans, babas and savarins, are coated with a fruit glaze, a liquid jelly made from finely sieved apricot jam or redcurrant jelly, usually with gelatine added. As well as being decorative, this prevents the fruit from drying out or oxidizing.

Food that is to be baked, particularly pastry, is coated with whole beaten egg, egg yolk only, milk or milk and sugar.

Hot cooked food, particularly vegetables, can be glazed either by cooking with butter, sugar and very little liquid or by brushing with melted butter when cooked.

Food coated with sauces that are rich in egg yolk, cream or butter is grilled (broiled) under, or baked in, a very high heat to form a shiny brown surface.

In France the term *glaçage* is also used for glazing cakes with icing (frosting) and for the preparation of many cold or frozen desserts and chilled drinks.

GLOUCESTER A traditional English cow's-milk cheese, with a firm, close texture. Double Gloucester is larger than Single Gloucester, which is seldom made now. The main difference is that Single Gloucester is made with skimmed evening milk and whole morning milk, while Double Gloucester is made with whole milk. Gloucester is compact and smooth, with a delicate and creamy flavour. It is used for making sandwiches and canapés, but it is also sometimes served as a dessert, with a salad or a fruit compote.

GLUCOSE The simplest of the carbohydrates and the end product when carbohydrates are digested by the body. Glucose is present in the blood and is

Glazing pastry with beaten egg

Beat the egg or egg yolk with a little water or milk and a tiny pinch of salt.

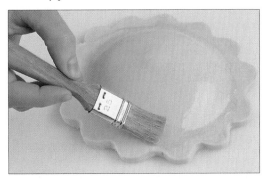

1 Brush the egg lightly and evenly over the pastry. Avoid brushing the cut edge of puff pastry: the egg prevents it from rising evenly.

2 For even browning, brush any excess egg from around the edge evenly over the pastry, or mop it off gently with a paper towel.

used as a source of energy by the body. It is found naturally in ripe fruit and honey.

Glucose is made industrially by heating starch with various acids. This produces dextrins first and then an impure form of glucose itself. Two forms of glucose are used commercially, viscous and semisolid. Glucose has many industrial uses, notably to increase the sugar content of wine and beer, and in the manufacture of syrup, confectionery and jam. Liquid glucose (corn syrup or clear corn syrup in America) is a clear syrup of glucose and other sugars. It is used in the preparation of sugar paste and to prevent sugar syrup from crystallizing.

GNOCCHI Small dumplings made of flour, semolina (semolina flour), potato or choux pastry. They are usually poached, then they may be cooked *au gratin* in the oven and served as a hot entrée. This dish is Italian in origin (the word means 'lumps') and is classified with pasta, but it is also found in Austro-Hungarian and Alsatian cookery in the form of knepfle, knödel, noques or quenelles, which are all quite similar.

Italian gnocchi *alla Romana* are made with semolina, egg and cheese; gnocchi *à la parisienne* are prepared from choux pastry with milk and cheese; and gnocchi *à la piémontaise* or *à l'alsacienne* are made with potato purée, eggs and flour. The basic ingredients can be varied by incorporating various cooked vegetables (pumpkin, spinach, green vegetables, beetroot), which colour the gnocchi; by varying the cheese (Emmental, Parmesan, Ricotta) or the flour (maize, wheat); and by including chicken liver or brains, herbs and condiments (nutmeg, fines herbes, paprika, oregano, parsley).

RECIPES

potato gnocchi

Cook 3 medium-sized potatoes in boiling salted water for about 20 minutes. Meanwhile grate 6–7 medium-sized peeled potatoes and squeeze them in a cloth to extract as much water as possible. Peel and mash the cooked potatoes, then mix them with the grated raw potatoes. Add 100–125 g (4–4½ oz, 1 cup) plain (all-purpose) flour, a little grated nutmeg, salt and pepper, then 2 whole eggs, one after the other. Mix thoroughly. Boil some salted water and use 2 spoons to shape the paste into small, round portions. Drop them into the water and leave to simmer for 6–8 minutes. Drain the gnocchi and place them on a cloth. Butter a gratin dish and arrange the gnocchi in it, coated with 200 ml (7 fl oz, ¾ cup) crème fraîche and sprinkled with grated cheese. Brown in a very hot oven.

gnocchi à la parisienne

Make some choux pastry using milk instead of water and flavour with grated nutmeg. Add 75 g (3 oz, ¾ cup) grated Parmesan per 500 g (18 oz) dough. Boil some salted water, using 1 teaspoon salt per 1 litre (1¾ pints, 4 cups). Push the dough through a piping (pastry) bag fitted with a large plain nozzle so that it drops into the water in pieces measuring about 3 cm (1¼ in). Poach for a few minutes, then drain and arrange on a cloth. Line a gratin dish with Mornay sauce, place the gnocchi in it, cover them with more sauce, sprinkle with grated Gruyère, and pour over melted butter. Brown quickly in a preheated oven at 250°C (480°F, gas 9).

gnocchi alla Romana

Pour 125 g (4½ oz, ¾ cup) semolina into 500 ml (17 fl oz, 2 cups) boiling milk and stir to obtain a very thick, smooth porridge. Add salt, pepper and grated nutmeg, then 100 g (4 oz, 1 cup) freshly grated Parmesan cheese and 25 g (1 oz, 2 tablespoons) butter. Allow to cool slightly and then beat in 1 lightly beaten egg and 1 yolk.

Spread the paste evenly on a moistened slab or in a tin (pan), leave to cool completely, then chill until firm. Cut with a pastry (cookie) cutter into rounds about 5 cm (2 in) in diameter. Arrange the rounds in a buttered gratin dish and sprinkle with extra grated Parmesan cheese. Pour over melted

butter and brown slowly in the oven. Alternatively, deep-fry small balls of this paste, drain on paper towels and serve immediately, with tomato sauce if liked. (The paste can also be made without butter or grated cheese.)

gnocchi with herbs and tomatoes

Wash 500 g (18 oz) potatoes and bake them in their skins in a preheated oven at 180°C (350°F, gas 4) for 40 minutes. Peel them while still hot and mash them to a purée. Arrange them with a well in the middle and allow to cool. Peel and seed 500 g (18 oz) ripe tomatoes and cut into small cubes. Chop up ½ onion, 1 shallot and 1 small celery stick. Heat some olive oil in a sauté pan and stir in the onion, shallot, celery and 1 garlic clove. Remove the latter when it is golden. Now add the tomatoes, fry for a few minutes, then add a little basil, rosemary, sage and mint. Season with salt and pepper and reduce the cooking juices. Then add 100 g (4 oz, 1 cup) plain (all-purpose) flour, 2 pinches nutmeg, 3 egg yolks and 50 g (2 oz, ½ cup) freshly grated Parmesan cheese to the potato purée. Add a little flour to make a ball that is neither too dry nor too moist. Divide into 100 g (4 oz) chunks and shape into cylinders on a floured surface. Cut the cylinders into small pieces and press them on to the back of a fork to make a slightly concave shape with ridges. Poach the gnocchi for 6–8 minutes in boiling, salted water.

GOAT A domestic animal bred mostly for its milk. In France, where a wide variety of goat's-milk cheese is produced, the main rearing areas are Poitou, Berry, Dauphiné and Touraine.

Goat's meat is fairly firm, with a pleasant flavour but a strong smell. It is consumed principally in the regions where the goats are bred; when the animal is young, it is eaten roasted or marinated, sometimes even smoked and dried (in the mountains). The male (*bouc*) is today eaten only when a kid, but for centuries, in spite of its leathery flesh and pungent smell, it was a basic meat of the poor; the word *boucherie* (butcher's shop) is derived from *bouc*.

GOAT'S-MILK CHEESES *chèvres* In France cheeses prepared exclusively from goat's milk contain at least 45% butterfat. *Mi-chèvre* cheeses are made from a mixture of cow's milk and goat's milk (at least 25%). Among the best known French goat's-milk cheeses are Cabécou, Chabichou, Chevreton, Crottin, Pouligny-Saint-Pierre, Sainte-Maure, Selles-sur-Cher, Valençay.

Goat's milk is increasingly being used in other countries to make both hard and soft cheeses in the French style. Examples of soft cheeses include Mine-Gabhar from County Wexford in Ireland; Perroche, Tymsboro, Vulscombe and Wigmore from England and Wales; and Coach Farm and Cypress Grove in the United States of America. Firm goat's-milk cheeses include Tickle More from Devon and Ribblesdale from Yorkshire in England; Pen y Bont from Wales; and Idaho Goatster in the United States of America.

GOBLET A wide-mouthed drinking vessel. Antique goblets were made of gold and silver, often exquisitely engraved and embellished with precious stones. See also *glassware*.

GOBO A root of a variety of burdock. It is long, thin and brown, and is commonly used in Japan as a condiment, finely chopped and usually blanched. Gobo has a flavour similar to that of cardoon and is used in cooking stocks and vegetable mixtures.

GOBY *gobie* A small sea fish, known in France as *goujon de mer*, of which there are numerous types. Its flesh has a delicate taste, but because it is so small it is usually served fried.

GODARD A classic garnish for large cuts of meat, poultry, and calves' sweetbreads. According to the *Dictionnaire de l'Académie des gastronomes*, it was dedicated to the farmer-general and man of letters Godard d'Aucour (1716–95), but other authorities say that it is named after the chef de cuisine of the Élysée Palace at the time of Sadi-Carnot. The garnish consists of quenelles, lamb's sweetbreads (braised and glazed), cockscombs and kidneys, small truffles and fluted mushroom caps. These are covered by a sauce made of white wine or champagne with a ham mirepoix.

RECIPE

Godard sauce
Cook 2 tablespoons ham mirepoix* in butter, add 200 ml (7 fl oz, ¾ cup) champagne, and boil down by half. Moisten with 200 ml (7 fl oz, ¾ cup) demi-glace* sauce and 7 tablespoons mushroom* essence and boil down again by one-third. Strain.

GODIVEAU The delicate forcemeat, consisting of veal and fat, used to make quenelles, which are served as a hot entrée or used to fill vol-au-vent or to accompany meat dishes. The word seems to be a corruption of *gogues de veau* (gogues of veal). Godiveau can also be made from fish (pike in particular) or poultry. The mixture, which must be very smooth, springy and yet firm, requires quite a long preparation time, because the raw meat and fat are pounded with cream or panada, eggs and seasoning.

RECIPES

godiveau lyonnais
Pound together in a mortar 500 g (18 oz) trimmed diced beef suet, 500 g (18 oz) frangipane panada* and 4 egg whites (these ingredients may first be put through a blender). Add 500 g (18 oz) pike flesh and season with salt and pepper. Work vigorously with a spatula, then with a pestle. Rub through a fine sieve, place in an earthenware dish and work with a spatula until smooth.

The forcemeat is shaped into quenelles and poached in salted water when served as a garnish for pike.

godiveau with cream
Chop up 1 kg (2¼ lb) fillet of veal and pound it. Also chop up and pound 1 kg (2¼ lb) beef suet. Mix these ingredients together and add 1 tablespoon salt, ¼ teaspoon pepper, a pinch of grated nutmeg, 4 whole eggs and 3 egg yolks, grinding vigorously with a pestle the whole time. Rub the forcemeat through a fine sieve and spread it on a board. Leave on ice or in the refrigerator until the next day. Put the forcemeat back in the mortar and pound it again, gradually adding 750 ml (1¼ pints, 3¼ cups) single (light) cream.

To test the consistency of the godiveau, poach a small ball and rectify if necessary, adding a little iced water if it is too firm or a little egg white if it is too light. Shape into quenelles and poach.

GOGUES Savoury black puddings (blood sausages) that are a speciality of Anjou. Made of vegetables, bacon, cream and blood, they are poached in boiling water, then cut into slices and fried.

RECIPE

gogues
Chop 250 g (9 oz) onions, 250 g (9 oz) spinach beet leaves, 250 g (9 oz) spinach leaves and 250 g (9 oz) lettuce leaves. Season with salt and pepper, leave to stand for 12 hours, then braise over a very gentle heat with 40 g (1½ oz, 3 tablespoons) lard in a casserole. Dice 250 g (9 oz) fat bacon and cook without browning. Add to the chopped vegetables and season with a pinch of cinnamon and mixed spice. Take off the heat and add 7 tablespoons double (heavy) cream and 250 ml (8 fl oz, 1 cup) pig's blood. Adjust the seasoning. Fill a pig's intestine with this mixture, twisting it every 10–15 cm (4–6 in) after filling. Poach the gogues in salted water, just below boiling point, for about 30 minutes. When they rise to the surface, prick them with a pin to prevent them from bursting. Drain and leave to cool. When they are cold, cut the gogues into thick slices and brown them in butter or lard in a frying pan.

GOLD A precious metal used for decorative tableware or as a veneer, in the form of silver gilt. Gold also has some culinary uses. In the Middle Ages pâtés and roast birds were wrapped in thin gold leaf. Even today, chocolates (*palets d'or*) are decorated with a tiny piece of gold leaf, and minute pieces of gold are suspended in the liqueur Danziger Goldwasser, which is used to flavour soufflé Rothschild. It is also an authorized food additive (E175), a colouring agent for charcuterie, confectionery and cake decorations.

GOMPHIDE A fleshy, viscous mushroom that grows under conifers. It is edible if peeled carefully, although its flesh turns black when cooked. It is usually sautéed in oil and served with noisette butter and a little fresh cream.

GONDOLE A decoration consisting of a stiffened white table napkin, reinforced by a sheet of greaseproof (wax) paper or foil and folded using a particular technique into the shape of a curved horn. In catering gondoles are used to decorate the two ends of a long dish when serving fish.

GOOSE A migratory bird originally prized as a game bird and later domesticated. The Romans practised the force-feeding of geese; the preparation of foie gras therefore has a long history.

All breeds of domesticated goose are probably descended from the greylag goose. In France geese providing foie gras may weigh up to 12 kg (26½ lb) after fattening; they are found mainly around Toulouse, Landes and Strasbourg. White geese, from Bourbon or Poitou, are descended from the snow goose, and they weigh less (5–6 kg, 11–13 lb). Laying birds may be kept until they are five or six years old; because the meat is by then very tough and dry, it is usually stewed or preserved (see *confit*). Table geese are killed at three months, by which time the breast is well developed and the meat has a delicate flavour. In areas where geese are bred primarily for foie gras, the remainder of the bird (the meat and carcass, called the *paletot*) is sold as it is, or cut up and preserved, or made into rillettes. The gizzard, heart, tongue, neck and giblets are all used in various savoury dishes. Today, in spite of competition from the turkey, roast goose is still the typical dish cooked at Christmas and New Year in Scandinavia and Germany. Formerly in Britain roast goose with sage and onion stuffing was served at Christmas and Michaelmas. Two famous recipes for cooking goose come from northern Europe: goose *à l'instar de Visé* from Belgium and smoked goose from Pomerania. Many of the recipes given for cooking turkey and chicken can be used for goose.

RECIPES

ballotine of goose with Savigny-lès-Beaune
Take a young goose weighing about 3.5 kg (8 lb) and cut off the wings and legs. Bone the legs and remove the meat from the wings to make the forcemeat. Remove the suprêmes from the carcass and refrigerate until required.
• *Stuffed goose legs en ballotines* Mince (grind) the reserved wing meat and the liver very finely. Place in a bowl over a dish of ice and work the mixture until smooth. Then blend in an egg white followed by 300 ml (½ pint, 1¼ cups) double (heavy) cream. Add salt, pepper and a pinch of cayenne pepper, and 50 g (2 oz, ½ cup) boiled diced chestnuts. Stuff the boned legs with this mixture, shape them into ballotines and tie them. Spread some sliced onion over the base of an ovenproof dish and lay the carcass of the goose on top. Then place the ballotines on top of the carcass and braise them in a preheated oven at 180°C (350°F, gas 4) for 45–60 minutes, basting frequently so that they remain moist. (The remainder of the stuffing can be used to make godiveau.)
• *Chestnut custards* Mix 300 ml (½ pint, 1¼ cups) single (light) cream, 3 whole eggs, 150 g (5 oz, ½ cup) chestnut purée and 100 g (4 oz, 1 cup) boiled diced chestnuts. Butter 8 small dariole moulds and divide the mixture among them. Cook in a bain marie in a preheated oven at 170° C (325° F, gas 3). Leave for a few minutes before unmoulding.
• *Onions stuffed with garlic purée* Blanch 8 medium-sized Spanish onions in fast-boiling salted water, refresh them and drain them carefully. Peel 500 g (18 oz) garlic cloves, cook them in milk, drain them and rub them through a fine sieve. Reheat them with a little cream. Stuff the onions with the garlic purée, filling them to the top.
• *Accompanying sauce* Remove the fat from the liquor in which the ballotines were braised and deglaze the pan with a bottle of Savigny-lès-Beaune. Reduce by one-third, strain and thicken the sauce with 200 g (7 oz, scant 1 cup) butter. Adjust the seasoning.
• *Fried suprêmes* Fry the suprêmes in the goose fat until the outside is golden brown but the inside is still pink.
• *Presentation* On each plate, place a thin slice of suprême, a slice of ballotine, a stuffed onion and a chestnut custard. Pour the sauce around the items without covering the sliced meat. Serve the rest of the sauce separately.

goose à la bourguignonne
Dice 100 g (4 oz) blanched lean bacon and fry it in 25 g (1 oz, 2 tablespoons) butter. Using the same pan, fry 20 small onions and then 20 sliced mushrooms. Remove them and brown the goose all over in the same butter. Remove the goose, deglaze the pan with 500 ml (17 fl oz, 2 cups) red wine, boil down to reduce it by half and then add 400 ml (14 fl oz, 1¾ cups) demi-glace* sauce (or reduced stock). Boil for 5 minutes and add a bouquet garni. Put the goose back into the pan. Start the cooking over a high heat, then reduce the heat, cover the pan and cook gently for 30 minutes. Add the bacon, onions and mushrooms and continue to cook over a moderate heat, with the pan still covered, for 45–60 minutes. Remove the bouquet garni, and either serve the goose and its accompaniments in the cooking dish or arrange it on a large serving dish and pour the sauce over it.

goose à l'alsacienne
Braise some sauerkraut with a small piece of lean bacon. Stuff a goose with sausagemeat seasoned with salt, pepper, a pinch of allspice and a little chopped onion and parsley. Truss and roast the goose as for roast goose with sage and onion

stuffing, basting it frequently. When the goose is half-cooked, add a little of the goose fat to the sauerkraut and continue cooking. Poach Strasbourg sausages gently in barely simmering water. Spread the sauerkraut over a long serving dish and place the goose in the centre. Cut the bacon into pieces and arrange them around the bird, alternating the bacon with the sausages. Keep everything hot. Skim the fat from the goose cooking juices and deglaze the pan with white wine and an equal quantity of stock. Boil down to reduce. Serve the sauce separately.

goose à l'instar de Visé

Take a 3.5 kg (8 lb) goose that has not yet started laying and poach it in white stock flavoured with 2 heads (bulbs) of garlic for 1½ hours. Drain it, cut into pieces and place these in a sauté pan. Moisten with goose fat and simmer, with the lid on, until cooked.

Meanwhile, prepare a velouté sauce using the goose fat (for the roux) and the cooking juices from the goose. Cook over a low heat for 1 hour. Thicken the velouté with 4 egg yolks, then pass it through a very fine strainer. Add a few tablespoons of cream and a purée of the garlic that was cooked with the goose.

Drain the pieces of goose and add to the sauce. Heat well and serve in a deep dish.

goose en daube Capitole

Stuff the goose with a fine forcemeat mixed with foie gras and diced truffles. Truss and braise it in the usual way. When it is almost cooked, remove the string used for trussing and pour the braising liquid through a fine strainer. Put the goose back into the pan with 250 g (9 oz) small mushrooms, an equal quantity of stoned (pitted) blanched olives and 250 g (9 oz) small fried chipolatas. Pour the cooking juices over the goose and finish cooking in a preheated oven at 180°C (350°F, gas 4).

goose hearts en papillotes

Cut 4 large squares of foil. Place 3 carefully cleaned goose hearts in the centre of each square together with 100 g (4 oz) cleaned and sliced cep mushrooms. Season generously with salt and pepper and fold the foil into parcels, sealing the edges thoroughly. Place them on a grill over very hot embers. Cook for about 20 minutes on each side.

goose in the pot

The day before it is required, stuff a young goose weighing about 3.5 kg (8 lb) with the following mixture: the chopped liver and heart, 2–3 diced apples and 3–4 desalted anchovy fillets pounded to a paste. Leave the goose in a cool place for 24 hours. The following day make a stock with 20 unpeeled garlic cloves, a bouquet garni and an onion studded with 2 cloves. Stud the goose all over with garlic and poach it in the stock for 1½ hours, skimming the pan when it comes to the boil.

Stew some dessert apples and add to them 2 desalted, pounded anchovies and 1 cup of the strained cooking stock. Prepare some small gougères: for every 2 eggs used for the dough, add 100 g (4 oz) Gruyère cheese and 1 puréed anchovy fillet.

Serve the goose very hot, accompanied by the apple and garnished with the gougères.

roast goose with fruit

Stuff a goose and roast it as for roast goose with sage and onion stuffing. While it is cooking, poach some quartered pears in boiling syrup until translucent. Peel and core some small apples and sprinkle them with lemon juice. Fill the centres with redcurrant jelly. Half an hour before the goose is cooked, place the apples around it and baste with the goose fat that has collected in the pan. Complete the cooking. Place the goose on a long serving dish and arrange the apples and the drained pear quarters around it. Keep hot at the front of the oven. Deglaze the cooking pan with a little of the pear syrup, reduce the liquid by half and pour it into a sauceboat (gravy boat).

roast goose with sage and onion stuffing

Roast 1 kg (2¼ lb) large unpeeled onions in the oven. Let them get cold, then peel and chop them. Soak an equal weight of crustless bread in milk, then press out as much milk as possible. Mix the bread with the chopped onion and season with 1½ teaspoons salt, a pinch of pepper, a little grated nutmeg and 3 tablespoons chopped fresh sage.

Stuff the goose with this mixture and sew up the vent. Calculate the cooking time at 40 minutes per 1 kg, 20 minutes per 1 lb, in a preheated oven at 180°C (350°F, gas 4). Drain off excess fat during roasting. Place it on a long serving dish, pour over the deglazed cooking juices and serve with unsweetened or very slightly sweetened apple sauce.

other recipes See *confit, rillettes*.

GOOSE BARNACLE A type of barnacle, which is permanently attached to a rock by a long, stalk-like foot. In Biarritz it is called *operne*; in Brittany it is called *poche-pez*; while in Saint-Jean-de-Luz it is known as *lamperna*. It is found in large numbers on rocky reefs battered by the sea but is so difficult and dangerous to harvest that it rarely appears on the dining table. However, the natives of Biarritz insist that it is delicious when cooked for 20 minutes in a court-bouillon (only the foot is edible). It is the emblem of a gastronomic society, Les Chevaliers de l'Operne, which is dedicated to increasing the consumption of seafood.

GOOSEBERRY The fruit of the gooseberry bush, a large berry with a slightly hairy, green, amber-green or pink skin. The French name, *groseille à maquereau*, derives from the use of the fruit to prepare a sauce traditionally served with mackerel. Gooseberries are grown on a small scale in France and on a larger scale in the Netherlands and Britain.

Depending on type, gooseberries may be eaten raw with sugar or used to make tarts, sorbets, fools, jellies and syrups. The larger, pink, fruit are sweeter than the small green varieties and are known as dessert gooseberries. They are used in puddings, chutneys and fruit salads and in sauces to complement fish and duck. They freeze well.

RECIPES

gooseberry jelly
Remove the stalks from 3 kg (6½ lb) gooseberries and put them in a pan. Cover and heat them, shaking them from time to time until the skins burst. Purée the fruit in a blender, then strain. Pour the juice obtained back into the pan. Add 2.5 kg (5½ lb, 11 cups) granulated sugar and the juice and grated rind (zest) of 2 lemons. Cook over a high heat for 5 minutes, then lower the heat and cook for 15 minutes. Skim and pot.

gooseberry sauce
Cook 500 g (18 oz) gooseberries in a saucepan with 500 ml (17 fl oz, 2 cups) water and 6 tablespoons sugar. When the pulp becomes very soft, strain and serve piping hot. If the gooseberries are very ripe, add a few drops of lemon juice.

gooseberry syrup
Mix a few tablespoons of water with 1 kg (2¼ lb, 4½ cups) caster (superfine) sugar and cook to the large ball stage (see *sugar*). Add 500 ml (17 fl oz, 2¼ cups) strained gooseberry juice. Bring to the boil once more and then leave to stand. Skim, then cook until the temperature reaches 103°C (217°F). Strain, bottle and seal.

GORENFLOT The name of one of Alexandre Dumas's heroes, a larger-than-life monk who appears in *La Dame de Monsoreau* and *Les Quarante-Cinq*. In the middle of the 19th century, this name was given to a large hexagonal baba, created by the Parisian pastrycook Bourbonneux, and also to a garnish for pieces of braised meat, consisting of a julienne of red cabbage, slices of saveloy sausage and stuffed potatoes.

GORGONZOLA A DOP Italian cow's-milk cheese (48% fat), white or light yellow and streaked with blue. Gorgonzola should be delicate and creamy with a natural grey rind, pitted with red. It has a distinct smell and can have a mellow, strong or sharp flavour, depending on its degree of maturity (it is ripened dry, in a cold, damp cellar). Cylindrical in shape, 25–30 cm (10–12 in) in diameter and 16–20 cm (6¼–8 in) high, it is wrapped in silver paper bearing its trademark. It is good to eat all the year round, its qualities being due to the special manufacturing technique: the hot curds from the morning milking are used to line the moulds, while the cold curds from the evening milking are placed

in the middle. Contrary to the normal manufacturing technique for blue cheeses, the mould *Penicillium glaucum* is not included.

The history of Gorgonzola is connected with the migration of cattle from the Alps to the south of the plains of the Po. Tired from their journey (*stracche* in the Lombard dialect), the cattle were rested in the small town of Gorgonzola in the region of Bergamo. Their milk was used to make a soft cheese, Stracchino di Gorgonzola. Apparently, it was not until the beginning of the 11th century that this cheese became blue-veined, although the exact circumstances of this innovation are not known. In Lombardy they still make Panerone, a cheese similar to Gorgonzola, but not a blue cheese.

Gorgonzola is served in small cubes with aperitifs, included in mixed salads, spread on canapés or presented on a cheese board. It can also be used to season sauces or forcemeats and to flavour gratins, soufflés and flaky pastries. In Lombardy hot polenta may be served with a piece of melted Gorgonzola in the middle. In the Trieste area a mixture of Gorgonzola, mascarpone (a fresh creamy cheese), cream, anchovy paste, cumin, chives and sweet mustard is served as a dessert.

GOTTSCHALK, ALFRED Swiss doctor and scholar (born Geneva, 1873; died Paris, 1954). Founder of the medical gastronomy review *Grandgousier* (1934–48), he also published *Histoire de l'alimentation et de la gastronomie* (1948) in two volumes. This is a lively and well-documented study, which describes the way in which people have eaten and cooked from prehistory up to the 20th century. He collaborated with Prosper Montagné in the first edition of the *Larousse Gastronomique*, published in 1938.

GOUDA A DOP Dutch cow's-milk cheese (30–40% fat) with a compressed paste. Firm to the touch, it is light yellow to yellow ochre, depending on whether it has matured for two or three months (waxed rind, tinged with yellow or colourless), has been semi-oven dried (golden rind) or oven dried (yellow rind). Its flavour can be mellow or pronounced. Gouda owes its name to a small Dutch port near Rotterdam, from which it was originally exported. It is made in flat rounds with a curved edge, 25–30 cm (10–12 in) in diameter and 7 cm (2¾ in) high, weighing 3–5 kg (6½–11 lb). In France and Belgium it is usually made in a rectangular block (*galantine*) weighing 2–3 kg (4½–6½ lb). 'Genuine' Gouda, originating in the south of Holland, is protected by a label. Imitated all over the world, factory-made Gouda is very similar to Edam both in taste and in the way it is used. The rare farmhouse cheese has a good fruity tang to its flavour.

GOUFFÉ, JULES French chef (born Paris, 1807; died Neuilly, 1877). At the age of 17, having been an apprentice pastrycook to his father in Paris, Jules Gouffé became a disciple of Carême, who took him on when he saw his skill in producing *pièces mon-tées* (decorative set pieces). Between 1840 and 1855 Gouffé ran a famous restaurant in the Faubourg Saint-Honoré. Later, although Gouffé was semi-retired, Emperor Napoleon III always called upon him to prepare banquets, and Alexandre Dumas and Baron Brisse managed to persuade him to become the head chef at the Jockey Club. It was at this time that he published various culinary works.

His most important work, *Livre de cuisine* (1867), was republished several times and eventually revised and enlarged by Prosper Montagné. His other works include *Le Livre des conserves* (1869), *Le Livre de pâtisserie* (1873) and *Le Livre des soupes et des potages* (1875).

His name has been given to a dish consisting of small pieces of sautéed meat coated with a Madeira-flavoured demi-glace sauce and garnished with potato nests filled with morels in cream and buttered asparagus tips.

GOUGÈRE Savoury choux, usually in round or ring shapes, flavoured with cheese (Gruyère, Comté or Emmental). In Burgundy cold gougères traditionally accompany wine-tasting in cellars. Individual or large gougères are also served warm as an entrée.

RECIPE

gougères
Make 500 g (18 oz) unsweetened choux* paste. After adding the eggs, blend in 100 g (4 oz, 1 cup) grated Gruyère cheese and a pinch of white pepper. Butter a baking sheet and shape the dough into small balls using a spoon or into a ring using a pip-ing (pastry) bag. Brush with beaten egg, sprinkle with flakes of Gruyère and cook in the oven at 200°C (400°F, gas 6) for about 20 minutes until golden brown. Leave to cool in the oven with the heat switched off and the door half-open.

gougères with celeriac, celery and cream of caviar ◆
Fit a piping (pastry) bag with a large, fluted nozzle. Prepare 250 ml (8 fl oz, 1 cup) gougère pastry (see above). Pipe 4 rings 10 cm (4 in) in diameter and bake in a preheated oven at 240°C (475°F, gas 9). Slice in half horizontally and cool on a wire rack.

Coarsely chop some frisée; season with salt, pepper and lemon juice. Cut celery and celeriac (celery root) into matchsticks. Mix the frisée, cel-ery and celeriac with 200 ml (7 fl oz, 1 cup) whipped whipping cream and 25 g (1 oz, 1 gener-ous tablespoon) caviar, working very gently with two forks in order not to damage the caviar.

Arrange a circle of lamb's lettuce on each plate and place the gougère bases in the middle. Spoon the cream mixture on to the bases and cover with the gougère tops. Serve freshly filled, garnished with diced tomato.

GOUJON Small strips of fish, typically plaice or sole, coated and fried. The name is derived from gudgeon, a small freshwater fish. The term is also used to describe strips of poultry coated in bread-crumbs and fried.

GOULASH A Hungarian beef soup named after the keepers of Magyar oxen (*gulyas*). The origin of this dish, which is now made with onions and paprika and garnished with potatoes, dates back to the 9th century, before the foundation of the Hun-garian state, when nomadic tribes prepared a meal that was in keeping with their way of life. At that time goulash consisted of chunks of meat stewed slowly until the cooking liquid completely boiled away. The meat was dried in the sun and could be used later to prepare a stew or a soup by boiling it in water.

Traditionally, goulash is made in a special caul-dron (*bogracs*). There are a number of regional vari-ants of the recipe according to the cut of beef and the cooking fat used (pork fat or lard), but purists agree that goulash should not include flour or wine, nor should soured (sour) cream be added just before serving. Hungarians regard Viennese *Goulasch* as a flour-thickened version of genuine goulash soup; in Hungary the latter is sometimes served with potatoes and *csipetke* (small quenelles of egg pasta, poached in stock).

RECIPE

Hungarian goulash
Peel 250 g (9 oz) onions and slice them into rings. Cut 1.5 kg (3¼ lb) braising steak (chuck beef) into pieces of about 75 g (3 oz). Melt 100 g (4 oz, ½ cup) lard in a casserole. When it is hot, put in the meat and onions and brown them. Add 500 g (18 oz) tomatoes, peeled, seeded and cut into quarters, then 1 crushed garlic clove, a bouquet garni, salt, pepper and finally 1 tablespoon mild Hungarian paprika. Add enough stock to cover the meat, bring to the boil, then reduce the heat, cover and cook very gently for 2 hours. Add 600 ml (1 pint, 2½ cups) boiling water and 800 g (1¾ lb) potatoes, peeled and cut into quarters. Again bring to the boil and continue boiling until the potatoes are cooked. Adjust the seasoning. Serve very hot.

GOUMI A wild berry that originated in the Far East but is now grown in the United States. The goumi has a fleshy red or orange skin covered with silvery dots. When raw, its flesh is rather sour; it is therefore usually cooked and used in compotes or as a filling for tarts.

GOURD (SQUASH) The fruit of several plants of the family *Cucurbitaceae*. Originating in tropical Asia and Africa, they have a thick skin and watery flesh and are used as vegetables. They include the summer and autumn pumpkins (yellow gourd), veg-etable marrows, courgettes (zucchini) and various squashes. Pumpkins are large, round fruits with yellow or red skin and flesh. They are eaten in winter in soups, gratin dishes, purées, soufflés and pies. The courgette is a summer vegetable, but can now be obtained all year round. Squash melons have firm flesh and a flavour rather like an artichoke. The very small varieties can be pickled in vinegar. Custard marrows are eaten mostly in the West Indies. Winter and muscat squashes (the latter do not keep well) are longer and wider, and tend to be more insipid and watery than courgettes, but they can be cooked in the same way. Their seeds must always be removed.

Calabashes and colocynths are grown as ornamentals because of their attractive colours, shapes and patterned skins.

RECIPES

marrow au gratin
Peel a large marrow (summer squash) and cut it into several medium-sized pieces. Blanch them in salted water for 4–5 minutes, drain and pat them dry. Place them in a greased gratin dish on a layer of grated cheese. Pour some melted butter over the top and brown them in a medium oven.

Marrow au gratin may also be prepared with alternating layers of pieces of marrow and sliced onions (softened in butter) or with rice cooked in meat stock.

marrow flower fritters
Pick very fresh marrow (summer squash) flowers and wash them only if really necessary. Pat them dry, dip them in a light batter and deep-fry them in hot fat at 180°C (350°F) until golden brown. Drain the fritters, sprinkle with salt and serve very hot as an hors d'oeuvre.

GOURD-MELON An Oriental plant, the fruit of which looks like a marrow (squash), tastes something like a cucumber and is eaten as a vegetable in South-east Asia and China. It is cooked in water and preserved in vinegar.

GOURMANDS AND GOURMETS Synonymous until the 18th century, these two words later became clearly differentiated: a gourmand merely enjoys good food, whereas a gourmet knows how to choose and appreciate it. In *Caractères*, La Bruyère describes the gourmand as follows: 'Above all, he has a discerning palate which is never deceived, and so he never experiences the ghastly problem of eating a bad stew or drinking a mediocre wine.' In fact, there is a hierarchy that starts at the bottom with the *goinfre* (greedyguts), progresses to the *goulu* (glutton), then the *gourmand*, the *friand* (epicure) and the *gourmet*, and finally the *gastronome* (see *gastronomy*).

GOÛTER A light meal eaten in France between lunch and dinner. Until the 18th century, *goûter* was eaten at about 5 p.m. and constituted a proper meal, generally cold, with cakes, cheese, fruit and wine. With the change in mealtimes following the Revolution, *goûter* was increasingly omitted, as noted by Grimod de La Reynière: 'Now that people dine at six o'clock, they hardly ever have a *goûter*, except children.' Indeed, nowadays the *goûter* or *quatre-heures* is eaten only by children, and consists of fruit juice, bread, chocolate, biscuits (cookies) and milk.

Even when it was a full meal, the *goûter* was always considered common and unstylish. It was replaced by the English meal of afternoon tea, with tea and cakes. But in the countryside, *goûter dinatoire* (high tea) was traditionally served at the end of the afternoon, when work in the fields was over. It was so substantial that it took the place of dinner, a simple snack of soup or milk and bread being served at night. In Spain, where mealtimes are later, 6 p.m. marks the middle of the afternoon and is the time for the *merienda*, which usually consists of a cup of coffee or chocolate and cakes (dinner is eaten at about 10 p.m.).

GOYÈRE A speciality of the north of France, particularly Valenciennes. Its origin dates back to the Middle Ages. It was originally a cheesecake made with cream cheese, eggs and cassonade (or honey) flavoured with orange-flower water. Today it is a Maroilles cheese flan: a mixture of matured and white Maroilles, or of Maroilles and drained cream or curd cheese. It is eaten very hot, as an entrée, with fairly strong beer or red wine. Some think that goyère owes its name to a pastrycook called Gohier (hence the old spelling *gohière*). Others maintain that the name is derived from the Old French *goguer*, meaning to enjoy oneself.

RECIPE

goyère
Make a short pastry with 250 g (9 oz, 2 cups) plain (all-purpose) flour, 1 egg, 125 g (4½ oz, ½ cup) butter and a generous pinch of salt. Roll it out to a thickness of 3 mm (⅛ in), line a flan (pie) dish with it and bake blind for 10–12 minutes. Leave to cool.

Remove the rind from half a Maroilles cheese, cut the cheese into cubes, and rub through a sieve with 200 g (7 oz, scant 1 cup) well-drained curd cheese. Add to this mixture 3 beaten eggs, 2 tablespoons crème fraîche and a pinch of salt. Season generously with pepper and mix well. Pour the filling into the flan case (pie shell), level the surface and bake in a preheated oven at 220°C (425°F, gas 7) for 20 minutes. Take the goyère out of the oven and trace a diamond pattern on the top with the tip of a sharp-pointed knife. Dot with cubes of butter and put back in the oven for about 15 minutes. Serve piping hot.

Gougères with celeriac, celery and cream of caviar, see page 569.

GOZETTE A small pocket made of puff, shortcrust or yeast pastry in which are placed slices of apple with cinnamon, fried in butter and sprinkled with soft brown sugar. The gozette pastry is closed and glazed with egg yolk, then baked (see *chausson*).

GRADIN A tiered plinth, usually cut from sandwich bread, used for the presentation of cold dishes (such as *chauds-froids*), particularly for buffets. In former times gradins were widely used for the presentation of set pieces of confectionery: they were carved wooden stands, decorated with sugarwork (*pastillage*), almond paste, sugar motifs and nougat. Carême describes this decoration:

'Let us suppose, for example, that you wish to decorate a gradin with laurel leaves. You first cut out a laurel wreath in paper. Next you give the base of the gradin a light coating of icing and stick the paper wreath to it. Now you cover the rest of the gradin with a medium grade of coarse sugar. When this is done, you remove the paper, after which you sprinkle the imprint of the leaves with green pistachio sugar. Now, you have a laurel crown surrounding the base of the gradin.

'For a large set piece with three gradins, each one can be individually decorated. This creates a graceful and elegant effect.

'I have also sometimes embellished my gradins with laurel crowns made from biscuit pastry shaped like laurel leaves and coloured green, or with garlands of spun sugar. This last decoration has both brilliance and elegance.

'I have also created gradins out of almond paste, moulded in basket moulds.'

But although he favoured the presentation of set pieces on gradins, Carême maintained that young practitioners should not forget 'that gradins of German or Italian waffles, of nougat, of glazed duchesse cakes, of puff pastry . . . of Genoese cake or of croquembouche are immensely effective and truly belong in the realm of the great pastry-making establishments'.

And, in fact, Carême was right: all the types of gradin mentioned above are edible, whereas the other types, regardless of how decorative they might be, were merely pieces of wood.

GRAHAM, SYLVESTER American nutritionist (born West Suffield, Connecticut, 1794; died Northampton, Massachusetts, 1851). He became the leader of a crusade against the bad eating habits of his compatriots, denouncing excessively spicy condiments and overindulgence in meat. For him, the cure-all was bran and it was essential to make bread exclusively from wholemeal (wholewheat) flour. Bread and biscuits (cookies) sold under his trademark have to be made with flour containing all the original bran. Graham bread, marketed in the United States and in Europe since the mid-19th century, was the first internationally consumed bread. It is a wholemeal bread with a very dense texture and it keeps extremely well. Graham crackers, still one of the most popular American biscuits (cookies), are made with wholemeal flour and are named after Sylvester Graham.

GRAINER The French word *grainer* applies to cooked sugar tending to crystallize and turn cloudy or to a fondant mixture that has been overheated. The word also describes whisked egg whites lacking cohesion and the property of holding air. Instead of becoming thick and foamy, the egg whites form a multitude of small particles when beating stops. This defect is often due to greasy equipment. It may be possible to correct this by adding 2–3 drops of vinegar just as the egg whites are beginning to form small bubbles before rising.

GRAMMONT A style of serving shellfish cold, usually reserved for lobster and crayfish. The shellfish are first cooked in court-bouillon, then cooled. The flesh of the tail is made into escalopes (scallops), garnished with slices of truffle and glazed with jelly. The shell is filled with a mousse made from the flesh of the claws and the coral. The escalopes are placed on top, alternating with poached, glazed oysters. The dish is decorated with lettuce hearts and parsley.

The word is also used for a classic preparation of poached chicken, from which the breasts and breast bone are removed. The cavity is filled with lark fillets, mushroom tops, and cockscombs and kidneys, bound together with a béchamel sauce flavoured with truffle oil, on which the breast fillets, cut into thin strips, are laid. The dish is then covered with *sauce suprême*, sprinkled with Parmesan cheese and browned in the oven.

GRAMOLATE Also known as gramolata. A type of sorbet made from a granita mixture. It is served between main courses or as a refreshment during an evening party. It should not be confused with *gremolata*, a condiment in Italian cookery, which is made of a mixture of orange and lemon rind (zest), chopped parsley and garlic and is used in ragoûts and, most often, in osso bucco.

GRANA PADANO Cooked pressed AOC Italian cheese made from partly skimmed cow's milk (32% fat), with a natural crust coated with oil. It is a slightly convex cylinder weighing 24–40 kg (53–88 lb). Known since the 12th century, it has a very hard, granular texture, and a smoky, slightly rancid taste. In cooking it is often used grated.

GRANCHER, MARCEL ÉTIENNE Gastronomic writer and chronicler (born Lons-le-Saunier, 1897; died Le Cannet, 1976). He settled in Lyon and founded the Académie Rabelais and the Académie des Gastronomes Lyonnais. In 1937, together with Curnonsky, he published a work called *Lyon, capitale de la gastronomie*. He also wrote a number of novels in which food plays an important part, such as *Le Charcutier de Mâchonville* (1942), and was a connoisseur of wines, which he describes in *Des vins* d'*Henri IV à ceux de Brillat-Savarin* (1952). In *Cinquante Ans à table* (1953), he describes the achievement of perfection in gastronomy, after centuries of cookery, in the following terms: 'We did not immediately come up with béarnaise, Bercy and poivrade sauces. It took more than a single attempt to discover reduced cream, marinade and forcemeat. We did not straightway invent barding fat, the touch of garlic, and the thin slice of truffle under the skin. . . . While genius is spontaneous, its manifestations nevertheless require the passage of time before glorious perfection is achieved. This is particularly true in the area of food and drink . . . Magical dishes, magical words: a great cook is, when all is said and done, a great poet . . . For was it not a visit from the Muses that inspired the person who first had the idea of marrying rice and chicken, grape and thrush, potatoes and entrecôte, Parmesan and pasta, aubergine (eggplant) and tomato, Chambertin and cockerel, liqueur brandy and woodcock, onion and tripe?'

GRAND-DUC The name given to various dishes created in the Parisian restaurants frequented by the Russian aristocracy during the Second Empire and at the turn of the 20th century. These dishes contain asparagus tips and truffles: poached fillets of sole covered with Mornay sauce, arranged in a ring around asparagus tips and crayfish tails and garnished with thin slices of truffle; soft-boiled (soft-cooked) or poached eggs covered with Mornay sauce, browned, garnished with a slice of truffle, placed on a bed of fried croûtons or puff-pastry croustades and surrounded by asparagus tips in butter; sautéed meat served with the cooking liquid mixed with Madeira and périgourdine sauce, topped with thin slices of truffle and surrounded with bundles of asparagus tips. Stuffed turkey grand-duc is a very elaborate recipe created in 1906 by M. Valmy-Joyeuse, while he was in charge of the kitchens of the Marquise de Mazenda.

RECIPE

stuffed turkey grand-duc
Slit open a turkey along the back and stuff with the following mixture: 500 g (18 oz) chicken rubbed through a fine sieve, 500 ml (17 fl oz, 2 cups) double (heavy) cream, 250 g (9 oz) foie gras poached in port wine and rubbed through a sieve. Mix all these ingredients thoroughly and season. Add 12 truffles, peeled and cooked for 10 minutes in a little liqueur brandy, and 24 chicken hearts with the blood vessels removed, which have been soaked in water, steeped in white Malaga wine, drained, dried in a cloth, stuffed with a purée of York ham and poached for 15 minutes in truffle essence.

Carefully reshape the stuffed turkey. Cover with slices of raw ham or bacon, and enclose in a large layer of lining pastry, taking care to keep the shape of the bird as far as possible. Bake in a preheated oven at 180°C (250°F, gas 4) for 2½ hours. During cooking, cover the turkey with greaseproof (wax)

paper folded into four, so that it will cook all through without browning the pastry too soon. Serve the turkey freshly cooked, with a demi-glace sauce flavoured with truffle essence.

GRAND MARNIER A liqueur evolved by the Marnier-Lapostolle family firm in 1880. It is based on oranges, and there are two types. Cordon rouge includes Cognac; cordon jaune is slightly lower in strength. Grand Marnier is often used in sweet dishes, such as soufflés, or with crêpes or in whipped cream.

GRAND-MÈRE Describing dishes similar to those called *bonne femme* or *en cocotte*. The term is applied particularly to a chicken casserole served with pieces of fried bacon, small brown-glazed onions, sautéed mushrooms and fried new potatoes. The same garnish can accompany fried entrecôte (sirloin) or rump steak.

RECIPE

entrecôte grand-mère
Prepare 12 small glazed onions, 12 blanched mushroom caps and 50 g (2 oz, ⅓ cup) diced blanched salt pork or bacon. Sauté the steak in butter, browning both sides, then add the vegetables and bacon to the pan and cook all together. Meanwhile, prepare and fry some small new potatoes until browned. Arrange the steak on the serving dish surrounded by the garnishes and keep hot. Dilute the pan juices with a little stock, bring to the boil and pour over the steak. Sprinkle with chopped parsley and serve with the potatoes.

GRAND VÉFOUR A Parisian restaurant situated in the Galerie de Beaujolais in the Palais-Royal. Founded by Aubertot in 1784 and initially called the Café de Chartres, it was first taken over by Charrier, who served English breakfasts and whose scallops with mushrooms were famous, and then (in 1820) by Jean Véfour. Bonaparte, Brillat-Savarin, Murat, Grimod de La Reynière, Lamartine, Thiers and Sainte-Beuve frequented this well-known restaurant and enjoyed chicken Marengo and poultry mayonnaise. Other proprietors succeeded Jean Véfour, but the restaurant kept his name. When, under the Second Empire, one of Véfour's brothers opened his own restaurant in the Palais-Royal, a distinction was made between the Grand Véfour and the Petit Véfour (which closed in 1920). At the end of the 19th century the Grand Véfour ran into difficulties, but after World War II Louis Vaudable (whose restaurant, Maxim's, closed) took it over and in 1948 went into partnership with a young chef, Raymond Oliver, who became the maître of the restaurant two years later. Jean Cocteau and Colette, to whom several recipes are dedicated, frequented the restaurant and helped to establish its excellent reputation; its 18th-century décor has remained intact.

GRAND VENEUR A term used to describe dishes of ground game, roasted or sautéed, covered with grand veneur sauce (also called venison sauce). This is a poivrade sauce (sometimes made with the blood of the animal) with redcurrant jelly and cream added. Grand veneur dishes are usually accompanied by chestnut purée.

RECIPES

grand veneur sauce
Prepare a poivrade sauce using the trimmings of a piece of cooked venison, and boil it down to obtain at least 200 ml (7 fl oz, ¾ cup). Strain, then blend it with 1 tablespoon redcurrant jelly and 2 tablespoons cream. Whisk. If the sauce is to accompany hare, mix 1 tablespoon hare's blood with 2 tablespoons strained marinade and add this mixture to the reduced and strained sauce.

saddle of roebuck grand veneur
Trim the saddle, then lard it with strips of bacon that have been marinated in Cognac with chopped parsley, salt, pepper and a little oil. Roast it and arrange on a serving dish surrounded by braised chestnuts or chestnut purée and dauphine potatoes. Serve with a grand veneur sauce.

GRANITA A type of Italian sorbet popularized by Tortoni in Paris in the 19th century. It is a half-frozen preparation with a granular texture (hence its name), made of a lightly sweetened syrup or of a syrup flavoured with coffee or liqueur. Unlike sorbet, granita does not contain any Italian meringue.

It is served in sundae dishes or a glass bowl, either between courses or as a refreshment.

RECIPE

granita
Make a light syrup with fruit juice (such as lemon, orange, tangerine, passion fruit or mango) or very strong coffee. Cool the syrup, then pour it into an ice tray and freeze for 3–4 hours without stirring. The granita will then have a granular texture.

GRAPE The fruit of the vine, which grows in bunches on a stalk. The skin, which may be green, yellow or purple, encloses a sweet pulp with one to four seeds. Both white and black varieties are used to make wine. There are also varieties cultivated as dessert grapes, which are served as fresh fruit or used in cooking, and other varieties are dried to produce raisins, sultanas (golden raisins) and currants.

It is known that in the Stone Age wild vines were already established in the Caucasus, where they originated, as well as in the Mediterranean region. Very early on people discovered how to make a fermented drink from grapes. The cults of Osiris and Dionysus, as well as the biblical story of Noah, are evidence of the antiquity of the cultivation of vines and the manufacture of wine. After the Greeks and Romans, who learned the technique of drying grapes, came the Gauls, inventors of the cask. The Gauls made great progress in the cultivation of vines, while later still monks throughout Europe became progressively more adept in the art of wine-making. Throughout this period, fresh and dried grapes were always available.

Grape juice, valued for its invigorating and purifying properties, gave rise to the cult of the 'grape cure' in France. A grape cure centre (called the Uvarium) was opened in Moissac in 1927; in 1930 a grape centre was set up at the Saint-Lazare station in Paris and sold the juice of 5 tonnes of grapes daily. The development of bottled fruit juices led to the disappearance of these public outlets, but in Avignon, Béziers and Narbonne freshly pressed grape juice is still sold during the grape harvest.

When buying dessert grapes, choose fruit that is clean, ripe, firm and not too closely packed on the stalk, which should be firm and crisp. The grapes should be of equal size, uniformly coloured and with the bloom still on. Ripe grapes do not keep well; they can, however, be stored for a few days in the centre of a refrigerator, wrapped in a perforated paper bag. They should be taken out an hour before they are required.

Before they are eaten, grapes should be carefully washed in water that has been slightly acidulated with lemon juice or vinegar. If served as a dessert, they can be arranged in a basket or dish, alone or with other seasonal fruits, together with a special pair of scissors designed for cutting off small bunches from the main stalk.

Grapes are also used in pâtisserie and other forms of cookery. Sole Veronique, created by Auguste Escoffier in 1903 and named after a comic opera, combines grapes with sole. Chicken is often served with grapes in a similar dish. Grapes are served with veal and duck livers, roast quails and thrushes and *boudin blanc*. They are used in fruit salads, tarts and flans, jams (including raisiné) and sweet rice dishes. Grapeseed oil, a table oil, is extracted from the seeds. See also *verjuice*.

RECIPES

duck foie gras with grapes
Skin and seed 8 large white Muscat grapes for each slice of foie gras. Slice the foie gras fairly thickly, season the slices with salt and pepper and sauté them rapidly in butter. Drain and keep hot. Deglaze the pan with a small glass of Sauternes, Monbazillac or a liqueur wine (or use half wine and half thickened veal stock), then add the grapes and shake them about in the pan. Adjust the seasoning. Pour the sauce and the grapes on to the foie gras and serve very hot.

grape jam
Pick the grapes off the stalk, removing any bad ones, and seed them if the grapes are large. Weigh the fruit. Weigh out 500 g (18 oz, 2¼ cups) granu-

lated sugar for every 1 kg (2¼ lb) grapes. Put the sugar into a pan with 120 ml (4½ fl oz, ½ cup) water per 1 kg (2¼ lb) grapes and dissolve it over a low heat. Bring to the boil and boil for 4 minutes, then add the grapes and a split vanilla pod (bean). Bring back to the boil and skim the pan. Cook for 10 minutes over a medium heat, then 15 minutes over a low heat. Take out the grapes with a slotted spoon and put them to one side. Boil the syrup to a temperature of 107°C (225°F), see *sugar*, then replace the grapes and bring the pan back to the boil. Take off the stove and pot in the usual way.

grape tart

Make a tart pastry with 250 g (9 oz, 2¼ cups) plain (all-purpose) flour, a generous pinch of salt, 100 g (4 oz, ½ cup) caster (superfine) sugar, 1 egg yolk, ½ glass water and 125 g (4½ oz, ½ cup) softened butter. Roll the dough into a ball and chill it for 1 hour. Wash and seed 500 g (18 oz) white grapes.

In a bowl mix 3 eggs with 100 g (4 oz, ½ cup) caster (superfine) sugar and 250 ml (8 fl oz, 1 cup) single (light) cream. Beat the mixture with a whisk and while whisking gradually add 250 ml (8 fl oz, 1 cup) milk, then 6 tablespoons kirsch.

Roll out the dough and use it to line a 24 cm (9½ in) tart tin (pan). Prick the bottom with a fork, spread the grapes over the tin and bake in a pre-heated oven at 200°C (400°F, gas 6) for 10 minutes. Pour the cream into the tart and continue to cook for 25–30 minutes (cover the tin with foil if the cream browns too fast). Leave the tart to get cold, then unmould it on to a serving dish and sprinkle with icing (confectioner's) sugar.

Muscat grape tartlets

Make a *pâte sablée* (see *short pastry*), roll it out very thinly, cut out 4 circles 18 cm (7 in) in diameter and use them to line 4 tartlet tins (pans). Prick the bottom of each lined tin, leave to rest, then bake blind for 15 minutes.

Mix together 250 ml (8 fl oz, 1 cup) black Muscat grape juice, 150 ml (¼ pint, ⅔ cup) single (light) cream, 100 g (4 oz, ½ cup) melted butter, 2 egg yolks, 2 whole eggs and 2 tablespoons sugar. Fill the tarts with this mixture and bake in a preheated oven at 180°C (350°F, gas 4) for 20 minutes.

other recipes See *foie gras, quail, raisiné.*

GRAPEFRUIT A large round citrus fruit, 11–17 cm (4½–7 in) in diameter, the most common varieties of which have a yellow skin and a refreshing, slightly acid-tasting pulp. There are also pink varieties, which have a pinkish-red tinge to the skin and pink flesh that is much sweeter. The grapefruit tree probably originated in the West Indies but a large percentage of the world's crop is now grown in the southern United States.

The grapefruit is popular as a breakfast food, usually cut in two, each segment being detached from the skin with a special serrated knife with a curved

GRAPEFRUIT

ruby or red grapefruit

pink grapefruit

grapefruit

seedless grapefruit

point designed to loosen the segments. It is eaten either plain and fresh, or quickly grilled (broiled) after being brushed with melted butter and/or sprinkled with sugar. Grapefruit is also an ingredient in cocktails and salads, and it goes well with some rich savoury poultry and meat dishes.

As a dessert, grapefruit can be used in ices, fruit salads, cakes and various sweet courses, in the same way as the orange.

The fruit is also used to make marmalade, and the juice is widely consumed as a drink.

RECIPES

grapefruit ices

Cut the tops off some grapefruit, hollow them out with a special grapefruit knife without piercing the rind and separate the segments. Press the segments (or put them through a blender, then strain) to obtain the juice and use this to prepare a grapefruit ice in the same way as an orange ice. Put the grapefruit skins in the freezer. When the ice has just started to freeze, fill the grapefruit skins with it. Place the caps on the fruits and return to the freezer until the ice has frozen. Transfer to the refrigerator 40 minutes before serving.

grapefruit salad

Mix grapefruit segments with fine slices of apple sprinkled with lemon juice, chopped celery and a few shredded lettuce leaves. Dress with a little yogurt or a light oil-based dressing.

GRAPPA A marc brandy made in Italy from the residue of grapes left after pressing. It should ideally be matured so that the harsh initial taste is refined. Grappa is made in various regions and may be used for certain dishes, such as the Piedmontese speciality, braised kid.

GRATER A flat, convex or cylindrical utensil with the surface perforated with holes of different sizes and shapes, some of them toothed. A solid substance is rubbed over the holes repeatedly to reduce it to coarse or fine threads (cheese, carrots, celery) or to powder or very fine fragments (coconut, nutmeg, rind of citrus fruits, Parmesan cheese). A nutmeg grater is the smallest, being 3 cm (1¼ in) long, while a cheese or vegetable grater may be 20 cm (8 in) long. Some graters are in the form of mechanical mills in which the interchangeable drums provide the grating surface. Food processors are equipped with grating accessories for large quantities.

GRATIN The golden crust that forms on the surface of a dish when it is browned in the oven or put under the grill (broiler). Usually the top of the dish has been coated with grated cheese, breadcrumbs or egg and breadcrumbs. Formerly, 'gratin' was the crust adhering to the cooking receptacle, which was scraped off (*gratté* in French) and eaten as a titbit.

The term has been extended to denote a method

Peeling and segmenting grapefruit

This method is used for preparing segments from all citrus fruit.

1 *Cut the peel off the top and bottom of the fruit, removing all pith. Stand the fruit on a board and cut the peel and pith off the sides, working from top to bottom in neat slices.*

2 *Hold the fruit in one hand (preferably over a bowl to catch the juice) and cut between the membranes to remove the segments.*

of cooking fish, meat, vegetables, pasta dishes and even sweets. The preparation is cooked or reheated in the oven so that a protective layer forms on the surface, improving the taste of the food and preventing it from drying up. This layer consists of strongly flavoured grated cheese (such as Gruyère or Parmesan) or breadcrumbs, sprinkled with melted butter. The length of cooking time depends on whether the dish is to be cooked from scratch or merely reheated or browned. In all cases a number of rules apply: use dishes that are flameproof and can be transferred directly to the table; butter them generously so that the preparation does not stick; if the dish is to be browned under the grill, it must already be very hot; for a gratin that is to be fully cooked, the dish must be set on a metal tray separating it from the oven shelf or placed in a bain marie.

Gratins are served straight from the dish they are cooked in. They are frequently made using minced (ground) leftover meat, pasta and poultry, but the method can also be applied to more elaborate preparations (lobster thermidor, scallops *à la parisienne*, sole *au gratin*, calves' sweetbreads *au gratin*, crayfish).

RECIPES

gratin dauphinois
Peel and thinly slice 1 kg (2¼ lb) potatoes and arrange them evenly in a generously buttered dish. Mix 2 whole eggs with a little milk, add 1 teaspoon salt, then whisk together with 600 ml (1 pint, 2½ cups) warmed milk or cream. Pour this mixture over the potatoes and dot with knobs of butter. Cook in a preheated oven at 220°C (425°F, gas 7) for about 50 minutes, if necessary protecting the top of the dish with foil towards the end of the cooking period.

The bottom of the dish can be rubbed with garlic, and a little grated nutmeg may be added at the same time as the salt. Grated Gruyère may also be added: one layer on the bottom of the dish and another on the top.

gratin languedocien
Half-cook in oil 4 peeled and sliced aubergines (eggplants), seasoned with salt and pepper, and 12 halved, seasoned tomatoes. Arrange them in alternate layers in a flameproof dish. Cover with a mixture of breadcrumbs, chopped garlic and parsley. Sprinkle with olive oil. Begin cooking on the top of the stove, then bake slowly in a preheated oven at 180°C (350°F, gas 4) until the top is well browned.

gratin of beetroot in verjuice
Slice 1 kg (2¼ lb) raw beetroot (beets) and cut into sticks. Cook in a white stock and drain without cooling. Gently heat 200 ml (7 fl oz, ¾ cup) single (light) cream without boiling, whisking all the time. Remove from the heat. Mix together half a glass of verjuice obtained by pressing a large bunch of sour white grapes, 2 egg yolks, 1 tablespoon chopped parsley, salt and pepper. Gradually add this mixture to the cream. Arrange the vegetables in a baking dish and cover with the sauce. Sprinkle with grated Cantal cheese, add very small knobs of butter and cook au gratin by placing the dish in a very hot oven for a few minutes until the top is browned.

gratin of sardine fillets with lemon juice
Wash 800 g (1¾ lb) sardines and wipe them dry with paper towels. Remove the fillets with a kitchen knife and place the fish in a buttered roasting tin (pan), skin side down. Put the rind (zest) of 1 lemon and 100 g (4 oz, ½ cup) crème fraîche in a bowl. Season with salt and pepper and add the juice of 2 lemons. Stir and pour over the sardines. Cook in a preheated oven at 240°C (475°F, gas 9) for 7–10 minutes. Serve with toasted bread.

gratin savoyard of frogs' legs
Allow 12 pairs of frogs' legs per person. Trim them, season with salt and pepper, dip in milk and then lightly flour. Fry in butter with shallots and a little chopped garlic, then drain and arrange them in a fairly large baking dish. Dilute the pan juices with Mandement wine (from the Côte de Mandement on the right bank of the Rhône, in the canton of Geneva) or with a fruity white wine; reduce and pour over the frogs' legs. Sprinkle with chopped chives and parsley, then squeeze the juice of a lemon over them. Mix together 250 ml (8 fl oz, 1 cup) double (heavy) cream, 75 g (3 oz, ¾ cup) grated Gruyère cheese and 2 egg yolks. Season with salt and pepper and pour over the frogs' legs. Brown under the grill (broiler) and serve garnished with a few fluted slices of lemon.

macaroni gratin
Bring 2.5 litres (4¼ pints, 11 cups) salted water to the boil. Add 300 g (11 oz, 2¾ cups) macaroni and cook for 5 minutes, stirring with a wooden spoon so that the macaroni do not stick. Remove from the water, drain and hold under cold running water to cool them. Place them in a bowl and cover with milk. Cover and place in the refrigerator for 12 hours. The following day, take out the macaroni. Season with salt and pepper. Stir well, pour into a gratin dish and smooth the top with a wooden spatula. Sprinkle with 75 g (3 oz, ¾ cup) grated Gruyère cheese and dot 25 g (1 oz, 2 tablespoons) butter, cut into small pieces, across the top. Bake in a preheated oven at 180°C (350°F, gas 4) for 10 minutes, then place under a medium hot grill (broiler) for 1 minute. Serve very hot.

polenta gratin
Dice 2 boneless chicken breasts. Chop 2 onions and 75 g (3 oz, ½ cup) olives very finely. Season with salt, pepper and chopped fresh coriander (cilantro) and fry until golden. Remove from the heat. Now brown 2 chopped onions and 2 tomatoes, peeled, seeded and crushed, and 250 g (9 oz, 1¾ cups) polenta (cornmeal) in the olive oil. In a roasting tin (pan), put a layer of chicken, then a layer of polenta. Continue this layering process until all the ingredients have been used up. Gratiné in a preheated oven at 240°C (475°F, gas 9) for 5 minutes and serve very hot.

GRATINÉE Onion soup poured into a tureen or individual casseroles made of ovenproof porcelain, topped with dried bread and grated cheese and cooked au gratin in a very hot oven. Gratinée is a Parisian speciality, traditionally served for late supper in the bistros of Montmartre and the district around the Halles.

In general, the cheese used is Gruyère, Comté or Emmental, but gratinée can also be made with Cantal or Bleu d'Auvergne (see *blue cheese*).

RECIPES

gratinée
Peel and finely slice 4 large onions. Heat 40 g (1½ oz, 3 tablespoons) butter and 4 tablespoons oil in a shallow frying pan. Add the onions and stir

with a wooden spatula until they are golden brown. Sprinkle with 25 g (I oz, ¼ cup) flour and stir until brown. Add 200 ml (7 fl oz, ¾ cup) dry white wine, reduce for a few minutes over a gentle heat, then pour in I litre (1¾ pints, 4⅓ cups) water or stock. Season with salt and pepper, add 2 small crushed cloves of garlic and a bouquet garni, then bring to the boil and cook very gently for I hour.

Meanwhile, in the oven dry some slices of bread cut from a long, thin French loaf. Mix 3 egg yolks with 6 tablespoons Madeira or port. Preheat the oven to 220°C (425°F, gas 7) and put a bain marie into it. When the onion soup is cooked, remove the bouquet garni, gradually add the mixture of egg yolks and Madeira, then divide the soup among 4 individual ovenproof soup bowls. Generously sprinkle the dried slices of bread with Gruyère and arrange on the surface of the soup. Place the soup bowls in the bain marie in the oven and cook until the top of the bread is well browned. Serve immediately.

gratinée de poires aux pistaches

Bring to the boil I litre (1¾ pints, 4⅓ cups) water with I vanilla pod (bean) cut in two, 200 g (7 oz, I cup) caster (superfine) sugar and 2 tablespoons lemon juice. Peel and core 6 ripe but firm pears. Poach gently. Allow to cool. Make a crème pâtissière (confectioner's custard) with 250 ml (8 fl oz, I cup) milk, I vanilla pod cut in two, 20 g (¾ oz, 2½ tablespoons) plain (all-purpose) flour, 3 egg yolks and 70 g (2¾ oz, 5 tablespoons) sugar. Place in a bowl, add I tablespoon pear brandy and, when it is almost cold, 3 tablespoons whipped cream. Beat I egg yolk with 25 g (I oz, 2 tablespoons) sugar until the mixture foams and turns a paler yellow. Incorporate I tablespoon chopped pistachio nuts and 2 tablespoons whipped cream. Drain the pears and cut them in the shape of a fan but still attached. Cut I vanilla pod into matchsticks. Put some crème pâtissière on to each plate and place a pear in the middle. Sprinkle icing (confectioner's) sugar on the pears without going over the edge. Place the plates under the grill (broiler) to brown the fruit. Pour some pistachio cream evenly around the pears and draw marbling patterns with the point of a knife. Now sprinkle the edge of the plate with icing sugar and chopped pistachio nuts. Place a spoonful of ice cream next to each pear, decorate with vanilla matchsticks and serve immediately.

GRATTE PAILLE A rich cow's-milk cheese (70% fat) made with both pasteurized and unpasteurized milk in the Île-de-France. Produced in brick shapes about 8 cm (3 in) high, the cheese has a beige mottled rind and an oily texture. The flavour is very rich and creamy.

GRATTONS Also known as gratterons. The name given in certain regions of France to the residue of melted pork or goose fat containing small pieces of meat, which is eaten cold as an hors d'oeuvre. (See also *friton*.) Grattons from Auvergne are strips of pork neck and fatty meat cooked together, then pounded or minced (ground) and pressed in a mould. Lyonnais grattons are formed into rissoles and not moulded. Bordeaux grattons combine melted pork fat and lean pork. In *Odeurs de forêt et Fumets de table*, Charles Forot gives the recipe for Vivarais grattons: 'The pork fat, cut into small pieces, is melted for 5–6 hours over a very low heat. When it has completely melted, it is put into jars. Salt, pepper, spices, chopped parsley and a pinch of grated garlic added to the remains of meat left on the bottom of the pan. This mixture is stirred for a long time so as to mix together the ingredients and flavours, then it is put in a stone jar.'

Goose grattons are obtained during the preparation of confit, by draining the residue of goose fat and the tiny fragments of flesh while they are still hot. They are then pressed, sprinkled with fine salt and eaten cold.

Grattons can also be pieces of fatty pork cooked until crisp (cracklings).

GRAVES Red and white AOC Bordeaux wines from the gravelly vineyards mostly to the south of the city of Bordeaux, along the left bank of the River Garonne and down into the Landes. The area was often considered as two regions: the northern part, particularly famous for red wines, and the southern region, abutting and enclosing the Sauternais. In 1987, however, an area of the Graves region, which included a number of the famous properties and the southern parts of Bordeaux, was formed into a new appellation: Pessac-Léognan (see *Pessac-Léognan*). The Graves region, which was named after the type of ground (gravel and sand), is possibly the oldest part of the Bordeaux vineyard to have been planted.

The red wines are made from the same grapes as other red wines of the Bordeaux area: Cabernet Sauvignon, Cabernet Franc and Merlot.

The white wines of the Graves, more numerous than the reds, are made from the same grapes as Sauternes – Sémillon, Sauvignon Blanc and Muscadelle – and they are basically of two types: the truly dry wines and Graves Supérieur, which are sweet wines. The dry whites are excellent accompaniments to fish.

GRAVES DE VAYRES Red and white AOC wines from the left bank of the Dordogne, in the Entre-Deux-Mers region, the whites being dry, the reds lighter in style. They should not be confused with the wines coming from the Graves region itself.

GRAVLAX Also known as gravad lax. This classic Scandinavian dish of salmon pickled with salt, sugar and dill, originates from an ancient method of preserving fish by burying it. Over a period of a few days the fish would ferment and become slightly sour, but when buried for weeks or months it would begin to decay.

Gravlax is prepared by filleting the fish and laying one fillet, skin side down, in a dish, then topping it with a pickle mixture of sugar, salt, pepper and dill before covering with the second fillet. The fish is weighted down and allowed to pickle for 4–10 days in the refrigerator. Every day the fish is turned and basted with the pickle liquid (which develops as the sugar and salt draw out the juices in the salmon and dissolve). The pickle mixture is scraped off before serving.

Gravlax may be served thinly or thickly sliced, usually with a slightly sweetened sauce of mustard and dill.

GRAVY Cooking juice, usually from meat, extended with stock or other liquid and thickened with a roux or another starch. The excess fat is removed and a small amount retained to make a roux before liquid is added. Alternatively, the pan can be deglazed with wine or other alcohol, or a little stock, then more liquid may be added and boiled until reduced to a slightly syrupy consistency. Gravy may also be thin, but full-flavoured.

GRAYLING *ombre* A freshwater fish similar and related to the trout; it is distinguished by its small mouth and its dorsal fin. Weighing about 1.12 kg (2½ lb) and 40–50 cm (16–20 in) long, it has a good flavour and is cooked in the same way as trout. It will not travel or keep, however, and must be cooked and eaten without delay.

GREASING The process of coating a baking sheet, cake tin (pan) or mould with cooking fat to prevent the preparation from sticking to the container during cooking and to enable it to be removed easily.

GREAT BRITAIN See *page 580*.

GRECQUE, À LA Describing dishes of Greek origin, but more loosely used for dishes inspired by Mediterranean cuisine. Vegetables *à la grecque* are cooked in a marinade flavoured with olive oil and lemon and served cold, either as an hors d'oeuvre or an entrée. Pilaf *à la grecque* consists of rice mixed with sausage, peas and cubes of pepper. Fish *à la grecque* is coated with a white wine sauce flavoured with celery, fennel and coriander seeds.

RECIPES

marinated fish à la grecque

Gently cook 100 g (4 oz, 1 cup) finely chopped onions in 150 ml (¼ pint, ⅔ cup) olive oil without browning them. Add 150 ml (¼ pint, ⅔ cup) white wine, 150 ml (¼ pint, ⅔ cup) water and the strained juice of a lemon. Add 2 finely shredded (bell) peppers, 1 crushed garlic clove and a bouquet garni (consisting of parsley, a sprig of thyme, a bay leaf and a sprig of fresh fennel). Season with salt and pepper and boil for 15 minutes. Pour piping hot over the selected fish, allow to cool and keep in the refrigerator. This quantity of sauce is sufficient for 500 g (18 oz) fish. Suitable fish include sardines and red mullet.

sauce à la grecque for fish

Heat a finely sliced quarter of a celery heart and 3 finely sliced onions in 3 tablespoons olive oil. Add a bouquet garni (including a sprig of fennel), 6 tablespoons white wine and 12 coriander seeds. Boil down by two-thirds and add 6 tablespoons thin velouté* sauce and the same quantity of single (light) cream. Boil down by one-third. Blend in 50 g (2 oz, ¼ cup) butter and strain before serving.

The velouté sauce may be replaced by an equal volume of strained fish fumet and 1 tablespoon beurre manié, added in small knobs to the boiling liquid, which is whisked for 1–2 minutes.

stuffed tomatoes à la grecque

Soak 125 g (4½ oz, scant 1 cup) sultanas (golden raisins) in a little tepid water until they swell, then drain. Heat 4 tablespoons olive oil in a saucepan and add 200 g (7 oz, 1 cup) rice; stir until the grains become transparent. Then add to the rice twice its volume of boiling water, a pinch of powdered saffron, 1 teaspoon salt, pepper, a pinch of cayenne and a bouquet garni. Bring to the boil and simmer gently until the rice is cooked. Slice off the tops of 6 large tomatoes, remove the seeds and pulp and lightly season the insides with salt. Place the tomatoes upside down in a colander to drain. When the rice is cooked, drain and cool, add the sultanas and adjust the seasoning. Dry the tomato cases, put 1 teaspoon olive oil in the bottom of each and fill them with the mixture of rice and sultanas. Replace the tops. Arrange the stuffed tomatoes fairly close together in a baking dish. Pour a little oil in the bottom of the dish and cook in a preheated oven at 240°C (475°F, gas 9). Remove the tomatoes from the oven before they become too soft and serve immediately.

vegetables à la grecque

Choose very fresh tender vegetables, such as aubergines (eggplants), cardoons, mushrooms, cauliflower, courgettes (zucchini), fennel, artichoke hearts and small onions. Small onions may be left whole, but the other vegetables should be washed thoroughly and cut into fairly small pieces so that they can be cooked properly. They should be sprinkled with lemon juice if there is a risk of discoloration. Make a court-bouillon by boiling 6 tablespoons olive oil, 750 ml (1¼ pints, 3⅛ cups) water and the strained juice of 2 lemons with a bouquet garni (consisting of parsley, celery, fennel, thyme and bay leaf), 12–15 coriander seeds and 12–15 peppercorns for 20 minutes. Lightly brown the vegetables in a little olive oil, then pour over the very hot court-bouillon and finish cooking. Add 2 tablespoons concentrated tomato purée (paste) to the court-bouillon if desired.

other recipes See *croustade, omelette (flat omelettes)*.

GREECE See *page 582*.

Great Britain

It is perhaps surprising to realize that British and continental cookery draw on a common tradition. The first British cookery book, *Forme of Cury* (Cooking Methods), attributed to the cooks of Richard II, is from the same period as *Viandier* by Taillevent. The French words *boudin, pudding, bacon, rosbif* and *bifteck* all have English origins.

British cookery retains some of the characteristics of its medieval origins, as shown by the predominance of cereals in foodstuffs, the sweet-and-sour contrasts (such as roast pork with apple sauce, roast lamb with redcurrant jelly or mint sauce) and the traditions of a large breakfast and of cheese served as a dessert.

Carême, and later Escoffier, who both worked in London, introduced French people to a number of great British specialities: turtle soup, oxtail soup, oyster soup, fried whitebait from the Thames estuary, John Dory with lobster sauce, curry and its numerous variants, eel pie, Irish stew and, of course, eggs and bacon, fruit cake and a wide range of puddings.

■ **Regional specialities** British cookery is full of highly characteristic regional specialities (see *England, Scotland, Wales*), which sometimes have surprising names: Hindle wakes from Lancashire (chicken stuffed with prunes, served cold with a lemon sauce), toad-in-the-hole (sausage in batter), angels on horseback (fried oysters on croûtons), petticoat tails (shortbread) and maids of honour (almond tartlets).

■ **Meat, vegetables and fish** The British are traditionally great meat eaters: John Bull, the archetypal Englishman, was based on a fictional 18th-century landowner whose diet consisted of beef and beer. Roast meat is the traditional Sunday lunch, and fresh or cooked meat is used in innumerable pies (chicken and ham, steak and kidney, ham and veal) and meat

puddings. Cooked vegetables are usually served with the main dish; leeks are traditionally associated with Wales and turnips with Scotland. Traditional main dishes are nearly always served with potatoes, whether or not there are other accompanying vegetables: they may be mashed, boiled, roasted, baked in their skins in the oven or fried.

Sea and freshwater fish, shellfish and seafood are important foods in the British diet. Fresh cod, plaice and haddock are often served fried with tartare sauce, sole is grilled, and crab is prepared mainly in salads. Mackerel is traditionally accompanied by gooseberry sauce. Halibut, herring and whiting are also popular. Fish is enjoyed simply poached and served with a complementary sauce, such as shrimp, oyster, fennel, parsley, horseradish, cucumber (especially with salmon) or mustard.

Game and venison have featured in festive cookery and have been eaten by the well-to-do since the Middle Ages. Then, the practice of poaching also led to some humble traditional dishes – rook pie (in the absence of pigeons and pheasants) and hare pie (with its numerous variants). Winged game is enjoyed roasted with bread sauce and cranberry or redcurrant sauce, and hare is jugged.

Poultry (turkey, goose and chicken in particular) are used in traditional recipes, including chicken pie, boiled chicken with oysters or parsley sauce, mulligatawny soup and the traditional roast turkey at Christmas, stuffed with chestnut stuffing and sausage meat, accompanied by bacon and small chipolata sausages.

■ **Fruit and desserts** Fruit has always played an important part in British cookery, particularly apples (including the well-known Bramley and Cox), strawberries and raspberries. Simple fruit desserts are served for family meals: stewed or poached fruit with hot custard sauce, fruit salad with yogurt or ice cream, or soft fruit with whipped or clotted cream. Fruit tarts,

crumbles, pies, jellies, fools and trifles (made with sponge cake, jam, fruit, custard and cream) are very popular. Fruit is also used in sweet and savoury preserves: jams, jellies, chutneys and pickles. The hot puddings, with their infinite variety, reign supreme among desserts. All the recipes have been carefully catalogued, particularly by Mrs Beeton in her famous cookbook; some of them have royal names (Coburg or Prince Albert); others are more traditional, such as bread and butter pudding, apple dumplings, cabinet pudding, plum pudding and the milk puddings (rice, semolina and tapioca).

■ **Modern British cooking** Traditional dishes may still be cherished and regional specialities appreciated, but across the country there is a wide variety of contemporary food eaten on a daily basis. Light dishes and uncooked foods in salads, influenced by European and Oriental styles, are everyday fare. Herbs, spices, fruit, vegetables and staples, such as bread, reflect the multi-cultural society that is modern Britain. The average cook is just as likely to serve rice, pasta or couscous as boiled potatoes, and a stir-fried dish is more popular for mid-week dinner than a traditional stew. Traditional flavours and food combinations are often retained in the context of quicker methods. This fresh approach to food and cooking complements the classics rather than replacing them completely.

WINE With traditions of wine-making dating from at least Roman times, the industry has seen considerable growth in recent years. The vineyards are mainly concentrated in Kent, Sussex and the south-west and are predominantly planted with Reichensteiner, Seyval Blanc, Bacchus, Schönburger and Madelaine Angevine. Whilst production is mainly white wine in a dry or medium dry, light, aromatic style, a few vineyards are making red and sparkling wines.

GREENGAGE A type of plum with a green skin, sometimes tinged with yellow, red or purple, and greenish-yellow, sweet flesh with good flavour; there are many different strains. Greengages are delicious eaten fresh and make good jam. They can also be bought canned in syrup.

The French name, *reine-Claude*, is an abbreviation of *prune de la reine Claude* (Queen Claude's plum), because the fruit was dedicated to Claude of France, wife of Francis I.

GREMOLATA A flavouring mixture used in Italian cooking, consisting of chopped parsley, grated lemon rind (zest) and finely chopped garlic. The fresh mixture is sprinkled over cooked dishes just before serving to introduce a fresh, zesty flavour. It is the classic final flavouring and garnish for osso bucco, the veal stew cooked on the bone.

GRENADIER Fish of the *Macrouridae* family, which lives in the deep waters of the Atlantic; it is fished from Greenland to the Bay of Biscay. It is identified by its tapered body, which ends in a point. The flesh is very white, and the boneless fillets are ideal for making fish mousse.

GRENADIN A small slice of fillet of veal, about 2 cm (¾ in) thick and 6–7 cm (2½–3 in) long, cut from the loin, the fillet or the chump end of the loin. Grenadins are usually interlarded with best larding bacon and then grilled (broiled), fried or even braised. A small unbarded grenadin of veal fried in butter is called a *noisette*. Grenadins may also be cut from white turkey meat.

RECIPES

braised veal grenadins
Trim four 100 g (4 oz) grenadins and interlard with bacon fat. Butter a casserole dish and line it with unsmoked bacon rinds or pork skin with the fat removed. Peel and finely slice a large carrot and a medium-sized onion and brown them in butter, with any trimmings of meat from the grenadins. Put the vegetables on top of the bacon rinds, arrange the grenadins on top, cover and cook gently for 15 minutes. Add 200 ml (7 fl oz, ¾ cup) white wine and boil down almost completely. Then add a little stock, bring to the boil, cover the casserole dish and cook in a preheated oven at 220°C (425°F, gas 7) for about 40 minutes, basting the meat several times. Arrange the grenadins on an ovenproof serving dish, coat them with a little of the strained cooking juice and glaze in the oven. Dilute the cooking juices in the casserole with consommé, strain and remove the fat. Boil down further if necessary and pour the sauce over the grenadins. Serve with buttered spinach.

fried grenadins in cream
Season four 100 g (4 oz) grenadins with salt and pepper and sauté them in oil until brown on both sides. Reduce the heat, cover and cook gently for about 15 minutes until tender. Drain the grenadins and keep them hot in a serving dish. Remove the cooking oil from the pan and add 200 ml (7 fl oz, ¾ cup) white wine or cider. Scrape the pan with a spatula, add a small sprig of tarragon and boil down to reduce by half. Remove the tarragon, add 200 ml (7 fl oz, ¾ cup) single (light) cream, and boil down, stirring continuously. Adjust the seasoning and pour the sauce over the grenadins.

GRENADINE A refreshing drink made of water and grenadine syrup. The latter was originally made from pomegranates only, but today it contains vegetable matter, citric acid and certain red fruits.

Grenadine syrup is used as a colouring agent for cocktails, diabolos and aperitifs.

GRENOBLOISE, À LA Preparations of fish *à la meunière*, garnished with capers and finely diced lemon flesh. Croûtons may also be added.

GREUBONS Residue made after gently rendering pork fat to make lard. These coloured fragments, also known as *rillons* or *grabons* in the Jura, are used in making a savoury.

GRIBICHE A cold sauce based on mayonnaise in which the raw egg yolk is replaced by hard-boiled (hard-cooked) egg yolk. Capers, fines herbes and the chopped white of a hard-boiled egg are added. Gribiche sauce is served with calf's head (*tête de veau*) or cold fish.

RECIPE

gribiche sauce
Thoroughly pound or mash the yolk of a hard-boiled (hard-cooked) egg and gradually add 250 ml (8 fl oz, 1 cup) oil, beating constantly and keeping the mixture smooth as for a mayonnaise. As it thickens, add 2 tablespoons vinegar, salt, pepper, 1 tablespoon each of capers, chopped parsley, chervil and tarragon, and the white of the hard-boiled egg cut into julienne.

GRIDDLE A flat cast-iron cooking plate, traditionally known as a bakestone or girdle. Used lightly greased to cook griddle cakes, such as Welsh cakes; some types of scones, including potato scones; small thick pancakes or drop scones; and crumpets. Heavy cooking plates of this type, varying in size and shape, are used in many countries. For example, in Britanny they are used to cook galettes and crêpes; in India they are used to cook flat breads, such as chapatis; and in Malaysia they are used to make murtabak, a filled roti made from finely stretched dough enclosing a savoury filling. A heavy frying pan is usually used instead of a griddle in modern kitchens.

GRIFFE A French cut of beef consisting of the muscle between the shoulder and the neck. When

GREECE

Contemporary Greek cuisine is dominated by fish, mutton and various Mediterranean vegetables flavoured with aromatic herbs, olive oil and lemon. The eastern European influence is apparent in the custom of eating mezze (small appetizers) with ouzo, the habit of drinking very strong, sweet, black coffee with cold water and in the sweet, rich pâtisserie.

■ **Fish** Abundant everywhere, fish is usually either brushed with olive oil, grilled (broiled) and garnished with lemon, or cooked in the oven with aromatic herbs (fennel, aniseed or coriander). Fish roe is used in the preparation of taramasalata.

■ **Lamb and mutton** Mutton is relatively abundant in the north; it is cooked in stews (often with leeks and herbs), in a sauce blended with eggs and lemon juice (*avgolemono*), on skewers or shaped as spicy meatballs. In the south, where meat is scarcer, offal is used in such dishes as *souvlakia* (kidney on skewers with tomatoes and peppers), grilled lamb's intestine on skewers and sausages made with lamb's liver, spleen and lungs (*kokoretsi*). Dried marinated meat is also popular (see *pastirma*).

■ **Vegetables** The originality of Greek cookery can be seen in the preparation of vegetables. Aubergines (eggplants) are used in a variety of ways: they are an essential ingredient in moussaka; they can also be stuffed, prepared *au gratin* and puréed to make *tarato*, a thick, cold soup including peppers and yogurt and seasoned with vinaigrette.

Other specialities include courgettes (zucchini) stuffed with minced (ground) mutton flavoured with saffron and marjoram; stuffed artichokes *à l'athénienne* and stuffed vine leaves or cabbage leaves (dolmas); and marinated vegetables *à la grecque*. Yogurt is used with cucumber and garlic to make *tzatziki*, a refreshing hors d'oeuvre.

Lemon is used extensively in Greek cuisine, in *avgolemono* soup (a consommé with rice, flavoured with egg and lemon), in garnishes for ragoûts, in marinated vegetables and in sweet desserts and cakes.

■ **Dairy produce** As in other Balkan countries, dairy products play an important part in Greek cuisine. Greek cheeses, made of ewe's or goat's milk, are quite varied. The hard cheeses include Agrafaou, Kefalotyri (highly salted), Kasseri and Skyros. Feta, the best known soft cheese, is a crumbly goat's-milk cheese, which is eaten fresh. There is also a blue cheese, Kopanisti. Cheese is often used in stuffings, gratins, sauces or mixed with minced vegetables, meat or fish to fill *bourekakia* (small pastries served as an entrée). Curd cheeses are flavoured with herbs, onion and soured (sour) cream, and tomato and cucumber salads are mixed with black olives and cubes of fresh salted cheese.

WINE Although the Greeks were not the first to make a drink fermented from the fruit of the vine, they were, nevertheless, the creators of viticulture, and their wines were highly esteemed throughout the ancient world. Greece continues to grow grapes, and vineyards are located on the mainland and on many of the numerous islands. The terrain is arid and mountainous with many vineyards at high altitudes up to 800 m (2,600 ft). In recent years there has been considerable investment in modern technology and training resulting in the production of a range of top quality wines. The industry is dominated by a number of big companies but, increasingly, smaller estates are also producing premium wines.

Wine laws conform to EU guidelines and often adopt the French appellation system. Wines entitled to the Quality status are either sweet wines from Mavrodaphne or Muscat grapes described as Controlled Appellation of Origin (OPE), or dry wines described as Appellation of Superior Quality (OPAP). Vin de Pays wines are from defined areas and allow for the inclusion of both indigenous Greek and foreign grape varieties. The Table Wines category includes brands as well as interesting wines made outside the strict appellation rules.

Red, white, rosé, sparkling and dessert wines are made. Perhaps the most famous are Retsina – where small pieces of resin from the *Pinus helepensis* pine are added to the grape must to give a dry white or rosé wine with distinctive pungent flavour – and the Muscat of Samos, a luscious dessert wine produced from Muscat Blanc à Petits Grains.

the fat is removed, it can be used with other more fatty or more tasty cuts to make soups and stews.

GRILL An item of kitchen equipment for grilling meat and fish; that is, equipment used for cooking food by radiant heat. The heat source may be gas, electricity, charcoal or coke. The best form of grill is heated from below, as in charcoal grilling. When the heat comes from above, the grill is referred to as a broiler in the United States and as a salamander in professional kitchens. One of the oldest grill models consisted of a wrought-iron grid with four legs and a handle. Food was placed on the grid, which was then rested on top of the glowing embers of a fire, the legs preventing the food from actually touching the embers. It was oiled before use and was suitable for cooking large pieces of meat, such as rib of beef or entrecôte. Another old model, which is still used in France, consists of two grids hinged together, the

In Greece, after the Lenten fast, lambs are roasted for an Easter feast.

food being placed between them. It is especially useful for sardines, sausages or small cutlets, which are often difficult to turn over on an ordinary grill. Some grills consist of a cast-iron or sheet steel plate that is placed in direct contact with the hotplate or burner of the stove.

Electric or gas grills consist of burners or infrared elements. They may be situated above the unit or in the roof of the unit. This type of grill is effective only if the heat radiation is intense.

GRILLADE
The French name for food that has been grilled (broiled), particularly meat.

A prime French cut of pork taken from along the blade bone or loins and usually grilled is also known as a grillade. These cuts are scarce, because there are only two per pig. Weighing 400–500 g (14–18 oz), a grillade is slightly fatty, tender and tasty and is characterized by long fibres, which are cut crossways before cooking. Grillades are fried or grilled over a medium heat. They may also be coated with egg and breadcrumbs, stuffed or rolled into large paupiettes.

GRILLÉ AUX POMMES
A rectangular puff pastry base topped with stewed apple, sometimes flavoured with vanilla, covered with a lattice of the same pastry and cooked in a very hot oven.

GRILLING
A method of cooking by intense heat, the nourishing juices being sealed into the meat by the crust formed on the surface. The fuel traditionally used for grilling is small charcoal (known as *braise* in France). The charcoal, when thoroughly alight, is spread out to form a bed in a grill pan with a well-regulated draught. This bed of charcoal varies in depth according to the size and kind of meat to be grilled. The food is cooked over the hot coals. When using a gas or electric grill, the food is usually cooked under the heat source.

The grill must be scrupulously clean and heated before the meat is laid upon it or under it. The food to be grilled must be basted with clarified butter, oil or fat, and seasoned. Meat should be gently flattened and trimmed before cooking.

Fish should be scored with a knife, well coated with butter and oil and seasoned. Fish that is rather dry has a tendency to stick to the bars of the grill and should, therefore, be floured before being coated with butter or oil. This will form a covering that will enable the fish to cook without becoming too dry. Turn grilling meat or fish over once or twice during cooking and baste frequently with the butter or oil, using a brush.

Grilled food is ready when it resists pressure if lightly touched with the fingertip. Tiny pinkish droplets appearing on the browned surface are another indication that it is fully cooked. Grilled white meat should be less browned than red meat and a less intense heat should be used. Grill fish at moderate heat and baste frequently.

Grill poultry first if it is to be cooked in breadcrumbs. When three-parts cooked, cover with butter or oil and roll in the breadcrumbs.

■ **Griddling** This is a form of cooking on a very hot, preheated surface, typically a heavy fluted griddle. In America this is known as grilling. The technique produces a result similar to that achieved by grilling and differs from frying in that the fat drains away into a ridge around the edge of a griddle; also the temperature is so fierce that the food seals and cooks rapidly.

GRILL-ROOM
Also known simply as a grill. A restaurant or room where, in theory, only grills are served. It is usually used to describe a restaurant in a large hotel, where the service is faster and the meals are less elaborate than in the large dining room. The name was first used in England in the 1890s.

GRIMOD DE LA REYNIÈRE, ALEXANDRE BALTHASAR LAURENT
French writer and gastronome (born Paris, 1758; died Villiers-sur-Orge, 1837). His father, who was a farmer-general, was himself the son of a pork butcher. Born disabled, with one hand shaped like a claw and the other like a goose's foot, the boy was rejected by his aristocratic mother and eventually rebelled against his entire family. While pursuing his law studies, his extravagant behaviour made him quite notorious.

■ **Taste for scandal** Shortly after becoming a qualified barrister, the young Alexandre, who had already published *Réflexions philosophiques sur le plaisir par un célibataire*, organized a memorable dinner at the end of January 1783. He sent the following invitation card to his guests: 'You are invited to attend the funeral procession and burial of a feast that shall be given by Master Alexandre Balthasar Laurent Grimod de La Reynière, Esquire, barrister to the high court, drama correspondent of the *Journal de Neuchâtel*, at his residence in the Champs-Élysées. You are invited to attend at nine o'clock in the evening and the meal will be served at ten.' Bachaumont, in his *Mémoires secrets*, relates the details of this curious dinner: 'In the middle of the table ... there was a catafalque ... We took our seats at the table. The meal was magnificent, consisting of nine courses, one of which was entirely of pork. At the end of this course, Monsieur de La Reynière asked his guests whether they had enjoyed it; after everyone had replied in chorus "excellent", he said: "Gentlemen, those cooked meats were from Mr So-and-so, the pork butcher, living at such-and-such a place, *who is the cousin of my father*." After another course where everything was prepared with oil, the host again asked his guests if they were pleased with the oil, then said: "It was supplied by Mr So-and-so, the grocer, living at such-and-such a place, *who is the cousin of my father*. I recommend him as highly as I do the pork butcher." ' By proclaiming the plebeian origin of his paternal forebears, Alexandre, who was indeed the grandson of a pork butcher, simply aimed to upset his mother, but at the same time he managed to gain a reputation as a madman, which he carefully fostered.

He held gatherings in his father's residence twice

a week. Besotted with literature, he invited not only Beaumarchais, Chénier and Restif de La Bretonne, but also would-be poets and public letter-writers. The sole qualification for admission was the ability to drink 17 cups of coffee, one after the other. The food served was simply bread and butter with anchovies and, on Saturday, sirloin. At this stage in his life, Grimod was passionately fond of the theatre; he became one of the best drama critics of his time.

■ **From retreat to the grocery business** Following a particularly shocking scandal, the young barrister's family obtained an order against him under the king's private seal. In April 1786 Alexandre was sent to a Cistercian monastery near Nancy, where he spent three years. It was at the table of the abbot that Grimod discovered the art of good eating, and his knowledge of this improved in Lyon and Béziers, where he next took refuge.

In order to make a living, he decided to set up in business. In the Rue Mercière, Lyon, he started a business selling groceries, hardware and perfumery. Then he travelled through the fairs in the south of France. But the death of his father in 1792 brought him back to Paris. He renewed his ties with his mother, whom he saved from the gallows, and endeavoured to pick up a few fragments of his father's estate, including the mansion in the Champs-Élysées, where he again organized extravagant dinner parties. At the same time he resumed his drama criticism. But Talma, whom he had often attacked, managed to have his review *Le Censeur dramatique* suppressed.

■ **A vocation for gastronomy** Banned from drama criticism, Grimod turned to writing about restaurants. This gave rise to the series *Almanach des gourmands* (1804–12), an anecdotal and practical guide to Paris, including a food guide that proved to be very successful. In 1808 Grimod published *Manuel des amphitryons* to instruct the new rich in the conventions and proprieties that they must observe. In his *Variétés nutritives* he wrote the following: 'Soup must be eaten boiling hot and coffee drunk piping hot – happy are those with a delicate palate and a cast-iron throat. The local wine, a dinner at your friends' house and music performed by amateurs are three things to be equally dreaded – cheese is the biscuit of drunkards.'

Grimod de La Reynière established his authority on gastronomic matters by setting up a 'jury of tasters', who awarded a kind of academic certificate called *légitimation* to various dishes or foods that were presented to them. The jury of tasters met at intervals at Grimod's home in the Champs-Élysées. There, they solemnly tasted the choice dishes sent by tradesmen who sought publicity by making known to their customers the judgement, always favourable, pronounced by this gastronomic Areopagus. Among the most influential members of this jury were Cambacérès, the Marquis of Cussy and Gastaldy, doctor and gastronome, who died at table when he was almost a hundred years old! Gastaldy conceived an original way of classifying Burgundy wines: the king – Chambertin; the queen – Romanée-Conti; the regent – Clos-de-Vougeot; the princes of the blood – Romanée, Romanée-Saint-Vivant, Clos-de-Tart, Musigny, La Tâche, Nuits-Échezaux, Bonnes-Mares; the first cousin of Chambertin – Richebourg. However, the jury of tasters soon had to give up its sittings because some of its judgements aroused protest. Grimod was even accused of partiality!

Threatened with lawsuits, Grimod had to suspend publication of the *Almanach*. His mother had died, and he inherited the remains of a vast fortune. He married the actress with whom he had been living for 20 years and retired to the country to live among his life-long friends the Marquis of Cussy and Doctor Roques. He died one Christmas Eve, during the midnight feast, and left, among other extravagances, the following recipe for an 'unparalleled roast', punctuated with references to the actresses of his time: 'Stuff an olive with capers and anchovies and put it in a garden warbler. Put the garden warbler in an ortolan, the ortolan in a lark, the lark in a thrush, the thrush in a quail, the quail in a larded lapwing, the lapwing in a plover, the plover in a red-legged partridge, the partridge in a woodcock – as tender as Mlle Volnais – the woodcock in a teal, the teal in a guinea fowl, the guinea fowl in a duck, the duck in a fattened pullet – as white as Mlle Belmont, as fleshy as Mlle Vienne and as fat as Mlle Contat – the pullet in a pheasant, the pheasant in a duck, the duck in a turkey – white and fat like Mlle Arsène – and finally, the turkey in a bustard.'

GRIS DE LILLE A soft cow's-milk cheese from Flanders (45% fat), also called Puant Macéré and Vieux Lille. It is very similar to Maroilles, with a pale pinkish-grey washed rind, and is matured by soaking in brine and washing with beer. It is sold in slabs 12–13 cm (5 in) square and 5–6 cm (2–2½ in) thick. It has a highly seasoned, salty taste and a very strong smell; it is known as 'the stinkes'.

GRISSINI Italian bread sticks. Long, thin and crunchy, they are made from a dough containing butter or oil and sometimes eggs or malt. They were first made in Turin and are either eaten as appetizers or served with soup or pasta dishes.

GROG A traditional winter drink, made with a mixture of boiling water, rum, sugar (or honey) and lemon. The rum may be replaced by Cognac, kirsch or whisky.

Originally, grog was simply a glass of rum topped up with water. Its name comes from 'Old Grog', a nickname borne by Edward Vernon, a British admiral, because of the grogram cloak he used to wear. In 1776 he ordered his crew to put water in their ration of rum.

The name may also be used informally (especially in Australia) for any alcoholic drink.

GROS-PLANT A white wine from the lower reaches of the River Loire, made from the grape of the same name (also called Folle Blanche). Pale in colour, it is light in character and very dry, a pleasant wine to drink with seafood and shellfish.

GROUNDNUT See *peanut*.

GROUPER *mérou* A large marine fish that can grow to a length of more than 1.5 m (5 ft) and weigh about 50 kg (110 lb). It is a member of the sea perch family. There are two closely related species: one is found in the Mediterranean; the other, also called stone bass or wreckbass (*cernier* in French), is more widespread, also occurring in the Atlantic. It is brown, speckled with yellow and has an enormous head (representing one-third of its weight), a wide mouth with a protruding bottom lip and numerous teeth. A peaceful fish that prefers the warm seas of the Caribbean and Mediterranean, it is a favourite catch of underwater fishermen. It is rarely sold by fishmongers, although its flesh is excellent. It is cooked like tuna but is particularly tasty when grilled over charcoal.

RECIPES

ceviche of grouper
Clean and trim 4 grouper steaks of 200 g (7 oz) each. Cut into 1 cm (½ in) cubes. Squeeze the juice from 4 limes. Place the diced fish in a large salad bowl sitting on a bed of ice cubes. Sprinkle the lime juice on the fish and allow to marinate for 2–3 hours, stirring several times to cook the grouper, which must remain pink in the middle. Drain and place in a large bowl. Peel and finely chop diagonally 4 spring onions (scallions) and their stems. Peel, seed and crush 3 cherry tomatoes. Add all these ingredients to the fish. Season with salt and add ½ teaspoon freshly grated ginger, 1 pinch turmeric, chives and chopped flat-leaf parsley. Pour olive oil on top and sprinkle with paprika. Stir well and serve.

grouper with corcellet sauce
Trim, gut and clean a small grouper, poach it in very concentrated court-bouillon, and allow it to cool in the stock. Take out the fish, remove the skin and garnish with blanched tarragon leaves and thin slices of tomato.

Finely chop 6 large, very ripe, peeled and seeded tomatoes and rub them through a sieve. Store the resulting fresh tomato purée in the refrigerator. Just before serving, add 2 generous tablespoons aniseed-flavoured Corcellet mustard to the tomato purée. Serve well chilled.

GROUSE Any of several game birds belonging to the same family. They resemble fowl and are mostly ground living. British species include the red grouse, the black grouse and the capercaillie. The common French species is the hazel grouse (*gelinotte*), and the pin-tailed grouse (*ganga*) is found in the south of France (this species has very delicate flesh and is usually spit-roasted). In North America there are many species, including the ruffed grouse, blue grouse and sage grouse.

Grouse may be roasted, braised or made into pâtés or terrines.

RECIPE

roast grouse
Mash 50 g (2 oz, ¼ cup) butter with 2 tablespoons lemon juice, salt and pepper. Wipe 2 plump or 4 small prepared grouse and place some of the butter inside each bird. Cover the breasts of the birds with bacon and tie in place, then wrap each bird in foil. Place the birds, breast side down, on a rack resting in a baking tin (pan) and roast in a preheated oven at 200°C (400°F, gas 6) for about 25 minutes for small birds and 35 minutes for the larger ones. While the birds are roasting, fry the grouse livers in butter, then mash together to make a paste. Fry 2–4 slices of bread, crusts removed, in a mixture of butter and oil until crisp and golden. Spread these croûtons with the liver paste. Unwrap the birds, baste each one well with hot fat, then dust the breasts with flour, baste again and return to the oven for about 5 minutes until well browned. Serve the grouse resting on the croûtons, garnished with watercress. Serve hot game chips and rowan or redcurrant jelly separately. The birds should be moist enough to serve without gravy.

GRUEL A liquid food made by boiling a cereal flour in milk, water or vegetable broth. Gruel is one of the oldest forms of nourishment. The Egyptians made gruel from millet, barley and wheat; the Greeks added olives, and the daily diet of the Roman legionaries was usually gruel made from wheat and the related cereal, spelt, together with onions, salted fish and cheese. The Germans and Franks ate gruel made from oats (see *porridge*). In the French provinces, the evening meal traditionally consisted of maize (corn) or buckwheat gruel (see *gaudes, kasha, polenta*).

GRUMEAU A French word meaning a small lump, also used to describe a clot of blood, a coagulum formed in milk or the lumps found in a lumpy sauce or batter.

GRUYÈRE A Swiss or French cow's-milk cheese (45% fat content) with a firm but pliable texture and a brushed and washed rind. It takes about six months to mature in a damp cellar and has a nutty flavour. It is ivory yellow or golden brown in colour.

Gruyère is made in Switzerland from unpasteurized milk in the cantons of Fribourg, Neuchâtel and Vaud; in France, it is manufactured in Savoy, Franche-Comté and Burgundy. By analogy, the word is often incorrectly used in France for all cooked compressed cheeses sold in large rounds, including Emmental, Beaufort and Comté.

According to the Swiss, Gruyère cheese is named after the Counts of Gruyère, whose coat of arms was embellished with a crane (*grue*) and who settled in the Gruyère valley in the canton of Fribourg at the beginning of the 9th century (in France, Swiss Gruyère is called 'Fribourg'). The French believe that the word comes from *agent gruyer*, an officer of the waterways and forestry authorities who, in the Middle Ages, used to collect certain taxes in the form of timber and cheese.

Gruyère cheese is made in rounds weighing 30–45 kg (66–100 lb), 50–65 cm (20–26 in) in diameter and about 11 cm (4 in) thick. It should not be confused with Emmental, which has larger holes.

The cheeses that are exported are less salty than those made for local consumption, and to enhance the pungent flavour of this excellent cheese the Swiss preserve it is a cloth soaked either in salt water or in white wine. The cheese is made in cheese factories in the mountains, close to the pastures. It keeps for a very long time if uncut. Some connoisseurs demand a very mature cheese; others prefer it to be fairly fresh. It is eaten at the end of meals or in sandwiches and is used to prepare many dishes, such as fondues, gratins, soufflés, croûtes, croque-monsieur and mixed salads; it also serves as a condiment for pasta and rice.

Gruyère is used to make processed cheese called Crème de Gruyère. This is also made from Comté cheese and is sold in small triangles wrapped in silver paper. Gruyère de Comté is one of a number of Gruyère-type cheeses made in the United States and all over Europe. For a long time, a type of Gruyère cheese was manufactured in the Jura, but Gruyère de Comté manufacturers themselves now insist that the *appellation* Gruyère de Comté be replaced simply by Comté.

GUACAMOLE A dip originating in Mexico and consisting of avocado, tomato, onion, lemon juice and spices. It is usually eaten with *totopos*, maize (corn) chips.

GUAVA A fruit originating in Central America and the West Indies but now grown in many tropical countries. There are several varieties: some are pear-shaped, some are apple-shaped, and some are shaped like walnuts. The thin yellow skin of the guava is dotted with black spots when ripe and sometimes mottled with green; it covers an orange-pink, white or yellow pulp. Highly flavoured and refreshing, yet rather sour, it contains a large number of hard seeds. The variety called 'pear of the Indies', which is the size of a hen's egg, is the most popular. It is imported from Brazil and the West Indies (December to January) or from India and the Ivory Coast (November to February). When it is ripe it is eaten on its own, after being peeled and seeded (it may be flavoured with sugar or a little rum). It is also used to make drinks, ice creams and jellies. In Brazil the pulp collected when making jelly is often used to make a firm jellied fruit paste or cheese, which is sliced and served as a dessert with fresh goat's-milk cheese. Guava is also preserved in syrup and is included in exotic fruit salads. In China there is a variety called the strawberry guava, which is the size of a walnut, with a white, black, yellow or red skin and a strong flavour.

GUDGEON A small freshwater fish with a large head, thick lips and very delicate flesh. Formerly abundant, gudgeon were a speciality of the small eating houses on the banks of the Seine and Marne that served fried food; Fulbert Dumonteil described it as 'that small fish – a crunchy tasty mouthful', and stated: 'In a good lunch, there is no second course more delicate than a splendid plateful of fried gudgeon, skilfully browned.'

Gudgeon must be gutted (cleaned), wiped but not washed, dipped in milk or beer, then drained, seasoned with salt and pepper, rolled in flour and deep-fried. As soon as they are crisp and golden, they are drained, sprinkled with fine salt and served with lemon as an hors d'oeuvre. If the fish are fairly large they are fried twice, first in oil that is at the correct temperature to cook them, then in very hot oil to brown them.

By extension, goujons or *goujonnettes* is the name given to fillets of sole and other fish cut diagonally into strips, coated, fried and served like gudgeon or used as a garnish.

GUÊLON A mixture consisting of eggs, milk and sugar, to which cream or buttermilk or even flour is sometimes added. It is used to enrich fruit tarts, combining with the cooking juices.

GUIGNOLET A cherry liqueur made from a specific variety of cherry, from around the River Loire. It is one of the liqueurs of Anjou and, in the region, is sometimes combined with kirsch. It is quite different from the cherry brandies of other areas and should not be confused with kirsch, which is a distillate of the fruit and an *alcool blanc*.

GUILLOT, ANDRÉ French chef (born Faremoutiers, 1908; died 1993). Apprenticed at the age of 16 in the kitchens of the Italian Embassy, Guillot later pursued his career in various private houses; his employers included Raymond Roussel, an extremely rich epicurean who had his early fruit and vegetables brought from the Côte d'Azur in a Rolls-Royce, and the Duke of Auerstaedt. From 1952 he worked at the Auberge du Vieux-Marly, which he turned into a restaurant of great renown. After retiring, he wrote about his experiences and recorded his expertise in *La Grande Cuisine bourgeoise* (1976) and in *La Vraie Cuisine légère* (1981).

He was outspoken and did not hesitate to attack well-established traditions: 'I am certain to annoy many restaurateurs when I say that all these flambé dishes set alight under the customers' noses are no more than play-acting. The flambé process must be carried out at the start of cooking, in the privacy of the kitchen.'

GUINEA FOWL A gallinaceous bird, all domesticated varieties of which are descended from an African species that was known and appreciated by the Romans, who called it Numidian hen or Carthage hen. Before the introduction of modern rearing methods in France, young guinea fowl (*pintadeaux*) – a speciality of the Drôme region – were sold at Whitsun (the seventh weekend after Easter) at about 11 weeks old, while adults, weighing over 1 kg (2¼ lb), were killed in the autumn.

Guinea fowl are now bred all the year round. In France they are sold with a red label guaranteeing their origin, feeding and rearing. The term *fermier* (free-range) is reserved for birds reared with access to runs, as opposed to those that are battery reared. The most tender and succulent birds are the young *pintadeaux*. They can be roasted and prepared in any way suitable for a young pheasant, partridge or chicken. The flesh of the adult guinea fowl is firmer and is usually fricasséed or prepared in any other way suitable for chicken, being well basted, barded and larded or casseroled to keep the flesh moist.

RECIPES

breast of guinea fowl with potatoes Alex Humbert

Prepare 800 g (1¾ lb) potatoes by the Alex Humbert method: slice thinly and soak in cold water for about 10 hours, then cook for approximately 20 minutes in 150 g (5 oz, ⅔ cup) clarified butter seasoned with salt and pepper. Drain off the excess butter and brown the potatoes in the oven.

Remove the breast meat from 2 guinea fowl, each weighing about 1.5 kg (3¼ lb), slicing along the breastbone. Season with salt and pepper. Heat 100 g (4 oz, 7 tablespoons) butter in a large flameproof casserole and brown the guinea fowl breasts on both sides (8 minutes in all), then remove. Add 4 chopped shallots to the casserole. Cook them for a few seconds and then mix in 50 g (2 oz, 1 cup) fresh breadcrumbs to absorb all the cooking butter. Brown slightly and stir in 3 tablespoons wine vinegar, then add 6 chopped basil leaves. Put to one side and keep warm.

On to each of 4 warmed plates, pour 2 tablespoons previously made brown gravy, place some of the potatoes in the centre and cover with a guinea fowl breast cut into 5 or 6 slices. Give one twist of the pepper mill and add a little salt. Finally, sprinkle with the breadcrumb mixture and serve immediately.

guinea fowl Catalan style

Blanch 30 peeled garlic cloves for 1 minute, having first removed any green part. Peel 3 lemons and remove all the pith. Cut 2 into quarters and slice the third one. Blanch them for 1 minute. Roast a guinea fowl, barded with a few thin slices of salted or smoked breast of pork. Cut the guinea fowl into pieces. Deglaze the roasting tin (pan) with 100 ml (4 fl oz, 2 cup) of Rancio or dry Banyuls. Add the crushed carcass of the bird and 200 ml (7 fl oz, ¾ cup) of veal stock. Simmer for 10 minutes, strain through a chinois, pressing in order to extract all the juices. Pour this sauce on to the garlic and lemons, and return to the heat for a few minutes. Season with salt and pepper. Place the pieces of guinea fowl in the sauce and cook over a low heat for 10 minutes. Serve with steamed or roasted new potatoes or with rice.

guinea fowl salad with fruit

Roast half a guinea fowl weighing about 1 kg (2¼ lb) for approximately 30 minutes. Leave to cool completely. Wash and dry some radiccio leaves, and cover the serving dish with them. Peel and finely slice 1 Granny Smith apple and 2 peaches. Sprinkle with lemon juice. Arrange these items on the bed of lettuce, together with the finely sliced meat of the guinea fowl and 25 g (1 oz, ¼ cup) blackcurrants. Blend 150 ml (¼ pint, ⅔ cup) plain yogurt with 1 tablespoon cider vinegar, seasoned with salt and pepper. Cover the guinea fowl with this dressing.

guinea fowl with chestnuts

Cut 2 small guinea fowl in half lengthways. Brown them in hot butter in a flameproof casserole, together with 150 g (5 oz, ¾ cup) diced belly of pork and 3 chopped shallots. Cook gently for approximately 40 minutes, turning occasionally, then dilute the meat juices with 250 ml (8 fl oz, 1 cup) red Burgundy. Add a bouquet garni and 300 g (11 oz) cooked chestnuts. Cook gently for a further 10 minutes. Remove the bouquet garni, bind the sauce with 75 g (3 oz, 6 tablespoons) butter, adjust the seasoning and serve hot straight from the casserole.

stuffed guinea fowl Jean Cocteau

Draw a guinea fowl weighing about 1 kg (2¼ lb) and put the liver and gizzard to one side. Soak 100 g (4 oz, 1¾ cups) fresh breadcrumbs in hot milk, then strain them. Mix with 1 raw egg, 1 chopped hard-boiled (hard-cooked) egg, a pinch of salt, pepper, nutmeg and cinnamon, 1 tablespoon chopped tarragon, chives, chopped parsley and chervil, then the liver and gizzard, also chopped. Stuff the guinea fowl with this forcemeat and season the outside lightly with salt and pepper. Sew it up, bard it and tie firmly, then fry in a flameproof casserole containing 15 g (½ oz, 1 tablespoon) butter and 1 tablespoon oil. When the guinea fowl begins to turn a golden colour, remove it from the casserole and place on a dish, then sprinkle with 100 ml (4 fl oz, ½ cup) heated Cognac and set alight.

In the same casserole place 3 carrots and 3 onions chopped into large pieces and 2 crushed garlic cloves. Leave to cook for a few moments, then return the guinea fowl to the casserole. Moisten with 250 ml (8 fl oz, 1 cup) each white wine and Cognac. Add 100 ml (4 fl oz, ½ cup) water, cover the casserole and cook for 45 minutes over a gentle heat.

Use a fork to prick 4 *boudins blancs* and 4 black puddings (blood sausages), place them with 1 tablespoon oil in a flameproof dish and grill (broil). Peel, quarter and core 4 apples and brown them in a sauté pan with a little butter. Season very lightly with salt. When the guinea fowl is ready, carve it and arrange on a warm dish. Cover with the strained cooking liquid, sprinkle with chopped herbs and surround with the grilled puddings and apple quarters.

GUINEA PEPPER The name is sometimes applied to cayenne pepper, but it is usually an alternative term for Melegueta pepper.

GUINEA PIG The guinea pig has long been a source of food in Peru, Ecuador and Bolivia where it is known as *cuy* or *cui*. Peruvian Incas kept domesticated guinea pigs as a source of food. European explorers named this rodent, a species of cavy (*Cavy porcellus*), the guinea pig and introduced it to Spain in the 16th century. It was considered a delicacy at first, but it did not become an established source of food. Guinea pig is cooked in South America, West Africa and the Philippines, by grilling or simmering in a rich stew.

GUINGUETTE A type of French suburban tavern, usually situated in pleasant surroundings, where people go to eat, drink and dance on public holidays. Some etymologists believe that the name is derived from *guinguet*, a rather sour wine cultivated in the Paris suburbs; others that it might be derived from the Old French *guinguer* (to jump), which has given rise to the French word *guincher* (to dance). In the 18th century *guinguettes* were spread out along the Seine, in the district of the Tuileries. Their name is especially linked to the Romantic period, when they were found outside the gates of Paris and on the hilltops of Belleville.

GULAB JAMUN An Indian speciality, a dessert or sweetmeat made from fresh, soft cheese or milk which is boiled until greatly reduced and condensed. A little flour is added and the mixture is rolled into small balls. These are deep-fried in ghee or oil until golden and then macerated in a syrup flavoured with rose water, cardamom or vanilla. The gulab jamun may be flavoured with spice or stuffed with a filling of nuts and dried fruit before being shaped.

GUM A viscous, translucent substance that exudes from certain plants.
• GUM ARABIC Secreted from acacia trees in Sudan and Egypt. The basic ingredient of chewing gum, marshmallow and liquorice, it is also used to glaze some items of confectionery and as a clarity stabilizer in the chemical treatment of wines.
• GUM TRAGACANTH The most mucilaginous kind of gum, extracted from shrubs of the genus *Astragalus*. It is used in the manufacture of stabilizers, emulsifiers and thickeners for the food industry. It prevents crystallization in ice cream and jam. Guar gum, produced by a leguminous plant, can be used for the same purposes as gum tragacanth.

Gums extracted from some algae are also used in cooking, as well as synthetic gums.

GUMBO An American stew or hearty soup featuring in Creole and Cajun cooking. A stew of mixed ingredients, including vegetables, okra in particular, with onions, (bell) peppers, tomatoes and garlic. Fish, crab, oysters, poultry, meat and/or spicy sausage may be added. The okra acts as a thickening agent (okra is also known as gumbo in West Africa) but it is not an essential ingredient in all recipes for gumbo (and there are many). File powder, made from ground sassafras leaves, may be added as well as or instead of okra to thicken and flavour gumbo.

GUMPOLDSKIRCHNER A wine town in Thermenregion, Austria, producing good white varietal wines, particularly from Zierfandler and Rotgipler grapes.

GURNARD *grondin* Also known as gurnet. Any of several European fish of the family *Triglidae*. The French name, meaning 'grunter', derives from the grunting sound the fish is said to make when it comes out of the water. In Britain it is also called sea robin. All gurnards have a cylindrical body, a spindle-shaped tail, a large head protected by bony plates, an elongated muzzle and a wide mouth. The pectoral fins are finger-shaped and are used to explore the muddy sea bed. They are 20–60 cm (8–24 in) long and their weight varies between 100 g (4 oz) and 1.25 kg (2¾ lb). There are several types of gurnard, which are mainly distinguished by their colour: the cuckoo gurnard is red mottled with green, the grey gurnard is brownish-grey, the red gurnard and the trigle lyre are pink or red, with lighter coloured bellies.

The fish should always be carefully trimmed with the fins removed. The flesh is lean, white, firm and sometimes rather tasteless, but it is rich in protein, iodine and phosphorus. It is usually poached or used in soups and bouillabaisse. It can also be cooked in the oven or even grilled (broiled), but in this case the fish must be protected, because the fragile skin is damaged by excessive heat.

Gurnard is often sold in France as red mullet, but although it has a delicate flavour it cannot really be compared with this fish. However, all recipes for red mullet are suitable for gurnard.

RECIPE

baked gurnard
Choose 2 good quality gurnards, each weighing about 400 g (14 oz). Draw, clean and dry them. Score oblique cuts on the back of each fish from the backbone outwards and pour in a few drops of lemon juice. Butter a gratin dish and spread in it a mixture of 2 large onions, 2 shallots and 1 small garlic clove, all very finely chopped. Sprinkle with chopped parsley. Place the fish in the dish and add 200 ml (7 fl oz, ¾ cup) white wine and 50 g (2 oz, 4 tablespoons) melted butter. Season with salt and pepper and sprinkle with a little thyme. Arrange slices of lemon along the backs of the fish and sprinkle with chopped fresh bay leaf. Bake in a preheated oven at 240°C (475°F, gas 9) for about 20 minutes, basting the fish several times during cooking.

Just before serving, flame the gurnards with 4 tablespoons heated pastis.

GUT To remove, by hand or mechanically, the innards, including the giblets, of an animal, bird or fish.

GYOZA Japanese name for Chinese-style dumplings. Circles of dough are folded into little pasties over the filling, which usually consists of well-seasoned minced pork with vegetables. The edges are pinched together to seal in the filling. The dumplings are fried in a little fat, then a small quantity of water is added and the pan is covered so that the dumplings are steamed until cooked through. The gyoza are served freshly cooked, with a dipping sauce. When cooked by frying and steaming, the dumplings are known as pot stickers or pan stickers. They may also be deep-fried, steamed or simmered in broth.

GYRO Greek spit-roast lamb. Minced (ground) lamb is shaped on a vertical spit and cooked in front of a heat source. The meat is sliced off the outside as it is cooked, then served in pitta bread, with onion, tomato, lettuce and tzatziki (cucumber in yogurt) or a yogurt sauce. Rolled up in the bread, with its accompaniments, gyro pita is a popular snack.

GYROCEPHALUS RUFUS *gyrocéphale roussâtre* A funnel-shaped mushroom, split at the side and orange-pink to reddish-brown. It grows in damp meadows and under conifers. Fleshy and tender, it is eaten raw in salads when unripe; otherwise it can be eaten only after thorough cooking.

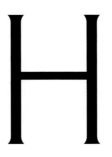

H

HACHÉE SAUCE A sauce of ancient origin, so called because all the ingredients are chopped and appear as separate pieces in the finished sauce. It can accompany roast red meat or venison. Carême gives this recipe:

'Put 2 tablespoons vinegar into a saucepan. Add 1 level tablespoon chopped mushrooms, half this quantity of parsley, 2 chopped shallots, a little garlic, a fragment of thyme and bay leaf, 2 cloves, a generous pinch of white pepper and a little grated nutmeg. Cook this seasoning over a low heat. Remove the thyme, bay leaf and cloves, and add 2 tablespoons consommé and 2 tablespoons espagnole* sauce. Boil down to reduce and transfer to a bain marie. Just before serving, stir in a small piece of anchovy butter, 2 small gherkins, chopped very finely, and some capers.'

HACHUA A Basque dish made from sirloin of beef and fat ham, braised for several hours in white wine with carrots, onions and a bouquet garni. *Hachua* is also the name of a ragoût of veal or beef braised with diced Bayonne ham, peppers and onions.

HADDOCK *églefin* A fish belonging to the cod family but generally smaller than cod: up to 1 m (3 ft) long and weighing 2–3 kg (4½–6½ lb). When sold whole and gutted (cleaned), fresh haddock can be recognized by its brownish-grey colour, with a dark lateral line and a black mark under its first dorsal fin. The flesh is white and delicate. Haddock is also sold in fillets.

Fresh haddock is prepared and cooked in the same way as cod, both fish lending themselves to a great number of culinary treatments.

Smoked haddock is prepared by splitting the fish lengthways as soon as it is caught, rubbing it lightly with salt, hanging it by the tail, and leaving it to smoke for 24 hours. Smoked haddock is usually poached in milk and served either with boiled potatoes and leaf spinach or with a poached egg and covered with a white cream sauce. Other members of the cod family, especially cod itself, may be lightly smoked in the same way as haddock, but they have neither the texture nor the subtle flavour.

The following recipes are for smoked haddock.

RECIPES

curried haddock
Soak the smoked haddock in cold milk for 2–3 hours. Prepare a curry sauce. Drain and dry the haddock thoroughly, then bone, skin, and dice the flesh. Cook thinly sliced large onions in butter, allowing 2 onions per 450 g (1 lb) fish. Cool. Add the haddock to the onions, moisten with the curry sauce, then cover and simmer for about 10 minutes. Serve with boiled rice.

grilled haddock
Place the smoked haddock in a dish, cover it with cold milk, and leave for 2–3 hours. Dry the fish thoroughly, brush with melted butter or oil, and grill (broil) gently. Serve with melted butter seasoned with pepper and lemon juice, but no salt, accompanied by boiled potatoes or buttered spinach.

haddock gâteau
Boil 1 kg (2¼ lb) potatoes in their skins. Clean and slice the white part of 5 leeks and braise them in a little water and 40 g (1½ oz, 3 tablespoons) butter for 8 minutes. Thinly slice 2 smoked haddock fillets

weighing about 350 g (12 oz) each. Clean 150 g (5 oz, 2 cups) mushrooms and slice them thinly. Peel the potatoes and cut them into thick slices. Spread two-thirds of the haddock in the bottom of a buttered ovenproof mould and cover with the mushrooms, potatoes, leeks and the remaining haddock. Top with 6 tablespoons crème fraîche. Sprinkle with pepper, but not salt. Cover the mould with foil and cook in a bain marie in a preheated oven at 240°C (475°F, gas 9) for 30 minutes. Unmould the gâteau and retain the juices that will have formed. Cook 1 chopped shallot in 10 g (¼ oz, 1½ teaspoons) butter, add the juices, and boil down until reduced by one-third. Add 6 tablespoons single (light) cream. Pour this sauce over the gâteau.

haddock rillettes
Poach 900 g (2 lb) smoked haddock in a mixture of unsalted water and milk for 3 minutes. Simmer very gently, but do not boil. Remove the fish and drain well. Using a food processor, mix together 5 hard-boiled (hard-cooked) eggs, 40 g (1½ oz, 3 tablespoons) butter, 3 tablespoons parsley and 2 tablespoons chopped chives. Then add the haddock, the juice of half a lemon and 6 tablespoons olive oil, and mix together very rapidly. Place the mixture in a bowl. Peel and seed 2 large tomatoes and place in a food processor or blender. Add the juice of half a lemon, 3 finely chopped shallots, 6 tablespoons olive oil, salt and pepper. Blend to a smooth sauce. Cover the bottom of each plate with 3 tablespoons of this sauce. Arrange 3 ovals of the haddock mixture (formed with a spoon) in a star pattern on the sauce. Serve with toast.

poached haddock
Soak the smoked haddock in cold milk for 2–3 hours, then remove it. Bring the milk to the boil, add the haddock, and poach without boiling (otherwise it will become stringy) for 6–10 minutes, depending on the thickness of the fish. Serve with melted butter strongly flavoured with lemon juice and chopped parsley, accompanied by boiled potatoes.

HAGGIS A Scottish national dish, a type of spicy offal sausage, traditionally consisting of a sheep's stomach stuffed with a spicy mixture of the animal's heart, liver and lungs, onions, spices, oatmeal and mutton fat. The haggis is poached in stock or water and served with mashed swede (rutabaga). The traditional accompaniment is malt whisky or strong beer. It is served on high days and holidays, such as the anniversary of the birth of the Scottish poet Robert Burns (25 January), who wrote an 'Address to a Haggis', and Hogmanay.

The name probably comes from the verb *haggen* (to hack), although some authorities suggest that it is derived from the words *au gui l'an neuf* (mistletoe for the New Year), the cry of the mistletoe sellers in the Middle Ages, possibly inspired by a vague memory of ancient Druidic ceremonies.

The best haggis are still prepared in a stomach casing, but good examples are commonly available in synthetic casing. Although its description is not immediately appealing, haggis has an excellent nutty texture and delicious savoury flavour. It is especially good with a simple velouté sauce of rich chicken or lamb stock flavoured with a generous quantity of whisky, refreshed by stirring in a handful of chopped parsley. This accompaniment may not be traditional but it complements the haggis and buttery swedes.

HAKE *merlu* A sea fish that has a long cylindrical body with two dorsal fins, one anal fin and no barbs. It belongs to the genus *Merluccius* and there are about ten species. In France the fish is called *colin* in many recipes and even by fishmongers. Small hake are called *merluchons*.

The hake can measure up to 1 m (39 in) and weigh up to about 4 kg (9 lb). The head and back are dark grey (hence the French name *colin*, which comes from the Dutch *koolvisch*, meaning 'coal fish'); the undersurface is silvery white. It has a mild flavour and few bones and these are easy to remove. Although it is intensively fished, it is always expensive. Before the opening up of North Atlantic fishing, hake was salted and used instead of salt cod in European markets. Medium-sized fish are sold whole (in which case there is 40% waste). Larger fish are sold in sections or steaks. The piece of hake just behind the head tastes the best, but its appearance is less pleasing. The head itself, which is cartilaginous, imparts a smooth texture to fish soups.

Hake should always be cooked for a short time, particularly when poached, and care should be taken to ensure that the flesh does not disintegrate. There are numerous ways of preparing hake, both hot au gratin with delicate sauces such as caper or Mornay, and cold with mayonnaise or *sauce verte*. All recipes for cod are suitable for hake.

RECIPES

hake à la boulangère
Season a piece of hake weighing 1 kg (2¼ lb), taken from the middle of the fish. Put it into a greased gratin dish and coat with melted butter. Arrange 800 g (1¾ lb) thinly sliced potatoes and 200 g (7 oz, 1¾ cups) sliced onions around the fish. Sprinkle with salt, pepper, thyme and powdered bay leaf. Pour 25 g (1 oz, 2 tablespoons) melted butter over the top. Place the dish in a preheated oven at about 200°C (400°F, gas 6) and cook for 30–35 minutes. Sprinkle the fish with a little water several times during cooking. Serve in the gratin dish garnished with chopped parsley.

hake cosquera
Cut a 1 kg (2¼ lb) hake into thick slices. Wash 24 clams. Heat 2–3 tablespoons olive oil in an earthenware casserole and cook the fish steaks for 6 minutes. Season with salt and pepper. As soon as

the juices from the fish become colourless, add the clams. Sprinkle with chopped garlic and parsley and continue to cook briefly until the shellfish open. Serve immediately.

hake mère Joseph

Dress a hake weighing about1 kg (2¼ lb). Remove the head and cut the body into 4 pieces. Dry them and rub each piece thoroughly with the cut surface of a lemon half. Sprinkle with pepper, and brown them in lard in a flameproof casserole. Add 3–4 chopped shallots and allow them to brown slightly. Blend 1 tablespoon tomato purée (paste) with 1 tablespoon brandy and add to the casserole. Season with salt, cover, and simmer gently for 15–20 minutes.

hake steaks à la duxelles

Clean and chop 500 g (18 oz, 4½ cups) button mushrooms and 2 shallots and mix together with 1 tablespoon lemon juice. Fry the mixture in 20 g (¾ oz, 1½ tablespoons) butter over a high heat for 5 minutes. Line a greased gratin dish with the mushroom duxelles and arrange 4 hake steaks on top. Add 250 ml (8 fl oz, 1 cup) white wine and 250 ml (8 fl oz, 1 cup) fish stock, or 500 ml (17 fl oz, 2 cups) fish fumet. Top with small pieces of butter, season and add a bouquet garni. Place in a preheated oven at 240°C (475°F, gas 9) and cook for 25 minutes. Moisten with small quantities of water during cooking. Drain the fish and keep warm. Reduce the cooking liquid, replace the fish in the dish, pour over some cream and return to the oven for 5–6 minutes.

hake steaks à la koskera

Flour 4 hake steaks. Heat 2 tablespoons olive oil in a deep, non-stick frying pan. Add the fish steaks and brown them on both sides, then add 2 chopped garlic cloves. Add 250 ml (8 fl oz, 1 cup) white wine, 250 ml (8 fl oz, 1 cup) of the liquid from a can of asparagus, 100 g (4 oz, 1 cup) petits pois cooked in water, 200 g (7 oz) clams and ½ chopped sun-dried red pepper. Simmer for about 15 minutes, or until the fish and vegetables are cooked. Add plenty of parsley and adjust the seasoning. Arrange in a dish, garnish with asparagus tips and quarters of hard-boiled (hard-cooked) eggs.

HALÉVY The name given to two dishes, one of poached or soft-boiled eggs, the other of poached fish (cod, turbot or halibut), both dedicated to the French lyric composer Jacques Halévy and his nephew Ludovic, who wrote the libretti for various comic operas (particularly by Offenbach). These dishes, now seldom prepared, are unusual in using two different sauces for the same dish. Eggs Halévy are served in pairs, sometimes in tartlet cases filled with chicken in a velouté sauce. One egg is coated with either allemande sauce or suprême sauce and garnished with chopped truffles; the other is coated with tomato sauce and garnished with chopped egg

yolk. Cod Halévy is surrounded by a border of duchess potatoes and served with the same sauces as for the eggs, each sauce covering one half of the dish. Turbot Halévy is also bordered with duchess potatoes, but one half is covered with a white wine sauce and chopped truffles and the other half with a Nantua sauce and chopped egg white.

HALIBUT *flétan de l'Atlantique* Flat sea fish, member of the *Pleuronectidae* family, which lives in cold, deep Atlantic waters. It can be up to 2.5 m (8 ft) long and weigh up to 350 kg (800 lb); the flesh is very lean, white and similar to turbot. It can be grilled (broiled) or poached like brill. The black halibut (*flétan noir*) has a white, boneless flesh.

HALICOT A mutton stew, whose name is derived from the Old French verb *halicoter* (to cut into small pieces). The dish is also known as *haricot de mouton* even though it did not originally contain beans: it is mentioned in the recipes of Taillevent and La Varenne before the haricot (navy) bean was introduced into France. Today the stew is made with chopped meat, turnips, onions, potatoes and sometimes haricot beans.

RECIPE

halicot of mutton

Cut about 800 g (1¾ lb) neck or breast of mutton into pieces. Season and put into a casserole with 4 tablespoons oil. Add a large sliced onion, 1 teaspoon granulated sugar and 3 level tablespoons plain (all-purpose) flour. Stir thoroughly. Then add 3 tablespoons tomato purée (paste) diluted with a little stock. Completely cover the meat with more stock, stir well, add a small crushed garlic clove and a bouquet garni, and cook for 45 minutes. Skim the fat from the sauce and add 500 g (18 oz) potatoes cut into quarters or neat oval shapes, 400 g (14 oz) small turnips and 200 g (7 oz) small peeled onions. Add sufficient stock to cover the vegetables and continue to cook for about 40 minutes.

HALLES, LES One of the main market places in central Paris, dating back to the reign of Philip Augustus in 1183. The other important markets were the corn and flour market (established in 1765) and the fresh fish and oyster market (in the Rue Montorgueil). Until 1969 all the wholesale food markets of central Paris were grouped together under metal pavilions that were constructed by the architect Victor Baltard in the reign of Napoleon III (1852–70). These pavilions, known as 'umbrellas', replaced the stalls and booths that had stood on this site, which was called Les Champeaux, since the time of Louis de Gros. In the 15th century the market halls of Les Champeaux were reserved exclusively for food trading. In 1958 an enquiry was opened into the possibility of moving Les Halles from their central position to a site on the outskirts of Paris, and in 1973 the wholesale markets for meat and poultry moved to Rungis.

HALVA Also known as halvah. An Eastern sweetmeat based on roasted sesame seeds, which are ground into a smooth paste and mixed with boiled sugar. It has a high fat content and, although very sweet, a slightly bitter taste. Other types of halva can be aerated and whipped, and cream or crystallized (candied) fruit may be added.

HAM A leg of pork, cured in various ways. The ham may be sold whole or sliced, cooked (for example, Paris ham or York ham) or raw – that is pickled in brine, dried, and sometimes smoked (for example, the hams of Bayonne, Auvergne, Westphalia, Parma, Prague). A good ham should be plump, with an ample, though not too thick, layer of fat under the rind. Pork shoulder is cured in the same way, but it is not entitled to be called 'ham'; the flavour is not as good, but it can be used in cooked ham dishes.

Ham is cut from the leg and then brined. Gammon is also from the leg but it is cured while still on the side of the carcass. It may be smoked separately or left unsmoked. In French cookery the term *jambon* means not only ham but also a leg of fresh pork. This cut can be cooked in a great many ways, either whole or divided into smaller cuts. It is also used as an ingredient for stuffing and in various manufactured pork products.

The salting and smoking of pork to produce ham is of French origin. It was the Gauls, great devotees of pork and efficient pig breeders, who first became renowned for the salting, smoking and curing of the various cuts of pork. After salting, the Gauls subjected the pork to the smoke of certain selected woods for two days. They then rubbed the meat with oil and vinegar, and hung it up to dry and preserve it. The Gauls ate ham either at the beginning of a meal to sharpen their appetites, or at the end to induce thirst.

Salting is also an ancient method of preserving meat all over Europe. Pigs, in particular, were ideal animals for home rearing and they were kept in town gardens as well as country cottages. The meat from animals slaughtered in early autumn was salted and hung for winter use. This method is also used in China, where Yunnan is known for fine-quality ham.

■ **Modern curing** Today the curing of ham involves two main operations, salting and smoking. The hams are salted in brine or dry salt; rubbed with dry salt, saltpetre and sugar and left for three days well covered with this mixture; or have brine injected into the veins before they are boned. The salted joints are then put into brine, washed, brushed and dried. Finally, the hams are smoked in special chambers, starting with a light smoke, which grows denser as the operation proceeds. This treatment varies according to the type of ham and whether it is to be eaten cooked or raw.

Formerly, the characteristic flavours of hams varied with the type of salt, the curing process and the breed, diet and age of the pig; hence their regional names. In many cases these names still designate a local product, but others merely describe a method of curing and are applied to hams from any breed of pig or place of origin. This is the case with York ham, Prague ham and even Bayonne ham.

■ **Ham served cooked** York ham is the best-known variety. After dry salting, it is lightly smoked. It is cooked on the bone either in stock or steamed. It can be served hot or cold.

Paris ham is pressed in a mould and steamed to give it its oblong or cylindrical shape. It is unsmoked and lightly salted, with a delicate flavour.

Prague ham is soaked in sweetened brine and may also be smoked. It is sold ready-cooked, or ready for cooking, either by poaching or by baking in a pastry case.

In the United States high-quality hams are referred to as 'country-cured', and most of them are produced in Georgia, Kentucky, Tennessee and Virginia. The best-known is Snutfield, a dark, lean Virginia ham. Mass-produced hams are called 'urban' or 'city' hams, and are not of the same quality.

■ **Raw hams** These hams are usually served finely sliced. They are cured, matured and dried; they may be smoked. Although they are suitable for serving raw, they may be used in cooked dishes. The various trade names are not usually protected. Traditionally the ham is treated by repeatedly rubbing salt into the meat, but not by injecting brine (though this may be done to certain 'mountain' or 'country' hams); the most important aspect of the curing process is the maturing period.

Bayonne ham is manufactured all over France, although the original product was made in that region and is still made at Orthez and Peyrehorade. The red seal guarantees that the ham comes from good-quality carcasses, has been rubbed with a mixture of salt from Salies-de-Béarn, saltpetre, sugar, pepper and aromatic herbs, and has been dried for 130–180 days.

Hams from the Alps, the Morvan, the Causses, Savoy and the Ardennes are all smoked to some extent, and are of varying quality. The injection of brine and polyphosphates along the length of the bone hastens the curing and the ham can be sold two months after processing, but its keeping quality is poor and the flavour insipid. If, however, it has been produced by local tradesmen supplied direct from the farms, then it is full of flavour. It is eaten in thin slices, either raw or fried with eggs, or it may form part of one of the regional dishes.

Parma ham (*prosciutto di Parma*) is particularly tasty, being matured for 8–10 months. Connoisseurs are very fond of the ham from San Daniele. It is eaten very thinly sliced, with melon or fresh figs.

Serrano ham, from Spain, is an unsmoked ham from white pigs.

Westphalian ham is protected by trademark. It is dry-salted, brined, desalted and cold-smoked over strongly resinous wood, then dried. Mainz ham is brined, desalted, soaked in brandy or wine lees, and smoked for a long period. Both these German products are excellent.

A leg of wild boar is also called a ham; it is soaked in a sweet-and-sour marinade, then braised in the same liquid, often with fruit such as prunes, raisins or candied orange peel.

Other specialities include Reims ham (prepared with pieces of cooked shoulder and ham, covered with aspic and pressed in a mould), which is traditionally sold coated with breadcrumbs; *jambon persillé* from Burgundy or the Morvan, also made with cooked shoulder and ham, with jelly and a large proportion of parsley added before moulding. According to Austin de Croze, the very best of all hams is from Artigues-de-Lussac, cooked but not smoked, fried with garlic and vinegar, left in the vinegar for 24 hours, and served very cold.

■ **Cooking ham** Hams to be served cooked and cured by traditional methods, with a high salt content, have to be soaked for several hours before cooking. However, the majority of hams cured by contemporary processes are far less salty and do not require soaking, which can make them tasteless. Check with the supplier or on the label for information.

The drained ham should be brought to the boil in fresh water. Just as the water boils, it should be drained away and fresh water added. When the water boils and scum has been skimmed off, flavouring ingredients, such as onions, vegetables, a bouquet garni, cloves, coriander seeds and peppercorns, are added. The ham is then simmered gently. Alternatively, many mild, lightly salted hams can be baked. A combination of boiling for half of the time and then baking gives excellent results. As a guide, cooking times are calculated at 40 minutes per 1 kg or 20 minutes per 1 lb, plus an extra 40 or 20 minutes.

RECIPES

braised ham
A few hours before cooking a fresh ham (or a corner or middle gammon), rub it with salt mixed with powdered thyme and bay leaf. When ready to cook, wipe the ham dry, then brown it lightly in 50 g (2 oz, ¼ cup) butter. Prepare a meatless matignon* with 250 g (9 oz, 1½ cups) peeled, finely diced and cored carrots, 100 g (4 oz) celery sticks with the strings removed, and 50 g (2 oz, ⅓ cup) coarsely chopped onions. Cook these vegetables gently in 50 g (2 oz, ¼ cup) butter, in a covered pan, with a bay leaf, a sprig of thyme, salt, pepper and a pinch of sugar, for about 30 minutes. Then add 200 ml (7 fl oz, ¾ cup) Madeira or 200 ml (7 fl oz, ¾ cup) Meursault or Riesling and let it reduce with the lid off until the vegetables are soft and all the liquid has been used up.

Put the ham in a roasting tin (pan), coat it with the matignon and sprinkle it with melted butter, then cover with buttered greaseproof (wax) paper. Cook in a preheated oven at 200°C (400°F, gas 6), allowing 20–25 minutes per 450 g (1 lb), basting frequently with the cooking butter (if this seems to

be getting too brown, add a few tablespoons of stock). When the ham is cooked, remove the greaseproof paper and the matignon and place the ham on a hot serving dish. Deglaze the roasting tin with a mixture of one-third Madeira and two-thirds stock, and reduce by half. Put the matignon and the cooking juices through a blender and pour this sauce over the ham.

braised ham à la bayonnaise
Soak a Bayonne ham in cold water for at least 6 hours to remove the salt, then poach it in salted water until it is three-quarters cooked (the meat should still resist a trussing needle stuck into it). Drain and skin it by removing the rind and excess fat, leaving about 1 cm (½ in) of fat on the ham. Complete the cooking as for braised ham. When it is cooked, put it on an ovenproof serving dish, with a little of the strained cooking juices poured over, and glaze in the oven.

Meanwhile, prepare a well-seasoned rice pilaf, adding chopped tomatoes (use slightly less water to cook the rice, as tomatoes are very watery). Sprinkle some cleaned button mushrooms with lemon juice and cook them gently in butter. Fry some very thin chipolata sausages in butter. Mix the rice and the mushrooms, and arrange this garnish around the ham, with the chipolatas around the edge of the dish. Serve the rest of the cooking juices separately in a sauceboat.

braised ham à la crème
Cover a fresh ham with water and cook until three-quarters done (the meat should still resist a trussing needle stuck into it). Remove the rind and surplus fat, leaving about 1 cm (½ in) of fat on the ham. Prepare a mirepoix* with 200 g (8 oz) peeled and cored carrots, 125 g (4½ oz) onions, 75 g (3 oz) celery sticks and 125 g (4 oz) raw ham or blanched belly pork. Melt 50 g (2 oz, ¼ cup) butter in a saucepan and add the mirepoix with a sprig of thyme and a few sprigs of chopped parsley; cook very gently with the lid on until the vegetables are quite soft.

Spread the mirepoix in a roasting tin (pan) and place the skinned ham on top; pour over 6 tablespoons stock, 50 g (2 oz, ¼ cup) melted butter and 200 ml (7 fl oz, ¾ cup) Madeira. Cover the ham with buttered greaseproof (wax) paper and cook in a preheated oven at 200°C (400°F, gas 6) for about 1½ hours, basting frequently with the cooking juices and adding a little stock if necessary to keep it moist. When cooked, drain the ham and place it on a hot serving dish.

Reduce the cooking liquid a little, then add 500 ml (17 fl oz, 2 cups) crème fraîche and reduce by one third. Put this sauce through a blender and serve it with the ham.

braised ham with pineapple
Put a fresh ham weighing about 5 kg (11 lb) into cold water, bring to the boil, and simmer very

gently for 2 hours. Drain the ham and leave until cold, then remove the rind, leaving a 1 cm (½ in) layer of fat on the ham. Stud the ham with cloves and sprinkle with 125 g (4½ oz, ½ cup) caster (superfine) sugar. Place in a roasting tin (pan) and bake in a preheated oven at 220°C (425°F, gas 7) for 1½ hours.

Heat about 12 canned pineapple slices in their syrup. Put 250 ml (8 fl oz, 1 cup) wine vinegar and 20 peppercorns into a saucepan, bring to the boil, and then add 500 ml (17 fl oz, 2 cups) stock. Prepare a pale caramel with 125 g (4½ oz, ½ cup) caster sugar and strain the flavoured stock on to the caramel. Add 2 glasses of sherry and reduce until syrupy; pour into a sauceboat. Put the ham on a hot dish and surround it with the drained slices of pineapple; serve the sauce separately.

cold ham mousse
Mince (grind) 500 g (18 oz) cooked lean ham, adding 200 ml (7 fl oz, ¾ cup) cold thick velouté* sauce. Purée in a blender, then put it into a bowl and stand it on ice; season and stir with a spatula for a few minutes, adding 150 ml (¼ pint, ⅔ cup) liquid aspic, a little at a time. Finally, gently fold in 400 ml (14 fl oz, 1¾ cups) double (heavy) cream whipped until fairly stiff. Pour into a mould lined with aspic, and chill until set. Turn out on to the serving dish and garnish with chopped aspic.

glazed ham
Soak a medium-sized ham in cold water for at least 6 hours, then scrub it and bone it at the loin end. Put it in a large saucepan with plenty of cold water but no seasoning. As soon as the water boils, reduce the heat and let it simmer very gently, allowing no more than 20 minutes per 450 g (1 lb). After draining and skinning the ham, put it in a roasting tin (pan), sprinkle with icing (confectioner's) sugar and glaze in a preheated oven at 180°C (350°F, gas 4) for about 30 minutes. As it caramelizes, the sugar turns into a sort of golden lacquer, enhancing the appearance and flavour of the ham.

glazed ham reine pédauque
Poach a middle or corner gammon in Meursault for 20 minutes per 450 g (1 lb). Cut it into thin slices and leave until cold. Spread each slice with a layer of foie gras mixed with diced truffle, and put the slices together to re-form the original shape. Coat with a port-flavoured chaud-froid sauce. Garnish with slices of truffle and glaze with port-flavoured aspic. Place the glazed ham on a long serving dish and surround it with little squares of aspic.

ham à la chablisienne
Remove the stalks from 1.5 kg (3¼ lb) spinach, wash the leaves and cook them briskly in salted boiling water until wilted. Cool them down in iced water, then squeeze out all the water. Finely chop

1 small shallot and sweat in a saucepan in 10 g (¼ oz, 1½ teaspoons) butter, without letting it brown. Add 200 ml (7 fl oz, ¾ cup) Chablis and reduce to 4 teaspoons. Add 200 ml (7 fl oz, ¾ cup) chicken stock and reduce by half. Pour in 200 ml (7 fl oz, ¾ cup) double (heavy) cream and cook until it thickens slightly. Season with salt and pepper. In another saucepan, heat 50 g (2 oz, ¼ cup) butter until it turns brown. Add the spinach and stir with a fork spiked with a peeled garlic clove. Adjust the seasoning. Place the spinach in an ovenproof dish. On top arrange 4 thick slices of ham previously warmed in stock and then drained. Pour the sauce on top and put in a preheated oven at 180°C (350°F, gas 4) for a few minutes.

poached ham in pastry à l'ancienne
Poach a York ham in water until it is two-thirds cooked, then drain. Remove the skin and glaze on one side with caramel, then let it get cold. Prepare 575 g (1¼ lb) lining pastry (see short pastry), about 225 g (8 oz) vegetable mirepoix and 3 tablespoons mushroom duxelles. Mix the mirepoix and the duxelles together, adding 1 chopped truffle.

Roll out the pastry to a thickness of about 4 mm (¼ in) and spread the vegetable mixture over an area in the centre about the same size as the ham. Place the ham on the vegetables, glazed side down, wrap it in the pastry and seal the edges. Put it in a buttered roasting tin (pan), sealed side down. Brush the top of the pastry with beaten egg yolk and garnish with shapes cut from the pastry trimmings. Make a hole in the top for the steam to escape and cook in a preheated oven at 180–200°C (350–400°F, gas 4–6) for about 1 hour. Place the ham on a serving dish. If liked, a few spoonfuls of Périgueux sauce can be poured in through the opening.

other recipes See *aspic, canapé, cornet, crêpe, fig, pâté, pea, porte-maillot, quiche.*

HAMBURGER Minced (ground) beef shaped into a flat round patty and grilled (broiled) or fried. The name is an abbreviation of Hamburger steak – beef grilled in the Hamburg style. Originally introduced into the United States by German immigrants, the American style of hamburger has been exported around the world. It is usually sandwiched in a round bread roll and may be garnished with tomato ketchup, mayonnaise, lettuce, pickles and slices of tomato. It may also be topped with various other foods, including cheese (a cheeseburger), olives (olive burger), mushrooms (mushroom burger) or chilli (chilli burger).

RECIPE

hamburgers
Mix 400 g (14 oz) best-quality minced (ground) beef with 50 g (2 oz, ⅓ cup) chopped onion, 2 beaten eggs, salt, pepper and 1 tablespoon

chopped parsley if liked. Shape the mixture into 4 thick flat round patties, and fry in very hot clarified butter or grill (broil). They are cooked when droplets of blood appear on the surface. Fry 100 g (4 oz, ⅔ cup) chopped onion in the same butter to garnish the hamburgers. Serve very hot in a round bun.

HANAP A large drinking goblet with no handle. Used in France in the Middle Ages, it was made of wood, pewter, silver or even hard polished stone.

HANGING The operation of leaving red meat, especially game, in a cool place for a varying length of time to make the flesh more tender and improve the flavour.

The French word is derived from *faisan* (pheasant). When it is fresh, pheasant is tough and without much flavour. It grows tender and its aroma develops after it has been hung, the length of time depending upon the temperature. In Brillat-Savarin's time, pheasant was not considered fit for the gastronome's table except in a state of complete putrefaction. This authority recommends, in effect, that it should be kept, unplucked, until its breast turns green, so that for roasting on the spit it has to be held together by a slice of bread tied on with string. Nowadays, game and meat are no longer hung until they are high.

Game that is wounded in the belly or damaged by lead shot should never be hung, as it will rot very quickly. Woodcock and certain other game birds are not drawn, but large game should be drawn as quickly as possible. Game birds are wrapped in muslin (cheesecloth) or a cloth and suspended by the legs in a cool, dry, and preferably well-ventilated place. Woodcock needs to be left for the longest time, followed by wild duck, pheasant and partridge. Small birds are generally not hung. Game animals are hung for 2–4 days. Both winged game and ground game when hung acquire a similar flavour to that of pheasant.

Meat should be hung in a cool, airy place. In theory, beef needs to be hung for 3–4 weeks at –1.5°C (29°F), 15 days at 0°C (32°F), 2 days at 20°C (68°F) or 1 day at 43°C (109°F). In practice, however, it is hung in a cold room at 2°C (35°F) for 5–6 days.

HARE A game animal belonging to the same family as the rabbit, but larger and having dark flesh. The male is called a 'buck', the female a 'doe'. The best French wild hares are found in Beauce, Champagne, Brie, Normandy, Poitou, Gascony and Périgord (the last being the region where the most famous French hare dish, *à la royale*, originated). The meat is highly flavoured and excellent, the mountain variety having a more delicate flavour than that of the plains.

Hare meat is cooked in different ways according to its age. A leveret (2–4 months) weighs about 1.5 kg (3¼ lb) and is usually roasted. A 1-year-old hare (called a *trois-quarts* in France) weighs 2.5–3 kg (5½–6½ lb) and yields excellent saddles for roasting and meat for sautéing. Hares more than 1 year old (known in France as *capucins*), weighing 4–6 kg (9–13 lb), are mostly made into civets (jugged hare). A year-old hare is best for the table. If it is much older, it should be made into a terrine or cooked *en daube*.

Hares are not hung, since they deteriorate after about 48 hours. A marinade based on a rough red wine is used for civets. Hare fillets and legs are sometimes used for specific recipes. Hare with cherries is a German speciality.

RECIPES

preparation of fillets of hare

Separate the saddle from the forequarters of a hare as far behind the ribs as possible, and place the saddle on its back. With a pointed knife, cut away the meat on both sides of the backbone. Ease off the flesh to halfway up the backbone, then place the blade of a very heavy knife against the backbone and, by tapping on the blade, complete the separation of the fillets. Do the same on the other side. Separate the fillets from each other, then lard them with fat bacon. Season with salt, pepper and a pinch of cayenne; pour over a dash of brandy and leave to marinate until the time for cooking.

fillets of hare on croûtes

Prepare the fillets and place them in a buttered roasting dish. Pour over melted butter and cook them in a preheated oven at 240°C (475°F, gas 9), covering them with foil once they are browned. Serve on bread croûtes fried in butter and coat with financière or Périgueux sauce, or a fruit sauce (cranberry or redcurrant).

hare cutlets with mushrooms

Finely chop a boned hare. Add one-third of its weight of bread soaked in cream and an equal quantity of chopped mushrooms, parsley and shallots. Season with salt and pepper, add a pinch of *quatre-épices* (a mixture of white peppercorns, nutmeg, cinnamon or ginger, and cloves), and blend all the ingredients together into a firm paste. Divide the mixture into portions of 50–65 g (2–2½ oz), roll into balls, then flatten into cutlets. Coat with flour and fry in clarified butter. Serve with a game sauce, such as poivrade.

hare mousse

Remove the sinews from 450 g (1 lb) hare meat and chop the meat very finely in a food processor. (A few chopped truffle skins may be added.) Sprinkle with 1¼ teaspoons table salt and a large pinch of white pepper. Gradually incorporate 2–3 egg whites, still in the processor, then rub the mixture through a sieve. Stir the sieved mixture in a shallow frying pan over a low heat until it is quite smooth, then transfer it to a bowl; refrigerate for 2 hours.

Stand the chilled bowl in a bowl of ice cubes and

gradually add 750 ml (1¼ pints, 3¼ cups) double (heavy) cream, stirring vigorously with a wooden spoon. Put it back in the refrigerator for 1 hour. Butter some dariole moulds and fill with the mousse. Put the moulds in a bain marie, bring to the boil, cover with foil, and cook them in a preheated oven at 200°C (400°F, gas 6) for 25–30 minutes (a fine needle inserted in the mousse should come out clean). Serve with a Périgueux sauce.

hare pâté

Bone a hare and set aside the fillets (including the filets mignons) and the thigh meat. Remove the sinews from these cuts, lard the meat, and season with salt, pepper and a little mixed spice. Then marinate them in brandy together with an equal weight of thin slices of lean unsmoked ham, fat bacon and quartered truffles. Prepare a game forcemeat with the rest of the meat; rub it through a sieve and then thicken it with the hare's blood.

Butter an oval hinged mould and line with lining pastry. Cover the pastry with very thin slices of fat bacon and spread a layer of foremeat over the bottom and up the sides. Arrange a layer of marinated hare fillets in the mould and cover with a layer of forcemeat. Continue to fill the mould with alternate layers of hare and forcemeat, finishing with a layer of forcemeat. Cover with slices of fat bacon, then with a layer of pastry, inserting a chimney in the centre to allow the steam to escape during cooking. Seal well around the edges. Shape the crust with a pastry crimper and garnish the top with pastry shapes. Brush with beaten egg and cook in a preheated oven at 190°C (375°F, gas 5), allowing 35 minutes per 1 kg (15 minutes per 1 lb).

Let the pâté cool in the mould. When it is cold, pour a few spoonfuls of Madeira-flavoured aspic through the central hole (or, if the pâté is to be kept for any length of time, a mixture of melted butter and lard). The pâté should be prepared at least 24 hours before serving.

hare with chocolate

Skin a hare, detach the saddle and thighs, season these with salt and pepper, and marinate for 3 days in oil. Break up the rib cage, the forelimbs and the offal, and marinate these for 3 days in a marinade made with 2 bottles of red wine, 2 onions, a garlic head (bulb) broken into cloves, 2 carrots and a leek (coarsely chopped), thyme, bay leaves, grated nutmeg, pepper, the juice of 1 lemon, chopped root ginger, cinnamon and cloves.

After 3 days, strain the marinade and sauté the pieces of carcass in olive oil until brown. Remove the fat. Add a little of the marinade and a calf's foot. Cook very gently for 4 hours, then remove the fat. Strain the sauce obtained and thicken it with 50 g (2 oz) bitter (bittersweet) chocolate and 100 g (4 oz, ½ cup) butter. Heat the juice of 1 lemon with 3 tablespoons poultry blood without boiling, and add to the sauce. Cook the saddle and thighs in butter in a casserole (the meat should remain pink). Cut into portions. Pour over the sauce and serve with spiced pears sautéed in butter.

roast hare en saugrenée

Let the hare hang, unskinned, in a cool place for 24 hours, then joint it and reserve the blood and liver. Place the joints in a dish containing 250 ml (8 fl oz, 1 cup) cider, 4 tablespoons olive oil, 1 onion and 1 carrot (finely chopped), 6 juniper berries, 12 shallots and a pinch of spice. Leave to marinate for 12 hours.

Blanch the shallots from the marinade and put them in a roasting dish with a slice of fat bacon. Place the hare on top and roast in a preheated oven at 200°C (400°F, gas 6) for 30–40 minutes. Prepare the hearts of 2 celery heads, wash them, blanch them in salted water and drain. Braise the celery for 40 minutes in a buttered dish, moistened with stock.

Place the cooked hare in a warm dish. Deglaze the roasting dish with 1 small ladle of stock and 1 tablespoon brandy. Remove from the heat and thicken carefully with the puréed liver of the hare and the reserved blood. Pour this sauce over the hare. Serve the celery separately.

other recipes See *cherry (savoury dishes), saddle*.

HARICOT See *halicot*.

HARICOT BEANS, DRIED Legume produced basically for its dry seed. (See *beans, dried*.) Some varieties, which are shelled and dried before they are sold, are very highly regarded.

• FLAGEOLETS Very delicate, white or green, and with little starch, these kidney-shaped beans are grown in the regions of Arpajon, Brittany, and in the north of France. Also known as *chevriers*, they are picked from April to September before they are mature; they are sold after they have been dried under cover, canned or frozen.

• LINGOTS Large, thin, very white beans grown in the north of France and the Vendée. Sold dried, they keep a long time.

Produced in smaller quantities, *soissons, rognons de coq* (cock's kidney beans), *suisse blancs* (Swiss white beans), and *cocos blancs* are all good as well. Like fresh beans, dried haricot beans are used in various characteristic regional dishes. Flageolets are a traditional accompaniment for leg or shoulder of pork, and are excellent with lamb.

■ **Cooking dried haricot beans** Soak the beans in plenty of cold water for at least 2 hours or, preferably, overnight. Drain them, put in a large saucepan and cover with plenty of cold water. Bring to the boil, then skim and boil for 10 minutes. Reduce the heat so that the water simmers. Add 1 bouquet garni, 1 peeled onion stuck with 2 cloves, 1 peeled garlic clove and 1 diced carrot. Cover and cook for 1½–2½ hours at a gentle simmer, until the beans are tender. Check the water level during cooking and add more, if necessary, to keep the beans covered. When the beans are thoroughly cooked, season them to taste. Do not add salt earlier in the cooking process, as this will harden the beans and prevent them from becoming tender.

HARICOT BEANS, FRESH See *beans, fresh*.

HARISSA A condiment from North Africa and the Middle East. It is a paste (*tabal*) made from chillies, oil, garlic and coriander, pounded with cumin or coriander and sometimes with dried mint or verbena leaves. The harissa must be left for 12 hours before using. Covered with olive oil, it keeps well in a sealed container. It is diluted with a little stock and added to couscous, soups and dried meat. It is also served as a table condiment.

HASH A preparation of finely chopped raw or cooked meat, poultry, fish or vegetables. Hashes are nearly always prepared from leftovers and usually either piled in the centre of a ring of duchess potatoes and browned in the oven, or accompanied by a pilaf of rice or a risotto. The classic example of this dish is *hachis Parmentier*, in which finely chopped beef is topped with mashed potato, then with breadcrumbs and butter, and browned in the oven.

A purée of vegetables, such as aubergines (eggplants), tomatoes, courgettes (zucchini) or pumpkin, can be substituted for the potato. Diced beef, mutton, rabbit or pork is sometimes enriched with mushrooms, and diced veal or poultry is often mixed with cream, béchamel sauce or Mornay sauce (see *moussaka*). Finely chopped or minced (ground) meat is also used for meatballs, croquettes and fricadelles. Pork is used for certain regional dishes, such as caillettes and attignoles.

Fish for hashes should be firm-fleshed (such as tuna, swordfish or cod) and it is best to use only one variety of fish.

RECIPES

Beef Hash
All the recipes for beef hash can also be used for mutton or lamb. They can also be used for leftovers of pork if the meat has been braised. If it has been boiled or roasted, use the recipes for veal hash.

beef hash à l'italienne
Sauté 3 tablespoons chopped onion in 3 tablespoons olive oil until slightly brown, sprinkle with 1 tablespoon flour and mix well. Then add 200 ml (7 fl oz, ¾ cup) water or stock, 3 tablespoons tomato purée (paste) diluted with 6 tablespoons stock, a bouquet garni and a crushed garlic clove. Cook gently for about 30 minutes. Remove the bouquet garni and allow to cool. Add some of this sauce to some finely chopped braised or boiled beef and reheat gently. Serve with tagliatelle and the remainder of the sauce.

beef hash with aubergines au gratin
Prepare and cook the sauce as for beef hash à *l'italienne*, then add the finely chopped beef together with 1 tablespoon chopped parsley. Slice some aubergines (eggplants) into rounds, sauté them in oil and arrange them in a buttered gratin dish. Pour in the beef in its sauce, smooth the surface, sprinkle with a mixture of grated Parmesan cheese and breadcrumbs, pour over a little olive oil and brown in a preheated oven at 230°C (450°F, gas 8).

boiled beef hash
Chop very finely (by hand or in a food processor) 500 g (18 oz) boiled beef. Cook 2 large finely chopped onions in 15 g (½ oz, 1 tablespoon) butter until tender. Sprinkle with 1 tablespoon flour and cook until golden brown. Add 200 ml (7 fl oz, ¾ cup) stock, season with salt and pepper, and bring to the boil, stirring constantly. Simmer for 15 minutes. Allow to cool, add the boiled beef, and cook in a covered dish in a preheated oven at 200°C (400°F, gas 6) for 25 minutes.

Chicken Hash
small hot entrées with chicken hash
Make one of the following sauces: allemande, béchamel, cream or velouté. Dice poached, braised or roast chicken meat very finely and mix it with the tepid sauce. Heat the mixture thoroughly in a saucepan. Chicken hash can be used to stuff mushroom caps, artichoke hearts or hard-boiled (hard-cooked) eggs (mix the crushed yolks into the hash): sprinkle with grated Gruyère cheese, cover with melted butter and brown in the oven. The hash can also be used to fill warmed croûtes, croustades or vol-au-vent cases.

Veal Hash
veal hash à l'allemande
Prepare an allemande sauce and allow it to cool. Mix it with finely diced leftover roast or sautéed veal. Pour the mixture into a sauté pan and heat gently but thoroughly. The hash may be served in a flaky pastry case or with fresh pasta.

veal hash à la Mornay
Finely dice leftover roast or sautéed veal. Prepare a well-seasoned béchamel sauce and add a little crème fraîche. Divide the sauce into 2 equal portions. Add some chopped *fines herbes* to one portion and some grated Gruyère cheese to the other. Mix the sauce containing the herbs with the diced veal and pour into a buttered gratin dish. Smooth the surface and cover with the cheese sauce. Sprinkle with more grated Gruyère, pour melted butter over the top, and brown in a preheated oven at 240°C (475°F, gas 9). Sliced mushrooms, braised in butter with a little lemon juice, can be added if desired.

HAUSER, GAYELORD (born *Helmut Eugene Benjamin Gellert Hauser*) American nutritionist (born Tübingen, Baden-Württemberg, 1895; died Los Angeles, 1984). He suffered from tuberculosis of the hip but was cured by following the advice of a Swiss doctor, who convinced him of the power of natural foods such as wholewheat flour, brewer's yeast, yogurt, dried pulses, cereals and soya. Having written *Message of Health* and a *Dictionary of Foods*, Hauser achieved worldwide recognition with *Live Young, Live Longer* (1950). In this book he propounds several basic theories concerning a balanced diet, discusses the importance of fruit diets and aromatic herbs, and suggests cooking methods that preserve vitamins and mineral salts. Various dietetic products have been marketed under his name.

HAUT-MÉDOC The southern part of the Médoc district of Bordeaux. Within this region – the birthplace of such world-famous clarets as Châteaux Lafite-Rothschild, Latour, Mouton-Rothschild and Margaux – there are various parishes, each having its own AOC. For example, the first three of the estates mentioned above are AOC Pauillac. Other parishes with their own AOC here are Margaux, St-Julien and St-Estèphe. Wines not included in these AOCs may be labelled under the Haut-Médoc appellation.

HAUT-POITOU WINES Red, white and rosé wines produced in the Vienne and Deux-Sèvre. Mainly produced by a local co-operative, the whites, made from either the Sauvignon Blanc or the Chardonnay grape, and the reds, from a blend of Gamay and Cabernets Sauvignon and Franc, are good value.

HAVIR A French culinary term that originally meant to cook the outside of a dish at a very high temperature to sear or seal it. Nowadays it is more likely that anything described as *havi* will be burnt on the outside and raw on the inside.

HAWTHORN A thorny shrub or small tree of the rose family that grows throughout Europe, North America and Asia. Its leaves and flowers are used for tisanes, as it is traditionally thought to have a calming action on the heart. A Mediterranean species of hawthorn, known as the Mediterranean or Neapolitan medlar, is very widespread in the south of France; its red fleshy fruits have a tart flavour and are used to make jellies and jams.

HAZEL GROUSE *gelinotte* A game bird of the grouse family. It is also called hazel hen or wood grouse and is about the size of a partridge. The hazel grouse has succulent flesh and is cooked like partridge; it can be hung briefly, but not until high. When the hazel grouse has fed on fir cones, its flesh tastes of resin. This flavour can be made less strong by soaking the bird in milk.

HAZELNUT A hard-shelled nut with an oval or round kernel that is produced by one of several species of hazel tree. Harvested in August and September, the nuts can be eaten fresh but are usually dried.

Hazelnut oil is extracted in small quantities for use as a flavouring (for example, in salad dressings) it should not be heated. Fresh hazelnuts are always sold in their green husks (*involucres*). The whole dried nuts should have shiny shells, not too thick and free from blemishes, holes and cracks; they can be broken only with a nutcracker. Once shelled, the kernels should be kept in an airtight container or they will become rancid. They can be served on their own, salted or toasted, as an appetizer; they are also used whole, grated or ground in many dishes (for example, stuffings, terrines, with chicken, and in fish meunière, in the same way as almonds). They make a good flavouring for butter as well. Their chief role, however, is in pâtisserie and confectionery: the *noisetier* (a cake from Pontarlier), hazelnut cake and *noisettine* (puff pastry with hazelnut-flavoured butter cream) are some examples.

The filbert (*aveline* in French) is a variety of large cultivated hazelnut, although the name is sometimes used loosely to describe dishes containing ordinary hazelnuts; for example, *truite aux avelines*.

RECIPES

chicken with hazelnuts

Cut an uncooked chicken into 4 pieces. Sprinkle the pieces with salt and freshly ground pepper, dip them in flour, then brown them in butter. Moisten with stock made from the giblets and cook with the lid on for 30 minutes. Keep hot. Lightly toast 150 g (5 oz, 1 cup) shelled hazelnuts under the grill (broiler), then grind them and blend with 150 g (5 oz, ⅔ cup) butter. Reduce the cooking liquid from the chicken, then add the nut butter and 4 tablespoons crème fraîche; cook for 5–6 minutes over a low heat. Pour this sauce, to which some whole nuts can be added, over the chicken.

hazelnut cake

Spread 50 g (2 oz, ½ cup) ground hazelnuts on a baking sheet and brown them lightly in a preheated oven at 140°C (275°F, gas 1). Whisk 5 egg yolks with 150 g (5 oz, ⅔ cup) caster (superfine) sugar for 5 minutes, then beat in 150 g (5 oz, 1¼ cups) sifted plain (all-purpose) flour and the ground hazelnuts. Melt 90 g (3½ oz, 7 tablespoons) butter over a very low heat, blend in the nut mixture, then carefully fold in 5 egg whites whisked to stiff peaks. Pour this mixture into a 20 cm (8 in) buttered, deep, round sandwich tin (layer cake pan) and bake in a preheated oven at 180°C (350°F, gas 4) for 30–35 minutes. Turn the cake out on to a wire rack and leave to cool.

Meanwhile, make butter cream using 4 egg yolks, 150 g (5 oz, ⅔ cup) caster sugar, 175 g (6 oz, ¾ cup) butter and 50 g (2 oz, ½ cup) ground hazelnuts. Then prepare the decoration: soften 50 g (2 oz, 4 tablespoons) butter and blend in 50 g

(2 oz, 4 tablespoons) caster sugar, I teaspoon vanilla sugar and I egg; using a whisk, beat in 50 g (2 oz, ½ cup) plain flour. Roll this dough out, cut it into small rounds with a biscuit (cookie) cutter, and place the rounds well apart on a lightly buttered baking sheet. Bake in a preheated oven at 240°C (475°F, gas 9). Remove the rounds when cooked and leave to cool.

Cut the cake into 3 equal layers, spread butter cream over each layer, then reassemble the cake. Coat the sides with the remaining butter cream and decorate with the baked rounds. The spaces between the rounds can be filled with toasted hazelnuts. Store in a cool place.

Jerusalem artichoke and hazelnut salad

Peel the required quantity of Jerusalem artichokes and cook them for about 10 minutes in salted white wine. Drain and slice. Put the slices into a salad bowl and season with oil, mustard and lemon juice. Chop lightly toasted hazelnuts and scatter them over the artichokes.

other recipes See *butter (flavoured butters), fond de pâtisserie*.

HEAD A gelatinous variety of white offal (variety meat). Certain parts of the head are particularly appreciated and prepared separately: brain, tongue, ears and cheeks, for example. Only calf's head is used whole in classic cuisine, although lamb's or sheep's head is prepared whole in certain regional dishes from Auvergne and south-western France.

Ox head (head of beef) is always sliced or prepared as a terrine (*museau de boeuf*, made of salted ox muzzle and chin, and served with vinaigrette).

Pig's head is quite widely used in charcuterie for *pâté de tête* (made with cooked boned head and cooked salted pork with the rind), *museau de porc* (boned pieces of head and tail that are cooked, pressed and moulded), *hure à la parisienne* (head and loin of pork), and *tête de porc roulée* (boned pig's head and tongue cut into cubes, then cooked, set in aspic, moulded and garnished with pressed pig's ears; it is sliced when cold and served with vinaigrette). It is similar to the British brawn, but in the latter the head is cooked and then the meat removed.

Calf's head is always cooked in a white court-bouillon. In France it is sold at the tripe butcher's already boned, wrapped and blanched (the flesh must be bright pink and there must be a marked contrast in colour between the flesh and the white gelatinous part). Calf's head has always been of major importance in French cookery and can be prepared in a wide variety of ways, either hot or cold, and served with such sauces as herb, Madeira, caper, ravigote, tomato, gribiche and piquante. It is also cooked stuffed, au gratin, or fried in batter. Traditionally, it was prepared *en tortue*, a prestigious dish with a rich garnish of truffled quenelles, cockscombs and kidneys, calves' sweetbreads and mushrooms.

preparation and cooking of calf's head

Clean the head thoroughly, soak it in cold water, then blanch it. Prepare a white court-bouillon: mix 3 tablespoons flour with 3 litres (5 pints, 13 cups) water in a saucepan. Season with salt and pepper, then add the juice of half a lemon, an onion studded with 2 cloves, and a bouquet garni. Bring to the boil and immerse the head wrapped in muslin (cheesecloth) in this court-bouillon. Simmer very gently for about 2 hours. Serve with the chosen garnish.

calf's head à l'occitane

Cut half a well-soaked calf's head into 8 uniform pieces and cook in a white court-bouillon with the tongue. Poach the brain separately in a highly flavoured court-bouillon. Put 4 tablespoons chopped onion, lightly fried in butter, into a shallow ovenproof dish and add a small quantity of grated garlic towards the end of cooking. Arrange the pieces of calf's head on top with the sliced tongue and brain. Garnish with black olives, 2 peeled, seeded tomatoes crushed and tossed in oil, and 2 hard-boiled (hard-cooked) eggs cut into fairly thick slices. Season with salt and pepper. Pour 6 tablespoons olive oil and the juice of half a lemon over the calf's head and sprinkle with chopped parsley. Heat in a bain marie, keeping the dish covered. Just before serving, baste the garnished head with the sauce in which it was cooked.

calf's head in crépinettes

Cut 500 g (18 oz) calf's head cooked in a white court-bouillon into medium-sized dice. Add one-third of its weight in diced mushrooms, lightly fried in butter, and 5 tablespoons diced truffles. Blend with concentrated Madeira sauce flavoured with truffle essence and allow to cool.

Divide the mixture into 50 g (2 oz) portions and enclose each of these in 100 g (4 oz, ½ cup) finely minced (ground) sausagemeat. Wrap each of these in a piece of pig's caul (caul fat), previously soaked in cold water, and roll into the shape of a flat sausage. Brush the crépinettes with clarified butter or melted lard, roll them in fine fresh breadcrumbs and sprinkle again with fat. Grill (broil) the crépinettes on both sides under a low heat and serve with Périgeux sauce.

other recipes See *lyonnaise, poupeton, tortue (en)*.

HEAD CHEESE See *brawn*.

HEART A type of red offal (variety meat) from various animals, which must be bright red and firm when bought. Remove the hard fibres and any clots of blood, if necessary, by soaking it in cold water. Heart is devoid of fat and inexpensive. It is considered to be an excellent dish despite its lack of gastronomic repute. Ox (beef) heart is eaten roasted or braised and may be stuffed. It may also be cut into cubes and grilled (broiled) on skewers (like *anticucho*, a popular Peruvian dish). Heifer's heart is more tender and is considered to be better than ox heart. However, calf's heart has the most flavour and may be either roasted whole or cut into slices and fried. Pig's or sheep's hearts are used to make a ragoût or a civet. Poultry hearts are grilled on skewers, used in terrines, incorporated in mixed salads or merely seared in butter.

RECIPES

casserole of calf's heart à bonne femme
Clean the heart, season with salt and pepper, and brown it in butter in a casserole, traditionally made of earthenware. Add pieces of potato, small glazed onions and strips of streaky bacon that have been lightly fried in butter. Cook over a gentle heat for about 30 minutes.

grilled calf's heart on skewers
Clean the heart and cut it into large cubes. Clean some small mushrooms and marinate the heart and mushrooms in a mixture of olive oil, lemon juice, chopped garlic, chopped parsley, salt and pepper. Thread the cubes of heart and the mushrooms, alternately on some skewers, finishing each skewer with a small tomato. Cook under a hot grill (broiler).

matelote of ox heart
Divide the heart into two and soak the halves in cold water. Remove the blood clots and sinews, wash and wipe. Cut the heart into large dice and marinate for 6 hours in vinegar containing salt, pepper, thyme, cloves and a bay leaf. Drain and lightly brown the diced heart in a casserole with 20 g (¾ oz, 4½ teaspoons) butter and 100 g (4 oz, ½ cup) streaky bacon, cut into small pieces. Add 15 small onions and cook until golden brown. Stir in 1 tablespoon flour with a wooden spoon. Cover the contents of the pan with good red wine and add salt, pepper, a bouquet garni and 1 garlic clove. Cook gently for 3 hours. Half an hour before the end of cooking, add a few strips of bacon and about 15 mushrooms. Remove the bouquet garni and serve very hot.

roast calf's heart
Clean the heart, season with salt and pepper, cover with oil and 1 tablespoon lemon juice, and marinate for 1 hour. Drain and remove the heart, cut it into large slices and wrap each slice in a piece of pig's caul (caul fat). Put the slices on a spit or skewers and roast for 30–35 minutes. Make a sauce from the juices in the grill (broiler) pan mixed with a little white wine. Reduce and pour over the pieces of heart.

sautéed calf's heart
Clean the heart and cut it into thin slices. Season with salt and peper. Sauté the slices quickly in butter in a frying pan. Remove, drain and keep warm. Brown some sliced mushrooms in the same butter and mix them with the slices of heart. Deglaze the frying pan with some Madeira. Reduce, add 15 g (½ oz, 1 tablespoon) butter, and pour the sauce over the heart and mushrooms.

sautéed lambs' hearts
Clean the hearts, cut them into slices and sauté them briskly in butter or olive oil in a frying pan. Add parsley sauce and 1 tablespoon wine vinegar for each heart.

stuffed calf's heart
Clean the heart, season with salt and pepper, and stuff with forcemeat (fine or mushroom). Wrap it in a piece of pig's caul (caul fat) and tie with string. Follow the recipe for casserole of calf's heart, but cook for an additional 30 minutes. Keep the heart hot on the serving dish and make a sauce with the pan juices and white wine. Reduce, then thicken with 15 g (½ oz, 1 tablespoon) beurre manié. Pour the sauce over the heart and serve with vegetables such as carrots, turnips and glazed onions, or a printanière of vegetables.

HEAT DIFFUSER A specially designed mat that is placed between a cooking utensil and the source of heat, either to slow down the heating process or because the material from which the vessel is made is not resistant to intense heat. It may be round or square, generally with a handle, and is made of wire gauze or a double thickness of perforated metal.

HEDGEHOG An insect-eating mammal, two varieties of which can be found in France: the dog hedgehog and the edible pig hedgehog. Boiled hedgehog was a common dish in Paris in the early 16th century, but nowadays it is eaten only by gipsies, who either roast it or stew it. The meat has a stronger flavour than wild rabbit. It is roasted by wrapping it in wet clay and cooking it in a pit full of hot embers. When the clay has hardened, it is broken open and the quills remain embedded in it. The hedgehog can also be skinned or scalded and then marinated to make a civet. The gipsy *niglo* is eaten with a purée of potatoes cooked in red wine with diced bacon.

HÉDIARD, FERDINAND A French grocer who lived in the 19th century. A carpenter by trade, Hédiard travelled around France as a journeyman. In 1853, while on his travels, he was inspired by the sight of foreign goods coming into the ports to set himself up as a grocer in Paris. His first establishment was in the Rue St Georges; later he moved to the Place de la Madeleine. Hédiard was the first Frenchman to sell cardamom from Ceylon, saffron from the island of Réunion (formerly Bourbon), okra from Turkey, annona (custard apple) from the West Indies, mangosteens from Indonesia and Chinese pork crackling. He was also the first regular importer of bananas.

HEIFER A young cow aged between 8 and 20 months. Its meat and liver are of good quality.

HELDER A dish of small pieces of sautéed meat garnished with noisette potatoes and a thick tomato sauce. Helder was the Dutch port that General Brune, commander-in-chief of the Dutch army, captured from the English in 1799. A Parisian café was named after the port; it became very popular with army officers and the students at Saint-Cyr, and it was in the Café du Helder that the dish was created. The name is also used for a dish of shaped chicken cutlets with tomato sauce but a different vegetable garnish.

RECIPES

shaped chicken cutlets Helder

Make a velouté from chicken carcasses (the white meat that has been removed is shaped into cutlets). Add tomato to the velouté and reduce over a gentle heat. Incorporate some butter and then strain the sauce. Season the cutlets with salt and pepper, brush with melted butter and place them in a buttered casserole. Sprinkle with a little lemon juice, cover and cook in a preheated oven at 240°C (475°F, gas 9) for 6–10 minutes. Braise some diced carrots in butter and boil some diced artichoke hearts and mushrooms in water. Arrange the cutlets on a warmed serving dish and garnish with the vegetables. Coat with the tomato sauce.

tournedos Helder

Prepare a béarnaise sauce and a very thick tomato fondue. Also prepare noisette potatoes. Brown the steaks in butter, drain them and keep warm. Deglaze the pan with white wine and consommé, and boil down to reduce to a thick syrupy consistency. Put a ribbon of béarnaise sauce on each steak with a little tomato fondue in the centre. Garnish with the noisette potatoes. Pour the reduced pan juices over the steaks.

HELIOGABALUS Roman emperor (born 204; died 222), who was notorious for his many excesses, particularly his culinary extravagances. It is said that his kitchens were equipped with silver utensils. A different-coloured dinner service appeared at every feast he gave and he served meals composed entirely of pheasant, chicken or pork. He also devised an itinerant feast moving around the city of Rome, eating the hors d'oeuvre at one house, the main course at another and the dessert at a third. These lengthy meals could take up an entire day! He also organized mock naval battles fought out on wine-filled canals and for a single feast he ordered 600 ostrich brains to be prepared.

HEN The female of various gallinaceous birds, particularly the domestic fowl but also the pheasant (hen pheasant). The word 'hen' normally denotes a chicken kept for laying.

Hens are slaughtered between 18 months and 2 years of age, weighing 2–3 kg (4½–6½ lb). Known as boiling fowl, they have firm flesh that is always a little fatty. They are usually cooked by gentle simmering, to make them tender.

HENRI IV The name given to a dish consisting of small pieces of grilled (broiled) or sautéed meat or offal (kidneys), garnished with potatoes *pont-neuf* and béarnaise sauce. The presentation of sautéed tournedos Henri IV is precisely defined: watercress in the centre of the dish, the steaks separated by potatoes *pont-neuf* arranged in pairs crisscross fashion, each pair resting across the one beneath, and the sauce in a ribbon across the steaks. Artichoke hearts stuffed with *noisette* potatoes sometimes replace the potatoes *pont-neuf*.

HERBS Various aromatic plants that are used in cookery. Among the most common herbs used for seasoning are chervil, thyme, rosemary, dill, tarragon, chives and parsley (see *aromatic* and *fines herbes*). Pot herbs traditionally include six vegetables: chard, lettuce, orache, purslane, sorrel and spinach. They are used not only to flavour soups and stews but also as vegetables, salad ingredients and a garnish. *Herbes à soupe*, which were traditionally used to flavour soups and stews, consisted of various green vegetables (carrot and celery tops, radish leaves, parsley stalks). *Herbes de Provence* consist of a mixture of aromatic plants (thyme, rosemary, bay, basil, savory), which are sometimes dried and are used especially to flavour grilled (broiled) food. *Herbs vénitiennes* are a mixture of aromatic herbs (tarragon, parsley, chervil and sorrel), which are finely chopped and incorporated into beurre manié.

In former times, the term 'herbs', when used in cookery, included all edible plants and vegetables that grow above ground; those growing below ground were called 'roots'.

HERMITAGE AOC red and white wines from the left bank of the Rhône, the vineyards being on the steepish slopes above Tain-l'Hermitage. The young red wine can be somewhat assertive, even rough-textured, but with time it mellows admirably and is justifiably esteemed as one of the great Côtes-du-Rhône wines. Red Hermitage is produced from Syrah alone, which endows the wine with a wonderful bouquet, a full but fine-textured flavour, and great length. The white wine, made mainly from the Marsanne grape, is full-bodied and aromatic. It is dry, with slight mineral overtones of taste (some describe its taste as that of a gun-flint). Hermitage – which appears in some reference books as 'Ermitage' – should not be confused with the nearby Crozes-Hermitage vineyards, which also make first-rate red and white wines.

HERRING Any of various sea fish of the family *Clupeidae*. The common herring (*Clupea harengus*)

HERBS

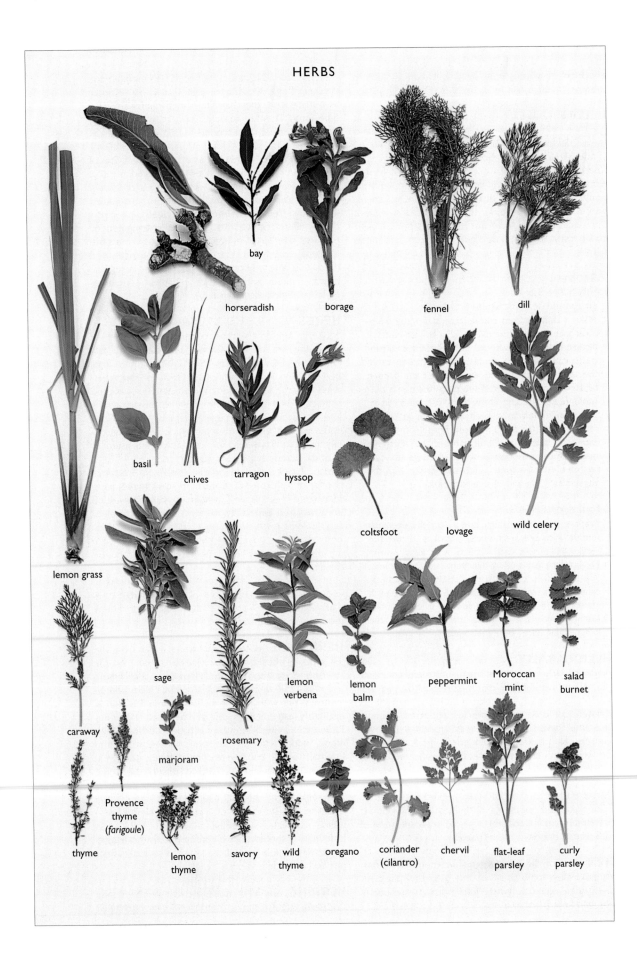

bay

horseradish

borage

fennel

dill

basil

chives

tarragon

hyssop

coltsfoot

lovage

wild celery

lemon grass

sage

rosemary

lemon verbena

lemon balm

peppermint

Moroccan mint

salad burnet

caraway

marjoram

Provence thyme (*farigoule*)

thyme

lemon thyme

savory

wild thyme

oregano

coriander (cilantro)

chervil

flat-leaf parsley

curly parsley

is seldom more than 30 cm (12 in) long; it has a tapering body, silvery bluish-green with a silver belly. The large scales are easily removed. Herring are found mainly in the cold waters of the Atlantic and the North Sea.

Herring was an essential part of the European diet in the Middle Ages, especially in northern Europe, where its economic importance rivalled that of spice. It was because of the herring that the first maritime fishing rights were established, and the herring trade was one of the reasons for the foundation of the Hanseatic League. It served many purposes: food, barter, ransom and gift.

There are many varieties of herring, each one confined to its own sea area: the North Sea and the Baltic, where the largest fish are caught; the Atlantic from Chesapeake Bay in the west to the north of France in the east, the Atlantic or Norwegian Sea, off the coast of Norway, and the Irish Sea. Each variety has its own spawning season, which influences the taste and nutritional value of the fish. A prespawning herring, caught from October to January while still carrying its eggs (hard roe) or milt (soft roe), has the most flavour, but also contains the most fat. When caught after spawning (January to March), the herring is said to be 'spent': it is only half the weight and the flesh is drier.

Fresh herring can be cooked in foil, grilled (broiled), fried, baked or stuffed. It can also be preserved in various ways.

• BLOATER Very lightly salted (for 1 day at most), then smoked until it becomes straw-coloured. It will keep for 10 days in a refrigerator.

• BUCKLING Salted for a few hours, then smoked at a high temperature, thus being partly cooked.

• GENDARME – PICKLED or RED HERRING Salted for 9 days and then smoked for 10–18 hours.

• KIPPER Slit open and flattened, salted for 1–2 hours, then lightly smoked on both sides over a wood fire. It is a traditional breakfast dish in Great Britain, where it sold fresh, frozen, canned or in ready-to-cook bags. It will keep for 24–48 hours in the refrigerator.

• ROLLMOPS AND BALTIC HERRING (formerly *Bismarck herring*) Slit open like a kipper, marinated in vinegar and spices, rolled up and secured with a sliver of wood. Baltic herring are sold as flat fillets.

• SALT HERRING Found in two forms – the small herring from Dieppe or Boulogne, which is salted at sea after the head is removed; and the large herring from the Baltic, cut into thick fillets and preserved in brine.

• SMOKED (OR DRIED) HERRING Salted for 2–6 days, then lightly cold-smoked. Smoked herring fillets are sold in packets.

All north European countries have a great many recipes for serving herring: it is an ingredient of zakouski in Russia and of smörgasbord in Scandinavia; in Berlin fresh herring is fried and eaten either hot or cold; in Norway it is prepared in a sweet-and-sour dressing of vinegar, mustard, sugar and ginger; and in Flanders smoked herring and warm potato salad is a classic dish, eagerly adopted by the French.

It was J.-K. Huysmans who praised the herring most highly: 'Your raiment, O herring, displays the rainbow colours of the setting sun, the patina on old copper, the golden-brown of Cordoba leather, the autumnal tints of sandalwood and saffron. Your head, O herring, flames like a golden helmet, and your eyes are like black studs in circlets of copper.'

RECIPES

preparation of herring
If fresh, scale the fish, but do not slit them in half. Gut (clean) them through the gills, leaving the hard or soft roes inside. Wash and dry them. If they are to be cooked whole, score the skin lightly on both sides. The fish is filleted by running a very sharp knife between the backbone and the fillets, starting from the tail end. The fillets can then be eased off the bone, trimmed, washed and dried.

If the herring is smoked, take out the fillets, then skin and trim them. Before cooking, soak them for a while in milk to remove some of the salt.

If the fish is salted, wash the fillets and soak them in milk, or a mixture of milk and water, to remove the salt. Drain, trim and dry them.

Fresh Herring
fried herring
Choose small herrings weighing about 125 g (4½ oz). Clean, trim, score and soak them in milk for about 30 minutes. Drain. Coat with flour and deep-fry in oil at 175°C (347°F) for 3–4 minutes. Drain well on paper towels. Sprinkle with salt and serve them with lemon quarters.

grilled herring
Clean and trim medium-sized herrings. Brush them with oil or melted butter, season with pepper and cook under a moderate grill (broiler). Sprinkle with salt and serve with maître d'hôtel butter or a mustard sauce.

marinated herrings
Clean and trim 12 small herrings, sprinkle them with fine salt and leave for 6 hours. Chop 3 large onions and 3 carrots. Choose a flameproof dish just big enough to hold the herrings and half-fill it with the chopped vegetables. Add a pinch of chopped parsley, a pinch of pepper, 2 cloves, a bay leaf cut into small pieces, and a little thyme. Arrange the fish in the dish and pour in enough of a mixture of half white wine and half vinegar to just cover the fish. Top with the remaining vegetables, cover the dish with foil and bring to the boil on the top of the cooker (stove). Then cook in a preheated oven at 220°C (425°F, gas 7) for about 20 minutes. Leave the herring to cool in the cooking liquid and refrigerate until ready to serve.

sautéed herring à la lyonnaise
Clean and trim 6 herrings. Chop 2 medium-sized onions. Season the fish with salt and pepper, coat

with flour and fry in butter until golden brown on both sides. Fry the onions until golden brown in a separate pan. Turn the herrings over, add the onions and continue cooking for about 10 minutes. Arrange the fish on a serving dish, cover with the onions and sprinkle with chopped parsley. Deglaze the frying pan in which the fish were cooked with a generous tablespoon of vinegar and pour the sauce over the fish.

Swedish herring balls

Fillet 3 fresh herrings. Boil 3 large floury (baking) potatoes in salted water, peel and mash. Cook 3 finely chopped onions slowly in a covered pan for about 10 minutes. Chop the herring fillets finely, add the potato, onions, salt, pepper and, if desired, a little grated nutmeg. Mix everything together thoroughly and form into small balls. Fry them in butter or oil and serve with hot cranberry sauce.

Smoked Herring

herring fillets à la livonienne

Remove the fillets from large smoked herrings, trim them and cut into dice. Boil potatoes in salted water peel and slice them into rounds. Peel and halve sweet crisp apples, core them, cut into slices and dip in lemon juice. Arrange the herring, potato rounds and apple slices in concentric circles. Sprinkle with vinaigrette and chopped parsley, chervil and fennel. Refrigerate until required.

herring fillets marinated in oil

Put lightly smoked herring fillets into an earthenware dish. Soak them in milk and leave in a cool place for 24 hours. Drain the fillets and wipe them dry. Wash the dish. Slice 2 onions for every 450 g (1 lb) fillets and spread half over the bottom of the dish. Arrange the fillets on top and cover with the rest of the onion, some sliced carrot, coriander seeds and half a bay leaf cut into pieces. Sprinkle a little thyme over the top, pour on some groundnut (peanut) oil, cover the dish with foil and leave to marinate for several days at the bottom of the refrigerator.

other recipes See *boulangère, canapé (cold canapés), devilled, forcemeat, russe.*

HERVE A Belgian AOP cow's-milk cheese with a fat content of 45%. It is soft, close-textured, pliable and cream-coloured, with a smooth pinkish-yellow washed rind. The cheese has been made since the 16th century on the plain of Herve, in the province of Liège. It tastes mild and creamy after 6 weeks of ripening, but after 8 weeks the taste becomes more pronounced. Cube-shaped, each side measuring 5–10 cm (2–4 in), it is in season in summer and autumn. The strong-flavoured cheese is best eaten with brown ale; red wine or even very sweet black coffee are good accompaniments to the mild cheese.

HIPPOCRAS A spicy drink based on red or white wine, popular during the Middle Ages and up to the 17th century. It was made by macerating various fruits and spices in wine: angelica and nutmeg; raspberries and brandy; juniper berries, fruit stones (pits), vanilla, wormwood, citrus fruits and violets; cinnamon, nutmeg, mace, cloves and ambergris. Hippocras was sweetened, then filtered, and could be served cool or iced as an apéritif or at the end of a meal. It was also used in cooking, particularly by Taillevent for his *partridge trimolette* (a sweet-and-sour salmis) and for poached pears. The word probably comes from a Greek verb meaning 'to mix', though an analogy has been suggested with the name Hippocrates, the father of medicine: the tammy cloth through which the wine was passed was called 'Hippocrates' sleeve'. Today hippocras is a home-made drink.

RECIPES

hippocras with angelica

Infuse 7 g (¼ oz) fresh angelica and a pinch of grated nutmeg in 1 litre (1¾ pints, 4⅓ cups) red or white wine for 2 days. Sweeten to taste and add a glass of brandy. Strain.

hippocras with juniper berries

Infuse 25 g (1 oz, ¼ cup) crushed juniper berries in 1 litre (1¾ pints, 4⅓ cups) red or white wine for 24 hours. Add a little powdered vanilla or vanilla essence (extract) and 75 g (3 oz, ⅓ cup) caster (superfine) sugar. Mix and strain.

HOB The name for the cooker (stove) top or independent cooking surface on which to cook in saucepans and other pans. The appliance may be heated by gas, electricity, oil or, less commonly, solid fuel. It may be an integral part of the cooker or range, or a separate appliance set in an area of work surface.

There is a wide choice of hobs, of different finishes and sizes, with space to accommodate from two to six pans in the average domestic appliances. Electric appliances offer various types of heating plates and gas hobs offer different pan stands. Combined gas and electric burners and rings are available in some appliances, with options for fast boiling or steady simmering. Flat or ridged griddles are a feature of larger hobs, allowing for traditional bakestone-type cooking or contemporary griddling, allowing fat to drain away between the ridges.

HOLLANDAISE, À LA The name given to a dish of poached eggs, boiled vegetables (artichokes, asparagus, chard, cauliflower) or poached fish, with hollandaise sauce either poured over or served separately. It also describes dishes of Dutch cuisine, such as eggs in cups *à la hollandaise.*

RECIPE

eggs in cups à la hollandaise

Butter the insides of 3 cups and coat them with

grated cheese. Put a layer of diced bacon in the bottom of each cup, pour in a beaten egg, cover with another layer of diced bacon and then with a thick layer of grated cheese. Cook in a bain marie for 10 minutes. Serve with a well-flavoured tomato sauce.

other recipes See *canapé (cold canapés), caroline.*

HOLLANDAISE SAUCE A hot emulsified sauce based on egg yolks and clarified butter. It is the foundation of several other sauces, including chantilly (or mousseline), maltaise, mikado and mustard sauce, depending on the ingredients added. It is served with fish cooked in a court-bouillon, or with boiled or steamed vegetables. The sauce should be made in a well-tinned copper or stainless steel sauté pan; an aluminium pan will turn it greenish. As it must not get too hot, hollandaise sauce should be kept warm in a bain marie. If it does curdle, it can be re-emulsified by adding a spoonful of water, drop by drop; use hot water if the sauce is cold, and cold water if the sauce is hot.

RECIPES

hollandaise sauce
Pour 4 tablespoons water into a pan with a pinch of salt and a pinch of ground pepper. Place the base of the saucepan in a bain marie of hot water: do not allow the water to approach boiling point, but keep it hot. In another saucepan, melt 500 g (18 oz, 2¼ cups) butter without letting it get too hot. Beat 5 egg yolks with 1 tablespoon water and pour into the pan containing the warmed water. With the pan still in the bain marie, whisk the sauce until the yolks thicken to the consistency of thick cream; add the melted butter slowly, whisking all the time, and then add 2 tablespoons water, drop by drop. Adjust the seasoning and add 1 tablespoon lemon juice. The sauce can be strained.

hollandaise sauce au suprême
Put 6 egg yolks in a saucepan; add about 50 g (2 oz, ¼ cup) best-quality butter, a pinch of salt and pepper, a pinch of grated nutmeg, 1 tablespoon alle-mande* sauce and 1 tablespoon chicken stock. Stir this sauce over a very low heat and, as it begins to thicken, gradually add a further 100 g (4 oz, ½ cup) butter, taking care to stir constantly.

Just before serving, pour in a little good quality plain vinegar and add a generous knob of butter.

HOMINY Dried, hulled corn (maize) kernels, ground to make hominy grits. Coarsely ground hominy is known as samp. An American speciality, hominy are available dried or reconstituted and ready to use. Hominy grits may be fine, medium or coarse and are cooked to make a thick porridge. This can be set and cut into pieces, then fried to be served as an accompaniment for main dishes.

Making hollandaise sauce

1 *Place a saucepan containing the water and seasoning in a bain marie. Beat the egg yolks with 1 tablespoon water and add them to the water and seasoning.*

2 *Whisk the sauce continuously until the yolks are lighter in colour and thickened to the consistency of thick cream.*

3 *Gradually add the melted butter, a little at a time, whisking in each addition before adding the next. When all the butter is incorporated, finish the sauce with a little water and lemon juice, whisking them in drop by drop.*

HONEY A sweet substance manufactured by bees from nectar and stored in the cells of the hive as food. Its flavour varies depending on the season, the species of flower from which it is derived, and when it is collected from the hive. Honey contains 17–20% water, 76–80% sugar (primarily glucose and fructose), small amounts of pollen and wax, and mineral salts (especially calcium, potassium, magnesium and phosphorus), but practically no vitamins. It is a valuable source of natural unrefined sugars in a

Principal types of pure honey

plant	French region/country	
acacia	Provence, Gironde, Rhone valley, Auvergne, Paris basin, Canada, Hungary, Romania	Liquid, very pale and very fine. Used mainly for serving at the table and also for sweetening drinks.
alfalfa	Many regions	Very crystalline, thick and yellow. Suitable for cooking.
buckwheat	Sologne, Brittany, Canada, USA (California)	Dark reddish-brown, coarsely crystalline, with a strong taste. Should be used for gingerbread.
clover	All regions of France, Canada, USA (California), Britain	Very pale, fairly oily and full of flavour. Used for serving at the table.
heather	Landes, Sologne, Auvergne, Britain	Reddish-brown and fairly thick, rich in mineral salts. Used mainly in baking (cakes, biscuits, gingerbread).
lavender, lavandin	Alps, Provence, Cévennes	Amber-coloured, aromatic and full of flavour, rich in iron. Used mainly for serving at the table.
lime blossom	All regions of France, Far East, Poland, Romania	Greenish-yellow and thick with a very pronounced flavour and aroma; crystallizes rapidly. Suitable for serving at the table and for cooking.
orange blossom	Algeria, Spain, South Africa	Very pale golden yellow, oily and smooth, and full of flavour. Suitable for serving at the table.
pine	Vosges, Alsace	Greenish (sometimes almost black), slightly aromatic, with a malted flavour. Almost exclusively used for serving at the table.
rosemary	Provence, Lower Alps, Narbonne, Spain	White or golden and fairly soft, with a fine delicate flavour when pure and a more pronounced flavour when mixed with thyme honey. Suitable for serving at the table.
sainfoin	Gâtinais, Beauce, Champagne	Pure sainfoin honey, which is very rare, is pale golden, finely crystalline and full of flavour. It should be reserved for serving at the table.
thyme	Provence, Larzac	Dark golden yellow, oily and aromatic, with a distinctive taste. Excellent for spreading.

NOTE: There are many other honeys, including colza honey (all regions except mountainous ones; pale and smooth, rich in sucrose, produced in large quantities for the table and for cooking); ling honey (Landes; full-flavoured, slightly bitter, with a strong floral scent); black alder honey (Auvergne; greenish-brown and aromatic); eucalyptus honey (North Africa, Spain, Australia and tropical regions; rare but very aromatic, dark brown); and hymettus (an aromatic Greek honey which combines the flavours of thyme, savory and marjoram, dark brown in colour).

form easily assimilated by the body.

Commercial honey is extracted centrifugally from the combs of the hive and then filtered and purified: this is 'cast' honey. 'Pressed' honey, which is rarer nowadays and does not keep so well, is obtained by crushing the honeycombs. Honey is specified as coming from a certain type of flower (for example, heather honey, lavender honey) or from a certain region or country.

A distinction is made between blended honey, which is derived from honeys from different parts of the world, and honey from a single variety of flower or from one country. Honey can be liquid or thick, but the liquid forms usually crystallize with age. The colour varies according to the flowers from which the honey nectar came: alfalfa, rape and clover honeys are white, heather honey is reddish-brown, lavender honey is amber, and acacia and saínfoin honey are straw-coloured.

Naturally, the flavour also depends on the flower source: honey from leguminous plants is relatively neutral, while honey from conifers, buckwheat and heather has a stronger flavour; aromatic plants such as thyme and lime blossom impart a distinctive flavour to the honey.

In ancient times honey was regarded as the food of the gods, a symbol of wealth and happiness used both as a food and as an offering. In the Bible, the Promised Land is described as 'the land of milk and honey'. In the Middle Ages honey continued to be regarded as a precious commodity and was used medicinally. As in Greek and Roman times, it was used for confectionery and as a condiment for savoury or sweet dishes, including pork with honey, dormouse *en sauce*, mead and honeyed wine, and gingerbread. Nowadays, honey plays a major role in pâtisserie, being used in gingerbread, *nonnettes*, *croquets*, oriental cakes and various types of confectionery. Grog, eggnog and certain liqueurs also contain honey, and it is used instead of saltpetre in pickling brine for fine delicatessen meats. But it also has a role in cooking meat dishes, particularly in North Africa (couscous, stuffed pigeons, roast lamb, chicken tajines with prunes, mutton tajine), in the United States (Virginia ham), and in China (duck).

RECIPES

aiguillettes of duckling with honey vinegar
Cut 2–3 aiguillettes* per serving (there are 2 per duckling). Season with salt and pepper. Cook a chopped shallot in butter over a gentle heat. When it begins to brown, add 1 tablespoon liquid honey

(preferably acacia honey); boil for about 2 minutes until it thickens. Grill (broil) the aiguillettes separately and arrange them on a warm dish. Pour the sauce over the top and serve immediately.

Serve with potato straws, rice or a mixture of sautéed carrots and turnips.

caramel cream with honey
Make a caramel* with 50 g (2 oz, 3 tablespoons) honey and 50 g (2 oz, ¼ cup) sugar and use to line the bottom and sides of a charlotte mould. Mix together 8 whole eggs and 350 g (12 oz, 1 cup) honey with a spatula. Pour 1 litre (1¾ pints, 4⅓ cups) boiling milk on to the egg and honey mixture, mix well and pour it into the mould. Cook in a bain marie in a preheated oven at 180°C (350°F, gas 4) for 1 hour.

honey pastry for tarts
Mix 3 tablespoons liquid honey with 100 g (4 oz, ½ cup) creamed butter, using a fork. Quickly blend in 1 tablespoon crème fraîche, followed by 200 g (7 oz, 1¾ cups) plain (all-purpose) flour. Set the dough aside to rest. Knead the dough again with a little flour, then roll it out on a well-floured working surface. Line a tart plate and bake blind. Fill the tart case with raw fruit. If the fruit is not sufficiently sweet, add a little honey. If it is too dry, add a little purée or jam made from the same fruit.

Landes ham with honey
Cook 450 g (1 lb, 2 cups) rice in salted water and drain. Coat 4 slices of slightly salted raw ham on both sides with a little liquid honey (such as chestnut honey). Butter an ovenproof dish, line it with the rice, top with the slices of ham and sprinkle with cinnamon. Grill (broil) for 10 minutes. Sprinkle with pepper and serve piping hot.

onion and honey tart
Peel and thinly slice 1 kg (2¼ lb) new onions. Cook in boiling water for 3 minutes and drain. Melt 25 g (1 oz, 2 tablespoons) butter in a thick-based saucepan, add the well-drained onions and cook without allowing them to brown. Add 3 generous tablespoons mixed-flower honey, salt, 1 teaspoon ground cinnamon and a little pepper. Stir thoroughly and remove from the heat.

Line a flan tin (pie pan) with 300 g (11 oz) thinly rolled out shortcrust pastry (basic pie dough). Fill with the onions and bake in a preheated oven at 230°C (450°F, gas 8). When the tart is half-cooked, cover it with foil. Serve the tart warm either as an entrée or as a dessert.

HONEY FUNGUS *armillaire couleur de miel* A mushroom (*Armillaria mellea*) that grows on old tree stumps from summer to early winter. The yellow cap has brownish scales and is edible only if young and cooked: it should be plunged in very hot oil and then cooked in butter on a low heat. The fibrous stalk should be thrown away.

HONGROISE, À LA Describing dishes that contain paprika. Hongroise (Hungarian) sauce is based on onion, paprika and white wine, with velouté or tomato purée (paste) added. Depending on what it is to be served with, it is finished with Mornay sauce (for eggs), a reduced fumet thickened with butter (for fish), demi-glace (for meat), or velouté or suprême sauce (for poultry).

Meat dishes *à la hongroise* are garnished with cauliflower florets coated with paprika-flavoured Mornay sauce, which are arranged in duchess potato cases or browned in the oven and served with potato fondantes.

RECIPES

gratin of potatoes à la hongroise
Bake the potatoes in their skins in the oven or in hot embers. Cut them in half and scrape out the insides; rub this through a sieve. Peel and chop some onions (use half the weight of the sieved potato) and soften them in butter in a covered pan. Season with salt, pepper and a sprinkling of paprika, then mix with the sieved potato. Stuff the potato jackets with this mixture and put the stuffed potatoes into a buttered ovenproof dish. Cover with breadcrumbs, moisten with melted butter and brown in a preheated oven at 240°C (475°F, gas 9).

Hungarian omelette
Fry 150 g (5 oz, generous ½ cup) diced lean ham in butter over a very low heat. Fry 150 g (5 oz, 1¼ cups) diced onions in butter. Season with salt, pepper and paprika. Lightly beat 8 eggs, season with salt and pepper, then pour over the onions. Add the diced ham. Cook as for a flat omelette, without folding. Serve immediately with Hungarian sauce.

Hungarian sauce
Peel and chop some onions and fry them in butter, without browning them. Season with salt and pepper and sprinkle with paprika. For 6 tablespoons cooked onion add 250 ml (8 fl oz, 1 cup) white wine and a small bouquet garni. Reduce the liquid by two-thirds. Pour in 500 ml (17 fl oz, 2 cups) velouté* sauce (with or without butter enrichment). Boil rapidly for 5 minutes, strain through a strainer lined with muslin (cheesecloth) and finish with 50 g (2 oz, ¼ cup) butter.

mushrooms à la hongroise
Clean and wash some mushrooms and cut off the stalks. If the mushrooms are very small, leave them whole; if they are larger, cut them in quarters and dip them in lemon juice. Gently sauté them in butter without letting them colour. Pour off the butter from the sauté pan and replace it with cream, lemon juice, paprika, salt and pepper. Reduce by half, sprinkle with chopped parsley and serve very hot.

other recipes See *cep, entrecôte, paupiette, sturgeon.*

HOP A vigorous climbing plant that grows in temperate regions. The female flowers are used mainly in the brewing industry to give the bitter taste to beer.

The flowers of the male plant, known in France as *jets de houblon* (hop shoots), are edible and are used particularly in Belgian cooking; dishes including hop shoots are termed *à l'anversoise*. The shoots are prepared in the same way as asparagus: they are first boiled in salted water with lemon juice added, then they can either be cooked in a covered pan in butter or simmered in cream, veal juices and so on. Hop shoots in cream are the classic accompaniment to poached eggs (plain or on fried croûtons, possibly with hollandaise sauce) and poached sole. Hops are particularly popular in central Italy, where they are called *luppoli*. In Rome they are made into soup.

RECIPE

hop shoots in cream
Put 350 g (12 oz) fresh hop shoots into salted boiling water; remove while they are still firm. Drain them, braise in butter in a covered pan, then add 200 ml (7 fl oz, ¾ cup) double (heavy) cream. Season with salt and pepper and simmer until cooked.

HORACE, QUINTUS HORATIUS FLACCUS

Roman poet (born 65 BC; died 8 BC). A friend of Virgil and Maecenas and one of the favourites of Augustus, he preferred the simple family pleasures of rural life to the tumult of Rome. When the fashion in cookery was for pretentious and complicated dishes, he advocated simple straightforward meals: farm-reared chicken, roast milk-fed kid, a salad from the garden and fruit from the orchard.

HORN OF PLENTY *craterelle* A common woodland mushroom, also called trumpet of death (in France its common names are *corne d'abondance* and *trompette-de-la-mort*). Resembling a smoke-grey or black funnel, it is not very fleshy and is slightly tough but is nevertheless highly edible. It is chopped and added to sauces (poivrade with red wine), mixed with blander mushrooms to enhance their flavour, or prepared in the same ways as the chanterelle. It can be dried easily and is ground for a condiment.

HORS D'OEUVRE The first dish to be served at a meal, particularly luncheon (dinner usually starts with soup). As the hors d'oeuvre is, by definition, additional to the menu, it should be light and delicate, stimulating the appetite for the heavier dishes to follow. The presentation of an hors d'oeuvre is very important: it should always look decorative.

There are two main types of hors d'oeuvre: cold and hot. Cold hors d'oeuvre include the following: fish or seafood, which can be marinated, smoked, in oil or in vinegar; vegetables *à la grecque*; various types of charcuterie; fish roes; various raw vegetables; stuffed or jellied eggs; mixed salads; and prawn (shrimp) cocktail. They are arranged in hors d'oeuvre dishes, on plates or in glass dishes. Hors-d'oeuvre dishes are small and usually oblong or rectangular; at least two are used together, so that different foods can be displayed without mixing them. These dishes can be arranged in fours or sixes in a ring or other pattern to present the hors d'oeuvre as attractively as possible.

Hot hors d'oeuvre include, for example, croquettes, fritots, fritters, kromeskies, rissoles and vol-au-vent. These are, in fact, more likely to be served at dinner after the soup, but they may also appear at lunch.

France has adopted and modified the Russian custom of serving an assortment of hors d'oeuvre as a small meal preceding the main one. Under the name of *hors d'oeuvre à la russe*, these snacks are arranged on trays and served to the guests at table.

HORSE A domestic animal used for centuries for transport and agricultural work, not sold in France as meat for human consumption until the nineteenth century. When it was first sold, draught animals were slaughtered and the cheap meat was sold in special horse butcher's shops in order to avoid any attempt to sell it as beef. Today Ardennes and Postier Breton horses are specially bred for meat. Colts are preferred, as their flesh is tender and full of flavour, although slightly sickly. Ass and mule meat may also be sold as horsemeat.

Horsemeat lends itself to all beef dishes, but is particularly suitable for raw dishes (such as the authentic steak tartare), as the animal is unaffected by tuberculosis and tapeworm. Nevertheless, it does not keep as well as other meats and its degree of freshness is difficult to assess. Some charcuterie products, such as Arles sausage, are based on horsemeat.

The consumption of horse flesh has been controversial for a long time, and was strictly prohibited in France until 1811, when it was decreed legal. Its fervent supporters included the naturalist Geoffroy Saint-Hilaire, Parmentier Cadet de Gassicourt (Napoleon's pharmacist) and Larrey (a surgeon during the Empire, who testified that horse flesh had saved a number of human lives during the Napoleonic campaigns). On 6 February 1865 a horse butchers' banquet was organized to prove that horse flesh was perfectly healthy and, furthermore, good to eat. The feast took place at the Grand Hôtel, under the supervision of a chef named Balzac. Among the guests were Dr Véron, Roqueplan, Flaubert and Dumas. The menu consisted of the following: horse-broth vermicelli, horse sausage and charcuterie, then boiled horse and horse *à la mode*, followed by horse stew and fillet of horse with mushrooms, potatoes sautéed in horse fat, salad in horse oil, and finally rum gâteau with horse bone marrow. The wine was Château Cheval-Blanc. At the time of this banquet, Edmond de Goncourt did not conceal his hostility towards this 'watery and brackish-red' meat.

Another ten years passed before statutory regulations controlled the butchery of horses in France; it was already strictly controlled in England,

Germany and Scandinavia. Today horsemeat is eaten in some European countries, including Belgium, France and Italy; in some parts of China and Japan; and in South America. It is not eaten in Britain or North America.

HORSE BEAN Large green bean from Quebec, an ingredient of several specialities of this province. Horse bean soup is traditional in the region of Saguenay. The beans are cooked for 3 hours with pieces of salt bacon, carrots, onions, savoury herbs (a mixture of herbs steeped in brine) and barley.

HORSE MACKEREL (JACK MACKEREL) *chinchard* A sea fish resembling mackerel, with a body 40–50 cm (16–20 in) long, a bluish-grey back and silvery sides. The lateral line on each side is studded with bony scales that become more pointed nearer the tail. It is widespread in temperate seas and plentiful in summer and autumn. It is prepared like mackerel and is very suitable for fish soups. It is also used for canning, plain or in a tomato sauce.

In the United States, jack mackerel, horse mackerel or California horse mackerel are names given to a fish found in the Pacific, from Canada to Chile. The Atlantic bluefish is also sometimes called horse mackerel.

HORSE MUSHROOM Large wild mushroom of *Agaricus* family, the *Agaricus arvensis*, which can have a cap size up to 20 cm (8 in). Gills turn from creamy white, through pink to dark brown as the cap develops and opens, from a button mushroom to a convex shape. The flesh is firm and white, with a slightly aniseed aroma and flavour resembling common cultivated mushrooms.

HORSERADISH A perennial plant originating in eastern Europe, where it grows wild; it is cultivated throughout Europe and in the United States for its root, which is used as a condiment.

Horseradish is a traditional condiment in Scandinavia, Alsace, Russia and Germany. The root has a grey or yellowish skin and white flesh, which is pungent, with a sharp, hot taste and a strong smell. Wear rubber gloves and hold the root submerged in a bowl of cold water while scrubbing and peeling it to reduce the irritation it causes to skin and eyes. After being washed, peeled and grated, it can be used either as it is, dressed with oil and vinegar, or with the flavour softened by cream or by breadcrumbs soaked in milk. It is sometimes grated and dried, and then has to be reconstituted before use. It can also be thinly sliced. It accompanies a wide range of dishes, such as beef and pork (boiled, braised or cold), fish (herrings and smoked trout), poached sausages and potato salad. Horseradish is also an ingredient in hot or cold sauces, relishes, vinaigrettes, mustards and flavoured butters, which are served with the dishes mentioned.

RECIPES

cold horseradish sauce
Soak some breadcrumbs in milk, then squeeze them dry. Add grated horseradish, salt, sugar, double (heavy) cream and vinegar (adjust the quantities of these ingredients to give the desired taste).

This sauce can be served with smoked fish, potatoes or beetroot (beet) salad.

hot horseradish sauce (or Albert sauce)
Cook 4 tablespoons grated horseradish in 200 ml (7 fl oz, ¾ cup) white stock. Add 250 ml (8 fl oz, 1 cup) English butter sauce*. Boil to reduce, then strain. Mix 3 tablespoons English mustard with 3 tablespoons wine vinegar. Bind the sauce with 2 egg yolks, then add the mustard.

This sauce is served with boiled or braised beef.

additional recipe See *butter (flavoured butters)*.

HOTCHPOTCH A Flemish stew that can be made with pig's ears and tails, breast of beef, oxtail, shoulder of mutton, salt bacon and all the usual pot vegetables (cabbage, carrots, onions, leeks and potatoes). However, it is more usually made with oxtail only. The vegetables are served whole or mashed into a purée. Formerly, hotchpotch was made with chopped meat, turnips and chestnuts cooked in an earthenware pot with stock, as described in *L'Agronome, ou le Dictionnaire portatif du cultivateur* (1760). The word *hochepot* is derived from the Old French *hottison* (to shake) and its origin is obscure, especially as the term can also be applied to a chicken cooked in a pot with cheap cuts of beef and vegetables.

RECIPE

oxtail hotchpotch
Cut an oxtail into uniform pieces and put them into a casserole with 2 raw quartered pig's trotters (feet) and a raw pig's ear. Cover the meat with water and bring to the boil. Skim, and simmer for 2 hours. Then add a firm round cabbage (cut into quarters and blanched), 3 diced carrots, 2 diced turnips and 10 small onions. Simmer for a further 2 hours.

Drain the pieces of oxtail and trotters, and arrange them in a large round deep dish with the vegetables in the centre. Surround with grilled (broiled) chipolata sausages and the pig's ear cut into strips. Serve boiled potatoes separately.

HOT DOG A long split roll filled with a frankfurter sausage (see *sausage*). The frankfurter was introduced to the United States by German immigrants. It is steamed, boiled or grilled, and eaten in a bun with various toppings – including mustard, onions, pickle relish, pickles, peppers, cheese, beans and sauerkraut – and has become an American national food. The name 'hot dog' was coined around 1900 by the

American cartoonist T.A. Dorcan, when he drew talking sausages resembling dachshunds.

HÔTELIÈRE, À L' The name given to grilled or sautéed meat and fish dishes that are served with hôtelier butter, a creamed butter to which lemon juice, chopped parsley and a dry duxelles are added.

HOTPLATE An electric heating device consisting of one or two heating rings sunk into an enamelled metal framework. It is used for keeping serving dishes and their contents warm at the table.

Hotplates were used in Roman times. Made of bronze, they were filled with embers and were used to cook or reheat dishes at the table. In the 13th century they were made from wrought iron and mounted on wheels. In the 18th century they were even made of silver and filled with boiling water.

Chafing dishes can also be used as hotplates.

HOT WATER CRUST PASTRY This close-textured, firm pastry is used as a crust for raised or moulded pies, such as pork or game pies, or as a casing for pâtés. It is cooked at a lower temperature than puff and shortcrust pastries, and often for a longer period. When used as a casing for large pies, it may be baked for 2 hours or more. The pastry absorbs the juices from the filling, becoming moist and full-flavoured on the inside with a crisp crust outside.

The dough is made from a mixture of hot milk and melted fat – traditionally lard, but often a mixture of lard and butter – combined with the flour to make a smooth dough that can be shaped and moulded while hot. It sets and becomes crumbly when cold. Once made, it is kept warm in a covered bowl over a bain marie until used.

RECIPE

hot water crust pastry

Mix 350 g (12 oz, 1½ cups) plain (all-purpose) flour with ½ teaspoon salt in a bowl. Heat 4 tablespoons milk and 4 tablespoons water with 100 g (4 oz, ½ cup) lard or 50 g (2 oz, ¼ cup) each of lard and butter over gentle heat until the fat has melted completely. Then bring the mixture to the boil and immediately pour it into the flour. Working quickly, stir the liquid into the flour to make a dough, then knead it lightly together by hand in the bowl. (Take care as the mixture is very hot.) Do not over-knead the dough or it will become greasy.

Press or roll out the dough as required. If the dough is rolled out into too large a sheet or too thinly, it breaks up easily, so for lining large moulds, begin by rolling out the dough, then press it into the mould, thinning it out evenly with the fingertips. For small pies, allow the dough to cool and set slightly (1–2 minutes is usually enough), when small portions can be rolled thinly and evenly to give a smooth result without breaking.

HUMMUS An Arabic and Greek dish made from cooked chick peas crushed with sesame paste (tahini), garlic and lemon. Spices and parsley may be added to season the dip. It usually accompanies hors d'oeuvre or crudités.

RECIPE

hummus

Soak 175 g (6 oz, 1 cup) chick peas overnight. Drain and bring to the boil in fresh water (not salted), cover and simmer for 2–2½ hours, until the chick peas are completely tender. Drain and purée in a food processor with 2 chopped garlic cloves until coarse, not completely smooth. Add 100 ml (4 fl oz, 7 tablespoons) tahini and 60 ml (2 fl oz, ¼ cup) freshly squeezed lemon juice, then process again, gradually adding 60 ml (2 fl oz, ¼ cup) olive oil. Transfer to a dish and stir in seasoning to taste with plenty of chopped parsley.

If a food processor is not available, the chick peas can be mashed and the garlic crushed, then the remaining ingredients can be beaten in by hand. The hummus can be seasoned with ground roasted cumin seeds or ground roasted coriander seeds.

HUNDRED-YEAR-OLD EGGS A Chinese speciality consisting of duck eggs that are enclosed in a coating made of lime, mud, saltpetre, fragrant herbs and rice straw, which preserves them for a very long time. They can be eaten after the third month, but their smell grows stronger with age. When they are broken out of their covering, the eggs are black and shiny. They are eaten cold as they are or with slices of ginger, cucumber or pieces of preserved chicken gizzard.

HUNGARY See *opposite page*.

HUNTING Once the means of providing an essential part of the human diet, hunting became – and continues to be – a popular sport. In France, until the abolition of such privileges, it was reserved strictly for the nobility. All the grounds around Paris devoted to the royal hunts were called 'the king's pleasures'. The game shot by the king, princes or noblemen was sold in the market known as La Vallée on the Quai des Grands-Augustins, and thus competed with other suppliers of meat. Official inspectors were commissioned to draw up a written return of all the items put up for sale, but that did not prevent poaching form flourishing.

By analogy, the term *chasse* was also given to a meat course consisting solely of roast game arranged on an enormous dish.

HURE The French word for a type of brawn (head cheese) made with boar's or pig's head.

The word is also used for the head of a pike or a salmon.

HUSK The tough outer casing of the seedlike fruits of cereal plants, such as wheat, barley, rye and oats.

HUNGARY

Hungarian cuisine is rooted in the ancient traditions of the nomad Magyar people, who used preserved foods, which could be prepared rapidly as soon as they made a halt on their journeys. In the 16th century *tarhonya*, a granulated dried pasta made from flour and eggs, was boiled and eaten with dried meat; today it is used to garnish dishes made with a sauce.

The principal ingredients in modern cuisine are lard and bacon, onions and soured (sour) cream. But it is undoubtedly paprika that characterizes present-day Hungarian dishes, although it was not introduced to the country until the 18th century. It is an essential ingredient in four typically Hungarian dishes: goulash, *pörkölt*, *tokány* and *paprikache*; these four main recipes can be adapted for cooking red and white meat, poultry and fish.

Other Hungarian dishes include a thick soup sometimes flavoured with caraway, garlic and paprika; *tarhonya* fried in lard; *galuska* (small dumplings made with flour); noodles with a sweet or savoury flavouring; ravioli filled with damson preserve; and *lecso*, a sort of ratatouille made from peppers, tomatoes and onions with pieces of bacon or sliced sausage.

■ **Freshwater fish** Freshwater fish are highly regarded, in soup, in aspic, filleted and cooked in a court-bouillon, in a ragoût or baked. They are often combined with green peppers and bacon, mushrooms, cream and dill. The *fogas*, a fish found in Lake Balaton, is worth special mention: unknown elsewhere, but closely related to the pike-perch and with very delicate flesh, it is grilled (broiled) or poached in white wine and served whole. Crayfish are frequently cooked in a ragoût, with paprika or cream, and used as a garnish for pancakes or flaky pastries.

■ **Meat** Meat is usually prepared according to one of the four main paprika recipes. Other noteworthy meat dishes include sauerkraut served with pork, bacon and smoked sausages, and flavoured with dill, and grills (*fatányeros*), which combine, on one large wooden platter, a fillet of beef, a veal escalope, a pork chop and smoked bacon, the whole garnished with crudités. Another dish that is typical of Hungarian cookery without paprika is entrecôte steak braised with marjoram, tomatoes and cumin, and garnished with peppers and semolina dumplings (*rostélyos*). However, paprika is often used in the cooking of pork chops, for which there is a great variety of recipes, many of them including lard and tomatoes.

■ **Salads and vegetables** Nowadays, rich and filling dishes are accompanied by various salads, such as salted cucumber, beetroot (beet) with cumin and horseradish, lettuce with vinaigrette dressing, and fresh or marinated green peppers. Vegetables are sometimes seasoned with paprika; for example, gratin of asparagus with cream; stewed mushrooms, frequently served with fried eggs; and potatoes, which are served with everything. Soured cream is nearly always used in the cooking of French (string) beans, cabbage, or marrow (squash) with dill.

■ **Pâtisserie** The national pâtisserie speciality is *rétès*, strudel pastry filled with apples, cherries, poppy seeds, morello cherries or nuts; it is sometimes filled with savoury mixtures. One of the many classics of the Hungarian pastrycook is *dobos torta*, made from seven layers of Savoy sponge cake filled with mocha cream and covered with a crisp caramel coating.

Other specialities include rissoles, stuffed pancakes (especially stuffed with cream cheese, jam and crushed nuts), soufflé fritters, tarts and quenelles made with curd cheese and sprinkled with melted butter.

■ **Famous names** Many classic dishes in Hungarian cuisine are named after famous people or historical events; examples are *Ujházi*, a chicken casserole named after an actor, and *Munkácsy*, jellied eggs on a macédoine in rémoulade with dill, named after a 19th-century painter. Poached eggs on a *pörkölt* of carp's roes is called *à la Kapisztrán*, in memory of a Franciscan monk, Capistrano, hero of the defence against the Turks, and the cake *Rigó Jancsi* (a famous gipsy violinist) is a pavé layered with chocolate mousse and covered with chocolate icing.

WINE Hungary is a huge producer of wine of many categories, including the world-famous Tokay (see *Tokaji*).

The wine regions are subdivided into 20 areas, each vineyard being registered and classified. A number of native grapes are grown, notably Furmint and Hárslevelü (important in making *Tokay*), as well as Kéknyelü, Ezerjó and others. Much use is also made of other varieties that are planted throughout Europe – Olaszrizling, Szürkebarat (Pinot Gris), Rheinriesling, Sylvaner, Gewürztraminer, Pinot Blanc and Sauvignon Blanc are among the white grapes; the black grapes include Kadarka (much planted in eastern European countries), Kekfrankos, Merlot, Cabernet Sauvignon and Cabernet Franc. On labels, the Hungarian versions of the names of some grapes and wines may look strange, due to use of the suffix -i: 'Tokaji', for example, for Tokay – the 'i' meaning 'from the region of'.

There is an enormous range of Hungarian white table wines from many regions, varying from light, crisp and fresh in style to fuller and rather aromatic ones. Among the reds, Egri Bikavér (Bull's Blood of Eger) is very well known, but there are many others. Hungary does a great deal of business exporting wines of good quality and value.

Gruau is the French for husk and the French expression *farine de gruau* is used for wholewheat flour.

HUSS Small shark, a member of the *Squalidae* family known as *chien de mer* ('sea dog') in France, from Boulogne to Sables-d'Olonne, and in Canada, but as *aiguiat* in the Mediterranean. It is called 'nursehound' in the United States, which is probably its original British name. It can be up to 1.20 m (4 ft) long and is identified by a venomous spine in front of each dorsal fin and by the absence of an anal fin. It is a close relative of the spotted dogfish (roussette) and, like it, is usually sold skinned. Having hardly any taste, it is eaten in fish stew, or cold with a generously seasoned vinaigrette.

HUSSARDE, À LA The name usually given to a dish of braised beef garnished with potatoes and stuffed aubergines (eggplants). It is masked with a sauce made from the pan juices deglazed with demiglace and served with grated horseradish.

Hussarde is also the name of a sauce and a garnish. The former is an espagnole sauce with tomatoes, shallots, sliced onions, diced ham, grated horseradish and chopped parsley. A hussarde garnish, which is served with sautéed meat, consists of halved tomatoes stuffed with a purée of onions and mushrooms stuffed with spinach purée, all moistened with a tomato-flavoured demi-glace.

HYDNUM *hydne* A mushroom characterized by soft spines or pegs under the cap. The various species grow in deciduous woods in autumn. The best are the *pied de mouton* and the pink hydnum, which is more delicate. They are prepared in the same way as chanterelles and should be cooked slowly for a long time. They go particularly well with stuffed tomatoes and ragoûts.

HYDRIA A Greek jar or pitcher made of ceramic or bronze, originally used by women to fetch water from the well. It has three handles: one vertical, on the neck of the vessel, the other two lateral, on the rounded portion. The hydria had various domestic uses, including that of wine container.

HYDROMEL A drink made from honey and water. It was very popular with the ancient Greeks, who regarded bees as a symbol of immortality, and was consumed in large quantities by the Romans. The Celts, Saxons, Gauls and Scandinavians drank as much hydromel as beer, calling it *met*. It was drunk up to the 18th century.

HYGROPHORUS *hygrophore* A mushroom of which there are many varieties, some of them edible. Some species grow in November or in March, when few other mushrooms grow. Of the edible varieties, the very delicate snow-white hygrophorus (*blanc de neige*) is recommended. These mushrooms should be peeled and cooked like cultivated mushrooms. Species that are not very fleshy or have a bitter smell are mixed with other mushrooms or used as a seasoning.

HYPHOLOMA *hypholome* A mushroom often found growing in clumps on old tree stumps. The edible variety is identifiable by the complete absence of green or yellow in the gills. It is vital to take expert advice when picking mushrooms to avoid any possibility of mistaking poisonous species for edible types.

HYSSOP An aromatic plant from the Mediterranean region, with a pungent taste and a strong, rather acrid smell. In ancient times and during the Middle Ages it was very popular as a flavouring for soups and stuffings. Nowadays its main use is in the distillation of liqueurs, such as Chartreuse, and the young leaves are also used as a seasoning for oily fish and to flavour stuffings, some charcuterie products, fruit salads and compotes.

I

IBEX Wild goat of the *Bovidae* family, which lives in the mountains of Europe and Asia. Ibexes are common in Italy and Switzerland, but they had almost disappeared from the French Alps. Swiss animals have now been reintroduced there, but they have not yet been re-established in the Pyrenees, although ibexes are numerous in the other mountainous parts of Spain.

ICE BOX A sealed insulated chest containing blocks of ice, maintaining a sufficiently low temperature to cool drinks and preserve foodstuffs for a relatively short time. This type of ice box was superseded by the refrigerator.

ICE CREAM See *ices and ice creams*.

ICE-CREAM CAKE A dessert made of alternate layers of different flavoured ice creams and/or a bombe mixture (a very light-textured ice cream), frozen in a brick-shaped mould (see *Neapolitan slice*) or suitable round cake tin (pan).

The same name is used to describe a round or oblong cake having a sponge cake or meringue base with ice cream, sorbet, parfait or a bombe mixture on top. It may be decorated with whipped cream, crystallized (candied) fruit or fruit in syrup, and chocolate vermicelli (chocolate sprinkles).

Comtesse-Marie cake is made in a special square mould lined with strawberry ice cream; the inside is filled with vanilla-flavoured whipped cream.

RECIPE

blackcurrant ice-cream cake

Trim some sponge-cake fingers to the height of a rectangular cake tin (pan). Prepare a sugar syrup flavoured with blackcurrant liqueur and allow to cool. Soak some whole sponge-cake fingers in the syrup and use to line the bottom of the tin. Repeat the process for the cut sponge-cake fingers and use these to line the sides.

To make about 675 g (1½ lb) filling, beat 6 egg yolks and 200 g (7 oz, ¾ cup) sugar until white and fluffy. Add 60 ml (2 fl oz, ¼ cup) blackcurrant liqueur and, if available, some blackcurrants macerated in sugar. Add 6 tablespoons cold milk to 400 ml (14 fl oz, 1¾ cups) very thick, cold double (heavy) cream and whip until the cream stands in peaks. Mix the whipped cream with the blackcurrant mixture and pour into the mould.

Place in the freezer until slightly set, then soak some more sponge-cake fingers in the syrup and cover the mixture with them. Leave in the freezer until completely set. Just before serving, turn out of the mould and pipe with whipped cream. This dish may be served with a hot or cold blackcurrant sauce.

ICE-CREAM MAKER *sorbetière* An electric appliance consisting of a container with a mixer or paddle blades driven by a motor and used to make ice creams and sorbets. Manual machines, which used crushed ice and salt as a freezing agent, are now rare. Modern electric ice-cream makers are free-standing or placed directly in the freezer. The motor drives the blades, which churn the mixture during freezing. Worktop appliances with integral freezing units are also available, reducing the freezing time and avoiding the need to adjust settings on the main freezer to reduce the temperature for fast freezing. Some ice-cream makers have two compartments so that two flavours can be made at the same time.

ICES AND ICE CREAMS Cold desserts made by freezing a flavoured mixture. Freezing is carried out commercially in an ice-cream maker or a churn freezer, mainly consisting of a refrigerated tank in which a number of electrically driven blades stir the mixture throughout the operation to incorporate air and make it smooth. The tank can act as a mould, but the ices are usually spooned into individual tubs or put into moulds after they are taken out of the ice-cream freezer. There are moulds of all shapes, made of metal or plastic, enabling flavours to be combined in various ways. The mould is filled, then frozen. To remove the ice cream from it, the mould is immersed briefly in warm water. The ice cream can be decorated in many ways, for example with fresh or crystallized (candied) fruit, Chantilly cream, coffee beans in liqueur, grated chocolate.

■ **History** The history of ice cream is linked with that of gastronomy and refrigeration. The Chinese knew the art of making iced drinks and desserts long before the Christian era. They taught this art to the Arabs, who began making syrups chilled with snow, called *sharbets* (hence the words 'sherbet' and 'sorbet').

At the court of Alexander the Great, and later under Nero, fruit salads and purées were served mixed with honey and snow. It was not until the 13th century, however, that Marco Polo is said to have brought back from the East the secret of cooling without ice, by running a mixture of water and saltpetre over containers filled with the substance to be cooled. Thus the great fashion for water ices began in Italy.

When Catherine de' Medici arrived in France to marry the future Henri II, she introduced iced desserts to the court, among other culinary novelties, but the Parisian public discovered them only a century later, when Francesco Procopio opened a café. People went there to read news-sheets, discuss politics and literature, and above all to sample drinks and delicacies, among which there were ices and sorbets (sherbets) that soon became all the rage. Procope (as he was now called) was soon imitated by his colleagues: in the 18th century, 250 *limonadiers* were selling ices in Paris, but only in summer. In about 1750 Procope's successor, Buisson, had the idea of selling ices all the year round. The fashion at the time was to walk under the arcade of the Palais-Royal where the fashionable cafés sold their iced specialities, but these were still of poor quality.

Around 1775, ices became more delicate in flavour, richer and with more body, so that they could be moulded into different shapes. Ices made with milk, cream and eggs appeared. In fact, they had been discovered in 1650 by a French cook of Charles I of England, who paid him to keep his method secret. The end of the 18th century saw the great fashion for *fromages glacés*. The manufacture of ices continued to develop. The ice bombe appeared and it became customary to serve it during a meal of any significance. Two Italians, Pratti and Tortoni, were especially famous for their fine ices; in particular, Tortoni launched the iced sponge cake in

1798. Under the Second Empire the *omelette surprise* was invented, then the first coupes, mousses and parfaits. Ices were served at the end of meals and also became common during balls and receptions. Very refined blends of flavours were invented, including apricot and wild cherries, Mignonne peaches, Malmsey wine from Alicante, angelica liqueur, the yolks of finch eggs, sugary melon, hazelnuts and mint liqueur, green tea and citron juice, pistachios and peach juice, according to the recipes in the *Préceptoral des menus royaux* of 1822. By the beginning of the 20th century, itinerant ice-cream vendors were selling in the streets. The United States has been particularly creative, inventing myriad new flavours and ways of eating ice cream, including sundaes (ice cream topped with flavoured sauces, whipped cream, chopped nuts and sometimes fruit), sodas (scoops of ice cream topped with flavoured syrup to which soda water is added), milk shakes (ice cream and flavoured syrup liquidized with milk), malts (milk shakes with malt added) and pie *à la mode* (pie with a scoop of ice cream).

Ancient recipes were gradually modified and adapted to the needs of industrial manufacture. Nowadays stabilizers are included, such as edible gelatine, egg white, agar-agar and carob.

RECIPES

Ice Creams
caramel ice cream
Whisk together 9 egg yolks and 300 g (11 oz, 1⅓ cups) caster (superfine) sugar until the mixture becomes white and foamy. Make caramel without water: warm 100 g (4 oz, ½ cup) sugar in a heavy based saucepan over a gentle heat, stirring with a wooden spoon. As soon as the sugar has melted and turned into a smooth mass, add a further 100 g (4 oz, ½ cup) sugar, melt, then blend in another 100 g (4 oz, ½ cup) sugar. Continue to stir until the caramel has turned brown. Add 1 teaspoon lemon juice or vinegar straight away, and remove from heat.

Boil 1 litre (1¾ pints, 4⅓ cups) milk. Mix with the hot caramel over a gentle heat, stirring with a wooden spoon. Pour this boiling mixture over the sugar and egg yolk mixture, whisking vigorously, then stir the mixture into the saucepan, over a low heat. When the mixture begins to coat the spoon, remove the saucepan from the heat and immerse the base in cold water. Continue to stir until the mixture is cold. Freeze in an ice-cream maker.

coffee and brandy bombe
Chill a 1 litre (1¾ pint, 1 quart) bombe mould in the freezer. Make a custard* with 500 ml (17 fl oz, 2 cups) milk, 6 egg yolks and 125 g (4½ oz, ½ cup) caster (superfine) sugar, then add 1 tablespoon instant coffee. Stir until the mixture is cold. Freeze in an ice-cream maker.

Bring to the boil a syrup made with 200 ml (7 fl oz, ¾ cup) water and 250 g (9 oz, 1 heaped cup) caster sugar. While still boiling, pour the syrup over 8 egg yolks and beat with an electric mixer until cool. Whip 6 tablespoons milk with 250 ml (8 fl oz, 1 cup) very cold double (heavy) cream. Blend the cream with the egg yolk mixture, flavour it with 3 tablespoons liqueur brandy and chill.

Line the mould with coffee ice cream. Fill with the brandy-flavoured cream, then freeze. Remove from the mould and decorate with coffee beans soaked in liqueur.

honey ice cream

Infuse 10 g (⅓ oz) mixed ground spices (such as black pepper, juniper, cloves, cinnamon) in 1 litre (1¾ pints, 4⅓ cups) milk. Beat 10 egg yolks with 400 g (14 oz, 1¼ cups) dark Yonne honey until pale and creamy. Add the boiling milk and cook gently at 85°C (185°F) until slightly thickened. Allow to cool and strain through a chinois. Freeze in an ice-cream maker.

strawberry ice cream

Make a custard with 500 ml (17 fl oz, 2 cups) milk, 6 egg yolks, 125 g (4½ oz, ½ cup) caster (superfine) sugar and little natural vanilla extract (essence). Cool, stirring, all the time. Purée 450 g (1 lb) strawberries with 4 tablespoons icing (confectioner's) sugar and stir into the custard. Freeze in an ice-cream maker.

other recipes See *banana bombe glacée, chocolate, coffee, mousse, parfait, plombières, vanilla.*

Water Ices

A light sugar syrup is required for the following recipes. The density is given and this can be measured using a saccharometer or syrup hydrometer (see *sugar*). As a guide, a translucent coating syrup boils at 100°C (212°F) or very slightly above – 100.5°C (213°F) – and has a density of 1.2407. To make a light syrup of this type, use 10% sugar to water: 100 g (4 oz, ½ cup) sugar to 1 litre (1¾ pints, 4⅓ cups) water.

Grand Marnier ice

Make 1 litre (1¾ pints, 4⅓ cups) clear, coating syrup (density 1.2407). Whisk in the juice of half a lemon and 6 tablespoons Grand Marnier. Freeze in an ice-cream maker.

liqueur ice

Mix cold, clear sugar syrup (density 1.1407) with the chosen liqueur, generally 6 tablespoons liqueur to 1 litre (1¾ pints, 4⅓ cups) syrup. Add a little lemon juice. (The density of the mixture must be between 1.1425 and 1.1799.) Freeze in an ice-cream maker.

mango ice

Choose mangoes that are very ripe and in perfect condition. Cut them in two, remove the stone, and put the pulp into a blender, adding the juice of half a lemon or lime. For about 500 ml (17 fl oz, 2 cups)

pulp reduced to a purée, prepare 400 ml (14 fl oz, 1¾ cups) clear, coating syrup (density 1.2407). Whisk the syrup and mango pulp together. Freeze the mixture in an ice-cream maker.

other recipes See *apricot, cherry, lemon, orange.*

ICING A preparation of icing (confectioner's) sugar used to coat sweet goods. Glacé and royal icing are the traditional types, but the term covers a variety of cake coverings, including American frosting – a whisked mixture of egg whites and sugar syrup, prepared over hot water to give a foamy, soft and sweet meringue-like mixture. Frosting sets slightly on the surface when cooled. Other types of icing can be made from boiled sugar mixtures, including fondant and fudge icing. Melted chocolate can be used as a main ingredient in icings. Butter cream is sometimes referred to as an icing, in the sense of being a cake covering.

■ **Glacé icing** Uncooked water icing, known as glacé icing, is a simple solution of icing sugar mixed with water: 200 g (7 oz, 1½ cups) sugar mixed with

Glacé icing

Glacé icing should be beaten to a thick pouring consistency. Use the icing as soon as it is prepared.

1 *Brush any loose crumbs from the item to be coated and place it on a wire rack. Pour the icing on to the middle of a sponge cake, allowing it to flow evenly over the top.*

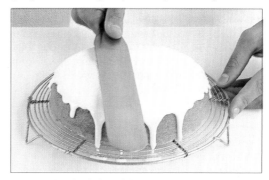

2 *Use a palette knife (spatula) and a circular movement to spread the icing out towards the edge of the cake, encouraging it to run evenly over the edge if there is enough to coat the side. Smooth the icing on the side with the same circular action, allowing the excess to run off through the rack.*

Île-de-France and Paris

Paris, the symbol and home of the whole gastronomic tradition of the Île-de-France, possesses culinary specialities that are particularly its own thanks to the magnificent work carried out by the master chefs of Parisian restaurants for more than 250 years.

Paris abounds with foodstuffs imported from abroad and brought in from every corner of France. The livestock reared in all the departments around the city provide it with fish, poultry, meat and game.

A vast range of vegetables is associated with the Île-de-France, including Argenteuil asparagus; Clamart green peas; the French beans of Bagnolet; the cauliflower of Arpajon; the carrots of Crécy-sur-Morin; Laon artichokes and asparagus; the white beans of Noyon; the lettuces of Versailles; the morels of the woods of Verrières, Viarmes and Rambouillet; the cultivated mushrooms of the Paris region, called *champignons de Paris*; onions, leeks, cabbages, carrots, turnips, cucumbers, shallots, various salads, spinach, sorrel, chervil, parsley, parsnips, horseradish and beetroot (beets).

The fruits long linked with this region include the peaches of Montreuil, the strawberries of the Bièvre valley, the Héricart strawberry, as well as pears, apples, plums, figs, apricots and nectarines.

Very good cheeses are made round about Paris, among which are Coulommiers, Brie, Brie de Melun and the Crémet of Fontainebleau.

On the hillsides of the Marne, which are an extension of the neighbouring champagne vineyards, the grapes gathered produce pleasant table wines. Excellent cider is brewed in the Aisne and Oise districts, and Noyau de Poissy is one of many liqueurs distilled in the Paris region.

■ **Culinary specialities** The following soups were invented in Paris, in Parisian restaurants by Parisian chefs, and may be classed among the culinary specialities of the region: Crécy, Saint-Germain, Parisien, bonne femme, cressonnière, santé, Bonvalet, Compiègne, Cormeilles, Briard, Soissonnais, Argenteuil, Ambassadeurs, Balvet, Faubonne, Germiny (invented by Dugléré at

The Le Moulin de la Vierge bakery, Rue Vercingétorix, Paris XVIe, retains both the décor and the wood ovens it had in 1908.

the Café Anglais), Darblay, Longchamp and Saint-Cloud.

Among the pork specialities of the Paris region are andouillettes, black and white puddings, petit-salé, veau piqué (misnamed since it is not made from veal but from pork), friands parisiens, pig's liver

120 ml (4 fl oz, ½ cup) water until a thick consistency is obtained. It can be flavoured with a fruit juice, a liqueur or coffee essence (extract). It is used mainly to cover soft sponge cakes and pastries, forming a glittering smooth coating that sets lightly.

■ **Royal icing** Royal icing, made with egg whites and icing sugar, is a completely different preparation to glacé icing, used for coating marzipan-covered fruit cake and for adding piped decoration. Royal icing dries to a fairly hard consistency and it keeps for several months.

RECIPE

royal icing

Gradually add icing (confectioner's) sugar to lightly whisked egg whites, stirring continuously and gently until it forms a mixture that is thick enough to spread without running. Stop stirring when the mixture is smooth. Strained lemon juice may be added (10 drops for 2 egg whites). Keep the icing cool, covered with damp greaseproof (wax) paper. To cover a Genoese cake 20 cm (8 in) in diameter, use 1 egg white, 175 g (6 oz, 1¼ cups) icing sugar and 1 teaspoon lemon juice. If a piped decoration is to be used, the icing must be firmer, so use 300 g (11 oz, 2¼ cups) icing sugar per egg white.

other recipes See *fondant, frosting.*

IDIAZABAL Unpasteurized DOP sheep's milk cheese from the Basque region of Spain. This cooked pressed cheese (45–50% fat content) is shaped into 13–18 cm (5–7 in) diameter wheels weighing around 2.5–4.5 kg (5½–10 lb). The firm paste is yellow-beige in colour, with tiny holes and a rich buttery flavour. Many of the cheeses are smoked in natural wood smoke.

ÎLE-DE-FRANCE AND PARIS See *above.*

ÎLE FLOTTANTE A very light dessert made from egg whites and sugar cooked in a bain marie, then

À la Mère de Famille, a traditional grocer's shop in Rue du Faubourg-Montmartre, Paris, was founded in 1761. The façade was redesigned in 1900 and today the shop is known particularly for its confectionery.

pâté, *fromage de tête de porc* (pork brawn), *hure de porc à la parisienne* (boar's head brawn), roulade of pig's head, *pâté de porc de Paris*, rillons and rillettes, saveloys, *jambon glacé de Paris* (glazed Paris ham), ribs of pork *à la charcutière* and pig's trotters *à la parisienne.*

The dishes made from other meat include beef miroton, shoulder of mutton *à la boulangère*, entrecôte Bercy and entrecôte marchand de vin, navarin of mutton, fillet of beef *à la béarnaise*, rib of veal *à la bonne femme*, calves' tendons *à la paysanne*, calf's head du Puits Certin, sauté of veal chasseur, mutton chops Champvallon, sheep's trotters *à la poulette*, and épigrammes of mutton or lamb.

Among the special poultry and game dishes of Paris are sautéed chicken Bercy, Boivin-Champeaux, chasseur, Durand, Lathuile and Parmentier; spring chicken *en cocotte, à la Clamart, à la bonne femme* and *à la diable*;

squab *à la crapaudine, en compote* and *en papillotes*; Rouen duckling *à la presse*; timbale of duckling Voisin; gibelotte of young rabbit; pheasant *à la Sainte-Alliance*, a majestic creation from the hands of Brillat-Savarin; snipe *à la fine champagne* and *à la Riche*; and pressed wild duck.

Vol-au-vent, flans and tarts filled in many different ways have also long been regarded as culinary specialities of Paris.

Special Parisian fish and shellfish dishes are lobster *à l'américaine*; the various stews, including *matelote du Moulin de la Râpée* and *matelote à la canotière*; eel *à la tartare*; carp *à la canotière*; bouillabaisse *à la parisienne*; whiting Bercy,

Colbert and au gratin; brill Dugléré; young turbot *au plat*; sole *à la normande* and Marguery; turbot *à la parisienne*; spring lobster *à la parisienne*; *coquilles Saint-Jacques* (scallops) *à la parisienne* and frogs' legs *à la poulette.*

The classic sauces in the Paris repertoire are numerous. Among the brown sauces mentioned elsewhere in this book are charcutière, chasseur, Colbert, hachée and Robert. Among the best-known white sauces the following are included in this book: béarnaise, Bercy, Bonnefoy, Chantilly, Choron, Laguipière, marinière, mousseline, mustard, poulette, ravigote, Riche and Véron.

unmoulded on to a custard cream and usually coated with caramel. Known in English as 'floating island', it can be decorated with toasted slivered almonds, chopped praline or very fine strips of lemon zest (the latter dessert is also called *dame-blanche*). See *floating islands.*

IMAM BAYILDI A Turkish dish of stuffed aubergines (eggplants) whose name means 'the imam fainted'. According to legend, when aubergines prepared in this way were offered to a certain *imam* (priest), he was so moved by the fragrant odour of the dish that he fainted from sheer gastronomical joy! The stuffing is made with a mixture of the aubergine pulp, onions and tomato. Cooked rice is sometimes added, as are various other ingredients (especially currants or raisins), spices and aromatic herbs, but not meat. The dish may be served hot or cold. Aubergines, stuffed or plain, are used a great deal in Turkish cooking as a garnish for roast lamb or mutton. In classic cuisine, the garnish *à l'imam bayildi* consists of slices of

fried aubergine, sautéed halved tomatoes and pilaf rice; it is served with tournedos steaks or noisettes of lamb.

RECIPE

imam bayildi

Soak 200 g (7 oz, 1 cup) currants in a little tepid water. Wipe 4 long aubergines (eggplants) and, without peeling them, slice them in half lengthways. Carefully remove the pulp without piercing the skin, cut it into small dice and sprinkle with lemon juice. Peel and chop 4 large onions; peel, seed and squeeze 8 large tomatoes; and chop a small bunch of parsley. Heat 4–5 tablespoons olive oil and brown the diced aubergine, tomato pulp, chopped onion and parsley. Add salt, pepper, a sprig of thyme and a bay leaf. Cover the pan and cook gently over a low heat for about 20 minutes. Then add 2 crushed garlic cloves and the drained currants. Mix everything together thoroughly and cook for a further 5 minutes. Grease an ovenproof dish remove the thyme and the bay leaf, arrange the aubergine halves in the dish, and fill them with the mixture. Pour some olive oil around the aubergines and add a little fresh thyme and some crumbled bay leaf. Cook in a preheated oven at 160°C (325°F, gas 3) for 2 hours.

IMBRUCCIATA Any of various Corsican pastries containing Broccio, a white cheese made from ewe's and goat's milk. The name is applied particularly to a savoury tart and sweet fritters.

RECIPE

fritters à l'imbrucciata
Sift 500 g (18 oz, 4½ cups) plain (all-purpose) flour into a bowl, add 3 eggs, a pinch of salt, 2 teaspoons baking powder and 3 tablespoons olive oil, and mix together. Add 250 ml (8 fl oz, 1 cup) water and mix to obtain a smooth batter. Cover the bowl with a cloth and leave the batter to stand for 3 hours at room temperature. Cut some fresh Broccio cheese into slices, dip them in a little of the batter, and deep-fry them in very hot oil until golden brown. Drain and sprinkle with sugar.

IMPÉRATRICE, À L' The name given to various sweet or savoury classic dishes characterized by the richness of their ingredients. Consommé *à l'impératrice*, made from chicken stock, is garnished with cockscombs and kidneys, chervil and asparagus tips. Chicken and sole *à l'impératrice* are finished with suprême sauce. However, the name is most commonly applied to a dessert made with rice, crystallized (candied) fruits and a Bavarian cream mixture. All fruit desserts *à l'impératrice* are based on this preparation.

RECIPE

rice à l'impératrice
Soak 15 g (½ oz, 2 envelopes) gelatine in 3 table-spoons warm water. Soak 125 g (4½ oz, ¾ cup) crystallized (candied) fruit in 3 tablespoons rum. Add 250 g (9 oz, 1⅓ cups) short-grain rice to 1 litre (1¾ pints, 4⅓ cups) boiling water and boil for 2 minutes. Drain, and then add the rice to 1 litre (1¾ pints, 4⅓ cups) boiling milk containing 1 vanilla pod (bean), a pinch of salt and 15 g (½ oz, 1 table-spoon) butter. Cook gently for about 20 minutes until the rice is just beginning to soften. Now add 200 g (7 oz, scant 1 cup) caster (superfine) sugar and cook for a further 5 minutes. Remove from the heat and add the crystallized fruit with the rum.

While the rice is cooking, prepare a custard* with 250 ml (8 fl oz, 1 cup) milk, half a vanilla pod, 4 eggs, 5 tablespoons caster sugar and a tiny pinch of salt. While the custard is still hot, add the soaked gelatine and stir until dissolved. Then rub the custard through a fine sieve and flavour with 1 tablespoon rum if desired. Leave the rice and the custard to cool.

Whip 250 ml (8 fl oz, 1 cup) double (heavy) cream with 3–4 tablespoons very cold milk until thick, then add 1 teaspoon vanilla sugar and 3 tablespoons caster sugar. Mix the custard into the chilled rice, then very carefully fold in the cream. Pour into a savarin mould or a deep sandwich tin (layer cake pan) and keep in the refrigerator until required. Unmould on to a serving dish and deco-rate with crystallized fruit or fruit in syrup.

IMPÉRIALE, À L' The name given to various dishes of grande cuisine, including a consommé gar-nished with small quenelles, cockscombs and kid-neys; fish dishes (such as sole or trout) garnished with crayfish tails, poached soft roes and finely sliced truffle; and chicken dishes garnished with foie gras and truffles.

INDIA AND PAKISTAN See *page 622.*

INDIAN CORN Quebec name for maize, unknown to Europeans until they set foot in Amer-ica. Thinking they were in India, they called it Indian corn. '*Épluchette de blé d'Inde*' (peeling the Indian corn) is a meeting of friends at harvest time, where corn-on-the-cob cooked in boiling water on a campfire is eaten with butter and salt. Among the Acadians, 'washed' (*lessive*) Indian corn is prepared with dried grains; these are soaked in cold water, then boiled with bicarbonate of soda (baking soda) to burst their husks and softened in several changes of water.

INDIENNE, À L' The name given to many dishes of curried fish, eggs, mutton or poultry. They are usually served with boiled rice. A curry or Indian sauce can be used to coat or as a base in which to cook main ingredients. With fish and shellfish, a fish fumet is used instead of the chicken stock.

A cold Indian or curry sauce is made with mayon-naise flavoured with curry powder and chives.

RECIPE

curry or Indian sauce
Cook 4 large sliced onions slowly in 5 tablespoons ghee, butter or oil. Add 1 tablespoon each of chopped parsley and chopped celery, a small sprig of thyme, half a bay leaf, a pinch of mace, salt and pepper. Sprinkle with 25 g (1 oz, ¼ cup) flour and 1 generous tablespoon good quality curry powder and stir. Then add 500 ml (17 fl oz, 2 cups) chicken stock, stir and bring to the boil, stirring. Reduce the heat, cover the pan and cook slowly for about 30 minutes. A quarter of the chicken stock can be replaced by coconut milk for a coconut-flavoured curry. Rub the sauce through a sieve, add 1 teaspoon lemon juice and 5 table-spoons cream, and reduce a little. Adjust the seasoning.

other recipes See *haddock, hash.*

INDONESIA

The staple food in the Indonesian archipelago is rice, which is accompanied by various ingredients or garnishes (some very rich, others less so) and a range of spices and sauces. Two famous rice dishes are *rijsttafel*, a classic of Dutch cuisine, and *nasi goreng*, a dish of rice garnished with chicken, lobster, peppers and tomatoes. Other dominant elements in this cuisine are chicken and pork, yams and palm hearts, and seafood.

Indonesian cuisine is characterized by its variety of spices and seasonings. These include not only such familiar items as onions, shallots, garlic, bay leaves, nutmeg, saffron and cloves, but also sambal (for seasoning rice, vegetables and meat), dried powdered roots, fruit such as *djerek purut* (a small aromatic lemon) and tamarind, red peppers and cooked seasonings such as *trasi*, a paste of fermented prawns (shrimp). The influence of Indian cuisine is evident in the use of curry powder, and the Chinese influence is seen in the use of rice vermicelli and soy sauce.

Fruits are eaten raw and in salads, especially in *rudjak*, a dish of pineapple, cucumber, green mango and *bengkuang* (a type of large juicy turnip), flavoured with sugar, tamarind, vinegar and *trasi*. But the great Indonesian speciality is *satay* (or *satai*): small pieces of meat threaded on to bamboo skewers, grilled (broiled) and dipped in a spicy sauce. Satay can be made with chicken, mutton or pork. In Jakarta, mutton satay is eaten with a thick sauce made with peanuts and various seasonings; Chinese pork satay is accompanied by a tomato sauce; and the chicken satay from Madura is served off the skewers with a thick purée of chopped meat. The garnish, of course, is rice.

Indonesians normally drink tea, coconut milk and fruit juices, but there are also locally made alcoholic drinks, such as *arak*, made from fermented vegetable fibres, and *bromi*, based on rice alcohol.

INDIGO CARMINE Also known as Indigotine. A blue food colouring (E132) originally extracted from plants, but now synthesized from aniline. It is used in food manufacture, mainly in cooked meats, pastries, ices, cheese, jams and confectionery. The colouring is either incorporated into the foodstuff or applied externally.

INDONESIA See *above*.

INFUSION The process of steeping an aromatic substance in a boiling liquid until the liquid has absorbed the flavour. The resulting flavoured liquid is also called an infusion; examples are tea and tisanes (herbal teas). White wine is infused with truffle peelings for flavouring sauces; red wine can be infused with cinnamon and cloves; and vanilla-flavoured milk is obtained by infusing a vanilla pod (bean) in boiling milk.

INN An establishment where, traditionally, travellers obtain food and lodging. The provision of lodging on a commercial basis started at the beginning of the 16th century; before this, it was undertaken free of charge by monasteries. Modern inns are small country hotels run on a family basis. Restaurants of rustic appearance, tastefully decorated and offering food and overnight accommodation, are also called inns. The term is used for some British pubs that no longer offer accommodation.

INSECT LARVAE Certain species of insect larvae are eaten as food in several tropical countries. In Cameroon about 20 species of larvae are sold in the markets. They are usually grilled (broiled) or they may be prepared in a sauce with peanuts or gourd seeds, cooked over charcoal, wrapped in banana leaves, or cooked on skewers. The Pygmies, who are very partial to them, crush them in palm oil and use them as a condiment. The Japanese eat grilled (broiled) mantis, wasp and dragonfly larvae, whereas in Latin America, agave grubs and bamboo caterpillars are popular.

The French anthropologist Claude Lévi-Strauss, writing in his book *Tristes Tropiques*, takes great delight in describing a larva known as *koro*: 'A stroke of the axe opens up thousands of channels deep down in the wood. In each one, there is a large cream-coloured animal, rather similar to the silkworm ... From its body comes a whitish fatty substance ... it has the consistency and fineness of butter and the flavour of coconut milk.' In the West Indies, palm grubs are a choice delicacy. They are grilled (broiled) on skewers and served sprinkled with breadcrumbs and lemon juice.

The French missionary Père Favaud recounts the following experience in China at the beginning of the 20th century: 'For centuries, our farmers in the Midi have devoted themselves to the rearing of silkworms, but never, to my knowledge, have they dreamed of using them as food. It is different in China. During my long stay, I have often seen people eat silkworm chrysalids and, indeed, I have eaten them myself. I can affirm that they make an excellent stomach medicine, both fortifying and refreshing, and often a successful remedy for those in poor health.

'After the cocoons have been spun, a certain number of chrysalids are taken and grilled in a frying pan so that the watery fluid runs out. The outer coverings come away easily, leaving behind a quantity of small yellow objects that resemble a mass of carp roe.

'These are fried in butter, fat or oil, and sprinkled with stock ... After boiling them for 5 minutes, they

INDIA AND PAKISTAN

Indian and Pakistani cookery is based on rice, spices, pulses and fruit and is influenced by the various religious practices of the subcontinent, including vegetarianism. Each area offers its own specialities: Kashmir is famous for its meat and chick peas, Delhi for its tandoori food, Mumbai (Bombay) for its pork in vinegar, Bengal for its intensely sweet desserts and its fish, and Madras for its vegetarian dishes, made with tamarind, semolina and coconut. British influence led to the spread of dishes and seasonings derived from Indian cuisine, particularly curries and chutneys.

■ **Basic ingredients** Indian cookery is based on rice, dried pulses (see *dal*) and spices such as cardamom, cinnamon, cloves, coriander, cumin, fennel seeds, mustard seeds, black pepper and, sometimes, chillies. Pineapple is used in dishes that need to be cooked for a long time; the pith of the banana tree is eaten as a vegetable in Bengal, while the bitter seeds of cucumber are popular as an hors d'oeuvre, and water chestnuts are crunched as a sweetmeat. Dates are cooked to a thick sugary paste, indispensable in confectionery making; figs are used mainly as a vegetable; leaves of the margosa, or bead tree, are served fresh or fried as a first course with rice, or they are dried and used as a condiment; mango and papaya are also cooked as vegetables. Ready-made curry powder is never used in India: each cook prepares spices as required at each stage in the cooking of a particular dish. There are two other ingredients that are traditional in Indian cuisine: ghee (a clarified butter) and a form of condensed milk called *khir*, in liquid or solid form, depending on how concentrated it is.

■ **Snacks and rice dishes** Indians are very fond of snacks, which may be savoury or sweet. Some examples are *chanachur*, made from split peas, peanuts, lemon, peppers and lentil flour, all the ingredients being fried separately; little meat pies; spiced fish balls; fritters of fish roe or aubergine (eggplant) served with chutney; lentil fritters with yogurt sauce; and little fried cakes spiced with fennel flower and covered with syrup. Indian bread is usually in the form of thin, flat cakes made from wheat flour, lentil flour or potato pulp; they are sometimes stuffed with different mixtures of spices, mutton or spinach, and cooked in ghee until golden brown in the *kodai*, a basic kitchen utensil shaped like a frying pan but without a handle.

Rice is served with all savoury dishes. It is never eaten plain but is either mixed with a sauce or mashed vegetables, or cooked with browned onions and spices. For special occasions a delicately flavoured long-grain rice called *basmati* is used, especially to make the dish pulao (basmati rice cooked with raisins, flaked almonds, small peas, cardamom, cinnamon and cloves, served with crayfish or meat) or *murghi biriani* (basmati rice with chicken marinaded in spices and yogurt, flavoured with nutmeg flowers, and served with vegetables).

■ **Fish and meat** Fish is prepared in many ways. Small slices of fried fish are coated in turmeric and served with dal; bass fritters are eaten with onion salad; gilthead is cooked with spices and yogurt; shad is cooked in aubergine sauce; boiled giant prawns (shrimp) are served with ginger, coconut or mint; spiced ragoût of mullet with mustard oil, garnished with aubergines, tomatoes and potatoes, is served with rice and freshly fried croûtons made with lentil flour. The latter is a typical Bengali dish.

The most commonly eaten meats are chicken, mutton and pork, either stewed with spices or marinated and then grilled (broiled). Examples are chicken pieces in a sauce made with yogurt, garlic and pepper, and chicken with coconut or vinegar, garnished with hard-boiled eggs. *Murghi tandoori* is a famous speciality: chicken pieces are marinated in chillies and spices, coated with saffron, grilled and served with a salad of raw vegetables. Pork is often served in a sweet-and-sour sauce. There are innumerable lamb and chicken curries; other curried dishes are made with offal (lamb's liver and sheep's kidneys) and vegetables (green cabbage, green papaya, spinach and aubergines).

■ **Vegetables** Contrasting flavours are combined in one dish. Examples are sour gherkins with potatoes and peppers; courgettes (zucchini) stuffed with prawns, ginger and turmeric; and *chachadi* – a sweet-and-sour ratatouille with mustard or coconut. True vegetarian dishes often contain cream cheese and lemons. To offset so many highly spiced dishes, there is an equally wide range of crudités (raw vegetables), such as onions, cauliflower and tomatoes, served with yogurt, coriander (cilantro) and tamarind sauces.

■ **Desserts** Popular desserts include *halva*, a cake made from semolina cooked in milk and decorated with raisins, almonds and cardamom seeds; vermicelli cooked in milk and flavoured with cinnamon and cashew nuts; curd cheese with pistachios, raisins or rose petals; green mangoes cooked in milk; and very sweet cakes made with banana, almonds or rice. *Sandesh*, made from casein (milk solids), sugar and milk, is flavoured with coconut and cooked like a fritter.

A fabulous display of citrus fruits, mangoes and papayas at the Cowford Market in Mumbai (Bombay).

are crushed with a wooden spoon and the whole mass is carefully stirred so that nothing remains at the bottom of the pan. Some egg yolks are beaten, in the proportion of 3 to every 100 chrysalids, and poured over them. In this way, a beautiful golden yellow cream with an exquisite flavour is obtained.

'This is the way the dish was prepared for the mandarins and the wealthy. On the other hand, the poor people, after grilling the chrysalids and removing their outer coverings, fry them in butter or fat and season them with a little salt, pepper or vinegar, or even eat them just as they are . . . with rice.'

INTERLARDING The process of inserting thin strips (lardons) of pork fat into lean cuts of meat using a larding needle. Interlarding is similar to larding, but the lardons are left protruding from the surface of the meat rather than pushed right into the flesh. Interlarding is usually done only on the top side of the meat. Its purpose is to keep the meat basted, and therefore moist, throughout the cooking time, as the lardons will melt in the heat of the oven.

Roasts that are interlarded include fillet of beef, leg of veal, saddle of mutton, haunch of venison, and baron of hare. Small cuts, poultry and game birds can also be interlarded, using very small lardons.

INTESTINE The intestines of slaughtered animals are used mainly as casings for various types of sausages. Pig's intestine is most commonly used. For large sausages, the large intestine and caecum are used; the small intestine is used for chitterlings and small sausages. The small intestine of sheep is used for some sausages, and ox intestines are used to make black pudding (blood sausage). Artificial intestines made from viscose are also used.

IRELAND See *opposite page*.

IRISH COFFEE An alcoholic drink made from black coffee, sugar and Irish whiskey, topped with cream. To prepare Irish coffee, warm a tall glass and pour in 1 good measure of Irish whiskey. Add about 2 teaspoons sugar, then fill the glass to within 2.5 cm (1 in) of the top with very strong hot coffee. Stir to dissolve the sugar, then carefully pour double (heavy) cream over the back of a teaspoon, which is just touching the surface of the coffee, so that the cream floats on the surface. Once the cream is added, do not stir.

IRISH STEW A stew of mutton and potatoes, which, according to Courtine, 'is witness, if not of the art of living, at least of the art of staying alive in difficult times, and has thus become a legendary dish'. The potato was introduced into Ireland in the 16th century and, together with mutton, became the staple food. Pieces of neck end of mutton are arranged in alternate layers with sliced potatoes and onions. Water is added, and the pot is left to simmer over a very low heat. The traditional accompaniment is pickled red cabbage.

IROULÉGUY An AOC red, rosé or white wine from the Basque country. The red wine is made from the Cabernet Sauvignon or Cabernet Franc and the Tannat grapes.

IRRORATEUR A type of spray gun, invented by Brillat-Savarin, which was used to perfume rooms, especially the dining room.

Brillat-Savarin writes in the preface to *La Physiologie du goût:* 'I submitted to the council of the Society for the Encouragement of National Industries my *irrorateur*, a piece of apparatus invented by me, which is none other than a compressor spray that can fill a room with perfume. I had brought the spray with me, in my pocket. It was well-filled. I turned on the tap and, with a hissing sound, out came a sweet-smelling vapour which rose right up to the ceiling and then fell in tiny drops on the people present and on their papers. It was then that I witnessed, with indescribable pleasure, the heads of the wisest men in the capital bending under my *irroration*. I was enraptured to note that the wettest among them were also the happiest.'

The pedantic name of this device comes from the Latin verb *irrorare*, meaning to sprinkle or to bedew.

ISSUES A term used in the French butchery trade to describe the inedible parts of animal carcasses, such as the skin, hair and horns. In some regions, the word *issues* can also mean both edible offal (variety meats) and also those parts of the animal that are forbidden by law to be sold for human consumption.

When the term is used in the flour industry, it refers to the by-products of milling, such as bran.

ITALIENNE, À L' In French classic cuisine, this name is given to dishes of meat, fish, vegetables or eggs that are either dressed with Italian sauce (based on a duxelles of mushrooms, ham and chopped herbs) or garnished with artichoke hearts or macaroni. It is also applied to pasta cooked *al dente* and to many other dishes typical of Italian cookery.

RECIPES

fried eggs à l'italienne
Prepare some Italian sauce, allowing 1 tablespoon for each egg, and keep it hot. Cook very small slices of ham in butter over a very low heat, taking care that they do not become tough. Fry the eggs in oil and arrange them in a circle, alternating them with the slices of ham. Pour the Italian sauce over the top.

Italian sauce
Clean and chop 250 g (9 oz, 2 generous cups) button mushrooms, 1 onion and 1 shallot. Heat 5 tablespoons olive oil in a saucepan, add the chopped vegetables and cook over a high heat

IRELAND

The food and cooking of Ireland is based on the simple use of good ingredients in hearty peasant-style dishes. This was a country that relied on grain, including wheat, oats, barley and rye, until the introduction of the potato, a vegetable that provided far greater yield and ready food for the people and their livestock. The poor communities relied so heavily on potatoes that the failure of the crop in the mid-19th century brought widespread disaster: the potato famine. As well as potatoes, cabbage and leeks were popular vegetables while dairy cows provided milk, butter and buttermilk, along with fresh and matured cheese. Pigs provided excellent bacon. Wild foods, including game birds and venison, nettles, seafood and fresh water fish all featured in the traditional diet. The same ingredients are still important in dishes enjoyed in Ireland and countries to which they have been introduced.

With its extensive coast, Ireland is known for excellent seafood. As well as the cockles and mussels that were traditionally sold on barrows through the streets of Dublin, the country is known for scallops and Galway oysters. Dublin Bay prawns – langoustine – acquired the name from being sold fresh from the fishing boats, but whether they were caught in the bay or brought from Norway waters is subject to debate. Mackerel, fresh or smoked, is local and good. Sorrel sauce is a traditional accompaniment for fish, particularly poached Irish salmon. Trout is another popular freshwater fish.

Sea vegetables are also important, including dulse; which goes well with potatoes and is also eaten dried as a snack. Carragheen, originally from the village of the same name, is also known as Irish moss and used for its setting properties, particularly to make desserts. Sloke is the Irish name for laver, the seaweed used to make Welsh laverbread, which is also cooked in Ireland.

Salty bacon, fine hams and tasty breakfast sausages all feature. There is good lamb and beef – ideal for rich steak and ale pies, made with the inimitable Guinness stout, and pickled to make excellent salt beef, particularly in preparation for Christmas. Drisheen is a blood sausage, made from sheep and beef blood, and cooked by poaching in milk with onion. It may also be fried or poached with tripe.

■ **Irish cheese** Traditional cheese-making in Ireland enjoyed a revival in the closing decade of the 20th century. Examples include Cashel Blue from County Tipperary; Crogan, raw goat's-milk cheese from County Wexford; Coolea, a Gouda-type cheese from County Cork; and Gubbeen and Milleens, both soft, washed rind cheeses also from County Cork.

■ **Traditional dishes and hearty meals** Potatoes feature in many traditional dishes, including breads, pastry and scones as well as savoury meals. Griddle scones, made from fluffy mashed potatoes, and moist breads are matched by a light yet satisfying pastry softened with potatoes. Pies are just as likely to have a thick crust of mashed potatoes as a pastry lid, especially seafood pies with shellfish as well as white fish. Mashed with milk and spring onions, potatoes make fluffy champ, or combined with cabbage, leeks and onions, they are the base for colcannon. Fried potato cakes are also a feature of traditional Irish breakfasts – a mixed grill with a variety of meats, eggs, mushrooms and tomatoes.

Traditional meat dishes include Irish stew, originally made from goat, but known as a lamb dish, with potatoes. Boiled bacon cooked with cabbage and served with plenty of potatoes is another old-fashioned favourite. A fine ham could just as well be baked as boiled, especially Limerick ham, a traditional smoked ham. Dublin Coddle is a hearty stew of sausages and bacon, simmered slowly with onions and potatoes.

Ireland is known for baked goods, for spicy boiled fruit cake and teabreads, including barm brack and treacle loaf, a dark fruity teabread enriched with treacle (molasses). Soda bread (wholemeal, white or with fruit) is traditionally made with buttermilk and bicarbonate of soda (baking soda) as the raising agent. Slashed with a deep cross on top, the soft bread rises high and tastes wonderful warm or fresh on the day it is baked. With added fruit it is buttered and served as an alternative to teabread or currant buns. Boxty bread is made from cooked and raw potatoes, and is more a scone than a bread.

until the juices from the mushrooms are completely evaporated. Add 150 ml (¼ pint, ⅔ cup) stock, 6 tablespoons tomato purée (paste), salt, pepper and a bouquet garni and cook gently for 30 minutes. Just before serving, add 1 tablespoon diced lean ham and 1 tablespoon chopped parsley.

lettuce à l'italienne
Braise some lettuce hearts, then drain them well and arrange them in a buttered gratin dish. Moisten with Italian sauce, using 1 tablespoon per lettuce.

Cover the pan and simmer over a gentle heat for about 20 minutes. Place the lettuce hearts in a ring and arrange some sautéed veal around the outside. If desired, the lettuces can be sprinkled with a little lemon juice.

sliced meat à l'italienne
Prepare some Italian sauce and keep it very hot. Cut thin slices of beef, mutton or veal that has been boiled or braised. Pour some of the sauce into a greased flameproof dish and arrange the slices of meat on top. Cover with the remaining

ITALY

Italian cuisine is one of the best-known outside its country of origin. Pasta, risotto, fritto misto and pizza are enjoyed practically worldwide, together with excellent charcuterie (including mortadella, salami, Parma ham and zampone) and cheeses, notably Gorgonzola and Parmesan, which goes so well with all pasta dishes. The fine quality of Italian ice cream and water ices is also widely acknowledged.

Italian cuisine is one of the oldest in Europe. It is derived from Greek gourmet traditions, these being derived in their turn from Oriental cuisine. Throughout the centuries these culinary traditions became firmly established and attained perfection in the country that had adopted them. Choose any ordinary Italian dish and it is the replica of one that was once enjoyed by gourmands in ancient Rome. Italian polenta, for example, is the same as the *puls* that the Romans prepared en route when they set out to conquer the world. They toasted grains of wheat, crushed them, and made a gruel from the result. The only difference is that polenta is now made from coarse maize (corn) flour, not wheat flour.

■ **Regional cooking** The great attraction of modern Italian cooking lies in the quality and variety of its ingredients and it is for this reason that the true Italian specialities are regional – even local.

Not so very long ago, a 'culinary frontier' separated northern Italy, with its butter, cow's-milk cheese, rice and Barolo or Valpolicella wines, from the south, the land of olive oil, pasta, Marsala and mare's milk. It was the Tuscans who forged the first link with the regions of the south, with the opening of restaurants where Lucca oil, entrecôte steak *à la florentine*, white haricot (navy) beans and Chianti could be enjoyed. Other regions followed

suit: pizzas became known in the north, while risotto and polenta were eaten in the south. However, regional cookery continues to dominate. Lombardy is still the home of dishes prepared *à la milanaise*, which are rich in butter, and of vegetable soups and osso bucco. Venice has its fish and seafood specialities and shows the influence of Austrian cuisine. Liguria specializes in highly seasoned stuffed food, and the province of Emilia-Romagna is dominated by Bologna, a city that is gastronomically to Italy what Lyon is to France. It is especially noted for its charcuterie and its endless range of *paste asciutte* (pasta with butter). Tuscany is the orchard and vegetable garden of Italy and is famous for its red meat.

Other regions are also known for their specialities: the Marches, for their game (wood pigeon with lentils) and olives; Latium, offering fried fish and stewed tripe; Campania, home of macaroni in tomato sauce; Apulia, where the figs and melons come from; Calabria, producing both aubergines (eggplants) and tuna; Sicily, land of citrus fruits and fish cooked *en papillote* with aromatic herbs; and Sardinia, renowned for its honey, wild boar ham and its thrushes.

■ **Rice and pasta** People who enjoy rice and pasta will find that the Italians have developed the preparation of dishes based on these simple foods to a fine art. Herbs are used extensively, especially basil, thyme, sage, oregano, rosemary and parsley. These herbs flavour the hearty minestrone soup from Lombardy, as well as delicate chicken consommés with vermicelli.

Rice will absorb any flavour: it may be cooked in a savoury stock, flavoured with saffron, prepared *à la milanaise* or *à la piémontaise*, used as a stuffing for tomatoes or (bell) peppers, flavoured with garlic and basil, and used as a garnish for fish and seafood. It can also be mixed with sautéed mushrooms or peas, as it is in the

famous *risi e pisi* of Venice.

Italian pasta has a worldwide reputation. In Italy it is served as a first course, sometimes mixed with butter and Parmesan cheese or covered with a thick tomato sauce, a meat sauce (*à la bolognaise*), a *carbonara* sauce (made with ham, eggs, cream, pepper and grated cheese), or any of a variety of other sauces. Pasta can be the basis of some delicately flavoured dishes, such as the Neapolitan spaghetti *alle vongole*, which is cooked in a fish fumet with clams, tomatoes and garlic. *Pesto* is a Genoese sauce made with basil, parsley and marjoram pounded with oil, Parmesan cheese and garlic; it is eaten with spaghetti or tagliatelle.

Everyone is familiar with cannelloni, ravioli and tortellini, but there are also *capelletti* from Emilia (cone-shaped pasta stuffed with minced (ground) chicken, cheese and eggs), *pansotti* from Rapallo (filled with spinach and served with a walnut sauce), macaroni *à la sicilienne* (braised with meat balls, mozzarella cheese and fried aubergines), and finally, pasta *con le sarde*, a gratin of macaroni in sardine sauce with fennel and raisins, topped with fresh sardines.

■ **Meat and fish** Italian cookery does justice to its meat. As with pasta, there are many regional variations and they do not begin and end with osso bucco. The Lombards, who are hearty eaters, are very fond of *bollito misto* (mixed boiled meats seasoned with sweet-and-sour sauce and vinegar) and *busecca* (a thick soup made from veal tripe, haricot beans and green vegetables). The Tuscans and people from Campania prefer roast baby lamb or a stew of kid, while Florentines remain faithful to *bistecca* (grilled entrecôte steak). Dishes described as *alla pizzaiola* are found all over Italy. They consist of beef or veal sautéed in very hot oil and then simmered with tomatoes, garlic and herbs. There is an amazing variety of recipes for veal: *saltimbocca* from Rome,

The wine-producing regions of Italy

- ◼ North
- ◼ Tuscany and the central region
- ◼ South and the islands
- ▬▬ Border
- - - - Regional boundary

involtini (thin slices of stuffed rolled veal with ham) from Milan, *picatta* (thin slices of meat with a lemon or Marsala sauce), loin of veal cooked *en papillote* with small artichokes, the celebrated *vitello tonnato* from Naples (veal in a tuna and anchovy sauce garnished with capers), veal with olives from Leghorn and, from

Sicily, *messicani* (very thin stuffed escalopes, threaded on skewers, sautéed in butter and deglazed with white wine and Marsala) and *farsumagru* (a terrine of veal with sausages and hard-boiled eggs, simmered with mozzarella and tomatoes). There are fewer recipes for cooking poultry, but two worth mentioning are chicken

breasts *à la Valdostana* (covered with white truffles and mozzarella cheese, sautéed and deglazed with white wine) and fried chicken *à la toscane* (small birds threaded on skewers and served on a bed of polenta).

Fish is prepared in a variety of ways. Examples of dishes made with freshwater fish are salmon ▶

◀ trout from the lakes cooked in a court-bouillon and served with a very fruity olive oil and lemon sauce, and lampreys braised with bacon and covered with a tomato and garlic sauce. However, sea fish predominate. They are cooked quite simply as they are, *en papillote, à la sicilienne* (stuffed with almonds and raisins), grilled or fried. The fish soups are less highly flavoured than those found in Provence.

■ **Vegetables** There is an abundance of vegetables and they are used in a wide variety of ways: chopped spinach with vinaigrette, marinated courgettes (zucchini), stuffed peppers and artichokes. Some less well-known recipes are worthy of note: cardoons *à la piémontaise* (mixed with a hot sauce made with oil, butter and garlic); *fagioli* (white haricot beans) with herbs, served warm in vinaigrette; asparagus served with fried eggs; and broad (fava) beans mixed with bacon, onion and bay leaf and simmered with a chiffonade of lettuce. *Capon magro* consists of slices of bread rubbed with garlic and covered with layers of cooked vegetables, which are then covered with boiled fish and a thick mayonnaise containing a mixture of chopped herbs. It is served with olives, prawns (shrimp), hard-boiled eggs and anchovy fillets.

■ **Cheese and desserts** An Italian meal will often end either with cheese, such as Gorgonzola, Provolone, Bel Paese or perhaps mozzarella with herbs, or fruit followed by very strong espresso coffee.

However, there are also many kinds of desserts and cakes including delicately flavoured Venetian lemon biscuits (cookies) called *bacioli*, Genoese marzipan, Florentine zabaglione, Sicilian *amaretti* (almond macaroons), *cassata Siciliana* is a sponge cake layered with ricotta cheese and candied fruit, *torta di ricotta* and zuppa inglese (trifle).

Panettone is the vanilla-scented, yeasted cake which is rich with eggs and butter, and studded with raisins and candied peel. It is made for Christmas and for Easter. Panforte is the other famous sweetmeat prepared for Christmas. It is a dense mixture of nuts – almonds, hazelnuts, walnuts – dried, candied and crystallized fruit, and spices, including ground coriander, cloves, mace and cinnamon. Bound by honey, this concoction is baked in a shallow tin lined with rice paper and allowed to cool. Panforte is dredged with icing (confectioner's) sugar, tightly wrapped and allowed to mature for a few days before it is served. It will keep for weeks.

WINE Italy is the second largest producer of wine in the world behind France and is a major exporter, although huge quantities of Italian wines are consumed in the home market. Vines are grown the entire length of the country from the Alps and Dolomites in the north to the island of Sicily in the south. Whilst there is a 10 degree difference in latitude, the great climatic variations are modified by the Appenine Mountains running the length of the country, and the Adriatic and the Mediterranean.

There are said to be over 2,000 native grape varieties with 20 recognized as being widely grown. The predominant variety planted is Sangiovese, the main component of Chianti from Tuscany, followed by the Sicilian white grape Catarratto, Trebbiano Toscano (the basis of many white wines from the central regions) and red varieties including Barbera, found in Piedmont, Negroamaro, from Apulia, Montepulciano and Primitivo (thought to be related to the Californian variety Zinfandel). International varieties such as Merlot, Cabernet Sauvignon, Syrah, Chardonnay and Gewürztraminer are being increasingly planted, particularly in the north-east – Trentino, Alto Adige, north Veneto and Friuli.

The wines complement the local cuisine and vary in style from crisp dry whites, as in Geco di Tufo, through light fruity reds, such as Valpolicella, to deep, concentrated, full-bodied, tannic Barolos. The latter are produced in Piedmont from the highly regarded Nebbiolo grape variety.

Good quality sparkling wines are also produced, notably the DOCs Moscato d'Asti and Asti Spumante, which are ideally drunk young. Dessert wines include Marsala, a fortified cask-aged wine available in dry to sweet styles, and Vin Santo, traditionally produced in Tuscany from grapes left to dry on racks throughout the winter.

The Italian wine laws encompass four qualities: at the highest level is Denominazione di Origine Controllata e Garantita (DOCG), followed by Denominazione di Origine Controllata (DOC), which is equivalent to the Appellation Contrôlée classification in France, Indicazione Geografica Tipica (IGT) – similar to Vin de Pays – and Vino da Tavola.

Other styles of drinks are produced in Italy, including grappa, vermouth and liqueurs.

Italy introduced the art of making fine ice cream (gelato) to the rest of the world and its ice-cream parlours are open from early morning to late evening. This gelateria in Florence offers ice creams of all flavours, including lemon, kiwi fruit, pineapple and mango.

sauce and sprinkle with grated Parmesan cheese. Reheat on top of the stove without allowing the sauce to boil.

Swiss chard à l'italienne

Remove the green parts of the leaves, then break off the veins and stalks (it is important not to cut them with a knife) and remove the stringy parts. Divide into 7.5 cm (3 in) lengths, put into boiling white stock, and cook for about 20 minutes. Drain the chard. Prepare enough Italian sauce to cover the chard. Put the chard and the sauce into a pan, simmer, mix well and adjust the seasoning. Before serving, sprinkle with chopped basil.

other recipes See *aubergine, chicken, hash, liver (chicken liver), macaroni, mullet.*

ITALY See *page 626.*

IVOIRE A variety of suprême sauce enriched with white meat glaze or reduced veal stock, used especially for poached chicken. It is used thick for a chaud-froid sauce.

RECIPE

chicken à l'ivoire

Poach a chicken in white stock; prepare 500 ml (17 fl oz, 2 cups) ivoire sauce. Make 24 small chicken quenelles. Clean and trim 24 button mushrooms, sprinkle with lemon juice, and place in a sauté pan with a little butter. Just cover with chicken consommé and cook for about 10 minutes.

Drain the chicken and arrange on a serving dish, surrounded by the mushrooms and quenelles. Coat with ivoire sauce; serve the remaining sauce in a sauceboat.

•*Ivoire sauce* Add 2 tablespoons reduced veal stock or meat glaze to 200 ml (7 fl oz, ¾ cup) suprême sauce.

IZARD A variety of the chamois found in the Pyrenees. Tender and full of flavour, the meat (particularly the haunch and the fillets) is much sought-after, being either roasted or stewed. As the animal is in danger of becoming extinct, it is now a protected species. Therefore mutton, from sheep slaughtered the day after they return from pasture, is marinated to produce a similar taste.

J

JACK This soft and mild cheese was created by David Jacks in the 1830s in America. It is matured for a week. Good examples come from Monterey and Sonoma in California. Dry Jack is Monterey Jack which has been aged for 7–10 months to give a much sharper, nutty flavour.

JACKFRUIT The fruit of a tropical tree that originated in India. Oval in shape and studded with small protuberances, a jackfruit can weigh up to 30 kg (67 lb). The skin is bluish, pale green, yellow or brown; the flesh is white or yellowish and full of large seeds. Blanched and then peeled, it is eaten in stews or baked in the oven as a vegetable. The seeds are cooked in the same way as chestnuts, either roasted or in a purée.

JACOB'S BÂTON *bâton de Jacob* A small stick-shaped éclair filled with confectioner's custard (pastry cream) and iced (frosted) with fondant icing.

JALOUSIE A small rectangular pastry consisting of a strip of puff pastry spread with vanilla-flavoured marzipan (almond paste) and topped with a slatted pastry lid resembling a Venetian blind (*jalousie* in French). Apple compote, apricot jam or a fruit preserve can be used instead of the marzipan. The jalousie can also be made in the form of one large pastry and fresh fruit fillings can be used.

RECIPE

jalousies with apricot jam
Roll out 500 g (18 oz) puff pastry* into a rectangle about 3 mm (⅛ in) thick and cut it into 2 equal strips about 10 cm (4 in) wide. Brush all round the edges of one of the strips with beaten egg and spread 500 g (18 oz, 1½ cups) apricot jam in the centre. Fold the second piece of pastry in half lengthways, and with a knife make slanting cuts from the folded side to within 1 cm (½ in) of the other edge. Unfold the strip and place it over the first one. Press the edges firmly together to seal them, trimming if necessary to a neat rectangle, then make decorative indentations with the point of a knife. Brush the top with beaten egg, put in a preheated oven at 200°C (400°F, gas 6), and bake for 25–30 minutes. When it is done, brush the top lightly with apricot jam that has been mixed with double its volume of water and boiled to reduce it slightly; finally, sprinkle the top with caster (superfine) sugar.

Cut the strip into 4 cm (1¾ in) slices and serve warm or cold.

JAMBALAYA A speciality of New Orleans, inspired by Spanish paella and made of highly spiced rice, chicken and ham. Various ingredients can be added; for example, sausage, peppers, tomatoes, prawns (shrimp) or oysters.

RECIPE

chicken jambalaya
Poach a chicken in stock, then drain. When it is quite cold, remove the skin and bones, weigh the meat, and dice it finely. Sauté half this weight of raw diced ham in 50 g (2 oz, ¼ cup) butter over a low heat, with the pan covered. While it is cooking, prepare some rice* *à la grecque* using 300–400 g (12–14 oz, 2 cups) uncooked rice and the stock from the chicken. When the ham is cooked, add the diced chicken together with some cayenne, salt

and pepper so that the mixture is highly seasoned. Finally, add the rice, mix everything together thoroughly, and serve very hot.

JAMBE DE BOIS The French term for shin or knuckle of beef (beef shank) left on the bone, when used as an ingredient of a pot-au-feu. In former times, the preparation of *potage à la jambe de bois* was a major undertaking; according to a recipe from 1855 it required a chicken, a brace of partridges, 1 kg (2 lb) boned fillet of veal and a variety of vegetables. The dish came originally from Lyon.

JAMBONNEAU The French name for the knuckle end of a ham or pork leg. It is eaten fresh, semi-salted or smoked. Braised or poached like ham, but for a longer time, it is served with sauerkraut and used in thick soups. It can be bought ready cooked and skinned.

The name *jambonneau* is also given to a preparation of stuffed chicken thigh, because of its similar shape. Bone plump uncooked chicken thighs, making only one cut so as to keep them as intact as possible. Spread with a little forcemeat and reshape the thighs so that they look like small ham knuckles. Tie them in shape and braise until cooked through.

JAMBONNETTE Cooked charcuterie made from pork shoulder (50–60%) and bacon (40–50%), chopped, seasoned and enclosed in rind to make a pear shape. A jambonnette can be garnished and glazed in the same way as a galantine.

JAM, JELLIES AND MARMALADES Sweet preserves in which the high sugar content acts as a preservative. Jellies and marmalades are set; the majority of jams are set but some are less firm than others and they may be less firm than jellies or marmalades. Some jams can be quite soft, of a thick flowing consistency, and in these are usually referred to as conserves. A home-made conserve has pieces of fruit in a thick, fruity syrup. (Commercially, conserve refers to a high-quality jam, usually with a high proportion of fruit.)

The art of jam making began in the Middle East. It was introduced into Europe by the Crusaders, who had discovered cane sugar and certain previously unknown fruits. In North America, jelly is generally used as the term for jam.

■ **Keeping quality** These preserves rely on the right balance of ingredients for a good set and to ensure that they keep well. Keeping quality depends on a high proportion of sugar to prevent the growth of moulds or fermentation. They are poured into sterilized pots and wax paper discs cover the surface of the preserve to exclude air. An airtight lid is used to prevent micro-organisms from entering the pots during storage. With the right ingredients and potting, preserves will keep for several months (or longer) in a cool, dark place without the need for refrigeration. Once the pots are open, the preserve is best stored in the refrigerator. Low-sugar preserves are prepared commercially but they are sterilized in their containers and once opened they do not have a long shelf life. It is not possible to produce this type of low-sugar preserve without the right processing.

■ **Setting quality** Pectin, a gum-like substance contained in the cells walls of plants, is essential for a good set. Cooking the fruit breaks down the cell walls to release the pectin. Acid, found naturally in some fruit or added in the form of lemon juice, helps to release the pectin. When boiled with sugar, the pectin forms a gel that sets. To achieve a good set there must be sufficient pectin, with enough acid and the right concentration of sugar. If there is too little or too much sugar, the preserve will not set.

The pectin content of the fruit can be checked by placing a teaspoonful of the cooked pulp (before the sugar is added) in a little methylated spirits and swilling it around in an old jar or container. Fruit with a high pectin content will clump together in one clot; that with a medium content will form a few clots; fruit with a low pectin content will clump in lots of small pieces rather than large clots. Commercial pectin is available as a powder, liquid or in combination with sugar. These products can be added to low-pectin fruits to make set preserves – follow the manufacturer's instructions for adding the pectin.

■ **The choice of fruits** Certain regions and towns in France have made a speciality of a particular jam; for example, redcurrant jam from Bar-le-Duc, bilberry (huckleberry) jam from Alsace, and green tomato jam from Provence. In Britain many types of fruit are grown for jam in the Vale of Evesham, Kent and Essex. Speciality jams, such as mulberry, quince and medlar, are grown and made in the Tiptree area.

To make good preserves, the fruit should be sound and not overripe. Fruit contains the maximum pectin when it is underripe, but its flavour is weak. Often the best solution is to combine a small proportion of underripe fruit with ripe produce. Overripe fruit has poor flavour and pectin content. Pears, peaches, apricots, strawberries and raspberries should be slightly underripe, while plums and cherries should be just ripe but still full-flavoured. Combining fruits rich in pectin with others low in pectin is a good way of achieving an interesting flavour and a good set. Examples of fruit with good pectin contents include cooking apples and crab apples, quinces, blackcurrants, redcurrants, physalis, lemons, Seville or bitter oranges and gooseberries. Plums, raspberries, blackberries, loganberries and grapes have a medium pectin content. Strawberries, apricots, peaches, pears, rhubarb, kiwi fruit, sweet oranges and cherries have a low pectin content. Fruit with a medium or low pectin content can still be used to make conserves with an excellent flavour, but they have a soft set or flowing texture. The same method should be used and the conserve should have a high proportion of sugar to ensure it keeps well. Similarly, the boiling time should be 5–8 minutes.

The flavour of jams can be enhanced by spices (vanilla and cinnamon), a little alcohol (rum and kirsch), caramel (for apples), or another fruit of more robust flavour (peaches, raspberries, cherries, redcurrants, mixed citrus fruits, rhubarb and strawberries). The colour may be deepened by adding blackberries or raspberries to peaches and melon. Watermelon, tomatoes, fresh walnuts, mango, guava and coconut can also be used, as well as small wild fruits, such as haws, elderberries, blackberries, bilberries and rosehips. At one time flowers (such as violets, roses and pumpkin flowers) and many spices (especially ginger) were used and rose petals are still an important ingredient for some sweet preserves. Lastly, there is milk jam, which does not contain fruit. Widely eaten in South America, where it is known as *dulce de leche* (milk sweet), it is made by slowly reducing sweetened vanilla- or cinnamon-flavoured milk.

■ **Utensils** In addition to the usual kitchen equipment, a large, wide preserving pan is useful for boiling large quantities of sweet preserves. It should be heavy and made of material that will not react with the acid in the fruit – stainless steel is ideal. Copper and aluminium should not be used as these metals react with the fruit and contaminate the preserve. (At one time, copper was favoured because the reaction between the metal and fruit produced a sparkling preserve, but this was before the risks of metal contamination were fully appreciated.)

As well as the ability to withstand boiling sugar at high temperatures without burning, the preserving pan should be deep enough to allow ample space for cooking significant quantities that rise to over twice their volume during rapid boiling. A wide pan allows a large surface area for evaporation, so that the excess water rapidly evaporates and the sugar concentrates quickly, which reduces the boiling time. This helps to give the preserve good colour and flavour, which are spoilt by prolonged boiling.

A long-handled spoon is useful for stirring in the initial stages of cooking. A wide-necked funnel makes potting far easier, allowing the preserve to be ladled into the pots with speed. The pots should be heat-resistant and have airtight, acid-resistant lids. They should be clean and freshly sterilized (a liquid sterilizing solution of the type used for cleaning baby feeding equipment is recommended). Wax paper discs are essential for covering the surface of the preserve – they come in sizes to match different jars.

A jelly bag is used to strain the cooked fruit for making jellies. This is fine enough to allow the juice through but not the fibres or pulp that spoil the clarity of the preserve. A special stand allows the bag to be hung with ease.

■ **Sugar** As a rule, for fruit with a good pectin content use an equal weight of sugar. The weight of sugar may be increased slightly for fruit with a very high pectin content. If too little sugar is used, the jam may ferment and will not keep. If there is too much sugar, the jam is too concentrated and tends to crystallize.

Ordinary white granulated sugar can be used. Preserving sugar has larger crystals that dissolve more slowly and produce less scum. Lump sugar or sugar cubes may be used and some cooks prefer these,

again for their slow dissolving and reduced scum. Sugar with added pectin is especially useful for setting fruit with a low to medium pectin content.

■ **Cooking stages** There are three key stages for the majority of sweet preserves – cooking the fruit, dissolving the sugar, then boiling. Testing for setting is important to determine whether the preserve has boiled down to the right sugar concentration. Following a few simple rules at each stage will help to ensure good results.

• Cooking the fruit The first stage is to cook the fruit until it is completely tender before adding sugar. This is essential as adding the sugar before the fruit is tender will toughen the skins. This stage is also essential for releasing the pectin in the fruit and, to assist this process, lemon juice is added to those fruit that are not naturally very acidic. Water may be added or a very little sugar may be sprinkled over some juicy fruit to help release the juice and prevent the fruit from burning.

The trimmings – peel, pith and seeds – are tied in a muslin (cheesecloth) bag and boiled with the fruit. They are a valuable source of pectin. When thoroughly cooked, the bag should be squeezed into the pan of fruit to extract all the juice from the trimmings.

When making marmalade, the rind may be prepared and cooked with the fruit juices in a large proportion of water for a fine result, or the chopped fruit may be used for a coarse marmalade. Citrus fruit require lengthy cooking until quite soft before the sugar is added, otherwise the rind becomes very tough during boiling.

• Adding the sugar When the fruit is completely tender, the sugar is added and the preserve is cooked slowly, stirring often, until the sugar has dissolved completely. A little additional lemon juice can be added at this stage as it helps to give the jam a good colour and sparkling appearance.

• Boiling When the sugar has dissolved, the preserve should be brought to a fast boil, known as a full rolling boil. It should not be stirred as this encourages the sugar to crystallize. The boiling is continued until setting point is reached. This depends on the concentration of sugar, which can be measured by checking the temperature using a sugar thermometer. This can take between 5 and 10 minutes, but it should not take more than about 15 minutes or the preserve will taste overcooked and have a poor colour.

■ **Testing for setting** Check the temperature of the preserve when it has been boiling for 3–5 minutes. Most preserves set at about 104°C (220°F). When this temperature is reached, remove the pan from the heat and try a saucer test. Place a little of the preserve on a cold saucer and leave it in a cool place for a few minutes. A distinct skin develops when the preserve has reached setting point – push the little puddle of preserve with your finger and the surface should wrinkle quite distinctly. The other useful sign that the preserve has reached setting point is when it forms flakes on the edge of a spoon – try dipping the stirring spoon into the preserve in the pan and then hold it at an angle and allow the preserve to run off. The last of the preserve should begin to set in flakes on the edge of the spoon and run off more slowly, forming wide drips.

Do not overcook the preserve – if it boils for too long, it will become syrupy and will not set. Over-boiled preserve has a dark colour, poor texture and poor flavour.

■**Potting** The clean pots should be sterilized and warm. Use a sterilizing solution to thoroughly clean the pots, then place them on a folded tea-towel (dish-towel), on a baking sheet or roasting pan, in a warm oven for a few minutes so that they are just too hot to hold.

The majority of preserves should be potted immediately they reach setting point. If the pan has been removed from the heat for any length of time while testing for setting, then return it to the heat and bring the preserve just back to the boil. Remove it from the heat immediately and pot the preserve. Ladle the preserve into the hot pots and cover immediately with discs of waxed paper, placing the waxed side down and ensuring there are no air bubbles between the preserve and paper. Cover immediately with airtight lids, screwing them on firmly.

Fine marmalade, with shreds of rind, should be cooled for a few minutes before potting, otherwise the rind will float. When a fine skin begins to form on the surface of the marmalade in the pan, stir it, and the shreds should disperse evenly and remain in suspension. The marmalade is ready for potting: ladle it into the heated pots and cover its surface with waxed discs but do not put lids on the pots. Leave the marmalade to stand undisturbed (moving or shaking the pots may cause the rind to float) until completely cold. Then cover with airtight lids. If lids are placed on the pots when the preserve has cooled slightly, condensation forms inside the jars and this provides the right environment in which mould will grow later.

Label the jars with the type of preserve and the date on which it was prepared. Store in a cool, dark place.

■**Jellies** Fruits with a good pectin content are essential for a jelly with a good set. Fruits with only a moderate pectin content will make a soft, floppy jelly. Since the fruit pulp is strained and the solids discarded, there is no need to prepare the fruit to the same extent as for other preserves. Some of the kernels from stone (pit) fruits, such as apricots, can be cooked with the fruit for the almond flavour they contribute, but only a small number should be added as they contain cyanogens, compounds that produce cyanide.

The fruit is cooked as for other preserves, sometimes with slightly more water added than usual. The pulp is then strained through a jelly bag for several hours or overnight. It is essential that the bag is not disturbed or squeezed as this will make the jelly cloudy. Although the juice looks cloudy at this stage, it clears when boiled with sugar.

The juice is measured and sugar added according to the volume – usually 450 g (1 lb, 2 cups) sugar to 600 ml (1 pint, 2½ cups) juice when fruit with a high pectin content has been used. The sugar is dissolved as when adding to other preserves and the preserve is boiled in the same way. Testing for setting and potting are also the same as for preserves with whole fruit.

■**Uses** Jams, jellies and marmalades are eaten with bread, toast, brioches or other types of rolls for breakfast and snacks. They are also used to accompany desserts (rice pudding, bread pudding, poached fruits, iced desserts, pancakes, waffles) and to fill or cover cakes, to flavour yogurt and soft cream cheese (such as fromage frais), and to make sauces for desserts. Jams also accompany meat: red fruits with game, orange with duck or pork, for example.

RECIPES

apple jelly

Take 3 kg (6½ lb) tart apples with a good flavour or a mixture of apples, such as crab apples, or cooking apples and dessert apples, including Braeburn, Cox's or Granny Smiths. Wash and quarter them without peeling or coring. Place the quarters in a saucepan containing 3 litres (5 pints, 13 cups) water. Bring to the boil, then cook gently for about 1 hour or until the fruit is pulpy. Then pour the contents of the pan into a jelly bag and let the juice run through for several hours or overnight, without pressing the fruit. Pour the juice back into the pan and add 3 kg (6½ lb, 13 cups) granulated sugar. Add the juice of 6 lemons, bring to the boil, and boil until setting point is reached. Pot and cover.

apricot conserve

For 1 kg (2¼ lb) ripe stoned (pitted) apricots, use 1 kg (2¼ lb, 4½ cups) sugar (granulated or lump) and 7 tablespoons water. Dissolve the sugar in the water in a pan, bring to the boil for 5 minutes, and then skim. Add the apricots and cook for about 30 minutes. A few half-kernels from the apricot stones may be added to the conserve in the final 5 minutes of cooking. Pot and cover.

greengage conserve

For 1 kg (2¼ lb) ripe stoned (pitted) greengages, allow 675 g (1½ lb, 3 cups) granulated sugar and 7 tablespoons water. Dissolve the sugar in the water in a pan, bring to the boil for 5 minutes, and then skim. Add the greengages and cook until the preserve reaches a temperature of 104°C (220°F). Pot and cover.

red fruit jam

Combine 450 g (1 lb) each of prepared raspberries, redcurrants and strawberries in a large pan. Weigh 1.4 kg (3 lb) preserving or granulated sugar and sprinkle a little over the fruit; set the rest of the measured sugar aside. Sprinkle 6 tablespoons water over the fruit and cook gently until it gives up its juice.

Continue cooking, stirring, until the fruit is soft. Add the sugar and heat gently, stirring often, dissolved completely. Bring to a full boil without stirring and boil until setting point is reached. Skim, pot and cover.

JAPAN See *page 636*.

JAPANESE QUINCE The fruit of an ornamental Japanese tree or shrub with clusters of red flowers. The Japanese quince is a juicy greenish oval fruit, which tastes rather like a lemon. The fruit is very hard and ripens in the autumn. It is not sold commercially and is edible only when cooked. Japanese quinces are usually mixed with apples to make a jelly, using three parts by weight of quinces to one part of apples.

JAPONAISE, À LA In classic French cuisine, this name is given to various dishes containing Chinese artichokes (called Japanese artichokes in French). It applies particularly to large cuts of roast meat garnished with Chinese artichokes braised in butter or cooked with the meat juices and demi-glace, or to a filled omelette. Francillon salad is known as Japanese salad when Chinese artichokes replace the potatoes, but there is another Japanese salad. This is served as an hors d'oeuvre and combines diced tomato, pineapple and orange on lettuce leaves, covered with crème fraîche to which lemon juice has been added, and sprinkled with sugar. Finally, there is a bombe glacée called japonaise, consisting of peach ice cream filled with tea mousse.

RECIPE

filled omelette à la japonaise
Clean 300 g (11 oz) Chinese artichokes and blanch for 3 minutes in boiling water; drain, rinse and wipe dry. Braise over a low heat in a covered pan without browning; add salt, pepper and a little cream sauce. Make an omelette with 8 eggs and fill it with the artichoke mixture. Fold the omelette and slide it on to the serving dish; sprinkle with chopped parsley. The rest of the cream sauce is served separately in a sauceboat.

JARDINIÈRE A mixture of vegetables, essentially carrots, turnips and French beans, served as a garnish for roast or sautéed meat, casseroled poultry, braised calves' sweetbreads, and similar dishes. Carrots and turnips are cut into chunks 3–4 cm (1¼–1½ in) long, trimmed to a regular shape, cut into slices 3–4 mm (⅛ in) thick, then cut again into matchsticks 3–4 mm (⅛ in) wide; the French beans are cut into chunks, sometimes diamond-shaped, 3–4 cm (1¼–1½ in) long. The vegetables are cooked separately, then mixed with garden peas and bound together with butter. The jardinière often also includes flageolet beans and small cauliflower florets. Meat juices or some clear veal stock can be added. A jardinière can also consist of a simple macédoine of vegetables.

Cutting vegetables for jardinière

Cut the vegetables into even-length chunks, then slice them before cutting them into batons.

RECIPE

flat omelette à la jardinière
Prepare a standard jardinière, cooking the ingredients in water or in consommé and making sure that they retain their crispness. Add some cooked peas and tiny cauliflower florets cooked in the same way. Brown gently in melted butter in a large pan, adding salt and pepper. Beat some eggs as for an omelette, adding a pinch of salt and pepper, and pour over the vegetables; cook like a thick pancake. Garnish with steamed asparagus tips and coat with cream sauce.

JARLSBERG This is an old Norwegian cheese which was revived in the 1950s. It is a cooked and pressed cheese, rather similar to Emmental, with a dry nutty taste but without the complexity of Emmental. The texture is quite soft and rubbery, and there are numerous large holes in the paste.

JASMINE A sweetly scented flower used mostly in the perfume industry. In the Far East, sambac jasmine is used to perfume tea, while Chinese jasmine is used in pastry-making and cooking.

RECIPE

red mullet with jasmine
Gut, trim and clean the mullet. Remove the backbone. Stuff the fish with a mousse made of whiting flesh bound with cream and flavoured with essence (extract) of jasmine. Wrap each fish in buttered paper and cook in a preheated oven at 180°C (350°F, gas 4) for 25 minutes. Take the fish out of their wrappings and arrange them on a hot dish. Cover with a tomato-flavoured white wine sauce.

JASNIÈRES An AOC dry white wine from the Coteaux-du-Loir in Touraine. It is made from the Chenin Blanc grape. Some dry or sweet botrytised wines are occasionally made.

JELLY A cold dessert made of fruit juice, wine or liqueur to which sugar and gelatine are added and left to set in a dish or dishes, or in a mould. There

JAPAN

To traditional Western palates, Japanese cooking seems frugal but refined. Although there are few basic ingredients, they are set out with great delicacy and elegance.

■ **Heritage of the past** The pantheistic worship of nature and its bounty – especially seafood, rice, soya and vegetables – is reflected in Japanese cookery by the term *sappari* (clarity, lightness, simplicity and order). Japanese gastronomy relies as much on the intrinsic flavour of ingredients, often subtly combined, as on the presentation of the food and the table setting. However, some important Western influences have filtered through, notably the technique of frying (*tempura*), introduced by Portuguese Jesuits in the 17th century, and the marked increase in meat consumption (especially chicken and pork), which was formerly condemned by Buddhist precepts. *Sukiyaki*, now the Japanese national dish, was formerly prepared in secret by peasants.

■ **Food and the seasons** One of the basic principles of classic Japanese cookery is that every product should be served in the right season.

Spring is celebrated with the 'nightingale cake', made from pounded sticky rice stuffed with a paste of sweetened haricot (navy) beans. April is the traditional time for raw squid; in May the Japanese drink *shincha*, the new season's tea (traditionally green but mellow and perfumed), and eat *ayu*, a small freshwater fish with delicate flesh, grilled (broiled) with salt and garnished with green vegetables. Also during spring the Japanese hold a 'children's feast', formerly for boys only. The dishes offered symbolize virility and courage: scampi presented with their claws erect, to look like a samurai warrior's helmet, and rice cakes wrapped in leaves from the oak tree, a symbol of vigorous growth.

Summer is the time for eel, grilled over charcoal and served with soy sauce; for soya bean paste, garnished with dried bonito, spring onions (scallions) and ginger; and for glazed buckwheat noodles. August is the hot season, when the food is particularly light and refreshing: fried chicken, cucumbers stuffed with prune paste, trout cooked in stock, and sea urchins.

Autumn is the season for mushrooms, especially the *matsutake*, which has a delicious flavour of grilled meat: these mushrooms are marinated in soy sauce and *sake*, then roasted or steamed with chicken, fish and nuts from the ginkgo (or maidenhair) tree. This is also the season of the *kaki* (or Japanese persimmon) and chestnuts, excellent with sweetened rice. September is the month of the moon, and the food is often symbolic: slices of abalone cooked with steamed cucumbers, boiled bamboo shoots, and rolled eel with hard-boiled (hard-cooked) eggs.

In winter the food is more substantial, with such dishes as terrine of octopus with *daikon* (a large white radish) or dried- mushroom soup. November heralds some particularly savoury dishes made with rice, the cornerstone of Japanese cookery and the symbol of good fortune. Its Japanese name is *gohan*, which means cooked rice (usually steamed) and, by extension, a meal. Winter is also the season for white fish, served raw, grilled or fried, in stews and in soups. Noodle soups containing meat and vegetables are eaten all year round, but are particularly fortifying against the rigours of winter. The mandarin orange (tangerine), a delicious symbol of the sun, is offered as a traditional New Year's Day gift.

■ **Basic ingredients of Japanese cooking** The basic ingredients are combined in a great variety of ways. At the head of the list are the soya bean (used in miso, tofu and sauces) and rice, which can be either savoury or sweet. The other most commonly used ingredients are *mirin*, a spirit-based liquid sweetener; rice wine (*saké*), a strong flavoured alcoholic drink; rice vinegar; sesame oil; green horseradish (*wasabi*); daikon, which is either cut up or grated; dried marrow (squash); burdock; *shirataki* (noodles made from the dried tubers of devil's tongue plant, a subspecies of the sweet potato); bamboo shoots and lotus roots. The Japanese are fond of the taste of marinades, and there is a wide range of pickles (including prune, radish, ginger and sea urchin). A great variety of noodles and vermicelli of all sizes are made from wheat, buckwheat or rice flour. Finally there is seafood, which includes the dried powdered and compressed

are also savoury jellies, made from fresh vegetable juice. Commercial jelly tablets and crystals are available for making jelly desserts but these contain mostly sugar, flavouring and colouring.

The term jelly is also used to describe a strained, clear, set fruit preserve. See *jam, jellies and marmalades*.

JEREPIGO A *vin doux naturel* produced in South Africa, usually from Muscadelle.

JERUSALEM ARTICHOKE A perennial plant cultivated for its edible tubers, which are cooked and eaten as a vegetable or used in distilling. The French name (*topinambour*) is the name of a small tribe in Brazil, but in fact the vegetable originated in North America and was introduced into France in the 17th century by Samuel de Champlain. Called *pommes de terre* by Nicolas de Bonnefons and *poires de terre* by Lemery, 'because they are born in the earth, attached to the branches of the root which bears them', the tubers are knobbly and quite difficult to peel.

seaweeds, added to sauces, soups and garnishes (such as *nori*, *konbu* and *wakame*). Dried bonito fish (*katsuobushi*) is used in a variety of ways. Ginger, pepper, pimientos, mustard, glutamate and all the spices and fresh herbs (including parsley and chives) are indispensable.

The preparation of food follows a characteristic pattern. Fish can be salted and grilled, or boiled in a strongly flavoured sauce, but it is often finely sliced and eaten raw (see *sashimi*). Chicken is grilled with salt or left in a sweet-and-sour marinade, then fried and sprinkled with the marinade. Cooking times are very precise, particularly for eggs. Beef is usually finely sliced, grilled, then rapidly immersed in a vegetable soup. Two typically Japanese culinary processes can be applied to many dishes: *nabemono* is food cooked at table, on a grill (broiler) or in a fondue pan; and *nimono* is food cooked in aromatic stock. Steaming is another common method; the food is then accompanied by sauces and various seasonings. Beef, pork and seafood may be cooked in coarse salt in a casserole. Fried marinated chicken, pork (either sliced and coated with breadcrumbs or threaded on skewers), and oysters coated with breadcrumbs are all highly esteemed. Frying is in fact the pride of Japanese cooking. More than one oil may be used in carefully measured proportions, especially for prawns (shrimp), fish, scallops, (bell) peppers, mushrooms and aubergines (eggplants), which are served separately with a galaxy of sauces. Finally, the Japanese excel in the art of presenting food decoratively, cut into rounds, squares, petals, filaments, small tongues, roses and other complicated shapes; this is skilled work, requiring special tools and great dexterity.

■ **Riches from the sea** Japan is one of the world's greatest consumers of seafood. Japanese coastal waters support a variety of fish, many edible seaweeds, cetaceans (whales and dolphins), and shellfish (including abalone, oysters, clams, crabs, lobsters and prawns). All these are present in huge numbers and are of exceptionally high quality. Tuna, bonito, gilt-head bream and cuttlefish are the current favourites, the most popular dishes being bite-sized slices of raw fish (*sashimi*) served with soy sauce sharpened with mustard and horseradish; *nigiri zushi*, small balls of *sushi* (rice flavoured with vinegar) topped with a small slice of seafood; and *maki zushi* (raw seafood rolled up in vinegar-flavoured rice and crisp seaweed). A speciality is blowfish (*fugu* or *diodon*), a fish whose organs contain a highly poisonous substance but whose flesh is much prized; it is served only in selected restaurants where the chef has a special licence guaranteeing the safety of the diners. Fried fish is eaten a great deal and, like other fried dishes, is accompanied by soy sauce with grated daikon and a pinch of ginger, or simply with salt and lemon.

■ **Eating at home** The Japanese breakfast normally consists of a bowl of rice and dried seaweed, a miso-based soup or eggs. Lunch, which is relatively light and is always eaten in a hurry, may be rice with eggs and meat – pork chops or minced (ground) steak – or noodles, either cold or in a soup. Dinner, on the other hand, is a more extensive and sophisticated meal. Traditionally, it consists of at least four different dishes combining liquid, crisp and simmered foods, some spicy and others bland: the alternation of consistencies and tastes is one of the golden rules of Japanese cuisine. Colour, texture and shape are as important as the taste. Tea and beer are the most common accompaniments to the meal.

Although the Western sweet dessert has become popular in Japan, traditionally sweets and cakes are reserved for feast days or enjoyed between meals, as is fresh fruit. Symbolic dishes are served on feast days and important occasions, such as clam soup at a Shinto marriage ceremony (the two halves of the shell symbolizing union); red rice (sticky rice cooked with *azuki*, small dried red beans that are also known as aduki beans) is a symbol of happiness. The most typical food for the New Year feast is *mochi*: pounded sticky rice formed into pancakes and simmered with vegetables (for savoury dishes) or with red beans and sugar (for dessert). In addition, there may be fish loaf, oranges, chrysanthemum leaves, chestnuts, carp and good-luck ferns. The culinary art and Japanese tradition reach their apogee in the tea ceremony and attendant *kaiseki*, a formal meal consisting of several courses, served in a symbolic tea house, representing a time-honoured ritual symbolizing great harmony.

Fairly firm in consistency, they have a taste similar to that of globe artichokes. They are boiled, steamed or braised with butter and can be served with cream or béchamel sauce, sprinkled with parsley, or used in salads, fried in batter, puréed or souffléed.

Recipes

Jerusalem artichokes à l'anglaise
Peel some Jerusalem artichokes, cut into quarters, and trim to egg shapes if they are large. Blanch for 5 minutes in boiling water, then dry them. Cook gently in butter in a covered pan for about 30 minutes. Stir in a few tablespoons of light béchamel sauce or double (heavy) cream and simmer for about 10 minutes. Serve as a garnish for veal, for example, sprinkled with chopped chervil and tarragon.

Jerusalem artichoke pie with foie gras and truffle ♦
Peel and finely cut 575 g (1¼ lb) pink Jerusalem artichokes into slices 3 mm (⅛ in) thick. Cook in

stock for 5 minutes, then drain. Slice 50 g (2 oz) truffles very finely. Cut very thin slices across the width of a lobe of foie gras. Season with salt and pepper, and add some nutmeg. Line the bottom and sides of a well-buttered medium-sized soufflé mould with the slices of Jerusalem artichoke. Place a thin layer of truffle on top, then a layer of foie gras. Repeat the layering until all the ingredients are used up and cover with foil. Press down with a smaller mould. Cook in a bain marie in a preheated oven at 180°C (350°F, gas 4) for 20 minutes. Unmould on to a serving dish and pour over a warm vinaigrette made with walnut oil and sherry vinegar, flavoured with chervil or flat-leafed parsley.

salad of Jerusalem artichokes

Prepare like a potato salad, using small new Jerusalem artichokes, cooked in water for 20 minutes, peeled and cut into uniform pieces. Dress with a sunflower oil vinaigrette seasoned with shallot and sprinkle with plenty of parsley.

additional recipe See *pork*.

JESSICA A garnish for poultry suprêmes, veal escalopes (scallops) or grenadins (small slices of fillet of veal interlarded with best larding bacon), and soft-boiled eggs. It consists of small artichokes braised in butter and filled with a salpicon of bone marrow with shallots, and morels sautéed in butter, both arranged on tartlets made from Anna potatoes. These are accompanied by an allemande sauce enriched with thickened veal stock and flavoured with truffle essence (extract). An omelette Jessica is filled with sliced morels and asparagus tips bound with cream, then folded and surrounded with a ribbon of Chateaubriand sauce.

JÉSUITE A small triangular puff pastry filled with marzipan (almond paste) and covered with royal icing (frosting). Formerly, these pastries were covered with a dark-coloured praline or chocolate icing shaped like the hat, with a rolled brim, worn by the Jesuits.

JÉSUS A large sausage made in Franche-Comté (especially at Morteau) and in Switzerland, consisting of coarsely chopped pork (or sometimes pork and beef) encased in the widest part of the gut. It has a small wooden hook inserted in the end so that it can be hung up to be lightly smoked. A *morteau* (or *saucisson de Morteau*) is one that is made in the same way in Alsace and the Jura. Both these sausages can be poached and used to garnish thick soups, but they are also used in particular regional recipes.

RECIPE

jésus à la vigneronne

Make a court-bouillon* with 2 litres (3½ pints, 9 cups) Arbois wine, 2 litres (3½ pints, 9 cups) water, 2 peeled onions each studded with 2 cloves, a bouquet garni, salt and pepper. Simmer for 1 hour.

Place a handful of vine shoots in the pan. Prick 1 or 2 jésus with a fork and rest them on the vine shoots so they are just above the surface of the liquid; leave them to cook in the steam from the court-bouillon. Serve with butter and baked potatoes.

Red wine can be used instead of the Arbois, and red or white haricot (navy) beans, according to the colour of the wine, can be substituted for the potatoes.

JEWISH COOKERY Jewish cookery is closely linked to religious feast days and the Sabbath, but it incorporates culinary specialities from all the countries of the Diaspora. It is a family-based art, with a unity derived from ancient traditions. The rules imposed by the *kashruth* do not in any way limit the variety of dishes; they merely ensure that food is completely fresh: meat (only beef and mutton) is carefully washed, then salted and seared to remove any blood (see *kosher*). Tradition plays a great part: for example, the fish prepared on Friday for Saturday's meal is eaten fried by eastern Jews and stuffed by European Jews; eggs, symbols of totality and death, are part of many feast-day dishes; honey is a reminder of the Promised Land. Plaited bread (*hallah*) is a reminder of the sacrificial bread. Even the shape of some foods can relate to a biblical character, like the 'ears of Haman', a cake served at the feast of Purim. Fasts (at least three of 24 hours' duration during the year) are the excuse for some splendid feasts before and after: although Jewish religious precepts forbid greed and drunkenness, they do not condemn good eating.

The cooking of the Sephardic Jews (from Mediterranean countries) and of the Ashkenazi Jews (from central Europe) is derived from a common source. For example, the *tchoulend* of the latter and the *tfina* of the former (meat and vegetable stews) are both cooked in the baker's oven so as to ensure a hot meal on Saturday, when the religious laws forbid the lighting of a fire. However, tastes have been strongly influenced by the foods that are available in the region and the local recipes. North African Jews enjoy couscous; Iranian Jews like to eat *gipa* (ox stomach stuffed with rice) and pilaf; Ashkenazi Jews cook potatoes, puddings (*kugel*) and pasta (such as *lockshen*, noodles made with water, and *kreplech*, pasta filled with meat), as well as Austrian and Russian dishes (borsch, strudel and torten). On the whole, Jewish cookery relies a great deal on frying, for example in stuffed carp, onions with sugar and meat (a dish served at Sephardic wedding feasts), and the Moroccan *pastelas*, pastry rissoles stuffed with meat, honey and vegetables.

Since Israel became an independent nation it has developed its own native cuisine. Each wave of immigrants tends to retain its ethnic cookery, but in

Jerusalem artichoke pie with foie gras and truffle, see page 637.

everyday life Israelis eat simply; their meals are based mainly on raw vegetables (particularly cucumbers and avocados), dairy produce and citrus fruits. Like their Middle Eastern neighbours, they are fond of vegetable purées and spiced meatballs. Israeli farmers rear large numbers of turkeys and ducks, of which they have developed a new breed. They also export foie gras.

JEW'S-EAR FUNGUS *auriculaire oreille-de-judas* A blackish mushroom shaped like an ear lobe that grows in clusters on old tree trunks. Its body is partly hard and partly jelly-like. It was originally eaten raw in salad, but is now mainly served in Chinese restaurants in France under the name of *champignon noir* (black mushroom).

JOHANNISBERG A world-famous white wine from the Rheingau, the best-known vineyard being that of Schloss Johannisberg. There is also a Swiss Johannisberg, made from the Sylvaner grape, whereas the great Rheingau wines are all Rhein-riesling. The term often used in California for the Rheinriesling is Johannisberger Riesling.

JOHN DORY An oval deep-sided fish found along rocky coasts. Only 30–50 cm (12–20 in) long, it has a large head with an enormous mouth and a prominent lower jaw, and the dorsal fin is extended into filaments; the other fins are spiky. On each side of the body, which is bronze-coloured with silvery glints, is a large black spot. This spot, according to tradition, is the thumbprint of St Peter, who seized the fish to throw it back into the water because it was moaning (which, in fact, it does when removed from the water). Tradition also has it that the apostle took a coin from the fish's mouth, on Jesus's instructions. (It should be pointed out, however, that the Sea of Galilee, which is a freshwater lake, does not harbour this fish.)

The John Dory rarely provides more than four servings, since the enormous head, the fins and the bones account for nearly 60% of its weight. Nevertheless, it is one of the best sea fish: its firm white flesh comes off the bone easily and can be used for many different dishes. It can be cooked like turbot or brill, is used in bouillabaisse and fish soups, and many chefs have created original recipes for it.

The English name is a corruption of one of its French nicknames, *Jean-doré*.

RECIPES

fillets of John Dory palais-royal
Poach some John Dory fillets in a mixture of white wine, fish fumet and the juice of a lemon. Boil some potatoes in their skins, peel them, mash them and put in a greased ovenproof dish. Place the fillets on top. Using part of the reduced court-bouillon, make some Mornay sauce, pour it over the fish and brown in a preheated oven at 220°C (425°F, gas 7).

grilled John Dory with deep-fried butter pats
Cut 8 rounds of very cold, slightly salted butter, each weighing 25 g (1 oz). Thickly coat them in breadcrumbs and chill them in the refrigerator. Fillet a John Dory, then grill (broil) it. Just before serving, carefully place the rounds of butter into hot deep fat. As soon as they are golden, drain on paper towels and quickly arrange on top of the portions of fish. Garnish the dish with fried parsley and serve straight away.

John Dory fillets in a soufflé
Steam 4 John Dory fillets, each weighing 150 g (5 oz), for 4 minutes. Sprinkle with salt and pepper. Whisk 8 egg whites until stiff and fold in 3 tablespoons mustard. Arrange the fillets in an ovenproof dish, pile up the egg whites on top, and cook in a preheated oven at 230°C (450°F, gas 8) for about 4 minutes.

John Dory fillets with lemon
Fillet a John Dory weighing about 1.25 kg (2¾ lb); this should provide 600 g (1 lb 6 oz) flesh. Remove the skin and cut the flesh into 1 cm (½ in) dice. Finely shred the zest of 2 lemons, blanch and refresh it, then cook it in a little water and 50 ml (2 fl oz, ¼ cup) olive oil. Remove the white pith from the lemons, break up the lemon segments and dice them. Cut 350 g (12 oz) courgettes (zucchini) into small pieces, trim them to the shape of olives and blanch them.

Lightly grease 4 pieces of foil large enough to wrap round a piece of fish and some vegetables. On each one place a quarter of the fish, courgettes, lemon dice and rind, 20 g (¾ oz, 1½ tablespoons) butter, and some salt and pepper. Seal the foil envelopes and bake in a preheated oven at 230°C (450°F, gas 8) for about 8 minutes. Open the envelopes and sprinkle with chopped chives.

John Dory fillets with melon
Fillet a John Dory weighing about 1.5 kg (3¼ lb) and quickly sauté the fillets in a nonstick frying pan without fat, allowing 2 minutes for each side. Keep the fillets warm. Blanch a julienne of 2 carrots and 1 leek for 1 minute in boiling water. Pat them dry and sauté briskly in 20 g (¾ oz, 1½ tablespoons) butter for 2 minutes. Sprinkle with salt and pepper and keep warm.

In another pan, fry slices of a 400-g (14-oz) melon in 25 g (1 oz, 2 tablespoons) butter, sprinkle with salt and pepper, and allow to caramelize slightly. Arrange a quarter of the melon slices and a John Dory fillet in a ring on each plate, place a spoonful of the vegetables in the centre, and sprinkle with fresh chopped mint.

John Dory fillets with red peppers
Fillet a John Dory. Braise the fillets in fish fumet: they should be just cooked. Arrange them on a dish and keep warm. Reduce the braising liquid, add

200 ml (7 fl oz, ¾ cup) double (heavy) cream, and reduce once again. Remove from the heat, add 3 tablespoons hollandaise* sauce, and adjust the seasoning. Bake 4 whole red (bell) peppers in a preheated oven at 240°C (475°F, gas 9) or put under the grill (broiler) until the skin blackens and blisters. Peel and seed them and purée the flesh in a blender. Season with salt and pepper and heat the purée. Coat the fish with the sauce and with 4 tablespoons pepper purée. Garnish with sprigs of chervil. Serve with French (green) beans.

John Dory steaks in whisky velouté sauce with vegetable julienne

Fillet 2 John Dorys, each weighing 1.25 kg (2¾ lb). Grease an ovenproof dish and sprinkle it with 2 finely chopped shallots. Season the fillets with salt and pepper and lay them in the dish. Moisten with 7 tablespoons dry white wine and 7 tablespoons whisky. Cover with buttered greaseproof (wax) paper and bake in a preheated oven at 180°C (350°F, gas 4) for 10–12 minutes.

Drain the fillets and reduce the cooking liquid by one-third. Remove from the heat, whisk in 50 g (2 oz, ¼ cup) butter in small pieces, then add 500 ml (17 fl oz, 2 cups) whipped double (heavy) cream. Mix well, still off the heat. Put the fish back in the oven or under the grill (broiler) for 2 minutes, then coat with the sauce.

Serve the fish with steamed potatoes and a vegetable julienne made with 2 carrots, 1 celery heart, the white parts of 2 leeks, a bulb of fresh fennel and 4 large mushroom caps.

John Dory with rhubarb

Fillet a John Dory weighing 1.5 kg (3¼ lb) and cook the fillets in a little butter over a gentle heat, allowing 1 minute for each side. Keep warm. Add 150 g (5 oz) rhubarb, peeled and thinly sliced, to the butter in which the fish was cooked, and cook for 30 seconds. Add 200 ml (7 fl oz, ¾ cup) double (heavy) cream and reduce by half. Season with salt and pepper and add a pinch of sugar and a pinch of chopped basil. Mix well and pour the sauce over the fish.

stuffed John Dory with sea-urchin cream

Bone a John Dory, keeping it intact. Stuff it with 300 ml (½ pint, 1¼ cups) leeks stewed in butter mixed with a duxelles of grey chanterelles. Place the fish in an ovenproof dish with chopped onion, thyme, bay leaf, 225 ml (8 fl oz, 1 cup) white Cassis wine and 7 tablespoons cream. Bake in a preheated oven at 180°C (350°F, gas 4) for 20 minutes.

Meanwhile, prepare the sauce: open up 4 sea urchins and put the coral into a small sauté pan. Beat together 2 egg yolks and 7 tablespoons double (heavy) cream in a bain marie. When this mixture is really frothy, add it to the sea-urchin coral, whisking vigorously, and season with salt and cayenne. Pour some of the cream sauce over the fish and put the rest into the sea-urchin shells heated in the oven. Arrange these shells around the fish.

JOINTING The process of cutting up meat and poultry into large pieces at the joints, using a very sharp knife.

JOINTOYER A French culinary term meaning to fill in any surface unevenness and to smooth the joined edges of cakes and pastries that are made up of several layers. Using a cream as the filling agent, the object is to ensure a smooth and uniform surface on the top and sides of the cake; this is essential if the cake is to look its best or if it is to be iced (frosted).

JOINVILLE The name of a dish of sole fillets arranged in a circle, which was dedicated to the third son of Louis-Philippe, the Duc de Joinville. The garnish for fillets of sole Joinville usually consists of prawns (shrimp), poached mushrooms and truffles, while the sauce is made from a sole velouté bound with cream and egg yolks with oyster liquor, mushroom essence (extract) and a purée of prawns and crayfish added to it. There are a number of simpler variations.

The name is also applied to a *normande* sauce with prawn butter, and to a prawn sauce with crayfish butter and a julienne of truffles when it is to accompany braised fish. Joinville garnish is also used to fill barquettes, tartlets, bouchées and an omelette, which is then surrounded with a prawn sauce. Finally, there is a gâteau Joinville, made from two squares of flaky pastry filled with raspberry jam.

RECIPE

fillets of sole Joinville

Clean 250 g (9 oz) mushrooms; dice them, sprinkle with lemon juice, and cook slowly in butter over a low heat. Fillet 2 sole. Make a fumet from the sole trimmings and poach the fillets in this for 6 minutes. Drain. Cook 8 giant prawns (shrimp) in boiling salted water for 4 minutes. Prepare 300 ml (½ pint, 1¼ cups) normande* sauce using the fish fumet and the mushroom cooking juices; add 15 g (½ oz, 1 tablespoon) prawn butter* to the sauce. Mix 100 g (4 oz, ⅔ cup) peeled prawns with a finely diced truffle and the mushrooms; bind with a little sauce. Arrange the sole fillets in a circle on a round dish; stick a prawn into each fillet. Put the garnish in the centre of the dish and cover with the sauce. Formerly, the fillets were arranged on a border of fish forcemeat and truffle slices, with the garnish in the middle.

JOULE Since 1980 this has been the official international unit of measurement for energy. The kilojoule is the metric replacement for the Calorie or kilocalorie (1 kJ = 0.24 Cal or kcal). Calories continue to appear without the metric equivalent on some information labels. When kilojoules are given, the calorific equivalent also appears and is generally expressed as *kJ/kcal*.

JUDIC A garnish for small or large cuts of meat, sautéed chicken, braised calves' sweetbreads and similar dishes, usually consisting of braised lettuce, small stuffed tomatoes and château potatoes. The accompanying sauce is made by deglazing the pan with Madeira and demi-glace sauce, or with a tomato-flavoured demi-glace. According to the *Dictionnaire de l'Académie des gastronomes*, tournedos Judic was supposed to have been named after the comedian Anna Damiens, known as Dame Judic: the steaks are garnished with braised lettuce and a ragoût of sliced truffle and cockscombs and kidneys, covered with a Madeira demi-glace. The name is also given to poached fillets of sole garnished with lettuce and fish quenelles, the whole dish being coated with Mornay sauce and browned.

JUDRU A short, thick, dry sausage made from pure pork, a speciality of Chagny in Burgundy. The meat is steeped in marc brandy and cut into small pieces rather than minced (ground) or chopped.

JUICE See *fruit juice, jus*.

JUICE EXTRACTOR An electrical appliance used to extract juice from vegetables and fruit by means of rapid rotation (citrus fruits, which are pressed, are an exception). A sieve retains the pulp, seeds and skin. Some models have a system for ejecting the waste and can operate continuously, producing large quantities of juice; others require frequent cleaning of the filter. The juices obtained are used in drinks, ices, sorbets and jellies.

JUIVE, À LA Describing a dish of carp, generally served cold. In the authentic Jewish recipe, the carp is cleaned with salt, quickly browned in hot oil, then braised in a white roux with the roe, garlic and parsley. This recipe is adapted in classic French cookery, the fish being sautéed in onion, then braised in white wine with herbs. This dish has many variations; for example, chopped almonds and saffron, or fresh parsley, raisins, sugar and vinegar, can be added to the cooking juices.

A dish of artichokes stuffed with breadcrumbs, chopped fresh mint and garlic, cooked in oil, is also described as *à la juive*.

RECIPES

carp à la juive (1)
(Jewish recipe) Scale and gut (clean) a carp weighing about 1 kg (2¼ lb), taking care to reserve the roe. Cut the fish into slices and rub it with coarse salt. Leave for 20–30 minutes, then drain the pieces, dry them with a cloth and add the roe. Mix 2–3 chopped garlic cloves with some parsley in a small bowl. Heat 3–4 tablespoons oil in a saucepan and sear the fish and the roe. Add enough water to almost cover the fish, then add salt and pepper, the parsley and garlic, and simmer for about 20 minutes. Take out the pieces of fish and the roe and arrange them in a deep dish.

Make a smooth paste with 3 tablespoons cornflour (cornstarch) and a little water, then mix in two-thirds of the liquid from the saucepan. Simmer the sauce until it has reduced by one-third. Pour it over the fish and leave in the refrigerator to set.

carp à la juive (2)
Cut a medium-sized carp into regular slices and cook them in 200 ml (7 fl oz, ¾ cup) oil with 100 g (4 oz, ⅔ cup) sliced onion and 50 g (2 oz, ⅓ cup) sliced shallots without browning. Sprinkle with 40 g (1½ oz, ⅓ cup) flour. Pour in enough white wine and fish fumet (or water) to almost cover the fish; add salt, a pinch of cayenne, 2 crushed garlic cloves and a bouquet garni. Moisten with a few tablespoons of oil and bring to the boil, then cook gently for 20 minutes. Drain the pieces of carp and arrange them on a long dish in the shape of the original fish. Boil down the liquor by two-thirds, take off the heat, and thicken by beating in 7 tablespoons oil. Pour this sauce over the carp and leave to cool.

JUJUBE An oval, olive-sized fruit with a smooth, tough red skin; soft, sweet, yellowish or green flesh; and a hard stone (pit). The jujube tree, which originated in China, was known to Homer, and the fruit (usually dried) was used medicinally for hundreds of years. The jujube is grown in the temperate zone from the Far East to the Mediterranean. The Far East exports large jujubes, either fresh or dried, known as 'red dates'. The jujube can be eaten as it is, either fresh or dried, and is also used in pastry-making (cakes and fritters) and in savoury dishes, such as meat stuffings and soups.

JULES-VERNE A garnish for large cuts of meat consisting of stuffed braised potatoes and turnips, arranged alternately with sautéed mushrooms. It was dedicated to the famous novelist by a 19th-century chef.

JULIÉNAS One of the ten classified growths of the Beaujolais, which in good years may have good keeping qualities, although most should be drunk within a couple of years of the vintage.

JULIENNE Foodstuffs, especially vegetables, that are cut into thin sticks. They are cut with a knife or a mandoline into even slices 1–2 mm (1/16 in) thick and then into strips 2.5 cm (1 in) long. The julienne is cooked in butter in a covered pan until quite soft and then used for various garnishes, particularly for soups and consommés.

Raw vegetables to be served as an hors d'oeuvre can also be cut as a julienne, such as carrots in vinaigrette and celeriac in spicy mayonnaise. Many other foods can also be cut in this way: gherkins, truffles, peppers, mushrooms, ham, tongue, chicken breasts and citrus-fruit peel, for example.

The origin of the word is obscure, but it appears in the 1722 edition of *Le Cuisinier royal*.

Cutting julienne strips

Cut the vegetables into pieces about 2.5 cm (1 in) or slightly longer, then slice them thinly. Cut the slices into fine strips.

RECIPES

bouchées à la julienne

Cut the following vegetables into fine strips: carrots (discarding any hard core), turnips, the white stem of leeks, celery sticks with the strings removed, and mushrooms sprinkled with lemon juice (use twice as much carrot as each of the other vegetables). Cook the julienne in melted butter, in a covered sauté pan over a low heat, so that the vegetables retain a little bite. Add 7 tablespoons double (heavy) cream for every 450 g (1 lb) vegetables, and reduce until the mixture is thick. Add Bayonne ham, also cut into strips (1 part ham to 5 parts mixture), and heat through without boiling. If liked, a little very fine julienne of truffle can be added. Adjust the seasoning.

Heat some small puff-pastry cases and divide the mixture between them. Serve immediately before the pastry goes soggy.

consommé julienne

Make a julienne of 100 g (4 oz) carrot (discarding any hard core), 75 g (3 oz) turnip, and 40 g (1½ oz) each of white of leek, onion and celery. Sprinkle with a pinch of salt and a pinch of sugar. Soften the vegetables in 50 g (2 oz, ¼ cup) melted butter over a low heat, with the pan covered, for 10 minutes. Cut 50 g (2 oz) white cabbage into julienne strips and blanch for 10 minutes in boiling water, then refresh and drain; do the same with the heart of a medium-sized lettuce; add these to the other vegetables.

Cook them all together, covered, for 15 minutes. Pour in 300 ml (½ pint, 1¼ cups) consommé* and simmer for 5 minutes; add 25 g (1 oz) sorrel cut into fine ribbons and 1 tablespoon fresh peas, and cook for a further 25 minutes. Add another 1.25 litres (2¼ pints, 5½ cups) consommé and boil for a few seconds; skim the pan, and at the last moment add some chervil leaves.

The consommé can be garnished with pearl barley, rice, semolina, tapioca or vermicelli, or with quenelles, profiteroles or royales.

julienne salad with orange and horseradish dressing

Pare the zest from ½ orange and cut it into fine julienne. Cook the strips of orange zest in boiling water for about 5 minutes or until tender. Drain and set aside. Squeeze the juice from the orange and place it in a large bowl. Add 1 teaspoon caster sugar, 2 teaspoons creamed horseradish, salt and pepper, and whisk until the sugar has dissolved. Gradually whisk in 4 tablespoons olive oil. Then stir in the orange zest.

Cut ½ celeriac into julienne and add to the dressing in the bowl, tossing well to coat the celeriac evenly and prevent it from discolouring. Cut 4 carrots into julienne and add to the celeriac. Finely chop 4 spring onions and add to the salad with 2 tablespoons chopped mint. Toss well and chill lightly before serving.

potage julienne à la cévenole

Prepare 450 g (1 lb) julienne of carrots, turnips, white of leek, celery and onions, in equal proportions; cook gently in butter for about 30 minutes. Pour in 1 litre (1¾ pints, 4⅓ cups) consommé* and cook for a further 30 minutes. Add 500 ml (17 fl oz, 2 cups) salted chestnut purée, mix thoroughly, and boil for 5 minutes. Just before serving, blend in 50 g (2 oz, ¼ cup) butter, cut into small pieces.

other recipes See *celeriac, Darblay, sea bream.*

JUMBLES Biscuits made from a rich dough, shaped into short ropes and then twisted into knots or 'S' shapes. Jumbles were originally flavoured with caraway seeds, lemon zest or rose water. The name is also applied to biscuits made from a coarse-textured mixture of dried fruit and nuts. The mixture is piled into clusters before baking and the name refers to the method by which the ingredients are all jumbled together.

JUNIPER BERRIES The darkish berries of the juniper tree, which are used in cooking and the manufacture of wines and spirits because of their pungent and slightly resinous flavour. Used either whole or ground, juniper berries are particularly appreciated in Scandinavian cookery. They are the indispensable seasoning for marinades and court-bouillon, dishes of game animals (wild boar) and birds (thrush, blackbird, woodcock), pork dishes (knuckle, pâtés) and sauerkraut. They are generally used in dishes *à la liègeoise* or *à l'ardennaise.*

A highly aromatic brandy, drunk mostly in northern Europe, is flavoured with juniper berries: it is known as *genièvre* in France, *genever* and *schiedam* in the Netherlands, and *péquet* in Belgium. English gin, as well as a number of schnapps and brandies, are also flavoured with juniper berries. In addition, the berries are used to flavour Scandinavian beers.

JUNKET An ancient dessert made by setting milk with rennet, originally made using warm milk fresh from the cow and served with clotted cream. The rennet sets the milk to produce a product similar to set, unstrained yogurt. The milk for junket may be flavoured with rose water and sweetened, then sprinkled with a little cinnamon or nutmeg. Junket takes its name from the French *jonquette*, a type of rush basket used to drain curds, which suggests that the curds of the first junkets were drained before they were served, rather than being left as a light dessert with a jelly-like texture.

JUNK FOOD A 20th-century term for inferior highly processed, ready-prepared fast foods and snacks. Junk food does not provide a well-balanced snack or meal in terms of nutrition. Junk foods often have high fat and salt contents; sweet junk foods have a high sugar content. Synthetic flavourings, flavour enhancers and colours may be used to disguise poor-quality ingredients.

JURANÇON One of the best-known wines from south-western France, produced in limited quantities in the foothills of the Pyrenees from vineyards that are difficult to work because of their steepness. The white wine has been famous since the day it was used to moisten the lips of the newborn future Henri IV. It is made from local grape varieties (Petit Manseng, Gros-Manseng and Courbu) that, in ideal conditions, may be picked late and affected by 'noble rot' (see *noble rot*). There are two *appellations contrôlées*: Jurançon, a sweet wine, and Jurançon Sec, which is traditionally drunk young. The other Jurançon grapes are Camaralet and Lauzet.

JUS This French word is roughly equivalent to 'juice', but has more specific meanings in French cookery than the English word.

It is used primarily for the gravy of a roast, made by diluting the pan juices with water, clear stock or any other suitable liquid, and then boiling it until all the goodness in the pan has been absorbed into the stock. Dishes described as *au jus* are prepared or served with this gravy.

It is also used for a thickened or clear brown stock, especially veal stock (*jus de veau*).

Finally, it is used for the juice squeezed from raw vegetables or fruit (see *fruit juice*).

JUSSLÈRE A garnish for small cuts of meat, consisting of stuffed onions, braised lettuce and château potatoes, sometimes with carrots cut into neat shapes and glazed.

K

KALE Also known as collard or kail, this member of the cabbage family is dark green, with large, coarse leaves on heads that do not form hearts. Originating in Mediterranean countries, this is the predecessor of the firm-headed or hearted cabbage. Curly kale is more popular than the plain-leafed variety. It can be prepared and cooked in the same way as cabbage, with tough stalks trimmed off and discarded. The flavour resembles strong cabbage.

KALTSCHALE A Russian dessert consisting of a fresh fruit salad that has been macerated in wine and is covered with a purée of red fruit (strawberries, raspberries and redcurrants). It is served in a large bowl that traditionally rests on a dish of crushed ice. The word *kaltschale* is German, and its literal meaning is 'cold cup'.

RECIPE

kaltschale
Rub 1 kg (2¼ lb, 7 cups) strawberries and 250 g (9 oz, 2 cups) very ripe redcurrants through a sieve. Bring 1 litre (1¾ pints, 4⅓ cups) light sugar syrup and ½ bottle of champagne to the boil, then allow to cool. Add the syrup mixture to the fruit purée. Peel and remove the seeds or stones (pits) from several different fruits, such as melon or watermelon, apricots, peaches, pears or fresh pineapple. Cut them into thin slices and sprinkle with lemon juice. Place all the fruit in a large bowl and pour the liquid purée over it. Chill until ready to serve. Add some raspberries at the last moment.

KANGAROO A marsupial native to Australia. Kangaroo meat has long been eaten by Aborigines and it was shot as game in Australia during the 19th century. It went out of fashion until the latter part of the last century, when its lean, dark meat again attracted attention as an alternative to beef. Farmed kangaroo is available in a variety of prepared cuts. The meat is lean, close-textured and dark, with a full, rich flavour, similar to venison. Depending on the cut, kangaroo meat can be grilled (broiled) or pan-fried, roast, braised or stewed. When using dry cooking methods, it is important not to overcook the meat: marinating, barding or larding are good methods of keeping it moist.

KASHA Also known as *kacha*. An eastern European dish, often a type of porridge or gruel, made from crushed or powdered buckwheat. There are several ways of preparing it: the simplest is to boil it, then serve it as an accompaniment for a savoury main dish in the same way as rice. In Russia it is baked in the oven, mixed with butter, rolled out and shaped into small pancakes. These are served with soups or stews, possibly flavoured with cheese, eggs or mushrooms, or cooked au gratin. In Poland, *kasha* is also the name for buckwheat, sold crushed and roasted, and for a type of sweet pudding made either from hulled barley (cooked in milk and served with cream) or from semolina (served with melted butter).

RECIPES

Polish kasha with barley
Pick over 350 g (12 oz, 1⅓ cups) pearl barley and blanch in boiling water for 2 minutes. Bring 3 litres (5 pints, 13 cups) milk and 65 g (2½ oz, 5 tablespoons) butter to the boil, then add the barley. Bring to the boil, reduce the heat so that the

mixture simmers and cook stirring frequently until the barley is soft – about I hour. Take the pan off the heat and add 200 g (7 oz, I cup) butter. Cool for about 10 minutes before stirring in 6 lightly beaten eggs and 100 ml (4 fl oz, 7 tablespoons) soured (sour) cream. Pour the mixture into a buttered charlotte mould and cook in a preheated oven at 200°C (400°F, gas 6) until set and golden on top. Serve it in the mould with double (heavy) cream served separately.

Russian kasha

Crush 500 g (18 oz, 3¾ cups) fresh buckwheat and soak in sufficient warm water to make a thick paste. Season with salt and put it in a deep cake tin (pan) or charlotte mould (traditionally an earthenware pot is used). Bake in a preheated oven at 180°C (350°F, gas 4) for 2 hours. Remove the thick crust formed on the surface and pour the remaining soft paste into a dish. Add 65 g (2½ oz, 5 tablespoons) butter and mix well with a spatula. Spread the paste out on a greased surface, cover it with a board, then press it until it is about I cm (½ in) thick. Cut into shapes with a pastry (cookie) cutter and fry in clarified butter until golden brown. Serve with soup.

Russian kasha with Parmesan cheese

Prepare a *kasha* of buckwheat as described. Spread a thin layer of the soft paste over the bottom of a buttered gratin dish. Sprinkle with grated Parmesan cheese and a little melted butter, alternating the layers until all the ingredients are used up. Smooth the final layer of *kasha* carefully, then sprinkle with Parmesan cheese, top with melted butter and brown in a preheated oven at 230°C (450°F, gas 8). Serve melted butter separately.

KEBAB A dish consisting basically of small pieces of meat threaded on to skewers and grilled or roasted. It originated in Turkey and eventually spread to the Balkans and the Middle East. The name is a shortened form of the Turkish *şiş kebab*, *şiş* meaning skewer and *kebab* meaning roast meat. *Şiş* (or shish) kebab consists of cubes of marinated mutton threaded on to wooden or metal skewers, traditionally alternating with cubes of mutton fat, but the latter is often replaced by large pieces of belly of pork (fat pork). The skewered meat is grilled over hot embers and usually served with quarters of lemon, yogurt or soured (sour) cream. There are many variations of this dish: it may be made with or without vegetables (tomatoes, peppers, onions), or with veal, lamb or even buffalo, or meatballs. Sometimes the kebabs are slipped off the skewers and served on a bed of rice with chick peas, raw onions and a salad of chopped raw vegetables.

RECIPES

dagh kebab

Cut boneless veal into even-sized cubes. Also cut very firm small tomatoes into quarters and seed them. Cut some onions into quarters. Marinate all these ingredients in a little oil containing aromatic herbs. Thread the meat on to skewers alternating with the quarters of tomato and onion. Season, sprinkle with crumbled thyme and grill (broil) under a less fierce heat than for shish kebab. Serve with rice pilaf, a green salad or okra.

shish kebab

Cut some shoulder or leg of mutton into cubes. Marinate the meat for 30 minutes in a mixture of olive oil and lemon juice seasoned with pepper and salt, thyme, powdered bay leaf and a little finely chopped garlic. Cut an equal quantity of belly of pork (fat pork) into cubes and blanch them. Thread the mutton and pork alternately on to skewers and grill (broil) them under a very high heat, or, preferably, over charcoal. Serve with quarters of lemon and either a green salad or saffron rice.

KEDGEREE An English dish that came originally from India. The word comes from the Hindi word *khicari*, from Sanskrit *khiccā*, the origin of which is obscure. It consists of a mixture of rice, cooked flaked fish and hard-boiled (hard-cooked) eggs. The fish is usually smoked haddock, but it may be salmon or even turbot. Peas may be added, or the ingredients can be bound with a curry-flavoured béchamel sauce seasoned with cayenne pepper and nutmeg.

The original Indian dish, known as *kadgeri*, consists of rice garnished with onions, lentils and eggs. Fish was added by the British.

KEFALOTIRI This well-flavoured ewe's-milk cheese is made throughout Greece and Cyprus. A similar cheese sold outside Greece is often made with cow's milk and has a milder flavour.

KEFIR The fermented product of camel's milk, also made from cow's milk, goat's milk or sheep's milk, whole or skimmed, consumed mainly in the Caucasus. With the addition of a yeast known as 'kefir seed', it is matured in bottles.

Young kefir is frothy and has a rather sour taste. 'Strong kefir' (*kéfir fort*) is a fizzy drink with a certain amount of alcohol (2.5% after fermenting for 3 days) and a piquant flavour. Easy to digest and rich in protein, kefir has the reputation of being responsible for the long life of the inhabitants of the Caucasus.

KELLOGG, WILLIAM KEITH American industrialist (born Battle Creek, Michigan, 1860; died Battle Creek, 1951). He worked as an assistant to his brother, who was a well-known nutritionist and the director of a hospital specializing in nutritional disorders. In 1894 he discovered a process for making flakes out of grains of maize (corn). These could be eaten as part of the vegetarian diet recommended by the Seventh Day Adventists, to which sect both brothers belonged. In 1898 the process was industrialized and in 1906 a company was formed to market cornflakes. Ever since then, they have been regarded as an integral part of both the English and American breakfast.

KETCHUP A sweet-and-sour condiment with one flavour predominating, usually based on tomatoes, but sometimes on mushrooms or walnuts. Tomato ketchup is very popular in Britain and North America and is the variety usually sold in France; it is used to flavour meat sauces or served with fish, hamburgers, eggs, rice and pasta. It is made from tomato purée (paste), vinegar, sugar and spices.

KETTLE A container with a spout, handle and lid, used for boiling water. Kettles are made of aluminium, stainless steel, chrome-plated copper, enamel, Pyrex, plastic and other materials. They may have steam whistles, which blow when the water boils.

Ancient kettles, known in French as *coquemars*, were often very large and were made of earthenware or, more usually, copper. These are now used only as ornaments.

A milk kettle or boiler is a cylindrical pot used for boiling milk. It has a perforated lid designed to stop the milk boiling over. See also *Fish kettle*.

KHOLODETZ A Russian dish of jellied meats. The meats – generally beef, veal and chicken, or perhaps pig's trotters (feet) and knuckle of veal – are cooked in stock, placed in a dish garnished with slices of carrot, tarragon and dill, then covered with aspic. When the aspic has set, the *kholodetz* is unmoulded and served with gherkins, plums or pears macerated in vinegar.

KID A young goat. Only the very young males (six weeks to four months old) are slaughtered for meat, as the females are reserved for milk production. They are available from mid-March until the beginning of May. Kid's meat is insipid and rather soft, similar to that of milk lamb. It is generally eaten roasted and, in most recipes (particularly in Corsica and Spain), well seasoned and spiced.

KIDNEYS A type of red offal (organ meat). Ox and calves' kidneys are multilobed, while pigs' and sheep's kidneys are shaped rather like a haricot (navy) bean. The kidneys of young animals, such as calves, heifers and lambs, have the most delicate flavour; pigs' kidneys are rather strongly flavoured, while those of the ox and sheep tend to be tough as well as strongly flavoured (it is best to boil the latter for a few minutes and drain them before preparing them for cooking).

In all cases, the transparent membrane that surrounds the kidneys must be removed so that they do not shrink when cooked. Any blood vessels, together with the central core of fat, must also be removed. When grilled (broiled) or sautéed, they should be served when still pink, otherwise they may become tough. They can also be braised in a medium oven. Calves' kidneys are particularly good when fried (whole or sliced) without trimming the surrounding fat, which gradually melts; they are ready when golden brown.

Cocks' kidneys, which are now rare, feature with cockscombs in several classic garnishes.

RECIPES

Calves' Kidneys
calf's kidney à la bonne femme
Fry 50 g (2 oz, ⅓ cup) coarsely diced streaky (slab) bacon and 4 small onions in butter in a small flame-proof casserole. Remove the bacon and onions from the casserole, and in the same butter toss a whole calf's kidney with most of the outer fat removed, just to stiffen it. Fry 12 small new potatoes in butter until they are three-quarters cooked, then add the diced bacon, the onions and the kidney, and season with salt and pepper. Continue the cooking in a preheated oven at 240°C (475°F, gas 9) for about 15 minutes. Just before serving, sprinkle with 3 tablespoons veal stock. Serve the kidney in the casserole. It may be garnished with mushrooms tossed in butter if desired.

calves' kidneys Ali-baba
Remove most of the surrounding fat from 4 small calves' kidneys, season with salt and pepper, and coat them with strong mustard. Arrange in a lightly buttered ovenproof dish and cook in a preheated oven at 220°C (425°F, gas 7) for 7–8 minutes.

Meanwhile, put 500 ml (17 fl oz, 2 cups) double (heavy) cream into a saucepan, together with some grated lemon rind and ½ teaspoon ground pepper. Bring to the boil, add the kidneys and cook very gently for a further 8 minutes. Drain the kidneys, put on a plate, cut each into 8 pieces and arrange in a hot serving dish. Pour the juices that have collected on the plate into the sauce and put the pan over a high heat. Finish the sauce with a few drops of brandy and finally beat in 75 g (3 oz, 6 tablespoons) butter, cut into small pieces. Adjust the seasoning and pour the sauce over the kidneys. Serve very hot.

calves' kidneys Collioure
Braise 4 calves' kidneys in a covered sauté pan on a bed of vegetables. When they are half-cooked, remove them from the pan and trim off the fat. Continue to cook the vegetables until they begin to brown, then deglaze the pan with 60 ml (2 fl oz, ¼ cup) white wine and boil down to reduce the cooking liquid by half. Put the kidneys into a small pan with 40 g (1½ oz, 3 tablespoons) butter, some chopped shallots and 12 well-pounded anchovy fillets. Simmer until cooked. Strain the cooking juices over the kidneys and heat through for a few moments. Serve sprinkled with chopped parsley.

calves' kidneys with chicken livers
Skin 4 calves' kidneys and remove the fat. Halve them and chop into small pieces. Slice 12 chicken livers. Using a tinned copper saucepan or a stainless steel saucepan with a copper base, fry the kidneys and the chicken livers in a knob of butter for about 5 minutes, taking care not to let them brown. While they are still pink, flame them with 5 tablespoons Armagnac and set aside, keeping them hot.

Pour 150 ml (¼ pint, ⅔ cup) port and 500 ml (17 fl oz, 2 cups) red Gigondas wine into the cooking liquor. Boil down to reduce, then thicken with 15 g (½ oz, 1 tablespoon) beurre manié. When the sauce is ready (about 15 minutes), strain it. Arrange the kidneys and chicken livers in the serving dish, then coat with the sauce, adjust the seasoning and sprinkle with chopped parsley.

grilled calf's kidney

Remove some of the fat from a calf's kidney, slit it lengthways without cutting it through completely, and keep it open and flat by threading it on to 2 small metal skewers. Season with salt and pepper, brush lightly with oil and cook rapidly under a hot grill (broiler). Serve with Bercy butter, maître d'hôtel butter or anchovy butter.

roast calf's kidney with mustard

Remove some of the fat from a calf's kidney, season with salt and pepper, and spread with mustard. Place it in a small greased flameproof casserole and roast it in a preheated oven at 240°C (475°F, gas 9) for about 15 minutes. Drain the kidney and keep it hot. Pour the fat from the casserole, add 100 ml (4 fl oz, 7 tablespoons) Madeira and boil down to reduce by half. Off the heat, mix in 1 tablespoon mustard, then heat and whisk vigorously without boiling. Replace the kidney in the casserole and heat through before serving.

sautéed calf's kidney with Madeira and three mustards

Remove some of the fat from a calf's kidney, season with salt and pepper, and cook for 10–15 minutes in a small pan with a little oil and butter (this is known as cooking à la coque). Drain all the fat away and flame the kidney with a generous liqueur glass of young good-quality Armagnac. Drain the kidney and slice it thinly on a plate; keep hot.

Pour 100 ml (4 fl oz, 7 tablespoons) Madeira into the pan and boil to reduce the liquid by half. Pour any kidney juices on the plate into the sauce, boil rapidly for a few minutes, add the kidney and place the pan over a very low heat. Do not let it boil again.

Blend 50 g (2 oz, ¼ cup) butter with a mixture of Dijon, Champagne and Bordeaux mustards. Add this mixture, a little at a time, to the pan, stirring constantly, so that the sauce becomes smooth and creamy. This is the most critical process in the whole preparation and should be carried out away from the heat. Serve the kidney with sautéed potatoes.

sautéed calf's kidney with wholegrain mustard ♦

Finely chop 1 large shallot and place in a pan with 1 bay leaf and a sprig of thyme. Add 200 ml (7 fl oz, ¾ cup dry white wine) and boil until reduced by half. Add 500 ml (17 fl oz, 2 cups) veal stock and 200 ml (7 fl oz, ¾ cup) double (heavy) cream. Reduce until the sauce has a coating consistency. Stir in 1 teaspoon Dijon mustard and strain the

sauce through a fine sieve. Then stir in ½ teaspoon wholegrain Meaux mustard. Taste for seasoning and dot the surface of the sauce with a little butter to prevent a skin from forming, then set aside in a bain marie to keep hot.

Remove the fat from 1 calf's kidney, slice it in half lengthways and trim away any core or remaining fat, then cut the kidney halves crossways into thick slices. Season with salt and pepper. Brown the pieces of kidney in a hot oil in a frying pan for 2 minutes on each side, then transfer to a sieve and leave to drain for about 10 minutes so that any blood drips away.

Reheat the kidneys in the sauce without boiling. Serve sprinkled with snipped chives. Serve with a potato galette, gratin dauphinois or tagliatelle and buttered spinach.

other recipes See *Bercy, bordelaise.*

Ox Kidneys

ox kidney with lardons

Slit an ox kidney (or preferably a heifer's kidney) in half and take out the central core. Cut the kidney into thin slices. Sprinkle 250 g (9 oz, 3 cups) washed sliced mushrooms with a little lemon juice. Cut 200 g (7 oz) rindless streaky (slab) bacon into thin strips; chop 2 shallots. Melt 25 g (1 oz, 2 tablespoons) butter in a sauté pan, add the sliced kidney and brown quickly over a high heat. Then add the mushrooms, the bacon lardons and the shallots, and cook until all the ingredients are lightly browned. Season with salt and pepper, lower the heat, cover the pan and cook for about 20 minutes. Then add a small glass of Madeira and 150 ml (¼ pint, ⅔ cup) crème fraîche and reduce the sauce over a high heat. Pour the preparation into a serving dish and sprinkle with chopped parsley.

Pigs' Kidneys

preparation of pigs' kidneys

To reduce the rather strong taste of these kidneys, skin them, cut them open without separating the halves, take out the white central core, wash them under running water, cover them with milk and leave them in a cool place for 3–4 hours. They can then be grilled (broiled) or sautéed (with bacon lardons or mushrooms) in the same way as calves' kidneys.

Lambs' Kidneys

lambs' kidneys à l'anglaise

Remove the skin of the kidneys and cut them in half without separating the halves completely. Remove the white central core and tubes. Thread the kidneys on skewers, pushing the skewer through each half of the kidney to keep them open. Season with salt and pepper, brush with melted butter and (if desired) roll them in fresh breadcrumbs. Grill

Sautéed calf's kidney with wholegrain mustard.

(broil) the kidneys under a high heat for about 3 minutes on each side, then arrange in a long dish with grilled rashers (slices) of bacon, small boiled new potatoes and fresh watercress. Put a pat of maître d'hôtel butter on each half kidney.

lambs' kidneys sautéed with mushrooms

Clean and slice 8 large button mushrooms and sprinkle with lemon juice. Clean 8 kidneys, cut them in half, season with salt and pepper, and sauté them quickly in very hot butter. (Do not overcook; ensure that they remain pink.) Drain and keep hot in a serving dish.

Sauté the sliced mushrooms in the same butter, drain them and arrange around the kidneys. Keep hot. Pour 250 ml (8 fl oz, I cup) stock into the pan and boil down to reduce by one-third; add 100 ml (4 fl oz, 7 tablespoons) Madeira, port, champagne or Riesling and again reduce by one-third. Thicken with I teaspoon arrowroot, then add 40 g (1½ oz, 3 tablespoons) butter. Pour the sauce over the kidneys and sprinkle with chopped parsley.

other recipes See *brochette, omelette (filled omelettes), steak and kidney pie, Turbigo.*

KIELBASA A term used for any fresh sausage in Poland, but also used elsewhere to describe a spiced, garlic-seasoned sausage, sold fresh, smoked or fully cooked.

KILKA A Russian fish similar to the sprat, three species of which are fished intensively in the Caspian Sea. It is sometimes eaten fresh, but is usually frozen at sea and then canned in oil, salted or marinated. It is served as a cold hors d'oeuvre with slices of lemon.

KINGFISH A member of the *Trevallie* family, the yellow tail (*Seriola grandis*) is the best of the Australian species and a prime angling fish, growing to a maximum length of 2.5 m (8 ft). It has fine yellow fins as well as the yellow tail, a blue-black back and a stripe along its body. Steaks are cut from larger fish, which can be coarse and dry if too large; the smaller fish are best and can be baked whole.

KIPPER Smoked herring, prepared by splitting and gutting, then salting the fish in brine before smoking, traditionally over oak. This British speciality originates from Northumberland, where the method of smoking was first used on kippers in the 1840s. Before then, 'kipper' was the term used to describe a male salmon that had just finished spawning, while 'kippering' was the term for the method used to smoke salmon. The kipper replaced the red herring in popularity, the latter being a Yarmouth speciality, highly salted and smoked until dry, a condition in which they kept well.

Kippers are traditionally prepared by jugging – by placing in a tall jug (pitcher) and having freshly boiled water poured over them. They are left to cook gently in the hot water for about 10 minutes, then drained and served. Poaching for about 5 minutes in simmering water is another method and kippers can also be grilled. They are usually served topped with a small pat of butter and accompanied by thinly sliced bread and butter. See *Herring.*

KIR Originally, a Burgundy mixture of dry white Aligoté wine and cassis (the blackcurrant liqueur for which Burgundy is famous). Referred to as *vin blanc cassis*, it became associated with the late Canon Félix Kir, a hero of the French Resistance, who, as Mayor of Dijon, insisted on it being the only drink offered at official receptions. Kir Royale was originally made with champagne, but like ordinary Kir is now based on any dry sparkling wine. Kir Communard is red wine plus cassis; in the Beaujolais region this mix is known as a *rince cochon.*

KIRSCH A white spirit (*alcool blanc*) and a true fruit brandy distilled from cherries; it should not be confused with the sweetened cherry brandies made by most of the great liqueur establishments. The type of cherry used depended originally on where the distillate was made, but nowadays firms reputed for their kirsch, such as those in Alsace, Franche-Comté and the Black Forest in Germany, may have to buy in fruit to supplement the local supplies. The kernels of the cherries are included in the 'mash'. As with many spirits that are widely used for culinary purposes, there are less expensive types of kirsch, which are used for flaming pancakes, incorporating with whipped cream and fillings for pastries and cakes, and in confectionery. The top-quality liqueurs are particularly appreciated as a *digestif.*

RECIPE

apples with cream and kirsch

Peel and core crisp sweet dessert (eating) apples, sprinkle them with lemon juice and cook them in boiling vanilla-flavoured syrup until transparent. Drain and leave to cool. Mix very cold fresh double (heavy) or whipping cream with a quarter of its volume of very cold kirsch, then whip until the whisk leaves a trail. Pour this over the apples.

KISS See *baiser.*

KISSEL A Russian dessert made from sweetened red fruit purée thickened with arrowroot or flour and sometimes flavoured with white wine. Kissel can be served warm or cold with crème fraîche.

RECIPE

kissel with cranberries

Put I kg (2¼ lb, 9 cups) cranberries through a vegetable mill. Mix with 2–2.5 litres (3½–4¼ pints, 9–11 cups) water, pour the mixture through a cloth into a bowl and wring out the cloth to extract the maximum quantity of juice. Alternatively, purée the fruit and water in a blender. Mix 50 g (2 oz, ½ cup) potato flour, cornflour (cornstarch) or tapioca into the juice and pour into a saucepan. Add 200 g (7 oz, 1 cup) caster (superfine) sugar and bring to the boil. Stir constantly until the mixture thickens and becomes transparent. Pour into a fruit bowl and serve warm or cold.

KISSING CRUST In baking, the kissing crust is the pale, slightly underdone, portion of a loaf of bread that was in contact with the loaf next to it during baking.

KITCHEN A room set aside for the preparation of food. The kitchen as a separate room in a house first appeared in about the 5th century BC, but in ancient times it was also associated with religious practices: the hearth where meat and vegetables were cooked was also the altar of the cult of the household gods. Roman kitchens in great residences were particularly well equipped, including a water tank, sink, cavities made in worktops for pounding spices and bronze tripods.

In chateaux in medieval France, the kitchen was one of the most important rooms and the scene of constant activity. Very spacious and endowed with one or several gigantic chimneys, particularly in abbeys (Fontevrault) and palaces (Avignon, Dijon), it extended into numerous annexes (including bread store, fruit store and cupbearer's room). In middleclass houses and farms, on the other hand, the kitchen was usually the communal room where guests were received, cooking was done and meals were eaten.

In the reign of Louis XV, when the culinary art underwent a true renewal, the kitchen of a noble house could be luxurious, as the Abbé Coyer proves (in *Bagatelles morales*, 1755, quoted by Franklin): 'I am dragged into kitchens and made to admire the taste of the master; it is the only room in the house which is pointed out to the curious. Elegance, solidity, cleanliness, conveniences of all kinds, nothing is missing from this vast workshop of Comus, a modern masterpiece where architecture has enjoyed displaying its resources.'

In the 19th century, technical progress (improved utensils and, above all, the range) transformed the kitchen into a veritable *laboratoire* (as great chefs called it). A room distinctly separated from the rest of the house, possessing a service entrance, it was sometimes situated in the basement (particularly in Victorian England) or at the end of a long corridor. In middle-class homes, it was the domain of the housewife, as epitomized by the German *hausfrau* in the cliché of the 'three Ks': *Kinder Kirche* and *Küche* (children, church, kitchen).

The 20th century saw progress in lighting and heating, improvements in interior decoration, and the introduction of refrigerators, freezers, dishwashers and various cooking appliances, including microwave ovens. For many people, the kitchen remains the symbol of the home.

KITCHEN EQUIPMENT *batterie de cuisine* All utensils and accessories used to prepare and cook food. Of widely varying shapes and materials, such utensils range from skewers, which are as old as the invention of fire, to the latest applications of modern technology.

■ **Origins** We know very little about the first kitchen utensils. The Egyptians, the Assyrians and the Persians principally used earthenware and bronze vessels, big-bellied in shape, with and without handles. They also used the spit and, for baking cakes and biscuits (cookies), they had baking dishes rather like those we use nowadays.

The Jews did not generally use earthenware vessels for cooking purposes; most of their pots and pans were made of metal. To extract the meat from the big pots in which food destined to be offered to God was prepared, they used a big two-pronged fork, the forerunner of the modern table fork, which did not make its appearance until the 17th century.

The Greeks, for their culinary preparations, used greatly improved bronze, iron or silver vessels. They also had some in earthenware. Almost all these vessels were conical and not very deep. They had lids and handles or detachable rings.

Among the principal kitchen utensils used by the Greeks was the *chytra*, a kind of earthenware pan used for cooking meats and stews. It may have been in this utensil that the famous Spartan broths were prepared. Or perhaps they were made in the *kakkabi*, a fairly large three-legged pot. The Greeks also had another pot, which can be considered as the prototype of the earthenware casserole. Filled with fruit that probably had been cooked in wine and sweetened with honey, this dish was carried to the altar of Dionysus, on the third day of the feast of Anthesteria, the famous festival in honour of the god.

The Greeks also had bronze casseroles, which resembled those now in use. For cooking pieces of meat and fish, they had a frying pan called a *teganon*. In order to place all these metal or earthenware receptacles on the fire, the Greeks used a triangular support, the tripod.

Kitchen utensils used by the Romans were similar to those of the Greeks, and it was Greek cooks who brought the art of cooking to Rome. The Romans, who were sensual, voluptuous people, with a great love of luxury in all things, made kitchen utensils not only of bronze but also of silver. Among the treasures of Bosco-Reale, which are kept in the Louvre in Paris, various kitchen utensils of this type can be seen. Kitchen utensils used by the Romans included the *clibanus*, an earthenware utensil with holes pierced in it, used for cooking various dishes, mainly pastry, in hot ashes; *craticula*, a grill for cooking meat and fish on the glowing embers of a fire; and the *apala*, a dish with cavities of varying sizes, which was used for cooking eggs.

The Gauls and the Gallo-Romans had earthenware and metal kitchen utensils somewhat similar to those of the Greeks and Romans. The Celts knew nothing of the refinements of the sumptuous cookery of Imperial

Rome and their pots and pans were rudimentary. With the coming of the Merovingian era, kitchen utensils began to improve. Some specimens of the magnificent bronze vessels in which the food was prepared have survived and can be seen in museums.

From reading Charlemagne's *Capitularies*, it seems evident that in succeeding centuries kitchen utensils were improved still further. After the Crusades, a great number of richly worked metal utensils – ewers, salvers, cauldrons – were brought to Europe and served as models for the artisans of the West in the manufacture of magnificent utensils.

Among the many utensils used was the horsehair sieve, or tammy; a large strainer with a handle, which was used for draining foods; iron hooks on which food was hung; pots and kettles of all sizes; baking tins (pans); saucepans; frying pans (skillets); a large metal vessel used as a water container; a pot with a handle and a long curved spout; funnels, mostly in copper; a grater used for grating nutmeg and cheese; gridirons; mortars; spice-grinders; various ladles; long-bladed knives; and various other utensils that are still in use in the present day.

■ **Modern times** Many of the basic utensils we know today already existed during the Renaissance, and about two centuries ago, Brillat-Savarin, who followed the latest developments of his era very closely, owned 'an economical cooking pot, a roasting shell, a pendulum spit roaster and a steamer'. Since then, technical improvements and the emergence of new materials (not to mention the imagination of manufacturers) have led to great variety in modern kitchen equipment.

Electrical appliances have completely transformed professional and domestic kitchens. Food mixers, blenders and food processors replace a battery of individual pieces of equipment. At a domestic level, smaller households and a less formal approach to food, meals and cooking has changed the type of food preparation carried out. This has led to a reduction in the number of items of equipment and, in general, the use of versatile appliances, pots, pans and dishes that can be adapted for many techniques or to prepare a variety of dishes.

KITCHEN SCALES An instrument used for measuring weight, essential for weighing ingredients and keeping to the correct proportions, especially in pastry making. In home cooking, the traditional balance with two pans and a series of weights was superseded by spring-balance scales. Modern electronic kitchen scales weigh with accuracy to 5 grams.

KIWANO Fruit of a plant from the *Cucurbitaceae* family, originally from South Africa. Also known as 'horned melon' or 'horned cucumber' after the little spines on its skin, the kiwano has a taste reminiscent of cucumber and melon. It is eaten cold or its flesh can be pulped and the juice then drunk.

KIWI FRUIT A fruit about the size of a large egg, with a greenish-brown hairy skin. The plant is a climber and belongs to the genus *Actinidia*. It originated in China, but is now cultivated chiefly in New Zealand (hence the name) and also in California, western France and Israel. The flesh is pale green, highly perfumed and juicy, with a slightly acidic taste. The fruit is ripe when soft to the touch. It is used in various ways: halved and eaten from the skin as a dessert; peeled and cut into cubes or slices for fruit salads and tarts; and as a garnish for roast quail, baked mackerel or fried pork chops. It is also an ingredient in a sweet-and-sour sauce served with cold meat or fish.

RECIPES

fruit salad with kiwi fruit
Choose the fruit according to the season. Divide oranges and grapefruits into segments, then peel and remove the pith. Peel, core and slice apples and pears, and sprinkle with lemon juice. Peel peaches and melon and cut into cubes; sprinkle the peaches with lemon juice. Hull strawberries and raspberries. Peel and slice the kiwi fruit, which should represent a quarter of the total volume of fruit.

Place all the fruit (except for the raspberries) in a large salad bowl, sprinkle with sugar and moisten with kirsch or another fruit-based liqueur. Leave in a cool place until ready to serve. Add the raspberries at the last moment.

The whole strawberries can be replaced by strawberry purée: put the fruit through a blender, sieve the purée, sweeten with sugar and pour it over the other fruit just before serving.

pork chops with kiwi fruit
Fry 4 pork chops in butter. Meanwhile peel 8 kiwi fruit, cut them into thick slices or quarters, and sprinkle with a little lemon juice. Drain the chops and keep them hot in the serving dish. Add the fruit to the frying pan, cover the pan and heat in the pan juices. Arrange the fruit around the chops. Deglaze the pan with 100 ml (4 fl oz, 7 tablespoons) pineapple juice and an equal quantity of stock. Boil down to reduce the sauce to a thick syrup. Add a generous pinch of pepper and pour over the chops.

KLÖSSE A German and Austrian dish consisting of spiced dumplings made from a mixture of flour, breadcrumbs or potato purée, eggs, milk and, sometimes, chopped ham. The dumplings are poached in boiling water and served on their own with melted butter and fried breadcrumbs or used as a garnish for soups or dishes in a sauce. A similar Polish dish, *klouskis*, consists of dumplings made from a mixture of flour, eggs, sugar and yeast, which are poached, coated with noisette butter and served as a dessert.

RECIPE

klösse à la viennoise
Remove the crust from 550 g (19 oz) brown bread, cut the crumb into small dice and soak the diced

bread in boiling milk. Cook 175 g (6 oz, 1 cup) chopped onions in 15 g (½ oz, 1 tablespoon) butter in a covered frying pan until soft. Add the onions to the bread, together with 1 tablespoon chopped chervil, 1 tablespoon chopped tarragon and 250 g (9 oz, 1½ cups) chopped ham. Bind with 1 tablespoon flour and 3 lightly beaten eggs, and season with salt, pepper and nutmeg. Divide the mixture into 50 g (2 oz) pieces and roll them into balls. Coat with flour and poach for about 12 minutes in a large pan of salted water. Fry some fine breadcrumbs in butter. Drain the dumplings and sprinkle them with the fried breadcrumbs.

KNACKWURST A type of fresh German sausage similar to a frankfurter, but shorter and thicker. It is made with 50% lean pork, 30% beef and 20% fat pork, finely minced (ground) and flavoured with cumin and parsley. Saltpetre is added to give it a pinkish colour and the sausage is eaten poached or grilled (brioled). The name is derived from the German *knacken* (to make a cracking sound), referring to the sound made when the sausage is bitten into.

KNEADING The process by which a mixture or dough is made smoother and, sometimes, more elastic. In bread doughs or other yeast doughs, made using strong flour with a high gluten content, kneading develops the gluten in the flour. This makes the dough tough and elastic, trapping gas produced by fermenting yeast and making the risen dough light in texture. Yeast doughs are usually kneaded by applying a firm pressing, turning and stretching action with the hand. They are usually kneaded for about 10 minutes, until quite springy. Light, brief kneading from a few seconds to a minute is enough to make a soft baking powder dough smooth, for preparing scones or soda bread. Over-kneading this type of dough will toughen it and spoil its texture. Pasta dough and similar stiff mixtures are kneaded firmly and for almost as long as yeast dough, until smooth.

KNEADING TROUGH The large wooden trough in which bread dough was kneaded. In the 19th century it was replaced in the bakery trade by the mechanical kneader. The latter is made of stainless steel and the dough is continuously stirred by rotating metal arms. Domestic electric food mixers and food processors have special attachments for kneading dough. Some electric hand mixers are fitted with attachments suitable for kneading light and semi-liquid dough or batter, but their motors are not powerful enough for thick doughs.

KNIFE A cutting instrument with a handle and a blade. The part of the blade that fits into the handle is called the 'tang' and is encircled with a thick band of steel called a 'bolster'. Between the tang and the blade there is a projection, the guard or rocker, which prevents the blade from touching the table surface when the knife is lying flat. When a knife has no bolster, the blade is held in place by two plates that form the handle. Before stainless steel came into general use, the blades were made of carbon steel, except for fruit knives and fish knives, which were made of silver. Table knives match the style of the forks and spoons.

The ancestor of the knife was a sharpened piece of flint, and the first blades were made of bronze and later of iron. In Greek and Roman times, knives were luxury articles, but were already fairly similar to modern knives. Until the end of the 16th century, knives were used both for cutting and for spearing food, particularly meat, and to cut bread. A knife was a personal object that the host would not necessarily make available to his guests. It was therefore worn on the belt. The colour of the handle could vary according to the time of year (ivory for Easter, ebony for Lent). The first round-ended knives appeared around 1630 as the social conventions of the time demanded that the knife should no longer be used as a toothpick. Handles were made of wood, hard stone, horn, shell or metal, and were often decorated with grotesque figures or fantastic animals. Later, they were made of gold and silver plate, and sometimes even of porcelain or china, especially in the 18th century. In the 17th century table knives began to differ according to their use.

Nowadays, a standard formal set of serving knives includes knives for cutting meat, for serving fish, for serving cheese (curved with a double-pointed end) and for serving cakes. Bread knives have teeth along one edge like a saw. There are also electric knives with sawlike edges that are used for cutting meat. In a traditional formal setting, each person at the table has a large knife (or table knife), sometimes a steak knife (with a serrated or special cutting edge), and small knives of various types according to the type of dish being served (grapefruit, fish, cheese, fruit or dessert). Butter knives are specially designed for spreading and have blunt edges and a rounded end.

■ **Kitchen knives** A set of knives is as personal to a chef as an instrument is to a musician; their weight, balance and shape are all important features. A standard chef's set comprises the following main items, many of which are also likely to be found in a domestic kitchen.

• ALL-PURPOSE KNIFE The smallest and most frequently used kitchen knife, with a narrow pointed blade, used for peeling vegetables and fruit and many other tasks.

• BONING KNIFE Used mostly by butchers but also by cooks, this is a small knife with a short blade that is wide near the handle and sharply pointed at the end.

• CARVING KNIFE Large, with a long, wide, sharply pointed blade.

• CHEF'S KITCHEN KNIFE With a very wide, stiff, sharply pointed blade, for carving, slicing, shredding and chopping.

• CHOPPING KNIFE With a heavy, strong, thick blade for breaking up and crushing bones and chopping meat.

• FILLETING KNIFE With a long, flexible, sharply

pointed blade for filleting fish.

• HAM KNIFE With a long, flexible blade rounded at the end, which may be smooth, pitted or fluted, for carving ham and cold or hot meat.

• SLICING KNIFE Specially designed for vegetables.

Various small tools complete the set: a potato peeler (or parer) for peeling vegetables and fruit; a tomato knife, with a very fine saw edge; an oyster knife, with a short thick pointed blade protected by a guard; a knife for scraping lemon zest; and a cannelle knife for fluting. Knives used in pâtisserie include a long round-ended spreading knife; a palette knife (spatula), pliable with no cutting edge, for lifting tarts and pancakes; and a saw-edged knife for cutting biscuits (cookies), cakes and brioches.

Many knives are designed specially for use in commercial cookery and butchery.

• CHEVALIER For drawing the sinews from meat.

• CHIP KNIFE With small perpendicular blades spaced at regular intervals, used for cutting potato slices into chips (French fries). (If the blades are closer together, it is a julienne knife.)

• CHOPPER With a very thick, rectangular blade for breaking up bones.

• CLEAVER With an almost rectangular blade, fine and rounded, used particularly for cutting up saddles and loins of mutton and pork.

• FISH KNIFE With a serrated edge for cutting large pieces.

• FROZEN FOOD KNIFE A strong knife or saw for frozen foods, with a thick serrated blade, irregularly indented on one or both sides, for sawing through frozen foods.

• LARDON KNIFE For cutting fat into bards and lardons, fitted with milled screws for adjusting the thickness of the slices.

• MEAT KNIFE In the form of a spatulate chopper, for separating minced (ground) meat and sausage meat.

• ONION KNIFE Possibly with a transparent plastic hood over the blade to prevent tears.

• SALAMI KNIFE With a saw-edged blade at an angle to the handle, used for thinly slicing all firm-textured charcuterie.

• SMOKED-SALMON KNIFE With a long, flexible, serrated blade.

KNOCK BACK (PUNCH DOWN) To briefly and lightly knead a yeast dough after the first proving or rising. By folding the dough over on to itself several times, the gas is knocked out and the dough flattened. It is then shaped and put to rise in its finished shape. This process is sometimes carried out twice during the preparation of the dough and improves the final result. Fast action easy-blend dried yeasts are used to make one-stage doughs, without any knocking back and a single rising process in the finished shape.

KNÖDEL Also known as *knödl*. A type of sweet or savoury dumpling found all over eastern Europe. In Alsace and Germany, *knödel* are small dumplings made from pasta dough and served with cream or melted butter. The dough may be enriched with bone marrow to produce *markknödel* or with puréed liver to form *leberknödel*. They are served as a hot entrée or as a garnish. In the Czech Republic and Slovakia, *knödel* may be made from breadcrumbs soaked in milk, from potato purée, or from yeast dough, mixed with chopped onions and meat.

The size and shape varies: some *knödel* are formed into sausages, which are poached and then sliced. The Austrian *zwetschenknödel* are large plum fritters eaten as a dessert. Another type of dessert *knödel* consists of squares of dough filled with stewed cherries or apricots, formed into dumplings and poached in boiling water. These are served with melted butter and sugar, and may be sprinkled with poppy seeds or chopped almonds.

KNORR, CARL HEINRICH German industrialist (born Meedorf, 1800; died Heilbronn, 1875). His second marriage, to a wealthy lady farmer, enabled him to set up, in 1838, a small industrial plant for roasting coffee and chicory. After his death, his two sons expanded the business and began to manufacture pea, lentil, haricot (navy) bean and sago flours, which were marketed in packets. These were the precursors of today's packet (dehydrated) soups.

KNUCKLE Also known as shin, that part of the leg of an animal carcass lying below the thigh or the shoulder. In France, shin of beef is called the *gîte-gîte*, and shin of mutton corresponds to the *manche de gigot* (see *gigot*). In veal, the fore or hind knuckle is gelatinous and lean; the bone is rich in marrow. Boned and cubed, it is added to sautéed and braised dishes and blanquettes; whole, it can be cooked in stock with vegetables or form part of a thick meat and vegetable soup. *Osso bucco* is made from slices of veal knuckle. Pork knuckle, or *jambonneau*, can be roasted, braised or boiled like a ham, but it is less tender. The fore knuckle can be braised, boiled or cut up and stewed; a semi-salted pork knuckle is an excellent addition to sauerkraut, meat and vegetable soups, and dishes that require a slightly salty flavour.

RECIPE

knuckle of veal à la provençale ♦
Cut about 800 g (1¾ lb) veal knuckle (shank) into slices 4 cm (1½ in) thick and season with salt and pepper. Brown in a sauté pan in 3 tablespoons very hot olive oil. Chop 150 g (5 oz) onions finely and fry until golden in the sauté pan; add 575 g (1¼ lb) peeled, seeded and coarsely chopped tomatoes – or 500 g (18 oz) tomatoes and 1 tablespoon tomato purée (paste) – together with 150 ml (¼ pint, ⅔ cup) dry white wine and a bouquet garni. Stir well, then add 100 ml (4 fl oz, 7 tablespoons) stock or consommé and 2 crushed

Knuckle of veal à la provençale.

garlic cloves. Cover the pan and cook gently for about 1¼ hours, then remove the lid and reduce the liquid for 10 minutes. Adjust the seasoning.

KNUSPER A large cinnamon-flavoured shortcake covered with chopped almonds and crushed lump sugar. An Austrian speciality, it is cut into squares or rectangles and eaten with tea or coffee. The name is derived from the German *knusprig*, meaning 'crunchy'.

KOFTA The term for a meatball or small meat patty which may be round, oval or sausage-shaped and large or small. They can be grilled (broiled), fried or baked, served plain or simmered in a sauce. Dishes of this type are made in North Africa, in Mediterranean countries, through Central Europe, Asia and India. *Kofta* is the general term and the one commonly used for Indian dishes, but a variety of names are used – in Greece they are known as *kefte* (or *kefthedes* in the plural); in Turkey they may be *kofte*; and in Morocco *kefta*.

Whatever the name, the mixture is likely to be finely minced (ground) meat, mixed with onions and spices. Grains, such as cooked rice, may be added to the mixture and egg may be used to bind it. The *kofta* may be stuffed; for example, a piece of cheese may be placed in the middle of the mixture as it is shaped, and Indian *nargisi kofta* consists of a spicy minced lamb mixture shaped around a hard-boiled (hard-cooked) egg.

Vegetable *kofta* are also made; for example, in Indian cookery there are excellent versions made with cooked pulses or with vegetables, such as cooked peas.

KOHLRABI A vegetable of the cabbage family whose fleshy stalk swells at the base like a turnip. The round swollen stem is the edible part. Tender when young, kohlrabi is prepared like turnip or celeriac and may be eaten raw or cooked.

KONBU Kelp, an edible seaweed frequently used in Japanese cookery. The large black leaves are dried; when rehydrated, they are widely used, for example, to flavour *dashi*, the light stock, or as a flavouring in many dishes. Kelp is also finely shredded and cooked or marinated, then served as an accompaniment or garnish.

KORMA A mildly spiced Indian dish thickened with poppy seeds and/or nuts, such as cashew nuts or almonds. Yogurt and/or cream enrich the sauce. Cubes of lean meat or chicken may be the main ingredients for a korma.

KOSHER Describing food that is permitted to be eaten according to Jewish dietary laws (the word is Hebrew meaning 'permitted', 'ritually correct'). Fruit and vegetables can be eaten without further preparation, but there are strict rules governing the eating of meat. The Old Testament distinguishes between *tahor* (authorized meat) and *tame* (prohibited meat). Rabbinical proscriptions forbid the eating of pork, game, horsemeat, shellfish, fish without scales (eels) and snakes, as well as camel, hippopotamus and bear. Fermented drinks are also forbidden except for wine, which is subject to certain rules. If a kosher food comes into contact with one that is forbidden, it becomes itself forbidden. Strictly Orthodox Jews therefore buy only foods that are certified kosher. In addition, the *kashruth* (the Jewish dietary laws) lays down two basic principles: no blood must be eaten, and 'the calf shall not be cooked in the milk of its mother'. Therefore meat can be eaten only if it comes from an animal that has been ritually slaughtered: its throat is cut and the meat is then salted and washed. Milking is also carefully supervised. Milk or dairy products must not be used to prepare meat dishes, or even appear at the same meal. Orthodox Jews usually have two sets of kitchen equipment so that accidental contamination can be avoided.

KOUING-AMAN A flat Breton cake from the Douarnenez region, the name meaning 'bread and butter'. It is made from bread dough enriched with butter (unsalted or slightly salted) or double (heavy) cream, cooked in a hot oven and caramelized with sugar. It is best eaten warm.

RECIPE

kouing-aman
Dissolve 15 g (½ oz, 1 cake) fresh (compressed) yeast in 2 tablespoons warm water and mix with 50 g (2 oz, ½ cup) plain (all-purpose) flour. Cover with a cloth and leave to rise in a warm place. When its volume has doubled, sift 200 g (7 oz, 1¾ cups) plain flour and a pinch of salt into a bowl and add the yeast, kneading it in with the tips of the fingers and adding just enough water to obtain a pliable dough. Knead it well, then leave it to rise again in a warm place.

When its volume has doubled, place it on a floured working surface and roll it into a large circle. Dot the surface with 125 g (4½ oz, ½ cup) softened butter cut into pieces and sprinkle with 50 g (2 oz, ¼ cup) caster (superfine) sugar. Fold the dough into three, roll it out and fold it again into three. Leave it for 15 minutes. Roll it out into a circle again, fold it into three and leave it to rest. Repeat the operation once more.

Shape the dough into a circle about 23 cm (9 in) in diameter and put it into a buttered and floured flan tin (pie pan). Score the top of the dough with diamond shapes and brush with egg. Bake in a preheated oven at 240°C (475°F, gas 9) for about 20 minutes, basting the top occasionally with the butter that will run out of the dough. Sprinkle with icing (confectioner's) sugar and continue to bake until the cake is cooked (it should still be fairly moist inside). Unmould straightaway and serve warm.

KOULIBIAC Also *coulibiac*, *koulibiaca* or *coulibiaca*, or *koullbiaca*. A Russian pie filled with fish, vegetables, rice and hard-boiled (hard-cooked) eggs. The filling is topped with *vésiga* (dried spinal marrow of the sturgeon), an essential element of an authentic *koulibiac*. European cooks have adapted and varied the recipe in many ways. It can be made with brioche dough or puff pastry, and it may be filled with rice, chicken and mushrooms or with salmon (or even turbot), onions, parsley and shallots. Hard-boiled eggs are an essential ingredient, but *vésiga* is now very rarely used. *Koulibiac* is often cooked without being enclosed in a dish, but traditionally it is baked in an earthenware dish shaped like a fish.

RECIPES

basic salmon koulibiac

Make some puff pastry* with 350 g (12 oz, 3 cups) plain (all-purpose) flour, 275 g (10 oz, 1¼ cups) butter, 200 ml (7 fl oz, ¾ cup) water and 1 teaspoon salt. While the dough is resting, prepare the filling. Hard-boil (hard-cook) 3 eggs, shell them and cut into quarters. Cook 100 g (4 oz, ⅔ cup) rice in boiling salted water, then drain. Skin about 400 g (14 oz) boned fresh salmon and poach it in salted water, adding 200 ml (7 fl oz, ¾ cup) white wine, a bouquet garni and 2 teaspoons paprika.

Cook for about 12 minutes, remove from the heat and allow the salmon to cool in its own cooking liquid. Chop 3 shallots and 350 g (12 oz, 4 cups) mushrooms, season with salt and pepper, and cook briskly in 15 g (½ oz, 1 tablespoon) butter. Finally, cook 3 tablespoons semolina in boiling salted water.

Roll out two-thirds of the dough into a rectangle 3 mm (⅛ in) thick. Leaving a narrow border free, spread over a layer of rice, then a layer of flaked salmon, the mushrooms and the semolina, then top with the hard-boiled eggs. Roll out the remaining dough and cover the pie. Pinch the edges to seal them, garnish with strips of pastry and brush with beaten egg. Cook in a preheated oven at 230°C (450°F, gas 8) for about 30 minutes. Serve the koulibiac very hot, with melted butter.

chicken koulibiac

Make 675 g (1½ lb) puff pastry*. Boil a chicken in stock. Hard-boil (hard-cook) 3 eggs, shell them and cut into quarters. Chop 250 g (9 oz, 3 cups) mushrooms, 2 shallots and a small bunch of parsley, and cook in 50 g (2 oz, ¼ cup) melted butter until all the moisture has evaporated. Set this mixture aside.

Put 100 g (4 oz, ⅔ cup) rice into the pan with 2½ times its volume of the strained chicken stock and a bouquet garni. Season with salt and pepper, mix, cover the pan, bring to the boil and cook for about 16 minutes. Add the cooked mushroom mixture and leave to get cold. Dice 400 g (14 oz, 2 cups) cooked chicken meat and the hard-boiled eggs and carefully mix them into the mushroom-flavoured rice.

Roll out the pastry, make and bake the koulibiac as for basic salmon koulibiac, piling the rice mixture on the pastry instead of layering the ingredients.

KOUNAFA A cake made in eastern countries, comprising alternating layers of pastry (cut into strips and browned in butter or sesame oil) and sweetened chopped almonds or hazelnuts (pistachios or pine kernels, or a mixture of these nuts, can be used instead). When cooked, the cake is moistened with a thick syrup flavoured with lemon and rose water. There are many variations.

• BASMA Very long pastry strips are arranged in a lattice pattern and the nuts are chopped more coarsely.

• GOUCH The pastry strips are very wide, moistened with syrup and covered either with whole toasted nuts or halves.

• LAKHANA The nuts are replaced with drained cream cheese, and the strips of pastry are rolled instead of forming flat layers.

The Arab *kounafa* is similar to the Turkish *kadaif*, which consists of long vermicelli-like strands of pastry and finely chopped nuts, saturated with a heavy syrup.

KRAPFEN A doughnut made with yeast dough, usually filled with apricot jam, raspberry jam or almond paste and served hot with a light custard cream or apricot sauce. Also known in France as a *boules de Berlin* or *berlines*, they originated in Germany and Austria.

KREPLACH Also known as *kreplech*. Jewish filled pasta or dumplings, with minced (ground) meat or chicken stuffing. Similar to tiny ravioli, kreplach are often served in broth.

KROMESKY A type of rissole or fritter, often served as a hot hors d'oeuvre and originating in Poland, but also traditional in Russia. It is made by binding the ingredients in a thick sauce and using as a filling for thin pancakes. The filled pancakes are coated in breadcrumbs and fried. Alternatively, the mixture may be coated in batter or breadcrumbs. Kromeskies may be made with a savoury or sweet filling. The following are some of the French terms for different types of kromesky.

• à l'ancienne The filling is enclosed in a thin layer of duchess potato purée and then in a very thin savoury crêpe.

• à la française The portions of mixture are floured and shaped into *pavés* or cork shapes.

• à la polonaise Each portion of mixture is wrapped in a very thin crêpe.

• à la russe The portions of mixture are wrapped in pieces of pig's caul (caul fat).

RECIPES

kromeskies à la bonne femme

Boil 500 g (18 oz) beef and retain the cooking stock. Soften 2 tablespoons chopped onion in 15 g (½ oz, 1 tablespoon) butter or lard and add 1 tablespoon flour. Brown lightly and then add 200 ml (7 fl oz, ¾ cup) very reduced beef stock. Stir well, then cook over a very gentle heat for about 15 minutes. Dice the beef very finely and mix it with the sauce. Reheat and then cool completely. Divide the mixture into portions weighing about 65 g (2½ oz), shaping them into cork shapes. Roll them in flour, dip them in batter and fry in very hot fat.

The beef may be replaced by pieces of cooked chicken or game.

kromeskies à la florentine

Cook some spinach slowly in butter and mix with a well-reduced béchamel sauce and grated Parmesan cheese. Enclose the mixture in some very thin savoury crêpes, dip them in batter and fry them in very hot fat.

KRUPNIK A simple Polish soup made from grain, usually barley or buckwheat, with vegetables, such as carrots, leeks, celeriac and cabbage.

There is also a potent drink of the same name, made from caramel with spices, including cinnamon, allspice, peppercorns and aniseed. The cooled spiced caramel is reheated with honey and then Polish spirit is added. The drink is served warm or cold.

KUGELHOPF A yeast cake from Alsace, of Austrian origin, containing raisins or currants and cooked in a special high, crownlike mould. The word is spelt in various ways (*kougelhof, gougelhopf* or *kouglof*) and is derived from the German *Kugel* (a ball). It is said that Marie Antoinette's fondness for this type of dough made such cakes very fashionable in France. However, some authorities consider that it was Carême who popularized the cake in Paris, when he was pastry chef at the Avice. He is reputed to have been given the recipe by Eugène, head chef to Prince Schwarzenberg, the Austrian ambassador to Napoleon. Others claim that the first pastrycook to make true *kugelhopfs* in Paris was a man named Georges, who was established in the Rue de Coq in 1840.

In Alsace, *kugelhopf* is eaten at Sunday breakfasts, and traditionally prepared the night before, as it is always better when slightly stale. It goes well with Alsace wines.

RECIPE

kugelhopf ◆

Soak 40 g (1½ oz, ¼ cup) currants in a little warm tea and soften 175 g (6 oz, ¾ cup) butter at room temperature. Mix 25 g (1 oz, 2 cakes) fresh (compressed) yeast with 3 tablespoons warm milk, add 90 g (3½ oz, scant 1 cup) strong plain (bread) flour and mix well. Add just enough warm milk to obtain a soft dough. Shape the dough into a ball, put it in a bowl, mark a cross on the top with a knife, cover it with a cloth and leave it to rise in a warm place, away from draughts.

Sift 250 g (9 oz, 2¼ cups) strong plain (bread) flour into a heap on the working surface, make a well in the centre and into this put 2 eggs and 1 tablespoon warm water. Mix these ingredients and knead the dough well. Dissolve 3 tablespoons caster (superfine) sugar and 1 teaspoon salt in a little water and add this to the mixture, together with the softened butter. Finally add 2 more whole eggs, one at a time, continuing to knead the dough. Roll this out on the board, put the yeast mixture on top, then mix it together by gathering the dough up, kneading it on the board and then repeating the procedure. Finally, add the currants. Put the dough into a bowl, cover it with a cloth and leave it to rise in a warm place until it has doubled in volume.

Butter a *kugelhopf* mould and sprinkle the inside with 100 g (4 oz, 1 cup) shredded almonds. When the dough is ready, shape it into a long sausage and put it into the mould, turning the mould as the dough is fed in (it should half-fill the mould). Leave it to rise again in a warm place until the dough reaches the top of the mould. Bake in a preheated oven at 200°C (400°F, gas 6) for at least 40 minutes. Unmould the *kugelhopf* on to a wire rack. When it is completely cold, sprinkle it lightly with icing (confectioner's) sugar.

KULFI Indian ice cream made from almonds and milk, flavoured with cardamoms and rose water. The milk is simmered with almonds for 5–6 hours, until it is reduced and thickened, then it is sweetened and frozen. Condensed milk and cream are used to shorten the preparation time. Kulfi is frozen in individual cone moulds.

KULICH A traditional Russian Easter cake, shaped like a tower. It is made from yeast dough and contains raisins, crystallized (candied) fruit, saffron, cardamom, mace and vanilla. The cake is sprinkled with icing (confectioner's) sugar, cut into slices crosswise, and traditionally eaten with hard-boiled (hard-cooked) eggs.

KUMISS Mare's, ass's or cow's milk fermented with yeast. This is an easily digestible drink, much enjoyed in Russia.

KÜMMEL A liqueur flavoured with caraway seeds, probably first made in Holland in the 16th century. Caraway is an ingredient of gripe water, the old remedy for treating wind in babies, and it was recommended for flatulence as long ago as ancient Egyptian times. Production of Kümmel was fairly widespread in the Baltic countries in the 19th century, some being made in Danzig, where the gold-flecked Danziger Goldwasser may be flavoured with both aniseed and caraway.

Today Kümmel is a speciality of the northern European countries: some versions are rather sweet and are therefore served on the rocks to make the drink more refreshing. Because of the pronounced flavour, its culinary uses are limited, although in

Kugelhopf.

English-speaking countries the old-fashioned seed cake, made with caraway seeds, can incorporate Kümmel as an addition.

KUMQUAT A citrus fruit originating in central China and now cultivated in the Far East, Australia and America. It resembles a small orange, the size of a quail's egg, and has a sweet rind and a sour flesh.

It may be eaten fresh (unpeeled) or preserved and is also used to make conserves and jams. Kumquats may be poached until tender and used in desserts or fruit salads. They may be sliced or used whole in savoury dishes.

KUZU Also known as *kuzo*, this is a type of starch obtained from the tubers of the kudzu vine. The vine, a rampant climber, is native to Japan and China, and cultivated elsewhere, including Hong Kong and the Philippines.

Starch extracted from the tubers is used as a thickening agent in the same way as arrowroot or cornflour (cornstarch), for example to thicken soups and glazes. In Japanese cookery kuzu is also used to make a type of noodle.

KVASS A Russian beer, made locally from rye and barley must or from soaked and fermented black bread, flavoured with mint or juniper berries. It is brown in colour, with a low alcohol content and a bitter-sweet taste. It is sold in the streets of Moscow in summer from the backs of small tankers. Kvass can be drunk either as it is, or mixed with spirits or tea it is also used in cooking, particularly for making soups.

L

LABELLING Modern food production, transportation and retailing have completely transformed the availability of ingredients. The second half of the last century brought a culinary revolution to Western countries, with international ingredients available at affordable prices and vast arrays of processed foods, seasonings and condiments. Whereas food labelling may have been arbitrary in the early days of supermarket shopping, it became the focus of national and international legislation. Not only is it essential that pre-packed items are clearly labelled, but displays and loose produce must also be clearly labelled to designated standards.

■ **Food labelling** The information given on the labels of food products sold in countries in the European Union must conform to EU regulations. As well as telling consumers what they are buying, labels on most foods give the weight or volume, a full list of ingredients and additives, the country of origin, and the name and address of the manufacturer. They also often give additional information, such as nutritional data, serving suggestions and the date after which the product must not be sold or used.

■ **Wine labelling** Wines produced within and those imported into the EU must conform to an increasing number of regulations, which in turn can be complicated by national, regional or local laws.

Wines produced in the EU have to state the quality of the wine – for example, Appellation Contrôlée, Vino da Tavola. The area of origin must be indicated and can be a country, as in Deutscher Tafel Wein, or a controlled appellation, such as Appellation Margaux Contrôlée. If the wine is from a European appellation, all the wine should originate from the region specified on the label. If the wine is from an American Viticultural Area (equivalent to a French

AOC) or from a specified area in Australia, at least 85% of the wine must come from that area. The volume and alcoholic strength must be included on the label, together with the year of vintage (an exception is made for European table wine), and a minimum of 85% of the wine should be from that year's harvest.

Producer information is required and, if a grape variety is specified, the bottle must contain at least 85% wine made from that variety. Certain countries also include health warnings on the back label and a list of additivies.

Within the EU, the use of product names on labels has been restricted so that the name 'sherry' is now used only for wines produced within the Jerez DO, while 'port' is the produce of the demarcated area of the Douro Valley and 'champagne' comes from the defined Champagne region in northern France.

LABSKAUS A dish from northern Germany, made with marinated minced (ground) beef, onions, and either herrings or anchovies, which are browned in lard (shortening) and then added to a potato purée seasoned with pepper and nutmeg. It is garnished with a poached egg, marinated beetroot (beet) and gherkins.

Labskaus is a variation on the old Norwegian dish *lapskaus* – salt cod with potatoes – which acquired its name from the nickname 'lobscouse', given to it by British seamen.

LACAM, PIERRE French pastrycook and culinary historian (born Saint-Amand-de-Belvès, 1836; died Paris, 1902). Lacam created many petits fours and desserts, notably puddings topped with Italian meringue. He is best known for his *masséna*, which he dedicated to the Duc de Rivoli: an oval of sweet shortcrust pastry (basic pie dough) and an oval-shaped base of sponge cake are sandwiched together with chestnut purée, covered with Italian meringue and then iced, half with chocolate and half with coffee icing (frosting). Lacam is also credited with the invention of the pastry crimper. Among his literary works are *Le Nouveau Pâtissier-Glacier français et étranger* (1865), the massive *Mémorial historique et géographique de la pâtisserie* (1890) and *Le Glacier classique et artistique en France et en Italie* (1893). He also edited a professional magazine, *La Cuisine française et étrangère*.

LACCARIA (*laccaire*) Generic term for a group of very small orange-red, pink or amethyst coloured mushrooms, with spaced-out fleshy gills and a spindly stalk. Edible laccaria are eaten as a side dish mixed with other mushrooms.

LA CHAPELLE, VINCENT French chef, born in 1703, who began his career in England in the service of Lord Chesterfield. His work *The Modern Cook* was published in 1733 in three volumes; it was subsequently reprinted several times. He returned to France to work for the Prince of Orange-Nassau, then for Madame de Pompadour and, finally, for Louis XV. His book was published in French (as *Le Cuisinier moderne*) in 1735 in four volumes. It was enlarged to five volumes in its final edition in 1742. *Le Cuisinier moderne* was praised by Carême and even in 1930 it was considered by Nignon to be perfectly up to date. La Chapelle's recipes were intentionally simple and are therefore eminently suitable for today's cooks. Among his dishes are sole stuffed with anchovies, parsley, shallots and spring (green) onions, cooked in white wine and sprinkled with orange juice; mackerel with fennel and gooseberries; and lamb *ratons*, paupiettes of leg of lamb stuffed with chicken and roasted on skewers.

LA CLAPE Red, rosé or white wine from a named terroir within the Coteaux du Languedoc appellation, produced in a village on a spur of the Corbières hills. The wines are typical of this part of the south of France – dry, aromatic, lightweight whites and full reds, most enjoyable while young, although a few can improve with some bottle age.

LACQUERED DUCK A traditional Chinese dish in which a duck is coated with a sweet-and-sour 'lacquer sauce', roasted and served, hot or cold, cut into small pieces. Pork is prepared in the same way. The sauce is a mixture of soy sauce, five-spice powder, liquid honey, oil, garlic, vinegar, flour, ginger, red colouring, rice wine, chilli oil and baking powder.

The duck is drawn, pierced in several places with a needle, left to marinate overnight in the sauce and then hung. It is then brushed with sauce several times and allowed to dry between each coat. This process makes the skin golden and crispy. The duck

is roasted on a spit and basted several times with the juice and lacquer sauce while cooking. Success depends on the degree to which the duck absorbs the sauce. If the duck is roasted in the oven and not on a spit, it must not lie in the dripping pan, otherwise the skin will be dry and shrivelled. Finally, the duck is cut across the grain of the meat into small pieces. These are served with fresh lettuce leaves and heads of sweet-and-sour leeks or gherkins.

LACROIX, EUGÈNE German chef (born Altdorf, 1886; died Frankfurt, 1964). He was the son of restaurant owners in Heidelberg and became apprenticed to one of the chefs of Napoleon III. He established himself and made his name in Strasbourg, but left the city in 1918. He moved to Frankfurt, where he created a foie gras *en croûte* and a clear turtle soup.

LACRYMA CHRISTI DEL VESUVIO An Italian DOC white, red, rosé or sparkling wine produced on the slopes of Mount Vesuvius. It gets its name, 'tear of Christ', from an old legend – when Lucifer was banished from Heaven, he fell to earth in what is now Campania, and the impact created the Bay of Naples. Sad to see such a beautiful country falling prey to the devil, Christ shed a tear which landed on Vesuvius. Where the tear fell, a vine sprang up. The wines have a minimum alcohol level of 12 degrees. Whites produced from Coda di Volpe, Verdeca, Falanghina and Greco grapes can be dry, sweet or sparkling. Red and rosé wines are made from Piedirosso, Sciascinoso and Aglianico grape varieties.

LACTARY *lactaire* Any mushroom of the genus *Lactarius*, which exudes a white or coloured milky juice when cut. Lactaries are bitter, with an unpleasant smell, and are frequently inedible. They should therefore be tasted when picked, and only those with a sweet-tasting juice should be retained. None of them is poisonous, but few are worth eating. The best is *Lactarius sanguifluus*, which has dark red juice; it should either be grilled (broiled) or cooked slowly with meat, particularly in a *gibelotte* of rabbit. The orange-coloured lactary, which smells of either crayfish or herrings, may be seasoned and eaten raw. The curry milk cap (*Lactarius camphoratus*) smells like celery and can be dried and used as a condiment. It can also be used to flavour omelettes. Lastly, the saffron milk cap (*Lactarius deliciosus*) has an orange-coloured juice that changes to green, and is usually pickled when it is small, or used to make a piquant sauce.

RECIPE

grilled saffron milk caps à la Lucifer
Blanch the caps from 575 g (1¼ lb) young saffron milk caps for 3 minutes, drain and blot dry.

Prepare 200 ml (7 fl oz, ¾ cup) devilled* sauce, boil down to reduce, then add 1 teaspoon paprika, 300 ml (½ pint, 1¼ cups) brown sauce and 2 tablespoons tomato purée (paste). Stir, cook over a moderate heat and season with salt. Add 1 tablespoon Worcestershire sauce and a generous pinch of cayenne. Strain through a sieve, return to the saucepan and keep hot in a bain marie.

Chop a small bunch of parsley and a little fennel. Brush the mushroom caps with olive oil and grill (broil) for 4 minutes. Then rub them with garlic and arrange them on a dish. Sprinkle them generously with the chopped parsley and fennel, together with about 100 g (4 oz, 1 cup) grated Parmesan cheese and some salt. Whisk the hot sauce and pour it over the mushrooms.

LADLE A large, bowl-shaped spoon with a long handle, used for serving soups and stews. A smaller ladle with a lip is used in cooking for basting and for spooning out cooking juices and sauces; it is made of metal. There is another kind of ladle for punch or mulled wine, which is also lipped and sometimes made of glass. The ladle used in cheese-making for pouring the curds into the moulds is known in France as a *poche*.

LADOIX-SERRIGNY A commune in the northern Côte de Beaune producing mainly red burgundy. The commune AOC name rarely appears on labels because the growers of the two villages understandably prefer to use the names of wines that may be classified as *premier cru* Aloxe-Corton. Le Corton and Corton-Charlemagne vineyards also extend into the commune. Commune wines are more usually sold as Côte de Beaune Villages.

LAGUIOLE-AUBRAC A cow's-milk cheese from Rouergue, containing 45% fat. It is a pressed, uncooked cheese with a natural, brushed rind that is either light or dark grey, depending on its storage time (3–6 months in a damp cellar). Made in Aubrac and protected by an *appellation contrôlée*, DOP Laguiole-Aubrac, or Fourme de Laguiole, is shaped into a cylinder 40 cm (16 in) in diameter and 35–40 cm (14–16 in) high. A straw-coloured, strong-flavoured cheese that is springy to the touch, it is very similar to Cantal. It is best in March or April. Laguiole-Aubrac is served at the end of a meal or as a snack and is also used in cabbage and bread soup. It is manufactured on a small scale in the mountain pastures.

LAGUIPIÈRE French chef (born mid-18th century; died Vilnius, 1812). He learned his trade in the household of Condé (descendants of the French general Condé the Great) and worked for Napoleon. Laguipière then moved into the service of Marshal Murat and accompanied him on the Russian campaign. He died during the retreat of the French army from Moscow and his body was brought back to France on the back of Murat's carriage. Carême, who had been one of Laguipière's pupils, wrote in his introduction to *Le Cuisinier parisien*: 'You were a man of outstanding gifts which brought you the hatred of those who should have admired your efforts to improve our existence. You should have died in Paris, respected by all for your great work'.

This great chef left no literary legacy, but his name lives on in several recipes, some of which may have been merely dedicated to him by other chefs: sauces; fillets of sole, turbot or brill (poached, then coated in a white wine or normande sauce, and sprinkled with a julienne of truffles marinated in Madeira); and a salmis of pheasant (part-roasted, jointed, then casseroled in a stock made from the bones, onions, bacon, red wine, Madeira and a little bouillon).

RECIPES

dartois Laguipière
Prepare some strips of puff pastry. Sandwich them together with a salpicon of braised calves' sweetbreads and truffles mixed with finely diced vegetables and bound together with a thick velouté sauce. Bake in a preheated oven at 220°C (425°F, gas 7) for 15–20 minutes, then cut into rectangles and serve.

Laguipière sauce
Put into a saucepan 1 large tablespoon butter sauce*, 1 tablespoon good consommé or a little chicken glaze, a pinch of salt, some nutmeg and either plain vinegar or lemon juice. Boil for a few seconds, then stir in a generous knob of fine butter. The sauce may also be made with fish glaze instead of chicken glaze.

This sauce is often known as *sauce au beurre à la Laguipière*.

Laguipière sauce for fish
Prepare some normande sauce. Infuse 3 tablespoons chopped truffles in 1 tablespoon Madeira. Mix the 2 preparations together thoroughly.

LALANDE-DE-POMEROL AOC red wine, fragrant and smooth, produced in the communes of Lalande-de-Pomerol and Néac. The best growths come from the eastern part of the region (see *Bordeaux*).

LAMB The male or female young of the sheep. Lambs killed for the market in France fall into three categories. The milk lamb, known in France as *agnelet*, is killed before being weaned, at the age of 30–40 days, and weighs 8–10 kg (18–22 lb). The meat of the milk lamb is very tender and delicate, if a little lacking in flavour. Milk collection areas for Roquefort cheese specialize in this type of lamb production, as the ewes must be freed as soon as possible after lambing for milking.

The second category is the *agneau blanc* or *laiton*, which is available mainly from Christmas to June and provides 70% of the lamb that comes into the French market. Slaughtered at the age of 70–150 days, it weighs 20–25 kg (44–55 lb). It has

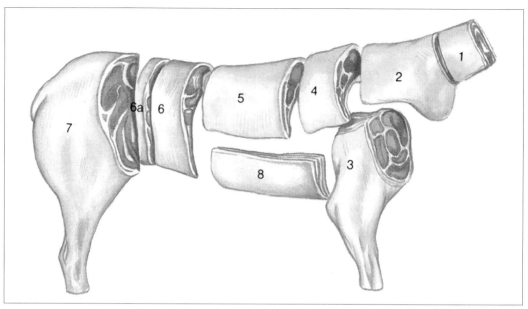

British cuts of lamb *1 scrag end of neck; 2 middle neck; 3 shoulder; 4 best end of neck; 5 loin; 6 chump; 6a chump chops; 7 leg; 8 breast.*

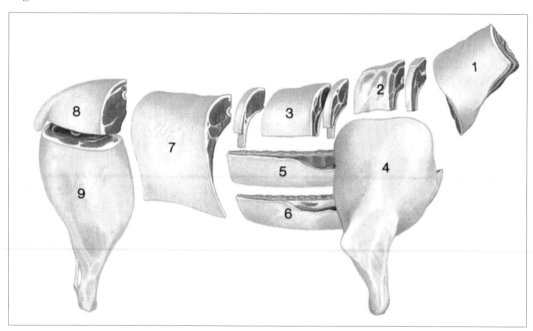

French cuts of lamb *1 collet (small animals) or collier (large animals); 2 carré de côtes découvertes; 3 carré de côtes premières: côtes premières and côtes secondes; 4 gigot; 5 haut de côtelettes; 6 poitrine; 7 filet; 8 selle de gigot; 9 gigot entier (with selle) or raccourci.*

had a rich milk-based diet and its dark pink meat, firm at the time of purchase, becomes very tender on cooking; its fat is white.

Lastly, the grazing lamb, known as *broutart*, is killed at 6–9 months and weighs 30–40 kg (66–88 lb). Its diet causes its fat to lose its whiteness, giving rise to its French name of *agneau gris* (grey lamb). Its flesh is fully developed, firmer and of a stronger flavour, and many gourmets prefer it to the *agneau blanc*. It is sold by butchers mainly from

September to December. (See also *salt-meadow sheep*.)

In Britain and the United States, milk lamb is known variously as sucking, milk-fed and baby lamb. The weaned lamb is usually referred to as 'spring lamb'. In Britain, animals over 1 year old are called 'hogget lamb' or 'yearling lamb', the latter being the term also used in the USA, while in both countries the meat of animals over 2 years old is called 'mutton'.

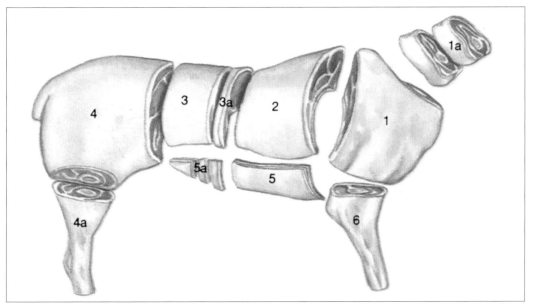

American cuts of lamb 1 shoulder; 1a neck slice; 2 rib; 3 loin; 3a loin chop; 4 leg; 4a hind shank; 5 breast; 5a riblets; 6 fore shank.

Lamb is cut up into neck, shoulder, breast, saddle and legs for roasting. The rib, which is composed of cutlets, and the loin, which provide chops, are roasted whole or cut into individual pieces for grilling (broiling). Various cuts of lamb are also diced for braising, stewing and grilling, and minced (ground) for use in stuffings, meatballs and other dishes.

The lamb often appears in the coats of arms of butchers' guilds, particularly in Paris.

RECIPES

Loin of Lamb
grilled loin of lamb
Shorten and trim the bones of a loin of lamb and lightly score its skin in a criss-cross pattern. Season with salt and pepper and brush with melted butter. Cook very slowly on both sides, either under the grill (broiler) or over a barbecue well away from the source of heat, until the meat is cooked through. Garnish with watercress or young vegetables and serve with maître d'hôtel butter.

loin of lamb à la bonne femme
Lightly brown a dozen button onions in melted butter and set aside. Cut 250 g (9 oz) potatoes into large olive-shaped pieces. Coarsely chop 50 g (2 oz) unsalted streaky (slab) bacon. Blanch the bacon for 1 minute in boiling water, then drain, pat dry and lightly fry in butter with the potatoes. Shorten and trim the bones of a 1 kg (2¼ lb) loin of lamb. Brown the meat on all sides in butter over a fairly high heat, then place it in a large casserole, season with salt and pepper, and add the onions, bacon pieces and potatoes. Spoon 1–2 tablespoons melted butter over the meat, cover the casserole

and cook in a preheated oven at 180°C (350°F, gas 4) for about 1 hour until the lamb is cooked. Serve the lamb in slices with the casserole vegetables and juices spooned round.

loin of lamb à la bordelaise
Cut 250 g (9 oz) potatoes into large olive-shaped pieces. Slice 225 g (8 oz) mushrooms (preferably cep mushrooms) and fry them quickly in a little oil. Shorten and trim the bones of a 1 kg (2¼ lb) loin of lamb, then brown on all sides in equal quantities of melted butter and oil. Place the meat in a large casserole with the mushrooms and potatoes, and season. Cover and cook the meat in a preheated oven at 180°C (350°F, gas 4) for about 1 hour, then add a small, crushed garlic clove mixed with several tablespoons stock and a little tomato purée (paste). Continue to cook until the lamb is tender.

loin of lamb Clamart
Shorten and trim a 1 kg (2¼ lb) loin of lamb, then brown it in butter in a flameproof casserole. Season with salt and pepper, then spoon over a little melted butter, cover and cook in a preheated oven at 180°C (350°F, gas 4) for about 1 hour. When the meat is cooked, add to the casserole 350 g (12 oz, 2½ cups) fresh garden peas cooked *à la française* and simmer for 5 minutes.

loin of lamb en crépine
Soak a pig's caul (caul fat) in cold water. Braise a trimmed 1 kg (2¼ lb) loin of lamb in a preheated oven at 180°C (350°F, gas 4) for about 1 hour until just cooked. Leave until cold, then thinly coat it on both sides with finely minced (ground) pork stuffing to which diced truffles have been added. Roughly

Preparing a rack of lamb

If the rack has not been trimmed, chop off the thin ends of the rib bones.

1 *Trim off the skin and excess fat from the rack of lamb, leaving a thin, even layer of fat covering the meat.*

2 *Turn the rack so that the fat side is underneath, then cut between and around the end of each rib to separate the ribs and backbone.*

3 *Cut the bones away from the meat, freeing the ribs from the backbone. Remove the backbone and leave the ends of the ribs in place.*

4 *Hold back the meat and rib ends, then cut off the strip of fat and nerve remaining when the backbone is removed.*

5 *Cut between the tops of the rib bones, about 2 cm (¾ in) down into the rack. Cut away all fat and meat, leaving the ends of the bones clean.*

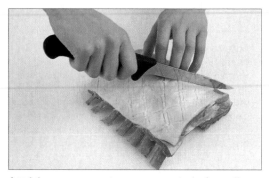

6 *Lightly score a neat criss-cross pattern in the fat to allow the fat to drain off as it melts and the seasonings to permeate the fat and meat.*

dry the caul, spread it out, place the loin on it, wrap it up and brush with melted butter. Slowly grill (broil) the wrapped meat on all sides to cook the stuffing.

roast loin of lamb

Shorten and trim the bones of a loin of lamb. Brown it on all sides in butter, then place in a roasting tin (pan) and season with salt and pepper. Add a little more melted butter, then roast in a preheated oven at 220°C (425°F, gas 7), allowing 25 minutes per 1 kg (11 minutes per 1 lb). When cooked, place the lamb on a serving dish and keep hot. Add 150 ml (¼ pint, ⅔ cup) white wine to the meat juices and boil vigorously to reduce; add 2–3 tablespoons jellied stock to make a gravy. Sprinkle the meat with chopped parsley to serve.

Note: the loin may also be spit-roasted, allowing the same time. Cooked by either method, the meat will be rare.

Milk Lamb

Kurdish milk lamb

Follow the recipe for stuffed milk lamb, but add cooked and chopped dried apricots to the stuffing.

roast milk lamb

Prepare as for stuffed milk lamb, but baste with melted butter and meat juices during cooking. It may be served as for stuffed lamb or surrounded by young vegetables. Instead of using a spit, the lamb may be roasted in a preheated oven at 180°C (350°F, gas 4); allow 20 minutes per 450 g (1 lb) plus 20 minutes to the total time.

saddle of suckling lamb prepared as carpaccio with a pistou sauce

Remove the fat from a saddle of suckling lamb. Season with salt and pepper. Put in a roasting tin (pan) with 1 peeled shallot, cut into pieces, 2–3 sprigs thyme, a little oil and butter. Cook in a preheated oven at 220°C (425°F, gas 7) for 8–10 minutes. Baste from time to time during the cooking.

To prepare the pistou sauce, remove the leaves from 1 bunch of basil and crush them in a mortar with 3 peeled garlic cloves. Emulsify this paste with 200 ml (7 fl oz, ¾ cup) olive oil.

Take the saddle out of the oven, still pink, and put to the side to allow the meat to rest. Bone the fillets and cut into long, thin slices.

Crush the bones finely and return them to the tin, then deglaze it with 120 ml (4½ fl oz, ½ cup) dry white wine and a little water. Reduce and add 2 teaspoons black and 2 teaspoons white coarsely ground peppercorns, 1 tomato cut into pieces, 3 chopped garlic cloves, and half of the pistou. Strain this syrupy juice and adjust the seasoning. Arrange the thin slices of lamb round large plates and coat with this juice. Meanwhile, cook 200 g (7 oz) fresh noodles, drain, and then mix with 1½ teaspoons salted butter, 60 ml (2 fl oz, ¼ cup) double (heavy) cream and the remaining pistou sauce.

Reheat the lamb in the oven. Place a 'nest' of noodles in the centre of each plate and sprinkle the edge of it with Parmesan cheese.

stuffed milk lamb

Ask the butcher to dress a whole baby lamb ready for stuffing and spit-roasting. Finely slice the liver, heart, sweetbreads and kidneys, and fry quickly in butter, seasoning with salt and pepper. Add these to half-cooked rice pilaf and loosely stuff the lamb cavity with the mixture. Sew up the openings and truss the animal by tying the legs and shoulders close to the body to give it a regular shape. Pierce the lamb evenly with the spit, season with salt and pepper, and cook over a high heat (20 minutes per 1 kg, 15 minutes per 1 lb). Place a pan under the lamb to catch the juices; blend sufficient stock into the pan juices to make a gravy and keep it hot. Remove the lamb from the spit, untruss it and place it on a long serving dish. Garnish with watercress and lemon quarters and serve the gravy separately.

Rack and Cutlets of Lamb

breaded lamb cutlets

Season the cutlets (rib chops) with salt and pepper and coat them with a beaten egg, then with breadcrumbs. Sauté on both sides in clarified butter, then arrange in a crown in a serving dish and sprinkle with noisette butter.

grilled lamb cutlets

Season the cutlets (rib chops) with salt and pepper, brush them with melted butter or groundnut (peanut) oil, and cook either over a barbecue or under the grill (broiler). Arrange on a serving dish: the protruding 'handle' bone may be covered with a white paper frill. Garnish with watercress or with a green vegetable, which may be steamed (and tossed in butter or cream if desired), braised, puréed or sautéed. Serve with noisette potatoes.

lamb cutlets Du Barry

Boil or steam small florets of cauliflower until just tender. Prepare some Mornay sauce. Butter a gratin dish and arrange the florets, well separated, in it. Coat each floret with Mornay sauce, sprinkle with grated Parmesan cheese and pour over a little melted butter. Brown the cauliflower quickly in a preheated oven at 220°C (425°F, gas 7). Grill (broil) or sauté the cutlets (rib chops) until cooked through, then arrange them in the serving dish with the cauliflower.

rack of lamb with thyme ♦

Sweat 100 g (4 oz) lean bacon in a sauté pan. Add 3 racks of lamb (6–8 chops), trimmed but with the bone still attached to the fillet. Seal for 4–5 minutes, then season with salt and pepper. Remove the lamb and bacon from the pan. Pour away the fat. Deglaze with 550 ml (18 fl oz, 2¼ cups) vegetable stock. Reduce to a quarter. Place the lamb in a cast-iron braising pan, then cover with a large bunch of green thyme, and bacon cut into small pieces to baste the meat. Cover. Make a long sausage with 200 g (7 oz) flour-and-water dough and put round the edge of the braising pan to seal it. Cook for 10 minutes in a preheated oven at 240°C (475°F, gas 9). Strain the juice and check the seasoning. Open the braising pan in front of the guests before cutting up the lamb. Serve the strained cooking juice with the lamb.

sautéed lamb cutlets

Season the cutlets (rib chops) with salt and pepper, then sauté on both sides in clarified butter, goose fat or olive oil. The sautéed cutlets may be served with any of the following garnishes: *à la financière, à la française, à la portugaise, à la romaine.*

other recipes See *ballotine, baron, blanquette, breast, brochette, curry, épigramme, gigot, kidneys, liver, noisette, pascaline, paupiette, sauté, shoulder, sweetbread, Villeroi.*

LAMBALLE The name given to various dishes in honour of the Princesse de Lamballe, a friend of Marie-Antoinette. These include a soup made from a purée of garden or split peas mixed with tapioca and cooked in consommé, as well as a dish of stuffed quails in paper cases.

RECIPES

Lamballe soup
Prepare 750 ml (1¼ pints, 3¼ cups) purée of fresh peas (see *Saint-Germain*). Add 750 ml (1¼ pints, 3¼ cups) consommé with tapioca cooked in it and mix well. Garnish with chervil leaves.

stuffed quails in cases à la Lamballe
Prepare the stuffed quails in cases (see *quail*), lining the base of each greaseproof (wax) paper case with a julienne of mushrooms and truffles blended with cream. Add some port to the pan juices in which the quails were cooked, blend in some crème fraîche and pour the resulting sauce over the quails.

LAMBIC A highly intoxicating, slightly bitter Belgian beer made with malt, uncooked wheat and wild yeast. Lambic is produced by spontaneous fermentation and may either be sold from the keg and pumped under pressure into the glass or it may be bottled. In the latter case, some new beer is added just before bottling. This induces a secondary fermentation, and the resulting beer is known as *gueuze*.

Cherry flavouring is added to make *Kriek-Lambic*.

LAMB'S LETTUCE A plant with rounded leaves in a rosette form, which is usually eaten raw in a salad. It is also known as corn salad and field lettuce and, in France, as *mâche, doucette, valérianelle potagère, raiponce* and *oreille-de-lièvre*. It grows wild in fields, usually in the autumn, but is cultivated in France from September to March and gives a good flavour to a winter salad. There are several varieties: Northern Green, with large leaves, is inferior to the round variety, which has smaller leaves and is juicy and tender; Italian corn salad has lighter leaves, slightly velvety and indented, and is less tasty. The lettuce must be carefully washed and dried, leaf by leaf, before it is eaten. It is used in mixed salads with potatoes, walnuts and beetroot (beet), and enriches poultry stuffings. It can also be cooked like spinach.

RECIPES

lamb's lettuce mixed salad
Peel and chop 200 g (7 oz, 1 cup) cooked beetroot (beet). Trim, wash and cut into rings 200 g (7 oz) chicory (endive). Wash 250 g (9 oz) lamb's lettuce. Peel, core and thinly slice an apple, then sprinkle with lemon juice. Place all these ingredients in a salad bowl. Prepare a vinaigrette, seasoning it with mustard, pour on to the salad and mix well. A small handful of coarsely chopped walnuts can be added to the salad, or a little Roquefort cheese can be mixed into the vinaigrette.

lamb's lettuce salad with bacon
Cut 150 g (5 oz) thick rindless streaky (slab) bacon rashers (slices) into pieces. Trim, peel and wash 400 g (14 oz) lamb's lettuce. Arrange in a salad bowl. Brown the bacon pieces in a little butter and add to the salad. Sprinkle with vinaigrette.

LAMINGTON A small Australian cake, made from a square of sponge cake coated in chocolate or chocolate icing (frosting) and dipped in desiccated coconut. The cakes were named after Lord Lamington, the governor of Queensland from 1896 to 1901.

LAMPREY An eel-like fish, up to 1 m (3 ft) long, with small fins and no scales. Using its sucker-like mouth, it attaches itself to other fish and feeds on their blood. The European species are marine, but they migrate upriver to spawn in fresh water. In France, they are caught in the lower reaches of the Gironde, Loire, Rhône and other large rivers. Lampreys have been a delicacy since ancient times. Roman patricians ate them, and Saint Louis had them brought from Nantes in barrels of water. Gloucester in England was famous for its lamprey pies, and in France, braised lamprey *à l'angevine* and lamprey *à la bordelaise* are still popular dishes. The fish is bled, washed and then scalded so that the skin can be easily removed. Next, the head and the dorsal nerve that runs down the body from it are removed. The lamprey can then be sliced and cooked in a similar way to eel. It is fatty like eel, but is considered to be superior.

RECIPE

lamprey à la bordelaise
Bleed a medium lamprey, reserving the blood to flavour the sauce. Scald the fish and scrape off the skin. To remove the dorsal nerve, cut off the lamprey's tail, make an incision around the neck just below the gills, then take hold of the nerve through this opening and pull it out. Cut the fish into slices 6 cm (2½ in) thick and put them into a buttered pan lined with sliced onions and carrots. Add a bouquet garni and a crushed garlic clove, season with salt and pepper, and add enough red wine to cover the fish. Boil briskly for about 10 minutes, then drain the lamprey slices.

Clean 4 leeks, cut each into 3 slices, then cook in a little butter with 4 tablespoons finely diced ham. Add the lamprey. Make a roux with 2 tablespoons butter and an equal quantity of flour. Add the cooking stock of the lamprey and cook for 15 minutes. Strain the sauce and pour it over the lamprey in the pan with the vegetables. Simmer very gently until the fish is cooked.

Rack of lamb with thyme, see page 667.

Arrange the lamprey slices on a round dish, stir the reserved blood into the sauce and pour over the fish. Garnish with slices of bread fried in butter.

LANCASHIRE CHEESE An English cow's-milk cheese containing 45% fat. It is a pressed, uncooked, soft-bodied cheese. Although it is delicious eaten on its own, it is equally good melted on toast, and its crumbly texture makes it suitable as a condiment in cooking. Lancashire cheese is increasingly mass-produced, but the farmhouse version made with unpasteurized milk can still be found and has a much stronger flavour. This is because a second or third quantity of fresh curds is added to a batch that has been prepared the previous evening.

LANCASHIRE HOTPOT A classic British dish, this hotpot of layered stewing lamb, sliced onions and potatoes originally contained oysters – at one time a cheap food for the Lancashire mill workers and often added to casseroles and stews to stretch a modest amount of meat – and mushrooms. Lamb kidneys were also added, giving the stew a rich flavour. The layer of potatoes on top forms a deep golden crust.

LANDAISE, À LA Describing dishes inspired by cooking techniques of the Landes region of France. The most common ingredients are Bayonne ham, goose fat and mushrooms. The name can be applied both to basic dishes such as potatoes and to more elaborate preparations such as goose or duck livers, as well as to such regional culinary classics as *confit d'oie* (preserved goose).

RECIPE

potatoes à la landaise
Fry 100 g (4 oz, ⅔ cup) chopped onions and 150 g (5 oz, 1 cup) diced Bayonne ham in goose fat or lard. When both are browned, add 500 g (18 oz) potatoes cut into large dice. Season with salt and pepper, cover and cook, stirring from time to time. Just before serving, add 1 tablespoon chopped garlic and parsley.

additional recipe See *confit.*

LANGOUSTE A crustacean also known as spiny lobster, thorny lobster, rock lobster and crawfish. It differs from the true lobster in having no claws. In addition, it is also sometimes known as crayfish, a cause of confusion with the freshwater crayfish, which resembles a diminutive lobster. To cap the confused nomenclature, in the United States the freshwater crayfish is also known as crawfish.

It takes five years for a langouste to grow to the regulation size (in France) for the table – 23 cm (9 in) long – during which time it sheds its shell more than 20 times. When it reaches its maximum size, it can weigh up to 4 kg (9 lb). Despite the fact that it produces up to 100,000 eggs at a time, the langouste is becoming scarcer. Attempts have been made to breed them near Roscoff, in Brittany.

Langoustes inhabit rocky seabeds at a depth of 20–150 m (65–492 ft) and are found in the Atlantic, the Mediterranean and around the coasts of the West Indies and South America.

• The red, Breton or common langouste, also known as thorny lobster, is considered to be the best, being fished in the English Channel, the Atlantic Ocean and the western Mediterranean. Its shell is reddish-brown or purplish-red and is covered with sharp spines. It has two light spots on each segment.

• The pink or Portuguese langouste is found in the seas off south-western Ireland and as far south as Senegal. It is the same length as the common variety, but its body is narrower and its shell is covered with light blotches.

• The green or painted langouste has the longest antennae, plus an additional elongated pair. Its carapace is bluish-green and there are a light-coloured stripe and two pale blotches on each segment.

• The brown or Cape langouste has a reddish-brown scaly shell and is usually sold frozen, sometimes as lobster tails.

• The Florida langouste is also brown and has large pale spots on its second and sixth segments. It is also usually marketed frozen and often sold as lobster tails.

Fresh langoustes should be bought live and undamaged, with all their legs intact and no holes in their shells. Inevitably, the antennae are sometimes broken, but this is unimportant. Females are considered to be superior, and they can be recognized by the egg sacs beneath the thorax. Like all shellfish, langouste should be cooked alive.

The pale, delicate, firm flesh has a milder flavour than that of the true lobster, but the same recipes can be used for both. However, the langouste is more suitable for highly seasoned recipes. The most visually appealing methods of preparing langouste are *en bellevue* and *à la parisienne*.

There are also two other delicious recipes worthy of mention, one from Spain and one from China. The Spanish recipe is for Catalonian langouste with unsweetened chocolate, cooked with a tomato-based sauce seasoned with chopped almonds and hazelnuts, red (bell) pepper and cinnamon chocolate. The Chinese speciality is langouste with ginger, in which the shellfish is sautéed in sesame oil with onions, chives and fresh ginger. Langouste is also a popular shellfish in the Caribbean.

RECIPES

grilled langouste with basil butter
Cut a langouste in two. Place the halves in a roasting dish, carapace side down. Season the cut surface with salt and pepper and moisten with olive oil. Grill (broil) for 10 minutes, turning once. Turn once more, so that the flesh faces upwards, and baste with a mixture of melted butter and coarsely

chopped fresh basil. Continue to baste at regular intervals until the langouste is cooked (about 20 minutes). Serve piping hot.

langouste à la parisienne
Most of the preparation for this dish should be carried out the day before. Prepare a court-bouillon with 4 carrots and 2 medium onions (chopped very finely), a bouquet garni, 175 ml (6 fl oz, ¾ cup) dry white wine, 2 teaspoons salt, some pepper and 3 litres (5 pints, 13 cups) water. Simmer for 20 minutes. Add a langouste weighing 1.8–2 kg (4–4½ lb) and simmer very gently for about another 20 minutes. Drain the langouste by making a small opening below the thorax, then tie it to a board to retain its shape. Leave it to cool completely.

Peel and finely dice 3 carrots and 3–4 turnips. Cut 200 g (7 oz) French (green) beans into small pieces. Cook the carrots, turnips and 100 g (4 oz, ⅔ cup) fresh garden peas separately in salted water. Cook the French beans in another saucepan of boiling water, uncovered, and do not add salt until they are half-cooked. All these vegetables should be slightly undercooked. Drain and leave to cool.

When the langouste is cold, cut through the membrane underneath the tail and carefully remove the flesh so that the shell is intact. Cut the tail flesh into 6–8 round slices and dice the flesh from the thorax very finely. Make some aspic and glaze the tail slices (several coatings are necessary). Place the shell on a serving dish and glaze it with aspic. Arrange the glazed slices in the shell, overlapping them slightly. Glaze this arrangement once more.

Make a mayonnaise with 2 egg yolks, 1 tablespoon mild mustard, 500 ml (17 fl oz, 2 cups) oil, 3 tablespoons tarragon vinegar, salt and pepper. Toss the cold vegetables and the diced flesh of the langouste in three-quarters of the mayonnaise and set this macédoine aside in a cool place. Hard-boil (hard-cook) 8 eggs and leave to cool.

The following day, halve the eggs and sieve the yolks. Add some tomato purée (paste) to the remainder of the mayonnaise, blend in the egg yolks and spoon this mixture into the egg-white cases. Cut the tops off 8 small tomatoes at the stalk ends, extract the seeds and juice, sprinkle the insides lightly with salt and turn upside down to drain in a colander.

One hour later, fill the tomato shells with the vegetable macédoine. Slice a truffle and place 1 slice on each slice of langouste. Surround the langouste with the stuffed tomatoes and eggs, and garnish the dish with a lettuce chiffonnade.

langouste with Thai herbs
Roast 4 tablespoons coriander seeds and the same amount of cumin in an ungreased frying pan. Allow to cool, then grind. Mix 4 tablespoons chopped galangal, 8 chopped stems lemon grass and 4 tablespoons chopped fresh coriander (cilantro) with 100 g (4 oz) chopped shallots, 100 g (4 oz) garlic cloves, 2 tablespoons pimento paste, 120 ml (4½ fl oz,

½ cup) sweet red pepper purée, 65 g (2½ oz) shrimp paste, 1 tablespoon saffron, 3 tablespoons turmeric, 1 tablespoon salt and the zest of 1 makrut lime. Place all these ingredients in a blender and liquidize, then strain through a sieve.

Blanch 2 langoustes weighing 800 g (1¾ lb) and cut in two lengthways. Remove the meat from the tail. Cook the meat for 2 minutes in 50 g (2 oz, ¼ cup) butter in a sauté pan without browning it. Take it out and put to one side. Now fry the Thai paste with 2 teaspoons grated fresh root ginger. Add 200 ml (7 fl oz, ¾ cup) white port, 20 g (¾ oz) apple julienne, 40 g (1½ oz) carrot julienne and 2 kafir lime leaves. Reduce until dry, then add 1 teaspoon turmeric and 50 g (2 oz, ¼ cup) butter. Remove from the heat and incorporate 200 ml (7 fl oz, ¾ cup) double (heavy) cream. Finally, pour in 2 tablespoons coconut liqueur and a similar amount of ginger wine. Place the langouste meat in soup bowls. Bring the sauce to the boil and pour over the lobster meat. Sprinkle with chopped parsley.

other recipes See *aspic, bisque, lobster, soup.*

LANGOUSTINE The French name for the Dublin Bay prawn or Norway lobster. This marine crustacean of the lobster family resembles a freshwater crayfish. In Britain, the shelled tail meat is known as scampi (after the Italian *scampo,* or *scampi* in the plural), popular as a prepared breaded seafood. The langoustine is 15–25 cm (6–10 in) long, with a yellowish-pink shell which does not change colour when cooked. Its pincers are characteristically ridged and, like the legs, are white-tipped. Langoustines cannot live for long out of water and they are therefore usually sold cooked, displayed on a bed of ice. When buying langoustines, look for bright black eyes and shiny pink shells. They can be poached and served whole, but many dishes require only the shelled tails. They are one of the ingredients of paella, and are often used instead of king prawns (jumbo shrimp) in European versions of Chinese and Vietnamese dishes.

RECIPES

langoustine fritters
Choose 12 medium langoustines and shell the tails. Marinate for 30 minutes in a mixture of 3 tablespoons olive oil, 1½ tablespoons lemon juice, 1 generous tablespoon chopped parsley, 1 small chopped garlic clove, 1 small teaspoon Provençal herbs, salt, pepper and a dash of cayenne. Prepare a fairly stiff batter by mixing 250 g (9 oz, 2¼ cups) plain (all-purpose) flour with a little water, then fold in 2 egg whites, stiffly whisked. Drain the langoustine tails, dip them in the batter and deep-fry until golden. Drain on paper towels and serve with lemon halves and tartare sauce.

Ninon langoustines ♦
Remove the large, green leaves of 4 leeks. Slice the remaining white part of each leek in two,

lengthways. Separate the leaves and wash. Remove the tails of 24 langoustines. Put the heads in a sauté pan with 1 tablespoon olive oil. Crush them slightly. Season with salt and cover with cold water. Bring to the boil, cover and cook for 15 minutes. Strain. Cut the zest of 1 orange into fine strips. Squeeze this orange and another one. Heat 25 g (1 oz, 2 tablespoons) butter in a sauté pan. Add the strips of leeks and cover with water. Cook, uncovered, over a high heat until the liquid has completely evaporated. Pour 350 ml (12 fl oz, 1½ cups) langoustine stock and 175 ml (6 fl oz, ¾ cup) orange juice in a saucepan. Add the orange zest. Bring to the boil and reduce by half. Incorporate 50 g (2 oz, ¼ cup) plain butter, cut into pieces, by whisking. Remove from the heat, then season with salt and pepper. Fry the langoustine tails for 2–3 minutes in 50 g (2 oz, ¼ cup) butter. Arrange the langoustine tails and leeks on a heated serving dish. Gently pour the orange sauce on top.

Peking-style langoustines

Soak 6 large diced shiitake mushrooms and 1 tablespoon Chinese lily flowers in hot water until soft. Drain and slice the mushrooms. Shell the tails of 12 langoustines without detaching them from the body. Sauté them in a frying pan in a little oil with 1 bunch of chopped spring (green) onions and 1 crushed garlic clove. Take them out and keep them hot. Blend 1 tablespoon cornflour (cornstarch), ½ teaspoon sugar and 2 tablespoons soy sauce with a little cold water. Brown some crushed tomatoes in the frying pan in which the langoustines were cooked, allow to reduce, then pour in the cornflour mixture to thicken the sauce. Add the mushrooms and drained lily flowers; bring to the boil, stirring, and simmer for 2–3 minutes. Pour this sauce over the hot langoustines.

poached langoustines

Add the langoustines to a cold court-bouillon, bring to the boil and simmer gently for 6 minutes, or until cooked. Drain and leave to cool.

The dressings are the same as for lobster or crayfish.

LANGRES
An AOP cow's-milk cheese (45% fat content) from Bassigny (Haute-Marne department) in the Champagne area of France. Langres is a soft cheese with a reddish-brown rind and is produced in rounds 10 cm (4 in) in diameter and 5 cm (2 in) deep, which are slightly hollowed out in the middle. It is springy to the touch, with a creamy yellow paste. It has a strong aroma and flavour, and is best served with a full-bodied wine or with beer.

LANGUE-DE-CHAT
A small, dry, finger-shaped biscuit (cookie), whose name (meaning 'cat's tongue') is probably derived from its shape. Langues-de-chat are thin and fragile, but they keep well and are usually served with iced desserts, creams, fruit salad, champagne and dessert wines.

langues-de-chat (1)
Cut 125 g (4½ oz, heaping ½ cup) butter into pieces and beat with a wooden spatula until smooth. Add 1 tablespoon vanilla sugar and 75–100 g (3–4 oz, ⅓–½ cup) caster (superfine) sugar; work for about 5 minutes with a wooden spatula. Blend in 2 eggs, one at a time. Finally, add 125 g (4½ oz, 1 generous cup) sifted self-raising flour a little at a time, mixing it in with a whisk. Lightly grease a baking sheet. Using a piping (pastry) bag with a round nozzle, pipe the mixture into strips 5 cm (2 in) long, leaving a space of about 2.5 cm (1 in) between them. Bake in a preheated oven at 220°C (425°F, gas 7) for about 8 minutes: remove as soon as the langues-de-chat have begun to turn golden.

langues-de-chat (2)
Work together in a mixing bowl 250 g (9 oz, 1 generous cup) caster (superfine) sugar, 200 g (7 oz, 1¾ cups) plain (all-purpose) flour and 1 tablespoon vanilla sugar. Gently fold in 3 stiffly whisked egg whites. Pipe the mixture and bake as described in the previous recipe. When the langues-de-chat are cooked, turn off the heat and leave them to cool in the oven.

LANGUEDOC See *page 674.*

LANGUEDOCIENNE, À LA
The name for various dishes that include tomatoes, aubergines (eggplants) and cep mushrooms, either individually or together. Fried eggs *à la languedocienne* are served on a bed of aubergine rings and accompanied by a tomato and garlic sauce. The languedocienne garnish for joints of meat and poultry consists of cep mushrooms fried in butter or oil, sliced or diced aubergines fried in oil, and château potatoes (or fried sliced ceps and aubergines with chopped tomatoes). The accompanying sauce is a demi-glace with tomatoes, often seasoned with garlic. The term *à la languedocienne* is also used to describe certain dishes that are typical of Languedoc cookery, in which the principal ingredients are garlic, ceps and olive oil or goose fat.

loin of pork à la languedocienne
Stick the loin with garlic cloves cut into sticks, sprinkle with salt and pepper, brush with oil and leave to stand for 12 hours. Roast it in a preheated oven at 220°C (425°F, gas 7) for 1 hour per 1 kg (25–30 minutes per 1 lb), or on a spit, and serve with its cooking juices accompanied by potatoes sautéed in goose fat.

Ninon langoustines,
see page 671.

Languedoc

This area of south-western France, which stretches from the Garonne to the Rhône and from the Lozère to the Mediterranean, is rich in arable land, natural resources and culinary traditions.

■ **A cornucopia of ingredients**
The fertile countryside around Toulouse yields garlic, asparagus, onions, tomatoes and plums, while the cereal crops support excellent poultry (geese, ducks and chickens). Some of the finest French lamb is produced on the limestone Causses, and the Gard is the site of many fruit orchards (cherries, peaches, apricots and figs).

Freshwater fish include pike, perch, tench, lampreys and eels, and the Mediterranean provides tuna, mackerel, anchovies and red mullet. Bouzigues is the place to find blue-ribbed oysters and mussels.

Game is also plentiful. The marshy coastal areas are visited by quail, woodcock and waterfowl, while hares, rabbits, thrushes and red-legged partridge are found in the Cévennes. The perfect complement to game, from the Lozère to the Haute-Garonne, the woodlands provide such mushrooms as ceps, morels and orange-milk agarics; truffles can be found in the Uzès region.

The principal cooking media for this wealth of food resources are lard, goose fat and olive or walnut oil rather than butter, and garlic is almost invariably used as a seasoning.

■ **Regional specialities** Languedoc has many regional specialities: pot-au-feu, made with stuffed chicken (in Toulouse) or with stuffed goose necks (in Albi), and garlic soups give way to fish soup, cockle soup, bourride and bouillabaisse on the coast. There are many varieties of pâté: goose or duck foie gras (Toulouse, Gaillac, Bédarieux, Quillan), thrush and hare (Lozère), lamb (Nîmes) and the sweet meat pâtés of Pézenas and Béziers.

Two of the most famous fish dishes of the region are brandade of salt cod from Nîmes and tuna tripe from Palavas. Snails are prepared in many different ways: à la *sommiroise*, *à la gayouparde*, *à la narbonnaise* or *à la lodévoise*. The same holds true for the famous cassoulet, which differs depending on whether it is prepared in Toulouse, Castelnaudary or Carcassonne. Other specialities worthy of note are the goose and duck confits (Toulouse), duck à *l'agenaise*, civet, tripe, gigot of lamb with juniper berries, and salted pig's liver (Albi), as well as thrushes *à la cévenole*, herb sausages from Mont Lozère, carbonade of veal, potatoes *à la persillade* and tomato and aubergine (eggplant) gratin.

■ **Pâtisserie** Pastries and

At Bouzigues, mussels are farmed on ropes along the north side of the pool of Thau.

confectionery are represented by crystallized violets from Toulouse, *caladons* and *croquants* (bonbons and cakes) from Nîmes, *minerves* from Nîmes and Uzès, Florac madeleines, *biscotins* from Bédarieux and Montpellier, Limoux *tourons* (petits fours), Castelnaudary *alléluias*, Uzès liquorice, almond *navettes*, *gimblettes* and *petits janots* from Albi, together with marrons glacés from Montpellier and Carcassonne.

WINE Languedoc is an increasingly important wine-producing region comprising the departments of Aude, Hérault and Gard in the south-west of France. Often linked with its southern neighbour Roussillon and named Languedoc-Roussillon, it includes the AOCs Fitou, Corbières, Minervois, St Chinian, Faugères, Clairette du Languedoc, Cabardès, Malpère, Limoux and Coteaux du Languedoc. It is a principal producer of table wine, but is gaining international acclaim for the quality of the Vin de Pays d'Oc wines. Traditional grape varieties include Carignan, Grenache, Syrah, Cinsaut and Mourvèdre, which produce intense, spicy red wines. However, there have been new plantings of Cabernet Sauvignon and Merlot, often sold as varietal wines. A small amount of rosé is produced. Sauvignon Blanc and Chardonnay are widely planted and more recently Rolle, Roussanne, Marsanne and Viognier. Limoux is the centre for the production of lively sparkling Blanquette and Crémant wines. A substantial amount of Vin Doux Naturel is also made.

At Lézignan-la Cèbe, the church and château dominate the landscape of lower Languedoc. The warm, dry climate encourages vine growing and the region is one of the largest producers of French table wine; it also yields several grand cru wines.

pheasant à la languedocienne

Cut a pheasant into 4–6 pieces; season with salt and pepper. Prepare 4 tablespoons mirepoix*; cook slowly in butter with a little thyme, powdered bay leaf, salt and pepper. Add the pieces of pheasant and lightly fry, then sprinkle with 1 tablespoon flour; cook until the flour turns golden. Moisten with 300 ml (½ pint, 1¼ cups) red wine and mix well. Add a few tablespoons of stock and a bouquet garni, then cover and cook for 20 minutes. Drain the pheasant and arrange it in a flameproof earthenware dish with 12 cep or button mushrooms and a truffle cut into fine strips; moisten with 3 tablespoons Cognac or marc. Strain the pan juice, add some butter, whisk and pour over the pheasant. Put the lid on the dish, seal it with flour-and-water paste and cook in a bain marie in a preheated oven at 190°C (375°F, gas 5) for 40 minutes. Serve in the cooking dish.

rack of lamb à la languedocienne

Lightly brown in goose fat a rack of lamb that has been trimmed and shortened. Add 12 small onions tossed in butter with 12 small pieces of raw smoked ham, 6 blanched garlic cloves and 200 g (7 oz) ceps or small mushrooms sautéed in oil. Sprinkle with salt and pepper. Arrange the meat and its garnish in a flameproof earthenware dish and cook in a preheated oven at 150°C (300°F, gas 2) for about 45 minutes, basting frequently. If necessary, cover with foil towards the end of the cooking time. Sprinkle with chopped parsley and serve in the cooking dish.

salt cod à la languedocienne

Completely desalt 1 kg (2¼ lb) salt cod, cut it into square pieces and poach in water, without boiling. Cut some potatoes into even-sized pieces, brown them in oil, sprinkle them with a spoonful of flour and fry for a few seconds, shaking the pan, until the flour has turned brown. Add a crushed garlic clove, the fish, a few spoonfuls of the fish cooking stock, a bouquet garni, pepper and very little salt, as the water in which the cod was cooked is already salty. Cook gently in a covered pan for 25 minutes. Take out the bouquet garni and pour the contents of the pan into a deep ovenproof dish, placing the cod in the centre. Sprinkle with chopped parsley, moisten with a little olive oil and finish cooking in a preheated oven at 230°C (475°F, gas 8) for about 5 minutes.

other recipes See *aubergine, sausage, tomato*.

LAOS Indonesian name for greater galangal.

LAPWING *vanneau* A bird with black, bright green and white plumage and a black crest. Through Brillat-Savarin it acquired a great gastronomic reputation, and as the Roman Catholic Church did not regard it as a meat, it was suitable for days of abstinence. As large as a pigeon, with fairly delicate flesh, the lapwing is usually roasted undrawn (except for the gizzard) for about 18 minutes, sometimes stuffed with stoned (pitted) olives.

Lapwing eggs came into fashion in Paris in the 1930s, imported at that time from the Netherlands, where the first egg from the nest is traditionally offered to the sovereign. They are prepared as hard-boiled (hard-cooked) eggs and are used in aspics or in mixed salads.

LA QUINTINIE, JEAN DE French horticulturalist (born Chabanais, 1626; died Versailles, 1688). He began his working life as a barrister in Poitiers, but left the bar to devote himself to the culture of fruit trees. By a process of trial and error, he perfected techniques of pruning and transplanting. He introduced the espalier method of training trees to grow against a wall by means of a trellis. He also created many famous kitchen gardens, including those at Versailles, Chantilly, Vaux and Rambouillet. The king's kitchen garden near the château of Versailles benefited from a remarkable irrigation and drainage system, in addition to cold frames and greenhouses introduced by La Quintinie. This garden supplied the royal table with asparagus in December, cauliflowers in March, strawberries in April and melons in June. His work *Instructions pour les jardins fruitiers* was published by his son in 1690.

LARD A cooking fat obtained by melting down pork fat. Lard is a fine white fat, which is not used as much now as formerly because of its high animal-fat content. It is used particularly for slow cooking, but also for deep-frying (it has a high smoking point) and for making pastry. It has a fairly pronounced flavour, which is associated traditionally with dishes from the north and east of France. It is used in the cookery of Alsace, Brittany, Britain, Scandinavia and Hungary, for ragoûts and dishes featuring cabbage, onion and pork, and also in specialities of the Auvergne region. Lard is also used a great deal in China.

LARDING The process of adding fat to cuts of meat or certain types of fish to make them more moist or tender. Larding consists of threading thin strips (lardons) of pork fat into a large cut of meat with a larding needle. The lardons can be seasoned with salt and pepper, sprinkled with chopped parsley and marinated in brandy for an hour in a cool place before use. Strips of ham or pickled tongue may also be used, but it is essential that the lardon is very firm (taken straight from the refrigerator) so that it can be threaded through the meat easily. Larding a roast with various ingredients improves both its flavour and its appearance when it is carved.

LARDING NEEDLE An implement used for larding cuts of meat, poultry and game. It consists of a hollow stainless steel skewer, pointed at one end and with the other slotted into a wooden or metal handle. A lardon is threaded into the needle, which is then pushed into the meat. When the needle is extracted, the lardon is left behind in the meat.

LARDONS Also known as lardoons. Strips of larding fat, of varying lengths and thicknesses, which are cut from the belly fat (*lard maigre*) of pork. Lardons about 1 cm (½ in) wide are used to lard lean meat before roasting. Lardons cut at right angles are used in the cooking of ragoûts, fried dishes, stews and fricassees, and as a garnish for certain vegetables and salads (dandelion leaves and endives). These lardons can also be cooked with potatoes, used in omelettes, and threaded on to skewers as an ingredient of kebabs.

LARK *alouette* A small passerine bird with delicate flesh, known as *mauviettes* in French cookery. There are several species, but it is mainly the crested lark and skylark that were shot for food. According to Grimod de La Reynière in his *Almanach des gourmands*, they are hardly more than 'a little bundle of toothpicks, more suitable for cleaning the mouth than filling it'. They were traditionally used mainly for making pies, and those from Pithiviers have been well known for centuries. According to tradition, when Charles IX was held to ransom in the forest of Orléans and then set free, he promised to spare the lives of his captors if they told him the provenance of the delicious lark pie they had shared with him. This brought fame to a pastrycook from Pithiviers, called Margeolet and known as Provenchère.

LARUE A Parisian restaurant founded in 1886 by a man named Larue on the corner of the Rue Royale and the Place de la Madeleine. In 1904 it was taken over by Édouard Nignon, one of the greatest chefs of his day. Marcel Proust and Abel Hermant were among his enthusiastic customers. The Club des Cent – a society of 100 gourmets – used the restaurant as its headquarters. When the establishment closed its doors for the last time in 1954, the club moved to Maxim's.

LASAGNE Italian pasta cut into wide flat sheets. Green lasagne is flavoured with spinach, pink lasagne with tomato. The pasta can also be made with whole wheat. The dish called lasagne is usually prepared with alternate layers of minced (ground) meat in tomato sauce, pasta and white sauce, topped with grated Parmesan cheese and baked in the oven until browned.

RECIPES

lasagne with Bolognese sauce
Make a Bolognese sauce. Cook 575 g (1¼ lb) lasagne in boiling salted water until tender, following the packet instructions. Spread the lasagne out on a clean cloth. Prepare a béchamel sauce. Butter a gratin dish and put a layer of Bolognese sauce on the bottom, then alternate layers of lasagne, béchamel sauce and Bolognese, ending with a thick layer of Béchamel sauce. Cook in a preheated oven at 200°C (400°F, gas 6) for 30 minutes. Serve with freshly grated Parmesan cheese.

LASSI An Indian drink made from yogurt thinned with water. Lassi may be served plain, seasoned with salt or flavoured with rosewater or fruit and sometimes lightly sweetened. Similar yogurt drinks are prepared in Middle Eastern countries. In Turkey, *ayran*, made by thinning yogurt with iced water to taste, is served as a refreshing drink with meals.

LAVALLIÈRE The name given to several great culinary dishes, although it is not known whether they were dedicated to Louise de la Vallière, mistress of Louis XIV, or to a famous actress in the Belle Époque. The dishes include: poultry or calves' sweetbreads garnished with trussed crayfish and truffles *à la serviette*; a cream soup of chicken and celery, garnished with a salpicon of celery and royale, served with profiteroles filled with chicken mousse; poached sole fillets garnished with poached oysters, fish quenelles and mushrooms, the whole dish being coated with a normande sauce; and grilled (broiled) lamb cutlets garnished with artichoke hearts stuffed with a purée of asparagus tips and served with a bordelaise sauce with beef marrow.

LA VARENNE, FRANÇOIS PIERRE French chef (born Dijon, 1618; died Dijon, 1678). He was in charge of the kitchens of the Marquis d'Uxelles, the governor of Chalon-sur-Saône, after whom mushroom duxelles were probably named, since this dish was perfected by La Varenne. This master chef is also remembered as the author of the first systematically planned books on cookery and confectionery, which revealed his attention to detail and showed how French cuisine, having been influenced by Italian cookery during the previous 150 years, had now developed a style all of its own. *Le Cuisinier français* was published in 1651, followed by *Le Pâtissier français* (1653), *Le Confiturier français* (1664) and *L'École des ragoûts* (1668). These books – especially the first – were reprinted several times before the end of the 18th century and marked a new direction in French cookery, a move away from the over-elaborate dishes of the past. His books are now rare, but they have been consulted for centuries and contain recipes that can still be used today.

La Varenne is particularly remembered for his *potage à la reine*, invented in honour of Marguerite de Navarre, the recipe for which is still usable, as well as his *soupresse* (terrine) of fish, his stuffed breast of veal and his *tourte admirable*, a marzipan (almond paste) base covered with a lime cream and preserved cherries, then topped with meringue. His name is still linked with various dishes that include mushrooms, either as a salpicon or as duxelles.

RECIPES

La Varenne sauce
To 225 ml (8 fl oz, 1 cup) mayonnaise* add 2–3 tablespoons duxelles* cooked in oil and cooled, then 1 tablespoon each of chopped parsley and chervil.

loin of lamb La Varenne

Trim and completely bone a loin of sucking (baby) lamb. Flatten it slightly and season with salt and pepper. Dip it in beaten egg and cover with finely crumbled fresh breadcrumbs (press the breadcrumbs well in to make them stick). Cook the loin in clarified butter, allowing it to turn golden on both sides. Prepare a salpicon of mushrooms bound lightly with cream and coat the serving dish with it; place the loin on top. Moisten with noisette butter and serve piping hot.

LAVER The Welsh name of a red sea weed, *Porphyra umbilicus,* with lettuce-type leaves which is almost identical to Japanese *nori.* It grows in inlets on the Atlantic coast of northern Europe, where some fresh water dilutes the salt, and is a capricious weed, moving its location.

When cooked it is called laver bread (*bara lawr*) in Wales, where it is sold ready-made in local markets on the south and west coasts. Well washed, then cooked for about 5 hours, it becomes a thick dark-green purée. Traditionally, it is mixed with a little oatmeal and shaped into small round cakes, which are then fried in bacon fat and served with bacon for breakfast. Called slake in Scotland and sloke in Ireland, laver is also eaten with potatoes, or as a sauce for roast lamb, with lemon or orange juice. Canned laver, available from some delicatessens, is vastly inferior to the fresh product.

LAVEUR A Parisian boarding house that opened in 1840 in the Rue Serpente. It was the model for the *pension* and its unpretentious but excellent cuisine attracted the custom of young writers and politicians. Its patrons included Victor Hugo (whose portrait was still hanging on the wall in 1925), Jules Vallès and Gambetta. In *Paris vécu,* Léon Daudet said: 'When we had something to celebrate, we would treat ourselves to a bottle of champagne, with the invariable plate of biscuits [cookies] and Gondolo gaufrettes [wafers].'

LEAVEN Loosely, any substance that can produce fermentation in dough or batter. In a bakery, this is a dough used to make bread rise. It is prepared by taking a piece of dough from a previous batch and 'refreshing' it by kneading it with flour and water until it has matured sufficiently to act as a raising (leavening) agent for the next batch of bread. As this is a long, finicky and laborious operation, many modern bakers have changed to much simpler processes, using yeast, for example.

LEBANON See *page 678.*

LEBKUCHEN A flat, hard, German gingerbread, shaped into hearts for hanging on ribbons, and made into gingerbread houses. Flavoured with the seven *lebkuchen* spices, including black pepper, cloves, star anise, cinnamon and nutmeg, and honey. Sometimes a little chopped candied peel is added and the gingerbreads are usually glazed, often with icing (frosting) decorations.

A special raising agent called *hirschhornsalz* (hart's horn salt) is used – actually carbonate of ammonia – which needs a very long rising time. This accounts for the Christmas smell of spices in many German homes in Advent.

Celebrated in Nuremberg, but made throughout Germany, it is perhaps the most famous type of gingerbread. It dates to about the turn of the 12th century, when local merchants started importing spices into a region of south Germany, already famous for its honey.

For several weeks after it is made, *lebkuchen* is too hard to eat and it must mature and soften. It is the origin of the cinnamon-and-spice Dutch *speculaas* (eaten on St Nicholas Eve, 5th December) as well as all the gingerbread men, trees and houses in Switzerland, Scandinavia, the United States of America and Britain.

LE BROUÈRE Essentially a variation of French Gruyère, this new cheese (45% fat content) is made in Alsace. The cheeses are made in not quite spherical wheels about 10 cm (4 in) in depth. Each cheese carries a number and signature. They have a light brown rind with a bright yellow paste; the flavour is sweet and buttery, with nutty tones.

LECKERLI Also known as *lecrelet.* A spiced biscuit (cookie) with a very distinctive flavour, sometimes coated with icing (frosting). It is a Swiss speciality, originating in Basle. The name is an abbreviation of *leckerli kuchen,* meaning 'tempting cake'.

RECIPE

leckerli

Sift 500 g (18 oz, 4½ cups) plain (all-purpose) flour into a bowl, add 350 g (12 oz, 1 cup) liquid honey and beat with a spoon. Add 75 g (3 oz, ½ cup) candied orange peel, 40 g (1½ oz, ⅓ cup) flaked (slivered) almonds, 20 g (¾ oz, ¼ cup) spices (half mixed spice, half ground ginger), and 1 teaspoon bicarbonate of soda (baking soda). (The candied peel and flaked almonds can be replaced with chopped hazelnuts and cinnamon.) Mix well until blended. Butter some square baking sheets and spread the mixture in them to a depth of 2.5 cm (1 in). Bake in a preheated oven at 180°C (350°F, gas 4), for about 20 minutes, or until well browned. When done, brush with milk and cut into even rectangles.

LE DOYEN A restaurant that opened in the gardens of the Champs-Élysées towards the end of the 18th century. The establishment was originally a fairly humble drinking house called Le Dauphin, near the Place de la Concorde. In 1791 it was rented by Antoine Nicolas Doyen, who numbered among his customers members of the National Convention, including Robespierre. In his *Mémoires,* Barras

LEBANON

Having its roots in European, Arabian and oriental cuisines, Lebanese cookery is characterized by a very cosmopolitan range of dishes, in which rice and Mediterranean vegetables predominate. However, the widespread use of sesame oil, together with cracked wheat (see *Bulgur*), makes Lebanese cookery quite distinctive. Chicken is a popular ingredient and is almost always served with rice. It may be stuffed with meat hash, pine kernels or almonds, or else chopped, marinated and grilled (broiled) on skewers; another common method is to grill the chicken whole, flavoured with garlic.

Mutton is widely used, as it is throughout the Middle East: roast, on skewers and in meatballs. The national dish of Lebanon is *kibbeh*: balls or patties of minced (ground) mutton mixed with bulgur, onion, parsley, pine kernels or almonds, and either baked or grilled, often on skewers. This dish is found in many Islamic countries, although the spelling varies – *kobba* in Syria and Jordan, *koubba* in Iraq.

Other typical dishes include *moghrabié*, a chicken couscous, prepared without vegetables, using quite large grains and seasoned with saffron; and *chawurma*, lamb grilled on a vertical spit, sliced thinly and served with a rice salad.

There are some very sophisticated dishes in the Lebanese repertoire, served for special occasions. One such dish is the classic pheasant *à la libanaise*: boned, stuffed with grated bacon fat, pine kernels, cloves and cinnamon, then wrapped in a cloth, boiled in stock and finished off on the spit. It is sliced and served with rice and a pepper sauce.

One of the most outstanding features of Lebanese cookery is the large selection of hors d'oeuvre, which can make a meal in themselves. These include lamb's tongue, brains, chicken livers, chopped kidneys and spinal marrow, dressed with vinaigrette. Puff-pastry cases may be filled with spinach or minced meat. Pulses are widely used, for example in *foul*, broad (fava) beans in a hot salad; *falafel*, chick peas or broad beans puréed, seasoned with sesame oil and formed into little balls or patties, then fried and served garnished with salad; or hummus. Vegetables come in so many guises, from simple spreads, such as a purée of aubergines (eggplants) known as *baba gannoj* or cucumber with mint and yogurt, to stuffed vine leaves; and courgette (zucchini) balls with cheese, coated in breadcrumbs and fried. Two salads that are characteristic of Lebanese cookery are *tabbouleh*, in which bulgur, mint, spices and tomatoes are marinated in oil and lemon, and *fattoosh*, a minted salad of finely chopped vegetables and bread, seasoned with sumac.

The Lebanese are extremely fond of very sweet pastries with an oriental flavour: crystallized (candied) dates, baklava, Turkish delight, halva and preserves made from whole figs or sliced quinces. They also enjoy some very subtle ice creams, made from milk and grape juice and flavoured with orange-flower water.

WINE The Lebanon is an historic wine-producing country making high quality, mainly red, wines from varieties including Cinsaut, Carignan, Cabernet Sauvignon, Mourvèdre, Merlot, Syrah and Grenache. Château Musar is perhaps the best known of the top producers.

---

mentions dining there, and Grimod de La Reynière, who was also a patron, wrote about Doyen's brother, who had a restaurant of his own in the courtyard of the Tuileries orangery. In about 1848, Le Doyen moved to a new location near the Rond-Point, taking over a house that is said to have belonged to Marie de' Medici. The restaurant became very fashionable during the Second Empire. A tradition grew up of dining at Le Doyen on the first day of the Paris Salon, when the customers could enjoy *sauce verte Le Doyen*, a herb mayonnaise. This sauce was created for Napoleon III by his chef, Balvay, in 1855, before he took over the ownership of the restaurant.

LEEK A vegetable believed to have originated from a Near Eastern variety of garlic. Leeks are usually eaten cooked, either hot or cold, though they can be finely shredded in a salad. The plant consists of a bulb and stem completely ensheathed by leaves, to form a cylindrical shaft. It is set deep in the soil so that most of the plant is blanched; this white and tender part is considered to be the best. Most of the green leaves are usually cut off and used in stews and for purées.

The leek was cultivated by the Egyptians and the Hebrews. The Romans believed that leeks had the property of imparting and maintaining the sonority of the voice. The emperor Nero had leek soup served to him every day, to develop a clear and sonorous voice for delivering his orations, and was nicknamed 'the Porrophage' (*porrum* meaning 'leek' in Latin).

The Romans may have introduced the leek to Great Britain, where it became the national emblem of Wales. In France it has been used for centuries to make soups, and the names *porreau* and *pourreau* eventually became *poireau* at the beginning of the 19th century.

Leeks must be bought when very fresh. They should be smooth, with a good fresh colour and erect foliage. To prepare, the roots and base are removed, then the green part is cut off and set aside. The white part must be washed several times and is then usually blanched in boiling salted water before further preparation. Leeks may be served cold with vinaigrette or mayonnaise, or hot with béchamel sauce, white sauce, melted butter or cream, au gratin, or braised. They are also used in soups, tarts (see *flamiche*), fritters, *à la grecque*, or even stuffed. They go equally well with beef, chicken, lamb and fish. The white part of the leek can also be cut or shredded for a brunoise or julienne and the green part used to flavour a court-bouillon or stock.

RECIPES

boiled leeks
Trim and clean some young leeks, keeping only the white parts. Cut these all to the same length, split them, wash well and tie together in bunches. Cook for about 10 minutes in boiling salted water until just tender (they must not fall to pieces). Untie them, drain thoroughly on a cloth or paper towels, and arrange them in a warm dish. Garnish with chopped parsley and serve fresh butter separately.

Alternatively, coat with melted butter seasoned and flavoured with lemon juice, or with reduced and seasoned cream.

braised leeks
Trim and wash 12 leeks, keeping only the white parts. Cut into slices and place in a casserole with 50g (2 oz, ¼ cup) butter, salt and pepper, and 5–6 tablespoons water or meat stock. Braise for about 40 minutes. Arrange the leeks in a vegetable dish and pour the braising liquid, enriched with an extra 15 g (½ oz, 1 tablespoon) of butter over them.

leek flan with cheese
Butter a 25 cm (10 in) flan ring (pie pan) and line it with 350 g (12 oz) unsweetened lining pastry (see *short pastry*). Prick the base and bake blind in a preheated oven at 200°C (400°F, gas 6) for 12 minutes. Allow to cool. Clean, trim and slice 800 g (1¾ lb) leeks (the white part only) and braise them gently for about 14 minutes in 40 g (1½ oz, 3 tablespoons) butter. Strain. Make 400 ml (14 fl oz, 1¾ cups) Mornay* sauce and allow to cool. Completely cover the base of the flan with half the sauce. Spread the leeks on top and cover with the remainder of the sauce. Sprinkle with 40 g (1½ oz, ⅓ cup) grated Parmesan cheese and 25 g (1 oz, 2 tablespoons) knobs of butter and place in a preheated oven at 240°C (475°F, gas 9) until brown.

leeks à la crème
Put the well-washed white parts of leeks into a buttered casserole. Add salt and pepper, cover and braise in butter for 15 minutes. Completely cover with crème fraîche, then continue to simmer, with the lid on, for 30 minutes. Arrange the leeks in a vegetable dish, add a few tablespoons of crème fraîche to the pan juices and pour over the leeks.

leeks à la vinaigrette
Use the white part of the leeks only, wash well and cook in boiling salted water. Drain on a cloth to remove any surplus liquid and arrange in an hors-d'oeuvre dish. Season with vinaigrette, containing mustard if liked. Sprinkle with chopped parsley and chervil or sieved hard-boiled (hard-cooked) egg yolk.

leeks au gratin
Trim the leeks and use only the white parts. Wash them well, blanch for 5 minutes in plenty of boiling salted water, drain them, then cook slowly in butter. Arrange the cooked leeks in an ovenproof dish, sprinkle with grated cheese (preferably Parmesan) and melted butter, and place in a preheated oven at 240°C (475°F, gas 9) until brown.

leeks with béchamel sauce
Blanch the white parts of some trimmed washed leeks for 5 minutes in boiling salted water. Drain thoroughly and braise in butter. Prepare a béchamel sauce that is not too thick. Arrange the leeks in a long dish, cover with the sauce and serve hot.

turbot with leeks
Lift the fillets from a young 900 g (2 lb) turbot. Trim and clean in fresh water and cut up into small pieces (*goujonnettes*). Make a fumet from the head and trimmings. Wash, trim and slice 6 small leeks and arrange them in a buttered ovenproof dish. Cover with the fumet, season with salt and pepper, and cook in a preheated oven at 220°C (425°F, gas 7) until they are just cooked but not soft. Drain the leeks, retaining the cooking liquid, and divide them among individual dishes. Keep warm.

Pour 200 ml (7 fl oz, ¾ cup) strained fumet into a pan, add 3 tablespoons crème fraîche, a pinch of sugar, white pepper (2 twists of the pepper mill) and 2 tablespoons dry vermouth. Boil down to reduce. Put the turbot pieces into the sauce. Poach for 5 minutes. Drain the fish and place on top of the leeks. Further reduce the cooking liquid, then pour it over the fish. Serve hot.

other recipes See *cream soup, monkfish, soup.*

LEES The deposits that settle in a cask or vat, consisting mainly of tartrates and yeasts. A wine bottled directly 'off the lees' (*sur lie*) may be slightly 'working' or lively. This is appreciated by some drinkers, notably those buying Muscadet. Normally, wine is pumped off its lees prior to bottling.

LEGRAND D'AUSSY, PIERRE JEAN BAPTISTE French historian (born Amiens, 1737; died Paris, 1800). He planned to write a massive work called *Histoire de la vie privée des Français, depuis l'origine de la nation jusqu'à nes jours*, dealing with the housing, dress, leisure activities and food of the French. However, only three volumes, all on the subject of food, were published (1782). They gave a detailed account of the diet, menus (especially at Versailles), table customs and regional traditions of former times. Legrand d'Aussy also included information about the guilds of the butchers, cooks and pastrycooks, together with a collection of proverbs illustrating the most popular customs of the times. After his appointment as chief librarian of the National Library, Legrand d'Aussy devoted his time to other topics of research.

LEICESTER This brightly coloured, English hard cheese used to be made from surplus milk left over from the production of Stilton cheese. Carrot juice was added to the curds to give the characteristic orange-red colour and it became known as Red Leicester. Today it is coloured with annatto dye and made into flat cartwheels. It is close-textured, with a light flavour enlivened by a touch of lemon piquancy.

LEIDEN A Dutch cow's-milk cheese (40% fat content) named after the city where it was originally made; it is also called Leidse Kaas and Leyde. The cheese is flavoured with cumin seeds or cloves and has a brushed, washed, waxy rind. It is shaped into a flattened globe weighing 5–10 kg (11–22 lb), and its mild flavour is dominated by the flavour of the relevant spice. Leiden is used in sandwiches and for canapés and croûtes as well as being served at the end of a meal.

LEMON A citrus fruit with an acid juicy pulp surrounded by an aromatic yellow peel of varying thickness.

Originally from India or Malaysia, the lemon was introduced into Assyria, and from there passed to Greece and Rome, where it was used as a condiment and a medicament. The Crusaders brought the lemon and other citrus fruits back from Palestine, and its cultivation became widespread in Spain, North Africa and Italy. The lemon reached Haiti with Columbus in 1493, while the Spanish and Portuguese were responsible for its introduction to various places in North and South America from the 16th century onwards. Until the 18th century, it was traditional for French schoolboys to give lemons to their masters at the end of the school year. The lemon was also used as a beauty product – it was thought to make the lips red and the complexion pale. Above all, it was a vital remedy against scurvy, being a good source of vitamin C, and was used in particular by sailors.

Lemons are available throughout the year. The different varieties are distinguished by shape, size, thickness of the skin and the number of seeds; the quality of flavour is fairly consistent. A good lemon should be heavy and fragrant, with a close-grained peel. As the lemon becomes very ripe, it gets less sour and more juicy. There are numerous uses for the lemon in cookery, especially in pâtisserie, confectionery and drinks.

■ **The juice** Obtained simply by hand-squeezing or with a lemon-squeezer, lemon juice serves firstly as a natural antioxidant, with which certain fruit and vegetables can be coated to prevent discoloration. It is

also an ingredient in numerous dishes, including blanquettes and ragoûts; it appears in marinades and courts-bouillons, and replaces vinegar in dressings for raw vegetables and salads; it seasons mayonnaises and certain sauces (butter or white); and large quantities are used in the preparation of ice creams, sorbets and various refreshing drinks. Finally, marinating raw fish in lemon juice is a method of 'cooking' widely practised in South America and the Pacific islands.

■ **The peel and the zest** As citrus fruits are often treated with diphenyl, it is preferable, if the peel is to be used, to choose untreated lemons, or failing this to wash and dry them carefully. The zest may be obtained by grating, peeling it with a special utensil, or by rubbing it with a sugar lump (sugar cube), depending on the intended use. It serves as a flavouring, usually in pâtisserie for creams, soufflés, mousses, tarts and flans; candied lemon peel is used for flavouring biscuits (cookies) and cakes.

■ **The fruit** Lemon slices are an essential accompaniment for a seafood platter, most fried food and savoury fritters, and many dishes coated in breadcrumbs. They are also a necessary ingredient of lemon tea. Lemon quarters may serve as a condiment for certain ragoûts and sautés (of veal or chicken) and also for *tajines*. Preserved lemons are widely used for flavouring fish and meat in North African cookery. Lemon is included in jams, compotes, lemon curd and chutneys. Finally, whole lemons are prepared frosted or iced.

■ **The extract** Lemon extract or flavouring is used in confectionery and in wines and spirits. It also flavours certain aromatic teas.

RECIPES

Savoury Dishes
chicken with lemon
Cut a chicken into portions. Squeeze 2 lemons and to the juice add salt, pepper and a dash of cayenne pepper. Marinate the chicken portions in this juice for at least 1 hour, then drain them, retaining the marinade. Wipe the portions, then brown them in butter in a flameproof casserole. Reduce the heat, sprinkle the chicken with crumbled thyme, cover and leave to cook gently for 30 minutes. Drain the chicken portions and keep them hot. Now add the marinade to the casserole along with 100 ml (4 fl oz, 7 tablespoons) double (heavy) cream. Stir well and heat, stirring constantly as the sauce thickens. Adjust the seasoning. Coat the chicken portions with this sauce.

chicken with preserved lemon
Cut a chicken into portions and sprinkle with salt and pepper. Finely slice 300 g (11 oz) onions; crush 3 garlic cloves. Grate at least 1 teaspoon fresh root ginger. Oil a flameproof casserole and spread the sliced onions over the bottom, then sprinkle with the crushed garlic, a pinch of powdered saffron, the grated ginger and 1 tablespoon coriander seeds.

Add a bouquet garni. Garnish with 8 slices of preserved lemon (see recipe below).

Arrange the chicken portions on top, sprinkle with 6 tablespoons olive oil, season with salt and pepper, and one-third cover the chicken pieces with chicken stock. Cover the casserole and cook over a moderate heat for about 1½ hours, or until the flesh comes easily away from the bones. Remove and drain the chicken, throw away the bouquet garni and reduce the pan juice until it is oily. Coat the chicken portions with it and serve very hot with rice à la créole.

duckling with lavender-honey and lemon

For 4 people, allow 2 ducklings, each weighing about 1.5 kg (3¼ lb), and their giblets. Soften 2 tablespoons mirepoix* in a shallow frying pan. Add the giblets and turn them over in the mirepoix. Barely cover with a mixture of half white wine and half water. Season with salt and pepper. Cover and leave to cook gently for about 30 minutes. Strain. Season the ducklings with salt and pepper. Fry them lightly in butter for 20 minutes, taking them out while they are still pale pink.

Discard the cooking butter and deglaze the pan with the juice of 2 lemons; then add 1 small teaspoon lavender honey to make a sauce. Leave to reduce almost completely. Then add 2 tablespoons strained duck giblet juices and finally stir in a knob of butter. Adjust the seasoning.

Cut the breast of the ducklings into long thin slices; grill (broil) the legs briefly on both sides. Coat with the seasoned sauce.

preserved lemons

Wash 1 kg (2¼ lb) untreated lemons, wipe and cut into thick round slices. (Small lemons can simply be quartered lengthways.) Dust with 3 tablespoons fine salt and leave them to discharge their juices for about 12 hours. Drain them, place in a large jar and cover completely with olive oil. Leave in a cool place for 1 month before use. Close the jar firmly after opening and keep in a cool place away from light.

sea bream with preserved lemon

Scale and gut (clean) a large sea bream and make a shallow incision in the back. Oil a gratin dish and in it place 6–8 slices of lemon preserved in oil. Arrange the bream on top and sprinkle with salt and pepper. Add a small handful of coriander seeds and garnish the bream with 6 more slices of preserved lemon. Sprinkle with 2 tablespoons lemon juice and several tablespoons of olive oil, then cook in a preheated oven at 230°C (450°F, gas 8) for about 30 minutes, basting the fish several times during cooking.

stuffed lemons

Remove the stones (pits) from about 30 black olives; put 6 olives aside and chop the rest together with a bunch of parsley. Cut the stalk ends off 6 large thick-skinned lemons; using a small spoon with a cutting edge, scoop out all the flesh, leaving the peel intact. Separate the pulp from the fibrous partitions and seeds. Crumble a medium-sized can of tuna or salmon and remove any skin and bones. Mix the lemon pulp and juice (or half the juice if the lemons are very sour) with the crumbled fish and the chopped olives and parsley, plus 4 hard-boiled (hard-cooked) egg yolks and a small bowl of aïoli. Adjust the seasoning. Fill the lemon shells with this stuffing, garnish each lemon with a black olive and place in the refrigerator until time to serve.

The tuna (or salmon) and aïoli mixture may be replaced by a mixture of sardines in oil-and-butter.

Sweet Preparations

confiture de citron

Allow 1.12 kg (2½ lb) sugar per 1 kg (2¼ lb) lemons. Wash the lemons (ideally untreated ones) and carefully remove the outer peel from one-third of them. Blanch the peel for 2 minutes in boiling water, then cool in cold water and cut into fine strips. Squeeze the peeled lemons to extract the juice and cut the remaining ones into thick slices.

Put the juice and slices of lemon in a preserving pan, bring to the boil and boil for 5 minutes, stirring all the time. Add three-quarters of the strips of lemon peel, the sugar, and 100 ml (4 fl oz, 7 tablespoons) water per 1 kg (2¼ lb) sugar. Stir and cook for 20 minutes over a gentle heat. When the jam is cooked, add the remaining peel, either mixing it in over the heat for 3 minutes, or adding it after straining the jam and reheating it (the jam is then clear like a jelly). Pour into scalded jars.

frosted lemons

Cut the stalk ends off some large thick-skinned lemons and reserve. Using a spoon with a cutting edge, remove all the pulp from the lemon without piercing the peel. Then chill the peel in the refrigerator. Press the pulp, strain the juice and use it to prepare a lemon sorbet. When the sorbet is set, fill the chilled peel with it and cover with the section that was removed. Freeze until time to serve. Decorate with leaves of marzipan (almond paste).

lemon meringue pie

Butter a baking tin (cake pan) 23–25 cm (9–10 in) in diameter and line it with 350 g (12 oz) shortcrust pastry (basic pie dough), see Short* pastry. Cook the pastry case (pie shell) blind in a preheated oven at 200°C (400°F, gas 6) for 10 minutes.

Boil 350 ml (12 fl oz, 1½ cups) water in a saucepan. In another saucepan put 65 g (2½ oz, ½ cup plus 2 tablespoons) plain (all-purpose) flour, 65 g (2½ oz, ½ cup plus 2 tablespoons) cornflour (cornstarch) and 250 g (9 oz, 1 cup) caster (superfine) sugar and gradually add the boiling water, stirring all the time. Bring to the boil, still stirring, then remove from the heat and leave to cool slightly.

Wash and wipe 2–3 lemons, grate the zest and squeeze the juice. Add the grated zest, the juice, 4 egg yolks and 25 g (1 oz, 2 tablespoons) butter to the cooled mixture and cook in a bain marie for 15 minutes, whisking from time to time. Pour the mixture into the pastry case, bake in a preheated oven at 200°C (400°F, gas 6) for 10 minutes, then leave to cool.

Add a pinch of salt to 4 egg whites, whisk into stiff peaks, then gradually fold in 125 g (4½ oz, ½ cup) caster (superfine) sugar and 20 g (¾ oz, 2 tablespoons) icing (confectioner's) sugar. Spread this meringue over the pie using a metal spatula, then return to the oven for 10 minutes, to brown lightly. Serve lukewarm or cold.

lemon sorbet

Cut away the zest from 3 lemons, chop it and add it to 500 ml (17 fl oz, 2 cups) cold light syrup with a density of 1.2850. Leave to infuse for 2 hours. Add the juice of 4 lemons, then strain. (The density should be between 1.1699 and 1.1799.) Complete by the usual method.

lemon soufflé

In a saucepan, work 100 g (4 oz, ½ cup) butter into a paste. Add 65 g (2½ oz, ⅓ cup) caster (superfine) sugar and 100 g (4 oz, 1 cup) plain (all-purpose) flour. Moisten with 300 ml (½ pint, 1¼ cups) boiled milk and stir well. Bring to the boil while stirring with a spatula, then dry the mixture as you would with choux pastry. Remove from the heat and add the juice of 2 lemons, 5 egg yolks, 6 egg whites whisked to stiff peaks, 40 g (1½ oz, 3 tablespoons) sugar and 2 tablespoons finely chopped, blanched lemon zest. Butter and coat a soufflé mould with sugar, pour in the mixture and cook in a bain marie in a preheated oven at 110°C (225°F, gas ¼) for about 40 minutes. Serve with a light egg custard with lemon zest and small almond cakes.

preserved lemon peel

Peel some fresh lemons and, using a spoon with a serrated edge, remove the pith, keeping only the zest. Blanch this zest for 5 minutes in boiling water, drain, place in a very concentrated sugar syrup and leave overnight. The next day, remove the zest and cook the syrup until it reaches a density of 1.2095; then return the zest and leave to macerate for 24 hours. Repeat this operation until the syrup reaches a density of 1.3319.

tarte au citron

Prepare a short* pastry using 200 g (7 oz, 1¾ cups) plain (all-purpose) flour, 100 g (4 oz, ½ cup) butter, 4 tablespoons caster (superfine) sugar, 1 egg and a pinch of salt. Use it to line a baking tin (pan) that has been well-greased with butter.

Break 2 eggs into a mixing bowl containing 50 g (2 oz, ¼ cup) caster sugar and beat the mixture until it turns white. Remove the outer peel from a lemon and chop it finely; squeeze the juice from the pulp. To the eggs and sugar, add 100 g (4 oz, 1 cup) ground almonds, the lemon peel and the juice. Mix

well. Fill the pastry case (shell) with this cream and bake in a preheated oven at 190°C (375°F, gas 5) for at least 30 minutes.

Meanwhile, wash 2 lemons and slice them very thinly. Measure into a saucepan 200 g (7 oz, 1 cup) sugar, 250 ml (8 fl oz, 1 cup) water and 1 tablespoon vanilla-flavoured sugar. Cook for 10 minutes, then add the lemon slices and cook for a further 10 minutes. Leave them to cool completely before using them and some glacé (candied) cherries to decorate the tart, which should also be cool.

other recipes See *butter (flavoured butters), cigarette, creams, custard, manqué, sponge cake.*

LEMONADE A refreshing drink made by a variety of methods, the simplest from lemon juice (3 tablespoons per glass), sugar and still or aerated (sparkling) water. The liquid is often left to infuse with the peel of the fruits before being passed through a cloth strainer (cheesecloth). *Citron pressé* (pressed lemon) is made in a glass just before serving. Alternatively, the lemon juice can be squeezed and set aside, then the peel cooked in water to extract all its flavour. The strained cooked lemon liquid is sweetened to taste and the juice is added and diluted with water.

LEMON BALM A lemon-scented herbaceous plant native to Europe and cultivated elsewhere. The leaves are used in salads, drinks, soups, stuffings and sauces and to flavour white meat and fish; fresh or dried leaves are also used in tisanes. The sweet-scented flowers are distilled to make melissa cordial, especially that known as *eau de Carmes*.

LEMON CURD An English speciality, made from a mixture of sugar, butter, eggs and lemon juice, used to fill tartlets or to spread on bread and butter. It should be kept in an airtight jar in the refrigerator.

RECIPE

lemon curd

Finely grate the peel of 2 large lemons. Squeeze them and reserve the juice. Melt 100 g (4 oz, ½ cup) butter in a double saucepan (double boiler) over a very gentle heat. Gradually add 225 g (8 oz, 1 cup) caster (superfine) sugar, 3 beaten eggs, the grated lemon zest, and the lemon juice. Stir until thickened. Put into sterilized jars while still hot and cover with wax paper, pressing the paper on the surface of the lemon curd. Leave until completely cold before covering the pots.

LEMON GRASS A variety of grass found in South-East Asia, this has a strong lemon-like flavour and it is a popular flavouring ingredient in Thai, Indonesian, Malaysian and Vietnamese cooking. Known as *sereh, sera, serai, takrai* or *vasanelalang,* lemon grass is available fresh, dried or ground to a powder for use as a spice.

The stems of the fresh grass are tough, but the lower 7.5 cm (3 in) of the grass is tender and edible. The trimmed grass should be chopped and bruised. Alternatively, the dried grass or tough stems can be bruised to release their flavour, used whole in cooking, then removed before serving.

LENT In the Roman Catholic calendar, 46 days of abstinence before Easter, intended as a time of penitence. The original strictures of Lent forbade people to eat meat, fat and eggs, so the diet comprised mainly vegetables – usually dried, since fresh ones were not in season – and fish, especially dried fish, such as herring and salt cod. However, in the past, the rules of abstinence were circumvented by various means. In France, for example, special alms enabled people to eat butter and eggs in measured quantities (the proceeds of these particular alms financed the construction of Rouen cathedral's 'Butter Tower'). Moreover, certain waterfowl were permitted, particularly teal and plover, because of a tenuous association with fish, as well as the beaver, because of its 'fishlike' scaly tail. In the kitchen, pâtés and pies were brushed with mashed pike's eggs, and carp meat was used instead of eggs as a thickening agent. Even the pastrycook got round the difficulty: *croquants*, *craquelins*, *échaudés*, and cakes of flour and honey boiled with almonds demonstrate this.

The rule of abstinence, which has almost disappeared now, did much to develop the cook's imagination: salt cod, served at many tables for 40 days on end, has probably more recipes than any other fish eaten in France. Fresh fish were also served, with a great variety of sauces.

LENTIL A small, annual leguminous plant with small, round, dry, flat seeds that are borne in pairs in a flat pod. They can be yellow, pink, brown, red, grey or green, and are always eaten shelled and cooked. Lentils have been cultivated since ancient times, originating in central Asia and forming the staple diet of the poor for many centuries. Ancient Rome imported whole shiploads from Egypt.

Red lentils, or split red lentils, are common. They cook quickly to a soft, powdery texture and are popular for soups and dishes made with lentil purées. Green and brown lentils retain their shape, becoming tender rather than mushy. They are popular for casseroles, particularly with pork, bacon or spicy sausages, and for salads, or as accompaniments to main dishes. Lentils are also a good source of vegetable protein, important in vegetarian diets, and are ofen key ingredients in main dishes. The green Puy lentil flourishes in the volcanic soil of the Velay in France. The seeds are dark green with blue marbling and have an excellent flavour.

Lentils do not have to be soaked before cooking, as they become tender after boiling for about 30 minutes. Once cooked, lentils are used as an accompanying vegetable (puréed, in gravy, creamed, with parsley), as well as for soup. They are the traditional

LENTILS

Puy lentils

red lentils

green lentils

yellow lentils

accompaniment for pickled pork and can also be used in salads.

Lentils have a mild glavour and they readily absorb the flavours of ingredients with which they are cooked or dressed. Most herbs, spices and citrus fruit zests go well with lentils. Citrus juice also contrasts well with them.

RECIPES

green or brown lentil purée

Pick over the lentils and place them in a large saucepan, cover with plenty of cold water, bring to the boil, then skim. Add salt, pepper, a bouquet garni, a large onion stuck with 2 cloves and a small diced carrot. Cover and simmer gently for 30–45 minutes (the cooking time will depend on the type and freshness of the lentils). Remove the bouquet garni and the onion. Reduce the lentils to a purée in a blender while still hot, then heat the purée through gently, beating in a knob of butter. If desired, add a little stock, water, boiled milk or cream before beating in the butter.

hot lentil salad

Cook green or brown lentils in boiling water for 30–35 minutes, until tender but still whole. Cut thick bacon rashers (slices) into strips and brown the strips in a little butter. Allow about 100 g (4 oz) bacon for 350 g (12 oz, 1½ cups) lentils. Prepare a vinaigrette and add to it 1 tablespoon red wine. Drain the lentils and place them in a warm dish. Add the pork, dress with the vinaigrette and sprinkle with plenty of chopped parsley. Mix the salad and serve hot or cold. A little finely chopped mild onion or a chopped bunch of spring (green) onions can be added, and the vinaigrette can be flavoured with a crushed garlic clove.

red lentil purée

Allow 450 ml (¾ pint, 2 cups) water for 225 g (8 oz, 1 cup) lentils. Add 1 finely chopped onion, 1 finely diced carrot and 1 bay leaf, bring to the boil, reduce the heat to the lowest setting and cover the pan tightly. Cook gently for 20–30 minutes, or until the water has been absorbed and the lentils are tender. Purée in a food processor or beat well, then press through a sieve, if required. Season and enrich with butter or cream.

L'ÉTOILE An AOC wine from the Jura. The parish of L'Étoile and the neighbouring communes of Plainoiseau and Saint-Didier produce a small quantity of good dry white wines, plus a little *vin jaune* and *vin de paille*. The white wines tend to be naturally 'lively' (*pétillant*).

LETTUCE A plant that grows wild all over the northern hemisphere and is cultivated in many varieties for its large edible leaves. It has been cultivated in Egypt and Asia for thousands of years, and was popular with the ancient Greeks and Romans because of the milky juice it exudes when cut (its Latin name, *lactuca*, is derived from *lac*, meaning 'milk').

Lettuce was introduced into France in the Middle Ages, some think by Rabelais, who is said to have brought some seeds back from Italy, although others believe that the popes in exile at Avignon were responsible. Until the time of Louis XVI, lettuce was eaten as a hot dish. Raw lettuce with a vinaigrette proved a great success in London when it was introduced by the Chevalier d'Albignac, a French nobleman who had emigrated to England. He made his fortune by visiting various private hotels and fashionable restaurants to dress the salads. Brillat-Savarin described him as a fashionable salad maker going from one dining room to another, complete with his mahogany tools and his ingredients, which included flavoured oils, caviar, soy sauce, anchovies, truffles, meat juices and flavoured vinegars.

Nowadays, many varieties of lettuce are available commercially. The most common are: *round (butterhead)* lettuce, which has a rounded head with a yellow heart and smooth or curled floppy leaves; *crisp* or *iceberg* lettuces, which are crisp and round, with very large firm hearts; *cos (romaine)* lettuce, which has long dark-green leaves with thick veins and a relatively open crisp heart; and *loose-leaved* lettuces, which have leaves sprawling out from the centre. Lettuces in the first three categories are various shades of green, while those in the last category can be green or red, or both.

Great care must be taken to clean lettuces thoroughly in plenty of water so that all the soil is removed. It is important to dry the leaves gently. The way lettuce is prepared depends on the size of the leaves. Lettuce can be seasoned and served raw in green or mixed salads, and the leaves are often used as a garnish. In addition it can be braised, stuffed, cooked with cream and used to prepare peas *à la française*.

RECIPES

braised lettuce au gratin

Braise the lettuces in meat stock or water and arrange in an ovenproof dish. Cover with Mornay sauce, sprinkle with grated cheese, top with melted butter and cook in a preheated oven at 220°C (425°F, gas 7) until brown.

creamed lettuce with spring onion soufflés

Clean and trim 4 lettuces, blanch them in salted water and leave to cool. Press dry in a cloth and cut *en chiffonade*. Melt 25 g (1 oz, 2 tablespoons) of butter. Peel and finely chop 1 onion and add to the butter. Add the chiffonade and sweat for 4–5 minutes. Pour in 1 litre (1¾ pints, 4⅓ cups) chicken stock. Cook for 5 minutes, blend and put to one side. Peel 30 small spring onions (scallions), keeping only the white part. Chop very finely and place in a saucepan. Add 2 tablespoons water and cook uncovered for 20 minutes. Purée the spring onions in a blender and then thicken 300 g (11 oz, 1½ cups) of the purée with 1 teaspoon cornflour (cornstarch) and 3 egg yolks; add salt. Whisk 5 egg whites and 25 g (1 oz, 3 tablespoons) albumen powder or powdered egg white until they form stiff peaks and carefully fold into the purée. Fill 6 buttered ramekins or ovenproof moulds with this mixture. Cook for 12 minutes in a preheated oven at 180°C (350°F, gas 4).

Reheat the creamed lettuce, add 100 ml (4 fl oz, 7 tablespoons) single (light) cream and 50 g (2 oz, ¼ cup) butter. Heat through without boiling and check the seasoning. Pour the creamed lettuce into bowls. Unmould the soufflés and place in the bowls. Add a slice of grilled, smoked streaky bacon to each soufflé.

lettuce à la crème

Braise the lettuces in stock or water. Divide each lettuce in two, folding each in half, and place in a buttered pan. Moisten with cream and simmer until the cream has reduced by half. Transfer to a serving dish and garnish with fried croûtons.

lettuce salad

Prepare a lettuce chiffonade, incorporating a julienne of unsmoked ham, breast of chicken, and either Gruyère or Emmental cheese. Dress with a vinaigrette made with walnut oil and sprinkle with chopped herbs.

TYPES OF LETTUCE

round (butterhead)

cos (romaine)

crisphead: batavia blonde

crisphead: batavia rouge

red oak leaf

oak leaf

iceberg

lollo rosso

little gem

stuffed lettuce

Trim the lettuces, blanch for 5 minutes, cool under running water and blot dry. Halve each lettuce without cutting through the base. Season them inside. Fill each lettuce with a generous tablespoon of fine forcemeat mixed with mushroom duxelles. Tie each lettuce back together and braise in meat stock or water.

Stuffed lettuce can be served on its own with fried croûtons, or it may be used as a garnish for roast or sautéed meat.

other recipes See *chiffonnade, italienne.*

LEVROUX A French goat's-milk cheese (45% fat content) from the province of Berry. Shaped like a truncated pyramid, it is made in the countryside around Levroux, in the Indre department. It is similar to Valençay, which some people say is derived from Levroux; they share the same characteristics.

LIAISON Any mixture used for thickening or binding sauces, soups, stews and similar dishes. Commonly used liaisons are beurre manié, egg yolks, arrowroot, cornflour (cornstarch), a roux and cream.

LIBATION An ancient religious ritual in which wine, milk, oil or blood was sprinkled on the ground or on an altar to honour the gods. A libation was made standing with cup in hand, looking up towards the heavens. A few drops of liquid were sprinkled and this was followed by a short prayer uttered with the arms extended towards the sky; finally, the offering was drunk from the cup. In ancient times, no one would dream of eating a meal without first performing a libation (see *symposium*). As well as being a display of deference to a deity, a libation was also intended to enlist help in times of need, especially before a battle or a journey. It was also used to seal a truce or a peace treaty.

In modern parlance, the word libation is used, often facetiously, to describe the act of taking an alcoholic drink.

LID A cover with a handle or knob, placed over cooking vessels, to prevent splashing and to reduce or stop the evaporation of water and juices. Some serving utensils, such as vegetable dishes and soup tureens, also have lids. Lids may be convex (for sauté pans) or concave (for holding water on certain types of casserole). For utensils without a purpose-made lid, so-called 'universal' lids are used. These have three concentric notches so they can fit on pans of different diameters. Other lids have special uses: a filter lid, made of double aluminium mesh, lets steam through but prevents fat from splashing and reduces cooking smells; an anti-vapour and anti-splash lid, with a row of small holes around the circumference, slows down evaporation and prevents fat from splashing; a strainer lid makes it possible to drain the cooking water while retaining the solid contents of the pan.

LIEBIG, JUSTUS, BARON VON German chemist (born Darmstadt, 1803; died Munich, 1873). Professor of chemistry at Giessen, Heidelberg and then Munich, he was particularly interested in the agricultural and industrial applications of organic chemistry; his most important work on this subject was published in 1823. Realizing that the transport of enormous quantities of meat imported from South America and Australia was proving expensive, he had the idea of extracting the nutritional part of the meat. In 1850 he produced the first meat extract; this was followed by concentrated stock powder.

In 1862 the Fray Bentos Giebert company was formed in Belgium, the forerunner of what was eventually to be a giant industrial concern. In 1865 Liebig was involved in founding Liebig's Extract of Meat Company in England, which later became part of Brooke Bond Oxo.

LIÉGEOISE, À LA Describing certain dishes that include alcohol and juniper berries. Kidneys *à la liégeoise* are casseroled, garnished with crushed juniper berries, potatoes and bacon, and served in a sauce made from the meat juices, gin and white wine. Small birds cooked *à la liégeoise* are flamed with gin and casseroled with juniper berries and Ardennes ham.

LIGHTS The lungs of certain animals, used as food. Calves' lights are usually used. After being beaten to expel the air, they can be cooked in a civet (with wine, mushrooms, strips of bacon and onions), *à la poulette* or *à la persillade* (cut into thin slices and sautéed in butter, with garlic and parsley).

LIGURIENNE, À LA Describing large cuts of meat garnished with small stuffed tomatoes alternating with a saffron risotto shaped in dariole moulds, and piped duchess potatoes brushed with egg yolk and browned in the oven.

LILY Lily bulbs and buds are used in Chinese and Japanese cooking. The tiger lily, *lilium tigrinum,* and white trumpet lily, *lilium brownii,* are both common. The bulbs are boiled and used as a vegetable or thickening agent.

Tiger lily buds, *fleur-de-lis* in French, are known as golden needles and used fresh or dried in Chinese cooking.

LIMA BEAN A bean plant grown in tropical countries and the United States, also known as Cape bean or pea, Siéva bean, sword bean, jack bean and Chad bean. The seeds are normally pale green and the same size as broad (fava) beans; they are prepared in the same way as fresh white haricot (navy) beans. Butter beans are a variety of Lima bean, grown in the southern United States.

LIMBURG Originally a Belgian cow's-milk cheese, although production has now largely been taken over by German cheesemakers. The brick-shaped cheese (40% fat content) has a soft, smooth, yellow paste and a crust varying in colour from reddish-yellow to brick red. It weighs 500–600 g (1–1⅓ lb) and has a strong aroma and a full-bodied flavour. Many people enjoy it with a glass of beer. It has been widely copied in the United States, where Leiderkranz is a milder version of the same cheese.

LIME A citrus fruit closely related to the lemon. Rounded, with bright-green peel and very sour pulp, it is smaller, more fragrant and juicier than the lemon. The lime is cultivated in tropical countries, including the Ivory Coast, Brazil and the West Indies, and is often used in Caribbean and Brazilian dishes, particularly fish or meat stews, marinated chicken, jams, sorbets, punches and cocktails. The zest is used like lemon zest and will keep for a long time steeped in caster (superfine) sugar or rum. Sugar lumps (cubes) rubbed with the zest are kept in an airtight jar for flavouring tea, creams or milk.

RECIPE

roast pork with lime sorbet and mint
Roast a 1 kg (2¼ lb) fillet of pork (pork tenderloin) for 70 minutes in a preheated oven at 220°C (425°F, gas 7) and leave to cool completely. To make the sorbet, dissolve 575 g (1¼ lb, 2½ cups) sugar in 200 ml (7 fl oz, ¾ cup) water, heat just sufficiently to dissolve the sugar completely and leave to cool. Squeeze enough limes to collect 500 ml (17 fl oz, 2 cups) strained juice. Add it to the syrup. Pour into ice trays and place in the freezer. After about 1 hour, stir and leave for at least 1 further hour until set completely .

Slice the roast thinly and arrange on the serving dish; garnish with sprigs of fresh mint. Prepare a lettuce salad and sprinkle it with chopped mint. Serve the sorbet in small sundae glasses alongside the cold roast meat and the salad.

LIME BLOSSOM The highly fragrant flowers of the lime tree, or linden, which are dried and used to prepare soothing infusions, sometimes to flavour creams, ices and desserts, and more rarely as an aromatic in cooking. Édouard Nignon made a powder of dried, crushed and sifted lime blossom to season sauces and stocks, and R. Lasserre created a recipe for chicken with lime blossom. Veal chops can also be flavoured with lime blossom, as can cream sauces and dishes cooked in white wine or cider. The most aromatic lime blossom comes from the Drôme in France, where a lime-blossom ratafia was formerly made. Lime-blossom honey has a pronounced aroma and flavour.

LIMONER A French word meaning to remove the skin, blood and impurities from certain foods (brains, fillets of fish, pieces of meat) by dousing them in water or holding them under running water. Certain freshwater fish are washed in this way to remove any slimy covering. The word is also a synonym for *écailler*, meaning to remove the scales of a fish or to open oysters.

LIMOUSIN AND MARCHE These two provinces, corresponding to the departments of Haute-Vienne, Corrèze and Creuse, have the same specialities and products, despite the differences in their climate and soil. The plateaux, with their grasslands and forests, provide game (hares and partridges) and mushrooms (ceps and chanterelles); they also provide pasture for rearing some very fine livestock (sheep and pigs, but mostly cattle). Where the fields are cultivated, these plateaux also yield excellent vegetables and many kinds of fruit and nuts (especially plums, cherries and chestnuts). The rivers and swamps sustain a variety of fish, including trout, carp, pike, gudgeon and sometimes crayfish.

The culinary specialities of the region include *bréjaude*, *miques*, and other hearty soups made with cabbage, pickled pork and beans; all these are traditionally finished off with red wine. The Limousin pigs are used for making pickled pork, confits and black pudding (blood sausage) with chestnuts, as well as ham, sausages and various pâtés. Among the excellent *farcidures* are stuffed cabbage and stuffed mushrooms. The great Limousin speciality is hare *encabessal*, but some excellent braised veal dishes are also cooked. Among the desserts, apart from the famous *clafoutis*, should be mentioned the Limousin fruit tarts, plum pies, marzipan (almond paste) and *cornues* (two-horned brioches made at Easter time), the rustic *tartes sèches* (cooked in water, covered with aniseed and finished in the oven), madeleines from Saint-Yrieix, *croquants* from Bort-les-Orgues and macaroons from Dorat. Special mention should be made of the Limousin chestnuts, which have formed a staple part of the diet of the rural population and are still enjoyed boiled (*boursadas*), roasted or blanched (shelled and braised).

The vineyards on the slopes of Corrèze and in the Vienne valley produce a modest amount of table wine, but the Limousin peasants also make cider and some very good fruit brandies, based on cherries, plums and prunes, as well as various home-made liqueurs, including walnut cordial.

LIMOUSINE, À LA Describing a method of preparing red cabbage. The cabbage is sliced very finely and cooked in lard with a little stock, a dash of vinegar and a pinch of sugar. When it is almost cooked, grated or finely diced potato and crushed raw chestnuts are added. This garnish is served with roast pork and other roasted meat. Chicken *à la limousine* is stuffed with sausagemeat and fried mushrooms, cooked in a casserole, coated with the pan juices mixed with veal gravy, and garnished with bacon and poached chestnuts. An omelette *à la limousine* is filled with fried diced ham and potato.

LIMPET *bernique* Sea mollusc of the *Patellidae* family, measuring 3–7 cm (1¼–2¾ in) in diameter, whose thick conical shell is a dull grey outside and yellow-orange inside. The shell of the Mediterranean limpet, or *arapede*, is iris blue inside. The limpet is abundant in the rocks of the Atlantic coast, where it is also known as the 'Chinese hat' or barnacle. Limpets are eaten raw, with lemon juice or vinaigrette, or grilled (broiled), with a little butter; chopped up, they are used as a stuffing.

LINE To cover the bottom and sides of a casserole, mould, terrine or baking dish with a thin layer of bacon, pork fat, flavouring ingredients or pastry. A braising pan can be lined by covering the bottom with such ingredients as sliced onions and carrots, thyme, bay leaf, parsley and garlic, which enhance the flavour, or with fatty or nutritious ingredients, such as bacon rind, bones and meat trimmings. A pâté terrine is lined with strips of pork fat or fatty bacon.

Lining pastry should be cut to match the size and shape of the container, either by using a pastry (cookie) cutter before lining, or by passing a rolling pin over the edges of the container after lining to cut off the excess. In general, pastry linings are placed on lightly greased surfaces. Lining a tart plate or flan ring often involves making a ridge around the top, which is pinched with a special tool or with the fingers to improve the final appearance.

Baking tins (pans) may be lined with greaseproof (wax) or other paper to ensure that mixtures are easily removed when cooked.

LING *lingue* A fish of the cod family, also called sea burbot or long cod. The common ling, found in the North Sea, can reach a length of 1.5 m (5 ft); a smaller variety, fished in the Mediterranean, is rarely more than 90 cm (3 ft) long. The ling is a slender olive-grey fish with a silver stripe along its length and a small barbel on its lower jaw. It is sold in fillets and is prepared in the same way as cod.

In the United States, the name ling is sometimes given to the freshwater burbot.

LING, BLUE *lingue bleue* Fish of the *Gadidae* family, also known as 'sling' (*élingue*) in Boulogne and Lorient. The blue ling usually lives at a depth of 350–500 m (1,148–1,640 ft) in the Atlantic as far north as Greenland, Norway and Iceland. Often sold as fillets, it is served in the same way as cod. Sometimes it is also salted like cod.

LINZERTORTE An Austrian pastry that takes its name from the town of Linz. It is made from a sweet shortbread dough flavoured with lemon and cinnamon, topped with raspberry jam, and decorated with a lattice of pastry.

RECIPE

linzertorte ◆
Leave 75 g (3 oz, 6 tablespoons) butter to reach room temperature. Remove the rind (zest) from a lemon and shred two-thirds of it into fine julienne

Lining a quiche tin with pastry

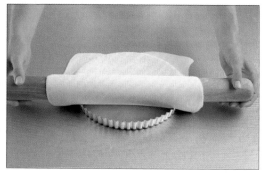

1 *Lift the rolled-out pastry by rolling it loosely over the rolling pin and lay it loosely over the quiche tin; do not press the rolling pin down firmly.*

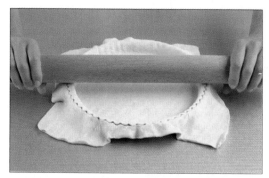

2 *Lift the edges of the pastry and ease the middle down into the tin without stretching and thinning it. Then roll the rolling pin across the top of the tin to cut off the excess pastry around the outside.*

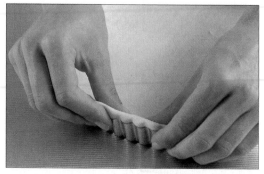

3 *Gently press the pastry down into the rim of the dish and against the side to neaten and raise the edge slightly.*

strips. Blanch, drain and chop these strips. Sift 175 g (6 oz, 1½ cups) plain (all-purpose) flour on to the work surface and add 75 g (3 oz, ¾ cup) ground almonds, 75 g (3 oz, 6 tablespoons) caster (superfine) sugar, 1 egg, 2 teaspoons powdered cinnamon, the softened butter, the lemon rind, and a pinch of salt. Knead the ingredients thoroughly and refrigerate the dough for 2 hours.

Linzertorte.

Butter a 23 cm (9 in) round flan tin (pie pan). Roll the dough out to a thickness of 3–4 mm (⅛–¼ in) and line the flan tin carefully, trimming off the excess around the top. Prick with a fork and fill with 125 g (4½ oz, ⅓ cup) raspberry jam. Gather the pastry trimmings together and roll them out into a rectangle about 3 mm (⅛ in) thick. Cut it into strips a little under 1 cm (½ in) wide and make a lattice pattern on top of the flan, pressing the ends into the top of the pastry case. Bake in a preheated oven at 200°C (400°F, gas 6) for about 30 minutes.

Remove the flan from the tin, place on a serving dish and allow to cool completely. The tart may be lightly brushed with an apricot glaze.

• *Variation* Instead of strips of pastry, a piped dough can be applied over the jam filling. Make a half quantity of the dough with an additional 50 g (2 oz, ¼ cup) butter and 1 egg yolk, creaming the ingredients in a bowl to a stiff piping consistency. Fit a piping (pastry) bag with a star tube and pipe the mixture on the tart.

LIPTAUER The German name for a Hungarian cheese spread; the base is a fresh cheese originally made in the province of Liptó and also called Liptai or Juhturó. This cheese is made with ewe's milk, sometimes mixed with cow's milk, and sold in small wooden cases. It has a creamy colour, a buttery consistency and a slightly spicy flavour. The spread is usually made by mixing the fresh cheese with cream, paprika, chopped capers, onions and anchovies; it is spread on wholemeal (whole-wheat) bread as a snack. It is also used as a stuffing for sweet peppers for an hors d'oeuvre: this dish is very popular in the Czech Republic and Slovakia, where it is called *liptovsky sir* and is usually accompanied by a glass of lager.

LIQUEUR An alcoholic drink of more than table-wine strength, usually incorporating some form of spirit. Liqueurs may be sweet or sweetish, herby (this type is often used as a *digestif* after meals), distillates of fruit (the *alcools blancs*), and flavoured spirits (such as fruit brandies). They are served at different times and in different ways – some as apéritifs, especially when poured 'on the rocks', some after a meal, some as between-times drinks, often as an ingredient of cocktails and mixes. Liqueurs are widely used in recipes for desserts, confectionery, cakes and pastries, and fruit dishes. A large number are made in France, and many formerly independent producers have now become part of a few huge organizations.

From very early times, compounded mixtures of herbs, spices and other ingredients were used for medicinal purposes. After the evolution of distilling, the monastic orders made many drinks with spirits and other ingredients to serve as remedies, preventives and ultimately as enjoyable drinks. In France, so rich in many of the ingredients required, the influence of immigrant Italians during and after the

15th century encouraged the practice of making liqueurs in many religious houses and subsequently by lay organizations, as a commercial concern. In regions where the basic materials for liqueur-making were cheap or free, the French often made such drinks in their own homes and many old recipes are still followed, especially when there is a glut of fruit or some other ingredient and when the necessary spirit is fairly cheap. It should be noted, however, that the process of distilling by the general public is illegal and those who wish to make liqueurs in their homes may only do so by macerating and/or infusing the ingredients in different forms of alcohol. There are many liqueur recipes, but the formulae for many of the most famous, such as Chartreuse, Bénédictine and Izarra, are closely guarded secrets, unlikely to be fathomed by the amateur and impossible to reproduce in the domestic kitchen.

The use of the word 'liqueur' as applied to certain spirits (liqueur brandy, for example) implies that it is a superior version of the product, usually intended for drinking without dilution.

RECIPES

apricot liqueur
Stone (pit) 30 apricots and put them in a preserving pan with 4 litres (7 pints, 4 quarts) white wine; bring to the boil. When boiling, add 1 kg (2¼ lb, 4½ cups) sugar, 1½ tablespoons cinnamon and 1 litre (1¾ pints, 4⅓ cups) 33° eau-de-vie. Take the pan off the heat, cover, and leave to infuse for 4 days. Strain, filter and bottle. Cork the bottles tightly and store in a dry place.

cherry liqueur
Crush 4 kg (9 lb) Montmorency cherries with their stones (pits). Place in an earthenware dish and leave to macerate for 4 days. Dissolve 1 kg (2¼ lb, 4½ cups) sugar in 4 litres (7 pints, 4 quarts) 22° alcohol and add it to the macerated cherries. Decant the mixture into a large jar, cork it and leave to infuse for 1 month. Then squeeze the mixture through muslin (cheesecloth) to extract the liquid. Filter and bottle. Cork tightly and store in a cool place.

orange liqueur
Wash 6 oranges, pare off the peel very thinly and chop it. Squeeze the oranges and pour the juice into a jar. Add 500 g (18 oz, 2¼ cups) sugar and stir until it dissolves. Add the peel, a pinch of cinnamon and a pinch of ground coriander. Pour in 1 litre (1¾ pints, 4⅓ cups) Cognac or white eau-de-vie, mix and leave to macerate for 2 months. Filter, bottle, cork and store in a cool place.

The same recipe may be used for lemons and for tangerines.

strawberry liqueur
Hull 1.25 kg (2¾ lb, 9 cups) very ripe strawberries, place in a large jar and cover with 4 litres (7 pints,

4 quarts) eau-de-vie. Cork and leave to infuse for 2 months, placing the jar in the sun whenever possible. Add 500 g (18 oz, 2¼ cups) caster (superfine) sugar and shake well. When the sugar has completely dissolved, shake again and filter. Bottle, cork tightly and store in a cool place.

Raspberry liqueur can be made using the same recipe with 1 kg (2¼ lb, 7 cups) ripe raspberries.

other recipes See *angelica, anise, cassis, orange blossom.*

LIQUEUR CABINET

In the past, an ornate wooden cabinet in which spirits were stored. Today this is outmoded, but any bottle of spirit should be kept upright, otherwise the spirit may rot the cork or stopper.

LIQUORICE

A shrub cultivated in temperate regions for its root, from which liquorice sticks for chewing are cut and liquorice juice is extracted. This juice, purified and concentrated, is used principally to make various types of confectionery; it is also used for flavouring medicines and apéritifs, and in brewing. The plant grows wild in Syria, Iran and Turkey; in France, it is cultivated mainly around Uzès in the Gard region. It was grown extensively around Pontefract in England during the 16th century and was used to manufacture Pontefract cakes, lozenges of liquorice sold as sweetmeats.

Depending on its origin, liquorice juice contains 5–10% glycyrrhizine, the ingredient responsible for its sweet taste and its reputed therapeutic properties, known since very early times. Assyrian tablets and Chinese and Indian papyruses give evidence of its early medicinal use. During the 19th century, liquorice began to be made into sweets, presented in elegantly decorated little boxes or given as a treat to children. There are two basic types.

• HARD LIQUORICE (in the form of sticks, pastilles and 'cakes'). Made from a mixture of liquorice juice, sweeteners, gum arabic and, perhaps, a flavouring (mint, aniseed, violet); liquorice sweets contain at least 6% glycyrrhizine.

• PLIABLE LIQUORICE (ribbons, laces and twists). Made from a paste of liquorice juice plus sweeteners, hard-wheat flour, starch and icing (confectioner's) sugar; this is cooked, then flavoured and extruded in a thread. Gums, pastilles and chewing gum made from liquorice are flavoured with at least 4% pure liquorice juice.

LIQUORICE WATER

A refreshing drink made from liquorice sticks soaked or infused in water with added lemon juice. The French name, *coco*, comes from the fact that the drink resembles coconut milk in appearance. It was popular in the 18th and 19th centuries, when it was sold in the streets and public gardens by the *marchand de coco*, who carried a small cask on his back from which he served it in goblets very cheaply.

RECIPE

orange-flavoured liquorice water
Cut 100 g (4 oz) liquorice root sticks into small slices and wash them; place in a saucepan with 2 teaspoons grated orange peel and 4 litres (7 pints, 4 quarts) water. Boil for 5 minutes, then strain and leave to cool. Serve very cold.

LIRAC

A wine from the southern Rhône with its own appellation contrôlée, produced in the Gard around Roquemaure. The most famous is Lirac rosé, which is similar to its neighbour, Tavel. It is made principally from the Grenache and Cinsault vines. The red wines are light and suitable for drinking young, and the whites are aromatic.

LISETTE

Fish of the *Scombridae* family, less than 1 year old. In summer, this small mackerel lives in shoals near the surface, and is found in the Bay of Biscay, where it is caught in seine nets, in the Mediterranean and in the North Sea, where it is trawled. The lisette is an excellent swimmer and has a tasty flesh less fatty than that of the mackerel. It is eaten grilled (broiled), marinated in white wine, or smoked.

LISTRAC-MÉDOC

A vigorous AOC red wine of the six communal appellations of the Haut Médoc of Bordeaux, with a beautiful ruby colour, pleasant bouquet and excellent structure. 'Listrac' became 'Listrac-Médoc' in 1986 (see *Bordeaux*).

LIVAROT

A cow's-milk cheese (40–45% fat content) from the Calvados region of Normandy. It has a soft, smooth paste and a washed, brownish-red rind, traditionally tinted with annatto (an orange dye from the fruit of a tropical American flowering tree). It is left to mature for 3–4 months in a damp cellar. Livarot is one of the earliest traditional Normandy cheeses. Thomas Corneille, in his *Dictionnaire universel géographique et historique* of 1708, mentioned its excellent qualities. It originated in the Auge, and it is still made only in the villages of the Livarot area. It is a cylindrical cheese, 11–12 cm (5 in) in diameter and 4–5 cm (1½–2 in) deep, and is sold boxed or unboxed, encircled by five thin strips of ribbon (the stripes left by this binding gained it the nickname 'colonel'), which were originally intended to maintain its shape. Livarot is at its best from November to June and has a fine firm elastic texture, with no holes. It has a distinctive but not overwhelming aroma, and a full-bodied flavour that is neither bitter nor spicy. It is protected by an *appellation d'origine*, now AOP, and is still made on farms by the traditional method, although there is some mass production and smaller versions of the cheese, known as *petits lisieux*, are made.

LIVER

Offal (organ meat) from carcasses of animals, poultry and game.

Apart from chicken liver, the most tender and

savoury variety is calf's liver, which is pale pink and firm, and cooked whole, larded with bacon and roasted; or in slices, grilled (broiled) or fried and served with a sauce. Next, in decreasing order of quality, is lamb's liver, which is often fried or grilled on skewers. Ox (beef) liver, which has a strong flavour and is usually tougher, is less expensive, and sheep's liver, which is mediocre, can also be fried or grilled. Pig's (pork) liver can be casseroled, but it is used mainly in the charcuterie and delicatessen trade, for pâtés, terrines and cooked sausages, because it has a slightly stronger flavour.

Chicken livers are widely used in cookery, particularly for cooking on skewers and for risottos, pilafs, pâtés and forcemeats, and for various garnishes. In France, Bresse chicken livers (*foies blonds*) are regarded as a delicacy and used in chicken-liver terrines. Duck's liver, even when the duck has not been fattened, is of very high quality, excellent when cooked with Armagnac brandy and grapes.

The liver of certain fish is also edible. Skate's liver (in fritters) and monkfish liver (poached) are especially used. Cod liver is smoked and preserved in oil, and then used to make cold canapés.

RECIPES

Calf's Liver
calf's liver à la bourguignonne
Fry some slices of calf's liver in very hot butter over a high heat. Keep hot on a serving dish. Deglaze the pan with red wine and stock (in equal proportions), and reduce. Pour this sauce over the slices of liver and surround with bourguignonne garnish.

calf's liver à l'anglaise
Cut some calf's liver into thin slices; fry in hot butter on both sides quickly over a high heat, allowing 25 g (1 oz, 2 tablespoons) butter to 4 slices. Drain and keep hot on the serving dish. Fry some thin rashers (slices) of bacon in the same pan, and use to garnish the liver. Sprinkle with chopped parsley, a squeeze of lemon juice and the cooking juices. Serve with small steamed potatoes.

fried calf's liver à la florentine
Braise some spinach in butter. Peel some large onions, cut into thick slices and separate into rings. Dip the onion rings in batter and fry in very hot oil until golden brown. Drain and keep hot. Lightly grease a serving dish, cover it with drained spinach and keep it hot. Quickly fry some very thin slices of calf's liver in very hot butter and arrange on the spinach. Deglaze the liver pan with white wine, reduce, then pour the juice over the slices. Garnish the liver with the fried onion rings and (if liked) with lemon wedges.

roast calf's liver
Cover the liver with thick rashers (slices) of bacon, season with salt, pepper, a pinch of fennel and some chopped parsley, then moisten with brandy. Soak a pig's caul (caul fat) in cold water, wiping it dry and

stretching it before use. Wrap the prepared liver in the caul and tie up with string. Cook on a spit or in a preheated oven at 200°C (400°F, gas 6) for 12–15 minutes per 450 g (1 lb). Dilute the pan juices with white wine or veal stock and pour over the liver. Serve with glazed carrots.

other recipes See *bacon, Bercy, bordelaise.*

Chicken Liver
Bresse chicken-liver terrine
Select 8 Bresse chicken livers (preferably white ones; ordinary chicken livers can be used instead, but will give a darker result); rub through a sieve together with 150 g (5 oz, ¾ cup) beef marrow. Add 50 g (2 oz, ½ cup) plain (all-purpose) flour. Mix thoroughly, then, one by one, add 6 whole eggs and 4 yolks, 2 tablespoons double (heavy) cream, and 750 ml (1¼ pints, 3¼ cups) milk. Season with salt, pepper and ground nutmeg. Add a generous pinch of chopped parsley and half a peeled crushed garlic clove. Place the mixture in a greased mould and cover with foil. Then cook in a bain marie in a preheated oven at 180°C (350°F, gas 4) for about 45 minutes or until set. Turn out of the mould just before serving.

Prepare a sauce by reducing some cream, port and fresh tomato purée, enriched with a little butter. Pour the sauce over the dish and garnish with a few slices of truffle. Serve warm or cold.

chicken-liver brochettes à l'italienne
Clean some chicken livers and cut each in half. Roll up each piece of liver in a thin slice of smoked bacon, then thread them on to skewers, with pieces of onion and sage leaves in between each piece. Moisten lightly with oil and season with salt, pepper and a little dried thyme. Leave to stand for 30 minutes. Grill (broil) the brochettes under a fierce heat for about 10 minutes, brushing them with oil when necessary. Serve with lemon halves and a green salad.

chicken-liver croustades
Make some small pastry cases. Clean the chicken livers (turkey or duck livers can be used instead), separate the pieces, season with salt and pepper, and fry quickly in very hot butter. Drain. Fry some sliced mushrooms and chopped shallots in butter, then season with salt and pepper. Warm the empty croustades in the oven.

Add enough Madeira sauce to the mushroom pan to make a filling for the croustades, then add the livers. Alternatively, deglaze the liver and mushroom cooking juices with Madeira, then thicken with a small amount of beurre manié. Heat up this mixture and use to fill the pastry cases. Serve very hot. The croustades can be garnished with slices of truffle poached in Madeira.

chicken-liver fritots
Trim about 500 g (18 oz) chicken or duck livers and purée by rubbing through a sieve or using a blender.

Peel 4 shallots and chop them finely. Separately, chop a small bunch of parsley and a small peeled garlic clove. Gently braise the shallots in 25 g (1 oz, 2 tablespoons) butter. Mix the liver purée, garlic, chopped parsley and braised shallots together in a bowl, together with 100 g (4 oz, 2 cups) fresh breadcrumbs, 2 beaten eggs, 2 tablespoons Madeira, 2 tablespoons cream, 1 tablespoon plain (all-purpose) flour and some salt and pepper. Knead together to obtain a smooth mixture and leave to rest for 1 hour. Divide the mixture into small pieces (about the size of a tangerine), roll into balls, flatten them slightly and dip in batter. Deep-fry in very hot oil. Drain well. Serve with a well-seasoned tomato sauce and some fried chopped parsley.

chicken-liver timbale
Prepare some chicken livers and mushrooms as in the recipe for chicken-liver croustades. Cook some shell-shaped pasta or macaroni *al dente*. Drain well. Add the chicken livers to the pasta, together with the mushrooms and some Madeira sauce (or a Madeira sauce thickened with blended arrowroot or beurre manié) and cream. Adjust the seasoning and serve very hot in a timbale mould or large dish.

Lamb's Liver
lamb's liver with garlic
Peel and chop very finely as many garlic cloves as there are slices of liver. Melt some butter in a frying pan and sauté the liver over a high heat, on both sides. Season with salt and pepper, drain and keep hot. Put the garlic in the frying pan, stirring well so that it does not brown. Immediately deglaze the pan with as many tablespoons of wine vinegar as there are slices of liver, and allow to reduce by half. Coat the liver with this sauce, sprinkle with chopped parsley and serve immediately.

Pig's Liver
pig's liver with mustard
Lard a pig's (pork) liver with strips of bacon and brush generously with strong mustard. Sprinkle with chopped parsley, crushed garlic and a little butter, and cook in a covered casserole in a preheated oven at 150°C (300°F, gas 2) for about 45 minutes. Cut and arrange the liver in slices on a hot dish. Deglaze the casserole with 1 tablespoon mustard and 2 tablespoons wine vinegar; coat the liver with this sauce.

LIVONIENNE Name given to a sauce based on fish velouté and thickened with butter, garnished with a fine julienne of carrot, celery, mushroom and onion sweated in butter, and finished with a julienne of chopped truffle and parsley. Livonienne is served in particular as an accompaniment to trout and salmon, or any seafood with lean flesh.

LOACH *loche* A freshwater fish with an elongated slimy body, greenish-grey or orange-yellow with black spots and covered with very delicate scales.

Three species are found in Europe. The *pond loach* can grow up to 35 cm (14 in) long and has ten barbels around the mouth. The *river loach,* 8–10 cm (3½–4 in), is the smallest species with six barbels and a spine beneath each eye. The *common loach*, 10–12 cm (4–5 in) long and the most popular, has six barbels and no spines. All these fish live in the mud, which sometimes gives them a somewhat earthy taste. They should be soaked for a few hours in vinegar and water before being cooked, either *à la meunière* or *en matelote*. They are considered to be at their best between October and March.

LOAF In addition to being the name for an item of bread, loaf is used to describe a variety of moulded mixtures. Typically, it is a preparation made from a moulded forcemeat, cooked in the oven in a bain marie. The basic ingredient of the forcemeat may be fish (such as pike, carp, salmon, whiting) or shellfish (lobster, crab, crayfish), poultry, meat, game or even foie gras.

Vegetable loaves may be made using green vegetables such as endive (chicory), spinach and lettuce, braised and mixed with beaten eggs; artichoke hearts; aubergines (eggplants); cauliflower or carrots.

Although long, deep loaf tins (pans) are usually used, loaf mixtures can be baked in any shape or size of mould. Delicate mixtures are cooked in a bain marie. Loaves do not have to be served hot – many are cooled before serving. Some are not even cooked and may be cold mixtures of fish, shellfish or chicken set in a mould lined with aspic.

LOBSTER A marine crustacean related to the crayfish, crawfish and crab, and found in cold seas. It is the largest and most sought-after shellfish. It has a thick shell and its small pointed head bears long red antennae. The abdomen is in seven sections and terminates in a fan-shaped tail. The first pair of claws, which are full of meat, end in large powerful pincers. The thorax contains a creamy substance (the liver), and hen lobsters frequently have a coral, often used in the sauces served with lobster. The abdomen, or tail, is filled with dense-textured white meat that can be cut into escalopes (scallops) or medallions.

There are two main types: the European lobster, found in British and Norwegian waters, and the Northern lobster, fished off the east coasts of Canada and the United States. When cooked, the lobster turns from blue or greenish to red, which is why it is sometimes called 'the cardinal of the seas' (Monselet). Although a prolific breeder, the lobster has had to be protected: since 1850 experiments in lobster farming have been carried out on both sides of the Atlantic, but it is still regarded as a rather special delicacy.

A live lobster, which can be identified by the reflex actions of the eyes, antennae and claws, should not show any signs of damage from fighting or have any pieces missing when it is bought, especially if it is to be boiled. A female is generally heavier and better value than a male of the same size and in the opinion of gourmets has a better flavour.

Cutting up an uncooked lobster

1 *Wash and scrub the lobster, then lay it on a flat surface with the head towards you. Stun the lobster by inserting the point of a sharp knife between the two antennae. With a sharp movement, separate the head from the abdomen.*

2 *Remove the claws and set them aside. (The claws may be cracked before cooking but left whole.) Hold the head firmly and use a large knife to cut it in half lengthways.*

3 *Use a teaspoon to scoop out and discard the gravel pocket. Remove and reserve the coral if there is any.*

4 *Cut the abdomen across into sections following the joints in the shell and taking care not to crack the shell.*

An average European lobster is about 30 cm (12 in) long and weighs 300–500 g (11–18 oz). Northern lobsters are larger, and are not uncommon at 1–1.5 kg (2¼–3¼ lb). Lobsters can reach a length of 75 cm (2½ ft), with a weight to match, but such specimens are very rarely sold on the open market.

The British Universities Federation for Animal Welfare has discovered that lobsters can be humanely killed by putting them in a plastic bag in the freezer, at a temperature at least as low as –10°C (14°F) for 2 hours. The lobster will gradually lose consciousness and die. It can then be plunged into boiling water. If a freezer is unavailable, make sure that at least 4.5 litres (1 gallon, 5 quarts) water per lobster is boiling fast over a very fierce heat before plunging the lobster in head first, ensuring it is totally immersed. Hold it under the water with wooden spoons for at least 2 minutes. The lobster should die within 15 seconds. If the recipe calls for uncooked lobster, remove it after 2 minutes.

■ **Lobster dishes** There are numerous methods of preparing lobster and a wide variety of dishes using the raw or cooked meat. These are some of the best-known: *à l'américaine*, *à la parisienne*, Thermidor, Newburg, grilled (broiled) or spit-roasted. Other dishes include lobster in scallop shells (hot or cold), soufflés and mousses.

RECIPES

grilled lobster (1) ♦
Plunge 2 lobsters, each weighing about 450 g (1 lb), head first into boiling salted water for about 3 minutes. Drain them, split in half lengthways and crack the claws. Season the meat with salt and pepper, sprinkle with melted butter or oil, and grill (broil) under a medium heat for about 25 minutes. Arrange each half lobster on a napkin. Serve with melted butter flavoured with lemon, maître d'hôtel butter or hollandaise sauce.

grilled lobster (2)
Plunge 2 lobsters, each weighing 400–500 g (14–18 oz), in boiling water for 1 minute. Take them out and cut in two lengthways. Remove the gravel pouch from the head and the intestine from the tail. Take out the greenish coral and, stirring gently, mix with 2 tablespoons crème fraîche, 1 egg yolk, 1 generous pinch paprika, salt, pepper, 1 teaspoon sherry and a small pinch of Provençal herbs or freshly chopped basil.

Season the lobsters with salt and pepper and

Grilled lobster (1).

place in a grill tin (pan) with the shell down. Spoon some of the coral mixture over the lobsters. Cook the lobsters under a preheated grill (broiler) for 1–2 minutes. Spoon a little more coral mixture over the lobsters, then grill again for about another 1–2 minutes. Repeat twice more, until all the coral mixture is used and the lobsters are cooked. Arrange 2 lobster halves on each plate and serve. Braised fennel with a little saffron and crushed tomato or broccoli are suitable accompaniments.

lobster à l'américaine

Cut a lobster weighing about 1 kg (2¼ lb) into even-sized pieces; split the body in two lengthways; crack the shell of the claws; reserve the liver and the coral, which will be used to thicken the sauce. Season all the pieces of lobster with salt and pepper. Heat 60 ml (2 fl oz, ¼ cup) olive oil in a pan. Put in the lobster pieces, brown quickly on both sides and remove from the pan. Finely chop a large onion and cook it gently in the oil; when it is nearly done add 2 finely chopped shallots and stir well. Peel, seed and chop 2 tomatoes and put them in the pan; add 1 tablespoon tomato purée (paste), a piece of dried orange peel, a small garlic clove and 1 tablespoon chopped parsley and tarragon. Arrange the pieces of lobster on this mixture. Pour over 100 ml (4 fl oz, 7 tablespoons) white wine, 100 ml (4 fl oz, 7 tablespoons) fish fumet* and 3 tablespoons brandy. Season with cayenne. Bring to the boil, then cover and cook over a gentle heat for a maximum of 10 minutes. Drain the lobster pieces and remove the flesh from the claws; arrange all the pieces in the split body halves in a long serving dish. Keep warm.

To prepare the sauce, reduce the cooking liquid by half. Chop the coral and liver and work them into 40 g (1½ oz, 3 tablespoons) butter, then add this mixture to the cooking liquid. Take the pan off the heat and blend the mixture well, then whisk in 50 g (2 oz, ¼ cup) butter cut into small pieces. Season the sauce with a pinch of cayenne pepper and a few drops of lemon juice. Pour the boiling sauce over the lobster and sprinkle with chopped parsley.

The chopped onion and tarragon can be replaced by 3–4 tablespoons finely chopped mirepoix*, added to the lobster while it is cooking.

lobster and crayfish with caviar

Gently simmer a lobster weighing about 800 g (1¾ lb) in a well-flavoured court-bouillon for 10 minutes. Remove the lobster, make an incision on the underside of the body between the antennae, then set aside. Boil about 20 crayfish for 2 minutes in the same stock and leave them to cool in the stock. Shell the lobster claws and tail; slice the tail into about 12 even rounds. Drain and shell the crayfish and remove the intestines. Keep hot.

Prepare some *beurre nantais*. Melt a little butter in a sauté pan and stiffen the claws, lobster rounds and crayfish tails. Add a little court-bouillon and 3 tablespoons double (heavy) cream. Heat, but do not let it boil. Place the lobster and crayfish in deep plates. Add a few tablespoons of *beurre nantais* to the sauce and, just before serving, add 4 teaspoons caviar. Cover the shellfish with this sauce and serve immediately.

lobster cardinal

Cook a lobster in a court-bouillon. Drain, cool a little and split it lengthways. Remove the flesh from the tail and cut it into slices of equal thickness. Cut off the claws, take out the flesh and dice it to make a salpicon. Add an equal quantity of diced truffles. Bind the salpicon with a lobster sauce. Fill the halves of the lobster shell with the salpicon. Place the slices of lobster interspersed with strips of truffles on top. Pour on some lobster sauce. Sprinkle with grated cheese and melted butter. Place the lobster halves on a baking sheet and brown them quickly in the oven. Garnish with curly parsley.

lobster en chemise

Plunge a lobster head first into boiling water to kill it and drain immediately. Season with salt and pepper and brush with oil or melted butter. Wrap it in a double thickness of oiled greaseproof (wax) paper, tie it securely and put it on a baking sheet. Cook in a preheated oven at 230°C (450°F, gas 8) for 40–45 minutes for a medium-sized lobster. Remove the string and serve the lobster in the paper in which it has been cooked.

It can be accompanied either by half-melted maître d'hôtel butter or by an américaine, béarnaise, Bercy, bordelaise, hongroise or curry sauce.

lobster escalopes à la parisienne

Cook a medium-sized lobster in a court-bouillon and leave to cool. Remove the shell and cut the meat into thick slices. Coat each slice separately with gelatine-thickened mayonnaise and garnish with a slice of truffle dipped in the half-set mayonnaise jelly; brush over with more jelly to give a glaze. Finely dice the rest of the lobster flesh and mix it with a salad; finely diced truffles can also be added. Bind with thickened mayonnaise and pack this salad into a dome-shaped mould. Turn the mould out into the centre of a round serving dish and arrange the lobster slices all around it in a border. Garnish with chopped jelly.

lobster Henri Duvernois

Split a lobster in half lengthways or, if it is large, cut it up as for lobster *à l'américaine*. Season with salt and paprika and sauté it in butter. As soon as it is well coloured, take it out of the pan. Add to the butter in the pan 4 tablespoons julienne of leeks and mushrooms that have been tossed in butter. Put the lobster back in the pan and add 150 ml (¼ pint, ⅔ cup) sherry and 2 tablespoons brandy. Reduce the liquid, pour in some single (light) cream, cover and simmer until cooked. Arrange the lobster on a long serving dish and garnish with a rice pilaf. Boil down the sauce, whisk in 40 g (1½ oz, 3 tablespoons) butter and pour over the lobster.

lobster in court-bouillon

Prepare a really well-flavoured court-bouillon – to 2 litres (3½ pints, 9 cups) water add the following ingredients: 2 medium carrots, 1 turnip, the white of a leek and 1 celery stick (all finely diced), a large bouquet garni, an onion stuck with 2 cloves, a small garlic clove, 500 ml (17 fl oz, 2 cups) dry white wine, 200 ml (7 fl oz, ¾ cup) vinegar, salt, pepper and a pinch of cayenne pepper. Bring to the boil and simmer for 30 minutes. Plunge the lobster head first into the boiling court-bouillon and let it simmer gently, allowing 10–15 minutes per 450 g (1 lb). Drain. If it is to be served cold, tie it on to a small board so that it keeps its shape and leave it to get completely cold.

A lobster weighing about 450 g (1 lb) should be split lengthways and served in 2 halves. If the lobster is large, take off the tail, remove the meat and cut it into medallions. Split the body in half lengthways and remove and crack the claws. Arrange the medallions on the tail shell and place the 2 halves of the body together to resemble a whole lobster again. Garnish with the claws. Serve with mayonnaise.

lobster in cream

Cut up a lobster as described in the recipe for lobster à l'américaine. Sauté the pieces of lobster in butter until they are completely red. Season with salt and pepper. Pour off the butter and deglaze the sauté pan with 3 tablespoons brandy. Flame the lobster. Then add 400 ml (14 fl oz, 1¾ cups) double (heavy) cream. Adjust the seasoning, add a pinch of cayenne pepper, cover the pan and cook gently for a maximum of 10 minutes. Drain the lobster pieces and arrange them in a deep serving dish; keep hot. Add the juice of half a lemon to the sauté pan and reduce the cream by half. Add 25 g (1 oz, 2 tablespoons) butter, whisk and pour over the lobster.

lobster sauce

Prepare 300 ml (½ pint, 1¼ cups) fish fumet* made with white wine. Reduce it by two-thirds, let it cool and add 4 egg yolks; whisk over a low heat until thick and light. Melt 250 g (9 oz, 1 cup) butter and blend it into the sauce, whisking constantly. Add 2 tablespoons lobster butter*. Still whisking, season with salt and pepper and add the juice of half a lemon. At the last moment, a little diced lobster meat can be added.

lobster sautéed à l'orange

Split a lobster in half lengthways, reserving the coral and the liver. Cut off the claws and crack them. Season the meat with salt. Crush and pound the small claws, which should be cut off close to the body. Brown them in a little oil with crushed garlic and a pinch of cayenne pepper. Add enough oil to just cover the contents of the pan and cook over the lowest possible heat so that the oil does not smoke.

Rub the mixture through a sieve and adjust the seasoning. Put 4 tablespoons of this oil into a sauté pan, slice 4 shallots and 1 onion, and brown them in the oil, together with half an orange cut into large dice, and some tarragon leaves. Push this mixture to the sides of the pan to leave the centre free and put in the lobster, flesh side down. Boil for 3 minutes to reduce the liquid.

Pour the juice of half an orange into the pan. Turn the lobster halves over on to the shell sides and add the claws. Purée the coral and the intestines with 2 tablespoons single (light) cream in a blender. Add a little brandy, a pinch of cayenne pepper and some chopped tarragon. Garnish the lobster halves with this mixture. Put under a preheated grill (broiler) for 3 minutes and serve at once.

spit-roast lobster

Plunge a large live lobster head first into boiling salted water for a few minutes, then put it on a spit. Season with salt, pepper, thyme and powdered bay leaf, then brush with melted butter or oil. Roast it over a dish or roasting pan containing a few tablespoons of dry white wine and baste frequently while cooking. A lobster weighing about 1.5 kg (3¼ lb) needs to be cooked for 40–45 minutes. Remove the lobster from the spit and arrange it on a long serving dish; serve the juice collected in the pan separately. Spit-roast lobster can be served with a curry or ravigote sauce.

other recipes See *aspic, bisque, border, butter (flavoured butters), gazpacho, soup.*

LOCUST A herbivorous insect living in desert areas, particularly in Africa, which is an important item of food in these regions. There are two edible species: the smaller one has green wings and a silver belly; the larger species has a red head and legs. Locusts are eaten grilled (broiled), roasted or boiled; dried and ground to a powder or a paste, they are also used as a condiment.

LOGANBERRY The loganberry is a cross between a blackberry and a raspberry. It is an American hybrid named after James H. Logan, who first grew it in California in 1881. The loganberry is a large, juicy, dark-red fruit, with a tart flavour, but is considered by some people to be less delicious than the raspberry. Loganberries can be eaten fresh or used in the same way as raspberries.

LOIN A cut of veal, lamb, pork or mutton that includes some of the ribs. It is usually roasted or braised whole, or can be divided into cutlets or chops.

Boned (boneless) veal loin is cooked with the bones placed alongside the roast to add their flavour to the meat. When cooking loin of mutton (or lamb, which is more delicate), the fat is lightly trimmed, the tops of the cutlet bones are scraped and the joint chined in order to make carving easier.

Although boned pork loin, tied up and lightly

barded, makes an excellent roast, the meat is tastier when cooked on the bone. The butcher should be asked to split the vertebrae and separate the top of each rib. Then tie all the ribs together to form a crown before roasting. Boned loin can also be cut into cubes and cooked on skewers.

LOIRE WINES For a little more than half its length, between Pouilly-sur-Loire and Nantes, the longest river in France is bordered by gently sloping hills where vines have been cultivated since Roman times. Different varieties of vines are grown on the different kinds of soil, the main ones being Cabernet Franc (and some Gamay) for red and rosé wines and Chenin Blanc (or Pineau de la Loire) and Sauvignon Blanc for whites. These produce a wide range of wines, ranging from sweet to dry, still to sparkling. Much rosé wine is produced. All the wines are inclined to be elegant and refreshing and some of the whites can attain a very high quality; most should be drunk while relatively young, although this depends on both the vintage and the maker.

From east to west, the Loire Valley is divided into nine main wine-producing areas of varying sizes. Upriver, producers in the small town of Pouilly-sur-Loire use Sauvignon Blanc grapes to make fine Pouilly Blanc Fumé, the more ordinary Pouilly-sur-Loire wines being made from Chasselas. Sancerre, nearby, produces many respected dry whites, made only from the Sauvignon Blanc, and some red and rosé wines, made from Pinot Noir. The small regions of Quincy and Reuilly make dry whites from Sauvignon Blanc. The extensive vineyards of Touraine produce all kinds of wine – red, white and rosé, still and sparkling. The reds include Chinon, Bourgueil and St-Nicolas-de-Bourgueil, and Champigny. The whites, which include Montlouis and Vouvray, range from still to fully sparkling, from dry to sweet and luscious. Slightly to the north, in the Sarthe, Jasnières makes dry and sweet whites. The Coteaux-du-Loir area is known mainly for its reds. Anjou, like Touraine, produces a huge range of wines, notably rosés and pleasant whites. The finest wines are the reds of Saumur-Champigny and the sparkling white and rosé Saumur wines. Further down the river, the sweeter wines of the Coteaux-du-Layon, including Quarts de Chaume and Bonnezeaux, are famous, and Savennières makes distinguished dry whites. Nearer the sea, the dry whites Muscadet and Gros Plant are made.

LOLLIPOP A sweetmeat made of boiled sugar mounted on a little stick, which is held in the hand for sucking. Lollipops, which appeared at the end of the 19th century, are flavoured with fruit, caramel or mint; some types are trimmed with strips of opaque sugar or combined contrasting colours.

The name is also used for a wide variety of ices frozen on a stick inserted in the freezing mould. The simplest frozen lollipops are fruit-flavoured, but there are many products made with ice creams as well as water-based mixtures.

LOLLO Generic name for several varieties of lettuce known for their small size, maximum 20 cm (8 in), and their shape without a firm heart. The soft, finely ribbed, divided leaves are more or less coloured at the tips. Lollo lettuce leaves are used in salad; they are tender and slightly crisp.

LONGAN An oval fruit about the size of a plum, originating in India and China. Its red, pink or yellow skin covers firm, white, translucent flesh which is quite sweet and surrounds a large black stone (pit) with a white eye-shaped marking (hence the Chinese name for the fruit – *lung-yen*, meaning 'dragon's eye'). The longan is somewhat similar to a lychee, but has a fainter aroma. In France it can be bought canned in syrup, or sometimes crystallized (candied). It is used in fruit salads and can be liquidized to make a refreshing drink.

LONGANIZA A half-dried, half-smoked Spanish sausage, rather like a fat chorizo sausage. Made from fatty sausagemeat, which is highly coloured and seasoned with hot peppers and aniseed, it is eaten fried, particularly with egg dishes, or uncooked.

LONGCHAMP The main racecourse of Paris, whose name was given to a thick soup, based on a pea purée.

RECIPE

Longchamp soup
Cut some sorrel into fine strips and soften it in butter in a covered saucepan. When well braised, add 4 tablespoons sorrel to 1 litre (1¾ pints, 4⅓ cups) puréed fresh peas. Add 500 ml (17 fl oz, 2 cups) stock with vermicelli and stir well. Heat up the soup and sprinkle with parsley.

LONGEOLE A sausage from Switzerland or Savoy, made with vegetables (spinach beet, cabbage, leeks), which are cooked, drained and pounded, then mixed with pork fat and pluck (heart, lungs and spleen). Longeoles are braised and can be preserved in oil.

LONZO An item of Corsican charcuterie prepared in the same way as coppa, but using the fillet instead of the faux-filet. The fillet is boned, rubbed with salt and coated with saltpetre, then washed with garlic-flavoured red wine, dried and dusted with paprika. It is then pressed into a pig's intestine and tied up with string. Lonzo is eaten in thin slices as an hors d'oeuvre.

LOQUAT The pear-shaped fruit of an ornamental evergreen tree that is native to China and Japan and is cultivated in the Mediterranean basin, as well as in Australia and North, Central and South America. The loquat, which is the size of a crab apple, is also called Japanese medlar or Japanese plum; it has a slightly downy skin and white, yellow or orange flesh that may be firm or soft, depending on the variety. The fruit may contain one or more seeds. The loquat is eaten raw as a dessert fruit when very ripe, having a slightly acid refreshing flavour. It can also be made into jam, jelly, syrup or a liqueur.

LORETTE A garnish for large joints of roast beef and smaller sautéed ones. It consists of chicken croquettes, small bunches of asparagus tips and sliced truffles. A demi-glace sauce is used for large roasts; for the sautéed steaks, the pan is deglazed with Madeira and demi-glace.

Lorette potatoes are deep-fried, cheese-flavoured dauphine potatoes. Lorette salad consists of lamb's lettuce, with a julienne of celeriac and cooked beetroot (beet).

RECIPE

lorette potatoes
Prepare a dauphine potato mixture and add grated Gruyère cheese, using 100 g (4 oz, 1 cup) for 675 g (1½ lb) potato mixture. Divide the mixture into portions of about 40 g (1½ oz, 3 tablespoons) and mould into crescent shapes, or use a piping (pastry) bag to make stick shapes or knobs. Allow to dry for 30 minutes in the refrigerator, then deep-fry until golden brown. Drain on paper towels.

LORRAINE This province comprises widely differing regions. The Vosges mountains are rich in forests and pastures. The rugged countryside of the Vôge – with its narrow steep valleys, numerous thermal springs (Vittel, Contrexéville, Plombières) and beautiful oak and beech forests – is famous for wild boar, mushrooms and bilberries (huckleberries), and for the rearing of horned cattle, whose milk is used for making some well-known cheeses (often strong or flavoured). The Lorraine plateau, with its fertile soil, is increasingly used for growing maize (corn) and animal feed for horned cattle – both beef and dairy breeds – and also for sheep and pigs. The slopes of the Meuse region, with its varied agricultural activities, are covered in vineyards (*vin gris de Toul*), orchards (mirabelle plums, quetsche plums and cherries) and pastures. The rivers – the Meuse, Moselle and Ornain – are rich in carp, pike and trout.

The Lorraine cuisine is based principally on pork, which is an important ingredient in *potée* (smoked ham soup), in the famous quiche, and in *tourte de porc et de veau* (marinated meats baked in a pie crust with egg custard), not to mention the *andouillettes* of Epinal, the black puddings (blood sausages) of Nancy, the sauerkraut of Saint-Dié, fresh pork liver, sucking pig in aspic, and the wide range of charcuterie from Jametz, Dannevoux and Vaucouleurs. Goose is often prepared *en daube*, and the pâtés de foie gras of Lorraine rival those of Alsace.

The local fish is used for delicious fish stews, while frogs and crayfish are served *en gratin*.

Lorraine pâtisserie has been famous ever since Stanislas Leszczyński ruled in Nancy, but even before then the province was renowned for its traditional specialities: the quetsche, mirabelle, bilberry and grape tarts, the biscuits (cookies) of Stenay, *chemitrés* (a kind of waffle), cream puffs from Pont-à-Mousson, macaroons from Nancy, madeleines from Commercy, and ginger cakes and gingerbread from Remiremont. Its confectionery is equally famous: bergamots, sugared almonds, barley sugar, kirsch chocolates from Charmes, redcurrant jam from Bar-le-Duc and bilberry jam from Remiremont.

Lorraine beer no longer enjoys the fame it once did, but mirabelle, raspberry, quetsche and cherry brandies are still, rightly, highly appreciated.

LORRAINE, À LA Describes a preparation of large cuts of meat, usually braised, which are garnished with red cabbage cooked in red wine, and apples. The braising juices are served as an accompanying sauce after the fat has been skimmed.

The term is also used to define other specialities from Lorraine, such as *potée* (smoked ham soup) and quiche, as well as various egg-based dishes, all of which include smoked bacon and Gruyère cheese.

RECIPES

baked eggs à la lorraine
Grease an ovenproof egg dish with butter and line it with 3–4 rashers (slices) of grilled (broiled) smoked bacon together with 3–4 thin slices of Gruyère cheese. Break 2 eggs into the dish and pour a ring of double (heavy) cream around the yolks. Bake in a preheated oven at 180°C (350°F, gas 4) for 10–15 minutes or until the eggs are just set.

flat omelette à la lorraine
For a 6-egg omelette, dice 150 g (5 oz, 6 slices) smoked bacon and sauté in butter. Shred 65 g (2½ oz, ½ cup) Gruyère cheese. Prepare 1 tablespoon finely chopped chives. Beat the eggs and add the rest of the ingredients, then season with pepper. Melt 15 g (½ oz, 1 tablespoon) butter in a frying pan; pour in the mixture. Cook on one side, then turn and cook the other side.

LOTUS An Asian plant related to the water lily. Its roots, leaves and seeds are used in cookery. The large, fan-shaped leaves are dried, then used as a wrapping for steamed foods, to which they give a delicate flavour, particularly to rice mixtures.

The young leaves are chopped and used in cooking as a herb or in the same way as spinach. In Java, lotus leaves are stuffed with prawns (shrimp) and rice; while in China they are stuffed with chopped meat and onion. In Vietnam, lotus seeds, which have a nutty taste, are used in a very popular sweet soup.

In Chinese cookery, the seeds are used dried, when they may be ground to a powder for thickening or simmered to make a sweet filling for steamed buns and other sweet specialities. The dried lotus seeds can be eaten as a snack or used in savoury braised dishes. The seeds are either pickled in vinegar or candied in syrup.

Lotus roots are the most striking and widely recognized parts of the plant. They are underwater stems, rather than roots, and when cut crossways the hollow channels that run along their length are revealed. Fresh roots have to be thickly peeled and they are often sliced before being boiled or stir-fried. The round holes resulting from the channels give the slices an attractive, flower-like appearance. The flavour is delicate, yet distinctive, and the texture is firm and slightly crunchy. Lotus root is known as *renkon* in Japanese cookery. In Europe and America fresh lotus roots are available in specialist markets and shops. Canned lotus root is available prepared and sliced.

LOUISIANE A chicken dish in which the bird is stuffed with a mixture of creamed sweetcorn and diced red and green (bell) peppers, browned on the hob (stovetop), then baked in the oven in a covered casserole, with a few herbs. It is basted frequently. When it is nearly cooked, some chicken stock and Madeira are added. The chicken is served with a garnish of sweetcorn in cream (sometimes in tartlets), rice moulded in darioles and thick fried slices of banana (possibly arranged on fried slices of sweet potato). The accompanying sauce consists of the strained and skimmed cooking liquid.

LOUP D'ATLANTIQUE Fish of the *Anarhichadidae* family, often confused with sea bass, known as 'wolf fish' (*loup*) in the Mediterranean. With a length of 1.2–1.5 m (4–5 ft), it is differentiated by its elongated body, its strong head, its rounded muzzle and its very large prominent canine teeth. The loup d'Atlantique lives in cold waters about 450 m (1,475 ft) deep, from the south of the British Isles to Greenland. Its flesh, similar to that of ling, is served in the same ways as cod.

LOUPIAC A sweet AOC white wine, from the right bank of the River Garonne, opposite Barsac, some 30 km (20 miles) south-east of Bordeaux. The wines are full-bodied and with a pronounced bouquet.

LOUQUENKA A small raw sausage from the Basque area, flavoured with pimiento and garlic. It is traditionally eaten grilled (broiled), with oysters.

LOVAGE An aromatic herb, which originally came from Persia but is now naturalized in many parts of Europe and North America. The leaves taste rather like celery, and the plant used to be popular in England. It is also used in Germany, where its leaves and seeds flavour salads, soups and meat dishes. The leafstalks are blanched and eaten in salads, but they can also be crystallized (candied), rather like angelica. The roots, too, are used as a salad vegetable (raw or cooked) and can be dried and ground for use as a condiment. Lovage is also added to cool summer drinks.

LOVING CUP *vidrecome* A large drinking vessel, usually with two handles, originating in Germany and used in the Middle Ages at banquets, when it was passed from one guest to another. The French name, which comes from the German *wieder* (again) and *kommen* (come), means literally 'to start drinking again'.

LUCULLUS, LUCIUS LICINIUS Roman general (106–56 BC), now remembered chiefly for the splendour and luxury of his feasts. After winning a brilliant victory over Mithridates, Lucullus retired to his country villa, where he lived on a grand scale. Each of his various dining halls was used according to the amount of money spent on the meals served there. Thus, surprised one day by the unexpected arrival of Caesar and Cicero, who wanted to share his meal but would not allow him to change anything on their account, he served them in the Apollo room, where the cost of meals had been fixed at 100,000 sesterces. One night, when he was on his own, he reprimanded his cook for preparing a less elaborate meal than when there were guests, and shouted at him: 'Today Lucullus is dining at Lucullus's!'

It was Lucullus who introduced the pheasant, the peach tree and the cherry tree to his native country.

The name Lucullus has been given to numerous classic dishes characterized by the richness of their ingredients. Pheasants, ortolans or quails Lucullus are stuffed with foie gras and truffles, cooked in a casserole, deglazed with Madeira and demi-glace sauce, then garnished with truffles poached in Madeira, cockscombs and cocks' kidneys. In tournedos Lucullus, the steak is sautéed, placed on a croûton, garnished with a thin slice of truffle and a poached mushroom cap, then coated with a sauce prepared by deglazing the pan with Périgueux sauce; the garnish consists of cockscombs and cocks' kidneys with asparagus tips. There are even poached eggs Lucullus, which are served on artichoke hearts stuffed with a salpicon of lamb's sweetbreads, cockscombs and truffle.

RECIPES

hot snipe pâté Lucullus

Bone 8 snipe and lay them out flat on a working surface. Prepare some fine forcemeat *à la crème* and mix with a third of its volume of foie gras and chopped snipe's entrails. Spread the forcemeat over the birds and place a piece of foie gras and a piece of truffle in the middle. Reshape the birds and pour some Cognac over them.

Line an oval mould with pastry and spread over it a layer of forcemeat *à la crème* mixed with half its volume of *à gratin* forcemeat. Place the snipe in the mould, packing them close together and filling in the gaps with the forcemeat. Top with a layer of forcemeat and cover with some rashers (slices) of bacon. Cover the mould with a lid of pastry, seal and crimp the edges, then garnish with pastry motifs. Make an opening in the middle and brush with beaten egg.

LUXEMBOURG

This country has some interesting gastronomic specialities, although it has been said, 'Luxembourg cuisine consists of French dishes with a few German additions.'

■ **Soups and vegetables**
Luxembourg used to be a poor country, where bread was once a rare commodity. The diet of farmers and peasants consisted of beans, peas and potatoes, the latter still remaining a staple food, in the same way as oats (in the form of gruel) and buckwheat (used to make cakes and *quenelles*).

Lunch and dinner often start with soup, lighter at lunchtime, made from vegetables. The most famous of these soups is *bounesschlupp*, made from green beans; when made with haricot beans and prunes, it is called *bohnensuppe*. Potatoes and cabbages are still the most important vegetables. Potatoes are consumed at every meal, either served on their own with the addition of diced bacon, in soups, or with meat or fish. Cabbage is also served with meat, but also with charcuterie and potatoes.

■ **Meat and fish** The pillar of Luxembourg cuisine is, without doubt, pork. In fact, beef was introduced into the country quite late in its history. Although tripe is very popular, the uncontested national dish is smoked neck of pork with broad (fava) beans (*Judd mat gaardebounen*). Pork may be roasted, cooked as chops, braised, grilled (broiled) or stewed. There are numerous recipes, and leftovers are used to make delicious dishes like the *tirtech*, which combines pork, potatoes and sauerkraut.

There is also a wide choice of different kinds of sausages and flavoured, smoked hams, such as Oesling ham, which is smoked over beech, oak and juniper wood.

Most of the fish are freshwater fish from the local rivers, such as pike, cooked in Riesling, and trout, cooked *au bleu* in a mixture of water, wine and vinegar. Freshwater crayfish, cooked *à la luxembourgeoise*, are traditional for special occasions. However, sea fish and shellfish are increasingly replacing freshwater fish, as a result of the growing international population.

Kachkéis, a cheese prepared with skimmed milk, curdled and drained, is very similar to Cancoillotte. It is used as a spread on buttered bread, sometimes with the addition of crème fraîche or egg yolk, and is traditionally accompanied by mustard.

Finally, desserts – crêpes, fruit dishes, tarts and whipped cream – are simple, with the conspicuous exception of *baumkuchen*, a cake baked on a spit according to an Austrian recipe of the late 18th century.

WINE The Moselle winds its way through beautiful vineyards, from Schengen, in the south, to Wasserbillig, in the north. There are a very few timid appearances of Pinot Noir, but most of the vines are white grape varieties: Elbling, Rivaner, Auxerrois, Pinot Blanc, Pinot Gris, Riesling and Gewürztraminer. These are used to produce classic white wines, some sparkling wines, and, since 1988, some crémants as well. The traditional Elbling, cultivated since Roman times, produces a rustic wine much enjoyed by connoisseurs for its original purity.

Place the mould in a bain marie, bring to the boil over a moderate heat, then cook in a preheated oven at 180°C (350°F, gas 4) for about 1 hour. Cut away the pastry lid, take off the layer of bacon and unmould the pâté. Add to it a ragoût of truffles bound with a few spoonfuls of Madeira-flavoured game stock. Replace the pastry lid and heat up the pâté in the oven. Serve immediately.

macaroni Lucullus
Boil some macaroni until cooked al dente. Prepare a very concentrated Madeira sauce, then add it to a salpicon of truffle and foie gras. Arrange alternate layers of macaroni and salpicon in a dish. Garnish with strips of truffle.

LUMPFISH A fish found in cold seas and therefore abundant in the North Sea and the Baltic. About 50 cm (20 in) long, it leads a sedentary life, attaching itself to the rocks by means of a sucker on its belly. It is fished mainly for its eggs. These are laid in large quantities in March and are yellow in their natural state. They are dyed black or red and sold as caviar substitute, but they do not have anything like the delicious flavour of sturgeon's eggs.

LUNCH The midday meal in many English-speaking countries. The word was introduced into France in the first half of the 19th century, and is used for a cold buffet served at a reception where a large number of guests have to be catered for. In addition to canapés, a lunch of this type consists of cheeses, fruit, petits fours, chilled puddings and a few larger dishes, such as fish in aspic and cold hams.

LUNCHEON MEAT A cooked meat eaten in Britain and the United States. Related to the sausage widely used in Germany for putting on bread, luncheon meat is made of a fine pork paste, often with the addition of chunks of lean meat, thickened with flour, and seasoned with salt, saltpetre and spices. The product is available canned or put inside a skin, which has been smoked and rubbed with olive oil. In the United States, the term 'luncheon meat' is also used for cold sliced meats used for sandwiches.

LUTE A mixture of flour and water, also known in France as *repère*, used to seal the lid on to an earthenware cooking pot. The lute hardens as it dries in the heat. This means that the food is cooked in a sealed container, avoiding evaporation.

Lyonnais

Lyon is a gastronomic centre of high repute, famous for its *mâchons* served with jugs of Beaujolais. It owes its place in French cuisine to its own local resources (notably, onions, fruit and vegetable produce, and a wide range of local charcuterie, some say the largest variety in France) as well as to imports from bordering provinces: beef from Charolais, fruit and vegetables from the Rhône valley, poultry from Bresse and freshwater fish and game from Dombes.

As an important communication point between Gaul and Cisalpine, Lyon (then called Lugdunum) enjoyed a reputation as a gourmet town even in times of antiquity. Its local fairs attracted craftsmen, tradesmen, moneylenders and, later, manufacturers and industrialists, who met together around sumptuously laden tables. Rabelais joined Erasmus in singing the praises of Lyon and its cuisine. The prosperous bourgeoisie of the

town ensured that the tradition of good food was perpetuated. The fame of their rôtisseurs and caterers spread as far as Paris, even before the first restaurants were established. Then there was the period of the Mères Lyonnaises (mothers of Lyon), before the great chefs of modern times turned Lyon, Roanne and other large towns of Lyonnais into the centres of the district's cuisine.

As well as being the home of great chefs, Lyonnais is also the cradle of a traditional hearty cuisine that is as delicious as the more elegant and refined cuisine that extended its reputation beyond its own borders. This dual tradition is upheld by a number of typically Lyonnais gastronomic societies, such as the Club Brillat-Savarin, which held its meetings at Morateur's; the Société des Amis de Guignol, which preserves the popular recipes of the Lyonnais; and the Académie Rabelais and the Francs-Mâchons, also enthusiasts for the traditional local cuisine.

■ **Lyonnais specialities** Lyonnais

cuisine is undoubtedly dominated by the onion, indispensable for the preparation of omelettes and other egg dishes, *miroton*, sautéed vegetables and many other dishes. However, it is an extremely varied cuisine, with a particularly wide range of charcuterie. These include the rosette, the sabodet and the *saucisson de Lyon* (a 'product with a gnarled uneven surface, held in tightly by its string casing, thus giving it a swollen appearance'). Then there are the *andouille* and *andouillettes* of Charlieu, *cervelas truffé* (truffled saveloy), *gras-double* (tripe), *tablier de sapeur*, roulade of pig's head, *grattons*, *paquet de couennes*, *jambonneau* (knuckle of ham), and the pigs' ears and tails that featured in the Rabelaisian snacks in the taverns of the town.

Typical Lyonnais soups are bone-marrow consommé, onion soup, pumpkin soup with cream, and egg yolk soup (thickened in a bain marie, like a baked custard). Lyonnais pike quenelles are famous, and local freshwater fish

The Lyonnais is known for its bouchons, *little restaurants where simple dishes are served at any time of day, as well as for the grand cuisine of the region. This appealing* bouchon *is located in the old part of Lyon, in Rue Leynaud.*

and crustaceans form the basis of both sumptuous and simple dishes: *matelote* (fish stew) with red wine, fried Rhône gudgeons, gratin and mousse of crayfish tails, trout and pike *au bleu*, braised carp with onion, and frogs with cream or garlic.

The peaks of culinary art have been reached with Lyonnais meat and poultry dishes: *grillades de boeuf à la moelle* (grilled beef with marrow), *farci de veau en vessie* (veal sausage), *poulet Célestine* and *poularde demi-deuil*, seven-hour braised *gigot, rouelle de veau roulé* and *potage à la*

jambe de bois are just a modest selection from the range of Lyonnais cuisine. Vegetable specialities include cardoons au gratin, with bone marrow or chicken, artichoke hearts with foie gras, *galette lyonnais* (made with potatoes and onions), dandelion salad with diced bacon, and sautéed green beans. Cheeses from neighbouring areas that are eaten in Lyon include Bleu de Bresse, Pélardon du Vivarais, Reblochon, Rigotte and Brique du Forez. But Mont-d'Or (once made exclusively from goat's milk) and Cervelle de canut are typically

Lyonnais.

The desserts, cakes and confectionery of the region show the same sort of range as the other products. For example, there is vacherin with whipped cream and strawberries, Bernachon chocolates, the *sablés* of Noirétable, as well as the more homely *bugnes du carnaval* (a sort of fritter), *matefaims* (a type of pancake, usually served with fruit or jam) almond and kirsch tart *à la lyonnaise, radisses* (large elongated brioches), pumpkin cakes, marrons glacés and mimosa blossom fritters.

LUXEMBOURG See *page 701.*

LUXEMBOURGEOIS Smooth macaroon, also called *macaron gerbet*, filled with cream or a ganache, which is the basis of various pastries.

LYCHEE A fruit that originated in China, and which is now grown there and in parts of India, South Africa, the West Indies and the United States. It is about the size of a small plum and has a thin, hard, knobbly shell that can be removed easily. The shell is green when unripe, but turns either pink or red. The white, juicy, translucent flesh surrounds a large dark-brown stone (pit); the fruit has a sweet rather musky flavour. In Chinese cookery, they are often served fresh with meat or fish. They can also be used to enhance a winter fruit salad. Lychees are sold canned, preserved in sugar syrup. If the fruit is allowed to dry in its shell, it eventually turns black like a prune. These 'litchi nuts' are very sweet with a slightly acid flavour.

LYONNAIS See *page 702.*

LYONNAISE, À LA Describing various preparations, usually sautéed, characterized by the use of chopped onions, which are glazed in butter until golden and often finished off with the pan juices deglazed with vinegar and sprinkled with chopped parsley. Preparations of leftover meats, cardoons and calf's head, are also described as *à la lyonnaise* if they are served with a lyonnaise sauce, which has an onion base.

RECIPES

calf's head à la lyonnaise
Blanch some pieces of calf's head. Line an oven-proof dish with a layer of sliced onions softened in butter, plus some chopped parsley, then arrange the pieces of meat on top. Cover with lyonnaise sauce. Sprinkle with breadcrumbs, moisten with clarified butter and cook au gratin.

calf's liver à la lyonnaise
Cut the liver into thin slices and season with salt and pepper. Coat the slices with flour and sauté quickly in butter. Keep them warm on a serving dish. Peel and slice some onions and soften in butter. Bind them with a few spoonfuls of meat glaze and place on top of the liver. Moisten the liver with a dash of vinegar heated up in the same frying pan and sprinkle with chopped parsley. Serve with green beans in tomato sauce.

cardoons à la lyonnaise
Clean some cardoons, cut them up and blanch them in white vegetable stock. Braise gently in butter. Add a few spoonfuls of lyonnaise sauce and simmer for about 10 minutes. Arrange the cardoons in a vegetable dish and serve very hot.

lyonnaise potatoes
Parboil some potatoes and slice them. Melt some butter in a frying pan and add the potatoes. When they start to turn golden brown, add some finely chopped onions that have been softened in butter; allow 4 tablespoons onion per 675 g (1½ lb) potatoes. Sauté the mixture well. Arrange in a vegetable dish and sprinkle with chopped parsley.

lyonnaise sauce
Cook 3 tablespoons finely chopped onions in 15 g (½ oz, 1 tablespoon) butter. When the onions are well softened, add 500 ml (17 fl oz, 2 cups) vinegar and 500 ml (17 fl oz, 2 cups) white wine. Reduce until almost evaporated, then add 200 ml (7 fl oz, ¾ cup) demi-glace*. Boil for 3–4 minutes, then strain the sauce or serve it unstrained. Add 1 tablespoon tomato purée (paste) to this sauce if liked.

Alternatively, sprinkle the cooked onions with 1 tablespoon flour and cook until golden, deglaze with 175 ml (6 fl oz, ¾ cup) vinegar and 175 ml (6 fl oz, ¾ cup) white wine, then add some meat stock or pan juices. Boil for a few minutes and serve as above.

omelette à la lyonnaise

Chop some onions finely. Brown them in butter and add some chopped parsley. Season with salt and pepper. Break the eggs into a bowl, add the onions and beat together (allow 1 tablespoon fried onion per egg). Cook the omelette and roll it on to a serving dish. Pour over it a few spoonfuls of vinegar heated up in the same frying pan and a little noisette butter.

salt cod à la lyonnaise

Prepare and cook some salt cod. Drain, separate the individual flakes and put them in a saucepan. Cover the saucepan and place over a low heat to dry out any water the cod might still contain. Dice 3 large white onions and cook them gently over a low heat in 225 g (8 oz, 1 cup) melted butter. As soon as they are golden brown, add the cod and sauté. Season with pepper, grated nutmeg and the juice of 1 lemon before serving.

sautéed veal à la lyonnaise

Take 4 loin chops or 4 escalopes (scallops) of veal and sauté in butter. When they are almost cooked, add 4 tablespoons sliced onions gently cooked in butter. Complete the cooking. Arrange the meat on a serving dish and keep warm. Add to the sauté dish 60 ml (2 fl oz, ¼ cup) wine vinegar, 1 tablespoon chopped parsley and 2 tablespoons meat stock. Reduce and pour over the meat.

other recipes See *andouillette, artichoke, bean (haricot beans), beet, civet, crapaudine (en), entrecôte, frog, godiveau, herring, mackerel.*

M

MACADAMIA NUT The fruit of an Australian tree. Also known as Queensland nut, it has a thin green fleshy husk; a very hard light-brown shell encloses the edible white kernel, which has a mild, yet rich, flavour. The nuts are rounded in shape and slightly larger than chick peas in size. In Asia the nut is used in curries and stews; in the United States it is a flavouring for ices and cakes, and is also eaten as a sweetmeat, dipped in honey or chocolate.

MACAIRE A flat potato cake used as a garnish for roast or sautéed meats.

RECIPE

macaire potatoes
Cook 4 large floury unpeeled potatoes in the oven. Cut in half and remove the pulp. Mash the potato pulp with butter until smooth, allowing 100 g (4 oz, ½ cup) butter per 1 kg (2¼ lb) potato. Season with salt and pepper. Heat some butter in a frying pan and add the mashed potato, spreading it out into a flat round cake. Cook until golden, then, with the aid of a plate, turn the potato cake over and cook the other side.

MACARONI Tubes of pasta, 5–6 mm (about ¼ in) in diameter, which originated in Naples. Macaroni is cooked in boiling water and may be served with grated cheese, tomato sauce, butter, cream or au gratin. It may also be put in a timbale mould or ring mould and served with, for example, seafood, vegetables or mushrooms. The word comes from the Italian *maccherone*, meaning 'fine paste'. In Rome the popular method of serving macaroni is *alla ciociara*, with sliced fried vegetables, smoked ham and slices of sausage. In Naples it is served *all'arrabbiata* (with a spicy sauce of pimientos) or with Mozzarella cheese, mushrooms, peas and giblets. Macaroni has been known since the 17th century and in Britain, in the 19th century when it was fashionable to give a British slant to Italian dishes, macaroni cheese became a traditional dish. It was also served as a dessert, showing Britain's fondness for milk puddings.

RECIPES

macaroni à l'italienne
Cook 250 g (9 oz) macaroni and drain thoroughly. Mix in 75 g (3 oz, ¾ cup) grated cheese (a mixture of Gruyère and Parmesan) and 75 g (3 oz, 6 tablespoons) butter, cut into small pieces. Season with salt, pepper and a pinch of grated nutmeg. Mix well together, pour into a serving dish and serve very hot.

macaroni calabrese
Rinse 1 kg (2¼ lb) ripe tomatoes. Cut them in half and press to remove the juice. Arrange the tomatoes in a gratin dish. Season with salt and pepper and sprinkle with a generous amount of extra virgin olive oil. Cook in a preheated oven at 180°C (350°F, gas 4) until almost roasted but not completely cooked. Halfway through the cooking process, add stoned (pitted) black olives and capers. Cook 575 g (1¼ lb) macaroni in plenty of boiling water, drain and garnish with the tomatoes. Sprinkle a little basil on top, pour on a dash of olive oil and serve very hot.

macaroni with cream
Boil the macaroni until it is three-parts cooked. Drain and put back in the saucepan over the heat

to evaporate all moisture. Moisten with 200 ml (7 fl oz, ¾ cup) boiled double (heavy) cream. Simmer slowly for 10–12 minutes. Season with a pinch of salt and a little grated nutmeg. Remove the pan from the heat and mix in 65 g (2½ oz, 5 tablespoons) butter, cut into small pieces.

macaroni with mirepoix
Prepare a vegetable mirepoix of equal weight to the cooked macaroni. Mix the mirepoix with the macaroni and put into a buttered gratin dish. Sprinkle with grated cheese, pour melted butter over it and brown in the oven.

macaroni with seafood
Prepare a seafood ragoût. Cook the macaroni in salted water and drain thoroughly. Place half the macaroni in a serving dish, cover with the ragoût and pile the remaining macaroni on top. Serve very hot.

MACAROON A small, round, biscuit (cookie) crunchy outside and soft inside, made with ground almonds, sugar and egg whites. Macaroons are sometimes flavoured with coffee, chocolate, nuts or fruit and then joined together in pairs.

The origin of this biscuit goes back a long way. The recipe originally came from Italy, particularly Venice, during the Renaissance: the name is derived from the Italian *maccherone* and the Venetian *macarone* (meaning fine paste), from which macaroni is also derived. Some authorities claim that the recipe for the macaroons of Cormery, in France, is the oldest. Macaroons have been made in the monastery there since 791 and legend has it that they used to be made in the shape of monks' navels. The macaroons of many French towns are famous, including those of Montmorillon (shaped like coronets and sold on their cooking paper), Niort (made with angelica), Reims, Pau, Amiens and Melun. The Nancy macaroons are probably the best-known. During the 17th century they were manufactured by the Carmelites, who followed Theresa of Avila's principle to the letter: 'Almonds are good for girls who do not eat meat.' During the French Revolution, two nuns, in hiding with an inhabitant of the town, specialized in making and selling macaroons. They became famous as the 'Macaroon Sisters' and in 1952 the street in which they had operated was named after them; macaroons are still made there today.

Ratafias are a similar biscuit, originally eaten with the liqueur of the same name (see *ratafia*). They are smaller, browner and now usually flavoured with ratafia essence. Amaretti are Italian biscuits which are much the same and flavoured with bitter almonds or apricot kernels.

RECIPES

classic macaroons
Line a baking sheet with rice paper or buttered greaseproof (wax) paper. Mix 350 g (12 oz, 1½ cups) caster (superfine) sugar with 250 g (9 oz, 2½ cups) ground almonds. Lightly whisk 4 egg whites with a pinch of salt and mix thoroughly with the sugar and almond mixture. If liked, a little finely chopped candied orange peel or cocoa powder can be added to the mixture before cooking. Pipe or spoon small heaps of this mixture on to the baking sheet, spacing them so that they do not run into one another during cooking.

Cook in a preheated oven at 200°C (400°F, gas 6) for about 12 minutes. Lift the macaroons off the baking sheet with a spatula, transfer to a wire rack and leave to cool completely. Macaroons can be stored in an airtight container for several days in the refrigerator, or for several months in the freezer.

soft macaroons
Mix together 250 g (9 oz, 2½ cups) ground almonds, 450–500 g (16–18 oz, 3⅓–3⅔ cups) icing (confectioner's) sugar, and 1 teaspoon vanilla sugar or a few drops of vanilla essence (extract) in a bowl with 4 lightly whisked egg whites. Whisk 4 additional egg whites into stiff peaks with a pinch of salt and fold very gently into the mixture. Place the mixture in a piping (pastry) bag with a smooth nozzle 5 mm (¼ in) in diameter. Pipe small amounts of the mixture on to a baking sheet lined with rice paper or greaseproof (wax) paper, spacing them so that they do not stick together during cooking. Cook in a preheated oven at 180°C (350°F, gas 4) for about 12 minutes. Finish as for classic macaroons. A little finely chopped angelica can be added to the almond mixture.

MACE A spice derived from the fibrous, lacy outer coating of the nutmeg seed. It is pressed, dried and used as it is or reduced to powder. The whole mace is known as a blade. It is golden brown when dried, with a distinct flavour similar to nutmeg, but stronger. Mace is widely used in savoury and sweet cooking. It is a popular seasoning for sausage meats and forcemeats, and it has an affinity with pork dishes. It can also be used to improve the flavour of sauces for meats and can replace nutmeg in omelettes, béchamel sauce and potato purée.

MACÉDOINE A mixture of vegetables or fruit cut into small dice. The name 'macédoine' is derived from Macedonia, the ancient royal kingdom formed from the various Balkan states united by Philip II, father of Alexander the Great.

A vegetable macédoine is usually composed of carrots and turnips, which are peeled and cut into slices 3–4 mm (⅛ in) thick, then into sticks, and finally into 3–4 mm (⅛ in) cubes. French (green) beans are cut into small pieces. The vegetables are cooked separately and then mixed together with some well-drained peas and possibly other vegetables. The macédoine is bound with butter and is served hot as a garnish for meat and poultry. Roast meat juices are often added, particularly veal, as are chopped herbs and crème fraîche. It can also be served cold, in aspic or bound with mayonnaise and used to stuff tomatoes or to accompany hard-boiled (hard-cooked) eggs or ham cornets.

A fruit macédoine consists of diced fruit soaked in fruit syrup which is served cold, often sprinkled with kirsch or rum. It can be used to decorate grapefruit and many other dishes.

RECIPE

vegetable macédoine with butter or cream

Peel and dice 250 g (9 oz) each of new carrots, turnips, French (green) beans and potatoes. Prepare 500 g (18 oz, 3½ cups) shelled peas. Add the carrots and turnips to a pan of boiling salted water. Bring back to the boil and add the beans, then the peas and finally the potatoes. Keep on the boil but do not cover. When the vegetables are cooked, drain and pour into a serving dish and add butter or cream (keep the cooking water for a soup base). Sprinkle with chopped herbs.

MACERATE To soak raw, dried or preserved foods in liquid (usually alcohol – liqueur, wine or brandy – or sugar syrup) so that they absorb the flavour of the liquid. Macerate is the term usually applied to fruit, as opposed to marinate, which is used for the same process in savoury cooking. Macerating imparts flavour to the fruit, softens it and draws out the fruit juices. Dried fruits for winter compotes and other dishes are often treated in this way.

To prepare some conserves and jams, the fruit may be macerated with the sugar in which it will later be cooked.

MACKEREL A common oceanic fish found in the waters of the Black Sea and the Mediterranean, the North Sea and the North Atlantic, from Spain to Norway and Iceland and off the coast of Labrador and New England on the American side. It can be fished throughout the year, in surface waters during the summer months and in deep waters during the winter months. They migrate in large shoals to specific breeding grounds each year. Mackerel caught by line are always fresher and tastier than those caught by trawler.

The mackerel has a streamlined body, greenish-blue with black and green bands on the back and a silvery underside. When freshly caught, the flesh is firm and the eyes are bright. The chub mackerel is common in the Mediterranean but also found off the Iberian and French Atlantic coasts and in New England waters. It is small, has less pronounced markings and larger eyes. Chub mackerel are sometimes known as Spanish mackerel but the term can also refer to similar fish found in tropical and semi-tropical waters around the world, particularly in South-East Asia, notably off Thailand and the Philippines, and the Caribbean.

Mackerel is an oily fish with a distinctive flavour. It can be prepared in many ways – grilled (broiled); classically served with gooseberry sauce, to set off its richness; stuffed; prepared *à la provençale* or with white wine; made into a soup (*cotriade*); or poached and served with mustard, horseradish, tomato or cream sauce. Mackerel fillets can also be smoked, sometimes crusted with peppercorns, or preserved in oil or tomato sauce.

RECIPES

Mackerel Fillets

fillets of mackerel à la dijonnaise

Fillet 4 large mackerel. Season the fillets with salt and pepper and coat with white mustard seeds.

Soften 2 chopped onions in 2 tablespoons oil in a saucepan. Add 1 tablespoon flour and mix well. Pour a glass of stock or fish fumet into the saucepan, together with a glass of dry white wine. Stir well, add a bouquet garni and cook for 8–10 minutes.

Arrange the fillets in a buttered ovenproof dish and add the sauce. Place the dish in a preheated oven at 200°C (400°F, gas 6) and cook for about 15 minutes. Drain the fish and arrange on a serving dish. Remove the bouquet garni from the sauce, add a little mustard, check the seasoning and pour the sauce over the fillets. Garnish with slices of lemon and sprigs of parsley.

fillets of mackerel à la lyonnaise

Fillet and season 4 large mackerel. Soften 4 chopped onions in melted butter, then add 1 tablespoon vinegar. Place half the onions in a buttered ovenproof dish, lay the fillets on top and cover with the remaining onions. Moisten with 3 tablespoons dry white wine. Sprinkle with breadcrumbs, dot with knobs of butter and cook in a preheated oven at 220°C (425°F, gas 7) for about 10 minutes. Sprinkle with chopped parsley.

fillets of mackerel in white wine

Add 5 tablespoons white wine to 500 ml (18 fl oz, 2¼ cups) fish stock and boil down to reduce by half. Fillet and season 4 large mackerel. Arrange the fillets in a buttered ovenproof dish, add the stock and cook in a preheated oven at 220°C (425°F, gas 7) for about 12 minutes. Drain the fish and keep warm on a serving dish. Strain the cooking juices and boil down to reduce by a third. Add 200 ml (7 fl oz, ¾ cup) double (heavy) cream and reduce by half. Coat the fish with the sauce and sprinkle with chopped parsley.

mackerel in cider Pierre Traiteur

Trim and wash the mackerel and season them thoroughly. Place them on a base of onions and chopped apples in a pan. Cover with cider, add 3 tablespoons cider vinegar and bring to the boil. Simmer for 5 minutes. Allow the fish to cool in the pan. Remove the fillets and arrange them on a serving dish surrounded by pieces of apple that have been fried in butter. Boil down the cooking liquid in the pan and pour over the mackerel while still hot. Sprinkle with pepper and chopped chives.

additional recipe See *piémontaise*.

Whole or Sliced Mackerel
mackerel à la boulonnaise
Clean some mussels and cook them in a little vinegar over a brisk heat. Prepare a butter sauce using the strained cooking juices from the mussels. Gut (clean) the mackerel, cut it into thick slices, and poach for about 12 minutes in a court-bouillon with a generous quantity of vinegar. Drain the fish, skin and arrange on a long serving dish; keep warm. Shell the mussels, arrange them around the fish and coat the mackerel and the mussels with the butter sauce.

mackerel à la nage
To 750 ml (1¼ pints, 3¼ cups) red wine, add 2 garlic cloves, 2 chopped shallots, a clove, a small piece of cinnamon and a bouquet garni. Boil down to reduce, then add 2 chopped carrots, a bulb of fennel cut into 6 pieces, and 3 celery sticks. Cook gently. Finally, add the white parts of 4 leeks (cut into thick slices) and the finely chopped green tops of the leeks. Season with salt and pepper and add a little sugar. Continue simmering until the vegetables are cooked but still firm.

Clean and gut 8 small mackerel. Place in an ovenproof dish, partially cover with the vegetable mixture and add a few slices of lemon. Cover the dish with foil and cook in a preheated oven at 180°C (350°F, gas 4) for 5–6 minutes. Serve very hot.

mackerel with noisette butter
Clean 6 medium mackerel and cut them into thick slices of a similar size. Poach for about 12 minutes in a court-bouillon made with vinegar. Drain, place on a serving dish, and keep warm. Sprinkle with a little vinegar. Prepare 100 g (4 oz, ½ cup) noisette* butter and add 1 tablespoon capers and chopped parsley. Pour the butter over the mackerel and serve very hot.

mackerel with sorrel
Trim 6 mackerel, slit them along the back and dry them. Melt a large knob of butter in a frying pan, place the fish in the hot butter and cook on one side for 5 minutes. Turn and cook the other side. Remove the fish from the pan, season and keep warm.

Pick over 500 g (18 oz) sorrel, wash it thoroughly and add it to the juices in the frying pan. Heat the mixture, stirring constantly, until the sorrel is reduced to a purée (do not allow it to dry out). Check the seasoning, then bind the mixture with butter and 1–2 eggs. Serve the mackerel on a long dish, garnished with the sorrel purée.

mackerel with two-mustard sauce
Wash and gut (clean) 8 small mackerel (*lisettes*). Place them in an ovenproof dish, season with salt and pepper, moisten with a glass of dry white wine, and cook in a preheated oven at 240°C (475°F, gas 9) for 8 minutes. Mix 1 tablespoon strong mustard with 1 tablespoon mild mustard in a saucepan. When the mackerel are cooked, add their cooking juices to the mustard mixture. Add 40 g (1½ oz, 3 tablespoons) butter, bring to the boil and cook for 2 minutes. Coat the fish with the sauce and serve with rice *à la créole*.

MÂCON The region between the southern end of the Côte de Beaune and the Beaujolais. It produces red, white and rosé AOC wines, of which the white Pouilly-Fuissé and St-Véran are well known. Although Mâconnais wines do not usually attain the character and quality of Côte d'Or Burgundies, they can be both agreeable and varied. Since Pouilly-Fuissé became popular in the United States, it is no longer reasonably priced.

MÂCONNAIS Unpasteurized goat's milk cheese from Burgundy (40–45% fat content), with a fresh body and natural bluish crust. Mâconnais is a small truncated cone 3–4 cm (1¼–1½ in) across, weighing 50–60 g (2–2¼ oz). It has a mildly goaty, nutty flavour and it is used in making fromage fort ('strong cheese') in Burgundy and Lyonnais.

MÂCONNAISE, À LA Describing dishes cooked with Mâcon wine, such as fish cooked in red Mâcon wine with herbs, garnished with small brown glazed onions, fried mushrooms, croûtons and shrimps.

MACROBIOTIC Denoting a system of diets inspired by the Zen sect of Japanese Buddhism, based on balancing the opposing principles of Yin (feminine) and Yang (masculine). It was founded by Sakurazawa Nyoiti, known as Oshawa (1893–1966). It comprises a dozen diets, adapted to the individual's physical and spiritual requirements, based on wholegrain cereals and dried vegetables. Some diets include some green vegetables and a little fish, but meats, fruits and alcoholic drinks are forbidden. The only beverage permitted is tea and then only in small quantities.

MACTRE Shellfish of the *Mactridae* family with a smooth triangular shell, related to the clam, which is collected on the Atlantic and North American coasts. About 10 cm (4 in) in size, they are sold cooked and frozen in the United States and Canada. They are also eaten raw.

MACVIN An AOC *vin de liqueur* and a regional speciality of the Jura, in France, reputedly dating from the late 9th century. Essentially it is spiced wine, sweet and fairly high in strength due to the addition of marc.

MADAGASCAR See *page 710*.

MADEIRA A fortified wine from the island of the same name, which belongs to Portugal. The vineyards are terraced and the vines trained vertically. The wine is produced by a process known as the *estufa*, in which the wine in the cask is very gradually heated and then allowed to cool down. The finest Madeiras are left to mature naturally in oak casks stored under the eaves of the lodges and are heated only by the sun. Quality Madeiras are named after the grapes that make them: Sercial is the driest, Verdelho is nutty and mellow, Bual (or Boal) and Malmsey are sweet and full-bodied. The wine from each Madeira establishment has its own distinctive character and there are in addition a few blends sold under brand names, such as Rainwater. Madeira is regaining its previous popularity. It can have a very long life in the bottle – there are 18th-century Madeiras still in existence, but these are exceptional vintage wines. Dry Madeiras are good drunk as apéritifs or with clear soup, while the sweeter wines may be drunk at any time, or with dessert and nuts.

RECIPES

braised ham with Madeira
Braise the ham and cut it into slices. Remove the fat from the meat juices, reduce them and add Madeira. Strain and then thicken with arrowroot or cornflour (cornstarch). Arrange the slices of ham in an ovenproof dish and cover with the Madeira-flavoured stock. Cover and heat through in the oven without boiling.

Madeira sauce (old recipe)
Add 3 tablespoons Madeira to 200 ml (7 fl oz, ¾ cup) reduced meat juices and warm.

Madeira sauce (modern recipe)
Put 1 kg (2¼ lb) crushed veal bones into an oven-proof dish and place in a preheated oven at 240°C (475°F, gas 9). Turn the bones over from time to time so that they colour evenly. Meanwhile dice 2 carrots and a large onion. When the bones are golden, add the vegetables and cook until golden, then drain the bones and vegetables and place in a large pan. Remove the fat from any juices in the cooking dish and add 1 litre (1¾ pints, 4⅓ cups) stock or water. Scrape the sides of the dish well and stir the residue into the liquid.

Quickly bring to the boil, skim, and add 2 finely chopped celery sticks, 200 g (7 oz) peeled and seeded tomatoes, 1 peeled crushed garlic clove, a bouquet garni and 1 tablespoon tomato purée (paste). Bring to the boil, cover and simmer gently for 2 hours. Strain and then add some tarragon and 100 g (4 oz, 1¼ cups) finely chopped mushrooms. Bring to the boil. Dissolve 1 tablespoon cornflour (cornstarch) in 200 ml (7 fl oz, ¾ cup) Madeira and pour in a stream into the boiling sauce, whisking it in. Strain and reheat before serving.

additional recipe See *foie gras (goose foie gras)*.

MADELEINE A small, individual, French sponge cake shaped like a rounded shell, made with sugar, flour, melted butter and eggs, flavoured with lemon or orange-flower water. The mixture is cooked in ribbed oval moulds which give the cakes their shell-like appearance.

The origin of this 'seashell cake so strictly pleated outside and so sensual inside' (Marcel Proust) is the subject of much discussion. It has been attributed to Avice, chef to Talleyrand, the French statesman, who had the idea of baking a pound-cake mixture in aspic moulds. Other authorities, however, believe that the recipe is much older and originated in the French town of Commercy, which was then a duchy under the rule of Stanislaw Leszczynski. It is said that during a visit to the castle in 1755 the duke was very taken with a cake made by a peasant girl named Madeleine. This started the fashion for 'madeleines' (as they were named by the duke), which were then launched in Versailles by his daughter Marie, who was married to Louis XV. The attribution of the cake to Madeleine Paumier, cordon-bleu cook to a rich burgher of Commercy, seems doubtful.

The name madeleine is also given to the small, individual, English sponge cake which is baked in a dariole mould, coated with jam and desiccated coconut and toppped with a glacé (candied) cherry and angelica.

RECIPES

classic madeleines
Melt 100 g (4 oz, ½ cup) butter without allowing it to become hot. Butter a tray of madeleine moulds with 20 g (¾ oz, 1½ tablespoons) butter. Put the juice of half a lemon in a bowl with a pinch of salt, 125 g (4½ oz, scant ⅔ cup) caster (superfine) sugar, 3 eggs and an extra egg yolk. Mix well together with a wooden spatula and then sprinkle in 125 g (4½ oz, scant 1¼ cups) sifted self-raising flour and mix until smooth; finally add the melted butter. Spoon the mixture into the moulds but do not fill more than two-thirds full. Bake in a preheated oven at 180°C (350°F, gas 4) for about 25 minutes. Turn out the madeleines and cool on a wire rack.

Commercy madeleines
Cream 150 g (5 oz, ⅔ cup) butter with a wooden spoon. Add 200 g (7 oz, scant 1 cup) caster (superfine) sugar and mix well. Add 6 eggs, one at a time, then 200 g (7 oz, 1¾ cups) plain (all-purpose) flour sifted with 1 teaspoon baking powder, and finally stir in 1 tablespoon orange-flower water. Butter and lightly flour some madeleine moulds and spoon in the mixture. Bake in a preheated oven at 220°C (425°F, gas 7) for about 10 minutes. Turn out the madeleines on to a wire rack to cool.

English madeleines
Cream 100 g (4 oz, ½ cup) butter with 100 g (4 oz, ½ cup) caster (superfine) sugar until pale and creamy. Stir in 2 eggs and a little self-raising flour

MADAGASCAR

Madagascan cuisine combines several traditions: African, Chinese, Indian, British and French. Its dishes tend to be highly spiced, combining a variety of spices and condiments such as garlic, cinnamon, cardamom, curry, ginger, pimento, chives, bay leaves and thyme.

Excellent soups, bouillons (*roumajava*) and stews are made from maize, manioc, sweet potatoes and rice, tomatoes and green vegetables – watercress, green beans, spinach – combined with meat (beef and mutton) or fish. A meal will often consist of just one of these comprehensive dishes, such as *vary amin*, a stew made with zebu meat, chayote, tomato and ginger. The

Madagascans are very partial to *kitoza*, which is beef rubbed with garlic and ginger, then dried and grilled. Seafood and fish are the staple diet, especially along the coast where lobster is part of most dishes. There, the fish is often cooked in coconut milk while on the high plateaus, it is cooked with ginger, curry and pimento. Tropical fruit is cooked as fritters, pies or flans to make delicious desserts.

taken from 100 g (4 oz, 1 cup). Then fold in the remaining flour. Divide the mixture between 10 well-greased dariole moulds and bake in a pre-heated oven at 180°C (350°F, gas 4) for about 20 minutes, until risen, golden and springy to the touch. Cool on a wire rack. When cold, coat each cake with a thin layer of warmed and sieved raspberry jam, then roll in desiccated coconut. Top each cake with ½ glacé (candied) cherry.

MADIRAN AOC red wine from south-western France. It has a pronounced character and may be rather tannic when young but ages well. The predominant grape variety is Tannat. Madiran is produced in the same area as the white wine Pacherenc du Vic-Bilh.

MADRILÈNE, À LA The name given to a poultry consommé enriched with tomato pulp, sometimes served hot but usually served chilled or iced, as in the Spanish tradition for soups.

RECIPE

consommé à la madrilène
Prepare a chicken consommé for 5 people. When clarifying, add 300 ml (½ pint, 1¼ cups) chopped fresh tomato pulp. Strain the soup through a very fine strainer, add a pinch of cayenne and leave to cool completely, then refrigerate. Serve cold in cups. The soup can be garnished with finely diced red (bell) pepper which has been cooked in stock.

MAFÉ Traditional Senegalese dish based on beef (silverside or top rump), vegetables, onion, garlic, tomato and groundnut paste, served with white rice. The beef may be replaced by chicken or shoulder of mutton.

MAGISTÈRE A very nourishing concentrated consommé invented by Brillat-Savarin to combat the effects of 'muscular, intellectual or sexual exhaustion'. There are two types: one for robust temperaments, based on a stock made with chicken (or partridge) and beef bones and meat; and one for weak temperaments, made from shin of veal (veal shank), pigeon, shrimps and cress. These dishes

were recommended by Ambroise Paré to nourish invalids without overexciting them.

MAGRET A portion of meat from the breast of a duck (mallard or Barbary, traditionally fattened for foie gras). Magrets are presented with the skin and underlying layer of fat still attached. For a long time they were used only for confits. A renewed interest came when the restaurateurs from the Landes region in France served magrets grilled in the traditional country way (skin side first so that the fat impregnates the flesh), so that the skin is crunchy but the meat remains bloody or very rare. The best magrets (the name means the lean portion of a fat duck) come from ducks boned the day after they are killed, and are served the day after that.

RECIPES

magrets of duck
Place 4 chopped shallots and 300 ml (½ pint, 1¼ cups) red wine in a small saucepan and reduce over a high heat until the wine has been absorbed. Then add 120 ml (4 fl oz, ½ cup) single (light) cream and reduce again until syrupy. Lower the heat. Remove from the heat and gradually whisk in one or two pieces of butter cut from 350 g (12 oz, 1½ cups), returning the saucepan to the heat for a few moments and then removing it. Continue in this way until all the butter has been incorporated. Keep the sauce warm in a bain marie.

Quickly brown 6 duck breasts (magrets) in a heavy-based saucepan, placing the fatty side down. Turn them over as soon as they are golden, cook the other side similarly and reduce the heat. Leave to cook for about 15 minutes. Remove the breasts from the pan and keep warm in a serving dish. Skim off the cooking fat and deglaze the pan with 7 tablespoons red wine. Reduce for a few minutes, then remove from the heat and thicken the sauce with 1 tablespoon of the butter sauce prepared earlier. Pour this sauce over the duck breasts and serve the remainder of the butter sauce separately.

Fish is an important source of food for those living near the Madagascan coast.

magrets with green peppercorns
Brown the duck breasts in butter or goose fat in a frying pan. Add ½ glass of stock, salt and some green peppercorns and cook, keeping the meat rare. Remove from the heat and add 2 tablespoons double (heavy) cream. Keep warm.

Cook some rice in the Oriental way (lightly brown the rice in butter or goose fat, then add stock and cook until the rice is tender and all the stock has been absorbed) and add an equal quantity of chopped mushrooms. Prepare a thick béchamel sauce (half the volume of the rice). Add the rice and mushrooms and form into flat cakes. Brown the cakes in a little hot oil. Serve the duck breasts with the rice cakes and coat with the sauce.

MAHON This semi-hard, pressed DOP cheese (40–45% fat content) from the island of Majorca is made by farmers from cow's milk. The cheeses are gathered from the farmers by *recogedores-affinadores* who ripen them in underground cellars for anything from two months to two years. Produced in irregular squares with round corners, the cheese has a tangy, nutty flavour. In Majorca it is served sliced with olive oil, salt and fresh tarragon.

MAIDENHAIR FERN A species of fern with aromatic and mucilaginous leaves that are used to make infusions and syrups to ease bronchial conditions. Maidenhair fern syrup was once used to sweeten hot drinks, particularly Bavarian cream. *Capilè*, a popular drink in Portugal, especially in Lisbon, is made of maidenhair fern syrup, lemon zest and cold water.

MAID OF HONOUR A small English tart with an almond filling. Tradition has it that Anne Boleyn created the recipe while she was lady-in-waiting to Catherine of Aragon and that an enchanted Henry VIII named the cake 'maid of honour'. The recipe was closely guarded until a lady from the court of George I gave it to a gentleman who opened a shop in Richmond to sell them. Originally small cheesecakes, with a curd cheese, almond and lemon filling, there are various recipes. Almond custard or jam topped with almond sponge are typical fillings.

MAILLE An 18th-century French mustard and vinegar manufacturer. In 1769 he succeeded Leconte as vinegar distiller to the king but his reputation had already been established. He had invented the famous 'four thieves' vinegar in 1720, the antiseptic qualities of which protected the doctors and nuns treating plague victims in the great epidemic in Marseilles.

A hundred varieties of vinegar for health or beauty and 53 varieties of flavoured table vinegars (for example nasturtium, caper, game, ravigote and distilled) were produced in his laboratories in Paris as well as mustards and fruits preserved in vinegar. These products were exported to Hamburg and Moscow. The name Maille is still used on a range of mustards and vinegars, the recipes of which date back to the 18th century.

MAINTENON The name given to a savoury dish made with mushrooms, onions and béchamel sauce, sometimes containing truffles, tongue and chicken breasts. This style of preparation is usually applied to delicate meats (such as lamb chops, veal and sweetbreads), but stuffed omelettes, poached eggs and stuffed potatoes can also be prepared in this way. Sweetbreads *à la Maintenon* are braised, arranged on croûtons, garnished with a slice of truffle and onion purée, and surrounded by a ring of suprême sauce.

Dishes *à la Maintenon* were probably created by a chef in the service of the Noailles family, who owned the Château de Maintenon, but Madame de Maintenon was also interested in cooking: she created lamb chops *en papillotes* for Louis XIV.

RECIPES

lamb (or mutton) chops Maintenon
Quickly brown the chops in butter on one side only. Coat the cooked side of each chop with 1 tablespoon Maintenon mixture, shape into a dome, and coat with breadcrumbs. Lavishly butter a baking dish and arrange the chops on it. Sprinkle with melted butter and cook in a preheated oven at 240°C (475°F, gas 9) until golden. Serve with Périgueux sauce.

Maintenon mixture
Clean and slice 150 g (5 oz, 2 cups) mushrooms and sweat in 15 g (½ oz, 1 tablespoon) butter. Prepare a Soubise* purée with 500 g (18 oz, 4½ cups) sliced onions blanched and sweated in butter and 500 ml (18 fl oz, 2¼ cups) thick béchamel sauce, salt and pepper, and a little grated nutmeg. Add the mushrooms and bind with 2 egg yolks. Check the seasoning.

stuffed omelette à la Maintenon
Prepare 4 tablespoons salpicon* made with chicken, mushrooms and possibly truffles and cooked tongue. Bind with thick velouté sauce. Prepare and cook a very soft 8-egg omelette. Arrange the salpicon on half the omelette, roll up, and slide on to an ovenproof plate. Coat with a light Soubise sauce, sprinkle with Parmesan cheese and melted butter, and brown quickly in the oven.

stuffed potatoes à la Maintenon
Bake some floury medium unpeeled potatoes in the oven. Cut in half and remove the pulp without breaking the skin. Prepare a salpicon with chicken, cooked tongue and mushrooms, bound with a light Soubise purée. Fill the potato skins with this mixture, forming a dome shape. Sprinkle the tops with grated cheese, breadcrumbs and melted butter. Brown in the oven.

MAISON This French term meaning house, when used honestly, indicates that the dish concerned has been prepared according to an original recipe and is served only in the establishment which claims it. It is more commonly used today to refer to a speciality of the house, or to a dish that is home-made to the chef's own recipe.

MAÎTRE D'HÔTEL

The French term for the person in charge of the dining room in a hotel or restaurant. Traditionally a man, the maître d'hôtel is assisted by a team of senior, junior and assistant waiters.

In the royal and noble households of France, the office of maître d'hôtel was always held by noblemen of the highest rank, sometimes princes of the blood royal. Although at that time the office was a sinecure, the maître d'hôtel was, at least nominally, in charge of all departments of the royal household, including the kitchens and cellars, and all the functionaries and servants. In *La Maison réglée* (1692), Audiger sets out the maître d'hôtel's duties in a private house: he should supervise the accounts, choose the cooks, buy the bread, wine and meat, and 'regulate and arrange the table settings of all the different services the nobleman might require'.

The maître d'hôtel's function has almost ceased to exist in private houses as it is rare to require someone's services just to arrange tables and buy provisions. However, in the large traditional restaurants it has lost none of its importance. He must be thoroughly familiar with details of the special work of the dining room, kitchens and cellars. He must also be able to advise his clients, to guide them in their choice of dishes, the wines to go with them, and the fruit to follow.

MAÎTRE D'HÔTEL BUTTER

A savoury butter containing chopped parsley and lemon juice and served with grilled (broiled) or fried fish, grilled meat or vegetables, either in liquid form or solidified, in rounds or slices.

RECIPES

maître d'hôtel butter
Work 200 g (7 oz, generous ¾ cup) butter to a smooth paste with a wooden spoon, add ½ teaspoon fine salt, a pinch of pepper, a squeeze (about 1 tablespoon) of lemon juice and 1 tablespoon chopped parsley. This butter can be kept in the refrigerator for 2 or 3 days.

maître d'hôtel French beans
String and slice the beans and place them in a large pan of boiling water. Cook at a rolling boil, uncovered, and season with salt halfway through cooking. Drain thoroughly and mix in 50 g (2 oz, ¼ cup) maître d'hôtel butter per 450 g (1 lb) cooked beans. Serve with a little chopped parsley.

additional recipe See *potato*.

MAIZE (CORN)

A cereal with white, yellow or rust-coloured grains, rich in starch, which are attached to a cob protected by layers of fibrous leaves with tasselled tops. Also known as corn (in the United States) and Indian corn, it originated in North America, being discovered by Christopher Columbus. There are several varieties.

- GRAIN MAIZE This is hard and bright yellow with a fairly small cob. It can be ground into flour, meal or semolina and used to make bread, pancakes, fritters, waffles, polenta, tortillas, milk puddings, biscuits and cakes. Cornflakes are also made with maize flour. Cornflour (cornstarch) is widely used as a thickening agent. This type of maize is also used to make Bourbon whiskey and certain types of beer, as well as corn oil. One variety of maize has blue-black grains, rather than yellow, and is ground to produce blue cornmeal.

- SWEETCORN Known as corn on the cob, this is grown as a vegetable. The grains are pale yellow and the cob is larger than that of grain maize. It is harvested while still unripe and must be eaten quickly as the natural sugar in the grains begins to turn to starch after picking, and it loses its sweetness. It should be chosen with plump, milky grains and covered with pale green leaves. It is sold either fresh, canned or frozen. The fresh cobs are cooked in boiling salted water or grilled (broiled). They are served with fresh or melted butter, lightly flavoured with lemon or cream. Sweetcorn can be served hot, on or off the cob, as an accompaniment to meat dishes or roast poultry. The grains can also be used in mixed salads. Baby sweetcorn is harvested when immature. Sold fresh, canned and pickled, it is eaten whole and often used in Oriental dishes.

- POPCORN This is prepared by heating the grains in oil until they pop (puff up and burst), forming soft white light masses which can be sprinkled with salt, coated in melted butter or caramelized. Popcorn is eaten as a snack or sweetmeat.

RECIPES

cornbread
Mix 500 g (18 oz, 3½ cups) cornmeal, 250 g (9 oz, generous 2 cups) wheat flour, 4 teaspoons sugar, 1½ tablespoons baking powder, 1½ teaspoons salt and 100 g (4 oz, ½ cup) butter in a bowl. Blend in 4 egg yolks beaten with 500 ml (17 fl oz, 2 cups) milk and 6 tablespoons double (heavy) cream, stirring as little as possible. Fold in 4 egg whites, whisked stiffly, and pour into well-buttered patty tins (muffin pans), filling them three-quarters full. Bake in a preheated oven at 220°C (425°F, gas 7) for 25–30 minutes. In the United States this bread is served hot, straight from the oven, at breakfast.

corn fritters
Make a smooth batter using 100 g (4 oz, 1 cup) plain (all-purpose) flour, 2 eggs and 100 ml (4 fl oz, 7 tablespoons) water. Add 225 g (8 oz, 1 cup) thawed frozen or drained canned sweetcorn. Stir well, adding seasoning to taste and a little nutmeg. Shallow fry spoonfuls of the sweetcorn in batter in

a mixture of sunflower oil and butter until golden underneath and set. Turn and cook the second sides until golden. Serve with deep-fried bread-crumb-coated chicken and fried bananas as American Maryland chicken.

fresh corn with béchamel sauce

Choose fresh cobs with tender grains. Leave only one layer of leaves on and cook in boiling salted water for about 15 minutes (be careful to keep the water on the boil). Drain the cobs and remove the leaves. Detach the grains from the cob and serve with a light béchamel sauce.

MÁLAGA A mainly fortified Spanish DO wine produced around the town of the same name in Andalusia. It is made according to a type of solera system, in which the casks of maturing wine are repeatedly topped up with younger wines to perpetuate the quality and character of the original. Sixteen types of wine are officially recognized, ranging from dry to sweet with alcohol levels of 15–23%.

MALAKOFF The name given to various classic cakes, often containing nuts. The most common type is made of two thick round dacquoise (nut meringue) cakes, each of which is coated in coffee mousse; the top is sprinkled with icing (confectioner's) sugar and the sides coated with chopped toasted almonds. Another version of malakoff is composed of a choux paste crown placed on a puff pastry or sponge cake base, the centre filled with ice cream containing crystallized (candied) fruits, Chantilly cream, or any other cold frothy filling.

MALANGA Also known as tannia, yautia or new cocoyam. A large, firm, starchy root vegetable with a brown skin and white flesh, which is used grated in the West Indies for the preparation of acras. The root vegetable is also baked or boiled and the leaves are used in cooking as well. Malanga belongs to the same family of plants as the taro, this being the arum lily family. Malanga should be cooked before eating as it may contain calcium oxalate crystals which are an irritant.

MALLARD Migratory wild duck of the *Anatidae* family, which has become more and more sedentary and which is easily found, even in the big cities. The adult male has multicoloured plumage: the head and neck are dark green with blue glints and often a white ring at the base of the neck; the back is metallic blue, the throat is red and the stomach is greyish white; the wings are ash blue. The female, a little smaller, has a more or less dark beige plumage, like that of the young. The mallard is prepared in the same way as duck.

MALLOW A common plant that grows in fields, hedgerows and on roadsides. There are about 20 different species found all over the world. Its leaves contain a mucilage used as an emollient and in infu-

sions. The leaves can also be eaten in salad or as a vegetable, like spinach. The flowers are soothing to chest troubles and sore throats.

MALT Barley that is prepared for brewing or distilling by being steeped, germinated, roasted and then crushed in a mill. The extent to which the malt is roasted determines the colour of the beer: the higher the caramelization, the darker the beer. The main constituent of malt is starch, which is converted to sugar by fermentation when the crushed malt is soaked and heated. This process, called saccharification, results in the production of wort, which is processed further to produce beer or distilled to produce whisky.

Malt extract – a concentrated infusion of germinated barley – is used as a sugar substitute.

MALTAISE, À LA The term used to describe sweet or savoury preparations which are based on oranges, particularly the Maltese blood orange. Maltaise sauce is a hollandaise sauce flavoured with blood-orange juice and shredded rind, served with poached fish or boiled vegetables (such as asparagus, Swiss chard and cardoons). The bombe glacée *à la maltaise* is coated in orange ice and filled with tangerine-flavoured Chantilly cream.

RECIPES

banana croûtes à la maltaise

Cut a large, day-old brioche into slices, and then cut the slices into rectangles a little longer and wider than the bananas. Arrange them on a baking sheet, sprinkle with sugar, and lightly glaze in a preheated oven at 220°C (425°F, gas 7). Meanwhile peel 6 bananas, cut them in half lengthways, and sprinkle lightly with lemon juice. Place the bananas on a buttered baking sheet and cook in the oven for 5 minutes. Arrange the bananas, alternating with slices of brioche, in a circle in an ovenproof dish. Fill the centre with a confectioner's custard (pastry cream) flavoured with orange zest (see *custard*). Sprinkle the whole dish with finely crushed macaroons and melted butter and brown in the oven. Before serving, decorate with candied orange peel.

maltaise sauce

Mix the juice of a blood orange with 200 ml (7 fl oz, ¾ cup) hollandaise* sauce. Add 1 tablespoon grated and blanched orange peel.

other recipes See *fruit salad, strawberry.*

MAMIROLLE Uncooked pressed cheese made from pasteurized cow's milk (40% fat content) with a washed, smooth, reddish crust. Mamirolle is a rectangular loaf-shaped cheese, 15 cm (6 in) long and 5–6 cm (2–2½ in) wide, weighing 500–600 g (18–21 oz). It is made in Franche-Comté, at the dairy industry's famous national school which is established in Mamirolle, to the east of Besançon.

MANCELLE, À LA The name given to dishes which originated in the French town of Le Mans and the surrounding area, notably poultry (roast capon, chicken fricassée), pork rillettes, wild rabbit, and an omelette in which the eggs are mixed with artichoke hearts and diced potatoes.

MANCHEGO A DOP Spanish cheese made from ewe's milk (45–50% fat content), which originated in La Mancha. It is cylindrical, 10 cm (4 in) deep and 25 cm (10 in) in diameter, and is sold either fresh (rare) or matured for two to three months (semicurado), one year (curado) or two years (veijo). The cheese is white and firm to the touch with an even distribution of small holes. The flavour is fairly mild and nutty even when very mature. The cheeses used to be pressed in plaited grass moulds which left a cross-hatch pattern on the rind; today plastic moulds are used. In Spain Manchego is served in characteristic triangular wafers as part of a selection of tapas or with honey and fruit as a dessert.

MANCHETTE A paper frill used to garnish the projecting bones of, for example, a leg of lamb, a ham or chops.

MANCHON The French term for muff, this is a small petit four made of almond paste. It is shaped like a muff, into a small tube, by rolling it around a wooden handle. It is filled with Chiboust cream or praline butter cream and the ends are dipped in ground almonds or in chopped pistachio nuts.

MANDARIN See *tangerine*.

MANDOLINE A vegetable slicer consisting of two adjustable stainless steel blades, one plain, one grooved, held in a wooden or metal frame. A folding support enables the mandoline to be tilted during slicing. It is used particularly to slice cabbage, carrots, turnips and potatoes.

MANGE-TOUT Also known as snow pea or sugar pea. A type of pea with flat pods, which are eaten whole before the seeds are fully formed, hence its French name, mange-tout ('eat all'). The pods have no membrane lining like common garden peas and are usually stringless, so they are crisp but tender. They are brilliant green in colour and can be stored for a few days in the refrigerator. Preparation entails topping and tailing; they taste best when used raw in salads or cooked only briefly – steamed, boiled or stir-fried. They can be used, either whole or sliced, for the same recipes as fresh peas, and are widely used in Oriental cuisine.

MANGO A large tropical fruit of which there are many varieties. Mangoes are typically oblong and greenish, ripening to yellow, red or violet (particularly on the side of the fruit which has been exposed to the sun). The skin should be slightly supple. The orange juicy flesh clings to a large flattish stone (pit); it is aromatic, soft and sweet with an acid aftertaste. Certain varieties are fibrous, others have a flavour of lemon, banana or mint.

The mango tree came originally from India and Malaysia and has been known in Asia for a long time; it was introduced into Brazil and the West Indies in the 18th century and into Africa, Mexico, Florida and Hawaii in the 19th century.

In Asia and the West Indies unripe mangoes, either raw or cooked, are used as an hors d'oeuvre or as an accompaniment to fish or meat. Mango chutneys are among the best-known chutneys. Ripe mangoes, which do not keep long, can be used as a garnish for chicken, as an ingredient in mixed salads, and to make sorbets, jams, marmalades and jellies. Fresh mangoes can be cut in two off the flat stone and eaten with a spoon; alternatively, the flesh can be removed and diced.

RECIPES

duck with mangoes
Choose mangoes that are not too ripe, peel them, and remove the stones (pits) over a plate to collect the juice. Put the fruit and juice in a saucepan with a little apricot or peach liqueur, cover and cook gently for a few minutes over a low heat. Strain the fruit, reserving the juice, and put to one side.

Pluck, draw, singe and truss a duck. Season with salt and pepper and coat lightly with fat. Roast in a preheated oven at 220°C (425°F, gas 7) with chopped onions, carrots, celery, a little thyme, a bay leaf and 2 tablespoons water. After about 35 minutes for a 1.12 kg (2½ lb) duckling, when the flesh is still pink, pour off the cooking juices into a pan and add 5 tablespoons white wine or stock. Keep the duck warm.

Make a dry caramel by heating 2 tablespoons granulated sugar, stirring with a wooden spoon. Add 1 tablespoon vinegar to the caramel, followed by the strained mango juice and then the pan juices. Cook the sauce gently for a few minutes. Carve the duck and garnish with the warm cooked mangoes. Serve coated with the sauce.

mango dessert with passion fruit and rum
Remove the pulp from 500 g (18 oz) passion fruit and discard the seeds. Whisk the pulp together with an equal quantity of sugar syrup and freeze to make a sorbet.

Cut some Genoese sponge cake into 4 rounds, 10 cm (4 in) in diameter and 1 cm (½ in) thick, and scoop out a slight hollow in each. Cut the flesh of 4 well-ripened mangoes into slices. Fill the hollows in the sponge rounds with the passion fruit sorbet and arrange the slices of mango in the shape of a fan over the top. Place in the coldest part of the refrigerator.

Prepare a zabaglione with rum: whisk 4 egg yolks with 7 tablespoons rum in a bain marie. When the mixture is light and fluffy, add 4 tablespoons whipped double (heavy) cream. Coat the slices of mango with the zabaglione, glaze for a short time under the grill (broiler), and decorate with Cape gooseberries.

mango sorbet

Choose ripe mangoes, peel them, and rub the flesh through a fine sieve. Add an equal volume of sugar syrup and some lemon juice – the juice of 2 lemons is needed per 1 litre (1¾ pints, 4⅓ cups) sorbet. Add a little extra lemon juice if the syrup is too heavy or some sugar if it is too light. Freeze and finish the preparation in the usual way (see *sorbet*).

sautéed chicken with mangoes

Cut a chicken into pieces and sauté in butter for about 20 minutes. Soften a chopped onion and a peeled crushed tomato in a mixture of 2 tablespoons oil and 20 g (¾ oz, 1½ tablespoons) butter with a pinch of ground ginger. Add the crushed pulp of 2 or 3 mangoes, a squeeze of lemon juice, the chicken pieces, a cup of water, salt, pepper and a pinch of cayenne. Cover and cook for about 30 minutes over a medium heat.

MANGOSTEEN A round ribbed fruit, the size of an orange, native to Malaysia. The thick, tough, dark red to brown skin covers a delicate juicy white flesh divided into five or six segments. The mangosteen is eaten fresh, peeled and cut in half. It is also used in jams, sorbets and exotic salads. In Indonesia it is made into a vinegar and a concentrated oil is extracted from the seeds to make *kokum* butter.

MANIOC The edible root of a tropical plant, also called cassava, tapioca or yuca. This has white starchy flesh beneath thick brown peel. It is used as a vegetable or to make tapioca, the washed and dried form of granular starch used to make puddings and in some baking. Originally from Brazil, the plant is cultivated throughout South and Central America and has been introduced into Africa, where it is now a basic foodstuff (ground into semolina, salted or sugared in flat cakes, or boiled in *foutou*). It is also grown in Asia.

There are two varieties of manioc: sweet and bitter. The root of sweet manioc is peeled, washed, cut into pieces, cooked in salted water and used like potatoes to accompany meat or fish. The root must be washed, peeled and cooked as it contains natural toxins. A flour is also extracted to make cakes, soups, stews, bread and biscuits. The starchy leaves are prepared like spinach (West Indian *brèdes*). Bitter manioc is used in the food industry. It contains larger amounts of the natural toxin, a poisonous juice which contains hydrocyanic acid, but this is eliminated by washing and cooking; the fresh roots are then grated and left to ferment. The starch is extracted by centrifugation, cooked, crushed, dried and made into tapioca.

MANQUÉ A type of sponge cake that is a speciality of Paris. It is said to have been invented by a famous 19th-century Parisian pastrycook called Félix, while preparing a Savoy sponge cake. When the egg whites would not whisk up, in order not to waste the mixture, he had the idea of adding melted butter and flaked (slivered) almonds, and covering the cake with praline when it was cooked. The customer who bought it thought it was so good that she ordered another and wanted to know the name of the mystery cake. The baker said it was a *manqué* (failure), but it became such a success that a special mould was invented.

The *moule à manqué* is a round deep-sided mould which is also used for other cakes. The original manqué mixture has been considerably modified since Félix first made it. It is now often flavoured with flaked hazelnuts, raisins, crystallized (candied) fruit, aniseed, liqueur and alcohol. It can be decorated with cream, jam, crystallized fruit or coated with fondant icing (frosting).

RECIPES

gâteau manqué

Melt 100 g (4 oz, ½ cup) butter without allowing it to brown. Separate 6 eggs. Put the yolks into a bowl with 200 g (7 oz, scant 1 cup) caster (superfine) sugar and 1 teaspoon vanilla sugar. Whisk until the mixture becomes light and frothy. Then fold in 150 g (5 oz, 1¼ cups) plain (all-purpose) flour, the melted butter and half a liqueur glass of rum, mixing until evenly blended. Whisk the egg whites together with a pinch of salt into firm peaks and gently fold them into the manqué mixture.

Grease a deep sandwich tin (layer cake pan) or a manqué mould with butter, pour in the mixture, and bake in a preheated oven at 200°C (400°F, gas 6) for 40–45 minutes. Leave for a few minutes in the tin, then turn out on to a wire rack to cool completely.

lemon manqué

Remove the peel from a lemon and blanch for 2 minutes in boiling water. Refresh in cold water, dry and shred very finely. Finely dice 100 g (4 oz, ½ cup) candied citron peel. Prepare the manqué mixture and add the shredded lemon peel and diced citron before incorporating the egg whites. Bake the cake, remove from the tin (pan) while still warm, and cool completely.

Lightly whisk 2 egg whites and mix in 1 tablespoon lemon juice, then some icing (confectioner's) sugar, until the mixture has a spreading consistency. Coat the cake with the icing (frosting) and decorate with small pieces of candied citron peel.

pineapple manqué

Prepare the manqué mixture, but add 100 g (4 oz, ½ cup) crystallized (candied) pineapple, finely chopped, before adding the egg whites to the mixture. Bake the cake.

When it is cold, ice (frost) with 100 g (4 oz) fondant* mixed with half a liqueur glass of rum heated to 35°C (95°F). Decorate the top with pieces of crystallized pineapple and glacé (candied) cherries.

MANZANILLA A type of sherry produced from around Sanlúcar de Barrameda, in Andalucia. It is crisp and dry and should be served chilled. It is a very good accompaniment to shellfish.

MAPLE One of about 200 species of tree or shrub which grow in temperate climates. The North American sugar maple has orange sap, which is collected from the trunk in the spring and yields a clear golden syrup. Rich in sugar, with an aromatic flavour, maple syrup is very popular in the United States and Canada. It is spread on roasts and ham, served with pancakes and puddings, and used to glaze carrots and caramelize sweet potatoes. Maple syrup tart is another favourite.

Centrifugation of maple syrup produces a 'butter'; an essence used as a flavouring in pâtisserie and confectionery is obtained by distillation. Concentrated maple syrup produces a type of candy sugar. Lastly, maple sap can be used to make a cider-like drink (especially in Louisiana) which, after fermentation, yields an aromatic vinegar.

RECIPE

maple syrup tart
Boil 7 tablespoons maple syrup with a little water for 5 minutes. Blend in 3 tablespoons cornflour (cornstarch) mixed with cold water, then 50 g (2 oz, ¼ cup) butter. Line a tart plate (pie pan) with shortcrust pastry (basic pie dough) and spread the lukewarm syrup mixture over it. Decorate with chopped almonds. Cover with a fairly thin pastry lid, pinch round the edge, prick with a fork, and bake in a preheated oven at 220°C (425°F, gas 7) for about 20 minutes.

MAQUÉE Uncooked soft cream cheese from the Walloon area of Belgium made from cow's milk and rennet, left in muslin (cheesecloth) to strain. After draining, it is lightly whipped and becomes creamy. Maquée is eaten spread on a slice of bread, or salted and accompanied with red radishes, or sweetened and sprinkled with soft brown sugar.

MARAÎCHERE, À LA Describing preparations that incorporate a selection of fresh vegetables. The term is applied particularly to large roast or braised cuts of meat that are garnished with glazed shaped carrots, small glazed onions, braised stuffed cucumber and quarters of artichoke heart cooked gently in butter. Another maraîchère garnish consists of Brussels sprouts in butter, salsify and château potatoes. The accompanying sauce consists of the deglazed and thickened meat juice or the strained skimmed braising liquid.

MARASCHINO A colourless liqueur made from the distillate of fermented Maraschino cherries. It originated in Dalmatia and is much used in flavouring sweet dishes.

MARBLE Marble working surfaces are used by professional pastry-cooks and confectioners when working with chocolate, sugar and pastries that need to be kept cool. A marble surface always remains clean and cool as it does not absorb fat or atmospheric moisture. However, the surface should not be exposed to acid substances, which will cause pitting. When making toffee at home, a small marble slab brushed with oil can be used.

MARBRADE A charcuterie speciality from southwestern France, similar to brawn (head cheese). It is made with pieces of pig's head loosely packed in aspic and served in a mould.

MARC A spirit distilled from the debris (skins and pips) left after the final pressings of grapes for wine. In Italy it is known as *grappa*. It can be used as brandy in cookery, although marc that has not been matured can be a fiery spirit and should be actually cooked or set alight, and not used neat. The marcs of several French regions are famous, notably the marc de Bourgogne. In Alsace there is one made from Gewürztraminer grape pressings.

MARCELIN A French cake consisting of a pastry base covered with strawberry jam, coated with a mixture of eggs and ground almonds and sprinkled with icing (confectioner's) sugar.

MARCHAND DE VIN The name for certain preparations that are made with red wine and shallots, especially a flavoured butter served with grilled (broiled) meat (usually entrecôte steak or kidneys). Whiting or sole *à la marchand de vin* are poached in red wine with chopped shallots, then coated with the cooking liquid, reduced and whisked with butter, and sometimes glazed in the oven.

RECIPES

entrecôte marchand de vin
Grill (broil) an entrecôte steak under a high heat. Season with salt and pepper and garnish with rounds of marchand de vin butter.

marchand de vin butter
Add 25 g (1 oz, ¼ cup) finely chopped shallots to 300 ml (½ pint, 1¼ cups) red wine and boil down to reduce by half. Add 300 ml (½ pint, 1¼ cups) beef consommé* and reduce further until almost dry. Cream 150 g (5 oz, ⅔ cup) butter and mix it with the reduced wine mixture. Add 1 tablespoon finely chopped parsley and a little lemon juice and season with salt and pepper. Chill well.

MARÉCHALE, À LA In classic cuisine, describing small cuts of meat (such as lamb chops or noisettes, veal escalopes (scallops) or cutlets, calves' sweetbreads, or poultry suprêmes) that are coated with breadcrumbs and sautéed. They are garnished with bundles of asparagus tips and a slice of truffle on each item and served in a ring of thickened chateaubriand sauce or veal gravy. They may also be served with maître d'hôtel butter. Fish *à la maréchale* are poached in white wine and fish fumet, with mushrooms and tomatoes. The sauce is made from the reduced cooking liquid mixed with meat glaze and butter.

RECIPE

lamb cut'ets à la maréchale

Braise some asparagus tips in butter. Cut a truffle into thin strips and braise in butter for 2 minutes. Prepare a liquid maître d'hôtel butter. Season the cutlets with salt and pepper, coat them with breadcrumbs, and sauté them in clarified butter. Arrange the cutlets in a crown, garnish each one with a strip of truffle, and place the asparagus tips between the cutlets. Serve with the maître d'hôtel butter in a sauceboat. Very finely chopped truffle parings may be added to the breadcrumb coating.

MAREDSOUS Pressed uncooked cow's milk cheese (45% fat content) with a washed crust. Maredsous is rectangular or square in shape and weighs 0.5–2.5 kg (1⅛ –5½ lb). It has a supple, dense texture and a sweetish taste.

MARÉE A French collective name for all sea fish, shellfish and seafood that are sold in a fish market.

MARENGO A dish of chicken or veal sautéed with white wine, tomato and garlic.

Chicken Marengo is named after the Battle of Marengo (14 June 1800), at which Napoleon Bonaparte defeated the Austrians; it was created on the battlefield itself by Dunand, Napoleon's chef.

Bonaparte, who on battle days ate nothing until the fight was over, had gone forward with his general staff and was a long way from his supply wagons. Seeing his enemies put to flight, he asked Dunand to prepare dinner for him. The master chef at once sent men of the quartermaster's staff and ordnance corps in search of provisions. All they could find were three eggs, four tomatoes, six crayfish, a small hen, a little garlic, some oil and a saucepan. Using his bread ration, Dunand first made a panada with oil and water, and then, having drawn and jointed the chicken, browned it in oil and fried the eggs in the same oil with a few garlic cloves and the tomatoes. He poured over this mixture some water laced with brandy borrowed from the general's flask and put the crayfish on top to cook in the steam.

The dish was served on a tin plate, the chicken surrounded by the fried eggs and crayfish, with the sauce poured over it. Bonaparte, having feasted upon it, said to Dunand: 'You must feed me like this after every battle.'

The originality of this improvised dish lay in the garnish, for chicken *à la provençale*, sautéed in oil with garlic and tomatoes, dates from well before the Battle of Marengo. In the course of time the traditional garnish was replaced by mushrooms and small glazed onions and the preparation was also used for veal.

Some authorities believe that the dish was created in the town of Marengo (now Hadjout) in Algeria.

RECIPE

sautéed veal Marengo

Cut 1 kg (2¼ lb) shoulder of veal into large even-sized cubes and sauté in 25 g (1 oz, 2 tablespoons) butter and 2 tablespoons oil in a flameproof casserole until lightly browned. Add 2 chopped onions and brown them, sprinkle with 1 tablespoon flour and cook until golden brown. Add 1 glass of white wine, scraping the bottom of the casserole to incorporate all the residue, then 500 g (18 oz) seeded chopped tomatoes, a bouquet garni, a crushed garlic clove, and salt and pepper. Add enough hot water to just cover the ingredients, bring to the boil, cover and simmer for 1 hour.

Meanwhile, glaze 24 small (pearl) onions in 1 tablespoon granulated sugar, 25 g (1 oz, 2 tablespoons) butter, salt and pepper. Keep hot. Sauté 150 g (5 oz, 1½ cups) finely sliced mushrooms in 20 g (¾ oz, 3 tablespoons) butter. Cut 2 slices of bread into croûtons and fry in 3 tablespoons oil until golden brown. Five minutes before the meat is cooked, add the mushrooms and complete the cooking.

Pour the sautéed veal into a deep warmed dish, sprinkle with chopped parsley and garnish with the glazed onions and the croûtons.

MARGARINES AND SPREADS Since the 1860s, margarine has played an important part in the diet of industrialized countries. The product was conceived by French research chemist Hippolyte Mège-Mouriès, to meet a pressing need for a longer lasting and economical alternative to butter to suit the population that had moved from the country and into the cities. Noticing its pearly sheen, he named his invention margarine, taken from the Greek word *margarites* meaning pearl. The Dutch company, Jurgens, initiated commercial production in the 1870s. The popularity of margarine soon grew on a worldwide scale, as it became recognized as a valuable and economical food product.

Margarine has a minimum fat content of 80% but less than 90%. Spreads, although similar to margarine in that they are made from vegetable oil, have varying fat levels.

Margarines and spreads can be made from a wide variety of vegetable oils, and those most commonly used include rapeseed (canola), sunflower, soya, palm and palm kernel. The oils are refined to purity and blended. Essential vitamins A, D and, sometimes, E, flavourings, salt and milk and/or whey are added and the final mixture is emulsified, pasteurized and chilled.

Over the years, a variety of technological innovations have taken place, resulting in products suitable for a number of uses. Examples include margarines and spreads sold in tubs which can be spread easily even when chilled. Some spreads are based on particular types of fat, others offer a 'buttery taste'.

Around a third of all British-produced margarine and related spread products are essential ingredients for catering, baking and commercial food processors. They are used in baking instead of butter or lard (shortening), for example to provide tender, short or soft textures and flavour; to incorporate air in cakes and creams; and to produce layers in puff pastry. For pastry, biscuits and bread baking, margarine or high fat spreads produce good texture. Margarines and other high-fat spreads are also suitable for frying.

Reduced-fat and low-fat spreads cannot be used in cooking as alternatives to butter or margarine, but special recipes have been created for them, giving similar results to those obtained from high-fat products. Spreads with a very low fat content are not suitable for cooking and should only be used for spreading.

MARGAUX

A parish (*commune*) in the Médoc region of Bordeaux, it has its own separate AOC, Margaux. Many fine wines are produced within the Margaux area, including a number of classed growths, such as Palmer, Issan, Lascombes, Rauzan-Ségla, Rauzan-Gassies, and the great first growth, Château Margaux.

MARGGRAF, ANDREAS SIGISMUND

German scientist (born 1709; died 1782). In 1747 he discovered that the root of sugar beet contained a white crystalline substance with a sweet taste. He envisaged that it could be used in the same way as cane sugar but was unable to find a practical application for his discovery. It fell to other researchers (Achard and Delessert) to perfect its manufacture.

MARGUERY, NICOLAS

French chef (born 1834; died 1910). He began his career as a dish-washer at the Restaurant Champeaux in Paris, during which period he married the owner's daughter. He then became an apprentice chef and eventually, in 1887, he opened a restaurant of his own. The Marguery became an elegant, opulent rendezvous for gourmets and was famous for its marvellous cellar and, especially, for its fillets of sole Marguery (cooked in white wine). Marguery invented a number of other dishes, particularly tournedos Marguery (served on artichoke hearts).

RECIPE

fillets of sole Marguery
Fillet 2 sole. Using the bones and trimmings, make a white wine fumet, adding a little chopped onion, a sprig of thyme, a quarter of a bay leaf and a sprig of parsley. Season with salt and pepper and boil for 15 minutes. Add to the fumet the cooking liquid from 1 litre (1 quart) mussels cooked in white wine. Season the sole fillets with salt and pepper and lay them in a greased dish. Pour over a few spoonfuls of the fumet and cover with a sheet of buttered greaseproof (wax) paper. Poach gently, then drain the fillets and arrange them in a oval dish; surround with a double row of cooked shelled mussels and peeled prawns (shelled shrimp). Cover and keep warm while the sauce is being made.

Strain the fumet and the cooking liquid from the sole, reduce by two-thirds, remove from the heat and, when slightly cooled, mix in 6 egg yolks. Whisk the sauce over a gentle heat, like a hollandaise sauce, incorporating 350 g (12 oz, 1½ cups) softened butter. Season the sauce with salt and pepper and strain it; pour over the fillets and their mussel and prawn garnish. Glaze quickly in a preheated oven at 230°C (450°F, gas 8) and garnish with pastry motifs pointing outwards.

MARIE-LOUISE

A garnish dedicated to the second wife of Napoleon I and served mainly with cuts of lamb or mutton. It consists of either noisette potatoes and artichoke hearts stuffed with a mushroom duxelles and onion purée, the sauce being made by deglazing the pan with demi-glace; or small tarts filled with peas and tiny balls of carrot and turnip.

MARIGNAN

A savarin cake spread with sieved apricot jam and covered with Italian meringue; it is traditionally decorated with a ribbon of angelica fashioned like the handle of a basket.

RECIPE

marignan
Soak 75 g (3 oz, ½ cup) raisins in warm water until plump. Weigh out 250 g (9 oz, 2¼ cups) strong plain (bread) flour. Dissolve 15 g (½ oz) fresh yeast (1 cake compressed yeast) in a very small amount of water, stir in a little of the flour, then cover the mixture with the rest of the flour and leave to rise. When cracks appear in the flour (after about 15 minutes), transfer the yeast and flour to a mixing bowl and add 25 g (1 oz, 2 tablespoons) caster (superfine) sugar, a pinch of salt and 3 very lightly whisked eggs; knead the dough well until it becomes elastic. Gradually incorporate about 4½ tablespoons water to make a very soft smooth dough. Let it stand for 30 minutes.

Melt 75 g (3 oz, 6 tablespoons) butter and add this to the dough, together with the drained and dried raisins. Turn the dough into a buttered and floured manqué mould or deep-sided cake tin (pan), 19 cm (7½ in) in diameter, and leave it to rise. When the dough has doubled in volume, bake in a preheated oven at 190°C (375°F, gas 5) for about 40 minutes.

Prepare a syrup with 100 g (4 oz, ½ cup) sugar,

250 ml (8 fl oz, 1 cup) water, and 6 tablespoons rum. Pour this over the warm cake. Spread the cake with warmed and sieved apricot jam (about half a jar is required). Prepare an Italian meringue mixture with 400 g (14 oz, 1¾ cups) caster sugar, 4 egg whites and 1 liqueur glass of rum. Completely cover the sides and top of the cake with this mixture. Bend a long strip of angelica over the cake to resemble the handle of a basket, and fix it to the cake at each end.

MARIGNY A garnish for small sautéed cuts of meat consisting either of fondant potatoes, peas and French (green) beans cut into sticks (buttered and arranged in tartlet cases) or artichoke hearts stuffed with sweetcorn in cream and small noisette potatoes. The sauce is made by deglazing the pan with white wine (or Madeira) and thickened veal stock. Marigny soup has peas and French beans as its basis.

RECIPES

marigny soup
Mix 1.5 litres (2¾ pints, 6½ cups) Germiny* soup (thinned with a little consommé) with 2 tablespoons sorrel chiffonnade gently cooked in butter and 1 tablespoon each of boiled peas and diced French beans. Garnish with 1 tablespoon chopped chervil.

tournedos marigny
Gently cook some artichoke hearts in butter. Prepare some buttered sweetcorn and some noisette potatoes. Sauté the steaks in butter and keep them warm. Deglaze the pan with a little white wine and reduce; complete the sauce by adding some thickened veal stock. Surround the steaks with the artichoke hearts stuffed with sweetcorn and noisette potatoes. Serve with the sauce.

MARIGOLD A garden plant with yellow flowers, the petals of which were once used to heighten the colour of butter. Traditionally they were used to enrich such dishes as Jersey conger soup (with cabbage, leeks and peas), to garnish green salads and to season vinegar. Alexandre Dumas proposed a herb soup à la dauphine, which included marigold flowers. Special care must be taken not to boil the slightly bitter petals.

MARINADE A flavoured liquid, cooked or uncooked, in which savoury ingredients, such as meat, offal (organ meats), game, fish or vegetables, are steeped for varying lengths of time. The process of soaking is known as marinating. Its principal purpose is to flavour the food, but it also makes certain meats more tender by softening the fibres and adding moisture. It is one of the oldest culinary procedures: wine, vinegar, salted water, herbs and spices not only counteract the strong taste of game, for example, but also increase the length of time that the meat can be preserved. The word is ultimately derived from the Latin *marinus* (marine), referring to the sea water or brine that was used for preserving foods in ancient times. Nowadays, foods are usually marinated to improve their flavour rather than to preserve them.

In Mediterranean countries, it is traditional to marinate vegetables and fish (for example, sardines, tuna, peppers, onions and mushrooms). In Sweden, goose is salted and marinated; other foods marinated in Scandinavia include pickled tongue, ham, damsons and mackerel (in white wine). In India, many ingredients are marinated in spiced curdled milk; in Peru, raw fish is marinated in lemon juice (see *ceviche*).

The length of time that foodstuffs should be left in a marinade depends on the nature and size of the food and this can vary from 30 minutes to several days. When the marinade is used for its preserving effect, the food should be completely submerged and not removed until required.

An essential distinction is drawn between cooked, uncooked, and quick marinades. The two former marinades (based on carrots, shallots, onions, pepper, salt, bouquet garni, parsley, vinegar, garlic and red or white wine) are used for meat and game. A cooked marinade must be cooled before use, whereas uncooked and quick marinades can be used immediately as they require no heating. Quick marinades are used to impart flavour and not generally for tenderizing, as this requires a longer marinating time. They are used for fish (lemon, oil, thyme and bay leaf), for the ingredients of fritters or fritots (lemon, oil, parsley, salt and pepper), and for the ingredients of terrines, pâtés and galantines (brandy, Madeira or port, salt, pepper and shallots).

In general, the food that is being marinated is turned over with a slotted spoon from time to time. Because of their high acid content, uncooked marinades are used in glass, porcelain or glazed earthenware dishes.

The food should be removed from its marinade just before cooking and drained well; in the case of grilled (broiled), fried or roasted items, the marinade may be used to baste the food during cooking, to deglaze the pan after cooking or to make the accompanying sauce.

RECIPES

Cooked Marinades
marinade for meat and venison
Take the same vegetables and herbs as listed for the uncooked marinade for large cuts of meat and game and brown them lightly in oil. Moisten with a mixture of 750 ml (1¼ pints, 3¼ cups) wine (red or white according to the recipe) and 6 tablespoons vinegar, then simmer gently for 30 minutes. Season the meat with salt and pepper and put it in a bowl; when the marinade is completely cold pour it over the top. Cover and chill for 2–6 days.

Uncooked Marinades
marinade for ingredients of pâtés and terrines

Season the ingredients with salt, pepper and mixed spice. Add a little crushed thyme and a finely chopped bay leaf. Moisten with brandy – about 150 ml (¼ pint, ⅔ cup) brandy for the ingredients of a duck terrine – and marinate for 24 hours in a cool place.

marinade for large cuts of meat and game

Season the meat with salt, pepper and mixed spice. Place in a dish just large enough to hold it. Add 1 large chopped onion, 2 chopped shallots, 1 chopped carrot, 2 crushed garlic cloves, 2–3 sprigs of parsley, a sprig of thyme, half a bay leaf (coarsely chopped) and a clove. (For a daube add a piece of dried orange peel.) Cover completely with red or white wine (according to the recipe) fortified with 1 liqueur glass of brandy. Cover and marinate for 6 hours to 2 days in a cool place, turning the meat 2 or 3 times so it is thoroughly impregnated with the marinade. The marinade can be used in the cooking if the meat is to be braised.

marinade for small cuts of meat, fish and poultry

Season the meat or fish with salt and pepper and sprinkle with the following: 1 large chopped onion, 2 chopped shallots, 1 finely chopped carrot, a sprig of thyme, a finely chopped bay leaf, 1 tablespoon chopped parsley, a small crushed garlic clove, a clove and 12 black peppercorns. Moisten with the juice of a lemon and 300 ml (½ pint, 1¼ cups) oil (preferably olive oil) and marinate in a cool place for 2–12 hours.

quick marinade for grilled fish

Season all the pieces to be marinated with salt and pepper. Add a few slices of peeled lemon and sprinkle with some thyme and ground bay leaves. Allow to rest for about 10 minutes.

MARINATE To steep ingredients in a seasoning mixture. The term refers to the preparation of savoury ingredients. Macerate is the term used for soaking sweet items. See *marinade* and *macerate*.

MARINIÈRE, À LA A method of preparing shellfish or other seafood, especially mussels, by cooking them in white wine, usually with onions or shallots. The term is also applied to certain fish dishes which are cooked in white wine and garnished with mussels. Marinière sauce is similar to a Bercy sauce made with mussel cooking juices, and the marinière garnish always includes mussels and sometimes also prawns (shrimp). Langoustines, crayfish, frogs and various types of seafood used to garnish, for example, croûtes, timbales and vol-au-vent are also cooked in this way.

crayfish or langoustines à la marinière

Sauté the shellfish in butter over a high heat. When they are really red, season with salt, pepper, thyme, a little crushed bay leaf and add enough white wine to almost cover them. Cook gently with the lid on for 10 minutes. Drain the shellfish and keep warm in a deep dish. Reduce the cooking liquid and thicken it with butter. Pour the sauce over the shellfish and sprinkle with chopped parsley.

marinière sauce

Prepare a Bercy sauce using the juices from moules marinière. Add 2 egg yolks per 150 ml (¼ pint, ⅔ cup) sauce and whisk continuously over a low heat until the sauce thickens.

moules marinière

Trim, scrape and wash some mussels. Peel and chop 1 large shallot per 1 kg (2¼ lb) mussels. Put the chopped shallots in a buttered pan with 2 tablespoons chopped parsley, a small sprig of thyme, half a bay leaf, 200 ml (7 fl oz, ¾ cup) dry white wine, 1 tablespoon wine vinegar and 2 tablespoons butter (cut into small pieces). Add the mussels, cover the pan and cook over a high heat, shaking the pan several times, until all the mussels have opened. Remove the pan from the heat and place the mussels in a large serving dish. Discard any mussels that do not open. Remove the thyme and bay leaf from the saucepan and add 2 tablespoons butter to the cooking liquid. Whisk the sauce until it thickens and pour it over the mussels. Sprinkle with chopped parsley.

MARIVAUX A garnish for large cuts of roast meat served with thickened veal stock. It consists of French (green) beans in butter together with oval nests of duchess potato, browned in the oven, filled with a mixture of finely chopped carrots, celery, artichoke hearts and mushrooms which have all been softened in butter and blended with a béchamel sauce; the nests are sprinkled with grated Parmesan cheese and lightly browned in the oven.

MARJORAM A herb of which there are various types, the most familiar being sweet marjoram, pot marjoram and wild marjoram (see *oregano*). Sweet marjoram is one of the most popular herbs in Mediterranean cookery; it has a strong aromatic scent but a fairly delicate flavour, which is good in salads and combines well with meat, game, poultry, pulses and some vegetables, particularly carrots, salsify and cucumber. To avoid losing its mild flavour, which is easily done in cooking, it is best added towards the end of the cooking period.

Pot marjoram can be used in the same way as sweet marjoram but, because it is not so sweet in flavour, it goes well with more strongly flavoured dishes such as those with onion, garlic and wine. It too is a Mediterranean herb and grows wild in

Greece where it is one of the plants they call *rigani*. There are many wild species of *rigani* and in Greece it is used frequently with lamb.

MARMALADE An orange jam invented by a manufacturer from Dundee in Scotland in about 1790. In domestic cookery marmalades can, in principle, be made with any fruit, but in 1981 the EEC issued a directive that limited the term to those items prepared with citrus fruit (sweet or bitter oranges, lemons and grapefruit). Originally marmalades were made with quinces: the word is derived from the Portuguese *marmelada*, quinces cooked with sugar or honey (see *melimelum*). See also *jams, jellies and marmalades*.

MARMELADE A thick sweet purée prepared from fruit that is stewed for a long time with sugar. The fruit, whole or cut into pieces, is first macerated in a sugar syrup – made with 450 g (1 lb) sugar per 450 g (1 lb) fruit – for about 24 hours. In a *marmelade*, unlike jam, the fruit is no longer identifiable.

MARMITE A French metal or earthenware covered pot with two handles, with or without feet, depending on whether it is used for cooking in a hearth or on the stove. Its large capacity makes it suitable for boiling large quantities of food such as soups, large cuts of beef, stews, pâtés, shellfish and various types of seafood. Catering establishments use even larger marmites that are fitted with a tap at the bottom for emptying. The tallest kind in France are called *pot-au-feu*, and the smallest, *fait-tout*. The *huguenote* is an earthenware marmite with short legs.

The word 'marmite' is derived from an Old French word meaning 'hypocrite', which was applied to the vessel because its contents were concealed. In France it was formerly known as *oille ouille*, or *oule* (see *Olla podrida*). From the 14th century onwards, the marmite was made of cast iron with a lid, a handle and three feet. It was suspended from the trammel of the chimney and used for boiling water amd washing laundry, as well as for preparing the soup. In the 17th century the marmite was reserved for making soups. Special silver marmites, decorated with coats of arms, medals and inscriptions, were manufactured to serve the soup at table.

Marmite is also the name of a product first made in England in 1902. It is a concentrated yeast extract, made from brewer's yeast with salt and spices, and is used as a spread or savoury flavouring.

MARMITE DIEPPOISE A fish soup from the Normandy coast of France made of sole, turbot and anglerfish cooked in white wine with vegetables (celery, leeks, onion, fennel), garnished with mussels, prawns (shrimp) and scallops, and blended with cream.

MARMITE NORVÉGIENNE The French name for a double cooking pot in which food is cooked very slowly and economically over a low heat. The inner container is an ordinary aluminium or stainless steel casserole. When its contents have been brought to the boil, it is taken off the heat and immediately placed inside the second container, which has double walls filled with an insulating material. The temperature of the food in the casserole falls very slowly – 30°C (86°F) in 6 hours – thus the food can continue to cook without using any more fuel.

MARMITE PERPÉTUELLE An establishment that was situated in the Rue des Grands-Augustins in Paris, near the old poultry market. It was very famous at the end of the 18th century, especially for capons and beef boiled in consommé, which could either be taken away or eaten on the premises. It is said that the fire under the marmite never went out, and that more than 300,000 chickens were cooked successively in the same stock, which the proprietor, Deharme, simply watered down every day.

MAROCAINE, À LA The name given to sautéed noisettes of mutton or lamb arranged on mounds of pilaf rice (lightly seasoned with saffron) and coated with a sauce made by deglazing the pan juices with tomato purée (paste). They are served with sautéed diced courgettes (zucchini) and sometimes braised green sweet peppers stuffed with chicken forcemeat.

MAROILLES A French cow's-milk cheese (containing 45–50% fat) with a soft yellow paste and a smooth shiny reddish-brown rind. Named after the Abbey of Maroilles (Thiérache), where it was first made around 960, it is a semi-hard, full-flavoured cheese with a strong smell. Its nickname is *vieux paunt* or 'old stinker'. Philippe Auguste, Louis XI, François I and Fénelon, in particular, greatly appreciated Maroilles cheese. It is manufactured in the towns of Vervins, Avesnes-sur-Helpe and Cambrai. Maroilles is excellent in summer, autumn and winter and is matured for 4 months in a damp cellar. It is sold in 13 cm (5 in) squares, 6 cm (2½ in) deep and weighing 800 g (1¾ lb). Sorbais, Mignon and Quart de Maroilles are related cheeses that benefit from the same DOP. All of them are good to eat at the end of a meal, especially with beer. They are also used in various regional recipes.

MARQUISE Any of various delicate desserts. Chocolate marquise is a glazed dessert halfway between a mousse and a parfait. It is based on chocolate, butter, eggs and sugar, chilled in a mould, and served with vanilla-flavoured custard cream or Chantilly cream. Another type of marquise is a granita (usually flavoured with strawberry, pineapple or kirsch), to which very thick Chantilly cream is added just before serving.

The name is also used for a chocolate dacquoise and for a Genoese sponge or almond cake filled with chocolate-flavoured confectioner's custard (pastry cream) and covered with chocolate fondant icing (frosting).

Formerly, marquise was the name for a refreshing drink made with sweetened white wine or champagne mixed with Seltzer water. It was served very cold with paper-thin slices of lemon.

RECIPES

chocolate marquise

Break 250 g (9 oz, 9 squares) plain (dark) chocolate into small pieces and melt it gently in a covered bain marie. Separate the yolks and whites of 5 eggs. Add 100 g (4 oz, ½ cup) granulated sugar to the yolks, beating the mixture until it becomes light and fluffy. Then add the melted chocolate and 175 g (6 oz, ¾ cup) melted butter and mix well. Whisk the egg whites with a little salt until very stiff, and carefully fold them into the chocolate mixture. Cool a deep sandwich tin (layer cake pan) or charlotte mould under running water and pour the mixture into it, smoothing it down well.

Chill for 12 hours in the refrigerator before removing from the mould.

marquise (the drink)

Dissolve 500 g (18 oz, 2¼ cups) sugar in a little water, then add a bottle of dry white wine and 1 litre (1¾ pints, 4⅓ cups) sparkling mineral water. Cut 2 lemons into thin slices, remove the pips (seeds) and add them to the drink. Store in the refrigerator and serve with ice cubes.

additional recipe See *punch*.

MARRONS GLACÉS

Chestnuts that have been poached in syrup and then glazed; they are packaged as sweetmeats and are also used in pâtisserie. Marrons glacés were created during the reign of Louis XIV and were formerly sold in the syrup in which they were prepared.

RECIPE

chocolate gâteau with chestnuts

Cut a chocolate sponge cake horizontally into three equal layers. Bring to the boil 200 ml (7 fl oz, ¾ cup) water with 150 g (5 oz, ⅔ cup) sugar and cook for 3 minutes. Remove from the heat and add 1 tablespoon rum. Soak the three layers of the chocolate sponge with this syrup after it has cooled down.

Bring 3½ tablespoons milk to the boil. Add 250 g (9 oz, 9 squares) grated plain (dark) chocolate and stir until the mixture is smooth. Add 25 g (1 oz, 2 tablespoons) butter, then cool before adding 250 ml (8 fl oz, 1 cup) whipped Chantilly cream. Coat the first layer of chocolate sponge with this chocolate mousse. Mix 200 g (7 oz, ¾ cup) chestnut purée with 50 g (2 oz, ¼ cup) soft butter. Beat vigorously and incorporate 1 tablespoon flamed rum, then 300 ml (½ pint, 1¼ cups) whipped Chantilly cream. Using a wide spatula, spread this chestnut mousse on the next chocolate sponge layer, arrange 75 g (3 oz, ½ cup) crumbled marrons

glacés on the mousse and cover with the third layer. Put the cake in the refrigerator for 1 hour. Bring 200 ml (7 fl oz, ¾ cup) milk to the boil and add 1½ teaspoons sugar. Now add 150 g (5 oz, 5 squares) grated plain chocolate, then 25 g (1 oz, 2 tablespoons) butter. Stir well and cool slightly. Coat the cake with this ganache, decorate with a few marrons glacés and store in a cool place.

MARROW See *gourd*.

MARSALA

A Sicilian fortified wine, made around the town of the same name. It is produced in a type of solera system (see *sherry*) and the finer examples are matured for some while – the type described as *vergine* must be at least five years old. Marsala tends to be full in character and brownish, and, surprisingly, it can be dry as well as sweet. There are also Marsalas that are flavoured with almonds, coffee, chocolate, tangerines and other fruits. Marsala *all'uovo* is a rich sweet drink consisting of Marsala enriched with egg yolks. Marsala is used in various savoury and sweet recipes, notably veal piccata and zabaglione.

MARSH MALLOW

A medicinal plant, related to the common mallow, with sweet-tasting roots used to make cough lozenges and syrup. The mucilage from the roots was formerly used to make the spongy sweets known as marshmallows. Now, however, marshmallows are prepared with sugar, flavouring, colouring, then either starch and gelatine or gum arabic and egg white.

Marshmallows are commonly eaten as a sweet but are also used as an ingredient in cooking to make cakes, icings (frostings) and sauces. This was a particularly popular fashion in the United States in the middle of the 20th century.

MARZIPAN

A product of almond paste, made with ground almonds and sugar or sugar syrup. The classic French and German marzipans have the ingredients cooked together (see *almond paste*). In Britain, an uncooked paste, made from ground almonds, sugar and egg, is sometimes called marzipan. Marzipan is used in making cakes and pastries, especially as a base for the icing (frosting) on a Christmas or wedding cake, and it can be coloured and flavoured and used in confectionery to make petits fours, usually coated with sugar or praline. Other marzipan sweetmeats are formed into shapes such as fruits and vegetables.

Marzipan sweetmeats are said to have been perfected by an order of nuns in France. The word marzipan is derived from the Italian marzapane, originally meaning a sweet box, and later its contents.

RECIPES

marzipan (1)

Blanch 250 g (9 oz, 1¾ cups) sweet almonds and 2 or 3 bitter almonds and pound them in a mortar (or use a food processor), moistening from time to time with a little cold water. When the almonds have been reduced to a fine and fairly firm paste, put them in a heavy-based pan with 500 g (18 oz, 2¼ cups) caster (superfine) sugar, a pinch of powdered vanilla or vanilla extract, and a few drops of orange-flower water. Dry out over a gentle heat, stirring with a wooden spoon.

Put the paste back into the mortar and grind it with the pestle, then work it with the hands on a marble slab until smooth, adding a small handful of icing (confectioner's) sugar, sifted through a fine sieve. Use the paste as required.

• *Marzipan sweets (candies)* To make sweets, roll the paste out to a thickness of 2 cm (¾ in), lay it out on a sheet of rice paper, and cut it up into various shapes with a cutter. Lay the pieces on a baking sheet lined with rice paper and dry out in a very cool oven.

marzipan (2)

Take 1.4 kg (3 lb) sweet almonds, blanch and peel them; drain and wipe them. Pound them in a marble mortar, sprinkling them from time to time with a little water, so that they do not become too oily (or use a food processor). When they are pounded to a smooth paste, cook 675 g (1½ lb, 3 cups) sugar to the small thread stage, 101°C (214°F). Add the almonds to the sugar and mix together with a spatula, carefully scraping the bottom and sides to prevent sticking, which may occur even when the pan is removed from the heat. The paste is ready when it does not stick to the back of the hand when touched. Place the paste on a board. Sprinkle with caster (superfine) sugar on both sides and leave it to cool.

• *Baked sweets* Roll out the paste to a moderate thickness and cut out different shapes with cutters, pressing them gently with the fingertips on to sheets of rice paper before baking. Cook on one side only, then ice (frost) the other side and bake in the same way.

MASA HARINA A specially processed cornflour, (cornstarch) also known as tamale flour, much used in Mexican food.

MASCARPONE This Italian speciality is made by mixing cream with lemon juice or citric acid. Originally, the curdled mixture was hung up to drain in muslin (cheesecloth); today it is made in factories using centrifugal equipment. It has a smooth creamy taste and texture. It is served on a cheese board or used to make Italian desserts, such as tiramisu.

MASCOTTE A Genoese sponge cake soaked in kirsch or rum, filled and coated with praline butter cream or coffee-flavoured butter cream, and decorated with praline or with caramelized or toasted shredded almonds.

RECIPE

mascotte

Make a Genoese mixture with 4 eggs, 125 g (4½ oz, scant ⅔ cup) granulated sugar, a pinch of salt and 125 g (4½ oz, generous 1 cup) plain (all-purpose) flour. Bake in a buttered round cake tin (pan) 23 cm (9 in) in diameter.

Prepare a syrup with 100 g (4 oz, ½ cup) granulated sugar and 6 tablespoons water. When it has cooled, blend in 6 tablespoons rum. Make a coffee-flavoured butter cream (see *creams*) with 4 tablespoons instant coffee powder, 250 g (9 oz, generous 1 cup) sugar, 6 egg yolks, 300 g (11 oz, scant 1½ cups) softened butter and 3 tablespoons rum. Divide into 2 equal portions and add 2 tablespoons toasted crushed almonds to one half.

Cut the cake horizontally into 2 halves and soak them in the rum-flavoured syrup. Sandwich together with the butter cream without almonds and coat the top and sides of the cake with the remaining butter cream.

MASCOTTE, À LA A garnish for small sautéed cuts of meat and poultry. It consists of olive-shaped pieces of potato and sliced artichoke hearts sautéed in butter, with a few slices of truffle and, sometimes, some small stewed whole tomatoes. The sauce is made by deglazing the meat juices in the sauté pan with white wine and thickened veal stock. Dishes *à la mascotte* were named after an operetta by Audran, 1880. They are usually served in an oven-proof casserole or an earthenware dish.

MASK To coat food with a sweet or savoury substance, usually just before serving but sometimes during preparation of, for example, aspic or a chaud-froid. The masking substance can be a sauce, a cream, a salpicon bound with a sauce, a purée, fondant icing (frosting) or aspic.

MASKINONGE American Indian name for the largest species of pike, which is found in Canadian lakes, particularly in the provinces of Quebec, Ontario and Manitoba. Varied in colour, maskinonge always has several light stripes. It is a very aggressive fish, a choice catch for anglers, who keep it to eat themselves.

MASSÉNA A method of preparing sautéed tournedos steaks or lamb noisettes, in which the pan is deglazed with Périgueux sauce and the garnish is artichoke hearts and slices of poached beef marrow bone. Soft-boiled (soft-cooked) eggs Masséna are served with artichoke hearts and béarnaise sauce and topped with slices of bone marrow.

RECIPE

tournedos masséna

Gently cook some medium artichoke hearts in butter and poach some slices of bone marrow

(2–3 per steak) in a court-bouillon. Prepare a thin Périgueux sauce. Sauté the steaks in butter and arrange them on a dish with the artichoke hearts. Garnish each of the steaks with 2–3 slices of bone marrow and pour a little of the Périgueux sauce over the artichoke hearts. Serve the remaining sauce separately.

MASSENET A garnish for large and small cuts of meat dedicated to the French composer Jules Massenet. It consists of Anna potatoes baked in individual moulds, small artichoke hearts filled with a salpicon of bone marrow, and French (green) beans in butter. The sauce is made from the meat juices or from a demi-glace sauce flavoured with Madeira. Massenet also gave his name to various egg dishes garnished with asparagus tips and artichoke hearts.

RECIPES

scrambled eggs Massenet
Cook some asparagus tips in butter. Boil or steam some artichoke hearts, dice them and sauté them in butter. Prepare some scrambled eggs, mix them with the diced artichoke hearts and garnish them with the asparagus tips.

soft-boiled or poached eggs Massenet
Prepare some individual croustades with Anna potatoes. Fill them with a salpicon of French (green) beans dressed with butter and keep hot. Cook the eggs and place one in each croustade. Coat with bone marrow sauce and sprinkle with chopped parsley.

Alternatively, place an artichoke heart in the bottom of each croustade and garnish the dish with very small asparagus tips.

MASSIALOT, FRANÇOIS French chef (born 1660; died 1733). He was chef de cuisine to various illustrious personages, including the brother of Louis XIV, the dukes of Chartres, Orléans and Aumont, Cardinal d'Estrées and the Marquis de Louvois. In 1691 he published anonymously *Le Cuisinier royal et bourgeois*. His name did not appear on the title page until the work was republished in 1712. He also wrote an *Instruction nouvelle pour les confitures, les liqueurs et les fruits*, published in 1692. These two works were relatively unknown to the general public but were held in great esteem by the professional cooks of the 18th century and certainly had an influence on the development of French cuisine. Massialot's recipes include chicken with green olives and herbs, ragoût of salmon's head with white wine, verjuice, capers and mushrooms, and also *benoiles* (soufflé fritters flavoured with orange-flower water and served very hot, sprinkled with sugar).

MASSILLON A petit four consisting of a barquette made of pâte sucrée filled with vanilla-flavoured almond paste and covered with almond glaze or with kirsch-flavoured fondant icing (frosting). This sweetmeat was dedicated to the preacher Massillon and was created in the French town of Hyères, where he was born.

MASTICATORY A substance of vegetable origin that is chewed simply for pleasure. These substances are popular in Asia, Africa and America and often contain flavoured substances or stimulants.

Among the most widely used are betel (nuts of the betel palm wrapped in leaves of the betel pepper and sprinkled with lime) in south and south-east Asia; chicle (sapodilla gum) in Mexico, which was originally chewed by the Mayas and once formed the basis of chewing gum; liquorice; and coca (the dried leaves of the coca tree), which contain cocaine and are chewed by the people of the Andes.

MATAFAN Also known as *matefaim*. A large thick nourishing pancake made in different regions of France. The dish was first named *matafan* in Franche-Comté when the province was occupied by the Spanish in the 15th century. The word is derived from the Spanish *mata hambre* (kills hunger), which in French became *mate le faim*, hence the frequent spelling *matefaim*. In the environs of Lyon and in the mountains, matafans are savoury and contain spinach, potatoes, pieces of bacon, or even lean pork. In Burgundy and Bresse, they are served as sweet desserts, dried fruit replacing the savoury ingredients.

RECIPES

Besançon matafans
Blend 5 tablespoons plain (all-purpose) flour, 1 egg, 2 egg yolks, a little caster (superfine) sugar, a pinch of salt and 1 teaspoon oil with a little milk. Flavour the batter with kirsch and let it stand at room temperature for 1 hour. Melt a little butter in a frying pan; when it starts to smoke, pour in some batter, tilting the pan so that the batter spreads out to cover the base. When the first side is cooked, turn the pancake over and brown the other side.

Savoy matefaim
Make a batter with 125 g (4½ oz, generous 1 cup) plain (all-purpose) flour, 200 ml (7 fl oz, ¾ cup) milk, 4 eggs, salt and pepper, and a little grated nutmeg. Then blend in 1 tablespoon melted butter. Melt 20 g (¾ oz, 4½ teaspoons) butter in a heavy-based frying pan and pour in the batter, tilting the pan so that the batter spreads out to cover the base. Cook gently until the pancake is set. Turn it out on to a buttered flameproof plate, sprinkle generously with grated Gruyère cheese, and brown under a grill (broiler).

MATÉ A beverage prepared from the leaves of a South American holly shrub. Both the shrub and the beverage are also known as yerba maté and Paraguay tea. The leaves – dried, roasted and powdered – are infused to produce a tonic drink, rich in caffeine, which is popular in Argentina, Brazil and other South American countries. It can be flavoured with lemon, milk or brandy. Originally, the South American Indians chewed the fresh leaves without any previous preparation.

MATELOTE A French fish stew made with red or white wine and aromatic flavourings. The term is generally applied to stews made with freshwater fish: eel in particular, but also carp, small pike, trout, shad and barbel. Matelote is a standard recipe in the regions of the Loire and the Rhône and in Langue-doc; there are also several regional variations (see *bouilleture, meurette, pochouse*). In Normandy a matelote is made with sea fish such as turbot, gurnard, conger eel and brill. It is flamed with Calvados, cooked in cider, bound with butter, and enriched with shrimps and mussels or oysters. All matelotes are usually garnished with small onions, mushrooms, rashers of bacon and sometimes with crayfish cooked in court-bouillon and fried croûtons.

By extension, the term matelote (originally *plat de matelots*, 'sailors' dish') is also used for a similar preparation of brains, sautéed veal, hard-boiled (hard-cooked) or poached eggs.

RECIPE

eel matelote

Skin 1 kg (2¼ lb) eels and cut them into thick slices. Cook them in 65 g (2½ oz, 5 tablespoons) butter until firm, then flame them in 1 liqueur glass of marc or brandy. Add 2 onions, 1 celery stick and 1 carrot, all thinly sliced. Cover with 1 litre (1¾ pints, 4⅓ cups) red wine and add salt, a bouquet garni, a crushed garlic clove, a clove and 4–5 peppercorns. Bring to the boil and simmer for about 20 minutes.

Meanwhile, glaze 24 pickling (pearl) onions in butter and keep them warm, then sauté 250 g (9 oz, 3 cups) thinly sliced mushrooms. When the eel is cooked, drain and keep warm. Put the cooking liquid through a blender together with 1 tablespoon beurre manié. Return the sauce to the pan, replace the eel, add the mushrooms, and simmer for 5 minutes.

Fry 12 small croûtons. Pour the matelote into a deep dish, add the glazed onions, and garnish with the fried croûtons. About 20 small fried pieces of sliced streaky bacon may be added just before serving.

additional recipe See *canotière*.

MATIGNON A vegetable mixture that is prepared *au gras* (with bacon) or *au maigre* (without bacon). It is used as a complementary ingredient in various braised or fried dishes. Matignon is also the name of a garnish for various cuts of meat, consisting of artichoke hearts stuffed with vegetable fondue, sprinkled with breadcrumbs and browned, accompanied by braised lettuce and sometimes Madeira or port sauce.

RECIPES

matignon mixture

For the *au maigre* (meatless) version, cook 125 g (4½ oz, 1¼ cups) sliced carrots, 50 g (2 oz, ½ cup) chopped celery, and 25 g (1 oz, ¼ cup) sliced onions gently in butter. Add salt, a sprig of thyme, half a bay leaf and a pinch of sugar. When the vegetables are very soft, add 6 tablespoons Madeira and boil to reduce until nearly all the liquid has evaporated.

For the *au gras* version (with meat), add 100 g (4 oz, ½ cup) lean diced bacon to the mixture with the onions.

fillet of beef à la matignon

Stud a fillet of beef with strips of pickled ox (beef) tongue (see *écarlate*) and truffle (optional). Cover with a matignon mixture and wrap in very thin slices of bacon. Secure with string. Put into a braising pan and add enough Maderia to cover one-third of it. Cover and braise in a preheated oven at 160°C (325°F, gas 3) until the meat is tender. Drain the fillet and remove the bacon and matignon. Skim the fat from the cooking liquid, strain it, pour a few tablespoons over the fillet, and put it into the oven to glaze. Serve surrounded with a matignon garnish and a little of the sauce. Serve the remainder of the sauce separately.

MATURATION The process of maturing a food or wine under controlled conditions in order to produce the required texture, colour, flavour, aroma and overall quality.

■**Cheese** The final stage in the manufacture of French cheese (except for fresh soft cheeses). In this stage the curds have set and been turned out of their moulds, the rind forms, and the cheese acquires its texture, aroma and flavour. The maturing takes place in a cellar, vault or similar place, at a particular temperature – 10–18°C (50–64°F) – and a specific degree of humidity, sometimes in the presence of bacterial flora. The lower the temperature and the larger the cheese, the longer is the maturing process (from four to eight weeks for a Brie; three to six months for a Cantal cheese).

During this process the cheese is subject to the action of micro-organisms that are present in the atmosphere or deliberately introduced into the cheese. In the case of blue cheese, the action progresses from the interior towards the outside, but for most cheeses, ripening starts at the rind. Meanwhile certain treatments are necessary: brushing of the cheese, washing of the rind, steeping, regular turning and coating with ash, grass or hay. When the maturing is complete, the cheese is said in France to be *fait* or, in the case of a soft cheese, *à coeur*. If it has overripened, it loses its characteristic qualities.

■**Sausages** Many varieties of continental sausages, being similarly fermented products, also go through the maturing process. They are subjected to a ripening and drying period which ensures their stability, taste and aroma.

■ **Wine** Most wines produced today are designed to be drunk young and would not benefit from ageing. Fine wine, vintage, single quinta and crusted ports and some sparkling wines, however, can develop more complex flavours and aromas by 'laying down'. A great number of factors need to be taken into account when assessing when best to drink a wine: the grape variety, area of production, wine-making method and whether the wines were fermented and aged in oak barrels. Full maturity is a mellow marriage of flavours and aromas before the wine starts to deteriorate. The wine will throw a sediment which will need decanting and gradually lose colour – red wines will turn from a rich deep garnet to brick red, whites will become more amber/tawny. Wines matured in half bottles age much faster than those stored in magnums. Cellar conditions also play a part. The bottle needs to be laid down with the cork always in contact with the wine so it does not dry out and shrink, thus letting in air, which would spoil the wine. It should be left undisturbed allowing the sediment to settle. Constant cool temperatures are best for longer slower maturation.

MATZO A Jewish unleavened bread which resembles a very thin, large, dry biscuit. The biscuits are crushed to make matzo meal, used in Jewish cooking as a thickener, to make dumplings and as an ingredient in puddings.

MAULTASCHEN A German speciality consisting of large ravioli stuffed with meat and spinach, flavoured with marjoram, nutmeg and onion, and poached in meat stock. They are used to garnish a type of vegetable soup made with fried chives and onion or a pot-au-feu. They may also be browned and covered with a layer of sautéed onions or coated with breadcrumbs, fried and served with tomato sauce, or used as filling for an omelette.

MAURY A *vin doux naturel* produced in Roussillon, mainly from Grenache grapes.

MAXIM'S A Parisian restaurant that opened in 1893 in the Rue Royale. Maxime Gaillard, who worked in Reynolds Bar nearby, bought the premises with his friend Georges Everaert, with the financial backing of the president of the Distillers' Union, a butcher and a champagne merchant. They converted the establishment into a café and ice cream parlour with the name Maxim's et George's; the second part of the name disappeared fairly rapidly.

After the death of M. Gaillard in 1895, his chef Henri Chaveau and his maître d'hôtel Eugène Cornuché became partners and took over the management of the business. Maxim's premises were modernized and became the meeting place for multimillionaires, princes and opera singers. The most famous cocottes of the era took over a small room nicknamed the *saint des seins*, to which only a favoured few were admitted. Maxim's was bought in 1907 by an English company, and its success continued. After World War I, it was acquired by Oscar Vaudable and thereafter classified as an historic monument. Maxim's retained its reputation, the eccentricities of the 1920s giving way to quiet dinners for the wealthy élite.

Several illustrious dishes have been created by the great chefs at Maxim's, including saddle of lamb Belle Otéro, soufflé Rothschild and fillets of sole Albert. The latter was dedicated to Albert Blazer, who was maître d'hôtel at Maxim's for 50 years.

MAYONNAISE A cold emulsified sauce consisting of egg yolks and oil blended together and flavoured with vinegar, salt, pepper and mustard.

There are four possible etymologies of its name, whose spelling has also changed several times. Some sources attribute the name to the Duke of Richelieu, who captured Port Mahon on the island of Minorca on 28 June 1756. Either the duke himself or his chef created the sauce during this period and named it *mahonnaise*. Others believe that the sauce was originally a speciality of the town of Bayonne, known as *bayonnaise* sauce, which has since become modified to mayonnaise. However, Carême claimed that the word is derived from the French verb *manier* (to stir) and called it *magnonnaise* or *magnionnaise*; in his *Cuisinier parisien: Traité des entrées froides* he wrote: '. . . it is only by stirring the liquids together that one can achieve a velouté sauce that is very smooth, very appetizing, and unique of its kind, as it does not bear any resemblance to the sauces that are obtained only by boiling and reducing on the stove.' Finally, Prosper Montagné suggested that the word was 'a popular corruption of *moyeunaise*, derived from the Old French *moyeu*, meaning egg yolk. Now when all is said and done, the sauce is simply an emulsion of egg yolk and oil.'

The incorporation of complementary ingredients into plain mayonnaise allows a very wide range of derivative sauces to be obtained: andalouse, italienne, tartare, verte, Cambridge, indienne, dijonnaise, gribiche, maltaise, rémoulade, russe or Vincent, depending on whether herbs, curry powder, tomato purée (paste), chopped watercress, caviar, anchovy essence, garlic, capers, gherkins (pickled cucumber), chervil or chopped truffle, respectively, are added.

In order to make a successful mayonnaise, it is important that all the ingredients should be at the same temperature. Some recommend that the egg yolk should be left to stand with some mustard for a few minutes before adding the oil. If a mayonnaise has curdled, this can be rectified by adding the mixture, a little at a time, to another egg yolk plus a pinch of mustard and a few drops of vinegar or water. Mayonnaise should be stored in a cool place, but not in the refrigerator.

Mayonnaise is served as an accompaniment to cold dishes such as hors d'oeuvre, eggs, fish and meat. It can also be used for garnishing (piped through a bag) or as a seasoning, for example in Russian salad, macédoines of fish, shellfish, poultry or vegetables. These dishes are, by extension, known as mayonnaises. When mixed with aspic, mayonnaise is used for coating cold food or binding the ingredients of a salad.

RECIPES

classic mayonnaise

Half an hour before making the mayonnaise, ensure that all the ingredients are at room temperature. Put 2 egg yolks, a little salt and white pepper, and a little vinegar (tarragon, if available) or lemon juice in a medium bowl. 1 teaspoon white mustard can also be added. Stir quickly with a wooden spoon or whisk and as soon as the mixture is smooth use a tablespoon to blend in about 300 ml (½ pint, 1¼ cups) olive oil. Add the oil drop by drop, with a few drops of vinegar, taking care to beat the sauce against the sides of the bowl. The whiteness of the sauce depends on this continued beating. As it increases in volume, larger quantities of oil can be added in a thin trickle and also more vinegar or lemon juice. It is essential to add the ingredients slowly and sparingly to avoid curdling.

anchovy mayonnaise

Add 1 teaspoon anchovy essence (paste) or 4 puréed anchovy fillets to 300 ml (½ pint, 1¼ cups) mayonnaise. Mix well.

aspic mayonnaise

Prepare 8 tablespoons meat aspic*. When cooled but before it sets, add 300 ml (½ pint, 1¼ cups) mayonnaise and whisk thoroughly. The sauce must be used promptly because it will set very rapidly. It can be flavoured in the same way as classic mayonnaise.

caviar mayonnaise

Pound 25 g (1 oz) caviar in a mortar and add 3 tablespoons mayonnaise. Continue to pound. Rub the mixture through a fine sieve and blend with 200 ml (7 fl oz, ¾ cup) classic mayonnaise.

Russian mayonnaise

Make 400 ml (14 fl oz, 1¾ cups) aspic* and leave to cool. Before it sets, add 300 ml (½ pint, 1¼ cups) mayonnaise and 1 tablespoon vinegar. Place the bowl in a larger one containing ice cubes and beat until the mixture becomes foamy.

shrimp or prawn mayonnaise

Mix 50 g (2 oz, ⅓ cup) shrimps or prawns into 3 tablespoons mayonnaise in a mortar or blender. Sieve the mixture and blend with 200 ml (7 fl oz, ¾ cup) mayonnaise. The sauce can be coloured by adding a drop of cochineal (red food colouring) or a little tomato ketchup.

watercress mayonnaise

Add 2 tablespoons very finely chopped watercress to 250 ml (8 fl oz, 1 cup) very thick classic mayonnaise. Mix well.

MAYTAG First made in 1941, this American blue cheese is produced in Iowa. The cheese comes in foil-wrapped wheels of various sizes. The paste is very white in colour with a thick, soft, crumbly texture and bright green veining. The flavour is smooth and nutty with a final lemon-like kick.

MAZAGRAN An earthenware goblet in which coffee and certain iced desserts are served (the name is also given to the dessert itself). Originally, iced coffee laced with brandy or rum was served in a mazagran and drunk through a straw. The name is derived from the town of Mazagran, in Algeria, where the French garrison withstood a memorable siege in February 1840. According to tradition, the Zouaves held their ground thanks to this drink! The goblet was created in their honour.

In classic cuisine, mazagran is the name of a case made with duchess potato mixture and filled with chopped or diced savoury ingredients; the filling is covered with duchess potatoes, piped on with a fluted nozzle. Mazagrans are baked in a hot oven and served hot with a suitable sauce. A single large mazagran can be prepared in a manqué mould or deep-sided cake tin (pan).

MAZARIN A two-layered cake made with dacquoise mixture and filled with praline mousse.

Formerly, a mazarin was a very large Genoese cake with a cone-shaped hollow in the centre. This was filled with crystallized (candied) fruit in syrup and topped with the cone-shaped piece of cake that had been removed, inverted, replaced and iced (frosted) with fondant. The cake was decorated with crystallized fruit. A third type of cake named mazarin was made with raised (leavened) dough and filled with a butter cream mixed with diced candied citron.

MAZARINE, À LA Describing preparations of small cuts of meat which are garnished with rice, button mushrooms and artichoke hearts stuffed with mixed diced vegetables cooked in butter.

MEAL A relatively fixed occasion at which food is consumed each day. The three principal meals of the day are breakfast, eaten at the beginning of the day and literally meaning breaking a fast, lunch, an abbreviation of luncheon, eaten in the middle of the day and dinner, the main meal of the day. A modest dinner is called supper. Other meals, eaten at other times of the day, are brunch, which is a combination of breakfast and lunch, and afternoon tea and high tea, both British institutions. At both occasions, tea, the beverage, is drunk and whereas afternoon tea is usually accompanied by a biscuit (cookie) or small cake, high tea is more substantial and would include a savoury dish. Religious feasts, such as Christmas, Easter or Ramadan, are commemorated by meals consisting of traditional dishes.

Meal is also a term used to describe a coarsely-ground grain or pulse.

MEAT The flesh of animals and birds used as food since ancient times. In the Western world, it refers to the flesh of ox (and calf), pig and sheep, known as beef (veal), pork and lamb or mutton. Beef, lamb and mutton are generally classified as red meats and veal and pork are white meats. The flesh from domesticated birds and wild animals, such as chicken, duck, turkey, rabbit and hare, is categorized as poultry or game. The edible internal organs of all the above are known as offal. In different countries of the world, the flesh of a wide variety of animals and birds is eaten, including camels, goats, horses, llama, reindeer (venison) and water buffalo.

There are numerous rites and customs concerning meat: the slaughtering of the animal, how it should be eaten, how it should be served, and how it should be preserved. Even today, in certain countries or rural communities, the slaughter of a pig or other animal is an important occasion in the life of the community. Festive meals (at Christmas and Easter) are still associated with copious meat dishes, or meat cooked according to special recipes, and the 'Sunday roast' remains a tradition if not for every weekend, then certainly for special occasions.

Meat is composed of small fibres, which are bound together in bundles to form muscles of the animal. These may be surrounded by thick sheaths of tendon or connective tissue (the fascia) and the various cuts of meat are classified into categories according to the amount of this connective tissue present. Cuts for roasting, grilling (broiling) and frying have almost none so are very tender and can be cooked quickly in dry heat. Cuts for pot roasting and braising have a moderate amount and so need gentle, moist cooking to make the meat tender. If there is a high proportion of connective tissue, or the tissues are thick because the animal is old or the muscle has had more active use, then the cut needs long, moist cooking, such as stewing or boiling.

The muscular tissue is enclosed in a layer of fat of variable thickness. If there is fat between the bundles of fibres making up the muscle, the meat is said to be marbled, a desirable quality particularly sought after in beef as it helps tenderize the flesh when cooked. In addition to the various cuts of meat, which vary from country to country and within

Grilling and frying times for meat

Suitable cut	Thickness	Grill (broil) time for each side	Shallow fry/Pan fry time for each side	Stir-fry strips per 225 g (8 oz)
BEEF				
Steaks Sirloin, Rump	2 cm (¾ in)	**Rare** 2½ minutes **Medium** 4 minutes **Well done** 6 minutes	**Rare** 2½ minutes **Medium** 4 minutes **Well done** 6 minutes	2–4 minutes, plus 2 minutes when vegetables added
Fillet	2–3 cm (¾–1¼ in)	**Rare** 3–4 minutes **Medium** 4–5 minutes **Well done** 6–7 minutes	**Rare** 3–4 minutes **Medium** 4–5 minutes **Well done** 6–7 minutes	–
PORK				
Fillet (Tenderloin), sliced	1–1.5 cm (½–⅝ in)	3–5 minutes	2–4 minutes, plus	2–4 minutes, plus 2 minutes when vegetables added
Chops Loin, Chump, Spare Rib **Steaks**	2–3 cm (¾–1¼ in)	8–10 minutes	8–10 minutes	–
Loin, Leg	1–2 cm (½–¾ in) 2 cm (¾ in)	6–8 minutes 8–10 minutes	6–8 minutes 8–10 minutes	2–4 minutes, plus 2 minutes when vegetables added
Escalopes (scallops)	5 mm (¼ in)	2–4 minutes	1–2 minutes	2–4 minutes, plus 2 minutes when vegetables added
Spare Ribs	2–3 cm (¾–1¼ in)	5–8 minutes	–	–
Belly Slices	1–2 cm (½–¾ in)	8–10 minutes	–	–
LAMB				
Neck Fillet, sliced	1–1.5 cm (½–⅝ in)	3–5 minutes	2–4 minutes	2–4 minutes, plus 2 minutes when vegetables added
Chops Loin, Chump	2 cm (¾ in)	6–8 minutes	6–8 minutes	–
Cutlets	2 cm (¾ in)	4–6 minutes	4–6 minutes	–
Steaks Leg, Chump	1–2 cm (½–¾ in) 2 cm (¾ in)	4–6 minutes 6–8 minutes	4–6 minutes 6–8 minutes	2–4 minutes, plus 2 minutes when vegetables added

regions, the breed of the animal, its feed and period of maturing also affect its tenderness as well as its flavour. There are also methods of tenderizing and flavouring meat before cooking. One way is to add fat by larding or barding, another is to cut the meat to break down the fibres by chopping, finely slicing or mincing (grinding), and also by marinating.

■ **The qualities of meat** Immediately after slaughter, the still warm meat is described as being *pantelante* (twitching) and is not edible; the muscles are soft, the water in the meat is strongly bonded to the proteins and the glycogen in the muscles is breaking down into lactic acid. After several hours, rigor mortis sets in and the muscles become stiff. At this stage the meat would be extremely tough after cooking; 24 hours after slaughter, the meat is hung to mature; once it is 'settled' it becomes suitable for eating.

There are five factors to consider when judging the quality of meat.

• COLOUR This – the first sign that the consumer is aware of – depends on the level of myoglobin in the blood, the breed and age of the animal, and possibly its feed. Beef is a vivid shiny dark red, with a fine network of yellow fat; veal is slightly pink with white fat; lamb is bright pink with white fat, mutton a little darker; pork is pale pink.

• TENDERNESS This depends on the following: the age and breed of the animal; its feed; the proportion of connective tissue around the muscle fibres; the treatment of the carcass (whether it was stored in a well-ventilated place and at the correct temperature);

the period of maturing; and correct butchery (cutting up) of the carcass into joints and cuts of meat. In addition to all these factors, the cooking method is also very important: boiling and stewing increase the tenderness, even of very poor cuts of meat; indeed, expensive first-category meat from a young animal, which is considered to be very tender, becomes tough if roasted for too long.

• WATER RETENTION This relies on the strength of the bond between water and proteins in the meat and is also an important factor, both when preserving meat and when eating it fresh.

• SUCCULENCE This depends on the ability of the meat to give up its juices on being chewed. Prolonged chewing of meat that is not very succulent causes salivation and leaves a sensation of dryness in the mouth, which is often attributed to the meat not being tender, which may not be the case. Succulence, or juiciness, is linked to the presence of intramuscular fat (marbled meat); however, some young meat (veal raised on the udder, for example) which has a high water content may also seem to be succulent if the water remains in the meat after it has been cooked.

• FLAVOUR This comes essentially from the fat and is therefore linked with the succulence, which itself is determined by the feed of the animal. The flavour is more pronounced in an adult animal that has been well reared for the table, often with more highly coloured meat.

The quality of the animal and the category of meat should not be confused. A piece of stewing steak

Times for methods of slow cooking meat

Cut	Pot Roast 180°C (350°F, gas 4)	Stew/Braise 160°C (325°F, gas 3)
BEEF		
Joints Silverside, Brisket	30–40 minutes per 450 g (1 lb), plus 30–40 minutes	–
Stewing Beef Shin, Leg	–	2–3 hours
Braising Steak Chuck, Blade	–	1½–2½ hours
PORK		
Joints Leg, Shoulder, Belly, Spare Rib Joint	30–35 minutes per 450 g (1 lb), plus 30–35 minutes	–
Cubes	–	1–1½ hours
Steaks Leg, Shoulder	–	1–1½ hours
Chops Loin, Chump, Spare Rib	–	1–1½ hours
Belly	–	1½–2½ hours
LAMB		
Joints Shoulder, Middle Neck, Breast	25–30 minutes per 450 g (1 lb), plus 25–30 minutes –	–
Chops Loin, Chump	–	1–1½ hours
Steaks Leg, Shoulder	–	1–1½ hours
Middle Neck	–	1–1½ hours

Roasting times for meat

Based on cooking in a preheated oven at 180°C (350°F, gas 4)

Type	Rare	Medium	Well done
Beef	20 minutes per 450 g (1 lb), plus 20 minutes	25 minutes per 450 g (1 lb), plus 25 minutes	30 minutes per 450 g (1 lb), plus 30 minutes
Pork	–	30 minutes per 450 g (1 lb), plus 30 minutes	35 minutes per 450 g (1 lb), plus 35 minutes
Lamb	20 minutes per 450 g (1 lb), plus 20 minutes	25 minutes per 450 g (1 lb), plus 25 minutes	30 minutes per 450 g (1 lb), plus 30 minutes

Note Weigh the meat with any stuffing to calculate the cooking time.

(a third-category cheaper cut) of high quality makes a delicious pot-au-feu, while a piece of rump steak (a first-category expensive cut) can be disappointing if it comes from an animal of mediocre quality.

The category of a cut of meat determines its culinary treatment: the first category comprises cuts for rapid cooking – grilling (broiling), frying, roasting – which mainly come from the back part of the animal; the second category includes the braising cuts, generally from around the legs at the front and (a few) at the back; the third category consists of what is left (neck, knuckle, shin, breast, tail), cuts that need to be boiled or stewed for a long time.

■ **Cooking meat** The choice of cooking method depends on the type and cut of meat. Quick, dry methods suit tender cuts; slow, moist methods tenderize tough cuts.

There are three techniques for rapid cooking: frying and stir-frying; grilling under a grill (broiler) or on a barbecue; and roasting in the oven, either on a spit or in a roasting pan.

There are three methods of slow cooking: braising (browning the meat, then cooking it covered in a small amount of well-flavoured stock); stewing in stock, wine, beer, cider or milk; and boiling (simmering or poaching, in fact) in a large quantity of liquid with vegetables and herbs.

Meat is most often eaten cooked and hot, but it is also served cold and there are examples of raw meat dishes, such as steak tartare.

■ **Preserving meat** Cooking the meat will only preserve it for a limited time and, once cool, it has to be chilled. Man discovered, very early on, various ways of preserving meat, quite apart from charcuterie. One method is cooking in fat, to make confits of goose, duck and pork. Coating cooked meats with aspic is another traditional way of preserving them, but only for a limited time.

Salting, practised since ancient times, is a method of preserving raw meat and examples include pickled pork, cured bacon, salt beef and pickled tongue.

Smoking is applied to pork and charcuterie, as well as to poultry; some cuts of beef were also traditionally treated in this way, although this meat does not adapt itself so well to the changes in flavour brought about by smoking.

The drying of meat takes place in some regions, for example, *brési* from Jura, Swiss *Bundenfleisch*, South American *charqui, pastirma* in the East and South African *biltong* are all dried meats. Drying was the traditional method used by the American Indians to conserve the meat of the bison (pemmican). Freeze-drying is a new method of preparing dried meat.

Canning is also a successful method of long-term preservation and there are many examples of processed meat products sold in cans.

Freezing is the most suitable method for preserving meat. A wide variety of commercially frozen cuts and meat products are readily available. Meat can also be frozen successfully in the domestic freezer.

MECCA CAKE A small sweet French bun, made with choux paste, glazed with egg and sprinkled with granulated sugar or shredded almonds. Mecca cakes are served without fillings, usually with tea.

MÉCHOUI A North African or Arab dish served on festive occasions, the cooking of which is traditionally supervised by men. It consists of a whole lamb or sheep that is roasted on a spit over the embers of a wood fire. Before cooking, the entrails are removed and the carcass is seasoned. Méchoui (*kharouf machwi* in Arabic) can also be prepared with a small camel, a gazelle or a wild sheep.

MEDALLION An item of food cut into a round or oval shape. The word is synonymous with tournedos when applied to small cuts of beef. Medallions of various thicknesses can be prepared from meat, poultry, fish, shellfish, and even from slices of foie gras. Medallions of veal or poultry are sautéed or fried and can be served hot or cold.

Médaillons composés are medallions made with various croquette mixtures. The mixture is shaped into rounds weighing about 75 g (3 oz), coated in breadcrumbs, then sautéed in butter.

RECIPES

chicken medallions Beauharnais
Remove the breasts from a large chicken and cut each into 2 or 3 slices of equal thickness; flatten them slightly and trim them into round or oval medallions. Season with salt and pepper and sauté

in butter. Prepare an equal number of artichoke hearts and cook them in butter.

Fry some round bread croûtes, the same size as the medallions, in butter. Arrange an artichoke heart on each croûton, cover with Beauharnais sauce, and top with a chicken medallion. Serve any remaining sauce separately.

chicken medallions Fédora

Prepare some medallions from the breast of a chicken. Peel some cucumbers, cut them into uniform pieces, and cook them in butter. Keep warm. Cut some slices of bread to the same size and shape as the medallions and fry them in butter. Cook the medallions gently in butter, and keep them warm.

Deglaze the pan in which the chicken was cooked with a mixture of wine and stock; boil until almost completely evaporated. Add some cream and reduce again until the sauce is smooth. Place a medallion on top of each croûton and arrange them in a circle on the serving dish. Coat with the sauce and place the pieces of cucumber in the centre of the circle.

medallions of veal Alexandre

Sauté the medallions of veal in butter in a sauté pan. Arrange them on a hot dish, place a sliver of truffle on each if wished, and keep warm. Cook some fresh artichoke hearts in white stock, brown them in butter, garnish with morels in cream, and arrange them in a circle around the medallions. Deglaze the sauté pan with 1 tablespoon brandy and 1 tablespoon Marsala, boil to reduce and pour the sauce over the medallions.

additional recipe See *égyptienne*.

MEDIANOCHE A Spanish word meaning midnight and used to denote a meal that was eaten in the middle of the night as soon as the fast of the previous day had finished. By extension, the term was also used for an exquisite meal that was eaten very late, on such occasions as New Year's Eve.

MÉDICIS A method of preparing sautéed noisettes of lamb or tournedos, which are either coated with béarnaise sauce or surrounded by a ring of sauce made by deglazing the meat juices with Madeira and a thickened stock. The garnish consists of noisette potatoes and artichoke hearts cooked in butter, with peas and tiny balls of carrots and turnips arranged alternately.

MEDLAR A yellowish-brown pear-shaped fruit, 3–4 cm (about 1½ in) in diameter, with greyish flesh enclosing five seeds (certain varieties are seedless). It is native to central Asia and south-eastern Europe and was known in ancient times. It sometimes grows wild in Britain and Europe. The medlar is edible only when overripe, after the first frosts if it is still on the tree, or after it has been left to ripen slowly

on straw. (The process is known as bletting.) It has a mildly acidic and rather wine-like flavour. The fruit is usually made into compotes or jellies.

MÉDOC One of the most important regions of Bordeaux. It runs from an area just north of the city of Bordeaux almost to the Pointe de Grave, the tip of a peninsula jutting into the Atlantic. The vineyard is divided into the Bas-Médoc in the north and the Haut-Médoc to the south, which includes some of the most famous of all the Bordeaux parishes (communes): Pauillac, St-Julien, St-Estéphe, Margaux, and certain others, such as Listrac and Moulis. Within these districts some of the greatest red wines of the world are made.

The term *cru classé* (classified growth) refers to the 1855 classification of many of the Médoc wines (and one red Graves) into five categories established by brokers for the Paris Exhibition, according to the price each was expected to fetch. Each of the parishes has its own special character, each of the great estates among the *crus classés* possesses considerable individuality, and these days the *crus bourgeois* and *crus artisans* can be extremely good wines too. Wines from the different parishes, both vintage and non-vintage, may be offered simply as 'generics', merely bearing the name of the commune. If wines from different communes are blended together they are labelled 'AOC Bordeaux' or 'AOC Bordeaux Supérieur' – denoting a higher alcohol content.

The great estates also produce 'second' and *sous marque* wines, which may not be quite up to the quality of their finest wines. It is up to the individual winemakers to decide whether they will declassify their wine – for example, in a very poor year, the château label may not be put on a wine that does not attain its usual high standard, but which may be acceptable as a 'second wine' or *sous marque*.

The red Bordeaux wines (clarets) are made from a blend of several permitted grapes, notably Cabernet Sauvignon, Cabernet Franc, Merlot and sometimes Petit Verdot, the proportions of each varying according to the estate.

MÈGE-MOURIÈS, HIPPOLYTE French scientist (born 1817; died 1880). Napoleon III commissioned him to perfect a cooking fat for the French navy that would be cheap and would keep well. In 1869 he obtained a fat from mutton suet which he named 'margarine' because of its pearly appearance (from the Greek *margaron*, 'pearl'). Later, margarine was manufactured from vegetable oils. As early as 1883, the chef Joseph Favre underlined the culinary advantages of Mège-Mouriès' invention: 'It is an excellent product for deep-frying, roasts and soups, but will never replace butter for sauces or vegetables.'

MEGRIM A large flat-fish of the *Pleuronectidae* family, also known as sail-fluke and whiff. It is trawled in the North Sea and around Ireland.

MELAGUETA PEPPER Also known as ginny pepper, Guinea pepper, alligator pepper, malagueta, malaguetta, manigetta or maniguetta. Part of the same family of plants as cardamom and ginger (*Zingiberaceae*), the small red-brown irregular-shaped seeds are contained in small oval pods. The seeds are used ground or whole and their flavour is reminiscent of a mixture of ginger and cardamom. The seeds are also known as grains of paradise; however, there are claims that the true grains are said to come from a related plant of the same species.

This spice is used in West African cooking, its country of origin. The Grain Coast, from which it was exported to Europe, took its name from the spice in the same way as the Gold and Ivory Coasts became famous for their exports. It was one of the flavouring ingredients for the ancient wine Hippocras and it is still used as a flavouring for drinks, including a Scandinavian spirit, although it is no longer widely used in European cooking.

MELBA The name of various dishes dedicated to Dame Nellie Melba, the famous 19th-century Australian opera singer. The best known is peach Melba, created in 1892 by Escoffier when he was chef at the Savoy, in London, at the time when Melba was starring in the opera *Lohengrin*. It was first served at a dinner given by the Duke of Orléans to celebrate her triumph: Escoffier conjured up a dish of a swan of ice bearing peaches resting on a bed of vanilla ice cream and topped with spun sugar. Escoffier first included peach Melba on a menu in 1900, for the opening of the Carlton, where he was in charge of the kitchens. In this version the peaches were coated with raspberry purée and the swan was omitted. Today peach Melba consists of poached stoned (pitted) peach halves placed on a bed of vanilla ice cream and coated with raspberry purée. The latter can be replaced by slightly melted redcurrant jelly flavoured with kirsch, and pears, apricots or strawberries can be substituted for the peaches.

Melba is also the name of a garnish for small cuts of meat consisting of small tomatoes stuffed with a salpicon of chicken, and mushrooms bound with velouté sauce.

RECIPES

lamb noisettes Melba
Stuff 8 very small tomatoes with a salpicon of chicken and mushrooms bound with velouté sauce. Brown them in the oven or under the grill (broiler) and then keep warm. Fry 8 croûtons cut the same size as the noisettes of lamb. Sauté the noisettes in butter and arrange them on the croûtons on a serving dish. Keep warm.

Deglaze the sauté pan with 350 ml (12 fl oz, 1½ cups) stock and boil down to reduce by three-quarters. Blend 1 tablespoon arrowroot with 175 ml (6 fl oz, ¾ cup) Madeira, pour the mixture into the sauté pan and whisk until the sauce thickens. Add 20 g (¾ oz, 4½ teaspoons) butter, cut into small pieces, and continue whisking. Pour the sauce over the noisettes and arrange the stuffed tomatoes in a circle around them.

peach Melba
Prepare 500 ml (17 fl oz, 2 cups) vanilla ice cream and 300 ml (½ pint, 1¼ cups) raspberry purée. Plunge 8 peaches into boiling water for 30 seconds, then drain, cool and peel them. Make a syrup with 1 litre (1¾ pints, 4⅓ cups) water, 500 g (18 oz, 2½ cups) sugar and 1 vanilla pod (bean). Boil for 5 minutes, then add the peaches and poach them in the syrup for 7–8 minutes on each side. Drain and cool completely.

Cut each peach in half and remove the stones (pits). Either line a large fruit bowl with the vanilla ice cream, lay the peaches on top, and coat them with the raspberry purée or spoon the ice cream into individual glasses, top with the peaches and Melba sauce, and serve scattered with flaked (slivered) almonds.

MELBA TOAST Fine, crisp toast. Made by lightly toasting medium-thick slices of bread, then cutting off the crusts and slicing each piece of toast horizontally into two thin layers. The uncooked sides are lightly toasted, making the bread curl slightly. Melba toast is served with light pâtés, such as fish pâté, or fine, smooth meat pâtés, and as an accompaniment for soups or first courses.

MELIMELUM In ancient Greece and Rome, a sort of jam made with honey and apples. The word comes from Latin *mel* (honey) and *malum* (apple) and is itself derived from the Greek *melimelon*, from *mel* (honey) and *mélon* (apple). The word *melimelum* also denoted a variety of sweet apple, similar to quince.

MELOKHIA A plant of the mallow family, with green slightly serrated leaves, several species of which are cultivated in Egypt and Israel as a green vegetable. The leaves may be eaten raw in a salad or cooked like spinach. *Molokhia*, a popular soup in Egypt, is made with fried onions, garlic and coriander, cooked in very fatty beef stock with chopped melokhia leaves. It can be served with lemon juice and is often thickened with rice. Dried melokhia leaves are also available.

MELON The roundish fruit of several types of climbing plants of which there are a very large number of different varieties. They range in size, shape and colour but all melons have a hard rind, and a juicy sweet flesh, usually with a mass of seeds in the centre. They are, in Western countries, usually eaten fresh at the beginning of a meal, as an hors d'oeuvre, or at the end, as a fruit. In Asia, some types of melon are cooked and eaten as a vegetable. Melons can also be used to make jams and pickles. The rinds of large melons can also be pickled. Melon seeds are dried and eaten as a snack, or used in cooking in China, Greece, and Central and South America. Watermelons belong to a different family of plants.

The melon originated in Asia and was known in China at least 1000 years BC. It has been cultivated in southern Europe for centuries and now grows in warm climates, or under glass, all over the world. Three main groups of melon varieties can be distinguished: musk, cantaloupe and winter melons.

Musk (or netted or nutmeg) melons (known as cantaloupe melons in North America) are oval or round with a net-veined, sometimes ribbed, rind and a green to pinkish or orange flesh. The Persian is a variety of musk melon.

The cantaloupe was named after the Italian town of Cantalupo where they were thought to have first grown in Europe. They usually have a warty rind and yellowish scented flesh. The French variety of cantaloupe is the charentais of which there are many types, usually small with a smooth, pale green or yellow rind. There are types of charentais with a rough, netted skin. Other types are the ogen, tiger and galia melons.

Winter melons, which are oblong, have a smooth or finely ribbed rind and a lightly scented yellow or greenish flesh. This type of melon, once picked, ripens slowly and is not ready until winter, hence its name. A common member of the group is the honeydew which has a smooth, yellow rind and pale green or slightly yellow flesh. Casaba and watermelon are also classed as winter melons.

The melon has a very high water content. A good-quality melon should feel heavy for its size and should have a thick unmarked rind that 'gives' slightly when pressed gently with the fingers at the stalk end. The 'female' melon is the most sought-after and can be distinguished when the end opposite the stalk has a large coloured circle that resembles the areola of a woman's breast.

Larger melons are usually cut into wedge-shaped slices for serving, but it is better to serve the smaller ones either whole with the top and the seeds removed or cut in half. It is considered wrong to serve melon with a fortified wine poured over it. However, a glass of port, served separately or drunk afterwards, is a pleasant accompaniment.

RECIPES

iced melon

Choose a large melon weighing about 2 kg (4½ lb) and cut a fairly large slice from the stalk end. Carefully remove the seeds and then scoop out the flesh without piercing the skin. Make a sorbet with the flesh. Put the empty melon shell and the top into the freezer. When the sorbet has set, but is still a little mushy, fill the empty case, pressing down well. Replace the top of the melon and store in the freezer until ready to serve. Serve the melon standing on a dish of crushed ice.

melon en surprise à la parisienne

Choose a good-quality ripe firm melon weighing about 2 kg (4½ lb). Remove a thick slice from the stalk end. Carefully remove the seeds and then scoop out the flesh without piercing the rind. Dice the flesh and place in the refrigerator. Select some fruit in season, such as apricots, peaches and pears, and cut it into cubes. Add some grapes, stoned (pitted) plums, strawberries, raspberries and pineapple cubes. Mix this fruit with the melon cubes, sprinkle with a little caster (superfine) sugar, and pour over some kirsch, Maraschino or other liqueur.

Sprinkle the inside of the rind with a little sugar, pour in a liqueur glass of the same liqueur, fill with the fruit, replace the top of the melon, and store in the refrigerator. Serve the melon in a dish containing crushed ice.

Alternatively, ripe small melons can be used. Cut them in half and prepare each half as above to serve as individual portions.

melon jam

Dice 1 kg (2¼ lb) melon flesh (net weight after peeling). Put in a large dish in layers, sprinkled with 800 g (1¾ lb, 3½ cups) sugar. Leave to macerate in a cool place for 3–4 hours. Then cook in a preserving pan until the setting point is reached. Pot and seal in the usual way.

melon with Parma ham

Arrange seeded and peeled, fine slices of melon on individual plates, allowing 3–4 per portion. Add 3–4 fine slices Parma ham, loosely folded to one side of the melon. The ham and melon are eaten together as a simple starter.

MELT To heat a product, such as sugar, chocolate or fat until it liquefies. To prevent it from burning, a bain marie or a heat diffuser is sometimes used, and the substance is stirred with a wooden spoon.

MÉNAGÈRE, À LA A French term meaning housewife's style. The name is given to various dishes in plain domestic cookery in which simple and relatively inexpensive ingredients are used, prepared according to recipes that are accessible to any good housewife.

RECIPES

entrecôte à la ménagère

Gently cook 250 g (9 oz) small carrots, 150 g (5 oz) small onions and 150 g (5 oz, 1½ cups) mushrooms in butter. Season the steak with salt and pepper and brown it in butter in a frying pan over a brisk heat. Add the vegetables and fry for a further 3–4 minutes. Arrange the entrecôte and the vegetables on a serving dish and keep hot. Make a sauce in the frying pan by adding 5 tablespoons white wine and 3 tablespoons stock. Boil down to reduce and pour it over the entrecôte.

MELONS

green winter melon

honeydew

yellow Cavaillon charentais

netted charentais

white Cavaillon charentais

smooth charentais

galia

ogen

fried eggs à la ménagère

Prepare enough tomato sauce to provide 1 tablespoon per person. Drain some stockpot vegetables, slice them and sauté them in butter. Fry the eggs in butter. Line a serving dish with the sautéed vegetables, arrange the eggs on top, surround with a ring of tomato sauce and serve immediately.

omelette à la ménagère

Cut some boiled beef into small dice and fry lightly in butter. Fry an equal quantity of diced onions in butter. Put the meat and onions in the same frying pan. Beat some eggs, add some chopped parsley and season with salt and pepper. Pour the beaten eggs into the frying pan and cook.

sole à la ménagère

Skin and prepare a sole weighing about 1 kg (2¼ lb). Break the backbone at the head and at the tail. Sauté 200 g (7 oz, 1¾ cups) chopped carrots, 150 g (5 oz, 1 cup) chopped onions, and 2 chopped celery sticks in butter until soft. Season with salt and pepper and sprinkle with a pinch of thyme, a little ground bay leaf and 1 tablespoon chopped parsley.

Place the vegetables in an ovenproof dish and arrange the sole on top. Add 150 ml (¼ pint, ⅔ cup) red wine, cover the dish and cook in a preheated oven at 240°C (475°F, gas 9) for about 10 minutes. Pour the wine from the cooking dish into a saucepan, thicken with 1 tablespoon beurre manié, then pour it back into the dish over the sole. Glaze in a hot oven.

additional recipe See *eel*.

MENDIANTS A dish consisting of four types of dried fruit and nuts: almonds, figs, hazelnuts and raisins, whose colours are those of the habits of the four Roman Catholic mendicant orders (Dominicans in white, Franciscans in grey, Carmelites in brown and Augustinians in deep purple). Mendiants was traditionally served at Christmas.

In Alsace, *mendiant* is the name of a type of moist fried bread (*pain perdu*) made with apples, crystallized (candied) fruit and cinnamon. This is also a very popular dessert in Germany, where it is known as *armer Ritter* (see *bettelman*).

MENETOU-SALON A wine from the Berry region, south-west of Sancerre. The Sauvignon Blanc grape makes pleasant dry white wines and there are also a few reds and rosés made from the Pinot Noir grape.

MENTONNAISE, À LA The name for various dishes inspired by the cuisine of the south of France. For fish prepared *à la mentonnaise*, the main ingredients are tomatoes, black (ripe) olives and garlic, while meat dishes are garnished with courgette (zucchini) halves stuffed with tomato-flavoured rice, small braised artichokes and château potatoes. Courgettes *à la mentonnaise* are stuffed with spinach.

RECIPE

courgettes à la mentonnaise

Cut the courgettes (zucchini) in half lengthways. Make an incision around the pulp, 1 cm (½ in) from the edge, and several smaller incisions in the centre of the pulp. Season the courgettes with salt and put them upside down on paper towels to remove the excess moisture. Dry, then sauté gently in olive oil until they are golden brown. Drain, remove the pulp from the centre without damaging the skin, and chop it.

Blanch some spinach in boiling water, then drain, cool, chop and cook it in butter in a covered pan. Mix the courgette pulp with an equal amount of cooked spinach and fill the courgette halves with this mixture. Sprinkle with 1 tablespoon grated Parmesan cheese and add a little garlic and some chopped parsley. Sprinkle with breadcrumbs and olive oil and brown in the oven.

MENU A list, in specific order, of the dishes to be served at a given meal. In French restaurants, all the dishes that are available are listed on the *carte*; the *menu* lists the dishes for set meals, the composition of which is decided by the restaurant manager. The word menu dates back to 1718, but the custom of making such a list is much older. In former times, the bill of fare of ceremonial meals was displayed on the wall and enabled kitchen staff, in particular, to follow the order in which dishes should be served.

MENU-DROIT A strip cut from a poultry fillet, 2.5 cm (1 in) wide and 2.5 cm (1 in) thick. Marinated in double (heavy) cream, menus-droits are grilled (broiled) for 2 minutes on each side and served with lemon juice and noisette butter. They can also be heated gently for a few minutes in a suitable sauce for poultry. Formerly, menus-droits denoted a ragoût made with the tongue, muffle and ears of a deer.

MERCÉDÈS A garnish for large cuts of meat, consisting of tomatoes, large grilled (broiled) mushrooms, braised lettuces and croquette potatoes. It is also the name of a chicken consommé with sherry, seasoned with cayenne, traditionally garnished with cockscombs and slices of cock's kidneys, and sprinkled with chervil.

MERCIER, LOUIS SÉBASTIEN French writer, critic and playwright (born 1740; died 1814). He is principally known for his *Tableau de Paris* in 12 volumes, published in 1781, to which six volumes (*Le Nouveau Paris*) were added in 1800. It is a series of short articles about everyday life in the French capital and contains valuable information on the history of food and catering, which was in its infancy at the time. The author also condemned certain culinary fashions, such as jellies, consommés, ragoûts and mousses, which were very much in vogue during the 18th century.

MERCUREY A wine from the Côte Chalonnaise in southern Burgundy, a region most famous for its reds, made from the Pinot Noir grape. A small amount of white wine, made from the Chardonnay grape, is also produced. These wines are excellent value.

MERGUEZ A beef sausage seasoned with red pepper, from which it gets its red colour and highly spiced flavour. It originated in North Africa, particularly Algeria, but became popular in France in the 1950s. It is small and fairly thin – 2 cm (¾ in) in diameter – and may be fried or grilled (broiled) and served with couscous.

MERINGUE A very light sweet mixture made from stiffly whisked egg whites and sugar that, when baked, becomes crisp and firm. Some historians of cookery believe that the meringue was invented by a Swiss pastrycook called Galasparini, who practised his art in the small German town of Meiringen. Others maintain that the word comes from the Polish word *marzynka* and that the preparation was invented by a chef in the service of King Stanislas I Leszczyński, who later became Duke of Lorraine. The king passed on the recipe to his daughter Marie, who introduced it to the French. Queen Marie Antoinette had a great liking for meringues and court lore has it that she made them with her own hands at the Trianon. Until the early 19th century, meringues cooked in the oven were shaped with a spoon; it was Carême who first had the idea of using a piping bag.

• MERINGUE SUISSE This simple meringue is made with whisked egg whites and sugar. It can be used as it is for making floating islands, baked Alaska or as a topping for various desserts and pies. When baked in the oven, it can be used for making meringue shells (which can be flavoured, coloured and filled in various ways) as well as vacherin cases. Ground almonds or hazelnuts can be added to produce progrès, succès or dacquoise mixtures. The addition of vinegar and cornflour (cornstarch) to this type of meringue makes it crisp on the outside and soft and sticky inside. It is sometimes called American meringue and is used to make pavlovas and layered cakes.

• ITALIAN MERINGUE This is made by pouring hot sugar syrup on to whisked egg whites. Rarely used on its own, this meringue mixture is used as a topping for tarts, flans and desserts, for finishing *zuppa inglese* (an Italian meringue-topped trifle), for coating Polish brioche and for folding into sorbets. It is also used in the preparation of icings (frostings), butter creams, iced soufflés and petits fours.

• MERINGUE CUITE This is prepared by whisking the egg whites and sugar over a gentle heat and then baking it in the oven. It is used principally by professional bakers for making meringue baskets and petits fours and to decorate desserts and cakes.

Making Italian meringue

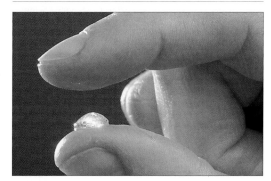

1 *The sugar syrup should be boiled to the soft ball stage, when a little forms a soft ball as it is rolled between the fingertips. The syrup should be boiling when it is added to the egg whites, so time its preparation carefully.*

2 *Whisk the egg whites until stiff, then pour in the syrup in a thin, steady stream while whisking continuously.*

3 *Continue whisking until the meringue has cooled. Italian meringue cannot be overwhisked and it is more stable than other types; it does not separate on standing.*

RECIPES

Italian meringue

Put 300 g (11 oz, scant 1½ cups) caster (superfine) sugar and 100 ml (4 fl oz, 7 tablespoons) water in a heavy-based saucepan and boil to the soft ball stage (see *sugar*). Whisk 4 egg whites until stiff and add the boiling sugar syrup in a thin stream, whisking continuously until the meringue is cold. It can then be stored in the refrigerator until needed.

meringues cuites

Put 8 egg whites and 500 g (18 oz, 4 cups) icing (confectioner's) sugar into a bowl resting on a pan of simmering water over a low heat and whisk the mixture until it is very stiff and holds its shape. Flavour with coffee essence, vanilla sugar or a little rum. Pipe the mixture into small mounds on a baking sheet either oiled or lined with non-stick baking parchment and bake in a very cool oven for about 2 hours.

Swiss meringues

Work 500 g (18 oz, 4 cups) icing (confectioner's) sugar with 2 egg whites, 3 drops of white vinegar, 1 teaspoon vanilla sugar and a pinch of salt. When the mixture is white and smooth, add 4 stiffly whisked egg whites. Mix well and pipe the mixture on to a buttered and floured baking sheet. Dry the meringues in a preheated oven on the lowest possible setting for 12 hours; if possible, prop the oven door slightly ajar to maintain a low temperature for drying out, rather than cooking, the meringues.

vanilla meringues with exotic fruit ♦

Whip 200 ml (7 fl oz, ¾ cup) whipping cream with 2 tablespoons caster (superfine) sugar and put in the refrigerator. Peel and dice 1 mango, 2 kiwis and 1 pineapple. Coat the fruit with 200 g (7 oz) crème pâtissière*. Add to this mixture the pulp of 8 passion fruit, the seeds of a vanilla pod (bean) and the seeds of a pomegranate. Fold in the whipped cream. Spoon the mixture into individual flame-proof bowls. Place a layer of thin slices of exotic fruit on top of the creamy mixture. Whisk 2 egg whites until they form stiff peaks and fold in 2 tablespoons caster sugar. Cover the fruit with the meringue, smooth the surface with a spatula, brown under the grill (broiler) and serve dusted with icing (confectioner's) sugar. The meringue can be piped on top of the fruit. if preferred.

MERINGUER A French verb meaning to top or decorate a dessert or item of pâtisserie with a meringue mixture. It is usually placed in the oven to brown the surface. In France, the part of the cake or dessert consisting of the cooked meringue mixture is called the *meringage*.

When applied to a sorbet mixture, *meringuer* means to add a certain amount of Italian meringue to make it more frothy.

MERLAN A French cut of beef from the thigh near the topside (beef round). It is so called because its long flat shape resembles that of a whiting (the French name for whiting is *merlan*). This cut of meat is very good for steaks.

MERLOT Grape variety with blue-black grapes, cultivated in the south-west and Languedoc–Roussillon regions of France, Italy, Spain, Portugal, Hungary, Romania, Bulgaria, California, the state of Washington, Argentina, Chile, Australia and New Zealand. Merlot is so-called from the colour of its grapes and after the blackbirds (*merles*) which are particularly fond of them.

The fifth most widely cultivated grape variety in France, it produces a fruity wine with a fine colour that is of exceptional richness.

MERVEILLE A traditional French pastry made from dough cut into different shapes and deep-fried. Merveilles are sometimes made with a raised (leavened) dough, and the mixture contains a large quantity of flour. The dough is rolled out and either cut into strips and formed into small plaits (braids) or cut with a pastry cutter into rounds, diamonds, heart or animal shapes. Merveilles are sprinkled with sugar and served hot, warm or cold. Closely related to roussettes and oreillettes, merveilles are made in several regions of southern France. Traditionally, they were made at Shrovetide.

RECIPE

merveilles

Make a dough with 500 g (18 oz, 4½ cups) plain (all-purpose) flour, 4 lightly beaten eggs, 150 g (5 oz, ⅔ cup) softened butter, a generous pinch of salt, 2 tablespoons sugar and 1 liqueur glass of orange-flower water, rum or Cognac. Roll the dough into a ball and leave it to stand for at least 2 hours, covered with a cloth. Roll it out to a thickness of about 5 mm (¼ in) and cut it into various shapes with fluted pastry (cookie) cutters. Deep-fry in oil (175°C, 347°F) until golden brown. Drain on paper towels, sprinkle with a mixture of icing (confectioner's) sugar and vanilla-flavoured sugar, and pile up on the serving dish.

MESCAL A Mexican spirit made from a distillate of the agave plant. In Mexico it is often drunk by itself, but for export markets the more complex spirit tequila, also made from the agave, is more familiar.

MESCLUN Also referred to as mesclum. A mixture of at least seven multi-coloured, multi-textured salad leaves. It originated in the south of France and the name is derived from the Latin word *misculare* (to mix up). Mesclun generally consists of various types of wild and cultivated chicory (endive), lamb's lettuce (corn salad) and dandelion, but it may also include rocket (arugula), groundsel, chervil, salsify, purslane and oak leaf lettuce. It is seasoned with vinaigrette made with olive oil and flavoured with herbs, garlic and even anchovies. This slightly bitter salad is sometimes served with croûtons, small baked goat's-milk cheeses, small pieces of bacon, preserved gizzards or chicken livers fried in butter.

A similar salad mixture is found in Rome where it is known as *misticanza*.

Vanilla meringues with exotic fruit.

MESENTERY A membrane covering the intestines of animals. In France calves' mesentery is usually used in cookery, although the mesentery of lambs and young goats can also be used. The mesentery is washed and poached in boiling water before being sold and must be white and firm to the touch. It may be cut into squares and eaten cold with a ravigote sauce or prepared as a hot dish in the same way as tripe *à la lyonnaise* or tripe *à la poulette*. It is also used as a filling for vol-au-vent.

METAL Any one of a number of dense opaque chemical elements or alloys that are insoluble in water and in normal solvents. Many metals can be highly polished and easily worked by smelting or forging when hot, or by rolling, stamping or embossing when cold. Because of these qualities, metals have been used for making plates and dishes from the earliest times. As metals are also good conductors of heat and electricity, they are used for most cooking utensils.

MÉTEIL The French term for a mixed crop of wheat and rye, sown and harvested together. The flour made from this crop is used for making various regional breads.

MÉTHODE CHAMPENOISE The method by which champagne is produced where secondary fermentation takes place within the bottle. Sparkling wines produced in the same way, but outside the designated Champagne region, may use the term *méthode traditionnelle* (traditional method) or *méthode classique* (classic method). The grapes are pressed with a maximum extraction rate of 100 litres of juice to 160 kg of grapes. The first pressing releases the *cuvée* which is acknowledged to be the best as it is highest in sugars and acidity and low in phenolics. The juice from the second pressing is known as the *premières tailles*. The harsher third pressing (*deuxième tailles*) has been abolished in a move to improve the quality of the base wines.

The juices settle, then ferment in the usual way – usually in tank but sometimes in oak casks. Champagnes are a blend made from grapes sourced from different vineyards within the demarcated area and in the case of non-vintage include a proportion of reserve wines from previous years. The next stage is *tirage*, when the wine is bottled with the addition of sugar and yeast (*liqueur de tirage*) creating a secondary fermentation. This produces carbon dioxide, generating a pressure of six atmospheres inside the bottle. The wines are laid down horizontally for a minimum of one year for non-vintage champagnes or three years for vintage champagnes.

The wines are regularly agitated and reracked during this period. The bottles are then placed in gyropalettes or *pupitres* to undergo the process known as *remuage* where they are rotated regularly to move the yeast sediment towards the neck. The sediment is frozen and removed by the process of *dégorgement*. The final stage is *dosage* when the bottle is topped up with a sweetening *liqueur d'expedition* which enables the degree of sweetness of the final champagne to be controlled.

METS The French word for any dish prepared for the table. It can be hot or cold, savoury or sweet. The word is derived from the Latin *missum* (that which is served on the table).

METTON Low-fat preparation (1% fat content) made with the skimmed milk left after making Comté cheese. It is cooked, then left to mature in a warm place. Metton is used in walnut-sized pieces as the basis of *cancaillotte*.

METTWURST A smoked sausage from Germany, made with pork and beef, and sometimes flavoured with sugar, paprika and nutmeg. Its consistency may be spreadable or coarse-cut, suitable for slicing.

MEULE Name given to very big cheeses, mostly pressed and cooked (such as Beaufort, Comté, Emmenthal and Gruyère), which are formed into large, thick discs looking like millstones. A *meule* of Emmenthal can weigh 130 kg (287 lb).

MEUNIÈRE, À LA A method of cooking that can be used for all types of fish (whole, filleted or steaks). The fish is always lightly floured (hence the name of the dish – *meunière* means miller's wife) and fried in butter. It is arranged on a long dish and sprinkled with lemon juice, then noisette butter and finally chopped parsley. Frog's legs, scallops, brains and soft roes can also be prepared *à la meunière*.

RECIPE

sea bream (or bass) à la meunière
Scale and gut (clean) the fish (each weighing less than 575 g, 1¼ lb) and make a few incisions along the back. Season with salt and pepper and coat with flour (shake the fish lightly to get rid of the excess flour). Heat some butter in a frying pan and brown the fish on both sides. Drain them, arrange on a long dish, sprinkle with chopped parsley and lemon juice, and keep them hot. Add some butter to the frying pan and cook until golden then pour the bubbling butter over the fish.

other recipes See *frog, Mont-Bry, salmon (hot salmon dishes), soft roe, sole.*

MEURETTE Any of certain dishes cooked in a red wine sauce, such as a matelote of river fish (for example eel, carp and pike) or a stew of veal or chicken. Apart from red wine, it is traditional to add strips of bacon and often baby onions and mushrooms. Meurette is usually served with fried croûtons. Eggs and brains *en meurette* are poached in this sauce.

RECIPES

eggs en meurette

Prepare enough bourguignonne sauce to poach the eggs. Fry some small croûtons and small strips of smoked streaky (slab) bacon in butter. Break the eggs one by one and poach them in the sauce. Arrange them in a dish, pour the sauce over the top and garnish with the strips of bacon and the croûtons.

meurette of fish

Clean 1.4 kg (3 lb) freshwater fish (such as small carp, young pike, small eels, perch and trout) and cut them into pieces. Brown them in butter in an flame-proof casserole, then flame them with marc (use at least 1 liqueur glass). Shred 1 carrot, 1 onion and a shallot and add them to the casserole. Stir thoroughly. Cover the contents of the casserole with red Burgundy wine, add a small crushed garlic clove and a bouquet garni, and season with salt and pepper. Cover and simmer very gently for about 20 minutes. Rub some small croûtons of bread with garlic and fry them in butter. Thicken the sauce with 1 tablespoon beurre manié, adjust the seasoning and serve garnished with the small fried croûtons.

MEURSAULT A village in Burgundy's Côte de Beaune, containing some outstanding vineyards – the finest of which are Les Perrières, Les Genevrières and Les Charmes. Most of the wine is white, made from the Chardonnay grape, but there are some reds, made from the Pinot Noir. There is much variation in the styles of the white wines, many of them being outstanding in quality and capable of long lives in bottle.

MEXICAINE, À LA Describing a dish prepared in the Mexican-style. Braised or roast meat is garnished with grilled (broiled) mushrooms stuffed with, for example, chopped tomato, sweet peppers and aubergine (eggplant) halves. The accompanying sauce is a tomato demi-glace to which finely shredded red (bell) peppers are added.

Paupiettes of fish *à la mexicaine* are poached and garnished with the stuffed grilled mushrooms only. They are served with a white wine and tomato sauce containing finely diced red peppers.

MEXICO AND CENTRAL AMERICA See *page 742*.

MEYERBEER A dish of shirred eggs dedicated to the German composer Giacomo Meyerbeer, whose operas were very successful in Paris during the Romantic era.

RECIPE

shirred eggs Meyerbeer

Cut a lamb's kidney in half without separating the halves completely. Clean, season with pepper and grill (broil). Sprinkle with salt. Cook 2 shirred eggs*, garnish them with the kidney and surround with a border of Périgueux sauce.

MEZE Also spelt mezze. An assortment of dishes consisting of (usually cold) simple snacks, served in Greece, Turkey, North Africa and the Middle East. Mezes almost take the place of a meal and dishes suitable for a meze table are numerous. Examples include taramasalata, stuffed vine leaves, böreks, green and black (ripe) olives, cold meats, dips, marinated vegetables and fish, salads, pulses and pitta bread.

MICHE A French wheat bread that was originally made for well-to-do citizens and then gradually became the daily bread of the rural areas. Originally a small loaf (the word comes from the Latin *micca*, meaning 'morsel' or 'crumb'), it became larger when used as the standard family loaf and is now a large, round country-style loaf.

MICROWAVE OVEN An electric cooking apparatus whose source of energy consists of high-frequency ultra-short waves. Ovenproof glassware and china are suitable for microwave cooking but all dishes with metallic trims should be avoided. Specially manufactured plastics are ideal but some thin plastics melt in the microwave, so these materials must be carefully selected. Metallic material reflects the waves, so dishes made of these materials should not be used as the energy will not pass through them. The dish is placed on a turntable or on the base of the cooker. The waves are absorbed by the food and produce heat by the agitation of the water molecules. Microwave cooking is a moist cooking method because of the steam created by heating the water molecules. It is this extremely rapid friction inside the food which creates the heat and cooks the food, and the cooking time is much shorter than in a conventional oven. However, the absence of radiated heat prevents food from browning or from developing a crisp outer crust.

The lack of browning, or crisp cooking, means that meat cannot be roasted as in a conventional oven and the speed of microwave cooking does not allow time for any tougher cuts of meat to tenderize.

However, fish, tender poultry and vegetables all cook very successfully in the microwave oven. Sauces, soups and fruit also cook well. The microwave oven can also be used to thaw and reheat foods quickly. Combination microwave ovens offer the facility for simultaneous use of conventional heat and microwaves.

MIDDLE EASTERN COOKING Middle Eastern cuisine is simple yet at the same time sophisticated. For thousands of years, the culinary heritage of each country in the region has been enriched by the contribution of travellers and also by the successive waves of invaders. Thus, the names of most Arab dishes are Persian in origin: *dolmeh* has become

MEXICO AND CENTRAL AMERICA

Mexican cookery, which has strongly influenced the cuisine of other Central American countries, combines old Indian traditions with the influence of the Spanish colonists. The latter introduced pig rearing, the cultivation of rice and a new method of cooking – frying. The cuisine of the indigenous population relied on steaming, cooking in a tightly covered pan with very little liquid, and braising, which explains the great diversity of ragoûts and sauces, which are also served with boiled or roast dishes.

The main contribution of the Aztec civilization was the cultivation of maize (corn), which together with red beans and rice constitutes the staple food throughout the whole of Latin America: tortillas (pancakes made of cornmeal) are eaten in a number of ways. They may be served plain, fried or baked, either flat or folded, and topped or filled with various stuffings. Crisply fried pieces of tortilla are used as a garnish or for dipping into sauces;

fried whole and piled high with a savoury assortment they are called *tostadas*. *Enchiladas* are folded stuffed tortillas, usually topped with a sauce and baked. *Tacos* are plain tortillas stuffed, rolled and sometimes fried. The grain of maize, cooked in water, is used as an accompaniment for stews and fish dishes, while maize leaves are stuffed with minced (ground) meat and seasonings (see *tamal*). The leaves are also used for cooking chicken with red peppers and banana leaves are used for cooking kid. Haricot (navy) beans (white, red and black) accompany pork and chicken. The fruits include avocado (used especially for *guacamole* sauce), bananas (of which there are over 20 varieties), pineapple and papaw; they are served both as desserts and as vegetables.

The most characteristic feature of Mexican and Central American cookery is the widespread use of chilli peppers. About 100 varieties exist, ranging from bright red to dark brown, most of which have a hot pungent taste. They are used in the famous dish chilli con carne, and one variety is ground to produce cayenne. Ground or crushed with tomato, they are used as an accompaniment to salt cod and chicken; larger varieties

are often cooked stuffed with meat, walnuts and almonds, mixed with soured (sour) cream. Goat's-milk cheeses are also sprinkled with ground chilli.

Meat is not very plentiful; apart from pork (especially in Guatemala, cooked with bananas), chicken is the main dish. *Mole poblano de guajolote*, a ragoût of turkey with spices and cocoa, is the Mexican dish par excellence.

The most popular drink is beer. Alcoholic drinks of various strengths are distilled from the yucca and the agave plants (see *mescal*, *pulque*, *tequila*). All Mexican cakes are very sweet.

The cookery of other Central American countries is very similar and includes tortillas, tamales and empanadas, omelettes, fried black beans, vegetable soups and fish soups (particularly in Nicaragua).

WINE Although Mexico is the oldest wine-producing country in the Americas, a great proportion of the grapes now grown are dried, table grapes or used for brandy. With recent investment in vineyards and cellar technology and training, good quality wines are being produced from varieties including Cabernet Sauvignon, Merlot, Petite Syrah, Colombard and Chenin Blanc.

dolma, and *polo*, pilaf. Similarly, the distillation of rose petals, a refined Persian speciality, spread to the entire Mediterranean where many desserts are flavoured with rose water. Today, Islam's influence is predominant in the Middle East, where the consumption of pork and alcohol are forbidden.

■ **Aromatic flavours** The subtlety of Middle Eastern dishes is mainly due to the numerous spices and aromatic herbs which are used in their preparation. Sesame seeds are grilled and puréed to produce *tahina*.

Middle Eastern cuisine is also based on the association of sweet and savoury: yogurt, for instance, is an essential ingredient in savoury preparations. Dried fruits are also much used in savoury dishes, as in *tarator* sauce, made from pine nuts, bread and garlic, often served with fish.

■ **Mixed appetizers** The tradition of *mezes* is very strong, as it is in the Mediterranean basin. Symbols of hospitality and conviviality, these dishes are served like hors d'oeuvre and every country in the Middle East practises the custom while varying the composition of the dishes.

The meal then continues, centred around a single dish which may be soup or stew: lentil soup, spinach soup or avocado soup, prepared the previous day so that the flavours blend and become stronger. Sweet and sour soup made with fruit is a popular Iranian speciality which has a very unusual taste.

■ **Vegetables and cereals** Courgettes (zucchini), spinach, gumbos, chick peas and peppers are popular ingredients in Middle Eastern dishes. Aubergines (eggplants) and tomatoes are the most important: in salads, puréed (separately or mixed with onion), simply fried or stuffed (*dolmeh*), they are used in all dishes, hot or cold, on their own or with other ingredients.

Bulgur is served as an accompaniment. It is the basic ingredient of *tabbouleh* and *kibbeh*. Rice, however, has the place of honour. Served plain, it accompanies all dishes. The Iranians prefer basmati

Mangoes, papayas and pineapples are piled high at this market in Yucatán, Mexico.

rice, which is more fragrant. It is sometimes cooked with saffron when it is called *tchelo*.

■ **Meat and fish** Mutton and lamb are extremely popular in Middle Eastern countries. Every part of the animal is eaten, including the offal (organ meats). The most tender cuts are used to make *kaba* or *sis kebab*, brochettes cooked on a wood fire. Before being cooked the meat is often left to marinate in spices. It is sometimes also minced (ground) to stuff vegetables or fruit or cut in chunks when cooked in stews: Iranian *khoreche*, a mixture of several kinds of meat (lamb, veal, poultry), is left to simmer for hours with vegetables, fresh fruit and dried fruit, nuts and aromatic herbs. Chicken, pigeon and quail are the basic ingredients of many dishes and they may be grilled (broiled) or stewed. Fish is particularly popular in coastal regions where they are often grilled and served with *tarator* sauce.

■ **Desserts** The art of pastry and confectionery has really surpassed itself in this region of the world, where marzipan and nougat were invented: *loukoums*, flavoured with orange-flower water or rose water, little cakes stuffed with dates, honey and nut pastries, aniseed-flavoured cakes, puff pastry with almonds and pistachios (*baklava*), and *halva*. There is an incredibly wide range of flavours and sugar is always a fundamental ingredient. These small pastries are served with coffee, Turkish or Arab, the latter being flavoured with cloves, cardamom, rose water or orange-flower water.

MIGNONETTE Coarsely ground pepper, particularly from the more flavoursome white peppercorns. Formerly, a mignonette was a small muslin (cheesecloth) sachet filled with peppercorns and cloves, used to flavour soups and stews.

The name is also used for elaborate preparations of, for example, noisettes of lamb, suprêmes of chicken and filet mignon. Potatoes cut into thick matchsticks are also called mignonettes.

RECIPE

mignonettes of milk lamb
Season 8 noisettes of lamb with salt and pepper, sprinkle them with a little thyme and rosemary, and marinate them for 24 hours in grapeseed oil. Drain them and coat lightly with strong mustard. Add 1 tablespoon chopped shallot to 5 tablespoons white wine vinegar mixed with 5 tablespoons white wine and an equal quantity of beef stock. Boil down over a brisk heat until almost dry, add 575 ml (19 fl oz, 2½ cups) double (heavy) cream, and season with salt and pepper. Grill (broil) the noisettes briskly for about 2 minutes on each side. Put them in the sauce and cook, uncovered, until reduced.

MIGNOT Parisian caterer of the 17th century, satirized as a poisoner by the critic and poet Boileau. Offended, he brought a legal action but it was rejected. To revenge himself, the caterer had the idea of selling his customers biscuits (cookies) wrapped in fine paper on which was printed a biting epigram against Boileau, written by the Abbé Cottin. The notion amused the Parisians and even Boileau himself. The biscuits made Mignot rich and famous.

MIKADO The name for various classic French dishes garnished or flavoured with ingredients that are reminiscent of Japanese cuisine. Escalopes of veal or chicken mikado are prepared by arranging the meat on croquettes of curried rice, coated with a curry sauce to which a little soy sauce has been added; the dish is served with tartlets filled with soya bean sprouts in cream. Tournedos or noisettes mikado are arranged on grilled (broiled) tomato halves, coated with a mixture of chopped tomatoes and a small quantity of tomato sauce and garnished with Japanese artichokes cooked in butter in a covered pan. Mikado sauce is made by adding the juice and shredded blanched peel of tangerines to a hollandaise sauce.

RECIPE

mikado salad
Boil 800 g (1¾ lb) unpeeled potatoes in salted water. Allow them to cool, remove the skin and dice them. Season 3 tablespoons mayonnaise with a little soy sauce. (If making the mayonnaise, use soy sauce instead of salt as the seasoning.) Remove the seeds from a green (bell) pepper and cut it into very fine strips. Peel, seed and dice the flesh of 3 firm tomatoes. Blanch 6–7 small chrysanthemum flowers for 2 minutes in boiling water, drain, dry and season lightly with vinaigrette. Mix the diced potatoes with the mayonnaise and 150 g (5 oz, scant 1 cup) peeled prawns (shelled shrimp). Arrange the mixture in a dome in a salad bowl and garnish the top of the salad with chrysanthemum petals. Surround the salad with clusters of finely shredded green pepper and diced tomato.

MILANAIS The French name for various cakes or biscuits (cookies).

The small biscuits known as milanais are made with lemon or orange-flavoured almond paste cut into various shapes and decorated with almonds or crystallized (candied) fruit. They can also be shaped by hand into rounds or plaits (braids), for example, and decorated with sliced almonds.

Milanais are also small cakes made of sponge or Genoese mixture flavoured with rum and raisins or with aniseed, covered with apricot glaze and sometimes iced (frosted) with fondant.

Milanais sablés are small round biscuits sandwiched together in pairs with jam and sprinkled with icing (confectioner's) sugar. They are more commonly known as *lunettes*, because the two small circles cut out of the top resemble spectacles.

RECIPE

milanais sablés
Using the fingers, blend 250 g (9 oz, 2¼ cups) plain (all-purpose) flour with 125 g (4½ oz, ⅔ cup)

softened butter. Add 1 egg, 125 g (4½ oz, ⅔ cup) sugar and ½ teaspoon vanilla essence (extract) or 1 teaspoon vanilla sugar. Knead the dough quickly, shape it into a ball, put it into a floured bowl, and place in the refrigerator for 1 hour.

Roll out the dough to a thickness of 5 mm (¼ in) and cut it with a 6 cm (2½ in) oval biscuit (cookie) cutter into an even number of sablés. Using a small round cutter about 1 cm (½ in) in diameter, cut out 2 circles of dough from half of the sablés. Place the sablés on a buttered baking sheet and bake in a preheated oven at 180°C (350°F, gas 4) for about 12 minutes: they should be just golden. Allow them to cool completely.

Sprinkle the pieces in which holes have been cut out with icing (confectioner's) sugar (these will form the tops) and spread the others with a layer of redcurrant jelly. Lightly press the tops and bottoms together.

MILANAISE, À LA Food prepared in the style of Milan is generally dipped in egg and breadcrumbs mixed with grated Parmesan cheese, then fried in clarified butter.

The name also describes a method of preparing macaroni (served in butter with grated cheese and tomato sauce), and a garnish for cuts of meat, made from macaroni with cheese, coarsely shredded ham, pickled tongue, mushrooms and truffles, all blended in tomato sauce.

Dishes cooked au gratin with Parmesan cheese are also described as *à la milanaise*.

RECIPES

celery à la milanaise
Cut the sticks from a head of celery into strips, chop them into small pieces, and cook them *au blanc* for 10 minutes. Drain thoroughly and place half of them in a buttered ovenproof dish. Sprinkle with grated Parmesan cheese, top with the remaining celery and sprinkle with more Parmesan cheese. Pour melted butter over the top and brown in a preheated oven at 240°C (475°F, gas 9). Just before serving, pour a few spoonfuls of noisette butter over the top.

fried eggs à la milanaise
Prepare some macaroni (cooked *al dente*) and some tomato sauce. Put the macaroni into a vegetable dish, fry the eggs and arrange them on the pasta. Surround with a ribbon of tomato sauce.

other recipes See *risotto, veal.*

MILANESE A dried Italian salami usually made of 50% lean pork, 20% fat pork and 30% beef. It is seasoned with garlic, salt and pepper and has a mild flavour.

MILK A white, opaque, slightly sweet, nutritious liquid secreted by the mammary glands. Milking animals was originally a religious ritual among the early human societies that raised livestock. Milk has always been a symbol of fertility and wealth: in the Bible the Promised Land is described as 'flowing with milk and honey', and Moses proclaimed that the milk of cows and ewes were gifts from God. In Asia and India, zebus' and water-buffalo's milk are sacred. Like the Greeks, the Romans were partial to goat's and ewe's milk, but they also drank mare's, camel's and asses' milk.

The composition of milk varies according to the type and breed of animal, its state of health and the diet on which it has been reared. In most Western countries the word 'milk' without specification means cow's milk, the most readily available kind. Cow's milk is a very nutritious food and a major source of protein and calcium.

Fermentation preserves milk and alters its flavour. Apart from spontaneous coagulation, due to the action of the lactic microbes in the milk producing curds and curdling by means of rennet, there are many other types of fermented milk. *Leben, kumiss* and *kefir* from the Middle East, Indian *khir* and *gioddu sarde*, and Icelandic *skyr* are examples.

■ Different types of European milk
• UNTREATED MILK This retains all its natural flavour. It must come from brucellosis accredited herds, be bottled on the farm where it was produced, and sold under licence. Untreated milk has to be labelled 'raw unpasteurized milk'. Some people advise boiling untreated milk for 5 minutes before drinking it. It is especially good in the spring and will keep for 24 hours in the refrigerator.

• PASTEURIZED MILK This undergoes mild heat treatment, which destroys any harmful bacteria and improves the milk's keeping qualities. A small amount of the vitamin content is lost in pasteurization; otherwise there is little significant change. It will keep for one to two days in a cool place, three to four in a refrigerator. Three types are available: *ordinary* milk has a visible cream line; *homogenized* milk has no cream line because the fat is broken up into small globules; *Channel Islands* milk has a marked cream line and is rich. Domestic boiling changes the flavour of milk and also produces a skin in which some of the nutritious substances are often lost.

• STERILIZED MILK Homogenized milk heated to about 150°C (300°F) for several seconds. Sterilization destroys all germs and increases the shelf life of an unopened bottle, which can be kept at room temperature for several weeks. Date-stamped plastic bottles and cartons have a shelf life of several months. After opening, it should be stored in the refrigerator. Its flavour is like caramel.

• UHT (OR LONG-LIFE) MILK Homogenized milk given ultra-heat treatment, then rapidly cooled. Unopened, it has a shelf life of six months, but once opened should be kept in the refrigerator. It tastes quite different from pasteurized milk.

• SKIMMED MILK Pasteurized milk from which nearly all the fat has been removed. The vitamin content is also reduced.

• SEMI-SKIMMED MILK Pasteurized milk from which some of the fat has been removed, with a consequent reduction in vitamin content.

• EVAPORATED MILK A concentrated homogenized milk, which is sterilized in the can and which, unopened, will keep almost indefinitely.

• CONDENSED MILK This is made from whole, semi-skimmed or skimmed milk, to which sugar is added. Unopened, it will keep almost indefinitely.

• POWDERED OR DRIED MILK This is made from skimmed or semi-skimmed milk to which vegetable fat has been added. Water is evaporated from the milk by heat to produce solids. Powdered milk is packed in airtight containers and can be kept for a long time if stored at a moderate temperature. It dissolves readily in water but once reconstituted should be treated as fresh milk.

■ **Uses of milk** Milk is a very versatile food: it is the basic ingredient of butter, cheese, buttermilk and yogurt, and it makes a delicious drink, either on its own or flavoured with, for example, fruit, vanilla or chocolate. It is stirred into tea and coffee and forms the basis for many hot drinks, notably chocolate. Milk shakes are popular, and this versatile liquid can even be used in cocktails.

Milk is an indispensable ingredient in cookery and is essential for many sauces. It may also be added to soups, used in gratin dishes, courts-bouillons for certain fish, and even in meat cookery. Milk can also be thickened and flavoured to produce various desserts. Custards and cooked creams require large quantities of milk, as do ice creams and batters for pancakes, waffles and fritters.

MILK CAP One name used for mushrooms of the genus *Lactarius*. The name derives from the milky juice the mushrooms yield when cut. See *Lactary*.

MILL A mechanical or electric implement used to reduce a solid foodstuff to a powder or paste. The hand-worked coffee mill has largely been replaced by the electric coffee grinder.

The pepper mill and the coarse-salt mill are mechanical crushers, with a serrated roller or grinding wheel, operated by a handle or by a rotating movement of the lid. Freshly ground pepper gives a more pronounced aroma and flavour.

A vegetable mill with a handle and interchangeable plates is often preferable to an electric blender or processor, particularly for preparing purées of starchy vegetables, which can easily be overworked in the electric appliance.

Small spice mills formed part of kitchen equipment as early as the 14th century, but the mortar was more commonly used. From the 18th century the spice mill was used mainly for coffee, while the pepper mill became part of the table service.

MILLAS Also known as millasse or millias. In the Languedoc region of France, a porridge made with either cornmeal or a mixture of wheaten flour and cornmeal. When cold, it is shaped into flat cakes and fried. The cakes are eaten like bread, either seasoned with salt or sweetened with sugar. The word is derived from the Old French *millet*, meaning fine-grained maize (corn).

In the Anjou region, *millière*, a porridge of sweet or savoury millet, is prepared with rice or maize.

RECIPES

millas porridge
Heat 1 litre (1¾ pints, 4⅓ cups) water in a large saucepan. When it boils, flavour it with orange-flower water and a small piece of lemon zest, and gradually add 300–350 g (11–12 oz, 2¾–3 cups) cornmeal. Cook over a gentle heat, stirring with a wooden spatula. When the porridge is thick, serve it on warm plates with caster (superfine) sugar. Alternatively, leave it to cool, cut into slices, and either fry in butter sprinkled with caster sugar or icing (confectioner's) sugar, or fry in lard or goose fat and serve with stews and casseroles.

millas with fruit
Cook the millas, flavouring it with kirsch or brandy. Put a layer of millas about 1 cm (½ in) thick in a buttered pie dish. Cover with drained cherries that have been cooked in a kirsch- or brandy-flavoured syrup. Then put a layer of millas on top of the cherries, smooth the surface carefully and decorate with a border of drained cherries. Sprinkle lightly with crushed macaroons, pour on some melted butter and bake in a preheated oven at 220°C (425°F, gas 7) until golden.

The cherries can be replaced by apricots, peaches, pears, apples, pineapple, plums or prunes, and rum can be used as a flavouring.

MILLE-FEUILLE A pastry consisting of thin layers of puff pastry separated by layers of cream (which may be flavoured), jam or some other filling. The top is covered with icing (confectioner's) sugar, fondant icing (frosting) or royal icing. Mille-feuilles are usually small rectangular pastries, but they can also be made as large gâteaux, which may be round. The origin of the mille-feuille dates back to the late 19th century. Savoury dishes may be prepared in a similar way using puff pastry with a filling of fish or shellfish. They are served as hot entrées.

RECIPES

chocolate mille-feuille ♦
Mix 1.5 kg (3¼ lb, 13 cups) plain (all-purpose) flour, 2 tablespoons fine salt and 575 g (1¼ lb, 2½ cups) butter. Add 3 tablespoons milk and 400 ml (14 fl oz, 1¾ cup) double (heavy) cream. Stir without giving too much shape to the dough. Rest for 4 hours.

Work 300 g (11 oz, 3½ cups) cocoa powder into 1.25 kg (2¾ lb, 5½ cups) butter. Roll out the dough

Chocolate mille-feuille.

into a square and put in a cool place. Now place the marbled butter in the middle of the square and fold the ends of the dough over the butter to enclose it. Roll out again, fold into three again, then allow to rest for 30 minutes. Repeat this operation 5 times, allowing the pastry to rest each time for 30 minutes between operations. Finally roll out the pastry to a thickness of 3 mm (⅛ in). Cut into 3 strips and allow to rest for 30 minutes. Trim the ends of the strips and place on a baking sheet. Bake in a preheated oven at 200°C (400°F, gas 6) for 5 minutes, then at 150°C (300°F, gas 2) for 1 hour 10 minutes. Cool on a wire rack.

Bring 750 ml (1¼ pints, 3¼ cups) milk to the boil. In a mixing bowl, beat 8 egg yolks with 100 g (4 oz, ½ cup) caster (superfine) sugar until the mixture turns a pale yellow. Add 50 g (2 oz, ½ cup) plain flour, then 150 g (5 oz, 1¾ cups) cocoa powder but without stirring. Pour the boiling milk into the egg mixture, stir, bring to the boil and cook for 3 minutes. Pour into a bowl and cover with cling film (plastic wrap). Allow to cool.

Assemble the mille-feuille by sandwiching the chocolate pastry together with the chocolate crème pâtissière, spreading it thickly. Decorate with mint leaves and cocktail cherries, and serve with a chocolate sauce.

mille-feuille gâteau

Prepare some puff pastry with 300 g (11 oz, 2¾ cups) plain (all-purpose) flour, a generous pinch of salt, 6 tablespoons water and 225 g (8 oz, 1 cup) softened butter. Divide the dough into 3 equal portions and roll them out to a thickness of 2 cm (¾ in). Cut out 3 circles 20 cm (8 in) in diameter, place them on a baking sheet and prick them with a fork. Sprinkle with 50 g (2 oz, ½ cup) icing (confectioner's) sugar and bake in a preheated oven at 220°C (425°F, gas 7) for 15 minutes.

Meanwhile, prepare 750 ml (1¼ pints, 3¼ cups) rum-flavoured confectioner's custard (pastry cream; see *custard*) and allow it to cool. Roughly chop 100 g (4 oz, 1 cup) blanched almonds and brown them gently in a frying pan. Leave the circles of pastry to cool completely. Use two-thirds of the custard to cover 2 circles of pastry, arrange them one on top of the other and cover with the third circle. Cover the entire gâteau with the remaining custard, sprinkle with the browned almonds and some icing sugar, and store in a cool place.

mille-feuille of salmon au beurre rosé

Cut some thinly rolled puff pastry into 4 rectangles measuring 10 × 7 cm (4 × 2¾ in) and bake them in a preheated oven at 220°C (425°F, gas 7) for 15 minutes. Arrange some thin slices of fresh uncooked salmon on 3 of the pastry rectangles and place them on top of each other, spreading each layer with a mixture of cream and lemon juice seasoned with chopped tarragon, salt and pepper. Cover with the fourth rectangle of puff pastry and bake for 5–10 minutes, then cool. Blend

some butter with cream and mix with cranberry compote. Coat the cold mille-feuille with this butter.

vanilla mille-feuille with a raspberry coulis

Prepare 3 rounds of puff pastry 22 cm (8½ in) in diameter and bake in a preheated oven at 220°C (425°F, gas 7) for 15 minutes. Bring to the boil 1 litre (1¾ pints, 4⅓ cups) milk with 2 vanilla pods (beans), slit open and scraped. Mix 10 egg yolks with 150 g (5 oz, 1¼ cups) icing (confectioner's) sugar. Add 50 g (2 oz, ½ cup) plain (all-purpose) flour, 50 g (2 oz, ¼ cup) custard powder and 2 teaspoons cornflour (cornstarch). Add the milk and stir well. Simmer gently for 2 minutes, stirring all the time. Allow to cool. Then place in the refrigerator. Soften 200 g (7 oz, 1 cup) butter and whisk in the milk mixture. Spread a layer of this mixture on one of the pastry rounds, using a spatula. Place the second round of pastry on top and spread another layer of creamy mixture on it before covering it with the third round. Sprinkle the latter lightly with icing sugar. Crush 500 g (18 oz, 3½ cups) strawberries with a whisk or in a blender or food processor, adding the juice of half a lemon and 100 g (4 oz, 1 cup) icing sugar. Serve with the mille-feuille.

MILLÉSIME The French word for the vintage year of a wine. Only certain wines are demarcated with a date (*millésimé*) when they are made; the bulk are non-vintage. A vintage date on a bottle of wine enables one to judge when it will be at its best (for a wine that is drunk young and fresh) or when it is approaching its prime (for a great wine, capable of long-term maturation and improvement).

MILLET Any of several varieties of cereal grain. The main types of millet include the common millet, used for flour milling or as a poultry feed, pearl millet, cultivated for food and for animal fodder in dry arid soils, Italian millet, cultivated for grain and animal fodder, and Japanese millet.

Millet has been cultivated from the earliest times; in ancient Rome a kind of milk porridge was made from the grains after removing the husks. This method of preparation is still used by certain African tribes. Millet continues to be important in the diet of many African and Asiatic countries, but in Europe and North America it is cultivated mainly as a pasture grass and fodder crop. Millet is sold in the form of grain, flakes and flour. It is easy to prepare, being cooked for 20 minutes in twice its volume of boiling water or milk.

RECIPE

millet tartlets

Put 200 g (7 oz, 1¾ cups) millet flour, 400 g (14 oz, 1¾ cups) caster (superfine) sugar and 8 beaten eggs into a bowl. Work the mixture well and add a generous pinch of salt and the finely chopped zest of 2 lemons. Add 1.5 litres (2¾ pints, 6½ cups) boiling milk and mix well. Pour the mixture into small plain round buttered moulds and cook in a preheated oven at 220°C (425°F, gas 7) for 25–30 minutes.

MIMOLETTE FRANÇAIS
A cow's-milk cheese (45% fat content), characterized by its orange colour and shaped like a flattened ball, 20 cm (8 in) in diameter. It is a compressed cheese with a dry hard grey or brown rind. Depending on its maturity (young, semi-matured, or matured up to 18 months), the cheese may be supple, dry, or hard and flaky; the nutty flavour of the young cheese gradually becomes more piquant. (The word *mimolette* comes from the French *mollet*, meaning fairly soft.) The cheese is eaten at the end of a meal, but may also be used in mixed salads and in the preparation of croûtes and cocktail snacks. The cheese can be steeped in port or Madeira for one week before eating. The Mimolette manufactured in France is sometimes called Boule de Lille or Vieux Lille.

MIMOSA
A plant whose yellow flowers can be made into fritters and used to garnish salads and prepare home-made liqueurs.

The name is also given to certain egg dishes using sieved hard-boiled (hard-cooked) egg yolk (which resembles mimosa flowers), particularly a cold hors d'oeuvre consisting of stuffed hard-boiled eggs. The yolks are sieved, mixed with mayonnaise and parsley, and piped in flower shapes into the egg-white cases. Mimosa salads are mixed salads sprinkled with sieved hard-boiled egg yolk.

RECIPE

mimosa salad
Boil some unpeeled potatoes, then peel them, cut into cubes and keep warm. Poach some artichoke hearts in salted water and cut them into quarters. Boil and chop some French (green) beans. Mix the ingredients and season them with a very spicy vinaigrette. Rub the yolks of some hard-boiled (hardcooked) eggs through a coarse sieve and sprinkle over the salad. Serve immediately.

MINCEMEAT
A spicy preserve in English cookery, consisting of a mixture of dried fruit, apple, beef suet, candied peel and spices, steeped in rum, brandy or Madeira. It is the traditional filling for individual mince pies served warm at Christmas.

In the 17th century, a mince pie was a huge covered tart filled with ox (beef) tongue, chicken, eggs, sugar, raisins, lemon zest and spices. Gradually, the small tartlets replaced the single large tart and the filling was reduced to a mixture of beef suet, spices and dried fruit, steeped in brandy.

Mincemeat, which can be stored in jars like jam, can also be used in various hot desserts; for example, mincemeat omelette, flavoured with brandy; steamed suet or sponge puddings and baked apples.

RECIPES

mincemeat
Combine the following ingredients in a large mixing bowl: 450 g (1 lb, 3 cups) shredded suet, 450 g (1 lb, 3 cups) currants, 450 g (1 lb, 3 cups) seedless white raisins, 450 g (1 lb, 4 cups) chopped apples, 450 g (1 lb, 2 cups) sugar, 450 g (1 lb, 3 cups) sultanas (golden raisins), 100 g (4 oz, ⅔ cup) chopped mixed candied fruit peel, 3 tablespoons brandy or rum, the juice and zest of 1 lemon and 1 teaspoon each of cinnamon, nutmeg, cloves and mace.

Pack closely in jars and cover tightly. This yields about 2 kg (4½ lb) mincemeat.

mince pies
Line some tartlet tins (moulds) with shortcrust pastry (basic pie dough) and fill with mincemeat. Cover with a thin layer of puff pastry and seal the edges. Make a small hole in the centre of each pie to allow the steam to escape. Brush with egg and bake in a preheated oven at 220°C (425°F, gas 7) for 15–20 minutes. Serve hot.

MINCING
Also known as grinding in the United States. The process of cutting or chopping food into very small pieces. This may be done manually with a knife, a manual or electric meat mincer, a blender or food processor.

MINERVOIS
Red, white or rosé AOC Languedoc wines. The area has been under vines since Roman times and, thanks to modern vinification methods and considerable investment, the wines (especially the reds) are acknowledged as being good quality.

MINESTRONE
An Italian mixed vegetable soup containing pasta or rice. Italians often start a meal either with *minestra* (a vegetable soup), *minestrina* (a lighter soup) or minestrone, which – with its garnish of pasta – virtually constitutes a meal on its own. Sometimes several types of pasta are used or it can be made with macaroni alone or with rice. The latter is usually used in minestrone in Milan.

Minestrone is characterized by the variety of vegetables it contains, which vary from region to region. In Tuscany it is always made with white haricot (navy) beans, together with peas, celery, courgettes (zucchini), leeks, onions, potatoes, tomatoes and carrots. It is generally thought that minestrone originated in Genoa, where it is made with pumpkin, cabbage, broad (fava) beans, courgettes, red (kidney) beans, celery and tomatoes and garnished with three sorts of pasta – *cannolicchi* (small cubes filled with meat and herbs), small finger-shaped *ditalini* and feather-like *penne*. It is mainly served with *pesto*, a thick sauce made with fresh basil, olive oil, garlic and grated Parmesan cheese. Elsewhere, minestrone is classically flavoured with garlic; grated cheese is served separately.

minestrone

Cook 300 g (11 oz, 1¾ cups) small white haricot (navy) beans in a large amount of water, seasoned with 1 garlic clove, 1 bunch sage and 1 tablespoon extra-virgin olive oil. Purée half the haricot beans by crushing through a sieve. Heat some olive oil in a large saucepan and fry in it 1 slice of chopped uncooked ham, 1 celery stick, 1 bunch parsley, 1 chopped onion and 1 sprig thyme. Add 2 sliced leeks and 2 courgettes (zucchini), cut into cubes, 1 cabbage, cut into thin strips, and 500 g (18 oz) spinach. Then, after 10 minutes, add tomato sauce. When everything has simmered, add all the haricot beans together with their cooking juices and the puréed haricot beans. Add 1 litre (1¾ pints, 4⅓ cups) stock to obtain an unctuous consistency. Simmer for another hour. Season with salt and pepper. Pour 1 glass olive oil into a small frying pan and add 2 crushed garlic cloves, 1 sprig thyme and 2 sprigs rosemary. Place over the heat and when the garlic starts to turn golden, pour this flavoured oil on to the minestrone through a sieve in order to prvent the herbs from getting into the minestrone. Serve hot or cold.

MINNOW A very small fish with a bluish back and pink belly, commonly found in streams and used mainly as a bait for trout. Although not much used in cookery, it may be eaten fried: the heads are removed and the fish soaked in cold milk until they swell up. If cooked in a court-bouillon, they may be used to fill an omelette.

MINT A very fragrant aromatic plant of the genus *Mentha*, used in infusions, to flavour liqueurs, sweets and syrups, and as a culinary herb. There are about 25 species, widely distributed in temperate and subtropical regions. Garden mint, or spearmint, is the most common. Its leaves are used to flavour sauces (particularly mint sauce, the traditional accompaniment for roast lamb in England) and salads, in cooking vegetables (especially peas and potatoes), and to season roast lamb and other meat dishes. Mint tea is made by infusing the leaves. Fresh mint can be dried and is also suitable for freezing.

Other species used in cookery are water mint and horsemint, both water-loving mints. The leaves of peppermint (*menthe poivrée*) produce a very pungent oil used mainly in confectionery and to flavour spirits, liqueurs and jellies. Bergamot or eau-de-Cologne mint is a Mediterranean species, which produces a lemon-scented essential oil similar to essence of bergamot. It is used to flavour drinks and marinades. Japanese mint is the species from which menthol is extracted. Crème de menthe is a peppermint-flavoured cordial made of mint syrup and used in cocktails.

mint sauce

Pour 150 ml (¼ pint, ⅔ cup) vinegar over 50 g (2 oz, 1 cup) very finely chopped fresh mint leaves in a bowl. Add 25 g (1 oz, 2 tablespoons) brown sugar or caster (superfine) sugar dissolved in 4 tablespoons boiling water, with a pinch of salt and a little pepper, and leave to marinate.

mint tea

Pour boiling water on to a mixture of equal quantities of Chinese green tea and finely chopped mint leaves, allowing 200 ml (7 fl oz, ¾ cup) boiling water for each tablespoon of the mixture. Immediately sweeten with caster (superfine) sugar, according to taste (the tea is usually drunk very sweet). Infuse for 2–3 minutes, strain and serve very hot.

Mint tea can also be made by the above method by adding 2 teaspoons finely chopped mint to the boiling water. Sweeten with sugar or honey and serve with a thin slice of lemon.

additional recipe See *pea.*

MINT JULEP An American cocktail made by placing crushed ice, mint leaves and sugar in a tall glass and pouring over Bourbon whiskey. Juleps are served decorated with mint leaves and sprinkled with sugar.

MIQUE A dumpling made in the countryside around Périgord, in France, since the Middle Ages. Originally made with flour and fat, miques today are prepared with a mixture of cornmeal and wheat flour, or wheat flour only, and either lard, goose fat or butter. Yeast and milk are sometimes added, as well as eggs. The dough can be used to make one large ball, which is cut into slices after being cooked, or several small balls. They are poached in salted boiling water or in stock and accompany such dishes as pot-au-feu, pickled pork with cabbage, soup or civet of hare or rabbit. They can be flattened before being poached and cooled and then fried and served as a dessert with jam or sugar. They can also be sliced, browned in goose fat, and served as an entrée with grilled (broiled) bacon.

Miques are also eaten in Béarn and in the Basque country of France, especially black miques, made from maize (corn) and wheat, poached in the cooking water of black puddings (blood sausages), and then grilled.

miques

Mix 250 g (9 oz, 2¼ cups) cornmeal, 250 g (9 oz, 2¼ cups) plain (all-purpose) flour, 1 generous tablespoon lard, a large pinch of salt and 175 ml (6 fl oz, ¾ cup) lukewarm water. When the dough is well kneaded, divide it into 100 g (4 oz) portions and shape them into balls by rolling them in floured hands. Drop the balls into a saucepan of salted boiling water and turn them twice so that they cook evenly. After boiling for about 25 minutes, strain the miques, put them on a cloth and keep them warm.

black Périgord mique made with yeast

Make a dough with 500 g (18 oz, 4½ cups) plain (all-purpose) flour, 3 eggs, 15 g (½ oz) fresh yeast (1 cake compressed yeast) or 2 teaspoons dried yeast (mixed with a little lukewarm milk and left to stand for 10 minutes before the dough is mixed), 100 g (4 oz, ½ cup) softened butter (or goose fat), a pinch of salt and 350 ml (12 fl oz, 1½ cups) milk. Knead the dough until it is firm and well-blended, shape it into a ball and let it rest in a bowl, covered with a cloth, for about 5 hours.

Prepare a pot-au-feu: 45 minutes before the end of the cooking time, put the mique into the stock so that it cooks with the vegetables (turn it halfway through cooking). Serve in slices with the vegetables and meat.

MIRABEAU A dish of grilled (broiled) meat (especially beef), fillets of sole or shirred eggs, garnished with anchovy fillets, stoned (pitted) olives, tarragon leaves and anchovy butter.

RECIPE

entrecôtes mirabeau

Stone (pit) about 15 green olives and blanch them in boiling water. Prepare 2 tablespoons anchovy butter*. Blanch a few tarragon leaves. Grill (broil) 2 thin sirloin steaks. Garnish with strips of anchovy fillets arranged in a criss-cross pattern, the tarragon leaves and olives, and anchovy butter, which may be piped into shell shapes.

MIRABELLE A small, yellow, French variety of plum with a firm sweet-tasting flesh. Mirabelle plums are stewed, made into jam, preserved in syrup and used to make a white brandy. They are also used in flans and tarts.

RECIPES

mirabelle custard pudding

Wash and stone (pit) 300 g (11 oz) mirabelle plums. Mix 4 eggs with 75 g (3 oz, 6 tablespoons) caster (superfine) sugar, then add 400 ml (14 fl oz, 1¾ cups) milk and a generous pinch of salt. Gradually add 100 g (4 oz, 1 cup) plain (all-pupose) flour and whisk well until smooth. Blend in 20 g (¾ oz, 4½ teaspoons) melted butter. Put the plums into a buttered ovenproof dish and cover them with the mixture, tilting the dish so that the mixture penetrates down between the fruit. Bake in a preheated oven at 220°C (425°F, gas 7) for 35–40 minutes. Remove from the oven, sprinkle with caster sugar and serve hot, warm or cold.

mirabelle jam

Stone (pit) the plums without separating the halves and weigh them. Place them in a bowl with an equal weight of caster (superfine) sugar. Mix well and leave to macerate for 24 hours, stirring several times during this period. Pour the plums and sugar into a preserving pan, bring to the boil and cook for 20 minutes. Pot and seal in the usual way.

other recipes See *compote (plum compote), plum.*

MIREPOIX A culinary preparation created in the 18th century by the cook of the Duc de Lévis-Mirepoix, a French field marshal and ambassador of Louis XV. It consists of a mixture of diced vegetables (carrot, onion, celery); raw ham or lean bacon is added when the preparation is with meat.

A mirepoix is used to enhance the flavour of meat, game and fish, in the preparation of sauces (notably espagnole sauce) and as a garnish for such dishes as frog's legs, artichokes and macaroni. When a mirepoix is used in braised or pot-roasted dishes, it should be simmered gently in a covered pan until all the vegetables are very tender and can impart their flavour to the dish. Mirepoix without meat is mainly used in the preparation of shellfish, for braised vegetable dishes and in certain white sauces.

RECIPES

mirepoix with meat

Peel and finely dice 150 g (5 oz) carrots and 100 g (4 oz) onions. Cut 50 g (2 oz) celery and 100 g (4 oz) raw ham (or blanched streaky bacon) into fine strips. Heat 25 g (1 oz, 2 tablespoons) butter in a saucepan and add the ham and vegetables, together with a sprig of thyme and half a bay leaf. Stir the ingredients into the butter, cover and cook gently for about 20 minutes until the vegetables are very tender.

vegetable mirepoix

This mirepoix is cooked in the same way as mirepoix with meat, but the ham or bacon is omitted and the vegetables are shredded into a brunoise.

other recipes See *artichoke, ear, macaroni.*

MIRIN A Japanese spirit-based liquid made from rice, usually referred to as rice wine. This is a sweet liquor (unlike sake, a dry rice liquor or wine). It is used in cooking, not as a table wine or drink. It is used as a sweetener for savoury dishes, particularly fish and meat.

MIRLITON A French puff-pastry tartlet filled with almond cream and decorated with three almond halves arranged in the form of a star.

Crisp petits fours flavoured with orange-flower water are also called *mirlitons*.

RECIPE

Rouen mirlitons
Roll out 250 g (9 oz) puff pastry to a thickness of about 3 mm (⅛ in). Line 10 tartlet tins (moulds). Mix 2 beaten eggs, 4 large crushed macaroons, 65 g (2½ oz, generous ¼ cup) caster (superfine) sugar, and 20 g (¾ oz, scant ¼ cup) ground almonds in a bowl. Three-quarters fill the tartlets with the almond mixture and leave to stand for 30 minutes in a cool place.

Halve 15 blanched almonds and arrange 3 halves on each tartlet. Sprinkle with icing (confectioner's) sugar and bake in a preheated oven at 200°C (400°F, gas 6) for 15–20 minutes. Serve warm or cold.

MIROTON A dish of sliced cooked meat (usually boiled beef or leftovers) reheated in a sauce with sliced onions.

RECIPE

beef miroton
Cook about 10 tablespoons finely sliced onions in 125 g (4½ oz, generous ½ cup) butter in a covered pan. Sprinkle with 1 tablespoon flour. Brown slightly, stirring continuously, then add 2 tablespoons vinegar and an equal amount of stock or white wine. Bring to the boil, then remove from the heat. Pour half the sauce into a long ovenproof dish. Cut 500 g (18 oz) cold boiled beef into thin slices and arrange them in the dish on top of the sauce. Pour the rest of the sauce over the top, sprinkle generously with breadcrumbs and pour on some melted butter (or dripping). Brown in a preheated oven at 220°C (425°F, gas 7) without allowing the sauce to boil. Sprinkle with chopped parsley and serve piping hot.

MISCHBROT Bread made from 70% rye flour and 30% cornflour (cornstarch). The leaven obtained with half (or more) of rye flour gives rye bread a slightly acidic taste and a crumb with little aeration. This bread is the kind most eaten in Germany, and it is sometimes flavoured with, for example, bacon or onions. It is eaten several days after it is made.

MISO A Japanese condiment consisting of a red or white paste of fermented soya, made from cooked soya beans mixed with rice, barley or wheat grains, and salt.

MISTELLE Grape juice to which spirits have been added in order to prevent fermentation from taking place, so that the natural sweetness of the fruit is retained. Mistelle is used in the making of various apéritifs and vermouths.

MITONNER A French cooking term that originally meant to simmer stale bread for a long time in soup or stock so that it absorbs the liquid and thickens the soup.

MIXED GRILL An assortment of various meats such as steak, lamb chops, sausages, bacon and kidneys, barbecued or grilled (broiled) and usually served with a garnish of watercress, grilled tomatoes and mushrooms. It is a popular dish in English-speaking countries.

MOCHA A variety of Arabian coffee bean grown on the borders of the Red Sea, named after the Yemenite port from which they were traditionally exported. Mocha is a strong coffee with a distinctive aroma, but some people find it bitter, with a musky flavour. It is normally served very strong and sweet in small cups.

Mocha is used as a flavouring for cakes, biscuits (cookies), ice creams and confectionery, and the word is used to describe various cakes with a coffee flavour, particularly a large Genoese sponge cake with layers of coffee or chocolate butter cream.

Mocha is also a term used to describe a combined coffee and chocolate flavour. For example, a cake or cream flavoured with both coffee and chocolate may be referred to as mocha.

RECIPE

mocha cake
Melt 90 g (3½ oz, 7 tablespoons) butter, taking care not to let it get too hot. Whisk 5 egg yolks with 150 g (5 oz, ⅔ cup) caster (superfine) sugar until the mixture has turned white and thick. Mix in 150 g (5 oz, 1¼ cups) plain (all-purpose) flour and 50 g (2 oz, ½ cup) ground hazelnuts, then incorporate the melted butter and fold in 5 stiffly whisked egg whites. Pour this mixture into a deep 22 cm (8½ in) buttered cake tin (pan) and bake in a preheated oven at 180°C (350°F, gas 4) for about 35 minutes. As soon as the cake is cooked, turn it out on to a wire rack and leave to cool completely. Then cover and refrigerate for at least 1 hour.

Dissolve 150 g (5 oz, ⅔ cup) sugar with 2 tablespoons water and very slowly bring it to the boil. Gently mix the boiling syrup with 4 egg yolks and beat briskly until it has cooled and is thick and mousse-like. Now whisk in 175 g (6 oz, ¾ cup) soft butter, cut into small pieces, and 1 teaspoon coffee essence (extract). Finely grind 150 g (5 oz, 1¼ cups) toasted hazelnuts. Cut the cake into 3 layers. Mix two-thirds of the ground nuts into half the cream and spread on 2 of these layers. Sandwich the cake together and cover it completely with half the remaining cream. Sprinkle the surface of the cake with the remaining ground hazelnuts, put the rest of the cream into a piping bag with a fluted nozzle and pipe a regular design of rosettes on the cake. Place a coffee bean covered in bitter chocolate at the centre of every rosette. Refrigerate the cake in a sealed container for at least 2 hours; serve very cold.

Mocha cake can also be filled and coated with coffee cream, then decorated with toasted flaked (slivered) almonds and crystallized (candied) violets and mimosa. Mocha cake is best eaten the day after its preparation.

MODE, À LA A French term describing a preparation of braised beef, to which diced leg of veal, sliced carrots and small onions are added when it is three-quarters cooked. Beef *à la mode* is eaten either hot or cold (in aspic).

Literally meaning 'in the style of', the term is also used to describe dishes that are a speciality of a particular town or region, such as tripe *à la mode de Caen*. In the United States, it is used to describe a sweet pie served with ice cream.

MODERNE, À LA A French term meaning 'in the modern style', used to describe a garnish of braised lettuce and cabbage (stuffed or plain) and other mixed vegetables, served with cuts of meat.

MOÏNA A French dish consisting of poached fillets of sole garnished with quartered artichokes braised in butter and morels *à la crème*.

MOISTEN To add a liquid to a culinary preparation, either in order to cook it (for example, for stews or braised dishes) or to make the sauce or gravy. The liquid, which may be water, milk, broth, stock or wine, usually just covers the items to be cooked but in certain cases (for example, baked fish) the ingredients are only half-covered.

MOLASSES The thick brown uncrystallized residue obtained from cane or beet sugar during refining. This dense viscous syrup can be used for various purposes. Only sugar-cane molasses, known as 'black treacle', is sold for domestic consumption. It is used in desserts, such as treacle tart, and in cakes and biscuits (cookies), and also for sweet-and-sour cooking. It is also used in confectionery and for the manufacture of rum. Sugar-beet molasses is used mainly for the production of industrial alcohol, baking powders and animal feeds.

MOLE POBIANO A festival dish in Mexican cookery (its full name is *mole poblano de Guajolote*), consisting of a turkey stew with a chocolate sauce. It is supposed to have been invented in the 16th century by nuns of the convent of Puebla. The story goes that the nuns were taken unawares by a visit from their bishop, so they cooked the local poulterer's only turkey in a sauce typical of Aztec cookery. Originally, the turkey was cooked in a casserole but it can also be roasted in the oven or fried.

The sauce (*mole*) is traditionally prepared by pounding various sweet and hot chillies, such as *ancho*, very aromatic; *mulato*, large and scented; and *pasilla*, very hot, in a little turkey stock. Onions, tomatoes, pieces of tortilla, garlic, crushed almonds, aniseed, sesame seeds, cinnamon, cloves and coriander are added. The mixture is thoroughly pounded, then strained and simmered with more turkey stock to which lard and plain (dark) chocolate are added. The cooked turkey is cut into pieces, liberally coated with the sauce, and served sprinkled with sesame seeds, sweetcorn or small tortillas.

RECIPE

turkey mole
Joint a small turkey into small portions and marinate them overnight in a mixture of the juice of 4 oranges, 100 ml (4 fl oz, 7 tablespoons) tequila, 2–4 chopped garlic cloves, 1 chopped onion, some chopped fresh oregano, a sprinkling of ground cinnamon and 6 whole cloves. The following day, grill (broil) a mixture of fresh chillies until just soft – try 250 g (9 oz) mulatto chillies, 300 g (11 oz) ancho chillies, 150 g (5 oz) pasilla chillies and 50 g (2 oz) chipotle chillies. Remove the cores and seeds, then rinse the chillies and chop finely.

Fry the chillies in a little oil, then add 6 chopped garlic cloves, 150 g (5 oz, 1¼ cups) chopped blanched almonds, 100 g (4 oz, 1 cup) unsalted peanuts 100 g (4 oz, ¾ cup) sesame seeds and 100 g (4 oz, ⅔ cup) raisins. Remove from the heat.

In a dry frying pan, lightly roast 6 black peppercorns, 10 coriander seeds, 4 cloves, 1 teaspoon aniseeds and 1 teaspoon ground cinnamon. Cool, then grind these spices and add them to the chilli mixture. Fry 450 g (1 lb) peeled, chopped tomatoes and 250 g (9 oz) peeled chopped tomatillos until all their excess liquid has evaporated, then purée them with the chilli mixture, adding a little turkey stock to make a smooth, thick paste. Transfer the paste to a pan and add a little salt, then cook over a low heat, stirring, until the oil rises to the surface. Add 200 g (7 oz, 7 squares) bitter chocolate and stir until it has melted into the sauce. Dilute the sauce with extra stock if necessary. Set aside off the heat.

Drain the turkey portions, reserving the marinade, and place in a large deep roasting tin (pan). Roast in a preheated oven at 200°C (400°F, gas 6) for 30 minutes. Pour the marinade over and continue cooking for a further 40 minutes, turning and rearranging the turkey occasionally. The turkey should be thoroughly cooked and the marinade evaporated to a glaze. Arrange the turkey on a dish and sprinkle with sesame seeds. Serve with the reheated mole sauce.

MOLLUSC A soft-bodied animal, usually with a shell. The bivalves (or lamellibranchs), which have a shell consisting of two valves hinged together, include mussels, oysters, cockles and scallops. The gastropods have a single spiral shell and include periwinkles, whelks, snails and limpets. Bivalves and gastropods are sold as shellfish. The third group of molluscs – the cephalopods – do not have shells; they include squid, octopuses and cuttlefish.

MOLOKHIA See *Melokhia*.

MOMBIN Name given to some *Spondias* genus fruits, which are yellow or dark red in colour when ripe, egg or pear shaped and 3–5 cm (1¼–2 in) long. The juicy flesh surrounds a hard central stone (pit). Mombins can be eaten fresh or dried, or used to make compotes, jams (preserves) or chutneys. Grown in central America, central Africa and Asia, mombins are known by a number of other names, including hog plums and Spanish plums.

MONACO A dish consisting of poached fillets of sole covered in a sauce made with white wine, tomatoes and mixed herbs and garnished with poached oysters and croûtons in the shape of wolves' teeth. The name is also applied to a chicken consommé thickened with egg yolks and garnished with slices of bread powdered with sugar. The latter dish is similar to consommé Monte-Carlo (chicken consommé thickened with arrowroot, sprinkled with small pieces of Genoese cake made with cheese and browned in the oven).

MONBAZILLAC An AOC white wine from southwest France, produced on the left bank of the River Dordogne not far from Bergerac. It is made from the same grapes and by the same methods as Sauternes. Monbazillac is a mellow dessert wine with a delicate bouquet.

MONÉGASQUE, À LA Describing a dish from Monaco of cold stuffed tomatoes, served as an hors d'oeuvre. The tomatoes are hollowed out, seasoned with salt and pepper, dressed with oil and vinegar, then stuffed with a mixture of mayonnaise, pieces of tuna, chopped onions, mixed herbs and (if desired) chopped hard-boiled (hard-cooked) eggs.

MONGOLIAN FIREPOT A metal cooking pot designed for tabletop use, consisting of a base, in which to burn charcoal, topped with a lidded ring-shaped cooking vessel formed around a central funnel. Modern versions may feature a central spirit burner rather than a charcoal-burning base. The pot is used in the same way as a Swiss fondue pot, but with different ingredients. Broth is prepared in the pot and kept simmering at the table. A selection of prepared uncooked foods, such as prawns and other seafood, sliced poultry, meat, vegetables and Oriental dumplings, are offered, sometimes marinated with garlic, ginger, wine, soy sauce, spring onions (scallions), herbs and/or spices. Diners select and cook ingredients in the broth using small wire baskets to add and remove the items. Dipping sauces and other condiments, such as pickles, are served to complement the cooked foods. Finally, the full-flavoured broth is served (sometimes thinned if it has become very rich and concentrated), usually with added vegetables and noodles.

MONKFISH An ugly-looking sea fish with an enormous head, a very large mouth and a scaleless brownish body. The head is unfamiliar to the consumer as usually only the tail is sold. The flesh is firm, dense, white and lean and can be grilled (broiled), fried, poached or baked. It is found in the Mediterranean and on both sides of the Atlantic.

RECIPES

escalopes of monkfish with creamed peppers

Take 500 g (18 oz) thoroughly cleaned monkfish and cut into 8 small escalopes. Season with salt and pepper. Coat them with breadcrumbs, roll in 50 g (2 oz, ½ cup) grated Parmesan cheese, then brown in butter. Cut open 3 green (bell) peppers and remove the seeds. Blanch for about 10 minutes in boiling water, then cut into pieces and purée in a blender or food processor. Enrich the purée with about 65–75 g (2½–3 oz, 5–6 tablespoons) butter. Season with salt and pepper and add a dash of Worcestershire sauce. Place 2 escalopes of monkfish on each plate and surround them with a ribbon of the green pepper purée.

fillets of monkfish braised in white wine

Lightly flatten 2 fillets and season with salt and pepper. Arrange the fillets in a buttered roasting dish just big enough to hold them and half-cover them with reduced fish stock mixed with white wine. Bake in a preheated oven at 220°C (425°F, gas 7) for 7–8 minutes. Turn the fillets over and bake for another 7–8 minutes, then cover with foil and bake for a further 5 minutes. Place them on a serving dish and keep warm. Add cream to the juices in the roasting dish and reduce until the sauce has thickened. Adjust the seasoning if necessary. Pour the sauce over the fish, sprinkle with chopped parsley and serve very hot accompanied by braised spinach or puréed broccoli.

fillets of monkfish with leeks and cream

Clean 300 g (11 oz) leeks (the white part only), 1 celery stick and 2 turnips. Peel 2 shallots. Shred all these vegetables finely. Melt 25 g (1 oz, 2 tablespoons) butter in a flameproof casserole, add the shredded vegetables and cook until golden, stirring all the time; then cover and cook gently for about 5 minutes, until soft. Take some fillets of monkfish – about 1 kg (2¼ lb) – and place them on top of the vegetable mixture, then turn them over carefully in it. Add 2 more chopped shallots, a chopped garlic clove, a small bouquet garni, 1 glass of dry white wine, 1 glass of water, salt and pepper. Cover the casserole. When the mixture begins to boil, turn the heat down and simmer.

Five minutes before cooking is completed, add 250 g (9 oz, 3 cups) mushrooms which have been cleaned, chopped, sprinkled with lemon juice and lightly fried in butter. Adjust the seasoning if necessary and cook until ready (the fish must remain slightly firm). Drain the fillets and keep them warm in a dish. Remove the bouquet garni from the casserole. Leave the juices on the heat and pour in 150 ml (¼ pint, ⅔ cup) double (heavy) cream. Reduce until the sauce is slightly thickened. Mix in another 25–50 g (1–2 oz, 2–4 tablespoons) butter, beating all the time. Pour this piping hot sauce over the fish.

medallions of monkfish with a red-pepper sauce

Prepare a court-bouillon with water and white vinegar, I carrot and I onion (thinly sliced), a bouquet garni, salt and pepper. Cook for 20 minutes. Halve a red (bell) pepper and remove the seeds. Cook slowly in olive oil, in a covered saucepan, for 6 minutes, then press through a fine sieve.

Cut 675 g (1½ lb) monkfish fillets into medallions I cm (½ in) thick. Soften 2 small chopped shallots in white wine and reduce until all the liquid is absorbed. Add 2 tablespoons double (heavy) cream and boil for 2 minutes, whisking all the time then, over a low heat, incorporate 150 g (5 oz, ⅔ cup) butter, whisking all the time. Add the puréed red pepper, season with salt and pepper and add a squeeze of lemon juice.

Arrange the medallions well separated in a gratin dish. Season with salt and pepper. Pour the court-bouillon over the fish and simmer for 4 minutes over a low heat. Remove from the heat and strain. Arrange the medallions on a serving dish and coat with the sauce.

medallions of monkfish with herbs

Skin 2 large tomatoes and remove the seeds, then dice the flesh and sprinkle with finely chopped chives, salt and pepper. Clean a piece of monkfish weighing 1.4 kg (3 lb), remove the backbone and skin. Cut into medallions I cm (½ in) thick. Place these in a heavy-based saucepan with 20 g (¾ oz, 4½ teaspoons) butter, I tablespoon Sauvignon white wine, I chopped shallot, a squeeze of lemon juice, salt and pepper. Bring to the boil, then simmer for I minute. Turn the medallions over and cook for another minute.

Remove the fish from the pan and keep warm and covered. Boil to reduce the cooking juices by half. Add 250 ml (8 fl oz, I cup) double (heavy) cream and reduce again by one-third. Add 25 g (I oz, ½ cup) watercress, 20 g (¾ oz, ¼ cup) sorrel, 20 g (¾ oz, ¼ cup) chervil and I lettuce heart, then purée in a blender or food processor. Reheat and check the seasoning. Pour the sauce into a warm dish. Arrange the monkfish medallions on top, cover with the warmed diced tomatoes and chives and serve.

monkfish à l'américaine ♦

Trim, wash and dry 1.5 kg (3¼ lb) monkfish and cut into even slices. Wash and dry the heads and shells of some langoustines (the tails of which may have been used to prepare brochettes, for example). Chop 4 shallots and crush a large garlic clove. Prepare a little chopped parsley and 2 tablespoons chopped tarragon leaves. Skin 500 g (18 oz) very ripe tomatoes, remove the seeds, then chop the flesh finely. Heat 6 tablespoons olive oil in a flameproof casserole or large saucepan and add the langoustine heads and shells and the sliced monkfish. As soon as the monkfish has started to brown, add the chopped shallots and cook until just

golden. Pour in I liqueur glass of Cognac and set it alight.

Add the crushed garlic, a strip of dried orange zest, the chopped tarragon and parsley, the chopped tomatoes, a small bouquet garni, I tablespoon tomato purée (paste) diluted with ½ bottle of very dry white wine, salt, pepper and cayenne (this dish must be strongly seasoned). Cover and leave to cook for about 15 minutes; the fish must remain slightly firm.

Drain the fish and keep it warm on a serving dish. Remove the bouquet garni, strain the sauce and pour over the fish. Garnish with tarragon sprigs and serve with rice.

roast monkfish

Prepare a tomato sauce. While this is cooking, fry some very small button mushrooms together with some chopped garlic in a little olive oil. Oil a roasting tin (pan) and place in it a piece of well-trimmed monkfish seasoned with salt and pepper. Bake in a preheated oven at 240°C (475°F, gas 9) for 10 minutes, then reduce the heat to 200°C (400°F, gas 6) and leave until cooked, basting from time to time. Serve the fish surrounded with mushrooms; the tomato sauce should be served separately.

whole monkfish roasted with caramelized shallots

Peel 200 g (7 oz) potatoes and finely slice with a mandoline. Wash and dry thoroughly. Season with salt and pepper. Put them in a bowl and sprinkle with 40 g (1½ oz, 3 tablespoons) melted butter. Arrange in a roasting tin (pan) in a very thin, even layer. Brown in a preheated oven at 240°C (475°F, gas 9). Gently brown a 350 g (12 oz) monkfish tail in 15 g (½ oz, I tablespoon) butter. Add 4 shallots in their skins and cook in a preheated oven at 240°C (475°F, gas 9) for 10 minutes. Take the monkfish out of the oven and keep warm. Pour 3½ tablespoons vegetable or fish stock over the shallots. Return them to the oven for 5–10 minutes or until they have become tender. Remove their pulp and put with the cooking juices in a saucepan. Thicken with 25 g (I oz, 2 tablespoons) butter. Add a few drops of lemon juice, salt and pepper. Arrange the potatoes in a crown on a hot dish and place the monkfish on top. Strain the sauce through a chinois and pour over the fish.

other recipes See *blanquette, brochette.*

MONOSODIUM GLUTAMATE A powder, used as a seasoning in Far Eastern and some Western cookery, developed in 1905 by a Japanese called Ikeda. Chemically extracted from the gluten of cereals, it is an additive used to enhance the flavour of foodstuffs.

MONSELET, CHARLES PIERRE French journalist and author (born 1825; died 1888). Of particular value among his numerous works is *La*

Cuisinière poétique (1859), a work on which Dumas, Banville and Gautier collaborated, among others.

A friend of numerous restaurateurs of his time, Monselet had many recipes containing artichokes and truffles dedicated to him, including poached oysters, steamed quarters of artichoke and truffle slices on skewers, coated with Villeroi sauce and breadcrumbs, and fried; and an omelette filled with a salpicon of artichoke hearts and truffles simmered in cream, garnished with slices of truffles cooked in butter, and served with a well-reduced Madeira sauce. Various other rich dishes are also dedicated to him.

RECIPES

partridge Monselet
Trim a partridge and stuff it with foie gras to which a truffle salpicon has been added. Truss it, season with salt and pepper, and brown in a small heavy flameproof casserole. Cover and cook in a pre-heated oven at 160°C (325°F, gas 3). After about 15 minutes, add 2 thin slices of artichoke hearts which have been tossed in lemon and butter. Cook for about a further 15 minutes. Cut a truffle into small dice and add to the casserole. Add 2 table-spoons warmed brandy and set alight. Serve in the casserole.

soft-boiled or poached eggs Monselet
Prepare a chicken velouté sauce and add to it a third of its volume of veal stock, the same amount of cream and a small glass of sherry. Reduce until the sauce is thick. Dice some truffles and braise them in butter; do the same with whole artichoke hearts cooked *au blanc*. Place a soft-boiled (soft-cooked) or a poached egg on each artichoke heart, cover it generously with sauce, and garnish with the diced truffles.

other recipes See *bombe glacée, quail.*

MONTAGNÉ, PROSPER French chef (born 1864; died 1948). Son of a hotelier from Carcassonne, he was to have studied architecture but adopted his father's occupation when his parents opened a hotel in Toulouse. He worked his way up through the kitchens of the most famous establishments in Paris, Cauterets, San Remo and Monte Carlo. He then returned to Paris, where he became chef first at the Pavillon d'Armenonville, then at Ledoyen, and finally at the Grand Hotel (where he had had his first job), finishing there as head chef. It was then that he published his first culinary work, with Prosper Salles, *La Grande Cuisine illustrée* (1900), to be followed by the *Grand Livre de la cuisine* (1929). With Dr Gottschalk, he published the *Larousse gastronomique*, the first edition of which dates from 1938.

During World War I Montagné organized the kitchens of the Allied armies. After the war he visited the United States, where he was adviser to the man-agement of the Chicago abattoirs. He then returned to Paris and opened a restaurant in the Rue de l'Échelle, which was considered by some to provide the best fare in the whole of France and was frequented by celebrities during the 1920s. Here he created numerous dishes, but management difficulties forced him to close this establishment. In addition to this, Prosper Montagné organized the first Concours de Cuisine and several gastronomic exhibitions. His name will live on, thanks largely to the Club Prosper Montagné, an association of gas-tronomes and professionals founded by René Morand in memory of the master. See also *Mont-Bry*.

MONTAGNY An AOC white Burgundy wine from the Côte Chalonnaise. The wines, made from the Chardonnay grape, can be very good, and the monks of Cluny are supposed to have enjoyed them. They usually represent excellent value.

MONTASIO A DOP cheese from Italy's Veneto, it is made from partially skimmed unpasteurized cow's milk. It is cooked and pressed to give a firm paste with small holes throughout. The cheese is 30–35.5 cm (12–14 in) in diameter and 7.5 cm (3 in) thick, and weighs about 7.5–11.5 kg (17–25 lb). It has a mild and nutty flavour with a light tang.

MONTBAZON A garnish for chicken, comprising lightly fried lamb's sweetbreads, quenelles, mush-room caps and slices of truffle.

MONT-BLANC A cold dessert made of vanilla-flavoured chestnut purée, topped with a dome of Chantilly cream and decorated. Alternatively, the cream may be surrounded by a border of sweetened chestnut purée and mounted on a base of sablé pas-try or meringue.

RECIPE

mont-blanc
Shell 1 kg (2¼ lb) chestnuts and simmer them until soft in 1 litre (1¾ pints, 4⅓ cups) milk with 150 g (5 oz, ⅔ cup) sugar, a pinch of salt and a vanilla pod (bean) split in two. Press the chestnuts through a potato ricer and pack the vermicelli-like chestnut purée into a buttered ring mould. Refrigerate for at least 30 minutes. Whisk together 400 ml (14 fl oz, 1¾ cups) double (heavy) cream, 1 teaspoon vanilla sugar and 25 g (1 oz, ¼ cup) icing (confectioner's) sugar to make Chantilly cream. Turn the chestnut ring out on to a dish and fill the centre with the Chantilly cream. Decorate with pieces of marrons glacés and crystallized (candied) violets. Refrigerate until served.

MONT-BRY The pseudonym of the chef, Prosper Montagné, used to name various dishes which he created or which were dedicated to him. The Mont-Bry garnish for small cuts of meat consists of little

Monkfish à l'américaine, see page 755.

cakes of spinach purée bound with Parmesan cheese and cep mushrooms cooked in cream; the meat pan juices are deglazed with white wine and thickened veal stock and used as a sauce.

RECIPES

fritters Mont-Bry

Prepare sweetened semolina as for a dessert, let it cool, then spread it on a buttered baking sheet in a layer 1 cm (½ in) thick. When completely cold, cut it into small rectangles 4 × 5 cm (1½ × 2 in). Boil down some apricot jam mixed with rum until reduced by half, then add a fine salpicon of walnuts and figs. Coat half the semolina rectangles with this mixture and cover with the remaining rectangles. Dip into batter and deep-fry at 175°C (347°F). Drain on paper towels, dust with caster (superfine) sugar and serve very hot.

omelette Mont-Bry

Prepare a salpicon of celeriac (celery root) braised in butter and a cream sauce. Beat some eggs together, adding salt, pepper, chopped parsley, a pinch of grated horseradish and chopped chives. Prepare 2 flat omelettes. Put one of them on a round buttered dish and keep warm. Mix the salpicon of celeriac with the cream sauce and season the mixture with paprika. Cover the omelette with this salpicon and put the second omelette on top. Cover with Mornay sauce, sprinkle with grated Parmesan cheese, moisten with melted butter and brown in a preheated oven at 240°C (475°F, gas 9).

sole meunière Mont-Bry

Prepare in advance 200 g (7 oz) thin noodles. Scald, peel and seed 6 tomatoes, then crush them to remove any liquid. Chop a medium onion and brown in butter. Add the crushed tomatoes, a pinch of salt, a pinch of caster (superfine) sugar and a small amount of crushed garlic; cover and cook slowly.

Then prepare 3 sole weighing about 300 g (11 oz) each. Remove the brown skin and carefully detach the fillets from the backbone. Season the fillets with salt and pepper, roll them in flour and cook in clarified butter in a frying pan until golden brown on both sides.

Using another frying pan, sauté the noodles in 5–6 tablespoons clarified butter until they are lightly browned and slightly crisp. Place the sole fillets in a hot long serving dish, sprinkle with lemon juice and chopped parsley, and arrange the tomato mixture around them. Pile mounds of noodles at each end of the dish. Baste the fish copiously with noisette butter, which should be bubbling and frothy.

additional recipe See chestnut (sweet dishes).

MONT-D'OR A French cheese made from goat's milk, a mixture of cow's and goat's milk, or (now increasingly common) from cow's milk only. Containing 45% fat, it is a soft cheese with a crust which is slightly blue with a hint of red in it. The best Mont-d'Or is made in the region around Lyon and is becoming rare. Sold in the form of small discs, 8–9 cm (3–3½ in) in diameter and 1.5 cm (½ in) thick, it has a delicate flavour, like that of a mature Saint-Marcellin. It is at its best in winter, eaten with Beaujolais. (Mont-d'Or cheese should not be confused with the Mont-d'Or Vacherin.)

MONT-DORÉ A method of preparing potatoes. The potatoes are puréed and mixed with egg yolks (and often cream) and grated cheese. The mixture is piled into a dome shape on a gratin dish, sprinkled again with grated cheese, and put in the oven to brown.

MONTER A French culinary term meaning to give body to or to increase in volume. Egg whites, cream and meringues or other sweet mixtures are whisked to increase their volume (by incorporating air) and thickness.

In making hot emulsified sauces, egg yolks are whisked over a low heat until the mixture has become thick and mousse-like. Egg yolks are whisked with fat or oil when making cold or hot emulsions (such as béarnaise sauce or mayonnaise).

The term is also used for stirring small amounts of butter into a sauce to make it smoother or creamier.

MONTGLAS A salpicon dedicated to the Marquis de Montglas, an 18th-century French diplomat. It consists of shredded pickled tongue, poached mushrooms, foie gras and truffles bound with thick Madeira sauce, and is used as a filling.

Lamb chops Montglas are cooked on one side, covered with this salpicon and breadcrumbs, browned in the oven, and surrounded with a border of demi-glace sauce. Lamb's sweetbreads and chicken Montglas are braised and covered with their deglazed pan juices mixed with the salpicon.

MONTHÉLIE AOC Burgundies from the Côte de Beaune. They are mostly red wines though some white is made and also some sparkling white wines. The still wines may be labelled Monthélie or Monthélie-Côte-de-Beaune-Villages. The Monthélie wines are akin to those of neighbouring Volnay but are usually cheaper.

MONTILLA Wines from near Córdoba in southern Spain that slightly resemble sherry, although they have their own specific controls. They are traditionally made in huge earthenware jars and range in style from very dry and light to rich and luscious. They may be naturally high in alcohol and so do not always require any fortification.

MONTLOUIS AOC white Touraine wines, still or sparkling, from the south bank of the River Loire, opposite Vouvray. Like the wines of Vouvray, they are made from the Chenin Blanc grape.

MONTMARTRE A tiny vineyard surviving in the heart of Paris, where much wine was produced. When the vintage (about 400 bottles annually) is sold, the proceeds go to charity. In 1961 vines from certain famous Bordeaux estates were planted here.

MONTMORENCY The name given to various savoury or sweet dishes that include the sour Montmorency cherries. Duck Montmorency, cooked with herbs in a frying pan, is garnished with stoned (pitted) cherries poached in a Bordeaux wine; the sauce is made by deglazing the pan with cherry brandy and adding strained veal stock. The classic gâteau called Montmorency is a Genoese sponge topped with cherries in syrup and covered with Italian meringue; the top is decorated with glacé or crystallized (candied) cherries. The ice creams, bombes, iced mousses, croûtes, tarts and tartlets called Montmorency all include cherries, which may be fresh, crystallized or macerated in brandy.

There are, however, other dishes in classic cookery dedicated to the Montmorency family, which do not include cherries. For example, the Montmorency garnish for cuts of meat consists of artichoke hearts stuffed with balls of glazed carrot and balls of noisette potatoes.

RECIPES

bombe glacée Montmorency
Coat a bombe mould with kirsch ice cream. Prepare a bombe mixture flavoured with cherry brandy and add cherries macerated in kirsch. Fill the mould with this. Finish the bombe in the usual way.

gâteau Montmorency
Separate the yolks from the whites of 3 eggs. Whisk the 3 yolks with 50 g (2 oz, ½ cup) ground almonds and 125 g (4½ oz, scant ⅔ cup) caster (superfine) sugar. Drain 400 g (14 oz) cherries in syrup, halve, stone (pit) and roll them in flour. Incorporate 50 g (2 oz, ½ cup) plain (all-purpose) flour and the cherries into the almond mixture, then carefully fold in the 3 egg whites stiffly whisked with a pinch of salt. Pour the mixture into a buttered cake tin (pan) and bake in a preheated oven at 200°C (400°F, gas 6) for about 30 minutes. Turn the cake out on to a wire rack and allow to cool.

Melt 200 g (7 oz) fondant* over a low heat, stirring all the time. Add a liqueur glass of kirsch and 2–3 drops of cochineal (red food colouring). Spread the fondant over the cake with a spatula and decorate with 12 glacé (candied) cherries and a few pieces of angelica.

Alternatively, the cake may be cut into 2 layers, steeped in kirsch, and sandwiched together with butter cream mixed with cherries in brandy.

additional recipe See *croûte*.

MONTPENSIER The name given to various savoury or sweet dishes that may have been dedicated to the Duchesse de Montpensier (1627–93), but were more probably dedicated to the fifth son of Louis Philippe. Gâteau Montpensier is a Genoese sponge enriched with ground almonds, raisins and crystallized (candied) fruit. By extension, cakes cooked in a tin (pan) lined with the ingredient which gives them their flavour are termed *à la Montpensier*.

The Montpensier garnish for small cuts of meat and poultry consists of artichoke hearts, asparagus tips, sliced truffles and Madeira sauce.

RECIPES

gâteau Montpensier
Steep 50 g (2 oz, ⅓ cup) crystallized (candied) fruit and 50 g (2 oz, ⅓ cup) sultanas (golden raisins) in 6 tablespoons rum. With the fingertips, work 125 g (4½ oz, generous 1 cup) plain (all-purpose) flour with 75 g (3 oz, 6 tablespoons) butter cut into small pieces. Beat 7 egg yolks with 125 g (4½ oz, scant ⅔ cup) caster (superfine) sugar until the mixture is white, then mix in 100 g (4 oz, 1 cup) ground almonds and finally 3 stiffly whisked egg whites. Drain the fruit and sultanas, then add them to the mixture, together with the flour-and-butter mixture. Work briskly with a wooden spoon for a short time.

Butter a 22 cm (8½ in) cake tin (pan) and sprinkle it with 50 g (2 oz, ½ cup) flaked (slivered) almonds. Pour the mixture into the tin and bake in a preheated oven at 200°C (400°F, gas 6) for 30 minutes. Turn out the cake on to a wire rack and allow to cool. Melt 150 g (5 oz, ½ cup) apricot jam over a low heat, strain and spread over the surface of the cake. Keep cold until serving.

MONTRACHET One of the most famous of all white Burgundies, produced by two parishes (communes) in the Côte de Beaune, Puligny-Montrachet and Chassagne-Montrachet. It is made from the Chardonnay grape and usually achieves great distinction. However, the specific vineyard is tiny and the wine is therefore scarce and expensive.

Also a soft goat's-milk cheese (45% fat content) from Burgundy with a natural bluish crust. It is cylindrical, 6 cm (2½ in) in diameter and 8–9 cm (3–3½ in) thick. Packed in a vine leaf, Montrachet has a goaty scent and a marked nutty taste.

MONTRAVEL Mainly AOC white wines, some of which are dry and others sweet, from vineyards on the right bank of the River Dordogne, about 130 km (80 miles) east of Bordeaux.

MONTREUIL A garnish for beef steaks and other small cuts of meat consisting of artichoke hearts braised in butter and stuffed with peas and tiny balls of glazed carrot. Poached fish Montreuil are covered with white wine sauce and garnished with balls of boiled potato coated with a shrimp velouté sauce.

MONTROUGE The name given to various dishes which include cultivated mushrooms. They are so called because of the mushroom beds which used to be at Montrouge, near the gates of Paris.

RECIPES

croquettes Montrouge
Prepare a dry mushroom duxelles and add half its volume of chopped ham and a third of its volume of bread soaked in milk and then dried. Add some chopped parsley and 2 egg yolks for each 250 g (9 oz) of mixture, mix well and season to taste. Shape the preparation into balls the size of tangerines. Flatten them slightly, coat with egg and breadcrumbs, and deep fry in oil at 190°C (375°F). Drain on paper towels and sprinkle with salt.

croustades Montrouge
Line some tartlet moulds with shortcrust pastry and bake blind. Fill them with a thick purée of creamed mushrooms. Sprinkle with fresh breadcrumbs, moisten with a little melted butter, and brown in a preheated oven at 240°C (475°F, gas 9).

escalopes of foie gras Montrouge
Prepare a thick mushroom purée. Cut some foie gras into slices and prepare an equal number of slices of bread of the same size. Fry the bread in butter. Sauté the foie gras in clarified butter and put each slice on a slice of fried bread. Arrange in a ring on a flat dish with the mushroom purée in the centre and keep warm. Deglaze the foie gras pan with Madeira and a little stock, boil down to reduce and thicken with a little arrowroot. Pour the sauce over the foie gras.

additional recipe See *eggs (sur le plat).*

MOOSE A member of the *Cervidae* family. A powerful and prolific animal, also known as American elk, which along with deer is the most hunted game in Canada. Although its meat is not sold commercially, it is often found on domestic tables in the autumn. Its meat is cooked in the same way as venison, accompanied by a spicy sauce and a preserve made of wild berries.

MOQUE A kind of earthenware cup used as a measure for liquids, particularly in northern France. Cider is traditionally served in a moque.

MOQUES A Belgian pâtisserie speciality from Ghent. A fat sausage of pastry made with brown sugar and cloves is rolled in granulated sugar, cut into thick slices and cooked in the oven.

MORAY A large eel, up to 1.3 m (4 ft) long, found in tropical seas. It is dark brown with yellow and black markings and its wide mouth is armed with several rows of strong pointed teeth; its bite is poisonous. The flesh of the moray is fatty but fairly delicate. The Romans bred morays in fish ponds and are said to have fed them on live slaves; they continued to be regarded as a delicacy until the Renaissance and history relates that Henry I of England died from indigestion caused by eating moray. Today, moray is hardly ever found but when eaten it is included in bouillabaisse, eaten cold with garlic mayonnaise, and it may also be prepared in all the same ways as eel.

MORBIER A cow's milk cheese (45% fat) from the French Jura. At first glance this cheese looks as though it has a band of mould running through the middle: in fact, it is a layer of ash. The cheeses are semi-soft with a natural brushed rind and sweet flavour. The best are made from unpasteurized milk.

MORCILLA A Spanish blood sausage made from pork and pig's blood. There are many different varieties, the most famous coming from Asturia, and may be flavoured with onion, aniseed, fennel, almonds, pine nuts, peppers and parsley.

MOREL A very tasty but rare mushroom which is found in the spring. Its globular or conical cap is deeply furrowed in a honeycomb pattern, and therefore the morel must be very carefully cleaned to get rid of any earth, sand or insects which may be inside. This can be done either by rinsing the mushroom several times in water and then draining it or by cleaning the cap with a fine brush so as not to destroy its delicate scent. Morels with dark caps (from dark brown to black) are the most highly prized ones. The paler (blonde) variety is less tasty, and mushrooms with a longer stalk and a conical cap are regarded as inferior.

All morels should be well cooked. A classic dish is morels braised in butter, the pan juices being thickened with cream or deglazed with Madeira. They can also be cooked au gratin, used in a forestière garnish for omelettes, chicken, red meat or calves' sweetbreads, or as a seasoning for soups and sauces. Morels may be preserved in oil or by drying.

RECIPES

chicken with morels
Carefully wash 4–5 morels and split them in two lengthways. Dredge 6–8 chicken fillets with flour and fry briskly in 25 g (1 oz, 2 tablespoons) butter in a shallow pan together with 1 chopped shallot. When golden brown, season with salt and pepper and add the morels. Cover the pan and cook gently for 7–8 minutes, then add 6 tablespoons Sauvignon wine and finish the cooking with the lid off. (A little grated nutmeg will further improve the flavour.) Add 1 tablespoon double (heavy) cream and cook for another 10–12 minutes. Serve in a hot dish.

morels à la crème
Clean 250 g (9 oz) morels. Wash them briskly in cold water and dry them thoroughly. Leave them

whole if they are small, cut them up if they are large. Put the morels in a shallow frying pan with 15 g (½ oz, I tablespoon) butter, I teaspoon lemon juice, I teaspoon chopped shallots, salt and pepper. Braise for 5 minutes, then cover with double (heavy) cream and reduce until the sauce has thickened. Just before serving, add I tablespoon cream and some chopped parsley.

morels in herb sauce
Put into a saucepan a pinch of rosemary, sage, thyme and basil, a quarter of a bay leaf, a clove, a little pepper and a little grated nutmeg. Add a shredded onion and a ladleful of good consommé and simmer for a few minutes, then strain through muslin (cheesecloth). Add about 30 cleaned morels to the strained liquid and bring to the boil, pour in some thick allemande sauce and reduce. Just before serving, add a little chicken stock, a little butter, some lemon juice and I tablespoon chopped chervil.

purses of lobster with morels ♦
Soak 2 calves' sweetbreads in cold water for I hour. Drain and cover with water. Blanch for 5 minutes. Cool in cold water, peel and press them. Put in the refrigerator until the following day.

Rehydrate 50 g (2 oz) dried morels in lukewarm water for 30 minutes. Drain and blanch in boiling water for 3 minutes. Gently brown 2 carrots, 4 shallots and 3 garlic cloves, all very finely sliced, 25 g (I oz, 2 tablespoons) butter. Add the diced sweetbreads and braise very gently for 10 minutes. Add 3½ tablespoons dry white wine and reduce. Now add 100 ml (4 fl oz, 7 tablespoons) shellfish stock and 2 seeded, crushed tomatoes. Season with salt and pepper. Cover and cook for 10 minutes. Drain the diced sweetbreads. Purée the contents of the sauté pan in a blender and keep the mixture warm. Set this sauce aside: reheat it when the purses are cooked.

Cook two 900 g (2 lb) lobsters in salted water for 5 minutes, remove the meat and cut into cubes. Add to the sweetbreads and coarsely chopped morels.

Make 6 lightly cooked, thin 20 cm (8 in) pancakes. Alternatively, use 6 sheets of brik pastry cut into 20 cm (8 in) squares. Top each pancake or square in turn with a little of the cooled lobster mixture, brush the edge with melted butter and fold the pancake or pastry around the filling to form a neat bundle or purse. Place on a greased baking sheet. Cook the purses in a preheated oven at 200°C (400°F, gas 6) for about 10 minutes or until golden. Serve with the reheated sauce.

MOREY-SAINT-DENIS
A red Burgundy, or more rarely a white wine, from the Côte de Nuits. The *grands crus* of the parish are sold under their own names: Clos de la Roche, Clos Saint-Denis, Clos des Lambrays, Clos de Tart and Les Bonnes Mares (the greater part of the latter being in the parish of Chambolle-Musigny). Morey-Saint-Denis is between Gevrey-Chambertin in the north and Chambolle-Musigny in the south. Its wines sometimes possess the vigour of the former and the delicacy of the latter.

MORGON
One of the ten *crus* of the Beaujolais region and considered to have longer ageing potential than many other *crus* Beaujolais.

MORNAY
A béchamel sauce enriched with egg yolks and flavoured with grated Gruyère cheese. It is used to coat dishes to be glazed under the grill (broiler) or browned in the oven, including poached eggs, fish, shellfish, vegetables and filled pancakes. The invention of this sauce and its use is attributed to Joseph Voiron, a chef of the 19th century, who is thought to have dedicated it to the cook Mornay, his eldest son.

RECIPES

fillets of sole Mornay
Season some fillets of sole with salt and pepper, place them in a buttered gratin dish, spoon over a little fish stock, and poach gently in a preheated oven at 200°C (400°F, gas 6) for about 7–8 minutes, until cooked. Drain them and cover with Mornay sauce, sprinkle with grated Parmesan cheese and clarified butter, and brown in a preheated oven at 240°C (475°F, gas 9).

Mornay sauce
Heat 500 ml (17 fl oz, 2 cups) béchamel* sauce. Add 75 g (3 oz, ¾ cup) grated Gruyère cheese and stir until all the cheese has melted. Take the sauce from the heat and add 2 egg yolks beaten with I tablespoon milk. Bring slowly to the boil, whisking all the time. Remove from the heat and add 2 tablespoons double (heavy) cream (the sauce must be thick and creamy). For browning at a high temperature or for a lighter sauce, the egg yolks are omitted. If the sauce is to accompany fish, reduced fish stock is added.

pannequets Mornay
Make some savoury crêpes. Chop some mushrooms, sprinkle with lemon juice and cook slowly in butter. Finely chop some ham. Prepare some Mornay sauce (2 tablespoons per pancake) and mix the chopped mushrooms and ham with half of this sauce. Cover the pancakes with this salpicon, roll them up and arrange them in a buttered gratin dish. Coat them with the rest of the sauce (slightly reduced if necessary), sprinkle with grated Parmesan cheese, moisten with melted butter and brown in a preheated oven at 220°C (425°F, gas 7).

soft-boiled or poached eggs Mornay
Soft-boil (soft-cook) or poach some eggs. Remove the crusts from some round slices of bread (one for each egg) and fry in butter. Prepare a Mornay

sauce. Place each egg on a slice of fried bread in a buttered gratin dish. Coat generously with Mornay sauce, sprinkle with grated cheese and melted butter, and brown in a preheated oven at 240°C (475°F, gas 9).

other recipes See *Brussels sprouts, cardoon, chicory, hash (veal), lobster, salsify, scallop, scallop shell.*

MOROCCO See *page 764.*

MORTADELLA
A lightly smoked Italian sausage served cold and very thinly sliced as an hors-d'oeuvre. A speciality of Bologna, the name by which it is sometimes called, it is traditionally made with different cuts of pork flavoured in various ways, particularly with coriander (cilantro) or parsley; originally it included myrtle (*mortella* in Italian), hence its name. (Another etymology suggests that the word is derived from *mortaio della carne*, a reference to the mortar used for pounding the meat.) It is also studded with pistachios or green olives. The authentic sausage is very large in diameter and appears in cross-section as a fine light-coloured paste, dotted with diced fat. The first recipe dates from 1484. Later on many different recipes were devised, not only in Italy but also in other countries, using a variety of different meats.

MORTAR
A bowl made of wood, earthenware, marble or stone in which foods are pounded or ground to a paste or powder, using a pestle. Mortars have been used in cookery since ancient times.

MORVANDELLE, À LA
A French term, meaning in the style of Morvan, used to describe various preparations. These include raw Morvan ham, soup, omelette, baked eggs, tripe and veal cutlets.

RECIPE

omelette à la morvandelle
Dice 100 g (4 oz, ½ cup) raw Morvan ham and fry it lightly in butter. Beat 8 eggs as for an omelette, season with pepper and add the ham. Cook the omelette in the usual way. Garnish with small thin slices of Morvan ham heated gently in butter and rolled up into cornets.

MOSAIC
In charcuterie, a garnish on the top of a terrine or a galantine using ingredients of various colours cut into shapes – circles, squares and stars.

In pâtisserie, a mosaic is a round Genoese sponge, filled with butter cream, glazed with apricot jam and iced (frosted) with white fondant. The top is decorated with apricot and redcurrant jam piped in parallel lines and scored with vertical lines, using the tip of a knife.

MOSCATEL
Also known as Muscat of Alexandria. Grape variety producing dessert wines. These grapes are grown in Spain, where wines include Moscatel de Málaga; Portugal, where they include Moscatel de Setúbal; Italy, where they include Moscato di Pantelleria; as well as in Australia, California and South Africa.

MOSCOVITE
Any of various cold moulded desserts similar to Bavarian cream. Moscovites were originally iced desserts made in special sealed, domed hexagonal moulds. Today the name is given to a Bavarian cream containing fruit, a plombières ice cream or a chilled sponge cake soaked in kirsch and topped with a dome of ice cream or fruits mixed with cream.

MOSCOVITE, À LA
Describing various preparations inspired by Russian cookery or perfected by French chefs who had worked in Russia in the 19th century. Salmon *à la moscovite* is poached whole, cooled, skinned, covered with jellied mayonnaise, garnished with slices of truffle, hard-boiled (hard-cooked) eggs, blanched tarragon leaves and, finally, glazed with aspic. The garnish includes artichoke hearts stuffed with Russian salad and halves of hard-boiled eggs filled with caviar. Sauce *à la moscovite*, served with game, is a poivrade sauce to which pine nuts, sultanas (golden raisins) and juniper berries have been added. Consommé *à la moscovite*, based on sturgeon and cucumber, is garnished with a julienne of Russian mushrooms (*gribouis*) and diced *vésiga* (sturgeon's spinal marrow). Eggs *à la moscovite* are poached and served either cold with Russian salad or hot with sauerkraut.

MOUCLADE
A preparation of cultured mussels from the Poitou-Charentes region. They are cooked in white wine with shallots and parsley, usually flavoured with curry or saffron, and coated with their cooking liquid enriched with cream and butter and thickened with egg yolks or cornflour (cornstarch).

RECIPE

mussel-farmers' mouclade
Clean and wash 2 kg (4½ lb) mussels. Toss them in a saucepan over a brisk heat until they open. Discard any that do not open. Remove the empty shells and place the ones containing the mussels in a dish; keep hot over a saucepan of boiling water. Strain the juice from the mussels through a fine sieve. Finely chop a garlic clove and a sprig of parsley and blend with 100 g (4 oz, ½ cup) butter. Warm the mussel juice in a saucepan over a gentle heat. Add the flavoured butter, a pinch of curry (or saffron), a pinch of ground celery seed, a dash of pepper and the mussels. Stir well, then simmer for 5 minutes. Sprinkle with 1 teaspoon cornflour (cornstarch), stir well and simmer for 2 minutes. Add 150 ml (¼ pint, ⅔ cup) double (heavy) cream and serve.

Purses of lobster with morels,
see page 761.

MOROCCO

Moroccan cuisine, original and sometimes complex, combines a multitude of influences: Berber, Egyptian, Spanish, French and Jewish. The everyday meals often consist of a large, single dish which may be a soup (*harina*) combining meat, chicken or fish and vegetables. Seasoned with subtle mixtures of spices (*ras al-hanout*), simmered for hours in a tajine or cooked in steam (*chaoua*), they acquire a surprisingly delicious flavour and tender texture.

The cuisine is characterized partly by the use of the various spices, condiments and aromatic herbs used in the preparation: garlic, aniseed, cinnamon, cardamom, caraway, coriander (cilantro), cumin, turmeric, rose water, orange-flower water, mace, mint, nutmeg, onion, parsley, pimento, pepper, liquorice, saffron, sesame, thyme, and so on. The cuisine also relies heavily on particular associations of tastes (sweet/salted); for example, tajine of mutton with quince and honey, or tajine with onions and almonds. Moroccans are very partial to preserved lemon which is used in dishes such as chicken tajine with preserved lemon and olives.

Along the coast, fish, such as bream, red mullet, sardine or tuna, is eaten every day. The fish is marinated, then grilled (broiled), as for instance in sardines *à la charmoula*, or it may be stuffed (bream stuffed with rice and spices), or cooked in the oven like *tagra*. As far as couscous is concerned, this is sometimes prepared with fish, but it is more often garnished with mutton or chicken. Normally its preparation is much simpler than in the other countries of the Maghreb (see *North Africa*): only one kind of meat is used, accompanied by a wide range of vegetables. For example, *Bidaoui* couscous includes seven vegetables – aubergine (eggplant), carrots, cabbage, turnips, peppers, pumpkin and tomato – and sometimes two kinds of bouillon.

In Morocco, the art of puff pastry reaches its peak of perfection with pastilla which alternates very thin layers of puff pastry, almonds and filling made from poultry (pigeon or chicken) or beef, very finely minced (ground) and highly spiced, the top then being sprinkled with cinnamon and sugar. When stuffed with almonds and crème pâtissière, *pastilla* is also a dessert. The principle is the same for the pasties, which are made with puff pastry, and filled with minced meat or almonds and honey. Moroccan pastries are less syrupy and also drier than those of other Mediterranean countries, though they are also made with almonds and sugar.

The most popular drinks in Morocco are fruit juices (lemonade, orangeade, watermelon juice, almond milk or water, flavoured with orange flowers), and the ubiquitous mint tea, a real institution which punctuates the day and which is a symbol of hospitality.

WINE A Roman colony in antiquity, Morocco was then a major producer of wine, which was exported in large quantities to Rome. But at the beginning of the 8th century, the country converted to Islam, which forbids the consumption of fermented drinks, so the vineyards producing grapes for wine-making were abandoned, leaving only those specializing in the growing of grapes for eating. It was only in the early 20th century, after Morocco became a French protectorate, that wine-producing vineyards were re-established. Most Moroccan wines are red or rosé, the climate being unsuited to white wines. The main varieties include Carignan, Cinsaut (producing pleasant *vin gris* – rosés), Grenache, with increased plantings of Cabernet Sauvignon, Syrah, Merlot and Mourvèdre.

MOUFLON A wild sheep from Corsica and Sardinia, now rare, ancestor of the domestic sheep.

MOULD A furry growth, consisting of very small fungi, which grows on foods such as meat, cheese, bread and preserves that are kept in warm, moist conditions. The growth usually indicates that the food is not fresh. However, some moulds are not harmful, such as those on certain cheeses. Moulds are responsible for the flavour and blue colour inside Roquefort, Gorgonzola and Stilton cheeses and the mould introduced to certain soft cow's milk cheeses, such as Camembert, forms a white, downy crust.

MOULDS AND TINS A mould is a hollow receptacle that holds a preparation in a certain shape while it sets, is baked or frozen so that it retains this shape when turned out. In France, tins (pans) for cooking cakes and pastries are also referred to as moulds. Moulds can be tall, shallow, shaped, plain or with patterned indentations. China or glass moulds are used where heat or cold retention is an important factor, but most moulds, unless they are to be used in a microwave, are made of metal because of its quick response to temperature change. The following list covers only a selection of those most commonly used.

■ **General moulds and tins**
• DECORATIVE MOULDS For jellies and mousses, both sweet and savoury; may be tall or shallow. They are often in the shape of fish or fruit to indicate the main ingredient of the dish.
• DEEP CAKE TINS Used to make deep cakes, which can be served whole or sliced into layers and

Piles of spices contribute to the aroma of the souk at Tinezouline, in the south of Morocco.

sandwiched, with a fixed or loose bottom or with flexible sides. They can be used for sponge cakes as well as heavier mixtures. Deep cake tins are available in a wide range of sizes and may be round, square, hexagonal, or heart-, number- or letter-shaped.

- FLAN TINS, DISHES AND RINGS These are usually round but can be square, rectangular or oval. The sides slope and may be fluted. The metal ones often have loose bottoms. They are available in many sizes.
- LOAF TINS AND BREAD MOULDS These are usually rectangular with deep sides.
- PIE MOULDS These may be rectangular or oval with hinged or loose sides which clip together for easy unmoulding.
- RING MOULDS Deep or shallow, plain or decorated, these are used for cakes, sweet or savoury mousses, and jellied desserts.
- SHALLOW CAKE TINS Used to make shallow cakes, sometimes loose-bottomed and with a non-stick coating. They are available in a large variety of shapes and sizes, round, square, rectangular and heart-shaped being the most common.
- SMALL CAKE TINS (PATTY PANS) These are in the form of trays containing six, nine or twelve indentations with rounded or sloping sides. Some have special shapes for baking particular items, such as éclairs or madeleines.

■ **Moulds and tins for special purposes**

- BARQUETTE TINS Boat-shaped tins in various sizes, used for sweet and savoury pastries.
- BRIOCHE TIN Available in large or individual sizes. It is deeply fluted.
- BUTTER MOULDS Traditionally made of wood, these should be dampened before use. They can be trough-shaped, to take a large slab of butter, or small and cylindrical in shape, with a decorative plunger, for individual butter pats.
- CHARLOTTE MOULD The shape is deep and round with slightly sloping sides and two small handles. The sloping sides facilitate the lining of the sides of the mould with fingers of bread or sponge. These moulds can also be used for Bavarian creams.
- CHEESE MOULDS These have holes in the bottom, and sometimes in the sides, for releasing whey when moulding soft cheeses or cheese-based desserts, such as pashka. They are available in various shapes and sizes.
- CHOCOLATE MOULDS These are made in two halves for easy unmoulding and held together by clips. They are usually in the shape of animals, eggs or figures for making festive hollow chocolate novelties.
- CONFECTIONERY MOULDS Small decorative moulds for making chocolates and fondants, either individual or in 'mats'.
- CREAM HORN MOULD Conical-shaped mould for forming individual pastry shapes for pâtisserie.
- CROQUEMBOUCHE TIN Conical-shaped tin which is filled with tiny caramel-dipped choux buns. When

the caramel is set the tin is removed to leave an impressive cake, which is served at festive occasions in France.
- DARIOLE MOULD A small flowerpot-shaped mould used to make individual steamed puddings, small cakes, timbales and savoury or sweet mousses.
- ICE-CREAM MOULDS For making iced bombes and layered iced desserts. They can be conical, square or shaped like a domed bombe.
- KUGELHOPF MOULD A deep ring mould with heavy patterning.
- MANQUÉ MOULD The classic French cake tin, 18–23 cm (7–9 in) in diameter; the sides are about 5 cm (2 in) deep and slope slightly to give the turned out cake an attractive shape.
- SAVARIN MOULD A shallow ring mould with a smooth rounded base in large or individual sizes for rum babas and savarins.
- SHORTBREAD MOULD A wooden mould usually engraved with a thistle pattern in which the short-bread dough is rolled to shape it before being turned out on to a baking sheet for cooking.
- SWISS (JELLY) ROLL TIN A rectangular tin, about 2 cm (¾ in) deep.
- TARTLET TINS Fluted individual tins in various shapes for petits fours and pâtisserie.

MOULIN-À-VENT One of the Beaujolais *crus*, where the wines can achieve considerable quality and, unlike most Beaujolais, can age for a longish period in certain vintages.

MOULIS An AOC vineyard region in the Haut-Médoc area of Bordeaux, making wines capable of achieving subtlety and finesse.

MOUSSAKA A dish common to Turkey, Greece and the Balkans, made with slices of aubergine (egg-plant) arranged in layers, alternating with minced (ground) mutton or lamb, onions, and sometimes tomatoes, often with the addition of a thick béchamel sauce. In some recipes, courgettes (zuc-chini), potatoes or spinach are used instead of aubergines. The dish is baked in the oven.

RECIPE

moussaka

Fry 1 large chopped onion, 2 crushed garlic cloves and 1 bay leaf in olive oil for about 15 minutes, until tender, but not browned. Add 450 g (1 lb) minced (ground) lamb and cook, stirring, until the lamb has browned. Add 1 teaspoon dried oregano, 1 teaspoon ground cinnamon and salt and pepper. Peel and chop 450 g (1 lb) tomatoes and add to the meat mixture with 250 ml (8 fl oz, 1 cup) lamb or beef stock. Bring to the boil, then reduce the heat and cover the pan. Simmer gently for about 30 minutes.

Meanwhile, slice 2 large aubergines (eggplants). Lightly fry the aubergine slices in olive oil until lightly browned on both sides. Do this in batches, setting aside the slices on a plate as they are cooked. Layer the aubergine slices and minced meat mixture in a large ovenproof dish, ending with a layer of aubergines. Beat 2 eggs with 2 tablespoons flour, salt, pepper and a little grated nutmeg. Stir in 600 ml (1 pint, 2½ cups) yogurt. Pour this mixture over the top of the moussaka. Bake in a preheated oven at 180°C (350°F, gas 4) for about 1 hour, until the topping is set and golden brown. Allow to stand for 15 minutes before serving to give the layers time to settle.

MOUSSE
A light soft preparation, either sweet or savoury, in which the ingredients are whisked or blended and then folded together. Mousses are often set in a mould and usually served cold. Savoury mousses, served as an hors d'oeuvre or entrée, may be based on, for example, fish, shellfish, poultry, ham or a vegetable; sweet mousses are usually based on fruit or a flavouring such as chocolate or coffee.

RECIPES

Savoury Mousses
chicken mousse
Prepare in the same way as fish mousse but use poached chicken meat instead of fish and season the mixture well using curry powder or ground nutmeg.

fish mousse
Clean 500 g (18 oz) fillets or steaks of either pike, whiting, salmon or sole and pound them in a mortar or put in a food processor. Sprinkle with salt and pepper, then blend in 2–3 egg whites, one after the other. Rub this forcemeat through a sieve and refrigerate for 2 hours. Then place the bowl in crushed ice and gradually add 600 ml (1 pint, 2½ cups) double (heavy) cream, stirring the mixture with a wooden spoon. Adjust the seasoning, pour the mousse into a lightly oiled plain mould, and poach gently in a bain marie in a preheated oven at 190°C (375°F, gas 5) for about 20 minutes. Wait about 10 minutes before turning out and serve the mousse warm, coated with a sauce for fish.

hare mousse with chestnuts ◆
Finely mince (grind) 500 g (18 oz) hare meat, having first removed all the nerves, and sprinkle with salt and white pepper. Slowly add 2 or 3 egg whites, then pass through a sieve. Put the meat in a sauté pan and stir over a low heat with a wooden spoon to obtain a smooth mixture. Then put the meat in a bowl and place it in the refrigerator for 2 hours.

Meanwhile, braise 400 g (14 oz) chestnuts and chop 300 g (11 oz) of them. Reserve the remaining whole chestnuts. Place the bowl of meat in a container filled with ice cubes and briskly but gradually incorporate 500 ml (17 fl oz, 2 cups) thick crème fraîche and the chopped chestnuts. Put back in the refrigerator for 1 hour.

Butter dariole moulds and put the hare mousse in them, pressing it down lightly. Place the moulds in a bain marie and bring it to the boil over the heat. Cover with foil and cook in a preheated oven at 200°C (400°F, gas 6) for 25–30 minutes. Serve on a bed of lightly cooked cabbage, on a truffle sauce, if liked. Garnish with sliced truffle and the reserved whole chestnuts.

individual crayfish mousses à la Nantua
Prepare a mixture similar to that for the fish mousse but replace a quarter of the fish with the same volume of crayfish à la bordelaise and add a salpicon of crayfish tails à la bordelaise to the mixture before incorporating the cream. Butter some dariole moulds. Pour the mixture into them and cook in a bain marie in a preheated oven at 190°C (375°F, gas 5) for about 20 minutes. Turn out the mousses, either directly on to the serving dish or into croûtes of puff or thin shortcrust pastry, baked blind. Serve the mousses with Nantua sauce.

shrimp or lobster mousse
Cook the shellfish as for crayfish à la bordelaise and shell them. Reduce the cooking mirepoix, then rub through a sieve (or put through a blender or food processor) with the flesh of the shellfish. For every 250 g (9 oz, generous 1 cup) purée obtained, add 5 tablespoons well-reduced fish velouté* and 6 tablespoons fish aspic (see aspic jelly). Cool but do not allow to set. Line a small charlotte mould with fish aspic. Add 100 ml (4 fl oz, 7 tablespoons) half-whisked double (heavy) cream to the shellfish purée, then pour the mixture into the mould. Pour over it a thin layer of aspic and refrigerate for at least 2 hours. Turn out on to a serving dish and garnish with prawns.

other recipes See *foie gras, forcemeat, ham, hare, tomato.*

Sweet Mousses
chocolate and strawberry mousse
Melt 500 g (18 oz) plain (dark) chocolate. Separate the whites from the yolks of 8 eggs. Add the yolks, one by one, to the cooled melted chocolate and then blend in 6 tablespoons double (heavy) cream. Place in the refrigerator. Very lightly cook 200 g (7 oz, 1½ cups) strawberries in 6 tablespoons sugar syrup. Drain and leave to cool. Stiffly whisk the egg whites with a pinch of salt. Fold them carefully into the chocolate cream. Serve the mousse in individual moulds, topped with a few strawberries.

chocolate mousse
Melt 150 g (5 oz) plain (dark) chocolate in a bain marie, remove from the heat and add 75 g (3 oz, 6 tablespoons) butter. When the mixture is very smooth, quickly blend in 2 large egg yolks. Whisk 3 egg whites with a pinch of salt until very stiff, then whisk in 25 g (1 oz, 2 tablespoons) caster (superfine) sugar and 1 teaspoon vanilla-flavoured

sugar. Carefully mix the chocolate preparation with the whisked egg whites, using a wooden spatula. Pour into a dish and chill for at least 12 hours.

fruit mousse

Weigh the pulp of the chosen fruits (for example, strawberries, raspberries, apricots) and rub it through a sieve. Measure the same amount of double (heavy) cream. Prepare a sugar syrup using half as much sugar as fruit pulp. Whisk the cream and quickly add first the syrup, then the fruit purée. Refrigerate until time to serve.

langues-de-chat mousse

Butter a charlotte mould and line the bottom and sides with langues-de-chat biscuits (cookies). Completely melt over a low heat 250 g (9 oz) chocolate with 2 tablespoons water and 200 g (7 oz, 1 cup) caster (superfine) sugar. Remove from the heat and add 200 g (7 oz, 1 cup) butter and 4 egg yolks, then fold in the 4 egg whites, stiffly whisked. Fill the mould with this preparation. Cover the top with langues-de-chat and refrigerate for at least 2 hours. Turn out and serve with coffee-flavoured whipped cream.

lemon mousse

Beat together 2 egg yolks and 5 tablespoons sugar. When the mixture is foamy, add 2 tablespoons cornflour (cornstarch) and then the heated juice of 6 limes and 2 lemons. Bring the mixture to the boil, stirring all the time. Stiffly whisk 2 egg whites and fold into the mixture. Pour this mousse into ramekin dishes and serve chilled with a salad of blood oranges and pink grapefruit.

strawberry mousse

Put 400 g (14 oz, 3 cups) strawberries through a blender or food processor and sweeten the purée with 150 g (5 oz, ⅔ cup) caster (superfine) sugar. Flavour with a small amount of strawberry liqueur and leave to stand. Stiffly whisk 4 egg whites and add 15 g (½ oz, 1 tablespoon) sugar. Carefully fold the whisked egg whites into the strawberry purée. Place the mixture in individual glass dishes and refrigerate. Serve with a strawberry sauce made by adding a little lemon juice to about 150 g (5 oz, ⅔ cup) strawberry purée.

Iced Sweet Mousses

iced cream mousse

Prepare a custard cream (see *custard*) with 500 ml (17 fl oz, 2 cups) milk, 350 g (11 oz, 1¾ cups) sugar, and some egg yolks (8 for a liqueur mousse; up to 16 for a fruit mousse). Leave to cool completely. Then add the chosen flavouring – vanilla, orange or lemon zest, liqueur, or 500 ml (17 fl oz, 2 cups) fruit purée – and 500 ml (17 fl oz, 2 cups) double (heavy) cream. Place the mixing bowl in a basin containing crushed ice and whisk the preparation well. Pour into a mould and put in the freezer for at least 4 hours to set.

iced fruit mousse

Prepare an Italian meringue with 300 g (11 oz, 1⅓ cups) sugar, 6 tablespoons water and 4 egg whites and put it in the refrigerator. Prepare a fruit purée – with 375 g (13 oz, 2½ cups) strawberries, for example. Whip 500 ml (17 fl oz, 2 cups) very cold double (heavy) cream with 150 ml (¼ pint, ⅔ cup) very cold milk until stiff. Mix the meringue and the fruit purée and then add the whisked cream. Pour into a mould and put in the freezer for at least 4 hours to set.

iced liqueur mousse

Make a syrup with 4 tablespoons water and 200 g (7 oz, 1 cup) sugar; while still very hot, pour it in a thin trickle over 7 egg yolks, whisking until the mixture has cooled. Then add 3 tablespoons liqueur, followed by 500 ml (17 fl oz, 2 cups) very cold double (heavy) cream, whisked with 150 ml (¼ pint, ⅔ cup) cold milk. Pour into a mould and put into the freezer for at least 4 hours to set.

MOUSSELINE Any of various mousse-like preparations, most of which have a large or small quantity of whipped cream added to them. This term is used particularly for moulds made of various pastes enriched with cream (poultry, game, fish, shellfish, foie gras, for example). Mousselines are served hot or cold. If cold, they are also known as small aspics.

Mousseline is used as an adjective to denote a sauce enriched with whipped cream (mayonnaise mousseline, hollandaise mousseline). It is also used to describe the paste or forcemeat used to make fish balls and mousses.

The term *mousseline* is much used in confectionery to describe certain cakes and pastries made of delicate mixtures (for example, brioche mousseline).

RECIPES

mousseline of apples with walnuts

Peel and core 8 medium dessert apples, cut into slices, and make a compote by stewing them until soft with 2 knobs of butter, 3 tablespoons caster (superfine) sugar, 1 teaspoon vanilla-flavoured sugar and a small piece of finely chopped lemon zest.

Peel and core 3 more apples and cut each into 8 pieces. Poach these pieces of apple slowly in a syrup prepared with 350 ml (12 fl oz, 1½ cups) water, 125 g (4½ oz, scant ⅔ cup) sugar and a vanilla pod (bean): the fruit should be just softened. Remove 15 pieces of apple and complete the cooking of the other 9. Drain the fruit and put the syrup to one side.

As soon as the compote is cooked, mash it with a fork and reduce it over a high heat, turning it over with a spatula until a thick fruit paste is obtained. Remove from the heat and cool. Thicken with 120 ml (4½ fl oz, ½ cup) whipped double (heavy)

Hare mousse with chestnuts, see page 767.

cream, 3 beaten eggs and 3 yolks. Add 2 tablespoons crushed walnuts and the half-poached apple pieces.

Butter a charlotte mould well and pour the mixture into it. Pile it up slightly and cook in a bain marie in a preheated oven at 190°C (375°F, gas 5) for about 40 minutes. Remove from the oven and turn out 15 minutes later on to a hot dish.

Prepare a sauce by reducing the syrup in which the apples were cooked to 120 ml (4½ fl oz, ½ cup), remove it from the heat, and add 50 g (2 oz, ¼ cup) butter and then 250 ml (8 fl oz, 1 cup) whipped double (heavy) cream. Flavour with Noyau liqueur. Coat the mousseline with this sauce and decorate with the 9 fully cooked pieces of apple. Serve some langues-de-chat biscuits (cookies) separately.

mousseline sauce

Prepare a hollandaise sauce. Just before serving, blend into it half its volume of stiffly whipped double (heavy) cream.

other recipes See *brioche, forcemeat, omelette (flat omelettes), potato, quenelle, sponge cake (orange sandwich cake).*

MOUSSERON The common French name for several species of small white or beige mushrooms with a delicate flavour, including St George's mushroom, the fairy-ring mushroom and blewits. They are cleaned and prepared like chanterelles.

MOUVETTE The French term for a round flat wooden spoon of varying size, used principally for stirring (or 'moving') sauces and creams and for mixing various preparations.

MOZART A garnish for small cuts of meat consisting of artichoke hearts, slowly cooked in butter and stuffed with celery purée and potatoes, cut into strips (called 'shavings') and fried.

MOZZARELLA An Italian cheese originating from Latium and Campania, still made with buffalo's milk in these areas but with cow's milk (40–45% fat content) in the rest of Italy. It is a fresh cheese, springy and white; the mild flavour has a slight bite. Mozzarella is kept in salted water or whey, shaped into balls or loaves of varying size – 100 g to 1 kg (4 oz to 2¼ lb). The buffalo's-milk cheese, which has a more delicate flavour, is eaten at the end of a meal; the cow's-milk cheese is used mainly for cooking, particularly for pizzas, but also (with the addition of Ricotta) for preparing a lasagne gratin or for stuffing fried rice croquettes. *Mozzarella in carrozza*, a popular Neapolitan snack, is a small sandwich filled with cheese, rolled in flour, dipped in beaten egg, fried in oil, and eaten very hot.

MUESLI (GRANOLA) A Swiss dish, originally consisting of apples, oats, milk and, often, nuts. Dr Bircher-Benner, who advocated the use of raw food, invented muesli (from the German *müesli*, meaning mixture). When the Bircher-Benner clinic was founded in Zurich in 1897, the fruit diet, as it was originally known, was served frequently and became popular long before it was described in detail in a little book, *Fruit Dishes and Raw Vegetables*, published in 1924. Dr Bircher-Benner died in 1947, so did not live to see all the vitamin and the nutritional discoveries that justified his work.

Many restaurants in Switzerland introduced muesli and it became known as *Birchermüesli*. Muesli has become a popular nutritious breakfast dish and mixtures of cereals and dried fruit are marketed with many variations. A standard mixture is rolled oats, wheat germ, roasted almonds, raisins and dried apple, served with milk. Other ingredients, such as pears, berries, banana, dried apricots, walnuts, pecans, hazelnuts, condensed milk, evaporated milk, yogurt, orange juice, sugar, honey or malt extract, may be added as required.

MUFFIN In Great Britain, a muffin is a traditional light-textured roll, round and flat, which is made with yeast dough. Muffins are usually enjoyed in the winter – split, toasted, buttered and served hot for tea, sometimes with jam. In the Victorian era muffins were bought in the street from sellers who carried trays of them on their heads, ringing a handbell to call their wares.

American muffins are entirely different, more like cake than bread. The raising (leavening) agent is baking powder and the muffins are cooked in deep patty tins (muffin pans). Cornmeal and bran are sometimes substituted for some of the flour.

RECIPE

English muffins

Prepare the yeast liquid: blend 15 g (½ oz) fresh yeast (1 cake compressed yeast) in 300 ml (½ pint, 1¼ cups) warm water. Alternatively, dissolve 1 teaspoon caster (superfine) sugar in the warm water and sprinkle in 1½ teaspoons dried yeast. Allow to stand until frothy (about 10 minutes).

Mix 450 g (1 lb, 4 cups) strong plain (bread) flour and 1 teaspoon salt together. Add the yeast liquid and mix to form a soft dough. Turn out on to a lightly floured surface and knead until smooth and elastic (about 10 minutes by hand). Shape into a ball and place inside an oiled polythene (plastic) bag; leave to rise until doubled in size. Remove from the polythene bag, knock back (punch down) and knead until the dough is firm (about 2 minutes). Cover the dough and rest it for 5 minutes. Roll out on a floured surface to a thickness of 1 cm (½ in). Cover again and rest for a further 5 minutes.

Cut into 9 cm (3½ in) rounds with a plain cutter. Place on a well-floured baking sheet and dust the tops with flour or fine semolina. Cover and prove in a warm place until doubled in size (about 15–30 minutes).

Heat a griddle, hotplate or heavy frying pan and grease lightly. Cook the muffins for about 3 minutes or until golden brown on each side, or bake in a preheated oven at 230°C (450°F, gas 8) for about 10 minutes, turning over carefully with a palette knife (spatula) after 5 minutes. Cool on a wire rack.

American muffins

Mix 225 g (8 oz, 2 cups) plain (all-purpose) flour, 2 teaspoons baking powder, 3 tablespoons soft brown sugar and 6 tablespoons bran in a bowl. Beat 1 egg with 100 ml (4 fl oz, 7 tablespoons) milk and 3 tablespoons melted butter. Pour the liquid over the dry ingredients and mix briefly. Do not beat or overmix the ingredients – it does not matter if there are patches of dry flour in the mixture. Divide the mixture between greased deep patty tins (muffin pans) and bake in a preheated oven at 200°C (400°F, gas 6) for about 20 minutes. The muffins should be well risen, cracked on top and firm to the touch. Leave in the tins for about 5 minutes, until firm enough to remove, then cool on a wire rack. Serve warm with butter and jam.

This basic mixture can be varied in many ways: all or part wholemeal flour can be used and the proportion of bran can be increased; dried fruit, such as raisins, sultanas (golden raisins) or mixed dried fruit are often added; also chopped candied peel; chopped walnuts or pecan nuts are good with dried fruit; or fresh fruit, such as blueberries, are popular in muffins – add about 150 g (5 oz, 1 cup) for the above quantity of mixture.

MULBERRY The fruit of the mulberry tree. The two most common varieties are the black and white mulberry. The fruit is similar in appearance to the blackberry and should be picked or allowed to fall from the tree when very ripe. The juice of the black mulberry is very staining. In China, the leaves of the white mulberry are fed to silkworms, which eat nothing else. Mulberries are usually eaten raw or can be used in the same way as blackberries.

MULLED WINE An aromatic alcoholic drink made with red wine, sugar and spices and served hot, traditionally in winter; examples are grog, punch and Bishop. Mulled wine is particularly popular in mountainous regions, in Germany and Scandinavia. It is traditionally prepared by slowly heating the contents of a bottle of Bordeaux, Burgundy or a similar red wine for about 10 minutes with lemon or orange zest, sugar or honey, and spices (cinnamon, cloves, mace), but this should never be brought to the boil; the liquid is strained and served in glasses or cups with handles. In the country it may be served in a pottery jug. To strengthen the aroma of the spices, these are sometimes left to infuse for half an hour in a glass of wine brought up to the boil, before the rest of the heated wine is added. If spirits are added or the wine is sufficiently high in alcohol, its vapours may be flamed.

MULLET One of several unrelated fish which can be divided into two broad groups.

■ **Grey mullet** These are found in coastal waters and there are several species. The largest is the striped mullet, which is up to 60 cm (2 ft) long, with a large head, silvery-grey back and brown sides. The golden mullet is the smallest – 20–45 cm (8–18 in); it has gold spots beside its eyes and a yellowish tint to the sides. The thick-lipped grey mullet has wide thick lips. The thin-lipped mullet resembles the golden mullet but is larger and lacks spots. The first two are the most highly prized and the most common. They are prepared like bass – cooked in court-bouillon, baked or grilled (broiled), after they have been carefully scaled. The flesh is lean, white and slightly soft; it contains few bones but sometimes smells of mud. Grey mullet roe is the traditional ingredient used to make taramasalata although cod's roe is now more frequently used.

■ **Red mullet (goatfish)** These fish are distinguished from the grey mullets by their smaller size – 40 cm (16 in) maximum length – reddish coloration and the pair of barbels beneath the chin. They are a lean fish with a delicate flavour. The best variety is bright pink streaked with gold and has a black striped front dorsal fin and two scales under its eyes. The sand mullet is inferior in quality. It is reddish-brown and has three scales under the eyes.

The *rouget de Sénégal* or Senegal red mullet is identified by its pinky-red body, and is about 30 cm (12 in) long, with yellow dots on its sides and blue ones on its cheeks. It is fished off the west coast of tropical Africa. This smaller fish is dry and more bony than the other varieties.

The colour of the red mullet is brighter if the fish is scaled as soon as it is caught. This is a difficult operation, however, as the skin is fragile. Mullet are therefore generally sold unscaled. The fish are extremely perishable and must be sold and consumed within a short time. An infallible guide to freshness is the colour: if this begins to fade, the fish is going off. The flesh should be quite firm, the body almost rigid, the skin tight, and the eyes prominent and clear.

Very fresh small red mullet do not need to be gutted (cleaned); if they are, the liver should be reserved. They can be grilled, after being dried and lightly salted. Mullet with drier flesh can be fried or baked. Medium-sized fish are grilled or cooked *en papillote* (taking care always to reserve the liver, which can be used in the sauce). Large mullet are cooked in the oven, *en papillote*, or on a bed of herbs, with butter or olive oil.

RECIPES

baked red mullet à la livournaise

Gut (clean) 4 red mullet, make some light incisions on their backs, season them with salt and pepper, and lay them head to tail in a buttered or oiled gratin dish. Cover with a reduced tomato fondue or sauce, sprinkle with breadcrumbs and 2 tablespoons oil or melted butter, and bake in a preheated oven at 240°C (475°F, gas 9). When the top is brown (after about 15 minutes), add some chopped parsley and a few drops of lemon juice. Serve from the cooking dish.

baked red mullet with fennel

Soften 25 g (1 oz, ¼ cup) chopped onion in oil, then add 1 tablespoon very finely chopped fresh fennel. Gut (clean) a mullet, make some light incisions on its back, and season with salt and pepper. Butter a small ovenproof dish, spread the base with the onion and lay the fish on top. Sprinkle with breadcrumbs and a little olive oil and bake in a preheated oven at 220°C (425°F, gas 7) for 25 minutes. Sprinkle with parsley and a little lemon juice.

baked red mullet with shallots

Peel and chop 40 g (1½ oz, ¼ cup) shallots. Boil them in 250 ml (8 fl oz, 1 cup) dry white wine until almost all the liquid has evaporated, then spread the mixture into a buttered gratin dish. Gut (clean) 3 red mullet, dry them, make some incisions on their backs, season with salt and pepper, and lay them in the dish. Pour over 6 tablespoons dry white wine and dot with about 25 g (1 oz, 2 tablespoons) butter. Cook in a preheated oven at 230°C (450°F, gas 8) for 15 minutes, basting several times with the juices; add a little more white wine if necessary. Sprinkle with chopped parsley and a little lemon juice, and serve from the cooking dish.

fillets of red mullet Girardet

Remove the fillets from 4 mullet weighing 225 g (8 oz) each. Reserve the livers. Heat 25 g (1 oz, 2 tablespoons) butter and brown the bones and the heads with 2 chopped shallots and some rosemary for 2 minutes. Moisten with a glass each of white wine and water and cook for 5 minutes. Strain this stock and reduce it by half. Stir in 250 ml (8 fl oz, 1 cup) double (heavy) cream and reduce again. Blend in the chopped livers, 20 g (¾ oz, 4½ teaspoons) butter, some salt and pepper, and the juice of half a lemon.

Heat a little butter in a clean frying pan. Put the fillets in, skin side down, cook for 45 seconds, then turn them and cook the other side for 30 seconds. Pour the sauce into a hot dish and place the fillets on top.

fried red mullet

Gut (clean) some small mullet, dry them and make a few shallow incisions on their backs. Soak them for 30 minutes in salted boiled milk, then drain them, dip in flour and fry at 175°C (347°F). Drain on paper towels, arrange in a dish and garnish with lemon slices and fried parsley.

grilled red mullet

Scale 800 g (1¾ lb) red mullet. Cook whole if they are small, but make some light incisions in the skin. Brush them with oil, applied with a small bunch of thyme or rosemary sprigs. Grill (broil) the fish under a moderate heat. Oil them lightly from time to time while cooking, using a herb brush. Turn them as few times as possible so as not to damage them. Sprinkle with salt and serve either as they are or accompanied by a béarnaise or Choron sauce or with melted butter. A traditional Provençal method is to grill them without any previous preparation, complete with scales and fins, and without salt. They should be eaten, unsalted, when still barely cooked.

grilled red mullet à l'italienne

Prepare 8 tablespoons Italian sauce (see *italienne, à l'*) and spread half of it over an oiled gratin dish. Clean and gut 4 red mullet, make some light incisions on their backs, season with pepper, grill (broil) them, then season with salt. Arrange them head to tail in the dish. Mask them with the rest of the sauce, sprinkle with breadcrumbs and a little oil, and brown under the grill. Sprinkle with parsley.

red mullet grilled in cases

Grill (broil) some red mullet. Cut pieces of greaseproof (wax) paper large enough to enclose the fish and spread them with mushroom duxelles. Put a fish on each piece of paper and pour over some duxelles sauce; sprinkle with breadcrumbs and melted butter and brown in a preheated oven at 240°C (475°F, gas 9) for a few minutes.

red mullet poached à la nage with basil

Prepare the sauce in advance: finely chop 20 fresh basil leaves, 5 tarragon leaves and 5 sprigs of parsley. Peel and chop a tomato. Marinate these ingredients with a little garlic in 250 ml (8 fl oz, 1 cup) extra-virgin olive oil. Add a few drops of wine vinegar and season with salt and pepper.

On the day of the meal, prepare an aromatic poaching liquid (see *nage*) for the fish and cook it for 30 minutes. Meanwhile, scale 4 red mullet, each weighing 175–200 g (6–7 oz), but do not gut (clean) them. Place a slice of orange, a slice of lemon and a bay leaf on each fish and wrap in foil. Cook the fish gently in the poaching liquid for about 10 minutes; they should still be firm and have retained their shape. Serve with the sauce.

striped mullet in a mille-feuille of cabbage with marrow ◆

Descale and clean 12 red mullet weighing 120–150 g (4¼–5 oz), keeping the livers to one side. Lift the bones with tweezers and remove the gills. Finely chop 1 garlic head, then scald, cool and drain it. Dry it lightly in the oven, then caramelize it with a knob of butter, a little sugar and salt.

Blanch and cool the leaves of 2 green cabbages. Drain and cut out 30 rounds, 7.5 cm (3 in) in diameter, avoiding the tough ribs. Cut the red mullet fillets into 2 or 3 thin slices. Cut 150 g (5 oz)

Striped mullet in a mille-feuille of cabbage with marrow.

blanched bone marrow into very fine slices. On each round of cabbage, arrange the equivalent of a fillet of fish and a slice of marrow. Season with salt and pepper. Allow 4 layers and 5 rounds of cabbage per mille-feuille, making 6 in all. Steam the 6 portions for 8–10 minutes.

Meanwhile, sweat the red mullet livers in 60 ml (2 fl oz, ¼ cup) olive oil and a little marrow. Pour a little fumet on top, correct the seasoning, add 50 g (2 oz, ¼ cup) butter and blend until smooth at the last moment. Place a mille-feuille in the middle of each plate and pour the juice around it. Sprinkle with a pinch of salt, pepper and garlic on top. Garnish with flat-leaf parsley.

other recipes See *Bercy, nantaise, niçoise, orientale, papillote.*

MULLIGATAWNY

A soup of Indian origin, adopted by the British and particularly popular in Australia. It is a chicken consommé to which are added stewed vegetables, such as onions, leeks and celery, highly seasoned with curry and spices (bay leaf and cloves), garnished with chicken meat and rice *à la créole.* In the original Indian preparation the garnish also includes blanched almonds and coconut milk (possibly replaced by cream). The Australians generally add tomatoes and smoked bacon.

MUNG BEAN

A bean plant, originating in the Far East, having small green, yellow or brown seeds. In India they are also known as green gram and are sometimes ground to make a flour used for savoury pancakes and dumplings. The hulled split beans are known as moong dal. Mung beans can be cooked and used as a dried pulse and are widely cultivated for their shoots. Commonly known as bean sprouts, they are eaten either raw or blanched. They can be served as a vegetable accompanying a main dish, in stir-fries, such as chop suey, or in mixed salads. Bean sprouts can be bought fresh or canned.

MUNSTER

An Alsatian cheese made from cow's milk (45–50% fat content); it has a soft yellow paste and a washed straw- to orange-coloured rind. After it has matured for 2–3 months and had regular washings it has a strong smell and a full-bodied flavour. It is eaten with Gewürztraminer in Alsace and with well-balanced red wines elsewhere. Created in the 7th century by monks – the name is derived from *monastère* (monastery) – it is protected by an AOP which applies to certain districts of the Haut- and Bas-Rhin, Meurthe-et-Moselle, the Haute-Saône, the Vosges and the Territory of Belfort.

Munster is best eaten in summer and autumn. It is a flat round cheese, 13–20 cm (5–8 in) in diameter and 2.5–5 cm (1–2 in) thick, and is sold unwrapped or boxed (when it is small). Cumin seeds are sometimes added to the paste, but it is better to serve them separately. In Alsace, Munster is often eaten young and is traditionally served with unpeeled boiled potatoes.

MURAT

A method of preparing fillets of sole, which are cut into small strips, cooked *à la meunière,* and arranged in a timbale with potatoes (boiled in their skins and peeled) and poached artichoke hearts, cut into dice and sautéed. The whole preparation, which may be garnished with slices of tomato sautéed in oil, is sprinkled with coarsely chopped parsley, mixed with lemon juice and moistened with noisette butter.

MURFATLAR

A region in Romania, not far from the Black Sea, producing dessert wines. The use of overripe grapes gives a golden liqueur-like wine, with a bouquet reminiscent of orange blossom.

MUSCADET

White AOC wine made from the Melon de Bourgogne grape variety in the region south of Nantes, close to where the Loire meets the Atlantic. There are four appellations: Muscadet, Muscadet de Sèvres-et-Maine, Muscadet des Coteaux de la Loire and Muscadet Côtes de Grand Lieu. The description *sur lie* means that the wines are left to mature on the lees (grape skins), thus gaining more complex flavours and a small amount of carbon dioxide before being bottled. The wines can be zesty and crisp and are a good accompaniment to seafood dishes.

MUSCAT

There are over 200 different types of Muscat vines recorded but the finest is acknowledged as the Muscat à Petits Grains or Muscat de Frontignan. Widely grown throughout the world the wines can be dry but are mainly sweet and luscious with pronounced grapey aromas. Wines produced include Beaumes-de-Venise, Asti, Muscat of Samos, liqueur Muscats from Australia and the renowned Vin de Constance from South Africa.

MUSHROOM

A type of fungus (a plant with neither chlorophyll nor flowers) generally found growing in cool damp places in woodland and meadows, where the soil is rich in humus. A mushroom usually consists of a stalk and an umbrella-shaped cap. Sometimes the whole mushroom may be eaten, in other cases just the cap. As well as wild fungi, there is also a variety of cultivated mushrooms.

■ **Wild mushrooms** In order to collect mushrooms, it is essential to be able to identify them properly. While some species are prized as food, many are very poisonous, to the extent that eating them may even be fatal in some instances. There is no empirical means of distinguishing poisonous species from edible ones. Therefore, it is wise only to use cultivated mushrooms and purchase wild mushrooms from reliable sources. Some experts provide fungi identification services and/or arrange forays. Although this may present a rather terrifying picture in a work dedicated to gastronomy, fatal accidents occur every year from eating poisonous mushrooms. Detailed encyclopedias are dedicated to the subject of fungi and it is worth investing in suitable reference sources when taking the subject seriously.

MUSHROOMS

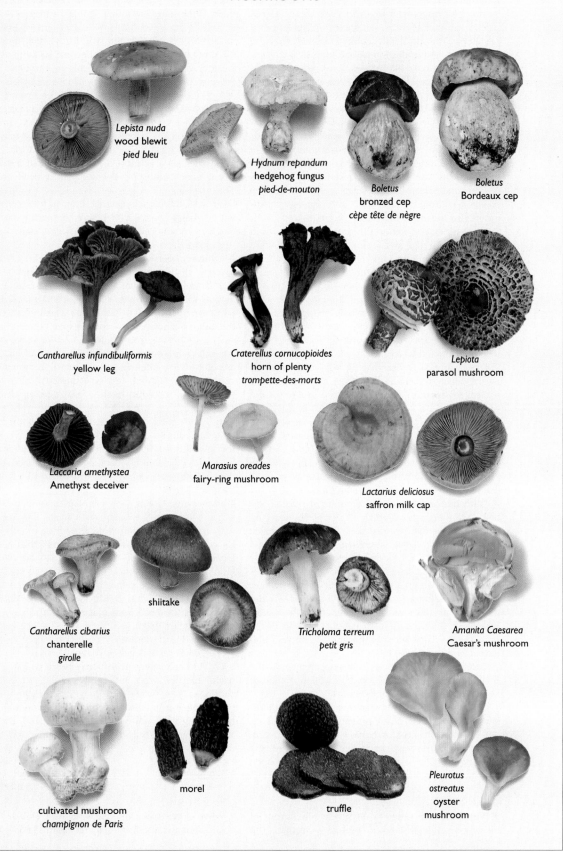

Lepista nuda
wood blewit
pied bleu

Hydnum repandum
hedgehog fungus
pied-de-mouton

Boletus
bronzed cep
cèpe tête de nègre

Boletus
Bordeaux cep

Cantharellus infundibuliformis
yellow leg

Craterellus cornucopioides
horn of plenty
trompette-des-morts

Lepiota
parasol mushroom

Laccaria amethystea
Amethyst deceiver

Marasius oreades
fairy-ring mushroom

Lactarius deliciosus
saffron milk cap

Cantharellus cibarius
chanterelle
girolle

shiitake

Tricholoma terreum
petit gris

Amanita Caesarea
Caesar's mushroom

cultivated mushroom
champignon de Paris

morel

truffle

*Pleurotus
ostreatus*
oyster
mushroom

Mushrooms must be bought fresh and young, and must not be maggoty. It is advisable to cook them as quickly as possible. Although some wild mushrooms are edible raw or lightly cooked, others must be properly cooked to destroy natural toxins.

Field mushrooms, like berries, have been gathered for food throughout history. In France in the Middle Ages, the most highly prized mushroom was the field mushroom belonging to the genus *Agaricus*, which was easily identifiable. (Ceps were not known to be edible until the 18th century.) *Agaricus campestris*, the common field mushroom found in Britain and throughout Europe, has a white or cream coloured cap with pink gills, darkening to brown as the cap opens from button stage to full width. The common cultivated mushrooms and chestnut mushrooms also belong to this family of fungi.

Separate entries cover the popular fungi, both wild and cultivated less-common species, including beefsteak mushroom; cep; chanterelle; chicken of the woods; Chinese black fungus; enokitake; fairy-ring mushroom; grisette; honey fungus; horn of plenty; *hydnum* or hedgehog fungus; milk cap; morel; oyster mushroom; puffball; shaggy ink cap; shiitake; shimeji mushroom; straw mushroom; *tricholoma terreum* or *petit gris* in French; truffle; wood blewit; and yellow leg.

The illustration of examples of wild and cultivated mushrooms also includes a member of the *Lepiota* or parasol mushroom family. The *lepiota procera* is not common, but it is a good edible species unlike some of its close relatives that can cause stomach upsets. The amethyst deceiver, *laccaria amethystea*, is the distinctively coloured member of the *Laccaria* family, which includes a wide variety of fungi. The *Amanita Caesarea* or Caesar's mushroom is an excellent fungi that has been enjoyed since Roman times.

■ **Cultivated mushrooms** The common mushrooms belong to the genus *Agaricus*, with a fleshy cap and pale pink gills that become dark brown at maturity. The erect stalk has a membranous ring of tissue about halfway up. These mushrooms are extensively cultivated around Paris (hence the French name – *champignon de Paris*) in two varieties: *blanc* (white) and *blond* or *bistre* (golden), of which the latter has more flavour. Chestnut mushrooms, with the darker brown cap and slightly fuller flavour, are part of the same family. They are sold throughout the year and have a firm soft flesh.

Other types of cultivated mushroom include the oyster mushroom (pale, brown or yellow), shiitake and enokitake or enoki mushrooms.

Common cultivated mushrooms are sold at different stages in their development: tiny or medium-sized button mushrooms have a tightly closed cap; closed cap mushrooms are larger with the 'veil' still covering the gills on the underside of the cap; open cup mushrooms are larger, with the gills showing; large cup or flat mushrooms are dark and wide, with slightly curved or flat caps.

■ **Preparation** In order to retain the full flavour of mushrooms, it is best not to peel or wash them, but simply to wipe them with a damp cloth and then dry them. If the stalks are tough, stringy or maggoty, they should be removed (tiny holes are signs of maggot infestation). Otherwise, the base of the stalk is sliced off. Only the mushrooms that become sticky in damp weather (including certain boletus mushrooms) and those with a bitter outer skin (*cortinae* and *pholiotae*) are peeled. The fleshy tubes of boletus mushrooms are removed if they are too spongy, and the gills of certain other mushrooms are trimmed if they are too ripe. If absolutely necessary, the mushrooms may be washed very quickly, but never allowed to soak.

Varieties such as morels, with a cap that is pitted like a honeycomb, are cleaned with a small brush. The flavour of delicate fungi is completely destroyed by blanching and only a few varieties with a bitter, peppery, resinous or earthy flavour (such as certain milk caps and *russulae*) stand up to this treatment.

■ **Culinary uses** Mushrooms are widely used in savoury dishes, as a flavouring ingredient or as vegetables in their own right. Dr Paul Ramain, author of an important *Mycogastronomie* (1954), was one of the first to treat field mushrooms from the culinary angle. A few species may be eaten raw, such as Caesar's mushroom (*Amanita caesarea*), coprinus and cultivated mushrooms; the majority are edible only after they are cooked. They may be stir-fried or sautéed, grilled (broiled), baked or braised. The cooking method and type of dish in which they are used depends on the variety of fungi; rare and expensive examples are often celebrated in simple creations or as the key flavouring for an otherwise plain dish. Some delicate mushrooms require brief cooking to preserve their flavour: they may be sautéed and added to a dish in the final stages.

■ **Preserving** Drying is a popular method for preserving wild mushrooms, particularly the species with dry flesh (chanterelle, craterellus, morel) and for ceps (the caps of which are cut into thin strips). Dried mushrooms and fungus are also popular in Oriental cuisines, particularly shiitake. Some dried mushrooms may be reduced to a powder and used as a seasoning. Dried mushrooms have an intense flavour that brings a particular character to dishes in which they are used. The fleshy types of mushrooms are bottled and sterilized. Mushrooms may also be preserved in oil, vinegar or brine.

Cooked cultivated mushrooms freeze well and are useful for flavouring sauces, casseroles, soups and stuffings. They should be finely sliced or chopped, then cooked in a little olive oil or butter until all the liquor they yield has completely evaporated. By this stage, they are greatly reduced in volume and their flavour is concentrated.

RECIPES

mushroom blanc
Bring 6 tablespoons water with 40 g (1½ oz, 3 tablespoons) butter, the juice of half a lemon and

I scant tablespoon salt to the boil. Add 300 g (11 oz, 3½ cups) mushrooms and boil for 6 minutes. Drain and retain the cooking stock to flavour a white sauce, fish stock or marinade.

mushroom croquettes

Clean and dice some mushrooms, sprinkle with lemon juice and sauté them briskly either in oil or in butter. Add some chopped shallot and parsley, a little thyme, or bay leaf, a chopped garlic clove, salt and pepper. Bind this salpicon with a thick béchamel sauce and leave to cool. Divide the mixture into equal portions and roll them into cylinders. Dip the cylinders in batter, plunge into very hot oil and brown. Drain and dry on paper towels. Serve very hot (possibly with a tomato sauce), either as an entrée or as a vegetable.

mushroom essence

Clean and dice about 450 g (1 lb) open-cap cultivated mushrooms, then place them in a saucepan and season with salt. Add a little white wine and water. Bring to the boil, stirring, then reduce the heat and cover the pan tightly. Cook for about 20 minutes, until the mushrooms are greatly reduced. Strain the liquor through a sieve, pressing or squeezing the mushrooms dry. Boil the liquor to reduce it to a full-flavoured essence.

mushroom purée

Prepare 200 ml (7 fl oz, ¾ cup) béchamel* sauce. Add to it 6 tablespoons double (heavy) cream and stir over a brisk heat until reduced by a third. Clean and chop 500 g (18 oz, 6 cups) mushrooms. Press through a sieve or blend in a food processor. Place the resulting purée in a shallow frying pan and stir over a brisk heat until the vegetable juice has completely evaporated. Add the béchamel, a pinch of salt, a little white pepper and a dash of grated nutmeg. Stir again over the heat for several minutes. Remove from the heat and blend with 50 g (2 oz, ¼ cup) butter.

mushroom salad

Clean some very fresh mushrooms. Slice them finely and sprinkle with lemon juice to prevent them from turning brown. They may be served with either a very highly seasoned vinaigrette dressing with added lemon juice and chopped herbs or with a mixture of cream, vinegar or lemon juice, salt, pepper and chopped chives. Keep in a cool place until ready to serve.

mushrooms à l'anglaise

Choose good-quality cultivated mushrooms. Trim, wash and remove the stalks. Season the caps with salt and pepper. Butter small round lightly toasted pieces of bread. Place a mushroom, hollow side up, on each slice, garnished with a little maître d'hôtel butter. Arrange the toast in a gratin dish, cover and bake in a preheated oven at 180°C (350°F, gas 4) for 12–15 minutes.

mushrooms cooked in butter

Cut some raw cultivated mushrooms into thin slices. Season with salt and pepper, sauté in butter in a frying pan over a brisk heat and serve in a vegetable dish, possibly with chopped herbs or thinly sliced onions softened in butter, à la lyonnaise.

mushrooms cooked in cream

Sauté the mushrooms in butter, cover them with boiling double (heavy) cream and simmer for 8–10 minutes, until reduced.

This preparation may be used as a filling for flans or vol-au-vent.

mushroom soufflés

Add 4 egg yolks to 400 ml (14 fl oz, 1¾ cups) mushroom purée, followed by 4 stiffly whisked egg whites. Butter some small ramekins and divide the mixture between them. Place them in a preheated oven at 190°C (375°F, gas 5) and cook for about 20 minutes without opening the oven door. The soufflés are cooked when they have filled the moulds and the tops have browned. Serve immediately.

mushroom stuffing

Clean some mushrooms, remove the caps and set them aside to use as garnishes. Chop the stalks and toss them in very hot butter (or olive oil) with chopped shallots, salt, pepper and (optional) a dash of grated nutmeg. Then add some fresh breadcrumbs, chopped parsley, 1 egg (either whole or just the yolk), salt and pepper.

The stuffing may be used to fill mushroom caps or other vegetables, such as tomatoes, aubergines (eggplants), courgettes (zucchini) and cabbage, and also as a fish or meat stuffing.

stuffed mushrooms

Choose large mushrooms of a similar size. Remove the stalks so that the cavities of the caps are fully exposed. Wash and wipe the caps, arrange them in a buttered or oiled dish and season with salt and pepper. Coat them with oil or melted butter and place them in a preheated oven at 200°C (400°F, gas 6) for 5 minutes. Stuff each one with duxelles. Dust with fine breadcrumbs, sprinkle with olive oil and brown.

Like all stuffed vegetables, mushrooms may be filled with different mixtures, such as chopped vegetables, forcemeat, mirepoix, salpicon or risotto.

MUSIGNY *Grand cru* vineyard producing red and white Burgundies from the village of Chambolle-Musigny in the Côte de Nuits. Mostly red, the wines are world-famous, being extremely fine and delicate and very expensive.

MUSK A strong-smelling secretion from the glands of the musk deer and Ethiopian civet or from various seeds (especially musk mallow, cultivated in Africa and in the West Indies). Musk was formerly used as a spice and to flavour certain African and

Oriental dishes. Today, smells are 'musky' when they recall the plants from which infusions are made, or the wines which combine the scent of dried apricots, white peaches, dried figs and honey.

MUSLIN (CHEESECLOTH) Loosely woven cloth used for straining thick liquids, such as sauces and purées. The liquid is either pressed through the cloth with a spatula or enclosed in the cloth, the two ends of which are twisted in opposite directions.

Small muslin bags are used to hold ingredients intended to flavour a dish. The flavouring ingredients are placed on a small square of muslin (or chiffon); the muslin is then drawn up and knotted to form a bag. In this way the flavouring material does not escape into the dish and can be removed when cooking is complete.

MUSSEL A bivalve mollusc found in seas all over the world, of which there are many species. European mussels have thin, rectangular shells, which are dark blue, almost black, and finely striped. The common European mussel is cultivated on the coasts of the Atlantic, the English Channel and the North Sea, especially between the mouth of the Gironde and Denmark. It is small, convex and tender. The mussels from Spain tend to be larger, brown in colour and with a tortoiseshell effect. The Toulon mussel, which is larger, flatter and less delicate, is found only in the Mediterranean. The main species of European mussels have spread to other areas through attaching themselves to the hulls of ships. Other varieties are found, such as the green-lipped mussel from New Zealand and a slightly larger variety found on the Pacific coast of North America.

Wild mussels are usually smaller and more leathery than mussels that have been cultivated. Care must be taken when gathering these because of their ability to absorb toxins, as with other shellfish.

In France, mussel culture has been practised since the 13th century although mussel beds date back to Roman times. The story goes that an Irish traveller, Patrick Walton, was shipwrecked in the region of La Rochelle in 1290 and then settled in the district. One day he noticed that the posts hung with nets which he set up in the sea to catch birds were covered with mussels. This gave him the idea of increasing the number of posts, placing them closer together, and joining them with bundles of branches (*bouches*). This is the origin of *bouchot*, the modern French word for the wooden stakes on which mussels are bred. Today the stakes are stocked with young mussels taken from lines for catching seed oysters. Mussel culture in France is practised mainly on the Atlantic coast, from Cotentin to the mouth of the Charente, and produces mussels which are small but full of flavour and very fleshy.

The most important modern method of mussel culture originates from the areas of north-west Spain. In suitable bays, rafts are anchored with many ropes suspended from them and on which the mussels grow. Another method of mussel culture, used in the

Trimming a cooked mussel

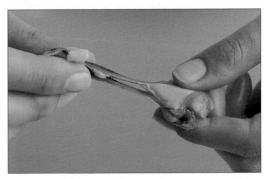

When removed from its shell, a cooked mussel may still have the rubbery edge of slightly frilly muscle attached. Gently pull this and the small, white and tough foot off the tender mussel as both are unpleasant to eat.

Netherlands and Denmark, consists of creating sheltered mussel beds. The mussels are first reared in dense, flat beds and then thinned out over a wider area to improve their feeding. Harvesting under this method is highly mechanized.

■ **Buying and cleaning** Mussels are sold alive, cooked, or cooked and shelled. They are also sold smoked and shelled, and preserved in oil or sauce. Mussels bought live must be known to have come from clean waters, be firmly closed and cooked within 3 days of being caught (mussels with cracked or half-opened shells which do not close when they are tapped must be thrown away).

The mussels must be completely cleaned of any beard-like filaments and parasites, which may be attached to them, before they are used. This is done by brushing and scraping under running water. To remove the beard – the cluster of fine dark hairs by which the shell attached itself to rocks – pull it firmly away from the shell. The beard should come away in one clump. If the mussels are consumed raw, they must be eaten the same day that they are bought. Cooked mussels may be kept for 48 hours in the refrigerator.

■ **Cooking** Mussels are often cooked very simply: *à la marinière* in cream, fried, au gratin or in an omelette. French regional mussel dishes include stuffed mussels from Ile de Ré, éclade and mouclade. Mussels also feature in a number of recipes from other parts of the world, including Spanish paella, *zuppa di cozze* from Liguria, Italy (soup made from garlic, celery and onion), English mussel broth (soup made from cider, milk, leeks, parsley and cream) and in various Belgian dishes, made with white wine or cream and parsley and *moules et frites*, a national dish.

RECIPES

fried mussels
Prepare some mussels *à la marinière*, remove from their shells and leave to cool. Marinate for 30 minutes in olive oil, lemon juice, chopped parsley and

pepper. Then dip in frying batter and cook in oil heated to 180°C (350°F). Drain them on paper towels and serve as an hors d'oeuvre (with lemon quarters) or with apéritifs (on cocktail sticks).

hors d'oeuvre of mussels à la ravigote

Cook some mussels à la marinière, remove from their shells and leave them to cool completely in a salad bowl. Prepare a well-seasoned vinaigrette and add to it some chopped hard-boiled (hard-cooked) eggs, parsley, chervil, tarragon and gherkins (pickled). Pour over the mussels and stir. Put in a cool place until time to serve.

iced mussel soup

Place a red (bell) pepper in a preheated oven at 240°C (475°F, gas 9) for a few minutes, to loosen the skin, then peel. Clean 1.5 kg (3¼ lb) mussels and cook over a brisk heat with half a glass of white wine for 2 minutes. Discard any mussels that do not open. Remove the shells and reserve the cooking liquid. Peel and seed a cucumber, cut it into dice, then place in a colander and sprinkle with coarse salt; leave to drain. Cut half a bunch of radishes into slices. Shell and skin 500 g (18 oz) broad (fava) beans. Wash and dice 5 mushroom caps (preferably wild) and sprinkle them with lemon juice.

Finely slice one half of the peeled red pepper and dice the other half. In a food processor, blend 6 peeled tomatoes, the slices of pepper, the mussel cooking juices, 2 tablespoons olive oil, a little sauce à l'anglaise and 10 drops of Tabasco sauce. Add the diced and sliced vegetables, the broad beans and the mussels. Adjust the seasoning. Refrigerate for several hours before serving.

mussel brochettes

Open some mussels over a brisk heat. Discard any that do not open. Remove the mussels from their shells and thread on skewers, alternating them with thin pieces of smoked bacon and tomato. Season with pepper. Cook under the grill (broiler) for about 1 minute.

mussels la bordelaise

Prepare 2 kg (4½ lb) mussels à la marinière, drain them, remove one shell from each mussel, and place them in a vegetable dish. Keep hot. Prepare 200 ml (7 fl oz, ¾ cup) meatless mirepoix*, moisten it with the strained liquid in which the mussels were cooked, and add 150 ml (¼ pint, ⅔ cup) fish velouté* and 2 tablespoons tomato purée (paste). Heat and reduce by one-third, then add the juice of half a lemon and whisk in 50 g (2 oz, ¼ cup) butter. Pour this hot sauce over the mussels, sprinkle with chopped parsley and serve immediately.

mussel salad

Prepare 1 kg (2¼ lb) mussels à la marinière, drain them and remove their shells. Set aside.

Boil, without peeling, 675 g (1½ lb) potatoes; peel while still hot and cut into cubes. Finely dice or shred 2–3 celery sticks. Peel and chop 1 shallot and 1 garlic clove and mix with plenty of chopped parsley. Mix all the ingredients together in a salad bowl.

Make a vinaigrette with 2 tablespoons hot vinegar, 6 tablespoons oil, 1 tablespoon Dijon mustard, salt and pepper. Pour this dressing over the salad and serve immediately.

mussels à la poulette

Prepare some mussels à la marinière, drain them, remove one of the shells from each mussel and place in a vegetable dish. Strain the cooking liquid through a fine sieve, reduce by half and add 300 ml (½ pint, 1¼ cups) poulette* sauce. Add a little lemon juice, pour over the mussels and sprinkle with chopped parsley.

mussel sauce

Prepare 500 g (18 oz) small mussels à la marinière with 300 ml (½ pint, 1¼ cups) white wine; remove from their shells and keep the mussels hot. Strain the cooking liquid and reduce it to 2 tablespoons. Let it cool until lukewarm, then beat in 2–3 egg yolks, followed by 100 g (4 oz, ½ cup) butter and a few drops of lemon juice. Add the mussels and adjust the seasoning. This sauce accompanies white fish or poached fillets of fish.

mussels in cream

Prepare 2 kg (4½ lb) mussels à la marinière, drain them, remove one of the shells from each mussel and place them in a vegetable dish. Keep hot. Strain the cooking liquid through a fine cloth. Prepare 300 ml (½ pint, 1¼ cups) light béchamel* sauce, add 200 ml (7 fl oz, ¾ cup) double (heavy) cream and the cooking liquid from the mussels, and reduce by at least one-third. Season with salt and pepper and pour this hot sauce over the mussels.

The béchamel cream sauce may be flavoured with curry or 1 tablespoon chopped onion, softened in butter.

other recipes See attereau, brochette, croquette, fritot, marinière, mouclade.

MUST Grape juice, skins, seeds and pulp before it has been acted on by the yeasts that convert the natural sugar in it to alcohol. See wine.

MUSTARD A herbaceous plant, originating from the Mediterranean region, of which there are numerous species. Several have edible leaves, some produce an edible oil and three provide seeds which are used to prepare the yellow condiment of the same name. The three varieties are black mustard (spicy and piquant), brown mustard (less piquant) and white, or yellow, mustard (not very piquant but more bitter and more pungent). These seeds contain two elements, myronate and myrosin: when crushed in the presence of water, they release a volatile and piquant essence which gives mustard its distinctive flavour.

Mustard has been known and used since ancient times. Black mustard seed is mentioned in the Bible; the plant, cultivated in Palestine, was introduced into Egypt, where its crushed seeds were served as a condiment (as they still are in the East). The Greeks and Romans used the seeds in the form of flour or mixed in tuna-fish brine (*muria*), for spicing meat and fish. Mustard also has an ancient history throughout Europe. The medicinal properties of the plant were also highly valued in the Middle Ages. Commercial production began in Dijon by the mid-14th century and in Britain in 1727.

French mustards are sold in the form of a paste; the main centre for production is Dijon, followed by Meaux, Orléans and Bordeaux. Dijon mustard is prepared with verjuice or wine must and white wine, Orléans mustard with wine vinegar, and Bordeaux mustard, which is milder, flavoured with herbs and brown in colour, with grape must. Meaux mustard, also known as *moutarde à l'ancienne*, owes its flavour and colour to coarsely crushed seeds of various colours and is prepared with vinegar. English mustard is sold either as a fine powder consisting of white mustard with turmeric added, which is mixed with water before use, or ready-mixed in jars or tubes. It has a strong flavour. German mustard is similar to Bordeaux mustard and American mustard is coloured with turmeric and is usually very mild and sweet in flavour.

Mustard is a condiment that can be flavoured in many different ways: for example with tarragon, garlic, mixed herbs, horseradish, chilli, honey, paprika and fruits. In addition to its uses as a condiment for meat and charcuterie, mustard is used in cookery for coating rabbit, pork, chicken and oily fish before cooking. It may be added to the cooking stock of a ragoût or a blanquette, and it is the basis of numerous dressings and sauces, both hot and cold (such as vinaigrette, mayonnaise, rémoulade, devilled sauce, dijonnaise, Cambridge). In English cookery, mustard sauce is often enriched with egg yolk or flavoured with anchovy essence, to accompany fish. Cremona mustard, from Italy, resembles chutney rather than mustard, as it is made from fruits macerated in a sweet-and-sour sauce containing mustard; it generally accompanies boiled meat.

RECIPES

mustard and dill dressing
Whisk 2 tablespoons Dijon mustard with 1 tablespoon caster (superfine) sugar and 3 tablespoons cider vinegar in a bowl. Add a little salt and pepper and whisk well. Gradually pour in 150 ml (¼ pint, ⅔ cup) olive oil, whisking continuously to make a thick dressing. Stir in 3 tablespoons finely chopped dill. Taste for seasoning and sweet-sour balance; add a squeeze of lemon juice to sharpen the dressing, if liked. Serve with fish salads, poached or smoked salmon, or gravlax. The dressing also goes well with poached eggs or cold hard-boiled (hard-cooked) eggs in salads.

mustard sauce
Melt 2 tablespoons butter in a small saucepan, then blend in 2 tablespoons flour and mix well. Pour in 250 ml (8 fl oz, 1 cup) milk, beat and leave to cook over a brisk heat until the sauce thickens. Lower the heat and simmer for 3 minutes, then add 4 tablespoons double (heavy) cream, 1 teaspoon white vinegar, 1 teaspoon English mustard powder, salt and a little pepper. Serve at once with poached fish.

mustard sauce (for cold fish)
Heat some cream to reduce it by one-third. Cool, then add to it a quarter of its volume of Dijon mustard and a squeeze of lemon juice. Whisk until light and foamy. Adjust the seasoning.

mustard sauce (for grills)
Peel and finely chop 50 g (2 oz, ⅓ cup) onions and soften them in butter. Add 150 ml (¼ pint, ⅔ cup) white wine, salt and pepper and reduce until almost dry. Then add 250 ml (8 fl oz, 1 cup) demi-glace* sauce and reduce by one-third. Blend in 1 tablespoon Dijon mustard, a squeeze of lemon juice and 1 tablespoon butter. Adjust the seasoning.

rich wholegrain mustard and red wine marinade (for meat)
In a small saucepan, mix 3 tablespoons mild wholegrain mustard with 1 finely chopped garlic clove and 2 tablespoons brandy. Add 1 finely chopped shallot and 2 bay leaves, crumpling them slightly. Pour in 250 ml (8 fl oz, 1 cup) red wine and season with salt and pepper. heat gently, stirring continuously, until the mixture boils. Simmer for 2 minutes, then remove the pan from the heat, cover the marinade and leave it to cool completely. When cold, use for marinating meat steaks of chops (beef, lamb or pork) prior to grilling or stewing meat before preparing a casserole. The mustard marinade also goes well with venison.

MUSTARD POT A small pot in which mustard is served at table; it sometimes forms part of a cruet. Its lid is notched to allow the mustard spoon to pass through. The oldest models, which are made of pewter and very large, date from the 14th century. In the 17th century mustard pots were made of silver, silver-gilt and even gold. It was only after the 18th century that mustard pots were manufactured in porcelain, pottery, glass or wood.

MUTTON The meat from sheep over a year old. The criteria of quality are firm, compact, dark-red flesh and hard fat, pearly white in colour and plentiful around the kidneys. Mutton is at its best at the end of the winter and in the spring; in summer (shearing time) the smell of wool grease tends to impregnate the flesh.

New Zealand is the greatest worldwide exporter of mutton and lamb. Australia and Great Britain are also large producers and exporters (largely to the halal market). Consumption of mutton in Great Britain was popular, as witnessed by such traditional dishes as Irish stew, mutton broth, haggis and Lancashire hotpot. Mutton is essential meat in North Africa, the Middle and Near East and also in the Indian subcontinent. Able to subsist in a rugged environment, the sheep is a most useful animal, supplying milk, leather, meat and wool. Mutton itself is eaten much less in Western countries than formerly because sheep are slaughtered much younger and people now prefer the more tender and succulent meat of lamb.

Mutton was highly prized in ancient times. For centuries the production of wool made it necessary to keep the animals for a long time before slaughter and the oldest mutton recipes are devised to tenderize the meat and eliminate the taste of wool grease. Examples include boiled leg of mutton in England, marinated and larded mutton in France, whole roast sheep in Mediterranean countries. Sautéed and braised ragoûts, which make up the majority of recipes for mutton, are usually accompanied by starchy foods, to counteract the fattiness of the meat. For roasts and grills it is generally better to use lamb.

■ **Cooking mutton** The joints for roasting are cut from the leg (shank or fillet end), the saddle (double unseparated loin), the best end, and the shoulder (sometimes boned). As well as being roasted, the leg may also be boiled as in the traditional English fashion and served accompanied by caper sauce.

The pieces for grilling (broiling) are essentially chops (chump, loin, or neck).

Pieces of mutton for cooking on skewers are cut from the breast, shoulder or neck.

Cuts for braising, sautéing, or stewing are supplied by the neck, the breast and the shoulder.

Certain items of sheep's offal are in great demand in France: the brains, kidneys, tongue and feet.

RECIPES

braised mutton cutlets
Trim some thick cutlets and season with salt and pepper. Butter a shallow frying pan, line it with bacon rinds from which all the fat has been removed and add some thinly sliced carrot and onion. Arrange the cutlets in the pan, cover and cook gently for 10 minutes. Add enough white wine to just cover, then reduce with the lid removed. Moisten with a few spoonfuls of brown gravy or stock, add a bouquet garni and cook with the lid on for about 45 minutes. Drain the cutlets and keep them hot on the serving dish. Surround with boiled Brussels sprouts (the garnish may also consist of chestnuts, sautéed potatoes or a vegetable purée). Reduce the braising stock, strain it, and pour it over the cutlets.

mutton broth
Finely dice a carrot, a turnip, the white part of 2 leeks, 1 celery stick and 1 onion. Soften this brunoise in butter, then add 2 litres (3½ pints, 9 cups) white consommé*. Add 300 g (11 oz) breast and collar of mutton and 100 g (4 oz, ½ cup) pearl barley blanched for 8 minutes in boiling water. Cover and cook gently for 1½ hours. Remove and dice the meat and put back in the soup. Sprinkle with chopped parsley just before serving.

mutton cutlets à la fermière
Season 6 thick cutlets with salt and pepper. Fry them lightly in butter in a shallow flameproof serving dish. Add 300 ml (½ pint, 1¼ cups) vegetable fondue*, 6 tablespoons fresh green peas and 150 ml (¼ pint, ⅔ cup) white wine. Reduce, then add a bouquet garni and 200 ml (7 fl oz, ¾ cup) brown stock and cook with the lid on for 20 minutes. Then add about 20 small potatoes and continue cooking with the lid on for a further 35 minutes. Serve in the cooking dish.

mutton cutlets à la Villeroi
Braise the cutlets and leave them to cool in their stock. Drain them, coat them in Villeroi sauce, then dip them in beaten egg and breadcrumbs. Fry until golden in clarified butter and serve with a Périgueux or a tomato sauce.

mutton cutlets chasseur
Sauté 6 cutlets in butter in a shallow frying pan, then drain and keep them hot. Place in the pan 1 tablespoon chopped shallots and 6 large thinly sliced mushrooms and stir for a few moments over a brisk heat. Sprinkle with 150 ml (¼ pint, ⅔ cup) white wine and reduce until almost dry. Pour in 250 ml (8 fl oz, 1 cup) thickened brown stock and 1 tablespoon tomato sauce, boil for a few moments, then add 15 g (½ oz, 1 tablespoon butter) and ½ teaspoon chopped chervil and tarragon. Coat the cutlets with this sauce.

mutton fillets in red wine
Cut the fillets of mutton into small squares. Season with salt and pepper, then cook them quickly in very hot butter, keeping them slightly pink inside. Drain them and put on one side. In the same butter quickly cook (for 6 fillets) 125 g (4½ oz, 1½ cups) thinly sliced mushrooms and add them to the meat. Make a sauce by adding 300 ml (½ pint, 1¼ cups) red wine to the pan juice, reduce, then add several spoonfuls of brown veal gravy. Reduce once again, add some butter and strain. Mix the meat and the mushrooms with this sauce and serve very hot.

ragoût of mutton à la bonne femme
Cut 800 g (1¾ lb) mutton into cubes, season with salt and pepper, and fry quickly in oil with a chopped onion. Skim off some of the oil in which the meat was cooked, dust the meat with a pinch of caster (superfine) sugar and 2 tablespoons flour

and mix. Then add a small crushed garlic clove and moisten with I litre (I¾ pints, 4⅓ cups) water or stock. Add 3 tablespoons tomato purée (paste) or 100 g (4 oz, ½ cup) fresh tomatoes, peeled and crushed, and a bouquet garni. Cook, covered, in a preheated oven at 220°C (425°F, gas 7) for I hour. Drain the meat and reserve the cooking stock (strained and skimmed).

Return the meat to the pan and add 400 g (I4 oz, 2½ cups) potatoes cut into olive shapes, 24 glazed baby (pearl) onions, and 125 g (4½ oz, ½ cup) streaky (slab) bacon (diced, blanched and lightly fried). Pour the cooking stock over the ragoût. Bring to the boil, cover and finish cooking in the oven for I hour. Arrange in a timbale or in a round dish.

This ragoût may also be prepared with celeriac (cut into small pieces and blanched), kohlrabi, haricot (navy) beans, or chick peas. Alternatively it may be served with a macédoine of vegetables, a ratatouille or boiled rice.

other recipes See *Champvallon, chick pea, couscous, feet and trotters, gigot, halicot, kidneys, lamb, Maintenon, moussaka, navarin, noisette, shoulder, tongue.*

MUZZLE The projecting nose and jaw of certain animals. The muzzle of an ox or pig is used chiefly in charcuterie. Both are prepared in the same way as ox tongue. In France, ox muzzle is usually sold ready prepared and it is used as a cold hors d'oeuvre, served in a herb-flavoured vinaigrette. Pig's muzzle is also sold as a cooked meat speciality, similar to brawn (head cheese); it is prepared using the whole head (and sometimes the tongue and the tail), which is boned, cooked, pressed and moulded. In Brazil, the most popular dish is *feijoada* which consists of pig's muzzle cooked in a stew.

MYCOPROTEIN A protein-rich type of manufactured fungi which is processed to make Quorn. See *Quorn.*

MYRTLE A Mediterranean shrub whose aromatic evergreen leaves and purple-black berries have a flavour like that of juniper and rosemary. Myrtle leaves are used particularly in Corsican and Sardinian cookery, to flavour roast thrushes, boar, charcuterie and bouillabaisse. The Romans used myrtle leaves and berries extensively for flavouring ragoûts and certain wines.

MYSÖST A Scandinavian cheese made from cow's-milk whey (20% fat content). Mysöst is a brown compressed cheese: the water from the whey is evaporated leaving only the whey albumen and lactose, which acquires the consistency of very hard butter and a slightly sweetish flavour. See also *Gjetöst.*

N

NAGE An aromatic court-bouillon in which crayfish, langoustes, small lobsters or scallops are cooked. They may be served either hot or cold in the cooking stock, which is either seasoned, or mixed with double (heavy) cream. Dishes prepared in this way are described as *à la nage* (literally, 'swimming').

RECIPES

crayfish à la nage
Prepare a nage as described, but keep it hot. Immerse 48 crayfish (either cleaned or not) in the boiling liquid and cook for 8 minutes, stirring occasionally. Season with a pinch of cayenne and leave the crayfish in the cooking stock until completely cold. Serve in a large bowl with the cooking stock.

Alternatively, drain the crayfish and prepare a sauce by reducing the cooking stock and stirring in some butter. Pour the sauce over the crayfish and sprinkle with chopped parsley. This method is described as *à la liégeoise*.

nage of scallops with lemon thyme ♦
Remove 2.5 kg (5½ lb) carefully cleaned scallops from their shells. Remove their beards. Wash again several times and put in the refrigerator. Finely snip a bunch of chives and dice the flesh of 1 lemon. Squeeze the juice of 1 lemon. Chop or dice 400 g (14 oz) carrots, 1 medium leek and 300 g (11 oz) celeriac or 2 celery sticks. Bring to the boil 400 ml (14 fl oz, 1¾ cups) fish stock, lightly seasoned with salt and pepper, with 200 ml (7 fl oz, ¾ cup) white wine. Add the vegetables, 4 sprigs lemon thyme and the lemon juice. Bring back to the boil, then reduce the heat. Add the scallops and 100 ml (4 fl oz,

7 tablespoons) double (heavy) cream and simmer gently for another 2 minutes (overcooked, the scallops would become hard). Remove from the heat, discard the thyme sprigs, and incorporate the chives and diced lemon. Arrange the scallops in soup bowls, and garnish with chervil or parsley.

NALESNIKI Stuffed pancakes from Russia or Poland. Soft cheese is a typical filling around which the pancakes are folded, then coated in egg and breadcrumbs or sometimes a thin batter and fried until crisp. The pancakes can also be stuffed with cabbage, chicken or meat and are a traditional accompaniment for borsch.

Although usually savoury, nalesniki are served as a dessert when filled with sweetened soft cheese or jam.

NAN Also known as naan, this Indian bread is soft, flat, pear-shaped and leavened. It is made from plain wheat flour and cooked in a tandoor oven. The term comes from the Persian word for bread and this type of bread is common in many Central Asian countries, including Pakistan and Afghanistan. The precise flour, mix, shape and cooking method varies according to the country or region of origin.

NANETTE The name given to a classic dish of lamb cutlets, veal escalopes (scallops) or calves' sweetbreads, garnished with small artichoke hearts and mushroom caps braised in butter. The former are stuffed with a chiffonnade of lettuce in cream, the latter with a salpicon of truffles blended with a reduced demi-glace. The dish is served with a sauce made from the pan juices deglazed with Marsala and blended with chicken velouté, cream and concentrated chicken stock.

NANTAIS A Breton cow's-milk cheese made with pressed curds (40% fat content). It has a smooth washed rind. The paste is springy to the touch, pale to deep yellow in colour, and has a pronounced flavour. Nantais is manufactured in 9 cm (3½ in) squares, 4 cm (1½ in) deep. It is also known as 'Curé' or 'Fromage du Curé' because it was first made in the 19th century by a priest from the Vendée.

NANTAIS A cake made of pâte sablée (similar to shortbread dough) mixed with ground almonds or chopped crystallized (candied) fruit and flavoured with kirsch or rum. It may be baked as a large flat cake or as small biscuits (cookies) cut out with a round fluted pastry (cookie) cutter and decorated with chopped almonds, chopped crystallized fruit or raisins.

RECIPE

gâteau nantais

Cream 150 g (5 oz, ⅔ cup) butter with a spatula. Mix 250 g (9 oz, 2¼ cups) plain (all-purpose) flour, 150 g (5 oz, ⅔ cup) sugar and a pinch of salt in a bowl. Add the butter, 3 egg yolks, 1 tablespoon rum and 125 g (4½ oz, 1 cup) diced candied angelica. Work these ingredients together to make a smooth paste, roll it into a ball, flatten it out with the palms of the hands, again roll into a ball, and leave in a cool place for 2 hours. Roll the paste out into a circle 2 cm (¾ in) thick and place it on an oiled baking sheet. Mix 1 egg yolk with 1 tablespoon water and brush it over the surface of the gâteau. Sprinkle with chopped almonds. Cook in a preheated oven at 200°C (400°F, gas 6) for 35 minutes. Serve when cold.

NANTAISE, À LA The name given to various dishes served with a white wine sauce enriched with butter. Scallops *à la nantaise* are poached, sliced and then reheated in white wine together with poached oysters and mussels. They are then served in the scallop shells with the sauce poured over, and glazed under the grill (broiler). Chopped mushrooms and peeled (shelled) shrimps coated with a mixture of velouté and hollandaise sauce can also be added. Grilled (broiled) fish *à la nantaise* is served with a sauce made with white wine and shallots and thickened with butter. Roast or braised meat *à la nantaise* is garnished with glazed turnips, garden peas and creamed potatoes.

RECIPE

red mullet à la nantaise

Put 150 ml (¼ pint, ⅔ cup) white wine and 2 or 3 finely chopped shallots into a pan and boil down to reduce. Trim and gut (clean) 4 mullet, but do not remove the livers. Wipe the fish, season with salt and pepper, brush with oil and grill (broil). Then remove the livers from the fish, mash them and beat them into the reduced sauce together with a few drops of lemon juice and about 50 g (2 oz,

¼ cup) butter. Pour the sauce into a long serving dish and arrange the grilled mullet on top. Garnish with slices of lemon.

NANTES CAKE A small, round, French cake flavoured with lemon or orange and cooked in a tin (pan) coated with slivered almonds. The baked cakes are glazed with apricot jam, iced (frosted) with fondant and dusted with coloured sugar grains.

RECIPE

Nantes cakes

Cream 100 g (4 oz, ½ cup) butter, 100 g (4 oz, ½ cup) caster (superfine) sugar, a pinch of salt, ½ teaspoon bicarbonate of soda (baking soda) and the zest of 1 lemon or 1 orange until pale and soft. Beat in 2 eggs and 125 g (4½ oz, 1 cup) sifted plain (all-purpose) flour, beating the mixture well. Butter some tartlet moulds and sprinkle with slivered almonds. Pour in the mixture and cook in a preheated oven at 190°C (375°F, gas 5) for about 20 minutes. Turn the cakes out on to a wire rack. Coat them with warmed apricot jam, then ice (frost) them with fondant flavoured with maraschino and dust with coloured sugar grains.

NANTUA, À LA The name given to various dishes containing crayfish or crayfish tails, either whole or in the form of a savoury butter, a purée, a mousse or a thick sauce. These dishes often contain truffles as well. Nantua is a town in Bugey, with a centuries-old reputation for gastronomy.

RECIPES

fillets of sole Nantua

Poach some fillets of sole in a little court-bouillon made with white wine or concentrated fish stock. Arrange them in a circle on a serving dish and garnish the centre of the circle with a ragoût of crayfish tails. Coat with Nantua sauce and garnish with mushroom slices.

Nantua sauce

Make 200 ml (7 fl oz, ¾ cup) béchamel* sauce. Add an equal volume of strained crayfish cooking liquor and single (light) cream. Boil to reduce by one-third. While the liquid is boiling, beat in 100 g (4 oz, ½ cup) crayfish butter*, 1 teaspoon brandy and a tiny pinch of cayenne pepper. Rub through a very fine sieve and use in the appropriate recipe.

ragoût of crayfish tails à la Nantua

Cook 150 ml (¼ pint, ⅔ cup) vegetable mirepoix* in a pan for about 10 minutes. Add 48 crayfish, season with salt and pepper, and cook until the crayfish turn red. Moisten with 200 ml (7 fl oz, ¾ cup) dry white wine, cover and cook for 8 minutes.

Nage of scallops with lemon thyme,
see page 783.

Drain the crayfish and shell the tails.

Pound the mirepoix and the shells in a mortar, then add 200 ml (7 fl oz, ¾ cup) béchamel* sauce to the resulting purée. Set the sauce aside.

Put the crayfish tails into a small sauté pan with 15 g (½ oz, 1 tablespoon) butter. Heat through without allowing them to brown, add 1 tablespoon flour and mix well. Stir in 2 tablespoons brandy and 6 tablespoons double (heavy) cream and cook over a low heat for 7–8 minutes. Then add either all or part of the prepared sauce. Remove from the heat and incorporate 65 g (2½ oz, 5 tablespoons) butter.

This ragoût may be used to fill vol-au-vent, a timbale, or pastry barquettes. Add more crayfish if necessary, depending on the recipe.

other recipes See *bouchée (savoury), choux paste, croûte, mousse.*

NAPOLITAIN A large cylindrical or hexagonal French cake with a hollow centre. It is made of layers of almond pastry sandwiched together with apricot jam, redcurrant jelly or other preserve, and usually lavishly decorated with marzipan (almond paste) and crystallized (candied) fruits. It was formerly used as the set piece of elaborate buffets. The name of the cake suggests that it originated from Naples, but it was more probably created by Carême, who made a number of elaborate cakes for set pieces and named them himself.

Although the large cake is rarely seen today, small biscuits (cookies) known as *fonds napolitains* are still made in France; they are decorated with butter cream or jam.

Napolitain or neapolitan is the name given to very small tablets of fine, often bitter, chocolate served with coffee. Miniature bars of milk chocolate are also sold as neapolitans.

RECIPES

Napolitain cake
Pound 375 g (13 oz, 2½ cups) sweet almonds in a mortar, together with 5 g (¼ oz, 1 teaspoon) bitter almonds, if desired. Gradually incorporate 1 egg white to prevent the almonds from becoming oily. Then add 200 g (7 oz, 1 cup) caster (superfine) sugar, the very finely grated zest of 1 lemon, 250 g (9 oz, generous 1 cup) softened butter and 500 g (18 oz, 4½ cups) sifted plain (all-purpose) flour. Work all the ingredients together in the mortar. Add 4 whole eggs, one by one, until the dough is very smooth but still firm.

Leave the dough in a cool place for 2 hours. Then roll it out to a thickness of 1 cm (½ in) on a lightly oiled surface and cut out circles 20–25 cm (8–10 in) in diameter. Leaving 2 rounds whole, cut out the centres of the remaining rounds with a pastry (cookie) cutter 6 cm (2½ in) in diameter. Place all the rounds on a baking sheet, in batches if necessary, and bake in a preheated oven at 200°C (400°F, gas 6) for 20–25 minutes.

When completely cold, cover one of the whole rounds with very reduced sieved apricot jam, then build up the cake by placing the rounds with the centres cut out one on top of the other, covering each of them with apricot jam. Place the remaining whole round on the top and cover it with apricot jam. Put the cake in a cool place. Finish by covering the cake with marzipan (almond paste) or royal icing and decorate the top with crystallized (candied) apricot halves.

Napolitain biscuits
Rub 250 g (9 oz, generous 1 cup) chilled butter into 250 g (9 oz, 2¼ cups) plain (all-purpose) flour until the mixture resembles breadcrumbs. Add 250 g (9 oz, 1 generous cup) caster (superfine) sugar, 250 g (9 oz, 2¼ cups) ground almonds and 2 or 3 egg yolks. Mix quickly without kneading and roll out to a thickness of about 1 cm (½ in). Cut into rounds with a pastry (cookie) cutter and bake in a preheated oven at 200°C (400°F, gas 6) for about 10 minutes. Decorate the biscuits (cookies) with butter cream or jam when cold.

NAPOLITAINE, À LA A method of serving buttered macaroni or spaghetti either in a tomato sauce or with peeled, chopped and seeded tomatoes, sprinkled with grated cheese. It can be served either as a main dish or as an accompaniment to small cuts of meat.

NAPOLITAINE SAUCE This sauce, invented by Carême, is made with horseradish, ham, Madeira, espagnole sauce, redcurrant jelly, raisins and (sometimes) candied citron.

This sauce has nothing in common with Neapolitan cooking, which is characterized by the famous pizzaiola sauce, consisting of peeled, chopped, seeded tomatoes; garlic, basil or marjoram; and olive oil. It is served with pasta, grilled (broiled) dishes and pizzas.

RECIPE

napolitaine sauce
Put 1 tablespoon grated horseradish, a little chopped lean ham, a seasoned bouquet garni, a little ground white pepper, some grated nutmeg and 120 ml (4½ fl oz, ½ cup) dry Madeira into a pan. Reduce over a very low heat. Remove the bouquet garni and stir in 2 tablespoons consommé and 2 tablespoons espagnole* sauce. When the sauce has reduced, strain and reduce it again, gradually adding 120 ml (4½ fl oz, ½ cup) Málaga and 3 tablespoons redcurrant jelly. Just before serving, add a little butter and game glaze.

This sauce goes well with game and venison. If well-washed sultanas (seedless white raisins) are added, the sauce can be served with braised or roast fillet (sirloin) of beef *à la napolitaine.* A little candied citron rind, diced and blanched, may also be added.

NAPPER The French term used to mean 'to mask or cover a food with a sauce'.

NASHI PEAR Also known as Asian pear, this fruit is round rather than pear-shaped, with crisp, white, very juicy flesh having a pearlike flavour. The brown-red speckled skin resembles that on russet apples in colour and has a coarse texture.

The Tientsin pear is another type of related Asian pear with a similar texture and flavour to the nashi pear, but an elongated shape and paler, speckled yellow skin.

NASI GORENG An Indonesian rice dish. Finely chopped onion, garlic and chilli are fried in oil, then cooked rice is added with diced cooked pork or chicken and peeled (shelled) cooked prawns (shrimp). The fried rice is served garnished with strips of freshly cooked plain omelette laid in a lattice pattern on top, accompanied by cucumber and roasted peanuts.

The Dutch adopted this dish during their colonial period and adapted it to European tastes; it is known in the Netherlands as *rijsttafel* (literally, 'rice table').

NASI KUNING Javanese festival dish. Rice coloured yellow is formed into a cone shape and presented as the centre of a buffet with fried chicken, sweetened raw vegetables, chopped-beef meatballs and potatoes. The whole is accompanied by various spicy condiments.

NASTURTIUM An ornamental plant with edible leaves, flowers and seeds. The leaves have a strong peppery, slightly hot flavour; the flowers are similar but far milder. Both can be used in salads or as a garnish. The seeds can be pickled and used as a condiment. The flower buds and seeds, picked when soft and pickled in tarragon vinegar, can be used as a substitute for capers. They are a little tougher, but peppery, slightly mustard-like and more aromatic. Tuber nasturtiums, which come from Peru, yield tubers that can be pickled and used to garnish hors d'oeuvre and cold meats.

NATURE A French term used to describe dishes which are served plainly cooked with no additions other than those necessary to make them edible.

The term is applied chiefly to boiled or steamed unseasoned vegetables, but also to meat or fish that has been grilled (broiled) *au naturel* (that is, without butter or sauce), plain omelettes without garnish or filling, and fresh fruit served either as a dessert (such as strawberries or raspberries) or as a first course (such as melon).

NAVARIN A ragoût of lamb or mutton with potatoes and/or various other vegetables, particularly young spring vegetables (when it becomes *navarin printanier*). The dish is popularly supposed to have been named after the Battle of Navarino, at which British, French and Russian ships destroyed the Turkish and Egyptian fleets on 20 October 1827, during the Greek War of Independence. However, the dish existed well before 1827, and was more likely to have been named after the *navet* (turnip), originally the main accompanying vegetable. Some chefs therefore use the name navarin, quite justifiably, for other types of ragoût (such as shellfish, poultry and monkfish) garnished with turnips.

RECIPE

navarin of lamb ♦
Cut 800 g (1¾ lb) shoulder of lamb into 6 pieces and 800 g (1¾ lb) neck of lamb into 6 slices. Heat 2 tablespoons oil in a large flameproof casserole. Brown the pieces and slices of lamb in it. Take out, drain and remove two-thirds of the fat. Put the meat back in the casserole and sprinkle with 1 teaspoon sugar on top. Stir well, sprinkle in 1 tablespoon flour and cook for 3 minutes while stirring all the time. Add 200 ml (7 fl oz, ¾ cup) white wine and season with salt, pepper and nutmeg. Cook over a moderate heat.

Peel, seed and crush 2 tomatoes. Peel and chop 2 garlic cloves. Add these ingredients to the casserole with a bouquet garni and enough water to cover the meat. As soon as it starts boiling, cover, reduce the heat and simmer for 45 minutes.

Peel and scrape 300 g (11 oz) new carrots and 200 g (7 oz) new turnips. Peel 100 g (4 oz) small white onions. Brown all these vegetables in 25 g (1 oz, 2 tablespoons) butter in sauté pan. Cut 300 g (11 oz) green beans into short lengths and steam for 10–12 minutes. Add the carrots, turnips, onions and 300 g (11 oz, 2 cups) shelled petits pois to the casserole. Stir and cover again. Continue cooking for 20–25 minutes. Add the green beans 5 minutes before serving and stir in very gently. Serve very hot.

NAVARRA Navarre in French, this is an historic wine region in the north of Spain producing good quality, mainly red, wines from Garnacha (Grenache) blended with Tempranillo, Cabernet Sauvignon, Merlot and Syrah.

NAVETTE A dry, boat-shaped cake made from butter, flour and sugar syrup flavoured with orange-flower water. In Marseille navettes are traditionally made at Candlemas and sold at the *four des navettes*, near the Abbaye Saint-Victor. They have been made to the same recipe for over a century.

The cake is believed to have originated in ancient Egypt, and its shape is thought to represent the boat that carried Isis, the goddess of fertility and harvests (the name comes from the Latin *navis*, a boat). However, another theory suggests that the shape represents the boat that brought the Virgin of the Sea to the Camargue, together with Lazarus, whom Jesus raised from the dead.

Navettes can also be found at Albi, where they are

sometimes made with crystallized (candied) fruit or almonds. In this region the shape represents the weaver's shuttle, which was the secret emblem of the Cathars, a medieval heretical Christian sect.

NEAPOLITAN SLICE
A slice of ice-cream cake made with mousse mixture and ordinary ice cream. Neapolitan ice cream consists of three layers, each of a different colour and flavour (chocolate, strawberry and vanilla), moulded into a block and cut into slices. Neapolitan ice-cream makers were famous in Paris at the beginning of the 19th century, especially Tortoni, creator of numerous ice-cream cakes.

NEBBIOLO
A black grape variety grown mainly in the Piedmont region in northern Italy and used in the production of one of Italy's finest wines, Barolo. There are some plantings in Victoria, Australia, and Argentina.

NECK
Also called 'scrag', this part of the neck, shoulder and ribs of slaughtered animals provides economical cuts of meat. The neck contains a lot of fat and gristle and must be cooked slowly. Neck of beef is used in stews and carbonades, and may be braised. Neck of veal, lamb or mutton is usually cut into fairly large cubes and used for braised dishes or stews such as blanquettes, navarins and Irish stew. Neck of pork is used only to make sausagemeat.

Stuffed neck of duck or goose is a speciality of south-west France. The bones are carefully removed from the neck, then the skin is sewn up at one end and stuffed with a mixture of chicken and pork meat, a little foie gras, Armagnac and truffle juice. It is cooked in duck or goose fat. The stuffed neck is eaten hot or cold, with a Périgueux sauce.

In poultry the neck forms part of the giblets. Goose necks may be eaten stuffed.

NECTAR
In Greek mythology, the drink of the gods, which conferred immortality on those who drank it. In the botanical sense, nectar is the sugary liquid produced by flowers and turned into honey by bees.

In the French soft-drinks industry, the term 'nectar of . . .' followed by the name of a fruit is applied only to sweetened fruit juices with added water, the juice being considered unpalatable in its pure state because it is too acid or too thick. The most common fruits from which nectars are made are apricots, peaches, pears, guavas, sour cherries and blackcurrants. In the United States, in particular, undiluted fruit juice is known as nectar, as are certain mixtures of fruit juices.

NECTARINE
A variety of peach with a smooth skin, reddish tinged with yellow, and firm sweet juicy flesh. The flavour is a mixture of plum and peach. Nectarines are eaten plain and can be used instead of peaches in desserts. They are often preferred to peaches as a dessert fruit or snack because of their smooth, rather than velvet-like, skin.

NÈGRE EN CHEMISE
A chilled chocolate dessert covered with Chantilly cream.

RECIPE

nègre en chemise
Melt 250 g (9 oz, 9 squares) chocolate in a double saucepan (boiler) with 1 tablespoon milk. Soften 250 g (9 oz, generous 1 cup) butter with a spatula. Mix the melted chocolate with the butter, beat thoroughly, and then add 5 tablespoons sugar and 4 or 5 egg yolks. Whisk 5 egg whites until very stiff and fold them carefully into the mixture. Oil a bombe or charlotte mould, pour in the chocolate cream and refrigerate for at least 12 hours.

Just before serving, make some Chantilly cream by whisking 200 ml (7 fl oz, ¾ cup) double (heavy) cream and 5 tablespoons very cold fresh milk, adding 40 g (1½ oz, ⅓ cup) icing (confectioners') sugar and either 1 teaspoon vanilla sugar or a few drops of vanilla essence (extract). Unmould the chocolate cream on to a serving dish, then pipe over Chantilly cream, taking care that the chocolate shows through in places.

NEIGE
The French term for egg whites whisked until they form stiff peaks. They are used to prepare many different desserts and pastries, such as meringues, soufflés and floating islands.

Neige is also a type of sorbet made with red fruit juice and sugar. *Neige de Florence* (Florentine snow) – feather-light flakes of pasta – is used in consommés and clear soup. It is served separately and stirred into the soup by the person eating it.

NÉLUSKO
An iced petit four consisting of a stoned (pitted) cherry steeped in brandy, filled with Bar-le-Duc redcurrant jelly and covered with fondant icing (frosting) flavoured with cherry brandy. Nélusko is also the name of a chocolate and praline bombe glacée flavoured with Curaçao.

According to the *Dictionnaire de l'Académie des gastronomes*, the name, which was given to one of the heroes in Meyerbeer's opera *L'Orientale*, was originally applied to a sweet soup made from coconut, arrowroot and almonds.

NEM
Fried Vietnamese pie consisting of a galette stuffed with vegetables, aromatic herbs and possibly eggs, meat or chopped crabmeat. In China nem is prepared with a galette made from maize.

NEMOURS
A garnish for small entrées, consisting of duchess potatoes, buttered garden peas, and shaped and glazed carrots. It is also the name of a dish of poached fillets of sole coated with shrimp sauce, topped with a slice of truffle and garnished with quenelles and small mushrooms in normande sauce. Nemours soup is made with potato purée moistened with consommé, thickened with cream and egg yolk, and garnished with tapioca.

Navarin of lamb, see page 787.

NEROLI A volatile oil extracted from orange blossom and used in perfumery. The name is derived from the family name of a 17th-century Italian princess, Anne-Marie de la Tremoïlle of Neroli, who is thought to have created the perfume. Neroli, which has a bland, though penetrating, scent, is also used in confectionery and in the manufacture of certain liqueurs.

NESSELRODE The name given to various cooked dishes and pastries, all containing chestnut purée, dedicated to Count Nesselrode, the 19th-century Russian diplomat who negotiated the Treaty of Paris after the Crimean War. Braised calves' sweetbreads or sautéed roebuck steaks in poivrade (pepper) sauce are served with salted chestnut purée. For consommé Nesselrode, the purée is used to fill profiteroles which are served with a game consommé.

Among the desserts, one of the best-known is Nesselrode pudding, created by M. Mouy, head chef to Count Nesselrode. It consists of custard cream mixed with chestnut purée, crystallized (candied) fruit, currants and sultanas (golden raisins) and whipped cream. In bombe Nesselrode, the bombe mousse mixture contains kirsch-flavoured chestnut purée and the mould is lined with vanilla ice cream.

RECIPES

consommé Nesselrode
Prepare some game consommé and make some small savoury choux buns. Mix some chestnut purée with one-third of its weight of onion purée and use the mixture to fill half of the choux. Fill the remainder with a very dry mushroom duxelles. Garnish the consommé with the profiteroles.

Nesselrode pudding
Mix 1 litre (1¾ pints, 4⅓ cups) crème anglaise (see *custard*) with 250 g (9 oz, 1 cup) chestnut purée. Macerate 125 g (4½ oz, ¾ cup) candied orange peel and diced crystallized (candied) cherries in Málaga, and soak some sultanas (seedless white raisins) and currants in warm water. Add all the ingredients to the crème anglaise together with 1 litre (1¾ pints, 4⅓ cups) whipped cream flavoured with maraschino. Line the base and sides of a large charlotte mould with greaseproof (wax) paper and add the mixture. Cover the mould with a double thickness of foil and secure it with an elastic (rubber) band. Place the mould in the freezer. When the pudding is frozen, unmould it on to the serving dish, peel off the paper and surround the base with marrons glacés.

NEST A small basket made with potato matchsticks and shaped like a bird's nest. Potato nests are used to hold small roast birds, such as thrushes or quails, the preparation being described as *au nid* (in a nest). The nests are built up and deep-fried in a special wire basket, called a *panier à nids* (nest basket), which is made up of two parts, one fitting into the other. Potato nests are sometimes lined with pancakes, particularly when the birds are served with a garnish and a sauce. The nests may be decorated with poached cherries and small bunches of parsley or watercress.

Other preparations described as *au nid* include soft-boiled (soft-cooked) or poached eggs placed in hollowed-out tomatoes or in 'nests' made of piped Montpellier butter garnished with chopped aspic and watercress.

See also *birds' nests*.

RECIPE

potato nests
Peel some firm potatoes. Using a mandoline, cut them into very fine strips (matchsticks). Line the larger nest basket with an even layer of potato matchsticks, overlapping them slightly. Press them against the sides and trim them. Place the smaller basket inside the larger one so that the matchsticks are held in position. Deep-fry in hot oil at 180°C (350°F) for 5–6 minutes. Open the basket and the nest should come out quite cleanly.

NETHERLANDS See *opposite page*.

NETTLE A plant whose leaves have stinging hairs which cause a rash on contact; because of this, people are generally unaware of its therapeutic qualities and its food value. The young leaves of the annual small nettle can be chopped and used in salads. The leaves of the perennial large, or common, nettle can be used in green vegetable soups, on their own or combined with sorrel, leeks, watercress or cabbage, thickened with broad (fava) beans or potatoes. Both types of nettle can be cooked like spinach.

NEUFCHÂTEL A cow's-milk cheese (45% fat content), with a white downy rind mottled with red, and a soft, smooth, creamy golden-yellow paste. It has a mild flavour and is sold in various shapes – rectangular, square, cylindrical or heart-shaped. It has been made in Neufchâtel, a small town in the Seine-Maritime region, since the Middle Ages and is now protected by a DOP, guaranteeing its source of manufacture. Several other cheeses are similar to Neufchâtel, such as Coeur de Bray, Bondon and Gournay.

NÉVA, À LA The name given to a dish of stuffed chicken coated with a white chaud-froid sauce and glazed with aspic. The reference to the River Neva, which flows through St Petersburg, is justified because it is served with Russian salad.

RECIPE

chicken à la néva
Prepare a chicken weighing about 3 kg (6½ lb) and remove the breastbone. Stuff the bird with a mixture of 800 g (1¾ lb, 3¼ cups) fine chicken

NETHERLANDS

Dutch cookery is closely related to that of Belgium and northern Germany. A country of rich pasturelands, it has an abundance of high-quality dairy produce, which goes into its famous cheeses. The best known of these are Gouda, a yellow cheese with a yellow or black rind, shaped like a flattened cylinder, and sometimes flavoured with cumin; Edam, a large spherical yellow-orange cheese with a red or yellow rind; and Leyden cheese, which is round and flat and flavoured with cumin or aniseed.

The Netherlands is a country of both fishermen and livestock farmers, so the Dutch table features a wide variety of salted and smoked meats and fish. Together with many different breads, these make up the famous *koffietafel*, a cold buffet which is served at lunchtime. The main meal of the day is served in the evening.

There is a Dutch proverb which says: *'Haring in't land, dokter aan de kant'* ('As long as the herring is there, the doctor stays away'). Herring is a popular food and the centrepiece of countless feasts. One of these is the 'New Hollanders' (first fishing of the year), celebrated in gaily decorated coastal villages. The first barrel of herring is offered to the reigning monarch.

Dutch cooking is quite filling. Winter dishes include split pea soup, *hutspot* (a stew served with a plate of chops), *balkenbrij* (brawn, or head cheese, served with an apple compote), *hazepepper* (jugged hare) and knuckle of veal with sauerkraut. Other typical dishes are *rolpens* (fried marinated meat served with potatoes and pineapple) and escalope of veal with a creamy cheese sauce, seasoned with nutmeg and served with green vegetables.

Rice is imported in large quantities from the former Dutch colonies in South-East Asia and is a frequent ingredient in both sweet and savoury dishes. *Rijsttafel* (literally, 'rice table') is a direct result of the influence of Indonesian cookery. It consists of rice garnished with different types of highly spiced meat, fish, sauces and vegetables, and is a typically Dutch dish.

In pâtisserie and confectionery, ginger, cinnamon and nutmeg are used a great deal; for example, in *spéculos* (tiny cakes) served at Christmas, spiced pancakes, *boterkoek* (butter cake) and the famous *hopjes* (coffee caramels).

From Indonesia come excellent coffee, tea and high-quality cocoa and chocolate. The Dutch love good coffee and drink it often, from small porcelain coffee cups. Apart from their own national beer, the Dutch drink French and Rhine wines. Two famous Dutch liqueurs are Curaçao and advocaat.

---

forcemeat*, small cubes of raw foie gras and truffles. Truss the bird, poach it in white stock and leave to cool in the liquid. When it is quite cold, wipe dry and coat with a white chaud-froid sauce prepared with some of the cooking liquor. Garnish with mushroom slices, glaze with aspic and allow to set firmly. Place the chicken on a long serving dish.

Prepare some Russian salad mixed with a thick mayonnaise, divide the mixture into two and shape each half into a dome. Garnish each dome with mushroom slices and place them on the serving dish at each end of the chicken. Garnish the edges of the dish with chopped aspic.

NEWBURG A method of cooking lobster created by a Mr Wenburg, a former head chef at Delmonico's, the famous New York restaurant. The first letters of Wenburg have been transposed to give Newburg. Lobster Newburg is basically lobster sautéed in cream, although there are many variations on both sides of the Atlantic.

Newburg sauce is made by preparing lobster *à l'américaine* and adding cream and fish stock. It can also be used to accompany fish, particularly sole or fillets of sole garnished with lobster medallions.

RECIPE

lobster Newburg
Wash 2 lobsters weighing about 450 g (1 lb) each and joint them as for lobster *à l'américaine*. Remove the coral and liver and keep for use later. Season the lobsters with salt and paprika and brown them in 75 g (3 oz, 6 tablespoons) butter. Cover the pan and cook with the lid on for 12 minutes. Drain off the butter, add 300 ml (½ pint, 1¼ cups) sherry and boil down over a high heat. Add 300 ml (½ pint, 1¼ cups) fish stock and an equal quantity of velouté* sauce. Cover the pan and simmer gently for 15 minutes. Take out the pieces of lobster and arrange them in a deep dish. (The tail pieces may be shelled if wished.)

Boil down the cooking liquid and add 400 ml (14 fl oz, 1¾ cups) double (heavy) cream. When the sauce is thick enough to coat the back of the spoon, add the coral and liver, rubbed through a fine sieve and blended with 100 g (4 oz, ½ cup) butter. Beat the sauce vigorously and pour it over the lobster.

NEW ZEALAND See *page 792*.

NEW ZEALAND SPINACH A climbing plant, *Tetragonia tetragonioides*, native to New Zealand and Australia, also called summer spinach. It is cultivated in many warm regions for its dark-green fleshy leaves, which have a pleasant though slightly acid flavour, and is eaten as a vegetable. It is prepared in the same way as spinach.

It was introduced into Europe from New Zealand by Sir Joseph Banks, who travelled with Captain Cook on his voyage around the world in 1771.

NEW ZEALAND

New Zealand cuisine consists of simple country dishes, based largely on the island's natural produce: sheep, vegetables and tropical fruit (especially kiwi fruit), dairy products, fish, shellfish and large game. Grilled (broiled) food and hot pots seasoned with aromatic herbs alternate on New Zealand dining tables as the main regional dishes of the country. Kiwi fruit is eaten at every meal, fresh as a dessert or in a salad. It is also used in pies and cakes as well as in some savoury dishes.

WINE Wine-growing in New Zealand started in the 19th century. At first only liqueur and sherry-style wines were produced, but in the 1950s and 1960s wine production became established on a large scale. There are vineyards planted on both the main islands. The climate is largely cool maritime, but with significant differences between regions in the warmer North Island and the cooler South Island. Rainfall can be high. New Zealand has established an international reputation with the excellent quality of the wines produced from Sauvignon Blanc and increasingly from Chardonnay, Riesling, Pinot Noir and Cabernet Sauvignon grapes. Other varieties grown include Merlot, Chenin Blanc, Gewürztraminer, Sémillon and Müller-Thurgau.

In the North Island, Gisbourne is renowned for Chardonnay wines with ripe tropical fruit flavours and for spicy Gewürztraminer. Hawkes Bay, situated on the east coast and often registering the highest sunshine hours in the country, produces top quality Chardonnay and Cabernet Sauvignon or Cabernet Sauvignon/Merlot/Cabernet Franc blends. The Sauvignon Blanc wines made here have a peach, stone (pit) fruit character.

New vineyards have been planted in the Auckland area at Waiheke Island and Matakana, giving high quality red wines. Wairarapa, which includes the Martinborough region at the southern end of North Island, has achieved great success with plantings of Cabernet Sauvignon and Pinot Noir.

Sauvignon Blanc is extensively planted in Marlborough in the north-east part of South Island, the largest of New Zealand's wine regions. The wines have tropical fruit, gooseberry and green pepper flavours. Chardonnay is the second most planted variety, some of which is made into sparkling wine. The area also produces good quality wines from Riesling; some are botrytised (see *noble rot*), making sweet, luscious dessert wines.

Nelson and Canterbury produce good Chardonnay wines, and in Central Otago the world's most southerly vineyards produce top quality wines from Pinot Noir.

NICE AND ITS ENVIRONS The city of Nice is situated on the French Riviera, in the south-eastern corner of Provence, close to the Italian border. Although influenced by both Provençal and Italian cooking, the cuisine of the region still retains its own specific characteristics. The Mediterranean provides the region with a variety of seafood.

Olive trees growing on the hills behind Nice provide both oil and the celebrated small black Nice olives. Oranges, especially bitter oranges, are a speciality of Nice. Cultivated or wild flowers are a source of honey. Other fruits and vegetables of the region include aubergines (eggplants), tomatoes, courgettes (zucchini) and (bell) peppers, combined in the famous ratatouille; as well as small purple artichokes, broad (fava) beans, and medlars, figs and strawberries. Among the cheeses, Cachat and Brousse de la Vésubie are highly esteemed.

Bellet AOC wines are made only in small quantities and are highly sought after. White wines are produced from the Rolle grape variety with some Chardonnay added; elegant rosés from Braquet; and reds from Folle Noir, often blended with Cinsaut and Grenache.

NIÇOISE, À LA The name given to various dishes typical of the cuisine of the region around Nice, in which the most common ingredients are garlic, olives, anchovies, tomatoes and French (green) beans.

Fish, such as mullet, sole or whiting, grilled (broiled) *à la niçoise* is served with coarsely chopped peeled, seeded tomatoes, anchovy fillets, olives and sometimes anchovy butter.

The niçoise garnish for large cuts of meat and poultry consists of tomatoes stewed in oil and flavoured with garlic, buttered French beans, or stewed courgettes (zucchini) and small artichokes, and château potatoes. The sauce that coats the meat is made by deglazing the pan with veal stock thickened with tomato.

Salade niçoise is a typical dish of southern France, containing tomatoes, cucumber, locally grown fresh broad (fava) beans or small artichokes, green (bell) peppers, raw onions, hard-boiled (hard-cooked) eggs, anchovy fillets or tuna, black Nice olives, olive oil, garlic and basil. Neither potatoes nor cooked vegetables should be added to this salad.

RECIPES

grilled red mullet à la niçoise
Clean, wash and dry the fish, season with salt and pepper, brush with olive oil and marinate for 30 minutes. Make a well-flavoured tomato fondue* and boil down until very thick. Grill (broil) the mullet gently for 15 minutes. Cover the bottom of the serving dish with the tomato fondue (capers may be added if desired) and place the grilled fish on top. Garnish with strips of anchovy fillets in oil arranged in a lattice, and small black olives. Place a slice of lemon on the head of each fish.

omelette à la niçoise

Beat some eggs lightly and add some concentrated tomato fondue* (I level tablespoon per 2 eggs), some chopped parsley and some chopped garlic. Make the omelette, garnish it with anchovy fillets arranged in a criss-cross pattern and sprinkle with noisette butter.

rack of lamb à la niçoise

Trim a rack of lamb and calculate the cooking time at 15 minutes per 450 g (1 lb). Brown the lamb lightly in butter in a flameproof casserole. Add a coarsely diced, peeled courgette (zucchini) fried quickly in olive oil, a large, peeled, seeded, chopped tomato fried in olive oil, and 20 or so small peeled and parboiled new potatoes tossed in olive oil. Season with salt and pepper and cook in a preheated oven at 230°C (450°F, gas 8) for the calculated time. Serve sprinkled with chopped parsley.

other recipes See *artichoke, attereau, chicken, courgette, sole, stockfish.*

NID D'ABEILLE Traditional cake very popular in Germany and Alsace. It is a round brioche, 5 cm (2 in) thick, covered with a mixture of butter, sugar, honey and almonds, split in two and covered with confectioner's custard (pastry cream).

NIGELLA Also known as love-in-a-mist and fennel flower, a plant grown for its black seed, which is used as a spice in India, Egypt and the Middle East. In France the seeds are sometimes known as four spices (quatre-épices), a confusing description as there is a spice mixture of the same name consisting of white pepper, ground ginger, cloves and nutmeg. The seeds have a mild peppery flavour and can be used as a substitute for pepper. They are scattered over bread and cakes. In India they are sometimes known as black cumin, but should not be confused with the true black cumin. Nigella seed is also often confused with onion seed, which it resembles, and even referred to as wild onion seed.

NIGNON ÉDOUARD French chef (born 1865; died c. 1934), regarded as one of the greatest masters of French cuisine. His apprenticeship and his exceptionally successful career took him to the most famous restaurants in France – Potel et Chabot, the Maison Dorée, the Café Anglais, Bignon, Magny, Noël Peter's, Paillard and Lapérouse – and also to Claridges in London and L'Ermitage in Moscow. He was head chef to the Tsar, the Emperor of Austria and President Woodrow Wilson. In 1918 he took over the management of the restaurant Larue, exchanging his white chef's waistcoat for the black suit of a maître d'hôtel, causing Sacha Guitry to comment: 'He spent two-thirds of his life dressed all in white or all in black.' He wrote three cookery books in which he recorded his experiences: *L'Heptaméron des gourmets ou les Délices de la cuisine française* (1919); *Éloges de la cuisine française* (1933), with a preface by Sacha Guitry; and *Les Plaisirs de la table* (1926). Some of his recipes, such as *beuchelle tourangelle* (rice, calves' kidneys, and morels in a cream sauce), are still much appreciated by gourmets.

NIMROD A biblical character, described as 'a mighty hunter before the Lord', to whom various classic game dishes were dedicated during the 19th century. The Nimrod garnish for ground game consists of small pastry barquettes or vol-au-vent filled with stewed cranberries, croquette potatoes and large grilled (broiled) field mushrooms stuffed with chestnut purée. Consommé Nimrod is made with game consommé mixed with port, thickened with arrowroot and garnished with small quenelles of game forcemeat enriched with chopped truffle. Finally, attereaux Nimrod consist of quenelles of game and ham forcemeat, mushrooms and hard-boiled (hard-cooked) lapwings' eggs threaded on to skewers and deep-fried.

NINON The name given to various classic French dishes dating from the 19th century. The Ninon garnish for small sautéed cuts of meat served with marrow sauce consists of small nests of duchess potato, filled with a salpicon of cockscombs and kidneys blended in a velouté sauce, together with asparagus tips in butter. This garnish is also used as a filling for Ninon canapés, which are cut from a round loaf and crisped in a very hot oven.

In a variation of the garnish, the meat is arranged on a base of Anna potatoes and covered with a sauce made with the pan juices deglazed with Madeira and concentrated veal stock. A small pastry case (shell), filled with asparagus tips cooked in butter and sprinkled with a finely shredded truffle, is arranged on each piece of meat.

The Ninon mixed salad consists of lettuce leaves and orange segments, flavoured with lemon and orange juice, salt and a few drops of oil.

NIOLO A Corsican cheese made either from ewe's milk or a mixture of goat's and ewe's milk (fat content at least 45%). Niolo has a soft texture and a natural greyish-white rind. After being soaked for 3–4 months in brine it is firm to the touch, with a sharp flavour and a strong smell. Niolo is a farmhouse cheese, made in 13 cm (5 in) squares, 4–6 cm (1½–2½ in) deep. It is best from May to December.

NIVERNAIS AND MORVAN The rich pastures of Nivernais and the meadows of Morvan are the home of a highly prized breed of beef cattle, the Charolais, yielding high-quality meat suitable for lavishly garnished roast or braised dishes. Sheep with delicately flavoured meat are reared, and the pork and poultry are of equally fine quality. Smoked ham from Morvan is a speciality. The forests of Morvan are full of winged and ground game, and trout, pike and perch are fished in the rivers. It is also well known for its root vegetables. There is a wide variety of cheeses, including those of Lormes, Toucy, Tracy and Dornecy.

NIVERNAISE, À LA Describing preparations of large roast or braised cuts of meat or braised duck garnished with glazed carrots cut into olive shapes, small glazed onions and, sometimes, braised lettuce. This garnish may also be arranged in croustades and it is usual to pour the braising liquid over the dish.

NOBLE ROT Also know as *edelfäule* in Germany, or *pourriture noble* in France, this is a fungus, *botrytis cinerea*, which can develop in certain humid climatic conditions. It attacks ripe white grapes, reducing their water content, concentrating the sugars and acids and creating other complex chemical changes. The resulting grapes are capable of making some of the great sweet wines of the world such as Sauternes and the great Trockenbeerenausleses of Austria and Germany. These are referred to as botrytised wines.

NOËL The surname of a pastrycook from Angoulême whose skill at making pâtés was discovered by Casanova. His son became head chef and maître d'hôtel to Frederick the Great, who was so impressed by this chef's creation called *bombe à la Sardanapale* that he wrote an ode in his honour entitled 'The Newton of cooking'.

NOËL PETER'S A Parisian restaurant that opened in the Passage des Princes in 1854 and became very popular during the period of the Second Empire. At first it was known simply as 'Peter's', after the proprietor, Pierre Fraisse. Having lived in the United States, he served dishes that were then new to France, such as turtle soup, roast beef sliced at the table to the customer's requirements and, above all, lobster *à l'américaine*, which he created. The restaurant was much patronized by journalists, including the writer Monselet, who was exempted from paying a cover charge. When the place was bought by Vaudable, father of the manager of Maxim's, it became known as Noël Peter's because of its association with a certain Noël. During the 1880s the restaurant pioneered the concept of a *plat du jour*: each day of the week was allotted its particular dish. When covered arcades fell out of fashion the restaurant declined and eventually closed.

NOISETTE A small round steak, usually of lamb or mutton, cut from the rib or loin. Surrounded by a thin band of fat, like a tournedos steak, noisettes are very tender and can be fried in butter and served with a variety of garnishes, including Anna potatoes and fried onions, morels sautéed with herbs, artichoke hearts, sautéed aubergines (eggplants) or cucumber shells, buttered French (green) beans or garden peas, or asparagus tips. The accompanying sauce often consists of the pan juices deglazed and reduced with Madeira, tomato sauce or wine.

The name 'noisette' is also given to a small round slice of beef fillet, fried in butter and served with the same garnishes; a small grenadin of veal, which can be cooked like a veal escalope (scallop); or the 'eye' of a roebuck cutlet, grilled (broiled) or sautéed in butter.

RECIPES

noisettes Beauharnais
Braise some small artichoke hearts in butter. In another pan, sauté some lamb noisettes in butter, arrange them on fried croûtons and keep hot. Prepare some noisette potatoes and a béarnaise sauce, and pour the sauce over the artichoke hearts. Deglaze the meat pan with Madeira, boil down to reduce and add some chopped mushrooms. Arrange the noisettes on a serving dish alternately with the artichoke hearts and the noisette potatoes and cover with the sauce.

noisettes chasseur
Sauté 8 lamb noisettes in a mixture of oil and butter, then drain. Add 100 g (4 oz, 1⅓ cups) finely sliced mushrooms and 1 tablespoon chopped shallots to the pan, deglaze with white wine and moisten with veal stock to which a little tomato sauce has been added. Arrange the meat on a hot dish, garnish with the mushrooms and pour the sauce over.

noisettes of the Tour d'Argent
Sauté some lamb noisettes in clarified butter and arrange them on a hot dish. Deglaze the cooking pan with a mixture comprising equal quantities of vermouth, sherry and veal stock. Thicken with butter. Put 1 teaspoon Soubise* purée on each noisette and grill (broil) for a few seconds. Serve the sauce separately.

noisettes Rivoli
Prepare some Anna potatoes and arrange them on a serving dish. Sauté some lamb noisettes in butter and place them on top of the potatoes. Deglaze the meat pan with Madeira and (if possible) with some demi-glace, then add some finely diced mushrooms. Pour this sauce over the lamb.

additional recipe See *Melba*.

NOISETTE BUTTER Butter heated until it becomes nut brown; it is used to add a finishing touch to a variety of dishes, particularly fish.

Noisette sauce is a hollandaise sauce to which a few spoonfuls of noisette butter are added. It is served with salmon, trout and turbot, cooked in a covered pan on top of the cooker (stove).

NOISETTE POTATOES Small potato balls, cut out with a melon baller, lightly fried and browned in butter. They are used as a garnish, usually for small cuts of meat.

NOIX The fleshy upper part of the fillet end of a leg of veal, cut lengthways. The meat is lean and tender, but tends to be rather dry. It can be sliced into escalopes (scallops) or grenadins, or it can be roasted. Various garnishes may be used to accompany it; for example, bouquetière, bourgeoise, Clamart, milanaise, or piémontaise. It can also be served with mushrooms, braised chicory (endive), buttered spinach, mixed vegetables or a risotto. The noix can also be braised, which enhances its tenderness.

The lean plump 'eye' of a veal cutlet (chop) is also known as the noix.

RECIPES

noix of veal Brillat-Savarin

Bone a whole noix of veal. Flatten it, then sew the cut parts together to re-form the noix. Chop 3 shallots. Cook 100 g (4 oz) black morels in cream. Spread a 1 cm (½ in) layer of *à gratin* forcemeat mixed with the shallots over the veal. Sprinkle on some of the cooked morels, then place a piece of duck foie gras weighing about 200 g (7 oz) in the centre. Roll up the noix and tie it securely. Bard with strips of fat pork, brown the veal in butter, then place in a flameproof casserole on a bed of mirepoix. Moisten with equal quantities of dry white wine and beef stock. Add some peeled, seeded, roughly chopped tomatoes and a bouquet garni. Cover the pan and cook slowly for 2 hours.

Take out the meat, then reduce and strain the cooking liquid. Serve the veal sliced, with a little of the sauce poured over, accompanied by leaf spinach and the remaining morels. Serve the rest of the sauce separately.

roast noix of veal

Heat some butter in a flameproof casserole. Lard a noix of veal with thin pieces of bacon and brown it on all sides in the butter. Sprinkle with salt and pepper, then cook in a preheated oven at 200°C (400°F, gas 6), allowing 16 minutes per 450 g (1 lb).

NONNETTE
A small, round, iced gingerbread cake from France. The cakes were originally made by nuns in convents, but today they are commercially produced. The nonnettes of Reims and Dijon have a good reputation.

NONPAREILLE
A small round caper pickled in vinegar. In France the name is also used for 'hundreds and thousands' (sprinkles), the multicoloured sugar crystals used as a decoration on cakes and pastries.

NOODLES
Term used to describe long pasta and believed to originate from the German *nudeln*, a general name for pasta. For Italian-style and other European pasta, 'noodle' is the term for tagliatelle and similar long, flat pasta or ribbon noodles. Jewish *lokshen* and Russian *lokshyna* are examples of egg noodles similar to tagliatelle.

In terms of Oriental pasta, noodles cover many types of long thin pasta, both flat and rounded, and made from various types of dough. In addition to wheat flour, the flours and starches used for noodles include those obtained from rice, mung bean, buckwheat and arrowroot. There is an incredible variety, as a visit to any well-stocked Chinese or Japanese supermarket will confirm. The following are a few examples.

■ **Wheat-flour noodles** Chinese-style egg noodles are well known, particularly as the main ingredient for chow mein. Made from wheat flour, these round noodles may include egg. White or yellow in colour, fresh or dried, they can be plain or slightly wrinkled. In dried or fresh form, noodles of this type are used throughout South-East Asia and Japan, where they are known as *ramen*.

Other Japanese wheat noodles include *somen* or *soumen*. There are various types; typically white in colour, round and fine, they are cut into lengths and sold in bundles (similar to the short versions of spaghetti). *Udon* are thicker than *somen* and usually sold fresh, when they are soft and white. (Dried wholewheat Japanese noodles are also known as *udon*, but they are typically a wholefood product.) *Hiyamugi* are medium-thick dried wheat noodles, between somen and *udon*, and served cooked and chilled in a cold dish of mixed ingredients, also known as *hiyamugi*.

■ **Rice-starch noodles** Rice sticks or rice noodles refer to pasta made from rice flour. These noodles take many forms, from fine semi-transparent vermicelli to thicker examples more than double the width of Italian tagliatelle. Rice sticks require soaking or brief simmering; they are used in casseroles and stir-fries. Fine vermicelli are added to soup or deep-fried (without pre-soaking) to make a crisp, light garnish.

A mixture of rice flour or cornflour (cornstarch) with wheat flour is used to make the thicker white Chinese noodles, cut into short lengths and known by a number of names, including *ho fun, hor fun, kua teaw* and *kway teow.*

Malaysian *laksa* are white rice noodles, slightly thicker than spaghetti and sold fresh. They are used in a dish of the same name, consisting of a spicy fish broth, typically garnished with cucumber, lettuce and chillies.

■ **Mung-bean noodles** Mung bean pasta are often known as cellophane or glass noodles because of their transparent, shiny quality. They may include other flours, such as pea starch, and other types of cellophane noodles can be made using flours ground from yam, buckwheat or wheat. The fine noodles are also known as bean-thread noodles. They may be soaked and stir-fried, added to soups or used in braised dishes.

■ **Buckwheat-flour noodles** Buckwheat flour is often used with wheat flour and other starches to make dark noodles, sometimes with a slightly coarse texture and wholemeal-type flavour. There are many types of Japanese *soba*, made using varying proportions of buckwheat flour, and they may include yam flour. Fine vermicelli-like Japanese noodles, known as *naeng myun*, are made from a combination of buckwheat, wheat and sweet-potato starch.

■ **Shirataki** These white Japanese noodles are made from the root of a plant known as the devil's tongue plant. The root is used to make a cake or loaf known as *konnyaku*, from which the noodles are cut. They are sold wet, stored in water in cans or sealed sausage-shaped plastic tubes.

■ **Noodle dishes** In European-style dishes, noodles may be served as an accompaniment to sauced dishes, tossed with a sauce or dressing or served very simply dressed, for example with olive oil, garlic and Parmesan cheese. They have a broader use in Oriental cooking: they may be served as a simple accompaniment, for example tossed with chopped spring onions (scallions) to complement Chinese sauced dishes or fried as a crisp cake or topping; or they may be the main ingredient for the dish, complemented by a modest proportion of various other ingredients.

As well as savoury use, noodles feature in sweet dishes. Famous examples include Jewish lokshen pudding and Polish Christmas Eve dessert, for which noodles are tossed with ground poppy seeds, often sweetened with honey.

RECIPES

fresh egg noodles
Sift 500 g (18 oz, 4½ cups) strong plain (bread) flour into a bowl and make a well in the middle. Dissolve 2 teaspoons salt (or less to taste) in 2 tablespoons water, put it in the middle of the flour, then add 3 beaten eggs and 6 egg yolks. Gradually work the liquids into the flour to make a firm dough. Knead the dough thoroughly, working it with the heel of the palm until the dough is smooth and firm. Wrap the dough in a cloth or cling film (plastic wrap) and leave it in a cool place, but not the refrigerator, for 1 hour so it loses its elasticity. Then divide the dough into pieces about the size of an egg and roll these into balls. Roll out each piece into a very thin pancake shape. Lightly dust with flour, roll up loosely, cut into strips 1 cm (½ in) wide, then unroll the strips on a flat surface.

To cook the noodles, plunge them into boiling salted water, using 2.5 litres (4¼ pints, 11 cups) water for every 250 g (9 oz) fresh noodles. Boil fast for about 3 minutes, drain and serve tossed with butter.

noodles au gratin
Prepare some buttered noodles. Mix with 50 g (2 oz, ½ cup) mixed grated Gruyère and Parmesan cheese and a little grated nutmeg. Pour into a buttered gratin dish, cover with more grated cheese, sprinkle with melted butter and brown under the grill (broiler).

NOQUE A small round quenelle (dumpling) from Alsace made from flour, eggs and butter. Also called *knepfles*, noques are poached and served as a first course or in soup. Noques *à l'allemande* are quenelles of flour with pork liver added, or are made with choux pastry and lean veal; they are served with meat and gravy or used as a garnish in soup.

Noques *à la viennoise* are small light balls made of dough containing eggs, cream and butter; they are poached in vanilla-flavoured milk and served with custard.

Using a pasta machine to roll out and cut noodles
A simple, hand-operated pasta machine can be used to roll out pasta dough and cut noodles.

1 *Begin with the rollers set as far apart as possible and feed in the lump of smooth dough, turning the rollers and coaxing the dough between them. Repeat this process, reducing the gap between the rollers each time to roll out the dough thinly and evenly.*

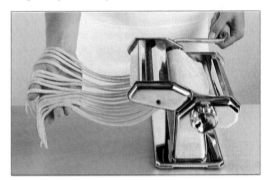

2 *Fit the noodle-cutting attachment, then feed manageable lengths of the rolled-out dough through the machine. Dust the noodles with flour to prevent them from sticking together.*

RECIPES

noques à l'alsacienne
Bring 250 g (9 oz, generous 1 cup) butter to room temperature, then cut into pieces and place in a bowl. Sprinkle with salt, pepper and a little grated nutmeg, then work to a paste using a wooden spatula. Blend in 2 whole eggs and 2 yolks, add 150 g (5 oz, 1¼ cups) sifted plain (all-purpose) flour all at once, and finally 1 stiffly whisked egg white. Scrape this mixture into a clean bowl and leave it in a cold place for 30 minutes. Shape the dough into walnut-sized balls. Poach them in simmering salted water, turning them so they puff up on both sides. Drain, turn into a deep serving bowl, sprinkle with Parmesan cheese and noisette butter, and serve as a first course or with soup.

noques à la viennoise
Cream 125 g (4½ oz, generous ½ cup) butter in a bowl and blend in a generous pinch of salt, 25 g (1 oz, ¼ cup) semolina (semolina flour), 5 egg yolks

(one by one) and 3 tablespoons double (heavy) cream. Beat the mixture until smooth, then add 100 g (4 oz, 1 cup) sifted plain (all-purpose) flour all at once and beat this in; then fold in 1 stiffly whisked egg white and finally 3 unwhisked egg whites, one by one.

Add 50 g (2 oz, ¼ cup) sugar and 1 teaspoon vanilla sugar to 500 ml (17 fl oz, 2¼ cups) milk and bring to the boil. Poach spoonfuls of the dough in the simmering milk, turning them so they puff up on both sides. Drain them, arrange in a bowl and allow to cool.

Prepare some custard by beating together 3 tablespoons double (heavy) cream and 5–6 egg yolks. Blend with the poaching milk and heat gently until the custard thickens. Strain it on to the noques.

NORI The Japanese name for edible seaweed used for centuries in Japanese cookery. In Wales nori is known as laver; in Scotland, slouk; and in Ireland, sloke. Nori covers several varieties that are grown along the Japanese coasts. Sometimes it is flavoured with saké or soy sauce, or even sweetened. The Japanese consume large amounts of nori – more than any other country worldwide – in a wide selection of dishes. It may be shredded for adding to soups and rice dishes or used in flakes. It is also available powdered, as a seasoning ingredient. However, it is best known as the fine dried sheets used to wrap rice in rolled sushi or little balls of rice as neat bundles. Plain thin sheets of dried nori are dark green-black – virtually black. They are toasted by passing over a gas flame for a few seconds on each side, when they become crisp and turn green. They are also sold as sushi nori; ready toasted and seasoned with soy sauce, these sheets are crisp and shiny.

NORMANDE, À LA Describing various dishes based on the cooking of Normandy, or made using typically Norman products, notably butter, cream, seafood, apples, cider and Calvados. The term can be applied to a host of fish, meat, poultry and egg dishes as well as to desserts, such as pancakes, omelettes, puff-pastry galettes, Genoese sponge cake and fruit salad.

Sole *à la normande* (a model for several dishes of fish braised in white wine) was in fact invented by a Parisian called Langlais, chef at the Rocher de Cancale at the beginning of the 19th century. The original dish was based on fish braised in cream and was prepared with cider, not white wine. However, it evolved to become an haute cuisine dish with an elaborate garnish – comprising oysters, mussels, prawns (shrimp), mushrooms, truffles, fried gudgeon and crayfish in court-bouillon – that was no longer typically Norman.

Normande sauce, which accompanies many fish dishes, is a fish velouté with cream and mushroom fumet. Small cuts of meat and chicken *à la normande* are sautéed, deglazed with cider, moistened with cream and sometimes flavoured with Calvados.

Partridge *à la normande* is cooked in a covered pan with Reinette apples and cream. Apples also accompany black pudding (blood sausage) *à la normande* and are used as the filling for pastries, pancakes and galettes *à la normande*. Cream is used as a dressing for French beans and for matelote normande (seafood flamed in Calvados and moistened with cider).

RECIPES

apple puffs à la normande
Roll out 575 g (1¼ lb) puff pastry* to a thickness of 2 cm (¾ in), cut it into two 20 cm (8 in) squares, prick them with a fork and place them side by side on a baking sheet. Blend 1 egg white with 75 g (3 oz, ¾ cup) icing (confectioner's) sugar for 2 minutes using a wooden spoon. Spread this icing (frosting) over one of the squares, then bake both squares for 12–15 minutes in a preheated oven at 200°C (400°F, gas 6).

Peel and slice 675 g (1½ lb) apples and cook them in 50 g (2 oz, ¼ cup) melted butter with 150 g (5 oz, ⅔ cup) caster (superfine) sugar for 15 minutes. Brown 25 g (1 oz, ¼ cup) flaked (slivered) almonds in a frying pan over a low heat, stirring them with a wooden spoon. Spread the cooked apples over the plain square, cover with the iced square and sprinkle with the toasted almonds. Serve warm.

filled genoese sponge à la normande
Bake a Genoese cake, allow to cool completely, then slice it into 2 rounds and sprinkle each half with a little Calvados-flavoured sugar syrup. Prepare a very dry apple compote, press it through a sieve, then add half its weight of warm confectioner's custard (pastry cream) flavoured with Calvados. Allow this to cool, then spread a thick layer over the bottom half of the cake. Replace the top half. Spread the surface with sieved apricot jam, then ice (frost) with fondant and leave to cool completely. Decorate with thin slices of apple cooked in very concentrated syrup, flaked (slivered) almonds and lozenge-shaped (diamond-shaped) pieces of candied angelica.

normande sauce
In a heavy-based saucepan heat 200 ml (7 fl oz, ¾ cup) fish velouté* sauce and 6 tablespoons each of fish fumet* and mushroom* essence. Mix 2 egg yolks with 2 tablespoons double (heavy) cream, add to the pan, and reduce by one-third. Just before serving, add 50 g (2 oz, ¼ cup) butter cut into small pieces and 3 tablespoons double cream. If necessary, pass the sauce through a very fine strainer.

An alternative method is as follows: mix 2 tablespoons mushroom peelings with 200 ml (7 fl oz, ¾ cup) fish velouté; add 6 tablespoons double cream and boil down by half. Then add 50 g (2 oz, ¼ cup) butter cut into pieces and 4 tablespoons double cream. Strain through a very fine sieve.

potatoes à la normande

Peel 800 g (1¾ lb) potatoes, slice them thinly, wash and dry them, and sprinkle with salt and pepper. Butter a flameproof casserole and put in half the potatoes. Clean and slice 3 large leeks and chop a small bunch of parsley. Spread the leeks and parsley over the potatoes in the casserole, then cover with the rest of the potatoes. Add sufficient meat or chicken stock to cover the potatoes and dot with 50 g (2 oz, ¼ cup) butter cut into small pieces. Cover the casserole, bring to the boil, then transfer to a preheated oven at 220°C (425°F, gas 7) and cook for about 45 minutes, or until the potatoes are tender.

sole à la normande

For a sole weighing about 400 g (14 oz), prepare a garnish of 4 debearded and poached oysters, 12 mussels cooked in white wine, 25 g (1 oz) peeled (shelled) shrimps, 4 fluted mushrooms cooked in white wine, 6 slices of truffle, 4 gudgeon (or smelt) coated with breadcrumbs and fried, 4 trussed crayfish cooked in court-bouillon, and 4 heart- or lozenge-shaped croûtons of bread fried in butter (or puff-pastry crescents).

Trim the sole, split it, skin one side only, and carefully raise the fillets a little. Break the backbone in 2 or 3 places to facilitate its removal after cooking. Poach the fish in a little fish fumet made with white wine, to which the cooking liquids from the oysters, mushrooms and mussels have been added. Drain the fish on paper towels and remove the backbone.

Arrange the fish on a long buttered serving dish together with the various garnishes and cover with normande sauce made from the fish cooking stock. The fish can be garnished with a ribbon of light fish aspic or meat glaze.

sweet omelette à la normande

Peel, core and slice 3 dessert apples. Cook them in 50 g (2 oz, ¼ cup) butter and some caster (superfine) sugar. Add 200 ml (7 fl oz, ¾ cup) double (heavy) cream and reduce to a creamy consistency, then flavour with 2–3 tablespoons Calvados.

Beat 10 eggs with a pinch of salt, sugar and 2 tablespoons double cream. Cook the omelette, fill it with the apple mixture, then place under a hot grill (broiler) to glaze.

other recipes See *black pudding, border (savoury rings), fruit salad, pheasant.*

NORMANDY See *opposite page.*

NORTH AFRICA See *page 800.*

NORVEGIENNE, À LA Describing several cold dishes of fish or seafood, usually glazed with aspic and garnished with such items as cucumber stuffed with smoked-salmon purée, hard-boiled (hard-cooked) eggs halved and topped with shrimp mousse, lettuce hearts and small tomatoes. The term is also used for various hot fish dishes, such as haddock and anchovy soufflé, and puff pastry filled with fish and anchovy butter and garnished with anchovy fillets.

Omelette norvégienne consists of ice cream covered with meringue and browned in the oven (see *Baked Alaska*).

NORWAY See *page 801.*

NOSTRADAMUS French physician and astrologer (born 1503; died 1566). Michel de Nostre-Dame, who was physician to Catherine de' Medici and Charles IX, is best known for his prophecies, set out in *Centuries astrologiques* (1555). But in the same year he published *Excellent et Moult Utile Opuscule à tous nécessaire qui désirent avoir connaissance de plusieurs exquises recettes* (An Excellent and Most Useful Little Work, essential to all who wish to become acquainted with some exquisite recipes). The first part is devoted to formulae for cosmetics, toilet waters and scents; the second part gives recipes for various jams 'using honey as well as sugar and cooked wine' and including such fruit as cherries, ginger, limes and oranges. There are also recipes for sugar candy, quince paste, marzipan (almond paste) and other sweets (candies).

NOUGAT A sweetmeat made from sugar, honey and nuts. Although the recipe for the Roman sweet *nucatum* (from the Latin *nux*, nut), described by Apicius, was based on honey, walnuts and eggs, nougat in its present form appears to have been invented in Marseille in the 16th century, also based on walnuts. In about 1650, following the introduction of almond trees to the Vivarais region of France by Olivier de Serres, Montélimar became the manufacturing centre of nougat based on almonds.

Nougat production is now entirely mechanized and no longer exclusive to Montélimar. A paste of sugar, glucose syrup, honey and invert sugar is beaten and usually lightened with egg white and gelatine (or egg albumen or milk), then mixed with nuts. When cold it is cut into pieces. Nougat remains a speciality of south-eastern France and is one of the traditional Provençal 'thirteen Christmas desserts'.

Several types of nougat are made in France and in other countries. Nougat (or white nougat) contains at least 15% nuts; traditional Montélimar nougat contains at least 30%, comprising toasted sweet almonds (28%) and pistachios (2%). Other regional speciality nougats are made to their own specification. The texture of the finished product is defined by the cooking temperature, and the quantity and type of sugar used.

Vietnamese nougat, hard or soft, is made from sesame seeds, peanuts and sugar. The Italian *torrone* and the Spanish *turrón* are similar forms of nougat.

RECIPE

white nougat

Cook 250 g (9 oz, ¾ cup) honey with the same amount of sugar to the 'soft crack' stage – 129°C

Normandy

This maritime and agricultural region, described by the chronicler Froissart as 'a rich and flavoursome country in all its aspects', possesses many resources, which are employed in a culinary tradition developed over many hundreds of years. The traditional foods include butter, cream, rich milk, duck, chicken and tripe, cooked *à la mode de Caen* and used in the tripe sausage known as andouillette.

The coastal waters teem with fish and shellfish, and shad, eel and trout are fished in the rivers. The rich pastures of the interior support herds of dairy cattle, while delicious mutton and lamb is obtained from sheep reared on the salt meadows of Avranchin. There is also a thriving pig-rearing industry.

Normandy apples provide the raw material for cider and Calvados and are also used in cooking and pâtisserie; dessert varieties, such as Colville, are also grown. Market gardening, too, is important in the region.

■ **A tradition for rich cooking**
The most famous dishes of Normandy cuisine are *canard au sang* (prepared using duck killed by smothering to retain the blood), tripe *à la mode de Caen*, chicken with cream and Calvados, and roast leg of mutton. Less well

known is *graisse normande*, which is used as a cooking fat (particularly for roast sirloin of beef) and as the basic ingredient of a rich vegetable soup. Although omelette *à la crème de la Mère Poulard* is famous, omelettes filled with cockles, mussels or shrimps (and sometimes topped with poached oysters) are just as delicious. And while the *tripe de Caen* are universally acclaimed, those of Ferté-Macé and Coutances are close rivals.

Helped by the ritual of the *trou normand* (a glass of Calvados taken between courses), traditional Normandy meals tend to be rich and plentiful. Poultry dishes include duckling *à la rouennaise*, sautéed chicken *yvetois*, flamed partridges with Reinette apples, and goose *en daube*. Rabbit is cooked with morels, in pâtés or *à la havraise* – stuffed with truffled pigs' trotters (feet); the blood is traditionally eaten seasoned and cooked in *sanguette* in Alençon (with pieces of fat pork and onions). Other meat dishes are sheep's trotters *à la rouennaise*, casseroled veal, larded calf's liver braised with carrots, and veal escalopes (scallops) in cream with mushrooms.

■ **Cheese** Normandy cheeses are mainly soft with bloomy rinds and a high fat content (many are made from double or triple cream). Besides Camembert, Livarot and

Racking enables the fermentation of the cider to be checked. This is carried out in metal tanks or in wooden casks, as here at Saint-Désir de Lisieux in Calvados.

Pont l'Évêque, there are also Neufchâtel, Gournay, Trappiste de Briquebec, Lucullus, Brillat-Savarin, Bouille, Excelsior, Coeur de Bray and Bondon. Particular mention must be made of *pain brié*, a white fine-textured bread that is a speciality of the Auge region.

■ **Rounding-off a meal** As for desserts and pastries, the region is noted for its butter brioches, puff-pastry galettes with jam, puff-pastry apple turnovers, tarts served with crème fraîche, madeleines, sablés, mirlitons, *fallues* and the traditional *terrinée*. The meal is rounded off with Benedictine or perhaps with coffee spiked with Calvados.

Famous for its cheeses, the Pont l'Évêque region of Calvados is typical of Normandy with its green pastures, orchards and half-timbered houses.

NORTH AFRICA

The cuisine of North Africa, perhaps more than any other, tells us as much about the history of the country as its geography. The African provinces were the granary of imperial Rome. They later came under the influence of the Turks (who gave the natives a taste for sweet cakes and pastry), as well as that of the Jews, whose religious ordinances often coincided with those of the Muslims, notably fasting, respect for ritual religious feasts and the exclusion from the diet of the pig and its products. Market gardening (truck farming), fruit growing and the introduction of the vine are due to the French and Italian colonists, who have influenced both the ancestral traditions of the 'cuisine of the desert' – based on cereals, vegetables, dried fruits and grilled meat – and gastronomic development in the towns, particularly in Fez and Algiers, where the science of spices, the art of pastry-making and the preparation of dishes served in sauce have reached a high degree of sophistication.

Food is always served in abundant quantities, for family life and the tradition of hospitality result in large numbers at the table. The custom of eating with the fingers is a symbol of brotherhood inspired by the Koran, which urges the appreciation of food.

Although they are neighbours, the three North African countries vary considerably in their cuisines, particularly where spices are concerned. Dishes are very highly seasoned in Algeria and Tunisia (see *Harissa*), but spiced with more subtlety in Morocco, where dried lemon is widely used. In the south, the Bedouins are very fond of spit-roasted whole sheep (see *Méchoui*); this may be replaced by gazelle or even camel, which supplies the Tuaregs with meat, milk, fat and cheese.

■ **Specialities of the Maghreb** One of the distinguishing characteristics of North African cuisine is the variety of soups, always highly aromatic and often associated with religious ordinances: *chorba* in Algeria, *brudu* in Tunisia, and *harira* in Morocco. Soups combine dried vegetables or cereals (lentils, beans, chick peas, unripe wheat) with meat (diced mutton, chicken with vermicelli) or fish.

The best-known North African culinary speciality is couscous, traditionally mixed with *smeun* fat, a sort of rancid butter. There are many kinds of couscous, with chicken, mutton, beef meatballs or even with fish or tripe. According to local custom, hard-boiled (hard-cooked) eggs, raisins, mint leaves, pumpkin or celery may be added, as well as the usual vegetables and the sauce (*marga*). Sweet couscous may also be served for dessert, embellished with fresh fruit, pomegranate, almonds and dates.

Another well-known speciality is tajine, a type of ragoût cooked very slowly. In Tunisia it is made of mutton or rabbit with prunes, accompanied by fennel with lemon; in Algeria chicken is combined with cinnamon and onions; and Moroccan tajines are made of mutton with quinces and honey. Meat is also often served in balls (*kefta* in Tunisia) or on skewers (see *Kebab*).

Vegetables are either cooked in a sauce (as ratatouille) and frequently served with scrambled eggs, as in *chakchouka*, or marinated and served in a salad (in the fanshaped Tunisian *kemia*, which are served with filled pancakes, or *trids*). They may also be stuffed – artichoke hearts, cabbage leaves, (bell) peppers. Fish may be grilled (broiled) or fried (sardines, red mullet), but can also be cooked in sauce (in pickle for tuna), or marinated (as in Moroccan *charmoula*) and cooked in the oven (stuffed sea bream, shad with olives).

■ **Pastry, cakes and drinks** Puff pastry of great delicacy is used in cooking and cake-making (particularly for baklava). In Tunisia, where it is called *malsouga*, it is the basis of egg or meat briks; while in Algeria its name is *dioul* and it is made into savoury turnovers. In Morocco it is used to make pastilla and *briouats*, which are stuffed with meat or with almonds and honey.

All the North African countries like sweetmeats (such as Turkish delight) and pastries (with walnuts, almonds, lemon or dates), soaked with honey and syrup in Algeria and Tunisia, but drier in Morocco (gazelle's horns). Cakes are eaten on special occasions and at large family gatherings rather than every day.

Since the Koran forbids alcohol consumption, coffee is very widely drunk, and tea made with mint, marjoram, basil or jasmine is served with great ceremony.

(264°F). Add 1 tablespoon orange-flower water and 1 stiffly whisked egg white. Melt over a very low heat, stirring constantly, and bring the temperature up to the 'soft ball' stage – 109°C (228°F). Now add 500 g (18 oz, 4½ cups) sweet almonds that have been blanched, dried, chopped and heated through. Put the mixture into a shallow baking tin (pan) lined with sheets of rice paper. Cover with more rice paper and place a wooden board and weight on top. While the nougat is still slightly warm, cut into squares or rectangles.

Nougat with hazelnuts, pine nuts or pistachios is prepared in the same way.

NOUGATINE A sweetmeat made from light caramel syrup and crushed almonds, sometimes also hazelnuts. Nougatine is rolled out on an oiled marble slab and cut into small pieces; alternatively, it can be moulded to form cups, eggs, cornets or other shapes for use as cake decorations.

Many sweets (candies) and chocolates have a nougatine filling – a mixture of honey, sugar, glu-

NORWAY

Gastronomy in this land of fishermen is based on cod, salmon, trout and herring. Fish may be served at every meal: fresh, smoked or salted. It is even eaten at breakfast, which is a substantial meal: salt or pickled fish, strong cheese, bacon, sauté potatoes, eggs, and various kinds of bread and brioches, eaten with bread and jam. By contrast, lunch normally consists only of sandwiches, especially in town. The most important meal of the day is dinner. As in the rest of Scandinavia, meals take the form of large buffets (*koldtbord*) which include salads, eggs, cooked meats, fish and bread (such as *knekkebrød*), sauces and soured (sour) cream.

■ **Meat and game** Reindeer and mutton are the meats most widely consumed in Norway. Reindeer meat is prepared in the same way as beef: roasted, boiled or grilled (broiled), but it can also be smoked and dried, as can mutton. A leg of mutton prepared in this way and cut into long, thin slices is called *fenalår*. There are countless recipes for mutton, such as salted chops grilled on a birch wood fire (*pinnekjøt*), smoked rib cooked in steam (*smalahoved*) and roast mutton head. Mutton is also used in more complete dishes, like mutton stew with cabbage and black pepper (*fårika*).

Game recipes include ptarmigan with cranberries, roast roe deer with goat's cheese, or smoked elk, all served with country vegetables: potatoes, beetroots (beets), cabbage (especially red cabbage), turnips, celery and mushrooms.

■ **Fish** Trout is eaten fresh or fermented, and salmon is often cooked in a court-bouillon and served cold with creamed horseradish and cucumber or dill sauce, or grilled, or smoked. Besides these, there are many other sea fish available.

Boiled salt cod is served with melted butter and egg sauce, or simmered with potatoes and yellow peas, accompanied by a mustard sauce. Traditionally for Christmas the cod was left to soak in water in a wooden vat to remove the salt (*lutefisk*). This water was changed every day.

After several days the tub was emptied and sprinkled with lime on which the cod was then placed and covered with lime and a soda solution. Finally, the *lutefisk* was wrapped in a napkin and boiled, then served with potatoes and cream sauce. The process of soaking is now greatly simplified as the fish is available ready for boiling.

As everywhere in Scandinavia, herring is prepared in all kinds of different ways. Mackerel is also very popular: marinated, grilled and served with tomato butter, aquavit and beer. Fish is a basic ingredient in many salads (with horseradish, dill and onions) or in soups (Bergen fish soup with green vegetables, soured cream and egg yolks).

■ **Cheeses and fruit** Gjetöst is a goat's cheese with a sweet yet salty taste, eaten in thin slices. Desserts are usually based on fruits such as apples and pears, but red fruits and berries – cranberries, blackberries and bilberries (huckleberries) – are also popular. Eaten fresh, poached, with cream or as a base for puddings, they make light desserts.

---

cose, almonds or hazelnuts, and egg white – which is cooked, then mixed with pistachios, almonds or preserved fruit.

Nougatine cakes usually consist of a Genoese sponge cake filled with praline or pralinized hazelnuts, brushed with apricot jam and decorated with almonds or toasted or chopped hazelnuts. The nougatine cake of Nevers, created in 1850 by one of the town's pastrycooks, was reputedly offered to the Empress Eugénie, who was passing through the Nivernais region in 1862. It consists of a Genoese sponge filled with praline cream and iced (frosted) with chocolate fondant.

RECIPE

nougatine
Put 200 g (7 oz, 1 cup) caster (superfine) sugar and 4 teaspoons liquid glucose into a copper pan. Melt over a fairly high heat, stirring constantly with a wooden spoon. When the mixture turns a light brown, add 100 g (4 oz, 1 cup) ground almonds. Stir well, then pour on to an oiled baking sheet. Keep this hot until it is to be used, by placing it at the front of an open oven. Then allow the nougatine to cool and set slightly. Using a lightly oiled rolling pin, roll out the nougatine on the baking sheet to the desired thickness and cut it into shapes with a biscuit (cookie) cutter. Alternatively, if the nougatine is to form the base of a cake, pour it into an oiled cake tin (pan) the same size as the cake, or cut it to shape with an oiled knife.

NOUVELLE CUISINE A movement in cookery started in 1972 by two food critics, H. Gault and C. Millau, with the aim of encouraging a simpler and more natural presentation of food. The movement combined a publicity campaign with novel recipes and a new ethic, although the idea itself was not new. Foreshadowing the apostles of nouvelle cuisine, Voltaire complained: 'I confess that my stomach does not take to this style of cooking. I cannot accept calves' sweetbreads swimming in a salty sauce, nor can I eat mince consisting of turkey, hare and rabbit, which they try to persuade me comes from a single animal ... As for the cooks, I really cannot be expected to put up with this ham essence, nor the excessive quantity of morels and other mushrooms, pepper and nutmeg, with which they disguise perfectly good food.'

Advocates of nouvelle cuisine rejected the over-rich, complicated and indigestible dishes that they considered were no longer suitable for a generation conscious of the health hazards of overeating, especially of fatty foods. To counter this – and the increasing use of processed food – they espoused authenticity and simplicity in cooking. The *nouveaux cuisiniers* upheld a concept – their theorists even talked of a world vision – that combined the professions of medicine and dietetics. Their guiding principles were: absolute freshness of ingredients, lightness and natural harmony in the accompaniments, and simplicity in the cooking method. This meant less fat, no flour liaisons, no indigestible mixtures and no 'disguised' dishes. Instead, they devised light sauces based on meat juices, stocks, essences and spices; vegetables prepared so that their natural flavours were retained; and rapid cooking without fat, allowing the food to retain some of its texture. This entailed dry cooking in the oven or under a grill (broiler), steaming, stewing, cooking in a bainmarie or cooking *en papillote*.

However, in practice, nouvelle cuisine at its peak was characterized by small portions, extensively arranged on large plates with elegantly presented sauces and minimal accompaniments. The crisp vegetables, resplendent in their natural colours and decorative shapes, flanked thinly sliced meat; airy mousses accompanied pink and firm fish; while vegetable purées became the stars of the culinary repertoire. Astonished gourmets scanned menus to find *gigot* applied to fish, not mutton; *darne* to meat, not salmon. They found gruels, rare produce, compotes not of fruit but of vegetables, and perhaps even soups as dessert.

Nouvelle cuisine, dedicated as it was to phasing out elaborate dishes, rigid formulae, and pompous and academic set pieces, suited the climate of the times in the same way that 'bourgeois' cookery suited the 19th century. It introduced the idea of less complex and lighter foods, served in a stylized manner. Its legacy is a broad awareness of the importance of food presentation rather than relying on unsuitable fussy garnishes as disguise for messy platefuls of overcooked ingredients.

NOYAU Any of several liqueurs, brandies and ratafias based on an infusion of the kernels of certain fruits, particularly apricots and cherries (*noyau* is the French word for the stone that encloses the kernel). The best known of these is Noyau de Poissy, a liqueur made from cherry kernels and drunk straight or with water; it is also used to flavour ice creams, sorbets, fruit salads and cocktails.

NUITS-SAINT-GEORGES A small town in the Côte de Nuits, in Burgundy, making mostly red wines, plus a few whites. The wines are world-famous but diverse – there are no *grands crus* but many exceptional fine wine vineyards and, as with other Burgundies, much depends on the grower and the shipper to establish character and quality.

NULLE A type of custard made with egg yolks, sugar and cream, and flavoured with musk or amber. It was in fashion at the time of Louis XIV. La Varenne gives the recipe in *Le Pâtissier français*: 'Take 4 or 5 egg yolks, some very fresh cream, a quantity of sugar, a grain of salt; beat all this well together and cook in a deep plate or a flat dish; brown the top with a salamander, sprinkle with perfumed water and serve with musk-flavoured sugar to sweeten.'

Nicolas de Bonnefons suggests its origin: 'I think I am right in saying that a certain Italian gentleman called Nullio, groom to the kitchen of a great princess, was the inventor of this dish' (reported by Franklin).

NUOC-MÂM A condiment used in Vietnamese cookery. Meaning literally 'fish water', it is made by marinating small fish in brine, then pounding them to a paste. Nuoc-mâm replaces salt in almost all culinary preparations; it is also used at table as a seasoning, served in a flask or small bowl. It has a strong taste and when heated the smell is very pronounced. Lemon juice or red pepper is sometimes added, or it can be garnished with very thinly sliced onion rings. It is a good flavouring for scrambled eggs, soups and stews, and it accompanies spring (egg) rolls.

NUTCRACKERS Implements used to crack walnuts and other hard-shelled fruits. They usually take the form of a chrome-plated steel pincer with two notches to accommodate shells of different sizes. There are also wooden nutcrackers, cylindrical in shape and made of olive wood with a large screw that cracks the nuts when tightened.

NUTMEG The seed of the nutmeg tree, native to Indonesia but widely cultivated in tropical Asia and America. There are numerous varieties, the best-known being the nutmeg tree of the Sunda Islands. The nutmeg is oval and rounded in shape, greyish-brown in colour and wrinkled. It has a spicy flavour and aroma and is always used grated; nutmegs should be stored in an airtight container. The crushed nuts are used to manufacture a 'nutmeg butter', crumbly and very fragrant, which may be used as cooking fat or as a flavouring for butters. The red weblike covering of the seed is the mace, also used as a spice (see *mace*).

Nutmeg is widely used as a spice in savoury and sweet cooking, especially for flavouring cakes and custards and dishes with a base of potatoes, eggs (omelettes and soufflés) or cheese. It may also be included in béchamel sauces, onion soup, snail dishes and minced (ground) meatballs. Grated nutmeg is used to spice numerous cocktails and punches and is used in the manufacture of some fortified wines and spirits.

NUTS The different types of nuts are discussed under their own headings: see *almond, Brazil nut, cashew nut, hazelnut, peanut, pecan, pistachio, walnut*, and so on.

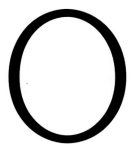

OATS A cereal that is well adapted for cultivation in cold, wet climates and, until the 19th century, was a basic food in Scotland, Wales, Scandinavia, Germany and Brittany. Oats are used mainly to make savoury or sweet broths and gruels, and porridge, eaten for breakfast with milk. They are also used for making biscuits (cookies) and pancakes, particularly in Anglo-Saxon countries. Numerous traditional Scottish, Welsh and Austrian recipes use oats in stews, ragoûts, stuffings for meat, a coating for herrings, and for charcuterie.

Oats are processed to make oatmeal, in various grades. The largest and coarsest is pinhead, then rough (coarse), medium, fine and superfine. Pinhead oatmeal can be used to make coarse porridge and in haggis; rough oatmeal, to make oatcakes and biscuits; and medium oatmeal, to make cakes and parkin. Fine oatmeal can be used for thickening soups and sauces, for stuffings, and for making Scottish brose and bannocks.

Rolled oats or oat flakes are made by steaming and rolling pinhead oatmeal, and instant or quick-cooking rolled oats are made by applying greater heat to the grains. Jumbo rolled oats are made by rolling the whole oat grain. Rolled oats are used in breakfast dishes, such as muesli, and to make biscuits, such as flapjacks.

OCTOPUS A fairly large cephalopod mollusc, measuring up to 80 cm (32 in). The octopus has a head with a horny beak and 8 equal-sized tentacles, each having 2 rows of suckers. Its flesh is fairly delicate in flavour, but it must be beaten for a long time and then blanched before use. Octopus can be prepared like lobster, cut into pieces and fried, or simmered *à la provençale* and served with saffron rice.

octopus à la provençale
Clean an octopus, remove the eyes and beak, and soak it under running water for a long time if it has not been prepared by the fishmonger. Drain it and beat well to tenderize the flesh. Cut the tentacles and body into chunks of the same length. Blanch the pieces in court-bouillon, drain them and pat dry. Then brown them in oil in a saucepan, with chopped onion. Season with salt and pepper, add 4 peeled, seeded and chopped tomatoes, and simmer for a few minutes. Moisten with ½ bottle of dry white wine and the same quantity of cold water. Add a bouquet garni and a crushed garlic clove. Cook, covered, for at least I hour. Sprinkle with chopped parsley and serve in a large bowl.

OENOLOGY The study of the manufacture and maturing of wines (from the Greek *oinos*, wine). In France the title oenologist was officially recognized by law on 19 March 1955, and it is possible to study for a diploma in the subject. An oenologist is a wine technician, whereas an oenophile is a wine lover, whose knowledge may or may not be as extensive. In France a wine shop that specializes in the local wines is known as an *oenothèque*.

OEUIL-DE-PERDRIX Used as a description, tasting term and name for pale pink wines, it means literally 'partridge's eye'. It can refer to a distinctive wine from Neuchâtel, Switzerland, produced from Pinot Noir.

OFFAL (VARIETY MEATS) The edible internal parts and some extremities of an animal, which are removed before the carcass is cut up. It therefore includes the head, feet and tail, and all the main internal organs. The offal from poultry is called the giblets.

The pig provides the greatest variety of offal used in cooking: brawn (a jellied mould made from the head and ears); various liver pâtés; sausages made from the chitterlings (small intestine) and the digestive tract; and black pudding (blood sausage). The lungs (lights), spleen (melts) and heart are less highly valued, but other offal provides simple and tasty dishes: pigs' trotters (breaded and grilled), kidneys (sautéed) and liver (fried).

The ox provides much edible offal, the commonest dishes being made from the tongue (boiled or pickled), stomach (intestines and tripe), and feet and tail (in pot-au-feu and ragoût). The brains are less delicate than those of calves or lambs. Heifer's liver can also be cooked, but the kidneys and spleen are less popular.

Veal offal is regarded as a delicacy: mainly brains, bone marrow, kidneys, liver and sweetbreads, but splendid dishes can also be made from the head and feet.

Lamb and sheep offal is also good and the kidneys, liver, testicles (see *animelles*), brains, heart, spleen, intestine, stomach and feet can be cooked in many ways.

OIL A fatty substance that is liquid at normal room temperatures. Although there are mineral oils, such as paraffin, and animal oils, such as whale oil, seal oil and cod-liver oil, it is the vegetable oils that are used in cooking. These are extracted either from seeds, such as sunflower, rapeseed, soya or cotton-seed, or from fruits, including olives, avocados and nuts.

Sesame and olive oils have the oldest origins. Records show that they were both used by the ancient Egyptians. The ancient Greeks, too, used olive oil and in Athens the olive was a sacred tree, symbol of the city's life. Oil was used not only for food but also as a fuel to provide light, and its use as a fuel continued for many centuries in Europe.

Most vegetable oils are low in cholesterol, being made up mainly of monounsaturated or polyunsaturated fatty acids. However, a few vegetable oils, such as palm oil and coconut oil, contain almost as much saturated fatty acid as animal fats. These oils solidify at normal room temperature in the same way as butter or lard (shortening).

Unsaturated fatty acids are considered less harmful to the body than saturated fatty acids, which may contribute to the incidence of coronary heart disease and other health problems. Some vegetable oils and some fish oils are also important for their essential fatty acid content. These are fats which the body cannot manufacture for itself; examples are omega 3, found in cod-liver oil and walnut oil, and omega 6, found in unrefined sunflower seed oil, olive oil and sesame oil.

Oils extracted from a single vegetable species are known as 'pure'; the term 'vegetable oil' indicates that the product is a mixture. Some mixtures may include oils with different fatty acid profiles. Most oils sold in shops have been refined, with the result that their flavour and smell have been removed, leaving them quite neutral. However, there are unrefined oils that have been obtained through cold pressing and these retain the flavour of their vegetable origin. The most widespread example is extra-virgin olive oil.

■ **Use** Oils, sometimes mixed with butter, provide the fatty medium for many cooking methods. They are an ingredient in salad dressings, cold sauces and condiments and they are also used to preserve foods, such as cooked and smoked fish, goat's cheese and sun-dried vegetables. They are used in marinades to moisten and flavour main ingredients, particularly poultry, game and meat.

Refined vegetable oils are the most suitable for heating to high temperatures, as they have the highest smoke points and can withstand the heat best. Grapeseed oil has the highest smoke point at 230°C (450°F) followed by rapeseed oil at 225°C (435°F). Corn oil, groundnut (peanut) oil, refined olive oil and soya oil are also all good frying oils, each with a smoke point of 210°C (410°F). The highest temperature needed to deep-fry potatoes is 190°C (375°F). It is best not to heat the same batch of oil to this temperature more than 8–10 times.

Refined vegetable oils are also widely used in food manufacture, particularly for margarine and high-fat products, such as biscuits (cookies and crackers), confectionery and prepared dishes.

Unrefined vegetable oils, particularly extra-virgin olive oil, are chosen for their flavour and can be used as flavouring ingredients in their own right. Such oils are used to dress hot and cold vegetables and to finish soups, stews and speciality dishes, such as ribollita or gazpacho. They are not recommended for frying as their smoke points tend to be fairly low. The following are the most commonly used oils worldwide.

• CORN (MAIZE) OIL Without a particular flavour, this is always sold refined. It is rich in polyunsaturates and is widely used in the United States and in northern Europe.

• COTTONSEED OIL No particular flavour and always sold refined. This oil has a high smoke point and good polyunsaturated fat content. It is widely used outside Europe as a cooking agent, and in the West it is used as an ingredient in margarine, baked goods and proprietary dressings.

• GROUNDNUT (PEANUT) OIL No particular flavour and always sold refined. It remains liquid at quite low temperatures, 5°C (41°F). It is widely used in Asian cooking and in the United States.

• OLIVE OIL Extra-virgin unrefined olive oil and refined olive oil are widely used in southern Europe and their use is widening to the rest of Europe, North America and Japan. See separate entry on *Olive oil.*

• RAPESEED (CANOLA) OIL No particular flavour and always sold refined. It has a high monounsaturated fatty acid content and high levels of omega 6. It is widely used in northern Europe and increasingly in North America.

• SOYA BEAN OIL This is a refined oil with a light neutral flavour, suitable for all seasonings. Widely used around the world.

• SUNFLOWER SEED OIL This refined oil has a light, almost neutral, flavour with a low solidification point. It has a high polyunsaturated fatty acid content and is widely used for that reason. The unrefined oil has a very definite, slightly earthy flavour.

Besides the above major oils, there are others which are more localized or less well known.

• AVOCADO OIL This is a relatively new oil, produced from fruit grown in California. Made from the flesh of the fruit without the aid of chemical solvents, it has a high monounsaturated fatty acid content.

• COCONUT OIL This has a high saturated fatty acid content and solidifies at much higher temperatures than other vegetable oils. It is used locally in India, Indonesia and the Philippines as a cooking medium and in the rest of the world in the manufacture of margarine and other mixed oils.

• GRAPESEED OIL This is produced mainly in the south of France and is sold refined. It has a very high smoke point and is recommended for deep-frying. It has a very high polyunsaturated fatty acid content.

• HAZELNUT OIL This is a relatively new oil and it was first manufactured in the 1970s. Small quantities are made in France with nuts from France, Italy and Turkey. It is used to contribute a nutty flavour to dressings and sauces.

• PALM OIL There are two kinds of palm oil – one made from the thick fibrous layer on the outside of the fruit and the other from the kernel inside. The oils are produced and widely used in West Africa and Indonesia. In the West the oil is used in the production of margarine, biscuits and other manufactured foods.

• POPPY-SEED OIL This has a very fine flavour when it is left unrefined. It is used in salads and for crudités, particularly in northern France. It is known as *huile blanche* in France.

• PUMPKIN (OR MARROW-SEED) OIL This has a strong, slightly sweet flavour and is not suitable for all dishes.

• RICE BRAN OIL This light refined oil with little flavour has a high unsaturated fatty acid content and good levels of antioxidants.

• SAFFLOWER OIL A refined oil with little flavour and a high unsaturated fatty acid content, this is widely used in Asia.

• SESAME OIL There are two types of sesame oil. One uses roasted seeds to produce a dark oil with an extremely strong flavour. This is widely used to give added flavour to Chinese and Asian dishes – a few drops will give a strong taste of sesame. The other uses unroasted seeds to make a well-flavoured, but much lighter, oil which can be used in much the same way as nut oils.

• WALNUT OIL This has a characteristic nutty taste and is used principally in dressings and seasonings.

France has a tradition of producing walnut oil and the best oils come from the nuts of native trees. However, walnuts may also come from Turkey, India or the United States. Walnut oil has a high polyunsaturated fatty acid, including omega 3. It has the disadvantage of turning rancid quickly.

• OTHER OILS Other oils include sweet almond oil, which is used in the manufacture of confectionery and in the pharmaceutical and cosmetic industries; pine seed oil and pistachio nut oil, both less common and used for dressings; mustard oil, which is used in India and the Far East in the same way as ghee (clarified butter); and paraffin oil, which is used to coat dried fruit thinly, to prevent it from sticking together. Paraffin oil is a hydrocarbon and not a vegetable oil – if consumed in quantity, it can act as a strong laxative.

OILLE Originally, a large stockpot; the word was then applied also to the contents of the pot. This sense is still preserved in Spain, with its *olla podrida*, and in certain regional dishes from south-western France, such as *ouillade*, *ouillat* and *oulade*.

Until the 19th century a *pot-à-oille* was a large silver pot in which a substantial soup was served.

OISEAU SANS TÊTE The French name, meaning literally 'headless bird', for a slice of meat (veal, beef or mutton) that is stuffed, rolled, tied, possibly barded, and usually cooked in a sauce or braised. In Flanders, *vogels zonder kop* (a literal translation of the French term) are slices of beef stuffed with sausagemeat (or a rasher or slice of bacon seasoned with spiced salt), simmered in stock flavoured with aromatic herbs, served with mashed potatoes, and coated with the cooking juices thickened with beurre manié. Alternatively, they may be cooked with onions and beer, as in a carbonade.

RECIPE

oiseaux sans tête
Bone a shoulder of mutton or lamb and cut it into 8 slices. Beat them, trim the edges and season with salt and pepper. Make a stuffing from breadcrumbs (soaked in milk and squeezed dry) and plenty of finely chopped parsley, chives, chervil and tarragon and a raw egg. Put some of this stuffing in the centre of each slice of meat and roll it up. Put a small sprig of rosemary on top of each roll and wrap it in a piece of caul fat, preferably lamb's. Fry 250 g (9 oz, 3 cups) chopped mushrooms in a mixture of butter and oil, drain them and spread them over the bottom of an ovenproof dish. Arrange the rolls side by side on top of the onions. Cover the casserole with buttered greaseproof (wax) paper and cook in a preheated oven at 220°C (425°F, gas 7) for 25 minutes.

Just before serving, mix ½ teaspoon curry powder with a little crème fraîche. Pour this sauce over the rolls and serve.

OKRA A tropical plant widely cultivated as a vegetable. The most widespread species, also known as ladies' fingers, gumbo and (in France) *bamia* or *bamya*, is grown for its pods, which have longitudinal ridges and are either elongated – 6–12 cm, (2½–4½ in) long – or short and squat – 3–4 cm (1¼–1½ in) long. It contains small seeds and a mucus substance, which gives okra its character. Another species, from New Guinea, is cultivated for its sorrel-like leaves.

Okra, which originally came from Africa or Asia and was introduced into the Americas by the black slaves, first appeared in Europe in the 17th century as a typical ingredient of Caribbean cookery.

Okra is used before it is ripe, when it is green and pulpy and the seeds are not completely formed (ripe seeds were formerly used as a substitute for coffee). It can be obtained fresh throughout the year and is also available dried and canned. When quickly fried in very hot oil, tender young okra retain their texture and do not become slimy, so stir-frying and deep-frying are useful methods. They can be cooked in butter or cream, braised with bacon, fried, puréed, or prepared with lime or rice. Okra are added to tajines, foutou and Caribbean ratatouille, and eaten with mutton in Egypt and chicken in the United States. When added early on in the cooking, the okra thicken the cooking liquor; added at the end, the young whole vegetables remain crisp.

RECIPE

okra à la créole
Wash the okra carefully. If using dried vegetables, soak them in cold water for about 12 hours. Top and tail (stem and head) and put in a saucepan. Cover them amply with cold water and cook for 10–25 minutes, skimming from time to time. Drain and dry them. Peel and finely slice 150 g (5 oz) onions and cook in 2 tablespoons oil until soft. Add the okra and brown very gently. Scald, peel and seed 4 large tomatoes. Crush them and add to the okra with 2 crushed garlic cloves, salt, pepper, a little cayenne and powdered saffron. Cover and leave to cook very gently for at least 1 hour (more if using dried okra). Adjust the seasoning. Serve in a dish with a border of rice *à la créole*.

OKROCHKA A Russian soup made from *kvass* (home-made beer) and vegetables, served cold with quartered hard-boiled (hard-cooked) eggs, chopped herbs and cucumber, and soured (sour) cream. The accompanying garnish may be a salpicon of leftover beef fillet, white chicken meat, pickled tongue and ham, or of diced crayfish tails and salmon.

OLEAGINOUS PLANTS Fruits, seeds and plants with a high fat content. They include walnuts, hazelnuts, almonds, pistachios, peanuts, olives and the seeds of sesame, safflower, poppy, soya, sunflower and rape. Besides their main use as a source of oil, oleaginous plants and seeds play an important role in cookery and gastronomy. They are served raw, grilled (broiled), 'roasted' (fried) or salted as snacks to eat with apéritifs and they feature in many exotic recipes, as well as in more mundane cooking. Like all fatty substances, oleaginous plants and seeds combine well with green vegetables and salads.

OLIVE The small oval fruit of the olive tree, widely cultivated in Mediterranean regions. The fruit ripens from green to black; the fleshy pulp, enclosing an oval stone (pit), is the source of olive oil; and the whole fruit, stoned (pitted) or stuffed, is used in cookery as a flavouring, ingredient or hors d'oeuvre.

Originating in the East, the olive tree is extremely long-lived; its history is bound up with that of the Mediterranean, which since biblical times has been its native habitat. Large quantities of olives were consumed by both the Greeks and the Egyptians, who credited the goddess Isis with the discovery of oil extraction. In Greek mythology, Pallas Athene struck the Acropolis with her spear and out sprang the olive tree; she then taught men how to cultivate it and make use of its fruits. The Romans, too, venerated the olive tree. Throughout ancient times, both olives and olive oil were essential in nutrition and food preparation.

The Romans took the olive tree to all the Mediterranean countries, together with the techniques of oil extraction and the preparation of table olives. It continues to be widely grown in all countries of the Mediterranean basin, where the fruity taste of the olive is very apparent in the cooking. Spain is the leading producer of table olives, followed by Turkey, Greece and Morocco. Small quantities are also produced in Italy, Portugal and in southern France. The olive tree was introduced into Latin America in the 16th century and from there into California in the 19th century. California is now an important producer of table olives.

Fresh olives have a very bitter taste and are not edible in the raw state. The bitterness must be removed in a curing process before the olives can be eaten. There are two basic types of table olive, green and black (ripe). Table olives are an ingredient of many hors d'oeuvre and Mediterranean dishes, including pizzas, *mezze* from Greece, tapas from Spain, dishes *à la niçoise* and *à la provençale* and so on. They are eaten widely as cocktail snacks, but are also used in cookery, either plain or stuffed, for preparing duck, daubes, paupiettes and many other dishes.

• GREEN OLIVES These are gathered before they are ripe, treated to remove the bitter taste, then rinsed and pickled in brine. In France, varieties of green olive include the Picholine from the Gard region, Corsica and the Bouches-du-Rhône; Lucques from the Hérault and Aude regions; and Salonenque from the Bouches-du-Rhône.

• BLACK (RIPE) OLIVES These are harvested when fully ripe; they are not treated with an alkali but are pickled in brine and then sometimes in oil. Two of the best varieties grown in France are the 'Nyons' from the Drôme and the Vaucluse, and the 'Cailletier' from around Nice.

• OTHER OLIVE PRODUCTS Olives are also marketed in many other ways. 'Cracked' green olives, called *cachado*, are pickled in brine seasoned with herbs and spices. Green olives in water (*à l'eau*) are repeatedly soaked in water to remove the bitterness; they have a strong fruity taste, but retain a slight bitterness. Green olives are often prepared stuffed with anchovies, sweet (bell) peppers, pimiento or almonds. Black olives pickled in wine vinegar (from Kalamata in Greece) are treated with brine mixed with oil and vinegar. Black olives preserved dry in salt have a good fruity, slightly bitter taste, but do not keep well. The black olives from Morocco, washed and dried in the sun, are lightly salted, then packaged or barrelled in oil. Finally, black olives can simply be dried in the sun. Today these traditional methods are supplemented by the mass production of table olives using faster chemical treatments which leave the olives with considerably less flavour. Some olives lose some of their black colour during this process and so they are dyed with ferrous gluconate.

RECIPES

cabbage charlotte with olives

Blanch a cabbage, then cook in water and put through a vegetable mill. To the resulting purée add 100 ml (4 fl oz, 7 tablespoons) water, I egg yolk and a little grated cheese. Stone (pit) and coarsely chop 30 black (ripe) olives and add them to the cabbage purée with a stiffly whisked egg white. Mix well. Butter a charlotte mould and sprinkle with dried breadcrumbs. Pour the mixture into the mould and cook in a preheated oven at 220°C (425°F, gas 7) for about 30 minutes.

cracked olives

Split some green olives, without crushing them, by giving them a light tap with a mallet on the top end. Cover with cold water and leave them for I week, changing the water every day. Then put them into brine, prepared using I kg (2¼ lb) salt per 8 litres (14 pints, 9 quarts) water, flavoured with bay leaf, fennel, the skin of an orange and some coriander seeds, and cover with fennel. Leave the olives for 8 days before eating.

duck with olives

Stone 250 g (9 oz, 1½ cups) green olives, blanch them for 10 minutes in boiling water, refresh them under cold water and drain. Rub salt and pepper on the inside and the outside of a duck weighing about 2 kg (4½ lb) and truss it. Slice 200 g (7 oz) slightly salted bacon into small strips, blanch for 5 minutes in boiling water, refresh and dry, then fry in 40 g (1½ oz, 3 tablespoons) butter. Drain.

Fry the duck until golden in the same butter, then remove it. Still using the same butter, brown 2 onions and 2 carrots, both finely chopped. Add 250 ml (8 fl oz, I cup) meat stock, I tablespoon

tomato purée (paste), a pinch of crumbled thyme and bay leaf, and I tablespoon chopped parsley. Season with salt and pepper, cook gently for about 20 minutes, then strain.

Pour this sauce into a large flameproof casserole, add the duck and the bacon, cover the pot and bring to the boil on top of the stove. Transfer the casserole to a preheated oven at 230°C (450°F, gas 8) and cook for 35–40 minutes, then add the olives and continue cooking for at least another 10 minutes. Arrange the duck on a hot serving dish, cover it with the sauce, and arrange the olives all around it.

olives stuffed with anchovy butter

Wash and dry some salted anchovies, remove the fillets and pound to a purée. Mix this with butter, using 65 g (2½ oz, 5 tablespoons) butter for 5 anchovies. Season with pepper and mix everything well together. Put the anchovy butter into a piping (pastry) bag with a very narrow plain nozzle and stuff the olives. Keep them in the refrigerator until ready to serve as appetizers or with crudités.

OLIVE OIL Olive oil has a history stretching back before the written word, but the first records of its use are found in ancient Egypt. Olive oil probably originated in the Middle East, from where its production gradually spread to other parts of the Mediterranean basin. Olive oil is now produced in all countries that have a Mediterranean-type climate, including parts of Australia, New Zealand, South Africa and South America. California is also becoming an increasingly important centre of production.

There are two main grades of olive oil: extra-virgin olive oil and olive oil. Extra-virgin olive oil is unique among cooking oils in that it is made directly from the fresh juice of the olive fruit. The fruit is picked, milled and pressed, and the resulting juice is separated into oil and water. If the oil meets the required standard, it is bottled and sold as extra-virgin olive oil; if the oil fails the chemical and taste requirements for extra-virgin status, it is refined and bottled as olive oil. Extra-virgin olive oil is virgin olive oil with less than 1% acidity. Ordinary olive oil has about 15% extra-virgin olive oil added to it to give it a mild flavour of olives.

Olive oil has always been valued for its flavour, but in recent years it has also been highlighted for its value in a healthy eating regime. Olive oil is rich in monounsaturated fatty acids, which are thought to be beneficial in protecting against coronary heart disease.

The olive oil with the best flavour is the freshest and youngest. The oil may be filtered to give a bright clear colour or it may be left unfiltered, when it may be quite cloudy. Unfiltered oil will deteriorate more quickly. Colour is no indication of quality or flavour. Olive oil varies in flavour from light and delicate to strong and pungent; it may be sweet, bitter or peppery. In general, the olive oils of Spain and France tend to be less aggressive than those of Greece or central Italy. However, northern Italy,

Sicily and Crete may also produce lighter styles of oil. Californian oils vary from very mild to quite pungent. Some oils carry the words 'first pressed' or 'cold pressed' on the label. These phrases do not mean very much today, as modern equipment (both hydraulic and centrifugal) is such that there is no second pressing and the extraction can be temperature controlled.

■ **Using olive oil** Olive oil is the traditional cooking medium of the Mediterranean and it can be used in almost any culinary application that requires fat. Ordinary olive oil is best for high temperature cooking and deep-frying as it has a high smoke point. Extra-virgin olive oil has a lower smoke point, but it will stand up to flash-frying, grilling, basting and pot-roasting. Extra-virgin olive oil is used to dress salads, cooked vegetables and fish dishes, and to finish soups and stews. It is also served at the beginning of the meal on its own with bread or crudités.

Its definite taste makes olive oil a flavouring ingredient in its own right and it is worth taking care to match the flavour and strength of the oil to the other ingredients in the dish. While mild and sweet oils, such as those from Provence or Liguria, are particularly good with fish, strong salad ingredients, such as rocket (arugula) or watercress, will need a more pungent olive oil from Tuscany or the Greek mainland. Olive oil can also be used in baking to make cakes, cookies and biscuits, and for the short-term preservation of roasted vegetables, wild mushrooms and goat's cheeses.

Olive oil should be used as soon after purchase as possible. If you need to store it, choose a cool, dark cupboard.

OLIVER, RAYMOND French chef (born Langon 1909; died Paris 1990). His father, who had been a chef at the Savoy in London, kept a hotel in Bordeaux, where Oliver started his apprenticeship. In 1948 he and Louis Vaudable, owner of Maxim's (which had been closed when France was liberated), reopened the Grand Véfour restaurant and restored it to its former glory. In 1950 Oliver became the manager of the restaurant and its success was assured.

Raymond Oliver can be regarded as one of the great innovators and reformers of French cuisine, as evidenced by such dishes as red mullet with basil butter in puff pastry, ragoût of pike and crayfish with aniseed, sautéed chicken in honey vinegar, stuffed guinea fowl Jean Cocteau, or the simpler lampreys *à la bordelaise* and other classic regional dishes. French cuisine has gained a great deal from his humour and his deep knowledge of the culinary arts, which he demonstrated in television programmes. He also lectured in other countries and was the author of various books.

OLIVET A small soft French cow's-milk cheese (40% fat), made in the small town of Olivet, in the Loiret. The skin is either bluish (Olivet Bleu) or ash-covered. The cheese is straw-coloured, with a fruity or spicy taste, and is made in flat discs 12–13 cm

(4½–5 in) in diameter and 2–3 cm (about 1 in) thick. Balzac liked to eat it with walnuts and chilled wine.

OLIVET CENDRÉ Soft cow's-milk cheese (40% fat) with a natural crust covered in ashes after being ripened for 3 months in a container filled with wood ash. Olivet cendré has a more pronounced, soapier taste than Olivet.

OLLA PODRIDA A Spanish soup whose name, literally translated, means 'rotten soup'. Numerous regional varieties are found using local produce. The ingredients include various pulses, vegetables, meat and sometimes fruit. This is a country dish that has evolved from the traditional Cocido.

OMBIAUX, MAURICE DES Belgian writer and gastronome (born Beauraing 1868; died Paris 1943). Nicknamed the 'Prince of Walloon story-tellers' and 'Cardinal of gastronomy'. He wrote many books which were published in the 1920s.

OMBRINE A sea fish found in the Mediterranean and the Bay of Biscay. It grows to a length of 1 m (39 in) and is silvery in colour, with golden or grey-blue stripes on the back and a marked lateral stripe. It has a short beard on the lower jaw. The flesh is as good as (if not better than) that of bass, and the same recipes can be used to cook it.

OMELETTE A sweet or savoury dish made from beaten whole eggs, cooked in a frying pan, and served plain or with various additions. The word comes from the French *lamelle* (thin strip) because of its flat shape; previously it was known as *alumelle* and then *alumette*, and finally *amelette*. (Some authorities claim that the word has a Latin origin, *ova mellita*, a classic Roman dish consisting of beaten eggs cooked on a flat clay dish with honey.)

The success of an omelette depends as much on the quality of the pan and the quantity and distribution of the butter as on the cooking. A large variety of different ingredients may be mixed with the omelette or added just before serving, with a ribbon of sauce. An omelette can be served, either flat or folded, as an entrée or a dessert, depending on whether it is savoury or sweet; it is nearly always served hot. It can also be used as a garnish for soup and some Chinese rice dishes.

Omelettes were known during the Middle Ages. In the 17th century one of the most famous omelettes was *omelette du curé*, containing soft carp roes and tuna fish, which Brillat-Savarin much admired. Nowadays, a particularly popular French omelette is the variety known as *Mère Poulard* (after the owner of the Hotel Poulard in Mont-Saint-Michel in the early 1900s). The omelette owes its fame to the high quality of the Norman butter and eggs as well as to a special knack in the making. Some chefs recommend beating the yolks and the whites separately to obtain a lighter and foamier omelette. Among the different types of savoury omelettes are:

• OMELETTES COOKED WITH A FLAVOURING The flavouring is mixed with the beaten eggs before cooking.

• FILLED OMELETTES The hot filling is spread on the omelette, which is then folded over and slipped on to the serving dish.

• GARNISHED OMELETTES Filled omelettes with some garnish placed on the top; if this garnish is accompanied by a sauce or bound with butter, it is poured into a slit made in the omelette. It is usual for a garnished omelette to be surrounded by a ribbon of sauce.

• FLAT OMELETTES Made like plain omelettes but with fewer eggs; they are cooked for a longer time and turned over in the pan halfway through cooking. The result is a sort of thick pancake which can be served cold, accompanied by the same garnishes as a plain omelette.

Sweet omelettes are usually filled with jam or poached fruit flavoured with a liqueur; they are sprinkled with sugar and glazed in the oven, or they may be flamed.

Soufflé omelettes are really a type of soufflé cooked in a shallow dish (rather than in a deep soufflé dish). They can be flavoured with liqueur, fruit or coffee.

RECIPES

plain omelette
Beat 8 eggs lightly and season with salt and (if liked) freshly ground pepper; 2–3 tablespoons milk or 1 tablespoon single (light) cream can be added to the beaten eggs. Heat 25–40 g (1–1½ oz, 2–3 tablespoons) butter in a scrupulously clean pan, preferably non-stick. Raise the heat and pour in the beaten eggs. Stir them with a fork, drawing the edges to the centre as soon as they begin to set. When the omelette is cooked, slide it on to a warm serving dish, folding it in three. Rub a piece of butter over the surface to make it shiny.

Filled Omelettes
chicken-liver omelette
Slice some chicken livers, sauté them quickly in butter and bind them with some reduced demi-glace sauce. Fill the omelette with this mixture and garnish with a ribbon of demi-glace flavoured with Madeira.

kidney omelette
Slice or finely dice some calf's or sheep's kidneys, sauté them in butter and bind them with some reduced demi-glace sauce flavoured with Madeira. Fill the omelette with this mixture. Garnish with a ribbon of Madeira-flavoured demi-glace.

omelette Argenteuil
Cook an omelette and fill it with 3 tablespoons asparagus tips cooked in butter. Fold it on to a hot serving dish. Pour some cream sauce around it.

omelette with black pudding
Grill (broil) some black pudding (blood sausage) and skin it while it is still hot. Mash the meat with a fork. Separate some eggs and whisk the yolks and whites separately, then fold them together. Cook the omelette and fill it with the black pudding before folding it.

salsify omelette with Brussels sprouts
Cook some salsify in white wine, dice it, braise it in butter and bind with some reduced velouté sauce. Fill an omelette with the mixture and serve it surrounded with noisette potatoes and Brussels sprouts sautéed in butter. Reduce some demi-glace sauce, stir in some butter and pour the sauce around the dish.

other recipes See *chasseur, châtelaine, duxelles, japonaise, Maintenon, portugaise, rouennaise, Saint-Hubert, shrimps and prawns.*

Flat Omelettes
courgette omelette
Slice some courgettes (zucchini) into thin rounds and sauté them in butter in a frying pan. Beat the eggs with chopped parsley, salt and pepper, pour them into the pan over the courgettes and cook the omelette on both sides like a thick pancake.

omelette à la grecque
Beat the eggs, adding some chopped onions softened in butter and diced sweet (bell) peppers. Make 2 flat omelettes. Put one of them on a round plate and spread with a layer of very hot finely chopped braised mutton or lamb; cover with the second omelette. Pour some tomato sauce seasoned with a little garlic round the omelette, sprinkle with chopped parsley and moisten with noisette butter.

omelette à la Sainte-Flour
Brown some sliced onions and blanched bacon strips in pork fat. Beat the eggs, adding the onions and bacon, and make 2 flat omelettes. Put one of them on a dish and spread with a layer of braised chopped cabbage. Cover with the second omelette and surround with a ribbon of tomato sauce.

omelette à la verdurière
Cut some sorrel and lettuce into very fine strips and cook them gently in butter. Beat the eggs and add the sorrel and lettuce with some chopped parsley, chervil and tarragon. Cook like a large pancake. Sprinkle with noisette butter.

omelette Du Barry
Steam some very small florets of cauliflower. Take them out while they are still a little crisp and fry them in butter. Pour on the eggs, beaten with salt, pepper and chopped chervil, and cook like a large pancake.

omelette Mistral

Brown 3 tablespoons diced aubergines (eggplants) in oil in a frying pan. Beat the eggs together with some diced tomato gently fried in oil, chopped parsley and a pinch of finely chopped garlic. Pour the eggs over the aubergines and cook like a large pancake.

omelette mousseline

Beat 6 egg yolks with 2 tablespoons double (heavy) cream and season with salt and pepper. Whisk the egg whites to stiff peaks and fold into the mixture. Cook like a large pancake.

omelette Parmentier

Finely dice some potatoes and fry them in butter. Beat the eggs and add the potatoes and some chopped parsley. Cook like a large pancake.

seafood omelette

Beat the eggs with chopped parsley and chervil, salt and pepper and make 2 flat omelettes. Put one on to a round ovenproof dish and cover it with a ragoût of mussels, prawns (shrimp), small clams or other shellfish, poached and bound with shrimp sauce. Cover with the second omelette. Coat with a cream sauce flavoured with shrimp butter and glaze in a hot oven.

spinach omelette

Braise enough spinach leaves in butter to provide 4 tablespoons cooked spinach. Mix with 8 beaten eggs and cook like a large pancake.

other recipes See *diplomate, jardinière, ménagère, Mont-Bry, niçoise, paysanne, romaine.*

Garnished Omelettes

omelette André-Theuriet

Fill an omelette with morels in cream. Turn it into a dish and garnish with bunches of asparagus tips cooked in butter. On top, arrange some slices of mushroom which have been tossed in butter. Surround with a ribbon of suprême sauce and serve at once while very hot.

omelette Feydeau

Make a very creamy omelette and fill it with mushroom duxelles. Slide it on to a flameproof dish, then garnish the top with poached eggs (one per person) – choose small eggs and keep them underdone. Mask with Mornay sauce to which finely shredded mushrooms have been added. Sprinkle with grated Parmesan cheese and brown quickly under a hot grill (broiler).

other recipes See *espagnole, fines herbes, hongroise, parisienne, Rossini, viveur.*

Omelettes Cooked with their Flavouring

anchovy omelette

Soak 3 anchovy fillets until free of salt and rub them through a sieve. Add the anchovy purée to 8 eggs and beat together. Cook the omelette as usual. Garnish with a criss-cross pattern of fine strips of anchovies in oil.

artichoke omelette

Slice 4 artichoke hearts and sauté them in butter until they are half-cooked, without letting them brown. Add the artichoke slices to 8 eggs and beat together; cook the omelette as usual. It can be garnished with a row of sliced sautéed artichoke hearts and surrounded with a ribbon of reduced veal stock.

aubergine omelette

Add 2 tablespoons diced aubergines (eggplants), sautéed in oil, to 8 eggs and beat together. Cook the omelette.

bacon omelette

Fry 3–4 tablespoons diced bacon in butter and beat into 8 eggs. Cook the omelette. It can be garnished with 6 thin strips of bacon fried in butter.

cep omelette

Brown 200 g (7 oz, 2 cups) sliced cep mushrooms in butter or oil and add them, with some chopped parsley, to 8 eggs, beating them all together. Cook the omelette. Garnish with a line of chopped ceps sautéed in butter or oil.

Any edible mushrooms can be used to flavour this omelette.

omelette jurassienne

Fry 4 tablespoons finely diced bacon in a large pan over a low heat. Add 1 chopped onion, 3 diced boiled potatoes and 1 diced tomato. In a large bowl, beat 4 eggs with 100 g (4 oz, 1 cup) grated Gruyère cheese and some chopped chives. Pour this mixture over the bacon and vegetables in the pan. Add a little salt and plenty of pepper and finish cooking the omelette.

sorrel omelette

Prepare 4 tablespoons finely shredded sorrel. Cook gently in butter or bind with cream, and beat it into 8 eggs. Cook the omelette. It may be served surrounded with a ribbon of cream sauce.

tuna omelette

For 6 people, wash 2 soft carp roes and blanch them for 5 minutes in lightly salted boiling water. Chop the roes together with a piece of fresh tuna about the size of a hen's egg so that they are well mixed. Put the chopped fish and roes into a pan with a small, finely chopped shallot and butter and sauté until all the butter is incorporated – this gives the essential flavour to the omelette.

Blend some fresh butter with parsley and chives, and spread it on to the dish in which the omelette will be served; sprinkle with lemon juice and keep warm.

Beat 12 eggs, add the sautéed roes and tuna, and mix well together. Cook the omelette in the usual way, keeping the shape long rather than circular, and ensure that it is thick and creamy. As soon as it is ready, arrange it on the prepared dish and serve at once.

This dish should be reserved for special luncheons for those who appreciate good food. Serve it with a good wine, and the result will be superb.

Notes on preparation: the roes and the tuna should be sautéed over a very low heat, otherwise they will harden and it will be difficult to mix them properly with the eggs. The serving dish should be fairly deep, and preferably fish-shaped, so that the sauce can be spooned up when serving. The dish should be heated enough to melt the maître d'hôtel butter on which the omelette is placed.

other recipes See *fermière, sea urchin.*

Sweet Omelettes
omelette à la dijonnaise
Beat 8 eggs with 2 tablespoons sugar, 2 or 3 finely crushed macaroons and I tablespoon double (heavy) cream. Make 2 flat omelettes. Put one of them on to a round ovenproof dish and spread it with 3 tablespoons very thick confectioner's custard (see *custard*) mixed with I tablespoon ground almonds flavoured with Cassis. Place the second omelette on top and completely coat with egg whites whisked to stiff peaks. Sprinkle with icing (confectioner's) sugar and glaze quickly in a very hot oven. Serve the omelette surrounded by a ribbon of blackcurrant jam.

omelette flambée
Beat the eggs with some sugar and a pinch of salt, then cook the omelette in butter, keeping it very creamy. Dredge with sugar, sprinkle with heated rum and set light to it immediately before serving. The rum can be replaced by Armagnac, Calvados, Cognac, whisky or a fruit-based spirit.

omelette Reine Pédauque
Beat 8 eggs with I tablespoon caster (superfine) sugar, I tablespoon ground almonds, I tablespoon double (heavy) cream and a pinch of salt. Make 2 flat omelettes. Place one of the omelettes in a round ovenproof serving dish. Mix 6 tablespoons thick apple compote with 2 tablespoons double (heavy) cream and I tablespoon rum. Spread this mixture over the omelette, put the second omelette on top, sprinkle with icing (confectioner's) sugar and glaze quickly in the oven or under the grill (broiler).

omelette with fruit compote
Prepare a compote of peaches, plums, apples or apricots: cook the fruit in vanilla-flavoured syrup, drain, bind with jam made from the same type of fruit and flavour with liqueur. Beat 8 eggs with I tablespoon caster (superfine) sugar and a pinch of salt. Cook the omelette in butter. Just before folding, fill with 4 tablespoons fruit compote. Fold the omelette, slip it on to a round plate and sprinkle with caster sugar. Glaze under the grill (broiler).

soufflé omelette
Mix together in a bowl 250 g (9 oz, generous I cup) caster (superfine) sugar, 6 egg yolks and I teaspoon vanilla sugar or I tablespoon grated orange or lemon zest. Beat until the mixture turns white and thick. Whisk 8 egg whites to stiff peaks and fold carefully into the yolk mixture.

Butter a long ovenproof dish and sprinkle it with caster sugar. Pour in three-quarters of the omelette mixture and smooth it into a low mound with the blade of a knife. Put the rest of the mixture into a piping (pastry) bag with a plain round nozzle and pipe an interlaced decoration on top of the omelette. Sprinkle with caster sugar. Cook in a preheated oven at 200°C (400°F, gas 6) for about 20 minutes. Dredge with icing (confectioner's) sugar and glaze under the grill (broiler).

The omelette can also be flavoured with chocolate, coffee or a liqueur.

soufflé omelette with wild strawberries
Clean, wash and drain some wild strawberries. Leave them to macerate in a few spoonfuls of Alsace framboise (raspberry-flavoured spirit) with a pinch of vanilla sugar. Whisk 4 egg whites to stiff peaks and separately beat the yolks with a little sugar. Mix the two carefully, then pour into a heavy frying pan containing very hot butter. When the eggs begin to set, add the strawberries, fold the omelette over and continue to cook over a low heat. Dredge very lightly with sugar and serve. A little fresh strawberry purée can be poured over the omelette.

other recipes See *Célestine, normande.*

OMELETTE SURPRISE A dessert based on the same ingredients as a baked Alaska – sponge cake soaked in syrup, ice cream and meringue – but with the addition of fruit. The base, which may be Genoa cake, Genoese sponge or madeleine cake mixture, is sprinkled with liqueur, covered with a bombe mixture, a fruit ice cream or a parfait mixture, mixed with preserved fruits or pralined violets. The whole is then masked with meringue and glazed in the oven. The dessert is surrounded by poached fruits or cherries in brandy.

ONGLET A French cut of beef consisting of two small muscles joined by an elastic membrane (the supporting muscles of the diaphragm). The butcher splits it open, trims it and removes all the skin and membrane. Onglet must be well hung; the meat is then tender and juicy. In the past it was not a popular cut, but it is now accepted that it makes a prime steak. Whether fried or grilled (broiled), it should be eaten rare, otherwise it becomes tough.

RECIPES

fried onglet with shallots
Make shallow criss-cross incisions on both sides of the meat. Peel and chop 3–4 shallots. Heat about

25 g (1 oz, 2 tablespoons) butter in a frying pan; when it is very hot, put in the meat and brown it quickly on both sides. Season with salt and pepper, drain it and keep it hot. Cook the shallots in the frying pan until golden. Add 2–3 tablespoons vinegar to the pan and reduce the liquid by half. Pour this gravy over the meat.

grilled onglet

Make shallow criss-cross incisions on both sides of the meat and rub it with a little oil and pepper. Cook under a very hot grill (broiler), seasoning with salt halfway through cooking, and serve rare.

ONION A plant, grown in many countries, whose bulb is probably the most common vegetable used in cooking. It is a member of the *Allium* genus and includes chives, garlic, leeks and shallots. The bulb is formed of white fleshy leaves covered with several layers of thin papery skin, red, brown, yellow or white in colour. Depending on the variety, its flavour varies from very mild to strong. It is eaten fresh or dried, raw or cooked, as an ingredient in other dishes, or as a seasoning.

Originating in northern Asia and Palestine, the onion has been cultivated for more than 5000 years. It was highly esteemed by the Egyptians and the Jews, who usually ate it raw, and the Greeks attributed great therapeutic values to it. In Europe it has been one of the mainstays of cooking since the end of the Middle Ages.

The following are examples of the popular varieties of onions.

• GLOBE OR BULB ONIONS are the common brown-skinned onions. There are many types with different strengths of flavour and some have a strong aroma with a sharp taste. They are grown in Britain, France, Italy, Holland, Spain, the United States, Australia, Chile, Egypt, Israel, Hungary, Poland and the Canary Islands. As a general rule, when buying British varieties, the smaller the onions, the stronger their flavour.

• SPANISH (YELLOW) ONIONS Originally from Spain, the name is now applied to the largest, brown globe onions. In America the name is given to the large red-skinned onions. They are mild, tender and sweet, suitable for eating raw or cooked.

• BERMUDA ONIONS These vary in skin colour and include red, white and yellow examples. Similar to Spanish onions, they are large and mild in flavour. These are enjoyed in Bermuda, the United States and the West Indies.

• WHITE ONIONS Fairly large onions with white skin, these are mild and sweet, and ideal for serving raw. They can be quite tough.

• RED ONIONS These have dark purple-red skins. The Italian red onion is smaller than the French equivalent and is usually oval and elongated in shape. They are mild and slightly sweet, with pink flesh, which looks attractive when served raw.

• PICKLING ONIONS These small brown onions are picked when the bulb has just been formed. They

ONIONS

globe onion: *rosé de Roscoff*

red onion

pickling onions

globe onions

white onion

spring or salad onions

silverskin onion

are aromatic, juicy and strongly flavoured. As their name indicates, they are pickled (in vinegar); they are also used in casseroles or they can be glazed and served as a vegetable dish.

• PEARL (BUTTON) ONIONS These small white onions are ideal for pickling, but they can also be added to stews and casseroles.

• SILVERSKIN ONIONS These are very small and, as their name suggests, they have silver skin and white flesh. They are used for pickling and are also sold cooked as 'cocktail onions', for use as a garnish, in hors d'oeuvre and adding to drinks.

• SPRING ONIONS (SCALLIONS OR GREEN ONIONS) These are also known as salad onions or bunching onions. These are picked either before the bulbs form or with small white bulbs. Originally these were the seedlings, picked in the spring to thin out the onion beds, but now they are available all the year round. They may be cooked or served in salads. They are ideal for quick methods and are often cooked in stir-fry dishes. Young spring onions are small and mild in flavour, but as they grow the flavour of the larger bulb becomes stronger.

• ORIENTAL ONIONS These are used extensively in China, Japan and Asia. They look like spring onions and grow in clusters. Their thickened stem bases never form bulbs. Both the green and white parts can be eaten and they have a mild flavour, which is between that of a spring onion and leek. Their leaves can be broken off for use, leaving the remainder of the plant growing, which is why they are also sometimes called 'everlasting onions'. Similar varieties include Welsh onions (scallions or green shallots), which originated in Japan not Wales, and Japanese bunching onions.

• EGYPTIAN ONIONS OR TREE ONIONS These vegetables look unusual as they have small bulbs towards the tops of their stems instead of flowers and larger bulbs at the roots. They taste similar to garlic.

■ **Buying and using onions** When buying onions, look for bulbs which are quite firm and store them in a cool, dry, airy place. When preparing onions, the substance which makes the eyes water (allyl sulphide) is released. To chop onions in comfort, put them into the freezer for 10 minutes or into the refrigerator for 1 hour before peeling; small pickling onions are easily peeled if they are boiled rapidly for 1 minute. Leaving the root end on also helps to prevent the volatile substance from being released. (It disappears during cooking.) Once peeled, onions oxidize rapidly and can eventually become toxic; peeled onions should therefore be kept covered.

The onion is a major ingredient in cooking, being used especially as a flavouring in many casseroled dishes, in which it may be chopped, sliced or left whole and studded with cloves. Onions are also used for stuffings and to make sauces and braised dishes. In many dishes they are the main ingredient; for example, in France they are used in onion tart from Alsace, pissaladière, tourin, salt cod *à la bretonne*, onion soup, beef miroton, tripe, Soubise purée and all recipes *à la Soubise*, and in many dishes cooked *à la lyonnaise*. From Asia come onion *bhaji* and from Britain, stuffed onions, which can be served as a hot main dish or as a garnish for roast or braised meat. Fried onion rings are used as a garnish for many dishes (sautéed or fried meat or fish), and finely chopped onion is an ingredient of vinaigrette, marinades and many cold garnishes. The onion is used with potatoes in many stews, gratins, and meat and vegetable soups, and it also goes well with cabbage and with many egg dishes. Small glazed onions are an essential ingredient for a range of meat and fish dishes (matelote, blanquette, chicken *en barbouille*, coq au vin and dishes *à la bourguignonne*). Pickled onions are used as a condiment.

RECIPES

fried onions
Peel some onions, slice them into rings 5 mm (¼ in) thick and separate the rings. Season with salt, dip in flour and fry in very hot oil. Drain them thoroughly on paper towels and sprinkle with fine salt. They can also be marinated in oil and lemon juice for 30 minutes, then dipped in batter and fried.

onion soup
Finely chop 250 g (9 oz, 1½ cups) onions and fry them in butter without letting them get too brown. When they are almost ready, sprinkle with 25 g (1 oz, ¼ cup) plain (all-purpose) flour. Continue cooking for a minute or two, stirring the onions with a wooden spoon, then pour on 2 litres (3½ pints, 9 cups) white stock and flavour with 2 tablespoons port or Madeira. Continue to cook for a further 30 minutes. Put some slices of bread, which have been dried in the oven, into a soup tureen and pour the soup over them.

onion tart
Line a buttered 28 cm (11 in) flan tin (tart pan) with 400 g (14 oz) shortcrust pastry (see *Short* *pastry*) and cook it blind. Meanwhile prepare a Soubise* purée with 1 kg (2¼ lb) onions. Spread this in the flan case, sprinkle with fresh breadcrumbs, dot with butter and brown it in a hot oven for about 15 minutes.

stuffed onions
Peel some large onions, taking care not to split the outer white layer; cut them horizontally at the stalk end, leaving about three-quarters of their total height. Blanch them in salted water for 10 minutes, then refresh and drain them. Scoop out the insides, leaving a thickness all round of 2 layers.

Chop the scooped-out onion finely and mix it with some finely chopped pork, veal, beef, lamb or mutton. Stuff the onions with this mixture, put them in a buttered flameproof casserole and moisten with a few tablespoons of slightly thickened brown veal stock. Start the cooking, with the lid on, on the hob (stovetop), then continue cooking in the oven, basting frequently to glaze the onions. A few minutes before they are cooked, sprinkle with breadcrumbs or Parmesan cheese, moisten with melted butter and brown the surface.

Onions can also be stuffed in the following ways.

• *à la catalane:* rice cooked in meat stock with sweet (bell) peppers fried in olive oil and chopped hard-boiled (hard-cooked) eggs.

• *à l'italienne:* rice cooked in meat stock with finely chopped onion, cooked lean ham and Parmesan cheese.

• *à la parisienne:* finely chopped onion mixed with a duxelles of mushrooms and chopped cooked lean ham.

other recipes See *crêpe, gratinée, Soubise, tourin.*

OPÉRA A garnish for noisettes of veal and sautéed tournedos steaks (filets mignons). It consists of small bunches of asparagus tips and tartlets or croustades filled with chicken livers sautéed in Madeira. The sauce, which is poured over the meat, is made by deglazing the cooking juices with Madeira and demi-glace.

This garnish is also used for shirred eggs; in this case the sauce consists of reduced veal stock enriched with butter.

The dessert *crème renversée Opéra* is a caramel custard turned out of its mould and served decorated with Chantilly cream, crushed meringue and strawberries in kirsch. Opéra gâteau is an elaborate almond sponge cake with a coffee and chocolate filling and icing.

ORACHE A garden plant whose green fleshy triangular leaves are used in soups and herb stocks. Orache leaves may also be cooked like spinach and used either as a vegetable or as a garnish. They may also be used to counteract the bitter taste of sorrel.

ORANGE The fruit of the sweet orange tree, cultivated widely in Mediterranean countries and other parts of the world. It is round with an orange or yellow skin and sweet juicy flesh, divided into segments which may or may not contain seeds. Originating in China and mentioned at the beginning of the Christian era in Indian and Chinese texts, this citrus fruit was probably known to the ancient world. Seville (bitter) oranges were brought to Europe by the Arabs into Spain and by the Crusaders into France. Sweet oranges did not arrive in Europe until later, coming from Arab lands via Genoese or Portuguese merchants; the latter also introduced them to America.

For centuries oranges were a rarity; they were usually made into preserves, used for a table decoration or offered as luxury gifts. Oranges come mainly from Spain, Morocco, Turkey, Sicily, Israel, Italy, Cyprus, Algeria, Tunisia, South Africa, Australia and the United States.

■ **Sweet oranges** The different varieties of sweet oranges are classified into four groups, available at different times of the year.

• NAVEL ORANGES Characterized by a navel-like depression enclosing a small internal embryonic fruit. They are seedless and appear from the end of October. The Washington navels, with a firm rough skin, are juicy and slightly sour. Navellate is closely related to the Washington navel, but smaller and sweeter. The navelina is slightly paler and more oval in shape than the Washington navel; its flesh is tart, becoming sweeter later in the growing season.

• BLONDES These winter oranges have pale flesh. The Shamouti or Jaffa variety is quite large, has a thick skin, seeds and a crisp, well-flavoured, juicy pulp. Salustianas are seedless, have a grainy peel and are very juicy.

• BLOOD ORANGES These small oranges have dark-red pulp and the skin may be veined with dark red. They are available from December to April. The Maltese orange, with seeds, is sour, very juicy and has an exceptionally good flavour. Moro oranges, with a rough skin, are very juicy.

• LATE ORANGES These pale-fleshed oranges have few seeds and a thin rind. They include the Valencia variety. Valencia oranges, with or without seeds, have smooth firm skins and are very sharp and juicy.

■ **Bitter orange**

• SEVILLE ORANGE A bitter orange with rough peel, mostly used for making marmalade, jams and jellies. Seville orange trees are cultivated mainly in Spain, and on a local scale in the south of France, where crystallized (candied) Seville oranges (*chinois confit*) are a speciality of Nice. The flower of the Seville orange is used in the preparation of orange-flower water. The aromatic oil extracted from the thick peel of Seville oranges is used in distilling to flavour Curaçao, Cointreau and Grand Marnier. A traditional French dish is pot-roast duck in bitter-orange sauce (not to be confused with duck *à l'orange*).

■ **Buying and using oranges** When buying oranges, choose fruit that are shiny and heavy for their size. They are not easily damaged and will keep for some days at room temperature. If the zest or peel is to be used, the oranges should be scrubbed in warm water.

Oranges are widely used in desserts, pâtisserie and confectionery, for fruit salads, mousses, dessert creams, frosted fruit, ices and sorbets, jams and marmalades, fritters, soufflés, filled sponges and biscuits (cookies). The candied peel is also used in numerous desserts and cakes, either as an ingredient or as a decoration. Oranges form the basis of an equally large range of drinks: syrups, sodas, juice, orangeade, punches, liqueurs and fruit wines.

Sweet oranges are today used in recipes which, in former times, used bitter oranges: duck which nowadays is described as *à la bigarade* (with bitter oranges) is in fact cooked with sweet oranges. Some of the traditional dishes that use oranges as an ingredient are: trout with orange butter (butter worked with orange juice, grated nutmeg and paprika); sole *à l'orange* (surrounded with peeled orange slices, butter sauce, crème fraîche and Curaçao); young partridge roasted *à l'orange* (garnished with peeled

ORANGES AND TANGERINES

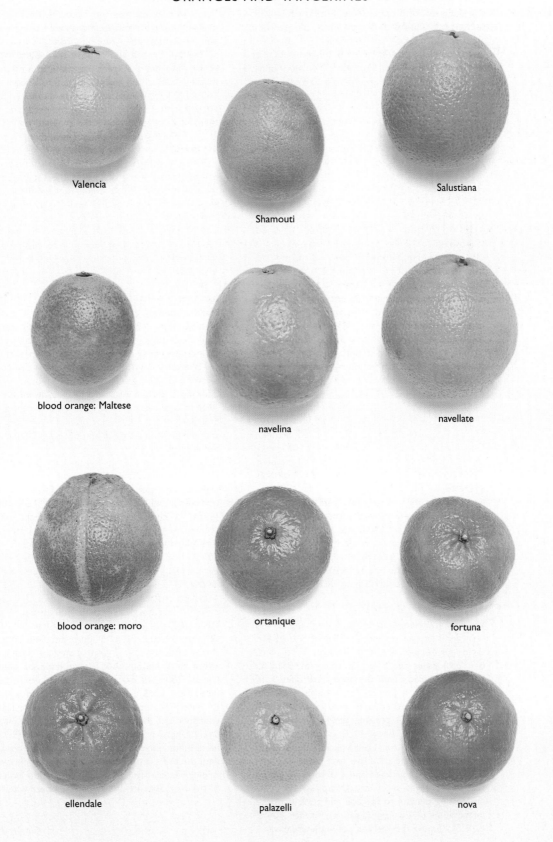

Valencia

Shamouti

Salustiana

blood orange: Maltese

navelina

navellate

blood orange: moro

ortanique

fortuna

ellendale

palazelli

nova

orange segments and grapes, the cooking juices being deglazed with orange juice); fried calf's liver *à l'orange* (garnished with orange slices, the pan being deglazed with orange juice); omelette *à l'orange* (a savoury omelette flavoured with tomato sauce and grated orange zest); veal knuckle *à l'orange* (braised with a julienne of orange zest, with orange juice added to the cooking liquid); sheep's tongues *à l'orange* (cooked in water, covered with a sauce made from vinegar roux, thickened with gooseberry jelly and garnished with orange segments); and salad of chicory (endive), beetroot (beets) and peeled orange segments, dressed with a tarragon-flavoured vinaigrette.

RECIPES

Sweet Oranges
candied orange peel

Choose thick-skinned oranges. Peel them, scrape off all the white pith from the peel and cut the peel into strips. For each orange, put 250 ml (8 fl oz, 1 cup) water, 125 g (4½ oz, scant ⅔ cup) sugar and 6 tablespoons grenadine syrup into a pan and bring to the boil. Add the peel, half-cover the pan and let it simmer gently until the syrup is reduced by three-quarters. Leave the peel in the syrup until it is quite cold, then drain it. Sprinkle a baking sheet thickly with icing (confectioner's) sugar, roll the pieces of peel in the sugar and dry off under the grill (broiler).

frosted oranges

Choose some unblemished thick-skinned oranges. Cut off the top of each orange at the stalk end. Using a sharp-edged spoon, scrape out all the pulp, taking care not to pierce the skin. Cut a small hole at the top of the orange caps, where the stalk was attached. Put the orange shells and the caps into the freezer. Make an orange sorbet with the pulp. When it begins to set, put it into the orange shells, smoothing the top into a dome shape. Replace the caps and insert a long lozenge-shaped piece of candied angelica into the hole, to resemble a leaf. Put back in the freezer until ready to serve.

orange and apple jelly

Weigh some ripe (but not overripe) apples and wash and slice them (without peeling or coring). Put them into a pan and add 1.5 litres (2¾ pints, 6½ cups) water per 1 kg (2¼ lb) apples. Bring to the boil and cook until the apples are quite soft. Pour them into a jelly-bag or a piece of muslin (cheesecloth) stretched over a basin and let the juice drain, without pressing the apples. Measure the juice obtained. Allow 10 large oranges per 1 litre (1¾ pints, 4⅓ cups) apple juice; squeeze them and strain the juice. Mix the two juices and add 900 g (2 lb, 4 cups) sugar and the coarsely grated zest of 3 oranges per 1 litre (1¾ pints, 4⅓ cups) juice. Bring the pan to the boil and cook until the temperature of the jelly (gelatine) reaches 104°C (219°F). Remove the peel and pot in the usual way.

orange conserve

Wash 16 juicy oranges and 3 lemons. Remove the peel without pith from 2 lemons and 4 oranges and chop it. Remove the white pith from this fruit. Cut all the fruit in half and remove the central white string. Take out the seeds, tie these in a piece of muslin (cheesecloth) and put them into a bowl with 250 ml (8 fl oz, 1 cup) water. Slice the halved fruit finely (the peel can be left on or removed) and put them into a large bowl with the chopped peel and 4 litres (7 pints, 4 quarts) water. Leave them to soak for 24 hours, turning the fruit two or three times.

Pour the contents of the bowl into a preserving pan and add the bag containing the seeds. Cover the pan and bring it to the boil. Remove the lid and simmer gently for 2 hours. Add 4 kg (9 lb) granulated or loaf sugar, bring the pan back to the boil, then reduce the heat and simmer, stirring constantly. Skim the pan and continue to cook for 30 minutes after bringing back to the boil. Pot in the usual way.

orange dessert ◆

Make a sponge* cake 24 cm (9½ in) in diameter with 4 eggs, 125 g (4½ oz, ⅔ cup) caster (superfine) sugar and 125 g (4½ oz, 1 cup) plain (all-purpose) flour. Bake and cool on a wire rack.

Make a syrup with 300 ml (½ pint, 1¼ cups) water and 200 g (7 oz, 1 cup) sugar. Wash 2 oranges. Cut in two and slice finely into even slices. Cook the orange slices in the syrup, drain and put them to one side. Remove the zest of 2 oranges, blanch it twice and cook for 10 minutes in the syrup.

Divide the remaining syrup into 3 amounts. Dilute one amount with 3½ tablespoons orange liqueur to moisten the sponge cake. Dilute the second amount with a little orange juice and add 100 g (4 oz, ⅓ cup) orange jelly to make the sauce accompanying the dessert, which is then strained through a fine chinois. Dilute the third amount with 100 g (4 oz, ⅓ cup) orange jelly and a little orange juice, adding 1 leaf of gelatine, melted, for the final glazing.

Make a custard* with 500 ml (17 fl oz, 2¼ cups) milk, flavoured with ½ vanilla pod (bean), 4 egg yolks, 100 g (4 oz, ½ cup) caster sugar and 60 g (2¼ oz, ½ cup) plain (all-purpose) flour. Add 2 sheets of dissolved leaf gelatine and cool it quickly. Whisk until smooth. Add 3½ tablespoons orange liqueur, 150 g (5 oz, 1 cup) candied orange zest, diced very small, and then gently fold in 300 ml (½ pint, 1¼ cups) double (heavy) cream, lightly whipped. Cut the sponge cake horizontally into 3 layers. Line the sides of a ring mould 24 cm (9½ in) in diameter, placed on iced (frosted) cardboard, with the half slices of candied orange, slightly overlapping. Place a layer of sponge cake at the bottom of the ring. Soak it with syrup and cover with half

Orange dessert.

the cream. Put the second layer of sponge cake on top, soak it again and cover with the remaining cream. Put the last layer of sponge cake on top, with the golden side facing upward. Press gently and soak with the rest of the syrup. Put in the refrigerator for a few hours. Glaze with the jelly and put it back in the refrigerator to set. Carefully remove from the ring. Pour a fine ribbon of sauce around and decorate with candied orange zest and sprigs of mint.

orange sorbet

Select 10 very large juicy oranges and remove the peel and pith. Put the pulp through a juice extractor to obtain the maximum amount of juice. Measure the juice and add 300 g (11 oz, 1⅓ cups) sugar per 1 litre (1¾ pints, 4⅓ cups) (more if the juice is very sour). Pour the juice into an ice-cream maker and leave it to set (see *sorbet*).

orange syrup

Select some ripe oranges and peel a few of them very thinly; put the peel to one side, as it will be used to flavour the syrup. Peel the rest of the oranges. Put the pulp through a vegetable mill, then strain it through a fine sieve or damp muslin (cheesecloth). Measure the juice. Add 800 g (1¾ lb, 3½ cups) sugar to each 500 ml (17 fl oz, 2 cups) juice, put into a preserving pan and bring slowly to the boil. While the syrup is heating, line a large conical strainer with muslin and put in the reserved orange peel. Pour the syrup over the peel as soon as it comes to the boil. Let it get completely cold before bottling and sealing.

orangine

Make a Genoese* sponge with 150 g (5 oz, ⅔ cup) caster (superfine) sugar, 6 eggs, 150 g (5 oz, 1¼ cups) plain (all-purpose) flour, 50 g (2 oz, ¼ cup) butter and a pinch of salt. Leave it to cool completely. Make 250 ml (8 fl oz, 1 cup) Curaçao-flavoured confectioner's custard (see *custard*) and mix in 250 ml (8 fl oz, 1 cup) double (heavy) cream, whisked with 1 teaspoon vanilla sugar and 25 g (1 oz, 2 tablespoons) caster sugar. Put this cream into the refrigerator. Slice the sponge into 3 equal layers. Soak each layer with 2 tablespoons Curaçao-flavoured syrup. Spread the cream over 2 of the layers and build up the cake again. Ice (frost) the top and sides with Curaçao-flavoured fondant. Decorate the cake with pieces of candied orange peel and angelica.

savoury orange and cucumber salad

Remove all the peel and pith from some oranges and slice them into rounds about 5 mm (¼ in) thick. Remove the seeds. Peel and finely slice some cucumber, sprinkle the slices with salt and leave them to drain. Rinse the slices in cold water and dry them. Arrange the slices of orange and cucumber alternately in a round glass dish. Serve with a well-seasoned vinaigrette as an entrée.

Alternatively, the oranges may be cut into small cubes and mixed with twice their volume of grated carrot. Season the salad with vinaigrette made with olive oil and raspberry vinegar and chill until ready to serve.

Bitter Oranges – Savoury Recipes
bitter orange sauce

Peel the rind (zest) of 1 Seville orange in strips running from top to bottom, ensuring that it is very thin: any pith left on it would make it bitter. Cut each strip into small pieces and place in a little boiling water. Allow to boil for a few minutes, then drain and put in a pan with some espagnole sauce, a little game extract, a pinch of coarsely ground pepper and the juice of ½ Seville orange. Boil for a few moments, then add a little good-quality butter.

brown bitter orange sauce for roast duck

Cut the rind of 1 Seville orange (or 1 sweet orange) and ½ lemon into thin strips; blanch, cool and drain. Heat 20 g (¾ oz, 1½ tablespoons) granulated sugar and 1 tablespoon good wine vinegar in a saucepan until it forms a pale caramel. Add 200 ml (7 fl oz, ¾ cup) brown veal stock (or well-reduced bouillon) and boil vigorously for 5 minutes. Add the juice of the orange and a dash of lemon juice. Strain and add the blanched rind. The sauce can be flavoured with a small amount of Curaçao added just before serving.

duck in bitter orange sauce

Cut the rind of 1 Seville orange (or 1 sweet orange) and ½ lemon into thin strips; blanch, cool and drain. Fry the duck in butter for about 45 minutes, until the flesh is just pink. Drain, untruss and arrange on a serving dish. Deglaze the cooking stock with 100 ml (4 fl oz, 7 tablespoons) white wine. Add 300 ml (½ pint, 1¼ cups) veal stock or a fairly light demi-glace sauce; otherwise use well-reduced chicken stock. Prepare some vinegar caramel, using 2 sugar lumps dissolved in 2 tablespoons vinegar and add to the sauce. Boil for a few moments. Add the juice of the orange and the lemon half, reduce, strain and add the orange and lemon rind. The duck can be garnished with peeled Saville orange segments, if liked.

fillets of wild duck in bitter orange sauce

Take the breast fillets from 2 wild ducks and place in an earthenware dish with salt, coarsely ground pepper, parsley, thyme, 1 bay leaf, chopped shallots, lemon juice and 3 tablespoons good oil. Marinate the duck in the mixture for 45 minutes, turning frequently. Lay the fillets on a spit rack, then skewer them loosely and sprinkle with the marinade. Cook until they are firm to the touch. Remove the skewers and place the duck in a sauté dish containing a melted knob of butter and the juice of ½ lemon. Serve with bitter orange sauce.

white bitter orange sauce for roast duck

Deglaze the dish in which the duck has been cooked with 175 ml (6 fl oz, ¾ cup) dry white wine. Cut the rind of 1 Seville orange (or 1 sweet orange) and ½ lemon into thin strips; blanch, cool and drain. When the sauce has almost completely reduced, add 150 ml (¼ pint, ⅔ cup) white consommé or stock and boil for 5 minutes. Thicken with 1 teaspoon cornflour (cornstarch) or arrowroot mixed with 2 tablespoons cold water. Add the juice of the orange and a dash of lemon juice. Strain, add the rind and adjust the seasoning.

Bitter Oranges – Sweet Recipes

orange marmalade

Wash and weigh 16 bitter oranges and 2 lemons. Peel them, including the pith, and separate them into segments. Scrape off the pith from half the peel and cut this peel into very fine strips. Put the fruit and the sliced peel into a pan and add an equal weight of water. Leave to soak for 24 hours. Pour into a preserving pan and cook until the fruit can be easily crushed; remove the pan from the heat. Weigh a pan large enough to contain the cooked fruit, pour in the fruit and weigh again to obtain the weight of the fruit. Leave to soak for another 24 hours. Pour the fruit back into the preserving pan, add an equal weight of sugar, bring to the boil and cook for 5–6 minutes. Pot in the usual way.

Seville orange jelly dessert

Peel the rind from 2 sound Seville oranges as thinly as possible, then squeeze the juice of 5 lemons on to the zest and strain the juice through a sieve. Mix with 400 g (14 oz, 1¾ cups) granulated sugar and 40 g (1½ oz) clarified gelatine. Finish the jelly and mould in the usual manner. Set over ice.

ORANGEADE A refreshing drink made from orange juice and sugar, diluted with plain or soda water. Orangeade is best served well chilled, with ice; a little lemon juice may be added or a trace of Curaçao or rum.

ORANGEAT A French petit four shaped like a flat disc, made from almond paste mixed with chopped candied orange peel, iced (frosted) with white fondant and decorated with orange peel.

ORANGE-BLOSSOM FLOWER WATER The fragrant flowers of the bitter (Seville) orange are macerated and distilled to produce orange-flower water. This is manufactured on an industrial scale and is widely used as a flavouring in pastries, puddings, cakes, syrups and confectionery. In Morocco it is used to flavour salads and some tajines. Orange blossom is also used to make orange-flower sugar, which is used to flavour pastries, cakes and custards. The essential oil of orange blossom, called neroli oil, is used in perfumery and for flavouring foods.

RECIPES

orange-flower liqueur

Add 250 g (9 oz) orange blossom, ½ teaspoon cinnamon stick and 1 clove to 1 litre (1¾ pints, 4⅓ cups) 22% alcohol (44° proof). Leave for 1 month, then filter. Prepare a syrup with 500 g (18 oz, 2¼ cups) sugar and 500 ml (17 fl oz, 2 cups) water. Boil, cool, then add the flavoured alcohol. Filter once more and pour into sterilized bottles. Store in a cool dark place.

orange-flower sugar

Dry some orange blossom, either in a closed container or in an oven, so as to obtain 250 g (9 oz) dry petals. Add 500 g (18 oz, 2¼ cups) caster (superfine) sugar to these petals and pound well in a mortar, then rub through a very fine sieve. Store in sealed airtight jars in a dry, dark place.

OREGANO Also known as wild marjoram, this is a herb with a pungent flavour. It grows mainly in Italy, where it is an important cooking ingredient, and also in Britain and parts of America, where its flavour is less pungent. It is popular in Mediterranean dishes such as pasta and pizza sauces and tomato dishes. In its dried form, in which it is often sold, it has a much stronger flavour.

OREILLER DE LA BELLE AURORE A large, square, raised pie dedicated to Brillat-Savarin's mother, Claudine-Aurore Récamier. It contains two different fillings (one of veal and pork, the other of chicken livers, young partridges, mushrooms and truffles), to which are added marinated veal fillets, slices of breast from young red partridge and duck, a saddle of hare, white chicken meat and blanched calves' sweetbreads.

OREILLETTES Pastry fritters traditionally made in the Languedoc region of France at carnival time. They are made from sweetened dough cut into long rectangles with a slit in the centre (sometimes one end is passed through this hole to form a sort of knot) and fried in oil. The oreillettes of Montpellier, flavoured with rum and orange or lemon zest, are famous.

RECIPE

oreillettes de Montpellier

Pour 1 kg (2¼ lb, 9 cups) plain (all-purpose) flour into a heap and make a well in the centre. Pour 300 g (11 oz, 1⅓ cups) melted butter into the well and work it in, gradually drawing the flour to the centre; continue to work in 5 eggs, 2 tablespoons caster (superfine) sugar, a few tablespoons of rum, a small glass of milk and the finely grated peel from 2 oranges. Knead well to obtain a smooth dough. Continue to work the dough until it becomes elastic, then form it into a ball and leave it to rest for 2 hours. Roll out the dough very thinly and cut it into rectangles 5 × 8 cm (2 × 3¼ in). Make 2 incisions in the centre of each rectangle. Fry the oreillettes in very hot oil at 175°C (345°F): they will puff up immediately and rapidly become golden. Drain them on paper towels, sprinkle with icing (confectioner's) sugar and arrange them in a basket lined with a napkin.

ORGANIC FARMING The term covers farming methods for cultivating land and growing crops without the use of artificial fertilizers or pesticides and for rearing animals and birds in a natural and humane way. The production of organic food varies with the different types of food and from country to country.

ORGANOLEPTIC Describing the qualities that determine the palatability or otherwise of a food. The organoleptic qualities of a food or drink can be defined by its flavour, smell, appearance, texture and colour.

ORGEAT A syrup made from sugar and milk of almonds, flavoured with orange-flower water; this is then diluted with water to make a refreshing drink. In former times it was made from barley (*orge* in French), hence its name.

ORGY A feast at which eating and drinking is indulged in to excess and which ends in debauchery. This modern sense of the word has lost its original religious overtones. To the ancient Greeks, and later the Romans, orgies were feasts held in honour of Dionysius, then of Bacchus, at which their followers, exalted by wine, dancing and music, became as if possessed by the god and lost all control of themselves.

ORIENTALE, À L' The name given to dishes inspired by the cooking of Turkey and the Balkans and containing numerous ingredients and spices from the Mediterranean region, such as aubergines (eggplants), tomatoes, rice, saffron, onions and (bell) peppers. The garnish *à l'orientale* for both large and small cuts of meat consists of small tomatoes stuffed with rice pilaf (sometimes flavoured with saffron), together with okra and peppers braised in butter; the sauce is a tomato-flavoured demi-glace.

RECIPES

red mullet à l'orientale
Clean some very small red mullet, season with salt and pepper, dip them in flour and fry quickly in oil. Arrange them in a flameproof dish. Cover with a fondue of tomato lightly flavoured with saffron, fennel, thyme, a crumbled bay leaf, a few coriander seeds, chopped garlic and parsley. Bring to the boil, cover, then finish cooking in a preheated oven at 220°C (425°F, gas 7), for 6–8 minutes. Leave the fish to get cold in their cooking sauce. Garnish with thin slices of peeled lemon and sprinkle with chopped parsley; serve cold.

salad à l'orientale
Cook some long-grain rice in salted water to which saffron has been added, keeping it fairly firm; drain thoroughly. Mix the rice with some peeled and finely chopped onion and season with vinaigrette well spiced with paprika. Pile the rice in a dome in a salad bowl. Turn some red and green (bell) peppers under a hot grill (broiler), then skin them, cut them open, take out the seeds and cut the flesh into strips. Peel, seed and chop some tomatoes. Garnish the rice with the peppers, tomatoes and some stoned (pitted) black (ripe) olives.

sauce à l'orientale
Make some tomato fondue and add saffron and a salpicon of red and green (bell) peppers. Make some very thick mayonnaise. Add the chilled tomato fondue to the mayonnaise and keep cold until ready to serve.

ORLÉANAIS AND SOLOGNE See *opposite page*.

ORLÉANAISE, À L' Describing large cuts of meat garnished with braised endive (chicory) and maître d'hôtel potatoes.

ORLÉANS The name given to tartlets of eggs (poached, soft-boiled or *sur le plat*) which are garnished with either a salpicon of bone marrow and truffle bound with Madeira sauce or with finely diced white chicken meat in tomato sauce. It also describes rolled sole fillets *en paupiettes*, garnished with a salpicon of shrimps and mushrooms, covered with white wine sauce and garnished with a slice of truffle.

ORLOFF The name given to a traditional recipe for cooking loin of veal: the meat is braised, sliced, stuffed with a purée of mushrooms and onions and possibly slices of truffle, then reshaped, covered with Maintenon sauce, sprinkled with Parmesan cheese and glazed in the oven. The chef who perfected this dish was undoubtedly Urbain Dubois, who was in Prince Orloff's service for over 20 years.

Orloff garnish for large cuts of meat consists of braised celery (or darioles lined with sticks of braised celery and filled with a mousse made from celery purée), château potatoes and braised lettuce.

RECIPE

veal Orloff
Peel and thinly slice 500 g (18 oz) onions, 1 large carrot and 800 g (1¾ lb) button mushrooms. Melt 50 g (2 oz, ¼ cup) butter in a casserole and brown 150 g (5 oz) bacon rinds, then a boned loin of veal weighing about 1.8 kg (4 lb). Add the sliced carrot, 1 large tablespoon sliced onions, a bouquet garni, salt and pepper. Add just enough water to cover the meat, put the lid on and cook over a low heat for 1 hour 20 minutes.

Orléanais and Sologne

The former province of Orléanais can be classed among the gastronomic centres of France. Val-de-Loire is extremely fertile, with a history of market gardening. The produce of its admirable market gardens and orchards is in great demand, especially Vendôme asparagus, carrots, Chinese artichokes, garden peas, strawberries, cherries and pears. The fertile plain of Beauce, the so-called 'granary of France', yields wheat producing one of the best-quality flours in the country. The poultry of the region is excellent. Perche is noted for its sheep and beef cattle; Gâtinais produces honey and poultry; and a variety of game and fish is found in the forests and lakes of Sologne.

■ **Vinegar and mustard** Orléans is a centre for vinegar production, originating from the days when wine transported up river from Anjou and Touraine, destined for Paris, did not survive the slow journey. By the time the casks reached Orléans, many were full of sour wine – *vin aigre*. Enterprising dealers fermented the wine to produce vinegar. Mustard is another condiment prepared to a high standard and with a long

The lakes of Sologne may be fairly small like this one at Ferté-Saint-Aubin, or very large. In all they cover an area of about 12,000 hectares (30,000 acres) and they are surrounded by forests of oak, chestnut, aspen and pine.

reputation for quality.

■ **Culinary specialities** Poultry and game pies, pâtés, pumpkin and leek soup are local specialities. Typical of the fish dishes are carp stuffed with bacon and onions, pike with saffron (which is grown round Pithiviers) or *à la marinière*, and matelote of eel. Soup made from *corbeau* (a fish like a small bass) and vegetables, sprinkled with **grated** cheese, is an old favourite in the region. Meat dishes include leg of mutton (not lamb) from Sologne, cooked in water with aromatic herbs and then deglazed with vinegar, and rabbit cooked with onions and venison cutlets.

■ **Cheese** Cheese production goes far beyond the Olivet beloved of Balzac. There are many other varieties, including Montoire (goat's milk), Papay (cow's milk), Pavé Blésois (goat's milk), Pithiviers, Selles-sur-Cher, Trôo (goat's milk) and Vendôme. The *tapinette* (a cheese tart) of Orléans is made with soft fresh cheese.

■ **Pâtisserie and confectionery** Pâtisserie is represented by the pithiviers, the tarte Tatin, and the financiers and croquets. The delicious confectionery includes cotignac (quince paste), fruit pastilles, honey sweets, spiced gingerbread, pralines and chocolates.

Meanwhile, melt 25 g (1 oz, 2 tablespoons) butter in a sauté pan and quickly brown the sliced mushrooms. Chop them, replace in the pan with salt, pepper, 1 tablespoon flour and a pinch of grated nutmeg, and cook for about 10 minutes. Put the rest of the sliced onions through a food processor or vegetable mill and cook in 40 g (1½ oz, 3 tablespoons) butter until golden. Then moisten them with water, cover the pan and cook for 20–25 minutes until puréed. Add the mushrooms and 200 ml (7 fl oz, ¾ cup) double (heavy) cream, then boil the cream down.

Cut the veal into thin even slices, cutting transversely from one long side to the other; spread each slice with a little of the onion and mushroom purée. Put the slices together again and reshape the loin. Tie it, place in a gratin dish and spread it with the rest of the purée. Mask it with Maintenon sauce, sprinkle with grated Parmesan cheese, dot

with butter and brown in a hot oven for 10 minutes. Skim the fat from the braising liquid, strain it and serve separately.

ORLY The name given to a method of cooking fish. The fish (eel, pike, whiting, sole, smelt or salmon), which may be filleted or whole according to their size, are dipped in batter or egg and breadcrumbs, then fried, drained and served with tomato sauce.

RECIPES

fried eels Orly

Take some eel fillets and slice them. Flatten the slices, season with salt and pepper, and dip them in a light frying batter. Deep-fry them, garnish with fried parsley and serve with a highly seasoned tomato fondue.

salmon fillets Orly with tomato sauce

Trim 14 salmon fillets. Put them into a dish with some salt, coarsely ground pepper, a little grated nutmeg, 2 finely sliced shallots, some sprigs of parsley, the juice of 2 lemons, 100 ml (4 fl oz, 7 tablespoons) olive oil, a little thyme and a bay leaf. Turn the fillets several times in this marinade and drain off the water which they produce. An hour before the meal, drain the fillets on paper towels, sprinkle with flour and turn them in this until they are quite dry. Pat them back into shape with the blade of a knife and dip them into 4 beaten eggs before frying them. When cooked, arrange them in a circle on a plate and serve a light tomato sauce separately.

ORMER (ABALONE) A large single-shell mollusc found off the Pacific coasts of Asia and Mexico, in the Mediterranean and off the European Atlantic coast. All the muscle is edible and has a chewy texture but unique flavour. To cook, remove from the shell, trim and beat well to tenderize, then slice thinly and fry very briefly. It can also be eaten raw. In Japan it is usually cooked by sake-steaming. Dried or canned abalone is used widely in Asia and, although cheaper than fresh, is still expensive. It is considered a delicacy in China, it is popular in California, and in New Zealand abalone is a Maori speciality called *pava pava*, which is sliced and barbecued on skewers.

RECIPE

ormeaux à la cancalaise

Place 8 large or 12 medium ormers, still alive, at the bottom of the refrigerator for 48 hours in order to weaken them. Remove them from their shells while still cold. Remove the beards and put them to one side. Scrape the ormers under cold running water to remove all traces of black. Put them on a damp cloth in the refrigerator for 24 hours. Before cooking them, massage gently to tenderize.

Carefully wash and dry the beards, then brown them in 100 g (4 oz, ½ cup) butter. Add 1 peeled and chopped shallot, 1 sliced carrot, 3 finely sliced mushrooms, 3½ tablespoons Coteaux-du-Layon, 1 roasted garlic clove, the stems of ½ bunch of parsley and 2 tablespoons chopped, dried nori. Add 100 ml (4 fl oz, 7 tablespoons) chicken stock. Cover and simmer gently for 1 hour, then strain. (This ormer stock is highly flavoured.)

Blanch 4 unblemished leaves of new cabbage in boiling salted water. Drain and put to one side. Heat 3½ tablespoons oil in a saucepan and briskly fry the leaves of 20 small sprigs of parsley. Remove from the oil, drain on paper towels and put to one side. Reheat the ormer stock and thicken with 50 g (2 oz, ¼ cup) butter. Brown the ormers for 2 minutes on each side. Allow to rest for 15 minutes to enable the meat to relax. Deglaze the pan with the stock and 4 teaspoons cider vinegar. Strain through a fine sieve. Reheat the cabbage leaves in a knob of butter and a little water.

Place a perfect warm shell on each plate with a cabbage leaf to one side. Finely shred 2 or 3 ormers and arrange on the cabbage leaf, with some on the shell. Sprinkle with finely chopped parsley, pour some ormer stock on top and garnish with a few leaves of fried parsley.

ORTOLAN The French name for a small migratory bird – a species of bunting – considered since early times to be the finest and most delicate of birds to eat. In Britain it is extinct and in France it is now officially protected, as it is becoming so rare in that country. However, the law is not strictly observed in south-western France, especially in the Landes, where they continue to be captured alive and fattened up for private consumption. The bird's diet (millet, buds, berries, grapes and small insects) gives its flesh flavour and delicacy. Weighing only 30 g (1¼ oz) when caught, it can quadruple its weight in a month.

Ortolans are usually roasted on spits or in the oven, cooked mainly in their own fat; the latter drips on to pieces of bread, which some recommend should be spread with Roquefort cheese.

ORVIETO A DOC predominantly dry, delicate white wine produced in Italy's Umbria region from Trebbiano blended with Verdello, Grechetto, Drupeggio and Malvasia Toscano grapes with a minimum alcohol level of 11.5%.

OSSAU-IRATY A French ewe's-milk cheese protected by an *appellation d'origine protégé* but often sold under the name 'Fromage de Brebis des Pyrénées'. With a fat content of at least 50%, the cheese has a creamy yellow, lightly pressed curd, a smooth orange-yellow to grey rind, and a pronounced flavour. It is made in the shape of a flat disc with straight or slightly convex sides, in two sizes: 24.5–28 cm (9½–11 in) in diameter, 12–14 cm (4¾–5½ in) deep, weighing 4–7 kg (9–15 lb); and 20 cm (7¾ in) in diameter, 10–12 cm (4–4¾ in) deep, weighing 2–3 kg (4½–6½ lb). It can be eaten at the end of a meal, on canapés, as a snack or as part of a mixed salad.

OSSO BUCCO An Italian dish, originally from Milan, whose name means literally 'bone with a hole'. It consists of a stew of pieces of veal shin braised in white wine with onion and tomato. It is generally served with pasta or rice. The variation called *alla gremolata* is prepared with the addition of a mixture of chopped garlic, orange and lemon peel, and grated nutmeg.

RECIPE

osso bucco à la milanaise

Season 8 veal shins, weighing about 1.6 kg (3½ lb), with salt and pepper, sprinkle with flour, then brown them in olive oil in a large flameproof casserole. Chop enough onions to give 5 level tablespoons; add these to the casserole and cook until golden. Moisten with 200 ml (7 fl oz, ¾ cup) white wine, reduce this, then add 4 large tomatoes, skinned, seeded and coarsely chopped. Pour in

250 ml (8 fl oz, 1 cup) stock. Finally add 1 large crushed garlic clove and a bouquet garni. Cover the casserole and cook in a preheated oven at 200°C (400°F, gas 6) for 1½ hours. Arrange the pieces of knuckle in a deep dish and cover them with the reduced cooking liquid. Squeeze on a little lemon juice and sprinkle with chopped parsley.

OSTRICH A large African bird, whose flesh and eggs have long been eaten. Its brain was considered to be a delicacy at the time of Nero. Ostrich is now farmed outside of Africa for its flesh, which is lean and tender. Its meat, the flavour of which is a mixture between beef and game, should be prepared and cooked in the same way as tender beef.

OUASSOU West Indian crayfish which lives in fresh water (*ouassou* in Creole means 'king of the springs'). It is served fried and also in a stew with many vegetables.

OUBLIE A small flat or cornet-shaped wafer, widely enjoyed in France in the Middle Ages, but whose origins go even further back in time. Oublies, which were perhaps the first cakes in the history of cooking, are the ancestors of waffles. They were usually made from a rather thick waffle batter and were cooked in flat, round, finely patterned iron moulds. Some authorities consider that the name comes from the Greek *obelios*, meaning a cake cooked between two iron plates and sold for an obol; others that it comes from the Latin *oblata* (offering), which also means an unconsecrated host.

In the Middle Ages oublies were made by the *oubloyeurs* (or *oublieux*), whose guild was incorporated in 1270. They made and sold their wares in the open street, setting up stalls at fairs and in the open space in front of churches on feast days. It was said that the most celebrated oublies were those from Lyon, where apparently they were rolled into cornets after being cooked. The *oubloyeurs* would put them one inside the other and sell them in fives, called a *main d'oublies* (a hand of oublies). Often they would play dice for them with their customers or draw lots for them on a 'Wheel of Fortune', which was in fact the cover of the large pannier – or *coffin* – in which they carried their wares. By the 16th century most of the Parisian pastrycooks were established in the Rue des Oubloyeurs in the Cité; by night and day the apprentices would set out laden with their panniers full of *nieules* (round flat cakes), *échaudés* (a sort of brioche), oublies and other small cakes, crying *Voilà le plaisir, mesdames!* ('Here's pleasure, ladies!'), which led to oublies being given the popular name of *plaisirs*. The last of these pedlars disappeared after World War 1.

RECIPE

oublies à la parisienne
Put 250 g (9 oz, 2¼ cups) sifted plain (all-purpose) flour, 150 g (5 oz, ⅔ cup) sugar, 2 eggs and a little

orange-flower water or lemon juice into a bowl. Work together until everything is well mixed, then gradually add 575 ml (19 fl oz, 2⅓ cups) milk, 65 g (2½ oz, 5 tablespoons) melted butter and the grated zest of a lemon. Heat an oublie or waffle iron and grease it evenly; pour in 1 tablespoon batter and cook over a high heat, turning the iron over halfway through. Peel the wafer off the iron and either roll it into a cornet round a wooden cone or leave it flat.

OUIDAD Traditional dish of Maghreb and, in particular, Moroccan cooking. Ouidad consists of hard semolina flour, like couscous, and fish, such as scorpion fish (rascasse) and gilt-head bream (daurade).

OUNANICHE Name of American Indian origin used in Quebec to describe the freshwater variety of the Atlantic salmon. Smaller than salmon, it lives only in Lake Saint Jean and its neighbouring rivers. It is prepared in the same ways as salmon or trout.

OURTETO A mixture of chopped spinach, sorrel, celery and leeks, boiled and flavoured with crushed garlic. It is eaten in Provence, in the south of France, on slices of bread cut from a large round white loaf, moistened with olive oil.

OUZO A spirit flavoured with aniseed, made in Greece and many of the Greek islands, including Cyprus. Like pastis, it turns cloudy when water is added, and it should always be served with iced water, though it should not be kept in the refrigerator for any length of time.

OVEN An enclosed cooking apparatus, derived from the bread oven, whose origins are lost in the mists of time. In domestic kitchens the oven is usually a source of dry heat, used for dry cooking methods, such as baking and roasting. There are many types of oven, fuelled by gas or electricity. Solid fuel, wood and oil-fired ovens are also available. Some ovens also have additional features, such as a rotisserie, fan or grill (broiler) element.

Standard oven temperature settings for domestic ovens are shown in the chart.

Oven temperature settings

Gas mark	°C	°F	Description
¼	110	225	very cool
½	120	250	
1	140	275	cool
2	150	300	
3	160	325	moderate
4	180	350	
5	190	375	moderately hot
6	200	400	
7	220	425	hot
8	230	450	
9	240	475	very hot

OVERLAP To arrange food so that each piece is partially covered by the next to achieve a decorative effect.

OXTAIL A cut of meat used to make many delicious dishes, notably oxtail soup and Flemish *hochepot* (see *hotchpotch*). It can also be braised and served with a flamande or nivernaise garnish, or it can be boiled, coated with breadcrumbs and grilled (broiled) *à la Sainte-Menehould*.

Oxtail soup is a classic English soup which, according to some authorities, could have been introduced into Britain by refugees from the French Revolution. It is a clear soup made from an oxtail and traditionally it is flavoured with basil, marjoram, savory and thyme, although these are often replaced by the classic braising vegetables: carrots, leeks and onions. Oxtail soup can be garnished with small vegetable balls or a brunoise, as well as with meat from the oxtail; it is flavoured with Madeira, brandy or sherry.

RECIPES

braised oxtail with horseradish croûtes

Cut 2 oxtails into chunks and trim off excess fat. Dust the pieces very lightly with a little well-seasoned flour, then brown them all over in a little butter, lard or oil in a large frying pan. Remove and set aside. Cook 2 large sliced onions, 2 diced celery sticks, 2 diced carrots, 2 bay leaves, 1 chopped garlic clove and 2 diced rindless bacon rashers (slices) in the pan, adding a little extra butter, lard or oil if necessary. When the vegetables are softened slightly remove the pan from the heat.

Layer the oxtail and vegetable mixture in a large deep casserole. Return the frying pan to the heat and deglaze it with a little brandy, stirring to remove all the cooking residue from the pan. Add a little water and bring to the boil, stirring. Pour this over the ingredients in the casserole. Add a bottle of red wine and plenty of salt and pepper. Cover the casserole and cook in a preheated oven at 160°C (325°F, gas 3) for about 3 hours or until the oxtail is completely tender.

Towards the end of the cooking time, beat a little creamed horseradish into softened butter. Cut slices off a baguette and spread them with the horseradish butter. Place on a baking sheet and cook in the oven until crisp and golden.

Taste the casserole for seasoning before serving. Stir in plenty of chopped fresh parsley and serve with the horseradish croûtes.

grilled oxtail Sainte-Menehould

Cut an oxtail into sections 6–7 cm (2½–3 in) long and cook them in stock prepared as for a pot-au-feu; stop cooking before the meat begins to come away from the bones. Drain the pieces, bone them without breaking them up, and leave them to cool, under a weight, in the stock (from which the fat has been skimmed). Drain and dry the pieces, spread them with mustard, brown them quickly in clarified butter, then roll them in fine fresh breadcrumbs. Grill (broil) gently and serve with any of the following sauces – diable, piquante, mustard, pepper, bordelaise or Robert – accompanied by mashed potatoes.

oxtail soup

Put 1.5 kg (3¼ lb) oxtail, cut into small chunks, into a casserole, on a bed of sliced carrots, leeks and onions. Sweat in the oven for 25 minutes. Cover with 2.5 litres (4¼ pints, 11 cups) stock made by cooking 1.5 kg (3¼ lb) gelatinous bones for 7–8 hours in 3.25 litres (5½ pints, 14 cups) water. Season. Simmer gently, so that the boiling is imperceptible, for 3½–4 hours. Strain the soup and skim off surplus fat. Clarify by boiling it for 1 hour with 500 g (18 oz, 2¼ cups) chopped lean beef and the white part of 2 leeks, finely sliced, first whisking both these ingredients with a raw white of egg. Strain the stock. Garnish with pieces of oxtail and 300 ml (½ pint, 1¼ cups) coarse brunoise of carrots, turnips and celery, sweated in butter and dropped into the stock. Add 1 tablespoon sherry.

OYONNADE A French goose stew with wine, thickened with the liver and blood of the bird and mixed with spirits. It used to be a traditional dish for All Saints' Day in the Bourbonnais region and was served with swedes (rutabaga).

OYSTER A saltwater bivalve mollusc, of which there are many edible varieties.

The oyster has been known to humans from the earliest times. The Celts, the Greeks (who reared oysters in beds) and the Romans all ate oysters in large quantities. Nowadays oysters are farmed, thus ensuring that they are not overfished and are free from pollution.

In the cultivation of oysters, seed oysters are affixed to tiles and reared in areas some way out to sea. When they have reached a certain size, they are transferred to the fattening beds, which are always situated at the mouth of a river, the mixture of fresh and sea water being essential to induce overgrowth of the liver, of which the fattening consists. The growing period lasts from three to four years and requires constant supervision. As the oyster grows, it needs more space and therefore a larger area is required for the bed. It must be protected from pollution and from its natural enemies – skate, winkles, crabs, starfish, octopus and sea birds.

The most important varieties are the European oyster, which is found off the coast of Essex and Kent in Britain, on the Atlantic coast of France, the coasts of Belgium and the Netherlands, and the southern coast of Ireland; the Portuguese oyster, which is larger than the European oyster and is a native of Portugal, Spain and Morocco; the American oyster, which is similar in size to the Portuguese oyster and is found along the Atlantic seaboard of Canada and the United States. The most famous

American oysters are the Cape, Long Island and Chesapeake Bay oysters. Amongst the Asian oysters, the largest is the giant Pacific oyster, which, because of its size, is generally cooked, dried or used for oyster sauce. Oysters are also found in Australia and New Zealand.

For generations oysters were supposed to be eaten only during the months containing the letter 'r' (from September to April). However, with modern methods of rearing and transport they can now safely be eaten at any time of the year. Oysters must always be bought live, with the shells closed or closing when tapped, and they should feel quite heavy, as they should be full of water. They are not opened until the last minute. To test whether an opened oyster is alive, prick the cilia, which should instantly retract.

Nowadays, as oysters have become more expensive, they are nearly always eaten live and raw, plainly dressed with lemon and accompanied by bread and butter, or with a vinegar dressing containing shallot and pepper. However, they can also be cooked and used in hot and cold dishes. Oysters can be poached, then chilled and served with various sauces, sometimes in barquettes; they can be browned in the oven in their shells; or they can be served with artichoke hearts or in croustades. Browning must always be done very rapidly and the preliminary poaching is often unnecessary. Oysters can also be cooked on skewers, made into fritters, croquettes, soups and consommés, and used as a garnish in fish recipes. English and American cookery in particular make good use of oysters – in soup, as a sauce, or as Angels on Horseback. Among the French regional specialities is one from Arcachon, where local oysters are served with grilled (broiled) chipolata sausages.

RECIPES

angels on horseback
Take some oysters out of their shells. Sprinkle them with a little white pepper and wrap each one in a thin slice of bacon. Thread them on skewers and grill (broil) for 2 minutes. Arrange on pieces of hot toast.

oysters à la Boston
Open 12 oysters; carefully take out the flesh from the shells and drain it. In the bottom of each concave shell, place a little white pepper and a generous pinch of fried breadcrumbs. Replace the oysters in the shells; sprinkle them with grated Gruyère cheese and a few breadcrumbs. Dot each with a small piece of butter. Brown under the grill (broiler) for 6–7 minutes. Serve with shrimp fritters or Parmesan cheese straws.

oysters à la Brolatti
Poach 12 oysters, drain them and remove the beards. Prepare a sauce with 2 chopped shallots tossed in butter, the oyster beards, 2 tablespoons

white wine and the strained liquid from the oysters. Reduce this sauce to about 3 tablespoons. Thicken the reduced sauces by whisking in 100 g (4 oz, ½ cup) butter. Season with pepper and lemon juice. Strain the sauce and keep it warm. Warm the oyster shells in the oven. Cook the oysters in butter in a covered pan for 1 minute and then return them to their shells. Cover with the sauce and serve.

oysters à la rhétaise
Open 24 oysters and put them in a saucepan with their own strained water, 2 shallots, 1 garlic clove and a knob of butter. Soften and reduce the liquid by half. Put this sauce into a pan with 4 tablespoons single (light) cream, a pinch of cayenne, a pinch of saffron and 2 teaspoons curry powder. Blend everything together and let it reduce. Add a few drops of lemon juice. Arrange the oysters in individual gratin dishes, cover with the sauce and put under the grill (broiler) for 10 seconds.

oyster fritters
Poach the oysters in their own water and let them cool in the cooking liquid. Drain them and dry in a cloth. Leave them to soak for 30 minutes in a mixture of oil, lemon juice, pepper and salt, then dip them in batter. Cook in very hot oil until the fritters are puffed and golden and drain them at once on paper towels. Sprinkle with fine salt and serve with lemon quarters.

oyster sauce
Open and poach 12 oysters. Prepare a white roux with 20 g (¾ oz, 1½ tablespoons) butter and 20 g (¾ oz, 3 tablespoons) flour, then moisten with 6 tablespoons oyster cooking liquid, 6 tablespoons milk and 6 tablespoons single (light) cream. Adjust the seasoning. Bring to the boil and cook for 10 minutes. Pass through a sieve. Add the debearded and sliced oysters and a pinch of cayenne.

oysters in their shells (hot)
Poach the oysters, replace them in their shells and set these firmly into a layer of coarse salt in a baking tin (pan). Brown in a preheated oven at 220°C (425°F, gas 7) for a few seconds (poaching can be omitted). They can then be served in the following ways.
• à l'américaine Sprinkle with a few drops of lemon juice and a pinch of cayenne.
• à la florentine Replace in their shells on a layer of buttered spinach, then mask with Mornay sauce, sprinkle with grated cheese and brown in the oven.
• à la polonaise Sprinkle with chopped hard-boiled egg yolk and chopped parsley, then moisten with noisette butter mixed with fried breadcrumbs.

oyster soup ♦
Open 24 oysters and put them into a sauté pan with the strained liquor from their shells. Add 200 ml (7 fl oz, ¾ cup) white wine. Bring just to the boil and take off the heat as soon as the liquid

begins to bubble. Use a draining spoon to transfer the oysters to a plate and set them aside. Skim any scum off the liquid, then whisk in 1 small, finely diced carrot, 1 finely chopped spring onion (scallion) and 3 tablespoons finely crushed water biscuits (crackers) and bring to the boil. Simmer for 1 minute, whisking, then add 200 ml (7 fl oz, ¾ cup) single (light) cream. Gradually whisk in 100 g (4 oz, ½ cup) butter cut into small pieces. The soup should be smooth and hot, but it must not simmer or boil as it will curdle. Replace the oysters and heat for a few seconds. Season with salt and pepper and a pinch of cayenne. Serve at once.

oysters Robert Courtine

Chop 2 shallots. Put them in a saucepan with 200 ml (7 fl oz, ¾ cup) champagne. Bring to the boil over a high heat and reduce the liquid by half. Let it cool slightly. Open 36 oysters and put them into a saucepan with their strained liquid. Add a few drops of champagne and bring just to the boil. Drain the oysters and pour the cooking liquid into the first pan. Gradually whisk in 200 g (7 oz, generous ¾ cup) butter. Add pepper and the juice of 1 lemon. Adjust the seasoning. Put the oysters into a serving dish or their shells, cover with the sauce and serve immediately.

oysters with cider and winkles

Open 24 oysters and keep the deep halves of the shells. Prepare a stock with 1 litre (1¾ pints, 4⅓ cups) water, 1 carrot, 2 celery sticks, 1 teaspoon salt and 200 ml (7 fl oz, ¾ cup) cider. Cook 200 g (7 oz) winkles in this stock for 10 minutes, then take them out of their shells. Skin 2 tomatoes and dice the flesh finely. Poach the oysters in their own water with 6 tablespoons cider. Remove the beards and keep the oysters warm. Prepare the sauce: chop 2 shallots and cook them in 200 ml (7 fl oz, ¾ cup) cider, then reduce this liquid by half. Add 6 tablespoons single (light) cream, reduce again and finish the sauce with 50 g (2 oz, ¼ cup) butter cut into small pieces. Add pepper, a few drops of lemon juice and the cooking liquid from the oysters. Adjust the seasoning. Snip the leaves from a small bunch of chervil. Heat the oyster shells, fill them with the poached and bearded oysters and the winkles, and cover with sauce. Sprinkle them with the diced tomato. Glaze them in a preheated oven at 240°C (475°F, gas 9) and just before serving add the chervil leaves.

poached oysters

Open the oysters and put them into a sauté pan and pour over them their own water, strained through a muslin (cheesecloth) sieve. Bring almost to the boil, removing the pan as soon as the liquid begins to simmer.

steak with oysters

Open 8 oysters. Slice through a piece of beef fillet (sirloin) weighing about 300 g (11 oz), without separating the 2 halves. Flatten it slightly, season with salt and pepper, brush the inside surfaces with a mild mustard and then sear it rapidly in a mixture of equal quantities of oil and butter. Flame it with brandy and keep hot. In another pan put the strained water from 4 oysters, 1 chopped garlic clove, 1 finely chopped shallot, a knob of butter, 3 tablespoons double (heavy) cream and 1 teaspoon brandy. Add pepper and reduce. Slip the oysters into the steak, press it closed and secure it with 1 or 2 cocktail sticks (toothpicks). In a small saucepan put the juices which have run from the meat, the reduced sauce, a few drops of Worcestershire sauce, pepper and 1 tablespoon brandy; reduce again. Cover the steak with this sauce. Arrange the last 4 oysters on top of the meat. Sprinkle with chopped parsley.

other recipes See *attereau, Colbert, devilled.*

OYSTER CRAB A tiny, soft-shell crab that lives in oysters and is considered to be a delicacy by oyster shuckers in New England. They may be stewed or fried.

OYSTER KNIFE A strong knife for opening oysters. The blade, which is thick and blunt, is short and wide, forming a diamond shape, with a blunt point and a sturdy handle. It is designed for sliding between the upper and lower shells, and for twisting them apart at the hinge.

OYSTER MUSHROOM An earlike grey or greyish-brown bracket mushroom, *Pleurotus*, which grows in clusters on deciduous trees and stumps. It is also cultivated to provide grey, dark brown and yellow oyster mushrooms with a delicate texture and flavour. Abundant in autumn and winter, the wild grey oyster mushroom, *P. ostreatus*, is firm with a good flavour. *P. pulmonarius*, the brown variety, is found wild in spring and autumn; its flavour is delicate and slightly musky.

RECIPE

oyster mushroom croutes

Use a zester to pare the zest off 1 lemon in fine shreds. Mix the lemon zest with 1 finely chopped garlic clove and 1 teaspoon finely chopped fresh tarragon. Cut fairly thick slices off a baguette or ciabatta loaf at an angle, brush them with a little olive oil and bake in a preheated oven at 200°C (400°F, gas 6) for about 20 minutes or until lightly browned and crisp.

When the croûtes are almost ready, heat a large knob of butter with a good layer of olive oil in a large sauté pan. Add 1 teaspoon fennel seeds and allow them to sizzle gently for 1 minute. Trim and wipe small to medium oyster mushrooms; if using

Oyster soup, see page 825.

large mushrooms, cut them in half or quarters. Add the mushrooms to the pan. Sprinkle in the lemon zest, garlic and tarragon, then cook for about 3 minutes over medium heat, turning the mushrooms occasionally. Stir about 2 teaspoons Dijon mustard into the pan juices between the mushrooms. Sprinkle with salt and pepper and a generous quantity of chopped fresh dill, then toss lightly.

Spoon the oyster mushrooms on to the baked croûtes. Add wedges of lemon so that they can be squeezed over the mushrooms just before they are eaten. Serve at once.

OYSTER NUT The seeds of a gourd from a tropical African vine of the *Telfairia* family. The large flat seeds are husked and eaten raw, boiled or roasted. They have a high fat content and their oil is extracted for use as a cooking medium.

OYSTER PLANT A name sometimes used for salsify.

OYSTER SAUCE A sauce used in Chinese and South-East Asian cooking as a marinade and seasoning ingredient. Originally made from whole fermented oysters ground to a thick paste, the modern oyster sauce is made from oyster extract and thickened with starch. Soy sauce, sugar and caramel are the other ingredients that go to make this rich, salty and sweet, dark-coloured sauce. Oyster sauce may be used to marinate meat or poultry, or it can be added to stir-fried meat, poultry, vegetables or noodles. It is also used to flavour dipping sauces.

OZANNE French chef (born 1846; died 1896). He was chef to the king of Greece and the author of *Poésies gourmandes*.

PACHADE A dessert that is a speciality of the Saint-Flour region of the Auvergne. Generally, *pachade* is made from a crêpe batter mixed with fruit (particularly plums or prunes) and baked in the oven in a deep buttered dish. Sometimes, however, it is simply a thick pancake.

PACHERENC-DU-VIC-BILH White AOC wines from the Adour Valley in south-western France. Like the red Madiran, they are traditionally made from grapes allowed to dry on the vine, so the juice is concentrated. The wines can be sweet or dry.

PACIFIC NORTH WEST Fine wine- and food-producing states of Washington, Oregon and Idaho in north-west United States.

PAELLA A traditional Spanish rice dish garnished with vegetables, chicken and shellfish. Its name is derived from that of the container in which it is prepared (*paellera*).

Paella originated in the region of Valencia. Its three basic ingredients are rice, saffron and olive oil. The garnish, which is cooked with the rice in stock, originally consisted either of chicken, snails, French beans (green beans), and peas or of eel, frogs and vegetables, but it became considerably enriched and varied as it spread throughout Spain and even beyond (see *jambalaya*). The garnish may now include chicken, rabbit, duck, lobster, mussels, langoustines, prawns (shrimp), squid, *chorizo*, French beans, peas, red (bell) peppers and artichoke hearts; chicken, *chorizo*, mussels, langoustines and peas are essential ingredients. Paella may be a rustic dish, cooked in the open air and eaten straight from the *paellera*, traditionally accompanied by small onions

(not bread), or a very elaborate preparation, presented with great care, the different-coloured ingredients contrasting with the saffron-flavoured rice and set off by the green peas.

RECIPE

paella
Cut a chicken weighing about 1.4 kg (3 lb) into 8 pieces and season them with salt and pepper. Place the crushed backbone and the giblets in a stewpan, cover with water, season with salt and pepper, bring to the boil and skim. Peel and chop 2 onions, cut the white part of a leek and a celery stick into fine strips and chop 3 garlic cloves. Add all the vegetables to the stewpan with a bouquet garni. Wait until the stock comes to the boil again, then simmer for 1 hour.

Wash 500 g (18 oz) squid, cut into thin strips and put in a saucepan with some cold water. Bring to the boil, leave to boil for 5 minutes, then cool and set aside.

Heat 4 tablespoons olive oil in a deep frying pan with a metal handle (or use a paella pan) and fry the chicken pieces in it until they turn golden. Drain them. Gently reheat the same oil and add 250 g (9 oz) *chorizo* cut into round slices, then the squid, 2 sweet (bell) peppers, seeded and cut into thin strips, and 2 chopped onions. Add a pinch of saffron and leave to soften, uncovered, for 5–6 minutes. Add 6 large tomatoes (peeled, seeded and crushed) and reduce for 5 minutes, still uncovered.

Measure the volume of 400 g (14 oz, 2 cups) long-grain rice, tip it into the pan and mix everything together. Place the chicken pieces on top, then add 12 scraped and washed mussels, 12 Venus clams (if available), a handful of brushed and washed cockles and 8–12 langoustines. Strain the giblet stock and measure two and a half times the volume of the rice, then pour into the pan. Cover with foil, bring to the boil over the heat, then cook in a pre-heated oven at 220°C (425°F, gas 7) for 25–30 minutes. Add 250 g (9 oz, 1¾ cups) frozen peas, stirring them into the mixture, and leave to cook for a further 5 minutes. Turn off the oven and leave the paella there for about 10 minutes before serving, to allow the rice to finish swelling.

PAILLARD A famous Parisian restaurateur of the 19th century. In 1880 he took over the establishment situated at the corner of the Rue de la Chaussée-d'Antin and the Boulevard des Italiens, kept since 1850 by the Bignon brothers. Frequented by all the élite of Europe, Paillard's restaurant became very fashionable. Favourite dishes were chicken Archduke, Georgette potatoes, calves' sweetbreads with asparagus tips, fillets of sole Chauchat and, above all, stuffed duck, rivalling the duck *au sang* of the Tour d'Argent. Paillard opened another luxurious restaurant, the Pavillon de l'Élysée, nicknamed 'Petit Paillard'.

Referring to one of the dishes created at Paillard's, the name *paillarde* was given to a thin escalope (scallop) of veal (or a thin slice of beef), well flattened and grilled (broiled) or lightly braised. This term is obsolete in France but is still used in Italy for a veal escalope.

RECIPE

paupiettes of sole paillard
Flatten some fillets of sole, season them with salt and pepper, and cover with a thin layer of fish forcemeat finished with mushroom purée. Roll them into paupiettes and place in a sauté dish lined with thinly sliced onions and mushrooms; add a bouquet garni and moisten with fish stock or dry white wine. Cook, covered, in a preheated oven at 220°C (425°F, gas 7) for 12 minutes.

Drain the paupiettes, arrange them on artichoke hearts in a deep buttered dish, cover them and keep them hot. Strain the cooking liquid through muslin (cheesecloth) or a fine sieve and add to it an equal volume of mushroom purée, 2 egg yolks, and 200 ml (7 fl oz, ¾ cup) crème fraîche. Bring to the boil, whisking all the time, and adjust the seasoning. Coat the paupiettes with this sauce, glaze in a preheated oven at 230°C (450°F, gas 8) and serve immediately.

PAIN AU CHOCOLAT A small rectangle of croissant dough folded over one or two chocolate bars and baked in the oven. This Viennese speciality is eaten cold.

PAK CHOI Also known as bok choy or bok choi or quing cai. A member of the *Brassica* family, this *B. rapa* has rounded leaves on wide, white stalks that grow in a rosette. The vegetable is shredded for use in stir-fries, soups and casseroles or braised dishes. Small heads may also be cooked whole. The tender leaves wilt rapidly on cooking (rather like spinach), but the stalks retain their crisp texture.

PAKORA A popular Indian snack and street food, these savoury fritters consist of vegetables in a spicy batter made from chick pea flour (besan). Onion bahjis or bajhias are very similar. They may be made from a single vegetable, such as aubergine (eggplant) or potato, or with a mixture of ingredients, such as cauliflower, onion, potato and peas.

PALATE An item of red offal (variety meat) consisting of the fleshy membrane at the back of the roof of the mouth of animals. Regarded as a delicacy until the 19th century, ox (and sometimes sheep's) palate was soaked in cold water, blanched, cooled, cut into slices or small sticks, then prepared as fritters, in a gratin or *à la lyonnaise*. It is now rarely used, except as a complementary item in the preparation of ox muzzle.

PALATINATE This wine region, a continuation of the Alsace vineyard to the north, extends along the left bank of the River Rhine and is one of Germany's main wine-growing areas. It includes the Pfalz and Rheinhessen wine regions. It produces a huge quantity of wine, mostly white, though some red is made; in the Mittelhaardt region, north of Neustadt, some truly fine wines are produced. They extend to all the quality ranges of German wines and are in general rather full and fragrant and can often be drunk even with quite robust food, unlike many of the other fine German wines from other areas. The various grapes associated with German wines are grown, including the Rheinriesling. Among famous wine villages the names of Forst, Deidesheim, Ruppertsberg and Wachenheim are especially notable. Other good wines are made around Bad Dürkheim, Kallstadt, Leistadt and Königsbach.

PALAY, MAXIMIN (known as Simin) French writer (born Casteide-Doat, 1874; died Gelos, 1965). A committee member of the Félibrige (a society of writers dedicated to preserving the Provençal language), Palay collected in his *Dictionnaire du béarnais* (1932) numerous culinary traditions of his native region. He also published *La Cuisine du pays* (1936), describing typical recipes of Armagnac, the Basque country, Béarn, Bigorre and the Landes, including *abignades, alicuit, armottes, cruchade, garbure, miques,* foie gras, *confits, piperade,* salmis of guinea fowl and *touron*. This work also includes details of the maxims, tricks of the trade, utensils and ingredients used in these regions.

PALERON A French cut of beef that includes the shoulder with some of the adjoining collar. It is a fleshy meat, providing cuts for braising or boiling. Neck or chuck are the nearest British and American equivalent cuts.

RECIPE

paleron ménagère

Cut 1 kg (2¼ lb) chuck steak into large dice and season with salt and pepper. Brown in hot oil in a saucepan for 5 minutes. Then pour off the oil, add a large, finely diced onion and cook until brown. Sprinkle with 1 tablespoon flour, stirring well to coat the meat and the onion, then moisten with 500 ml (17 fl oz, 2 cups) dry white wine. Add 2 whole tomatoes, 2 chopped garlic cloves and a bouquet garni. Cover with a mixture of half water and half stock, add 1 tablespoon coarse salt and cook gently with the lid on for 1 hour, stirring from time to time. Add 400 g (14 oz, 3 cups) carrots and 200 g (7 oz, 1½ cups) turnips cut into small sticks. Leave to simmer for 10 minutes. Finally add 20 button (pearl) onions, which have been cooked in salted water, and adjust the seasoning. Sprinkle with coarsely chopped parsley and serve very hot.

PALET A small crisp petit four flavoured with rum, aniseed, vanilla or brown sugar; ground almonds, candied peel or other ingredients may be added. *Palets de dames* are traditionally made with currants.

RECIPE

palets de dames

Wash 75 g (3 oz, ½ cup) currants and macerate them in a little rum. Mix 125 g (4½ oz, ½ cup) softened butter and 125 g (4½ oz, ½ cup) caster (superfine) sugar. Work with a whisk, then blend in 2 eggs, one after the other, and mix well. Next add 150 g (5 oz, 1¼ cups) plain (all-purpose) flour, the currants with their rum and a pinch of salt. Mix thoroughly. Butter a baking sheet, dust it lightly with flour and arrange the mixture on it in small balls, well separated from each other. Cook in a preheated oven at 220°C (425°F, gas 7) for 25 minutes or until the edges of the palets are golden.

PALETOT The French term for a partly boned carcass of a web-footed bird (goose or duck). After removing the neck and wings, the bones of the thoracic cage, the vertebral column and the pelvis and the wishbone are removed through an opening in the back. The bird then looks like a knitted jacket (*paletot*). The fatty skin is cut into small pieces and cooked; it provides the fat that covers and preserves the pieces as a confit. Chopped very finely, it is sometimes used in certain charcuterie products to enhance the flavour.

PALETTE A French cut of pork corresponding to the shoulder blade (butt) with the adjoining muscles. It is a tender meat that is especially suitable for stews; it is particularly good with sauerkraut, when it is salted and sometimes smoked. Uncured, it is good for roasting and is so rich in fat that there is no need to lard it. It may also be sautéed.
■ **Palette – the wine** A Provençal AOC wine region around Mont Sainte Victoire. Very attractive red, white and rosé wines are made, predominantly produced by Château Simone.

RECIPES

palette of pork with haricot beans

Soak a salted blade or butt of pork in cold water to remove the salt, changing the water once. Stud the meat with pieces of garlic and place it in a saucepan. Cover it generously with cold water, add a bouquet garni and leave to simmer for about 2 hours. Cook separately some dried or fresh white haricot (navy) beans or lentils. When the beans are half-cooked, add the meat (drained), adjust the seasoning and complete the cooking gently with the lid on. Alternatively, the cooked shoulder may be lightly fried in lard (shortening) before being added to the beans.

palette of pork with sauerkraut

Soak a salted blade or butt of pork in cold water to remove the salt, changing the water once. Prepare some sauerkraut, place the drained shoulder in it and cook for about 2 hours over a very low heat or in a preheated oven at 180°C (350°F, gas 4). The sauerkraut may be garnished with a few vegetables (potatoes, carrots, turnips and small onions) added 45 minutes before the end of the cooking time.

PALETTE KNIFE See *spatula*.

PALM HEARTS (HEARTS OF PALM) The terminal buds of certain palm trees, in particular the West Indian cabbage palm, also called 'coconut cabbage', 'glug-glug cabbage' or 'ti-coco cabbage'. The tender parts are eaten raw, thinly sliced in salad; the firmer parts are cooked and used to prepare *acras*, gratins or fillings for omelettes. The taste is similar to artichoke. Canned palm hearts are also available.

RECIPES

braised palm hearts

(Creole recipe) Rinse some palm hearts in water and wipe well. Melt some pork dripping (fatback) in a shallow frying pan. Cut some pieces of palm hearts about 5 cm (2 in) long, tie them together in bunches and lightly brown them in the fat over a gentle heat for 30 minutes. Add 1 teaspoon flour, blending it in, then mix in 1 tablespoon tomato purée (paste) and some very concentrated chicken stock. Bring to the boil, stirring and cook for several minutes, then simmer gently until the sauce is reduced. Serve with a little of the sauce.

palm hearts in salad

Drain a can of palm hearts, refresh them in cold water, wipe them and cut them into round slices. Peel a cucumber, remove the seeds and cut the pulp into dice. Peel, seed and dice 4 ripe firm tomatoes. Using a melon baller, scoop out some small balls from the pulp of an avocado. Mix together 200 ml (7 fl oz, ¾ cup) double (heavy) cream, some chopped chives,

2 tablespoons vinegar and 1 tablespoon lemon juice. Season liberally with salt and pepper. Combine the other ingredients with the sauce. Garnish some individual dishes with a lettuce chiffonnade. Divide the preparation between them and chill until time to serve.

palm hearts mille-feuille with smoked marlin

Using a blender, make a vinaigrette with 200 ml (7 fl oz, ¾ cup) groundnut (peanut) oil, 100 ml (4 fl oz, 7 tablespoons) wine vinegar, 1 teaspoon prepared mustard and 1 egg. Cut 250 g (9 oz) smoked marlin (billfish) into 12 slices. Wash 200 g (7 oz) tomatoes and cut into small cubes. Make roses with 4 cherry tomatoes. Cut 4 black olives into fan shapes (3 per olive). Squeeze the juice of 1 lemon. FInely slice 1 palm heart and coat the slices in the vinaigrette and lemon juice to prevent them from going black. Put a ring 7.5 cm (3 in) in diameter and 4 cm (1½ in) high in the centre of each plate. Put a slice of marlin in the bottom and add a thin layer of finely sliced palm heart. Cover with another slice of marlin and a thin layer of palm heart. Finish with a slice of marlin. Place a cherry tomato rose in the centre and arrange 3 of the olive fans. Remove the ring carefully. Place some diced tomatoes round the edge of each plate and garnish with a little parsley.

palm hearts with shrimps

Thoroughly drain some canned palm hearts, refresh them in cold water, then wipe and coarsely shred them. Prepare a light well-seasoned mayonnaise coloured either with tomato ketchup or with a very reduced strained tomato sauce. Peel some cooked shrimps. Scald some bean sprouts, refresh them in cold water and dry them. Mix all the ingredients together and put in a cool place. Line some individual dishes with a lettuce chiffonnade, divide the mixture among them and serve chilled.

PALMIER A small pastry made of a sugared and double-rolled sheet of puff pastry cut into slices, the distinctive shape of which resembles the foliage of a palm tree. First made at the beginning of the 20th century, palmiers are served with tea or as an accompaniment to ices and desserts.

RECIPE

palmiers

Prepare some puff pastry and give it 4 extra turns, dusting it generously with icing (confectioner's) sugar between each rolling. Roll it out to a thickness of 5 mm (¼ in), into a rectangle 20 cm (8 in) wide (the length will depend on the quantity used). Dust again with icing sugar. Roll each of the long sides to the centre and flatten slightly, then fold the strip in half. Cut this into sections 1 cm (½ in) thick and place on a baking sheet, leaving enough space between them so that they do not stick to each other during cooking. Cook the palmiers in a pre-

heated oven at 220°C (425°F, gas 7) for about 10 minutes, turning them over halfway through cooking to colour both sides.

PALM TREE Any of numerous tropical trees belonging to the family *Palmae*. Many species are commercially important as a source of food, notably the date palm, coconut palm and sago palm. Some palms, especially the cabbage palm, have edible terminal buds (see *palm hearts*), and others yield sugar, oil and vegetable 'butter'. The sap of some species is fermented to produce wine.

PALMYRA A palm tree (*Borassus flabellifer*) of Asia and Africa with edible buds and young shoots. The pulp of the fruit is made into a kind of flour used in numerous local dishes; in Sri Lanka, it is also used to make a popular jam. The fruit may be eaten either raw or roasted. The sap can be used in the preparation of fermented drinks.

PALOISE, À LA Describing preparations of small cuts of grilled (broiled) meat garnished with French (green) beans in cream and noisette potatoes. The *paloise* garnish for large grilled cuts (which is rare) consists of glazed carrots and turnips, French beans in butter, sprigs of cauliflower coated with hollandaise sauce and croquette potatoes. True *paloise* sauce is a béarnaise sauce with mint (rather than tarragon), but grills à la *paloise* may be accompanied by either demi-glace sauce or a classic béarnaise sauce.

RECIPE

grilled lamb cutlets à la paloise

Prepare some noisette potatoes and some French (green) beans in cream (see *bean*) and keep them hot. Season some lamb cutlets (chops) that have the bone end exposed with salt and pepper, coat them very lightly with olive oil and grill (broil) them quickly on both sides. Garnish the bone ends with white paper frills and arrange the cutlets in a crown on a large round serving dish. Place the beans in the centre and arrange the potatoes in clusters between the cutlets.

PANACHÉ A mixture of two drinks in approximately equal quantities. It usually refers to beer and fizzy lemonade, but the term may also be used to describe other drinks. In cooking and pâtisserie *panaché* also means a mixture of two or more ingredients with different colours, flavours or shapes.

RECIPE

panaché of lobster and crayfish with caviar

Prepare a well-flavoured court-bouillon. In it cook a lobster of 800 g (1¾ lb) for 12 minutes with the liquid gently bubbling. Remove the lobster, cut it under the chest, between the antennae, and set aside. Put about 1 kg (2¼ lb) crayfish (about 20) in the same liquid, boil for 2 minutes and leave to cool

in the liquid. Remove the shell of the tail and pincers of the lobster; slice the tail flesh into 12 even
rounds. Drain the crayfish and shell them (do not
forget to remove the inestines). Make a *beurre blanc
nantais*. When ready to serve, put a little butter in
a sauté pan and cook the rounds of lobster tail, the
pincer meat and the crayfish tails to make them
firm. Add a little court-bouillon and 3 tablespoons
double (heavy) cream. Let it heat without coming
to the boil. To serve, arrange the lobster and crayfish in shallow plates. Keep the plates warm in the
oven. Add a little *beurre blanc nantais* to the sauce
(to taste) and, at the last minute, 4 teaspoons
caviar. Cover the shellfish with the sauce.

PANADA A paste of variable composition used to
bind and thicken forcemeats. A flour panada is used
to thicken quenelle forcemeats; the flour is added all
at once to boiling salted and buttered water, and the
mixture is beaten well over the heat until it thickens
(as for a choux paste). A frangipane panada (made
with flour and egg yolks) is used for poultry and fish
forcemeats; bread panada for fish forcemeats; potato
panada for quenelles of white meat; and rice panada
for various forcemeats.

Panada is also the name of a type of soup or gruel
made from bread, stock, milk (or water) and butter.
It has to simmer for a certain time and is served piping hot. The basic recipe may be enriched with eggs
(whole or just yolks) or crème fraîche and seasoned
with nutmeg or tomato sauce.

RECIPES

bread panada

Soak 250 g (9 oz, 4½ cups) fresh white breadcrumbs in 300 ml (½ pint, 1¼ cups) boiled milk
until the liquid is completely absorbed. Pour this
mixture into a saucepan and let it thicken over the
heat, stirring it with a wooden spoon. Pour into a
buttered dish and leave to cool.

flour panada

Place 300 ml (½ pint, 1¼ cups) water, 50 g (2 oz,
¼ cup) butter and ½ teaspoon salt in a saucepan
and bring to the boil. Add 150 g (5 oz, 1¼ cups)
plain (all-purpose) flour, beat well over the heat
with a wooden spoon, then cook until the mixture
comes away from the edges of the saucepan. Pour
the panada into a buttered dish, smooth the surface,
cover with buttered paper and leave it to cool.

frangipane panada

Put 125 g (4½ oz, 1¼ cups) plain (all-purpose) flour
and 4 egg yolks in a saucepan. Mix well, stirring with a
wooden spoon, then add 90 g (3½ oz, ⅓ cup) melted
butter, ½ teaspoon salt, some pepper and a pinch of
nutmeg. Thin the mixture by blending it with 250 ml
(8 fl oz, 1 cup) boiled milk, poured in gradually. Cook
for 5–6 minutes, beating vigorously with a whisk.
Pour the panada into a buttered dish, smooth the surface, cover with buttered paper and leave to cool.

panada soup based on meat stock

Remove the crusts from 250 g (9 oz, about 10 slices)
stale bread and reduce it to crumbs. Peel and seed
500 g (18 oz) tomatoes, then crush the pulp. Peel and
chop a large onion. Heat 2 tablespoons oil in a
saucepan and cook the onion until golden, then add
the tomatoes and leave to cook for 5 minutes with
the lid on. Add 1 litre (1¾ pints, 4⅓ cups) stock and a
pinch of powdered marjoram, adjust the seasoning
and leave to cook for about 30 minutes. Pour 500 ml
(17 fl oz, 2 cups) stock over the breadcrumbs, leave
them to soak, then add the mixture to the soup and
let it cook for a further 10 minutes. Press the soup
through a sieve (or purée in a blender) and serve piping hot. A tablespoon of oil and some coarsely chopped herbs may be added to the soup just before serving.

panada soup with milk

Remove the crusts from 250 g (9 oz, about
10 slices) stale bread and pour over it 1 litre
(1¾ pints, 4⅓ cups) boiling milk. Leave to soak,
then cook gently for 15 minutes. Pureé in a blender
and season with salt.

This panada may be sweetened, sprinkled with
nutmeg or enriched with an egg yolk beaten with
crème fraîche.

potato panada

Boil 300 ml (½ pint, 1¼ cups) milk seasoned with
½ teaspoon salt, a pinch of pepper and a pinch of
grated nutmeg until it has reduced by one-sixth.
Add 20 g (¾ oz, 1½ tablespoons) butter and 250 g
(9 oz, 1¼ cups) thinly sliced boiled potatoes. Cook
gently for 15 minutes, then mix well to obtain a
smooth paste. Use this panada while still warm.

rice panada

Add 200 g (7 oz, 1 cup) short-grain rice to 600 ml
(1 pint, 2½ cups) white unclarified consommé to
which 20 g (¾ oz, 1½ tablespoons) butter has been
added and cook in a preheated oven at 160°C
(325°F, gas 3) for about 50 minutes. Mix the
cooked rice well with a wooden spoon to obtain a
smooth paste. Leave to cool in a buttered dish.

PAN-BAGNAT Also known as *pan bagna*. A
speciality of Nice consisting of a kind of sandwich
sprinkled with olive oil and filled with onion,
anchovy, celery and black (ripe) olives; its name
means literally 'bathed bread' (bathed in oil). Some
people spread the bread with garlic-flavoured
anchovy purée before garnishing it. Originally, this
preparation was a salade niçoise in which stale
bread was crumbled an hour before serving.

RECIPE

pan-bagnat

Split a round bread roll in two and open it out
without separating the two halves. Remove two-
thirds of the crumb. Rub the remaining crumb with
garlic and sprinkle it with a little olive oil. Fill with

slices of tomato, onion and hard-boiled (hard-cooked) eggs, thin strips of sweet (bell) pepper, stoned (pitted) black olives and anchovy fillets in oil. Sprinkle with olive-oil vinaigrette and close up the roll.

PANCAKE A flat product, savoury or sweet, made by frying batter with the minimum of fat. The most popular pancake is of the French crêpe variety, made from a thin batter, cooked in a thin layer on a lightly greased pan. The size and thickness may vary, but the pancake is thin enough to roll or wrap around a filling.

Thicker, smaller pancakes are made from leavened batter, typically with baking powder, yeast or folded-in whisked egg white acting as a raising agent. Ingredients such as fruit may be added.

Indian pancakes, for example dosas, are made from a batter of ground pulses. Chinese pancakes are very thin, made from a rolled-out wheat flour and water dough. They are lightly cooked in pairs, then peeled apart and lightly cooked on their second sides. These pale, soft pancakes are heated in a steamer and served with Peking duck. See *crêpe*.

PANCETTA An Italian speciality, this spiced, cured belly of pork is similar to high quality streaky (slab) bacon. It may be eaten raw, in thin slices, and also used in making various dishes.

PANDORA A spindle-shaped fish closely related to the sea bream, caught in the Mediterranean and in the Bay of Biscay. It is 30–50 cm (12–20 in) long, has a grey-green back and a white belly and weighs up to 1 kg (2¼ lb). Pandora is prepared like sea bream but does not have as much flavour.

PANEER Also known as panir. Indian fresh cheese with a firm texture and a very light flavour. It is used in savoury and sweet dishes. Fried cubes of paneer, which form a golden crust and soften slightly in the middle, may be added to pilau or cooked with peas.

PANETIÈRE A small openwork cupboard, hanging on the wall or from the ceiling, which was formerly used, particularly in Brittany and Provence, for keeping bread.

PANETIÈRE, À LA Describing various preparations which, after cooking, are arranged in a round, hollowed-out loaf of bread, which has been lightly browned in the oven. Lamb's sweetbreads, chicken livers, salpicons, various ragoûts, scrambled eggs, small birds and fillets of fish in sauce may be presented in this way.

RECIPE

fillets of sole à la panetière
Cut the top off a large, round loaf and remove three-quarters of the crumb. Butter the inside and lightly brown in a preheated oven at 200°C (400°F,

gas 6). Season some fillets of sole with salt and pepper, fold them in two, coat with flour and cook them in butter. Prepare a ragoût of mushrooms in cream. Drain the fillets of sole and arrange them in a crown in the bread. Pour the mushroom ragoût into the centre and heat in the oven for about 5 minutes.

PANETTONE A large, round Italian cake which is a speciality of the city of Milan but is made anywhere between Milan and Venice. Panettone is made from a raised dough enriched with egg yolks (which give it its colour) and contains raisins and candied orange and lemon peel. The dough is traditionally kneaded three times a day for several days to give the characteristic light texture, then it is placed in a cool oven to rise and cooked in a cylindrical mould. Traditional Christmas fare, this cake is also eaten for breakfast, with coffee, and it is sometimes served as a dessert, accompanied by a liqueur wine.

The word is derived from *pane* (bread). According to one legend, it is a contraction of *pane de Tonio*: Tonio, a poor baker from Milan, had a pretty daughter with whom a young nobleman was in love. As she could not be married without a dowry, Tonio provided all the ingredients necessary to make an excellent cake. Tonio made a fortune with his *pane* and his daughter made a good match.

RECIPE

panettone
Mix 3 tablespoons water, 50 g (2 oz, ¼ cup) butter and 75 g (3 oz, ½ cup) soft brown sugar in a saucepan and place over a moderate heat, making sure the mixture does not come to the boil. Sift 300 g (11 oz, 2¾ cups) plain (all-purpose) flour and 20 g (¾ oz, 3 packages) dried yeast at least four times. Put into a mixing bowl. Add 25 g (1 oz, 2 tablespoons) raisins and 50 g (2 oz, ⅓ cup) diced candied citron peel. Mix together thoroughly and incorporate 2 egg yolks. Slowly add the butter–soft brown sugar mixture. Work the dough thoroughly with a wooden spoon until it leaves the sides of the bowl. Then place the dough on a lightly floured work surface and knead it for another 1–2 minutes. Mould the dough into the typical dome shape of panettone, making an incision in the shape of a square with a cross in the middle. Leave to rest in a warm place for 30 minutes. Bake in a preheated oven at 180°C (350°F, gas 4) for 45 minutes, wrapping the panettone in foil for the first part of the cooking process to prevent the dough from spreading. Just before the end of the cooking, spray a little water over the incision in the panettone, which will give it a glossy surface.

PANFORTE An Italian Christmas speciality from Siena, it is a highly spiced, sweet mixture of dried fruit and nuts bound with honey and baked on a rice-paper base in a shallow round tin. Ground coriander, mace, cinnamon, cloves and white pepper are included; candied fruits and peel are also added. Panforte is dredged with icing (confectioner's) sugar and tightly packed, then allowed to mature for at least a few days before eating. In airtight wrapping panforte has a long shelf life.

PANINI An Italian hot sandwich made with very white bread, with a crust that is sometimes lightly brushed with olive oil. The sandwich is filled with crudités, charcuterie, tapenade or olive paste, small white (pearl) onions, or herbs. It is then lightly grilled (broiled).

PANNEQUET A sweet or savoury pancake filled with chopped ingredients, a purée or a cream.

Pannequets (the name is derived from the English word 'pancake') are generally served as a small entrée, as a hot hors d'oeuvre, as a soup garnish or as a dessert course. They are spread with the chosen filling, rolled up or folded into four, then browned or glazed under the grill (broiler) or sometimes coated with breadcrumbs and fried.

Fillings for savoury pannequets include: anchovies in béchamel or tomato sauce, spinach in Mornay sauce, melted cheese, soft roes with mushrooms, mushrooms with paprika or ham, chopped mutton with aubergines (eggplants), shrimps in Aurora sauce, game purée, puréed chicken in cream, and crayfish in Nantua sauce.

Sweet pannequets may be filled with confectioner's custard (pastry cream) flavoured with crystallized (candied) fruits, syrup, praline or liqueur, or with chestnut cream or jam. They may be browned under the grill (broiler) or flamed.

RECIPES

preparation of pannequets
Make a batter with 250 g (9 oz, 2¼ cups) plain (all-purpose) flour, a pinch of salt, 3 beaten eggs, 250 ml (8 fl oz, 1 cup) milk, 250 ml (8 fl oz, 1 cup) water and 1 tablespoon melted butter. For sweet pancakes, add 1 tablespoon caster (superfine) sugar mixed with the eggs. Prepare some fairly thick pancakes. Pile them in a covered dish and keep hot over a saucepan of boiling water.

Savoury Pannequets
anchovy pannequets
Prepare 8 savoury pannequets and 300 ml (½ pint, 1¼ cups) fairly thick béchamel* sauce without salt. Soak 8 anchovies in water to remove some of the brine, take out the fillets and reduce them to a purée. Cut 8 anchovy fillets canned in oil into small pieces. Mix the béchamel sauce and the anchovy purée and adjust the seasoning. Spread each pannequet with anchovy béchamel sauce and sprinkle with small pieces of the fillets. Fold in four and arrange in a buttered ovenproof dish. Sprinkle with fresh breadcrumbs fried in butter and place under the grill (broiler) for 3–4 minutes or in a preheated oven at 230°C (450°F, gas 8) for 10 minutes.

cheese pannequets
Prepare 8 savoury pannequets and 300 ml (½ pint, 1¼ cups) thick béchamel* sauce, to which 100 g (4 oz, 1 cup) grated Gruyère or Parmesan cheese has been added.

Proceed as for anchovy pannequets but add grated cheese to the fried breadcrumbs before placing under the grill (broiler) or in the oven.

fried pannequets
Fill some savoury pannequets, roll them into cigar shapes and cut into sections about 3 cm (1¼ in) long. Coat with egg and breadcrumbs and fry just before serving. Garnish with fried parsley. Fried pannequets may be filled like other savoury pannequets or in any of the following ways:
• *à la brunoise, à la hongroise* With a salpicon of onions and mushrooms softened in butter mixed with paprika-flavoured béchamel sauce.
• *à la grecque* With a salpicon of chopped braised mutton and sautéed aubergine (eggplant), bound with very thick tomato sauce.
• *à l'italienne* With mushroom duxelles, lean ham cut into small dice and tomato sauce.
• *à la Saint-Hubert* With roebuck purée thickened with game fumet.
• *à la strasbourgeoise* With foie gras purée and chopped truffles.

pannequets à la florentine
Prepare 8 savoury pannequets and 200 ml (7 fl oz, ¾ cup) thick béchamel sauce. Cook 400 g (14 oz) spinach in salted water, dry it thoroughly, chop it coarsely and mix it with the béchamel sauce. Add 75 g (3 oz, ¾ cup) grated Gruyère or Parmesan cheese. Proceed as for anchovy pannequets.

pannequets à la reine
Prepare 8 savoury pannequets and 150 ml (¼ pint, ⅔ cup) chicken purée* with cream. Add a little salpicon of truffle to the purée. Spread the filling on the pannequets and fold them into four. Cover each pannequet with 1 tablespoon very reduced chicken velouté* made with cream and sprinkle with a mixture of fried breadcrumbs and grated Parmesan cheese. Proceed as for anchovy pannequets.

pannequets for soup
Prepare some savoury pannequets (allow 6 for 8 people) and a vegetable brunoise, a cheese béchamel sauce or a very dry mushroom duxelles. Cover half of the pannequets with the chosen garnish and cover with the remaining pannequets. Press each pair together firmly, then cut out rounds with a fluted cutter. Place these in boiling consommé just before serving.

pannequets with soft roes
Poach some soft roes, drain, cool and cut them into a salpicon. Prepare 8 savoury pannequets, 4 tablespoons mushroom duxelles* and 300 ml (½ pint, 1¼ cups) well-reduced béchamel* sauce or

thin velouté*. Mix the duxelles with the béchamel sauce and add the soft roes. Proceed as for anchovy pannequets but add grated Parmesan cheese to the fried breadcrumbs.

other recipes See *brunoise, Mornay, shrimps and prawns.*

Sweet Pannequets
apricot pannequets
Prepare 8 sweet pannequets. Make 250 ml (8 fl oz, 1 cup) confectioner's custard (pastry cream) flavoured with rum (see *custard*) and add to it 12 very ripe apricots (or drained canned apricots), stoned (pitted) and cut into dice, and 75 g (3 oz, ¾ cup) coarsely chopped almonds. Spread the pannequets with this preparation and roll them up. Arrange them in a buttered ovenproof dish, dust them generously with icing (confectioner's) sugar, and place them in a preheated oven at 230°C (450°F, gas 8) for 8–10 minutes.

pannequets à la cévenole
Prepare 8 sweet pannequets. Mix 250 ml (8 fl oz, 1 cup) sweetened chestnut purée flavoured with kirsch with 3 tablespoons crème fraîche and 3 tablespoons fragments of marrons glacés. Spread the pannequets with this mixture and finish as for apricot pannequets.

pannequets à la créole
Prepare 8 sweet pannequets. Mix 300 ml (½ pint, 1¼ cups) confectioner's custard (pastry cream) flavoured with rum (see *custard*) with 4 slices of canned pineapple cut into a salpicon. Spread the pannequets with this mixture and finish as for apricot pannequets.

pannequets with crystallized fruit
Prepare 8 sweet pannequets. Cut 250 g (9 oz, 1½ cups) crystallized (candied) fruit into small dice and macerate them in 100 ml (4 fl oz, 7 tablespoons) brandy or rum. Mix 4 egg yolks with 125 g (4½ oz, ½ cup) caster (superfine) sugar, add 65 g (2½ oz, ½ cup) plain (all-purpose) flour, and mix well. Sprinkle with 500 ml (17 fl oz, 2 cups) boiling milk, whisking quickly. Pour into a saucepan and boil for 2 minutes, beating with a whisk. Combine the crystallized fruit and the macerating spirit with this mixture, then leave until lukewarm.

Spread each pannequet with a generous tablespoon of the fruit cream mixture, roll them up and arrange in a buttered ovenproof dish. Dust with 100 g (4 oz, ¾ cup) icing (confectioner's) sugar and caramelize in a preheated oven at 220°C (425°F, gas 7). Serve as soon as they are taken out of the oven. The pannequets may be flamed with rum just before serving.

praline pannequets
Prepare 8 sweet pannequets. Prepare 300 ml (½ pint, 1¼ cups) confectioner's custard (pastry cream) flavoured with liqueur (Cointreau or Grand Marnier) or with Armagnac (see *custard*) and mix with 100 g (4 oz, ½ cup) crushed praline*. Spread the pannequets with this mixture and finish as for the apricot pannequets, but sprinkle with 8 finely crushed macaroons before putting in the oven.

PANTLER'S OFFICE Under the Ancien Régime, an important office of the department of the *bouche du roi* in charge of the bread supply. At the beginning of the 15th century it consisted of: one head pantler and six other pantlers; six gentlemen carvers, to prepare the trenchers; three butlers, to move the furniture, linen and table cutlery; three *portechappes*, responsible for looking after the bread bins, cutting the bread and laying part of the table; an *oubloyer*, to prepare the wafers (*oublies*); a *baschonier*, to drive the horses loaded with bread; a launderer, to wash the tablecloths; and five tablecloth servants, to look after the linen.

The pantler's office dealt not only with the bread but also with everything associated with the king's table – the linen, the plates and dishes, and sometimes the fruit and certain cakes. The senior pantler, in addition to his court duties, exercised certain legal rights over the guild of bakers; among other things, he sold masterships to apprentice bakers at prices he determined himself. The *installation* ceremony included handing over to the senior pantler a pot of rosemary with titbits hanging from the branches. In 1650 the pot of rosemary was replaced by a 20-franc piece. The rights of the pantler, which dated from Philip Augustus, were abolished in 1711. The Duc de Brissac, last of the great pantlers, was given more than 100,000 francs in compensation for the loss of his office.

PANZAROTTI Rice fritters prepared in Corsica especially for religious festivals, rice being the symbol of life, abundance and immortality. The rice, cooked in milk, is mixed with brandy, oil and yeast, then egg yolks, grated lemon and stiffly whisked egg whites. The fritters are served hot, dusted with sugar.

PAPAW A slightly elongated and curved tropical fruit (*Asimina triloba*), native to North America. It has a smooth, yellowish skin and juicy, pale yellow flesh with numerous seeds. Its flavour and aroma are reminiscent of a banana and a pear. Not to be confused with pawpaw, the alternative name for papaya; the two are not related.

PAPAYA Also known as pawpaw. A large, pear-shaped, tropical fruit (*Carica papaya*) with a smooth, yellowish skin; its orange-coloured flesh has a central gelatinous cavity filled with edible black seeds. Originating in Malaysia, the papaya is now cultivated in South America, Asia and Africa. It can be cooked as a vegetable when green and unripe, or eaten ripe as a fruit. It is often used to make jam or pickles.

The green papaya is 'bled' (to get rid of the white

acid juice) and seeded. It may then be grated like a raw carrot, cooked like a vegetable marrow (squash), prepared as a gratin or in gruel, or fried in slices (as is done in Vietnam).

When it is completely ripe, the papaya is served as an hors d'oeuvre like melon, in a salad or as a dessert with sugar and cream. Its juicy and refreshing pulp is improved by flavouring with a little rum.

PAPER A material often used in cookery for the preparation, cooking, serving or preserving of foods and dishes. Greaseproof (wax) paper withstands a certain amount of heat and provides insulation; it is used to wrap dishes to be cooked *en papillote*, to cover preparations while they are cooked in the oven so that they do not brown too quickly and to line cake tins (pans). Cellophane paper is used to cover jams when they are put in jars.

Lace doileys, of various shapes and patterns, are used for presenting sweets (candies) and cakes. Plain doileys with a crinkled edge are used for serving fried food. Iced petits fours and bouchées are presented in little cases of pleated paper which are also used for baking small cakes. Paper towels are widely used in the kitchen for cleaning and wiping foodstuffs and for draining fried dishes.

PAPET A traditional Swiss soup from the Vaud canton. It consists of leeks and potatoes and is often accompanied by a piece of smoked pork. It is usually served with a sausage ring.

PAPETON A speciality of Avignon based on puréed aubergines (eggplants) and eggs, cooked in a mould that was originally shaped like a papal crown.

The creation of the *papeton* might have arisen after a quarrel between the cooks of Avignon and those who had come from Italy with the papal court and who therefore claimed to be superior. The local cooks, wishing to prove the contrary, devised an original dish, which pleased the pope.

RECIPE

aubergine papeton
Prepare 500 ml (17 fl oz, 2 cups) very reduced tomato fondue*. Peel 2 kg (4½ lb) aubergines (eggplants), cut them into cubes, sprinkle with fine salt and leave them to exude their juice for 1 hour. Wash them in cold water, wipe thoroughly, then flour them lightly and cook very gently in 4 tablespoons olive oil until soft. Sprinkle with salt and leave to cool, then purée in a blender. Mix 7 large eggs, beaten as for an omelette, with 100 ml (4 fl oz, 7 tablespoons) milk, 2 finely crushed garlic cloves, some salt, pepper and a pinch of cayenne. Add the aubergine purée and pour into a buttered manqué mould. Place this mould in a bain marie, bring it to the boil on the top of the stove, then cook in a preheated oven at 180°C (350°F, gas 4) for 1 hour. Turn out on to a warmed serving dish and coat with the hot tomato fondue.

PAPILLOTE A small decorative paper frill used to garnish the bone end of a lamb or veal chop, or the drumstick of a chicken.

The term *en papillote* is used to describe a preparation cooked and served in a wrapping of greaseproof (wax) paper or foil. Veal chops, whole stuffed fish, fish fillets and potatoes can be prepared en papillote. The dish is generally cooked with herbs, a sauce, chopped onions or mushrooms. The paper is buttered or oiled, wrapped around the food and folded tightly so that the food is completely enclosed. The wrapping swells in the oven during cooking, and the dish is served piping hot, before the wrapping collapses.

The name *papillote* is also given to a sweet (candy) or chocolate wrapped in brightly coloured shiny paper with fringed ends. The *papillote lyonnaise* contains a riddle or a motto wrapped up with the sweet: its name is attributed by some to a confectioner called Papillot, but it more probably derives from *papillon* (butterfly). The *cosaque* is a papillote in the form of a cracker made with two papers of different colours, one of them gold. Formerly sold at fairs, these crackers have practically disappeared.

Cooking en papillote

1 *Cut a piece of greaseproof (wax) paper large enough to enclose the food completely with plenty to spare around the edge. Brush the paper with oil or melted butter and place the prepared ingredients on one half. Fold the other half of the paper over to enclose the food completely.*

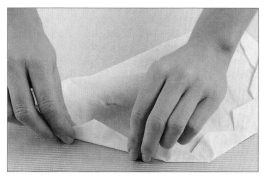

2 *Working around the edge, make small, sharp folds holding both layers of paper together securely to seal in the ingredients. Place on a baking sheet ready for cooking.*

RECIPES

fillets of fish en papillotes

Cut out some rectangles of greaseproof (wax) paper large enough to wrap up each fillet (such as sole, whiting, fresh cod, sea bream) folded in two. Spread 1 tablespoon double (heavy) cream in the centre of each papillote and season with salt and pepper. Place on top a fish fillet seasoned with salt and pepper, sprinkled with a little lemon juice and folded in two. Cover with a little cream and scatter with coarsely chopped herbs. Close the papillotes, folding the edges together. Cook in a preheated oven at 230°C (450°F, gas 8) for about 15 minutes.

A little julienne of vegetables cooked in butter may be placed under and over the folded fillet.

papillotes à la chinoise

Cut some fillets of fish (such as whiting, fresh cod, sea bream, haddock) into pieces about 2.5 × 5 cm (1 × 2 in). Season with salt and pepper, sprinkle with Chinese rice wine or a little sherry and leave to marinate for 30 minutes. Cut out some rectangles of greaseproof (wax) paper large enough to wrap up each piece of fillet and oil them. Place a piece of fish in the centre of each rectangle and sprinkle with ½ teaspoon chopped ginger and 1 tablespoon chopped spring onion (scallion). Close up the papillotes and fry in very hot oil (180°C, 350°F) for 3 minutes. Drain them, arrange on a serving dish and serve with spring onions cut into a julienne.

papillotes of lobster and scallops

Separate the tail from a lobster and set it aside. Open the body and take out the stomach. Crush the carcass and heat the pieces in a thick-based saucepan with some chopped shallot. Add 250 ml (8 fl oz, 1 cup) vermouth and reduce by half, then add 150 ml (¼ pint, ⅔ cup) double (heavy) cream and reduce again by half. Add the lobster tail, cook for 4 minutes, then remove the pan from the heat. Shell the tail and cut the flesh into 8 slices. Cut a truffle into 8 thin slices. Open 8 scallops and take out the kernel and the coral. Strain the sauce.

Prepare 4 pieces of oiled greaseproof (wax) paper. Place 2 slices of lobster on each piece of paper and top them with 2 scallops and 2 slices of truffle. Coat with the sauce and sprinkle with chopped fresh herbs. Close up the papillotes tightly, folding the edges together, and cook them in a preheated oven at 230°C (450°F, gas 8) for a maximum of 5 minutes. Serve in a very hot stainless steel dish so that the papillotes do not collapse.

potatoes en papillotes

Wash some large potatoes thoroughly under cold running water, but do not dry them. Wrap each potato in a piece of foil and cook for 40–45 minutes, either in a preheated oven at 230°C (450°F, gas 8) or in the hot ashes of a fire.

red mullet en papillotes

Clean 8 small red mullet, but leave the liver inside. Prepare a forcemeat with 5–6 slices of white bread dipped in milk, some parsley and 4 tablespoons anchovy butter*. Season the fish with salt and pepper, stuff them with the forcemeat, brush with olive oil and leave to marinate in a cool place for 1 hour. Place each mullet on a rectangle of oiled greaseproof (wax) paper and close up the papillotes. Cook in a preheated oven at 230°C (450°F, gas 8) for 15–20 minutes.

veal chops en papillotes

Sauté some veal chops in butter until they are cooked through and golden. Cut out some squares of greaseproof (wax) paper, big enough to wrap up each chop, and oil them. Place on half of each square of paper 1 slice of ham cut to the dimensions of the chop, 1 veal chop, 1 tablespoon mushroom duxelles* and another slice of ham the same size as the first. Fold over the paper and press the edges together. Place the papillotes in a preheated oven at 240°C (475°F, gas 9) until the paper turns golden.

other recipes See *fruit, pigeon*.

PAPIN, DENIS French physician and inventor (born Chitenay, near Blois, 1647; died London, 1714). Famous for his work on the properties of steam, he invented the original Papin marmite, forerunner of the pressure cooker, which he described in a treatise published in 1682 in Paris: *How to dress bones and to cook all kinds of meats in a very short time and at little cost, with a description of the machine which must be used.*

PAPRIKA A spice ground from one or more varieties of sweet red pepper (*paprika* in Hungarian), used to season ragoûts, stuffings, sauces and soups, to flavour fresh cheeses and for garnishing. Paprika is a distinctive feature of Hungarian cookery, into which it was introduced only in the 19th century, for seasoning goulash, *paprikache*, *pörkölt* and *tokany*. Paprika was probably invented by the Turks and has been known in Europe since the time of Christopher Columbus. The Palffy brothers of Szegd, Hungary, invented a machine to strip stalks and seeds from peppers, and the spice is still at its most sophisticated in Hungary. Kalossa, south of Budapest, is the main growing area, and Szeged, in the south of Hungary, is the main centre for producing paprika; the best variety is the 'pink' or 'sweet' pepper, which has a piquant flavour but no bitter aftertaste.

The original shrub that produces this pepper is native to America. Its pods, 6–13 cm (2½–5 in) long and 3 cm (1¼ in) wide, are harvested at the end of the summer, when they are red; they are then dried and crushed. There are, in fact, many types of paprika made from a range of peppers, from the long, tapering, mild varieties to the round, hot, cherry peppers. Paprikas labelled 'noble sweet' (in

PARAGUAY and URUGUAY

The cuisines of Paraguay and Uruguay are very similar to that of Argentina, and grilled beef is extremely popular in all three countries.

As in the whole of South America, maize (corn), rice, haricot (navy) beans and red kidney beans are widely used, often in stews that bring together vegetables, cereals, meat and numerous spices. Thus *bori bori*, also common in Argentina, combines seasoned meat balls, vegetables, chunks of fresh cheese and maize.

An abundance of freshwater fish and game brings some variety to the menus. Fish is often grilled (broiled) but is also sometimes cooked in a lemon-based marinade. In addition to the traditional sweet (bell) peppers and tomatoes, palm hearts are also used extensively. There is a great range of desserts, mainly based on tropical fruit.

the commercial description) are likely to be Hungarian. Spain is another centre for paprika production, where the peppers are smoked before being made into paprika. Jarandilla, in the west, and the River Vera valley are famed for Spanish paprikas.

Professor Szent-Györgyi, who was awarded the Nobel prize for medicine, considered this pepper to be the plant with the highest content of vitamin C. It develops the best flavour when it is cooked with onion and lard (shortening). It should be added to the preparation away from the heat or with liquid, otherwise the sugar it contains may caramelize and impair the flavour and colour of the dish.

RECIPE

sauté of lamb with paprika
Cut 1.5 kg (3¼ lb) lamb cutlets (chops) or boned shoulder into cubes and sauté them in butter. When they are brown, add 150 g (5 oz, ⅔ cup) chopped onions to the sauté dish. Season with salt and sprinkle with 2 tablespoons flour. Stir for a few minutes, then blend in 1 teaspoon paprika away from the heat. Moisten with 200 ml (7 fl oz, ¾ cup) white wine, reduce by half, then add 300 ml (½ pint, 1¼ cups) stock and 2 tablespoons tomato purée (paste). Add a bouquet garni and cook, covered, for 30 minutes. Drain the pieces of lamb and put them in a sauté dish with 250 g (9 oz, 3 cups) mushrooms, thinly sliced and quickly fried in butter. Add to the sauce 200 ml (7 fl oz, ¾ cup) crème fraîche and 1 teaspoon paprika, reduce and strain, then pour it over the lamb. Simmer gently with the lid on for 25 minutes.

PAPRIKACHE A Hungarian stew made with paprika, soured (sour) cream and either white meat or fish (whereas goulash is made with beef), cooked with chopped or thinly sliced onions and garnished with tomatoes, sweet (bell) peppers or potatoes.

PARAFFIN WAX A mixture of solid neutral hydrocarbons. White, translucent, tasteless, odourless and melting easily, paraffin wax is used for coating fruit and vegetables and for glazing the crust of cheeses. It can also be used for sealing jars of jam.

PARAGUAY AND URUGUAY See *above*.

PARASOL MUSHROOM A mushroom, of *Lepiota* family, found in copses and clearings, whose cap is usually covered in large scales. All the large varieties are edible, but the long woody stems surrounded by a thick ring are best discarded. Of the smaller species, one is poisonous. The two best species for eating are the common parasol (*Lepiota procera*) and the shaggy parasol (*Lepiota rhacodes*). They are brown or brownish-grey with many gills, which stand away from the stalk. The white flesh is rather soft and insubstantial and turns pink or reddish when exposed to the air. They cook quickly and can be deep-fried, shallow-fried, grilled (broiled) or even served raw in a salad.

RECIPE

parasol mushrooms à la suprême
Prepare the caps of 1 kg (2¼ lb) young parasol mushrooms, without washing them. Make a white roux with 25 g (1 oz, 2 tablespoons) butter and 40 g (1½ oz, ⅓ cup) flour and then add 500 ml (17 fl oz, 2 cups) hot chicken stock. Let it cook over a low heat for 15 minutes. Turn the heat up and thicken the sauce with 1 egg yolk mixed with 4 tablespoons double (heavy) cream. Season with salt and mild red paprika and keep warm in a bain marie. In a shallow frying pan, cook 65 g (2½ oz, ¼ cup) chopped onions seasoned with ½ teaspoon paprika in butter. When the onions start to turn pale golden, add the mushroom caps and sauté them briskly for 5 minutes, then season with salt, a little grated nutmeg and a bouquet garni to which extra basil and tarragon have been added. Cover the pan and cook for 10 more minutes over a high heat. Drain the mushrooms and keep them hot in the pan with a little butter. Whisk the suprême sauce and add to the mushrooms; check the seasoning. Serve piled up on small slices of white bread which have been fried golden brown in noisette butter.

PARATHA Indian fried, flat, wheat-flour bread with a flaky texture. The texture is achieved by rolling and folding the dough several times, brushing with ghee to create a flaky-pastry type product. Parathas may be plain or stuffed with a savoury or sweet filling. A spicy mixture of vegetables or minced (ground) meat may be used for the filling;

grated carrot, sugar, raisins and nuts may be lightly spiced to make a sweet filling.

PARFAIT An iced dessert made with double (heavy) cream, which gives it smoothness, prevents it from melting too quickly and enables it to be cut into slices. Originally the parfait was a coffee-flavoured ice cream; today, the basic mixture is a flavoured custard cream, a flavoured syrup mixed with egg yolks or a fruit purée, which is blended with whipped cream and then frozen. There is a special parfait mould in the shape of a cylinder with one slightly rounded end. The parfait can be served by itself or used as a base for preparing an iced cake, an iced soufflé or a vacherin.

In Britain and the United States a parfait is also the name of a whipped cream dessert.

RECIPE

iced parfait
Mix 4 tablespoons water with 200 g (7 oz, ¾ cup) caster (superfine) sugar and cook to the fine thread stage (110°C, 230°F). Place 8 egg yolks in a bowl and pour the boiling syrup over them, little by little, whisking all the time. Continue to whisk until the mixture has cooled. Then add the chosen flavouring from the suggestions below.

Whip 200 ml (7 fl oz, ¾ cup) double (heavy) cream with 100 ml (4 fl oz, 7 tablespoons) milk (both chilled) until very firm. Blend the whipped cream with the cooled mixture of egg yolks and syrup and pour into a parfait mould. Place in the freezer and leave to set for at least 6 hours.
• *Suggested flavourings* Add 3–4 tablespoons brandy or liqueur; 4–5 tablespoons coffee essence (extract); 200 g (7 oz, 7 squares) melted plain (dark) chocolate; 150 g (5 oz, ⅔ cup) powdered almond praline; or about 10 drops of vanilla extract.

PARFAIT AMOUR A liqueur of Dutch origin, flavoured with lemon (or citron), cloves, cinnamon and coriander. It originated in the 18th century and was very popular between the two world wars. The liqueur was coloured red or violet and perfumed with violets.

PARIS-BREST A large, ring-shaped cake of choux pastry, filled with praline-flavoured cream and sprinkled with shredded (slivered) almonds. It was created in 1891 by a pastrycook whose shop was situated in the suburbs of Paris on the route of the bicycle race between Paris and Brest: he had the idea of making large, ring-shaped éclairs resembling bicycle wheels. The Paris-Nice is a variation without almonds, filled with Saint-Honoré cream.

RECIPE

Paris-Brest
Sprinkle 100 g (4 oz, 1 cup) flaked (slivered) almonds over a baking sheet and cook them in a preheated oven at 200°C (400°F, gas 6) until golden. Prepare a choux paste* with 100 g (4 oz, ½ cup) butter, 2 tablespoons caster (superfine) sugar, a generous pinch of salt, 200 g (7 oz, 1¾ cups) plain (all-purpose) flour, 350 ml (12 fl oz, 1½ cups) water and 5 or 6 eggs, according to their size. Fill a piping bag, fitted with a nozzle 1.5 cm (¾ in) in diameter, with this mixture and pipe 2 rings, 18 cm (7 in) in diameter. Glaze them with beaten egg, sprinkle them with the flaked almonds and cook in a preheated oven at 180°C (350°F, gas 4) for 35–40 minutes. Turn off the oven and leave the rings to cool with the door ajar, then remove from the oven and leave them to get completely cold.

Prepare a confectioner's custard (see *custard*) with 65 g (2½ oz, ½ cup) plain flour, 175 g (6 oz, ¾ cup) caster sugar, 15 g (½ oz, 1 tablespoon) butter, 4 whole eggs, a generous pinch of salt and 500 ml (17 fl oz, 2 cups) boiling milk. In another bowl make a praline-flavoured French butter cream (see *creams*) with 200 ml (7 fl oz, ¾ cup) milk, 6 eggs, 200 g (7 oz, 1 cup) caster sugar, 400 g (14 oz, ¾ cup) butter and 75 g (3 oz, ⅓ cup) praline. Finally, prepare 150 g (5 oz) Italian meringue*.

Leave the three preparations to cool thoroughly, then mix them together. Cut the choux rings in half horizontally and fill the lower halves with the meringue mixture using a piping bag with a large fluted nozzle.

Replace the top halves of the rings, dust with icing (confectioner's) sugar and put in a cool place until time to serve.
• *Individual Paris-Brest* ◆ Instead of making large pastries, pipe rings measuring about 7.5 cm (3 in) in diameter. Bake as above, allowing about 30 minutes. Fill and serve with a custard sauce, if liked. Hazelnuts can be used instead of almonds in the praline (with chopped hazelnuts on top of the choux rings) and the dessert can be decorated with a few whole caramelized nuts.

PARISIEN A lemon-flavoured sponge cake filled with frangipane and crystallized (candied) fruits, covered with Italian meringue and lightly browned in the oven.

RECIPE

parisien
Beat 3 egg yolks with 100 g (4 oz, ½ cup) caster (superfine) sugar. When the mixture is white and thick, add 25 g (1 oz, ¼ cup) plain (all-purpose) flour, 25 g (1 oz, ¼ cup) potato flour, ½ teaspoon vanilla sugar and the grated zest of 1 lemon. Whisk 3 egg whites into stiff peaks and fold them carefully into the mixture. Pour this batter into a buttered manqué mould, 23 cm (9 in) in diameter, and cook in a preheated oven at 180°C (350°F, gas 4) for about 35 minutes.

Individual Paris-Brest.

While the cake is cooking, prepare a frangipane: over a very low heat, warm 400 ml (14 fl oz, 1¾ cups) milk with a vanilla pod (bean) split in two. Beat 3 egg yolks in a basin with 75 g (3 oz, 6 tablespoons) caster sugar, until the mixture is white. Add 25 g (1 oz, ¼ cup) cornflour (cornstarch), stir well and slowly pour in the boiling milk, mixing with a wooden spoon. Return the mixture to the saucepan and bring to the boil, whisking all the time, then pour into a bowl. When lukewarm, add 75 g (3 oz, ¾ cup) ground almonds and mix well.

Take the cake out of the oven and leave it to cool. Prepare an Italian meringue by boiling 3 tablespoons water with 175 g (6 oz, ¾ cup) caster sugar to the soft ball stage (see *sugar*). Place the saucepan in a bain marie to keep the syrup hot. Whisk 3 egg whites into stiff peaks, then gradually pour in the syrup in a trickle, whisking continuously. Continue to whisk for 2–3 minutes. Cut the cooled cake into layers 1 cm (½ in) thick and spread each layer with frangipane. Chop 100 g (4 oz, ¾ cup) crystallized (candied) fruits and sprinkle over the frangipane. Reassemble the cake.

Fill a piping bag fitted with a fluted nozzle with the meringue and cover the cake completely. Dust with icing (confectioner's) sugar and cook in a preheated oven at 180°C (350°F, gas 4) until golden. Leave to cool completely before serving.

PARISIENNE, À LA Describing preparations that are typical of the classic repertoire of Parisian restaurants. The term is particularly applied to meat and poultry dishes garnished with potatoes *à la parisienne* (noisettes with herbs) and accompanied by braised lettuces or artichoke hearts; the latter may be garnished with a julienne of pickled tongue and mushrooms bound with velouté, decorated with a thin slice of truffle.

Cold preparations of fish or shellfish *à la parisienne* are made with thick mayonnaise and the garnish often includes artichoke hearts garnished with macédoine in mayonnaise, stuffed hard-boiled (hardcooked) eggs or cubes of aspic.

The term *à la parisienne* is also applied to dishes containing chicken breasts, button mushrooms (*champignons de Paris*), pickled tongue or vegetable macédoine. Soup *à la parisienne* is made with leeks and potatoes, finished with milk and garnished with chervil leaves.

RECIPES

canapés à la parisienne
Cut some slices of white bread into rectangles and remove the crusts. Spread them with chervil butter. Coat some very thin slices of chicken breast (cooked in a white stock) with mayonnaise and garnish with a pattern of sliced truffle and tarragon leaves. Arrange the chicken slices on the canapés and surround them with a border of chopped aspic jelly.

chicken à la parisienne
Remove the breastbone from a chicken, stuff it with 500 g (18 oz) forcemeat* (cream or fine), truss it and poach in veal stock. Drain and leave to cool. Take off the chicken breasts. Remove the forcemeat, cut it into dice and mix with about 400 g (14 oz) cold chicken mousse*. Replace this mixture in the chicken and round it out well to reshape the breast of the bird. Coat the chicken with chaudfroid sauce.

Cut the breasts into thin slices, coat them with chaud-froid sauce, garnish with truffle and pickled tongue and place them on the chicken. Glaze with aspic jelly. Arrange the chicken on the serving dish. Mix some vegetable macédoine with mayonnaise and pour into small dariole moulds. When set, turn them out on to the serving dish around the chicken, placing a thick slice of truffle on each dariole. Garnish the spaces between with chopped aspic.

cold salmon cutlets à la parisienne
Poach some thick slices of salmon in court-bouillon and allow them to cool. Cut each slice into two. Cover the serving dish with a macédoine of vegetables in mayonnaise, arrange the half-slices on it and coat them with mayonnaise thickened with gelatine. Between the cutlets arrange some bunches of asparagus tips, some carrots cut into pod shapes and some chopped French (green) beans, all these vegetables being first cooked in salted water and well drained. A thin slice of truffle may be placed on each cutlet.

glazed salmon à la parisienne
Place a whole salmon in a fish stock, bring to the boil and simmer for 7–8 minutes. Leave it to cool in the cooking stock, then drain it and remove the skin and bones without breaking the flesh. Pat dry with paper towels. Coat it several times with half-set aspic jelly (prepared from the cooking stock), putting the fish in the refrigerator between applications. Cover the serving dish with a layer of aspic. When the aspic is firmly set, arrange the salmon on top.

Prepare some vegetable macédoine mixed with thick mayonnaise and use it to stuff some small round tomatoes. Hard-boil (hard-cook) some eggs and cut in half; sieve the yolks and mix with some mayonnaise. Pipe the mixture into the whites. Garnish the border of the dish with the tomatoes and eggs and slices of lemon.

omelette à la parisienne
Beat 8 eggs with 2 tablespoons chopped onion softened in butter and 2–3 tablespoons chopped mushrooms quickly sautéed in butter. Cook the omelette and roll it up on a warmed serving dish; cover it with grilled chipolata sausages. Surround with a thin ribbon of reduced veal stock mixed with butter.

Parisian salad
Prepare a vegetable macédoine and add to it a salpicon of langouste and truffles. Mix with mayon-

naise thickened with gelatine, then pour it into a domed mould coated with aspic and lined with thin slices of langouste and truffle. Put in a cold place to set, then turn it out.

Alternatively, the ingredients may be mixed together, turned into a salad bowl lined with lettuce leaves and garnished with slices of truffle and quarters of hard-boiled (hard-cooked) eggs.

Parisian sauce

Beat 2–3 Petit-Suisse cheeses in a mixing bowl. Alternatively, use 50–75 g (2–3 oz, ¼–⅓ cup) cream cheese. Season with salt and sprinkle with paprika. Add 2 tablespoons lemon juice, then beat the sauce like a mayonnaise, adding to it, in a thin trickle, 250 ml (8 fl oz, 1 cup) oil. Finally add 1 tablespoon chopped chervil. This sauce is served mainly with cold asparagus.

other recipes See *chartreuse, consommé (hot consommés with garnishes), langouste, lobster, melon, oublie, petite marmite, salt cod, tomato.*

PARMENTIER, ANTOINE AUGUSTIN Military pharmacist and French agronomist (born Montdidier, 1737; died Paris, 1813). Contrary to popular legend, Parmentier did not 'invent' the potato, which had been known and cultivated in France since the 16th century, but he was an enthusiastic propagator of it. While he was a prisoner-of-war in Westphalia during the Seven Years' War, he discovered the nutritional value of this vegetable, which was highly prized by the local population but considered by the French at that time as unwholesome and indigestible, fit only as a food for cattle or the destitute. In the few provinces in France where it was eaten, it was usually used in the form of flour, mixed with wheat and rye to make bread.

In 1772 the Academy of Besançon offered a prize for the discovery of plants likely to be of use to man in the event of famine. Parmentier, who had become an apothecary, then head pharmacist, at Les Invalides, was one of the seven competitors who recommended the use of the potato, which had already been grown for a long time in the Franche-Comté region. He won the prize in 1773. In 1778 he published *Examen chimique de la pomme de terre*, in which he described with enthusiasm the nutritional qualities of the tuber. This work won him the support of Turgot, Buffon, Condorcet, Voltaire and even the king, Louis XVI, who personally encouraged Parmentier in his efforts.

In 1786, after the famine of the previous year, he was granted a plot of land at Neuilly, in the Plain of the Sablons. Later he also obtained permission to have potatoes planted in the Plain of Grenelle, the present Champ-de-Mars. The king had begun to sport a potato flower in his buttonhole, so the aristocracy were already won over, and several noblemen had potatoes planted on their estates. A ruse gained support for the potato from the rest of the population, who until then were still distrustful. The Parisian crops were guarded by the army – proof that the experiments performed there concerned some precious commodity – but the guards were present only during daytime: thieves from the neighbouring district came secretly by night to obtain supplies and thus became the most effective propagandists of this new vegetable. The last prejudices vanished during a dinner at Les Invalides given for Benjamin Franklin; Parmentier had a menu prepared entirely of potatoes to ensure their gastronomic promotion.

Parmentier encouraged the spread of the potato throughout the whole of France by publishing booklets about its cultivation and its uses. His works also extended to other fields. An expert at milling, he founded a school of baking in Paris; he brought out numerous reports on the Jerusalem artichoke, maize (corn), the sweet chestnut, wines, syrups, preserves and food hygiene. He was appointed Inspector of Public Health and eventually ennobled as a baron. For a time the potato itself was known as the *parmentière* in his honour, and he gave his name to various culinary preparations based on potatoes, especially *hachis Parmentier* – chopped beef covered with puréed potatoes and browned in the oven. Other dishes named after him include a cream of potato soup, various egg dishes (omelettes filled with diced fried potatoes, scrambled eggs mixed with sautéed cubes of potato, eggs cooked in nests of potato purée) and a garnish for lamb and veal.

RECIPES

casserole of veal chops à la Parmentier

Season 2 fairly thick veal chops with salt and pepper and brown them on both sides in 25–40 g (1–1½ oz, 2–3 tablespoons) butter in a flameproof casserole. Finish the preparation as for loin of lamb Parmentier, but cook in a preheated oven at 200°C (400°F, gas 6) for 1 hour.

eggs sur le plat Parmentier

Line some small buttered dishes with diced potatoes fried lightly in butter. Break 2 eggs into each dish and cook in the usual way (see *egg*).

hachis Parmentier

Dice or coarsely chop 500 g (18 oz, 4½ cups) boiled or braised beef. Melt 25 g (1 oz, 2 tablespoons) butter in a shallow frying pan and cook 3 chopped onions in it until they are golden. Sprinkle with 1 tablespoon flour, cook until lightly brown, and then moisten with 200 ml (7 fl oz, ¾ cup) beef stock (or braising stock with water added to it). Cook for about 15 minutes, leave to cool, then add the beef and mix well. Place the beef and onions in a buttered gratin dish, cover with a layer of potato purée, sprinkle with breadcrumbs and moisten with melted butter. Brown in a preheated oven at 230°C (450°C, gas 8) for about 15 minutes.

Although it is not traditional, a small cup of very

reduced tomato sauce can be added to the chopped meat and a little grated cheese may be mixed with the breadcrumbs.

loin of lamb Parmentier

Brown a trimmed loin of lamb in 25–40 g (1–1½ oz, 2–3 tablespoons) butter in a flameproof casserole. Add 400 g (14 oz, 2 cups) peeled, diced potatoes, 3 tablespoons melted butter and season with salt and pepper. Place the casserole in a pre-heated oven at 220°C (425°F, gas 7) and cook for about 45 minutes. Drain the meat and the potatoes and keep them hot in the serving dish. Deglaze the casserole with 4 tablespoons white wine and the same amount of stock (traditionally veal stock); reduce. Pour this sauce over the lamb and sprinkle with chopped parsley.

PARMESAN *Parmigiano reggiano* is the DOP Parmesan cheese. The 'King of Italian cheeses' made from skimmed cow's milk (28–32% butterfat content) mixed with rennet and cooked for 30 minutes. It goes through several processes of draining and drying before being coated. Hard, yellow and with a crumbly, granular consistency (hence the generic name of *grana* given in Italy to grating cheeses of the same type), Parmesan cheese has a very fruity, even piquant, flavour. It was known in Parma in the 13th century (it may have originated there or in Tuscany in the 11th century) and by the 14th century was being used grated on pasta. It was introduced into France by a Duchess of Parma who married a grandson of Louis XV.

The true DOP Parmesan cheese (*parmigiano reggiano*) is manufactured from 15 April to 11 November in the province of Parma and also in the provinces of Bologna and Mantua. Known and appreciated throughout the world, Parmesan cheese is formed into cylindrical millstone shapes with slightly convex sides, 35–40 cm (14–16 in) in diameter, 18–24 cm (7–9½ in) in height and weighing about 24–40 kg (53–88 lb). It takes at least one year to mature to qualify as *vecchio* (old); the best, called *stravecchio* (very old), takes more than three years. Some enthusiasts prefer it when it is ten years old (the cheeses are then extremely hard). The cheese experts judge the cheese millstones by tapping them with a little hammer; those with a doubtful sound are sold grated. Parmesan cheese is principally used grated in cookery, for soups, pasta, soufflés, gratins and stuffed vegetables, particularly aubergines (eggplants). It is always preferable to grate the cheese just before using it. Parmesan is rarely included on a cheeseboard, although it is sometimes served cut into small pieces with aperitifs.

The term *à la parmesane* is used to describe preparations which include Parmesan cheese, usually gratins. (See *polenta*.)

PARSLEY A herb originating in southern Europe and cultivated mainly for its aromatic leaves, which are used to flavour or garnish many dishes.

Before the reign of Charlemagne parsley was thought to have magic powers, but since then it has become one of the most commonly used plants in cookery. There are three types of parsley: flat-leaf parsley, which has large, flat, relatively smooth leaves, has a strong flavour; curly-leaf parsley, which has bright green, crinkly leaves and good flavour; and turnip-rooted parsley, which is cultivated for its swollen root, which is cooked like celeriac and used in soups. It is eaten in eastern Europe, particularly in Austria, Germany, Hungary and the former Soviet Union. In France a number of other plants are known as parsley. Neapolitan or celery-leaf parsley (*persil noir*) is a type of wild celery; coriander (cilantro) is known as Arabian or Chinese parsley; and dill is commonly called Russian or Swedish parsley.

In cookery fresh parsley is an ingredient of a bouquet garni and is used in marinades and stocks. When mixed with chopped garlic it is often served with sautéed or fried dishes (see *persillade*). Chopped parsley is frequently added during the final preparation of a dish or is sprinkled over food just before serving to give a fresh flavour. It is also useful in salads, either coarsely chopped or broken into small sprigs. Deep-fried parsley is used as an accompaniment and garnish for fried items, particularly fish and seafood. Finely chopped parsley is used to flavour butter, sauces (particularly ravigote, green, Italian, maître d'hôtel and poulette sauces) and vinaigrettes. Parsley freezes well, and it can be dried, but drying spoils the flavour and has been superseded by freezing as a preservation method for herbs that lose their flavour when dried.

In former times meat was 'larded' with parsley (parsley was inserted into it); in *Le Bourgeois Gentilhomme* (1670), Molière mentions 'a loin of mutton rich with parsley'.

RECIPE

fried parsley

Wash, drain and dry some curly-leaf parsley and separate it into little sprigs. Place these in a wire basket and deep-fry in very hot oil for a few seconds. Drain on paper towels and use immediately. Fried parsley is used as a garnish for skate with black butter sauce.

PARSNIP A vegetable cultivated for its white or yellowish, sweet-tasting root. Widely grown by the Greeks and enjoyed in the Middle Ages and during the Renaissance, the parsnip has become a rarity in contemporary French cookery, although it is popular in other countries.

The parsnip is used in the same ways as other root vegetables and is often preferred to turnips as it has more flavour. Parsnips may be boiled, steamed, roast or baked. They are excellent mashed or puréed and make good soup either on their own or with mixed vegetables, poultry and meat. Creamed parsnips can be cooled, shaped, coated in egg and breadcrumbs, then deep-fried to make croquettes. They are complemented by curry spices and marry well with celery and cauliflower in vegetable curries. In traditional British cookery they are a favoured accompaniment for roast beef when par-boiled and then roasted in the fat and cooking juices from the meat.

PARSON'S NOSE A British nickname for the fleshy part of the tail of some poultry, especially chicken and turkey; the French equivalent is *bonnet-d'évêque* (this term is also used for a table napkin folded into the shape of a mitre). (See *croupion*.)

PARTRIDGE A highly prized game bird, which is hunted throughout France and in Britain. In France the word *perdreau* is used for partridges of either sex up to the age of one year. They have tender, succulent flesh that needs very little cooking. The bird is barded or wrapped in vine leaves and roasted with juniper berries or grapes. It may also be stuffed. Young birds can be recognized by their flexible beaks and by the pointed first feather on the wing, which has a white tip. Very young partridges, found at the beginning of the season, are known as *pouillards* in France. One young partridge per serving is sufficient.

The principal species found in France are the red-legged partridge and the common or grey partridge. The former has a red back and breast, a white throat and a red beak and feet. It is more often seen in south and south-western France.

The smaller and more common grey partridge, the main type found in Britain, has a reddish-grey back and an ash-grey breast. The male has a conspicuous brown horseshoe mark on the breast. The meat of the grey partridge is fuller in flavour and superior to that of the red-legged bird.

The rock partridge is also found in France and has a high gastronomic reputation, although it has become extremely rare.

The American partridge, which has been introduced to France, is also highly regarded. In the United States the word 'partridge' is also used for other game birds, especially the bobwhite quail and the ruffed grouse.

The mature partridge (known as *perdrix* in France) needs to be cooked for longer than the young bird. The cooking time for young and tender birds is about 45 minutes, but older birds need to be braised for at least 1 hour. When really tough, they must be simmered in a covered pan for 2 hours, usually with cabbage, or they can be boiled as for a *pot-au-feu*. Young partridges can be prepared in a ragoût, in a soufflé, as a pâté with truffles, in a casserole, in a caul, braised, in aspic, in a mousse or in a chaud-froid. The classic dish for mature birds is *chartreuse* of partridge prepared with lentils or with cabbage, but they can also be used for forcemeats, purées and thick soups. Charles Monselet, however, knew only one recipe worthy of the partridge:

'Gourmets! serve the bird roasted, with pink feet,
A strip of bacon to cover its modesty,
The breast sprinkled with lemon drops.'

RECIPES

partridge à la coque
Gut (clean) and singe a young partridge, season with salt and pepper, spread foie gras in the cavity and truss. Fill a saucepan with salted water and lay a stick across the top. Bring the water to the boil and hang the partridge by its feet from the centre of the stick so that it is suspended in the water. Boil briskly for 20 minutes, then remove the bird and allow it to cool. When cold, keep it in the refrigerator until ready to serve.

partridge croustades
Completely bone 4 young partridges. Reserve the breast fillets and marinate them for 24 hours in 750 ml (1¼ pints, 3¼ cups) red wine. Mince (grind) the meat from the thighs with the liver and season with salt and pepper. Place the bowl of minced meat over a dish of ice and gradually work in 2 eggs, followed by 150 ml (¼ pint, ⅔ cup) crème fraîche. Refrigerate the resulting mousse and then shape it into small quenelles.

Prepare a game stock with the partridge trimmings, the carcass and the marinade. Boil until reduced by half, then add 300 ml (½ pint, 1¼ cups) demi-glace*. Strain this stock, bring it to the boil, add the quenelles of partridge mousse and poach them for 6 minutes.

Make 4 rectangular croustades with puff pastry. Fry 4 sliced cep mushroom caps in butter and season with salt and pepper. When the quenelles are cooked, remove from the stock and keep hot. Reduce the stock to make about 400 ml (14 fl oz, 1¾ cups) sauce, removing any scum that rises to the surface. At the last minute, thicken the sauce with 50 g (2 oz, ¼ cup) foie gras. Fry the partridge fillets in butter, season with salt and pepper and cook for 2 minutes only on each side, so that they are still pink.

Fill the croustades with the quenelles, the fried mushrooms and the partridge fillets. Add a little sauce and place in a preheated oven at 150°C (300°F, gas 2) for 3 minutes. Serve the remaining sauce separately.

partridge cutlets Romanov
Soak 2 pigs' cauls (caul fat) in cold water. Pluck 4 young partridges, singe them, gut (clean) them and set aside the livers and hearts. Bone the breasts and remove the skin. Remove the feet, but keep them whole except for cutting off the claws. Marinate the breasts in a mixture of 4 tablespoons port, 1 tablespoon brandy, salt and pepper.

Prepare a forcemeat by finely mincing (grinding) 100 g (4 oz, 1 cup) pork, 100 g (4 oz, 1 cup) fat bacon, 50 g (2 oz, ½ cup) chicken livers and the hearts and livers of the partridges. Sauté 2 chopped shallots in butter, then place in a bowl and mix with an egg yolk, some spiced salt and a little truffle juice.

Prepare the sauce by first browning the partridge

bones in a saucepan together with 1 onion and 1 carrot. Then add some powdered thyme, a peeled, crushed tomato, 250 ml (8 fl oz, 1 cup) white wine, the marinade and a ladleful of veal stock. Add 6 juniper berries and cook for 1 hour (the liquid should then be syrupy).

Spread the cauls out on the worktop, wipe them and cut each into 2 rectangles measuring 20 × 15 cm (8 × 6 in). Spread a thin layer of forcemeat on each rectangle and put a partridge foot at the end. Place a partridge breast on the forcemeat and add a thin slice of foie gras and a slice of truffle. Cover with a thin layer of forcemeat. Fold the caul over the stuffing and shape it into a cutlet, using the partridge foot as the bone. When four 'cutlets' have been prepared, roast them in a preheated oven at 230°C (450°F, gas 8) for 15–20 minutes (they should still be slightly pink).

Arrange the cutlets on a dish and garnish the ends of the feet with a little white paper frill. Strain the cooking juices, add 150 ml (¼ pint, ⅔ cup) double (heavy) cream, and thicken with 100 g (4 oz, ½ cup) butter. Adjust the seasoning and pour the sauce over the cutlets. Serve with either chestnut purée or fried fresh cep mushrooms.

partridge Monselet ♦
Stuff 2 cleaned partridges with foie gras, adding a little diced black truffle. Truss and season well, then brown the birds all over in butter in a small flameproof casserole. Cover the casserole and continue to cook gently for 15 minutes. Turn 4 lightly cooked artichoke hearts in a little lemon juice and melted clarified butter, then add them to the casserole and cook for a further 15 minutes. Add a finely diced black truffle. Heat 2 tablespoons brandy, add to the casserole and flambé. Lightly cook some chanterelles in butter in a separate pan. Arrange the partridges with the artickoke bottoms and sliced foie gras used as stuffing, with the cooking juices poured over. Add the chanterelles and serve at once.

partridge salad with cabbage
Select a large Savoy cabbage with a good heart. Remove about 8 of the leaves and wash them in plenty of water after removing the thick midribs. Blanch for 5 minutes in boiling salted water, cool and drain. Pluck 6 partridges, gut them and retain the livers. Cut the birds into quarters and use the breasts only (the thighs can be made into a terrine). Bone the breasts and season them with salt and pepper. Wipe 500 g (18 oz, 6 cups) small firm cep mushrooms with a damp cloth and chop them coarsely.

Brown 6 slices of belly of pork in a frying pan and add the partridge breasts and livers. Cook for 6 minutes and then add the mushrooms. Cover the pan and braise for a further 5 minutes. Remove the contents of the pan and keep hot. Deglaze the pan with 100 ml (4 fl oz, 7 tablespoons) sherry vinegar, add some crushed peppercorns, boil down to

reduce and then thicken the sauce with 100 ml (4 fl oz, 7 tablespoons) hazelnut oil. Dip the cabbage leaves in the sauce and lay them out on the serving dish. Arrange the slices of pork, the partridge and livers, and the sliced mushrooms on the top and sprinkle with chopped chives.

partridges en vessie
Soak 4 small pigs' bladders in salt water and vinegar for 24 hours, then squeeze thoroughly. Gut (clean) 4 young partridges. Prepare a forcemeat with 250 g (9 oz, 1 cup) fine sausagemeat, the finely minced (ground) partridge livers, 150 g (5 oz, 2½ cups) breadcrumbs soaked in milk and squeezed thoroughly, 2 tablespoons crème fraîche, salt, pepper and an egg. Stuff the birds with the mixture, adding a large sprig of thyme to each portion.

Truss the partridges and place each in a pig's bladder. Add a pinch of coarse salt and a dash of brandy and port to each bladder, squeeze to release any air, tie them up with string and prick with a needle. Cook for 30 minutes in simmering veal stock and leave to cool in the liquid for 12 hours. Remove the partridges from the bladders, untruss and serve cold.

partridges with grapes
Pluck, singe and gut (clean) some young partridges. Season them with salt and pepper. Also season some large grapes with salt and pepper. Place 2 grapes and half a Petit-Suisse cheese (or 1 tablespoon cream cheese) inside each bird. Quickly brown the birds in 50 g (2 oz, ¼ cup) butter in a heavy-based saucepan for 6 minutes. Cover the pan and cook gently for a further 10–15 minutes (the wings should be white and the thighs pink near the bone). Drain the partridges and keep them hot.

Skim the fat from the cooking juices, add some green grapes and 3 tablespoons Armagnac and simmer over a low heat. Add a glass of red Banyuls wine and boil for 5 minutes to reduce. Strain the sauce and thicken with a Petit Suisse cheese (or 2 tablespoons cream cheese). Season generously with salt and pepper. Spoon over the partridges and serve with potatoes *à la dauphinoise* and red cabbage *à la flamande*.

partridge with cabbage
Clean a large cabbage, cut it into 8 pieces, blanch for 8 minutes in boiling water, cool and drain. Place the cabbage in a buttered heavy-based saucepan with a 500 g (18 oz) piece of lean bacon, an onion studded with 2 cloves and a bouquet garni. Add 175 ml (6 fl oz, ¾ cup) stock, cover and cook gently for 1 hour.

Pluck, gut (clean) and truss 2 partridges. Lard the breasts with thin rashers (slices) of bacon. Brown them in a preheated oven at 230°C (450°F, gas 8), then add them to the saucepan containing the

Partridge Monselet.

cabbage, together with 1 boiling sausage and 2 sliced carrots. Continue cooking for at least another hour (or more, if the partridges are old). Untruss the birds and slice the bacon and the sausage. Place the cabbage in a deep dish; cut the partridges in half and arrange them on top. Garnish with the slices of bacon, sausage and carrot. Pour the cooking liquid over the top.

Alternatively, the cooked partridges can be arranged en gâteau: cover the bottom of a round buttered timbale with the sliced carrots, sausage and bacon, then add a layer of cabbage, the partridges and finally the rest of the cabbage. Press down the cabbage, warm in a preheated oven at 160°C (325°F, gas 3) for 5 minutes and turn it out on to a round dish. Pour a few tablespoons of game fumet, demi-glace sauce or brown veal stock around the base of the 'gâteau'.

partridge with lentils
Roast 2 partridges in 50 g (2 oz, ¼ cup) lard for 20 minutes. Then place them in a heavy-based saucepan with 100 g (4 oz, 1 cup) bacon pieces, 2 sliced onions, 2 sliced carrots, 175 ml (6 fl oz, ¾ cup) white wine, 175 ml (6 fl oz, ¾ cup) stock, some salt and a bouquet garni. Simmer gently for 1½ hours. In the meantime, boil in water until tender 250 g (9 oz, 1¼ cups) lentils (previously soaked for 2 hours and drained) with 200 g (7 oz) fat bacon, 4 small onions, 2 carrots (cut into quarters), 1 boiling sausage weighing 200 g (7 oz) and a pinch of salt. Arrange the lentils in a deep dish, place the partridges on top and surround with the sliced sausage. Spoon over the cooking juices.

stuffed partridges in aspic
Bone some young partridges from the back. Cut them open and season with salt and pepper. Stuff each bird with 100 g (4 oz, ½ cup) truffled game forcemeat* wrapped around a piece of raw foie gras and a small peeled truffle. Season with salt, pepper and mixed spice and sprinkle with brandy. Close up the partridges, truss them and wrap each one in thin bacon barding or a piece of pig's caul (caul fat).

Prepare an aspic stock with Madeira, the partridge carcasses and trimmings, knuckle of veal and fresh bacon rind. Cook the partridges in this stock, then drain, remove the barding, untruss, wipe and arrange them in an oval terrine. Leave them to cool, then chill them. Clarify the aspic, adding gelatine if necessary for a good set, and cover the partridges completely with it. Chill again until ready to serve.

other recipes See Brillat-Savarin, chartreuse, Monselet, pistache, Souvarov, terrine.

PASCALINE A method of preparing lamb formerly traditional on Easter Day. Dumas gives a recipe, which he describes as being common in France until the reign of Louis XVI: the lamb, stuffed and roasted, is served whole, like the paschal lamb sacrificed by the Jews for the feast of Passover. Monselet gives the same version and claims that he tasted it during a journey in Provence. Simon Arbellot, on the other hand, mentions a completely different pascaline of lamb, made by Montagné, who had found the recipe in the papers of Talleyrand and Carême. In this recipe lambs' heads are stuffed with liver, bacon and herbs, lightly fried in fat, then arranged in a round dish with lambs' feet cooked in white stock, lambs' sweetbreads larded with bacon, croquettes of tongue and brain, and fried croûtons; the whole is coated with a velouté sauce to which finely sliced onions have been added.

RECIPE

pascaline
Truss a 6-month-old lamb to give a neat shape. Stuff with a forcemeat made of pounded lamb's flesh, yolks of hard-boiled (hard-cooked) eggs, stale breadcrumbs and chopped herbs, seasoned with quatre epices. Cover the lamb with thin strips of bacon, roast it over a brisk fire and serve it whole as a main dish following the soup, either with a green sauce or on a ragoût of truffles with ham coulis.

PASHKA A traditional Russian Easter dish made of curd cheese, sugar, soured (dairy sour) cream, and butter, filled with raisins, crystallized (candied) fruits, and walnuts or almonds, then pressed in a pyramid-shaped mould. The pashka mould is usually wooden, with the sides carved with symbols representing the Passion and with drainage holes in the base. The cake is decorated with crystallized fruits forming the letters X and B (initials, in the Cyrillic alphabet, of Khristos Voskress, meaning 'Christ is risen').

PASSION FRUIT The edible fruit of the passionflower, a climbing plant, also known as granadilla, originating in tropical America, but also grown in the West Indies, Africa, Australia and Malaysia. The fruit, which is the size of a hen's egg, has yellowish-green or brownish-red leathery skin, which is smooth and shiny when unripe and wrinkled when mature. The orange-yellow flesh, which is slightly acid and very fragrant, contains small, edible, crunchy, black seeds. It can be eaten simply: cut in half and scooped out of the shell with a small spoon, eaten raw, or the pulp can be pressed through a sieve and the juice made into sorbets, drinks, jellies and creams. Passion-fruit pulp is used as a filling for the classic dessert pavlova.

RECIPE

passion-fruit sorbet
Scoop out the flesh from some very ripe passion fruit and press it through a fine sieve. Add an equal volume of cold sugar syrup and a little lemon juice (the density should then be about 1.075, see sugar). Use an ice-cream maker to freeze the mixture. As

a simpler alternative, granulated sugar can be added to the pulp, together with just enough water to reach a density of about 1.075; press the pulp through a fine sieve before setting in the ice-cream maker.

PASTA There are many forms of pasta, most of which can be categorized as Italian-style or Oriental. Italian-style pasta is primarily wheat-based. Oriental pastas are prepared from a variety of flours and starches, and they often take the form of long strands or strips of pasta (see *noodles*).

■ **Italian-style pasta** This consists of a dough made from durum-wheat flour (of the type used for semolina), water and sometimes eggs. Pasta is shaped in various ways and can be flavoured. It is sold dried or fresh, ready to cook in boiling salted water or it may be sold ready stuffed and cooked, simply needing to be heated.

The term 'Italian-style' is used here because this type of pasta is made in other countries. For example, noodles similar to tagliatelle are prepared throughout Europe, and filled pastas resembling Italian tortellini or ravioli are popular in Eastern European countries. Polish *uska* are little filled pasta (usually containing a dried mushroom stuffing) traditionally served in beetroot soup and *varenyki* or *varieniky* are semi-circular filled dumplings (similar to ravioli) from Russia.

Durum wheat is grown in Italy, the Mediterranean, the Middle East, Russia and North and South America. It is a hard wheat, high in gluten, which is ground into semolina. British semolina is a coarse product and not suitable for pasta. Pasta flour is milled from the same wheat but to a finer degree; although the term 'semolina' is often used to describe pasta flour, it refers to the type of wheat used.

It is a popular belief that the 14th-century explorer Marco Polo introduced pasta into Italy from China, but the first known reference to pasta can, in fact, be traced to Sicily in the Middle Ages. It had been a basic food in Italy for many years, particularly in Naples and Rome, before Catherine de' Medici introduced it into France, although it became really popular throughout France only under the Empire.

Until the early 20th century, macaroni and vermicelli were the pastas most commonly used in France, mainly to make timbales, gratins and sweet desserts and to garnish soups. After 1840 pasta was manufactured on an industrial scale.

Pasta is made by kneading semolina flour with water, adding various other ingredients (such as eggs, flavouring, vegetable purées) and then shaping it.

There are hundreds of different shapes of dried pasta, but they can be loosely grouped into two types. Flat pastas are made industrially by rolling the dough between rollers into thin sheets, which are cut into various shapes with a punch, a stamp or some other suitable machine. The shapes include rectangles or squares with straight or wavy edges and flat ribbons of various widths. Cylindrical forms

of pasta are made by extruding the dough or forcing it through a pierced plate. The hole through which the dough is forced may be straight, curved, notched or fluted to produce solid or hollow tubes of variable size and shape. Drying is an important operation, and care must be taken to ensure that the pasta will mature and keep well.

Fresh pasta is the same type of product that has not been dried. It must, however, be eaten within a few days.

• BAKING PASTA Traditional dried and fresh pasta must be boiled before it can be used in baked dishes. Examples include large shapes for stuffing and lasagne (sheets or large squares). Modern types of lasagne and cannelloni are manufactured to be stuffed or layered dry and cooked in generous proportions of sauce; some are more successful than others. Pasta for baking includes lasagne (smooth or wavy-edged), tortiglioni, bucatini, conchiglie and cravattine.

• FILLED PASTA Fresh or dried, a wide variety of filled pastas is produced, including ravioli, tortellini and tortelloni (fairly large), agnolotti (small 'slippers') and cappelletti (little hats). Fillings range from traditional meat, cheese or mushroom mixtures to innovative fish, poultry and vegetable blends. These are also popular with home cooks and are often prepared in larger shapes for speed and ease. Dried or fresh pasta shapes that can be boiled, filled and sauced, then baked include cannelloni (tubes), lumache (large shells) and manicotti (large-ribbed tubes).

• FLAVOURED PASTA A wide variety of ingredients are used to flavour pasta, both fresh and dried. Herbs, spices and vegetables are popular individually or in combination; spinach and tomato are traditional, beetroot gives a strong colour with a mild flavour, and ceps or porcini give a full flavour. Squid ink is a traditional flavouring ingredient, which turns the dough black.

• NON-WHEAT PASTA There is a good range of Italian-style dried pastas made from corn (maize) and other non-wheat flours. These are produced mainly for the healthfood market for those who are allergic to wheat.

• SOUP PASTA Very small and made in various shapes, soup pasta is added to soups towards the end of cooking. These tiny shapes are also useful for filling vegetables or for adding to starters and salads. They include vermicelli, linguine (small grains), pennette (small quills), stelline (little stars), risoni (rice grains), conchigliette (little shells) and anellini (little rings, sometimes serrated).

• WHOLEWHEAT AND BUCKWHEAT PASTA Both types are well established, with buckwheat being traditional in some Oriental pasta as well as Italian-style doughs. These are usually dried.

■ **Cooking and serving pasta** Even when cooking a small quantity of pasta, a large pan must be used because plenty of boiling water is needed for the pasta to swell and move freely. Otherwise, the released starch makes it sticky. A tablespoon of oil added to the water can help prevent this. Sprinkle small pasta into briskly boiling water. Long pasta, such as spaghetti, is gradually pushed into the boiling water (without breaking the strands), until it softens and bends. It is by 'sealing' the pasta in fast-boiling water in this way that one obtains the degree of cooking known as al dente.

The cooking time depends on the quality of the pasta, its size and the hardness of the water. Even if the cooking time is indicated on the packet, it is advisable to test the pasta early to avoid overcooking. As a guide, dried vermicelli takes 4–5 minutes, flat pasta and spaghetti take 11–12 minutes and large macaroni takes 15 minutes; in each case timing begins when the water comes back to the boil. Fresh pasta cooks far more quickly and may need only 2–3 minutes.

If the pasta is to be served in a salad, drain it, rinse in cold water and immediately mix with a little oil so that it will cool without sticking. When serving hot, the chosen sauce should be poured boiling hot on to the hot pasta. Stir quickly and serve immediately with grated cheese, with the rest of the sauce served separately, if necessary.

The range of sauces for pasta is very large. The most commonly used are thick sauces based on tomatoes and often containing ham, minced (ground) meat, seafood, cheese, anchovies, chicken breasts, mushrooms, sliced vegetables or pickled ox (beef) tongue. Bolognaise and milanaise sauces are the most traditional. Pasta can also be served in a timbale, a gratin or a salad, with scrambled eggs, with mussels, in a ring or with peas, for example. Fillings include minced meat, spinach with béchamel sauce, chicken livers, cheese and herbs, sausagemeat and mushrooms. In Italy the pasta dish (*pasta asciutta*) is usually served as an entrée, whereas in France it is an accompaniment to the main dish.

■ **Oriental-style pasta** Noodles (see separate entry) are the predominant type, but similar types of dough are filled to make bite-sized dumplings served as dim sum. Chinese dumplings may be filled with meat, such as well-seasoned and slightly spicy pork, or seafood, such as minced prawns; a combination of pork and prawns is also used. Steaming is the usual cooking method for Chinese dumplings, which are often served with a dipping sauce (for example, soy sauce flavoured with garlic). Pot stickers are slightly larger dumplings cooked first by pan frying, then by simmering.

Wontons are small filled squares of wheat-flour dough made with egg. A tiny portion of full-flavoured filling is pinched into the middle of the dough, then the corners are free, making tiny bundles. These are simmered in broth or deep-fried and served coated with sauce.

RECIPE

cooking pasta
Plunge the pasta into a large quantity of boiling water – 2 litres (3½ pints, 9 cups) per 250 g (9 oz, 4 cups) pasta – containing 1 tablespoon salt per

1 litre (1¾ pints, 4⅓ cups), unless any additional ingredients are to be very highly seasoned. Gently stir the pasta so that it does not stick together and keep the water boiling at a constant rate. Drain the pasta completely when it is cooked and season immediately. If the pasta is not to be used straight away, drain it and keep it hot mixed with 1 tablespoon oil. When ready to use, plunge it into boiling water, drain once more and add the other ingredients.

other recipes See *macaroni, noodles, spaghetti.*

PASTEUR, LOUIS French chemist and biologist (born Dole, 1822; died Villeneuve-l'Étang, 1895). His work in microbiology is widely known, but less is known about his contribution to the field of nutrition. His studies on lactic, alcoholic and butyric fermentations enabled him to perfect a method of keeping milk, beer, wine and cider. Pasteurization is a heat treatment, intended to destroy the pathogenic bacteria that are found in a fermenting liquid and to allow foodstuffs to be kept for longer. Pasteurization is of prime importance in the dairy industry, whether the milk is intended for drinking or for manufacturing butter and cheese. It is also applied to beer and cider, more rarely to wine. Prepackaged foods, such as baby foods, are also pasteurized.

According to the *Dictionnaire de l'Académie des gastronomes*, on the evidence of his son-in-law, Vallery-Radot, Pasteur cared little for gastronomy: his favourite dish was a mutton cutlet with sautéed potatoes, which he ate every day except Thursdays, when he had hot sausage garnished with red kidney beans.

PASTILLAGE A paste, used in confectionery, made from a mixture of icing (confectioner's) sugar and water with the addition of gelatine or gum tragacanth and powdered starch. It is kneaded by hand or by machine until firm enough to be rolled out and shaped easily; it may be coloured during kneading.

The pieces shaped from the pastillage are left to dry and then attached to the cake (or built up into shapes) with royal icing or softened pastillage.

In the hands of a skilled confectioner, pastillage can be used to create decorative preparations closely resembling sculpture. Artistic pastrycooks paint pictures on pastillage plaques.

PASTILLE A small, round, flat sweet (candy) manufactured in different ways. One type of pastille is made from a cooked sugar syrup to which icing (confectioner's) sugar, a flavouring and a colouring have been added. The syrup is then dripped through a funnel to form 'drops', which are sometimes coated with chocolate. Another type of pastille is made from a mixture of icing sugar and gum tragacanth or gum arabic, which is rolled and then stamped into various shapes. These pastilles are flavoured with mint, lemon, aniseed or with salts extracted from a mineral water (such as Vichy pastilles); they are rarely coloured.

The word *pastille* comes from the Spanish *pastilla*, derived from a diminutive of the Latin *panis* (bread). However, some authorities claim that these sweets were invented by and named after Jean Pastilla, a confectioner appointed by Marie de' Medici.

PASTIRMA Also known as pasterma, pastarma or pastourma. Mutton, beef or goat meat marinated with spices and garlic and then dried. Distinguished by a very strong taste, *pastirma* forms part of Turkish and Greek *mezze* and is eaten like dried ham.

Popular pastrami of New York Jewish deli fame is a comparatively modern product adapted from the traditional wind-dried beef. This is cured, highly seasoned, dried and cooked. It is known as a sandwich filling or topping (hot or cold), particularly on rye bread.

PASTIS In the south of France, an aniseed-flavoured, rather strong drink, somewhat similar to the famous Pernod in the north. The formula does not now, in fact, contain any of the absinthe that originally made this type of aperitif distinctive. The name 'pastis' is a local dialect word meaning 'confused' or 'mixed', a reference to the cloudy appearance of the drink when diluted with water (in which form it is always drunk). Sometimes the water is dripped on to the spirit through a piece of sugar held in a perforated spoon. The people of the region will spend hours sipping pastis while watching the local game of *boule* or *pétanque*. Some regional recipes include pastis, because the herby aniseed flavour is especially useful in fish dishes. There are many brands of pastis, two well-known names being Ricard and Berger.

■ **Pastis – the pastry** The term is also used for various pastries made in south-western France (the name is derived from the word *pâté*, meaning pie). At Andernos-les-Bains (in the Gironde region) the pastis is a kind of brioche, called *landaise*. In Béarn *pastis bourrit* is made from raised dough. The Gascon pastis is difficult to make because the dough must be spread over the whole work surface (itself covered by a large cloth) to dry for an hour. It is then saturated with goose fat and cut into rounds. Half of these are spread with thin slices of apple macerated in Armagnac brandy, then covered with the other rounds, cooked in the oven and sprinkled with Armagnac. This method of making puff pastry seems to have been brought from Spain by the Moors and is reminiscent of the Moroccan *pastilla*.

RECIPES

Béarn pastis
Break 12 eggs into a mixing bowl and add 1 tablespoon orange-flower water, 3 tablespoons brandy, 400 g (14 oz, 1¾ cups) caster (superfine) sugar, a little milk and 100 g (4 oz, ½ cup) melted butter. Beat quickly, then beat in 25 g (1 oz) fresh yeast (2 cakes compressed yeast) dissolved in a little water and sufficient flour to make a soft dough. Gather the dough into a ball in the bowl, sprinkle with flour, cover with a cloth and leave it to rise in a warm place for 12 hours. Place the risen dough in a buttered mould and cook in a preheated oven at 220°C (425°F, gas 7) for about 45 minutes.

pastis bourrit
Make some leaven with 25 g (1 oz, ¼ cup) plain (all-purpose) flour, 7 g (¼ oz) fresh yeast (½ cake compressed yeast) and 100 ml (4 fl oz, 7 tablespoons) water. Leave to rise. Make a well in 1 kg (2¼ lb, 9 cups) plain flour in a very deep mixing bowl and add 150 g (5 oz, ⅔ cup) melted butter, a pinch of salt, 250 g (9 oz, 1 cup) sugar, 6 egg yolks, 4 teaspoons vanilla-flavoured sugar and 3 tablespoons rum or anisette cordial. Stir and add 7 g (¼ oz) fresh yeast (½ cake compressed yeast) and the leaven. Beat everything well. Whisk 6 egg whites into stiff peaks and add them to the dough. Leave to rise.

When the dough has doubled in size, butter some moulds, half-fill them with dough (this quantity of dough is enough for 2 or 3 pastis) and leave to rise to the top. Cook in a preheated oven at 220°C (425°F, gas 7) for 45 minutes until the pastis are golden. This cake is served with caramel custard or at a wedding. Cut into slices and toasted, it may also be served with foie gras.

PASTRAMI See *pastirma*.

PASTRY A mixture of flour and liquid, usually enriched with fat, forming a light dough. Pastry is used for savoury and sweet recipes, to partly or completely encase a filling before cooking. Alternatively, pastry cases may be baked and filled, topped or layered after cooking. When flavoured or sweetened, the pastry may be baked to make a variety of items, such as cheese straws or *palmiers*.

■ **Types of pastry** Depending on the ingredients and the proportions in which they are used, a variety of different pastry doughs can be made. Pastry doughs can be grouped according to their texture when cooked. As a rule, all ingredients should be chilled for pastry, and the mixture must be handled lightly and swiftly.

• CHOUX PASTE OR PASTRY Choux paste differs from the pastries in that it is a paste, not a dough. It is sometimes included in the pastry category, probably because it rises, becomes crisp and crusty, and forms a case or shell when cooked.

• FINE LAYERED PASTRIES These have little or no fat but consist of a flour and water dough, sometimes with egg added. The dough is first rolled, then stretched until paper thin or even finer. The pastry is assembled in several layers, each brushed with a little fat. The fat makes the layers of pastry stick together during shaping and also prevents the pastry from drying out and disintegrating. The fat gives the pastry a crisp texture and golden colour. Filo (phyllo) and struedel pastries are two examples.

• HOT WATER CRUST PASTRY This is a close-textured, firm pastry, which is used as a casing for raised pies, including individual pork pies, and to enclose pâtés and terrines. Traditionally, it is made with lard, but a mixture of butter and lard or white vegetable fat can be used. The proportion of fat to flour is small – about a third – and equal quantities of milk and water are used to make a soft dough. The fat is melted in the liquid, which is then brought to the boil and added to the flour. The pastry is gently kneaded and shaped while hot; on cooling, it sets and becomes firm. Hot water crust can be baked at a moderate to low temperature for the long cooking time necessary to cook heavy meat or game fillings. The pastry absorbs juices from the filling during cooking to become moist and well flavoured inside, firm outside.

• LAYERED FLAKY PASTRIES Instead of a short and crumbly texture, these pastries rise during cooking and become crisp. They are light and made up of fine layers, which flake, rather than crumble, when cut. They have a high proportion of fat, only a small amount of which is rubbed into the flour. A higher proportion of water is added to make a softer dough. The remaining fat is incorporated by rolling it into the dough in stages. The higher proportion of water (and sometimes a little lemon juice) strengthens the dough, which is more elastic than short pastry.

Puff pastry has equal weights of fat and flour. A small proportion of fat – about an eighth – is rubbed into the flour before mixing with water. The remainder is shaped into a thin block, which is wrapped in the rolled pastry. The pastry is then rolled and folded at least six times to incorporate the butter. When baked, the pastry rises well and sets into many fine, crisp layers.

Rough puff pastry contains slightly less butter than puff pastry. A small proportion – about an eighth – is rubbed into the flour and the rest is added in lumps. Water is used to bind the mixture into a lumpy dough, which is rolled and folded up to six times. Rough puff rises well and has good flaky layers, similar to puff pastry.

Flaky pastry has less fat – usually three-quarters fat to flour – and a quarter of the weight of fat is rubbed in before the dough is bound with water. The remaining fat is incorporated in three rolling stages, by dotting it over the dough, which is then folded over it. The dough is rolled and folded an additional time, without any added fat. Flaky pastry rises during cooking, but not as high as puff or rough puff, and the layers are closer and more flaky.

• SHORT PASTRIES There are several types of short pastry, with a crumbly texture when baked. These pastries do not rise during cooking. A medium to high proportion of fat is incorporated with the flour and a small amount of liquid is used to bind the mixture. The fat is mixed with the flour, either by rubbing in with the fingertips or by gently pressing the flour and lumps of fat together, adding the liquid at the same time, then very lightly kneading the dough. When the fat is rubbed in, the dough should just clump together, so that, when a little water is added, the lumps have to be pressed together gently with the fingers. Too much water (or liquid) and heavy handling or kneading makes a heavy, tough pastry.

The higher the proportion of fat, the more fragile and crumbly the pastry; for a crisp surface and crumbly texture, the dough must have the right proportion of fat and liquid, and it should be baked at a fairly high temperature.

Standard shortcrust pastry (basic pie dough), *pâte à foncer* and *pâte brisée* are made with half fat to flour. Butter, margarine, lard or white vegetable fat (shortening) may be used: traditional British shortcrust is made with half butter to half lard or white vegetable fat. Butter gives the best flavour; lard or white vegetable fat produces a good short texture; and margarine is often the popular choice as it gives a reasonable flavour and short texture. These may be plain, for savoury or sweet use; flavoured with ingredients, such as herbs or grated hard cheese; or sweetened.

Rich shortcrust pastry has a higher proportion of fat, and this is usually butter. A slightly rich pastry is often used to make rich quiche or mince pies. To further enrich the pastry, egg yolk replaces some or all of the water. Rich short pastries are often sweetened for making tarts and flans.

Short pastry can also be made using oil instead of solid fat. For example, olive oil makes a rich short pastry with a soft texture. These pastries are often very crumbly, and they can be difficult to handle or roll out.

• SUET PASTRY This is different from the other doughs. It is made with self-raising flour, mixed with shredded suet (traditionally beef suet, but a vegetable 'suet' alternative is often used). Half fat is used to flour and a comparatively high proportion of water is added to mix the ingredients to a soft dough. Suet pastry rises during baking, and it has a light, spongy texture. It is known particularly as a lining for steamed puddings, both savoury and sweet, and for British dumplings, either boiled or steamed. It may also be baked, either wrapped in foil or covered, when it browns lightly but retains the soft texture achieved when steamed, or uncovered, when it forms a deep-golden, crisp and risen crust.

See *choux paste, filo pastry, hot water crust pastry, puff pastry, short pastry, suet pastry*.

PASTRY BAG See *piping bag*.

PASTRY BRUSH A brush used for coating food or culinary utensils with liquid. For example, for brushing food with butter or oil (especially meat for grilling); for greasing moulds and dishes; and also for brushing pastries or similar items with beaten egg or milk before they are cooked.

PASTRY CREAM See *custard*.

PASTRY (COOKIE) CUTTER A round, semi-circular, oval or triangular utensil, with a straight or

fluted cutting edge, for cutting sheets of pastry into various shapes and sizes. Pastry cutters are made of tin or stainless steel. An *emporte-pièce à colonne* (pastry cutter column) is a cylindrical tin containing a set of pastry cutters with high edges and decreasing diameters, fitting into each other.

PASTRY, FLAKY

PASTRY, FLAKY A layered pastry similar to puff pastry, but with fewer layers and not as rich. The dough is made with three-quarters fat to flour and it is rolled and folded four times. Traditionally, a mixture of butter and lard is used, but the dough can be made with all butter.

The pastry is used as for puff pastry, but it does not rise high enough for making deep pastry cases, such as bouchées or a vol-au-vent. It is the traditional choice for sausage rolls, pie crusts and apple turnovers. Flaky pastry is cooked at a high temperature, so that it rises and sets into crisp layers.

RECIPE

flaky pastry

Mix 75 g (3 oz, ⅓ cup) butter with 75 g (3 oz, ⅓ cup) lard or white vegetable fat (shortening) by chopping both types of fat together in a basin. Divide into quarters and chill well. Rub a quarter of the fat into 225 g (8 oz, 2 cups) plain (all-purpose) flour, then mix in 7–8 tablespoons cold water to make a soft dough.

Knead the dough lightly on a floured surface, then roll it out into a long rectangle measuring about 15 × 35 cm (6 × 14 in). Mark the pastry across into thirds. Dot another quarter of the prepared fat in lumps over the top two thirds of the pastry. Fold the bottom third over the fat on the middle third, then fold the top third down. Press the edges together and give the pastry a quarter turn in a clockwise direction. Chill the pastry for 15 minutes, then roll it out as before and dot with another portion of fat. Fold and chill the pastry for 30 minutes. Repeat the rolling and folding twice more – once with the remaining portion of fat and once without any additional fat. Chill the pastry for 15–30 minutes between each rolling and at the end, before rolling it out and using as required.

PASTRY WHEEL

PASTRY WHEEL A small fluted wheel, made of wood, steel or plastic, mounted on a handle. It is used to cut pastry into strips or serrated narrow bands, for decorating the top of tarts, or to cut out shapes for fritters or ravioli.

PÂTÉ

PÂTÉ This word is used in three ways in French: *pâté*, *pâté en terrine* and *pâté en croûte*. In France the word *pâté* on its own should, strictly speaking, be applied only to a dish consisting of a pastry case (shell) filled with meat, fish, vegetables or fruit, which is baked in the oven and served hot or cold. The best English translation of this word is 'pie', although many of these dishes are much richer and more elaborate than the sort of pie usually eaten in Britain and the United States and are often prepared in moulds rather than pie dishes.

Pâté en terrine is a meat, game or fish preparation put into a dish (*terrine*) lined with bacon, cooked in the oven and always served cold. The correct French abbreviation of this is *terrine*, but in common usage the French also call it *pâté*. The English have adopted both names.

Pâté en croûte is a rich meat, game or fish mixture cooked in a pastry crust and served hot or cold.

Pâté was known to the Romans, who used to make it chiefly with pork but also used all types of marinated spiced ingredients (especially birds' tongues). In the Middle Ages there were numerous recipes for *pâtisseries* (meats cooked in pastry) made with pork, poultry, eel, burbot, carp, sturgeon, cod, venison, capon and sheep's tongues. Throughout the centuries, pâtés have been dedicated to famous people; some examples are pâté *à la mazarine* (in honour of Cardinal Mazarin), pâté *à la cardinale* and pâté *à la reine*. In his *Grand Dictionnaire de cuisine*, Alexandre Dumas names a dozen, with numerous variants. Today there are many varieties of pâté inspired by French regional cookery, notably pâté de Chartres (made with partridge), pâté d'Amiens (duck), pâté de Pithiviers (larks), pâté de Pézenas (mutton, spices and sugar), pâté de Brantôme (woodcock), pâté de Ruffec (foie gras with truffles), Corsican blackbird pâté, Dieppe sole pâté, pâté de Lorraine and pâté bourbonnais.

Most pâtés sold in delicatessens are actually terrines, based on pork meat or offal, in pieces or minced (ground) and bound with eggs, milk and jelly. Among the best French pâtés are *pâté de campagne*, particularly that from Brittany (pure pork pâté containing offal, rind, onions, spices and herbs); also *pâté de volaille* and *pâté de gibier* (chicken and game pâtés, containing 15% of the animal); *pâté de foie* (containing 15% pork liver and 45% fat); and *pâté de tête* (containing boned cooked pig's head mixed with cooked, salted meat with the rind still on).

The pastry most often used for *pâté en croûte* is *pâte à pâté*, which is an ordinary lining pastry made with lard (shortening), but a fine pastry made with butter is also used, as well as puff pastry and unsweetened brioche dough. *Pâte à pâté* must be made well in advance, as it is easier to work after a good rest and does not brown so quickly when cooking. The pastry lid, which is sealed at the edges so that the filling cannot escape, is golden and often decorated. The centre is pierced with a 'chimney' – a small hole (often two in large pâtés) is made in the pastry, and sometimes a small nozzle or cone is inserted to enable the steam to escape and prevent the pâté from splitting.

The pâté mould, which has deep sides and hinges or clips, may be round, oval or rectangular. Dariole moulds are sometimes used for very small pâtés.

The fillings are based on pork, pork and veal, ham, chicken, fish, game and sometimes vegetables. All the ingredients are generally minced (ground) quite finely, but some of them may be cut into matchsticks, small strips or dice. The ingredients may be marinated separately. They are mixed with the filling or alternated with layers of filling. The pâté is sometimes lined with bacon barding before the filling is added.

In general, baking starts in a preheated oven at 200–220°C (400–450°F, gas 6–7), which is then turned down to about 150°C (300°F, gas 2). The total cooking time is relatively long: 35–40 minutes per kg (15–18 minutes per lb). Some hot pâtés have a little sauce, gravy or juice poured into them through the chimney before serving; for others, the sauce is served separately in a sauceboat. For pâtés that are served cold, aspic flavoured with Madeira or port can be poured through the chimney when cold to fill up the spaces made during cooking (the aspic should be ready to set). The pâté is not turned out of the mould until the aspic has set, and it is kept cool until served. Hot or cold pâtés are cut into thick slices and served as an entrée. Small individual pâtés are arranged on plates, sometimes with aspic croûtons.

RECIPES

Pâtés en Croûte

butter pastry for pâté en croûte
This pastry can be used for hot or cold pâtés. Put 500 g (18 oz, 4½ cups) sifted plain (all-purpose) flour in a heap on the worktop and make a well in the centre. Add 2 teaspoons salt, 125 g (4½ oz, ½ cup) butter, 2 whole eggs and about 3 tablespoons water. Mix together, then knead lightly. Roll into a ball, cover and keep cool for 2 hours before use.

lard pastry for pâté en croûte
Particularly used for pork pâtés, this dough is made by the same method used for butter pastry, but with 500 g (18 oz, 4½ cups) flour, 125 g (4½ oz, ½ cup) softened lard (shortening), 1 whole egg, 200 ml (7 fl oz, ¾ cup) water and 3 teaspoons salt.

ham pâté (cold)
This is prepared like veal and ham pâté, but lean minced (ground) ham or thin ham matchsticks are added to the forcemeat.

lamprey pâté à la bordelaise (hot)
This is made with lamprey fillets and fish forcemeat with herbs, which are layered in the pastry-lined mould with leeks sweated in butter.

pâté en croûte 'pavé du roy'
Cut 300 g (11 oz) lean fillet of veal and 300 g (11 oz) lean fillet of pork into small cubes and marinate for 12 hours in 175 ml (6 fl oz, ¾ cup) white wine and 175 ml (6 fl oz, ¾ cup) Cognac, salt, pepper and a pinch of allspice. Mince (grind) 500 g (18 oz) lean boneless pork and season. Add 100 g (4 oz, ¾ cup) foie gras to the marinated meat.

Make an extra-rich butter pastry with 500 g (18 oz, 4½ cups) plain (all-purpose) flour, 300 g (11 oz, 1⅓ cups) butter and 2 eggs and use to line a pâté mould, reserving enough for the lid. Cover the bottom with bacon and add half the meat mixture. Cover with a thin layer of bacon and use the remaining pastry for the lid. Make two holes in the lid and brush with beaten egg.

Cook in a preheated oven at 220°C (425°F, gas 7) for 15 minutes, then reduce the temperature to 180°C (350°F, gas 4) and continue to bake for 1¼ hours. If necessary, cover the top of the pâté en croûte loosely with foil to prevent the crust from becoming too brown. Leave to cool and pour some cold aspic jelly through the holes in the lid to top up the filling. Place in the refrigerator for 12 hours.

pâté with calves' sweetbreads (hot)
Braise 2 calves' sweetbreads in a thin white sauce until half-cooked. Clean and slice 300 g (11 oz, 3½ cups) mushrooms and lightly fry in butter (with some thin slices of truffle, if desired). Line a shallow oval pâté mould with butter pastry. Coat the bottom and sides with 250 g (9 oz, 1 cup) cream forcemeat*. Pour half the mushroom and truffle mixture into the mould, cover with the sweetbreads, then add the remaining mushroom and truffle mixture. Sprinkle with melted butter. Cover with pastry and finish as for veal and ham pâté. Bake in a preheated oven at 190°C (375°F, gas 5) for about 1½ hours.

The same recipe can be followed using 6 lambs' sweetbreads.

pheasant pâté (cold)
This is prepared like woodcock pâté.

pork pâté à la hongroise (hot)
Cut 300 g (11 oz, 1½ cups) pork loin into strips and leave in a cold marinade for ingredients of pâtés and terrines for 5–6 hours (see marinade). Peel and dice 150 g (5 oz, ¾ cup) onions, wash and slice 200 g (7 oz, 2½ cups) mushrooms, then sweat both vegetables in butter with salt, pepper and paprika. Bind with 2–3 tablespoons velouté* sauce.

Line a pâté mould with pastry for pâté en croûte. Coat the bottom with 200 g (7 oz, 1 cup) cream forcemeat* containing chopped chives and paprika. Add the mushrooms and onions and press down gently. Drain the strips of pork, stiffen them slightly in hot butter, then put them on top of the vegetables. Cover with 200 g (7 oz, 1 cup) forcemeat and then with pastry (which can be pastry for pâté en croûte, shortcrust or puff pastry). Finish the pâté in the same way as veal and ham pâté and bake in a preheated oven at 180°C (350°F, gas 4) for 1½ hours. Pour some Hungarian sauce – see hongroise, à la – into the pâté through the chimney.

salmon pâté (hot)
Prepare 600 g (1¼ lb) pike forcemeat* and add a chopped truffle. Finely slice 575 g (1¼ lb) fresh salmon and marinate it for 1 hour in a little oil with

some salt, pepper and chopped herbs. Line a shallow oval pâté mould with pastry for pâté en croûte made with butter. Cover the bottom with half the pike forcemeat, then add the salmon slices (drained) and the remaining forcemeat. Top with a piece of pastry. Finish as for veal and ham pâté. Bake in a preheated oven at 190°C (375°F, gas 5) for 1¼ hours.

veal and ham pâté (cold)

Remove the sinews from 300 g (11 oz) noix of veal and cut into matchsticks about 10 cm (4 in) long. Prepare 300 g (11 oz) lean pork and 200 g (7 oz) ham in the same way. Put all these meats into a terrine, sprinkle with 1 tablespoon spiced salt, add 100 ml (4 fl oz, 7 tablespoons) Madeira and leave to marinate for 6–12 hours (some herbs and chopped shallots can also be added to the marinade).

Line a round or oval pâté mould with pastry for pâté en croûte made with butter. Coat the bottom and sides with very thin strips of fatty bacon (200 g, 7 oz) and cover this with a layer of about 250 g (9 oz, 1 cup) fine forcemeat*. Fill up with layers of the veal, pork and ham matchsticks, separating them with thin layers of forcemeat. If desired, add 1 or 2 truffles cut into quarters or a few pistachio nuts. Finish with a layer of 200 g (7 oz, ¾ cup) forcemeat. Place a sheet of pastry over the top and pinch all round to seal.

Glaze the top with egg and garnish with shapes cut out from leftover pastry (rolled out thinly). Make a hole in the centre and insert a small smooth metal piping nozzle. Glaze the top again.

Bake the pâté in a preheated oven at 190°C (375°F, gas 5) for about 1¼ hours. Pour a few tablespoons of melted butter, lard (shortening) or aspic in through the 'chimney'. Turn the pâté out of the mould when completely cool.

woodcock pâté (cold)

Prepare about 575 g (1¼ lb) game forcemeat* à gratin. Remove the wings from 2 large woodcocks, season with salt and pepper and roast for about 10 minutes in a preheated oven at 230°C (450°F, gas 8) (they should still be very pink). Remove the flesh from the thighs and carcass and mince (grind) in a food processor with the liver and intestines. Add this minced (ground) meat to the forcemeat and adjust the seasoning.

Line an oval pâté mould with butter pastry. Coat the bottom and sides of the mould with a layer of forcemeat, then add the 4 wings. Cover with thick slices of truffle lightly fried in butter, spread the remaining forcemeat on top and cover with pastry. Finish as for veal and ham pâté and bake in a preheated oven at 190°C (375°F, gas 5) for about 1½ hours. Leave to cool completely, then pour in some chicken aspic through the 'chimney'. Keep the pâté cool until it is served.

other recipes See *duck, foie gras (goose foie gras), hare, quail.*

PÂTÉ PANTIN A variety of pâté en croûte, rectangular or oblong in shape, that is not cooked in a mould. The filling (meat, chicken, game or fish) is placed in the centre of the pastry, the edges are folded over and sealed, and the pâté is placed on a baking sheet and baked in the oven. The pâté may be baked with the sealed edges underneath or a second layer of pastry may be placed over the join and the edges sealed by pinching them together. It is served hot or cold as an entrée.

RECIPE

chicken pâté pantin

Prepare the chicken (or use duck or young turkey) as for a ballotine. Half-cook it in a light chicken stock, drain it and leave it to cool. Roll out about 575 g (1¼ lb) brioche* dough and divide it into 2 equal portions. Coat one of the halves with very thin strips of bacon, place the chicken in the centre and turn up the edges of the dough all around the sides. Place some more thin strips of bacon on top of the filling and cover with the second piece of dough. Seal the edges and make a small hole in the centre of the top to allow steam to escape. Bake in a preheated oven at 190°C (375°F, gas 5) for about 70 minutes and serve hot.

PÂTISSERIE Sweet or savoury pastries and cakes generally baked in the oven. The term also applies to the art of the pastrycook as well as to the place where pastries are made and sold. The pastrycook (*pâtissier*), however, usually makes sweet things: hot, cold or iced desserts, all types of cakes, gâteaux, petits fours and the highly decorated sweet creations that were traditional centrepieces, known as *pièces montées* in French. Quiches, vol-au-vent, pâtés en croûte (in pastry), tarts, bouchées, rissoles and savoury crêpes are generally made by the chef or cook (*cuisinier*). Pâtisserie is closely linked with the manufacture of ice cream and confectionery, which includes working with sugar, crystallized (candied) fruits, almond paste, nougatine and decorations, and uses sweetened creams and sweet sauces.

Prehistoric man made sweet foods based on maple or birch syrup, wild honey, fruits and seeds. It is thought that the idea of cooking a cereal paste on a stone in the sun to make pancakes began as far back in time as the Neolithic age. The Egyptians, Greeks, Romans and then the Gauls prepared pancakes with maize (corn), wheat or barley, mixed with poppy seeds, aniseed, fennel or coriander. Gingerbread and puddings date back to antiquity, and the Greek *obolios* (ancestors of wafers and waffles) gave their name to the first French pastrycooks (who were known as *obloyers* or *oubloyers*) and wafers (*oublies*). In the Middle Ages in France the work of bakers overlapped with that of pastrycooks: bakers made gingerbread and meat, cheese and vegetable pies. Apple fritters (*beugnets*, now known in France as *beignets*) and custards were also available. However, it was the Crusaders who gave a decisive impetus to pâtisserie, by discovering sugar cane and puff pastry in the East. This led to pastrycooks, bakers and restaurateurs all claiming the same products as their own specialities, and various disputes arose when one trade encroached on the other. Louis IX (1226–70) tried to create some order by giving status to the 'master *oubloyers* and the varlets of the *oubloiries*'. In 1351 an order from King John the Good (1350–64) listed the goods coming under the description of 'pâtisserie': wafers, *estrées*, supplications, *nieules*, *échaudés*, fritters (made of beef bone marrow, pikes' eggs, rice, almonds or sage), tarts, *gohières*, *popelins*, marzipan, darioles, *flanets*, *casse-museaux*, *talmouses*, *ratons*, tarts made with frangipane, pistachio, young pigeon and lark. Another order, in 1440, gave the sole rights for meat, fish and cheese pies to *pâtissiers*, this being the first time that the word appeared. Their rights and duties were also defined, and certain rules were established: prohibition of the use of spoiled meat, bad eggs, sour or skimmed milk and the sale of reheated pies. The proprietor could not take on a worker who was not capable of an output of a thousand *nieules* per day. Wafers were not made on feast days.

The 1485 statutes declared the statutory feast days and that of Saint Michel (the patron saint of the corporation) to be holidays. The final merger between *pâtissiers* and *oubloyeurs* took place in 1566; at the same time they obtained the monopoly for the organization of weddings and banquets. The corporation lasted until 1776, when Turgot abolished the trade corporations.

In the 16th century pâtisserie products were still quite different from the ones we know today. Choux pastry is said to have been invented in 1540 by Popelini, Catherine de' Medici's chef, but the pastry-cook's art truly began to develop only in the 17th century and reached its peak in the 18th and 19th centuries. Some landmarks are important: 1638, the invention of almond tartlets by Ragueneau; 1740, the introduction of the baba into France by Stanislas Leszczynski; 1760, the creation of toasted choux and ramekins by Avice; and 1805, the invention of the horn decoration by Lorsa, a Bordeaux pastrycook.

The greatest innovator at the beginning of the 19th century was indubitably Carême, to whom tradition attributes nougat, meringue, the *croquem-bouche*, vol-au-vent and the perfecting of puff pastry. Other great 19th-century pastrycooks include Rouget, the Julien brothers, Chiboust, Coquelin, Stohrer, Quillet, Bourbonneux and Seugnoy, who enriched the pâtisserie repertoire with the mille-feuille, Saint-Honoré, *bourdaloue, napolitain,* Genoa cake, mocha cake, *trois-frères*, savarin, *gorenflot* and many other creations.

There were about a hundred pastrycooks in Paris at the end of the 18th century. This number vastly increased over the next 200 years.

PATTE A Canadian term for leg of pork. The pork ragoût typical of Quebec is characterized by being thickened with toasted flour.

PAUILLAC A communal appellation in the Haut-Médoc region of Bordeaux. Many good and some very great clarets come from the estates here, as well as a number of small-scale wines. The most famous of all are the superb first growths – Châteaux Lafite-Rothschild, Latour and Mouton-Rothschild. All of these are AOC Pauillac.

PAULÉE A feast at the end of the harvest or the grape gathering, which used to be traditional in all regions of France. The word *paulée* comes from Burgundy; in other regions of France the feast is known by other names. In the Mâconnais, Dauphiné and Lyonnais regions, for instance, it is referred to as the *revolle*, in the Bordeaux region as the *pampaillet*, in Champagne, Lorraine and Franche-Comté as the *tue-chien,* and in central France as the *gerbaudes*.

Today, the *Paulée de Vendanges* (the feast after the grape harvest) survives only at Meursault and is celebrated at the end of November on the third day of the *Trois Glorieuses* (the 'Three Glorious Days') of the Côte de Beaune. The first day is devoted to the great annual chapter of the Chevaliers du Tastevin at the Clos de Vougeot, and the second to the auction of the Hospices de Beaune wines that takes place in the fermenting room of the Hôtel-Dieu.

PAUPIETTE A thin slice of meat spread with a layer of forcemeat and then rolled up. Paupiettes may be barded with thin rashers (slices) of fat bacon and tied up with string or secured with small wooden cocktail sticks (toothpicks). They can be braised in a little liquid or fried. Veal is most often used, but beef, lamb and turkey escalopes, or even slices of calves' sweetbreads, are also suitable. (See *oiseau sans tête*.)

Paupiettes can also be made with cabbage (the leaves are blanched, stuffed in various ways, then rolled up, tied and braised) or with fish (thin slices of tuna, or fillets of sole, whiting or anchovy, are stuffed, rolled up and cooked in stock).

RECIPES

braised paupiettes of beef

Flatten some thin slices of beef fillet, sirloin or chuck steak, season with salt and pepper, and spread with a layer of well-seasoned sausagemeat. Roll them up, wrap in thin rashers (slices) of fat bacon and tie with string. Braise the paupiettes in white wine or Madeira, drain them, untie the string, remove the bacon and arrange them on a heated dish. Coat with the cooking juices (reduced and strained).

All the accompaniments for small cuts of braised meat are suitable for these paupiettes: noisette potatoes, braised vegetables, vegetable purée, stuffed artichoke hearts, risotto, rice pilaf. Some garnishes (bourgeoise or chipolata) can be added to the casserole halfway through the braising time.

Paupiettes of beef can also be braised in red

wine. In this case, the accompaniments (baby onions, bacon and mushrooms) can also be added while the paupiettes are cooking.

paupiettes of beef à la hongroise
Prepare beef as for braised paupiettes of beef, but stuff with veal forcemeat mixed with chopped onion fried in butter, then wrap in thin slices of bacon, place in a pan on a bed of more fried onion and season with salt and paprika. Cover the pan and simmer for 10 minutes. Moisten with dry white wine, allowing 200 ml (7 fl oz, ¾ cup) for 10 paupiettes. Boil down, then add about 400 ml (14 fl oz, 1¾ cups) light velouté* sauce. Put a bouquet garni in the middle of the dish. Bring to the boil, cover the pan and cook in a preheated oven at 220°C (425°F, gas 7) for 25 minutes, basting frequently.

When the paupiettes are nearly ready, drain them, remove the barding, put back into the pan and add 20 small mushrooms lightly tossed in butter. Add some double (heavy) cream to the sauce, boil down a little, strain and pour over the paupiettes. Cook until they are done.

Serve on croûtes fried in butter, covering them with the sauce and mushrooms.

paupiettes of beef Sainte-Menehould
Braise some beef paupiettes until three-quarters cooked. Leave to cool in their strained cooking juices, then drain, pat dry and spread with French mustard mixed with a little cayenne. Moisten with melted butter, roll in fresh breadcrumbs and gently grill (broil) them. Arrange the paupiettes on a serving dish garnished with watercress. Reheat the cooking juices and serve, strained, in a sauceboat.

paupiettes of braised calves' sweetbreads
Blanch and clean some calves' sweetbreads and cook them gently for 15 minutes, with a little dry white wine, on a bed of carrots, celery and leeks that have been softened in butter. Drain the sweetbreads, cut them into slices and roll up in blanched spinach leaves. Keep hot on a serving dish. Reduce the cooking juices in the pan, thicken with beurre manié and add a little curry powder, a dash of mustard and a little double (heavy) cream. Adjust the seasoning. Strain the sauce over the paupiettes on the serving dish.

paupiettes of chicken with cabbage
Blanch some large leaves of green cabbage for 15 seconds. Drain and wipe them. Remove the legs, wings and breast from an uncooked chicken and season them with salt and pepper. Wrap the chicken pieces in cabbage leaves to make 5 large paupiettes and tie them up tightly with string. Brown some chopped carrots and onions in goose fat or dripping in a pan, add the paupiettes and cook them until they brown. Add 400 ml (14 fl oz, 1¾ cups) water, cover the pan and cook for about 1½ hours.

The chicken pieces may be boned and skinned before use, if preferred.

paupiettes of lamb à la créole
Cut 6 even slices from a leg of lamb. Flatten them well and season with salt and pepper. Peel and chop 6 large onions. Seed, then chop 1 large green (bell) pepper into very small dice. Gently cook half the onions and all the pepper in 25 g (1 oz, 2 tablespoons) butter. Add 350 g (12 oz, 1¾ cups) fine pork forcemeat* and season with salt and pepper. Spread the forcemeat evenly over the slices of lamb, roll them up and tie with string. Brown the paupiettes in a casserole with 25 g (1 oz, 2 tablespoons) butter and the remaining onions, cook until brown, then add 3 peeled tomatoes (seeded and chopped), some chopped parsley, 1 small crushed garlic clove, 1 piece of lemon rind, some salt and pepper and a little cayenne. Cover and cook in a preheated oven at 200°C (400°F, gas 6) for 45 minutes.

Drain the paupiettes, arrange them in a circle on a serving dish and keep warm. Reduce the pan juices until thickened, add 1 tablespoon rum, strain and coat the paupiettes with the sauce. Fill the centre of the dish with rice à la créole.

paupiettes of turkey à la crécy
Flatten some slices of turkey breast, roll them into paupiettes and cook as for paupiettes of veal braised à brun. Drain the paupiettes and return to the pan with the strained braising liquor. Add 1 kg (2¼ lb) glazed carrots and heat through. Serve the paupiettes coated with their sauce and surrounded with the carrots.

paupiettes of veal braised à brun
Coat some flattened veal escalopes (scallops) with a pork forcemeat mixed with dry mushroom duxelles and chopped parsley and bound with egg. Roll them up, bard them with thin rashers (slices) of fat bacon and tie with string. Arrange them in a buttered flameproof casserole lined with pieces of pork skin or bacon rinds and sliced onions and carrots browned in butter. Place a bouquet garni in the middle. Season with salt and pepper. Cover and cook over a gentle heat for 10 minutes.

Add some dry white wine or (depending on the accompaniments) Madeira – 200 ml (7 fl oz, ¾ cup) per 10 paupiettes. Reduce almost completely, then pour in some thickened veal stock until the paupiettes are two-thirds covered. Cover and braise in a preheated oven at 200°C (400°F, gas 6), basting frequently, for 45–60 minutes. Drain the paupiettes and remove the barding, then glaze them in the oven. Arrange them on the serving dish and coat with their braising liquor, reduced and strained. Serve with braised buttered vegetables or with vegetable purée.

other recipes See *cabbage, sole, whiting*.

PAUVRE HOMME, À LA Describes preparations of leftover meat served with a type of clear miroton sauce made by deglazing a roux with vinegar, reducing it and adding stock, chopped shallots, chives or onions, and chopped parsley. In the original recipe breadcrumbs were used instead of flour.

The term is also used for fried noisettes or cutlets of venison coated with a sauce made by deglazing the pan with vinegar and any marinade from the meat, thickening it with beurre manié and adding sliced gherkins. The name of the sauce (meaning poor man's sauce) derives from the fact that it was originally made with leftovers (stale bread and stock).

RECIPE

poor man's sauce
Make a golden roux with 1 tablespoon butter and 1 heaped tablespoon flour. Deglaze with 3 table-spoons vinegar, boil to reduce and add 200 ml (7 fl oz, ¾ cup) stock (or use water with a little added meat glaze or extract). Season with salt and pepper and boil for a few minutes. Just before serving, add 1 tablespoon chopped blanched shallots, 1 tablespoon chopped parsley and 2 tablespoons dried white breadcrumbs.

Chives can be used instead of shallots or a mixture of both can be used.

PAVÉ This word, which literally means slab or block, is applied to several dishes but most commonly to a square-shaped cake or dessert made from Genoese sponge cake sandwiched with butter cream or squares of rice or semolina pudding.

It is also used for a cold entrée, usually a mousse, set in a square or rectangular mould, coated with aspic jelly and garnished with slices of truffle.

Pavé also describes a square block of gingerbread and a thick piece of prime grilled (broiled) beef.

RECIPE

fried rice pavés
Make a thick rice pudding using 125 g (4½ oz, ½ cup) short-grain rice and 600 ml (1 pint, 2½ cups) milk, sweetened to taste (the grains must be completely soft and the mixture sticky). Butter a baking sheet and spread with a layer of rice about 1 cm (½ in) thick. Smooth the surface, sprinkle with a little melted butter and leave to cool completely. Cut the rice into 5 cm (2 in) squares.

Stew 800 g (1¾ lb) fruit with a little sugar until reduced to a purée (use apricots, apples, plums, oranges or greengages). Strain the pulp into a pan, add some chopped canned pineapple and boil to reduce by one-third. (Chestnut purée could also be used.)

Spread half of the rice squares with the fruit and top with the remaining squares. Press them together, coat in breadcrumbs and deep-fry in hot oil at 175–180°C (347–356°F) until golden brown. Drain them on paper towels and serve very hot with strawberry sauce or custard cream.

PAVÉ D'AUGE A Normandy cow's-milk cheese (50% fat content) with a soft straw-coloured centre and a washed crust. A firm cheese with a strong flavour, it is sold in 11 cm (4 in) squares, 5 cm (2 in) deep. Pavé d'Auge (or Pavé de Moyaux) resembles Pont-l'Évêque, but is more full bodied and contains more fat.

PAVLOVA A meringue basket or case, the best being of beautiful appearance, with a crisp and soft texture, filled with cream and fruit. This is the national dessert of both Australia and New Zealand. The meringue is made from egg whites whisked with vinegar and a little cornflour (cornstarch) as well as sugar to give the crisp crust concealing a marshmallowy inside. The whipped cream filling is topped with sliced or diced fruit, including peaches and kiwi. Passion fruit seeds ornament the top.

The dessert was named for the Russian ballerina Anna Pavlova on her visit to Australia in 1929 and honours her most famous role as the dying swan. First winning a newspaper prize in New Zealand, the recipe was perfected by Bert Sachse in Perth.

PAYSANNE A mixture of vegetables (potatoes, carrots, turnips and cabbage), cut into small squares and used to make soups known as *potages taillés* or to garnish meat, fish or omelettes. Potatoes and carrots prepared *en paysanne* are first cut into small sticks 8–10 mm (⅓ in) thick, which are in turn cut across into thin slices. Cabbage leaves are cut into strips 8–10 mm (⅓ in) wide, and each strip is then cut into small squares. Leeks are cut in half lengthways, if large, or slit lengthways and washed if small; they are then sliced evenly.

By extension, the term *à la paysanne* describes various braised dishes cooked with softened vegetables; the vegetables need not necessarily be cut *en paysanne*. Potatoes *à la paysanne* are cut into rounds and simmered in a herb-flavoured stock. Omelette *à la paysanne* is a potato omelette flavoured with sorrel and herbs.

Cutting vegetables for paysanne

Cut vegetables into even-sized sticks or lengths and then across into thin slices.

RECIPES

casserole of veal chops à la paysanne

Prepare a vegetable fondue with 4 carrots, 2 onions, 2 leeks (white part), a turnip and 4 celery sticks, all diced and softened in 25 g (1 oz, 2 tablespoons) butter. Add 1 tablespoon chopped parsley and season with salt and pepper. Fry 2 firm diced potatoes in a mixture of 20 g (¾ oz, 1½ tablespoons) butter and 2 tablespoons oil. Brown 200 g (7 oz) diced smoked streaky (slab) bacon in butter. Mix all these ingredients together. Fry 4 veal chops in butter, place them with the other ingredients in a casserole, season with salt and pepper, reheat thoroughly and serve.

omelette à la paysanne

For an 8-egg omelette, prepare 3–4 tablespoons sorrel braised in butter, 200 g (7 oz) potatoes boiled in their skins, skinned, sliced and browned in butter, and 1 tablespoon chopped parsley and chervil. Beat the eggs and add the garnish. Pour the mixture into a large frying pan and make a flat omelette.

potatoes à la paysanne

Peel and slice 1 kg (2¼ lb) waxy potatoes. Braise 100 g (4 oz, 3 cups) chopped sorrel in 25 g (1 oz, 2 tablespoons) butter with a crushed garlic clove, 1 tablespoon chopped chervil and some salt and pepper. Put a layer of potatoes in a buttered sauté pan, then a layer of the cooked sorrel and top with the remaining potatoes. Sprinkle lightly with salt, add a generous quantity of pepper and pour in sufficient stock to just cover the contents of the pan. Sprinkle with 25 g (1 oz, 2 tablespoons) butter cut into small pieces. Cover the pan and bring to the boil. Then transfer to a preheated oven at 200°C (400°F, gas 6) and cook for 50–60 minutes.

sole à la paysanne

Thinly slice a carrot, an onion, a celery stick and the white part of a small leek. Braise in butter, seasoning with salt and a pinch of sugar. When cooked, add enough warm water to just cover. Then add 1 tablespoon diced French (green) beans and an equal quantity of fresh peas. Finish cooking all the vegetables together, then boil the liquid to reduce it by one-third.

Place a trimmed sole weighing about 300 g (11 oz) in a buttered, oval, earthenware dish, season with salt and pepper and cover with the vegetables and their cooking liquor. Poach the fish in a preheated oven at 180°C (350°F, gas 4). When cooked, remove most of the cooking liquor from the dish, boil to reduce and then whisk in 2 tablespoons butter. Coat the sole with the sauce and glaze in a very hot oven. Serve immediately.

soup à la paysanne

For 4 servings, peel and dice the following ingredients and place them in a large pan: 200 g (7 oz, 1¾ cups) carrots, 100 g (4 oz, 1 cup) turnips, 75 g (3 oz, ¾ cup) leeks (white part), 1 onion and 2 celery sticks. Cover the pan and sweat the vegetables in 40 g (1½ oz, 3 tablespoons) butter.

Add 1.5 litres (2¾ pints, 6½ cups) water and bring to the boil. Blanch 100 g (4 oz, 1½ cups) cabbage cut into small squares; refresh, drain and add them to the pan. Leave to cook gently for 1 hour, then add 100 g (4 oz, ⅔ cup) diced potatoes and 100 g (4 oz, ¾ cup) small fresh peas. Cook for a further 25 minutes.

Crisp a long French stick in the oven. Just before serving the soup, add 25 g (1 oz, 2 tablespoons) butter and sprinkle with chopped chervil. Serve with the hot French bread.

additional recipe See *celeriac*.

PEA The small round green seed of the plant *Pisum sativum*, up to eight of which are enclosed in a long green pod.

Peas have been cultivated as a vegetable since ancient times, but they did not become widely appreciated in France until the 17th century, when Audiger introduced a new Italian variety to the French court. However, Taillevent had already made known his recipe for *cretonnée de pois* (a type of spiced purée of peas and milk, mixed with chicken breast and bound with eggs). Madame de Maintenon, in a letter to the Cardinal of Noailles in 1696, wrote: 'The question of peas continues. The anticipation of eating them, the pleasure of having eaten them and the joy of eating them again are the three subjects that our princes have been discussing for four days . . . It has become a fashion – indeed, a passion.'

Peas can be frozen, canned, bottled and dried. Frozen peas can be used in the same way as fresh peas. In France a distinction is made between early fresh garden peas (*lisses*) and the late varieties (*ridés*).

When buying peas, make sure that the pods are smooth and bright green. The peas should be shiny and not too large, tender but not floury. The sooner peas are eaten after picking, the better they taste. Peas can be boiled or cooked in butter (*à la française*), with lettuce and small onions. They can also be cooked with bacon (*à la bonne femme*) or carrots (*à la fermière*) or flavoured with mint. The cooking time is quite short for freshly picked peas, but longer for those picked a few days previously. Peas are regarded as the classic accompaniment for veal, lamb and poultry (especially duck and pigeon); they are often served with asparagus tips or artichoke hearts, as well as in a *jardinière* or a macédoine. Peas can also be puréed, made into soup or used to garnish soups and broths. When cold, they can be incorporated into mixed salads and vegetable terrines.

RECIPES

boiled peas

Shell the peas and cook them in boiling salted water in an uncovered saucepan. They should be tender without becoming mushy or losing their colour (10–20 minutes depending on size and freshness). Drain them thoroughly and serve with butter. The peas can be flavoured by cooking them with a sprig of fresh fennel or mint and serving them sprinkled with chopped fresh fennel or mint.

peas à la bonne femme
Melt some butter in a frying pan and lightly brown 12 baby (pearl) onions and 125 g (4½ oz, ½ cup) diced lean bacon. Remove the onions and bacon from the pan, add 1 tablespoon flour to the hot butter and cook for a few minutes, stirring with a wooden spoon. Moisten with 300 ml (½ pint, 1¼ cups) white consommé, boil for 5 minutes, then add 675 g (1½ lb, 4½ cups) fresh shelled peas. Add the onions and bacon together with a bouquet garni and cook, covered, for about 30 minutes.

peas à la crème
Boil 800 g (1¾ lb, 5¼ cups) fresh peas, shelled, drain them and put them back in the saucepan. Dry out a little over a brisk heat, then add 150 ml (¼ pint, ⅔ cup) boiling crème fraîche and boil until reduced by half. Adjust the seasoning and add a large pinch of sugar. Just before serving, add 2 tablespoons crème fraîche, blend well and serve sprinkled with chopped herbs.

peas à la fermière
Clean 500 g (18 oz) baby carrots and peel 12 baby (pearl) onions. Brown them in butter in a saucepan. When the carrots are brown but still firm, add 800 g (1¾ lb, 5¼ cups) fresh peas, shelled, a coarsely shredded lettuce and a bouquet garni composed of parsley and chervil. Season with salt and sugar, moisten with 2 tablespoons water, cover the pan and simmer gently for about 30 minutes. Remove the bouquet garni. Blend in 40 g (1½ oz, 3 tablespoons) butter just before serving.

peas à la française
Place 800 g (1¾ lb, 5¼ cups) fresh peas, shelled, in a saucepan together with a lettuce shredded into fine strips, 12 new small (pearl) onions, a bouquet garni composed of parsley and chervil, 75 g (3 oz, 6 tablespoons) butter cut into small pieces, 1 teaspoon salt, 2 teaspoons caster (superfine) sugar and 4½ tablespoons cold water. Cover the pan, bring gently to the boil and simmer for 30–40 minutes. When the peas are cooked, remove the bouquet garni and mix in 1 tablespoon fresh butter just before serving.

peas in butter
Cook the peas in boiling salted water, drain them, and put them back in the saucepan over a brisk heat, adding a pinch of sugar and 100 g (4 oz, ½ cup) fresh butter per 1 kg (2¼ lb, 6¾ cups) fresh peas, shelled. Serve hot, sprinkled with chopped herbs.

peas with ham à la languedocienne
Cut a medium onion into quarters and brown in goose fat with 125 g (4½ oz) lean unsmoked raw ham. Add 800 g (1¾ lb, 5¼ cups) fresh shelled peas and brown lightly. Sprinkle with 1 tablespoon flour and cook for a few minutes. Then add 300 ml (½ pint, 1¼ cups) water, season with salt and caster (superfine) sugar, add a small bouquet garni and cook, uncovered, for about 45 minutes. Remove the bouquet garni and serve hot.

peas with mint
Proceed as described in the recipe for peas in butter, but cook the peas with a few fresh mint leaves. Arrange in a vegetable dish and sprinkle the peas with scalded chopped mint leaves.

other recipes See *asparagus, duck, pigeon*.

PEACH The fruit of the peach tree, with a velvety skin, juicy sweet flesh, which can be white or yellow in colour, and a single stone (pit). The peach tree originated in China, where it has been grown since the 5th century BC. It was introduced to Japan and then to Persia, where it was discovered by Alexander the Great. He in turn introduced it to the Greeks. The English name comes from the French *pêche*, and the Latin name, *Prunus persica* (literally Persian plum) is an indication of its origins. Throughout the centuries, the peach has been highly regarded as a table fruit and has been used as an ingredient in many delicate desserts. In the reign of Louis XIV splendid varieties of peach were grown in France by La Quintinie, and the peach was nicknamed *téton de Venus* (Venus' breast). It was also much in favour during the Empire and the Restoration. The peach forms the basis of various refined dishes, including peach Bourdaloue, cardinal, Condé, *à l'impératrice* and the internationally famous peach Melba.

Peaches are harvested from the end of May to September. In France peaches come mainly from the southeast and the southwest. White peaches have a delicate, fine-textured flesh, which is full of flavour. They make up 30% of the total crop and are used for jams, compotes, sorbets and soufflés, as well as being a table fruit. The majority of the crop consists of yellow peaches, which generally mature later than the white forms and are less aromatic and not as juicy. They are best suited for jams, tarts, fritters and for decoration.

Alberge is a type of peach particularly esteemed in Touraine. Balzac considered jam made from alberges to be unrivalled. The fruit has a wrinkled skin, and its juicy flesh, which has a tart flavour, clings to the stone. It was traditionally used in Anjou in certain ragoûts. Lesser known today, its principal role is in jam making.

When buying peaches, ideally make sure that they are ripe and have a fine, unblemished skin; however, this is not always practicable when supermarkets stock under-ripe fruit. Before eating, ripen the fruit at room temperature, if necessary, otherwise the

Traditional peach varieties

variety	characteristics
white peaches	
Charles-Roux	fine succulent flesh, full of flavour (excellent for jam-making)
Michelini	colourful skin, good quality
Redwing	colourful skin, firm flesh, sweet and juicy
Ribet	greenish-yellow skin, sweet juicy flesh
Robin	red skin, pleasant flavour, sweet flesh
Springtime	colourful skin, sweet aromatic flesh
yellow peaches	
Cardinal and Earlired	skin almost red, firm aromatic flesh
Dixired	juicy, but little flavour; plentiful on the market
Loring	pale, very large and succulent (ideal for tarts and for decoration)
Merrill Gemfree	very firm flesh, medium flavour (good for poaching in wine)
Pavie	good firm flesh; ideal for jam-making, conserves, poaching and for fritters (named after a town in Gers where it has been produced since the 16th century)
Red Haven	good colour, firm flesh, pleasant flavour
Suncrest	good colour, very good quality

flavour is weak. To peel peaches, they are plunged into boiling water for 30 seconds so that the skin can be easily removed. Although peaches are used mainly for desserts and pastries, they can also serve as an accompaniment for savoury dishes (calf's liver, duck and crab in particular). They make excellent ices and sorbets and are delicious simply poached in syrup or wine. Peach liqueur and brandy are very popular after-dinner drinks, and the fruit can also be crystallized (candied) as a confection.

RECIPES

chilled peaches with raspberries
Poach some peaches in a vanilla-flavoured sugar syrup, leave to cool completely, then chill. When ready to serve, drain and arrange them in a glass dish. Prepare a fresh raspberry purée, add a little of the reduced sugar syrup and flavour with a few drops of raspberry liqueur. Cover the peaches with the purée and decorate with fresh raspberries.

crown of peaches with Chantilly cream
Prepare an egg or caramel custard (see *custard*) or a Bavarian cream in a 1 litre (1¾ pint, 4⅓ cup) ring mould. Bring a mixture of 1 litre (1¾ pint, 4⅓ cup) and 575 g (1¼ lb, 2½ cups) granulated sugar to the boil, add a vanilla pod (bean) and simmer gently for 5 minutes. Plunge 6 ripe peaches into boiling water for 30 seconds. Drain, peel and remove the stones (pits). Poach the fruit gently in the sugar syrup for 15 minutes, then drain thoroughly.

Unmould the custard (or Bavarian cream) on to a round dish. Arrange the peaches in the centre of the ring and chill. Whip 300 ml (½ pint, 1¼ cups) double (heavy) cream with 100 ml (4 fl oz, 7 table-spoons) very cold milk, 65 g (2½ oz, ⅓ cup) caster (superfine) sugar and 1 teaspoon vanilla sugar. Pipe this whipped cream in a dome over the peaches, using a piping bag fitted with a star (fluted) nozzle.

Decorate with glacé (candied) cherries and pieces of angelica.

peach conserve
Plunge 1 kg (2¼ lb) peaches into boiling water for 30 seconds. Drain, peel and remove the stones (pits). Poach the fruit in a pan with 100 ml (4 fl oz, 7 tablespoons) water and the juice of 1 lemon for about 30 minutes. Then add 900 g (2 lb, 4 cups) granulated sugar. Bring back to the boil and cook until setting point is reached (about 20 minutes). Pot and cover in the usual way.

peaches à la bordelaise ♦
Plunge 4 peaches into boiling water for 30 seconds. Drain, peel and remove the stones (pits). Sprinkle the fruit with sugar and leave to steep for 1 hour. Boil 300 ml (½ pint, 1¼ cups) Bordeaux wine with 8 lumps of sugar and a small piece of cinnamon stick. Place the peach halves in this syrup to poach for 10–12 minutes. When the fruit is cooked, drain, slice and place in a dish. Boil the syrup to reduce it, pour over the peaches and leave to cool. Serve with vanilla ice cream, decorated with wild strawberries and mint.

peaches Pénélope
Prepare a strawberry mousse as follows. Wash and hull 1 kg (2¼ lb) ripe strawberries and purée them in a blender. Add 300 g (11 oz, 1½ cups) caster (superfine) sugar, the juice of 1 lemon and 1 teaspoon vanilla sugar. Stir to dissolve. Prepare some Italian meringue* with 100 g (4 oz, ½ cup) caster sugar and 2 egg whites and set aside to cool completely. Whip 250 ml (8 fl oz, 1 cup) double (heavy) cream with 150 ml (¼ pint, ⅔ cup) very cold milk. Add the Italian meringue to the strawberry purée, then carefully fold in the whipped cream. Put the mousse into individual 10 cm (4 in) soufflé moulds and place in the refrigerator to set.

In the meantime, poach some peaches as for crown

of peaches with Chantilly cream, allow them to cool, then place in the refrigerator. To serve, turn out the mousses into sundae dishes, place either a half peach or slices of peach on each mousse and decorate with fresh raspberries. Sprinkle with a little icing (confectioner's) sugar and serve with zabaglione flavoured with Parfait Amour liqueur.

peach jam

Plunge the peaches into boiling water for 30 seconds. Drain, peel and remove the stones (pits). Weigh the fruit. Using 800 g (1¾ lb, 3½ cups) sugar and 100 ml (4 fl oz, 7 tablespoons) water per 1 kg (2¼ lb) peaches, boil the sugar and water for 5 minutes, add the fruit and simmer gently, stirring occasionally. The jam is ready when it coats the back of a wooden spoon (about 40 minutes). Pot and cover in the usual way.

peach sorbet

Prepare a sugar syrup with 350 g (12 oz, 1½ cups) sugar and 300 ml (½ pint, 1¼ cups) of water. Bring to the boil, simmer for 3 minutes and cool. Plunge 1 kg (2¼ lb) ripe peaches into boiling water for 30 seconds. Drain, peel and remove the stones (pits). Reduce the fruit to a purée in a blender and add the juice of 1 lemon. Mix the cold sugar syrup and the peach purée together, pour into an ice-cream maker and freeze (see *sorbet*).

peach sundaes

Prepare 500 ml (17 fl oz, 2 cups) vanilla* ice cream. Plunge some peaches in boiling water for 30 seconds (allow 6 peaches for 4 sundaes). Drain, peel and remove the stones (pits). Reserve a few slices of peach for decoration and chop the remainder. Sprinkle with 1 tablespoon lemon juice and 2 tablespoons fruit liqueur (preferably strawberry). Whip 200 ml (7 fl oz, ¾ cup) double (heavy) cream. Chill 4 sundae glasses in the refrigerator, put a quarter of the peaches into each cup, cover with a layer of ice cream and pipe the whipped cream on top, using a piping bag fitted with a star (fluted) nozzle.

Decorate with a few thin slices of raw peach, which have been soaked in liqueur.

other recipes See *compote, duck, Melba*.

PEACOCK A bird of the same family as the pheasant, originating in the Middle East. Greatly prized in ancient times for its beauty, the peacock appeared on the tables of Europe under Charlemagne, essentially as a banquet dish. Throughout the Middle Ages it enjoyed considerable prestige, but more for the beauty of its plumage than for the succulence of its flesh. For several centuries now, it has practically disappeared from cookery.

The peacock was served with great ceremony, roasted and entirely reconstituted, sometimes spitting fire (the beak covered with camphor). It was skinned, roasted (the head wrapped in a wet cloth to protect the crest), then re-covered with its skin (still bearing the plumage), and its feet were gilded. The task of carving it was allotted to the most eminent guest, who did so to the applause of the company present and then made a vow to perform some exceptional deed – for example, in a war or in the service of his lady or of God.

PEANUT The edible seed of a widely cultivated tropical plant. Originating in South America, the plant was introduced into Africa by Portuguese slave traders and was widely grown from the colonial era onwards. It is also grown in India and the United States. Each pod matures underground and contains from two to four seeds, also called groundnuts or sometimes ground pistachios.

In Africa the seeds may be made into a paste, grilled (broiled) or served in a variety of dishes. In Egypt they are made into cakes. However, they are now primarily an oil crop. Groundnut oil, which has a neutral flavour, is one of the most widely used cooking oils as it is very stable. The same oil can be used for frying over and over again, and it can be heated to high temperatures without losing its qualities. It is also suitable for mild-flavoured salad dressings. Furthermore, groundnut oil plays an important role in the canning industry and in the manufacture of margarine. Raw groundnuts have a high energy value.

Roasted and salted peanuts are served as cocktail snacks. They can replace pine nuts in salads, and almonds and pistachios in pâtisserie. They are made into smooth or crunchy peanut butter, which is used in sandwiches and snacks, and also used in making some biscuits (cookies).

PEAR The fruit of the pear tree, which narrows towards the stalk and has a yellow, brown, red or green skin, a fine white slightly granular flesh and a central core. The tree is native to Asia Minor and grew wild in prehistoric times. It was known to the Greeks and was even more popular with the Romans, who ate it raw, cooked or dried. They also used to prepare an alcoholic drink with the fruit.

Today there are countless varieties of pears (*Pyrus communis*), produced by progressive selection of cultivated varieties.

A distinction is made between summer, autumn and winter pears, which can be either dessert or cooking varieties.

The first pears ripen in mid-July, but the main season is between September and January. The pear is the third most popular fruit in France. Most French varieties come from the south-east, Lot-et-Garonne, Normandy and Maine-et-Loire. Pears are also imported from Argentina, South Africa and Australia. In Britain many of the same varieties are grown or imported.

Dessert pears can be eaten raw as a table fruit or used in fruit salads and desserts. They can be used as a decoration, in which case they should be

Peaches à la bordelaise, see page 861.

PEARS

Docteur Jules Guyot

Williams' Bon Chrétien

conference

doyenné du Comice

beurré Hardy

General Leclerc

Louise Bonne of Jersey

passe Crassane

sprinkled with lemon juice to prevent discoloration as the flesh oxidizes quickly. Many of the cooking varieties have now disappeared and dessert pears are used instead. Nevertheless, the flavour of the Curé and Belle Angevine becomes apparent only when they have been cooked.

Pears are used in numerous desserts, including mousses, charlottes, soufflés, tarts, ice creams, sorbets and compotes and in a number of specialities (*bourdaloue, cardinal*, Condé, Belle-Hélène, *à l'impératrice*). Pears can also be cooked with poultry and game (duck, hare) and can be prepared as hors d'oeuvre (filled with Roquefort butter, for example). Dried pears are used especially for compotes and to accompany savoury dishes. The most common variety of pear that is canned in syrup is the Williams' Bon Chrétien, which is also used for making pear brandy and pear liqueur. The brandy (sometimes called 'Williamine') is allowed to mature for a few months in an earthenware jar or bottle; it develops a delicate bouquet, very much like the natural fragrance of the fruit, which is intensified by serving it in chilled glasses. Pear liqueur, which is not as highly regarded, is made either from diluted sweetened brandy or from a mixture of steeping and distillation. Both may be drunk as digestives and used in a number of desserts (ice creams, soufflés and fruit salads).

RECIPES

baked pears with Sauternes
Make some walnut ice cream with a custard base made from 1 litre (1¾ pints, 4⅓ cups) milk, 150 ml (5 fl oz, ⅔ cup) walnuts ground to a purée with a little milk, 150 g (5 oz, ⅔ cup) caster (superfine) sugar and 6 whole eggs. Peel, core and halve 2 Doyenné du Comice pears. Put 200 g (7 oz, ¾ cup) butter and 300 g (11 oz, 1⅓ cups) sugar in a sauté pan over a medium heat. As soon as the caramel begins to thicken, add the pears, then a bottle of Sauternes and cook slowly until the fruit is tender. Serve coated with the ice cream.

Bourdaloue pear tart
Roll out some shortcrust pastry (basic pie dough) thinly. Use to line a buttered pie dish, making a little crest along the edge. Cover the pastry with a layer of frangipane cream and arrange thinly sliced pears in syrup on top. Cook in a preheated oven at 190°C (375°F, gas 5) for 30 minutes. Leave to cool, then coat with apricot glaze.

pear charlotte
Put 15 g (½ oz, 2 envelopes) gelatine to soften in 5 tablespoons cold water. Press 350 g (12 oz) drained canned pears through a sieve and warm the pulp gently in a saucepan. Add the softened gelatine to the pear purée and stir to dissolve. Cut 350 g (12 oz) drained canned pears into 1 cm (½ in) cubes. Whip 250 ml (8 fl oz, 1 cup) whipping cream with 3 tablespoons icing (confectioner's) sugar.

Traditional pear varieties

variety	characteristics
Beurré Hardy	delicate fruit, excellent quality
Clapp or Clapp's Favourite	American pear, green with red blush; juicy; does not keep well
Comice, Doyenné du Comice	fruit often very large; aromatic, melting, juicy and sweet
Conference	juicy, aromatic and firm flesh; elongated shape
Docteur Jules Guyot	small fruit; sweet, white and juicy flesh, slightly granular near the core
General Leclerc	large aromatic fruit
Louise Bonne of Jersey	slightly juicy and slightly acidic
Passe Crassane	fruit often very plump; flesh tender, very juicy, sometimes gritty and firm
Williams' Bon Chrétien (Bartlett)	sweet, juicy and fragrant; stands up very well to cooking

Whisk 2 egg whites with 50 g (2 oz, ¼ cup) caster (superfine) sugar until they form stiff peaks.

Line a charlotte mould with a ring of greaseproof (wax) paper. Line the bottom and the sides with sponge fingers (ladyfingers) trimmed at the ends to the height of the mould. Pour the pear and gelatine mixture into a large bowl, add the diced pears and 1½ tablespoons pear brandy, then incorporate the cream and the egg whites, using a spatula. Pour this mixture into the charlotte mould and chill in the refrigerator for about 10 hours until set.

Turn out the charlotte on to a serving dish and surround it with a ring of raspberry sauce. Serve the remainder of the sauce in a sauceboat.

pears in wine

Peel 8 fine Williams' Bon Chrétien or Passe Crassane pears, but leave the stalk on and brush them with lemon juice. Put the pear peelings in a large saucepan and add 1 litre (1¾ pints, 4⅓ cups) red wine (Côtes du Rhône or Madiran), 100 g (4 oz, ⅓ cup) honey, 150 g (5 oz, ¾ cup, firmly packed) soft brown sugar, the zest of 1 lemon (previously blanched), a little white pepper, a few coriander seeds, a pinch of grated nutmeg and 3 vanilla pods (beans), slit in two. Bring to the boil and simmer. After 10 minutes, add the pears, stalks upright. Cover the pan and cook slowly for 20 minutes. Leave to cool before putting in the refrigerator for 24 hours. Serve coated with the gelled juice.

pears Joinville

Line a 23 cm (9 in) savarin mould with caramel. Boil 1 litre (1¾ pints, 4⅓ cups) milk with half a vanilla pod (bean). Beat 12 eggs with 200 g (7 oz, ¾ cup) caster (superfine) sugar until thick and pale. Add the boiling milk gradually, whisking all the time, then strain the mixture through a fine sieve and pour it into the caramel-lined mould. Put the mould into a baking dish filled with enough water to reach halfway up the sides. Cook in a preheated oven at 200°C (400°F, gas 6) for 20 minutes or until the custard has set. Remove from the oven and allow to cool completely before turning out.

Drain the contents of a large can of pears. Melt 200 g (7 oz, ⅔ cup) apricot jam over a gentle heat and flavour with 100 ml (4 fl oz, 7 tablespoons) kirsch or pear brandy. Make a Chantilly cream by whipping together 200 ml (7 fl oz, ¾ cup) double (heavy) cream, 5 tablespoons iced milk, 50 g (2 oz, ½ cup) icing (confectioner's) sugar and 1 teaspoon vanilla sugar. Cut the pears into thin slices and arrange them in the centre of the caramel mould. Put the Chantilly cream in a piping bag fitted with a star (fluted) nozzle and decorate the pears.

Serve immediately with the warm apricot sauce.

pears Wanamaker

Cut 6 madeleines in half and arrange them on a buttered dish, spacing them out slightly. Soak with kirsch and coat with a thick, sweetened, pear purée mixed with a little redcurrant jelly. Poach 6 peeled pears in vanilla-flavoured syrup, cut in half, remove the cores and place a pear half on each half-madeleine. Prepare a vanilla soufflé mixture and cover the pears with it. Brown in the oven.

If desired, serve with a kirsch zabaglione.

poirissimo

This dessert consists of pear compote, pear conserve, pears in wine, pear tart and pear granita, a small portion of each being carefully arranged on individual plates. For all the recipes, the pears must be peeled quickly just before they are required, to prevent discoloration.

• *Compote* Peel the pears, cut them into quarters and cook them for 10 minutes over a brisk heat in a covered saucepan with sugar, lemon juice and a little water.

• *Conserve* Allow 800 g (1¾ lb, 3½ cups) sugar and 100 ml (4 fl oz, 7 tablespoons) water per 1 kg (2¼ lb) fruit. Boil the sugar and water until the syrup coats the back of a spoon. Add the sliced pears to the syrup, together with vanilla extract to taste, and cook until the fruit is tender.

• *Pears in wine* Boil a mixture of wine and honey, reducing it by half. Peel some small ripe pears without removing the stalks and cook them in the honey-and-wine mixture for 15 minutes. Cool and add some cassis (blackcurrant liqueur).

• *Tart* Roll out some shortcrust pastry (basic pie dough) into a circle and cover with slices of pear sprinkled with lemon juice. Sprinkle with sugar and bake for 20 minutes in a preheated oven at 220°C (425°F, gas 7). Serve warm.

• *Granita* (to be prepared the day before) Make a

purée with some very ripe pears and a little lemon juice and place it in the freezer. When it begins to solidify, purée in a blender, adding sugar, lemon juice and a little pear liqueur to taste. Return to the freezer and repeat the operation once. The resulting granita must have the colour and consistency of snow.

wild duck with pears

Pluck, draw and season a small wild duck. Roast it for about 30 minutes so that the flesh remains pink and leave it in its cooking dish. Make a caramel with 2 tablespoons caster (superfine) sugar and add 150 ml (¼ pint, ⅔ cup) red wine, a small stick of cinnamon, 6 coriander seeds, 6 black peppercorns and the zest of an orange and a lemon. Bring it to the boil and cook 2 peeled pears in it for no longer than 15 minutes.

Remove the breast fillets of the duck, bone the legs and put the carcass and bones to one side. Cut the pears in half, slice them and keep them warm. Dilute the duck cooking juices with 150 ml (¼ pint, ⅔ cup) red wine. Add the carcass and the pear cooking syrup. Bring to the boil, reduce and then strain. Cut the duck fillets and leg meat into thin slices. Cover with the sauce and surround with slices of pear (the finished dish may be warmed up for 30 seconds in a microwave cooker just before serving, if desired).

other recipes See *charlotte (cold charlottes), compote, pie, sorbet.*

PECAN NUT The fruit of a tall tree found in the north-eastern United States. It has a smooth brown fragile shell enclosing a bilobed brown kernel, which looks and tastes similar to a walnut but has a slightly softer texture. Pecan nuts are eaten as a snack or widely used in cooking for cakes, biscuits, in ice cream or as a topping. They are also versatile for savoury dishes. Pecan pie is a popular American sweet dish.

PÉCHARMANT A red AOC wine from the Bergerac region of the Dordogne, for which the same grape varieties as those in the Bordeaux vineyard are used, especially Merlot.

PECORINO An Italian ewe's-milk cheese. Pecorino is hard-pressed with a yellow crust when mature (those made in Siena have a red crust). The name is derived from the Italian word for ewe (*pecora*). The cheese was praised by Pliny and his contemporary Columella, who described its manufacture in *De re rustica*. Pecorino cheese has a white, cream or straw-yellow centre, depending on its degree of maturity. It is produced from October to June in southern Italy. There are several varieties, the best known being Pecorino Romano, a cooked cheese from Lazio. It is matured for at least eight months and contains 36% fat. It is manufactured in cylinders 20–25 cm (8–10 in) in diameter and 15–25 cm (6–9 in) high. It has a strong, salty flavour and is used as a table cheese or, when sufficiently aged, as a condiment, like Parmesan cheese. Pecorino Siciliano and Pecorino Sardo, the Sicilian and Sardinian varieties, contain more fat and are uncooked cheeses. They have an equally strong flavour.

PECTIN A natural gelling agent found in plants. It is a polysaccharide and is especially abundant in certain fruits (apples, quinces, redcurrants, bitter oranges and lemons). Pectin can be extracted on an industrial scale from dried apple marc.

Pectin is an essential ingredient in making set preserves, such as jams and jellies. When making jellies and marmalades, a small muslin (cheesecloth) bag containing the seeds and skins of apples, quinces and citrus fruit is boiled with the sugar and fruit juice; the pectin from the seeds and skins is released and helps set the jelly.

PEDIMENT An element of food presentation which was once very popular but is not often used today. Pediments of rice shaped in dariole moulds to accompany eggs or small pieces of meat remain a classic method. In catering, pediments are used for cold dishes (whole fish, poultry suprêmes, medallions of foie gras), which have been set in a mould with milk and gelatine and are cut as desired.

In decorative cookery, pieces of meat, poultry and fish used to be arranged on elaborate pediments. Turkey was served on a pediment made from 'a mixture of ordinary very white lard with a proportionate quantity of kidney and mutton fat, which must be very pure and very fresh. All filaments, fibres and pieces of skin must be removed; it should then be cut into small pieces and soaked in water for at least four hours' (Urbain Dubois and Émile Bernard). Like *pièces montées*, pediments were influenced by architecture and by the animal and floral world; their shapes and ornamentation were very varied: 'bastions, crowns, satyrs, angels' heads, peasants, sailors, swans, wings, dolphins, claws, animals and flowers moulded in lard, butter, and wax, etc.' Carême left many designs for pediments.

PEELING The action of removing the skin of fruits and vegetables. The French term, *épluchage*, is also used for the removal of stalks, ribs, wilted leaves and roots of salad plants, spinach and cabbage.

Peeling is generally done by hand, using a knife or peeler, although sometimes in restaurants an electric peeling machine is used; this reduces waste to 5%, whereas up to 25% can be wasted in peeling by hand. When peeling potatoes in this way, however, any 'eyes' have to be picked out afterwards. The peelings are not always thrown away: cabbage stalks are kept for soups; cucumber peel is sometimes used to decorate cocktail glasses; and truffle parings are as precious as the truffle itself.

PEKING DUCK A famous dish from classical Mandarin cookery. Its preparation is intricate and involved. The duck should be drawn, washed, rapidly scalded and dried. An air pump is used to separate the skin from the flesh, so that the skin swells outwards. The duck is then stuffed with a mixture of spring onions (scallions), aniseed, ginger, celery and sesame oil, sewn up, then hung, preferably in a draught, where it is coated every half hour with a mixture of honey and flour. After 3 hours it is roasted in the oven and basted with its own juice and a little sesame oil.

There is a precise ritual for serving Peking duck: the skin is cut into 3 × 4 cm (1¼ × 1½ in) rectangles, which, in theory, are the only parts of the bird to be eaten, the meat being saved for other uses. In common practice, however, the meat is also cut into pieces and rolled in pancakes. Using chopsticks, a rectangle of the skin is placed on a small hot savoury pancake; to this is added a piece of spring onion (scallion), which has been dipped in a sauce with a sour plum base; the pancake is covered with a little sugar and garlic, rolled up, still using the chopsticks, and eaten. Apart from requiring that only the skin is served, tradition also dictates that the carved re-formed duck is presented in advance to the diners.

PÉKINOISE, À LA

A method of preparing pieces of fried fish or scampi in batter served with a sweet-and-sour sauce, inspired by Chinese cookery. The sauce is made with chopped garlic and onions mixed with slivers of ginger. These are braised in butter, then sprinkled with sugar. Soy sauce is added, followed by fresh tomato juice. The mixture is thickened with cornflour (cornstarch) and flavoured with Chinese mushrooms.

PELAMID

Another name for the bonito, one of the smallest members of the *Scombridae* family, that includes mackerel and tuna. The pelamid is no more than 70 cm (28 in) long and lives in warm seas. All recipes for tuna can be prepared with pelamid. Its flesh is considered to have a finer flavour and to be less dense than that of the albacore, the long-fin tuna.

PÉLARDON

A small goat's-milk cheese from Cévennes (45% fat content), with a soft white centre and a very fine natural crust. Its full name depends on the region where it is produced: in Cévennes it is known as Pélardon des Cévennes; in the Ardèche as Pélardon de Ruoms; and in Gard, where it is often steeped in white wine, it is called Pélardon d'Anduze (or sometimes Péraldou). It measures 6–7 cm (2¼–2½ in) in diameter and is 2.5–3 cm (1–1¼ in) thick. This cheese is made on the farm and has a delicious nutty flavour.

PELLAPRAT, HENRI PAUL

French chef (born Paris, 1869; died Paris, 1950). After serving his apprenticeship with Pons, a Parisian pastrycook, Pellaprat obtained work at the Champeaux and then became assistant chef to Casimir Moisson at the Maison Dorée, where he eventually became the chef. In the army he was assigned to the officers' mess at Verdun. Pellaprat became a cookery instructor at the Cordon-Bleu schools in Paris and wrote many books on the culinary art that are still considered to be important today: *L'Art Culinaire moderne* (first edition 1935), *La Cuisine familiale et pratique* and *Le Poisson dans la cuisine française*.

PELLE

The French name for various kitchen utensils designed for lifting foods: tart or pie slice, fish slice, flour scoop and oven shovel. Tart or pie slices can be made of porcelain, earthenware, stainless steel or silver-plate and are often manufactured to match the cutlery or crockery. They can also be used for cakes and ice creams. Fish slices are made of stainless steel or silver-plate. They are sometimes slightly concave and may be slotted for lifting large fish. Flour scoops are used for scooping up flour, sugar and other dry ingredients. Oven shovels are made of wood and have handles 2 metres (6½ ft) long. They are used in bakeries and large kitchens to remove large baking sheets of pastries from the oven.

PELMIENI

A type of Russian ravioli originating from Siberia, made with noodle dough and stuffed with minced (ground) meat, potato purée with cheese, or with chicken. The *pelmieni* are cooked in boiling salted water and served with melted butter poured over them. Soured (dairy sour) cream, or meat juice mixed with lemon juice, can be served separately.

PELURE D'OIGNON

A French term, meaning literally 'onion peel', that is sometimes used to describe the shade of red that certain wines acquire with age and that other rosé wines possess naturally.

PEMMICAN

A North American Indian cake of dried and pounded meat mixed with melted fat, a food product famous since the early explorations of North America. It is no longer in demand.

Pemmican could be kept for a long time, did not deteriorate and took up little space. It was first made from the meat of bison (wild ox, now almost completely extinct) or from venison. The rump of the animal was cut into thin slices, dried in the sun and pounded finely. This meat powder was then mixed with melted fat in the proportion of two parts meat to one part fat and enclosed in bags made from the animal's skin. It was eaten raw or boiled in water.

The word comes from the Algonquian *pime*, meaning fat or grease.

PEPERONE

Also known as peperoni. A spicy Italian salami or sausage of pork and beef, which may be eaten raw. It is a popular topping for pizza.

PEPINO

The fruit of a shrub of the *Solanaceae* family, cultivated in New Zealand and in Central and South America. Also known as the pepino melon, the pepino has a firm, juicy and slightly sweet flesh under golden skin streaked with purple. The fragrant flesh is eaten like a melon.

PEPPER (BELL PEPPER)

The vegetable known as sweet or bell pepper, this is a large, fleshy capsicum with a mild flavour. Green, pale cream-yellow, yellow, orange, red, purple or black, these are widely used in cooking. Choose peppers that are firm and glossy; avoid any with wrinkles or soft spots. Peppers are an excellent source of vitamin C.

The flavour varies slightly according to the colour and type: green peppers are strong with a distinct edge to their flavour, making them slightly bitter; red peppers are sweet, with a 'rounded' flavour; and orange or yellow peppers are often lightly flavoured by comparison.

Peppers are used raw in dishes such as salads or salsas. They feature in a wide variety of cooked dishes, including fish, meat, poultry, egg, rice and pasta recipes. They may be stuffed with meat or rice and cooked in a sauce. Classic dishes with peppers include gazpacho, ratatouille, piperade and peperonata; they are also characteristic ingredients in dishes prepared *à la basquaise, à la portugaise, à la turque, à l'andalouse* and *à la mexicaine*.

■ **Preparing peppers** Halve the pepper or cut around the stalk to remove the core, seeds and white fibrous ribs from inside.

To peel peppers, grill (broil) them close to the heat, turning as necessary, until the skin blackens and blisters all over. Alternatively, spear on a long fork or skewer and run in a gas flame until blackened. Place in a polythene bag or wrap in foil until cool enough to handle, by which time the skin will have loosened and can be removed easily by peeling and/or scraping off with a knife.

RECIPES

grilled pepper salad

Cut some green (bell) peppers in half, removing the stalks and the seeds. Oil them very lightly and cook in a very hot oven or under the grill (broiler), skin side up, until the skin blisters and blackens. Peel them and cut into strips. Make a vinaigrette with olive oil, very finely chopped garlic, chopped parsley, lemon juice and a very small quantity of vinegar. Sprinkle over the pepper strips while they are still warm, marinate at room temperature for at least 2 hours, then chill in the refrigerator. Serve as a cold hors d'oeuvre with toast spread with tapenade, shrimps, small octopuses in salad and so on.

langoustines royales with sweet red peppers

Shell 20 large langoustines. Brown 1 sugar lump (dry) in a saucepan, then add 1 tablespoon vinegar and the juice of half a Seville (bitter) orange. Reduce to a thick syrup, then add 2 glasses red port wine and 3 strips of orange peel. Reduce by half, leave to cool slightly, then whisk in 60 g (2 oz, ¼ cup) butter.

Cook 2 red (bell) peppers for 10 minutes in a very hot oven or grill (broil) them, turning until the skins blister and blacken. Peel the peppers, remove the seeds and cut the flesh into strips.

Steam the langoustine tails for 3 minutes. On each of 4 ovenproof plates pour 1 tablespoon sauce and arrange 5 langoustines in a circle, alternating with strips of pepper. Place in the oven for a few minutes to heat through.

mille-feuille of scallops with sweet peppers

Prepare some puff pastry. Roll out thinly and divide into 16 equal rectangles, about 10 × 7 cm (4 × 2½ in). Cook in a preheated oven at 220°C (425°F, gas 7) under golden. Trim the edges and keep warm. Cook 6 peeled and crushed garlic cloves in 250 ml (8 fl oz, 1 cup) whipping cream. Strain, season with salt and pepper and add 25 g (1 oz, 2 tablespoons) butter. Keep warm.

Clean, peel and remove the seeds from 3 red peppers and 3 green peppers. Cut into strips and cook in 3 tablespoons olive oil. Sauté 32 walnut halves and 16 scallop corals in butter. Keep all prepared ingredients warm.

Construct 8 mille-feuilles by layering the puff pastry, red pepper, 4 walnut halves, 2 scallop corals, a little garlic cream, green pepper and, finally, a rectangle of puff pastry. Glaze the mille-feuilles with hot melted butter and arrange on a serving dish. Serve with scalloped mushrooms sautéed in butter and beurre blanc.

peppers à la piémontaise

Grill (broil) some peppers or cook in a very hot oven until the skins blister and blacken. Peel them, remove the seeds and cut into strips. Make a risotto *à la piémontaise*. Arrange alternate layers of peppers and risotto in a buttered gratin dish. Finish with a layer of peppers, sprinkle with grated Parmesan cheese and melted butter, and brown in a hot oven.

peppers à l'orientale

Cut the stalk ends off 500 g (18 oz) green peppers and remove the seeds. Grill, peel and cut into large dice. Gently fry 100 g (4 oz, 1 cup) chopped onions in a saucepan, without allowing them to brown, then add the peppers, a pinch of powdered garlic, 150 ml (¼ pint, ⅔ cup) clear stock and pepper. Simmer for 30–35 minutes, then adjust the seasoning and serve very hot as a garnish for white meat or mutton.

stuffed peppers

Cut the stalk ends off 12 very small green peppers. Remove the seeds and blanch for 5 minutes in boiling salted water. Prepare a stuffing by coarsely chopping 2 handfuls of very fresh sorrel leaves, 4 peeled seeded tomatoes, 3 Spanish onions, 3 green peppers and a small sprig of fennel. Place in a saucepan with 2 tablespoons warm olive oil and cook gently, stirring, until soft but not brown. Strain to remove the liquid and mix with an equal

A SELECTION OF PEPPERS

yellow

green

red

orange

long green peppers

volume of rice cooked in meat stock.

Stuff the peppers with this mixture. Pour a little oil in a deep frying pan and arrange the stuffed peppers in it, closely packed together. Half-fill the pan with thin tomato sauce to which lemon juice and 200 ml (7 fl oz, ¾ cup) olive oil have been added. Cook for about 25 minutes with the lid on. Arrange the peppers in a shallow dish together with the liquid in which they have been cooked. Leave to cool and then refrigerate for at least 1 hour. Serve as an hors d'oeuvre.

stuffed pepper fritters

Peel and seed some very small green peppers, as for stuffed peppers *à la turque*. Marinate for 1 hour in a mixture of olive oil, lemon juice and chopped garlic, seasoned with salt, pepper and a pinch of cayenne. Peel and chop equal quantities of onions and mushrooms. Gently fry them in butter, add an equal volume of well-reduced tomato sauce, then some chopped garlic and parsley. Cook this mixture until it has the consistency of a thick paste. Drain and dry the peppers and stuff them with the mixture. Dip them in a light fritter batter and fry in very hot fat (180°C, 350°F) until golden. Drain and serve with a well-reduced tomato sauce.

stuffed peppers à la turque

Cut away a small circle around the stalks of some (bell) peppers and place them in a very hot oven or under the grill (broiler) until the skin has blistered and blackened. Peel them, cut off the stalk ends and remove the seeds. Blanch for 5 minutes in boiling water. Cool, drain and dry thoroughly. Mix equal quantities of rice cooked in meat stock and cooked coarsely chopped mutton. Add some crushed garlic, chopped parsley and well-reduced tomato sauce; a handful of raisins soaked for 1 hour in warm water may also be added. Slightly widen the opening in the peppers and stuff them with the rice-and-mutton mixture.

Peel and chop some onions and fry them gently in olive oil in a casserole without allowing them to brown. Then add the stuffed peppers, packing them tightly together. Pour in a mixture of equal proportions of stock and tomato sauce to come a quarter of the way up the peppers. Adjust the seasoning. Bring to the boil, then cover and cook in a preheated oven at 230°C (450°F, gas 8) for 30–35 minutes. Arrange the stuffed peppers in a serving dish and pour the cooking liquid over them.

additional recipe See *espagnole.*

PEPPERCORNS AND PEPPER

The berry-like fruits of the pepper plant (*Piper nigrum*), a climbing vine native to India, Java and the Sunda Islands. The peppercorns ripen from green to red and finally to brown. Peppercorns harvested at various stages of maturity provide different types of pepper. Black pepper is whole red peppercorns sold dried; it is very strong and pungent. Unripe green peppercorns are sold dried or pickled in vinegar or brine; they are less pungent than black pepper and more fruity. White pepper is ripe peppercorns with the outer husk removed; it is less spicy and particularly suitable for seasoning white sauces. Grey pepper is a mixture of black and white pepper.

The name 'pepper' is also used loosely for several other seasonings and condiments, notably cayenne, paprika and chilli powder (all derived from varieties of capsicum).

■ **Whole or ground pepper** Pepper is sold either as peppercorns or ready-ground. The peppercorns must be solid, compact and of uniform colour, and they must not crumble. Ground pepper quickly loses its flavour and aroma; it is therefore best to buy whole peppercorns and grind or crush them yourself as required.

Historically, pepper has been the most popular and most widespread spice in the world. It had been in general use in India and China for centuries before Alexander the Great introduced it into Greece. The Romans used to adulterate pepper by adding juniper berries to it. Apicius even recommended its use in sweet desserts, but more importantly he suggested using it to disguise the insipid taste of boiled dishes and to hide the overpowerful taste of gamey meats (as Taillevent did at a later time). Although it occupied an important place in cooking as early as the Middle Ages, it was still rare and expensive, and several times it served as exchange currency, to pay taxes or ransoms. The voyages of the great explorers were undertaken primarily to find a sure supply of spices. The struggle between the Venetians and the Dutch for the monopoly of pepper lasted until the end of the 18th century. Over the course of the centuries, pepper became so popular that mixtures of pepper and other spices were developed. Although the craze for exotic spices died down after the Renaissance, pepper remained in favour with the cooks of the western world and came into general use, as a complement to salt, for the majority of seasonings. In the 1770s the aptly named Pierre Poivre, governor of Fort-de-France (Martinique), introduced pepper plant cultivation on the island of Bourbon (Réunion); until then it had been practised solely in Asia. Today, the annual consumption of pepper in France is about 100 g (4 oz) per person.

Pepper owes its piquant flavour to essential oils, a sharp resin and a crystalline substance, piperin. Rich in mineral salts, it stimulates the appetite and enhances digestion but is an irritant when taken in large quantities.

■ **Pepper in cooking** Several dishes take their name and character from pepper: the French poivrade sauce, steak *au poivre*, the German *Pfefferkuchen* (gingerbread, literally pepper cake) and the Dutch 'pepper pot' (a spicy ragoût of mutton with onion). Whenever a recipe states 'adjust the seasoning', salt and pepper are added at the discretion of the cook. Pepper is required in practically all savoury dishes, whether they are served hot or cold. Whole peppercorns are used in court-bouillons, marinades and pickles; crushed pepper for grills, certain raw vegetable dishes, forcemeats and hashes; and freshly ground pepper for salads and cooked dishes. A 'turn of the pepper mill' produces a very spicy fresh seasoning, whereas a 'pinch of pepper' gives a more discreet flavour to sauces and stews. Green peppercorns are used in specific dishes, such as *canard poêlé*, fish terrines and avocado salad.

PEPPERMINT A mint liqueur made from various kinds of mint steeped in alcohol. The infusion is then filtered and sweetened. Peppermint is drunk on its own, with ice cubes, with water or poured over crushed ice and sucked through a straw.

PEPPERY A word defining a slightly piquant taste combined with an aromatic flavour, as is found in 'pepper' mint or some boletus mushrooms. As long as it remains tolerable, the sensation in the mouth is reminiscent of pepper.

PERCH A freshwater fish belonging to the genus *Perca*. The common or river perch (*Perca fluviatilis*) is considered in France to be one of the best freshwater fish. It is usually 25–35 cm (10–14 in) long, but can grow to 50–60 cm (1½–2 ft) and weigh up to 3 kg (6½ lb), which is exceptional, as the fish grows slowly. It has a humped, greenish-brown back marked with dark bands and bearing two dorsal fins, the first of which is spiny; the remaining fins are red. Perch must be scaled as soon as they are caught, otherwise the task becomes impossible. Small perch are fried, medium ones are prepared *à la meunière* or in a stew, and large ones can be stuffed, like shad.

Other spiny-finned fish nicknamed 'perch' by the French include the sunfish, which is imported from the United States; the black bass; the small gudgeon, which is usually fried; and the sea bass.

RECIPE

perch fillets milanese
Make a risotto *à la piémontaise* with 250 g (9 oz, 1¼ cups) rice. Wash the fillets of 4 perches and pat dry with paper towels. Coat the fillets in breadcrumbs and fry on both sides in butter. Butter an oval serving dish and put the risotto in it. Arrange the perch fillets on top. Garnish with lemon quarters.

PÈRE LATHUILE A small suburban café established in 1765 by Lathuile, near the Porte de Clichy in Paris, which was in vogue for a while because of its cellar, its sautéed chicken and its tripe *à la mode de Caen*. It became famous on 30 March 1814, at the time of the fall of the Empire, when Marshal Moncey installed his command post there in a last attempt at resisting the opposing forces. Père Lathuile distributed all his food and drink provisions to the soldiers, 'so as to leave nothing for the enemy'.

This episode aroused people's interest, and when the fighting was over the restaurant became twice as successful: sautéed chicken with potatoes and artichoke hearts, covered with noisette butter and garnished with fried onion rings and parsley, became a classic. The establishment became a café-concert in 1906.

PÉRIGNON, DOM PIERRE French Benedictine monk (born Sainte-Menehould, 1638; died Épernay, 1715) whose name is associated with champagne of fine quality. While in charge of the wine cellars at the Abbey of Hautvillers, near Épernay, he evolved a method of blending the different wines from various plots to produce a harmonious whole or cuvée; this was a major development. Dom Pérignon is also credited with the rediscovery of the use of cork for sealing bottles, thereby retaining in the bottle the natural effervescence so pronounced in the wines of the Champagne region. He was also able to control its force by adding sugar to the wine. The results were so successful that in his own lifetime customers began to ask specifically for Pérignon wines. It is sometimes erroneously claimed that he discovered champagne (until 1660 the region was noted for its red wines); nevertheless, the importance of his work in developing it cannot be overestimated. Unfortunately, the records of Hautvillers were lost at the time of the French Revolution. Dom Pérignon's name is attached to the luxury cuvée made by Moët et Chandon, which now own the abbey.

PÉRIGORD See *page 872*.

PÉRIGOURDINE, À LA Describing egg, meat, poultry or game dishes served with périgourdine sauce or Périgueux sauce. Périgourdine sauce consists of a demi-glace sauce enriched with a little foie gras purée and truffles cut into large slices (or diced).

Many other dishes from the Périgord region are described as *à la périgourdine* despite the fact that they contain neither foie gras nor truffles.

RECIPES

calves' sweetbreads à la périgourdine
Clean some calves' sweetbreads, blanch them in boiling water, then cool and press them in the usual way. Stud them with small pieces of truffle and braise in brown stock. Drain and keep hot. Make a Périgueux sauce with the reduced cooking liquor. Coat the sweetbreads with some of the sauce and serve the remainder separately.

eggs en cocotte à la périgourdine
Butter some ramekins and line them with a purée of foie gras. Break I egg into each ramekin, place a knob of butter on top of each yolk and cook in a bain marie in the oven. When serving, surround the yolks with a ring of Périgueux sauce.

Périgord

Although some gourmets regard the cuisine of this region as one of the best regional cuisines in France, it owes its reputation as much to the natural resources of the region as to the native talent of its cooks. The low limestone plateaux, planted with chestnut trees, walnut trees and common oaks, is ideal terrain for finding truffles, ceps, chanterelles and other types of mushroom, and it provides good shelter for game. The wide alluvial valleys of the Dordogne and its tributaries have fields full of cereal crops, vegetables and market garden produce, as well as orchards and vineyards, while the plains provide pasture for the sheep and cattle of Périgord. The poultry of the region is particularly famous, especially the geese and ducks. The pork of Périgord has an excellent flavour and can be prepared in many delicious ways.

The rivers and pools abound with fish, and crayfish can still be found. Among the notable fish dishes are carp stuffed with foie gras, trout (grilled, marinated, stuffed, cooked with truffles, or *en papillote* in the ashes), eel in red wine, and fried gudgeon with vinegar or gudgeon *aux gardèches* in an omelette. Traditional salt cod dishes include salt cod brandade, salt cod salad and salt cod with tomato.

The three outstanding features of the cuisine of Périgord are foie gras, confit of goose, duck or pork (served with sorrel purée, new peas and dried or preserved apples) and, of course, truffles. The last in particular are used as a filling for omelettes, or are served with larks or quail, but can also be cooked in the ashes, *à la serviette*, or in white wine. The cuisine of this region also makes much use of walnut oil, goose fat and lard.

■ **Wonderful soups** The soups of Périgord are usually seasoned with the classic *fricassée périgourdine*

or enriched with a forcemeat. The traditional chabrot (a little red wine) is added to the last few spoonfuls of soup in the dish. The most popular soups include haricot (navy) bean or broad (fava) bean soup from Thiviers, sometimes garnished with bacon rind; blanched sorrel soup; *tourin*; *bouillon de noces* made with four kinds of meat; veal *pot-au-feu*; stuffed chicken in the pot; *bougras* (a cabbage, leek and potato soup cooked in a *fricassée périgourdine*); *sobronade* (a country soup made with salt and fresh pork, haricot beans, leeks, celery and root vegetables); and soups made with goose or turkey giblets, pigs' heads, *miques*, cabbage, oxtail, hare, rabbit or partridge.

■ **Meat, poultry and game** The range of charcuterie is impressive: in addition to the famous pâtés de foie gras, there are ballotines of turkey or partridge, goose or pig's *rillons*, stuffed goose necks, preserved pork rind and Périgord

At La Roque-Gageac, one of the most beautifully sited villages in the valley of the Dordogne, the houses nestle at the foot of imposing limestone cliffs, flanked by a dense forest.

black puddings (blood sausages made from blood mixed with meat from the pig's neck or head) cooked in stock with vegetables and herbs.

The poultry (turkey or goose) is excellent with truffles but may also be stuffed with ceps or chestnuts or grilled, roasted or stewed. Turkey giblets are made into tarts. Chickens are prepared with rouilleuse sauce (made with blood), spatchcocked, fried with verjuice or cooked *à la mode de Sorges* or in *pot-au-feu*. The traditional dish known as *sanguette* is becoming increasingly rare. Omelettes can be flavoured with foie gras fat or garnished with various mushrooms (especially ceps, chanterelles or morels) and also with black salsify or sorrel.

Of the game dishes, hare *à la royale* is highly regarded, although some people believe that it originated in Poitou. Hare can also be cooked *en cabessal*, made into *civets* or served with cornmeal porridge. Rabbits may be stuffed, roasted, braised or simmered in white wine (especially young rabbits). Partridges are stuffed with foie gras, and larks are grilled (broiled) with chestnuts.

Beef is made into succulent dishes, such as fillet steak *à la sarladaise*, grilled entrecôte *à la périgourdine*, braised loin of beef (braising steak) with cornmeal porridge or onions, beef in red wine, braised oxtail or ox (beef) tongue with tomato sauce or gherkins.

Veal is cooked in the usual ways, but there is also a speciality made with veal tripe. Pork specialities of Périgord include *enchaud* (with or without truffles), roast pork with chestnuts and stuffed sucking pig. Mutton is enjoyed in the form of gigot 'with sixty garlic cloves' or with mixed beans and as stuffed shoulder.

■ **Vegetables** The vegetables of Périgord are imaginatively prepared. Cep mushrooms are cooked *à la périgourdine* (stuffed or *en cocotte*); Caesar's mushrooms are grilled (broiled);

Truffles grow in the limestone rocks and are sold in the markets of Périgord in December, January and February.

morel mushrooms are braised in verjuice; and chanterelle mushrooms are served with parsley. Potatoes are cooked *à la sarladaise*, with ceps, stuffed or as croquettes or potato cakes. The following vegetables may also be stuffed: artichoke hearts, onions, tomatoes, cabbage, courgettes (zucchini), and cucumbers.

French (green) beans *à la périgourdine*, French beans with tomatoes, purée or ragoût of broad (fava) beans and chestnut purée are among the many other succulent vegetable dishes of this region. Salads, which are seasoned with walnut oil, include dandelion salad with fresh walnuts, endive (chicory) with *chapons*, purslane with hard-boiled (hard-cooked) eggs, cabbage salad and truffle salad.

■ **Cheese** The best known Périgord cheeses are the Cujassous cheeses of Dubjac, the Thiviers cheeses (dried on hay or wrapped in chestnut leaves) and Échourgnac Abbey cheese. There are also the Cabécou cheeses, which are rolled in vine leaves and steeped in jars with wine vinegar.

■ **Desserts and confectionery** The large range of desserts includes blanched chestnuts or chestnut gâteau, aniseed tarts,

crêpes or waffles, apple pancakes (called *Jacques*), mimosa-flower fritters, *merveilles* and *cornuelles*. The Périgord marzipans, Périgueux *millasses* (tarts filled with almond-flavoured egg custard), Bergerac macaroons and walnut or aniseed biscuits are less rustic specialities. Fruits are used for flans, tarts, *flaugnardes* and clafoutis. Other notable desserts are *rasimat* (a gâteau made with walnuts, grapes, lemon and quinces), set custards and crème caramel.

The confectionery of the region includes stuffed prunes and walnuts, marrons glacés, sugar-coated chestnuts and chocolate truffles (the last is a Périgord speciality).

■ **Wines, spirits and liqueurs** Nearly all Périgord wines come from the vineyards of Bergerac. The whites include Monbazillac, Bergerac, Côtes de Bergerac, Saussignac, Montravel and Rosette, and the reds Pécharmant, Bergerac and Côtes de Bergerac.

Private distillers make some good-quality brandies from plums, grapes, cherries and pears. Finally, there are some excellent home-made liqueurs, such as walnut cordial, and quince, gin, plum or blackcurrant ratafias.

salpicon à la périgourdine
Fry some diced truffles gently in butter, add some diced duck or goose foie gras, season with pepper and blend with a little Périgueux sauce. The ingredients should barely be coated with sauce.

other recipes See *baron, bouchée (savoury), chicken, fillet, quail, suprême, truffle, woodcock.*

PÉRIGUEUX A Madeira sauce containing finely diced or chopped truffles. It is served with small cuts of meat, poultry or game and with bouchées; these preparations are described as *Périgueux* or *à la périgourdine.*

RECIPES

périgueux sauce
Clean, peel and dice some truffles and gently braise them in butter for 10 minutes. Then add them to some Madeira sauce just before mixing in the cornflour (cornstarch) and Madeira.

pheasant Périgueux
Pluck, singe and gut (clean) a pheasant. Season the carcass inside and out with salt and pepper, then insert some slices of truffle between the skin and flesh. Fry the truffled pheasant in butter in a heavy-based saucepan and arrange on a slice of bread fried in butter. Prepare some Périgueux sauce with the cooking juices and serve separately. The dish can be garnished with large quenelles of truffled game forcemeat.

other recipes See *soufflé (savoury soufflés).*

PERMIT An official document that must accompany wines and spirits in circulation within France, attesting that the required excise tax has been paid before the wine was put on the market. Wines intended for export must be accompanied by a paper known as an *acquit.*

PERNAND-VERGELESSES AOC white and red Burgundies of the Côte de Beaune. Sections of the famous vineyards of Corton and Corton-Charlemagne lie within its limits, and the Pernand wines are perhaps best known for these great whites, although the red wines can also be very good.

PERNOD See *absinthe, pastis.*

PERRY A fermented drink made like cider but with pear instead of apple juice. It has been made since ancient times in western France: Normandy, Brittany and Maine-et-Loire. Sparkling perry is an inexpensive alcoholic drink in the UK.

The French word *poiré* should not be confused with the pear *alcool blanc*, referred to in full as Poire William.

PERSANE, À LA Describing a preparation of mutton or lamb noisettes or chops garnished with slices of fried aubergine (eggplant), fried onions and tomato stewed with peppers. The cooking juices are flavoured with tomato and spooned over the garnishes. Pilaf *à la persane*, more obviously influenced by Iranian cuisine, consists of a mixture of rice and diced mutton fried with onions, which is simmered in stock with pepper and various condiments. The dish is finally sprinkled with melted mutton fat.

PERSILLADE A mixture of chopped parsley and garlic, which is added to certain dishes at the end of the cooking time.

Beef *persillade* is a piece of leftover boiled beef sautéed in oil and seasoned with *persillade*. *Persillade* mixed with fresh breadcrumbs provides the finishing touch to a loin of lamb *persillé* and stuffed tomatoes *à la provençale*. It is also a basic ingredient in snails *à la bourguignonne*.

The word *persillé* is also used to describe dishes finished off with *persillade* or with chopped fresh parsley (for example, potatoes or sautéed tomatoes) and for dishes in which a large quantity of chopped parsley is used, such as ham with parsley (*jambon persillé*).

PERSILLÉ The French term to describe certain cheeses veined with bluish-green moulds. The term is often included in the name of the cheese. For example, Persillé des Aravis, Persillé de Thônes and Persillé du Grand-Bornand are Savoyard goat's-milk cheeses (45% fat content) with pressed centres and brushed natural crusts. They have a strong flavour and are manufactured in cylinders 8–10 cm (3–4 in) in diameter and 12–15 cm (5–6 in) high. Persillé du Mont-Cenis is made with a mixture of cow's and goat's milk (45% fat content) and has a lightly pressed centre and a natural crust. It also has a strong flavour and is sold in cylinders 30 cm (12 in) in diameter and 15 cm (6 in) high.

The word *persillé* is also used to describe dishes prepared with *persillade* and a piece of top-quality beef flecked with fat.

PERSILLÉ DES ARAVIS A soft cow's-milk cheese (45% fat content) from Savoie, with green veining and a natural crust. It is a cylinder, 8–10 cm (3–4 in) in diameter and 12–15 cm (4–6 in) tall, weighing 1 kg (2¼ lb). Its near neighbours, Persillé de Thônes and Persillé du Grand-Bornand, are also farm-made cheeses, which have the same spicy flavour.

PERSIMMON The fruit of a tree of Japanese origin that has been cultivated for centuries in China and Japan and is now cultivated commercially in Italy and other Mediterranean countries and also in the Middle East and the United States. The Japanese persimmon resembles an orange tomato, with soft, sweetish, orange-red flesh and up to eight seeds, depending on the variety. It should be eaten when very ripe, otherwise it has a bitter taste. When it ripens, the skin becomes transparent. The flesh is

PERU

Peruvian cuisine has been strongly influenced by the Spanish colonization. Onions and rice, imported by the conquistadors at the beginning of the 16th century, are today as much a part of Peruvian cuisine as the potato, a native plant. Tomatoes, which were cultivated by the Incas, are now included in many dishes and are often served with fish.

A typical Peruvian dish, *ceviche* is made with fish marinated in lemon juice, sometimes seasoned with chilli pepper (*agi*). Fish is also often served with *anticuchos*, brochettes of heart of beef, grilled on bamboo skewers, served with potatoes and a spicy sauce or with *butifarras*, small rolls garnished with raw onion, ham and salad. There is a great variety of breads: of all shapes and sizes, they are sold in large baskets in markets and on street corners.

On the Andean plateau the only meal of the day consists of small, dehydrated potatoes, *chuños* and grilled maize (corn). Sometimes, as a luxury, this basic meal is accompanied by *charki*, salted llama meat dried in the sun, or, on very special occasions, by *cuy*, guinea-pig whose tender meat is much appreciated; *picante de cuy* is very popular.

To cool the heat of the *agi* (chilli pepper), which is used without moderation, meals are accompanied by a sauce made from milk and fromage blanc. Desserts are very sweet: *suspiro de monja* (nun's sigh) or *ranfañote*, made with bread, nuts, candied fruit and generously soaked in cane syrup.

In addition to sodas, Peruvians drink *chincha*, alcohol distilled from maize and sweetened with honey, which is the national drink. It is drunk on special occasions but is also an everyday drink. South of Lima some wines are produced, such as Ocucaje, Tacama and Vista Alegre; these are usually served in restaurants or at Creole festivals.

---

usually eaten fresh, but it can be made into compotes, jams or sorbets or cooked *à l'impératrice*.

The Sharon fruit is similar to a persimmon, but the flesh is sweeter, even when firm and slightly underripe. It can be used in the same recipes as the persimmon.

RECIPE

iced persimmon à la créole
Cut a hole in the fruit around the stalk and scoop out the pulp with a teaspoon, taking care not to break the skin. Sprinkle a little marc brandy or liqueur into each fruit and leave to macerate for 1 hour. Mix the fruit pulp with some pineapple ice (1 tablespoon pulp to 3–4 tablespoons pineapple ice). Press the mixture through a fine sieve and fill the fruit shells with the cream. Freeze for about 1 hour before serving.

PERU See *above*.

PESSAC-LÉOGNAN AOC red or white wine produced on the left bank of the Garonne, near Bordeaux. It includes all of the estates listed in the Graves 1959 classification and other renowned châteaux, notably Haut-Brion, La Mission-Haut-Brion and Pape-Clément.

PESTLE A utensil used for crushing or pounding food in a mortar. It can be used for such items as garlic, tomatoes, butter, coarse salt, spices, nuts, parsley or bay leaves. The rounded head may be integral with a short stem or may fit on to a separate handle. The purée pestle, nicknamed *champignon* (mushroom) in French, has a relatively long handle ending in a large, solid head made of boxwood, beech or *lignum vitae* or sometimes of perforated metal. It is used for pressing purées and forcemeats through a sieve and for pressing poultry carcasses in a strainer to extract the juices.

PESTO A cold Italian sauce from Genoa. Large quantities of basil are ground with garlic, pine nuts and Parmesan cheese, and olive oil is added gradually to make a bright green, aromatic and full-flavoured sauce with a thick pouring consistency. In its simplest presentation, pesto is tossed with freshly cooked pasta to make a fabulous meal; it may be served to complement a wide variety of other foods, including fish, poultry, meat and vegetables. Many variations have been created from this classic sauce using different herbs and ingredients, such as sun-dried tomatoes.

PÉTÉRAM A well-known speciality from Luchon in the Haute-Garonne. It is a stew of sheep's trotters (feet) and tripe, ham, calf's mesentery, bacon, potatoes, garlic and herbs, cooked slowly over a period of 10 hours in dry white wine.

PÉTILLANT The term used to describe wine with a slight sparkle. This is sometimes naturally present, but may also be encouraged and regulated.

PETIT-BEURRE A small square or rectangular biscuit (cookie) with fluted edges. The dough is made with flour, sugar and butter, but contains no eggs. Petits-beurres are a speciality of Nantes, where they are manufactured on an industrial scale. They are eaten for afternoon tea or served with various desserts; they are also used as an ingredient in a number of desserts.

PETIT DÉJEUNER The traditional French, or continental, breakfast consists of a cup of tea, coffee, café au lait or hot chocolate, with buttered croissants, bread or *biscottes* spread with jam or honey.

There is, however, a growing trend, particularly in French hotels, to provide buffet-style breakfasts, similar to those in Germany or Scandinavia, which may include boiled eggs, cheeses, sausages, cold meats, compotes, plain and flavoured yogurts and fruit juices.

Known simply as *déjeuner* (meaning literally 'to break one's fast'), the first meal of the day originally consisted of a bowl of soup sometimes accompanied by wine and meat (for the men). The main meal (*dîner*) was taken at midday. At the time of the Revolution, however, it became customary to eat *dîner* at the end of the afternoon, when the business of the day was completed, and a second 'breakfast' was needed to bridge the gap between the two meals. So the midday meal became known as *déjeuner* and a smaller *petit déjeuner* was consumed early in the morning.

PETIT-DUC A garnish for small pieces of meat, consisting of tartlets filled with chicken purée with cream, little bunches of asparagus tips and slices of truffle. *Petit-duc* dishes are less prestigious versions of *grand-duc* dishes.

PETITE MARMITE A type of *pot-au-feu* served in the receptacle in which it was cooked (originally an earthenware pot but now often small individual dishes made of flameproof porcelain). The *petite marmite* was created in Paris in 1867 by Modeste Magny in his famous restaurant. In theory it should contain lean beef, oxtail, chicken, marrow bone, stock-pot vegetables and small cabbage balls. The soup is usually served with grated cheese, croûtons spread with rounds of marrow and sprinkled with pepper, or slices of a long thin French loaf crisped in the oven and sprinkled with fat from the stew.

RECIPE

petite marmite à la parisienne

Pour 2.5 litres (4½ pints, 11 cups) cold consommé* into a pan. Add 500 g (18 oz) rump roast (standing rump) and 250 g (9 oz) short rib of beef. Bring to the boil and skim. Then add 100 g (4 oz, ¾ cup) chopped carrots, 75 g (3 oz, ⅔ cup) chopped turnips, 75 g (3 oz) leeks (white part only, cut into chunks), 2 baby (pearl) onions browned in a dry frying pan, 50 g (2 oz) celery hearts (cut into small pieces and blanched) and 100 g (4 oz) cabbage (blanched in salted water, cooled and rolled into tight balls). Simmer these ingredients for 3 hours, occasionally adding a little consommé to compensate for the evaporation.

Lightly brown 2 sets of chicken giblets in a preheated oven at 200°C (400°F, gas 6), add them to the pan and cook for a further 50 minutes. Finally, add a large marrow bone wrapped in muslin (cheesecloth) and simmer for another 10 minutes. Skim off the surplus fat, unwrap the marrow bone and replace it in the pan. Serve the soup hot with small slices from a long thin French loaf that have been crisped in the oven and sprinkled with a little fat from the stew. Spread some of the bread with bone marrow and season with freshly ground pepper.

PETIT FOUR A small fancy biscuit (cookie), cake or item of confectionery. The name, according to Carême, dates from the 18th century, when ovens were made of brick and small items had to be cooked *à petit four* (at a very low temperature), after large cakes had been taken out and the temperature had dropped.

After the bonbons, dragées, marzipans, pralines and crystallized (candied) fruits that were in vogue during the Renaissance and in the reign of Louis XIV, other titbits were created. They required imagination and flair by the pastrycooks to reproduce the large-scale decorations in miniature. Carême himself attached great importance to the petits fours known as *colifichets* – part of the *pièces montées*, which decorated the table and buffets. A *colifichet* is really a dry cake made for the birds, but pastrycooks use the term to distinguish the *pièces montées* from the proper dishes. The elder Paul Coquelin, who became established at Passy in 1897, created 30 different types of petits fours, each one given a female Christian name. Today, petits fours constitute an important part of pâtisserie. They are served mainly at buffets, lunches or with cocktails, but also with tea, ice creams and some desserts. At a sophisticated meal in France, an assortment of petits fours (sometimes known as *mignardises*) may be served either with or after the dessert.

■ **Plain petits fours** These are dry biscuits (cookies) that keep well and are served with dessert custards, ice creams and sorbets, and also with tea, liqueur wines or dessert wines. They include *tuiles, cigarettes, bâtonnets, palets, langues de chat*, macaroons, small meringues, sponge fingers (ladyfingers), *croquettes*, small *galettes, milanais* and *rochers*.

■ **Fresh petits fours** This category constitutes petits fours proper. It can be divided into three groups. First, there are miniature reproductions of individual cakes (miniature éclairs, *duchesses*, choux, tartlets, *barquettes* and babas).

Iced or glazed petits fours are the largest and most diverse group. Some consist of small, geometric shapes of Genoese sponge cake filled with butter cream, *ganache*, confectioner's custard (pastry cream) or jam, glazed with apricot jam, iced (frosted) and decorated. Others are made with a base of almond paste, chocolate, nougatine, *dacquoise* or meringue, topped with a square of Genoese sponge soaked in liqueur, a spoonful of cream or diced crystallized (candied) or glacé fruit. They are then coated with fondant and decorated with piped icing (frosting), coated with chocolate or dipped in boiled sugar and decorated with crystallized fruits, chopped almonds or coconut.

The third group includes sugar-coated fruits such as prunes, dates and cherries filled with almond paste and glazed with sugar; morello cherries and grapes coated with fondant icing; orange quarters or pineapple cubes glazed with caramel; aboukir almonds; and green walnuts *en surprise*.

■ **Savoury petits fours** These are served with aperitifs and cocktails and at receptions or lunches. They are also referred to as *amuse-gueule* (cocktail snacks). They are made of a pastry base (matchsticks, straws, miniature turnovers, croissants, barquettes, *bouchées*, quiches, pizzas) and filled with a savoury filling, such as anchovy paste, flavoured butter, shellfish or foie gras mousse, cheese, smoked salmon, mayonnaise, vegetable or game purée.

PETIT-LAIT The French name for a by-product of milk, such as skimmed milk, buttermilk (liquid residue after butter has been separated from milk) or whey (the transparent pale yellow watery liquid that separates from the curd when milk is curdled).

PETIT MAURE A cabaret that opened in Paris in 1618, on the corner of the Rue de Seine and the Rue Visconti. It was frequented by Voiture, Théophile de Viau, Colletet, Tallemant des Réaux and, most notably, the poet Saint-Amant, who is said to have died there in 1661, after a violent beating occasioned by a rather biting epigram. In the following century, another Petit Maure was fashionable for a time. This was a small suburban restaurant at Vaugirard, where one could enjoy the strawberries and petits pois that grew in the surrounding district, drink the local wine and eat the home-bred turkeys.

PETIT POIS See *pea*.

PETIT-SUISSE A French cheese made with cow's milk enriched with cream, giving it a high fat content (60–75%). It is a fresh cheese, unsalted, smooth and soft, sold in the form of 30 g (about 1 oz) wrapped cylinders. Originally, it weighed 60 g (about 2 oz) and was called Suisse. In spite of its name, it was first made not in Switzerland but in Normandy, in 1850, when a Swiss employee of a cheesemonger in Auvilliers had the idea of adding cream to the milk used to make the fresh Bondon cheeses. The larger cheeses are now known as double Petits-Suisses.

The cheese is served as a dessert, with sugar, honey, jam or poached fruits, or as a savoury with salt, herbs and pepper. It is also used to prepare cold emulsified sauces, to spread on canapés (mixed with paprika, chopped herbs or raisins), and is added to the forcemeat for some poultry (such as turkey and guinea fowl), to help make the flesh more tender.

PETS-DE-NONNE Soufflé fritters made of choux pastry, about the size of walnuts. They are fried in oil that is hot but not smoking so that the pastry swells up considerably into a light, puffy ball. The name means literally 'nun's farts' and the fritters are therefore sometimes called *soupirs de nonne* (nun's sighs), thought to be less disrespectful, or *beignets venteux*. When they are cooked and golden brown, the fritters are sprinkled with sugar and served hot, sometimes with a fruit sauce. They can also be filled with cream or jam.

RECIPE

pets-de-nonne
Make some choux paste* with 250 ml (8 fl oz, I cup) water, a pinch of salt, 2 tablespoons caster (superfine) sugar, 65 g (2½ oz, 5 tablespoons) butter, 125 g (4½ oz, I cup) plain (all-purpose) flour and 3 or 4 eggs. Heat up some oil in a deep-fat fryer to 180°C (356°F). Drop teaspoonfuls of the paste into the hot oil; when golden brown on one side (after about 2½ minutes), turn them over, if necessary, to cook the other side (another 2 minutes). Drain the fritters on paper towels and sprinkle with icing (confectioner's) sugar.

PÉZENAS PIE A small, round pastry filled with a mixture of minced (ground) mutton, sheep's kidney fat, brown sugar and lemon zest. It is served very hot as an entrée or even as a dessert (as recommended by Prosper Montagné). The recipe comes from Languedoc but is also claimed by Béziers, where small meat pies were being sold in the streets as early as the 17th century. According to A.-P. Alliès, a local historian, Lord Clive, viceroy and governor of India, spent the winter of 1766 at Pézenas for health reasons. During this period his Indian cook baked him some sweetened spiced mutton pies, and the pastrycooks of Pézenas were inspired to make them themselves. They soon became popular throughout the region.

PFEFFERNÜSSE Small, round, domed, dark, strongly flavoured German 'peppernut' biscuits (cookies), seasoned with black pepper (and/or ginger), made with honey and often coated with icing (frosting). The successful combination of pepper with honey was discovered in the monasteries of Austria and Germany around the 11th century. Returning crusaders subsequently brought back ginger and a taste for spices. The name is probably an allusion to Nuremberg's *Pfeffersake* ('pepper sacks' or spice merchants). There is a German saying 'Without peppercakes, no Christmas feast', and they are part of the *bunter Teller*, the biscuit display.

PFLUTTERS Also known as Floutes. These Alsatian dumplings are made with potato purée, beaten egg and flour or semolina, sometimes moistened with milk; they are poached in boiling water and served as an entrée with melted butter. *Pflutters* can also be made into cakes and fried. In this case, the dough is rolled out and cut into shapes with a pastry (cookie) cutter, and they are served with a roast.

RECIPE

pflutters
Prepare 500 g (18 oz) very fine potato purée and mix with 2 eggs and about 75 g (3 oz, ¾ cup) plain flour (all-purpose flour) to obtain a fairly stiff dough. Season with salt, pepper and nutmeg. Shape the dough into balls and drop them into a saucepan

of boiling salted water. Poach for 8–10 minutes, drain and arrange in a buttered dish. Sprinkle with hot noisette butter in which fine stale breadcrumbs have been browned to give a crumbly topping.

PHEASANT A long-tailed game bird introduced into Europe from Asia in the early Middle Ages. In many countries shooting has considerably reduced the pheasant population, in spite of the periodic supply of reared birds. These are either released in January and allowed to breed in the wild or they are liberated just before the shoot. In the latter case, the flesh of the birds has less flavour than that of the truly wild pheasant. Hens and young cock pheasants can be roasted without being barded, but barding fat on the back and breast is necessary for old male birds. True connoisseurs prefer the hen pheasant to the cock because the hen has finer flesh. The male bird is larger than the female. It is also more brightly coloured, with iridescent blue and green feathers, bright fleshy wattles, longer tail feathers and large leg spurs. Pheasants should be hung for a period of between three days and two weeks, depending on taste and the weather, in a cool, dry, airy place. A bird has usually been hung for long enough when the tail feathers can be pulled out easily. Reared birds should not be hung but cooked immediately, like poultry.

The young pheasant can be distinguished from an old bird by the first wing-tip feather, which is pointed in a young bird and rounded in an old one. The upper part of the beak of a young bird is pliable to the touch. It is best roasted or casseroled and flavoured with wine or spirits. A stock can be made from the carcass and used as a basis for sauce or consommé. A fricassée of pheasant can be made by cutting it into quarters (two suprêmes and two legs) or into six pieces (two wings, two legs and two pieces of breast). Older birds can be prepared as a *chartreuse* (a mould made from game birds, cabbage and other vegetables) or a salmi, accompanied by braised cabbage, cep mushrooms, fresh pasta or apples with bacon and onions. Very old birds should be casseroled or made into pâtés or terrines. But the most decorative method of preparing pheasant is *à la Sainte-Alliance*, in which it is presented in all the glory of its magnificent plumage.

RECIPES

preparation of pheasant

Keep the pheasant in the refrigerator for a few hours as this makes it easier to pluck. Begin by twisting the large wing feathers to remove them. Then pluck the remaining feathers in the following order: the body, legs, neck and wings. Draw the bird in the same way as a chicken. Season the inside of the carcass with salt and pepper. Bard if necessary and truss the bird with the legs pressed as tightly as possible against the breast, especially if the bird is to be roasted.

Cold Pheasant Dishes

ballotine of pheasant in aspic

Take a Strasbourg foie gras. Soak in cold water and (from Carême's recipe) blanch. Cut each half into 4 fillets and trim. Pound 2 of these fillets in a mortar with the trimmings and the meat of a red partridge with an equal weight of pork fat. Season the mixture very well. Add 2 egg yolks and some cultivated mushrooms tossed in butter. Pound the lot thoroughly. Press the stuffing through a quenelle sieve.

Carefully bone a well-hung fat pheasant. Lay it on a cloth and season very well. Lay on top of it half the stuffing and then 3 fillets of foie gras, interspersing these with halved truffles. Add as much spiced salt as required. Cover the whole with half the remaining stuffing. Lay on top the rest of the foie gras and the halves of truffle. Season and cover with the rest of the stuffing.

Fold the pheasant into shape. Wrap in a cloth. Tie and cook in aspic stock flavoured with Madeira, to which have been added the bones and trimmings of the pheasant and partridge. Leave the ballotine to cool under a light weight. Glaze with aspic in the usual way.

chaud-froid of pheasant

Cook a prepared trussed pheasant in butter in an ovenproof casserole, taking care that the meat remains pinkish. Joint (cut) the bird into 4 or 6 pieces. Skin the pieces, trim them and allow them to cool completely. Place in the refrigerator for about 1 hour. Prepare a brown chaud-froid sauce with some game stock, flavoured with truffle essence. Also prepare some Madeira-flavoured aspic jelly. Place the chilled pieces of pheasant on a rack and pour the chaud-froid sauce over them twice, refrigerating between the 2 applications. Prepare various ingredients for a garnish; for example, thinly sliced pieces of truffle cut into fancy shapes, tarragon leaves, thinly sliced carrots and leeks, and pieces of hard-boiled (hard-cooked) egg white. Coat each item in aspic before arranging them on the joints of pheasant. Finally, coat the pheasant with the remaining aspic and place in the refrigerator to set. To serve, arrange on a serving dish garnished with chopped aspic or slices of aspic. Alternatively, arrange in a glass bowl and coat the entire arrangement with clear seasoned aspic.

Hot Pheasant Dishes

casserole of pheasant

Brown a trussed pheasant in 25 g (1 oz, 2 tablespoons) butter in a flameproof casserole. Cover and continue to cook gently for 45 minutes. Add some Cognac (or other brandy) and 2 tablespoons boiling water or stock. Season with salt and pepper. Cook for a further 5–10 minutes. Cut the pheasant into joints and serve with, for example, puréed celery.

Alternatively, halfway through the cooking time add 12 mushroom caps and some small shaped potato pieces to the casserole. Then deglaze with cream, reducing the sauce by half.

A third method is to add 250 ml (8 fl oz, 1 cup) single (light) cream to the casserole two-thirds of the way through the cooking time, basting the pheasant frequently with the cream. Just before serving, add a squeeze of lemon juice.

grilled pheasant à l'américaine

This recipe is particularly suitable for young pheasants. Split the pheasant along the back and flatten it gently. Season with salt and pepper, then fry in butter on both sides until the flesh is firm. Coat both sides with freshly made breadcrumbs seasoned with a large pinch of cayenne. Grill (broil) the pheasant slowly. Place on a dish and cover with grilled bacon rashers (slices). Garnish with grilled tomatoes and mushrooms, bunches of watercress and potato crisps (chips) or game chips. Serve with maître d'hôtel butter.

pheasant à la douro

Stuff the bird with boiled and peeled chestnuts, foie gras and prepared truffles. Tie, truss and bard the pheasant and brown in butter in a flameproof casserole. Add a few rashers (slices) of streaky bacon and 325 ml (11 fl oz, 1⅓ cups) white port. Season with salt and pepper, cover and cook over a very low heat for about 50 minutes.

pheasant à la géorgienne

Clean, bard and truss a young or hen pheasant. Place it in a saucepan with about 30 shelled walnuts. Add the juice of 3 oranges and 675 g (1½ lb) grapes, crushed and strained. Add 175 ml (6 fl oz, ¾ cup) Madeira or Malmsey and an equal quantity of very strong strained green tea. Then add 40 g (1½ oz, 3 tablespoons) butter. Season with salt and pepper. Cover the saucepan, bring to the boil, then reduce the heat and simmer for 45 minutes. Drain, untruss and discard the barding. Cook the pheasant in a preheated oven at 230°C (450°F, gas 8) for 15–20 minutes until brown. Place it on a serving dish with the walnuts arranged around it and pour over the reduced, strained cooking liquid or brown veal gravy.

pheasant à la normande

Brown the pheasant in butter in a flameproof casserole. Peel and slice 4 firm apples and fry quickly in butter. Place them in the bottom of the casserole with the pheasant on top. Cover and cook in a preheated oven at 240°C (475°F, gas 9) for about 45 minutes. Five minutes before serving, pour 100 ml (4 fl oz, 7 tablespoons) double (heavy) cream and 1 tablespoon Calvados over the pheasant. Untruss, carve into joints and serve very hot with the apples.

pheasant with port

Cut 2 young pheasants, preferably hens, into 4 or 6 pieces each. Season with salt and pepper and brown in 50 g (2 oz, ¼ cup) butter in a frying pan. Soften 4 peeled, chopped shallots in 20 g (¾ oz,

1½ tablespoons) butter in a flameproof casserole. Add the pheasant pieces and 250 ml (8 fl oz, 1 cup) port. Cover and simmer for 20 minutes. Fry 300 g (11 oz, 3½ cups) chanterelle mushrooms in butter. Remove the pheasant pieces and deglaze the casserole with 250 ml (8 fl oz, 1 cup) double (heavy) cream. Add a little juice from the pan in which the chanterelles were cooked and boil down to reduce. Finish the sauce by gradually whisking in 65 g (2½ oz, 5 tablespoons) butter, cut into small pieces. Adjust the seasoning. Replace the pheasant pieces and the chanterelles in the hot sauce and allow to bubble for a few seconds. Arrange on a dish and serve with spätzle, Italian potato gnocchi or noodles tossed in butter.

pheasant with truffles

At least 24 hours before cooking, insert some large slices of prepared truffle under the skin of a pheasant. Make a forcemeat with 250 g (9 oz) diced truffles and 350 g (12 oz) fresh pork fat and use it to stuff the pheasant. Cook in a preheated oven at 220°C (425°F, gas 7) for 50–55 minutes or for 55–60 minutes on a spit. (The pheasant may also be fried rather than roasted.) Place it on a large croûton, arrange some balls of game forcemeat around it and serve with Périgueux sauce.

roast pheasant

Truss and bard a young pheasant, brush with melted butter and season with salt and pepper. Roast in a preheated oven at 240°C (475°F, gas 9) for 30–40 minutes, depending on the size of the bird, basting 2 or 3 times. Fry some croûtons until golden brown. Untruss the pheasant and remove the barding fat. Place it on top of the croûtons and keep warm. Deglaze the roasting tin (pan) with a little poultry stock and serve this gravy separately. (The pheasant can be stuffed with truffles before roasting and the croûtons can be spread with a small amount of forcemeat made with the minced liver of the pheasant.)

salmi of pheasant ◆

Pluck, draw, prepare and truss a young pheasant. Roast in a preheated oven at 240°C (475°F, gas 9) for only 20 minutes so that it is still rare. Set the roasting tin (pan) aside. Cut the pheasant into 6 pieces as follows: remove the legs; remove the wings, leaving sufficient white meat on the breast bone; cut the breast into 2 pieces, widthways. Trim each piece carefully and remove the skin. Place the portions of pheasant in a buttered sauté pan and add a dash of good quality Cognac. Season with pepper. Cover and keep warm.

Crush the bones of the carcass, the skin and trimmings, and brown briskly with 1 unpeeled garlic clove in the roasting tin in which the pheasant was roasted. Reduce the heat and add 3 finely chopped shallots; cover and sweat the shallots gently for 5 minutes, then spoon or pour off excess grease. Deglaze with a dash of Cognac and add 500 ml

(17 fl oz, 2 cups) good red wine. Season the mixture and add a bouquet garni. Cook the wine, uncovered, for a few minutes and then add a generous ladle of game stock. Simmer for 30 minutes, uncovered. Skim thoroughly. Strain the sauce through a chinois, pressing the mixture to extract as much of the juice as possible. Pour the liquor into a clean pan and bring back to simmering point. Correct the seasoning. Flavour the sauce with a little truffle juice and thicken with 50 g (2 oz, ¼ cup) foie gras pressed through a sieve and pour over the pheasant. Fry a few sliced button mushrooms in butter, add to the pheasant and heat through gently, but thoroughly. Garnish with a few slices of truffle. Serve with garlic croûtons.

sautéed pheasant

Cut a young tender pheasant (preferably a hen) into 4 or 6 pieces. Season with salt and pepper, brown in butter and continue to cook gently in an open pan. Arrange the pieces of pheasant on a warmed, covered serving dish. Deglaze the sauté pan with 4 tablespoons white wine and a little veal stock, reduce the sauce by half and add some butter. Pour the sauce over the pheasant and serve very hot.

slices of pheasant with orange juice

Remove the flesh from a pheasant. Make a sauce as follows. Crush and pound the carcass and place it in a saucepan with some veal stock and a bottle of flat champagne. Add salt and pepper, bring to the boil and leave over a low heat to reduce. Press through a fine sieve and return to the heat. Add the minced (ground) heart and liver; cook for another 10 minutes. Cut the pheasant flesh into long, thin slices and sauté these in butter for 10 minutes, adding a handful of chopped parsley, chervil and chives. Arrange the slices on a dish. Add the cooking juice from the pheasant to the sauce, together with the strained juice of an orange. Stir and pour the hot sauce over the slices of pheasant.

other recipes See *alsacienne, languedocienne, Périgueux, Sainte-Alliance.*

PHILIPPE A Parisian restaurant established in the 19th century in the Rue Montorgueil, near Les Halles, on the site of an old post house. It began as a modest public house, but when Magny was installed as head chef in 1842, followed by Pascal, ex-chef of the Jockey Club, in 1848, the Philippe became very fashionable. It was famous for entrecôte steaks, onion soup, Normandy sole and *matelote.* Its clientele was not as sophisticated as that of the neighbouring Rocher de Cancale, but people went to Philippe mainly to eat well. In the 1870s the Club des Grands Estomacs used to meet there and it is said that their Gargantuan meals could last as long as 18 hours!

PHYSALIS See *Cape gooseberry.*

PIC, ANDRÉ French chef (born Saint-Péray, 1893; died Valence, 1984). He began his career at the auberge Le Pin, the family inn near Valence, with his mother Sophie, who was herself a famous cook. He then became an apprentice chef at various houses in the Rhône Valley. In 1924 he returned to Le Pin, which became a renowned stopping place on the road to the Midi. In 1936 he opened a restaurant in Valence itself, and in 1939 it was awarded three stars in the Michelin Guide. André Pic, Alexandre Dumaine and Fernand Point were the three greatest French chefs in the period between the wars.

In the 1950s, however, Pic's health deteriorated and his son Jacques took over. Jacques began by reviving his father's great specialities: *poularde en vessie* (chicken in a bladder), crayfish gratin, Grignan truffle turnover and *boudin de brochet à la Richelieu* (made with pike) – in a style similar to that of Escoffier. His own creations include bass fillets with caviar, *cassolette* of crayfish with morel mushrooms, calves' kidneys with sorrel or mint and fishermen's salad with sherry.

PICARDY See *page 882.*

PICCALILLI An English pickle consisting of small florets of cauliflower, sliced gherkins, shallots and other vegetables cooked and preserved in a spicy mustard and vinegar sauce, flavoured with turmeric, which also gives a bright yellow colour. It may be strong or mild and is eaten with cold meats, particularly ham and roast pork.

PICCATA In France a small round veal escalope (scallop) cut from the noix or the *sousnoix* and fried in butter. Three *piccatas* per person is usually sufficient. It was originally an Italian dish, most often served with Marsala or lemon.

RECIPE

veal piccata with aubergines and tomatoes

Cut a fillet of veal weighing about 1.4 kg (3 lb) into 12 round slices (*piccatas*). Cut an aubergine (eggplant) into round slices and dust them with flour. Fry the piccatas in a frying pan in 50 g (2 oz, ¼ cup) clarified butter and drain them. Fry the aubergine slices in the same butter. Sauté 2 sliced white onions gently in a covered pan. Cut a sweet red (bell) pepper into strips and fry them in butter for about 15 minutes. Crush 450 g (1 lb) ripe tomatoes.

Arrange the piccatas on an ovenproof serving dish, alternating them with small strips of cooked ham and the aubergine slices. Garnish with the onions, the strips of red pepper and the tomatoes.

Salmi of pheasant, see page 879.

Picardy

The region of France formerly known as Picardy incorporates the Nord, which extends from the Belgian frontier to the Ile-de-France and from the North Sea coast to Champagne. The Nord-Picardy region is particularly rich in food resources. Corn, sugar beet and potatoes bring a fundamental robustness to the cuisine which makes full use of the seafood and high-quality livestock of the area. Beyond the clichés – beer and strong cheeses, mussels with chips – the cuisine of the Nord has a variety that is not widely recognized, with such original specialities as *caudière* (fish soup), *hochepot* (vegetable soup), *flamiche* (leek and cheese tart) and *cramique* (buns with raisins).

■ **Versatile vegetables** While vegetables, such as leeks, onions, turnips, cabbages, peas, green beans, spinach, carrots and potatoes, are fundamental ingredients, pink garlic, hop shoots (cooked in cream, to accompany fish), pumpkin and watercress contribute their individual flavours. Chicory is particularly popular – in salad with potatoes and beetroot; as a gratin with ham; or as a *chiffonnade* with cream. The description *à la flamande* is applied to dishes accompanied by cabbage, glazed carrots and turnips, steamed potatoes and salt pork.

■ **Excellent fish** With its great fishing harbours, the Nord supplies the whole of France with fish and the local cooking reflects the wealth of fish available. Herring is popular and there are also mackerel, hake, gurnard, skate and turbot. The dishes range from stuffed fish, through fish simmered in white wine or beer, to fish stew. Freshwater fish is not forgotten, notably used in the celebrated *waterzooï*, a stew with vegetables and herbs, cooked with butter and cream.

■ **Meat, poultry and game** Lamb from the salt marshes in the bay of the Somme is excellent and Picardy produces fine charcuterie, with andouilles and sausages, boudins and smoked ham, as well as such specialities as the smoked tongue of Valenciennes and the andouillettes of Cambrai. Poultry is distinguished by the turkeys of Licques.

Picardy is famous for its wildfowl. The reputation of the legendary Amiens duck pâté (now made with farmed duck) has been perpetuated by the Maison Degand, which was founded in Amiens in 1643. Madame de Sévigné extolled this dish in one of her letters: 'The bird lay as if in a casket, embalmed with peppers and herbs, the secret of which doubles the pleasure.' Another well-known speciality is mallard *à la picarde* (cooked in a casserole and garnished with apples sautéed with diced duck's liver), and traditional dishes make use of teal, thrushes and even bustard.

■ **Cheese, beer and cider**
Excellent cheeses, all having a strong flavour, are made in Picardy: Maroilles, Rollot, Guerbigny, Manicamp and Saint-Winocq. Daussade, on the other hand, is a cream cheese that is steeped in vinegar and flavoured with herbs.

Beer is the standard drink in the north and east of the region, whereas cider and perry are traditionally drunk in the west, together with *frénette*, made from the fermented leaves of the ash tree.

The beer from Nord is made with locally grown hops, which are fermented in cellars for two to seven days before being filtered and bottled. It is still the everyday drink and is often used in cooking.

■ **Pâtisserie** The pâtisserie is abundant: *rabottes* and *taliburs* are similar to the *douillons* of Normandy, and *gâteau battu* is much appreciated, so are the rice and prune tarts. The region boasts a very varied range of confectionery. Amiens macaroons, Arras caramels and gingerbread hearts, Berck chocolate shells and chiques, *mignonnettes sablées* from Péronne, and chocolate slices (*tuiles*), *gaillettes, briquettes* and *brindinettes* from Douai prove that, as A. de Croze wrote in *Les Plats régionaux de France*, 'of all French provinces, Picardy is possibly the one that has best preserved the old recipes of its popular dishes'.

Old Lille, with its Grand'Place, is a lively part of the town, where there are pleasant street cafés and beautiful 17th- and 18th-century buildings.

Cook in a preheated oven at 200–220°C (400–425°F, gas 6–7) for 5 minutes. Sprinkle with noisette butter and garnish with parsley just before serving.

PICHET An earthenware pitcher used in France for serving water, fruit juice, cider or carafe wine (but not good-quality wine). In restaurants, *vin au pichet* is an unbottled medium-quality wine served in large quantities.

A *pichet* is also an old measure for salt and liquids. Made of tin, with or without a lid, it is one of the most handsome regional utensils.

PICKLE A condiment consisting of vegetables or fruit (or a mixture of both) preserved in spiced vinegar. Of Indian origin, pickles are a milder version of the *achars* of Madras and Bombay. Pickles are sold in jars, sometimes arranged decoratively, but can also be made at home. They are served with cold meats, cheese and curries with aperitifs and in mixed hors d'oeuvre.

The vegetables used for pickling – cauliflower, cucumber, cabbage, marrow (squash) and courgettes (zucchini), mushrooms, small onions and unripe tomatoes – are sliced if necessary and soaked in brine or in cold water. They are then rinsed, put into jars and covered with spiced vinegar. They can also be cooked in vinegar with spices. Fruits (plums, cherries, apples, pears, peaches) are cut into small pieces and usually cooked for a short time so that they will soak up the vinegar. Eggs and walnuts can also be pickled. The best salt to use is coarse sea salt, as this gives the optimum flavour.

Malt, wine, cider or spirit vinegars may be used. The spices enhance the flavour and also act as preservatives. The classic formula is as follows: to 1 litre (1¾ pints, 4⅓ cups) vinegar, add a 5 cm (2 in) stick of cinnamon, 1 teaspoon cloves, 2 teaspoons fennel seeds, 1 teaspoon black pepper, 1 teaspoon mustard seeds (or 5 teaspoons whole pickling spice) and 2 or 3 bay leaves. Bring the mixture to the boil and then steep for 3 days. The vinegar is then strained and used either cold (for vegetables, which should remain crisp) or hot (for fruit, which should be a little softer). Mixed pickles may combine any number of vegetables, such as onion, cabbage, cucumber, green beans, carrots and green peppers. But some vegetables and fruits are pickled on their own; for example, beetroot (red beet) with dill, red cabbage with white wine vinegar, sweet (bell) peppers with thyme and bay leaf, lime with pepper and peaches with spices and lemon zest.

RECIPE

cauliflower and tomato pickle
Divide 2 medium-sized cauliflowers into florets and arrange them in layers in a terrine together with 675 g (1½ lb) firm tomatoes (quartered), 4 coarsely chopped onions and a chopped cucumber. Sprinkle each layer with an equal quantity of salt – a total of about 200 g (7 oz, 1 cup). Cover completely with cold water, place a sheet of foil over the top and leave in a cool place for 24 hours.

The next day place the vegetables in a strainer and rinse them thoroughly under running water to wash away the excess salt. Drain and place them in a large saucepan. Sprinkle with 1 teaspoon mustard powder, 1 teaspoon ground ginger and 1 teaspoon black pepper. Then add 250 g (9 oz, 1½ cups, firmly packed) brown sugar. Pour in 750 ml (1¼ pints, 3¼ cups) white wine vinegar and bring to the boil over a medium heat, stirring frequently. Then simmer for 15–20 minutes, continuing to stir, until the vegetables are just beginning to soften but are still firm when pricked with the tip of a knife.

Remove the pan from the heat, put the vegetables in clean jars and completely cover with vinegar. The proportions given will make 3 kg (6½ lb) pickle. The jars should be stored in a cool, dry place away from the light.

PICKLED Describing pork or beef that has been preserved by steeping in brine to which saltpetre has been added, and then boiled. For recipes using pickled tongue, see *écarlate*.

The word is also used to describe vegetables and fruit preserved in brine or vinegar.

PICNIC 'An informal meal in which everyone pays his share or brings his own dish,' according to the Littré dictionary. That was the original meaning of the word, which is probably of French origin (the French *piquer* means to pick at food; *nique* means something small of no value). The word was accepted by the Académie française in 1740 and thereafter became a universally accepted word in many languages.

From the informal picnic, the outdoor feast developed. In Victorian Britain picnics may not have been as formal as country-house dinners, but they were often elaborate affairs. Weekend shooting parties and sporting events were occasions for grand picnics, with extensive menus and elaborate presentation. Comparatively formal picnics are still served on some occasions, notably during the evening intervals at the Glyndebourne opera festival and at Henley regatta. Traditional fare, such as smoked salmon sandwiches, raised pies, dressed salmon, chicken chaud-froid and strawberries and cream, are often complemented by contemporary alternatives.

The popular family picnic is still an informal meal in the open air; the dishes are usually cold and easy to carry: for example, hard-boiled (hard-cooked) eggs, salads, pâtés, cold meats, sandwiches, cheeses, tarts and fruit. These days, however, with the aid of vacuum flasks, camping stoves and portable barbecues, picnics can take on whole new dimensions with as much hot food as cold on the menu!

PICODON An AOP goat's-milk cheese (45% fat content) with a soft centre and a fine natural crust that is bluish, golden or reddish, depending on the ripeness of the cheese. Picodon – the name comes from the Languedocian word *pico* (to sting) – has a strong or nutty flavour. It is produced in several regions and is in season between May and December. Picodon de Dieulefit (in Dauphiné) is 6–7 cm (2½ in) in diameter and 2–3 cm (¾–1¼ in) thick; it is steeped in white wine. Picodon de Saint-Agrève (in Langue-doc) is slightly larger and has a less pronounced flavour. Picodon de Valréas is eaten when half-ripe.

PICON Very similar to Cabrales, but reputed by some to be even better, this DOP blue cheese from Cantabria in northern Spain may be made with cow's, ewe's or goat's milk. It has a sharply piquant flavour with a lingering complexity.

PICPOUL DE PINET A white wine, one of the named *crus* from the Coteaux du Languedoc, made exclusively from the Picpoul Blanc grape, which is attracting a lot of interest.

PIE The French have adopted the English word for the classic British and American pies. A pie consists of a filling topped with a crust and baked. Pastry is the usual crust, and the filling can be savoury or sweet. The name is said to originate from magpie, the bird notorious for collecting items and hiding them in its nest, reflecting the idea that a mixture of ingredients could be combined under the pie crust.

Confusion often arises over the terms pie and tart. Traditionally, the British pie is made in a deep dish and has a pastry lid, but not a pastry base. The tradi-tional pie dish has a wide rim on which to place a strip of pastry to which the top crust can be attached once the filling is in place. A pie funnel, placed in the middle of the dish to support the pastry lid once the filling has cooked and reduced, allows steam to escape during cooking.

Raised pies are served cold. They consist of pastry completely enclosing a savoury filling, and they stand alone without a dish or container. Hot water crust pastry is used for the crust. Small pies are traditionally raised by hand, by shaping a ball of pastry over the fist, then placing the filling in the hollow and attach-ing a lid. Pork is a classic filling for small raised pies. Alternatively, the pastry crust may be shaped over jam jars, placed upside down, and it is left until set before removing and filling. Pie moulds are used to shape small or large pies and many are very elabo-rate. The sides of the mould are removed towards the end of baking. The tops of raised pies are garnished with pastry trimmings, and a hole is left to allow steam to escape. Aspic is poured into the cooled pie and left to set before serving. Game and pork are typ-ical fillings for large raised pies; in Scotland, small raised pies are filled with lamb in gravy.

A British tart is shallow, baked on a tart plate, which is deeper than a standard dinner plate, with a pastry base and a lid. When a lattice of pastry strips replaces the lid, the tart becomes a lattice tart. British tarts are usually sweet. An apple tart, or plate tart, dif-fers from an apple pie in being shallow and having a pastry base. The French open tart, with a pastry base but no lid, is now accepted as a tart, particularly when the filling is cooked; individual jam tarts or strawberry tarts are traditionally open. In Britain the word flan is often used to describe tarts that consist of a baked pastry case that is filled when cooled. American pies can have a bottom crust but no lid, and they would generally be known as tarts in Britain.

A pie can also have a mashed potato topping, as in shepherd's pie or fish pie.

Savoury pies are usually served as a main course. The best known are chicken pie, steak and kidney pie, game pie, and pork and apple pie. Buffalo and beer pie (made with buffalo meat, vegetables, spices and beer), oyster pie, clam pie and salmon pie are American specialities.

The classic dessert pies are apple pie and plum pie, but almost any stone (pit) fruit can be used as well as pears, blackcurrants, redcurrants, blackber-ries, gooseberries and rhubarb. American specialities include pecan pie, pumpkin pie and blueberry pie. These dessert pies are traditionally served with cus-tard or cream.

RECIPES

British-style apple pie
Make shortcrust (basic pie) pastry using 225 g (8 oz, 2 cups) plain (all-purpose) flour and 100 g (4 oz, ½ cup) butter. Instead of all butter, half white veg-etable fat (shortening) and half butter can be used. Roll out a small portion of pastry into a strip and press this on to the dampened rim of a deep pie dish. Peel, core and slice 900 g (2 lb) cooking apples, such as Bramleys, and place them in the dish, adding 100 g (4 oz, ½ cup) sugar between the layers. Dis-tribute 6 whole cloves among the layers of apple.

Roll out the remaining pastry and use to cover the top of the pie, dampening the pastry rim with water and pressing the edge firmly to seal in the fruit. Make several slits or a hole in the middle of the pie and decorate the top with pastry trimmings. Brush with milk and bake in a preheated oven at 200°C (400°F, gas 6) for 15 minutes. Reduce the oven temperature to 180°C (350°F, gas 4) and cook for a further 30 minutes, until the top of the pie is browned. Sprinkle with caster (superfine) sugar and cool slightly before serving.

chicken pie
Cut a raw chicken weighing about 1.25 kg (2¾ lb) into pieces. Sprinkle the pieces with 100 g (4 oz, ⅔ cup) finely chopped onions and shallots, 150 g (5 oz, 1¾ cups) sliced mushrooms and some chopped parsley. Season with salt and pepper. Line a buttered pie dish with 200 g (7 oz) very thin slices of veal seasoned with salt and pepper. Place the chicken in the dish, first the thighs, then the wings and finally the breasts. Cover with 150 g (5 oz) bacon cut into very thin rashers (slices). Add 4 hard-boiled (hard-cooked) egg yolks cut in half.

Pour in some chicken stock to three-quarters fill the dish.

Press a strip of puff pastry around the rim of the pie dish, brush with water, then cover the whole dish with a layer of pastry. Seal the edges, then flute with the back of a knife. Brush the whole surface with beaten egg and make a hole in the centre. Bake for 1½ hours in a preheated oven at 190°C (375°F, gas 5). Just before serving, pour 2–3 tablespoons concentrated chicken stock into the pie.

French-style double-crust apple pie

Rub 100 g (4 oz, ½ cup) butter into 200 g (7 oz, 1¾ cups) plain (all-purpose) flour. Add ½ teaspoon salt and gradually add about 4 tablespoons water. Knead to form a soft ball of dough that does not stick to the bowl. Allow the pastry to rest in a cool place for at least 20 minutes, then divide it into 2 unequal pieces.

Butter a china manqué mould or deep ovenproof dish. Roll out the larger piece of dough and line the bottom and the sides of the mould. Mix 2 heaped tablespoons plain flour, 2 heaped tablespoons soft brown sugar, a pinch of vanilla powder, ½ teaspoon ground cinnamon and a pinch of grated nutmeg. Sprinkle half of this mixture over the pastry. Peel 800 g (1¾ lb) pippin (eating) apples, cut into quarters, then into slices. Arrange these on the pastry, forming a dome in the centre. Add a dash of lemon juice and sprinkle with the remaining spice mixture. Roll out the second piece of pastry and cover the pie, sealing the edges with beaten egg. Make an opening in the centre. Glaze the top with the beaten egg. Put in a preheated oven at 230°C (450°F, gas 8). After 10 minutes, reduce the oven temperature to 180°C (350°F, gas 4), glaze again with the egg and return to the oven. It may be glazed again a third time if desired. Cook for a total of 50 minutes. Serve on its own, with crème fraîche, blackberry coulis or some ice cream.

pear pie

Peel and core 4 pears, cut into slices and sprinkle with lemon juice. Arrange the pear slices in a buttered pie dish and sprinkle with 2 tablespoons caster (superfine) sugar; a little ground cinnamon may also be added. Dot with 25 g (1 oz, 2 tablespoons) butter.

Prepare some shortcrust (basic pie) pastry (see *short pastry*) and put a border around the rim of the dish, brush it with beaten egg and cover the dish with a lid of pastry. Press down to seal the edges, then crimp between finger and thumb, brush with beaten egg and bake in a preheated oven at 180°C (350°F, gas 4) for 1 hour. When cooked, dust with sugar and serve very hot.

other recipes See *pâté, rhubarb*.

PIÈCE MONTÉE A large ornamental item of pâtisserie, formerly very popular, used to decorate the table at a banquet or party. It usually reflects the theme of the other decorations. Such set pieces are much rarer today than in the past, often now being replaced by arrangements of flowers, especially on sideboards. In France the *pièce montée* is still popular for a wedding or baptism and displays the artistic skills of the confectionery trade.

The *pièce montée* can be made of various ingredients: layers of sponge cake or Genoese sponge; nougat; shaped or blown sugar; flowers, ribbons and leaves made out of drawn or twisted sugar; baskets of woven sugar; inedible decorative sugarwork; crests and pompons of spun sugar; crisp petits fours; crystallized (candied) fruit; dragées; items of almond paste; and chocolate shavings. Classic *pièces montées à la française* are constructed on a metal framework with a central pivot that enables trays to be stacked one above the other in tiers. *Pièces montées à l'espagnole*, on the other hand, consist of separate trays of confectionery arranged in layers one on top of the other, each supported by pillars resting on the outer edges of the tray beneath. Whichever style is chosen, the confectioner may give free rein to his or her imagination, working on various subjects, some of which have become standard since the great era of *pièces montées* when Carême reigned supreme: the harp, the lyre, the globe, the Chinese pagoda, the horn of plenty, the ship, the chapel, the bandstand, the waterfall, the Louis XV carriage, the dolphin on the rock, the harvester's basket, the temple and the cart. Today a simple and popular type of *pièce montée* is the *croquembouche* made of profiteroles filled with sweetened cream, glazed with sugar and arranged on top of one another with glazed fruit.

Pièces montées were very popular in the Middle Ages, when they were very spectacular, of gigantic proportions and often made in the shape of an animal, such as the peacock. But it was in the 18th and 19th centuries that the *pièces montées* reached their greatest heights, depicting allegorical subjects (for which Chiboust and Frascati were famous) and pastoral or historic subjects, such as 'The Great St Bernard Pass' or 'The Episode of the Lodi Bridge'. However, these sumptuous items were rarely edible, and their function was first and foremost a decorative one. Today's *pièces montées* are more modest but combine pleasure to the eye with pleasure to the taste.

One 'literary' set piece has remained famous. It was conceived by Flaubert for the wedding reception of Madame Bovary: 'At the base was a piece of blue cardboard representing a temple with porticoes, colonnades and stucco statuettes all around in tiny niches, embellished with gold stars. Above this, on the second tier, stood a castle keep of Savoy cake, surrounded by tiny fortifications made out of angelica, almonds, currants and pieces of orange. Finally, on the top tier, was nothing less than a verdant meadow where there were rocks, pools made of jam and boats made out of nutshells. The tiny figure of Cupid could be seen, playing on a chocolate swing, the posts of which were tipped with two real rosebuds.'

PIEDMONT A quality wine-producing region in northern Italy making intense, full-bodied wines from the renowned Nebbiolo grape variety including DOCG Barolo, Babaresco and Gattinara. DOC wines includes those produced from Barbera, the lighter style Dolcetto, Bonarda, Cortese and Moscato. Sparkling wines are also produced, notably Moscato d'Asti – sweet, aromatic and sometimes with a delicate spritz, and Asti or Asti Spumante, produced through natural bottle or tank fermentation and ideal drunk with desserts.

PIEDS ET PAQUETS A speciality of Provence, consisting of stuffed sheep's tripe tied up to form small packets (*paquets*) and simmered in white wine and stock with bacon and sheep's trotters or feet (*pieds*). Sometimes called *pieds-paquets* or *pieds-en-paquets*, the dish apparently originated in the Restaurant de la Pomme, on the outskirts of Marseille.

RECIPE

pieds et paquets de la pomme

Clean a sheep's tripe and cut it into 8–10 cm (3–4 in) pieces. Make a slit in one corner of each piece. In the middle of each place a spoonful of a minced (ground) mixture of 100 g (4 oz) raw ham, 100 g (4 oz) lamb's mesentery, a garlic clove and a bunch of parsley. Roll each piece of tripe around the stuffing and form a packet (*paquet*) by pushing one corner of skin into the slit; tie if necessary.

Clean, blanch and singe some sheep's trotters (*pieds*). In a flameproof casserole place 100 g (4 oz, ¾ cup) diced bacon, 1 leek and a thinly sliced onion. Brown them, then add a sliced carrot and 2 tomatoes, peeled, seeded and crushed. Cover with 500 ml (17 fl oz, 2 cups) white wine and 2 litres (3½ pints, 9 cups) meat stock, then add the trotters and the 'packets'. Add a bouquet garni, 2 crushed garlic cloves, salt, pepper and 2 cloves. Cover and seal the lid with a flour-and-water paste. Simmer very gently for 6–7 hours.

Open the casserole, remove the 'packets' (untie them if necessary) and remove the bones from the trotters. Skim off excess fat from the stock and reduce to the desired consistency by simmering with the lid off until ready to serve.

PIÉMONTAISE, À LA Describing various dishes that incorporate a risotto, sometimes accompanied by white Piedmont truffles. Arranged in a variety of ways – in darioles, in timbale moulds or as *coquettes* – the risotto is used to garnish poultry, meat and fish. The term *à la piémontaise* also refers to dishes of the Piedmont region of northern Italy that do not necessarily feature truffles, such as polenta, ravioli and macaroni. Pastries *à la piémontaise* are usually based on hazelnuts, another famous product of Piedmont.

RECIPES

artichoke hearts à la piémontaise

Cook some artichoke hearts in butter. Prepare a risotto *à la piémontaise* and garnish each artichoke heart with a dome of 2 tablespoons risotto. Sprinkle with grated Parmesan cheese and a little melted butter and brown in a very hot oven. Serve with tomato sauce.

attereaux à la piémontaise

Prepare some polenta; season with salt and pepper. Spread it over a lightly oiled square baking sheet and allow to cool completely. Cut into 4 cm (1½ in) squares and thread on to skewers. Coat in breadcrumbs and deep-fry in hot oil at 175–180°C (347–356°F) until brown. Drain on paper towels and arrange on a dish garnished with fried parsley. Serve with a well-reduced tomato sauce.

fillets of mackerel à la piémontaise

Prepare a risotto* *à la piémontaise* using 200 g (7 oz, 1 cup) rice. Fillet 4 mackerel; wash and pat them dry with a clean cloth or paper towels, then dip in breadcrumbs and fry in butter on both sides. Butter a long serving dish, cover with the risotto and arrange the fillets on top. Garnish with quarters of lemon. Serve with a slightly thickened tomato sauce.

piémontaise sauce

(from Carême's recipe) Finely dice 2 large onions and brown in clarified butter. Strain, then cook in a good stock, skimming off all the fat. Blend in enough béchamel sauce to accompany an entrée, together with 225 g (8 oz, 2 cups) diced Piedmont truffles and 2 tablespoons pine nuts (kernels). After the sauce has boiled for a short while, add a little chicken glaze, a little garlic butter and the juice of 1 lemon. (The quantity of truffles can be reduced without affecting the recipe.)

spring chickens à la piémontaise

Prepare a risotto* *à la piémontaise*, using 250 g (9 oz, 2¼ cups) rice. Chop 75 g (3 oz) onions, soften in butter, then mix with 400 g (14 oz, 2 cups) finely minced (ground) sausagemeat and the minced livers of 4 spring chickens (poussins). Season the chickens with salt and pepper, stuff with the forcemeat, truss, and cook in a casserole containing 50 g (2 oz, ¼ cup) butter in a preheated oven at 180°C (350°F, gas 4) for about 50 minutes. Place the risotto in a ring on a heated serving dish, arrange the chickens in the centre and keep warm. Deglaze the casserole with 300 ml (½ pint, 1¼ cups) white wine and 3 tablespoons tomato purée (paste). Reduce by half, thicken with 1 tablespoon beurre manié, add 2 tablespoons freshly chopped parsley and pour this sauce over the chickens.

veal chops à la piémontaise

Season 4 veal chops with salt and pepper; dip them in flour, beaten egg and, finally, fresh breadcrumbs mixed with grated Parmesan cheese – 40 g (1½ oz,

⅓ cup) Parmesan to 50 g (2 oz, 1 cup) bread-crumbs. Cook gently in 40 g (1½ oz, 3 tablespoons) clarified butter. Serve with squares of risotto* *à la piémontaise*, prepared with 200 g (7 oz, 1 cup) rice, and a well-reduced tomato sauce.

other recipes See *border (savoury rings), capsicum (sweet peppers), chicken, risotto, timbale, tomato.*

PIERRE-QUI-VIRE

A soft cow's-milk cheese (45% fat content) from Burgundy with a reddish, washed crust. Pierre-qui-Vire is a disc, 10 cm (4 in) in diameter and 2.5 cm (1 in) thick, weighing 200 g (7 oz). Made by the monks of the abbey of the same name, it has a taste similar to Époisses. Badly formed cheeses are reshaped and flavoured with *fines herbes* to make Boulette de la Pierre-qui-Vire.

PIG See *pork.*

PIGEON

A domesticated or wild bird of which several species are eaten as poultry or game. Young pigeons (squabs; *pigeonneaux* in French) are particularly tender and are usually roasted. The rock dove, which still lives in the wild in Brittany, Provence and in mountainous regions of southern Europe, is the ancestor of all the varieties of domestic pigeon. The most common wild pigeon in France is the wood pigeon or ring dove. Its flesh is denser and more highly flavoured than the domestic pigeon, although both are prepared in the same way. Most recipes for woodcock are applicable to pigeons. Casseroles, stews, ballotines, pâtés and ragoûts are suitable for older birds, whereas younger and more tender birds are good roasted, grilled (broiled), *à la crapaudine*, sautéed and *en papillotes*. It is customary to leave the liver inside when dressing the bird since pigeon's liver does not contain bile. Otherwise it is drawn and prepared like other poultry. Young pigeons are only very lightly barded, if at all, whereas it is essential for adult birds.

Pigeon has been a popular dish since the Middle Ages and was much in vogue during the reign of Louis XIV, especially served with peas. The French cook La Varenne gives a recipe for pigeon and green-pea stew in which the birds are poached in stock and then garnished with lettuce, peas and pieces of bacon.

RECIPES

dressing roasting pigeons

To pluck the birds more easily, chill for a few hours in the refrigerator: the flesh will tighten and there will be less danger of tearing. Pluck each bird beginning with the large wing feathers, then the tail and proceed upwards to finish at the head. Singe and draw. Place a thin rasher (slice) of bacon on the back and breast of the bird. Truss by folding the head down between the wings.

pigeon compote

Season 4 pigeons with salt and pepper, inside and out, then place 3–4 juniper berries and 1 tablespoon marc brandy in each bird. Turn the birds over so that the brandy is evenly distributed inside. Put a thin strip of bacon over the breast and truss. Brown the pigeons in a flameproof casserole containing 50 g (2 oz, ¼ cup) butter, then remove, drain and keep warm.

In the same butter, brown 20 small (pearl) onions and 100 g (4 oz, ⅔ cup) smoked streaky bacon, cut into small pieces. Then add 150 g (5 oz, 1⅔ cups) thinly sliced mushrooms. When these have turned a good golden colour, add a bouquet garni, 200 ml (7 fl oz, ¾ cup) white wine and the same quantity of chicken stock. Reduce by two-thirds, return the pigeons to the casserole, cover and bring to the boil. Then cook in a preheated oven at 230°C (450°F, gas 8) for 30 minutes. Remove the bouquet garni, untie the pigeons, arrange them on a heated serving dish and spoon the cooking liquid over.

pigeons à la niçoise ♦

Peel 18 small pickling (pearl) onions. Put them in a flameproof casserole with 20 g (¾ oz, 1½ tablespoons) butter. Season with salt and pepper. Add 3 tablespoons water, cover and cook for 20 minutes over a moderate heat. Melt 40 g (1½ oz, 3 tablespoons) butter in a braising pan, add 6 pigeons, turning them over so they brown on all sides. Add 1 crumbled bay leaf and 2 pinches of winter savory. Pour over 100 ml (4 fl oz, 7 tablespoons) dry white wine and incorporate the drained onions. Simmer for 15 minutes. Add 200 g (7 oz) small black olives and cook for another 5–10 minutes. Steam 1 kg (2¼ lb) sugarsnap (snow) peas. Put them in a serving dish and arrange the pigeons on top, garnished with the olives, onions and a few fresh bay leaves and sprigs of savory.

roast pigeons, shallot vinegar

Debone 2 pigeons, each weighing about 575 g (1¼ lb). In a medium saucepan, prepare a stock with the carcasses, 1 carrot and 2 onions cut into slices, a bouquet garni, 150 ml (¼ pint, ⅔ cup) white wine, salt and pepper. Add just enough water to cover and cook for 30 minutes. Strain the stock and boil down to reduce by a third to a half; the exact volume of stock will depend on the size of the pan and volume of water added.

Fry the pieces of pigeon in 1 tablespoon of olive oil, turning occasionally, until just cooked; deglaze with 2 tablespoons shallot vinegar, then add the pigeon stock.

Boil 800 g (1¾ lb) potatoes in their skins. Peel them, then mash with a fork, adding 100 g (4 oz, ½ cup) butter and 2 teaspoons ground cumin. Use two spoons to scoop the potatoes into quenelle shapes. Arrange the pieces of pigeon on 4 plates, surround with the quenelles and pour over the sauce.

squab à la minute

Split the bird in half lenghways. Remove the small bones, gently flatten the 2 halves and fry quickly in butter. When the squab is almost cooked, add 1 tablespoon chopped onion lightly fried in butter. Finish cooking. Arrange the squab on a dish and keep warm. Dilute the pan juices with a dash of brandy, thicken with a little dissolved meat essence and add 1½ teaspoons chopped parsley. Pour the sauce over the bird.

squabs en papillotes

Take 4 squabs and split each in half lengthways. Remove as many bones as possible, especially the breastbone. Season each half with salt and pepper, and fry in a casserole containing 50 g (2 oz, ¼ cup) butter to seal them. Prepare a duxelles* from 40 g (1½ oz, ½ cup) mushrooms and 200 g (7 oz, 1¼ cups) raw unsmoked ham. Cut out 8 heart-shaped pieces of greaseproof (wax) paper, oil each piece lightly on one side and spread with the duxelles. Place a pigeon half on each and fold over the edges of the papillotes to seal. Cook in a preheated oven at 230°C (450°F, gas 8) until the paper cases have swollen and browned (about 15 minutes).

squabs with peas

Season 4 squabs with salt and pepper inside and out. Truss, then brown on all sides in 50 g (2 oz, ¼ cup) butter in a flameproof casserole. Remove and drain. Dice 150 g (5 oz, ¾ cup) slightly salted streaky bacon, scald for 5 minutes in boiling water, then drain and cool. Peel 12 small (pearl) onions. Brown the bacon and onions in the butter in which the pigeons were cooked, then, without removing them, deglaze the casserole with 175 g (6 fl oz, ¾ cup) white wine and 175 ml (6 fl oz, ¾ cup) stock. Reduce by half.

Return the pigeons to the casserole and add 800 g (1¾ lb, 3½ cups) fresh peas, shelled, 1 lettuce heart and a bouquet garni. Season with salt and pepper, cover and cook in a preheated oven at 220°C (425°F, gas 7) gently for about 30 minutes. Adjust the seasoning, remove the bouquet garni and serve from the casserole. The peas may be flavoured with savory if wished.

stuffed pigeons with asparagus tips

Starting at the backbone, bone 4 pigeons, each weighing about 400 g (14 oz). Prepare a forcemeat with 250 g (9 oz) noix of veal, 250 g (9 oz) fat bacon, 250 g (9 oz) calves' sweetbreads and 250 g (9 oz) foie gras. Chop all these ingredients very finely and add 25 g (1 oz, ¼ cup) broken truffle pieces and 1 whole egg. Blend together. Stuff the pigeons and then wrap each in a caul (caul fat), which will prevent the skin from drying while they are cooked.

Place the pigeons in a flameproof casserole, cover and cook over a gentle heat for about 15 minutes. Remove the pigeons, deglaze the casserole with 4 tablespoons vermouth and reduce over a brisk

heat before pouring the sauce over the pigeons.

Serve with a gratin of asparagus tips prepared as follows: boil 32 asparagus tips in plenty of salted water, spread on a buttered gratin dish, cover with 100 ml (4 fl oz, 7 tablespoons) crème fraîche blended with 1 beaten egg yolk and brown under the grill (broiler).

PIGEON PEA Also known as Angola pea and cajan. A pulse vegetable consisting of pale green to dark red seeds enclosed in long pods; the shrub itself is native to Asia but is also cultivated in Africa and the West Indies. The peas are used either fresh or dried, in purées or as a base for sauces. A type of flour made from the peas is used to prepare fritters and cakes.

PIGOUILLE A soft cheese from Poitou made from sheep's milk, goat's milk or cow's milk (45% fat content), lightly crusted with mould. Pigouille is a small, round cheese weighing about 250 g (9 oz). It has a mild, creamy flavour, like Caillebotte. The word *pigouille* originally referred to the long pole used to steer the flat-bottomed boats of the Poitou marshes.

PIKE *brochet* A freshwater fish with a long head and strong jaws equipped with hundreds of small sharp teeth. The body is long and thin, marbled with green or brown, and the belly is silvery. Nicknamed *grand loup d'eau* (great water wolf) in the Middle Ages because of its voracious nature, pike was much appreciated at the royal table and was reared in the Louvre fish ponds. It measures from 40 cm (16 in) – the minimum size below which it is not allowed to be fished – to 70 cm (28 in); exceptional fish may reach up to 1.5 m (5 ft) and weigh up to 25 kg (55 lb) but, over 4 kg (9 lb), the flesh is good only for quenelles and mousses.

In addition to the traditional preparation *au beurre blanc*, pike is prepared with white wine, *à la juive* or roasted. At spawning time the roe and eggs are slightly toxic (but they are eaten in some countries, especially Romania). River pike are better than those from ponds.

RECIPES

pike au beurre blanc

Gut (clean) the pike, clean it carefully and cut off the fins and tail. Prepare a court-bouillon in a fish kettle and boil for about 30 minutes. Add the pike. As soon as the court-bouillon starts to boil again, reduce the temperature to keep it at a barely perceptible simmer. After 12–20 minutes remove the fish kettle from the heat.

Meanwhile, prepare the *beurre blanc*: boil down some vinegar containing 2–3 chopped shallots and freshly ground pepper (one turn of the pepper mill); when it has reduced by half remove from the

Pigeons à la niçoise, see page 887.

heat. Soften a large piece of butter – about 225 g (8 oz, 1 cup) to 2 tablespoons reduced vinegar – on a plate using a spatula and incorporate it gradually into the vinegar, beating vigorously with a whisk. It will turn frothy without becoming liquid and will acquire its characteristic whiteness. Drain the pike, arrange on a long dish and coat with the *beurre blanc*, adding fresh sprigs of parsley. Alternatively, serve the *beurre blanc* separately in a sauceboat.

• *Alternative recipe* Wash the pike in plenty of water, sprinkle with fine salt and leave for about 15 minutes. Wash again and place in the fish kettle, surrounded with parsley, 2 sliced onions, 2 quartered shallots, 2 garlic cloves, 8–20 chives or the green part of a leek, a sprig of fresh thyme, a bay leaf and a few slices of carrot; season with salt and pepper. Cover with sprigs of parsley and add enough dry white wine to cover the whole fish. Leave to marinate for 1 hour. About 35 minutes before serving, place the fish kettle over a high heat; as soon as it begins to bubble, reduce the heat and simmer as gently as possible.

While it is cooking, prepare a *beurre blanc* as in the first recipe, using 250 g (9 oz, 1 cup) slightly salted butter. Keep the *beurre blanc* warm in a bain marie and do not allow to boil. Trim the pike, drain for a few seconds on a cloth and place on a long, very hot dish. Using the blade of a knife, quickly slit the middle of the side, from the head to the tail, following the lateral line. Detach and remove the main bone, holding the head in the left hand, then reshape the fish. Quickly stir the *beurre blanc* with a spatula to mix the shallots in well, pour over the pike and serve.

pike au bleu

This method is used mostly for cooking young or very small pike. Cook the fish in a court-bouillon prepared as for trout *au bleu*. Drain, place on a napkin and garnish with fresh parsley. Serve with melted butter or with one of the sauces recommended for poached fish. To accompany the fish serve boiled potatoes, various purées (celery, turnip, onion), leaf spinach or broccoli.

pike du meunier

Scale, beard, gut (clean), remove the heads from, and wash 3 young pike, each weighing 675–800 g (1½–1¾ lb). Cut into pieces and season; dip in milk and then flour. Cook gently in a sauté pan with 200 g (7 oz, ¾ cup) butter and 1 tablespoon oil. Separately, soften 4 medium chopped onions in butter. When the pieces of pike are lightly coloured, add the onions and 3 tablespoons very good white wine vinegar. Reduce by half. Season with salt and pepper and serve each portion with 2 croûtons cooked in butter.

pike in vinegar

Take a pike weighing about 1.5 kg (3 lb). Remove the fillets and season with salt and pepper, then dust with flour. Cook them *à la meunière*, but then deglaze with white wine vinegar; reduce, add 3 tablespoons fresh double (heavy) cream, and bind with a little béchamel. Pour the sauce over the fillets. Serve with a sprinkling of chopped parsley.

terrine of pike with Nantua sauce

Cut the fillets from a pike weighing about 1.5 kg (3¼ lb) and remove the skin. Cut the fillets from the belly into narrow strips, then into dice.

Prepare a frangipane by mixing 100 g (4 oz, 1 cup) plain (all-purpose) flour, 40 g (1½ oz, 3 tablespoons) butter and 3 egg yolks with 200 ml (7 fl oz, ¾ cup) hot milk. Work this mixture over the heat, until the dough collects in a ball around the spatula. Then spread the frangipane on a buttered plate and allow to cool.

Clean and finely chop 100 g (4 oz, 1⅓ cups) button mushrooms and chop 4 or 5 shallots.

Brown the diced pike in butter in a frying pan, then add the mushrooms and brown; finally add the shallots, but do not allow them to change colour. Remove all ingredients with a skimming spoon and pour 100 ml (4 fl oz, 7 tablespoons) good dry white wine into the frying pan, stir with a spatula to deglaze, then replace the ingredients and add 25 g (1 oz, ½ cup) chopped parsley. Remove from the heat.

Pound or finely chop the remaining flesh of the pike (about 500 g, 18 oz); season liberally with salt and pepper. Add the cooled frangipane in small pieces, then 3 unwhisked egg whites. Mix well, then pass twice through the mincer (or chop finely in a food processor). Beat the mixture with 350 ml (12 fl oz, 1½ cups) double (heavy) cream and add the diced fish, mushrooms and shallots.

Generously butter a flameproof pâté dish and heap the mixture into it. Cover and place in a bain marie. Bring to the boil on top of the stove, then place in a preheated oven at 180°C (350°F, gas 4) and cook gently for about 1½ hours. The top of the terrine should turn pale gold, but not brown. Serve the terrine in the container in which it was cooked, with Nantua sauce.

other recipes See *godiveau, mousse (fish mousse), quenelle.*

PIKE-PERCH *sandre* A large fish of the perch family, living in rivers and lakes, which can reach a length of 1 m (39 in) and a weight of 15 kg (33 lb). Its back is greenish-grey, striped with dark bands; the gills and dorsal fins have hard spines, which are difficult to remove, as are the scales, which are light and tend to fly around and adhere to the hands when scraped. The delicate flesh is firm and white and has few bones; it is prepared in the same way as pike or perch. The pike-perch comes from central Europe; in France it is caught in the Doubs, the Saône and in the small lakes into which it has been introduced.

Smaller than the European pike-perch, the fish is called doré in Canada because of its golden scales. There are blue, green and yellow varieties, particularly appreciated by fishermen for their fighting spirit. It is cooked like perch or other firm-fleshed fish.

RECIPES

fillets of pike-perch with cabbage

Trim and clean a pike-perch weighing about 1.5 kg (3¼ lb). Remove the 2 fillets, trim and wash them, then cut each in half.

Prepare the flavourings for a court-bouillon: a carrot, a celery stick, 2 small white young onions, a shallot, a garlic clove, a bouquet garni with a sprig of tarragon, a sage leaf and the green part of a leek added, and a muslin (cheesecloth) bag containing 3 lightly crushed peppercorns, a clove, a star anise and 2 coriander seeds. Put all these ingredients in a large saucepan with 1½ teaspoons coarse sea salt and 500 ml (17 fl oz, 2 cups) water, boil for 5 minutes and leave to cool.

Cut away the thick ribs from the leaves of a small green cabbage weighing 675–800 g (1½–1¾ lb), wash the leaves and blanch for 8 minutes in boiling water. Drain, squeeze in a sieve and keep warm.

Prepare the sauce: in a large bowl put ½ teaspoon table salt, a pinch of freshly ground pepper and 4 tablespoons wine vinegar; beat in 150 ml (¼ pint, ⅔ cup) olive oil and keep in a warm place.

Arrange the pike-perch fillets in a fish kettle, on top of the vegetables from the court-bouillon, and just cover with the cooled court-bouillon; add 100 ml (4 fl oz, 7 tablespoons) spirit vinegar and the juice of half a lemon. Bring to the boil, cover, remove from the heat and leave to poach for 5–8 minutes. Arrange the cabbage leaves in the serving dish. Lift out the fillets with a fish slice, removing any vegetables, and arrange on top of the cabbage. Pour the sauce over and sprinkle with 3 small young onions, finely chopped, and 1 tablespoon chopped chives.

marinated pike-perch with cardoons ◆

Finely chop 5 garlic cloves, a small bunch of parsley and 2 thyme sprigs. Mix with the juice of 2 lemons and 150 ml (¼ pint, ⅔ cup) olive oil in a large shallow dish. Lay 4 pike-perch cutlets in the dish, turning them once in the marinade to make sure they are well coated. Cover and leave in a cold place for 2–3 hours.

Trim 2 kg (4½ lb) cardoon stalks and cut them into 2.5–5 cm (1–2 in) lengths. Cook the cardoons in boiling salted water, adding a little lemon juice, for 1 hour. Peel 300 g (11 oz) pickling onions and brown them gently in butter, turning occasionally so that they are evenly glazed. Set the onions aside to keep hot. Drain the cardoons and return them to the pan; add a knob of butter and keep them hot.

Remove the fish cutlets from the marinade. Pour the marinade into a saucepan and heat it gently,

then cover and leave to infuse over a low heat for about 30 minutes, stirring occasionally. Grill (broil) the fish cutlets until golden on both sides. Arrange the buttered cardoons on a serving platter or individual plates and top with the fish cutlets. Add the glazed onions, then spoon the sauce over the fish and vegetables.

pike-perch and oyster-mushroom salad

Peel and wash 675 g (1½ lb) oyster mushrooms; slice thinly, sauté briskly in 100 ml (4 fl oz, 7 tablespoons) olive oil with salt and pepper and drain. Gently heat 2 tablespoons vinaigrette with 2 tablespoons cream until warm; add the mushrooms and a vegetable julienne made from 1 carrot, ¼ celeriac, 100 g (4 oz) French (green) beans and 1 turnip, all stewed in butter. Season 4 fillets of pike-perch, each weighing 200 g (7 oz), and cook in a covered dish in a preheated oven at 180°C (350°F, gas 4) for about 20 minutes. Serve with the oyster-mushroom salad, pouring a few drops of vinegar over each fillet just before serving.

PILAF Also known as *pilau*. A method of preparing rice that originated in the East. The word is Turkish and is related to the Persian *pilaou* (boiled rice). In the basic recipe the rice is browned in oil or butter with onion, then cooked in stock; halfway through cooking, vegetables, meat or fish may be added. Pilaf is always spiced, sometimes with saffron, particularly in paella.

There are many variations of pilaf, including garnishes of seafood, shrimps, prawns, lobster, foie gras, sautéed chicken livers, lambs' sweetbreads, sheep's kidneys, fish in sauce, minced (ground) meat or thinly sliced chicken. The rice is often moulded in the shape of a crown and the garnish in its sauce is arranged in the centre. Pilaf rice can also be moulded in darioles, as a garnish for meat, fish or poultry.

RECIPES

chicken pilaf

Prepare some pilaf rice as in the recipe for garnished pilaf. Select a chicken weighing about 1.25 kg (2¾ lb) and divide it into 8 pieces. Season with salt and pepper and cook in a flameproof casserole containing 50 g (2 oz, ¼ cup) butter. Remove with a draining spoon. Add to the casserole 1 tablespoon chopped onion, 175 ml (6 fl oz, ¾ cup) dry white wine, 200 ml (7 fl oz, ¾ cup) chicken stock, 1 tablespoon well-reduced tomato sauce, a crushed garlic clove and a bouquet garni. Cook this sauce for 5 minutes, stirring, then strain and return it to the casserole with the pieces of chicken; reheat thoroughly. Shape the pilaf rice into a ring on the serving dish and pour the chicken and its sauce into the centre. Serve hot.

garnished pilaf

Thinly slice and chop 1 large onion. Heat 3 tablespoons olive oil in a flameproof casserole. Measure

250 g (9 oz, 1¼ cups) long-grain rice. Test the temperature of the oil by tossing a grain into it; when the grain begins to change colour, pour in all the rice at once and stir with a wooden spoon until the grains are transparent. Incorporate the chopped onion and stir. Add to the rice 2½ times its volume of stock or boiling water and season with salt, pepper, a small sprig of thyme and half a bay leaf. Stir, cover, reduce the heat and cook gently for 16–20 minutes. Turn off the heat, remove the thyme and bay leaf, then place a cloth under the lid to absorb the steam. Butter may be added just before serving.

Mould the rice to form a ring and fill the centre with any of the following garnishes: slices of foie gras and truffles, sautéed in butter and sprinkled with their cooking juices deglazed with a little Madeira; poultry liver and mushrooms, sliced, sautéed in butter and flavoured with garlic, shallots and parsley; halved lambs' kidneys sautéed in butter and sprinkled with their cooking juices deglazed with white wine and enriched with butter; or fish in sauce (bream in white wine or *à l'américaine*, tuna *en daube* or monkfish *à l'américaine*.)

shellfish pilaf

Dice 150 g (5 oz) cooked crab, lobster or langouste meat. Shell 150 g (5 oz) cooked shrimps and toss in butter. Cook 500 ml (17 fl oz, 2 cups) mussels (or cockles or clams) *à la marinière**, allow them to cool in the cooking juices, then remove the shells and keep warm. Strain and measure the cooking juices and dilute with boiling water to obtain 680 ml (23 fl oz, 2¾ cups) liquid. Wash and drain 300 g (11 oz, 1½ cups) long-grain rice. Heat 4 tablespoons olive oil in a frying pan; add the rice and stir. When it is transparent, add the diluted mussel juice, salt and pepper; cover and cook for 15 minutes. Then add the shellfish meat (bound with lobster or langouste butter), the shrimps and the mussels. Serve piping hot.

PILCHARD A small fish related to the herring and sprat; young pilchards are called sardines. Pilchards are often sold canned in oil or tomato sauce.

PILI-PILI A small, hot-tasting African pepper, the name of which is a corruption of the Arabic *felfel* (strong pepper). Its use is virtually confined to Africa (especially Senegal) and Réunion Island. Crushed with gourd seeds and tomato pulp, it is a basic ingredient of *rougail* and numerous sauces. In Africa *pili-pili* is eaten with semolina, *foutou*, meats and griddle cakes.

PIMBINA Algonquin Indian name used in Canada to describe the fruit of the *trifoliate viburnum*, a shrub of the *Caprifoliaceae* family. These berries, which remain hanging by their stalks all winter, are much appreciated by game birds such as grouse, whose flesh it flavours. The berries become soft in severe frost, and this is when they are picked to make a bright, rather bitter red jam or jelly, which is a perfect accompaniment to game.

PINCER A French culinary term meaning to brown certain foods, such as bones, carcasses or flavouring vegetables, in the oven with the addition of very little or no fat, before moistening them to make a brown stock. The word also means to caramelize meat juices slightly in their cooking fat before skimming off the fat and diluting the juices to make gravy.

The word also means to crimp up the edges of pies or tarts before cooking to improve their appearance.

PINEAPPLE A tropical plant whose fragrant fruit, weighing 1–2.5 kg (2¼–5½ lb), resembles a large pine cone and is topped with a cluster of green leaves. When the fruit is ripe the skin colour changes from yellow-green moving towards brown. When quite yellow-brown, the fruit may be over-ripe. Its russet skin, covered with lozenge-shaped scales, encloses the juicy yellow flesh. Spines, or short prickly spikes, on the skin are firmly implanted in the flesh and have to be cut out with the point of a knife. A hard core runs down the centre of the fruit.

Discovered in Brazil by Jean de Léry in the 16th century, the pineapple was introduced first into England and then France. The earliest pineapples ripened under glass were presented to Louis XV in about 1733. Still rare and expensive at the beginning of the 19th century, this fruit is now widely grown in the West Indies, Africa and Asia and is common in European markets, particularly in winter. There are many varieties, ranging from miniature fruit suitable for one or two portions to very large specimens. Some are quite tart and mild in flavour, others are sweet, fragrant and luscious. There are a few pineapple products: it is widely consumed canned in syrup or juice and as pineapple juice. Semi-dried pineapple is available for use in sweet dishes and baking and candied pineapple is very sweet.

Pineapple may be served plain or with kirsch, in salads and in numerous sweets and desserts. It can also be used to dress fatty meats (pork and duck, as in Creole, Asian and West Indian recipes).

Because fresh pineapple deteriorates in temperatures lower than 7°C (45°F), it is not advisable to store it in the refrigerator. When served plain, it is better to cut it along its length, as it is sweeter at the base. Round slices are always served with the tough central core removed.

RECIPES

Savoury Dishes
Caribbean chicken with pineapple and rum

Season a large chicken inside and out with salt and pepper. Brown in a flameproof casserole in chicken fat, butter or oil and dust with a pinch of ginger and cayenne. Chop 2 large onions and 1 shallot and soften them in the fat around the chicken. Pour

Marinated pike-perch with cardoons, see page 891.

3 tablespoons rum over the chicken and set light to it. Then add 60 ml (2 fl oz, ¼ cup) pineapple syrup and I tablespoon lemon juice. Cover and cook in a preheated oven at 180°C (350°F, gas 4) for 45 minutes. Dice 6 slices of pineapple and add them to the casserole. Add salt and pepper and cook for about 10 more minutes.

duck with pineapple
Prepare a young duck, season its liver with salt and pepper and replace inside the carcass. Slowly brown the duck in butter in a flameproof casserole for 20 minutes, add salt and pepper, and then flame it in rum. Add a few tablespoons canned pineapple syrup, I tablespoon lemon juice and I tablespoon black peppercorns. Cover the dish and finish cooking (50 minutes altogether). Brown some pineapple slices in butter and add them to the casserole 5 minutes before the end of the cooking time. Check the seasoning. Cut the duck into pieces and arrange on a warm plate. Garnish with the pineapple and pour the cooking juices over the top.

loin of pork with pineapple
Brown a loin of pork in a flameproof casserole with a little butter and oil. Add salt and pepper, cover the casserole and cook gently for about 1½ hours, either on the top of the stove or in a preheated oven at 200°C (400°F, gas 6). Brown some pineapple slices and apple quarters in butter and add them to the casserole 5 minutes before the end of the cooking time. Place the pork with the apples and pineapple on a warm plate and keep hot. Deglaze the casserole with a little hot water or rum and serve this separately as a sauce.

Sweet Dishes
apple and pineapple jam
Dice 450 g (I lb) peeled and cored cooking apples and 450 g (I lb) peeled pineapple. Simmer the fruit in 4 tablespoons water until soft. Stir in 900 g (2 lb, 4 cups) preserving sugar until dissolved. Boil the jam rapidly until setting point is reached. Pot and cover as usual.

iced pineapple à la bavaroise
Choose a large, well-shaped pineapple with a good cluster of fresh leaves. Cut off the top I cm (½ in) below the crown and set aside. Scoop out the flesh, leaving an even I cm (½ in) thickness around the outside. Fill the inside with a mixture of pineapple Bavarian cream and a salpicon of pineapple soaked in white rum. Leave to set in a cool place or on ice. Replace the top of the pineapple before serving.

iced pineapple à la bourbonnaise
Prepare a large pineapple, scooping out the flesh as for iced pineapple à la bavaroise. Soak the chopped flesh in rum. Sprinkle the inside of the pineapple case with 2 tablespoons white rum and leave in a cool place for about 2 hours. Just before serving, fill the pineapple case with alternate layers of rum ice

cream and the soaked flesh. Replace the top and arrange the pineapple on a napkin or in a fruit bowl, surrounded with crushed ice.

iced pineapple à la Chantilly
This dish is prepared in the same way as iced pineapple à la bourbonnaise, but the rum ice cream is replaced with a mixture of vanilla ice cream and whipped cream.

iced pineapple à la parisienne
This dish is prepared in the same way as iced pineapple à la bourbonnaise, but with banana ice cream. Each layer of ice cream is scattered with blanched sliced almonds.

pineapple ice
Add the crushed flesh of half a fresh pineapple to 500 ml (17 fl oz, 2 cups) sugar syrup and leave to soak for 2 hours. Reduce to a purée in a blender and flavour with rum. Measure the density with a syrup hydrometer and adjust the sugar content as necessary to achieve a density of 1.609. Freeze in an ice-cream maker.

pineapple surprise ◆
Cut a pineapple in half lengthways through the whole fruit, including the leaves, and scoop out the flesh carefully, making sure you do not damage the skin. Cut the flesh into small, equal-sized cubes and macerate in 100 g (4 oz, ½ cup) caster (superfine) sugar and 3 tablespoons light rum for 2 hours.

Bring 600 ml (I pint, 2½ cups) milk to the boil with a vanilla pod (bean), cut in half. Beat I whole egg and 3 egg yolks with 100 g (4 oz, ½ cup) caster sugar. When the mixture is white and foamy, add 65 g (2½ oz, ½ cup) plain (all-purpose) flour and stir to obtain a very smooth mixture. Pour the hot milk on to this mixture, very slowly so as not to cook the yolks and make the mixture curdle. Return to a low heat and whisk briskly until the custard has thickened. Remove from the heat. Drain the pineapple and add the rum-flavoured syrup to the crème pâtissiere. Chill the mixture in the refrigerator. Reserve a few pieces of pineapple for decoration, then add the rest to the crème pâtissière. Fold in 3 very stiffly whisked egg whites and 100 ml (4 fl oz, 7 tablespoons) crème fraîche. Fill the pineapple halves with this mixture. Decorate with the reserved pineapple and a few wild strawberries. Add a little finely pared lime rind if liked. When they are available, small pineapples can be used, allowing ½ per portion.

other recipes See *attereau, compote, fritter, manqué.*

PINEAU DES CHARENTES A sweet aperitif made in the Charentais by 'stopping' grape juice

Pineapple surprise.

from fermenting by the addition of Cognac. It varies according to the maker, in both colour and style, and is said to date from the time of François I. It can be served with melon or even with foie gras and features in some regional recipes.

PINE NUT Also known as pine kernel. The small oblong edible seed of the stone pine, which grows in the Mediterranean region. Surrounded by a hard husk, pine nuts (or *pignoles*, as they are known in the south of France) are extracted from between the scales of the pine cones.

Pine nuts taste a little like almonds but are sometimes more resinous and spicy. Pine nuts are sometimes eaten raw or used in a variety of dishes, but they are often lightly browned in a dry frying pan to bring out their flavour. They are often used to garnish rice dishes in India and in Turkey, where they are also used in stuffed mussels, poultry forcemeats and mutton balls. In Italy pine nuts are used in sauces for pasta, fish forcemeats, fillings for omelettes and to flavour sautéed chicken. In Provence they are used in charcuterie, in *tourte aux bettes niçoise* and in raw vegetable salads dressed with olive oil. They are also used in pâtisserie – for macaroons and biscuits (cookies) – and in other recipes.

RECIPES

pine-nut crescents
Boil 4 tablespoons water with an equal quantity of sugar in a small saucepan, then remove the syrup from the heat. In a mixing bowl blend 50 g (2 oz, ½ cup) plain (all-purpose) flour with 150 g (5 oz, 1¼ cups) ground almonds, 200 g (7 oz, ¾ cup) caster (superfine) sugar and 3 egg whites. When the dough is quite smooth, divide it into 30 pieces and shape into small crescents. Cover a baking sheet with lightly oiled greaseproof (wax) paper. Dip the crescents in beaten egg, then roll them in 200 g (7 oz, 2 cups) pine nuts. Arrange the crescents on the baking sheet and bake in a preheated oven at 200°C (400°F, gas 6) for 8–10 minutes. Remove from the oven and brush the crescents with the sugar syrup. Transfer to a wire rack to cool.

pine-nut flan
Spread 2 tablespoons blackcurrant jelly over a base of sweetened rich shortcrust pastry. Cover with equal quantities of confectioner's custard and ground almonds. Scatter 100 g (4 oz, 1 cup) pine nuts over the top. Cook in a preheated oven at 200°C (400°F, gas 6) for about 20 minutes.

pine-nut omelette
Remove the husks from 150 g (5 oz, 1½ cups) pine nuts and grind half of them. Brown the other half in a frying pan containing 1 tablespoon oil and 25 g (1 oz, 2 tablespoons) butter. Beat 8 eggs and add the ground pine nuts. Pour the mixture over the browned pine nuts. Cook the omelette and turn it out on a warmed serving dish.

pine-nut sauce à l'italienne
(from Carême's recipe) In a saucepan put about 50 g (2 oz, ¼ cup) brown or caster (superfine) sugar, 2 tablespoons vinegar, 2 tablespoons veal stock, a seasoned bouquet garni, a pinch of grated nutmeg and a pinch of coarsely ground pepper. Reduce over a moderate heat, then add 2 tablespoons espagnole* sauce and 175 ml (6 fl oz, ¾ cup) red Bordeaux. Reduce further, then strain the sauce through coarse muslin (cheesecloth) and mix in 1 tablespoon pine nuts. Just before serving, boil the nuts rapidly in the sauce.

PINION The wing tip or terminal segment of a bird's wing. It can be prepared in various ways: sautéed or braised, or stuffed if it is large enough, but it is used principally for making consommé.

RECIPES

stuffed braised turkey pinions
Singe and clean 6 turkey pinions and remove the bones carefully without tearing the skin. Stuff them with finely minced (ground) pork forcemeat or a poultry or quenelle forcemeat. Wrap each pinion in a thin rasher (slice) of bacon and tie in place with kitchen thread. Line a buttered sauté pan with bacon rind, 50 g (2 oz, ¼ cup) chopped onions and 50 g (2 oz, ⅓ cup) thinly sliced carrots; add a bouquet garni and the pinions. Season with salt and pepper, cover and cook gently for 15 minutes. Moisten with 200 ml (7 fl oz, ¾ cup) dry white wine or Madeira and cook uncovered until the liquid has evaporated. Add 400 ml (14 fl oz, 1¾ cups) poultry or veal stock, bring slowly to the boil, then cover and cook in a preheated oven at 180°C (350°F, gas 4) for 40 minutes. Drain the pinions, remove the bacon and brown the pinions quickly in a preheated oven at 240°C (475°F, gas 9). Arrange them on a serving dish. Remove the fat from the cooking liquor, reduce and strain it, and pour it over the pinions.

Serve with one of the following garnishes: *Choisy, financière, forestière, Godard, jardinière, languedocienne, macédoine, milanaise, piémontaise*, rice pilaf or risotto. Braised pinions may also be garnished with all kinds of braised or boiled vegetables, coated with butter or cream.

turkey pinion fritters
Stuff and braise small turkey pinions as in the recipe for stuffed braised turkey pinions. Strain the hot cooking liquor, then pour it back over the pinions and leave until cool. Remove the pinions from the liquor, pat dry, then marinate for 30 minutes in olive oil, lemon juice, salt, pepper and chopped parsley.

Drain and dry the pinions, then dip them in batter and fry in very hot deep fat until crisp and golden. Drain and sprinkle with salt. Serve the pinion fritters on a doiley or napkin, garnished with fried parsley and lemon quarters or, more originally, with fresh mint leaves. A well-seasoned tomato sauce may be served with this dish.

turkey pinions à la fermière

Prepare and braise the pinions as in the recipe for stuffed braised turkey pinions. Cooked chopped onions and parsley may be added to the finely minced (ground) pork forcemeat. Arrange the drained pinions in a casserole with a fermière vegetable garnish. Remove the fat from the reserved cooking liquor, reduce and strain it into the casserole over the vegetables. Cover and cook in a preheated oven at 200°C (400°F, gas 6) for about 25 minutes or until piping hot.

other recipes See *giblets, Sainte-Menehould.*

PINOT One of the great grape families, used for making classic wines and grown in many countries. The Pinot Noir makes the finest red Burgundies; it and the Pinot Meunier are two of the black grapes used in champagne. The Pinot Blanc and the Pinot Gris are two of the white varieties of Pinot.

PINOT BLANC Pinot Blanc is widely planted in Germany, Italy, Hungary, Austria and parts of California. It is also cultivated in Alsace where it is blended with Auxerrois to make the AOC Pinot Blanc, also known as Klevner, and Crémant d'Alsace.

PINOT GRIS A permutation of the well-known grape variety Pinot Noir, from which it is distinguished by the bluish-grey colour of its grapes, producing white wines. Grown in Alsace, Germany (Graver Burgunder or Ruländer), Italy (Pinot Grigio), Austria, Hungary (Szürkebarát), California, Oregon, Australia and New Zealand, it produces full, dry wines that partner food well.

PINOT NOIR A high quality red grape variety that is notoriously difficult to grow. Pinot Noir has small, compact bunches of grapes that are bluish with a thick skin, rich in colouring matter, protecting a colourless flesh. It has made the reputation of the great red wines of Burgundy, such as Romanée-Conti, La Tâche, Musigny, Chambertin, Clos-de-Vougeot, Pommard and Corton. It is also one of the traditional champagne grape varieties, together with Chardonnay and Pinot Meunier. For champagne, pressing is carried out very rapidly so that the skins do not colour the juice. In a favourable climate Pinot Noir can produce the richest, silkiest wines in the world, especially on calcareous soil. Excellent wines are also being produced in Switzerland, Oregon, New Zealand and some estates in South Africa.

PIPE To force a paste, icing (frosting), cream, stuffing or similar substance from a piping (pastry) bag. The operation must be carried out steadily, holding the nozzle in the bag at an angle. The shape of the

Piping

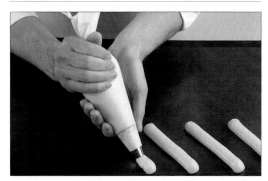

When filling the piping bag, allow enough space to twist the top closed and grip the bag firmly. Support the bag at the required angle with one hand, then apply steady pressure with the other to squeeze out the mixture while moving the bag slowly and evenly. When enough mixture has been piped, stop squeezing before lifting the nozzle away with a short swift movement. When piping some mixtures, the end can be cut from the piping nozzle with a knife before lifting the bag away.

nozzle and the way it is handled determine the final shape of the preparation – éclairs are made by piping out choux pastry into finger shapes, the mixture for *langues de chat* is piped out in thin tongue shapes, while the mixture for duchess potatoes is forced out into large spiral rosettes.

PIPERADE A Basque speciality consisting of a rich stew of tomatoes and sweet (bell) peppers (*piper* in Béarnais), sometimes seasoned with onion and garlic, cooked in olive oil or goose fat and then mixed with beaten eggs and lightly scrambled. A garnish of Bayonne ham may also be added or piperade may be eaten with slices of fried ham on the side.

RECIPES

eggs à la piperade

Peel and seed 1 kg (2¼ lb) tomatoes and cut into quarters. Seed 500 g (18 oz) red and green sweet (bell) peppers and cut into strips. Gently fry the peppers and tomatoes, seasoned with salt and pepper, in a large frying pan in 2 tablespoons olive oil for 30–40 minutes. Dice 150 g (5 oz, ⅔ cup) Bayonne ham and add to the fried vegetables. Beat 8 eggs and pour them gently into the frying pan, stirring until they have coagulated but are still quite soft. Serve piping hot.

piperade with poached eggs

Melt a little fat (preferably ham fat) in a large sauté pan. Finely slice 1 kg (2¼ lb) onions and 1 kg (2¼ lb) seeded green sweet (bell) peppers and cut into four, lengthways. Add to the ham fat in the sauté pan. Add 8 crushed garlic cloves, a little diced ham and a bouquet garni. Add 2 kg (4½ lb) peeled, seeded, coarsely chopped tomatoes. Season with salt and pepper. Add a little sugar if the tomatoes are too acid and 1–2 pinches of paprika. Cook over a high heat, stirring often until the liquor from the tomatoes has evaporated. Correct the seasoning. Serve topped with poached eggs.

PIPING (PASTRY) BAG A cone-shaped bag fitted with nozzles of different sizes and shapes. The bag may be made of coarse linen or nylon. The nozzles, made of plastic or metal, have large or small apertures that may be plain, starred, fluted, slitlike or serrated.

Small piping bags can be made from greaseproof (wax) paper or other cooking parchment – these are used for fine work, such as intricate cake decorating or piping chocolate. Piping bags are used extensively in confectionery and pâtisserie for creating decorative designs of icing (frosting) and cream. They are also used for shaping certain pastries, notably éclairs, and for piping potato or meringues. They are also used in savoury cookery, for example to pipe creamed potatoes or to hand-fill sausage skins.

A rigid syringe may also be used for piping icing instead of a piping bag, but it has a restricted capacity and is not as easy to handle.

PIQUANT The term used to describe an acid flavour. In France *il pique*, it may also be said of a fizzy drink, meaning that it creates a prickly sensation in the mouth. In general use, the term describes a mildly spicy acidity and a more complex flavour than simple acid. For example, sauces that are piquant usually combine the merest hint of a hot flavour with a little acidity – this may be the result of using chilli with lemon, mustard with vinegar or a complex condiment based on slightly hot spices with acid ingredients. It can also be used to describe a positive quality in matured ingredients, as, for instance, in a well-matured cheese that combines a rich spiny tone with remnants of immature acidity.

PIQUETTE A home-made drink obtained by soaking the residue from grape-pressing in water. By extension, the word denotes a sour wine of poor quality with a low alcohol content.

PIROSHKI Also known as *pirozki*. In Russian and Polish cooking, small filled pastries served with soup or as a hot entrée. They are made of choux pastry, puff pastry, or a yeast or brioche dough; the savoury filling may be based on fish, rice, game, poultry, meat, brains, cream cheese or chopped vegetables. They can be baked or deep-fried.

RECIPES

Caucasian piroshki
Spread a thin layer of cheese-flavoured choux pastry on a large baking sheet and cook in a preheated oven at 180°C (350°F, gas 4) for about 25 minutes. Turn the pastry out on to the work surface and cut

in half. Coat one half with a layer of thick béchamel sauce to which grated cheese and cooked sliced mushrooms have been added. Cover with the other half and seal the edges well. Cut into 6 × 3 cm (2½ × 1¼ in) rectangles. Coat completely with more cheese-flavoured béchamel sauce and then with breadcrumbs. Deep-fry in very hot oil or fat, drain on paper towels and arrange on a napkin.

cheese piroshki
Butter 8 dariole moulds and line them with unsweetened brioche dough. Mix 225 g (8 oz, 1 cup) curd cheese with 75 g (3 oz, 6 tablespoons) creamed butter and 3 beaten eggs; season with salt, pepper and nutmeg. Fill the moulds with this mixture and cover with a thin layer of brioche dough. Trim this flush with the edge and press firmly on to the base. Leave to rise at room temperature away from draughts for about 1 hour, then cook in a preheated oven at 220°C (425°F, gas 7) for 25–30 minutes. Turn out and serve very hot.

Moscow piroshki
Prepare some unsweetened brioche dough and cut out small ovals, 6–7 cm (2½ in) wide and 10 cm (4 in) long. Prepare the filling: chop and mix 125 g (4½ oz) cooked white fish fillets (whiting or pike), 75 g (3 oz) cooked *vesiga* (dried spinal marrow of the sturgeon) and 2 hard-boiled (hard-cooked) eggs. Season with salt and pepper. Put a large knob of this mixture on each oval. Moisten the edges of the ovals slightly, fold over to cover the filling and press to seal tightly.

Leave for 30 minutes in a warm place for the dough to rise, then brush with beaten egg and cook in a preheated oven at 220°C (425°F, gas 7) for about 25 minutes. When ready to serve, drizzle with a little melted *maître d'hôtel* butter.

puff-pastry piroshki
Make 400 g (14 oz) puff* pastry. Prepare 5 tablespoons finely diced cooked game (wild duck, pheasant, young rabbit or partridge) or the same amount of white fish (fillets of whiting or pike) poached in a court-bouillon. Add to the diced meat 2 chopped hard-boiled (hard-cooked) eggs and 5 tablespoons long-grain rice cooked in meat stock. Mix this hash thoroughly and adjust the seasoning.

Roll out the pastry very thinly and cut out 12 rounds, about 7.5 cm (3 in) in diameter. Pull slightly into oval shapes. Put a small amount of hash on to half of each piece, without going right to the edge. Brush the other half of each oval with beaten egg and fold over, pressing the edges together firmly. Score the top and brush with beaten egg. Cook in a preheated oven at 220°C (425°F, gas 7) for about 20 minutes until crisp, puffy and golden. Serve piping hot.

PIROT A speciality of Poitou consisting of pieces of sautéed kid goat seasoned with fresh garlic and sorrel leaves.

PIS A French butchery term denoting the breast and belly meat of cattle, equivalent to brisket and flank in Britain, and to plate in the United States. There is no direct translation as French cuts of meat differ from those of the English and American.

The word is also sometimes used for the udder of the cow, ewe, goat or sow, but this is more frequently referred to as *tétine* in French.

PISSALADIÈRE A speciality of the Nice region, consisting of a flan filled with onions and garnished with anchovy fillets and black olives. It is traditionally coated with the condiment *pissalat* before being cooked, hence the name. A good *pissaladière* should have a layer of onions half as thick as the base if bread dough is used; if the flan is made with shortcrust pastry (basic pie dough), the layer of onions should be as thick as the flan pastry. It can be eaten hot or cold.

RECIPE

pissaladière

Prepare 675 g (1½ lb) bread* dough, and work into it 4 tablespoons olive oil. Knead it by hand, roll it into a ball and leave to rise for 1 hour at room temperature. Soak 12 salted anchovies for a short while in cold water (or use 24 drained canned anchovy fillets).

Peel and chop 1 kg (2¼ lb) onions and fry them gently until soft in a covered frying pan with 4–5 tablespoons olive oil, a pinch of salt, a little pepper, 3 crushed garlic cloves, 1 sprig of thyme and 1 bay leaf. Fillet the anchovies. Strain 1 tablespoon pickled capers, pound them into a purée and add to the softened onions.

Flatten three-quarters of the dough to form a circle. Place on an oiled baking sheet and spread with the onion and caper mixture, leaving a rim around the edge. Roll up the anchovy fillets and press them into the onions, together with 20 or so small black (ripe) olives. Shape the rim of the dough to form a wide border that will retain the filling. Roll out the remainder of the dough and cut it into thin strips. Place these in a criss-cross pattern over the filling, pressing the ends into the border. Brush the dough with oil and cook in a pre-heated oven at 240°C (475°F, gas 9) for about 20 minutes.

The strips of dough may be replaced by anchovy fillets arranged in a criss-cross pattern if preferred.

PISSALAT Also known as *pissala*. A condiment originating from the Nice region, made of anchovy purée flavoured with cloves, thyme, bay leaf and pepper and mixed with olive oil. Originally *pissalat* was made from the fry of sardines and anchovies, but because this is not readily available outside the Mediterranean area, anchovies in brine may be used instead. *Pissalat* is used for seasoning hors d'oeuvre, fish, cold meats and the regional dish *pissaladière*.

RECIPE

escalopes of red mullet with pissalat

Fillet 3 red mullet, each weighing about 200 g (7 oz). Season with salt and pepper and cook in a frying pan in 2–3 tablespoons olive oil and 25 g (1 oz, 2 tablespoons) butter. When cooked, remove and drain on paper towels. Arrange the fillets in a ring on a round serving dish. Prepare some beurre blanc and mix with some *pissalat* to taste. Coat the fillets lightly with this sauce and garnish with small sprigs of chervil or cress.

PISTACHE A method of preparation from Languedoc, characterized by the presence of garlic cloves in the cooking liquid; it is used particularly for marinated and braised mutton (*pistache* of mutton or mutton *en pistache*) and also for partridges and pigeons.

The Saint-Gaudens *pistache*, a speciality of Comminges, is a somewhat richer variation, consisting of a mutton ragoût with garlic cloves to which are added haricot (navy) beans cooked with a shin of pork, fresh pork rind and a bouquet garni.

RECIPES

partridge en pistache

Stuff a partridge with a forcemeat of its liver, breadcrumbs, raw ham, parsley and garlic, all chopped and bound with 1 egg. Truss the partridge, bard it, season with salt and pepper and place in a flameproof casserole containing 3 tablespoons heated goose fat. Cook until the partridge becomes a good golden colour, then remove it.

Place 1 tablespoon diced raw ham in the casserole, brown it, dust with 1 tablespoon flour and cook for a few minutes. Add 3 tablespoons dry white wine, then 100 ml (4 fl oz, 7 tablespoons) giblet or chicken stock. Add 1 tablespoon tomato purée (paste), a bouquet garni and a small piece of dried orange peel. Cook for 10 minutes. Remove the ham and the bouquet garni. Strain the sauce.

Return the partridge to the casserole, together with the ham and bouquet garni, then pour on the sauce. Bring to the boil, cover and cook for 10 minutes. Then add 12 garlic cloves (blanched in boiling salted water, drained and peeled) and simmer for a further 30 minutes. Remove the bouquet garni and serve the partridge straight from the casserole.

shoulder of mutton en pistache

Roll up and tie a boned shoulder of mutton and place it in a flameproof casserole lined with a large slice of raw unsmoked (boiled) ham, 1 sliced onion and 1 sliced carrot. Add salt, pepper and 2 tablespoons goose fat or lard. Cook over a very gentle heat for 20–25 minutes. Remove the mutton and ham and add 2 tablespoons flour to the casserole. Stir and cook for a few minutes, then add 200 ml (7 fl oz, ¾ cup) white wine and the same amount of stock. Mix thoroughly, strain and set aside.

Dice the ham and return to the casserole, together with the mutton. Add 50 garlic cloves (blanched in boiling water and peeled), a bouquet garni and a piece of dried orange peel. Add the strained cooking liquid, cover the casserole and cook in a preheated oven at 220°C (425°F, gas 7) for about 1 hour. Remove and drain the shoulder, untie it and arrange on a warm plate. Cover with the sauce (bound with breadcrumbs if necessary) and serve the garlic cloves as a garnish.

PISTACHIO The seed of the pistachio tree, native to western Asia and reputedly introduced to Rome by Vitellius during the reign of Tiberius. The tree is now cultivated widely in Mediterranean countries and the southern United States. The pistachio nut is about the size of an olive and the pale green kernel is surrounded by a reddish skin. It is enclosed in a smooth, pale reddish-brown shell, which is easy to break and is covered by a brownish husk. Sweet and delicately flavoured, the kernel is used chiefly for decorating pastries, cakes and confectionery. It is also used to flavour charcuterie and is eaten roasted and salted in cocktail snacks.

In Mediterranean and Oriental cooking, pistachios are used in poultry sauces and stuffings and also in hash. In classic cuisine they garnish galantines, brawn (head cheese) and mortadella. In India pistachio purée is used to season rice and vegetables. Pistachios go best with veal, pork and poultry. Their green colour (often accentuated artificially) makes them popular for creams (especially for filling cakes, such as the *galicien*) and also for ice creams and ice-cream desserts. In confectionery it is especially associated with nougat.

RECIPES

loin of pork with pistachios
Marinate a loin of pork – or unsmoked (fresh) ham – for 24 hours in white Bordeaux wine. Soak 800 g (1¾ lb) prunes in warm white Bordeaux. Stud the pork joint with garlic and pistachios. Place it in a flameproof casserole, add 500 ml (17 fl oz, 2 cups) of the marinade, cover and cook for 3 hours over a moderate heat. Then add the strained prunes, cook for a further 45 minutes and serve very hot.

pistachio brawn
Clean and scrape a pig's head; remove the tongue, brains and the fat portion of the throat. Cut off the ears at their base. Put the head, ears, tongue and 2 calves' tongues to soak in brine for 3–4 days. Drain. Wrap the head in a cloth, put it in a flameproof casserole together with the ears, also wrapped, and braise gently for 4–5 hours. After 2 hours, add the tongues.

Remove the best part of the skin and spread it on a linen cloth or napkin. Cut the flesh of the head into strips as thick and as long as possible, leaving out the parts tinged with blood. Sprinkle all the meats with *quatre épices* spice mixture and add about 10 chopped shallots. While still hot, arrange the meats and shallots on the skin, mixing the various meats and interspersing them with pistachios. Strips of raw truffle may also be added. Fold the skin over the contents, wrap it in the napkin and tie with string.

Return it to the cooking liquid, bring to the boil and simmer for 1 hour. Drain, remove the string and place the galantine in a brawn (headcheese) mould. Cool, putting a weight on top so it is well pressed. Chill before serving sliced.

PISTOLE A small, clear yellow plum, which is cultivated and prepared in the region of Brignoles. The *pistole* is stoned (pitted), pressed flat, then rounded and dried.

PISTOLET A small, round Belgian roll, made from a very light, crusty dough, eaten for breakfast, particularly on Sunday. *Pistolets* are the equivalent of French croissants. They are served also during the day, cold and filled with cold meats or cheese, or even raw minced (ground) beef fillet.

PISTOU A condiment from Provence, made of fresh basil crushed with garlic and olive oil. The word (derived from the Italian *pestare*, to pound) is also used for the vegetable and vermicelli soup to which it is added. The condiment, sometimes supplemented by Parmesan cheese and tomatoes, is similar to the Italian *pesto*.

RECIPE

pistou soup
Soak 500 g (18 oz, 3 cups) mixed white and red haricot (navy) beans for 12 hours in cold water. Drain and place in a large saucepan together with 2.5 litres (4½ pints, 11 cups) cold water and a bouquet garni. Bring to the boil, boil rapidly for 10 minutes, then add a little salt, reduce the heat and cook gently. String 250 g (9 oz) French (green) beans and cut into pieces. Dice 2 or 3 courgettes (zucchini). Scrape and dice 2 carrots and peel and dice 2 turnips. When the haricots have been cooking for 1½ hours, add the French beans, carrots, salt and pepper. After a further 15 minutes, add the courgettes and turnips. Cook for another 15 minutes, then add 200 g (7 oz) large vermicelli and cook for a further 10 minutes.

Meanwhile, pound together the pulp of 2 very ripe tomatoes, 5 peeled garlic cloves, 3–4 tablespoons fresh basil leaves and 75 g (3 oz, ¾ cup) grated Parmesan cheese, gradually adding 4 tablespoons olive oil. Add this mixture to the soup while it is still boiling, then remove from the heat and serve piping hot.

Quartered artichoke hearts or potatoes may be added 30 minutes before the end of cooking, if wished.

PITA A traditional Middle Eastern dish. It consists of a round base of unleavened bread, cut in two, heated and then covered with a mixture of maize (corn) and puréed sesame seeds, grated raw vegetables and chick peas. See *pitta bread*.

PITAHAYA
The pink or red fruit of one of the species of the *Opuntia* cactus, originally from the American tropics. Its thick scales conceal a white flesh sprinkled with small seeds, which is eaten raw. The pitahaya is sometimes acid, sometimes sweet.

PITCHER
A pot-bellied vessel, cylindrical or truncated in shape, made of stoneware, glass or pottery and having one or two handles and a pouring spout (or a slanting neck). Pitchers (*cruches*) are usually used for serving cold drinks (water and fruit juices). A small pitcher (*cruchon*) is sometimes used in France for serving local wines.

PITHIVIERS
A cow's-milk cheese from the Orléans area, with a high fat content (40–45%), a soft texture and a greyish-white, furry crust. Ripened under a thin layer of hay, it is a supple creamy-yellow cheese when ripe, with a strong flavour. Very similar to Coulommiers, it is shaped into rounds, 12 cm (5 in) in diameter and 2.5 cm (1 in) thick.

PITHIVIERS
A large, round, puff-pastry tart with scalloped edges, filled with an almond cream. A speciality of Pithiviers, in the Orléans region, it traditionally serves as a Twelfth Night cake, when it contains a broad (fava) bean. The town of Pithiviers is also renowned for another cake, again made of puff pastry, but filled with crystallized (candied) fruit and covered with white fondant icing (frosting). The classic Pithiviers has been interpreted in various ways, the almond cream being replaced by such fillings as creamed rice, kidneys and even chicken liver in a sauce.

RECIPE

Pithiviers
Cream 100 g (4 oz, ½ cup) butter with a spatula and mix with 100 g (4 oz, ½ cup) caster (superfine) sugar. Then beat in 6 egg yolks, one at a time, 40 g (1½ oz, ¼ cup) potato flour, 100 g (4 oz, 1 cup) ground almonds and 2 tablespoons rum. Mix this cream thoroughly. Roll out 200 g (7 oz) puff* pastry and cut out a circle 20 cm (8 in) in diameter. Spread this with the almond paste, leaving a 1 cm (½ in) border all round. Beat 1 egg yolk and brush it around the rim of the circle.

Roll out a further 300 g (11 oz) pastry and cut another circle the same size as the first but thicker. Place it on the first circle and seal the rim. Decorate the edge with the traditional scalloped pattern and brush with beaten egg. Score diamond or rosette patterns on the top with the point of a knife. Cook in a preheated oven at 220°C (425°F, gas 7) for 30 minutes. Dust with icing (confectioner's) sugar and return it to the oven for a few minutes to glaze. Serve warm or cold.

PITTA BREAD
The English name for Middle-Eastern flat yeasted bread (see *bread*). The bread puffs slightly during cooking to form a hollow pocket that can be filled to make a type of sandwich. Originating from the Greeky name *plakous* for a thin bread, 'pitta' evolved into pizza in Italy. Turkish *pide* is a similar flat bread, plain or topped and baked as for Italian pizza.

Pitta is internationally popular filled or as an accompaniment to salads or dips.

PIZZA
A popular Italian dish originating from Naples. In its simplest form it consists of a thin slab of bread dough spread with thick tomato purée (paste) and Parmesan or Mozzarella cheese, seasoned with herbs and garlic, then baked in an oven. There are countless varieties of pizza, garnished with vegetables (small artichoke hearts, peas, olives, mushrooms, peppers, capers), slices of smoked sausage, ham, anchovy fillets, seafood or mussels. It can be served as an entrée, a savoury or a snack.

The word 'pizza' derives from an Italian verb meaning to sting or to season. From the same origin comes *à la pizzaiola*, a piquant mixture of tomato sauce, shreds of pepper, herbs (thyme, marjoram, bay leaf) and garlic, which is suitable for pasta, pork chops or grills.

Léon Gessi in *Rome et ses environs* describes pizza as 'a blossoming flower, noble and full of fragrant odours; Mozzarella bubbles in the heat of the fire, revealing spots of oil and touches of tomato. Rust-coloured streaks soften the bright red of these touches, but it is the anchovy purée which strengthens the taste on the palate . . . which is difficult to define because it subtly covers a range extending from a sweet kiss to a sharp bite.'

Neapolitan pizza went around the world with migrating Italians, who opened pizzerias in the major cities of Europe and North America. These are typically small popular restaurants offering Italian pastas, pizzas and other specialities.

In classic French cuisine, a pizza is prepared as a tartlet of shortcrust pastry (basic pie dough) or puff pastry garnished with a purée of tomatoes, olives and anchovies. Miniature pizzas are served as cocktail snacks.

RECIPES

pizza dough
Crumble 15 g (½ oz) fresh baker's yeast (1 cake compressed yeast) into 3 tablespoons warm water containing a little sugar and leave until frothy (about 15 minutes). Alternatively, sprinkle 2 teaspoons dried yeast into the same amount of water and sugar, stir until dissolved and leave in a warm place until frothy.

Sift 350 g (12 oz, 3 cups) strong plain (bread) flour, make a well in the centre and pour in 300 ml (½ pint, 1¼ cups) warm water and 4 tablespoons olive oil. Add the yeast and 1 teaspoon salt. Work the dough with the fingers, then knead on a floured board until the dough becomes smooth and elastic (about 10 minutes). Roll it into a ball, dust with flour and leave in a covered bowl in a warm place away from draughts until it has doubled in volume (about 1½ hours).

Knead for a further minute, then roll out into a circle about 25 cm (10 in) in diameter. Raise the edge with the thumbs to form a rim. The pizza is ready for filling and baking in the oven.

Neapolitan pizza
Spread 6 large spoonfuls of well-seasoned passata or tomato concassée on a base of pizza dough. Add 400 g (14 oz) Mozzarella cheese, cut into fine slivers, 50 g (2 oz) anchovy fillets and 100 g (4 oz) black olives and spread evenly on the pizza. Sprinkle with oregano to taste. Season with salt and pepper and pour 4 tablespoons extra-virgin olive oil over the top. Cook in a preheated oven at 240°C (475°F, gas 9) for 30 minutes.

pizza Mario
Make some fairly short pastry with 500 g (18 oz, 4½ cups) plain (all-purpose) flour, 175 ml (6 fl oz, ¾ cup) good-quality olive oil and a large pinch of salt. Leave overnight. Then flatten the dough by hand and line a lightly oiled tart (pie) plate with it. Open some mussels over the heat, then remove from their shells. Add them to a mixture of chopped shallots, salt, pepper, 5–6 pounded anchovies and 2–3 crushed tomatoes. Spread this mixture over the dough and garnish with 2 anchovy fillets arranged in a cross and a few black olives. Sprinkle with grated Parmesan cheese and a dash of olive oil and cook in a preheated oven at 230°C (450°F, gas 8) for 12 minutes.

PLAICE A flat-fish of the *Pleuronectidae* family, which lives in coastal waters from Norway to Morocco. It is abundant in the Atlantic, the English Channel and the North Sea, but rare in the Mediterranean. It is 25–60 cm (10–24 in) long, with both eyes on the uppermost side, which is grey-brown in colour with orange spots (which are very distinct and bright in fresh fish). The blind (lower) side is pearly grey.

Plaice is available all the year round, but is best from November to April. Allow a 175–225 g (6–8 oz) whole fish per portion, because of waste. The flesh, which has a delicate taste and texture, can be prepared like sole or brill; it is particularly suitable for frying, grilling (broiling), poaching and preparing *à la bonne femme* and even *à la Dugléré*; according to tradition, it was for plaice that the chef Dugléré of the Café Anglais originally created this dish.

RECIPE

plaice à la florentine
Clean a large plaice, put it into a buttered dish, add equal quantities of concentrated fish stock (or court-bouillon) and white wine, and bake in a pre-

heated oven at 160°C (325°F, gas 3) for about 35 minutes, basting frequently. Remove from the dish and drain. Completely cover the bottom of an ovenproof serving dish with spinach braised in butter. Lay the plaice on the spinach, cover with Mornay sauce, sprinkle with grated cheese and clarified butter, and glaze quickly in a preheated oven at 240°C (475°F, gas 9).

PLAISIR A popular name, meaning literally 'pleasure', formerly given to wafers (*oublies*) rolled into a cone, which street vendors offered 'for pleasure'.

PLANTAGENÊT The name describing the specialities created by the association of pastrycooks of the Loire region, known for their use of morello cherries and Cointreau, based on biscuits (cookies), parfaits, ice creams or cakes, and recognizable by a label carrying this appellation. There is also a Plantagenêt bonbon with chocolate (white, dark or milk), which is square, filled with praline and orange zest, and lightly flavoured with Cointreau.

PLANTAIN Any of various species of common herbaceous plants found growing in the wild. The young leaves may be used in salads or soups.

For plantain bananas, see *banana*.

PLATE A piece of crockery used to hold food, the size and shape varying according to the nature of the food it is meant to contain. In this sense, the French word *assiette* replaced the term *écuelle* (bowl) in the 16th century. The name *assiette* derives from the fact that it marked the position where the eater was seated (*assis*) at the table. The word denoted the action of placing an eater or a guest at the table, then the action of putting the plates on the table, then the serving of a meal (by a tavern-keeper who *tenait assiette*, offered food to customers), and finally it came to mean the complete range of dishes served during the course of a meal.

In ancient times, plates, either flat or bowl-shaped, were made of terracotta, wood or precious or non-precious metal. The Romans also moulded them from glass paste. By the end of the 15th century silver plates had become a symbol of wealth in France, and up to the 17th century the tables of the rich bourgeoisie were covered with magnificent gold plate and silverware. But following the disastrous wars in the reign of Louis XIV, faïence and porcelain replaced precious metal in such homes. Nicolas de Bonnefons commented in 1653 on the novelty of the individual soup plate, or *assiette à l'italienne*, introduced into France by Mazarin and given the name of *mazarine*: 'The plates are hollowed out so that one can be offered soup and serve oneself with the quantity one wishes to consume, without taking it spoonful by spoonful from the dish, and without the distaste that some might feel about the spoons of others being taken out of the mouth and dipped into the dish without first being wiped.'

The centre of a hollowed-out plate is called the

ombilic (navel). The edge is called *marli* (raised rim) or *talus* (slope), but some modern soup plates do not have this feature. A complete table service includes, in descending order of size: flat plates, soup plates, cheese plates, dessert plates, fruit plates, buffet plates and bread plates. The salad plate may be half-moon-shaped. Other special plates complete the service: plates with six or twelve compartments for snails and oysters, plates for *fondue bourguignonne* with compartments for the sauces, suitably shaped bowls for avocados, corn-on-the-cob and artichokes, and draining plates that are used to serve strawberries or asparagus. Presentation plates are a particular refinement: very flat and sometimes made of silver or silver-gilt, they are placed underneath a second, slightly smaller flat plate. They remain on the table when each plate is changed and are removed only at the cheese course.

■ **Correct use of plates** Traditional etiquette requires that two plates should never be placed on top of each other (except for presentation plates). The table is first laid with flat plates, which are replaced when the guests are seated by those for the first course. This custom is now limited to some catering establishments. It is advisable to have heated plates ready to serve hot dishes.

Although the use of plates is widespread in most western countries, this is far from being the case in other parts of the world. In the Far East bowls are most often used. In Africa it is often the custom to eat out of the main dish with the fingers, while in the Middle East flat breads are sometimes used instead of plates.

PLATINA (born Bartolomeo Sacchi) Italian humanist (born Platina, 1421; died Rome, 1481), known as 'Il Platina'. Born near Cremona, he became the Vatican librarian after publishing in Venice in 1474 a book in Latin on the culinary art entitled *De honesta Voluptate ac Valetudine* ('Honest Pleasure and Health'). This highly successful work was reprinted six times in 30 years and translated into French by the prior of Saint-Maurice, near Montpellier, with the help of a famous cook of the time, Nony Comeuse. Il Platina defended the then novel idea that delicacy is more important than quantity in cooking. He protested against the abuse of spices and recommended seasoning with lemon juice or wine. Furthermore, he suggested starting a meal with fresh fruit, such as melon or figs. His collection of recipes, which also contains a wealth of medical advice, is one of the first to describe regional specialities of the south of France.

PLEUROTE French name for *Pleurotus ostreatus*, the oyster mushroom. See *oyster mushroom*.

PLOMBIÈRES An ice cream made with custard cream prepared with almond-flavoured milk and usually enriched with whipped cream and mixed with crystallized (candied) fruit steeped in kirsch. Formerly, *plombières* cream was a type of custard cream, usually prepared with milk enriched with ground almonds and whipped cream, served with melted apricot jam sauce or in a pastry shell. Balzac writes in his novel *Splendeurs et Misères des courtisanes* (1847): 'After supper, ices by the name of *plombières* were served. Everyone knows that this type of ice is arranged in a pyramid with small, very delicate crystallized fruit placed on the surface. It is served in a small glass dish and the covering of crystallized fruit in no way affects the pyramid shape.'

It has been said (incorrectly) that *plombières* ice cream was invented at Plombières-les-Bains, in the Vosges, at a time when Napoleon III was taking a cure there. During his visit, he entertained the Italian statesman Cavour, who persuaded him to intervene in the War of Liberation between Italy and Austria (1859). However, it had already been mentioned by Balzac before this, so one must assume that the etymology of *plombières* is connected with the lead (*plomb*) moulds in which it was originally made. The addition of crystallized fruit to the recipe, which is the distinctive feature of this dessert, dates from the beginning of the 19th century.

RECIPES

chestnut plombières ice cream
Proceed as in the recipe for *plombières* ice cream, but instead of the crystallized (candied) fruit add 250 g (9 oz, 1 cup) sweetened chestnut purée, obtained by cooking the chestnuts in vanilla-flavoured sweetened milk. (Alternatively, use a can of sweetened chestnut purée.)

plombières cream
Place 8 egg yolks and 1 tablespoon rice flour in a saucepan. Add 500 ml (17 fl oz, 2 cups) full cream (whole) good milk, which is almost boiling. Place the saucepan over a moderate heat, stirring continuously with a wooden spoon. When the mixture begins to thicken, remove it from the heat and stir thoroughly until it is perfectly smooth. Then cook it over the heat for a further few minutes. This cream must have the same consistency as a confectioner's custard (pastry cream). Then add 175 g (6 oz, ¾ cup) caster (superfine) sugar and a minute pinch of salt.

Pour the mixture into another pan and set it on ice, stirring from time to time: it will thicken as it cools. When it is completely cold, just before serving, mix in 4 tablespoons of a liqueur (kirsch or rum, for example) and then a small quantity of whipped cream; the finished product should be light, velvety and perfectly smooth. Serve in a silver dish, in small pots, in a pastry case, a biscuit (cookie) crumb case or a dish-shaped base of almond paste.

plombières ice cream
Pound thoroughly in a mortar (or use a blender or processor) 300 g (11 oz, 2 cups) blanched fresh almonds and (if desired) 15 g (½ oz, 1½ tablespoons)

ground bitter almonds, gradually adding 4 table-spoons milk. Then add 1.5 litres (2¾ pints, 6½ cups) scalded single (light) cream and mix thoroughly. Press through a fine sieve. Place 300 g (11 oz, 1½ cups) caster (superfine) sugar and 12 egg yolks in a large bowl and beat until the mixture becomes white and thick. Bring the almond milk to the boil and pour it on to the egg and sugar mixture, whisking continuously. Place over the heat and stir gently until the cream coats the back of the spoon. Then immerse the base of the saucepan in cold water to stop the cooking process and continue to whisk until the cream has cooled. Place in an ice-cream freezer.

When the mixture is partially frozen, mix in 200 g (7 oz, 1 cup) finely chopped crystallized (candied) fruit soaked in kirsch or rum, 400 ml (14 fl oz, 1¾ cups) whipped double (heavy) cream and 150 ml (¼ pint, ⅔ cup) milk, both very cold. Then place in an ice-cream mould and freeze.

PLOVER A migratory wading bird of which several species winter in western Europe. In the Middle Ages the plover was considered to be a delicate and delicious food, served at winter feasts and in the best houses. The ringed plover frequents the marshlands and water meadows near the sea, while the golden plover, which is the more sought-after, inhabits moorlands. Plovers are considered to be excellent game, and certain gastronomes insist that they should be cooked undrawn. This tradition is an old one: in the 16th century, according to Lucien Tendret, only three kinds of birds – larks, turtledoves and plovers – could be roasted without 'breaking into them'. Plover can be prepared in the same way as woodcock or lapwing, but it is usually roasted. Its eggs are used in the same way as those of the lapwing.

PLUCHES The French name for the fresh leaves of some herbs, such as chervil, tarragon and parsley, used to flavour salads and hot dishes. Chervil *pluches*, for example, are used to flavour several sauces and soups, the leaves being cut with scissors rather than chopped, and added to the dish at the last minute to give maximum flavour. It is important not to boil these herbs and thus impair their flavour, although for certain recipes the leaves may be quickly blanched in boiling water before use.

PLUCK The heart, spleen, liver and lungs of a slaughtered animal. The components of ox (beef) and calf's pluck are cooked separately. Lamb's or sheep's pluck is prepared as a ragoût with red or white wine in several regions. Pig's pluck is a speciality of Vendée, where it is made into a ragoût together with the animal's blood and skin and sometimes the head.

At one time, all these pieces of offal (organ meat) were made into a ragoût. The French potter and writer Bernard Palissy made the following remark: 'In my time I have found that people did not want to eat sheep's feet, heads, or stomachs, yet at the moment this is what they prize most highly.'

PLUCKING The process of removing the feathers from a fowl or a game bird. It is usual to start at the tail and work towards the head; care must be taken not to tear the skin. The feathers are easier to remove if the bird is put into the refrigerator to firm the flesh (especially in the case of a small bird). Poultry is usually sold ready-plucked, but small feathers often remain on the wing tips, and these should also be plucked before singeing, which burns off any residual down. Any remaining vestiges of the feathers, such as the tube-like remnants of the shafts, can be removed with the point of a knife.

PLUM A yellow, green, red or purple stone (pit) fruit, which is eaten fresh from July to September as a dessert fruit and has numerous uses in pâtisserie and confectionery. It is also dried (see *prune*), preserved in brandy and distilled to produce a spirit.

Originating in Asia, the plum tree (*Prunus domestica*) was cultivated in Syria and grafted by the Romans, who preserved plums (particularly damsons) by drying. It was the Crusaders who introduced the plum to western Europe. The fruit was particularly prized after the Renaissance. From the 16th century plums were widely cultivated and many varieties were developed in France. Among these were the Catherine, the Impériale, the Perdrigon, the Goutte d'Or and the Plum de Monsieur (the favourite of Louis XIII's brother).

Plums selected for eating should be ripe but not soft, wrinkled or blemished; a very slight matt white bloom on the surface proves that they have not been handled too much. The main plum-producing regions of France are in the south-west, the south-east and the east. They are also grown in abundance in Britain, and imported varieties are available most of the year.

• Japanese varieties are available during June and July. Fairly mediocre in quality, they are large, round and juicy, either purplish-red with orange-coloured flesh or orange-yellow with yellow flesh.

• Bonne de Bry, a small, blue and rounded plum, with a juicy and very sweet, greenish-yellow flesh, is available in July. Greengages, which are yellowish-green, with firm, very juicy, sweet and fragrant flesh, are abundant in July.

• A reddish-purple greengage appears in August and September. This is as good as the green variety. It is followed by the Ente plum (elongated, purplish-red, with sweet but not very juicy flesh), the Alsatian quetsch (small, oblong and purple-black, with very sweet, fragrant, yellow flesh), the Nancy early mirabelle and, at the end of August, the Vosges mirabelle (small, round and orange-red, with very fragrant, sweet, juicy flesh).

• Brignole, a dark red plum from Brignole in France, is a comparatively new species valued as a cooking fruit.

In Britain there are several varieties of plum, in addition to the greengage and the damson.

• Czar is ready in early August. A large dark-blue plum with golden flesh, it is suitable for cooking or as a dessert variety.

• Pershore is also available in August; it is a conical-shaped dessert fruit with a yellow skin and rather pulpy flesh.

• Victoria plums ripen in late August and are very popular fruit. They are large and oval with a yellowish-scarlet skin. Sweet and juicy, they are perfect for bottling or eating as a dessert fruit.

• Kirke's Blue is ready in late August; it is a large fruit with deep purple skin with a distinct bloom and dark, sweet, juicy flesh; suitable for cooking or eating as a dessert fruit.

Later varieties include Warwickshire Drooper, the cherry plum and the Monarch. In the United States the Santa Rosa and Burbank plums are tart and juicy and are grown especially in California. They are also known as Japanese plums and are exported throughout Europe. Dark purple beach plums grow wild in the United States, especially around Cape Cod; they are mostly used to make beach-plum jelly.

A distinction is made between the varieties of plums used for cooking, preserves, jams and distillery, and those varieties that are enjoyed as dessert fruits. The Metz mirabelle and the quetsch, for example, are both used for distilling. The damson is used for bottling and jam-making and for making damson cheese. This traditional English preparation is a very thick damson pulp, boiled with sugar, which stores well and is served with biscuits (cookies) or used to fill tartlets.

RECIPES

flambéed plums
Stone (pit) some greengages or mirabelle plums and poach them in a vanilla-flavoured syrup until just tender. Drain them and place in a flameproof casserole. Add a little arrowroot blended with water to the cooking syrup, pour a little of this syrup over the plums and heat. Sprinkle with quetsch or mirabelle brandy heated in a ladle, flame and serve immediately.

plum conserve
Stone (pit) some plums, weigh the pulp and weigh out 675 g (1½ lb, 3 cups) sugar per 1 kg (2¼ lb) pulp. Put the fruit in a preserving pan with 100 ml (4 fl oz, 7 tablespoons) water per 1 kg (2¼ lb) fruit. Bring to the boil and leave to cook for about 20 minutes, stirring with a wooden spoon. Purée the fruit in a blender, return the purée to the pan and add the sugar. Cook until the conserve coats the wooden spoon. Pot in the usual way.

plums in brandy
Choose some very ripe, sound plums or greengages, prick them in 3 or 4 places with a large needle and weigh them. In a preserving pan, prepare a sugar syrup with 250 g (9 oz, 1 cup) sugar and 3 tablespoons water per 1 kg (2¼ lb) fruit, bring it to the boil and leave to boil for 2 minutes. Add the plums, stirring so that they are evenly coated with syrup, then transfer them to jars with a skimmer.

Leave to cool completely, then add some fruit spirit – 1 litre (1¾ pints, 4⅓ cups) per 1 kg (2¼ lb) plums – to cover the plums. Seal the jars.

Leave to stand for at least 3 months before consuming.

plum tart
Prepare a lining pastry with 200 g (7 oz, 1¾ cups) plain (all-purpose) flour, 90 g (3½ oz, 6½ tablespoons) softened butter, a pinch of salt, 1 egg and 1 tablespoon water. Roll the dough into a ball and refrigerate for 2 hours. Wash 500 g (18 oz) ripe plums and stone (pit) them without separating the halves completely. Roll out the dough to a thickness of 5 mm (¼ in) and use it to line a buttered tart tin (pan). Trim off the excess pastry and mark the edge with a criss-cross pattern. Prick the bottom with a fork, sprinkle with 40 g (1½ oz, 3 tablespoons) caster (superfine) sugar, and arrange the plums in the tart, opened out with curved sides downwards. Sprinkle the fruit with 40 g (1½ oz, 3 tablespoons) caster sugar. Cook in a preheated oven at 200°C (400°F, gas 6) for 30 minutes. Remove from the oven, leave until lukewarm, then coat the top with apricot jam.

plum tart à l'alsacienne
Prepare a sweet pastry with 125 g (4½ oz, ½ cup) softened butter, 250 g (9 oz, 1 cup) caster (superfine) sugar, 1 whole egg, 250 g (9 oz, 2¼ cups) plain (all-purpose) flour and 250 g (9 oz, 2 cups) ground almonds. Add just enough very cold water to bind the dough, roll it into a ball and place in the refrigerator for 2 hours.

Set aside a quarter of the dough and roll out the rest to a thickness of 5 mm (¼ in). Use it to line a tart tin (pie pan) 23 cm (9 in) in diameter. Roll out the remaining dough very thinly and cut it into long narrow strips. Spread a thick layer of quetsch or mirabelle plum jam over the tart and arrange the strips of pastry in a criss-cross pattern over the top. Cook in a preheated oven at 220°C (425°F, gas 7) for 30 minutes. Dust with icing (confectioner's) sugar and serve the tart hot, with whipped cream.

other recipes See *compote, fruit paste, jams, jellies and marmalades.*

PLUM CAKE A traditional British cake, flavoured with rum and containing currants, raisins, sultanas and candied peel.

RECIPE

plum cake
Soften 500 g (18 oz, 2¼ cups) butter until creamy and beat until it turns very pale. Add 500 g (18 oz, 2¼ cups) caster (superfine) sugar and beat again for a few minutes. Then incorporate 8 eggs, one at a time, beating well after each addition. Add 250 g (9 oz, 1½ cups) chopped candied peel (orange,

citron or lemon), 200 g (7 oz, 1¼ cups) seedless raisins, 150 g (5 oz, 1 cup) sultanas (golden raisins) and 150 g (5 oz, 1 cup) currants. Mix in 500 g (18 oz, 4½ cups) plain (all-purpose) flour sifted with 1½ teaspoons baking powder, the grated zest of 2 lemons and 3 tablespoons rum.

Line a 25 cm (10 in) round cake tin (pan) with greaseproof (wax) paper so that the paper extends 4 cm (1½ in) above the rim. Pour the mixture into the tin, taking care not to fill it above two-thirds. Bake in a preheated oven at 180°C (350°F, gas 4) for about 2 hours or until a skewer inserted in the centre of the cake comes out clean. Cover with a piece of foil if the cake is browning too much during cooking. Leave to cool in the tin for 10 minutes, then turn out on to a wire rack to cool completely.

PLUM PUDDING A traditional British pudding made with suet, raisins, currants, sultanas, prunes, almonds, spices and rum. It is boiled or steamed in a pudding basin (mould) and traditionally served flamed with brandy or rum and accompanied by brandy butter or sauce.

RECIPE

plum pudding
Put the following ingredients in a large mixing bowl: 125 g (4½ oz, 1 cup) suet, 175 g (6 oz, 1½ cups) chopped blanched almonds, 250 g (9 oz, 1½ cups) each of raisins and currants, 100 g (4 oz, 1 cup) sifted plain (all-purpose) flour, a generous pinch of salt, 250 g (9 oz, 1 cup) caster (superfine) sugar, 125 g (4½ oz, 1 cup) fairly dry white breadcrumbs, 250 g (9 oz, 1½ cups) chopped candied peel, the grated zest of ½ lemon and ½ teaspoon each mixed spice, ground cinnamon and grated nutmeg.

Beat 4 eggs with 4 tablespoons milk and the same quantity of rum. Add to the mixing bowl.

Boil 150 g (5 oz, ⅔ cup) granulated sugar with 4 tablespoons cold water until golden brown, then stir in 250 ml (8 fl oz, 1 cup) boiling water. Add this caramel to the mixing bowl. Stir the mixture thoroughly for 15 minutes.

Butter a large pudding basin (mould) and place a circle of greaseproof (wax) paper at the bottom. Place 125 g (4½ oz, ¾ cup) stoned (pitted) prunes (previously soaked in cold tea or water, then drained) in the basin and pour the pudding mixture on top. Cover with a circle of greaseproof paper, then with a pudding cloth or double thickness foil. Place the basin in the basket of a pressure cooker and add enough water to reach halfway up the basin. Cook for 1½ hours, beginning the timing from the moment that steam begins to escape. Alternatively, cook for 4 hours in a steamer or on an old saucer in a saucepan with enough boiling water to reach halfway up the basin. Remove the basin, wrap in foil and store in a cool place.

Steam for 1 hour more in a pressure cooker, or

2 hours in a steamer or saucepan, before serving. Then turn the pudding out on to a serving dish and sprinkle with 3 tablespoons sugar. Pour 4 tablespoons warm rum over the pudding and set it alight. The pudding can also be served cold.

PLUTARCH Greek biographer, essayist and philosopher (born Chaeronea, Boeotia, AD 46; died Chaeronea, AD 120). His main source of inspiration was Platonism and he wrote about 250 essays, of which about a third have survived in the form of his *Parallel Lives* (a series of biographies) and the *Moralia*. Among the latter are a few fragments from a *Symposium*, which deals with cooking and dietetics. The translation in 1572 by Jacques Amyot, a French bishop and classical scholar, made Plutarch the most widely read and influential ancient author in France until the 19th century. The *Symposia* were published in France under the title *Règles et Préceptes de santé de Plutarque* (Plutarch's rules and precepts about health).

POACHING A method of cooking food by gently simmering it in liquid. The amount of water or stock used depends on the food to be poached.

Red meat is poached in a white stock with vegetables. It is usually immersed in simmering stock, so that it is sealed and retains its juices and flavour. White meat is seldom poached.

Large poultry to be poached is put into cold white stock with vegetables; the liquid is then brought to the boil, skimmed and seasoned. The poultry is then simmered very slowly in the stock. Poultry for poaching can be stuffed or not and trussed. It can be larded with best lardons or studded with pieces of ham, tongue or truffles cut into the shape of little pegs. To protect the breast while cooking, poultry should be barded. To test whether the poultry is ready, prick the thigh. When the juice that runs out is white, the bird is cooked. After cooking, drain and untruss the poultry and remove the barding. Serve on fried bread, surrounded with an appropriate garnish. The stock, strained and skimmed, is boiled down and added to the sauce to be served with the dish.

Large fish can be poached whole or in slices, and moistened with concentrated fish stock or court-bouillon. Thick slices of fish are prepared in the same way. Fillets of fish (brill, whiting, sole, turbot) to be poached are put in a buttered baking dish, seasoned, moistened with a few tablespoons of concentrated fish stock and cooked in the oven.

Poached eggs are cooked in simmering salt water to which a few drops of vinegar have been added.

Fish or meat balls are put into a buttered pan, covered with boiling salted water and very slowly simmered.

Fruit is poached in a sugar syrup to cook it while still retaining its shape.

Some foods are poached on the bain marie principle, including mousses, mousselines, moulds and puddings. They are put in baking tins or pans half-full of hot water and cooked in a very slow oven.

POCHOUSE Also known as *pauchouse*. A Burgundy *matelote* (fish stew) made from a selection of pike, gudgeon, eel, perch or carp; it should also include burbot, which is now very rare. The Bresse *pochouse* often includes tench, carp and catfish. *Pochouse* is cooked with white wine and thickened with beurre manié.

The name is probably derived from the French *poche*, a fisherman's game bag, which in the local patois along the banks of the Doubs and the Saône is also known as a *pochouse*. The recipe comes from the Lower Doubs and is a very old one, appearing in the dispensary registers of the hospital of Saint-Louis de Chalon-sur-Saône as early as 1598. It was introduced into Burgundy by the fish merchants from Bresse. The dish is a speciality of Verdun-sur-le-Doubs where there is an association, the *Confrérie des Chevaliers de la Pochouse*, which is dedicated to preserving it.

RECIPE

pochouse
Butter a flameproof casserole generously and completely cover the bottom with 2–3 large peeled sliced onions and 2 carrots cut into rings. Clean 2 kg (4½ lb) freshwater fish and cut into uniform pieces: use 1 kg (2¼ lb) eels (skinned) and 1 kg (2¼ lb) burbot, tench, pike or carp. Place the pieces of fish in the casserole with a bouquet garni in the centre. Cover with dry white wine and add 2 crushed garlic cloves. Add salt and pepper, cover, bring to the boil, reduce the heat and allow to simmer for about 20 minutes.

Meanwhile, dice 150 g (5 oz) unsmoked streaky bacon and blanch for 5 minutes in boiling water. Strain. Glaze 20 small (pearl) onions. Clean and slice 250 g (9 oz, 3 cups) mushrooms and sprinkle with lemon juice. Toss the bacon and mushrooms in butter in a sauté pan. Strain the pieces of fish and add them to the sauté pan, together with the onions.

Thicken the cooking liquid from the fish with 1 tablespoon beurre manié, strain and pour into the sauté pan. Simmer for a few minutes, then add 200 ml (7 fl oz, ¾ cup) crème fraîche. Boil, uncovered, for 5 minutes to reduce. Pour the *pochouse* into a deep serving dish and garnish with garlic-flavoured croûtons.

POÊLON A small, long-handled saucepan, often with a lid. It was formerly made of earthenware (glazed or not) and was suitable for slow-cooking, simmering or braising foods. It is still used for the same purposes but is now made of stainless steel, black or enamelled cast iron, or enamel plate. It can also be used for browning mushrooms, making sauces and cooking *paupiettes* or peas with pieces of bacon. The *caquelon*, used for preparing *fondue savoyarde* (a baked cheese fondue), is a type of *poêlon*, as is the pan used for making Burgundy fondue, which is deeper, fitted with a lid and rests on a table warmer. The sugar *poêlon* is made of copper and is used for cooking sugar and syrups.

POGNE Also known as *pognon* or *pougnon*. A type of brioche, sometimes filled with crystallized (candied) fruit, served either hot or cold, often with redcurrant jelly. It is a speciality of the Dauphiné. The *pogne de Romans* is well known, but *pognes* are also made in Crest (mainly for Easter), Die and Valence. In certain parts of the Lyonnais and Franche-Comté regions, *pognes* can be brioches or tarts, made either with fruit or, in winter, with gourd or pumpkin. The word originates from *pougna* or *pugne*, a patois word for the handful of dough left over from bread-making, which housewives used to enrich with butter and eggs to make pastries.

RECIPE

pogne de romans
Arrange 500 g (18 oz, 4½ cups) plain (all-purpose) flour in a circle on the worktop. In the middle of this circle put 1½ teaspoons salt, 1 tablespoon orange-flower water, 25 g (1 oz) fresh yeast (2 cakes compressed yeast), 250 g (9 oz, 1 cup) softened butter and 4 whole eggs. Mix together thoroughly, working the dough vigorously to give it body. Add 2 more eggs, one after the other, and finally incorporate 200 g (7 oz, ¾ cup) caster (superfine) sugar, little by little, kneading the dough all the while. Place this dough in a bowl sprinkled with flour, cover with a cloth and leave it to rise for 10–12 hours at room temperature away from draughts.

Turn the dough out on to the table and knock it back (punch down) with the flat of the hand. Make into 'crowns': shape two-thirds of the dough into balls, then use the remainder to shape smaller balls to place on top, like brioches. Place these crowns in buttered baking tins (pans). Leave the dough to rise for a further 30 minutes in a warm place. Brush with beaten egg and bake in a preheated oven at 190°C (375°F, gas 5) for about 40 minutes. Serve with redcurrant jelly.

POINT, À The French term describing a grilled (broiled) or sautéed steak (or other small cut of meat) that is cooked to the medium stage – between medium-rare and well-done.

By extension, a dish is referred to as *à point* when cooking has reached the desired stage and must be stopped immediately (green vegetables and pasta cooked *al dente*, fish in court-bouillon). The expression is also used to describe a dish that is ready to be served, all preparations being completed to the chef's satisfaction.

POINT, FERNAND French chef (born Louhans, 1897; died Vienne, 1955). His parents kept the station buffet at Louhans, where both his mother and grandmother were in charge of the cooking. He studied in Paris (as sauce chef at Foyot's, the Bristol and the Majestic), then at the Hôtel Royal in Évian, where he was the fish chef. In 1922, when the Paris–Lyon–Mediterranée railway company refused to recognize officially the Louhans station buffet as a restaurant, Auguste Point (his father) decided to move to Vienne, where he opened a more conventional restaurant. Two years later he left it to his son, who renamed it La Pyramide. Fernand Point concentrated on producing a cuisine based on good-quality food enhanced by careful cooking and meticulous preparation. The restaurant soon became well known to gastronomes on their way to the south of France. All the famous people of the time came to sample what Curnonsky regarded as the pinnacle of culinary art. Fernand Point's personality also had a lot to do with the popularity of the restaurant: his humour, his intransigence, the warmth of his welcome, his anecdotes, his eccentricities and his massive size, all contributed to make him one of the great French chefs. After his death, the kitchens of La Pyramide were supervised first by Paul Mercier and then by Guy Thivard, still under Madame Point's administration.

The great chef was also a first-class teacher, and his pupils, namely Thuilier, Bocuse, Chapel, the Troisgros brothers, Outhier and Bise, bear witness to the value of his training. Point's cuisine was in the great classical mould: truffled Bresse chicken *en vessie*; stuffed salmon trout braised in port wine; *délices de Saint-Antoine en feuilleté*, a dish of pig's trotters (feet) in puff pastry, which he made especially for Albert Lebrun; and the famous *marjolaine*, which took him several years to perfect (a light almond and hazelnut sponge cake filled with three different creams: chocolate, butter and praline).

'The pharaoh of the Pyramide at Vienne' (in the words of his biographer Félix Benoît) is also remembered for his maxims, some of which can be found in his book *Ma gastronomie*: 'Garnishes must be matched like a tie to a suit' and 'A good meal must be as harmonious as a symphony and as well-constructed as a Norman cathedral.' He considered that the most difficult preparations were often those that appear to be the easiest: 'A béarnaise sauce is simply an egg yolk, a shallot, a little tarragon vinegar and butter, but it takes years of practice for the result to be perfect.'

POIRE A French cut of beef that is part of the topside. It is a round, lean, very tender cut and is cooked as steak. It weighs about 500 g (18 oz).

POITOU The variable quality of the soil has not prevented Poitou from having solid culinary traditions. The prosperity of the region is based on its cereal crops, cattle, sheep, goats, pigs and poultry. The ground and winged game (hare, rabbit, quail, thrush and partridge) are plentiful, and the produce of the lakes and rivers provides excellent fish dishes: tench *à la poitevine*, lamprey simmered in wine and eels sautéed in garlic, grilled (broiled) or prepared as a *bouilleture*. The marshland of Poitou provides frogs, and the nearby coastline of the Vendée is a source of sea fish (especially for *chaudrée*)

and shellfish (especially mussels and oysters).

The cultivated marshlands are very fertile, yielding onions, artichokes, asparagus, melons, peas, white beans (*mojettes*, cooked with cream) and French (green) beans, leeks (which are made into a succulent vegetable loaf), cauliflowers and cabbage. Orchards are planted with apples (especially the 'Clochard' variety), cherries, peaches and walnuts, as well as the chestnuts for which the region is famous.

Soups typical of the region include a wine soup, served either hot (known as *rôtie*) or cold (*migé*), and a pig's head potée. Charcuterie specialities include the famous *pâté de Pâques en croûte*, a pie filled with meat, poultry, meatballs, and hard-boiled (hard-cooked) eggs; duck-liver pâtés; and the confits of Civray and Sauzé-Vaussais. Snails (*lumas*) are cooked stuffed or in wine, and frogs' legs are prepared as a blanquette or *à la luçonnaise* (sautéed in butter and garnished with fried garlic cloves). Among the most characteristic dishes of Poitou are the *sauce de pire*, pig's liver and lung simmered with onions, shallots, red wine and spices; the *gigorit* of pork and poultry; the Vendée *fressure*, pigs' fry with bacon, eaten cold; the *pirot*, prepared with goat meat, young fresh garlic and sorrel; the Poitou *biftecks*, chopped beef bound with bone marrow, eggs, breadcrumbs, onions and white wine; and also the *far*, a rum-flavoured tart, and forcemeats.

Poitou produces some good fresh cheeses, such as caillebottes and small caillés, but it is best known for its wide variety of goat's-milk cheeses, including the famous Chabichou, the Bougon, La-Mothe-Saint-Héray, Lusignan, Parthenay, Saint-Loup, Saint-Saviol, Saint-Varent, Sauzé-Vaussais, Trois-Cornes and Xaintray.

Among the desserts should be mentioned the *tourteau* (made with goat's-milk cheese), *clafoutis*, *grimolle* (a fruit pancake baked in the oven) and plum pie. Butter is used to prepare *broye* and *fouée* (a circle of bread dough covered with cream and butter and baked in the oven). *Millas*, *échaudés* and *craquelins* are common in the west of Poitou. Some noted local products are the *berlingolettes* of Châtellerault, the macaroons of Montmorillon and Lusignan, the biscuits (cookies) of Parthenay, the nougatine of Poitiers and the candied angelica of Niort (a famous liqueur is also made from the plant).

Poitou produces some pleasant red, white and sparkling wines.

POIVRADE Any of various sauces in which pepper plays a more important role than that of a simple condiment. The best known *poivrade* is a *mirepoix* mixed with vinegar and white wine, reduced, blended with a roux and white wine, and seasoned with crushed peppercorns. It is served with marinated meat and ground game. The other *poivrade* sauces are based on vinegar and shallots (hot) or vinaigrette (cold).

Poivrade is also the name of a small artichoke, which is eaten *à la croque au sel* (with salt as the only accompaniment).

RECIPES

Carême's poivrade sauce

Put 2 sliced onions and 2 sliced carrots in a saucepan. Add a little lean ham, a few sprigs of parsley, a little thyme, a bay leaf, a generous pinch of *mignonette*, a little mace, then 2 tablespoons good vinegar and 2 tablespoons clear stock. Simmer over a gentle heat until the vegetables are very soft. When well reduced add 2 tablespoons clear stock and 2 tablespoons well-blended *espagnole*** sauce. Boil for a few minutes, then press the sauce through a sieve and boil again to reduce to the desired consistency.

Add a little butter to the sauce just before serving.

poivrade sauce

Finely dice 150 g (5 oz) scraped or peeled carrots with the cores removed, 100 g (4 oz, ⅔ cup) onions and 100 g (4 oz) green (unsmoked) streaky bacon. Cut 50 g (2 oz, ½ cup) celery into thin strips. Sweat very gently for about 20 minutes with 25 g (1 oz, 2 tablespoons) butter, a sprig of thyme and half a bay leaf. Add 500 ml (17 fl oz, 2 cups) vinegar and 100 ml (4 fl oz, 7 tablespoons) white wine, then reduce by half.

Make a brown roux with 40 g (1½ oz, 3 tablespoons) butter and 40 g (1½ oz, ⅓ cup) plain (all-purpose) flour. Add 750 ml (1¼ pints, 3¼ cups) beef or chicken stock and cook gently for 30 minutes. Skim the fat from the mirepoix and add to the roux. Deglaze the mirepoix pan with 100 ml (4 fl oz, 7 tablespoons) white wine and add to the sauce, together with 2 tablespoons finely chopped mushrooms.

Cook gently for a further hour, adding a little stock if the sauce reduces too much. Crush about 10 black peppercorns, add to the sauce and leave to simmer for 5 minutes. Then strain the sauce through coarse muslin (cheesecloth) or a very fine strainer.

If this sauce is to be served with a marinated meat, use the strained marinade to deglaze the cooking pan and dilute the roux. If it is to be served with game, cut the trimmings from the game into small pieces and add to the mirepoix.

POJARSKI A way of serving veal chops in which the meat is detached from the bone, chopped with butter and bread soaked in milk, seasoned, reformed on the bone and fried in clarified butter. By extension, it has come to mean a cutlet made up of white chicken meat or salmon, covered with flour or breadcrumbs and sautéed in clarified butter.

Kotliety pojarskie is a classic Russian dish of meatballs named after its creator, an innkeeper called Pojarski. Originally made of beef, they were a great favourite of Tsar Nicolas I. When the tsar arrived at Pojarski's unexpectedly one day, he was served with veal meatballs instead and enjoyed them just as much, so they became popular too.

RECIPES

salmon cutlets Pojarski

Chop 300 g (11 oz) fresh salmon flesh, then add 65 g (2½ oz, ⅔ cup) stale breadcrumbs (soaked in milk and strained) and 65 g (2½ oz, 5 tablespoons) fresh butter. Season with salt and pepper and sprinkle with a pinch of grated nutmeg. Divide the mixture into 4 equal portions and shape into cutlets. Coat with breadcrumbs and brown on both sides in clarified butter. Arrange on a serving dish, sprinkle with the cooking butter and garnish with canelled slices of lemon.

veal chop Pojarski

Bone a veal chop and keep the bone. Weigh the flesh and chop finely. Add an equal weight of stale breadcrumbs soaked in milk and strained, a quarter of its weight of butter and a little chopped parsley. Season with salt and pepper and add a pinch of grated nutmeg. Stir the mixture thoroughly until smooth. Scrape the chop bone thoroughly and blanch in boiling water for 5 minutes. Cool and wipe dry. Press the meat mixture along the bone and reshape the chop. Leave to dry for 30 minutes, then cover with flour and cook in clarified butter for about 15 minutes until brown on both sides and cooked through. Arrange the chop on a serving dish, garnish with a canelled slice of lemon, sprinkle with a little noisette butter and serve with an appropriate vegetable cooked in butter.

POLAND See *page 910.*

POLENTA A cornmeal porridge that is the traditional basic dish of northern Italy (both Venice and Lombardy claim to have invented it). The Greeks used to eat various cereal porridges called *poltos*, but maize (corn) did not arrive from America until the beginning of the 16th century.

Polenta is traditionally made with water in a large copper pot, stirred with a big wooden spoon. The porridge is cooled in a round wooden tray and then cut into squares or diamond shapes. It can also be made with milk (for desserts), stock or with a mixture of white wine and water. Like rice and pasta, polenta is very versatile and is used for a large number of dishes: fritters, croquettes, gratins, croûtes and timbales. Served plain, with butter and cheese, in a sauce, or even flavoured with vegetables, ham or white truffle, polenta may accompany fish stews, meat ragoûts or brochettes of small birds. In Italy the large-grained Bergamo and Verona varieties of maize, which take a long time to cook, are preferred for making polenta.

Gastronomic societies have been formed to promote polenta and its dishes: the Académie des Polentophages was founded at the beginning of the 18th century, and the P.P.P.P. Society (*Prima Patria Poì Polenta*, 'First the homeland, then polenta!') a century later.

POLAND

A country with a harsh climate and subject to numerous invasions throughout its history, Poland has a cuisine showing very diverse influences. In spite of this, it is dominated by pork, cabbage, potatoes and spirits, not to mention an abundant and varied pâtisserie, introduced into France by Stanislas Leszczynski.

A number of Slavonic dishes, notably soups, patties and ravioli, show Russian influence, while the feasts of the Catholic Church and the cookery of the Jewish community have also had their effect. The marriage beween the King of Poland and an Italian princess in the 16th century also brought italian culinary skills.

■ **Substantial meals** The Poles have a reputation for being solid eaters and great drinkers. Traditionally, the morning meal often includes cold meat or charcuterie, while the evening meal consists of potatoes with curdled milk, *klouski* (a kind of savoury dumpling), patties and large ravioli served in soup. Any of the following may be served: *piroshki*, *cyrniki*, *kromeskies* and other *varieniki* (of Russian origin); also *uszka*, small pastries stuffed with mushrooms; *kolduny*, types of ravioli stuffed with raw minced (ground) beef, prepared with bone marrow and oregano; and *paszteciki* (meat patties).

The traditional Polish meal (*obiad*) takes place at about 2 p.m. and consists of several courses. The soups are always impressive, especially *barszcz* (the Polish borsch), a clear beetroot (red beet) soup; the version eaten at Christmas is *barszcz wigilijny*, made with beetroot and mushrooms. Other soups include *zupa szczawiowa*, with sorrel and smoked bacon; *chlodnik*, with beetroot, soured (dairy sour) cream and crayfish; *rassolnick*, with cucumber; *krupnik*, cream of barley soup with vegetables (krupnik is also a liqueur with honey and spices, which is drunk warm with the dessert); *kapusniack*, with cabbage, celery and bacon; and *stchi*, a broth of beef, tongue and pig's ears, flavoured with fennel.

■ **Fish dishes** Many of Poland's fish dishes are derived from Jewish cooking, including marinated herrings, herrings in cream, jellied carp in sweet-and-sour sauce or in horseradish sauce with sour cream, and sweet-and-sour mackerel. Trout *à la cracovienne* is poached and served with chopped hard-boiled (hard-cooked) eggs, lemon juice and melted butter.

■ **Meat, poultry and game** Meat is usually braised or cooked in ragoûts (see *bigos*). Stuffed dishes, which are also very popular, include braised beef stuffed with mushrooms and *paupiettes* stuffed with *kasha*. The pig provides a wide range of savoury charcuterie, including smoked and marinated ham, smoked and braised bacon, *kabanosy* (long thin sausages smoked with juniper wood) and *kielbasa tatrzanska* ('wrinkled' sausages from the Tatras).

Game is served with fruit; for example, roasted partridge with bilberries (huckleberries), apples, lemon and cinnamon, or wild boar (smoked loin of pork) with stewed apples. Poultry is usually roasted: *ges* (goose) and *indyk* (turkey) are equally popular.

■ **Vegetables** Cabbage is the most commonly used vegetable, especially in sauerkraut with apples and carrots. Boiled vegetables, such as asparagus, cauliflower, salsify and cabbage, are prepared with chopped hard-boiled eggs and melted butter. Sweet-and-sour preparations are common, for example in salads (onions with apples in mayonnaise, cucumber with cream and sugar, peppers with walnuts) and in pickled and spiced plums.

■ **Sumptuous pâtisserie** Polish pâtisserie is sumptuous: *babka* is a kind of baba (but not soaked in rum); the *babka wielkanocna*, with raisins and richly decorated, is eaten at Easter. Other cakes include *chrust* (a very sweet sponge cake); honey and ginger cakes (Poland is a great producer of honey); *mazurek*, resembling a Linzertorte and sometimes topped with chocolate meringue; *makowiec*, a yeast cake sprinkled with poppy seeds, eaten at Christmas; *tort orzechowy*, a walnut cake with coffee icing (frosting); *paczki*, fritters filled with jam; and *nalesniki*, pancakes filled with cream cheese.

■ **Refreshing and invigorating drinks** Beer is usually drunk during the meal, and tea is served at the end. Vodka is drunk at the beginning of the meal with *zakuski* as in Russia: *zubrowka* (vodka flavoured with 'bison herb', a very strong scented grass) is a particular favourite. Poles also appreciate iced coffee or coffee with the skin of boiled milk.

RECIPE

Parmesan polenta
Boil 1 litre (1¾ pints, 4⅓ cups) water with 1–2 teaspoons salt (or to taste), then add 250 g (9 oz, 2 cups) cornmeal and mix together thoroughly. Cook for 25–30 minutes, stirring continuously with a wooden spoon. Then add 50–65 g (2–2½ oz, 4–5 tablespoons) butter and 75 g (3 oz, ¾ cup) grated Parmesan cheese. Pour the porridge on to a damp plate, spreading it out in an even layer, and leave to cool completely. Cut into squares or diamond shapes and fry in butter until golden. Arrange on a serving dish and sprinkle with grated Parmesan cheese and noisette butter.

POLIGNAC The name of various classic French dishes dedicated to members of the Polignac family.

Suprêmes of chicken Polignac are covered with suprême sauce enriched with thinly sliced truffles and mushrooms. Flat-fish are poached, dressed with a sauce made with white wine and cream, and served with a mushroom julienne. Eggs Polignac are either cooked in moulds, on thin slices of truffle or soft-boiled and covered with Périgueux sauce.

RECIPE

eggs Polignac in a mould
Butter some small round moulds and line the bottom with a thin slice of truffle. Break an egg into each mould. Bake in a preheated oven at 180°C (350°F, gas 4) in a bain marie. Turn each egg out on to a croûton of bread fried in butter. Heat some meat glaze and add to it an equal volume of *maître d'hôtel* butter. Cover the eggs with this sauce.

POLKA A gâteau consisting of a ring of choux pastry on a base of shortcrust pastry (basic pie dough), filled with confectioner's custard (pastry cream) or frangipane cream, then dusted with sugar and caramelized with a red-hot skewer forming a criss-cross pattern. Small polkas can also be made.

Polka bread (*pain polka*) is a traditional French bread, particularly popular in the Loire Valley. Usually round and flat, weighing 2 kg (4½ lb), it has deep criss-cross grooves in the top, which enable the bread to be divided without using a knife. It is always highly baked with a thick, brown crust.

In both cases, the name is derived from the dance of the same name, the criss-cross pattern resembling the figures of the dance.

RECIPE

gâteau polka
Make a short pastry with 50 g (2 oz, ¼ cup) softened butter, 125 g (4½ oz, 1 cup) plain (all-purpose) flour, 1 tablespoon caster (superfine) sugar and 1 egg yolk. When smooth, roll it into a ball and chill in the refrigerator.

Make a confectioner's custard (pastry cream; see *custard*) with 1 litre (1¾ pints, 4⅓ cups) milk, 6 eggs, 200 g (7 oz, ¾ cup) caster sugar, 175 g (6 oz, 1½ cups) plain flour and 100 ml (4 fl oz, 7 tablespoons) rum. Leave to cool.

Roll out the dough thinly into a circle 20 cm (8 in) in diameter. Place it on a buttered baking sheet and prick with a fork. Make some choux* pastry with 120 ml (4½ fl oz, ½ cup) water, 25 g (1 oz, 2 tablespoons) butter, 1 tablespoon caster sugar, a pinch of salt, 65 g (2½ oz, ⅔ cup) plain flour and 2 beaten eggs. Place in a piping bag with a plain nozzle 1.5 cm (⅝ in) in diameter. Brush the rim of the pastry circle with beaten egg and pipe the choux pastry in a border 5 mm (¼ in) from the edge. Brush this border with beaten egg.

Bake in a preheated oven at 200°C (400°F, gas 6) for 20 minutes, covering the centre of the circle with foil if the pastry browns too quickly. Leave to cool completely, then pour the confectioner's custard into the centre. Sprinkle with granulated sugar.

Carefully heat a metal skewer in a flame until it is red hot and then mark a criss-cross pattern on the top of the custard.

POLLACK Either of two large sea fish (up to 70–80 cm (28–32 in) long), related to the whiting. The yellow pollack is found in the Atlantic as far south as the Bay of Biscay, while the black pollack can be found as far north as Norway and rarely further south than Brittany.

The black pollack has a grey underside and a grey-green or dark-green back; the yellow pollack is more of an olive colour, and its underside is coppery or silvery. Both varieties are very lean fish (1% fat), but the yellow variety has a finer texture. Both are sold whole, in steaks or filleted. Black pollack is often deep-frozen. Pollack can be prepared in the same way as cod or whiting, but the black pollack tends to disintegrate and should not be cooked for as long. In Scandinavian countries dried pollack is called *klippfisch*; when dried and salted, it is referred to as *stockfisch*.

POLO, MARCO Venetian voyager (born Venice, 1254; died Venice, 1324). He travelled through Armenia, Persia and the Gobi Desert, was lavishly entertained in Peking, then returned to Europe at the end of a 16-year voyage via Sumatra and the Persian Gulf. While imprisoned by the Genoese, he wrote an account of his voyage, *The Book of the Wonders of the World*. He is given credit for the discovery and spread of rice and pastas, but more importantly he enabled Venice to trade in spices and exotic goods from the Far East. In memory of this great voyager, an annual gastronomy prize, Marco-Polo-Casanova, is awarded by a panel of journalists and restaurateurs to the best Paris restaurant specializing in foreign cooking.

POLONAISE, À LA Describing a classic dish of vegetables, especially cauliflower and asparagus. The vegetables are cooked in boiling water, then sprinkled with chopped hard-boiled (hard-cooked) egg yolk and parsley (or *fines herbes*) and finally with breadcrumbs fried in butter. The description also refers to other recipes derived from Polish cooking.

RECIPES

asparagus à la polonaise
Clean some asparagus and trim to the same length. Tie into small bunches and cook for 25 minutes in plenty of boiling salted water (to which may be added 1 tablespoon flour to help the asparagus keep its colour). Drain thoroughly and arrange in a long buttered dish, in staggered rows, so that the tips show clearly. Sprinkle with sieved hard-boiled (hard-cooked) egg yolk and chopped parsley. Lightly brown some breadcrumbs in noisette butter and pour over the asparagus. Serve immediately.

beetroot salad à la polonaise

Peel some cooked beetroot (beet) and cut into thin slices. Season with a highly spiced vinaigrette, pile in a salad bowl and sprinkle liberally with chopped parsley and sieved hard-boiled (hard-cooked) egg yolk. Thin apple slices sprinkled with lemon juice may be added.

cauliflower à la polonaise

Divide a cauliflower into large florets and cook in boiling salted water until just cooked (the cauliflower should stay slightly firm). Reshape it in a round serving dish, sprinkle with 2–3 chopped hard-boiled (hard-cooked) eggs and chopped parsley, and keep in a warm place. Crumble 75 g (3 oz, about 3 slices) stale bread in 75 g (3 oz, ⅓ cup) melted butter in a frying pan. Fry until golden and sprinkle over the cauliflower; serve immediately.

Swiss chard à la polonaise

Trim away the green parts of the leaves from the white central stalks of the Swiss chard, cut the white stalks into strips, remove the strings, then cut into pieces of the same length. Cook, covered, for about 1 hour in a white stock for vegetables. Drain and finish the dish as for asparagus à la polonaise. Cook the green part of the leaves like spinach for a separate dish.

other recipes See *chicken, salsify*.

POLONAISE Also known as *brioche polonaise*. A brioche soaked in rum or kirsch, sliced and layered with crystallized (candied) fruits mixed with confectioner's custard (pastry cream), and then covered with meringue and decorated with sliced almonds before browning in the oven. Small individual brioches may be hollowed out and filled with the custard and fruit mixture and are sometimes arranged on little pastry bases or in paper cases before being covered with meringue.

RECIPE

brioche polonaise

Make a brioche* weighing about 800 g (1¾ lb). Dice about 200 g (7 oz, ¾ cup) crystallized (candied) fruit and steep in kirsch. Make a syrup with 200 g (7 oz, ¾ cup) granulated sugar, 250 ml (8 fl oz, 1 cup) water and a liqueur glass of kirsch. Prepare a confectioner's custard (pastry cream; see *custard*) with 50 g (2 oz, ½ cup) plain (all-purpose) flour, 4 egg yolks, 100 g (4 oz, ½ cup) caster (superfine) sugar, 1 teaspoon vanilla sugar and 500 ml (17 fl oz, 2 cups) milk. Mix 40 g (1½ oz, 3 tablespoons) butter with the custard, then incorporate the drained fruit.

Cut the brioche horizontally into slices, after removing the top. Dip the slices in the syrup and spread each with a thick layer of the fruit custard. Reshape the brioche and put the top back in position. Stiffly whisk 4 egg whites, incorporating 50 g (2 oz, ¼ cup) caster sugar. Completely cover the brioche with the meringue, then sprinkle with icing (confectioner's) sugar – no more than 2 tablespoons – and scatter about 100 g (4 oz, 1 cup) shredded (slivered) almonds over the surface. Brown in a preheated oven at 230°C (450°F, gas 8) for 5 minutes. Cool completely before serving.

POLYPORE A generic term for a very large number of mushroom species growing on tree trunks. The *polypore en touffe* or *poulet de bois* and the umbel polypore are highly valued in the East for their consistency and flavour, which makes them excellent accompaniments for chicken and fish.

POMEGRANATE A shrub of Asiatic origin, cultivated for its large, edible fruit. The fruit has a tough reddish-yellow or green skin enclosing many red seeds surrounded by sweet, pinkish, juicy pulp. The ancient Egyptians fermented pomegranates to make a heady wine. The fruit was regarded as a symbol of love and fertility because of its numerous seeds: it is mentioned in Greek mythology as well as being depicted in Christian symbolism. The dried seeds were used as a condiment by the ancients, and the fruit was used mainly as a medicine until the Renaissance. Recipes featuring the pomegranate began to appear at the time of Louis XIV, especially those for sauces and soups.

It is cultivated in many tropical countries, including Central America, Lebanon, Pakistan and India, and it also grows in the south of France. The fruit is usually eaten fresh or used to make refreshing drinks (see *grenadine*), but in some countries it is also used as an ingredient or as a condiment: pomegranate concentrate is used in some Lebanese dishes (meatballs and stuffed fish); fresh seeds are used in salads, aubergine (eggplant) purées, sweet couscous and almond creams in Oriental cookery; and crushed seeds are used in meat dishes in India and Pakistan.

RECIPE

lemonade with pomegranate juice

Choose 6 very ripe pomegranates, squeeze out the juice from the seeds using a vegetable mill or blender, and then strain. Add the juice of 2 lemons and 2 oranges and the zest of 1 lemon and 1 orange. Add water (twice the volume of the fruit juice) and sugar as required. Steep for several hours or up to 36 hours in the refrigerator, pass through a very fine strainer and chill before serving.

POMELO The largest of the citrus fruits, sometimes known as shaddock. The pomelo is pear-shaped, 20–30 cm (8–12 in) long, with a thick skin and a bitter, coarse flesh similar in flavour to the grapefruit. It can be eaten on its own or used in the same recipes as grapefruit.

POMEROL A Bordeaux wine region, slightly north-west of Saint-Émilion. There is some gravel in the soil, which makes the finer Pomerol wines, produced predominantly from the Merlot grape, very elegant. The most famous estate is Château Pétrus, but there are many other well-known ones, including Châteaux Lafleur, Le Pin, L'Eglise-Clinet and La Fleur de Gay.

POMIANE, EDOUARD POZERSKI DE
French doctor and gastronome (born Paris, 1875; died Paris, 1964). Head of the food physiology laboratory at the Pasteur Institute, where he spent his entire career, Dr de Pomiane conducted research into digestion and dietetics, which led him to take an interest in cooking. He invented *gastrotechnie*, a study of the physico-chemical processes to which foods are subjected during cooking. Himself a gourmet, he cooked to perfection, with an emphasis on simplicity and the harmonization of flavours. He wrote in a lively, humorous and pleasant style and is still one of the most popular of 20th-century French gastronomical writers.

We are particularly indebted to him for *Bien manger pour bien vivre* (1922), *La Cuisine en six leçons* (1927), *Le Code de la bonne chère* (1924), *Radio-Cuisine* (1936; based on radio broadcasts in 1932–33 and 1934–35, on his culinary discoveries, his travels, his own creations and his favourite recipes). In *Cuisine juive, ghettos modernes* (1929) he traced his Polish family back to its origins (his father emigrated to France in 1845). His other works include *La Cuisine pour la femme du monde* (1934), *Réflexes et Réflexions devant la nappe* (1940) and *Cuisine et Restrictions* (1940), in which Pomiane dealt humorously with subjects in which cooking and contemporary life are closely associated.

POMMARD
An AOC wine from a village in the Côte-de-Beaune in Burgundy. The red wines, produced from Pinot Noir, are deep in colour, with good structure, and are capable of long ageing.

POMME DE PIN
A tavern established in the 16th century on the Île de la Cité in Paris. Made famous first by François Villon, then by Rabelais, it was associated for three centuries with the world of literature, being frequented by the poets of La Pléiade and later by the classical poets. In the 17th century writers were allowed to get drunk free of charge, which helped the establishment to enjoy a long period of popularity.

Other taverns of the same name existed in Paris, Rome and Copenhagen. The symbol of the pine cone, from which the tavern derives its name, is probably a survival of the worship of Dionysus, the god of wine, whose symbol was a stick surrounded with vine shoots and topped with a pine cone.

POMPADOUR, JEANNE POISSON, MARQUISE DE
French royal favourite (born Paris, 1721; died Versailles, 1764). The wife of Charles le Normant d'Étiolles, a farmer-general, she became Louis XV's mistress in 1745 and was made a marquise. She played an important role in the king's life and was a notable influence in the field of the arts.

Like many other courtesans of the period, she was very interested in cookery. Several dishes were named after her (dishes of apricots, lamb chops, pheasant croquettes and small iced petits fours), both during her lifetime and in the 19th century (especially by Escoffier and Urbain Dubois). Other dishes appear to be her own creations, such as fillets of sole with truffles and mushrooms, chicken breasts *en bellevue* and tendrons of lamb *au soleil* (cooked in a white veal stock with thin escalopes and truffles). Monselet also credits her with a sauce for asparagus containing butter and egg yolks, bound with cornmeal and seasoned with verjuice.

In classic cookery Pompadour is the name of a dish of noisettes of lamb or tournedos fried and coated in Choron sauce, then surrounded with Périgueux sauce and artichoke hearts stuffed with lightly browned noisette potatoes.

Salpicon Pompadour (diced foie gras, pressed tongue, mushrooms and truffles bound with a Madeira sauce) is used to fill timbales and vol-au-vent.

RECIPES

Savoury Dishes
lamb cutlets Pompadour
Braise the cutlets, which should be taken from the fillet end and trimmed of fat; drain and allow to cool thoroughly. Mask with a well-reduced Soubise purée and leave to dry. Coat with fine breadcrumbs and then beaten egg. Lightly brown the cutlets in clarified butter. Serve with lemon quarters and small buttered turnips.

rissoles Pompadour
Roll out some rough puff pastry to a thickness of 5 mm (¼ in) and cut out an even number of circles 5–6 cm (2–2½ in) in diameter. Prepare a salpicon of pickled tongue, truffles and mushrooms cooked in butter and bound with a very thick demi-glace sauce; coat half the pastry circles with this mixture (not completely to the edge) and cover with the remaining circles. Seal the rissoles tightly and leave for 30 minutes. Fry in hot oil at 180°C (350°F) until golden brown. Drain on paper towels and serve with fried parsley.

Sweet Dishes
attereaux of apricots Pompadour
Thread slices of stale brioche on skewers, alternating with halved apricots, which have been cooked in syrup and thoroughly drained. Dip them in fried custard flavoured with rum or kirsch. Coat them with breadcrumbs and deep-fry quickly in hot oil at 180°C (350°F). Drain on paper towels, sprinkle with caster (superfine) sugar and serve with hot apricot sauce.

rice cakes Pompadour
Prepare 175 g (6 oz, ¾ cup) short-grain rice*, cooking it until all the milk has been absorbed and

the grains begin to burst; allow to cool slightly. Butter a baking sheet and spread the warm rice to a thickness of about I cm (½ in). Dot the surface with butter and allow to cool completely. Prepare 200 ml (7 fl oz, ¾ cup) thick confectioner's custard (pastry cream) flavoured with rum (see *custard*). Chop 150 g (5 oz, I cup) crystallized (candied) fruits into small pieces. Cut the rice into 5 cm (2 in) squares. Mix the custard and crystallized fruits and coat the underside of the squares with this mixture; stick the squares together in pairs, coat twice with breadcrumbs and deep-fry in hot oil at 180°C (350°F). Drain the cakes on paper towels and serve with hot apricot sauce.

POMPANO An Atlantic fish of the *Carangidae* family, this is *Trachinotus carolinus*, related to the round pompano (*Trachinotus ovatus),* which is found in the Mediterranean. Pompano is derived from the Spanish name for vine leaf (*pampana*). The fish is blue-green with a silver belly and grows to about 45 cm (18 in) in length. The flesh is firm and delicate in flavour, making excellent eating; the round pompano (*Trachinotus ovatus*) is not considered to be the same culinary delicacy.

POMPE A sweet or savoury pastry, popular in many parts of Auvergne, Lyon and Provence. *Pompe aux grattons*, from the Bourbonnais area, is a type of tart or crown-shaped brioche containing lardons or *grattons*, which is served as an entrée or with an aperitif (a white Saint-Pourçain). In the Nivernais it is called *pompe aux grignaudes; pompe aux poires*, a fruit tart or pie, is also found here.

In Auvergne, *pompe* (or *pompo*) *aux pommes* is a traditional dish for family celebrations, Christmas and Easter. It is made of buttery rough puff or flaky pastry, spiced with cinnamon and filled with jam, plums or even cream cheese.

In Provence, *pompe à l'huile* is a flat Christmas cake of leavened dough made with olive oil, flavoured with orange-flower water, lemon zest or saffron, and sometimes studded with sugared almonds (dragées). The *pompe à l'huile* is an essential element of the 13 desserts of the Provençal Christmas, which are eaten with mulled wine. Its variants are numerous and include *flamado, gibassier, girodo, resseto* and *toca.*

RECIPE

Christmas pompes
Place I kg (2¼ lb, 9 cups) plain (all-purpose) flour in a bowl and add 250 g (9 oz) bread-dough leaven cut into small pieces, 250 g (9 oz, 1½ cups, firmly packed) brown sugar, ½ teaspoon salt, 4 tablespoons olive oil and 3–4 whole eggs. Mix well. Add the grated zest of an orange and a lemon. Knead the dough thoroughly and 'throw' it on the table. When it is very soft, roll the dough into a ball, wrap it in an oiled plastic bag and leave to rise in a warm, draught-free place for about 6 hours. Knead

the dough again, divide into 8 pieces and shape into crowns. Place the crowns on a buttered cloth and leave for a further 2 hours. Then place in a preheated oven at 230°C (450°F, gas 8) and bake for 25 minutes. Remove from the oven, moisten with orange-flower water and return to the oven for 5 minutes with the oven door left open.

POMPONNETTE A small round rissole, filled with forcemeat or a finely minced salpicon, which is fried and served as a hot hors d'oeuvre. The name is a diminutive of *pompon.*

RECIPE

pomponnettes
Prepare 400–500 g (14–18 oz) lining pastry (see *short pastry*) and leave in a cool place for about 2 hours. Prepare 250 g (9 oz, I cup) gratin or game forcemeat*, mushroom duxelles* or a ham and mushroom salpicon* bound with a very thick béchamel sauce. Roll out the pastry to a thickness of 3–4 mm (⅛ in) and cut into circles 7.5 cm (3 in) in diameter. Place a small amount of filling on the centre of each circle. Moisten the edges, draw up together towards the middle like a small pouch and pinch firmly to seal. Deep-fry the pomponnettes in hot oil heated to 180°C (356°F) until golden. Drain on paper towels and serve very hot.

PONCHON, RAOUL French poet (born La Roche-sur-Yon, 1848; died Paris, 1937). He wrote some 150,000 verses on the themes of eating and drinking, which were published in daily newspapers (the best of these appeared in the collection *La Muse au cabaret*, 1920). He proclaimed the bottle superior to the saucepan ('One must eat to drink, not drink to eat') and proved to be a worthy heir of Saint-Amant, Basselin and Béranger. He was elected to the Goncourt Academy in 1924.

PONT-L'ÉVÊQUE An AOP soft cow's-milk cheese (45–50% fat content) from Normandy, with a washed or brushed crust, matured for six weeks in a damp cellar. Sold either wrapped in waxed paper in a wooden box or unwrapped, it is 10 cm (4 in) square and 3 cm (1¼ in) thick. It should have a smooth crust, golden-yellow or orange in colour and never sticky, hard or greyish. The interior should be soft but not runny. It has a pronounced flavour and should 'smell of the earth, not manure': if it smells too strong, it can be unpacked and wrapped in a damp cloth for half a day.

Pont-l'Évêque is served at the end of a meal with a full-bodied red wine. The name comes from the chief market town of Calvados, where it is made. Probably one of the oldest cheeses of Normandy, it was mentioned by Guillaume de Lorris in the *Roman de la Rose*, when it was known as *angelot* (from *augelot*, meaning 'cheese from Auge'). It is at its best in the autumn and winter. The cheese should be cut first in half through the centre, then progressively towards the edges, keeping the remaining portions together so that the interior does not dry out. It is still often farm-produced. The Pavé d'Auge is similar but thicker.

PONT-NEUF A small Parisian pastry consisting of a tartlet of puff or shortcrust pastry, filled with frangipane or a mixture of choux pastry and confectioner's custard (pastry cream) flavoured with rum or with crushed macaroons, topped with a pastry cross and glazed with apricot jam or redcurrant jelly after baking. This name is also given to a type of talmouse decorated with a lattice of pastry.

RECIPE

ponts-neufs
Prepare a lining pastry with 200 g (7 oz, 1¾ cups) plain (all-purpose) flour, a pinch of salt, 25 g (1 oz, 2 tablespoons) caster (superfine) sugar, 100 g (4 oz, ½ cup) melted butter and 1 whole egg. Roll the dough into a ball and put it in the refrigerator. Prepare a confectioner's custard (pastry cream; see *custard*) with 400 ml (14 fl oz, 1¾ cups) milk, 4 eggs, 50 g (2 oz, ¼ cup) caster sugar, half a vanilla pod (bean) and 25 g (1 oz, ¼ cup) plain flour; add 25 g (1 oz, ¼ cup) crushed macaroons and leave to cool. Prepare a choux* paste with 100 ml (4 fl oz, 7 tablespoons) water, 25 g (1 oz, 2 tablespoons) butter, a pinch of salt, 65 g (2½ oz, ⅔ cup) plain flour, 3 eggs and ½ teaspoon caster sugar. Leave to cool.

Roll out the lining pastry very thinly, cut into 10 circles and line sections of patty tins (muffin pans) of a slightly smaller diameter. Roll the remaining pastry into a ball. Mix the choux pastry with the confectioner's custard and fill the tartlets. Glaze the tops with egg yolk. Roll out the remaining pastry very thinly and cut into 20 thin strips; use to make a pastry cross on each tartlet. Cook in a preheated oven at 190°C (375°F, gas 5) for 15–20 minutes and cool on a wire rack.

Melt 100 g (4 oz, ⅓ cup) redcurrant jelly over a gentle heat; coat the opposite quarters of each tartlet with the jelly and dust the remaining quarters with icing (confectioner's) sugar. Keep cool until ready to serve.

PONT-NEUF POTATOES A dish of fried potatoes, cut into sticks twice as thick as matches. Pont-neuf potatoes are generally used to garnish small cuts of grilled (broiled) beef, especially tournedos Henri IV (the name may come from the statue of the king on the Pont-Neuf in Paris). In English they are popularly known as chips (French fries).

RECIPE

pont-neuf potatoes
Peel some large waxy potatoes, wash them and cut into sticks 1 cm (½ in) thick and 7 cm (2¾ in) long. Wash well and dry in a cloth, deep-fry in oil heated to 170°C (338°F) for 7–8 minutes, until they begin to colour, then drain. Just before serving, fry again in the oil, reheated to 180°C (350°F), until golden. Drain and sprinkle with fine salt.

POPCORN Aerated grains of a type of maize (corn) that explodes when cooked in a little hot oil in a covered pan. The moisture in the grain causes the starch to soften and swell when heated. As the moisture content evaporates, the corn pops, leaving the grain dry and crisp. They may be coated with caramel, sprinkled with sugar or seasoned with salt.

POPPADOM Also known as *pappadum*, *papadum*, *papad* and by various other spellings. This Indian savoury, a crisp, thin wafer, is usually classed as a type of bread. The dough is made from lentil or chick pea flour, rolled out very thin and fried. A raising agent in the dough makes it puff up during brief cooking, expanding in size and browning rapidly.

Poppadoms may be plain or spiced, for example with cumin and/or peppercorns. Chilli-spiced poppadoms have a hot flavour. They are sold dried ready for cooking in a little hot oil, or they can be cooked under a hot grill (broiler). Authentically, poppadoms are served throughout or at the end of a meal, but they are often eaten as an appetizer, with raita and/or fresh chutneys, in restaurants. Tiny cocktail poppadoms are available dried, and these are ideal for serving with drinks.

POPPY Any plant of the genus *Papaver*. The red poppy (*coquelicot* in French) has blazing red petals. These are used as colouring in confectionery, notably for *coquelicots de Nemours*, flat, rectangular sweets (candies) made from cooked and flavoured sugar, coloured red. Poppy leaves used to be eaten as a vegetable, much in the same way as sorrel. When in season, they are traditionally added with the flowers to the *caillettes* (flat sausages) made in Viviers.

Varieties of the opium poppy are cultivated for their blue-grey seeds, which are rich in oil (40–50%); these seeds are not narcotic. Poppy-seed oil is extracted from varieties grown in the Balkans, Germany, Poland, the Netherlands and (more rarely) in northern France. The oil is pale and has a pleasant taste, and it is used in cooking and to dress or flavour dishes in the same way as olive oil; in Paris and northern France it is known as *huile blanche* (white oil), *olivette* and *petite huile*.

Poppy seeds, which have a rather nutty taste, are used mainly in pâtisserie in Turkey, Egypt and central Europe, where they are used to flavour a cream filling for some gâteaux or are sprinkled over bread rolls (also very popular in Britain). They are also used as a condiment for cream and curd cheeses, to flavour Chinese rice-flour noodles and as an ingredient in Indian curries.

PORBEAGLE A fish of the shark family, known as *taupe* or *touille*. It can reach a length of 3.7 m (12 ft).

It is fished by the fishermen of the Île-d'Yeu off Vendée throughout the year, but especially from May to September, when it migrates towards the coast. It is sold as 'sea calf', or as slices like tuna, and it is cooked in the same way as tuna.

PORCHÉ A Breton speciality from Dol-de-Bretagne. Based on pig's trotters (feet), bones and rinds, flavoured with various condiments and sorrel, it was formerly cooked overnight in the local baker's oven.

PORÉE A fairly thick purée or soup, made in the Middle Ages with green vegetables, spinach, Swiss chards, leeks and watercress. Depending on whether times were bad or not, these leaves were cooked in water, meat stock or almond milk.

RECIPE

porée of Charente
Chop the whites of 1.5 kg (3¼ lb) leeks and soften them in 100 g (4 oz, ½ cup) slightly salted butter in a frying pan. Add 200 ml (7 fl oz, ¾ cup) fish stock, 200 g (7 oz, ¾ cup) crème fraîche, a pinch of coarse salt and the same of pepper. Arrange 6 fillets of turbot or John Dory, 6 pieces of monkfish, 6 scallops and 6 langoustine tails. Cover and poach for 8 minutes. Serve the fish on the bed of leeks. Thicken the liquid with 2 egg yolks and pour it over the fish. Garnish with chervil.

PORK The flesh of the domestic pig. The male pig is called a boar, the female a sow, and the young a piglet, porker or sucking pig, according to age. The wild boar is the ancestor of the domestic pig. It became domesticated living on refuse near human settlements, which is why pork is regarded as unclean in some religions. From the Middle Ages the killing of a pig, an abundant source of food, was the occasion for a feast day.

Selective breeding has produced a high-meat carcass, with a thin coat of fat and large hams. In the past pigs had long legs, were fattened on potatoes and chestnuts and were butchered at about 10 or 12 months. Modern breeds have shorter legs and provide more meat; they are fattened in six or seven months on cereal flours and weigh between 90 and 100 kg (200–220 lb). Their meat is in general less tasty and not always of the same quality. The Large White Yorkshire, Western White, Danish Landrace and the Belgian Piétrain, which is white with black patches, are among the most common breeds. Pork is a widely consumed meat in France, Germany, Scandinavia and Britain.

■ **Cuts of pork** Good-quality pork is identified by firm pink flesh, which shows no trace of moisture; whitish and damp flesh comes from a factory-farmed pig and is bland; meat that is flaccid, too red or too fat comes from an older animal of mediocre quality. In northern and eastern France white meat is preferred; elsewhere, pink is more sought-after. In Paris pork from a butcher is paler than that used for charcuterie because pink meat absorbs water better, which is an advantage in making pâtés, hams and galantines. Some cooks prefer the former as being finer and more delicate, others the latter as having more flavour. Pork is eaten fresh, slightly salted, cured or smoked. There is an old French saying that all parts of a pig can be eaten and an English one that all parts can be eaten except the squeak. It is true that even the ears, feet, offal (variety meats) and tail, has a culinary use, either fresh or in charcuterie.

After slaughter, the offal and head are removed and the pig is cut in half; the leg and shoulder are cut from each half-carcass for separate treatment. It is mainly the back of the pig that is sold for fresh meat, although in Britain the leg and shoulder are also sold fresh. A wide variety of names is used for different cuts, and many prepared meats are labelled according to their suitability for specific cooking methods rather than the area of carcass from which they originate. The following is a guide to some of the traditional cuts and carcass sections.
• The spare rib and bladebone (shoulder butt) are roasted or braised in a casserole. More moist than fillet (loin), soft and slightly fatty, they can also be made into a stew, grilled (broiled) or fried as chops, cut into cubes for kebabs or used for home-made sausagemeat.
• The foreloin and the unboned middle fillet give succulent roasts but can also be prepared as chops and grilled (broiled) or fried; this is lean and rather dry meat.
• The hind loin is more succulent and less fatty than the sparerib; it is usually roasted.
• The tenderloin is the middle part of the fillet, which consists the tender juicy noisette.
• *Grillades* is the French name for thin blade steaks cut in a fan shape, which are flat and excellent for grilling (broiling); they are tasty but rather rare.
• The leg is sometimes eaten fresh: the fillet end can be cut into thick slices and grilled (broiled) or used for kebabs; it can also be braised or roasted. The knuckle end is usually boiled in stock.
• The hand (picnic shoulder) is often braised on the bone; when chopped, it makes a fine meat for pâtés. It can also be roasted or sautéed and is often used in a *potée* or with sauerkraut.
• The thick end of belly consists of the top ribs; formerly eaten only as salt pork, it can also be grilled (broiled) as spare ribs or cooked in a sweet-and-sour sauce, Chinese style. It is from the belly of the animal that the fat and skin are removed to make lardons and strips for barding and larding.

■ **Pork in cookery** Pork has been enjoyed in France since the time of the Gauls. It was, however, a meat of the common people: Grimod de La Reynière saw the pig as 'an encyclopedic animal, a meal on legs' that did not provide roasts for aristocratic tables; he considered only sucking pig to be of value. The same is true of Britain, where pigs were economical to feed and easy to rear in small spaces, such as the back gardens of town houses as well as country cottage gardens.

British cuts of pork

1 spare rib;
1a blade;
2 loin;
3 leg fillet end;
3a leg knuckle end;
3b hock;
4 belly;
5 hand;
5a trotter.

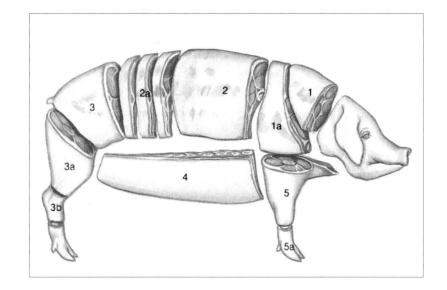

American cuts of pork

1 blade shoulder;
2 loin;
2a tenderloin;
3 leg;
4 side;
4a spare rib;
5 arm shoulder;
5a hock.

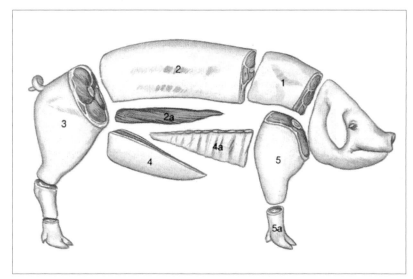

French cuts of pork

1 tête (head);
2 lard gras (pure pork fat);
3 échine;
4 palette;
5 carré de côtes or côtes premières;
6 côtes de filet;
7 pointe;
8 jambon;
9 jambonneau arrière;
10 poitrine (belly);
10a travers (spare ribs);
11 épaule (palette and jambonneau);
12 plat de côtes;
13 jambonneau avant;
14 pieds (feet);
15 gorge;
16 queue (tail)

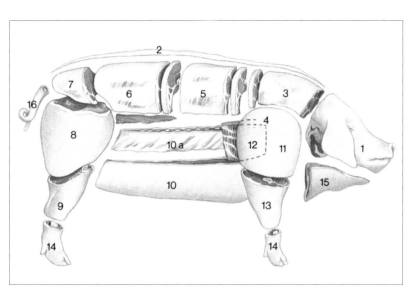

A rich and fatty meat, pork goes well with fruit (pineapple, apples, prunes) and vegetable purées. It can be enlivened with green sweet (bell) pepper, mustard, fried onions, pepper sauce, garlic or a Roquefort sauce. Garnished with beans and lentils, it makes a substantial winter meal. Aromatic herbs (especially sage) are often used to flavour roasts and grills.

The base of all French regional *potées*, pork is also used in recipes inspired by Chinese, Caribbean and Danish cookery.

RECIPES

grilled pork chops
Season the chops with salt and pepper, brush with melted butter or oil and grill (broil) under a moderate heat, turning once. Arrange on a serving dish and garnish with watercress. Serve with lemon wedges.

loin of pork à l'alsacienne
Salt and pepper a loin of pork and cook in a preheated oven at 200°C (400°F, gas 6), allowing 50 minutes per 1 kg (22 minutes per 1 lb) and turning it over halfway through the cooking time. Prepare a braised sauerkraut with a garnish of bacon and sausages. Drain the loin, place in the centre of the sauerkraut and continue cooking for a further 15 minutes. To serve, cut the bacon into slices and separate the loin chops. Arrange on the sauerkraut with the sausages and boiled potatoes.

loin of pork bonne femme
Salt and pepper a loin of pork. In a flameproof dish heat 15 g (½ oz, 1 tablespoon) butter or lard per 1 kg (2¼ lb) meat. Brown the meat on all sides, then place the dish in a preheated oven at 200°C (400°F, gas 6) and cook according to the weight of the meat, allowing 50 minutes per 1 kg (22 minutes per lb). About 25 minutes before the end of the cooking time, add 500 g (18 oz) peeled potatoes per 1 kg (2¼ lb) meat and 20 small (pearl) onions fried in butter. Season with salt and pepper, cover and finish cooking. Separate the loin chops and serve very hot, sprinkled with chopped parsley.

loin of pork with red cabbage
Prepare a braised red cabbage while roasting a loin of pork. Arrange the pork on a hot serving dish; surround with red cabbage and boiled potatoes or braised chestnuts. Serve very hot.

mother's cretons
In a heavy-based saucepan place 500 g (18 oz, 2¼ cups) minced (ground) shoulder of pork, 1 chopped onion, 2 crushed garlic cloves, 1 cup breadcrumbs, 1 cup milk, 1 cup chopped parsley, salt, pepper and cinnamon. Mix thoroughly, cover and cook for 2 hours over a gentle heat, stirring frequently. Leave to cool, then process in a blender or food processor for 2 minutes. Pour into a buttered terrine and refrigerate until firm.

neck of pork with broad beans
Soak 1 kg (2¼ lb) smoked neck of pork for 12 hours in fresh water, changing the water two or three times if the meat seems too salty. Place the pork in a braising pan and cover with cold water. Bring to the boil and skim. Add 1 leek, 1 carrot, 1 onion, 1 celery stick, 1 bay leaf, 6 peppercorns, 3 cloves and 200 ml (7 fl oz, ¾ cup) Rivaner or Riesling. Cover and cook for 2–3 hours. Prepare a roux with 50 g (2 oz, ¼ cup) butter and 2 tablespoons plain (all-purpose) flour. Dilute with stock from the braising pan to make a sauce. Cook 1 kg (2¼ lb) broad (fava) beans with a few sprigs of summer savory. Serve the meat, sliced, with the beans and boiled potatoes.

pork chops à la bayonnaise
Stud the chops with slivers of garlic. Season with salt, pepper, powdered thyme and bay leaf and sprinkle with oil and a dash of vinegar. Leave to marinate for 1 hour, then sauté briskly in lard. When the chops are browned on both sides, surround them with small new potatoes tossed in goose fat and cep mushrooms fried in oil. Cook in a preheated oven at 200°C (400°F, gas 6) for 20 minutes. Arrange on a hot dish and sprinkle with chopped parsley.

pork chops à la gasconne
Marinate the chops as for pork chops *à la bayonnaise*. Fry quickly in butter or goose fat. Place in a pan with 6 peeled and slightly blanched garlic cloves per chop and finish cooking over a gentle heat for 20 minutes. When the chops are almost cooked add 8 stoned (pitted) blanched green olives per chop. Arrange the chops in a crown and put the garnish in the centre. Deglaze the pan juices with 4 tablespoons white wine, add a few tablespoons of meat juice (or stock) if required and reduce. Pour the sauce over the chops and sprinkle with chopped parsley.

pork chops à l'alsacienne
Salt and pepper the pork chops and either sauté in a little butter or lard or braise them. Arrange in a turban on a heated serving dish and garnish as for loin of pork *à l'alsacienne*. Coat the chops with their deglazed cooking juices or, if braised, with the strained braising juices.

pork chops charcutière
This dish is found ready-cooked in some French pork butchers' shops, prepared as follows. Sauté the pork chops (they may be coated with breadcrumbs) in lard, then simmer in charcutière sauce with thinly sliced gherkins.

In restaurants the preparation is as follows. Flatten the chops slightly, season, coat with melted butter and breadcrumbs and gently grill (broil). Arrange them in a crown and fill the centre of the dish with mashed potato. Serve separately, in a sauceboat, a charcutière sauce to which chopped gherkins have been added at the last minute.

pork chops pilleverjus

Trim and slightly flatten 4 pork chops, season with salt and pepper, and fry in lard until both sides are golden. Place 4 tablespoons finely chopped onions, lightly cooked in butter, in the frying pan. Add a bouquet garni, cover and cook gently for about 30 minutes. Meanwhile, shred a spring cabbage heart and cook in butter. Moisten with a few tablespoons of boiling cream, then stir. Arrange the cabbage julienne in a dish, place the chops on top and garnish with boiled potatoes if required. Deglaze the pan juices with 1 tablespoon vinegar and 4 tablespoons meat glaze and pour over the chops.

pork chops with Robert sauce

Season the chops with salt and pepper, grill (broil) gently and serve with Robert sauce and mashed potatoes or haricot (navy) beans.

Alternatively, sauté the chops in butter or lard; when half-cooked, add 100 g (4 oz, ⅔ cup) finely chopped white onions (for 4 chops). Drain the chops, arrange on a serving dish and keep warm. Deglaze the pan juices with 200 ml (7 fl oz, ¾ cup) white wine and reduce almost completely. Moisten with 300 ml (½ pint, 1¼ cups) demi-glace* sauce or 200 ml (7 fl oz, ¾ cup) stock and boil for 5 minutes. Add 1 tablespoon concentrated tomato purée (paste) and thicken with 1 tablespoon beurre manié. Remove from the heat and add a pinch of caster (superfine) sugar and 1 tablespoon mustard to the sauce. Pour the sauce over the chops and serve very hot.

roast loin of pork with various garnishes

Season a loin of pork with salt and pepper 2 hours before cooking. In an ovenproof dish heat a maximum of 15 g (½ oz, 1 tablespoon) lard per 1 kg (2¼ lb) meat. Brown the meat on all sides, place the dish in a preheated oven at 200°C (400°F, gas 6) and cook for about 50 minutes per 1 kg (22 minutes per 1 lb). Baste the loin with its cooking juices and turn it several times during cooking.

Serve with the cooking juices, skimmed of fat, and any of the following garnishes: potatoes (boulangère, dauphinoise, or puréed), a vegetable purée (celery, turnips, lentils or chick peas), braised vegetables (celery, endive, cabbage, Brussels sprouts, chicory, artichoke hearts or lettuce) or fruit (apples, pears or pineapple). The skimmed cooking juices can also be used to make various sauces, such as charcutière, piquante, Robert or tomato.

roast pork with Jerusalem artichokes

Peel 800 g (1¾ lb) Jerusalem artichokes per 1 kg (2¼ lb) meat. Trim them into large bulb shapes and blanch for 5 minutes in boiling salted water. Rinse in cold water and drain. Melt 20 g (¾ oz, 1½ tablespoons) lard in a pan and brown the piece of pork gently. Cook in a preheated oven at 200°C (400°F, gas 6) allowing 50 minutes per 1 kg (22 minutes per 1 lb). About 30 minutes before the end of the cooking time, add the artichokes and season with salt and pepper.

Serve the roast pork surrounded by the artichokes; the deglazed cooking juices should be served separately.

salt pork with lentils

Soak 500 g (18 oz) slightly salted spare ribs, 1 slice slightly salted knuckle end of ham, 400 g (14 oz) slightly salted loin and 200 g (7 oz) slightly salted belly of pork streaked with fat in cold water for at least 2 hours. Rinse all the pieces, place in plenty of cold water, bring to the boil, skim thoroughly and simmer for 1 hour. Pick over 500 g (18 oz, 2½ cups) Puy lentils, then wash, drain and cook for 15 minutes in plenty of water. Drain again and add to the meat with 1 large onion stuck with 2 cloves, 2 carrots, 2 leeks, a bouquet garni and a few black peppercorns. Simmer for 45 minutes, skimming from time to time. Add 1 cooking sausage and continue cooking for another 40 minutes. Remove all the meat and reserve in a warm place. Discard the bouquet garni and drain the lentils. Place in a large serving dish and arrange the sliced meat on top.

sautéed pork chops

Trim and flatten 4 pork chops and season with salt and pepper. Heat 25 g (1 oz, 2 tablespoons) butter or lard in a frying pan and brown the chops on both sides. Cover the pan and cook for about 15 minutes. Remove the chops and arrange on a hot dish. Coat with the deglazed cooking juices and serve with any of the garnishes suggested for roast loin of pork.

shoulder of pork with five spices

In a mortar crush 2 garlic cloves and 2 shallots with 2 teaspoons sugar and the same amount of nuoc-mâm and soy sauce, ½ teaspoon five spices and a little black pepper. Fry the shoulder of pork, with its rind, on all sides, then add the spice mixture. Cover and cook for 30 minutes over a moderate heat, turning the meat halfway through the cooking time. Remove the lid and reduce, turn the meat in its cooking juices, then remove and slice; arrange the slices on a plate and pour over the reduced juices. Serve with plain boiled rice.

other recipes See ballotine, boulangère, brochette, ear, feet and trotters, kidneys, languedocienne, liver, pâté, pineapple, salting, sauerkraut (sauerkraut à l'alsacienne), spare ribs, zampone.

PORK BUTCHERY See charcuterie.

PORK FAT The fatty tissue lying just beneath the skin of a pig. At one time a staple item of the diet, pork fat today is used mostly as a seasoning or a cooking fat. In France a distinction is made between pure pork fat (lard gras) and belly fat (lard maigre).

Pure pork fat is usually used fresh and occurs in two layers. The layer closest to the flesh is used mostly for making lard and is called 'melting fat'. The layer next to the skin, called 'hard fat' (leaf lard), is firmer and melts less readily; it is used mostly for barding.

Belly fat consists of fat streaked with muscular tissue. It has many more culinary uses than pure pork fat and can be salted or smoked, as well as used fresh (see *lardons, larding*). Thinly sliced belly pork – or streaky bacon – is often served with eggs (see *bacon*).

The thick fat found especially around the fillet and the kidneys is known in France as *panne*. When melted, it yields a high-quality lard, used for preparing fine forcemeats and white sausage. In Lorraine, the residue (*chons*) obtained by gently melting this pork fat in a stewpan is used to flavour a large, crusty, flat cake, which is served with a dandelion salad and a rosé wine.

PÖRKÖLT One of the four great Hungarian dishes seasoned with paprika. Also flavoured with onions, *pörkölt* is made with meat that is too fat for goulash, cut into larger pieces. Mutton, game, pork, goose and duck are served in this way, as are veal or even fish (carp) and sometimes shrimps (in white wine).

PORK RIND Pork rind is generally thick, hard and very fatty. When scalded or singed and scraped, it is used to line casseroles and stewpans, adding its fat to the preparation. It is an ingredient of pork brawn (headcheese), *bréjaude* soup, *zampone, cassoulet*, and various items of charcuterie, such as *coudenou*. Along with calves' feet, it can be used to give the gelatinous element required in the preparation of meat aspics. After boiling in a flavoured stock, pork rind may be used to prepare ballotines (meat loaves) and roulades.

PORRIDGE A dish of rolled oats or oatmeal cooked in boiling water or milk, which can be eaten, with or without sugar, with hot or cold milk or cream. It is a traditional breakfast dish in Anglo-Saxon countries. The name is derived from French *potage*. An ancient food of Celtic origin, it has always been popular in Scotland's changeable climate, where it is eaten with salt instead of sugar, and in Ireland and Wales. Its reputation has spread throughout Britain and it is especially enjoyed with brown sugar and cream.

RECIPE

porridge
Add 1 tablespoon salt to 1 litre (1¾ pints, 4¼ cups) water and bring to the boil. Sprinkle 250 g (9 oz, 3 cups) rolled oats into the water and boil gently, stirring continuously with a wooden spoon, until the mixture thickens (about 15 minutes). Each serving may be sprinkled with sugar or salt and eaten with milk or cream poured over it.

PORT One of the great dessert wines of the world. It is produced from a demarcated region in the Upper Douro valley in northern Portugal and is usually matured and blended in the *amarzens* (wine lodges) of the shippers in Vila Nova de Gaia opposite Oporto (the wine takes its name from this seaport). Traditionally, in order to qualify as true port, the wine had to be shipped over the bar or the point where the Douro meets the Atlantic. However, producers are now able to export wines direct from the vineyards, thus opening up the market to smaller growers who previously had to sell their wines to the larger companies.

The name 'port' is protected within the EU, although many other countries produce 'port-style' wines. The wine is made from a blend of grape varieties, including Touriga Nacional, Touriga Francesa, Tinta Cão and Tinta Roriz, and the fermentation is arrested by the addition of grape spirit. Depending on when the spirit is added, the resulting port varies in sweetness because of the natural sugars retained in the wine. There are various styles of port. White port is produced from white grapes and is ideal chilled as an aperitif – it is often drunk in Portugal with a tonic water mixer. Ruby port is perhaps the simplest wine. It is a blend of young wines from different vintages, aged in bulk for a few years and bottled. It is a deep ruby in colour and full and fruity. The name given to Vintage Character ports is misleading: in essence they are premium ruby ports and are often sold under brand names.

Tawny ports are variable in quality, but the finer wines and those with an indication of age – 10, 20, 30 or over 40 years – are blended wines that have matured for longer in wooden casks, thus taking on a mellow tawny colour. They become elegant and smooth with aromas and flavours of nuts and raisins.

Colheitas are tawny ports from a single harvest and aged for at least seven years in wood. Late bottled Vintage ports (LBV) are a blend of wines from one harvest and bottled after four to six years. LBVs labelled 'Traditional' are not filtered before bottling and so will throw a sediment, which will need decanting. The wines are ready for drinking when bottled.

Vintage port is made only in exceptional years, which are 'declared'. Only grapes picked from the top quality vineyard sites are used. The wines are matured in cask for around two years, then bottled without filtering. They develop slowly, becoming more harmonious and complex, and are suitable for ageing for at least 15 years.

Single Quinta ports are wines from a single estate (*quinta*) and are produced in very good years when there is no vintage declaration. The method of production is similar to Vintage port. Both styles require decanting, as does Crusted port, which is produced from a blend of harvests and bottled young.

Port may be enjoyed at any time – more unusual food pairings are drinking Tawny with soft cheese or fruit cake, and LBVs with chocolate. The classic combination is with cheese, particularly strong Cheddar or Stilton.

PORTEFEUILLE, EN Describing dishes in which the food is stuffed, folded or placed in layers one on top of the other. The term is applied to the following dishes: veal chops split, stuffed and cooked in a caul (caul fat) or coated with breadcrumbs; a gratin of sautéed potatoes *à la lyonnaise*; and minced (ground) meat layered with sauce and topped with puréed potatoes. An omelette *en portefeuille* is folded in three, first towards the side opposite the handle of the pan, then towards the centre of the pan.

RECIPES

grilled veal chops en portefeuille
Soak a pig's caul (caul fat) in cold water for 2 hours. Take thick veal chops from the loin, cut open the lean meat and season the pocket with salt and pepper; fill with mushroom duxelles or with a salpicon of pressed tongue and mushrooms cooked slowly in butter, bound with a thick béchamel sauce. Wrap each chop in a piece of caul and grill (broil) gently. Serve with buttered spinach.

sautéed veal chops en portefeuille
Prepare the chops as for grilled veal chops *en portefeuille*, then cook in butter in a frying pan. Arrange the chops on a round dish with small braised carrots. Keep warm. Deglaze the cooking juices with white wine and stock, bind with beurre manié and pour over the chops.

veal chop cussy en portefeuille
Cut a pocket in a thick veal chop taken from the middle of the loin. Stuff with a salpicon of mushrooms, carrot and lean ham bound with a thick, seasoned béchamel sauce. Secure with a wooden cocktail stick (toothpick). Coat the chop with beaten egg and breadcrumbs and cook in clarified butter until golden on both sides. Prepare a risotto and add cream, grated cheese and a salpicon of truffles. Arrange the chop on a round dish garnished with the truffle risotto. Pour a ring of brown veal gravy, flavoured with tomato, around the dish; sprinkle the chop with noisette butter.

PORTE-MAILLOT Also known as *maillot*. A garnish for large pieces of braised meat, consisting of carrots, turnips, onions and green beans. Braised lettuce or cauliflower is sometimes added to the mixture.

RECIPES

braised beef porte-maillot
Cut 100 g (4 oz) fat (slab) bacon into thin strips and marinate for 12 hours in a mixture of oil and brandy (one-third brandy, two-thirds oil), mixed herbs, chopped garlic, and salt and pepper. Interlard 1.5 kg (3¼ lb) trimmed beef aiguillettes with the bacon strips. Braise the meat in a flameproof casserole with 200 ml (7 fl oz, ¾ cup) white wine, the same amount of stock and the ingredients of the marinade.

Glaze 250 g (9 oz) small (pearl) onions, 250 g (9 oz) small turnips and 500 g (18 oz) new carrots. Cook the beef for at least 2¾ hours; 10 minutes before the end of the cooking time add the onions, carrots and turnips and finish cooking. Steam some green beans until just tender and drain. Arrange the meat on a long serving dish (platter) and surround with the vegetables in separate piles. Keep warm.

Skim the fat off the cooking juices, strain and reduce. Sprinkle with chopped parsley and serve the sauce separately in a sauceboat.

braised ham porte-maillot
Braise, drain and dress the ham. Place it in a small braising pan, pour over 500 ml (17 fl oz, 2 cups) Madeira, cover and simmer gently for 30 minutes. Prepare a garnish of glazed carrots and onions, green beans cooked in salted water and braised lettuce. When the ham is cooked, glaze it in the oven. Arrange on a long serving dish (platter), surrounded by the vegetables in separate piles and keep warm. Skim the fat off the cooking juices, strain and serve separately.

PORT-SALUT A trademark granted by the monks of Port-du-Salut Abbey at Entrammes in Mayenne to a commercial enterprise making Saint-Paulin cheese. Like all Saint-Paulins, Port-Salut is made from pasteurized cow's milk (45–50% fat content). The cheese is pressed, but not cooked and has a washed crust. It is round, about 20 cm (8 in) in diameter and 7.5 cm (3 in) deep, and has a soft, creamy texture. It is served at the end of a meal or on toast and is used to make *croque-monsieur*. The Trappist monks of Entrammes produce a similar cow's-milk cheese in the same way.

PORTUGAISE, À LA Describing various dishes (eggs, fish, kidneys, small pieces of meat and poultry) in which tomatoes predominate.

RECIPES

Portuguese omelette
Fill an omelette with a very thick spicy tomato sauce or concassée and surround it with a ring of the same sauce.

Portuguese sauce
Finely chop 2 large onions and cook in 1 tablespoon olive oil until soft. Peel, seed and crush 4 tomatoes and add to the onions, together with 2 crushed garlic cloves. Bring to the boil, cover and cook slowly for 30–35 minutes, stirring from time to time, until the tomatoes are reduced to a pulp. Moisten with 150 ml (¼ pint, ⅔ cup) stock and season with ground pepper. Leave to cook for a further 10 minutes. Bind with 2 teaspoons beurre manié and sprinkle with chopped parsley.

PORTUGAL

Portuguese cookery must not be confused with that of Spain: its characteristic flavours are more varied, strong spices are less dominant, but fresh herbs and spices are more abundant. There are a number of general traits: the use of four predominant ingredients (cabbage, rice, potato and cod), a marked taste for soups, a wide range of fish and seafood dishes, a notable selection of pork products such as black pudding (blood sausage), *andouille*, smoked ham, and sausages flavoured with chilli peppers, and a predilection for very sweet desserts, often made with eggs.

■ **Regional specialities** The regions, however, preserve their own traditions. The north is famous for *caldo verde*, lamprey from the Minho cooked with curry, and many rice dishes accompanied by rabbit, duck or roast partridge, with ham and lemon juice. Other classics are the *açordas* (stale-bread soups) – bread soaked in olive oil, flavoured with crushed garlic and herbs, and cooked in boiling water. These soups are garnished with vegetables, pork, chicken, fish or snails. Seafood *açorda*, garnished with coriander (cilantro) and poached eggs, is particularly well known. There are several ewe's-milk cheeses (usually fresh), notably Azeitão, Serra and Évora.

Oporto, famous for its wine (see *port*), also specializes in stewed tripe, cooked with haricot (navy) beans, chilli sausage, onions and chicken, and served with rice. Along the coast fish and seafood dishes naturally predominate: fried skate with vegetables, grilled (broiled) sardine and red mullet, shellfish *escabèche* and stewed cuttlefish. *Caldeirada*, a type of *bouillabaisse*, is the best example: at Aveiro this is made with freshwater fish and sea fish with oysters, mussels and carrots, flavoured with coriander. The convent at Aveiro is also famous for *ovos moles*, sweetmeats made of egg yolk and sugar cooked in rice water.

The cookery of Coimbra is substantial: steak *à la portugaise* originated here. Served with a purée of garlic and pepper, topped with lemon slices and grilled (broiled) ham added at the last minute, it is accompanied by sautéed potatoes. This *bife com batatas* (steak and chips) is very popular. More typical dishes are *canja* (a poultry consommé garnished with lemon and mint and sometimes also with almonds, ham and onion rings) and salted pig's trotters (feet) with young turnip tops.

The national fish is salt cod (*bacalhau*), for which there are said to be a thousand recipes. The best known of these are: fried salt cod croquettes (flavoured with coriander, mint and parsley) topped with poached eggs; salt cod poached in layers, garnished with mussels cooked in wine and tomatoes, then simmered in the oven in the cooking liquid of the mussels; and salt cod poached and cooked in the oven on a bed of potatoes and onions, garnished with black (ripe) olives and quartered hard-boiled (hard-cooked) eggs.

In Portuguese cookery there are some surprising combinations of ingredients: pickled pork served with shellfish stuffed with lardons; chicken and eel stew with shrimps; roast duck with ham and chorizos; and red sweet (bell) peppers, onions, smoked ham, sausages, oysters, tomatoes and parsley

sole à la portugaise

Lightly butter a long ovenproof dish and cover with a thick tomato sauce flavoured with garlic. Trim, prepare and season a 675 g (1½ lb) sole and lay it in the dish. Moisten with 2 tablespoons olive oil, 1 tablespoon lemon juice and 2 tablespoons fish stock. Cook in a preheated oven at 230°C (450°F, gas 8) for about 10 minutes, basting the sole from time to time with its cooking juices. Sprinkle with breadcrumbs, brown under the grill (broiler), then sprinkle with chopped parsley.

tournedos à la portugaise

Prepare very small stuffed tomatoes and brown them with some château potatoes. Fry the steaks in a mixture of butter and oil, drain and keep warm. Deglaze the cooking juices with white wine and thick tomato sauce and thicken with a little beurre manié. Arrange the tournedos on the serving dish with the tomatoes and the potatoes. Serve the sauce separately.

other recipes See *anchovy, artichoke, bass, chicken, sauté.*

PORTUGAL See *above*.

POT Formerly in France, a *pot* was a large cooking vessel. The word survives in the dishes *poule au pot* (stewed chicken) and *pot-au-feu*. It is still used in Britain too, in 'stockpot' and 'hot-pot'.

POTATO A starchy tuber, native to America, which is a major food in the form of a vegetable (always cooked); it is also processed in a wide variety of ways and used in distilling, the starch industry and the biscuit (cracker) trade.

■ **History** The potato, which was originally grown by the Incas, was discovered in Peru by Pizarro and brought to Europe in 1534. Fifty years later Sir Walter Raleigh made the same discovery in Virginia and brought the potato to England. The English name, like the Spanish (*batata*), is derived from *patata*, the American Indian name for the sweet potato (due to early confusion between the two vegetables). The Spaniards introduced it to Italy, where it was called *tartufola* (little truffle). It was soon planted all over Europe: in Germany it was called *Kartoffel*, in Russia *kartoschka* and in France *cartoufle* or *tartoufle*, being simmered together in a *cataplana* (a deep cooking pot with a handle and lid).

In Lisbon and the south seafood is always on the menu, especially lobster cooked in stock and served with tomato and pimiento sauce. In the *cervejarias* (small brasseries) the Portuguese enjoy a variety of freshly caught shellfish, including mussels, prawns and squid grilled with scrambled eggs. Coffee is the most widely consumed beverage in Lisbon, but lemonade and cordials are also enjoyed (through a straw), as well as an aniseed drink with candy sugar. The desserts and pastries are always highly sweetened: *pudim flan*, a thick creamy dessert rich in eggs; rice with milk and cinnamon; baked caramelized figs; doughnuts with syrup; and marzipans. The most original Portuguese cake is the *lampreia de ovos*, made with egg yolks, cooked in a lamprey-shaped mould, decorated with crystallized (candied) fruits and served on a special egg yolk custard (*ovos moles*).

The delicate cookery of the extreme south includes calves' liver marinated in red wine, *sarapatel* (a mixed lamb and kid stew), figs stuffed with almonds and chocolate, and a cake called *lardo celeste* made with almonds, lemon and cinnamon.

WINE Portugal has a wealth of indigenous grape varieties, and in recent years it has made great improvements in the vineyards and in the wineries, which are producing some excellent wines.

The Minho region is best known for Vinho Verde – fresh, zesty wines, sometimes slightly *pétillant*, which are meant for drinking young. The Douro Valley, renowned for port, produces top-quality table wines predominantly from Touriga Nacional and Tinta Roriz (Tempranillo). Mateus Rosé and Lancers – a rosé wine particularly popular in the United States – are also produced in the north. The Dão region produces very good red and white wines: Bairrada, long-lived, concentrated reds from the Baga grape; lighter, fruitier red and white from Estremadura and Ribatejo on the banks of the Tejo (Tagus) River; and a wide range of wines from the Alentejo region south of Lisbon. Traditionally, wines were a blend, but varietal wines are emerging, such as Alfrocheiro Preto (deep coloured wines with ripe berry fruit flavours); Castelão Frances, also known as Periquita or João de Santarém; Tinta Roriz (Aragonez); Trincadeira; and particularly Touriga Nacional, which is recognized as one of Portugal's best grape varieties. Some Chardonnay has been planted, but some very good white wines are made from native varieties, including Alvarinho from Moncão in the north, Roupeiro from Alentejo, Arinto (fresh, fruity wines with good balance) and Fernão Pires, a very adaptable variety producing aromatic, sparkling wines, oak-aged dry whites and even a botrytised (see *noble rot*) sweet wine in the Ribatejo.

In addition to port there are two other renowned fortified wines – Madeira, which is produced on the Portuguese island, some 850 km (530 miles) from Lisbon, and Moscatel de Setúbal.

Wine laws are in line with other EU countries. Denominação de Origem Controlada (DOC) is equivalent to Appellation Contrôlée, and Indicação de Proveniencia Reulamentada (IPR) to Vin de Pays. Vinho Regional embraces larger regions and Vinho de Mesa is a table wine.

---

eaten there in the 16th century in the form of regional dishes, such as the *truffade* and the *truffiat*. Long regarded in France as food fit only for the poor, the potato was popularized by Parmentier and became one of the staple foods at the beginning of the 19th century. It lends itself to the most comprehensive range of recipes of all vegetables, from the popular mash and chips (French fries) to the elaborate potato straw nests, duchess potatoes and soufflé potatoes.

■ **Types** There are numerous varieties of potatoes available, varying according to country and season, but with a broad choice throughout the year. They fall into two main categories – early or new potatoes and main crop or old potatoes. Modern cultivation methods and food transportation mean that early or new potatoes are now available throughout the year. In addition to these two categories, salad potatoes are small, waxy vegetables with a thicker skin than new potatoes (but this is not as thick as that on main crop or old potatoes). Salad potatoes have the texture and fuller flavour of new potatoes.

Fine-skinned early potatoes, traditionally harvested in the spring and early summer, do not keep well. Main crop potatoes can be stored in a dry, dark and cool environment for several months – traditionally from the end of the picking season in autumn through to the following spring. Thick brown paper bags are the best form of container because polythene makes the vegetables sweat and rot.

Main crop potatoes are classed according to their texture and cooking qualities. Although they are never as firm and waxy as early or salad potatoes, they are described as waxy or floury, suitable for boiling and moist methods or for baking, roasting and frying. Some traditional types fell between the categories and were traditionally labelled as good cooking potatoes for general use; many popular cultivars tend to be produced for this quality, and they are unlikely to disintegrate with careful boiling but are also good for baking.

Potatoes may have white or red skins, or a mixture of both. The colours vary from creamy white to yellow-cream; from pink, through light red to deep red, purple, mauve, blue or virtually black. The flesh of the purple and dark-skinned varieties is often a similar colour to the skin. Colour is not necessarily an indicator of cooking quality, and there are waxy or floury examples of each type.

Examples of early or new varieties include Jersey Royals, Home Guard, Arran Pilot or Piper and Maris Piper. Main crop potatoes include the well-known Pentland Squire, Golden Wonder, King Edward, Maris Piper, Ailsa, Desiree and Wilja. Salad potatoes include Linzer Delicatesse and Pink Fir Apple. When buying, the description of texture and cooking qualities is the most useful guide.

■ **Storage** Potatoes should be stored in a cool, dry, well-ventilated place at 8–10°C (46–50°F) to prevent them from sprouting or freezing. It is particularly important that the storage place is dark and cool, to prevent the development of solanine, a substance normally present in small amounts. When the level rises, the potatoes turn green, and the high solanine content is toxic so the vegetables should be discarded immediately.

■ **Preparation and use** Numerous utensils have been designed for preparing potatoes, including the potato peeler, potato holder (for peeling a potato boiled in its skin without burning oneself), knife-guide (for producing regular slices), special knives for potato straws, waffles and chips, the chip cutter, chopping and shredding board, scoop and masher.

Potatoes can be served with most meats, poultry, fish and even eggs. Many combinations are standard: gigot *à la boulangère*, chateaubriand with *pont-neuf* potatoes, hachis Parmentier, Francillon salad, poached fish and steamed potatoes, and numerous garnishes (*à la bourgeoise*, *flamande*, Henri IV, *maraîchère*, Montreuil, Parmentier). The potato also forms the basis of many traditional and regional dishes, both in France and other countries: *aligot, gratin dauphinois* or *savoyard*, goulash, Irish stew, *criques, rosti, saladier lyonnais* and *pflutters*.

Its flavour can be complemented by grated cheese, bacon, onion, cream, herbs, garlic and spices. Potatoes are also used to give body to a number of dishes, including quenelles, gnocchi, vegetable and meat loaves, stews, soups, croquettes and panada. Carême even had the idea of making a small pastry with it, and the potato can be used, very successfully, mixed with wheat flour, in pastry, bread dough and scones.

RECIPES

baked potatoes with garlic

Peel 1.5 kg (3¼ lb) potatoes, cut into slices, wash and pat dry. Heat a mixture of oil and butter in a flameproof casserole, then add 4 chopped garlic cloves and 3 thinly sliced onions. Fry gently, stirring until soft. Add the potatoes and mix well. Cover and cook in a preheated oven at 200°C (400°F, gas 6) for about 1 hour, until the potatoes are tender. Sprinkle with chives.

baked stuffed potatoes

Peel some large potatoes, trim off the ends and carefully scoop out the inside to leave cylinder shapes. Blanch the potato cylinders, drain and pat dry. Season them with salt and pepper inside and out, fill them with the chosen stuffing, then arrange them closely packed together in a buttered flameproof dish. Half-cover them with clear stock. Bring to the boil, then cover and cook in a preheated oven at 200°C (400°F, gas 6) for 30–35 minutes.

Drain the potatoes and arrange in a buttered ovenproof dish. Sprinkle with breadcrumbs or grated cheese (or a mixture of both), pour melted butter over them and brown in a preheated oven at 230°C (450°F, gas 8). The cooking juice may be used as the base for a sauce to go with the potatoes.

• *potatoes stuffed with duxelles* Fill the potatoes with a highly seasoned duxelles.

• *stuffed potatoes à la charcutière* Fill the potatoes with sausagemeat mixed with plenty of chopped parsley and garlic and, if desired, chopped onion fried in butter.

• *stuffed potatoes à la provençale* Mix equal amounts of canned tuna in oil and chopped hard-boiled (hard-cooked) egg yolks. Bind with well-reduced tomato fondue or a rich tomato sauce and adjust the seasoning; this stuffing must be highly spiced.

deep-fried potatoes

Peel or scrub the potatoes, slice or cut into fingers for making British-style chips. Cut fine fingers for French fries. Rinse, then dry the potatoes thoroughly. Heat the oil for deep-frying to 180°C (350°F). This temperature will drop to 150°C (300°F) when the potatoes are added and the oil should be reheated to 180°C (350°F). Continue cooking, uncovered, until the potatoes turn golden. Shake the basket or rearrange the potatoes occasionally so that they cook evenly.

Thick and fine chips (French fries), known as *pont-neuf* potatoes in French, should be drained when they are tender before they have turned brown. Reheat the oil and then add the potatoes again and cook until crisp and brown. This double-frying process gives chips a crisp, light finish.

When potatoes are cut very finely into potato straws, they will cause only a small drop in the temperature of the fat and will therefore need to be immersed only once.

hashed potatoes

Boil some potatoes in salted water, drain and chop up roughly. Sauté them well in butter in a frying pan. Add salt and pepper. Press them well down into the form of a cake, leave to brown and then turn out on a warm dish. Chopped onions fried in butter may be added to these hashed and browned potatoes, which are typical of American cooking.

mashed potatoes

Peel and quarter the potatoes or cut them into large chunks. Boil in salted water for about 15 minutes or until tender. Drain thoroughly, then return

Neat ropes of golden onions glow in the sunshine in this Oporto market place. They are an important ingredient in Portuguese cooking, so they are selected with care.

them to the pan. Heat, shaking the pan, for a few seconds to evaporate moisture. Then remove from the heat and add 75 g (3 oz, 6 tablespoons) butter per 800 g (1¾ lb) potato. Mash, then add a little milk and beat with a wooden spoon until smooth. Adjust the seasoning, adding freshly ground white pepper.

The mash may be flavoured with grated cheese 75 g (3 oz, ¾ cup) per 800 g (1¾ lb) mash or placed in a buttered dish, sprinkled with a little melted butter and browned in the oven or under the grill (broiler).

Alternatively, a potato ricer, mouli grater or vegetable mill may be used to make the mash instead of a hand masher.

potato cocotte

Cut some peeled potatoes into finger shapes, then trim into oblongs 4–5 cm (1½–2 in) long (keep the trimmings for a soup). Wash and drain the potatoes, place in a saucepan, cover with cold, unsalted water and bring rapidly to the boil. Drain the potatoes.

Heat a knob of butter and a little oil in a sauté pan big enough to hold the potatoes in a single layer. As soon as the fat is hot, add the potatoes, seal them over a brisk heat, then sauté them gently for about 15 minutes. Cover and place them in a preheated oven at 200°C (400°F, gas 6) and continue cooking for about 10 minutes. Check the potatoes while cooking and remove from the oven as soon as they have browned. Drain and season them with fine salt. Serve in a vegetable dish or next to the meat to be garnished, sprinkled with chopped parsley.

potatoes à la boulangère

Prepare 800 g (1¾ lb) peeled potatoes, cut into slices and brown them in 40 g (1½ oz, 3 tablespoons) butter. Slice 400 g (14 oz) onions and brown in 20 g (¾ oz, 1½ tablespoons) butter. Arrange alternate layers of potatoes and onions in a buttered ovenproof dish. Season with a little salt and pepper, then cover completely with stock. Cook in a preheated oven at 200°C (400°F, gas 6) for about 25 minutes, then reduce the oven temperature to 180°C (350°F, gas 4) and leave to cook for a further 20 minutes.

If required, add a little stock while they are cooking.

potatoes à la crème

Boil some firm, unpeeled potatoes in salted water. Peel them immediately, cut into thick slices and arrange them in a lightly buttered casserole. Cover with crème fraîche, season with salt, pepper and nutmeg, and cook them in a preheated oven at 200°C (400°F, gas 6) until the cream has completely reduced and the potatoes are tender. Add a little extra cream just before serving and sprinkle with chopped herbs.

potatoes à la maître d'hôtel

Put some potatoes in a saucepan of cold salted water, bring to the boil and boil until cooked. Peel and cut into thin slices. Place in a sauté pan and cover with boiling milk or water. Add 40 g (1½ oz, 3 tablespoons) butter per 800 g (1¾ lb) potatoes. Season with salt and pepper. Cover the pan and boil until the liquid has reduced. Turn into a vegetable dish and sprinkle with chopped parsley.

potatoes à la sarladaise

Peel and wash 1.5 kg (3¼ lb) potatoes. Cut in half lengthways, then cut each half into quarters. Heat 2 tablespoons goose fat in a flameproof casserole until it turns a beautiful rich brown colour. Add the potatoes and cook over a high heat, stirring often. Remove the excess fat. Season with salt and pepper. Crush 4 garlic cloves, whole but not peeled, and add to the potatoes. If in season, add the stalks of 2 fresh ceps, cut into quarters. Cover and cook in a preheated oven at 200°C (400°F, gas 6) for 40 minutes.

potatoes au jus

Peel some potatoes and cut into quarters. Butter a flameproof casserole and arrange the potatoes in layers. Half-cover with meat glaze or stock. Season with salt and pepper. Cover the pan and bring to the boil, then cook in a preheated oven at 200°C (400°F, gas 6) for about 40 minutes, adding a little stock if necessary (these potatoes must be very soft). Sprinkle with chopped parsley.

potatoes émiellées

Sauté some thinly sliced peeled potatoes in butter in a heavy-based frying pan, together with some small pieces of bacon and a bay leaf. Cover the pan when the potatoes are half-cooked so that they remain soft. When they are brown and well cooked, bring the pan to the table, break 1 egg per person into it and stir together so that the eggs coagulate quickly. Serve with a salad.

potatoes Mère Carles

Peel some waxy potatoes and cut out of them 28 large cork shapes about 5 cm (2 in) long. Remove the rind from 14 rashers (slices) of smoked streaky bacon (about 225 g, 8 oz) and cut each rasher in half. Pack the potato shapes tightly in a sauté pan and completely cover with cold salted water. Bring to the boil to blanch the potatoes, then drain.

Brown 50 g (2 oz, ¼ cup) butter in a sauté pan, then add the drained potato shapes, season with pepper and cover. Leave to brown for about 20 minutes, stirring frequently. Remove from the heat, leave to cool, then roll each potato shape in a half-rasher (slice) of smoked bacon. Arrange these in a sauté pan and cook, uncovered, in a preheated oven at 180°C (350°F, gas 4) for 10 minutes. Drain the cooking fat from the sauté pan and replace with 25 g (1 oz, 2 tablespoons) fresh butter. Roll the potatoes in this butter before serving.

potatoes vendangeurs de bourgogne

Place in a cast-iron or copper terrine 175 g (6 oz) smoked streaky bacon rashers (slices) with the rinds removed, then 225 g (8 oz) thinly sliced raw potatoes. Sprinkle with grated Gruyère cheese. Then add 150 g (5 oz) slightly salted belly pork, blanched and thinly sliced, and cover with 225 g (8 oz) potatoes, 50 g (2 oz, ½ cup) grated Gruyère cheese, then a further 150 g (5 oz) slightly salted belly pork prepared in the same way. Finish with 225 g (8 oz) potatoes, 50 g (2 oz, ½ cup) grated Gruyère cheese and a further 175 g (6 oz) smoked streaky bacon rashers with the rinds removed. Season lightly with pepper, scatter with a few knobs of butter and cook in a preheated oven at 200°C (400°F, gas 6) for 1¼ hours or until cooked through. Unmould and serve piping hot.

potatoes with bacon

Heat 25 g (1 oz, 2 tablespoons) butter or lard in a flameproof casserole and sauté in it 125 g (4½ oz, ⅔ cup) diced blanched bacon together with 10 small (pearl) onions. Drain and remove from the casserole. Cut some potatoes into oval shapes or cubes and brown them in the casserole. Season with salt and pepper, replace the bacon and onions, cover and cook gently for about 15 minutes. Sprinkle with chopped parsley and, if desired, finely chopped garlic.

potato fondantes

Peel some potatoes and trim them to the shape of small eggs. Fry gently in butter for 5 minutes, then drain. Add more butter, cover and finish cooking in a preheated oven at 200°C (400°F, gas 6). When cooked, remove from the oven, add 4 tablespoons white stock and leave until the potatoes have absorbed the stock. Serve in a vegetable dish, without parsley.

Alternatively, fry the potatoes in butter in a sauté pan. When cooked, remove the potatoes, wipe out the pan with paper towels, then add fresh butter – 100 g (4 oz, ½ cup) per 1 kg (2¼ lb) potatoes. Replace the potatoes, cover and keep warm over a very gentle heat or in a preheated oven at 150°C (300°F, gas 2) until all the butter is absorbed.

potato mousseline

Bake some unpeeled potatoes in the oven, peel them and rub the pulp through a sieve. Stir this mash over the heat, adding 200 g (7 oz, ¾ cup) butter per 1 kg (2¼ lb) mash, then 4 egg yolks. Season with salt, white pepper and grated nutmeg. Remove from the heat and add 200 ml (7 fl oz, ¾ cup) whipped cream. Heap the mixture in a buttered ovenproof dish, sprinkle with melted butter and brown in a preheated oven at 230°C (450°F, gas 8).

potato pancakes

Peel and wash some potatoes, pat them dry and grate coarsely. Drain on paper towels, then place in a bowl. Add salt and pepper, and for every 500 g (18 oz, 2½ cups) potatoes add 2 eggs beaten with 100 ml (4 fl oz, 7 tablespoons) milk and 1½ tablespoons melted butter. Mix thoroughly. Fry spoon-fuls of the potato mixture in a buttered frying pan, distributing the potato evenly to make small, thick pancakes. When set and golden underneath, turn the pancakes and fry until golden on the second side. Keep cooked pancakes hot until the entire batch of batter is cooked. Serve in a warm dish.

A little grated cheese or grated garlic and chopped herbs can be added to this mixture. These pancakes may be served with coq au vin, roast veal or roast venison.

roast potatoes

Peel some potatoes and cut into fairly small, evenly-sized pieces (leave them whole if they are small). Melt some butter or lard in a flameproof casserole – 100 g (4 oz, ½ cup) per 1 kg (2¼ lb) potatoes – and put the potatoes into it (in a single layer only). Roll the potatoes in the fat, season with salt, then cook at the top of a preheated oven at 190°C (375°F, gas 5) for 40 minutes or more, frequently basting with the fat until they turn golden and are cooked through. Sprinkle with chopped parsley to serve.

sautéed cooked potatoes

Boil 15 unpeeled potatoes in salted water until almost tender. Drain and leave to cool, then peel and cut into slices. In a sauté pan heat a mixture of equal amounts of butter and oil; or use butter only: 50 g (2 oz, ¼ cup) per 800 g (1¾ lb) potatoes. Brown the potatoes evenly for 12–15 minutes, first over a brisk heat, then over a gentle heat, uncovered, turning them often. Season with salt and pepper and sprinkle with chopped parsley.

sautéed raw potatoes

Peel and cut 800 g (1¾ lb) waxy potatoes into slices or small cubes. Wash, pat dry and season with salt and pepper. Fry for 25 minutes in a frying pan in butter or oil – 50 g (2 oz, ¼ cup) butter or 4 tablespoons oil per 800 g (1¾ lb) potatoes – or in a mixture of equal amounts of butter and oil. Cover when brown, but toss frequently so that they cook evenly. Serve in a vegetable dish, sprinkled with chopped parsley.

soufflé potatoes

Peel some large waxy potatoes, wash and pat dry. Cut into slices 3 mm (⅛ in) thick. Wash and dry once again. Deep-fry in oil at 150°C (300°F) for about 8 minutes. Drain on paper towels and leave to cool. Reheat the oil to 180°C (350°F) and replace the potatoes in it. Cook until puffy and brown, then drain on paper towels. Serve in a very hot dish, sprinkled with salt.

stuffed baked potatoes

Bake some large unpeeled potatoes in a preheated oven at 200°C (400°F, gas 6) for 1¼–1½ hours, until tender. Cut a slice off the top lengthways and scoop out the potato without breaking the skins. Press the pulp through a sieve and mix it with butter, a little milk or single (light) cream, salt and pepper. Fill the empty potato skins with the potato mixture, sprinkle with breadcrumbs or grated cheese (or a mixture of the two) and brown in the oven.

The sieved potato mixture can be enriched by using double (heavy) cream instead of milk or single cream. Fromage frais or yogurt can be used for a creamy, yet light, result. Grated Gruyère, Parmesan or mature (sharp) Cheddar cheese can be added. Chopped fresh parsley, dill, fennel or basil are good; snipped chives are excellent with other flavourings or on their own.

stuffed baked potatoes à la cantalienne
Prepare some baked potatoes. Add an equal volume of braised chopped cabbage to the pulp and adjust the seasoning. Fill the potato skins with this mixture, sprinkle with grated cheese and a little melted butter or lard (shortening) and brown in a preheated oven at 230°C (450°F, gas 8).

stuffed baked potatoes à la florentine
Prepare some baked potatoes. Mash half of the potato pulp and mix with twice its volume of spinach cooked in butter and chopped. Fill the potato skins with this mixture. Cover with Mornay sauce, sprinkle with Parmesan cheese and brown in a preheated oven at 230°C (450°F, gas 8) or under the grill (broiler).

stuffed baked potatoes chasseur
Prepare some baked potatoes. Mix the pulp with an equal volume of thinly sliced chicken livers and mushrooms sautéed in butter. Adjust the seasoning and add a small quantity of chopped herbs. Fill the potatoes with this mixture, sprinkle with bread-crumbs and then with melted butter, and brown in a preheated oven at 230°C (450°F, gas 8).

stuffed baked potatoes with ham and mushrooms
Prepare some baked potatoes. Keep the pulp. Pre-pare equal amounts of chopped cooked ham, chopped mushrooms lightly fried in butter and chopped onions fried in butter. Mix together, then bind with a little béchamel sauce. Adjust the sea-soning, adding paprika if desired. Stuff the potatoes, sprinkle with breadcrumbs and melted butter and brown in a preheated oven at 230°C (450°F, gas 8).

Other recipes See *Anna, basquaise, berrichonne, château potatoes, dauphine potatoes, duchess pota-toes, galette, hongroise, landaise, lorette, lyonnaise, macaire, Maintenon, noisette potatoes, normande, panada, papillote, Parmentier, paysanne, pont-neuf potatoes, salpicon (vegetable salpicons), soubise, soufflé (savoury soufflés), subric.*

POT-AU-FEU An essentially French dish that pro-vides at the same time soup (the broth), boiled meat (usually beef) and vegetables (root and leaf). 'The

foundation of empires,' according to Mirabeau, *pot-au-feu* is an ancient dish with innumerable varia-tions. Like *potée* and *poule au pot*, it is prepared in a huge pot in which the ingredients are cooked together in water, with added flavourings. *Pot-au-feu* (which can also be made with poultry) is served in restaurants or at home as a warming winter dish.

For a successful *pot-au-feu* many flavours and tex-tures are needed: lean cuts of meat, such as shin; fatter cuts, such as belly or flank; gelatinous cuts, such as oxtail; and thick slices of meat with marrow bone.

To improve the flavour of the broth, the meat may be put into cold water, brought to the boil, then skimmed when the first bubbles appear. The broth will be light and tasty, but the meat will lack flavour. To maintain the flavour of the meat, it should be put into boiling water, so the juices are sealed in and do not escape into the water. Alternatively, strongly flavoured meats may be put into boiling water while others (such as rolled boned breast) are put into cold water.

A *pot-au-feu* is tastier when it is cooked the day before and the fat is skimmed from the surface before reheating. The classic vegetables are carrots, turnips, onions (often studded with cloves), leeks, celery (cut into even lengths and tied in bundles) and parsnips. A bouquet garni and aromatic herbs are also added. Potatoes are cooked separately; if a cabbage is to be used, it should be blanched before it is added to the broth so that its flavour does not overpower that of the meat.

A *pot-au-feu* is a meal in itself. The skimmed broth is served with toasted croûtons sprinkled with cheese, then the bone marrow on toast, and finally the sliced meat and vegetables, with fresh sea salt and freshly ground pepper, and accompanied by gherkins, grated horseradish, various mustards, pick-les, small beetroot (red beet), pickled onions and redcurrant jelly, as in eastern France.

The leftover meat from a *pot-au-feu* can be eaten hot or cold: in a salad with gherkins, potatoes or shallots in oil; as boiled beef with sauce; or made into shepherd's pie, meatballs or croquettes.

RECIPE

broth from the pot-au-feu
Strain the broth from a *pot-au-feu* through a fine sieve. Leave to cool and refrigerate. Several hours later, skim off the fat from the surface. Thoroughly brown a chopped onion and add it to the broth to give colour. Strain again and adjust the seasoning. Bring to the boil gently and serve very hot in cups or bowls with toasted croûtons. A little port or Madeira may be added to the broth.

Pot-au-feu,
see page 930.

pot-au-feu ◆

Place 800 g (1¾ lb) flank (flank or short plate) in a large stockpot and pour in 3 litres (5 pints, 13 cups) cold water. Heat until just simmering, then skim the water, cover and continue to simmer for 1 hour. Stud 1 onion with 4 cloves and add it to the pan with 4 coarsely crushed or chopped garlic cloves, a bouquet garni, 1 teaspoon salt and pepper. Add 800 g (1¾ lb) each of sirloin and chuck steak. Bring back to simmering point, skim the soup, then cover and simmer gently for 2 hours.

Cut 6 carrots, 6 turnips and 3 parsnips into large even-sized pieces, turning them into neat ovals if liked. Cut the white parts of 3 leeks and 3 celery sticks into similar lengths. When the pot-au-feu has cooked for 3 hours, add the celery and leeks, then simmer for 10 minutes before adding the carrots, turnips and parsnips. Continue to cook for a further 1 hour.

Towards the end of the cooking time, poach 4 sections of marrow bone in lightly salted water for 20 minutes. Drain the meats and vegetables, and place on a large serving platter. Drain the marrow bone and add to the platter. Skim the fat off the broth and spoon a little over the meat and vegetables. Serve at once, with coarse salt, gherkins, mustard and toasted French bread on which to spread the marrow.

other recipes See *petite marmite, poule au pot.*

POT-BOUILLE In the *Grand Dictionnaire universel* Pierre Larousse defines this word as 'everyday household cooking'. It was used in this sense by Flaubert, Richepin, Huysmans and Vallès. Zola used the expression as the title for one of his books (1882). The term *pot-bouille* is no longer in use, but the more colloquial *tambouille*, derived from *pot-en-bouille*, is still found.

POTÉE Any dish cooked in an earthenware pot. The term generally applies to a mixture of meat (mainly pork) and vegetables (especially cabbage and potatoes), which is cooked in stock and served as a single course. Potée is a very old dish and is found throughout rural France, often under other names (*hochepot, garbure* and *oille*); similar dishes exist in most other parts of the world. Each region has its own traditional recipe; the following are examples of ingredients used.

• POTÉE ALBIGEOISE Leg of beef, hock of veal, raw smoked ham, preserved duck, sausage, carrots, turnips, celery, leeks, white cabbage and haricot (navy) beans.

• POTÉE ALSACIENNE Smoked bacon fat, white cabbage, celery, carrots and haricot (navy) beans. The vegetables are sweated in goose fat before the liquid is added.

• POTÉE ARTÉSIENNE Pig's head, unsmoked (slab) bacon, breast of lamb, *andouille*, carrots, green cabbage, turnips, celery, white beans and potatoes.

• POTÉE AUVERGNATE Fresh or salt pork, sausages, half a pig's head, cabbage, carrots and turnips.

• POTÉE BERRICHONNE Knuckle of ham, sausages, and red beans cooked in red wine.

• POTÉE BOURGUIGNONNE Bacon, shoulder of pork, hock of pork (ham hock), cabbage, carrots, turnips, leeks and potatoes. Also, in the spring, green beans and peas.

• POTÉE BRETONNE Shoulder of lamb, duck, sausages and vegetables. An eel potée is also made in Brittany.

• POTÉE CHAMPENOISE Called the grape-pickers' potée: unsmoked streaky bacon, salt pork, cabbage, turnips, celeriac and potatoes, sometimes sausages or smoked ham, and perhaps chicken.

• POTÉE FRANCHE-COMTOISE Beef, bacon, Morteau sausage, mutton bones and vegetables.

• POTÉE MORVANDELLE Ham, dried sausage, smoked sausage and various vegetables.

RECIPE

potée lorraine

Soak a pickled shoulder of pork in cold water to remove the salt. Clean and blanch a green cabbage and rinse in cold water. Line a stewpot with bacon rinds and add the pork shoulder, the cabbage, 500 g (18 oz) fat belly pork, 1 uncooked pig's tail, 6 peeled halved carrots, 6 peeled turnips, 3 leeks (cleaned, sliced and tied in bunches), 1 or 2 celery sticks (strings removed) and a bouquet garni. Cover with water and bring to the boil; cook for 3 hours. About 45 minutes before the end of the cooking time add a boiling sausage and some peeled potatoes. Adjust the seasoning. Serve the cut-up meat and vegetables together and the broth separately.

POTJEVFLEISCH Also known as *pot-je-vleese*. A Flemish speciality, well known around Dunkirk. It is a terrine of three meats (veal, bacon and rabbit) to which calves' feet are sometimes added. The name means literally 'pot of meat'.

RECIPE

potjevfleisch

Trim and bone 200 g (7 oz) loin of pork, 200 g (7 oz) rabbit meat, 200 g (7 oz) chicken meat and 200 g (7 oz) leg of veal. Cut into pieces 5 × 2 cm (2 × ¾ in). Peel and blanch 5 large garlic cloves. Place in a bowl, then add 1 diced celery stick, 3 sprigs of thyme, ¼ bay leaf, 2 tablespoons juniper berries and 750 ml (1¼ pints, 3¼ cups) light beer. Add the pieces of meat, cover and leave to soak for 24 hours in a cool place.

Soften 3 sheets of leaf gelatine in cold water. In a medium-sized terrine arrange the drained meat in three layers, each one covered with a sheet of gelatine. Strain the marinade and pour on top. Cover the terrine and seal the lid with flour and water paste. Cook in a preheated oven at 150°C (300°F, gas 2) for 3 hours. Leave to cool and rest at room temperature. Chill until set. Arrange a slice of *potjevfleisch* on each plate and garnish with *fines herbes*. Serve with onion or rhubarb chutney or a herb salad.

POT-ROASTING
Slow cooking by moist heat in a covered flameproof casserole after first browning in butter or other fat, then adding seasoning and a little water, stock or wine. This may be carried out in the oven or on top of the stove. Pot-roasted meat, poultry or fish should be frequently basted during cooking. The meat is usually cooked on a bed of vegetables. When it is ready, the meat is removed from the casserole and the fat is skimmed from the rich, full-bodied cooking liquid, which is used as a sauce. Suitable items for pot-roasting include white meat (such as rib and noix of veal and loin of pork); brisket, topside or silverside of beef; leg or shoulder of lamb; and also poultry (particularly duck, chicken and small turkeys).

POTTED CHAR
An old English speciality consisting of a fish paste that was traditionally served at breakfast. The fish is cooked in stock with herbs and spices, then puréed, placed in shallow earthenware dishes and covered with a layer of clarified butter. It keeps for several weeks.

POUILLY-FUISSÉ
An AOC white wine from the Mâconnais district in southern Burgundy, made from the Chardonnay grape. Good quality wines with ageing potential are to be found in Solutré-Pouilly, Vergisson, Fuissé and Chaintré.

POUILLY-FUMÉ
Also known as Pouilly Blanc Fumé and Blanc Fumé de Pouilly. An AOC white wine produced from Sauvignon Blanc grapes on the slopes above the River Loire between Pouilly and Sancerre. Internationally renowned, the wines are to be distinguished from Pouilly-sur-Loire wines, which are made from the Chasselas grape variety.

POULAMON
A small fish of the *Gadidae* family, which normally lives in the sea, but in Quebec in winter it swims up the Saint Lawrence river to breed. This is the occasion for popular festivals, notably at Sainte-Anne-de-la-Pérade. As soon as the ice begins to break up, hundreds of little cabins are set up on the river banks for fishermen. The poulamon, which is also called the 'little fish of the flume', is usually fried.

POULARD, MÈRE
(born Annette Boutisut) French restaurant owner (born Nevers, 1851; died Mont-Saint-Michel, 1931). Chambermaid to Édouard Corroyer, an architect in charge of restoring historic monuments, she accompanied her master when he undertook the restoration of the Abbey of Mont-Saint-Michel. There she married Victor Poulard, the local baker's son, and the couple took over the management of the hotel-restaurant, the Tête d'Or.

Mme Poulard made her name with her omelette, the secret of which has been attributed to a long-handled pan placed on a hot wood fire; the quality of the butter and eggs; a glass of cream added to the eggs; a very short cooking time; and the proportion of whisked egg whites. Visitors crossing by boat from the mainland to Mont-Saint-Michel would work up a hearty appetite, for which Mme Poulard prescribed her omelette at any time of the day.

POULE AU POT
A *pot-au-feu* made with beef and a stuffed chicken. There are numerous variations on the stuffing ingredients and the choice of stewing vegetables. The historian Jacques Bourgeat quotes a text dating from 1664 in which Hardouin de Péréfixe, the archbishop of Paris, recounted a conversation between Henri IV of France and the duke of Savoy, to whom the king is reputed to have uttered his famous words: 'If God grants me a longer life, I will see to it that no peasant in my kingdom will lack the means to have a chicken in the pot (*une poule dans son pot*) every Sunday.'

RECIPE

poule au pot à la béarnaise
For a chicken weighing 2 kg (4½ lb) make a forcemeat with 350 g (12 oz, 1½ cups) fine sausagemeat, 200 g (7 oz) chopped Bayonne ham, 200 g (7 oz, 1¼ cups) chopped onions, 3 crushed garlic cloves, a small bunch of parsley (chopped) and 4 chopped chicken livers. Season with salt and pepper and work these ingredients together well to make a smooth paste. Stuff the chicken and carefully sew up the openings at the neck and parson's nose (tail). Then continue as for the recipe for petite marmite using the same vegetables. Cut the chicken into portions, slice the forcemeat and serve with the vegetables.

POULETTE, À LA
The term applied to various dishes served with poulette sauce, which is made by adding lemon juice and chopped parsley to allemande sauce. It was originally served with fricassee of chicken (*poulet*), hence its name. Nowadays the sauce is more often used with fish (eel), mussels, offal (variety meats), snails or mushrooms.

RECIPES

calves' brains à la poulette
Soak 2 calves' brains in cold water with a little vinegar added, then clean them and poach for 6–7 minutes in a court-bouillon. Drain and leave to cool. Cut into thick slices and heat them very gently in some poulette sauce. Sprinkle with chopped parsley and serve very hot.

Lambs' brains, cut in half, are prepared in the same way.

mushrooms à la poulette
Clean some mushrooms by rinsing them under water several times and draining well; then stew them in butter, without letting them colour. Add

just enough poulette sauce to bind the mushrooms; check and adjust the seasoning if necessary. Serve the mushrooms sprinkled with chopped herbs in a warmed vegetable dish.

poulette sauce

Whisk 2 or 3 egg yolks with 400 ml (14 fl oz, 1¾ cups) white veal or poultry stock (or fish fumet* if the sauce is to be used with fish or mussels). Heat for about 10 minutes, whisking all the time, adding lemon juice (from a half or a whole lemon) and 50 g (2 oz, ¼ cup) butter. Remove from the heat when the sauce coats the spoon. Keep the sauce warm in a bain marie until needed, stirring from time to time to stop a skin from forming.

other recipes See *mussel, snail.*

POULIGNY-SAINT-PIERRE A goat's-milk cheese from Berry (45% fat content), with a smooth curd and a fine natural rind with a bluish tinge. It is firm but smooth, with a pronounced flavour, and is shaped like an elongated pyramid (hence its nickname 'Eiffel Tower'). It is farmhouse-made, at its best from April to November and protected by an AOC (which limits its production to the district of Blanc, in the department of Indre). It is sometimes matured in its mould, between plane leaves, with a little marc brandy.

POULTRY The generic term for farmyard birds, notably chicken, turkey, duck, goose and guinea fowl. The French term *volaille* is used in cookery to indicate chicken when used in basic preparations such as stocks, minced (ground) or thinly sliced meat in sauces, salpicons, consommes, croquettes and salads; recipes using a particular bird will name it specifically.

Chicken is by far the most popular poultry; next comes turkey, more widely eaten since it has been sold in portions (escalopes, legs, roasts). France is the leading world producer of guinea fowl. Geese bred in France are raised nowadays mainly for the production of foie gras, but in Britain they are fattened for the table, especially for Christmas. They remain fairly expensive and uneconomical. The breeding of ducks, on the other hand, has developed in France under the dual impetus of a fashion for duck foie gras and *magrets* (duck fillets). In Britain duck has become increasingly popular for special occasions, both whole and as fillets sold separately. The commercial production of poultry, particularly chickens and turkeys, has transformed what was once a farmyard enterprise into a huge industry, a fact regretted by some breeders and consumers, who prefer traditional methods. This has allowed prices to fall and a constant supply to be provided for the market.

In the Middle Ages poultry (together with small game) was sold in France by *rôtisseurs-oyers* and *poulaillers* and in Britain by poulterers. They sold geese, capons, chickens and ducks. During the time

of the Renaissance poultry started to be fattened in the coop. The turkey was still rare (one of the first occasions it was served in France was at the marriage of Charles IX on 26 November 1570), but the guinea fowl, forgotten since Roman times, reappeared thanks to the Portuguese, who brought it back from Guinea. From the 17th century a distinction was made between free-range farmyard chickens and those that had been specially fattened. Mme de Sévigné mentions the chicken of Caen and Rennes; in Paris Le Mans chickens were prized above all others, while at Lyon those of Bresse were preferred. Turkey was still a luxury and Barbary ducks and geese were both sought-after. In the 18th century goose had become a bourgeois dish, but Rouen ducks were highly prized.

Until the end of the 19th century the poultry market in Paris was situated at La Vallée, around the Quai des Grands-Augustins and the neighbouring streets. La Vallée, 'whose floor is the leading and inexhaustible source of all the fur and feathers sold in Paris' (Grimod de La Reynière), was still encumbered in 1900 with 'crates full of live poultry and square hampers in which rows of dead poultry lay in deep beds. ... On the ground, the large birds – geese, turkeys, ducks – squelched about in the dung: higher up, on three rows of shelves, flat latticed boxes contained hens and rabbits.' (Zola, *Le Ventre de Paris*).

■ **Poultry in cooking** In the past birds that today would be roasted were poached or boiled, and vice versa. Nowadays, the classic ways of cooking poultry are roasting (the most usual method), boiling or steaming, braising (particularly for birds that are rather old or very large, as well as for giblets) and sautéing. Forcemeat is often an essential complement to the dish. Chicken livers, gizzards (and, more rarely, cockscombs and kidneys) are also used in several ways in cooking.

Poultry can be served in hot or cold dishes but is never eaten raw. In home cooking the commonest dishes are casseroles, fricassées, pilaf, hashes, blanquettes, curries and gratin dishes; French regional dishes also include salmis, *poule au pot*, fritters, *crépinettes, kromeskis* and gratin dishes. Among more elaborate recipes are chicken in aspic, ballotines, chauds-froids, medallions, suprêmes, *turbans*, soufflés, bouchées and vol-au-vent, as well as dishes *à la reine*.

POUND CAKE A simple, plain cake made with equal weights of flour, sugar, butter and eggs. The mixing method and the order in which the ingredients are added varies according to the recipe. The cake can be flavoured with vanilla, lemon or orange.

RECIPES

pound cake

Butter and flour a cake tin (pan). Weigh 3 eggs, then weigh out the same amount of caster (superfine) sugar, butter and sifted plain (all-purpose) flour. Break the eggs, keeping whites and yolks separate. Beat the yolks with the sugar and a pinch of salt until the mixture becomes white and creamy. Beat in the butter, which should be melted but not hot, then the flour and finally 3 tablespoons rum or brandy. Whisk the egg whites to stiff peaks and fold them in carefully. Pour the mixture into the cake tin and bake for about 45 minutes in a pre-heated oven at 200°C (400°F, gas 6); the temperature can be increased to 220°C (425°F, gas 7) when the cake has risen. Turn the cake out of the tin as soon as it is removed from the oven and leave it to cool on a wire rack.

Instead of mixing in the yolks and whites separately, the whole eggs can be lightly beaten and mixed directly with the sugar: the result is not quite so light.

orange pound cake
Mix up a pound cake according to the basic recipe, flavouring it with 3 tablespoons Cointreau, Grand Marnier or Curaçao. In addition, add the blanched, finely grated rind from 2 oranges or 75 g (3 oz, ½ cup) chopped candied orange peel. Bake the cake and let it cool.

Heat 400 g (14 oz, 1¼ cups) orange marmalade, boil until it is reduced to three-quarters of its volume, then pour it over the cake. Leave until cold, then refrigerate for 1 hour before serving.

POUNTARI A speciality of Auvergne, consisting of a hash of bacon, onions and aromatics rolled up in a cabbage leaf (or a piece of pig's intestine), tied at both ends like a sausage and cooked in a vegetable soup. It is served in slices with the soup.

POUNTI A speciality of Auvergne, consisting of a hash of bacon, onions and Swiss chard bound with milk beaten with eggs and cooked in a cool oven in a casserole greased with lard. This rustic dish can be enriched with ham, cream, raisins or prunes, as well as potherbs.

POUPELIN An old-fashioned gâteau consisting of a large, flat, bun made of choux pastry and filled with sweetened whipped cream, ice cream or a fruit mousse just before serving.

POUPETON A traditional method of preparing meat or poultry by boning, stuffing and rolling it into ballotines or *paupiettes* ready for braising. *Poupeton* of turkey, which Brillat-Savarin liked, was originally stuffed with ortolans (buntings) arranged on slices of foie gras.

RECIPES

calf's head in a poupeton
Cook a whole calf's head in a court-bouillon, drain it and flatten it out on a large piece of pig's caul (caul fat). Remove part of the lean meat, as well as the ears and tongue, cut them into small dice and mix with a stuffing made from equal quantities of à gratin forcemeat and veal forcemeat; also add 150 g (5 oz, 1⅓ cups) chopped mushrooms. Season with salt and pepper and sprinkle with mixed spice, then add 2 liqueur glasses of brandy. Mix until all the ingredients are combined.

Spread the stuffing over the calf's head, then roll it up into a ballotine; wrap in the caul and tie it up. Cook gently in a preheated oven at 180°C (350°F, gas 4) in some braising stock made with Madeira, Bayonne ham, knuckle of veal, carrots, onions and a bouquet garni until firm and cooked through. Drain and untie the *poupeton*, slice it and arrange the slices on a large serving dish. Pour over a few tablespoons of braising stock and glaze it in the oven.

Surround with a garnish made up of braised lambs' sweetbreads or slices of calves' sweetbreads, cockscombs and kidneys stewed in Madeira, calf's-brain fritters and stuffed olives, blanched and dipped in Madeira demi-glace. Arrange 12 trussed crayfish, cooked in a court-bouillon with white wine, in rows on either side of the dish. Pour over a few tablespoons of braising stock, strained and reduced to a good consistency. Serve the rest of the sauce separately.

poupeton of turkey Brillat-Savarin
Prepare a turkey in the same way as for a ballotine. Stuff it with a smooth mixture of fine veal forcemeat, à gratin forcemeat, lambs' sweetbreads braised à blanc and diced foie gras and truffles. Roll the turkey into a ballotine; wrap it in a pig's caul (caul fat), then in muslin (cheesecloth) and tie it up.

Line a greased flameproof casserole with diced raw ham and slices of carrot and onion. Place the turkey in this and cook gently, covered, for 15 minutes, then add 3 tablespoons Madeira. Reduce by half, add some gravy (or chicken stock) and continue cooking, covered, in a preheated oven at 190°C (375°F, gas 5) for 1½ hours. Skim the fat from the cooking liquid, strain, season and serve in a sauceboat.

The *poupeton* can also be served cold, as it is or in aspic.

POURLY A goat's-milk cheese from Burgundy (45% fat content) with a soft curd and a natural rind, which is fine and bluish. It is fairly smooth, with a flavour of hazelnuts and a goaty smell, and is made exclusively in Essert (Yonne). Moulded into a small cylinder with convex sides, 10 cm (4 in) in diameter, 6 cm (2½ in) high and weighing about 300 g (11 oz), it is at its best between April and November.

POUSSE-CAFÉ A French slang term for a spirit, brandy or liqueur served at the end of a meal, in a small glass or in an empty coffee cup, which is still warm enough to allow the flavour and aroma to develop.

In cocktail language, a *pousse-café* is a drink made by pouring one layer after another of liqueurs and spirits of differing colours and densities, which do not mix, into a tall glass. This kind of drink is called a *pousse-amour* when an egg yolk is used in the middle of these layers.

POUTINE A dish from the south of France, consisting of a mixture of tiny young fish, particularly sardines and anchovies, which are fried like whitebait. The name comes from the dialect of Nice, from the word *poutina* (porridge). *Poutine* can also be made with poached fish sprinkled with lemon and oil, and can be used to garnish a soup or fill an omelette.

PRALINE Traditionally a confection consisting of almonds coated with caramelized sugar. The granulated appearance results from the technique used in its manufacture: the almonds are heated in sugar syrup (with the addition of a little glucose) to the hard crack stage so that sugar crystals form around the nut. The almond is then coated several times with the sugar syrup, the last coating being coloured and flavoured, traditionally providing pink, beige or brown pralines flavoured with chocolate or coffee.

The praline is a speciality of Montargis, where its inventor, Lassagne, who was *chef de bouche* (master of the household) to the Comte du Plessis-Praslin, came to retire. Legend has it that his creation came about in this way: seeing a kitchen boy nibbling at leftovers of caramel and almonds, Lassagne had the idea of cooking whole almonds in sugar. The sweetmeat that resulted had a great success and even, it is said, contributed to certain diplomatic triumphs, for which the Comte du Plessis-Praslin, minister to Louis XIII and Louis XIV, took all the credit (he also gave his name to the sweets). Lassagne finally retired to Montargis in 1630 and there founded the Maison de la Praline, which exists to this day.

Pralines have also become a traditional fairground sweet, cooked in the open air in a copper 'shaker'; the almonds are sometimes replaced by peanuts, which are cheaper. The following verse was composed in honour of the 'true' praline, at about the time of its creation:

The sweet, when created, was certainly rare;
Dented all over, its colour was brown.
Its subtle aroma delighted the nose;
You'd think it was made of a nectar divine.

Other towns in France have also made this product a speciality, notably Aigueperse (where the almonds are coated in soft sugar) and Vabresl'Abbaye (where they are sold in paper cones). Pralines are also used for decorating brioches and soufflés.

■ **Caramelized nuts** In modern culinary use the term refers to almonds coated with caramel, or cooked with sugar until caramelized, and set in a thin layer on a baking sheet. Praline is used in pâtisserie and confectionery, for flavouring creams and ice creams, and for filling sweets and chocolates. When home-made it spoils very quickly and will keep for only a day or two, stored in an airtight jar or wrapped in foil. When cold, the nuts and caramel are finely or coarsely crushed. Hazelnuts may be used instead of, or as well as, almonds. (See also *dragée*).

brioche with pralines
Make some leavening dough with 250 g (9 oz, 2¼ cups) strong (bread) flour and 20 g (¾ oz) fresh yeast (1½ cakes compressed yeast) or 2 teaspoons dried yeast dissolved in 150 ml (¼ pint, ⅔ cup) warm water. Roll this dough, which will be fairly soft, into a ball and leave it to rise for at least 30 minutes; it should double in volume.

In the meantime, mix together 800 g (1¾ lb, 7 cups) plain (all-purpose) flour, 1 tablespoon salt, 65 g (2½ oz, 5 tablespoons) sugar and 6 whole eggs. Knead vigorously and then add 900 g (2 lb, 4 cups) good-quality softened butter, a little at a time. Then mix in the leaven and roll the dough into a ball again. Leave this to rise at room temperature for 6–7 hours.

Mix some pink pralines (or candied rose petals) into the dough, then put it into a large brioche mould and bake in a preheated oven at 200°C, 400°F, gas 6) for about 1 hour. When cooked, decorate the surface of the brioche with a few crushed pralines.

praline
Blanch 200 g (7 oz, 1½ cups) almonds and toast them under the grill (broiler) or in a frying pan without fat (they should be golden brown but not burned). Put 200 g (7 oz, ¾ cup) granulated sugar and 1 tablespoon water into a copper pan and melt over a brisk heat. When the sugar bubbles, add a few drops of vanilla extract; as soon as the sugar has turned brown, add the almonds and mix all together briskly for 1 minute. Pour on to a greased baking sheet, spread out and leave to cool. Pound the praline very finely in a mortar as required.

additional recipe See *île flottante*.

PRALINÉ A delicate filling for sweets (candies) or chocolates, consisting of lightly roasted almonds or hazelnuts mixed with sugar, then crushed with cocoa or cocoa butter.

Praliné is also the name of a cake consisting of layers of Genoese sponge separated by a layer of praline butter cream and covered with a layer of the same cream, sprinkled with chopped almonds.

PRAWNS See *shrimps and prawns*.

PRÉCUISSON The French term meaning precooking and referring to the first very rapid cooking of a food, which changes its appearance. This includes browning (cooking over or at a high heat to colour the food), blanching by rapid boiling in water or deep-frying.

PRESERVATION OF FOOD The keeping of perishable foods in a consumable form. Most of the processes of preservation, learned by trial and error, have been handed down through the ages; the necessity of guarding against want by stocking surplus food is almost as old as human life itself. The biological discoveries of the end of the 19th century and the vast improvements in techniques have meanwhile improved and diversified methods considerably.

The principle of preservation, whether it be on an industrial or small domestic scale, is to prevent or slow down the development and action of natural micro-organisms and enzymes and to avoid exterior deterioration.

• DEHYDRATION This draws much of the water (which encourages biological reactions) from the food. Drying and smoking have been practised since antiquity and small-scale processes can still be found coexisting beside the great industrial ovens. In everyday practice, exposure to fresh air or the sun is sufficient for the dehydration of vegetables, aromatic plants and mushrooms, and the kitchen oven will suffice for fruit.

• SATURATION This also results, albeit indirectly, in the elimination of water. This is the principle of preservation by cooking in sugar (jams, confectionery) or by salting (raw meat submerged in dry salt or put into a saturated brine solution). Salting is also used to preserve butter. Preserving with oil (aromatic plants and fish) is a very old method, used by the ancients.

• COATING A method that protects the food from the action of oxygen. The gastronomic practice most common nowadays is the preserving of meat in its own fat (see *confit*), although this is of limited value if not accompanied by sterilization.

• PRESERVATIVES These create a medium incompatible with all microbial life, hence their use among the authorized additives. Classic methods employ either vinegar, sweet-and-sour preparations (gherkins, pickles, chutneys) or alcohol (for fruit). Alcoholic fermentation (wine, beer, cider, spirits) and acidic fermentation (sauerkraut) are, in varying degrees, preserving agents.

• HEAT This destroys enzymes and micro-organisms as long as the temperature is sufficiently high and the period of treatment sufficiently long. Pasteurization (milk, semi-preserved products) is an industrial practice allowing only short-term preservation (from a few days to several months) and foodstuffs have to be kept in the refrigerator. Sterilization (preserves, UHT milk) enables food to be kept for long periods at room temperature (see *appert*). These two processes, however, result in the destruction of certain vitamins sensitive to heat (C, B). Sterilization can be carried out in the kitchen, but it must be done with care and only with a pressure cooker.

• REFRIGERATION This is a very old practice, but for centuries natural ice and snow had to be used. The activity of enzymes and bacteria is reduced (but germs are not destroyed) at temperatures of –8 to –10°C (18 to 14°F). Refrigeration enables vegetables, milk products, opened drinks and fresh meat, to be preserved for several days. Very low temperatures, such as those used for freezing, enable foods to be preserved for longer periods (up to several months or even a year for some foods); the nutritive value remains the same, and the taste of the food is best preserved by this method.

In everyday practice the length of time food can be kept depends on the type of food itself and the storage methods available. A cellar enables foodstuffs to be preserved in greater quantity; a pantry, refrigerator or freezer will give successively longer periods of preservation. Packaging also plays an important role, from airtight tins for dry biscuits (crackers and cookies) to plastic film and foil, which are especially suited to refrigeration.

PRESERVATIVE An additive intended to stop deterioration (fermentation, mould, decay) in foods. Many preservatives are natural products such as salt, sugar and vinegar; others are synthetic and are used extensively in commercial products.

PRESERVES Food preparations with a long shelf life. These are prepared by methods and/or using ingredients that prevent attack by micro-organisms that cause decay or spoilage. Preservation methods include drying, pickling or cooking with sugar, sterilization and freezing. The term generally refers to jams and similar sweet preserves and to chutneys and pickles. These are popular products for home preparation; commercial preserves often rely on sterilization and/or the addition of chemical preservatives to ensure lengthy shelf life and food safety in the commercial and retail environment.

PRESERVING JAR A wide-necked glass container, usually hermetically sealed with either a metal screw-ring or with a glass lid fitted with a rubber seal and a metal clasp. These jars are used for bottling and sterilizing: preserving fruit and vegetables in their own juice, other liquor or syrup. Jars for sterilized food should not be too large, because once they are opened, their contents must be used quickly. Also, the sterilization process is more difficult for large quantities. Home bottling is an old-fashioned method of preserving, replaced by freezing as a domestic means of storing vegetables and plain fruit. The process of sterilizing and sealing jars is one that requires close attention, with exact temperatures and timing used to ensure food safety.

PRESS A utensil used for producing a liquid or purée from solid ingredients. Citrus fruit squeezers made from glass, plastic or wood allow fresh fruit juice to be squeezed from oranges and lemons. Cast-aluminium fruit squeezers, with perforated bowls, are also sometimes used for other types of fruit, but produce only small quantities of juice (for fruit cocktails). The 'half-slice' squeezer, made of metal, is used for flavouring lemon tea or for squeezing over fish or hors d'oeuvre where a wedge of lemon is needed.

Small presses made from enamelled steel are used for making jellies, jams and wine: these crush the fruit very rapidly by the action of a screw against a face-plate. A vegetable mill (or purée press) is used to rub cooked vegetables or fruit through a sieve to reduce them to a purée. All these have mostly been replaced by electrically operated machines with a centrifugal action. Meat presses are used to extract the juice from raw or slightly cooked meat. The carcass (or duck) press is a piece of equipment used mainly for extracting the fatty juices from the carcass of a duck (see *Tour d'Argent*).

Some terrines, pâtés and meats (such as tongue) need to be chilled under a press to be smoothly integrated, well moulded or well flattened. The food is left in a cool place, covered with a small board with a heavy weight on top, or a special press with a screw-down lid can be used. In old French cookery, the term *soupresse* ('under press') was applied to a sort of fish pâté in which the crushed flesh of the fish was wrapped in a piece of muslin (cheesecloth) and pressed down hard.

PRESSING The process of making pressed cheese, cooked or uncooked. It consists of accelerating the draining of the cut-up curds by putting them in a press, which is operated either by hand or mechanically. It makes it possible to produce cheeses that can be kept.

PRESSURE COOKER A sealed saucepan in which food is cooked under pressure at a higher temperature and therefore much more quickly than in an ordinary pan. Temperatures range from 112–125°C (234–257°F) instead of a maximum of 100°C (212°F), the boiling point of water at atmospheric pressure.

A type of autoclave, the pressure cooker is made of thick aluminium or stainless steel; its lid has a watertight seal that can usually be closed hermetically, either with a screw and clamp or a bayonet-type locking mechanism. A valve controls the escape of the steam once the desired pressure is reached (a safety device is included in case the valve becomes blocked). It is essential to allow the pressure to fall before opening the lid, either by letting all the steam escape through the valve, or by cooling the pressure cooker with cold water. Modern pressure cookers are simple to use, with automatic valves, timers and pressure-releasing devices to speed up the final stages of pressure cooking.

The pressure cooker is designed for cooking in steam or in water or stock (often with a reduced quantity of liquid). It has the advantages of saving time, especially for cooking ingredients that take several hours by traditional methods. However, in the opinion of gourmets, the pressure cooker cannot replace the traditional method of simmering. In such opinion, meat has a tendency to be noticeably softer, with less flavour, and the flavours of various ingredients in a dish are indiscriminately mixed.

PRETZEL A crisp biscuit (cracker) from Alsace, traditionally served with beer. It is usually shaped like a loose knot and is made of dough poached in boiling water, sprinkled with coarse salt and cumin seeds and hardened in the oven. The ancient origins of this pastry are linked to the cult of the sun: it was originally made in the shape of a ring encircling a cross. Since this was too fragile, it evolved into its present shape, which is a traditional motif of bakers and pastrycooks. Originally, the pretzel was not necessarily the crisp biscuit known today, but a chewy product. Pretzels of all sizes are now made as aperitif biscuits.

Sweet pretzels are also made, particularly in Germany and Austria; they may be flavoured with vanilla or aniseed and iced with a hard sugar coating.

PRICKLY PEAR The edible orange-red pear-shaped fruit of a species of cactus. The fruit has a thick skin covered with large prickles and must be handled with care, preferably wearing gloves. The prickles can be removed by rubbing the skin with a thick, rough cloth. The fruit is peeled and eaten raw, sprinkled with a little lemon or lime juice. It can also be cooked and puréed for use in desserts and preserves. An oil can be extracted from the seeds, and the seeds can be sprouted to produce edible shoots, which are used mainly as animal feed.

PRIMROSE A meadow and woodland plant whose pale yellow flowers appear in spring. Its young tender leaves can be eaten as a salad and its flowers are used for garnishing salads and for herb teas. Primrose flowers are also used in several recipes, including a dish of roast veal cooked in butter with sliced onions, carrots and a bouquet garni, moistened with white wine, to which primrose flowers are added 30 minutes before cooking is finished; the cooking liquid is deglazed with port and thickened with cream.

PRINCE ALBERT A method of preparing fillet of beef, which was named in honour of the Prince Consort, husband of Queen Victoria. The meat is stuffed with raw foie gras with truffles, braised in a vegetable fondue and then moistened with port; the garnish consists of whole truffles.

RECIPE

fillet of beef Prince Albert
Marinate a raw goose foie gras studded with truffle in a little Cognac with salt and pepper for 24 hours in a cool place. Lard a piece of beef cut from the middle of the fillet with fine strips of bacon. Slice the meat along its length without separating the 2 halves completely. Drain the foie gras, place it in the meat and tie together firmly to keep the liver in place. Fry the meat in butter in a braising pan over a brisk heat until it is well browned on all sides, then cover it with a layer of *matignon*, wrap in very thin rashers (slices) of bacon and secure with string.

Prepare a braising stock with a calf's foot and aromatic herbs, adding the liver marinade; pour into the braising pan and add the beef. Pour on a little port, cover, bring to the boil, then transfer to a preheated oven at 200°C (400°F, gas 6) and cook for 1 hour. Untie the fillet, remove the bacon and the *matignon*, but leave the string holding the foie gras in place. Strain the braising stock, pour some over the meat and glaze quickly in a very hot oven. Untie the meat, place it on a serving dish and garnish with whole truffles, stewed in butter or poached in Madeira. Serve the braising stock, skimmed of fat and strained, in a sauceboat.

PRINCESSE A rich garnish for poultry, salmon steaks, calves' sweetbreads, vol-au-vent or egg dishes, distinguished by the inclusion of asparagus tips and slivers of truffle.

RECIPES

calves' sweetbreads princesse
Slice some calves' sweetbreads and braise them in white stock; drain and keep warm. Prepare an allemande sauce with the braising stock. In separate pans, cook some green asparagus tips in butter and heat through some slivers of truffle in butter. Arrange the slices of sweetbread in the serving dish and garnish with the slivers of truffle and bunches of asparagus tips. Serve the sauce separately.

chicken princesse
Poach a chicken in white stock. Bake some barquette cases (shells) blind and cook some green asparagus tips in butter. Drain the chicken and place it on a serving dish and keep warm. Prepare an allemande sauce with the cooking liquid. Arrange the asparagus tips in the barquettes and use to garnish the dish. Sprinkle the barquettes with slivers of truffle heated through in butter. Pour some sauce over the chicken and serve the remainder in a sauceboat.

fillets of sole princesse
These are prepared in the same way as salmon steaks princesse, but they are poached folded in half. The asparagus tips are sometimes cut very short and arranged in barquettes made from fine lining pastry. Both the barquettes and the fillets are garnished with slivers of truffle cooked in butter.

salmon steaks princesse
Ask the fishmonger to cut some steaks of equal thickness from a large fresh salmon. Prepare some fish fumet, leave it to cool and strain. Lay the steaks in a fish kettle with a small amount of fumet and poach them gently for 6 minutes from the time that the fumet starts to simmer. Drain and skin the steaks and arrange on a serving dish; keep warm. Use the cooking liquid to make a normande sauce. Garnish the steaks with slivers of truffle warmed through in butter and with green asparagus tips, also cooked in butter (these can be arranged in barquettes made of fine lining pastry). Serve the sauce separately.

scrambled eggs princesse
Prepare some scrambled eggs and pour into a bowl. Garnish with green asparagus tips stewed in butter, a julienne of white chicken meat bound with suprême sauce and some slivers of truffle heated through in butter.

soft-boiled or poached eggs princesse
Prepare some soft-boiled or poached eggs, arrange them on slices of fried bread and coat with suprême sauce; garnish with silvers of truffle heated through in butter. Garnish the dish with bunches of freshly cooked asparagus tips dressed in butter and a julienne of white chicken meat bound with suprême sauce.

other recipes See *consommé (hot consommés)*.

PRINTANIÈRE, À LA Describing various dishes (meat, poultry, eggs) that are garnished with a mixture of vegetables (in theory, spring vegetables), usually tossed in butter.

Navarin of mutton and spring vegetable soup are usually described as *printanier*.

RECIPE

vegetable ragoût à la printanière
Generously grease a large flameproof casserole with butter. Prepare and wash the following new vegetables: 250 g (9 oz) baby carrots, 250 g (9 oz) baby turnips, 12 button onions, 250 g (9 oz) very small new potatoes, 2 lettuce hearts, 250 g (9 oz) finely sliced French (green) beans, 250 g (9 oz, 1½ cups) shelled peas and 3 trimmed artichoke hearts quartered and sprinkled with lemon juice. Separate half a very white cauliflower into tiny florets.

Put the carrots, beans, artichoke hearts and onions into the buttered casserole; just cover with chicken stock and bring to the boil. After it has boiled for 8 minutes, add the turnips, potatoes, peas, cauliflower and lettuce hearts; adjust the seasoning and continue cooking for about 20 minutes. Drain the vegetables and arrange them in a vegetable dish. Reduce the cooking liquid, whisk in 50 g (2 oz, ¼ cup) butter and pour over the vegetables.

additional recipe See *navarin*.

PROCOPE The oldest café in Paris, which is still in existence in the Rue de l'Ancienne-Comédie. The establishment was founded in 1686 by Francesco Procopio dei Coltelli, who changed his name to Procope; he had previously worked with the Armenian Pascal, who ran a coffee stall at the Saint-Germain Fair and thus introduced the beverage to the capital.

Procope opened the first permanent establishment devoted to the consumption of coffee; his café was richly decorated with chandeliers, wood panelling and mirrors.

The Procope rapidly became the most famous centre of Parisian literary and intellectual life. From the 17th to the 19th century it was patronized by writers, actors (the Comédie-Française was situated opposite from 1687 to 1770), Encyclopedists and later by Revolutionaries and Romantics. His syrup drinks, ice creams, confectionery and cakes were also popular. Procope had the original idea of pasting up a news-sheet on the chimney of the stove that heated the room; his café thus became 'the true speaking newspaper of Paris' and a celebrated forum for the exchange of ideas.

The founder retired in 1716 and his son Alexandre succeeded him. In 1753 a certain Dubuisson bought the establishment, then later sold it to the Italian Zoppi (a friend of Marat and Danton), who managed it during the time of the Empire. The focus of literary life during the Romantic period, the Procope later began to suffer the effects of competition from the Café de la Régence. It was sold in 1872 to Baroness Thénard and closed in 1890; it reopened in 1893 as a literary club, then became, successively, a vegetarian restaurant and an eating house for poor students, before being used by the French administration. It reopened as a restaurant in 1952 but never recaptured its former glory.

PROFITEROLE A small, filled sweet or savoury bun made of choux paste. Savoury profiteroles are filled with a cheese mixture or game purée and are generally used as a garnish for soup.

Sweet profiteroles are filled with confectioner's custard (pastry cream), Chantilly cream, ice cream or jam; they are the basic ingredient of *croquembouches* and gâteaux Saint-Honoré. Chocolate profiteroles are filled with vanilla or coffee ice cream or Chantilly cream and are coated or served with hot chocolate sauce. Profiteroles can also be filled with Chantilly cream combined with fruit purée and can be served with zabaglione flavoured with syrup of the same fruit. The name comes from the word *profit* and originally meant a small gratuity or gift.

RECIPE

chocolate profiteroles
Prepare some choux* paste with 250 ml (8 fl oz, 1 cup) water, a pinch of salt, 2 tablespoons sugar, 125 g (4½ oz, 1 cup) plain (all-purpose) flour and 4 eggs. Using a piping bag with a plain nozzle, pipe out balls of dough the size of walnuts on to a greased baking sheet and brush them with beaten egg. Cook in a preheated oven at 200°C (400°F, gas 6) for about 20 minutes until crisp and golden; allow to cool in the oven.

Meanwhile melt 200 g (7 oz, 7 squares) plain (semisweet) chocolate with 100 ml (4 fl oz, 7 tablespoons) water in a bain marie; add 100 ml (4 fl oz,

7 tablespoons) double (heavy) cream and stir well. Prepare some Chantilly cream by whipping 300 ml (½ pint, 1¼ cups) double cream with 100 ml (4 fl oz, 7 tablespoons) very cold milk, then 75 g (3 oz, 6 tablespoons) caster (superfine) sugar and 1 teaspoon vanilla sugar. Split the profiteroles on one side and fill them with the Chantilly cream, using a piping bag. Arrange in a bowl and serve with the hot chocolate sauce.

additional recipe See *consommé (hot consommés)*.

PROGRÈS A light and crunchy cake base made from a mixture of stiffly whisked egg whites, sugar and ground almonds and/or hazelnuts, which is piped out in a spiral to form discs and baked in the oven. The cake is built up by placing the discs one on top of the other, sandwiched together with praline butter cream or with coffee or chocolate cream. The cake is topped with flaked (slivered) or roasted almonds, sprinkled with icing (confectioner's) sugar, and iced (frosted) with fondant or decorated with butter cream, which is piped with a fluted nozzle or with a small plain nozzle to write the word 'progrès' on the top.

RECIPE

coffee progrès
Grease 3 baking sheets, dust with flour and trace a circle, about 23 cm (9 in) in diameter, on each of them with a spoon. In a bowl mix together 150 g (5 oz, ⅔ cup) granulated sugar, 250 g (9 oz, 2 cups) ground almonds and a pinch of salt. Whisk 8 egg whites until stiff with 100 g (4 oz, ½ cup) granulated sugar and gently fold into the first mixture with a wooden spoon. Put this mixture into a piping bag with an 8 mm (⅜ in) nozzle and fill the 3 circles, piping in a spiral from the centre to the edge. Bake in a preheated oven at 180°C (350°F, gas 4) for 45 minutes. Gently ease the cooked discs off the sheets and let them cool on a flat surface.

While the oven is still hot, roast 150 g (5 oz, 1 cup) flaked (slivered) almonds for 5 minutes. Put 250 g (9 oz, 1¼ cups) granulated sugar in a saucepan with 3 tablespoons water and bring to the boil. Beat 6 egg yolks in a bowl, then gradually pour over the boiling syrup, beating hard until the mixture cools. Dissolve 2 tablespoons instant coffee in 1 tablespoon boiling water. Cream 350 g (12 oz, 1½ cups) butter and gradually beat in the egg–syrup mixture; then pour in the dissolved coffee and beat well. Reserve one-quarter of this butter cream; cover each disc with one-third of the remaining cream. Then put the discs one on top of the other and cover the sides with the reserved butter cream. Decorate the top with the flaked almonds. Place in the refrigerator for about 1 hour.

Cut out some strips of thick paper 1 cm (½ in) wide and 25 cm (10 in) long. Place them on top of the cake without pressing, leaving a gap of 2 cm (¾ in) between each, and dust the cake with sifted icing (confectioner's) sugar. Carefully remove the paper strips and put the *progrès* back in the refrigerator for at least 1 hour before serving.

PROSCIUTTO The Italian word for ham, used in the names of raw hams coming from Italy, in particular *prosciutto di Parma* and *prosciutto di San Daniele*.

PROTEIN Any of a large group of nitrogenous compounds, present in all animals and plants, consisting of linked amino-acid units. Foods of animal origin are rich in proteins: fish, poultry, game, meat, eggs, milk and cheese. Plant proteins occur in a variety of foods, including pulses, bread and pasta.

PROVENÇALE, À LA Describing numerous preparations inspired by (or arising directly from) the cookery of Provence, in which olive oil, tomato and garlic predominate. The Provençal garnish for cuts of meat or poultry includes either peeled and slowly cooked tomatoes and large mushrooms garnished with *duxelles* seasoned with garlic, or crushed garlic-flavoured tomatoes with stoned (pitted) olives (black or green), or aubergines (eggplants) stuffed with a tomato fondue, French (green) beans in butter and château potatoes. Provençal sauce (made with tomato, onion, garlic and white wine) is used to dress vegetables, eggs, poultry and fish.

RECIPES

bass or brill à la provençale
Prepare a Provençal sauce. Scale some bass or brill, weighing about 400 g (14 oz). Cut off the fins and make an incision in the top of the back, on either side of the backbone. Wash and wipe the fish. Sprinkle them with salt and pepper, dust them with flour and brown them quickly in olive oil in a frying pan. Mask an ovenproof dish with a little Provençal sauce. Arrange the fish in it and just cover with Provençal sauce. Sprinkle with fresh breadcrumbs, moisten with a little olive oil and cook in a preheated oven at 200°C (400°F, gas 6) for about 20 minutes. Sprinkle with chopped parsley and serve piping hot in the cooking dish.

fried eggs à la provençale
Prepare a garnish of fried tomatoes and aubergines (eggplants) and a tomato fondue as for the soft-boiled eggs *à la provençale*. Mask a dish with the vegetables. Lightly fry some eggs in olive oil and arrange them in the dish. Coat them with tomato fondue and sprinkle with chopped parsley and garlic.

Provençal sauce
Heat 2 tablespoons olive oil in a heavy-based saucepan. Soften in it without browning 3 tablespoons peeled and chopped onions, then add 800 g (1½ lb, 3 cups) peeled, seeded and crushed toma-

toes and cook gently for about 15 minutes. Add a crushed garlic clove, a bouquet garni, 200 ml (7 fl oz, ¾ cup) dry white wine and 200 ml (7 fl oz, ¾ cup) meat stock. Leave to cook, covered, for 15 minutes, then adjust the seasoning, remove the lid and reduce the sauce by half. Add some fresh chopped parsley or basil just before serving.

sautéed veal chops à la provençale
First prepare a garlic-flavoured tomato sauce and then some small round tomatoes stuffed with mushroom duxelles and browned in the oven. Quickly brown some veal chops in olive oil in a frying pan. Season with salt and pepper, cover, reduce the heat and leave to complete cooking for about 15 minutes. Drain the chops and arrange them in the serving dish surrounded by the stuffed tomatoes. Keep hot in the oven with the door ajar.

Pour the oil out of the frying pan, add the tomato sauce and 3–4 tablespoons white wine, stir well and reduce by half over a brisk heat. Pour the sauce over the chops, sprinkle with chopped parsley or basil and serve piping hot.

soft-boiled or poached eggs à la provençale
Prepare a garlic-flavoured tomato fondue. Cut some very large firm (beefsteak or Marmande) tomatoes in half horizontally, remove the seeds and fry gently in olive oil. Fry some slices of aubergines (eggplants) or courgettes (zucchini) in olive oil. Prepare the same number of soft-boiled or poached eggs as there are tomato halves.

Place the eggs in the tomato halves and arrange the latter in a crown in a round, heated serving dish. Coat with tomato fondue. Arrange the sliced vegetables in the centre and sprinkle with chopped herbs.

other recipes See *beans (fresh), brain, brandade, cep, courgette, daube, eel, knuckle, octopus, potato, salsify, salt cod, scallop shell, tomato, tuna.*

PROVENCE See *page 940.*

PROVE (RISE) Of dough, to increase in volume through the action of a raising (leavening) agent. To make a leavened dough rise, it should be placed away from draughts in a warm atmosphere – 25–30°C (77–86°F) – to encourage fermentation; this results in the production of carbon dioxide gas, which puffs up the dough. While it is proving, the dough is covered with a cloth to stop a crust forming. If brioche or bread dough has not risen sufficiently, it remains heavy and solid; when proving goes on for too long, the dough becomes acid.

PROVOLONE A *pasta filata* or cooked and stretched paste cheese from southern Italy. The plastic curd lends itself to improvisation, and so Provolone comes in all shapes and sizes. The shaped cheeses (45% fat content) are brined and hung up to

Provence

A vast region with a favourable climate, Provence possesses a great variety of natural resources, reflected in its colourful gastronomy, which began to be known in Paris at the time of the Revolution. The specialities were listed in *Le Cuisinier Durand*, which appeared in Nîmes in 1830, and by Maître Reboul, at the end of the 19th century. Dishes *à la provençale* are extremely varied, but all are characterized by the presence of tomato, garlic and olive oil.

■ **Fish and seafood** The Mediterranean coast supplies a number of fish (especially local species of rockfish) and seafood, and the inland waters provide such fish as trout, bleak, pike, tench, char and carp.

Fish and seafood predominate in the gastronomy of the coastal region, which includes the *bourride* of Sète, *oursinade* (dish of sea urchins), *sartagnano*, the *esquinade* of Toulon (crabs stuffed with mussels and browned in the oven), *favouilles* (crabs) with rice, sardines stuffed with spinach or cooked *au gratin*, fried *supions* (small cuttlefish), octopus sautéed with garlic and sea-anemone fritters or omelettes. Dried salt cod is cooked *en raito* and stockfish is prepared *à la niçoise* (see *estofinado*). Small snails are eaten *à la sucarelles, à l'arlésienne* or in bouillabaisse (as *limaçons*).

■ **Meat and game** The raising of sheep (particularly the famous Sisteron lambs) and goats produces savoury meat as well as local cheeses. The excellent Arles sausage has an age-old reputation. The game of the region includes young rabbits from the Garrigue, snipe, plovers (in the vicinity of Arles) and thrushes (in the Basses-Alpes).

Among the best known meat dishes are the excellent *daube* of beef *à la provençale*, with tomatoes and olives; gigot *à l'avignonnaise; gayettes* with pig's liver; the *pieds et paquets* of Marseille; and *sou-fassum*.

■ **A cornucopia of produce** Truffles are gathered in Tricastin (the principal market is Carpentras), but market-garden produce and fruit dominate the market. The valleys of the Rhône

Olives, green or black, are pickled in brine before being eaten.

and Durance are the largest fruit- and vegetable-producing areas of France; Vaucluse is the principal producer of dessert grapes. Another speciality is the lavender honey of Vaucluse. Rice is cultivated in the Camargue, figs (those of Solliès are well known) and almonds near Aix, and oranges, lemons and even thick-skinned citrons in the Alpes-Maritimes region.

In the Gorges du Verdon, as everywhere in Provence, the air is fragrant with the scent of lavender, thyme, savory, rosemary, bay and sage that flourish in the favourable climate.

Cultivation of the olive tree provides an oil that gives Provençal cookery its fruity flavour, often accentuated by aromatic herbs.

■ **Colourful cooking** Typical Provençal soups include the following: *aïgo boulido* and *aïgo sau d'iou* (dominated by garlic); bouillabaisse with its numerous variations; and soups garnished with *pistou, poutine, fielas* (conger eel), mussels and *favouilles* (crabs).

Vegetables are often stuffed and seasoned with many spices. Some typical Provençal vegetable dishes are stuffed gourd flowers, gratins prepared with *herbes de Provence* and garlic, tarts made with Swiss chard or courgettes (zucchini), *tians, papeton* of aubergines (eggplants) and *panisse*. Gnocchi, ravioli, macaroni and cannelloni

are very common in the Midi.

Provence has long been known for its original sauces and condiments, such as aïoli, *rouille, pissalat* and the similar *melet* (typical of Martigues), *tapenade, boutargue, aillade* and *anchoyade*.

Provençal cheeses, both goat's- and ewe's-milk cheeses, are characterized by their very strong taste; they include Banon, Brousse, Bossons macérés, Cachat and Picodon.

■ **Pâtisserie** Pâtisserie specialities include the crisp biscuits (cookies) and *calissons* of Aix, the *bugnes* of Arles, the *pompe*, the *échaudés* of Draguignan, the *fouaces*, the *navettes* of Marseille and the soufflé cakes and croissants with pine nuts, which are included among the so-called 'thirteen desserts' of the Provençal

Christmas. The confectionery of Provence includes crystallized (candied) fruits from Apt, Digne, Valréas and Grasse, crystallized or caramelized flowers, nougat from Saint-Tropez, *berlingots* from Carpentras and fig sausages.

WINE The wines of Provence include Côtes de Provence, Coteaux d'Aix-en-Provence, Cassis, Bellet, Bandol, Les Baux de Provence and Coteaux Varois. The region makes mainly delightful rosés, which go well with the local cuisine, but there are an increasing number of red wines being produced. Thirteen grape varieties are allowed under Appellation laws in Côtes de Provence wines, including Cinsaut, Grenache, Mourvèdre, Carignan, Tibouren, Ugni Blanc, Clairette, Rolle and Semillon.

---

dry to give a firm paste with a thin, natural rind. They may be sold after two months or up to six months. As the cheese matures, the paste develops small cracks or fissures and the flavour strengthens until it becomes rich and spicy. Provolone is usually used in cooking, but it can be sliced and served as an appetizer or in sandwiches. Provolone has been extensively copied in North America, where the best version is made in Wisconsin.

PRUNE A dried red or purple plum, which keeps for a long time. The preparation of prunes has been known since Roman times. Traditionally the plums are dried in the sun, but most prunes today are prepared by progressive desiccation in the oven; there is also a technique of dehydration through immersion in hot syrup, producing Karlsbad plums, which taste strongly of the fruit and are packed in wooden boxes for Christmas.

Several varieties of plums are processed into prunes, the finest being the Ente (or Agen) plum, the large damson of Tours and the Catherine. The Perdrigon plum, peeled, stoned (pitted), dried in the sun and flattened, is sold under the name of *pistole*. The same plum, unpeeled, unstoned, scalded, then dried in the shade, is called *brignole* (named after the town of Brignoles, of which it is a speciality) or *pruneau fleuri*; it was very popular during the Renaissance, being the favourite delicacy of the Duc de Guise.

When purchased, it must be quite black, shiny and soft, but not sticky or excessively sweet. Its pulp should be amber-yellow, not caramelized. Sold loose or packaged, prunes should be stored in a place that is neither too damp nor too dry (which would cause

blooming, a sugary crystallization on the surface).

Before use, traditional prunes must be washed, then soaked (for a minimum of 2 hours but preferably overnight) in cold or tepid weak tea. However, they may also be cooked directly in water or red wine, particularly if they are to be made into a compote or a purée. Ready-to-use prunes that do not require soaking are now readily available. They are tender but will swell and become soft when soaked.

Stoned prunes are included in numerous pastries, either whole or boiled to a pulp with sugar (for tarts, puddings and turnovers). They may also be used for ices, fruit salads or fruit compotes, or served soaked in liqueur or brandy, then flamed. In confectionery, they are stuffed in various ways (often with almond paste) and sometimes glazed; they can also be preserved in brandy.

Prunes are used as a condiment in cookery, particularly for rabbit and pork, but also for game, goose and turkey; they are also used to stuff *paupiettes* of fish. Prunes also feature in international cuisine: lamb preserved with prunes and cinnamon in Algeria; roast pork with prunes in Denmark and Poland; sweet-and-sour carp in the former Czechoslovakia; and bacon lightly fried with prunes in Germany.

RECIPES

compote of prunes

Soak the prunes in tepid weak tea for at least 2 hours. When they are swollen, drain them, stone (pit) them and put in a saucepan. Just cover with cold water (or red or white wine) and stir in some sugar to taste – a maximum of 100 g (4 oz, ½ cup) per 500 g (18 oz, 4 cups) prunes – 2 tablespoons lemon juice and I teaspoon vanilla-flavoured sugar. Bring to the boil, then cook gently for about 40 minutes. Serve lukewarm or cold. When well-reduced and strained, this compote may be used to fill puff-pastry cases, turnovers or tartlets.

The prunes may be left unstoned (unpitted) and the quantity of water or wine can be increased; the prunes are then served with all their juice.

marzipan and sugar-coated prunes

Heat in a saucepan 4 tablespoons water, 200 g (7 oz, ¾ cup) caster (superfine) sugar and 20 g (¾ oz, 1½ tablespoons) powdered glucose, until the temperature reaches 115°C (240°F). Remove from the heat and add 100 g (4 oz, 1 cup) ground almonds. Stir well with a wooden spoon until the mixture has the consistency of cooked semolina. Cut 40 semi-dried Agen prunes lengthways, without separating the halves, and take out the stones (pits).

Knead the cooled almond paste by hand; when it is soft, add 3 or 4 drops of red or green food colouring and I tablespoon rum. Knead the paste on a smooth worktop, gather it into a ball, roll it out into a very thin long cylinder and cut into 40 equal sections. Roll the sections into olive shapes and insert into the prunes, making 2 or 3 slanting cuts in the visible part of the almond paste. Arrange the prunes in little pleated paper cases.

The prunes may also be glazed with sugar syrup.

prunes in Rasteau with fresh cream

Soak 36 prunes overnight in 500 ml (17 fl oz, 2 cups) light red Bordeaux wine and the same amount of Rasteau (a sweet wine of the Rhône Valley). The following day cook them in the wine together with a lemon and an orange cut into thick slices: bring to the boil, reduce the heat and simmer for 15 minutes. Leave to cool, then cover and chill for 3 days in the cooking liquid. Remove the slices of fruit and serve the prunes coated with double (heavy) cream.

prunes stuffed with Roquefort cheese

Stone (pit) about 30 Agen prunes and flatten them with the blade of a knife. Crumble 100 g (4 oz) Roquefort cheese with a fork and crush 30 hazelnuts. Mix the Roquefort cheese with the hazelnuts, some pepper, 2 tablespoons crème fraîche and I tablespoon port. Place a small ball of this mixture in the centre of each prune. Reshape the prunes and put in a cool place for several hours before serving as a cocktail snack.

prunes with bacon

Stone (pit) some semi-dried Agen prunes by splitting them lengthways. Insert a shelled pistachio in place of the stone, then roll up each prune in half a thin rasher (slice) of bacon. Secure the bacon around the stuffed prunes by means of a wooden cocktail stick (toothpick). Arrange the prunes in an ovenproof dish, and place in a preheated oven at 230°C (450°F, gas 8) until the bacon is crispy (about 8–9 minutes). Serve piping hot as a cocktail snack.

other recipes See *brochette, rabbit, turnover.*

PRUNE DE CYTHÈRE French name for ambarella (see *fruit, exotic fruit*) also known as *pomme cythère*, the fruit of a spiny shrub of the mango family, it comes from South-east Asia and the Pacific islands.

PRUNIER, ALFRED French restaurateur (died 1898). In 1872 he founded a restaurant in Paris, in the Rue Duphot, serving oysters, grills and judiciously chosen wines, which quickly became successful. Among the customers were Sarah Bernhardt, Oscar Wilde, Clemenceau and the great Russian dukes.

His son Émile succeeded him and the establishment became known for its fish and seafood specialities, notably bass *à l'angevine*, Boston fillet (beef with oysters), *marmite dieppoise*, lobster Newburg and *thermidor*, and, of course, oysters and shellfish. He opened a second restaurant, Prunier-Traktir, in the Avenue Victor Hugo and also took an active interest in oyster culture and fishing, particularly sturgeon farming in the Gironde region (for French caviar).

On his death in 1925, his daughter Simone continued his work and opened a third restaurant in London, which closed in 1976.

PUB A public house. An establishment in Britain licensed for the sale and consumption of alcoholic drinks. In older pubs there are often several rooms known as bars. The public bar is usually the most crowded room, providing drinks at the bar and possibly snacks. The saloon bar, lounge bar and sometimes a private bar offer varying degrees of comfort, elegance and privacy. Many pubs also have restaurants renowned for their high standard of food.

One of the much debated features of British pubs is their restricted hours of opening and closing. Furthermore, customers go to the bar to order and pay for drinks, rather than being waited on at tables.

PUCHERO A Spanish or Latin American stew, highly seasoned, made with beef, mutton, sausage, ham and vegetables. In Latin American countries it is garnished with corn on the cob.

PUDDING Any of numerous dishes, sweet or savoury, served hot or cold, which are prepared in a variety of ways.

English suet puddings consist of a sweet or savoury filling (for example, apples or steak and kidney) completely enclosed in a suet dough and steamed or boiled in a pudding basin (mould). Most other puddings of English origin are served as desserts, usually baked or boiled in a mould.

In the past the word 'pudding' applied to all boiled dishes; it has the same origin as the French *boudin* (black pudding, blood sausage). However, the sweet pudding that is known today did not assume its modern form until the 17th century.

Some English puddings have now become traditional in Continental Europe, with their own variations. Among these are diplomat and Nesselrode puddings, bread pudding, apple or pear pudding (in a suet crust) and semolina, tapioca and rice puddings. Soufflé pudding is made with choux pastry enriched with sugar, butter, egg yolks and whisked egg whites and flavoured with vanilla, chocolate or orange.

Iced puddings are made by lining the mould with sponge cake or finger biscuits and filling it with ice creams, sometimes combining several colours.

In France, the name 'pudding' is also given to a cake made from dry bread or stale brioche, sweetened and mixed with milk, raisins, rum, eggs and candied orange peel, cooked in a small brioche mould, then lightly covered with fondant icing (frosting). It is similar to the English bread pudding, though much more elaborate.

RECIPES

American pudding
Put in a large bowl 75 g (3 oz, ¾ cup) stale breadcrumbs, 100 g (4 oz, 1 cup) plain (all-purpose) flour, 100 g (4 oz, ⅔ cup, firmly packed) brown sugar and 75 g (3 oz, ⅓ cup) chopped beef suet. Add 100 g (4 oz, ⅔ cup) finely diced crystallized (candied) fruit, 1 tablespoon blanched finely shredded orange zest and the same amount of lemon zest. Bind the mixture with 1 whole egg and 3 yolks. Add a generous pinch of cinnamon, the same amount of grated nutmeg and 1 liqueur glass of rum. Mix well and pour into a buttered and floured charlotte mould. Cook in a bain marie in a preheated oven at 200°C (400°F, gas 6) for about 50 minutes until firm. Leave to cool and turn out on to the serving dish. Serve with rum-flavoured zabaglione.

biscuit pudding with crystallized fruits
Soak 125 g (4½ oz, ⅔ cup) currants in rum. In a saucepan, moisten 200 g (7 oz, 2½ cups) crumbled sponge finger biscuits (ladyfingers) with 600 ml (1 pint, 2½ cups) boiling milk to which 150 g (5 oz, ⅔ cup) caster (superfine) sugar has been added. Work the mixture over the heat, then add 150 g (5 oz, ¾ cup) diced crystallized (candied) fruits, the currants, 3 egg yolks and 125 g (4½ oz, ½ cup) melted butter. Finally, fold in 3 egg whites whisked into very stiff peaks. Butter a smooth, round mould, sprinkle it with breadcrumbs, pour the mixture into it, and cook in a bain marie in a preheated oven at 200°C (400°F, gas 6) for 50–60 minutes. Serve with a pineapple or cherry sauce.

cabinet pudding
Prepare 600 ml (1 pint, 2½ cups) vanilla-flavoured egg custard (see *custard*). Cut 100 g (4 oz, ⅔ cup)

crystallized (candied) fruits into a salpicon. Wash 100 g (4 oz, ⅔ cup) seedless raisins, then moisten them with 3 tablespoons rum. Pour another 3 tablespoons rum over 150 g (5 oz, 2 cups) sponge finger biscuits (ladyfingers) broken into pieces. Butter a charlotte mould and fill it with alternate layers of sponge fingers, raisins and crystallized fruit. Pour the egg custard over. Place in a bain marie and cook in a preheated oven at 220°C (425°F, gas 7) for about 45 minutes. Leave the pudding until lukewarm before turning it out. Serve with a vanilla-flavoured custard cream (see *custard*) or an apricot sauce.

Capucine iced pudding
Prepare a Genoese sponge and cook it in a charlotte mould. Leave it to cool completely, then slice a thin layer of sponge from the top (to serve as a lid). Scoop out the rest of the sponge, leaving a lining crust and fill it with alternate layers of tangerine-flavoured iced mousse and Kümmel-flavoured iced mousse. Cover with the sponge lid and put in the freezer for 6 hours. Just before serving, decorate with Chantilly cream, using a piping bag. Traditionally, this iced pudding is set on a base of nougatine and decorated with flowers and ribbons made of sugar.

chocolate pudding
Soften 150 g (5 oz, ⅔ cup) butter at room temperature and 125 g (4½ oz, 4½ squares) plain (dark) dessert chocolate in a bowl over a pan of simmering water. Work the butter with a wooden spoon in a warm mixing bowl, then beat in 75 g (3 oz, 6 tablespoons) caster (superfine) sugar and 1 tablespoon vanilla-flavoured sugar. When the mixture is white and creamy, add 8 egg yolks, one after the other. Mix the softened chocolate with 1 tablespoon flour and 1 tablespoon potato flour, then blend it with the mixture. Finally, add 5 stiffly whisked egg whites. Pour into a buttered and floured charlotte mould, place in a bain marie, and cook in a preheated oven at 200°C (400°F, gas 6) for about 50 minutes until firm. Turn out the pudding while still lukewarm and coat with vanilla- or coffee-flavoured custard cream (see *custard*).

English almond pudding
Cream together 125 g (4½ oz, ½ cup) softened butter and 150 g (5 oz, ⅔ cup) caster (superfine) sugar in a basin. Add 250 g (9 oz, 2 cups) almonds, blanched and finely chopped, a pinch of salt, 1 tablespoon orange-flower water, 2 whole eggs and 2 yolks, and 4 tablespoons double (heavy) cream. Work the mixture well, then pour it into a buttered soufflé dish and cook in a preheated oven at 200°C (400°F, gas 6) for at least 45 minutes. Serve from the dish.

English apple pudding
Mix together the following ingredients: 400 g (14 oz, 3½ cups) plain (all-purpose) flour, 225 g (8 oz,

1½ cups) finely chopped beef suet, 2 tablespoons caster (superfine) sugar, a little salt and 100 ml (4 fl oz, 7 teaspoons) water. Knead thoroughly, then roll out the dough to a thickness of 8 mm (⅜ in).

Butter a 1 litre (1¾ pint, 5 cup) pudding basin (mould) and line it with half of the dough. Fill with finely sliced apples, sweetened with caster sugar and flavoured with the grated zest of a lemon and some ground cinnamon. Cover with the remaining dough and press the edges together firmly. Wrap the basin in a cloth and tie it up firmly at the top. Place the pudding on an old saucer in a saucepan with enough boiling water to come halfway up the sides of the basin. Cover and cook for about 2 hours over a gentle heat, topping up with boiling water as necessary.

This pudding can be prepared with pears in the same way.

French bread pudding

Crumble 14 slices of stale milk bread. Pour over the top 4 beaten eggs mixed with 100 g (4 oz, ½ cup) caster sugar (superfine) sugar; add 400 ml (14 fl oz, 1¾ cups) tepid milk, then 4 tablespoons raisins which have been soaked in weak tea, 3 tablespoons chopped crystallized (candied) fruit, the same amount of rum, a pinch of salt and sieved apricot jam. Mix everything together well.

Butter a pudding basin (mould) or a charlotte or manqué mould and pour half the mixture into it. Arrange 4 finely sliced canned pears over the surface, then pour in the remaining mixture. Place the mould in a bain marie containing boiling water. Put in a preheated oven at 200°C (400°F, gas 6) and cook for about 1 hour until set. Dip the bottom of the mould in cold water, then turn the pudding out. Serve with blackcurrant sauce.

German bread and fruit pudding

Finely dice 150 g (5 oz, about 5 slices) white bread and fry lightly in butter. Put in a bowl and pour on 200 ml (7 fl oz, ¾ cup) boiled milk. Mix, then add 2 apples cut into small cubes and cooked in butter, 50 g (2 oz, ⅓ cup) diced candied orange peel, 50 g (2 oz, ½ cup) ground almonds and the same amount of seeded raisins, which have been soaked in water and drained. Add 75 g (3 oz, 6 tablespoons) caster (superfine) sugar, 1 tablespoon blanched and finely chopped lemon peel and 3 egg yolks. Mix well, then blend in 3 egg whites whisked into very stiff peaks.

Pour this mixture into a buttered charlotte mould, place in a bain marie, and cook in a preheated oven at 200°C (400°F, gas 6) for about 50 minutes. Turn out the pudding while still lukewarm and coat with a sauce made by mixing 200 ml (7 fl oz, ¾ cup) red wine with 2 tablespoons sieved and warmed apricot jam.

lemon soufflé pudding

In a saucepan, work 100 g (4 oz, ½ cup) butter into a soft paste with a wooden spoon. Add 100 g (4 oz,

½ cup) caster (superfine) sugar and 100 g (4 oz, 1 cup) plain flour (all-purpose flour), then moisten with 300 ml (½ pint, 1¼ cups) hot milk and mix well. Bring to the boil, stirring all the time, then beat until the mixture leaves the sides of the pan clean. Remove from the heat and beat in the juice of 2 lemons and 5 egg yolks, then fold in 6 egg whites whisked into stiff peaks and 2 tablespoons blanched and finely chopped lemon peel.

Turn the mixture into a buttered 1.5 litre (2¾ pint, 6 cup) pudding basin or soufflé mould, place in a bain marie, and cook in a preheated oven at 200°C (400°F, gas 6) for 40 minutes until well risen and golden brown. Serve with a lemon-flavoured custard cream (see *custard*).

rice pudding

Wash 250 g (9 oz, 1½ cups) round-grain rice and blanch it in boiling water. Drain it and place in a flameproof casserole, then add 1 litre (1¾ pints, 4⅓ cups) milk boiled with 150 g (5 oz, ⅔ cup) caster (superfine) sugar, half a vanilla pod (bean) and a pinch of salt. Add 50 g (2 oz, ¼ cup) butter, stir and bring slowly to the boil. Then cover the casserole and finish cooking in a preheated oven at 220°C (425°F, gas 7) for 25–30 minutes.

Remove from the oven and beat in 8 egg yolks, mixing carefully, then 7–8 egg whites whisked into very stiff peaks. Use this mixture to fill about 10 small moulds which have been buttered and sprinkled with fine breadcrumbs. Cook in the oven in a bain marie for 30–35 minutes. Turn out and serve with a rum-flavoured zabaglione, a custard cream or a fruit sauce flavoured with liqueur.

The mixture may be flavoured with 50 g (2 oz, ½ cup) cocoa per 500 g (18 oz, 3 cups) cooked rice.

Scotch pudding

Place 500 g (18 oz, 9 cups) fresh breadcrumbs in a bowl with rum. Work the mixture together thoroughly and pour it into a smooth buttered mould, filling it up to 1 cm (½ in) from the brim. Place in a bain marie and cook in a preheated oven at 200°C (400°F, gas 6) for 1 hour. Serve with a rum-flavoured zabaglione or a Madeira-flavoured custard cream (see *custard*).

semolina pudding

Sprinkle 250 g (9 oz, 1¾ cups) semolina into 1 litre (1¾ pints, 4⅓ cups) boiling milk in which has been dissolved 125 g (4½ oz, ½ cup) caster (superfine) sugar, a generous pinch of salt and 100 g (4 oz, ½ cup) butter. Mix and cook over a very gentle heat for 25 minutes. Leave to cool slightly, then add 6 egg yolks, 1 small liqueur glass of orange-flavoured liqueur and 4 egg whites whisked into a very stiff peaks. Pour this mixture into a savarin mould, buttered and dusted with semolina. Place in a bain marie and cook in a preheated oven at 200°C (400°F, gas 6) until the mixture is slightly elastic to the touch. Leave the pudding to stand for 30 minutes before turning it out. Serve with custard or an orange sauce.

other recipes See *Christmas pudding, Nesselrode.*

PUFFBALL A globular or pear-shaped mushroom. The giant puffball is globular and its short stalk is almost unnoticeable. It is edible when young and unripe, while the flesh is still white, but the tough skin must be discarded. It can be eaten sliced, covered in breadcrumbs and fried, or as a filling for an omelette. Other varieties of puffball are pear-shaped and some are edible. *Lycoperdon echinatum*, recognizable by its brownish colour and clusters of hairs, is not edible.

PUFF PASTRY *Pâte feuilletée* or *feuilletage* in French, this is a rich and delicate pastry made up of very thin layers. It is said by some historians to have been invented by Claude Gellée, better known as the 17th-century landscape painter Claude Lorrain, who was said to have served a pastrycook's apprenticeship. Others say it was invented by a chef called Feuillet, who was chief pastrycook to the house of Condé. Carême praises Feuillet, who was undoubtedly a great pastrycook, and in his *Pâtissier royal* writes: 'Richard spurred me on to work twice as hard by speaking to me often of the great Feuillet.' But Carême stops there and nowhere in his learned treatises on pastry does he say that Feuillet was the inventor of puff pastry. But Joseph Favre is definite on this subject. In his *Dictionnaire universel de cuisine* he states that Feuillet was 'the inventor of puff pastry'.

It appears, however, from the study of documents of a much earlier date, that puff pastry was known not only in the Middle Ages, but also in ancient Greece. In a charter drawn up by Robert, bishop of Amiens (1311), puff-pastry cakes are mentioned. It therefore seems more likely that this pastry was perfected and brought back into fashion by Claude Lorrain and Feuillet in their own times.

■ **Preparation** The preparation of puff pastry is a lengthy and complicated procedure. Butter is incorporated into a rolled-out dough of flour and water. The dough is then folded, turned at right angles, rolled out and folded again. The turning, rolling out and folding is repeated a number of times and the dough is left to stand and chill between each turning. The more turns there are (up to eight), the greater the number of layers in the finished pastry.

This basic preparation can be varied. Margarine, lard or white vegetable fat (shortening), oil or goose fat may be substituted for butter, and egg yolks can be added (as in Viennese puff pastry).

Commercially prepared puff pastry is more popular with most domestic cooks than home-made pastry. It may be purchased chilled or frozen, in blocks or ready rolled. Bought pastry varies widely in quality, with the poorest examples being extremely tasteless and fatty. Better examples are to be found, made with all butter and usually sold chilled in blocks.

■ **Use** Puff pastry is light, golden and crisp, but not usually sweetened. It is used for pies, tarts, allumettes, bouchées, vol-au-vent, *mille-feuilles* and many other dishes. Creative cooks are experimenting by adding flavouring ingredients. Chocolate pastry for mille-feuille (see *mille feuille*) is a good example: cocoa powder is mixed with the butter.

Puff pastry is baked at a high temperature so that the air trapped during rolling expands. This separates the layers and makes the pastry rise. The melting fat content and heat set the layers and give the pastry its characteristic crisp texture.

Puff pastry can also be deep-fried successfully, for example when used as a covering for fritters. The pastry should be rolled thinly and the oil for deep-frying should be very hot. When frying, puff pastry is suitable only for ready cooked fillings or those that cook quickly. As soon as the pastry has puffed and turned golden, it should be drained in a basket or on a draining spoon, then transferred to a dish lined with kitchen paper or a clean napkin so that any remaining cooking fat is mopped up. Then it must be served immediately.

The French name *demi-feuilletage* is given to any leftover pieces of dough that may then be rolled out and used, for example, to line barquettes or tartlets, or to make *fleurons* and other decorative items.

■ **Rough puff pastry** The so-called rough puff pastry can be made in a much shorter time by incorporating all the butter in lumps with the dough, rolling the dough fewer times and omitting the resting periods between each turning.

■ **Flaky pastry** A layered pastry similar to puff pastry, but with fewer layers and not as rich. The dough is made with three-quarters fat to flour and it is rolled and folded four times. Traditionally, a mixture of butter and lard is used, but the dough can be made with all butter. The pastry is used as for puff pastry, but it does not rise high enough for making deep pastry cases, such as bouchées or a vol-au-vent. It is the traditional choice for sausage rolls, pie crusts and apple turnovers. Flaky pastry is cooked at a high temperature, so that it rises and sets into crisp layers. See *pastry, flaky.*

RECIPES

puff pastry

Put 500 g (18 oz, 4½ cups) plain (all-purpose) flour on a board in a circle, making a well in the middle. Since flours differ, the exact proportion of water to flour is variable. Into the centre of this circle put 1½ teaspoons salt and about 300 ml (½ pint, 1¼ cups) water. Mix and knead until the dough is smooth and elastic. Form into a ball and leave to stand for 25 minutes.

Roll out the dough into square, mark a cross in the top and roll out the wedges to form an evenly thick cross shape. Put 500 g (18 oz, 2¼ cups) softened butter in the middle of this dough. (The butter should be softened with a wooden spatula until it can be spread easily.) Fold the ends of the dough

Rolling and folding puff pastry

Prepare the dough and the butter. Roll out the dough into a square of the same size as the pat of butter. Follow the rolling and folding stages, chilling the dough between rolling to prevent the butter from melting and making the dough sticky.

1 *Score a cross in the top with a knife. Roll each segment of dough to form an evenly thick cross.*

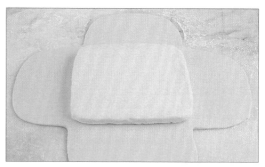

2 *Place the pat of butter on the dough, making sure that it fits neatly in the middle of the cross.*

3 *Fold the dough extensions over the butter to enclose it completely.*

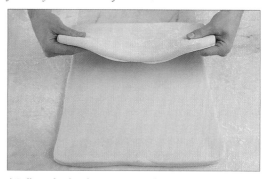

4 *Roll out the dough into a rectangle and fold a third of the dough over the middle.*

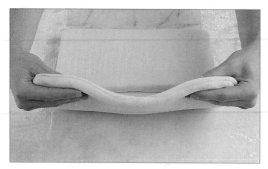

5 *Fold the remaining third (single layer) of the dough over the top.*

6 *Give the folded dough a quarter turn and press the edges of the dough.*

7 *Repeat the folding and rolling 6 times, keeping the dough neat and even.*

8 *Chill after each folding, making fingerprints to indicate the number of turns completed.*

over the butter in such a way as to enclose it completely. Leave to stand for 10 minutes in a cold place, until rested and firmed slightly.

The turning operation (called *tournage* in French) can now begin. Roll the dough with a rolling pin on a lightly floured board in such a way as to obtain a rectangle 60 cm (24 in) long, 20 cm (8 in) wide and 1.5 cm (⅝ in) thick. Fold the rectangle into three, give it a quarter-turn and, with the rolling pin at right angles to the folds, roll the dough out again into a rectangle of the same size as the previous one. Again fold the dough into three and leave to stand for about 15 minutes and chill if too sticky. Repeat the sequence (turn, roll, fold) a further 4 times, leaving the dough to stand for about 15 minutes after each folding. After the sixth turn, roll out the dough in both directions and use according to the recipe.

puff pastry case for flans
Prepare some puff pastry and roll it out to a thickness of about 5 mm (¼ in). Cut it into a rectangle twice as long as it is wide. Then cut 4 small strips about 3 cm (1¼ in) wide, two of which are the same length as the width of the rectangle, and two the same as its length. Cut the ends of these strips at right angles so that they form corners. The remaining rectangle of the pastry forms the base of the tart. Brush some beaten egg around the edge of the base and stick the strips to it to form the sides of the pastry case. Trim the edges with a knife and mark the top edge with a decorative criss-cross pattern. Prick the base to prevent the pastry from rising during cooking. Bake in a preheated oven at 230°C (450°F, gas 8) for about 20 minutes. Fill the flan case with drained poached or cooked fruit covered in a fruit glaze.

puff pastry made with oil
Make the flour and water dough as described in the traditional recipe for puff pastry (see above), then incorporate 200 ml (7 fl oz, ¾ cup) groundnut (peanut) oil. Roll out the dough into a 20 cm (8 in) square and brush it generously with oil. Then proceed in the usual way except that the dough is brushed with oil each time it is rolled out. Allow a total of about 350 ml (12 fl oz, 1½ cups) oil for 500 g (18 oz, 4½ cups) plain (all-purpose) flour.

rough (fast) puff pastry
Mix 400 g (14 oz, 3½ cups) plain (all-purpose) flour, 300 g (11 oz, 1⅓ cups) butter cut into pieces, 1 tablespoon salt and 200 ml (7 fl oz, ¾ cup) very cold water in a bowl to form a soft smooth dough. Roll it out into a rectangle measuring about 60 × 20 cm (24 × 8 in). Fold it into three, turn and roll it out again into a rectangle of the same size. Repeat twice more without allowing it to stand between turns. Use immediately.

PUGLIA WINES Puglia or *Apulia*, on the heel of the boot of Italy, produces large amounts of wine. The majority was traditionally sold for blending or for use in the manufacture of vermouth, but with modern wine-making techniques some good quality wine is made.

PUITS D'AMOUR A small pastry made of two rounds of rolled-out puff pastry placed one on top of the other, the second being hollowed out. After cooking, the centre is filled with jam or vanilla- or praline-flavoured confectioner's custard (pastry cream), which is sometimes caramelized. This pastry was probably created in 1843, after the success of a comic opera entitled *Le Puits d'amour*.

RECIPE

puits d'amour
Roll out 500 g (18 oz) puff* pastry into a 25 × 18 cm (10 × 7 in) rectangle. Cut out from it 12 circles, 6 cm (2½ in) in diameter. Place 6 of them on a buttered baking sheet and brush with beaten egg. Cut out the centres of the other 6 circles with a 3 cm (1¼ in) pastry (cookie) cutter; place these rings on the circles of pastry and brush with beaten egg. Cook in a preheated oven at 230°C (450°F, gas 8) for 15 minutes. Allow them to cool, then dust with icing (confectioner's) sugar and fill the centres with redcurrant jelly or vanilla-flavoured confectioner's custard (see *custard*).

PULIGNY-MONTRACHET A vineyard region in the Côte de Beaune in Burgundy, most famous for its white wines from the Chardonnay grape, but also making some reds. There are several AOC *grand* and *premier cru* wines, of which the best known is probably Le Montrachet.

PULQUE A Mexican alcoholic drink obtained by fermentation of the juice of the maguey plant, a species of agave (see also *tequila, mescal*). This very popular drink is consumed in large quantities on farms, as well as in the *pulquerías*, small popular taverns.

PULSES Leguminous plants whose seeds are used as a vegetable; they include peas, beans, lentils, soya (soy) beans and peanuts. One of the characteristics of pulses is their very high energy value and very low water content compared with fresh vegetables (which means they can be stored for long periods). They are also an important source of vegetable protein and form a vital part of a vegetarian diet along with a mixture of grains and vegetables.

Pulses form one of the staple foods in India (see *dal*), many North African countries (particularly chick peas) and South America (red kidney beans).

PUMPERNICKEL Rye bread originating from Westphalia and now manufactured throughout Germany and sometimes in Alsace. Very solid and almost black in colour, pumpernickel is made with leaven and coarsely crushed pure rye; abroad, it is often sold, packaged, in very thin slices. As it has a fairly pronounced flavour, it is eaten mostly with smoked sausages, marinated fish and cheese.

There are several explanations of its etymology: *pumper* could be an onomatopoeic reference to the action of the yeast, and *nickel* an abbreviation of the Christian name Nikolaus (often used in Germany to designate a halfwit); the word would therefore mean 'a coarse bread suitable for a halfwit'. According to another explanation, the word originated in the 1450s: as a severe famine was threatening the inhabitants of Osnabrück, the municipality baked a 'good bread' (*bonum panicum*) for the poor; its success was so great that it continued to be made and its name developed into *bumponickel*, then into *pumpernickel*.

PUMPKIN A vegetable of the marrow (squash) family, which is round, with a flattened top and base. The orange or yellow pulp is surrounded by a green, yellow or orange ribbed rind. There are several varieties, weighing up to 100 kg (220 lb). Once the seeds and fibres have been removed, the flesh is eaten cooked, often as a soup, in a gratin or as a purée. It is also used as a pie filling (*à la citrouille*), mixed with onion, especially in northern France, where pumpkin pie is as popular as in the United States. The pumpkin is cultivated in southern France, especially in the south-east, where it is harvested from October to December and keeps throughout the winter. When bought in slices, preferably cut from a small, juicy, fresh-coloured pumpkin, it does not keep long.

In French recipes pumpkin is sometimes called *citrouille*, rather than *potiron*.

RECIPES

pumpkin au jus
Peel a pumpkin and remove the seeds and surrounding fibres. Cut the pulp into slices and blanch in boiling salted water for about 10 minutes. Drain thoroughly and put into a frying pan with some veal stock. Cover and simmer gently for about 20 minutes. Serve sprinkled with chopped parsley.

pumpkin gratin à la provençale
Peel a fine ripe pumpkin and remove the seeds and their surrounding fibres. Cut the pulp into small dice and blanch for 10 minutes in boiling salted water; refresh in cold water and drain. Peel some onions (a quarter of the weight of the pumpkin), chop and sweat them gently for 5–6 minutes in butter. Rub the inside of a gratin dish with garlic and butter; arrange a layer of cut drained pumpkin pieces, then the onions, then the rest of the pumpkin, in the dish. Sprinkle with grated cheese and olive oil and brown in a preheated oven at 220°C (425°F, gas 7).

pumpkin purée
Sweat the pulp of a pumpkin in butter and reduce to a purée, as for pumpkin soup. Cook some

potatoes (one-third of the weight of the pumpkin) in boiling salted water and reduce to a purée. Mix the two purées, add a little boiling milk, and stir thoroughly. Remove from the heat and beat in some fresh butter.

pumpkin soup
Peel and seed a pumpkin to obtain 800 g (1¾ lb) pulp. Cut the pulp into small pieces and place in a saucepan with 50 g (2 oz, ¼ cup) butter and 8 tablespoons water. Add salt, cover the pan and sweat for about 20 minutes. Purée the pulp, pour into the rinsed-out saucepan and add 1 litre (1¾ pints, 4⅓ cups) stock or consommé. Bring to the boil, adjust the seasoning and whisk in 50 g (2 oz, ¼ cup) butter cut into small pieces. Serve with small croûtons fried in butter.

Alternatively, the purée can be diluted with 1 litre (1¾ pints, 4⅓ cups) boiling milk and sweetened to taste. Thicken with 2 tablespoons ground rice blended with a little milk.

sautéed pumpkin with spices
Melt 50 g (2 oz, 1 cup) salted butter in a frying pan and add 1 tablespoon clear honey and 4 crescent-shaped pieces of fresh pumpkin, each weighing about 200 g (7 oz). Fry until golden. When they have finished cooking, sprinkle with 1 teaspoon allspice, 1 teaspoon curry powder, the chopped zest of 1 unwaxed mandarin, 2 teaspoons freshly chopped mint leaves, the juice of half a lemon and some good quality salt. Serve hot with chicken or sweetbreads.

PUNCH An iced or hot drink, sometimes flamed, which can be made with tea, sugar, spices, fruits and rum or brandy, or with rum and sugar syrup. The word originally described a British colonial drink, in which, theoretically, five ingredients had to be included (*pānch* means 'five' in Hindustani). In France in the 18th century, the word changed to the form *ponche* or *bouleponche* (from the English punch bowl in which the drink was served).

About 1830 the ban on the importation of rum into France from the West Indies was lifted; it had been prohibited so as not to compete with Cognac. At the same time a fashion for English things introduced the vogue for punch. A forerunner of the cocktail, it has been made according to various recipes. English punch consists of boiling tea poured over slices of lemon, with sugar, cinnamon and rum (it was formerly flamed before being drunk). In French punch, the quantity of tea is smaller and the rum is sometimes replaced by brandy, poured in last and flamed. Marquise punch, which is served hot or iced, is made with Sauternes wines and with sugar, lemon peel and cloves; it may be flamed. Roman punch is a sorbet made with dry white wine or champagne with orange or lemon slices, mixed with Italian meringue, over which a glass of rum is poured at the time of serving. Planter's punch is a mixture of white rum, sugar-cane syrup and orange or lemon juice, sometimes enlivened with a dash of Angostura bitters. Brazilian batida punch, which appeared more recently in Europe, has a base of brandy, rum and lime, guava or mango juice.

RECIPES

iced punch
Dissolve 200 g (7 oz, ¾ cup) sugar with the grated zest of a lemon in 1 litre (1¾ pints, 4⅓ cups) sweet white wine. Heat gently, then add 1 tablespoon tea leaves and leave to infuse for about 10 minutes. Strain, then add an orange and a lemon, peeled and cut into slices, and 200 ml (7 fl oz, ¾ cup) warmed flaming rum. Leave to cool. Strain and put in the freezer for 3 hours until slushy, then stir and serve in sundae dishes.

kirsch punch
Infuse 1 tablespoon tea leaves for 8 minutes in 1 litre (1¾ pints, 4⅓ cups) boiling water. Put 500 g (18 oz, 2¼ cups) caster (superfine) sugar in a punch bowl. Pour in the strained hot tea and stir until the sugar has dissolved. Flame 750 ml (1¼ pints, 3¼ cups) kirsch and add to the punch. Serve in punch cups. The kirsch may be replaced by rum.

marquise punch
Put in a copper pan 1 litre (1¾ pints, 4⅓ cups) Sauternes (or similar sweet white wine), 200 g (7 oz, ¾ cup) caster (superfine) sugar, and the grated zest of a lemon, tied in muslin (cheesecloth) with a clove. Heat until a fine white foam has formed on the surface, then pour into a punch bowl. Add 250 ml (8 fl oz, 1 cup) flaming Cognac. Serve in punch cups decorated with a thin slice of lemon.

West Indian punch
Mix in a shaker 250 ml (8 fl oz, 1 cup) pineapple juice, 250 ml (8 fl oz, 1 cup) orange juice and 4 tablespoons orgeat* or grenadine syrup. Add 500 ml (17 fl oz, 2 cups) white rum and shake thoroughly. Pour over ice cubes in frosted glasses.

PURÉE A creamy preparation obtained by pressing and sieving cooked foods (or by using a blender or food processor).

Vegetable purées used as a garnish or condiment are fairly thick. For making soups, they are diluted with a liquid. Certain vegetables which are too watery to give a sufficiently thick purée are thickened with a binding agent – potato purée, cornflour (cornstarch) or potato flour, thick béchamel sauce. The following vegetables may be puréed: artichoke, asparagus, aubergine (eggplant), beetroot (red beet), cardoon, carrot and other root vegetables, celery, mushrooms, endive, cauliflower, courgette (zucchini), chicory, spinach, broad (fava) beans, red or white haricot (navy or kidney) beans, green beans, lettuce, lentils, chestnuts, onions (Soubise), sorrel,

split peas, green peas (Saint-Germain), potato and pumpkin. Puréed garlic, watercress and tarragon are usually used as condiments.

Purées of meat, game or fish, often mixed with a brown or white sauce, are usually used as fillings for vol-au-vent, bouchées or barquettes, or as a stuffing for hard-boiled (hard-cooked) eggs, artichoke hearts and pancakes.

Fruit purées, either cold or hot, are used for making ices, mousses, soufflés and dessert sauces.

RECIPES

anchovy purée (for cold dishes)
Desalt 75 g (3 oz) anchovies, remove the fillets and reduce them to a purée in a mortar or in a blender with 4 hard-boiled (hard-cooked) egg yolks and 40 g (1½ oz, 3 tablespoons) butter. Add 1 tablespoon chopped herbs. Mix well.

This purée is used to stuff hard-boiled eggs, artichoke hearts and fish (red mullet), for serving cold.

anchovy purée (for hot dishes)
Desalt 75 g (3 oz) anchovies, remove the fillets and pound them into a purée in a mortar or with a blender. Add to this purée 150 ml (¼ pint, ⅔ cup) thick béchamel* sauce and, if desired, 2–3 sieved or pounded hard-boiled (hard-cooked) egg yolks and some coarsely chopped herbs.

This purée is used to fill bouchées, tartlets or rissoles that are to be served hot.

calf's or chicken liver purée
Quickly fry the diced calf's liver or whole chicken livers in butter, then reduce to a purée in a blender. Season and flavour with Madeira if desired.

This purée is used for *à gratin* forcemeats.

chicken purée
This is prepared like game purée.

game purée
Remove the sinews from the cooked meat of pheasant, duck, young rabbit or partridge and reduce the flesh to a purée in a blender or food processor. Incorporate the same weight of rice cooked in meat stock and purée again quickly. Adjust the seasoning.

This purée is used as an *à gratin* forcemeat.

potato and turnip purée
Peel 800 g (1¾ lb) turnips and 800 g (1¾ lb) potatoes. Cut them separately into cubes. Put 8 juniper berries, 4–5 slices fresh root ginger, 1 teaspoon rosemary leaves and 1 teaspoon black peppercorns in a small linen bag. Peel and chop 2 medium-sized onions. Peel and chop 2 garlic cloves. Heat 3 tablespoons goose fat or duck fat in a flameproof casserole. Add the diced turnips. Season lightly with salt and a pinch of sugar, then brown. Add the potatoes and sauté them, then add the onion and garlic. Add a little chicken stock and

cook over a low heat until the stock has evaporated. Meanwhile, heat I tablespoon fat and fry 12 croûtons on both sides.

Remove the linen bag from the vegetables, purée the vegetables in a food processor and adjust the seasoning. Sprinkle with a little roasting juice if desired and serve garnished with the croûtons.

salmon purée

Purée 250 g (9 oz) skinned and boned fresh salmon cooked in a court-bouillon (or well-drained canned salmon with bones and skin removed). Add to this purée 100 ml (4 fl oz, 7 tablespoons) very thick béchamel sauce. Heat, stirring well, then whisk in 50 g (2 oz, ¼ cup) butter. Adjust the seasoning. If desired, add a quarter of its weight of mushroom duxelles.

This purée is used to fill barquettes, pannequets, croustades and hard-boiled (hard-cooked) eggs.

shrimp purée

Pound in a mortar some shelled shrimp. Add an equal volume of béchamel sauce mixed with cream and reduced. Adjust the seasoning.

This purée is added to stuffings and sauces for fish and shellfish.

smoked-salmon purée

Using a blender or a food processor purée 200 g (7 oz) smoked salmon together with the juice of half a lemon and 4 egg yolks. Add 50 g (2 oz, ¼ cup) butter and work the mixture until smooth.

This purée is used for garnishing canapés, barquettes, cold pancakes or slices of smoked salmon rolled into cornet shapes.

PURI Also known as poori. This Pakistani and Indian bread (made particularly in northern India) is made from wheat flour. The basic dough is the same as for chapati, the flat, wholemeal bread cooked on a bakestone, but it is rolled into small, thin rounds. The freshly prepared rounds of dough are deep-fried in hot oil so that they puff up into golden, crisp hollows. They are served to accompany a meal, particularly with a selection of mixed dishes served on a thali. They are sometimes stuffed or topped with a savoury mixture when cooked.

PURSLANE A hardy plant (*Portulaca oleracea*), which originated in India, was known by the Romans and was used in the Middle Ages, particularly for pickling. There are several species, including the golden purslane with large leaves and the *claytone de Cuba* (cultivated in the north of France and in Belgium). Rich in magnesium and with a slightly spicy flavour, this purslane can be eaten as a salad, flavoured with burnet. The fleshy young leaves and the tender stalks can be cooked like spinach and cardoons (particularly with gravy, butter or cream). The leaves can also be used as garnish for soups, omelettes and cuts of meat (instead of watercress) or to flavour sauces (béarnaise or paloise).

PYRAMIDE The name of a goat's cheese with a shape similar to Valençay, made in a cheese factory in central France from frozen curds and milk powder.

Q

QUADRILLER A French culinary term meaning to mark the surface of grilled (broiled) food (usually meat or fish) with a criss-cross pattern of lines. These scorings can be produced by contact with very hot (but not scorching) single grill bars, which brown the surface of the food. Alternatively, very hot skewers can be used to mark the surface.

Food that has been coated in egg and bread-crumbs, such as fish or escalopes (scallops), can be marked before cooking, using the back of a knife to trace squares or diamond shapes on the surface to improve the appearance of the cooked dish.

In pastry- and cake-making a criss-cross pattern is achieved by placing narrow strips of pastry over an open tart. A red-hot skewer can be used to mark a dessert cream or a meringue-topped dessert. For savoury dishes, a criss-cross pattern can be made with anchovy fillets on a pissaladière, a pizza or a mixed salad.

QUAIL A small migratory game bird found in Europe, in flat open country, from April to October. It has become very scarce. (A breed from the Far East is raised like poultry in France.) In the autumn the bird is plump and round and its flesh is full of flavour. Wild quail should never be allowed to get 'high'. Quail fattened in captivity has less flavour. The bird is drawn and usually barded with bacon. Weighing 150–200 g (5–7 oz), quails may be roasted (especially on skewers), grilled (broiled), sautéed, braised (with grapes) or stuffed and served on a canapé. They can be served chaud-froid (jellied) and can also be used in a pâté or terrine. Quails' eggs are plum-shaped and yellowish-green with brown markings: they may be served hard-boiled (hard-cooked), *en cocotte* or in aspic. One can also buy hard-boiled quails' eggs preserved in vinegar or brine for use as a cocktail snack.

RECIPES

grilled quails
Pluck, draw and singe the quails. Split them down the centre of the back from the base of the neck to the tail and flatten them slightly. Season with salt and pepper, brush with flavoured oil or melted butter and grill (broil) lightly for about 20 minutes. (Before cooking, the quails may be coated with fresh breadcrumbs.)

grilled quails petit-duc
Coat the quails with melted butter and bread-crumbs and grill (broil). Arrange them on a bed of Anna potatoes and place a large grilled mushroom on each quail. Heat a few tablespoons of game fumet with a little Madeira and butter and sprinkle this over the quails.

jellied stuffed quails à la périgourdine
Prepare and stuff the quails as described for stuffed quails in cases, adding diced foie gras to the force-meat. Reshape the quails and wrap each one in a piece of muslin (cheesecloth) tied at both ends. Poach for 20–25 minutes in liquid meat aspic stock, flavoured with Madeira. Leave the quails to cool in the stock, but drain them before it sets. Unwrap them and dry with a cloth. Arrange them in a round, fairly shallow terrine. Clarify the aspic jelly and pour over the quails. Chill in the refrigerator before serving.

minute quails
Pluck, draw and singe the quails. Split them down the centre of the back from the base of the neck to the tail, flatten slightly and season with salt and

pepper. Sauté them briskly in butter. After 15 minutes add a small chopped onion, some parsley and some melted butter. Cover the pan and continue cooking for a further 5 minutes. Cut some mushrooms into thin slices, allowing 150 g (5 oz, 1½ cups) for 4 quails. Drain the quails and arrange them on a serving dish while still hot. Brown the mushrooms in the sauté pan. Add a dash of brandy and, optionally, a few tablespoons of game stock. Boil for 3–4 minutes and add a dash of lemon juice. Pour this sauce over the quails.

quail casserole
Pluck, draw and singe the quails. Smear the inside of each carcass with a knob of butter kneaded with salt and pepper, then truss each bird. Melt some butter in a flameproof casserole and fry the quails until golden. Add salt and pepper, cover the dish and place it in a preheated oven at 240°C (475°F, gas 9) for 12–18 minutes. When the birds are cooked, deglaze the dish with a little brandy.

quail casserole à la bonne femme
Pluck, draw, singe and truss the quails. Fry them in butter in a flameproof casserole until golden. Dice some potatoes and scalded bacon, and cook in butter in a separate pan. Add the fried potato and bacon to the quails and complete the cooking in the oven, as for quail casserole.

quail casserole Cinq-Mars
Pluck, draw, truss and singe the quails. Cut some carrots, onions and celery sticks into thin strips. Soften the strips in butter over a low heat, then add salt and pepper. Fry the quails in butter until golden, season with salt and pepper and cover with half the vegetable strips. Add 2–3 tablespoons sherry, cover and leave to cook in a preheated oven at about 240°C (475°F, gas 9) for 10 minutes.

Untruss the quails and arrange them in an ovenproof dish that can be taken to the table. Top with thinly sliced mushrooms (wild mushrooms if possible) and either thinly sliced truffles or truffle peel. Cover with the rest of the vegetables and add the cooking juices, 2 tablespoons brandy and some knobs of butter. Cover the dish and seal the lid with a flour-and-water paste. Place the dish in a bain marie and bring to the boil. Then place the bain marie in the oven at 200°C (400°F, gas 6) and leave to cook for another 30 minutes. Remove the lid and serve very hot in the same dish.

quail casserole with grapes
Pluck, draw and singe 8 quails. Wrap each one in a vine leaf and a very thin rasher (slice) of bacon, truss and fry in butter until golden. Add salt and pepper, cover the pan and leave to cook for another 10 minutes. Peel and seed about 60 large white grapes. Untruss the quails, arrange in an ovenproof dish (which can be taken to the table) and add the grapes. Sprinkle with the quails' cooking juices. Place the dish, without a lid, in a pre-

heated oven at 240°C (475°F, gas 9) for 5 minutes. Just before serving, 2–3 tablespoons brandy can be added to the dish.

quail pâté
Bone the quails. Stuff each with a piece of *à gratin* forcemeat about the size of a hazelnut, and the same amount of foie gras, studded with a piece of truffle, the whole well seasoned with salt, pepper and nutmeg, and sprinkled with a dash of brandy. Wrap each quail in a very thin rasher (slice) of bacon.

Line a hinged oval or rectangular mould with fine pastry, then with thin rashers of bacon. Cover with a layer of finely pounded forcemeat made of veal and lean and fat pork in equal proportions, bound with an egg, well seasoned, sprinkled with a little brandy and mixed with diced truffles. Over this forcemeat put a layer of *à gratin* game forcemeat, then half the stuffed quails, pressing down well. Cover with another layer of forcemeat, put in the rest of the quails and follow with a layer of forcemeat. Cover this with a layer of truffled forcemeat, flatten it and cover again with a layer of thin rashers of lean bacon. Seal with a pastry lid. Garnish with pieces of pastry cut in fancy shapes. Make a hole in the middle of the lid to allow steam to escape and brush the top with beaten egg. Bake in a preheated oven at 180°C (350°F, gas 4) for about 1½ hours.

When cooked, leave the pâté to get cold and pour liquid game aspic stock through the hole in the top.

quails' eggs in aspic with caviar
Prepare an aspic jelly with 1 litre (1¾ pints, 4⅓ cups) well-reduced consommé, 20 g (¾ oz, 3 envelopes) gelatine and 100 ml (4 fl oz, 7 tablespoons) port. Boil 24 quails' eggs for 1½ minutes in salted water, cool and remove the shells.

Evenly coat the bottom and sides of 6 ramekins with aspic jelly. Garnish each ramekin with 1 teaspoon caviar, cover with a small amount of aspic and leave to set. Arrange 4 boiled quails' eggs in each ramekin with the tops pointing downwards. Add 50 g (2 oz, ¼ cup) caviar to the rest of the aspic and cover the eggs with it. When the aspic has set, remove from the moulds and arrange on a chiffonnade of lettuce.

Make a mousse by mixing together 1 tablespoon concentrated tomato soup, 250 ml (8 fl oz, 1 cup) whipping cream, salt, pepper and a dash of brandy. Whip the mixture and add a few grains of caviar. Serve this mousse separately.

quails in vine leaves ◆
Wash and dry 4 large fresh vine leaves; if they are canned, rinse in plenty of water, sponge dry and remove the stalks. Draw 4 quails and season with salt and pepper. Generously butter the breast and

Quails in vine leaves.

legs. Put a vine leaf on the breast of each quail and fold the edges down under the bird. Wrap 2 thin rashers (slices) of bacon around the quails and secure with string. Wrap each one tightly in foil. Cook en papillote in a preheated oven at 220°C (425°F, gas 7) for 20 minutes or in the ashes of a wood fire, or roast on a spit for 15 minutes. Remove the string and bacon rashers and serve the birds, cut in two lengthways. Serve with potato chips (French fries) and watercress or small mushroom brochettes.

quails with rice

Pluck, draw and singe the quails. Season with salt and pepper, truss them and cook them in butter. Arrange them on a bed of rice pilaf. Dilute the pan juices with a dash of brandy and either game stock or game fumet. Pour the sauce over the quails.

The rice pilaf can be replaced by cheese risotto, risotto *à la piémontaise* or polenta.

roast quails

Wrap the quails in vine leaves and then in thin rashers (slices) of larding bacon. Secure with string. Roast on a spit before a lively fire or in a preheated oven at 200°C (400°F, gas 6) for 15–20 minutes. Arrange each quail on a canapé. Garnish with watercress and lemon quarters. Serve the diluted pan juices separately.

stuffed quails à la gourmande

Pluck, draw and singe the quails. Season with salt and pepper, and stuff each bird with a mixture of butter, lean ham and chopped truffles (or truffle peel). Truss them and brown them in butter in a sauté pan. Cover the pan and finish cooking. Drain the quails, dilute the pan juices with champagne and reduce. Adjust the seasoning. Arrange the quails in a circle on a warm serving dish. Garnish the centre of the dish with boletus or chanterelle mushrooms sautéed in butter. Pour the pan juices over the birds.

stuffed quails à la Monselet

Pluck, draw and half-bone the quails. Stuff them with a salpicon of truffles and foie gras. Wrap each bird separately in a piece of muslin (cheesecloth) and poach them in a Madeira-flavoured game stock prepared from the bones and trimmings of the quails. Drain the birds, then unwrap and place them in an earthenware casserole together with a garnish of sliced artichoke hearts tossed in butter, cultivated mushrooms and thick slices of truffles. Strain the stock, add an equal quantity of crème fraîche and reduce. Pour this sauce over the birds. Cover the dish and place in a preheated oven at 180°C (350°F, gas 4) for 10 minutes. Serve the quails in the casserole.

stuffed quails à la Souvarov

Pluck, draw and singe the quails. Stuff them with a salpicon of foie gras and truffles seasoned with salt and pepper and sprinkled with a dash of brandy. Truss the birds and fry briskly in very hot butter for 5 minutes. Season with salt and pepper. Cook some very small truffles in butter and place them in a casserole that is large enough to hold the quails. Arrange the quails in the casserole. Dilute the pan juices with Madeira (and possibly game stock), reduce, add a dash of brandy and pour the sauce over the birds. Cover the casserole and seal the lid with a flour-and-water paste. Cook in a preheated oven at 230°C (450°F, gas 8) for 15–18 minutes.

stuffed quails in cases

Pluck, draw and remove the bones from 8 quails. To 175 g (6 oz, ¾ cup) *à gratin* forcemeat*, add 3 or 4 chicken livers and 1 tablespoon chopped truffle peel. Stuff the quails, reshape and wrap each one in buttered greaseproof (wax) paper. Arrange them in a buttered dish so that they are tightly packed together and add a little melted butter, salt and pepper. Cook (without a lid) in a preheated oven at 240°C (475°F, gas 9) for 18–20 minutes. Remove the quails from the dish and unwrap them. Place each bird in an oval paper case. Deglaze the cooking juices with some Madeira and pour over the quails. Put the cases in the oven for 5 minutes before arranging on a serving dish.

stuffed quails in nests

Pluck, draw and bone the quails. Stuff them with game forcemeat mixed with chopped truffles. Wrap each bird in a small piece of muslin (cheesecloth) and make into a roll. Poach for 18 minutes in a stock prepared from the bones and trimmings, with added veal stock and Madeira. Drain the birds, unwrap and glaze lightly in the oven. Reduce the stock. Arrange each quail in a nest of straw potatoes and pour a little reduced stock over the top.

other recipes See *chemise, cherry, financière, Lamballe, romaine, terrine.*

QUAIL, BOBWHITE A species of quail, *Colinus virginianus*, a member of the *Phasianidae* family, originally from North America and found also in some parts of tropical Africa. Recently introduced into France, the bobwhite is one of the species that may be shot for sport; it has therefore become the object of breeding. It is prepared in the same way as the common quail, which it resembles.

QUARTS DE CHAUME A sweet white wine produced from Chenin Blanc grapes grown within the Coteaux-du-Layon appellation of the Loire Valley. It took its name from the fact that a former owner of that particular section of the vineyard used to retain a quarter (*un quart*) of the vintage for his own use. The wines are made only in the best vintages and usually only with grapes affected by noble rot (botrytis). They are capable of long ageing.

QUASI A French cut of veal taken from the rump (corresponding to rump steak in beef). In Anjou it is called the *cul-de-veau* and is used to make many savoury dishes. It can be sliced into escalopes (scallops) – more stringy and tougher than those taken from the leg – or into thicker slices for roasting, or it can be roasted whole. This cut can also be braised, sautéed or made into a *blanquette* or a *fricandeau*. As it is lean and slightly tough, it is advisable to lard or bard it, but it is full of flavour when cooked.

The origin of the word, which is applied only to veal, is obscure; it began to appear in the culinary vocabulary at the end of the 18th century.

QUASSIA A tree or shrub, found in tropical areas of America and in Malaysia, the wood of which was traditionally used to make aperitifs and tonics.

Fizzy drinks and bitters are flavoured with quassine, the bitter extract of quassia.

QUATRE ÉPICES A spice mixture used in French and Middle Eastern cookery. Literally meaning 'four spices', the mixture consists of ground white pepper, nutmeg, ginger and cloves. Cinnamon may be used instead of ginger and allspice may be used instead of white pepper. The proportions of the spices vary.

QUEBEC See *Canada*.

QUEEN OF SHEBA A chocolate gâteau, usually round, made from a sponge mixture lightened by the addition of whisked egg whites. The cake is lighter still if the flour is replaced by potato flour or ground almonds (or a mixture of the two). It is served cold with a crème anglais (see *custard*).

QUEEN SCALLOP A European bivalve mollusc resembling a small scallop. Measuring 4–8 cm (1½–3½ in) across, the queen scallop has a creamy white shell marked with brown, with fairly wide ridges radiating from the top, and two small lugs.

QUENELLE A dumpling made with a spiced meat or fish forcemeat bound with fat and eggs, sometimes with panada added; it is then moulded into a small sausage or egg shape and poached in boiling water. The most common types are veal quenelles, made from a *godiveau* forcemeat, and pike quenelles, a speciality of the Lyon region of France. They are served as an entrée with a sauce or au gratin. Small quenelles may also form part of a garnish (*financière*, *Godard*, *toulousaine*), particularly for poultry, or they can be added to ragoûts and salpicons as a filling for vol-au-vent or croustades. Quenelles are sometimes used as a garnish for soups. The name comes from the German *Knödel* (dumpling).

RECIPES

pike quenelles
Fillet a pike weighing about 1.25 kg (2¾ lb). Remove the skin and take out the bones, then weigh the flesh – there should be about 400 g (14 oz). Finely mince or pound the flesh, then put it in the refrigerator.

Shaping fish quenelles

1 *Use a pair of spoons to shape the quenelle mixture – traditional dessertspoons are ideal. Dip a spoon in hot water, then scoop up a portion of the mixture.*

2 *Dip the second spoon in water and scoop the mixture from the first spoon, smoothing the mixture. Repeat the process, keeping the spoons hot, to form a neat oval.*

Prepare a panada: bring 300 ml (½ pint, 1¼ cups) water to the boil, adding a generous pinch of salt. Remove from the heat and sift in 150 g (5 oz, 1¼ cups) plain (all-purpose) flour through a sieve; stir vigorously until smooth, then continue to stir over heat until the mixture dries out, taking care that it does not stick to the bottom of the pan. Remove from the heat and beat in 1 whole egg; leave the mixture to get cold, then refrigerate. When the panada is well chilled, process in a blender until it is quite smooth.

Cream 200 g (7 oz, ¾ cup) butter. Put the pike flesh into a bowl placed in another bowl full of crushed ice; season with salt and pepper, then work it with a wooden spoon until it is smooth. Now mix in the panada, 1 whole egg and 4 yolks (one by one), and finally the butter: the mixture should be uniformly blended and smooth. (If all the ingredients are really cold, this last stage can be carried out in a blender, as long as it is powerful enough to work quickly without heating; the blender goblet itself should have been cooled in the refrigerator.) Chill the mixture for 30 minutes. Shape the quenelles, using 2 spoons dipped in hot water, and place on a lightly floured surface. Bring 2 litres (3½ pints, 9 cups) salted water to the boil and poach the quenelles for 15 minutes, without letting the water boil. Drain them and leave to get cold, then proceed according to the recipe.

pike quenelles à la florentine

Prepare some pike quenelles, spinach in cream, and a béchamel sauce enriched with cream: 100 ml (4 fl oz, 7 tablespoons) crème fraîche to 400 ml (14 fl oz, 1¾ cups) béchamel sauce; the sauce should be very thick. Butter a gratin dish and spread the spinach over the bottom of the dish. Arrange the quenelles on top, mask them with the béchamel sauce, sprinkle with grated cheese and dot with pieces of butter. Brown in a preheated oven at 230°C (450°F, gas 8).

pike quenelles à la lyonnaise

Prepare 575 g (1¼ lb) *godiveau* *lyonnais* and use it to make some quenelles. Make a béchamel* sauce with 100 g (4 oz, ½ cup) butter, 1.5 litres (2¾ pints, 6½ cups) milk, 100 g (4 oz, 1 cup) plain (all-purpose) flour, a pinch each of grated nutmeg, salt and pepper, and 200 ml (7 fl oz, ¾ cup) double (heavy) cream.

Butter a gratin dish and pour in a quarter of the béchamel sauce. Arrange the quenelles on top, cover them with the remaining sauce and dot the surface with very small pieces of butter. Cook the quenelles in a preheated oven at 190°C (375°F, gas 5) for 15 minutes (they will swell a great deal). Serve at once.

pike quenelles mousseline

Work 500 g (18 oz) pike flesh, 1 teaspoon salt, a pinch of white pepper and a pinch of grated nutmeg in a blender, then add 3 egg whites one by one. When the mixture is smooth, pour into a bowl and refrigerate. Also refrigerate 600 ml (1 pint, 2½ cups) crème fraîche and the blender goblet. When the fish mixture is cold, pour it back into the blender goblet, add 250 ml (8 fl oz, 1 cup) of the chilled crème fraîche and blend for a few seconds until it is thoroughly incorporated. Add a further 200 ml (7 fl oz, ¾ cup) crème fraîche, blend again, then repeat the process with the remaining crème fraîche. Shape the mixture into quenelles and poach as for ordinary pike quenelles.

quenelles Nantua

Make some pike quenelles and poach them. Melt 40 g (1½ oz, 3 tablespoons) butter in a flameproof casserole and add 40 g (1½ oz, ⅓ cup) plain (all-purpose) flour. Cook for 1 minute, stirring with a whisk, without allowing the mixture to colour. Season 500 ml (17 fl oz, 2 cups) milk with salt, pepper and nutmeg and bring to the boil. Add 250 ml (8 fl oz, 1 cup) double (heavy) cream. Add this mixture to the cooled butter-flour mixture. Add 1 medium-sized onion, studded with 2 cloves. Simmer for 30 minutes over a low heat. Strain and add 75 g (3 oz, 6 tablespoons) crayfish or lobster butter* and whisk to incorporate.

Wash 250 g (9 oz) mushrooms and cut into quarters. Cook for 4–5 minutes in a little lemon-flavoured, salted water. Pour the sauce into a gratin dish (or individual gratin dishes). Arrange the quenelles and add some shelled crayfish or prawns (shrimps). For a crisp crust, sprinkle with breadcrumbs and pour 50 g (2 oz, ¼ cup) melted butter on top. Bake in a preheated oven at 180°C (350°F, gas 4) for about 15 minutes.

Alternatively, the freshly cooked quenelles can be served with crayfish or prawns in the hot sauce without the gratin topping and mushrooms. Part-shelled crayfish and a little mayonnaise may be added as a garnish.

salmon quenelles

These are made in the same way as pike quenelles, but using salmon instead of pike. Poach, arrange on a dish, then cover them completely with Nantua sauce, cream sauce, shrimp sauce or white wine sauce.

veal quenelles

Make a *godiveau* with cream and chill it for at least 30 minutes. With floured hands, roll the mixture into balls. Press these into the shape of large olives, poach them, then proceed as in any of the recipes for pike quenelles; for example, cook them in a béchamel sauce enriched with crème fraîche.

Chicken meat can be used to make quenelles in the same way.

QUERCY This French region, and its capital Cahors, is renowned for cuisine similar to that of its neighbour, Périgord.

The soups are outstanding: *tourin* with garlic and onion; cabbage soup accompanied by *miques* (cornmeal dumplings); and vegetable soups, of which the remains, after all the bread and vegetables have been eaten, are drunk with red or white wine (this is known as *le chabrot*).

For many, however, Quercy is best known for its truffles: these may be eaten rolled in bacon rashers (slices); enclosed in puff pastry; in salads with hardboiled (hard-cooked) eggs, sprinkled with verjuice, lemon juice and walnut oil; or added to pâtés, poultry and game dishes, and omelettes.

There is a great variety of charcuterie: *boudin blanc*, tripe with saffron, pig's trotters (feet) *à la vinaigrette*, liver sausages and smoked ham from the Causses make delicious introductions to a meal.

Quercy cooks have devised succulent recipes for goose, such as stuffed and preserved neck. Other poultry dishes include *alicot* (giblets stewed with cep mushrooms and chestnuts); pies made with chicken, potatoes and salsify; roast guinea fowl, flambéed and arranged on a piece of bread spread with foie gras (known as *pharaonne*); chicken in a pastry case; and ballotine of turkey and chicken, in a pie or steamed. Not much fish is eaten, although it does appear in such dishes as stuffed pike and crayfish and trout in white wine (which Pierre Benoît mentions in *Le Déjeuner de*

Sousceyrac) and *stoficado* (smoked cod with walnut oil and eggs).

Gigot of lamb or mutton is served crowned with garlic, not merely studded with it, garlic being an indispensable ingredient of all Quercy cooking. Other specialities of the region are veal with ceps, *estouffat* of pork with haricot (navy) beans, *farcidures* (small vegetable dumplings), *porcellous* (cabbage leaves stuffed with veal, bacon, pork and herbs) and beef hotchpotch (cooked with chestnuts and turnips, flavoured with saffron). Mushrooms are highly esteemed, particularly ceps, a valued product of the Lot region.

The most common cheeses of the region are blue cheeses and Cabécou. For dessert, there are various types of local brioches, especially the *coques de Pâques*, flavoured with citron, and the *fouassous*, made with eggs and butter and glazed with sugar. There are also fritters (*gougnettes*) and thick pancakes, made either from wheat flour and filled with fruit (*pescajounes*) or from buckwheat flour (*bourriols* and *tourtous*). The plums, peaches, strawberries, melons and grapes grown in Quercy are all of excellent quality, as are the walnuts from which oil is pressed and a liqueur and jams made. As for wines, the most famous is the 'black' AOC wine from Cahors, where the 16th-century poet Clément Marot was born. In his *Remède contre la peste* Marot praises the cooking and the wine, recommending his readers to eat 'plenty of young pheasants' and to drink the 'delicious wines'.

QUESO The Spanish word for cheese. Numerous cheeses in Spain and Latin America are called simply *queso*, followed by a qualifying adjective. For example, there is the *queso añejo* of Mexico, a dry crumbly cheese made from goat's or cow's milk, served with cornmeal pancakes and sometimes sprinkled with red pepper (it is then known as *enchilado*); the *queso de bola* of Mexico and Spain, made from cow's milk and resembling Edam; the Chilean *queso de cabra*, a round, white, fresh goat's-milk cheese; the Spanish *queso de cabrales*, a type of blue goat's- or ewe's-milk cheese; the *queso de crema* of Costa Rica, a cow's-milk cheese with a pressed curd; the Spanish *queso de Mahón*, a pressed cow's-milk cheese; the *queso de puna* from Puerto Rico, made from skimmed cow's milk and eaten fresh; and the *queso de mano* from Venezuela, a round cow's-milk cheese wrapped in banana leaves, with a pressed and rubbery curd.

QUETSCH A type of plum with mauve skin and sweet, well-flavoured, yellow flesh. It is grown mostly in Alsace, from where it gets its original German name (*Zwetsche*). It is particularly suitable for tarts, compotes and jams and is the source of a well-known brandy, which is smooth and fruity.

QUICHE An open tart filled with a mixture of beaten eggs, crème fraîche and pieces of bacon, served hot as a first course or hors d'oeuvre.

Originating in Lorraine (the name comes from the German *Küchen*, meaning 'cake'), it has become a classic of French cuisine and is also widely enjoyed in other countries.

Its origins go back to the 16th century; in Nancy, where it is a speciality, its local name is *féouse*. Quiches used to be made from bread dough, but now shortcrust or puff pastry is used. In some areas of Lorraine any pastry tart filled with *migaine* (eggs and cream) mixed with onions, cream cheese or pumpkin is called a quiche, and elsewhere quiches can be made with cheese, ham, bacon, onion, mushrooms, seafood and various other ingredients.

A *quiche tourangelle* is filled with rillettes and beaten eggs, sprinkled with chopped fresh parsley and served warm.

RECIPES

quiche lorraine
Make some lining pastry (see short* pastry) with 250 g (9 oz, 2¼ cups) plain (all-purpose) flour, 125 g (4½ oz, ½ cup) butter, a generous pinch of salt, 1 egg and 3 tablespoons very cold water. Roll it into a ball and chill in the refrigerator for a few hours. Then roll it out to a thickness of 5 mm (¼ in) and line a buttered and floured tart tin (pan), 23 cm (9 in) in diameter, bringing the edges of the pastry up to extend slightly beyond the tin edge. Prick it all over and cook blind in a preheated oven at 200°C (400°F, gas 6) for 12–14 minutes. Leave to cool.

Cut 250 g (9 oz) slightly salted pork belly into flat strips and blanch for 5 minutes in boiling water. Refresh and pat dry, then brown very lightly in butter. Spread the pork strips over the pastry case. Beat 4 eggs lightly and mix in 300 ml (½ pint, 1¼ cups) double (heavy) cream; add salt, pepper and nutmeg, then pour the mixture into the pastry case. Cook for about 30 minutes in a preheated oven at 200°C (400°F, gas 6). Serve very hot.

mussel quiche
Cook 450 g (1 lb) mussels and remove them from their shells. Reserve the mussel cooking liquor.

Make a shortcrust pastry (basic pie dough; see short* pastry) with 200 g (7 oz, 1¾ cups) plain (all-purpose) flour, 100 g (4 oz, 1 cup) butter, 4 tablespoons water and 3 pinches of salt. Roll out the dough to a thickness of 3 mm (⅛ in) and use it to line a 23 cm (9 in) tart tin (pan). Spread the mussels over the base. Mix 1 whole egg with 50 g (2 oz, ½ cup) plain flour, 2 egg yolks, 150 ml (¼ pint, ⅔ cup) double (heavy) cream, 250 ml (8 fl oz, 1 cup) milk diluted with some of the mussel cooking liquor, and salt and pepper; pour over the mussels. Cook the quiche in a preheated oven at 220°C (425°F, gas 7) for 30 minutes and serve with a well-chilled white wine.

small ham and cheese quiches
Prepare the lining pastry and the filling as for a quiche lorraine, but substitute 150 g (5 oz, ⅔ cup)

ham cut into strips for the bacon and add 100 g (4 oz, 1 cup) grated Gruyère cheese. Line 6 tartlet moulds, 10 cm (4 in) in diameter, with the pastry, divide the filling among them and bake in a preheated oven at 180°C (350°F, gas 4) for about 18 minutes.

QUIGNON A piece of bread, usually the end crust of a loaf. The word is a modification of *coignon*, from the Latin *cuneolus* (a small coin). In Flanders, at Christmas, they make *cougnous*, little cakes of yeast dough in the shape of a swaddled child; in Provence these are known as *cuignots*.

QUINCE The yellow fruit of a tree native to Asia, but widely cultivated in temperate regions. Round or pear-shaped, it is covered with a fine down when ripe. It is an aromatic fruit, and its flesh, which is very hard and tart when raw, is rich in tannin and pectin. Quince is too hard to be palatable raw, but it is used to make some fragrant and delicate dishes. In Europe it is used to make confectionery, liqueurs and jam (the word marmalade comes from the Portuguese *marmelo*, meaning quince).

The quince tree is native to the Caucasus and Iran and was known as the pear of Cydonia. It was very popular with the Greeks, who ate it hollowed out, filled with honey and cooked in a pastry case. The Romans extracted an essential oil from the fruit that was used in perfumery. It has been known in France for centuries and has been used not only in cookery but also in perfumery and medicine. In the 14th-century *Ménagier de Paris*, there is a recipe for quince paste (see *Cotignac*), and there is an equally ancient recipe in Spain, where it is called *dulce de membrillo*. Quince is used in the preparation of compotes and jellies, as well as in ratafia and fruit pastes. In the East it may be eaten with salt, or stuffed, or used in tajines and stews. It may even be used as a garnish for roast poultry, such as quail or chicken.

RECIPES

baked quinces
Generously butter an ovenproof dish. Peel 4 very ripe quinces and hollow them out carefully with an apple corer. Mix 100 ml (4 fl oz, 7 tablespoons) double (heavy) cream with 65 g (2½ oz, 5 table-spoons) caster (superfine) sugar and fill the quinces with the mixture. Sprinkle the fruit with 125 g (4½ oz, ½ cup) caster (superfine) sugar and bake in a preheated oven at 220°C (425°F, gas 7) for 30–35 minutes, basting several times.

quince liqueur or ratafia
Cut the quinces into quarters and remove the seeds. Shred the fruit without peeling. Place in a bowl, cover and leave to stand in a cool place for 3 days. Squeeze them through muslin (cheese-cloth) and collect the juice. Add an equal volume of spirit or vodka to the juice. For each 1 litre

(1¾ pints, 4⅓ cups) of the mixture, add 300 g (11 oz, 1½ cups) caster (superfine) sugar, 1 clove and a small piece of cinnamon stick. Infuse in a jar for 2 months, then strain through muslin (cheese-cloth) and bottle.

tajine of chicken with quince
Cut a prepared chicken into 8 pieces. Peel and chop 3 onions. Brown the chicken in a flameproof casserole in 3 tablespoons olive oil. Add the onions, stir, season and add a pinch of paprika, a generous pinch of ground ginger, a few parsley and coriander (cilantro) leaves and 175 ml (6 fl oz, ¾ cup) chicken stock. Cook gently for 30 minutes with the casserole half-covered.

Meanwhile, cut 2 large quinces into 8 pieces, remove and discard the seeds and fry them in oil or butter over a high heat until golden. Place the pieces of chicken and quince in a tajine (an earth-enware dish). Pour the cooking liquid over the top and cover the dish with a piece of perforated greaseproof (wax) paper. Cook in a preheated oven at 220–230°C (425–450°F, gas 7–8) for about 30 minutes. Serve very hot.

other recipes See *compote, cotignac*.

QUINCY A dry white AOC wine from Berry, in the upper reaches of the River Loire. It is made from the Sauvignon grape, is of high quality and somewhat similar to white Sancerre.

QUINOA Seeds of *Chenopodium quinoa*, a plant cultivated by the South-American Incas for the leaves and seeds. Quinoa is a staple in the highlands of South America, including Argentina, Bolivia, Chile, Colombia, Ecuador and Peru. The seeds are also grown to a small extent in the USA and Britain. Quinoa is used as a grain or milled to produce a variety of products, including flours for baked goods, breakfast cereals and animal feed. Quinoa flour is combined with wheat flour for breadmaking since it does not contain gluten.

QUINQUINA Any of various wine-based aperitifs containing a certain proportion of crushed cinchona bark; the flavour is slightly bitter, due to the quinine in the bark. Quinquina bitters can be made at home by macerating together the zest of a Seville (bitter) orange, some cinchona bark and some gentian root in spirits and white wine. Alternatively, the peel of a Seville orange, raisins and cinchona bark can be macerated in 90° alcohol, red wine and cassis.

QUORN The trade name for mycoprotein, a protein-rich, manufactured fungi. Cultivated from a starter based on egg white (albumen) and processed to form chunks, slices or 'mince', Quorn is available as a plain ingredient or in prepared foods. Its texture is similar to tender chicken and its flavour is bland. It absorbs the flavours of ingredients, aromatics and seasonings with which it is cooked.

RABBIT A small burrowing mammal, closely related to the hare, that has been regarded as a pest for many years, because of the damage it inflicts on crops and also as a result of its prolific breeding habits. An old name for the rabbit is coney or cony (in French, *connil* or *connin*), derived from the Old French *conis*, from the Latin *cuniculus*. Rabbit was regarded as a fertility symbol, especially in Germany, and was often included in Easter menus. Rabbits have been domesticated for many generations, and in 17th-century France the practice of rearing rabbits for the table was widespread. The meat was prepared as a *civet*, in a mustard or a poulette sauce, with onions or prunes, jellied, or made into *rillettes*. The tastier wild rabbit was roasted, grilled (broiled), or fried.

Domestic rabbits, which are raised not only for their meat but also for their fur, are distinguished by their size, the colour and texture of their fur, and the quality of their meat. Some notable French varieties are the Burgundy tawny, the silver field rabbit and the Bouscat giant. Efforts have been made to introduce the cottontail rabbit (*sylvilagus floridanus*), a native of North America, to France to raise it commercially for its meat.

A really large rabbit can weigh up to 10 kg (22 lb), but the average weight of a commercially reared specimen is 1.12–1.4 kg (2½–3 lb). The meat of the domestic rabbit is always tender and should be eaten young. The animal should be well-covered in meat, with a rounded back, pink flesh, a pale unspotted liver, and pure white fat around the kidneys (the latter should be clearly visible). The French Angevin rabbit has a superior flavour because it is fed on a special diet, but it is scarce nowadays, even on the French market, as is the wild rabbit. Myxomatosis decimated wild rabbit numbers both in France and in the UK in the 1950s.

A medium rabbit should be jointed into six pieces: two front legs, two hind legs and the two halves of the saddle. Marinating in wine seasoned with shallots, carrots, parsley, garlic and thyme improves a commercially reared rabbit before it is made into a pie or a stew, and the addition of pig's blood brings about an even greater improvement. Rabbit can be deep-frozen either raw or cooked.

RECIPES

rabbit coquibus

Joint a rabbit into small portions and marinate it overnight in 250 ml (8 fl oz, 1 cup) white wine with a bouquet garni, including a sprig of savory. Drain and wipe, reserving the marinade. Peel 24 small onions. Blanch 24 strips of slightly salted belly pork or bacon. Heat 40 g (1½ oz, 3 tablespoons) butter in a large flameproof casserole and lightly brown the pieces of rabbit in it, together with the onions and bacon. Sprinkle with a little flour and cook until golden. Pour in the reserved marinade with the bouquet garni. Add enough stock to cover the pieces of rabbit and sprinkle with salt and pepper. Bring to the boil, reduce the heat and cover the casserole. Simmer for 15 minutes. Then add 500 g (18 oz) peeled new potatoes, cover and continue cooking for 45 minutes. Taste for seasoning before serving.

rabbit roasted in a caul

Soak a large pig's caul in fresh water. Joint a rabbit weighing 1.25 kg (2¾ lb); season the pieces with salt and pepper, sprinkle with a little dried thyme

Jointing a rabbit

This method is also used to joint a hare. The head should be removed from the cleaned carcass.

1 *Cut the forequarters from the saddle by cutting between the ribcage and through the backbone.*

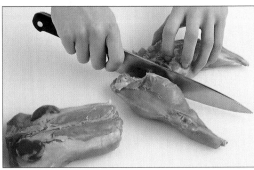

2 *Cut between the ribcage and through the backbone to separate the hind legs from the saddle. Then cut between the legs to separate them.*

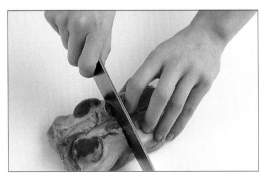

3 *Cut the saddle across into 2 or 3 portions according to the size of the rabbit.*

4 *Cut the front legs and ribcage in half. To give smaller portions, the front legs can be cut from their rib sections and the rear legs can be cut into thigh and lower leg portions.*

and plenty of mustard powder. Wipe the caul, stretch it on the worktop without tearing it, and cut it into 6 pieces. Wrap each piece of rabbit in a piece of caul and place the pieces in a roasting tin (pan) just large enough to hold them. Add 3 tablespoons water, put the tin in a preheated oven at 220°C (425°F, gas 7) and cook for 30 minutes, turning the pieces every 7–8 minutes. Add a little boiling water if necessary. Arrange the pieces on a warmed serving dish and keep hot.

Skim the fat from the cooking juices remaining in the roasting tin and add 60 ml (2 fl oz) white wine and 200 ml (7 fl oz, ¾ cup) double (heavy) cream; scrape the bottom of the tin to release the juices and boil until reduced by half. Adjust the seasoning and pour the sauce over the rabbit. Serve with buttered noodles.

rabbit sautéed à la minute

Joint a rabbit weighing about 1.25 kg (2¾ lb). Sprinkle the pieces with salt and pepper and brown them in smoking hot butter, over a very brisk heat, stirring thoroughly so that all the pieces are evenly coloured. Arrange them in a pie dish and keep hot. Dilute the pan juices with 150 ml (¼ pint, ⅔ cup) white wine and add 1 chopped shallot. Boil down the sauce until it is very concentrated, then moisten with a few tablespoons of stock. Reduce again, then mix in 1 tablespoon butter and a squeeze of lemon juice. Pour the sauce over the rabbit and sprinkle with chopped parsley.

rabbit with mustard

Joint a rabbit weighing about 1.25 kg (2¾ lb). Spread the pieces with a mixture of 2 tablespoons strong mustard, 1 tablespoon oil, salt and ground pepper. Place the pieces in a flameproof dish and put in a preheated oven at 230°C (450°F, gas 8). After 5 minutes, sprinkle with 60 ml (2 fl oz, ¼ cup) water. Continue cooking, basting with the pan juices every 5 minutes. When the pieces of rabbit are cooked, arrange them on a heated serving dish and keep hot. Skim the fat from the cooking juices and add 2 tablespoons white wine to the pan; reduce slightly, stirring with a wooden spoon. Then add 60 ml (2 fl oz, ¼ cup) single (light) cream and some salt, stirring all the time; do not boil. Pour this sauce over the rabbit. Serve with pasta.

sautéed rabbit chasseur

Joint the rabbit and prepare exactly like sautéed chicken chasseur, with mushrooms and strips of larding bacon. Serve with steamed potatoes.

sautéed rabbit with prunes

Soak 350 g (12 oz, 2 cups) prunes in tea until swollen, then drain them. Sauté a rabbit of about 1.25 kg (2¾ lb) as in the recipe for rabbit sautéed *à la minute*. Pound the rabbit's liver with 1 tablespoon vinegar (or put through a blender). When the rabbit is cooked, keep hot in a serving dish. Dilute the pan juices with 150 ml (¼ pint, ⅔ cup) white wine, add the prunes, then reduce a little. Mix in the pounded liver and adjust the seasoning. Pour the prunes and gravy over the rabbit.

wild rabbit with Hermitage wine

Joint a rabbit weighing about 1.25 kg (2¾ lb) and season the pieces with salt and pepper. Cut 150 g (5 oz) fat bacon into dice. Peel 12 small white onions. Pound the rabbit's liver. Put the fat bacon in a saucepan and brown it with the onions. Place the pieces of rabbit in the saucepan and sauté them over a brisk heat; dust with flour and leave to brown slightly. Flame with 60 ml (2 fl oz, ¼ cup) Hermitage marc and moisten with (500 ml, 17 fl oz, 2 cups) of red Crozes-Hermitage. Add a little warm water or stock. Adjust the seasoning and add a bouquet garni made of thyme, bay leaf, parsley stalks and a garlic clove. Cook gently for about 1 hour. When the rabbit is cooked, take it out of the saucepan and keep it hot. Remove the pan from the heat and add the liver and blood (to which a little vinegar has been added); blend with the pan juices away from the heat. Return the pan to the hob (stove top) over a very moderate heat, so that the blood cooks without boiling. Strain the sauce and keep it hot. Arrange the rabbit in a deep earthenware dish and pour the sauce over it. Some fried croûtons may be arranged around the dish.

RABBIT, COTTONTAIL North American rodent, *sylvilagus floridanus*, intermediate between the hare and the wild rabbit, although it is not a close relation of either and it differs from them in its ability to climb trees.

RABELAIS, FRANÇOIS French humanist and writer (born Chinon, *c.* 1483; died Paris, 1553). He became successively a monk, a doctor and a professor of anatomy before ending his days as the parish priest of Meudon. He is best known, however, as the author of the comic satires *Pantagruel* (1532), *Gargantua* (1534), *Tiers Livre* (1546) and *Quart Livre* (1552). This powerful and original body of work, which one has to 'crack like a bone' to get to the 'real marrow', is very much occupied with eating and drinking. The terms 'pantagruelian' and 'gargantuan' are used to describe an appetite, meal or stomach of gigantic size, worthy of a well-laden festive board.

In the *Quart Livre* (chapter XI) Rabelais gives us 'the names of the valiant and worthy cooks who, as in the Trojan horse, entered into the sow'. He mentions numerous cookery terms and dishes common in his time; for example: *Saulpicquet* (saupiquet), *Paimperdue* (pain perdu), *Carbonnade, Hoschepot* (hotchpotch), *Gualimafré* (gallimaufry), *Croquelardon* (bacon on bread), *Salladier* (salad bowl), *Macaron* (macaroon), *Cochonnet* (suckling pig) and *Talemouse* (a pastry case with a cheese filling).

In Book IV of *Pantagruel* (chapters LIX and LX), Rabelais makes a long list of dishes and foods, giving us some idea of what was eaten in the 16th century: '. . . soups made with prime cuts of meat, bay-leaf soups, soups *lionnoise* (with onion and cheese); olives pickled in brine, caviar, *boutargue* (a paste of dried salted pressed mullet or tuna roes), stockfish (salted and dried cod); roast capons with their cooking juices, cockerels, hens and turkey-hens, ducks *à la dodiné* (boned and served with a sauce), pigeons, squabs, geese, swans, herons, cranes, partridges, francolins, turtledoves, rock pigeons, pheasants, quails, plovers, blackbirds, woodcocks, hazel grouse, loons, etc.; leverets, fawns, young rabbits; sausages, black puddings (blood sausage), saveloys, *andouilles* spread with fine mustard, potted boar's head; bleaks, eels, barbels, pike, young carp, loach, tench, trout, shad, white *apron* (small perchlike fish), whales, plaice, dolphins, sea bream, sturgeons, lobsters, oysters in their shells, fried oysters, lampreys in hippocras sauce, dabs, *laveret* (salmon-like lake fish), salted hake, Moray eels, sea anemones, sea urchins, bonito, skate, salmon, turtles, turbot, sardines, dogfish; pork cutlets with stewed onions, young goat, shoulder of mutton with capers, pigs' and calves' fry, smoked ox tongue, cold roast loin of veal sprinkled with *zinziberine* powder (mustard and ginger); cabbage with beef marrow, artichokes, spinach, rice, salads, purée of peas, salted broad beans; almond butter, raised meat pies, puff-pastry cakes; lark pâtés, chamois, capons, quinces, bacon rashers, or venison; *poupelins* (pastry cakes filled with whipped cream, etc.), tarts, wafers, curds, pancakes, *jonchées* (fresh sheep's- or goat's-milk cheeses), *neige de beurre* (shallots and vinegar, or Muscadet, whipped up with butter), figs, pistachio nuts, Corbeil peaches, grapes, prunes, white bread, soft bread, *bourgeois* bread, wheaten bread; eggs fried, lost, suffocated, boiled, dragged over the coals, thrown into the chimney, smeared with something or other, etc.'

RABOTTE Also known as *rabote*. An apple or pear enclosed in pastry, cooked in the oven and served warm or cold. It is the name used in Picardy, Ardennes and Champagne for the Norman *douillon* or *bourdelot*. In Picardy it is also called *talibur*, and in Ardennes and Champagne the name *boulaud* is sometimes used. The name *rabotte* comes from the word *rabote*, which was the old term for the ball used in real tennis.

RACAHOUT A culinary starch used in the Middle East and Arab countries. It is a greyish powder, consisting of salep, cocoa, sweet acorns, potato flour, rice, flour, sugar and vanilla, which is mixed with water or milk to make a drink or soup.

RACHEL The stage name of the great tragic actress Élisabeth Félix (1821–58). She was the mistress of the famous gastronome Doctor Véron, whose dinners are still a byword, and many dishes in classic cuisine have been named after her. The Rachel garnish – for small grilled (broiled) or sautéed cuts of meat, braised calves' sweetbreads, or poached or soft-boiled eggs – consists of artichoke hearts stuffed with thin slices of beef marrow, with a bordelaise or beef marrow sauce. Artichoke hearts are also used in the Rachel mixed salad. Whiting (or turbot) Rachel is poached, masked with Nantua sauce and garnished with a julienne of truffle.

RECIPE

Rachel salad
Clean and string some celery sticks and cut them into chunks. Cook some potatoes and some artichoke hearts in salted water and cut them into small dice. Mix equal amounts of these ingredients and dress them with a well-flavoured mayonnaise. Pile into a salad bowl and garnish with asparagus tips, cooked in salted water and well drained. If desired, the salad can be garnished with slices of truffle.

RACK A trellis or grid of varying shape, size, material and function.

Round or rectangular wire racks, usually with small legs, are used to cool cakes and pastries after they have been taken out of the oven and removed from their tins (pans). This allows the steam to be released during cooling; otherwise, the cakes would retain too much moisture. A similar rack is also used in a roasting tin. By roasting the meat on the rack, the joint is prevented from lying in its cooking juices.

Wooden racks serve for storing fruits or vegetables; wicker trays are used for drying crystallized (candied) fruits; and racks of stainless steel or plastic-covered wire form storage units in refrigerators and larders.

RACLETTE A cheese fondue from the canton of Valais in Switzerland. It is prepared by holding a half-round of the local cheese close to the fire; as it melts, the softened part is scraped off and eaten (the word *raclette* means literally 'a scraping'). Traditionally, the cheese should be grilled in front of a wood fire: it is held slantwise over a plate and the runny part is scraped off together with part of the grilled rind (after several scrapings, when the rind becomes coated with the melted cheese, it is called a *religieuse* and is a much-coveted morsel). The melted cheese is shared between the guests and is eaten hot, with boiled potatoes, freshly ground pepper, gherkins and pickled onions. Raclette should be accompanied by Fendant, a white wine from Valais, and must be made from a fatty and highly flavoured cheese: Bagnes, Conches or Orsières. It is now possible to buy a 'raclette oven' for the table, which is fitted with a support for the cheese while it is exposed to an electric element.

RADICCHIO A variety of chicory (endive) of Italian origin, now also cultivated in the south of France and other countries throughout the world. Radicchio keeps well. Its small hearts, red with white veins, are round and crunchy and have a taste which is at once bitter, peppery and slightly acid. It is sweetest late in the year, most bitter in the summer. It is generally used in salads, mixed with other salad vegetables, and looks particularly attractive when mixed with curly endive (chicory) and green lettuce or lamb's lettuce (corn salad). It is often served with terrines, pies and pâtés; a suitable dressing is walnut-oil vinaigrette. It is also used in some cooked dishes; for example, as a topping for pizza.

RADISH A cruciferous plant, cultivated for its edible root, which is generally eaten raw in European dishes, as an hors d'oeuvre or in salads. In East Asian dishes, the long white radish is used both raw and cooked, as a vegetable in its own right, as well as for garnishing or as a relish to accompany main dishes.

There are many varieties of radish, differing in size, shape and colour, the main types being 'small pink' and 'large black'. The radish has been grown in China for more than 3000 years and was esteemed by the Greeks and the Romans. In France, it was not cultivated until the 16th century and is now grown principally in the Loire region, being available throughout almost the whole year.
- RED RADISHES These are small, flattish, round or slightly elongated, and pink or scarlet, with or without a white tip. Their flavour is particularly good in March–April and September–October, when they are not too hot (in summer they may be too strong).

There are pale pink or yellow radishes, round or slightly elongated. There are also some traditional regional varieties: the Strasbourg – small, white and top-shaped, 5 cm (2 in) across; the turnip radish – very long and narrow, with a red skin and juicy scented flesh – which is found in eastern France and in Nice; and the golden-yellow radish – with flesh of this colour, 3–4 cm (1¼–1½ in) long – which is grown in Alsace.
- WHITE RADISH These large, elongated radishes are also known as mooli or daikon. They are milder in flavour than the small red ones and are popular as a raw or cooked vegetable in East Asian cooking. The leaves may also be used in cooking. The large white radishes are also carved into elaborate garnishes.
- BLACK RADISH The black-skinned radishes, also known as the Spanish black or Spanish radish, are old varieties. They are still cultivated, especially in Spain as well as in Italy, and they may be round or elongated. The coarse black skin conceals white flesh with a strong flavour.

RADISHES

round red radish

black radish

white radish or mooli

elongated red radish with white tip

■ **Using radishes** Radishes must be eaten when very fresh, smooth and firm, with an unblemished brightly coloured skin (if they are red or pink varieties); the leaves should be rather short, bright green and stiff.

Really fresh pink radishes do not need to be peeled; the root tip and nearly all the leaves are cut off, then the radishes are washed in plenty of cold water and thoroughly dried; they are served as they are, with fresh butter and salt. Larger pink radishes are better sliced into thin rounds and added to a salad; they can also be cooked in the same way as small new turnips. Radish leaves can be added to potato soup or a sorrel or spinach purée.

The black radish, which has a more pungent flavour than the small pink variety, can also be eaten raw with salt after it has been peeled and sliced; the slices may be salted and left to stand so that some of their water is drawn out before being rinsed and dried. They can be used in the same way as celery, added to a rémoulade mayonnaise or used in salad with a yogurt and shallot dressing.

RECIPES

black radish as an hors d'oeuvre
Peel a black radish and slice it very thinly; soak the slices in a bowl with a small handful of table salt for an hour. Wash thoroughly, dry well and serve in an hors d'oeuvre dish accompanied by rye bread or wholemeal (whole wheat) bread with fresh or slightly salted butter.

pink radishes à l'américaine
Wash the radishes and cut all the leaves to the same length. Wash and then split the radishes in four from tip to leaf end without cutting through the bases; put them in a bowl of water and ice cubes. When they open out like flowers, drain and serve in an hors d'oeuvre dish, with fresh butter and table salt.

radish-leaf soup
Cut off the leaves from a bunch of fresh radishes and cook them gently in butter in a saucepan. Pour in some chicken stock. Add 3 peeled potatoes, salt and pepper. Cook over a low heat for 25 minutes, then pass the soup through a vegetable mill. Add 2 tablespoons crème fraîche, mix, then adjust the seasoning. Sprinkle with coarsely chopped chervil. This soup can be served with baked croûtons.

RAGOÛT A stew made from meat, poultry, game, fish or vegetables cut into pieces of regular size and shape and cooked – with or without first being browned – in a thickened liquid, generally flavoured with herbs and seasonings.

The French word *ragoût* dates from 1642; in

classic French it was used to describe anything which stimulated the appetite or, in a figurative sense, awoke interest. The verb *ragoûter* meant to bring back someone's appetite. Ragoûts have been enjoyed for many centuries and were even known in ancient times; up to the Middle Ages they were probably very highly spiced.

Today there are two basic types of ragoût – brown and white. For a brown ragoût, of which the best known example is ragoût of mutton, the meat is first browned in fat, then sprinkled with flour, cooked a little and finally moistened with clear stock or water (or thickened meat juices, if the meat has not been floured). For a white ragoût (as for a fricassée), the meat is cooked until firm but not coloured, then sprinkled with flour and diluted with stock. (A white ragoût should not, however, be confused with a blanquette.)

If fish is to be made into a ragoût, its flesh must be firm enough to withstand the cooking (such as carp, monkfish or eel). Meat should be chosen from cuts which are suitable for braising or stewing (such as shoulder, chuck or neck of beef; rib, breast, or knuckle of veal; shoulder, breast, collar or middle neck of mutton; poultry giblets; and knuckle, chine or blade of pork).

Vegetables for a ragoût – chicory (endive), celery, mixed root vegetables, mushrooms – are usually browned, then cooked in their own juices, with herbs and tomatoes (peeled, seeded and coarsely chopped).

'Ragoût' is also the name of a plain or mixed garnish, thickened with a white or brown liaison, with a meat or vegetable stock. It is used to fill croustades, tarts and vol-au-vent, to embellish a fish or poultry dish, to garnish scrambled eggs and to fill omelettes. These ragoûts are made from such ingredients as crayfish tails (ragoût *à la Nantua*), cock's kidneys and cockscombs, asparagus tips, truffles, mushrooms, calves' sweetbreads, bone marrow and even snails or seafood; they appear in such garnishes as banquière, cancalaise, cévenole, financière, marinière, périgourdine and printanière.

RECIPES

ragoût of celeriac
Peel a celeriac root and cut it into small oval-shaped pieces. Blanch these for 5 minutes in boiling water, then place in a flameproof casserole with butter, salt and pepper and let it stew gently, with the lid on, for about 30 minutes. Bind with cream sauce, sprinkle with coarsely chopped parsley and serve as a garnish to roast or braised white meat.

ragoût of mushrooms
Clean and slice 500 g (18 oz, 6 cups) large cultivated mushrooms, sauté them in butter or oil, then add a small glass of Madeira and some cream sauce. Reduce over a low heat until thick and creamy, sprinkle with coarsely chopped parsley and serve as a garnish for roast or braised white meat or for braised fish.

West Indian ragoût
Cut 800 g (1¾ lb) shoulder of beef or neck of mutton into small pieces. Chop 3 onions and slice 3 carrots, 6 potatoes and 3 ripe tomatoes. Brown the meat in oil or butter in a flameproof casserole, add the vegetables and mix together. Then pour in 175 ml (6 fl oz, ¾ cup) water and simmer over a low heat, stirring occasionally. When the ragoût has been cooking for 45 minutes, take out the vegetables, drain them and keep warm.

Add 1 small chopped chilli, salt and pepper, 3 tablespoons vinegar and 1 tablespoon peanut butter to the casserole.

Bone a herring and grill (broil) it gently, turning once, until cooked through. Mash the flesh and mix it into the sauce, adding a little hot water if necessary. Cover the casserole and simmer for a further hour. Transfer the vegetables and the meat to a deep dish, pour the sauce over and serve very hot with rice *à la créole*.

other recipes See *asparagus, cancalaise, cévenole, espagnole, mutton, Nantua, printanière.*

RAGÙ The name for the celebrated Bolognese meat sauce, commonly served with spaghetti, the principal ingredients of which are minced (ground) meat, usually beef, cooked with chicken livers, unsmoked bacon, onion, celery, tomato purée (paste) and wine. Curiously, given the popularity of the pairing elsewhere, meat sauce in Bologna is never served over spaghetti, but with tagliatelle or lasagne.

RAGUENEAU, CYPRIEN Parisian pastrycook (born Paris, 1608; died Lyon, 1654). He established himself in the Rue Saint-Honoré, displaying the sign 'Amateurs de Haulte Gresse', where he created the *tartelettes amandine* (almond tarts) mentioned by Edmond Rostand in *Cyrano de Bergerac*. He kept open house for half-starved poets and bohemians, who paid in poetry. He was renowned for his tarts, marzipan confections, savoury pies flavoured with musk and amber, puff pastries, fritters and biscuits (cookies). Charles d'Assoucy relates that he would give away these delicacies to anyone who flattered him by calling him 'Apollo reborn as a pastrycook'.

Ragueneau's shop became a sort of academy, where the pastries and tartlets served as attendance tallies. Drawn into writing, Ragueneau gradually neglected his work as a pâtissière and his business. He was very proud of his tragedy *Don Olibrius, occiseur d'innocents* and – hoping that Molière would produce it – he went to Béziers to join the playwright's group of actors. His prolific attempts at writing were not successful. He was given a few bit-parts to play, but finally resigned himself to being a candle snuffer and eventually died in extreme poverty. After his death it was found that he had written 456 sonnets, 4 elegies, 63 odes and 19 comic-heroic plays.

RAIL Any of a large family of wading birds. Two species are regarded as delicacies in France – the corncrake, found in wet meadowland, and the water rail, living in marshland. The corncrake is particularly valued; its size and the influence that it is supposed to have on quail migration has resulted in its nickname of 'the king of quails' in France. It is cooked in the same ways as quail.

RAISINÉ A jam made without sugar, by simmering grape juice (or even sweet wine) with various fruits cut into pieces. It is a speciality of Burgundy. Raisiné is usually spread on slices of bread; it does not keep as well as jam.

RECIPE

Burgundian raisiné
Select some very sweet grapes, either black or white, discarding any which are marked or bad. Put them into a preserving pan over a low heat and crush them with a wooden spoon. Strain the pulp through a cloth and collect the juice in a bowl. Pour half of this juice into a saucepan and boil briskly, skimming the pan carefully. When the juice rises in the pan add some of the reserved juice; do this each time the juice boils up. Stir constantly.

When the must has reduced by half, add the fruit (such as pears, quinces, apples, peaches and melon), peeled, seeded or stoned (pitted), and cut into small pieces; add at least the same quantity of fruit as there were grapes. Cook until the jam becomes quite thick (a drop taken up between the thumb and index finger should form a sticky thread when the fingers are separated). The jam may be passed through a sieve (if desired) and then potted in the usual way.

RAISINS See *dried vine fruits*.

RAISSON, HORACE-NAPOLÉON French writer and gastronome (born Paris, 1798; died Paris, 1854). Under different pseudonyms, one of which was A. B. de Périgord, he published several cookery books, notably a *Nouvel Almanach des gourmands* (1825–30), borrowing this title from Grimod de La Reynière. His *Code gourmand* went through several editions. In 1827 he published a *Nouvelle Cuisinière bourgeoise* under the name of 'Mlle Marguerite'. This book remained popular for quite a long time, the last edition being published in 1860.

RAITA An Indian side dish based on raw vegetables, such as cucumber, or fruits, mixed with plain yogurt and salt (in the case of vegetables) or sugar (for fruits).

RAÏTO Also known as *raite* or *rayte*. Provençal condiment which may have originated in Greece. The sauce consists of olive oil and red wine, with tomatoes, onions, crushed walnuts and garlic, flavoured with bay leaf, thyme, parsley, rosemary, fennel and a clove, and sometimes garnished with capers and black (ripe) olives; the mixture is simmered for a long time until very thick, and then strained. It is served very hot with certain fried or sautéed fish dishes, often cod.

RAKI A Turkish aniseed-flavoured apéritif, very similar to the Greek ouzo. The best rakis, with 45–50° alcohol, are made from selected aged brandies; some, like the Greek mastika, have mastic (resin of the mastic tree) added. Raki should be served cold. Traditionally, it is drunk neat from a small glass in small sips, alternated with mouthfuls of iced water.

RAMADAN The ninth month of the Muslim lunar year, during which the faithful must fast from dawn until dusk. During this period, a Muslim must not drink (except to rinse the mouth out), eat, smoke, have sexual relations or apply perfume during the daytime. A meal is eaten at sundown, usually consisting of soup (*harira*), hard-boiled (hard-cooked) eggs, dates and sweet cakes. After evening prayer and before it is time to fast again, just before dawn, a second meal is eaten; this may include pancakes, honey and sometimes also soup (*bazine*, made from semolina with butter and lemon juice added, or *halalim*, made of pulses and herbs and containing sausages, lamb or veal and dumplings made from leavened semolina). Halfway through the month, a traditional meal is served; in Morocco, for instance, this consists of *pastilla*, roast chicken with lemon, and a sweet pastry. The end of Ramadan is celebrated by a feast, during which a sheep is ritually roasted.

RAMAIN, PAUL French doctor (born Thonon, 1895; died Douvaine, 1966). He liked to describe himself as an 'independent provincial gastronome' and was a great connoisseur of wines, choosing for his motto 'Jamais en vain, toujours en vin!'

A well-known mycologist, he was the author of *Mycogastronomie* (1953), which is still regarded as an authority and which gives some very good, little-known mushroom recipes. Writing on the best wines to accompany meals, he suggests that all good meals could well be accompanied solely by 'excellent authentic champagnes', ranging from the blanc de blancs to the blanc de rouges or the *oeil de perdrix* (pink champagne). But he also recommends locally grown wines and mentions a meal he ate in Aveyron of an 'extremely high gastronomic standard', accompanied by an old Cahors wine; apparently the wine and the food together created 'a faultless gustatory and olfactory symphony'.

Ramain offers this last admonition: 'Between each wine and each dish one should drink a mouthful of pure fresh water, preferably not (or only slightly) aerated.'

RAMBUTAN A fruit, belonging to the same family as the lychee, originating in Malaysia and very common throughout South-East Asia. Crimson, green, orange or yellow in colour, the thick shell is covered with hooked hairs and has a translucent sweet pulp that is more acidic but also more aromatic thanthat of the lychee. The fruit is available fresh in November and December and can be bought canned in syrup all the year round. The rambutan is eaten peeled, in fruit salads, but can also accompany poultry or pork.

RAMEKIN A small, round, straight-sided soufflé dish, 8–10 cm (3–4 in) in diameter, in ovenproof china or glass; it is used to cook and serve individual portions of a variety of hot entrées: small cheese, seafood or fish soufflés, eggs *en cocotte à la crème*, or *aux fines herbes*. It is equally useful for serving aspics (particularly eggs *en gelée*, served unmoulded), as well as for cold creams and custards, which may or may not be unmoulded.

In former times, a ramekin was a slice of toasted bread spread with 'meat, kidneys, cheese, onions, or garlic cloves' (according to La Varenne), moistened with cream, and, as was often done with various dishes, 'sprinkled with soot from the chimney'. Nowadays, the word is still used in the Swiss canton of Vaud for a type of toasted cheese. The word is derived from *ramken*, the diminutive of the German *rahm* (fresh cream): thus it came to mean 'a little dish with cream'. Later on, it denoted either a tartlet filled with a cream cheese or a type of gougère (choux pastry) sometimes made in a small mould.

Two French regional specialities are still called 'ramekin', used in its old sense: the *ramequin douaisien* (baked bread rolls, stuffed with a mixture of chopped kidney, breadcrumbs soaked in milk, eggs and herbs) and the *ramequin du pays de Gex* (a blue cheese – Bleu du Haut Jura – and Gruyère cheese melted together in a saucepan with stock, red wine, butter, garlic and mustard, served like a fondue with cubes of bread).

RECIPES

ramekin

Pour 250 ml (8 fl oz, 1 cup) milk into a saucepan and season with a generous pinch of salt, a small pinch of sugar and a little white pepper. Add 25 g (1 oz, 2 tablespoons) butter and bring to the boil. As soon as the milk begins to boil, move the pan half off the heat and mix in 100 g (4 oz, 1 cup) sifted plain (all-purpose) flour. Return to the heat and stir vigorously with a wooden spoon, as for choux paste, until the mixture has dried out. When it is quite dry, take the pan off the heat and add 3 eggs, one by one, and 50 g (2 oz, ½ cup) finely diced Gruyère cheese. Put this paste into a piping (pastry) bag with a plain nozzle and pipe small buns on to a baking sheet. Brush with beaten egg and sprinkle with tiny pieces of Gruyère. Bake the ramekin in a preheated oven at 190°C (375°F, gas 5) for 15 minutes.

jellied eggs in ramekins

Arrange 2 blanched leaves of tarragon in a cross shape in the bottom of each ramekin dish. Coat the inside of each ramekin with a little tarragon-flavoured meat aspic and leave in the refrigerator to set. Then put in a small slice of very good ham, cut to the shape of the dish. Arrange a shelled soft-boiled (soft-cooked) egg on top, fill the dish with aspic and leave to set in the refrigerator. Unmould just before serving.

ramekin vaudois

Cut some thin slices from a large white loaf and slice some Gruyère cheese – 300 g (11 oz) of each. Arrange alternate slices of bread and cheese in a buttered gratin dish. Beat together 2 eggs and 500 ml (17 fl oz, 2 cups) milk, season with salt, pepper and nutmeg, and pour the mixture over the bread and cheese (the liquid should half-fill the dish). Dot with butter and cook in a preheated oven at 190°C (375°F, gas 5) for 25 minutes.

RAMPION A plant of the campanula family with edible roots. These may be eaten raw in salads, for which they are cut into pieces and usually mixed with beetroot (red beet) or celery; or they can be cooked in the same way as salsify or turnips. The leaves, which have a refreshing taste, can also be eaten in salads or cooked like spinach. Rampion is rarely used in cooking today.

RAMPONEAUX, JEAN Also known as Ramponneau. Parisian innkeeper and restaurateur (born Vignol, 1724; died Paris, 1802). As his wine cost 1 sou per pint less than that sold by his fellow innkeepers in the Courtille du Temple, at the lower end of Belleville, he attracted a lot of 'curious idlers hoping for a cheap drink', as Grimm commented in 1760. A number of prints from that period show the interior of the Tambour Royal, as his inn was called, and it was the subject of poems and songs.

His son took over this flourishing business, and Jean opened a restaurant in the Chaussée d'Antin, with tables for 600 diners, called La Grand-Pinte. Filled with confidence over his successful ventures, Ramponeaux tried to make a name for himself in the world of the theatre; here, however, he failed. La Grand-Pinte was closed in 1851.

A restaurant in the Avenue Marceau is named after Ramponeaux.

RANCID Describing stale fat or fatty foods which have developed a strong smell and an acrid taste, due to oxidation of the fat. Rancidity is accelerated by exposure to light, high temperatures and metallic contamination.

RANCIO Term used to describe wines of the *vin doux naturel* type, which owe their special taste to ageing in cask over several years, in theory under the sun; the resulting oxidation produces a very smooth wine.

RANGE A large stove with hotplates or burners and one or more ovens, heated by solid fuel, oil, gas or electricity. The range was originally made of masonry, and then of either thick sheet metal or cast iron. It is the main basic piece of equipment in a kitchen, especially in the restaurant trade. The range often has a polished cast-iron hotplate and pans can be moved along easily to the desired position. A hot-water boiler may also be heated by this type of stove. There are also models modified for use in a large kitchen: 'browning' ranges, 'live-fire' ranges and 'simmering-plate' ranges.

The first ranges appeared in the 18th century and caused a revolution in the kitchen by replacing the large fireplace, which, until then, was the only source of heat available. The introduction of the range meant that several sources of heat at different temperatures were available, and several dishes requiring different temperatures could be cooked at the same time, so items could be roasted, boiled, simmered or simply kept warm. It is no accident that the 18th century is noted for the invention of so many new dishes. Another decisive development occurred at the end of the 18th century, when the cast-iron range, which burned coal, replaced the wood-burning stove. However, the problem of ventilation was still causing concern and led Carême to comment, 'Coal is killing us.' In the 1850s in London, the chef Soyer introduced the gas cooker, and today most stoves are heated by either gas or electricity.

RAPE A plant related to the cabbage that is widely cultivated for the oil contained in its seeds, although they also contain toxins that have to be removed. Rapeseed oil cannot be heated to very high temperatures, but it keeps well and remains in a liquid state down to freezing point. The flower buds of rape may be eaten in the same way as broccoli.

RASCASSE See *scorpion fish*.

RAS EL HANOUT A complex mixture of twenty or more ground spices, used mainly in Morocco, Algeria and Tunisia. The mixture varies but may typically include cardamom, cumin, ginger, cinnamon, cloves, black pepper, turmeric, coriander, nutmeg, chilli and wild herbs. The Tunisian version is generally less hot and is perfumed with dried rosebuds. The literal meaning is 'head' or 'top of the shop'.

Ras el hanout is used to season soups and stews, and is known as a flavouring for the broth which accompanies couscous. It is also used in many other North African dishes.

RASPBERRY The fruit of the raspberry cane, which grows wild in the woods or can be cultivated in the garden. In Europe and America, it is cultivated in open soil or under frames.

The raspberry has been known since prehistoric times and the Ancients attributed its origin to divine intervention: the nymph Ida pricked her finger while picking berries for the young Jupiter and thus raspberries, which had been white until then, turned red. Raspberries have been cultivated since the Middle Ages; although cultivation methods were improved in the 18th century, the fruit did not become widely cultivated until the 20th century.

Raspberries are oval or conical in shape, rather small, and have a sweet, slightly acid, flavour. They are usually fairly dark red, but yellow-coloured varieties have also been produced, as have orange, pink, purple and black. Greenhouse raspberries are marketed from mid-April onwards but do not have the delicious flavour of those grown in open soil from mid-June to October. Raspberries must always be firm, plump and ripe when they have a delicious flavour. The fruits are delicate and must be handled carefully: they do not keep for very long.

Regarded as a dessert fruit *par excellence*, the raspberry can be eaten with sugar or cream. Raspberries are used to make flans, desserts, jam, compotes, jellies, syrups, fermented drinks, liqueurs and brandy, and raspberry juice can be used to flavour ice creams and sorbets. The fruit can be preserved in syrup or brandy, and can also be frozen, although the fruit becomes soft once it is defrosted. It is best to freeze raspberries by open-freezing on trays or by freezing them in sugar (dry pack), or making the bruised or slightly poor-quality ones into purée, made in the same way as strawberry purée.

The loganberry is a cross between a blackberry and a raspberry. It is an American hybrid named after James H. Logan, who first grew it in California in 1881. The loganberry is a large, juicy, dark-red fruit and is marketed in September and October. It also has a tart flavour, but is considered by some people to be less delicious than the raspberry.

Other hybrids of more recent origin include the tayberry (named after a river in Scotland) and the boysenberry (named after its inventor).

RECIPES

raspberry barquettes
Prepare some barquettes (boat-shaped tartlets) of shortcrust pastry (basic pie dough) and leave them to cool. Spread a little confectioner's custard (pastry cream) in each tartlet and top with fresh raspberries. Coat the fruit with some warmed redcurrant or raspberry jelly.

raspberry charlotte
Line a charlotte mould with sponge fingers (ladyfingers) soaked in raspberry-flavoured syrup. Whip some fresh cream with caster (superfine) sugar and vanilla sugar. Add an equal quantity of raspberry purée made with either fresh or frozen raspberries. Fill the lined mould with the mixture and cover with a layer of sponge fingers, also soaked in raspberry syrup. Press the sponge fingers down, put a plate over the mould and chill for at least 3 hours. Invert on to a plate just before serving.

raspberry jam

Select firm ripe fruit and remove the stems. Put them into a preserving pan. For each 1 kg (2¼ lb) fruit, make a syrup with 1 kg (2¼ lb, 4½ cups) sugar, boiled to the 'soft ball' stage. Pour the syrup over the raspberries, bring back to the boil, cook gently for 5–6 minutes, then remove from the heat. Put the jam into clean, sterilized jars, cover, seal, label and store.

raspberry jelly

This is made with equal quantities of redcurrants and raspberries. Pour the redcurrants into a pan and add 120 ml (4½ fl oz, ½ cup) water per 1 kg (2¼ lb) fruit. Boil until the berries soften and the juice comes out. Leave to cool, then place the redcurrants and raspberries in a cloth over a bowl and twist the cloth to extract the juice (for a very clear jelly, pour the fruit into a jelly bag and leave to drip overnight). Pour the juice into a pan, add 1 kg (2¼ lb, 4½ cups, firmly packed) sugar per 1 litre (1¾ pints, 4⅓ cups) fruit juice, and boil quickly until setting point is reached. Remove from the heat and pour immediately into clean, sterilized jars. Cover, seal and label.

other recipes See *compote, fig, peach, sorbet, soufflé, tart.*

RASSOINICK A Russian soup made from poultry stock flavoured with cucumber, thickened with egg yolk and cream, and garnished with cucumber cut into shapes and finely diced pieces of poultry meat (classically duck). A richer version is made by adding brisket of beef and vegetables, such as beetroot (red beet), leeks and cabbage to the stock. The soup is thickened with cream and beetroot juice, seasoned with fennel and parsley, then garnished with the diced meat and possibly small grilled (broiled) sausages.

RASTEAU A village in the southern Rhône producing red, white and rosé wines sold as Côtes-du-Rhône Villages. The AOC relates to *vins doux naturels* made from Grenache.

RASTEGAÏ A small, oval, Russian patty made of puff pastry and normally filled with a mixture of sturgeon spinal marrow, hard-boiled (hard-cooked) egg and fresh salmon. It is served with melted butter as a hot entrée or as part of the *zakuski* (hors d'oeuvre).

RATAFIA A home-made liqueur produced by macerating plants or fruit in sweetened spirit; some traditional ingredients are: angelica, cherries, blackcurrants, quinces, raspberries, walnuts, oranges and cherry kernels.

The name is also given to a sweet apéritif made in the French provinces: this is a mixture of two-thirds fresh grape juice (must) and one-third brandy. These liqueurs are mostly intended for home consumption, but some have achieved a higher status, such as Pineau from Charentes, the Floc of Gascony and the Ratafia Champenois from the Champagne region.

The word is of Creole French origin; it formerly referred to the alcoholic drink which clinched an agreement or a business transaction and is said to be derived from the Latin phrase *rata fiat* (let the deal be settled).

RATATOUILLE A vegetable stew typical of Provençal cookery, originally from Nice, which is now found all over south-east France and is popular abroad. The word, derived from the French *touiller* (to mix or stir), at first designated an unappetizing stew.

A ratatouille from Nice (*ratatouille niçoise*) is made from onions, courgettes (zucchini), aubergines (eggplants), sweet (bell) peppers and tomatoes simmered in olive oil with herbs. It accompanies roasts, sautéed chicken or small cuts of meat, as well as braised fish, omelettes and scrambled eggs. According to the purists, the different vegetables should be cooked separately, then combined and cooked together until they attain a smooth, creamy consistency.

RECIPE

ratatouille niçoise

Trim the ends of 6 courgettes (zucchini) and cut them into rounds (do not peel them). Peel and slice 2 onions. Cut the stalks from 3 green (bell) peppers, remove the seeds and cut them into strips. Peel 6 tomatoes, cut each into 6 pieces and seed them. Peel and crush 3 garlic cloves. Peel 6 aubergines (eggplants) and cut them into rounds. Heat 6 tablespoons olive oil in a cast-iron pan. Brown the aubergines in this, then add the peppers, tomatoes and onions, and finally the courgettes and the garlic. Add a large bouquet garni containing plenty of thyme, salt and pepper. Cook over a low heat for about 30 minutes. Add 2 tablespoons fresh olive oil and continue to cook until the desired consistency is reached. Remove the bouquet garni and serve very hot.

RATON The former name for a small tartlet filled with either sweetened cream cheese or confectioner's custard (pastry cream). A *raton* can also be made with a mixture of flour, sugar, crushed macaroni, pounded almonds, eggs and milk; this is cooked in a pie dish, turned over halfway through cooking and served hot.

Nicolas de Bonnefons, in his *Délices de la campagne* (1650), gives another recipe using puff pastry (quoted by P. Androuet in *La Cuisine au fromage*): during the last turn and rolling, a well-drained cream cheese is incorporated into the dough, which is rolled out, cut into small rectangles, brushed with beaten egg, sprinkled with grated cheese and baked.

RAVE In France, the word *rave* is used loosely for several vegetables regarded as having a low culinary status, such as kohlrabi, turnips, swedes and black radishes. In former times, the name was applied to all root vegetables (*racines*), as opposed to *herbes* (leaf vegetables).

RAVIGOTE A spicy sauce served hot or cold but always highly seasoned. Cold ravigote is a vinaigrette mixed with capers, chopped herbs and chopped onion. The hot sauce is made by adding veal velouté sauce to equal quantities of white wine and wine vinegar, reduced with chopped shallots; it is finished with chopped herbs and served particularly with calf's head and brains and boiled fowl. Savoury butter and mayonnaise *à la ravigote* are flavoured with chopped herbs and shallots, and sometimes with mustard.

RECIPE

ravigote sauce (cold)
Prepare 120 ml (4½ fl oz, ½ cup) plain vinaigrette* with mustard. Add ½ teaspoon chopped tarragon, 1 teaspoon chopped parsley, 1 teaspoon fines herbes, 2 teaspoons chervil, 1 finely chopped small onion and 1 tablespoon dried and chopped capers.

RAVIOLE Also known as *raviolle*. A dish from Nice and Corsica consisting of small square pockets of pasta stuffed with chopped spinach, Swiss chard or cream cheese and cooked in water. The word may come from the Latin *rapum* (turnip), as a *raviole* was formerly a small meat and turnip pie, but it seems more likely that it has the same derivation as ravioli, which is a very similar dish.

*Raviole*s also exist in Savoyard cookery: these are small dumplings made of spinach, Swiss chard, flour, fresh Tomme cheese and eggs, poached in water, then browned and served with tomato sauce.

RAVIOLI An Italian dish consisting of small square envelopes of pasta dough enclosing a meat or vegetable stuffing, cooked in boiling water and usually served with tomato sauce and grated cheese. Very small ravioli may be used as a garnish for soup. Agnolotti, a variation from Piedmont, are cut into rounds. The stuffing may be made from chopped veal or beef, chicken livers, calves' sweetbreads, or vegetables only, especially spinach.

It is said that ravioli originally came from Liguria and were invented as a means of using up leftover food, hence their original name, *rabiole* (bits and pieces, odds and ends, in Genoese dialect), which later became 'ravioli'. Whether or not leftovers are used, the ingredients of good ravioli must always be varied: one Genoese recipe includes lean bacon, basil, carrots, celery, finely sliced roast chicken, chopped loin of veal, mortadella and Parmesan cheese. Ravioli is one of the best-known stuffed pasta dishes, famous well beyond the shores of Italy. Fresh ravioli can be bought, ready to poach and serve with a sauce, and it is also available ready-prepared.

RECIPES

preparation and cooking of ravioli
Make some pasta dough with eggs and roll it out thinly into 2 equal rectangles. Using a piping (pastry) bag, pipe small quantities of the chosen stuffing on to one of the rectangles of dough, placing them in rows about 4 cm (1½ in) apart. Moisten the dough between the heaps of stuffing with the fingertips. Place the second rectangle of dough over the first and gently press them together around the heaps of stuffing. Using a pastry (cookie) wheel or ravioli cutter, cut down and across the rows, producing small square envelopes of dough enclosing the stuffing. Dry in a cool place for 3–4 hours, then cook in boiling salted water for 8–10 minutes. Drain them and either treat them as a gratin or warm them through in tomato sauce.

stuffings for ravioli
• *chicken liver* Sauté 150 g (5 oz) chicken livers in butter with 1 chopped shallot, a little garlic and a pinch of salt, then finely chop and mix with 100 g (4 oz, 1 cup) blanched and pressed spinach, 1 desalted anchovy fillet, and 50 g (2 oz, ¼ cup) butter. Mix these ingredients well together, working in 1 lightly beaten egg and a pinch each of dried basil, salt, pepper and nutmeg. The chicken livers can be replaced by braised veal and the spinach by Swiss chard leaves (blanched, pressed and stewed in butter).
• *meat and cheese* Finely chop 200 g (7 oz) cooked veal or chicken, 100 g (4 oz) mortadella and 100 g (4 oz) lettuce leaves, blanched, pressed and braised in butter. Add 50 g (2 oz, ½ cup) grated Parmesan cheese, 1 egg, a pinch of salt, a pinch of pepper and a little grated nutmeg. Stir well.
• *meat and vegetable* Finely chop 150 g (5 oz) beef en daube* or à la mode*, or braised beef. Add 100 g (4 oz, 1 cup) blanched spinach, pressed and chopped; 50 g (2 oz) veal brains, lightly cooked in butter; 1 shallot and 1 large onion, chopped, then softened in butter; 1 egg; and 50 g (2 oz, ½ cup) of grated Parmesan cheese. Stir well. Season with salt, pepper and nutmeg.
• *spinach* Chop 300 g (11 oz) raw spinach and braise in 25 g (1 oz, 2 tablespoons) butter. Season with salt, pepper and nutmeg. Add 50 g (2 oz) ricotta and stir. Add 50 g (2 oz, ½ cup) grated Parmesan cheese and 1 egg yolk. Stir well.

foie gras ravioli ♦
Finely dice 75 g (3 oz) carrot, 65 g (2½ oz) celery and just over 25 g (1 oz) black truffle as for a brunoise. Set aside a little carrot, celery and truffle for the garnish, then sweat the remainder of the ingredients in a little goose fat. Remove from the heat. Add 1 teaspoon truffle-flavoured oil, 1 teaspoon truffle juice and 25 g (1 oz) chopped parsley. Set aside. Blanch the reserved vegetables with 1 tablespoon finely diced courgette (zucchini) for a few seconds, drain and set aside. Reduce 2 litres

(3½ pints, 9 cups) chicken consommé to half its original volume.

Prepare 32 squares of pasta, each measuring 10 cm (4 in). Cut 250 g (9 oz) raw foie gras into 4 evenly thick escalopes, then cut each into quarters. Fill the ravioli with the foie gras. Poach the ravioli in simmering salted water for about 5 minutes, then drain and arrange on soup plates or bowls. Stir the sweated vegetables into the reduced consommé and taste for seasoning, then ladle it over the ravioli. Garnish with the reserved diced vegetables and serve.

lobster ravioli with a glazed coral sauce
Stuff 20 squares of pasta with a mixture of diced lobster and a duxelles of mushrooms, bound with 250 ml (8 fl oz, 1 cup) lobster bisque*. Reduce 250 ml (8 fl oz, 1 cup) bisque and 500 ml (17 fl oz, 2 cups) white wine sauce, and bind with 200 ml (7 fl oz, ¾ cup) hollandaise* sauce and 200 ml (7 fl oz, ¾ cup) whipped cream. Sweat 1 kg (2¼ lb) spinach in butter. Poach the stuffed ravioli for 2 minutes in simmering salted water. Put the spinach in 4 soup bowls or gratin dishes. Arrange the ravioli on top, cover with sauce and brown under a grill (broiler). Garnish each plate with 1 medallion of lobster and 3 claws.

ravioli of daube of duck with red wine
Cook 1 duck in a casserole in 60 ml (2 fl oz, ¼ cup) oil with 2 chopped onions and 2 thinly sliced carrots. Add 1 litre (1¾ pints, 4⅓ cups) red wine, salt, pepper and 1 bouquet garni halfway through the cooking. Reserve the duck in a warm place and finish the sauce by thickening it with a mixture of 25 g (1 oz, ¼ cup) plain (all-purpose) flour and 25 g (1 oz, 2 tablespoons) butter. Joint and debone the duck. Chop coarsely. Incorporate 20 g (¾ oz) chopped, stoned (pitted) olives and a little sauce. Brush 10 x 10 cm (4 x 4 in) squares of pasta with egg white. Put the stuffing on the moistened sides of half the squares and cover with the remaining squares, moistened sides down. Press the edges together. Cook the ravioli for 2 minutes in simmering salted water. Pour the remaining sauce on top and garnish with chervil. Serve immediately.

ravioli with herbs
Pour 1 kg (2¼ lb) strong plain (bread) flour into a circle. In the middle put 4 eggs, 2 teaspoons salt (or to taste), 100 ml (4 fl oz, scant ½ cup) olive oil and 500 ml (17 fl oz, 2 cups) of water. Gradually mix the flour with the other ingredients: the dough should be quite soft. Cover and leave it to rest for at least1 hour.

Blanch 1 kg (2¼ lb) Swiss chard, 500 g (18 oz) spinach and 100 g (4 oz) parsley for 5 minutes, refresh, then drain thoroughly. Sauté 250 g (9 oz) chanterelles in oil, add the vegetables and 3 garlic cloves, then chop everything finely and season with salt and pepper.

Make the ravioli. Bring a large saucepan of salted water containing 1 tablespoon olive oil to the boil, drop in the ravioli and poach gently. Drain them on a cloth and serve with melted butter and grated cheese. They can also be accompanied by a sauce made with raw tomato pulp, chopped chives, lemon juice and olive oil.

small ravioli for soup
Make some ravioli, fill with chicken-liver or calf's-brain stuffing, then cut into 2 cm (¾ in) squares. After poaching, divide them among plates of clear soup or consommé just before serving.

RAZOR-SHELL Also known as razor clam. A sand-burrowing bivalve mollusc with an elongated tubular shell. It can be made to come to the surface of its burrow by placing a little coarse salt at the opening of the hole. The two main types are the straight razor-shell, which is 10–20 cm (4–8 in) long, and the curved razor-shell, which is 10–15 cm (4–6 in) long. They may be eaten either raw or cooked (after cleaning).

REBIBES Thin shavings of cheese with an extra-hard crust from the Swiss Pré-Alps.

REBLOCHON A cow's-milk cheese made in Savoy (50% fat content), with a pressed uncooked curd and a washed rind, yellow, pink or orange in colour. It is very pliable, creamy and fine-textured, with a sweet nutty taste, and was known in the 15th century. Its name comes from the French verb *reblocher*, meaning 'to milk a second time', because the cheese used to be made in the Alpine meadows from the last milk to be drawn from the cow, which is very rich in fat. Since 1958 it has been protected by an AOC, now AOP, applying to the districts of Annecy, Bonneville, Saint-Julien-en-Genevois and Thonon (in the department of Haute-Savoie), and Albertville and Saint-Jean-de-Maurienne (in the neighbouring department of Savoie). It is shaped like a flat disc 13 cm (5 in) in diameter and 2.5 cm (1 in) thick; there is also a smaller version, 9 cm (3½ in) in diameter and 3 cm (1¼ in) thick. It is made both on farms and in dairies and can be eaten from May to October.

REBOUX, PAUL French writer and journalist (born Henri Amillet, Paris, 1877; died Nice, 1963). He was the author of several recipe books, including *Plats nouveaux, 300 recettes inédites ou singulières* (1927), *Plats du jour* (1936) and *Le Nouveau Savoir-Manger* (1941), which were much criticized by chefs of the classic cuisine; he was, however, a pioneer and an enlightened lover of good food. He wrote a memorable homage to mustard: 'A touch of these mustards brings out the flavour of Gruyère cheese, seasons a salad, gives a lift to white sauces, and

Foie gras ravioli, see page 969.

gives style to a ragoût. The hors d'oeuvre is the first dish to feel their good effect, which ceases only with the dessert.'

RÉCHAUD 18th-century French chef. He was praised by Grimod de La Reynière in the *Manuel des amphitryons* (1808), who mentioned his spinach with goose fat and placed him in the same rank as the 'great Morillon', his father's head chef. He also gave this biographical detail: 'The late M. Réchaud, famous chef to the last Prince of Condé, founder of one of the foremost schools of the last century.'

REDCURRANT A shrub of the genus *Ribes* that is cultivated for its fruit – small, red, acid-tasting berries growing in clusters of 7–20. (The white currant is a variety producing slightly sweeter white berries – it is prepared and used in the same way as the redcurrant.) Redcurrants were introduced into France from Scandinavia in the Middle Ages. In France they are now cultivated principally in the Rhône valley and (on a smaller scale) on the Côte d'Or and in the Loire valley.

Redcurrants are rich in citric acid (which gives them their acid taste) and pectin. They are mostly used to make jams and jellies. The fruit can also be eaten raw, sprinkled with sugar, either alone or in fruit salads. It freezes well and is also used to make sauces, syrups, cold desserts and tarts. A speciality in France is Bar-le-Duc jelly, made with red- and white currants: the pips are removed from the fruit by hand with a quill – a technique invented in the 14th century.

RECIPES

redcurrant jelly (1)
Use either all redcurrants or two-thirds redcurrants and one-third white currants. Weigh 100 g (4⅔ oz) raspberries for each 1 kg (2¼ lb) currants.

Crush the currants and raspberries together and strain them through a cloth which is wrung at both ends. Measure the juice. Allow 1 kg (2¼ lb, 4½ cups) granulated sugar for each 1 litre (1¾ pints, 4⅓ cups) fruit juice. Heat the sugar in a pan with a little water – just enough in which to dissolve the sugar. Add the fruit juice and cook until setting point is reached, then pot and cover as usual.

redcurrant jelly (2)
Put the prepared and weighed currants in a pan, add a small glass of water for each 1 kg (2¼ lb) currants, then heat them gently until the skins burst and the juices come out. Add raspberries (the same proportion as in the recipe above) and boil for a few seconds only. Strain the fruit and filter the juice. Continue as described above.

redcurrant sorbet
Slowly dissolve 175 g (6 oz, ¾ cup) granulated sugar in 450 ml (¾ pint, 2 cups) water. Bring the syrup to the boil and boil steadily for 10 minutes.

Cool. Mix 500 ml (17 fl oz, 2 cups) filtered redcurrant juice with 500 ml (17 fl oz, 2 cups) sugar syrup. Add a few drops of lemon juice and mix well. Then freeze the sorbet in the usual way (see *sorbet*).

redcurrants in a tulip ♦
Using a spatula, spread 250 g (9 oz) tuile* dough in circles 12 cm (4¾ in) in diameter. Cook in a preheated oven at 230°C (450°F, gas 8) until lightly coloured, then shape by pressing on to an upturned bowl. Leave to cool. Soak 1½ sheets of gelatine in cold water. Finely chop ¼ bunch of basil. Heat 300 g (11 oz, 1¾ cups) strawberries with 40 g (1½ oz, 3 tablespoons) sugar and bring to the boil. Simmer for 8–10 minutes, crushing the fruit coarsely with a fork. Incorporate half the basil and put in a cool place. Whip 300 ml (½ pint, 1¼ cups) whipping cream to make a Chantilly*, adding 25 g (1 oz, 2 tablespoons) caster (superfine) sugar. Then, very delicately, add 300 g (11 oz, 1½ cups) redcurrants and the rest of the basil. Pour a little basil-flavoured strawberry coulis on to each plate and garnish with a tulip filled with redcurrant cream. Decorate with peaks of crème fraîche and a few redcurrants.

additional recipe See *compote*.

REDFISH A fish, also called Norway haddock, related to the scorpion fish. There are two main varieties: the smaller one lives in the Mediterranean and in the Atlantic as far north as the River Loire; the larger one is found in the North Atlantic and in colder waters. The redfish has a large spiny head, like the scorpion fish, but lacks spines on its fins. It is bright pink with a silvery sheen and the inside of its mouth is black or bright red. The fish is plumper than the scorpion fish and there is less waste (40–50%) when it is prepared for cooking. It has lean firm flesh and is tastier than the scorpion fish. It yields very good fillets which taste like crab.

RED KIDNEY BEAN Variety of bean eaten widely in the USA, Spain and the West Indies in its dried form. Red kidney beans accompany chilli con carne, the beef ragoût typical of the cooking of the pioneers of Texas. In France, where they are cultivated a little, they are often cooked with red wine and bacon. Dried red kidney beans have to be soaked, boiled for 10 minutes and then simmered in unsalted water for about 1 hour or until tender.

RECIPE

red beans à la bourguignonne
Soak and drain red kidney beans, then boil them for 10 minutes and drain. Cook the beans with a little streaky bacon in equal quantities of water and red wine until tender. When the beans are cooked,

Redcurrants in a tulip.

drain them a little and place in a deep sauté pan. Cut some bacon into dice, cook gently in butter, then add to the pan. Thicken with beurre manié and season to taste.

REDUCE To concentrate or thicken a liquid such as a sauce or stock by boiling, which evaporates some of the water and reduces the volume. The time required will depend on the quantity of liquid and the degree of concentration desired. It takes longest to reduce a liquid to a glaze, thick and shining, so that it will coat the back of a spoon. The aim of reducing a sauce is to improve its flavour, smoothness and consistency.

For some sauces, reduction is a preliminary operation and precedes the main preparation; it is designed to obtain a concentrated essence of white wine or vinegar (sometimes both together) or of red wine with chopped shallots or a herb such as tarragon: béarnaise and bordelaise sauces and beurre blanc are prepared in this way.

When deglazing a roasting pan to prepare a sauce or gravy to accompany the meat, the fat is skimmed off and the caramelized juices are diluted with wine or double (heavy) cream; when white wine is used, it is essential to reduce the liquid so as to remove the acidity. Clear or thickened stock is then poured into the pan and the reduction is continued until the gravy or sauce has reached the desired consistency and taste.

RED WINE See *wine*.

RE-EMULSIFY To restore a homogeneous consistency to a sauce which has curdled. Mayonnaise can be re-emulsified by adding it drop by drop to any one of the following: an egg yolk, a little mustard or a few drops of vinegar or water, while constantly beating the sauce. Hollandaise or béarnaise sauce can be reconstituted in the same way by adding a little water – hot if the sauce is cold, cold if the sauce is hot.

REFORM SAUCE An English sauce, originating from the Reform Club in London, based on an espagnole sauce well seasoned with black pepper and with the addition of gherkins, hard-boiled (hardcooked) egg whites, mushrooms, pickled tongue and truffle. It is traditionally served with lamb cutlets or may be used to fill an omelette. The sauce can also be prepared using the same ingredients but with a base of game sauce (half poivrade and half demi-glace with redcurrant jelly added); it is served with game cutlets and small single cuts of venison.

REFRESH To run cold water over food which has just been blanched or cooked in water, in order to cool it down rapidly and prevent further cooking or softening in texture.

RÉGALADE, À LA Describing a method of drinking which consists of pouring the liquid into the mouth without letting the container (usually a flask or a long-necked wine bottle) touch the lips. The word originates from the Old French *gale* (making merry), from which *régaler* (to regale, entertain) also derives.

RÉGENCE The name given to various elaborate dishes associated with the style of cooking of the Regency period in France. Régence garnish consists of quenelles (fish, poultry or veal, according to the main dish), poached mushroom caps and slivers of truffle. Poached oysters may be added for fish dishes, and slices of foie gras for meat, offal (variety meats) or poultry dishes; fish dishes are masked with normande sauce flavoured with truffle essence, and meat dishes with a suprême or allemande sauce. Régence sauce was formerly served with calves' sweetbreads and poached or braised fowl.

RECIPES

calves' sweetbreads régence
Prepare the sweetbreads, stud them with truffles and braise them in white stock. Meanwhile, make some large chicken quenelles with truffles and sauté some slices of foie gras in butter. Prepare an allemande sauce using the reduced braising liquor from the sweetbreads. Arrange the sweetbreads on a hot dish and surround them with the quenelles and foie gras slices. Garnish with slivers of truffle tossed in butter and coat with the sauce.

régence sauce
Coarsely dice 100 g (4 oz, ¾ cup) lean ham and cut 1 onion into quarters; melt 50 g (2 oz, ¼ cup) butter in a saucepan and cook the ham and onion without letting them brown. When the onion is almost cooked, add 1 sliced shallot. Deglaze the pan with 100 ml (4 fl oz, 7 tablespoons) Graves wine; reduce by two-thirds, then add 200 ml (7 fl oz, ¾ cup) white chicken stock. Reduce further until the sauce coats the back of a spoon, then strain.

RÉGNIÉ AOC Beaujolais growth, the most recent of the ten growths of the region, with red berry bouquet, supple and elegant (see *Beaujolais*).

REGRATER A person who used to buy food from great houses and restaurants for resale. The food might consist of cooked dishes, leftover meat and pieces of pastry or cake. The word comes from the French *gratter* (to collect); it is now obsolete in English. In his book *La Vie privée d'autrefois*, Alfred Franklin describes this ancient trade, originally an honourable one, which had by the 19th century fallen to dealing in restaurant surplus and scraps. During the 14th century the regraters were almost comparable to modern grocers: 'If the housewife is in a hurry, and will put up with having less choice and paying a little more, she can get nearly all her shopping from the same place by going to the regraters, who sell everything and who are supplied by the residents and the convents of the district. There she can buy bread, salt, eggs, cheese, vegetables, sea fish, poultry and game.' It was only with the introduction of restaurants in the 18th century that regraters began to specialize in the resale of leftover cooked dishes.

REHEAT To bring a food back to the correct temperature for eating when it has already been cooked, but has been chilled or cooled. A bain marie heated either on top of the stove or in the oven can be used for this purpose. Some cooked foods, vegetables for instance, can be reheated by putting them in a strainer and immersing them for a few minutes in salted or unsalted boiling water. Other foods (such as gratins or quenelles) may be reheated in the serving dish in a cool oven; stewed foods can be reheated in a saucepan over a low heat, and sautéed dishes over a high heat with added fat.

A liquid or semi-solid food (soup, sauce or salpicon) can be warmed up over a moderate heat, with a wire gauze between flame and pan, and stirred constantly. It is extremely important when reheating food to ensure that it is thoroughly reheated right through, at the same time paying close attention to ensure that it does not boil, dry, stick to the pan or overcook in the oven. Some dishes requiring long, slow cooking improve when reheated and can be prepared one or two days in advance (such as *daubes* and braised dishes).

REIMS BISCUIT A small, light, crunchy, rectangular biscuit (cookie), generously dusted with sugar, 'created at the end of the 18th century by bakers wishing to make use of a hot oven after baking bread. The biscuit was originally white; it was only later that biscuit manufacturers decided to colour it pink and flavour it with vanilla. Note that the natives of Reims disdain to use the pink biscuits, preferring the white ones which retain all their natural flavour' (Charles Sarrazin, *La France à table*). The Reims biscuit was intended to accompany champagne, which at that time was very sweet.

RECIPE

Reims biscuits
Whisk 300 g (11 oz, 1⅓ cups) caster (superfine) sugar, 10 egg yolks and 12 egg whites together in a saucepan and boil over a pan of hot water until pale and thick. Fold in 175 g (6 oz, 1½ cups) sifted plain (all-purpose) flour and 1 tablespoon vanilla sugar. Using a plain piping nozzle, pipe the mixture on to buttered greaseproof (wax) paper into finger shapes, well separated from each other. Bake in a preheated oven at 180°C (350°F, gas 4) for about 10 minutes.

REINDEER A large deer found in Arctic regions. Reindeer milk, like whale milk, has a very high fat content; it is used to make cheese in Lapland, Norway and Sweden. The Lapps rear reindeer, under free-range conditions, for both their milk and their meat. Venison from wild reindeer is cooked in the same way as roebuck; the meat from animals fed on grain and hay has a sweeter taste. The meat is also used to make meatballs and is cooked as steaks or in stews.

REINE, À LA A term applied to a number of elegant and delicate dishes from classic French cuisine, characterized by the presence of chicken (often with calves' sweetbreads, mushrooms and truffles) with suprême sauce. *Reine* is the traditional name for a bird classed between a *poulet de grain* (a medium to large battery chicken) and a *poularde* (caponized hen).

The term *à la reine* is also applied to a very light milk-bread roll.

RECIPES

chicken à la reine
Prepare 500 g (18 oz) panada forcemeat* with butter and use it to stuff a chicken weighing about 1.8 kg (4 lb). Poach it gently in white stock. Bake some puff-pastry tartlet cases and fill them with chicken purée with cream; garnish with sliced truffles. Make a suprême sauce with the chicken stock. Arrange the chicken on a large hot serving dish and place the tartlets round it. Serve the suprême sauce separately.

consommé à la reine
Make some chicken consommé and some plain royale. Then poach some chicken breasts in court-bouillon and shred the meat finely. Thicken the consommé with tapioca. Garnish the soup with the royale cut into dice or lozenges and the shredded chicken.

croûtes à la reine
Prepare some chicken purée with cream. Cut some slices from a white loaf and lightly fry in butter. Spread the croûtes with the purée, sprinkle with white breadcrumbs and clarified butter, then brown in a preheated oven at 240°C (475°F, gas 9).

scrambled eggs à la reine
Make some very thick chicken purée and some suprême sauce. Bake a large vol-au-vent case and keep it hot. Make some scrambled eggs, cooking them gently until creamy. Fill the vol-au-vent case with alternate layers of chicken purée and scrambled eggs. Serve hot, offering the suprême sauce in a sauceboat.

soft-boiled or poached eggs à la reine
Make some tartlet cases using puff pastry or shortcrust pastry (basic pie dough) and cook them blind. Prepare some chicken purée and some suprême sauce. Soft-boil (soft-cook) or poach 1 egg per tartlet. Reheat the tartlets and fill them with the purée; arrange an egg on each one and mask with the suprême sauce.

stuffed tomatoes à la reine

Slice the tops off some large firm tomatoes; scoop out the seeds and core without breaking the skin. Make a salpicon of equal quantities of chicken breast poached in white stock and mushrooms sweated in butter; add a little diced truffle and thicken with some very thick velouté sauce. Stuff the tomatoes with this mixture and place in a buttered gratin dish. Sprinkle with fresh breadcrumbs and clarified butter and cook in a preheated oven at 240°C (475°F, gas 9) for 10–15 minutes.

other recipes See *bouchée (savoury), pannequet.*

RÉJANE The stage name of the great actress Gabrielle Réju (born Paris, 1856; died Paris, 1920), which has been given to various dishes. The Réjane garnish (for small pieces of sautéed meat or braised calves' sweetbreads) consists of cassolettes of duchess potatoes (which act as containers for the meat), buttered leaf spinach, quarters of steamed artichokes and slices of poached bone marrow; the sauce consists of the braising stock or the pan juices deglazed with Madeira.

In a Réjane salad, sliced potatoes are mixed with asparagus tips and a julienne of truffles. Paupiettes of whiting Réjane, arranged on a base of duchess potatoes, are each garnished with a small metal skewer bearing an oyster, a mushroom cap, a slice of truffle and a prawn (shrimp).

RELIGIEUSE A cake classically consisting of a large choux pastry filled with coffee- or chocolate-flavoured confectioner's custard (pastry cream) or Chiboust cream surmounted by a smaller choux pastry, similarly filled; the whole is iced (frosted) with fondant (the same flavour as the filling) and decorated with piped butter cream. The *religieuse* can be made either as a large cake or as small individual cakes. In one former version, the choux pastry was cooked in the form of éclairs, rings or buns, filled with coffee or chocolate cream, and stacked on top of each other or arranged in a pyramid on a base of sweet pastry; the whole was then decorated with piped butter cream. *Religieuse* is a fairly recent invention, which originated in Paris. The name comes from the colour of the icing, which resembles the homespun robe worn by nuns.

Less frequently, the name is given to a puff-pastry tart filled with apple and apricot jams and raisins, and decorated with a lattice of pastry strips, recalling a convent grille.

RECIPES

coffee religieuses

Make some choux* paste with 250 ml (8 fl oz, 1 cup) water, a pinch of salt, 65 g (2½ oz, 5 tablespoons) butter, 1 teaspoon sugar, 125 g (4½ oz, 1 cup) plain (all-purpose) flour and 3–4 eggs. Pipe bun shapes on to a baking sheet so that half of them are twice the size of the others. Bake in a preheated oven at 200°C (400°F, gas 6) for 30 minutes, then leave to cool in the oven with the door ajar.

Make some butter cream with 4 egg yolks, 125 g (4½ oz, ½ cup) caster (superfine) sugar, 60 ml (2 fl oz, ¼ cup) water, 125 g (4½ oz, ½ cup) creamed butter and 1 teaspoon vanilla sugar.

Prepare some Chiboust* cream with 6 egg yolks, 200 g (7 oz, 1 cup) caster sugar, 75 g (3 oz, ¾ cup) flour or 50 g (2 oz, ½ cup) cornflour (cornstarch), 1 litre (1¾ pints, 4⅓ cups) milk, 4 leaves of gelatine and 4 egg whites. Flavour it with ½ teaspoon coffee essence (strong black coffee) and allow to cool completely. Fill all the choux pastries with the Chiboust cream.

Melt 400 g (14 oz) fondant* icing (frosting), flavour it with ½ teaspoon coffee essence and use it to ice all the choux pastries. Before the icing sets, stick the small buns on to the larger ones. Using a piping (pastry) bag with a fluted nozzle, decorate the top of each cake with a rosette of butter cream, then run a ribbon of butter cream around the joint of the 2 buns. Keep in a cool place until ready to serve.

grande religieuse à l'ancienne

Make some sweet pastry with 125 g (4½ oz, 1 cup) plain (all-purpose) flour, 1 egg yolk, a pinch of salt, 40 g (1½ oz, 3 tablespoons) caster (superfine) sugar and 50 g (2 oz, ¼ cup) butter cut into small pieces (see *short pastry*). Roll the pastry into a ball and leave it in a cool place.

Make some choux* paste with 250 ml (8 fl oz, 1 cup) water, 65 g (2½ oz, 5 tablespoons) butter, a pinch of salt, 1 teaspoon sugar, 125 g (4½ oz, 1 cup) plain flour and 3–4 eggs. Using a piping (pastry) bag with a smooth nozzle, 1 cm (½ in) in diameter, pipe on to a baking sheet 12 strips 10 cm (4 in) long, 1 small round bun, and 4 rings decreasing in size from a diameter of 15 cm (6 in). Bake in a preheated oven at 200°C (400°F, gas 6) for 30 minutes, then leave to cool in the oven with the door ajar.

Meanwhile, butter a deep 19-cm (7½-in) sandwich tin (layer cake pan), using 25 g (1 oz, 2 tablespoons) butter. Roll out the sweet pastry to a thickness of 3 mm (⅛ in) and use it to line the sandwich tin; prick the bottom, cover with dried haricot (navy) beans and bake blind for 10 minutes. Remove the beans, leave to cool, then turn it out of the tin.

Prepare some butter cream by boiling 60 ml (2 fl oz, ¼ cup) water with 125 g (4½ oz, generous ½ cup) caster sugar; when the temperature reaches 110°C (225°F), pour slowly on to 4 egg yolks and whisk briskly until the mixture is cold; then whisk in 150 g (5 oz, ⅔ cup) softened butter.

Prepare some Chiboust* cream with 6 egg yolks, 200 g (7 oz, 1 cup) caster sugar, 75 g (3 oz, ¾ cup) cornflour (cornstarch), 1 litre (1¾ pints, 4⅓ cups) milk, 4 leaves of gelatine and 4 egg whites. Mix half of this cream with 50 g (2 oz, 2 squares) melted chocolate and the other half with ½ teaspoon coffee essence (strong black coffee). Slit all the cooked choux pastries: into half of them pipe a filling of the chocolate cream and into the other half pipe the coffee cream.

Put 200 g (7 oz) fondant* icing (frosting) into a saucepan with 1 tablespoon water and heat to 40°C (104°F), stirring constantly; add 50 g (2 oz, 2 squares) melted chocolate. Prepare the same quantity of fondant flavoured with ½ teaspoon coffee essence. Ice the éclairs, rings and bun with the fondant corresponding to their filling. Boil 150 g (5 oz, ⅔ cup) caster sugar in 60 ml (2 fl oz, ¼ cup) water; when the temperature reaches 145°C (293°F), brush the syrup over the bottom of the éclairs. Stick these together side by side vertically inside the pastry base, alternating the flavours, then put the 4 rings on top, beginning with the largest; place the bun at the very top. Using a fluted nozzle, pipe the butter cream along the joints of the éclairs, the rings and the bun.

RELISH A highly flavoured condiment which resembles chutney, usually with a hot or piquant flavour, served to pep up plain foods. A relish may take many forms; for example; it may be a sweet-and-sour purée made from sour fruits and vegetables, with the addition of small pickled onions, gherkins and spices (such as ginger, chilli pepper, cinnamon, white pepper, cloves and nutmeg), simmered with soft brown (coffee) sugar and vinegar.

Alternatively, the term can describe a thin sauce with a strong mustard flavour underpinning a sweet or fruity content. Chunky vegetable relishes are often eaten in generous quantities, for example with hamburgers, cold meats or cheese. Relishes are also served with curries and other Oriental dishes.

REMOUDOU A Belgian cow's-milk cheese with a fat content of 45%; it has a soft curd and a very strong flavour. The name is derived from the German *rahm*, meaning 'fresh cream'. The cheese is made in the town of Battice and dates from the time of Charles V. La Confrérie du Remoudou undertakes the promotion of all dairy products from the plain of Herve. The German cheese Romadur is similar, as is Romalour from Lorraine, which Zola mentions in *Le Ventre de Paris*: 'the Romantour (*sic*) wrapped in its silver paper.'

RÉMOULADE A cold sauce made by adding mustard, gherkins, capers and chopped herbs to mayonnaise; it is sometimes finished with a little anchovy essence, and chopped hard-boiled (hard-cooked) egg may be included. Its name may originate from the Picardy word *rémola*, meaning 'black radish', even though radish is not an ingredient. Rémoulade can accompany cold meat, fish and shellfish; it sometimes appears as a simple mustard-flavoured mayonnaise spiced with garlic and pepper, and in this version is the traditional accompaniment of grated celeriac and various mixed salads.

RECIPE

rémoulade sauce
Make some mayonnaise* with 250 ml (8 fl oz, 1 cup) oil, replacing, if desired, the raw egg yolk with 1 hard-boiled (hard-cooked) egg yolk rubbed through a fine sieve. Add 2 very finely diced gherkins, 2 tablespoons chopped herbs (parsley, chives, chervil and tarragon), 1 tablespoon drained capers and a few drops of anchovy essence (optional).

additional recipe See *celeriac*.

REMOVE In the days when food was served in the grand manner, this was a dish which 'came to remove' (in other words, followed) another, usually the soup. Grimod de La Reynière distinguishes between ordinary entrées and 'grosses' (large) entrées. The latter came to be called relevés, he says, because 'when they arrived, the soup was removed, being at each end of the table'. As examples, he gives stuffed top loin of veal with cream, calf's head *à la financière*, and a large freshwater fish, served with sauce and garnish. This was the order of a classic menu: hors d'oeuvre; soups; relevés of the soups; fish (providing that fish was not one of the relevé dishes); relevés of fish (later eliminated); roasts, sometimes followed by relevés of roasts; and finally desserts.

RENAISSANCE, À LA A cookery term describing either a large braised or roast cut of meat or a roast or poached chicken that is garnished with small heaps of different vegetables, such as glazed carrots and turnips (cut out with a melon baller and sometimes arranged on artichoke hearts), fondant or fried potatoes, braised lettuce, French (green) beans, asparagus tips and cauliflower florets. The accompanying sauce is made from the meat juices or the braising stock; suprême sauce is served with chicken poached in white stock.

RENNET An extract from the stomach (abomasum) of calves and lambs, containing the enzyme rennin, which brings about the coagulation of milk. Rennet is indispensable in the manufacture of cheese and for making junket. For some cheeses, of both traditional and vegetarian varieties, vegetable alternatives are used: these are milk-coagulating substances obtained from certain plants, such as the cardoon.

REPÈRE A soft paste made from flour and water, used to make an airtight seal between casserole and lid prior to cooking (see *lute*).

The term also means a mixture of flour and egg white that is used to stick decorations on to a cake or dish (it is advisable to warm the dish before sticking on the decorations).

RÉSERVE A word that is applied to any wine of quality in France, although as yet it has no legal definition. In some wine-producing areas, such as Spain and Italy, *reserva* or *riserva* refer to specific ageing periods. Reserve wines in Champagne are wines held over from a particular vintage for blending – usually to make a non-vintage champagne.

RESERVE To put aside ingredients, mixtures or preparations, either hot or cold, for later use. Food can be kept hot in a bain marie, over a low heat, or in a cool oven. The refrigerator is the best place to keep items cold. To ensure that food is not spoiled, it may be wrapped in greaseproof (wax) paper, foil, or a cloth. To prevent a skin forming on a cream or a sauce, the surface is covered with buttered paper or with fat (see *tamponner*). Pastry dough is covered with a cloth and kept cold to prevent a crust from forming. Certain cooked vegetables can be put in a dish and covered with a cloth to keep warm. Peeled potatoes can be kept immersed in cold water for a short time before cooking.

REST To put a dough or batter to one side in a cool place as part of its preparation. Pastry must be left to rest for at least an hour before it is used: it is rolled into a ball and wrapped in a cloth or foil, then left in the refrigerator or in a cool place away from draughts.

RESTAURANT An establishment where meals are served between set hours, either from a fixed menu or *à la carte*. The word appeared in the 16th century and meant at first 'a food which restores' (from *restaurer*, to restore), and was used more specifically for a rich, highly flavoured soup thought capable of restoring lost strength. The 18th-century gastronome Brillat-Savarin referred to chocolate, red meat and consommé as *restaurants*. From this sense, which survived until the 19th century, the word developed the meaning of 'an establishment specializing in the sale of restorative foods' (*Dictionnaire de Trévoux*, 1771).

Until the late 18th century, the only places for ordinary people to eat out were inns and taverns. In about 1765, a Parisian 'bouillon-seller' named Boulanger wrote on his sign: 'Boulanger sells restoratives fit for the gods', with a motto in dog Latin: *Venite ad me omnes qui stomacho laboretis, et ego restaurabo vos* (Come unto me, all you whose stomachs are aching, and I will restore you). This was the first restaurant in the modern sense of the term. Boulanger was followed by Roze and Pontaillé, who in 1766 opened a *maison de santé* (house of health). However, the first Parisian restaurant worthy of the name was the one founded by Beauvilliers in 1782 in the Rue de Richelieu, called the Grande Taverne de Londres. He introduced the novelty of listing the dishes available on a menu and serving them at small individual tables during fixed hours.

One beneficial effect of the Revolution was that the abolition of the guilds and their privileges made it easier to open a restaurant. The first to take advantage of the situation were the cooks and servants from the great houses, whose aristocratic owners had fled. Moreover, the arrival in Paris of numerous provincials who had no family in the capital created a pool of faithful customers, augmented by journalists and businessmen. The general feeling of wellbeing under the Directory, following such a chaotic period, coupled with the chance of enjoying the delights of the table hitherto reserved for the rich, created an atmosphere in which restaurants became an established institution.

To a certain extent, the restaurateurs guided their customers' tastes, as shown by Grimod de La Reynière's *Almanach des gourmands*, with its 'good addresses'; it was the first gastronomic guide of Paris and listed about a hundred restaurants. Fashion favoured various parts of the capital in turn: after the Palais-Royal (with such establishments as Méot, the Boeuf à la mode, the Frères Provençaux, and the Grand Véfour) came Les Halles (with the illustrious Rocher de Cancale); then it was the turn of the Grands Boulevards (Very, Hardy, Riche), the Madeleine (with Larue, Voisin, Maxim's), the Champs Élysées (Fouquet's, Laurent), the Villette, Bercy, then Montparnasse and the Left Bank (Lapérouse, the Tour d'Argent, Allard), along with Clichy and the heights of Montmartre.

Nowadays, a distinction can be made between the large restaurants, which employ a chef, and those with an owner-manager who does the cooking himor herself.

In Paris, as in the provinces, the 20th century saw a tendency towards standardization and even Americanization of the restaurant trade, as evinced by snackbars, motorway pull-ins (highway rest-stops), cafeterias and takeaways. In spite of this, restaurants still offer great scope for creativity. They provide both a testing ground for new ideas and a haven for more traditional recipes.

The great regional restaurants were established, in many cases, at former mail staging posts. Still near to tourist routes, and rediscovered by such gourmets as Curnonsky and M. Rouff, these establishments counterbalance the reputation of the temples of *haute cuisine*, which are the pride of Paris. In his book *Voyages gastronomiques au pays de France* (1925), J.-A. P. Cousin classifies Parisian restaurants into categories: 'perfection' (Foyot, Larue, Lapérouse, the Tour d'Argent, Voisin, and Paillard); 'the last word' (Prosper Montagné); 'very high class' (Café de Paris, Pré Catelan, Ritz); 'smart' (Laurent, Maxim's, Noël Peters, the Cascade); 'reliable' (the Boeuf à la Mode, Drouant, Lucas, Maire, Marguery); 'savoury and plentiful' (Dagorno, Jouanne, L'Escargot Montorgueil, Pharamond); and finally 'good little places' and 'good atmosphere' (the Bon Bock, the Boeuf sur le Toit, the Lapin Agile, Ramponneau, the Rotonde). He also lists wine merchants, grillrooms, inns, regional and foreign restaurants (Chinese, British, Greek, Dutch, Italian, Mexican, Russian, Swedish and Swiss), and finally the fish bars (Prunier). In modern guides these categories are signified by means of symbols, such as crowns, stars, or crossed knives and forks. Nowadays, however, great chefs are also found in the provinces, especially since the reign of the 'three greats' (Point, Pic and Dumaine). Tradition is giving way to new methods, such as the *service à l'assiette* (plate service) introduced in the 1960s.

There are also plenty of bistros, bars and cafés, many of them extremely modest, where the food is simple and honest and which often specialize in one or two dishes – for example, pike *au beurre blanc de la mère Michel* or omelette *de la mère Poulard*. Other such specialities may include pieds et paquets *à la marseillaise*, tripe *à la mode de Caen* and entrecôte *marchand de vin*.

Today, restaurants are developing along two lines: on the one hand, they are attempting to fulfil their original function by feeding more and more city workers, many of whom do not go home during their lunch hour. The catering offered by works canteens and restaurants is supplemented by bars, cafés, self-service restaurants and pizzerias. On the other hand, the top-ranking restaurants continue to provide their customers with luxurious surroundings, great wines, rare delicacies and all the refinements of the culinary art.

RÉTÈS A Hungarian pastry similar to the Austrian strudel. The dough is made from strong high-gluten flour and is stretched until very thin (the saying goes that it should be possible to read a faded love letter through the dough). It is then covered with any of various fillings, rolled up, baked and cut into slices, which are served dusted with icing (confectioner's) sugar. Suitable fillings include: cream cheese with raisins and beaten egg whites; apple jam flavoured with cinnamon; cooked cherries or plums; grated walnuts with sugar, lemon, raisins and milk; and a cream made from poppy seeds cooked in milk and sugar, with grated apple, lemon zest and sultanas.

RETICULUM The second compartment of the stomach of ruminants, situated between the rumen and the psalterium. The reticula of beef cattle are one of the components of tripe and *gras-double* (a dish made with three stomachs). That of sheep is most notably used in mutton tripe. Like the other parts of the stomach, the reticulum, having been emptied of material being digested, is scalded, scraped, cleansed of all impurities and left to soak in running water before being finished.

RETSINA A wine made in Greece and the Greek islands, either white or rosé and strongly flavoured with pine resin – hence its name.

REUILLY A small region, producing AOC wines, in Berry, around the upper reaches of the River Loire, where white, red and rosé wines are made. The white wines are made from the Sauvignon Blanc grape, the red and rosé wines from the Pinot Noir and Pinot Gris grapes.

RÉVEILLON See *Christmas*.

RHINE WINES See *Germany*. Rhine wines include some from the finest wine-producing regions of West Germany: the Rheingau, the Rheinhessen and the Palatinate (or Pfalz), all in the central region of the River Rhine's course. Nearly all the wine is white, the most famous grape being the Riesling, although the renowned German wine institutes have evolved many successful crosses (such as the Müller-Thurgau and Scheurebe, now very widely planted), which are both resistant to disease and able to withstand the cold of this northern vine-growing region.

• RHEINGAU This region has sometimes been called the German Riviera, and the vineyards, mostly in the finest sites on south-facing slopes and planted with Riesling grapes, produce many remarkable white wines. Some of these, in the higher-quality categories, have been affected by the noble rot (*Botrytis cinerea*) and are outstanding and delicately luscious, the drier wines being markedly fruity and all having a wonderful bouquet. In the Ahr Valley, some red wines are made, the most famous being produced at Assmannshausen, on the Rhine itself.

• RHEINHESSEN Some very fine wines are produced here, but many are only of good average quality. This is the place of origin of much Liebfraumilch, and in addition to the Riesling grape, the Müller-Thurgau and Kerner are also grown.

• PALATINATE (PFALZ) 'Cellar of the Holy Roman Empire' is the tag sometimes given to this region. A small amount of red wine is made, but the majority is white and some outstanding estates and growers have made their wines famous. In this region, as with the others, a wide range of different categories of wine are made, but in general many of the finer Palatinate wines have a substance, combined with delicacy, that makes it possible to drink them with food.

RHÔNE A river which rises in the Swiss Alps and flows through several very important wine regions before it meets the Mediterranean. In the Valais, in Switzerland, vines are planted on the very steep slopes of the valley. However the name is perhaps most associated with wines made in the Rhône valley in France. The region subdivides into northern and southern zones and produces the greatest amount of appellation contrôlée wine after Bordeaux. Côtes-du-Rhône applies to red, rosé and the small amount of white wines from both zones, although they are predominantly from the south. Sixteen villages may add their name to the more highly regarded Côtes-du-Rhône-Villages appellation.

Top quality wines are produced from Syrah in the steep, northern part of the valley, which includes the appellations St-Joseph, St-Péray, Cornas, Hermitage, Crozes-Hermitage and Côte Rôtie. Château Grillet and Condrieu are made from the very elegant Viognier grape. The southern Rhône valley is broader and flatter and is more influenced by the Mediterranean climate, although it can be affected by the cold Mistral wind. The wines are mainly red, although a number of rosés are made from blends of grapes including Syrah, Grenache, Carignan, Mourvèdre and Cinsaut. Appellations include Châteauneuf-du-Pape, Gigondas, Tavel, Lirac and Vacqueyras. Dessert wines are made at Beaumes-de-Venise and Rasteau.

RHUBARB A hardy perennial plant, originally from northern Asia, whose fleshy stalks are used to make cooked desserts, such as pies, jams or compotes. It was the English who first introduced rhubarb to the kitchen: until the 18th century it was regarded as a medicinal and ornamental plant. The normal growing season lasts from May to July, but early forced rhubarb is delicious, bright pink and tender; it is available from January to April. Rhubarb is very sour and must always be sweetened. The leaves contain a large amount of oxalic acid and should not be eaten.

There are many varieties of rhubarb, with stalks ranging from green to varying shades of mauve. The stalks should be firm, thick and crisp, releasing sap when snapped. They will keep for some days in a cool place, but quickly become soft; however, rhubarb freezes well.

Rhubarb jams and compotes are often flavoured with lemon zest or ginger. The compote may also accompany savoury dishes, such as fish, and rhubarb can be made into chutneys. An Italian apéritif, Rabarbaro, is made from rhubarb.

RECIPES

rhubarb compote with strawberries
Peel 1 kg (2¼ lb) rhubarb, carefully removing all the stringy parts, and cut into even chunks 4–5 cm (1½–2 in) long. Place in a large bowl and sprinkle generously with vanilla sugar. Leave to soak for 3 hours, stirring occasionally. Put the rhubarb in a saucepan and cook for 15 minutes over moderate heat. Wash, hull and quarter 300 g (11 oz, 2 cups) ripe strawberries. Add to the rhubarb and cook for another 5 minutes. Transfer to a fruit bowl and allow to cool. Serve in bowls, on its own or with vanilla ice cream and small warm madeleines.

rhubarb jam
Carefully strip the stringy fibres from some fresh rhubarb stalks, then cut up the stalks. For every 1 kg (2¼ lb) rhubarb, put 800 g (1¾ lb) granulated sugar and 100 ml (4 fl oz, 7 tablespoons) water into a saucepan and bring to the boil. Cook for 8 minutes, then add the rhubarb and poach it very gently until the pieces disintegrate. Then bring to a fast boil and cook until setting point is reached. Pot and seal in the usual way.

rhubarb pie
Make 300 g (11 oz) shortcrust pastry (see *short pastry*), shape it into a ball, and leave it to rest for at least 2 hours. Roll it out to a thickness of about

3 mm (⅛ in) and cut out a piece to cover the pie dish, and also a strip to go around the edge of the dish. Remove any stringy fibres from the rhubarb and cut it into pieces 4 cm (1½ in) long. Put the rhubarb in the buttered pie dish and sprinkle with caster (superfine) sugar or soft brown (coffee) sugar, using about 250 g (9 oz, 1 cup) sugar for 800 g (1¾ lb) rhubarb; moisten with 2–3 tablespoons water.

Cover the edge of the pie dish with the strip of pastry, brush it with beaten egg, then place the pastry lid over the dish, pressing down at the edges. Decorate the lid with a diamond-shaped design, brush with egg, then sprinkle lightly with caster sugar. Insert a small pie funnel in the lid for the steam to escape and bake the pie in a preheated oven at 200°C (400°F, gas 6) for 40–45 minutes.

Take the dish out of the oven, remove the funnel and pour in some double (heavy) cream. Alternatively, the cream can be served separately or crème anglaise can be served with the pie. Vanilla ice cream also goes well with rhubarb pie.

RHYTON An antique drinking vessel made in the shape of the horn, head or forepart of an animal, in use as long ago as 2000 BC. It was filled through a hole in the upper part, and the drinker could direct a stream of the drink from this hole into his mouth; more often, the contents were poured into a cup or other receptacle. It lacked a flat base, so the drinker was obliged to drain it before putting it down. Rhytons were also made of pottery, bronze or some other metal; the finest were made of silver (in Crete) and gold (in Persia).

RIBBON STAGE The stage in beating together egg yolks and caster (superfine) sugar when the mixture is sufficiently smooth and homogeneous for it to flow from the spoon or whisk in a continuous ribbon.

RIBERA DEL DUERO An important and prestigious wine region in Castile and León, north of Madrid. The wines, produced from Tinto Fino (also known as Tinto del Pais, and a variant of Tempranillo) have Denominación de Origen status and are deep, concentrated and capable of long ageing. More recently Cabernet Sauvignon, Merlot and Malbec may be included in the blend.

RICE Apart from wheat, this is the most widely cultivated cereal in the world, growing in tropical, equatorial and temperate zones. Rice is always eaten cooked, either hot or cold, as a sweet or savoury dish. The largest consumers worldwide are China, India, Indonesia, Japan and Bangladesh, followed by Latin America and Africa.

■ **History** Growing both on dry land and on swampy or irrigated land, rice was known and cultivated in China more than 3000 years ago. It seems, however, that the rice plant (*Oryza sativa*) may have originated in southern India, then spread to the north of the country and to China. Later it arrived in Korea, the Philippines (about 2000 BC), Japan and Indonesia (1000 BC). The Persians imported rice to Mesopotamia and Turkestan, and Alexander the Great, who invaded India in 327 BC, brought it to Greece. Arab travellers encouraged the use of rice in Egypt, Morocco and Spain. Portugal and Holland introduced it into their colonies in West Africa from the 15th century onwards, and it reached North America towards the end of the 17th century. Another species, *Oryza glaberrina*, was cultivated around 1500 BC in West Africa, from Senegal to the banks of the Niger, but it has been replaced by the Asian species.

It was the Crusaders who introduced rice into France, and various attempts were made to grow the cereal without much success, in spite of an edict issued by Sully in 1603. Since 1942, a relatively prosperous rice-growing area has been established in the Camargue, supplying about 20% of the national requirement. Piedmont, in Italy, is also a major rice-producing area.

■ **Types and treatment** There are two main types of rice: the subspecies *indica* (long-grain), which has long grains that remain separate when cooked, and the subspecies *japonica* (short-grain), with round grains that tend to stick together when cooked. Round-grain rice is also referred to as pudding rice in Britain because of its use as the main ingredient in a milk pudding. There are also various intermediate types, such as risotto rice, with medium-length grains. Rice is classified according to the type of processing it receives after harvesting. Processing techniques influence the flavour, food value and cooking qualities of the rice. Highly processed grains – part-cooked, steamed or fully cooked – are sold as 'convenience' forms, requiring minimum cooking and/or ensuring that the grains remain separate and quite 'dry' when cooked. Highly refined types often lack the flavour of less-processed grains.

• BROWN RICE Also known as husked or whole rice or in Italy as *semigreggio*. Rice with the outer husk removed, but still retaining the bran, having a characteristic beige colour, a very chewy texture and a mild nutty bran flavour.

• CAMOLINO RICE Polished and lightly coated with oil.

• GLACÉ RICE Polished rice covered with a fine layer of French chalk suspended in a glucose solution and specially processed to give it an attractive sheen.

• PADDY RICE Unhusked rice in its raw state, with no further treatment after threshing (contains 20–25% moisture).

• POLISHED RICE White rice that has been passed through machines that remove any flour still adhering to the grain.

• PRECOOKED OR INSTANT RICE Rice that has been husked or blanched, soaked, boiled for 1–3 minutes, then dried at 200°C (400°F).

• STEAMED OR PRETREATED RICE Paddy rice that has been meticulously cleaned, soaked in hot water, steamed at a low pressure (leaving some of the nutritive elements), and then dehusked and blanched.

• WHITE RICE Brown rice from which the germ and the outer layers of the pericarp have been removed by passing the grains through machines that rasp the grain; it is also called unpolished rice.

■ **Varieties** There are many varieties, identified by species and/or country of origin, as well as by shape and cooking qualities. The following are examples of grain available from supermarkets or specialist food shops.

• BASMATI RICE Indian rice with very small but long grains, with a distinctive flavour; 'old' Basmati, which is rarely available, is much prized by Indians and Pakistanis.

• CAMARGUE RED RICE Taking its name from the region in the South of France where it is grown in comparatively small amounts, this is relatively expensive and favoured for its flavour and firm texture. The long grains are covered by a red husk.

• CAROLINA RICE The name is no longer used to describe a particular variety; it used to be imported from the United States and was of a high quality.

• GLUTINOUS OR STICKY RICE Long-grain rice with a very high starch content. This is suitable for Chinese dishes of shaped rice, such as rice balls or sticky rice cakes, and it must not be confused with rice that has been badly cooked.

• PERFUMED RICE Also known as Thai fragrant or jasmine rice. Long-grain rice from Vietnam and Thailand, with a distinctive taste; in Asia it is reserved for feast days.

• RISOTTO RICE There are several types, including Arborio and Carnaroli. Risotto rice is characterized by high absorbency and a firm, but 'clinging' texture. These characteristics are ideal for achieving a moist, slightly sticky risotto in which the grains retain their separate identity with a little bite.

• SURINAM RICE Very long thin grains from Surinam; sought after by connoisseurs.

• SUSHI RICE Varieties used for Japanese sushi cling together when cooked, without becoming sticky and heavy.

• WILD RICE The seed of an aquatic grass, related to the rice plant, which comes from the northern United States. The seeds grow one by one up the stalk and resemble little black sticks; it is very expensive and is sometimes mixed with brown rice.

■ **Rice products**

• FLAKED RICE Rice that is steamed, husked, then flattened into thin flakes. In Asia, it is used for stuffing poultry or for making sweets; elsewhere, it is turned into breakfast cereals, snacks and confectionery.

• POPPED OR EXPANDED RICE Short-grain rice cooked in sugar, then subjected to high pressure which is suddenly released; it resembles popcorn.

• PUFFED RICE In India it is roasted and fried on hot sand; in the United States it is subjected to heat at high pressure and then at low pressure.

• RICE DRINKS Rice is also the foundation of various alcoholic drinks: *choum* in Vietnam, *samau* in Malaysia, *sake* in Japan, *chao xing* in China (Chinese yellow or rice wine). Broken rice may sometimes be used to replace some of the malt in brewing.

• RICE OIL Rice bran yields an oil similar to groundnut (peanut) oil.

• RICE SEMOLINA, GROUND RICE AND RICE FLOUR These are made by grinding fragments of very white rice; they are used in making cakes and pastries and to thicken sauces.

■ **Cooking and preparation** The amount of uncooked rice required per serving is 65 g (2½ oz, ⅓ cup) for a main dish, 25 g (1 oz, 2 tablespoons) for an hors d'oeuvre, and 40 g (1½ oz, 3 tablespoons) for a dessert. Rice is normally cooked in water, meat stock or milk. Long-grain rice and pretreated rice are best cooked in water (the grains remain separate and retain their flavour). The former can also be sautéed in fat, but pretreated rice should not be fried, as it is too dry. Round-grain rice is best reserved for dessert dishes, as it has thickening properties and holds together.

Rice can absorb a great deal of liquid and will soak up water, milk, oil or stock according to the recipe. The whole art of cooking rice is to ensure that the grains remain a little firm (*al dente*) but not hard, that they are separate and that they retain their flavour (these criteria do not apply to rice cooked in milk). Unless it is precooked or pretreated, rice should always be washed in running water and drained well before being cooked. There are four different methods of cooking rice:

• IN WATER The rice is poured into the pan with twice its volume of cold water, brought to the boil and cooked with the pan covered until all the water is absorbed. Alternatively, it can be poured into a large quantity of boiling water – 3 litres (5 pints, 13 cups) per 1 kg (2¼ lb, 5 cups) rice – and brought back to the boil, cooked uncovered, then drained. Yet another method is to pour the rice into boiling salted water, simmer for 10 minutes, wash in cold water, drain and put in a covered dish in a cool oven until cooking is complete. Rice cooked in water, termed *à la créole* or *à l'indienne*, is particularly suitable for mixed salads and as a garnish for meat or fish.

• STEAMED The rice, previously washed in cold water, is placed in a steamer over boiling water for 20–40 minutes (according to the variety); sometimes it is blanched for a few minutes before being placed in the steamer. Alternatively, the rinsed rice may be put into a saucepan with 1½ times its volume of water, brought to the boil and cooked with the pan tightly sealed until all the water has been absorbed. Steamed rice is eaten plain or as a garnish.

• AU GRAS This method of cooking rice is used for pilaf, risotto, paella or rice *à la grecque*; the rice is first gently fried in fat, then twice its volume of stock or water is added and cooking is continued until all the liquid is absorbed.

• IN MILK This is the standard way of cooking all rice desserts. The rice is blanched in boiling water, rinsed, drained and cooked slowly in milk, which may be flavoured in some way, until it attains the

consistency of a creamy paste. It is then garnished, moulded or flavoured in various ways.

■ **Rice dishes** There are numerous recipes based on rice. The most important rice dishes are risotto, pilaf, paella and biryani, but rice is also the traditional garnish for grilled (broiled) fish, kebabs and other preparations cooked on skewers, blanquette of veal, and chicken poached in white stock (where the rice is cooked in the same stock). Rice is also an ingredient of mixed salads, garnished with fish, seafood, raw vegetables, black (ripe) olives and ham, and is used as a stuffing for vegetables such as tomatoes, aubergines (eggplants), (bell) peppers and vine leaves. It may be used to garnish or thicken soups and, of course, it is the basis of the Dutch *rijsttafel*.

Among the desserts are rice cakes and rings garnished with fruit (Condé, *à l'impératrice*), rice tarts and moulds, and rice pudding. It may also be an ingredient in croquettes, subrics and other desserts.

RECIPES

Savoury Rice Dishes
boiled rice with butter
Put 250 g (9 oz, 1¼ cups) washed and drained long-grain rice into a saucepan, cover with cold water and add 2 teaspoons salt per 1 litre (1¾ pints, 4⅓ cups) water or to taste. Bring to the boil, cover the pan and simmer for a maximum of 15 minutes. Drain and refresh the rice under running water, drain again, and pour it into a casserole. Add 50–75 g (2–3 oz, 4–6 tablespoons) butter cut into small pieces and mix gently with the rice. Cover the dish and place in a preheated oven at 200°C (400°F, gas 6) for 15 minutes. Serve very hot, as a garnish.

pilaf rice
Sweat some very finely chopped onions in butter without browning. Add the unwashed rice and stir until it becomes transparent. Add 1½ times its volume in boiling water. Season with salt and add a bouquet garni. Put some greaseproof (wax) paper over the rice and cover with a lid. Cook for 16–18 minutes in a preheated oven at 200°C (400°F, gas 6). Remove from the oven and allow to stand for 15 minutes. Add butter and stir to separate the grains.

rice à la créole
Thoroughly wash 500 g (18 oz, 2½ cups) long-grain rice and pour it into a sauté pan. Add salt and enough water to come 2 cm (¾ in) above the level of the rice. Bring to the boil and continue to boil rapidly with the pan uncovered. When the water has boiled down to the same level as the rice, cover the pan and cook very gently until the rice is completely dry (about 45 minutes). The second part of the cooking process may be carried out in a cool oven.

rice à la grecque
Heat 3 tablespoons olive oil in a pan until very hot, add 250 g (9 oz, 1¼ cups) unwashed long-grain rice and stir with a wooden spoon until the grains

become transparent. Then add 2½ times its volume of boiling water, a handful of raisins, salt and pepper, a small bouquet garni, a chopped onion and a small chopped garlic clove. Lower the heat, cover the pan and leave to simmer for 16 minutes. Remove the bouquet garni. If wished, 2 tablespoons finely diced red (bell) pepper (which has been cooked in butter or oil) and 150 g (5 oz, 1 cup) peas (cooked in water and well drained) may be added to the rice.

rice à l'iranienne

Rinse 400 g (14 oz, 2 cups) basmati rice in cold water until the water runs clear. Soak for 12 hours in water with 40 g (1½ oz, 2½ tablespoons) salt. Bring 1.5 litres (2¾ pints, 6½ cups) water with 2 tablespoons of salt to the boil in a non-stick saucepan. Drain the rice and put in the saucepan, a little at a time. Boil vigorously for 7 minutes, stirring twice. Drain and rinse in lukewarm water. Heat 50 g (2 oz, ¼ cup) butter with 2 tablespoons of water in a pan. Transfer the rice to it and shape into a pyramid. Make 7 chimneys (openings) with the handle of a wooden spoon. Now sprinkle 2 tablespoons water and 50 g (2 oz, ¼ cup) butter over it. Wrap the lid in a cloth and place on the pan. Cook for 7 minutes over a moderate heat, then 45 minutes over a heat diffusing mat. Before serving, soak the bottom of the pan in icy water to unstick the *tah digue* – the golden crust that will have formed at the bottom of the pan. Delicately remove the rice with a skimming ladle and serve garnished with a few saffron coloured rice grains.

rice au gras

Pour 250 g (9 oz, 1¼ cups) long-grain rice into boiling salted water, leave for 5 minutes, then drain and refresh under cold running water. Heat 25 g (1 oz, 2 tablespoons) butter in a flameproof casserole, add the rice and mix well. Then cover with twice its volume of rather fatty stock (beef or chicken). Bring to the boil over a moderate heat, then cover the casserole and place it in a preheated oven at 220°C (425°F, gas 7) for 20 minutes.

wild rice à l'indienne

Carefully rinse 150 g (5 oz, ¾ cup) long-grain rice and 150 g (5 oz, ¾ cup) wild rice. Soften 100 g (4 oz, ¾ cup) chopped onion and 100 g (4 oz, ¾ cup) chopped celery in 7 g (¼ oz, 1½ teaspoons) butter and 1 tablespoon oil. Add the rice and 40 g (1½ oz) raisins and stir. Add 1 litre (1¾ pints, 4⅓ cups) chicken or vegetable stock. Bring to the boil, cover and cook until the rice is tender. Incorporate 40 g (1½ oz, 3 tablespoons) grilled pine nuts or chopped nuts, and allow to rest for 5 minutes.

other recipes See *border (savoury rings), chicken, consommé (hot consommés), croquette, croustade, pilaf.*

Sweet Rice Dishes

rice cooked in milk

Cook 200 g (7 oz, 1 cup) washed round-grain rice for 2 minutes in boiling salted water. Drain and pour it into 900 ml (1½ pints, 1 quart) boiling milk. Add 75 g (3 oz, 6 tablespoons) caster (superfine) sugar, a pinch of salt and either a pinch of ground cinnamon or a vanilla pod (bean). Cover the pan and cook over a very low heat for 30–40 minutes. Add 50 g (2 oz, ¼ cup) butter, and, if desired, 2 or 3 egg yolks. Serve either warm or chilled.

rice cooked in milk for ring moulds and cakes

Blanch 200 g (7 oz, 1 cup) round-grain rice in boiling water for 2 minutes. Drain, refresh under cold running water and drain again. Bring 900 ml (1½ pints, 1 quart) milk to the boil, add ½ teaspoon salt and a vanilla pod (bean), then add the rice, together with 75 g (3 oz, 6 tablespoons) caster (superfine) or granulated sugar and 25 g (1 oz, 2 tablespoons) butter. Cook either over a very low heat in a covered pan for 30 minutes without stirring, or in a preheated oven at 200°C (400°F, gas 6) for 35 minutes. Remove the vanilla pod. Mix 4–6 egg yolks with a little of the rice, then pour it into the pan and stir well. If liked, 4 egg whites, whisked until stiff, may be added.

rice gâteau with caramel

Prepare some plain rice cooked in milk. Remove the vanilla pod (bean), if one has been used, and add 175–200 g (6–7 oz, 1–1¼ cups) caster (superfine) sugar and 3 egg yolks. Gently mix, then add the 3 egg whites whisked to stiff peaks. Place 100 g (4 oz, ½ cup) granulated sugar, the juice of half a lemon and 1 tablespoon water in a saucepan, then cook until the mixture turns brown. Pour it immediately into a charlotte mould with a diameter at the top of 20 cm (8 in). Tilt the mould to line the bottom and sides with caramel. Pour the rice mixture into the mould, press it down and place the mould in a bain marie. Bring to the boil, then bake in a preheated oven at 200°C (400°F, gas 6) for about 45 minutes. Leave the gâteau to cool, then turn it out on to a serving dish.

Heat a little hot water in the mould to dissolve the remaining caramel and pour it over the gâteau. Serve with crème anglaise or a purée of red fruits. Crystallized (candied) fruit and raisins, soaked for 2 hours in a small glass of rum, can be added to the rice before the whisked egg whites.

rice tart

Cut 200 g (7 oz, 1 cup) crystallized (candied) fruit into small dice and macerate in 2 tablespoons rum. Prepare some sweet pastry with 250 g (9 oz, 2¼ cups) sifted plain (all-purpose) flour, 125 g (4½ oz, ¾ cup) caster (superfine) sugar, 1 egg, a pinch of salt and 125 g (4½ oz, ½ cup) softened butter. Roll the pastry into a ball and chill.

Boil 400 ml (14 fl oz, 1¾ cups) milk with a vanilla

pod (bean). Add 100 g (4 oz, ⅔ cup) washed round-grain rice to the boiling milk, together with a pinch of salt and 75 g (3 oz, 6 tablespoons) caster sugar, cover the pan and cook over a very low heat for 25 minutes. When the rice is cooked, allow it to cool slightly, then add a beaten egg, stirring it in thoroughly. Then add 2 tablespoons crème fraîche and the crystallized fruit with the rum. Mix thoroughly.

Roll out the pastry and use to line a sponge tin (cake pan). Prick the pastry base and then put in the filling. Pour 50 g (2 oz, ¼ cup) melted butter over the top and sprinkle with 5 crushed sugar cubes. Cook in a preheated oven at 200°C (400°F, gas 6) for 30 minutes. Serve either warm or cold.

rice with almond milk and citrus fruit jelly ◆

Cook 75 g (3 oz, ½ cup) round-grain Camargue rice in 250 ml (8 fl oz, 1 cup) milk and 25 g (1 oz, 2 tablespoons) sugar. Incorporate a mixture of 200 ml (7 fl oz, ¾ cup) double (heavy) cream, 1 egg, 1 egg yolk and 1 teaspoon almond milk. Place this mixture in 4 ovenproof dishes and cook for 15 minutes in a preheated oven at 120°C (250°F, gas ½). Place in a cool place. Remove the skin and pith of 4 oranges and 3 pink grapefruit, then quarter lengthways and cut the segments across into slices. Collect the juice of the oranges and grapefruit, warm slightly and add 2 sheets of soaked and drained gelatine, heat gently, stirring until the gelatine has dissolved. Put in a cool place. Decorate each dessert with the slices of orange and grapefruit and cooked sheds of finely pared zest. Pour the still syrupy jelly on top.

other recipes See *border (sweet rings), croquette, impératrice, pavé, pudding, saffron, subric.*

RICE PAPER A white, smooth, glossy, edible paper made from the pith of a tropical tree, *Tetrapanax papyrifera*, used as a base for macaroons and other sweetmeats.

RICHE, À LA A term applied to two of the most famous dishes created during the 19th century at the Café Riche: roast woodcock on fried bread and sole fillets in sauce. Riche sauce exists in two versions: a velouté made from the sole fumet, flavoured with mushroom and oyster cooking liquor, bound with cream and egg yolks, then finished with the fish juices or with lobster butter; or a normande sauce made with lobster butter and truffles, seasoned with cayenne and flavoured with Cognac – this is also called diplomat sauce and may accompany any fine fish, such as turbot, John Dory or sole.

RECIPES

fillets of sole à la Riche
Make a Riche sauce: prepare 250 ml (8 fl oz, 1 cup) normande* sauce and add to it 2 tablespoons lobster butter*, 1 tablespoon chopped truffle skins, a

pinch of cayenne pepper and 2 tablespoons Cognac. Keep warm.

Cook a small lobster in a well-seasoned court-bouillon, drain and shell it, then cut the meat into a salpicon. Fold 8 sole fillets in half and poach them for 5 minutes in fish fumet. Drain and arrange them in a ring on a hot serving dish. Fill the centre with the lobster salpicon and mask everything with the hot Riche sauce.

woodcock à la Riche
Prepare à gratin forcemeat. Truss a woodcock and roast it in a preheated oven at 240°C (475°F, gas 9) for 10–12 minutes. Cut a slice of white bread large enough to hold the woodcock, fry it until golden, then spread it thickly with the forcemeat. Warm a liqueur glass of fine liqueur brandy, set it alight and immediately pour it into the pan in which the woodcock was roasted to deglaze it. Add a purée consisting of 25 g (1 oz, 2 tablespoons) foie gras pounded with the same amount of butter, and mix with the pan juices until the sauce is quite smooth. Place the woodcock on the fried bread and pour the sauce over it.

RICHEBOURG One of the most celebrated red wines of Burgundy, produced in the parish (commune) of Vosne-Romanée, in the Côte de Nuits area. It is classified as a *grand cru*.

RICHELIEU A number of dishes, garnishes and methods dedicated to the Duc de Richelieu (the Cardinal's great-nephew), whose patronage figures prominently in the culinary world. For example, *boudins à la Richelieu* – small ramekins filled with chicken forcemeat and a salpicon *à la reine*, turned out and served with Périgueux sauce and a garnish of truffles. There was also a Richelieu sauce.

A garnish for large cuts of meat (baron, leg) comprising stuffed tomatoes and mushrooms (sometimes browned), braised lettuce and fried new potatoes or château potatoes. The name is also applied to a method of cooking sole, in which the fish is cut open, dipped in egg and breadcrumbs, and cooked in butter; the backbone is removed and the fish is garnished with maître d'hôtel butter and sliced truffle. Fillets can also be prepared in the same way.

The Richelieu cake is large, made of several layers of almond sponge cake, usually flavoured with Maraschino, and sandwiched together with apricot jam and frangipane. The Richelieu is then covered with fondant icing (frosting) and decorated with crystallized (candied) fruits. It is reputed to have been invented by the chef of the Duc de Richelieu, great-nephew of the Cardinal.

Rice with almond milk and citrus fruit jelly.

RECIPE

Richelieu sauce

(from a recipe by Carême) Dice 4 onions and fry them in clarified butter without letting them colour; drain, then continue cooking them in 2 tablespoons consommé with a little caster (superfine) sugar, a pinch of grated nutmeg and some coarsely ground white pepper.

When the onions are cooked, add 2 tablespoons allemande* sauce, a little chicken glaze and a little butter. Rub the sauce through a sieve. Just before serving, add ½ tablespoon chopped and blanched chervil.

RICOTTA An Italian curd cheese made from the whey produced as a by-product in the manufacture of various cow's- and ewe's-milk cheeses. Soft and rindless, with a granular crumbly texture and mild flavour, ricotta is used mainly in cooking, to spread on canapés and sandwiches, in mixed salads, for pancake fillings, in sauces for pasta, in forcemeats and stuffings, in fritter batters, or as an ingredient for gnocchi.

Ricotta cheese may also be served as a dessert with sugar or jam, or blended with Marsala, or with vinaigrette. It is an ingredient of two famous sweet Italian specialities: Sicilian *cassata*, a cake made with chocolate, ricotta and crystallized (candied) fruit; and *crostata di ricotta*, a kind of tart filled with a mixture of ricotta, grated orange and lemon rind, sugar, raisins, almonds, pine nuts, candied orange peel and egg yolks.

RIESLING A white grape variety, also known as Weisser Riesling, Rheinriesling, Johannisberger, Riesling Renano and Rhine Riesling. It can produce a variety of styles of wine from dry to sweet, as well as wines that can either be drunk young or kept for 20 years or more. The grapes are susceptible to botrytis (see *noble rot*), making exceptional sweet, luscious dessert wines. The wines have honey, floral and, when mature, petrol notes, and a crisp, citrus acidity. It is grown mainly in Germany, Alsace, Australia (particularly in the cooler Eden and Clare Valleys), Spain, Austria and New Zealand.

RIGOTTE Rigotte is a local name for cheese in the regions of Isère, Rhône and the Loire. Now mostly made in factories, and almost always from cow's milk, it is allowed to drain for a week before it is sold. Rigotte des Alpes, produced in the Dauphiné, is often macerated in white wine. Rigotte de Condrieu is a farm cheese from the Lyon district – made exclusively from goat's milk, it is quite rare.

RIJSTTAFEL Originally from Indonesia, this dish has become a classic of Dutch cooking. The name literally means 'rice table'; 20 or more different items are arranged around a large plate of spiced rice, including *sajur* (highly seasoned soup), *satay* (small skewers of grilled meat), *oppordagni* (thin slices of fried beef, seasoned with coconut), fried ox (beef) liver, pork in soy sauce, curried chicken, shrimps and scrambled eggs.

RILLETTES A preparation of pork, rabbit, goose or poultry meat cooked in lard, then pounded to a smooth paste, potted and served as cold hors d'oeuvre.

Pork rillettes from Tours and Anjou are renowned for their fine texture and deep colour because they are almost caramelized by the cooking process. Balzac praised this 'brown jam' in his book *Le Lys dans la vallée*. Rillettes from Le Mans and La Sarthe, also of pork, are characterized by larger pieces of meat in the fat and by their paler colour (they are cooked very slowly). Formerly, rillettes were made from the loin of old breeding sows, whose meat was rather dry; the prolonged cooking in lard tenderized the meat so that it acquired the smooth, soft texture that is the hallmark of well-made rillettes.

The goose rillettes described as *pure oie* (pure goose) are prepared in the same way as the pork rillettes, but they are more fatty and softer (they are sold fresh only in winter). There are also *rillettes d'oie* (made from half goose and half pork meat) and *rillettes porc et oie* (containing more pork than goose).

Rillettes of rabbit (or wild rabbit, particularly in the Orléans region) often include some veal, to make them less dry. Rillettes can also be prepared from sardines or tuna; the fish is cooked in butter and pounded to a paste with fresh butter. Outstanding among fish rillettes are those made from eels or salmon using a mixture of poached fresh fish and smoked fish.

Rillettes are always served cold, sometimes with toast; they can also be used in sandwiches and canapés.

RECIPES

goose rillettes

These are made in the same way as *rillettes de Tours* from boned birds whose liver has been made into foie gras. Pot them as for rabbit rillettes, but use goose fat to seal the pots.

rabbit rillettes

Bone 4 wild rabbits, weigh the meat and cut it into large dice. Dice 1.4 kg (3 lb) fat streaky (slab) bacon. Melt 50–75 g (2–3 oz, 4–6 tablespoons) lard in a large frying pan and fry the bacon along with 8 peeled garlic cloves and a sprig of thyme; add the rabbit and cook until golden. Pour in 750 ml (1¼ pints, 3¼ cups) water and 1½ tablespoons salt for every 1 kg (2¼ lb) meat. Cover the pan and simmer gently for 3 hours. Adjust the seasoning. When cooked, shred the meat using 2 forks and pour the mixture, still boiling hot, into small stoneware pots which have previously been scalded. Leave to cool. Fill the pots to the brim with melted lard, cover and chill until ready to serve.

rabbit rillettes en terrine with Parma ham

Cook 3 young rabbits in stock, seasoned with aromatic herbs. Remove the meat and shred it. Reduce the cooking juice by two-thirds, then strain it through a fine sieve and add it to the rabbit meat, together with 3 egg yolks and 2 tablespoons each of chopped fresh sage and marjoram. Season the mixture. Line a terrine with long, thin slices of Parma ham. Arrange a first layer of rillettes, then a row of preserved duck's gizzards, and cover with rillettes. Fold the ends of the Parma ham slices over the top and cook for 45 minutes in a bain marie in a preheated oven at 150°C (300°F, gas 2). Serve with thin slices of pear, marjoram leaves and some slender chives.

rillettes de Tours

Select some pieces of fat and lean pork from various cuts, such as blade, neck, belly and leg. Separate the fat from the lean meat and remove any bones. Chop the bones, cut the lean meat into strips and coarsely chop the fat.

Put the fat into a large saucepan, arrange the chopped bones on top, then add the strips of lean meat. Tie 4 or 5 cloves and about 12 black peppercorns in a small piece of muslin (cheesecloth) and place it in the pan, then add salt, using 5 teaspoons per 1 kg (2¼ lb) meat. Cover the saucepan, bring to the boil, and simmer gently for 4 hours.

Remove the lid, turn up the heat and remove the bones, stripping off any adhering meat and returning it to the pan to continue cooking. Stir constantly until all the liquid has evaporated. Remove the bag of spices.

Pour the rillettes into stoneware pots, which have previously been scalded, stirring well so as to mix the fat and lean; leave to cool. The fat will rise to the top so there is no need to add lard. Cover with greaseproof (wax) paper and then foil and store in the refrigerator.

RILLONS A speciality of Touraine, made from pieces of belly or shoulder of pork. The meat is first sprinkled with salt, then cooked in lard and browned with caramel. Balzac described them in *Le Lys dans la vallée*: 'Pork trimmings sautéed in their own fat, which look like cooked truffles.'

Rillons are also known as *rillauds, grillons* or *rillots*; they are served as a first course, with various other pork products.

RECIPE

rillons

Cut some pieces of fat belly of pork into 6 cm (2½ in) cubes, without removing the rind. Sprinkle with salt – 1½ tablespoons salt per 1 kg (2¼ lb) meat – and leave for 12 hours.

Put one-third as much lard as there is meat into a saucepan, heat and then brown the pieces of pork. Lower the heat and simmer gently for

2 hours. Finally, add 2 tablespoons caramel per 1 kg (2¼ lb) meat, heat through quickly and drain. The rillons may be served either very hot or thoroughly chilled.

RINCETTE A small quantity of brandy poured into a coffee cup just after it has been emptied and is therefore still warm. This residual warmth helps to release the bouquet of the brandy. The French word is an informal one, as is the practice it describes.

RIOJA A leading wine-producing area in north-east Spain divided into three areas: Rioja Alta, Rioja Alavesa and Rioja Baja. Both red and white wines are made and conform to strict regulations. The region has a DOC quality status. White wines are mainly from Viura (Macabeo), sometimes with Malvasia added. They integrate well in oak making rich, full-bodied dry white wines. Crianza, Reserva and Gran Reserva wines must spend a minimum of six months wood ageing, with a further year, two years or four years respectively ageing in bottle or tank before they can be released for sale. Tempranillo is the main grape variety used in the production of red wines, usually with the addition of Garnacha, Mazuelo (Carignan) and Graciano. As with the white wines, there are strictly defined regulations for the quality categories: Crianza and Reserva have to spend at least a year in oak barrels and a further one or two years respectively ageing in tank or bottle before release. Gran Reservas, made only in the best vintages, spend two years in barrels and a further three years in bottle. The barrels (*barricas*) are 225 litres capacity and are mainly made from American oak, giving hints of vanilla to the wines.

RIOLER A French culinary term meaning to arrange straight or serrated strips of pastry on the top of a cake, tart or flan to form a crisscross pattern, as on a *linzertorte*.

RIPAILLE An informal French name for a hearty feast, where the food is abundant and the wine flows freely. The origin of the expression *faire ripaille* (to have a good blowout) is traditionally linked to the Château de Ripaille, on the shores of Lake Geneva, where in about 1449 Amédée VIII, Duke of Savoy (the antipope Félix V) retired to indulge to excess in the delights of the table. This would be a plausible explanation if the expression had not been found in earlier texts, more than 150 years before the duke's exploits. In fact, the word comes from the Dutch word *rippen* (to scrape), undoubtedly referring to a well-laden table on which, after the meal, hardly a crumb is left!

There is also a white wine called Ripaille, which is dry and fruity and comes from Haute-Savoie.

RISOTTO An Italian rice dish (the name means literally 'little rice') which exploits the properties of certain Italian rice varieties. The rice is gently sautéed in butter (or sometimes olive oil), often with chopped onion, then hot stock is added, a ladleful at a time. The rice is stirred frequently until the liquid has disappeared, partly through absorption and partly through evaporation. The result should be rice that is *al dente*, with a rich, creamy and moist consistency. Risottos can be served as a starter, accompaniment or main course, depending on the ingredients they contain. When only cheese or saffron is added, it is served as an accompaniment to meat (particularly veal), eggs or even fish. Risotto can be based on fish and/or seafood, poultry, meat or vegetables (especially mushrooms); a combination of ingredients may be used, but the essential texture of firm rice in a moist dish must be retained. For some recipes, risotto is set in moulds.

RECIPES

black risotto with langoustines and Thai herbs

Carefully wash 175 g (6 oz) black Thai rice and leave to soak for at least 12 hours. Drain, wash again, then steam for 45 minutes in a steamer. Now place the rice in a saucepan, add salt and incorporate 50 g (2 oz, ¼ cup) butter with a fork. Cover and place in a warm place. Cook chopped shallots, 1 teaspoon minutely sliced ginger, 1 stem lemon grass (trimmed and chopped) 2 garlic cloves and 100 ml (4 fl oz, 7 tablespoons) white wine in a small sauté pan. Reduce until all the liquid has been absorbed. Add 200 ml (7 fl oz, ¾ cup) coconut milk and simmer gently to reduce the liquid by half. Now add 3 tablespoons single (light) cream, 2 teaspoons grated fresh turmeric root and ½ teaspoon green curry paste. Cook until the sauce begins to coat the spoon. Pour 4 teaspoons olive oil in a non-stick frying pan and fry 24 langoustines, previously salted, for 30 seconds on each side. Remove from the heat and keep in a warm place. Pour the sauce into a small saucepan and bring to the boil. Correct the seasoning, then add 25 g (1 oz, 2 tablespoons) butter, a little lime juice, 2 tablespoons minutely chopped red (bell) pepper, 40 leaves of Thai basil and the cooking juices of the crustaceans. Arrange the rice in a dome in the middle of each plate with the langoustines around and pour the sauce on top.

risotto à la milanaise

Heat 40 g (1½ oz, 3 tablespoons) butter or 4 tablespoons olive oil in a saucepan and cook 100 g (4 oz, ¾ cup) chopped onions very gently, without browning. Then add 250 g (9 oz, 1¼ cups) rice and stir until the grains become transparent. Add twice the volume of stock, a ladleful at a time, stirring with a wooden spoon and waiting until all the liquid has been absorbed before adding more. Adjust the seasoning, add a small bouquet garni, then add 200 ml (7 fl oz, ¾ cup) thick tomato fondue*, 500 g (18 oz) pickled ox (beef) tongue, ham and mushrooms (in equal proportions, all chopped), and a little white truffle. Keep hot without allowing the rice to cook further.

risotto à la piémontaise

Prepare the rice as for risotto *à la milanaise*, but omit the tomato fondue, tongue, ham and mushrooms, adding instead 75 g (3 oz, ¾ cup) grated Parmesan cheese and 25 g (1 oz, 2 tablespoons) butter. Some saffron may also be added.

risotto with chicken livers

Make a risotto *à la milanaise*, but omit the final garnish. While it is cooking, prepare 150 ml (¼ pint, ⅔ cup) very thick tomato fondue*. Sauté 200 g (7 oz, 1 cup) diced chicken livers and 250 g (9 oz, 3 cups) sliced cultivated mushrooms in butter. Add salt and pepper and a small grated garlic clove. Mix the tomato fondue, the chicken livers and the mushrooms with the rice and serve very hot. If liked, 75 g (3 oz, ¾ cup) grated Parmesan cheese may be added.

spring risotto

Clean, then cook separately in some oil and a few drops of water 2 small purple artichokes, cut into quarters, 200 g (7 oz, 2⅓ cups) mushrooms, finely chopped and seasoned with oil and a few drops of lemon juice, and 2 small onions with their root stems intact, and 2 tablespoons each sugar and salt. Blanch 1 bunch green asparagus, wild if possible, then fry lightly in butter. Now gently reheat all the vegetables together, except for the asparagus, so that their flavours blend. Gently sauté 500 g (18 oz, 2½ cups) rice in a little oil in a casserole, then bring 1.5 litres (2¾ pints, 6½ cups) stock to the boil and pour 1 ladle on to the rice, stirring until the liquid is completely absorbed. Repeat the operation several times until the rice is completely cooked. After 15 minutes, add the vegetables, except for the asparagus. Grate 25 g (1 oz, ¼ cup) Parmesan cheese. Remove the rice from the heat, add 50 g (2 oz, ¼ cup) butter and the Parmesan cheese and stir well. Garnish with asparagus tips.

additional recipe See *seafood*.

RISSOLE A small sweet or savoury pastry, usually in the form of a turnover, that contains any of various fillings and is usually deep-fried.

Puff pastry is usually used, but rissoles can also be made with lining pastry or brioche dough.

Savoury rissoles may contain chopped meat, sliced poultry, foie gras, duxelles, oysters, prawns, a salpicon bound with a sauce, a flavoured butter or a cheese cream. They are served very hot, as an hors d'oeuvre or a small entrée. Very small rissoles (for example, *pomponettes*, shaped like tiny purses) may be served as appetizers, or used to garnish large joints of meat.

Sweet rissoles are filled with cooked fruit, a cream or jam. They are eaten very hot, sprinkled with sugar and accompanied by a fruit sauce.

In former times, rissoles (or *roissoles* as they were called) were a very popular dish in France. Originally in the form of small fried pancakes, they later came to be filled with chopped meat or fish.

Rissoles de Bugey are a famous French regional speciality that were traditionally served at Christmas time. They are little oblong puff-pastry pies filled with a mixture of roast turkey and ox tripe, seasoned with onion, thyme, chervil and currants, and baked in the oven.

RECIPES

preparation of rissoles

Make some puff pastry or some lining shortcrust pastry and roll it out to a thickness of 3–4 mm (⅛ in). Using a round or oval fluted pastry (cookie) cutter, cut out 2 pieces of pastry for every rissole required. Put a small amount of filling (about the size of a walnut) in the centre of half of the pieces of pastry, moisten the edges, cover with the second piece of pastry and press the edges firmly together.

If the rissoles are to be made from ordinary brioche dough, cut the latter into small pieces and flatten them with the palm of the hand. Place the filling on top and leave them to rise in a warm place, away from draughts, for 30–45 minutes.

Deep-fry the rissoles, whatever dough is used, in very hot oil (175°C, 347°F) until golden brown, then drain them well on paper towels. Arrange the rissoles on a dish covered with a napkin; if the filling is a savoury one, garnish with fried parsley.

rissoles à la chalonnaise

Cut circles 7.5 cm (3 in) in diameter from some puff pastry. Fill with a salpicon of calves' sweetbreads braised in white stock, fried mushrooms and truffles, blended with a thick chicken velouté sauce.

rissoles à la dauphine

Make rissoles in the shape of turnovers from some brioche dough. Fill them either with a purée of foie gras (possibly mixed with a little chopped truffle) or with a salpicon of lobster blended with lobster butter.

rissoles à la fermière

Cut some fluted circles, 7.5 cm (3 in) in diameter, from some shortcrust pastry. Fill them with equal quantities of a salpicon of cooked ham and a mirepoix of vegetables cooked in butter, binding the mixture with a small quantity of concentrated Madeira sauce.

additional recipe See *Pompadour.*

RITZ, CÉSAR Swiss hotelier (born Niederwald, 1850; died Küssnach, 1918). The son of a shepherd, he rose to become the owner of some of the grandest establishments of his time. After an obscure beginning in an hotel in Brigue, he arrived in Paris in 1867, where he became a waiter at Voisin's. Ten years later, he was appointed manager of the Grand Hôtel in Monte Carlo, where he became very friendly with Escoffier. Between them, they established the reputation first of the London Savoy

(1890–93) and later of the Carlton. On 15 June 1898, César Ritz opened the palatial building in Paris, in the Place Vendôme, which bears his name; at the same time he continued to manage the other great hotels – Claridge's and the Hyde Park Hotel in London, the Grand Hôtel in Rome, the Frankfurter Hof in Frankfurt, the Villa Egeia in Palermo and the Hôtel National in Lucerne. The splendid London Ritz was opened in 1906. There are always some of Escoffier's creations on the menu of the Paris Ritz; for example, fresh foie gras with port. One of the innovations at the Ritz was to seat diners at small tables, as in a restaurant, as opposed to the traditional table d'hôte.

RIVESALTES One of two appellations in the Roussillon region – Rivesaltes and Muscat de Rivesaltes – both *vins doux naturels.*

RIVIERA Cake created by the French pâtissier Lucien Peltier. This summer pâtisserie, cool and colourful, consists of a lime mousse and a strawberry mousse, separated by a Genoese sponge, on an almond biscuit (cookie) base. The Riviera is decorated with lime and strawberries.

ROACH Small fish of the *Cyprinidae* family, which usually lives in fresh water with weeds. It can reach a length of 30 cm (12 in), and it has a greenish brown back and silvery belly. It is most often served fried, and its taste is similar to that of the gudgeon.

ROASTING Cooking meat, poultry, game or fish by exposing it to the heat of a naked flame or grill (spit-roasting) or to the radiant heat of an oven (oven-roasting).

Spit-roasting is considered best, but it is more difficult. Some cooks consider that oven-roasted meat is spoilt because it is subjected to humidity. It is a mistake to add water to the roasting pan, because when this evaporates it tends to give a boiled taste to the meat. To ensure that the roast does not dry out or get too brown, particularly when it is to be cooked for a long time, it may be barded. The other preliminary processes are interlarding and larding. Many joints can also be stuffed before roasting.

Whichever method is used, the meat is first exposed to a high heat, which produces a surface crust and concentrates the juices inside the meat, conserving all its flavour. The meat should not be pierced while it is cooking or the juices will run out. The cooking temperature will depend on the type and the size of the joint.

■ **Spit-roasting** The intensity of the heat must always be proportionate to the type of meat to be cooked: red meat, full of juices, should first be seized and then cooked at a steady heat to make sure that it is cooked right through. For white meat and poultry, the heat must be regulated so that the inside is cooked without the outside getting too brown. The meat should be basted frequently with the fat which collects in the drip tray, but not with the meat juices underneath the fat. Cooked in this way, the meat will be tender and a good colour.

■ **Oven-roasting** The meat should be put into a very hot oven to seal the surface. It should rest on a rack, to keep it out of its own fat and juices, and should be basted as for spit-roast meat.

If roast beef, mutton and game are to be served rare, a few drops of deep pink blood should be emitted when the surface is lightly pricked; for a medium-rare roast, the blood should be pale pink. With veal, young lamb and pork, the juices should run clear. Poultry should be lifted from the pan and tilted over a plate: it is done when the juice runs out clear; if there are still traces of pink, the bird is not sufficiently cooked.

As a rule, a roast should be served, with its strings and barding removed, as soon as it is taken out of the oven or off the spit; in the case of red meat, however, it is better to leave the roast to rest for a few minutes in a warm place before serving. The meat is then easier to cut.

The accompanying gravy is made by pouring into the roasting pan either a little water or a little light stock and scraping and mixing in all the juices and bits adhering to the pan. Some of the fat is poured off and the gravy is then served separately in a sauceboat with a special spout which retains the remaining fat when the gravy is poured.

ROBERT A sauce based on white wine and vinegar, which is the classic accompaniment to pork chops and other grilled (broiled) meats. It is wrongly attributed to a cook named Robert Vinot active at the end of the 16th century, but its origins are older than this. Rabelais, in *Le Quart Livre* (1552), mentions 'Robert, the inventor of Robert sauce, which goes so well with roast rabbit, duck, fresh pork, poached eggs, salt cod and a thousand other such foods'. *Le Grand Cuisinier* (1583) mentions a sauce known as *Barbe Robert*, the recipe for which had already appeared in *Le Viandier* under the name of *taillemaslée* (fried onion, verjuice, vinegar and mustard), to be served with roast rabbit, fried fish and fried eggs.

RECIPE

Robert sauce
Cook 2 finely chopped onions until golden brown in 25 g (I oz, 2 tablespoons) butter or lard. Sprinkle with I tablespoon flour and continue to cook until the mixture browns. Add 200 ml (7 fl oz, ¾ cup) white wine and 300 ml (½ pint, I¼ cups) stock, or 100 ml (4 fl oz, 7 tablespoons) white wine, 200 ml (7 fl oz, ¾ cup) vinegar and 100 ml (4 fl oz, 7 tablespoons) water, then boil until reduced by one-third. Adjust the seasoning. Mix together I tablespoon mustard and a little of the sauce, then add it to the rest of the sauce, mixing thoroughly away from the heat.

ROBIOLA This is the general name given to creamy fresh cheeses (50% fat content) made in the

Asti region of Piedmont in Italy. Cow's, ewe's or goat's milk is used according to availability. One of the best known, with AOP status, comes from the town of Roccaverano. The cheeses are shaped into rough rounds and wrapped in paper. The paste is very white and soft, and the flavour is milky with a sour tang.

ROCAMADOUR Soft AOP goat's cheese from Quercy with a natural bluish crust. It is a small disk 5–6 cm (2–2½ in) in diameter and 1.5 cm (¾ in) thick, weighing about 25 g (1 oz). It has a lactic flavour, sweet and nutty, which sharpens and strengthens as the cheese matures. Macerated in olive oil or plum brandy, it is used to make Picadou.

ROCAMBOLE A variety of garlic cultivated in the French Midi, also known as 'Spanish garlic' or 'red Provençal garlic'. The large wine-red bulbs are less pungent than those of the common garlic. La Chapelle, in a recipe for sole *à la sauce aux rois* (1733), recommends using rocambole instead of shallots: the fish are fried in butter and stuffed with a forcemeat of rocambole, anchovies and spring onions (scallions), all cooked in a fish fumet over a gentle heat and sprinkled with orange juice. The name 'rocambole' comes from the German *rockenbolle*, meaning distaff bulb, referring to its shape.

ROCHAMBEAU A garnish for large cuts of braised or roast meat, consisting of croustades of duchess potatoes filled with Vichy carrots, alternating with stuffed lettuces, cauliflower florets *à la polonaise* and Anna potatoes.

ROCHER An item of pâtisserie or confectionery with an irregular outline and (often) a granular texture, resembling that of a rock (hence the name). Usually with a base of sugar and beaten egg whites, they can be made with almonds, coconut (*congolais*), chocolate and raisins, and vary in size. For a *pièce montée* (a large structured cake), *rochers* are made from soufflé sugar – boiled sugar beaten with royal icing (frosting), cut into irregular pieces and sometimes coloured – or from sponge cake (coloured pink, green or with chocolate).

ROCHER DE CANCALE A Parisian restaurant that opened in 1795 in the Rue Montorgueil and was taken over in 1804 by Alexis Balaine; he made it the centre for oyster connoisseurs, where their favourite food was available throughout the year. At that time, the oyster beds of Cancale supplied the markets of Rouen, Paris and even England; in about 1775, the oysters produced there were estimated to be in the region of 100 million. The restaurant, which also served sumptuous dishes of game, fish and poultry, was richly decorated with carpets, wall hangings and crystal. Dining clubs were founded at the Cancale (Les Dîners de Vaudeville in 1796, followed by the Caveau moderne), and Grimod de La Reynière's 'Jury of Tasters' regularly met there. It was here that the chef Langlais created *sole normande* in 1837.

Borel succeeded Balaine. He, too, was an excellent chef, but the popularity of the nearby Restaurant Philippe proved damaging to the Rocher, and in 1860 it was obliged to close down. Eventually a certain M. Pécune opened a second Rocher, called Le Petit Rocher de Cancale, on the old site in the Rue Montorgueil.

ROCKET (ARUGULA)

A Mediterranean plant, which also grows wild in Asia, with a pungent taste and smell, whose young leaves are eaten as a salad or used for flavouring salads and other dishes. They should be gathered before flowering, when smooth and hairless, as later the taste becomes too mustardy. Rocket is one of the traditional ingredients of the Provençal mesclun.

ROCKLING

A Mediterranean fish, 10–40 cm (4–16 in) long, with three barbels on the head and an elongated, slimy, reddish-brown body speckled with black on the back. The rockling has a lean and very delicate flesh, but it is only consumed locally as it does not travel well. It may be prepared in the same way as whiting.

RODENT

A mammal with long, cutting, incisor teeth. Some herbivorous rodents have quite well-flavoured meat; rabbits and hares are good examples. Other rodents have been assiduously hunted in the past and recipes for these animals, including squirrel, marmot and beaver, are still used in some remote regions.

In some tropical countries the meat of rodents forms prime roasts: the *agouti* from South America and the West Indies (called *acouchi* in Guyana) is cooked in the same way as a sucking pig. There is a Guyanese proverb which says, 'He who eats *acouchi* will always return.'

During the siege of Paris in 1870, the citizens ate rats which were sold for 10–15 sous each in the Place de l'Hôtel de Ville. In 1859, Monselet noted in *La Cuisinière poétique* that the Bordeaux coopers traditionally feasted on grilled (broiled) rat with shallots. Thomas Genin, cook and organizer of the first culinary competition (1884–89), considered rat meat to be of excellent quality.

RODGROD

A Danish dessert made from the juice of mixed red fruit (raspberries, redcurrants, blackcurrants, cherries), thickened with potato flour or cornflour (cornstarch), and diluted with white wine. It is served very cold in a fruit dish, sprinkled with sugar and sliced almonds, and accompanied by double (heavy) cream.

ROE

The reproductive glands of male or female fish, containing the sperm and eggs respectively. This article deals with the uses of fish eggs, or hard roe; for culinary uses of the male gland, or milt, see *soft roe*. Traditionally, hard roes have been preserved and served as a luxury, both for their texture – the larger eggs pop most satisfactorily in the mouth – and for their flavour. Preservation methods include salting and smoking, which add an extra dimension to the taste. Brining briefly, pasteurizing and vacuum-packing have been added to modern options for preservation.

Caviar, from sturgeon, is the king of all roes, followed by botargo, correctly the salted and pressed grey mullet roe, but also made with blue-fin tuna and bonito eggs. Pike and grey carp roes are eaten in the Danube delta by those who cannot afford caviar. Fannie Farmer, at the end of the 19th century, thought shad roe one of the finest American delicacies. The list of roes available include some with a regional history, restaurant discoveries (such as sea bream, burbot and hake eggs) and new industries, such as that for lumpfish, developed in the 1950s, and snails' eggs, developed in the 1980s.

• COD AND LING Large and solid, cod's roe is eaten fresh, poached or fried in slices. But it is best-known smoked and pressed (sold in delicatessens or canned). This is used to make taramasalata and for sauces and garnishes. A similar cream is sold ready-prepared in Sweden and exported as *kales kaviar*. Dyed and salted cod's roe in Japan is called *hontarako*. The related ling makes another close-textured, red, salty appetizer.

• HERRING Spain packs glossy, black, undyed pasteurized herring roes.

• LUMPFISH A nearly inedible fish, widely available in the Atlantic, yields a tiny, well-known and cheap roe, dyed black or a garish orange. Denmark makes the best-quality, mildly salted one: it can be obtained an undyed, grey-green.

• SALMON AND TROUT The female salmon roe gives red caviar in Europe and the golden caviars of California. Bigger than any sturgeon egg, salmon eggs have a transparency and colour that adds to their appeal as a garnish. The industry in north-west America dates back to the first decade of 20th century. Keta salmon 'pearls' come from the keta or dog salmon fished in Canadian and Siberian rivers flowing into the Pacific, while salmon eggs from Lakes Michigan and Superior are exported chiefly to Sweden and Japan. The most suitable come from the coho, pink and chum salmons.

Trout eggs are a late-20th century development from Scandinavia and Belgium. Dry cured with salt or wet cured in brine, with a delicate taste, they are banana-yellow from wild trout and orange from farmed trout.

• SHELLFISH ROES are normally used fresh, crab berries garnish salads and soups, and lobster coral, which turns pink when cooked, is used for sauce turbot and included in the classic sauce for lobster americaine. Prawn (shrimp) roe is frequently included in sauce rouille.

• WHITEFISH From the Baltic seas come several roes from fish that are freshwater elsewhere, called *löjrom* in Sweden. The most popular is from the bleak fish, a crunchy roe called *crème d'ablette* in France, eaten on toast, with blinis, with hard-boiled (hard-cooked) eggs and in salads. The lavaret roe is also popular. From the fish called vendace in Britain comes a pink roe with very tiny eggs, which seem pastelike. Under the name 'whitefish caviar', these roes are also preserved in North America and are exported from northern Europe.

RECIPES

barquettes with roe
Prepare some very small barquettes, bake them blind and leave them to cool completely. Skin a smoked cod or grey mullet roe and mix it with an equal quantity of butter. Add some finely grated lemon peel, using 1 lemon for 250 g (9 oz, 1 cup) roe mixture. Fill the barquettes with the mixture and garnish with fluted half-slices of lemon. Chill for 1 hour before serving.

grilled roes
Season some fish roes (whiting, cod or salmon) with salt and pepper. Brush with oil, sprinkle with a little lemon juice and leave them for 30 minutes. Then either brush them with clarified butter and grill (broil) gently, or fry in butter over a gentle heat. Serve with rye bread, butter and lemon.

ROEBUCK A small deer common in Eurasian forests, where it is increasingly popular as game (particularly in Germany). It is called a fawn up to 6 months, a yearling up to 18 months, and then a brocket. The flesh of young roebucks is dark red and is delicate, and does not need to be marinated (cooking should leave it pink inside). The best pieces are the cutlets and noisettes, taken from the loin, and fillets of saddle or noix of leg, which are most often sautéed; the saddle and the leg (or haunch) are on the whole eaten roasted. Stews are also made from it, accompanied by chestnut purée, poivrade sauce, cherries, redcurrant jelly or pears in syrup.

RECIPES

haunch of roebuck with capers
Trim the haunch and prepare a marinade with a bottle of red wine, 1½ tablespoons olive oil, pepper, 2 onions and 2 shallots (both thinly sliced), parsley, salt (in moderation) and pepper. Add the haunch and leave to marinate for at least 24 hours, basting it from time to time.

After draining, lard the meat with small strips of streaky (slab) bacon (250 g, 9 oz). Baste with melted butter, cook in a preheated oven at 200°C (400°F, gas 6) for at least 2 hours, basting occasionally with butter. Meanwhile, simmer the marinade, also for 2 hours. When the meat has finished cooking, mix 2 teaspoons cornflour (cornstarch) or arrowroot with a small cup of beef stock and add this mixture and the meat juices to the reduced marinade. To serve, add 1 tablespoon capers and about 40 g (1½ oz, 3 tablespoons) fresh butter to the sauce.

roast haunch of roebuck
Skin and trim the haunch of young roebuck, pulling off the fine membrane which covers it. Lard with long strips of streaky (slab) bacon and place in an ovenproof dish; moisten with clarified butter, or brush with butter softened to room temperature, and sprinkle with salt and pepper. Roast the haunch in a preheated oven at 220°C (425°F, gas 7), basting several times, for 12–15 minutes per 1 kg (6–8 minutes per 1 lb); as soon as the meat is browned on all sides, add 250 ml (8 fl oz, 1 cup) boiling water to the dish. Serve it with a poivrade sauce and chestnut purée, together with baked apples filled with cranberry compote, or small mushroom croûtes.

roast saddle of roebuck with poivrade sauce
Remove the sinews from a saddle of roebuck and lard it with thin strips of bacon. Before roasting the saddle, it may be coated with olive oil to which pepper and herbs have been added and left to marinate for 3–4 hours. Roast the meat on a spit or in a preheated oven at 220°C (425°F, gas 7), allowing 12–15 minutes per 1 kg (6–8 minutes per 1 lb).

Serve with a poivrade sauce, braised chestnuts, and either dauphine potatoes, potatoes sautéed in butter, or potatoes scooped out and filled with a cranberry compote and baked in a buttered dish for about 15 minutes.

roebuck filets mignons
In principle, filets mignons are thin, tongue-shaped strips of meat situated beneath the saddle bone, but they may also be taken from the large fillets of the saddle. Trim these fillets, flatten them slightly and lard them with fat bacon. They may then be either quickly sautéed in oil or butter, like cutlets, or oiled and grilled (broiled) under a high heat. They are served with a poivrade sauce, a chestnut purée, a fruit compote (especially of peaches) or a cherry or redcurrant sauce, according to choice. Generally speaking, all cutlet recipes may be applied to them.

roebuck noisettes with red wine and roast pear
Pour 500 ml (17 fl oz, 2 cups) red Burgundy into a saucepan and bring to the boil. Add 1 peeled, chopped shallot and reduce the liquid by three quarters. Stir in 100 g (4 oz, ¾ cup) puréed cooked carrots and stir well. Season with salt and pepper. Peel and core 4 firm pears. Cut in a fan shape. Melt 25 g (1 oz, 2 tablespoons) butter in a frying pan. Add the pears and cook gently. Heat 25 g (1 oz, 2 tablespoons) butter in a sauté pan until it starts foaming. Add 12 roebuck noisettes, weighing 50 g (2 oz) each. Season with salt and pepper. Cook over a high heat for 2 minutes on each side, keeping the inside pink. Reheat the red wine sauce. Incorporate 150 g (5 oz ⅔ cup) butter, cut into pieces and whisk vigorously to obtain a smooth

mixture. Season with salt and pepper. Remove the noisettes from the pan. Drain on paper towels. Deglaze the cooking juices in the pan with 1 small glass of water. Reduce for 1 minute and add to the red wine sauce. Drain the pears. Pat dry with paper towels. Pour the sauce on to 4 plates. Place the noisettes on top and surround with the roast pears.

saddle of roebuck à la berrichonne

Trim a saddle of roebuck, removing the sinews and keeping the trimmings. Lard it with very thin strips of fat bacon and season with salt, pepper, thyme and a crushed bay leaf. Clean and finely dice 100 g (4 oz, ⅔ cup) carrots and 100 g (4 oz, ⅔ cup) onions. Brown the game trimmings in oil, then add the diced vegetables, 40 g (1½ oz) shallots, 25 g (1 oz) celery, 2 garlic cloves, a bouquet garni, 8 peppercorns and 2 cloves. Add 1.5 litres (2¾ pints, 6½ cups) red wine, and cook gently for 1 hour.

Drain the saddle, skim the cooking liquid and pass it through a conical strainer lined with coarse muslin (cheesecloth), then thicken with 50 g (2 oz) brown roux. Beat the sauce with 150 g (5 oz, ⅔ cup) butter, salt, pepper and finally 3 tablespoons pig's blood; keep hot in a bain marie.

Cook 4 pears in 500 ml (17 fl oz, 2 cups) red wine flavoured with a generous pinch of powdered cinnamon, then braise gently in butter some quarters of celeriac cut into half-moon shapes. Keep the pears and celeriac hot, and roast the saddle in a preheated oven at 220°C (425°F, gas 7). Coat the bottom of the serving dish with sauce and arrange the saddle on it, garnishing it with pears and celeriac quarters alternately. Serve the remaining sauce separately.

sautéed roebuck cutlets

Trim and flatten the cutlets slightly, sprinkle with salt and pepper, and sauté briskly in 2 tablespoons very hot oil and a knob of butter. Arrange them in a crown, alternating with croûtons of bread cut into the shape of hearts and fried in butter. The eye of the cutlets may be larded with a few thin strips of fat bacon arranged in a star.

sautéed roebuck cutlets à la crème

Season some roebuck cutlets with salt and pepper, dust with paprika and sauté them briskly in butter. Add a little lemon juice to a cream sauce and pour it over the cutlets. Serve with a chestnut purée or, better still, braised chestnuts.

sautéed roebuck cutlets à la minute

Prepare a marinade with 2 tablespoons olive oil, 1 very small crushed garlic clove, 2 teaspoons lemon juice, 2 teaspoons blanched and chopped lemon peel, 2 teaspoons chopped parsley, and salt and pepper. Marinate 8 roebuck cutlets in this mixture for 30 minutes, turning them over three or four times.

Clean 500 g (18 oz, 6 cups) small mushrooms (preferably wild) and sauté them briskly in butter, adding 1 chopped shallot and 1 small chopped onion. Drain the cutlets without wiping them and sauté them briskly in about 25 g (1 oz, 2 tablespoons) hot butter. Moisten them with a liqueur glass of Cognac and flame. Arrange the cutlets in a crown in a round dish, with the mushrooms in the centre. Serve with a lemon-flavoured apple compote and, if desired, a poivrade sauce.

sautéed roebuck cutlets à la mode d'Uzès

Prepare some croûtons fried in oil and some dauphine potatoes. Cut some blanched orange zest and pickled gherkins into fine strips. Sauté the cutlets briskly in oil and keep them hot. Make a sauce from the pan juice, vinegar, brown gravy and crème fraîche, then add the strips of orange zest and gherkins and a few shredded almonds. Coat the hot cutlets with this sauce and serve with the croûtons and the dauphine potatoes.

sautéed roebuck cutlets with cherries

Place 1 glass of port with the same amount of sweetened cherry juice and redcurrant jelly in a small saucepan. Add salt and pepper, ½ teaspoon lemon juice, a pinch of powdered ginger and, if desired, a dash of cayenne pepper. Heat gently for about 10 minutes, then add a large glass of cherries in syrup and reheat. Sauté the cutlets and coat with the cherry sauce; serve very hot.

sautéed roebuck cutlets with grapes

Fry some croûtons in oil and prepare a poivrade sauce. Macerate some large skinned and seeded grapes in Cognac. Sauté the cutlets briskly, then heat the grapes in the same frying pan. Serve the cutlets with the grapes, fried croûtons and poivrade sauce.

sautéed roebuck cutlets with juniper berries

Sauté the cutlets briskly and coat with a sauce made from the pan juice flavoured with juniper berries. Serve with an unsweetened apple purée (apple sauce).

shoulder of roebuck with olives

Bone a shoulder of roebuck, leaving the knuckle bone, and marinate. Cut 200 g (7 oz) fat bacon into strips, roll them in salt and pepper, and lard the shoulder with them. Roll it up and tie fairly tightly. Heat 25 g (1 oz, 2 tablespoons) butter, 2 teaspoons oil and 2 tablespoons diced fatty bacon in a casserole. Brown the shoulder in the casserole, then cover and leave to cook gently for a good hour. Meanwhile stone (pit) some green and black (ripe) olives; blanch and drain the green ones. When the shoulder is cooked, skim the fat from the cooking liquid, add the olives and bring to the boil. Mix 2 teaspoons arrowroot with very little water, add it to the casserole and stir until it thickens. Pour the sauce over the shoulder and serve very hot, with a celery purée if desired.

three-hour leg of roebuck

Trim a leg of roebuck weighing 2.5–3 kg (5½–6½ lb). Cut 300 g (11 oz) fat bacon into thin strips and lard the leg with them. Brown on all sides in a braising pan containing 25 g (1 oz, 2 tablespoons) butter and 2 tablespoons oil. Heat a small glass of Cognac, pour it over the leg and flame. Cover and leave to cook for 1 hour over a gentle heat. Add 250 ml (8 fl oz, 1 cup) red wine, the juice of a lemon, 1 garlic clove, 1 or 2 small dried chilli peppers, salt and pepper, and leave to cook gently for another hour, keeping the lid on. Then mix 2 teaspoons flour and 2 teaspoons strong mustard with 250 ml (8 fl oz, 1 cup) red wine, pour over the leg and cook for a third hour. When time to serve, strain the sauce and thicken it with 4 teaspoons raspberry jelly. Blend 1½ tablespoons double (heavy) cream with 1 litre (1¾ pints, 4⅓ cups) thin chestnut purée and serve the leg, purée and sauce together.

additional recipe See *grand veneur.*

ROEBUCK SAUCE An English sauce to accompany venison or meats *en chevreuil.*

RECIPE

roebuck sauce

Brown in butter 1 tablespoon thinly sliced onions and 40 g (1½ oz, ¼ cup) ham cut into small dice. Add 100 ml (4 fl oz, 7 tablespoons) vinegar and a bouquet garni, and reduce almost completely. Then add 200 ml (7 fl oz, ¾ cup) espagnole* sauce and reduce for 25 minutes, skimming off the scum which forms. Remove the bouquet garni and add 3 tablespoons port and 2 teaspoons redcurrant jelly. Reheat, stirring well.

ROGNONNADE A loin of veal from which the kidney has not been removed. The loin is boned and the sinews removed, then it is beaten flat. Some of the fat is removed from the kidney, which is cut into two lengthways; the two halves are placed end to end in the centre of the loin over the filet mignon. The loin is then rolled and tied securely and roasted.

It is advisable to baste the joint frequently during cooking and not to add salt until it is carved.

ROHAN, À LA The name of a garnish for braised or sautéed poultry, consisting of artichoke hearts topped with slices of foie gras and truffle, arranged alternately with tartlets filled with cock's kidneys in suprême sauce. When the poultry has been arranged with the garnish on a large dish, cockscombs cooked gently in butter are placed between the artichoke hearts and tartlets.

ROLLING PIN A smooth cylinder, 20–50 cm (8–20 in) long and 5–6 cm (2–2½ in) in diameter, sometimes fitted with handles, used to roll out pastry (dough). Made from hardwood (beech or box), china, stainless steel or glass, some rolling pins can move on an axis connecting the two handles. There are also aluminium rolling pins with a nonstick surface, and hollow plastic models, closed by a screw handle, which can be filled with hot water to soften a dough that is too hard or with iced water to firm up dough that is too soft.

Professional pastrycooks use various specialized rolling pins: fluted metal pins to pattern the surface of caramel or almond paste; fluted wooden pins to roll out puff pastry (this keeps the pieces of butter separate and ensures uniform distribution); pins covered in wickerwork to imprint a pattern on pastry; croissant-cutting rolling pins, which cut regular triangles to make into croissants; and rolling pins fitted with adjustable wheels of different sizes at either end, which automatically regulate the thickness of the dough.

ROLLMOP A boned herring fillet, marinated in spiced vinegar, rolled around chopped onion and a piece of gherkin *à la russe*, and secured with a cocktail stick (toothpick). The name comes from the German *rollen* (to roll) and *mops* (a pug dog). Before being rolled up, the fillets are sometimes spread with mustard and sprinkled with capers; the marinade, flavoured with juniper berries, cloves and black peppercorns, is poured cold over the rolled fillets. The rollmops are left to marinate for five or six days in a cold place and then served as a cold hors d'oeuvre, with parsley and onion rings. They can be bought ready-prepared, imported from Denmark or Germany.

ROLLOT A soft, highly flavoured cow's-milk cheese from the Picardy region (45% fat content), with a washed reddish or orange-yellow rind. It was already a popular cheese in the reign of Louis XIV. Rollot is either heart-shaped or wheel-shaped, about 4 cm (1½ in) thick, and is made by small dairies, especially those in the region around Rollot, Amiens and Beauvais. It is at its best between November and June.

ROMAINE, À LA The name given to various French dishes inspired by the cuisine of the Italian region of Latium; these dishes include eggs with spinach, anchovies and Parmesan cheese; small birds casseroled with peas and ham; spinach loaf or soufflé. Sauce *à la romaine* is the classic sauce to serve with roast venison; it is a sweet-and-sour sauce made with dried vine fruits, game stock and pine kernels. Gnocchi *à la romaine* are made from semolina and grated cheese and usually served as a first course. When used to garnish large joints of meat, they are put into tartlet cases (shells) and browned in the oven; they may be accompanied by small spinach loaves with a light tomato sauce or veal stock thickened with tomato.

RECIPES

omelette à la romaine

Prepare some spinach with anchovies as for scrambled eggs *à la romaine*. Make 2 flat 5-egg omelettes garnished with chopped onions cooked in butter and chopped parsley. Spread the spinach mixture over one of the omelettes and place the second one on top. Spoon some light Mornay sauce over the omelettes, sprinkle with grated Parmesan cheese and melted butter, and brown in a preheated oven at 230°C (450°F, gas 8) or under a grill (broiler).

quails à la romaine

Brown 12 chopped small new onions and 100 g (4 oz, ⅔ cup) diced cooked ham in 25 g (1 oz, 2 tablespoons) butter. Add 1 kg (2¼ lb, 7 cups) shelled petits pois, a pinch each of salt and sugar, and a small bouquet garni. Cover and braise gently for 20 minutes. Dress, trim and truss 8 quails and brown them in butter over a high heat in a flameproof casserole. Tip the vegetables on to the birds, cover and cook in a preheated oven at 230°C (450°F, gas 8) for 20 minutes. Serve directly from the cooking dish.

sauce à la romaine

Put 1 tablespoon each of sultanas (golden raisins) and currants in warm water to soak and swell. Cook 4 lumps of sugar to a pale caramel in a saucepan, add 1 tablespoon vinegar, then 200 ml (7 fl oz, ¾ cup) demi-glace*, and finally 4 tablespoons game stock. Boil for a few minutes and strain. Brown 1 tablespoon pine nuts either in the oven or in a frying pan with no fat. Strain the sauce and add the pine kernels, currants and sultanas.

scrambled eggs à la romaine

Cook 800 g (1¾ lb) spinach in butter and scramble 8 eggs with 50 g (2 oz, ½ cup) grated Parmesan cheese. Cut 8 anchovy fillets in oil into small pieces, add them to the spinach and spread the mixture over the base of a buttered gratin dish. Arrange the scrambled eggs on top and sprinkle with 25–40 g (1–1½ oz, ¼–⅓ cup) grated Parmesan cheese and some melted butter. Brown under the grill (broiler).

other recipes See *gnocchi, soufflé (savoury soufflés)*.

ROMANÉE-CONTI
One of the most famous grand cru red wines of Vosne-Romanée, in the Côte de Nuits in Burgundy. It is considered by many to be outstanding. Only small quantities are made. Romanée-Saint-Vivant, also from Vosne-Romanéec, is a slightly larger vineyard that also makes fine wines.

ROMANIA See *page 996*.

ROMANOV
The name given to various dishes of classic French cooking, which were dedicated at the beginning of the 20th century to the Russian Imperial family. The Romanov garnish for meat consists of pieces of cucumber stuffed with duxelles and then browned in the oven and duchess potato cases filled with a salpicon of mushrooms and celeriac bound with thick velouté sauce and seasoned with horseradish. Strawberries Romanov are macerated in Curaçao and arranged in sundae dishes with a decoration of Chantilly cream.

RONCAL
Ewe's milk DOP cheese from Navarre in northern Spain. This hard cheese is pressed and aged for a minimum of 3 months, during which it forms a hard, inedible rind. The paste is beige in colour, becoming amber as it ages, and the flavour is rich and nutty.

RONDEAU
A cooking utensil used in restaurants. It is a round shallow pan with straight sides, a lid and two curved handles (not one long handle as in a sauté pan, though it is used in a similar way). Food can also be reheated or stewed in the pan. In confectionery, it is used mainly in the preparation of marrons glacés. It may be made of aluminium, stainless steel, tinned cast iron or hammered copper.

Deep two-handled pans are also available.

ROQUEFORT
A French ewe's-milk cheese (45% fat content) made in the Rouergue district. The cheese is blue-veined, smooth and creamy, with a naturally formed rind, and has a strong smell and pronounced flavour. Roquefort is one of the oldest known cheeses: it was mentioned by Pliny the Elder; it was Charlemagne's favourite cheese; and in 1411 Charles VI signed a charter giving the inhabitants of Roquefort-sur-Soulzon, a village in the Aveyron, sole rights to the maturing of this soft cheese.

Roquefort was the first cheese to benefit from an *appellation d'origine* now AOP, conferred by a statute of 26 July 1926. The cheese is matured in natural caves in the mountains of Cambelou. Most of the milk comes from the Aveyron region, then from Tarn, Lozère, Hérault and Gard; the Pyrenees and Corsica make up any shortfall, but the only place where the cheese can be matured is the commune of Roquefort. After being seeded with the spores of *Penicillium roqueforti*, the cheese is matured for 3 months in a damp cave, where the *fleurines* (humid currents of air) encourage the development of the blue veins. The best season is from June to December.

A Roquefort cheese is shaped like a cylinder, 19–20 cm (7½–8 in) in diameter and 8.5–10.5 cm (3¼–4¼ in) high, wrapped in foil. It can be bought in slices, portions or even creamed, but it is always better to take a piece from the whole cheese, particularly when it is to be served at the end of a meal. It should then be accompanied by a really full-bodied red wine (such as Châteauneuf-du-Pape or Madiran) or even an old port or a Sauternes. Curnonsky recommended a Clos de Vougeot or Haut-Brion. Roquefort is also used in a number of recipes: mixed salads, sauces and flavoured butters (for spreading on canapés or to serve with a grill or roast meat), soufflés, pancakes, puff pastries and soups.

ROMANIA

Traditional Romanian cuisine shares many characteristics with that of the other Balkan countries influenced by regional produce and Ottoman rule. Fish is an important ingredient because of the country's proximity to the Black Sea and the fact that the Danube flows through it. Maize is one of the main crops and the country also produces sunflower and poppy seeds. The diet of the ordinary Romanian consists of the traditional fish soup (*ciorba*), veal-based dishes and poultry.

Like their Bulgarian neighbours, the tradition of the hors d'oeuvre buffet is well established: puréed aubergine (eggplant) with olive oil and lemon, *mittei* (small grilled sausages), often served with fermented grape juice, a wide range of salads, and meat balls. Carp, crayfish and bream are prepared in the same way as in Austria (stuffed or fried). Cabbage leaves or vine leaves are stuffed and braised as they are in Greece.

Romania produces several ewe's cheeses (*brandza*, *katshkawalj*), some mellow and refined, others strong and matured in pine bark; also cheeses made from cow's milk, which are sometimes eaten with the maize gruel (*mamaliga*), whose methods of preparation are as varied as those of polenta in Italy. Turkish occupation has left its mark in the shape of a wide range of sweet pastries and rose-petal jam. See *Balkan states*.

RECIPES

pears savarin

Peel 12 pears, cut them in half, remove the cores and fill the space with Roquefort cheese blended with a little butter. Arrange the pears on a plate, mask with 300 ml (½ pint, 1¼ cups) double (heavy) cream and sprinkle with paprika. Serve chilled, as an hors d'oeuvre.

Roquefort balls

Mix a good portion of Roquefort with an equal quantity of butter. Add pepper, a pinch of cayenne pepper and 1 tablespoon Cognac for every 100 g (4 oz, ½ cup) mixture. Shape it into little balls about the size of walnuts, roll them in golden breadcrumbs mixed with a little paprika, and chill until ready to serve, spiking each one on a cocktail stick (toothpick).

Roquefort rolls

In a food processor, blend 250 g (9 oz) Roquefort with the same amount of Cheddar cheese. Add 250 ml (8 fl oz, 1 cup) béchamel* sauce, together with salt, pepper and 1 teaspoon mustard. Melt this mixture down in a bain marie, then spread it on thin slices of bread cut lengthways through the loaf, after removing the crust. Roll up each slice, bake until golden in the oven, then cut into sections 1 cm (½ in) thick.

Roquefort sauce

Mash 75 g (3 oz) Roquefort with a fork, blend in 6 Petits Suisses or 175 g (6 oz, ¾ cup) cream cheese, and mix well. Add 3 tablespoons crème fraîche and 1 tablespoon Cognac, then season with pepper and salt (if necessary). Stir well and chill; serve with crudités.

other recipes See *butter (flavoured butters), crêpe, diablotin, feuilleté, prune.*

ROQUEPLAN, JOSEPH French journalist and theatre administrator (born Louis Victor Nestor Rocoplan, Montréal, Aude, 1804; died Paris, 1870). Editor-in-chief of *Figaro*, he directed successively the Opéra-Comique, the Théâtre des Nouveautés, the Théâtre des Variétés and the Châtelet. He was a well-known figure on the Boulevard and a regular customer of the Café Riche and of the Maison Dorée. In *La Vie parisienne* (1853), he described the salons, restaurants and cafés of his period, often adding opinionated judgments of his own: 'The only cooks in the civilized world are French cooks. ... Other nations understand food in general; the French alone understand cooking, because all their qualities – promptitude, decision, tact – are employed in the art. No foreigner can make a good white sauce.'

ROQUES, JOSEPH French doctor (born Valence, now Valence d'Albigeois, 1771; died Montpellier, 1850). A friend of Grimod de La Reynière, he was a member of the latter's Jury of Tasters. He was the author of various works, the most important of which is a *Histoire des champignons comestibles et vénéneux* (1832), in which he deals with the botanical, medicinal and culinary aspects of mushrooms. In the four volumes of his *Nouveau Traité des plantes usuelles* (1837–38), he points out the medicinal value of various fruits and vegetables.

ROSE The flower of the rose bush, whose perfumed and coloured petals are used for flavouring cakes, creams and confectionery. Rose-petal jam, very popular in the Middle East and the Balkans, is made from damask rose petals macerated in sugar. In France, Provins is the centre of rose-flavoured confectionery: petal jam, rose-flavoured bonbons, rose jelly and crystallized (candied) rose petals.

Rose water and rose essence are used like orange-flower water to flavour creams, jellies and ices, as well as liqueurs and flower wines (very popular in the 17th century, particularly Rosolio). Rose honey is made by boiling rosebuds with honey, and rose vinegar by macerating the petals in wine vinegar in the sun. Essence of roses is found in many pastries and cakes from the East, such as *loukoum*. Dried and powdered rosebuds are used as a spice, either alone or with other ingredients (see *ras el hanout*). In North Africa, chicken is often flavoured with rose combined with jasmine.

ROSE-HIP The red berry-like fruit of the rose, used for making jam. The hip is not a true fruit but the swollen receptacle of the plant, containing small hard seeds (the true fruits) with stiff hairs attached. When topped and tailed (stemmed and headed), the hips are placed in a dry pot to soften for a few days, then boiled in water and put through a food mill several times or puréed in a blender. Finally, an equal volume of sugar is added, and they are cooked like jam. A white eau-de-vie can also be made from them.

ROSELLE A species of tropical hibiscus (*Hibiscus sabdariffa*), also known as Jamaica sorrel, used as a condiment. The petals, which have a bitter taste, are used to flavour fish and meat sauces in India and Jamaica, while the red fruits are made into jam and into a refreshing sour drink called *karkade*, which is very popular in Egypt.

ROSEMARY An aromatic evergreen shrub native to Mediterranean countries. The name comes from the Latin *rosmarinus* (rose of the sea). The sprigs or spiky leaves are used either fresh or dried. As they have a strong flavour, only a few sprigs are needed to flavour a marinade, a ragoût, a game dish or a grill. The herb complements veal; it is also used in some tomato sauces and with baked fish. In northern Europe it is used to flavour sausagemeat, sucking pig and roast lamb. In addition, a sprig of rosemary gives a delicate flavour to the milk used for a dessert. The flowers can be used to garnish salads and they can be crystallized (candied) in the same way as violets. Rosemary honey, a speciality of Narbonne in France, is much esteemed.

ROSETTE A dry pure-pork sausage, originating in the Beaujolais region of France. Its name comes from the part of the pig's entrails into which it is stuffed – the spindle-shaped part of the intestine terminating in the rectum and commonly known as the *rosette*, because of its pink colour. The sausage is in the shape of a trussed spindle, about 30 cm (12 in) long, with a medium-coarse filling. It is cut into thin slices and eaten as an hors d'oeuvre or a snack.

ROSETTE WINE An AOC wine from south-west France, grown on the slopes to the north of Bergerac. It is produced from Sauvignon Blanc, Sémillon, and Muscadelle grapes and is usually a semi-sweet wine. It is very rarely seen outside the locality.

ROSÉ WINE A pink wine, usually best when young and drunk cool. It should never be a blend of red and white wines, except in the Champagne region, where makers can use certain of the local reds for this purpose, as well as make the wine pink

by contact with the grape skins. Some rosé wines made from both black and white grapes are produced by allowing the black grapes (such as Grenache, Pinot Noir, Cabernet Franc, Gamay, Carignan and Syrah) to ferment on their skins: the juice is then run off when a satisfactory colour has been obtained. Some well-known rosés include Tavel, Marsannay (Burgundy) and Cabernet d'Anjou, and those from Alsace, Béarn and Provence. Rosé wines are made in many other countries throughout the world.

ROSSINI, GIOACCHINO Italian composer (born Pesaro, 1792; died Paris, 1868). A prolific operatic composer, he is equally well known in the field of gastronomy as a lover of good food. In his own words: 'To eat, to love, to sing and to digest; in truth, these are the four acts in this *opéra bouffe* that we call life, and which vanishes like the bubbles in a bottle of champagne.'

Dishes named after Rossini generally include foie gras and truffles and demi-glace sauce. The first and best-known dish to be named after him was tournedos Rossini (Rossini is said to have given the recipe to the chef at the Café Anglais). Other dishes that bear his name are scrambled eggs, soft-boiled (soft-cooked) or poached eggs, an omelette, roast chicken, chicken breasts, sole fillets and a sautéed chicken dish. Truffles also feature in a salad dressing for which Rossini himself gave the recipe: 'Take some Provençal oil, some English mustard, some French vinegar, a little lemon, some pepper and salt; beat everything together; then throw in a few truffles, which should be cut up very small. The truffles lend a certain aura to this dressing which will send a gourmand into ecstasies . . . The truffle is the Mozart of mushrooms.'

The cook and historian Lacam writes that Rossini invented a way of stuffing macaroni with foie gras by means of a silver syringe.

RECIPES

omelette Rossini
Just before beating the eggs, add a salpicon of foie gras and truffle. Cook the omelette and fold it over on to a hot plate. (Instead of adding the salpicon, the omelette can be garnished with small slices of foie gras sautéed in butter and sliced truffle cooked in butter.) Pour some Madeira-flavoured demi-glace sauce round the omelette.

roast chicken Rossini
Using lining or shortcrust pastry, line 1 tartlet tin (pan) per serving and bake them blind. Roast a chicken weighing 1.8 kg (4 lb) and keep hot in a serving dish. Cut 2 slices of truffle per serving and sauté the slices in butter. Place 1 slice of foie gras and 2 slices of truffle in each tartlet case. Deglaze the roasting pan with Madeira and demi-glace sauce made from the truffle cooking liquor and pour the sauce over the chicken. Surround it with the filled tartlets.

scrambled eggs Rossini

Make some scrambled eggs. Sauté some thin slices of foie gras in butter. Cook some sliced truffle in butter. Pour the scrambled eggs into a serving dish, garnish with the foie gras and truffle, then coat with a very reduced Madeira-flavoured demi-glace sauce.

soft-boiled or poached eggs Rossini

Arrange each cooked egg on a slice of foie gras sautéed in butter. Pour over some Madeira-flavoured demi-glace sauce and place 2 slices of truffle, cooked in butter, on each egg.

tournedos Rossini

Sauté 1 slice of foie gras and 2 slices of truffle per steak in butter. Fry some slices of bread trimmed to the shape of the steaks. Fry the fillet steaks (filets mignons) in butter and place each steak on a croûton. Arrange the foie gras and truffle slices on top. Deglaze the pan in which the steak was cooked with Madeira and pour the sauce over the meat.

RÖSTI Also known as *roesti*. Swiss recipe of potatoes parboiled in their skins, then coarsely grated and fried in a pan until golden to make a large cake. The genuine rösti of Bern have bacon and chopped onions added.

RECIPE

rösti

Peel and grate (or finely slice) 800 g (1¾ lb) potatoes which have been parboiled in their skins the night before. Add 1 teaspoon salt and, if liked, 100 g (4 oz, ½ cup) diced bacon. Melt 4 tablespoons lard in a frying pan and add the potatoes, turning them several times so that they become impregnated with the lard. Cook over a medium heat, stirring frequently. (If the potatoes seem a little dry, cover the pan; if they start to disintegrate, leave uncovered.) When they are cooked, draw together in the pan and raise the heat until a golden crust forms underneath. Turn this cake out on to a plate, with the crust upwards. It can be served with *longeoles* (coarse Savoy sausages).

RÔT An obsolete French word for a piece of meat or fish cooked directly in front of the fire; with the pot-au-feu, it formed the basis of most meals in former times. The equivalent today is *rôti*, roast.

ROTHOMAGO A dish of eggs *sur le plat* apparently invented by a cook from Rouen, the Latin name for which was *Rotomagus*. It should not be confused with dishes *à la rouennaise*.

RECIPE

eggs sur le plat Rothomago

Prepare a very thick tomato sauce. Grill (broil) 2 chipolata sausages per serving. Brown some small slices of ham in butter and use them to garnish the dishes in which the eggs are to be served. Break 2 eggs into each dish and cook them *sur le plat*. Garnish each plate with 2 chipolatas and pour a ribbon of tomato sauce round them.

ROTHSCHILD The name of the famous banking family has been given to a soufflé made from confectioner's custard (pastry cream) and crystallized (candied) fruit macerated in Danziger Goldwasser (a liqueur containing suspended particles of gold). Classically, this soufflé is decorated with a border of fresh strawberries.

RECIPE

soufflé Rothschild

Cut 150 g (5 oz, 1 cup) crystallized (candied) fruit into small pieces and macerate in 100 ml (4 fl oz, 7 tablespoons) Danziger Goldwasser for at least 30 minutes.

Whisk together 200 g (7 oz, 1 cup) caster (superfine) sugar and 4 egg yolks until the mixture turns white and thick. Then mix in 75 g (3 oz, ¾ cup) plain (all-purpose) flour and 500 ml (17 fl oz, 2 cups) boiling milk. Pour into a saucepan and bring to the boil, stirring constantly, then cook for 1–2 minutes. Pour the confectioner's custard (pastry cream) into a bowl and add 2 raw egg yolks, the pieces of fruit, and their macerating liquid. Whisk 6 egg whites to stiff peaks with a pinch of salt and fold them carefully into the cream.

Butter 2 soufflé dishes (for 4 servings each) and sprinkle the insides with 1½ tablespoons caster sugar. Divide the mixture between the 2 dishes and bake in a preheated oven at 200°C (400°F, gas 6).

After 25 minutes, sprinkle the tops of the soufflés with icing (confectioner's) sugar, taking care to leave the oven door open for the shortest possible time, then continue to cook for another 5 minutes.

RÔTI-COCHON The title of a book for children, published by Claude Michard at Dijon in about 1680. This 'very easy method of teaching children to read Latin and French' is of great interest because of the light it throws on the history of gastronomy. Many of its passages are inspired by cookery, greed and the way of life of the period: 'After eating pears, you must drink something.' 'Sweet wafers, fritters, crackling waffles, buttered pancakes, and loaf sugar – these foods have a whiff of Lent about them.' 'Long live hot roast pork crackling.' 'Boiled capon is fine for those who have no teeth.' 'In a calf's head, the eyes and the ears are the tastiest morsels.' 'The modern way to serve salad is with the vegetables on one plate, the oil and vinegar in another.' 'Broth to take the edge off large appetites, roast meat to eat on feast days.'

ROTISSERIE A rotating spit, designed for spit-roasting meat or poultry. The large spit is sometimes replaced by four or six skewers or by a container which avoids having to skewer the meat.

A rotisserie is also a shop or restaurant where spit-roast meat (especially chicken) is prepared and sold. In France, the term *rôtisseur* began to be used in about 1450. Before this time, the sellers of roast game and poultry were known as *oyeurs*, taking their name from the Rue des Oues (the present Rue aux Ours), in Les Halles district.

Under the Ancien Régime, the body of servants who were responsible for the king's food included an *hâteur*, a kitchen official who directed the operation of roasting. In recent times, in large restaurants the rôtisseur is in charge of all spit- or oven-roasting, as well as grilled (broiled) and fried foods (meat, fish, poultry, game and vegetables). According to custom, he also supplies the other staff with chopped parsley and fresh breadcrumbs, when required. He also slices the potatoes for frying.

ROUELLE A thick round slice of veal cut across the leg; it is roasted or braised. Shin of veal (veal shank) is also cut across into rounds; for example, for osso bucco.

ROUENNAISE, À LA A description applied mainly to preparations of duck or duckling, for which Rouen is famous. Some typical preparations are pressed duck, invented in Rouen at the beginning of the 19th century, and stuffed duck, roasted and served with rouennaise sauce (a highly spiced bordelaise sauce to which chicken liver has been added). This sauce may also be served with poached eggs. The description *à la rouennaise* is applied to many recipes which include duck or duckling liver, as well as other specialities of Rouen, such as duck pâté, stuffed sheep's trotters (feet), fish with red wine or cider, and chicken with cream.

RECIPES

croûtes à la rouennaise
Fry 4 slices of bread in butter. Prepare 150 g (5 oz) *à gratin* forcemeat* using Rouen duckling livers, grill (broil) 4 large mushroom caps and make 2 tablespoons very thick bordelaise* sauce. Spread the croûtes with the forcemeat and heat them through for 10 minutes in the oven. Garnish each with a grilled mushroom cap, filled with 1½ teaspoons bordelaise sauce.

eggs en cocotte à la rouennaise
Lightly butter some small ovenproof cocotte dishes, then spread *à gratin* forcemeat made with Rouen duckling livers over the base and sides of each dish. Break 2 eggs into each dish and put a knob of butter on the yolks. Cook in a bain marie. When the eggs are done, surround the yolks with a ribbon of red wine sauce thickened with butter.

omelette à la rouennaise
For an 8-egg omelette, prepare 4 tablespoons red wine sauce* and reduce until it is very thick. Whisk in 1 tablespoon butter. Prepare a purée of Rouen duckling livers. Cook the omelette and fill it with the purée. Place it on a serving dish and pour the sauce round it.

rouennaise sauce
Pound 150 g (5 oz) duck livers in a mortar. Peel and chop 75 g (3 oz, ½ cup) shallots and cook until golden in 20 g (¾ oz, 1½ tablespoons) butter. Pour 325 ml (11 fl oz, 1⅓ cups) red wine into the pan and boil until the liquid is reduced by half. Add 25 g (1 oz, ¾ cup) chopped parsley and 2 litres (3½ pints, 9 cups) demi-glace* sauce. Adjust the seasoning and put aside. Just before serving, add the pounded duck livers and mix well to obtain a smooth sauce.

stuffed duck à la rouennaise
Draw, singe and truss a duck weighing 1.5 kg (3¼ lb). Prepare a forcemeat: melt a little butter and oil in a saucepan and in this brown 25 g (1 oz, 2 tablespoons) chopped onion, 2 duck livers, a few sprigs of parsley and 100 g (4 oz, ⅔ cup) chopped bacon fat. When all the ingredients are golden brown, take the pan off the heat and leave it to cool.

Stuff the duck with the cold forcemeat, sprinkle it with salt and pepper, and bard it. Put it in a roasting pan with a little butter and some coarsely chopped vegetables – 1 onion, 2 carrots, 1 celery stick. Cook for 1 hour in a preheated oven at 240°C (475°F, gas 9). Towards the end of the cooking time, remove the barding. When the bird is done, remove from the pan and keep hot.

Strain the cooking juices and pour off the fat. Replace the duck in the pan, sprinkle it with Madeira, bring to the boil, add the cooking juices, bring to the boil again, cover the pan and leave it to cook for a few minutes. Place the duck on a hot serving dish and serve with either rouennaise sauce or the cooking juices, strained again and thickened with a little beurre manié.

additional recipe See *feet and trotters (sheep's)*.

ROUERGUE A former French province in the south-east, now part of the departments of Aveyron and Tarn-et-Garonne. The great specialities of its capital, Rodez (in Aveyron), are typical of the cooking of the whole region: veal tripe (*trénels à la ruthénoise*), game pâtés and fricassée of pig's trotters (feet) are particularly famous.

Among the soups common to the whole Aveyron region are cabbage soup, *aïgo bouilido*, *ouillade* and the very rich *mourtayrol*.

Specific to the Rouergue region are sheep's tripe (called *manouls*), the dried hams from Naucelle and Najac, preserved goose, truffle omelette, stuffed pancakes from Ségala, thrushes from the Causses and *stoficado* (dried salt cod) from the Lot valley.

Puff pastries are flavoured with Roquefort, while Laguiole, Bleu des Causses and Cabécou cheeses can be counted among the best. Wine from Gaillac (best when it is slightly sparkling: Gaillac Perlé) goes well with the cakes and pastries of the region, of which *fouace*, flavoured with lemon, orange-flower water or bergamot, and sprinkled with sugar, is most representative. In the past, *fouace* was sprinkled with dragées (sugared almonds) for weddings and baptisms, and at Easter it takes the form of an enormous circular cake called *coque*, which is the centrepiece of an annual procession at Najac. Other cakes surviving from a past tradition are the decorative *soleil* of Marcillac (made from yeast dough with almonds, relic of an ancient sun-worshipping cult), prune rissoles, gâteau *à la broche* and *flônes*.

ROUFF, MARCEL

French journalist and writer (born Geneva, 1887; died Paris, 1936). He was a colleague and friend of Curnonsky, whom he accompanied on a gastronomic tour of France, seeking out and recording her culinary resources. They published their findings in 28 little guides, written in a lively and humorous style, under the collective title of *La France gastronomique*.

Rouff is best known for his novel *La Vie et la Passion de Dodin-Bouffant, gourmet* (1924), in which he created the archetypal perfect gastronome who sacrifices everything to the epicurean pleasures of the table.

ROUGAIL

A highly spiced seasoning used in the cooking of the West Indies and Réunion. Made from vegetables, shellfish or fish and pimientos, it is simmered in oil and can be eaten hot or cold, with rice-based West Indian dishes.

RECIPES

rougail of aubergines

Remove the stalks from 2 or 3 aubergines (eggplants) weighing in total about 300 g (11 oz) and cook them for 20–25 minutes in a preheated oven at 220°C (425°F, gas 7). Meanwhile, in a food processor, purée 1 small new onion, a small piece of fresh root ginger, half a red chilli pepper, ½ teaspoon salt, the juice of half a lemon and 3–4 tablespoons olive oil. Halve the aubergines and remove the pulp with a spoon. Mix this pulp with the other ingredients and blend well to obtain a fine paste. Chill until ready to serve.

rougail of salt cod

Soak 300 g (11 oz) salt-cod fillets in cold water for 24 hours, changing the water 2 or 3 times. Dry the fish, cut into small pieces and dip in flour. Heat 3 tablespoons olive oil – or oil and lard – in a flameproof casserole and cook the fish until golden. Add 3 finely sliced onions, then cover and cook gently until the onions are soft. Then add 4 peeled tomatoes, seeded and coarsely chopped. In a food processor, purée a small piece of fresh root ginger, 1 garlic clove, 1 small red chilli, 1 teaspoon chopped parsley and a few leaves of fresh thyme.

Mix this purée into the fish, cover the casserole and cook in a preheated oven at 180°C (350°F, gas 4) for 50 minutes. Serve either hot or cold.

rougail of tomatoes

Using either a food processor or a mortar, make a purée of 1 large onion (chopped), a small piece of fresh root ginger, ½ teaspoon salt, 4 peeled, seeded and coarsely chopped tomatoes, the juice of lemon and 1 small red chilli. Serve cold.

ROUILLE

A Provençal sauce whose name (meaning rust) describes its colour, due to the presence of red chillies and sometimes saffron. The chillies are pounded with garlic and breadcrumbs (or potato pulp), then blended with olive oil and stock. Rouille is served with bouillabaisse, boiled fish and octopus. Lemon juice and fish liver may be added to it.

RECIPE

rouille

Pound 2 small red chillies and 1 garlic clove in a mortar (if the chillies are dried, soak them first for a few hours in cold water). Add 1 teaspoon olive oil if liked, but this is not essential and may change the taste of the sauce. Pound 2 scorpion-fish livers and 1 small potato, cooked either in the bouillabaisse or in a little fish fumet, and add the chillies. When the mixture is smooth, gradually blend it with some strained broth from the bouillabaisse (use enough to make it up to 7 times the original volume). If the sauce is to accompany a chicken bouillabaisse rather than a fish one, replace the scorpion-fish livers with chicken livers.

ROULADE

Any of various savoury or sweet preparations which are stuffed or filled and then rolled.

A pork or veal roulade consists of a fairly thin slice of meat, spread with forcemeat and rolled up, then usually braised. Veal roulade can also be made using a slice from the leg or breast, slit open to form a pocket, filled with a forcemeat mixed with a salpicon, then rolled into a galantine and poached in white stock. A roulade of pig's head is prepared from the boned head with the rind left on, which is salted and washed, stuffed (usually with the ears, tongue and filets mignons), and cooked in a cloth. It is served as a cold hors d'oeuvre.

The term is also used for baked goods, again savoury or sweet; for example a rolled sweet sponge with a cream filling, or similar. A savoury roulade, based on a baked cheese or vegetable mixture, may be prepared as for a sweet roulade, but with a savoury filling. Savoury roulades may be served hot or cold.

ROUND OF BEEF

A cut of beef taken from the top of the hind leg of the animal. Topside (top round), which forms part of the cut, gives a lean and fairly tender roasting joint with a good flavour. Silverside (bottom round) and rump are also part of the round.

Roussillon

This part of Languedoc, lying to the east of the Pyrenees, with its Côte Vermeille bathed by the Mediterranean, has many gastronomic resources.

■ **From fine game to good vegetables** Game, including chamois, snow partridge, capercaillie, wild pigeon and even bear, are prepared in ways which date from the Renaissance. The river trout are as well known as the snails, which are cooked over charcoal. Among other well-known dishes are shoulder of mutton *à la catalane* (with pistachio nuts), young partridge with morels, and pigeons simmered in a casserole with Rancio wine and flavoured with orange peel.

• SEAFOOD DISHES Civet of langouste, monkfish and salt cod *à la catalane* are justly famous on this coast, as are the anchovy pâtés, the mussels and the clams. The *bouillinada*, a local form of bouillabaisse, is accompanied by *crémat* of garlic (puréed and diluted with stock), and the most common way of cooking fish is *à la catalane* – heavily flavoured with (bell) peppers, aubergines (eggplants) and tomatoes.

• EGG DISHES Eggs are prepared in many different ways:

The great wines of Banyuls are aged in oak for over two years to develop their ruby or mahogany colour.

à la causalade (with slices of fried local ham), scrambled with aubergines or ceps, hard-boiled (hard-cooked) with anchovies, or in an omelette with sausage or black pudding (blood sausage).

• VEGETABLES The excellent early vegetables of the region are used in salads and especially in soups: *escuedella de nadal*, *ouillade*, soups with mint and thyme and *braoubouffat*. Broad (fava) beans are stewed *à l'étouffée* (with wine and herbs), haricot (navy) beans are prepared as an *estouffat*, and onions are ingredients in many spicy dishes simmered in olive oil, which make the cooking of Roussillon so

typical of the Mediterranean region.

■ **Specialities to complete a menu** Several varieties of ewe's-milk cheese are made in Roussillon, but their reputation is surpassed by that of the region's fruit: peaches and apricots are of prime quality, followed by raspberries, grapes, figs and pomegranates.

The pastries and sweetmeats of the region include tartlets filled with pears, apples, dried figs or prunes, brioche rings (or *bistortos*), pancakes with honey or bilberry or strawberry jam, *turrón*, honey and nougat. The old traditions are kept alive with *biscotins* (sweet biscuits or cookies), *rosquilles*, and aniseed bread.

■ **Wines and liqueurs** A good ratafia is made from quinces, and some vigorous red wines are produced (Corbières-du-Roussillon and Côtes-du-Roussillon), but it is the liqueur wines and the sweet fortified wines which are considered the best (Banyuls, Muscat de Rivesaltes and Maury).

When the fruit trees are in flower, Roussillon takes on a Japanese air. These orchards of apricot and peach trees are near Thuir, at the foot of Mount Canigou, the highest peak of the Pyrénées-Orientales.

ROUT An archaic name for a large party, social gathering or reception. The English word is derived from the French *route*, which used to mean 'company'. The modern French word (*raout*) is derived from the English and first appeared in 1804. In the 1920s, when everything to do with the English was fashionable, the word was used to describe a cocktail party or an evening reception (Proust used it). The word has now fallen into disuse.

ROUX A cooked mixture of equal amounts of flour and butter, used to thicken many sauces. The cooking period varies, depending on the colour of roux required (a white or blond roux for a white sauce; a brown roux for a brown sauce).

A white roux should, in theory, remain white. However, as it must also be cooked long enough to lose its floury taste, it is advisable to cook it until it is just beginning to take on a golden colour (blond). Blended with milk, a white or blond roux is used for a béchamel sauce; blended with white veal stock, it makes a veal velouté; with chicken stock, a chicken velouté; and with fish stock, a fish velouté.

A brown roux, cooked just long enough to obtain a light brown colour, is used to thicken espagnole and demi-glace sauces.

RECIPES

white roux

Melt the butter in a heavy-based saucepan, then clarify it. Add the same weight (or a little more) of sifted plain (all-purpose) flour – up to 125 g (4½ oz, 1 cup) flour for 100 g (4 oz, ½ cup) butter. To make 1 litre (1¾ pints, 4⅓ cups) béchamel sauce, the roux should contain 75 g (3 oz, ¾ cup) flour and the same weight of butter; to make 1 litre (1¾ pints, 4⅓ cups) velouté sauce, use 50–65 g (2–2½ oz, ½–⅔ cup) flour and the same weight of butter.

Mix the butter and flour, stirring constantly with a wooden spoon and covering the whole bottom of the saucepan, so that the roux does not colour unevenly and become lumpy. Continue to cook in this way for 5 minutes, until the mixture begins to froth a little. Take the pan off the heat and leave it to cool until time to add the liquid (milk, white stock, fish stock). To avoid lumps forming this must be poured boiling on to the cold roux. Use a whisk to mix the roux and heat gradually while whisking constantly. (Alternatively, the cold liquid may be whisked gradually into the warm roux.)

blond roux

Make a white roux, but cook it gently for 10 minutes, stirring constantly, until it becomes a golden colour.

brown roux

Make a white roux, but cook it very gently for 15–20 minutes, stirring constantly, until it becomes a light brown colour.

ROWANBERRY An orange-red berry the size of a small cherry. It is the fruit of the mountain ash tree, a species of *Sorbus*. The berries are used when almost overripe to make jam or jelly (good with venison) and, on a small scale, brandy. They have a tart flavour.

ROYALE A moulded custard which is cut into small dice, lozenges (diamonds) or stars, and used as a garnish for clear soup. Made from consommé and eggs, or a vegetable or poultry purée thickened with eggs, it is cooked in dariole moulds in a bain marie. When it is cooked, it is unmoulded and cut into the desired shapes.

The word *royale* (royal) is also used to describe a type of icing (frosting) made from egg whites and icing (confectioner's) sugar.

RECIPES

plain royale

Add a generous pinch of chervil to 150 ml (¼ pint, ⅔ cup) boiling consommé* and leave it to infuse for 10 minutes. Beat 1 whole egg with 2 yolks and add the consommé gradually, stirring constantly. Strain through a sieve lined with muslin (cheesecloth), skim and cook in a bain marie as for royale of asparagus.

royale of asparagus

Cook 75 g (3 oz) asparagus tips and 5 or 6 fresh spinach leaves in boiling water for a few minutes, then drain them. Add 1½ tablespoons béchamel* sauce and 2 tablespoons consommé*. Press through a sieve. Bind the mixture with 4 egg yolks, pour into dariole moulds and cook in a bain marie in a preheated oven at 200°C (400°F, gas 6) for 30 minutes.

royale of carrots à la Crécy

Cook 75 g (3 oz) carrots in butter over a low heat, adding salt and a pinch of sugar. Stir in 2 tablespoons béchamel* sauce and the same amount of cream, and press through a sieve. Bind with 4 egg yolks and cook in the same way as royale of asparagus.

royale of celery

Cook 75 g (3 oz, ¾ cup) finely sliced celery sticks in butter; add 1 tablespoon béchamel* sauce and 2 tablespoons consommé*. Bind with 4 egg yolks and cook as for royale of asparagus.

royale of chicken purée

Poach 50 g (2 oz) white chicken meat and pound it finely. Add 2 tablespoons béchamel* sauce and the same amount of cream and press it through a sieve. Bind with 4 egg yolks and cook in a bain marie as for royale of asparagus.

royale of tomatoes

Mix 100 ml (4 fl oz, 7 tablespoons) concentrated tomato purée (paste) with 4 tablespoons consommé*. Add salt and pepper, bind with 4 egg yolks and cook in a bain marie as for royale of asparagus.

ROYALE, À LA Describing clear soups garnished with a royale; the term is also applied to various other dishes which have a light and delicate garnish.

Fish *à la royale* (salmon, turbot, trout) are poached and served hot, garnished with quenelles, mushrooms, poached oysters and truffles, accompanied by a mousseline sauce. Poultry *à la royale* is poached, garnished with quenelles and mushrooms (sometimes with the addition of slices of foie gras), and covered with royale sauce (a thick velouté to which cream and chopped truffles are added). Hare *à la royale* is a famous dish claimed by Périgord and Orléanais. The description *à la royale* may also apply to hot or cold desserts – puddings, soufflés, stuffed pineapple, ice cream sundaes – which are made from unusual ingredients and are presented with sophistication.

RECIPES

consommé à la royale
Make some meat or chicken consommé; prepare a plain or herb-flavoured royale. Let the royale get completely cold, unmould it on to a cloth (this will absorb any moisture) and cut it into small cubes, circles, stars or leaves. Just before serving, add this garnish to the hot soup.

hare à la royale
Collect the blood from a good-sized skinned hare, reserve the liver, heart and lungs, and remove the head. Carefully grease the bottom and sides of a very large stewpot with goose fat. Make a bed of bacon rashers (slices) in the pot, place the hare (on its back) on top and cover with bacon rashers. Add 1 sliced carrot, 20 garlic cloves, 40 shallots, 4 onions studded with cloves, and a bouquet garni. Pour in 250 ml (8 fl oz, 1 cup) wine vinegar and a bottle and a half of Burgundy. Season with salt and pepper. Put the pot over a low heat, cover it and cook for 3 hours.

Finely chop 125 g (4½ oz) bacon, the hare's offal (variety meat), 10 garlic cloves and 20 shallots. Mix all these together very thoroughly. Remove the stewpot from the heat. Lift out the hare very carefully and put it on a dish, leaving the bacon and vegetables in the stewpot. Tip the contents of the pot into a strainer, pressing to extract as much liquid as possible. Add this to the chopped bacon, offal and vegetables and pour in half a bottle of heated Burgundy. Pour this mixture into the stewpot, replace the hare and cook over a low heat for 1½ hours. Skim off the surface fat. About 15 minutes before serving, add the blood, well whisked and diluted with Cognac. When cooking is complete, arrange the hare on a serving dish and pour the sauce around it. Serve the same type of wine that was used to cook the hare.

royale sauce
Mix together 200 ml (7 fl oz, ¾ cup) chicken velouté* sauce and 100 ml (4 fl oz, 7 tablespoons) white chicken stock. Reduce by half, adding 100 ml (4 fl oz, 7 tablespoons) double (heavy) cream during the reduction. Just before serving, add 2 tablespoons finely chopped raw truffle, then whisk in 50 g (2 oz, 4 tablespoons) butter, and finally add 1 tablespoon sherry.

salpicon à la royale
Prepare 3 tablespoons chopped mushrooms and 1 tablespoon chopped truffle. Cook the mushrooms in butter, then add the truffle and 4 tablespoons chicken purée. Mix well and use as a filling for bouchées or barquettes.

RUB IN To mix fat into dry ingredients, usually flour, using the fingertips to achieve a crumbly consistency similar to breadcrumbs. This is done fairly rapidly by pinching or rubbing the small pieces of fat with the flour, allowing it to drop back into the bowl. The technique is quick, cool and light; the palms of the hands should remain clean. The aim is to incorporate some air as well as combining fat with flour, without melting it or reducing the mixture to a paste. If the rubbed-in mixture is to be bound together, for example into a dough, a little liquid is added after rubbing in. A food processor is often used for this technique, but care must be taken to avoid overprocessing the mixture into a paste.

RUBENS Sauce made from a brunoise of vegetables combined with white wine and then reduced; fish stock is added and the sauce is then simmered, sieved, degreased and reduced again. This preparation is then flavoured with Madeira, combined with egg yolks, thickened with beurre rouge (see *butter*) and finished with a dash of anchovy essence.

RUDD *rotengle* A freshwater fish, known also in France as *gardon rouge* (red roach), as it is similar to the roach in appearance and habitat. It is cooked in the same ways as the roach: fried, grilled (broiled) or *meunière*.

RUE A perennial herbaceous plant with small, greyish-blue, bitter-tasting leaves. It is an ancient herbal remedy, and during the Middle Ages was among the plants used for making liqueurs. Traditionally it was used to flavour the herb-based hippocras. In Italy it is used to flavour grappa (a marc brandy) – a small bunch of fresh rue sprigs is put into the bottle to macerate. In eastern Europe, it is an ingredient of meat stuffings and is added to flavour cream cheeses and marinades.

RUIFARD A dessert typical of the Dauphiné region of France, particularly the Valbonnais area. It is a large pie made from yeast dough, filled with sliced pears, apples and quinces cooked in butter, sweetened and flavoured with Chartreuse.

ruifard

Dissolve 15 g (½ oz) dried yeast (2 packages active dry yeast) in 2 tablespoons warm water. Sift 250 g (9 oz, 2¼ cups) strong plain (bread) flour into a heap and pour the dissolved yeast into a well in the centre. Mix in a little of the flour to make a thick cream. Leave it to rise for 10 minutes. Then add 1 whole egg, 20 g (¾ oz, 1½ tablespoons) softened butter, 1 tablespoon oil, 100 ml (4 fl oz, 7 table-spoons) double (heavy) cream, 15 g (½ oz, 1 table-spoon) sugar and ¼ teaspoon salt. Work with the hands to incorporate all the flour and knead until the dough leaves the fingers cleanly, then put it in a bowl and leave to rise for 30 minutes at 25°C (77°F).

Peel and slice 5 large apples, 5 pears and 2 small quinces. Cook them for 10 minutes with 50 g (2 oz, ¼ cup) butter and 150 g (5 oz, ⅔ cup) sugar; flavour with 2 tablespoons Chartreuse. Butter a 20 cm (8 in) sandwich tin (layer cake pan) and roll out half the dough to a thickness of 5 mm (¼ in). Line the base and sides of the tin with this dough and pour in the cooked fruit. Roll out the remain-ing dough a little more thinly and cover the fruit, sealing the edges with a little cold water.

Leave to rise for a further 10–15 minutes, then brush the surface with egg yolk. Bake in a pre-heated oven at 190°C (375°F, gas 5) for 30 minutes.

RULLY A village in the Côte Chalonnaise area of Burgundy producing red and white wines. Nineteen vineyards have *premier cru* status. Sparkling Cre-mant de Bourgogne is also made.

RUM A spirit distilled from sugar cane. The origin of the word is disputed: it may be a corruption of the Spanish *ron*; it may derive from the Latin *sac-charum* (sugar); or it may be a contraction of *rum-bustion* or *rumbullion*, formerly meaning 'strong liquor'. The Oxford English Dictionary prefers the latter etymology and dates the use of the word 'rum' from 1654.

■ **History** According to legend, sugar cane was brought to the West Indies by Christopher Columbus from the Canaries, where it had been introduced from the Orient. Distillation from sugar cane or its by-products was taking place in Hispaniola around the start of the 17th century, but these rough spirits were drunk by colonists only in the absence of imports of anything better: a contemporary descrip-tion of them is 'hot, hellish, and terrible'. Gradually, rum became more refined: sea-farers acquired a taste for it and introduced it into Europe, particularly western England, France and Spain, and it eventually spread all over the known world.

Historically, rum was powerful and strong in flavour. The cane juice, or diluted molasses (the residue after cane has been pressed), would ferment violently in hot climates when in contact with nat-ural yeasts, producing an alcoholic wash. From this rum was distilled, and often redistilled, in pot-stills (alembics). There were improvements in techniques – cultured yeasts were discovered, filtration improved and the value of maturing appreciated – but no basic change took place in rum production until the invention in Britain of continuous (patent, or column) distillation, which was perfected in the 1830s. Patent stills were soon in operation in the Caribbean region and they were to have a profound effect. Continuous distillation permitted increased volume with less labour and gave improved control over the final product's strength and degree of flavour.

■ **Types of rum** Some de-luxe rums are wholly from pot-stills, but most of the rums of normal commerce come from the column stills at very high strength and as almost flavourless spirit. They are either left as white rum or coloured and flavoured in various ways. Blending of rums of diverse origins is com-monly practised.

Since all distillates are initially colourless, regard-less of absence or presence of natural flavour, it is necessary to adjust dark rums to the required colour, ranging from pale golden, through amber, to deep brown, by the addition of caramel. Certain premium rums are matured in oak casks long enough to acquire some natural tint from the wood. Colour is, however, principally a matter of style; it has nothing to do with taste and only marginally with quality. The consumer has come to associate a dark hue with a pungent rum and white rum with virtual lack of flavour. Yet there are excellent full-flavoured rums that are almost colourless.

In speciality rums, there are two outstanding types. *Rhum agricole* is particularly relished in France and there is some demand for it in the United States. This 'agricultural rum' is made not from molasses but entirely from straight cane juice: this confers prestige in the opinion of some drinkers. The best-known (Clément) comes from Martinique and is aged for six years. British Navy Rum (Pusser's), from the British Virgin Islands, is rela-tively new to general commerce: formerly it was exclusively sold to be used as the Royal Navy's offi-cial daily issue of powerful, highly aromatic rum. The issue was stopped in 1970.

Rum of sorts is made wherever sugar cane flour-ishes, often for purely local use. In world terms, by far the largest producer is Puerto Rico. All styles are made there, including some unusual *añejos* (aged) rums. However, white rum predominates, typified by Ron Bacardi, progenitor of 'Cuban' rum, whose largest distillery is in Puerto Rico. The next most important rum island is Jamaica. Jamaican rum is tra-ditionally double-distilled in pot-stills and distinctly pungent, but Jamaica also produces light white rums by continuous distillation. Martinique is principally noted for rich fragrant rum. Other important produc-ers are Guyana (Demerara), which distils heavy, sometimes exceptionally strong, rums, but also white varieties; Barbados, famous for Mount Gay, a smoothly medium-rich rum; and Trinidad.

■ **Uses of rum** White rum is best for punches, daiquiris and other cocktails, while the stronger and darker rums are used in grogs, flamed dishes, cooking and pâtisserie. Old rums can be drunk as liqueurs.

There are many uses for rum in cooking, from soaking sponge cakes (for desserts and charlottes) to flavouring pancake batters, dessert creams, mousses, zabaglione, sorbets and fruit salads, or sprinkling on babas and savarins, flaming pancakes and omelettes, and macerating crystallized (candied) or dried fruit.

Rum combines particularly well with sweet potatoes, pineapple and bananas and the meat and fish dishes that these accompany (pork, sautéed chicken, turkey, scampi or monkfish kebabs, kidneys, roast duck). The aroma enhances sauces and marinades. Rum is suitable for flaming only very tender meat, such as offal (variety meats) and spring chicken.

RUMEN The first compartment of the stomach of ruminants, the three others being smaller. Before it is used, the rumen is emptied, heated in water at 70°C (158°F), then scraped, to remove any food particles which may be sticking to its lining. It is then 'hardened' in boiling water: this results in *boeuf blanc* (white beef). This is used to make tripe or for preparing *gras-double* (a dish made with three stomachs), *à la lyonnaise*, *à la florentine*, or even as *tablier de sapeur* (fireman's apron). *Tripous* of the Auvergne are made from lamb rumen and other internal organs.

RUMFORD, BENJAMIN THOMPSON, COUNT American physicist (born Woburn, Massachusetts, 1753; died Paris, 1814). He came to Europe to reorganize the army of the Elector of Bavaria, and during this period became interested in the problems of nutrition; in particular, how to extract the maximum benefit from food while using the minimum of fuel. As a result, he invented a brick cooker, with separate adjustable burners, which made the cook's job very much easier and also saved fuel. He also invented a pressure cooker and a kitchen stove.

Having discovered that the volatile oils in coffee were responsible for its taste, he suggested making coffee in a closed container, over a constant heat which kept the liquid just below boiling point and so avoided destroying the aroma; he could thus claim to be the inventor of the percolator. He is often credited with the invention of baked Alaska.

RUMOHR, KARL FREDERICK VON German writer and patron of the arts (born Dresden, 1785; died Dresden, 1843). Rich and independent, writer of novels and travel books, he is best known as the author of a cookery book, *Der Geist der Kochkunst*, which appeared in 1823, two years before Brillat-Savarin's *La Physiologie du goût*. Karl von Rumohr was an enlightened amateur, a fastidious connoisseur, a historian, even a dietician; his book deals with the nature of food, the origins of cookery and cooking methods, and the preparation of meat and fish, sauces, pâtés and conserves. It then goes on to discuss vegetables, herbs, spices, sugar and jams. The third volume is devoted to table manners and how to receive guests. The book relates remarkably well to modern culinary practice.

RUMP STEAK A cut of beef taken from between the buttock and the sirloin. Less tender than fillet but with a better flavour, the cut yields steaks for rapid grilling (broiling) or frying; when cut into pieces it can be used for kebabs or a fondue bourguignonne. It can be cooked as a roast, for which a piece at least 7 cm (2¾ in) thick is required, usually from the top rump, which is treated in the same way as a fillet or sirloin; the meat, which is dense and lean, should be lightly barded.

RUNNER BEAN A climbing bean plant widely cultivated for its edible green pods, which are cooked and prepared in the same way as French beans. A famous variety is the scarlet runner (*haricot d'Espagne*), named after its red flowers.

RUSK A slice of bread made from a special kind of dough (containing flour, water, salt, yeast, fat and sugar) and rebaked in the oven. Rusks are widely consumed in France (as *biscottes*) and also in other countries, such as Germany (as *Zwieback*) and the Netherlands. The bread is first baked in a mould, then sliced. The stale slices are rebaked in the oven, giving them a golden colour. They must have a crumbly texture with very small holes.

Rusks were originally considered as diet food. Now they are commonly eaten in France for breakfast and with meals. The composition may be modified for certain diets (salt-free, gluten-enriched, with bran). French 'toast', marketed in oblong slices, contain less fat and sugar than rusks.

Rusks are sometimes used in cookery and pastry-making, either soaked in milk for stuffings, as a garnish for gratin dishes, or powdered for use as breadcrumbs.

In Britain, rusks are generally thought of as something given to babies when they are teething.

RUSSE, À LA Describing preparations of shellfish coated in aspic jelly, covered with a chaud-froid sauce or a thick mayonnaise, and accompanied by a Russian salad (a macédoine of vegetables bound with mayonnaise, set in an aspic-lined mould or served in glass dishes). Russian sauce (*sauce russe*), served with crudités or cold fish, is made from mayonnaise mixed with caviar and possibly the creamy parts of lobster or crayfish.

All these dishes are inspired by the classic cuisine as practised at the time of the tsars, particularly by French chefs, and are not really representative of true Russian cookery. However, some recipes described as *à la russe* are based on Slav traditions, including those featuring cucumbers and gherkins, *bitoke*, herrings, stuffed (bell) peppers, fillet of beef, *kacha* and *piroshki*.

RUSSIA

Russia, with its seas frozen over for ten months of the year in the north and its Mediterranean climate in the south, has inherited diverse culinary traditions, influenced by Scandinavian, Mongol, Germanic and French cuisines.

■ **History** The dynasty of the Riourikides, who arrived from Scandinavia in the 9th century, introduced smoked fish and meats, grain alcohol and the use of soured cream (*smetana*) in many dishes. In the following century, Russia saw the arrival of Vladimir the Great who introduced Eastern culinary traditions: aubergines (eggplants), mutton and raisins shared plates with cereals and turnips, basic ingredients of the Russian diet. Soon sauerkraut arrived from the north and curdled milk with the Tartars. In the 16th century, the banquets of Ivan the Terrible and his boyars were famous. At the end of the 17th century, Peter the Great fell in love with France. During the 18th and 19th centuries, great French chefs, such as Antonin Carême and Urbain Dubois, visited the imperial court, and they in turn introduced the great Russian classics in France. At the beginning of the 20th century, Russian emigrants brought with them other specialities such as caviar, blinis, *vatrouchka* and *zakuski*.

■ **Three great gastronomic occasions** Russian culinary art reaches a peak with Easter and the culinary rituals of *zakuski* and tea.

• THE FEAST OF EASTER After the midnight mass preceding Easter day, the table prepared for the occasion is covered with a wide range of pâtés, side dishes, main course dishes and pastries. The menu often includes a roast lamb or sucking pig, cold ham in jelly, *koulibiac*, a roast turkey or game, coloured eggs, *paskha, koulitch* and traditional Easter cakes, such as the babas, made from yeast dough. The food is seasoned with blessed salt and served with Polish flat cakes of unleavened dough.

• THE TRADITION OF ZAKUSKI This ritual, linked to the traditional hospitality of the Russian home, is still practised. While waiting for dinner, the guests are offered herrings which may be marinated, smoked or served with cream, a range of *pirojki, pelmieni, cyrniki, cromesqui, rastegais, varieniki* and *sausseli* (sweet or savoury puff pastry), *nalizniki* (crêpes stuffed with fromage blanc), stuffed eggs, aubergine caviar, marinated fruit and vegetables, cucumber in soured cream and salt (*molossols*), as well as cheese specialities. Washed down with vodka, the *zakuski* are served with a wide range of bread: *balabouchki* made from sour dough, *boubliki*, made from hard dough, *boulotchki* made with milk, very white *korj*, plaited *krouchenik*, black rye bread, *katachapouri* made with cheese, cheese *none*, *tcherek* with sesame seeds, and *oukrainka*, very brown and wheel-shaped.

• THE RITUAL OF TEA All day long, the samovar keeps the water boiling to make a very strong tea, sometimes flavoured and usually drunk unsweetened. It is sometimes served with pastries and confectioneries: *gozinakhi* (sweets with nuts and honey), *fromage blanc* fritters, *pampouchki* (nun's farts), *krendiel* (very sweet pretzel-shaped brioches), lemon waffles, *vatrouchki* (fromage frais tartlets), *zavinaniets* (croquettes stuffed with fruits and nuts), nougat with hazelnuts.

■ **The core cuisine** Apart from the feasts of the wealthy and regional specialities, the majority of the cooking is simple and peasant-style. Cabbage, cereals, root vegetables, potatoes, sour soups garnished with fish or meat (often served cold), tarts and fruit desserts are key, with regional variations on these themes.

The repertoire of soups includes *borsch, chtchi, botvinya, okrochka, rassolnick, solianka* (cucumber, onion and tomato, garnished with

---

RECIPES

canapés à la russe

Remove the crusts from slices of white bread and cut into small rounds, squares or triangles. Spread with butter flavoured with herbs, cover with Russian salad and then coat with a thin layer of aspic. Refrigerate and serve as an hors d'oeuvre. A small slice of truffle may be placed in the centre of each canapé.

fillets of herring à la russe

Boil some potatoes in their skins, then peel and slice them. Take some large herring fillets in oil and slice them very thinly. Reshape them, placing a slice of potato between each slice of herring. Arrange on a long serving dish and dress with a herb vinaigrette (made with parsley, chervil, tarragon and chives) to which some finely chopped fennel and shallots have been added.

Russian mayonnaise

Melt 400 ml (14 fl oz, 1¾ cups) aspic* jelly, but do not let it get too warm. Mix with 300 ml (½ pint, 1¼ cups) mayonnaise and 1 tablespoon wine vinegar. Pour the mixture into a bowl placed over crushed ice and beat with a whisk until it becomes frothy (never use a wooden spoon). This sauce can be used to bind a dry macédoine of vegetables, which is then set in aspic-lined moulds.

Russian salad

Boil and finely dice some potatoes, carrots and turnips; boil some French (green) beans and cut into short pieces. Mix together equal quantities of these ingredients and add some well-drained cooked petits pois. Bind with mayonnaise and pile up in a salad bowl. Garnish with a julienne of pickled tongue and truffles and add some finely diced lobster or langouste meat.

meat or fish), the famous Bagration soup, and *spass* (made with barley and yogurt, flavoured with herbs).

Fish recipes include sturgeon in aspic with horseradish sauce; fish fillets, either smoked or grilled (broiled) on skewers; smoked or fried *sigui, kilki* and *silki* (small fish similar to sprats), accompanied by onions; carp, lamprey or pike-perch in sweet-and-sour preparations; and eel or salmon koulibiaca. Caviar (*ikra*) is lightly salted (*molossol*) or pressed into bricks (*paiousnaia*).

Among the meat and poultry specialities are *kournik* (a croustade of chicken with rice), *kholodetz, solonina* (salted rolled beef, poached and garnished with sauerkraut and potatoes, served with horseradish sauce), and stuffed shoulder of veal, marinated with juniper berries, then simmered and served with sautéed cucumbers.

Authentic Russian desserts include *halva,* a walnut custard sprinkled with toasted walnuts), *gourieva kacha,* semolina pudding containing walnuts and crystallized (candied) fruit; *kissel*; and *mazurek,* a walnut sponge cake covered with an icing (frosting) made with walnuts, lemon and vinegar. *Charlotka* is of French origin, being based on the iced charlottes made by French chefs working in Russia.

There is a wide range of pastries and sweets, including *gozinakhi* – walnut and honey sweets; fritters made with cream-cheese pancakes or with yeast dough; *pampouchki,* soufflé fritters; *krendiel,* very sweet brioches shaped like pretzels; lemon waffles; *vatrouchki;* cream-cheese tartlets; *zavyvaniets,* little balls made from fruit and walnuts, covered in sweet pastry; and hazelnut nougat.

Any survey of Russian gastronomy would be incomplete if it omitted to mention vodka, which may be flavoured with aniseed, herbs (*zubrowka*), lemon zest, blackcurrant leaves, caraway seeds, peppercorns or even lichen. Among other traditional Russian alcoholic drinks are *kvass, hydromel,* Caucasian wines and *krupnikas* (a honey-based liqueur).

One other aspect that should be mentioned is the originality of Russian Jewish cookery. Typical dishes are iced soups with hard-boiled (hard-cooked) eggs or sorrel; sweet-and-sour stuffed carp and mackerel, *petchia,* jellied calves' feet; and *klops,* minced (ground) beef pâté with veal fat and herbs, cooked on a bed of onions and herbs. Saturday is the day for *tcholent* (brisket of beef cooked in the oven with onions, kasha and potatoes). Other favourite dishes are stuffed goose

neck and *gribenes* (pieces of goose skin fried with onions, served with sorrel fritters). Sauerkraut is eaten hot with smoked beef sausages or roast goose or cold, as an hors d'oeuvre. *Tsimes,* consisting of carrot or beetroot (beet) in a sweet-and-sour sauce, is served as a first course or as a garnish for meat. There are numerous flour-based dishes, including *lokschen* (vermicelli with eggs and cream cheese) and *kendlachs* (little dumplings of flour, egg, goose fat and ginger, which are poached or fried). The pastries resemble those typical of Austria, many being based on dried fruit, cinnamon and poppy seeds. Jams are prepared from black radish and honey and from quetsche plums and walnuts.

WINE Russia is a historic wine-producing country. Most of the vineyards are situated in the North Caucasus, with the best dry table wines produced in the valley of the Don, on the Black Sea coast of the Caucasus, in the foothills of the Stavropol area and in South Degestan, mainly from Aligoté, Riesling and Cabernet Sauvignon. Dessert wines are produced, as are sparkling wines. About 100 grape varieties are allowed for commercial cultivation, with Rkatsiteli predominant.

For a more elaborate dish, the ordinary mayonnaise can be replaced by thickened mayonnaise and the salad is poured into mould lined with aspic and garnished with slivers of truffle and pickled tongue. Chill in the refrigerator for 4 hours and remove from the mould just before serving.

Russian sauce (cold)
Mix equal quantities of caviar and the finely sieved creamy parts (liver) of lobster. Make some mayonnaise and add the caviar mixture: use 1 part mixture to 4 parts mayonnaise.

This sauce may be seasoned with a little mild mustard.

salmon cutlets à la russe
Cut fresh salmon steaks in two lengthways to make the cutlets; poach them for 5 minutes in a court-bouillon. Let them cool completely in their juices, then drain, dry and glaze them with aspic.

To serve place a layer of shredded lettuce dressed with vinaigrette on a large serving dish and arrange the salmon cutlets on top. Garnish with very small lettuce hearts, quartered hard-boiled (hard-cooked) eggs, black (ripe) olives, capers and anchovy fillets in oil.

sauce à la russe
(from a recipe by Carême) Chop and blanch 1 tablespoon parsley, chervil and tarragon, drain it, and mix with a fairly thick velouté sauce. Just before serving, add 1 tablespoon fine mustard, 1½ teaspoons caster (superfine) sugar, a pinch of finely ground pepper and some lemon juice.

This sauce can be served with large joints of meat.

other recipes See *cigarette, cucumber, fillet, gherkin.*

RUSSIA See *above.*

RUSSULA A short, brightly coloured mushroom with granular, crumbly flesh. There are numerous species, not all of which are edible. They can be differentiated by colour or more reliably by tasting a very small fragment of the raw mushroom: if it has a bitter or a hot taste it should not be eaten; mild-tasting species can be eaten, but experience is needed to select the edible varieties. The best species, which are cooked in the same way as cultivated mushrooms, are the green russula (*russule verdoyante* or *palomet*), with a green-patched whitish cap, which is excellent for grilling (broiling), and the variety known in France as *charbonnier* or *charbonnière*, with a purple, violet or green cap and a pleasant but rather insipid taste.

RUSTER AUSBRUCH An Austrian white wine, produced near Rust in the Burgenland, from Late-picked grapes. It is therefore somewhat concentrated and sweet – the term *ausbruch*, in the context of Austrian wines, signifies that the gapes are not picked until very ripe.

RYE A cereal native to western Asia, which appeared in Europe before the Iron Age and is grown mainly in Nordic regions, in the mountains and on poor soil. Rye flour can be made into bread; because it does not have a high gluten content it is usually mixed with wheat flour. This results in bread with a fine crumb and dense texture. The higher the proportion of wheat flour, the better the gluten content and elasticity of the dough, and the lighter the bread. Ryebread rolls are popular served with oysters and seafood. Rye flour is also used to make gingerbread and certain cakes (*nieules* and *pain de Linz*), as well as Russian and Scandinavian pies and crispbreads. Some spirits can also be made based on rye; for example, vodka and whiskey.

RYE WHISKEY An American whiskey, produced and consumed mainly in Pennsylvania, Maryland and Canada. It is made from nonmalted rye and barley or rye malt. It is not matured for as long as Scotch or Bourbon and it has a more pungent taste.

S

SABAYON French name for zabaglione. The name is also given to a savoury mousseline sauce made with champagne and served with fish or shellfish. See *zabaglione*.

SABLAGE In former times, a table decoration made with sands of different colours, which were spread on the tablecloth so as to form various patterns, such as flowers, landscapes, coats of arms and monograms.

SABLÉ A crumbly biscuit (cookie) of varying size, usually round and often with a fluted edge. Sablés are made from flour, butter, egg yolks (these are sometimes omitted) and sugar, mixed rapidly until of a sandy texture. The mixture is kneaded quickly, then either rolled out thinly and cut out with a pastry (cookie) cutter, or rolled into a thick sausage shape and sliced, as for so-called Dutch sablés, which are made with two mixtures, one coloured with chocolate or cinnamon, the other flavoured with vanilla. Sablés can be flavoured with lemon, flaked (slivered) almonds or raisins, and iced (frosted) with chocolate or topped with jam (see *milanais*). Shortbread and Austrian *Knusper* are other varieties of sablé. Sablé pastry is also used for making tartlets and barquettes, often filled with cream or strawberries.

RECIPES

Milan sablés
Place 250 g (9 oz, 2¼ cups) plain (all-purpose) flour in a bowl. Add the grated zest of 1 lemon, 125 g (4½ oz, ½ cup) softened butter cut into small pieces, 125 g (4½ oz, ½ cup) sugar, 4 egg yolks, a pinch of salt and 1 teaspoon brandy or rum. Knead these ingredients together quickly, roll the dough into a ball and chill for 30 minutes. Then roll out the dough to a thickness of 5 mm (¼ in) and cut out the sablés with a round or oval pastry (cookie) cutter. Arrange the sablés on a greased baking sheet, brush them with beaten egg and score lightly with a fork. Bake in a preheated oven at 200°C (400°F, gas 6) for 15 minutes, when the sablés should be scarcely golden.

vanilla and cinnamon sablés
Mix 250 g (9 oz, 2¼ cups) sifted plain (all-purpose) flour with 125 g (4½ oz, ½ cup) butter until crumbly. Add 125 g (4½ oz, ½ cup) caster (superfine) sugar and 1 egg. Work together quickly, roll the mixture into a ball, then chill for 1 hour. Cut the dough in half; sprinkle one half with 1 teaspoon ground cinnamon and the other with 1 teaspoon vanilla sugar. Knead each half until the flavourings are well blended, then roll each out into a rectangle, 5 mm (¼ in) thick. Brush the vanilla dough with water and lay the cinnamon dough on top. Roll up the 2 layers into a sausage shape. Brush with water, sprinkle with 3 tablespoons sugar and cut into slices 5 mm (¼ in) thick. Arrange on a greased baking sheet and bake in a preheated oven at 200°C (400°F, gas 6) for about 15 minutes. Allow the sablés to cool completely, then store in an airtight container.

additional recipe See *short pastry*.

SACCHAROMETER An instrument, also called a syrup hydrometer, for measuring the density of a solution of sugar in water, in order to obtain the correct concentration. The saccharometer consists of a sealed tube with a weighted bulb at one end. A second tube is three-quarters filled with the syrup solution to be tested. The saccharometer works on the principle that any body immersed in a liquid displaces its own weight by volume, so when plunged into the syrup, the graduated tube sinks vertically and the density of the syrup is indicated by the reading at the level to which the saccharometer sinks. The saccharometer can only be used when preparing syrups at the lower temperatures – up to the light (small or soft) crack stage, 129–135°C (265–275°F). See *sugar*.

SACHERTORTE

SACHERTORTE A famous Viennese gâteau, created at the Congress of Vienna (1814–15) by Franz Sacher, Metternich's chief pastrycook. Sachertorte (literally, 'Sacher's cake') is a sort of chocolate Savoy sponge cake, filled or spread with apricot jam (preserve), then covered with chocolate icing (frosting); it is traditionally served with whipped cream and a cup of coffee.

For years, Vienna was divided into two camps by the sachertorte controversy. The supporters of sachertorte as it was served at the Sacher Hotel – two layers separated by jam, the top being iced – were led by the descendants of Franz Sacher, who regarded their version as the only authentic one. On the other side were the customers of the famous Demel pâtisserie, who based their claim on the rights acquired by Édouard Demel from Sacher's grandson, who authorized the so-called 'true' recipe (the cake is simply spread with jam, then covered with the icing), as published in *Die Wiener Konditorei* by Hans Skrach. The Sacher Hotel finally won the court case that fascinated Vienna for six years. Demel replied by claiming that his was the *Ur-Sachertorte* (the original cake).

RECIPE

sachertorte
(from Joseph Wechsberg's recipe in *Viennese Cookery*, Time-Life) Line two 20 cm (8 in) round sandwich tins (layer cake pans) with buttered greaseproof (wax) paper. Melt 200 g (7 oz, 7 squares) plain cooking (semisweet) chocolate, broken into small pieces, in a bain marie. Lightly beat 8 egg yolks and mix in 125 g (4½ oz, ½ cup) butter, melted, and the melted chocolate. Whisk 10 egg whites until stiff with a pinch of salt and add 150 g (5 oz, ⅔ cup) caster (superfine) sugar, slightly vanilla-flavoured, beating all the time until the mixture stands up in stiff peaks. Fold one-third of the egg whites into the chocolate mixture, then gradually fold in the remaining whites. Add 125 g (4½ oz, 1 cup) sifted plain (all-purpose) flour, sprinkling it on gradually and lightly mixing and folding together all the ingredients until all traces of white disappear. Pour equal quantities of the mixture into the 2 tins and bake in a preheated oven at 180°C (350°F, gas 4) for about 45 minutes, until the cakes are well

risen and a skewer inserted in the centres comes out clean. Turn out the cakes on to a wire rack and allow to cool completely.

To make the icing (frosting), put 150 g (5 oz, 5 squares) plain cooking chocolate, broken into pieces, in a saucepan together with 250 ml (8 fl oz, 1 cup) double (heavy) cream and 200 g (7 oz, ¾ cup) vanilla sugar. Stir over a moderate heat until the chocolate has melted, then cook for 5 minutes without stirring. Beat 1 egg, mix in 3 tablespoons of the chocolate mixture, and pour this back into the saucepan. Cook for 1 minute, stirring, then leave to cool at room temperature.

Spread 175 g, (6 oz, ½ cup) sieved apricot jam over one of the halves of the chocolate cake, then put the other half on top. Cover the whole cake with the chocolate icing, smoothing it out with a metal spatula. Slide the cake on to a plate and chill in the refrigerator for 3 hours, until the icing hardens. Remove 30 minutes before serving.

SACRISTAIN A small biscuit (cookie) made from a stick of twisted puff pastry, often sprinkled with flaked (slivered) or chopped almonds. Classically, it is one of the assortment of biscuits served with tea.

SADDLE A cut of meat consisting of the two joined loins. The saddle of a hare or rabbit extends from the lower ribs to the tail. It is a fleshy piece of meat that can be roasted whole, often larded or barded and marinated. It can also be cooked with mustard or with cream (sautéed in a casserole); braised and served with mushroom purée, chestnuts and poivrade sauce; or sautéed and garnished with cherries, with a soured (sour) cream sauce. When it is not cooked whole, the saddle is cut into two or three pieces and made into a civet, stew or sauté with the rest of the animal.

A saddle of venison comprises the part of the animal between the loin and the haunch (see *roebuck*).

RECIPES

roast saddle of hare
Insert some small strips of fatty bacon into the saddle. Sprinkle it with salt and pepper, brush with oil and roast it in a preheated oven at 240°C (475°F, gas 9) for about 20 minutes (the meat should still be pink). It can also be spit-roasted.

Garnish the serving dish with fluted half slices of lemon and watercress. Serve the saddle either with its own cooking juices – by deglazing the roasting tin (pan) with white wine – or with a poivrade sauce; the tin can also be deglazed using a mixture of equal proportions of white wine and double (heavy) cream.

saddle of hare à l'allemande
Insert some small strips of fatty bacon into the saddle and sprinkle it with table salt. Cut 1 carrot and 1 onion into slices; chop 1 shallot, 1 celery stick and 1 garlic clove. Put some of these vegetables

Carving a saddle of lamb

The style of carving varies: the British method is to cut the meat across the grain at right angles to the backbone. The French method, shown here, is to slice the meat lengthways. For traditional buffet serving, the slices should be reassembled into shape for neat presentation.

1 *Separate the thin, fatty section of meat from the underside of the saddle along one side and cut it into thin slices. Cut off and slice the same portion of meat from the other side of the saddle in the same way.*

2 *Turn the meat over. Cut the first slice at a slant along one side of the backbone, cutting down into the meat. When this first slice is cut, the following cuts are horizontal.*

3 *Cut between the meat and the bone, as close to the bone as possible, to separate the meat from the bone, then cut horizontal slices of meat off one side of the saddle.*

4 *Turn the saddle around and cut the meat in slices from the second side. Finally, cut off the small fillets of meat that run close to the backbone.*

into a deep bowl and lay the saddle on top. Pour in 250 ml (8 fl oz, 1 cup) oil, sprinkle with coarsely chopped parsley, powdered thyme, 1 bay leaf cut into pieces and 12 peppercorns, and add 1 small onion studded with 2 cloves. Cover the saddle with the remaining vegetables and pour in just enough white wine to cover everything. Leave to marinate for 6 hours, turning the meat once.

Oil a roasting tin (pan) and place in it the vegetables from the marinade; place the saddle on top and cook in a preheated oven at 240°C (475°F, gas 9) for 20–25 minutes (the meat should still be pink). Drain the saddle and keep it hot. Pour the marinade into the roasting tin, add 200 ml (7 fl oz, ¾ cup) double (heavy) cream, and boil to reduce by half. Adjust the seasoning with the juice from half a lemon; strain and pour over the saddle. Serve with unsweetened apple sauce and redcurrant jelly.

additional recipe See *wild boar*.

SADE, DONATIEN ALPHONSE FRANÇOIS, MARQUIS DE French writer (born Paris, 1740;

died Charenton, 1814). Taking as his principle that 'nature created men only in order that they should take pleasure in everything on earth', Sade was a firm believer in the importance of good food, as well as the pleasures and pains of love. From the prisons where he spent several decades, he wrote to his wife – whom he sometimes called 'fresh pork of my thoughts' – with precise and insistent requests for food. He organized a ball in Marseilles, at which he distributed among the ladies pastilles that were supposed to be chocolate but were in fact made of cantharidine, an alkaloid aphrodisiac. The marquis was also a regular at the 'chez Méot dinners' organized by Grimod de La Reynière.

SAFFLOWER A plant originating from Africa and Asia but cultivated in the south of France, North Africa, the USA and India for its seeds, which yield a low-cholesterol oil used in cooking oils and margarines. The petals of its flowers are sometimes used as a saffron substitute (another name for it is 'bastard saffron'), but their taste is a little more bitter. They are mainly used to add colour and flavour to rice dishes. In Jamaica, safflower is used as a spice, mixed with chilli peppers and cloves.

SAFFRON A spice consisting of the dried stigmas of the saffron crocus, a bulbous plant originating in the East, introduced into Spain by the Arabs, and later cultivated in Mediterranean regions and elsewhere in Europe. In France it has been grown by the *safraniers* in the Gâtinais and the Angoumois regions since the 16th century. In England, the Essex town of Saffron Walden became the centre of saffron cultivation.

The spice, which takes the form of an orange-yellow powder or dried brownish filaments called strands or threads, has a pungent smell and a bitter flavour. The best saffron comes from Valencia in Spain, but it is also cultivated in Italy, Greece, Turkey, Iran, Kashmir and Morocco. Since between 70,000 and 80,000 stigmas are required to make 500 g (18 oz) saffron, it is very expensive and various substitutes are often used, for example safflower (or 'bastard saffron') and turmeric (or Indian saffron).

Until the Middle Ages, saffron played an important role in cooking, magic and medicine. It was widely used before the Renaissance as a perfume and colouring agent, in baking and cookery, but had lost much of its popularity by the 19th century (Dumas noted that this flower was used 'to colour cakes, vermicelli and butter').

Saffron today has a privileged place in cookery, particularly in bouillabaisse, paella, the *mourtayrol* (a chicken soup) of Périgord, risotto, some recipes for mussels, white meats and tripe, as well as in Persian-influenced Indian dishes such as pilau and biryani. In desserts, it is used to flavour rice cooked in milk, semolina puddings and some brioches. Saffron should be blended into hot liquid, never fried quickly in very hot fat.

RECIPES

saffron ice cream with rose water ♦
Whip 150 ml (¼ pint, ⅔ cup) milk with 150 ml (¼ pint, ⅔ cup) double (heavy) cream. Place in the freezer to harden.

Beat 3 egg yolks in a bowl with 75 g (3 oz, 2 cup) caster (superfine) sugar until the mixture foams. In a saucepan, bring to the boil 450 ml (¾ pint, 2 cups) milk, 150 g (5 oz, generous ⅔ cup) crème fraîche and ½ teaspoon vanilla essence (extract). Reduce the heat so that the mixture does not even simmer. Slowly incorporate the egg yolk mixture, stirring all the time. Remove from the heat. Pound ½ teaspoon saffron, then stir in a little hot water and pour into the saucepan with 1 tablespoon rose water. Stir well and leave to cool completely, stirring occasionally. Chill well, then transfer to an ice-cream maker and freeze until firm. Remove the frozen whipped cream from the freezer and scoop it into small pieces using 2 teaspoons. Return the scoops to the freezer.

Remove the ice cream from the freezer 30 minutes before serving. Keep in the refrigerator until ready to serve. Serve in bowls, decorated with the scoops of cream and slivers of pistachio nut.

saffron rice à la néerlandaise
Wash about 175 g (6 oz, ¾ cup) short-grain rice. Blanch it for 2 minutes in boiling water. Drain, rinse in cold water and drain again. Boil 1 litre (1¾ pints, 4⅓ cups) milk with ½ teaspoon salt and 1 generous tablespoon soft light brown sugar. Add the rice and cook for 35–40 minutes until very soft. Then add 1 tablespoon lemon juice and a generous pinch of powdered saffron and mix well. Pour the rice into individual sundae dishes and leave to cool completely. Serve as a cold dessert, sprinkled with brown sugar, accompanied by cinnamon or ginger biscuits (cookies).

SAGAN A garnish for escalopes (scallops), calves' sweetbreads or poultry suprêmes, which consists of risotto and mushroom caps filled with a purée of calf's brain mixed with a salpicon of truffle. An accompanying sauce is made by deglazing the meat residue with Madeira and thickened veal stock. Truffles, mushrooms and calf's brain are also ingredients of Sagan flan, while scrambled eggs Sagan comprise eggs scrambled with Parmesan cheese, arranged in a timbale and garnished with slices of brain and truffles. All these dishes are dedicated to Charles de Talleyrand-Périgord, Prince of Sagan.

SAGE A perennial herb widely cultivated in temperate climates for its leaves, which have an aromatic slightly peppery flavour and are used for flavouring fatty meats (such as pork), forcemeats, marinades, certain cheeses (including the English Sage Derby) and various drinks. Sage is traditionally considered to have curative properties: the name comes from the Latin *salvus* (safe, in good health).

In France, sage is used mainly in Provence, for cooking white meat and certain vegetable soups. It is used more frequently in Italian cuisine: *saltimbocca*, *osso bucco*, paupiettes and rice minestrone are flavoured with sage. In Britain and Flanders, sage and onion are used for poultry and pork stuffings and to flavour sauces. In Germany, ham, sausages and sometimes beer are flavoured with sage, and in the Balkans and the Middle East it is eaten with roast mutton. In China, tea is flavoured with sage.

RECIPE

sage and onion sauce
Cook 2 large onions for 8 minutes in salted boiling water. Drain them and chop them. Put the chopped onion into a saucepan with 100 g (4 oz, 2 cups) fresh white breadcrumbs and 25 g (1 oz,

Saffron ice cream with rose water.

2 tablespoons) butter. Season with salt and pepper and add 1 tablespoon chopped fresh sage. Cook for 5 minutes, stirring constantly. Just before serving, add 3 tablespoons pan juices from the roast pork or goose that this sauce is served with.

additional recipe See *stuffing*.

SAGO A starch made from the pith of the sago palm and other palms cultivated in the tropics. Sago comes in the form of small whitish, pinkish or brownish grains, which are very hard and semi-transparent and have a sweetish taste. Sago has been known in Europe from the time of the Renaissance. At the end of the 17th century, it was one of the most popular forms of starch in the West, used for garnishing veal or chicken broth, for thickening soup, for making soft rolls, or cooked in milk with spices. In Europe, it is now little used – only for thickening and to make puddings. It is more widely used in tropical areas. In Indonesian cookery, for example, it is reduced to a paste with coconut pulp and milk and used for making fritters, cakes, ravioli and desserts. In India, it is boiled with sugar to make a dessert jelly.

SAINGORLON A French blue cheese from Bresse made from pasteurized cow's milk (50% fat content) with a natural crust. It is a cylinder weighing 6–12 kg (13–26 lb). It was created at the beginning of World War II to replace Gorgonzola, which the Italians no longer exported. Smooth, with a pronounced flavour, it is the origin of Bresse Bleu.

SAINT-AMANT, MARC ANTOINE GIRARD, SIEUR DE French poet (born Quevilly, 1594; died Paris, 1661). The author of lyrical, satirical and realist poems, he became famous for his ode *La Solitude* (1618). He divided his time between Paris, where he frequented the taverns in the company of Cardinal de Retz, and his birthplace, taking part in military campaigns in Catalonia and Flanders as chief administrator of the artillery. He also stayed in Poland for a time and it is thought that he visited America.

He left a large body of poems about eating and drinking, which figure in the best Baroque anthologies. His witty compositions were inspired by all aspects of food and drink, including cider, Brie cheese, the vine and the melon.

Although his words lose something in translation they are worth reading:

'The dear apricot which I love,
The strawberry cover'd with cream,
The manna which falls down from heav'n,
The savour of honey's pure food,
The heavenly pear grown in Tours,
The sweetness of any green fig,
The plum with its delicate juice,
The very grape of Muscat
(A very strange title to me),
All are mere sourness and mire
Compar'd with this melon divine.'

It is said that he died in the company of a certain Montglas, tavern-keeper at the Petit More, where he obviously enjoyed the hospitality.

SAINT-AMOUR The AOC of the northernmost of the Beaujolais classified growths. It is a relatively light wine, with a beautiful ruby colour.

SAINT-AUBIN A village in the Côte-de-Beaune, Burgundy, producing mainly red wines. A high proportion of the vineyards have *premier cru* status.

SAINTE-ALLIANCE, À LA This description, evoking the festivities surrounding the signing of the Treaty of Paris (1815) by the sovereigns who had conquered Napoleon I, is given to several dishes: foie gras poached with truffles and champagne; a chicken stuffed with truffles cooked in Madeira, then fried and surrounded with slices of foie gras cooked in butter; and roast pheasant stuffed with woodcock, served on a canapé spread with woodcock purée. Brillat-Savarin supplied the recipe for the last dish in his *Physiologie du goût*, but without this name (which was later attributed to it by Prosper Montagné).

RECIPE

pheasant à la Sainte-Alliance
(from Brillat-Savarin's recipe) Hang a pheasant until it is very high, then pluck it and lard it with fresh firm bacon. Bone and draw 2 woodcock, separating the flesh and the offal. Make a stuffing with the flesh by chopping it with steamed beef bone marrow, a little shredded pork fat, some pepper, salt, herbs and truffles. Stuff the pheasant with this mixture.

Cut a slice of bread 5 cm (2 in) larger than the pheasant all round, and toast it. Pound the livers and entrails of the woodcock with 2 large truffles, 1 anchovy, a little finely chopped bacon and a moderately sized lump of fresh butter. Spread this paste evenly over the toast. Roast the pheasant in a preheated oven at 230°C (450°F, gas 8); when it is cooked, spoon all the roasting juices over the toast on a serving dish. Place the pheasant on top and surround it with slices of Seville (bitter) orange. This highly flavoured dish is best accompanied by wine from Upper Burgundy.

SAINTE-BEUVE, CHARLES AUGUSTIN French writer (born Boulogne-sur-Mer, 1804; died Paris, 1869). One of the greatest literary critics of his time, he was also one of the most famous gourmets. He founded, together with the Goncourts, Gavarni, Renan and Turgenev, the 'Magny dinners'; he was also one of the regulars at Alexandre Dumas's 'Wednesday suppers'.

SAINTE-CROIX-DU-MONT AOC sweet white wine produced on the right bank of the River Garonne, opposite the Sauternes region, using the same grapes and the same methods (see *Bordeaux*).

SAINTE-FOY-BORDEAUX An AOC region east of Bordeaux on the River Dordogne. Sweetish white and some red wines are made, all well worth trying by visitors to the region.

SAINTE-MAURE A French goat's-milk AOP cheese from Touraine (45% fat content), with a soft curd and a thin natural bluish rind, sometimes marked with pink and sometimes coated in ash. The best source is the Sainte-Maure plateau, where the cheese is farmhouse-made and has a particularly good flavour in summer and autumn. It is firm and creamy with a fairly pronounced goaty smell and a well-developed bouquet. It is cylindrical in shape, 15 cm (6 in) long and 4 cm (1½ in) in diameter. Sometimes a straw is inserted through the centre, running the length of the cheese. Ligueil, another cheese from the Tours area, is similar to Sainte-Maure and has the same shape.

SAINTE-MENEHOULD Describing dishes in which the main ingredient is cooked, cooled, coated with breadcrumbs and grilled (broiled), then served with mustard or Sainte-Menehould sauce (made with mustard, onion, vinegar and herbs). The term is typically applied to pig's trotters (feet), a speciality of the town of Sainte-Menehould in the Marne region of France, where the recipe was developed, but it can also be used for skate, pigeon, chicken, oxtail, pig's ears, *crépinettes* and poultry wings.

RECIPES

Sainte-Menehould sauce

Melt 15 g (½ oz,1 tablespoon) butter in a saucepan. Add 15 g (½ oz, 2 tablespoons) finely chopped onion, cover and cook very gently for 10 minutes until soft. Season with salt, pepper, a pinch of thyme and a pinch of powdered bay leaf and add 100 ml (4 fl oz, 7 tablespoons) white wine and 1 tablespoon vinegar. Reduce until all the liquid has evaporated, then moisten with 200 ml (7 fl oz, ¾ cup) demi-glace* sauce. Boil over full heat for 1 minute, then add a pinch of cayenne pepper. Remove from the heat and blend in 1 tablespoon each of mustard, very finely diced gherkins, chopped parsley and chervil.

turkey wings Sainte-Menehould

Braise some small turkey wings with herbs and flavourings, but do not let them get too soft (about 50 minutes). Drain and leave to cool. Pour a little melted butter or lard over them, roll them in fresh breadcrumbs and chill for 1 hour. Coat with melted butter and bake in a preheated oven at 230°C (450°F, gas 8) until golden (about 15 minutes). Serve with mustard or Sainte-Menehould sauce.

other recipes See *oxtail, paupiette.*

SAINT-ÉMILION A very attractive historic town and centre of a prestigious region for red wine production on the right bank of the River Gironde. The vineyards are reclassified every ten years – the most famous being Château Ausone and Cheval Blanc. The wines are mainly made from Merlot and Cabernet Franc grape varieties and can be full-bodied, with good concentration and capable of long ageing. The satellite appellations Lussac St-Émilion, Montagne St-Émilion, Puisseguin St-Émilion and St-Georges-St-Émilion lie on the outskirts, to the north and east of the town.

SAINT-ESTÈPHE A parish (commune) AOC in the Haut Médoc. Five châteaux figure in the 1855 classification: Cos (formerly Cos-d'Estournel) and Montrose as second growths, Calon-Ségur as a third, Lafon-Rochet as a fourth, and Cos-Labory as a fifth. Saint-Estèphe wines tend to be somewhat astringent when young, but they can develop impressively.

SAINT-ÉVREMOND, CHARLES DE French writer (born Coutances, 1615; died London, 1703). A famous gourmet, he formed the trio of the Coteaux with his two friends, the Marquis de Bois-Dauphin and the Comte d'Olonne. It was said that he started the day with oysters and had his rabbits sent from La Roche-Guyon, where they had a very high reputation at the time. In his *Comédie des friands*, he mentions a soup with stuffed onions to which he was very partial. Only the veal of Normandy, the partridges of Auvergne and the wines from the coteaux of Ay, Hautvillers and Avenay found favour in his eyes.

SAINT-FÉLICIEN A French soft cow's-milk cheese (60% fat content), with a natural bluish crust. Made in Dauphiné, Saint-Félicien is a small flat disc, weighing 150 g (5 oz). It has a slightly nutty taste.

SAINT-FLORENTIN A French cow's-milk cheese (45% fat content) with a soft curd and a smooth reddish-brown washed rind. Saint-Florentin is a wheel-shaped cheese, 12–13 cm (4½–5 in) in diameter and 3 cm (1¼ in) thick. It is best from November to June and has a fairly strong flavour. However, it is often sold unmatured, as a soft cheese, which tastes very sweet and milky.

The small town in the Yonne region from which the cheese comes has also given its name to a trout dish known as *à la Saint-Florentin*, which was described by Fulbert-Dumonteil as 'flavoured with nutmeg and cloves, cooked over a clear flame in a Chablis wine which, when well heated, gives it a crown of fire'.

Saint-Florentin is also the name of a square Genoese sponge cake, which is split in half, soaked with kirsch and filled with a cream made with Italian meringue, melted butter, kirsch and glacé (candied) cherries or fresh strawberries. The top of the cake is iced (frosted) with pink fondant and the sides are left uncovered, to show the fruit in the filling.

SAINT-GERMAIN The name given to various dishes containing green peas (also known as

Clamart) or split peas; they are all named after the Comte de Saint-Germain, war minister under the French king, Louis XV. Saint-Germain purée, which is fairly thick and sometimes bound with egg yolk, is served with joints of meat and accompanied by a sauce made of clear veal stock. The purée is served separately in a vegetable dish or heaped up on top of artichoke hearts around the meat. When diluted to the required consistency with white stock or consommé, this purée becomes Saint-Germain soup, for which there are various garnishes.

The term is also applied to a method of preparing fillets of sole or brill, which are dipped in melted butter, coated with breadcrumbs, grilled (broiled), and served with a béarnaise sauce and a garnish of noisette potatoes.

RECIPES

fillets of sole Saint-Germain
Fillet 2 soles. Flatten them out and sprinkle with salt and pepper. Brush with melted butter, dip in fine fresh breadcrumbs, spoon over 50 g (2 oz, ¼ cup) melted butter and grill (broil) gently on both sides. Arrange on a long dish, surround with 575 g (1¼ lb) small noisette* potatoes, and serve with béarnaise sauce in a sauceboat.

Saint-Germain purée
Prepare in the same way as Saint-Germain soup, but add 100–150 ml (4–5 fl oz, ½–⅔ cup) double (heavy) cream to the peas after they have been sieved.

Saint-Germain soup
Shell 800 g (1¾ lb) fresh peas and put into a saucepan with a lettuce heart, 12 small new onions, a bouquet garni with chervil added, 50 g (2 oz, ¼ cup) butter, 1 teaspoon salt and 1 tablespoon granulated sugar. Add 250 ml (8 fl oz, 1 cup) cold water, bring to the boil and cook gently for 30–35 minutes. Remove the bouquet garni and rub the vegetables through an ordinary sieve, then a fine one. Add a little consommé or hot water to obtain the desired consistency of soup and heat through. Add 25 g (1 oz, 2 tablespoons) butter, beat well and sprinkle with chopped herbs. If desired, a few peas and croûtons can be added to garnish.

SAINT-HONORÉ A gâteau consisting of a layer of shortcrust pastry (basic pie dough) or puff pastry, on top of which is arranged a crown of choux paste, which is itself garnished with small choux balls glazed with caramel. The inside of the crown is filled with Chiboust cream (also known as 'Saint-Honoré cream') or Chantilly cream.

A Parisian gâteau, Saint-Honoré takes its name from the patron saint of bakers and pastrycooks. It is also said that its name may come from the fact that the 19th-century pastrycook Chiboust, who created the cream which is used in it, set himself up in the Rue Saint-Honoré in Paris.

RECIPE

Saint-Honoré
Prepare the dough for the base with 125 g (4½ oz, 1 cup) plain (all-purpose) flour, 1 egg yolk, 50 g (2 oz, ¼ cup) softened butter, a pinch of salt, 15 g (½ oz, 1 tablespoon) granulated sugar and 2 tablespoons water. When the mixture is smooth, put it in the refrigerator.

Make some choux paste by heating 250 ml (8 fl oz, 1 cup) water, 50 g (2 oz, ¼ cup) butter, 15 g (½ oz, 1 tablespoon) caster (superfine) sugar and a pinch of salt until the butter has melted, then bring to the boil. Immediately add 125 g (4½ oz, 1 cup) plain (all-purpose) flour, stirring, and remove from the heat. The paste should form a ball, leaving the sides of the pan clean. Cool slightly before beating in 4 beaten eggs, one by one.

Roll out the dough for the base into a circle 20 cm (8 in) in diameter and 3 mm (⅛ in) thick. Place on a buttered baking sheet, prick with a fork and brush the edge with beaten egg. Fit a piping (pastry) bag with a smooth nozzle the diameter of a finger and fill it with one-third of the choux paste. Pipe a border around the base 3 mm (⅛ in) from the edge. Brush this border with beaten egg. On a second buttered baking sheet, pipe 20 small choux balls, about the size of walnuts. Bake the base and choux balls in a preheated oven at 200°C (400°F, gas 6) for about 25 minutes, then leave to cool completely.

Prepare a light caramel sauce by cooking 250 g (9 oz, 1 cup) granulated sugar with 100 ml (4 fl oz, 7 tablespoons) water until it reaches 145°C (293°F). Dip the choux balls in the caramel and stick them on top of the choux border so that they touch each other.

To make the cream filling, soften 15 g (½ oz, 2 envelopes) gelatine in 5 tablespoons cold water. Boil 1 litre (1¾ pints, 4⅓ cups) milk with a vanilla pod (bean). Beat 6 egg yolks with 200 g (7 oz, 1 cup) caster (superfine) sugar until the mixture turns white and thick and then add 75 g (3 oz, ¾ cup) cornflour (cornstarch). Remove the vanilla pod from the milk and pour the milk over the mixture, beating hard. Return it to the saucepan and bring to the boil, whisking all the time. Stir in the softened gelatine until it has completely dissolved. Stiffly whisk 4 egg whites in a bowl. Bring the custard back to the boil and pour it over the egg whites, folding them in with a metal spoon. Leave until cold and on the point of setting, then fill the centre of the cake with this mixture, sprinkle with icing (confectioner's) sugar and grill (broil) rapidly until golden.

Put in a cool place until ready to serve, but do not keep for too long.

SAINT-HUBERT The name of various dishes, usually based on game or including game, which take their name from the patron saint of hunters. Quails Saint-Hubert are casseroled with a piece of truffle in each bird and coated in a sauce made by deglazing the meat residue with Madeira and game stock. The name is most often used for dishes that include game purée: for filling large mushroom caps served with saddle of hare and poivrade sauce; in tartlets with poached or soft-boiled (soft-cooked) eggs coated with poivrade sauce; in vol-au-vent, timbales or omelettes; or for making a consommé.

RECIPES

consommé Saint-Hubert
Make some game consommé, thicken it with tapioca, then garnish it with an ordinary royale and a julienne of mushrooms poached in Madeira.

omelette Saint-Hubert
Prepare an omelette and fill it with a game purée thickened with a reduced demi-glace sauce, flavoured with game fumet. Arrange some sliced mushrooms, sautéed in butter, on top.

Saint-Hubert timbales
Grease some dariole moulds, garnish them with slivers of truffle and some chopped pickled tongue, then line them with a layer of game forcemeat. Prepare a salpicon of game meat, truffles and mushrooms, bound with demi-glace sauce made with game fumet, and divide it between the darioles. Cover with game forcemeat. Place the darioles in a bain marie and cook in a preheated oven at 200°C (400°F, gas 6) for 18–20 minutes. Allow to rest for a few moments before turning out of the moulds. Serve as a hot starter, coated with poivrade sauce.

SAINT-JOSEPH Also known as *St-Joseph*. Appellation red and white wines produced in the Ardèche region of France, on the right bank of the River Rhône, opposite the Hermitage vineyard. Saint-Joseph AOC wine, produced from Syrah, may often be a robust, highly coloured red, whose bouquet emerges after it has aged in the bottle for a few years. The whites are lighter in character than the white Hermitages and are produced from Marsanne and Roussanne varieties.

SAINT-JULIEN Also known as *St-Julien*. A parish (commune) of France's Haut-Médoc region, having its own AOC. The wines are varied and some of the finest have an appealing velvety character. There are five second growths, two third growths and four fourth growths.

SAINT-MALO A sauce for grilled (broiled) fish (brill or turbot) for which there are several recipes: Prosper Montagné recognizes at least two. The most common version is a fish velouté with the addition of reduced white wine with shallots; it can be thickened with egg yolk and may include the juice from cooked mushrooms. This sauce often has butter added, the final touch being a little mustard and/or a trickle of anchovy essence (extract) or Worcestershire sauce. Saint-Malo sauce does not in fact have anything to do with the town of Saint Malo.

RECIPE

Saint-Malo sauce
Cook 40 g (1½ oz, ¼ cup) chopped onion in a little butter until soft but not coloured. Add 100 ml (4 fl oz, 7 tablespoons) white wine, a sprig of thyme, a piece of bay leaf and a sprig of parsley. Reduce by two-thirds. Moisten with 250 ml (8 fl oz, 1 cup) velouté* sauce made with fish stock, and 100 ml (4 fl oz, 7 tablespoons) fish fumet. Add 100 ml (4 fl oz, 7 tablespoons) mushroom cooking juices and reduce by one-third. Strain through muslin (cheesecloth), and mix in 1 teaspoon mustard, a trickle of Worcestershire sauce and 15 g (½ oz, 1 tablespoon) butter.

SAINT-MANDÉ A garnish for small cuts of sautéed meat, consisting of peas and French (green) beans tossed in butter, and small Macaire potatoes.

SAINT-MARCELLIN A French cow's-milk (formerly goat's-milk) cheese from the Dauphiné (50% fat content), with a soft curd and a thin natural rind, which is bluish-grey. It has a sweet but slightly acidic taste, and is marketed as small discs, 6–7.5 cm (2½–3 in) in diameter and 2 cm (¾ in) thick. Saint-Marcellin goes well with a light fruity Beaujolais. In Lyon, it is also used for making *fromage fort*, crushed and marinated with ingredients such as oil, wine, cream and herbs for about a week or it may be left for up to a month.

Saint-Marcellin is said to have been 'discovered' by the future Louis XI when he was governor of the Dauphiné; when he came to the throne; he had it included on the royal table.

SAINT-NECTAIRE A French cow's-milk cheese (45% fat content) from Auvergne, with a pressed curd and a natural rind; it is matured for 8 weeks on a bed of rye straw. Saint-Nectaire, which is best in summer and autumn, is soft but not flabby, with a musty smell and an earthy flavour, giving it a pronounced bouquet. It is marketed unwrapped in the form of a flat disc 20 cm (8 in) in diameter, 4 cm (1½ in) thick, weighing 1.5 kg (3¼ lb). It has a greyish rind which is sometimes marked with yellow and red. Since 1957 the cheese has been protected by an AOC, now AOP (covering the Saint-Flour, Mauriac, Clermont-Ferrand and Issoire districts).

This very old cheese was introduced to the table of Louis XIV by Henri de Sennectere, marshal of France and lord of Saint-Nectaire.

SAINT-NICOLAS-DE-BOURGUEIL The AOC of red or rosé wines from Touraine in France, similar to Bourgueil. Like the latter, it is made mainly from the Cabernet Franc grape. It is a fruity wine with a pronounced bouquet.

SAINT-PAULIN A pasteurized cow's-milk cheese (45% fat content) with a pressed curd and a washed smooth orange rind, which shows traces of the muslin (cheesecloth) in which it is wrapped when pressed. Now made all over France, it is derived from the monastery cheeses, particularly that of Port-du-Salut (the best come from Maine, Anjou and Brittany). Saint-Paulin is soft and smooth, with a sweet taste. It looks like a small millstone, 20–22 cm (8–8½ in) in diameter and 4–6 cm (1½–2½ in) thick. It is served at the end of the meal, but can also be used for croûtes, croques-monsieur and mixed salads.

SAINT-PÉRAY A white wine from Côtes-du-Rhône vineyards opposite Valence, on the right bank of the River Rhône, with its own AOC. The still wine is not as well known as the sparkling version, which is one of the quality French sparkling wines.

SAINT-POURÇAIN A red, rosé or white wine from the Bourbonnais.

SAINT-RAPHAËL Aromatic wine made with grape juice and alcohol (see *mistelle*), barrel-aged for 2 years and diluted with red or white wine to a strength of 15% by volume. This mixture is then scented with an infusion of roots and plants – quinine bark, zest of lemons and Seville (bitter) oranges, Colombo root and berries – which have been macerated in alcohol. Saint-Raphaël then undergoes a further period of ageing before being filtered and bottled.

SAINT-ROMAIN Red and white AOC Burgundy wines from the Côte-de-Beaune. They can be extremely agreeable and offer good value.

SAINT-SAËNS The name of the famous composer has been given to a garnish for poultry suprêmes, which is typical of the rich cooking of the Second Empire in the time of Napoleon III. It consists of small truffle and foie gras fritters, cock's kidneys and asparagus tips, accompanied by a suprême sauce flavoured with truffle essence.

SAINT-VÉRAN An AOC white wine from southern Burgundy, made from the Chardonnay grape.

SAKE Also known as saké or saki. A Japanese alcoholic drink brewed from rice. It is clear or pale straw in colour and styles can range from dry, light and crisp to fuller and slightly sweet. Sake should be drunk young except for the specially aged Koshu, and served chilled or, if desired, warm (not hot). It is closely associated with rituals and ceremonies and the Japanese religion Shinto. It is often drunk as an aperitif, served with crudités or used in cookery, especially in shellfish and white fish dishes.

SALAD A dish of raw, cold or warm cooked foods, usually dressed and seasoned, served as an appetizer, side dish or main course.

• GREEN SALADS These consist of green-leaved raw vegetables, such as lettuce, curly endive (frisée), chicory (endive), watercress, dandelion leaves, spinach, Nice mesclun, purslane, rocket (arugula), sorrel and lamb's lettuce (com salad). These salads are served as appetizers or as an accompaniment to dishes such as grills, omelettes, meat, poultry, game or fish. They are usually dressed with vinaigrette, which can be flavoured (according to the natural flavour of the vegetable) and mixed with croûtons, strips of bacon, cheese, shallots and garlic.

• PLAIN SALADS These consist of a basic ingredient, either raw or cooked, but always served cold with a cold dressing (such as mayonnaise, vinaigrette, mustard, *gribiche*, *ravigote*, *rémoulade*, Roquefort and soft cheese dressing). The basic ingredient can be a vegetable, meat or shellfish, and the range is very varied: for example, French (green) beans, carrots, celery, cauliflower, lentils, red or white cabbage, potatoes, rice, crayfish, crab and cold chicken.

• MIXED SALADS These are more elaborate dishes combining various ingredients of contrasting (but complementary) flavours, textures and colours. Mixed salads can include exotic ingredients, such as truffle or lobster medallions, or simple ones (as in salade Niçoise), but should always be decorative. The accompanying dressing should blend with (rather than mask) the flavour of the ingredients. Mixed salads are served as appetizers or main courses, but can also accompany hot or cold roast meats. In addition to the many regional specialities, chefs often create their own salads, producing an immensely wide range.

RECIPES

Dressings
basic vinaigrette
Prepare a basic vinaigrette with 1 tablespoon wine vinegar, 3 tablespoons olive oil (or chosen salad oil), salt, pepper and, if desired, 1 teaspoon mustard. This vinaigrette can be varied in many ways.
• *Indian style* For cooked vegetables, rice or pasta. Add 1 small crushed garlic clove and 1 tablespoon finely chopped onion, fried until soft in 1 tablespoon oil with 1 teaspoon curry powder.
• *with anchovies* For raw salads, potato, pasta, roasted (bell) peppers or tomatoes. Thoroughly soak 4 anchovies to remove the salt and fillet them, if necessary. Purée them with 1 teaspoon capers; add this mixture to the vinaigrette.
• *with herbs* Chop a bunch of chives, chervil and parsley with a few tarragon and mint leaves. Make the vinaigrette and mix in the chopped herbs.
• *with nuts* Chop 50 g (2 oz, ½ cup) walnuts, peanuts or hazelnuts, or a mixture of all three types. Prepare a salad. Make the vinaigrette and add the chopped nuts just before tossing the dressing into the salad and serving.

cheese dressing
Mash 50 g (2 oz) Roquefort or Fourme d'Ambert cheese and mix in 1 Petit Suisse cheese or 2 table-

spoons cream cheese and 2 tablespoons single (light) cream. Add a few drops of Tabasco sauce and 1 teaspoon brandy, season with a very little salt and pepper if desired, and mix well. Pour this mixture over the salad and toss just before serving.

cream dressing

For round or cos (romaine) lettuce. Follow the recipe for basic vinaigrette; replacing the oil of the vinaigrette with 4 tablespoons whipping cream.

hot bacon dressing

For curly endive, red cabbage, lamb's lettuce (corn salad) or dandelions. Fry 100 g (4 oz, ⅔ cup) diced fairly fatty streaky (slab) bacon. Put the salad in a bowl and season with salt and pepper; add 1–2 tablespoons vinegar to the bacon in the pan, then pour over the salad while still hot, and toss.

mustard and cream dressing

For beetroot (red beet), macédoine, celeriac, chicory (endive) or potato. Blend 1 tablespoon French mustard with 3 tablespoons single (light) cream; add 1 teaspoon (or more) vinegar and season with salt and pepper.

yogurt dressing

For fish and seafood, poultry, root vegetables, pasta. Mix 1 teaspoon mild mustard with 1 teaspoon caster (superfine) sugar, salt and pepper. Stir in 1 tablespoon lemon juice, then add 150 ml (¼ pint, ⅔ cup) mild yogurt. Stir in 1–2 tablespoons chopped parsley. The lemon juice can be omitted for a less tangy dressing.

Mixed Salads

alienor salad

Mix 2 tablespoons grated horseradish with enough crème fraîche to give a smooth sauce with a strong flavour. Trim 2 smoked trout and remove the fillets, taking out all the bones. Cover 4 plates with lettuce. Cut a large avocado – stone (pit) removed – into thin slices; arrange the slices on the plates and sprinkle them with lemon juice. Arrange 2 fillets of trout, coarsely shredded, on each plate. Coat with the horseradish sauce. Sprinkle with a few flaked (slivered) almonds and complete with slices of gherkin. (The avocado may be replaced by pickled red cabbage.)

American salad

Line individual salad bowls with lettuce leaves. For each serving, mix together 1 tablespoon diced pineapple, 2 tablespoons sweetcorn, either canned or cooked in boiling water, 1 tablespoon thinly shredded chicken breast poached in white stock, and 1 tablespoon peeled, seeded and diced cucumber. Dress with 2 tablespoons vinaigrette flavoured with tomato ketchup and pile up in the bowls. Garnish each bowl with quarters of hard-boiled (hard-cooked) egg and tomato.

Arles salad

Slice some boiled potatoes and quarter some boiled artichoke hearts. Mix together and dress with vinaigrette, sprinkle with chopped chervil and tarragon, and garnish with curly endive (frisée) and tomato quarters. Garnish the top with drained canned anchovy fillets arranged in a criss-cross pattern, with a stoned (pitted) black (ripe) olive placed in the centre. Pour some vinaigrette (seasoned with very little salt because of the anchovies) over the garnish just before serving.

beef salad

Cut 250 g (9 oz) cooked beef into slices less than 5 mm (¼ in) thick. Thinly slice 6 small boiled potatoes. Sprinkle with salt and pepper while still warm and pour 150 ml (¼ pint, ⅔ cup) white wine and 1 tablespoon oil over them. Turn the slices over so that they become well impregnated with this dressing. Thinly slice 3 or 4 tomatoes. Slice an onion very finely. Arrange the potatoes heaped up in a salad bowl, with the slices of beef all around. Surround with the tomato slices. Garnish with the sliced onion and 1 tablespoon chopped chervil. Season with vinaigrette flavoured with mustard.

carrot salad with orange

Put 500 g (18 oz, 3¾ cups) grated carrots in a salad bowl. Remove the peel and pith from 4 oranges and dice the flesh finely. Thinly slice 2 large mild onions and break the slices up into rings. Pour some lemon vinaigrette over the diced carrots just before serving, and add the diced orange. Toss and garnish with the onion rings.

Chinese-style duck salad

Shred 200 g (7 oz) roast duck meat (with the skin if it is crisp). Soak 7–8 black Chinese dried mushrooms and 2–3 dried shiitake mushrooms in hot water for 30 minutes. Drain and squeeze dry, then cut into quarters.

Make a dressing by mixing together 1 teaspoon each of mustard and sugar, 1 tablespoon tomato purée (paste). 1 tablespoon each of soy light sauce and cider or rice vinegar, a pinch of black pepper, ½ teaspoon ground ginger, a pinch each of thyme and powdered bay leaf, 1 small crushed garlic clove, 3 tablespoons sesame oil and, if desired, 1 tablespoon rice wine.

Mix the duck, mushrooms and 500 g (18 oz) bean sprouts together in a large bowl and pour over the dressing. Toss well, sprinkle with 1 tablespoon chopped fresh coriander (cilantro) and serve at once.

cockle salad with fresh broad beans

Heat some cockles until they open, remove the walnut-sized pieces of flesh and keep warm. Peel some fresh broad (fava) beans, blanch them for 5 minutes in boiling salted water, then rinse in cold water. Pour some vinaigrette mixed with chopped herbs into a salad bowl. Add the beans and the cockles, toss quickly and serve.

fiddlehead fern and Matane prawn salad ♦

Cook 575 g (1¼ lb) fiddlehead ferns for 3 minutes in boiling water. Drain well and set aside. Prepare a vierge sauce*, made with 250 ml (8 fl oz, 1 cup) extra-virgin olive oil, the juice of 2 lemons, salt and pepper.

Brown 1 chopped onion in 100 ml (4 fl oz, 7 tablespoons) extra-virgin olive oil. Add 6 ripe tomatoes, peeled, seeded and crushed. Cook for 5 minutes over a high heat, stirring, then add 3 tablespoons sherry vinegar. Cook for 3 minutes to reduce then season to taste. Add 2 tablespoons snipped chives. Spoon the tomato mixture on to serving plates and top with fiddlehead ferns. Add 100 g (4 oz) peeled, cooked. Matane prawns (shelled Matane shrimp). Garnish with unpeeled prawns (unshelled shrimp). Serve immediately with the vierge sauce.

German salad

Coarsely chop 400 g (14 oz, 2⅓ cups) boiled potatoes and 200 g (7 oz, 1⅓ cups) tart eating apples and mix with 2 tablespoons mayonnaise. Place in a salad bowl; garnish with a large shredded gherkin and 2 herring fillets. Sprinkle with chopped parsley. Garnish with slices of cooked beetroot (red beet) and onion. Pour a mustard-flavoured vinaigrette over this garnish just before serving.

leafy truffle salad

Prepare a vinaigrette by whisking together salt, 2½ teaspoons aged wine vinegar and 2½ teaspoons sherry vinegar, 5 tablespoons groundnut (peanut) oil, pepper and 1 tablespoon truffle juice.

Wash and trim 20 g (¾ oz) curly endive (frisée), 20 g (¾ oz) oak leaf lettuce, 20 g (¾ oz) lollo rosso, 20 g (¾ oz) red chicory (endive), 20 g (¾ oz) Batavia lettuce, 20 g (¾ oz) Nice mesclun, 20 g (¾ oz) lamb's lettuce (corn salad), 20 g (¾ oz) rocket (arugula), 10 g (⅓ oz) watercress, 7 g (¼ oz) marjoram, 10 g (⅓ oz) chervil, 10 g (⅓ oz) flat-leafed parsley, 7 g (¼ oz) sage, 10 g (⅓ oz) dill, 10 g (⅓ oz) tarragon, 4 small mint leaves and 4 small celery leaves. Place the herbs and salad leaves, except for the celery and mint, in a large salad bowl and toss. Add 10g (⅓ oz) chopped truffle, toss again, then add the prepared vinaigrette. Toss gently again to coat all the leaves. Arrange the salad in a pile on each of 4 plates. Sprinkle each with a little more chopped truffle and garnish with a celery leaf and a mint leaf. Sprinkle a few drops of aged wine vinegar on top and serve.

maharajah salad

Prepare some rice à la créole and flake some crabmeat. Mix together, dress with Indian-style vinaigrette, then pile up in a salad bowl. Around

this, arrange some shredded celeriac, alternated with blanched and diced courgettes (zucchini) and tomato quarters. Sprinkle with sieved hard-boiled (hard-cooked) egg yolk and chopped chives. Pour some more of the same vinaigrette over the garnish just before serving.

Montfermeil salad

Put the juice of 1 lemon in a saucepan with 2 tablespoons flour, a generous pinch of salt and 2–3 litres (3½–5 pints, 9–13 cups) water. Peel 500 g (18 oz) salsify, cut into small pieces and cook for about 1 hour in this liquid – it should be tender but not disintegrating. Scrub 250 g (9 oz) potatoes and boil them. Drain and peel while still warm, then leave to cool completely and cut into dice. Leave the salsify to cool in its cooking liquid, then drain and refresh. Wash and chop a small bunch of parsley and a few sprigs of tarragon and mix with 2 roughly chopped hard-boiled (hard-cooked) eggs. Drain and dice 400 g (14 oz) canned artichoke hearts and put them in a salad bowl. Add the diced potatoes and the salsify. Pour over a vinaigrette flavoured with mustard and sprinkle with the chopped eggs and herbs.

new turnip salad

Peel and quarter 1 kg (2¼ lb) small new turnips. Blanch them for 6 minutes in boiling water, drain, then cook in stock, preferably chicken stock, for about 10 minutes. Drain and leave to cool, then sprinkle with chopped herbs. Add some strips of smoked haddock poached in milk (1 part haddock to 2 parts turnips) and dress with olive oil and vinegar.

octopus salad

Clean an octopus and plunge it into a saucepan filled with boiling water and a cork, which according to tradition will tenderize its meat. Season with pepper and simmer for 20 minutes. Check the octopus is cooked using a fork, then drain and allow to cool. Retaining the skin, cut the octopus into 1 cm (½ in) slices. Put 3 tablespoons olive oil, 2 crushed garlic cloves, flat-leaf parsley and pepper into a serving bowl. Add the pieces of octopus and stir carefully. Chill for 30 minutes befor serving.

Port-Royal salad

Mix together slices of boiled potato, chopped cooked French (green) beans, and slices of peeled apple lightly sprinkled with lemon juice. Add some mayonnaise to this mixture. Heap up in a salad bowl, pour over some more mayonnaise and garnish with whole French beans arranged in a star shape. Surround with small lettuce hearts and quarters of hard-boiled (hard-cooked) eggs.

Raphael salad

Line a shallow salad bowl with shredded lettuce dressed with mayonnaise and seasoned with

Fiddlehead fern and Matane prawn salad.

paprika. Arrange on top slices of peeled cucumber (previously sprinkled with salt and left to stand, then rinsed and drained), white asparagus tips (boiled and well drained), small tomatoes (peeled, seeded and cut into quarters), small lettuce hearts and sliced pink radishes. Just before serving, dress with vinaigrette made with olive oil, lemon juice and chopped chervil.

raw vegetable salad

Wash and thinly slice 2 tomatoes, 3 celery sticks and 1 head of fennel. Peel and finely dice 1 beetroot (red beet). Halve 2 sweet (bell) peppers, remove the seeds and cut the flesh into thin strips. Wash and chop a small bunch of parsley. Wash 1 lettuce and line the base of a shallow dish with the lettuce leaves. Place on top small heaps of fennel, beetroot, celery and peppers. Arrange 10 green and black (ripe) olives in the centre and the tomato slices all around the side. Pour over some vinaigrette and sprinkle with the chopped parsley.

Reine Pédauque salad

Mix together 200 ml (7 fl oz, ¾ cup) double (heavy) cream, 2 tablespoons oil, 1 tablespoon mustard, 2 tablespoons lemon juice, ½ teaspoon paprika and a little salt. Pour this mixture over a border of 12 lettuce-heart quarters arranged around a shallow dish. Garnish the centre with shredded lettuce dressed with vinaigrette and sprinkled with fresh stoned (pitted) cherries. Place a slice of peeled orange with the pith removed on each lettuce-heart quarter.

salade à d'Albignac

Heap some shredded celeriac, dressed with mayonnaise, in a salad bowl. Sprinkle the top with thinly sliced black truffle and around the edge arrange the following: thin slices of poached chicken breast dressed with lemon vinaigrette, prawns (shrimp) dipped in tomato ketchup, slices of white truffle dipped in olive oil seasoned with salt and pepper, tiny lettuce hearts, and quarters of hard-boiled (hard-cooked) eggs dressed with vinaigrette.

salade gourmande ♦

Cook 175 g (6 oz) fine French (green) beans topped and tailed, in plenty of salted water until *al dente*. Remove the beans with a slotted spoon and plunge them into icy cold water for 10 seconds, then drain thoroughly. Using the same cooking water, cook 12 asparagus tips for 5–6 minutes.

Using a small whisk, mix together salt, pepper, 1 teaspoon olive oil, 1 teaspoon lemon juice, 1 teaspoon groundnut (peanut) oil, 1 teaspoon sherry vinegar, 1 teaspoon chopped chervil and 1 teaspoon tarragon. Season separately the French beans, asparagus tips and 20 g (¾ oz) sliced truffle.

Place a few leaves of radicchio, frisée or other salad leaves on each plate and arrange the beans on top. Add a little chopped shallot and the asparagus

tips. Cut 50 g (2 oz) foie gras into fine slices and place on the vegetables. Garnish with the slices of truffle.

salade Niçoise

Separate the leaves of 1 lettuce and wash. You may also use 100 g (4 oz) mesclun (mixed salad greens). Wash and cut 10 very firm tomatoes into 8 equal wedges. Place in a colander in the refrigerator, over a plate, and sprinkle with salt to extract the water. Hard boil (hard cook) 6 eggs, then cool, shell and cut into quarters. Peel 2 small mild salad onions and chop very finely. Wash and fillet 6 anchovies preserved in salt. Rinse 1 (bell) pepper, seed and cut into strips. Wash 3 celery sticks with their leaves, dry and chop finely. Sprinkle 3 Provençal artichoke hearts with lemon juice and slice very finely. Place at the bottom of a shallow serving dish a few lettuce leaves, a layer of tomatoes, slivers of artichoke hearts, a few strips of pepper, shredded tuna, chopped celery and onions. Repeat until all these ingredients have been used up. Prepare a vinaigrette with oil, vinegar and pepper. Season the salad, toss and add a little salt if necessary. Garnish with the quarters of hard-boiled egg, some black (ripe) olives and anchovy fillets.

seafood salad

Roast and shell 8 king prawns (jumbo shrimp). Cook 1 kg (2¼ lb) mussels and 1 kg (2¼ lb) cockles in a tightly covered pan with a little water over a brisk heat for about 5 minutes, shaking the pan occasionally, until the shells have opened. Discard the shells and any closed shellfish. Cook 4 scallops and cut into thin strips. Cook 1 crab and crumble the meat.

Wash a white curly endive (frisée), a little purslane and 1 lettuce. Mix the leaves together and season with wine vinegar, salt, lemon juice and olive oil. Arrange the salad leaves on 4 plates. Season the seafood and sprinkle on top. Garnish each plate with 2 asparagus tips, thin slices of avocado, seasoned, snipped chives, chopped parsley and chervil.

skate salad

Poach a wing of skate weighing 800 g (1¾ lb) in simmering water, with vinegar, pepper and thyme added, for 6–8 minutes. Dress some mesclun (mixed salad greens) with 1 tablespoon wine vinegar, 3 tablespoons olive oil, 2 finely chopped shallots and some chopped herbs. Warm in a preheated oven at 110°C (225°F, gas ¼). When the skate is cooked, peel it, flake the flesh and mix with the salad. Add the finely grated zest of 1 lemon and 2 crushed tomatoes; toss all the ingredients lightly together and serve warm.

tomato salad with mozzarella

Wash, peel and slice 4 tomatoes. Thinly slice 200 g (7 oz) mozzarella cheese. Divide the sliced tomato

Salade gourmande.

between 4 plates and cover with slices of mozzarella. Sprinkle with salt, pepper and chopped fresh basil, pour over a few drops of vinegar, then a trickle of olive oil, and serve at room temperature.

Toulouse salad
Using a melon baller, scoop balls of melon from the flesh of a medium-sized melon. Cook 2 artichoke hearts in water and lemon juice, cool, then cut into thin strips. Thinly slice the white and green parts of a very tender leek; shred a thick slice of unsmoked ham. Mix together all these ingredients. Make a well-seasoned vinaigrette, adding chopped parsley, chives and sage, and blend it with 1 teaspoon cream. Pour over the salad and toss gently. Place a large leaf of raw spinach, washed and patted dry, on each plate. Divide the salad between the plates; just before serving, grate a little fresh root ginger over them.

SALAD BOWL A deep bowl for serving salad (called *saladier* in French), traditionally with matching servers in wood, horn or silver. A salad bowl should be chosen to match the salad. For example, olive-wood salad bowls are often reserved for highly seasoned green salads, which need to be tossed easily, whereas mixed salads, with ingredients of different colours, are best displayed in a fairly shallow transparent bowl. Individual salad bowls may be used for serving portions of side salad.

SALAD BURNET A hardy perennial herb whose serrated grey-green leaves have a cool cucumber-like flavour. It is used to season omelettes, cold sauces, marinades and soups and its tender young leaves can be used in salads like watercress. Burnet can also be used, like borage, in cooling drinks and for flavouring vinegar.

SALAMANDER A type of oven in which the heat is directed down from the roof, used by professional cooks for glazing, browning or caramelizing some savoury or sweet dishes. It is named after the legendary animal that was resistant to fire and lived in the bowels of the earth. Many chefs favour this method of cooking, which according to André Guillot, 'keeps all flavours intact, in the best conditions of speed and hygiene'. A grill (broiler) can be used instead of a salamander.

A salamander is also an iron, a metal instrument, which is heated over a flame or in a fire until red hot and then held over dishes, especially crème brûlée, to brown or caramelize the surface.

Small hand-held blow torches are a popular alternative for browning or caramelizing foods.

SALAMI A charcuterie product of Italian origin, which takes the form of a sausage usually made of finely minced (ground) pork, or a mixture of meats, interspersed with pieces of fat. Beef, goose, wild boar or veal may also be used. The mixture can be flavoured with red wine, smoked, or spiced with peppercorns, garlic and herbs such as fennel or parsley.

In Italy, salami is made particularly in Milan and Bologna under various official names, including *salame Milanese, fiorentino, di Felino, di Fabriano, di Secondigliano* and *Calabrese.* Salami made in France must bear a label in French, giving the place of origin, to avoid confusion. A notable example is *salami de Strasbourg* (Strasbourg salami or Alsatian sausage), a smoked and fairly thin sausage usually made with beef (for the lean meat) and pork (for the fat). Salami is also made in the United States, Germany, Austria, Switzerland, Denmark and Hungary. The best known of these are probably Danish salami (highly coloured, salted and smoked) and Hungarian salami (coloured with paprika, smoked and sometimes wrapped in horse or ox intestines).

Salami is often served thinly sliced as a cold appetizer; it is also used in sandwiches and canapés, and in cooked dishes such as pizza.

SALAMMBÔ A small French cake made from choux paste, filled with confectioner's custard (pastry cream) flavoured with kirsch, and iced (frosted) with green fondant; one end is sprinkled with chocolate vermicelli (sprinkles). Originally the salammbô was decorated with chopped pistachio nuts, pressed on to both ends, and glazed with caramel. Created at the end of the 19th century, the cake takes its name from the opera by Reyer, based on Flaubert's novel *Salammbô*, which was very popular at the time.

SALEE Sweet pastry from the French-speaking part of Switzerland, consisting of leavened dough formed into a flat round cake, with cream and plenty of sugar in the middle.

SALEP A type of starch extracted from the tubers of a variety of orchid and used like tapioca and sago as a thickening agent. In the Middle East and parts of Asia, salep is boiled in water or milk to make a jelly used for preparing desserts, including ice cream and drinks. Known in France and England since the 17th century, it was formerly considered an aphrodisiac, and was popular in the form of a drink flavoured with orange-flower water. In domestic cookery it has now largely been replaced by tapioca and potato flour, but it is available in certain delicatessens. Arrowroot is sometimes known as 'West Indian salep' and potato flour as 'poor man's salep'.

SALERS A French cheese from Auvergne made from untreated whole cow's milk (45% fat content), with a firm curd, pressed twice, and a greyish-brown natural brushed rind. It is protected by an AOP status, which defines the area of its production as well as its shape and conditions of manufacture. Farmhouse Salers is similar to Laguiole and Cantal. The cylindrical cheese has a strong flavour, is 38–48 cm (15–19 in) in diameter, and weighs 30–40 kg

(66–88 lb). Formerly, the milk used for this cheese came exclusively from Salers cows.

SALINITY The amount of salt contained in a liquid, such as wine or water. Salinity is indicated on the labels of bottled water.

SALLY LUNN Round English teacake made from a rich yeast dough, by the Bath pastrycook of the same name in the 1780s, who sold her cakes to the fashionable people who came to take the local waters. The Sally Lunn is sliced while still warm and spread generously with butter or clotted cream. (See *Solilemme*.)

SALMAGUNDI Also known as Salmagundy. An elaborate salad laid out on a large flat dish with each ingredient minced (ground), shredded or sliced, and arranged attractively in small rings of contrasting colour. Cold meats, fish, cooked vegetables, salads and pickles – anything can be used. The word is also used figuratively to mean a miscellaneous collection of things.

In France, *salmigondis* is an old dish which, according to the *Dictionnaire de Trévoux*, was a 'type of ragoût made from various cooked meats, reheated in a sauce'. The word would appear to come from Old French *sal* (salt) and *condir* (to season), which implies that it was a highly flavoured dish. André Guillot suggests a very appetizing recipe for game *salmigondis* (see *salmis*): pieces of wild rabbit, partridge, pheasant and venison, browned in butter, stewed in wine with herbs, then coated in their reduced cooking juices flavoured with garlic and cream.

The term *salmigondis* was also used, during the reign of Louis XIV, to denote a supper attended by several people, or several families, each bringing his or her own dish.

SALMIS A game stew. The word is an abbreviation of *salmigondis* (see *salmagundi*), and the dish is usually made with woodcock, wild duck, pheasant or partridge, but domestic duck, pigeon or guinea fowl can also be used. The bird is two-thirds roasted, jointed and then cooked in a saucepan, with mushrooms, for the remaining cooking time. It is served coated with salmis sauce, a kind of espagnole sauce made with the carcass and the cooking juices diluted with wine (dry white for woodcock, port for guinea fowl, Chambertin for duck).

RECIPE

woodcock salmis
Pluck and singe 2 woodcock; truss them and roast in a preheated oven at 220°C (425°F, gas 7) until two-thirds cooked.

Melt 50 g (2 oz, ¼ cup) butter in a sauté pan and add a carrot and an onion (both diced), a pinch of dried thyme and a pinch of powdered bay leaf. Cover and cook gently for 15 minutes. Then add a generous pinch of pepper and remove from the heat. Divide each woodcock into 4 joints, then skin them and arrange in a shallow heatproof serving dish; cover and keep warm.

Chop the skin and crush the bones of the carcasses; add to the diced vegetables, together with the roasting juices. Mix well with a wooden spoon for 4–5 minutes over a gentle heat. Then moisten with 200 ml (7 fl oz, ¾ cup) dry white wine and 400 ml (14 fl oz, 1¾ cups) thickened brown veal stock. Bring to the boil and cook gently for 15 minutes.

Meanwhile, clean 150 g (5 oz, 1⅔ cups) very small button mushrooms and cook, covered, in the juice of half a lemon, 2 tablespoons water and a pinch of salt, for 10 minutes. Drain and spoon the mushroom over the joints of woodcock, then flame with 2 tablespoons warmed brandy. Continue to keep warm.

Strain the sauce through a fine sieve, pressing the bones hard against the sides. Thicken with 1 tablespoon beurre manié, boil, then pour over the meat. Garnish with triangles of bread fried in butter.

SALMON A migratory fish living mainly in the sea but spawning in fresh water. True salmon are found only in the northern hemisphere. Fish referred to as 'salmon' elsewhere are, in fact, different species.

Young salmon remain in fresh water for about two years; at this age, when they are 15–20 cm (6–8 in) long and are called smolt, they begin to migrate towards the sea, where they reach maturity. The duration of their stay in the sea is variable as it depends on when they become sexually mature; spawning takes place in the winter following their journey upstream.

Smaller salmon, measuring 50–60 cm (20–24 in), remain in the sea for one year and migrate upstream in June or July; spring salmon, measuring 70–80 cm (28–32 in), remain for two years, migrating from March to May. The great winter salmon, which measures 90 cm to 1 m (about 3 ft), remains in the sea for three years and moves upstream from October to March. The migrating salmon at this stage is known as a grilse and its lower jaw becomes hooked as it fights against the current to return to the spawning ground. After spawning, the fish (known as kelts) either die or return to the sea. After a second migration the salmon reaches its maximum weight – up to 30 kg (66 lb) in Norway.

Salmon under three years of age are best for eating. They have pink, fatty, highly nourishing flesh, which can be cooked fresh, smoked or sometimes eaten raw. The salmon has a silvery-blue back with small, scattered black markings that turn orange when spawning. The sides and abdomen are golden.

Salmon were among the most popular fish in Europe in the Middle Ages: they were cooked in stock, potted, braised, served in ragoûts, pâtés or soups, or salted. When salmon became rare, it came to be regarded as one of the luxury foods. Pollution, overfishing and the construction of dams have considerably reduced salmon fishing generally. This is despite the construction in some places of specially designed 'lifts' to help the fish migrate upriver and counteract the effect of dams. Most commercially available salmon comes from the Pacific (Canada) and the North Sea (Scotland, Denmark and Norway). Salmon breeding in the Norwegian fjords, on the Scottish coasts and elsewhere has become big business. Although gourmets are not happy about the quality of farmed salmon, most consumers cannot tell the difference between farmed and wild salmon, and the increase in production of this 'king of fish' has made it a common food.

Nordic salmon, particularly the Greenland salmon (similar to French salmon), are usually eaten smoked. Canned salmon, sold in segments with the skin still attached, is mostly Canadian and includes the red salmon (considered to be the best), the sockeye and the chum.

■ **Cooking and serving** Salmon is prepared whole, or cut into segments, steaks or slices. The middle, which is the best part, is known in France as the *mitan*. Fresh salmon, whole or cut into steaks, is usually cooked in court-bouillon and served with a hot sauce, such as anchovy, butter, caper, prawn, lobster, mousseline, Nantua or ravigote. Cold salmon is accompanied by various cold sauces, such as mayonnaise, tartare, green, rémoulade or Vincent. Salmon can also be braised whole (stuffed or otherwise), or it can be cooked on a spit (whole or in segments). Salmon steaks are cooked in court-bouillon, grilled (broiled), fried in butter or braised, as are salmon fillets, escalopes (scallops) and 'cutlets' (trimmed steaks or shaped flesh). In Russia, Germany and Scandinavia, salmon is used in many traditional dishes, such as Russian *koulibiaca* or Swedish *gravadlax* (raw salmon marinated in pepper, dill, sugar and salt).

■ **Smoked salmon** This is delicious served cold with lemon juice, fresh cream or horseradish sauce, eaten with bread, toast or blinis. Smoked salmon is also used in various hot and cold recipes: aspics, canapés, filled cornets and scrambled eggs. The fish is smoked over a mixture of different types of wood (beech, birch, oak, ash and alder) and various aromatic essences (juniper, heather and sage).

• SMOKED WILD SALMON Fish that is smoked by traditional methods and sliced as required is the most highly prized. The best is Scotch salmon, with tender orange-pink flesh. Danish smoked salmon, which is pale golden brown, is also tasty but has less flavour, whereas Norwegian smoked salmon, which is a peachy pink colour, has a more pronounced flavour. Canadian smoked salmon is less highly prized; it is a deeper red in colour and drier in texture, the best being the salmon which are frozen when caught, before being smoked.

The best smoked salmon comes from fish that have been recently smoked; it is therefore best to buy from a shop with a high turnover. The middle of the fish yields the best portions; slices near the tail are drier and saltier. If a smoked salmon is bought whole, it is better to select a side weighing 1.25–1.5 kg (2¾–3¼ lb) – it will have a softer finer flesh than a smaller fish.

• INDUSTRIALLY SMOKED SALMON This is packaged as whole sides or in slices, either vacuum-packed or frozen. It is almost always prepared from the Canadian king salmon and the flesh is sometimes stringy. It should ideally be used for mixed salads or certain recipes in which the fish is incorporated into a mixture or a forcemeat.

RECIPES

Cold Salmon Dishes
cold poached salmon

Poach a whole salmon (or some salmon steaks) in a court-bouillon or a fish fumet and leave to cool in the liquid. Drain the fish, wipe it and arrange on a large dish, garnished with parsley. Alternatively, the skin can be removed and the fish garnished with lettuce hearts, hard-boiled (hard-cooked) eggs or stuffed vegetables, such as cherry tomatoes or slices of cucumber.

The following garnishes are also suitable: small pieces of aspic, prawns (shrimp) or crayfish tails, lobster medallions, a macédoine of vegetables, or small barquettes or cooked artichoke hearts filled with caviare, mousse or a seafood filling.

Cold poached salmon may be served with the following sauces: andalouse, Chantilly, gribiche, mayonnaise, ravigote, rémoulade, verte or Vincent.

The poached salmon can be drained and served hot, with the skin removed, and accompanied by hot melted butter, beurre blanc or a white wine sauce.

escalopes of raw salmon with pepper

Brush a cold plate lightly with olive oil and lay some thin raw escalopes (scallops) of salmon on it. Brush the escalopes with olive oil. Season with two turns of a pepper mill and one turn of a salt mill, then sprinkle with crushed green peppercorns. Serve very cold.

glazed salmon cutlets with a vegetable macédoine

Prepare, cook and glaze some salmon cutlets as in the recipe for glazed salmon cutlets with Chambertin, but replace the Chambertin with white wine or champagne. Arrange the cutlets in a circle on a round dish and fill the centre with a macédoine of vegetables in thick mayonnaise.

Strips of anchovy fillets or small green asparagus tips may be added to this salad.

glazed salmon cutlets with Chambertin

Cut the salmon into slices about 2.5 cm (1 in) thick and divide each slice in half. Shape the halves into cutlets and arrange on a buttered dish. Season with salt and pepper and add some fish aspic stock made with Chambertin (use enough stock to cover the cutlets.) Poach very gently for 8–10 minutes, then drain and wipe. Allow to cool completely. Clarify the stock, then cool it, but do not allow it to set. Arrange the cutlets on a rack over a dish and coat them with several layers of aspic, placing the dish in the refrigerator between each application. Put a thin layer of aspic to set on the serving dish and lay the cutlets on top.

marinated salmon
Fillet a fresh Scotch salmon and cut the fillets into very thin escalopes (scallops). Prepare a marinade with 1 part olive oil to 2 parts lemon juice and add some salt, pepper and 1 tablespoon chopped herbs (chives, chervil and tarragon). Marinate the escalopes for a maximum of 3 minutes. Make a sauce with a little whipped crème fraîche, some salt and pepper, and 1 teaspoon Meaux mustard. Drain the slices of salmon and arrange them on a serving dish. Serve the sauce separately.

raw salmon with red new potatoes ♦
Cover a 2 kg (4½ lb) salmon fillet with coarse salt and leave for a few hours. Rinse well and pat dry. Place in a large dish. Mix 500 ml (17 fl oz, 2 cups) groundnut (peanut) oil, 500 ml (17 fl oz, 2 cups) olive oil, 4 chopped red onions, 2 thinly sliced carrots, 15 juniper berries, 10 black peppercorns and 5 small bay leaves. Pour the oil over the salmon. Cover and leave for at least 24 hours.

Cook 500 g (18 oz) red new potatoes in boiling water. Slice them and season with coarse salt and thyme leaves. Drain the salmon and cut into slices across the grain. Arrange these on plates with the potato slices. Dress with a little of the marinade and garnish with thyme sprigs.

rillettes of salmon
Put a bouquet garni, some salt and pepper, a sliced carrot and a sliced onion in a saucepan with a little water. Boil gently for 20 minutes. Add a thick piece of fresh salmon and poach very gently in the stock for 10 minutes. Leave to cool, then drain. Trim the fish and flake it with a fork.

Cut 100 g (4 oz) smoked salmon into dice. Mix both types of salmon thoroughly with 1 egg yolk, 125 g (4½ oz, ½ cup) butter and 1 tablespoon olive oil. Place in an earthenware dish and leave overnight in the refrigerator before serving.

salmon mayonnaise
Cut some cooked salmon into thin escalopes (scallops) and season with salt, pepper, oil and either vinegar or lemon juice. Shred some lettuce leaves and arrange in individual dishes. Cover the lettuce with the salmon escalopes, coat with mayonnaise and garnish with capers, anchovies, black (ripe) olives and quarters of hard-boiled (hard-cooked) eggs. Serve well chilled.

terrine of salmon
Remove all the flesh from a small well-trimmed salmon and marinate it in dry white wine with salt and pepper. Prepare a forcemeat as follows: blend the flesh from 1 kg (2¼ lb) white fish and 300 g (11 oz) unpeeled shrimps in a blender or food processor. Then add 12 eggs, 175 ml (6 fl oz, ¾ cup) whipped cream, and some salt and pepper. Blend the ingredients thoroughly.

Butter a long terrine dish; spread a layer of forcemeat on the bottom, then add a layer of salmon and repeat the procedure, ending with a layer of forcemeat. Cover the dish and cook in a bain marie in a preheated oven at 180°C (350°F, gas 4) for about 1½ hours. Allow to cool completely and serve with green sauce (see vert).

other recipes See bellevue, chaud-froid, parisienne, purée, russe.

Hot Salmon Dishes
colombines of salmon Nantua
Rub the following ingredients through a sieve: 125 g (4½ oz) raw pounded salmon, 125 g (4½ oz) bread soaked in milk and squeezed, 2 whole eggs and 120 ml (4½ fl oz, ½ cup) whipping or double (heavy) cream. Mix them together over ice, season with salt and pepper, and add a little grated nutmeg. Prepare large dumplings with the mixture and poach them in Nantua sauce.

escalope of salmon with Gigondas
Gently boil 500 ml (17 fl oz, 2 cups) Gigondas wine until reduced by three-quarters. Then add 500 ml (17 fl oz, 2 cups) well-reduced fish fumet*, 1 chopped tomato, 1 thinly sliced mushroom and 2 thinly sliced shallots. Reduce again until almost dry, then whisk a large piece of langouste butter into the liquid. Prepare a fondue* with 150 g (5 oz) spring onions (scallions). Poach 1 very large escalope of salmon, weighing about 150 g (5 oz), until just cooked. Drain it and then fry it in butter. Arrange the onion fondue on a plate, lay the salmon escalope on top and pour a ribbon of sauce around it.

escalopes of salmon
Cut some raw salmon fillets into escalopes (scallops), weighing about 100 g (4 oz) each. Flatten them lightly and trim if necessary. Any of the recipes using salmon cutlets and steaks can be followed for escalopes.

escalopes of salmon with carrots
Cook 2 sliced carrots in a frying pan with some fish fumet, a little dry vermouth and some paprika. When cooked al dente, remove the carrots and set aside. Add 1 tablespoon green peppercorns and 200 ml (7 fl oz, ¾ cup) double (heavy) cream to the frying pan, season with salt and pepper, then boil to reduce. Arrange some raw escalopes (scallops) of salmon with the carrots on hot buttered plates. Coat with the hot sauce and serve at once.

fried salmon steaks
Season some salmon steaks, 2 cm (¾ in) thick, with salt and pepper. Dust well with flour and deep-fry

quickly in oil at 180°C (350°F) until golden brown. Serve with lemon or lime wedges.

grilled salmon steaks

Season some salmon steaks, 2.5–5 cm (1–2 in) thick, with salt and pepper. Brush them with olive oil and cook them gently under a moderate grill (broiler). Serve with maître d'hôtel butter, béarnaise sauce or gooseberry sauce.

minute steaks of salmon with aigrelette sauce

Butter some small ovenproof plates and sprinkle with salt and pepper. Place a salmon escalope (scallop) on each plate (the escalopes should be large enough to cover the plates completely). Just before serving, put the plates into a very hot oven for 2–3 minutes. Meanwhile, prepare a mayonnaise with wine vinegar and lemon juice, dilute it with fish fumet and season with salt, pepper, chopped chives and tarragon. Serve the cooked escalopes with this sauce.

poached salmon steaks

Place some salmon steaks, 4 cm (1½ in) thick, in enough court-bouillon or fish fumet to cover them. Bring to the boil, simmer for 5 minutes, then remove from the heat and drain. Serve the steaks topped with pats of butter flavoured with lemon, parsley, chives or tarragon. Alternatively, dress with melted clarified butter flavoured with lemon, maître d'hôtel butter or beurre blanc.

salmon aiguillettes

Cut some raw salmon fillets into thin strips (aiguillettes) and cook them as for salmon cutlets, steaks or escalopes (scallops). The strips can also be dipped in batter and deep-fried.

salmon brochettes with fresh duck liver

Prepare the brochettes by threading cubes of raw salmon and slightly larger cubes of fresh duck liver alternately on to skewers. Arrange the brochettes, without overlapping, on a julienne of vegetables in an ovenproof dish, and season with salt and pepper.

Boil some dry white wine and some shallots in a saucepan until reduced by half. Add an equal quantity of double (heavy) cream and boil for 5 minutes. Pour the sauce over the brochettes and cook in a preheated oven at 190°C (375°F, gas 5) for 10 minutes. Drain the brochettes and put them on a hot dish. Reduce the sauce and add some truffle juice. Then whisk the sauce with 3 egg yolks, as for zabaglione, and pour it over the brochettes.

salmon cooked in champagne

Prepare a fish fumet with 1 carrot, 1 onion, 25 g (1 oz, 2 tablespoons) butter, 400 g (14 oz) fish bones (preferably without skin), a bouquet garni, 300 ml (½ pint, 1¼ cups) white wine and 200 ml (7 fl oz, ¾ cup) water. Simmer for 30 minutes and then strain.

Prepare a blond roux with 50 g (2 oz, ¼ cup) butter and 40 g (1½ oz, ⅓ cup) plain (all-purpose) flour and then add the fish stock. Bring the sauce to the boil, stirring continuously, and cook for 15 minutes over a low heat.

Gut (clean) a salmon weighing about 2 kg (4½ lb). Butter a large flameproof dish and sprinkle it with salt, pepper and 3 chopped shallots. Place the salmon in the dish and add 500 ml (17 fl oz, 2 cups) champagne. Begin cooking the fish on the hob (stove top) and then transfer to a preheated oven at 220°C (425°F, gas 7) and cook for 20 minutes. Drain the salmon and place it on an ovenproof serving dish.

Boil the cooking juices until reduced by one-quarter and add to the sauce. Heat through, remove from the heat and beat in 2 egg yolks mixed with 2 tablespoons double (heavy) cream. Season with salt and pepper and strain. Coat the salmon with some of the sauce and glaze it in a very hot oven for about 5 minutes. Serve at once with the remainder of the sauce in a sauceboat.

salmon cutlets

Trim some halved salmon steaks into the shape of cutlets and fry them in butter, with or without a coating of breadcrumbs. Serve them as they are, sprinkled with the butter in which they were cooked, or serve with a sauce and garnish.

Salmon cutlets can also be made with a croquette mixture fashioned into the shape of cutlets. Coat these cutlets with beaten egg and breadcrumbs, fry in butter and serve coated with a sauce and garnished.

Salmon cutlets can also be prepared with a salmon quenelle mixture, put into cutlet-shaped moulds and poached. They are served as a hot appetizer coated with sauce.

salmon cutlets à l'anglaise

Trim some halved salmon steaks into cutlet shapes and season with salt and pepper. Dust with flour, dip into egg beaten with 1 tablespoon oil and some salt and pepper, and coat them with fresh white breadcrumbs. Brown the cutlets on both sides in clarified butter. Arrange them on a serving dish and coat them with slightly softened maître d'hôtel butter. Place a slice of lemon (with the peel removed) on each cutlet, and surround them with cannelled half-slices of lemon.

salmon cutlets à la bourguignonne

Poach some salmon cutlets, together with some button mushrooms, in a fish fumet made with red wine. Drain the fish and arrange it on a serving dish with the mushrooms. Garnish with glazed baby (pearl) onions. Reduce the cooking liquid and thicken it with beurre manié. Strain the sauce and pour over the fish.

Raw salmon with red new potatoes, see page 1027.

salmon cutlets à la florentine

Cook some salmon cutlets in reduced fish stock (just enough to cover them). Coarsely chop some spinach and cook gently in butter; season with salt and pepper. Drain thoroughly and place on a flame-proof serving dish. Drain the cutlets and arrange them on the bed of spinach. Coat the cutlets with Mornay sauce, sprinkle with some grated cheese and a little melted butter and brown under a hot grill (broiler). Serve immediately.

salmon cutlets with mushrooms à la crème

Season 6 cutlets with salt and pepper to taste, dust with flour and cook in 25 g (1 oz, 2 tablespoons) butter for 6–7 minutes. Add 3 mushroom caps (or 3 slices of truffle) per cutlet and continue to cook for a further 6–7 minutes. Drain the cutlets and keep them hot in a serving dish. Deglaze the pan with 150 ml (¼ pint, ⅔ cup) Madeira, add 200 ml (7 fl oz, ¾ cup) double (heavy) cream and reduce until creamy. Pour the sauce over the cutlets and serve immediately.

salmon cutlets with white wine

Poach some salmon cutlets for 5 minutes in fish fumet made with white wine (just enough to cover them). Drain the cutlets and arrange them in a circle on a round dish. Place some spinach cooked in butter in the centre. Coat with white wine sauce mixed with the reduced cooking liquid. Serve immediately.

salmon en croûte

Make some puff* pastry with 575 g (1¼ lb, 5 cups) plain (all-purpose) flour, 300 ml (½ pint, 1¼ cups) water, 1 teaspoon table salt and 425 g (15 oz, 2 cups) butter.

Trim the salmon and cut off all the fins except the tail fin. Cut off the gills and scale the fish, starting from the tail and working towards the head. Gut (clean) the salmon and remove any clots of blood. Wash the inside of the fish in plenty of water, arching its back slightly. Remove the skin from one side of the fish by making an incision along the back and separating the skin from the flesh on one side of this line, beginning at the tail and working towards the head, lifting it with the thumb. Wipe the salmon.

Divide the pastry into 2 equal portions. Roll out one of them into a long rectangle and place it on a large buttered baking sheet. Lay the salmon on the pastry, skin side down, and season with salt and plenty of pepper. Cut the pastry around the salmon to within 4 cm (1½ in) of the fish, leaving a large piece around the tail. Fold the pastry in towards the tail, tucking in the corners, and brush the edges of the pastry with 1 egg yolk beaten with 1 tablespoon water. Roll out the second portion of pastry like the first and place it over the fish. Seal the edges of the pastry together and trim to within 2 cm (¾ in) of the fish. Fold the projecting top edge of the pastry around the tail over the bottom piece. Using a sharp pointed knife, lightly score the position of the head, draw a line from the head to the tail along the backbone, and trace some oblique lines from this line down the side of the fish to mark it into portions. Glaze the pastry evenly with more beaten egg yolk, paying particular attention to the sealed edges. Bake in a preheated oven at 220°C (425°F, gas 7) for 1 hour. To serve, cut the pastry along the line marking the head, then cut along the median line and finally cut along the oblique lines.

Serve only the top layer of pastry, as the bottom layer will be soft and will have stuck to the salmon.

salmon fritters with apple sauce

Beat 4 egg yolks with 2 tablespoons double (heavy) cream and 2 tablespoons cornflour (cornstarch). Pour the mixture into a saucepan containing 250 ml (8 fl oz, 1 cup) boiling (hard) cider and thicken over a gentle heat. Remove from the heat and add 300 g (11 oz, 1¾ cups) diced salmon and then 2 stiffly whisked egg whites. Put to one side.

Prepare the sauce as follows. Brown 2 sliced shallots and 6 sliced apples in a pan and add 250 ml (8 fl oz, 1 cup) cider. When cooked, purée the mixture in a blender or food processor and keep hot.

Form the salmon purée into balls using 2 teaspoons and deep-fry them in hot oil, until they have puffed up and are golden brown. Serve with the apple sauce.

salmon steaks à l'américaine

Cook a whole langouste à l'américaine. Split it in half without damaging the shell, then remove the flesh and reserve the entrails.

From the middle of a salmon, cut some steaks, 4–6 cm (1½–2½ in) thick, and season them with salt and pepper. Place the steaks in a buttered flameproof sauté dish with 2 tablespoons raw matignon* per steak. Add 2 tablespoons melted butter per steak, fry quickly for 1–2 minutes, then cover the dish and transfer to a preheated oven at 230°C (450°F, gas 8). Baste frequently with the butter, but do not add any liquid. Remove the steaks from the dish and keep hot.

Dice the langouste meat and mix with an equal volume of braised diced mushrooms. Bind the mixture with 100 ml (4 fl oz, 7 tablespoons) reduced allemande* sauce flavoured with chopped tarragon and chervil. Stuff the 2 halves of the langouste shell with this mixture, smooth the surface and sprinkle with grated cheese and clarified butter. Place the shell halves on a baking sheet and brown in a very hot oven, 10 minutes before serving.

For the sauce, mix the cooked matignon with the langouste cooking liquid and then add 300 ml (½ pint, 1¼ cups) fish fumet* and 100 ml (4 fl oz, 7 tablespoons) velouté* sauce. Reduce this sauce by one-third over a high heat, stirring all the time. Remove from the heat and bind the sauce with the langouste entrails, rubbed through a sieve and mixed with 100 g (4 oz, ½ cup) butter. Add some chopped parsley, chervil and tarragon and the juice of half a lemon; adjust the seasoning.

Arrange the salmon steaks on a serving dish with the stuffed langouste shells at either end. Coat the salmon with the sauce.

salmon steaks à la meunière

Season some salmon steaks, 2.5 cm (1 in) thick, with salt and pepper and lightly dust with flour. Fry them on both sides in very hot butter. Arrange the steaks on a long dish, sprinkle with chopped parsley and add a dash of lemon juice. Just before serving, sprinkle the steaks with the cooking butter (very hot) and surround them with cannelled half-slices of lemon.

salmon steaks à la Nantua

Poach some salmon steaks in fish fumet, drain and place them on a serving dish. Surround with shelled crayfish tails and coat with Nantua sauce mixed with a little of the reduced fish fumet.

other recipes See *fritot, koulibiac, Orly, pâté, princesse, quenelle, soufflé*.

SALPICON Ingredients that are diced, often very finely, then bound with sauce (in the case of vegetables, meat, poultry, game, shellfish, fish or eggs) or with syrup or cream (for a fruit salpicon). The word comes from Spanish *sal* (salt) and *picar* (cut).

Savoury salpicons are used for filling or garnishing barquettes, vol-au-vent, canapés, croustades, croûtes, small meat pies, rissoles and tartlets. They are also used for making shaped cutlets, kromeskis and croquettes, and for stuffing or garnishing eggs, poultry, game, fish and some cuts of meat.

Fruit salpicons are made with fresh, raw or crystallized (candied) fruit or with fruit cooked in syrup, usually macerated in a liqueur. They are used for decorating or filling various desserts and pastries.

RECIPES

Fish and Shellfish Salpicons

Salpicons based on fish or shellfish can be hot or cold. The following are examples.
• *à l'américaine* Diced lobster or langouste flesh, bound with américaine sauce (hot).
• *with anchovies* Diced desalted fillets, bound with tarragon vinaigrette (cold) or with béchamel sauce (hot).
• *à la cancalaise* Poached oysters and raw mushrooms, thinly sliced, marinated in lemon juice and bound with normande sauce or fish velouté sauce (hot).
• *à la cardinal* Diced lobster flesh, truffles and mushrooms, bound with cardinal sauce (hot).
• *with crayfish* Peeled tails, bound with béchamel or Nantua sauce (hot) or with vinaigrette or mayonnaise (cold).

• *à la dieppoise* Peeled (shelled) prawns or shrimps, *moules marinière* and sliced mushrooms, stewed and bound with normande sauce (hot).
• *with fish* Diced poached fillets of fish, bound with béchamel, normande or white wine sauce (hot) or with vinaigrette or mayonnaise (cold).
• *with lobster or langouste* Diced flesh, bound with béchamel or Nantua sauce (hot) or with vinaigrette or mayonnaise (cold).
• *with mussels* Cooked mussels bound with allemande, poulette or white wine sauce (hot) or marinated and bound with vinaigrette or mayonnaise (cold).
• *with prawns or shrimps* Peeled (shelled), bound with béchamel sauce (hot) or mayonnaise (cold).
• *with skate liver* Slices of skate liver in butter, bound with velouté sauce made with fish stock (hot) or with vinaigrette (cold).

Meat, Poultry, Game, Offal and Egg Salpicons

Cooked meat or egg salpicons can be hot or cold.
• *with brains* Diced poached brains, bound with allemande, béchamel or velouté sauce (hot).
• *à l'écossaise* Pickled tongue cut into small cubes and diced truffles, bound with reduced demi-glace (hot).
• *with foie gras* Finely diced foie gras, bound with Madeira, port or sherry sauce or game fumet (hot), or with aspic (cold); sautéed chicken livers can be added.
• *with game* Finely diced game meat bound either with white or brown sauce made with game fumet (from the same game as the salpicon) or with aspic.
• *with ham* Diced York, Prague or Paris ham, bound with demi-glace (hot), or with vinaigrette or mustard-flavoured mayonnaise (cold).
• *with hard-boiled (hard-cooked) eggs* Diced whites and yolks, bound with allemande, béchamel, cream or velouté sauce (hot), or with vinaigrette or mayonnaise with herbs (cold).
• *with lamb's or calf's sweetbreads* Sliced sweetbreads cooked in butter, bound with allemande, béchamel, demi-glace, Madeira or suprême sauce (hot).
• *with meat* Finely diced leftover beef, veal, mutton or pork, bound with white or brown sauce (used particularly for croquettes and kromeskis and for filling pies).
• *with poultry* Diced white poultry meat, bound with allemande, béchamel, cream, velouté, brown or demi-glace sauce or with veal stock (hot, for filling vol-au-vent, barquettes, croustades and poached eggs, and for croquettes), or with vinaigrette with herbs for filling cold barquettes or hard-boiled eggs.
• *à la reine* Diced white chicken meat, mushrooms and truffles, bound with allemande sauce (hot).
• *à la Saint-Hubert* Diced game meat, bound with reduced demi-glace made with game fumet (hot).
• *with veal* Diced cooked veal, bound with allemande, béchamel or demi-glace sauce or with veal stock (hot).

Vegetable Salpicons

salpicon of truffles with cream sauce (hot)

Cut fresh truffles (raw or cooked in Madeira) or canned truffles into large or small dice, according to requirements. Sprinkle with salt and pepper. Cook gently in butter and bind with a few tablespoons of velouté or cream sauce.

vegetable salpicon with cream sauce (hot)

Cut vegetables into large or small dice, according to requirements and partially cook as below. Finish cooking the salpicon in a little butter and bind with a few tablespoons of thick cream sauce or reduced velouté sauce.

- *artichoke hearts* Half-cooked in white stock.
- *aubergines (eggplants)* Half-cooked in butter or olive oil.
- *carrots* Three-quarters cooked in water and butter.
- *celeriac* Half-stewed in butter.
- *ceps or button mushrooms* Half-stewed in butter or oil.
- *green asparagus or French (green) beans* Half-cooked in salted boiling water.
- *onions* Half-cooked in butter.
- *tomatoes* Blanched for 1 minute and peeled.
- *Jerusalem artichokes or salsify* Half-cooked in salted water.

vegetable salpicon with mayonnaise (cold)

Cook the chosen vegetable completely and leave to cool. Cut into small dice and bind with classic mayonnaise, which may be flavoured, coloured or thickened. Use any of the following vegetables: artichoke hearts cooked in white stock, patted dry and diced; asparagus tips or French (green) beans cut into short pieces, boiled in salted water and patted dry; peeled, diced celeriac, boiled in salted water and patted dry; mushrooms cooked in butter, drained and diced; or potatoes, boiled in their skins, peeled and diced.

vegetable salpicon with vinaigrette (cold)

Cook the chosen vegetable completely. Leave to cool, dice and dress with seasoned vinaigrette flavoured with finely chopped aromatic herbs. Use any of the following vegetables: diced cooked beetroot (red beet) with chervil and parsley; raw cucumber, sprinkled with salt, left to stand, rinsed, patted dry and diced, with fresh mint or tarragon; tomatoes, blanched for 20 seconds, peeled, seeded and diced, with basil or tarragon.

SALSA Spanish for sauce, either hot or cold. The term is usually applied in Spain and Mexico to spicy sauces, often hot with chillies (chiles), and particularly to uncooked sauces or dips.

SALSIFY A root vegetable, also called oyster plant or vegetable oyster, of which there are two varieties:

the true salsify, which is white and thick, with numbers of rootlets; and the black salsify, or *scorzonera*, which is black, longer and tapering and has no rootlets. The word *scorzonera* comes from Catalan *escorso* (viper), since the plant was formerly used in Spain to treat snake bites. Black salsify is easier to peel than true salsify and is cultivated for canning. Both varieties have a fairly strong and slightly bitter flavour and tender flesh; they are prepared in the same way. Both vegetables are in season between mid-autumn and early spring. They are particularly suitable for garnishing white meat.

Wild salsify, known as 'goat's beard', grows in slightly damp meadows. Its young shoots can be eaten in salad and can also be prepared like spinach; the roots are cooked like those of black salsify.

RECIPES

preparing and cooking salsify

Scrape or peel the salsify with a potato peeler, cut it into chunks 7.5 cm (3 in) long, and put them as they are prepared into water with a little lemon juice or vinegar added to prevent discoloration. Cook in boiling vegetable stock, covered, at a steady gentle simmer for 1–1½ hours, according to the quality of the vegetable, then drain and pat dry before final preparations for serving. (Alternatively, cut the salsify into pieces and cook the pieces with the skin on. It will then be easier to peel the vegetable after cooking.) If the salsify is not to be used immediately, it can be stored in its cooking liquid in the refrigerator for 1–2 days, but it will lose some of its nutritional value.

buttered salsify

Cook the salsify. Just before serving, make some noisette butter. Drain the salsify thoroughly while it is still very hot, quickly pat dry, then place on a heated dish and pour the noisette butter over it.

salsify à la polonaise

Cook the salsify in white stock, drain and dry, then stew in butter for about 10 minutes. Arrange in a deep dish and sprinkle with chopped hard-boiled (hard-cooked) egg yolks and parsley. Fry some fresh breadcrumbs in noisette butter – 25 g (1 oz, ½ cup) breadcrumbs to 100 g (4 oz, ½ cup) butter – and pour over the salsify.

salsify au gratin

Wash, scrape or peel, and roughly chop 1 kg (2¼ lb) salsify. Plunge into water with lemon juice added, then cook for 1 hour, or until tender, in salted white stock. Drain and dry. Cook 2 chopped shallots in butter until soft. Pour over 500 ml (17 fl oz, 2 cups) double (heavy) cream and reduce. Add the salsify and a little stock. Season with salt and pepper and pour into a gratin dish. Sprinkle with grated Gruyère cheese and breadcrumbs and brown in a preheated oven at 220°C (425°F, gas 7) for 20 minutes.

salsify fritters

Cook 1 kg (2¼ lb) salsify, drain and purée. Add 100 g (4 oz, ½ cup) butter and season with salt and pepper. Roll the purée into little balls, coat them in flour and deep-fry in hot oil at 180°C (350°F) until golden all over. Remove with a slotted spoon and drain on paper towels. Arrange on a warmed dish and garnish with fried parsley.

salsify in stock

Wash, peel and cook the salsify, then drain and dry. Pour over some slightly thickened white veal stock or meat gravy. Cook in a preheated oven at 180°C (350°F, gas 4) for 15–20 minutes.

salsify Mornay

Cook the salsify, drain, dry, then arrange in a gratin dish lined with a layer of Mornay sauce. Coat with boiling Mornay sauce, sprinkle with grated Parmesan cheese, pour over some melted butter and brown in a preheated oven at 230°C (450°F, gas 8).

salsify salad with anchovies

Cook some salsify in white stock, drain thoroughly and dry. Mix in some light, well-seasoned mayonnaise and chopped, drained, canned anchovy fillets (or whole filleted anchovies that have been soaked to desalt them). Sprinkle with chopped herbs.

salsify sautéed à la provençale

Cook some salsify in white stock, drain, dry and sauté in olive oil. Just before serving, add a little chopped garlic and parsley or some well-seasoned tomato sauce.

salsify with béchamel sauce

Cook, drain and dry 800 g (1¾ lb) salsify. Lay the salsify on a buttered ovenproof dish and cover with a fairly thin béchamel* sauce, made with 25 g (1 oz, 2 tablespoons) butter, 25 g (1 oz, ¼ cup) plain (all-purpose) flour and 450 ml (¾ pint, 2 cups) milk. Cook in a preheated oven at 190°C (375°F, gas 5) for 20 minutes, then pour over 2–3 tablespoons cream and reheat before serving.

salsify with mayonnaise

Cook the salsify and leave to cool, then drain thoroughly and dry. Add some well-seasoned mayonnaise or vinaigrette. Sprinkle with chopped herbs and serve with a cold white meat dish, such as rabbit in aspic.

sautéed salsify

Cook some salsify in white stock, drain, dry and fry in butter. Sprinkle with salt, pepper and chopped herbs just before serving.

other recipes See *fritter, omelette (filled omelettes), salad (Montfermeil salad)*.

SALSIZ Small dried sausage originally from the canton of Grisons in Switzerland. With a rectangular cross-section, and 6–15 cm (2½–6 in) long, salsiz consists of lean beef, pork and pork fat, roughly chopped. Traditionally, it is cut into fairly thick slices and served with gherkins and small pickled onions.

SALT A white, crystalline, odourless, sharp-tasting substance, which is used as a condiment and preserving agent. In its pure state, salt consists of sodium chloride and is abundant in nature. There are two basic types: sea salt, which is extracted from sea water by evaporation (30 kg per cubic metre/66 lb per cubic yard); and rock salt, which is found in a crystalline state in the ground – as a surface deposit at the site of dried salt lakes or, more commonly, as underground deposits from ancient oceans.

Since ancient times, salt has been a precious commodity. The Hebrews used it in sacrifices and ceremonies. Homer described nations as poor when they did not mix salt with their food. Salt is often a symbol of friendship and hospitality and in some countries is still traditionally offered with bread to strangers. The Romans used salt to preserve fish, olives, cheese and meat, and it formed part of the soldiers' wages (hence the etymology of the word 'salary'). In the Middle Ages, the salt routes were used for a solid flow of trade, both in France (especially from Saintonge) and Scandinavia, where dried salt fish was the basic food. There was a salt measurers' guild in France as early as the 13th century. Its members had the task of counting the salt fish and quantities of butter arriving in Paris by boat, and they also supervised the measuring of salt and grain. In medieval Britain, salt was an essential commodity – even for peasants. It was collected from the coastline where sea water had evaporated and left a crystalline deposit, and then stored in a box near the fire.

Since salt was essential to life and to the long-term preservation of foodstuffs, and since its production could be easily supervised, many governments taxed it. In France, the *gabelle* tax, created in the 14th century and abolished in 1790, obliged private individuals to purchase a certain amount of salt from the king's storehouses every year at a fixed price, even if they were not going to use it.

Salt is an essential condiment and remains an essential raw material in the food industry, for canned foods, salted meat and fish, charcuterie and cheese in particular. The function of salt is to enhance the flavour of food, to bring out the taste and to stimulate the appetite. It is essential for the body and contributes to maintaining the osmotic pressure of the body's cells.

• CELERY SALT A table salt mixed with dried ground celeriac. It is used to season tomato juice cocktails and other vegetable juices and also some stocks and consommés.

• COARSE SALT Refined or unrefined, this is available in large crystals. Unrefined salt contains traces of valuable minerals and is grey in colour; it is therefore best to use it in cooking and to reserve the white salt for the table. It can be used in its large crystal form or ground in a salt mill.

• COOKING SALT This comes in the form of small crystals and is used to season food while cooking. It should be kept within easy reach in a vessel with a lid, to prevent it from becoming damp.

• GARLIC SALT A table salt flavoured with dried ground garlic.

• HICKORY SALT An American condiment consisting of sea salt mixed with smoked, finely powdered hickory wood. It has a slightly nutty taste and is used for barbecues.

• IODIZED SALT A mixture of table salt and sodium iodide, sold as table salt.

• LOVAGE SALT A table salt flavoured with dried ground lovage root. It has more body than celery salt and is used in soups and sauces, particularly in Germany.

• SPICED SALT A mixture of dry table salt, white ground pepper and mixed spices in the proportions 10:1:1. It is used to season forcemeats, pies and terrines.

• TABLE SALT This is always refined and is used as a table condiment (in a salt cellar), in pâtisserie, for seasoning and to finish sauces. It is used by the pinch. To help keep it free-flowing, various products are added to it (for example magnesium carbonate or sodium silicoaluminate), the proportion of which must never exceed 2%.

• TENDERIZING SALT Ordinary salt containing 2–3% papain, used for tenderizing meat.

SALT BOX A wooden or earthenware box with a hinged lid, traditionally attached to the wall near a cooking surface, for easy access. Coarse and fine salt may be kept in two different boxes.

SALT CELLAR A small receptacle used for serving salt at the table. Made from various materials in several different shapes, such as a sprinkler or a tiny bowl and spoon, salt cellars are often incorporated in a cruet with pepper and mustard pots. Originally, salt cellars were simply hollowed-out lumps of bread; then silver salt cellars and rich gold-plated articles appeared, often fitted with a lock, as salt was once an extremely expensive commodity.

SALT COD Cod that has been salted and dried – not to be confused with stockfish, which is simply dried cod. For centuries, salt cod has been a basic food in some European countries and was particularly favoured by Catholics for days of abstinence. As it keeps so well, salt cod was also a valuable food in times of siege and on long sea voyages.

Today, salt cod is most popular in Portugal, Spain, France, Italy and in parts of Latin America and Africa subjected to colonial influence. In Spain and Portugal, there are specialist shops that sell only salt cod (*bacalao* in Spanish, *bacalhau* in Portuguese) and offer a large choice. The fish is sold by the cut (for example, loin) and often labelled with the dish for which it might be used. European cod is preferred to Newfoundland cod. Norwegian (followed by Scottish) cod is the choice for compact cuts that are cooked in the oven; tender Icelandic cod is best for recipes involving raw or macerated salt cod.

Before any preparation, the fish must be carefully desalted. (Most authorities favour soaking it in several changes of cold water, but some prefer to leave it under cold running water.) It can then be used raw, or poached and served cold (in vinaigrette, with mustard, in a gribiche sauce, with mayonnaise or in a salad with potatoes) or hot (in a white or Mornay sauce, au gratin, in scallop shells, as a soufflé or a fish loaf, in croquettes or in a cassoulet). Of the many recipes that use salt cod (Portugal has hundreds), one of the oldest is the muleteers' dish from Aragon in Spain, *bacalao al ajo arriero* (salt cod with garlic and tomato sauce). Another Spanish favourite is the Lenten dish of salt cod with chick peas (garbanzo beans) and spinach. Other classics include poached salt cod served with aioli and France's *brandade*, a rich purée of salt cod. Raw salt cod is very sophisticated – on a par with smoked salmon – and features in two popular Spanish dishes: *xató*, salt cod, tuna and anchovies with salad leaves and a chilli and hazelnut dressing; and *esqueixada* salt cod with grilled red (bell) pepper and tomato strips.

RECIPES

desalting and poaching salt cod

Wash the dried fish thoroughly under cold running water, then either leave it whole or cut it into sections, which speeds up the desalting process. Place it in a colander, with the skin uppermost, in a bowl of cold water, so that the fish is completely covered. Soak for 18–24 hours (12 hours for fillets), changing the water several times; the fish must be almost or totally free of salt (according to preference) before it is cooked.

Drain the cod and place it in a saucepan with plenty of cold water. Add a bouquet garni, bring the water to the boil and keep it simmering for about 10 minutes. Drain well and prepare according to the chosen recipe.

fillets of salt cod maître d'hôtel

Desalt the fillets whole, then drain and cut them into small tongue shapes. Flatten them slightly, coat with breadcrumbs and cook in butter. Arrange the pieces in a serving dish and coat with half-melted maître d'hôtel butter. Serve with boiled potatoes.

fried salt cod

Desalt the cod, cut it into small tongue shapes and soak for 1 hour in milk that has been boiled and cooled. Drain the fish pieces, flour them and fry in oil heated to 175°C (347°F). Place on paper towels and sprinkle with fine salt. Serve with lemon quarters.

salt cod à la créole

Desalt and poach 800 g (1¾ lb) salt cod. Prepare a fondue* with 1 kg (2¼ lb) tomatoes, some olive oil, plenty of garlic and onion, and a dash of cayenne pepper. Cut 6 tomatoes in half and remove the seeds. Seed 2 green (bell) peppers and cut them into small tongue-shaped pieces. Sauté the tomatoes and peppers in oil. Spread the tomato fondue in an oiled gratin dish, arrange the drained and flaked cod on top, then cover it with the tomato halves and the pieces of pepper. Sprinkle with a little oil and cook in a preheated oven at 230°C (450°F, gas 8) for 10 minutes, moistening with a little lime juice. Serve piping hot with rice à la créole.

salt cod à la florentine
Desalt and poach 800 g (1¾ lb) salt cod; drain and flake it. Blanch 1 kg (2¼ lb) spinach for 5 minutes in salted boiling water, then drain and press it to extract the water. Cook the spinach slowly in 50 g (2 oz, ¼ cup) butter for about 10 minutes. Line a gratin dish with this spinach. Arrange the cod on top, coat with Mornay sauce, sprinkle with grated Parmesan cheese and moisten with a little melted butter. Brown in a preheated oven at 230°C (450°F, gas 8).

salt cod à l'anglaise
Desalt and poach some salt cod, then arrange it in a dish, garnished with fresh parsley. Serve with boiled vegetables and melted butter, to which lemon juice, chopped hard-boiled (hard-cooked) egg and coarsely chopped parsley have been added.

The butter may be replaced by a sauce such as bâtarde, cream, hollandaise, caper, fines herbes, curry or mustard, or the cod can be served cold with mayonnaise.

salt cod à la parisienne
Desalt 800 g (1¾ lb) fillets of salt cod, cut them into pieces and poach them. Hard boil (hard cook) 3 eggs, shell them and chop them coarsely. Chop a small bunch of parsley. Drain the pieces of cod, arrange them in a serving dish and sprinkle with the egg and parsley. Keep hot. Fry 4 tablespoons fine fresh breadcrumbs in 100 g (4 oz, ½ cup) butter, sprinkle them over the cod and serve immediately.

salt cod à la provençale
Prepare 500 ml (17 fl oz, 2 cups) tomato fondue* with olive oil and season with garlic. Pour this fondue into a shallow frying pan and add 800 g (1¾ lb) desalted cod, cut into pieces, poached and drained. Simmer gently for about 10 minutes, adjust the seasoning, then pour into a serving dish and sprinkle with coarsely chopped parsley.

salt cod with flageolet beans
Desalt 1 kg (2¼ lb) dried salt cod cut into quarters. Soak 400 g (14 oz, 2½ cups) dried green flageolet beans in plenty of cold water for 24 hours. Cook the beans in water for 30 minutes with an onion stuck with cloves, 1 thinly sliced carrot, 1 bouquet garni and 3 crushed garlic cloves. Drain the cod and season with pepper. Heat some groundnut (peanut)

oil in a frying pan and lightly brown the cod on both sides. Arrange in a buttered ovenproof dish, sprinkle with 3 finely chopped garlic cloves, then cover with the drained flageolets. Coat with 250 ml (8 fl oz, 1 cup) crème fraîche and cook in a preheated oven at 200°C (400°F, gas 6) for 20 minutes. Sprinkle with coarsely chopped chervil just before serving.

tongues of salt cod in pistou
Thoroughly desalt 800 g (1¾ lb) salt cod tongues. Poach them for 6 minutes in a mixture of equal quantities of water and milk. Drain, lightly flour and fry quickly in olive oil. Crush 2 blanched garlic cloves and some basil in a mortar. Mix with olive oil, add some fresh puréed tomato and sprinkle with pepper. Sauté this pistou and the tongues in a non-stick frying pan and serve piping hot.

other recipes See *acra, bamboche, Bénédictine, bouillabaisse, brandade, croquette, languedocienne, lyonnaise, rougail.*

SALTIMBOCCA An Italian dish that is a speciality of Rome but originally came from Brescia, where the name literally means 'jump into the mouth'. It consists of fine slices of veal fried in butter, topped with small slices of ham, flavoured with sage and gently braised in white wine.

SALTING A preserving process used mainly for pork and certain types of fish. It is sometimes combined with smoking and drying. A very ancient technique, used by the Romans for fish, olives, shrimps and cheese, it became very much more sophisticated in the Middle Ages, for cod, herring and other fish. Salting is now less common than previously, especially in domestic cookery, where the main preserving method is freezing. It is confined to specific foods, using dry salt or brine (salt in solution).
• CHEESE Salting is an important operation in the manufacture of cheese. It accelerates drainage in soft fresh curd cheeses when sprinkled on by hand, and encourages rind formation on cooked and uncooked pressed curd cheeses immersed in brine; the more the brine is renewed, the thicker and harder the rind becomes. Some soft cheeses are salted to varying extents (slightly salted) or preserved in a light brine, as are the goat's- and ewe's-milk cheeses of Mediterranean countries.
• FISH Anchovies are cleaned and put into salt for 6–8 months. Herrings, sprats, salmon and eels are salted in dry salt or brine, then smoked. Cod are split in half, flattened and boned, then stacked between layers of salt with the addition of sulphurous anhydride (or one of its derivatives, E220), which keeps the flesh white. They are left for at least 30 days. (See *salt cod.*)
• FRUIT, VEGETABLES AND NUTS Salting is sometimes used to preserve French (green) beans and herbs, but is particularly associated with sauerkraut, peanuts, cashews, almonds, walnuts and hazelnuts,

as well as crisps (potato chips).

• MEAT Raw ham and bacon are rubbed with a mixture of salt and saltpetre, then the pieces are piled into salting tubs. The exuded water forms a supersaturated brine, in which the pieces are moved around every 10–15 days; salting lasts for 40–60 days.

Cooked ham is placed in vats, covered with brine and left there for 30–40 days, at a temperature of 3–5°C (37–41°F). It may also be smoked. Other traditional salted meats include beef in brine and salted tongue. Pork is also salted in brine without being cured.

RECIPES

home-salted pork
Choose fairly even-sized pieces of belly pork, knuckles of ham, spare rib or shoulder chops, and trimmed rind. Rub them with fine salt and lay in a salting tub, putting the largest pieces at the bottom: start with the pieces of belly pork, pressing them down well. Cover with cooking salt, making sure that there are as few air pockets as possible. A few garlic cloves, peppercorns and a bay leaf may be added, but not to excess. Then pile on the knuckles of ham, filling up the holes with the spare rib or shoulder chops. Cover each layer with salt, pressing down well, and finish with the rinds. Preservation time is 2–3 weeks for spare rib chops, 1 month for knuckles of ham, and much longer for belly of pork. Knuckle, brushed and wiped, can be stored hung up in a cool, airy place.

rolled salt belly pork
Choose a piece of streaky belly pork that is not too fatty. Trim it, cut into a rectangle and slash the inside. Rub with salt mixed with chopped garlic, then sprinkle with chopped thyme. Roll up the belly and tie tightly. Rub the outside – the rind side – with fine salt for some time, so that it penetrates thoroughly. Cut the belly into 2 or 3 pieces, according to the size of the salting tub.

SALTING TUB A container used for salting pork. Formerly a large wooden tub, it is now a cement, earthenware or plastic vat.

SALT-MEADOW SHEEP *mouton pré-salé* A French sheep or lamb raised and fattened on the pastures close to the sea, which are impregnated with salt and iodine. In this way, the flesh acquires a unique flavour and provides high-quality meat.

SALTPETRE The common name for potassium nitrate, derived from Latin *sal* (salt) and *petrae* (stone). Saltpetre takes the form of small white crystals, formerly obtained by scraping desposits from the walls of cellars and storerooms, but now manufactured industrially. A powerful bactericide, saltpetre has been used since ancient times to preserve food, especially raw and cooked meats, since it

strengthens the action of fermenting agents, while giving a characteristic flavour to the product being treated. Its oxidizing action produces the characteristic bright pink colour of salt beef, ham and pickled tongue. It is used in conjunction with salt in all types of brine, with the addition of at least twice its weight of sugar since it has a very bitter taste. If used excessively it can be harmful, so its use is controlled by very strict regulations.

SALT PORK A piece of pork (loin, knuckle, shoulder or hand) that has been salted in brine or dry salt and is sold raw (labelled *demi-sel*, or slightly salted, in France). Before being cooked, it is desalted by soaking in water for 1–12 hours, depending on the degree of salting.

Salt pork has more flavour and cooks more quickly than unsalted meat. The classic French recipe for salt pork is *potée* (a type of stew), but it can also be boiled and served with cabbage, pease pudding or with lentils and carrots.

RECIPE

boiled salt pork with pease pudding
Boil a piece of salted belly pork with some carrots, turnips, celery, leeks, onions and parsnips. Meanwhile, prepare a very smooth purée of split peas (preferably yellow) using 500 g (18 oz, 2¼ cups) split peas, 100 g (4 oz, ½ cup) butter, 3 eggs, grated nutmeg, salt and pepper. Butter a pudding basin (mould) and pour the mixture into it. Place the basin in a roasting tin (pan) containing 2.5 cm (1 in) boiling water and cook in a preheated oven at 190°C (375°F, gas 5) for 40 minutes. Drain the cooked pork, place in a serving dish and surround with the well-drained vegetables. Turn out the pease pudding and serve separately.

SAMARITAINE, À LA A term applied to large braised cuts of meat garnished with rice timbales, dauphine potatoes and braised lettuce.

SAMBAL A condiment (originally Indonesian) made with red chilli peppers, grated onion, lime juice, oil and vinegar. The name may also be used to describe the dish that it accompanies.

SAMBUCA A colourless anise-flavoured Italian liqueur, sometimes drunk *con la mosca* ('with the fly'): with one or two coffee beans floating in the glass, after it has been set alight. Sambuca is very strong but has a sweetish taste; the coffee beans are crunched as it is drunk.

SAMOS Wine from the Greek island of Samos, which has its own AOC. Samos wines are made from Muscat Blanc à Petits Grains.

SAMOSA An Indian pastry snack, and popular street food, consisting of a filling in a fine layered pastry. The pastry is of the filo (phyllo) type and the filling may be based on meat or vegetables or a mixture of both. Samosas are triangular and are deep-fried until crisp and brown. Vegetable fillings usually include diced potatoes and roasted whole spices, such as mustard seeds and black cumin, which give a crunchy texture. Minced (ground) meat is popular, cooked with whole spices, onions and vegetables.

SAMOVAR A Russian kettle, which provides a permanent supply of boiling water for domestic purposes. The word comes from *samo* (itself) and *varit* (to boil). Originally made from brass or copper, but now of aluminium or stainless steel and electrically heated, the samovar is the traditional Russian wedding gift. It consists of a pot-bellied container with two handles and a central chimney, which rests on a grid on which embers are placed. Cold water is added at the top and heated by contact with the chimney; the boiling water is drawn off through a small tap at the bottom of the container. Since this water is used, among other things, for making tea, the name 'samovar' has also been applied to a simple silver container heated by a small spirit lamp, which provided boiling water for adding to tea, during large gatherings.

SAMPHIRE The common name for *Crithmum maritimum*, a perennial herb, also called rock samphire, which grows on clifftops in cracks in the rocks or on dry stony ground. Its fleshy leaves are rich in iodine and are used principally to flavour soups and salads. The leaves can also be pickled in vinegar like gherkins or cooked in butter or cream, like purslane.

Samphire is used in an original way in Sarah Bernhardt's recipe for larks: 'Pound in a mortar the flesh of two larks; add some butter, some chopped samphire, some breadcrumbs soaked in milk, some Malaga raisins and some crushed juniper berries. Stuff a third lark with the mixture and roast it on a spit covered with samphire leaves and a strip of fat bacon. Serve on a croûton soaked in gin, and then toasted and buttered.'

See also *glasswort (marsh samphire)*.

SAMPIGNY-LÈS-MARANGES AOC mainly red Burgundies from the extreme south of the Côte-de-Beaune. Much of the wine from this area, whose production is limited, may be blended with that of neighbouring parishes (communes) and sold as *Maranges* or *Maranges Côte-de-Beaune*.

SAMSOË A Danish cow's-milk cheese (45% fat content), originally from the island of the same name and now produced in creameries all over Denmark. It has a pressed curd and a golden yellow rind coated with paraffin wax. Mild and firm, with a few round holes, it acquires a nutty flavour after a few months' maturing. It is made in round discs, 46 cm (18 in) in diameter and weighing about 15 kg (33 lb).

SANCERRE AOC wines from the upper reaches of the River Loire. The vineyards are around the picturesque little hill town of Sancerre, which stands above the river. The dry, crisp, fragrant white wines are especially famous and are made from the Sauvignon Blanc grape. The Pinot Noir grape is used to make light fruity reds and rosés.

SANCIAU A large, rustic pancake or fritter. Sweet or savoury, sanciaux are made from flour, milk and butter and sometimes with eggs. They are cooked in a frying pan as thick pancakes (in Berry and Nivernais, where they are also called *sauciaux*) or as batter fritters (in Bourbonnais). They are related to *grapiaux*, *chanciaux*, *matefaims* and other traditional flour-based dishes of rural areas of central France.

SAND EEL Generic name for various species of fish of the *Ammodytidae* family, identified by their elongated shape and pointed head. They are sold fresh and prepared by frying in oil.

SAND, GEORGE (born Aurore Dupin) French writer (born Paris, 1804; died Nohant, 1876). Together with the other great Romantic writers in Paris, she frequented the Procope, Mère Saguet's open-air café, and praised the sheep's trotters (feet) *à la poulette* served at Magny's. A cordon-bleu cook, she extolled *omelette nohantaise*, feasted on Chavignol (a soft goat's-milk cheese), and was not averse to 'fairy potatoes' (truffles). She also appreciated the wines of Berry and owned a vineyard in Mers-sur-Indre.

SAND-SMELT A small sea fish, also called silverside, living in shoals along coasts and in estuaries. The sand-smelt is about 15 cm (6 in) long and has a conspicuous silvery stripe down each side of the body. It is sometimes passed off as smelt, but its flesh is less delicate. It is generally deep-fried, but may also be eaten smoked. The French name, *athérine*, is derived from the Greek word *ather*, meaning 'beard of an ear of grain', as its bones resemble an ear of barley. Similar species are found in the Mediterranean.

SANDWICH In its simpest form, two slices of bread enclosing a plain or mixed filling based on cooked meats or fish, raw vegetables or cheese, cut into thin slices or small pieces. Sandwiches are made with virtually any type of bread (which can be used as whole slices, with or without crusts, and sometimes cut into triangles or rectangles after filling), or rolls, spread with pllain flavoured butter. Various condiments may complete the filling, including gherkins, herbs and black (ripe) olives.

■ **History** Sandwiches are named after John Montagu, 4th Earl of Sandwich, an inveterate gambler who acquired the habit of sending for cold meat between two slices of bread so that he would not have to leave the gambling tables to eat. Although the name is relatively recent, dating from the beginning of the 19th century, the concept itself is

Sandwich surprise

The simple sandwich can be adapted to make a sophisticated picnic loaf. Use a large loaf of the best-quality bread, with a close, firm texture and small crumb. The filling should be full flavoured and one or more fillings can be used. A fine mixture is essential if the loaf is to be thinly cut. Chunky, country style fillings – such as diced roasted vegetables dressed with garlic-flavoured olive oil – are ideal for a rustic loaf.

1 *Slice the crusts off the top and bottom of a round loaf or both ends of a long loaf.*

2 *Cut around inside the crust, taking care to keep it whole and leaving a thin layer of bread inside.*

3 *Remove the middle of the loaf in one piece, then slice it horizontally – thinly for fine fillings; thickly for chunky mixtures. Sandwich the slices back together with the filling. Spread the inside of the crust with filling and replace the sandwich stack. Spread the crusts with filling and replace them. Press the loaf together well and wrap tightly in cling film (plastic wrap). To serve, cut a round loaf into wedges or slice a long loaf vertically, as usual.*

ancient. It has long been the custom in rural France, for example, to give farm labourers working in the fields meat for their meal enclosed in two slices of brown bread. In south-western France, it was customary to provide those setting out on a journey with slices of cooked meat (especially pork or veal), sprinkled with their juices, sandwiched between two pieces of bread.

■ **Types of sandwich** There must be as many variations on the sandwich as there are hungry people, inspired to combine different bases and/or coverings with whatever filling is available and appetizing. The following is a summary of the main types.

• CLASSIC CLOSED SANDWICH A simple sandwich, consisting of a filling between two slices of bread. Dainty, crustless sandwiches, cut into neat triangles, are traditional for British afternoon tea, particularly with a filling of lightly seasoned, finely sliced cucumber. The nickname 'doorstep' is often applied to untrimmed, thick slices of bread sandwiched together with a substantial quantity of filling.

• FILLED BREADS AND ROLLS Chunks of baguette, individual country-style French or Italian breads, bagels, pitta bread or other flat breads, split rolls or wedges of Irish soda bread can all be filled. These are usually grouped with sandwiches, with occasional references to 'filled rolls'. Examples include the American 'submarine', or 'sub', the nickname for a filled long roll or length of French bread, usually laden with a mixture of different ingredients. 'Poor boy' and 'torpedo' are other nicknames for the submarine.

As well as filling individual breads, whole loaves can be scooped out and stuffed or sliced horizontally and layered with fillings, then tightly packed so that the loaf is firmly re-formed when it can be sliced vertically for serving.

• MULTI-LAYERED SANDWICHES Closed sandwiches can be made up of several layers. The club sandwich consists of three slices of bread (plain or toasted) with two different fillings. Originating in the United States, New York's Carnegie deli is renowned for offering sandwiches up to 900 g (2 lb) in weight, held together with cocktail sticks (tooth picks). Pastrami, bacon, cooked poultry or meat, lettuce, tomatoes and mayonnaise are typical filling ingredients for club sandwiches.

• OPEN SANDWICHES The Danish open sandwich or *smørrebrød*, meaning 'smeared bread' is the classic, with attractive and appetizing arrangements of ingredients neatly displayed on each thin slice. As for any other type, many varieties are prepared on thin or thick slices of bread, split rolls or flat breads. The open sandwich should provide a large proportion of filling and it should be eaten with a knife and fork.

• COOKED SANDWICHES The toasted sandwich is a popular alternative to the plain and simple sandwich. The filled bread is toasted on both sides, usually in a sandwich toaster, so that the bread is browned and crisp outside and the filling hot. Cheese and ham are basic fillings. Sandwiches can be fried rather than grilled (broiled) as for *croque* monsieur, the French cheese and ham sandwich, fried until crisp and golden. Baked or grilled, filled or topped breads are also sometimes grouped with sandwiches.

RECIPES

Alsatian sandwich
Spread 2 thin slices of rye bread with butter mixed with grated horseradish. Fill with thin slices of poached Strasbourg sausage, peeled and cut diagonally. Thin slices of black radishes can be added.

basil sandwich
Lightly toast 2 slices of bread and spread with butter mixed with chopped fresh basil. Fill with chopped hard-boiled (hard-cooked) eggs, sliced black (ripe) olives, and a few strips of sweet red (bell) pepper marinated in oil and well drained.

club sandwich
Remove the crusts from 3 large slices of bread. Lightly toast them and spread with mayonnaise. On 2 slices place a lettuce leaf, 2 slices of tomato, some thin slices of skinned cold roast chicken breast and sliced hard-boiled (hard-cooked) egg. Coat with more mayonnaise mixed with a little tomato ketchup or chopped herbs and put one slice on top of the other. Top with the third slice.

SANGIOVESE A quality grape variety that is widely planted in Italy. It is used solely in the production of Brunello di Montalcino and as the base of blends in Chianti, Vino Nobile di Montepulciano, Umbria's Torgiano and Rosso Piceno and Rosso Conero from the Marche. The wines produced range from those that are light and suitable for early drinking to those that are intense, full-bodied and with good tannins.

SANGLER A French culinary term meaning to pack crushed ice and cooking salt around a watertight mould placed inside a container. This process was traditionally used with ice-cream churns for freezing and for temporarily preserving bombe mixtures.

SANGRE DE TORO The registered name of one of the red wines of the Torres winery in the Penedès area of northern Spain.

SANGRIA The Spanish version of a cup, a mixed drink based on red or white wine with added fruit and mineral water, sometimes with a spirit as well. It is served chilled. Since red wine is the most usual base, the drink takes its name from sangre, Spanish for 'blood'.

RECIPES

sangria with brandy
Mix together 1 lemon and 1 orange, both sliced, 1 quartered apple, 5 tablespoons sugar, 1 bottle red wine, 60 ml (2 fl oz, ¼ cup) Spanish brandy, and 750 ml (1¼ pints, 3¼ cups) carbonated mineral water. A pinch of cinnamon may be added.

sangria with peaches
Strain a large can of peaches and cut the fruit into pieces. Pour them into a large glass bowl, together with their syrup. Remove the peel and pith from 4 oranges and 2 lemons; slice them and add to the peaches. Pour over 2 litres (3½ pints, 9 cups) Spanish or Algerian wine, 1 litre (1¾ pints, 4⅓ cups) lemonade and 2 liqueur glasses of Grand Marnier or Cointreau. Mix well and chill for at least 3 hours.

SANGUE DI GUIDA A *Denominazione di Origine Controllata* Lombardy red wine, known also as 'Judas' blood', from the Oltrepò Pavese region of Italy.

SANSHO A Japanese spice made from the berries of a tree in the prickly ash family. This is closely related to the tree which provides the berries for sichuan pepper. The berries are dried and their bitter black seeds removed before they are ground to make sansho. This spice is valued as a seasoning for fatty foods, such as grilled eel, or chicken.

The leaves, known as *kinome*, are used as a herb in Japanese cooking, chopped, whole, pickled or ground to a paste. See *Sichuan pepper*.

SANTÉ A thick soup derived from Parmentier soup, with sorrel stewed in butter and sprigs of chervil added. Nicolas de Bonnefons, however, wrote in *Les Délices de la campagne*: 'Santé soup should be good honest soup, full of choice meats and well reduced, without chopped vegetables, mushrooms, spices or other ingredients: it should be simple, since it bears the name *santé* (health).'

RECIPE

santé soup
Prepare 1.5 litres (2¾ pints, 6½ cups) fairly thin potato and leek soup*. Cook 4 tablespoons shredded sorrel in butter until soft. Mix together and thicken with 3 egg yolks blended with 100 ml (4 fl oz, 7 tablespoons) double (heavy) cream. Beat in 50 g (2 oz, ¼ cup) butter, cut into small pieces, and sprinkle with chervil. Serve with thin slices of French bread, dried out in the oven.

SANTENAY AOC Burgundy from the Côte-de-Beaune, from the southernmost parish in the Côte-d'Or, producing mainly red wines from Pinot Noir and some white wines.

SAPODILLA The fruit of a Central American tree cultivated in many tropical countries. It is about the size of a lemon and covered with a rough grey or brown skin. Its reddish-yellow flesh, which tastes similar to the apricot, is eaten almost overripe, peeled and with the seeds removed; or boiled to make a syrup.

SARD A sea fish related to the sea bream, found only off the coast of Provence, France. Known as *lou sar* in Provençal cookery, it may be grilled (broiled), boiled or deep-fried.

RECIPE

sard with chive butter
Choose a sard weighing about 800 g (1¾ lb); sprinkle with salt and pepper. Grill very rapidly over charcoal or on a preheated serrated griddle until the marks of the grill begin to show, then turn the fish through 90° and repeat so that a criss-cross pattern is formed. Carefully fillet the fish and place the fillets in a roasting tin (pan) with 2 tablespoons olive oil and 1 head of garlic previously cooked in its skin, split into cloves and peeled. Bake the fillets in a preheated oven at 230°C (450°F, gas 8) for 5 minutes, then dry on paper towels. Alternatively, fillet the raw fish and prepare for the oven in the same way, but increase the cooking time slightly to compensate for not grilling first.

Arrange on a dish and pour over beurre blanc mixed with chopped chives. Place a walnut-sized piece of crushed tomato on top. Surround with the garlic cloves and heart-shaped croûtons spread with tapenade.

SARDE, À LA Term used to describe cuts of meat coated with a sauce made by deglazing the pan juices with a tomato demi-glace, garnished with rice croquettes, and served either with mushrooms and beans cooked in butter, or with pieces of cucumber and stuffed tomatoes.

SARDINE A small fish – maximum length 25 cm (10 in) – related to the herring, various species of which are found worldwide. With a blue-green back, and silvery sides and belly, it may take its name from Sardinia, where it was once fished abundantly. The sardine is still fished intensively and is eaten fresh or canned.

Fished in spring and summer, the sardine starts growing in early spring and reaches its maximum size towards the end of summer. These large sardines are fat and full of flavour, and may be known as pilchards (not to be confused with canned herrings, which are also known in French as pilchards). In Europe, distinction is made between the small Italian sardine, 13–15 cm (5–6 in) long, which should be deep-fried since it is never very oily and dries out easily; the medium-sized sardine, 18–20 cm (7–8 in) long, with more compact and flavoursome flesh, for grilling (broiling) or frying; and the large Brittany sardine, 25 cm (10 in) long, which is grilled in its own fat and has a fine flavour. Fresh sardines can also be prepared as an *escabèche* or in a bouillabaisse, coated with breadcrumbs and fried, or stuffed and baked; they can even be eaten raw, in pâtés, or marinated.

Before cooking, the scales should be removed, the sardine gutted (cleaned) and wiped, and the head cut off, unless the fish is to be grilled (it is less likely to break up when turned if whole). Very fresh small sardines do not need to be gutted, but simply wiped. Their freshness can be judged by their rigidity, the brilliance of their eyes and the absence of bloodstains at the gills.

■ **Preserving sardines** Sardines can be smoked or salted, frozen or preserved in oil and canned. Breton sardines were salted and pressed as long ago as the Middle Ages. In the Nantes region of France, they were preserved in stoneware pots with vinegar and butter or oil. The first canning factory in France dates from 1824.

Sardines may be canned in olive oil, vegetable oil, oil and lemon juice, tomato sauce or a vinegar marinade; boneless sardines are also available, but they have very little flavour. Since they improve with age, canned sardines can be stored for several years in a cool place, turned regularly, but never in the refrigerator, as the oil solidifies and can no longer penetrate the fish.

Canned sardines are eaten mainly as a cold hors d'oeuvre with various raw vegetables. They can also be served on canapés and toast and in vol-au-vent, and can be used to make a flavoured butter.

SARDINIA See *page 1042.*

RECIPES

baked sardines
Wash and gut (clean) 12 good sardines. Grease an ovenproof dish and sprinkle the bottom with 2 or 3 chopped shallots. Lay the sardines on the dish and pour over a little lemon juice and 60 ml (2 fl oz, ¼ cup) white wine; dot with 25 g (1 oz, 2 tablespoons) butter, cut into small pieces. Bake in a preheated oven at 220°C (425°F, gas 7) for 10–12 minutes until just cooked through. Sprinkle with chopped parsley.

fried sardines
Scale, wash and gut (clean) the sardines; open out and remove the backbones. Sprinkle the fish with lemon juice and leave to marinate in a cool place for 30 minutes. Wipe dry, coat in breadcrumbs and oil and deep-fry in hot oil at 180°C (350°F) for about 3 minutes. Drain the fish, sprinkle with a little lemon juice and serve very hot.

raw sardines
Lay the sardines on a wicker tray, without removing the scales or gutting (cleaning) them. Put a generous pinch of mixed salt and pepper on each head. Refrigerate for 2 days. Remove the heads and gut the sardines, then skin and serve with toast and slightly salted butter.

raw sardine terrine
Remove the scales from the sardines, fillet them and wipe dry. Pour a layer of olive oil into a terrine,

add the zest of 1 orange, 1 clove, 1 small piece of bay leaf, 1 thinly sliced white onion, pepper and a few drops of brandy. Cover with a layer of fish fillets, another layer of spices and chopped onion, and a second layer of fish. Leave to marinate. Serve with farmhouse bread, toasted and buttered, and freshly ground sea salt.

sardine escabèche

Scale, wash and gut (clean) the sardines; remove the heads and wipe thoroughly. Heat in a frying pan enough olive oil to half-cover the sardines. Fry the fish, turning them when golden; drain and place in a deep dish. Add to the cooking oil an equal quantity of fresh oil and heat. Add to this mixture one-quarter of its volume of vinegar and one-eighth of water, some peeled garlic cloves, thyme, rosemary, bay leaves, parsley, Spanish chilli peppers, salt and pepper. Boil for 15 minutes, then remove from the heat and leave to cool. Marinate the sardines in this mixture for at least 24 hours before serving.

sardine fritters

Remove the scales from the sardines, fillet them and dry thoroughly. Dip in batter and fry for a few seconds in grapeseed oil.

sardines gratinées

Slice 1.5 kg (3¼ lb) aubergines (eggplants); place in a colander and sprinkle with a little salt. Peel and remove the seeds from 1 kg (2¼ lb) tomatoes. Fillet 14 large fresh sardines and clean thoroughly. Wash and dry the aubergines and brown them in a frying pan with a little very hot olive oil. Drain on paper towels. Purée the tomatoes in a blender with 2 garlic cloves, 3 basil leaves, salt, pepper and ½ teaspoon olive oil. Lay the aubergines and the sardine fillets in an ovenproof dish, in alternate layers, with grated Parmesan cheese between the layers. Cover with the puréed tomatoes. Bake in a preheated oven at 220°C (425°F, gas 7) for about 20 minutes.

souffléed sardines with sorrel

Scale, wash and gut (clean) 6 good sardines and remove the backbones. Shred a large bunch of sorrel and cook in butter with salt and pepper until soft; leave to cool and add a little raspberry vinegar. Make 6 very thin savoury crêpes. Whisk 2 egg whites until very stiff and spread over the crêpes. Stuff the sardines with the sorrel purée and lay a sardine on each crêpe. Roll up loosely, arrange in a wide dish, dot with a few small pieces of butter and bake in a preheated oven at 230°C (450°F, gas 8) for about 10 minutes.

stuffed sardines with white wine

Scale, wash and gut (clean) 12 large sardines. Remove the heads, then open out and remove the backbones. Stuff with a little fish quenelle forcemeat. Close them up again and place in a greased roasting tin (pan). Sprinkle with salt and pepper and moisten with 100 ml (4 fl oz, 7 tablespoons) white wine. Start cooking on the hob (stove top) and continue in a preheated oven at 220°C (425°F, gas 7) for 8–10 minutes until just cooked through. Drain the sardines, arrange on a long dish and pour over a few tablespoons of white wine sauce mixed with the strained cooking liquid.

additional recipe See *bouillabaisse*.

SARGUS A fish similar to and related to the sea bream, and prepared and cooked in the same way. It has an oval, squat, silvery body, large eyes, a spiny dorsal fin and a black mark on the tail fin. There are species found in the Mediterranean and in the Atlantic, south of the Bay of Biscay.

SARLADAISE, À LA The name given to a method of preparing potatoes in the Périgord region. The thinly sliced potatoes are sautéed (without parboiling) in goose fat. When they are cooked, they are sprinkled with chopped parsley and garlic, covered and left to sweat. In restaurants, truffles are often added, but this is incorrect; truffles are, however, an ingredient of sarladaise sauce, a cold emulsified sauce flavoured with brandy, served with grilled (broiled) or roast meat.

RECIPE

sarladaise sauce

Mash 4 hard-boiled (hard-cooked) egg yolks and blend with 2 tablespoons double (heavy) cream. Add 4 tablespoons very finely chopped fresh truffles and beat the sauce with olive oil as for mayonnaise. Add 1 tablespoon lemon juice, salt and pepper, and 1 tablespoon brandy.

additional recipe See *confit*.

SARRASINE, À LA Term for a method of preparing large joints of meat garnished either with small buckwheat pancakes or with rice cassolettes filled with tomato and green pepper fondue, topped with fried onion rings and served with a fairly thin demi-glace sauce.

SASHIMI A Japanese dish of raw fish, shellfish and molluscs. The fish (which must always be very fresh) is trimmed, boned and cut with a long thin knife. Precise cutting techniques are used according to requirements and/or type of seafood. For example, slices may be very fine or thick, straight or slanting; strips may be fine or thick; and decorative cuts may be applied. Tuna, bonito, abalone, bass, sole and plaice are cut into thin slices; cuttlefish and shellfish are cut into thin strips. The pieces are arranged attractively on a plate, garnished with ingredients such as shoots of young white radish known as daikon, sliced daikon, seaweed, slices of fresh ginger and slices of lemon. Dipping sauces, such as flavoured soy sauce, and a Japanese

SARDINIA

This island has a culinary tradition of Phoenician origin, influenced by Arab and African styles as well as local tradition.

Livestock farming is important and provides for such specialities as kid-goat tripe, roasted, grilled (broiled) or boiled, and served with peas and haricot (navy) beans; and a famous open air dish: sucking pig, lamb or kid cooked on a spit over a juniper or olive wood fire or on live charcoal in a ditch. Partridge are cooked whole, wrapped in myrtle leaves; Sardinian wild boar is renowned

for its delicate meat. Other typical dishes are beef braised in white wine and Sardinian veal braised with tomatoes and black (ripe) olives.

Sardinian bread is often made in the shape of thin pancakes, called *fogli di musica* or *carta da musica* ('sheet music'), marked with cracks.

Two pasta specialities are ravioli stuffed with ricotta cheese, spinach and eggs, flavoured with saffron and served with tomato sauce and cheese; and a gratin of layers of pasta, minced (ground) meat, ham, cream cheese and eggs, coated with tomato sauce.

Langoustes and sardines (which

gave the island its name) feature prominently in Sardinian cookery, as do tuna and swordfish. Dried tuna eggs (*bottarga*) are served as an hors d'oeuvre. The best-known Sardinian cheeses are *casu marzu* (a 'rotten' cheese with a strong smell) and *fiore sardo*, a ewe's-milk cheese for grating.

WINE A small number of producers are making good wines, notably Vermentino di Gallura, Carignano di Sulcis and the dry almost 'sherry-like' Vernaccia di Orestano. The red grape variety Cannonau is showing great potential for the production of quality red wines.

horseradish paste, known as wasabi, are typical accompaniments or condiments for the seafood.

SASSER A French culinary term meaning to wrap thin-skinned vegetables, such as carrots, new potatoes and Japanese artichokes, in a cloth with a little coarse salt, and to shake them for a few moments. This process cleans the vegetables by friction.

SATAY Also known as saté, this is the name for small kebabs of fish, poultry or meat on short bamboo skewers. The ingredients are marinated before being skewered and cooked over charcoal, then they are served with a dipping sauce. The marinade is usually slightly spicy and sweet, typically with lime and garlic, and the popular accompaniment is a spicy peanut sauce. Found all over South-East Asia, particularly as a street food but also served as an appetizer in restaurants, satay is thought to have originated in Indonesia.

SAUCE A hot or cold seasoned liquid either served with, or used in the cooking of, a dish. The word comes from the Latin *salsus* (salted), since salt has always been the basic condiment. The function of a sauce is to add to a dish a flavour that is compatible with the ingredients. Talleyrand claimed that England had 3 sauces and 360 religions, while France had 3 religions and 360 sauces. In an editorial of *Cuisine et Vins de France*, Curnonsky declared: 'Sauces comprise the honour and glory of French cookery. They have contributed to its superiority, or pre-eminence, which is disputed by none. Sauces are the orchestration and accompaniment of a fine meal, and enable a good chef or cook to demonstrate his talent.'

Medieval French sauces, such as cameline, dodine, poivrade or Robert, which relied on such ancient condiments as garum and spikenard, were either very hot or sweet-and-sour. They consisted mainly of

spicy stocks based on wine, verjuice and cooking juices, sometimes blended with toasted breadcrumbs. It was not until the 17th and 18th centuries that more refined and aromatic preparations appeared, such as béchamel, Soubise, mirepoix, duxelles and mayonnaise sauces.

■ **Classification of sauces** It was Carême who began to classify sauces. The hot sauces, which are by far the more numerous, are subdivided into brown sauces and white sauces. The great, or basic, brown sauces, from which many others are derived, are espagnole, demi-glace and tomato sauces. The basic white sauces are béchamel and velouté, and they too have innumerable derivatives. Cold sauces are usually based on mayonnaise or vinaigrette, and they also have many variations. The classical repertoire was gradually increased by sauces from other countries, often introduced by French chefs who had worked abroad (for example Cumberland, Albert, reform and Cambridge sauces, sauce *à la russe, à l'italienne* and *à la polonaise*). The diversity of resources from the French countryside contributed to a variety of recipes based on a particular ingredient: fresh cream (normande sauce), garlic (aïoli), fresh butter (beurre blanc), mustard (dijonnaise sauce), shallots (bordelaise sauce), red or white wine (bourguignonne sauce), and onions (lyonnaise sauce). Since Escoffier's time, there has been a tendency towards making lighter sauces. Nowadays, many chefs use mixtures based on curd cheese and yogurt for example.

A sauce may be thick or thin; it may be strained or it may contain visible ingredients. It can be used to season raw food (tomatoes with vinaigrette, celery with rémoulade), it may be served with a cold dish (hake with mayonnaise) or a hot dish

A cheese factory in Cagliari, Sardinia producing uncooked pecorino or pecorino sardo.

Basic sauces and some examples of sauces derived from them

White	
velouté	allemande, andalouse, aurore, Breton, caper, cardinal, chaud-froid, ivoire, mushroom, poulette, suprême, tarragon
white sauce (roux with milk)	béchamel, butter (British), cheese, egg (British), Mornay, mushroom, mustard, onion, oyster, parsley, Soubise
Brown	
espagnole	bordelaise, chateaubriand, Colbert, demi-glace, devilled, financière, Godard
Emulsion	
béarnaise	Choron, Foyot
hollandaise	mikado, mousseline, waterfisch (hot)
mayonnaise	aïoli, rouille, rémoulade, tartare
vinaigrette	anchoyade, gribiche, ravigote

(chateaubriand béarnaise, venison Saint-Hubert, sole normande). Some sauces are part of the dish itself (ragoûts, civets, coq au vin, chicken chasseur), rather than being made separately as an accompaniment. Such sauces may, however, be served separately in a sauceboat or used to coat some other preparation, such as chauds-froids or fish in scallop shells.

■ **Equipment and preparation** The choice of equipment is very important. Deep heavy-based saucepans should be used, to ensure the proper distribution of heat to prevent the sauce from burning or curdling. The bain marie is an essential accessory, as well as a metal whisk and a spatula for scraping the residue from the bottom of the pan. A fine, perfectly smooth and glossy sauce can be obtained by rubbing it through a sieve (known as 'tammying').

The preparation of sauces requires a certain amount of skill, as well as such techniques as deglazing; reducing; thickening; preventing a skin forming; emulsifying; thinning with milk, stock or alcohol; enriching with cream and/or egg yolks; and the judicious use of flavourings. This is why the sauce chef of the kitchen staff was traditionally considered to be such a great technician. According to Fernand Point, 'In the orchestra of a great kitchen, the sauce chef is a soloist.'

• CLASSIC METHODS There are four traditional basic methods for making a sauce, ranging from a simple one-stage procedure to complex methods.

1 Mixing together cold ingredients is the simplest method, used, for example, for making vinaigrette and ravigote sauce.

2 Emulsification means mixing two liquids that do not normally stay mixed. An emulsifying agent is used to hold the liquids together. This 'agent' is a solid that dissolves or disperses in both liquids so that the mixture will remain stable for a certain period of time. This method is used for cold sauces, such as mayonnaise and its derivatives, aïoli, gribiche, rouille and tartare sauces; and hot ones, including hollandaise, mousseline, béarnaise and beurre blanc.

3 Making a roux is a widely used starting point. This involves heating together butter and flour to make a paste. This method is used for béchamel sauce and its various derivatives (Mornay, Soubise).

4 Cooking a stock (veal, game, chicken or fish) and adding a white or brown roux or some other mixture (a mirepoix, marinade or cooked mushrooms) is the first stage for a wide variety of sauces. This produces velouté and espagnole sauces and their derivatives. These sauces may be thickened with butter, cornflour (cornstarch), blood or egg yolk, or flavoured with meat, chicken or fish glazes.

• A VARIETY OF INGREDIENTS Depending on the type of dish for which the sauce is intended, the most varied ingredients, herbs and spices can be used. Some dishes are classically accompanied by particular sauces: for example, mutton or fish with curry sauce, salt cod with garlic sauce (aïoli), duck with bigarade (orange) sauce, game with Cumberland sauce and beef with piquante sauce. Other ingredients include grated cheese, crushed tomatoes, anchovies, duxelles, chopped ham, foie gras, chopped truffles, shellfish, vinegar, cream, red or white wine, and alcohol.

The name of a sauce often reveals its ingredients: Périgueux sauce (truffles), Hungarian sauce (paprika) and Nantua sauce (crayfish); but sometimes the sauce is named after its creator, for example Mornay, Choron and Foyot.

■ **Dessert sauces** These may be hot or cold, either served separately or poured over the dessert. Many of these are based on fruit (in the form of a purée or jelly) and may be flavoured with vanilla or alcohol. Custard cream (flavoured or plain) is a popular dessert sauce, usually served with puddings and fruit pies. Chocolate sauce and zabaglione are also used.

RECIPES

anchoyade

Peel 3 garlic cloves and scrape them on the prongs of a fork over a plate. Rinse and chop the leaves of 6 sprigs of parsley. Remove the salt from 10 anchovies and fillet them or use drained canned anchovy fillets. Add them to the garlic and shred them, using 2 forks. Make the sauce by incorporating 100 ml (4 fl oz, 7 tablespoons) olive oil into the anchovy paste, whisking all the time. Still whisking, add the chopped parsley and a few drops of vinegar.

Andalusian sauce (cold)

Add 5 teaspoons very reduced and rich tomato fondue to 75 g (3 oz, ⅓ cup) mayonnaise. Finally, add 75 g (3 oz, ½ cup) sweet (bell) peppers, seeded and very finely diced.

Andalusian sauce (warm)

Add 4 tablespoons passatta or finely chopped ripe tomatoes to 3 tablespoons reduced velouté. Add 2 teaspoons sweet (bell) peppers, seeded, cooked and finely diced, ½ teaspoon chopped parsley and, if liked, a little crushed garlic.

aniseed sauce

Aniseeds are grey-green in colour but when they are old and stale, or have been incorrectly stored, they turn brown (this is usually after about 2–3 years). Avoid stale aniseeds, especially when making this sauce. Cook 2 lumps of sugar and 3 tablespoons vinegar to a caramel. Add 100 ml (4 fl oz, 7 tablespoons) white wine and 1 teaspoon aniseeds, bring to the boil and strain. Boil again and reduce by two-thirds. Add 300 ml (½ pint, 1¼ cups) thickened brown veal stock. Boil quickly again and strain. This sauce is particularly good with roast venison.

apple sauce

Cook pieces of peeled apples with a small quantity of sugar until they are soft; flavour with a little ground cinnamon or cumin. In northern Europe, this sauce is served with roast pork as well as roast goose and duck.

barbecue sauce

Mix 500 ml (17 fl oz, 2 cups) tomato* sauce with 60 ml (2 fl oz, ¼ cup) olive oil, 2 tablespoons brandy, a few drops of Tabasco sauce, ½ teaspoon curry powder, 1 tablespoon chopped herbs (chives, tarragon, parsley and chervil), and 1 tablespoon very finely chopped spring onion (scallion). Mix all the ingredients thoroughly, season with salt and sprinkle generously with pepper. This sauce is served with grilled (broiled) meat and sausages.

basic white sauce

Make 100 g (4 oz, ½ cup) pale blond roux using 50 g (2 oz, ¼ cup) butter and 50 g (2 oz, ½ cup) plain (all-purpose) flour. Blend in 1 litre (1¾ pints, 4⅓ cups) white stock (chicken or veal). Bring to the boil and cook gently for 1½ hours, skimming from time to time.

bâtarde sauce

Mix 20 g (¾ oz, 1½ tablespoons) melted butter, 20 g (¾ oz, 3 tablespoons) plain (all-purpose) flour and 250 ml (8 fl oz, 1 cup) salted boiling water. Whisk the mixture vigorously, adding 1 egg yolk mixed with 1 tablespoon ice-cold water and 1 tablespoon lemon juice. Over a very low heat, gradually incorporate 100 g (4 oz, ½ cup) butter

cut into small pieces, stirring constantly. Season with salt and pepper, and strain if necessary. This sauce is served with boiled vegetables and fish.

bread sauce

(from Carême's recipe) Chop 2 shallots and cut 1 thin slice of lean ham into small pieces. Place in a saucepan with 2–3 tablespoons white veal stock and a little pepper. Simmer and reduce over a low heat. Remove the ham and add 1½ tablespoons very fine dried breadcrumbs, a little fresh butter, 2 tablespoons consommé and the juice of 1 lemon. Boil for a few minutes and serve.

bread sauce à l'ancienne

(from Carême's recipe) Chop 1 garlic clove, 1 shallot and some parsley. Put into a saucepan with 4½ tablespoons white wine. Reduce by half, then mix in 2 tablespoons very fine fresh breadcrumbs, a little butter, a pinch of pepper, some grated nutmeg, 120 ml (4½ fl oz, ½ cup) consommé and 60 ml (2 fl oz, ¼ cup) white veal stock. Reduce by half and add the juice of 1 lemon.

butter sauce (1)

Proceed as for bâtarde sauce, but use 25 g (1 oz, 2 tablespoons) butter and 25 g (1 oz, ¼ cup) plain (all-purpose) flour. Do not thicken with egg yolk. This sauce is served with fish and boiled vegetables.

butter sauce (2)

(from Carême's recipe) Put 1 scant tablespoon flour and a little butter into a saucepan over a gentle heat. Blend them together with a wooden spoon, remove from the heat and add 4½ tablespoons water or consommé, a little salt, some grated nutmeg and the juice of half a lemon. Stir constantly over a brisk heat, and as soon as it comes to the boil, remove the sauce. Stir in a large piece of butter. The sauce should be velvety and very smooth, with a rich but delicate flavour.

chateaubriand sauce

Mix 100 ml (4 fl oz, 7 tablespoons) white wine with 1 tablespoon chopped shallots and reduce by two-thirds. Then add 150 ml (¼ pint, ⅔ cup) demi-glace* sauce and reduce by half. Remove from the heat and add 100 g (4 oz, ½ cup) fresh butter, 1 tablespoon chopped tarragon, a few drops of lemon juice and a little cayenne pepper. Mix well but do not strain. This sauce is served with grilled (broiled) meat.

cream sauce

Add 100 ml (4 fl oz, 7 tablespoons) double (heavy) cream to 200 ml (7 fl oz, ¾ cup) béchamel* sauce and boil to reduce by one-third. Remove from the heat and add 25–50 g (1–2 oz, 2–4 tablespoons) butter and 60–100 ml (2–4 fl oz, ¼–scant ½ cup) double (heavy) cream. Stir well and strain. This sauce is served with vegetables, fish, eggs and poultry.

Matching sauces to main ingredients and dishes

food		sauces
croustades, vol-au-vent		allemande, banquière, financière, marinière, normande, périgourdine, Soubise, suprême, toulousaine, sherry
eggs	hard-boiled (hot)	allemande, aurore, béchamel, curry, duxelles, lyonnaise, Mornay, Soubise, tomato, white
	hard-boiled (cold)	aïoli, mayonnaise, ravigote, rémoulade, tartare, verte, vinaigrette
	soft-boiled or poached	américaine, andalouse, aurore, banquière, bourguignonne, bretonne, chasseur, chaud-froid, Chivry, Choron, cream, cressonnière, curry, écossaise, hongroise, ivoire, marrow, matelote (eel), Mornay, Nantua, périgourdine, portugaise, printanière, provençale, rouennaise, royale, Soubise, suprême, tarragon, vénitienne
	omelettes	chasseur, Madeira, normande, prawn, Reform, tomato, Worcestershire
fish	braised or baked	américaine, bourguignonne, bourguignotte, bretonne, cardinal, Chambertin, Chambord (carp), crayfish, diplomat (John Dory, sole and turbot), genevoise, génoise (salmon and trout), grecque, gooseberry, hongroise, italienne, Joinville, Laguipière, matelote (eel), meurette, normande, Newburg, prawns, portugaise, red wine, Riche (John Dory, sole and turbot), rougail, tyrolienne, Véron, Victoria, white wine
	fried	nuoc-mâm, pékinoise, raïto
	smoked	cold horseradish, cream
	grilled	anchovy, Bercy and Gascony butters; flavoured oils, pissalat; bâtarde, Beauharnais, bone-marrow, Choron, Colbert, fennel (mackerel), italienne, mustard, Saint-Malo (brill, skate and turbot), tapenade
	marinated	escabèche, italienne, tomato
	meunière	Bonnefoy sauce, noisette butter
	poached or boiled (hot)	melted, creamed or noisette butter (skate); allemande (made with fish stock), anchovy (hot), aromatic, bâtarde, béchamel, Bercy, butter, brandade (salt cod), caper, chervil, chaud-froid (white), cream, curry, prawn, écossaise, egg, française, hollandaise, oyster (fresh cod), maltaise, marinière, Mornay, mousseline, mustard, Nantua, oursinade, parsley (mackerel and salmon), poulette, rouille, sabayon, Thermidor, truffle, turtle, vénitienne, waterfisch (hot), white (made with fish stock), white butter sauce (shad and pike)
	poached (cold)	aïoli, anchovy (cold), cinghalaise, gribiche, La Varenne, mayonnaise, Montpellier butter, Oriental, ravigote, rémoulade, Russian, sorrel, tartare, tomato, verte, vinaigrette, Vincent, waterfisch (cold)
frogs		aïoli, poulette
game		aniseed, apple, chaud-froid (brown), Cumberland (cold), dried cherry, grand veneur, moscovite, napolitaine, onion, pauvre homme, périgourdine, pignole, poivrade, Reform, roebuck, romaine, saupiquet (hare), smitane, Victoria
game birds		bread, chaud-froid (brown), moscovite, port, salmis
gratins		béchamel, bolognaise, duxelles, Mornay
meat	lamb	mint, Reform
	leftovers, boiled beef	bread, devilled, hachée, italienne, lyonnaise, pauvre, piquante, Robert, verjuice
	large roast or braised joints	Albert (hot with horseradish), anglaise, aromatic, bread, cooking juices, Godard, gravy (roast veal), Madeira, poivrade, Régence, Richelieu, Russian, sarladaise, Talleyrand
	ham	Cumberland (cold), Madeira, saupiquet, sherry
	mutton	Cumberland (cold), curry, harissa, onion
	pieces of sautéed or fried meat	béarnaise, bone-marrow, bordelaise, bourguignonne, chasseur, Choron, duxelles, financière, herb, hongroise, hussarde, italienne, Madeira, périgourdine, portugaise, provençale, roebuck, sherry, sweet-and-sour, Talleyrand, tarragon, tomato, Valois, zingara
	pork	apple, charcutière (grilled pork), nuoc-mâm, piquante, Robert, sage, Sainte-Menehould, sambal, suédoise, sweet-and-sour
	white meat	aurore, bretonne, cinghalaise, cream, hongroise, italienne, meurette, parsley, romaine (braised veal), Soubise, tarragon, truffle, villageoise, zingara
	cold meat	aïoli, anchovy butter, avocado, Cambridge, chaud-froid (brown), dijonnaise, horseradish (cold), mayonnaise, mousquetaire, ravigote, rémoulade, tomato

food		sauces
	grilled meat	butters: bercy, Chivry, Colbert, maître d'hôtel, marchand de vin (entrecôte steak), snail; sauces: barbecue, béarnaise, Beauharnais, Bonnefoy, Bontemps, bordelaise, chateaubriand, Colbert, Foyot, harissa, morel, mustard, oyster, paloise, ravigote, Robert, sarladaise, tyrolienne
	fried meat in breadcrumbs	tomato, Villeroi
	grilled meat in breadcrumbs	devilled, mustard, Sainte-Menehould
mussels		marinière, poulette, ravigote
offal	braised, deep- or shallow-fried	allemande (made with meat stock), banquière, bretonne, chaud-froid (white), écossaise, hongroise, ivoire, meurette, noisette butter, ravigote, Soubise, sweet-and-sour, suprême, tartare, Villeroi, sherry
	ox tongue	piquante, romaine, tomato
	pig's feet	devilled, mustard, Sainte-Menehould
	braised calves' sweetbreads	Albufera, aurore, Chantilly, financière, Foyot, Godard, Nantua, périgourdine, Régence, tarragon
	grilled or fried kidneys	Madeira, marchande de vin butter, portugaise, tyrolienne
	calf's head	gribiche, mayonnaise, parsley, turtle
oysters		flavoured vinegars, shallot, tartare
pasta		bolognaise, duxelles, financière, ketchup, noisette butter, poulette, stufatu, vinaigrette (with salad)
poultry	braised	Albufera, celery, duxelles, financière, Godard, onion, piémontaise, provençale, sherry, Talleyrand, villageoise
	duck	apple, bigarade, chaud-froid (brown), dodine, rouennaise
	goose	apple, sage, suédoise
	poached or shallow-fried	Albufera, allemande (made with meat stock), aurore, avocado (cold), banquière, bretonne, chevil, Chantilly, chaud-froid (white), Chivry, cream, curry, écossaise, financière, herb, ivoire, mayonnaise, Mornay, Nantua, Périgueux, parsley, printanière, ravigote (cold), Richelieu, royale, suprême, tarragon, toulousaine, vénitienne
	grilled chicken	Bontemps, devilled (also for pigeon), paloise, Sainte-Menehould, tyrolienne
	roast	anglaise, bread, cooking juices, cranberry (turkey), sweet-and-sour
	sautéed	bourguignonne, chasseur, curry, duxelles, hongroise, périgourdine, portugaise, salmis, zingara
quenelles		aurore, Nantua, Soubise, tomato
rice	hot	chasseur, curry, duxelles, mustard, Richelieu, tomato
	cold	mayonnaise, tartare, vinaigrette
shellfish	hot	américaine, curry, lobster, Nantua, Newburg, prawn, Victoria
	cold	gribiche, kiwi, mayonnaise, rémoulade, verte
snails		aïoli, poulette, snail butter
soft roe		noisette butter
vegetables	asparagus	bâtarde, Chantilly, maltaise, Pompadour, truffle, vierge
	boiled vegetables	sauces: aïoli, allemande, bâtarde, béchamel, Chantilly, hollandaise, mikado, Mornay, mousseline, tomato, white; butters: creamed, Gascogne, maître d'hôtel, melted, noisette
	cardoons	lyonnaise, marrow
	crudités and salads	anchovy, curry (cold), dijonnaise, horseradish (cold), kiwi, mayonnaise, rémoulade, Roquefort, Russian, verdurette, vinaigrette, yogurt
	haricot beans	bretonne, cream
	leeks	vierge, vinaigrette
	potatoes	cold horseradish (jacket potatoes), cream cheese, tartare (pont-neuf)
	green salad	flavoured oils, flavoured vinegars, Rossini and vinaigrette sauces
	sautéed, braised	bohémienne, Colbert, cream, italienne, poulette (mushrooms), provençale, Soubise, suprême, tomato

dried-cherry sauce

(from Carême's recipe) Wash 225 g (8 oz, 1 cup) dried cherries. Pound them in a mortar and place them in a saucepan with 1½ tablespoons icing (confectioner's) sugar, 350 ml (12 fl oz, 1½ cups) good-quality Burgundy wine, 2 tablespoons vinegar, a pinch of ground coriander and a little grated lemon zest. Bring to the boil and simmer for 20–25 minutes. Then stir in 4 tablespoons espagnole* sauce and the juice of 1 lemon and mix well. Reduce the sauce, stirring continuously over a brisk heat, and then rub through a sieve. This sauce is served with venison.

English bread-and-butter sauce

(from Carême's recipe) Bring to the boil 1 tablespoon breadcrumbs in 2 large tablespoons consommé, adding 1 small onion cut in half and 1 clove. Add a little salt, grated nutmeg and cayenne pepper. Simmer for 10 minutes, remove the onion and the clove, and mix in 1 tablespoon English butter sauce. Before serving, whisk in a little more butter. This sauce is served with roast game birds.

English butter sauce

Make a white roux with 25 g (1 oz, 2 tablespoons) butter and 25 g (1 oz, ¼ cup) plain (all-purpose) flour. Then whisk in vigorously 250 ml (8 fl oz, 1 cup) salted boiling water. Season with salt and pepper, and whisk in 100 g (4 oz, ½ cup) butter cut into pieces.

English cream sauce

Make a white roux with 50 g (2 oz, ¼ cup) butter and 25 g (1 oz, ¼ cup) plain (all-purpose) flour. Add 350 ml (12 fl oz, 1½ cups) white consommé*, 2 tablespoons mushroom ketchup and 100 ml (4 fl oz, 7 tablespoons) double (heavy) cream. Bring to the boil, add a small bunch of parsley and 1 small onion, and simmer gently for 20 minutes. Remove the parsley and onion. Strain before use. This sauce is traditionally served with roast loin of veal.

fennel sauce

Prepare 250 ml (8 fl oz, 1 cup) English butter sauce and add 1 tablespoon chopped blanched fennel. This sauce is served with boiled or grilled (broiled) fish.

François Raffatin sauce

Put 2 egg yolks, 1 tablespoon strong mustard and some salt and pepper in a saucepan. Beat the ingredients and then add 175 ml (6 fl oz, ¾ cup) dry white wine. Cook gently over a low heat, stirring with a wooden spoon, until the sauce thickens. Sprinkle with chopped chervil. This sauce is usually served with leftover meat.

French sauce

(from Carême's recipe) Heat some béchamel sauce in a saucepan. When almost boiling, add a little garlic, a little grated nutmeg and some mushroom ketchup. Immediately before serving, bring to the boil, then add some crayfish butter to colour it pink. (Shelled crayfish tails and button mushrooms may also be added.) This sauce is served with fish.

hachée sauce

Cook 1 tablespoon chopped onion in 15 g (½ oz, 1 tablespoon) butter for about 15 minutes. Then add 1½ teaspoons chopped shallots and cook for a further 5–10 minutes. Add 100 ml (4 fl oz, 7 tablespoons) vinegar, reduce by three-quarters and add 150 ml (¼ pint, ⅔ cup) demi-glace* sauce and 100 ml (4 fl oz, 7 tablespoons) fresh tomato purée. Boil for 5 minutes. Just before serving, add 1 tablespoon lean chopped ham, 1 tablespoon dry mushroom duxelles*, 1 tablespoon chopped capers and gherkins and 1 tablespoon chopped parsley. Do not strain. This sauce is served with slices of cooked meat or a boiled joint.

musketeer sauce

Prepare 500 ml (17 fl oz, 2 cups) mayonnaise* and add 2 tablespoons chopped shallots (cooked in white wine until the liquid has completely reduced) and 1 tablespoon dissolved meat glaze. Mix together and season with a little cayenne pepper. This sauce is served with grilled (broiled) foods.

mustard sauce with butter

Prepare 200 ml (7 fl oz, ¾ cup) butter sauce or hollandaise* sauce. Add 1 tablespoon mustard and strain. This sauce is served with boiled or grilled (broiled) fish.

mustard sauce with cream

Mix 1 part Dijon mustard with 2 parts double (heavy) cream. Season with a little lemon juice and some salt and pepper. Whisk thoroughly until the sauce becomes slightly mousse-like. This sauce is served with white meat, poultry and fish.

onion sauce

Cook 100 g (4 oz, ¾ cup) chopped onions in 300 ml (½ pint, 1¼ cups) milk seasoned with salt, pepper and nutmeg. As soon as the onions are cooked, strain and use the milk in which the onions were cooked to make a white sauce by stirring it into a roux made with 20 g (¾ oz, 1½ tablespoons) butter and 20 g (¾ oz, 3 tablespoons) plain (all-purpose) flour. Bring to the boil, add the chopped onions and cook gently for 8 minutes.

This typically English sauce is poured over mutton, chicken, braised game or rabbit.

The onions can also be cooked in milk, then the liquid thickened with beurre manié, using the above proportions of butter and flour.

parsley sauce (1)

Prepare a sauce with 25 g (1 oz, 2 tablespoons) roux and 250 ml (8 fl oz, 1 cup) freshly cooked fish stock that is strongly flavoured with parsley. Cook for 8 minutes and strain. Just before serving, add

1 tablespoon chopped blanched parsley and a dash of lemon juice. This sauce is particularly suitable to serve with salmon and mackerel.

parsley sauce (2)

Make 250 ml (8 fl oz, 1 cup) butter sauce, add 1 tablespoon chopped blanched parsley and a little lemon juice. This sauce is served with poached chicken, boiled rabbit, boiled ham and braised veal.

piquant sauce

Prepare 250 ml (8 fl oz, 1 cup) devilled* sauce with wine vinegar. Just before serving, add 3 tablespoons coarsely chopped gherkins and 1 generous tablespoon chopped parsley. This sauce is served with pork chops, boiled tongue or slices of beef.

port wine sauce

To 100 ml (4 fl oz, 7 tablespoons) port add 1½ teaspoons chopped shallots, 1 sprig of thyme and a piece of bay leaf. Reduce by half and then add the juice of 1 orange and half a lemon, together with a pinch of grated orange zest. Add 200 ml (7 fl oz, ¾ cup) thickened veal stock and boil for a few minutes. Strain through muslin (cheesecloth). This English sauce is served hot with game birds, especially wild duck.

printanière sauce

Add 50 g (2 oz, ¼ cup) green butter* sauce to 200 ml (7 fl oz, ¾ cup) allemande* sauce and strain. Serve with soft-boiled (soft-cooked) or poached eggs or poached chicken.

red wine sauce

Select the fish of your choice and cook it in 150 ml (¼ pint, ⅔ cup) mirepoix* cooked in butter, 500 ml (17 fl oz, 2 cups) red wine, 1 garlic clove and some mushroom skins. Remove the fish, then reduce the liquid by one-third. Thicken with beurre manié, add a few drops of anchovy essence, season with a pinch of cayenne pepper and strain. This is a suitable sauce for stuffed, hard-boiled (hard-cooked) or poached eggs and fish.

saffron rouille

Peel 3 garlic cloves, slit them lengthways and remove the green part. Grind with 1 pinch of coarse salt and add 2 pinches of white pepper, 1 pinch of saffron, 2 pinches of cayenne pepper and 2 egg yolks. Whisk vigorously to obtain a smooth paste. Allow to rest for 5 minutes. Make the sauce by incorporating 250 ml (8 fl oz, 1 cup) olive oil, a little at a time, into this paste.

sorrel sauce

Cook 2 chopped shallots in 4½ tablespoons dry vermouth, then reduce by half. Add 175 ml (6 fl oz, ¾ cup) double (heavy) cream and reduce again until the sauce is thick and smooth. Add 150 g (5 oz, 2 cups) finely shredded sorrel leaves, season with salt

and pepper, boil again briefly and allow to cool. Just before serving, add a few drops of lemon juice. This sauce is especially good with fish.

verjuice sauce

(from Carême's recipe) Wash 30 verjuice grapes, pound them and press out the juice through muslin (cheesecloth), or use a little ready-pressed verjuice. Boil 2 generous tablespoons allemande* sauce with a little chicken glaze, a little butter, a pinch of grated nutmeg, a pinch of finely ground pepper and enough verjuice to make the sauce sharp and appetizing. It is particularly good served with grilled (broiled) or roasted white meat or poultry.

vierge sauce

Beat 125 g (4½ oz, ½ cup) butter until soft, then beat in 2 tablespoons lemon juice and some salt and pepper. Continue to beat well until the mixture becomes fluffy. This sauce is served with asparagus, leeks and other boiled vegetables.

white wine sauce

Boil 150 ml (¼ pint, ⅔ cup) fish fumet* made with white wine, until reduced by two-thirds. Allow to cool slightly and add 2 raw egg yolks. Whisk over a gentle heat, as for hollandaise. As soon as the yolks thicken to a creamy consistency, whisk in, a little at a time, 150 g (5 oz, ⅔ cup) clarified butter. Season with salt and pepper; add ½ teaspoon lemon juice and some mushroom skins and stalks if wished. Rub through a fine sieve and reheat, but do not boil. This is a suitable sauce to serve with fish.

other recipes See *aillade, aïoli, Albufera, allemande, anchovy, andalouse, anglaise, aromatic, aurore, avocado, banquière, béarnaise, Beauharnais, béchamel, Bercy, bone-marrow, bordelaise, bourguignonne, brandade, bread sauce, bretonne, Cambridge, caper, cardinal, celery, Chambertin, Chambord, charcutière, chasseur, chaud-froid, chervil, Chivry, Choron, Colbert, cranberry, crayfish, cressonnière, Cumberland, devilled, dijonnaise, diplomate, duxelles, écossaise, egg sauce, espagnole, financière, fines herbes, Foyot, genevoise, Godard, grand veneur, grecque, gribiche, hollandaise, hongroise, horseradish, indienne, italienne, ivoire, Laguipière, La Varenne, lobster, lyonnaise, Madeira, maltaise, marinière, mayonnaise, mint, morel (morels in herb sauce), Mornay, mousseline, mussel, mustard, Nantua, napolitaine, normande, orange (Bitter Oranges – Savoury Recipes), orientale, parisienne, Périgueux, piémontaise, pine nut, poivrade, portugaise, poulette, provençale, ravigote, Reform, Régence, rémoulade, Richelieu, Robert, roebuck (roebuck sauce), Roman, Roquefort, rouennaise, royale, russe, sage, Sainte-Menehould, Saint-Malo, sarladaise, sea urchin, shallot, shrimps and prawns, Soubise, soy sauce, sweet and sour, Talleyrand-Périgord, tarragon, tartare, tomato, truffle, venison, vénitienne, Véron, vert, Victoria, villageoise, Villeroi, vinaigrette, Vincent, waterfisch, yogurt, zingara.*

Dessert Sauces

apricot sauce (1)

Stone (pit) 12 apricots and reduce to a pulp in a blender or food processor. Put the pulp in a thick copper saucepan and add 500 ml (17 fl oz, 2 cups) light syrup. Bring to the boil, skim and remove the pan from the heat when the sauce coats the back of a spoon. Strain. Flavour with 1 tablespoon kirsch or brandy.

Apricot sauce, which is served with hot or cold desserts, can itself be served hot or cold. If served hot, it can be made smoother by adding a little fresh butter. When stewed apricots (fresh or preserved) are used, the syrup can be used to dilute the sauce.

An apricot sauce can also be made by mixing about 3 tablespoons of the very best apricot jam (preserve), 1 tablespoon lemon juice and a few spoonfuls of water. Heat, strain and flavour with kirsch or brandy, as described above.

apricot sauce (2)

Purée 500 g (18 oz) stoned (pitted) apricots in a blender or food processor. Put the purée in a saucepan with 500 ml (17 fl oz, 2 cups) water and 500 g (18 oz, 2¼ cups) granulated sugar and boil for 5 minutes. Add 1 tablespoon cornflour (cornstarch) mixed with cold water. Bring to the boil again, stirring. Remove from the heat and add 3 tablespoons kirsch.

blackcurrant sauce

Put 10 lumps of sugar into a saucepan with 5 tablespoons water. Heat to dissolve the sugar and then boil to make a syrup. Wash 250 g (9 oz, 2 cups) blackcurrants in cold water, wipe them and reduce to a purée in a blender or food processor. Rub the purée through a fine sieve. Mix the syrup with the fruit purée and add the juice of 1 lemon. Pour the sauce into a bowl and chill in the refrigerator.

Chilled blackcurrant sauce can be served with baked apples, floating islands, pineapple water ice or fruit salad. It can also be served hot with a rice dessert, apple charlotte or cold lemon mousse.

Blackcurrant sauce can also be made quickly by mixing 500 ml (17 fl oz, 2 cups) blackcurrant cordial with 2–3 liqueur glasses of raspberry or plum brandy. A generous handful of whole blackcurrants may be added if in season. This sauce can be used to pour over sorbets or ice cream sundaes.

caramel sauce

Make a pale caramel with 150 g (5 oz, 1 cup) icing (confectioner's) sugar and 120 ml (4½ fl oz, ½ cup) water. Boil 500 ml (17 fl oz, 2 cups) milk with a vanilla pod (bean), remove the pod and whisk the milk into the caramel. Put 3 egg yolks into a bowl and whisk in the caramel mixture. Pour the sauce back into the saucepan and heat gently, stirring, until it thickens. When the sauce has reached a pouring consistency, remove from the heat and allow to cool, stirring continuously. This sauce is traditionally served with soufflé fritters.

peach sauce (1)

Plunge some peaches in boiling water for 30 seconds, peel them and remove the stones (pits). Weigh the flesh and immediately sprinkle with lemon juice – the juice of 1 lemon is sufficient for 1 kg (2¼ lb) fruit. Purée the peaches in a blender or food processor, then add one-third of their weight of caster (superfine) sugar and, if desired, some fruit liqueur. This sauce can be poured over fruit salads and charlottes.

peach sauce (2)

Prepare some peach purée as in the previous recipe. Put the purée into a heavy-based saucepan together with half its weight of sugar, and cook over a brisk heat for 7–8 minutes, stirring continuously. Allow to cool, then flavour with a fruit liqueur, according to taste. This sauce is used particularly for pouring over rice or semolina desserts.

pineapple sauce

Poach some fresh pineapple in sugar syrup, or use the syrup from some canned pineapple. Thicken the syrup with arrowroot and flavour it with rum, kirsch, brandy or a liqueur. This sauce can be poured over various hot or cold desserts – for example, pies, rice or semolina puddings.

other recipes See chocolate, gooseberry.

SAUCEBOAT Part of a dinner service used for serving sauce or gravy. Sauceboats are usually oval in shape with a handle and one or two lips. A spoon or ladle is often used to serve the sauce and the sauceboat may have a matching saucer-like base. Some sauceboats, used for the gravy of roast meat, have two lips and a double bottom. The latter enables the fat to be poured off one side, leaving the gravy to be poured from the other lip afterwards. From the Middle Ages until the 18th century, sauceboats were made of tin or silver.

SAUCEPAN A cylindrical cooking utensil with a handle and usually a lid. The first copper saucepans appeared in the 14th century, but their tin plating was far from perfect and they were little used. However, the long handle made them more manageable than a cooking pot. With the advent of the modern cooker (stove), the use of saucepans became widespread. They are made in many materials: aluminium (with or without non-stick finishes), stainless steel, cast iron, enamelled steel, copper, ceramic or flameproof porcelain.

Saucepans are mainly used to heat liquids, to cook food in liquid and to reheat prepared dishes – for which a double saucepan (boiler) is often used. They are frequently sold in sets of three, five or more, but it is not always sensible to buy saucepans in sets since one or two sizes will probably be little used, and it is often preferable to have at least two of certain sizes. A small milk pan is particularly useful. Some pans are ovenproof and may be used as a casserole.

The features of a saucepan depend on the material used: the type of base must be considered, especially when cooking with electricity; the stability; the weight and ease of handling (the handle should be sturdy, long enough, insulated if metal and, if desired, removable); the ease of pouring, either by a lip or better still by a pouring rim that runs around the circumference, enabling you to pour from any point on the rim; and finally, ease of cleaning.

SAUERKRAUT White cabbage that has been finely sliced, dry-salted and fermented. Sauerkraut requires some cooking before eating, although less cooking time is needed for commercially available canned and bottled sauerkraut, which is pasteurized and therefore already partly cooked. Sauerkraut is popular in parts of France (particularly in Alsace and Lorraine), Germany, Austria, Switzerland, Russia, Poland and the Balkans.

■ **Preparation** Remove the core and any green or damaged outer leaves from some white cabbages. Using a knife with a broad blade or a special shredder or food processor, cut the cabbages into very fine strips. Wash and drain thoroughly. Line the bottom of an earthenware crock with large cabbage leaves or vine leaves and arrange the shredded cabbage in layers, covering each layer with coarse salt, and sprinkling with juniper berries or other flavourings, if liked. Continue until the crock is two-thirds full. Put a handful of coarse salt on the final layer. Cover with a cloth to help exclude air, then with a wooden lid that fits down inside the crock. Place a heavy weight on this lid. By the next day, the weight should have forced out sufficient liquid (water drawn out of the cabbage by the salt) to cover the lid. Make sure that there is always enough liquid to keep the weighted lid covered. Keep in a cool place, skimming off scum or foam.

After at least three weeks, when no more scum or foam forms above the cabbage, the sauerkraut is ready to eat. Each time some sauerkraut is taken out, ladle off the covering liquid, replace the cloth, the lid and the weight, and add fresh water to cover.

Sauerkraut is best eaten fresh and should be pale in colour and crunchy. It should not be kept too long; eventually it turns yellow and acquires a more pronounced flavour.

■ **Serving sauerkraut** Sauerkraut is often cooked in white wine – only a small amount is used so as not to accentuate the sourness of the cabbage; it can also be flavoured with a small glass of kirsch, and is sometimes served with juniper berries, which aid digestion.

Sauerkraut has been popular in Alsace since the Middle Ages, where it is typically served in the form of *choucroute garnie* – sauerkraut with assorted

pork sausages, including those from Colmar or Strasbourg, plus smoked, grilled (broiled), blood or liver sausages, as well as various cuts of pork, such as smoked or unsmoked bacon, smoked loin of pork, liver dumplings and boiled pork belly, accompanied by potatoes. The German version is similar but uses Nuremberg and Frankfurter sausages, together with various pork cuts and apples. In Germany, sauerkraut is often served as an accompaniment to knuckle of pork, leg of pork and leg of veal.

Another variation is sauerkraut with fish. Raw sauerkraut, moistened with Riesling or Sylvaner, is cooked in chicken stock or wine, then served with smoked salmon, haddock, salt cod, turbot, scallops, monkfish or fish sausages, with a white butter or mousseline sauce.

■ **The symbol of Alsace** Hansi, the famous artist from Alsace, considered Colmar's way of serving sauerkraut the only true one:

'In a thick-sided metal (or earthenware) casserole, lightly brown some finely chopped onion in two good soupspoons of goose dripping or lard. Add 1 pound of sauerkraut, unwashed or very lightly washed and absolutely fresh. Add a generous glass of white wine, a dessert apple cut into pieces, then about ten juniper berries tied up in a little cloth. Pour in some stock until the sauerkraut is almost covered. Put on the lid and leave to cook for 2 to 3 hours. One hour before serving, add 1 pound of smoked belly bacon. Half an hour before serving, add half a small glass of kirsch. Arrange the sauerkraut on a warmed round dish. Surround with bacon cut into little pieces, cutlets and Colmar sausages, first heated for a good 10 minutes, either in the sauerkraut, or in almost boiling water. Serve with a few potatoes, baked in their jackets until very floury and quite dry.'

Apart from being the central ingredient in many Alsatian dishes, sauerkraut is used in preparing other French dishes, often named *à l'alsacienne*, based on poultry, red meat, or even fried eggs, snails, omelettes, fish and soup.

RECIPES

chicken au gratin with sauerkraut
Peel and dice 1 leek (white part) and 2 carrots. Stick an onion with 2 cloves. Tie up in a small piece of muslin (cheesecloth) 1 tablespoon juniper berries, 1 teaspoon peppercorns and 2 peeled garlic cloves. Wash 1.5 kg (3¼ lb) raw sauerkraut in plenty of water, then squeeze and disentangle it with your fingers.

Grease a large flameproof casserole with 40 g (1½ oz, 3 tablespoons) goose fat and pile half the sauerkraut in it. On top, arrange the vegetables and a large bouquet garni augmented with 1 celery stick and the muslin bag of spices. Cover with the remaining sauerkraut. Over the contents, pour 200 ml (7 fl oz, ¾ cup) dry white wine and 300 ml (½ pint, 1¼ cups) chicken stock. Season lightly with salt, cover and bring to the boil. Then transfer to a preheated oven at 190°C (375°F, gas 5) and cook for 1 hour.

Season a 1.5 kg (3¼ lb) chicken with salt and pepper inside and out, and place it in the middle of the sauerkraut. Return to the oven for a further 2 hours. Then take the chicken out, cut it up and bone it. Grease a gratin dish with goose fat. Press the sauerkraut and pile it in the dish, having removed the bag of spices, the cloves and the bouquet garni. Cover with the chicken, moisten with 300 ml (½ pint, 1¼ cups) crème fraîche, sprinkle 100 g (4 oz, 1 cup) grated Gruyère cheese on top and brown in a very hot oven.

sauerkraut à l'alsacienne ♦

Thoroughly wash 2 kg (4½ lb) raw sauerkraut in cold water, then squeeze and disentangle it with your fingers. Peel 2 or 3 carrots and cut into small cubes. Peel 2 large onions and stick a clove in each.

Coat the bottom and sides of a flameproof casserole with goose fat or lard. Pile in half the sauerkraut and add the carrots, onions, 2 peeled garlic cloves, 1 teaspoon ground pepper, 1 tablespoon juniper berries and a bouquet garni. Add the rest of the sauerkraut, a raw knuckle of ham and 1 glass of dry white Alsace wine and top up with water. Season lightly with salt, cover and bring to the boil. Then transfer to a preheated oven at 190°C (375 °F, gas 5) and cook for 1 hour. Add a medium-sized smoked shoulder of pork and 575–800 g (1¼–1¾ lb) smoked belly (salt pork). Cover, bring to the boil on the hob (stove top), then cook in the oven for a further 1½ hours.

Meanwhile, peel 1.25 kg (2¾ lb) potatoes. After 1½ hours, remove the pork belly from the casserole and add the potatoes. Leave to cook for a further 30 minutes. During this time, poach 6–8 Strasbourg sausages in barely simmering water. When the sauerkraut is cooked, remove and discard the bouquet garni and the cloves and return the pork belly for 10 minutes to reheat it. Arrange the sauerkraut in a large dish and garnish with the potatoes, sausages and meat cut into slices.

sauerkraut au gras for garnish

Follow the recipe above for sauerkraut *à l'alsacienne*, but replace the water with unskimmed stock and do not add meat. Cook gently for 3 hours. It is served as a garnish for poultry or meat.

sauerkraut salad à l'allemande

Thoroughly wash 1 kg (2¼ lb) raw sauerkraut, squeeze and disentangle it with your fingers. Place it in a saucepan along with 2–3 large whole onions, salt and pepper, then cover with either stock or water to which 1 tablespoon cooking oil has been added. Cook over a gentle heat for about 2½ hours, then drain and leave to cool. Dice the onions and return them to the sauerkraut, which is then pressed, seasoned with vinaigrette and piled into a deep dish. Garnish with quarters of hard-boiled (hard-cooked) eggs and cubes of cooked beetroot (red beet).

SAUMONETTE The name under which the lesser spotted dogfish is sold in France, usually skinned and without the head. This name reflects the salmon-pink colour of its flesh. (In Britain, it is called 'rock salmon'.)

SAUMUR A town on the left bank of the River Loire, lending its name to several appellations and a wine region. The most important wine is Saumur Mousseaux, which is mainly made from Chenin Blanc grapes and produced by the traditional method (see *méthode champenoise*). Saumur Blanc, from Chenin Blanc, and Saumur Rouge, from Cabernet Franc, Cabernet Sauvignon or Pineau d'Aunis, are also produced. However, Saumur-Champigny is an increasingly significant appellation for fruity red wines made from Cabernet Franc. Small amounts of rosés and Coteaux de Saumur, medium sweet white wines, are made.

SAUPIQUET In French medieval cookery, a spiced sauce made with red wine, verjuice and onions, which was served with roast lamb or wildfowl. Just before serving, it was thickened with toasted bread. In the Languedoc and Rouergue regions, saupiquet is a dish of roast hare served with a highly seasoned wine sauce containing the animal's liver and blood and sliced onions. The term is used by certain cooks for variations of this dish (particularly those made with duck), which have a sauce flavoured with wine and vinegar.

Saupiquet des Amognes is a speciality of Nivernais and Morvan. Said to have been created by Jean Reynier, a culinary author of the 16th century, it consists of slices of fried ham coated with a sauce made of reduced vinegar, peppercorns, shallots, juniper berries and tarragon, moistened with espagnole sauce and cream. In another version of this ham saupiquet, the meat is coated with a very spicy velouté sauce, which is finished off with cream.

The word saupiquet comes from *sau* (salt) and *piquet* (to season). It has no connection with Saupiquet, chef of the Baron de La Vieuville, who is thought to have created puff pastry.

RECIPES

duck saupiquet

Grill (broil) or roast 300 g (11 oz) sliced duck breasts and arrange them in a hot dish. Gently cook 2 small chopped garlic cloves in 2 tablespoons vinegar and 2 tablespoons white wine. Leave to cool, then put through a blender or food processor with 1½ tablespoons cream cheese, 100 g (4 oz) duck's liver and 1 tablespoon olive oil flavoured with herbs. Cover the duck with this sauce.

Sauerkraut à l'alsacienne.

ham saupiquet

Cut 8 thick slices of boned ham, which has been thoroughly desalted, and fry them in lard over a brisk heat. Make a roux with 25 g (1 oz, ¼ cup) plain (all-purpose) flour and 25 g (1 oz, 2 tablespoons) butter, then add 200 ml (7 fl oz, ¾ cup) white wine and 200 ml (7 fl oz, ¾ cup) ham, chicken or veal stock. Add the ham trimmings, 7 or 8 juniper berries and some chopped tarragon and reduce for 15 minutes. Reduce some wine vinegar seasoned with 10 crushed peppercorns. Pour the sauce over this and simmer for another 15 minutes. Thicken with 200 ml (7 fl oz, ¾ cup) crème fraîche, then rub through a very fine sieve. Drain the slices of ham, arrange them on a hot dish and pour the sauce over them.

SAUSAGE Typically, a mixture of minced (ground) seasoned meat, enclosed in a tube-like casing. Sausages may be fresh, cured, air-dried, smoked or precooked – there are numerous types and many regional variations and specialities. The word 'sausage', is derived from the Latin *salsicia*, from *salsus*, meaning 'salted'. In French terminology, a *saucisse* is usually small and fresh, while a *saucisson* is usually larger and may be fresh or dried.

The sausage casing or 'skin' can be made from a natural material, such as pig's or sheep's intestine, or an artificial casing made of cellulose or a synthetic material.

The term is so widely used that there are many types of sausage outside this typical description. For example, fish, poultry or vegetables may be used as the main ingredients; the sausages may be large and round rather than tube-like (Scottish haggis is a good example); and the mixture is not always encased in a skin, a flour or egg-and-breadcrumb coating being used instead.

■ **Fresh raw sausages** These sausages require cooking by grilling (broiling), frying, poaching or boiling, or a combination of more than one of these methods. They generally consist of pork and/or beef meat and fat, but can be made from other meats or contain added veal, mutton, poultry or offal (fish and vegetable are usually fresh and raw). They are seasoned with various herbs, spices, condiments and other flavourings, and sometimes bound with breadcrumbs or cereal. The ingredients are minced (ground) or chopped and funnelled into a casing; some varieties are then twisted into links. Like fresh meat, fresh sausages should be eaten within a few days of purchase. Cook sausages slowly so as not to burst their skins and to ensure they are cooked through as well as browned on the outside.

Fresh sausages include the British chipolata and link sausages (at one time commonly called 'bangers') and Cumberland sausage, which comes in a long coil and is sold in lengths; France's Toulouse sausage (*saucisse de Toulouse*) and flat sausages (*crépinettes*), with a caul fat casing. Various French regional specialities include the small Bordeaux sausage, which is cooked with white wine and

oysters; the small country sausages called *diots*, from Savoy; and white sausages from Alsace, for deep-frying. Other fresh sausages include the spicy *merguez*; the Corsican *figatelli*, made of pork liver; the *sabodet* (or *coudenat*), made of offal; the Mexican *chorizo*; South African *boerewors*; Polish *kielbasa*; *Bratwurst* from Germany; and the lengths of Italian *luganega* from northern Italy.

Known as 'black' sausages, black pudding and blood sausages often contain cereal and derive their colour and rich, offal-like flavour from pig's blood. Examples are France's *boudin noir* (see also *boudin blanc*), Germany's *Blutwurst*, Spain's *morcilla* sausages and the Irish drisheen. The best examples are often well spiced, may contain morsels of diced fat, and have an even texture.

■ **Cured sausages** These are sausages, generally raw, preserved by drying, salting or smoking. The traditional preparation of dried sausages involves a series of processes, varying according to country, region and type of ingredients used. These methods give them their characteristic aroma, texture and flavour. They include boning and trimming the meat, pounding or chopping the fat and lean meat with spices and other flavourings to form the mixture, funnelling the mixture into the casing, predrying the sausage to a careful degree at specific temperatures to ensure thorough preservation and then further drying and maturing under closely monitored conditions for at least 4 weeks. The sausage may also be smoked.

Typically, a good dry sausage is firm (hard even) to the touch and has a pronounced aroma. Some varieties have a 'bloom', which is a sign that maturing has been carried out correctly; some are bare, without a coating of plastic, flour or ash. In ideal circumstances, cured sausages should be kept hanging in a cool place, but it is more usual to store them in the refrigerator. The cut surface should be protected by covering it with foil. The sausage is cut into thin slices and peeled (if this is not done before slicing); it may be served as an appetizer, as a filling for sandwiches or canapés, or as a snack with drinks. A device called a *gibet* is sometimes used for hanging up several sausages at the table so that diners can help themselves; it comes with a small cutting board.

Examples of cured sausages include salami, Spanish *chorizo*, *kabanos* from Poland and the French *saucissons secs*, such as *saucisson de Lyon*, *saucisson de montagne*, *saucisson d'Arles*, *rosette* and *jésus*.

■ **Cooked and/or smoked sausages** Some sausages require part cooking or thorough reheating, by boiling or poaching. A well-known example is the German frankfurter, a smoked sausage made of finely minced (ground) pork and/or beef and sold fully cooked, ready for reheating. A French variety of frankfurter, called *francfort*, may contain beef and veal and is sold dried and smoked, for poaching. Other French sausages for poaching include the large *saucisse de Morteau*, made of pure pork, which can be hung up for smoking; the *Montbéliard* sausages; and the *cervelas de Lyon* (see *saveloy*), which are made of good-quality pure pork and contain pistachio nuts or truffles. *Gendarmes* are very dry, heavily smoked sausages from Switzerland and Austria; they can be eaten uncooked, but are often included in stews.

Other types of cooked or lightly smoked sausage are sliced and served as a cold appetizer (for example, mortadella), or have other cooking uses. For example, the French *saucisson de Paris* is used as a garnish for sauerkraut, and *saucisson de foie* (liver sausage), which consists of finely minced (ground) liver together with pork or veal, is spread on toast or canapés.

■ **German sausages** The greatest variety of sausages – well over 1,000 – is found in Germany. There are sausages of all types, from those sold cured or cooked ready for serving cold, to part-cooked examples for grilling (broiling) or baking, and others requiring lengthy simmering or stewing. Apart from the frankfurter, the best-known German sausages include the *Plockwurst*, made of beef and pork with a brown shiny skin, for poaching; the *Bierwurst*, for eating with beer; Holstein pork and beef sausages, for cooking; the *Bratwurst* and its many variations, for frying or grilling; the *Zungenwurst*, a cooked sausage containing coarsely diced lean pork, blood and tongue, for eating cold; the smoked *Schinkenwurst*, containing beef and thick-grained lean pork, for poaching; the thin Nuremberg sausages, made with herbs, for grilling; the Westphalian *Brägenwurst*, a long, thin, lightly smoked sausage made with pork fat, pig's brain, oatmeal and onions; the Munich *Weisswurst*, a white steamed sausage made from veal, beef and pork; and the Stuttgart *Presskopf*, made of pork, veal and beef.

RECIPES

grilled sausages
Use chipolatas, crépinettes or a piece of Toulouse sausage. Lay the sausages side by side in a grill (broiler) pan (long Toulouse or similar long sausages should be twisted into a coil and secured with skewers). Grill (broil) gently so that they cook right through without the outside burning. Serve with mashed potato or a purée of fresh vegetables or haricot (navy) beans.

sausage à la languedocienne
Twist 1 kg (2¼ lb) Toulouse sausage into a coil and secure with 2 crossed skewers. Heat 3 tablespoons goose fat or lard in a sauté pan and place the sausage in it. Add 4 chopped garlic cloves and a bouquet garni; cover the pan and cook for 18 minutes, turning the sausage halfway through. Drain the sausage, remove the skewers, arrange it in a serving dish and keep hot. Deglaze the pan with 2 tablespoons vinegar, then add 300 ml (½ pint, 1¼ cups) stock and 100 ml (4 fl oz, 7 tablespoons) fresh tomato purée. Boil for a few minutes, then add 3 tablespoons pickled capers and 1 tablespoon

chopped parsley. Pour this sauce over the sausage and serve with an aubergine (eggplant) gratin or tomatoes stuffed with rice.

sausage in brioche à la lyonnaise ♦
Select a boiling sausage of pure pork, weighing about 1 kg (2¼ lb) and about 30 cm (12 in) long. Boil it for 40 minutes in stock and allow to cool completely.

Dissolve 20 g (¾ oz, 1½ cakes) fresh (compressed) yeast in 3 tablespoons water. Mix 500 g (18 oz, 4½ cups) strong plain (bread) flour with 1½ tablespoon table salt, 20 g (¾ oz, 1½ tablespoons) caster (superfine) sugar, 5 eggs and the yeast in a food processor. When the dough begins to come away from the sides of the bowl, incorporate 250 g (9 oz, 1 cup) butter. Roll the dough into a ball, place it in a bowl, cover and put in a warm draught-free place to rise. (Its volume should double.) When risen, knock back (punch down) the dough, flatten and knead it four or five times. Then replace it in the bowl, cover and chill until ready to use.

Roll out the dough into a rectangle on a lightly floured surface. It should be a little longer than the sausage. Skin the sausage, dust it lightly with flour and roll it up in the dough. Fold the ends over and seal the edges firmly together. Place it in a long narrow terrine dish and leave it to rise. When the brioche fills the mould, glaze it with egg and bake in a preheated oven at 200–220°C (400–425°F, gas 6–7) for 25–30 minutes. Turn it out of the mould and serve hot, with a chicory (endive) salad, if desired.

sausages with cabbage
Braise some green or white cabbage. At the same time, grill (broil) some Toulouse sausages. Place the cabbage in a heated serving dish and arrange the sausages on top.

Alternatively, the sausages can be braised in white wine and the cooking juices poured over the cabbage.

additional recipe See *catalane*.

SAUSAGEMEAT A mixture of equal parts of lean pork (with the sinews and gristle removed) and pork fat, chopped finely and salted. Sausagemeat is used, with various seasonings, to stuff vegetables, meat (paupiettes) or poultry, and in terrines and pâtés. In charcuterie it is used to make crépinettes. However, a range of other meats may be used in the manufacture of sausages, including lean veal, beef, mutton, poultry or game, with different spices and seasonings, and even truffle and pistachio.

RECIPES

sausagemeat
Weigh out equal quantities of lean pork and fat bacon. Mince (grind) finely and add 3 tablespoons salt per 1 kg (2¼ lb) mince. Chopped truffle or

truffle peelings may be added, or the mince may be seasoned with finely chopped onions, garlic, salt, pepper and herbs. Chopped mushrooms, wild or cultivated, may also be added.

fine sausagemeat or fine pork forcemeat
Using the same mixture as for the sausagemeat recipe, finely mince (grind) the ingredients twice, or chop once and sieve. The seasonings are the same.

SAUSAGE ROLLS Traditional British pasty made by enclosing long thin rolls of sausagemeat in thinly rolled puff (or flaky) pastry. The long rolls are cut into lengths (bite-size or longer), glazed with egg and baked. Cooked chopped onions may be added to the sausagemeat and the pastry may be brushed with mustard before the sausagemeat is placed on it. Served hot, warm or cold as a snack, finger buffet fare or picnic food. See *friand*.

SAUSSELI A small puff pastry in Russian cookery, related to the French dartois. Sausselis, which are served as a first course or canapé, have various fillings, but the traditional filling is a mixture of cabbage braised in lard, onions and chopped hard-boiled (hard-cooked) eggs.

SAUTÉ To cook meat, fish or vegetables in fat until brown, using a frying pan, a sauté pan or even a heavy saucepan. Small items are cooked uncovered, but slightly thicker pieces (chicken, for example) sometimes need to be covered after browning, to complete the cooking. The process sometimes consists of frying food (which may be already cooked) while vigorously shaking the pan, which prevents it from sticking and ensures it is cooked on all sides. A sauce or gravy may be made by deglazing the cooking pan.

Sautéed potatoes are made with slices of raw or cooked potato, fried in butter or oil until golden. They are usually flavoured with parsley or garlic, or mixed with truffles (*à la sarladaise*) or sweated sliced onions (*à la lyonnaise*).

Sautés of meat or fish are dishes in which the meat is cut into uniform pieces, sautéed over a brisk heat, and then moistened and covered until the cooking is completed. The cooking liquid is reduced, thickened and sometimes strained to form the sauce. A garnish may be added during cooking.

RECIPES

minute sauté of lamb
Cut 800 g (1¾ lb) shoulder of lamb into small pieces and sauté in butter or oil over a brisk heat for 8 minutes. Season with salt and pepper. When the meat is well browned, add the juice of half a lemon, turn into a hot dish and sprinkle with chopped parsley.

minute sauté of veal
Using veal instead of lamb, proceed as for minute sauté of lamb, but cook the veal for about 15

minutes. When serving, keep the meat hot in a serving dish and deglaze the pan with 175 ml (6 fl oz, ¾ cup) white wine. Reduce, add the juice of half a lemon and whisk in 25 g (1 oz, 2 tablespoons) butter. Pour the sauce over the meat and sprinkle with chopped parsley.

sauté of lamb à l'ancienne
Clean 250 g (9 oz) calves' sweetbreads, blanch them for 5 minutes in salted boiling water and drain. Cook them gently for about 5 minutes in 40 g (1½ oz, 3 tablespoons) butter in a saucepan without allowing them to brown. Clean 250 g (9 oz, 3 cups) small button mushrooms and add them to the sweetbreads; braise together for another 10 minutes.

Remove all the contents of the pan; melt 25 g (1 oz, 2 tablespoons) butter in the same saucepan and brown about 1 kg (2¼ lb) best end of neck cutlets and pieces of boned shoulder of lamb (in equal proportions), seasoned with salt and pepper.

Drain the meat, pour the butter from the pan, then replace the meat together with the sweetbreads and mushrooms. Heat them, then sprinkle with 1 teaspoon flour. Mix together, then stir in 200 ml (7 fl oz, ¾ cup) Madeira and 200 ml (7 fl oz, ¾ cup) stock. Add a bouquet garni, cover and cook gently for about 20 minutes. Reduce by half with the lid off, then add 200 ml (7 fl oz, ¾ cup) double (heavy) cream mixed with 2 tablespoons lemon juice, and reduce again until the sauce is creamy. Adjust the seasoning.

Pour into a heated dish, sprinkle with chopped parsley and serve very hot, possibly with small croûtons fried in butter.

In the traditional preparation of this recipe, the quantity of sweetbreads was reduced and cockscombs and kidneys were added.

sauté of lamb or veal chasseur
Cut 800 g (1¾ lb) shoulder of lamb or veal into 50 g (2 oz) pieces and brown in a mixture of 20 g (¾ oz, 1½ tablespoons) butter and 2 tablespoons oil. Add 2 peeled chopped shallots, some stock – 200 ml (7 fl oz, ¾ cup) for lamb, 300 ml (½ pint, 1¼ cups) for veal – and 2 tablespoons tomato sauce. You could also add 175 ml (6 fl oz, ¾ cup) dry white wine to the stock if liked. Season with salt and pepper, add a bouquet garni, cover, then leave to simmer for 50 minutes (lamb) or 1¼ hours (veal). When the meat is cooked, add 250 g (9 oz, 3 cups) sliced mushrooms fried in oil. Heat all the ingredients through, put into a serving dish and sprinkle with chopped herbs.

sauté of lamb or veal with artichokes
Sauté 800 g (1¾ lb) best end of neck (rack) of lamb or boned shoulder of lamb or veal, cut into pieces.

Sausage in brioche à la lyonnaise, see page 1055.

Season with salt and pepper, then lower the heat, cover the pan and continue cooking until tender. Put the meat in a dish and keep hot. Blanch 4 artichoke hearts, cut into large dice or thin slices and sauté in butter or oil. Add to the meat in the dish. Deglaze the cooking pan with 100 ml (4 fl oz, 7 tablespoons) white wine, reduce by half, then add 200 ml (7 fl oz, ¾ cup) veal gravy. Stir well and pour over the meat and artichokes. Sprinkle with chopped parsley.

sauté of lamb or veal with aubergines

Cut 1.5 kg (3¼ lb) best end of neck (rack) of lamb or shoulder of veal into pieces. Season with salt and pepper and brown in a saucepan with half butter, half oil. When the meat is cooked, arrange it in a dish and garnish with 3 aubergines (eggplants), peeled, cut into small dice and fried in oil. Deglaze the pan juices with white wine, then mix with brown veal gravy and tomato purée (paste) flavoured with a little garlic. Reduce, strain and pour over the meat and vegetables. Sprinkle with chopped parsley.

sauté of lamb or veal with cep mushrooms

Proceed as for sauté of lamb with aubergines, but replace the aubergines (eggplants) with 300 g (11 oz, 3½ cups) cep or morel mushrooms, which have been fried in butter or oil.

sauté of lamb or veal with tomatoes

Proceed as for sauté of lamb with artichokes, but replace the artichokes with 8 small tomatoes, which have been peeled, seeded and fried in olive oil. A little finely chopped garlic may also be added.

sauté of veal clamart

Cut 1 kg (2¼ lb) shoulder of veal into uniform pieces. Season with salt and pepper and brown in a heavy-based saucepan with 25 g (1 oz, 2 tablespoons) butter or 3 tablespoons oil. Drain the meat, pour the fat out of the pan, deglaze the pan with 175 ml (6 fl oz, ¾ cup) white wine, then replace the meat and add 300 ml (½ pint, 1¼ cups) stock. Bring to the boil over a brisk heat, then reduce, cover and leave to cook for about 1 hour. Add 1 kg (2¼ lb, 7 cups) shelled peas and 12 baby (pearl) onions. Bring back to the boil and continue cooking for another 30 minutes. Adjust the seasoning, pour into a hot dish and sprinkle with chopped parsley.

sauté of veal with red wine

Cut 1 kg (2¼ lb) shoulder of veal into 50 g (2 oz) pieces and brown in 25 g (1 oz, 2 tablespoons) butter. Add 1 large sliced onion and season with salt and pepper. Then add 300 ml (½ pint, 1¼ cups) red wine, 150 ml (¼ pint, ⅔ cup) stock, 1 bouquet garni and 1 crushed garlic clove. Cover and leave to cook gently for 1¼–1½ hours. In the meantime, glaze 20 baby (pearl) onions until brown and fry

150 g (5 oz, 1¾ cups) sliced mushrooms in butter. Drain the pieces of meat, strain the sauce and thicken it with 1 tablespoon beurre manié. Return the meat to the sauté pan and add the onions, mushrooms and sauce. Reheat gently for 10–15 minutes.

veal sauté à la portugaise

Cut 1 kg (2¼ lb) shoulder of veal into 50 g (2 oz) pieces. Season them with salt and pepper and brown them in 3–4 tablespoons olive oil. Add 1 very large chopped onion and 1 crushed garlic clove. Deglaze the frying pan with 175 ml (6 fl oz, ¾ cup) white wine, then add 300 ml (½ pint, 1¼ cups) veal or chicken stock and 200 ml (7 fl oz, ¾ cup) tomato sauce. Add 1 bouquet garni and leave to simmer for about 1¼ hours. Drain the meat. Strain the sauce and reduce it by half. Return the meat to the sauté pan and add 8 tomatoes, which have been peeled, seeded and fried in oil, 1 tablespoon chopped parsley and the reduced sauce. Cover and leave to simmer for another 20 minutes. Arrange in a hot dish.

other recipes See *Marengo, paprika.*

SAUTÉ PAN A round shallow pan with straight or slightly flared sides and a handle. It is used to fry meat, fish and vegetables, often cut into pieces. The sides are slightly higher than the sides of a frying pan and enable the ingredients to be stirred easily, in order to coat them with fat and ensure that they cook evenly, especially when cut up into small dice or chopped and seasoned with herbs.

To make sautés in the correct sense of the word (especially those with sauce), a type of sauté pan called a *sautoir* or *plat à sauter* is preferred. It is a shallow pan with vertical sides, a handle and a lid. Made of aluminium, cast iron, stainless steel or tin-plated copper, it is used to make sautés of meat, poultry or fish. The pan is covered in order to finish the cooking, sometimes in the oven.

SAUTERNES A famous white wine from the Bordeaux region of France, south of the city of Bordeaux, on the left bank of the River Garonne. On account of its location, the grapes (the usual permitted varieties for white Bordeaux wines) can be affected in some years by 'noble rot' (*Botrytis cinerea*). This acts on the ripe and eventually overripe fruit and concentrates the juice in each grape. Because of the variation in the rate of ripening and the formation of noble rot, the grapes can seldom be picked a bunch at a time, but rather must be picked in small clusters or sometimes even grape by grape, the harvesters needing to work through each vineyard several times. The resulting wine is rich, very fragrant and luscious.

The most famous Sauternes of all is undoubtedly Château d'Yquem, but there are a number of other estates making excellent Sauternes. These wines should all be drunk chilled; although they are usually served at the end of a meal with dessert or fruit, some enthusiasts recommend serving Sauternes with melon and also with foie gras earlier in the meal, or with Roquefort blue cheese.

SAUVIGNON BLANC White grape variety widely grown in Bordeaux, the Loire Valley, Italy, New Zealand, Chile, Australia, South Africa, California, Portugal, Spain and Hungary. It has small bunches of golden yellow grapes, and flavours of gooseberries, green (bell) peppers, grass and tropical fruits.

SAVARIN A large, ring-shaped gâteau made of baba dough without raisins. After cooking, it is soaked with rum-flavoured syrup and filled with confectioner's custard (pastry cream) or Chantilly cream and fresh or crystallized (candied) fruit. The savarin was created by the Julien brothers, famous Parisian pastrycooks during the Second Empire. It was named after Brillat-Savarin, who gave Auguste Julien the secret of making the syrup for soaking the cake. Small individual savarins can also be made.

Savarin moulds can also be used for other mixtures, both sweet and savoury, such as hot or cold rice mixtures; meat, fish or vegetable loaves; or mousses, jellies and cakes.

RECIPES

preparing savarin batter in a food processor or mixer
Instead of making savarin batter by hand – an arm-aching task involving a cross between first kneading and then beating a heavy batter using the palm of the hand – a suitable food processor or mixer can be used. Follow the manufacturer's instructions for the choice of attachments and maximum quantities that can be mixed in the machine. This method is also suitable for dried fast-action, easy-blend types of yeast.

Put 1 teaspoon vanilla essence (extract), 25 g (1 oz, 1 tablespoon) acacia honey, 25 g (1 oz, 2 cakes) crumbled fresh (compressed) yeast, 1½ teaspoons salt, finely grated rind (zest) of ½ lemon and 3 eggs in the bowl of a food processor or mixer, fitted with a kneading attachment. Mix well, then add 250 g (9 oz, 2¼ cups) strong plain (bread) flour and mix or process until the mixture comes away from the sides of the bowl. Add another 3 beaten eggs and continue in the same way. Then add a further 2 beaten eggs and continue mixing for 10 minutes, before gradually adding 100 g (4 oz, ½ cup) butter, at room temperature and cut into small pieces, without stopping the machine. When the dough is very light, smooth and elastic, allow to rise at room temperature for 30 minutes.

savarin filled with confectioner's custard
Melt 50 g (2 oz, ¼ cup) butter. In a bowl, mix 125 g (4½ oz, 1 cup) strong plain (bread) flour, a good pinch of salt, 15 g (½ oz, 1 tablespoon) sugar and

1 egg. Dissolve 7 g (¼ oz, ½ cake) fresh (compressed) yeast in 1 tablespoon lukewarm water and add to the dough. Add another egg and work the dough by hand, using a combination of kneading and beating in the bowl, slapping the mixture from the palm of the hand against the side of the bowl. The mixture should be light, smooth and elastic. Beat in the melted butter by hand until well blended. Pour the batter into a buttered savarin mould, 20–23 cm (8–9 in) in diameter, and leave to rise in a warm place for 30 minutes. Bake in a preheated oven at 200°C (400°F, gas 6) for 20–25 minutes. Turn out on to a wire rack and leave to cool. Pour some syrup over the savarin, made with 500 ml (17 fl oz, 2 cups) water, 250 g (9 oz, 1 cup) sugar and a vanilla pod (bean).

Prepare some confectioner's custard (pastry cream, see custard) with 250 ml (8 fl oz, 1 cup) milk, 3 egg yolks, 50 g (2 oz, ¼ cup) sugar, 100 g (4 oz, 1 cup) plain (all-purpose) flour and 2½ tablespoons rum. Spoon into the centre of the savarin and serve well chilled.

fruit savarin
Prepare a savarin, leave it to cool and pour some rum-flavoured syrup over it. Peel 2 white peaches, 1 pear, 1 orange and 1 banana. Dice the fruit and sprinkle with the juice of half a lemon. Wash a small bunch of seedless green grapes, about 75 g (3 oz, ½ cup). Clean 50 g (2 oz, ½ cup) raspberries and 50 g (2 oz, ⅓ cup) wild strawberries (if available). Wash and hull 50 g (2 oz, ½ cup) large strawberries. Put all this fruit in a bowl, pour over the rest of the syrup used to soak the savarin, and leave to steep for 1 hour. Melt 200 g (7 oz, ⅔ cup) apricot jam (preserve) over a low heat and coat the savarin with it. Fill the centre of the savarin with some of the fruit and serve the rest separately.

savarin with red fruit sauce and whipped cream
Make a savarin as above and leave it to cool. Prepare a syrup by boiling 500 ml (17 fl oz, 2 cups) water with 250 g (9 oz, 1 cup) sugar and a vanilla pod (bean). Put the savarin in a deep dish and pour the hot syrup over it. Leave to cool and sprinkle with 150 ml (¼ pint, ⅔ cup) rum. Crush 250 g (9 oz, 2 cups) raspberries, then sieve. Mix the raspberry purée with 250 ml (8 fl oz, 1 cup) well-reduced cherry juice and add the juice of half a lemon. Whip 200 ml (7 fl oz, ¾ cup) double (heavy) cream with 2½ tablespoons very cold milk and 2 teaspoons vanilla sugar. Fill the centre of the savarin with the cream and pour over the cherry and raspberry sauce. Serve well chilled.

SAVELOY *cervelas* A short thick sausage made with pork meat and a varying amount of pork fat, and seasoned with pepper or garlic. It may be smoked and is sold either cooked or raw. The saveloy formerly contained brains (*cervelles*) as well, hence its French name. Most saveloys, also called 'cooking

Savoy

The cuisine of Savoy (*Savoie*), the Alpine region of south-eastern France, is dominated by butter, cream, milk and cheese. Fish from the lakes and mountain streams, game from the forests, mushrooms from the woods, meat (veal in particular) and charcuterie also play an important part in the fine cooking of the region. The orchards are planted with cherry, apple, pear and walnut trees, and strawberries and raspberries are plentiful, too.

■ **Dairy produce** Dairy foods combine with much of the produce of the area in a cuisine that is often rich.

The Savoyard cheeses include Beaufort, Reblochon, Tommes de Bonneville, Revard, Bauges and Boudane (the latter matured in grape marc brandy), Tamié (made by Trappist monks), Toupin and Chevrotin and Persillé des Aravis.

Cheese fondue, probably the best-known traditional cheese dish from this region, is made with dry white wine and kirsch. Eggs and cheese are used together in many recipes, including the ancient Pont-des-Andrieux omelette, which is associated with a sun rite; goat's-milk cheese pastries; cheese pancakes; and soufflé montagnard.

■ **From local rivers and lakes**
The rivers provide resources for a number of Savoyard specialities: fricassee of frogs' legs (with garlic, onions and vinegar); Léman perch with red wine; *lavaret* (similar to trout) with white wine or capers; and *féra* (a type of salmon) meunière, quenelles or *à la thononaise* (with white wine, or with a mushroom and ham sauce). Trout are cooked *au bleu*, meunière or stuffed and braised in the local dry white wine, Apremont.

■ **High-quality vegetables** In this cheese-producing region, gratins are a popular method of preparing vegetables, notably cep mushrooms, leeks, cardoons and marrows. Soups are made with sorrel, split peas, pumpkins, nettles or leeks, as well as with cheese. Other traditional dishes are vegetable or mushroom tarts with ham or bacon and little béchamel and oyster mushroom pies. There is a broad choice of typical vegetable dishes, such as *salade de mouraillons* (a salad made with dandelions and bacon, dressed with crème fraîche), potato *matafan* (flavoured with bacon, ham or spinach), potato and dried fruit forcement, *rambollets* (potato croquettes with prunes), gratin savoyard (without milk), *crozets* and polenta.

Made from cow's milk in the Beaufortin and Tarantaise regions, the rounds of Beaufort cheese weigh 40–60 kg (88–132 lb) and have a concave circumference.

■ **Favourite pâtisserie** The pâtisserie, which is rich and varied, includes some well-known traditional specialities, such as *suisses*, Saint-Genis brioche; and *biscuit de Savoie* (Savoy sponge cake), potato bread; pear rissoles; and prune, rhubarb or bilberry (huckleberry) tarts.

■ **Home-made drinks and country wines** There are various home-made drinks and country-style wines, such as mulled wine, raspberry wine, cherry ratafia and wormwood liqueur. The white brandies are also famous, as well as Chambéry vermouth.

■ **Traditional specialities** Less well-known specialities include a rustic black pudding (blood sausage) called *sang de caion*; *diots* with onion fondue and white wine; civet of fresh pork with red wine; *potée savoyarde* (made with belly of pork, knuckle of pork and sausages, together with stockpot vegetables and chestnuts); pork ribs with Chambéry vermouth; meatballs with cheese; veal ribs *à la marmotte* (larded with anchovies and bacon and braised with onions); and leg of kid goat

At this Savoyard chalet in the Beaufortin region, wood is stored to be burnt in winter in the great hearth, round which it is so pleasant to eat fondue.

with mushrooms. There are some original Savoyard recipes for poultry, such as chicken blanquette, chicken with cep mushrooms or crayfish, and coq *au Crépy*. Some delicious recipes for game birds include roast partridges stewed in white wine, then cut up and arranged in layers in a terrine with bacon, Gruyère cheese and vermicelli browned with garlic; thrushes

cooked with juniper berries; and pheasant or grouse cooked in Chartreuse.

WINE The French Alpine vineyards of Savoy have a long history, the wines being praised by both Pliny the Elder and Columella. The AOCs include Crépy, Seyssel, Seyssel Mousseux, Pétillant Vin de Savoie Mousseaux and Vins de Savoie, the latter

including red as well as still white and sparkling wines. The grapes used include some of the classic varieties, as well as a number of those with purely local names, such as Altesse (Roussette), Jacquère, Mondeuse Noir and Mondeuse Blanc. The white wines are very crisp and delicate and the reds are usually at their most enjoyable when drunk young and fresh.

sausages', are intended to be simmered with vegetables.

RECIPES

saveloys in salad
Cut some cold cooked saveloys into slices. Slice a cucumber and several seeded tomatoes into half rounds. Cut the heart of a head of celery into small rounds, and quarter some artichoke hearts that have been cooked in a court-bouillon. Arrange all the ingredients in a salad bowl, moisten with a well-seasoned vinaigrette containing white mustard, sprinkle with chopped parsley and chives, and serve chilled.

stuffed saveloys with spinach
Cook either 1.5 kg (3¼ lb) fresh spinach or 800 g (1¾ lb) frozen spinach in salted boiling water. Place 4 saveloys in a saucepan of cold water and heat them gently without boiling, so that they do not burst. Drain and press the spinach and reheat it with 25 g (1 oz, 2 tablespoons) butter. Scramble 6 eggs with 20 g (¾ oz, 1½ tablespoons) butter, salt, pepper and 1 tablespoon cream. Cover the serving dish with spinach. Drain the saveloys; split them along three-quarters of their length and stuff them with the scrambled eggs. Arrange the saveloys on the spinach.

SAVENNIÈRES An AOC of the Anjou region in the Loire valley. All white, these wines are made from the Chenin Blanc, have considerable elegance and charm, and can live long in bottle. Two subappellations are Savennières-La Roche-aux-Moines and Savennières-Coulée de Serrant.

SAVIGNY-LÈS-BEAUNE AOC mainly red and some white wines from the Côte-de-Beaune. They can be charming wines, although they are not particularly suited to long ageing.

SAVORY An aromatic herb, originating from southern Europe, with a scent resembling mint and thyme. Its name is derived from the Latin *satureia* (satyr's herb), a reference to the aphrodisiac qualities once attributed to it. There are two species. The

annual summer savory, with silvery-green leaves, is the species usually used in cooking. The perennial winter savory, with narrower stiffer leaves, is used mostly for flavouring soft goat's- or ewe's-milk cheeses and certain marinades; in Provence, it has the nickname of *poivre d'âne* (ass's pepper). Dried or fresh savory is the most popular herb for flavouring pulses. Fresh savory is also used to flavour Provençal salads, grilled (broiled) veal, roast lamb and loin of pork. When dried, it is used to flavour peas, ragoûts, soups, forcemeats and pâtés.

SAVOURY A small savoury item, English in origin, which was served at the end of the meal, after or sometimes instead of the dessert in late Victorian and Edwardian times. The range of savouries included Welsh rarebit, angels on horseback (see *oyster*), cheese straws, cheese soufflé, filled tartlets, poached eggs, various devilled items and hot or cold canapés.

SAVOY See *opposite page*.

SAVOYARDE, À LA The term used to describe a gratin of potatoes with milk and cheese, as well as several egg dishes: poached or soft-boiled (soft-cooked) eggs arranged on potatoes *à la savoyarde*, coated with Mornay sauce and glazed in the oven; eggs *sur le plat* cooked with sautéed potatoes, Gruyère cheese and cream; and flat omelettes with sautéed potatoes and cheese.

RECIPE

flat omelette à la savoyarde
Slice 250 g (9 oz) potatoes and sauté them in 40 g (1½ oz, 3 tablespoons) butter. Season with salt and pepper. Beat 8 eggs seasoned with salt and pepper and add 100 g (4 oz, 1 cup) Gruyère cheese in thin shavings. Add the potatoes to this mixture and pour it into a large frying pan. Proceed as for a flat omelette.

SAVOY SPONGE CAKE A sponge cake that is extremely light due to the large proportion of stiffly whisked egg whites in the recipe. It was probably made for the first time for Amadeus VI of Savoy in about 1348. The recipe has been handed down from generation to generation, and the small town of Yenne near Lake Bourget has become famous for this speciality.

This cake is not to be confused with the Savoy gâteau, a name sometimes given to the Saint-Genix brioche, another speciality of Savoy, made from brioche dough stuffed before baking with pink pralines and cooked in the shape of a hemisphere.

RECIPE

Savoy sponge cake
Beat 500 g (18 oz, 2¼ cups) caster (superfine) sugar, 1 tablespoon vanilla-flavoured sugar and 14 egg yolks until the mixture is pale and thick. Add 175 g (6 oz, 1½ cups) potato flour or cornflour (cornstarch). Finally, fold in 14 egg whites stiffly whisked with a pinch of salt until they stand in peaks. Pour the mixture into Savoy cake tins (pans), which have been buttered and dusted with potato flour, filling them only two-thirds full. Bake in a pre-heated oven at 180°C (350°F, gas 4) for about 40 minutes.

SBRINZ A Swiss unpasteurized cow's-milk cheese (45% fat content), produced mainly in the cantons of Lucerne, Schwyz, Uri and Unterwald. It has a cooked pressed centre and a washed, brushed, smooth crust, which is dark yellow or brown. Sbrinz is the oldest known Swiss cheese (it is the *caseus helveticus* mentioned by Pliny). Hard and brittle and with a strong flavour, this cheese is marketed in wheel shapes, 60 cm (24 in) in diameter and 14 cm (5½ in) deep, weighing 20 kg (44 lb). It can be eaten at the end of the meal and is also used to make canapés and toasted cheese; it can be grated like Parmesan.

SCABBARD FISH A very long Mediterranean fish, flattened like a ribbon, which can reach up to 2 m (6½ ft) in length. Its shiny silvery or black skin has no scales and its pointed snout is armed with several sharp teeth. It is usually sold in pieces and is particularly suitable for fish soup, since its rather soft flesh disintegrates easily.

SCALD To dip fruit or vegetables in boiling water to remove surface impurities or eliminate tartness. Jam jars (preserving jars) are also sterilized by scalding before they are filled.

Scald can also refer to dipping tripe into boiling water to remove the mucous membranes and prepare it for cooking. The head and feet of animals are also scalded to facilitate removal of the hair.

SCALE To remove the scales from a fish. This task is made easier by using a scaler, which is a scraping device with vertically toothed blades, but a scallop shell can also be used.

SCALLOP A bivalve mollusc, which moves by successively opening and closing its shell. In general, one side of a scallop's shell is flat and the other is rounded; both are marked with fan-shaped deep grooves and ridges. The hinge is framed by triangular lugs.

Fresh scallops may be sold live in their shells (which are tightly closed) or already cleaned and shelled; they are also available frozen or canned. Scallops comprise firm white flesh, which is the muscle that holds the shells together and which is a great delicacy, and the orange or pale red coral, or roe. This part is eaten in Europe, but not in North America.

To open a scallop shell, scrub it thoroughly and, if preferred, place the rounded side on an electric hotplate or in the oven at a low heat for a few minutes before opening it with a knife. Rinse the flesh and halve or slice it as required. Discard the beards or use them in the preparation of a fumet.

Scallops are generally eaten cooked, but require very little cooking or they will quickly toughen. They can be baked, grilled (broiled), fried or sautéed, cooked *à l'américaine*, with champagne or au gratin and served in the shell, curried, poached with various sauces, cooked on skewers, or eaten cold with a salad.

■ **Scallop species** There are hundreds of different species of scallops around the world. Some inhabit shallow sandy or weedy seabeds along the coast, other species prefer deeper waters. Most sea scallops are harvested by dredging and are normally cleaned on board as soon as they are caught. Large varieties of scallop include the large deep-water Atlantic sea scallop, which can grow to 20 cm (8 in) across, with the muscle sometimes reaching 5 cm (2 in), and the Pacific sea scallop. Other North American species include the smaller, sweet and delicate bay scallop, the tiny calico scallop, the weathervane scallop and the pretty pink and spiny (singing) scallops.

• KING SCALLOPS These are found in the North Atlantic and are also known as *coquille saint-jacques* and the pilgrim scallop. These names derive from the fact that this scallop used to be found in great numbers on the coast of Galicia in Spain, where it served as an emblem for medieval pilgrims who travelled a long way to reach nearby Santiago de Compostela (the shrine of St James). The shell is 10–15 cm (4–6 in) in diameter.

• QUEEN SCALLOPS Familiarly known as 'queenies', these are smaller, colourful scallops with a regular rounded shell. The queen scallop is fished in the English Channel, the Atlantic and the Mediterranean by trawling or dredging. It is very popular in Canada and the United States, where it is noticeably larger than the European variety. It is eaten raw, or cooked in a pan with a good *persillade* of parsley and garlic or shallots and flambéed. It is also used in many seafood dishes.

RECIPES

Cold Scallop Dishes
marinated sea bass, salmon and scallops ◆
Peel and grate into strips 1 fresh ginger root. Soak for 2 or 3 days in a bowl filled with 100 ml (4 fl oz, 7 tablespoons) olive oil. Thinly slice 250 g (9 oz)

Opening and trimming a scallop

1 *Scrub the shell thoroughly and rinse. Holding the shell, with the slightly cupped side down, in a thick cloth, insert a sturdy knife between the shells at the hinged end. Slide the knife around the edge between the top and bottom shells, keeping it close to the flat shell to loosen the scallop.*

2 *Discard the empty flat shell. Hold the cupped shell, with the scallop attached, over a bowl or dish. Use a knife to loosen the scallop from the cupped shell, then scoop the scallop and its juice into the bowl or dish using a spoon.*

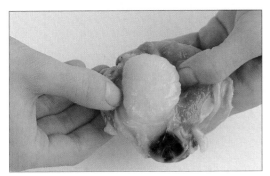

3 *Carefully remove all the membrane and beige-grey frilly edge around the scallop to leave a clean nugget of white meat and the red roe or coral.*

4 *Trim or gently pull away any membrane from the white meat and coral. Trim off any tough or dark bits of tissue from the end of the coral.*

sea bass, 250 g (9 oz) fresh salmon fillet and 4 shelled scallops. Arrange decoratively on 4 plates. Season with 1 teaspoon each sea salt and pepper. Sprinkle ½ bunch of fresh dill, very finely chopped, on top. Allow to marinate for 1 hour. Then add 1 tablespoon ginger oil (or olive oil marinated with sliced fresh root ginger) and a dash of lemon juice and serve.

raw scallops

Open the scallops, remove them from their shells, wash thoroughly (after removing the beards) and pat them dry. Cut the scallops into thin slices and lay them on a cold plate that has been lightly oiled. Cover with olive oil using a brush and give one turn of the pepper mill. Garnish with thin slivers of the coral.

scallop salad

Clean 1 lettuce heart, ½ bunch of watercress and the white part of 2 leeks. Slice the lettuce and the leeks and cook all these vegetables very gently in 1 tablespoon oil with salt and pepper until well reduced. Slice the flesh and corals of 12 scallops and seal them by steaming. Place the sliced

scallops on the tepid vegetable mixture and sprinkle with a little olive oil and the juice of 1 lemon.

scallops in mayonnaise

Line the rounded halves of some scallop shells with a little shredded lettuce seasoned with vinaigrette. Poach the white scallop meat in court-bouillon for 4 minutes, then drain well. Thinly slice the poached white flesh, dip the slices in the vinaigrette, then roll in chopped parsley. Place the slices on the lettuce and cover with mayonnaise. Garnish each scallop with the coral, an anchovy fillet and a few capers or black (ripe) olives.

scallops in salad

Hard boil (hard cook) some eggs, then quarter them. Shape the flesh of a cucumber into little ovals. Poach some scallops and let them cool. Shred some lettuce and season it with vinaigrette, then line the rounded halves of the scallop shells with this. Slice the scallops thinly, put them in a bowl with the cucumber, add some vinaigrette and mix well. Place the scallop slices and the cucumber into the lettuce-lined shells. Garnish with the egg quarters and corals, and sprinkle with mixed herbs. Crème fraîche with a little ketchup may be added to the scallop slices, in addition to some lemon juice, salt and pepper.

other recipes See *dieppoise, nage.*

Hot Scallop Dishes
fried scallops Colbert

Quickly poach the white flesh of the scallops in a court-bouillon for 4 minutes, then cut into slices if they are very large. Marinate them with the corals (as in the recipe for scallop brochettes), then drain, dip into batter and fry in plenty of fat. Drain and serve with Colbert butter. (The meat may also be covered in breadcrumbs before frying.)

queen scallops and oysters sautéed in Canadian whisky

Remove 12 queen scallops from their shells. Season, then brown on both sides in a frying pan over a high heat. Set aside. Melt 15 g (½ oz, 1 tablespoon) butter in a large saucepan. Add 1 teaspoon chopped shallots and 12 oysters and sauté for 30 seconds. Remove from the heat. Add the scallops and 200 ml (7 fl oz, ¾ cup) Canadian whisky. Flame at once. Using a slotted spoon, remove the scallops and the oysters and keep them warm. Pour 150 ml (¼ pint, ⅔ cup) white wine and 150 ml (¼ pint, ⅔ cup) fish stock into the saucepan, bring to the boil and reduce by half. Add 150 ml (¼ pint, ⅔ cup) crème fraîche and reduce by half again. Incorporate 25 g (1 oz, 2 tablespoons) butter, then 75 g (3 oz, ¾ cup) cornflour (cornstarch). Add salt and pepper to taste and reheat without boiling. Arrange the scallops and oysters on a bed of risotto made with wild rice. Pour over the sauce and garnish with peeled, seeded, chopped tomatoes and chopped chives.

scallop brochettes

Marinate the flesh and corals of 12 good scallops in a mixture of olive oil, garlic and chopped parsley, with a little lemon juice, salt and pepper. Leave for 1 hour, turning the ingredients at least once during this time. Clean 12 small mushrooms. Remove the seeds from a large sweet (bell) pepper and cut into squares. Cut 200 g (7 oz) smoked brisket into small pieces. Thread all these ingredients on 4 skewers, always placing a piece of meat on either side of the scallop flesh and its coral. Dip into the marinade and grill (broil) for 15–18 minutes under a moderate heat.

scallops Mornay

Poach the white flesh of the scallops with the corals. Fill the rounded halves of the shells with Mornay sauce. Slice the poached flesh and place the slices, with the corals, in the shells. Cover with more Mornay sauce. Sprinkle with grated cheese, baste with melted butter and brown in a preheated oven at about 240°C (475°F, gas 9).

steamed scallops

Place the flesh of some scallops and their corals into the basket of a steamer. Slice the flesh if the pieces are very large. Pour a well-spiced court-bouillon into the lower part and steam for 2–3 minutes. Finely sliced vegetables, such as the white part of a leek, fennel or celery, may be placed in the basket and steamed for about 10 minutes, before adding the scallops. Alternatively, the scallops and corals may be put into a dish with a lid, seasoned with salt and pepper and cooked in the oven in their own juice.

SCALLOP SHELL A preparation consisting of a salpicon, purée or ragoût, thickened and covered with an appropriate garnish, and presented in a scallop shell (especially for fish and shellfish) called a *coquille*, or in a receptacle of the same shape made of metal, tempered glass or heat-resistant porcelain. Scallop shells are normally cooked *au gratin* or with a savoury glaze, and served hot as a light first course. They can also be served cold. A number of preparations can be served in a scallop shell, including brill with shrimps, crayfish tails or skate livers *au beurre blonde*, devilled oysters, soft roes with spinach, *viande de desserte* with a tomato sauce, minced (gound) chicken, mussels, lambs' sweetbreads and fish pieces with a Mornay sauce.

It was once popular to garnish the border of the hot scallop shell with duchess potatoes piped through a fluted nozzle, or with thin rounds of boiled potatoes, which helped retain the various elements in the shell. A border is sometimes still made with chicken, veal or fish forcemeat, depending on the dish, or with spinach purée or rice.

Cold scallop shells are normally prepared with pieces of fish in mayonnaise – cold salmon, shrimps, thin slices of lobster, oysters – or simply with shellfish in a cold sauce. They are often presented on a bed of shredded lettuce, garnished with a mayonnaise piping, with slices of lemon perhaps or with black (ripe) olives.

■ **Preparation of hot scallop shells** Fill the bottom of the scallop shell with the appropriate sauce. Add the desired filling, which should be hot and well seasoned, and cover with sauce. Sprinkle with breadcrumbs or with grated cheese, then baste with melted butter. Place the shells in a roasting tin (pan) partly filled with water. Brown under a grill (broiler) or in a preheated oven at 240°C (475°F, gas 9).

RECIPES

scallop shells of fish à la Mornay

Mix some cooked fish – allow about 450 g (1 lb) for 4 people – with 300 ml (½ pint, 1¼ cups) Mornay* sauce and some chopped parsley. Season to taste. Fill the scallop shells with this mixture. Sprinkle

Marinated sea bass, salmon and scallops, see page 1062.

with grated Gruyère cheese, add a few knobs of butter and brown in a preheated oven at 240°C (475°F, gas 9).

scallop shells of fish à la provençale

Mix 400 g (14 oz) cooked fish with 400 ml (14 fl oz, 1¾ cups) well-seasoned Provençal sauce (see *à la provençale*) to which 1 tablespoon capers has been added. Distribute the mixture evenly among the scallop shells and sprinkle with some grated cheese according to taste. Baste each scallop shell with ½ teaspoon olive oil and heat in the oven.

scallop shells of shrimps

Shell some mussels, which have been cooked *à la marinière*, and strain the juice. Wash and thinly slice 250 g (9 oz, 3 cups) mushrooms, then sauté briskly in butter with 1 chopped shallot. Prepare a béchamel sauce, add the juice from the mussels and season. Mix all these ingredients, adding 150 g (5 oz, ¾ cup) peeled (shelled) shrimps. Butter 4 scallop shells and distribute the mixture evenly. Sprinkle with fresh breadcrumbs and a little grated Parmesan cheese, baste with melted butter and brown in a preheated oven at 240°C (475°F, gas 9).

SCAMORZE An Italian cheese (44% fat content), originally made from buffalo's milk in the centre of the peninsula, but now made from cow's and sometimes goat's milk throughout Italy. A pressed cheese with a natural crust, it is white or cream in colour with a nutty flavour. This cheese is related to Caciocavallo, but it is not matured as long. It is moulded into the shape of a narrow gourd with four little 'ears' at the top for handling. It is often eaten fresh and can be used in cookery like mozzarella.

SCAMPI Italian name (singular *scampo*) widely used for a shellfish that bears a number of other names, for example Dublin Bay prawn or Norway lobster. Scampi is usually applied to the tails only, while the French word *langoustine* is used for the shellfish when sold whole. Scampi can be cooked in the oven, fried or sautéed with garlic, grilled (broiled) on skewers, rolled up in small slices of ham, made into a ragoût with other seafoods, or boiled and served cold with lemon vinaigrette. *Scampi fritti* (fried in batter) is the best-known preparation.

SCANDINAVIA See *page 1068*.

SCAPPI, BARTOLOMEO Italian chef of the mid-16th century, who served several popes, in particular Pope Pius V. Informed by many journeys, Scappi edited an enormous culinary treatise on cooking, which was published in Venice in 1570, entitled *Opera* ('Works') and consists of six books, illustrated with fine engraved plates. The first is devoted to general instruction on cooking, the fourth contains a list of 113 menus created by him for official banquets, and the other two describe various different ingredients and dishes.

SCHABZIEGER A Swiss cheese made of skimmed cow's milk, which is very hard and has no rind. Sharp and strong, it is flavoured with dried sweet clover, which gives it a greenish colour. The French-speaking Swiss call it *Sapsago*, and the German-speaking Swiss call it *Kräuterkäse* (herb cheese). It is shaped like a truncated cone, 7.5 cm (3 in) wide at the base and 10 cm (4 in) high. When completely dry, it is used like Parmesan cheese to flavour rice, pasta, polenta or eggs.

SCHENKELE Also known as Schenkela. An Alsatian biscuit (cookie), traditionally eaten at Christmas (the name comes from the German *schenken*, meaning 'to offer'). Schenkeles are made from a fairly firm dough of flour, sugar, butter, eggs and ground almonds, flavoured with brandy or some other spirit. The dough is cut up into sticks, fried and liberally sprinkled with sugar.

SCHNAPPS Also known as schnaps. A spirit made in various forms in Germany (the word means literally a 'snatch' or a 'gasp') and also in the Scandinavian countries and the Netherlands. Aquavit is a schnapps. Often used as a chaser with beer, schnapps can accompany smoked meats and fish and cold cuts. It should be served ice cold.

SCHNECK Viennese pastry from Alsace, France, made from a leavened dough, rolled into a snail shape and filled with crème patissière flavoured with kirsch and preserved fruits.

SCHWEPPE, JACOB German industrialist (born Witzenhausen, 1740; died Geneva, 1821). He set up in Geneva as a jeweller, but soon began experiments in making artificial mineral water. His research led, in 1790, to the perfecting of an industrial process. In 1792, working with two engineers and a Genevan chemist, he set up a factory in London, then continued to run it on his own, producing sodas and imitations of Seltzer, Spa and Pyrmont waters, which were very popular at the time. The famous Schweppes Indian Tonic and Schweppes Ginger Ale were perfected in 1860 by Schweppe's successors, who made Seltzer water even more popular by adding quinine, bitter orange peel or ginger to it. These mixtures were extremely popular in the British colonies, where malaria was rife, and it became the custom there to add gin and drink them as 'tonics'. Today the firm is known internationally for these and a wide range of similar drinks.

SCONE (BISCUIT) A small round cake made of raised dough, which may be sweet or savoury. Originating in Scotland, it is soft and light inside and has a brown crust. Scones are eaten at breakfast or for tea, usually served hot, split in half and buttered. Traditionally cooked on a griddle (or girdle), a thick flat iron with a handle, placed on the fire or on top of the stove, they are now more often baked in a hot oven.

SCOOP OUT To remove the pulp from a fresh fruit or a raw vegetable before using it in a particular recipe. The cavity is usually stuffed with a filling consisting of the pulp mixed with other ingredients.

When preparing melon balls, the seeds are removed from the melon halves and then the flesh is scooped out with a melon baller; the melon balls can then be macerated in wine, replaced in the hollowed out rinds and served chilled.

In the preparation of fruit sorbets served in their skins (lemon, orange, tangerine or pineapple), the principle is the same; the sorbet is made with the fruit pulp and when the shell has been refilled, it is served chilled.

Apples can be hollowed out with an apple corer, before baking them in their skins or slicing them into rings for fritters.

SCORING Making a shallow incision, using a small knife or cutter in the skin of a fruit, vegetable or nut. Scoring an apple around its circumference prevents it from bursting during baking, while scoring chestnuts makes them easier to peel.

For a vol-au-vent, the lid is marked by scoring the pastry with a pastry (cookie) cutter or small knife before cooking.

Designs can be scored with the point of a knife or the prongs of a fork on top of a cake, pie or biscuit that has been brushed with beaten egg and is ready to bake. A puff-pastry galette is usually scored with diamond shapes, *pithiviers* with a rose pattern, and sablés, croquets and almond biscuits with criss-cross or parallel lines.

SCORPION FISH A fish found in warm temperate waters worldwide. In the Mediterranean it is often known by its French name, *rascasse*. It has a thick body and an enormous spiny head, marked with a transverse ridge and with loose skin hanging above and in front of the eyes. The dorsal fin is dotted with large spines. The small so-called brown scorpion fish is 30 cm (12 in) long and grey with a pink belly; scarce and expensive, it is much sought-after and cooked like sea bream. The red scorpion fish is 50 cm (20 in) long and a pinkish-bronze colour; it is much more common and has rather tasteless and tough flesh. It is an essential ingredient of fish soups and bouillabaisse. Species found in Australia include red rock cod and red scorpion cod.

RECIPE

fillets of scorpion fish à l'antillaise
Cut 800 g (1¾ lb) brown scorpion fish fillets into strips 2 cm (¾ in) wide. Peel and seed 1 kg (2¼ lb) very ripe tomatoes and rub the pulp through a sieve. Peel and slice 800 g (1¾ lb) potatoes and cook until golden in 4 tablespoons oil. Take the potatoes out of the pan and cook the fish until golden. Remove from the pan and set aside. Put 2 large sliced onions into the pan, then the tomato pulp, some salt and pepper and 1 small red (bell) pepper. Bring to the boil, then add the potatoes and 1 bay leaf. When the potatoes are almost cooked (but still firm when pierced with a knife), add the fish and continue to cook for 7–8 minutes. Serve very hot with rice *à la créole*.

SCORZONERA See *salsify*.

SCOTCH BROTH A Scottish soup, also known as barley broth. The ingredients are neck or shoulder of mutton, barley and various vegetables, including carrots, turnips, onions, leeks, celery, and sometimes green peas and cabbage. It is served sprinkled with parsley. Sometimes the broth (not strained) is served first, followed by the meat with caper sauce.

SCOTCH EGG A traditional British snack or picnic food, thought to have originated in Scotland. This consists of a hard-boiled (hard-cooked) egg covered in an even layer of sausagemeat, coated in egg and breadcrumbs and deep-fried. When cold, the Scotch egg is cut in half before serving. Originally, the sausagemeat was hand chopped and the Scotch egg was served hot as well as cold. When home-made, with excellent sausagemeat, the combination is a very successful one and ideal picnic fare.

SCOTLAND See *page 1071*.

SCOVILLE SCALE A scale by which to compare the pungency of chillies (chili peppers). Developed in 1912, the scale applies units of heat according to the amount of capsaicin present in the fresh chillies. See *chilli (chili pepper)*.

SCREWPINE Also known as kewra or pandanus, the leaves of tropical trees of the family are used as a spice in the cooking of India, Indonesia, Malaysia and other countries of South-East Asia. They contribute a delicate fragrance and slightly scented flavour to rice, pulses, chicken, vegetables and pickles. The fresh leaves are also used for their green colour.

The flowers are used to make kewra essence or water, a flavouring that is widely used in Indian cooking in the same way as vanilla is in Western dishes, to flavour desserts and drinks. It is also occasionally used in festive rice dishes, such as biriani.

SCROLLS Light pastry confections in the shape of little scrolls. The name is also given to a chocolate decoration obtained by shaving the edge of a block of chocolate with a knife, or by pouring some melted chocolate on to marble and scraping it off when it has hardened. This type of decoration is often called *caraque* and is used on Black Forest gâteau.

SEA ALMOND A small bivalve mollusc, about 5 cm (2 in) long, living on the sandy seabed. Its concentrically ribbed shell is cream, spotted with brown. Inside the shell are numerous small parallel teeth. The sea

SCANDINAVIA

The culinary repertoire of the Scandinavian countries relies on fish, potatoes, pork, beetroot (red beet), cucumber, fruit, dill, phorseradish, cream and butter; it preserves the distant heritage of the Vikings, who ate mutton, shellfish, wild birds, reindeer and bear, and were adept at making butter and beer.

The natural isolation of the Scandinavian countries has contributed to the survival of some very old recipes, notably raw salmon marinated with pepper, dill, sugar and salt and served with mustard sauce. Bread is traditionally made at home, hence the variety of Scandinavian barley or rye cakes and breads. In addition, the climate is conducive to the widespread practice of drying, smoking and marinating; cod and herring have therefore become the mainstays of the Scandinavian diet. One particularly typical dish is *surströmming* – sour herrings pickled in the sun in a barrel of brine, a strong sharp dish eaten with sour black bread and potatoes.

Within the Arctic circle, whether in Sweden, Norway or Finland, the meat is primarily reindeer meat. Smoked to the bone and then dried, it can be kept for a long time, but it is also cooked fresh, traditionally stewed with marrow bones. The Lapps maintain some old traditions, such as salted black coffee into which they dip reindeer-milk cheese.

Dairy products play an important role in Scandinavian cookery. Double (heavy) cream or soured (sour) cream, butter and cottage cheese or whey are much used in sweet and savoury recipes, and there are numerous cheeses, including Danish Blue and Samsoë (the best known), the Swedish Kumminost with cumin, Norwegian Gammelost, Gjetost, Nökkelost, Mysost and Pultost, which are often very strong, the Finnish Kreivi, Munajuusto and reindeer-milk cheese.

Each of the Scandinavian countries has its own culinary characteristics. Denmark relies heavily on pork and potatoes, and is renowned for its *smørrebrød* and pastries. Norway has a wilder terrain and consequently fish, reindeer and mutton are important here. Finland uses rye and potatoes, pork, fish and wild mushrooms and berries of the forest in its dishes, while Sweden has the most varied cuisine of the four, including the well-known *smörgasbord*.

■ **Denmark** Solid, plentiful and mild, Danish cookery makes much use of butter and cream. Pork and potatoes are traditionally the predominant foods. Two great classics are loin of pork stuffed with prunes and apples and roast leg of pork with crackling. Stews are also popular, especially *frikadeller*, meatballs of minced (ground) veal and pork with onion; as well as stuffed cabbage and *hakkebiff*, minced beef with onion, in a brown sauce. Poultry dishes, which are reserved for special occasions, include chicken stuffed with parsley, and roast goose. The offal specialities include a famous black pudding (blood sausage), calf's head *en tortue*, and stuffed ox heart with cream sauce. Liver pâté is also very popular and is one of the main items in the cold buffet, the traditional Danish lunch which includes salads, herrings, scrambled egg with bacon and cheese on slices of buttered wholemeal or black bread, together with various foods which are easy to slice, such as *rullepoelse* (spiced rolled belly of pork).

In terms of vegetables, in addition to potatoes, cabbage is widely used, especially braised red cabbage with apples, which is served with pork, goose or duck. Boiled kale, chopped and combined with a cream sauce, is a favourite garnish for ham.

• FAMOUS SWEET DISHES The best known items of Danish cookery are the pastries and desserts, ranging from simple pancakes filled with vanilla ice cream, fruit puddings and *rodgrod*, to the more elaborate apple cake, made of several layers of sweet pastry interspersed with jam and breadcrumbs mixed with melted butter and topped with whipped cream. There are also 'peasant maidens in veils', with a base of crumbled rye bread, apples, chocolate and cream.

Home-made biscuits (cookies) include the *brune kage,* made with spices, almonds; and brown sugar; gingerbread; and butter shortbreads. Some Danish pastries are very popular, such as the soft flaky turnovers of various shapes, filled with cream, jam or dried fruits. The most impressive set piece is the *kransekage*, eaten on birthdays and at weddings. As high as 80 cm (30 in), it is made of tiered rings of pastry decorated with crystallized (candied) fruit, studded with little flags and patterned with icing (frosting) designs.

• TRADITIONAL SIMPLICITY A less rich culinary tradition does exist in Denmark, going back to the rural origins of the country; some examples are milk porridge topped with butter and salt-pork gravy, and *ollebrod*, a thick soup made with beer and rye bread.

■ **Norway** The traditional Norwegian breakfast is based on salt or marinated fish, strong cheese, bacon, fried potatoes, eggs and various types of bread, together with butter and jam. The midday meal is often only sandwiches, except in the country, where the two main foods of Norway, mutton and fish, are often eaten. The main meal of the day is dinner.

Soured cream is widely used: in soups and sauces, porridge, waffles and with salt meat, pork products and salads. The natural taste of foods is appreciated, with such dishes as salt mutton chops grilled over a birch-wood fire and served with kohlrabi purée; fried trout coated with cream and sprinkled with parsley; fish salad with horseradish, dill and onions; and ham with *surkål*, a sort of sauerkraut with cumin.

The old Norwegian national dish is *rommegrot*, a porridge made with soured cream, flour and milk, dusted with cinnamon and sugar, and served with melted butter and redcurrant or blackberry juice; it has now given way to the more popular rice pudding.

• MEAT AND GAME Meat is often dried, salted and smoked. Leg of mutton prepared in this way is called *fenalår* and is cut into long thin slices. *Spekeskinke* is a dried ham eaten in the spring with new vegetables. In the winter more fortifying foods are eaten, such as *får i kål*, a mutton and cabbage stew with black pepper. There are some original recipes for game, including ptarmigan casserole with cranberries; roast venison with goat's-milk cheese sauce; and smoked elk.

• POPULAR FISH There are numerous ways of preparing fish. Trout is preserved by pickling as well as by the other methods. Salmon is grilled (broiled), smoked, or cooked in stock and served cold, for example with horseradish butter and cucumber.

Sea fish are widely used. Boiled salt cod is served with melted butter and egg sauce or cooked with potatoes and young peas with mustard sauce. Another very popular ingredient is cods' tongues, which are often mixed with different types of fish in aspic. As in other Scandinavian countries, herrings are prepared in many different ways. Mackerel are also highly prized: marinated and then grilled, they are often served with tomato butter, aquavit and beer. There is also a fish pudding, made with smoked haddock and cod, served with shrimp sauce. Fish soup from Bergen is made with green vegetables and enriched with soured cream and egg yolks.

■ **Sweden** Swedish cuisine is more open to external influences than its neighbours and, as well as *husmanskost* (plain cooking), it prides itself on a courtly culinary tradition with, for instance, dishes such as *slottsstek* (braised beef à la royale, served with cranberries and potatoes) or fillet of beef Oskar (served with asparagus and sauce béarnaise). Although the impressive buffet of food, *smörgasbord*, is still popular, ordinary everyday dishes are simpler, seasoned with a variety of herbs such as dill, marjoram, horseradish and thyme.

• MAIN DISHES These are often based on a rich combination of tastes. As in the rest of Scandinavia, fish is extremely important in Sweden, especially herring. *Surströmming* is herring from the Baltic that has been salted and allowed to mature, and whose taste is as strong as its smell. It is eaten with barley bread, raw onions and small potatoes. Freshwater crayfish is very popular and often cooked in dill-flavoured water.

Beef and pork are the most popular meats. Here too, the combinations of tastes are interesting: beef ragoût with beer; Lindström beef, minced beef with beetroot (red beet) juice, capers and onions; shoulder of pork with cranberries. Other interesting foods include: sausages, black pudding and even soup made with blood.

Goose and duck are often eaten on special occasions, such as the feast of St Martin in November. Goose is often served stuffed with prunes and apples.

Potato is much loved in Sweden. There are countless extremely inventive recipes for preparing potatoes: potato croquettes stuffed with pork; potatoes, halved, smothered in crème fraîche and topped with cod's roe; small potato pancakes with chives and pepper; *pytt i panna*, diced potato and cubed meat, sautéed with onions and parsley, and served with a raw egg yolk; and Janssen's temptation, a gratin of potatoes with anchovy or sprat and onions.

• CHEESE AND DESSERTS Sweden boasts 200 kinds of cheeses, made from cow's or goat's milk, including Västerbotten, which is rather strong, and Kryddost, flavoured with cumin.

There is a very wide range of pâtisserie, often flavoured with saffron and cardamom. Apples and berries (elderberries, blackberries and bilberries) are very popular and are used in many Swedish desserts and pastries.

■ **Finland** Finnish cuisine is characterized by foods with robust flavours, such as *vorshmack* – a hash of mutton, beef and salt herring, spiced with garlic and onion – accompanied by *ryyppy*, a very strong grain alcohol, which is drunk chilled.

Soup that is made of lake fish together with potatoes and onions is served with a hunk of buttered rye bread. A rich soup made of chopped offal cooked with carrots and potatoes is thickened with blood and garnished with barley balls.

The Finns are fond of swedes (rutabaga), raw salmon (*loki*) and strong liqueurs, such as *lakka*, based on Arctic cranberries. Other typical foods are burbot roe, smoked reindeer tongues and crayfish cooked in stock with fennel.

Milk is used a great deal, in the form of a fairly thick buttermilk or in puddings and porridge; these include puddings made with rye, malt, treacle and bitter-orange peel, and barley porridge served with rose-hip purée, raisins or melted butter.

• WILD FOODS Mushrooms from the forests are widely used in soups, sauces, stews, pickles and salads. tiny berries – cranberries, blackberries and tiny strawberries – are made into purées, mousses and cream desserts.

• THE RUSSIAN INFLUENCE This is significant, with borsch, pashka and blinis being common dishes. In Karelia (once part of Finland, now Russia) rye pastries, local versions of piroshki and koulibiaca, are the typical dishes as are *piirakka*, with a rice and fish filling, served with melted butter and hard-boiled (hard-cooked) eggs, and the famous *kalakukko*, filled with small

▶

<table>
<tr><td>

◄freshwater fish and minced (ground) pork.

■ **The Christmas season**
Throughout Scandinavia, Christmas festivities begin early. On 13 December, St Lucia's Day, the young girls dress in white and wear crowns of candles. They prepare the morning coffee and serve it with saffron biscuits (cookies). The main Christmas meal is served on Christmas Eve in the evening, and comprises the traditional dishes: ham pie (made with rye pastry) and turnip purée in Finland; braised caramelized ham with apples, red cabbage and

</td><td>

mustard in Sweden; roast pork or pork ribs and sauerkraut with cumin in Norway; and roast pork, duck or goose stuffed with apples and prunes and served with caramelized potatoes in Denmark. The pastries include petits fours flavoured with cloves and ginger, leavened dough fritters with brandy, Christmas loaves containing crystallized (candied) fruits, and cinnamon, butter and almond porridges.

Meals on Christmas Day itself are served as large cold buffets. Christmas breakfast sometimes includes some special foods, such

</td><td>

as the Swedish *julhög*, consisting of a ball of rye bread, a small wheat bun sprinkled with large sugar crystals, a heart-shaped piece of shortbread and a red apple placed on top of each other. The Danes are particularly fond of rice pudding made with whipped cream and almonds, topped with cherry sauce. The traditional punch is *glögg*, a mixture of red wine, Muscat, vermouth and angostura bitters in which raisins, orange peel, cardamom, cloves and cinnamon are steeped. This is served very hot with chopped almonds.

</td></tr>
</table>

almond may be eaten raw with lemon, but is usually stuffed, like the scallop, although it is not as good.

SEA BREAM A broad category of marine fish with gold or silvery scales; generally narrow bodied and oval in silhouette. The ancient Greeks and Romans liked it cooked with seasoned sauces and accompanied with fruits. There are many different species worldwide.

• *Couch's sea bream*, known as red porgy in the United States and *pagre* in France, is found in the Atlantic (south of the Bay of Biscay) and in the Mediterranean (especially on the Spanish coast). Up to 75 cm (30 in) long and weighing about 1.25 kg (2¾ lb), it has an oval body with large scales, a grey and pink back, silvery sides and fins marked with reddish-brown. Its flesh, although less delicate than that of the other species, is full of flavour.

• *Gilthead bream* is fished in the Mediterranean and the Bay of Biscay. It is 30–50 cm (12–20 in) long and weighs up to 3 kg (6½ lb); it has silvery scales, a gold-spot on each cheek and a golden crescent between the eyes. The shine of the scales is a good indication of freshness; its soft, white, dense flesh is excellent.

• *Grey sea bream*, 20–40 cm (8–16 in) long and weighing 300–500 g (11–18 oz), has flesh of a slightly coarser texture. It is much cheaper, both because of its less attractive appearance and its greater availability.

• *Pink sea bream* comes mainly from the Atlantic. It is gold-coloured with clear pink fins and a black mark near the gills. The flesh is less dense and has a drier texture, but is nevertheless tasty. It weighs up to 3 kg (6½ lb).

■ **Buying and cooking** Fresh sea bream are sold whole, usually gutted; the scales are numerous, wide and sticky and are preferably removed by the fishmonger. The percentage of waste is very high (up to 50%), so allow 300 g (11 oz) per person. Deep-frozen fillets of sea bream are also available. The backbone comes away easily, even when raw, and the fish is often cooked stuffed.

Sea bream can be grilled (broiled) – slit beforehand if very large and marinated if desired – roasted, poached in a court-bouillon or steamed with seaweed. In Mediterranean countries, it is often roasted on a spit and accompanied by chick peas or haricot (navy) beans and lardons of bacon. Sliced, it can be made into soup. It is also a good fish for making *sashimi*, provided it is absolutely fresh.

RECIPES

braised gilthead bream with apples
Remove the scales from a gilthead bream weighing about 800 g (1¾ lb), clean it through the gills and wipe it. Retain the liver. Peel and chop 3 shallots, 1 small fennel bulb and 1 onion. Peel and crush 2 garlic cloves. Remove the zest from 1 lime and blanch, cool and dry it. Arrange a bed of fresh fennel sprigs in a long flameproof casserole. Add the shallots, fennel, onion, garlic, lime rind and some parsley stalks; moisten with 250 ml (8 fl oz, 1 cup) fish fumet*, 1 tablespoon olive oil and 2 tablespoons white rum. Bring to the boil.

Place the bream on this bed, make 3 slits in the uppermost surface and insert lemon or orange slices and diced streaky (slab) salted bacon. Coat with olive oil and sprinkle with pepper and salt. Around it arrange the liver, cut into quarters, and 2 apples, also cut into quarters. Cover with foil and cook in a preheated oven at 180°C (350°F, gas 4) for 20–30 minutes. Arrange on a serving dish. Strain the reduced cooking juices, adjust the seasoning and serve separately in a sauceboat.

fillets of sea bream with vegetable julienne
Fillet a sea bream weighing about 1.7 kg (3¾ lb). Prepare a julienne of vegetables comprising the white parts of 2 leeks, 4 sliced celery sticks, ½ fennel bulb and 2 young turnips. Arrange it in a buttered gratin dish. Season the fillets with salt and pepper, fold them in half and place them in the dish.

SCOTLAND

Surrounded on three sides by water, Scotland has the resources of sea, the mountains, and also the mild, lush farmlands, where Aberdeen Angus, the world's finest beef cattle, graze and where raspberries are an important crop. The country has a record of fine cooking that goes back to the Auld Alliance with France in the 16th century. This French tradition continues in the elegant sauces, as well as many words in common usage – like *gigot* for a lamb's leg.

Breakfast and high tea (a combination of tea and supper) are elevated to full meals, with a variety of bannocks, baps (large soft rolls), Dundee marmalade or home-made jam. Steaming bowls of creamy porridge, sprinkled with brown sugar, and lightly poached kippers, topped with butter, are likely to feature on the Scottish breakfast menu. Old-fashioned high tea is more feast than meal, particularly during winter, when substantial meals compensate for bleak highland weather. A combination of a hot or cold savoury dish, the type of recipe often referred to as a supper dish, may be followed by a sweet pudding or fruit pie, a cake or scones. Simple but tasty potato dishes or light savouries on toast may be served. Cold meats and cheese with pickles are also suitable. The ubiquitous Scotch egg is excellent when home made. The finest sausagemeat or minced (ground) meat is wrapped around a hard-boiled (hard-cooked) egg, which is coated with breadcrumbs and deep-fried until golden.

■ **Fish** This is of the freshest, for nowhere is more than 65 km (40 miles) from the sea. Traditionally, herrings and trout are fried in oatmeal, while herring roe cakes are enjoyed in the Shetlands. The fattest herrings, nicknamed Glasgow magistrates, from Loch Fyne, are rolled up, then cooked in vinegar, to be served hot or cold. Simple shellfish dishes include limpet stovies (stewed with sliced potato), mussels cooked with onions in milk and wine, and *partan bree*, a crab soup made with cream and cooked rice. Codling is used for *cabbie claw* (with grated horseradish, served with mashed potatoes), while there is a long tradition of haddock preparation on the Aberdeenshire coast, particularly with Arbroath smokies. These are cooked in a milk and potato broth to make *cullen skink* in the north-east and Moray Firth. *Crappit heid* is the head stuffed with fish liver and oatmeal. On the west coast, farmed and smoked salmon have earned it the nickname of the 'salmon lands', and combinations of the smoked and fresh fish are the signature dishes here. There are also some fine shellfish, including langoustines and squat lobsters.

■ **Poultry, game and meat** Among the excellent game there are four types of grouse, including the red grouse, arguably the finest game bird in the world. The venison is roast, while Blair Atholl venison chops are cooked in butter with whisky. Excellent beef, such as that from the Aberdeen Angus and the Belted Galloway, are made into traditional dishes like *Forfar bridies*, a pasty of rump steak with onions. Lamb may be soaked in brine with allspice to make mutton hams and it is used in Scotch broth and the humbler *hotchpotch*, made with neck of lamb and vegetables and in the islands also with nettle tops and shemis (*Ligusticum scoticum*). Lamb is also the meat for the national dish, haggis, a type of offal sausage.

Howtowdie with *drappit* eggs is stuffed, poached chicken surrounded by spinach and poached eggs, served with a liver sauce. Cock-a-leekie, a much-loved chicken and leek dish, is cooked in beef stock enlivened with prunes and herbs.

■ **Vegetables and cereals** A fondness for strong tastes, one theme of Scottish cooking, is seen in the vegetable choice of swede (rutabaga), and turnips, eaten mashed as *bashed neeps*. Wild mushrooms are picked in quantity in central Scotland.

Oats are to Scotland what the potato is to England. Traditional dishes include parkin (made from porridge oats, treacle and spices), Scottish bannocks (flat scones without yeast) and last, but not least, porridge.

■ **Sweet specialities** The ladies' tearoom owes its origin to Glasgow's Kate Cranston in 1884, and baked goods are popular. Examples include shortbreads, such as petticoat tails (wedge-shaped, with an outside flounce); Dundee fruit cake (decorated with rings of almonds); Twelfth-Night cake; and black bun, a large pastry round filled with a fruited Christmas cake mixture.

Desserts include *cloutie dumpling*, a spiced boiled suet pudding with dried fruit, and several well-known creams. *Atholl brose*, known since 1475, is a cream of oatmeal, honey and whisky; *cranach* (cream crowdie) is made with cream or cream cheese, oatmeal and a soft berry garnish; and Edinburgh fog is a mixture of cream with ratafias and almonds. The Scots' fondness for caramel and ginger is reflected in confectionery such as butterscotch.

■ **Variety of cheeses** Traditional cheese-making in Scotland is having something of a comeback with farmhouse Cheddar from the Isle of Mull and farmhouse Dunlop (very similar in style to Cheddar) from Ayrshire. The isles of Arran and Orkney are also producing farmhouse cheeses similar to Dunlop. Other interesting Scottish cheeses include Lanark Blue; Crowdie, a traditional cottage cheese and Caboc, a buttery double cream cheese.

■ **Scottish spirit** Whisky is a national passion, from single malts to popular blends. Pubs have whisky menus and may stock 50 types. The Scots also have a tradition of laying down exceptional wine cellars.

Add some crème fraîche and a little lemon juice and cook in a preheated oven at about 220°C (425°F, gas 7) for about 30 minutes, covering the dish with a sheet of foil.

gilthead bream with lemon in oil

Remove the scales from 1 large gilthead bream; clean it and make small cuts in its back. Oil a gratin dish and line it with 8 slices of lemon preserved in oil. Place the sea bream on top and season with salt and pepper. Add 1 small handful of coriander seeds. Garnish with 6 slices of lemon preserved in oil. Pour over 2 tablespoons lemon juice and a few spoonfuls of olive oil. Cook in a preheated oven at 230°C (450°F, gas 8) for 30 minutes, basting several times.

sea bream stuffed with fennel

Remove the scales from a sea bream weighing about 1.5 kg (3¼ lb). Clean it through the gills, wash, wipe and season it with salt and pepper. Cut along both sides of the backbone, then cut through the backbone at the head and tail and remove it. Moisten 250 g (9 oz, 2½ cups) dry breadcrumbs with milk. Clean and thinly slice 1 fennel bulb. Squeeze the breadcrumbs and mix with the fennel plus 2 tablespoons pastis, 1 tablespoon lemon juice, and a little crumbled bay leaf and thyme. Fill the bream with this stuffing and tie it up like a ballotine.

Butter a gratin dish, sprinkle with chopped shallots and place the bream on top. Pour in white wine (or a mixture of wine and fumet) to a third of the depth of the fish, sprinkle with olive oil and cook in a preheated oven at about 240°C (475°F, gas 9) for about 30 minutes, basting from time to time. If necessary, protect the fish with a piece of foil towards the end of the cooking.

additional recipe See *meunière*.

SEA CUCUMBER Known as *bêche-de-mer* or less appealingly as a sea slug, there are many types of this sea creature, but only a few are valued as food. The edible types belong mainly to the *Holothurioidea* species. They resemble short cucumbers in shape and there are different types, varying in length, thickness and colour (which may be pale, yellow-brown to brown or very dark green).

Sea cucumber is popular in South-East Asia and China; it is exported from Australia (where it is rarely eaten) to the Oriental countries. It is extensively processed, by gutting, blanching, drying and sometimes smoking. The dried sea cucumber is soaked (and gutted if this was not part of the original preparation) before being cooked.

SEAFOOD A collective term for shellfish and other small edible marine animals (*fruits de mer* in French), such as spider crabs, mussels, shrimps, winkles, clams, sea urchins, oysters and langoustines. Seafood is often served as an hors d'oeuvre, perhaps on a bed of crushed ice and fresh,

clean seaweed and accompanied by butter and rye bread. It is also an ingredient of omelettes, risottos, vol-au-vent, pasta dishes and many more.

RECIPES

seafood bouchées

Prepare and cook some savoury bouchée cases. Prepare a seafood ragoût. Warm the bouchée cases in the oven (if prepared in advance), fill with the hot seafood ragoût, cover with the bouchée tops and serve immediately.

seafood ragoût

Peel and chop 2 shallots and 1 large onion. Clean 800 g (1¾ lb) mussels and 12 langoustines. Scald and peel 5 or 6 tomatoes, remove the seeds and crush the pulp.

Place the mussels in a pan with 200 ml (7 fl oz, ¾ cup) dry white wine, 1 bouquet garni and half the chopped shallots and onion. Season with pepper. Cover the pan and cook until the shells just open, then remove the mussels and strain the cooking liquid through fine muslin (cheesecloth).

Place the flesh of 15 scallops and the strained mussel liquid in a saucepan, cover and poach very gently for 5 minutes. Remove the scallops from the liquid. Remove the mussels from their shells.

Sauté the langoustines in oil in a flameproof casserole. When they have turned red, add some pepper and the remaining chopped shallots and onion; cook until golden. Add a liqueur glass of warm brandy and flame. Add the crushed tomatoes and the cooking liquid used for the mussels and scallops; cover, cook very gently for 5–6 minutes, then remove and drain the langoustines. Continue cooking the tomatoes for about 10 minutes.

Meanwhile, shell the langoustine tails, crush the shells and add them to the casserole to flavour the mixture. Cut the langoustine tails into chunks and slice the scallop flesh. Heat 50 g (2 oz, ¼ cup) butter in a sauté pan until it foams, then add the langoustines, scallops, mussels and 100 g (4 oz) peeled prawn (shelled shrimps). Press the tomato sauce through a fine sieve, add 200 ml (7 fl oz, ¾ cup) double (heavy) cream, adjust the seasoning and reduce until the mixture just starts to thicken. Pour over the seafood.

seafood risotto

Clean and cook 2 litres (3½ pints, 2 quarts) mussels and 1 litre (1¾ pints, 4⅓ cups) cockles or clams separately in white wine seasoned with spices and herbs. Drain the shellfish and remove from their shells. Put them in a casserole with 200 g (7 oz) peeled prawn (shelled shrimp) tails and 4 shelled scallops, previously poached in white wine and sliced. Prepare 400 ml (14 fl oz, 1¾ cups) fish velouté* sauce, using a white roux and the combined cooking liquids. Cook this sauce for 25 minutes, or until very smooth; add 6 tablespoons double (heavy) cream and reduce. Then mix in 40 g

A SELECTION OF SEAFOOD

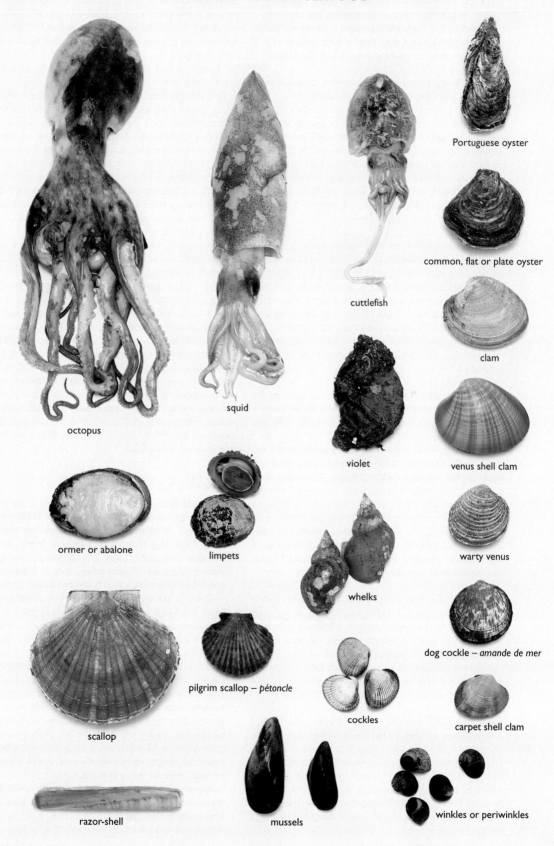

octopus

squid

cuttlefish

Portuguese oyster

common, flat or plate oyster

clam

violet

venus shell clam

ormer or abalone

limpets

whelks

warty venus

scallop

pilgrim scallop – *pétoncle*

cockles

dog cockle – *amande de mer*

carpet shell clam

razor-shell

mussels

winkles or periwinkles

(1½ oz, 3 tablespoons) butter and press through a sieve. Pour the sauce over the shellfish and keep hot without boiling. Meanwhile, prepare a risotto *à la piémontaise* and arrange it to form a large border in a deep dish. Pour the seafood mixture into the centre.

other recipes See *brochette, cannelloni, croûte, feuilleté, flan, macaroni, omelette* (flat omelettes).

SEAKALE A European plant that grows wild in coastal districts, but can be cultivated elsewhere. Seakale has broad, fleshy, pale-coloured leaf stalks, topped with tiny green leaves. It may be treated like asparagus – boiled or steamed and served with a seasoned sauce or melted butter; or blanched and braised, or sautéed with garlic, or eaten cold with a vinaigrette dressing.

SEAL *Loup marin* ('sea wolf') is the name given on the east coast of Canada to the seal, a sea mammal of the *Phocidae* family, which was once regularly hunted. Recent attempts have been made to commercialize it, but success has been limited. The seal's extremely nutritious flesh must first be removed from its fat, which has an extremely strong taste. It is floured and seared, then simmered for a long time in a casserole. The fins make a choice dish when braised.

SEAL, TO To begin cooking meat or poultry by dry-frying or frying in a small amount of fat over a high or moderate heat until firm outside, but not necessarily brown.

The edges of two layers of raw pastry, are moistened with water or glaze and sealed by pressing them gently together before baking. This operation is used when making tarts, pies, turnovers, rissoles and timbales.

Bottles of wine or preserves may be sealed with wax to help exclude air. The cork is pushed in until it is flush with the top of the bottle. Then the top of the bottle is plunged into melted wax, which hardens in about 20 minutes.

SEASONING The addition of various ingredients (salt, pepper, spices, condiments, aromatics, oil and vinegar) in variable quantities to a culinary preparation, either to give it a particular taste or to increase its palatability without changing the nature of the foods it contains. Seasoning is a delicate art that requires a precise knowledge of basic substances to bring out the best in the different flavours by blending them.

SEA SQUIRT A small, marine, invertebrate animal whose body is surrounded by a 'tunic', or sac-like membrane. The edible variety resembles a large purple-brown fig, hence its French nickname, *figue de mer*. It has two orifices through which it siphons water in and out, and attaches itself to rocks or the seabed. Found in the Mediterranean, it is split in half and the yellow part inside eaten raw, like the sea urchin.

SEA URCHIN A spiny, marine invertebrate comprising a spherical shell (called test), made of chalky platelets, which bears mobile spines. The shell encloses the digestive system, the locomotory system (the 'feet' pass through the shell) and the five yellow or orange genital glands. The latter form the edible portion (the coral).

There are numerous species of sea urchins worldwide, ranging in diameter from 2.5 cm (1 in) to 25 cm (10 in). Sea urchin is a popular delicacy in countries around the Mediterranean and in Japan. *Paracentrotus lividus*, found in the Mediterranean and off the coasts of Brittany and Ireland, is the species most commonly eaten in Europe. Japan imports sea urchins (whole or roe only) from North and South America and Korea, for use primarily in *sushi*. The Japanese consider the red sea urchin, *aki uni*, to be the best and generally eat it raw.

When fresh, the sea urchin should have firm spines and a tightly closed mouth orifice. It is opened by cutting into the soft tissue around the mouth, using pointed scissors or the specially designed French tool, *coupe-oursin*; by continuing right round, halfway up the shell, the top can be removed and the digestive system taken out and discarded. (Wear gloves when opening sea urchins.) The coral smells of iodine. It can be eaten raw, simply sprinkled with lemon juice, or crushed into a paste to flavour sauces, soufflés and scrambled eggs, to fill omelettes, to accompany fish or seafood or to garnish croûtes (toast). *Oursinade* is a thick sauce which, in Provence in France, is served as an accompaniment to poached fish; it is also the name of a fish soup of sea urchins.

RECIPES

langoustines in sea urchin shells
Dip 4 large tomatoes into boiling water for 2 minutes; peel, halve and seed them, then dice them finely. Heat 25 g (1 oz, 2 tablespoons) butter in a saucepan and gently cook 2 small finely chopped shallots. Add the diced tomato, salt and pepper, cook for 15 minutes, then set the pan aside.

Open 12 sea urchins and extract the edible part; strain the liquid and put it aside. Thoroughly clean the empty shells and set aside. Cut 12 langoustines in half; cook them in a little oil over a very high heat for 2 minutes, then shell them.

Put the sea urchin liquid and 2 tablespoons Cognac into a saucepan with 100 ml (4 fl oz, 7 tablespoons) dry white wine and 2 small chopped shallots; reduce by half. Add the tomatoes and reduce again for 2 minutes. Add 4 tablespoons double (heavy) cream, reduce again for 2–3 minutes, then whisk in 65 g (2½ oz, 5 tablespoons) butter. Heat the langoustines and the sea urchin corals through, without letting them boil.

To serve, heat the reserved sea urchin shells in the oven for a minute or two. Fill each with 1 tablespoon very hot sauce, langoustine and coral. Arrange on hot plates. Sprinkle with chervil leaves.

oursinade sauce

Melt 100 g (4 oz, ½ cup) butter in a heavy-based saucepan and add 6 egg yolks. Mix together and moisten with 2 or 3 glasses of the poaching liquid from the fish that the sauce is to cover. Beat until the mixture forms a smooth cream. Put into a bain marie, add the corals from 12 sea urchins and beat again until they are well blended.

sea urchin omelette

Lightly beat 12 eggs in a bowl; add a little pepper, then the juice of ½ lemon, and beat again. Add the corals from 12 sea urchins and mix them into the eggs. Heat a few drops of olive oil in a frying pan and cook the omelette. Serve it set, or slightly runny, with lemon juice.

sea urchin purée

Open the sea urchins, take out the corals and press them through a sieve. Add an equal quantity of very reduced béchamel sauce (or hollandaise sauce); heat the mixture while stirring and then beat in 25 g (1 oz, 2 tablespoons) butter.

This purée can be used to fill puff-pastry cases or tartlets. It can also be spread on slices of fried bread and then sprinkled with grated cheese and browned under the grill (broiler) or in the oven.

soupe oursinade

Clean 2 kg (4¼ lb) rockfish and small green crabs and cut the fish into pieces of about 5 cm (2 in). Make a roux with 50 g (2 oz, ¼ cup) butter and 75 g (3 oz, ¾ cup) plain (all-purpose) flour. Pour 150 ml (¼ pint, ⅔ cup) olive oil into a large saucepan. Clean and finely slice 1 leek, 1 fennel bulb and 1 celery stick; peel and crush the cloves from 1 small head (bulb) of garlic; peel and finely slice 2 or 3 onions. Put all the vegetables into the hot oil and cook over a low heat, adding 3 sprigs of parsley.

When the vegetables are soft, add the fish and the crabs and turn the heat up to its maximum. Add 1 sprig of thyme, 3 bay leaves, 5 fresh tomatoes (peeled, seeded and coarsely chopped) and 100 g (4 oz, ½ cup) tomato purée. Cook all these ingredients for about 10 minutes, until their juices run. Add the roux, then stir in 1 bottle white wine and finish with 4 litres (7 pints, 4 quarts) water. Bring to the boil. Add salt and pepper and cook, covered, over a moderate heat (or in a preheated oven at 180°C, 350°F, gas 4) for 30 minutes.

Then put everything through a vegetable mill or blender. Bring the soup to the boil again and add the liquid and corals from 24 sea urchins, 300 ml (½ pint, 1¼ cups) double (heavy) cream and 100 g (4 oz, ½ cup) shrimp butter*. Boil for 5 minutes, then pour the soup through a fine strainer and serve immediately.

SEAWEED Various marine plants, much used in Japanese cookery in particular. Most seaweeds form a single botanical group and are arranged in four large families – brown, red, blue (seaweeds that are entirely of a marine environment) and green (originating from land-based plants). Various seashore plants such as glasswort, whose habitat is the shoreline, are sometimes associated with seaweeds.

Seaweeds may be eaten fresh or used in a processed form – dried, compressed into sheets or powdered, for use as a seasoning.

SECHE Small, crumbly cake made in the French-speaking part of Switzerland from puff pastry, decorated with lardons, cumin or even sugar.

SEDUM A fleshy plant that grows in dry, sunny sites in parts of Europe, two common species being the wall pepper and the white stonecrop. The plants used to be eaten as vegetables and were recommended in particular by Olivier de Serres in the 17th century. Sedum leaves may be eaten raw in salads, or cooked with other leafy vegetables; or the leaves may be dried and ground to a powder for use as a seasoning.

SEELAC The French name for the black pollack (and sometimes also for hake) when it has been salted, smoked and marinated in oil. The name appears to come from the German *See* (lake) and *Lachs* (salmon).

SEIZE To cook meat, poultry or vegetables in hot fat or oil in a sauté pan, frying pan or saucepan until the surface is brown. Meat is seized in the preliminary stages of cooking to seal the juices. A joint to be roasted is sometimes treated in this way before being put into the oven.

SEKT The name often used for sparkling wines in Germany. The word was first used in the 19th century by the Berlin actor Ludwig Deurient, when ordering sack in the role of Falstaff. As he was also very fond of champagne, he would use the same word to describe his favourite drink in the restaurants. After this, German sparkling wines began to be referred to as 'Sekt'.

SELLES-SUR-CHER An AOP goat's-milk cheese from the Loire Valley, it is named after the village of Selles-sur-Cher near to Orleans. Produced in small 7–9 cm (3–3½ in) diameter discs, the cheese is always coated in ash. The white interior is firm, yet moist, with a sweet nutty flavour which sharpens as it matures.

SELTZER WATER A naturally sparkling mineral water or water that is charged with carbon dioxide gas under pressure. The name Seltzer is a corruption of Niederselters, a village in west Germany in the Taunus, whose mineral springs have been famous since the 18th century. Seltzer water is an ingredient in the preparation of many cocktails.

SÉMILLON White grape variety from Bordeaux. Originally from the region of Sauternes, it is the main grape used in all the great AOC wines of the Gironde, Dordogne and Lot-et-Garonne. It is also widely grown in Australia, Chile, Argentina, California and South Africa. Sémillon has medium-sized, compact bunches of grapes, juicy with a slightly musky flavour.

SEMOLINA A food obtained by coarsely grinding a cereal, mainly hard (durum) wheat, into granules. White semolina is ground from rice, semolina for polenta from maize (corn), and semolina for *kasha* from buckwheat. Yellow semolina is made from wheat and coloured with saffron; it resembles cornmeal in appearance.

The grains are first moistened, then ground, dried and sieved. Both light and nourishing, semolina (from the Latin *simila*, meaning 'flower of flour') is used to make pasta and to prepare soups, garnishes and dishes such as couscous, tabbouleh, gnocchi, puddings, rings, cakes, custards and soufflés.

High-grade semolina is made by grinding the wheat kernel, whereas ordinary semolina contains more of the peripheral part of the grain (and therefore a higher percentage of minerals). Fine semolinas are generally used to make pasta, whereas medium and coarse semolinas are used in soups and desserts. Very fine semolinas are used in baby foods.

RECIPES

baked semolina pudding
Bring to the boil in a flameproof casserole 1 litre (1¾ pints, 4⅓ cups) milk containing 150 g (5 oz, ⅔ cup) caster (superfine) sugar, a pinch of salt and a vanilla pod (bean) split in half. Mix in 250 g (9 oz, 1½ cups) semolina and 75–100 g (3–4 oz, 6–8 tablespoons) butter, then cover the pan and cook in a preheated oven at 200°C (400°F, gas 6) for 25–30 minutes.

semolina subrics
Make a baked semolina pudding as above, remove from the oven and mix in 6 egg yolks. Leave to cool a little, then spread it in a layer 2 cm (¾ in) thick over a buttered baking sheet. Brush the surface with melted butter to prevent a crust forming and leave to cool completely. Cut out rounds using a 6 cm (2½ in) pastry (cookie) cutter and brown them in a frying pan in clarified butter. Arrange them in a ring in a round dish and fill the centre with redcurrant jelly or with another red jelly or jam (preserve).

other recipes See *croustade, pudding*.

SENDERENS, ALAIN French chef (born 1939). A native of south-western France, he went to Paris at the age of 21 after his apprenticeship in Lourdes. He progressed from pantry-keeper to head roasting chef at the Tour d'Argent, then joined Marc Soustelle's staff at Lucas-Carton as sauce cook. After serving as head fish chef at the Berkeley, he became assistant chef at the newly opened Orly Hilton. In 1973 he opened his own restaurant in Paris; he named it L'Archestrate, in honour of the ancient Greek poet and gourmet Archestratus. Since 1985 he has been in charge of the renowned and innovative cuisine at Lucas-Carton.

Well read in gastronomy, Senderens has created imaginative new dishes using 'thousands of combinations and mixtures which have not yet been tried'. He combines ingredients, flavours and cooking methods, creating some of the most original recipes: salads of crayfish with mango, duck and basil or of warm calves' sweetbreads with raw cep mushrooms; veal ribs (chops) with tea and cucumber; turbot with broad (fava) beans; magrets of duck with honey and thyme blossom; hot guava charlotte with kiwi fruit sauce; millefeuille with medlars; and melon fritters with strawberry sauce. However, he has also been inspired by ancient recipes to create such dishes as hare quenelles, eel broth, hot oysters with leeks, and leg of mutton.

SÉRAC White cheese made from cow's milk, strained and ground, with little fat, made by hand in Savoy and the French-speaking part of Switzerland. A version of this cheese is made from the residues left in whey after the curds have been removed from Beaufort cheese. Sérac is mixed with melilot, a strong-smelling clover, to make Schabzieger, a cheese typical of the Glarus Alps.

SERDEAU An officer of the king's household in France, who disposed of the leftover food cleared away by the maître d'hôtel. The term was also used for the place where the leftovers were sold. At the French court, it was the custom to keep food ready for those whose duty or business called them to the king; dishes cleared from the royal table were taken to a special room for this purpose. When the custom of serving food to the king's guests was abandoned, the king's leftovers were taken straight to the serdeau and sold by auction. This practice was still in existence during the reign of Louis XVI, and many households were provisioned in this way. The servants of the serdeau traded from the *baraques du serdeau*, next to the barracks of the French Guards at Versailles.

SERGE, À LA Term for a dish of calves' sweetbreads or veal escalopes coated with a mixture of fresh breadcrumbs, truffles and chopped mushrooms, then fried and garnished with small artichoke quarters stewed in butter and a coarse julienne of ham warmed in Madeira. The sauce is a demi-glace flavoured with truffle essence.

SERRA-DA-ESTRELA Soft Portuguese DOP ewe's-milk cheese (45–60% fat content) with washed crust. It is a cylinder 15–20 cm (6–8 in) in diameter and 4–6 cm (1½–2½ in) thick, weighing 1–1.7 kg

(2¼–3¾ lb). Made in the mountainous region of the same name, the flowers and leaves of wild thistles are added to the curds. It has a sweet flavour when young, which becomes piquant after more than 6 weeks of maturing.

SERRER

A French culinary term that means to finish whisking egg whites with a quick circular movement of the whisk, making them very stiff and homogeneous.

A sauce is described as *serrée* when its consistency is thick enough (for example, béchamel sauce to be used for binding salpicons) or when it is reduced to make it creamier and increase its flavour.

SERRES, OLIVIER DE

French agronomist (born Villeneuve-de-Berg, 1539; died Villeneuve-de-Berg, 1619). He studied at the university of Valence, then at Lausanne, where his Calvinist convictions had forced him to take refuge. His estate at Pradel, near Privas, became a model farm, where he was the first to grow plants and cereals on a rationalized economic basis. He introduced maize (corn), sugar beet, hops and rice into France and also experimented with madder and silkworms. Encouraged by Sully, he also gained the support of the king, Henri IV, to whom he suggested the recipe for *poule au pot.*

In order to revive domestic gardening and animal husbandry, he published *Théâtre d'agriculture et mesnage des champs* (1600), which popularized agronomy and was highly successful (19 successive editions during the 17th century). The book offered a detailed and comprehensive study of rural farming methods and country life, covering grapes, cereals, winter stores, hunting and fishing, poultry, kitchen gardens and even bread-making. In addition, it provided information on the culinary uses and gastronomic qualities of animal and vegetable foodstuffs – describing for the first time the tuber that was later to be called the potato, and mentioning a process for the extraction of sweet juice from sugar beet. Serres also advocated the introduction of American poultry, such as the turkey, into France and gave a number of recipes for jam (preserve) and for 'everything that can be made with wheat flour alone: biscuits, brassadeaux, cache-museaux, échaudés, fougasses, macaroons, oublies, popelins and tourtillons'. His dictum was:

> *Provision faite en saison*
> *Et gouvernée par la raison*
> *Fait devenir bonne la maison.*

('A thriving household depends on the use of seasonal produce and the application of common sense.')

SERVERY

office A room in a restaurant, generally adjoining the kitchen, where all the items of table service are kept, and where certain dishes (cold hors d'oeuvre and salads) may be prepared. Wines are also placed there to reach room temperature.

In classic French cuisine, the word *office* was used for the branch of the culinary art that involved, according to Carême, 'the preparation and making of all the delightful delicacies that are offered as dessert at the tables of the wealthy'.

SERVICE

Originally, the group of dishes comprising each part of a formal meal. There were at least three services. The term also indicated the manner in which they were presented to the guests. Service *à la française* lasted until the end of France's Second Empire, when it was replaced by service *à la russe*.

■ **Service à la française** This was a continuation of the ceremony of the *grand couvert* observed during the reign of Louis XIV. Because it was so costly, it was practised only by grand houses on important occasions. A meal served *à la française* was divided into three (or four) parts: the first service covered the menu from the soup to the roasts, including the hors d'oeuvre and entrées; the second from the roasts, cold second roasts and vegetables to the sweet dishes; and the third consisted of pastries, set pieces, petits fours, sweets, ices and fruit. The order of the menu depended on the number of entrées; the number of dishes in the first service had to be equal to that of the second service. The dishes of the first service were arranged on the table (on hotplates or under covers, if necessary) before the arrival of the guests. A dazzling display of silverware, candelabra, glasses and flowers completed the effect.

The arrangement and order of the dishes on the table was very important. The service of a dinner for six to eight, for example, consisted of 'a main dish, two medium dishes and four smaller dishes' (from Massialot's *Le Cuisinier royal et bourgeois*, 1691). The first service comprised: at the centre, a piece of beef garnished with small pies and sweetbreads; two soups arranged symmetrically on each side (pigeon bisque and capon soup with lettuce and asparagus tips); four other entrées arranged two by two (spit-roasted chicken and fillet steaks with lettuce on one side, hot rabbit pâté and goslings with asparagus tips on the other). During the second service, three roast dishes were arranged along the centre of the table: two chickens, two hares and eight pigeons, with two salads and two sauces in separate dishes on either side. The centrepiece of the third service was a spit-roasted ham with a cream tart and a dish of choux pastries placed at each end; a ham loaf and skewered sweetbreads on the left faced a ragoût of mushrooms and asparagus on the right. Fruit was served with the dessert.

This service has often been criticized for sacrificing everything to ostentation and extravagance; the guests' appetites were not assuaged as they could not enjoy the food hot, in spite of the hotplates and covers, which appeared in the 18th century. In fact, the dishes did not remain long on the table; Massialot specified that they should be left for only a quarter of an hour or a little longer. Also, as all the food was placed on the table, the guests could serve themselves immediately without having to wait for dishes to be passed. But why was it thought that so many different dishes should be offered at each service? *L'Art de bien traiter* (1674) suggests an answer: 'Many people reject and condemn good things for which they have never developed a taste . . . it is therefore necessary to provide a choice.' The former service *à la française*, which depended on a large and experienced staff (if only to avoid wasting the leftovers, some of which were often reusable), treated the guests with courtesy by offering a variety of dishes.

Horace Raisson's *Code gourmand* (1829) is a good illustration of the latter days of the service *à la française*:

'*Article 1* – A grand dinner is composed of four services. The first should be the most substantial, as the appetite is sharpest; it comprises relevés and entrées. The roasts, escorted by salads and complementary vegetables, appear next. The third service consists of dishes hot from the oven arranged around an impressive cold dish. A dessert to delight the pretty ladies' eyes comes later.

Art. 2 – The hors d'oeuvre remain on the table until the third service, to whet the appetite.

Art. 3 – After each act of this gastronomic drama the table should be bare, but only for a moment, until the new dishes of the next service make their entrance.

Art. 4 – If it is impossible for the host to serve all the dishes himself and look after each guest individually, he should place carefully those of his friends on whose goodwill he can count.

Art. 5 – Dishes which do not require carving and which can be served with a spoon are available to all; each guest can serve himself and pass the dish on to whoever asks for it.

Art. 6 – The servants retire after the savoury courses. During the dessert each guest serves himself with whatever takes his fancy, asking his neighbour to pass him dishes that are out of reach.

Art. 7 – Jams, compotes and ice creams are the only dishes that require a spoon (which should be gilded). Other dishes are served by hand.

Art. 8 – Ordinary wines are placed in orderly profusion along the table, but the host should pour the choice wines for his neighbours and then circulate the bottle until empty.'

■ **Service à la russe** It was Prince Alexander Borisovitch Kourakine, the tsar's ambassador to Paris during the Second Empire, who introduced service *à la russe* into high society, from where it spread throughout the catering world. For the grand dinners he gave at the embassy he launched a new form of service, which Urbain Dubois popularized around 1880 and introduced to middle-class homes. It was characterized by less formality, less ostentation and fewer displays of silverware; flowers and pyramids of fruit were used in their place as table decorations. The aim was to eat hot dishes as hot as possible and, instead of leaving guests to choose from a variety of dishes, the order was arranged in advance and the dishes presented one after the other. Luxury and extravagance were replaced by the principle that everything should proceed as quickly as possible, so

that dishes would not lose their flavour. The presentation and appearance of the food, however, remained important (especially for cold dishes, aspics, chilled chicken, and so on). It was easier to serve dishes hot, as a set time for the meal allowed the chef to calculate cooking times accordingly.

In service *à la russe*, the guests are divided into groups of 8, 10 or 12, each of which is served by a maître d'hôtel who is instructed in advance which guests to serve first. Dishes are served from the left of a seated person and the plates are taken away or put down from the right. The wine is served from the right in the same order as the food, but the first drops are poured into the host's glass. In a less formal meal, the master of the house carves and serves the meat himself and passes the filled plates round the table, beginning with the person on his right.

■ **Catering services** In catering there are four types of service which are rarely, if ever, undertaken in private households. In the 'simple' service the food is placed directly on the plates or the dishes are placed on the table (service *à l'assiette*). In service *à la française* each guest serves himself from a dish with serving spoons. In service *à l'anglaise* the waiter places the food on the diner's plate. Finally, in service *à la russe*, also known as *à l'anglaise avec guéridon* or *au guéridon*, the dish is first offered for the guests' admiration and then the food is placed on the plates at a pedestal table (*guéridon*) beside the dining table.

SERVIETTE, À LA This describes a way of serving certain foods, particularly truffles. Truffles *à la serviette* are poached, then arranged in a timbale mould or a casserole, which is placed on a napkin folded into the shape of a pocket. If they have been cooked *en papillote* in hot ashes, they are placed directly on the napkin. Potatoes baked in their skins can also be served *à la serviette*, as can boiled asparagus, which is arranged without dressing on a white folded napkin.

Rice *à la serviette* is cooked in simmering salted water, drained, rinsed under cold running water and wrapped in a napkin to dry out in a cool oven. Ham and duck liver wrapped in a cloth and tied with string are known as *à la serviette*, but should more correctly be called *au torchon*.

SESAME An annual plant grown in hot countries for its seeds, from which an odourless light-coloured oil is extracted. Sesame oil has a sweet flavour, which resembles that of hempseed oil, and keeps well without turning rancid. It is widely used in Middle- and Far-Eastern cookery as a cooking oil or, more often, as a condiment or seasoning, although it loses its flavour quite quickly.

Sesame seeds have a nutty taste, which is more pronounced when they are toasted, and have many uses in cooking. They can be sprinkled over bread (for example, burger buns) and sweet and savoury biscuits (cookies and crackers). In the Middle East, sesame seeds are ground with sugar and almonds to make a sweet compressed bar called halva; they are also ground to an oily savoury paste called tahina or tahini, which is an important ingredient in hummus, a Middle-Eastern dip.

In China, a syrupy nourishing drink is made from the seeds; they are used to make prawn toast, an open deep-fried sandwich of sesame seeds and ground prawns (shrimp) on bread; and are sprinkled over Chinese toffee apples. In Japan, *gomasio* is a popular seasoning, comprising lightly toasted sesame seeds and sea salt.

In the American South, the seeds are called benne seeds. In parts of Africa and Asia, they are called *ajonjoli*, and are reddish in colour and eaten roasted, like peanuts.

SÈTOISE, À LA Describing a dish of monkfish, a fish much used (usually in bourride) in the cookery of Sète, a town in southern France. The fish is cooked briskly with a julienne of vegetables stewed in olive oil and white wine; it is then drained and coated in a thick mayonnaise mixed with the reduced cooking juices.

SÉVIGNÉ, MARIE DE RABUTIN-CHANTAL, MARQUISE DE Parisian woman of letters (born Paris, 1626; died Grignan, 1696). In letters written to her daughter, Mme de Grignan, she gave detailed accounts of meals enjoyed and culinary or gastronomic novelties, such as the first new peas of spring, chocolate and Amiens duck pâté. She described regional specialities (melons, figs and Muscat grapes from Grignan; poulardes from Rennes; fruit pâté from Apt, a town she called a 'cauldron of jams'; and calissons from Aix, sent to her by her daughter), as well as good stopping places encountered during her travels, such as the Auberge du Dauphin at Saulieu, and M. de Chaulnes' table at Vitré: 'There is an excess of good food, whole roasts are returned to the kitchen, and the pyramids of fruit are so high that the doorways have to be raised.' In her letter of 24 April 1671 she even mentions the death of the 'great Vatel', a famous Swiss maître d'hôtel.

A dish of soft-boiled (soft-cooked) or poached eggs on a bed of braised lettuce, covered with suprême sauce and topped with a slice of truffle, was dedicated to her.

SEYSSEL AOC dry and light white wines of Savoy. They are made from the Altesse (or Roussette) grape, but sparkling Seyssel, known locally as Bon-Blanc, is made from the Molette, Chasselas and Roussette grapes.

SHAD A migratory fish belonging to the herring family, which lives in the sea and travels upriver to spawn. The allis shad, which can measure up to 60 cm (2 ft) in length, and the smaller twaite shad are the main species found in Europe. The American shad is found in both Pacific and Atlantic waters.

Shad flesh is tasty and quite rich, but quickly deteriorates and is full of small fine bones. It was popu-

lar with the Romans and frequently appeared in recipes in the Middle Ages. Traditionally served with sorrel, shad is often stuffed and may be grilled (broiled) or baked.

RECIPES

preparing shad
Carefully scale and gut (clean) the shad, keeping the roe. Using plenty of cold water, wash the fish well on the outside to remove the remains of the scales, and on the inside to wash away the blood. Dry it with paper towels.

fried shad
Cut the fish into slices and soak in milk. Coat them with flour and plunge into hot fat. Fry the fish until golden, then drain and arrange on a napkin with fried parsley and lemon quarters.

grilled shad with sorrel
Gut (clean), scale, wash and dry a shad, weighing about 1 kg (2¼ lb). Make regular slits in the fleshy part of the back and both sides. Season with salt and pepper and marinate for 1 hour in oil, with a little lemon juice, chopped parsley, thyme and a bay leaf. Drain the fish, grill (broil) under a medium heat for 30 minutes or until tender, then arrange the fish on a long dish, surrounded by lemon quarters or slices. Serve with maître d'hôtel butter and a garnish of lightly braised sorrel.

shad au plat
Choose a shad weighing 675–800 g (1½–1¾ lb). Gut (clean) the fish and fill the cavity with a mixture of 50 g (2 oz, ¼ cup) butter kneaded with 1 tablespoon chopped parsley, 1½ teaspoons chopped shallot, salt and pepper. Place the shad on a long buttered ovenproof dish. Season with salt and pepper, sprinkle over 100 ml (4 fl oz, 7 tablespoons) dry white wine, dot with small pieces of butter and cook in a preheated oven at about 200°C (400°F, gas 6) for 15–20 minutes. Baste frequently during cooking. If the liquid reduces too quickly, add a little water. Serve on the cooking dish.

Shad may also be cooked *à la provençale* and *à la bonne femme*.

stuffed shad à la mode de Cocherel
For a 2 kg (4½ lb) fish, prepare a stuffing by crushing in a mortar or processing in a blender 300 g (11 oz) whiting flesh. Add 1 egg white, salt, pepper and grated nutmeg, then 350 ml (12 fl oz, 1½ cups) double (heavy) cream. Mix together well with a wooden spatula, preferably standing the bowl in a large container of ice to prevent the cream from turning. Finally, add 4 teaspoons blanched, drained and snipped chives and 2 teaspoons finely chopped parsley.

Stuff the shad with this mixture and wrap very thin strips of bacon around it. Then tie it up to hold its shape and cook in a preheated oven at 180°C (350°F, gas 4) or on a spit over a high heat for 30–45 minutes. Remove the bacon strips and cook for another 5 minutes to brown the fish. Deglaze the dripping pan with 175 ml (6 fl oz, ¾ cup) dry white wine, add 400 ml (14 fl oz, 1¾ cups) double (heavy) cream, and reduce, finally adding salt and pepper. Arrange the shad on a long dish and surround with small new potatoes cooked in butter, quarters of small artichokes blanched and gently cooked in butter, and some small glazed onions.

Shad may also be stuffed *à la portugaise*.

SHAGGY CAP An edible mushroom with a bell-shaped cap covered with shaggy hairs, also known as ink cap and lawyer's wig. It should be picked when young and firm and eaten soon afterwards, since the flesh is extremely delicate (it quickly becomes black and liquefies). It may be eaten raw with salt or sautéed in oil or butter with a touch of garlic.

SHAKER A stainless steel or silver-plated utensil shaped like a tall goblet, slightly wider at the top and with a closely fitting lid, in which the ingredients for a cocktail are mixed by shaking them with ice. Small models contain 500 ml (17 fl oz, 2 cups) liquid, large ones 1 litre (1¾ pints, 4⅓ cups). A shaker is especially recommended for cocktails based on cream or a syrupy liqueur, or those containing egg, milk or fruit juice.

SHALLOT A small bulb vegetable related to the onion, whose name is derived from Ascalon, an ancient port in Palestine, suggesting that the plant originated in the Middle East. It was already being grown in France at the time of the Carolingians (AD 751–987). The flavour of the shallot is more subtle than that of onion and less harsh than that of garlic. Varieties include grey shallots, with a small bulb and a pronounced but fine flavour; Jersey shallots, round and red and akin to the onion; pear hallots, with a large elongated bulb; Simiane shallots, grown in the south of France, with a large bulb; and the long pink banana shallots.

When wrapped in a cloth, put under cold water, and then pressed, the shallot loses some of its pungency. As with onion and garlic, it is unwise to keep shallots in the refrigerator, as other foods may be pervaded by the smell.

The shallot is widely used in French cooking, especially for flavouring sauces (Bercy, béarnaise, red wine and white butter sauce in particular), as well as vinegar (1 head of shallot is steeped for 2 weeks in wine vinegar) and flavoured butters.

Finely chopped shallot bulbs are served raw with salads and crudités, and with fish and grilled (broiled) or fried meats (such as red mullet and lamb's liver). Young shallot leaves, finely chopped, can also be added to salads.

As well as being a standard ingredient in French cookery, shallots are used extensively in Vietnamese,

SHALLOTS

semi-long Jersey or Brittany

long Jersey or Brittany

round Jersey or Brittany

grey

Thai, Malaysian, Indonesian, Chinese, Indian and Creole cookery. In China, fresh or pickled shallots are served with preserved eggs as a snack.

RECIPE

shallot sauce
Peel some shallots and chop them very finely. Add to a good wine vinegar and season with salt and pepper. This sauce is traditionally served with oysters or raw mussels.

SHANDY A mixture of two drinks in almost equal quantities. The equivalent French term, *panache*, can mean a mixture of coffee and alcohol, but the British term is usually used to describe a mixture of beer and lemonade or ginger beer.

SHAPING Process of giving cheese its shape after the curds have been broken up.

Fresh cheeses are shaped after the curds have drained, while soft cheeses with a mould crust are shaped before draining, and are then salted and coated with a culture of bacteria. Soft cheeses with a washed crust and blue cheeses are put in perforated moulds, while wooden and cloth moulds, which make pressing easier, are used for cooked and uncooked pressed cheeses. Goat's cheeses are drained in moulds of various kinds. Shaped curd (*pasta filata*) cheeses are moulded by hand and the plasticity of the curds enables them to be given original shapes (pear shapes in particular).

SHARK An edible cartilaginous fish with an elongated body, a pointed snout and a broad mouth. There are numerous species of shark, ranging in size from the small dogfish, with a maximum length of 1.5 m (5 ft), to the gigantic whale shark, which can reach 18 m (60 ft).

Shark has boneless, firm, meaty white flesh, which has a tendency to smell of ammonia. It is available fresh, frozen, smoked and dried-salted, and eaten in many countries around the world. Some of the smaller sharks may be sold whole, but fillets or loin steaks are more commonly available. The smaller species of dogfish, such as the smooth hound and the spur dog (often marketed as huss and 'rock salmon' in Britain, as flake in Australia and *saumonette* in France) are usually sold skinned with head and tail removed, thus looking most unshark-like. Dogfish may be prepared and cooked like cod or other large fish, and much of it is used in the British fish-and-chip trade. In general, shark meat can be tough and often benefits from being marinated before cooking; shark's fins are an ingredient of a famous Chinese soup.

Some of the more popular edible shark species from around the globe include mako (called *yoshikirizame* in Japan); porbeagle, which is popular in countries around the North Atlantic and the Mediterranean; the blue shark, found in temperate and tropical waters worldwide; the soupfin shark, the preferred species for producing dried shark's fin; the leopard shark, a uniquely patterned shark with excellent meat, caught off the Californian coast; whiskery, a stocky dogfish caught off the southern and western coasts of Australia; the thresher shark, found in all warm seas; and tope.

RECIPE

shark à la créole

Slice the flesh of a small shark and marinate it for several hours in the juice of 2 limes diluted with water, garlic, salt, pepper and 1 chilli pepper. Slice 2 onions and 4–5 shallots and wash 3 tomatoes; brown all these in a saucepan along with 2 chilli peppers, 3 garlic cloves and 1 bouquet garni. Drain the fish pieces, place them on top of the vegetables and cook with the pan covered. To serve, sprinkle with lime juice, chopped parsley and a little grated garlic. Serve with rice *à la créole* and red kidney beans.

SHARK'S FINS Fins and cartilaginous terminal segments of the tail of certain species of shark, sold dried whole or as long yellowish-white needles. This rare and costly product, reputed to be an aphrodisiac, is widely used in Chinese cooking. Probably the best-known dish is shark's fin soup, traditionally served to the mandarins at their banquets. The dried fins must be soaked overnight in chicken stock, then boiled for about 3 hours. The soup is made from shrimps, sweet-smelling mushrooms, ginger, onions and soy sauce and is garnished with the shark's fins, along with sliced ham, crabmeat and very thin slices of bamboo.

SHASHLYK A Russian dish, originating from Georgia, made of skewered raw mutton taken from a well-hung leg, cut into cubes and marinated in vinaigrette flavoured with thyme, nutmeg, bay leaf and onions. The skewers of meat are grilled (broiled), then served with rice moistened with melted butter. Raw ham and onion rings may be inserted between the cubes of meat.

SHEA A tree from tropical Africa with oval fruit containing oily seeds. When the seeds are dried and crushed, they yield a white butter-like fat called shea butter. This is used instead of cooking fat in some African countries, and can also be used to make soap and candles.

SHELDUCK A large duck resembling a goose in shape. This and a closely related species, the ruddy shelduck, are now protected by law. Formerly, they were prepared like wild duck and regarded as Lenten fare. Their flesh has a pronounced fishy taste, since they eat shellfish and roe.

SHELLFISH Aquatic invertebrates, with a shell or carapace, many of which are edible. There are two main classes of shellfish: crustaceans and molluscs.

■ **Crustaceans** These are arthropods and most of them are marine. The marine crustaceans include lobsters, langoustes (spiny lobsters), crabs and shrimps; the only freshwater crustacean used in cookery is the crayfish. Crustaceans must be bought very fresh and are best bought live if you are to prepare them yourself. Crustaceans are available ready cooked, frozen and canned. The heaviest crabs and lobsters are the best; they should still have their claws on.

Crustaceans can be prepared and cooked *à l'américaine*, as bisque soup, fried, poached in court-bouillon or grilled (broiled), depending on the species. They are also served in cold hors d'oeuvre – the large ones are shelled (legs, claws and trunks), while small ones are left whole or served in the form of tails by themselves, shelled.

■ **Molluscs** This group includes bivalves (clams, cockles, mussels, oysters and scallops), gastropods (winkles, whelks, ormers and limpets) and cephalopods (squid and octopus). Unless they are bought where they are caught, only shellfish that come from reputable areas and which are subject to some sort of quality control should be used.

Only molluscs with closed shells or that close on touching should be retained. Molluscs that are cooked in their shells and which remain closed after cooking should not be eaten. Similarly, only live gastropods, with a healthy smell of the sea, should be consumed.

See also *seafood*.

CRUSTACEANS

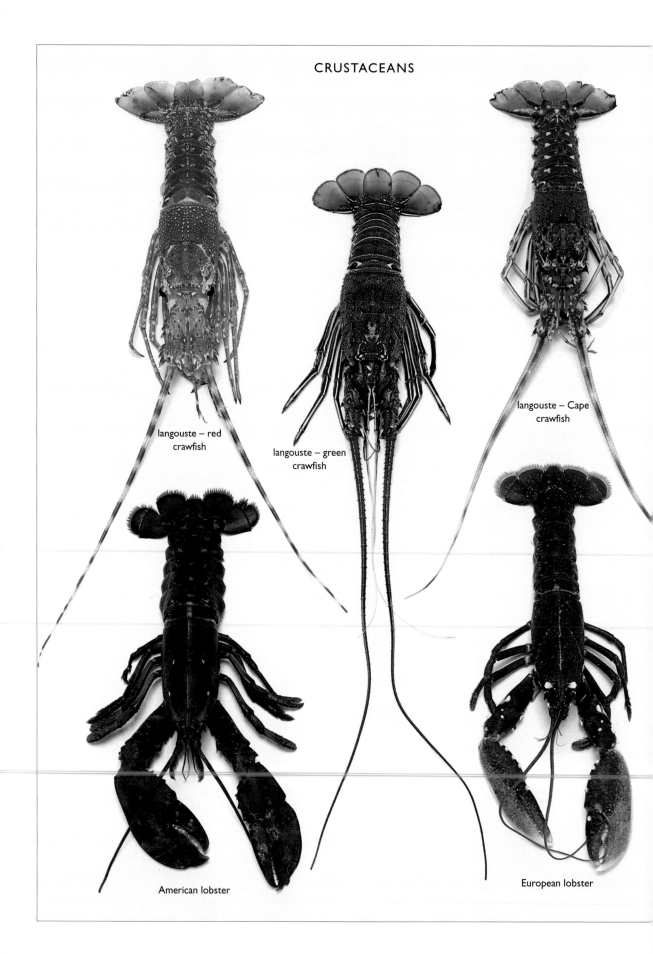

langouste – red
crawfish

langouste – green
crawfish

langouste – Cape
crawfish

American lobster

European lobster

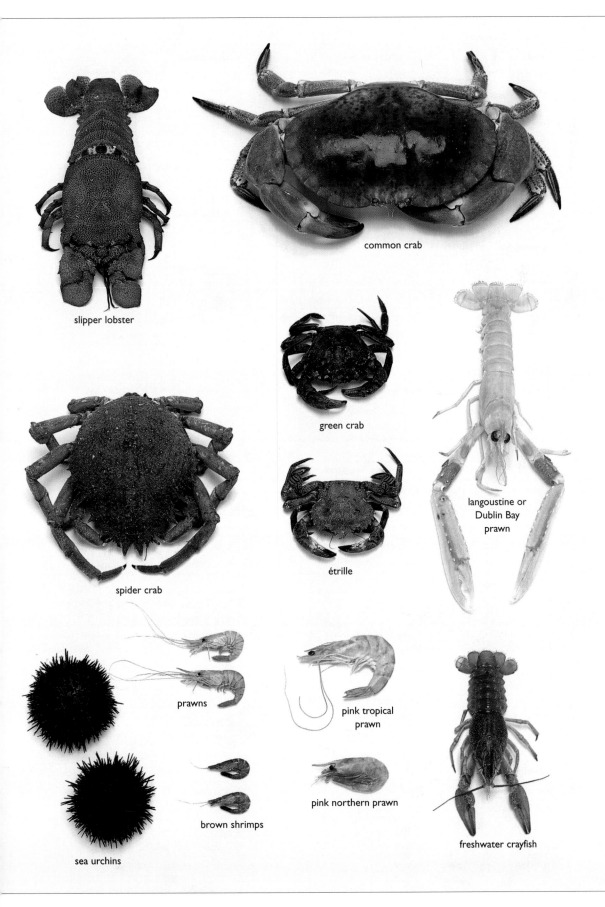

slipper lobster

common crab

green crab

langoustine or
Dublin Bay
prawn

spider crab

étrille

sea urchins

prawns

brown shrimps

pink tropical
prawn

pink northern prawn

freshwater crayfish

Bivalves and gastropods

name	where found	appearance
bivalves		
clam	Atlantic, Pacific	large, smooth, brown shell
clam, carpet shell	Atlantic	ridged, yellow-brown shell
cockle	English Channel, Atlantic	oval, white shell
dog cockle – amande de mer	English Channel, Atlantic	velvety, brown shell
queen scallop (black)	Atlantic, Mediterranean	ears of unequal size, brown shell
queen scallop (white)	English Channel, Atlantic	ears of unequal size, white shell
razor shell	English Channel	rectangular, dark beige shell
venus shell clam	Atlantic, Mediterranean	large, smooth, tawny-brown shell
warty venus (small clam)	English Channel, Atlantic	concentric sides, grey-white shell
gastropods		
lambis	West Indies	mother-of-pearl inside, pink shell
limpet	Atlantic, English Channel	regular, oval, raised, brown shell
ormer or abalone	English Channel, Mediterranean	oval, grey shell
whelk	English Channel, Mediterranean	conical, bulbous, spiral, brown shell
winkle	Atlantic, Ireland	globular, brown or white shell

Crustaceans

name	where found	appearance
langoustine or Dublin Bay prawn	Europe	pink, first claws prism-shaped
sea urchin	rocky coasts of the Atlantic and Mediterranean	6–8 cm (2½–3½ in), flattened shell, long spines, sharp, greenish brown or violet
crabs		
common crab	Atlantic, English Channel	stocky, large claws, chestnut brown
green or enraged crab	Atlantic, Mediterranean	small, green-brown
slipper lobster	Mediterranean	stocky, foreshortened, red-brown
small swimming crab – étrille	Atlantic, English Channel	small, flat, brown, smooth, fine meat
spider crab	Atlantic, English Channel	12–20 cm (5–8 in), long feet, fine meat
shrimps and prawns		
bouquet prawn	Brittany, Vendée	5–10 cm (2–4 in), pinky-grey (uncooked) or red (cooked)
brown shrimp	Atlantic, English Channel, North Sea	5 cm (2 in), grey (uncooked) or brown (cooked)
pink northern prawn	North Atlantic, North Pacific	5–7 cm (2–3 in), pinky-grey (uncooked) or pink (cooked)
pink tropical prawn	tropical West Africa, Indonesia, Thailand, Guyana, and farmed	9–15 cm (4–6 in), pinky-grey (uncooked) or pink (cooked)
lobsters		
American lobster	east coast of Canada, United States	brown with green reflections, clawed rostrum
European lobster	Atlantic, Mediterranean	dark or bright blue, straight 'beak', white meat
crawfish – langouste		
Cape crawfish	South Africa	scaly, brown-red
Cuban crawfish	West Indies	brown-red, light touches
green crawfish	West Africa	long antennae with antennules, blue-green
pink crawfish	Atlantic	stocky, starred with little light touches
red crawfish	Europe	stocky, brown-red or purplish red

SHEPHERD'S PIE A British dish consisting of a minced (ground) meat sauce topped with mashed potato, baked until crisp and golden on top. Shepherd's pie differs from cottage pie in that it is made with minced lamb, unlike cottage pie, which is made with minced beef. The meat sauce should be made with fresh mince, cooked with carrots and onions, but the pie is also a traditional way of using leftovers from the Sunday roast, when minced or diced cooked lamb (or beef in the case of cottage pie) is combined with leftover gravy, cooked onions and carrots.

SHERRY The best-known fortified wine of Spain, which gets its name from the town of Jerez de la Frontera in Andalucia. The name 'sherry' is now restricted to fortified wines produced within the Jerez Denominación de Origen. Wines of the 'sherry-type' originating from other areas or countries, at least within the European Union, may no longer use the name.

The main grape is Palamino Fino, which grows in the porous, white albariza soils of the demarcated vineyards. Some Moscatel Gordo Blanco (Muscat of Alexandria) and Pedro Ximénez (PX) is grown for sweetening.

The wine is started in the same way as other wines and undergoes a vigorous fermentation, after which it goes into the *bodegas* (wine stores) of the shippers. At this stage, all sherry is a completely dry wine, fully fermented so that the sugar in the original must is transformed into alcohol by the yeasts. The wine is fortified with brandy. Maturation takes place in the *bodegas* in what is known as the *solera* system. This varies from company to company, but essentially consists of a series of casks graded by age. It is a fractional blending system whereby *flor* (Spanish for 'flower'), a yeast growth on the surface of the wine in the cask that affects its character and maturation, can be nourished by the addition of the nutrients of young wines. When a consignment of sherry is required, wines are drawn off from the casks according to age and character and then blended. The arrangement and proportions in which the wines are drawn off and the casks refreshed from other wines is both complex and individual to the particular sherry house concerned. The name *solera* is given to both the process and the casks.

In the early stages, the various sherries are categorized according to whether or not they will develop *flor*. Those that do are the *finos*, those that do not are the *olorosos*. From this time onwards, the different sherries progress through the *solera* at varying rates, sometimes skipping a stage, sometimes going steadily from one cask to another. It is not always the case that, in the rows of high-piled casks in a *bodega*, the ones on the top row are gradually decanted off to the row beneath until they get to the bottom. Nor is it necessarily true that the dates on the sherry butts or huge casks in a *bodega* refer to the age of the wine inside: they usually refer to the year when the *solera* or the particular cask was first laid down.

Sherry of all types is completely dry when first made; the sweetening takes place later to suit the various demands of the markets. Thus, although a *fino* will normally be dry, the *fino* of certain establishments may quite legally receive some sweetening to suit their customers. Similarly, *oloroso* is a naturally dry sherry that is slightly or definitely sweetened if required. A matured *fino,* where the *flor* dies, will turn into an *amontillado.* Certain commercial sherries may be made up from a blend of different wines (not from the wines of a single *solera*), which can make them more appealing to many people and slightly cheaper. *Manzanilla* is the sherry matured at Sanlúcar de Barrameda on the coast, where the cooling sea breezes encourage the development of thicker *flor.* Puerto Fino is matured at Puerto de Santa Maria and again benefits from a cooler, more humid climate. Both *manzanilla* and *fino* are at their most enjoyable when young, fresh and crisp and make excellent aperitifs. Sweet sherries described as 'cream' or 'milk' are hardly known in Spain; they were evolved for the northern markets where, in the colder climates, sweetness is still enjoyed.

Although the production of sherry is strictly controlled, each establishment makes sherries according to its own standards and to the taste of its customers as described above. The term dry sherry is thus very broad, depending on the establishment and certainly on how much is paid for the wine! This also applies to medium sherry, which can be a magnificent *amontillado,* or an agreeable but inexpensive version of this category.

Very light, delicate *fino* sherry should be lightly chilled and will cease to be at its best if the bottle is not finished within a day or two of opening. The sweeter wines should be drunk within 7–10 days. The remains of any bottle can be be used up in cooking. Always serve sherry in a goblet or *copita* glass, shaped like an elongated tulip, and never fill this to the brim – sherry has a bouquet that deserves to be appreciated.

RECIPE

chicken with sherry
Cut a 1.25 kg (2¾ lb) chicken into quarters. Slightly brown 50 g (2 oz, ¼ cup) butter in a flameproof casserole and thoroughly brown the chicken pieces in it. Season with salt and pepper, cover and cook for about 35 minutes, adding 1 finely chopped shallot 10 minutes before the end of cooking. Remove the chicken pieces and keep hot on a serving dish. Blend 1 teaspoon arrowroot with 150 ml (¼ pint, ⅔ cup) medium sherry. Pour this mixture into the casserole and stir well while heating. Add a pinch of cayenne pepper, then pour the sauce over the chicken pieces and serve.

SHIITAKE Widely grown Asian mushroom, whose European name is the edible 'lentin'. It has a brown convex cap and tight, whitish-beige gills. It is cultivated in Japan, China, Korea and parts of the United States and Europe. Shiitake have a strong meaty flavour. They go well with meats, can be grilled (broiled), or used in rich sauces, stir-fries and other Oriental dishes. Dried shiitake need rehydrating in warm water before use.

SHIRAZ See *Syrah*.

SHORTBREAD
A biscuit (cookie), rich in butter, which is served with tea and is traditionally eaten at Christmas and New Year. Originating from Scotland and traditionally made with oatmeal, it is now made with wheat flour. For special occasions, it may be decorated with candied lemon or orange peel or flaked (slivered) almonds. In the Shetland Isles it is flavoured with cumin. Shortbread is traditionally baked in a large round and served cut from the centre into triangular wedges; it is a relic of the ancient New Year cakes that were symbols of the sun.

RECIPE

shortbread
Cream 175 g (6 oz, ¾ cup) butter with 75 g (3 oz, ⅓ cup) caster (superfine) sugar until very soft and pale. Gradually work in 250 g (9 oz, 2¼ cups) plain (all-purpose) flour to make a firm dough. Divide among two 15 cm (6 in) round greased sandwich tins (layer cake pans), pressing the dough out evenly, and chill well. Mark into wedges and bake in a preheated oven at 160°C (325°F, gas 3) for 50–60 minutes, until pale golden. Dust with caster sugar and cut the wedges, but leave in the tins for 15 minutes, until set, then transfer to a wire rack to cool.

SHORT PASTRY
Shortcrust pastry (basic pie dough) is the popular type used for savoury and sweet dishes, such as pastry cases and pies. Short pastries have a medium to high proportion of fat to flour and a low moisture content. They are handled lightly and quickly, with the minimum of rolling, to give a crumbly – or short – texture when baked. This type of pastry does not rise during cooking.

There are several types, with different proportions of fat: the higher the proportion of fat, the more fragile and crumbly the pastry. Standard shortcrust pastry uses half fat to flour. Butter, margarine, lard or white vegetable fat (shortening), or a mixture of these may be used; rich short pastries are made with butter. Short pastry may be sweetened or flavoured with savoury ingredients (such as cheese) and enriched by binding with egg yolk as well as a little water. The addition of a small proportion of water to shortcrust pastry gives the characteristic crisp surface, which is different from a very rich short pastry with a fine 'melt-in-the-mouth' texture right through to the top.

Oil can be used instead of solid fat to make short pastry. The resulting pastry is crumbly which can make it difficult to roll out; when cooked it tends to be quite soft.

RECIPES

Shortcrust Pastries
basic shortcrust pastry
Sift 225 g (8 oz, 2 cups) plain (all-purpose) flour into a bowl and stir in a pinch of salt, if required. Add 50 g (2 oz, ¼ cup) chilled butter and 50 g (2 oz, ¼ cup) chilled lard or white vegetable fat (shortening). Cut the fat into small pieces, then lightly rub them into the flour until the mixture resembles breadcrumbs. Sprinkle 3 tablespoons cold water over the mixture, then use a round-bladed knife to mix it in. The mixture should form clumps: press these together into a smooth ball. Chill the pastry for 30 minutes before baking. Roll out and use as required.

cheese pastry
Follow the recipe for shortcrust pastry, adding 50–100 g (2–4 oz, ½–1 cup) grated Cheddar or Gruyère cheese and 4 tablespoons grated Parmesan cheese to the rubbed-in mixture. Use for savoury dishes or to make cheese straws or savoury biscuits. For the latter, use the larger quantity of cheese and season the pastry with a generous pinch of cayenne pepper; chopped tarragon or thyme, caraway seeds or grated nutmeg may be added to season the pastry.

rich shortcrust pastry
Follow the recipe for shortcrust pastry, using 175 g (6 oz, ¾ cup) butter instead of butter and lard or white vegetable fat (shortening). Bind with water or beat 1 egg yolk with 1 tablespoon water and use to bind the pastry, adding a further 1 tablespoon water if necessary.

French Short Pastries
pâte à foncer
This is a lining pasty for flans and tarts; it is a basic shortcrust made by the French method. Sift 250 g (9 oz, 2¼ cups) plain (all-purpose) flour on to a board. Make a well in the centre and add ½ teaspoon salt and 125 g (4½ oz, ½ cup) butter (softened at room temperature and cut into pieces). Start to mix the ingredients and then add 2 tablespoons water (the quantity of water required may vary depending on the type of flour used). Knead the dough gently, using the heel of the hand, shape it into a ball, wrap it in foil and set aside in a cool place for at least 2 hours if possible.

A richer pastry can be made by increasing the quantity of butter to 150 g (5 oz, ⅔ cup) and by adding 1 small egg and 2 tablespoons caster (superfine) sugar.

pâte brisée
This is the French equivalent of shortcrust pastry (basic pie dough) which can be made with, or without, a little sugar. Sift 250 g (9 oz, 2¼ cups) plain (all-purpose) flour into a bowl or on to a board. Add a pinch of salt and 1½ tablespoons caster

(superfine) sugar (to taste). Spread the mixture into a circle and make a well in the centre. Add 125 g (4½ oz, ½ cup) softened butter and a beaten egg, and knead the ingredients together as quickly as possible with 2 tablespoons very cold water. Form the dough into a ball, even if there are still some whole pieces of butter visible. Wrap it in foil and leave it to rest for at least 1 hour in the refrigerator. Knead the dough, pushing it down gently with the heel of the hand, and roll it out on a lightly floured worktop to the required thickness.

pâte sablée

This is a rich, sweetened short pastry, flavoured with vanilla and used for sweet flans and tarts. Sift 250 g (9 oz, 2¼ cups) plain (all-pupose) flour. Cream 125 g (4½ oz, ½ cup) butter. Quickly mix the flour and butter by hand, draw the mixture together and make a well in the centre. Add 1 whole egg, 125 g (4½ oz, ½ cup) caster (superfine) sugar and a few drops of vanilla essence (extract). Quickly blend the ingredients together, roll the pastry into a ball and chill for 1 hour.

Alternatively, the pastry can be made by first mixing the egg and sugar, then rubbing in the flour, and finally kneading in the butter.

pâte sucrée (dite 'sèche')

Another sweet, short pastry. Heap together 250 g (9 oz, 2¼ cups) plain (all-purpose) flour, a pinch of salt and 75 g (3 oz, ⅓ cup) caster (superfine) sugar and make a well in the centre. Add 1 large egg (or 2 small ones), 100 g (4 oz, ½ cup) softened butter and 1½ teaspoons orange-flower water and work all the ingredients together, drawing the flour into the centre. Knead the dough quickly and gently with the heel of the hand, form it into a ball, cover and keep cool.

SHOULDER The part of the body to which the front leg is attached. In butchery, shoulder of beef yields cuts for braising or boiling, and blade or shin (shank) is especially suitable for the stockpot. Shoulder of veal gives cuts for braising, frying, roasting, stewing (fricandeau, veal blanquette) and even for escalopes (scallops), but it can also be cooked whole, after boning and stuffing, rolled into a ballotine and braised or roasted. Shoulder of mutton or lamb yields pieces for stewing, navarin, braising or kebabs. It can also be cooked whole (boned or unboned), studded with garlic, roasted, grilled (broiled), braised or rolled up and stuffed. Shoulder of venison can be treated like haunch, but it is usually stewed.

Making pâte sablée

1 *Mix the softened butter into the flour by hand until evenly distributed. The mixture should resemble breadcrumbs.*

2 *Make a well in the middle of the dry mixture and add the egg, sugar and vanilla. Use your fingertips to draw the ingredients together.*

3 *Continue working the mixture with the fingertips until the egg is evenly mixed and the dough begins to clump together.*

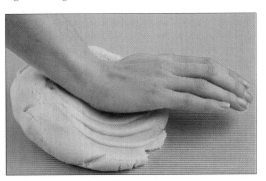

4 *Press the dough together into a ball, then knead it lightly, pressing with the hand until the dough is smooth.*

RECIPES

Lamb

braised shoulder of lamb

Bone a shoulder of lamb, trim it, season with salt and pepper, roll it up and tie with string. Crush the bones and brown them in butter with the trimmings. Trim the fat off some pork rind and line a braising pan with the rind. Peel and finely slice 2 carrots and 1 onion, cook in butter for 10 minutes, then add to the braising pan. Put the shoulder in the braising pan and season with salt and pepper. Add 150 ml (¼ pint, ⅔ cup) white wine and reduce. Add 250 ml (8 fl oz, 1 cup) thickened gravy, 100 ml (4 fl oz, 7 tablespoons) tomato purée, 1 bouquet garni and the bones and trimmings. Cover and cook in a preheated oven at 220°C (425°F, gas 7) for about 1–1½ hours, depending on the size of the joint. Drain it, glaze in the oven, then arrange it on a serving dish.

The usual garnish consists of green or white haricot (navy) beans, vegetable purées, artichoke hearts or haricot bean purée à la bretonne. It can also be served with mushrooms à la bordelaise, together with cooking juices deglazed with red wine and demi-glace and flavoured with shallot, thyme and bay leaf.

grilled shoulder of lamb

Trim the bone, make incisions in the flesh on both sides, brush with melted butter or oil, and grill (broil) the lamb under a medium heat for 20–25 minutes. Sprinkle with breadcrumbs and melted butter and brown under the grill. Garnish with bunches of watercress.

roast shoulder of lamb en ballotine

Bone a shoulder of lamb and season with salt and pepper; insert small pieces of garlic, if desired, then roll it up as for a ballotine and tie with string. Roast, either in a dish or on a spit, in a preheated oven at 240°C (475°F, gas 9) for about 50 minutes. The skin should be crisp and the centre pink. Remove the string and serve with just the cooking juices.

stuffed shoulder of lamb à la gasconne

Bone a shoulder of lamb and season with salt and pepper. Soak 4 slices of bread in some milk. Chop up 3–4 slices of raw ham, 1–2 onions, 2–3 garlic cloves and a small bunch of parsley. Squeeze the bread and add to this mixture, together with 1 egg and some salt and pepper. Mix well and spread it over the meat. Roll up the shoulder, tie with string as for a ballotine, and place in a roasting tin (pan). Brush with 1 tablespoon goose fat and brown quickly in a preheated oven at 240°C (475°F, gas 9).

Scald about 800 g (1¾ lb) green cabbage, cool in cold water and squeeze dry. Peel and dice 2 carrots; peel 1 onion and stick it with cloves. Transfer the joint to a braising dish, add the cabbage, diced carrots, onion and 1 bouquet garni, then half-cover the shoulder with stock (do not skim the fat off first). Cover and cook in a preheated oven at 190°C (375°F, gas 5) for 45 minutes. Then add 800 g (1¾ lb) peeled potatoes cut into quarters, or small whole potatoes, and cook for a further 20–25 minutes. Remove the onion and bouquet garni before serving.

stuffed shoulder of lamb à l'albigeoise

Bone a shoulder of lamb and season with salt and pepper. To make the stuffing, mix 350 g (12 oz) sausagemeat with 350 g (12 oz) chopped pig's liver, 2–3 garlic cloves, a small bunch of parsley (chopped) and some salt and pepper. Cover the shoulder with this stuffing, roll it up and tie it like a ballotine. Peel 800 g (1¾ lb) potatoes and cut into quarters. Peel 12 garlic cloves and scald for 1 minute in boiling water. Heat 2 tablespoons goose fat in a flameproof casserole, add the ballotine and brown all over, then add the potatoes and garlic, coating them well with the fat. Season with salt and pepper and cook in a preheated oven at 230°C (450°F, gas 8) for at least 50 minutes (longer for a large shoulder). When the joint is cooked, sprinkle with chopped parsley and serve from the casserole.

Mutton

shoulder of mutton en ballon

Bone a shoulder of mutton and season with salt and pepper, then spread it out on the worktop. Prepare a stuffing comprising 200 g (7 oz) fine sausagemeat, 150 g (5 oz, 1⅔ cups) cep mushrooms chopped up with a small bunch of parsley, 1 shallot, 2 peeled garlic cloves, 1 beaten egg, a little crushed thyme and some salt and pepper. Make this stuffing into a ball and place it in the centre of the meat. Fold the meat into a ball around the stuffing and tie with string.

Heat 3 tablespoons olive oil in a round flameproof casserole, add the joint and brown it all over. Then add 175 ml (6 fl oz, ¾ cup) white wine and the same amount of strong stock. Cover and cook in a preheated oven at 200°C (400°F, gas 6) for about 1¾ hours. Remove the string and cut the meat into segments, rather like a melon. Skim the fat off the cooking juices, then add 4 tablespoons thick tomato fondue*; reduce if necessary. Sieve and serve in a sauceboat to accompany the meat.

shoulder of mutton with garlic ♦

Bone and roll a shoulder of mutton into a ballotine and tie it neatly in place. Place the mutton in a large flameproof casserole with a slice of unsmoked ham, 1 chopped onion and 1 diced carrot. Season with salt and pepper and add 3 tablespoons goose fat or lard. Cover the casserole and sweat for 20–25 minutes, basting occasionally.

Remove the mutton and the ham and set aside.

Shoulder of mutton with garlic.

Stir in 2 tablespoons plain (all-purpose) flour and cook for a few minutes. Pour in 200 ml (7 fl oz, ¾ cup) white wine and 400 ml (14 fl oz, 1¾ cups) stock, stirring. Bring to the boil, then remove from the heat. Press the sauce through a sieve and set aside.

Replace the mutton ballotine in the casserole. Dice the ham and sprinkle it over the mutton. Peel and blanch 50 garlic cloves, then add them to the casserole with a bouquet garni and a piece of dried orange peel. Pour in the sieved sauce and cover. Cook in a preheated oven at 220°C (425°F, gas 7) for 1 hour. Serve the ballotine sliced and arranged on a platter or plates, coated with the sauce and garnished with the garlic cloves. Serve a potato cake or gratin of potatoes with the mutton.

Veal
stuffed shoulder of veal
Bone a shoulder of veal weighing about 1.5 kg (3¼ lb), flatten it out carefully, then season it with salt and pepper. Mix 450 g (1 lb) fine sausagemeat with 200 g (7 oz) mushrooms, 1 garlic clove and some chopped herbs and season with salt and pepper. Cover the meat with this stuffing, roll it up and tie with string. Braise as for shoulder of lamb (see above). Cook until the juices run clear when the meat is pricked. Remove and drain the meat and untie. Reduce the cooking juices, strain and pour over the joint. Glaze the joint in a very hot oven, then arrange on a serving dish and pour more juice over it. Serve the rest of the cooking juices in a sauceboat. Aubergines (eggplants) fried in oil or glazed vegetables (carrots, turnips or onions) make an ideal garnish.

stuffed shoulder of veal à l'anglaise
Bone a shoulder of veal weighing about 1.5 kg (3¼ lb). Prepare a stuffing consisting of one-third chopped calf's or ox kidney, one-third chopped breast of veal or veal fat and one-third breadcrumbs soaked in milk, then squeezed. Season well and bind using 1 egg per 450 g (1 lb) stuffing. Season the veal with salt and pepper and cover it evenly with the stuffing; roll it up and tie with string. Braise or roast, as preferred. Serve with the reduced cooking juices and garnish with slices of boiled bacon, cabbage and boiled potatoes.

SHRIMP NET A small hanging net used for catching shrimps and crayfish.

SHRIMPS AND PRAWNS Shellfish that live in fresh and salt water and range in size from tiny insect-like species to giant varieties almost 30 cm (12 in) long – these tend to come from warmer waters. The larger species are commercially important as food. In general terms, 'shrimp' is the name used in Britain for the smaller varieties, while 'prawn' refers to specific, larger species. In the United States, 'shrimp' is used in the majority of cases. (The French word, *crevette*, is the Picardy form of the word *chevrette*, meaning a kid goat, an allusion to their bounding movements in the water.)

There are numerous species of edible shrimps and prawns. The species living in tropical waters carry their eggs inside the rather large third pair of legs; those inhabiting temperate and cold waters do not have claws on the third pair of legs and the eggs are carried outside, attached to the abdominal legs.

There is widespread demand for, and consequently a large international trade in, these popular shellfish. Shrimp and prawn fishing (via nets or trawling) is highly industrialized, while prawn aquaculture (commercial 'fish farming') is practised worldwide, in both salt and fresh waters, and involves various different species. For example, species of tiger prawns are farmed in parts of Asia and Latin America; freshwater prawns in India and the Far East.

■ **Common species of shrimps and prawns**
• COMMON OR BROWN SHRIMP (*Crangon crangon*) Found in Europe, this is about 3–6 cm (1¼–2½ in) long. Fiddly to peel because of its size, it is greyish-brown when raw, and brown when cooked. It is fished intensively off the English Channel and North Sea coasts, and is also found in the Mediterranean. A related species fished in waters around the United States is the Californian, bay or grey shrimp (*Crangon franciscorum*).
• COMMON PRAWN (*Palaemon serratus*) Found in the North Atlantic and Mediterranean waters, this reaches a maximum length of 10 cm (4 in).
• DEEP-WATER PRAWN (*Pandalus borealis*) Found in northern waters on both sides of the Atlantic, this is almost always sold cooked.
• RED PRAWN AND PINK PRAWN The red is known as *crevette rouge* in French, or *gambero rosso* in Italian, and the pink prawn is *caramote* in French or *mazzancolla* in Italian. These are highly regarded Mediterranean species, both of which can grow to about 20 cm (8 in).
• WHITE, PINK-GROOVED AND BROWN SHRIMPS The white shrimp (*Penaeus setiferus*) and the pink-grooved shrimp (*P. duorarum*) from the Gulf of Mexico, and the brown shrimp (*P. aztecus*) of the Atlantic are the most important commercially fished species in waters near the United States, and can reach 20–23 cm (8–9 in) in length.
• TIGER OR KING PRAWNS These are found in the warm waters of the Indo-Pacific. The black, or giant, tiger prawn, also known in Australia as leader prawn (*Penaeus monodon*), is distributed over most of the Indian Ocean and reaches the western Pacific from southern Japan to northern Australia. *P. semisulcatus* is another tiger prawn fished off the coasts of northern Australia, and can reach 28 cm (11 in) in length. Considered the best in terms of taste and body weight, it is very important commercially and is exported in large quantities to Japan.
• BANANA PRAWN This is another warm-water variety found in the Indo-Pacific and is related to the tiger prawn. The common banana prawn (*Penaeus merguiensis*) is harvested in the tropical climates of Aus-

tralia and is widely available in the domestic and Pacific Rim fish markets.

• GIANT FRESHWATER PRAWN (*Macrobrachium rosenbergii*) This occurs in freshwater rivers in the tropical Indo-Pacific region, extending to northern Australia, and is farmed by aquaculture in a large number of countries.

■ **Preparation and cooking** Shrimps and prawns may be sold fresh, canned or frozen. They are often sold cooked; when fresh, the shell is very shiny, the flesh is firm and it is easy to peel (shell) them. They are sometimes coloured artificially. Some large prawns are sold raw, with or without their shells. All but the smallest shrimps require removal of the dark, threadlike intestinal vein that runs along their backs. Shrimps and prawns can be peeled and deveined before or after cooking.

Shrimps and prawns require only brief cooking or they will toughen. They can be prepared for eating in numerous different ways, for example in salads, curries and stir-fries, in the British-style prawn cocktail and in Mediterranean seafood dishes. They can be cooked in seawater or salted water and served with just butter, plain or flavoured with garlic. *Gambas*, which appear in Spanish and West Indian cuisine, are often fried or grilled on skewers. In South-East Asia, small shrimps are used to produce a fermented shrimp paste called *blachan* or *terasi*. Prawn crackers are another Asian speciality, made by pounding prawns into a paste, drying it in the sun and cutting it into petal shapes. These are then fried in very hot oil to make them swell up. They are served as a snack or as an accompaniment to various Oriental dishes.

See also *scampi, langoustine*.

RECIPES

fried prawns or shrimps
Wash and drain some raw prawns or shrimps and fry them in hot oil for about 1 minute. Drain, season with salt and serve with aperitifs.

prawn omelette
Bind some peeled (shelled) prawns (shrimp) with prawn sauce and use them to fill an omelette. When serving, pour a thin line of sauce around the omelette.

prawn pannequets
Bind some peeled (shelled) cooked prawns (shrimp) with some well-reduced prawn sauce. Prepare some savoury pannequets, fill each of them with prawns – about 500 g (18 oz, 3 cups) for 12 pannequets – and roll them up. Arrange them in a buttered dish, brush them with a little melted butter and reheat them in the oven.

prawn salad
Season some peeled (shelled) cooked prawns (shrimp) with vinaigrette or mayonnaise. Arrange them in a dish or a salad bowl garnished with quarters of hard-boiled (hard-cooked) eggs and lettuce hearts.

prawn sauce
Add ½ teaspoon anchovy essence (extract) to 250 ml (8 fl oz, 1 cup) English butter sauce (see sauce). Mix 40 g (1½ oz, ¼ cup) peeled (shelled) cooked prawns (shrimp) with the sauce and season with a pinch of cayenne pepper.

prawn sauce (for fish)
Blend 200 ml (7 fl oz, ¾ cup) normande* sauce with 2 tablespoons shrimp butter*. Season with a pinch of cayenne pepper and press through a sieve or mix in a blender. If the sauce is to be served separately, add to it 1 tablespoon peeled (shelled) cooked prawns (shrimp) just before serving.

shrimps in cider
Heat 50 g (2 oz, ¼ cup) slightly salted butter and a dash of olive oil in a frying pan. As soon as the mixture begins to foam, add some raw shrimps and cover immediately. Stir well. After 3 minutes of cooking, add 100 ml (4 fl oz, 7 tablespoons) dry farm (hard) cider. Reduce the liquid. Put the shrimps in a cloth. Season with coarse sea salt and pepper and shake well. Eat while still lukewarm with bread and butter and cider.

Alternatively, prepare a fish stock with 1 litre (1¾ pints, 4⅓ cups) dry cider, 1½ tablespoons coarse sea salt, thyme, bay leaves, 10 black peppercorns and 1 thinly sliced apple, and reduce for 10 minutes. Throw in the live shrimps and boil for 30 seconds. Put the shrimps in a cloth, season with salt and pepper and shake well.

shrimps sautéed in whisky
Wash, drain and sauté some raw shrimps in oil in a frying pan. Add some pepper, a pinch of cayenne pepper and either whisky, Cognac or marc–6 tablespoons per 500 g (18 oz, 3 cups) shrimps. Flame and serve very hot.

other recipes See *aspic, barquette, bouchée (savoury bouchée), butter (flavoured butters), Canapé, Caroline, croissant, egg (scrambled eggs), forcemeat, mayonnaise, mousse, pilaf, purée, salpicon (fish and shellfish salpicons), scallop shell, soufflé (crab soufflé), soup.*

SHROPSHIRE BLUE This British blue cheese does not have any connection with the county of Shropshire; in fact, it was invented in Scotland and is now made by some of the Stilton cheese producers. It is made in a very similar way to Stilton, except that annatto is added to the milk with the starter culture. The end result is a bright red cheese with blue veining. It has a sharper taste than Stilton, but it is equally distinctive.

SICHUAN PEPPER Also known as anise pepper or Chinese pepper, this hot, slightly peppery, spice is prepared from the dried berries of a tree of the prickly ash family. The berries contain tiny black seeds that have a bitter taste and they are removed from the split dried berries to make the best-quality spice. Sichuan pepper originated in Sichuan and is a popular seasoning in dishes of the region. See *sansho*.

SICILIAN COOKERY The cookery of this Mediterranean island is Greek in origin, with traces of Arab and African influence and certain ancient local traditions.

Sicily produces citrus fruit, early vegetables, olives, almonds and wheat. Its cakes are a source of pride and include *cannoli*, which are filled with cream cheese and crystallized (candied) fruits, and cassata, the Sicilian festive gâteau. Other specialities include Sicilian ice cream (*gelati*) and *Martorana* fruit (marzipan confectionery). There are numerous varieties of bread and pizza. A typical Sicilian speciality is *vasteddi* – small rolls sprinkled with cumin seeds and filled with ricotta, pork fried in lard and smoked ham; another is *arancine*, fried rice balls stuffed with meat or cheese. Pasta is also important, especially *pasta con le sarde* (with a tomato and sardine ragoût). Caponata, a type of cold ratatouille, is served as a first course or with fish or seafood, which have a special place in Sicilian cookery – notably grilled (broiled), swordfish, stuffed mussels and rockfish either stuffed or *en papillote*. Speciality meat dishes include veal *alla marsala*, and others traditionally made with lamb or goat.

■ **Wine** A producer and exporter of wine, Sicily was traditionally famous for such liqueur wines as Marsala and such dessert wines as Mamertino, which was known in Julius Caesar's day. A great proportion of the wines were exported for blending or for making into grape concentrate but increasngly producers are making quality wines. Some choose to market their wines outside the DOC systems as Vino da Tavola. White grape varieties are dominant in the vineyards – the better varieties are Inzolia and catarratto – whilst Nero d'Avola is considered to be a red variety with enormous potential for quality wines. Luscious sweet wines are still being produced with Moscato of Pantelleria and Malvasia della Lipari continuing Sicily's historic tradition.

SICILIENNE (À LA) Describing small pieces of meat or poultry, which are fried and garnished with stuffed tomatoes, rice timbales and croquette potatoes.

SIEVE A utensil used for sieving, sifting, draining or straining. Fine sieves made of silk, horsehair or nylon, supported on a frame, are used to sift flour or icing (confectioner's) sugar. Fine wire sieves are also used to sift dry ingredients, depending on how fine a result is required. Wire sieves are also used for sieving moist ingredients such as fruit purées or cooked vegetables to improve their consistency and texture, or to purée fruit and vegetables. Coarse

Sieving

The traditional method of sieving is by squeezing the ingredients in a cloth. This gives a very fine result and is useful for fine coulis. The mixture should be placed in the centre of the cloth and held over a basin. Both ends are twisted to squeeze all the moisture out of the mixture.

Pressing mixtures through a fine sieve is a practical method of removing lumps or ingredients that are no longer required in a liquid. A ladle, large spoon or spatula should be used to press the mixture through the mesh.

sieves are used for draining some ingredients or for straining liquids to remove unwanted solids. Fine sieves are also used for straining liquids, for example to remove lumps.

SIKI Commercial name for the shagreen shark, a fish of the family of *Squalidae*, which lives in the Atlantic, from Iceland to Senegal. It is sometimes confused with dogfish (spur dog or smooth hound), although it is much larger. The siki, boned, is served as a stew, sautéed, fried or braised.

SILVER GILT Material used in the manufacture of gold and silver plate. It can take the form of a thin layer of gilding (gold applied by electrolysis to silvered metal) or gilded silver (solid silver covered with a fine layer of gold). Cutlery, plates and serving dishes made in silver gilt are rarely suitable for practical use, with the exception of small coffee spoons or teaspoons.

SILVERWARE Tableware made of solid silver, silver gilt or silvered metal. Silver plate (made from a single strip of plated metal) can include not only cutlery, plates and serving dishes, but also accessories such as candelabras, table mats, hand bells, salt cellars and knife rests. Silver plates and dishes were used in ancient times. In medieval Europe, their use spread among the nobility and rich merchants, until this mass of immobilized precious metal began to worry the monarchs. In 1310 Philip the Fair, in an attempt to solve a monetary crisis in France, prohibited the manufacture of gold and silver dishes. But this measure had no effect, and the custom of using silver tableware continued until the French Revolution. It was nevertheless increasingly restricted to display items, after Louis XIV had the royal tableware melted down to replenish the coffers and encourage the development of porcelain and faience.

In 1840, the Englishman Elkington and the Frenchman Ruolz simultaneously invented electroplating, thus putting silverware within the reach of the less wealthy, who were able to replace their galvanized iron cutlery with silvered metal.

To prevent silver cutlery from going black, it should be stored away from contact with the air, either in cases or wrapped in special materials or tissue paper. It must be cleaned regularly with special cleaning materials applied with a very soft cloth.

SIMMER To cook food slowly and steadily in a sauce or other liquid over a gentle heat, just below boiling point, so that the surface of the liquid bubbles occasionally. When cooking poached dishes the liquid should be kept simmering. Meat for simmering or stewing comprises the tougher cuts, which become tender and tasty when cooked for a long time in seasoned stock, wine or beer.

SIMNEL CAKE A British cake made for Easter. It was originally made for Mothering Sunday, the fourth Sunday in Lent, when children in service were allowed time off to return to their homes. The fruit cake was taken as a gift.

The present fruit cake has evolved from various ancient and regional specialities, often consisting of dried fruit and spices, sometimes made with bread dough. Today's simnel cake has a layer of marzipan baked in the middle and it is covered with marzipan on top, then decorated with small balls of the paste. The topping is glazed under the grill (broiler) or in a hot oven until lightly browned. The balls of paste are thought to represent the twelve apostles and their number is usually reduced to eleven to represent the betrayal by Judas.

SINGAPOUR A large Genoese sponge cake, filled with jam (preserve) and fruit in syrup, coated with apricot jam and generously decorated with crystallized (candied) fruits.

RECIPE

singapour
Bring 750 ml (1¼ pints, 3¼ cups) water to the boil with 575 g (1¼ lb, 2½ cups) granulated sugar. Drain

a large can of pineapple slices, add the slices to the mixture and simmer for 1½ hours. Leave the slices to cool, then drain them.

Whisk 4 eggs with 125 g (4½ oz, ½ cup) granulated sugar in a bain marie until the mixture reaches 40°C (104°F), then remove from the heat and cool completely. Mix in 125 g (4½ oz, 1 cup) plain (all-purpose) flour, stirring with a wooden spoon, then add 50 g (2 oz, ¼ cup) melted butter. Pour the batter into a buttered and floured 23 cm (9 in) cake tin (pan). Bake in a preheated oven at 200°C (400°F, gas 6) for about 20 minutes, or until the cake is well risen and golden and the centre springs back when lightly pressed.

Meanwhile, melt 250 g (9 oz, ¾ cup) apricot jam (preserve) over a gentle heat and grill (broil) 150 g (5 oz, 1¼ cups) chopped almonds. Prepare a syrup with 300 ml (½ pint, 1¼ cups) water and 300 g (11 oz, 1⅓ cups) granulated sugar and allow to cool, then add 3 tablespoons kirsch.

Cut the sponge in half horizontally and let it soak up the kirsch syrup. Spread the lower half with some of the apricot jam; cut the slices of pineapple into small dice, set a few aside and sprinkle the rest over the jam. Place the upper half of the sponge in position and coat the whole cake with more of the jam. Sprinkle with chopped almonds and decorate the top with the remaining diced pineapple, together with glacé (candied) cherries and candied angelica. Serve on the day it is made.

SINGEING The process of rotating poultry or game birds over a spirit lamp or gas flame in order to burn off any feathers or down that remain after plucking.

SINGER A French culinary term meaning to sprinkle ingredients browned in fat with flour before adding liquid (such as wine, stock or water) to make a sauce. The flour must cook for several minutes before the liquid is added in order to thicken the sauce.

The term previously meant to colour a sauce with caramel, which was familiarly called *jus de singe* ('monkey juice').

SIPHON A bottle made of thick glass or aluminium containing water that has been made effervescent with carbonic gas under pressure (see *soda water*). It is closed with a screwed-on plastic or metal top provided with a lever, which, when depressed, allows the liquid to flow through an interior tube. The siphon is used to jet the water directly into the glass; it is refilled with water by unscrewing the top, into which gas cartridges are placed. Until World War II, siphons made of thick glass, sometimes engraved or coloured (blue or green), were often covered with wicker or metal basketwork; they were refilled with Seltzer water.

The siphon for Chantilly cream also uses gas cartridges and provides white, fluffy, Chantilly-like cream that lacks the richness and flavour of a classic whipped cream. It is not recommended to fill the siphon more than three-quarters full, using an equal quantity of double (heavy) cream and sweetened milk.

SIRLOIN A prime cut of beef from the lumbar region, which extends from the last rib to the sacrum. The sirloin includes the fillet (tenderloin), contre-filet or faux-filet (sirloin), rump steak and *bavette* (top of the sirloin). Cooked whole, the sirloin makes a display piece. It is, however, more usually cut into several large joints.

RECIPES

braised sirloin
Ask the butcher to prepare a piece of sirloin 2–3 kg (4½–6½ lb) in weight, cut along the grain of the meat. Lard the joint with lardons of bacon that have been marinated for at least 1 hour with a little brandy, pepper, spices, chopped parsley, sliced carrot and sliced onion. Tie up the sirloin, brown it on all sides in hot fat, then place it in a large braising pan on a mirepoix of vegetables. Add a bouquet garni and pour over about 600 ml (1 pint, 2½ cups) stock. Cover the pan and braise the joint in a preheated oven at 150°C (300°F, gas 2) for about 4 hours, or until the meat is very tender. After braising, the meat may be sliced and served with the cooking liquid, deglazed, reduced and strained.

roast sirloin
This very large joint is not normally cooked whole except by professional chefs. They trim off the top a little to give the joint a more regular shape, then cut the ligament that runs along the chine into regular sections and remove part of the fat that surrounds the fillet. The joint is then seasoned with salt and pepper and generally roasted in the oven or on a spit – allowing 10–12 minutes per 1 kg (5–6 minutes per 1 lb); it should be pink on the inside. It is served surrounded with watercress or with a bouquetière or printanière garnish.

SIROPER Also known as *siroter*. A French culinary term meaning to put a cake of leavened dough (baba or savarin) to soak in a warm syrup or to pour syrup over it several times until it is thoroughly impregnated. The term also means to pour a trickle of syrup over a sponge cake to lightly moisten it, flavour it and soften it before decoration.

SKATE AND RAY Virtually interchangeable names for cartilaginous, flat seawater fish of the *Rajidae* family, found in cold and temperate waters. These flat fish live at the bottom of the sea, camouflaged against the seabed by their colouring. The pectoral fins are enlarged in the form of wings and the tail is long and thin. The upper side of the fish is greyish-brown and bears two eyes and a short snout; on the underside, which is lighter coloured, there is a large mouth with pointed, slashing teeth. The cartilaginous skeleton is easily removed.

The best flavoured skate is probably the thornback, or roker, which is caught off the Mediterranean coast, as well as in the Atlantic, Pacific and Indian Oceans. It is 60–120 cm (2–4 ft) long and marked with pale spots, and owes its name to the cartilaginous spines scattered over the back and wings (and sometimes the belly). Other edible species include the spotted ray, pale brown with large black spots; the blonde ray; the white skate; the blue, or common, skate; and the thorny skate, which is found in Arctic waters.

The skin of a skate is covered with a viscous coating. Since this will regenerate for about 10 hours after death, the freshness of a skate can be judged by rubbing it with a cloth and observing whether the coating reappears. It is usually only the wings of a skate that are sold, or the fish may be sold in slices; it is sometimes skinned. The pinkish-white flesh is meaty and has a fine texture. It should be washed several times to get rid of the smell of ammonia, which is most marked when the fish is quite fresh. Skate liver is considered to be a delicacy by some gourmets, as are the 'cheeks'.

The traditional accompaniment for skate is black butter (or even better, noisette butter) as in the French classic dish, *raie au beurre noir*, but it may also be served with hollandaise sauce, vinaigrette with herbs or meunière sauce; it may be fried (especially good for small skate), grilled (broiled), served as a gratin or with béchamel sauce (particularly the Breton version of the sauce, with leeks).

RECIPES

fried skate
Select some very small skinned skate (or the wings from a small or medium fish). Pour some cold milk over them and soak for 1 hour, then drain, coat with flour and deep-fry at 180°C (350°F). When cooked, drain on paper towels, sprinkle with salt and arrange on a serving dish. Garnish with fluted lemon halves.

skate au gratin
Butter a flameproof casserole and sprinkle the bottom with 2 tablespoons chopped shallots and the same amount of chopped parsley. Add 150 g (5 oz, 1⅔ cups) finely sliced mushrooms. Season 2 skate wings with salt and pepper and arrange them in the dish. Moisten with 5 tablespoons white wine, dot with 25 g (1 oz, 2 tablespoons) butter cut into small pieces, and cook in a preheated oven at 230°C (450°F, gas 8) for 10 minutes. Remove the skate and drain it. Add 1 tablespoon crème fraîche to the cooking liquid and reduce it by half. Return the skate to the dish, pour over the cooking juices, sprinkle with breadcrumbs, dot with butter and brown under the grill (broiler).

skate liver fritters
Poach some skate liver for 6 minutes in courtbouillon, then drain it and leave it to cool. Make

some fritter batter. Slice the liver and marinate it in salt, pepper, oil and a little lemon juice for 30–60 minutes. Drain the slices of liver, dip them into the batter and deep-fry them at 180°C (350°F). Drain on paper towels, sprinkle with salt and serve with fluted lemon halves.

skate liver with cider vinegar

Poach 400 g (14 oz) skate liver very gently in court-bouillon for 5 minutes. Leave it to cool in the stock. Peel and core 4 firm apples (preferably Cox's Orange Pippins or Granny Smiths), slice them and cook over a low heat in 15–20 g (½–¾ oz, 1–1½ tablespoons) butter. Season with salt and pepper. Slice the liver and brown in a little butter. Drain and arrange the slices on a hot dish. Pour the butter from the pan in which the livers were cooked, then add 2 tablespoons cider vinegar to the pan, boil for 1–2 minutes and pour over the liver. Surround with the cooked slices of apple and sprinkle with chopped chives.

skate with lemon

Poach a skate wing, about 150 g (5 oz), in a little salted water with 1 chopped shallot. Peel 1 lemon, removing all the pith, and divide it into segments. Peel and grate 1 apple. Mix the apple and the lemon segments and add them to the fish halfway through cooking. Just before serving, add 1 tablespoon crème fraîche, a little pepper and a pinch of grated nutmeg.

skate with noisette butter ◆

Cut the skate into chunks, leaving the wings whole. Poach in court-bouillon or in water to which have been added 200 ml (7 fl oz, ¾ cup) vinegar and 1 teaspoon salt per 1 litre (1¾ pints, 4⅓ cups) water. Bring to the boil, skim the pan and simmer for 5–7 minutes, according to the thickness of the fish. Make some noisette butter. Drain the fish and arrange it on a hot dish. Sprinkle with lemon juice and, just before serving, pour over the noisette butter. Sprinkle with capers and garnish with a little parsley; serve at once with plain-cooked potatoes.

SKIM To remove the scum that rises to the surface of a stock, soup, sauce or ragoût when it is boiled. The skimming is carried out with a spoon, a special skimmer or a small ladle.

Skimming is also the term for removing cream from unhomogenized milk. The process occurs spontaneously after 24 hours if whole fresh unhomogenized milk is allowed to stand; the cream rises to the surface and can be easily removed, particularly for use in home baking. In the dairy industry, centrifugal skimming machines are used. Milk is widely sold as full cream, semi-skimmed or skimmed.

SKIMMER A large, flat or slightly concave perforated spoon with a long handle, used for skimming. For skimming sauces and stocks, the skimmer is made of stainless steel, aluminium, enamelled metal or tin. For jam (preserve) making, it should be made of untinned copper. A skimmer made of galvanized wire is used for removing deep-fried foods from hot oil and a concave wire skimmer is used for lifting poached items from their cooking water.

SKIRT A butchery term for the diaphragm of a beef animal or a horse, which is a long flat band of dark fibrous muscle. If the membranes are carefully removed and the meat is flattened out, the skirt can be cut into steaks which, although rather tough, are full of flavour. It is usually used for moist stews and casseroles, cooked slowly to allow the meat to become tender.

SKOAL The Scandinavian drinking toast, equivalent to 'good health' or '*à votre santé*'. The word has its roots in the old Norse *skalle* (skull), commemorating an ancient warrior custom of drinking from the vanquished enemy's skull.

SLIPPER LOBSTER *cigale de mer* Also known as squat or flat lobster, there are over 50 species of these lobster-like creatures of the family *Scyllaridae*. They have small claws at the ends of their legs, but they do not have the large, long pincers typical of lobsters. Their shells range in colour from rust-red or chestnut to green-tinged. The powerful ridged tail is wide and the two fine antennae are reduced in size. A more conspicuous pair are widened into shovel shapes, which are useful for digging in search of food. Only the tail is eaten.

The *grande cigale* of the Mediterranean can weigh as much as 2 kg (4½ lb); the smaller one is only 7–10 cm (3–4 in) and is used in soups. The French name comes from the snapping, cricket-like noise they make, audible underwater. In northern Spain the *santagüino*, St James' lobster, has a mark like a cross on its back. Another species is fished in Scottish waters. Called a slipper lobster in the United States, it is fished off Hawaii (and is imported from Thailand, Singapore and Australia). Called bay lobster in Australia (and popularly, 'bugs'), the best and largest – up to 23 cm (9 in) – is the Moreton bay bug; the Balmain bug is also well-known.

RECIPE

skewered saffron-dressed flat lobster tails
Remove the shells from the tails (discarding the heads and legs), rinse and blot dry. Marinate the tails in the following mixture: 1 pinch saffron threads and 1 chopped garlic clove per 500 g (18 oz) tails, mixed with olive oil, lemon juice, parsley, crumbled thyme, salt and pepper. Thread them on to skewers and grill (broil) briefly until the meat is firm and cooked through: time depends on size.

SLIT To open a fish slightly so that the cooking heat can penetrate the flesh more quickly (while also preventing it drying out), or to cut a pocket in a piece of meat or chicken breast for inserting an ingredient, such as garlic.

SLIVOVITZ A plum brandy made throughout central and eastern Europe, also known as *slivovica*. The name comes from the Serbo-Croat *Slijiva* and Russian *Sliva* (plum). It is the national drink of the Bosnians and the Serbs, who also call it *prakija*. It is made from purple plums, the stones (pits) of which are usually crushed and fermented with the pulp. Slivovitz is a true *alcool blanc*, not just a brandy flavoured with plums. It is usually served as a digestive.

SLOE The fruit of the blackthorn, a thorny shrub common throughout Europe. The sloe resembles a very small blue plum, with firm greenish flesh, which is juicy and very sour; it is edible only after the first frosts. Sloes are used to make jam (preserve) and jelly, sloe gin, sloe wine and other alcoholic drinks, such as the Spanish *pacharán*.

SLOKE A name used by the Irish and the Scots for the seaweed laver, which is also called 'sea spinach'. In former times it was cooked to make a traditional dish, also called sloke; it is now used as a base for soups and a sauce served with mutton. It is particularly popular with the Welsh, who boil it to a purée, then mix it with oatmeal to make laverbread, which is fried and served with bacon for breakfast.

SMALLAGE An umbelliferous plant, also called wild celery and known as *ache des marais* in French, from which cultivated celery originated. This was used as a seasoning in Greek and Roman times. This wild plant can be included in salads and also serves as an ingredient in medicinal syrups and tisanes.

SMELT A small marine fish of the salmon family, with fine delicate flesh. It grows up to 20 cm (8 in) long, is silvery in colour and has a second dorsal fin, which distinguishes it from similar but poorer quality fish, such as bleak and *athérine*, which are often used as substitutes. It spawns in estuaries but seldom travels upriver beyond the tideline.

The classic method of preparation is frying. The fish are gutted (cleaned), washed, dried and stored in the refrigerator (they also freeze very well). Besides frying, they can also be marinated, grilled (broiled), cooked in white wine, coated with flour and fried, or cooked *au gratin*. In Scandinavian countries, smelt are used in the manufacture of fish oil and fishmeal.

RECIPES

brochettes of fried smelt
Dip the prepared smelt in salted milk, then roll them in flour and shake off any excess. Impale them on metal skewers (6–8 fish per skewer) and deep-fry in very hot oil.

cold marinade of smelt
Prepare the smelt, roll them in flour and shake off any excess. Brown them in oil in a frying pan. Drain, season with salt and pepper, then arrange in a dish. Peel and slice some onions and scald them for 1 minute in boiling water. Cool, then wipe dry and arrange over the fish. Add some peppercorns, cloves (2–3 for every 30 smelt), thyme and bay leaves. Add vinegar and soak for at least 24 hours before serving as a cold hors d'oeuvre.

The vinegar in the marinade can be replaced by white wine boiled with 2 chopped shallots, 1 bouquet garni and some salt and pepper.

fried smelt
Dip the prepared smelt in salted milk, then roll them in flour and shake off any excess. Deep-fry in very hot oil at 175–180°C (347–350°F), then drain the fish on paper towels and sprinkle with fine salt. If desired, arrange in a cluster and garnish with fried parsley. Serve with lemon quarters.

grilled smelt à l'anglaise
Prepare the smelt, split them lengthways along the back and remove the backbone. Gently open them out and season with salt, pepper and a little cayenne pepper. Dip them one by one in melted butter and in fresh breadcrumbs, then grill (broil) them quickly. Sprinkle with fine salt and serve with maître d'hôtel butter.

smelt velouté soup à la dieppoise
Prepare a velouté soup* using 75 g (3 oz, ⅓ cup) white roux, 750 ml (1¼ pints, 3¼ cups) fish stock and 100 ml (4 fl oz, 7 tablespoons) mussel cooking liquid. Cook 250 g (9 oz) cleaned smelt and 1 tablespoon chopped onion in butter. Fillet the smelt and reduce to a purée. Add this to the velouté, then sieve. The mixture can be thickened with 1 or 2 egg yolks, if desired. Garnish the soup with 12 poached mussels and 12 peeled prawns (shelled shrimp).

SMETANA A soured (sour) cream, used extensively in central and eastern Europe. Produced by bacterial fermentation, it does not keep well. It is mainly used with fish, borsch, and as a sauce for stuffed cabbage leaves, sauerkraut and Hungarian meat stews. The similar *sauere Sahne* of Germany has a milder taste but is used in the same ways and also in horseradish sauce with herrings.

SMEUN Also known as *smen* or *smenn*. Clarified butter used in Arabic and Maghrebi cookery. Europeans loosely describe it as rancid, but this is incorrect. Smeun is made with the butter from ewe's milk or occasionally cow's milk (even buffalo's milk in Egypt), which is liquefied, clarified and mixed with a

Skate with noisette butter, see page 1095.

little salt (or sometimes semolina). It is stored in earthenware or stoneware pots. The traditional preparation of smeun came from the need to preserve fats in hot climates. As it ages, the butter becomes refined and develops an almond taste. It is used in pastries and in the preparation of couscous, broths and *tajines*.

SMOKING A traditional method of preserving fresh food, such as meat and fish, using prolonged exposure to smoke from a wood fire. Smoking tends to dry the food, kills bacteria and other micro-organisms on the food's surface, deepens its colour and impregnates it with a smoky flavour. Nowadays, smoking (or smoke-curing) is rather less a means of preserving than a process for giving flavour to meat or fish.

Smoked meat is traditional in many countries. *Bresil*, from Franche-Comté in eastern France, is made from lean beef, salted and hardened, and served in very thin slices; South American *charqui* is beef, mutton or llama cut into long strips and dried; *grisons* meat (lean beef soaked in brine and dried in the open to give a very close texture) comes from Switzerland; and *pastirma* from Turkey is smoked leg or shoulder of mutton.

Smoking is mostly performed on certain cuts of pork (ham, belly, bacon), sausages (for example, frankfurters), poultry (goose, raw or cooked chicken, cooked turkey pieces), some game (wild boar, pheasant) and some fish (salmon, eel, sturgeon). It is often preceded by salting or soaking in brine. For fish, there are two techniques. In cold smoking (20–30°C, 68–86°F), the fish is exposed to the smoke from a slow-burning wood fire; in hot smoking, it is first exposed to a draught of hot air (60–80°C, 140–176°F) emitted by a fast-burning fire, then placed in the thick smoke from a fire covered with sawdust. This second type of smoking involves a limited degree of cooking of the fish. Meat and pork products are hot-smoked, directly over an open fire.

The duration of smoking varies from 20 minutes to several days. The most commonly used woods are beech, oak and chestnut, to which aromatics (juniper, heather, laurel, sage and rosemary) can be added. In the United States, hickory is often used. In France, sausages in Savoy are smoked over fir wood, while in the Charente, mussels are cooked in the smoke from pine needles. (In general, however, resinous woods perform badly and produce an acrid taste.) In Brittany, gorse is used for ham. In Andalucia in Spain, chorizo is smoked over juniper, a plant also used by the Sicilians to smoke ewe's-milk cheese. The Chinese smoke eggs over fennel, cinnamon and poplar sawdust fires.

A smoky flavour can be produced using a concentrate extracted from carbonized wood. The concentrate is sprayed over the surfaces of the foods, but the food is not thoroughly impregnated, as in true smoking. This smoky flavour is mostly given to foods that cannot undergo traditional smoking, such as biscuits (crackers) and cheese.

SMOOTH HOUND Small shark of the family of *Triakidae*, of which there are species worldwide. In France, the smooth hound (*émissole*) is sold skinned under the name *saumonette*. It has a flesh that is much appreciated, particularly in Normandy, where it is cooked *à la crème*.

SMÖRGASBORD An abundant assortment of hot and cold dishes served in Sweden as hors d'oeuvre or a full buffet meal, related to the Russian zakuski. The literal meaning of the word is 'table of buttered bread' and it is a vast buffet from which guests serve themselves according to their appetite. A traditional order is observed: the first course is herrings, as this is the king of Scandinavian foods. On the first plate one might mix *hareng du verrier* (herrings marinated in sugar, vinegar, carrots and spices) with some fried marinated herring, herring with soured (sour) cream and smoked herring with raw sliced onion or cucumber. The herring dishes are followed by other fish dishes: salmon and smoked eels; jellied trout; cod roes with fennel; hard-boiled (hard-cooked) eggs with caviar or salmon roe; lobster salad; crab with shrimps, peas and mushrooms; or the typical smörgasbord speciality *fagelbö*, a salad of sprats, lettuce, onions, capers, sliced beetroot (red beet) and raw egg yolk. Then plates are changed for the third course, which consists of cold meats and Swedish charcuterie: veal in aspic, pressed tongue, roast beef and liver pâté, with vegetable macédoine in mayonnaise or cold pasta salads. The fourth course includes several traditional Swedish hot dishes: 'Janssen's temptation', an anchovy or sprat gratin with potatoes, cream and onions; stuffed onions; and meatballs with (bell) peppers and so on.

Several varieties of ryebread and crisp pancakes are served with the meal; there are also several types of cheese, both strong and mild (which are often eaten first, before the herrings). The desserts are usually fruit-based; for example, baked apples, cheesecake, cakes made with berries or fruit salad. Beer and aquavit are served for drinks.

Traditionally, smörgasbord was a sumptuous and carefully prepared buffet, at which the hostess could employ all her skills. It is now only really available in restaurants rather than in the home. Historically, it dates back to the ancient Norse custom of putting all the dishes for a meal on the table together. The present form dates from the 19th century, when catering helped its development considerably.

SNAIL A terrestrial gastropod mollusc characterized by a spiral shell. Some species are highly prized in gastronomy, particularly in France, where the snail is called *escargot* and where two native species are most commonly eaten.

• BURGUNDY OR ROMAN SNAIL Also called vineyard snail or large white, it is 4.5 cm (1¾ in) long. It has a slightly mottled or veined body and a tawny-yellow shell streaked with brown; the aperture of the shell is smooth or barely rimmed. It has a slow rate of growth, taking two to three years to reach maturity.

Rearing them is difficult, but wild snails may be collected in Burgundy, Franche-Comté, Savoy and Champagne.

• PETIT-GRIS This is the common snail or garden snail. It is 2.5 cm (1 in) long, with an unpatterned body and a brownish shell with a spiral of fawn-grey; the aperture has a rimmed edge. In the wild, it is found mostly in Provence, Roussillon and Languedoc, but also in Charente and Brittany. Its flesh is delicate, fruity and slightly firm.

■ **Buying snails** These snails are sold either live or freshly cooked in France (by pork butchers, caterers and fishmongers), or frozen.

The French species are becoming increasingly rare and, although the *petit-gris* is reared on snail farms in various parts of the world, imports of other varieties have increased to meet the demand. These include large snails from Algeria and Turkey, which have a striped shell, and snails from central Turkey, which are imported either live, canned or frozen. Giant 'Achatine' snails, less delicate and sold preserved, come from China, Indonesia and Africa. These are commercially reared and can reach 450 g (1 lb) in weight.

The types of live snail available depend on the season: spring and autumn for the *coureurs* ('runners'); summer and winter when they are *operculés* (the shell's aperture is sealed off for hibernation) or *voilés* ('veiled' – these are the best and, because they have fasted, the leanest). In France, the collection of both Burgundy and *petit-gris* snails is governed by regulations.

■ **History** Snails were among the first animals to be eaten by man, on the evidence of the heaps of shells found in prehistoric sites. It was the Romans who first prepared them for cooking. They had 'snaileries' where the snails were fattened on wine and bran, and Pliny speaks of grilled (broiled) snails, eaten with wine as a snack before or after meals. The Gauls, it seems, enjoyed them as a dessert. In the Middle Ages, the Church permitted consumption of snails on days of abstinence. They were fried with oil or onion, cooked on skewers or boiled. But Nicolas de Bonnefons was 'astonished that the odd tastes of man have led him as far as this depraved dish in order to satisfy the extravagance of gluttony'.

In the 17th century, the consumption of snails was appreciably reduced. But Talleyrand brought them back into fashion in the early 19th century by asking Carême to prepare some for the dinner he gave for the tsar of Russia.

■ **French gastronomy** All the regions of France have their own name for the snail; it is called *cagouille* in Saintonge, *lumas* in Poitou, *caracol* in Flanders, *carnar* in Lorraine, *carago* or *cacalau* in Provence, *carcaulada* in Roussillon and *cantaleu* in Nice. In the south, it is usually prepared in wine, with bacon or ham, spices, garlic and olive oil; it is also included in tarts, pastries and turnovers, cooked in broths, fricassées or on skewers, or grilled on a wood fire. For the classic entrée, snails are stuffed with butter à la bourguignonne and served piping hot in their shells or in tiny individual pots, 6–12 at a time, on a special grooved dish, the *escargotière*; they are eaten using a special pair of tongs and a small two-pronged fork.

Suçarelle is a typical regional dish from southeastern France: small snails (preferably) are cooked in court-bouillon with fennel and rosemary, then browned in olive oil with onion, tomatoes, bay leaf, garlic and pepper; they are then floured, sprinkled with stock and lemon juice, and simmered for a long time; the bottom of the shell is pierced and the flesh sucked through the hole.

Grimod de La Reynière gives recipes that use only the shells: 'In the season when snails are unobtainable, we sometimes divert ourselves by deceiving the senses through a semblance which is not unamusing. We make an excellent fine forcemeat, either of game or of fish, with anchovy fillets, nutmeg, delicate spices, herbs and a binding of egg yolks. Well-washed and very hot snail shells are used. Each one is filled with the forcemeat and they are served burning hot.' The recipe for *escargots simulés Comtesse Riguidi* is as follows: 'In large well-washed snail shells (from which, naturally, you will have expelled any undesirable inhabitant) you place rounds of lambs' sweetbreads sautéed in butter. Fill the cavity of the shells with a fine forcemeat of creamed chicken, to which some chopped white truffle has been added. Place the snails disguised in this way in an ovenproof dish or a snail dish; sprinkle with breadcrumbs and cook for a few minutes in the oven.'

Snails served with butter in their shells may be prepared à l'alsacienne (using flavoured aspic, garlic butter and aniseed), à l'italienne (maître d'hôtel butter and Parmesan cheese) or à la valaisane (chilli-flavoured gravy, garlic butter and chives). Snails served with sauce may be prepared à la poulette; other sauces include garlic-flavoured mayonnaise and béarnaise sauce. They can also be cooked in red wine or white wine, flamed in Armagnac or lightly fried.

■ **Preparation** Snails collected from the wild need to be starved for about 10 days to ensure they are rid of any poisonous leaves they may have eaten. (In Provence, instead of fasting, they are put on a diet of thyme, which helps the molluscs to eliminate poisonous material and also flavours their flesh.) Some authorities recommend that snails should not be purged with salt, because that risks spoiling their gastronomic quality. If they are purged, a small handful of coarse salt is required for 48 large snails, together with 5 tablespoons vinegar and a pinch of flour. Cover the vessel containing the snails and place a weight on top: leave to soak for 3 hours, stirring from time to time. Next, wash the snails in several changes of water to remove all the mucus, then blanch them for 5 minutes in boiling water. Drain and rinse in fresh water. Shell them and take out the black part (cloaca) at the end of the 'tail', but do not remove the mantle, comprising the liver and other organs, which represents a quarter of the total weight of the animal and is the most delicious and nutritious part. Cultivated snails do not require the purification period but should be used on the day of purchase.

RECIPES

butter for snails

Finely chop 40 g (1½ oz) shallots and enough parsley to fill 1 tablespoon. Crush 2 garlic cloves. Add all these ingredients to 350 g (12 oz, 1½ cups) softened butter, 1 tablespoon salt and a good pinch of pepper. Mix well. (This quantity is sufficient to fill about 50 snail shells.)

snail broth

(from an ancient recipe) Prepare 36 snails. Shell them and put them in a saucepan containing 3 litres (5 pints, 13 cups) water. Add 400 g (14 oz) calf's head, 1 lettuce (cleaned and quartered), a handful of purslane leaves and a little salt. Heat, then skim. Bring to the boil, then reduce the heat and simmer for about 2 hours. Adjust the seasoning and strain.

snails à la bourguignonne

Put the shelled snails in a saucepan and cover them with a mixture of equal parts of white wine and stock. Add 1 tablespoon chopped shallot, 15 g (½ oz) onion and 75 g (3 oz) carrot per 1 litre (1¾ pints, 4⅓ cups) liquid and 1 large bouquet garni. Add salt, allowing 1 teaspoon per 1 litre (1¾ pints, 4⅓ cups).

Simmer for about 2 hours, then leave to cool in the cooking liquid. Meanwhile, boil the empty shells in water containing 1 tablespoon soda crystals per 1 litre (1¾ pints, 4⅓ cups). Drain them, wash in plenty of water and dry in the oven, without letting them colour. Prepare some butter for snails; at least 50 g (2 oz, ¼ cup) is required for 12 snails. Remove the snails from the cooking liquid. Place a little butter in the bottom of each shell, insert a snail and fill up the shell with more butter. Arrange in snail dishes and heat without letting the butter brown. Serve piping hot.

snails à la poulette

Cook 48 shelled snails as for snails à la bourguignonne, then drain. Prepare a white roux using 25 g (1 oz, 2 tablespoons) butter and 25 g (1 oz, ¼ cup) plain (all-purpose) flour. Add 250 ml (8 fl oz, 1 cup) chicken stock, 250 ml (8 fl oz, 1 cup) white wine and 1 bouquet garni. Cook briskly for about 15 minutes, or until the sauce is reduced by a third. Soften 1 large chopped onion in 20 g (¾ oz, 1½ tablespoons) butter in a saucepan. Add the snails and the sauce and cook for 5 minutes.

Meanwhile, mix 2 egg yolks and the juice of 1 lemon; chop a small bunch of parsley. Remove the bouquet garni from the saucepan. Blend a little of the hot sauce with the egg yolks and lemon juice,

then add to the saucepan. Stir briskly and remove from the heat. Sprinkle with chopped parsley and serve piping hot.

snails grilled à la mode du languedoc

Arrange some shelled snails on a grid (grill). Prepare a fire of vine shoots; as soon as the embers form a light ash, place the grid on top, sprinkle the snails with salt, pepper, thyme and crushed fennel and grill. Meanwhile, cook some diced fatty bacon in a frying pan until soft. Tip the cooked snails into a dish and baste with the sizzling bacon fat. Serve immediately with farmhouse bread and red wine.

SNAKE Practically all snakes, poisonous or not, are edible: the boas of South America, the pythons of Africa, the cobras of Asia, the rattlesnakes of Mexico and the grass snakes and adders of Europe. Until the 18th century, adder-based diets were very fashionable in France for their beneficial effects on health and beauty. Mme de Sévigné, who obtained her adders from Poitou, advised her daughter to go on a month's adder diet once a year. Recipes of the period are full of suggestions: the adders should be skinned and gutted (cleaned), cooked with herbs, used to stuff a capon, cooked in stock, jellied or made into oils.

In China, an ancient recipe mentions the three cobras necessary to make a very complex dish called 'the meeting of the tiger, the phoenix and the dragon'. In Cameroon, a ragoût of adder and spices is prepared. In a recipe for python stew, the snake is skinned, cut into pieces, dusted with flour, and sealed in a frying pan with palm oil, then flamed with Armagnac and stewed for 5 hours in a rich tomato and onion sauce (fondue) flavoured with shallots, thyme, bay leaf and (bell) peppers. This dish is considered to taste like sautéed chicken.

SNAPPER The name given to a wide number of different tropical sea fish, the best known of which is probably the red snapper, also known as mangrove jack, an Indo-Pacific fish, popular from Australia to America. The name 'red snapper' is also applied to a number of different tropical fish of that colour; specific examples include the humpback red snapper, Malabar red snapper and emperor red snapper. Other popular snappers from the Atlantic waters off the United States, include the grey, yellowtail, mutton and schoolmaster snappers.

Snappers take their name from their large, often pointed heads and sharp-toothed mouths capable of a sharp snapping action. Their eating quality varies from good to excellent.

SNIPE A migratory game bird, similar in appearance to the woodcock but smaller, having a wing span of 50 cm (20 in); it is found in marshes, ponds and water meadows. Snipe are hunted from August to April (but are best in the autumn) in the northern hemisphere and are more easily shot than woodcock. The plumage is brownish-black on the head and back and white underneath. It is prepared in the same way as woodcock. See also *Lucullus*.

SNOEK The South African name, also used in Australia (where it is more commonly known as barracouta), for an elongated, blue-backed, carnivorous fish (*Leionura*) with a maximum length of 135 cm (4 ft 6 in). Abundant in the southern Pacific and Atlantic, it was much canned and exported during World War II.

SNOWBALL An ice cream dessert – *boule-de-neige* in French – made using a spherical (bombe) mould. The mould is lined with chocolate ice cream, filled with a mousse mixture and, when turned out, covered with Chantilly cream.

SNOW PEA See *mange-tout*.

SOAK To immerse a foodstuff in water for a variable length of time. Soaking is carried out to reconstitute dried vegetables or fruits, to facilitate the cooking of dried vegetables (lentils, beans), to desalt salt fish (especially salt cod), or to clean and wash vegetables or preserve them in the short term.

SOAVE AOC dry white wine produced in the Veneto region using 70–90% Garganega, the remainder being Chardonnay, Pinot Blanc or Trebbiano. It can be one of Italy's best wines.

SOBRESSADA A speciality of Spanish charcuterie, this is an unsmoked spreading sausage that consists of small pieces of lean meat in a fatty stuffing, highly seasoned and coloured with sweet (bell) pepper. The name *sobressada de Mallorca* is protected so no imitations can be made.

SOBRONADE A rustic soup from Périgord in France, made from haricot (navy) beans, potatoes, root vegetables, celery, and flavourings, garnished with both fresh and salt pork or sometimes ham.

RECIPE

sobronade
Soak 800 g (1¾ lb, 4½ cups) dried haricot (navy) beans in cold water for 12 hours. Peel 2 turnips and cut into thick slices. Brown one third of these in a pan with 100 g (4 oz, ½ cup) chopped fat bacon. Drain the beans and put them into a large saucepan, cover completely with cold water and add 250 g (9 oz, 1¼ cups) diced ham and a piece of fresh pork (fat and lean), weighing about 800 g (1¾ lb). Bring to the boil and skim; add all the turnip, 1 bouquet garni, 1 onion studded with 2 cloves, 4 carrots, 2 sliced celery sticks, 1 bunch of parsley and 2 chopped garlic cloves. Boil for about 20 minutes, then add 250 g (9 oz) potatoes cut into thick slices and leave to cook for about another 40 minutes. Garnish a soup tureen with slices of dried bread and pour the soup on top.

SOCCA A flour made from chick peas in the Nice region of France. A thick porridge is made from it, which can be cooked au gratin, used to fill a tart, or sliced (when cold), fried in olive oil and served with sugar. The latter is a popular delicacy, which is sold in the streets.

RECIPE

socca
Mix 125 g (4½ oz, 1 cup) chick pea flour with 250 ml (8 fl oz, 1 cup) water, salt, pepper and 1 tablespoon olive oil. Whisk vigorously. Pour this mixture into 2 large buttered gratin dishes. Cook in a preheated oven at 240°C (475°F, gas 9) for 20 minutes. Using a fork, prick the bubbles that have formed on the surface of the socca, then grill (broil) until golden under a preheated grill (broiler).

SODA BREAD A type of non-yeast bread, leavened with bicarbonate of soda (baking soda), of Irish origin. The bread was traditionally cooked in a covered pot over a peat fire. It is always served freshly baked, preferably still warm. Bicarbonate of soda and acidic sour milk or buttermilk, left after churning butter, react to make the bread rise. The solid loaf, with only a little butter, has a deep cross cut in the top to ensure that it cooks evenly. The bread can be made with white or wholemeal flour, or a mixture of both. See *bread*.

RECIPE

Irish soda bread
Sift 450 g (1 lb, 4 cups) plain (all-purpose) flour, 1 teaspoon bicarbonate of soda (baking soda) and 1 teaspoon salt into a bowl. Rub in 25 g(1 oz, 2 tablespoons) butter, then mix in about 300 ml (½ pint, 1¼ cups) buttermilk to make a soft but not sticky dough. Knead the dough briefly and quickly for a few seconds on a well-floured surface, then shape it into a ball and flatten it slightly. Place the loaf on a floured baking sheet and cut a deep cross in the top. Bake in a preheated oven at 220°C (425°F, gas 7) for about 40 minutes, until risen, browned and firm. Cool on a wire rack. Serve the loaf on the day it is baked.
Variation Fresh milk and 1 tablespoon lemon juice can be used instead of the buttermilk.

SODA WATER Effervescent mineral water formerly sold in a siphon but now usually bottled. Soda water is used to dilute spirits, syrups and fruit juices.

SOFT ROE The sperm, or milt, of a male fish. Soft roe is white and smooth. Roes can be used fresh, smoked or preserved in oil. Herring roes are the most widely available variety, followed by carp (one of Brillat-Savarin's favourite dishes when used as an omelette filling) and mackerel. Whether poached in a court-bouillon or cooked *à la meunière*, they can be served as hot hors d'oeuvre (barquettes, bouchées, canapés and fritters) or used as a garnish in fish dishes. Poached roes can be cooked briefly in butter or oil, with herbs or lemon zest, and then served on toast or croûtes as a snack or light meal.

RECIPES

poached soft roes in court-bouillon
Soak the roes in cold water for 2 hours, then remove the small blood vessels that run down the sides. Prepare a simple court-bouillon with cold water, a little lemon juice, salt and oil – 2 table-spoons for every 500 ml (17 fl oz, 2 cups) water. Put the roes in this liquid, bring slowly to a very gentle simmer and poach for about 4 minutes. Drain and cool.

soft roes à la meunière
Soak the roes and blot them dry with paper towels Coat them with flour, shake off any excess and fry in butter seasoned with salt and pepper. Sprinkle with lemon juice.

soft roes à l'anglaise
Poach the roes in a court-bouillon and allow to cool. Coat them in flour, then dip them in egg and breadcrumbs. Fry in butter, browning on both sides. Arrange on a serving dish and sprinkle with a mixture of melted butter and lemon juice. Garnish with half slices of lemon.

soft roes in noisette butter
Poach the roes in a court-bouillon, dry on paper towels and arrange on a long dish. Sprinkle with capers and chopped parsley, together with a little lemon juice. Top with a few tablespoons of noisette butter.

The lemon juice may be replaced with a few drops of vinegar, and the chopped parsley with 2 tablespoons chervil added to the noisette butter.

soft roes in scallop shells à la normande
Poach the roes in a court-bouillon and drain them. Put them in scallop shells edged with a border of duchess potatoes, previously browned in the oven. Top the roes in each shell with a poached drained oyster, a cooked mushroom and 1 scant tablespoon shrimps and mussels. Coat with normande, Mornay or butter sauce, and garnish each shell with a generous strip of truffle.

other recipes See *barquette, fritter, pannequet.*

SOLE A flat sea fish, almost a perfect oval in shape, found in the waters around western Europe. There are no true soles found in American waters, although the name may be used for some flounder-like fish. Soles have eyes on the right-hand side of their head (which is grey or brown, the blind side being creamy white). Soles range in weight from 200–800 g (7 oz–1¾ lb).

The sole was the favourite fish in the cookery of ancient Rome, where it was called *solea Jovi* (Jupiter's sandal). In former times it was preserved (marinated in salt), sweated, fried, made into pâté or soup, stewed or roasted. During the reign of the French king, Louis XIV, it became a 'royal dish', since when the fillets have been used in a number of elaborate dishes, one of which was created by the Marquise de Pompadour. The great French chefs of the 19th century, especially Dugléré and Marguery, exercised all their skill in preparing sole dishes.

■ **Types of sole** As a general rule, the finest sole are fished in deep, rather than coastal waters; cold-water varieties are better than those of warmer seas. Since about 50% of the weight is lost in trimmings, sole is often bought gutted (cleaned) and skinned or filleted. Its freshness is indicated by a very white blind side, coloured gills and, above all, by a very sticky skin.

• DOVER SOLE Also called Channel sole, this is the best-known and tastiest sole. It is brown or grey in colour and reaches a maximum length of 50 cm (20 in). Fished in the English Channel, the Atlantic, the Baltic and the North Sea, Dover sole is exported from The Netherlands, Belgium, Denmark and England. The flesh is firm and delicate with an exquisite taste, which is best when grilled (broiled) or pan-fried whole and served plainly. Alternatively, it can be filleted into 4 for serving with sauces.

• SAND SOLE Also called partridge, or French, sole, this has dark stripes and is smaller (up to 35.5 cm/ 14 in long) and less tasty than Dover sole. It is fished in the English Channel and the Atlantic, as far as Nantes on the west coast of France.

• THICKBACK SOLE This is smaller and thicker than the sand sole, and again not as tasty as Dover sole.

• CÉTEAU OR SÉTEAU This is a very small species of sole, common off the west coast of France between the Loire and Arcachon, but also caught off African coasts. It is known as *langue de chat* (cat's tongue) or *avocat* (lawyer) in the south-west of France. It has a clear brown skin and is seldom longer than 25 cm (10 in). It is usually cooked by very quick frying in hot oil.

• WITCH OR TORBAY SOLE This is not a true sole but a variety of plaice with a reasonable flavour. It is an inexpensive substitute for Dover sole, as is the lemon sole (see *dab*).

■ **Preparing and cooking** There are very few bones in the flesh, but there is a long fin armed with straight sharp spines all around the fish, which should be carefully removed with a fish knife. The large bones linked to the backbone are easily removed.

Usual cooking methods are deep-frying for the smallest fish; steaming, pan-frying or grilling (broiling) for medium sole or sole fillets (200–250 g/ 7–9 oz); and poaching in stock for larger fish. Stuffed sole are braised or cooked in the oven. Fillets, rolled into paupiettes or left flat, are poached and served with a sauce or coated with breadcrumbs and fried.

There are more recipes for sole than for any other fish: *à l'amiral*, *à la bonne femme*, *au gratin*, *à la dieppoise*, Colbert, Dugléré, Mornay, Joinville, Nantua and *à la normande*. Fillets lend themselves to even more recipes: *à la bâtelière*, *à la bordelaise*, *en goujonnettes*, *à la hongroise*, *à la Riche* and *à la Walewska*, not forgetting aspics, kebabs, croquettes, fritters, pâtés, timbales and vol-au-vent fillings.

Undoubtedly the most popular classic dish is a succulent sole meunière, as described by Proust in *À l'ombre des jeunes filles en fleurs*: ' . . . from the leathery skin of a lemon we squeezed a few golden drops on two sole, which soon left their bones on our plates, light as a feather and sonorous as a zither.'

RECIPES

preparing sole and fillets of sole
To skin a sole, take hold of the tail fin with a cloth and cut the black skin at a slight angle just above the fin. Gently detach the skin with your thumb, then take hold of it with the cloth and remove it with one sharp pull towards the head. Remove the head and, for the white side, pull the skin from the head towards the tail. Cut the side fins close to the flesh with scissors. The head can also be cut in half at an angle. To remove the fillets, cut the flesh down to the bones on each side of the backbone with a filleting knife. Detach the flesh with the knife, from the backbone to the sides, to make 4 fillets. Remove any debris attached to the flesh and flatten slightly. Wash under running water.

fillets of sole à la cantonnaise
Trim 2 good fillets for each guest. Sprinkle each one with a very small pinch of ground coriander, cinnamon, mixed spice, nutmeg and chopped onion. Add 2 slices of fresh root ginger and fold the fillets in half. Sprinkle with oil and a little more seasoning, then steam for 10–12 minutes. Arrange on a warm plate and season with salt and pepper.

Prepare the sauce separately. Heat 4 tablespoons oil in a pan and add 2 large chopped green (bell) peppers, 50 g (2 oz, ⅔ cup) sliced mushrooms, 8 thin strips of smoked pork, a slice of ham cut into strips, 100 g (4 oz, ¾ cup) chopped shrimps and a drained 225 g (8 oz) can of crabmeat. Cook for 5 minutes, stirring continuously. Beat 2 eggs with 1 tablespoon soy sauce; stir into the pan and dilute with a little stock blended with 2 tablespoons tomato purée (paste). Reheat and pour over the fillets of sole.

fillets of sole à l'anglaise
Coat 8 fillets of sole with egg and breadcrumbs and cook them in clarified butter. Arrange on a long plate and cover with maître d'hôtel butter. Serve with potatoes or a boiled or steamed green vegetable such as leeks or spinach.

Fillets of sole poached in salted water and milk are also known by this name. They are served with boiled potatoes and melted butter. Whole sole can be cooked in the same way.

fillets of sole au gratin
Butter a gratin dish and coat the base with 4 tablespoons dry mushroom duxelles*. Arrange 8 seasoned fillets of sole on top. Garnish with sliced mushrooms around the dish and place 2 mushroom caps cooked in butter on each fillet. Coat with a little duxelles sauce to which some concentrated fish fumet has been added, sprinkle with breadcrumbs and clarified butter, and cook in a preheated oven at 230°C (450°F, gas 8) until brown. Sprinkle with the juice of half a lemon and serve in the cooking dish.

fillets of sole Cubat
Poach fillets of sole in mushroom stock and butter. Place on a long ovenproof dish and cover with a thick mushroom duxelles. Place 2 slices of truffle on each fillet. Coat with Mornay sauce and brown in the oven. (This dish is named after Pierre Cubat, chef at the court of Russia in 1903.)

fillets of sole Drouant
Arrange trimmed fillets of sole in a buttered dish. Season with salt and pepper, sprinkle with 1 finely chopped shallot and moisten to the level of the fish with white wine and mussel stock. Cover and cook in a preheated oven at 220°C (425°F, gas 7) for 7 minutes. Drain the fillets and reduce the cooking juices by half. Add an equal amount of crème fraîche. Remove from the heat and add 100 g (4 oz, ½ cup) butter and the same amount of américaine sauce (prepared as in the recipe for lobster* *à l'américaine*). Strain and pour over the fillets. Glaze quickly in a preheated oven. Serve the fillets surrounded with shelled mussels and peeled prawns (shelled shrimp).

fillets of sole homardine
Fillet 3 × 800 g (1¾ lb) sole. Prepare a fish fumet* with 500 g (18 oz) lean fish trimmings, 200 ml (7 fl oz, ¾ cup) Chablis, 200 ml (7 fl oz, ¾ cup) water, 1 onion, 1 shallot, 1 lemon, 1 bouquet garni, a bunch of parsley, salt and pepper.

Prepare a lobster *à l'américaine* as follows: peel, seed and chop 5 tomatoes; make a mirepoix* of 1 onion, 2 shallots, 2 garlic cloves, 1 carrot and ¼ celery stick. Remove the leaves from a tarragon sprig and chop it. Remove the lobster's tail. Split the shell in half and reserve the juices (greenish parts) and the coral. Cook the lobster halves and the tail in a pan with 100 ml (4 fl oz, 7 tablespoons) olive oil until red; add the mirepoix, mix and pour over 100 ml (4 fl oz, 7 tablespoons) brandy. Flame, then add the chopped tomatoes, ½ teaspoon concentrated tomato purée (paste), 300 ml (½ pint, 1¼ cups) Chablis, some tarragon and 1 bouquet garni. Add just enough water to cover the lobster. Season with salt, pepper and a pinch of cayenne pepper. Cover and cook for 20 minutes.

Prepare some beurre manié by mixing the reserved coral and juices of the lobster with 75 g (3 oz, 6 tablespoons) butter and 1 tablespoon flour. Drain the cooked lobster and reduce the cooking juices by half.

Strain the fish fumet and poach the fillets of sole in it for about 10 minutes. Drain the fillets, reduce the fumet and strain.

Cover the bottom of an ovenproof dish with 300 g (11 oz, 3½ cups) sliced mushroom caps; put the fillets and shelled sliced lobster tail on top. Cover the dish with foil and place in a preheated oven at 140°C (275°F, gas 1) to keep warm.

Make a hollandaise* sauce with 100 g (4 oz, ½ cup) butter, 3 eggs, juice of half a lemon, salt and pepper. Mix the beurre manié into the reduced cooking juices, stir for 3 minutes, then add the fish fumet and the hollandaise sauce. Mix well and add 2 tablespoons crème fraîche. The sauce should be rich and smooth. Coat the fillets with the sauce, garnish with little puff-pastry flowers and glaze in a very hot oven. Serve immediately.

fillets of sole Marco Polo

Roughly chop some tarragon, fennel and 1 celery stick. Crush some lobster or langouste shells and put them in a frying pan. Flame with brandy and add the trimmings from 4 sole. Moisten with 300 ml (½ pint, 1¼ cups) white wine and simmer, allowing the liquid to reduce slightly.

Place 50 g (2 oz, ¼ cup) butter, ½ chopped shallot, and half a peeled, seeded and crushed tomato in a saucepan and moisten with 200 ml (7 fl oz, ¾ cup) champagne. Season with salt and pepper. Poach the fillets of sole in this mixture for 5–6 minutes.

Sieve the cooking juices of the shells, crushing the latter firmly, then strain through muslin (cheesecloth). Add 100 g (4 oz, ½ cup) butter and whisk in 2 egg yolks and 100 ml (4 fl oz, 7 tablespoons) crème fraîche.

Serve the fillets in their cooking juices, well reduced, separately from the lobster sauce.

fillets of sole Robert Courtine

Fillet 2 × 675 g (1½ lb) sole. Sprinkle with lemon juice and keep cool. Sweat 2 chopped shallots in a knob of butter over a gentle heat, moisten with 100 ml (4 fl oz, 7 tablespoons) white wine and add a pinch of salt and pepper. Reduce slightly and add 250 ml (8 fl oz, 1 cup) soured (sour) cream. Reduce by a third, remove from the heat and whisk in 150 g (5 oz, ⅔ cup) butter cut into small pieces. Strain into a sauceboat and keep warm in a bain marie. Reserve the shallots for the forcemeat.

Flake 200 g (7 oz) white fish in a bowl, mix with the reserved shallots and season with salt and pepper. Place the bowl over crushed ice and work in 150 ml (¼ pint, ⅔ cup) double (heavy) cream. Lay the fillets of sole skin-side up and season lightly. Spread the forcemeat along the fish and fold into 3. Steam (on seaweed, if possible) for 7–8 minutes.

Arrange on a dish and sprinkle with a little sevruga caviare. Add the remaining caviare – about 75 g (3 oz) altogether – to the sauce, mix gently and pour over the fillets.

Garnish with chunks of peeled, blanched, steamed cucumber bound with soured (sour) cream or, better still, make a garnish of small potato pancakes: rub 250 g (9 oz) boiled potatoes through a fine sieve into a basin. Add 3 tablespoons plain (all-purpose) flour and 2 tablespoons double cream, mix with a fork and beat in 5 whole eggs, one at a time. Heat a heavy pan over a gentle heat, lightly cover the bottom with oil and pour in the mixture to make small pancakes, which require about 3 minutes cooking on each side. The potato pancakes can be made in advance and kept warm.

fillets of sole with apples

Boil 2 teaspoons green peppercorns with 2 tablespoons fish fumet in a pan. Add 3 tablespoons crème fraîche, pepper and a pinch of salt. Reduce, add 2 sliced tart apples and cook for a few seconds. Gently poach 4 fillets of sole in a little fish fumet for 2 minutes. Drain, arrange on a plate and surround with the apples. Add the cooking juices of the fish to the peppercorn mixture and bring to the boil. Pour over the fish and serve.

fillets of sole with basil

Cover the bottom of an ovenproof dish with a mixture of 4 finely chopped shallots, 1 tablespoon basil and 1 tablespoon olive oil. Arrange the seasoned fillets of 2 × 800 g (1¾ lb) sole on top. Moisten with 5 tablespoons fish stock and an equal amount of white wine. Cover with foil and bring to the boil over a brisk heat, then place in a preheated oven at 230°C (450°F, gas 8) for 5 minutes. Drain the fish and keep warm on 2 plates. Reduce the cooking juices to a third. Whisk in 125 g (4½ oz, ½ cup) butter in small pieces, adjust the seasoning and add the juice of half a lemon. Plunge a tomato into boiling water for 30 seconds, peel, seed and dice, then place the tomato on the fillets and coat with the sauce. Sprinkle with chopped basil.

fillets of sole with mushrooms

Fold each fillet of sole over 2 large mushroom caps and cook over a gentle heat in a fish fumet prepared with white wine. Carefully invert the drained fish on to a long dish so that the mushrooms face upwards. Add an equal quantity of crème fraîche to the cooking juices and reduce by half. Whisk in 25 g (1 oz, 2 tablespoons) butter, strain and pour over the fish.

fillets of sole with noodles

Lay 8 fillets of sole in a buttered dish. Sprinkle them with chopped shallots and season. Moisten with white wine and fish fumet (made with the skin and bones of the sole). Add a crushed tomato and cook in the oven for 8 minutes.

Meanwhile, make a hollandaise sauce. Cook

some fresh noodles *al dente*; refresh them, turn into a buttered gratin dish and bind with 100 ml (4 fl oz, 7 tablespoons) crème fraîche. Place the drained fillets on top; reduce the cooking juices and add to the hollandaise sauce with a little crème fraîche. Adjust the seasoning, coat the fillets and glaze in a very hot oven.

fillets of sole with vermouth

Place the fillets of sole in a buttered pan. Moisten with 100 ml (4 fl oz, 7 tablespoons) fish fumet and 100 ml (4 fl oz, 7 tablespoons) dry vermouth. Poach gently for 10 minutes. Remove the fish and keep warm. Cook 125 g (4½ oz, 1⅓ cups) sliced mushroom caps in butter over a brisk heat for 4 minutes, with salt, pepper and lemon juice. Strain both cooking juices into a pan and reduce to 4 tablespoons; add 400 ml (14 fl oz, 1¾ cups) double (heavy) cream and boil. Remove from the heat and bind with 3 egg yolks. Reheat, stirring, without allowing the mixture to boil. Garnish the fillets with the mushrooms and coat with the sauce.

fried fillets of sole en goujons

Cut 2 large fillets of sole diagonally across in slices about 2 cm (¾ in) wide. Dip in salted milk, drain, coat with flour and fry in hot fat or oil at 180°C (350°F). Drain on paper towels, sprinkle with fine salt and arrange in a heap on a napkin. Garnish with fried parsley and lemon wedges. The fillets, also known as *goujonnettes*, can be used as a garnish for large braised fish and for sole *à la normande*.

grilled fillets of sole

Season the fillets of sole, baste with oil or clarified butter and grill (broil) each side for 4 minutes. Arrange on a long dish surrounded by lemon slices and fried parsley. Serve with melted butter flavoured with lemon juice.

grilled sole

Skin a sole of at least 400 g (14 oz). Lightly season, soak in oil and drain well. Grill (broil) on both sides. Serve with half slices of canelled lemon, fried parsley and any sauce suitable for grilled fish.

grilled sole à la niçoise

Arrange a grilled sole on a warmed dish and surround with a tomato fondue seasoned with tarragon and mixed with a little anchovy butter (½ teaspoon butter to 3–4 tablespoons fondue). Finish with capers and stoned (pitted) black (ripe) olives.

paupiettes of sole

Prepare a forcemeat from 500 g (18 oz) puréed whiting, salt, pepper and 200 ml (7 fl oz, ¾ cup) crème fraîche, working in a bowl over crushed ice.

Remove and prepare the fillets from 2 × 800 g (1¾ lb) sole. Lightly flatten them on a damp worktop and season both sides. Spread the forcemeat over the 8 fillets, roll them up and tie loosely, so that the forcemeat does not escape. Butter a flameproof dish large enough to hold the fillets upright, side by side, then sprinkle it with 2 or 3 chopped shallots and arrange the fillets in it. Season. Moisten with 175 ml (6 fl oz, ¾ cup) each of white wine and fish fumet. Cover with foil, bring to the boil, then place in a preheated oven at 230°C (450°F, gas 8) and cook for 10–15 minutes. Drain the paupiettes and arrange on a serving dish. Keep warm.

Strain the cooking juices into a small saucepan and whisk in 1 tablespoon butter. Pour this on to 2 egg yolks beaten with the juice of half a lemon, then return it to the saucepan and whisk until thick, without allowing it to boil. Pour over the paupiettes and serve very hot.

paupiettes of sole à l'ancienne

Cover 8 fillets of sole with a thin layer (250 g, 9 oz) whiting forcemeat (prepared as in the previous recipe) mixed with 75 g (3 oz) dry mushroom duxelles. Roll up the fillets, coat with egg and breadcrumbs and cook in 40 g (1½ oz, 3 tablespoons) clarified butter. Shape some small cutlets of whiting forcemeat and cook separately. Arrange the paupiettes and cutlets alternately in a ring. Garnish with a ragoût of shrimp tails, mushrooms and truffles, flavoured with Madeira.

sole à la dieppoise ♦

Poach 4 soles, each weighing 350 g (12 oz), in a mixture of 100 ml (4 fl oz, 7 tablespoons) white wine and 100 ml (4 fl oz, 7 tablespoons) fish stock, seasoned with salt and pepper. Keep warm. Cook 100 g (4 oz) button mushrooms in white stock. Cook 100 g (4 oz) prawns (shrimp) in salted water. Remove their shells and keep them warm. Cook 500 ml (17 fl oz, 3 cups) mussels with a bouquet garni over a high heat to open them. Remove them from their shells and keep warm. Prepare a roux with 40 g (1½ oz, 3 tablespoons) butter and 40 g (1½ oz, 6 tablespoons) plain (all-purpose) flour; add some of the reduced cooking liquid from the soles, and the strained cooking liquid from the mussels and that of the mushrooms. Bind with 100 ml (4 fl oz, 7 tablespoons) double (heavy) cream and 25 g (1 oz, 2 tablespoons) butter. Arrange the soles on a dish, surround with the prawns, mussels and mushrooms and pour the hot sauce on top.

sole à la meunière

Skin, gut (clean), wash and trim 4 sole, each weighing 250–300 g (9–11 oz); lightly flour and season with pepper. Heat 75–100 g (3–4 oz, 6–8 tablespoons) clarified butter and 1 tablespoon oil in a frying pan. Brown the sole for 6–7 minutes on each side. Drain and arrange on a heated serving dish. Pour over 75 g (3 oz, 6 tablespoons) butter melted in a saucepan with the juice of 1 lemon. Sprinkle with chopped parsley. Serve with sliced vegetables fried in oil or butter.

Suitable vegetables include aubergines (eggplants)

and courgettes (zucchini) fried in oil, chunks of cucumber sweated in butter, sliced artichoke hearts fried in butter, mushrooms (especially ceps) fried in butter or oil, and red or green (bell) peppers cut into thick julienne strips and sweated in oil.

sole à l'arlésienne
Poach 2 sole for 5–6 minutes in a fish fumet. Arrange on a serving dish and garnish with 4 small peeled tomatoes, cooked in butter, and 4 steamed sliced artichoke hearts to which 100 ml (4 fl oz, 7 tablespoons) reduced double (heavy) cream has been added. Then reduce the fish cooking juices and add 1 tablespoon tomato purée (paste). Add a little crushed garlic and 50–75 g (2–3 oz, 4–6 tablespoons) butter to the sauce. Pour over the sole.

sole and mushroom brochettes
Cut the fish into square pieces of equal size. Sandwich them together two by two with a stuffing made from hard-boiled (hard-cooked) egg yolks, fresh breadcrumbs and chopped parsley. Thread them on skewers, alternating them with mushrooms tossed in melted butter. Season with salt and pepper and baste with clarified butter. Cover with white dried breadcrumbs and grill (broil).

sole bagatelle
Prepare a salpicon from a lobster à l'américaine, mushrooms and truffles. Bind with very thick américaine sauce with a little added cream – 100 ml (4 fl oz, 7 tablespoons) double (heavy) cream to 300 ml (½ pint, 1¼ cups) sauce. Lay out the fillets of sole and spread with the salpicon; fold the fillets over the stuffing and coat with egg and breadcrumbs. Lightly brown them in a frying pan and arrange on a long dish, garnished with sliced truffles. Keep warm.

Cook 1 tablespoon grated shallot in butter without allowing it to colour. Moisten with 175 ml (6 fl oz, ¾ cup) dry white wine and reduce by half. Then double the volume with fish fumet and season. Add chopped parsley and the juice of 1 lemon. Thicken with 50 g (2 oz, ¼ cup) beurre manié. Cook for 10 minutes; finish with 25 g (1 oz, 2 tablespoons) butter and some finely chopped chives. Pour over the sole.

sole sur le plat
Open a sole as for stuffing. Put 25 g (1 oz, 2 tablespoons) seasoned butter inside and place in a buttered gratin dish. Moisten with fish fumet with added lemon juice to the level of the fish and dot with knobs of butter. Cook in a preheated oven at 230°C (450°F, gas 8) for about 15 minutes, basting frequently (the cooking juices should become syrupy and glaze the surface of the fish). Serve in the cooking dish.

sole with orange
Brown a trimmed floured sole in a knob of butter until cooked through on both sides. Place on a hot serving dish and season with pepper. Garnish with thin slices of peeled orange with the seeds removed. Melt a little butter in a bain marie, season with salt and add a little crème fraîche and Curaçao. Pour over the sole.

sole with thyme
Cook a small sole in butter in a frying pan for 2 minutes each side. Season with salt and pepper and add ¼ teaspoon dried thyme and 2 tablespoons white wine. Cook for 30 seconds, then remove the fish. Reduce the juices by half and add 2 tablespoons double (heavy) cream and a peeled slice of lemon, chopped. Boil the sauce until thick and pour over the fish. Garnish with small steamed courgettes (zucchini).

stuffed sole Auberge de l'Ill
Remove the black skin from 2 × 800 g (1¾ lb) sole and cut off the heads at an angle. Cut along the backbone and open out. Remove the bone, taking care that the fillets remain attached.

Put 100 g (4 oz) whiting fillets, 1 egg white, salt, pepper and a pinch of grated nutmeg in a blender or food processor. With the motor running, add 250 ml (8 fl oz, 1 cup) very cold double (heavy) cream, a little at a time. Mix the forcemeat with 150 g (5 oz) diced salmon fillets and 50 g (2 oz, ½ cup) chopped pistachios in a bowl. Stuff the sole with the mixture, season and arrange on a buttered ovenproof dish. Sprinkle with chopped shallots and moisten with 250 ml (8 fl oz, 1 cup) Riesling and 250 ml (8 fl oz, 1 cup) fish fumet. Cover with foil and cook in a preheated oven at 220°C (425°F, gas 7) for 25 minutes. Arrange on a plate and keep warm.

Pour the cooking juices into a pan, add 250 ml (8 fl oz, 1 cup) double cream and reduce by half. Whisk in 100 g (4 oz, ½ cup) butter, a little at a time. Add the juice of 1 lemon. Adjust the seasoning and pour over the sole. Garnish with slices of truffle glazed in butter and puff-pastry flowers.

SOLFERINO Sauce based on reduced tomatoes, to which is added meat glaze, a pinch of cayenne pepper and lemon juice. The sauce is finished with tarragon maître d'hôtel butter and shallot butter.

SOLILEMME Also known as *solilem*. A type of brioche, rich in eggs, butter and cream, which is cut in half after cooking, while still warm, and sprinkled with melted salted butter. Solilemme is usually served with tea, but it can also be served in slices with smoked fish. It is thought to have originated in Alsace and is similar to, though richer than, the English tea bread Sally Lunn.

Sole à la dieppoise,
see page 1105.

RECIPE

solilemme

Mix together 125 g (4½ oz, 1 cup) sifted plain (all-purpose) flour and 15 g (½ oz, 1 cake) fresh (compressed) yeast, creamed with 2–3 tablespoons warm water. Leave to rise for about 2 hours at room temperature, away from draughts. Break up the dough, mix in 2 eggs and 3 tablespoons crème fraîche, then add 375 g (13 oz, 3¼ cups) sifted plain flour. Knead the dough. Mix 125 g (4½ oz, ½ cup) butter cut into small pieces, 3 tablespoons double (heavy) cream and 2 eggs into the dough. Knead thoroughly, adding a little more cream if necessary (the dough should be fairly soft). Place in a buttered charlotte mould and leave to double in volume, away from draughts. Cook in a preheated oven at 220°C (425°F, gas 7) for 40 minutes. Turn out the solilemme and cut horizontally into 2 layers. Sprinkle each with 40 g (1½ oz, 3 tablespoons) melted slightly salted butter and sandwich together again.

SOLOGNOTE, À LA Term for a preparation for duck. The bird is stuffed, preferably the day before, with its liver, which has been marinated in Armagnac and herbs, then finely minced (ground) with fresh soft breadcrumbs. The duck is then pot-roasted.

Gigot *à la solognote* is a leg of lamb marinated in white wine and wine vinegar with flavourings, then roasted. The marinade, well reduced, is used as a sauce.

SOMMELIER Originally, the monk who had charge of the crockery, linen, bread and wine in a French monastery – in other words; the cellarer. During the Ancien Régime, the king's household had several sommeliers, whose primary function was to receive the wine brought by the *sommiers* (from French *bêtes de somme*, 'beasts of burden'). The name 'sommelier' was also applied to the officials who took care of royal furniture; later, it was used for any bearer of burdens. During the reign of Louis XIV, the sommelier was the official in charge of the transport of baggage when the court moved. In the household of a great lord he was the official who chose the wines, table settings and desserts.

Nowadays, the sommelier of a large restaurant is the specialist wine waiter, a job that requires extensive knowledge of the subject and the ability to choose the appropriate wine for a dish. The sommelier may also be responsible for buying, storing and cellaring the wine and advising on the wine list. The *caviste* (cellarman) is responsible for supervising the wines in the cellar.

SORB APPLE The berry-like fruit of the sorb tree. Native to southern Europe, and related to the rowan, it is also called the service tree, but is a different species from the American service-berry. Sorb apples resemble small greenish or reddish pears; they are gathered after the first frosts and become pulpy and sweet when they are overripe. They can then be eaten without further preparation, like medlars, though they have a more delicate flavour; or they can be made into a jelly to accompany game or fowl.

In Spain and the west of France, they are also used to make a fermented drink, which is a little like (hard) cider.

SORBET A type of water ice that is softer and more granular than ice cream as it does not contain any fat or egg yolk. The basic ingredient of a sorbet is fruit juice or purée, wine, spirit or liqueur, or an infusion (tea or mint). A sugar syrup, sometimes with additional glucose or one or two invert sugars, is added. The mixture should not be beaten during freezing. When it has set, some Italian meringue can be added to give it volume.

Historically, sorbets were the first iced desserts (ice creams did not appear until the 18th century). The Chinese introduced them to the Persians and Arabs, who introduced them to the Italians. The word *sorbet* is a gallicization of the Italian *sorbetto*, derived from Turkish *chorbet* and Arab *charab*, which simply meant 'drink'. Sorbets were originally made of fruit, honey, aromatic substances and snow. Today, the sorbet is served as a dessert or as a refreshment between courses; at large formal dinners in France, sorbets with an alcoholic base are served between the main courses, taking the place of the liqueurs (*trou normand*) formerly served in the middle of the meal. Sorbets are usually served in sundae dishes or tall glasses; they are sometimes sprinkled with a liqueur or alcohol to match their flavour (for example, vodka on lime, clear spirits on the appropriate fruit). Other ingredients, such as raisins or pine nuts, can be incorporated into the mixture before freezing.

RECIPES

fruit sorbet

For soft fruit, prepare a syrup using 200 g (7 oz, 1 cup) granulated sugar and 150 ml (¼ pint, ⅔ cup) water per 500 g (18 oz) fruit. Poach the fruit in the syrup, then purée in a blender or food processor: the density of the mixture should be 1.1513. For citrus fruit use 100 g (4 oz, ½ cup) sugar and 150 ml (¼ pint, ⅔ cup) water for every 3–4 fruit. Finely grate the zest, then squeeze the juice from the fruit and mix with the syrup: the density of the mixture should be 1.1697. Correct the density by adding more sugar if it is too weak or more water if it is too strong. Pour into an ice-cream maker and allow to freeze. Halfway through the cycle some Italian meringue (one third of the volume of the sorbet) can be added.

honey sorbet with pine nuts

Mix 900 g (2 lb, 2½ cups) orange-blossom honey, the juice of 1 lemon, a few drops orange-flower water and 1 litre (1¾ pints, 4⅓ cups) water. After processing in an ice-cream maker, add some lightly toasted pine nuts, then pour into a mould and place in the freezer until required.

passion fruit sorbet ♦

Halve some ripe passion fruit, strain the pulp through a vegetable mill, then through a fine sieve. Measure the pulp and add an equal volume of cold syrup made from 500 ml (17 fl oz, 2 cups) mineral water and 675 g (1½ lb, 3 cups) caster (superfine) sugar. The density of the mixture should be 1.135; add a little lemon juice, the density then being 1.075. Pour the mixture into an ice-cream maker and freeze until set. It is also possible – and easier – to add caster sugar to the pulp and add enough water to obtain a density of approximately 1.075, and then strain the mixture through a fine sieve before putting it in the ice-cream maker. Serve scoops of the sorbet with a fan of mango slices and a little passion fruit pulp.

peach sorbet

Prepare a syrup by boiling 100 ml (4 fl oz, 7 table-spoons) water with 300 g (11 oz, 1⅓ cups) granulated sugar and allow to cool. Peel 1 kg (2¼ lb) white peaches, cut into quarters and purée in a blender or food processor. Add the juice of 1 large lemon and mix the purée with the cold syrup. Pour into an ice-cream maker and set in operation for 1 hour. When the sorbet has frozen, switch off the machine and put the container in the freezer, together with 4 sorbet glasses, for about 1 hour. To serve: place 2 balls of sorbet in each glass and pour over some well-chilled champagne (½ bottle for the 4 glasses).

pear sorbet

Peel 4 juicy pears and cut into quarters. Remove the pips and dice the flesh. Sprinkle with the juice of 1 lemon. Reduce to a fine purée, with 300 g (11 oz, 1⅓ cups) granulated sugar, in a blender or food processor. Pour the purée into an ice-cream maker and operate for 1½ hours, or until the sorbet freezes. Put the container into the freezer until required or serve immediately.

raspberry sorbet

Prepare a syrup by boiling 250 g (9 oz, 1 cup) granulated sugar and 400 ml (14 fl oz, 1¾ cups) water. Allow to cool. Pour in 400 g (14 oz, 2¾ cups) raspberries and the juice of half a lemon. Purée in a blender or food processor and then rub through a sieve if wished. Pour the mixture into an ice-cream maker and set in operation for about 1 hour. When the sorbet begins to freeze, pour into a mould and place in the freezer until required.

sorbet of exotic fruits

Peel 1 very ripe pineapple, cut it into 4, remove the centre and dice the pulp, retaining the juice. Cut 2 mangoes in half, remove the stones (pits) and scoop out the flesh with a spoon. Peel and slice 1 banana. Put the fruit into a blender or food processor with the juice of 1 lemon and purée it. Measure the juice obtained. Add 75 g (3 oz, ⅓ cup) caster (superfine) sugar per 250 ml (8 fl oz, 1 cup) juice. Mix with a fork and add 1 teaspoon vanilla sugar and a pinch of cinnamon. Pour into an ice-cream maker and set in operation for 1½ hours. When the sorbet begins to freeze, place in the freezer until required.

sorbet with Calvados

Dissolve 200 g (7 oz, 1 cup) caster (superfine) sugar in 325 ml (11 fl oz, 1⅓ cups) water. Add a vanilla pod (bean) cut in half. Bring to the boil to obtain a light syrup. Remove from the heat and discard the vanilla pod. Add the juice of 1 lemon and a pinch of cinnamon. Mix well. Whisk 3 egg whites to stiff peaks and mix them gently into the syrup. Pour into an ice-cream maker. When the sorbet begins to freeze, add 4–5 liqueur glasses aged Calvados. Beat for a few moments, turn into a mould and freeze until required.

strawberry sorbet

Wash and hull 1 kg (2¼ lb, 8 cups) strawberries and purée in a blender or food processor. Add 300 g (11 oz, 1⅓ cups) caster (superfine) sugar. Mix well to dissolve, then add the juice of half a lemon and 1 orange. Pour into an ice-cream maker. Set in operation for about 1 hour. Pour the sorbet into a mould and place in the freezer for a further 1½–2 hours to allow the sorbet to freeze completely.

other recipes See *blackcurrant, lemon, mango, tomato*.

SORGHUM A cereal that is grown in hot, dry areas worldwide. In some countries, it is grown only for animal fodder. Also known as Indian millet, guineacorn or durra, sorghum has a slightly nutty taste. It can be cooked and eaten like rice, or ground into flour, which is used for making porridges and flat, unleavened breads. Fermented drinks are also made from its seeds, and sorghum syrup is extracted from some varieties of sorghum, and is used in baking.

Sorghum has been grown in Africa since prehistoric times and records of sorghum cultivation in India date back to 1900 BC. It was grown in Italy in the days of Pliny and was possibly named *surgo* ('I rise') at this time; the name could also be derived from Latin *syricus* (from Syria). Its cultivation was abandoned in Europe at the end of the 15th century, but it remains a staple food crop today in Africa, India and China, and is gaining increasing importance elsewhere in the world. Examples of sorghum's many culinary uses include cakes made from sorghum and served with spicy sauces or milk and butter; a type of couscous made from sorghum in Mali; and *sohleb*, a traditional sorghum porridge with ginger, sold in the streets in Tunisia. In China, such porridges are a staple food: sorghum appeared

3000 years before rice. *Pombé*, a beer made with sorghum and okra, is traditionally brewed by women in the Sudan. An alcohol flavoured with rose petals, called *caoliang* or *kaoloang*, is made from sorghum in China; it is also used in cookery for marinades and sauces.

SORINGUE An eel dish typical of 15th-century French cookery. Skinned steamed pieces of eel were simmered in a thick sauce of toasted breadcrumbs mixed with verjuice and flavoured with ginger, cinnamon, cloves and saffron, with added fried onion rings and chopped parsley. Finally, the dish was enhanced with wine, verjuice and vinegar.

SORREL A culinary plant originating in northern Asia and Europe; its edible green leaves have a slightly bitter taste (from the oxalic acid they contain). When sorrel is for sale, it should be shiny and firm; it will keep for some days in the bottom of the refrigerator. It is prepared and cooked in the same way as spinach; when made into a purée or shredded, it can be given extra smoothness by adding a white roux or some cream. Sorrel is a traditional accompaniment for fish (shad, pike) and veal (topside, breast). It can also be used as a filling for omelettes, as an accompaniment to eggs *en cocotte*, and to prepare soup and velouté sauce. When the leaves are very young and tender they can be eaten in a salad.

RECIPES

chiffonnade of sorrel
Pick over the sorrel leaves and remove the hard stalks. Wash and dry the leaves and shred them finely. Melt some butter in a saucepan without letting it colour – allow 25 g (1 oz, 2 tablespoons) butter for 200 g (7 oz, 3½ cups) leaves. Add the sorrel, three-quarters cover the pan with a lid and let it cook gently until all the vegetable liquid has disappeared. The chiffonnade can be used as it is as a garnish; it can also be mixed with double (heavy) cream and reduced. A 'mixed' chiffonnade is a combination of sorrel and lettuce.

preserved sorrel
Prepare and clean some sorrel as above, shred it finely and cook it in butter until it is completely dry. Pack it into a wide-mouthed jar. When it is quite cold, seal the jar and sterilize it. The sorrel can also be packed into containers and frozen. It is advisable to prepare only small quantities at a time.

sorrel purée
Prepare and clean some sorrel as above. Put the leaves into a large saucepan and pour in boiling water, allowing 1 litre (1¾ pints, 4⅓ cups) water per 1 kg (2¼ lb) sorrel. Bring to the boil, cook for 4–5 minutes, then remove from the heat and drain in a sieve. In a flameproof casserole, make a white roux using 65 g (2½ oz, 5 tablespoons) butter and 40 g (1½ oz, 6 tablespoons) plain (all-purpose) flour. Add the sorrel and mix well together. Pour in 500 ml (17 fl oz, 2 cups) white stock and add salt and a pinch of sugar.

Cover the casserole, bring to the boil on top of the stove, then transfer it to a preheated oven at 180°C (350°F, gas 4) and cook for 1½ hours. Purée the sorrel in a blender or food processor and return it to the hob (stove top) to reheat. Bind it with 3 whole eggs beaten with 100 ml (4 fl oz, 7 tablespoons) double (heavy) cream. Finally add 100 g (4 oz, ½ cup) butter, cut into small pieces.

other recipes See *fricandeau, omelette (omelettes cooked with their flavouring), shad, soup.*

SOT-L'Y-LAISSE The small piece of chicken meat in the hollow of each of the iliac bones, just above the tail. The French name for this delicacy, which literally means 'the fool leaves it there', confirms its choiceness. Its English name is the oyster.

SOUBISE The name given to dishes containing an onion sauce (a béchamel to which onion purée has been added) or an onion purée (usually thickened with rice). These preparations were named in honour of Charles de Rohan, Prince of Soubise and Marshal of France, an 18th-century French aristocrat. It is particularly applied to dishes of eggs, served on the purée or sometimes covered with the sauce. The purée may also be used to garnish cuts of meat or as a stuffing for vegetables.

RECIPES

hard-boiled eggs à la Soubise
Hard boil (hard cook) some eggs; cool and shell them. Prepare 2 tablespoons Soubise purée per egg and pour into a buttered dish. Place the eggs in the purée at regular intervals and coat with cream sauce.

Soubise purée
Peel and thinly slice 1 kg (2¼ lb) white onions and place in a saucepan with plenty of salted water. Bring to the boil, then drain the onions and place in a saucepan with 100 g (4 oz, ½ cup) butter, salt, pepper and a pinch of sugar. Cover and cook over a gentle heat for 30–40 minutes (the onions should not change colour). Then add to the onions a quantity of boiled rice or thick béchamel sauce equal to one quarter of the volume of the onion. Mix thoroughly and cook for a further 20 minutes. Adjust the seasoning, press through a very fine sieve and stir in 75 g (3 oz, 6 tablespoons) butter.

Passion fruit sorbet,
see page 1109.

Soubise sauce

Prepare a Soubise purée with béchamel sauce. When it is well thickened, add 100 ml (4 fl oz, 7 tablespoons) whipping cream. Blend thoroughly.

stuffed potatoes Soubise

Bake some firm unpeeled potatoes in the oven, then scoop out the insides of the potatoes into a bowl. Prepare a well-reduced Soubise purée. Add one quarter of its volume of double (heavy) cream and reduce still further until the mixture is extremely thick. Beat into the scooped-out potato until well blended. Stuff the potato skins with this mixture, arrange them in an ovenproof dish and sprinkle with breadcrumbs and small knobs of butter. Brown in a very hot oven.

SOUCHET
Also known as Suchet. Sauce made with a julienne of vegetables stewed in butter, to which white wine and fish stock are then added. It is reduced and finished with butter.

SOU DU FRANC
A former practice whereby the housekeeper or cook responsible for buying food, was given a cash discount of 5%. It was officially accepted by the employers that this profit, which could be quite considerable, should be kept by the housekeeper or cook over and above their basic wages. On the other hand, any servant caught trying to make an illicit profit by falsifying the accounts was immediately dismissed.

SOU-FASSUM
A whole cabbage stuffed with a forcemeat of Swiss chard, bacon, onions, rice and sausagemeat, typical of Nice, in France. Traditionally wrapped in a net known as a *fassumier*, it is cooked in the stock of a mutton pot-au-feu. In a variation of this dish, the cabbage leaves are arranged alternately with the forcemeat in a terrine lined with slices of streaky bacon. The sou-fassum, which is said to be of Greek origin, is thought to date back to the founding of Antibes.

RECIPE

sou-fassum

Trim a large green cabbage, blanch for 8 minutes in boiling salted water, then cool and drain. Detach the large leaves, remove their ribs and spread them out flat on a net or a piece of muslin (cheesecloth), soaked and wrung out.

Chop the remainder of the cabbage and set aside. Make the forcemeat by mixing 250 g (9 oz) blanched chopped Swiss chard leaves; 200 g (7 oz, 1 cup) lean bacon, diced and browned; 100 g (4 oz, ⅔ cup) chopped onions, fried in butter; 2 large tomatoes, peeled, seeded and crushed; 100 g (4 oz, ⅔ cup) blanched rice; and 800 g (1¾ lb, 3 cups) sausagemeat with 1 crushed garlic clove added.

Layer the forcemeat and chopped cabbage on the laid-out leaves. Then fold the cabbage leaves around to enclose the stuffing in a neat ball. Tie up the net

or muslin, plunge the cabbage into a mutton pot-au-feu stock and boil very gently for about 3½ hours. Drain the cabbage, unwrap and arrange on a round dish. Pour over a few tablespoons of stock and serve hot.

SOUFFLÉ
A hot preparation that is served straight from the oven, so that it is well risen above the height of the mould in which it is cooked.

■ **Types of hot soufflé** There are two basic types: savoury soufflés, which are served as hors d'oeuvre or light meals, and sweet soufflés, which are served as desserts.

• SAVOURY SOUFFLÉS These are made from a thick béchamel sauce or a purée, bound with egg yolks, to which are then added stiffly whisked egg whites. Ingredients added to the basic mixture (in the form of a salpicon or purée), which determine the name of the soufflé, include vegetables, ham, cheese, white poultry meat or poultry livers, fish or shellfish, or a game or offal salpicon. During cooking, the air trapped in the egg whites expands and increases the volume of the preparation, which must be served immediately, before it collapses. A soufflé must never be left to stand, but the basic mixture can be prepared in advance and kept in a bain marie or in a cool place until the stiffly whisked egg whites are added, just before cooking. The egg whites are whisked with a pinch of salt until stiff and folded in very gently. First a little of the egg white is beaten with the mixture to slacken it, then the remainder is folded in quickly, a little at a time, until the mixture is smooth.

The cooking mould is cylindrical, so that the preparation can rise evenly; it is buttered and often covered with flour, and filled only three-quarters full. For individual soufflés, ramekins are used. Special care must be taken not to open the oven door while the soufflé is cooking. As the soufflé is served straight from the mould, the latter is made of an attractive material that withstands high temperatures, such as fireproof porcelain (the material most frequently recommended), enamelled cast iron (which guarantees good distribution of heat) or fireproof glass (which takes longer to heat). The classic fluted white French soufflé dish (and ramekins or individual dishes in the same style) are made of a heatproof porcelain called aluminite.

• DESSERT SOUFFLÉS These are based either on a milk mixture or a fruit purée and a cooked sugar mixture. For the former, a confectioner's custard (pastry cream) (see *custard*) is used, which is bound with egg yolks and flavoured (with vanilla, liqueur or spirit) before folding in the stiffly whisked egg whites. Alternatively, a blond roux can be used: it is mixed with boiling sweetened vanilla-flavoured milk and bound with yolks (or yolks and whole eggs) before adding the stiffly whisked egg whites and the flavouring. These soufflés are cooked in buttered, sugar-coated moulds. Dessert soufflés may be filled with pieces of sponge finger (ladyfinger) or Genoese cake (soaked in liqueur or spirit), which are either sandwiched in three layers in the soufflé mixture or placed all together in the centre of the soufflé. The top is smoothed or sometimes grooved.

Soufflés made from a fruit mixture have a base of sugar cooked to the 'hard crack' stage, to which a fruit purée is added. The mixture is then reheated just to the 'soft ball' stage. The egg whites are whisked into the hot mixture, which is poured over them. The fruit flavour is enhanced by a little alcohol or liqueur. Fresh fruit soufflés are usually prepared using this recipe, but can also be made with confectioner's custard, in which case very dense fruit purée is added to the custard before the egg whites are incorporated.

The appearance of a dessert soufflé can be enhanced by sprinkling it with icing (confectioner's) sugar a few minutes before the end of cooking: the icing sugar caramelizes to give the soufflé a glossy surface.

■ **Cooking soufflés** Before cooking a savoury or sweet soufflé, it is advisable to stand it for a few minutes in a bain marie of very hot water. Alternatively, put the soufflé in a preheated oven at 220°C (425°F, gas 7), then immediately reduce the heat to 190°C (375°F, gas 5) and cook for 25–30 minutes (for a large soufflé) or 12 minutes (for small individual soufflés). The soufflé is served by placing it, still in its mould, on a plate, which in classic cuisine is covered with a dish paper (for a savoury soufflé) or a paper doily (for a sweet dessert soufflé).

■ **Iced soufflés** These are frozen desserts that superficially resemble genuine soufflés. The mixture is placed in a soufflé mould or a timbale whose height is increased by a band of paper around the mould. After freezing, the paper is removed so that the soufflé rises above the level of the mould, like a baked soufflé.

An iced soufflé is made either of a simple ice cream or, more frequently, of alternate layers of mousse and ice cream, parfait or bombe mixture, variously flavoured and coloured. These layers may be separated by layers of sponge cake soaked in liqueur, thick sweetened fruit purée, and fruit in syrup or crystallized (candied) fruits. The top is often decorated with Chantilly cream, coffee beans in liqueur or any other sugar decoration. These soufflés are also made in ramekins. Iced soufflés are usually served with champagne or a dessert wine.

■ **Set or chilled soufflés** Chilled soufflés can also be made in the same way as iced soufflés, but dissolved gelatine is incorporated in the mixture. The soufflé is then placed in the refrigerator to set rather than the freezer.

RECIPES

Dessert Soufflés

banana soufflé
Mix together in a saucepan 1 tablespoon sifted flour and a pinch of salt with 100 ml (4 fl oz, 7 tablespoons) milk, which has been boiled with 2 tablespoons caster (superfine) sugar and ½ vanilla pod (bean) and then cooled. Boil the mixture for

Making individual iced soufflés

Place a collar of greaseproof (wax) paper inside each soufflé dish, overlapping it neatly and securing it firmly on the outside near the top. Spoon the mixture into the middle of the mould without disturbing the paper until it is level with the top of the collar. Smooth the mixture with a palette knife.

2 minutes, whisking all the time, then remove from the heat and add the pulp of 4 finely sieved bananas, 2 egg yolks and 20 g (¾ oz, 1½ tablespoons) butter. Flavour, if required, with kirsch or rum. Fold in 3 stiffly whisked egg whites. Pour the mixture into a 20 cm (8 in) buttered soufflé mould (or small ramekins) coated with caster sugar. Cook in a preheated oven at 200°C (400°F, gas 6) for 30 minutes for a large soufflé or about 12 minutes for ramekins.

chestnut soufflé
Place 300 g (11 oz) peeled chestnuts in a saucepan with 200 ml (7 fl oz, ¾ cup) milk, 1½ tablespoons sugar and a pinch of salt. Boil for 10 minutes with the lid on, then remove the lid and continue to boil for a further 5 minutes to allow the milk to evaporate. Set 4 whole chestnuts aside and rub the remainder through a sieve or put in a blender or food processor. Blend the purée with 400 ml (14 fl oz, 1¾ cups) double (heavy) cream and place in a bain marie of very hot water.

Butter a 20 cm (8 in) soufflé mould and coat with flour. Whisk 5 egg whites until stiff, together with a pinch of salt. Return the chestnut purée to the heat and, when it is just boiling, remove from the heat and mix in 3 egg yolks. Stir thoroughly. Add one quarter of the stiffly whisked egg whites and mix thoroughly. Crumble 2 of the reserved chestnuts and add them. Carefully fold in the remaining egg whites using a metal spoon. Pour this mixture into the prepared mould and smooth the surface. Sprinkle with the 2 remaining chestnuts cut into 12 pieces. Place in a preheated oven at 180°C (350°F, gas 4). Turn off the oven and leave to cook for 15–20 minutes without opening the door. Serve immediately with a tangerine sorbet.

chocolate soufflé
Follow the recipe for coffee soufflé, but dissolve 75 g (3 oz, 3 squares) dark (semisweet) chocolate

in the milk instead of instant coffee and sweeten with 75 g (3 oz, ⅓ cup) caster (superfine) sugar.

coffee soufflé

Over a low heat, dissolve 2 tablespoons instant coffee in 1 tablespoon milk taken from a 250 ml (8 fl oz, 1 cup). Then add the remainder of the milk and bring to the boil. Beat 2 egg yolks with 2 tablespoons) caster (superfine) sugar until the mixture turns thick and white, then incorporate 25 g (1 oz, ¼ cup) plain (all-purpose) flour in a trickle. Gradually pour the boiling coffee-flavoured milk into the mixture, beating briskly. Pour the mixture into a saucepan and bring to the boil, stirring all the time. Once it has boiled, transfer it to a large bowl and allow to cool. Butter a 20 cm (8 in) soufflé mould and sprinkle it with 2 tablespoons caster sugar. Whisk 6 egg whites until they are stiff. Incorporate a further 2 egg yolks into the coffee preparation, then carefully fold in the whites using a metal spoon. Pour the mixture into the mould and cook in a preheated oven at 190°C (375°F, gas 5) for 20 minutes. Then sprinkle the soufflé with icing (confectioner's) sugar and return to the oven for 5 minutes to glaze the surface. Serve immediately.

Curaçao soufflé

Whisk 250 g (9 oz, 1 cup) granulated sugar with 8 egg yolks until the mixture turns pale and thick. Incorporate 100 ml (4 fl oz, 7 tablespoons) Curaçao (or another liqueur), then fold in the whites of 12 eggs very stiffly whisked with a pinch of salt. Pour the mixture into a large buttered soufflé mould coated with sugar, place in a preheated oven at 200°C (400°F, gas 6) and bake for 15 minutes. Sprinkle icing (confectioner's) sugar over the top and return to the oven for 5–6 minutes to glaze the surface. Serve immediately.

fruit soufflé made with sugar syrup

Mix 1 kg (2¼ lb, 4½ cups) granulated sugar with 100 ml (4 fl oz, 7 tablespoons) water and boil until the temperature reaches 140°C (284°F). Then add 1.12 kg (2½ lb) finely sieved fruit purée. Fold in 12 stiffly whisked egg whites and cook in a large soufflé mould in a preheated oven at 190°C (375°F, gas 5) for about 35–40 minutes.

Use strawberries and raspberries raw. Cook apricots, cherries, pears and apples with sugar beforehand; apples should be reduced until very dry before being sieved.

lime soufflé

Boil 120 ml (4½ fl oz, ½ cup) milk together with the zest of 1 lime. Whisk together 50 g (2 oz, ¼ cup) granulated sugar, 2 egg yolks, 25 g (1 oz, ¼ cup) cornflour (cornstarch) and 120 ml (4½ fl oz, ½ cup) lime juice. Pour the boiling milk on to this mixture, then return to the heat and bring to the boil, whisking all the time. Leave to cool.

Butter 4 ramekins liberally and coat with sugar. Add 2 egg yolks to the confectioner's custard (pastry cream). Stiffly whisk the whites of 6–8 eggs (depending on their size), blend in 75 g (3 oz, ⅓ cup) caster (superfine) sugar and fold the mixture into the confectioner's custard. Pour the mixture into the prepared moulds and place in a preheated oven at 200°C (400°F, gas 6). After 12 minutes, place a thin slice of lime on each soufflé, cover with a sheet of greaseproof (wax) paper and cook for a further 3 minutes. Serve immediately with a warm custard cream (see custard) flavoured with blanched lime zest.

soufflé Ambassadrice

Prepare a confectioner's custard using 1 litre (1¾ pints, 4⅓ cups) milk, 8 egg yolks, a generous pinch of salt, 100 g (4 oz, 1 cup) plain (all-purpose) flour (or 4 tablespoons cornflour or potato flour) and 300 g (11 oz, 1⅓ cups) granulated sugar. Add 1 teaspoon vanilla essence (extract), 8 crushed macaroons and 50 g (2 oz, ½ cup) shredded (slivered) almonds soaked in rum. Fold in 12 stiffly whisked egg whites, turn into a large prepared soufflé dish and cook in a preheated oven at 200°C (400°F, gas 6) for about 30–35 minutes.

soufflé lapérouse

Prepare a confectioner's custard using 250 ml (8 fl oz, 1 cup) milk (see custard). Add 65 g (2½ oz) praline*, 100 ml (4 fl oz, 7 tablespoons) rum and 50 g (2 oz, ⅓ cup) crystallized (candied) fruit. Stiffly whisk the whites of 5 eggs (whose yolks have been used for the custard) and fold them into the mixture. Butter a 20 cm (8 in) soufflé mould, then coat with caster (superfine) sugar. Pour in the mixture. Place in a preheated oven at 180°C (350°F, gas 4) and bake for 15 minutes. Sprinkle with icing (confectioner's) sugar and allow to cook for a further 5 minutes, so that the top of the soufflé is caramelized.

soufflé Simone

Generously butter a 20 cm (8 in) soufflé mould. Melt 100 g (4 oz, 4 squares) cooking (semisweet) chocolate in 2½ tablespoons milk. Add 2 tablespoons confectioner's custard and 50 g (2 oz, ¼ cup) caster (superfine) sugar and bring to the boil. Remove from the heat and add 2 egg yolks, mixing thoroughly. Stiffly whisk the whites of 5 eggs and sweeten very slightly. Lightly sprinkle the buttered mould with 2 tablespoons caster (superfine) sugar. Fold the egg whites into the chocolate mixture and pour into the mould. Bake in a preheated oven at 200°C (400°F, gas 6) for about 25 minutes. Serve with lightly whipped cream.

strawberry or raspberry soufflé

Prepare a confectioner's custard as in the recipe for soufflé Ambassadrice. Add 300 g (11 oz, 2–3 cups) puréed wild strawberries, large strawberries soaked in sugar or raspberries. Fold in 12–14 very stiffly whisked egg whites. Pour the mixture into a well-buttered large soufflé mould coated with sugar. Bake in a preheated oven at 190°C (375°F, gas 5) for 20–25 minutes.

other recipes See *chestnut (chestnut desserts), Rothschild, vanilla, violet.*

Iced Soufflés
iced fruit soufflé

Cook 300 g (11 oz, 1⅓ cups) caster (superfine) sugar in 100 ml (4 fl oz, 7 tablespoons) water to the soufflé stage (see *sugar*). Pour this syrup over 5 very stiffly whisked egg whites, whisking until completely cold. Purée 350 g (12 oz, about 2 cups) fresh strawberries or raspberries, or apricots, peaches or pears cooked in sugar. Fold the purée into the egg white and sugar mixture together with 500 ml (17 fl oz, 2 cups) stiffly whipped cream.

Cut a strip of greaseproof (wax) paper or foil 23 cm (9 in) wide and longer than the circumference of the soufflé mould. Fold in half to reduce its width to 11.5 cm (4½ in). Surround the mould with this double strip so that it comes well above the edge and keep it in place with an elastic band or adhesive tape. Pour the soufflé mixture into the mould until it reaches the top of the paper, smooth over the surface and freeze until firm (about 4 hours). Remove the paper to serve.

iced raspberry soufflé

Sort and clean 400 g (14 oz, 2¾ cups) raspberries. Put the best 20 to one side; crush the others and press through a sieve. Mix this purée with an equal amount of caster (superfine) sugar and add 500 ml (17 fl oz, 2 cups) Chantilly* cream. Whisk the whites of 2 eggs very stiffly, whisking in 50 g (2 oz, ¼ cup) caster sugar. Fold lightly into the purée and cream mixture, then pour it into a 15 cm (6 in) soufflé mould, around which has been wrapped a band of oiled greaseproof (wax) paper 6 cm (2½ in) higher than the mould. Place in a freezer for at least 8 hours. When the soufflé is firm, remove the paper. Decorate with the reserved raspberries and serve immediately, with a lightly sweetened purée of fresh raspberries and almond tuiles. Serve with a dry champagne.

Savoury Soufflés
basic recipe

Make a béchamel sauce using 40 g (1½ oz, 3 tablespoons) butter, 40 g (1½ oz, 6 tablespoons) plain (all-purpose) flour and 200 ml (7 fl oz, ¾ cup) cold milk. Season with salt, pepper and nutmeg and incorporate the chosen flavouring. Then add 4–5 egg yolks (use fairly large eggs) and fold in 4–5 egg whites whisked to stiff peaks. Preheat the oven for 15 minutes at 220°C (425°F, gas 7). Butter a soufflé mould 20 cm (8 in) in diameter and coat with flour. Pour in the mixture and bake in the preheated oven at 200°C (400°F, gas 6) for 30 minutes, without opening the door during cooking, until well risen and a deep golden-brown on top.

cheese and poached egg soufflé

Mix 250 ml (8 fl oz, 1 cup) milk with 50 g (2 oz, ½ cup) plain (all-purpose) flour and an equal amount of softened butter. Bring to the boil, stirring continously, then beat in 5 egg yolks and 100 g (4 oz, 1 cup) grated Gruyère cheese. Gently fold in 6 stiffly whisked egg whites. Pour half the mixture into a 20 cm (8 in) buttered soufflé mould and cook in a preheated oven at 200°C (400°F, gas 6) for 10 minutes. Meanwhile, poach 4 eggs in vinegar water for 4 minutes, then drain, plunge into fresh water, drain again and trim. Take the soufflé out of the oven and place the eggs in it. Add the remaining soufflé mixture, return to the oven and continue cooking at the same temperature for a further 10–15 minutes.

cheese soufflé

Follow the basic recipe, adding to the béchamel sauce 75–90 g (3–3½ oz, ¾ cup) grated Gruyère cheese or 50 g (2 oz, ½ cup) grated Parmesan cheese and a pinch of grated nutmeg. Proceed as in the basic recipe.

chicken liver soufflé

Clean 250 g (9 oz) chicken livers, cut into pieces and sauté in butter together with 2–3 chopped shallots and a small bunch of parsley. Add salt and pepper, then put the mixture into a blender or food processor, together with 25 g (1 oz, 2 tablespoons) butter. Blend this purée with the béchamel sauce in the basic recipe and proceed as directed.

chicory soufflé

Prepare 250 g (9 oz) braised or stewed chicory (endive), dry it over the heat and rub through a sieve. Incorporate 150 ml (¼ pint, ⅔ cup) béchamel sauce and 40 g (1½ oz, ⅓ cup) grated Parmesan cheese if desired. Sprinkle with nutmeg, add 3 egg yolks, then the stiffly whisked whites, and finish off as in the basic recipe, cooking for about 25 minutes.

crab soufflé

Prepare a béchamel sauce from 40 g (1½ oz, 3 tablespoons) butter, 40 g (1½ oz, 6 tablespoons) plain (all-purpose) flour, 150 ml (¼ pint, ⅔ cup) milk and 100 ml (4 fl oz, 7 tablespoons) reduced crab cooking liquid. Incorporate 200 g (7 oz, 1 cup) crab purée and adjust the seasoning. Add 4–5 eggs (the yolks, then the stiffly whisked whites) and cook as in the basic recipe. (Shrimp or lobster soufflés may be prepared in the same way.)

game soufflé with Périgueux sauce

Pound in a mortar 250 g (9 oz) cooked pheasant or partridge meat together with 150 ml (¼ pint, ⅔ cup) thick béchamel sauce flavoured with game stock. Season with salt and pepper. Add 3 egg yolks one by one, rub through a sieve, then incorporate 3 stiffly whisked egg whites. Bake in a preheated oven at 200°C (400°F, gas 6) for about 25 minutes. Serve with Périgueux sauce.

ham soufflé

Process 150 g (5 oz, 1 cup) chopped lean ham in a food processor, or finely mince (grind) twice. Prepare a cheese soufflé mixture, add the ham and proceed as directed.

potato soufflé

Bind 400 g (14 oz, 1⅔ cups) mashed potato with 60 ml (2 fl oz, ¼ cup) double (heavy) cream. Add 3 egg yolks, then fold in 4 stiffly whisked egg whites. Cook as in the basic recipe.

Chestnut, sweet potato or Jerusalem artichoke soufflés may also be made in this way. They can be flavoured with 75 g (3 oz, ¾ cup) grated Gruyère cheese or 50 g (2 oz, ½ cup) grated Parmesan cheese.

salmon soufflé

Skin a salmon and remove all the bones with a small pair of tweezers – you need 400 g (14 oz) flesh. Pass this flesh through a blender or food processor very quickly so as not to heat it. Add 4 whole eggs and 250 ml (8 fl oz, 1 cup) crème fraîche. Stir this mixture with a spatula for 15 minutes, keeping the bowl standing in ice. Rub through a sieve and adjust the seasoning. Whisk 4 slightly salted egg whites until stiff and fold gently into the salmon mixture. Pour into a buttered soufflé mould and bake in a preheated oven at 200°C (400°F, gas 6) for about 25 minutes. (This recipe can also be made using salmon trout or brown trout.)

soufflé à la romaine

Proceed as in the recipe for spinach soufflé, but add 5 diced desalted anchovy fillets to the spinach.

spinach soufflé

Proceed as in the recipe for chicory soufflé, but replace the chicory with 250 g (9 oz) spinach, blanched, drained and pressed, then chopped or sieved and simmered in butter.

tomato soufflé

Prepare a béchamel sauce as in the basic recipe. Add to it 250 ml (8 fl oz, 1 cup) thick fresh tomato purée and 75 g (3 oz, ¾ cup) grated Parmesan cheese. Proceed as for the basic recipe, extending the cooking time by 5 minutes.

woodcock soufflé with chestnuts

Pluck, singe and draw 2 woodcock. Remove the drumsticks and seal them quickly in butter, bone them and cut the flesh into small dice. Thinly slice the white meat of the wings and the breast, seize in butter and leave to cool.

Make the sauce as follows: prepare and cut into small dice 1 small carrot, 1 small onion and 1 stick thinly sliced celery. Place these vegetables in a saucepan with 25 g (1 oz, 2 tablespoons) butter and with the small bones and intestines of the woodcock. Fry together, flame with 1½ tablespoons brandy, then add some brown stock and 1 bouquet garni and boil gently, skimming several times. After cooking for 2 hours, strain it through some muslin (cheesecloth), return to the boil, skim and strain once again. Keep in a warm place.

Peel 675 g (1½ lb) chestnuts, steam them and reduce to a purée in a blender or food processor. Then blend in 6 egg yolks, 50 g (2 oz, ¼ cup) butter, salt, pepper, a pinch of cayenne pepper and the diced flesh of the woodcock. Whisk 6 egg whites until stiff and fold them into the mixture. Butter a 20 cm (8 in) soufflé mould and pour this mixture into it, layering it alternately with the slices of white meat, finishing with a layer of soufflé mixture. Bake in a preheated oven at 200°C (400°F, gas 6) for about 30 minutes. Serve the soufflé with the sauce.

SOUMAINTRAIN A French soft-textured cow's-milk cheese (45% fat content) with a washed, reddish, damp rind. A speciality of the Yonne region, it has a penetrating odour and a spicy flavour. It is sold unwrapped in a round slab; 12–13 cm (4½–5 in) in diameter and 2.5–3 cm (1–1¼ in) deep. Farm made, it is at its best from the end of spring until autumn, accompanied by a full-bodied Burgundy.

SOUP A liquid savoury food served at the beginning of a meal or as a light meal in itself. There are many soups that make heavy meals, including Italian minestrone and chunky seafood chowder.

Originally in France, the *soupe* was the slice of bread on which was poured the contents of the cooking pot (*potage*). *Soupe* and *potage* are now often synonymous, although the former is also used to designate unstrained vegetable, meat or fish soups garnished with bread, pasta or rice; it is also used for regional or classical soups with bread added to them, such as French onion soup (*soupe à l'oignon gratinée*).

Soups can be classified into two broad groups: clear soups and thick soups. Clear soups are discussed in the entries on bouillon and consommé. Thick soups can be further subdivided according to the type of thickening used.
- *purée soups* Vegetable soups thickened with the starch contained in the puréed vegetables.
- *bisques* Made with puréed shellfish and usually enriched with cream.
- *cream soups* Thickened with béchamel sauce or a roux; enriched with milk and/or cream.
- *velouté soups* Thickened with egg yolks, butter and cream.

In addition to these, there are soups and broths thickened with arrowroot, rice and tapioca.

RECIPES

artichoke velouté soup

Prepare a white roux with 40 g (1½ oz, 3 tablespoons) butter and 40 g (1½ oz, 6 tablespoons)

Asparagus velouté soup, see page 1118.

flour. Moisten with a generous 750 ml (1¼ pints, 3¼ cups) chicken consommé*. Blanch 8 small artichoke hearts, cut into slices, and simmer in 40 g (1½ oz, 3 tablespoons) butter for about 20 minutes. Add them to the consommé, bring to the boil and cook until the vegetables break up. Reduce the mixture to a purée in a blender or food processor. Dilute with a little consommé to obtain the desired consistency and heat. Remove from the heat and thicken the soup with a mixture of 3 egg yolks beaten with 100 ml (4 fl oz, 7 tablespoons) double (heavy) cream. Finally, whisk in 75 g (3 oz, 6 tablespoons) butter. Reheat but do not boil.

asparagus velouté soup ♦
Prepare a thickened chicken consommé as described in the recipe for artichoke velouté soup. Cut 400 g (14 oz) washed asparagus into pieces, blanch for 5 minutes in boiling water, drain and then simmer with 40 g (1½ oz, 3 tablespoons) butter for about 10 minutes. Purée in a blender or food processor and add to the consommé. Finish as for artichoke velouté soup. Garnish with cooked asparagus tips and parsley.

celeriac velouté soup
Proceed as for artichoke velouté soup, but use 300 g (11 oz) celeriac, blanched, sliced and simmered in 40 g (1½ oz, 3 tablespoons) butter, instead of artichokes.

chicken velouté soup
Thicken a generous 750 ml (1½ pints, 3¼ cups) chicken consommé* with a white roux made with 40 g (1½ oz, 3 tablespoons) butter and 40 g (1½ oz, 6 tablespoons) plain (all-purpose) flour. Add a small young chicken and simmer gently until the bird breaks up with a fork. Drain and bone the chicken, reserve some breast meat for a garnish and reduce the remainder to a purée in a blender or food processor, adding a little of the cooking liquid. Mix with the rest of the cooking liquid and complete as for artichoke velouté soup. Cut the reserved meat into very fine strips and add to the soup just before serving.

Game or any other meat can be used instead of chicken to make a game or meat velouté soup.

crayfish velouté soup
Proceed as for shrimp velouté soup, but use 12 crayfish instead of shrimps. The soup may be thickened with 65 g (2½ oz, 5 tablespoons) crayfish butter* instead of fresh butter.

fish soup with mussels
Shred the cleaned white part of 3 leeks, 2 carrots, and 1 celery stick and fry in 100 ml (4 fl oz, 7 tablespoons) olive oil. Add a pinch of saffron, a sprig of thyme, 1 bay leaf, 1 crushed garlic clove and 250 g (9 oz, 1 cup) crushed fresh tomatoes. Add 150 g (5 oz) each of fillets of brill, monkfish, red mullet and weever (sand lance), together with 1.5 litres

(2¾ pints, 6½ cups) fish fumet*. Simmer for 15 minutes. Season with salt and pepper and add 500 g (18 oz) shelled mussels. Serve piping hot.

fish velouté soup
Proceed as for chicken velouté soup, using fish instead of chicken. The chicken consommé may be replaced by fish fumet.

Hungarian soup with liver dumplings
Cut 150 g (5 oz) calves' or chicken liver into dice and sauté briskly in 15 g (½ oz, 1 tablespoon) lard. Season with salt and pepper. Braise 50 g (2 oz, ⅓ cup) thinly sliced onions in butter. Put these ingredients through a blender or food processor, together with 1 tablespoon chopped parsley, 1 large egg, 50 g (2 oz, ¼ cup) butter, salt, pepper, 1 teaspoon paprika and a generous pinch of grated nutmeg. Shape the mixture into small dumplings and simmer them in stock for 15 minutes. Prepare 1.5 litres (2¾ pints, 6½ cups) chicken consommé* and serve garnished with the dumplings.

iced avocado velouté soup
Using a melon baller, scoop out some balls of pulp from a small peeled and seeded cucumber. Blanch them rapidly in boiling water. Peel a firm ripe tomato after dipping it in boiling water, and cut the flesh into very small dice. Halve 3 avocados, remove the stones (pits) and scoop out all the pulp with a spoon. Put the pulp through a blender or food processor, adding the juice of 1 lemon, 4 tablespoons crème fraîche and 100 ml (4 fl oz, 7 tablespoons) milk. Season with salt and dust with cayenne pepper. Place in the refrigerator to chill. Pour the soup into 4 bowls and garnish with the cucumber balls, the diced tomato and 6 finely chopped mint leaves. Serve ice cold.

langouste velouté soup
Proceed as for shrimp velouté soup, but use 1 small langouste instead of shrimps.

lobster velouté soup
Proceed as for shrimp velouté soup, but use 1 small lobster instead of shrimps. The soup may be thickened with 65 g (2½ oz, 5 tablespoons) lobster butter* instead of fresh butter.

mushroom velouté soup
Proceed as for artichoke velouté soup but use 400 g (14 oz, 4½ cups) cultivated mushrooms, sliced and simmered in 40 g (1½ oz, 3 tablespoons) butter, instead of artichokes.

oyster velouté soup
Poach 24 oysters in their own juices and add the cooking liquid to a generous 750 ml (1¼ pints, 3¼ cups) fish velouté soup. Complete the cooking and thicken as for artichoke velouté soup. Trim the oysters, steam them quickly to reheat and add them to the soup just before serving.

potato and leek soup

Cut off the green part of 12 leeks and remove the withered leaves. Peel and quarter 4 large potatoes. Thinly slice the cleaned green parts of the leeks and fry in 25 g (1 oz, 2 tablespoons) butter. Add 1.5 litres (2¾ pints, 6½ cups) boiling water, bring back to the boil, then add the potatoes. Season with salt and pepper and leave to cook gently with the lid on for about 1 hour. Put through a blender or food processor and pour into a soup tureen. Sprinkle with chopped parsley and serve piping hot with small slices of bread dried in the oven.

purée of Brussels sprout soup

Trim 500 g (18 oz) Brussels sprouts and blanch them for 2 minutes in boiling water. Rinse in cold water and drain thoroughly, then sweat gently in 50 g (2 oz, ¼ cup) butter. Finish as for purée of celery soup.

purée of celery soup

Scrub 500 g (18 oz) celery sticks. Chop the celery or the same weight of blanched peeled celeriac and sweat in 50 g (2 oz, ¼ cup) butter. Purée the cooked celery in a blender or food processor. Pour the purée into a saucepan and add 1.75 litres (3 pints, 7½ cups) chicken stock and 250 g (9 oz) floury potatoes, cut into quarters. Bring to the boil and cook for about 30 minutes. Rub through a sieve and add sufficient stock to obtain the desired consistency. Adjust the seasoning. Just before serving, beat in 50 g (2 oz, ¼ cup) butter, cut into small pieces.

purée of chestnut soup

Peel 575 g (1¼ lb) chestnuts and cook in a saucepan with 1.5 litres (2¾ pints, 6½ cups) stock or consommé until they begin to disintegrate. Peel 200 g (7 oz) celeriac, cut it into slices and blanch for 2 minutes in boiling water. Drain and pat dry. Sweat in 25 g (1 oz, 2 tablespoons) butter with 1 tablespoon finely chopped onion. Add the celeriac to the cooked chestnuts and cook together for a further 10 minutes. Put through a blender or food processor. Dilute with a little stock or boiled milk and whisk in 50 g (2 oz, ¼ cup) butter cut into small pieces. Serve with small croûtons fried in butter.

purée of tomato soup

Peel and chop 50 g (2 oz, ⅓ cup) onions. Sweat them in 25 g (1 oz, 2 tablespoons) butter, then add 800 g (1¾ lb) peeled tomatoes, 1 crushed garlic clove, 1 small bouquet garni, salt and pepper. Cook gently for 20 minutes, add 100 g (4 oz, ⅓ cup) long-grain rice and stir. Add 1.5 litres (2¾ pints, 6½ cups) boiling stock, stir, cover and leave to cook for 20 minutes. Remove the bouquet garni. Reduce to a purée in a blender or food processor, then return to the saucepan and whisk in 50 g (2 oz, ¼ cup) butter cut into small pieces. Sprinkle with chopped parsley or basil. Serve with croûtons flavoured with garlic and fried in olive oil.

shrimp velouté soup

Thicken a generous 750 ml (1¼ pints, 3¼ cups) chicken consommé* or fish fumet* with a white roux made with 40 g (1½ oz, 3 tablespoons) butter and 40 g (1½ oz, 6 tablespoons) plain (all-purpose) flour. Cook 400 g (14 oz, 2⅓ cups) peeled (shelled) shrimps with a mirepoix. Then rub through a sieve or put through a blender or food processor and add this purée to the thickened consommé. Finish as for artichoke velouté soup; the 65 g (2½ oz, 5 tablespoons) fresh butter may be replaced by an equal quantity of shrimp butter.

soissonnais soup

Soak 350 g (12 oz, 2 cups) dried white haricot (navy) beans in cold water for 12 hours. Put them in a saucepan with 1.5 litres (2¾ pints, 6½ cups) cold water and bring to the boil. Add 1 onion studded with 2 cloves, 1 peeled diced carrot, 1 bouquet garni and 75 g (3 oz, ⅓ cup) slightly salted belly of pork or unsmoked streaky (slabs) bacon, blanched, diced and fried in butter. Cover, bring to the boil and cook until the beans break up. Remove the onion and the bouquet garni. Put the beans and some of the liquid through a blender or food processor. Return the purée to the saucepan, dilute with stock or consommé and adjust the seasoning. Bring to the boil and whisk in 50 g (2 oz, ¼ cup) butter. Serve with croûtons fried in butter.

Solferino soup

Wash, trim and chop the white part from 100 g (4 oz) leeks and 100 g (4 oz) carrots and sweat in 25 g (1 oz, 2 tablespoons) butter for 15 minutes. Make about 20 potato balls using a melon baller, and cook in salted boiling water for 15 minutes, without allowing them to break up. Set aside. Peel, seed and crush 800 g (1¾ lb) tomatoes and add the pulp to the sweated vegetables with 1 bouquet garni and 1 garlic clove. Season, cover and cook gently for 15 minutes, then add 1.5 litres (2¾ pints, 6½ cups) stock and 250 g (9 oz) peeled potatoes cut into pieces. Cook for 30 minutes.

Remove the bouquet garni and purée the vegetables in a blender or food processor. Dilute with a little stock if necessary and reheat. Remove from the heat, whisk in 50–75 g (2–3 oz, 4–6 tablespoons) butter in small pieces, then add the potato balls. Serve with chervil.

sorrel velouté soup

Proceed as for artichoke velouté soup, but use 250 g (9 oz) sorrel instead of artichokes. Blanch the sorrel in salted boiling water for 3–4 minutes, drain and dry thoroughly. Sweat in 40 g (1½ oz, 3 tablespoons) butter for about 15 minutes, then add to the consommé and finish as for artichoke velouté soup.

soupe à la bonne femme

Heat 40 g (1½ oz, 3 tablespoons) butter in a saucepan, but do not let it brown. Add the cleaned white part of 4 finely sliced leeks and cook gently until quite soft. Then add 3 litres (5 pints, 13 cups) ordinary consommé* and bring to the boil. Add 350 g (12 oz, 1¾ cups) thinly sliced potatoes, bring to the boil again, season with salt and pepper, then lower the heat and leave to cook for 1 hour. Just before serving, remove the saucepan from the heat and whisk in 50 g (2 oz, ¼ cup) butter and 1 tablespoon chervil leaves.

soupe albigeoise

Fill a large flameproof casserole with salted water and boil some beef flank (flank steak), calf's foot, salt pork and cooking sausage, together with vegetables such as cabbage, carrots, turnips, leeks and potatoes. Add 1 whole head of garlic per 6 servings. Brown some thin slices of goose confit in butter and garnish the soup with them.

soupe alsacienne à la farine

Mix 20 g (¾ oz, 3 tablespoons) sifted plain (all-purpose) flour with a few tablespoons cold consommé and pour on to this mixture 1.5 litres (2¾ pints, 6½ cups) boiling consommé*, beating continuously. Adjust the seasoning and add plenty of grated nutmeg. Leave to simmer for 5 minutes, then remove the saucepan from the heat, add 100 ml (4 fl oz, 7 tablespoons) crème fraîche and whisk in 15 g (½ oz, 1 tablespoon) butter.

soupe hollandaise

Peel 1 onion, wash 1 small celery stick and chop together. Lightly brown these vegetables for 10 minutes in 15 g (½ oz, 1 tablespoon) butter over a gentle heat. Add 3 tomatoes, peeled, seeded and cut into quarters. Continue cooking for 10 minutes. Purée the vegetables in a blender or food processor and return to the saucepan. Add a pinch of pili-pili and bring to the boil. Dilute with 1.5 litres (2¾ pints, 6½ cups) water and cook for 15 minutes.

Cut 200 g (7 oz) stale bread into very small pieces and place in a soup tureen with 150 g (5 oz, 1¼ cups) grated Gouda cheese. Remove the saucepan from the heat, add 100 ml (4 fl oz, 7 tablespoons) crème fraîche and pour into the tureen. Cover and leave to stand for 5 minutes before serving.

stracciatella soup

Pour into a bowl 100 g (4 oz, 2 cups) fine fresh breadcrumbs and add 2 eggs, lightly beaten. Mix, then add 50 g (2 oz, ½ cup) grated Parmesan cheese, salt, pepper and nutmeg. Pour this mixture into 1.5 litres (2¾ pints, 6½ cups) boiling chicken consommé*, whisking vigorously. Cook very gently for 8 minutes. Give a final whisk just before serving.

veal soup with quenelles

Prepare small veal quenelles. Make a roux with 40 g (1½ oz, 3 tablespoons) butter and 40 g (1½ oz, 6 tablespoons) plain (all-purpose) flour. Pour on to it 1.5 litres (2¾ pints, 6½ cups) well-seasoned veal

stock, whisk well and reheat. Pour the soup into a tureen, add the quenelles, garnish with chopped herbs and serve piping hot.

Viennese sour cream soup

Prepare 1.5 litres (2¾ pints, 6½ cups) thin velouté* sauce and add 1 onion studded with a clove, 1 bouquet garni, a pinch of ground cumin and grated nutmeg. Cook gently for 20 minutes, then rub through a fine sieve. Add 100 ml (4 fl oz, 7 tablespoons) soured (sour) cream, or double (heavy) cream mixed with 2 tablespoons lemon juice, and serve with small fried croûtons.

SOUP TUREEN A wide deep bowl, fitted with two handles, used for serving soup. A lid, sometimes with a notch to accommodate the ladle, keeps the soup warm. For a formal dinner, most soups are served directly in soup dishes or cups, and the soup tureen does not appear on the table. However, it is used for serving bisques and velouté and cream soups, for which it may be made of gold- or silver-plate or fine porcelain (the first such tureens appeared in the 18th century). Thick substantial soups with solid ingredients tend to be served in tureens made of earthenware, glazed clay or fireproof porcelain. Gratinées are often served in small individual soup tureens made of fireproof porcelain.

SOUR Term expressing a sensation of acidity when it is abnormal (a sauce, milk or wine becomes sour when it has 'turned'), or when it seems less pleasant (sour cherries, which are not edible in their natural state, become edible when they have been preserved in alcohol).

This word also describes a complex sharp/pungent sensation in the mouth, caused by a combination of an acid taste and aromas. Lactic acid makes milk products pleasantly sour, and acetic acid produces vinegar; other aromatic molecules give a 'sharpish' and frequently refreshing note to certain products, including fromage frais, yogurt and some cheeses.

SOURIS The small, sweet, rounded piece of meat at the knuckle end of a leg of lamb or mutton. Stronger-tasting than the noix, it can be eaten on its own, with a thin strip of grilled (broiled) skin, or accompanied by a slice of rare meat from the rest of the joint, the contrasting flavours being delicious.

SOUTH AFRICA See *page 1121*.

SOUTH AMERICA See *page 1122*.

SOUTH-EAST ASIA See *page 1124*.

SOUVAROV A method of preparing pheasant, partridge, woodcock or quail, which is also suitable for chicken. The bird is stuffed with foie gras and truffle, fried until three-quarters cooked, then finished off in a casserole together with the frying pan juices

SOUTH AFRICA

The cuisine of South Africa shows a variety of influences. Although among much of the black population maize (mealie) meal and stewed meat or sausage is the staple diet, the food eaten by the other groups reflects the diversity of their origins: Dutch, German, English, French Huguenot, Indian, Malay and Chinese. See entry on *black Africa.*

South Africa is a meat-eating country, but there is also a high consumption of both fish and shellfish. A favourite snack food is biltong – dried, salted and spiced beef, antelope or ostrich meat. *Boerewors* are the spiced sausages made from various meats and most often cooked over a *braai* (barbecue).

Dishes of East Indies origin, such as *sosatie* (marinated lamb or mutton grilled on a skewer) and *bobotie* (a meat stew flavoured with cumin, coriander and cardamom, and mixed with raisins and yellow rice) are found mainly in restaurants specializing in Cape Dutch cookery. Cape fruit including citrus fruit and grapes is world famous and is eaten in abundance, and vegetables are prolific and of high quality.

WINE South Africa has a long tradition in winemaking – vines were first planted in the Cape in 1655. Only about half the annual harvest is used for wine, the rest goes for distillation, grape spirit or concentrate for fruit juice. The winelands fan out from Cape Town. Some of the more recognized cultivation areas include: Constantia, historic centre of the wine industry and home to the renowned dessert wine of the same name, and Stellenbosch, producing very good quality red and white wines. Paarl's wineries make red, white, sparkling and fortified wines, brandies, and liqueurs. Worcester produces mainly brandies, but some estates are now making white wines for everyday drinking from Colombard and Chenin Blanc. Good quality white wines, particularly from Chardonnay, and an increasing number of reds are made in the hot, arid Robertson region, whilst excellent Pinot Noirs and Chardonnays are made in the cool maritime region of Walker Bay.

White grape varieties dominate in the vineyards with Chenin Blanc (locally known as Steen) most widely planted. Other varieties include Chardonnay, Sauvignon Blanc, Colombard, Semillon, (Weisser) Riesling, Gewürztraminer and various Muscats, including Hanepoot (Muscat of Alexandria).

Red grape varieties are being increasingly planted: Cabernet Sauvignon, Merlot and Cabernet Franc making very attractive Bordeaux-style blends; Shiraz (Syrah), Zinfandel and Grenache. Pinotage (South Africa's 'own' grape variety) a crossing of Pinot Noir and Cinsaut, is gaining in popularity and produces top quality red wines.

---

deglazed with demi-glace sauce, truffle fumet and Madeira. Foie gras Souvarov is seized in butter, then cooked in a sealed terrine with truffles and a truffle-flavoured demi-glace sauce.

These dishes were named after a certain Prince Souvorov, who used to frequent Paris restaurants and was a descendant of the governor of the Crimea. His name, corrupted to Souvarov, Souvaroff or Souwaroff, has also been given to a petit four made of two small sablés sandwiched together.

RECIPES

foie gras Souvarov
Season a goose foie gras weighing 500 g (18 oz) with salt and pepper and leave to steep for 24 hours in Cognac. Drain off the excess liquid, then seize the foie gras in 25 g (1 oz, 2 tablespoons) butter. Place it in a terrine just large enough to contain it, surrounded by quartered truffles. Half-cover it with reduced demi-glace sauce flavoured with truffle. Cover the terrine and seal the lid with a strip of dough. Cook for 40 minutes in a preheated oven at 200°C (400°, gas 6). Serve in the terrine.

partridge à la Souvarov
Stuff a partridge with fois gras and truffles cut into large dice, seasoned with salt and pepper and sprinkled with a dash of brandy. Truss the bird and seize it in butter, then place it in a small oval terrine, surrounded by diced or whole truffles, peeled and seasoned with salt and pepper. Moisten with 100 ml (4 fl oz, 7 tablespoons) Madeira-flavoured game fumet to which the pan juices, diluted with Madeira, have been added. Sprinkle with a dash of brandy. Cover the terrine, seal the lid with a strip of dough and cook in a preheated oven at 190°C (375°F, gas 5) for 45 minutes. Serve in the terrine.

Woodcock and chicken can be prepared in the same way, but fry chicken in butter until it is three-quarters done, then finish cooking in the oven for 30 minutes.

petits fours Souvarov
Make a sablé mixture using 675 g (1½ lb, 6 cups) plain (all-purpose) flour, 400 g (14 oz, 1¾ cups) butter, 200 g (7 oz, 1 cup) caster (superfine) sugar, and 1 tablespoon double (heavy) cream. Leave to stand for 1 hour in a cool place.

Roll out the dough to a thickness of 5 mm (¼ in) and cut out shapes using a round or fluted oval pastry (cookie) cutter. Place on a baking sheet and cook in a preheated oven at 200°C (400°F, gas 6) for 15 minutes. Leave to cool, then spread the sablés with thick sieved apricot jam (preserve), sandwich together in pairs and sprinkle with icing (confectioner's) sugar.

SOUTH AMERICA

The highly spiced cuisine of the South American countries betrays its Spanish or Portuguese origin – in stews, fish and seafood dishes, with an emphasis on fried food. By another route, the African slaves introduced their own dietary habits, as did the European colonists: the Italians to Argentina, where pasta is very popular; the Germans to Bolivia, where more beer is drunk than in other Latin American countries; and the French to Guyana and Venezuela, where the cuisine is more delicate. A lot of meat is eaten in livestock-breeding regions, sometimes dried (*charqui*) but more often grilled since open-air cooking is popular everywhere. Local recipes remain colourful, however; armadillo is still eaten, as well as iguana eggs and large grilled ants. All South American countries use beans, potatoes, rice and, above all, maize (corn) – its flour, leaves and ears (see *empanada, tamal*). Tropical fruits are extremely varied and are eaten with vegetables, in salads, as juice or as jellies. Desserts are primarily sweet dishes such as mashes and milk jellies. (For drinks, see *aguardiente, coffee, chicha, maté, pulque, tequila*.)

Where applicable, separate entries give a more specific view of the countries; however, the following provides an overview of the cooking of South America by comparing their individual traditions.

■ **Argentina** Argentinians eat a lot of meat, particularly beef (the country has the highest beef consumption per capita in the world), either roast (*asado*) or grilled (*churrasco*). But this does not exclude more elaborate dishes, such as beef broth garnished with pumpkin and ears of maize. *Matambre* ('hunger-killer') is typically Argentinian, made from marinated beef stuffed with vegetables and hard-boiled (hard-cooked) eggs, roasted and boiled, and served cold at the beginning of a meal. Another Argentinian meat dish is *carbonada criolla*, a stew simmered in a hollowed pumpkin. This renowned livestock-breeding country also produces such cheeses as Tafi, which is like Cantal, and *dulce de leche*, a sweet, fudge-like spread made from aromatized condensed milk and eaten throughout South America. See *Argentina* entry.

■ **Bolivia** With Peru, Bolivia is the country of origin of the potato, and prides itself on producing more than 300 varieties. Particularly popular are *chuños*, freeze-dried potatoes, which are very light and are soaked before using. Bolivian cuisine offers highly spiced stews and small fried dishes cooked in the open air; it uses vegetables and freshwater fish, and a particular speciality is *conejo estirado*, a dish made from rabbit that has been stretched to make its flesh very tender.

Good quality wines are being produced from varieties including Pinot Blanc, Syrah, Cabernet Sauvignon, Merlot and Moscatel (Muscat of Alexandria). The vineyards are at a high altitude – around 1,800 –2,500 m – benefit from high ultra-violet exposure and have an average of 20ºC difference in day/night temperatures giving more elegance or finesse in the wines. Singani, a local brandy is distilled from Moscatel.

■ **Brazil** Influenced by the Portuguese, Brazilian cuisine is, with that of Peru, the most varied and refined in South America. Portuguese influence accounts for the use of olives, almonds, dried shrimp, garlic, onions and salt cod; the native Indians have contributed cassava flour, cocoa, sweet potatoes and peanuts; the descendants of the African slaves have bought yams, bananas, okra, coconuts and, above all, palm oil (*dende*), which gives its flavour to all fried dishes.

The national dish is *feijoada*, traditionally preceded by a *batida*, a cocktail shake of eau-de-vie mixed with lime. There are many local variants of the national dish, since the cultural and historical personality of each region of Brazil is reflected in its cuisine. Fish and seafood are widely consumed in the north-east. *Fritada de mariscos* is a dish of mussels, oysters and pieces of crab coated in fritter batter and fried; large shrimps are prepared in many ways – in sauces, with coconut for *vatapa*, in balls; fried with red beans; and even in *xinxin de galinha*, a chicken fricassée with peanuts and cassava. The cakes and pastries of this region are highly prized and include flavoured custards, cakes made with coconut or prunes, and egg yolks beaten with sugar and given picturesque names such as angel's cheeks, young girl's saliva and mother-in-law's eye. The typical dish of central Brazil is *churrasco* (grilled meat), and everywhere cream cheese is eaten with guava jelly. The south has a copious and abundant cuisine with such dishes as offal in

---

SOVIETSKI A Russian pasteurized pressed cow's-milk cheese (50% fat content), which is elastic in consistency and has a rather piquant taste. After it has been ripening for a few months, small holes appear in it. It comes in a rectangular slab, 50 × 20 cm (20 × 8 in), weighing 12–16 kg (26–35 lb). It is usually eaten for breakfast and is also used in cooking.

SOW THISTLE (MILKWEED) A plant with something of the flavour of both chicory (endive) and lettuce. It exudes a copious white sap when cut. The young leaves of the cultivated sow thistle are used in salads, while the tougher more leathery ones are cooked in salted boiling water like spinach. The stalks can be boiled and served as a vegetable. In winter, the roots can be eaten and are cooked in the same way as salsify.

ragoûts and fruit-stuffed poultry. The basic dish is a purée of black beans, cassava flour and bacon pieces. Amazonian fauna provides some culinary curiosities – pickled peccary and sea cow cooked in coconut milk – and there is also an impressive range of fruits.

There has been considerable investment in vineyards and wineries by international companies with varieties including Chardonnay, Semillon, Gewürztraminer, Cabernet Sauvignon, Cabernet Franc and Merlot planted. Red, white and also sparkling wines are produced.

■ **Chile** The quality of the meat is excellent, particularly the grilled mutton, and there is a great variety of *empanadas* (meat pies). The abundance of seafood is reflected in the cuisine, which is invariably seasoned with chilli (chili pepper) and onion. *Congrio* (cusk eel) soup is a famous speciality. Stews (*chupes*) are made from offal, vegetables (beans and squash in particular) or dried meat. See *Chile* entry for wine information.

■ **Colombia** The geography of the country (two coasts plus mountains) accounts for distinctive regional cooking styles and ingredients. Scrambled eggs with tomatoes and onions are served from breakfast onwards and *tamales* and *empanadas* are nibbled all day. Stews are very substantial – *ajiaco* is made from meat or poultry, maize, potatoes and avocado, and seasoned with chilli, while *sancocho* is made from meat or fish, with cassava and unripe bananas. Maize biscuits (*arepa*) are used as bread. Coconut is very popular and may be found as often in sauces as in

desserts. Strawberries and oranges are as plentiful as papaya, guava and passion fruit.

■ **Ecuador** Varieties of banana are particularly numerous in this country, and so bananas occur in a great many recipes. Other typical ingredients include potatoes, peanuts (groundnuts), chillies and almonds. As well as *tamales*, soups and filled pies, a lot of marinated raw fish is eaten. All Saints' Day is the major holiday of the year and hundreds of little decorated sugar cakes are made for the occasion.

■ **Guyana, French Guiana and Surinam** Some authentic native Indian dishes are eaten in this region, such as armadillo ragoût, alligator kebabs and roast peccary. Much of the cooking is based on the Creole style. Typical ingredients include cassava, corn, chillies, okra, sweet potatoes and plantain, and shellfish on the coast.

■ **Paraguay and Uruguay** Here the food is the same as in Argentina, with the addition of freshwater fish and abundant game. Palm hearts (terminal buds) are mainly produced in this region. The national dish is again a stew, *bori bori*, made of meat balls, vegetables, pieces of cream cheese and maize.

Whilst Uruguay is becoming known for producing a good range of wines from Pinot Blanc, Chardonnay, Sauvignon Blanc, Cabernet Sauvignon, Merlot and Cabernet Franc, Tannat is gaining a reputation as 'the' grape variety in the international market place.

■ **Peru** Peruvian cooking, as highly spiced as that of Mexico, has kept up the tradition of the *pachamanca*, an oven dug out of the earth in which is cooked a pig,

goat or chickens with corn on the cob, potatoes and aromatic herbs. Peru is the country of *ceviche*, marinated raw fish served with sweet limes, onions, tomatoes and maize. Peruvian *chupes* (thick stews), more liquid than the Chilean variety, have milk added to them and are garnished with vegetables or poached eggs. Potatoes are prepared in various ways: with cream cheese, onions and orange juice; mashed with shrimps, olives and hard-boiled (hard-cooked) eggs; as an accompaniment to dried meat; and, of course, in all the stews. Another Peruvian speciality is *anticucho*, kebabs of highly spiced ox or calf hearts. Among sweetmeats, Lima nougat is renowned.

Peru has a long history of winemaking – the first vines were planted by the Spanish conquistadors in the 16th century. Whilst around half the total grape production is for table grapes, Peru is making good quality red, white and sparkling wines from Semillon, Sauvignon Blanc, Chenin Blanc, Malbec, Cabernet Sauvignon, Merlot and Cabernet Franc.

■ **Venezuela** This country has the mildest cuisine in South America, again featuring beef, red and black beans mixed with rice, and maize, bananas and cassava. The *arepa*, or maize biscuit, accompanies every dish. *Hayaca*, the typical dish prepared traditionally at Christmas, consists of maize pancakes filled with meat or fish, eggs, olives, raisins, almonds and condiments, and is cooked in banana leaves. *Sancocho* is the classic stew of meat, offal or fish. Papaya jelly is the favourite dessert but, like bananas, it is also served with savoury dishes.

SOYA BEAN (SOY BEAN) A pulse that probably originated in Manchuria, which the Chinese call *dadou* (big bean) and the Japanese *daizu*. This staple food is known for its products rather than the bean itself, and is used worldwide. There are over a thousand varieties of soya bean, varying in size and colour (white, yellow, red, green, brown and black). Extremely nutritious, the bean is low in carbohydrates and high in protein, and therefore an important source of protein for those whose diet includes little or no meat.

The soya bean was known in China as a basic foodstuff well before our era. It was introduced to Japan in the 6th century, where it was called the 'meat vegetable'. European travellers discovered it in the 17th century and introduced certain soya-based

SOUTH-EAST ASIA

The cuisines of China's neighbouring countries resemble Chinese cooking in many ways. China's influence is particularly noticeable in Korea (as is Japan's; for example, *sashimi*), Vietnam, Laos and Cambodia; in Myanmar (formerly Burma) and Thailand, the cuisine is influenced by the proximity of India and includes variations on curry.

As in China, the dishes of a meal, often a great number of them, are served all together. The concepts of hors d'oeuvre and desserts are unknown, and between meals the Indo-Chinese eat sweetmeats and small snacks, such as *nems* (stuffed and fried rice pancakes) and spring rolls.

Typical Vietnamese dishes are *bi-thanh,* scooped-out gourd, steamed and filled with sliced chicken, lotus seeds, dried mushrooms, ham, crab and ginger; pork ribs with lemon balm (marinated, then grilled); and *vit-tim,* steamed duck stuffed with prunes, mushrooms and shallots. There is also a vast range of filled omelettes. *Lap* (crushed and spiced raw meat), fried crab's claws and chicken with spices are specialities in Laos and Thailand, while *bahmi* (a mixture of meat, fish and noodles) and *bahuri* (ragoût of pork and salted fish

mixed with pineapple and mango) are special Thai dishes. Pickled cabbage with ginger and turnips and *bulgogi* (marinated beef) are popular Korean dishes.

Malaysian and Singaporean cuisines epitomize the cross-culture styles of South-East Asia. Not only do Chinese and Indian cooking exist separately, but they meet and mix. The high-class Nonya home cooking of Malaysia uses indigenous herbs and spices with pork as well as seafood, bean curd, bean sprouts, dried mushrooms and noodles. Popular street food stalls and markets impart the same mix of Indo-Chinese aromas and flavours

■ **Spices and aromatics** The spices and aromatics used in South-East Asia are those found all over the East (chilli, black pepper, ginger, saffron and cinnamon), but many fresh plants are also used, such as shallots, lemon balm and coriander (cilantro). Turmeric, with which curry is made, is widely used in Myanmar, but it is *nuoc-mâm,* or *nam pla,* in particular (unknown in China) that gives Indo-Chinese cooking its characteristic flavour.

■ **Soups** Garnished stocks and soups are prominent everywhere; for example, the Vietnamese *pho* (spiced stock garnished with noodles, vegetables and very thin slices of meat), the acid-flavoured Thai *tom yam,* or the *hincho* from Myanmar, with vegetables. They take the place of breakfast, and

are served with or at the end of the main meals.

■ **Meats, seafood and vegetables** The most common meats are pork and chicken. Beef is also eaten (particularly in Vietnam and Korea), but never mutton. Duck and duck eggs are popular. A great deal of fish is eaten, and crabs and prawns (shrimp) are even more popular. Vegetables – turnips, cabbage, cucumbers and many varieties of mushrooms – are cooked in small pieces. They are also served raw in salad, which never happens in China.

Rice is a traditional accompaniment throughout the region, together with very fine vermicelli noodles used in soups and ragoûts. Whether food is simmered, marinated, fried or braised, the dishes are generally less elaborate and lighter than those of China.

■ **Fruit and sweetmeats** The most widely grown fruits are pineapple, lychee, mandarin (tangerine), papaya, rambutan, ginkgo, jujube, kumquat and mango. They may be eaten fresh or preserved, but are also used to garnish savoury dishes and may be mixed with raw vegetables in certain recipes. Durian, with its very distinctive 'rotten' smell, is much appreciated in Vietnam. Popular sweetmeats include little cakes made of almonds, lotus cream or sesame, and other specialities include preserved ginger and gourds.

dishes – soups, cakes and porridges – on their return. A century later, the first seeds arrived in Paris at the Jardin des Plantes; only after World War I did the United States and Europe become interested in commercial production of the soya bean for forage and oil.

Soya beans are now used in a variety of forms. Fresh soya beans are rarely used in their natural state, but dried soya beans, soaked and boiled, are eaten in soups or salads. In Japan, dried black soya beans are cooked for a long time with cloves and sugar, flavoured with soy sauce and served with rice. Soya beansprouts are the seeds of the bean and their shoots. Mung and alfalfa seeds and sprouts are milder and more tender than the true soya and more common in Europe. Beansprouts are used in stir-fries and spring rolls, in salads and as a sweet-and-sour vegeatable.

■ **Soya bean products** There are many important products obtained from processing the soya bean. These include:

• SOYA BEAN CURD Known as tofu or bean curd, this is popular in Chinese, Japanese and South-East Asian cooking.

• SOYA BEAN OIL This is used in cooking and for making margarine.

• SOYA BEAN PROTEIN Available in many forms, including chunks, granules and even steaks, this is used by vegetarians as an alternative to meat. It is also used in the manufacture of some products to extend their meat content.

• SOYA FLOUR (twice as rich in protein as wheat flour) is used in cakes and to bind sauces. In Japan, it is used to coat sticky rice pâtés.

• SOYA MILK This has always been drunk by the

Chinese, and is a useful substitute for anyone with an intolerance to cow's milk. Soya milk can be used in cooking, although it has a tendency to curdle when added to hot liquids, and can be used to make soya milk yogurt.

• SOY SAUCE AND BLACK BEAN SAUCE These are condiments made from fermented soya beans, both of which are widely used in Oriental cooking.

In ancient China, soya beans were regarded as one of the essentials of daily life, and have always played a large part in Chinese cuisine. Japanese cookery, too, has always made extensive use of soya-based products: *natto* is a product of fermented soya beans, used as a garnish for rice dishes and dishes for special occasions; *tofu*, or soya cheese, with its many uses; and *miso*, made of rice, barley or soya, which is fermented and used in broths and soups, or as a garnish for fish with vegetables. The Vietnamese enjoy pancakes of soya flour and soya milk, served plain or with honey, while Indonesians make great use of *tempeh*, a thin cake made from fermented soya beans.

RECIPES

shellfish and soya bean sprout salad
Cook a large crab in stock and 200 g (7 oz) prawns (shrimp) in salted water. Shell the crab and the prawns and flake the crabmeat. Place 500 g (18 oz, 4½ cups) soya bean sprouts in cold water, remove the debris that comes to the surface, drain and blanch for no more than 1 minute in salted boiling water. Drain and refresh in very cold water, then wipe them.

Place the flaked crab, prawns and bean sprouts in a salad bowl. Finely slice 2 spring onions (scallions) and add ½ teaspoon soy sauce, ½ teaspoon mustard, a pinch of sugar, 1 tablespoon brandy or sherry, 1 tablespoon vinegar, 2–3 tablespoons oil, pepper, a little salt and a few drops of Tabasco (or a small pinch of cayenne pepper). Pour the sauce on to the salad, mix well and sprinkle with chopped fresh coriander (cilantro).

soya bean sprout salad
Prepare 500 g (18 oz, 4½ cups) soya bean sprouts as for the recipe above and lightly fry with 3 tablespoons hot oil. Drain and allow to cool completely. Hard boil (hard cook) and shell 4 eggs. Turn the beansprouts into a salad bowl and dress with a spicy vinaigrette seasoned with a touch of cayenne pepper. Add a few slices of white chicken meat or cold roast duck. Mix and garnish with the quartered hard-boiled eggs.

SOYER, ALEXIS
French cook (born Meaux, 1810; died London, 1858). He started out at the age of 16 at Grignon's in Paris and became the deputy chef in the kitchens of the Ministry of Foreign Affairs. After the July Revolution, he emigrated to England, where he was chef at the Reform Club, whose kitchens he installed. After the sudden death of his wife, an English actress called Emma Jones, he devoted himself to charity, opening canteens for the underprivileged in London and Dublin.

He worked for the British government during the Crimean War and designed an 'economical bivouac and camp kitchen' for the army. He also invented a 'magic oven', the ancestor of the table hotplate, which was heated by a spirit lamp. Soyer, who had a sense of publicity, launched Soyer sauce (for meat dishes) and Soyer nectar (based on fruit juice and aerated water).

He wrote several books, both for wealthy gourmets and for the less fortunate, including *The Gastronomic Regenerator* (1846), *The Poor Man's Regenerator* (1848) and *A Shilling Cookery* (1854).

SOY SAUCE
A basic condiment from China, South-East Asia and Japan (it is called *shoyu* in Japan and *jiang yong* in China). The sauce is made from a fermented mixture of soya (soy) bean, wheat, water and salt. Other ingredients can be used: chopped pork in Canton, ginger and mushrooms in Peking. Sometimes *nuoc-mâm* or anchovy paste is added. There are light and dark varieties of soy sauce; tamari is a dark soy sauce made without wheat. Soy sauce has the same nutritional value as meat extract and improves with age.

In Japanese cooking, it is used mainly to season grilled kebabs, tofu, cold vegetable and fish salads, fritters and sashimi. It can be enriched with grated daikon, taro, ginger, horseradish sauce or finely sliced vegetables. In China, soy sauce is mainly used in marinades and stewed dishes, while in Indonesia it is mainly a table condiment and goes by the name of *kecap*.

RECIPE

soy sauce
The following is taken from a traditional Chinese recipe. Boil 2.5 kg (5½ lb, 13 cups) soya beans in water until they are reduced to a purée. Add 1 kg (2¼ lb, 9 cups) plain (all-purpose) flour and knead well to produce a thick dough. Leave in a cool dark place for 2 days, then hang the container in a draught for a week. When a yellow mould appears on the dough, place a jar containing 5 litres (8½ pints, 5½ quarts) water and 1.5 kg (3¼ lb, 5⅔ cups) salt in a sunny place. When the water is warm to the touch, put the dough into the jar. Leave this uncovered for a month, pounding the mixture vigorously every day with a stick. The mixture will turn black as it ages.

Leave for 4–5 months without stirring or covering the jar, unless the weather is bad, in which case the jar should be covered. Decant and store the sauce in hermetically sealed bottles.

SPAGHETTI
Long solid threads of pasta (*spago* means string), and one of the most popular of Italian pasta products. Originating in Naples, it spread to other parts of Italy (especially to the kitchens of Rome and Liguria) and then abroad. Originally made

in the home, spaghetti began to be marketed in the Renaissance period, at the same time as macaroni. Outside Italy it is usually prepared *alla napoletana,* with a tomato sauce base; *alla bolognese,* with a sauce based on minced (ground) meat and tomato; and *alla carbonara,* with bacon, Parmesan cheese and eggs.

Cooked al dente, spaghetti is traditionally served with tomato sauce and Parmesan cheese, as an accompaniment for poultry or veal. There is a large number of other original recipes, especially in Latium (west central Italy): *a cacio e pepe,* with cheese and pepper; *alla carrettiera,* with mushrooms and tuna; *con le vongole,* with clams and chopped parsley; and *all'amatriciana,* with tomatoes, onion, bacon and Pecorino cheese. In Naples, it is eaten with mushrooms, peas and mozzarella cheese, or *alla zappatora,* with sweet (bell) and chilli (chili) peppers. In Capri it is cooked with squid, and in Umbria it is served with chopped white truffles marinated in olive oil with garlic and anchovies.

RECIPES

spaghetti à la ligurienne

Peel and crush 2 garlic cloves. Strip and chop 2 sprigs of basil. Place these ingredients in a mortar together with 40 g (1½ oz, ⅓ cup) dry crumbled Pecorino Romano cheese and 25 g (1 oz, ¼ cup) pine nuts. Cover with 60 ml (2 fl oz, ¼ cup) olive oil and leave to soak for 2 hours. Then pound all these ingredients with a pestle to obtain a fluid paste. Cook the spaghetti *al dente*, drain, pour into a heated serving dish and cover with the basil sauce. Stir and serve immediately.

spaghetti alla botarga

Cook 575 g (1¼ lb) spaghetti al dente. In a frying pan, brown 1 red chilli (chili pepper) and 2 crushed garlic cloves in 60 ml (2 fl oz, ¼ cup) extra-virgin olive oil. Drain the spaghetti and add to the frying pan. Stir the mixture thoroughly. Remove from the heat and add 150 g (5 oz, ¾ cup) crumbled salted and pressed tuna or mullet roe, some chopped parsley and a few drops of lemon juice. Stir and serve immediately.

spaghetti alla carbonara

Cook 250 g (9 oz) spaghetti al dente. Meanwhile, cut 100 g (4 oz) rindless streaky (slab) bacon into small pieces and fry over a gentle heat until crisp. Beat 2 eggs in a bowl, adding 50 g (2 oz, ½ cup) grated Parmesan cheese and salt and pepper to taste. When the spaghetti is cooked, drain, return it to the pan and stir in the beaten egg and hot bacon. (The heat of the pasta is sufficient to cook the eggs.) Serve immediately, with 50 g (2 oz, ½ cup) grated Parmesan cheese in a separate dish for sprinkling on top.

spaghetti all'amatriciana

Cut 200 g (7 oz) pancetta into small cubes and brown in a frying pan with a little extra-virgin olive oil

and 1 red chilli (chili pepper). Over a high heat, add 60 ml (2 fl oz, ¼ cup) dry white wine and 1 kg (2¼ lb) peeled tomatoes, crushing them with a fork. Allow the water to evaporate completely. Cook 575 g (1¼ lb) spaghetti al dente. Drain and add to the saucepan. Stir and sprinkle with 100 g (4 oz, 1 cup) grated Pecorino Romano cheese. Serve very hot.

spaghetti with basil

Cook 250 g (9 oz) spaghetti al dente. Meanwhile, peel and crush 3 garlic cloves, then strip and chop 3 sprigs of basil. Pound these ingredients in a mortar and form a fine paste by gradually adding 3 tablespoons olive oil. Drain the spaghetti and tip into a heated serving dish, add 50 g (2 oz, ¼ cup) butter cut into small pieces, the pounded basil mixture, then 100 g (4 oz, ⅔ cup) stoned (pitted) black (ripe) olives cut into small dice. Mix thoroughly and serve piping hot, with grated Parmesan cheese in a separate dish.

SPAIN See *page 1128*.

SPALLA A speciality of Italian charcuterie, made in the same way as coppa but with shoulder of pork (*spalla* in Italian), boned, trimmed and salted, then wrapped and tied in a casing, steamed and only partially dried.

SPARASSIS CRISPA A mushroom with a thick stalk, divided into a large number of flattened branches. It looks like a large yellowish curly endive (frisée) and grows near the trunks of conifer trees. It has a hazelnut taste and is best eaten young.

SPARERIB (SHOULDER BUTT) A cut of pork taken from the back of the animal, near the head. This part yields a soft, slightly fatty meat. Chops are cut from here, as well as pieces for grilling (broiling) on skewers and roasting on a spit (they do not need to be barded). It is also used for stews. The sparerib kept whole, either boned or not, is a roasting joint.

SPARE RIBS The upper part of the pork belly, cut in long narrow strips; the flesh and fat surrounding the pieces of bone and ribs. The appearance of this cut justifies its French nickname of *cartouchière* (cartridge belt). The best spare ribs are the fleshiest and the leanest. They are either boiled (in *potées*, as a sauerkraut garnish or processed as salt pork) or grilled (broiled). Spare ribs of pork, marinated in spices and soy sauce, then grilled, make a popular Chinese dish. In the United States, spare ribs are marinated in a mixture of soy sauce, ketchup, sugar, ginger and often garlic, then grilled or barbecued.

RECIPE

spare ribs

Prepare a marinade with 1 tablespoon sugar, 1 teaspoon salt, a pinch of ground ginger, 60 ml (2 fl oz,

¼ cup) soy sauce and the same quantity of ketchup, I chopped garlic clove and some black pepper. Marinate the spare ribs for at least 30 minutes, then drain and grill (broil) briskly on one side. Baste with a little marinade and grill the other side. Baste once more and grill the ribs until they are stickily glazed on both sides. The ribs may also be baked in a pre-heated oven, and require basting occasionally.

SPARKLING WINES *mousseux* A fully sparkling wine may be produced by several methods. The finest are made according to the procedure followed for making champagne (see *méthode champenoise*). Very good sparkling wines are made according to a process known as *charmat* or *cuve close*; others, which may be pleasant inexpensive wines, can be made by carbonating a still wine. Most sparkling wines are white, varying from dry (*brut*) to sweet, but a number of rosés are also made and there are some red sparkling wines, notably from Touraine, Burgundy, Australia and Argentina.

SPATCHCOCK A small bird, split in half down the back and flattened. The term was popular in 18th-century cooking and is similar to spitchcock, an earlier term for prepared eel. It may have evolved from 'dispatch cock' meaning to grill a bird. The method of splitting and flattening the bird was used to speed up the cooking so it is possible that 'dispatch cock' was originally a demand for a speedy meal, perhaps for unexpected guests.

In modern use, small chickens and small game birds are spatchcocked, secured in shape with long metal skewers and grilled (broiled), spit-roasted or barbecued. The French equivalent is *en crapaudine*.

SPÄTLESE One of the quality wine categories in the QMP (*Qualitätswein mit Prädikat*) classification defined by German wine law. Meaning 'late harvest', the grapes should be picked at least a week later then the first picking of less ripe grapes. Wines can be dry (*trocken*) or sweeter in style.

SPATULA Any of several types of kitchen utensil with a flat blunt blade.
• *The palette knife* has a long, flexible, stainless steel blade with a rounded end, mounted on a short handle. It is used to ice (frost) cakes, to loosen pastries from the baking sheet or to smooth the surface of a preparation. This and other types of spatula are used for loosening or turning over fried or braised foods in the pan and for transferring them to the serving dish.
• *The fish slice* has a wide flat blade, sometimes perforated, and is fitted with a flat handle. It is especially designed for turning over and serving whole fish and large fillets.
• *The wooden spatula* is designed for mixing and stirring various mixtures, liquids or sauces while they are cooking, to prevent them from sticking and to avoid scratching receptacles with a non-stick surface. It has the advantage over the wooden spoon of doubling up as a turning and lifting instrument.

Flattening a bird for grilling

The following is the French method of spatchcocking a poussin by part-splitting the bird horizontally and flattening it: this is known as *en crapaudine*. The alternative method is to turn the bird breast down and split it along the back using poultry shears and a sharp knife, then opening it out flat as in steps 2 and 3.

1 *To flatten a small bird, cut at an angle between the thighs and wings. Use a sharp knife and a pair of poultry shears, if necessary, to cut down as far as the back, leaving the breast whole. (Alternatively, place the bird breast down and cut it in half along the back, then cut out the broken backbone with poultry shears or a knife.)*

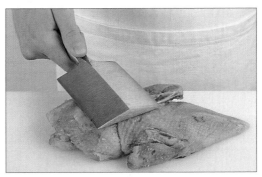

2 *Fold back the breast and wings and turn the bird cut side down. Use a meat mallet, steak bat or rolling pin to flatten the bird evenly. (The same method is used for flattening a bird split down the back.)*

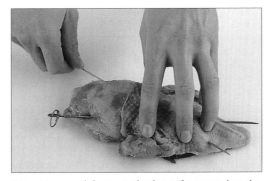

3 *Insert two metal skewers in the shape of a cross to keep the bird flat during grilling. (If the bird is flattened from back to front, insert the skewers parallel across the spatchcock, one through the wings and the other through the thighs.)*

SPAIN

A combination of influences created the varied cooking that is Spanish cuisine. Between North Africa and France, with its Mediterranean coast on the east and the Bay of Biscay to the north, the climate, geography and culture make Spanish cooking regional and colourful.

The Romans developed the cultivation of olives and production of olive oil for which Spain became renowned. The colour in Spanish cooking came not from the Romans but from the Moors. During their reign of nearly a thousand years between the 8th and 15th centuries, the Moors developed Spanish agriculture, building irrigation systems and introducing citrus groves, pomegranates, almond trees, pistachios, vegetables such as aubergines (egg plants) and asparagus, and rice. They also included warm spices and sweet flavours in savoury dishes, and created a foundation for modern Spanish cooking.

Explorers returning from their travels in the Americas made their unmistakable mark on Spanish cookery by introducing tomatoes, chillies (chili peppers), sweet (bell) peppers and potatoes – all ingredients that were eventually to pass through Spain to France and onwards to northern Europe.

■ **Regional styles** Straightforward cooking is the common theme that runs through the very distinct regional cuisines that make the best of local produce: seafood from the Mediterranean; rice from Valencia in the east; or ham from the mountainous regions of Andalusia or Extremadura. Galicia, a region on the north-west corner and considered to be individual in culture and cuisine, is known for Celtic influences. Catalonian cooking is traditionally seasonal, high-quality and frugal.

Then there is the Basque country linking France and Spain, in the shade of the Pyrenees and coasting the Bay of Biscay in the North Atlantic. The Basque country is known for traditional cooking based on long-established classic skills and using seafood – fresh tuna and cod, as well as the popular salt cod.

■ **Local and national specialities** Authentic dishes in the south (rice and pork) differ from those in the north (beef and potatoes), while people in the central provinces traditionally ate lean mutton and chick peas. Fish and shellfish are caught all along the coast, and are often deep-fried in olive oil.

One well-known dish is *olla podrida*, a soup of meats and vegetables. Other good Spanish soups and stews are *puchero*, which is often a substitute for *olla podrida*; *cocido*; and *gazpacho*, the model for all cold soups.

Paella is a hearty rice dish, best known in its Valencia form, made with chicken and seafood. There are as many versions as regions and home cooks vary their paella to suit the ingredients available. These may include pork, chicken, duck, chorizos, fish, shellfish, frogs, snails, a large number of vegetables, pulses and cereals.

Other special Spanish dishes are *empanadas*, roast sucking pig and various egg dishes, including tortillas (omelettes) and eggs *à la flamenca,* cooked in the oven on a spiced mixture of chopped meat and vegetables and garnished with peas, asparagus and chillies. The Spaniards discovered how chillies could be used in cooking and introduced them to the rest of Europe, together with various dishes based on tomatoes.

Fish and shellfish have always been popular and this is reflected in the many ways these ingredients are used. Examples of recipes include *bacalao à la biscaïenne,* salt cod served with tomatoes, onions, green peppers and hard-boiled (hard-cooked) eggs; escabèches; and shellfish ragoûts, such as *calderata* from Asturias and *zarzuela* from the Basque region. Canned seafood products are a particularly Spanish delicacy.

■ **Refinements and subtleties** Sherry is often used for cooking veal escalopes (scallops), crab and kidneys. Cooking with chocolate is a memento of the days when Mexico was a colony, and is used to prepare rabbit, pigeon and crayfish.

Game, such as partridge, boar and chamois, is highly prized and is used in certain top-class dishes. The regional cuisines are more basic, with such foods as *serrano* ham and spicy pimiento-seasoned sausages such as the *chorizo*, *longaniza* and *boutifar*.

The streets of busy Spanish towns are filled with the smell of *churros* (hot fritters) and of sweet *turrón* (a kind of nougat). Orange trees grow in the heart of many cities, and water melons are sold in the public squares in summer, while there is usually an aroma of cinnamon-flavoured chocolate or aniseed liqueur. Beer and *sidra* (cider) are manufactured in addition to wine, and other specialities include *horchata*, a thirst-quenching drink made from orgeat, and sangria, a popular punch based on red wine. Pâtisserie often contains large quantities of sugar and almonds and includes flaky pastries, jam-filled Swiss (jelly) rolls, biscuits (cookies) flavoured with cinnamon and aniseed, quince paste, orange flans and the curious speciality of Avila, *yemas de Santa Teresa* (soft creamy confectionery balls made from egg yolk and sugar).

■ **Spanish ham** Air-dried ham is extremely important in Spain, a country that produces and eats about 10 kg (22 lb) per head annually. The premier hams come from the wild pig (*pata negra*) and are sold with the black hoof attached, but these account for a small percentage of the production. Hams are graded by the pigs' diet and rearing, with those living outdoors yielding better hams; *bellota* is the term for pigs fed on acorns. The key hams are *Jabugo* and *Trevélez* in Andalucia; *Teruel* in Aragon; and *Montánchez* in Extremadura.

Unlike hams in other countries, Spanish hams are carved with the grain and they have threads of fat running through them. They are distinctly chewy and said to have more flavour than Parma ham. *Serrano* (short for *jamón serrano*) means from the mountains and refers to air-dried ham, which is salted for 4–10 days before being hung to dry for about 6 months.

The front shoulders (*paletilla*) and loins (*lomo embuchado*) are also cured, with those from famous producers being valued products.

■ **Spanish cheese** Goat's and ewe's milk is used for cheesemaking and some cheeses are made from cow's milk. Burgos, a type of fresh cheese sold in its whey, is nationally available and typical of a very popular type of cheese. Cabrales is a blue cheese to rival Roquefort and made the same way. At home it is packed in maple leaves, but this is not for export. Other blue cheeses included Picón cheeses like Afuega'l pitu and Gamonedo. Manchego, made from ewe's milk, is well known – sold at all ages and with rinds of different colours, the splendid matured cheese is expensive and exported as Iberico. Mahón is a much exported, square, orange cheese. Roncal, from the Pyrenees border, is admired by the French. ▶

The wine-producing regions of Spain

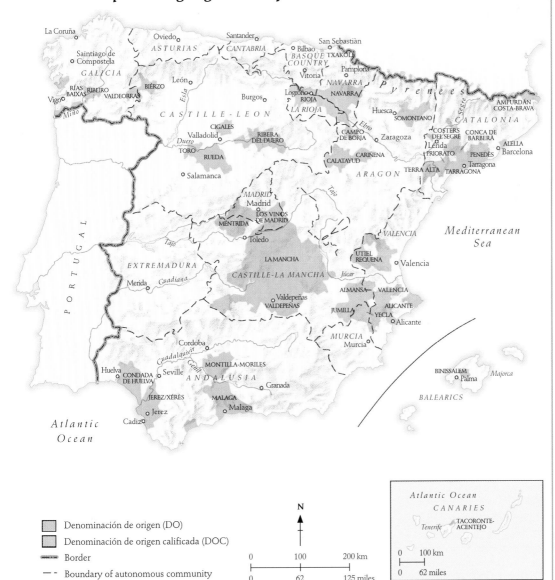

Legend:
- Denominación de origen (DO)
- Denominación de origen calificada (DOC)
- Border
- Boundary of autonomous community

0   100   200 km
0   62   125 miles

Atlantic Ocean
CANARIES
Tenerife   TACORONTE-ACENTEJO
0   100 km
0   62 miles

◀ San Simón, a smoked and pear-shaped cheese from Galicia, is popular with tourists; Tetilla is a Galilician fresh cheese.

■ **Spanish rice** The Spanish planted medium-grain rice in Italy in the 14th century, but the subsequent development of its cultivation was very different in the two countries. Spain is Europe's major rice grower and the Spanish are the continent's most frequent rice eaters. Valencia is the main area for cultivation and much is grown in Andalucia. The famous brand is *Calasparra*, grown on the River Segura which exits in Murcia.

Whereas Italian risotto is stirred to encourage the release of starch and create a creamy dish, Spanish rice is washed before cooking and it is prepared in such a way that every grain is separate after cooking. The Spanish divide rice dishes into wet and dry dishes. Paella is dry, called an *arroz* when cooked outside Valencia, in a shallow open pan. The wet dishes are made in a *caldero*, a cauldron or pot, and include many fish dishes for which the fish broth is used to cook the rice, which is then served first, followed by the broth; for example, *arroz abanda* (meaning 'rice apart') is a two-course dish.

■ **Tapas** Little snacks served with sherry or cider, especially during the early evening, are a feature of Spanish eating. From pieces of cheese or a little ham to fried snacks, seafood, potato specialities, tortillas or any number of local specialities served in sampler-sized portions – the tapas bars provide a mosaic of different dishes. All this originates from slices of bread laid on top of glasses to cover drinks and prevent flies from getting in; later they were topped with a little cheese or ham and served as a complimentary snack with the drink.

WINE The country has the largest area of land under vines in the world, but ranks third in importance as a producer. The first vines were probably planted by the Phoenicians around 1100 BC and the Romans subsequently improved and consolidated the methods of cultivation and winemaking. Spain is a very diverse country producing a wide range of wines.

In the north, in Rias Baixas, elegant Albariños are produced and are highly sought-after. Rioja is well known for making top quality wines, with its neighbour Navarra following close behind. Somontano, close to the French border, in the foothills of the Pyrenees, is producing crisp, fruity wines, while Penedès continues to produce an exciting range of wines. Priorat is best known for making excellent, full, concentrated red wines mainly from Garnacha (Grenache), often including varieties such as Cabernet Sauvignon, Syrah and Merlot. Ribera del Duero, Toro and Rueda all straddle the River Duero – Toro produces good red wines, while Rueda makes delightful, crisp, fruity white wines, the best being from the Verdejo grape variety, sometimes blended with Sauvignon Blanc. The central and east coast areas of Spain, in general, produce red and white wines for everyday drinking.

Tempranillo is the main red grape variety planted, and together with Garnacha is predominant in the north of the country, with Bobal and Monastrell (Mourvèdre) dominating production in the south.

Airen, the most widely planted white variety and traditionally used in brandy production, is now being made into light, fruity dry wines. Other white grapes include Palamino Fino, the sherry grape, and Pedro Ximénez, with some Chardonnay and Sauvignon Blanc

grown too. Maccabeo (Viura) is also grown, particularly in Catalonia and Penedès, where together with Xarel-lo and Parrellada it is used to make Cava sparkling wine. The wines are of very good quality and are produced by the traditional method (see *méthode champenoise*).

Spain is well known for its fortified wines – sherry and the dry to sweet, rich, nutty Malaga made from Moscatel and Pedro Ximénez grapes. Wines from Montilla, which are generally not fortified, range from dry to sweeter styles and are traditionally aged like sherry in a solera system. There is a new classification system of Joven Afrutado – younger fruitier wine.

Wine classification in Spain conforms to that of the EU. *Vino de Mesa* (VdM) is equivalent to *Vin de Table*, *Vino de la Tierra* (VdT) to *Vin de Pays* and the quality *Denominacion de Origen* (DO) is the same as *Appellation Contrôlée*. The highest category, *Denominacion de Origen Calificada* (DOCa), equates to Italy's DOCG and to date has been awarded only to wines from Rioja.

The wine laws have been standardized throughout Spain to ensure that Crianza, Reserva and Gran Reserva wines conform to the same minimum ageing rules. Vino Joven is wine for immediate drinking, Crianza wine must have two years' ageing, including at least six months in oak, and may be released in its third year. Reserva wine spends 12 months in *barricas* (225-litre oak barrels) and a further two years in the bodega, while Gran Reservas, produced only in excellent years, spend two years in *barricas* and three years in bottle before release in their sixth year. Some regions stipulate longer ageing periods.

Very fine Brandy de Jerez, aged in soleras, is also produced.

At a charcuterie in Valencia, a wide variety of sausages and salamis is displayed alongside the air-dried hams.

There are also rubber or plastic spatulas for scraping out batter, sauces or other mixtures from the sides of the mixing bowl (these should not be used over heat).

SPÄTZLE A speciality common to Alsace in France and southern Germany, consisting of small dumplings made of flour, eggs and cream poached in boiling water. They are used to garnish sauced meat dishes (especially game) or are eaten as an entrée, au gratin, with cream or noisette butter, or with small fried croûtons. In Würtemberg, spätzle are similar to small quenelles and are made with liver purée or cheese. The word literally means 'little sparrow'; in Alsace, it is also spelt *spatzele* or *spetzli*.

RECIPE

spätzle with noisette butter
Blend together 500 g (18 oz, 4½ cups) sifted plain (all-purpose) flour, 4 whole eggs, 2 tablespoons double (heavy) cream and 1 tablespoon fine salt. Season with pepper and grated nutmeg. Boil plenty of salted water in a large pan. Drop small spoonfuls of the dough into the boiling water, using a second spoon to shape them into little dumplings. Leave the spätzle to poach until they rise to the surface. Drain on paper towels and serve piping hot, liberally coated with noisette butter. (They may be fried in butter before being coated with noisette butter.)

SPÉCULOS Also known as *speculaas*. A Dutch and Belgian speciality consisting of small, flat, spicy, ginger biscuits (cookies) made in the shapes of legendary and traditional characters. Spéculos are traditionally made in carved wooden moulds and sold at Flemish fairs; they are also found in southern Germany (as *Spekulatius*). The name comes from the Latin *speculator* ('he who sees'), the nickname for St Nicholas, the original model for these cakes.

RECIPE

spéculos
Put 500 g (18 oz, 4½ cups) sifted plain (all-purpose) flour in a pile on the worktop. Make a well in the centre and add a pinch of salt, 1 teaspoon bicarbonate of soda, 1½ teaspoons ground cinnamon, 3 eggs, 4 finely crushed (or ½ teaspoon ground) cloves, 300 g (11 oz, 1¾ cups) brown sugar and 200 g (7 oz, 1 cup) softened butter. Mix these ingredients thoroughly, gradually incorporating the flour. Roll the dough into a ball and leave in a cool place overnight. Divide into several pieces and roll them out. Mould them in spéculos moulds coated with flour. Turn out on to a lightly buttered baking sheet and bake in a preheated oven at 190°C (375°F, gas 5) until the biscuits (cookies) have browned (about 20 minutes).

SPELT An ancient variety of wheat, quite unlike modern varieties, with small brown grains that adhere strongly to the chaff. Widely grown until the beginning of the 20th century, especially in upland regions of Germany, Switzerland and France, spelt is now grown only in parts of central and eastern Europe. Its nutritional value is comparable with soft wheat and it does not need rich soil. After threshing, spelt can be cooked like rice; it is still an ingredient in certain country soups, especially in Provence, and is used to make bread.

RECIPE

spelt broth
Place either 1 kg (2¼ lb) shoulder or leg of mutton (on the bone) or 1 large cooking sausage in a saucepan and add 3 litres (5 pints, 3 quarts) water. Bring to the boil, then skim. Add 1 onion studded with 2 cloves, 2 carrots, 1 turnip, 1 leek, 1 stick celery, 1 garlic clove and 1 bouquet garni. Season with salt, add 4 small handfuls of spelt, then simmer gently for 3 hours. When ready, remove the meat and vegetables and serve together. The remaining swollen spelt makes a smooth and creamy broth.

SPICE Any of the many aromatic substances derived from plants, that have a fragrant or sharp flavour and are used to season food.
■ **The spice route** Most spices come from the East, and the first spice to be introduced to Europe was pepper, from India, which long remained a rare and expensive commodity. Roman food was always liberally spiced, ginger being a particular favourite, and the practice of adding spices continued through the Middle Ages and remained common until the 18th century.

The use of spices in cooking was originally introduced by the Byzantines. Foodstuffs were preserved in spiced sauces, sometimes to hide the fact that the meat was 'high', sometimes to replace the flavour lost after lengthy boiling.

Supplies increased as a result of the Crusades, and control of the 'spice route' aroused much rivalry. Venice managed to obtain a near-monopoly over the distribution of spices in Europe, and the quest for alternative sources of supply was one of the reasons for the great voyages of discovery to America and the West Indies. Spices became more plentiful and less expensive, with British and Dutch companies in particular trading in them. Meanwhile, belief in the miraculous properties of spices waned, and spices were used in cookery with much greater discretion. Nowadays, only saffron can be considered a genuinely precious spice.

Because of their rarity and value, spices were highly esteemed as gifts. It is reported that in the 16th century, a German banker called Fugger, wishing to honour Charles V, had a faggot of cinnamon burnt in his honour. Taxes, ransoms or customs dues were sometimes paid in spices. Thus, the French word *épice* had a special meaning under the Ancien Régime. It was the gift that litigants, especially successful ones, would make to the judge; it consisted at first of confectionery, and later of coin of the realm. Subsequently, *épices* became a compulsory tax, paid to the judge as remuneration. The poor were exempted from this tax, but on certain documents one could read: 'Justice will not be rendered to those who do not pay *épices*.' The practice was abolished by the Revolution.

■ **Spices in French cookery** The word *épice* was originally applied to sugary items as well as to spices. There was a distinction between *épices de chambre* – fennel or aniseed dragées, nougat, marzipan, jams (preserves) and crystallized (candied) fruits – and *épices de cuisine*. The latter term covered products no longer considered to be spices, such as milk, sugar and honey, as well as others that have totally disappeared (galingale, amber and musk).

Taillevent gave a list of the spices he thought were necessary in a well-stocked kitchen: ginger, cinnamon, cloves, cardamom, chillies (chili peppers) and peppercorns, spikenard, cinnamon flower, saffron, nutmeg, bay leaves, galingale, mastic, orris, cumin, sugar, almonds, garlic, onions, chives, and shallots, to which should be added 'green-colouring spices' (parsley, *salmonde*, sorrel, vine leaves, redcurrant leaves and green wheat) and 'steeping spices' (white wine, verjuice, vinegar, water, fatty stock, cow's milk and almond milk). Thus, 'spice' covered both liquids and solids used in cookery. Taillevent also referred to *poudres* (powders, which would now be called spices) without indicating their composition. In the Middle Ages and up to the 17th century, *poudre* meant 'powder made of ground spices'. *Poudres forts* (strong powders) were distinguished from *poudres douces* (mild powders), according to whether the spices were sharp or not. *Le Trésor de santé* (1607) gives the composition of the 'powder' used for sauces and soups: ginger, 4 ounces; cinnamon, 3½ ounces; peppercorns, 1½ ounces; chilli, 1 ounce; nutmeg, 2 ounces; cardamom and galingale, 1 ounce each; cloves, 1 ounce. The author added: 'All the powders will keep for one month, or even 40 days, without spoiling. They must be kept in leather bags, to avoid exposure to the air, since they have already been overexposed on the long journey from their place of origin. From Spain to Calcutta (India), where pepper and ginger come from, is 4000 leagues by sea, and from there to the Spice Islands and nearby islands, where cloves and nutmeg come from, is 2000 leagues.'

Carême regarded the abuse of spices as one of the enemies of good cookery, and in his memoirs he recalls that before his arrival at the court of King George IV of England, the cooking was 'so strong and over-flavoured that the prince often had pains lasting all day and night'.

Spices were widely reputed to have aphrodisiac qualities, as well as being the mark of refined and high-class cuisine. Baudelaire's response to Flaubert's Pécuchet, who was afraid of spices because they might 'set his body on fire', was that spices ennoble food. He scorned 'simple meats and insipid fish' and also summoned 'the whole of nature's pharmacy to the aid of the kitchen'. 'Peppers, English powders, saffron-like substances and exotic dusts' seemed essential to him to make a dish elegant and attractive.

■ **Spices in contemporary cookery** Spices are fundamental to the food of the many countries where they are grown, including Indian, South-East Asian, African and Caribbean cooking. Being affordable in Western countries, spices are now readily available and their use has moved on from the conspicuous consumption practised by early cooks.

There are two styles of Western spice cookery. With broader knowledge of world cuisines and a wide variety of international ingredients displayed in most supermarkets, spices are often used in the context of authentic cooking styles, such as Indian, Chinese or South-East Asian. There is better understanding of the preparation and use of spices to achieve subtle or pronounced results and less crass over-spicing or inappropriate mixing of clashing flavours. Much spice cookery relies on classic combinations, even when they are applied to different main ingredients from those for which they were originally intended.

Knowledge has inspired experimentation. Individually or carefully blended, spices are now used to complement ingredients and dishes that are far removed from traditional cuisines. Referred to as fusion food, many dishes marry the spices of one culture with the produce and methods of another. Individual, complementary flavours are allowed to run in parallel in a dish, providing excitement as they alternately surprise the palate, rather than blending in a depth of flavour that may be elusive in specific identity.

The flavours of spices are better appreciated – refreshing aniseed, fennel or cardamom; warming cinnamon, nutmeg or cloves; or the variety of heat and complex flavour of chillies. Cooks are just as likely to introduce a few roasted seeds to a simple leafy salad as they are to prepare a paste for simmering in a stew.

Spices play a vital role in flavouring savoury preserves, such as chutneys, pickles, sauces and condiments. They enhance simple or light produce and combine well with sweet and piquant ingredients; when matured, they become rich and complex, giving many preserves their inimitable characters.

As well as savoury cooking, spices are important in sweet dishes ranging from light fruit salads to baked cakes and breads. While many sweet dishes rely on single spices, others are characterized by spice mixtures – Italian panforte, a rich confection of nuts and dried fruit; the gingerbreads of Eastern Europe; and Christmas cakes and puddings are good examples.

• FRESH SPICES Chillies and ginger are popular examples of spices that are used fresh – often referred to as aromatics – as well as dried and processed. The flavour of the fresh spice is very different from that of the dried or processed product

• GROUND SPICES Bought ready ground or prepared just before use, these are popular. Ground spices are cooked by a wide variety of methods, from pan frying or grilling (broiling) to roasting and moist cooking. Spices that are roasted, then ground, are sometimes sprinkled over cooked dishes as a final seasoning – garam masala, the Indian spice mix, is a good example.

• SPICE PASTES These may be based on ready ground spices or spices that are roasted and then ground with the other ingredients that make up the paste. Indian cookery is known for its spice pastes, made with onions, garlic, ginger and yogurt as well as dried spices. Pastes of spices in oil are also popular – for example, fiery harissa, the chilli and spice paste used in Tunisian cooking, is well-known as a condiment for couscous.

• WHOLE DRIED SPICES Many spices are used whole, roasted or plain, to bring light flavour to a dish. Whole spices are often used in marinades to impart their flavour to food before cooking. They may be added to the cooking water for rice or pulses, or used in other moist dishes, such as casseroles and stews. When roasted or lightly fried in a little oil, small seeds are used to dress cooked vegetables or enliven salads.

SPICE BOX A small cylindrical or rectangular box with a lid, usually forming part of a set. The containers may vary in size and are designed to store, within easy reach, the ingredients that are frequently used in cooking. They were very common in kitchens until the 19th century and were usually arranged in a line on the mantel shelf. Spice boxes in contemporary kitchens, as decorative as they are functional, may be made of wood, enamelled or painted metal, porcelain or pottery. Spices keep better, however, in airtight opaque bottles.

Restaurant chefs tend to keep a metal spice box within easy reach. This is a rectangular box with compartments containing pepper, nutmeg, and so on.

SPIDER CRAB The name given to several species of crab having a spiny shell, slender hairy legs and long claws. The most common spider crab in Europe is the *maia*. Its shell is about 20 cm (8 in) across, compared with the giant spider crab, which lives on the coasts of Japan and has a body 40 cm (16 in) wide and a claw span of nearly 3 m (10 ft). Considered by some to be the finest of all shellfish, the spider crab is perhaps best prepared in a court-bouillon and traditionally served cold, accompanied by mayonnaise.

SPIKENARD A bitter and highly scented aromatic extract obtained from certain valerianaceous plants. It was highly esteemed in ancient and medieval cookery, being used in sauces, meat dishes and wines. Indian spikenard, which tastes of ginger and verbena, is still used in Malaysian and Sri Lankan cooking.

SPINACH A vegetable with dark-green curled or smooth leaves, generally cooked, but also eaten raw in salads when young and tender.

Spinach originated in Persia and was brought to Europe in the 11th century via the Arab invasion of Spain. It was very fashionable in the 17th century,

when it was often cooked with sugar and used in sweet dishes.

Nowadays, spinach is available all the year round. The winter varieties have much larger and lighter-coloured leaves than the summer ones. Scalded, drained and served with fresh butter, spinach is a classic accompaniment to veal and poultry, as well as eggs; it is also used in tarts and pâtés, for stuffings (mixed with other vegetables, particularly sorrel), soufflés, purées, gratins and for colouring pasta. It is an essential ingredient for Florentine dishes. Spinach is also available preserved in jars (whole, chopped or as purée) and deep-frozen.

Because of its pronounced bitter-sweet flavour, people either love or hate spinach. Le Prudhomme in Flaubert's *Dictionnaire des idées reçues* declared: 'I dislike it, and am happy to dislike it because if I liked it I would eat it, and I cannot stand it.'

A Mexican shrub known as giant Mexican spinach has large leaves that are cooked and eaten like spinach. Similarly, New Zealand (tetragonian) spinach, although unrelated to spinach, is another substitute.

RECIPES

preparing and cooking spinach
Cut off the stalks, wash the spinach in plenty of water and remove any yellowing or wilting leaves. The flavour and nutritional qualities are best preserved if it is cooked very quickly and served immediately. Boil a large quantity of water in a saucepan and add the prepared and drained spinach. Boil briskly for 8 minutes. Check if the spinach is cooked by pinching a piece between your fingers. More mature leaves take longer than younger ones. Drain in a large colander or sieve, refill the pan with cold water and replace the spinach. Repeat this several times to cool the spinach quickly. Then, taking handfuls at a time, squeeze hard to extract all the water. If the spinach is not to be served immediately, keep it in an earthenware dish in the refrigerator or in a cool place.

scallop broth with spinach
Cut 12 prepared scallops into slices, 5 mm (¼ in) thick, and place in a buttered frying pan. Add salt and 120 ml (4½ fl oz, ½ cup) fish stock, poach for 2 minutes, then remove and drain. Add 200 ml (7 fl oz, ¾ cup) crème fraîche to the stock and reduce until it is the consistency of a light soup. Add 500 g (18 oz, 3½ cups) chopped fresh spinach and heat for 2 minutes. Then bind with a mixture comprising 100 ml (4 fl oz, 7 tablespoons) double (heavy) cream, 2 egg yolks and the juice of 1 lemon. Then add the scallop slices and adjust the seasoning. Serve in hot dishes garnished with hot roughly chopped tomatoes.

spinach and potato soup with poached eggs
Wash and trim 1 kg (2¼ lb) spinach, cook for 5 minutes in boiling water, cool and drain. Squeeze with your hands to extract all the water, then chop.

Place 150 ml (¼ pint, ⅔ cup) olive oil in a flame-proof casserole, add 1 chopped onion and brown lightly, then add the spinach and stir over a low heat for 5 minutes. When the spinach is dry, add 5 potatoes cut into slices. Season with salt and pepper and a little saffron. Add 1 litre (1¾ pints, 4⅓ cups) boiling water, 2 chopped garlic cloves and 1 sprig of fennel, and cook, uncovered, over a low heat. When the potatoes are cooked, break 4 eggs, one by one, on to the surface, and allow to cook very gently. This dish can be served straight from the casserole.

spinach au gratin

Wash, thin, parboil and dry some spinach. Lightly butter a gratin dish and spread out the spinach leaves in it. Cover with a light béchamel sauce flavoured with nutmeg and grated cheese. Sprinkle with more grated cheese and then with melted butter, and brown in a preheated oven at 230°C (450°F, gas 8). Hard-boiled (hard-cooked) egg halves may be arranged on top of the sauce before sprinkling with cheese, if desired.

spinach croquettes

Mix 2 parts chopped spinach cooked in butter with 1 part duchess potato mixture. Shape this mixture into balls the size of tangerines and gently flatten. Coat with beaten egg and breadcrumbs, deep-fry in oil heated to 180°C (350°F) until golden, then drain on paper towels. Serve with grilled (broiled) or roast meat or poultry.

spinach in butter

Wash, trim and parboil some spinach, then drain and dry in a cloth. Melt a little butter in a frying pan and add the spinach. Season with salt, pepper and a little grated nutmeg. When all the moisture has evaporated, add more butter, allowing 50 g (2 oz, ¼ cup) butter to 500 g (18 oz, 3½ cups) cooked spinach. Arrange in a vegetable dish and garnish with fried croûtons. The spinach may also be sprinkled with noisette butter, if desired.

spinach in cream

Wash, trim, parboil and dry some spinach. Arrange it in a warm vegetable dish and pour heated crème fraîche or cream sauce over the top; stir before serving. The spinach may be slightly sweetened, and served with fried croûtons cut into the shape of sponge fingers (ladyfingers).

spinach purée

Wash, trim, parboil and dry some spinach, then rub it through a sieve or use a blender to form a purée. Add 50 g (2 oz, ¼ cup) butter for every 500 g (18 oz, 3½ cups) cooked spinach. If desired, add one-third of its volume of potato purée, or bind with one-quarter of its volume of béchamel sauce.

spinach salad

Plunge some prepared spinach into boiling water for a few seconds. Cool under running water, then drain and dry in a cloth. Arrange in a salad bowl, sprinkle with chopped hard-boiled (hard-cooked) eggs and dress with oil, vinegar, salt and pepper.

Raw spinach may be finely sliced and mixed with flakes of smoked haddock, sliced scallops or new potatoes.

other recipes See *crêpe, omelette (flat omelettes), saveloy, soufflé, subric, tendron.*

SPINY LOBSTER See *langouste.*

SPIT A pointed iron rod with which a piece of meat or a whole animal is speared for roasting, either horizontally or vertically, traditionally over or in front of a fire.

When all cooking was carried out at the hearth, the roasting spit was a most important piece of equipment. It is used much less nowadays, although this method of cooking provides excellent roasts. According to Escoffier, 'Cooking a roast on a spit is performed in the open air, in a dry atmosphere, which leaves the joint with all its unique flavour.'

Spit-roasting owes its perfect cooking to the regular and constant rotation of the spit. From the technical point of view, this method of cooking, which is closer to grilling (broiling) than oven-roasting, comprises two phases. In the first, the meat is cooked quickly at a high temperature to seal the outside (particularly for red meat and juicy game, which require rapid sealing before actual cooking); the second phase, which requires a lower temperature and skill on the part of the roaster, is intended to cook the inside of the joint to the required degree. White meat and poultry, on the other hand, require simultaneous cooking of the inside and the outside, at a lower temperature than for red meat. While it is cooking, the meat is basted with the drippings.

SPLIT PEAS Small, pale green or yellow dried peas that are split in two. Picked in summer, they are obtained from mature peas that are mechanically stripped of their cellulose skins and then split in two, dried and often polished by friction. Certain varieties of peas, such as Rondo, are specially grown for producing split peas.

Split peas can be stored in a dry place for several months and are always soaked before being cooked. They can be used for preparing soups, stews and purées, especially as a garnish for preparations cooked *à la Sainte-Menehould*, and also with roast pork or veal. They can also be served as a vegetable with boiled ham.

RECIPES

cooking split peas

Soak some split peas for 1½ hours in cold water, drain, then place them in a saucepan with 2 litres (3½ pints, 9 cups) fresh cold water per 500 g (18 oz, 2⅓ cups) peas. Add 1 carrot, 1 celery stick, the white part of a leek and 1 onion, all chopped as for a mirepoix. Then add 1 bouquet garni including the green part of the leek and, if possible, a knuckle of ham and some lettuce leaves. Bring slowly to the boil, skim and season with salt and pepper. Simmer gently with the lid on for about 2½ hours. Then remove the bouquet garni and the ham. Strip the meat off the bone and discard the skin. Dice and serve with the peas if wished.

split pea purée

Rub some cooked split peas through a fine sieve or reduce to a purée in a blender or food processor. Pour the purée into a heavy-based saucepan and heat, stirring continuously with a wooden spoon and slowly pouring in a little of the strained cooking liquid. Blend in some cream, remove from the heat, add a knob of butter and serve piping hot.

split pea soup

Rub some cooked split peas through a fine sieve or reduce to a purée in a blender or food processor, together with the vegetables they were cooked with. Add equal amounts of the cooking liquid and milk (or use one-third of this volume of cream instead of milk and replace the cooking liquid with consommé). Stir well and adjust the seasoning. Sprinkle with chervil. Fry some croûtons in butter or oil and serve separately. The ham used for cooking the split peas may also be added after being finely diced.

SPONGE CAKE A cake that is usually lightened with baking powder or whisked egg whites. There are many varieties, the best known being the French Savoy sponge cake, Swiss (jelly) roll and pound cake. They are often enriched with almonds and flavoured with lemon zest, vanilla, chocolate or liqueurs, and can be filled with jam (preserve) or butter cream.

RECIPES

basic sponge cake mixture

Using a large bowl and a spatula, beat 500 g (18 oz, 2¼ cups) caster (superfine) sugar with 2 tablespoons vanilla sugar and 10 egg yolks until the mixture is very pale and thick enough to form a ribbon trail. Then carefully fold in 125 g (4½ oz, 1 cup) plain (all-purpose) flour and an equal quantity of cornflour (cornstarch), 10 stiffly whisked egg whites and a pinch of salt.

Alternatively, a slightly heavier mixture can be made using 250 g (9 oz, 1 cup) granulated sugar, 8 eggs (separated), 125 g (4½ oz, 1 cup) plain flour and a pinch of salt.

Large Sponge Cakes
almond sandwich cake

Prepare a sponge cake mixture using 500 g (18 oz, 2¼ cups) caster (superfine) sugar, 1 tablespoon vanilla sugar, 12 egg yolks, 175 g (6 oz, 1½ cups) sifted plain (all-purpose) flour and an equal quantity

of cornflour (cornstarch). When the egg and sugar mixture is very pale, and thick enough to form a ribbon trail, add the flour and cornflour, then 200 g (7 oz, 1¾ cups) blanched almonds (with 4 or 5 bitter almonds if desired), which have been pounded to a paste with 2 egg whites and a few drops of orange-flower water. Whisk 10 egg whites until stiff and fold into the mixture. Butter a very large round cake tin (pan) and dust the inside with caster sugar. Pour in the mixture, which should fill only two-thirds of the tin. Bake in a preheated oven at 160°C (325°F, gas 3) until risen and springy to the touch – about 1–1¼ hours depending on the size of the tin. Turn the cake out on to a cooling rack and, when cool, slice horizontally into 3 equal layers. Spread the bottom round with apricot jam and the middle round with raspberry jelly. Reassemble the cake and coat the top and sides with apricot glaze. It may be iced (frosted) with vanilla fondant icing (frosting) and decorated with chopped almonds on the top and sides, if desired.

Italian sponge cake

Using a large bowl and a spatula, beat 500 g (18 oz, 2¼ cups) caster (superfine) sugar with 1½ teaspoons vanilla sugar and 10 egg yolks. Whisk 10 egg whites with a pinch of salt until stiff and fold into the mixture. Quickly fold in 125 g (4½ oz, 1 cup) plain (all-purpose) flour and 125 g (4½ oz, 1 cup) cornflour (cornstarch) sifted together. Butter a charlotte mould and dust the inside with caster sugar and cornflour. Pour the mixture into the mould, no more than two-thirds full. Bake in a preheated oven at 160°C (325°F, gas 3) until risen, golden and firm to the touch – about 1¼ hours depending on the size of the mould.

orange sandwich cake ♦

Prepare the same mixture as for Italian sponge cake. Butter a charlotte mould and dust generously with icing (confectioner's) sugar. Pour the mixture into the mould, no more than two-thirds full. Bake in a preheated oven at 160°C (325°F, gas 3) until risen, golden, and firm – about 1¼ hours depending on the size of the mould. Turn the cake out on to a wire rack and leave until just warm. Cut horizontally into 2 rounds of equal thickness. Pour a little Curaçao on to the bottom half and spread with a thick layer of orange jam (preserve) or marmalade. Place the other half on top. Coat the top and sides with orange jam or warmed sieved marmalade. Coat with fondant icing (frosting) flavoured with Curaçao. Decorate with candied orange and mint sprigs, and serve with a coulis of blackcurrant and raspberry. Instead of making a large cake, the mixture can be baked in individual moulds or soufflé dishes.

Orange sandwich cake.

Swiss roll

Prepare a sponge cake mixture using half the quantities for almond sandwich cake. Line a rectangular baking sheet with greaseproof (wax) paper and brush with clarified butter. Spread the mixture evenly using a metal spatula until it covers the whole buttered area to a thickness of about 1 cm (½ in). Cook in a preheated oven at 180°C (350°F, gas 4) for 10 minutes. The top of the cake should be just golden. Meanwhile, prepare a syrup using 75 g (3 oz, ⅓ cup) granulated sugar, 60 ml (2 fl oz, ¼ cup) water and 3 tablespoons rum. Lightly toast 125 g (4½ oz, 1½ cup) flaked (slivered) almonds. When the cake is cooked, turn it out on to a cloth and sprinkle with the syrup. Spread it with apricot jam or raspberry jelly. Using the cloth, roll up the cake and trim the ends. Cover the whole Swiss (jelly) roll with apricot glaze and decorate with the toasted almonds.

Sponge Drops and Small Sponge Cakes

chocolate soufflé biscuits

Melt 300 g (11 oz, 11 squares) plain (semisweet) chocolate and stir in 2 egg yolks. Beat 500 g (18 oz, 2¼ cups) caster (superfine) sugar with 10 egg whites in a small saucepan over a very low heat or in a bain marie. When the meringue mixture is fairly firm, add the chocolate mixture. Grease and flour a baking sheet and pipe the biscuit (cookie) mixture on to it, in the shape of macaroons or sponge fingers (ladyfingers). Bake in a preheated oven at 180°C (350°F, gas 4) for about 10 minutes.

Geneva sponge fingers

Beat 125 g (4½ oz, ½ cup) caster (superfine) sugar with a little grated lemon zest, a pinch of salt, 1 whole egg and 3 egg yolks until the mixture is thick enough to form a ribbon trail. Add 50 g (2 oz, ¼ cup) clarified butter, 40 g (1½ oz, ⅓ cup) ground almonds, 125 g (4½ oz, 1 cup) plain (all-purpose) flour and 3 stiffly whisked egg whites. Pour into finger-shaped moulds that have been buttered and dusted with caster sugar and cornflour and bake in a preheated oven at 180°C (350°F, gas 4) for about 10 minutes. Turn the sponge fingers out of the moulds and leave to dry at the front of the oven with the oven door open. Leave to cool and store in an airtight container.

Italian sponge drops

Put 250 g (9 oz, 1 cup) granulated sugar into a small saucepan with 500 ml (17 fl oz, 2 cups) water and boil until the syrup reaches the 'hard ball' stage (see *sugar*). Partially cool, then add 4 egg yolks and 125 g (4½ oz, 1 cup) plain (all-purpose) flour. Whisk 4 egg whites stiffly with a pinch of salt and add to the mixture. Pipe into small flat rounds and finish as for lemon sponge drops.

lemon sponge drops

Using a large bowl and a spatula, beat 250 g (9 oz, 1 cup) caster (superfine) sugar with 8 egg yolks until the mixture is thick enough to form a ribbon trail. Add the grated zest of 1 lemon, 125 g (4½ oz, 1 cup) sifted plain (all-purpose) flour, 75 g (3 oz, ¾ cup) cornflour, 1½ tablespoons ground almonds and 8 egg whites stiffly whisked with a pinch of salt.

Using a piping (pastry) bag with a smooth nozzle, pipe small flat rounds, 2.5 cm (1 in) in diameter, on to a baking sheet and dust with caster sugar. Bake in a preheated oven at 180°C (350°F, gas 4) for about 10 minutes, or until lightly browned and set. Cool completely before storing in an airtight container.

punch cakes

Using a large bowl and a spatula, beat together 375 g (13 oz, 1⅔ cups) caster (superfine) sugar, 1½ teaspoons orange-flavoured sugar, 1½ teaspoons lemon-flavoured sugar, 3 whole eggs and 12 egg yolks until light and fluffy. Continue beating and add 3 tablespoons rum and 375 g (13 oz, 3¼ cups) sifted plain (all-purpose) flour, then 8 stiffly whisked egg whites and 300 g (11 oz, 1⅓ cups) clarified butter. Butter some small paper cases and fill them with the mixture. Bake in a preheated oven at 180°C (350°F, gas 4) for about 15 minutes, until risen and golden.

sponge biscuits

Make a basic sponge cake mixture. Flavour with Curaçao and add chopped candied orange peel. Using a piping (pastry) bag with a smooth nozzle, pipe the mixture on to a sheet of greaseproof (wax) paper in figures of 8. Dust with icing (confectioner's) sugar. Bake in a preheated oven at 180°C (350°F, gas 4) for about 10 minutes. Remove the biscuits (cookies) from the paper while still warm and allow to cool completely before storing them in an airtight container.

SPONGE FINGER (LADYFINGER) A small elongated sponge cake made of a mixture similar to that used for Savoy sponge cake, but lighter. Sponge fingers, also called sponge biscuits and boudoir biscuits, are served with fruit creams and purées and are often used as a border for cold charlottes or served with ice creams. They can be kept for 2–3 weeks in an airtight container.

RECIPE

sponge fingers

Beat 250 g (9 oz, 1 cup) caster (superfine) sugar with 8 egg yolks until the mixture is thick enough to form a ribbon trail. Flavour with 1 tablespoon orange-flower water. Add 200 g (7 oz, 1¾ cups) plain (all-purpose) flour and fold in 8 egg whites stiffly whisked with a pinch of salt. Using a piping (pastry) bag with a smooth nozzle, pipe short lengths of the mixture on to baking sheets lined with greaseproof (wax) paper. Dust with icing (confectioner's) sugar and gently lift and tap the sheets of paper to remove any excess sugar. Bake in a preheated oven at 160°C (325°F, gas 3) for about 10 minutes, or until pale golden.

The mixture can be flavoured with orange or lemon zest, if liked.

SPOOM A type of frothy sorbet, which used to be a great favourite in England, made with a lighter syrup than that required for a true sorbet. As it begins to set, it is mixed with half its volume of Italian meringue. Like sorbet, it is made from fruit juice, wine, sherry or port and served in a tall glass. The name comes from the Italian *spuma* (foam). In Italy, *spumone* is a light frothy ice cream made with egg whites, a flavouring and whipped cream.

SPOON A utensil comprising a hollow part (the bowl) and a handle of varying length. The French word for a spoon, is *cuillère*, derived from the Latin *cochlea* (snail), since a *cuillère* was originally a spatula used for eating snails.

The spoon is as old as the knife and was used both to prepare and to eat the meal. The first spoons were cut in a simple fashion out of wood, sometimes sweet-smelling wood, such as juniper or box. During the Middle Ages and the Renaissance, however, the spoon became a luxurious table utensil, made of crystal, serpentine or cornelian, but always with a fairly short handle studded with precious stones or enamels. In the 17th century, chased silver was used for the first time and the handle became longer. Ever since then, the sizes and shapes of spoons have varied according to their uses.

■ **Table spoons** These are usually made of metal (silver, silver plate or stainless steel), or at least the bowl is. A table setting includes three sizes of spoons: the serving spoon (tablespoon), the soupspoon and the dessertspoon. In addition to these basic spoons, there are many others with specific uses, according to the dish to be consumed: grapefruit (serrated edge), oysters (which some people prefer to eat with a fork), boiled eggs, sauces, ice cream and coffee. Other spoons of various shapes complete this individual set: spoons for breakfast, cocktails or syrups (with a very long handle) and for tea.

Table settings may also include specific spoons for serving salad, often made of wood, horn or plastic. The spoon specifically for serving sauce has a bowl with two compartments (with fat and without). Other serving spoons of special shape include those used for salt, mustard, sugar, jam, honey (often of a material to match the serving container), fruit salads (with a pouring spout), olives (made of wood pierced with holes), strawberries and ice cream (in the shape of a spatula or a paddle).

■ **Kitchen spoons** The shape and material used for cooking spoons are suited to their uses. For example, basting spoons are small ladles with a lateral pouring spout for basting roasts; ragoût spoons have a straight lip; and spoons for tasting are made of porcelain so that one does not burn oneself. Spoons for stirring and mixing are usually made of wood, which is strong and a poor conductor of heat. Some

have a corner on the bowl for reaching into any awkward areas in the bottom of a pan. There are also sets of spoons for measuring. The ice-cream spoon is used for filling bombe moulds and the ice-cream scoop for shaping balls for sundaes and cornets. Finally, the melon baller, which has a small oval, fluted or round bowl, is used to make decorative ball shapes out of potatoes, carrots and fruits (apples or melons).

SPRAT This is a small fish related to the herring, 11.5–15 cm (4½–6 in) long, with a bluish-green back and silvery sides. It is most common in the Baltic and North Seas and in the English Channel, but is also found in the Atlantic. Rich and oily, fresh sprats can be cooked like sardines and are good grilled (broiled) or dusted with flour and pan-fried. However, they are more often sold smoked (Kiel sprats are a well-known German speciality), preserved or marinated. Sprats are much used in Scandinavian cooking (in gratins, open sandwiches and salads), where confusingly, smoked sprats are called 'anchovies' and canned sprats may actually be young herrings.

RECIPE

sprats à la vinaigrette
Remove the heads and skin from some fresh sprats. Arrange them in a small bowl and sprinkle liberally with chopped shallots and parsley. Coat with oil and shallot-flavoured (or white distilled) vinegar. Leave to marinate in a cool place for 10 hours. Serve with parsley, rye bread and shallot butter.

SPRING ONION (SCALLION) Also known as salad or green onion. A variety of onion that produces small white mild-flavoured bulbs with a long neck of stiff leaves. Spring onions are usually eaten raw and thinly sliced in salads, although they may be cooked and are often used in stir-fries.

SPRING ROLL An Oriental preparation, so-called because it is often served during the New Year celebrations, known in China and Vietnam as the Spring Festival. The Chinese spring roll differs slightly from the Vietnamese version; it consists of a square of dough made with eggs and wheat flour, rolled around a filling of pork, onions, prawns (shrimp), bamboo shoots or beansprouts, flavoured mushrooms, chives and sometimes water chestnuts. The filling is bound with egg and a seasoning based on soy sauce, ginger, pepper and rice wine. The rolls are deep-fried, served with soy sauce flavoured with garlic and lemon, and garnished with lettuce leaves, raw beansprouts, mint leaves, parsley or fresh coriander (cilantro).

The Vietnamese spring roll is called a *nem*. Chicken can be used in the filling instead of pork and crab instead of prawns, but the distinctive feature is that the filling is seasoned with *nuoc-mâm* and wrapped in a very thin rice pancake. These spring rolls are either deep- or shallow-fried and served with lightly peppered *nuoc-mâm*, mint leaves and lettuce leaves. Very tiny spring rolls are known as *cha gio*.

SQUASH The edible fruit of various members of the gourd family, which are cooked and served as a vegetable. Squashes vary widely in size, shape and colour (white, yellow, orange and green) and feature in many cuisines. They can be roughly divided into two categories – summer squash and winter squash (although there are some anomalies).

■ **Summer squash** In general, these are varieties picked when immature and tender, with thin, edible skins and soft seeds. The mild-flavoured flesh has a high water content and requires little cooking. Summer squash varieties include the crookneck squash (yellow with a bulbous base and a long, curved neck); the pattypan squash (small, round and flattish with a scalloped edge, also called custard marrow); the silk squash (a long, thin, tapering and ridged squash, favoured in Oriental cooking and also known as Chinese okra); the courgette (zucchini) and the vegetable marrow (very large, green and oval in shape, which can grow to the size of a watermelon). Summer squashes can be cooked by steaming, boiling, baking, sautéing, deep-frying and grilling (broiling).

■ **Winter squash** These tend to be mature squashes with hard, thick skins and seeds that are generally inedible. Their flesh is deep yellow to orange in colour; it is firmer than that of summer squash and so requires longer cooking. Winter squashes are often halved and baked (sometimes stuffed), or peeled, chopped into chunks and cooked in stews or by steaming or boiling. Two popular treatments include baking squash with butter and brown sugar or maple syrup, and boiling, then mashing squash with butter and a little orange juice. Very small squashes can be pickled in vinegar. Many recipes for pumpkin are suitable for squashes.

Winter squash varieties include butternut squash (an elongated pear shape, smooth-skinned and yellow-orange in colour with sweet, nutty-tasting flesh); acorn squash (oval-shaped with a thick, ribbed, dark green or orange skin); spaghetti squash (a pale, melon-shaped squash, also called vegetable spaghetti since its flesh separates when cooked into spaghetti-like strands); hubbard squash (very large with a dark green to bright orange, thick, bumpy, hard skin and grainy-textured flesh); and turban squash (a family of colourful winter squashes with hard, bumpy skins and turban-like formations at the blossom end). Other winter squashes include the kabocha squash (streaked green skin with smooth, sweet-tasting flesh); the delicata squash (also called sweet potato squash, for its similarity in taste to sweet potato); the golden nugget squash (small pumpkin-shaped squash with bright orange skin); the calabaza (round pumpkin-like squash, also called West Indian pumpkin, popular throughout the Caribbean and in Central and South America and similar in taste to butternut squash); and the cushaw

squash (a family of squashes popular in Cajun and Creole cooking).

■ **Squash flowers** The flowers from both summer and winter squash are edible. They come in varying shades of yellow and orange and may be used as a garnish or in salads. Squash blossom fritters – flowers coated in a light batter (sometimes stuffed with ingredients such as soft cheese) and fried – are a popular cooked dish.

SQUEEZE OUT To use pressure to extract the juice of a fruit or vegetable or to remove excessive liquid from a food. The liquid and seeds may be removed from tomatoes by halving them and pressing them in a colander with a spoon before crushing the flesh. Excess liquid in blanched drained spinach is squeezed out by hand. A special lemon squeezer is used to squeeze the juice from citrus fruits.

SQUID A marine mollusc of the cephalopod family, related to the cuttlefish. Squid is found worldwide and there are numerous species. Also called calamari, squid has a spindle-shaped body, which varies in size according to species. It has two triangular fins, or 'wings', at the tail end and its head bears ten arms, or tentacles, two of which are longer than the others. Like cuttlefish, the squid has an ink sac situated near its heart. Squid are sold fresh, whole or ready-cleaned and sliced, as well as frozen and sometimes dried.

Young, tender squid may be used whole and require less cooking than larger ones. However, squid should never be overcooked or it will become rubbery. Its tubular body is ideal for stuffing with various ingredients. Alternatively, squid may be thinly sliced into rings and, together with its tentacles, used in stir-fries, cooked in sauce *à l'américaine* or in a white wine sauce, battered and deep-fried (a component of the Italian dish, *fritto misto*) or served cold in salad or with aïoli. A classic Spanish speciality is to cook squid *en su tinta*, in a black sauce made from its own ink; the ink is also used in some Italian pasta and risotto dishes. In Japan, squid may be eaten raw, cooked as tempura or used in its dried form.

RECIPES

fried or sautéed squid
Wash and dry 1 kg (2¼ lb) very small cleaned squid. Put them in a frying pan with 60 ml (2 fl oz, ¼ cup) cold olive oil. Heat and cook over a brisk heat for 10 minutes, turning continually. Season with salt and pepper, cover the pan, reduce the heat and cook for 15 minutes more. Add 2–3 chopped large garlic cloves and 1 tablespoon chopped parsley. Increase the heat and stir. Serve very hot.

squid à l'andalouse
Wash and dry 1 kg (2¼ lb) white squid flesh and cut it into thin strips. Fry the strips in very hot olive oil. Place 3–4 (bell) peppers in a very hot oven

for a few minutes so that the skin swells. Peel, remove the seeds and cut the flesh into thin strips. Peel 3 onions and slice them into rings. Peel 4–5 tomatoes, remove the seeds and crush the pulp. Dice 100 g (4 oz) farmhouse bread and brown in very hot olive oil. Add the strips of pepper to the squid, then the onions and finally the tomatoes. Brown the mixture, add 120 ml (4½ fl oz, ½ cup) very dry white wine and cook for 35–45 minutes over a low heat. Chop and mix together the diced fried bread, a small bunch of parsley and 3–4 large garlic cloves. Add a pinch of saffron, 75 g (3 oz, ¾ cup) ground almonds and 2 tablespoons oil. Pour this mixture over the cooked squid, mix well and adjust the seasoning. Serve piping hot with well-drained rice.

stuffed squid ♦

Separate the tentacles from the bodies of 12 small squid, 10 cm (4 in) long. Remove the guts from inside the bodies and the blackish membranes and skins from the outsides and rinse the squid thoroughly under cold running water. Pat them dry and season with salt and pepper.

Chop the tentacles and brown them in olive oil in a heavy-based saucepan. Add 4 chopped onions and cook gently for 10 minutes until all of the liquid has completely evaporated. Add ½ bunch of parsley, chopped, 50 g (2 oz, ½ cup) fried cubes of bread, 1 chopped garlic clove and a pinch of cayenne pepper. Stuff the squid with this mixture and secure using wooden cocktail sticks (toothpicks). Brown the squid in more olive oil.

Peel 4 large green or red (bell) peppers, or a mixture of both, remove their cores and seeds, then slice them. Peel and roughly chop 8 tomatoes; remove the stones (pits) from 12 black (ripe) olives and halve them, or leave them whole if they are small. Place the vegetables in a casserole, adding seasoning to taste. Arrange the stuffed squid on top. Cover and cook in a preheated oven at 200°C (400°F, gas 6) for 1½ hours, basting frequently. Adjust the seasoning to taste, sprinkle with chopped parsley and serve with rice.

stuffed squid à la marseillaise

Buy some small cleaned squid complete with their tentacles. Chop the tentacles finely, together with 2 large onions. Soak 100 g (4 oz, 4 slices) stale bread in milk, then squeeze it out. Chop and mix together some garlic and parsley. Brown the chopped tentacles and onions in olive oil, then add 2 peeled and crushed tomatoes. Mix all the ingredients together. Add 2–3 egg yolks, salt, pepper and a pinch of cayenne pepper, and blend well. Fill the squid with this stuffing, sew them up and pack tightly together in an oiled baking dish. Sprinkle with chopped garlic and parsley, add 1 coarsely crushed onion, salt, pepper, 120 ml (4½ fl oz, ½ cup) white wine and an equal amount of hot water. Cover the dish with oiled greaseproof (wax) paper. Start the cooking on the hob (stove top),

then transfer the dish to a preheated oven at 180°C (350°F, gas 4) for about 30 minutes. Uncover the dish to reduce the liquid, then sprinkle the squid with olive oil and dried white breadcrumbs and brown under the grill.

additional recipe See *basquaise*.

SQUILLA MANTIS *squille* Known as the mantis shrimp, this is one of the many different crustaceans in the *Squillidae* family. It is a large shrimp-like crustacean living on the muddy bed of the Mediterranean; members of the same family are also found in South-East Asia and off the Atlantic and Pacific coasts of America (but they are not fished commercially in America). The mantis shrimp has a pair of large, grasping appendages like those of a praying mantis and it grows up to 25 cm (10 in) long. It is prepared in the same way as scampi, but is less of a delicacy.

STALE Term for food, particularly bread, that is no longer fresh, being rather dry and hard. For some dishes (croûtes and pain perdu), the bread or brioche should be slightly stale. (Bread can be kept fresh if it is stored in the freezer.)

STANLEY The name of various onion dishes seasoned with curry powder, named after the British explorer Sir Henry Morton Stanley. Eggs Stanley, soft-boiled (soft-cooked) or poached, are arranged on tartlets filled with Soubise purée and coated with curried sauce. Chicken Stanley comprises chicken sautéed with onions, then coated with a Soubise sauce spiced with curry powder. This sauce may also accompany poached chicken.

RECIPE

sautéed chicken Stanley

Cut a chicken into 6 pieces and sauté them in butter in a flameproof casserole without allowing them to brown. After 30 minutes, add 2 large finely sliced onions, cover and finish cooking over a low heat (about 20 minutes). Cook some mushrooms in butter. Arrange the chicken and mushrooms in a serving dish and keep warm. Deglaze the casserole juices with 200 ml (7 fl oz, ¾ cup) double (heavy) cream, reduce by a quarter and press through a sieve. Add ½ teaspoon curry powder and a pinch of cayenne pepper, then whisk in 40 g (1½ oz, 3 tablespoons) butter. Cover the chicken with this sauce and, if desired, garnish with a few strips of truffle.

STAR ANISE The reddish-brown fruit of an evergreen shrub native to the Far East. It is shaped like an eight-pointed star and contains seeds with a slightly hot aniseed flavour. The spice can be used whole or ground. In the West, it is used in confectionery, in the preparation of liqueurs (anisette) and in pastry- and biscuit-making. Star anise is commonly used in Oriental cuisine and is an ingredient in Chinese five spices or five-spice powder. In

China, it is used as a seasoning for fatty meats (pork and duck) and sometimes as an ingredient of scented tea. In some Eastern countries, the spice is chewed as a breath freshener.

STARCH A type of carbohydrate stored in the seeds, stalks, roots and tubers of numerous plants. Fruits and vegetables that are rich in starch include potatoes, chestnuts, sweet potatoes, bananas, cassava and yams.

Starch for culinary uses is extracted from the roots or tubers of certain plants (such as cassava, yam or potato) or from the grain of wheat, rice or maize (corn). It takes the form of a fine, white powder that swells and forms a gelatinous paste in a hot liquid. Potato starch is used in large quantities in the food industry. In the domestic kitchen, starch is used to thicken purées, broths and sauces. The main types used are cornflour (cornstarch), potato flour, arrowroot and tapioca.

STEAK A slice of meat. When the term is not qualified, it refers to a cut of beef; without description of a suitable cooking method, it is assumed to be a tender cut for grilling (broiling) or frying. Steak can also be used as a term for tougher cuts, such as braising or stewing steak, and it can be used for all types of meat as well as for a portion of fish.

Introduced to France after the Battle of Waterloo by the occupying English forces, steak was originally cut from the fillet, rump or sirloin. It later became customary to cut steaks from all roasting joints and subsequently from braising joints as well. The fact that butchering techniques vary between countries and even regions explains the differences in the names and shapes of cuts of meat. However, fillet is acknowledged as the best cut, from which come chateaubriand, *filet mignon* and tournedos. Sirloin and rump provide first-class steaks that are tender and full of flavour, and steaks cut from topside are almost as tender. Popular steaks include porterhouse, T-bone, entrecôte (rib steak) and *fiorentina* (an Italian steak cut from the sirloin and fillet). Beef steak may be cooked to varying degrees according to taste – from 'blue' to well done.

Steak tartare is a preparation of raw chopped fillet, with an egg and various seasonings. The origins of steak *au poivre,* a steak coated with crushed peppercorns or served with a peppercorn sauce, are controversial. Chefs who claim to have created this dish include E. Lerch in 1930, when he was chef at the Restaurant Albert on the Champs-Élysées; and M. Deveaux in about 1920, at Maxim's. However, M.G. Comte certifies that steak *au poivre* was already established as a speciality of the Hôtel de Paris at Monte Carlo in 1910, and O. Becker states that he prepared it in 1905 at Paillard's!

RECIPES

steak au poivre
Generously sprinkle a thick steak (preferably rump steak) with coarsely ground black pepper. Seal the steak in hot clarified butter or oil in a sauté pan; when half-cooked, season with salt. When it has finished cooking, remove from the pan and keep hot. Skim the fat from the sauté pan and dilute the cooking juices with white wine and brandy. Boil down a little, then add 2 tablespoons demi-glace* sauce or thick veal stock. Reduce further until the sauce becomes thick and glossy. Finish off with fresh butter and adjust the seasoning with salt.

Serve the steak coated with the sauce. Some cooks flame the steak with Cognac, Armagnac, whisky or liqueur brandy, and it is standard practice to finish the sauce with cream. It has also become common practice to prepare this dish using whole green peppercorns.

steak Dumas
Poach 12 rounds of beef marrow in some court-bouillon. Sauté 4 sirloin steaks in butter in a frying pan, season with salt and pepper and garnish with the marrow slices; remove from the frying pan and keep warm. Add 100 ml (4 fl oz, 7 tablespoons) dry white wine and 2 tablespoons chopped shallots to the frying pan and reduce by three-quarters. Add 100 ml (4 fl oz, 7 tablespoons) stock, bring to the boil, stir in 100 g (4 oz, ½ cup) butter and adjust the seasoning. Coat the steaks with the sauce and sprinkle with chopped parsley.

other recipes See *andalouse, cheval.*

STEAK AND KIDNEY PIE A British speciality consisting of a hot pie with a filling of lean beef and kidney, to which are added onions and mushrooms, or sometimes potatoes, hard-boiled (hard-cooked) eggs, or oysters (for steak, kidney and oyster pie).

Steak and kidney pudding has the same filling, which is packed raw into a pudding basin (mould) lined with suet dough and cooked by boiling or steaming for several hours.

RECIPE

steak and kidney pie
Make some puff* pastry, using 225 g (8 oz, 2 cups) plain (all-purpose) flour and 225 g (8 oz, 1 cup) butter. (Traditionally, steak and kidney pie can also be made with flaky or shortcrust pastry.)

Cut 675 g (1½ lb) stewing steak into cubes. Clean an ox (beef) kidney and cut it into small pieces. Season 25 g (1 oz, ¼ cup) plain flour with salt and pepper to taste and coat the steak and kidney with the mixture. Finely chop 1 onion. Melt 50 g (2 oz, ¼ cup) butter in a saucepan, add the meats and onion and fry until golden. Stir in 600 ml (1 pint, 2½ cups) beef stock. Continue to stir until the mixture boils and thickens, then cover the pan, reduce the heat and simmer for about 1½ hours,

Stuffed squid,
see page 1141.

until the meat is almost tender.

Spoon the mixture into a 1.15 litre (2 pint, 5 cup) pie dish, reserving excess liquid for gravy. Wet the rim of the pie dish and put a strip of pastry around it; brush with water, then cover the dish with pastry. Trim, knock up and flute the edges with the back of a knife and brush with beaten egg. Make a small hole in the centre of the pie crust to allow steam to escape, and bake in a preheated oven at 190°C (375°F, gas 5) for about 45 minutes. Cover the pastry with foil if overbrowning. Serve piping hot in the pie dish.

STEAK BATT Also known as a steak mallet or meat mallet. A culinary hammer, originally made of wood but now usually stainless steel. There is usually one side plain and the other ridged. Relatively heavy in proportion to its size, the steak batt is used for tenderizing and/or flattening meat, including steaks, cutlets and escalopes (scallops).

STEAMING A method of cooking whose origins are believed to predate the discovery of fire, using the stones of hot springs. Fish, vegetables and poultry in particular may be cooked in this way, as well as grains such as rice and couscous. The essential factor in steaming is the perfect quality of the ingredients used, since the slightest doubtful quality is accentuated. In Britain, suet and sponge puddings are also steamed.

In Western cookery, the classic process for steaming consists of quarter-filling a saucepan or casserole with water or stock flavoured as desired, then placing the item to be cooked in a perforated container or basket, the base of which is just above the level of the boiling liquid. The saucepan or steamer is covered and the item is cooked gently in the steam from the water or stock, which must be kept topped up. Several baskets may be stacked one above the other and steamed simultaneously.

Foods may also be cooked in their own steam without any liquid, in a heavy-based saucepan or casserole over a low heat or enclosed in foil in the oven. Steaming foods in their own moisture is different from steaming over liquid as the food sits in the moisture in the base of the container. This method is usually referred to as sweating. Pot roasting is based on a similar combination method, but using dry cooking (roasting) and steaming with the moisture evaporating from a small quantity of liquid in the bottom of the pot.

Steaming is also used in Oriental cookery, particularly in Chinese cooking, to prepare *dim sum*, little snacks. These include bite-sized dumplings cooked in bamboo steamers stacked on large woks. The method is also used for fish, poultry and meat dishes, usually with the careful use of aromatics, such as fresh root ginger, and full-flavoured sauces. Filled buns, savoury or sweet, are also steamed.

The aim when steaming is to retain and magnify the natural flavour of the main ingredients, enhancing them by well-chosen complementary seasonings or aromatics. As a moist method, it is suitable for tenderizing tough meats as well as ensuring that tender fish and chicken remain succulent.

RECIPES

steamed fillets of sole in tomato sauce
Arrange 6–7 sprigs of basil in the basket of a steamer and place on top 4 sole fillets folded in half. Season with salt and pepper. Pour a little water into the lower pan, bring to the boil and cook, covered, for about 8 minutes. Keep the sole fillets hot.

Poach 1 egg for 3 minutes in boiling water with vinegar added; mash well. Cook 1 chopped shallot gently in olive oil in a saucepan. Away from the heat, add the mashed poached egg, a dash of French mustard, the juice of 1 lemon, salt and pepper, as well as some basil leaves, finely chopped. Place over a low heat and whisk the mixture. While whisking, gradually add 100 ml (4 fl oz, 7 tablespoons) olive oil to thicken the sauce to the consistency of a hollandaise. Then add 3 tomatoes, peeled, seeded and diced, and 1 tablespoon chopped chervil.

Serve the sole fillets coated with the sauce.

steamed turbot steaks
Cut a turbot into steaks; season with salt and pepper and steam for 12 minutes. Chop some shallots and put them in a saucepan with a drop of vinegar and 100 ml (4 fl oz, 7 tablespoons) single (light) cream beaten with 2 mashed bananas. Reduce. Glaze in butter 2 unpeeled garlic cloves per turbot steak. Serve the fish coated with the sauce and surrounded with the garlic cloves and sprigs of parsley.

veal steamed with vegetables
Cut a shoulder of veal into 24 pieces and place in a heavy-based casserole, together with 18 small trimmed carrots, 18 olive-sized turnip pieces, the white part of 18 leeks cut into 2 cm (¾ in) pieces and 18 small young onions. Cover and cook over a very low heat without fat or liquid, shaking the pan occasionally to prevent sticking. After 20 minutes, remove the turnips, season them with salt and keep hot. Ten minutes later, remove and season the leeks; after a further 10 minutes, do the same with the carrots and onions. Continue to cook the veal over a very low heat, so that it does not burn, for a further 20 minutes. Moisten with 120 ml (4½ fl oz, ½ cup) white wine and reduce until almost dry. Then add 500 ml (17 fl oz, 2 cups) whipping cream and leave to cook for 10 minutes. Replace the vegetables in the casserole and bring to a final boil. Serve the veal with its vegetables piled into a dish.

STEELS AND SHARPENERS A steel is a cylindrical grooved rod made from high-carbon steel, used for honing knife blades. The handle usually has a ring on the end for hanging it up. A steel gives only a temporary edge, and sharp knives, especially butcher's and kitchen knives, should be ground periodically on a grindstone to sharpen them.

Electric sharpeners have slots for knives and kitchen scissors. When the motor is switched on, a wheel spins fast, putting a sharp edge to the knife.

Oilstones are made of a very hard silicon carbide. The very fine grain gives a good edge to the knife, making it extremely sharp.

STEEP To saturate certain cakes with syrup, alcohol or liqueur to make them moist and to add flavour. Babas, savarins, plum pudding, sponge fingers (ladyfingers) and Genoese sponge may be treated in this way.

STEGT SILD I LAGE Scandinavian cold herring dish. The fish is boned, cleaned, brushed with a mixture of mustard and parsley, folded head-to-tail, then floured and fried. It is left to marinate for a few hours in a mixture of vinegar, water, pepper, sugar and bay leaves. *Stegt sild i lage* is eaten cold with capers and onions.

STERLET A small freshwater sturgeon, less than 1 m (3 ft) long, common in Eastern Europe and Western Asia. It is prized for its delicate flesh and used as a source of high-quality caviar. Eaten fresh, dried or marinated, it may be prepared in the same way as salmon, salmon trout and larger sturgeon, but is most frequently braised in white wine.

STEWING The term for long slow cooking in liquid. This may be carried out on the stove top or in the oven, but in either case the temperature should be kept low enough to prevent the liquid from doing any more than barely simmering. The ingredients are covered with liquid and a generous proportion of flavouring ingredients, such as onions and root vegetables, are added with aromatics. This is a method for tenderizing tough meats and firm ingredients, such as pulses and root vegetables. The cooking time may range from 1 hour to 4–5 hours, according to the type of food used.

Stews should always be rich, an intensity resulting from the mingling of flavours, extraction of juices and breaking down of connective tissue and gelatinous subtances. The extended cooking time results in significant evaporation even at a controlled temperature may be increased (or pan uncovered) towards the end of cooking to encourage reduction. Stews also have a good colour, from the sediment forming around the rim of the pot as well as from colourful root vegetables.

STILTON An English cheese made from cow's milk (48–55% fat content). It is firm and cream-coloured, uniformly mottled with bluish veins, and has a natural brushed rind. Considered one of the best cheeses in the world, some say it was originally made in the village of Stilton in Huntingdonshire, where its production dates back to 1730. Others say it was first served at the Bell Inn, Stilton, in the 18th century. However, it was – and still is – made in parts of Leicestershire, Derbyshire and Nottinghamshire, and its production is tightly protected. Stilton is moulded in a cylinder, 15 cm (6 in) in diameter by 25 cm (10 in) high, and weighs 4–4.5 kg (9–10 lb). It is at its best from autumn to spring and is particularly popular in Britain at Christmas.

Stilton is traditionally accompanied by a glass of port or Burgundy, together with fresh walnuts or grapes. Some people soak it in port, Madeira or sherry, by pouring the wine into a hollow cut out of the centre of the cheese, which is eaten after a week or two with a small spoon. This is not considered advisable by cheese enthusiasts, who recommend cutting it across into rounds and working gradually down the cheese. To revive a slightly drying cheese, simply wrap it in a moistened cloth and leave it until the dampness has restored the proper consistency.

STIR To agitate ingredients with a spatula, wooden spoon or whisk, either before or during cooking, to ensure that the mixture is smooth and free from lumps and/or that it does not stick to the pan while cooking.

Rice and pasta need to be stirred as soon as they are immersed in boiling water.

STIR-FRYING A method of cooking over high heat in a large pan while stirring continuously, originating from Oriental cooking methods and particularly Chinese cooking in a wok. The method is very quick and the ingredients are finely cut into even pieces, typically strips of small, very thin slices, then cooked briefly. Ingredients are added at different stages, according to how quickly they cook, but the entire process takes no more than a few minutes. Food may be cooked in batches and combined at the end before serving in order to avoid creating too much cooking juice which will slow down the method and result in braising rather than frying. See *frying*.

ST-JEAN-DE-MINERVOIS A *vin doux naturel* with delicate orange and grape aromas, produced in the Languedoc region from the quality Muscat à Petits Grains.

STOCK A flavoured liquid base for making a sauce, stew or braised dish. A white stock is prepared by placing the ingredients directly into the cooking liquid; in a brown stock, the ingredients are first browned in fat. Sauces made from white stock are always called white sauces, whether they are basic or variation sauces (for example, allemande, poulette, aurore or suprême); all sauces made from brown stock are called brown sauces (for example, espagnole, bordelaise, Bercy or piquante).

Stocks can be used in thickened or unthickened form. They are based on veal, beef, poultry, game, vegetables, aromatic ingredients or fish. Other basic cooking stocks include velouté, consommé, aspic jelly, marinade, matignon and court-bouillon.

White and brown stocks, which used to be

essential bases for almost all the great classic sauces, take a long time to make and are often expensive. In practice, they belong to the realm of the restaurant and their use has been considerably reduced in domestic cookery. The advent of stock (bouillon) cubes and of commercial ready-made stocks have reduced the use of traditional stocks.

- FISH STOCK This is made with fish trimmings, including bones, skin and heads (excluding the gills as they are bitter). They are simmered for 30–45 minutes with aromatic vegetables and herbs. Overcooking spoils the flavour of fish stock.
- WHITE STOCK This is made with white meat or poultry, veal bones, chicken carcasses and aromatic vegetables. It is used to make white sauces, blanquettes, fricassées and poached chicken dishes.
- BROWN STOCK This is made with beef, veal, poultry meat and bones, and vegetables that have been browned in fat and then had the liquid added to them. It is used to make brown sauces and gravies, braised dishes and brown stews, for deglazing fried meats and for making glazes by reduction.
- VEGETABLE STOCK This is made by boiling vegetables and aromatic herbs that have first been gently fried in butter.

In general, stocks are aromatic but not salty, since they have to remain unseasoned until the sauce is perfected. Nevertheless, an optional pinch of salt enhances the blending of ingredients and the liquid.

RECIPES

brown veal stock
Bone 1.25 kg (2¾ lb) shoulder of veal and the same amount of knuckle of veal. Tie them together with string and brush with melted dripping. Crush 500 g (18 oz) veal bones as finely as possible. Brown all these ingredients in a large flameproof casserole or saucepan. Peel and slice 150 g (5 oz) carrots and 100 g (4 oz) onions, then add them to the pan. Cover and leave to sweat for 15 minutes. Add 250 ml (8 fl oz, 1 cup) water and reduce to a jelly-like consistency. Repeat the process. Add 3 litres (5 pints, 13 cups) water or white stock and bring to the boil. Skim and season. Leave to simmer very gently for 6 hours. Skim off the fat and strain through a fine sieve or, better still, through muslin (cheesecloth).

game stock
Tie together 1.5 kg (3¼ lb) shoulder, breast and other pieces of venison. Draw and truss 1 old partridge and 1 old pheasant. Brush all the meat with butter and brown in the oven in a roasting tin (pan). Slice 150 g (5 oz) carrots and 150 g (5 oz) onions. Line a large flameproof casserole with fresh pork rind, then add the carrots and onions, 1 kg (2¼ lb) hare or wild rabbit trimmings and the rest of the game. Deglaze the roasting tin with 500 ml (17 fl oz, 2 cups) red wine and 500 ml (17 fl oz, 2 cups) water and reduce to a jelly-like consistency. Pour into the casserole, add 2.5 litres (4¼ pints,

11 cups) water, bring to the boil, then skim and season lightly. Add 1 large bouquet garni, 1 sprig of sage, 10 juniper berries and 1 clove. Simmer for 3 hours. Skim off the fat, then strain through a fine sieve or, better still, through muslin (cheesecloth).

light brown stock
Scald 150 g (5 oz) fresh pork rind and 125 g (4½ oz) knuckle of ham for 4–5 minutes. Bone 1.25 kg (2¾ lb) lean stewing beef (leg or blade) and cut into cubes, together with the same amount of knuckle of veal. Peel 150 g (5 oz) carrots and 150 g (5 oz) onions, cut into slices, then brown on the hob (stove top) in a large flameproof casserole with all the meat, 500 g (18 oz) crushed veal or beef bones and the pork rind. Add 1 bouquet garni, 1 garlic clove, 500 ml (17 fl oz, 2 cups) water and reduce to a jelly-like consistency. Add another 500 ml (17 fl oz, 2 cups) water and reduce to a jelly again. Add 2.5–3 litres (4¼–5 pints, 11–13 cups) water and 2 teaspoons coarse salt; bring to the boil and simmer very gently for 8 hours. Skim off the fat and strain through a fine sieve or, better still, through muslin (cheesecloth).

thick veal stock
Reduce 2 litres (3½ pints, 9 cups) brown veal stock by a quarter. Thicken with 2 tablespoons arrowroot blended with 3 tablespoons clear cold veal stock. Strain through muslin (cheesecloth) or a fine sieve and keep hot in a bain marie.

tomato veal stock
Add 200 ml (7 fl oz, ¾ cup) fresh tomato purée to 2 litres (3½ pints, 9 cups) brown veal stock. Reduce by a quarter. Strain through a fine sieve or, better still, through muslin (cheesecloth).

white chicken stock
Prepare in the same way as for ordinary white stock, but add a small chicken (which can be used afterwards in another recipe) or double the quantity of giblets.

white stock
Bone an 800 g (1¾ lb) shoulder of veal and a 1 kg (2¼ lb) knuckle of veal, then tie them together with string. Crush the bones. Place the bones, meat and 1 kg (2¼ lb) chicken giblets or carcasses in a saucepan. Add 3.5 litres (6 pints, 3½ quarts) water, bring to the boil and skim. Add 125 g (4½ oz) sliced carrots, 100 g (4 oz) onions, 75 g (3 oz) leeks (white part only), 75 g (3 oz) celery and 1 bouquet garni. Season. Simmer gently for 3½ hours. Skim off the fat and strain through a very fine sieve or, better still, through muslin (cheescloth).

STOCKFISH Cod that has been dried until stiff and hard. Stockfish is traditionally produced in Norway where freshly caught cod are decapitated and gutted (cleaned), then hung from timber frames and dried in the open air for 6–12 weeks. The name comes from the German *Stock* or Dutch *stoc* (stick) and *Fisch* or *vis* (fish). Stockfish was an important food in early Medieval times, but was later replaced in popularity by salt cod. Stockfish is particularly popular today in Italy, especially in Liguria and Veneto. Here, confusion arises from the fact that stockfish, *stoccafisso*, is also referred to by Venetians as *bacaalà*, which is the name for salt cod elsewhere in Italy. Stockfish keeps well and requires long soaking in water before use.

RECIPES

stockfish à la niçoise

Soak 1 kg (2¼ lb) stockfish in water for 48 hours, then chop it into pieces. Prepare 750 ml (1¼ pints, 3¼ cups) rich tomato fondue* flavoured with garlic. Put the stockfish and the tomato fondue in a saucepan, cover and let it poach gently for 50 minutes. Then add 400 g (14 oz) thickly sliced potatoes and 250 g (9 oz, generous 2 cups) pitted black (ripe) olives. Cook for a further 25 minutes. Five minutes before it is ready, add 1 tablespoon chopped fresh basil.

stockfish and turnip soufflé

Poach 300 g (11 oz) well-soaked stockfish in champagne without boiling, then rub it through a sieve or purée in a blender or food processor. Make a béchamel sauce using 40 g (1½ oz, 3 tablespoons) butter, 40 g (1½ oz, ⅓ cup) plain (all-purpose) flour, 400 ml (14 fl oz, 1¾ cups) milk and salt and pepper. Add to this 50 g (2 oz, ½ cup) grated Gruyère cheese and the stockfish purée. Thinly slice some young turnips and cook gently in butter over a low heat. Add 4 egg yolks to the béchamel sauce and then fold in 5 very stiffly whisked egg whites. Pour the mixture into some buttered ramekins, arranging layers of turnip slices between layers of soufflé mixture. Cook in a preheated oven at 200°C (400°F, gas 6) for 20 minutes.

STOCKPOT A fairly deep, cylindrical, two-handled pan with a heavy close-fitting lid. Such pans are usually made of hardened aluminium, but some are of stainless steel, enamel or cast iron. The translation of the French name *fait-tout* (literally 'do-all') is a good description of this type of pan, which is used for cooking food with or without liquid. Two handles are needed as the pan is very heavy when full.

STOEMP Flemish mixture of potatoes and one or two types of finely chopped vegetables, such as Savoy cabbage, red cabbage, carrots, leeks, spinach or celery, boiled together, then mashed and seasoned. Fried diced bacon is often added to the mixture.

STOLLEN Similar to brioche and made with dried fruits, this is a German speciality traditionally eaten at Christmas. There are several recipes, the best known being that from Dresden. Some stollens have a filling of marzipan.

RECIPE

Dresden stollen

Make a well in the centre of 800 g (1¾ lb, 7 cups) sifted plain (all-purpose) flour. Add 20 g (¾ oz, 1½ cakes) fresh (compressed) yeast, 1 tablespoon caster (superfine) sugar and 250 ml (8 fl oz, 1 cup) warm milk. When bubbles form in the mixture, knead it thoroughly, incorporating the flour to make a smooth dough. Cover with a cloth and leave to rise in a warm place free from draughts.

Soak 200 g (7 oz, 1⅓ cups) currants in 3 tablespoons rum. Soften 500 g (18 oz, 2¼ cups) butter at room temperature, then beat it with 150 g (5 oz, ⅔ cup) granulated sugar and 3 eggs until light and creamy; add the currants and the rum, 200 g (7 oz, 1⅓ cups) chopped mixed peel (candied peel), a pinch of powdered vanilla or a few drops vanilla of essence (extract) and 1 teaspoon grated lemon rind (zest).

Add this mixture to the dough with just enough milk to keep it soft but not sticky. Knead it well, knocking it back (punching it down) several times, as for a brioche dough, and leave it to rise again under a cloth. When it has doubled in size, turn it on to a floured work surface, stretch it into a thick sausage shape and fold it in half lengthways. Put this on a buttered baking sheet and leave it to rise again for 15 minutes in a warm place. Brush with clarified butter and bake in a preheated oven at 180°C (350°F, gas 4) for 50 minutes.

When cooked, brush again with clarified butter, dust with icing (confectioner's) sugar and leave to cool before serving.

STONEWARE Dense hard pottery that is fired at a very high temperature. It may be brown, red, yellow or grey, depending on the colour of the clay. Fine stoneware consists of a mixture of clay and feldspar and is usually enamelled. It is generally used for ovenware and serving dishes but is also traditional for preserving jars.

STOPPER *bouchon* A piece of cork, glass, plastic or rubber, usually in the shape of a cylinder or truncated cone, which is inserted into the neck of a bottle, carafe or flask to form a more or less airtight seal. The French word *bouchon* comes from the Old French *bousche*, meaning a bunch of hay, corn or leaves to be used as a stopper.

■ **For wine** Originally, wine was protected by a layer of oil poured on to the surface; then wooden pegs covered with hemp soaked in oil were used. Its elasticity, flexibility and durability make cork ideal for stopping wine bottles. Wines that are to be drunk young are given a softer cork than wines that are laid down for several years, allowing the young wine to 'breathe' more readily. Corks must be 4–4.5 cm (about 1¾ in) long; for champagne, sparkling, wine and cider they are held in place with wire. Sometimes the cork is sealed with wax or covered with foil or a plastic capsule.

■ **Special stoppers** There are several different kinds of stopper that allow an opened bottle to be resealed or to facilitate pouring from a bottle.

• *glass pourer* For serving aperitifs.

• *chrome-plated metal pourer* To measure out syrups or liqueurs.

• *dropper* To measure out a dash of spirit or bitters into a cocktail.

• *pressure cork* To close an opened bottle of champagne.

• *spring stopper* To close a bottle of sparkling mineral water or an opened bottle of beer.

STORZAPRETI A Corsican speciality, particularly associated with Bastia, consisting of dumplings made of chopped green vegetables (spinach, Swiss chard or both), mixed with fresh Broccio cheese and bound with eggs, grated cheese, salt and pepper. They are poached in salted boiling water, drained and browned in the oven.

STOUT A strong dark English and Irish beer with a high proportion of hops. Some roasted barley is added to the malts and give the beer its distinctive taste. Probably the best-known stout is Ireland's Guinness.

ST NICHOLAS'S DAY A traditional feast day in northern Europe, celebrated on 6 December. The legend goes that a butcher had cut up three children into pieces and put them into a salting tub. Nicholas, suspecting the crime and passing by the place, insisted on tasting the criminal's salted meat. Faced with refusal, he resuscitated the little victims. On the night between 5 and 6 December, it is traditional for children to hang stockings full of hay, oats and bread on the fireplace, to feed the saint's donkey.

From the culinary point of view, St Nicholas's Day is celebrated with aniseed biscuits (cookies), gingerbread, chocolate and red sugar candy in the shape of the saint, who was the bishop of Myra, in Asia Minor, in the 4th century. In Alsace, bakers used to celebrate the feast day by making a special kind of bread called *männela* (literally 'little man').

STRACCHINO An Italian cow's-milk cheese (48% fat content) with a washed rind and a soft centre. Traditionally made on the return of the cows from the Alpine pastures (when they are 'tired', *stracche* in Italian), Stracchino is a speciality of the Lombardy region.

STRAINER A utensil used to filter drinks, liquids and sauces or to drain raw or cooked foods. Strainers are of various sizes and shapes according to their uses. Small strainers generally have a handle to enable them to be held under a pouring spout. Examples are the tea or infusion strainer, made of stainless steel or aluminium and perforated with small holes, and the milk strainer, made of fine metal netting, to retain the milk 'skin'. The finest strainer, used for pressing sauces, straining broths and

creams is the conical chinois. The vegetable strainer, which is much larger, is made of metal or plastic netting. Colanders are strainers with a base for standing in the sink.

Cloth strainers of horsehair, wool, silk or yarn were formerly used for sieving, sifting or filtering. Today, they are usually made of linen, cotton or nylon and are used particularly in confectionery for the preparation of fruit jellies and syrups.

STRASBOURGEOISE, À LA Term for a dish consisting of large cuts of meat or poultry, braised or lightly fried and garnished with braised sauerkraut, thin strips of streaky (slab) bacon cooked with the sauerkraut, and thin slices of foie gras sautéed in butter; the pan juices are used to make the sauce.

The term *à la strasbourgeoise* is also used to describe sautéed tournedos served on thin slices of foie gras and coated with a sauce made by deglazing the pan juices with Madeira-flavoured demi-glace. Consommé *à la strasbourgeoise* is seasoned with juniper berries, thickened with starch and garnished with a julienne of red cabbage and slices of Strasbourg sausage; grated horseradish is served separately.

STRAW A hollow tube of straw, glass, plastic or waxed paper, used for sipping cold drinks, such as milk shakes, soda and cocktails, from tall glasses. Curved straws are used to drink cocktails served in small glasses. Straws may accompany coffee and chocolate liégeois and other iced desserts served in tall glasses.

STRAWBERRY Red, roughly conical, fruit, which has its seeds on the outside. Strawberries are cultivated in numerous varieties throughout Europe and America. The strawberry was valued in Roman times for its therapeutic properties and the alchemists of the Middle Ages considered it to be a panacea.

In Europe, strawberries began to be cultivated from the wild varieties in the 13th century. The scarlet Virginia strawberry (*Fragaria virginiana*) was introduced into Europe from America early in the 17th century, and the French explorer Frézier later imported some strawberry plants from Chile (*F. chiloensis*). Both of these strawberries were larger than the European hautbois strawberry (*F. moschata*) and crossed naturally to produce the cultivated strawberry known today. Hundreds of modern varieties are derived from this and are constantly being added to by cross-breeding.

Strawberries grow well in temperate areas; peak season is from late spring to early summer, although the season can be extended by growing under glass. Spain, Israel and the United States are major exporters. In some countries 'pick your own' (PYO) is popular, allowing people to pay the farmer for what they pick themselves from his fields.

The strawberry is both refreshing and full of flavour. Although available frozen and canned, strawberries are best when fresh and uncooked.

Fresh strawberries should be red, shiny, unbruised, firm and fragrant. They need not necessarily be large; in fact, the larger ones are often full of water and have less flavour. Strawberries are delicate and do not keep long (a maximum of 48 hours in the refrigerator, loosely covered, if not too ripe). They should be rinsed quickly if dirty before hulling them. They should never be soaked, handled too much or exposed to heat and should be eaten within an hour after preparation. They are often served as a dessert with sugar and cream (a British favourite), or sometimes sprinkled with black pepper; they may also be steeped in wine, champagne or kirsch. Strawberries feature in many dessert recipes – in fruit salads, sundaes, flans, soufflés, sauces, Bavarian creams, mousses and ice creams – and in jams (preserves) and liqueurs.

■ **Wild strawberries** These can be found growing in woods, while alpine varieties may be found in mountainous regions. The berries of wild strawberries are small, up to 1 cm (½ in) long, very dark red and matt and do not have to be hulled. The flavour and scent of really ripe wild strawberries far surpass those of cultivated ones. All the recipes given for cultivated strawberries can be prepared using wild strawberries.

RECIPES

iced strawberry mousse

Dissolve 900 g (2 lb, 4 cups) granulated sugar in 500 ml (17 fl oz, 2 cups) water and boil until a thick syrup is obtained (104.5°C, 220°F). Add 900 g (2 lb, 4 cups) sieved freshly prepared strawberry purée, then fold in 1 litre (1¾ pints, 4⅓ cups) very stiffly whipped cream. Freeze in the usual way. (Raspberry mousse can be prepared in the same way.)

strawberries à la maltaise

Cut some oranges in half and scoop out the flesh. Trim the bases of the orange halves so that they can stand upright. Place them in the refrigerator. Squeeze the pulp and sieve it to obtain the juice. Wash, wipe and hull some small strawberries. Add some sugar and a little Curaçao or Cointreau to the orange juice, and pour the mixture over the strawberries. Store in the refrigerator. To serve, fill the orange halves with the strawberries and arrange them in a dish on a bed of crushed ice.

strawberry jam

Select perfect, unblemished fruit. Wash the strawberries carefully only if necessary; otherwise wipe and hull, then weigh them. Use 675 g (1½ lb, 3 cups) preserving or granulated sugar and 100 ml (4 fl oz, 7 tablespoons) water per 1 kg (2¼ lb) fruit. Dissolve the sugar and water in a preserving or large pan over a gentle heat, then cook to the 'soft ball stage' or 116°C (241°F). Skim the syrup, add the prepared strawberries and cook for a few minutes so that the juice is released. Remove the strawberries and boil the syrup again until it is at the soft ball stage once more. Return the strawberries to the pan and cook for another 5–6 minutes, until the jam reaches the jelling stage (101°C, 214°F). To enable the jam to keep longer, boil until the temperature reaches 104°C (219°F), 'thread stage'. Put into sterilized jars, seal and store.

strawberry purée (bottled)

Prepare the purée as for freezing, place in sterilized jars and seal. Put the jars in a large preserving pan, separating them with either paper or cloths. Cover the jars with cold water and bring to the boil for 10 minutes. Leave in the pan to cool, then wipe, label and store in a cool dry place.

strawberry purée (frozen)

Wash and wipe the strawberries carefully, hull them, mash to a purée and strain the purée through a fine sieve. Add 300 g (11 oz, 1⅓ cups) granulated sugar per 1 kg (2¼ lb) fruit. Place in special freezer containers, leaving a 2 cm (¾ in) space between the top of the purée and the lid.

Close the container, label and freeze. The purée must be defrosted at room temperature or in the refrigerator, before opening the container.

strawberry syrup

Wash, wipe and hull some very ripe strawberries. Crush them and squeeze through a cloth. Pour the strained strawberry juice into a bowl and check the density, which depends on the sugar content of the fruit and determines the amount of sugar to be added. This will range from 1.7 kg (3¾ lb, 7½ cups) granulated sugar per 1 kg (2¼ lb) fruit if the density at boiling point is 1.007, to 1.12 kg (2½ lb, 5 cups) if the density at boiling point is 1.075. Boil the sugar and the juice from the strawberries for 2–3 minutes. The density of the syrup should then be 1.3319. Pour the strawberry syrup into sterilized jars, seal and store in a cool and dry dark place.

other recipes See *cardinal, Condé, fruit paste, liqueur, soufflé.*

STRAW POTATOES Potatoes cut into long, very thin strips and deep-fried. Cooked, they resemble straw and are served mainly with grills.

RECIPE

straw potatoes

Peel some large firm potatoes, cut them into very thin strips and leave them to soak in plenty of cold water for 15 minutes. Drain and wipe them thoroughly, then cook them in deep-frying oil at 180–190°C (350–375°F) until they are golden (about 5 minutes). Drain them on paper towels, dust them with fine salt and serve them piping hot.

STRENGTHEN To reinforce the flavour and aroma of a preparation by adding concentrated substances (meat glaze to a sauce, for example) or strong and piquant ingredients (spices or condiments). The flavour of a liquid preparation can also be strengthened by reducing it (by boiling).

STREUSEL Crumbly topping for cakes and desserts, popular in central European cooking, the name for which comes from the German word *streusen* (to scatter). Streusel comprises flour, butter and sugar with possible additional ingredients such as ground cinnamon, vanilla essence (extract), lemon zest, ground almonds or other nuts.

Streusel is also the name for a round brioche from Alsace in France, which is covered with a sweetened shortcrust pastry made without eggs and flavoured with vanilla and cinnamon, and possibly ground almonds. The Alsace streusel is sometimes cut in half and filled with cream.

STRING Fine cord made of hemp or flax used to truss poultry and to tie joints of meat or poultry before roasting or braising. Fine thread is also used to sew up meat and poultry after they have been stuffed, and to secure such dishes as paupiettes and stuffed cabbage. *Gigot à la ficelle* is leg of lamb roasted in front of a hot fire suspended by a piece of string that allows it to be rotated as it is roasting. This method of preparation (more picturesque than gastronomic) is attributed to Alexandre Dumas.

STROGANOV A dish of thinly sliced beef, coated with a cream-based sauce and garnished with onions and mushrooms.

This traditional dish of classic Russian cookery has been known in Europe, in various forms, since the 18th century. The Stroganovs were a family of wealthy merchants, financiers and patrons of the arts, originally from Novgorod. They set up trading posts as far as the Netherlands; one of them, raised to the nobility by Peter the Great, employed a French cook, who might have given his master's name to one of his creations. (Some authorities give an etymology derived from the Russian verb *strogat*, 'to cut into pieces'.)

Thin strips of beef (fillet, sirloin or rump steak), seasoned with salt, pepper and paprika, are sautéed over a brisk heat, then coated with a sauce made by deglazing the pan juices with white wine, cream and thickened veal stock, to which onions sautéed in butter have been added. The dish is served with pilaf rice and sautéed mushrooms. In one version, regarded as more 'Russian', the onions and mushrooms are sautéed together and then added to the thin strips of sautéed meat; the whole mixture is then coated with a sauce made by blending a roux with soured (sour) cream and seasoning it with mustard and lemon juice. Alternatively, the meat may be marinated, then sautéed, flamed and coated with a sauce made from the reduced marinade blended with cream.

RECIPE

beef Stroganov
Cut 800 g (1¾ lb) fillet of beef into fine strips 2.5 cm (1 in) long. Sprinkle with salt and pepper and place in a small ovenproof dish with 4 sliced onions, 3 chopped shallots, 1 large carrot cut into slices, 1 crushed bay leaf and a small sprig of crumbled fresh thyme. Add just enough white wine to cover the meat and leave to marinate in a cool place, covered, for 12 hours. Drain and dry the meat; reduce the marinade by half and set it aside.

Sauté 2 thinly sliced onions in a shallow frying pan in 25 g (1 oz, 2 tablespoons) butter until soft and lightly brown; set aside. Lightly brown 200 g (7 oz, 2⅓ cups) thinly sliced mushrooms in the same pan with 25 g (1 oz, 2 tablespoons) butter, then add them to the onions. Wipe the pan and melt 50 g (2 oz, ¼ cup) butter in it; when hot, add the meat and sauté over a brisk heat, turning it frequently. When the meat is well browned (about 5 minutes), sprinkle it with 3 tablespoons warmed brandy and flame it. Keep warm in a serving dish.

Tip the onions and mushrooms into the frying pan together with the reduced and strained marinade and 150 ml (¼ pint, ⅔ cup) double (heavy) cream; stir over a brisk heat until thickened. Adjust the seasoning and coat the meat with the sauce. Sprinkle with chopped parsley and serve piping hot.

STRUDEL Sheets of wafer-thin pastry rolled around a sweet or savoury filling (the name literally means 'whirlwind'). Strudel is one of the most famous Viennese pastries; inspired by the Turkish baklava made from the related filo (phyllo) pastry, the recipe was apparently created by a Hungarian. The dough, which must be made with strong (high-gluten) flour, is difficult to prepare and to handle. It is stretched so thin as to be almost transparent; it is then sprinkled with breadcrumbs and ground almonds, spread with the chosen filling and rolled up. The usual filling is apples and raisins flavoured with cinnamon and grated lemon zest. Other classic fillings include stoned (pitted) morello cherries, sugar, lemon zest, and ground almonds; and cream cheese mixed with egg yolks, lemon zest, raisins, cream and stiffly whisked egg whites. In Austria, savoury strudels can be filled with chopped boiled beef with bacon, onions, paprika and parsley; another version uses chopped cabbage, baked with fat and sugar.

RECIPE

apple strudel
Mix 150 ml (¼ pint, ⅔ cup) tepid water in a bowl with a pinch of salt, 1 teaspoon vinegar and 1 egg yolk; add 1 tablespoon oil. Make a well in 250 g (9 oz, 2¼ cups) strong plain (bread) flour in a mixing bowl; pour the egg mixture into the centre, mix with the blade of a knife, then knead until the dough is elastic. Gather it into a ball and place it on

a floured board; cover it with a scalded basin and leave it to stand for 1 hour.

Peel and finely dice 1 kg (2¼ lb) cooking apples; sprinkle them with 3 tablespoons caster (superfine) sugar. Wash and wipe 200 g (7 oz, 1⅓ cups) raisins.

Spread a large floured tea towel (dish cloth) over the worktop and place the dough on it. Stretch the dough carefully using your knuckles; working from underneath it, brush with melted butter, then keep on stretching it until it is very thin, taking care not to tear it. Trim the edges to the shape of a large even rectangle.

Lightly brown a handful of breadcrumbs and 100 g (4 oz, 1 cup) chopped fresh walnuts in 75 g (3 oz, 6 tablespoons) melted butter; spread this mixture evenly over the dough. Sprinkle with the prepared apples and raisins, then dust with 1 teaspoon cinnamon and 8 tablespoons caster sugar. Roll up the dough carefully to enclose all the ingredients, then slide the strudel on to a buttered baking sheet. Brush with 2 tablespoons milk. Cook in a preheated oven at 200°C (400°F, gas 6) for 40–45 minutes. When golden, take it out of the oven, dust it with icing (confectioner's) sugar and serve it lukewarm.

STUD Typically, to insert one or more cloves into a large raw onion, which is then added to a preparation to flavour it during cooking.

A piece of meat, poultry or game can also be studded – with small thin sticks cut from truffle, cooked ham, anchovy fillets or gherkins; the meat thus flavoured is usually braised. Large joints of firm meat are most often treated in this way.

STUFATU Also known as *stufato*. A Corsican ragoût of meat with tomatoes and onions, which is generally served with pasta. It is prepared with braising beef, loin of pork and diced ham, browned in oil with tomato, onion, garlic and parsley. The mixture is sprinkled with white wine and flavoured with bay leaves, rosemary and thyme. Stufatu (the word literally means 'slowly cooked in a closed container') can also be prepared with mutton, pigeons or partridges, rabbit or chicken giblets. It is commonly served in a soup tureen, in alternating layers with pasta cooked *al dente* and sprinkled with cheese.

STUFF To fill the interior of poultry, game birds, prepared joints of meat, fish, shellfish, hollowed-out vegetables, eggs, fruit or other preparations (pancakes, croquettes) with a stuffing, a forcemeat, a salpicon, a purée or any other appropriate mixture. This is usually carried out before cooking except in the case of certain cold dishes.

Practically all poultry and game birds can be stuffed, unless they are very small. Cuts of meat that are suitable for stuffing include boned shoulder, leg and breast, paupiettes (rolled-up fillets) and chops; whole milk-fed lamb and sucking pig can also be stuffed. Most types of river and sea fish can be stuffed: round fish are stuffed whole, while fillets of flat fish are wrapped around the stuffing. Scallops,

mussels, clams and snails are also suitable for stuffing. The most suitable vegetables are tomatoes, large mushrooms, cabbage (whole or leaves), aubergines (eggplants), courgettes (zucchini), (bell) peppers, potatoes, onions, chicory, vine leaves and lettuce hearts. The best fruits for stuffing are avocados, citrus fruits (scooped out and filled with ice cream sorbet, and frozen), melon, pears and apples.

STUFFING A mixture used as a filling for an ingredient. Stuffings may be made from bread, rice or other grains, vegetables or fruit. They can be coarse or fairly fine in texture and are usually well flavoured. A wide range of forcemeats and fine mixtures are also used as fillings: forcemeats may be based on fine fish, poultry or meat mixtures and the term is used for mixtures that are more refined or complex than stuffings. See *forcemeat or stuffing*.

RECIPES

chestnut stuffing

Boil and peel 450 g (1 lb) chestnuts, then coarsely chop them. Finely chop 1 large onion, 1 celery stick and 1 garlic clove, and sweat with 2 crumbled bay leaves in a covered pan in butter 50 g (2 oz, ¼ cup) butter for about 30 minutes, until thoroughly softened but not browned. Stir in the grated zest of 1 lemon, 2 tablespoons lemon juice and 4 tablespoons brandy or sherry. Remove from the heat. Discard the bay leaves, then add 2 tablespoons thyme leaves, 1 tablespoon chopped fresh tarragon and a good handful of parsley, chopped. Stir in the chestnuts and season with salt, pepper and freshly grated nutmeg.

herb and lemon stuffing

Follow the method for sage and onion stuffing, using 1 onion and reducing the cooking time to 10 minutes. Instead of sage, add the grated zest of 1 lemon, 4 tablespoons chopped parsley and 3–4 tablespoons chopped thyme or tarragon.

rice stuffing

Cook 100 g (4 oz, ½ cup) long grain rice in 300 ml (½ pint, 1¼ cups) fish, poultry, meat or vegetable stock, depending on the use for the stuffing. Cook 1 finely chopped onion, 2 finely chopped garlic cloves and 2 finely diced celery sticks in olive oil until soft but not browned. Add 2 tablespoons chopped capers and 1 teaspoon very finely chopped fresh rosemary. Remove from the heat and mix in the rice.

Add seasoning to taste and extra finely chopped herbs to complement the main ingredient: coriander (cilantro) leaves, marjoram, oregano, fennel or dill are all suitable. When using delicate herbs, such as dill, it may be necessary to omit the rosemary. Chopped raisins, currants, ready-to-eat dried apricots or prunes, or peeled and diced dessert apple or pear can be added. Chopped walnuts or lightly roasted pine nuts also go well in rice stuffing.

Stuffing whole boned fish

This method is excellent for small whole fish. If necessary, scale the fish first, before it is gutted and cleaned. Instead of using cocktail sticks (toothpicks), depending on the cooking method, fine ham (such as Parma ham) or thin bacon can be wrapped around the fish to keep the stuffing in place during cooking. Alternatively, the fish may be wrapped in foil or cooked en papillote.

1 Use a fine-bladed, sharp knife to cut along the line of the back, separating the top fillet from the bones without cutting through the edge of flesh and skin on the opposite side of the fish. Keep the knife close to the bones. Leave the fillet attached at both ends.

2 Turn the fish over and repeat on the second side. The bones should be free from the flesh and in one piece. Use a pair of scissors to snip the bones at the head and tail, then remove them in one piece. Check for, and remove, any remaining bones.

3 Use a small spoon to insert the stuffing into the fish, pressing it in neatly and allowing a small gap for the stuffing to expand during cooking. Use wooden cocktail sticks (toothpicks) to secure the opening.

Stuffing poultry

Prepare the stuffing, allowing any cooked ingredients to cool completely. For reasons of food hygiene, the bird should not be stuffed more than 1–2 hours in advance and, once stuffed, it should be kept chilled until it is cooked. The bird should be thoroughly trimmed, especially of any lumps of fat and remains of internal organs or tubes, rinsed well with cold water and patted dry. There are many methods of stuffing a bird, including loosening the skin covering the breast and inserting stuffing under it. The cavity of a large bird, such as a turkey, is often stuffed with a whole onion, studded with cloves, or cut citrus fruit and herbs, and a small amount of stuffing inserted at the neck end. The following is suitable for smaller birds, such as a chicken or pheasant.

1 Truss the wings and neck end of the bird before inserting the stuffing. Use a trussing needle to pass the string through the thighs and truss the wings tightly in place.

2 Holding the legs firmly in one hand, use a spoon to insert the stuffing just inside the body cavity. Slide the stuffing in and press it firmly in place, but do not overfill the bird.

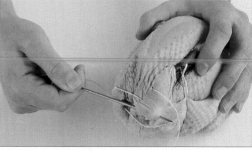

3 Tuck the ends of the legs into the opening and use a trussing needle to sew up the opening and tie the legs neatly in place.

sage and onion stuffing

Finely chop 3 onions and cook in 50 g (2 oz, ¼ cup) butter in a covered pan for 20–30 minutes, until thoroughly softened and reduced but not browned. Stir occasionally so that the onions cook evenly. Add 4 tablespoons milk and cook for a few seconds, then remove from the heat. Chop the leaves from 4 large fresh sage sprigs and add to the onions. Leave to cool. Mix the sage and onions with 225 g (8 oz, 4 cups) fresh white breadcrumbs, made from good country-style bread. Add salt and pepper to taste. Bind with a little extra melted butter or milk, if necessary.

STURGEON A very large migratory fish found in the northern hemisphere, which lives in the sea and migrates upriver to spawn. Almost prehistoric-looking, the sturgeon has a long tapering body with pointed, platelike scales running along its length and fleshy barbels around its mouth. Once plentiful in certain European and American rivers, it is now mainly fished in the Volga Basin and the Caspian Sea, essentially for its roe (see *caviare*), rather than its flesh. Overfishing and destruction of habitat have caused the decline in numbers of sturgeon; however, sturgeon farming is having some success.

Among the several species of sturgeon, the largest is the beluga (*Huso huso*), which grows up to 9 m (30 ft) long, weighs up to 1400 kg (3086 lb) and provides the costliest caviare. Other species of sturgeon found in European waters are the sevruga (*Acipenser stellatus*) and oscietra (*A. gueldenstaedti*); the smallest is the sterlet (*A. ruthenus*). The white sturgeon (*A. transmontanus*) is the largest North American species.

Sturgeon flesh is white, firm and rich. It may be cut into steaks or thick slices and braised like veal (fricandeau of sturgeon), grilled (broiled), sautéed or roasted. One luxurious recipe is sturgeon poached in champagne. The traditional Russian method of preparing sturgeon is called *en attente* (waiting): the fish is cooked in court-bouillon for several hours with aromatic vegetables. It is served cold with cooked parsley, olives, mushrooms, crayfish tails, horseradish, lemon and gherkins, or hot with a tomato sauce finished with crayfish butter. Sturgeon is also very good when smoked.

RECIPES

fricandeau of sturgeon à la hongroise

Brown a thick slice of sturgeon in butter with finely diced onions. Season with salt, paprika and a bouquet garni. Moisten with 200 ml (7 fl oz, ¾ cup) white wine. Boil down. Add 300 ml (½ pint, 1¼ cups) velouté* sauce based on fish stock. Finish cooking in a slow oven. Add butter to the sauce and pour it over the fish. Serve with boiled potatoes, cucumber balls or a purée of sweet (bell) peppers.

sturgeon à la brimont

Fillet a medium-sized sturgeon. Trim the fillets and thread anchovy fillets through them. Place in a baking dish lined with a fondue of carrots, onions and celery, finely sliced and cooked slowly in butter until very tender. Cover with 2 peeled, chopped and seeded tomatoes mixed with 4 tablespoons coarsely diced mushrooms. Surround with potatoes cut into little balls with a ball-scoop, three-quarters cooked in salted water and drained. Moisten with 100 ml (4 fl oz, 7 tablespoons) dry white wine. Dot with 50 g (2 oz, ¼ cup) butter, cut into tiny pieces. Bake in a preheated oven at 150°C (300°F, gas 2), basting frequently, for about 40 minutes, depending on the size and thickness of the fish. Gently ease the flakes apart at the thickest part to see if the fish is cooked. Five minutes before the end of cooking sprinkle with breadcrumbs and brown lightly.

ST VINCENT'S DAY The feast day of the patron saint of wine growers (22 January). St Vincent was a Spanish deacon and martyr whose remains are said to have been taken to Burgundy and then to Champagne. The feast day used to be celebrated with gargantuan 'pig feasts', a custom revived by the Chevaliers du Tastevin during the 1930s. The Confrérie des Vignerons de Saint-Vincent de Bourgogne et de Mâcon was founded in 1950.

SUBRIC A small croquette sautéed in clarified butter and served as an hors d'oeuvre, a hot entrée or a garnish. It is usually garnished with fried parsley and accompanied by a fairly highly seasoned sauce. Subrics are made from ready-cooked ingredients (leftover meat, diced chicken livers, fish, vegetable purée or cooked rice) bound with allemande or béchamel sauce, beaten eggs and flour, or cream and grated cheese. They are never coated in egg and breadcrumbs and deep-fried like most croquettes. Sweet subrics, made with rice or semolina, are served with jam or poached fruit as a dessert.

In ancient times, subrics were cooked *sur les briques* – on hot bricks from the kitchen fire – hence their name.

RECIPES

potato subrics

Finely dice 500 g (18 oz) potatoes and blanch for 2 minutes in salted boiling water. Drain and wipe, then cook slowly in butter. Remove from the heat and bind them with 250 ml (8 fl oz, 1 cup) thick béchamel* sauce. Add 3 egg yolks and 1 whole egg and season with salt, pepper and grated nutmeg. Proceed with moulding and cooking as for spinach subrics.

spinach subrics

Cook some well-washed spinach gently in a covered saucepan without water. Drain and cool it. For 500 g (18 oz, 3½ cups) pressed chopped spinach, add 150 ml (¼ pint, ⅔ cup) very thick béchamel* sauce, 1 whole egg and 3 yolks, lightly beaten as for an omelette, then 2 tablespoons double (heavy) cream. Season with salt, pepper and grated nutmeg, then leave to cool completely. Mould this mixture into small balls and cook in 40 g (1½ oz, 3 tablespoons) clarified butter in a frying pan until golden (about 3 minutes). Serve piping hot, with a cream sauce well seasoned with nutmeg.

sweet rice subrics

Cook 800 g (1¾ lb, 3½ cups) round-grain rice* in milk. Blend with it 100 g (4 oz, ⅔ cup) chopped crystallized (candied) fruits soaked in liqueur and spread the mixture over a buttered baking sheet, in a layer 2 cm (¾ in) thick. Brush the whole surface with 40 g (1½ oz, 3 tablespoons) melted butter and leave to cool, then chill lightly.

Cut the rice into rounds, rings or squares and cook in clarified butter in a frying pan until golden on both sides. Arrange in a serving dish and decorate each subric with 1 teaspoon redcurrant or raspberry jelly, apricot purée, or an apricot half-poached in syrup.

additional recipe See *semolina*.

SUCCÈS A French round cake made from two layers of meringue mixture containing almonds, separated by a layer of praline-flavoured butter cream and topped with a smooth layer of the butter cream. It is decorated with flaked (slivered) almonds, sugar, hazelnuts, marzipan leaves and, traditionally, by a rectangle of almond paste with the word 'succès' piped in royal icing (frosting).

The succès mixture is also used for making petits fours, usually filled with butter cream, as well as various pastries.

RECIPE

succès base

Crush 250 g (9 oz, 2 cups) blanched almonds with 250 g (9 oz, 1 cup) sugar until reduced to a powder. Fold in 350 g (12 oz) egg whites (about 8) whisked into very stiff peaks with a pinch of salt. Pour this mixture into two 18–20 cm (7–8 in) flan rings set on buttered and floured baking sheets; it should form a layer about 5 mm (¼ in) thick. Cook in a preheated oven at 180°C (350°F, gas 4). for 12–15 minutes. Cool on a wire rack after removing the rings.

SUCHET Description for a method used for preparing and serving crustaceans, which are first cooked in a court-bouillon. The tail shell is removed and the flesh cut into escalopes (scallops) or medallions, which are gently heated in white wine with a julienne of carrots, celery and leeks. The seafood and vegetables are arranged in the half-shells and coated with a sauce made from the cooking liquid, usually enriched with white wine. Alternatively, a Mornay sauce may be used. The sauce is glazed under a grill (broiler).

SUCKING PIG Also known as suckling pig. A very young piglet, usually slaughtered at less than two months old, when it generally weighs less than 15 kg (33 lb). Usually roasted whole, it forms a sumptuous dish for special occasions; it is also cooked in a blanquette and in a ragoût. Its succulent pale flesh has been appreciated throughout Europe since the Middle Ages; the grilled skin and ears were once a choice dish. Sucking pig is most popular now in Spain and Portugal.

Sucking pig roasted *à l'anglaise* (stuffed with onions and sage, moistened with its own juice and Madeira, and served with a purée of apples and raisins) was well known in the 1890s in restaurants of the Paris Boulevard. Another speciality, sucking pig in aspic, was particularly famous in the East. In *Madame Bovary*, sucking pig is the main attraction of the wedding breakfast: 'The table was set up inside the cartshed. On it there were four sirloins of beef, six fricassées of chicken, casseroled veal, three legs of mutton and, in the centre, a beautiful roasted sucking pig, flanked by four chitterlings with sorrel.'

RECIPES

roast sucking pig

Clean out the animal as for stuffed sucking pig *à l'occitane*, without boning or stuffing it. Sew it up and tie up the trotters. Marinate the pig, following that same recipe, then cook the pig on a spit over a high heat for about 1¾ hours: the skin should be golden and crisp. Baste the pig with a little of the marinade during cooking. Serve on a dish garnished with watercress.

stuffed sucking pig à l'occitane

Clean out the sucking pig through an incision in the belly. Bone it, leaving only the leg bones. Season the inside with salt and four spices, sprinkle with brandy and leave for several hours.

Prepare a forcemeat: slice the pig's liver and an equal amount of calves' or lambs' liver, season and brown briskly in very hot butter. Drain and set aside. In the same butter, still over a high heat, lightly brown the pig's heart and kidneys and 150 g (5 oz) calves' sweetbreads (trimmed, blanched, rinsed in cold water and sliced). Drain these ingredients and add to the liver. Add 40 g (1½ oz, 3 tablespoons) butter to the same pan and brown 200 g (7 oz, 1½ cups) finely chopped onions, then add 2 tablespoons chopped shallots and 75 g (3 oz, 1 cup) shredded mushrooms and cook for a few moments. Add a pinch of powdered garlic, cover with dry white wine and reduce, then add 400 ml (14 fl oz, 1¾ cups) stock and boil. Add 150 g (5 oz) fresh bacon rinds, cooked and cut into small pieces, and 100 g (4 oz, ¾ cup) blanched pitted green olives. Cook for a few minutes, then add the reserved liver mixture and heat without boiling. Mix well and leave to cool. Then add an equal amount of fine sausagemeat and bind with 4 whole eggs. Add chopped parsley and 60 ml (2 fl oz, ¼ cup) brandy, mix well and adjust the seasoning.

The day before the sucking pig is to be cooked, stuff it with this mixture. Sew it up, truss and marinate in a mixture of oil, brandy, sliced carrots and onions, crushed garlic cloves, chopped parsley, thyme, bay leaf and pepper.

On the day of cooking, lay the pig out in a large braising pan lined with bacon rinds and sliced carrots and onions (those from the marinade, with others if necessary). Do not hesitate to add plenty of vegetables, as they will be used as a garnish; small carrots and onions may be used whole. Brush the sucking pig with melted lard, cover and cook on the hob (stove top) until the vegetables begin to fry. Moisten with 300 ml (½ pint, 1¼ cups) dry white wine, reduce, then add a few tablespoons stock and a bouquet garni. Finish cooking in a preheated oven at 200°C (400°F, gas 6). The total cooking time should be about 2½ hours, when the skin will be slightly crisp.

Drain and untruss the sucking pig and lay out on a serving dish. Garnish with pork crépinettes with mixed herbs and small black puddings (blood sausages) cooked in butter. Add the sliced onions and carrots from the braising pan and pour over the strained cooking juices. Serve with a celery purée or mashed potatoes.

SUÉDOISE

A cold dessert, made of fruits cooked in syrup, arranged in layers in a mould or an earthenware dish, then covered with a jelly flavoured with fruit, wine or liqueur. When set, the suédoise is turned out and served with fresh whipped cream or a fruit sauce.

SUÉDOISE, À LA

A term describing various dishes reminiscent of Scandinavian cookery. Mixed salads à la suédoise combine vegetables, fruit, mushrooms, cheese and shellfish or fish, dressed with a herb-flavoured vinaigrette. Mayonnaise à la suédoise is mixed with grated horseradish and apple sauce, made with white wine but no sugar. Roast pork à la suédoise is stuffed with stoned (pitted) prunes and served with apples stuffed with prunes.

RECIPE

anchovy salad à la suédoise
Peel and dice 500 g (18 oz) cooking apples and sprinkle with lemon juice. Dice the same weight of cooked beetroot (beet). Mix these ingredients with a vinaigrette seasoned with mild mustard. Heap in a salad bowl and garnish with desalted anchovy fillets, the whites and yolks of hard-boiled (hard-cooked) eggs chopped separately and thin slices of blanched mushrooms.

SUET

The hard fat from around the kidneys and loin of beef (which tastes best) and other animals. It has a very high melting point and it has influenced British cooking considerably. One of its more famous uses is in fish-and-chip shops, to fry chips and battered fish. The traditional domestic alterna-

tive to suet as a cooking fat is dripping (rendered-down fat from roasting beef), used to roast potatoes and bake Yorkshire pudding.

Suet is better known as the fat in suet crust pastry, used to make dumplings and steamed puddings, both savoury and sweet. These include suet pastry rolled up with a filling (jam or currants), or used to line a bowl with savoury or sweet filling (Sussex pond pudding has cut lemons inside). Alternatively, suet is mixed with crumbs and dried fruit, to make plum duff, New College pudding, the Scots cloutie dumpling (which also has black treacle) and the plainer 'brown George'. Suet is also traditional in mincemeat and Christmas pudding.

Suet is sold trimmed, shredded and dredged with fat to prevent the shreds from sticking together. Vegetarian alternatives to proper suet are readily available and known as vegetable suet; they are based on vegetable fat.

SUET PASTRY

A traditional British pastry, made by mixing shredded suet with flour and water. This differs from other pastries, particularly short pastries, in that self-raising flour and a higher proportion of water are used. The pastry rises during cooking and has a spongy texture when cooked.

Suet crust pastry can be cooked by boiling, steaming or baking. It is used to make savoury and sweet steamed or boiled puddings and dumplings. It is also used for baked pastry dishes, such as roly-poly, a pastry roll filled with jam or a savoury mixture. When baked as a topping or shaped into dumplings, the pastry becomes golden brown and crusty on the outside.

RECIPES

suet crust pastry
Sift 225 g (8 oz, 2 cups) self-raising flour into a bowl. Stir in a pinch of salt and 100 g (4 oz, ¾ cup) shredded suet. Mix in 175 ml (6 fl oz, ¾ cup) cold water to make a soft dough. Turn the dough out on to a floured surface and shape into a smooth ball, then roll out fairly thickly or use as required.

suet dumplings
Prepare the suet crust pastry. Divide it into 8 equal portions and roll each into a ball on a lightly floured surface. To cook the dumplings, add them to barely simmering broth and cook for 15 minutes, until risen, light and fluffy. Alternatively, bake the dumplings on the surface of a stew in a covered casserole for about 40 minutes.

SUGAR

Any of a class of sweet-tasting carbohydrates, formed naturally in the leaves of numerous plants, but concentrated mainly in their roots, stems or fruits. The plants' energy reserve may be in the form of simple sugars or high-molecular-weight polymers of simple sugars (known as starch). Sugar can be extracted from the maple tree; the toddy, palmyra, coconut and date palms; and from sorghum and grapes among others. However, the two main commercial sources of sugar are sugar cane, a giant bamboo-like grass, in tropical regions and sugar beet, a root vegetable, in temperate regions.

The term 'sugar', in the singular, usually denotes cane sugar or beet sugar, the scientific name for which is sucrose (or saccharose). It consists of a molecule of glucose combined with a molecule of fructose. In the plural, 'sugars' denotes the class of soluble simple carbohydrates to which sucrose belongs. Other simple sugars include glucose (or dextrose), which occurs naturally in fruit and vegetables; glucose syrup (partially hydrolysed starch); fructose (or levulose), which is the sugar of fruit and honey; and galactose, found in dairy products.

The different sugars vary in sweetness or sweetening powder. Fructose is sweeter than sucrose and its 'sweetening power' in culinary use is greater. Glucose is not as sweet as sucrose. Honey is a mixture of glucose and frutose and therefore sweeter then pure sucrose.

■ **History** A few thousand years ago, sugar was already being used in Asia, in the form of cane syrup, whereas in Europe at that time honey and fruit were the only source of sweetening. According to legend, the Chinese and Indians have always known how to manufacture granulated sugar. In about 510 BC, at the time of the expedition of Darius to the valley of the Indus, the Persians discovered a 'reed which yields honey without the assistance of bees'. They brought it back with them and jealously guarded the secret of how this sugary substance could be obtained, and traded it as a rarity. In the 4th century BC, Alexander the Great also brought back the 'sweet reed', from which was extracted *çarkara* (a Sanskrit word meaning 'grain'), a crystal obtained from the juice of the plant. Cultivation of this reed gradually extended to the Mediterranean basin (Venice became an important trade centre for sugar) and to Africa. A new food had just been created: *saccharose* for the Greeks, *saccharum* for the Romans, *sukkar* for the Arabs, then *zucchero* in Venice, *çucre* (then *sucre*) in France, *sugar* in England, *azúcar* in Spain, *Zucker* in Germany.

In the 15th century, the Spanish and Portuguese introduced cultivation of the cane into their Atlantic possessions (the Canary Islands, Madeira and Cape Verde islands), so as to free themselves from the monopoly of the Mediterranean producers. Lisbon soon superseded Venice as the principal European city of refining. The discovery of the New World and other colonial conquests led to the extension of sugar-cane cultivation, firstly in the Caribbean, Brazil and Mexico, next in the islands of the Indian Ocean, then in Indonesia, and finally as far as the Philippines and Oceania. The West Indies, which had become known as the 'Sugar Islands', provided sugar for the refineries of the European ports. Growing European demand for sugar, later increased even more by the fashion for tea, coffee and chocolate, was a major reason for the slave trade, which kept the American sugar plantations supplied with labour.

Sugar beet remained initially unexploited, although French botanist Olivier de Serres had drawn attention to its high sugar content as early as 1575. It was not until 1747 that the German chemist Marggraf succeeded in extracting sugar from beet and solidifying it. In 1786, a former student of his called Achard tried to produce it on an industrial basis, but the output was still small, with a very high cost. In 1800, Chaptal published some conclusive findings and blockades of France during the Napoleonic Wars cut off continental Europe from supplies of cane sugar and gave an additional impetus. In 1811, Delessert perfected the industrial extraction of beet sugar in his Passy refinery; on 2 January 1812, he offered Napoleon I the first sugar loaf. France later became the first large-scale beet sugar producer in Europe.

Today, sugar beet is grown extensively in Russia, the Ukraine, Germany, France, Poland and northwestern USA. Sugar cane is grown in Brazil, India, China, the southern states of the USA, Thailand, Australia, Mexico, southern Africa and Pakistan.

■ **Manufacture of raw sugar** Once harvested, the beets and cane must be converted quickly to crystalline raw sugar. This is to ensure there is no microbiological degradation and no loss of their rich sugar content. For this reason, raw sugar factories are established close to the growing areas and work without a break during the whole harvesting campaign, which lasts several months.

The principle of raw sugar production from both beet and cane consists of extracting the sucrose by successively eliminating the other constituent parts of the plant.

The root of the beet is sliced and the sweet juice is extracted by diffusion in hot water. The juice, which contains 13–15% sugar, is then treated with milk of lime and carbon dioxide. This results in the production of chalk, trapping much of the insoluble non-sugar material, which is filtered off to give a clear juice.

In the case of cane sugar, the cut cane is shredded, crushed and sprayed with hot water. The juice is heated, treated with lime and then filtered.

Both clarified cane and beet juices are then concentrated by evaporation under reduced pressure until crystallization is induced. The concentrated crystallized mass is transferred to mixers (crystallizers), where crystal growth continues. The crystalline raw sugar is then separated from the remaining syrup by centrifugation. Not all of the sugar may have been extracted from the juice at this stage, so the remaining liquid may be recycled. When it is no longer economically practical to extract more sugar, the remaining syrupy liquid is called molasses. Cane molasses is called blackstrap and has various uses in food and drink processing; beet molasses is unfit for human consumption and is used in animal feed.

Some raw cane sugars are prepared with extra care and to recognized standards; these sugars are marketed for consumption as unrefined brown sugars and include such sugars as raw cane demerara and muscovado sugars (see below). In the main, however, raw sugars require further refining. Raw sugar is a stable product, which may be handled, stored and transported to wherever it is to be refined.

Unlike the production of raw sugar, refining may continue all year and need not be in the country of origin. Cane refineries tend to be in the importing country, while raw beet is often refined adjacent to the raw beet sugar factory.

■ **Refining raw cane sugar** Refining raw cane sugar removes all impurities, leaving an end-product of pure natural sucrose. This product contains no artificial colourings, preservatives or flavourings of any kind. White refined sugar contains 99.9% pure sucrose; brown sugars contain a small proportion of molasses, which imparts colour and flavour.

The raw sugar consists of brown sugar crystals containing many impurities and covered with a coating of molasses. The outer layers are first softened with a warm syrup solution to create a batter-like mixture called magma. This is passed into centrifugal machines to separate the molasses film from the crystals. The crystals are rewashed to remove remaining impurities and treated again with lime and carbon dioxide. The emerging liquid, which is a clear amber colour, is passed over bone charcoal or another decolorizing agent (such as resin) to remove nearly all the soluble impurities and any nonsweetening colouring matter. The liquid is now colourless and clear and ready for recrystallization.

The liquid is boiled in a vacuum to avoid colouring or destroying the sugar by heat. When the liquid reaches the correct consistency, crystallization is started by adding to the liquid a controlled quantity of very small crystals known as 'seeds'. When the tiny crystals have grown to the required size, they are separated from the mother liquid in centrifugal machines and dried in granulators. The boiling and crystallization process is repeated several times before the sugar starts to discolour. This liquid is then used to make other sugar products, such as golden syrup, or is boiled and crystallized again together with syrup separated from the raw sugar magma. The final syrup is called 'refinery molasses'.

Different sizes of sugar crystals are normally produced by variations in boiling technique and duration. The crystals are graded by screening before being packed. Just under half the sugar produced is used in direct form; the remainder is sold to food industries or to specialists producing items containing sugar.

■ **Sugars and sugar products** White sugar is refined beet or cane sugar containing 99.9% sucrose and less than 0.06% moisture, having been oven-dried at 105°C (221°F). It has the highest purity and may be sold as granulated, caster (superfine), grain or lump sugars (see below).

Brown sugar is unrefined, or raw, cane sugar (no brown sugar is made from beet because of the inedible molasses), containing 85–98% sucrose and certain impurities, which account for the varying shades of brown. Natural brown sugar possesses a distinctive flavour. There are various types, ranging from the very dark, moist, soft molasses sugar and muscovado, through a pale muscovado to the large, crystallized demerara (see below). Some essential minerals and vitamins may be present, but probably in insufficient quantities to substantiate claims that brown sugar is nutritionally superior to white. Some commercial brown sugars are, in fact, refined white sugar with caramel or molasses added to colour and flavour them. This is indicated on the label under 'Ingredients'; the natural raw product will have no such list.

Organic sugars are those made from organically grown sugar beet and sugar cane.

• CASTER (SUPERFINE) SUGAR Comprising fine, small-grained crystals. Caster (sometimes spelt 'castor') sugar dissolves faster than granulated and is particularly used in baking, for making meringues and for sweetening fruits and ices. Golden caster sugar, again derived from unrefined cane sugar, is also available.

• GRANULATED, OR 'REGULAR', SUGAR Produced directly from crystallization of the syrup; it forms fairly coarse crystals. It is the most common all-purpose sugar – for use on the table and in cooking. Golden granulated sugar, a free-flowing brown sugar derived from cane sugar molasses, is very pale brown in colour and has the same general uses.

• ICING (CONFECTIONER'S) SUGAR OR POWDERED SUGAR Granulated sugar milled into a very fine powder, mixed with starch, calcium phosphate or cornflour (cornstarch) to prevent it caking. The fastest dissolving sugar, it is used for dusting, decorating and icing (frosting) cakes and is included in many kinds of confectionery. Golden icing sugar, very pale brown in colour, is derived from unrefined cane sugar.

• LUMP (LOAF) SUGAR Obtained by moulding moistened granulated sugar while hot, then drying it in order to fuse the crystals together (agglomerated sugar). Invented in 1854 by Eugène François, a Parisian grocer, lump sugar takes the form of cubes, tablets or irregular chunks. Quick-dissolving cubes are compressed only, to give an open texture and quicker dissolution. Larger quantities are usually packaged in cartons to preserve the shape of the sugar lumps; two or three lumps, wrapped in paper, are often served in cafés and restaurants for sweetening hot drinks. Some recipes call for lump sugar to be used to rub the zest from citrus fruit.

• PRESERVING SUGAR Large sugar crystals designed for jam (preserve) making because they dissolve quickly without forming too much scum. Some jam sugars (gelling sugars) consist of caster or granulated sugar, with added natural pectin and citric and/or tartaric acid, which helps produce a good-quality set in jams and jellies, particularly for fruit low in pectin. This sugar is useful for reducing boiling time, thereby giving a better colour and retaining the aromatic flavour of the fruit.

• SUGAR LOAF Mainly used in Arab countries, this is sugar moulded into a cone shape, with its base wrapped in blue paper.

• Sugar nibs (crystal sugar) Rounded grains, obtained by crushing pieces of blocks of white sugar, sorted for size in a sieve. This sugar is used in the manufacture of sweetened products and for decorating pastries such as Bath buns.

• Vanilla sugar Caster sugar to which has been added at least 10% powdered essence (extract) of natural vanilla. Used for flavouring sweet dishes and pastries, it is sold in small quantities in sachets available from specialist shops.

• Demerara sugar Raw or partly refined cane sugar with relatively hard, large, golden-coloured sugar crystals. Some demeraras are simply white sugar with added molasses.

• Jaggery Moist, dark brown, coarse unrefined sugar, extracted by traditional methods from the sap of palm trees. It tastes strongly of molasses and is used in India and South-East Asia.

• Muscovado sugar Another raw cane sugar. Dark muscovado (called Barbados sugar) is similarly good for baking rich cakes, while light muscovado sugar goes particularly well in cooking with banana, toffee and butterscotch flavours.

• Soft molasses sugar or black Barbados sugar Soft, fine, moist, raw cane sugar. Very dark in colour, it has a high molasses content and a strong flavour. It is often used for making gingerbread, rich dark fruit cakes, Christmas cakes and Christmas puddings, and for chutneys and pickles.

• Candy sugar Very large crystals of white or brown sugar (the latter being white sugar sprayed with caramel colour), obtained by means of slow crystallization on wire-mesh frames. This is often served with coffee.

• Fondant Sugar syrup worked when cool into a thick white paste with a quantity of glucose syrup or cream of tartar, used for flavouring and decorating pâtisserie and confectionery. Fondant can also be made with icing (confectioner's) sugar, egg white and glucose syrup worked together. A ready-mixed dry fondant can also be bought (which requires the addition of just water) and ready-to-roll fondant in blocks is also marketed.

• Invert sugar A sugar obtained by the action of acids and an enzyme (invertase) on sucrose, which comprises a mixture of glucose and fructose with a little non-inverted sucrose. It is used mainly by professional pastrycooks and industries (brewing, confectionery), in the form of 'invert sugar solution' (62% dissolved solids, of which 3–5% is invert sugar) or 'invert sugar syrup' (62% dissolved solids, of which over 50% is invert sugar and syrups); for example, golden syrup (see below).

16• Liquid caramel Liquid sugar ready for use without cooking, sold in small bottles or sachets for flavouring yogurts, desserts and ices.

• Liquid sugar (sugar syrup) Literally, a sugar solution, normally prepared by dissolving white sugar in water. In industry, however, it is more closely defined. It is a colourless or golden solution of cane sugar containing at least 62% dissolved solids (usually 66% for better microstability), of

which not more than 3% consists of invert sugar. The cane industry has a wide range of liquid sugars, most of which are prepared from intermediate liquids from the refinery process. Cane molasses has a pleasant flavour, unlike beet, hence there is no equivalent to these products in the beet industry. Liquid sugars are used in the food and brewing industries and also for preparing punches or desserts – 1 coffeespoon is equivalent to 3 g (⅛ oz) sugar.

• Syrups, molasses and black treacle Some syrups, such as maple syrup and palm syrup, occur naturally, but golden syrup (slightly sweeter than sugar) is a byproduct of sugar refining, which undergoes its own refining process. It is used a great deal in biscuit (cookie) manufacture and in the brewing industry, as well as having a useful role in home baking for melted mixtures (such as brandy snaps and flap-jacks) and in cakes and desserts. Corn syrup, produced from sweetcorn (maize), can be light or dark (the darker one being more strongly flavoured). It is used in the same way as golden syrup.

Molasses and black treacle are dark and viscous, with a strong distinctive flavour, and are less sweet than honey. Molasses is the natural syrup drained from sugar cane or a blend of refinery syrups obtained during the refining of white sugar. Black treacle is a refined molasses-like sugar syrup. They are interchangeable in cooking for such recipes as gingerbread, rich fruit cakes, treacle toffee and the American speciality Boston baked beans. Treacle is also used in the pharmaceutical industry for lozenges and linctuses.

• Turbinado sugar Similar to demerara, but more refined and lighter in colour.

• Vergeoise Solid residue from refining beet or cane sugar, giving a product of soft consistency, golden or brown, with a pronounced flavour. It is used mostly in Flemish pâtisserie and found mainly in France.

■ **Sugar in industry and cooking** Sugar is widely used in the industrial preparation of foods and beverages: confectionery, chocolates, biscuits (cookies), manufactured desserts, cakes, dietetic foods, yogurts, jellied milks, dessert creams and ice cream, evaporated and powdered milks, jams, canned fruits and vegetables, fizzy drinks (sodas), fruit juices, squashes, syrups, cordials, beers, ciders, champagnes, sparkling wines, liqueurs and creams, fortified wines and aperitifs. Sugar is also used in the manufacture of some pharmaceutical products.

In cookery, sugar is an important ingredient for sweetening, as well as having a number of other functions.

• Sweetening Sugar is added to numerous hot or cold drinks, the flavour of which it completes, strengthens, improves or just sweetens – for example in coffee, tea, chocolate, infusions, fruit juices and sodas. It performs the same function with numerous dairy products, fruit salads and compotes. It is also one of the essential ingredients of pâtisserie and sweet dessert dishes.

- FLAVOURING Sugar is used in a number of savoury dishes, such as glazed onions, carrots and turnips, caramelized brown sauces, glazed ham, carbonades, ragoûts and sweet-and-sour dishes.
- PRESERVING Versatile and highly soluble, sugar plays an important part as a preservative for jams, jellies and marmalades, fruit jellies, preserved or glacé (candied) fruits and crystallized (candied) flowers.
- BULKING Sugar can serve to provide bulk and texture, particularly in ice creams and confectionery.
- WORKING WITH YEAST Sugar acts as a 'food' for yeast in baking and brewing.

■ **The properties and cooking of sugar** White, shining, odourless and with a particularly sweet flavour, granulated sugar in its pure state is in rhomboidal prisms; its true density is 1.6 by volume but its practical density is about 1.2 by volume. Its degree of solubility in water depends on the temperature: 1 litre (1¾ pints, 4⅓ cups) water can dissolve 2 kg (4½ lb, 9 cups) sugar at 19°C (66°F) and nearly 5 kg (11 lb, 22 cups) at 100°C (212°F). It is not easily dissolved in alcohol. Heated when dry, it begins to dissolve at about 160°C (320°F); rapid cooling at this stage produces barley sugar. Sugar caramelizes above 170°C (338°F) and burns at about 190°C (374°F).

Beaten with egg yolks, it forms a creamy foam used in numerous recipes for desserts; when added to stiffly whisked egg whites it provides the basis for meringues.

The cooking of sugar should be carried out progressively, in a heavy-based pan made of untinned copper or stainless steel, which must be absolutely clean and without traces of grease; a simple heavy-based saucepan can be substituted. Use refined white sugar (granulated, caster or, better still, lump), which is barely moistened – a maximum of 300 ml (½ pint, 1¼ cups) water per 1 kg (2¼ lb, 4½ cups) sugar. Since refined sugar is the purest, there is less risk of crystallization (massing) under the action of an impurity, which would render it unusable; for greater precautions, 50–100 g (2–4 oz, ⅓–⅔ cup)

glucose (powder or liquid) is added per 1 kg (2¼ lb, 4½ cups) sugar. The sugar must never be stirred during cooking, but the container can be shaken. Cooking begins over a low heat until the sugar is dissolved; the heat is then increased and the sugar should be constantly watched, as the different stages of cooking, which correspond to specialized uses, follow very closely on each other. When a cooking stage is reached, the pan must be removed quickly from the heat; a few drops of cold water can be added in order to lower the temperature of the syrup naturally, but when the syrup begins to turn golden, this is then irreversible. The physical characteristics of the sugar indicate the point reached and the degree of cooking is measured manually, either with a saccharometer (also called a syrup hydrometer), which measures the density, or with a sugar (candy) thermometer, graduated up to 200°C (392°F).

■ **The different stages of cooking sugar**
Definitions of stages and temperatures vary slightly. Specialist chefs adjust the cooking for delicate procedures according to the precise results required and their experience of handling the syrup. The following are typical stages and temperatures.

- COATED 100°C (212°F) Absolutely translucent syrup about to come to the boil. When a skimmer is dipped in it and withdrawn immediately, the syrup coats its surface. It is used for fruits in syrup.
- SMALL THREAD OR SMALL GLOSS 103–105°C (217–221°F) Professional chefs test the consistency of this sugar by plunging the fingers first in cold water, then quickly in the sugar syrup, which has become thicker; on parting the fingers carefully, short threads will form, about 3 mm (⅛ in) wide, which break easily. It is used for almond paste.
- LARGE THREAD OR LARGE GLOSS 106–110°C (223–230°F) The thread obtained between the fingers is now stronger and about 5 mm (¼ in) wide. This syrup is used in recipes requiring 'sugar syrup' (without any further qualification) – for butter creams and icings (frostings).

The stages of cooking sugar

name	degrees Centigrade	degrees Fahrenheit	density	manual assessment
coated	100	212	1.240	translucent coating
small thread or small gloss	103–105	217–221	1.251	2–3 mm (⅛ in) thread
large thread or large gloss	106–110	223–230	1.262	5 mm (¼ in) thread
small pearl	110–112	230–234	1.296	rounded bubbles
large pearl or soufflé	113–115	235–239	1.319	bubbles with skimmer, 2 cm (¾ in) thread
small or soft ball	116–118	241–244	1.344	soft ball
large or hard ball	121–124	250–255	1.357	harder ball
light (small or soft crack)	129–135	264–275		hard but sticky ball
hard crack	149–150	300–302		brittle but not sticky ball
light caramel	151–160	304–320		
brown or dark caramel (blackjack)	166–175	331–374		

Cooking sugar

1 *To check the cooking stage of the sugar, take a little from the saucepan, put it on the the end of the fingers, then dip it in a bowl of iced water.*

2 *Small thread: when pulled between the thumb and index finger, it makes a thread.*

3 *Small or soft ball: when put on the end of the finger, it makes a little flat pearl.*

4 *Large or hard ball: when pressed between the fingers, it makes a ball which does not subside any more.*

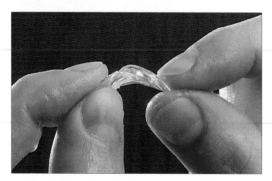

5 *Light, small or soft crack: when pressed between the fingers, it remains supple.*

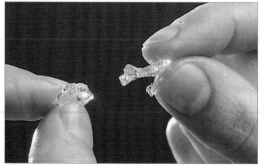

6 *Hard crack: it breaks easily between the fingers.*

• SMALL PEARL 110–112°C (230–234°F) A few minutes after the large thread stage, round bubbles form on the surface of the syrup; when a little is collected on a spoon and taken between the fingers, it forms a wide solid thread. It is used in jams and *torrone* (a type of nougat).
• LARGE PEARL OR SOUFFLÉ 113–115°C (235–239°F) The thread of sugar between the fingers may reach a width of 2 cm (¾ in); if it drops back, forming a twisted thread (at 1° higher) it is described as 'in a pigtail'; when one blows on the skimmer after plunging it into the syrup, bubbles are formed on the other side. It is used in jams, sugar-coated fruits, marrons glacés and icings.

• SMALL OR SOFT BALL 116–118°C (241–244°F) When a little syrup, which has obviously thickened, is removed with a spoon and plunged into a bowl of cold water, it will roll into a soft ball; if one blows on the skimmer dipped into the syrup, bubbles break loose and blow away. It is used in jams and jellies, soft caramels, nougats and Italian meringue.
• LARGE OR HARD BALL 121–124°C (250–255°F) After several boilings, the previous operation is repeated and a harder ball is obtained; if one blows through the skimmer, snowy flakes are formed. It is used in jams, sugar decorations, Italian meringue, fondant and caramels.

• LIGHT, SMALL, OR SOFT CRACK 129–135°C (264–275°F) A drop of syrup in cold water hardens immediately and will crack and stick to the teeth when chewed. (A saccharometer cannot be used above these higher temperatures.) It is used mainly for toffee.

• HARD CRACK 149–150°C (300–302°F) The drops of syrup in cold water become hard and brittle (like glass), but not sticky; the sugar acquires a pale straw-yellow colour at the edges of the saucepan; it must be watched carefully to avoid allowing it to turn into caramel, which would spoil it at this stage. It is used for boiled sweets and candies, spun sugar decorations, icings, sugar flowers and candy floss.

• LIGHT CARAMEL 151–160°C (304–320°F) The syrup, which now contains hardly any water, begins to change into barley sugar, then into caramel; yellow at first, it becomes golden and then brown. It is used in the caramelization of crème caramel, sweets and nougatine and for flavouring sweet dishes, puddings, cakes, biscuits (cookies) and icings.

• BROWN OR DARK CARAMEL (blackjack) 166–175°C (331–347°F) When it has turned brown, sugar loses its sweetening power; extra sugar is added to preparations with a basis of dark caramel. As the last stage of cooked sugar before carbonization (sugar burns and smokes at about 190°C, 375°F), brown caramel is used mainly for colouring sauces, cakes and stocks.

■ **Sugar for decorating** In addition, there are several methods for fashioning sugar, for making confectionery and decorating pastries and cakes.

• BROWN SUGAR Cooked to nearly 145–150°C (293–302°F), which may be coloured and is blown like glass.

• FASHIONED, DRAWN OR PULLED SUGAR Cooked so that it loses its transparency. It is then cooled, poured on to a greased marble slab or other cold surface, and then pulled, kneaded or moulded into flowers or sweets (candies) with a satinized finish. (These should be stored in an airtight container.)

• POURED SUGAR (SUCRE COULÉ) Cooked to cracking point, possibly coloured, then moulded into cups, pompons, little bells and other decorative shapes.

• ROCK SUGAR (SUCRE ROCHER) Cooked to nearly 125°C (257°F), emulsified with royal icing (coloured or otherwise), then used especially to give a rocky effect. It keeps well when exposed to the air.

• SPUN SUGAR (SUCRE FILÉ OR ANGELS' HAIR) Cooked to nearly 155°C (311°F). The pan is taken off the heat and left to cool for 1–2 minutes, then placed in a saucepan of hot water to keep the syrup hot. Two forks are dipped into the syrup and flicked quickly backwards and forwards above a lightly greased rolling pin; the threads obtained are then spread over a marble slab and flattened lightly with the blade of a knife in order to make 'ribbons', or collected and used decoratively like a veil. The spun sugar may be coloured. The strands should be used within an hour, otherwise they will melt.

These types of sugar are used in pâtisserie, mainly for constructing *pièces montées*: flowers and leaves, ribbons, knots and shells of drawn and coloured

Making spun sugar

1 *Cook the sugar until it forms threads. Remove from the heat and let the caramel thicken. Dip two forks in the mixture, holding them back to back. Pull the threads and move them rapidly to and fro over a rolling pin.*

2 *Lift the threads carefully with your fingers but quickly enough to prevent them getting sticky.*

3 *Roll these threads on to themselves and arrange on the confectionery to form a veil.*

sugar; flowers of fashioned or pulled sugar (rolled out into thin sheets); moiré ribbons (in strips shaped over a spirit lamp and flattened by hand on a board); various types of baskets of plaited sugar (sugar spun into the shape of small cords, plaited and cooled); objects made of cut, compacted or pressed sugar (moistened and moulded, then dried out in a closed container); and plumes of spun sugar. Coloured sugars are made from granulated or coarse caster (superfine) sugar, which is heated, then sprinkled with colourings soluble in alcohol.

For making biscuits (cookies), pastries and petits fours, sugar may be flavoured with the zest of citrus fruits, cinnamon, aniseed, clove, ginger or dried and pounded flower petals (orange blossom, thyme, lime, violet or rose).

RECIPES

aniseed sugar

Dry out 50 g (2 oz) aniseed wrapped in paper in a cool oven. Pound it finely in a mortar with 500 g (18 oz, 2¼ cups) caster (superfine) sugar. Sift through a sieve. Store in a tightly corked jar, in a dry place. Use as required.

cinnamon sugar

Chop 1 thin stick of cinnamon, mix with 1 tablespoon caster (superfine) sugar, then pound with another tablespoon of sugar. Sift through a fine sieve. Pound the cinnamon remaining in the sieve with another tablespoon of sugar and sift. Store as for aniseed sugar.

clove sugar

Proceed and store as for aniseed sugar, using 20 g (¾ oz) whole cloves and 500 g (18 oz, 3 cups) caster (superfine) sugar.

ginger sugar

Proceed and store as for aniseed sugar, using 25 g (1 oz) fresh root ginger and 500 g (18 oz, 2¼ cups) caster (superfine) sugar.

glacé icing

Mix some icing (confectioner's) sugar with a little water. Flavour it with coffee; melted chocolate; a liqueur; vanilla essence (extract); or finely grated orange, tangerine or lemon zest. The quantity of water should be increased if a softer icing (frosting) is desired. Use it to coat small and large cakes and biscuits (cookies).

orange sugar

Take some sweet oranges with fine skins. Rub sugar lumps over the zest, but take care not to reach the white pith immediately under the zest, since this is extremely bitter and would spoil the orange flavour. As the surface of the sugar becomes coloured, scrape off the layer of zest that becomes attached to it through repeated rubbing. Continue until all the zest is removed, then dry the sugar in a sealed container or in a cool oven. Crush the sugar lumps and sift through a fine sieve.

The procedure is the same for Seville (bitter) orange, lemon or tangerine sugars. Store as for aniseed sugar.

vanilla sugar

Split 50 g (2 oz) vanilla pods (beans) and chop them finely. Pound them finely in a mortar with 500 g (18 oz, 5 cups) lump (loaf) sugar and sift through a fine sieve. Store as for aniseed sugar.

additional recipe See *orange-blossom flower water*.

SUGAR BOWL A container for serving sugar at table. It may be made of porcelain, earthenware, glass or crystal, stainless steel, silver or silver plate and sometimes forms part of a tea or coffee service. Bowls for lump (loaf) sugar are accompanied by a pair of sugar tongs and often fitted with a lid. Prototypes of sugar bowls, called 'sugar pots', appeared in the 18th century. Caster (superfine) sugar can be served in a sugar bowl with a small ladle, but a sugar sprinkler (dredger) is more practical.

SUGAR CANE A plant, originating in Indonesia, widely cultivated in tropical and subtropical regions for its sugar-rich stems, which contain 14% sucrose. References to 'an Indian reed with juice sweeter than honey' occur in Roman literature; however, widespread cultivation of sugar cane did not develop until after the discovery of America, where it was planted on a large scale.

A cane known as 'eating cane' is grown by the local people, who remove the husk and chew it to extract the sweet juice.

Industrial cane juice, obtained by crushing the stems, is used to make sugar. It also ferments spontaneously and can be distilled to produce various spirits, particularly rums.

SUGAR DREDGER A small cylindrical container with a screw top pierced with small holes, used for sprinkling icing or caster (confectioner's or superfine) sugar over the top of cakes, waffles and desserts, or dishes to be caramelized.

SUGARED ALMONDS See *dragée, praline*.

SUGAR SNAP PEA A type of pea similar to but distinct from the mange-tout (snow pea), in that the pod is similarly wholly edible but is lumpy rather than flat because the peas inside have swollen and matured. Sugar snap peas actually resemble normal garden peas in appearance when harvested and are therefore often sold labelled as 'edible podded'. Sugar snap peas are thicker than snow peas and can be broken or snapped like green beans. They can be stored in the refrigerator for a few days and are prepared by topping and tailing; some varieties have strings that need removing. Like mange-tout, sugar snap peas should be served raw or only briefly cooked in order to retain their crisp texture.

SUISSE A traditional pastry of Valence (from the Drôme region of France) in the shape of a little man, made of sweetened brioche dough flavoured with orange. The original suisse was said to have been modelled on the Emperor Napoleon, whose legendary hat was, over the years, confused with the cocked hats of the Swiss Guard at the Vatican. However, a different explanation exists: 'As a prisoner of the republican army, Pope Pius VI . . . came to end his days at Valence. It was the picturesque costume of the soldiers of his Swiss Guard (designed, it is said, by Michelangelo), soon a familiar sight to the inhabitants of Valence, which inspired an astute pastrycook to make little men from crisp pastry flavoured with orange, to which he gave the name of *suisses*, which they have kept to this day.' (Ned Rival, *Traditions pâtissières de nos provinces*.)

Suisses were formerly baked as a speciality for Palm Sunday, but are now sold all the year round.

SUKIYAKI A typically Japanese dish, of the type described as *nabemono* (cooked directly on the table). Its origin goes back to the era when religion banned the consumption of meat. In country districts, however, the peasants used to cut birds and game into fine strips and grill them secretly out in the fields (*sukiyaki* means literally 'grilled on a ploughshare').

Nowadays, sukiyaki usually consists of thin slices of beef, chopped vegetables, vermicelli or small noodles and tofu, sautéed in a copper pan over a table hotplate, then dipped in raw egg just before being eaten. Pork, chicken and fish are also prepared in this way. In Japan, each guest serves himself directly from the pan, as the cooking proceeds.

RECIPE

sukiyaki
Before proceeding with the cooking, which is done in the course of the meal, prepare the ingredients: 450 g (1 lb) lean beef (fillet or sirloin), cut into very fine strips; 250 g (9 oz) shirataki (vermicelli made with starch), dipped in boiling water and drained (this may be replaced by fresh small noodles); 100 g (4 oz, 1⅓ cups) thinly sliced mushrooms; 150 g (5 oz, 1 cup) canned bamboo shoots, drained and finely sliced; 4 large leeks, thinly sliced; 150 g (5 oz, ¾ cup) bean curd cut into small dice; 100 g (4 oz, 1½ cups) blanched shredded Chinese cabbage; and (optional) a few coarsely shredded spinach leaves.

Heat a large heavy-based pan on a table hotplate, over a brisk flame, and grease it lightly with a piece of beef fat, which should be removed before cooking begins. Place one-third of the strips of meat in the pan, heat through, then add 60 ml (2 fl oz, ¼ cup) soy sauce and 2 tablespoons sugar; turn over the meat, cook for 1–2 minutes, then push towards the edge of the pan. Next, add one-third of the vegetables, together with some shirataki and bean curd, and sprinkle with 60 ml (2 fl oz, ¼ cup) sake; leave to cook for 4–5 minutes. Distribute the vegetables and meat between the plates (the proportions given are for 4), and repeat the operation until the ingredients are used up.

Sukiyaki is eaten with chopsticks: each mouthful is dipped in raw beaten egg before being eaten; each guest breaks an egg into a small bowl for this purpose. Sukiyaki is served with plain boiled rice.

SULTANAS Type of dried fruit. Sultanas are dried grapes, lighter in colour and flavour than raisins, and

seedless. Sultanas, also referred to as sultana raisins or golden raisins, are tender, delicate and very sweet. Used in baking, in sweet dishes and in some savoury cooking in the same way as raisins. See *dried vine fruits*.

SULTANE, À LA A term describing various preparations characterized by pistachio nuts, either in the form of a flavoured butter to finish a chicken velouté or to accompany fish, or chopped, or used as a flavouring for ice cream or for fruit-based desserts (apricots, pears and peaches). The sultane garnish, for suprêmes of chicken served on a chicken forcemeat, consists of small tartlets filled with truffle purée and studded with peeled pistachio halves. There is, however, another sultane garnish, for large cuts of meat, which does not contain pistachio nuts: it consists of duchess potatoes cut into the shape of Islamic crescents (to which it owes its name) with a julienne of stewed red cabbage.

SUMAC Also known as sumach or shoomak. A shrub originating in Turkey, certain varieties of which are cultivated in southern Italy and in Sicily. Its fleshy petals and small berries are dried and reduced to purple powder, which has an acid taste and is very popular in Middle Eastern cookery. Mixed with water, it can be used in the same way as lemon juice, particularly in preparations of tomatoes and onions, chicken forcemeats, marinades of fish and dishes with a lentil base.

Varieties of sumac cultivated in Britain are ornamental and not used in cookery. The dried and ground leaves are also used in tanning and dyeing.

SUMMER PUDDING A British pudding or dessert of mixed summer fruit moulded in a pudding basin lined with overlapping slices of bread. The dish is said to have originated in spas and nursing homes, where it was served to patients as an alternative to heavy puddings made with pastry, and it was known as 'hydropathic' pudding. Before bread was dosed with additives to prevent it from drying out, and the home freezer was commonplace, summer pudding was a popular dish for using up day-old or slightly stale bread and a glut of summer fruit. It is still a popular, fabulous dessert, and it has the advantage of being light but full of flavour.

RECIPE

summer pudding
Cook some redcurrants and blackcurrants with sugar until their juice runs and they are just tender. Add a mixture of strawberries (halving or quartering any that are large) and raspberries; blackberries can be added for an autumn pudding, when available. Taste the fruit mixture and add enough caster (superfine) sugar to sweeten it and create a generous amount of syrup.

Line a deep basin (bowl) with medium-thick slices of bread, trimmed of crusts, overlapping them evenly. Place a neat slice in the bottom of the bowl first, so that it will look neat when the pudding is turned out. Fill with the fruit mixture, pressing it down well, then cover with bread slices. Stand the basin in a shallow dish and cover the top with a saucer or plate. Place a heavy weight on top to press the pudding and chill overnight. (The shallow dish will catch any juice that seeps from the pudding.) Reserve any leftover fruit juices to spoon over the pudding before it is served.

Ease a knife between the pudding and the basin before inverting it on to a serving dish. Spoon any reserved juices over the top, especially if there are any white patches of bread, and serve at once, with clotted cream or whipped cream.

SUMPTUARY LAWS Government regulations issued to keep down expenses in banquets and also designed to control personal extravagance. In ancient Rome, the sumptuary laws forbade the consumption of very young animals and the slaughter of certain species. They also put a stop to ostentatious displays of luxury, and once even decreed that everyone should eat with their doors wide open so that the laws could be enforced. This type of controlling legislation was also introduced during the *Ancien Régime* in France (pre-1789), when it was extended to customs and traditions, notably to wedding feasts: 'To put an end to ruinous extravagance . . . members of the upper classes shall no longer be allowed to serve more than eight courses at table; these will include the entrée, entremets and set pieces; as for wedding feasts, the number of dishes will henceforth be restricted to a maximum of six.'

SUNDAE A dessert that originated in the United States, consisting of ice cream and fruit coated with jam or syrup and topped with nuts, confectionery and cream. Originally, it was reserved for the family meal on Sundays: at the end of the 19th century, North America was fairly puritanical and the consumption of sweets and delicacies was still frowned upon. But the fashion for ice-creams, encouraged by the first manually operated ice-cream freezers, was increasing and gradually the nickname 'sundae' was given to the traditional ice which could be served on Sundays 'without offending God'. Today, there is a wide variety of sundaes.

Henri Troyat, in *La Case de l'oncle Sam*, describes it thus: '. . . I shall remember that sundae all my life. In a sumptuous confectioner's shop, light, airy, full of fragrance, we were served with a mountain of coffee ice cream, sprinkled with cream and scattered with walnuts, honey, peanuts and various fruits. When I carried the first spoonful to my mouth . . . my taste buds experienced a violent ecstasy. A whole opera of sensation rolled off my tongue . . .'

(See *coupe* for recipes for sundaes.)

SUNFLOWER An annual plant, originally from Mexico and Peru, also known as helianthus. Nowadays, it is widely cultivated both for ornament and for its seeds, from which an oil is extracted. Sun-

flower is a good all-purpose oil for cooking as well as for use in salad dressings and for making mayonnaise. Sunflower seeds can be nibbled, raw or roasted as a snack, and are an excellent source of energy.

SUPERSTITIONS OF THE TABLE There have always been superstitions associated with eating. Some have a rational explanation; others remain a mystery.

Spilt salt is supposed to bring bad luck. The origins of this superstition go back to the times when it was very expensive (and therefore not to be wasted). In addition, salt has been a symbol of friendship and welcome from the earliest times: to offer salt and bread remains a traditional gesture of greeting in a number of countries. On the other hand, the act of throwing a pinch of salt over one's shoulder to ward off bad luck arises purely from superstition; as Léon de Fos wrote: 'Upon my faith, the essential thing is for no salt to be dropped into the stewed fruit or custard!'

Crossed knives, another bringer of bad luck, evoke both the cross on which St Andrew was crucified and the murderous gesture of crossing swords with an enemy.

Ought one to break the shell of an egg after eating the contents? This custom has its roots in the past; it is referred to by ancient and modern writers. The Romans attached great importance to it. The egg was regarded as an emblem of nature, a substance that was both mysterious and sacred. People were convinced that magicians used eggs in their incantations, emptying them and drawing magic characters from inside the shell. These had the power to cause much harm. One crushed the shell to destroy the evil spell. Occasionally it was enough to pierce it with a knife, or to rap it three times.

Why will you marry within the year (or, if you are already married, why will you have a daughter) if the last drop of a bottle of wine is poured into your glass? This has been seen as an allusion to the poverty that befalls the married man, or the one who has too many daughters to marry off and provide with dowries. On the other hand, wine spilt over the table is an omen of good luck, in memory of the ancient libations.

The presence of 13 people at table is regarded as unlucky because of its association with the Last Supper, where the 13 participants included Judas Iscariot, who betrayed his master and hanged himself. This superstition was shrugged off by Grimod de La Reynière, who said that it is dangerous to be 13 at table only if the dinner is prepared for 12.

There are various popular superstitions attached to the food itself. Cabbage is not supposed to be eaten on St Stephen's Day, because the saint, according to the legend, hid in a cabbage field to try and escape from his persecutors. Melon was said to cause fever in autumn, and jams (preserves) were supposed to ferment when the fruit trees begin to blossom. The custom of throwing handfuls of rice over newly married couples as they come out of the church is supposed to symbolize abundance and prosperity.

SUPPER A light meal taken in the evening. Originally the only evening meal (now called dinner), supper usually consisted of soup (hence the name) and was eaten relatively early. The fashion for supper as an intimate late dinner became established in French high society in the 18th century. Saint-Simon recalls the famous suppers of the Regent hotel: 'For small suppers, dishes were prepared in kitchens specially set up on the same floor, using utensils made of silver. The roués often gave the cooks a hand.' Rich and extravagant dishes were prepared, including marinated wild boar kidneys, oysters with cream, followed by cakes, tarts, salads and entremets (pig's trotters Sainte-Menehould, peas with poached eggs, apples *à la chinoise*).

Until the middle of the 19th century, supper was the essential conclusion of any successful high-society evening. At a ball, the orchestra gave the signal for supper by means of a fanfare. Gradually, however, the supper was abandoned (one reason was the expense). It was sometimes replaced by buffets or refreshments brought on trays, and sometimes, very late in the evening, by a punch and pastries. At dawn, the guests were revived with tea, broth, chocolate, coffee, sandwiches and wines. However, private households continued to hold quiet suppers: 'When only a chosen few are left in the drawing room, the master of the house gathers them together quietly around a table concealed in some cosy nook, and there they see in the day, chatting about the events of the past night. Wit and appetite normally find their best openings in these private suppers, which have a certain smack of the forbidden fruit' (E. Briffault, *Paris à table*). The supper vogue also became established with restaurateurs of the time, especially those who had private rooms.

SUPRÊME The breast and wing of a chicken or game bird; the term is also used for a fine fillet of fish (sole or brill, for example). Suprêmes of chicken or game (traditionally garnished with truffles, a delicate and stylish preparation, hence their name) are usually cooked rapidly: they may be brushed with butter, sprinkled with lemon juice and baked quickly in the oven in a covered casserole or wrapped in foil, or poached in a very little liquid (without boiling), or browned quickly in butter, or coated with breadcrumbs and fried or grilled (broiled).

Suprêmes are usually served with fresh green vegetables bound with butter or cream, but the classic garnishes for fried or poached chicken can also be used. The accompanying sauce is white or brown, depending on the method of cooking and the garnish. Fillets of turkey and duck can be cooked in the same way.

Suprêmes of fish are generally poached and served with a garnish and a white wine, shrimp, Nantua, américaine or normande sauce.

The term is also applied to preparations of luxury foods (suprêmes of foie gras, for example). Suprême sauce, which accompanies poached and fried poultry, is a reduced velouté mixed with chicken stock and fresh cream, sometimes finished with mushroom essence and lemon juice.

RECIPES

preparing suprêmes
Pull the leg of the bird away from the body; slice down to where the thigh joins the carcass. Cut through the joint and remove the whole leg. Repeat with the other leg and set both legs aside for use in another recipe. Separate the flesh on either side of the breastbone, cutting down towards the wing joints. Then sever the joints of the wings from the body, without separating them from the breast meat. Finally, cut through each wing at the second joint to remove the pinion (wing tip). Carefully ease off the skin.

garnishes for suprêmes of chicken
Prepare the suprêmes *à blanc* or *à brun*. The following garnishes can be used: diced aubergines (eggplants) sautéed in butter, braised lettuce or chicory (endive), pieces of cucumber slowly cooked in butter, spinach in butter or gravy, artichoke hearts slowly cooked or sautéed in butter, French (green) beans or macédoine of vegetables in butter, peas *à la française*, asparagus tips in butter or cream, or a vegetable purée.

suprême sauce
Prepare a velouté with a white roux, comprising 40 g (1½ oz, 3 tablespoons) butter and 40 g (1½ oz, 6 tablespoons) plain (all-purpose) flour and 750 ml (1¼ pints, 3¼ cups) well-seasoned and well-reduced chicken consommé. Add 500 ml (17 fl oz, 2 cups) white chicken stock and reduce it by at least half. Add 300 ml (½ pint, 1¼ cups) crème fraîche and reduce the sauce to about 600 ml (1 pint, 2½ cups), at which point it should coat the spoon. Remove from the heat and stir in 50 g (2 oz, ¼ cup) butter. Strain through a very fine sieve and keep warm in a bain marie until ready to use.

suprêmes of chicken à blanc
Season the suprêmes with salt and pepper, brush with clarified butter, arrange in a buttered casserole and sprinkle with a little lemon juice. Cover the casserole and cook in a preheated oven at 220°C (425°F, gas 7) for about 15 minutes. Drain the suprêmes and arrange them on a serving dish with the chosen garnish.

suprêmes of chicken à brun
Season the suprêmes with salt and pepper, coat them in flour and cook them in clarified butter in a sauté pan until golden on both sides. Arrange on a serving dish with the chosen garnish.

suprêmes of chicken à l'anglaise

Season the suprêmes with salt and pepper, then coat them with beaten egg and breadcrumbs. Cook in clarified butter in a sauté pan until golden and cooked through. Arrange on a bed of Anna potatoes, surround with grilled (broiled) tomatoes and garnish each suprême with a grilled rasher (slice) of bacon.

suprêmes of chicken à la périgourdine

Cook some suprêmes *à brun* and arrange them on a serving dish. On each suprême place a slice of foie gras fried quickly in butter and a thin slice of truffle. Coat with Périgueux sauce.

suprêmes of chicken with mushrooms

Cook some suprêmes *à blanc*. Garnish them with mushrooms that have been slowly cooked in butter and coat them with suprême sauce (see above) mixed with the pan juices.

Alternatively, cook the suprêmes *à brun*, garnish with sautéed mushrooms and coat with Madeira sauce or demi-glace flavoured with Madeira.

suprême of chicken with Sauternes and preserved lemon ♦

Season 4 prepared chicken suprêmes. Use a flame-proof casserole in which the suprêmes will fit snugly, overlapping slightly if necessary. Cook the suprêmes gently in a mixture of butter and olive oil, skin-side down, until browned. Turn the suprêmes over and half cover the casserole, then continue to cook gently until the chicken is cooked through.

Meanwhile, trim and clean 500 g (18 oz) chanterelles and sweat them gently in a covered frying pan. Drain and set aside. Finely chop 3 shallots. Remove the chicken from the pan. Degrease the juices and stir in half the shallots. Add 200 ml (7 fl oz, ¾ cup) Sauternes and reduce by half. Stir in 300 ml (½ pint, 1¼ cups) single (light) cream and a pinch of mignonette – a mixture of ground black and white pepper – then reduce for 2 minutes. Sieve the sauce.

Return the sauce to the pan and stir in a dash of lemon juice with the finely diced zest of 1 preserved lemon. Then replace the chicken and reheat thoroughly but gently, without boiling. In a separate pan, cook the remaining shallot in butter with the chanterelles. Season with salt and pepper. Arrange the suprêmes on plates, partly slicing the meat, if liked, with their sauce. Add the chanterelles and garnish with a little shredded lemon zest and parsley.

other recipes See *ambassadeur, chicken, duck, financière, florentine, hollandaise sauce.*

SURATI An Indian cheese made from buffalo milk, sometimes also from cow's milk, with a soft whitish centre and a slightly sour yet salty flavour. It is matured and sold in its whey in large terracotta containers. It takes its name from the city of Surat, where it is manufactured.

SURPRISE, EN A term describing certain dishes that are presented in such a way as to give a false impression of their flavour or consistency, or which are revealed, when they are eaten, as a delightful surprise. The most obvious example of such a dish is baked Alaska, in which ice cream is hidden inside a meringue that has been placed for a short time in a hot oven.

The term *en surprise* is generally given to fruits that have been scooped out and filled with ice cream or sorbet and frozen, or filled with a soufflé, mousse or other preparation and chilled. Good examples are oranges, tangerines, melons and pineapples, all of which can have their 'lids' replaced to hide what is inside. Sugar-coated fruits are also described as *en surprise*.

In one of his *Lettres gourmandes* to the playwright Émile de Najac, Charles Monselet mentions eggs *en surprise*, for which he gives an ancient recipe from the royal château of Marly: 'Take 12 fine eggs; in each one, make two small holes at the ends. Pass a straw through one of these holes to burst the yolk, then empty the eggs by blowing through one of the ends. Rinse the shells in water, drain them and dry in the open air. Fill up one of the holes in each egg with a mixture of flour and egg yolk and leave to dry, then fill the eggs through the remaining hole with chocolate custard cream mixture, coffee custard cream mixture or orange-blossom custard cream mixture (made with the blown-out egg); for this purpose, use a very small funnel. Stop up the holes of the eggshells with the flour and egg yolk mixture and cook them in plenty of hot water (which should not be allowed to boil) to set the custard cream. Remove the "plugs" from the two ends of the eggs, wipe the eggs and serve them under a folded napkin as a dessert.'

RECIPE

pineapple en surprise

Cut the top off a choice pineapple close to the leaves and hollow it out carefully, without splitting the skin. Cut the pulp into dice and macerate it with 100 g (4 oz, ½ cup) caster (superfine) sugar and 2 tablespoons rum for 2 hours.

Boil 600 ml (1 pint, 2½ cups) milk in a saucepan with a vanilla pod (bean) split in two. In a mixing bowl, beat 1 whole egg with 3 yolks and 100 g (4 oz, ½ cup) caster sugar; when the mixture is white and thick, blend in 50 g (2 oz, ½ cup) plain (all-purpose) flour to obtain a very smooth paste. Pour the boiling milk over the paste fairly slowly to avoid cooking the yolks, whisking rapidly all the time. Return the mixture to the pan, place over a gentle heat and stir until the cream has thickened. Then remove from the heat and add the juice in which the pineapple has been macerated.

Suprême of chicken with Sauternes and preserved lemon.

Cool this cream in the refrigerator, then mix it gently with the diced pineapple, 3 egg whites whisked to very stiff peaks, and 100 ml (4 fl oz, 7 tablespoons) crème fraîche. Fill the pineapple with this preparation, replace its top and refrigerate until ready to serve.

other recipes See *chartreuse, melon, tangerine, walnut.*

SUSHI Japanese speciality comprising rice mixed with a dressing when freshly cooked. A round-grain rice that remains whole when cooked but becomes slightly sticky is used. The moist grains barely cling together so that the mixture can be shaped in a mould or by rolling. Additional ingredients include fresh or cooked raw fish or seafood or vegetables. Layers of sushi rice and prepared ingredients are pressed in a mould to make rice 'cakes' or wrapped in a sheet of nori seaweed and served in slices. Dipping sauce and pickled ginger are typical accompaniments.

Sushi can also be a mixture of prepared rice with other ingredients, served in bowls, or the mixture can be rolled into small cones of nori by diners just before it is eaten.

SUZETTE A type of sweet pancake flavoured with tangerine and coated with a tangerine-flavoured sauce. In the recipe given by Escoffier, tangerine juice and Curaçao are used to flavour both the pancake batter and the melted butter and sugar (to which tangerine zest has been added) used to mask the pancakes.

Henri Charpentier, who was Rockefeller's cook in the United States, falsely claimed to have invented crêpes Suzette in 1896, at the Café de Paris in Monte Carlo, as a compliment to the Prince of Wales and his companion whose first name was Suzette; in actual fact, at that date Charpentier was not old enough to be the head waiter serving the prince. Back in the United States he introduced the fashion for flamed crêpes Suzette. Elsewhere, Léon Daudet, in *Paris vécu* (1929), speaks of pancakes called Suzette which in about 1898 were one of the specialities of Marie's Restaurant (famous for its oeufs Toupinel and its entrecôte bordelaise): they were made with jam and flavoured with brandy 'which improved them greatly'.

RECIPE

Crêpes Suzette ◆
Prepare a crêpe batter with 250 g (9 oz, 2¼ cups) plain (all-purpose) flour, 3 whole eggs, 250 ml (8 fl oz, 1 cup) milk and a pinch of salt. Add the juice of 1 tangerine, 1 tablespoon Curaçao and 2 tablespoons olive oil. Leave to stand for 2 hours at room temperature. Work 50 g (2 oz, ¼ cup) butter with the juice and grated zest of 1 tangerine, 1 tablespoon Curaçao and 4 tablespoons caster (superfine) sugar.

Make some thin crêpes in a heavy-based frying pan (never washed, but wiped each time with clean paper towels). Coat them with a little of the tangerine butter, fold them in four, return them one by one to the frying pan and heat them. Arrange them in a warm dish, slightly overlapping, to serve.

SWAN A large, aquatic, web-footed bird with oily leathery flesh, now regarded purely as an ornamental bird. From the Middle Ages to the Renaissance, however, it ranked with the peacock in providing a sumptuous roast at banquets. On some occasions, the bird was carefully plucked and roasted on a spit, then dressed in its feathers and brought ceremoniously to the table with a piece of blazing camphor or wick in its beak.

SWEAT To cook vegetables (generally cut up small) in their own juices in a covered pan over a gentle heat, so that they become soft (but not brown). A little fat is usually used to begin the cooking process or more can be added for a rich result. The pan is covered during cooking, so the ingredients retain a certain amount of their natural moisture. Sweating is a popular alternative to sautéing or frying as a low-fat cooking method.

SWEDE (RUTABAGA) A root vegetable with orange-yellow flesh. Related to the turnip and one of the brassicas, the swede is also known as the Swedish turnip. Originally from Scandinavia (where it is called *rotabagge*), it can be cooked in the same way as potatoes or turnips (baked, roasted, boiled and mashed). It is not as watery as turnip and it has a distinctive flavour similar to other brassicas. Swede is often mashed with potatoes and/or carrots, used in soups or stews. It is sometimes referred to as a turnip.

SWEET Term describing a sugary taste. The sweet taste that man craves was provided by the various fruit sugars and honey until the use of sugar (extracted from sugar cane or sugar beet) became widespread. In cooking, sweetness is provided by substances giving a sweet character to the dish.

SWEET AND SOUR The association of two contrasting flavours, acid and sweet, in the same dish is a very old culinary practice. Honey with vinegar and verjuice were among the basic ingredients of the seasonings used in Roman times and in medieval cooking, with its sauces and ragoûts. Many meat, game or fish (particularly river fish) dishes, marinated or boiled in wine or beer, have dried fruit in the sauce, or the jelly of red berries as an accompaniment: this is one of the distinguishing features of Russian, Scandinavian, German, Alsatian, Jewish and Flemish cooking. Fruits (such as grapes, quinces,

Crêpes Suzette.

plums, cherries and cranberries) preserved in vinegar or acetomel, a syrupy mixture of honey and vinegar whose name is derived from the Latin *acetum* (vinegar) and *mel* (honey), are a typical example of the sweet-and-sour combination; there is a large range, too, of cooked condiments – chutneys, sweet mustards, achars – some of which are of exotic origin (from India and the West Indies) and were introduced into Europe by British colonialists. It is undoubtedly in China, however, that sweet-and-sour cooking is at its finest, particularly for pork and duck.

RECIPE

sweet-and-sour sauce

Soak 1 tablespoon raisins in water. Using a small heavy-based saucepan, cook 3 lumps of sugar moistened with 2 tablespoons vinegar until they caramelize slightly. Add 150 ml (¼ pint, ⅔ cup) dry white wine and 2 teaspoons chopped shallots; cook briskly until the liquid has evaporated. Add 250 ml (8 fl oz, 1 cup) demi-glace* sauce and boil for a few moments. Press the sauce through a fine sieve, then return to the pan and slowly bring to the boil. Drain the raisins and add them to the sauce with 2 teaspoons capers. This sauce can be served with poultry or roast pork.

SWEETBREAD The culinary term for the thymus gland (in the throat) and the pancreas (near the stomach) in calves, lambs and pigs, although the latter are not much used. Thymus sweetbreads are elongated and irregular in shape; pancreas sweetbreads are larger and rounded. Lambs' and calves' sweetbreads are cooked in the same way, but the latter are considered to be superior; they can be used in fillings and ragoûts for moulds and vol-au-vent. Sweetbreads need to be blanched, refreshed and cooled before use; they can then be fried, braised, roasted, grilled (broiled), poached, cooked *au gratin* or on skewers.

RECIPES

preparing lambs' or calves' sweetbreads

Soak the sweetbreads in cold water until they become white, changing the water from time to time until it remains clear (at least 5 hours). Put them into a saucepan with cold salted water to cover and bring them slowly to the boil. At the first sign of boiling, remove and drain the sweetbreads and refresh them under cold running water. Then drain and wipe dry, remove the skin and fibres and press them between 2 cloths under a board with a weight on top. Leave for 1 hour.

Depending on the recipe chosen, they can be studded with thin pieces of bacon, truffle, tongue or ham.

fried sweetbreads

Blanch, cool and press some sweetbreads. Cut each one into 3 or 4 slices and season with salt and pep-

per. Dip each slice in flour and fry in butter until brown. Alternatively, clean the sweetbreads well and dry them thoroughly. Put them into a sauté pan with some melted butter, add salt and pepper to taste, cover the pan and let them cook gently for 30–35 minutes.

Serve fried sweetbreads sprinkled with chopped parsley on top of Anna potatoes, with a thick béarnaise sauce served separately.

grilled sweetbreads

Blanch, cool and press some sweetbreads. Brush them with oil or clarified butter, season with pepper and grill (broil) slowly, either whole or sliced, under a moderate heat. Serve with a green salad; with a seasonal vegetable, steamed and tossed in fresh butter; or with a purée of carrots, peas or turnips.

poached sweetbreads

Blanch, cool and press some sweetbreads, put them into a sauté pan, barely cover them with white stock and let them simmer very gently for 35–40 minutes, according to their thickness. Drain them and keep hot. Reduce the cooking liquid and pour this over the sweetbreads. Serve with buttered green beans, young broad (fava) beans, or a macédoine of spring vegetables.

roast sweetbreads

Blanch, cool and press some sweetbreads, and lard them if wished. Season with salt and pepper and wrap each one in a small piece of pig's caul (caul fat). Thread them on to a skewer and roast in a preheated oven at 220°C (425°F, gas 7) for about 30 minutes.

sweetbread fritters

Blanch, cool and press some sweetbreads. Cut into slices and dip them first in flour, then in a light fritter batter, and deep-fry at 180°C (350°F) until golden brown on both sides. Drain the fritters on paper towels. Serve with quarters of lemon and either a well-reduced tomato fondue or a herb mayonnaise.

sweetbreads braised in white stock

Blanch, cool and press some sweetbreads. (They may be larded, studded or left plain, depending on the recipe.) Put some bacon rinds and some finely sliced onions and carrots into a buttered flameproof casserole and lay the sweetbreads on top. Add salt and pepper and a bouquet garni. Cover the casserole and begin the cooking slowly over a gentle heat. Then moisten with a few tablespoons of white stock. Transfer the covered casserole to a preheated oven at 220°C (425°F, gas 7) and continue the cooking for 25–30 minutes, basting frequently with the stock. When the sweetbreads are cooked, they can be glazed very lightly by removing the lid and leaving the casserole in the oven for a further 5–6 minutes, basting with the fat in the stock. Serve with one of the following garnishes: anversoise, Nantua, princesse or Régence.

sweetbreads in breadcrumbs

Blanch, cool and press some sweetbreads. Cut them into slices, dip in beaten egg and then in breadcrumbs, and sauté them in butter. Alternatively, after dipping them in beaten egg, roll them in a mixture of minced (ground) ham and mushrooms, or in a mirepoix or in grated Parmesan cheese. When cooked, serve with braised chicory (endive) or sweetcorn.

sweetbreads with grapes

Prepare either I large sweetbread or 2 medium ones, and lard them with 100 g (4 oz, ½ cup) strips of pork fat. Heat 50 g (2 oz, ¼ cup) butter in a saucepan and cook the sweetbreads gently until they are golden brown. Add 8 small onions, salt, pepper, I bouquet garni and 4 chopped mushrooms. Cover the pan and simmer until the sweetbreads are cooked (about 20 minutes). Arrange them in a dish and keep hot.

Deglaze the pan with 100 ml (4 fl oz, 7 tablespoons) fresh grape juice and add some white Muscat grapes and 4 tablespoons Madeira. Work I tablespoon flour with 50 g (2 oz, ¼ cup) butter to a smooth paste or beurre manié and use the mixture to thicken the sauce.

terrine of sweetbreads

Blanch and cool 4 sweetbreads. Stud them with slices of truffle and press them under a light weight for 24 hours. Brown a finely chopped mirepoix of onions, carrots, shallots and I garlic clove in some butter. Season the sweetbreads, then sauté them with the mirepoix, without allowing them to brown. Pour in 175 ml (6 fl oz, ¾ cup) white wine, 175 ml (6 fl oz, ¾ cup) Madeira and 6 tablespoons port. Add a bouquet garni and braise gently for 40 minutes. Take out the sweetbreads and reduce the cooking liquid by a quarter. Strain and set aside.

Make a fine forcemeat using 250 g (9 oz, I cup, firmly packed) minced (ground) fat pork, an equal quantity of minced noix of veal, 75 g (3 oz, ⅓ cup) minced ham, 100 ml (4 fl oz, 7 tablespoons) crème fraîche, I egg, I tablespoon foie gras, salt and pepper. Line a terrine with thin strips of bacon. Fill the dish with alternate layers of sweetbreads and forcemeat, covering each layer of forcemeat with very thin rindless bacon rashers (slices). Pour a little of the strained reduced cooking liquid on to each layer. Finish with a layer of forcemeat topped with bacon rashers.

Cover the terrine and cook gently in a bain marie in a preheated oven at 180°C (350°F, gas 4) for 1½ hours. Before it becomes completely cold, cover with port-flavoured aspic jelly. Chill for 1–2 days before serving.

other recipes See *feuilleté, financière, pâté.*

SWEETCORN See *maize (corn).*

SWEETEN To reduce the sharpness, tartness, bitterness, sourness, acidity or excessive seasoning in a dish by adding to it a little water, milk, cream or sugar, or by prolonging the cooking time considerably. A pinch of sugar will sweeten crushed tomatoes, and the acidity of a sauce may be lessened by first boiling up the wine that is added to the meat juices in the pan.

SWEETENER A chemical substance with a high sweetening power but no nutritional value and containing no calories. The best known are saccharin and aspartame. Sweeteners are used in the food industry, in sugar-free diets and by those aiming to reduce calorie intakes by using sweeteners instead of sugar, particularly in hot drinks.

SWEET LIME A small citrus fruit that is often confused with other varieties of lime, but which constitutes a separate species. It is spherical, 2.5–4 cm (1–1½ in) in diameter, greenish-yellow, strongly scented and produces a large quantity of juice. It is used for making sharp-tasting sauces in exotic cookery, notably Brazilian duck with rice, Peruvian ceviche, Indian saffron rice, Tunisian dried vegetable soup, and also certain Oriental salads, stews and grilled (broiled) fish dishes. Its grated zest is an ingredient in certain chutneys, and lime syrup is sprinkled on some pastries.

SWEET PEPPER See *pepper.*

SWEET POTATO An edible tuber originating in South America and gradually introduced to New Zealand, the Pacific islands, Europe, Africa and Asia. It has a reddish, violet or grey skin and a sweet and floury flesh, white, orange-yellow, pink or violet in colour, which is usually eaten cooked – as a vegetable, a garnish or as the basis for a dessert.

When bought, it should be really firm, with no bruises or smell. It is prepared like the ordinary potato (although unrelated), but is much sweeter. Sweet potatoes may be boiled, baked or puréed, cooked in their skins, in cream, as croquettes, in gratins and in soufflés. Caribbean cookery probably offers the most original recipes for them.

In the United States, the sweet potato is often wrongly referred to as a yam, which is a different plant.

RECIPES

sweet potato cake

Soak 150 g (5 oz, I cup) seedless raisins in some rum. Boil 5 unpeeled sweet potatoes in unsalted water. When they are cooked, peel them and purée finely in a blender or food processor. Blend I teaspoon vanilla-flavoured sugar and I tablespoon flour with the potato purée and beat the mixture hard. Soften with a little milk, then add 3 whole eggs, one by one, and finally I egg yolk. Whisk I egg white into stiff peaks and blend it with the purée to produce a smooth light mixture. Add the raisins and pour the mixture into a buttered charlotte mould. Place the mould in a bain marie, bring the water to the boil, then cook in a preheated oven at 200°C (400°F, gas 6) for about 40 minutes. Turn out on to a wire rack, leave to cool and serve with a custard cream.

sweet potatoes à l'impériale

Place equal quantities of sliced sweet potatoes, sliced dessert apples and thinly sliced bananas in a well-buttered gratin dish. Mix everything together well, add salt and sprinkle with paprika. Dot the surface with tiny pieces of butter and cook in a preheated oven at 150°C (300°F, gas 2) until tender.

This gratin is served as an accompaniment for meat, roast poultry or game; it may be coated with redcurrant jelly.

SWEETS (CANDIES) Items of confectionery based on sugar. Sugar is dissolved in water, then boiled, and goes through different stages from soft to hard in the crystallization process. This, together with various additional ingredients, determines the type of sweet produced. Typical of soft, or crystalline, sweets (smooth, creamy and easily chewed) are fondants and fudge; typical hard, non-crystalline sweets are toffees and caramels. Besides chocolates, other popular confections include boiled sweets, nougat, marshmallows, pastes and marzipan, crystallized (candied) fruits, fruit jellies, sugared almonds and liquorice. The principal raw materials used in the manufacture of sweets are sucrose, glucose syrup, milk, gum arabic, gelatine, nuts, vegetable fat, fruit, honey and butter. Artificial flavourings, acidulation and colourings also play a part.

In ancient times, confections of fruit and nuts candied in honey were prepared by the Arabs and the Chinese (similar sweets are still produced in the Middle East today). The ancient Egyptians, too, made such confections and offered them to their gods. Although the French word *bonbon* dates from 1604, sweets were actually made in Europe before this time, using fruit, honey or grain, flavoured with cinnamon. The true sweet appeared in Europe from the 12th and 13th century onwards, when sugar cane was brought back from the Orient by the Crusaders. However, the high cost of sugar in Europe initially made sugar confectionery a luxury available only to the wealthy. Almond and fruit pastes, apple sugar and marzipan were specialities in the 14th century. Sugared almonds and pralines date from the Renaissance period. In the 17th and 18th centuries, Parisian confectioner's shops became the meeting place of the bourgeois rich, and marrons glacés, pastilles, twists, crystallized fruits, lollipops and liqueur-filled sweets were sold; in 17th-century England and the American colonies, boiled sweets were particularly popular and remain so today.

With the discovery of sugar-beet juice and the advance of mechanical appliances, sweet-making developed rapidly into an industry during the early 19th century and the first factories were opened in Europe and in North America. Today, the manufacture of sweets is a large branch of the confectionery industry worldwide. Different types of sweets have their own traditions and specific origins – for example, Britain is known for its toffee, and Montélimar in France for its nougat. Eastern France specializes in sugared almonds, Turkish delight is popular in the Middle East and the Dutch passion for liquorice, which is available in many variations in the Netherlands and consumed in vast quantities, is well known.

With continuing technological advances, there is a growing move towards sugar-free confectionery, which relies on sweeteners and newly developed, blended natural ingredients.

■ **Boiled sweets** The standard method of manufacture consists of heating a mixture of sucrose and glucose, which is then flavoured and coloured. This is then cooled, and either shaped to make solid sweets or moulded for filled sweets.

Solid sweets, such as acid drops, caramels, barley sugars, lollipops and humbugs, are shaped between two cylinders, set in pill-shaped moulds or in a press. Rocks are sweets with relief patterns of flowers or fruits.

Filled sweets consist of an outside mould with a creamy or liquid centre. The filling may comprise fruit pulp, praline, coffee cream, liqueur or honey.

The flavour is a very important aspect of the quality of a sweet and accuracy is essential in this respect: a sweet with a 'pure fruit' centre contains only the pulp of the fruit indicated. If it is simply a 'fruit centre', it contains the pulp of several fruits and natural flavouring. If it has a 'fruit-flavoured' filling, then this is a syrup containing natural or concentrated flavouring.

SWIMMING CRAB A type of crab with paddle-shaped back legs that enable it to swim. The main family of swimming crabs, *Portunidae*, includes several edible species. The velvet swimming crab is a small brown crab particularly common on the shores of the Atlantic and the English Channel. It is covered with short fine hairs, which give it a velvety texture. When cooked in a court-bouillon, the flesh is full of flavour, although difficult to remove from the shell.

The blue crab is a North American swimming crab of great commercial importance. Blue crabs are harvested as 'hard-shell', 'peeler' (just prior to moulting) and 'soft-shell' (immediately after moulting). In Indo-Pacific waters, large edible species of swimming crabs include the blue swimmer crab, the mask crab and the mangrove, or mud, crab.

SWISS CHARD A variety of beet whose leaves and stalks are eaten as a vegetable. Swiss chard is also known as spinach beet. The leaves, which have prominent and broad tender white midribs, have a slightly less pronounced flavour than spinach and are prepared in the same way. The stalks are usually boiled or steamed.

Swiss chard often appears in regional French dishes, especially in Lyon, Provence and Corsica – tarts, stuffings and soups using the green leaves, and gratin dishes and garnishes using the stalks. Swiss chard tart is a speciality of Nice and is served as a dessert.

RECIPES

preparing Swiss chard
Remove the green parts of the leaves, then break the veins and leaf stalks (it is important not to cut them with a knife) and remove the stringy parts. Divide these into sections 5–7.5 cm (2–3 in) long and cook in salted water or, better still, in a white vegetable stock. Once drained, these sections are ready for use in various recipes. Wash the green parts, blanch for 5 minutes in boiling water (salted or unsalted), rinse in cold water, drain and pat dry.

Swiss chard au gratin
Prepare Swiss chard in béchamel sauce and pour into an ovenproof dish. Smooth the surface, sprinkle with grated cheese and melted butter, and brown at the hottest possible temperature in the oven or under the grill (broiler).

Swiss chard in béchamel sauce
Cook 800 g (1¾ lb) Swiss chard veins in a court-bouillon and drain. Place in a deep frying pan with 400 ml (14 fl oz, 1¾ cups) fairly liquid béchamel* sauce; cover and cook for about 5 minutes. Mix with 50 g (2 oz, ¼ cup) butter and serve in a vegetable dish.

Swiss chard in butter
Cook 1 kg (2¼ lb) Swiss chard veins thoroughly in salted water or white stock. Drain, place in a deep frying pan with 75 g (3 oz, 6 tablespoons) fresh butter, cover and cook gently for 15–20 minutes. Place in a vegetable dish, pour over the butter in which the chard was cooked and sprinkle with chopped parsley. Alternatively, the chards may be blanched for 5 minutes in salted water, drained and then cooked in a deep frying pan with 75 g (3 oz, 6 tablespoons) butter and 200 ml (7 fl oz, ¾ cup) water. Arrange in a vegetable dish and pour over the cooking liquid.

Swiss chard in cream
Boil 800 g (1¾ lb) Swiss chard veins in white stock and drain. Fry for 5 minutes in 25 g (1 oz, 2 tablespoons) butter. Moisten with 300 ml (½ pint, 1¼ cups) boiling double (heavy) cream and cook until the volume has reduced by half. Place in a vegetable dish and pour over the cooking liquid.

Swiss chard pie
Marinate 100 g (4 oz, ¾ cup) raisins in a little brandy. Make the pastry using 500 g (18 oz, 4½ cups) strong plain (bread) flour, a pinch of salt, 4 tablespoons sugar, 1 sachet easy-blend dried yeast (1 package active dry yeast), 1 egg yolk and 200 ml (7 fl oz, ¾ cup) oil. Mix the dough, adding a few teaspoons of very cold water, knead until smooth and leave to stand, covered, in a warm place until light and risen – about 1 hour.

Blanch 500 g (18 oz) Swiss chard leaves in salted water, dry very thoroughly and chop coarsely. Peel 2 cooking apples, slice thinly and sprinkle with lemon juice. Cut 2 dried figs into quarters; crumble 1 macaroon. Mix these ingredients (including the chopped chard leaves) with the raisins, 2 whole eggs, a little grated lemon zest, and about 40 g (1½ oz) pine kernels (nuts).

Grease an ovenproof flan dish, 28 cm (11 in) in diameter. Line with half the pastry, spread the filling over the pastry base and coat with 3 tablespoons redcurrant jelly. Cover with the remaining pastry and pinch the edges together to seal the pie. Place a small pastry funnel in the lid. Bake in a preheated oven at 200°C (400°F, gas 6) for 30–40 minutes. Dust with icing (confectioner's) sugar and serve hot or cold.

other recipes See *italienne, polonaise*.

SWISS ROLL (JELLY ROLL) A thin sponge cake, spread with jam (jelly) and rolled up. There are many variations on the plain sponge and filling, including cream fillings, chocolate-flavoured sponge with chocolate cream filling. Plain Swiss roll can be served as a cake or used in desserts, for example as a basis for British trifle or to line a charlotte mould. See *sponge cake*.

SWITZERLAND See *page 1174*.

SWORDFISH A very large game fish, 2–5 m (6–16 ft) long and weighing 100–500 kg (220–1102 lb), which is abundant in all warm seas. It has an elongated upper jaw, which is about three times the length of the lower jaw and resembles a sword. Its firm flesh is considered excellent and is similar to that of tuna. Swordfish is available fresh or frozen, and is best grilled (broiled) or barbecued.

SYLLABUB An English cream or dessert of sherry or wine with lemon, possibly with brandy, with whipped double (heavy) cream. Syllabub is served in a wineglass so that the liquid and cream separate, and the liquid is drunk or spooned through the cream. The name is obscure, most credibly derived from 'bubbly', and/or 'silly' meaning merry.

The recipe goes back at least to Tudor times, when it was made of new milk and cider, with the cows milked directly into an ale pot, to give a frothy (cappuccino) effect. This was also achieved in the kitchen by using a 'wooden cow'. An everlasting syllabub was allowed to stand for several days for the cream to rise and thicken. There are variations all over England; the Somerset version mixes port and

SWITZERLAND

Swiss cookery reflects the multinational origins of the country. The French-speaking cantons are familiar with the dishes of the Jura and Savoy, the German-speaking cantons share the German and Austrian traditions, while the cookery of Ticino (Tessin) is related to that of northern Italy. Grisons (Graubünden) has a relatively original cuisine, while central Switzerland boasts a number of ancient sweet-and-sour recipes. The common feature of all these regions is the charcuterie: an assortment of sausages of all types (especially smoked), salted or cured meats and bacon, which are used to garnish sauerkraut or Swiss potée – national dishes on a par with rösti, cheese fondue and raclette.

■ **Cheese** Switzerland produces some 150 cheeses, some of which are solely for local consumption. Among the best-known hard cheeses are Gruyère, Emmental, Sbrinz and cheeses à rebibes (for scraping into fine shavings); semi-hard ones include Tilsit, Vacherin de Fribourg, Appenzell and raclette cheeses; while the Mont d'Or Vacherin is outstanding among the soft varieties.

■ **Chocolate** Just as famous as Swiss cheese is Swiss chocolate, and the chocolate industry deserves its reputation for producing a vast range of fine bars, particularly of milk chocolate.

■ **Regional traditions** Although there is no typically Swiss cuisine, each of the 23 cantons (most of which are mentioned below in alphabetical order) has its own culinary traditions.

The pâtisserie of Basle is distinguished by the honey-rich, spicy *leckerli*, and the *brünsli*, little Christmas biscuits (cookies) made with almonds, hazelnuts and chocolate. Berne is famous for its *Bernerplatte*, an assortment of meats and charcuterie (served with sauerkraut in winter and French beans in summer) and also for its version of rösti; among Bernese pastries and confectionery are *leckerli* made with hazelnuts, honey and cinnamon, meringues (said to have been invented by a pastrycook from Meiringen), and a plaited loaf eaten throughout the country.

Specialities of Fribourg include Vacherin fondue served warm with potatoes; chalet soup, made of vegetables, wild herbs, pasta, cheese, milk, cream and butter; and *cuchaule*, a brioche spiced with saffron.

Geneva is the home of longeole, fresh sausage made from pork meat and rinds; *attriaux*, small sausages of pig's liver with herbs), cardoons with bone marrow or *au gratin*; and fillets of perch, fried or meunière. Veal *boudin blanc* (served with creamed potatoes, prunes and an onion sauce) and pear bread are specialities of Glarus. Grisons is well known for its cured meat, salt beef dried in the open air and pressed (similar to Italian *bresaola*); *capuns*, stuffed Swiss chard; ragoût of mutton with potatoes (very like Irish stew); and the famous walnut tart of the Engadine.

In the Swiss Jura, the feast of St Martin of Ajoie in November is the occasion for a meal that includes *grelatte* – aspic of pig's trotters (feet), tail, head and ears, with knuckle of ham – and a meat and leek pie. The area can also boast wild trout, mushroom stews, an unusual ragoût of mutton with milk, *floutes* made of potatoes moistened with noisette butter and all kinds of tarts.

In Lucerne, people enjoy *chügelipastete* (a timbale of rice and veal) and a dish of fried potatoes, dried pears and bacon. Fondues vary from canton to canton according to the local cheese. The version from Neuchâtel, which uses the local wine, is probably best known. Also from Neuchâtel come boiled tripe, served with vinaigrette, mayonnaise and pickles; duck in red wine; and a soup of lake fish.

St Gallen produces its famous veal sausages (roasted and served with onions) and smoked pork sausages, while Thurgau is known for its apple tart, in which the fruit is cut in half and pressed into the surface of a raised dough. In Schaffhausen, a famous onion tart and a delicious sausage roll are produced; the traditional dish in Schwyz is a cheese soup, simmered with stale bread and stock. In Solothurn (Soleure), the inhabitants feast on roast beef that has been marinated in red wine and vinegar.

Ticino has the atmosphere of northern Italy, with its tripe soup; *minestrone ticinese*, with vegetables and white haricot (navy) beans; osso bucco; ravioli; and *torta di pane* (a cake with a base of stale bread). From Unterwald comes *stunggis*, a traditional stew made with pork, garden vegetables and potatoes. Specialities of the Valais are raclette, a dish based on melted cheese; and a tart containing potatoes, leeks, bacon and cheese. This region also preserves the traditions of the *sil*, a dessert formerly served at weddings, consisting of crumbled rye bread sprinkled with red wine, then heated with elder syrup, raisins and fresh cream until thick; and Cardinal Schiner's stew, made with roast beef, knuckle, oxtail, quails, partridges and vegetables, served with a sauce thickened with breadcrumbs.

The canton of Vaud possesses a multitude of specialities, including *papet*, leek stew thickened with mashed potatoes; sausages with cabbage or liver, Payerne smoked sausage; the *pote de la Broye*, pig's snout stuffed with a tenderloin and then braised; as well as *malakoffs* (cheese puffs) and cakes containing white or red wine. Zug is noted for its small salmon trout, prepared *au bleu* or meunière, and its kirsch-flavoured tarts.

Finally, Zurich is famous for its *Geschnetzeltes*, thinly sliced veal served with a Stroganov-style sauce made by deglazing the pan with white wine and cream; and its kebabs of calves' liver and bacon flavoured with sage.

WINE Wine is produced in all of the 23 cantons, with the majority being made in the French-speaking part, the Suisse-romande. Whilst the country is very mountainous, the warm Föhn winds, the warming influence of the lakes and the long hours of sunshine, particularly in the Valais, help the grapes to ripen fully.

White wines are produced predominantly from Chasselas grapes, giving light, delicate wines. The variety is called Gutedel in German-speaking Switzerland, Fendant in the Valais, Perlan in Geneva, and used to be known as Dorin in the Vaud.

Other white varieties planted include Sylvaner (Johannisberg) in the Valais, Riesling-Sylvaner (Müller-Thurgau) in German Switzerland, Pinot Gris (Malvoisie), Pinot Blanc, Gewürztraminer and Chardonnay.

Pinot Noir (Blauburgunder, Clevener) is the most widely planted red grape throughout Switzerland, with Gamay dominating in the Vaud and Geneva and Merlot in Ticino/Tessin. In the Valais, Pinot Noir and Gemay are blended, with Pinot Noir dominating to make Dôle; Dôle Blanche is a similar blend with the grapes vinified to make a white wine. Pinot Noir and/or Gamay, if approved by a tasting panel, can make Salvagnin in the Vaud. Top-quality Merlot wines

produced in Ticino may be awarded the VITI seal.

There is a vast wealth of indigenous grape varieties producing serious, quality wines that are highly sought-after: Amigne, Petite Arvine, Marsanne Blanche (Ermitage), Muscat du Valais and Païen or Heida (Salvagnin Blanc) and for red wines Cornalin and Humagne Rouge. The Vin des Glaciers from the Val d'Anniviers, traditionally produced from the rare grape variety Rèze, is a speciality.

Swiss wine laws have adopted an Appellation Contrôlée system. In the Vaud, for example, there are six wine regions with 26 villages each having their own appellation and two *grands crus*, Dézaley and Calamin, on the shores of Lake Geneva.

The wine-producing regions of Switzerland

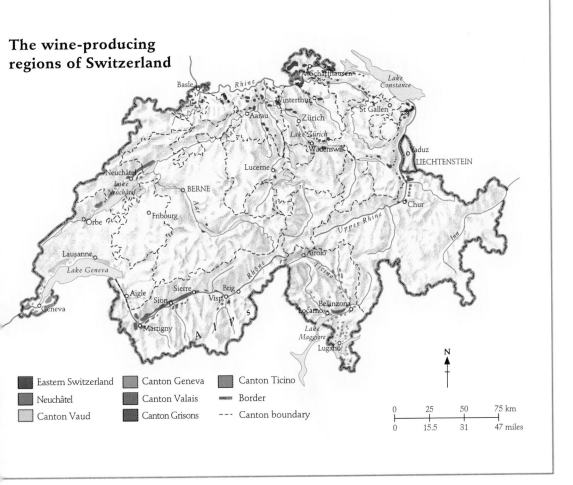

Eastern Switzerland · Canton Geneva · Canton Ticino
Neuchâtel · Canton Valais · Border
Canton Vaud · Canton Grisons · Canton boundary

| 0 | 25 | 50 | 75 km |
| 0 | 15.5 | 31 | 47 miles |

sherry with clotted cream, which then stands for 20 minutes, to be topped with more cream.

■ **Similar creams** A variety of similar creams are related to the syllabub. Possets started as warmed ale curdled with boiling milk, to be drunk or eaten, but by the mid-18th century these were made with cream and sack (sweet sherry), often with lemon, and thickened with grated Naples biscuits and/or ground almonds. They also have a history as invigorating invalid food (served in a china dish with a lid), but are better known in Elizabeth Moxon's version, from *English Housewifery* (1749), as a whisked cream flavoured with lemon zest and white wine, lightened with whisked egg whites.

Fools, in the 17th and 18th centuries, were desserts of boiled, or fresh, cream mingled with sack, ground almonds or fresh fruit. The latter version now predominates – fresh fruit and cream blended together – for 'a dessert that any fool can make'.

The best-known version of flummery is probably white wine or sherry, with lemon syrup, egg yolks and brandy, set with gelatine; but flummery also covers milk-and-cereal creams, made with semolina (also called flamri), sometimes even rice, enriched with cream, set with gelatine and flavoured with nutmeg or lemon. The latter version points to flummery's history (in Wales and Ireland) as an oatmeal dish, soaked and then cooked. Frumenty is the wheat version, eaten as a solid gruel with spices and raisins (and the origin of Christmas pudding). The liquid strained from these cereals is gelatinous, and a base to which cream and fruit could be added.

These creams added a touch of sophistication at the end of supper and special glasses were designed for syllabubs. The Georgian invention of the hand whisk changed such recipes by making possible light, whipped cream, which could be folded into mixtures. The introduction of ice houses for the rich, at the end of the 18th century, and the coming of ice cream, began their demise in popularity.

SYLVANER

SYLVANER A white-wine grape cultivated in many countries. It is grown in particular in Germany and Alsace.

SYMPOSIUM

SYMPOSIUM In ancient Greece, a symposium was a continuation of dinner, during which it was customary to serve wine accompanied by fresh and dried fruit, cheeses, salted cakes or even preserved cicadas, which provoked a thirst and therefore maintained the desire to drink – the word is derived from the Greek *sumposion* (banquet), from *syn* (with) and *potes* (drinkers). Women, with the exception of slaves, dancing girls and courtesans, were excluded from the symposium, which could provide the opportunity for philosophical discussion, as in Plato's *Symposium*. More often, however, it was an occasion for musical pageants and dancing, acrobatic and similar displays: the symposiasts, who arrived at the end of the dinner, joined the diners in drinking goblets of wine.

The symposium traditionally began with a libation from the master of the house, who opened the session by striking up a 'symposiacal paean', a hymn in honour of Dionysius. A 'symposiarch' was appointed to decide the number of goblets to be drunk, the quantity of wine they would contain, and the proportion of water to wine (Greek wine, at that time, was very thick and highly alcoholic). The servants drew the wine from the bowl, prepared the mixtures and served them to the guests in goblets (*cyathae*). It was customary to dilute the wine more as the night progressed. In Xenophon's *Symposium*, Socrates expresses a wise precept regarding this: 'If the servants cause a fine and frequent rain to fall into our small goblets of wine . . . we shall not reach a state of drunkenness under the influence of alcohol, but its sweet persuasion will lead to more gaiety.' The tradition of the symposium continued into Roman times, but often degenerated into a drinking bout.

SYRAH OR SHIRAZ

SYRAH OR SHIRAZ Red grape variety producing bluish-black grapes with a soft juicy flesh. These make powerful, heady, tannic, rich fruity wines, which can improve with age. In France it is known as Syrah and is mainly grown in the Rhône Valley and the Languedoc. It is also widely planted in Australia (and used in the production of the renowned Penfold's Grange), South Africa, Argentina and California, where the wines are usually labelled Shiraz.

SYRINGE

SYRINGE A small hollow metal or plastic cylinder with a plunger, a handle and a threaded tip to which various nozzles can be attached. The rigidity of the syringe makes it more manageable than a piping (pastry) bag, but its capacity is limited. It is used for decorating cakes and pastries.

The basting syringe, which is made of plastic and has a bulb at one end, is for sucking up cooking fat to baste a roasting joint. Unfortunately, it sucks up all the juices, not just the fat, which is not conducive to a good roast, which should be basted with the fat only, leaving the juices moist in the tin (pan) for making a flavoursome gravy.

Other syringes are used in charcuterie to inject brine into salted meat.

SYRUP

SYRUP A solution of sugar in water, which can be used hot or cold in the preparation of jams and ices with syrup and for many operations in pâtisserie and confectionery – for example, soaking babas and savarins, dipping biscuits and working fondant. Information on cooking sugar syrup to different levels measured by boiling temperature and/or density is included under *sugar*.

■ **Simple syrups** For pâtisserie and sugar work, or when preparing sorbets and other mixtures for which syrup of a precise concentration is required,

Harvest time on the cliffs of Lavaux, above Lake Geneva in the canton of Vaud.

the temperature and/or density of the syrup is measured. For simple home cooking and preparation of dishes for which such detail is not essential, light, medium or heavy syrups can be made without lengthy boiling and testing. Measure sugar and water by volume (for example, with a cup), and for a light syrup use 1 part sugar to 3 parts water; for medium syrup use 2 parts sugar to 3 parts water; and for heavy syrup use 3 parts sugar to 3 parts water. Dissolve the sugar in the water, stirring frequently, without allowing it to boil. Stop stirring and bring to the boil when the sugar has dissolved completely. Boil for about 2 minutes until clear, then cool or use as required. These syrups are useful for sweetening fruit salads or poaching soft fruit (light syrup); for soaking sponge cakes or baba (medium syrup flavoured with spirits); or for making compotes of sharp fruit, such as plums or rhubarb (heavy syrup).

■ **Flavoured syrups** Concentrated syrups flavoured with fruit or other flavourings can be diluted with water to make a refreshing drink. Fruit syrups are usually based on the juice of red fruit (strawberry, raspberry, blackcurrant), to which sugar is added – 1.8 kg (4 lb) cube sugar to the juice of 1 kg (2¼ lb) fruit in 1.5 litres (2¾ pints, 6½ cups) water. They are cooked over full heat until they reach 32°C (90°F) on a sugar (candy) thermometer, then cooled and bottled. For long-term storage, these are sterilized and sealed.

Some syrups are a mixture of a sugar syrup and an essence or concentrate (mint, grenadine, aniseed, orange or lemon). These are diluted in a proportion of 5:8 with a still or sparkling water, lemonade or milk. They are also used in numerous cocktails.

Simple flavoured syrups make versatile ingredients for sweet sauces and dessert toppings. The pared zest from lemons, oranges or limes is ideal for flavouring syrups. Citrus syrup combines well with liqueurs or spirits in dressings for crêpes, waffles or fruit fritters. Spiced syrups are excellent for bringing the flavour of the spice to sweet dishes, for example in compotes and fruit salads. Cinnamon sticks, whole cloves, a piece of nutmeg or whole green cardamoms can be added to the syrup during cooking, then left in the jar or bottle to infuse. Citrus zest, particularly from oranges, complements the warm flavour of the spices. Herb syrups can be delicate and delicious with lightly flavoured fruits, such as melon, papaya or pears. Bay leaves, mint and lavender complement sweet dishes.

Syrups were once more popular as refreshments than they are today and violets and roses were used, in addition to fruits. The word has the same origin as *sorbet*, from the Arabic *charab* (drink).

T

TABASCO A proprietary American sauce, popular in cookery the world over, that consists of chilli peppers marinated in spirit vinegar with salt. This hot-flavoured condiment is used to season a wide variety of foods, including meat, egg and red kidney bean dishes and sauces. It is also used in cocktails.

TABBOULEH A popular Middle Eastern salad and speciality of Lebanon, from where it is thought to have originated. There are many versions, from simple mixtures of soaked wheat flavoured with herbs to vegetable-rich varieties with a comparatively small proportions of wheat to tomatoes, onions and peppers. Essentially, tabbouleh is made of bulgur wheat mixed with aromatic herbs, tomatoes and spring onions (scallion) or chopped onion. Sometimes sweet (bell) pepper and lemon are added. Tabbouleh is traditionally served with or in cos (romaine) lettuce leaves and eaten with the fingers. The lettuce is used to scoop up the salad.

RECIPE

tabbouleh
Put 250 g bulgur wheat (9 oz, 2½ cups) into a bowl. Add plenty of cold water to cover and leave to soak for 20 minutes; drain thoroughly in a fine sieve. Place the bulgar in a large salad bowl. Add 500 g (18 oz, 3 cups) finely diced juicy tomatoes with their juice, 250 g (9 oz, 1½ cups) finely chopped onions, 2 tablespoons of both chopped fresh mint and parsley. Season with salt and pepper. Mix in 100 ml (4 fl oz, 7 tablespoons) olive (or sesame) oil and the juice of 3 lemons. Leave in a cool place for 2–3 hours, stirring occasionally. Just before serving, garnish with 8 spring onions (scallions) and leaves of fresh mint.

TABIL A mixture of spices in Arab cookery, consisting of three parts fresh (or dried) coriander (cilantro) to one part caraway (fresh or dried), crushed with garlic and red pepper. Tabil is dried in the sun, finely ground and stored in a dry place. In particular, it is used to spice semolina dishes, mutton ragoût and purée of broad (fava) beans in oil. It is also used to season vinaigrette for crayfish cooked in court-bouillon and as a sauce to accompany snails – two popular Arab dishes.

TABLE A piece of furniture on which food is served. In a wider sense, the word can also refer to the meal itself.

■ **Tableware through the years** At the beginning of the 17th century, the usefulness of items still took precedence over their decorativeness. The conventional plate had a wide raised rim and in France was called a 'cardinal's hat'; the fork, which was still rare, had only two prongs. The drinking glass was beginning to replace the metal goblet, although pewter ewers were very common.

The beginning of the 18th century saw the introduction of more elaborate silverware. Forks and spoons were adorned with architectural motifs; forks had four prongs, but the knives still did not match the forks and spoons. The plate evolved into its modern shape and the drinking glass came into general use. The flat pewter candlestick became a sconce. New items appeared, such as the sugar sprinkler, the egg cup and the salt cellar.

The Regency period and the reign of Louis XV were the heyday of silverware. Decoration became more complex, with mouldings and borders. Fork, spoon and knife formed a matching set. The sconce became a candelabrum with several branches. The broth bowl on its stand appeared, soon followed by the soup plate. Glasses became more and more delicate. The fashion for coffee and drinking chocolate gave rise to the coffee pot and sets of coffee cups. The '*oille* pot' was used to serve soups and ragoûts of game.

From the time of Louis XVI to the First Empire, neoclassical decoration replaced the rococo style. The heavy silver or pewter plate gave way to porcelain and the newly invented silver- or gold-plated metal (*pomponne*). Industrial processes influenced shapes: for example, glasses were moulded rather than blown. More new objects appeared, including oil and vinegar cruets, sauceboats and pepper pots.

It was under Napoleon III that the decorative craze reached its peak. Styles were at their most ornate and heaviest. On the same table Empire plates, rococo cutlery, a Renaissance pitcher and Venetian glassware could be found clustered around enormous and elaborate centrepieces.

At the end of the 19th century, a reaction began: craftsmanship reasserted itself and many older styles disappeared. The revolution in the arts at the beginning of the 20th century inspired such designers as the Art Nouveau exponent Van de Velde (1900) and Puiforcat (1920s) and led to the appearance of the Tiffany and Scandinavian styles.

■ **Decorating the table** The fashion for complicated 'pâtisserie' decorations, candelabra or monumental flower arrangements went out long ago; nowadays, one or two candles or a vase of flowers is considered an elegant and practical decoration. For special occasions *chemins de fleurs* in little crystal jardinières, arranged end to end, make a charming border of roses, violets or nasturtiums. Also attractive are sprays of autumn leaves on the tablecloth. Bowls or baskets of fruit can replace floral decorations. Low fruit dishes, plates or baskets with handles that are easy to hold are preferable to symmetrical pyramidal arrangements on high dishes, which might impede conversation with guests sitting opposite. Fruit should be arranged without too much fuss, interspersed, if necessary, with clusters of leaves, and should please the eye as well as the appetite.

Nowadays, the tendency is towards simplicity. Whereas at one time the fork had to be placed prongs down on the tablecloth, so that the figure engraved on the back of the handle was visible, the fork is now almost always placed prongs uppermost. Also, it is better to have just two glasses, one for water and one for wine, the latter being changed when a different wine is poured.

TABLE D'HÔTE
Formerly, a large communal table at an inn, where people sat as and when they arrived and where everyone could be served meals that were prepared throughout the day. A communal table d'hôte was also the rule in boarding houses, where meals were served at a set time. They still exist in provincial areas, in certain hotels for commercial travellers. In Paris, in a few restaurants with regular customers, they are again fashionable. When the inn was superseded by the restaurant, customers were served at separate tables.

At the end of the 18th century, Sébastien Mercier gave this description: 'Tables d'hôte are intolerable for outsiders, but they have no choice. They have to take a knife and fork and go and eat in the midst of a dozen strangers. Those who are polite and shy do not manage to get enough to eat for their money. The centre of the table, near what are called the *pièces de résistance*, is occupied by the regular customers, who seize these important seats . . . Equipped with tireless jaws, they devour the food without ceremony. Unhappy are those who are slow eaters.'

Originally, when restaurateurs were permitted to invite customers into their dining room, table d'hôte meant that the owner allowed the customer to sit 'at his own table' to eat the cooked dishes he had purchased on the premises, instead of taking them home.

TABLE ETIQUETTE AND MANNERS
A set of rules which govern the serving and eating of a meal; the strictness with which they are adhered to depends on the degree of formality of the meal, lunch generally being rather less formal than dinner. Brillat-Savarin said: 'To invite someone to one's table is to assume responsibility for his happiness during the time he is under your roof.' The guest's enjoyment will be increased if a tasteful arrangement of the table and a flawless service are added to the good quality of the food.

■ **Etiquette through the centuries** With the Greeks, etiquette required that shoes were exchanged for light sandals before entering the dining room. The best place was given to the stranger and it was customary to offer him, before the meal, a bath or a foot wash. Roman diners, who used to eat reclining and crowned with flowers, changed not only their shoes but also their clothes, putting on a woollen tunic provided for this purpose. It was essential to make the first step into the *triclinium* with the right foot. The dishes were presented first to the master of the house, accompanied by music, by a servant executing a dance step.

Under the Merovingian kings an elaborate ceremony, inspired by the Byzantine court, was introduced and honorific duties were created, such as that of the *mapparius*, who presented a tablecloth to the monarch. At the time of Charlemagne, the ceremonial became even more complicated: the emperor was seated on the highest chair, while dukes, chiefs and kings of other nations passed him the dishes to the sound of fifes and oboes. These lesser ranks did not eat themselves until the imperial meal was finished; they were served in their turn by counts, prefects and dignitaries, who did not themselves dine until after this second service; the people of the lowest ranks usually had to make do with leftovers, towards the middle of the night. From feudal times, the king usually dined alone and it was a rare honour to be admitted to his table.

The table of François I was magnificent, but the

preoccupation with eating well, strengthened by the arrival of the Florentine cooks, took precedence over formal presentation. Henri III, on the other hand, reintroduced a strict etiquette and his enemies accused him of multiplying the 'idolatrous bows' not only to himself but also to his personal belongings.

When Louis XIV dined *au grand couvert*, he ate alone but in public, and the courtiers were allowed to watch him eat while each victualling officer carried out his duties according to a complicated ceremonial. At the *petit couvert*, in intimate surroundings, the etiquette was relaxed and the Duc de Luynes relates that the king threw little balls of bread to the ladies and allowed them to throw them at him. The *grand couvert* was maintained under Louis XV (who aroused admiration through the skill with which he removed the top from a boiled egg with a single stroke of the fork) and under Louis XVI. Marie-Antoinette, anxious to withdraw from the obligation of eating in public, appeared only once a week at this meal, which, according to Arthur Young, 'had more peculiarity than magnificence'. Before the 17th century, it was the custom to keep a hat on one's head while eating. Under the Empire and until the end of the monarchy, etiquette imposed strict rules.

■ **A question of manners** Table manners have developed through the ages and attitudes towards them vary in every country. The Gauls used to eat sitting down, and the Romans lying down, while the Japanese traditionally squat on their heels at the table. The French are taught to keep their hands over the table throughout the meal, whereas English etiquette requires that they should be placed in the lap when not actually eating. Belching, regarded as the grossest indelicacy in western countries, was a sign of politeness in ancient Rome and still is in the Middle East.

One of the first collections of the rules of etiquette was compiled by Robert de Blois, since the rules of chivalry extended to good table manners. His advice was always to have clean hands and fingernails, not to eat bread before the first course, not to take the largest pieces of food, not to pick one's teeth or scratch oneself with one's knife, not to talk with one's mouth full, and not to laugh too loudly. Washing one's hands before and after the meal was a compulsory ritual, for which servants would bring a copper basin full of perfumed water and a towel. When we realize that there were no forks at that time, that a bowl and goblet were shared by several guests, and that meals could last for hours, these precautions were not negligible.

Erasmus wrote a *Treatise on Manners* in 1526, in which he too advised his readers to wash their hands and clean their fingernails before going to the table. We also read: 'Starting a meal by drinking is for drunkards: one begins to drink only with the second course, after the soup, and first one must wipe one's lips with one's handkerchief. It is coarse to put your fingers in your soup, and it is unseemly to put chewed items back on your plate. It is absolutely not done to throw your bones under the table or to lick your plate.'

An important turning point came at the beginning of the 17th century, when the Italian influence on French society as a whole was reflected in the refinement of both table manners and the vocabulary of the menu. *Soupe* became *potage* and the *plat de chair* became a *plat de viande*. This concern for refinement became affectation in the next century, with the *petits soupers*, *médianoche* and *ambigu* (new French names for snacks taken at various times of the day). Nevertheless, advice on good manners was still plentiful: in 1765 Antoine Le Courtin wrote a *Traité de civilité*, in which he prohibits 'lapping like an animal', while La Bruyère, in his *Caractères*, describes what one does not do at table by depicting Gnathon the guzzler, 'for whom the table is a hay rack'. After the French Revolution, treatises multiplied, although manners were still sometimes slow to develop. It was not until the middle of the 19th century that people stopped eating chicken with their fingers and stopped mixing the salad with their hands, and that table cutlery in a well-to-do house began to include leg-of-mutton and cutlet holders.

■ **The placing of guests** Today, table arrangement and the places allotted to guests are still subject to a number of rules for formal occasions such as state banquets.

At very formal meals, the guests will enter the dining room in couples, or the women will be asked to enter the dining room first. When there are eight or fewer guests, the mistress of the house shows each one where to sit. Above that number, it is a good idea to provide small cards. For a party meal, a table plan must be prepared. The subtleties of French etiquette sometimes present problems of precedence (whereas, in Britain, Burke's *Peerage* makes provision for all cases).

In the United States and in Britain, it is customary for the man of the house to place himself at the end of the table, in order to leave the best places for the guests, a custom sometimes practised in France. The lady of the house may preside with her chosen guest opposite her or, in the case of a royal guest, let the guest preside in her place.

In ancient times, the place of honour was on the left of the master of the house, on the side of the heart. In the Middle Ages, the table hierarchy was much less precise, but the master of the house honoured his guest by having a choice morsel brought to him, inviting him to cut off a piece of meat, or drinking to his health (see *toast*). In China, the place of honour is situated opposite the door of the dining room and, if possible, facing south. Precedence is determined by age, degree of relationship and social rank, rarely by sex.

■ **Rules for guests** All meals to which guests are invited are social occasions which require mutual deference and courtesy. Guests should not arrive before the indicated time, but custom dictates that a guest should not keep his host waiting for more than a quarter of an hour.

When the guests are taken into the dining room, they should wait to be seated by the hostess; it is she who, when each course is served, gives the signal to take the first mouthful. It is also she who rises first from the table when the meal is over.

At formal lunches, ladies wearing hats may keep them on (a custom which crossed from England to France at the beginning of the 20th century).

Nothing is touched with the fingers except bread, which is broken up into pieces and never cut with a knife, and a few foods, such as globe artichokes and certain seafoods, which are usually reserved for less formal gatherings.

The cutlery should be handled without any noise, and the knife should never be put in the mouth. When a dish is offered to guests, they should serve themselves with moderation, taking the portion closest to them without ostensible selection. At family meals, the dish may be placed in the middle of the table.

It is the custom to wait a little before beginning to drink. The master of the house will pour (or order the pouring of) the first few drops of each bottle of wine into his own glass, in case it is corked. Wine glasses are filled only two-thirds full, to bring out the bouquet of the wine.

When a course is over, the guest should leave his cutlery on his plate, side by side (never crossed). The person who clears the table should remove the plates one by one, without stacking them up. Clean cutlery must be used after shellfish and fish.

In certain countries it is polite for the guest to leave a little food on his plate to indicate that he has had enough to eat, although in many parts of the world, it is good manners to clear one's plate as a compliment to the quality of the food.

Fingerbowls usually appear on the table with the fruit course, but sometimes also after a platter of seafood or artichokes. The guests should dip their fingers into the bowls discreetly.

To smoke during a meal is extremely bad manners and ashtrays should never be placed on the table.

■ The rules of etiquette

• ARTICHOKES These are eaten leaf by leaf, the leaves being detached with the fingers. However, at formal meals only the hearts are served, garnished or stuffed.

• ASPARAGUS The tips are cut off with a fork and the rest is left, unless the hostess invites the guests to use their fingers. It is, however, acceptable these days to eat the whole thing with the fingers, leaving any woody stalk on the side of the plate afterwards.

• BOILED EGGS In France the top should be removed with the spoon and the egg should never be taken out of the egg cup. Once empty, the shell should be crushed. In England the top may be cut off (never peeled) and the shell left intact.

• CHEESE It is preferable to serve cheese already cut, in order not to embarrass the guests, who would hesitate to start a new cheese. Rectangular cheeses are cut lengthways in even strips, round cheeses (like Camembert) are cut along the radius into small wedges, Brie-shaped cheeses are usually served in a wedge and are cut diagonally, ensuring that not only crust is left for the next diner. In France, cheese is eaten in small pieces, placed with the knife on a fragment of bread (never use your fork or eat the cheese from the tip of your knife). Lastly, the cheeseboard is rarely offered a second time (to take a second helping would indicate that you had not had enough to eat). This custom is, of course, deplored by certain cheese-lovers.

• COFFEE AND LIQUEURS These are served in the drawing room, not at the dining-room table. The hostess should never be complimented on the success of the meal, as this could possibly imply that one is surprised that it was good. But at informal meals with close friends compliments are perfectly acceptable.

• FRUIT This is peeled with a small knife with a silver blade, while being held with a fork (not the fingers). If you require only half a large fruit (at an intimate gathering), you should leave the part with the stalk attached and the stone (pit), if any, in the bowl. (Melon is generally eaten with a spoon, but certain gourmets recommend using a fork, or a knife and fork.)

• SALAD This is sometimes served in a small individual dish to the left of the diner. Salad is never cut with a knife as, in theory, it is prepared so that the leaves can be eaten in small mouthfuls.

• SOUP The soup should be sipped from the side of the spoon. Any sucking noises should be avoided. In France, the bowl is never tilted to spoon up the last mouthfuls though it is acceptable to do so in England and many other countries.

Whatever blunders he or she may commit, the guest is always treated with respect: the ultimate courtesy, on the part of the host or hostess, consists of voluntarily committing the same mistake as the guest, to show that it is quite all right.

TABLE NAPKIN An individual piece of linen which is used to protect the clothing or to wipe the mouth during a meal. On a set table the napkins are folded, sometimes with a bread roll inside, and placed on the plate. Decorative folding is sometimes used in restaurants or at formal dinner parties. It is good manners to wipe the mouth before drinking and whenever a trace of sauce or other food remains on the lips. Tying the napkin around the neck is regarded as inelegant, unless the dish consists of shrimps or seafood which require peeling. (That said, the Serviette au cou, a gastronomic society, was founded in Paris in 1934 by Paul Colombier; it had a monthly dinner, served at a precise time, at which there was no place of honour and tying the napkin round the neck was compulsory!)

The Romans used a *sudarium* (cloth) to mop the forehead and face while slaves brought round basins of water for washing. The use of napkins was not widespread at the beginning of the Middle Ages, although tablecloths did exist. Guests wiped their hands and mouths on the cloth or on the *longuière*, a band of linen running along the edge of the table for this purpose. Around the 13th century *touailles* came into use: these were cloths hung on the wall for guests to use as required; they were also used to cover the remains of the food. This led to individual napkins of cotton or linen, sometimes embroidered, which were worn on the shoulder or over the left arm. With the fashion for ruffs during the reign of Henri III, it became acceptable to tie the napkin around the neck.

In catering establishments, the maître d'hôtel traditionally carries a folded napkin on his left arm as a mark of office, as do waiters.

It is customary to arrange certain dishes on white napkins instead of dish papers or doilies: a 'gondola' for a whole fish served on a long dish, for example, or a folded napkin for hot toast or a bombe.

TABLE SETTING

The linen, crockery and cutlery laid out for a meal. For formal occasions, everything should coordinate, with matching tablecloth and napkins, all the crockery of same design, or at least toning, and matching sets of wine glasses. A few flowers, not strongly scented, may be arranged in small clusters or in a single flower bowl. The tablecloth, white or of an unobtrusive pattern, is placed on a table felt, to deaden the sound; table mats placed directly on the table are suitable for less formal meals. Each guest must have sufficient elbow and leg room – about 60 cm (2 ft). The places are laid symmetrically: fork on the left of the plate, soup spoon and main knife on the right, together with the fish knife or oyster fork (if required); the knife rest, which is now rarely seen, should not be used for a formal dinner. According to the number of wines, several glasses (not more than three), of decreasing size, are placed in front of the plate. The napkin, folded in the simplest possible manner, is put on the plate. Salt cellars and carafes are placed at either end of the table, or possibly in the centre if the table is round. The wine, uncorked in advance, remains in its original bottle, but clarets may be decanted into a carafe; fresh water is also provided in a carafe.

The setting may also include several pieces designed to be used together for a particular dish. An asparagus set comprises a cradle or draining dish, in which the boiled asparagus is placed, and tongs or a scoop for serving. A fondue set has a heater, a pan, long-handled forks and, sometimes, dishes with compartments for various sauces. A cake set has a serving plate (round or long), a cake slice, matching plates and cake forks. A fish set has a long plate, sometimes a sauceboat, and fish knives and forks. A cheese set has a cheeseboard, small plates and a cheese knife. The strawberry set, with its drainer, small plates and scoop, and the snail set, with its dimpled plates and pincers, are also worth mentioning. Finally, there is the carving set, a large knife and fork (sometimes with a holder) used to cut joints of meat, poultry or game at the table. As for drinks, a liqueur or port set consists of small glasses and a decanter. A tea or coffee service comprises cups and saucers of the appropriate size, small spoons, small plates, a teapot or coffeepot, a sugar basin and a milk jug, sometimes on a tray. The *tête-à-tête* is a tea, coffee or breakfast service for two people.

TABLE SONG

The ancient custom of singing at table at the end of a meal arose from the natural tendency of the guests to express their satisfaction. According to Ecclesiastes: 'There is nothing under the sun better for man than to eat, drink and be merry. Go, therefore, eat your bread with joy and drink your wine with cheer.' Greek and Roman banquets usually ended with great spectacles, and in the Middle Ages all feasts were punctuated by interludes of song or mime, but the table song, or rather, the drinking song, began in the 15th century with Olivier Basselin, creator of the *vau de vire*, from which the term vaudeville is derived.

The custom was at its peak at the time of the Empire and the Restoration. E. Briffault notes in *Paris à table* (1846): 'Under the Empire, part of the old freedom of the past returned: people used to sing at table during dessert, sometimes drinking songs, most often fashionable ballads; there were also verses to celebrate festivals and weddings. It was then that singing dinners were formed, dinners for bachelors, dinners for friends, dinners for corporations, etc.' As early as 1804, Grimod de La Reynière complained of patriotic songs ('true signs of carnage') sung during the Revolution and rejoiced in the return of drinking songs and love songs, symbols of 'healthy French gaiety' composed by Désaugiers, Pannard, Collé, Favart and others. Practising what he preached, he published drinking and eating songs in the successive editions of his *Almanach des gourmands*.

The tradition of singing during dessert was upheld through the ages, but came to be regarded as a rather vulgar habit. As early as 1830, Henri Monnier ridicules it through the character of Monsieur Prudhomme, singing at table being a sign of the lower middle classes.

TABLIER DE SAPEUR

A speciality of Lyon, made of pieces of tripe cut from the so-called 'honeycomb', dipped in beaten egg and covered with breadcrumbs. They are then fried or grilled (broiled) and served piping hot with snail butter, gribiche sauce or tartare sauce.

TABOUREAU

A chef who probably lived at the beginning of the 16th century. He is the author of a *Viandier*, which is similar in some ways to that written by Taillevent. Taboureau's manuscript, dating from the 1550s, contains recipes which date back to the 14th century as well as the *escriteaux* (menus) of banquets given by the Comte d'Harcourt in honour of the king of France in 1396.

TÂCHE, LA

Red AOC *grand cru* of the Côte de Nuits. Made in the commune of Vosne-Romanée, this robust wine with its powerful bouquet of red berry fruits and violet notes is rated by some as the best in the commune (see *Burgundy*).

TACO In Mexican cookery, a cornmeal pancake (tortilla) filled with a thick sauce, minced (ground) meat seasoned with chilli pepper, black beans, or avocado purée with onion. When filled, the pancake is rolled and eaten straight away or fried gently. Tacos are a popular snack or hot entrée.

TAFIA Originally, the name given to rum by the natives of the French West Indies. The word is now used to mean a second-rate form of the spirit.

TAGLIATELLE Italian egg ribbon noodles, about 5 mm (¼ in) wide and golden or green in colour (green tagliatelle contains spinach). Tagliatelle is a speciality of Emilia-Romagna, where, according to legend, its invention was inspired by a nobleman's love for the hair of Lucrezia Borgia. Tagliatelle literally means 'small cut-up things'. In Italy, there are variant forms: taglierini, which are narrower (3 mm, ⅛ in); and tagliolini, which are shorter. Fettucine is a wider ribbon pasta.

Tagliatelle may be served in a wide variety of ways, with many sauces, including a simple dressing of olive oil and garlic; a cream and ham sauce; a light seafood dressing; or a rich meat sauce.

TAHINI Beige-coloured, oily and thick paste of sesame seeds. Used in Middle-Eastern cooking, both savoury and sweet, and a popular product for vegetarian dishes. The oil floats and the thick paste must be stirred thoroughly before use.

TAHITI See *above*.

TAHITIENNE, À LA A term for raw fillets of fish (gilt-head bream, monkfish, grouper or turbot) cut into thin strips or small dice, marinated for several hours in lemon juice and oil with salt and pepper, then served with seeded tomato quarters or tomato pulp and sprinkled with grated coconut. Fish *à la tahitienne* can also be included in a mixed salad along with avocado, grapefruit quarters and a chiffonnade of lettuce and tomatoes, all seasoned with lemon mayonnaise.

TAIL The caudal appendage of an animal, classed as a cheap cut of meat.

The most widely used is oxtail, which makes many delicious dishes, notably oxtail soup (see *oxtail*). Lamb's or sheep's tail is not often used, although it can be boiled and then grilled (broiled) or braised with curry. Pig's tail can be cooked in the same way as pig's trotters (feet), boned and stuffed, braised or boiled, coated with breadcrumbs and grilled (broiled); it can also be pickled in brine.

The tail of prawns (shrimps), scampi, crayfish and similar crustaceans is often the only edible portion after shelling.

TAILLAULE A pastry from Neuchâtel, Switzerland, made from a leavened dough to which chopped candied orange peel and rum have been added. Baked in a rectangular mould, *taillaule* is cut up when cooked, using scissors.

TAILLÉ A pastry from the French-speaking part of Switzerland, savoury and slightly flaky, to which pork pieces known as *greubons* are added. The *taillé* is a hearty traditional snack.

TAILLEVENT, GUILLAUME TIREL A French cook (born Pont-Audemer; *c.* 1310; died Pont-Audemer, *c.* 1395) author of *Le Viandier*, one of the oldest cookery books written in French. Four manuscripts were discovered by Baron Jérôme Pichon, who, assisted by Gabriel Vicaire, published the book in 1892 and included some information about the author's life and career.

The name Guillaume Tirel is found in a manuscript dated 1326 describing the coronation of Jeanne d'Évreux – the young Tirel was in the service of the latter as a kitchen boy. In 1346 he entered the service of Philippe de Valois (who later gave him a house in Saint-Germain-en-Laye), then he joined the household of the Dauphin, as squire, becoming cook in 1355. He subsequently held the same position in the households of the Duke of Normandy (1359–61) and of Charles V (1368–73). Finally, in 1381, he entered the service of Charles VI, who ennobled him and under whom, in 1392, he was elevated to master of the king's kitchen provisions, the crowning title of his career. Guillaume Tirel, known as Taillevent (or Taillevant), a nickname apparently inspired by the length of his nose, was buried in the priory of Notre-Dame, in Hennebont.

It is thought that *Le Viandier*, the first professional cookery treatise written in France, predates 1380. It was commissioned by Charles V, who was anxious to have the specialists of his time write about various 'learned' subjects. For expertise concerning cookery, Taillevent was an obvious choice – at the pinnacle of his career and in charge of the royal kitchens. The full title of the work (translated into English) is: 'Hereafter follows the Viandier describing the preparation of all manner of foods, as cooked by Taillevent, the cook of our noble king, and also the dressing and preparation of boiled meat, roasts, sea and freshwater fish, sauces, spices, and other suitable and necessary things as described hereafter.' The word *viande* in the original French means all foodstuffs, not simply meat, and one of the most interesting features of the work is that it details the foodstuffs eaten in the 14th century: some of the more unusual meats include *connins* (rabbits), wild boars, plovers, swans, peacocks, storks, herons, bustards, cormorants and turtledoves. Lamprey, loach, eel, pike, carp and other freshwater fish were common, whereas sea fish were less numerous (conger-eel, dogfish, mackerel, sole, herring, cod, turbot, sturgeon, mussels and oysters, not forgetting whales). Green vegetables were uncommon, but spices, eggs, milk and cheeses were all important.

Numerous copies of the *Le Viandier* circulated among noblemen and chefs before the printing press popularized this 'dispensatory'. The author of *Le Ménagier de Paris* (1393) quoted extensively from it, and Villon mentions it in his *Testament*: 'See Taillevent – the chapter on fricassees.' First printed around 1490 and enlarged with notes, new recipes and banquet menus, *Le Viandier* was published several times up to the beginning of the 18th century. Its predecessors included *Traité où l'on enseigne à appareiller et à assaisonner toutes viandes* (1306) and *Le Grand Cuisinier de toute cuisine*, which appeared anonymously in 1350, but *Le Viandier* provides a complete synthesis of all aspects of cookery in the 14th century. Its influence was felt until the advent of the Florentine chefs under Catherine de' Medici, and the publication of *Le Cuisinier français* by La Varenne in 1651, which introduced a new perception of culinary art. The main contribution of *Le Viandier* lies in its emphasis on spicy sauces (predominantly saffron, ginger, pepper and cinnamon), soups and ragoûts, which included the preparation not only of meat, poultry and game, but also fish.

Also noteworthy is the common use of verjuice and liaisons with toasted breadcrumbs.

Another aspect of 'gothic' cookery was the popularity of sweet-and-sour dishes throughout Europe: German gruel with almonds, onion and larding bacon; rice with milk and fatty bouillon; pies of meat with raisins and sugar; eels with prunes; goose with apples and cinnamon; and not forgetting hippocras and wines flavoured with honey or herbs. The principal cooking methods were roasting and boiling. Stuffed dishes and pies and flans based on minced (ground) meat were numerous. Furthermore, cookery often had to conform to the strictures of the Church, and considerable attention was given to the cookery of the days of abstinence (in Lent, for example).

The cookery of Taillevent is often depicted as a series of heavy, complex and overspiced dishes. Nevertheless, the recipes in *Le Viandier* also include simpler preparations, for example *aigo boulido* from Provence, *tourin* from Périgord, *bouilleture* of eels, *saupiquet*, hotchpotch, Pézenas pâtés, Pithiviers gâteau with frangipane, and pears in wine. Some of the recipes can be prepared quite easily today, almost without changing anything: *cretonnée* of new peas, almond blancmange, watercress soup and Bourbonnais tart, for instance.

Moreover, the late 20th-century move towards *nouvelle cuisine* took inspiration from Taillevent, updating such old dishes as salmon pâté with sorrel, *civet* of hot oysters and fresh ham with leek.

TAJINE A deep glazed-earthenware dish with a conical lid that fits flush with the rim. It is used throughout North Africa for preparing and serving a range of dishes that are cooked slowly in a flavoured basting liquid; these preparations themselves are also called tajines and are made with vegetables, such as potatoes and courgettes (zucchini); fish; chicken with quinces or dates; meat; or even fruit. Mutton with prunes, or veal with tomatoes and aubergines (eggplants) are typical.

RECIPES

tajine of beef with cardoons

Pour 60 ml (2 fl oz, ¼ cup) olive oil into a tajine and brown 1 kg (2¼ lb) cubed beef, 2 sliced onions, 2 chopped garlic cloves, ½ teaspoon cumin, ½ teaspoon ginger, 2 pinches saffron strands, ½ teaspoon grey pepper (mixed ground black and white peppers) and 1 teaspoon salt. Cover with water and simmer gently for 1 hour. Peel 1.5 kg (3¼ lb) cardoons, cut into strips, placing them in water and lemon juice to prevent discoloration. Add to the tajine and cook for 30 minutes, then add the juice of 1 lemon and cook for 10 minutes.

tajine of carrots

Put 1 kg (2¼ lb) sliced carrots into a tajine or saucepan. Add 5 tablespoons olive oil, then add 450 g (1 lb) finely sliced onions, a bouquet of coriander (cilantro), the same amount of parsley, 2 chopped garlic cloves, 1 teaspoon ginger, a pinch each of cumin, paprika and saffron powder, 2 turns of the pepper mill and a large pinch of salt. Mix together, put on the lid and cook over a very low heat for 1½ hours (using a heat diffuser). Just before serving, add 150 g (5 oz, 1 cup) black (ripe) olives and sprinkle with lemon juice.

tajine of mutton with prunes and honey

In a tajine (or saucepan) put 1 kg (2¼ lb) mutton cut into pieces, 5 tablespoons olive oil, a pinch of salt, 1 finely sliced onion, a pinch of ginger, a bouquet of coriander (cilantro), a pinch of saffron powder and 1 cinnamon stick. Cover with water, put on the lid and simmer over a very low heat for 2 hours (using a heat diffuser). When the meat is cooked, take off the lid and allow the sauce to reduce and thicken. Remove the coriander, meat and cinnamon. Add 450 g (1 lb) prunes to the sauce and cook for 20 minutes. Then pour in 5 tablespoons honey and simmer for a further 10 minutes. In a frying pan, brown 1 tablespoon sesame seeds. Return the meat to the tajine along with 1 teaspoon orange-flower water. Replace the lid, reheat and serve very hot. Just before serving, sprinkle with the fried sesame seeds.

tajine of spring lamb ♦

Cut a boned shoulder of lamb into pieces. Chop 200 g (7 oz) onions and 3 garlic cloves. Heat 6 tablespoons olive oil in a tajine. Add the pieces of meat and onion and brown them. Cut 4 tomatoes into quarters. Peel 6 potatoes and cut into large cubes. Add to the tajine with the tomatoes, 1 teaspoon cinnamon and 1 teaspoon ground cumin. Season with salt and pepper and add 200 ml (7 fl oz, ¾ cup) water. Cover and simmer for 1 hour.

Shell and skin 250 g (9 oz) broad (fava) beans. Cut 4 preserved lemons into quarters, discarding their seeds. Add the beans and lemons to the tajine with 4 artichoke hearts, cut in half. Continue cooking for 30 minutes. Wash and remove the tough stalks from 1 bunch coriander (cilantro). Chop the leaves and sprinkle on the tajine just before serving.

TALEGGIO A DOP Italian cow's-milk cheese (48% fat content); pressed, uncooked, and white or creamy yellow, it has a soft texture and a washed, thin, pale-pink rind. The fruity taste is accompanied by a pronounced smell. Originally from Taleggio (a province of Bergamo), it is now made throughout Lombardy and is sold as slabs, 20 cm (8 in) square by 5 cm (2 in) thick, in silver paper. It is best between June and November.

TALLEYRAND-PÉRIGORD, CHARLES MAURICE DE French statesman (born Paris, 1754; died Paris, 1838), who not only managed to retain high office and good fortune throughout the Revolution until the Restoration, but was also a celebrated host and connoisseur of good food, whose table was considered one of the finest in Europe. He employed the famous pastrycook Avice and the great chef Antonin Carême, whose fortune he made. He also stole from Cambacérès, his rival in gastronomy, a cook who invented for him snails *à la bourguignonne*, which Talleyrand made fashionable.

With his head cook Bouchée, who came from the Condé household, Talleyrand (for whom lunch was of little importance) devised some epoch-making dinners. His menu regularly consisted of two soup courses, two removes (including one of fish), four entrées, two roasts, four sweets and dessert – a menu which became the rule for all the best tables. Talleyrand himself would carve the meat and poultry and he used to serve his guests according to their status. In his eyes, however, the culinary art was not simply a question of gastronomic pleasure; it was above all an invaluable aid in government and diplomacy. 'Sire, I have more need of saucepans than instructions,' he said to Louis XVIII as he left for the negotiations at the Congress of Vienna, and it was at the meal table that he secured great advantages for France.

In classic cuisine, Talleyrand's name is associated with numerous preparations: veal chops, calves' sweetbreads, tournedos, large pieces of beef or veal, and poultry – garnished with buttered macaroni flavoured with cheese and served with a julienne of truffles, diced foie gras and Périgueux sauce. His name is also given to various other dishes, such as stuffed anchovy fillets rolled into paupiettes, a curried omelette filled with calves' sweetbreads, and semolina croquettes stuffed with a salpicon of poultry, pickled tongue, truffles and mushrooms and covered with demi-glace sauce. Talleyrand sauce (chicken velouté sauce with Madeira, mirepoix, truffles and pickled tongue) is used in the same way as Périgueux sauce. (See *Sagan*.) Finally, a *talleyrand* is a savarin cake made with chopped pineapple, soaked in syrup, covered with apricot glaze and decorated with pineapple pieces.

RECIPE

Talleyrand sauce
Prepare 200 ml (7 fl oz, ¾ cup) chicken velouté* sauce and add 200 ml (7 fl oz, ¾ cup) white stock. Mix and reduce by half. Add 4 tablespoons double (heavy) cream and 3 tablespoons Madeira. Boil for a few moments. Remove from the heat and blend in 50 g (2 oz, ¼ cup) butter. Strain the sauce and add 1 tablespoon vegetable mirepoix, then the same amount of finely chopped truffles and pickled tongue.

TALMOUSE A small savoury pastry made with soft fresh cheese and dating back to the Middle Ages. The Saint-Denis *talmouses*, which used to be

Tajine of spring lamb.

made for the Archbishop of Paris, are mentioned by François Villon and referred to by Balzac in *Un début dans la vie*: 'On entering Saint-Denis, Pierrotin stopped in front of the door of the innkeeper who sells the famous talmouses and where all travellers alight . . . Georges bought them some talmouses and a glass of Alicante wine.' *Le Viandier* and *Le Ménagier de Paris* both give a recipe for them (at that time, the spelling was *talmous, talmose* or *talemouse*): 'Made with fine cheeses, cut into squares as small as beans. A generous amount of eggs are added and it is all mixed together. The pastry case is coated with eggs and butter.'

In 1742, Menon recommended that the moulds used for making talmouses should be lined with puff pastry in such a way that it hangs over the edge; the pastry cases should then be filled with cheese béchamel sauce, after which the corners of the pastry should be folded over to form a tricorn shape. *Le Cuisinier gascon* (18th century) advocates rolled-out puff-pastry bases, which are filled with soft cheese blended with eggs, then 'trussed, brushed and cooked in the oven'. *Le Cuisinier des cuisiniers* (1882) gives the following variant: soufflé-fritter batter mixed with well-drained soft cheese, divided into small shapes, brushed and puffed up in the oven. The name 'Saint-Denis talmouses' is also given to tartlets made of shortcrust pastry (basic pie dough) filled with a mixture of soft cheese, rindless Brie, whole eggs and whisked egg whites.

As can be seen, recipes for talmouses have varied through the ages. Several kinds of talmouse are made today. The type known as a *pont-neuf* is a tartlet made of puff or lining pastry, filled with choux pastry mixed with thick cheese-flavoured béchamel sauce, with two thin strips of pastry forming a cross on top; it is brushed with egg and baked in a hot oven. In the Bagration talmouse, the tartlet is filled with cheese-flavoured choux pastry; after cooking it is covered with cheese-flavoured béchamel sauce piped through a piping (pastry) bag. For the *talmouse marquise*, the tartlet is masked with cheese-flavoured béchamel sauce, filled with choux pastry, then brushed and cooked. These talmouses are served piping hot with sprigs of parsley, as hors d'oeuvre.

Another variety, known as *talmouses en tricorne*, is based on an older recipe: they take the form of circles or squares of puff pastry, which are brushed with egg, filled with a thick béchamel sauce bound with egg yolks and flavoured with cheese, then shaped into tricorns or crowns by folding the corners inwards; they are baked in a hot oven. Various ingredients may be added, including spinach purée and diced ham. These talmouses are again served as hot hors d'oeuvre.

There are also sweet talmouses made with frangipane: tartlets or barquettes of puff pastry are filled with a mixture of confectioner's custard (pastry cream) and frangipane cream, covered with granulated sugar or shredded (slivered) almonds, then baked in a moderate oven and sprinkled with icing (confectioner's) sugar.

RECIPE

talmouses à l'ancienne
Roll out some puff pastry to a thickness of 5 mm (¼ in) and cut it into 10 cm (4 in) squares. Brush with egg yolk and in the centre of each square place 1 large tablespoon cheese soufflé* mixture, then on top sprinkle a little diced Gruyère cheese. Fold the corners of each square to the centre, keeping the filling in the middle. Put the talmouses on a buttered baking sheet and bake in a preheated oven at 200°C (400°F, gas 6) for 12 minutes. Serve piping hot.

TAMAL An ancient Mexican dish consisting of a bed of ground corn mixed with lard (this is traditional, but some cooks use butter) steamed in the husk of a corn cob. The corn mixture may be coarse or fine, soft or stiff. It is placed on the husk or on banana leaves and topped with a spicy filling of poultry, mealt or vegetables. The dough and husks are folded around the filling and tied, then cooked in a steamer. There are many regional variations. Tamales are served hot as an entrée and are also a popular street food.

TAMARILLO Fruit of a tree of the *Solanaceae* family, originally from Peru. Tamarillos grow in bunches of 30; they must be peeled before their juicy pulp is eaten.

TAMARIND The fruit of a leguminous evergreen tree, which originated in West Africa but is now grown in the West Indies, India, tropical Africa and South-East Asia. The brown pods, 10–15 cm (4–6 in) long and 7.5 cm (3 in) wide, contain a bittersweet pulp dotted with a few hard seeds. Tamarinds are mostly used for preparing jams, sorbets, chutneys, drinks and condiments. In India, the pulp of dried tamarind – a major ingredient in spice mixtures – is also used in salads, broths and purées of dried vegetables. The juice of fresh tamarind is used to season crudités. In China, crystallized (candied) tamarind is used to garnish certain sweet-and-sour soups.

TAMIÉ A cow's-milk cheese from Savoy (40–45% fat content), made by the Trappist monks of the monastery of Tamié. Pressed and uncooked, with a soft and elastic texture, Tamié has a washed, smooth, clear rind, a fairly pronounced lactic taste, and is made in the form of rounds, 18 cm (7 in) in diameter and 4–5 cm (1½–2 in) thick. Also called Trappiste de Tamié, it is served at the end of the meal or grilled (broiled) on croûtes.

TAMPONNER A French culinary term meaning to carefully place flecks of butter on the surface of a hot preparation, such as a sauce (especially béchamel) or a soup; as the butter melts, it forms a thin film of grease over the sauce, which prevents a skin forming while it is kept hot.

TANDOORI In Indian cookery, particularly in the Punjab and Pakistan, a method of cooking chicken or other meat. The pieces of chicken are skinned, then coated in yogurt mixed with chilli powder, turmeric, ginger, spices, onion and chopped garlic. After marinating overnight, the chicken is sprinkled with saffron or chilli powder and cooked on a bed of embers in a special cylindrical clay oven called a *tandoor*, until the flesh is tender, but the outside crispy. Tandoori chicken is served with salads: onions and tomatoes with tamarind juice and coriander (cilantro); cucumber with yogurt and cumin; or grated cabbage with pepper and lemon juice. Fish and galettes can also be cooked in the *tandoor*.

TANGELO A citrus fruit produced by crossing a tangerine and a grapefruit. It can be peeled as easily as a tangerine. Irregular in shape, the tangelo (an American hybrid) is bigger and more acid than an orange, but it is used in the same way – as fresh fruit, for fruit salad and for fruit juice.

TANGERINE A citrus fruit resembling a small slightly flattened orange. Also known as mandarin. There are many types of tangerine but their linking characteristics are sweet, fragrant flesh and loose skin, therefore they are easy to peel. This citrus fruit originated in China, with the fruit from North Africa first taking the name 'tangerine'. Many varieties have been produced and the same names are often used for different types, confusing the subject and making identification difficult. As in the cultivation of most fruit, new examples are often available, and seedless types are particularly popular. The following are some of the names used.

- *Clementine* Small fruit with orange-tangerine flavour. Originally from Algeria, it was discovered in a priest's garden (Father Pierre Clementine) where it was an accidental cross between a mandarin and an orange.
- *Malaquina* Originally from Uruguay, this fruit is a cross between a mandarin and an orange.
- *Mandarin* An alternative name for tangerine, and indicative of the Chinese origin of the fruit.
- *Mikan* This small, sweet fruit is popular for canning and rarely available fresh.
- *Minneola* This fruit is a cross between a tangerine and a grapefruit. It has strong-coloured skin with a little bump or nipple at the stalk end. The orlando is very similar.
- *Murcott* This fruit is a cross between a tangerine and an orange. Also known as murcott honey orange.
- *Ortanique* Originating from Jamaica, this is an orange–tangerine cross with fine, slightly rough skin and a sweet juicy flesh.
- *Satsuma* Originally of Japanese origin, these fruit are sharp as well as sweet.
- *Tangelo* An alternative name for fruit of minneola type, a cross between the tangerine and grapefruit or pomelo.
- *Tangerine* Originally the name for the North African fruit, or fruit imported to Europe through Tangier.
- *Tangors* Name for types of fruit resulting from an orange–tangerine cross.

■ **Use** Tangerines have a distinctly different flavour from oranges. Usually eaten fresh for dessert, they can also be preserved and used in cooking and pâtisserie in the same way as oranges; in sweet preparations their flavour can be enhanced with kirsch or liqueur brandy. The peel is used to flavour liqueurs.

In France, the word *tangerine* is used for the hybrid produced by crossing an orange with a tangerine.

RECIPES

frosted tangerines
Choose fine even-sized tangerines with thick skins. Cut off the tops and remove the segments without breaking the peel. Place the empty shells and tops in the freezer. Squeeze the pulp, strain the juice and add 300 g (11 oz, 1⅓ cups) caster (superfine) sugar for every 500 ml (17 fl oz, 2 cups) juice. Dissolve the sugar completely in the juice. Add a little more juice if too thick or a little more sugar if too thin. Place in an ice-cream maker, but stop the process before the ice sets. Fill the frosted shells with the iced pulp and cover each with its top. Return to the freezer to allow the ice to set.

tangerine gâteau
Grind 125 g (4½ oz, 1 cup) shelled almonds in a mortar and add 4 eggs, one by one. Add 4 pieces of candied tangerine peel, finely chopped, as well as 125 g (4½ oz, ⅔ cup) icing (confectioner's) sugar, 3 drops vanilla essence (extract), 2 drops bitter almond essence (extract) and 2 tablespoons apricot jam, strained through a fine sieve. Stir well.

Roll out some shortcrust pastry (basic pie dough) to line a flan ring mould. Spread a layer of tangerine compote on the bottom and cover with the almond mixture. Smooth the top. Bake in a preheated oven at 200°C (400°F, gas 6) for about 30 minutes. Take out of the oven and allow to cool. Press 3 tablespoons apricot compote through a sieve and spread over the top of the cake. Decorate with a few fresh mint leaves, quarters of tangerine cut in half horizontally, and flaked (slivered) almonds, briefly grilled (broiled) to colour them. Put in a cool place. Just before serving, place the cake on a serving dish and cut a few slices so as to reveal the inside.

- *Individual tangerine barquettes* ◆ Instead of making a large gâteau, line barquette or boat-shaped moulds with the pastry and fill as above. Reduce the cooking time to about 20 minutes. Decorate with flaked almonds. Serve with a scoop of tangerine sorbet or ice cream on a strawberry or raspberry coulis feathered with fine lines of single (light) cream.

tangerines en surprise
Prepare some frosted tangerines, but do not fill completely with the sorbet mixture and do not

cover. When they are completely frozen, top up with a tangerine-flavoured soufflé, sprinkle with icing (confectioner's) sugar and brown in a pre-heated oven at 220°C (425°F, gas 7).

tangerine syrup
Remove the peel from 4 tangerines, cut it into julienne strips and steep in a syrup made with 100 ml (4 fl oz, 7 tablespoons) water and 300 g (11 oz, 1⅓ cups) sugar. Add a sprig of fresh mint and allow to cool completely: leave the mint to infuse in the syrup for 2 hours. Carefully remove the white pith from the tangerine segments and cut them into small pieces. Remove the mint from the syrup and pour this on to the fruits. Keep in a cool place until time to serve.

TANNIN A substance contained in some vegetable matter, such as tea, and oak or walnut bark, and also in the skin, pips (seeds) and stalks of grapes. In wine-making tannin dissolves in the alcohol and is one of the main constituents of red wine, responsible for its character and longevity. It is particularly abundant in Bordeaux wines, which explains why they take so long to mature. Excess tannin makes wine astringent and leads to the formation of a deposit in the bottle.

TANSY A common European plant with tall stems and golden-yellow aromatic flowers. Its leaves have a bitter flavour and were included in the pharmacopoeias compiled by monks in the Middle Ages. In former times, a highly flavoured household liqueur was made with tansy. When Stanislas Leszczyński 'invented' the baba, he sprinkled it with tansy water.

TANT-POUR-TANT A mixture comprising equal proportions of caster (superfine) sugar and ground almonds, used by professional pastrycooks and confectioners to make biscuit (cookie) batters, almond cream and petit-four bases.

TAPAS In Spain, an assortment of hors d'oeuvre or cocktail snacks, traditionally served to accompany Málaga, sherry, Manzanilla or cider. The custom of nibbling tapas while drinking apéritifs, particularly in the evening, is widespread in bars and restaurants. The word comes from *tapa* (lid), since it originally meant a slice of bread which was used to cover a glass of wine to protect it from flies. Once confined only to Spain, tapas bars can now be found in many of the world's cities.

Tapas can sometimes take the place of dinner because they are so varied and abundant; they may include cubes of ham garnished with sweet red (bell) pepper; white haricot (navy) beans with vinaigrette; squares of thick filled omelettes; seafood in sauce; sautéed kidneys; fried shrimps; black (ripe) olives in brine; tuna rissoles; cauliflower in vinaigrette; small eels fried with sweet red pepper; squid *en su tinta* (in their ink); stuffed sweet peppers; and even snails in a piquant sauce, pigs' trotters (feet)

with tomato, or chicken fricassée with mushrooms. These tapas are served in small earthenware dishes, into which people dip using their fingers or cocktail sticks (toothpicks).

TAPENADE A condiment from Provence, made with capers (from Toulon), desalted anchovies and stoned black (pitted ripe) olives, pounded in a mortar and seasoned with olive oil, lemon juice, aromatics and possibly a drop of marc brandy. Tapenade is sometimes augmented by small pieces of tuna, mustard, garlic, thyme or bay leaf. It accompanies crudités (in particular, celery, fennel and tomato), meat or grilled (broiled) fish, is spread on slices of toast, and can garnish hard-boiled (hard-cooked) eggs (mixed with yolk).

The word is derived from the Provençal *tapeno* (caper).

RECIPE

tapenade
Desalt 100 g (4 oz) canned anchovy fillets, peel 4 garlic cloves and stone (pit) 350 g (12 oz, 3 cups) black (ripe) olives. Blend, using a food processor, 100 g (4 oz) tuna canned in oil, drained, the anchovy fillets, 100 g (4 oz, 1 cup) capers, the juice of 1 lemon, the olives and the garlic. Press the ingredients through a very fine sieve, then pound the purée in a mortar (or use a food processor), gradually adding 250 ml (8 fl oz, 1 cup) olive oil and the juice of 1 large lemon. The finished tapenade should be thick and smooth.

TAPIOCA A starchy food extracted from the roots of the manioc plant, which is hydrated, cooked, then ground. It is used mainly for thickening soups and broths and making milk puddings and other desserts. True tapioca (the word is derived from the Tupi-Guarani *tapioca*) comes from Guyana, Brazil and the West Indies.

RECIPES

tapioca consommé
Sprinkle 75–100 g (3–4 oz, ⅔–¾ cup) tapioca in 1.5 litres (2¾ pints, 6½ cups) boiling consommé* and cook for 10 minutes. Serve piping hot.

tapioca dessert
Boil 500 ml (17 fl oz, 2 cups) milk with a pinch of salt, 25 g (1 oz, 2 tablespoons) sugar and 1 teaspoon vanilla sugar. Sprinkle in 75 g (3 oz, ⅔ cup) tapioca, stir, then add 2 beaten egg yolks. Continue mixing, then blend in 3 egg whites whisked to stiff peaks with 75 g (3 oz, ⅔ cup) icing (confectioner's) sugar. Serve thoroughly chilled.

Individual tangerine barquettes,
see page 1189.

tapioca with milk

Boil 1 litre (1¾ pints, 4⅓ cups) milk with a pinch of salt, 2 tablespoons sugar and, as desired, either a vanilla pod (bean) or ½ teaspoon orange-flower water. Sprinkle in 75–100 g (3–4 oz, ⅔–¾ cup) tapioca, mix, then cook for 10 minutes, stirring regularly. Remove the vanilla pod.

TARAMASALATA Also known as *taramosalata*, particularly with reference to the authentic Greek dish. This Greek speciality is traditionally served as one of the *mezze* dishes or as a starter. It consists of a smooth, creamy paste of fish roe (botargo) crushed with breadcrumbs soaked in milk, egg yolk, lemon juice, a little vinegar, salt and pepper, then emulsified with olive oil. This is now a popular international dip, widely available as a commercial preparation, varying both from the original recipe and in quality.

TARO A perennial plant grown in tropical regions for its large starchy tuberous rhizomes, which have twice the calorific value of the potato. Taro originally came from India (where it is called *katchu*). It is known as *chou-chine* or *chou caraibe* in Martinique, *malanga* in Cuba and Haiti, *songe* in Réunion and *madère* in Guadeloupe. Up to 40 cm (16 in) long, the roots have a smooth skin and are variously coloured – white, purplish-blue, red or yellowish, according to the variety. They are scrubbed and peeled, then used in the same way as the potato: boiled, fried or cooked *au gratin*. In China, balls of steamed taro are stuffed with meat, then fried. In Japan, it is used in vegetable stews. In Haiti, the grated raw pulp is used to prepare *acras*. Taro is also used in desserts.

TARRAGON An aromatic perennial plant originating in central Asia. Its name is derived, via the Arabic *tarkhūn*, from the Greek *drakontion* (a serpent-eating bird) – the herb was formerly reputed to cure snakebite.

French tarragon is the plant used as a culinary herb for its pronounced, yet delicate, aniseed-like flavour. Russian tarragon is lighter in colour and more piquant, but does not have such a delicate taste. The narrow, elongated leaves of French tarragon have a fine flavour and are used to season salads, sauces and pickles. Tarragon is one of the herbs used in fines herbes. It is also a traditional aromatic for flavouring chicken dishes, fish and eggs. Tarragon vinegar is a classic ingredient for salad dressings and sauces. Tarragon leaves are used fresh or they may be preserved by drying or freezing.

RECIPES

tarragon cream

Boil 100 g (4 oz, 2 cups) chopped fresh tarragon with 150 ml (¼ pint, ⅔ cup) dry white wine. When almost completely dry, add 350 ml (12 fl oz, 1½ cups) thick béchamel* sauce, season with salt and pepper, bring to the boil for a few seconds, then rub through a sieve. Reheat and add a little butter.

This purée is used as a filling for small vol-au-vent, barquettes or canapés and also for stuffing certain vegetables such as artichoke hearts or mushrooms.

tarragon purée (cold)

Blanch 100 g (4 oz, 2 cups) tarragon leaves and cool under running water. Wipe them and pound in a mortar (or use a blender) with the yolks of 6 hard-boiled (hard-cooked) eggs, 2 tablespoons butter, salt and pepper.

tarragon purée (hot)

This is prepared in the same way as tarragon cream, but with a very reduced béchamel sauce. It can also be made by adding a purée of tarragon leaves (blanched, cooled under running water, drained, pounded in a mortar and sieved) to twice its volume of mashed potatoes.

tarragon sauce for poached fowl

Add a large handful of tarragon to the white stock in which the chicken was poached. Skim the fat from the stock, strain, reduce and thicken with arrowroot. Add some freshly chopped tarragon just before serving.

tarragon sauce for small cuts of meat

Sauté the meat in butter, then remove from the pan. Make a sauce from the pan juices by adding 100 ml (4 fl oz, 7 tablespoons) white wine, 1 tablespoon chopped tarragon leaves and 200 ml (7 fl oz, ¾ cup) stock. Boil down by half, adjust the seasoning and thicken with beurre manié.

tarragon sauce for soft-boiled or poached eggs

Coarsely chop 100 g (4 oz, 2 cups) washed and wiped tarragon leaves, add 100 ml (4 fl oz, 7 tablespoons) white wine, then boil down. Add 200 ml (7 fl oz, ¾ cup) demi-glace* or thickened brown veal stock and boil for a few moments. Strain through a very fine sieve. Add 1 tablespoon fresh coarsely shredded tarragon just before serving.

other recipes See *chaud-froid, chicken, egg (eggs en cocotte), vinegar.*

TART A pastry case (shell) filled, before or after baking, with savoury or sweet ingredients. The words 'tart' (*tarte*) and 'flan' are often used interchangeably in Britain and France to designate a pastry filled with fruit, jam, custard or some other filling. The American term often used is open pie. Most such dishes are cooked and served in the United States in a pie dish, whereas in Britain and France a metal flan or pastry ring, placed on a metal baking sheet, is used.

Savoury tarts are served as hot entrées, and

include flans; quiches; onion, tomato or cheese tarts; *pissaladière*; *flamiche*; and *goyère*. Sweet tarts are usually filled with fruit or a flavoured cream; they are one of the commonest and most varied pastries.

To prepare a tart, a flan ring, pie dish or tin (pan) is lined with suitable pastry – shortcrust (basic pie dough), puff or sablé – and the filling is placed in it. If the fruit (particularly strawberries and raspberries) is to remain uncooked, the case is baked blind and filled after baking. When the case is to receive a liquid filling, it is half-baked, then filled. Tarts of the galette type (which can be rectangular or square) are baked directly on a baking sheet without a tin: these are filled with narrow strips of fruit and sprinkled with sugar.

Tarts baked with their filling are usually made of shortcrust or puff pastry. Those baked blind and filled afterwards are made with sablé or shortcrust pastry. Some puff-pastry tarts are baked blind as rectangles edged with puff-pastry strips; they are then usually filled with confectioner's custard (pastry cream) and poached fruit, then glazed. Other varieties include: upside-down tarts, modelled on tarte Tatin; tarts decorated with crisscrossed pastry strips, known in France as *alsaciennes* and including the Austrian Linzertorte; and *tartes à l'anglaise*, which are similar to fruit pies in that they are covered with a pastry lid. The British fruit tart is baked in a tart plate, not a flan dish. The tart plate is slightly deeper than a standard dinner plate but not quite as deep as a classic soup plate. Tart pastry may be enriched with ground almonds or cinnamon, and the filling may be glazed with apricot or covered with meringue.

Since the Middle Ages, there have been innumerable tart recipes from all parts of France. The *tarte bourbonnaise* cited in Taillevent's *Viandier* ('fine cheese mixed with cream and preserved plums' in a case 'moulded with eggs') is still a speciality of the Bourbonnais, now called *gouéron*. The tarts of Alsace are well-known for the variety of their fillings: strawberries, cherries, bilberries (huckleberries), blueberries, redcurrants, mirabelle plums, quetsches and rhubarb. Everyday tarts are usually made with ordinary pastry, whereas those for feast days are made with a richer pastry. In northern and eastern France, fresh-cheese tarts are a traditional speciality; this tart is found in Corsica under the name of *imbrucciata*. A simple mixture of beaten eggs, sugar, milk and cream is used as a filling for the *tarte au goumeau* of Franche-Comté and the *tarte en quemeu* of Chaumont. Confectioner's custard is used as a bed for fruit in some tarts (pears for the *tarte Bourdaloue*, cherries or plums in Alsace). In northern France and Switzerland, rice or sugar tarts are made, similar to the Canadian maple syrup tarts. In western France, apples and pears are the most popular filling.

In Germany and Austria, tarts are called *Torte* (for example, *Linzertorte*) or *Küchen* (for example, *Kirschenküchen*, or cherry tart); they are frequently made with apples, cherries, plums or mixed fruits

and are often decorated with whipped cream. Also worth mentioning are the Russian *vatrouchka*, the American pecan pie and the Swiss wine tart.

RECIPES

Savoury Tarts

curd cheese tart
Mix 500 g (18 oz, 2¼ cups) well-drained curd cheese with 5 tablespoons plain (all-purpose) flour, the same amount of crème fraîche, 2 eggs, salt and a very little pepper. Pour this mixture into an unbaked tart case (pie shell) made of shortcrust pastry (basic pie dough), sprinkle with knobs of butter and bake in a preheated oven at 200°C (400°F, gas 6) for about 45 minutes. Serve cold.

spinach tart
Quickly blanch 1.5 kg (3¼ lb) young fresh spinach. Chop coarsely and blend with 40–50 g (1½–2 oz, 3–4 tablespoons) butter. Season with salt and pepper. Line a 20 cm (8 in) tart tin (pie pan), preferably made of cast iron for more rapid and even baking, with puff pastry rolled out to a thickness of 5 mm (¼ in). Fill it with the spinach. Drain 4 anchovy fillets canned in oil and lay them on top of the tart in a criss-cross pattern. Sprinkle the tart with a few knobs of butter and bake in a preheated oven at 220°C (425°F, gas 7) oven for 20 minutes. The anchovy fillets may be replaced by fresh sardines cooked very rapidly in a frying pan with a little olive oil.

tomato tart
Make some puff pastry, roll it out and use it to line a greased flan tin (pie pan); gently prick the bottom. Mix together 6 whole eggs, 100 ml (4 fl oz, 7 tablespoons) crème fraîche, 25 g (1 oz, 2 tablespoons) butter and 50 g (2 oz, ½ cup) grated Gruyère cheese. Add 1 kg (2¼ lb) tomatoes, peeled, seeded and crushed. Mix well and season with salt and pepper. Fill the tart with this mixture and bake in a preheated oven at 180°C (350°F, gas 4) for about 45 minutes.

additional recipe See *asparagus*.

Sweet Tarts

Alsace tart
Beat 1 whole egg with 250 g (9 oz, 1 cup) caster (superfine) sugar, then add 125 g (4½ oz, ½ cup) melted butter. Work the mixture together. Gradually blend in 250 g (9 oz, 2¼ cups) sifted plain (all-purpose) flour, then 250 g (9 oz, generous 2¼ cups) ground almonds. Knead thoroughly, adding 1–2 tablespoons water if the dough is difficult to work. Roll out three-quarters of the dough to form a circle 1 cm (½ in) thick; place this on a buttered baking sheet. Roll out the remaining dough very thinly and cut it into narrow strips. Surround the pastry circle with one of the strips and arrange the others crisscross fashion on the disc.

Fill each section with a different sort of jam (strawberry, plum or apricot, for example) and bake in a preheated oven at 200°C (400°F, gas 6) for 20 minutes. Serve lukewarm or cold.

apple tart

In a food processor blend 250 g (9 oz, 2¼ cups) plain (all-purpose) flour, 125 g (4½ oz, ½ cup) butter cut into pieces, and a large pinch of salt until the dough sticks to the sides of the bowl. Add 3 tablespoons water (or a little more) and operate the food processor again until the dough begins to bind together. Quickly shape the dough into a ball, wrap it in foil and chill for 2 hours.

Peel and finely slice 800 g (1¾ lb) apples and sprinkle with lemon juice. Roll out the dough to a thickness of 5 mm (¼ in) and use it to line a buttered and floured 25 cm (10 in) tart tin (pie pan). Arrange the slices of apple over the pastry base in concentric circles; sprinkle generously with granulated sugar and 50 g (2 oz, ¼ cup) melted butter. Bake in a preheated oven at 220°C (425°F, gas 7) for about 30 minutes, until the apples caramelize slightly. Serve lukewarm, accompanied by crème fraîche.

apricot tart

Make 350 g (12 oz) shortcrust pastry (basic pie dough, see *short pastry*) Roll it out to a thickness of 5 mm (¼ in) and use it to line a 24 cm (9½ in) buttered and floured flan tin (pie pan). Chill for 30 minutes. Prick the bottom with a fork. Stone (pit) 800 g (1¾ lb) very ripe apricots and arrange the halves on the bottom of the tart case, with the cut sides against the pastry. Sprinkle with 5 tablespoons caster (superfine) sugar. Bake in a preheated oven at 200°C (400°F, gas 6) for about 40 minutes. Turn out on to a wire rack. Spread the top with 3 tablespoons apricot compote, sieved and boiled down. Serve cold.

Basque tart

In a mixing bowl blend 300 g (11 oz, 2¾ cups) sifted plain (all-purpose) flour, 4 egg yolks, a pinch of salt, 2 teaspoons baking powder, 100 g (4 oz, ½ cup) caster (superfine) sugar and 50 g (2 oz, ¼ cup) softened butter; gradually add sufficient milk to obtain a pliable yet firm dough. Put aside for 1 hour. Roll out the dough and line a buttered 25 cm (10 in) flan tin (pie pan). Prick the base with a fork and bake blind in a preheated oven at 200°C (400°F, gas 6) for 20 minutes.

Meanwhile, peel and quarter 12 apples. Remove the cores and sprinkle with lemon juice. Melt 100 g (4 oz, ½ cup) butter in a saucepan, cook the apples to a pale golden colour, sprinkle with 100 g (4 oz, ½ cup) caster sugar and gently stir. Arrange the apples on the tart base in a rosette and sprinkle with the butter they were cooked in. Sprinkle with 2 tablespoons granulated sugar and glaze for 5 minutes, either in a very hot oven or under the grill (broiler).

cherry tart

Line a flan tin (pie pan) with shortcrust pastry (basic pie dough) and fill with ripe stoned (pitted) cherries. Whisk together 100 g (4 oz, ½ cup) caster (superfine) sugar and 2 whole eggs, then blend in 200 ml (7 fl oz, ¾ cup) milk and 50 g (2 oz, ½ cup) plain (all-purpose) flour. Pour this cream over the cherries and bake the tart in a preheated oven at 200°C (400°F, gas 6) for about 30 minutes.

Alternatively, use the same method as for apricot tart.

chocolate tart

Prepare a chocolate sablé pastry with 125 g (4½ oz, ½ cup) butter, 50 g (2 oz, ⅓ cup) icing (confectioner's) sugar, 50 g (2 oz, ½ cup) ground almonds, 1 whole egg, 175 g (6 oz, 1½ cups) plain (all-purpose) flour and 3 tablespoons sifted cocoa powder (see *short pastry*). Allow to rest for 2 hours in a cool place. Roll out the pastry and line a flan tin (pie pan). Bake in a preheated oven at 180°C (350°F, gas 4) for about 40 minutes and leave to cool. Bring 250 ml (8 fl oz, 1 cup) single (light) cream to the boil with 100 g (4 oz, ⅔ cup) glucose. Pour on to 200 g (7 oz, 7 squares) cooking chocolate with 80% cocoa content, broken up into small pieces, and 50 g (2 oz, ¼ cup) pure cocoa paste. Add 50 g (2 oz, ¼ cup) butter. Allow to cool but not thicken. Sprinkle 25 g (1 oz, ¼ cup) toasted chopped almonds on the bottom and pour the chocolate ganache on top.

curd cheese (me'gin) tart à la mode de Metz

Prepare a shortcrust pastry (basic pie dough) tart base (shell). Mix 200 g (7 oz, 1 cup) well-drained curd cheese (called *fremgin* or *me'gin*), 100–200 ml (4–7 fl oz, ½–¾ cup) crème fraîche, 3 beaten eggs, 2–3 tablespoons caster (superfine) sugar and a pinch of salt; flavour, if desired, with 1 teaspoon vanilla sugar or some vanilla essence (extract). Fill the base with this mixture and bake in a preheated oven at 200°C (400°F, gas 6) for about 35 minutes.

German cherry tart

Prepare some puff pastry and roll it out to a thickness of 5 mm (¼ in). Use it to line a flan tin (pie pan), moistening the edges of the pastry and pinching them to make a border. Prick the base with a fork. Sprinkle with a little caster (superfine) sugar and a pinch of powdered cinnamon. Over the base arrange some stoned (pitted) cherries (fresh or canned, well-drained) and bake in a preheated oven at 200°C (400°F, gas 6) for about 30 minutes. Allow to cool, then coat the top with a generous layer of sweetened cherry purée, prepared by cooking some cherries in sugar. To finish, bake some fine breadcrumbs to a pale golden colour in the oven and sprinkle them over the tart.

The cherries may be replaced by apricot halves if desired.

German gooseberry tart

Clean some large ripe gooseberries. Prepare a puff-pastry tart base and bake blind. Mix the gooseberries in a saucepan with an equal weight of sugar cooked to the crack stage (see *sugar*): when the sugar has melted, drain the fruit and boil down the juice until it sets into a jelly. Put the gooseberries back into the syrup, boil together for a moment, then pour into a basin. When cool, use it to fill the tart; mask with whipped cream.

lemon tart

Make a tart case (shell) of shortcrust pastry (basic pie dough) and bake blind until the pastry is crisp but not completely cooked. Mix together 3 eggs, 100 g (4 oz, ½ cup) sugar, 75 g (3 oz, 6 tablespoons) melted butter, the juice of 5 lemons and their grated zest. Whisk and pour into the tart case. Bake in a preheated oven at 240°C (475°F, gas 9) for 10–15 minutes.

This recipe can be made using 3 oranges or 7 tangerines instead of the lemons.

pineapple tart

Prepare some short pastry with 150 g (5 oz, 1¼ cups) plain (all-purpose) flour, 75 g (3 oz, 6 tablespoons) softened butter, a pinch of salt and a little cold water. When it is pliable and well-mixed, roll it out and use it to line a 22 cm (8½ in) buttered flan tin (pie pan); prick the base with a fork. Leave in a cool place for 2 hours, then bake blind in a preheated oven at 200°C (400°F, gas 6) for 20 minutes.

Meanwhile, mix together 2 egg yolks, 75 g (3 oz, 6 tablespoons) caster (superfine) sugar, 1 teaspoon flour and 175 ml (6 fl oz, ¾ cup) milk. Stir this mixture over a low heat until it thickens, then add the juice of half a lemon and 60 ml (2 fl oz, ¼ cup) reduced pineapple syrup. Take the tart case (shell) out of the oven, allow it to cool, then pour in the pineapple cream and arrange on top 6 slices of canned pineapple, well-drained. Whisk 2 egg whites to stiff peaks, pour over the fruit and sprinkle with 25 g (1 oz, 2 tablespoons) caster (superfine) sugar. Return to the oven at the same temperature and cook for 10 minutes to brown the meringue mixture. Leave in a cool place until just before serving.

puff-pastry apple tart

Prepare an apple compote with 800 g (1¾ lb) apples, the juice of half a lemon, 150 g (5 oz, ⅔ cup) caster (superfine) sugar and 1 teaspoon vanilla sugar. Sieve, heat gently to dry off the excess liquid. Prepare 400 g (14 oz) puff* pastry. Roll it out to form a rectangle 30 × 13 cm (12 × 5 in). Make a border with a small strip of pastry about 1 cm (½ in) wide. Bake blind. Thinly slice 500 g (18 oz) crisp apples and sauté them in 50 g (2 oz, ¼ cup) butter until they are brown but still intact. Spread the apple compote over the cooked base, decorate with the slices of apple and sprinkle with 2 tablespoons icing (confectioner's) sugar, then glaze in the oven or under the grill (broiler).

raspberry tart

Prepare some short pastry (basic pie dough) using 300 g (11 oz, 2¾ cups) plain (all-purpose) flour, 1 egg, a pinch of salt, 125 g (4½ oz, ½ cup) butter and 5 tablespoons water. Roll it into a ball and leave it in a cool place for 1 hour. Then roll it out to a thickness of 3–4 mm (about ¼ in) and use to line a 24 cm (9½ in) tart tin (pie pan). Prick the base and bake blind. Prepare some confectioner's custard (pastry cream, see *custard*) using 50 g (2 oz, ½ cup) plain flour, 20 g (¾ oz, 1½ tablespoons) butter, 175 g (6 oz, ¾ cup) sugar, 4 eggs, 500 ml (17 fl oz, 2 cups) milk and a vanilla pod (bean). Leave to cool. Pick over 500 g (18 oz, 3½ cups) raspberries, but do not wash. Cover the cooled tart with the confectioner's custard, put the raspberries on top and coat them with melted redcurrant and raspberry jelly. Serve chilled.

rhubarb tartlets

Roll out 250 g (9 oz) of puff* pastry and cook between two baking sheets in a preheated oven at 200°C (400°F, gas 6). Cut into rectangles 12 × 7.5 cm (4½ × 3 in). Sprinkle soft brown sugar on top and brown under the grill (broiler). Peel 500 g (18 oz) rhubarb and cut into pieces of the same length as the puff-pastry rectangles. Cook in the oven at 150°C (300°F, gas 2) until just tender, add a little water and 2 tablespoons caster (superfine) sugar, and continue cooking under a sheet of foil. Drain. Prepare a brown caramel sauce with 100 g (4 oz, ⅔ cup) icing (confectioner's) sugar and water. Add 50 g (2 oz, ¼ cup) butter: the caramel sauce must coat the spoon. Place the pieces of rhubarb on the puff pastry and put in a lukewarm oven for 1 minute. Using a pastry (piping) bag, pipe some very cold cream lengthways, then pour the lukewarm caramel in threads widthways.

strawberry tart

Sort, wash and hull 1 kg (2¼ lb, 7½ cups) strawberries. Put them in an earthenware bowl and sprinkle with the juice of 1 lemon and 50 g (2 oz, ¼ cup) caster (superfine) sugar. Prepare short pastry using 300 g (11 oz, 2¾ cups) plain (all-purpose) flour, 150 g (5 oz, ⅔ cup) softened butter, a pinch of salt and 2 tablespoons water. Roll it into a ball and leave it in a cool place for 2 hours. Then roll out the pastry and use it to line a buttered and floured 28 cm (11 in) tart tin (pie pan). Prick the base with a fork and bake blind. When the tart is cool, fill it with the strawberries. Mix 60 ml (2 fl oz, ¼ cup) redcurrant jelly with the juice drained from the strawberries and pour this syrup over the tart. The top can be decorated with whipped cream.

Swiss wine tart

Mix 350 g (12 oz, 3 cups) plain (all-purpose) flour, a pinch of salt and 1 tablespoon caster (superfine) sugar. Add 75 g (3 oz, 6 tablespoons) softened butter and 15 g (½ oz, 1 cake) fresh (compressed) yeast mixed with 3 tablespoons milk. Alternatively, sprinkle 1½ teaspoons dried (active dry) yeast over the milk, whisk with a balloon whisk until dissolved and leave in a warm place until frothy before adding it to the other ingredients. Rapidly work the ingredients, then roll the dough into a ball and set aside for 2 hours. Roll it out and use it to line a buttered tart tin (pie pan). Beat 3 eggs with 100 g (4 oz, ½ cup) sugar until the mixture becomes thick and creamy, then add 100 ml (4 fl oz, 7 tablespoons) dry white wine. Pour the mixture into the tart case (shell). Bake in a preheated oven at 220°F (425°F, gas 7) for 20 minutes. Take out the tart, sprinkle with caster sugar and knobs of butter, then return it to the oven for a further 15 minutes. Serve lukewarm.

three tatins with fresh pineapple and kiwi coulis

Cut 3 large fresh pineapples into quarters, then into slices 3 mm (⅛ in) thick. Make a brown caramel sauce with 125 g (½ oz, ½ cup) caster (superfine) sugar and 60 ml (2 fl oz, ¼ cup) cold water. Pour the mixture into 18 tatin moulds or shallow individual tart tins (pans). Allow to cool, then fill with pieces of pineapple, gently pressing them down. Put a knob of butter and a pinch of sugar on top of each. Cook in a preheated oven at 200°C (400°F, gas 6) for 10 minutes. Remove from oven, and cool slightly, then cover with puff-pastry lids of the same size as the mould. Continue cooking at 220°C (425°F, gas 7) for about 15 minutes, or until the pastry is cooked.

Meanwhile, peel 6 kiwis and carefully crush the flesh. Press this purée through a sieve and add the juice of a lemon. Remove the small tatins from their moulds when cold. Pour kiwi coulis in the centre of each plate and arrange three tatins around it. Add a few pieces of fresh fruit and a spoonful of pineapple sorbet in the middle. Decorate with a sprig of fresh mint.

other recipes See *cassonade, fig, grape, plum, rice, Tatin.*

TARTAR *tartre* A crystalline deposit left inside wine casks after racking. This by-product of wine consists mainly of crude potassium acid tartrate, which, when purified, gives cream of tartar, used in baking.

Tartaric acid is one of two principal acids found in grapes, the other being malic acid. If the must lacks acidity, some tartaric acid may be added to it if the relevant wine laws allow for this. Acidity helps to preserve wine and affects its stability and colour.

TARTARE, À LA A term originally describing dishes covered with breadcrumbs, grilled (broiled) and served with a highly seasoned sauce, but now usually used for a sauce or a raw meat dish. Tartare sauce is a mayonnaise made with hard-boiled (hard-cooked) egg yolks, onion and chives and is served with fish, calves' feet, oysters and pont-neuf potatoes. Steak tartare is made with minced (ground)

beef (or horse meat, according to the purists) served raw with egg yolk and seasoning. In Belgium, this dish is called *filet américain.*

The expression *à la tartare* is also applied to various highly seasoned cold or hot dishes: paupiettes of anchovies spread with horseradish butter, or fried eggs on a bed of minced (ground) beef seasoned with paprika, for example.

RECIPES

anchovy fillets à la tartare

Thoroughly desalt 12 anchovy fillets. Mix 1 tablespoon finely grated horseradish with the same amount of butter. Mask each fillet with a little of this flavoured butter and roll it into a paupiette. Cut some cooked beetroot (beet) into slices 5 mm (¼ in) thick and trim them with a fluted cutter. Place 1 anchovy paupiette on each slice. Garnish with a little sieved hard-boiled (hard-cooked) egg and chopped parsley, then a few capers. Sprinkle with vinaigrette and serve thoroughly chilled.

steak tartare

Mince (grind) 150–200 g (5–7 oz) lean beef (rump steak, sirloin or top rump). Season with salt and pepper, a little cayenne and a few drops of Worcestershire sauce or Tabasco. Shape the meat into a ball, place it on a plate, hollow out the centre and put a raw egg yolk in the hollow. Around the meat arrange 1 tablespoon each of chopped onion, chopped parsley and chopped shallots and 1 teaspoon drained capers. Serve with tomato ketchup, olive oil and Worcestershire sauce.

tartare sauce

Prepare some mayonnaise, replacing the raw egg yolk with hard-boiled (hard-cooked) egg yolk. Add some finely chopped chives and chopped spring onion (scallion).

Alternatively, a mixture of raw egg yolk and hard-boiled egg yolk can be used, and chopped herbs can replace the chives and onion.

additional recipe See *egg (eggs en cocotte).*

TARTE AU SUCRE Brioche pastry case covered with a cooked mixture of sugar or verjuice, nuts of butter and beaten egg. This speciality of northern France is eaten warm.

TARTINE The French word for a slice of bread spread with butter, jam or any other suitable substance of spreading consistency.

Le Dictionnaire de l'Académie des gastronomes refers to *fripe,* which, in the west of France, is any substance that can be spread on bread (such as butter, cheese or jam); in *Le Lys dans la vallée,* Balzac writes: 'Rillettes from Tours are the best of *fripes'.*

TARTINER The French verb meaning to spread butter, paste and the like, on a slice of bread; a special knife with a rounded edge (a *tartineur*) is used for this purpose. The word is also used to describe spreading forcemeats or fillings in escalopes, crêpes and cakes, and for lining or coating dariole or charlotte moulds.

TARTLET A small individual tart made in the same way as a large tart and with the same fillings. Tartlets filled with fruit, creams or other sweet mixtures are served as a dessert; savoury tartlets are served as hors d'oeuvre or small entrées.

RECIPES

coffee or chocolate tartlets
Line some greased tartlet tins (pans) with sablé pastry. Prick the bottom with a fork and bake blind for about 10 minutes. Allow to cool. Then, using a piping (pastry) bag, fill some of the cases with French coffee butter cream and the remainder with Chantilly cream flavoured with chocolate and rum.

walnut and honey tartlets
Line some greased tartlet tins (pans) with short-crust pastry (basic pie dough). Sprinkle them with crushed walnuts and arrange some narrow strips of pastry in a crisscross pattern on the top. Brush with beaten egg and bake in a preheated oven at 220°C (425°F, gas 7) for about 15 minutes. When they are cooked, coat them with acacia honey.

other recipes See *Agnès Sorel, blackberry.*

TASSAU A meat dish that is typical of West Indian and Central American cookery. It is made by steeping some pieces of meat (beef, veal or poultry) for several hours in a chilled and very spicy court-bouillon containing pepper, cloves, thyme, chilli, onion, limes and chives. The meat is then poached rapidly in the court-bouillon, drained and then either grilled (broiled) or fried. Tassau is served either with boiled bananas or with fried sweet potatoes.

TASTE The sense by which the flavours of food are perceived, the organ used being the tongue, which is equipped with taste buds. It is possible to distinguish four basic tastes: salt, acid, sweet and bitter, which, combined in different ways, determine the taste of everything we eat. From a gastronomic point of view, the sense of taste is closely associated with the sense of smell. The aroma of a dish provides a good deal of information about its taste, and the sense of smell contributes greatly to the sense of taste while actually eating – this is why food seems tasteless to anyone who has a cold.

TASTER A specialist who judges the quality of a drink or a food by its taste. No instrument has been devised to rival a properly trained human palate, particularly in the area of wine tasting, where the test consists of savouring the wine by rolling it in one's mouth so that all its qualities are brought out.

In Paris there is still a Compagnie de Courtiers-Gourmets-Piqueurs de Vins, which dates back to the time of Philip the Fair (1285–1314); the duties of these officials include the tasting of wines at the request of the courts or authorities. The word *piqueur* derives from a tool called a *coup de poing*, a sort of gimlet used to puncture (*piquer*) the barrel to take a sample. The food industry often makes use of professional tasters. Tea, coffee, butter, foie gras and oil, are tested by panels, which consist of groups of tasters whose opinions are cross-checked.

TASTING The critical appraisal of a food or drink via its impression on the senses. Although many foods are tasted, from basic items such as butter, oil and tea to the luxury foods, such as foie gras and fine chocolates, the word is usually applied to the tasting of wines and spirits.

The professional taster adopts the same procedure for both wines and spirits, but a spirit, whether on its own or 'broken down' with water, is seldom actually put in the mouth: it is mainly sniffed. In 'blind tasting' the identity of the liquid is not known. There are three main stages in tasting: looking, sniffing and appraising the liquid in the mouth. The taster will look at the colour and limpidity of the liquid (in wine the colour is known as the 'robe') and will then sniff at it. Then a small quantity is taken into the mouth, usually with a certain amount of air, which is drawn through the liquid; the sample is pulled around to make contact with the top and sides of the mouth and the tongue.

The registering of impressions conveyed by the smell is of great importance and much may be learned from this stage of tasting, although only experience can enable one to interpret the messages received by the nose from a wine or spirit. When the wine gets into the mouth, another set of impressions are registered – flavours associated with particular grapes, regions and even makers – and, with both the smells and the tastes, certain faults in the wine can be picked out. Each part of the mouth can often contribute to the overall impression, although it should be remembered that tasting young wines, before they are ready to drink, is an experience that the beginner can find unpleasant: time is needed before the development of a wine can be judged, except by the very experienced. In general, though, wine should be a unified harmonious beverage, each element being in balance with the others – fruit, acidity, alcohol.

A professional taster will usually spit out a wine – to taste and drink a number of assorted ones, even those that have reached the stage of being agreeable drinks, can be highly confusing as well as intoxicating when several dozen or more samples have to be tasted. With the fortified wines, the number that can be judged at one session is fairly small, even for the professionals. When the wine has either been swallowed or spat out, the taster breathes sharply out through the mouth; this process circulates the aromas within the facial cavities and registers the aftertaste, which can be very revealing. A wine that leaves the palate clean, refreshed and with a definite impression of interest and quality is said to have a good finish.

TÂTE-VIN Also known as *taste-vin*. A small receptacle made of pewter, silver or silver plate with a handle surmounted by a support for the thumb; it is used for examining and tasting wine. Known also as a *coupole* or simply (as in Burgundy) a *tasse*, its shape varies from region to region: the *tâte-vin* from Burgundy has rounded sides that are ornamented with bosses to reflect the colour of the wine, while those of Bordeaux have smooth funnel-shaped rims.

TATIN The name given to a tart of caramelized apples that is cooked under a lid of pastry and then inverted to be served with the pastry underneath and the fruit on top. This delicious tart, in which the taste of caramel is combined with the flavour of apples cooked in butter under a golden crispy pastry crust, established the reputation of the Tatin sisters, who ran a hotel-restaurant in Lamotte-Beuvron at the beginning of the 20th century. However, the 'upside-down' tart, made with apples or pears, is an ancient speciality of Sologne and is found throughout Orléanais. Having been made famous by the Tatin sisters, it was first served in Paris at Maxim's, where it remains a speciality to the present day.

RECIPE

tarte Tatin ◆
Mix 200 g (7 oz, scant 1 cup) sugar with 225 g (8 oz, 1 cup) butter. Smear this over the bottom and sides of a 23 cm (9 in) tarte Tatin tin (pan) or flameproof shallow baking tin or dish.

Peel and core 800 g (1¾ lb) apples and cut them into quarters or wedges, if large. Trim the pointed ends off the pieces of apple, then arrange them in concentric circles in the tin, adding the trimmed-off corners to fill in the gaps. When the apples are neatly packed in place, cook over a fairly high heat until the butter and sugar form a golden caramel. The mixture will rise as it boils and coats the apples: remove the tin from the heat to prevent it from boiling over. Leave until completely cold.

Make about 350 g (12 oz) shortcrust pastry (basic pie dough), roll it into a ball, and leave it in a cool place for 2 hours (see *short pastry*). (Alternatively, puff pastry can be used instead.) Roll out the pastry into a circle 3 mm (⅛ in) thick.

Cover the apples with the pastry, tucking it inside the edge of the tin so that the fruit is contained. Bake in a preheated oven at 200°C (400°F, gas 6) for 20–30 minutes.

Place a serving dish on top of the tin and turn the tart upside down. Remove the tin. Serve warm, with crème fraîche.

TAVEL A rosé wine which has its own AOC and comes from the southern Rhône valley, in the vicinity of Avignon. It is made from several different grapes, including Grenache and Cinsaut, and there are estate Tavels as well as the wines produced by the co-operative. Refreshing and always dry, the wines are best when drunk young and fresh.

TAVERN Originally, a tavern in France was simply a wine shop, as distinct from the cabaret, which also provided meals. In 1698, tavern-keepers were given permission to serve meat, provided that it was prepared elsewhere, at the rôtisserie or the charcuterie. Ten years later, they were allowed to cook meat on the premises, but they were still forbidden to cook ragoûts, which were the prerogative of the *traiteurs*. Nowadays, a tavern is usually a brasserie or a restaurant with traditional décor.

TAVERNE ANGLAISE The name given to several Parisian restaurants that specialized in English food. The first Taverne anglaise, which was also known as the Grande Taverne de Londres, was opened by Beauvilliers at the Palais-Royal in 1782. Later, he founded another establishment in his own name. There was also a Taverne anglaise in the Rue Taranne, in Saint-Germain-des-Prés.

The Englishman Richard Lucas opened a Taverne anglaise in 1832 and the menu included roast beef and Yorkshire pudding. This establishment became the Restaurant Lucas and subsequently the Lucas-Carton. A fourth Taverne anglaise opened in 1870 in the Rue de Richelieu; it served rare meat, rib of beef and rhubarb tart.

TCHORBA A thick soup from Arab cookery made with pieces of sheep's tail and mutton cutlets. The meat is browned in oil with onions and tomatoes, mixed with courgettes (zucchini), garlic, thyme and bay leaves, then cooked in plenty of water with white haricot (navy) beans or chick peas, and seasoned with red pepper, black pepper and saffron. Before serving, some macaroni or vermicelli or dried fruit are added to the soup.

Similar dishes are found in Balkan cookery: *corba*, beef soup with sweet (bell) pepper and onion, thickened with rice, from the former Yugoslavia, and Romanian or Bulgarian *ciorba*, a sharp-tasting soup made with beef and vegetables (or sometimes fish), which may be seasoned with lemon.

TEA The most universally consumed beverage, made by infusing the dried leaves of an Asiatic evergreen shrub, *Camellia sinensis*. There are two main varieties of tea plant, that of China and that of India, with numerous local varieties and hybrids. Climate, soil, altitude and orientation all affect the growth and quality of the plants, and therefore the colour, fragrance and taste of the tea. The best plants are cultivated at an altitude of about 2000 metres

Tarte Tatin.

A scoop of Assam tea. The scoop is made of cherry wood and the decorative pewter tea caddy is late 19th century.

(6500 ft) and are picked in the spring. Growing areas are situated at latitudes between 42°N and 31°S, in regions with a hot humid climate and winters that are neither too cold nor too dry.

It is thought that tea cultivation originated in China around 3000 BC and spread to Japan in about AD 780. It was not grown in India until the 1840s, and in Ceylon (now Sri Lanka) the first tea estate was planted in 1867. The beverage was brought to Europe in the 17th century by the Dutch, and reached England in 1644. It arrived in America in the early 18th century. At first regarded primarily as a medicinal beverage, tea drinking soon became fashionable with the aristocracy and then popular at all levels of society.

Today the principal tea producers are India, Sri Lanka, China, Japan, Indonesia, East Africa, Latin America and parts of Russia. In Britain, tea is mostly taken with milk and sometimes sugar, and drunk at regular intervals throughout the day. The drinking of tea is important in China and in Japan, where the tea ceremony (*kaiseki*) has influenced social life, art, religion and philosophy.

In the wild, the plant can reach a height of 10 m (32½ ft), but in cultivated plantations the shrubs are limited to a height of 1.2 m (4 ft), so that the leaves can more easily be picked by hand. The downy

terminal bud (the 'pekoe', from the Chinese *pa ko*, meaning down) and the top two leaves are plucked from each stem. The smaller and younger the leaves, the better the tea. The different grades of tea are *orange pekoe* (the tip of the bud is yellowish-orange), *pekoe* (shorter leaves without buds), *pekoe souchong* (even shorter, coarser and older leaves), and *souchong* (leaves older still and rolled into balls). The broken leaves are sold under the same names but preceded by the word 'broken'.

There are three types of tea, depending on the treatment of the leaves: *green tea*, which is unfermented and roasted immediately after harvesting and gives a strong, bitter, although quite clear infusion; *black tea*, by far the most common, which is fermented and dried; and *oolong tea*, which is semi-fermented and intermediate between green and black tea.

■ **Green tea** A speciality of China and Japan prepared by subjecting the leaves to fierce heat, green tea forms the basis of the Japanese tea ceremony, an important part of Japanese social life and culture. It is also highly favoured by the Chinese and Muslims, who are forbidden to drink fermented tea. The varieties are: Gunpowder (known as *Chao Chen* in China), the rolled leaves of which are similar to small shot about 3 mm (⅛ in) long; *Tychen* (also known as Coarse Gunpowder or Imperial Tea), having larger pellet-sized rolled leaves; Moroccan mint tea, which is very refreshing; and Japanese tea (*Shincha*), which gives a highly coloured infusion.

■ **Black tea** Whether from China or elsewhere, there are five stages in its preparation: withering, when the leaf is dried and softened; rolling, during which the cells of the leaves are broken down to release and mix the constituents; moist fermentation for 2–3 hours at 27°C, (81°F); desiccation for 20 minutes at 90°C (194°F); and sorting or grading. The three main types of black tea come from Sri Lanka (Ceylon), India and China.

• CEYLON TEAS These are quite strong infusions, with a natural simple taste, and can be drunk at any time. Among the best varieties are: Superior Orange Pekoe (large very fragrant leaves, with a delicate taste, giving an amber-coloured infusion, served preferably without milk); Flowery Orange Pekoe (rolled leaves which open out fully during infusion, giving a fragrant tea, blending well with lemon); Uva Highland (a great growth, obtained from large leaves, drunk without milk); Medium Grown Broken Orange Pekoe (a full-bodied tea, usually drunk with milk); and High Grown (a coloured very fragrant tea, excellent in the morning).

• INDIAN TEAS These are particularly fragrant teas, the most prestigious of which are Darjeeling (fruity, delicious with pastries, the taste varying depending on the soil, altitude and weather conditions of the estates where they are grown – Selimbong, Sington, Jungpana, for example) and Assam (small broken leaves with golden tips, producing a full-bodied tea often drunk with a little milk). Bengal tea has large leaves, giving a delicate tea with an almond taste, suitable for breakfast.

• CHINA TEAS There are two types: ordinary teas (which does not mean ordinary quality) and steamed teas. Among the former are: Yunnan, known as the 'mocha' of teas, stimulating and with a full-bodied taste (well-formed leaves with golden tips); Caravan, fragrant, low in caffeine, recommended for drinking in the evening; Keemun, with digestive properties; and Great Mandarin, flavoured with jasmine and a perfect accompaniment to oriental cookery. Steamed teas include Imperial Souchong (young tender leaves blended with jasmine flowers), suitable for the afternoon; Lapsang Souchong (a well-formed broad-leaved tea with a smoky taste and aroma), steamed more than Imperial Souchong; and Tarry Souchong (broad leaves), with a very pronounced smoky flavour.

■ **Oolong** This tea from Taiwan is made from semi-fermented leaves. Its quality varies from season to season (it is at its best in the summer). It is very popular in the United States, where it is divided into eight grades ranging from 'choicest' to 'common'. The best is Fancy Grade Oolong, characterized by well-formed whole leaves and giving a unique mellow infusion best drunk without milk. Other varieties taste of honey.

■ **Scented teas** Apart from the classic teas, there is a large variety of teas perfumed with flowers or fruits, the most famous of which is Earl Grey. A black unsteamed China tea to which oil of bergamot is added, it is named after the 2nd Earl Grey, for whom it was created. There is also Georgia tea, flavoured with citrus fruits and flowers. Vanilla, mulberry, raspberry, coconut, grapefruit, apple, apricot, ginger, cinnamon, passion fruit and many others, make various scented teas that may be drunk either hot or iced. However, apart from the traditional flavourings of jasmine, rosehip, bergamot, orange flower and lotus, other fragrances produce infusions which, for tea-lovers, have little to do with tea. See also *tisane*.

In addition, a number of classic, blended, unscented teas are available. Companies have also marketed instant tea, freeze-dried tea, decaffeinated tea and scented tea in powdered form.

■ **Tea and health** The many beneficial qualities of tea have been recognized since ancient times: it stimulates the nervous system because of its caffeine (or theine) content, it aids digestion, stimulates the circulation and heartbeat (by means of theophylline), and is a diuretic; it is rich in manganese, iodine and copper.

The properties and flavour of tea can be preserved by storing it in a dry airtight tin away from the light. Tea stored in this way will keep for up to about 18 months.

■ **To make tea** Tea is made according to a few simple rules.

• Use water that is as lime-free as possible (purists avoid tap water, which makes the tea cloudy). The water should be free from iron, which would precipitate tannins in the cup, and should not be chlorinated. In the absence of spring water, connoisseurs choose a light mineral water. Do not use water that has already been boiled in order to save time.

• Rinse out the teapot with boiling water just before putting in the tea. The general rule is one teaspoon of tea per person and one 'for the pot'. The better the tea, the smaller the quantity required, but you can never compensate for an insufficient quantity of tea by letting it infuse over a longer period.

• Pour the water on to the tea just as it reaches boiling point, taking the pot to the kettle.

• The infusion time is 3–5 minutes, depending on whether the tea leaves are whole or broken. After this time, the flavour does not improve, and the tannins spread and make the infusion more bitter and darker. (Because of this, tea balls or tea infusers are recommended.)

• Just before serving, stir the tea in the teapot with a spoon; if the tea leaves are left in the pot, use a strainer when pouring.

A good-quality tea is generally drunk on its own, or sometimes with a dash of milk (always cold). Tea-lovers avoid lemon, which denatures the flavour of tea, and they often do without sugar. Some, however, like tea sweetened with honey.

There are various traditions associated with the preparation and tasting of tea in different countries. Russian tea is quite dark and strong and is served in glasses. Sometimes a lump of sugar is placed in the mouth and the tea is sipped and allowed to filter through it. The reserve of boiling water in the samovar enables tea to be prepared continuously, and it is traditionally offered to all visitors. China tea is served in small fine porcelain cups without handles. It is sometimes flavoured with bergamot or jasmine, and can be drunk at any time of the day, except during meals. According to Vietnamese tradition, tea is drunk in cups with a closely fitted lid, which retains the flavour and heat. In Arab countries, tea is infused with mint and drunk very sweet, out of small glasses. The Japanese drink tea in accordance with an elaborate ceremony, governed down to the minutest detail and requiring years of experience.

Tea is also used as an aromatic in the cooking of certain exotic dishes.

RECIPES

China tea
Boil 1 litre (1¾ pints, 4⅓ cups) water in an enamel kettle. When the water starts to boil vigorously, pour a little into a teapot (made of earthenware or porcelain). Shake the teapot for 30 seconds so that it is heated evenly. Pour the water away. Put 2 teaspoons black tea into the teapot, fill with boiling water, put on the lid and leave for 2 minutes. Pour the tea into a large cup, then immediately pour it back into the teapot (this operation brings out the fragrance of the tea). Allow to infuse for a further 2 minutes, then serve.

duck with tea leaves – Chinese
Draw a duck weighing about 1.4 kg (3 lb). Rub the inside and outside of the carcass with salt, then with sugar. Place the duck in a deep ovenproof dish sprinkled with 3 tablespoons fresh root ginger cut into thin strips, 2 tablespoons crushed cinnamon, and 2 tablespoons star anise. Sprinkle with 175 ml (6 fl oz, ¾ cup) Chinese rice wine or dry sherry. Add 100 ml (4 fl oz, 7 tablespoon) water, cover and cook in a bain marie for 2 hours. Drain the duck and leave to cool on a plate. Heat a deep cast-iron pan and pour in 75 g (3 oz, ¾ cup) green tea. Place over a moderate heat until a light white smoke is given off. Then put the duck in the hot pan, cover and leave it to absorb the smoke for 4 minutes, then remove from the heat. Heat a little groundnut (peanut) oil in a large deep frying pan and brown the duck on all sides over a brisk heat for 5 minutes. Carve and serve piping hot, garnished with braised broccoli.

eggs with tea leaves – Chinese
Put 6 eggs into a saucepan with 500 ml (17 fl oz, 2 cups) cold water. Leave the pan uncovered and simmer for 20 minutes. Allow to cool. Remove the eggs and crack the shells by tapping with the back of a spoon over the entire surface. Put the eggs back into the saucepan with 500 ml (17 fl oz, 2 cups) cold water, 1 tablespoon salt, 2 tablespoons soy sauce, 1 star anise and 2 teaspoons black China tea. Bring to the boil, then reduce the heat as much as possible and cook gently for 2 hours. The eggs must always be covered with liquid (add boiling water as necessary). Remove the saucepan from the heat and allow the eggs to steep in the cooking liquid for 8 hours. Just before serving, shell the eggs. Cut them in half lengthways and serve them with thin strips of cold roast pork and a salad of sprouted soya beans with mushrooms, seasoned with soy sauce vinaigrette.

iced tea
Prepare an infusion of green tea and add a sprig of fresh mint. Strain the tea, pour it into a carafe, sweeten it slightly, allow it to cool, then chill it for at least an hour.

Just before serving, add 4 tablespoons rum per 1 litre (1¾ pints, 4⅓ cups) tea.

Indian tea with milk and spices
Pour 500 ml (17 fl oz, 2 cups) milk into a saucepan and add 1 cinnamon stick, 2 crushed cloves, 2 crushed cardamon seeds and 1 piece of fresh root ginger (peeled and chopped). Bring to the boil, then add 1½ tablespoons tea and some caster (superfine) sugar, according to taste. Boil for 1–2 minutes, cover, remove from the heat and allow to infuse for at least 7–8 minutes. Strain the infusion and serve very hot.

lamb with prunes, tea and almonds – Algerian
Bone 1 kg (2¼ lb) shoulder of lamb, remove the fat and cut the meat into large dice. Sprinkle with finely ground salt and cook it in a casserole with butter until golden brown. Drain. Add to the butter in the casserole 250 ml (8 fl oz, 1 cup) water, 1 cinnamon stick chopped into pieces, 50 g (2 oz, ½ cup) blanched almonds, 200 g (7 oz, 1 cup) caster (superfine) sugar and 2 tablespoons orange-flower water. Bring this mixture rapidly to the boil, stirring continuously. Replace the meat, cover the pan and allow to simmer over a low heat for 45 minutes. Meanwhile, soak 350 g (12 oz, 2 cups) stoned (pitted) prunes in very strong green tea. Add the prunes and tea to the casserole and cook for a further 10 minutes.

tea sorbet
Prepare quite a strong infusion of tea according to taste. Add sugar in the proportion of 300 g (11 oz, 1⅓ cups) per 1 litre (1¾ pints, 4⅓ cups) and allow to set in a churn freezer. Prunes cut up into tiny pieces may be added to the sorbet. Green tea flavoured with jasmine gives excellent results.

tuna fish in tea – Vietnamese
Brown a bluefin tuna steak, weighing about 800 g (1¾ lb), in oil in a frying pan. Meanwhile, prepare an infusion of fairly strong tea (black China tea or lotus tea). Put the tuna into a saucepan together with 100 g (4 oz, ½ cup) diced fresh unsalted belly

of pork. Add a piece of fresh root ginger cut into thin strips, pepper, 1–2 teaspoons *nuoc-mâm* (Vietnamese fish sauce), a lump of sugar and the tea (ensure that the liquid just covers the fish). Simmer over a gentle heat for 1 hour.

additional recipe See *mint*.

TEAL A small wild duck, several species of which are hunted in France, including the common teal, which rarely migrates and is found in France and Britain all year round, and the summer teal, which comes from Africa, as well as the Baikal teal, the marbled teal and the sickled teal. In the United States there are various species, the most common being the green-winged teal. The teal is more difficult to hunt than the mallard because of its jerky flight, but is cooked in the same way. Its brownish and rather bitter meat is much sought-after by connoisseurs. In the Middle Ages it was considered to be a lean meat; that is, one that could be eaten on fast days. Teal, like all wild ducks, is roasted blood-rare and seldom braised.

TEAPOT A receptacle with a lid, a spout and a handle, used to prepare and serve tea. Teapots come in various sizes and can be made of various different materials, including porcelain, faïence, earthenware and metal.

An innovation appeared in the 19th century: a trellis, or a screen pierced with small holes, placed inside, at the base of the spout, thereby preventing the leaves from pouring into the cup with the infusion. However, this does not mean that a strainer need not be used. Some models also have an internal strainer, which is fitted to the opening of the teapot. The tea leaves are placed in it before the water is poured in. The first metal teapots appeared in France at the end of the 17th century. Those made of porcelain and faïence came initially from China and Japan, then later from Meissen and Sèvres.

TEA ROOM An establishment in which tea, hot chocolate, coffee, soft drinks and cakes (and sometimes savoury pastries or egg dishes, salads, sandwiches, croque-monsieur and so on) are served in the afternoon or at lunch time. Nowadays, tea rooms are usually part of a baker's shop or a large store. The luxurious tea rooms found in larger cities in the first half of the 20th century, where society ladies met for 'five o'clock tea', are now disappearing.

TEA – THE MEAL A light meal in the afternoon, at which sandwiches, pastries and cakes are served with tea. A rather more substantial meal is high tea (or meat tea), which is taken particularly in Scotland and the north of England, where the evening meal is replaced by tea served with cold meat, fish and salads; as well as buttered rolls, toast and cakes. Afternoon tea taken at five o'clock was launched by the Duchess of Bedford in about 1830 (at that time lunch was served quite early and dinner was served late). It provided an opportunity to display tea services made

of porcelain or silver plate, to create recipes for cakes and biscuits (cookies), and to lay down rules of etiquette associated with the occasion (the correct way in which to hold the cup, put down the spoon, and so on). The most common items of an English tea are bread-and-butter, scones, muffins, crumpets, buns, cakes, biscuits, gingerbread and shortbread, with jams and jellies, lemon curd and other spreads.

On the Continent, tea was adopted during the period of Anglomania at the end of the 19th century, especially in towns. It was also served as a kind of buffet during balls and soirées. 'A prefect was reproached for bribing the electors of his *département* by inviting them to dine at his sumptuous table. He announced that henceforth he would confine himself to offering them tea. ... The precious infusion with a dash of cream was served on magnificent trays with small dry crispy pastries. The country electors ... could not understand people liking this insipid beverage, which, to them, was like hot water. The prefect's secretary discreetly led them to the back of the room. There, sideboards had been arranged, suitably decked with cold items, capable of satisfying the heartiest of appetites. They found pâtés, fish, galantines and venison, with wines to match. And so these worthy folk then understood what tea was. In France, tea is the supper of the salons.' (Eugène Briffault, *Paris à table*)

TELFAIRIA A plant of the gourd family, resembling a water melon, grown in Réunion. The telfairia, or oyster nut, contains numerous flat seeds which enclose the kernels. A light yellow oil, of good quality for cooking, is extracted from them and they are also pleasant to eat.

TELLIER, CHARLES French engineer (born Amiens, 1828; died Paris, 1913), nicknamed 'the father of refrigeration' in 1908 by d'Arsonval. In 1856 he developed the first industrial refrigerator, and in 1876 the first plant to produce ice consistently for preserving foodstuffs. In the same year an attempt was made to transport meat preserved by refrigeration from Rouen to Buenos Aires on board the steamship *Frigorifique*, which had been specially fitted out for that purpose. The experiment was successful and marked the first victory for the refrigeration industry.

TEMPRANILLO Spanish red grape variety, cultivated particularly in the production region of classic red Rioja, of which it usually forms 70%. In other areas, Tempranillo is known as 'Aragonez', 'Tinta Roriz', 'Tinta del Pais', 'Cencibel', 'Ojo de Liebre', 'Tinto Fino' or even 'Ull de Liebre'. It is also an important variety of Argentina, with increasing plantings in Australia, Portugal and Venezuela.

TEMPURA Typically Japanese shrimp or vegetable fritter, using a light batter made with wheat flour, water and eggs. Tempura is traditionally accompanied by a lightly sweetened sauce and a white radish purée sprinkled with ginger. It is perhaps the most important Japanese dish, now known and enjoyed throughout the western world.

TENCH A European freshwater fish found in ponds and quiet waterways. It is 15–30 cm (6–12 in) long, with a barbel on each side of the mouth, and has tiny olive-green to reddish-brown scales covered with thick mucus. Fish caught in clear water are delicious, especially since tench do not have too many bones. But ones caught in muddy waters may be tainted, which is why fishermen pour a spoonful of vinegar into their mouths as soon as the fish is caught, then soak them in water. Tench is generally used in matelotes and can also be fried or prepared *à la meunière*. In the past it was more popular, being cooked in court-bouillon or *à la bonne femme* and used in soups, ragoûts and pies.

TENDE-DE-TRANCHE A French cut of beef taken from the top of the thigh. Classified as second-category beef, it nevertheless provides cuts for steaks: *dessous-de-tranche* (rather firm), *merlan* (long and flat), *poire* (round and fleshy) and *morceaux du boucher* (delicious tender cuts of meat). Tende-de-tranche can also be roasted.

TENDERIZING Even good-quality meat may be tough for several hours after slaughtering. The storage or hanging of meat at low temperatures, 0–2°C (32–36°F), enables it to mature and become tender before it is sold.

The cook can also encourage tenderizing during preparation and by using the appropriate cooking method. Meat can be beaten or flattened with a steak mallet, which helps to make it more tender. Meat may also be tenderized by soaking it in a marinade. Lengthy marinating in acidic ingredients, such as yogurt or citrus fruit juice, for 1–2 days, encourages tender results. Papain, an enzyme found in plants, and fruit in particular, is useful for culinary purposes, breaking down protein, effectively 'digesting' it and making it tender. The texture of the meat changes – it becomes tender but dry rather than succulent. Over-long marinating of poultry with papain-rich fruit makes the poultry crumbly, dry and quite unpleasant in texture; it becomes almost curdled.

Papaya and pineapple are both rich in papain, and using them in marinades produces tender meat. The enzyme is destroyed at high temperatures, so canned fruit does not have the same effect and cooking meat with the fruit, without marinating, will provide only a short period, during the initial brief heating, when the enzyme can take effect before being destroyed.

Generally, the effect of low, slow and moist cooking is the one relied on to tenderize tough meats. Tender cuts do not require lengthy cooking – dry methods and shorter times make them palatable.

TENDRET, LUCIEN French lawyer and gastronome (born Belley, 1825; died Belley, 1896). He was a compatriot and distant relative of Brillat-Savarin and a scholar who was passionately interested in food. In 1892, he published *La Table au pays de Brillat-Savarin*, in which he recorded, among others, the recipe for the famous chicken Celestine, a Lyonnais speciality, as well as recipes for the three famous *pâtés en croûte* of Belley: the *oreiller de la Belle Aurore*, the *toque du président Adolphe Clerc*, and the *chapeau de monseigneur Gabriel Cortois de Quincey*, rich in game, poultry, truffles and foie gras.

The following aphorism is attributed to him: 'Gourmandism seeks out all the courtesies and all the refinements. It is the only passion that does not leave behind any remorse, sorrow, or suffering.' Rouff undoubtedly modelled his character Dodin-Bouffant upon Lucien Tendret.

TENDRON A piece of beef or veal cut from the extremities of the ribs, from the point at which the chops are generally cut, to the sternum. Tendrons of veal, which contain a few small cartilages, are streaked with fat and are very smooth. They are used for blanquette, braised or sautéed veal, or veal Marengo. If they include sufficient lean meat, they can be cut into slices, potroasted or braised as *côtes parisiennes*, and then garnished with fresh pasta, risotto, braised spinach in butter or braised carrots. Tendrons of beef are streaky pieces of meat used for braising and for pot-au-feu.

RECIPES

braised tendrons of veal à la bourgeoise
Braise 4 tendrons of veal; when half-cooked, add 12 small glazed onions, 12 shaped and glazed carrots, and 50 g (2 oz, ¼ cup) diced streaky (slab) bacon (blanched and fried). Finish the cooking, drain the tendrons and arrange them on an ovenproof serving dish. Sprinkle them with a little of the cooking juices and glaze in a preheated oven at 230°C (450°F, gas 8). Serve piping hot, garnished with the vegetables and the diced bacon.

tendrons of veal chasseur
Cook 4 tendrons in a shallow frying pan with 25 g (1 oz, 2 tablespoons) butter (10 minutes on each side). Drain them and keep them hot on a serving dish. Add 200 g (7 oz, 2⅓ cups) finely sliced mushrooms to the pan, brown them, and then add 3 tablespoons each of stock, white wine and tomato* sauce. Add 2 chopped shallots, then boil down by at least half. Pour the mushrooms and sauce over the tendrons, sprinkle with chopped herbs and serve piping hot.

tendrons of veal with spinach or sorrel
Braise some tendrons of veal and some spinach (or sorrel) in butter in separate pans. Drain the tendrons, arrange them on a hot dish and sprinkle with the cooking juices. Garnish with the drained and buttered vegetables.

TEQUILA A spirit made in several Mexican states from the plant *Agave tequilana*. The pulp of this plant is chopped up and baked to extract the sap. Then it is shredded and pressed, so that the juice runs out and begins to ferment. Subsequently it undergoes a double distillation. Some tequila is aged in wood, gaining colour; the best is usually five years old and golden in tone. Unless tequila is part of a cocktail, it is traditionally drunk from a small glass; the drinker puts some salt in the join of his thumb and forefinger, licks a slice of lime or lemon, and knocks the reflex of the wrist so that the salt jumps up to the mouth. (One can, alternatively, just lick the salt.) The tequila is then drunk in a single gulp.

TERIYAKI Japanese dish of grilled food glazed with a sauce of soy sauce, mirin or sake and sugar to give an excellent flavour and rich colour. The food – fish, chicken, meat or vegetables – may be marinated before cooking. Teriyaki sauce is available as a commercial product.

TERRINE A fairly deep dish with straight sides, grips or handles, and a tightly fitting lid that rests on an inner lip. Terrines are manufactured in a wide range of sizes; they can be made of glazed earthenware (with the lid sometimes shaped like an animal) or of porcelain, ovenproof glass or even enamelled cast iron. The food cooked or served in such a container is also known as a terrine.

The word terrine in France is also the name of a stoneware utensil shaped like a truncated cone with a wide rim and, sometimes, a pouring spout; it is used to hold milk or cream, to work a forcemeat or a paste or to steep a foodstuff. A terrine may also be a simple serving utensil used to present dishes such as pickled herring fillets or mushrooms *à la grecque*.

The preparations known as terrines are numerous and varied. They are usually made with mixed meats, but can also be made with fish, seafood and even vegetables. They are served cold in the container in which they are cooked (or in slices taken from the latter), accompanied by gherkins, pickled onions and cherries or grapes as a sweet-and-sour garnish. Fish or vegetable terrines are sometimes served with a sauce and may be eaten warm. They are generally prepared with cooked ingredients set in aspic jelly, or ingredients reduced to a mousse and cooked in a bain marie.

The majority of meat terrines contain a certain amount of pork (fat and lean), or sometimes veal, mixed with the meat that gives the dish its name: chicken, chicken liver, game or foie gras, for example. The ingredients are used in varying proportions and are cut up in different ways, depending on the recipe (reduced to a forcemeat; cut into strips, dice or fillets; or coarsely chopped). Seasoning always plays an important part in the preparation, as does marinating the ingredients in alcohol. The containers are usually lined with bacon fat and the preparation covered with jelly or lard. They are often autumn dishes, as this is the game season, and may be garnished with mushrooms, nuts (walnuts, almonds) and aromatic herbs such as thyme, bay leaf or juniper berries.

This is how René Boylesve describes the terrine in *L'Enfant à la balustrade*: 'She took us to the dining room and ran to the sideboard. She took out a brown glazed earthenware terrine, which had a recumbent animal roughly moulded on the lid . . . The contents formed an egg-shaped dome which was reddish-bronze in colour, decorated with strips of bacon fat, glazed and half-melted, which still seemed to sizzle, and small bay leaves, also cooked, like greenish copper ornaments. A snow-white grease enshrined it all like a crackled wall, milky-blue in colour. It was a pâté made with game from the *bourriche* (game bag).'

Terrines, which are cooked covered in the oven, in a bain marie, are often rustic dishes, suitable for slicing; others, however, are sophisticated preparations, such as terrine de Nérac (red-legged partridge, chicken livers, ham and truffles), terrines of goose liver (very much in vogue in the 18th century, before goose liver pâté was created), and terrines of vension, wild rabbit or thrushes with juniper berries. Contemporary chefs have a preference for terrines of fish and shellfish: crayfish with small vegetables, scorpion fish, red mullet, burbot, pike, as well as vegetarian varieties.

Terrines are also prepared as desserts made with fruit set in jelly, which are served with cream or a fruit sauce.

RECIPES

terrine de Body

Cut 575 g (1¼ lb) veal escalopes and 400 g (14 oz) smoked belly of pork into fine strips. Finely chop 16 shallots and a bunch of parsley and season with 2 teaspoons ground black pepper. Arrange the ingredients in a terrine as follows: first a layer of pork belly, then a layer of veal, then a layer of shallots and parsley, continuing this way until the ingredients are used up, finishing with a layer of pork. Moisten each layer with a little dry white wine and press down hard.

Cover the terrine and place it in a bain marie. Bring to the boil on the hob (stove top), then cook in a preheated oven at 180°C (350°F, gas 4) for 1 hour. Place a small board with a weight on the terrine before allowing it to cool. Chill for at least 24 hours before serving.

terrine de l'océan

Scale, gut and clean a 1 kg (2¼ lb) turbot, a 1 kg (2¼ lb) pike, 500 g (18 oz) fresh salmon and 2 large red mullet. Lift out the fillets and ensure that no bones remain. Reserve the trimmings.

Cut an 800 g (1¾ lb) lobster in half, seal it in 40 g (1½ oz, 3 tablespoons) slightly salted butter, then remove the shell and put it to one side. Clean 1 kg (2¼ lb) mussels and cook in a covered pan until they open. Remove the flesh and retain the cooking juices.

Prepare the forcemeat as follows: wash 500 g (18 oz) leeks and finely slice the white parts; chop 2 garlic cloves and 4 shallots. Soften all these vegetables in 40 g (1½ oz, 3 tablespoons) slightly salted butter. Add 200 g (7 oz, 3 cups) coarsely chopped sorrel, then the leaves of a sprig of tarragon. Use a coarse grater to shred the fillets of pike and then the lobster flesh. Blend in the leek and sorrel mixture. Season with salt and pepper; add a pinch of 'four spices', 2 tablespoons mustard and 3 whole eggs. Mix thoroughly, then add the mussels.

Now prepare the terrine: line a white porcelain ballotine mould with bards, leaving the ends hanging over the side of the dish, and brush with egg white, then spread in it the first layer of forcemeat and cover with the fillets of turbot and salmon. Add a second layer of forcemeat, then the flesh and corals of 1 kg (2¼ lb) scallops, pointing the corals towards the centre of the mould. Chop 1 large truffle and sprinkle over the scallops, then add another layer of forcemeat, then the red mullet fillets and finally the rest of the forcemeat. Put a bay leaf in the centre. Dissolve 7 g (¼ oz, 1 envelope) powdered gelatine in 4 tablespoons water; pour over the terrine. Fold down the bards to seal the terrine, cover and cook in a bain marie in a preheated oven at 190–200°C (375–400°F, gas 5–6) for 1¼ hours.

Prepare an aspic with the fish trimmings, the shell of the lobster, the juice of the mussels, the green parts of the leeks and some gelatine. Pour this over the terrine when it has cooled. Keep cool until just before serving. To serve, stand the mould in a little hot water, then turn it out on to a serving dish. Garnish with lettuce leaves and parsley. Serve some herb-flavoured mayonnaise separately.

terrine of duckling
Bone a duckling weighing about 1.25 kg (2¾ lb) without damaging the breast meat. Cut the latter into even strips, together with 300 g (11 oz) bacon fat. Put the meat into a bowl with salt, pepper, ½ teaspoon 'four spices', 4 tablespoons brandy, a chopped bay leaf and a small sprig of fresh thyme with the leaves removed. Thoroughly soak the meat in this mixture and marinate for 24 hours in a cool place. Put the rest of the duck in the refrigerator. Soak an intact pig's caul (caul fat) in cold water, then squeeze and wipe it dry.

Prepare a duxelles* with 250 g (9 oz, 3 cups) button mushrooms, 2 or 3 shallots, salt and pepper.

Finely chop 350 g (12 oz) fresh belly of pork, 1 onion, the remaining duck meat and the blanched zest of an orange. Mix the duxelles and the chopped meat in a bowl with 2 eggs, pepper and salt. Work the mixture well to make it homogeneous, adding the marinade in which the strips of bacon fat and duck were steeped.

Line the terrine with the caul. Arrange half of the forcemeat in an even layer. Cover with alternating strips of the marinated duck and bacon fat. Cover

with the rest of the forcemeat. Press down the caul on the contents of the terrine and trim. Place a bay leaf and 2 small sprigs of fresh thyme on top and then put on the lid.

Place the terrine in a bain marie, bring to the boil on the hob (stove top), then cook in a preheated oven at 180°C (350°F, gas 4) for 1½ hours. Remove from the oven and allow to cool. When lukewarm, take off the lid and replace with a weighted board. Allow the terrine to cool completely.

An aspic flavoured with port can be poured into the terrine and allowed to set. To preserve the terrine, cover with a fine layer of melted goose fat.

terrine of fruit with honey jelly
You will need 2 rectangular terrines for this recipe. Add 2 tablespoons honey, 500 g (18 oz, 2¼ cups), caster (superfine) sugar, some orange and lemon peel and a few leaves of lemon-balm to 1.5 litres (2¾ pints, 6½ cups) water in a pan. Boil for 30 minutes, then strain through coarse muslin (cheesecloth). Soak 75 g (3 oz, 12 envelopes) powdered gelatine in a little cold water, add to the strained liquid, then chill. Meanwhile, clean some strawberries, raspberries and alpine strawberries, cut some peeled pears into quarters, seed some grapes and dice some candied orange and lemon peel. Pour the half-set jelly on to the fruit and gently mix together. Put into the terrine and leave to set in a cool place for at least 2 hours. Serve with raspberry purée decorated with a band of honey.

terrine of leeks and fresh goat's cheese
Wash and tie into a bundle 1.25 kg (2¾ lb) leeks and cook in boiling salted water. Cut off the green part so that the white part is the same length as the terrine. Cool quickly in ice-cold water and drain for 2 hours under a press. Wash and trim 200 g (7 oz) tomatoes and cut into small cubes. Season with olive oil and chopped chives and chervil. Heat 500 ml (17 fl oz, 2 cups) of ready-made stock and melt in it 10 sheets of leaf gelatine, previously soaked in cold water. Allow to cool. Coat the terrine with cling film (plastic wrap). Pour a little jelly over the bottom and line the sides with leeks, alternating green and white. Put a first layer of tomatoes with 5 small fresh goat's cheeses in the middle. Continue with a layer of jelly, a layer of tomatoes and then fill the mould with the remaining leeks and the jelly. Press to remove excess liquid. Place in the refrigerator for 14 hours. Unmould the terrine on a board and cut into slices. Pour some vinaigrette on top. Sprinkle with some fresh diced tomato, sprigs of chervil and chopped chives.

terrine of oxtail in tarragon jelly
Degrease and trim a 1.5 kg (3¼ lb) oxtail. Cut into three. Marinate for 24 hours with 2 carrots, 1 onion and half a bunch of tarragon in 1 litre (1¾ pints, 4⅓ cups) red wine made from the Syrah grape. Put the oxtail, half a calf's foot and the boiled, filtered marinade in a large saucepan. Cover

with water, salt and bring to the boil. Skim regularly during the first 5 minutes, then add 1 bouquet garni with a few sprigs of tarragon, 1 small celery stick, the white part of 3 leeks, 1 garlic clove, 150 g (5 oz) green beans and 1 bunch of spring onions (scallions). Allow to simmer for 1½ hours, gradually removing the vegetables as they are cooked. Take the oxtail out and remove the bone. Filter the cooking liquid, reduce by half, add 100 ml (4 fl oz, 7 tablespoons) red port and 6 sheets of leaf gelatine, previously soaked in cold water. Filter again. Arrange the vegetables at the bottom of the terrine, pour some jelly on top, then a layer of meat. Repeat the process and finish with a layer of meat and jelly. Sprinkle with a few tarragon sprigs. Chill for 6 hours before serving.

terrine of pheasant, partridge or quail

Proceed as for terrine of duckling, but arrange the forcemeat in 3 layers, one separated by strips of meat, and the next by a thin layer of foie gras and diced truffle.

terrine of veal with spring vegetables ♦

Poach 500 g (18 oz) lean, boneless loin, fillet or leg of veal in a well-seasoned court-bouillon until very tender. Allow to cool in the stock. Cut half of the meat into neat, even, rather thick strips or cubes. Prepare a jelly with the clarified cooking stock.

Shell 40 g (1½ oz) petits pois and cook in salted boiling water until tender. Drain and refresh in cold water; drain well. Thinly slice 250 g (9 oz) baby carrots and cook in boiling salted water until just tender. Drain, refresh and drain well. Blanch and drain 4 sliced courgettes (zucchini).

Line the bottom of a terrine or mould with plenty of dill. Add layers of the vegetables, alternating them with the meat until the terrine or mould is almost full. Season each layer with pepper and sprinkle with a few dill leaves. Press to settle the contents. Pour in the cooled, but not set, jelly. Allow to set in the refrigerator for a few hours, unmould and serve chilled.

terrine of vegetables Fontanieu

Cook separately, in very lightly salted water, 7 fluted carrots, 300 g (11 oz) French (green) beans, and 150 g (5 oz, ¾ cup) petits pois. Cut the following vegetables into sticks and cook separately: 500 g (18 oz) turnips, 500 g (18 oz) courgettes (zucchini) and 1 small root of celeriac. Peel, halve and seed 3 tomatoes. Cool the vegetables and dry them thoroughly.

Bring 1 litre (1¾ pints, 4⅓ cups) double (heavy) cream just to the boil, then blend in 500 g (18 oz, 6 cups) shredded button mushrooms. Season with salt and pepper. Remove the mushrooms after 5 minutes and chop them. Do not boil down the cream, but blend in, while it is still hot, 25 g (1 oz, 4 envelopes) powdered gelatine, 5 tablespoons dry vermouth and the chopped mushrooms. Keep the mixture warm, ready for assembling the terrine.

Pour a thin layer of this mixture into the bottom of a china mould. Arrange the French beans lengthways, covering the whole of the bottom of the terrine, then mask them with a little of the mushroom cream. In this way, build up the terrine, alternating the layers of vegetables according to colour. (The purpose of the cream mixture is simply to bind the ingredients – it should not take precedence over the vegetables.) Place the tomato halves in the middle. When the terrine is full, settle the ingredients by lightly tapping the bottom and refrigerate for at least half a day. When serving, turn out of the mould and serve with small diced tomatoes sprinkled with chopped basil. Sprinkle the terrine with a dash of raspberry vinegar and olive oil. Season with salt and pepper.

other recipes See *cep, foie gras, pike.*

TERRINÉE

A cold dessert that is a speciality of Normandy. It was formerly an indispensable item of food at village fêtes and on special occasions and still remains a traditional family dish. It consists of rice cooked in milk in a glazed earthenware terrine, with sugar and a little salt, traditionally flavoured with cinnamon and sometimes with nutmeg. The cooking process lasts at least 5 hours (formerly it was cooked in the baker's oven) and the finished dish has a thick tasty golden crust. It is particularly nourishing, especially as it was often eaten with a slice of *fallue* (brioche). *Terrinée* is also commonly called *teurt-goule, teurgoule, torgoule* or *bourre-gueule*.

TÊTE-DE-MOINE

A Swiss cow's-milk cheese (40% fat content) from the canton of Berne. Pressed and uncooked, it is a firm yet pliable cheese with a washed brownish-yellow rather sticky rind. It has a spicy flavour and a pronounced aroma. The cheese is creamy yellow and becomes reddish as it matures. It is sold unwrapped in cylinders that are as high as they are wide (9–12 cm, 3½–4¾ in). The best Tête-de-Moine comes from Bellelay, where, long ago, it was customary for the prior of the abbey to receive one cheese *par tête-de-moine* (per monk) each year as a fee. Nowadays, it is produced on a small scale, as a cottage industry, and is in season between September and March.

This cheese is served at the end of the meal. Traditionally, the upper layer is sliced off and kept as a cover and the inside is sliced off in small frilly curls with an implement known as a *girotte*. It is also used for sandwiches and canapés. (It should not be confused with Tête-de-Mort or Tête-de-Maure, the name given in France to Dutch Edam cheese.)

TÊTE DE NÈGRE

A ball-shaped confection, consisting of two meringues sandwiched together with chocolate-flavoured butter cream. The ball is then coated with more cream and covered with grated chocolate or, more rarely, with grated coconut (or coconut on one half and cocoa powder on the other).

The name is also given to a dome-shaped rice cake entirely coated with chocolate sauce and surrounded with a ring of whipped cream, and to a small patty made of very light sweet pastry arranged on a wafer and coated with chocolate (this confection is also called *baiser de nègre*).

TÊTE MARBRÉE A pig's head pickled in brine, cooked, cut into dice, rolled into a rectangular shape and covered with jelly.

TÊTE PRESSÉE A method of preparing cold pork using a half-head, two trotters (feet) and one ear. After cooking in a court-bouillon, the meat is removed, put in a hollow dish and covered with the sieved, reduced cooking liquid. When cold and solidified, the preparation is turned out on to a plate and served in slices.

TETILLA Looking like a child's spinning top, this conical cow's-milk cheese (45% fat content) comes from Galicia in northern Spain. It has a thin, yellow rind and a pale yellow paste with some small holes. The elastic paste has a milky flavour with a lemon tang. It is served with Serano ham and fino sherry.

TFINA A slowly cooked ragoût of Arab cuisine, made with brisket of beef, calf's foot, chick peas or white haricot (navy) beans, peeled potatoes and whole eggs in their shells, arranged in layers with olive oil, garlic, paprika and honey. Meatballs and spices may also be added. Tfina must simmer for several hours. Traditionally, the meat is served in one dish and the vegetables and eggs in another. In wheat tfina, the potatoes are replaced by wheat or pearl barley and the eggs are omitted: this is the typical Sabbath dish of Algerian–Jewish cookery. Tfinas are also made with spinach or vermicelli.

THAILAND See *page 1210*.

THERMIDOR The name of a lobster dish created in January 1894 at Maire's, a famous restaurant in the Boulevard Saint-Denis in Paris, on the evening of the premiere of *Thermidor*, a play by Victorien Sardou (according to the *Dictionnaire de l'Académie des Gastronomes*). Other authors attribute it to Léopold Mourier of the Café de Paris, where the chef Tony Girod, his assistant and successor, created the recipe used today: cubes or escalopes of lobster mixed with Bercy sauce (or cream) seasoned with mustard and served in the two halves of the shell, either sprinkled with grated cheese and cooked *au gratin*, or covered with Mornay sauce and glazed in the oven or under the grill (broiler). Sometimes small mushrooms or truffles are added.

The name 'thermidor' is also given to a dish consisting of sole poached in white wine and fish fumet, with shallots and parsley, and covered with a sauce made from the reduced cooking liquid thickened with butter and seasoned with mustard.

RECIPE

lobster thermidor
Split a live lobster in two, lengthways, Crack the shell of the claws and remove the gills from the carcass. Season both halves of the lobster with salt, sprinkle with oil and roast in a preheated oven at 220°C (425°F, gas 7) for 15–20 minutes. Remove and dice the flesh from the tail and claws.

Prepare a stock using equal proportions of meat juices, fish fumet and white wine, flavoured with chervil, tarragon and chopped shallots. Boil it down to a concentrated consistency, then add a little very thick béchamel sauce and some English mustard. Boil the sauce for a few moments, then whisk in some butter (one-third of the volume of the sauce). Pour a little of this sauce into the two halves of the shell. Fill the shells with the flesh of the lobster, cover with the remainder of the sauce, sprinkle with a little grated Parmesan cheese and melted butter, and brown rapidly in a preheated oven at 240°C (475°F, gas 9).

More simply, the lobster can be split into two and grilled (broiled). The two halves of the shell are then emptied out, lined with a little cream sauce seasoned with mustard, and the sliced lobster flesh is put back, covered with the same sauce and glazed in the oven. Arrange the lobster on a long dish and serve piping hot.

THERMOMETER An instrument used to measure temperature. The graduation is in degrees Celsius (centigrade) or Fahrenheit on a scale varying according to the use intended: monitoring the temperature of a freezer, cooking sugar syrup, deep-frying, and so on. Most thermometers used in the kitchen consist of a glass tube containing a liquid which expands as the temperature increases. For roast meat, there are bimetallic thermometers, consisting of metals with different expansion coefficients. The meat thermometer has a pointed end and is graduated from 30°C (86°F) to 120°C (248°F) and has markings, often in colours, for well-done, medium and rare meat. It is implanted in the centre of a joint of meat to measure the internal temperature. The frozen meat thermometer is graduated from –30° to +30°C (–22° to +86°F).

THICKEN To give a liquid or liquid mixture more 'body', making it slightly less runny and not as fine or thin in texture. The techniques and ingredients used to thicken foods vary considerably according to the type of food and recipe. Starches are the most common ingredients for thickening cooked dishes; protein foods, such as eggs, are also widely used. Starches thicken mixtures by absorbing moisture and swelling; eggs thicken by setting. Uncooked mixtures can also be thickened, often by different methods, such as the formation of an emulsion, as when

Terrine of veal with spring vegetables, see page 1207.

THAILAND

Thai cuisine is vibrant. Flavours mingle without forfeiting individuality – hot spices, zesty citrus, vegetables and cooling fruit come together with deceptive simplicity. Contrasting textures complement each other, with tender rice, fine broths or moist sauces and crunchy vegetables carefully blended in a meal. Presentation is important and simple garnishes or elaborate carved vegetables ensure that the food always looks appealing.

■ **Exciting flavours and aromas** Chillies (chili peppers) are widely used, with the tiny bird's eye variety making some dishes extremely hot. Limes – both fruit and leaves – coriander (cilantro), lemon grass and coconut – milk and flesh – are also characteristic. Fresh root ginger and the slightly milder galangal, known as *kha* (*laos* in Indonesia and *lengkuas* in Malaysia) are used, as are the pink-tinged ginger flower buds. Thai basil and mint contribute their inimitable flavours alongside other herbs and spices.

Condiments include dried shrimps ground to a pungent paste known as *kapi*, and *nam pla* is the salty, fermented fish sauce that is used in Thai cooking to the same extent that soy sauce is in Chinese dishes. *Nam prik* is a spicy sauce of dried shrimps and fish, slightly sweetened and sharpened with lime or lemon, that often accompanies mild dishes. Garlic, tangy tamarind, warm spices such as cumin and coriander, sweet-sour and curry flavours combine with aromatics, herbs and spices in sauces that are the basis for a wide variety of dishes.

■ **All-important rice** Rice is the basis for main meals that may include a soup and several other dishes to be eaten as accompaniments to the rice. Fish, seafood, chicken, pork and beef are all prepared. The variety of vegetables includes cabbages, greens, carrots, bean sprouts, bamboo shoots, white radishes, spring onions (scallions), water chestnuts and lotus roots. They may be cooked with fish, poultry or meat, in mixed vegetable dishes, with noodles or eggs.

Salads are an important feature and they may include cooked meat or poultry, fruit and vegetables. Crunchy peanuts contribute flavour and texture to salads and many other dishes.

■ **Soups and noodles** Soups can be simple, clear and spicy or packed full of seafood, poultry, meat, vegetables and noodles. Noodles are popular for a light meal or snack, in broth or soup, or stir-fried with a variety of ingredients. The first dish of the day for breakfast may be a light soup or a bowl of noodles and both are just as acceptable for a lunchtime snack as they are for a satisfying meal.

■ **Fruit and desserts** Bananas, pineapple, mango, papaya and watermelon are plentiful and they are served simply or used with coconut, sticky rice, tapioca, mung-bean flour and palm sugar to create colourful desserts. There are many sweet cakes and flans or lighter colourful jellies, often made from coconut milk.

Fresh vegetables for sale in the colourful surroundings of a Chiangmai market place.

---

preparing salad dressing or hot sauces of the mayonnaise type.

THICKENING There are several different methods, depending on the thickening agent used. Thickening may be carried out at the beginning of cooking or at the end.

• BEURRE MANIÉ This thick paste of butter and flour is added in small knobs to simmering liquid. The liquid must be stirred vigorously or whisked until the butter has melted and the flour is evenly incorporated before another knob of mixture is added. The liquid is brought to the boil and simmered briefly to reach maximum thickness. This method is used for thickening soups, sauces, casseroles and similar dishes in the final stages of cooking.

• BREADCRUMBS Fresh breadcrumbs are used for thickening hot or cold dishes, such as sauces or hot soups and cold soups. The breadcrumbs have to be whisked into hot dishes and the mixture stirred until it boils. For cold soups and sauces, the ingredients are puréed with breadcrumbs, then allowed to stand until thickened.

• BUTTER Whisking small knobs of butter into a small amount of hot, reduced liquid creates an emulsion. This method is used for many classic sauces and for thickening fine cooking liquor just before serving. The mixture must not be overheated or allowed to boil or it will curdle.

• CREAM Adding cream to fine, thin sauces or soups thickens them very slightly and enriches them. The cream is added at the end of cooking and the mixture is heated gently and briefly. Overheating the mixture will make it curdle.

• EGG YOLK, BLOOD OR LIVER These are used to create an emulsion which has the effect of thickening a liquid. Soups and sauces thickened in this way should never be allowed to boil, as they curdle at a high temperatures. It is best to keep the temperature below 80°C (175°F).

• EGGS AND FLOUR This combination is used when making confectioner's custard (pastry cream). Mix egg yolks with cornflour (cornstarch) or flour and a little liquid; is this a method for lightly thickening and enriching soups or sauces. The egg yolks may be used on their own, but they curdle with prolonged heating or at too high a temperature. Mixing with a little cornflour or flour helps to stabilize the mixture, but the liquid should not be boiled.

• REDUCING Vigorously boiling cooking liquor in an open pan until most of the excess moisture has evaporated is a method of producing a sauce with a

syrup-like texture. This is used for cooking liquor remaining after pan-frying, then simmering or braising, or for long-braised casseroles. The cooking residue from main ingredients is important in producing the required syrupy consistency.

• ROUX Flour cooked with butter in the first stage of preparing a sauce or liquid to be thickened is known as a roux. Liquid is gradually added to the roux, stirring continuously, to make a smooth, thin mixture. Stirring the mixture over the heat until it comes to the boil and then simmering for a few minutes completes the thickening process. The same principle is involved when flour is sprinkled on to ingredients that have been sautéed in fat, before the stock is added (see *braising, ragoût*).

• STARCH Cornflour (cornstarch), arrowroot, ground rice or similar starches are used to thicken by the action of heat. The thickening agent is blended with water to make a thin paste and then added to the hot or boiling liquid that needs to be thickened. The mixture is stirred constantly over the heat until it boils and thickens. Slaking, or blending the starch with cold liquid before adding it to a hot liquid, is essential to avoid lumps. Depending on the type of thickening agent, the mixture may need simmering, or other cooking, for 3–5 minutes or longer after boiling so that it provides maximum thickening and is free from any 'raw' flavour. However, arrowroot provides maximum thickening at boiling point and thins down with further cooking; it is important to remember this when preparing fruit glaze or similar mixtures that are intended to be thickly set when cold.

RECIPES

thickening with arrowroot
Mix 1 teaspoon arrowroot with 2–3 tablespoons cold stock. Pour this mixture into 500 ml (17 fl oz, 2 cups) boiling stock or juice and whisk until it thickens. Strain.

thickening with beurre manié
To thicken 500 ml (17 fl oz, 2 cups) stock or sauce, work together 25 g (1 oz, 2 tablespoons) butter and 25 g (1 oz, 4 tablespoons) plain (all-purpose) flour. Add this paste to the boiling liquid and whisk over the heat for 2 minutes.

thickening with blood
Add 1 tablespoon vinegar to a small bowl of liquid blood (rabbit, hare, pork or duck) to prevent it curdling. To thicken the sauce, remove it from the heat and add this mixture, whisking continuously. Do not let it boil again. Sometimes the puréed liver of the animal can be added as well.

thickening with butter
Heat the strained sauce or stock. Cut the butter into small pieces and add it all at once to the hot liquid. Whisk well. 1 tablespoon liquid can absorb up to 50 g (2 oz, ¼ cup) butter.

thickening with cream
Mix the cream with a little of the sauce, stock or soup to be thickened and then pour it back into the preparation. Whisk until it begins to boil, then lower the heat and let it reduce until it has reached the desired consistency.

thickening with liver
Clean the liver of the appropriate animal and purée it finely. Add one-quarter of its weight of double (heavy) cream and mix well. Remove the boiling liquid from the heat and whisk in the cream and liver mixture at once.

THIGH The upper fleshy part of the leg of animals.

A thigh of beef provides choice pieces of meat for roasting, such as topside (beef round), rump, silverside (bottom round) and also steak.

A thigh of veal provides the fillet (round) and the rump, which may be roasted whole or cut into paupiettes or escalopes. (For thighs of mutton or lamb, see *gigot*; for pork thigh, see *ham*.)

In poultry, the thigh ends in the drumstick. Both thigh and drumstick are used for ragoûts and fricassees. The thigh may be boned and stuffed. In France, a thigh of turkey, together with the drumstick, is sold under the name of *gigolette* of turkey.

The thigh of a frog's leg is the only edible part of the animal.

THIN To add a liquid (such as broth, stock, milk, consommé or water) to a sauce, purée or stuffing, to render it less thick. For example, mayonnaise is thinned by adding a mixture of boiling water and vinegar.

THOUARSAIS WINES White, red and rosé wines of the Loire valley. The whites are made from the Chenin Blanc, the reds and rosés from the Cabernet Franc.

THREAD-FIN A sea fish related to the mullet, sometimes called *grand pourceau* ('great swine') in France. About 50 cm (20 in) long, it inhabits coastal regions of West Africa and can be found in the estuaries and rivers. Caught in large numbers, it has tasty flesh and is an important local food, particularly in Senegal, where it is used in *tié bou diéné*.

THRUSH A small bird belonging to the same family as the blackbird. There are a dozen species in France, which for centuries have been hunted in autumn and winter for their delicate flesh, the flavour of which depends on their diet (grapes, juniper berries or peas), although this practice is at last dying out throughout Europe. The song thrush makes excellent eating. The larger mistle thrush feeds on mistletoe berries, which make its flesh taste rather bitter. The smaller redwing is also highly prized; the fieldfare, imported from northern Europe, has a rather insipid flavour but firmer flesh.

All thrushes are prepared in the same way as

quails and there are, in addition, certain regional specialities, particularly pies and terrines. They are often cooked with juniper berries. Once common in Britain and the United States, thrushes have become rarer in recent years. For this reason they are now protected birds in Britain and may not be killed.

THYME A perennial plant with small grey-green aromatic leaves and small purplish flowers, much used as a culinary herb and also to prepare infusions. Thyme contains an essential oil, thymol, which has a very aromatic odour and antiseptic properties. Thyme is one of the basic herbs used in cooking. Alone or in a bouquet garni, fresh or dried, it is used in stuffings, casseroles, stews, soups and baked fish. Fresh thyme is particularly good for flavouring scrambled eggs, salads, tomato dishes and lentils. It is also used in the preparation of certain home-made liqueurs.

Wild thyme (called *serpolet* in France) has clusters of rose-pink flowers and a less pronounced flavour than garden thyme. It is used mostly with chicken or white meats, and in Provençal cookery (where it is called *farigoule* or *farigoulette*) it is traditionally used to flavour trout, mutton and rabbit. It is also used in the production of a liqueur.

TIAN An earthenware ovenproof dish from Provence. Square or rectangular, with slightly raised edges, it is used to prepare all kinds of gratin dishes, which are also called tians. Potato tian (a speciality of Apt) consists of alternate layers of sliced potatoes and chopped onion with sliced tomato, sprinkled with thyme, salt and pepper, covered with grated cheese and sprinkled with olive oil. Prepared in the same way are tians of artichoke hearts with anchovies, aubergines (eggplants) with tomatoes, salt cod (especially in Carpentras), white haricot (navy) beans and spinach. In Corsica, the *tianu* is a type of small earthenware saucepan used for preparing ragoûts (red kidney beans in wine, garnished with slices of preserved sausage and leeks). Rice is also cooked in it.

TIÉ BOU DIÉNÉ A Senegalese dish consisting of chunks or steaks of lean fish (conger eel, gilt-head bream, thread-fin, cod or hake), sometimes stuffed with chopped onion, parsley and red (bell) pepper. Browned in groundnut (peanut) oil, the fish is simmered on a bed of vegetables – onions, tomatoes, sweet potatoes, aubergines (eggplants), turnips, shredded cabbage – that have been sautéed in oil, then seasoned with chilli powder and pepper, and mixed with pieces of dried fish. Also called *tiep dien* or *tiébédienne*, the dish is served with steamed rice and the sauce it is cooked in.

TILAPIA A name for freshwater fish, including several species. Known as a food source since biblical times, with references to them in the context of the parting of the Red Sea, tilapia is usually a grey fish, with firm, white flesh of a good flavour. The species native to Africa is farmed in the United States.

TILSIT A Swiss cow's-milk cheese (45% fat content) from the cantons of Saint-Gall and Thurgovie. It is pressed, uncooked, pliable and golden yellow, with small regular holes and a polished yellow-brown rind. It has a very fruity flavour and a strong odour and takes the form of a small round slab about 35.5 cm (14 in) in diameter and 7–8 cm (2¾–3¼ in) high.

Originally from Holland, the cheese was imported several centuries ago into Tilsit, in the former east Prussia. It was not until the end of the 19th century that it was introduced into Switzerland. It is also made in northern Germany and central Europe, but has a stronger taste and is sometimes flavoured with aniseed. Used for canapés and toasted croûtes, it is also served at the end of a meal and may replace Emmental in gratin dishes and soufflés, which it flavours more strongly. When it has matured for more than four months, it is used like Parmesan cheese.

TIMBALE This word is used in various senses. Originally a timbale was a small metal drinking goblet; such timbales are now usually made of silver or silver plate and are purely decorative, being given to babies at birth or as christening presents.

The word also refers to a serving dish similar to a vegetable dish, made of silver-plated metal, stainless steel or heatproof porcelain, in which vegetables, scrambled eggs or ragoûts are served.

Today, however, the word is applied chiefly to a plain, round, high-sided mould and the preparation cooked in it – a pie crust baked blind and then filled with meat of various kinds, forcemeat or pasta, blended with a sauce. The crust is often garnished with patterns cut out with a pastry (cookie) cutter. The filling may be breast of chicken, calves' or lambs' sweetbreads, fish or seafood (fillets of sole, crayfish or scampi), truffles, quenelles, or any of the fillings for vols-au-vent or bouchées. Sometimes layers of meat or forcemeat are alternated with layers of pasta (as in timbale *à la milanaise*).

The name timbale is also given to small preparations moulded into darioles, consisting of various salpicons, vegetables and risotto, served as an entrée or a garnish.

Finally, a timbale can also be a dessert: a pastry case (shell) baked blind, then filled with various fruits, creams or ice cream.

RECIPES

large timbale case

Butter a large timbale or charlotte mould. Garnish the inside with little shapes of very firm noodle paste (slightly moistening them so that they will adhere to the pastry used to line the mould).

Prepare 400 g (14 oz) lining pastry (see *short pastry*) and roll it out into a circle 20 cm (8 in) in diameter and 5 mm (¼ in) thick. Sprinkle lightly with flour and fold in half, then bring the ends into the centre until they meet. Roll out again to smooth away the folds. Place this round of pastry in the mould and press it firmly against the base and sides without disturbing the noodle-paste decorations. Cut off any excess pastry.

Line the pastry case (shell) with buttered paper (buttered side inwards), then fill it up with dried beans. Place a circle of paper on top of the dried beans (which should be heaped into a dome) and then, on top of this, a round sheet of pastry 1 cm (½ in) thick. Join the edges of the pastry together by pressing them between the fingers, then make the rim of the pie by pinching this border with pastry pincers.

Moisten the lid with water and garnish with little shapes (leaves, rosettes, fluted rings) cut from a thin sheet of pastry. Make a chimney in the centre of the lid. Brush with egg and bake in a preheated oven at 190°C (375°F, gas 5) for 35–40 minutes.

Take the timbale out of the oven, cut round the lid with a sharp-pointed knife, then remove it. Take out the paper and dried beans and brush the inside of the pastry case with egg. Put the timbale back in the oven with the door open, to dry for a few minutes, then remove it, turn it out of the mould on to a wire rack and keep it hot together with the lid. Fill as desired and replace the lid. Serve immediately.

small timbales as an entrée
Butter some dariole moulds and sprinkle with truffle, pickled tongue or lean ham (chopped or cut into decorative shapes). Line evenly with a layer 5 mm (¼ in) thick of fine poultry or fish forcemeat, rice *au gras* (cooked in a meat stock) or vegetable brunoise. Fill the middle with a cooled salpicon or a barquette filling. Cover with a layer of the forcemeat used to line the moulds and cook in the oven, in a bain marie, for 15–18 minutes. Leave for a few moments, then turn the timbales out of the moulds on to a dish or on to rounds of fried bread or artichoke hearts. Serve with a sauce in keeping with the main ingredient.

small timbales à la fermière
Butter some dariole moulds and garnish with vegetable brunoise braised in butter. Line the moulds with a thin layer of quenelle forcemeat. Fill with a macédoine of vegetables bound with thick béchamel sauce. Cook in the same way as timbales à l'épicurienne. Turn out of the moulds and serve with a herb-flavoured cream sauce.

small timbales à la piémontaise
Butter some dariole moulds and line them with a salpicon of pickled tongue. Fill with saffron rice mixed with finely shredded white truffles and cook in the same way as timbales à l'épicurienne. Serve as a garnish for quails or small roast birds on skewers.

small timbales à l'épicurienne
Sprinkle some buttered dariole moulds with dried breadcrumbs and line them with an even layer, 5 mm (¼ in) thick, of rice *au gras* (cooked in meat stock) mixed with chopped truffle. Fill with a salpicon of lamb's sweetbreads, truffle and pickled tongue, blended with mushroom purée. Cover with a layer of rice *au gras*. Cook in a preheated oven at 190°C (375°F, gas 5) for 10–15 minutes (without a bain marie), then leave to stand for 5 minutes before turning out. Serve with tomato sauce.

timbales élysée
Prepare 8 pastry cups from a short biscuit-type (cookie-type) pastry made by thoroughly blending 100 g (4 oz, 1 cup) plain (all-purpose) flour, 100 g (4 oz, ½ cup) sugar, 1 egg and 50 g (2 oz, ¼ cup) rather soft butter. Flavour with vanilla. Divide the dough into 8, then roll into very thin rounds and arrange on a buttered and floured baking sheet. Bake in a preheated oven at 200°C (400°F, gas 6) for 6–8 minutes.

While the pastry rounds are still hot, mould each of them into a cup shape. Place a small slice of sponge cake soaked in a kirsch-flavoured syrup at the bottom of each pastry cup. Add a spoonful of vanilla ice cream and cover with fresh fruit, such as strawberries or raspberries. Coat this with a spoonful of kirsch-flavoured redcurrant jelly, then pipe rosettes of Chantilly cream round the inside edge of the cup.

Cover each of the filled cups with a cage of spun sugar: cook 200 g (7 oz, scant 1 cup) sugar and 40 g (1½ oz, ¼ cup) glucose to the 'hard crack' stage (see *sugar*). Thread this sugar in a delicate lattice over the bowl of a ladle. Slide the sugar cage off the ladle when set.

other recipes See *Agnès Sorel, Bagration, Beauvilliers, Brillat-Savarin, crayfish, liver, Saint-Hubert, woodcock*.

TIRAMISU Italian dessert invented during the 1970s, based on plain cake or a yeasted sweet bread soaked in spirits or liqueur and coffee, topped with a mascarpone mixture, sometimes containing beaten egg yolks lightened with whisked egg whites.

TISANE An infusion of herbs and dried plants that is drunk hot, on its own or slightly sweetened. The word derives from the Greek *ptisanê* (barley water) and originally designated a decoction of this cereal.

Today, most tisanes are made from medicinal plants. Digestive infusions, which are said by some to be beneficial at the end of a meal, can include the following: aniseed, a stimulant and sedative; camomile, effective against neuralgia, migraines and fever pains; corn poppy, a sedative and supposed to be effective against asthma; ground ivy, antitussive (good for coughs); marjoram, for spasms and insomnia; lemon balm, for giddiness, palpitations, migraines and sleep disorders; mint, a tonic and stimulant; meadowsweet, a sudorific and diuretic, effective against influenza and rheumatism; rosemary, beneficial to the liver; sage, a tonic, stomachic and digestive; wild thyme, an antiseptic, good for the respiratory tract and the stomach; lime blossom, an antispasmodic and sudorific; verbena, a digestive; and violet, an antitussive, expectorant, sudorific and diuretic. Tisanes can combine two plants blended together: for example, lime blossom and mint, or lime blossom and star anise.

The expression *tisane de champagne* used to refer to a lighter sweeter champagne than classic champagne. Nowadays, in colloquial usage, tisane is simply a bad champagne. Formerly, *tisane de Richelieu* was a colloquial name for Bordeaux wine.

TISANIÈRE A tall cup used for making an infusion. Made of porcelain, faïence or stoneware, it is fitted with an internal strainer (in which the leaves are placed before the boiling water is poured in) and a lid. The infusion is prepared directly in the cup, with the lid closed, so that it can be drunk from a hot vessel. The forerunner of the tisanière, the *timbale à tisane*, was already in existence in the 17th century. It had a lid to keep the tisane – at that time a very popular beverage – hot.

TIVOLI The name given, in the 18th and 19th centuries, to several Parisian establishments providing illuminations, fireworks and other attractions, together with refreshments (including ice cream), and evoking the famous Villa d'Este with its water gardens, built in Tivoli, not far from Rome, in the 16th century. In classic cookery, the name Tivoli has been given to a garnish for small cuts of meat, consisting of bunches of asparagus tips and grilled (broiled) mushroom caps, filled with a salpicon of cockscombs and kidneys blended with suprême sauce.

TOAD-IN-THE-HOLE A traditional British dish. It originally consisted of pieces of cooked meat mixed with smoked bacon, covered with batter and baked in the oven. In 1861, Mrs Beeton gave an excellent recipe for steak and kidney pieces cooked in batter, but specified that any leftover meat could be used instead. This was indicative of the status of the dish as a simple, family recipe for an economical meal. Nowadays, it is made with fresh sausages, lightly baked in a shallow dish, covered with pancake batter and then cooked in a hot oven. The resulting crisp, well-risen batter and golden sausages are served hot. Good onion gravy is often served with toad-in-the-hole.

TOAST A slice of bread grilled (broiled) on both sides in a toaster or under the grill (broiler) and served hot. Pieces of toast can be served in a toast rack, which will keep them crisp; they can also be served in a basket, loosely wrapped in a napkin to keep them warm.

Buttered toast is traditionally eaten for breakfast or tea, often spread with marmalade, honey or jam. It is also an accompaniment to caviar, foie gras, smoked fish and pâtés, and is used as a base for various other savoury preparations: cheese; flavoured but-

ters; poached, fried or scrambled eggs; grilled kidneys; mushrooms; asparagus tips with béchamel sauce; and grilled bacon. Slices of toast spread with forcemeat are served with roast game birds, especially woodcock and snipe.

A toast is also a proposal to drink someone's health. This sense of the word derives from the old habit of placing a slice of toast in a glass of hot spiced wine: the glass of wine was passed round among the guests and the slice of toast was offered to the guest of honour.

RECIPE

garlic toast
Cut some slices 5 mm (¼ in) thick from a loaf of brown or white bread and grill (broil) them lightly. Spread them with garlic purée and sprinkle with a thin layer of breadcrumbs and a little olive oil. Brown quickly in a hot oven and serve very hot with a salad of endive (chicory), cherry tomatoes or mesclun (mixed green salad).

TOFFEE A Canadian sweet invented in the 16th century by Marguerite Bourgeoys, who had come from Troyes in France to open the first school in French Canada. To attract the 'little savages', she made a syrup from molasses which she left to cool down with the first snow of winter. This happened on 25 November, and toffee is still a traditional delicacy on St Catherine's day. In Britain, toffee is homemade or produced on a small scale in many establishments. The basic sugar and butter syrup is flavoured with nuts, chocolate, mint, liquorice or treacle or left plain. The American 'taffy' is a little different, and usually 'pulled'.

TOFU Also known as bean curd. A basic foodstuff of Far Eastern cookery, especially Japanese, prepared from soya (soy) beans, which are soaked, reduced to a purée, then boiled, sieved and set in blocks. In recent years, Westerners have found tofu to be a good alternative to dairy produce in a vegetarian diet, as well as an excellent source of protein for vegans. With an appearance and colour reminiscent of fresh cheese, tofu can be used as a meat or fish substitute in a variety of modern dishes.

Originally from China, where it is said to have been prepared as early as the 2nd century BC, Mongolian *doufu* was introduced into Japan during the 8th century by Buddhist priests. It traditionally constituted the basis of vegetarian dishes. Western travellers referred to tofu as early as the 17th century, but it is only since the 20th century that its method of manufacture and its uses have become familiar in the west.

Relatively neutral in taste and very rich in vegetable proteins, tofu is used in a wide variety of Japanese recipes: combined with sweet and sour sauces in vegetable and seaweed salads; diced with noodle dishes; crumbled and cooked like scrambled eggs, with mushrooms and aromatics. It is used in *sukiyaki*, in fish and shellfish dishes and in soups; garnished with spring onions (scallions) or onions, it is shaped into small patties or fried in balls; it is coated with *miso* and grilled on skewers. It can also be cut into cubes, fried and eaten with grated ginger and soy sauce. In summer, it is served chilled, in a salad with spring onions, dried bonito, grated daikon and sesame seeds. In winter, it is scalded and accompanied by *konbu* (a type of seaweed).

Chinese *doufu* is firmer than Japanese tofu. It is usually used in steamed dishes, soups and broths. Cut into dice or strips, it also accompanies fish. *Doufu* can also be pressed, plain or flavoured in various ways with curcuma, green tea, or red (bell) pepper, and fried with vegetables or added to marinated dishes. Fermented *doufu*, which has quite a strong flavour, is often seasoned with pepper and used to garnish *riz gluant* (sticky rice) and potées.

In Vietnam, the Philippines, Indonesia and Korea, tofu is prepared with various condiments: dried shrimps, mint and rice spirit.

TOKANY A Hungarian beef stew, in which paprika is not the principal seasoning (unlike goulash or *paprikache*). The meat is cut into thin strips, which are lightly cooked with onions in lard. The basting liquid is white wine and the seasoning is based in particular on pepper and marjoram. Sometimes, halfway through cooking, some pieces of fried smoked larding bacon are added; the stew is finished off with soured (sour) cream.

TOKAY Also known as Tokaji. A world-famous sweet white wine produced in the Tokaji-Hegyalja region in northern Hungary. The area extends into Slovakia, but the predominant production is in Hungary. The main grape varieties are Furmint, blended with Hárslevelu and sometimes Muscat Blanc à Petits Grains. The local climate encourages the development of noble rot (*botrytis cinera*) in some years, but the grapes' naturally high sugar levels at picking qualify them as Aszú. There are different styles of wine made – those without Aszú may be made into a base wine for Tokaji Aszú or a varietal, for example Tokaji Furmint. Where a mix of Aszú and non-Aszú grapes have been harvested together the resulting wine is labelled *Szamorodni* ('as it comes'). The famous and historic wines are produced from Aszú grapes. They are stored until the base wine has fermented, then added as a paste in controlled amounts measured in hods called *puttonyos*. Each hod contains 20–25 kg (44–55 lb) of paste; the higher number of *puttonyos*, the sweeter the wine. Tokaji Aszú may be sold as 3, 4, 5 or 6 *puttonyos*.

Tokaji Esszencia is a rarity and made only from the free-run juice seeping from the stored Aszú berries.

The production of Tokay is complex and lengthy. Any visitor to the strange cellars underground in the region will be astounded by the thick blanket of mould that covers the walls and which must obviously have a marked effect on the wines that mature

many years in the small casks known as *gönci*. The bottles for the sweet wines are 50 cl, slightly dumpy in shape with elongated necks. Although the dry wines can be enjoyed on many occasions, the sweet ones are possibly best served at the end of a meal, lightly chilled.

TOMATE An apéritif made in Corsica with the local and excellent pastis (aniseed-flavoured) and grenadine, which results in a drink looking exactly like tomato juice.

TOMATO An annual plant cultivated for its red fruits, which are widely used, cooked or raw, as vegetables, in salads, or to make a sauce or juice. Originally from Peru (the name comes from the Aztec *tomatl*), the tomato was imported into Spain in the 16th century. Until the 18th century, it was thought to be poisonous and remained an ornamental plant (called 'Peruvian apple' or 'acacia apple'). In the south of France it was nicknamed 'love apple' or 'golden apple', a name also used in Italy (*pomodoro*). When its properties as a vegetable-cum-fruit were discovered, the tomato became established in Spain, then in the Spanish kingdom of Naples, then in the north of Italy, the south of France, and Corsica. It was not until 1790 that it reached the Paris area and the north of France. In an edition of *Encyclopaedia Britannica*, published in an 1797, it was stated that the tomato was at that time in daily use in Britain, but in fact it took until the 19th century for it to be really established. Nowadays, it is grown and cultivated throughout the British Isles.

■ **Types** The numerous varieties of tomato are distinguished according to shape and size: round, ribbed and flattened, elongated or oval, huge or tiny. Some are used while still green or yellow.

• BEEFSTEAK OR MARMANDE TOMATOES There are many types of large tomatoes. Depending on type and ripening method, they can have an excellent flavour and a firm, fairly thick layer of flesh. Some types have a thin layer of flesh, with watery seeds and minimal flavour. The best are excellent for all culinary uses – cut up in salads and cold dishes; in cooked dishes; and stuffed and baked.

• CHERRY TOMATOES These miniature tomatoes have a full, sweet flavour. Unfortunately, many of the types available also have tough skins. They are useful with crudités and flavoursome in salads, either whole or halved. They can be skewered on kebabs or braised in cooked dishes.

• PLUM TOMATOES These elongated, oval or pear-shaped fruit have firm flesh and a comparatively small core of seeds. When sun-ripened, they have a full flavour that is valued in the preparation of purées, passata and sauces. They are excellent for cooking as well as for use in salads. Miniature plum tomatoes, about the same size as cherry tomatoes, are a novelty and useful for salads or for stuffing.

• ROUND TOMATOES These may be small, medium or large and their texture, flavour and sweetness varies

TOMATOES

medium tomatoes on the
stalk or vine

small tomatoes on the
stalk or vine

large or beefsteak
tomatoes

plum tomato

small yellow plum
tomatoes

medium round
tomatoes

small plum tomatoes

cherry tomatoes

small cherry
tomatoes

according to type and to growing and ripening conditions. They are the popular 'all-round' choice for general cooking.

Fresh tomatoes must be firm, fleshy and shiny, without wrinkles or cracks, and preferably of uniform colour. Tomatoes that are rather green ripen quickly in a warm place such as a sunny windowsill. They can be kept for 10 days or so in the salad drawer of a refrigerator.

■ **Tomato products** Tomatoes are also available in many preserved forms, including: canned peeled whole or chopped tomatoes, passata or Italian-style sieved tomatoes, concentrated tomato purée (paste) in cans or tubes, condiments and sauces, and tomato juice. From the 1830s, the production of tomato ketchup in American factories led to this humble sauce becoming known as the USA's national condiment – and finding worldwide popularity.

Sun-dried tomatoes are a comparatively new product away from countries where they have been prepared for generations. They are sold dried; in a ready-to-use form that does not require soaking; bottled in oil or dressings; or in a variety of pastes.

■ **Tomatoes in cookery** Iberian, Italian, Provençal, Basque and Languedocian cookery are unimaginable without the tomato, and it is also used in the cookery of most other European countries. The tomato is also indispensable in classic French cookery (chicken Marengo, stuffed tomatoes, Aurora, américaine and Choron sauces). Crushed or diced tomato pulp is used to season a number of stocks and garnishes, and raw tomato is used in various salads and garnishes for cold dishes.

Tomato blends perfectly with many seasonings (garlic, shallot, basil, tarragon, even cumin), and its association with olives, sweet (bell) peppers and aubergines (eggplants) is by now classic. It is also a good accompaniment to tuna fish, salt cod, sardines and red mullet, as well as beef, veal, chicken and eggs.

Green or red tomatoes are used in pickles and chutneys, and the fruit can also be made into jam (red or green) and even sorbets.

RECIPES

cold tomato mousse

Lightly fry in butter 500 g (18 oz, 2½ cups) coarsely chopped tomato pulp (net weight after skinning and seeding). When it is well dried out, add 100 ml (4 fl oz, 7 tablespoons) velouté* sauce in which 4 leaves of gelatine (softened in cold water and drained) have been dissolved. Strain this mixture through coarse muslin (cheesecloth), then put in a bowl and whisk until smooth. When cool, add half its volume of fresh whipped cream. Season with salt, pepper and a little cayenne pepper and add a few drops of lemon juice. Mix well, then pour into a glass dish.

The mousse can also be used as a garnish for cold dishes (particularly fish). In this case, pour into dariole moulds lined with aspic jelly, set in the refrigerator, then turn out of the moulds.

concentrated tomato glaze

Immerse some ripe tomatoes in boiling water for 30 seconds, then peel them. Pound in a mortar and cook over a brisk heat until they are boiled down by half, then press through a fine strainer. Cook once more very gently until the pulp thickens and becomes syrupy. (It can be made even smoother by straining it twice in the course of cooking.) This tomato glaze keeps well in the refrigerator. It is used in the same way as tomato purée (paste).

fresh tomato pulp

Pound and press raw, ripe, perfectly sound tomatoes through a sieve to remove the seeds and skin. Put this pulp into a saucepan and boil for about 5 minutes. Strain through muslin (cheesecloth) and collect the thick pulp remaining in the cloth: this can be used to flavour hot or cold sauces. The fine liquid can be used in stock.

green tomato jam

Select some green tomatoes and prepare them in the same way as for red tomato jam, but steep for 24 hours and use preserving sugar with added pectin. The cooking time is 4 minutes after the syrup has come to the boil.

grilled tomatoes

Cut a circle around the stalk of some round, firm, sound tomatoes. Remove the seeds with a teaspoon. Lightly season the tomatoes with salt and pepper, brush with olive oil and grill (broil) them rapidly so that they do not collapse.

red tomato jam

Choose some very ripe firm tomatoes that are free of blemishes. Remove the stalks and plunge them in boiling water for 1 minute. Peel, cut into small pieces, then steep for 2 hours with their weight of granulated sugar and the juice of 2 lemons per 1 kg (2¼ lb) tomatoes. Put the mixture in a pan and bring to the boil. Cook very gently until the syrup reaches the jelling stage: this takes 1–1¼ hours. Seal and pot in the usual way.

To help the jam to set, either add 300 ml (½ pint, 1¼ cups) apple juice per 1 kg (2¼ lb) tomatoes or replace the granulated sugar with preserving sugar with added pectin. The cooking time, after boiling, is then reduced to 4 minutes.

sautéed tomatoes à la provençale

Remove the stalks from 6 firm round tomatoes. Cut them in two, remove the seeds, then season with salt and pepper. Heat 3 tablespoons olive oil in a frying pan and put in the tomato halves cut-side downwards. Brown them, then turn them over. Sprinkle the browned sides with a mixture of chopped parsley and garlic (3 heaped tablespoons). When the other side is browned, arrange the tomatoes on a hot serving dish. Add some breadcrumbs to the frying pan and brown lightly in the oil, then pour the contents of the pan over the tomatoes.

Alternatively, the breadcrumbs can also be added to the chopped parsley and garlic mixture; the stuffed tomatoes are then arranged in a gratin dish and the cooking finished in a hot oven.

soufflé tomatoes

Remove the seeds from some firm, regular-shaped tomatoes. Sprinkle with oil or clarified butter and cook for 5 minutes in a preheated oven at 240°C (475°F, gas 9). Allow to cool and fill with tomato soufflé mixture. Smooth the surface, sprinkle with grated Parmesan cheese and put back in the oven at 200°C (400°F, gas 6) for 15 minutes.

stuffed tomatoes

Choose some ripe but firm tomatoes, of medium size and regular shape. Cut a circle round the stalk end and, with a teaspoon, remove the seeds and juice. Still using the spoon, enlarge the hole slightly until it is large enough to receive the stuffing. Lightly season the inside with salt and turn the tomatoes upside down on a cloth to drain (if preferred, lightly season the inside with salt and pepper without draining). Arrange the tomatoes on an oiled baking sheet and warm them for 5 minutes in a hot oven. Drain again, then stuff them, heaping up the stuffing to form a dome. Complete according to the recipe.

Hot stuffed tomatoes are usually sprinkled with breadcrumbs and oil or clarified butter before being cooked.

stuffed tomatoes à la bonne femme (hot)

For 8 medium tomatoes, mix together 250 g (9 oz, 1 cup) sausagemeat, 75 g (3 oz, ½ cup) onion lightly fried in butter, 2 tablespoons fresh breadcrumbs, 1 tablespoon chopped parsley, 1 crushed garlic clove, and salt and pepper. Stuff the tomatoes with this mixture. Sprinkle with breadcrumbs and oil or clarified butter and cook in a preheated oven at 220°C (425°F, gas 7) for 30–40 minutes.

The stuffing can be precooked very gently in a frying pan for 15 minutes. The tomatoes are then stuffed and cooked au gratin. If this method is used, the tomatoes will not collapse.

stuffed tomatoes à la languedocienne (hot)

These are prepared in the same way as tomatoes à la bonne femme, but a chopped hard-boiled (hard-cooked) egg is added to the stuffing. Use olive oil.

stuffed tomatoes à la niçoise (hot)

Make a stuffing consisting of equal proportions of rice cooked in meat stock and aubergine (eggplant) diced very small and tossed in olive oil. Add chopped parsley, garlic and breadcrumbs fried in olive oil. Stuff the tomatoes, put them in an oven-proof dish, sprinkle them with breadcrumbs and olive oil and cook in a preheated oven at 220°C (425°F, gas 7) for 30–40 minutes.

stuffed tomatoes à la parisienne (hot)

Mix some fine sausagemeat with a salpicon of truffles and mushrooms cooked in butter. Stuff some cooked tomatoes, sprinkle with breadcrumbs and clarified butter and cook in an ovenproof dish in a preheated oven at 220°C (425°F, gas 7) for about 30 minutes.

stuffed tomatoes à la piémontaise (hot)

Stuff some large raw tomatoes, seasoned with salt and pepper, with risotto mixed with thick tomato sauce. Put them in a buttered gratin dish, sprinkle with melted butter and cook in a preheated oven at 220°C (425°F, gas 7) for about 30 minutes. Sprinkle with chopped parsley and serve with a thick tomato coulis.

stuffed tomato nests (hot)

Prepare some tomatoes for stuffing and cook them in the oven. Break an egg into each tomato. Lightly season with salt and pepper, place a small knob of butter on top and cook in a preheated oven at 230°C (450°F, gas 8) for 6 minutes.

tomatoes stuffed with cream and chives (cold)

For 6 medium-sized tomatoes, mix together 200 ml (7 fl oz, ¾ cup) double (heavy) cream and 2 tablespoons chopped chives, 2–3 very finely chopped garlic cloves and 2 tablespoons vinegar or lemon juice (or a mixture of the two). Season with salt, pepper and a little cayenne. Drain the tomatoes, lightly season with salt and pepper, pour in 1 teaspoon oil and leave to stand for at least 30 minutes. Fill the tomatoes with the cream stuffing, replace the tops and chill for at least 1 hour. The cream can be replaced by cream cheese, well-beaten until smooth.

tomatoes stuffed with tuna (cold)

Mix together equal amounts of rice pilaf and flaked canned tuna. Add 1 tablespoon mayonnaise for every 4 tablespoons rice/fish mixture and mix in some chopped herbs and finely diced lemon pulp. Stuff the tomatoes, garnish each with a black (ripe) olive and chill until just before serving; serve with sprigs of parsley.

tomatoes with mozzarella

Wash, peel and slice 4 tomatoes. Cut 200 g (7 oz) mozzarella into thin slices. Arrange the tomato slices on 4 plates and cover with slices of cheese. Season with salt and pepper. Sprinkle with fresh, chopped basil. Add a dash of vinegar, then a little olive oil. Serve at room temperature.

tomato loaf

Boil down some tomato pulp over a low heat until it becomes very thick. Blend in some beaten eggs – 6 eggs per 500 g (18 oz, 2 cups) purée. Season with salt, pepper and a pinch of mixed spice. Fill a round well-buttered tin (pan) or dariole moulds with this mixture and cook in a bain marie in a preheated oven at 180°C (350°F, gas 4) for 40 minutes. Allow the loaf to stand for a few moments before unmoulding. Serve coated with tomato sauce mixed with butter.

tomato salad

Immerse some ripe, firm, sound tomatoes in boiling water for 30 seconds. Peel them, cut into slices and place in a colander to drain off the liquid. Arrange the slices in a salad bowl. Add some finely chopped mild onion – 100 g (4 oz, ⅓ cup) onion per 1 kg (2¼ lb) tomatoes – and dress with a tarragon-flavoured vinaigrette. Leave in a cool place. Just before serving, sprinkle with chervil, parsley, basil or chopped tarragon.

tomato sauce

Cut 100 g (4 oz, 6 slices) fresh streaky (slab) bacon into small dice. Blanch, drain and lightly cook in 3–4 tablespoons oil. Add 100 g (4 oz, ¾ cup) each of diced carrots and diced onion. Cover and lightly fry for 25–30 minutes. Sprinkle in 50 g (2 oz, ½ cup) sifted plain (all-purpose) flour and lightly brown. Add 3 kg (6½ lb) fresh tomatoes, peeled, seeded and pounded, 2 crushed garlic cloves, a bouquet garni and 150 g (5 oz) blanched lean ham. Add 1 litre (1¾ pints, 4⅓ cups) white stock. Season with salt and pepper, add 1½ tablespoons sugar and bring to the boil while stirring. Cover and leave to cook very gently for 2 hours. Strain the sauce into a basin. Carefully pour some tepid melted butter on the surface to prevent a skin forming.

tomato sorbet

Peel 1 kg (2¼ lb) very ripe tomatoes, press them and filter the juice. Measure the volume, 250 ml (8 fl oz, 1 cup) is needed. Make a cold syrup with 150 ml (¼ pint, ⅔ cup) water and 300 g (11 oz, 1⅓ cups) preserving sugar. Mix the syrup with the tomato juice and add 2 tablespoons vodka, then pour into an ice-cream mould and freeze for at least 1 hour. Whisk 1 egg white with 50 g (2 oz, ⅓ cup) icing (confectioner's) sugar over a pan of water at about 60°C (140°F). When the sorbet begins to set, whisk it, gently fold in the beaten egg white and put back in the freezer until it sets (about 2 hours).

other recipes See *beans (fresh), coulis, fondue, grecque, reine, rougail, royale, salpicon, sauté, soup, tripe*.

TOMBE Fish of the *Triglidae* family, also called 'pearl gurnard' (*grondin perlon*) on the Atlantic coast and *galinette* in the Midi.

With a maximum length of 75 cm (30 in), it is distinguished from other gurnards by its large blue pectoral fins and its smooth lateral line. Fished throughout the year from Norway to Senegal and in the Mediterranean, it has a firm white flesh which is perfect cooked *à la normande*, in the oven, on a bed of potatoes and onions.

TOMBER A French term meaning to cook watery vegetables, either whole (such as spinach) or cut up (as with chiffonade of sorrel, finely sliced onions), over a low heat with or without fat. Under the action of the heat, they cook in their own juices without browning.

In the terminology of old French cookery, *tomber* referred to a method of cooking meat in a saucepan, without any liquid other than that produced by the meat itself. The reduced syrupy meat juices were used for the sauce. The expression *tomber à glace* still means to boil down a cooking liquid (stock or juice) until it is syrupy.

TOMME Also known as Tome. The generic name of two large families of cheeses: one made from goat's or ewe's milk, especially in south-eastern France and the Dauphiné and sometimes in Savoy; the other from cow's milk, pressed and uncooked, typical of Savoy and Switzerland. Tomme is also the name given to Cantal and Laguiole at the first stage of their preparation, when they are still fresh.

■ **Goat's- or ewe's-milk Tommes** The soft goat's-milk cheeses are usually made in small discs of various sizes. They include Tommes des Allues from the Haute Tarentaise and the similar Tomme de Courchevel; Tomme de Belley from Franche-Comté; Tomme de Brach from Limousin, sometimes blue-veined; Tomme de Camargue flavoured with thyme and bay; Tomme de Comnovin and Tomme de Corps from the Dauphiné; Tomme de Crest from Valence; and Tommes de Sospel from the Alpes Maritimes.

Toma is the Italian name given to similar soft, bloomy rind cheeses in Italy, but here they are mainly made from pasteurized cow's milk. Examples include Toma della Valcuvia from Lombardy and Toma de Carmagola from Piedmont.

■ **Cow's-milk Tommes** These are usually made with skimmed milk and are well pressed, uncooked and have a natural polished rind. Tomme de Boudane (from Savoy) and Tomme de Revard are variants of Tomme de Savoie (20–40% fat content), pliable and homogeneous, with a uniform yellow or red rind, a pronounced smell of mould and a nutty flavour; they are best from June to November and eaten at the end of the meal and in sandwiches. They are sometimes flavoured with fennel. Tomme au marc has a strong smell of alcoholic fermentation and a fairly piquant taste: the cheeses are dried slightly, then arranged in layers with marc brandy, in a cask sealed with clay, then left to ferment (it should not be confused with Tomme au raisin, a kind of processed cheese, coated with roasted grape seeds). Tomme de Romans (from the Dauphiné), shaped like a flat disk, is thoroughly pliable, with a mild to nutty flavour and a lactic smell. Tomme vaudoise (or de Payerne) is a soft, almost rindless Swiss cheese, white and springy, with a creamy taste; it is sometimes flavoured with cumin. Finally there is Tomme de Sixt, which is eaten very dry, and Tomme de Vivarais, which Charles Forot recommends kneading with rapeseed (canola) oil, a little vinegar, salt and pepper, and serving with baked jacket potatoes.

TOM-POUCE A small pastry consisting of two squares of shortcrust pastry (basic pie dough) sandwiched together with a cream made of butter, crushed nuts, sugar and coffee essence (extract); it is iced (frosted) with coffee fondant and decorated with a grilled (broiled) hazelnut.

TONGS A utensil comprising two arms made of metal, wood or plastic. They are either pivoted or connected by a spring and are used for grasping a variety of foods, including asparagus, gherkins, snails, salads, ice cream, sugar and ice (sugar and ice tongs sometimes have claws to help grasp the cubes). Lobster tongs are used for crushing the claws to extract the flesh. Working on the same principle, the pastry crimper is used for pinching the edges of pastries.

TONGUE Fleshy organs from the heads of slaughtered livestock, which are classed as offal (variety meat) for culinary purposes. Ox (beef) tongue, weighing up to 2 kg (4½ lb), calf's tongue (considered to be superior in quality and quicker to cook), pig's tongue and lamb's tongue are all used and can be prepared in many different ways: in ragoûts, stewed, boiled and served with highly seasoned sauces (charcutière, piquante, Italian), in fritters, *au gratin*, and often cold, with a vinaigrette. In earlier days, tongue was cooked with verjuice or chestnuts, made into small sausages, or grilled on skewers. Pickled ox tongue (*à l'écarlate*) is preserved in brine and can be used in many ways, sometimes as a garnish for other meats. It can also be smoked.

Pink flamingo tongues were considered to be a delicacy in ancient Rome, and blackbird tongues were popular in the Middle Ages. Deep-fried saltcod tongues served with tartare sauce are a Canadian speciality.

RECIPES

preparation of tongue
Soak the tongue in plenty of cold water for 12 hours, renewing the water 2 or 3 times. Then trim it, removing the fat parts, and dip it in boiling water. Skin it by making an incision in the skin at the base and on the top and pull the skin towards the tip. Wash and wipe the skinned tongue, then sprinkle it with fine salt and leave it in a cool place for 24 hours. Wash it again, then wipe it.

Calf's Tongue
boiled calf's tongue
Calf's tongue prepared in this way is always served with calf's head. Prepare and skin the tongue. Prepare a cooking stock separately: blend flour with cold water, using 1 tablespoon flour per 1 litre (1¾ pints, 4⅓ cups) water, until smooth. Strain the mixture and pour into a large saucepan. Season with 1 teaspoon

salt and add 1 tablespoon vinegar per 1 litre (1¾ pints, 4⅓ cups) water. Bring to the boil, then add 1 large onion stuck with 2 cloves and a bouquet garni. Put in this stock the tongue and the calf's head, weighing about 1 kg (2¼ lb), well tied up with string. Add about 200 g (7 oz, 1 cup) chopped veal fat, bring back to the boil and cook for 2½ hours.

The tongue may be served with a simple vinaigrette or with various other sauces, such as caper, fines herbes, hongroise, piquante, ravigote or Robert.

braised calf's tongue
Prepare the tongue and brown it in 50 g (2 oz, ¼ cup) butter; drain. Brown 1 kg (2¼ lb) crushed veal knuckle bones in the oven. Blanch 1 boned calf's foot. Peel and dice 2 large onions and 3 carrots, cook them in butter in a pan until golden, then take them out. Line this pan with a large piece of pork rind with the fat removed, add the diced onion and carrot, the veal bones, the boned calf's foot, the tongue, a bouquet garni and a crushed garlic clove.

Blend 2 tablespoons tomato purée (paste) with 300 ml (½ pint, 1¼ cups) white wine and the same quantity of stock (the wine may be replaced by Madeira, cider or beer); pour over the tongue. Add 2 tablespoons brandy, season with salt and pepper, cover and bring to the boil. Place the pan in a preheated oven at 200°C (400°F, gas 6) and leave for about 2½ hours to finish cooking.

Drain the tongue and cut it into slices. Cut the flesh of the calf's foot into dice. Take out the bouquet garni, the remainder of the rind and the bones. Purée the stock and vegetables in a blender and coat the tongue with the mixture.

calf's tongue à l'italienne
Braise the tongue as in the previous recipe, adding some crushed tomatoes to the pan at the same time as the bouquet garni. Blanch 200 g (7 oz, 1½ cups) green olives in boiling water, add them to the puréed braising stock and spoon them over the tongue.

Lambs' or Sheep's Tongues
devilled lambs' or sheep's tongues
Braise the tongues and leave to cool in their stock. Cut them in half and spread each half with mustard seasoned with cayenne pepper. Baste with butter. Dip in breadcrumbs, pour butter over them and grill (broil) slowly. Serve with devilled sauce.

lambs' or sheep's tongue brochettes
Prepare some lambs' or sheep's tongues and braise them as for calf's tongue, taking care that they remain slightly firm. Allow them to cool completely, then cut them lengthways into thin tongue-shaped slices. Marinate them for 30 minutes with some mushroom caps in a mixture of olive oil and lemon juice, with a crushed garlic clove. Cut some smoked belly bacon into strips. Roll up the tongue

slices and thread them on to skewers, alternating with the strips of bacon and the mushroom caps. Soak once again in the marinade and grill (broil) slowly.

The marinade may be omitted: in this case, lightly brown the mushrooms and the strips of bacon in butter before skewering them, then baste the skewers with melted butter and coat with breadcrumbs. Sprinkle again with a little melted butter and grill (broil) gently. Serve with a tomato sauce.

lambs' or sheep's tongues au gratin

Braise the tongues and cut them in half lengthways. Put them in an ovenproof dish masked with Mornay sauce. Garnish each half tongue with a cooked mushroom. Cover with Mornay sauce, sprinkle with breadcrumbs and pour on melted butter; brown slowly. Sprinkle with chopped parsley.

lambs' or sheep's tongues en crépinette

Braise the tongues and leave to cool in their stock. Cut them in half, enclose each half in fine pork forcemeat with truffles, then wrap in a piece of pork caul. Baste the crépinettes with melted butter. Dip in breadcrumbs and grill (broil) slowly. Serve with Périgueux sauce.

Ox Tongue

ox tongue à la bourgeoise

Prepare the tongue and braise it as for a calf's tongue. Prepare a bourgeoise garnish with 500 g (18 oz) carrots cut to uniform size and half-cooked, about 20 small onions glazed and half-cooked, and 20 or so strips of larding bacon (slightly salted belly bacon) blanched and lightly fried in butter. About 15 minutes before the end of cooking, drain the tongue and strain the braising stock. Return the tongue to the braising pan, add the bourgeoise garnish and pour the strained braising stock over everything. Finish cooking in a preheated oven at 180–200°C (350–400°F, gas 4–6).

ox tongue à l'alsacienne

Prepare the tongue and poach it in stock as for calf's tongue until it is half-cooked (about 1½ hours). Prepare some sauerkraut à l'alsacienne with its aromatic garnish and a piece of blanched larding (belly) bacon. Line a braising pan with rinds of smoked bacon and pour the sauerkraut into it, together with its garnish and the bacon. Place the tongue in the middle, cover the pan and poach for another hour, or until cooking is completed. Prepare some boiled potatoes; poach some Strasbourg sausages for 10 minutes in boiling water. Arrange the sauerkraut on a hot dish. Cut the tongue and the bacon into slices, place them on the sauerkraut and surround them with the potatoes and the sausages.

valenciennes stuffed ox tongue

Trim a smoked tongue and cut it into thin slices. Prepare a mixture consisting of two-thirds foie gras and one-third fine-quality butter; work it with a glass of port, some finely chopped fresh truffles, salt and pepper. Coat the slices of tongue with this preparation and reshape the tongue; wrap it in muslin (cheesecloth) and keep it in a cool place. To serve, unwrap the tongue, glaze it with clear aspic and arrange it on a bed of aspic.

other recipes See *devilled, écarlate*.

TONKINOIS An almond manqué cake sliced into two and filled with praline butter cream. The sides are masked with this cream and decorated with grilled (broiled) shredded (slivered) almonds; the top is iced (frosted) with orange fondant and sprinkled with grated coconut.

The name is also given to a square petit four made of nougatine and filled with frangipane flavoured with praline. The top is iced with chocolate and decorated with chopped pistachios.

TOPKNOT A marine flatfish, 20–50 cm (8–20 in) long, which has two eyes side by side, a large mouth and fins with long filaments. Its dorsal side is greyish, marked with brown or pink, and it has a very clear lateral line. The thick firm white flesh is lean and comes away easily from the bones. Sometimes also known as megrim, the topknot can be used for many dishes, particularly when filleted.

TOP RUMP Part of the leg of beef consisting of the group of three muscles situated in the front, in the femoral region. The *rond* (round), *plat* (flat) and *mouvant* (moving) muscles provide very good roasts and tender tasty steaks, which are fairly lean. The *rond* is less homogeneous than the other two cuts. The top rump also provides meat for spit-roasting or minced (ground) beef (for hamburgers or steak tartare).

TORRÉE Speciality of the canton of Neuchâtel, Switzerland, a region in which the sausage is king. It is cooked with other charcuterie under the ashes. The meal which follows, called by the same name, is eaten round the fire.

TORSK Fish of the *Gadidae* family, which lives in the waters off the north-west of Scotland, northern Europe and the east coast of Canada, at depths of 150–450 m (492–1476 ft). Having the particular characteristic of a single dorsal fin, it is known as *loquette* in Boulogne and *pousse-morue* in St-Malo. It is fished from April to July.

TORTEIL Also known as *tourteau*. A typically Catalan pastry, the authentic name being *tortell*. This crown-shaped brioche is a speciality of Villefranche-de-Conflent and Arles-sur-Tech, where it is flavoured with aniseed. In Limoux, where it is traditionally eaten on Twelfth Night, it is decorated with crystallized (candied) citron, raisins and pine nuts, then flavoured with orange, lemon and rum.

TORTELLINI Italian pasta made with small pieces of thinly rolled dough, filled with a stuffing, folded and shaped into rings. They exist in different sizes and shapes (rolled-up narrow strips or small rounded turnovers) and are called *tortelli, tortelletti* (mentioned in a 13th-century recipe book), *tortellini, tortelloni* and *tortiglioni*. All these words derive from *torta* (tart), with various diminutives and augmentatives.

The pasta used may be made simply with eggs or coloured with tomato or spinach. The stuffing is usually made from chicken or ham, chopped with lemon zest, nutmeg, egg yolks or Parmesan cheese. Tortellini is a speciality of the Bolognese Christmas dinner (filled with turkey, ham and sausage forcemeat). Poached in a consommé or cooked in water, tortellini and tortelloni are served with melted butter or in a sauce – tomato or cream (sometimes with mushrooms) – and with Parmesan cheese. This stuffed pasta is of ancient origin: legend has it that a young apprentice pastrycook made them in the shape of a navel out of love for his mistress.

TORTILLA A thin pancake made of cornmeal, which forms an important part of the diet in Latin American countries and has gained recognition in Britain and the United States. It was named by the Spanish conquistadors: in Spanish cookery, a tortilla is a flat omelette, usually filled with salt cod or potatoes, which is cut into quarters like a cake (the word has the same origin as *torta*, a tart).

Cornmeal has been used since time immemorial for preparing pancakes, which are traditionally grilled (broiled) on earthenware utensils. They are used as bread or as tart bases and are stuffed for turnovers and sandwiches. The old Indian method of preparation consists of kneading the cornmeal dough, or *masa*, on a stone called a *metate*, then shaping it into circles about 20 cm (8 in) in diameter and 3 mm (⅛ in) thick, which is quite a delicate operation. Nowadays, *tortillerias* provide ready-made tortillas, which can be bought cooked or uncooked. Grilled tortillas, lightly browned, have a thin but tough crust on each side. They can also be puffed up like soufflé potatoes, then stuffed. Tortillas are always eaten hot, either on their own (as bread) or filled with various ingredients, usually with a piquant sauce.

The range of condiments and stuffings used include *guacamole*, avocado purée with red (bell) pepper; chopped raw onion; red pepper; green tomato coulis; grated *queso* (cheese); or thin strips of chicken breast. The main dishes prepared with tortillas are *tacos*, a very popular type of sandwich; *echiladas*, tortillas rolled around their filling (fried sausages or pieces of roast chicken), then coated with a sauce and cooked in the oven; *tostadas*, small very crisp tortillas, covered with sautéed or fried red kidney beans and sometimes embellished with chopped meat, served as a hot hors d'oeuvre; *chilaquiles*, thin strips of fried tortilla covered with a highly spiced sauce and cooked in the oven; and *quesadillas*, tortillas filled with meat in sauce or vegetables with cheese, folded into turnovers, then fried in lard.

The tortilla even forms part of the Mexican breakfast, which basically consists of *huevos rancheros*: fried eggs arranged on fried tortillas and garnished with tomatoes crushed with red pepper and slices of avocado. At lunch, the soup is sometimes thickened with small pieces of tortilla. *Sopa seca* is a dish consisting of pieces of tortilla generously coated with sauce and served piping hot. Equally popular are *sopes*, tortillas filled with meat, beans and highly spiced sauce. Among the specialities of Yucatán, mention should be made of the *papatzul* (literally, food of lords): tortillas stuffed with pieces of pork or hard-boiled (hard-cooked) eggs, served with a sauce made from ground pumpkin seeds, tomato purée (paste) and pumpkin-seed oil. In Venezuela, cornmeal pancakes are found in the form of *arepas*. These are thicker than tortillas and are often raw in the middle, even after cooking. Butter, eggs, spices or fried maize (corn) grains are sometimes added to the dough.

TORTILLON A dry petit four, usually made of twisted puff pastry (like a sacristain) with crystallized (candied) or dried fruits or shredded (slivered) almonds; alternatively it is made of choux pastry moulded into a zigzag shape.

Tortillon is also another name for the *brassadeau*.

RECIPE

tortillons
Fill a medium-sized piping (pastry) bag with choux paste. Holding the bag at 45° and making a zigzag pattern, pipe on to a baking sheet some sawtooth shapes 15 cm (6 in) long. Sprinkle each tortillon with 12 currants steeped in rum. Dust very lightly with icing (confectioner's) sugar and bake in a preheated oven at 180°C (350°F, gas 4) for 25 minutes.

TORTONI A café, restaurant and ice-cream parlour opened in Paris in 1798, at the corner of Rue Taitbout and Boulevard des Italiens, by a Neapolitan called Velloni. Shortly afterwards, it was purchased by his head clerk, Tortoni, who gave the place its name. It closed in 1893. Every celebrity in Paris climbed the steps of the famous ice-cream parlour, which was also a highly regarded restaurant, well known for its cold buffets. Its meats in aspic, papillotes of young hare and salmon escalopes attracted as many customers as the ice-cream cakes, sorbets and granitas, Italian specialities that Tortoni made fashionable in Paris. A *Tableau de Paris*, dated 1834, quoted by R. Héron de Villefosse in *Histoire géographique et gourmande de Paris*, describes the activity of the establishment: 'In the morning, its excellent cold lunches brought in the stockbrokers, bankers and the fashionable set from the Chaussée d'Antin. At four o'clock, the speculators from the Stock Exchange met in front of its façade . . . Finally, in the evening, the regular customers from the Boulevard came to savour the imperial tea and the flavour of the iced pyramids in the shape of fruits and plants.'

TORTUE, EN A method of preparing calf's head. It is cooked in white court-bouillon, simmered with the tongue and sweetbreads in a white wine sauce with olives, mushrooms and gherkins added, then heaped on a platter in a mound usually garnished with small quenelles of veal forcemeat and fried croûtons. This French dish, which dates back to the Middle Ages, is also highly esteemed in Belgium.

Calf's head *en tortue* was once a large and spectacular entrée: the head was surrounded by small quenelles of veal forcemeat, cockscombs and kidneys, cooked mushrooms, stuffed poached olives, slivers of truffle and escalopes of calf's tongue. Small fried eggs, small slices of calf's brain cooked in court-bouillon, gherkins shaped like olives, dressed crayfish and fried heart-shaped croûtons completed the garnish.

Nowadays, calf's head *en tortue* is usually prepared using pieces of head, simmered in tortue sauce and arranged on fried croûtons, surrounded by a more modest garnish. When served whole, it is stuffed and cooked in a braising stock seasoned with 'turtle herbs', a mixture of basil, thyme, bay leaf, sage, rosemary and marjoram, with coriander seeds and peppercorns, inside a muslin (cheesecloth) bag.

Tortue sauce, made with white wine, mirepoix, a roux and stock and flavoured with tomato, traditionally accompanies calf's head *en tortue*; it was originally intended for turtle, hence its name, and is also used for fish and offal.

RECIPES

calf's head en tortue
Prepare a white court-bouillon and cook the calf's head and, separately, the tongue and sweetbreads. Cut all this offal (variety meat) into pieces and keep warm in their stock.

Make some tortue sauce. Cook in butter, without browning, 250 g (9 oz, 3 cups) diced mushrooms. Stone (pit) 150 g (5 oz, 1¼ cups) green olives, blanch for 3–4 minutes in boiling water and dice them. Also dice 7–8 gherkins. Strain the sauce and add the gherkins, olives and mushrooms. Heat thoroughly and adjust the seasoning by adding a pinch of cayenne.

Drain the pieces of offal and cover them with the sauce. Garnish the dish with small quenelles of veal forcemeat and croûtons fried in butter.

tortue sauce
Infuse a bouquet garni and a few sprigs of basil in 500 ml (17 fl oz, 2 cups) dry white wine. Lightly cook in butter 150 g (5 oz) smoked ham, 3 onions and 3 carrots (both cut into dice). Sprinkle with 3 tablespoons flour and brown. Add the strained white wine and 300 ml (½ pint, 1¼ cups) beef stock. Add 2–3 tablespoons concentrated tomato purée (paste), cover and cook very gently for at least 30 minutes.

TOSCANE, À LA A term used in France to describe various dishes prepared with Parmesan cheese and ham, specialities of Emilia-Romagna. True Tuscan cookery, however, is characterized by grilled beefsteak, bean dishes and Chianti. Macaroni *à la toscane* is bound with a purée of foie gras and sprinkled with diced truffles sautéed in butter.

RECIPES

allumettes à la toscane
Cut some puff pastry into strips 7.5 cm (3 in) wide and 5 mm (¼ in) thick. Mix equal amounts of cooked ham cut into small dice and poultry forcemeat, season and add a little chopped truffle. Completely coat the strips of puff pastry with this mixture. Cover with a very little béchamel sauce, sprinkle with grated Parmesan cheese and cook in a preheated oven at 240°C (475°F, gas 9 for 12–15 minutes).

soufflé fritters à la toscane
Mix a little grated nutmeg, 50 g (2 oz, ½ cup) grated Parmesan cheese, 50 g (2 oz, ¼ cup) cooked ham cut into small dice and a little chopped truffle with 300 g (11 oz) choux* paste. Shape into balls. Fry the fritters in boiling oil and serve very hot as an entrée.

TOULOUSAINE, À LA Describing a garnish for poached or pot-roasted poultry or a filling for croustades, tarts or vol-au-vent. It consists of a ragoût of small quenelles of poultry, lamb's sweetbreads or cockscombs and kidneys, mushrooms and truffles, bound with allemande sauce (or toulousaine sauce, which is a suprême sauce thickened and enriched with egg yolks and cream). Nowadays, the expression is more frequently applied to various dishes from south-western France.

TOULOUSE-LAUTREC, HENRI DE French painter (born Albi, 1864; died Château de Malromé, 1901). This great artist, noted for his drawings, paintings, lithographs and posters, was also an excellent amateur cook, the creator of recipes in which originality vied with soundness of taste (chick peas with spinach, perch with anchovies, plums in rum) and also with humour (grilled grasshoppers, seasoned with salt and pepper). Thanks to his friend Maurice Joyant, the traditional and regional recipes that he cooked were collected in *La Cuisine de Monsieur Momo*, of which 100 copies were printed in 1930; the work was republished in 1966 under the title *L'Art de la cuisine*, with illustrations of menus by Lautrec.

TOUPIN An earthenware pan or small stewpot, used in Savoy to prepare soups, fondues and ragoûts. Its name has been given to a pressed cow's-milk cheese (45% fat content), in the shape of a tall cylinder, made in the Vallée d'Abondance. It is firm and homogeneous, with a fruity flavour, and has a thin, rather rough, rind.

TOUPINEL A poached egg dish, said to have been created in the restaurant Maire at the end of the 19th century. It apparently owes its name to a vaudeville by A. Bisson, *Feu Toupinel*, which was playing at that time on the boulevards. Eggs Toupinel are presented in scooped-out baked potatoes. The potato pulp is mashed with butter and cream, seasoned with salt and nutmeg, then put back into the potatoes, which are coated with Mornay sauce. Finally, a poached egg is placed on top of each potato, also covered with Mornay sauce, and the dish is glazed in the oven or under the grill (broiler). Celery purée or shredded lean ham is sometimes added to the mashed pulp. Eggs Toupinel are traditionally served with fried parsley.

TOURAINE See *page 1226*.

TOURANGELLE, À LA Describing large pieces of roast lamb or mutton served with their thickened juices and a garnish of French (green) beans and flageolet beans bound with butter. The expression is also applied to poached or soft-boiled (soft-cooked) eggs arranged on tartlets filled with flageolet bean purée and coated with cream sauce.

TOUR D'ARGENT The oldest Parisian restaurant. It originated in 1582, as an inn on the Quai de la Tournelle, standing on the remains of a castle, built by Charles V, of which a white stone tower still remained. A certain Rourteau (or Rourtaud) used to prepare heron and wild duck pies, which Henri III himself ate there. Later, Richelieu enjoyed goose with prunes at the inn, while his great-nephew, the Duke of Richelieu, had his 'all beef' menu prepared there. Madame de Sévigné praised its chocolate and Madame de Pompadour its champagne. Under Napoleon I, Lecoq, head of the imperial kitchens, took over the restaurant, which had suffered during the Revolution. Roast duck and leg of lamb were at that time the best-known dishes. Paillard succeeded Lecoq, and George Sand and Musset were among the restaurant's regular customers.

It was after 1890 that the Tour d'Argent acquired the prestige that it retains to this day, with the renowned Frédéric, first maître d'hôtel and then manager, who invented the recipe for *canard au sang* and had the idea of attributing a serial number to each bird served (see *duck*). The tradition has continued and the *canardiers* in white aprons officiate on the small stage of the *théâtre du canard*, where two magnificent presses occupy the place of honour. The great Frédéric, who made the Tour d'Argent the 'Bayreuth of cookery' (according to Jean Cocteau), was succeeded by André Terrail, then by his son, Claude Terrail. Apart from pressed duck, other specialities are lobster Lagardère, lamb chops

Tour d'Argent, fillets of sole Frédéric, lemon, chocolate or violet soufflés and many great classics of French and foreign cookery. The Tour d'Argent vies with the Procope as to which serves the freshest coffee.

TOURER A French term meaning to give the necessary turns to puff-pastry dough to make it puff up during baking. This entails successive operations of folding, rolling out, turning the dough through 90°, then refolding, and so on. Professional pastrycooks do this on a *tour de pâtisserie*, which is a refrigerated marble or metal slab.

TOURIN Onion soup, sometimes with garlic or tomato, prepared with lard or goose fat; it is common to the Périgord and Bordeaux areas. The food historian Jean-Jacques Dubern writes: 'Tourin is onion soup made with good fat and a little garlic, bound with egg yolk in a trickle of vinegar and poured over slices of stale home-made bread. When there is no more bread left in the soup bowl, a good glass of strong red wine of the year is poured in. The colour is certainly not attractive, I admit, but we are on our own, and this warm beverage, flowing and generous, is an exceptional tonic.'

Tourin, which is also spelled *tourain, thourin, tourrin, touril* (in Rouergue) or *touri* (in Béarn), was traditionally taken to newly weds on the morning after their wedding and bore the name *tourin des mariés* or *tourin des noces* (with vermicelli added). In Quercy, some variants are *tourin à l'aoucou* (cooked with a preserved goose leg), *tourin à la poulette* (onion and flour browned in goose fat before adding the liquid) and *tourin aux raves* (shredded kohlrabi, browned in lard). In Périgord, a crushed clove of garlic and a little tomato purée (paste) or fresh tomatoes are usually added.

RECIPES

Périgord tourin

Lightly brown in goose fat, in a frying pan, 150 g (5 oz, 1 cup) finely chopped onion. Sprinkle with 1 tablespoon flour and add 2 crushed garlic cloves and a few tablespoons of boiling water. Stir to avoid lumps. Cook 2 large seeded tomatoes in 2 litres (3½ pints, 9 cups) stock. Drain, crush and return to the stock. Add the contents of the frying pan and boil for 45 minutes. Just before serving, blend in 2 egg yolks mixed with a few tablespoons of stock. Pour into a soup tureen over some thin slices of farmhouse bread.

tourin des noces

Brown in lard or goose fat 1 large grated onion and 6 quartered tomatoes. Add 1.25 litres (2¼ pints, 5½ cups) hot water. Season well with salt and pepper. When the vegetables are cooked, rub them through a sieve. Add 1 tablespoon vermicelli and

Touraine

Homeland of Gargantua and known as the 'garden of France', Touraine produces an abundance of delicious vegetables and fruits. As well as fish from the Loire, the Cher and the Indre, this region is known traditionally for the breeding stocks in the ponds and abundant wild fowl. Its poultry has been famous since the Middle Ages, and cattle from the nearby department of Maine provide quality animals.

The imposing château of Montrésor dominates the tiny village and the peaceful Indrois river – the epitome of the relaxed, harmonious atmosphere of Touraine.

■ **A fine and ancient cuisine** Rich in resources, this province has a simple and delicate cuisine, with many ancient recipes, such as green walnuts in verjuice, *bijane*, megrim with cream, noisettes of pork with prunes, braised veal in red wine, and the *fouaces* enjoyed by Rabelais. In addition, the long periods spent by the court in the Loire valley established a tradition for sumptuous dishes, such as carp *à la Chambord* and game pâtés.

■ **Impressive menus** The meal may start with *rillons, rillettes, andouillettes* and black puddings (blood sausages) from Tours, Vouvray or Chinon (*quiche tourangelle* with *rillettes* should also be mentioned). Alternatively, there are choices ranging from leek and turnip soup garnished with bacon and peas to pâtés and hams of game, and poultry from Richelieu.

• Fish, POULTRY OR MEAT Marinated shad, grilled (broiled) or roasted; matelotes of eels in Chinon wine with lardons; pike with shallot butter; perch stuffed with mushrooms or sorrel; and lamprey sautéed in walnut oil and simmered in red wine all bear witness to the wealth of fish recipes. Meat is prepared in a number of delicate dishes, particularly *cul de veau* (chump end of loin of veal) with spring onions (scallions), fricassée of chicken and hare *à la chinonaise*. *Sanguette* with onions and the rustic *sagourne* should also be mentioned.

The famous prunes of Tours, which were introduced into the Loire Valley from Damascus by the Crusaders, are widely used in cooking to garnish wild hare, roast pork, matelote of eel or lamprey.

• VEGETABLES Touraine is famous for its asparagus, celery, chicory (endive), lettuce, leeks and beans, particularly broad (fava) beans *à la tourangelle* (with ham and onions, bound with egg yolks and sprinkled with chervil), French (green) beans with béchamel sauce and peas with savory.

• CHEESE AND FRUIT There are numerous goat's-milk cheeses: Sainte-Maure, Saint-Loup, Ligueil, Loches and Chouzé (which sometimes contains cow's milk). Chasselas grapes from the slopes above the Loire, Williams and Passe-Crassane pears, Reinette and Golden Delicious apples, and greengages and plums from Rochecorbon are all well known.

• PÂTISSERIE AND CONFECTIONERY Apart from the traditional pastries – *fouaces, cassemuseaux* and *gâteaux cordés* and *russeroles* (similar to *pets-de-nonne*) – there are stuffed prunes, biscuits (cookies) and barley sugar from Tours, dried pears from Rivarennes, croquets from Sully-sur-Loire and crystallized (candied) walnuts and macaroons from Cormery.

WINE Many writers (including Rabelais) and poets (such as Ronsard) have praised the wines of Touraine: a combination of soil and climate, together with very old-established traditions of winemaking, have resulted in the region's wines being among the most charming of the Loire valley. Among the best known, each with an AOC, are Vouvray and Montlouis (white), and Chinon, Bourgueil and St Nicolas de Bourgueil (red), but there are many others and also some rosés. The grape varieties for the white wines are dominated by the Chenin Blanc (known locally as the Pineau de la Loire) and those for the reds by the Cabernet Franc (its regional nickname being Breton), but other varieties are grown, including Gamay, Cabernet Sauvignon, Grolleau and Cot (Malbec). A great deal of sparkling wine is also made, mainly white, according to the traditional method (see *méthode champenoise*).

The Renaissance gardens of the château of Villandry have a vegetable garden where cucurbits and medicinal plants are grown.

some small grilled (broiled) croûtons to the soup and boil for a few minutes more. Season with pepper and serve.

TOURNEBRIDE An obsolete name for an inn situated near a château or country residence, where visitors' servants and horses were lodged. Already old-fashioned at the beginning of the 20th century, the word *tournebride*, which originally meant 'turnabout', is, however, still used to describe a quiet welcoming country inn in France.

TOURNEDOS (FILET MIGNON) A small round slice, about 2.5 cm (1 in) thick, taken from the heart of a fillet of beef and sautéed or grilled. In French butchery, the classic presentation of the tournedos, barded and tied up, enables other roasting cuts to be used in the same way as fillet; these cuts are called *au façon tournedos* (tournedos style).

The *Dictionnaire de l'Académie des gastronomes* explains the etymology of the word, which appeared around 1864, as follows: 'In the last century, the stalls backing on to (*tournant le dos*) the central alleys of the fresh fish pavilion, in the Paris Halles, were assigned fish of doubtful freshness. By analogy, the name *tournedos* was given to pieces of fillet of beef that were kept for a few days in storage. An indiscretion is said to have led to the word's appearing on a restaurant menu one day; the public, not knowing its origin, adopted it.' Another explanation is connected with the dish ordered by Rossini (with foie gras and truffles), which surprised the head waiter so much that he had the dish served behind the backs (*dans le dos*) of the other customers. This cut of meat has one of the largest varieties of garnishes and sauces.

RECIPES

sautéed or grilled tournedos
Sauté the tournedos very rapidly in butter, oil or a mixture of both, so that the interior remains pink. They can also be grilled (broiled). Depending on the choice of garnish, or to prevent the garnish from masking the tournedos, the steaks are sometimes arranged on fried or grilled croûtons, potato cakes, artichoke hearts or rice. The following are a few suggestions for garnishes and sauces.
• *à la béarnaise* Grill and garnish with château potatoes; serve béarnaise sauce separately.
• *à la d'abrantès* Season with paprika, sauté in oil, then arrange on a grilled slice of aubergine (eggplant); add to the cooking juices some lightly fried onion, a salpicon of sweet (bell) pepper and tomato sauce.
• *à la périgourdine* Sauté in butter; place on a fried croûton; garnish with slices of truffle tossed in butter; pour over a sauce made from the pan juices mixed with Madeira.
• *archiduc* Sauté in butter and arrange on a potato cake; garnish with croquettes of calves' brains and slivers of truffle; cover with the pan juices diluted

with sherry, crème fraîche and veal stock, and flavoured with paprika.
• *Clamart* Sauté in butter and garnish with artichoke hearts filled with peas or fresh pea purée; pour over a sauce made from the pan juices mixed with white wine and veal stock.
• *Saint-Germain* Sauté in butter, place on a fried croûton and garnish with thick pea purée.
• *with anchovies* Sauté in butter and arrange on a slice of fried bread; pour over a sauce made from the pan juices mixed with thickened veal stock, white wine and a little anchovy butter; garnish with half fillets of anchovies in oil, placed in a crisscross pattern on the tournedos.
• *with mushrooms* Sauté in butter; pour over a sauce made from the pan juices mixed with thickened veal stock and Madeira; garnish with mushrooms sautéed in butter.

tournedos au lissé fermier
Cut off the base of the stalks of 800 g (1¾ lb) button mushrooms. Wash, sprinkle with lemon juice, slice thinly and brown gently in a frying pan with 50 g (2 oz, ¼ cup) butter. Set aside.

In another frying pan, melt 40 g (1½ oz, 3 tablespoons) butter with 2 tablespoons oil. As soon as it starts to boil, put in six 175 g (6 oz) tournedos and seal on both sides. Season with salt and pepper and cook for 5–8 minutes, according to the thickness of the meat. Drain, place in a hot serving dish, surround with the mushrooms and keep warm.

Stir into the second pan 250 g (9 oz) smooth cream cheese and reduce for 1 minute. Heat 100 ml (4 fl oz, 7 tablespoons) Calvados in a frying pan, reduce and add to the cheese. Add 1 tablespoon crème fraîche and reduce by half. Adjust the seasoning and pour over the tournedos. Sprinkle with chopped chives and serve immediately.

tournedos Brillat-Savarin
Wash 250 g (9 oz) fresh morels, cut off the stems and make small cuts in the caps. Simmer them in a little water for 15 minutes, then drain. Brown a chopped shallot in butter in a frying pan. Add the morels with a little mustard and a few tablespoons of double (heavy) cream. Finish cooking over a low heat. Adjust the seasoning and keep warm.

Gently fry the tournedos in butter. Remove and keep warm. Stir into the pan 175 ml (6 fl oz, ¾ cup) port and 5 tablespoons gravy and heat. Remove from the heat and thicken the sauce with butter. Adjust the seasoning. Arrange the morels around the tournedos and pour over the strained sauce.

other recipes See *bordelaise, Helder, Masséna, portugaise, Rossini.*

TOURTE A round pie or tart, which can be savoury or sweet. The name originally designated a round loaf (from the Latin *tortus*). A tourte consists of a shortcrust or puff pastry case (shell), filled either with a mixture of meat, poultry, game, fish or vegetables (with aromatics and additional ingredients) or with fruit and cream, covered with a lid of the same pastry. Some sweet tourtes do not have lids: these are high-sided tarts. Large rustic brioches are also called tourtes.

Similar to English pies, tourtes nowadays derive from rustic or regional cookery. They once played a major role as classic entrées or desserts: tourtes with truffles, oysters, pigeons, foie gras, *béatilles* and *godiveaux*, very fashionable until the 17th century, gave way to the lighter vol-au-vent, croûtes and timbales, as Carême pointed out in his *Traité des entrées chaudes*: 'The tourte is no longer elegant enough to appear on our opulent tables, because its shape is too common; even the middle classes scorn it and eat only hot pâtés and vol-au-vent, whereas rich merchants and their families used to regale themselves with the humble tourtes.'

In medieval cookery and during the Renaissance, it was one of the commonest dishes and was sometimes highly decorative: mention should be made of the frangipane tourte, similar to the Pithiviers gâteau, and the *tourtes panneriennes* of Taillevent (large round tall pies filled with mutton, veal or pork, with spices and raisins, coloured with saffron, and with castellated edges in which small flags bearing the guests' coats of arms were placed).

Tourte specialities of the French provinces include the tourte of Poitou (chicken, rabbit and pork belly meatballs); the salmon tourte of Brioude; the tourte of Nice, with Swiss chard, sugar and raisins; the *tourte bitteroise*, mutton fat, cassonade, lemon rind, and crystallized (candied) melon rind, and the Rouergue tourte, made with Roquefort and Laguiole cheeses. Among the fruit tourtes, the *poirat* of Berry, the *picanchagne bourbonnais*, the *ruifard valbonnais* and the *croustade* of Languedoc are worthy of mention.

RECIPES

apricot tourte

Place some thinly rolled-out shortcrust pastry (basic pie dough) in a *tourtière* or deep flan dish lightly moistened in the middle. Trim it to size, prick the base and moisten the edge, fixing around it a band of puff pastry 3 cm (1¼ in) wide and 1 cm (½ in) thick to form the rim. Fill the tourte with stoned (pitted) fresh apricots, without letting the fruit touch the pastry rim (which would prevent it from rising evenly during cooking). Brush the upper surface of the rim with egg and score it lightly with the point of a knife. Bake in a preheated oven at 190°C (375°F, gas 5) for about 45 minutes. About 5 minutes before it is cooked, sprinkle lightly with icing (confectioner's) sugar to provide a glaze.

Many other fruits can be used, cooked or uncooked, whole or cut up: pineapple, cherries, nectarines, pears, apples or plums.

tourte of veal with Parmesan cheese

Make 400 g (14 oz) shortcrust pastry (basic pie dough, see *short pastry*). Soak a pig's caul (fat) in cold water. Cut into strips 250 g (9 oz) noix of veal, a large slice of smoked ham and 200 g (7 oz) bacon fat; marinate in a bowl with 100 ml (4 fl oz, 7 tablespoons) white wine, 2 tablespoons Cognac, thyme, salt and pepper.

Meanwhile, chop up 200 g (7 oz) breast of veal, a large slice of smoked ham, 200 g (7 oz) bacon fat, 300 g (11 oz) calf's liver and 3–4 shallots. Add 100 g (4 oz, 1 cup) grated Parmesan cheese and mix with 2 beaten whole eggs, salt and pepper.

Roll out two-thirds of the pastry and line a buttered *tourtière* or deep flan dish with it. Lay the caul inside, letting the edges overhang. Spread half of the forcemeat on top; add the strips of meat, then the remaining forcemeat. Fold over the edges of the caul. Roll out the remaining pastry and place it on top of the flan dish, sealing the edges by moistening and pinching them. Make a small hole in the middle and slide a funnel made of foil inside to let the steam escape. Brush the top of the tourte with beaten egg and bake in a preheated oven at 220°C (425°F, gas 7) for 1½ hours.

tourtes à la mode béarnaise

Melt 500 g (18 oz, 2¼ cups) butter and pour it over 100 g (4 oz, 8 cakes) fresh (compressed) yeast in a bowl. Mix together. Add 500 g (18 oz, 2¼ cups) caster (superfine) sugar, 12 eggs, 1 small glass rum, the grated zest of 2 lemons, a pinch of salt and enough flour to obtain a firm mixture. Leave to rise for 24 hours. Divide into balls and put into buttered moulds. Bake in a preheated oven at 220°C (425°F, gas 7) for about 45 minutes.

additional recipe See *truffle*.

TOURTEAU A French name for the common edible crab, the biggest European crab, fished both in the Atlantic and in the Mediterranean, where it lives on rocks and stones at depths of up to 100 m (328 ft). Its oval yellowish-brown carapace is wider than it is long and is lightly scalloped around the edge. The first pair of legs, which are highly developed and have large black-tipped pincers, contain a delicate flesh.

TOURTEAU FROMAGÉ In Poitou and Vendée, a gâteau made with goat's-milk cheese; it is shaped like a slightly flattened ball with a smooth, almost black, surface. It is prepared by filling a deep pastry case (pie shell) with a mixture of fresh goat's-milk cheese, eggs, crème fraîche, sugar and flour, flavoured with Cognac. There are numerous variants, which sometimes incorporate candied angelica. This gâteau, originally from Lusignan, is also found in Niort, Poitiers and as far away as Ruffec. The prune torteau of the same region is a puff-pastry tart filled with prune purée and covered with a pastry lattice.

RECIPE

tourteau fromagé

Make some short pastry (basic pie dough) using 250 g (9 oz, 2¼ cups) plain (all-purpose) flour,

125 g (4½ oz, 9 tablespoons) butter, 1 egg yolk, 1–2 tablespoons water and a pinch of salt. Leave in a cool place for 2 hours, roll out to a thickness of 5 mm (¼ in) and line a buttered *tourtière* (or deep flan dish) 20 cm (8 in) in diameter. Bake blind for about 10 minutes. Mix 250 g (9 oz) well-drained fresh goat's-milk cheese with 125 g (4½ oz, ½ cup) caster (superfine) sugar, a pinch of salt, 5 egg yolks and 25 g (1 oz, ¼ cup) potato starch. Mix well, then add 1 teaspoon brandy or 1 tablespoon orange-flower water. Whisk 5 egg whites to very stiff peaks and gently fold them into the mixture. Pour into the pastry case (shell) and bake in a preheated oven at 200°C (400°F, gas 6) for about 50 minutes. Serve warm or cold.

TOURTIÈRE A round mould of variable diameter, slightly wider at the top, with high fluted or smooth sides. Made of ovenproof white porcelain, earthenware or ovenproof glass, sometimes with a removable base, it is used for cooking and serving tourtes, tarts or pies.

The word is also used in France for any kind of pie dish, tart mould or flan ring.

TOURTOU Also known as *tourton*. A small buckwheat pancake, the Limousin equivalent of the Breton galette, traditionally cooked in a frying pan greased with pork fat. Tourtous are a speciality of the Tulle region, where they are still made at home by housewives and taken to the local village shops to be sold.

In Périgord, Quercy and Rouergue, *tourteaux* are small cornmeal pancakes (not to be confused with the *tourteau fromagé*).

TRAIT A small quantity of a spirit or liqueur used for making a cocktail. It is generally measured by means of a measuring cap.

TRAPPISTE A generic name for various cheeses made by monks, particularly in the Trappist monasteries of Cîteaux, Belval, Briquebec, Mont-des-Cats and Tamié, as well as in certain Belgian monasteries (for example, Orval). They bear the name of the abbey where they are made, sometimes preceded by the words 'Trappiste de . . .'. Made from cow's milk (40–45% fat content), they take the form of discs of varying sizes. Trappiste de Belval, originating in Picardy, is a pressed uncooked cheese with a smooth washed rind, straw yellow to greyish in colour. Pliable and delicate, the ivory yellow cheese has a mild flavour. Trappiste de Cîteaux (Burgundy), with the same characteristics, has a more fruity flavour. Trappiste d'Echourgnac (Périgord), an ivory yellow cheese pierced with very small holes, which has a mild flavour, and Trappiste d'Entrammes (Maine), which has a fruity flavour, are also worth mentioning.

Trappisten is an Austrian cheese made from cow's milk (sometimes mixed with ewe's or goat's milk), matured to a varying degree; pale yellow, with a mild flavour, it is also made in Bosnia and Hungary.

TRAVAILLER A French verb meaning to beat or mix together the elements of a dough, batter or any liquid preparation, in order to blend in various ingredients, to make it homogeneous or smooth, or to give it body. Depending on the type of preparation (forcemeat, purée, dough, cream or sauce), the process is carried out either on the stove or away from the heat, sometimes on ice, with a wooden spatula, a manual or electric whisk, a blender, a mixer or even with the hand.

The intransitive form of the verb *travailler* is applied to rising dough or fermenting alcohol.

TRAY A large, flat, low-rimmed container, sometimes with handles, used for presenting and carrying to table various foods. It may be made of wood, wicker, glass or metal. A *plateau de fruits de mer* ('seafood platter') is an assortment of shellfish served on a tray garnished with crushed ice or seaweed.

TREACLE An alternative term for heavy syrup or golden (corn) syrup but more usually used in the context of black treacle, which is a dark (almost black), thick product of molasses and sugar syrup. It has a strong, bitter flavour. Black treacle is used in some baking, such as dark gingerbreads, and in some savoury dishes, including Boston baked beans.

TRENCHER Formerly, a wooden board used for carving meat. In the Middle Ages, the trencher was a thick slice of bread which was used as a plate. When the bread became too impregnated with sauce or broth at the end of the meal, it was given to the poor. Parisian trencher bread, according to the *Ménagier de Paris*, was a fairly coarse loaf made in Corbeil and sold in the Place Maubert.

TRICHOLOMA A genus of fleshy robust mushrooms with white or pink gills, indented near the stalk, and without a ring (or volva). They are available from spring to the end of autumn and most species are edible; the tastiest are *Tricholoma gambosum* (St George's mushroom, also called *mousseron* in French), which is white or buff (and sometimes a little indigestible), and the wood blewit (*pied-bleu*), which is a brownish-violet colour (the fibrous base of its stalk must be cut off and the rather sticky skin of its cap must be removed). Both of these are excellent when prepared like chanterelles and can be eaten raw. The wood blewit also grows in winter and can be cultivated. Other species worthy of note are *Tricholoma argyraceum*, which is brownish-grey with a very delicate flavour after cooking; *Tricholoma equestre* (firewood agaric or *jaunet*), which tastes like a carnation; the pinkish-white *Tricholoma columbetta*; and *Tricholoma terreum* (or *petit-gris*).

TRICLINIUM In ancient Rome, a dining room containing three couches arranged parallel to three sides of a table, the fourth side remaining free for the service. Each couch accommodated three guests.

Rich patricians had three tricliniums: one for summer, one for winter and one for spring and autumn.

TRIFLE A favourite English dessert – despite its name meaning 'of no account' – eaten on festive occasions. Also called tipsy cake, it is usually made of sherry-soaked sponge cake with custard and often jam, decorated with cream and sometimes fruit; however, recipes go back to the 16th century with many variations. Naples biscuits (see *sponge fingers*), macaroons and ratafia biscuits (cookies) formed the bottom layer in the 18th century, covered with custard and syllabub, the latter later becoming cream. Old versions of the Scottish whim-wham include syllabub, layered with sponge and redcurrant jelly. The dean's cream (from Trinity College, Cambridge) contains crumbled ratafias or macaroons with sherry, cream and crystallized (candied) fruit, while the duke's custard has brandied morello cherries and custard over Naples biscuits. There are also consciously non-alcoholic versions from the 1860s: 'church' trifle was made with sherry and 'chapel' without it, but jam instead. Jelly is a modern addition.

Zuppa inglese is a direct copy, created in Naples to honour Lord Nelson in 1798, but the world has many similar desserts.

TRIGGERFISH A flat, lozenge-shaped fish from warm seas. Its French name, *baliste*, comes from the name of a Roman war machine (*balista*) and derives from the dorsal trigger which it displays in times of danger. The best-known species is the Mediterranean triggerfish, which is prepared in the same way as tuna and has a similar flavour.

TRIM To remove all the inferior, unsuitable or inedible parts from food before cooking.

Some cooked items or dishes are trimmed to improve their appearance before serving. For example, poached eggs are trimmed after cooking to remove the rough edges.

TRIMALCHIO A character created by Petronius, a Roman writer of the 1st century AD, in the *Satyricon*, an account of the wanderings of a young dissolute Roman. Trimalchio is a typical parvenu who exhibits vulgar ostentation in his private life, particularly at table. Trimalchio offers his friends and courtesans a gargantuan feast with a multiplicity of courses: fish, plump chickens, wild boars, sow's udders, pigs stuffed with sausages and black puddings (blood sausages), oysters and snails. In Trimalchio, Petronius caricatures the nouveaux riches: the habits described are not representative of the usual Roman practice of the time. The expression *festin de Trimalcion* (Trimalchio's feast) is sometimes used to describe a magnificent meal, but in view of its true meaning it is hardly a compliment.

TRIPE The stomach of ruminants (especially ox, calf or sheep) used as food. It is usually sold specially prepared or cleaned for cooking, but is also available ready-cooked or pickled.

■ **Tripe in French cooking** Tripe can be prepared in a variety of ways and it is used in a large number of regional French dishes, usually highly seasoned. The best-known French dish is *tripes à la mode de Caen*, the authenticity of which has been defended by the Norman Confrérie de la Tripière d'Or since 1952; each year they award a prize to the best manufacturer. Tripe can also be marinated and then fried or grilled (broiled); sautéed with onions; slowly stewed with tomatoes; cooked *au gratin*; cooked in a sauce with vegetable flavourings; or cooked in broth, wine or cider. Particular mention should be made of tripe *en meurette*, cooked with vinegar, shallots and crème fraîche; Bugey tripe, sautéed, flamed with marc brandy and slowly stewed in white wine with tomatoes and spices; and tripe *à la dauphinoise* (slowly stewed with bacon rinds, pork skin, tomatoes, garlic and spicy stock).

■ **International tripe dishes** Tripe dishes of other countries include *busecca* from Lombardy, a soup made with calf's-tripe and green vegetables; Spanish *tripes à la madrilène*, highly spiced and garnished with chorizo, chilli peppers, garlic and thin strips of sweet red (bell) pepper; Bulgarian *tchorba*, tripe soup; the Arab *annrisse*, tripe and pluck boiled with cumin, pepper and orange and lemon rind and *barbouche*, or tripe couscous, tripe simmered with oil, garlic, cumin, caraway, white haricot (navy) beans and beef sausage; and the British tripe and onions, simmered in milk with bay leaves.

RECIPES

tripes à la mode de Caen

Line the bottom of a marmite or flameproof casserole with 500 g (18 oz, 2½ cups) finely sliced onions and 500 g (18 oz, 3 cups) sliced carrots. On top of these put 2 calves' feet, boned and cut into pieces, together with their long bones split in half lengthways. Add a mixture of 2 kg (4½ lb) ox (beef) tripe, consisting of the psalterium (or manyplies), rennet (or reed), reticulum and rumen, cut into 5 cm (2 in) pieces. Insert among the tripe 4 garlic cloves, a large bouquet garni (mostly thyme and bay leaf) and 300 g (11 oz) leeks, tied in a bunch. Season with 3 teaspoons coarse salt, 1 teaspoon freshly ground pepper and a pinch of 'four spices'. Cover with a few slices of beef fat, then pour in enough cider, mixed with a few tablespoons of Calvados, to cover.

Begin cooking on the stove without a lid, then cover and seal with a flour-and-water luting paste. Cook in a preheated oven at 140°C (275°F, gas 1) for about 10 hours. Before serving, remove the layer of fat, drain the tripe and take out the bouquet garni, all the bones and the leeks. Put the tripe into a serving dish and pour over the cooking stock, strained and skimmed of fat. Keep as hot as possible until serving. Serve on heated plates or in small earthenware bowls, with steamed potatoes.

tripe soup à la milanaise

Cut into julienne strips 500 g (18 oz) calf's tripe, which has been blanched, cooled and drained. In a flameproof casserole heat 100 g (4 oz, ½ cup) bacon cut into small cubes, a medium-sized onion and the shredded white part of a leek. Add the julienne strips of tripe and brown for a few minutes on the stove. Sprinkle with 1 tablespoon flour. Add 2 litres (3½ pints, 9 cups) stock or water and bring to the boil. Cut the heart of a medium-sized cabbage into small pieces, blanch for 6 minutes in boiling water, then drain. Peel and seed 2 tomatoes and crush the pulp. Add to the boiling soup the cabbage, the tomatoes, 5 tablespoons peas and a few small sprigs of broccoli. Season with salt and pepper and cook rapidly for at least 1½ hours.

TRIPERIE In France, all the offal (variety meat) of slaughtered animals, which is sold mainly by the tripe butcher. However, kidneys and liver may be sold at an ordinary butcher, and pig's offal is sold and processed by the pork butcher. In the Middle Ages, the tripe butchers' corporation was founded in Paris by six families, who purchased white or red offal from butchers on a wholesale basis. They prepared the offal and resold it to merchants, who peddled it about the streets, in copper containers, especially ox (beef) tripe with saffron.

TROIS-FRÈRES A pastry created in the 19th century by the three Julien brothers, celebrated Parisian pastrycooks, for which a special mould, in the shape of a large twisted crown, was invented. A mixture of rice flour and melted butter is poured on to eggs whisked with sugar, flavoured with vanilla or Maraschino, cooked, then set on a base of sweet pastry. Trois-frères is traditionally glazed with apricot and decorated with candied angelica. A variant of this pastry is made with ground almonds, sugar, eggs and whipped cream, flavoured with orange, iced (frosted), then decorated with fruit. The special mould is sometimes replaced by a savarin mould.

RECIPE

trois-frères

Make 250 g (9 oz) pâte sablée (see *short pastry*). Put 7 whole eggs into a heatproof basin and whisk on the hob (stove top), over hot water, with 250 g (9 oz, 1 cup) caster (superfine) sugar. When the mixture is thick and creamy, pour in 225 g (8 oz, 2 cups) rice flour, 200 g (7 oz, 1 cup) melted butter and 2 tablespoons Maraschino or rum. Mix thoroughly, then pour into a well-buttered trois-frères mould. Roll out the dough to a round shape 5 mm (¼ in) thick and a little larger than the mould. Place on a buttered and floured baking sheet. Bake both the pastry dough and the egg mixture in a pre-heated oven at 200°C (400°F, gas 6) at the same time, the former for 45 minutes and the latter for 20 minutes. Remove from the oven, turn out the

mould and allow to cool. Set the crown-shaped cake on the pastry base, cover generously with apricot syrup, sprinkle with chopped shredded (slivered) almonds and decorate with diamond shapes of candied angelica.

TROISGROS, JEAN AND PIERRE French chefs and restaurateurs: Jean (born 1926, Chalon-sur-Saône; died 1983, Roanne) and Pierre (born 1928, Chalon-sur-Saône), the sons of Jean-Baptiste Troisgros, a café-owner who later became proprietor of the small station hotel at Roanne (Loire), where his sister and his wife were in charge of the kitchens. The two brothers were sent to Lucas-Carton in Paris for their apprenticeship, then to Fernand Point in Vienne. In 1954 they began to practise their trade in the family hotel, then took over the management; thereafter their progress was continuous (one star in the Michelin guide in 1955, two in 1965, three in 1968).

Their cookery was inspired by recipes handed down from past generations, sometimes almost peasant in character: for example, pigeons *à la gouse d'ail en chemise*, snails *en poêlon* with green butter, and foie gras fried with spinach. But they also brought family dishes to a peak of perfection, notably their famous escalope of salmon with sorrel and their *mosaïque* of vegetables stuffed with truffles. Pierre proved to be the meat specialist, whereas Jean was a wine connoisseur. Together they created rib of beef *au fleurie* and *à la moelle*, accompanied by a gratin of potatoes *à la forézienne* (without cheese), aiguillettes of mallard with St George's mushroom, or, in a more modern vein, scallops *en croûte* with Nantes butter, and *salade riche* (foie gras, lobster and truffle).

TROMPETTE-DES-MORTS See *horn of plenty*.

TROPÉZIENNE A round of brioche pastry, cooked, then filled with a cream mousseline enhanced with rum, and sprinkled with icing (confectioner's) sugar. This speciality of Saint-Tropez is now known all over France.

TROQUET A popular term in France for a drinking establishment (synonymous with *bistro*). It is a shortened form of *mastroquet* (wine retailer), which appears to come from the Dutch *meesterke* (small employer), allied to the slang word *stroc* (a measure of wine).

TROTTERS See *feet and trotters*.

TROU NORMAND The former custom, also called *coup de milieu*, of drinking a small glass of spirits in the middle of a large meal to aid digestion and stimulate the appetite for the remaining courses. The spirit was Calvados (hence the name, Calvados being distilled in Normandy), but Cognac, kirsch or a fruit brandy could also be drunk, usually after the entrées and before the roasts. Nowadays, in place of the *trou normand*, a fruit sorbet is sometimes served, sprinkled with an appropriate spirit: orange and Cognac, pineapple and kirsch, pear and pear brandy, or lemon and vodka.

TROUSSER A French term meaning to arrange fowl or winged game in the appropriate form before trussing, with the legs straight out for roasting and folded in for braising or poaching. The term *troussé* is particularly applied to a bird with a small incision made in its sides for inserting the leg and thigh joint. For some small fowl, *troussage* may make trussing unnecessary.

Crayfish (and sometimes langoustines) are often *troussé* for a particular garnish: the process consists of sticking the ends of the pincers into the base of the 'tail' (that is, the abdomen).

TROUT A fish of mountain streams, lakes and rivers, highly sought-after by fishermen. This carnivorous fish, with tasty flesh (its name comes from Greek *troktes*, meaning 'voracious'), is also bred on a large scale in trout farms. Since 1961, when the Guillon law was passed, only specially bred rainbow trout have been sold in fish shops or served in restaurants in France, whereas the majority of regional trout dishes are, in principle, intended for trout caught locally.

• BROWN, SEA AND SALMON TROUT The common brown trout constitutes 5% of bred trout, but young fish are rapidly reintroduced into their natural environment to restock well-oxygenated rivers. Adult trout are a golden colour, with spots on the top half of the body, but the degree of colouring depends on habitat, sex and age; they can grow as long as 60 cm (2 ft). Highly esteemed in the Middle Ages, trout was then cooked in a court-bouillon or a pie. A variety called the lake trout, living in lakes and fast-flowing streams, can grow as long as 1 m (39 in). Its diet, rich in shellfish, turns its flesh pink; it is then called salmon trout. The same is true of the sea trout, which lives in coastal rivers near the English Channel and swims down to the sea, returning to the rivers in autumn. In France fishing for the brown trout, lake trout and sea trout requires a permit; the fish are reserved for private consumption.

• RAINBOW TROUT The rainbow trout is a species imported from the United States (where it lives in open water); it is bred in fish farms on a large scale. It is a silvery fish, sometimes with a purplish-blue band down its side. It has spots over its entire body, including the fins.

• SPECKLED TROUT The speckled trout is a fish of the *Salmonidae* family, imported from Labrador and introduced into the lakes of the Alps and the Vosges. Often wrongly confused with the char, the speckled trout is particularly identifiable by the many zebra stripes of its colouring. This fine, much sought-after species is fished in spring.

■**Trout farming** The brown trout was the first fish to be bred successfully by artificial insemination, as early as the 15th century. At the Réome monastery (Côte-d'Or), Dom Pinchon took and fertilized some trout eggs, put them in boxes on a bed of sand and replaced the fish in the river. Known to a number of fishermen and kept secret, this method was rediscovered in 1842 by two Vosgians. But the expansion of trout farming did not occur until the beginning of the 20th century, when the rainbow trout was imported. The milt of stud males is poured on to the eggs of selected females; the eggs are left to incubate in water rich in oxygen at a constant temperature. The alevins are then placed in tanks; while they are growing, they are sorted into batches of uniform size. At about five months, the alevin measures 6 cm (2½ in) and already has the general shape of a trout. Between 6 and 16 cm (2½ and 6¼ in), or 40–75 g (1½–3 oz), it is called a troutlet (*truitelle*), which becomes a *truite-portion* between 18 months and 2 years, when it measures 28 cm (11 in) and weighs 150–300 g (5–11 oz). It can live for a further 10 years and reach 6–8 kg (13–18 lb), but this only happens to those specimens selected for reproduction.

The diet of the bred trout – fish meal and soya (soy) flour – is carefully measured; the trout cannot be force-fed in order to make it grow. Furthermore, it needs space, otherwise it will die. The defects attributed to trout from breeding farms (tasteless or flaccid flesh) are usually caused by the treatment they receive at the fishmonger or at the restaurant, where the water in which they are kept may be too warm or insufficiently oxygenated.

■**Smoked trout** Smoked trout are also sold whole or in skinned fillets (rainbow or sea trout, sometimes salmon trout). In Norway, in particular, salmon trout bred in fjords are smoked, frozen or bottled.

■**Trout cookery** Trout *à la meunière* and *au bleu* are well-known dishes, which are succulent when made with freshly caught brown trout. There are, in addition, a variety of tasty ancient recipes from the French provinces. In Auvergne, trout is fried with chopped bacon and garlic; stuffed *à la montdori-enne* (with breadcrumbs, cream, herbs and mushrooms); cooked in a fumet and coated with cream sauce; or poached in fillets and served on a julienne of cabbage simmered in cream. Trout *à la d'Ussel* is poached, then, the next day, rolled in breadcrumbs and cooked *au gratin*. In south-western France, trout (known as *trouéte* or *truchet*) is fried or braised in white wine with cep mushrooms or stuffed with whiting flesh ground with duck foie gras and cooked *en papillote*. In Savoy, trout is cooked *au bleu*, *à la meunière* (a speciality of Lake Annecy), in a court-bouillon (served with a mousseline sauce), or stuffed and braised *à l'apremont*. In Corsica (where Corte is a major river-fishing centre), it is traditionally cooked with aromatics and red wine in a *poêlon* (a long-handled metal pan). In Normandy, trout is pot-roasted with bacon *à la mode de Vire*; cooked in a matelote with cider (in the Andelys); cooked *en papillote*, with apple, herbs, cream and Calvados; or made into a hot pie (a traditional dish of the bishops of Rouen). Mention should also be made of trout *à la beauvaisienne* (roasted with peppercorns); trout *à la montbardoise* (stuffed with spinach and shallot and cooked in a court-bouillon), also called *caprice de Buffon* (in honour of the naturalist Buffon, who was born in Montbard); trout pâté *à la lorraine* (fillets ground with nutmeg and herbs, mixed with chopped morels and garnished with whole fillets); trout flambé from Périgord, served with melted butter; and plain grilled (broiled) trout, as described by Austin de Croze: 'The trout were gutted, scraped, and washed, while some broad flat pebbles were being heated in a hole with burning twigs. The hot pebbles were removed with forked branches; on each was placed a few drops of oil or a tiny piece of butter, followed immediately by the seasoned trout, in which some diamond-shaped incisions had been made: hot pebbles were used to seal the other side of the trout . . ., which were eaten *au naturel* on large hunks of bread.' Jean Giono, a great connoisseur, denounces trout with almonds, a classic restaurant dish that is despised by many gourmets: 'Never with butter, never with almonds. That's not cookery, it's cardboard-making. . . . Apart from trout *au bleu*, people don't know how to cook trout.'

Despite the prejudice against them, bred trout are widely used in restaurants in various dishes, hot or cold, some more elaborate than others. Chefs have prepared them in a variety of imaginative ways. Laguipière served the Emperor Napoleon grilled trout, which had been marinated in olive oil and lemon, with a maître d'hôtel sauce seasoned with nutmeg. Fernand Point devised a recipe for trout stuffed with mushrooms, truffle, carrots and celery, sealed in a court-bouillon, sprinkled with port, and finished off in the oven *en papillote*, coated with the cooking juices thickened with beurre manié. Classic preparations include trout poached in a court-bouillon and served with a hollandaise sauce; cooked in red wine *à la bourguignonne*; fried *à la Colbert*; or cold, in aspic, with various garnishes. In addition, any salmon recipe can be used for trout.

RECIPES

fried trout
Clean, gut and dry some very small trout. Season with salt and pepper and dust with flour. Deep-fry in sizzling oil, then drain and arrange on a napkin. Serve with a green salad and slices of lemon.

medallions of trout with chive butter
Blanch 100 g (4 oz) spinach for 1 minute. Rinse in plenty of cold water, dry well and chop very finely. In a blender, combine 150 g (5 oz) scallops without their corals, the spinach, 5 tablespoons whipping cream and 3 tablespoons white wine. Season with salt and pepper. Cover 6 good trout fillets with this mixture, then roll them up on themselves. Wrap each trout roll in foil, carefully sealing the ends. Cook in steam for 8–10 minutes. Put to one side. Reduce almost completely 120 ml (4½ fl oz, ½ cup) good white wine with 1 very finely chopped shallot in a saucepan. Add 250 g (9 oz, 1 cup) very

cold butter, cut into pieces, and incorporate vigorously. Add 3–4 tablespoons finely chopped chives. Correct the seasoning. Put this chive butter on the plates and place the rolled trout fillets, cut into medallions, on top. Garnish with the vegetables, cooked *al dente*.

salmon trout Beauharnais
Stuff a salmon trout weighing about 900 g (2 lb) with 250 g (9 oz) forcemeat of whiting and cream mixed with 4 tablespoons vegetable mirepoix lightly cooked in butter. Place on the buttered grid of a fish kettle, half-cover with fish fumet made with white wine and cook in a preheated oven at 230°C (450°F, gas 8), or place the fish kettle on the hob (stove top) across two burners or hotplates, for about 20 minutes. Drain the trout, place in a serving dish and garnish with noisette potatoes cooked in butter and small artichoke hearts cooked in butter and filled with béarnaise sauce.

Strain the cooking liquid; reduce, thicken with butter and serve with the trout.

salmon trout with salad
Clean and fillet 4 salmon trout. Slice the fillets into thin strips, lay on a porcelain dish, season with salt and pepper and sprinkle with olive oil. Turn them over and repeat the operation. Leave to marinate overnight in a cool place.

On the day of the meal, cook some small artichokes, keeping them crisp, peel 2 very ripe avocados, poach 3 quails' eggs per guest and prepare a very fine julienne of orange zest and ginger. Cook 3 crayfish per person in a highly flavoured court-bouillon.

Arrange the raw trout fillets in a fan shape on the plates. Place the crayfish, with their tails shelled, at the base of the fan, then complete the fan with avocado slices, artichoke quarters and quails' eggs. Sprinkle with the julienne of orange and ginger, then season with a dash of lemon juice and a little olive oil.

In autumn, make the garnish with thin strips of Caesar's mushrooms, a boletus cap marinated with the trout fillets, small shaped pieces of beetroot (red beet), crisp French (green) beans, artichoke hearts, poached quails' eggs and a julienne of orange zest and fresh ginger.

trout à la bourguignonne
Clean and dry 4 trout and season with salt and pepper inside and out. Finely slice 250 g (9 oz) cleaned mushrooms, 1 carrot and 1 onion, lightly cook in butter and use to line a buttered ovenproof dish. Place the trout in the dish and add a bouquet garni and just enough red Burgundy to cover the fish. Bring to the boil on the hob (stove top), then cover and cook in a preheated oven at 220°C (425°F, gas 7) for about 10 minutes. Glaze 12 small (pearl) onions. Drain the trout and place in a heated serving dish, with the onions as a garnish. Keep hot. Strain the cooking liquid, thicken with

1 tablespoon beurre manié, and put back on the heat for 2–3 minutes. Add 2 tablespoons unsalted butter, whisk and pour over the trout.

trout à la nage Jean Giono

Clean and rinse the freshly killed trout. Pour into a dish 1 glass vinegar and season with salt and pepper; put the trout in the dish, turning them over several times, then leave to marinate for 15 minutes.

Heat a little vinegar in a large sauté pan or flameproof casserole (large enough to hold the trout), then pour in 1 glass olive oil beaten with 5 glasses water. Add 1 carrot, 1 leek and 1 onion (all sliced), 1 small chopped celery stick, 3 crushed garlic cloves, 5 crushed juniper berries, a pinch of powdered thyme, salt, pepper and a dozen fennel seeds. Boil rapidly, until the liquid has reduced to about 1 cm (½ in).

Add the trout. Cover, bring to the boil, then cook at maximum heat for 1 minute and over a low heat for a further 4 minutes.

trout au bleu

For true trout *au bleu*, the fish must be extremely fresh – killed about 10 minutes before cooking and serving. Take the fish out of the water and kill them with a hard blow on the head; gut and clean rapidly, without wiping. Sprinkle with vinegar, then plunge into a boiling court-bouillon containing a high proportion of vinegar. Simmer, allowing 6–7 minutes for fish weighing about 150 g (5 oz). Drain and arrange on a napkin. Garnish with fresh parsley and serve with melted butter or hollandaise sauce.

trout with almonds

Clean and dry four 250 g (9 oz) trout. Season with salt and pepper and dust with flour. Melt 50 g (2 oz, ¼ cup) butter in a large oval frying pan and brown the trout on both sides, then lower the heat and cook for 10–12 minutes, turning once. Brown 75 g (3 oz, ¾ cup) shredded (slivered) almonds in a dry frying pan or in the oven and add to the trout. Drain the cooked trout and arrange on a serving dish. Sprinkle with 2 tablespoons lemon juice and some chopped parsley. Keep warm. Add 20 g (¾ oz, 1½ tablespoons) butter and 1 tablespoon vinegar to the frying pan, heat, then pour over the trout with the almonds.

trout with leeks

Remove the backbone from an uncooked trout, season with salt and pepper, and stuff with a fine forcemeat of whiting and cream. Roll up in blanched whole leaves of young leeks. Cook in a buttered dish with a little white wine and shallots. Drain the fish. Reduce the cooking liquid, if necessary, and thicken with cream; adjust the seasoning and pour over the trout.

additional recipe See *Berchoux*.

TROUVILLE The name given to a recipe for lobster. After being cooked in a court-bouillon, it is removed from its shell and cut into salpicons, then mixed with thin slices of mushrooms sautéed in butter, oysters and mussels (poached and trimmed), and slices of truffle. This mixture is arranged within a circle of risotto with sauce *à la normande*; the whole is covered with a light sauce Mornay, sprinkled with grated cheese and glazed under the grill (broiler).

TRUFFADE Also known as *truffado*. A speciality from Auvergne, made of cooked potatoes, peeled, coarsely shredded, then fried in lard over a brisk heat, with thin strips of Tomme (fresh Cantal cheese) added. The mixture is stirred until the cheese melts and combines with the potato to form a thick pancake, which is turned over, covered, cooked for a few more minutes over a low heat and then served as a hot entrée. Connoisseurs of this dish consider that the best Tomme for truffade is that of la Planèze, which is particularly high in fat. Fried lardons or chopped garlic are sometimes added. The name comes from *truffe*, or *troufle*, a former name for 'potato' in country areas.

TRUFFER A French culinary term meaning to impart the aroma of truffles to a dish by incorporating pieces of truffle. It is mainly foie gras, forcemeats (for pâtés, poultry, quenelles and black puddings), salpicons and ragoûts that have diced or chopped truffle added to them. A chicken can be 'truffled' by sliding strips of truffle between the flesh and skin. As Grimod de La Reynière stated: 'Maraschino can be "truffled" as well as turkey.' But overuse is not recommended, as the *Dictionnaire de l'Académie des gastronomes* makes clear: 'Let us be truffophiles, even truffivores at times, but let us refrain from truffomania!'

TRUFFLE A subterranean fungus which lives in symbiosis with certain trees, mainly the oak but also the chestnut, hazel and beech. A highly esteemed foodstuff, the truffle (from the Latin *tuber*, meaning 'outgrowth' or 'excrescence') is rounded, of variable size and irregular shape, and black, dark brown or sometimes grey or white in colour; it is found especially in chalky soil or clay, quite near the surface, less than 30 cm (12 in) deep. French truffle production (particularly in the south-west and south-east) has drastically declined since the beginning of the 20th century, because of deforestation, the deterioration of suitable land and the use of pesticides. Before 1914, some 1740 tons of truffles were harvested each year in Périgord alone. Now less than 200 tons are harvested in the whole of France. Methodical truffle cultivation has not yet given conclusive results.

■ **Mysterious origins** The truffle has been known and appreciated since ancient times. The Egyptians ate truffles coated in goose fat and cooked *en papillote*. The ancient Greeks and Romans attributed therapeutic and aphrodisiac powers to them: the latter quality was still recognized in the 19th century, when Alexandre Dumas wrote, 'They can, on certain occasions, make women more tender and men more lovable.' Up to the beginning of the 18th century, their origin was shrouded in mystery: 'Since, during storms, flames leap from the humid vapours and dark clouds emit deafening noises, is it surprising that lightning, when it strikes the ground, gives rise to truffles, which do not resemble plants?', asked Plutarch. In the Middle Ages, when they were looked upon as a manifestation of the devil, they fell into oblivion. Having returned to popularity during the Renaissance, they subsequently suffered a further eclipse, but came back into favour under Louis XIV and have reigned supreme since then. La Varenne recommended ragoût of dried or fresh truffles as an entrée: washed, cooked in wine, seasoned with salt and pepper and served on a napkin or in a dish garnished with flowers. In 1711, Claude Joseph Geoffroy, a French botanist, published a paper entitled *Végétation de la truffe*, which definitively classified the truffle among the mushrooms.

Preparing truffled chicken

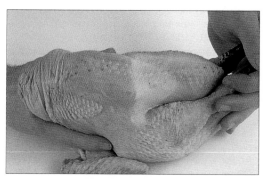

1 *Slip the point of a knife under the skin at the neck end of the chicken. Once the edge of the skin is loosened but carefully cutting the membrane, slip your fingers between the skin and meat, sliding them up over the breast to create a pocket. Loosen the skin over the thighs as well as the breast.*

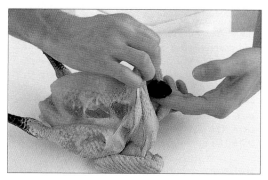

2 *Finely slice the truffles and dip them in clarified butter, turning them to coat both sides of each slice. Insert the slices of truffle one at a time: place a buttered slice on the tip of the finger and carefully slide it between the meat and skin, gently easing it into position.*

The practice of using muzzled pigs to seek out truffles was common in the 17th century; in 1705 Lémery wrote: 'There are dogs which can detect them as well as pigs. Some peasants, in areas where truffles are found, have taught themselves through long experience to recognize the places where they are hidden.' Nowadays, the many varieties of truffles are always gathered with the assistance of an animal (pig or dog) that can detect their presence. In some cases, the movement of a fly may reveal that truffles are nearby. With the animal on a leash, the 'digger' closely follows its footsteps and unearths the truffles as soon as the animal begins to root in the ground. He then carefully replaces the clods of earth so that no traces remain – the other truffles must be left to mature and the curiosity of potential poachers must not be aroused. Truffle cultivation remains essentially empirical and small-scale: truffles are neither sown nor planted. They spring up spontaneously when the fungal spores or mycelia encounter the rootlets of an oak tree (or another symbiotic species) and form a mycorrhiza, which takes its nutrients from the tree; the truffle itself is the fruiting body of the fungus and does not appear to be connected by any filaments to the mycorrhiza.

■ **Varieties of truffles** There are 70 varieties of truffles, 32 of which are found in Europe. The most highly esteemed is the black truffle of Périgord, which matures after the first frosts: it has black flesh streaked with whitish veins and gives off a strong aroma. In fact, it mainly comes from Tricastin, Vaucluse, Lot, Quercy and Gard, but it retains the prestigious appellation which established its reputation (it is also found in Piedmont, Tuscany and Aragon). The *truffe d'été*, or *truffe de Saint-Jean*, dark brown and white-veined, the grey truffle of Champagne and Burgundy, and the truffles of Alsace and Vaucluse, brown with black veins, have less of an aroma, like the *terfez* (the snow-white truffle, which grows in North Africa, in the Atlas mountains).

The white truffle of Piedmont enjoys a measure of popularity. It has a delicate aroma, especially marked in the truffle of the Alba region, and is in season from October to December. In cookery, it is served with capon, veal and sometimes langouste. It is also eaten cooked in Asti, sprinkled with Parmesan cheese, and seasoned with lemon vinaigrette. A sauce made with Piedmont truffles, butter, cream, garlic and anchovy is poured over spaghetti or vegetables served cold. The truffle is also used raw, grated or cut into thin strips (with a *coupe-truffe*, a special utensil), as a garnish for grilled meat, chicken, agnolotti or risotto.

■ **Truffles in cookery** A good black truffle must be well rounded and in a single piece. It is not at its best until ripe, which prompted Grimod de La Reynière to say: 'Truffles are only really good after Christmas. . . . So let us allow ignorant fops, beardless gourmands and inexperienced palates the petty triumph of eating the first truffles.'

Although its use in cookery is more restrained than in the past, because of its rarity and high price, the prestige of the truffle remains intact and the superlatives attributed to it bear witness to its almost mythical quality: 'diamond of cookery' (Brillat-Savarin), 'fairy apple' (George Sand), 'black queen' (Émile Goudeau), 'gem of poor lands' (Colette), 'fragrant nugget' (J. de Coquet), 'black pearl' (Fulbert Dumonteil) and 'holy of holies for the gourmet' (Alexandre Dumas). Regarding their cost, J.-L. Vaudoyer is said to have observed: 'There are two types of people who eat truffles: those who think truffles are good because they are dear and those who know they are dear because they are good.'

Truffles are eaten raw or cooked, cut into strips or slices, diced or shredded, in the form of juice, fumet or essence, or simply for their fragrance: 'When you feel like eating boiled eggs, if you have some truffles in the house, put them in a basket with the eggs and the next day you will have the best boiled eggs you have ever tasted in your gastronomic life' (M. des Ombiaux). Truffles occur, frequently associated with foie gras, in all recipes called *Périgueux* or *à la périgourdine*; these can include game, meat, poultry, pâté, forcemeat, black puddings (blood sausages), egg dishes and salads. They also feature in various sauces (diplomat, financière, Joinville, régence and riche) and garnishes (banquière, Belle-Hélène, Berny, cardinal, Chambord, Demidof, favorite, Frascati, Godard, Lorette, Lucullus, réforme and Rohan). Other prestigious dishes including truffles are: fillet of beef Prince Albert; timbale Talleyrand; chicken *à la d'Albufera*, demi-deuil and Edward VII; fillets of sole *à l'impériale* and Renaissance; lobster with Victoria sauce; and tournedos Rossini.

However, as Colette says, 'You pay its weight in gold for it, then in most cases you put it to some paltry use. You smear it with foie gras, you bury it in poultry overloaded with fat, you chop it up and drown it in brown sauce, you mix it with vegetables covered in mayonnaise. . . . To hell with thin slices, strips, trimmings and peelings of truffles! Is it not possible to like them for themselves?' Indeed, the true connoisseur enjoys truffles whole and fresh, either raw, with butter or salad, or cooked (in embers, braised with white wine or champagne or in a puff-pastry case).

Colette also gives us a delicious recipe: 'Steep in good very dry white wine (keep your champagne for banquets; the truffle does very well without it), lightly seasoned with salt and pepper. Cook in a covered black cocotte. For 25 minutes it dances in the boiling liquid with 20 or so lardons – like Tritons playing around a black Amphitrite – which give substance to the cooking juices. No other spices whatsover! And to hell with the pressed napkin, tasting and smelling of chlorine, the final bed of the cooked truffle! Your truffles should come to the table in their court-bouillon. Take a generous helping: the truffle whets the appetite and assists the digestion.'

■ **Canning** Truffles can be bought in cans, peeled or scrubbed, ripe and whole. They are graded: *surchoix* (with firm flesh, black and of a uniform size

and colour), *extra* (with firm flesh, more or less black and slightly irregular in size), *premier choix* (with more or less firm flesh, sometimes light in colour, of irregular size and possibly with abrasions). They are also canned in pieces, at least 5 mm (¼ in) thick, dark in colour, with up to 2% impurities; peelings, of variable colour, with 20% cracks at most and up to 3% impurities; and fragments, with up to 5% impurities.

■ **Truffle products** Truffle-flavoured oils, vinegars, pastes and sauces are available. The oils and vinegars are useful and provide a comparatively inexpensive way of bringing the flavour of truffles to pasta, sauces and similar dishes. It is a good idea to check the list of ingredients on pots of paste and sauces as they may include flavour enhancers and a large proportion of seasoning, that can limit their use in some recipes.

RECIPES

ragoût of truffles

Peel 8 fresh 40 g (1½ oz) truffles, cut into quarters, and season with salt and pepper. Add 100 ml (4 fl oz, 7 tablespoons) dry Banyuls and marinate for 20 minutes at room temperature.

Reduce by half 200 ml (7 fl oz, ¾ cup) good full-bodied red wine in a flameproof casserole, lightly rubbed with garlic. Blend in 1 teaspoon flour mixed with 2 teaspoons butter, bring to the boil, then add the truffles and the marinade.

Cover with foil and put on the lid, bringing the edges of the foil over the top; cook in a preheated oven at 180°C (350°F, gas 4) for 10 minutes.

Cut some stale bread into 3–4 cm (1½ in) croûtons, dry them slightly in the oven, then rub with garlic and spread the soft side with goose or duck fat. Serve the ragoût in its casserole, with the croûtons in a separate dish.

sauté of Piedmont truffles

White or black truffles may be used for this recipe, which can be prepared at table as follows. Finely slice the truffles. Put in a silver dish a few tablespoons of olive oil or butter and some good meat glaze, the size of an egg, cut into small pieces. Place the truffles on top with a little salt, white pepper and grated nutmeg. Sprinkle with a few tablespoons of oil or a few pieces of fine butter. The silver dish, covered with its lid, is placed on a spirit heater in front of the host, who frequently stirs the truffles with a spoon, replacing the lid of the dish each time. About 8 minutes' cooking should be sufficient. The host then adds the juice of a lemon and serves his or her guests.

truffle ice cream

Boil 3 large well-scrubbed truffles in 1 litre (1¾ pints, 4⅓ cups) milk for about 1 hour. In the meantime, whisk 8 egg yolks with 250 g (9 oz, 1 cup) sugar. Drain, dry and trim the truffles. Pour the milk over the sugar and egg mixture to make a custard; cook until it forms ribbons when the spoon is lifted, then add the chopped truffle trimmings. Allow to cool, then leave to set in an ice-cream maker. Cut the truffles into julienne strips. Fill tulip glasses with alternate layers of ice cream and truffle, finishing with a decoration of julienne strips. This ice cream is served as a dessert.

truffle salad
Clean some raw truffles and slice finely or cut into julienne strips. Make a vinaigrette with oil, vinegar, salt, pepper and lemon juice, but without aromatic herbs. (When fresh truffles are not available, preserved truffles can be used.)

The truffles may be mixed with sliced boiled potatoes (demi-deuil salad) or sliced artichoke hearts (impératrice salad).

truffle sauce
Cook a very black fresh truffle in a mixture of half Madeira, half meat stock, with a little tomato purée (paste), for 10 minutes. Drain and cut into julienne strips. Cover the pan tightly and reduce the liquid to a few teaspoonfuls, then add 2 egg yolks and the julienne. Thicken with 200 g (7 oz, ¾ cup) clarified butter, as for a béarnaise sauce. Season with salt and pepper.

This sauce is served with poached fish, white meats and Lauris asparagus.

truffles for garnishes
Depending on the dish to be garnished, fresh raw truffles are peeled, then cut into strips or dice of varying size, or into quarters, or shaped like olives. Cook gently in butter for a few minutes only, so as not to impair their flavour or texture. Add a few tablespoons of dessert wine and keep hot, but do not boil.

Sterilized truffles or truffles in goose fat, which have already been cooked, need only be heated with the dish that they are to accompany.

truffle tourte à la périgourdine
Line a pie dish, 4–5 cm (1½–2 in) deep, with lining pastry (see *short pastry*) and place on a baking sheet. Arrange on the bottom a layer of uncooked foie gras cut into large dice, seasoned with salt and pepper and sprinkled with 'four spices' and Cognac, covering the pastry to within 1 cm (½ in) of the edge. Top with scrubbed and peeled whole truffles, seasoned with salt and pepper and sprinkled with 'four spices' and Cognac. Place small slices of foie gras, seasoned with salt and pepper, on the truffles. Cover with a thin layer of pastry and seal the edges. Garnish the top with cut-out shapes of pastry and place a funnel in the centre. Brush with egg and bake in a preheated oven at 200°C (400°F, gas 6) for 40–45 minutes. Pour through the funnel a few tablespoons of reduced demi-glace sauce, flavoured with Madeira and truffle essence. The tourte is served hot or cold.

TRUFFLE, CHOCOLATE See *chocolate truffle*.

TRUSS To thread one or two pieces of trussing twine through the body of a poultry or game bird with a trussing needle to hold the legs and wings in place during cooking. This is done after dressing the bird (that is, when it has been plucked, cleaned, trimmed and singed); if the bird is to be braised, poached or fried whole (rather than roasted), the legs are tucked under the skin before trussing.

A well-trussed bird sits better on its roasting or cooking dish. It is easier to baste and turn and easier to cook and prepare, especially if it is to be served whole. It is always untied after cooking so that the parts which are protected by the legs can be checked to see that they are properly cooked.

TRUSSING NEEDLE A very large needle, usually of stainless steel, 15–30 cm (6–12 in) long and 1–3 mm (about ⅛ in) in diameter, pointed at one end and having an eye at the other. It is used to pass one or two strings of thread through the body of a chicken or game bird in order to keep the legs and wings in place or for sewing up stuffed boned meat. Trussing needles are often sold in a case containing an assortment of needles of different sizes.

TSARINE, À LA A term that describes poached poultry garnished with olive-shaped pieces of cucumber in cream, or poached fish (sole or brill) garnished with cucumber cooked in butter and coated with Mornay sauce seasoned with paprika. The expression also refers to various dishes directly inspired by classic Russian cookery: cream of hazel grouse and celery, garnished with a julienne of celery; poached eggs arranged on tartlets filled with hazel grouse purée, coated with cream and mushroom sauce; soft roes poached in white wine and garnished with chopped vesiga and caviar.

TUILE A crisp thin biscuit (cookie), so named as it was considered to resemble the shape of a curved tile. The basic mixture consists of sugar, shredded (slivered) or ground almonds, eggs and flour, sometimes with added butter and flavoured with vanilla and orange. This is spread on to a baking sheet. The tuile acquires its characteristic shape by being laid over a rolling pin while still hot, then left to set until cool and crisp. Flat round tuiles (called *mignons*) are stuck together in pairs with meringue, then dried in the oven.

RECIPE

tuiles
Whisk together 100 g (4 oz, ½ cup) caster (superfine) sugar, 1 teaspoon vanilla sugar, 75 g (3 oz, ¾ cup) plain (all-purpose) flour, 2 eggs and a small pinch of salt. Blend in 25 g (1 oz, 2 tablespoons) melted butter and 75 g (3 oz, ¾ cup) shredded (slivered) almonds (optional). Using a teaspoon, place small quantities of the mixture, well apart from one

Trussing poultry

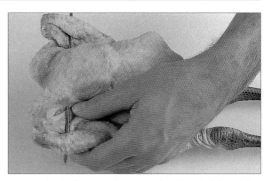

1 The bird should be cleaned and any stray feathers should be removed. Herbs or aromatic vegetables can be placed in the body cavity. Place the bird on its back, with the neck towards the left. Using a scalded trussing needle threaded with 50 cm (20 in) cooking twine, pierce between the bone and the fleshy part of the thigh. Pass the thread through from one side of the bird to the other.

2 Turn the bird on to its breast, neck still to the left. Hold the wing tips together and wrap the loose neck skin neatly over the back to cover the neck cavity. Insert the needle into the first joint of the wing, then over the wing tip, through the neck skin and body, over the next wing tip, through the wing joint and out on the other side. Tie the two pieces of twine securely together and cut off the ends (not too short).

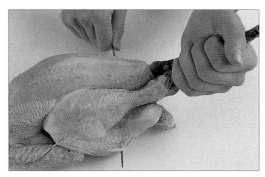

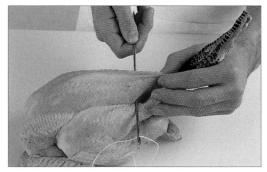

3 Replace the bird on its back. Fold the legs tightly along the body and insert the needle close to the join with the fleshy part of the thigh, then push it through to the other side.

4 Return the needle over the thigh, through the belly and out over the leg. Pull the ends of the twine firmly to hold the legs against the body and tie tightly in place. Trim the twine.

another, on a buttered baking sheet. Spread them out slightly with the back of a fork dipped in cold water. Bake in a preheated oven at 240°C (475°F, gas 9) for about 4 minutes – the edges of the tuiles should be golden brown, the centres remaining white. Take out of the oven, remove from the baking sheet and bend them, while still hot, over a rolling pin or a very clean bottle; leave to cool.

TULIP Light biscuit (cookie) made of butter, icing (confectioner's) sugar, flour and egg whites. The mixture is spread on greased baking sheets, well apart in circles, using a spoon or a palette knife (spatula). The mixture spreads during cooking to make thin biscuits. The hot, soft biscuits can be shaped when first removed from the oven by putting them in individual brioche moulds. The mixture quickly becomes firm and crisp as it cools and sets. They are served cold and crisp, filled with Chantilly cream, fruit or ice cream. The biscuits should be stored in an airtight container to prevent them from softening. They should be filled shortly before being served, otherwise they become soft. The biscuits can

be rolled around wooden spoon handles, rolling pins or cream horn tins (pans) to make different shapes.

TUNA *Thunnus thymus* A good source of the omega-3 fish oils so highly valued by modern nutritionists, tuna was also highly appreciated in ancient times. The Phoenicians used to salt and smoke it. Archestratus recommended the great tuna of Samos and that of Sicily, but he said, 'If one day you go to Hippone, a town in illustrious Italy (in North Africa), the tuna there are better than all the rest.' When using the female tuna, he recommended cutting the tail into pieces, roasting it, sprinkling it with salt and oil and pickling it in a strong brine. In the Middle Ages, pickled tuna was appreciated, particularly *tonnine* (cut up, roasted or fried in olive oil, then salted and strongly spiced). In the time of Louis XIV, the grocers still traded in pickled tuna. From the 19th century, tuna fishing gradually extended to the Atlantic.

Tuna are migratory fish which travel in dense shoals. As early as the 2nd century BC, the Greeks

Setting a tulip biscuit in a mould

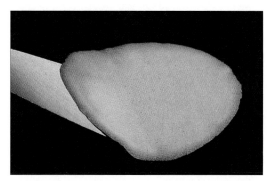

1 *Remove the biscuit mixture from the baking sheet using a spatula. The trick is to allow the biscuit to remain on the baking sheet to cool for a few seconds, so that it is just firm enough to be lifted without disintegrating.*

2 *Gently press the biscuits into little brioche moulds and leave to cool and set before removing.*

knew of their migratory habits, and ancient fishing methods have been practised for a long time in Sicily and the former Yugoslavia. In Provence, at the end of the 19th century, the approach of shoals of tuna was still heralded by lookouts blowing their horns. At the outbreak of World War I, fishing for bluefin tuna was still on a small scale and restricted to the Mediterranean, whereas fishing for albacore, which had been modernized around 1850, was thriving in the Bay of Biscay. The first boat designed for fishing tuna for the canning industry was built in 1906. Around 1930, a few shipowners in Saint-Jean-de-Luz fitted their boats with refrigerated holds. Today tuna fishing is industrialized and scientific: locating the migrating shoals by helicopter or even satellite. In the final decades of the 20th century, the fishing methods of certain countries caused controversy because it was found that other marine life, including dolphins, were perishing alongside the tuna. Such was the outcry that many manufacturers now label their cans 'dolphin friendly'.

■ **Types of tuna** Five species of tuna are now fished: the albacore, yellowfin tuna, bluefin tuna, blackfin tuna and skipjack, which represents the third grade of canned tuna found in supermarkets.

• ALBACORE OR WHITE TUNA Called *germon* or *thon blanc* in France, this is widely used for canning. For-

merly much more abundant than it is today, it weighs 10–30 kg (22–66 lb) and is fished from the Azores to Ireland. Its white flesh, slightly rose-tinted and very tasty, resembles veal and is cooked in a similar way. Formerly, it was nicknamed 'veal of the Carthusians', as it could be eaten on days of abstinence. Breton *germon* is sold fresh from the end of May to the beginning of October. It is sliced and braised (after marinating) or grilled (broiled).

• YELLOWFIN TUNA Called *albacore* in France, this is bigger and heavier than the albacore, up to 2.5 m (8 ft) long and 250 kg (550 lb) in weight; it has a steel blue back, greyish sides and a silvery belly (like the albacore), but its fins are yellow and its flesh pale pink. It is fished practically throughout the year in tropical and equatorial waters. Rarely sold fresh, it is widely used by the canning industry.

• BLUEFIN TUNA Fished in the Mediterranean, the Bay of Biscay, and a few tropical seas. In Australia, it is known as the southern bluefin to distinguish it from the northern variety. When it is young, its belly has green stripes and its flesh is white. The flesh of adult fish is dark red. The average weight of a bluefin tuna is 100–125 kg (220–275 lb), but some very old fish are more than 3.5 m (11½ ft) long and weigh 700 kg (1545 lb). The bluefin tuna is almost always sold fresh. In France it is prepared by Basque, Sicilian or Provençal cooking methods: cut into slices, marinated, then braised or cooked *en daube*, rather than grilled. The flesh of the bluefin tuna is best when it has been kept for about eight days: by that time it is shiny and bright red, with a more pronounced taste than that of the albacore. When its colour is verging on light brown, the fish has gone bad.

• BLACKFIN TUNA Called bigeye in the United States, this is caught in the same areas as the yellowfin. It does not exceed 100 kg (220 lb) and is usually eaten fresh, but it does not have the flavour of albacore.

• SKIPJACK This is a bonito. Its flesh is as good as that of the bluefin tuna but less firm. It is used mostly in canning for tuna-based preparations.

Several other fish resemble tuna and are prepared in similar ways: the *pelamide* (pelamid or bonito), which is cooked in steaks like albacore but does not have its quality and taste; *melva* (frigate mackerel), a small fish found in warm seas, with a dark blue back and often smoked; *thonine* (little tunny), a bonito with a speckled belly and brown flesh, used in canning.

■ **Preserved tuna** Tuna is consumed in a wide range of preserved forms, which are used to fill sandwiches; and make mixed salads; stuffed vegetables, including avocados, (bell) peppers and tomatoes; and various hors d'oeuvre.

Tuna is available canned in water, brine, various oils or sauces. Canned tuna is presented either whole (the slab is in fact composed of pieces tightly packed together), in small fragments or in fillets (long strips taken from the belly of the fish).

Cans labelled 'tunny' or 'tuna fish' almost always contain tropical tuna (yellowfin, skipjack or blackfin). Those labelled 'albacore', 'white tuna' or 'germon' must contain that variety, which is more expensive and of better quality.

RECIPES

grilled tuna

Mix some olive oil with lemon juice, salt, pepper, a little cayenne pepper, some finely chopped parsley and, if desired, a crushed garlic clove. Marinate some steaks of white tuna (albacore) 4–5 cm (1½–2 in) thick in this mixture for at least 30 minutes. Grill (broil) the drained steaks under a low heat for 10 minutes on each side. Serve with a flavoured butter – sweet (bell) pepper or anchovy.

tuna en daube à la provençale ♦

Stud a slice of bluefin tuna with anchovy fillets. Marinate in olive oil, lemon juice, salt and pepper for 1 hour.

Brown the fish in olive oil in a flameproof casserole, remove and set aside. Add 1 chopped onion and cook for 10 minutes, until softened but not browned. Stir in 2 large peeled, seeded and crushed tomatoes, a small crushed garlic clove and a bouquet garni. Replace the tuna, cover and cook for 15 minutes. Pour in 150 ml (¼ pint, ⅔ cup) white wine and finish cooking in the oven, basting often, for 40 minutes. Drain the fish and place on a serving dish. Add the concentrated cooking liquor and serve with a little timbale of ratatouille and a fan of sautéed courgette (zucchini).

tuna rouelle with spices and carrots

Brown a 1 kg (2¼ lb) tuna rouelle in butter in a flameproof casserole. Surround it with 6 peeled tomatoes, cut into quarters, 10 small, peeled whole onions and 1 kg (2¼ lb) baby carrots, peeled and sliced. Mix with 500 ml (17 fl oz, 2 cups) chicken stock and season with 2 teaspoons fresh root ginger, a pinch of grated nutmeg, ½ teaspoon ground cinnamon, 4 saffron strands, ½ teaspoon ground cumin and salt. Cover, bring to the boil and simmer for 1 hour. Serve very hot.

TUNISIA See *page 1242.*

TURBAN A word used to describe certain foods arranged in a circle on the dish: fillets of fish, crown of lamb, for example. The term also refers to a preparation of forcemeat or a salpicon, cooked in a ring mould: *turban* of fish, shellfish, poultry, rice or game; these are generally served as a hot or cold entrée, coated with sauce. Mousses and ice creams are also moulded in a turban.

RECIPES

iced turban

Pour into a ring mould some vanilla ice cream mixed with a salpicon of crystallized (candied) fruits steeped in rum. Freeze until set. Turn out of the mould on to a layer of nougatine and fill the centre with vanilla-flavoured Chantilly cream.

turban of poultry

Line a buttered ring mould with thin slices of raw poultry cut from the breast, so that the slices slightly overhang both edges. Mask with a thin layer of poultry forcemeat, then fill the mould with a salpicon of cooked poultry, mixed with truffle and mushrooms, and bound with allemande sauce. Cover with a thin layer of forcemeat and fold the overhanging slices over the top. Cook in a bain marie in a preheated oven at 180°C (350°F, gas 4) for about 40 minutes, then leave to stand for 10 minutes before turning out of the mould on to a round dish. Fill the centre of the turban with braised slices of calves' sweetbreads and sautéed morels. Coat with suprême sauce.

TURBIGO A dish consisting of lamb's kidneys cut in half, sautéed, garnished with grilled (broiled) chipolatas and sautéed mushrooms and covered with a sauce made from the cooking juices mixed with white wine and tomato-flavoured demi-glace sauce. This recipe, named after the Lombardy town where the French won two victories over the Austrians under the First and Second Empire, dates back to an era when restaurateurs and cooks named their creations after military victories or generals.

RECIPE

lamb's kidneys Turbigo

Cut the kidneys in half; remove the thin skin that surrounds them and the white central part. Season with salt and pepper and fry briskly in butter. Arrange them in a circle on a round dish, possibly on a bed of croûtons browned in butter, and keep hot.

Cook some small button mushrooms in the butter used to cook the kidneys and grill (broil) as many small chipolatas as there are kidney halves. Arrange the chipolatas between the kidney halves and place the mushrooms in the centre. Mix the cooking juices with white wine and tomato-flavoured demi-glace sauce; reduce and pour over the kidneys.

TURBOT A flatfish living on the sandy pebbly beds of the Atlantic (called *berdonneau* or *triboulet* in France) and the Mediterranean (nicknamed *rombu* or *clavelat*). It is one of the best sea fish. Both eyes are on one side of its body, which is brownish, dotted with black and white marks. The blind side is sometimes pigmented as well, which is unusual with flatfish. Its lozenge-shaped body, which is broader than it is long and made round by its fins, has led to the invention of a special turbot kettle (*turbotière*).

Tuna en daube à la provençale.

TUNISIA

The gastronomy of Tunisia is well seasoned with history, from the rich cultural legacy of Carthage, the ancient city of Phoenician traders, through Roman, Ottoman, Arab, Spanish, Italian and French influences. The cuisine shares characteristics with other countries of the Maghreb, the North African region which also includes Algeria and Morocco.

Fish and seafood are no longer in the abundant and inexpensive supply they once were from the Mediterranean but they are still important ingredients – squid, octopus or prawns (shrimp) are used in main dishes or appetizers. Chicken, mutton or lamb and beef are eaten with a wide variety of vegetables. Spicy *merguez* sausages are grilled and added to stews or couscous. Pulses, simple types of pasta and couscous in particular are satisfying ingredients. Olives and olive oil from the country's groves of trees are widely used. There are flat breads and fine pastries or crunchy, chunky breadstick rings, known as *kaaki*, sold from large baskets by street hawkers.

The food is spicy and sometimes tongue-numbingly hot.

Harissa, a fiery condiment of chilli, oil and other ingredients, such as caraway, cumin, coriander, garlic and tomatoes, is used in cooking and served at the table to make dishes even hotter according to individual taste.

It addition to its spicy nature, savoury cooking is also a mélange of contrasting flavours that are evident without dominating. Dried fruits, such as prunes or dates, or fresh quinces and honey make some dishes distinctly sweet. Nuts, warm spices and zesty lemon complement and balance the sweet flavour of many dishes.

■ **Popular dishes** Marinated vegetable salads are served with an assortment of dishes as part of *kemia*, a mixed hors d'oeuvre, which also includes stuffed crêpes, known as *trids*. *Briks* are probably the most famous Tunisian starters or snacks. Made from the circles of fine *malsouqa* pastry, prepared from batter set on a hot griddle, filled with lightly spiced meat or vegetables and a lightly cooked egg, the crisp-fried *briks* are irresistible. Eating these large semi-circular pasties without spilling any of the perfectly cooked egg is a tasty task: the knack of preparing the pasties is the real challenge.

Couscous is well known as the

national dish. The name applies to both the starchy ingredient and the finished dish with its accompanying stew of chicken or lamb, a mixture of vegetables and chick peas in a harissa-seasoned tomato sauce.

Tajine is another stew that takes the name of the cooking vessel. The tajine is a comparatively shallow pot with a conical lid fitting inside the rim of the base and designed to allow steam to condense.

Chakchouka is a stew of mixed vegetables, similar to ratatouille but cooked in a spicy broth, then served with eggs.

■ **Pâtisserie and desserts** There is an extensive variety of sweet pastries, cakes and desserts that are rich with nuts, scented with rose water and sweetened with honey or syrup. Little triangular, round or square pastries; nut pastes; and dried fruit preparations all feature. Semolina is used to make desserts and cakes, such as *makroud*, a cake flavoured with cinnamon and orange and filled with dates.

■ **Beverages** Sweet mint tea is sipped at any time of day and particularly at the end of a meal. *Bhouka* is a strong and aromatic brandy, distilled from figs, and *thibarine* is a sweet date liqueur.

Its tough skin lacks visible scales but is covered with small bony tubercles (hence its name, which derives from the Scandinavian word for a thorn).

Highly esteemed since ancient times and nick-named *roi du carême* (king of Lent) for centuries, turbot has been prepared in the most sumptuous ways. For Napoleon, Laguipière created turbot *à l'impériale* (cut into slices, poached in milk, arranged with crayfish tails and coated with a truffle sauce). The way in which it was cut up at table, with a silver fish slice, was formerly governed by precise rules.

Turbot is sold whole and gutted (cleaned) or in chunks, depending on its size. Most fish measure 40–50 cm (16–20 in) and weigh between 2 and 4 kg (4½ and 9 lb), although some, which are not necessarily less delicate, reach 90 cm (3 ft) and 20 kg (44 lb). Chicken turbot (*turbotin*) is the name given to small turbot weighing 1–1.5 kg (2¼–3¼ lb), which are often cheaper than large turbot, although they have the same qualities. There is always a large amount of waste: about 50% of the weight (slightly less for the biggest fish).

Its white firm flaky flesh, which is particularly delicate and tasty, makes turbot an expensive fish. Whether it is poached (in milk, to ensure that its flesh remains white), braised, grilled (broiled) or pot-roasted, its cooking must be carefully controlled. If it is cooked for too long, the flesh loses its flavour and texture. All recipes for brill and John Dory are suitable for whole turbot, and all recipes for fillets of sole are suitable for fillets of turbot.

As in the past, the great chefs give turbot pride of place in their creations. Some classic preparations for turbot are Dugléré, *à l'amiral*, Bercy, *à la cancalaise*, Saint-Malo and Victoria, while cold dishes include turbot in scallop shells or with mayonnaise, green sauce, tartare, remoulade or gribiche sauce. In turbot *à la pèlerine*, created by Prosper Montagné, the fish is sprinkled with melted butter and cooked on a baking sheet lined with onion lightly cooked in butter, coated with the cooking juices mixed with white wine, cream and butter, then glazed in the oven and garnished with fried scallops arranged *en buisson*. Such a large fish is rarely deep-fried, but

Brillat-Savarin recommended this method to his cook, La Planche: 'You tried my hellish idea and you were the first to have the glory of offering the startled world a huge fried turbot. That day, there was great jubilation among the lucky guests.' Notable creations of 20th-century chefs include turbot braised in vermouth (Fernand Point); *suprême de turbot de ligne*, studded with anchovies, roasted with parsley and steeped in a champagne sauce (Alain Chapel); *blanc de turbotin* with sorrel fondue (Roger Vergé); blanquette of turbot (André Guillot); chicken turbot with grapes and tea (Alain Senderens); and chicken turbot studded with anchovies and steamed with saffron (Michel Guérard). But many gastronomes consider that turbot should simply be grilled or poached on its own.

RECIPES

escalopes of turbot with buttered leeks

Slice some fillets of turbot into escalopes and make a fumet with the trimmings. Seal the escalopes in butter on both sides, then cover with the fumet. Simmer for 5 minutes. Drain the fish. Mix the cooking juices with an equal amount of double (heavy) cream. Arrange the escalopes on a hot dish and pour over the sauce. Serve with an *embeurrée* of leeks: cook 1 kg (2¼ lb) shredded white parts of leeks in a preheated oven at 190°C (375°F, gas 5) with 200 g (7 oz, 1 cup) butter and 175 ml (6 fl oz, ¾ cup) water, covered, for 20 minutes; season with salt and pepper.

fillets of turbot with leek fondue and beef marrow

Soften some shredded leeks with a knob of butter for 20 minutes, over a very low heat. Season with salt and pepper. Add some crème fraîche and cook for a further 5 minutes, then set aside. Steam the turbot for 8 minutes. Reduce for 1 minute half a shallot (finely chopped) in 100 ml (4 fl oz, 7 tablespoons) red wine. Add 2 tablespoons meat glaze. Reduce, then remove from the heat and thicken with 25 g (1 oz, 2 tablespoons) butter cut into small pieces. Line the plates with this sauce, put the fillets of turbot on top, then surround with the leek fondue, alternating with a *concassée* of tomatoes (2 very ripe tomatoes, peeled, seeded, diced and lightly cooked in a little butter with a chopped shallot). Finish off with slices of beef marrow, soaked in cold water for 2–3 hours, then poached for 3 minutes in boiling water. Garnish with parsley.

turbot en papillote with crispy vegetables and champagne sauce ◆

Fillet a 1.5 kg (3¼ lb) turbot and cut into 12 escalopes of equal thickness. Chill. Meanwhile, prepare a fish stock with the bones. Peel and cut 2 medium-sized carrots, 1 celery heart, 1 small turnip and the white part of leek into a coarse julienne. Cut 75 g (3 oz) green beans in half. Cook the vegetables for 3 minutes in the fish stock with 20 g (¾ oz, 1½ tablespoons) butter. Season when almost cooked. Drain and reserve the cooking liquid. Sweat 2 peeled and chopped shallots in 2 teaspoons butter. Deglaze with 200 ml (7 fl oz, ¾ cup) brut champagne and the reserved cooking liquid. Reduce by half.

Fold 2 sheets of foil 30 × 60 cm (12 × 24 in) in half to make 2 double-thick squares. Cut these into semi-circles, leaving the folded edge uncut. Place 6 fish escalopes, lightly seasoned with salt, pepper and cayenne pepper, on one half of each foil semi-circle. Put the vegetables on the fish and fold the other half of foil over. Seal the edges.

Add 200 ml (7 fl oz, ¾ cup) crème fraîche to the champagne reduction and bring to the boil, then cook for a few seconds. Whisk in 125 g (4½ oz, ½ cup) butter, cut into small pieces. Cook the papillotes in a preheated oven at 220°C (425°F, gas 7) for 7 minutes. Take out of the oven and open the parcels in front of the guests. Pour a little sauce on each plate and place 2 escalopes on top.

turbot with morels

For 5 or 6 servings, soak 300 g (11 oz) dried morels in plenty of water (or use fresh morels when in season). Remove the stalks and wash thoroughly. Cook in salted water, strain, squeeze gently and brown in a saucepan, adding 2 finely chopped shallots at the last moment. Add 200 ml (7 fl oz, ¾ cup) double (heavy) cream and bring to the boil. Adjust the seasoning and simmer for about 10 minutes.

Fillet, skin and trim a 3–4 kg (6½–9 lb) turbot and cut into 100 g (4 oz) escalopes. Season with salt and pepper on both sides. Garnish half the escalopes with small piles of morels and cover with the remaining escalopes. Cook in a frying pan with a little butter, then in a preheated oven at 180°C (350°F, gas 4) for about 10 minutes. Arrange in a dish and coat with Américaine sauce. Put a medallion of lobster on each escalope.

TURBOT KETTLE A square- or diamond-shaped fish kettle, provided with a grid with handles and a lid. Made of smooth or hammered aluminium, copper, tin-plated iron or stainless steel, the turbot kettle is designed for cooking large whole flatfish: turbot, brill and skate.

TURINOIS A cake that does not require cooking, made from chestnut purée, sugar, butter and grated chocolate and flavoured with kirsch. The purée is poured into a buttered square mould lined with greaseproof (wax) paper at the bottom, then pressed down firmly and left to cool for several hours. The cake is then turned out of the mould, cut into slices and served.

The name *turinois* (or *turin*) is also given to a square petit four made of sweet pastry, garnished with chestnut purée flavoured with kirsch, then spread with apricot syrup and decorated with chopped pistachios.

TURKEY A farmyard bird raised for its delicate flesh. The size of the bird will vary according to its variety and breeding. Although the traditional large birds are still available, particularly at festive seasons, medium-sized and small birds have been developed which are suitable for smaller gatherings all the year. Large turkeys are still produced for cutting up into joints and for charcuterie. The flesh of turkey cocks is drier and it is advisable to lard it with bacon strips. The word *dindonneau* (meaning young turkey) is often used on French menus.

The turkey was called 'Indian chicken' by the Spanish conquerors, who thought they were still in the Indies when they discovered it in Mexico (hence the French name – a contraction of *poule d'Indes*). It first appeared on a French table in 1570, at the marriage feast of Charles IX, but it was not commonly used in cooking until about 1630. In England, it eventually replaced the Christmas goose and is still the main part of the traditional Christmas meal, stuffed and served with bread sauce, cranberry jelly and a variety of accompaniments. The turkey still lives in the wild in the United States and Mexico, but it was already domesticated in Mexico at the time of the Aztecs; prepared with a sauce containing chocolate, it constitutes the national dish (*mole poblano de guajolote*). In the United States, turkey is the traditional dish on Thanksgiving Day, since the arrival of the first colonists who were saved from famine by the wild turkey. It is stuffed with corn bread, roasted and served with chestnuts and orange and cranberry sauce.

Brillat-Savarin, who proclaimed himself a 'dindonophile' (turkey-lover), dedicated a long paragraph in *The Sixth Meditation* to the 'Indian chicken': 'The turkey appeared in Europe towards the end of the 17th century; it was imported by the Jesuits, who raised a large number of them, particularly in a farm they owned near Bourges; it was from there that they gradually spread over the whole of France. This is why the colloquial name for a turkey is still *jésuite* in many places.'

■ **Selecting and preparing turkey** A good turkey should be young, plump and short-necked, with a supple windpipe. If the bird is old, its feet are reddish and scaly. The sinews must be drawn from the legs (it is best to ask the butcher to do this). The bird may be easier to carve if the wishbone is removed. Usually, the entire breast is barded so that the flesh is protected from drying out during cooking.

Apart from dishes using turkey joints or giblets, turkey is usually stuffed and roasted. However, it is sometimes braised or cooked in a ragoût (like goose) and garnished *à la bourgeoise* or *à la chipolata*. Turkey meat may also be grilled (broiled), cooked in a fricassée like chicken, or casseroled and garnished with such vegetables as aubergines (eggplants), artichokes, mushrooms, small onions or browned potatoes. Skinned and boned turkey meat is sold cut into escalopes, strips or dice, or minced (ground) for use in many types of recipes.

RECIPES

braised turkey legs
This recipe uses the legs of young turkeys; the wings or suprêmes can be used for another dish. Bone the legs, fill with a suitable poultry stuffing, then roll them into small ballotines. Braise in white or brown stock, then drain and glaze in the oven. Arrange on a serving dish and coat with the cooking stock. Serve with a vegetable purée, braised vegetables (such as carrots or celery), rice or creamed potatoes.

daube of turkey à la bourgeoise
This dish is made with a very tender turkey hen, rather than a young turkey cock. Braise the bird in a suitable brown stock; when three-quarters cooked, drain. Strain the braising stock. Replace the bird in the braising pan and surround with a bourgeoise garnish. Add the strained braising stock, cover the pan and finish cooking over a gentle heat.

roast turkey
Season and truss a small turkey and bard the breast and back with bacon. Roast either on a spit, allowing 20 minutes per 450 g (1 lb), or in a preheated oven, allowing 25 minutes per 450 g (1 lb) at 160°C (325°F, gas 3). Remove the bacon before the bird is completely cooked so that it browns. Serve with the skimmed strained cooking juices and garnish with watercress.

roast turkey stuffed with chestnuts
Scald and peel 1 kg (2¼ lb) chestnuts. Half-cook them in stock, drain and wrap in a large piece of soaked pig's caul, if available. Enclose them in the boned turkey, tie it up neatly and roast in the usual way.

roast turkey stuffed with dessert apples
Season the turkey and, if desired, insert some slices of truffle between the skin and the flesh. Remove the gall bladder from the liver and pound the liver with a small can of goose foie gras mousse, 40 g (1½ oz, 3 tablespoons) butter and 2 tablespoons port. Peel and remove the seeds from 800 g (1¾ lb) dessert (eating) apples, cut them into thick slices and brown them in a frying pan in 75 g (3 oz, 6 tablespoons) butter. Mix half the apples with the liver mixture and use to stuff the turkey. Keep the remaining apples hot. Place a very thin strip of bacon on the breast and on the back of the bird and tie up firmly.

Cook the turkey in a preheated oven at about 200°C (400°F, gas 6) for about 2 hours for a 3 kg (6½ lb) bird. The bird is cooked if the juices released when the skin is pricked are clear. Remove the bacon slices and quickly brown the turkey breast, if necessary, in a very hot oven. Carve in the

Turbot en papillote with crispy vegetables and champagne sauce, see page 1243.

TURKEY

Midway between Europe and the East, Turkish cookery draws equally on Muslim, Jewish and Christian traditions. In turn, it has left its mark on the cuisine of numerous countries: Russia, Greece, North Africa, the Middle East.

In France, a number of dishes of Turkish origin were adopted centuries ago, such as pilaf, lamb kebabs, stuffed aubergines (eggplants) and dried figs, not to mention coffee and pâtisserie. The Turks also invented *mezze*, *böreks*, *halva*, *baklava*, *kadaïf* (a shredded wheat dough used for pastries), Turkish delight, and all kinds of confectionery with picturesque names (such as beloved's lips, vizier's fingers and lady's navel).

The national drink is coffee – the average person drinks 10 cups per day. *Raki*, a kind of anisette drunk alternately with mouthfuls of cold water while nibbling *mezze*, is also worth mentioning.

At the end of the 19th century, Istanbul was described as a city where people ate day and night and where itinerant merchants sold cooked rice, chick peas, lamb or chicken tripe kebabs, curd cheese and grilled (broiled) fish, tea, coffee, salep and ice cream, pancakes, melons and watermelons. This atmosphere continues today in small popular restaurants with their *djindjères* – large round pans made of tin-plated copper – in which stews

and soups simmer all day long, and their spits, on which whole lambs and *döner kebabs*, dripping with fat, are continously cooking.

■ **Small specialities** Turkish cookery gives pride of place to hors d'oeuvre and small entrées. Apart from soup (meat or vegetable *chorba*), there is *cacik* (cucumber in yogurt); mussels stuffed with rice, pine nuts, chopped onion, raisins and spices; sheep's trotters (feet) in aspic; *pastirma* (dried and spiced beef) and a whole range of *dolmas* (stuffed vine leaves or cabbage leaves).

■ **Fish** The most sought-after fish are gilthead bream, mackerel, sardine, tuna, turbot and eel, often cooked in a court-bouillon and served with an aubergine (eggplant) and honey sauce. Also popular are fillets of salt cod (soaked in milk to remove the salt), coated with unsweetened almond milk, bound with cream and sprinkled with shredded (slivered) almonds.

■ **Favourite meat dishes** Among Turkish meat dishes, mutton reigns supreme, being used in a great variety of preparations. The *döner kebab* consists of layers of meat and fat placed on top of one another on a vertical spit, forming a large distaff which revolves in front of the flame and from which long thin strips are carved when they are cooked to the right degree. There is also *adjem pilaf*, diced roast shoulder of mutton with finely sliced onion, rice and broth; *unkar beyendi*, pieces of leg of mutton, sheep's tails and

fat, threaded on to skewers, grilled (broiled) and served on aubergine (eggplant) purée; meatballs, mixed with courgette (zucchini) pulp, onion and grated cheese, then fried and eaten hot or cold; not forgetting shish kebab, frequently served with shredded almonds and soured (sour) cream. Young goat is favoured, as is chicken – *à la circassienne*, with a red (bell) pepper and walnut sauce – and beef (particularly in meatballs).

■ **Vegetables and grains** The main vegetable is the aubergine, indispensable for the famous *imam bayildi* and moussaka, but Turkish recipes also include courgettes and stuffed (bell) peppers (these are generally eaten half-cooled in their cooking juices), okra, cabbage, spinach and mange-tout (snow peas), often cooked in water or butter and served with one of many spicy sauces, such as a sauce made from crushed anchovies in lemon juice, mixed with stock and oil. Bulgur wheat and rice are also basic ingredients, the former being used in stuffings and soups, the latter used in the famous pilaf (mixed with raisins, pine nuts or almonds).

■ **Sweet specialities** Apart from very sweet pastries, the Turks sometimes serve puddings, such as *azure* (made from chick peas, rice, flour, milk, sugar and dried fruit, flavoured with rose water or orange-flower water). Roses are also used in the preparation of jams and to flavour *loukoum*.

usual way. Put the remaining hot apples into a small vegetable dish, sprinkle them with the cooking juices from the bird and serve with the slices of turkey.

stuffed roast turkey

Stuff the turkey with a sage and onion stuffing prepared as follows: bake the onions in their skins in the oven, peel and chop them, then toss in butter. Season with plenty of chopped fresh sage. Mix with an equal quantity of fresh breadcrumbs and half their quantity of chopped suet. Bind with a little milk. Roast the turkey in the usual way, weighing it and calculating the cooking time with the stuffing.

Put it on a serving dish surrounded with slices of bacon or grilled sausages. Serve with gravy made from the cooking juices and bread sauce.

truffled turkey

Draw the turkey, leaving the skin of the neck very long so that the opening in the bird can be secured firmly when trussing. Insert beneath the skin some large slices of truffle that have been seasoned and soaked in brandy.

Prepare the stuffing as follows: dice 500 g (18 oz) fresh pork fat and mix with 250 g (9 oz) uncooked foie gras. Reduce to a purée in a mortar or a blender and add any parings from the truffles. Season with salt, pepper and a pinch of dried fennel. Press the stuffing through a sieve, add a little crushed thyme and bayleaf, and cook very gently in a heavy-based saucepan, stirring, for about 10 minutes. Add 2 tablespoons brandy and allow to cool completely.

Stuff and truss the turkey and wrap it in a sheet of buttered greaseproof (wax) paper. Leave it in a cool place for at least 24 hours. Bard the truffled turkey, wrap it again in the buttered paper and roast, uncovered, in a preheated oven at 160°C (325°F, gas 3), allowing 20–25 minutes per 450 g (1 lb). Unwrap the turkey, remove the barding and replace in the oven to brown. Place on the serving dish and keep hot. Deglaze the pan, reduce the gravy and serve separately. Alternatively, serve with a Périgueux sauce to which the cooking juices have been added.

other recipes See *ballotine (of chicken), chicken (chicken casserole), fricassée (of chicken), giblets, grand-duc, pâté pantin, paupiette, poupeton, Sainte-Menehould.*

TURKISH DELIGHT A Middle Eastern confectionery made of sugar, honey, glucose, syrup and flour – usually cornflour (cornstarch). It is flavoured and coloured, usually either pink or green, and often decorated with almonds, pistachio nuts, pine nuts or hazelnuts. Turkish delight (*loukoum*, or *rahat loukoum*, meaning literally 'rest for the throat') has a rubbery consistency and is presented as large cubes covered in icing (confectioner's) sugar.

TURMERIC A tropical herbaceous plant with an aromatic underground stem which resembles fresh root ginger in shape and form, but with a bright yellow colour and dark skin. The dried, ground spice is used to flavour savoury dishes and to produce a colourant. The extract is known as curcumine (E100) and is used to colour certain dairy products, confectionery, drinks and mustards.

Turmeric is an ingredient in curry powder. It is used mainly in the cuisines of India and South-East Asia. The dried spice has a warm, earthy flavour that goes well with citrus fruit, ginger and cardamom. Its flavour (and colour) diminishes as the spice ages and becomes stale.

TURNED VEGETABLES A basic culinary technique which is carried out after peeling vegetables, to give them a regular shape making them easier to cook, and for presentation.

Turning is generally done by hand, with a cook's knife, a peeler or a mandoline; but, for large quantities, electrical appliances are used today.

TURNIP A fleshy root vegetable, yellow or white in colour and often tinged with purple near the leaf bases. European in origin, the vegetable has been cultivated in India for centuries. It was always a popular pot vegetable in Britain and France, espe-

Turning vegetables

The trimmings from turned mushrooms, carrots and similar vegetables can be used in stocks and to flavour soups, casseroles or sauces.

To turn a small, closed-cap mushroom, work around the vegetable, making evenly spaced shallow curved cuts from the centre to the outside edge of the cap. Work around the mushroom once more, making a second cut into each curve and removing a fine wedge from the surface. A cannelle knife can be used for this technique.

To turn carrots, cut the prepared vegetables into equal lengths. Use pieces of roughly the same thickness. While turning a piece of carrot, pare off fine layers, making the ends slightly narrow to create a neat oval shape. All the pieces should be pared to the same size and shape.

cially in soups and stews, principally in northern and coastal regions. The turnips of certain parts of France (Nantes, Meaux, Belle-Île-en-Mer and Orleans) have been famous for centuries, as have those from Teltow in Berlin, which were even praised by Goethe.

The turnip's distinctive flavour makes it suitable for a garnish, purée and soup (Freneuse). It can even be eaten raw, grated and flavoured with lemon juice. Some chefs are now rediscovering its virtues and are preparing stuffed turnips, braised turnips in cider, turnip mousse with sorrel and chives, and sautéed turnips.

Among the varieties of garden turnip are purple top Milan (Milan), which is round and white with a purple collar and is available as a spring vegetable, and golden ball (boule d'or), a round yellow winter variety with a very good flavour. The French varieties Nantais and Croissy are elongated and white and are sold in spring and summer. There is also a black variety, which may be elongated or round.

Turnips should be firm and heavy with an unblemished smooth shiny skin. Spring turnips are often sold complete with their leaves, which can also be cooked (like spinach). Spring turnips must be used within a short time of purchase; winter turnips, on the other hand, will keep for 2 months in a cool place.

Turnips should be peeled and washed just before they are cooked, otherwise they will darken; small new turnips need only be scrubbed. Winter turnips are improved by blanching for 10 minutes before further preparation to reduce their very strong flavour. An essential ingredient of pot-au-feu and hearty meat soups, turnips can also be prepared in the same way as carrots (glazed *à l'anglaise*, sautéed in butter or cooked with cream), or puréed, used in a vegetable loaf or in a soufflé. They have the property of absorbing large quantities of fat, and for this reason they are traditionally served with fatty meat such as mutton or duck.

RECIPES

stuffed turnips à la duxelles
Peel and hollow out some medium-sized young turnips. Cook them for 8 minutes in boiling water, then drain and refresh in cold running water. Drain again and lightly sprinkle the hollows with salt. Cook the scooped-out flesh in butter and rub it through a sieve. Prepare a mushroom duxelles (1 tablespoon per turnip), add the purée and fill the turnips with the mixture. Arrange the stuffed turnips in a buttered gratin dish. Add a few tablespoons of beef or chicken stock, sprinkle with breadcrumbs and pour on some melted butter. Cook slowly in a preheated oven at 200°C (400°F, gas 6); the cooking time will depend on how tender the vegetables are – test by pricking with a skewer.

stuffed turnips à la piémontaise
Cook as for stuffed turnips *à la duxelles*, but use risotto for the stuffing. Sprinkle with grated Parmesan cheese before browning in the oven.

stuffed turnips braised in cider
Peel and blanch 575 g (1¼ lb) small round young turnips. Slice off and reserve the tops, then scoop out a shallow hollow in each and cook the scooped-out flesh in boiling salted water. When soft, reduce to a purée in a blender. Sauté the hollowed-out turnips and tops in equal quantities of olive oil and butter and cook until browned. Sprinkle with salt and pepper.

Meanwhile, boil half a bottle of dry (hard) cider and reduce to half its original volume. Drain the turnips and tops well and add them to the cider. Pour in a little stock and braise in a preheated oven 190°C (375°F, gas 5) for 15 minutes. Drain them, reserving the cooking juices. Add the purée to the

liquid to thicken it, and adjust the seasoning. Add 50 g (2 oz, ¼ cup) butter, beat the mixture and keep hot.

Mix together 100 g (4 oz, ½ cup) sausagemeat, 25 g (1 oz, 2 tablespoons) *à gratin* forcemeat*, some basil, rosemary and thyme flowers. Shape the mixture into balls and cook in butter over a low heat. Place one ball into each hollow turnip, adding the tops to form lids. Pour the sauce over and serve very hot.

turnips au gratin
Peel some turnips and slice them into rounds. Blanch them in boiling salted water, drain and refresh under cold running water and braise in butter. Place the turnip rounds in a buttered gratin dish, smooth the top and coat with Mornay sauce. Sprinkle with grated cheese and brown in a preheated oven at 240°C (475°F, gas 9).

TURNOVER A pastry in the shape of a semicircle, made from a thinly rolled round of puff pastry folded over a filling of stewed fruit, traditionally (but not necessarily) apples. Most are individual, but large turnovers, using a simple shortcrust pastry (basic pie dough), may be prepared for several people. All these pastries are eaten warm or cold.

Turnovers can also be savoury. They are usually small and served very hot, as an hors d'oeuvre or entrée, with various fillings such as fish, poultry, game, ham or mushrooms. See *empanada, rissole*.

RECIPES

preparing turnovers
Whether savoury or sweet, the method is the same. Roll out some puff pastry to a thickness of about 3 mm (⅛ in). Cut out circles 5–15 cm (2–6 in) in diameter. Place a fairly dry filling on half of each circle, without going right up to the edge, fold the free half back over the filled half and join the two edges firmly, pinching them to prevent the filling from oozing out during cooking. Decorate with lines made with the tip of a knife and glaze with egg yolk.

Savoury Turnovers
turnovers for light entrées
Following the method for preparing turnovers, use any of the following savoury fillings.
• *à la lyonnaise* Creamed pike with butter and crayfish tails, truffle and Cognac.
• *à la Nantua* Ragoût of crayfish tails *à la Nantua*.
• *à la périgourdine* Salpicon of foie gras and truffle sprinkled with Cognac.
• *à la reine* Purée of chicken mixed with diced truffles and mushrooms.

Sweet Turnovers
apple and prune turnovers
Soak 250 g (9 oz, 1¾ cups) stoned (pitted) prunes in tepid water and 50 g (2 oz, ⅓ cup) washed

currants in 4 tablespoons rum. Peel and thinly slice 4 good apples, then place in a stewpan with 5 tablespoons water and 50 g (2 oz, ¼ cup) caster (superfine) sugar. Leave to cook for 20 minutes, then blend and return to the pan with the drained currants and 25 g (1 oz, 2 tablespoons) butter; stir over a gentle heat to dry out. Put the drained prunes in another pan with 100 ml (4 fl oz, 7 tablespoons) weak tea, 50 g (2 oz, ¼ cup) sugar and the grated zest of a lemon; boil gently for 10 minutes, then blend and return to the pan to dry uncovered over a gentle heat.

Roll out 500 g (18 oz) puff pastry thinly on a floured board. Cut out 8 rounds, using a cutter 15 cm (6 in) in diameter, and elongate them slightly. Brush over the edges of the rolled-out pastry with beaten egg and fill half of each round with stewed apples and stewed prunes, without mixing them. Fold over the pastry and join the edges together, tucking them over each other and pressing down well. Arrange the turnovers on a moistened baking sheet and brush with beaten egg. Trace light diamond-shaped cuts in the pastry. Bake in a preheated oven at 220°C (425°F, gas 7) for about 25 minutes and serve them either warm, or cold and dusted with icing (confectioner's) sugar.

TURNSPIT (ROASTING JACK) A mechanism for rotating a roasting spit in front of a heat source. The modern turnspit is an oven or barbecue accessory, usually operated by electricity.

In the Middle Ages, turnspits were operated by *galopins* (urchins), young apprentice rôtisseurs, who turned the handles of heavy spits in front of glowing fires. Subsequently, dogs were used to turn the spit by running inside a wheel. Self-turning spits appeared at the end of the 16th century; Montaigne, in his *Voyage en Italie*, describes these appliances 'operating by a spring or a system of weights and counterweights'. In the 18th century, when clockwork mechanisms were perfected, turnspits could function automatically for 1–2 hours. A bell sounded when they needed to be reset. There were also spits operated by the heat of the fireplace, which turned a bladed wheel. In some restaurants, there were giant spit-roasters for cooking several dozen chickens at the same time.

TURQUE, À LA A term that describes various dishes inspired by Oriental cookery, particularly rice pilaf, either arranged in a ring with a garnish in the centre, or moulded in darioles as an accompaniment to shirred eggs, omelette or lamb noisettes, served with sautéed aubergines (eggplants).

The term refers specifically to a dish of chicken livers, sautéed with chopped onion and tomato-flavoured demi-glace sauce added; or aubergines, or sweet (bell) peppers, stuffed with minced (ground) mutton, rice and duxelles, baked with tomato-flavoured onion fondue. Vegetables stuffed *à la*

turque can be used to garnish pot-roasted loin or saddle of lamb.

RECIPES

lamb noisettes à la turque
Prepare some rice pilaf and sauté some diced aubergine (eggplant) flesh in oil. Fry the lamb noisettes in butter and arrange in a serving dish; garnish with the aubergine and the rice pilaf moulded in darioles. Keep hot. Dilute the pan juices with tomato-flavoured veal stock and pour over the noisettes.

stuffed peppers à la turque
Put some (bell) peppers in a preheated oven at 230°C (450°F, gas 8) until the skin blisters and blackens, so that they can be peeled easily. Cut open at the stalk end and remove the seeds, then blanch in boiling water for 5 minutes. Make a stuffing from two-thirds minced (ground) cooked mutton and one-third rice pilaf. Season with salt and pepper and add a little chopped garlic and just enough reduced tomato sauce to bind the stuffing. Fill the peppers with this mixture, to which some fairly dry mushroom duxelles can be added.

Peel, finely slice and lightly cook in oil enough onions to cover the bottom of a flameproof casserole. Pack the stuffed peppers into the casserole, add a few tablespoons of light tomato sauce and cover. Bring to the boil on the hob (stove top), then cook in a preheated oven at 220°C (425°C, gas 7) for about 30 minutes.

TURRÓN Also known as *touron*. Confectionery of Spanish origin, made from ground almonds, egg whites and sugar. Of various colours and flavours, it can also contain pistachios, whole almonds, walnuts or dried fruit. There are numerous varieties, which are all southern specialities.

• The Spanish turrón, also called *jijona* (from the name of the town where it is a speciality), is made from honey and sugar, with walnuts, hazelnuts, pine nuts, and sometimes coriander and cinnamon. The Alicante turrón, a traditional Christmas sweetmeat, is more crunchy. Both are made in the form of slabs, which are cut into slices.

• The Catalan turrón, which resembles the black nougat of Provence, contains hazelnuts but no almonds.

• The Basque turrón, made simply from almond paste, coloured red, takes the form of small balls similar to arbutus berries.

• The Bayonne touron is similar to almond paste. It looks like a chequerboard, with squares of different colours and flavours, with or without almonds.

• The honey touron of Gap, made from sugar and honey, contains almonds and hazelnuts.

The name *touron* is also given to a round petit four, made from almond paste, royal icing (frosting), chopped pistachios and orange zest.

RECIPE

tourons

Pound 250 g (9 oz, 2 cups) blanched almonds with 2 egg whites; add 200 g (7 oz, 1 cup) caster (superfine) sugar and knead the mixture on a marble worktop. Sprinkle with 2 tablespoons icing (confectioner's) sugar and roll out to a thickness of 5 mm (¼ in). Mix 100 g (4 oz, 1 cup) chopped pistachios with 200 g (7 oz, 1 cup) caster sugar and the zest of half an orange, very finely chopped. Add 100 g (4 oz) royal icing (frosting) and 2 whole eggs. Mix well with a spatula. Spread this mixture evenly over the almond paste. Cut into circles or rings and arrange on a buttered and floured baking sheet. Dry in a very cool oven.

TURSAN Wine from Landes in south-western France. It has been known since Gallo–Roman times and was exported even in the Middle Ages. Tursan is best known as a dry, white wine, made from a local vine called the Baroque. There are red and rosé versions, the former being fairly full-bodied. They are mostly made from the Tannat grape.

TURTLE A short-legged reptile, amphibious or terrestrial, whose body is enclosed in a scaly carapace. There are several edible varieties, but they are increasingly rare and protected, so their preparation for the table is chiefly a matter of gastronomic curiosity. The hawksbill turtle, which is quite small, used to be common on the east coast and islands of tropical America. Sought-after for its shell, it also provides highly esteemed meat and eggs. The loggerhead, the largest turtle, is considered to be leathery, with a taste of the sea. The diamondback turtle or terrapin, which lives in fresh water, is bred in the United States. Boiled in salted water and boned, it is prepared according to local recipes in Maryland.

At the beginning of the 19th century in New York, a popular entertainment was barbecuing turtles imported live from the West Indies. West Indian cookery has the greatest variety of dishes prepared from turtle, particularly the green turtle, which provides excellent flesh; the head, legs, tail, intestines and eggs are also edible. In addition, its fat provides very good oil. It is traditionally made into soup, daubes, fricassee, stew and colombo. Turtle steaks, marinated in vinegar, oil and garlic, are cooked like beef and served highly seasoned with pepper. In Egypt, turtle meat is prepared in a stew, with onions and pomegranate juice. The flippers make a special braised dish, served with a spicy sauce. In Europe, turtle soup was, at one time, a speciality: this was a British contribution to classic French cookery. Queen Victoria and Prince Albert were known to have begun their Christmas dinner at Windsor Castle in 1840 with turtle soup. It was being made in France as early as the 16th century, since, as stated by Delamare (quoted by Franklin), 'the blood of turtles, even live turtles, is cold. Therefore, the turtle is a true fish, and can be eaten without qualm on days of abstinence.'

■ **Mock turtle soup** Mock turtle soup, made from calf's head, was invented in Britain. This rather strange dish was created as a cheap alternative to the expensive and luxurious, genuine turtle soup, which was something of a sign of affluence on the dinner party menu. Imported turtles were extremely costly, so canned turtle was used but that also was too pricey for many budgets. The recipe for mock turtle soup is included here for its 'novelty' value.

RECIPE

mock turtle soup

Boil a boned calf's head in a white court-bouillon for 1½ hours, with carrots, an onion studded with cloves, celery, a bouquet garni, salt and pepper. Drain the head and discard the ears; trim the rest of the meat and put it under a press between 2 plates. When it is quite cold, cut it into small round or square pieces and reheat in a little of the stock.

While the calf's head is cooking, make a clear brown gravy in a stewpan, by adding some stock to slices of salt leg of pork, veal knuckle and a half-roasted chicken. When these meats are almost cooked and the gravy reduced, add the calf's head cooking juices and vegetables and simmer gently for about 2 hours.

Strain, thicken with a little arrowroot diluted with cold stock, then add an aromatic infusion of basil, spring onion (scallion), marjoram, thyme and bay leaf in Madeira or port.

Strain the soup and pour it into a soup tureen; garnish with pieces of calf's head and, if desired, small quenelles made from sausagemeat mixed with mashed hard-boiled (hard-cooked) egg yolks.

TURTLE HERBS A mixture of aromatic herbs (basil, marjoram, chervil, savory and fennel), used to flavour turtle soup and also turtle sauce, which is served with calf's head and boiled ox (beef) tongue.

TUSCANY A renowned wine-producing region in central Italy best known for Chianti produced mainly from Sangiovese. Further south the grape is used in making Brunello di Montalcino and Vino Nobile di Montepulciano, giving fuller, richer, more intense wines. Some white wines are produced from Trebbiano, but the region's reputation for quality is based on the excellence of the red wines. See *Italy*.

TUTTI-FRUTTI An expression of Italian origin, meaning 'all the fruits'. It is used to describe various desserts that combine the flavours of several fruits or contain mixed fruits, crystallized (candied), poached or fresh, generally cut into small pieces.

Tutti-frutti ice cream contains diced crystallized fruits steeped in kirsch. A tutti-frutti bombe may be coated with strawberry ice cream, with a lemon ice cream mixed with diced crystallized fruit inside.

Tutti-frutti is also a pastry made of a thin layer of sweet pastry covered with a layer of crystallized or poached fruit, finely diced, then a second layer of pastry. The top is covered with apricot syrup, iced (frosted) and generously sprinkled with shredded (slivered) almonds or pieces of candied orange peel.

RECIPE

tutti-frutti bombe
Line a bombe mould with 1 litre (1¾ pints, 4⅓ cups) pineapple* ice and harden in the freezer. Then make a sugar syrup using 250 g (9 oz, 1 cup) sugar and 100 ml (4 fl oz, 7 tablespoons) water, pour into a saucepan in a bain marie and blend in 8 egg yolks. Whisk on the hob (stove top) until thick and frothy. Strain, then whisk again in a basin. Blend in 400 ml (14 fl oz, 1¾ cups) Chantilly* cream. Flavour with 1 tablespoon kirsch and add a salpicon of 400 g (14 oz, 3 cups) crystallized (candied) fruits steeped in kirsch, together with 100 g (4 oz, ⅔ cup) raisins soaked in rum and well drained. Pour the mixture into the mould and freeze for 4 hours. Turn out of the mould and decorate with glacé (candied) cherries, candied angelica and shredded (slivered) almonds.

TVAROG In Russian cookery, a mixture of drained and sieved curd cheese, softened butter or soured (sour) cream and beaten eggs, usually seasoned with salt and pepper. It is used to stuff small patties, which are served cold as an hors d'oeuvre. *Tvarog* can also be used to fill tartlets, pastry cases (shells) or rolled pancakes.

TVP The abbreviation for textured vegetable protein, a manufactured product made primarily from soya beans. The vegetable protein is processed to form a variety of foods, including some resembling meat in texture, colour and flavour, such as dried granules, intended as an alternative to minced (ground) meat, and chunks. When they were first promoted, the flavoured dried TVP items were aimed at the vegetarian market, to replace meat-filled sausages, burgers and grilled bacon. They were also highlighted as an inexpensive alternative to meat for making stews and meat sauces. As well as dried foods, canned products resembling meat stews were also manufactured. Although dried textured vegetable protein shapes and granules are still sold, vegetable protein is more often used in commercial production as an extender for poultry and meat products.

TWELFTH-NIGHT CAKE A traditional cake eaten on the day of Epiphany. A bean is inserted in the cake before cooking, and the person whose portion contains the bean is appointed 'king' or 'queen' for the occasion. This ceremony probably dates back to Roman times. During the Saturnalia the 'king of the day' was chosen by lot, using a bean concealed in a galette. It was only in the Middle Ages that this cake ceremony began to be associated with the festival of Epiphany. From this time, the Church attached a different significance to it – the sharing of the holy bread – but the tradition of the 'elected king' survived. Formerly, in many French provinces, the cake was cut according to a particular ritual, with songs and processions of children collecting alms. During the Revolution, an unsuccessful attempt was made to replace the Twelfth-Night cake with a cake of Equality or Liberty, shared out during a 'good neighbour' festival.

In Britain, Queen Victoria's Twelfth-Night cake of 1849 was described by *The Illustrated London News* as being of 'regal dimensions, being about 30 inches in diameter, and tall in proportion'.

Nowadays, France has two major traditional Twelfth-Night cakes: in the north, in Lyon and in the Paris area, the cake is a puff-pastry galette, sometimes filled with frangipane; in the south, the cake is like a brioche, often decorated with crystallized (candied) fruit or flavoured with brandy or orange-flower water. In Provence and Auvergne, the Twelfth-Night cake is like a crown-shaped brioche and in Bordeaux and Limoux the cake is flavoured with citron. The bean is replaced by a china figurine of a baby or animal.

RECIPE

Bordeaux Twelfth-Night cake
Make a well in 500 g (18 oz, 4½ cups) plain (all-purpose) flour and crumble in 20 g (¾ oz, 1½ cakes) fresh (compressed) yeast and 2 teaspoons salt. Work in 8 whole eggs, one by one, the zest of a grated lemon, 200 g (7 oz, 1 cup) caster (superfine) sugar in small quantities, and 200 g (7 oz, 1 cup) butter softened until creamy. Knead the dough well until evenly blended, then leave it to rise in a warm place for 10 hours.

Knock back (punch down) the dough as for brioche dough and divide it into 4 equal parts. Shape each one into a crown and place these crowns, after inserting the bean on the underside of one of them, on a piece of buttered paper. Allow to rise in a very cool oven, then leave to cool. Brush the crowns with beaten egg. Decorate with thin slices of citron and crystallized (candied) sugar. Bake in a preheated oven at 200°C (400°F, gas 6) for about 40 minutes.

Traditionally, the 4 crowns are placed on top of each other.

TYROLIENNE, À LA A term given to preparations of meat, chicken, grilled kidneys, soft-boiled or poached eggs, or baked brill, garnished with fried slices of onion and a tomato fondue (or crushed tomato). Tyrolienne sauce is a tomato-flavoured béarnaise sauce, thickened with oil instead of butter.

grilled chicken à la tyrolienne

Prepare a 1 kg (2¼ lb) chicken *en crapaudine* or spatchcocked. Season with salt and pepper, brush with flavoured oil and grill (broil) for 25–30 minutes. Meanwhile, peel and slice 2 large onions and separate into rings. Dust the rings with flour and deep-fry in oil at 180°C (350°F). Cut 4 medium-sized tomatoes into quarters, seed and lightly fry in 25 g (1 oz, 2 tablespoons) butter. Arrange the grilled chicken on a hot dish, surrounded by the onions and tomatoes. Season with salt and pepper and garnish with parsley.

TYROPITA Also spelt *tiropita*, these are Greek cheese pies, puffs or turnovers. They are made from filo pastry with a filling of feta cheese, often mixed with a mild cheese or soft cheese. The pastry is cut into strips and the filling is placed at one end, then the pastry is folded over the filling several times to make a small triangular pie. The pastries are brushed with melted butter and baked until crisp and golden. They are served warm as a snack. For a main course, large versions of the pie are prepared in deep baking trays. *Spanakopita* are cheese and spinach pies.

TZATZIKI Greek dish, a type of salad or dip, served as a first course or with a selection of *mezze* as a snack or hors d'œuvre. Tzatziki consists of finely cut or grated cucumber in yogurt, usually seasoned with garlic and sometimes with mint; it may be topped with a trickle of olive oil.

tzatziki

Peel 1 cucumber (English cucumber) and cut it in half lengthways. Scoop out and discard the seeds from the middle, then coarsely grate the remainder of the vegetable. Place the grated cucumber in a sieve and sprinkle it lightly with salt. Leave to drain over a bowl for about 30 minutes. Squeeze the excess liquid from the cucumber, then place it in a bowl. Add 1 crushed garlic clove and a squeeze of lemon juice. Stir in 300 ml (½ pint, 1¼ cups) Greek yogurt. Finely chop the leaves from 2–3 sprigs of mint and add them to the tzatziki. Season with a little cayenne pepper and chill for about 1 hour before serving. Offer warm crusty bread with the tzatziki.

TZIMMES Jewish stew of vegetables, typically potatoes and carrots, often with beef, sweetened with sugar or honey, sometimes flavoured with cinnamon. Fresh or dried fruit, such as apples, prunes or raisins, may be added. Tzimmes is served for Rosh Hashanah, the New Year, when sweet foods are eaten to symbolize hope for sweetness and happiness in the year to come.

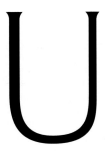

UDDER The mammary gland of an animal, especially that of a cow. Its gastronomic role is now fairly limited, in contrast to former times. Cow's udder should first be sliced, soaked in cold water, blanched and cooled. It can then be braised (possibly studded with small pieces of bacon fat) in the same way as noix of veal and served with mushrooms or rice. It can also be used in pâtés and terrines. Apicius gives a recipe for a puff-pastry pie of sow's udders, fish and chicken spiced with pepper and pine kernels. In the Middle Ages people enjoyed cow's udder with verjuice, while heifer's udder was quite a common constituent of forcemeat.

UDE, LOUIS-EUSTACHE French cook, a contemporary of Carême, who was one of the first to introduce the French culinary art into Britain.

Having been Louis XVI's head cook, then Princess Letizia Bonaparte's maître d'hôtel, he became chef to Lord Sefton, then to the Duke of York and finally director of St James's Club in London. An annuity bequeathed by Lord Sefton, a gourmet and epicurean, enabled Ude to retire and write *The French Cook or the Art of Cookery developed in all its various branches* (1813, republished several times up to 1833). This is a 'practical good cookery course' for organizing 'elegant and inexpensive dinners', with anecdotes, advice on choosing menus and a list of 'several new French recipes'.

UKRAINE See *below.*

UGLI A tropical plant, originally from eastern India, similar to the lemon tree and having fragrant fruit resembling medium-sized oranges. The Indians (who call them *bilva* or *mahura*) cook ugli fruit in ashes because of their leatheriness, then eat them with sugar. They can also be made into jam.

UKRAINE

The Ukraine shares the culinary characteristics of neighbouring countries, including Poland and Hungary. Many dishes are also reminiscent of German cuisine, with *galouchki* (thick, soft egg-based quenelles), cabbage leaves stuffed with rice and mushrooms, *nakypliak* (a kind of cabbage soufflé, cooked in steam) and *lekchyna* (egg noodles with spinach or nuts). The region's abundance of cereals led to it being called the 'bread basket of the Soviet Union' and is reflected in the wide range of bread such as *kalatch*, a very rich white bread, the small *balabouchki*, which is made with sour dough, and numerous *kacha*-based trimmings. *Kacha* is a preparation made with buckwheat. The traditional Christmas dish is *koutia*, a semolina cake with poppy seeds and dried fruit.

WINE The republic produces red and white wines mainly from the Crimea, Odessa, Kherson, Nikolayev, Transcarpathian and Zaporozh'ye regions. While some foreign grape varieties have been introduced, Ukraine has a wealth of indigenous vines. Sherry-style and Madeira-style fortified wines are produced in the Crimean wineries. Sparkling wines made from Pinot Blanc, Aligoté, Riesling and Fetiaska grapes play an important part in the economy.

UNITED STATES OF AMERICA

Far too vast and varied to be comprehensively described in a few paragraphs, the food of the United States is as rich and diverse as its people. The culinary traditions of the European pioneers have been enhanced and enriched by the contributions of myriad Italian, Chinese, African and Jewish immigrants, but there are still a few basic ingredients that have remained firmly anchored in American traditions.

Maize is one of the best examples: popular in the form of popcorn or corn on the cob, it is also eaten boiled as hominy grits and mixed with haricot (navy) beans to make succotash. Maize flour (corn flour) is also used in New Mexico to prepare tortillas, bread and cakes. Pumpkin or squash is eaten in soup, in pies, as a cake and puréed. Rice is also a mainstay throughout the country and is the basic ingredient of New Orleans's jambalaya, dirty rice (rice with giblets) and hoppin' John (rice, bacon and black-eyed beans).

■ **Traditional home cooking**
Western films have always emphasized the image of the pioneer's wife busying herself with her saucepans and frying pans, and many traditional recipes are indeed stews and fry-ups. The New England boiled dinner, Boston baked beans (baked beans with bacon), chilli con carne from Texas, Philadelphia pepperpot (very spicy), burgoo from Kentucky (porridge with meat and vegetables), Creole gumbo (meat and shellfish stew) and last but not least the soups, especially fish-based (chowders) or fruit-based, which can be eaten hot or cold: all these dishes are cooked slowly in a saucepan. Frying pans were used for frying eggs and bacon, but also for frying codballs, fanny dodies (clams) and hang-town fry (fried oysters and eggs).

The rituals of the barbecue and planked meat (meat or fish cooked in the oven on a plank of oak or hickory on which the food is then served) reflect the American fondness for simple but hearty country dishes: fish, shellfish and meat (spareribs, hamburgers and T-bone steaks) are grilled in the open and eaten with the minimum of ceremony.

The classic dishes eaten on special occasions and Thanksgiving are also part of the American tradition: turkey garnished with cornbread, served with cranberries and an orange-based sauce, clove- and whisky-flavoured ham, fried chicken and pecan pie.

The trends in contemporary cuisine are reflected in two characteristic types of dishes: the wide range of mixed salads, of which Caesar salad is one of the most famous: cos (romaine) lettuce, hard-boiled (hard-cooked) eggs, croûtons, anchovy and Parmesan cheese; and the numerous dips, thick sauces (with fromage blanc, clams, tuna, celery, avocado and so on) and spreads, thicker sauces, used as fillings for huge and imaginative sandwiches.

■ **Sweet specialities** Cakes and pastries are an important feature of traditional home cooking. Buns, rolls, cookies, brownies, pancakes, doughnuts and numerous other cakes and desserts, such as apple pandowdy (apple pie), pound cake (a sponge cake similar to British Madeira cake), strawberry shortcake, upside down cake (upside down pineapple cake), gingerbread, lemon chiffon pie (lemon meringue), Brown Betty (apple pudding) and cheesecake. Last but not least come all the iced puddings, including ice creams, sundaes, banana splits and iced soufflés of many flavours.

■ **Regional specialities** New England retains the tradition for making fabulous soups, roasts and pies, inherited from the Old Country. Fish and seafood (clams, lobster and cod) are very popular. In Pennsylvania and

Wisconsin German traditions are still present, as is reflected in the sweet-and-sour dishes, pickled meats and dairy products, while a strong Scandinavian influence is found in Minnesota (smörgasbord, herring and Danish pastries). In Michigan there is typical Dutch food, such as vegetable and potato stews and waffles. Oklahoma still has a range of Indian specialities such as squaw bread and jerky, which is smoked meat. In the mid-eastern seaboard fish is an important ingredient in many regional dishes. The South still bears the mark of French colonial occupation of Louisiana, as shown in the range of regional pastry. In Florida turtles, crabs and shrimps play an important part in the regional cuisine, while Virginia is famous for its hams and chicken. The main culinary influences in the south-west are Spanish and Mexican (chicken and rice, tamales, *picadillo* and tacos). On the west coast, in California, fish and seafood are vital ingredients in a wide range of regional dishes (such as *cioppino*) and fruit is cultivated everywhere. Game in Oregon is so abundant that it is sufficient to feed the whole country, while the state of Washington is famous for its salmon and crayfish.

WINE Wine is produced in 46 of the 50 states of the USA, although most of the production is based in California, New York, Oregon, Washington and Texas. The USA is a very significant producer and consumer of wine, particularly of fine wines. The industry increased dramatically after the repeal of Prohibition and again in the 1970s following the introduction of the Farm Winery Acts, which eased restrictions on wine growers and producers. The traditional American hybrid grape varieties (including Concord, Delaware and Catawba) are gradually being replaced by French hybrids (including Seyval Blanc, Baco Noir and Chambourcin) and more recently *Vitis vinifera* vines.

The wine-producing regions of the United States and Canada

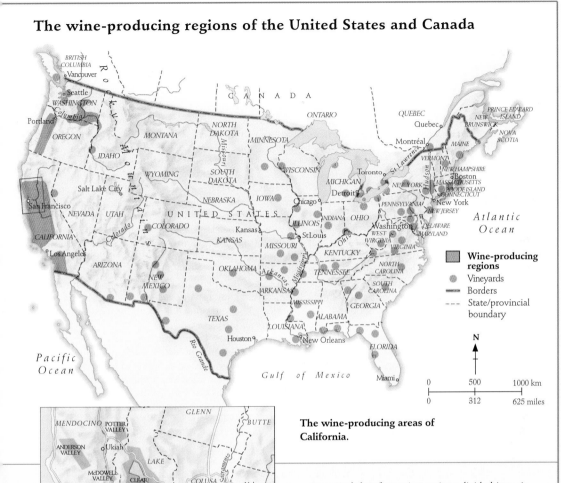

The wine-producing areas of California.

New York has four wine regions divided into six American Viticultural Areas (AVAs): Finger Lakes, with Riesling, Pinot Noir and Cabernet Franc producing good quality wines; Lake Erie, producing grapes for grape juice and table grapes in addition to wine; Hudson River, where the French hybrid Seyval Blanc is prominent; and Long Island, where Merlot and Cabernet Franc flourish in the temperate climate.

In Oregon, in the Pacific North West, the best known area for wine production is the Willamette Valley. The climate is cool and ideally suited to the production of very fine wines made from Pinot Noir and Chardonnay. Also in the Pacific North West, Washington is an important wine-producing state. The eastern area is the most predominant, with virtually all the vineyards to be found in the Columbia Valley. The climate embraces hot dry summers and sometimes bitterly cold arctic winters, and vineyard areas are defined by the availability of irrigation. Riesling, Semillon and Chardonnay are very successful in these northern regions, but there are also smaller plantings of Sauvignon Blanc and Chenin Blanc as well. Cabernet Sauvignon, Merlot, Cabernet Franc and Syrah grapes all produce good quality red wines.

ULLUCO Also known as ullucus. A plant from western South America, cultivated in Bolivia and Peru for its small, pinkish, edible tubers. Attempts to introduce the ulluco into Europe as a substitute for the potato have not been successful.

UMBRIA A quality wine-producing region in Central Italy best known for the white wine Orvieto and red wines Torgiano and Rosso di Montefalco made from Sangiovese. Recent investment in the vineyards and wineries has led to an exciting range of wines being produced from Merlot, Cabernet Sauvignon, Pinot Noir and Chardonnay, as well as Sangiovese.

UNITED STATES OF AMERICA See *page 1254.*

UNLEAVENED BREAD Describing a dough that is without leaven, or yeast. Unleavened bread plays an important role in Jewish ritual, as Orthodox Jews consider fermented bread to be profane. According to tradition, unleavened bread symbolizes absolutely pure food, the fermentation brought about by the leavening agent marking the beginning of the process of decay. Each year biblical Jews made *matzo* (from a verb meaning 'to extract'), round ritual bread resembling the offertory cakes of the Mediterranean peoples. Later, *matzo* was eaten in place of bread during the seven days of Passover, to commemorate the deliverance of the children of Israel (see Exodus XII: 33).

In earlier times the rabbis ordained that three women should work simultaneously in making *matzo*: one to knead the dough, another to shape the biscuits (cookies), and the third to put them into the oven. The custom of making patterns and interlaced designs on the *matzo* was abandoned, however, and the biscuits are now crisp, round or square, and of varying thickness and size. They may sometimes be shaped in moulds with geometric patterns. In England, in 1875, *matzo* was first made industrially under rabbinical control.

The composition of unleavened bread for religious purposes must be scrupulously respected: water and wheat flour (harvested in a prescribed way), without salt, sugar or fats. Barley, spelt, oats or rye may also be used. Sometimes the dough is flavoured with wine or fruit, but only 'pure' *matzo* is eaten on the first night of Passover. A whole cuisine has built up around the use of unleavened flour (*matzo* meal), including traditional soups containing *matzo* balls, fritters and cakes. Some of these recipes may account for the name 'celestial bread' in the Cabbala.

UNMOULD To turn out a cake, jelly, ice cream and the like from a tin or mould. This is often a delicate operation and should be carried out with care.
• Aspics and jellies Plunge the base of the mould in hot (but not boiling) water for a few seconds. Remove and shake lightly from side to side. Loosen the jelly around the edge with the blade of a knife, place a serving plate on top of the mould, turn over quickly and lift off the mould steadily, keeping it vertical. The same procedure can be used for cream desserts and flans.
• Sponge cakes Unmoulding is made easier if the mould or tin has a non-stick surface. Otherwise, it needs to be greased and lightly dusted with flour before adding the mixture. Another alternative is to line the tin or mould with greaseproof (wax) paper. Turn out on to a wire rack immediately after removing from the oven.
• Unmoulding ice cream Dip the mould briefly into cold water and then into lukewarm water. Loosen the ice cream with the blade of a knife, taking care not to cut into it. Place a napkin or a paper doily and then the serving dish on top of the mould. Turn over quickly and lift off the mould, keeping it vertical.

URUGUAY See *Paraguay and Uruguay,* and *South America.*

VACHERIN A cold dessert, made of a ring of meringue or almond paste filled with ice cream or whipped cream (or both). It owes its name to its shape and colour, which resemble the cheese of the same name. The classic vacherin is made of rings of meringue placed on top of each other, filled with ice cream of one or more flavours, to which may be added fresh or crystallized (candied) fruit, sponge biscuits soaked in liqueur, marrons glacés and so on, on a base of sweetened pastry. Whipped cream is piped over the top, and the dessert is decorated with crystallized flowers, sugar-coated 'pearls' or fruit.

Sometimes the name vacherin is given to rounds of meringue layered with cream or ice cream.

RECIPES

iced chestnut vacherin

Whisk 8 egg whites to stiff peaks, then mix in 500 g (18 oz, 2¼ cups) caster (superfine) sugar with a spatula. Make a round layer of meringue by piping a flat spiral on greased greaseproof (wax) paper on a baking sheet. Pipe 2 rings of the same diameter on to baking sheets. Cook in a very low oven, then leave to cool.

Cook 400 g (14 oz) peeled chestnuts in milk for 40 minutes, drain them and reduce to a purée. When the purée is cold, add 1 liqueur glass of rum, 3 stiffly whisked egg whites, 25 g (1 oz, 2 tablespoons) melted butter and 3 coarsely chopped marrons glacés. Freeze for 4 hours in the freezer. Place the rings of meringue on to the flat round to form a shell, then pile the ice cream into this meringue shell. Decorate with Chantilly cream and a few marrons glacés. Return to the freezer until ready to serve.

iced vacherin

Prepare 3 layers of meringue: draw 3 circles on sheets of greaseproof (wax) paper, marking their centres. Grease the paper on the side on which the circles have been drawn, then place the ungreased side on baking sheets. Whisk 8 egg whites to very stiff peaks with a pinch of salt; towards the end of this operation scatter in 500 g (18 oz, 2¼ cups) caster (superfine) sugar (the mixture will be pearly). Fill a large piping (pastry) bag fitted with a large, smooth nozzle with this meringue mixture, then, starting from the centre of the circles, cover these with meringue, forming a flat spiral. Place the baking sheets in a preheated oven at 110°C (225°F, gas ¼), or at the coolest setting, close the door, turn off the oven and cook for 1½–2 hours as it cools. Allow the meringues to become completely cold.

Prepare some vanilla ice cream: make a light custard cream (see *custard*) with 5 egg yolks, 150 g (5 oz, ⅔ cup) sugar, 100 ml (4 fl oz, 7 tablespoons) milk, a vanilla pod (bean) and 400 ml (14 fl oz, 1¾ cups) double (heavy) cream. Freeze this cream in an ice-cream maker, making sure that it remains soft. Prepare 500 ml (17 fl oz, 2 cups) soft strawberry ice* cream in the same way.

To assemble the vacherin, remove the greaseproof paper from the meringue layers with the point of a knife. Place a ball of vanilla ice cream in the centre of one layer, then place the second layer on top, pressing sufficiently to allow the ice cream to come to the edges of the layer. Replace in the freezer to harden the ice cream, then remove and repeat the process with the strawberry ice cream between the second and third layers. Replace the vacherin in the freezer and prepare the decoration.

Heat 100 g (4 oz, ½ cup) sugar with 400 ml (14 fl oz, 1¾ cups) water and boil for 1 minute. Whisk 2 egg whites to very stiff peaks, pour the boiling syrup over them and whisk until the mixture is cold. Add 500 ml (17 fl oz, 2 cups) double (heavy) cream and whisk until the mixture has set. Chill in the refrigerator, then put into a piping bag with a fluted nozzle and pipe it decoratively on the top of the cake. Alternatively, simply apply a smooth covering over the top and sides of the vacherin, giving it the appearance of a cheese. The vacherin may also be decorated with crystallized (candied) fruits or violets.

mocha vacherin

Place a 20 cm (8 in) flan ring, 5 cm (2 in) deep, on a cardboard base. Put a baked succès base in the ring and place it in the freezer for 20 minutes; this is the mould to be filled.

Prepare a mocha ice cream: coarsely grind 50 g (2 oz) good-quality coffee beans and add to 500 ml (17 fl oz, 2 cups) milk sweetened with 100 g (4 oz, ½ cup) caster (superfine) sugar. Bring to the boil, then cover and leave to infuse, away from the heat, for 10 minutes. Pour the milk through a fine strainer and replace it in the pan over a gentle heat. Whisk 6 egg yolks in a bowl with 100 g (4 oz, ½ cup) caster sugar. When the mixture is white and thick, add a little of the hot coffee-flavoured milk, whisking, then pour the contents of the bowl into the milk saucepan. Heat gently, stirring constantly with a wooden spoon. When the custard mixture coats the spoon at 83°C (180°F) withdraw the pan from the heat and stir occasionally until cold. Then add 250 ml (8 fl oz, 1 cup) double (heavy) cream and freeze in an ice-cream maker.

Fill the mould with this ice cream, gently mixing into it 20 coffee beans that have been steeped in liqueur. Smooth the surface with a palette knife, put the mould back in the freezer and leave to freeze for 3 hours. Place a serving dish in the refrigerator for 30 minutes, then carefully remove the flan ring and place the vacherin on the plate.

For the decoration, prepare coffee-flavoured Chantilly* cream, made with 200 ml (7 fl oz, ¾ cup) double cream, 60 ml (2 fl oz, ¼ cup) milk, 3 tablespoons icing (confectioner's) sugar and 1 teaspoon instant coffee powder. Put this mixture in a piping (pastry) bag; first decorate the sides of the vacherin with vertical bands of cream, then decorate the top, piping 8 spirals around it to indicate the portion for each guest. Finish with a rosette in the centre. Place 1 liqueur-soaked coffee bean in each whirl. Replace in the freezer until ready to serve.

VACHERIN CHEESES The name given to several cow's-milk cheeses (45% fat content) from Switzerland or France (Savoy or Franche-Comté), having a soft texture and a washed rind.

Vacherin d'Abondance, a Savoyard farm cheese, is in the shape of a thick pancake, 25 cm (10 in) in diameter and 4 cm (1½ in) deep, encircled by a thin strip of spruce bark and set into a box, adhering to the base. A soft, runny, sweet-tasting cheese with a smooth red or pink rind, it should be served with a fruity white wine from Savoy or Burgundy, and the rind should not be discarded (the flavour is exceptional). Vacherin des Bauges (or des Aillons) is similar but sometimes creamier. These traditional cheeses were made as long ago as the 12th century, when they were called *vachelins*. Finally, Vacherin Mont-d'Or, made on the farms in the Joux district of Franche-Comté from unpasteurized milk and in Switzerland from unpasteurized milk in the canton of Vaud (where it is also called Mont-d'Or de Joux), comes in the form of a flat cylinder, 15–30 cm (6–12 in) in diameter and 3–5 cm (1¼–2 in) deep, also in a box and encircled by a strip of resinous sapwood. Excellent at the end of autumn and in winter, this creamy cheese has a sweet, slightly aromatic flavour; the rind is smooth and pink, slightly damp, and the cheese is soft, almost liquid in the case of Swiss Vacherin (which is not cut into portions but served with a spoon after the rind has been removed).

A good Vacherin may be recognized by the colour and appearance of its rind. Before being broached it should be stored in a cool damp place. Once started, a block of wood should be placed against the cut surface to prevent it running too much, but it is a cheese which should be eaten quickly, as it rapidly loses its fragrance and flavour.

These soft cheeses should not be confused with Vacherin Fribourgeois, which is a Swiss cooked cheese. It is shaped like a small millstone, 40 cm (16 in) in diameter and about 8 cm (3 in) deep (it is similar to Tomme d'Abondance); it is a soft cheese with a smooth, yellowish-grey or pink rind, smelling a little of resin and with a slightly acid taste. It is used particularly to make *fondue fribourgeoise*.

VACQUEYRAS AOC red, white or rosé wines from the southern part of Côtes-du-Rhône, robust and concentrated, produced from Grenache, Syrah, Mourvèdre and Cinsaut (see *Rhône*).

VALENÇAY A goat's-milk cheese from Berry (45% fat content), also made in Touraine and the Charentes. It has a soft texture and a natural rind that is dusted with charcoal if it comes from a farm (in which case it is in season from April to November); otherwise the rind may have bloomed surface (it is sometimes also dusted with charcoal if the cheese is industrially produced). Made in the shape of a truncated pyramid, 7.5 cm (3 in) across by 6–7 cm (2½ in) high, it is firm to the touch, with a musty smell and a nutty flavour.

VALENCIENNE, À LA The term applied to a rice dish inspired by Spanish cooking and prepared in the Valencian style, cooked in meat stock and garnished with a salpicon of peppers and smoked ham, sometimes with peeled and seeded tomatoes; peas and green beans may also be added to the rice. It may accompany noisettes of lamb, sautéed tournedos steak (filet mignon) or fried chicken, which are coated with a demi-glace sauce.

These dishes *à la valencienne* should not be confused with those described as *à la Valenciennes*, which are typical of northern France, notably rabbit *à la Valenciennes* (with prunes and raisins) and tongue *à la Valenciennes* (slices of smoked tongue covered with foie gras purée).

In France the name *valence* is often used to designate Spanish oranges and, by extension, all oranges.

VALESNIKI In Russian or Polish cookery small savoury pancakes, coated with a mixture of cream cheese, beaten eggs and butter, then folded, rolled and fried in very hot oil. They are served as a hot hors d'oeuvre.

VALOIS The name of a garnish for fried or sautéed poultry or small cuts of meat. It consists of Anna potatoes and sliced artichoke hearts sautéed in butter, sometimes with the addition of stuffed olives. The sauce is made by deglazing the pan with white wine and butter-enriched veal stock.

The name Valois is also given to béarnaise sauce mixed with meat glaze.

VALPOLICELLA A well-known DOC red wine from the Veneto region of Italy, mainly using the Corvina grape variety. At its best, it has a charming colour, a certain distinctive fragrance and a full, appealing taste. Recioto della Valpolicella, a sweet wine, is also produced. The word *recioto* means 'ears', and it is the outer bunches of the grapes that become ripe first; these are sometimes picked separately, although selected whole bunches are usually picked and then dried before being pressed. Valpolicella is traditionally supposed to have been the wine of the lovers of Verona, Romeo and Juliet.

VANDYKE To embellish a decorative feature of a dish: usually applied to tomato, lemon or orange halves with their edges cut into zigzags. These decorations are often used to garnish poached, grilled (broiled) or fried fish, platters of oysters or seafood and so on.

The French term, *historier*, also means to cut lemons into basket shapes, with a strip of peel forming the handle, and to flute or otherwise shape mushroom caps, which are then poached and used chiefly to decorate dishes served in a sauce. In a more general sense, *historier* can mean to embellish a dish with small items of garnish; for example, dishes in aspic or covered with a chaud-froid sauce are garnished with small pieces of truffle or pieces of pickled ox (beef) tongue fixed in place with egg white. Finally, the word can be used to describe metal moulds with an inlaid decorative pattern.

VANILLA A climbing orchid native to Mexico and Central America (where it was discovered by Cortés) and now also cultivated in some islands of the

Vandyke technique

1 *Trim off both ends of the fruit or vegetable so that the halves will stand evenly. Use a fine knife to make a zigzag cut all around the middle.*

2 *Make the cuts even in size and in as far as the centre of the fruit or vegetable. Pull the halves apart gently, cutting any bits that are still attached.*

Indian Ocean and the West Indies for its pods (beans). The word derives from the Spanish *vainilla* (little sheath), referring to the long, thin shape of the pod. Harvested when barely ripe, it is plunged into boiling water and dried, or exposed to the sun (under covers) until it is dark brown; the pod becomes frosted with vanillin crystals, which give it its characteristic smell and flavour. According to its appearance, it is graded into *fine vanilla*, with a black, frosted and very fragrant pod 20–30 cm (8–12 in) long; *woody vanilla*, 13–20 cm (5–8 in) long, reddish-brown with a dry, dull surface and not very frosted; and *vanillon*, with thicker, flatter pods, 10–13 cm (4–5 in) long, which are brown and soft, partly opened and rarely frosted, having a stronger slightly bitter smell. Finally, there is a variety of yellowish, almost odourless vanilla from the West Indies.

Mexican vanilla (*ley* or *leg*) is the most highly prized; next comes that from the Indian Ocean (Bourbon vanilla), followed by that from Guyana, Guadeloupe, Réunion, Tahiti and so on. Vanilla is sold in various ways: in pods; in powdered form (the pods are dried and ground, giving a fine dry, dark brown powder, sold pure or sugared); as an essence (a liquid obtained by maceration in alcohol, then percolation or by infusion in sugar syrup of varying concentrations); or in the form of vanilla sugar (with at least 10% vanilla, obtained by mixing dried vanilla extract with sucrose).

Vanilla is used particularly in pâtisserie and confectionery, to flavour creams, cake mixtures, ices, compotes, poached fruit, desserts, sweets (candy) and chocolate, for example. It is also used in distillery and flavours punch, hot chocolate, mulled wine and sangria. In cookery a trace of vanilla is sometimes used to season fish soup, the cooking juices of mussels, certain white meats and even creamed vegetables.

RECIPES

vanilla ice cream

Prepare a crème anglaise (see *custard*) with 100 ml (4 fl oz, 7 tablespoons) milk and a vanilla pod (bean) cut in two, 5 or 6 egg yolks, 150 g (5 oz, ⅔ cup) caster (superfine) sugar and 400 ml (14 fl oz, 1¾ cups) double (heavy) cream. Pour the custard cream into an ice-cream maker and allow to set in the freezer for 4 hours. Pile up the mixture in a mould and replace in the freezer to complete the setting of the ice cream.

It may be unmoulded on to a serving dish and decorated with crystallized (candied) fruit or fruit poached in syrup or coated with cold fruit purée (strawberry, peach or mango, for example), or else used in balls in sundaes or to fill profiteroles.

vanilla soufflé

Pour 250 ml (8 fl oz, 1 cup) milk into a saucepan and add a vanilla pod (bean). Heat gently until boiling, stirring occasionally, then cover and remove from the heat. Leave to infuse until completely cold, or for at least 30 minutes. Remove the vanilla pod.

Mix 4 egg yolks with 3 tablespoons caster (superfine) sugar and 25 g (1 oz, ¼ cup) plain (all-purpose) flour. Gradually stir in a little of the vanilla-flavoured milk to make a smooth paste. Then stir in the remaining milk and pour the mixture into the saucepan. Bring to the boil, stirring continuously, until smooth and thick. Remove from the heat and cover the surface of this crème pâtissière with wet greaseproof (wax) paper or cling film (plastic wrap) and leave to cool.

Butter a 20 cm (8 in) soufflé dish and sprinkle it with caster sugar. Whisk 6 egg whites until stiff, but not dry, then beat a spoonful of them into the crème pâtissière to soften it slightly. Fold in the remaining whites and turn the mixture into the dish. Run your fingertip or end of a mixing spoon around the inside of the rim of the dish to make a shallow channel in the mixture, then bake the soufflé in a preheated oven at 190°C (375°F, gas 5) for 20 minutes. Working quickly, dust the surface of the soufflé with icing (confectioner's) sugar and cook for a further 5 minutes to glaze the surface. Serve at once.

other recipes See *charlotte (iced charlottes), sugar.*

VANILLIN A chemical substance responsible for the aroma of vanilla pods (beans). It may also be produced synthetically by using eugenol, an essence extracted from the clove tree. This consists of colourless crystals with a strong smell and a pronounced vanilla flavour. Synthetic vanillin competes widely with natural vanilla, being used in pâtisserie, confectionery and chocolate-making, but its flavour is harsh and inferior to that of natural vanilla and it is avoided by discriminating cooks.

VANNER A French culinary term meaning to stir a hot cream, sauce or mixture, with a wooden spatula or a whisk until it is cold, to keep it smooth and particularly to prevent a skin forming on its surface. This process also shortens the cooling time.

VARIENIKI In Russian cooking, a large form of ravioli filled with a mixture of drained curd cheese, butter and beaten eggs, seasoned with pepper and nutmeg, poached in boiling water and served as an entrée with soured (dairy sour) cream or melted butter. Lithuanian varieniki are stuffed with chopped cooked beef, onion and suet, bound with a parsley sauce; they are served in the same way as the Russian version.

VARIETY MEATS See *offal.*

VATROUCHKA A Russian cheesecake consisting of a sablé base, covered with a mixture of eggs, sugar, crystallized (candied) or sometimes dried fruits and curd cheese, usually topped with a lattice of pastry and dusted with sugar after cooking. Another Russian culinary speciality are *vatrouchki*, small turnovers made of ordinary brioche dough and filled with a savoury curd cheese filling.

RECIPE

vatrouchka

Macerate 200 g (7 oz, 1 generous cup) diced crystallized (candied) fruits in 2 tablespoons Cognac, Armagnac or rum.

To prepare the pastry, beat together in a bowl 3 egg yolks and 1 egg white with 200 g (7 oz, 1 cup) caster (superfine) sugar until the mixture is thick and creamy. Whisk in 125 g (4½ oz, ½ cup) softened butter, then sprinkle with 350 g (12 oz, 3 cups) sifted plain (all-purpose) flour. Form the pastry into a ball and chill for about 1 hour. Cut the pastry in half. Use one portion to line a 25 cm (10 in) round, fairly deep, loose-bottomed flan tin (pan). Prick the pastry with a fork and bake blind in a preheated oven at 200°C (400°F, gas 6) for 12–15 minutes, then leave to cool.

Meanwhile prepare the filling: combine 4 whole eggs and 5 yolks with 400 g (14 oz, 1¾ cups) caster sugar in a bowl until the mixture is thick and creamy; add the crystallized fruits with the alcohol in which they have been macerating and 1 kg (2¼ lb, 4½ cups) curd cheese; mix well together.

Pour the filling into the cooled pastry and smooth the surface. Roll out the reserved pastry into a rectangle and cut it into narrow strips. Arrange these in a lattice pattern on top of the filling sealing the ends on the sides of the pastry case. Glaze the filling and the pastry strips with beaten egg and bake in a preheated oven at 180°C (350°F, gas 4) for 40–50 minutes. Take out the *vatrouchka*, dust with icing (confectioner's) sugar and leave until completely cold before serving.

VDQS See *appellation d'origine*.

VEAL The meat of a calf up to one year old, specially reared for slaughter when weaned. Veal is a white, tender and delicate meat, highly prized in cooking, but its quality varies considerably according to the method of rearing.

■ **Grass-fed and yearling veal** Pink veal comes from grass-fed, loose-housed animals 4–5 months old; so-called 'grey' veal is from older animals and the meat is sometimes hung for 2–3 days. The meat does not have the quality of white veal, which is from animals under 3 months old. It contains more water and it also lacks the mature flavour of well-hung beef, but it is suited to light dishes, such as blanquette. Yearling veal is a comparatively new category of meat, known as *añejo* in Spain where it outsells beef. The French name for these older animals is *broutart* (which also includes lamb as well as calves), from the years after World War II, when the demand for meat was too urgent to let young animals reach maturity.

■ **High-quality veal** When the calf has been fed exclusively on its mother's milk (the most ancient and natural method), it gives a very pale pink meat smelling of milk, with satiny white fat having no tinge of red (which would indicate that the animal had eaten cereals or grass). In certain regions of France, including Normandy, the calf used to be 'finished' for the market by giving it up to 10 eggs daily, the yolks of which coloured its mouth: it was then said to have a *palais royal* (royal palate). According to *L'Art culinaire*, published at the beginning of the 20th century: 'The calf of the Seine valley, or river calf, so esteemed for the whiteness of its meat, is the product of special breeding. Its diet . . . consists only of milk and raw eggs, sometimes barley flour mixed with milk, and échaudés.' The Pontoise calf, also fed on biscuits soaked in milk, had an equally high reputation. Today the best localities for veal include Corrèze and Lot-et-Garonne, where the calves are raised *au pis* (on the udder), and the delicately grained flesh is slightly pink.

When the meat is reddish or greyish-white and rather soft and damp with thick, shiny tendons, the animal has been fed not with its mother's milk but with reconstituted milk; at the worst, it may have received hormone treatment (totally prohibited since 1976); the meat, of mediocre quality, cooks badly, gives off water and reduces in volume, whereas 'white' or 'pink' veal remains moist and does not dry

out. Among the best products of French breeding is the Saint-Étienne calf (not weaned, but fed supplements of protein-rich flours), whose pink meat is very tender, as well as the Lyon calf (weaned and intensively fattened indoors), which provides roasting and grilling (broiling) joints of excellent flavour. The Limousin milk calf, raised exclusively at the udder, is the only one to have been awarded that seal of approval, the *label rouge*.

■ **Cuts and cooking methods** The cutting up of the calf in the so-called 'Parisian' manner, which is the most widespread, provides for the following: first-category cuts, consisting of the chump (rump) end of loin, the leg – giving the parts known in French as the *noix, sous-noix* and *noix-pâtissière* and escalopes (scallops) cut from the noix or the noix-pâtissière – the loin, and the fillet, as well as the best end of neck (ribs and shortened best end of neck); second-category cuts, consisting of the shoulder, breast, tendron (not usually sold separately from the breast in Britain and the United States), flank and upper ribs; and, finally, third-category cuts, the scrag end (neck) and the knuckles.

Calf's offal is the most prized animal offal, particularly the liver, sweetbreads, kidneys and spinal marrow, but the head, brains, tongue, feet and mesentery are also valued. Calf's foot is used to prepare stocks, stews and braised dishes.

The best known classic veal dishes are fried escalopes, fried or casseroled grenadins (small thick fillet steaks) and chops, stuffed paupiettes (called *oiseaux sans tête*), roast joints, fricandeaux, braised tendrons (cut from the breast), blanquettes and sautés. Garnishes often call for pronounced flavours: fricandeau with sorrel, Foyot veal chops with onion, rump of veal *à l'angevine* accompanied by Soubise purée and loin of veal stuffed with mushrooms. Aubergines (eggplants), tomatoes or spinach go equally well with this meat, which is often prepared with cream, wine and spirits or cheese: veal chop vallée d'Auge (with cream and Calvados) or *à la Dreux* (larded with ox tongue, fat bacon and truffle, simmered in Madeira); veal steamed in red wine; Lorraine veal with pork rind (sliced almost through, interleaved with the pork rind and simmered in marc brandy); escalopes Franche-Comté (browned, then cooked *au gratin* with Franche-Comté cheese and cream); and so on. In the past, famous recipes were perfected for this 'chameleon of cooking', as Grimod de La Reynière called it, notably stuffed breast of veal, cutlets *en surprise*, brésolles, saddle of veal Orloff, feuilleton and veal sauté Marengo. Regional dishes are equally numerous, particularly for veal offal: casse of Rennes, veal mesentery *au gratin*, tripoux (a tripe dish), calf's head Sainte-Menehould and calf's lung bourguignon.

Outside France, it is in Italy that the widest variety of veal dishes is found: osso bucco, piccata, saltimbocca and veal with tuna-fish sauce, for example; also worthy of mention are the Hungarian *pörkölt* with paprika, the Austrian *Wiener schnitzel* (breaded escalopes), and the British veal and ham pie.

British cuts of veal

1 scrag end
2 middle neck
3 best end
4 loin
5 fillet
6 leg
6a knuckle
7 breast
8 shoulder

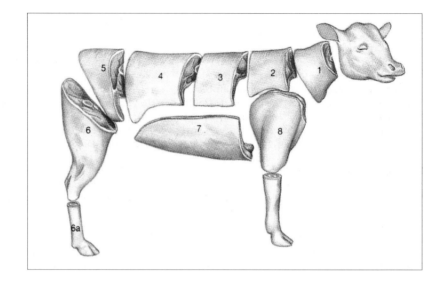

French cuts of veal

1 collier
2 bas de carré
3 côtes secondes
4 côtes premières
5 longe
6 quasi
7 cuisseau
7a noix-pâtissière
7b sous-noix
7c noix
8 jarret
9 flanchet
10 tendron
11 poitrine
12 épaule
13 queue (tail)

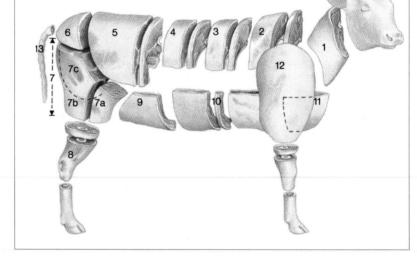

American cuts of veal

1 shoulder
1a blade
2 rib
3 loin
4 sirloin
5 leg (round)
5a boneless rump roast
5b round steak
6 breast
7 fore shank

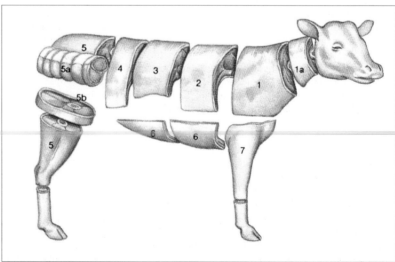

RECIPES

braised veal chops à la custine
(from Carême's recipe) Braise some veal chops; coat them first with 1 generous tablespoon duxelles*, then with breadcrumbs, then dip in beaten egg and finish with another coating of breadcrumbs. Fry in well-browned butter and serve with a light tomato sauce.

breaded veal chops à la milanaise
Flatten the chops and season with salt and pepper. Dip in beaten egg and coat in a mixture of half breadcrumbs and half grated Parmesan cheese. Cook gently in clarified butter in a sauté pan, then arrange on a serving dish garnished with cannelled lemon slices and sprinkled with noisette butter. Serve macaroni à la milanaise separately.

casseroled veal chops
Season some veal chops with salt and pepper and cook gently in 20 g (¾ oz, 1½ tablespoons) butter or 2 tablespoons oil per chop, at first uncovered, then covered, until they are browned. Deglaze the sauté pan with 2 tablespoons each of veal stock and white wine per chop, reduce by half and pour over the chops.

Alternatively, half-cook the chops, remove them from the pan, put in the chosen accompanying vegetable (also half-cooked), replace the chops in the pan and complete the cooking. The accompanying vegetables could include: diced aubergine (eggplant) sautéed in butter or oil; glazed carrots, turnips or small (pearl) onions; Vichy carrots; mushrooms sautéed in butter; celeriac, cucumber or artichoke hearts cut into quarters and cooked in butter; or green beans.

Alternatively, the chops may be completely cooked and garnished with vegetables cooked separately, either by braising, sautéeing or steaming.

Other vegetables that may be used are chicory, Brussels sprouts, cauliflower, endive, spinach, hop shoots, beans, lettuce, chestnuts, sorrel, peas or tomatoes. Buttered noodles or rice can also be served.

casseroled veal chops à la bonne femme
Sauté the chops in a flameproof dish until they are half-cooked. Add the bonne femme garnish, consisting, for each chop, of 4 small pieces of bacon, 5 small onions and 6 small new potatoes, all well browned. Cover and complete the cooking in a preheated oven at 220°C (425°F, gas 7).

casseroled veal chops à la dreux
Choose thick veal chops and stud them with strips of pickled tongue and truffle, so that the studding shows. Fry gently in butter on both sides until completely cooked. Arrange on a serving plate and surround with a financière garnish; keep warm. Deglaze the pan with Madeira and veal stock and reduce; use this sauce to coat the chops.

cold best end of neck of veal
Trim a shortened best end of neck (rib) of veal and season it with salt and pepper. Cook in a preheated oven at 220°C (425°F, gas 7), allowing 30–40 minutes cooking time per 1 kg (2¼ lb). Allow to cool completely, then glaze with aspic jelly. Chill until ready to serve. Garnish with watercress and artichoke hearts stuffed with asparagus tips, glazed with aspic if desired.

cold veal à l'italienne
Cook some small white (pearl) onions in olive oil in a flameproof casserole and set aside. Using the same pan, brown a noix of veal; then add to the casserole 300 g (11 oz) canned tuna in oil, 100 g (4 oz) desalted anchovy fillets, 2 peeled and diced lemons, salt, pepper and a bouquet garni. Replace the onions in the casserole. Moisten with an equal mixture of white wine and veal stock, cook for 1½ hours, then allow to cool in the casserole. Remove the veal and pass the rest of the contents of the casserole through a blender or processor. Prepare a mayonnaise, add the strained sauce to it and serve with the veal.

filets mignons of veal with lemon
Pare the zest of half a lemon and cut into fine strips. Put into a saucepan with 6 tablespoons cold water and bring to the boil, then drain and rinse in cold water. Put the lemon strips back into a saucepan with 1 tablespoon water and 1½ teaspoons sugar; cook until the water has evaporated, then set aside.

Heat 20 g (¾ oz, 1½ tablespoons) butter in a frying pan. When it starts to sizzle, add 4 veal filets mignons, each weighing 75 g (3 oz), sprinkled with salt and pepper on both sides. Brown them for 5 minutes on each side, then keep hot on a plate.

Pour off the butter from the pan and deglaze with 4 tablespoons dry white wine, reducing to 1 tablespoon liquid. Mix in 40 g (1½ oz, 3 tablespoons) butter, then 1 tablespoon chopped parsley.

Transfer the filets mignons to hot serving plates. Pour any meat juices into the sauce and coat the fillets with the sauce. Garnish each fillet with a peeled slice of lemon and a little of the shredded zest cooked in sugar.

grilled veal chops
Flatten the chops and season with salt and pepper; coat with tarragon-flavoured oil and leave to marinate for 30 minutes. Grill (broil) gently until the meat is cooked through (about 15 minutes), turning over once. Serve the chops with a green salad, a mixed salad or green beans, steamed and served with green butter.

sautéed veal chops à la crème
Brown some veal chops, seasoned with salt and pepper, in a frying pan using 1 tablespoon oil per chop; cover and finish cooking over a low heat (about 15 minutes). Strain off the oil from the pan

and add 1 chopped shallot per chop; cook, uncovered, until browned. Remove the chops and shallots and keep hot. Add to the pan 2–3 tablespoons cider or white wine and 1 tablespoon double (heavy) cream per chop; boil over a brisk heat until the sauce is reduced and smooth. Adjust the seasoning and coat the chops with the sauce.

All garnishes suggested for escalopes of veal may accompany sautéed veal chops.

veal grenadins with salsify ♦

Interlard 8–12 grenadins with strips of bacon fat. Cover the base of a flameproof casserole with pork or bacon rind. Finely slice 1 onion and 1 carrot, then brown them together in butter and place in the casserole. Add the grenadins, cover the casserole and cook gently for 15 minutes. Pour in 200 ml (7 fl oz, ¾ cup) dry white wine and bring to the boil, then continue cooking until the wine has almost dried up. Pour in enough stock to come a short way up the meat, add seasoning, bring to the boil and cover. Cook in a preheated oven at 220°C (425°F, gas 7) for about 40 minutes, basting the grenadins occasionally.

Meanwhile, scrub 675 g (1½ lb) salsify and cook in boiling water for 10 minutes. Allow to cool, then drain, peel and trim. Cut the salsify into fine strips and toss in lemon juice, seasoning and a little melted butter. Cover and set aside.

When the grenadins are cooked, transfer them to a gratin dish or ovenproof serving dish or plates. Spoon a little of the cooking juices over the meat. Then arrange the strips of buttered salsify around the edge and place the dish or plates in the oven until the meat and salsify are lightly glazed. Sprinkle with chives and serve.

vitello tonnato

Bone a 2 kg (4¼ lb) loin of veal and tie it neatly with string. Chop the bones into short lengths and set aside. Season the meat with salt and pepper. Brown it on all sides in a sauté pan in 2 tablespoons olive oil, then remove the roast from the pan. Put the bones in the bottom of a large roasting tin (pan), then place the meat on top and dot with 50 g (2 oz, ¼ cup) butter. Cook in a preheated oven at 220–230°C (425–450°F, gas 7–8) for 20 minutes. Add 1 diced carrot, 1 chopped onion and 2 garlic cloves in their skin, then continue cooking for a further 10 minutes. Season the meat and allow it to cool. Discard the bones, then degrease the cooking juices in the pan and reduce them by half. Deglaze the pan with 100 ml (4 fl oz, 7 tablespoons) white wine and 200 ml (7 fl oz, ¾ cup) water. Reduce, then strain the juice and set aside.

Purée 150 g (5 oz) cooked or drained canned tuna, with 3 preserved anchovies (desalted and boned), 40 g (1½ oz) drained capers and 2 tablespoons of the meat cooking juices. Mix with 450 ml (¾ pint, 2 cups) mayonnaise*. Add seasoning to taste and, if necessary, thin the sauce with up to 4 tablespoons chicken stock.

Cut the meat into 2–3 cm (¾–1¼ in) thick slices. Arrange on a platter and pour the tuna sauce over. Sprinkle with sprigs of flat-leafed parsley and 25 g (1 oz) capers. Serve with quartered radicchio hearts, dressed with olive oil and lemon juice.

VEAU DE MER The commercial name for porbeagle or taupe. This is a shark sold as steaks, fillets or in slices, like tuna.

VEGANISM A strict form of vegetarianism in which the diet is based on cereals, fruit, nuts, fresh and dried vegetables and vegetable oils. It excludes all animal products, even eggs, milk and honey.

With the ready availability today of a wide variety of fresh fruit and vegetables and modern production of items like soya (soy) milk, vegetable protein products and pure vegetable margarines, it is possible to have a reasonably varied and nutritious vegan diet. It is, however, still difficult to maintain a good balance of essential nutrients, and vegans must take great care to avoid dietary deficiencies in protein, calcium, iron, and vitamin B12.

VEGETABLES Herbaceous plants cultivated for food. According to the species, different parts of the vegetable are eaten: the fruit of courgettes (zucchini), aubergines (eggplants), sweet peppers and tomatoes, for example; the seeds of peas, lentils and beans; the leaves of spinach, lettuce and cabbage; the bulbs of onions, shallots and fennel; the tubers of potatoes and yams; the germ of soya; or the roots of carrots, turnips, parsnips and radishes. Mushrooms and other fungi are also usually regarded as vegetables. For culinary purposes, a distinction is made between fresh vegetables (including greens), dried vegetables (such as beans and pulses) and salads.

Cultivation, refrigeration and transportation have influenced the choice of vegetables available in Western supermarkets in the same way that they have broadened the choice of fruit. There seems to be an ever-expanding choice of exotic vegetables and markets in multi-cultural communities offer an excellent variety. As well as roots and tubers, the fruit-vegetables, pods and pulses, summer and winter squashes are increasingly popular.

■ **Vegetables in cooking** Some vegetables are fundamental to the majority of savoury cooking for the essential flavour they contribute. The humble onion brings essential character to a vast range of dishes; it is also an excellent vegetable in its own right. Carrots and celery are also widely used in the same way as onions. Some vegetables are used in modest proportions to complement the main ingredients in many dishes. The other vegetable-fruit that is as important as the onion in many cuisines is the tomato, which forms the basis for many sauces.

Veal grenadins with salsify.

A SELECTION OF EXOTIC VEGETABLES

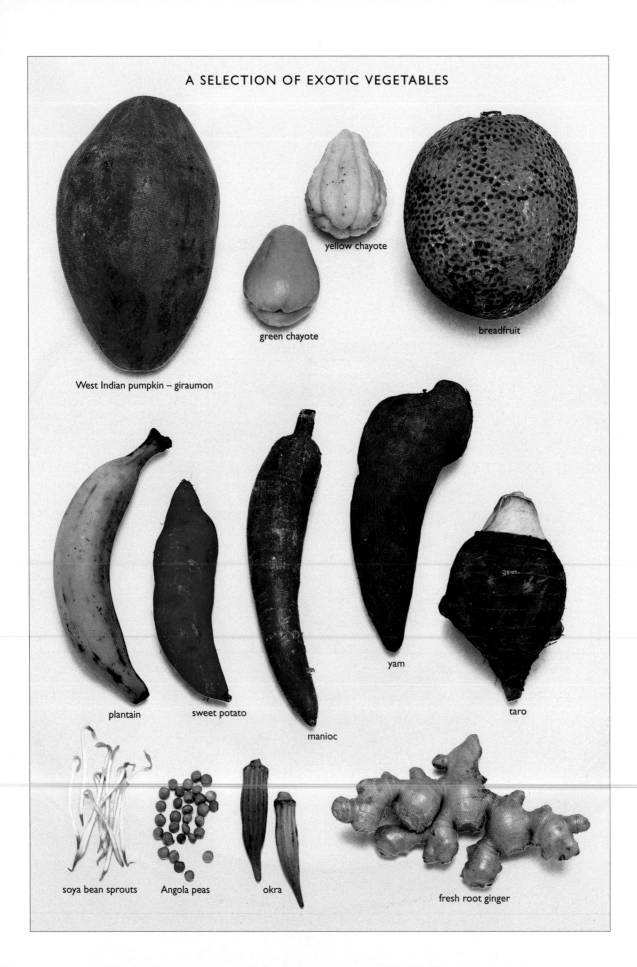

yellow chayote

green chayote

breadfruit

West Indian pumpkin – giraumon

yam

plantain

sweet potato

manioc

taro

soya bean sprouts

Angola peas

okra

fresh root ginger

Apart from their roles as flavourings, vegetables are cooked by all methods, singly or in various combinations, in dishes that are served as a separate course in some culinary cultures or to accompany fish or poultry and meat dishes.

Vegetables are also the main ingredients in many dishes and they are often the primary focus for a menu. As main dishes, they may be vegetarian or contain animal foods in a supporting capacity, for example as a stuffing.

■ **Preserved vegetables** Vegetables are widely used in chutneys, pickles and relishes. In addition, they are often preserved individually, as for example in sauerkraut or pickled onions. Bottling vegetables in brine has been replaced by freezing as a practical method of preserving them. The same is also true of drying: those vegetables that are dried are the ones that develop a particular flavour or intensity, such as mushrooms, sun-dried tomatoes or sun-dried peppers. Peas and other pulses are dried. Freezing is the most practical method because it conserves the fresh flavour of produce and the vitamin content.

■ **Vegetable products** There is an incredible array of vegetable products. Items that are regarded as basic ingredients include various vegetable starches, such as potato flour or starch; and tomato products, including purée (paste) and ketchup. Canned and dehydrated products are numerous, as are commercial pickles, sauces and condiments based on vegetables, such as mushroom ketchup.

■ **Buying and storing vegetables** The best choice and method of storage depends on the type of vegetable. The general rule is that vegetables should be as fresh as possible, in good condition and without any sign of ageing or decay. Some vegetables, particularly root vegetables, can be stored for long periods in the right conditions, but the modern heated home rarely offers ideal storage facilities for over-wintering produce. The least cold area of the refrigerator is the best place for keeping vegetables fresh. Therefore, it is best to buy vegetables often and in small amounts that can be consumed quickly.

VEGETARIANISM A type of diet that totally excludes meat, poultry and fish, but permits eggs, milk and butter. By including a wide variety of vegetables, grains, pulses and their products and dairy foods, the vegetarian diet can be well balanced.

VEINE A French cut of beef from the neck, subdivided into fat *veine* (or *saignée*) and lean *veine* (or second clod), both rich in connective tissue. This meat is used for braising and stewing (daube, carbonade and so on).

VELOURS The name given to a carrot soup to which consommé, substantially thickened with tapioca, is added. This gives the soup a thick, velvety consistency.

VELOUTÉ SAUCE One of the basic white sauces, made with a white veal or chicken stock or a fish fumet, thickened with a white or golden roux. Numerous other sauces are derived from it: allemande, caper, poulette and mushroom sauces (from veal velouté); ivoire, suprême and aurore sauces (from chicken velouté); and bretonne, cardinal and Nantua sauces (from fish velouté). The basic velouté can also be used as a basis for making smooth, fine but rich soups.

RECIPES

basic velouté sauce
Stir 2.75 litres (4¾ pints, 12 cups) white veal or chicken stock into a pale blond roux made with 150 g (5 oz, ⅔ cup) butter and 150 g (5 oz, 1¼ cups) plain (all-purpose) flour. Blend well together. Bring to the boil, stirring until the first bubbles appear. Cook the velouté very slowly for 30 minutes, skimming frequently. Strain through a cloth. Stir until it is completely cold.

Velouté may be prepared either in advance or just before it is required. As the white stock used for making it is seasoned and flavoured, it is not necessary to add other flavourings. An exception is made for skins and trimmings of mushrooms, which may be added when available, this addition making the sauce yet more delicate.

velouté sauce based on fish stock
Make in the same way as basic velouté sauce, replacing the veal or chicken stock with fish stock.

VELOUTÉ SOUP See *soup.*

VENACO A Corsican cheese made from goat's or ewe's milk (45% fat content), with a soft texture and a greyish scraped natural rind. It comes from Venaco and Corte and is made on only a small scale as a cottage industry. In season from June to September, it is made in the form of a 13 cm (5 in) square slab, 6 cm (2½ in) high. Venaco is a whitish, fatty cheese, firm to the touch, with a strong smell and sometimes a piquant flavour. It is served with a full-bodied red wine. Sometimes the cheese is crumbled and soaked in wine and marc brandy.

VENDACE A fish of the *Salmonidae* family, related to the *féra.*

VENDÉE The coastal strip of Poitou is known as the Vendée, and the cuisine of this region combines the resources of the sea with the culinary traditions of the hinterland.

The pastureland of the Vendée is stock-breeding country, and many cattle are raised, providing excellent meat. Cereals and vegetables are also grown, including the famous Vendée green cabbages and *mogettes,* white haricot (navy) beans, which are cooked in the usual way and dressed with butter and cream. Other popular dishes are broad (fava) bean purée in stock, *chouée* (green cabbage boiled in salted water, drained, pressed and mixed with

VENEZUELA

Venezuelan cuisine is the least hot of all South American countries, with mild spices and seasonings, rather than chillies, dominating. Haricot (navy) beans play a major part in many dishes, such as in the traditional ragoût (*sancocho*) of beef, tripe or fish, also served mixed with rice or maize (corn). These stews often also include large, green plantain and/or cassava.

Arepas are eaten at all meals. They are like Mexican tortillas but made from a different kind of maize. The typical Christmas dish, *hyaca*, consists of crêpes made from maize and stuffed with meat or fish, eggs, olives, raisins, almonds and condiments, cooked in banana leaves.

Papaya jam is the Venezuelans' favourite dessert, but, like bananas, it is also served with savoury dishes.

WINE An increasing number of good quality wines and sparkling wines are being produced, mainly from Chenin Blanc, Malvoisie, Maccabeo, Syrah, Tempranillo, Cabernet Sauvignon and Petit Verdot. The vineyards are located at higher altitudes near Mérida and on the cooler slopes of the Sierra de Barragua, near the historic town of Carora. The vines do not have a dormant period because of the high average temperatures and produce two, and in Maracaibo three, harvests a year. Beer is also made.

plenty of butter) and also buttered cabbage. The channels of the marshland, which extend from Challans to Beauvoir-sur-Mer, are famous for ducks, which are bred for the markets of Nantes and Paris.

Rivers and ponds provide cells for fish stews; frogs' legs are prepared *à la luçonnaise* (cooked in water flavoured with vinegar, then sautéed in butter and garnished with fried garlic cloves, and snails are grilled (broiled) or prepared *à la mode d'Oléron* (cooked in boiling water with fennel, then simmered in a white sauce with potatoes).

Rabbit and hare are cooked in particularly interesting ways; for example, rabbit pâté (a terrine with alternate layers of fillets of wild rabbit and a forcemeat of the remaining flesh mixed with onion and shallot) and hare *à la vendéenne*, a speciality of La Roche-sur-Yon, birthplace of the poet Raoul Ponchon. Pork from this region also has an excellent flavour, and specialities include boar's-head stew and *fressure vendéenne* (chopped pork offal and bacon mixed with congealed pig's blood and cooked slowly for a long time).

The recipes for fish and seafood are many and varied and include *cotriade*, *chaudrée*, *mouclade*, salt cod soup and oyster soup. The langoustes of the island of Yeu, sardines of Les Sables-d'Olonne and mussels from L'Aiguillon-sur-Mer are justly famous.

The cheeses, pâtisserie and sweets of Poitou are also found in the Vendée, but there are some additional specialities, such as brioche vendéenne, *alize pâquaude*, *bottereaux*, fouaces, caillebottes and *flan maraîchin* (eggs in milk under a caramelized crust).

VENEZUELA See *above*.

VENISON The meat of any kind of deer. In French, however, the term is used not only for deer meat but also for the meat of any large game animal (including wild boar). Hare and wild rabbit are known in French as *basse venaison*. The word venison comes from the Latin *venatio* (hunt).

Haunch or quarter of venison is generally a leg and loin of deer, which is roasted after being marinated or hung.

There are also various venison sauces to accompany game meat, of which the classic is a poivrade (pepper) sauce mixed with fresh cream and redcurrant jelly.

RECIPE

Burgundy sauce for venison
(from Carême's recipe) Pour into a saucepan a glass of old Burgundy wine, 2 tablespoons ordinary vinegar, 2 tablespoons sugar, the flesh of half a seeded lemon, and half a pot of redcurrant jelly. Boil to reduce and add 2 tablespoons espagnole* sauce. Reduce again, gradually mixing in the contents of a second glass of Burgundy. When the sauce has reached the correct consistency, rub it through a sieve.

pan-fried venison with pears ◆
First prepare a red wine sauce: bring 500 ml (17 fl oz, 2 cups) red Burgundy to the boil and flame it to evaporate the alcohol. Add 1 chopped shallot and reduce the sauce by three-quarters. Cook and purée 100 g (4 oz) carrots, then add them to the sauce with salt and pepper. Remove from the heat and set aside.

Peel and core 4 firm cooking pears, tossing them in lemon juice as they are ready. Quarter the pears lengthways and slice them into fine fans, leaving the slices just attached at the narrow ends. Melt 25 g (1 oz, 2 tablespoons) butter in a pan and add the pears, then cook gently until tender and browned around the edges.

Meanwhile, season 12 lean noisettes or medallions of venison steak, each weighing about 50 g (2 oz), with salt and pepper. Melt 25 g (1 oz, 2 tablespoons) clarified butter in a frying pan until foaming. Add the venison and cook over high heat

Pan-fried venison with pears.

for 2 minutes on each side, until well browned outside and still slightly pink in the middle.

Reheat the sauce and add 150 g (5 oz, ⅔ cup) butter, cut in small pieces, whisking hard continuously. Drain the venison on paper towels. Deglaze the pan with a little water and reduce for 1 minute, then whisk this into the sauce and add seasoning to taste. Drain the pears on paper towels. Coat warmed plates with the sauce, then arrange the venison and pears on top.

additional recipe See *roebuck*.

VÉNITIENNE, À LA The name given to poached fillets of sole, slices of conger eel sautéed in butter, poached chicken or soft-boiled (soft-cooked) or poached eggs when accompanied by vénitienne sauce. This sauce is made with a mixture of vinegar, tarragon and allemande sauce, reduced, mixed with green butter, strained and garnished with herbs. Fish served with a normande sauce mixed with herbs and chopped capers may also be called *à la vénitienne*.

RECIPES

fillets of sole à la vénitienne
Fold the fillets of sole in half and poach them in a fish fumet made with white wine. Drain and wipe them and arrange them in a ring on a serving dish, alternating with heart-shaped croûtons fried in butter. Coat them with vénitienne sauce mixed with the reduced cooking liquid from the sole.

vénitienne sauce
(from Carême's recipe) Boil together in a saucepan 2 tablespoons allemande* sauce, a generous pinch of chopped tarragon blanched and drained in a fine silk strainer, 1 tablespoon chicken glaze, a little Isigny butter, a pinch of grated nutmeg and a few drops of good tarragon vinegar.

VENTADOUR The name given to a dish of tournedos steaks or noisettes of lamb, garnished with slices of bone marrow and truffle and served with artichoke purée and potato cocotte.

VENTRÈCHE Belly of pork, salted, then rolled (and sometimes dried and sold prepared), a speciality of south-west France. Completely boned and skinned, the belly is salted for about ten days, then washed, drained and braised. Sprinkled with ground pepper, it is rolled, fitted into a cellulose casing, then dried for one to four weeks. Ventrèche is used in the same ways as salted belly of pork.

VERBENA, LEMON Also known as lemon vervain. The leaves of this evergreen shrub, *Aloysia triphylla*, have a distinct lemon flavour. They are narrow and bright green, and may be used whole or finely chopped. An infusion of the leaves and flowers of lemon verbena, sweetened with honey, is recommended for liver and kidney ailments and for soothing the nerves. Fresh verbena leaves contribute their lemony fragrance to stocks, sauces and moist dishes. Whole sprigs can be added to the cooking water for vegetables, rice or pasta, or thye can be used to flavour steamed foods. When finely chopped, the leaves are also suitable for dry mixtures, such as forcements.

Dried powdered verbena leaves can be added to meat and fish stuffings to give a delicate flavour.

VERDIER The name given to a dish of hard-boiled (hard-cooked) eggs stuffed with foie gras, placed on a bed of cooked sliced onions, coated with a béchamel sauce containing truffles, sprinkled with Parmesan cheese and browned in the oven. The dish is attributed to the proprietor of the Maison Dorée.

RECIPE

hard-boiled eggs Verdier
Hard-boil (hard-cook) the eggs, shell and halve them. Remove the yolks, rub them through a sieve and mix with one-third of their volume of foie gras cut into very small dice. Fill the halves of egg white with the mixture. Slice some onions, gently soften them in butter, blend them with a very little béchamel sauce seasoned with curry powder and spread in a layer in a gratin dish. Place the stuffed eggs on top, and coat with béchamel sauce mixed with a julienne of truffles. Sprinkle with Parmesan cheese and brown in a very hot oven.

The foie gras may be replaced by diced chicken livers sautéed in butter and the truffles with a julienne of sweet peppers, but in this case the dish should not be called by the classic name.

VERDURE A term used in French cuisine to describe a green salad or a mixture of green pot herbs. Chopped verdure is used especially to make forcemeats or purées. The name *verdurette* is given to a vinaigrette sauce mixed with chopped chives, hard-boiled (hard-cooked) eggs, chervil, tarragon and parsley. Kitchen staff in the times of the Ancien Régime included a *verdurier*, whose job was to provide the herbs and vinegar (see *vert*).

VERGEOISE A type of French soft brown sugar (beet or cane) crystallized from a syrup remaining at the end of the refining process, the colour and smell of which is determined by the components of the raw material used. Its name is taken from the old sugar moulds, the *vergeoises*, in which large sugar loaves were made.

There are two kinds of vergeoise, light and dark brown: the former is obtained by recooking the syrup removed at the first stage of the sugar-refining process; dark brown vergeoise, with a more unusual smell, results from recooking the syrup removed at the second stage of sugar refinement.

In northern France and Belgium, vergeoise is commonly used to make pastries, especially *tarte au sucre* (sugar tart), and also to sprinkle on or fill crêpes and waffles.

VERJUICE The acid juice extracted from large unripened grapes or crab-apples, which was formerly widely used as a sauce ingredient, a condiment and in deglazing until eventually superseded by the instruction to add a dash of lemon juice in recipes. In the Middle Ages *vertjus* (literally 'green juice') was an acid-tasting stock prepared with the juice of unripe grapes, sometimes mixed with lemon or sorrel juice, herbs and spices. It was used in most sauces and liaisons.

In the latter years of the 20th century the use of verjuice experienced a revival. It is in general use in Middle Eastern cookery.

RECIPE

soft roes of herring with verjuice
Soak 800 g (1¾ lb) soft roes of herring for 1 hour in cold water with 100 ml (4 fl oz, 7 tablespoons) white wine vinegar. Drain and wipe. Season with salt and pepper, coat with flour, shaking off any excess, then prick with a needle to prevent them from bursting during cooking. Heat 40 g (1½ oz, 3 tablespoons) butter and 3 tablespoons oil in a frying pan. Carefully place the roes in the hot fat and cook for 3–4 minutes on each side.

Heat 75 g (3 oz, 6 tablespoons) butter in a separate frying pan and brown 75 g (3 oz, 1 cup) diced mushrooms and an equal quantity of diced sour apples for 4 minutes. Then add 75 g (3 oz) diced tomatoes, cook for 1 minute and add 50 g (2 oz) capers, salt and pepper. Arrange the roes on warmed plates, sprinkle with 50 g (2 oz, 1 cup) small sprigs of parsley and garnish with the browned vegetables.

Remove the fat from the pan in which the roes were cooked and add, over a brisk heat, 3 tablespoons cider vinegar and an equal quantity of verjuice. Bring to the boil and pour over the roes.

additional recipe See *sauce.*

VERMICELLI A pasta made in the form of fine strands (the name means 'small worms'), often used in soups but also served like spaghetti. 'Angel's hair' is a very fine variety of vermicelli, used only in consommés and clear soups. Vermicelli is also used to make certain puddings and soufflés.

Chinese vermicelli, prepared with soya flour, comes in long, lustrous skeins. Boiled or fried, it is used in soups, vegetable mixtures, forcemeats and so on. In the Far East there is a type of vermicelli made with rice flour. It consists of long, flat, whitish strands and is cooked in the same way as noodles.

VERMOUTH An aromatized wine whose name is derived from the German word *Wermut* (wormwood

or absinthe), this being an ingredient of many recipes for vermouth.

Vermouth is now made in many regions where wine is made, although commercial production began in Turin in the 18th century. Before this, various versions of wine incorporating herbs, spices, barks and peels were made, often for semi-medicinal purposes; records of these drinks exist from about the 5th century BC. By the end of the 18th century establishments for making vermouth were established in Marseille and Chambéry in France, and these places, with Turin, remain the world centres for production.

There are several main methods of producing vermouth: the ingredients may be infused, macerated or even distilled in the base wine, or a combination of all these processes can be followed. Any good vermouth is subject to a certain maturation period.

Each of the great vermouth establishments makes a range of vermouths, the main types being dry and white, sweetish and red and rosé. An Italian speciality is Bianco, or white vermouth, which is slightly sweet (although many drinkers suppose it to be dry on account of the pale colour). It is a common error to categorize Italian vermouth as sweet and French as dry, as may be noted from the fact that the world's most famous cocktail, the dry martini, is thought to have been originally made with the Italian vermouth of the world-famous firm, Martini Rossi. However, because of the obviously different methods of production and the secret formulae of the great establishments, French vermouth is, overall, different from Italian. Chambéry vermouth, from Savoy, is very delicate and aromatic and traditionally always served straight. There is a 'strawberry vermouth', also made in Chambéry. There are hundreds of vermouth producers, as well as Noilly Prat, Cinzano and Gancia, and many chains of wine retailers have their own-label brands of vermouth in the main types.

In the kitchen vermouth is extremely useful, because the herby ingredients make it suitable for stuffings, seasonings, sauces and poaching stock, notably for fish and shellfish. Although vermouth, like wine, will decline in quality after the bottle has been opened and the contents exposed to the air (in a few weeks for the dry versions), it will remain usable for culinary purposes almost indefinitely.

VERNIS A bivalve mollusc that inhabits the sandy ocean bed and belongs to the same family as clams – it is cooked in the same way. Its shells, 6–10 cm (2½–4 in) long, are smooth, shiny and brown, marked with dark radiating stripes.

VERNON The name of a dish of sautéed small cuts of meat, which are garnished with artichoke hearts topped with asparagus tips, turnips stuffed with mashed potato and hollowed-out apples filled with peas in butter.

VÉRON, LOUIS DÉSIRÉ French doctor and journalist (born Paris, 1798; died Paris, 1867). After practising medicine in fashionable circles, he became a critic and the editor of various literary reviews, then administrator of the Opéra and finally a political journalist at the head of *Constitutionnel*, which supported the cause of Louis-Napoléon and the Empire. He owes his place in the history of gastronomy to his role as a lavish host, at first in his apartment in the Rue de Rivoli, then at Auteuil. Among his guests, Sainte-Beuve, Nestor Roqueplan and Arsène Houssaye rubbed shoulders with Halévy, Auber, Trousseau, Velpeau and a number of famous actresses, including Rachel, his mistress. On Fridays dinner was more formal, and guests included certain political personalities, sometimes even the Prince-President himself.

The reputation of Véron's table depended heavily on the talents of his cook-housekeeper, Sophie, who is said to have surpassed herself with such dishes as duck with olives and braised leg of lamb with beans. During his lifetime Véron gained a reputation with some for ostentatious luxury and gourmandism, but the doctor was, in fact, a sober and moderate man: 'He eats only two courses, and his normal drink is very old Bordeaux, greatly diluted with water,' a journalist wrote of him. Véron thanked the writer of the article and even added: 'At the Café de Paris, they would charge to me everything that was being eaten and drunk around me.' However, in a novel entitled *Cinq Cent Mille Livres de rente*, Véron contributed a menu consisting of a fabulous collection of dishes, including chicken suprêmes reine scattered with pickled tongue and truffles, Lake Geneva trout *au bleu* with green sauce, Alpine rock partridges *sur piédestal*, ortolans *en litière*, Swiss mousse and Italian cascade.

In classic cuisine Véron's name has been given to a normande sauce with herbs mixed with veal fumet or stock, served with breaded or grilled (broiled) fish.

RECIPES

fillets of brill Véron
Cut the fillets in half lengthways, season with salt and pepper, dip in melted butter and breadcrumbs, sprinkle with more melted butter and cook gently under the grill (broiler). Arrange the fillets on a hot serving dish and coat with Véron sauce.

Véron sauce
Prepare a reduced herb mixture as for a béarnaise sauce. Then add 200 ml (7 fl oz, ¾ cup) normande* sauce and 2 tablespoons very concentrated brown veal stock or fish glaze. Season with a pinch of cayenne, rub through a sieve and add 1 tablespoon snipped chervil or tarragon.

VERONICA A genus of plants of which there are numerous species found throughout temperate regions. *Veronica officinalis*, common speedwell, nicknamed the 'tea of Europe' in France, was used as long ago as the early 18th century as a substitute for tea. *Veronica beccabunga*, brooklime, is often confused with watercress and can be eaten raw in salads or cooked like spinach.

VERT In Flemish cooking the name *au vert* (literally, green) is given to a dish of eels cooked with numerous herbs (up to 15), which vary according to the season and may include sorrel, spinach, salad cress, white deadnettle, parsley, chervil, tarragon, mint, sage, salad burnet and lemon balm.

Sauce verte (green sauce) is a mayonnaise containing a purée of herbs. In former times the sauce was more of a vinaigrette, which the Parisian *sauciers* in the reign of Louis XII used to sell in the streets:

> *Do you need any green sauce?*
> *It's for eating with carp or dabs,*
> *For those who want it, let them ask for it,*
> *While my pot is open.*

The modern recipe was perfected by Balvay, formerly chef to Napoleon III, then chef at the restaurant Le Doyen, where it became a speciality, particularly when served with sea trout. Beurre vert (green butter) is a flavoured butter made with chopped herbs.

RECIPE

green sauce
For 400 ml (14 fl oz, 1¾ cups) sauce, prepare 300 ml (½ pint, 1½ cups) mayonnaise* and 100 ml (4 fl oz, 7 tablespoons) purée of green herbs (spinach, watercress, parsley, chervil and tarragon), blanched for 1 minute in boiling water, cooled under the tap, thoroughly dried and then pounded in a mortar. Mix the 2 preparations together and rub through a sieve.

Use the sauce like classic mayonnaise, especially to accompany cold poached fish.

VERT-CUIT A French culinary term used when food is cooked very lightly and served almost raw – by analogy with fruit, which is described as *vert* (green) before it has ripened. Duck *au sang* and woodcock, in particular, are served *vert-cuits*.

VERT-PRÉ The term describing preparations of grilled (broiled) meat (kidneys, steaks, chops, noisettes and so on) garnished with straw potatoes and watercress and served with *maître d'hôtel* butter, which is either placed on the meat in rounds or melted and served in a sauceboat. The name is also given to preparations of white meat, duckling, vol-au-vent, for example, garnished with a mixture of peas, asparagus tips and green beans, tossed in butter. Chicken or fish coated with green sauce are also called *vert-pré*.

VIARD A 19th-century French chef, author of a collection of recipes entitled *Le Cuisinier impérial, ou l'Art de faire la cuisine et la pâtisserie pour toutes les* *fortunes, avec la manière de servir une table depuis vingt jusqu'à soixante couverts* (1806). This 'dispensatory' was published in at least 32 successive editions, with titles that varied according to the prevailing political circumstances; in 1817, at the time of the Restoration, it became *Le Cuisinier royal* (with a supplementary chapter on wines, by Pierhugue), and in 1852, in its 22nd edition, *Le Cuisinier national de la ville et de la campagne*, whose authors were given as Viart (*sic*), Fouret and Délan. In 1853, published as *Le Cuisinier impérial de la ville et de la campagne*, it included 200 new articles by Bernardi. This culinary encyclopedia continued to be the basic reference book for professional chefs throughout the 19th century.

VICAIRE, GABRIEL French poet (born Belfort, 1848; died Paris, 1900). In a collection appearing in 1884, entitled *Les Emaux bressans*, he sang the praises of his native Bresse, the cuisine of which is among the most famous. He also published gastronomic articles. His writing was deliberately anti-Symbolist, as is shown by this verse extracted from *Victime du réveillon* (he is writing of the pig):

> *And good people, what joy*
> *When the good pig*
> *Suddenly comes back again*
> *In the shape of a black pudding.*

VICAIRE, GEORGES French scholar (born Paris, 1853; died Chantilly, 1921). A cousin of the poet Gabriel Vicaire, he wrote a *Manuel de l'amateur de livres au XIX' siècle* (in eight volumes) and also a study of Balzac as a publisher and printer. However, he is best known to collectors of books on cuisine for his valuable *Bibliographie gastronomique* (1890), which records and describes some 2,500 works on gastronomy and cuisine, from the time when printing first began up to 1890. The work is dedicated to Baron Jérôme Pichon, with whom he published Taillevent's *Viandier* in 1892.

VICHY The name given to a dish of sliced carrots cooked over a low heat (traditionally with sugar and bicarbonate of soda or 'Vichy salt') until all the moisture is absorbed. To justify the name, the water used for cooking should be Vichy Saint-Yorre mineral water. Vichy carrots, or carrots *à la Vichy*, with fresh butter and parsley, are often served with veal cutlets and sautéed chicken, coated with a sauce made by deglazing the cooking pan with veal stock.

RECIPE

Vichy carrots
Peel 800 g (1¾ lb) young carrots and cut into thin rounds. Place in a sauté pan and just cover with water, adding 1 teaspoon salt and a generous pinch of sugar per 500 ml (17 fl oz, 2 cups) water. Cook gently until all the liquid is absorbed. Serve the carrots in a vegetable dish, sprinkled with small pieces of butter and chopped parsley.

VICHYSSOISE A leek and potato soup thickened with fresh cream and served cold, garnished with chopped chives. Vichyssoise was created in the United States by Louis Diat, a French chef who named the soup after his local town. As a child, he had eaten the soup for breakfast when he lived in a village near Vichy in France. The name vichyssoise is also given to any cold soup based on potatoes and another vegetable, such as courgettes (zucchini).

RECIPE

vichyssoise
Slice 250 g (9 oz) leeks (white part only) and cut 250 g (9 oz) peeled potatoes into quarters. Soften the leeks in 50 g (2 oz, ¼ cup) butter in a covered pan without allowing them to brown. Then add the potatoes, stir and pour in 1.75 litres (3 pints, 7½ cups) water. Add salt, pepper and a small bouquet garni. Bring to the boil and cook for 30–40 minutes. Purée the potatoes and leeks in a blender or food processor and return to the pan. Blend in at least 200 ml (7 fl oz, ¾ cup) crème fraîche and return just to the boil, stirring frequently. Allow the soup to cool and chill in the refrigerator for 1 hour. Serve sprinkled with chopped chives in consommé cups.

VICTORIA There are a number of dishes and sauces dedicated to Queen Victoria, all characterized by their rich ingredients or elegant presentation. Barquettes and bouchées, fillets of sole, poached and soft-boiled (soft-cooked) eggs and filled omelette Victoria all contain a salpicon of lobster and truffle, bound in various ways. Scallop shells of fish Victoria, with mushrooms and truffles, are coated with Nantua sauce and garnished with slices of truffle.

Salad Victoria is a mixed salad of diced cucumber, a salpicon of langouste, sliced celeriac, sliced artichoke hearts, sliced potatoes and thin strips of truffle, dressed with pink mayonnaise.

Victoria garnish consists of small tomatoes stuffed with mushroom purée and browned under the grill (broiler) and quartered artichoke hearts cooked in butter. It is served with small sautéed pieces of meat coated with a sauce made by deglazing the pan juices with either Madeira or port and thickened veal stock. Victoria sauces are served with poached fish (white wine sauce with lobster butter and a salpicon of lobster and truffles) or with venison (espagnole sauce flavoured with port, redcurrant jelly, orange juice and spices).

Bombe Victoria has a plombières ice cream centre coated with strawberry ice cream, and Victoria cake is a kind of rich fruit cake with spices and glacé (candied) cherries (instead of dried fruit).

Victoria sandwich cake was also named after the queen. After the death of her husband, Prince Albert, in 1861, Queen Victoria used to spend time every year in retreat at Osborne House on the Isle of Wight. She was encouraged to give tea parties, during which the Victoria sandwich, a plain cake made by the creaming method, cut in half and spread with jam and cream, was served. Its popularity soon spread throughout England.

RECIPES

scallop shells of salmon Victoria

Fill the scallop shells with a mixture of salmon poached in fumet, sliced mushrooms cooked in butter and small diced truffles. Coat with Nantua sauce, dust with grated Parmesan cheese, sprinkle with clarified butter and brown in a very hot oven. Garnish each scallop shell with a slice of truffle heated in butter.

Victoria sauce for fish

Prepare 250 ml (8 fl oz, 1 cup) white wine sauce*. Add 2 tablespoons lobster butter*, a dash of cayenne, and 2 tablespoons diced lobster flesh and truffles.

Victoria sauce for venison

Prepare 250 ml (8 fl oz, 1 cup) espagnole* sauce; add 150 ml (¼ pint, ⅔ cup) port and 3 tablespoons redcurrant jelly. Then add 8 peppercorns, 2 cloves, a small stick of cinnamon and the blanched zest of an orange. Boil until reduced by one-third, add the juice of the orange and a little cayenne, and rub through a sieve.

VIDELER A French culinary term meaning to make a border around the edge of a piece of pastry by gently easing it with the fingers a little at a time, upwards then towards the centre, to form a rolled edge. The rim of a tart case (shell) is treated in this way before being cooked in a flan ring to give a neat, even edge.

VIENNOISE, À LA The description *à la viennoise* is given to veal escalopes or to fillets of poultry or fish coated with egg and breadcrumbs, sautéed and served with chopped hard-boiled (hard-cooked) egg (white and yolk separated), fried parsley and capers; the meat or fish is usually topped with a slice of lemon with skin and pith removed and with a stoned (pitted) green olive surrounded by an anchovy fillet. The serving dish is coated with thickened veal stock, and noisette butter is served separately.

This dish is a French interpretation of the classic Austrian dish *Wiener schnitzel*, which is made with veal coated with egg and breadcrumbs, cooked in lard and served with a slice of lemon and a potato salad or with a green salad and browned or mashed potatoes.

Spring chickens or chicken joints coated with breadcrumbs and sautéed or fried are also described as *à la viennoise*.

RECIPES

chicken à la viennoise

Quarter a young chicken weighing 800–900 g (1¾–2 lb), sprinkle the joints with salt and pepper, then coat with egg and breadcrumbs. Cook in a frying pan in 60 g (2 oz, ¼ cup) clarified butter, turning once, or deep-fry in fat at a temperature of 180°C (350°F) until golden and cooked through. Drain on paper towels and serve with fried parsley and lemon quarters.

escalopes à la viennoise

Flatten 4 escalopes well and sprinkle with salt on both sides. Put 4 tablespoons flour with a little salt on one plate, 175 g (6 oz, 2 cups) dried breadcrumbs on another and 2 beaten eggs on a third. Melt 100 g (4 oz, ½ cup) lard in a large frying pan. Dip the escalopes into the flour so that they are completely covered with a very fine coating, then in the beaten egg and finally in the breadcrumbs, coating them evenly on both sides. Place in the lard when it is on the point of smoking and cook gently for 8 minutes on each side. Serve well browned.

VIENNOISERIE A French term taking its name from Vienna and the local baking traditions. This is used to describe bakery products other than bread, traditionally consisting of croissants, milk-bread rolls, fruit buns, brioches and so on – that is, items made from raised dough or puff or rough-puff pastry – and excluding biscuits (cookies), sablés and so on, which come into the category of pâtisserie. Fancy breads, such as Viennese, granary and large brioche, for example, grouped under the term *panasserie*, are sometimes also included in viennoiserie. See *bread*.

VIETNAM See *page 1276*.

VIEUX PANÉ A soft cow's-milk cheese (50% fat content) with a washed crust. It is a flat, square cheese weighing 2.25 kg (5 lb). Recently invented, it is factory-made and has an honest, earthy flavour.

VIGNERONNE, À LA The description given to dishes prepared with grapes or autumn produce or in 'wine-growers' style'. Salad *à la vigneronne* consists of dandelion leaves (sometimes also lamb's lettuce) and browned, chopped bacon, dressed with walnut oil. The bacon pan is deglazed with vinegar, and this is used to season the salad. Small birds *à la vigneronne* are usually cooked in a casserole with grapes. Snails *à la vigneronne* are shelled, sautéed with garlic and shallots, coated in batter containing chives, then fried.

RECIPE

partridge à la vigneronne

Pluck, clean and truss a partridge. Cook it in butter in a saucepan for about 30 minutes, then drain and untruss it. Put into the saucepan 24 skinned and seeded grapes, 3 tablespoons game fumet and 1 tablespoon flamed brandy. Cover the pan and cook gently for 5 minutes, then replace the partridge on top, heat through and serve.

VILLAGEOISE, À LA The description given to poached white meat or poultry accompanied by villageoise sauce. This is either a béchamel sauce mixed with onions softened in butter, veal or poultry stock and mushroom essence, which is strained, thickened with egg yolk and finished with butter, or a light velouté sauce mixed with onion purée, thickened with egg yolk and cream and finished with butter.

Leek consommé, usually garnished with pasta, is also called *villageois*.

RECIPE

villageoise sauce

Slice 400 g (14 oz, 2½ cups) onions and cook gently for 20 minutes with a piece of butter – about 50 g (2 oz, ¼ cup). Add 300 ml (½ pint, 1¼ cups) very thick béchamel* sauce, then 200 ml (7 fl oz, ¾ cup) veal or poultry stock and a little mushroom essence. Continue to cook over a low heat, stirring constantly. Strain the sauce and thicken it with an egg yolk. Away from the heat, beat in 40 g (1½ oz, 3 tablespoons) butter cut in small pieces.

VILLEROI The name of a sauce used to coat various foods that are then covered with egg and breadcrumbs and deep-fried. These preparations are described as *à la Villeroi* and include attereaux of offal, brochettes of seafood, fish steaks, sweetbreads, chicken pieces or mutton cutlets; they are served with a tomato, devilled, chasseur or mushroom sauce.

Villeroi sauce (dedicated to Marshal de Villeroi, mentor of Louis XV) is an allemande sauce, made either with meat stock (for coating meat) or fish stock (for coating fish), mixed with white stock and mushroom essence and then reduced; the sauce may be finished with truffle essence or purée of tomatoes or onions, or mixed with chopped truffles or mushrooms or a mirepoix.

When the sauce has reached the right consistency, it should be left to cool before being used to coat the food.

RECIPES

attereaux of lamb's brains à la Villeroi

Cook the lamb's brains in white stock, leave them to get cold under a press, then cut into pieces. Marinate for 30 minutes in oil with a few drops of lemon juice, chopped parsley, salt and pepper. Thread the pieces on to skewers and coat with Villeroi sauce. Then coat with egg and breadcrumbs and deep-fry in hot oil at 180°C (350°F) until golden. Drain, dust with fine salt and arrange on a serving dish.

scallop and oyster brochettes à la Villeroi

Poach the white flesh and the coral of the scallops in water, then the shelled oysters in their own water; allow to cool. Drain and thread alternately on to skewers; coat with Villeroi sauce, then breadcrumbs; fry and serve as for attereaux of lamb's brains *à la Villeroi*.

Villeroi sauce

Prepare 200 ml (7 fl oz, ¾ cup) allemande* sauce, dilute with 4 tablespoons white stock flavoured with a little mushroom essence, then reduce until it coats the spoon. Put through a strainer and stir until the sauce is barely tepid.

other recipes See *cockscomb, mutton.*

VINAIGRETTE A cold sauce or dressing made from a mixture of vinegar, oil, pepper and salt, to which various flavourings may be added: shallot, onion, herbs, capers, garlic, gherkins, anchovies, hard-boiled (hard-cooked) egg or mustard, for example.

Vinaigrette is used especially for dressing green salads. The choice of oil (olive, sunflower, walnut and so on) and vinegar is made according to the nature of the salad; the vinegar may be replaced by lemon juice or is sometimes flavoured with it. Vinaigrette is also used to dress various other cold dishes: vegetables (such as tomatoes, asparagus, cauliflower, leeks or artichoke hearts), meat – sheep's trotters (feet), brawn, boiled beef, calf's head – and fish in court-bouillon. It is considered to be a typically French sauce and is often called 'French dressing' in Britain. It was a French émigré, Chevalier d'Albignac, who started the fashion in London high society for salads dressed in this way.

RECIPE

vinaigrette

Dissolve a little salt in 1 tablespoon vinegar (salt does not dissolve in oil). Add 3 tablespoons oil and some pepper. The vinegar can be replaced by another acid, such as the juice of a lemon, orange or grapefruit. In that case, the ratio is half lemon, half oil. The oil can be replaced by crème fraîche.

Other flavourings, such as herbs, mustard or garlic, may be added to taste. The mixture may also be placed in a screw-top jar and shaken vigorously to form an emulsion.

additional recipe See *salad.*

VINALGRIER The French name for the small glass bottle, usually with a glass stopper, used for serving vinegar at the table; it forms a pair together with the oil bottle as part of a cruet.

In France the name is also given to a large earthenware or stoneware cask traditionally used to make home-made vinegar. Shaped like a bottle or jug, usually with a capacity of 5 litres (9 pints, 5½ quarts), it has a tap at its base, allowing the vinegar to be drawn off as required.

VINCENT The name of a mayonnaise that contains chopped herbs or herb purée as well as chopped

VIETNAM

Vietnamese cuisine reflects Indian and French influences in addition to its individual identity based on the country's culture, geography and rural traditions. The cooking of the north echoes the Chinese use of soy sauce. The Chinese influence in northern cooking is also evident in stir-fried dishes. Fish sauce – *nuoc nam* – is the seasoning used in the same way as soy sauce in the majority of Vietnamese cooking. Chillies bring heat to southern dishes where herbs and vegetables are important, and where curries are also popular.

■ **Rice and noodles** Rice, mostly cultivated in the plains, is one of the five offerings made by the Vietnamese to the gods and ancestors because of its great importance as a source of food. Sticky or glutinous rice, used in combination with other ingredients, and fragrant, long-grain rice (*gao tam thom*), a northern speciality, play the same role as bread traditionally does on European tables. Not only is rice eaten as an accompaniment to other dishes or as a food in its own right, but it is also used as an ingredient in cooking: for example, to make rice bread, pasta (noodles and vermicelli) and flat rice cakes. Fine, dried wrappers made from rice are moistened and rolled around finely cut ingredients to make spring rolls, which are eaten raw; the same wrappers make *nems*, rolls which are fried.

Noodles are the other staple, especially for the less affluent, for whom they may be the main ingredient for every meal. For breakfast, lunch or dinner, noodles are inexpensive and satisfying. Fine or thick, moist or dry, with seasonings, a tasty sauce or in broth, noodles are the popular street food.

■ **Seasonal and full-flavoured** Vietnamese cooking is enlivened with spices, herbs and aromatics used in many ways, often for subtle and sophisticated results. These include garlic, dill, basil, spring onions (scallions), lemon balm, coriander (cilantro), shallots, ginger, mint, onions, water pepper (*daun kesom* or smartweed), pimiento and pepper. The dishes are served with complementary sauces. *Nam nem pha san* is a delicious dipping sauce accompanying fried or grilled fish: it is made from a thick fish paste or sauce, called *mam nem*, with pineapple, sugar and chilli. *Mam tom* is a sauce made with prawns, and *nuoc mam*, the salty sauce made from fermented fish and salt (of which there are several qualities) is also used in dipping sauces and accompaniments.

Presentation is important and the food is attractively served. The custom of offering several dishes at the same meal is common to South-East Asian countries and typical of the more sophisticated Vietnamese menus. Small portions of flavoursome dishes are served with rice.

Soup is one of Vietnam's traditional offerings. Hanoi's regional soup, *pho*, the most famous of Vietnamese soups, is made with vegetables and pieces of beef or chicken. But the most popular one is called *chao*; made with rice and water, it is eaten throughout the day. Soups, such as chicken soup, are often served with salads including lettuce, soya, mint, coriander and chives.

Lightly sautéed (*sao*) or braised (*ca bung*) vegetables, including aubergine, mushrooms, courgette (zucchini), water spinach and tomato, are served on their own or as an accompaniment.

■ **Fish and meat** Fish, shellfish and crustaceans are more common than meat. They are usually steamed or cooked by the *kho* technique: slow cooking with salt, *nuoc mam* and caramelized sugar. However, pork also plays an important part in Vietnamese cuisine, because bullocks are regarded as too important in the workplace to be used for food. Shoulder and knuckle of pork are used to prepare a very typical dish, *gio lua*. This is a meat paste, wrapped in fresh banana leaves, then boiled in water. Cut into pieces, it is served as an appetizer or as part of a buffet. Pork may be minced (ground), cut into thin slices or diced before being sautéed. Meat and poultry are also marinated in a mixture of spices and aromatic herbs and grilled on a barbecue. These ways of cooking pork are also used for beef and chicken. Less tender meat is often flavoured with ginger and allowed to simmer for hours (*dim*).

Meat, fish and crustaceans are combined in a very convivial dish: the fondue (*nhung dam*), in which the oil is replaced by vinegar-sharpened stock.

■ **Fruit and desserts** The range of fruit is as varied as the climate: apricot, pineapple, banana, mangosteen, mango, guava, persimmon, lychee, mandarin, grapefruit, papaya, peach, durian, rambutan, *mammee sapota* and so on. They are the basic ingredients of desserts but are also used in savoury dishes. There are numerous cakes made from sticky rice flour, filled with lotus cream or other sweet mixtures. *Che*, a sweet dish made with maize, and soy custard tart are much appreciated.

■ **Drinks** Tea is the popular drink, but the Vietnamese also drink *canh*, the water in which food has been cooked. The only alcoholic drink produced in the country is *ruou dê*, a rice alcohol with an alcoholic volume of 50–60%.

Pork with crackling and crisp duck are aromatic offerings from this stall on a busy Hanoi street.

hard-boiled (hard-cooked) egg. It is served with crudités, cold meat and fish.

RECIPE

Vincent sauce
Prepare a mayonnaise* with I egg yolk, I teaspoon white mustard, I tablespoon white-wine vinegar, 250 ml (8 fl oz, I cup) oil, salt and pepper. Blanch the following herbs for I minute in boiling water: chervil, chives, watercress, sorrel and parsley (a little mint, sage or burnet may also be added). Rub the mixed herbs through a sieve and add I generous tablespoon of the resulting purée to the mayonnaise. Mix in I finely chopped hard-boiled (hard-cooked) egg and adjust the seasoning.

VIN DE LIQUEUR The term adopted by the EU for all fortified wines, such as port, in which fermentation has been arrested by the addition of spirit.

The term *vin de liqueur* or *vin liquoreux* also signifies a sweet wine, where the spirit has been added earlier so that in the resultant drink the spirit is more pronounced. Ratafia, Pineau des Charentes, Macuin and Floc de Gascogne are all included in this category.

VIN DE PAILLE A dessert wine, coming mainly from the vineyards of the Jura and also from a small number of producers in Hermitage, Arbois and L'Étoile, which is made from grapes that are slightly dried after picking, either by being laid on straw mats (hence the name *paille*) or hung on racks. This drying before pressing concentrates the juice, and the wines are luscious and sweet in style and capable of long ageing. Very little is produced.

VIN D'HONNEUR A wine offered at receptions, as on certain civic occasions. Historic examples, quoted by Renouil and Traversay in their *Dictionnaire du vin*, include the following: the medieval *vin de bourgeoisie*, offered to the mayor and municipal magistrates by anyone who became a burger of the town; the *vin de coucher*, offered by newly-weds to the wedding guests; the *vin de curé*, offered to the priest by a family whose child had been baptized; and the *vin du clerc*, offered to the clerk of the court by a litigant, if the judgement had gone in his favour.

VIN DOUX NATUREL In France a wine that has been fortified with brandy, which increases its strength to more than that of table wines and arrests the working of the yeasts, so that some of the natural sweetness in the grapes remains in the finished wine. Both red and white examples are made, and the majority come from the Grand Roussillon region in the south, on the Franco-Spanish border, others come from the mouth of the Rhône. The grapes are predominantly Muscat, as in the well-known Beaumes-de-Venise and Muscat de Frontignan. But other grapes used include the Malvoisie and the Grenache, as in Rasteau.

The Muscats in particular are best served chilled and young and can be drunk as aperitifs. They are less well known than they deserve in Britain because their strength makes them liable to higher duty than table wines. However, they are enjoyed in the holiday regions of Banyuls (which makes a reputable *vin doux naturel*) and the French-Spanish hinterland from Collioure.

VINEGAR A sour liquid, widely used as a condiment, consisting of a dilute solution of acetic acid obtained by natural fermentation of wine or any other alcoholic solution. Vinegar (the French word, *vinaigre*, literally means 'sour wine') has been produced and used since the Gallo-Roman era; vinegar diluted with water was a common drink of the Roman legionaries. Orléans, an important centre for wine transport on the Loire, soon became the vinegar capital, and half the French wine vinegar is still produced there. The vinegar merchants' corporation was created in this city in 1394, and in 1580 Henri IV ordered that the profession of vinegar and mustard merchant should be a 'recognized occupation in the town and its suburbs', which resulted in the perfection of carefully developed production methods.

In 1862 Pasteur discovered that acetification was caused by a bacterium. Acetification takes place on contact with air; it produces a good vinegar if the wine – red or white – is light, acid and thoroughly strained to get rid of any residue. The operation takes place at a temperature of 20–30°C (68–86°F). The fermentation is caused by bacteria present in an even, velvety grey film, which forms on the surface and slowly sinks into the liquid in a folded sticky mass; this is the vinegar mother (*mère de vinaigre*). The quality of vinegar always depends on the quality of the wine or other alcohol used to make it; it must contain at least 6% acetic acid and be clear, transparent and colourless if it comes from white wine or differing shades of pink if it comes from red wine. Spirit or wine vinegars are mostly used in France, but in Britain and the USA malt and cider vinegars are also widely used. Vinegar may also be made from champagne or even honey. There are also differently flavoured or coloured vinegars, such as those using beetroot (red beet) or caramel.

■ **Types of vinegar**

• BALSAMIC VINEGAR A dark, richly flavoured wine vinegar originating from Modena in Italy, where there is a long tradition of making this vinegar that was thought to be a tonic and 'health giving', the meaning of its name.

Authentic balsamic vinegar is made from selected grapes, reduced to a must and concentrated, then fermented for a year. This is the comparatively quick part of the process – the technique that makes balsamic vinegar so special is the long maturing in wooden casks for at least 10 years. The vinegar is not set aside indefinitely, but transferred from one cask to another, each carefully selected for the wood and the flavour it imparts. During the maturing, the vinegar evaporates during the warm summers and rests in the cool winters, to become rich, full-bodied and mellow. The finest vinegars are aged for well over ten years and they can be nurtured for anything from thirty to a hundred years.

Factory-produced balsamic vinegar is not led lovingly through this process of transformation. It is particularly important to check information on inexpensive bottles to ensure that they do, at least, contain matured vinegar. Some mixtures sold as balsamic-style vinegar are no more than ordinary wine vinegar with flavouring and colouring ingredients added.

Balsamic vinegar is not harsh in flavour and therefore it is versatile in cooking. It is used sparingly in salad dressings and for dressing charcuterie and vegetables; it can be used to deglaze a pan after cooking meat or roasting vegetables; or to enrich and slightly sharpen sauces. The best balsamic vinegar should be treated like a precious wine and used with care.

• CIDER VINEGAR Cider vinegar is milder than malt or wine vinegars. It is golden in colour and useful for dressings, sharpening drinks and sauces. It can be used in pickling and for making cooked chutneys but it does not have the preservative qualities of the more acidic malt vinegar. However, this is not a problem when cider vinegar is used in sweet-sour combinations with sugar.

• MALT VINEGAR Malt vinegar is obtained from malted barley. It is a type of 'beer vinegar' compared to wine vinegar. Caramel gives it the dark colour. Malt vinegar is slightly milder than wine vinegar. Distilled malt vinegar or white vineger is clear and used for pickling light-coloured ingredients. In Britain malt vinegar forms part of the traditional accompaniment to fish and chips.

• RICE VINEGAR Chinese and Japanese vinegars are made from rice. They are generally lighter in flavour and in colour (there are dark rice vinegars). As for wine vinegars, they vary in quality and sharpness. Japanese rice vinegar is sweetened and seasoned to make sushi dressing (commercial sushi vinegars are often ready sweetened).

• SHERRY VINEGAR Sherry vinegar, also made by craftsmen, is a little more full-bodied.

• WINE VINEGAR Some vinegars traditionally produced by craftsmen are still made, including *vinaigre vieux à l'ancienne* and *vinaigre d'Orléans*; these are obtained by pouring red or white wine into oak casks already containing the *souche*, a small quantity of vinegar always kept in the cask. The vinegar drawn off is filtered and bottled, sometimes after ageing in a cask; it is fresh and perfumed, acid but without bitterness.

■ **Industrial producton** Industrially produced wine vinegar is made in 24 hours with red or white wine, which is brewed with beechwood shavings soaked in vinegar, a quick method (called the 'German method'), which gives a pungent, unperfumed product. Spirit vinegar is obtained by forcing air into a mixture of vinegar and beetroot alcohol; it is colourless or tinted with caramel.

■ **Uses of vinegar** Essential in the preparation of mustards, cold sauces and vinaigrettes (in which it is sometimes replaced by, or mixed with, lemon juice), vinegar also plays a major role in cooked reduced sauces and in deglazing. It is indispensable for sweet-and-sour preparations and for marinades and conserves, such as pickles or fruit and vegetable chutneys.

Different types of vinegar have different uses. Spirit vinegar is used to clean fish and mushrooms; it is also used to prepare cocktail onions and gherkins. White-wine vinegar is suitable for seasoning endive, cos (romaine) lettuce and chicory, for meat, game and fish marinades, to prepare *beurre blanc* (white butter sauce) and hollandaise and béarnaise sauces, and to finish noisette butter, as well as for deglazing. The traditional French white-wine vinegar is preferred for making aromatized vinegar at home.

Red-wine vinegar is preferable for seasoning delicate or rather flavourless salads (such as lettuce), as it has a more pronounced taste. It is used to cook red cabbage, and a trickle of this pink vinegar also improves fried calf's liver, sanguette, red meat dishes, pepper sauce or even eggs *sur le plat*.

Cider vinegar, like white-wine vinegar, is used in fish and shellfish court-bouillons; it is also used for chicken in vinegar, dressings and even in stewed apples. Malt vinegars are often preferred for marinated mackerel or herring, chutneys and salads in which fruits and vegetables are mixed (sweetcorn, grapefruit, apples and walnuts, for example).

■ **Home-made vinegar** The method consists of pouring some good-quality white or red wine into a cask and placing delicately on the surface a piece of vinegar mother. The vessel is then sealed with a paper stopper (to allow air to pass) and left at room temperature for a minimum of one month and a maximum of two months. The vinegar may then be drawn off as required and replaced by an equal quantity of wine. If a vinegar mother is unobtainable, wine vinegar should be mixed with red wine in equal proportions (or cider vinegar with non-pasteurized cider) and then left, as before, for acetification to take place; in this case, however, it will take at least three or four months for the vinegar to be produced. The vinegar mother should always stay on the surface and not mix with the alcohol. The cask should never be placed in a wine cellar.

■ **Flavoured vinegars** The traditional wine vinegars are often aromatized, using tarragon, basil, garlic, shallot, lemon, raspberry or even rose and elderflower (making *rosat* and *surard* vinegars).

A wide variety of traditional and contemporary spiced, sweetened and flavoured vinegars of excellent quality are produced commercially. From fungi, such as truffles, and mixtures of pickling spices, to fruit and herb mixtures, they reflect a history of seasonings. Home-made flavoured vinegars are easily prepared with dried spices and herbs. Fresh herbs give an excellent flavour when they are simply crushed with or added to vinegar in a bottle; however, there is a risk of contamination from

Clostridium botulinum (causing botulism) present on the herbs. This bacteria may be found on fresh uncooked produce and although it may be destroyed, its spores are highly resistant and they may develop in anaerobic conditions, that is without air, when the vinegar is stored for any length of time. Boiling the herbs separately or in the vinegar before leaving them to infuse is the safest method, but this does spoil the flavour of some herbs.

RECIPES

herb vinegar
Peel and slice 2 small onions and 2 shallots and blanch for 30 seconds in boiling water with 5 chives. Cool and wipe them and place in a 1 litre (1¾ pint, 1 quart) bottle of traditional French wine vinegar. Leave to macerate for a month before use.

raspberry vinegar
Pour into a stoneware jug 2 litres (3½ pints, 9 cups) red-wine vinegar and as many cleaned raspberries as it will hold. Leave to macerate for 8 days, then strain through a very fine sieve or jelly bag, without pressing the fruit, and decant into bottles.

rose vinegar
Put 100 g (4 oz) red rose petals in 1 litre (1¾ pints, 4⅓ cups) red-wine vinegar and leave to macerate for 10 days. Strain and bottle.

tarragon vinegar
Blanch 2 sprigs of tarragon for 10 seconds in boiling water; cool, wipe dry and place in a 1 litre (1¾ pint, 1 quart) bottle of white-wine vinegar. Leave to macerate for 1 month before use.

VIN GRIS A very pale rosé wine made only in small quantities from black grapes.

VINHO VERDE Red or white wine made from a wine-growing area between the Minho and Douro rivers in northern Portugal. Traditional Vinho Verde wines are low in alcohol, between 8.5 and 11.5%. The whites are light, crisp, sometimes spritzy, with lean acidity and are good as aperitif or picnic wines. The reds are lean and slightly peppery and make an excellent accompaniment to rich, oily food. Wines qualifying under the Vinho Regional Minho (Rios do Minho) appellation, which has the same demarcated area as Vinho Verde, may now be made in a fuller style with higher alcohol levels.

VIN JAUNE An AOC wine from the Jura, coming from Château-Chalon, Arbois, L'Étoile and several other regions. The grapes, all Savagnin, are picked late and the wine is put into oak casks, which are then sealed. The wine stays in the casks for a minimum of six years, during which time a yeast film forms on the surface, similar to *flor* on sherry. This method results in an unusual dry wine, yellow in colour, of slightly more than table-wine strength and

with a nutty flavour. Good vintages will 'fill out' in the mouth. Vin Jaune keeps admirably, even for many years. In cooking it may be best known for *coq au vin jaune*, a speciality of Franche-Comté.

VIN MUTÉ Also known as *vin mutage*. Wine to which a certain quantity of alcohol or sulphur dioxide is added in the course of fermentation. The purpose of this practice is to obtain sweet wines by preserving a certain amount of sugar.

VIN SANTO 'Holy Wine'. A dessert wine ranging from a straw-like to deep amber colour, produced throughout Tuscany mainly from Trebbiano and Malvasia grapes, although in some areas other varieties, including Chardonnay, Pinot Gris and Pinot Blanc, may be used. There is a pale pink to intense rose-coloured wine known as Vin Santo Occhio di Pernice, which is made from Sangiovese and Malvasia Nera grapes. Production methods vary depending on the producer. The grapes are laid to dry on racks or mats under the rafters, then pressed and stored for a minimum of three years in small oak or chestnut casks. The barrels are sealed and not topped up. The better producers age their wines for longer. The resulting wine can be dry, semi-sweet or sweet.

VINTAGE (*vendange*) The harvesting of grapes whenthey are at an optimum balance – that is, when the grape sugar and acidity are in balance. A vintage wine is made from the produce of a single harvest.

VIOLET Known in French as the *figue de mer*, the *Microcosmus sulcatus* is a member of the *Pyuridae* family. The violet looks like a gnarled shellfish, but its outer covering is a leathery coat. It can grow to about 8 cm (3½ in) in size. Its habitat is the seabed or rocks. The violet is cut in half to reveal the edible, soft yellow centre, which looks like scrambled egg. Scooped out and eaten raw, in Provence it is considered to be a delicacy. In Italy the violet is known as *uovo di mare* or *limone de mare* and in Spain it is *probecho*.

VIOLET FLOWERS Purple flowers from a small perennial plant. When newly opened, they may be used to decorate salads or in stuffings for poultry or fish. The sweet violet, a common European species, was formerly used in a cough medicine; nowadays, it is used mainly in confectionery and preserves. Crystallized (candied) violets are a speciality of Toulouse and are popular in Britain: the complete flowers are immersed in sugar syrup, sometimes coloured, which is allowed to come to the boil. After crystallization they are drained and dried, then used as decoration or to aromatize desserts, sometimes with crystallized mimosa flowers. Sweets (candies) can be made with cooked sugar perfumed with essence of violets and coloured and moulded in the shape of violets. Soufflés, cream and similar desserts can be flavoured with essence of violets.

VIROFLAY The name of a spinach dish consisting of subrics (a kind of croquette) made with spinach purée, wrapped in blanched spinach leaves, then coated with Mornay sauce and browned in the oven. Spinach subrics also feature in the Viroflay garnish to accompany large joints of roast meat served with thickened gravy, quartered sautéed artichoke hearts and château potatoes.

VISITANDINE A small round or boat-shaped cake, made of a rich mixture of egg whites, ground almonds, butter and sugar. After cooking, it is sometimes glazed with apricot jam and iced (frosted) with fondant flavoured with kirsch. Visitandines, which were first made in monasteries, were invented as a means of using up surplus egg whites.

RECIPE

visitandines
Mix 500 g (18 oz, 2¼ cups) caster (superfine) sugar and 500 g (18 oz, 4½ cups) sifted plain (all-purpose) flour, then mix in 12 very lightly beaten egg whites little by little, stirring in well, and finally 800 g (1¾ lb, 3½ cups) melted butter (barely tepid). To finish, add 4 stiffly whisked egg whites. Fill buttered barquette moulds with small quantities of the mixture, using a piping (pastry) bag with a large smooth nozzle. Cook in a preheated oven at 220°C (425°F, gas 7) for about 10 minutes or just long enough for the cakes to be browned with the insides remaining soft.

VIVANEAU A tropical fish of the West Indies and Africa, similar to sea bream (*dorade*). It is a brightly coloured fish weighing up to 2 kg (4½ lb), with a triangular head and pointed muzzle. Its flesh is fine and firm, very suitable for marinading in lime and spices, but it is also often prepared with coconut milk or simply grilled.

VIVEUR Now a synonym for 'reveller' or 'lover of the high life', this term was used, mainly in the 19th century, to describe various fairly rich or spiced culinary preparations: viveurs or des viveurs soup is a chicken consommé seasoned with cayenne, garnished with fine strips of celery and served with paprika diablotins. It may also be coloured with beetroot (red beet) juice and garnished with small poultry quenelles. Viveur omelette is made with celeriac, artichoke hearts and beef cut into small dice.

RECIPE

viveur omelette
Cook 2 artichoke hearts in white stock, drain them and cut into dice. Boil 2 tablespoons diced celeriac in salted water and drain. Cut 100 g (4 oz) beef fillet into small cubes, salt them and dust with cayenne. Sauté all these ingredients in butter in a large frying pan and pour over them 8 beaten eggs, seasoned with salt and pepper. Make into a flat omelette and serve very hot.

VLADIMIR A name given to various dishes dating from the Edwardian era, probably dedicated to a grand duke of this name. Turbot or sole Vladimir is poached, coated with white-wine sauce containing crushed tomatoes and poached clams, then glazed in the oven. Small cuts of meat Vladimir are sautéed, garnished with small pieces of braised cucumber and diced sautéed courgettes (zucchini), and covered with a sauce made of the cooking liquid deglazed with soured (dairy sour) cream and seasoned with paprika and grated horseradish; this preparation is reminiscent of Russian cookery. Eggs *sur le plat* Vladimir are fried, then sprinkled with Parmesan cheese and garnished with diced truffles and asparagus tips.

VOANDZEIA A type of bean, also called groundnut or (in French) *pois arachide*, with yellow pods containing round edible seeds, very rich in starch and protein. It has considerable economic importance in tropical Africa, where it is widely used as food, being one of the most nutritive vegetable products. It has also been introduced into Central America.

VODKA An alcoholic drink made from grain, molasses, potatoes or various other vegetables that are available for distillation. It probably originated in Poland (although countries of the former Soviet Union often dispute this) and is now made in many countries, including Britain. Vodka (a Russian word derived from *voda*, 'water') goes through distillation and rectification in a continous process. It is a neutral spirit and basically has neither taste nor smell. It is mainly appreciated for the stimulus given by the alcohol.

Various vodkas may be flavoured with spices (such as pepper), plants, leaves or fruits (such as lemons). From Poland, for example, comes *zubrowka*, made of a maceration of grasses called 'bison grass', mentioned by Somerset Maugham in his novel *The Razor's Edge* as a drink that 'smells of freshly mown hay and spring flowers'.

Vodka is now an international drink, often served with caviare and smoked fish (especially herring). It is also used to flame various fish preparations and a special sweet omelette and to deglaze certain dishes, particularly poultry.

The West was slow to take to vodka, but in recent years it has become enormously popular in the United States. It is used in a variety of mixes, including Bloody Mary (vodka and tomato juice).

VOILER A French cookery term meaning to coat certain pastries or iced desserts with a veil of sugar, consisting of fine threads of sugar cooked to the hard crack stage.

VOISIN A restaurant in the Rue Saint-Honoré in Paris, considered to be one of the foremost in the capital between 1850 and 1930.

Its first manager was Bellanger, who set up a

cellar of reputable Burgundies. The menu for the Christmas Eve midnight feast in 1870, consisting of the choicest meat of animals from the Paris Zoo, has remained famous: elephant consommé, civet of kangaroo, haunch of wolf with roebuck sauce, antelope terrine with truffles and so on. Taken over by Braquessac, who came from Bordeaux, the restaurant kept up its reputation with its chef, Choron, who created, among other things, a béarnaise sauce with tomatoes. Daudet, the Goncourts and Zola were regular customers, as was the Prince of Wales.

In his book *Un gastronome se penche sur son passé*, S. Arbellot mentions the Voisin as the most exclusive restaurant in Paris: 'Rumours were put about well calculated to discourage undesirables: only whole animals are served, Château-Lafite is drunk only in magnums.' In his *Guide des restaurants de Paris* (1925), Cousin classifies it in his 'perfection' class, with the note: 'No specialities, everything is recommended', but several enthusiasts selected its partridge salmi with sherry and its saddle of lamb as being particularly worthy of mention. Its name is still used for a timbale of duckling fillets with truffles in aspic.

RECIPE

duck voisin

Roast a duckling so that the meat remains slightly pink – about 30 minutes in a preheated oven at 230°C (450°F, gas 8). Let it get completely cold, then remove the fillets. Break up the carcass and trimmings and use these to prepare a salmi. Strain the salmi, remove the fat, and add to it an equal quantity of meat aspic. Reduce and strain. Place a layer of this sauce in a timbale mould; when it has set, place on top a layer of finely sliced duckling fillets. Coat them with more of the sauce, then cover with a layer of sliced truffle. Continue to fill the timbale with alternating layers of duck and truffle, coating each layer with a little half-set aspic. Finish with a layer of aspic. Chill in the refrigerator until set. Turn out and serve very cold.

VOL-AU-VENT A round case of puff pastry, 15–20 cm (6–8 in) in diameter, having a pastry lid. The vol-au-vent is filled after baking and served as a hot entrée or hors d'oeuvre. Its invention is attributed to Carême, who had the idea of replacing a shortcrust pastry case with puff pastry of such delicacy that 'it flew away in the wind (*s'envola au vent*) on coming out of the oven'. The celebrated chef also said: 'This entrée is attractive and undoubtedly very good; it is almost always eaten with pleasure on account of its extreme delicacy and lightness.'

The filling for a vol-au-vent is bound with sauce; there are many different kinds: *à la financière, à la reine, à la bénédictine, à la toulousaine, à la Nantua*, seafood, mushrooms in béchamel sauce, sole fillets, poultry or veal quenelles, veal sweetbreads or escalopes, sliced chicken fillets, lobster escalopes, salmon and so on. Purées of shellfish,

chicken or game finished with a salpicon of the basic ingredient can also be used, and even spaghetti in tomato sauce with diced ham. The classic presentations, however, are vol-au-vent *financière* and *marinière*.

Both the filling and the pastry case must be very hot, and the filling takes place at the last moment, to avoid soaking the pastry. The vol-au-vent is served immediately, although it may be placed briefly in the oven to reheat after filling.

The classic vol-au-vent has been adapted to modern tastes. Individual ones are now popular, and bite-size cocktail ones are often made to serve with drinks (see *bouchée*).

RECIPE

vol-au-vent case

Prepare 500 g (18 oz) fine puff* pastry. Divide it in half and roll out each half to a thickness of 5 mm (¼ in). Cut out 2 circles, 15 cm (6 in) in diameter. Place 1 pastry circle on a slightly dampened baking sheet. Using a 12–13 cm (4¾–5 in) round cutter, remove the centre of the second circle. Dampen the top of the pastry circle and place the outer ring from the second one on top. Turn the ring over as you place it on the circle so that the slightly floury underside is uppermost.

Roll the central circle of pastry from the ring to the same size as the vol-au-vent. Dampen the border of the vol-au-vent and place this third layer on top. Glaze the top with beaten egg top then use a small knife to score around the inside of the border. This marks the lid covering the well in the vol-au-vent; scoring it without cutting through completely makes it easier to remove when cooked. Mark a pattern on top of the lid by lightly scoring it in a criss-cross pattern.

Bake in a preheated oven at 220°C (425°F, gas 7) for about 15 minutes until well-risen and golden-brown. After taking it out of the oven, place the vol-au-vent on a wire rack; carefully cut out the lid without breaking it, place it on the wire rack, and remove the soft pastry from the inside of the vol-au-vent. Keep hot. Reheat the filling, fill the case with it, place the lid on top and serve very hot.

vol-au-vent financière ◆

Blanch 50 g (2 oz) sweetbreads, rinse under cold water, then dry. Remove the skin and cut into large chunks. Cut 200 g (7 oz) chicken quenelles into medum-sized cubes. Blanch 12 cockscombs and cook in butter for 2 minutes. Season with salt and pepper. Cut 300 g (11 oz) mushrooms into quarters and sauté in butter in a frying pan and then drain. In the same pan, sauté the sweetbreads, seasoned with salt and pepper, for 2 minutes. Remove and set aside with the mushrooms. Deglaze the pan with 100 ml (4 fl oz, 7 tablespoons) Madeira,

Vol-au-vent financière.

reduce a little and return the mushrooms and sweetbreads to the frying pan. Cover and simmer for 3–4 minutes.

Make a golden roux with 40 g (1½ oz, 3 tablespoons) butter, 40 g (1½ oz, 6 tablespoons) flour and 500 ml (17 fl oz, 2 cups) chicken stock. Add salt, pepper, nutmeg, 1 chopped white truffle and 100 ml (4 fl oz, 7 tablespoons) Madeira. Cook gently for 10 minutes.

Place the sweetbreads, mushrooms and their juice, the diced quenelles, cockerels' kidneys and 12 shelled crayfish in a saucepan. Pour the sauce on top and allow to simmer for 4–5 minutes. Just before serving, remove from the heat and add 1 egg yolk mixed with 100 ml (4 fl oz, 7 tablespoons) double (heavy) cream. Fill the vol-au-vent with the stuffing and place the lids on top.

VOLIÈRE, EN Describing a decorative method of presenting game birds, particularly pheasant and woodcock. This method was in common use up to the 19th century but is now obsolete. On the cooked bird, the head, tail and outspread wings were placed in position and held with small wooden pegs. In the Middle Ages peacocks, swans and herons were presented *en volière*, and a piece of burning flax was placed in their beaks. Under the Ancien Régime various game birds, complete with their feathers, were served on a large silver dish and presented as *chasse royale* (royal hunt).

VOLNAY An AOC red Burgundy wine from the Côte de Beaune. The favourite wine of Louis XI, Volnay is famous for its elegance, quality and charming bouquet.

VOSNE-ROMANÉE A village in the Côte de Nuits area of Burgundy, producing very fine wines from Pinot Noir. There are six *grand cru* vineyards: Romanée-Conti, La Romanée, La Tâche, Richebourg, Romanée-St-Vivant and La Grande Rue, as well as wines produced at *premier cru* and *village* level.

VOUVRAY AOC white wines from the Loire Valley near Tours. Made from the Chenin Blanc and Arbois grapes (mostly the former), Vouvray is dry to sweet, may be still, *pétillant* (slightly sparkling) or *mousseux* (fully sparkling). It often ages in cellars dug into the limestone.

VUILLEMOT, DENIS-JOSEPH French chef (born Crépy-en-Valois, 1811; died Saint-Cloud, 1876). The son and grandson of *maîtres d'hôtel*, he started his apprenticeship under Véry, became the pupil of Carême, then set up on his own account at Crépy and later at Compiègne. He then assumed the management of the Restaurant de France at the Place de la Madeleine in Paris and finished his career at the Hôtel de la Tête-Noire, at Saint-Cloud.

A long-standing friend of Alexandre Dumas, he was his technical associate for the recipes in the *Grand Dictionnaire de la cuisine* (1873). He also organized a banquet in the novelist's honour on his return from Russia, which has remained famous for its culinary creations, all bearing names evoking the titles of Dumas' works: soups *à la Buckingham* and *aux Mohicans*, trout *à la Henri III*, lobster *à la Porthos*, fillet of beef *à la Monte-Cristo*, bouchées *à la reine Margot*, bombe *à la dame de Monsoreau*, salad *à la Dumas*, gâteau *à la Gorenflot* and crème *à la reine Christine*.

W

WAFER A small, crisp, light biscuit with waffle-like marks from the cooking plates used for the dough. Wafers are mainly produced industrially. They can be plain, shaped like a fan, rolled up like cigarettes or filled with jam or praline cream. Wafer dough is also used to make ice-cream cornets.

WAFFLE A thin, light batter cooked on the stove between the two buttered and heated plates of a waffle iron. The waffle batter is made of flour, butter, sugar, eggs and water or milk, sometimes with a flavouring, such as vanilla, or orange-flower water, cinnamon, aniseed, brandy or citrus fruit zest.

The ancient Greeks used to cook very flat cakes, which they called *obelios*, between two hot metal plates. This method of cooking continued to be used in the Middle Ages by the *obloyeurs* who made all sorts of *oublies*, which were flat or rolled into cornets. The *oublie* became the waffle in the 13th century, when a craftsman had the idea of forging some cooking plates reproducing the characteristic pattern of honeycombs, which at that time were called *gaufres* (from the Old French *wāfla*).

Waffles, like fritters and pancakes, were one of the most common foods in country cooking. Sometimes they were simply made of flour and water or milk. The richer country people added eggs, *cassonade* (semi-refined sugar) or honey, sugar and aromatized wine. Each area has its own recipe for waffles – they can be savoury, made with ham, cheese or pumpkin, or sweet. The batter can be enriched with fresh cream or butter, or made lighter with whisked egg whites.

Waffles from the central regions of France are delicate and crunchy and can be kept in a tin. In Champagne and Franche-Comté the waffles are very crisp and sprinkled with sugar. The waffles of northern France, called *étrennes*, are thick and greasy and eaten hot. The batter contains a lot of butter and fresh cream, and the flour is mixed with milk rather than water.

Waffles, like pancakes, are traditionally sold in the street and at fairs, particularly in the northern provinces of France and Flanders. They are extremely popular in the United States, especially served with maple syrup for breakfast. It is thought that the Pilgrim Fathers brought them from England in 1620.

Waffles are usually eaten hot, sprinkled with sugar and accompanied by whipped cream or jam.

RECIPES

waffles

In a large earthenware bowl sift 500 g (18 oz, 4½ cups) plain (all-purpose) flour with 2 teaspoons bicarbonate of soda (baking soda), 4 teaspoons baking powder and 2 teaspoons salt. Add 30–40 g (1–1½ oz, 2–3 tablespoons) caster (superfine) sugar, 150 g (5 oz, ⅔ cup) melted butter, 5 beaten eggs and 750 ml (1¼ pints, 3¼ cups) milk (or more, if very light waffles are preferred). Mix well until the batter is runny and completely smooth.

Heat and, if necessary, grease a waffle iron. Pour a small ladle of batter in one half of the open waffle iron. Close the mould and turn it over so that the batter is distributed equally in both halves. Leave to cook. Open the waffle iron, take out the waffle, sprinkle with icing (confectioner's) sugar and serve.

bricelets vaudois

Beat 65 g (2½ oz, 5 tablespoons) butter with 100 g (4 oz, ½ cup) caster (superfine) sugar into a foamy

Piping hot, crisp, golden waffles ready to be topped with melted butter and warm honey, maple syrup or a dusting of sugar.

mixture. Add 1 whole egg plus 1 yolk, 250 ml (8 fl oz, 1 cup) crème fraîche, a pinch of salt and the grated zest of 1 lemon. Mix together, then add 200 g (7 oz, 1¾ cups) sifted plain (all-purpose) flour. Work together quickly to make a runny batter. Using a ladle or spoon, pour small quantities into a waffle iron. Close and cook, then remove and serve hot.

filled waffles

Mix 15 g (½ oz, 1 cake) fresh (compressed) yeast or 1½ teaspoons dried yeast with 300 ml (½ pint, 1¼ cups) tepid water. Blend in 500 g (18 oz, 4½ cups) strong plain (bread) flour, then add 125 g (4½ oz, generous ½ cup) butter, 40 g (1½ oz, 3 tablespoons) caster (superfine) sugar and 2 teaspoons salt, and knead to obtain a smooth dough. Leave to prove (rise) under a cloth overnight, then shape it into little balls and again leave to rise on a floured board for 1–2 hours.

When the balls have doubled in size, heat a waffle iron, grease it if necessary, place a ball of dough in it, close it and leave to cook. As soon as the waffle has browned, take it out, slice it in two horizontally and leave to cool completely. Do the same with the remaining dough.

In a warm basin, cream 250 g (9 oz, generous

1 cup) butter, 200 g (7 oz, 1½ cups) icing (confectioner's) sugar and 200 g (7 oz) praline. Use to fill the waffles.

Liège waffles

Take 500 g (18 oz, 4½ cups) sifted strong plain (bread) flour. Mix 15 g (½ oz, 1 cake) fresh (compressed) yeast or 1½ teaspoons dried yeast with 125 ml (4 fl oz, ½ cup) tepid water and blend with a quarter of the flour. Leave to rise until doubled in size. Then add the rest of the flour, a generous pinch of salt, 125 g (4½ oz, generous ½ cup) caster (superfine) sugar, 4 beaten eggs and 200 g (7 oz, scant 1 cup) softened butter. Mix well.

Work the dough with the palm of the hand. Divide it into balls, each the size of an egg. Roll into sausage shapes and leave to stand on a floured board for 30 minutes. Heat a waffle iron and, if necessary, grease it. Put a piece of dough between the plates, close the waffle iron and leave to cook. Repeat with the remaining dough. Serve the waffles lukewarm or cold, sprinkled with icing (confectioner's) sugar.

WAFFLE IRON A hinged cast-iron mould, consisting of two honeycomb-patterned plates between which waffle batter is cooked.

Hand-operated waffle irons, of which the oldest date from the 15th century, are sometimes veritable masterpieces, richly adorned with designs and engraved with coats of arms, crosses and religious or magic symbols. They are placed over a heat source (glowing embers, electric hotplate or burner) and turned over halfway through cooking. For this purpose they are equipped with long handles.

Traditional waffle irons are still used but the majority are electric, with a thermostat and non-stick plates. Some models have interchangeable plates so that toasted sandwiches, grills and even pancakes can also be cooked in them.

WALDORF

A mixed salad consisting of diced apple and celery and walnuts, dressed with a thin mayonnaise. It is named after the prestigious New York hotel, the Waldorf Astoria, where it originated as a simple apple and celery salad, dressed with mayonnaise.

This name has also been given to a dish of marinated conger eel fillets, floured, grilled (broiled) and sprinkled with melted butter. It is served with small baked potatoes and a mayonnaise Américaine (with mustard and the coral of a lobster or langouste added).

WALES See *page 1288*.

WALEWSKA, À LA

The name given to fish poached in a fumet, garnished with slices of lobster (or other crustacean) and thinly sliced truffle, coated with Mornay sauce finished with lobster butter and glazed in the oven. This dish, typical of the rich cuisine of the Second Empire, appears to have been dedicated to Count Walewski, natural son of Napoleon I and Marie Walewska, who was ambassador in London and minister for foreign affairs under Napoleon III.

RECIPE

fillets of sole à la Walewska
Poach some sole fillets in a fish fumet for 5 minutes, using very little liquid. Arrange on a long ovenproof dish and on each fillet place a slice of lobster or langouste flesh (cooked in court-bouillon) and a slice of raw truffle. Coat with Mornay sauce containing 1 tablespoon lobster or langouste butter* to every 150 ml (¼ pint, ⅔ cup) sauce. Glaze quickly in a very hot oven.

WALNUT

The fruit of the walnut tree, consisting of a hard-shelled nut surrounded by an outer green fleshy husk, called a shuck. The delicious kernel is shaped like the two halves of a brain (which is why the ancient Greeks and Romans believed that walnuts cured headaches). The kernel is 35–50% of the total weight, depending on the quality of the nut. It is covered with a fine skin, light to dark yellow in colour, and the kernel is white, turning greyish with age. Some thin-shelled varieties can be crushed in the hand, but normally nutcrackers are required.

Grown originally on the shores of the Caspian Sea and in northern India, walnuts were valued by the Greeks for their oil. The Romans extended cultivation of the walnut tree to other parts of Europe, and from the 4th century it was cultivated in the Grésivaudan region of France. Nowadays, French walnuts are grown mainly in Périgord and Dauphiné. The name 'noix de Grenoble', an *appellation d'origine*, can be applied to any of the three best known varieties – Franquette, Mayette or Parisienne (delicate and fruity, the most sought-after dessert walnut) – and guarantees their place of origin, quality and flavour. The main variety grown in Périgord is Corne; others are Marbot and Grandjean. They are usually sold shelled.

From mid-September to around All Saints' Day (1 November), dehusked fresh walnuts are sold in France: they should be kept in a wicker basket in a cool place, never in the refrigerator, where the oil they contain would harden and destroy their flavour, and eaten within a fortnight of harvesting. Later in the season, as they mature, the husk falls off and the nuts are sold dried. If the kernels are soaked in milk overnight they will regain their fresh flavour. Walnuts have a very high calorific content and are an important item in vegetarian diets.

Walnuts are used chiefly in cakes and pastries, either as an ingredient (ground or chopped) or as decoration (half kernels). But they are also used in salads; with meat, poultry or fish dishes (especially with chicken, salt cod and snails); and for flavouring sauces (for pasta), forcemeats (for pâtés or rissoles) and savoury butter. They can also be prepared with verjuice or preserved in vinegar (pickled walnuts). Walnut oil, with its fruity taste, is reserved for flavouring salads. Ratafias and liqueurs (especially *brou de noix*) are made from the shucks, and there are also walnut-flavoured wines.

RECIPES

cream soup with walnuts
Blend 1 egg yolk into 1 litre (1¾ pints, 4⅓ cups) chicken stock. Peel some fresh walnuts, pound them in a mortar and add them to the soup. Finish with a little double (heavy) cream.

green walnuts in verjuice
Clean some fresh green (unripe) walnuts without breaking them, place them in cold water, drain and dry them, sprinkle with coarse salt, then pour over some verjuice (the acid juice of unripe grapes). Scatter some chopped herbs over the walnuts and serve with cold meat, such as roast veal or pork.

pheasant with walnuts
Pound together 60 peeled fresh walnut kernels, 3 Petit-Suisse cheeses (or 3 oz cream cheese), ½ wine glass grape juice, the juice of 1 lemon, a

WALES

Best known for lamb, leeks and laverbread, Wales has more to offer. The traditional home cooking was based on the agricultural lifestyle prevalent in most rural areas, where a hearty cooked breakfast followed the early morning milking; a substantial main mid-day meal provided energy for an afternoon's work; and a relaxed supper provided an opportunity for lingering over bread, cheese, salad (when seasonal), simple dairy dishes and pickles, often served with wonderfully crunchy fried potatoes (the leftovers from lunch). In the farmhouse kitchens there was always a welcome – with home-made cake, fruit pie, bread and butter, cheese – and local gossip.

■ **Coastal specialities** It is rare to find a seaweed as a national food, but hand-gathered laver is sold ready-cooked in markets near the South Wales coast, ready to be made into cakes with rolled oats. Little cakes – or patties – of laverbread are traditionally fried in bacon fat and served with bacon for breakfast. Other traditional coastal seafood dishes include Gower oyster soup (made with mutton broth) and mussel stew. Another old recipe, *pastai gocos*, a double-crust cockle and bacon pie, has been replaced by cockles with pasta, influenced by the many Italians who live in Wales. Fine salmon are netted in the Teifi estuary; grilled or roast, they are served with Teifi sauce, made with port, anchovy and butter. There are also sewin or sea trout and big catches of skate. Mackerel

are particularly good, especially when caught young in the early months of summer, and shellfish are excellent, especially crab and lobster.

■ **Succulent, full-flavoured meat** The slow-maturing mountain lamb is renowned for its fabulous flavour. It may be served simply, with mint sauce, new potatoes and bright spring cabbage, or in more elaborate style. Adventurous chefs offer lamb as a honey-roast with laverbread sauce, or in a pie with small new carrots. Mutton is traditionally cured as hams, served boiled with a prune sauce that contains fresh blackcurrants. Other old-fashioned meat dishes included spiced beef (like that of Ireland), 'planked' steak and roast veal fillet, served with a 'veal' sauce of grated horseradish, lemons, vinegar and cayenne.

Other good dishes are roast goose eaten with apple, and the Hermit of Gower's salted-then-boiled duck served with onion sauce.

■ **Leeks and soups** Wales is a Celtic country, a culture that extends along Europe's Atlantic fringe. The simmering meat pot called a *caldo* in Spain is *cawl* here. A wonderful pot of soup, it is made with whatever meat, vegetables and grain, such as pearl barley, are good and fresh. Lamb, beef or a joint of boiling bacon often bring full flavour, and leeks (*cennin*) are a traditional feature along with potatoes, carrots, swede and cabbage. Lobscouse is a northern seaman's dish (shared with Liverpool), containing salt pork or mutton with any available roots and vinegar.

St David's Day, 1 March, is

associated with leeks, the national emblem. They are worn as badges or at least eaten in many dishes, and daffodil flowers (the other national emblem) are tucked into the buttonhole instead. Leek tart with chicken and bacon is excellent.

■ **Cheese dishes** Welsh rarebit is the famous savoury of melted cheese grilled on toast, and there are other cheese tarts and puddings. Glamorgan sausages (originally made from a Glamorgan cheese) are made of grated cheese, breadcrumbs, onions or leeks and mustard, shaped and crumbed, then grilled or fried. Wales is known for an old cheese, Caerphilly, no longer produced in the town of that name, and there are many local cheeses from small producers, especially goat's-milk cheeses as well as hard and soft cheeses from cow's milk.

■ **Sweet specialities** Many tea-time treats are traditionally made with buttermilk: thick pancakes (*crempog*) are served hot with butter or piled high with a filling, then cut in wedges. Oatmeal is used for traditional oat cakes. A heavy griddle is used to make simple, but good, Welsh cakes. Based on a short pastry, sweetened with currants and with added spice, Welsh cakes are served buttered or sprinkled with sugar. Scones are popular, plain or fruited, baked or made on the griddle. *Bara brith*, meaning 'speckled bread', is a yeasted fruit loaf with currants and other dried fruit; quick versions are made as teabreads, without yeast. Border tart (also called Chester pudding) has raisins and sultanas in a pastry case covered with meringue.

few drops of port, ½ cup very strong tea, salt and pepper. Stuff a pheasant with this mixture. Brown the pheasant in butter, then season with salt and pepper, cover the pan and cook until tender (about 40 minutes).

pickled walnuts
Choose fairly large green walnuts with husks that can be easily pierced with a pin. Wipe them and prick deeply all over. Marinate the nuts for 3 days in

brine, made with 100 g (4 oz, 1 cup) salt per 1 litre (1¾ pints, 4⅓ cups) water, then bring them to the boil. Repeat this operation 3 times, marinating the nuts for 3 days between each boiling. Then drain the walnuts and put them into jars. Boil 5 litres (8½ pints, 5½ quarts) vinegar for 15 minutes with 75 g (3 oz, ¾ cup) black peppercorns, 40 g (1½ oz, ⅓ cup) fennel seeds, 40 g (1½ oz, ⅓ cup) cloves, 40 g (1½ oz, ⅓ cup) mace and 40 g (1½ oz, ¾ cup) crushed fresh root ginger. Fill the jars to the top with boiling spiced vinegar, making sure that the walnuts are completely covered. Seal the jars and store them in a cool place. Serve with cold meats.

scampi with walnuts

Soak the walnut kernels in cold water overnight. Dry, peel and fry quickly in hot oil, then drain them and keep hot. Season some shelled scampi with white wine, fresh root ginger juice, salt and pepper. Roll them in flour and fry in very hot oil. In another pan, quickly fry some green onion stalks. Turn all these ingredients out on a hot dish, mix together and sprinkle with stock to which white wine, soy sauce and ground ginger have been added.

walnut cake

Cream 125 g (4½ oz, generous ½ cup) butter, then beat in 300 g (11 oz, 1½ cups) caster (superfine) sugar, 5 eggs (one by one), 125 g (4½ oz, generous 1 cup) ground almonds and 125 g (4½ oz, generous 1 cup) ground green walnut kernels. Then fold in 2 tablespoons rum and 75 g (3 oz, ¾ cup) sifted self-raising flour and mix well until smooth.

Butter a 20 cm (8 in) sandwich tin (layer cake pan), line the base with a circle of buttered grease-proof (wax) paper and transfer the mixture to the tin. Bake in a preheated oven at 200°C (400°F, gas 6) for 35–40 minutes. Allow the cake to cool in the tin before turning it out. Decorate the top with walnut halves.

walnut surprises

In a heavy-based saucepan heat 250 g (9 oz, 1 cup) granulated sugar, 750 ml (1¼ pints, 3¼ cups) water and 25 g (1 oz) glucose. When the temperature reaches 115°C (240°F), take the pan off the heat and add, all at once, 125 g (4½ oz, 1 cup) ground almonds. Stir until the mixture acquires a sandy texture, then knead it by hand, blending in 5 drops of coffee essence (strong black coffee). Roll the paste out into a long thin sausage and cut it into 50 equal slices; roll each slice into a ball and flatten it slightly; moisten each side and press in a walnut half. Store in a cool place. To serve, put each petit four into a pleated paper case.

other recipes See *crêpe (sweet crêpes), diablotin, fond de pâtisserie.*

WARBLER A small songbird of which there are many species, including the garden warbler and blackcap. During the autumn migration, they cross the south of France when the figs and grapes are ripe and eat the seeds. Brillat-Savarin was particularly enthusiastic about them, although they were already appreciated in Roman times. Once hunted to excess, they are now a protected species.

WASABI A Japanese plant, *Wasabia japonica*, found growing wild on river banks or cultivated in running water for its root (a rhizome, in fact). It is related to watercress, but the root has a hot flavour, similar to

horseradish but not as harsh. Fresh wasabi root, which is green in colour, is grated and used in sushi or mixed with soy sauce and served as a condiment for sashimi. Fresh wasabi is expensive, as is the true dried and ground root. The common dried or paste product sold as wasabi outside Japan is often made from horseradish, mustard and colouring.

WASHINGTON A garnish for poached or braised chicken consisting of boiled sweetcorn bound with very thick cream. The name is somewhat paradoxical, because although maize (corn) is considered the national cereal of the United States, George Washington is renowned for having encouraged the growing of wheat!

WATER CARRIER Large houses and princely residences were the first to have private water sources, at least their own wells, but the rest of the population had to make do with public fountains, which were few and unevenly distributed. It was not until 1860, under the auspices of Baron Haussmann, that these fountains began to be systematically sited in Paris, heralding the gradual installation of running water to buildings. Before this, people relied on the services of the water carriers.

A team of 58 water carriers was mentioned in a fiscal document of 1292. They bore a yoke on their shoulders, at the ends of which hung two buckets. When a customer replied to their cry of 'Who wants water? It's everyone's right, it's one of the four elements', they carried the water upstairs to him. They used the water of the Seine but were not allowed to draw water between the Place Maubert and the Pont-Neuf 'because of the infection and impurity of the stagnant water'.

In the 18th century the yoke was replaced by a diagonal strap, with a lattice to hold the bucket in place away from the body; a round piece of wood floated on the surface of the water to reduce its movement while the carrier walked. The corporation had about 20,000 members. Two buckets of water cost two sous for the first two floors and three sous for higher floors. The office of water carrier was worth about 1,200 French livres at the time.

WATER CHESTNUT The tuber of an aquatic plant originating in South-East Asia under similar conditions to those for rice cultivation. The water chestnuts are corms that form on the runners from the rhizomes from which the plants grow. They have dark brown skin enclosing crunchy white flesh, which is edible raw or cooked. One of the characteristics of the water chestnut is the fact that it does not become soft or tender during cooking, but retains its pleasing crunchy texture. The flavour is delicate and slightly nutty.

Water chestnuts are sold either fresh or canned and are used in Chinese and Vietnamese cooking in hot dishes and to give texture to stuffings. They are often combined with vegetables and bamboo shoots. A popular dish is lotus leaves stuffed with water chestnuts and rice. The rhizome can also be used fresh as a dessert or preserved in sugar.

WATERCRESS See *cress.*

WATERFISCH A hot or cold sauce for freshwater fish, of Dutch origin. Hot waterfisch sauce (mainly for pike and perch) is made by cooking a julienne of vegetables in white wine until reduced, then moistening with court-bouillon, reducing once more, then adding hollandaise sauce and parsley.

Cold waterfisch sauce is an aspic jelly prepared with the court-bouillon of the fish it is accompanying, with the addition of a julienne of vegetables, sweet red pepper, gherkins and capers; the fish is coated with the aspic, then decorated with thin strips of anchovy and served with rémoulade sauce.

RECIPES

cold waterfisch sauce

Prepare a julienne of vegetables as for hot waterfisch sauce; moisten with 200 ml (7 fl oz, ¾ cup) of the court-bouillon used to cook the fish that the sauce is to accompany and simmer until the liquid has evaporated. Dissolve 2 leaves or 7 g (¼ oz, 1 envelope) gelatine in 200 ml (7 fl oz, ¾ cup) fish court-bouillon, add the vegetable julienne while still hot, then allow to cool. Add 1 tablespoon each of chopped gherkins, chopped sweet red pepper and capers; mix together.

hot waterfisch sauce

Cut into very fine strips 50 g (2 oz) carrots, 25 g (1 oz) white part of leeks, 25 g (1 oz) celery, 25 g (1 oz) Hamburg parsley roots and 2 teaspoons grated orange zest. Place the julienne in a saucepan, moisten with 200 ml (7 fl oz, ¾ cup) dry white wine and boil until all the liquid has evaporated. Add 200 ml (7 fl oz, ¾ cup) fish court-bouillon made with white wine and reduce completely once again. Prepare 500 ml (17 fl oz, 2 cups) hollandaise* sauce and mix the vegetables into it, together with 1 tablespoon blanched, chopped, parsley sprigs. Keep hot in a bain marie until ready to serve.

WATERMELON A large spherical or oval fruit, weighing 3–5 kg (6½–11 lb), with a dark green rind and pink flesh, which is sweet and very refreshing but slightly insipid; the pulp is studded with large, flat black seeds.

Of tropical origin and known since antiquity, the watermelon is grown in many countries, particularly Spain and parts of the United States. When it is bought, it should be heavy and not sound hollow. It is generally cut into slices and eaten just as it is, to quench the thirst (it is sold in the streets in Mediterranean countries). When the seeds have been removed, watermelon pulp may be included in fruit salads (possibly served in the empty rind). In some countries, it is picked when green and unripe and prepared like a vegetable marrow (squash).

RECIPE

watermelon à la provençale

Make a circular incision around the stalk of a ripe watermelon. Cut off the end and scoop out some flesh. Shake the fruit so that some of the seeds fall out. Fill the watermelon with Tavel wine, stop it up with the cut-off end and seal it with wax. Chill in the refrigerator for at least 2 hours. Just before serving, take off the end, strain the wine, cut the watermelon into slices and serve it with the wine.

WATER PARSNIP A perennial herb with tuberous roots, which are prepared like salsify, and leaves, which can be eaten in salads. Cultivated in Japan and China, water parsnips were introduced into Europe in the 16th century and were once highly esteemed as a vegetable; they have now practically disappeared.

WATERZOOÏ Also known as waterzootje. A Flemish speciality consisting of freshwater fish and eel cooked in a court-bouillon with herbs, Hamburg parsley roots and vegetables. The preparation is finished with a generous amount of butter and crème fraîche and is sometimes thickened with breadcrumbs. Waterzooï (the word is formed from 'water' plus *ziedem,* to simmer) is also made in Ghent, using chicken.

RECIPES

chicken waterzooï ♦

Poach a chicken until three-quarters cooked (about 40 minutes) in a white stock containing an onion stuck with 2 cloves, a bouquet garni, 1 celery stick and 1 leek, both sliced. Slice 1 leek, 1 carrot and 1 celery stick and cook in a flameproof casserole with some of the chicken stock, as for fish waterzooï. Cut the chicken into 8 pieces and arrange them on the vegetables. Add sufficient stock to cover the chicken and cook for a further 30 minutes.

Remove the chicken pieces and the vegetables with a slotted spoon. Add 200 ml (7 fl oz, ¾ cup) double (heavy) cream to the casserole and reduce to a smooth sauce; adjust the seasoning. Replace the chicken and vegetables and serve from the casserole, accompanied with bread and butter or buttered toast.

fish waterzooï

Cut 200 g (7 oz) white part of leeks and the same quantity of celery into fine strips; butter a large flameproof casserole and cover the base with the vegetables; add salt, pepper and a bouquet garni containing 4 sage leaves. Add sufficient fish fumet (or court-bouillon) to cover 2 kg (4½ lb) freshwater fish (about 1.25 litres, 2¼ pints, 5½ cups)

Chicken waterzooï.

and add 100 g (4 oz, ½ cup) butter in small pieces. Cover and cook gently for about 30 minutes, then allow to cool. Meanwhile, clean the fish and cut into sections. Place them in the cold cooking liquid, adding a little more court-bouillon if necessary, partly cover the pan, bring to the boil, and poach for at least 20 minutes. Remove the fish with a slotted fish-slice, discard the bouquet garni and mix 200 ml (7 fl oz, ¾ cup) double (heavy) cream into the cooking liquid. Reduce this sauce, then replace the fish and reheat. Serve from the casserole, accompanied with bread and butter or slices of buttered toast.

WEDDING FEAST The ceremonial meal that follows a wedding – traditionally known as the wedding breakfast in Britain, no matter when it is served – has an important role. According to the New Testament, it was at a wedding feast (in Cana) that Jesus performed the miracle of turning water into wine; this illustrates the importance of the wedding feast as a social gathering from the earliest times.

In former times, the festivities of the wedding feasts of the nobility and royalty lasted for several days. On these occasions, roast meat, cakes and public fountains of wine were offered to the people. Marriages with princes or princesses from foreign lands were also occasions when new kinds of food were introduced into France (fruit and vegetables from Italy, chocolate from Spain and so on).

The most outstanding feature of wedding feasts is the cake or cakes, which are remarkable either for their size, the number of tiers, their richness or their beauty. Ornamental tiered cakes (*pièces montées*), topped by figurines representing the bridal couple, or featuring their names, are still very fashionable, but the wedding cakes of bygone days were more varied. In some parts of France the emphasis is on the variety and number of cakes: fruit, jam or cheese tarts; small cakes and fritters (particularly in the south of France and in Corsica); brioches, crystallized (candied) fruit and filled pastries; piles of wafers and waffles; and so on.

In other regions it is the spectacular size or nature of the cake that is important. In south-eastern France and Burgundy, *a pièce montée* of considerable size might be constructed using marzipan (almond paste) and Savoy sponge cakes. In the Pyrenees and in Rouergue, the traditional wedding cake is a *gâteau à la broche*, constructed with great difficulty on a wooden cone turned in front of the fire. The wedding cake of the Vendée is the *gâtais*, a huge brioche presented by the godfathers and godmothers of the bridal couple. Weighing up to 35 kg (77 lb) and either round – up to 1.2 m (4 ft) in diameter – or rectangular – 2.5 × 0.8 m (8 × 2½ ft) – this monumental cake is carried in by bearers who execute a kind of dance step to demonstrate that the cake is not too heavy. After the cake has been 'danced', the bride cuts it up and distributes a piece to each guest, setting aside portions for relatives who have not attended the wedding. Sharing and distribution rituals are found in all regions. Often the cake is eaten several days later when the guests are at home, so that they are reminded of the ceremony.

This custom is similar to the British tradition of sending pieces of the wedding cake in small decorative boxes specifically designed for the purpose to relatives and friends who, for various reasons, could not attend the ceremony.

WEDGE-SHELL A small marine bivalve mollusc with a pastel-coloured wedge-shaped shell, 3–4 cm (1¼–1½ in) long, which lives in the sand at the water's edge. In France it is known as *haricot-de-mer*, *flion* or *vanneau*. It is eaten in the same way as cockles, either raw or cooked, after having been soaked to clean it; it has a very good flavour.

WEEVER A sea fish that often lies buried in the sand on the sea bed. It is appreciated for the quality of its flesh but feared for its poisonous spines; the spines and the fins should therefore be cut off before any other preparation and the fish handled with gloves on. The greater weever, which is usually 25 cm (10 in) long but may reach 40 cm (16 in), has a long body (brown back striped with blue, yellow sides, and white belly) and a short head, with a wide mouth and large eyes close together. Its flesh is firm and fragrant, and fillets are cooked in the same way as sole fillets. Whole and cleaned, it may be grilled (broiled) or prepared like red mullet. Weever steaks can be used in a matelote made with white wine. The lesser weever (the size of a sardine) has hardly any flavour.

A related fish, the star-gazer (called *uranoscope*, *rat* or *rascasse blanche* in French), is found only in the Mediterranean and is used in bouillabaisse.

RECIPE

grilled weever
Gut and clean the weevers. Make shallow slits on the back of each fish and on each side of the central fin. Marinate them for an hour in a mixture of oil, lemon juice, salt, pepper and chopped parsley, with a little chopped garlic. Then gently grill (broil) them for about 15 minutes, turning once.

Serve with melted butter strongly flavoured with lemon and mixed with chopped herbs or with a mixture of olive oil and raw, crushed tomato pulp.

WEISSLACKER A German cow's-milk cheese produced in foil-wrapped blocks weighing about 1.5 kg (3¼ lb). Golden-yellow right through, with a dense texture and a washed rind, it has a pronounced flavour and smell. It originated in Bavaria and is also called *Bierkäse* (beer cheese). It is traditionally served with rye bread and *Doppelbock* beer.

WELSH RAREBIT A Welsh speciality consisting of a slice of toasted bread covered with a mixture of Caerphilly, Cheshire or Cheddar cheese melted in pale ale with English mustard, pepper and sometimes a dash of Worcestershire sauce and an egg yolk. It is then grilled (broiled) and served very hot. In Britain Welsh rarebit (also known as Welsh rabbit) can consist of slightly simpler versions of those ingredients, the most important components being toast and cheese, and it is served as a quick and delicious snack, often accompanied by beer. On the Continent, where this dish was popular in 'English taverns' in the 19th century, it is more usually served as a hot entrée.

RECIPE

Welsh rarebit
Grate 250 g (9 oz, 2¼ cups) Cheddar or Caerphilly cheese and place in a saucepan. Add 200 ml (7 fl oz, ¾ cup) pale ale, I large teaspoon prepared English mustard and a pinch of pepper. Heat gently, stirring constantly, until the mixture is smooth and runny. Toast 4 slices of sandwich bread and butter them. Put each slice on an individual flameproof plate, also buttered, and coat with the cheese mixture without spilling any over the edges of the bread. Brown under the grill for 3–4 minutes. Serve very hot.

WENSLEYDALE Originally made from ewe's milk and now from cow's milk, this English cheese from the Yorkshire dales is uncooked and pressed into small or medium-sized drum shapes. It is cloth-bound or waxed. The cheese has a thin, dry natural rind and a firm, but crumbly, paste. The taste is sweet and milky, with a tangy finish. The white version is a traditional accompaniment for apple pie or fruit cake. There are also blue and smoked versions.

WEPLER A brasserie that opened in the Place Clichy in Paris in 1891, not far from the Père Lath-uile, whose declining custom it hoped to capture. In its early days it was particularly well known as a place for wedding feasts and banquets. In 1906 its proprietor switched to the formula pioneered by the Duval restaurants, and in about 1930 the Wepler reverted to a brasserie. It was in this 'sad and freez-ing aquarium' (R. Crevel), enlivened by a gypsy orchestra, that the American author Henry Miller set up house. For the price of a cup of coffee with cream, never reordered, he had at his disposal writ-ing paper, envelopes, ink and pen: 'All that for free! This can only happen in Paris.'

WEST-INDIAN PUMPKIN Local varieties of win-ter squash, also known as giraumon, green pumpkin, toadback, Cuban squash or calabaza. They vary in skin colour and size, but the flesh is orange-yellow. It can be prepared and cooked as for ordinary pumpkin or other squashes, such as butternut squash.

WHALE A large aquatic mammal hunted for its fat in some parts of the world (the far north of Canada, Norway and Japan), in spite of increasingly strict measures intended to protect it from complete extinction.

Throughout the Middle Ages, when whales were still to be found off the coasts of Europe, in particu-lar the Bay of Biscay, they were also hunted for their oil (which was used for lighting) and for their flesh which, since it came from a 'fish', was considered a suitable food during Lent. According to Ambroise Paré, 'The flesh has no value, but the tongue, which is soft and delicious, is preserved in salt. The same applies to the blubber, which is eaten with peas dur-ing Lent.' This blubber, known as *craspols* or *lard de carême* ('Lenten fat'), was the main diet of the poor during the Easter period. However, the tail, and partic-ularly the tongue, were considered to be delicacies.

Nineteenth-century cookery books suggested recipes for grilled flipper escalopes (scallops), poached brains or slices of liver grilled in anchovy butter. Whale meat is very red and contains more protein than beef. Eskimos eat it dried, and Norwe-gians eat grilled whale meat. A traditional Icelandic dish is cooked whale blubber preserved in vinegar. The Japanese are the largest consumers of whale meat and eat it raw, cooked with ginger or marinated. Meat from the tail or throat is particularly prized. The blubber is cut into thin strips and served with *sake*. It is also used in the manufacture of preserved foods such as soups, canned meat and edible fat.

WHEAT A cereal used to produce flour and semolina that can also be eaten cooked, crushed and so on.

Wheat was cultivated in Neolithic times and was used in girdle – griddle – cakes and broth. The Egyptians, followed by the Greeks and Romans, used it to make bread, and it is in this form that wheat has mostly been used in southern and west-ern Europe. It has virtually replaced other cereals in this part of the world, whereas other civilizations have grown up on rice or maize.

Each grain of wheat consists of a husk (bran) and a kernel. The latter is made of starch and a mixture of proteins called gluten, which varies according to the particular type of wheat. Inside the kernel is the seed or embryo (known as wheat germ), the area rich in nitrogenous material and fatty substances.

There are several varieties of wheat with different uses within the food industry. Gluten-rich hard wheat is used for making semolina, especially for pasta and couscous. Soft wheat is ground for flour of varying degrees of whiteness, depending on how much of the husk is removed.

Growing interest in vegetarian cookery has led to the rediscovery of the use of wheat as a natural food. Ground whole wheat is used to make gruel, croquettes, biscuits (cookies) and the like.

Wheat grain can be cooked and used in the same way as rice. Cracked wheat is the uncooked grain, which is crushed. It is added to breads, to give a crunchy texture, or used as a topping to give an attractive crust. It can be cooked in boiling water and used as for rice, or added to soups.

Bulgur is a different product which is processed and cooked, then dried before being packed and sold. It does not require further cooking, but can be soaked and drained, then used as a cold ingredient for salads. See *bulgur*.

RECIPE

germinated wheat
Place wheat grains in a flat container and cover them with water. Leave for 24 hours. Wash the grains in running water, then replace in the container, without water, for another 24 hours. The grains must, however, remain moist. Wash again the next day. The grains now have a little white point (this is the germ) and are ready for use. They do not keep and must be used the same day. They are eaten either in their natural state or dried and ground and then added to soups, salads or purées.

WHELK A marine gastropod of the *Buccinidae* family, with a whitish, conical, pointed shell, very common on the coasts of the English Channel and the Atlantic. It is known as *ran* or *buccin*, while on the Mediterranean coast it is known as *casque épineux* ('spiny helmet'). Cooked in salted water for just 8 to 10 minutes – so as not to make them tough – whelks are eaten with buttered bread and, sometimes, mayonnaise.

WHISK A kitchen utensil made of tinned or stainless steel wire bent into loops and held together in a handle.

An egg whisk, which is short and rounded, with flexible wires attached by a ring to a wooden or metal handle, is used for whisking egg whites. It is also used to make potato purée, to beat egg yolks with sugar (especially for zabaglione) and to whisk crème fraîche.

A sauce whisk, which is longer and has stiffer wires and a metal handle, is used to beat and emulsify sauces and also to beat custards and various mixtures so that they will not be lumpy.

Nowadays electric beaters, fitted with steel or plastic attachments, are often used instead of hand whisks. Whisking is made much easier, especially for egg whites and mayonnaise, but the results are inferior for delicate mixtures, such as hollandaise and béarnaise sauces and Chantilly cream.

WHISKY A spirit originating from Scotland and made from malted grain. It is spelled 'whiskey' in Ireland and the United States, but Irish whiskey is different from American whiskey, which is made from rye or maize (corn).
* SCOTCH WHISKY The Scottish national drink is made from malted barley and has changed little over the centuries. After germination, the malted barley is dried over the heat of peat fires: it is the aroma of the peat that gives the whisky its particular flavour. The barley is then ground and mixed with water to form the wort; the wort is fermented and goes through two distilling operations, according to the methods of the craft. Malt whisky is obtained in this way; it is called single malt when it comes from one distillery only and pure malt when it is a blend of different malt whiskies.

Grain whisky is made from a mixture of any malted and unmalted cereals. A long maturation period is the key to the mellow flavour of Scotch whisky. Law requires that it be matured in oak casks in Scotland for a minimum of three years before becoming Scotch whisky. This is true of malt and grain whiskies. In fact, most Scotch whisky is matured for five or six years or longer. The label frequently states the age of a brand. In the case of a blended Scotch whisky, law demands that the age of the youngest individual whisky in the blend is stated.

Constantly increasing demand since World War I led producers to develop the market for blended whiskies, resulting from blends of malt and grain whisky. The latter, produced in a much more industrial way, has a less distinctive flavour. The blend takes its aroma mainly from the malt whisky, of which the proportion in the composition of the blend may vary from 15 to 40%. Extremely widely drunk, blended Scotch whiskies are now recognized throughout the world; there are about ten great brands, each corresponding to a particular blend of different whiskies and with its own fine and full-bodied aroma. Although connoisseurs may remain attached to malt whisky, it is blended whisky that has given rise to most imitations abroad.
* IRISH WHISKEY This was for a long time produced and consumed on a small-scale family basis. Made from barley, but also from wheat, rye and oats, it is not dried over peat. Distilled three times, it undergoes, like Scotch whisky, various blends before being sold.
* CANADIAN WHISKY Made from cereals, this is marketed under numerous names and has a fairly light taste. Maize (corn) is found in large proportions in the mixtures, which are fermented under the action of malted barley as for other whiskies.
* CORN WHISKEY This is an American grain spirit, produced from a mixture of cereals containing at least 80% maize (corn).
* BOURBON WHISKEY The most widely drunk of the American whiskies, this originated from Kentucky and is made from a mixture of maize (at least 51%), rye and malted barley; it is aged for at least two years in oak casks charred inside.
* RYE WHISKEY An American grain spirit produced from rye.

Many countries produce different spirits under the name of 'whisky' or 'whiskey', which covers all sorts of products. But, whatever the results of the various attempts and researches, none has been able to equal the particular delicate flavour of the original Scotch whisky.

Whisky is generally drunk as an aperitif, on ice, either neat or with plain or soda water; the Scots drink it with a glass of plain water beside it. This spirit is also used to make numerous cocktails, such as whisky Collins, whisky sour and Bourbon sour (see *Irish coffee*). It is also an ingredient in various cookery recipes (for chicken and shellfish, particularly), and some enthusiasts prefer it to Cognac or Armagnac for flamed dishes.

In Geneva there is a Confrérie du Bon Vieux Whisky, and in France, Britain and the United States, an Academy of Pure Malt Whisky. In France this Academy bestows the Glenfiddich Award each year.

WHITEBAIT The young of herrings, sprats, and so on, which are very common along coasts and in river estuaries. These small fish are usually fried and eaten whole.

The French word, *blanchaille*, is also used to describe various small freshwater fish.

WHITE FISH This anodyne term is accepted for lake fish of the family Corigonidae in the United States of America and Europe (see also *char*). They are beloved by restaurateurs in areas with no coast line, because simple service (fried, with lemon, or poached) suits the fresh fish best. They are also good smoked. The Lake of Geneva has its *bondelle* and Lake Garda in Italy the *coregone* (*lavaret* in France). Called a houting, skelly or powan in Britain, this fish is found throughout northern Europe, including the Baltic, and is reared in Germany. The vendace or pollan also extends across Europe; in Sweden it is *löja* (fished for its roe), in the United States of America it is called cisco and sold at about 500 g (18 oz) in weight. A bigger relation is fished at about 1.8 kg (4 lb) from Lake Superior and features in Chicago restaurants.

WHITE PUDDING (SAUSAGE) See *boudin blanc*.

WHITING A sea fish similar to haddock and cod but without barbs. The whiting is 25–40 cm (10–16 in) long, with a greenish-grey back, golden-coloured sides and a silvery belly with a line of small brownish-yellow streaks above the pectoral fin. It lives near the coast and is fished mainly in the Atlantic, from the north of Norway to Spain. Available most of the year, it is sold whole or in fillets.

Whiting flesh is fine-textured and friable and contains less than 1% fat, making it easy to digest. It must be cooked carefully because the flesh tends to fall apart easily. Whiting is an essential ingredient in some regional soups along the French coast. It dissolves in the soup, giving a velvety texture. It can be prepared in many ways: fried, grilled (broiled), fried in breadcrumbs or poached in wine. It can also be stuffed, rolled into paupiettes or used in forcemeats, fish loaves or mousses. However, it needs to be well-seasoned (with flavoured butter, lemon and herbs), as the flesh is rather tasteless.

The Australian whiting, a species of the *Sillago* family, is not botanically related to the European whiting. Generally of much better quality, it appears regularly in Australian markets and is one of the country's best fish for eating and angling.

RECIPES

fried whiting en colère

Soak the whiting for 10 minutes in milk or pale (light) ale. Drain, pat it dry, season with salt and pepper and roll it in flour. Shape the fish into a circle by putting the tail into the mouth and clenching the jaws so that it remains in this position during cooking. Deep-fry in hot (but not smoking) fat, making sure that it is evenly browned on both sides. Drain it on paper towels and serve with fried parsley, slices of lemon and tartare sauce. Whiting can also be fried flat, but in this case a shallow incision should be made along its back.

fried whiting en lorgnette

Make a deep incision in the fish along each side of the backbone. Do not separate the fillets from the head. Remove the backbone, starting at the tail and breaking it off at the base of the head. Season with salt and pepper and dip in egg and breadcrumbs. Roll up the fillets on either side of the head and secure each of them with a small wooden skewer so that they stay in position. Deep-fry in very hot (but not smoking) fat. Arrange on a napkin and garnish with fried parsley and slices of lemon.

paupiettes of whiting

Fillet 3 whiting and remove the skin. Put the bones and heads into a saucepan together with 2 grated carrots, 1 shredded onion, 2 chopped shallots, 350 ml (12 fl oz, 1½ cups) dry white wine, a large glass of water, a bouquet garni, salt and pepper. Boil gently for 30 minutes, then strain the fumet and boil it down by half. Leave it to cool.

Prepare a fish mousse in the following way. Reduce 2 whiting fillets to a purée in a blender and put it into a basin. Place the basin in a bowl containing crushed ice. Gradually add 200 ml (7 fl oz, ¾ cup) crème fraîche, working the mixture briskly until it becomes mousse like. Flatten the 4 remaining fillets, season with salt and pepper and coat evenly with the fish mousse. Roll the fillets up tightly and tie them with string. Arrange the paupiettes in a buttered flameproof dish, pour the reduced stock over the top and cover. Bring to the boil on top of the stove, then cook in a preheated oven at 220°C (425°F, gas 7) for 20–25 minutes.

Make some beurre manié by mixing 1 tablespoon butter with an equal quantity of flour. Drain the paupiettes and keep them hot on a serving dish. Thicken the cooking liquid with the beurre manié. Untie the paupiettes, coat them with the sauce and serve piping hot.

poached whiting with melted butter

Put a large whiting into a cold court-bouillon in a pan. Bring to the boil, cover and poach gently for 10 minutes. Drain the fish and arrange it on a serving dish. Pour a little melted butter over the top and sprinkle with chopped parsley. Serve any remaining butter in a sauceboat. Garnish with steamed potatoes, rice, cucumber slices, spinach or leeks cooked in butter or sautéed courgettes (zucchini) or aubergines (eggplants).

stuffed whiting with cider

Remove the backbone from 4 whiting, each weighing about 300 g (11 oz). Gut (clean) them through the back and season with salt and pepper. Cut 2 carrots, 2 celery sticks and the white parts of 2 leeks into very fine slices. Cook very gently for 5 minutes in a covered pan with 25 g (1 oz, 2 tablespoons) butter, salt and pepper. Leave to cool. Stuff the fish with the vegetables and place them in a large ovenproof dish with 1 tablespoon olive oil. Pour 350 ml (12 fl oz, 1½ cups) dry (hard) cider and 175 ml (6 fl oz, ¾ cup) fish stock over the fish. Cook in a preheated oven at 220°C (425°F, gas 7) for 15–20 minutes or until cooked. Remove the fish, boil down the stock until it is almost dry, then add 250 g (9 oz, generous 1 cup) curd cheese and heat gently, stirring, without boiling. Pour this sauce over the whiting, sprinkle with chopped chives and serve very hot.

whiting à l'anglaise

Open the fish from the back and remove the backbone. Season with salt and pepper, roll in flour, dip in egg and breadcrumbs and brown in butter on both sides. Arrange it on a dish and coat with slightly softened maître d'hôtel butter. Serve with boiled potatoes.

whiting à l'espagnole

Dip the whiting in egg and breadcrumbs, brown it in oil and serve on a bed of tomato fondue seasoned with a little crushed garlic. Garnish with fried onion rings.

whiting hermitage

Remove the bone from a large whiting and gut (clean) it through the back. Stuff it with a mixture of breadcrumbs, creamed butter, chopped shallot, egg, chopped herbs, salt and a pinch of cayenne. Put it into a buttered gratin dish with a little cream and some fish stock. Cover with buttered greaseproof (wax) paper and bake in a preheated oven at 220°C (425°F, gas 7) for 15 minutes. Drain the whiting and keep it hot. Boil the cooking liquid to reduce and add some butter, cream, salt and pepper. Bring to the boil again and pour over the fish.

whiting in white wine

Gut (clean) 2 large whiting and season with salt and pepper. Butter a flameproof gratin dish, line it with a layer of chopped onions and shallots and place the fish on top. Add equal quantities of white wine and fish stock so that the fish are half-covered. Cover the dish, begin the cooking on the top of the stove, then place in a preheated oven at 220°C (425°F, gas 7) for about 20 minutes. Drain the fish and keep them hot in a serving dish. Boil the cooking liquid to reduce by half and add 200 ml (7 fl oz,

¾ cup) single (light) cream. Boil down further and pour the sauce over the fish. Glaze for 5 minutes in a very hot oven.

additional recipe See mousse (fish mousse).

WIENER SCHNITZEL See viennoise.

WILD BOAR

The ancestor of the domestic pig, which has been hunted since ancient times and is now increasingly rare. It is known in French hunting terms as bête noire. The young animals have delicate flesh, but the flavour of the meat becomes more pronounced with age and is very strong in the adults.

Horace was one of the first to acclaim wild boar as a noble, highly flavoured dish: 'If you shun insipid meat, let a wild boar from Umbria, fed on ilex acorns, make your table bend under its weight.' Martial was equally enthusiastic: 'May your joyful aroma fill my home, may the wood burn in my kitchen as on a feast day. But my cook must use plenty of pepper and must be generous with the Falernian wine and the mysterious garum.' During and after the Middle Ages wild boar continued to be popular, particularly 'wild boar tails in hot sauce' (Ménagier de Paris), boar's head, stewed shoulder, roast loin and pâtés.

Up to the age of six months, the wild boar is known in France as a marcassin; its light coloured fur is striped with dark bands from head to tail (it is said to be 'in livery'). It is forbidden to hunt an animal younger than three months. From six months to a year it is called bête rousse (red beast) because of its colour, and from one to two years bête de compagnie. At that age its flesh is excellent for cooking. Then its black coat appears. At the age of two years the wild boar is called ragot; at three, it is a tiers-an; at four, a quartenier; older, a porc entier. An animal of advanced years (it can reach the age of 30) is called a solitaire or ermite. In an eight-year-old male the flesh, although tough and very strongly flavoured, is still edible. The delicate flesh of the marcassin does not need to be marinated. The bête rousse and bête de compagnie should be marinated in red wine for two to three hours, older animals for five to eight hours; at this stage long, slow cooking is essential.

Most recipes for pork are suitable for wild boar, apart from roasting (marcassins excepted). The cutlets, whether marinated or not, can be fried; slices cut from the tenderest parts can be cooked like escalopes (scallops). The leg, or ham, should be braised in sweet-and-sour sauce with its marinade, with the possible addition of raisins, prunes or orange peel. Marcassin fillet can be barded and roasted in a moderate oven, allowing 20–25 minutes per 450 g (1 lb), basting frequently. Wild boar fillet can be cooked in a daube: it is first browned, then simmered on a layer of pork rind with the marinade, allowing 30–45 minutes per 450 (1 lb), according to age. The best cuts are usually cooked in a civet. There is also a variation in which curry powder is sprinkled over the pieces after they have been browned. With or without curry spices, they are then cooked in a covered pan with onions, carrots, garlic and white wine; the sauce can be thickened with cream. Wild boar meat can also be minced (ground) and cooked in a pie with prunes.

Wild boar is readily available in the mountainous regions of Spain as well as in central and southern Italy. Boar are also reared or managed and bred with domesticated pigs to produce a slightly more manageable animal that still yields meat of the same flavour.

RECIPE

boar's-head brawn (head cheese)
Cook in court-bouillon 4 pigs' tongues, which have been blanched, peeled and soaked in brine for 4–5 days. Singe a boar's head weighing about 5 kg (11 lb), scrape it out carefully, and bone it completely, without tearing the skin. Cut off the ears and set aside; remove the tongue and the fleshy parts attached to the skin. Cut the pieces of lean meat into large, evenly sized cubes; leave them, with the tongue and the skin of the head, to marinate for 10 hours with 5 carrots, 4 chopped onions, thyme, bay leaf, salt, pepper and 1 teaspoon mixed spice.

Cut into dice 2 cm (¾ in) square the boar's tongue, the cooked pigs' tongues, 500 g (18 oz) pickled tongue, 800 g (1¾ lb) ham, 1 kg (2¼ lb) boned and trimmed chicken meat and 500 g (18 oz) fat bacon. Add 400 g (14 oz) truffles (peeled and coarsely diced), 150 g (5 oz, 1 cup) shelled pistachio nuts and the pieces of lean meat from the head. Marinate for 2 hours in brandy, salt, pepper and ½ teaspoon mixed spice. Add 4.5 kg (10 lb) fine pork forcemeat* and 4 whole eggs; mix all together well.

Spread out the skin of the head, with the outside underneath, on a cloth that has been soaked in cold water and wrung out. Lay the stuffing in the middle and fold the skin over the mixture. Wrap the head in the cloth, reshaping it into its original form, and tie it firmly.

Cook in aspic-jelly stock to which the bones and trimmings from the boar's head and the carcass and trimmings from the chicken have been added; simmer very gently for about 4½ hours. One hour before it is ready, put the ears into the stock to cook. Drain, leave to stand for 30 minutes, then unwrap the head, wash the cloth and wring it out well. Roll the head in the cloth again and bind with wide tape, taking care to keep the shape (start binding at the snout end). Leave to cool for at least 12 hours, then unwrap and wipe dry.

Using thin wooden cocktail sticks (toothpicks), fix the ears, coated with a layer of brown chaud-froid sauce or dissolved meat glaze, in their correct positions. Place the head on a rack and coat with the same sauce; put the tusks back in their sockets and make eyes with hard-boiled (hard-cooked) egg white and truffles. Lay the head on a large dish, gar-

nish with truffles and shelled pistachio nuts and glaze with the aspic (which should have the consistency of unbeaten egg white). Chill in the refrigerator. In domestic cookery, where the truffles are omitted, the cooled head is simply covered with golden breadcrumbs. The ears are diced and added to the rest of the stuffing.

cutlets of marcassin with quinces
Peel and finely dice 100 g (4 oz) carrots, an equal quantity of onions, the white part of a leek and a stick of celery. Place in a saucepan with 450 g (1 lb) bones and trimmings of a *marcassin*, a garlic clove and a small bouquet garni and cook until well browned. Pour 1 bottle of a robust red wine into the pan and add 100 g (4 fl oz, 7 tablespoons) single (light) cream. Add salt, stir and cook very gently for 1½ hours.

Skim off the fat, rub through a fine sieve and boil to reduce until about 300 ml (½ pint, 1¼ cups) liquid remains. Put this sauce on one side.

Prepare a stuffing: cook 400 g (14 oz) peeled, diced salsify in boiling water with a little lemon juice. Cook 200 g (7 oz, 1½ cups) thinly sliced onions and 200 g (7 oz, 2 cups) diced pears in a covered pan with a knob of butter for 30 minutes. Add the cooked salsify and adjust the seasoning. Prepare 6 crêpes. Spread the stuffing over the crêpes, roll them up, place in a greased gratin dish and bake in a preheated oven at 200°C (400°F, gas 6) for 15 minutes.

Peel 300 g (11 oz) quinces, cut into dice or segments and boil in water with lemon juice until tender but slightly firm. Fry 12 *marcassin* cutlets like pork chops until they are just slightly pink. Cover them with the quinces and add a dash of rum. Bring the sauce to the boil and blend in 100 g (4 oz, ½ cup) butter, stirring over a low heat. When the sauce becomes glossy, pour it over the cutlets. Serve with the stuffed crêpes.

This recipe can also be used for cutlets and noisettes of venison or adult wild boar.

saddle of wild boar with quince sauce
Cook 2 perfect quinces al dente in 1 litre (1¾ pints, 4⅓ cups) water, sweetened with 100 g (4 oz, ½ cup) caster (superfine) sugar. Peel and hollow them. Poach 100 g (4 oz, generous ½ cup) lentils in stock; 200 g (7 oz) cubed celeriac in vegetable stock; and 1 diced beetroot (red beet) in chicken stock.

Roast a saddle of wild boar in 50 g (2 oz, ¼ cup) goose fat, basting often. Add the vegetables half way through cooking. Take the meat out, degrease the roasting pan and deglaze with the quince cooking juices, 1 litre (1¾ pints, 4⅓ cups) brown wild boar stock and 1 teaspoon quince jelly. Reduce by four-fifths. Filter through a fine sieve and thicken with 25 g (1 oz, 2 tablespoons) butter. Roast the quinces, cut into quarters, in 20 g (¾ oz, 1½ tablespoons) butter, adding a little caster (superfine) sugar to caramelize them. Heat the lentils, celeriac and beetroot separately. Garnish the edge of the plates with these vegetables, add 2 quarters of quince and the wild boar aiguillettes, and pour the sauce on top.

sweet-and-sour leg of marcassin

Soak the following ingredients separately in cold water: 12 prunes, 175 g (6 oz, 1 cup) currants and 175 g (6 oz, 1 cup) sultanas (golden raisins). Braise a leg of *marcassin* in the same way as a leg of pork. Drain and place in a long ovenproof dish. Strain the braising liquid and pour a few spoonfuls over the meat. Sprinkle 1 tablespoon sugar over the meat and brown in a preheated oven at 220°C (425°F, gas 7). To make the sauce, first prepare a caramel using 4 sugar lumps, then add 4 tablespoons wine vinegar and 400 ml (14 fl oz, 1¾ cups) game stock. Boil for 10 minutes, then strain. Bake 4 tablespoons pine nuts, chop them coarsely and add to the sauce, together with the drained currants, sultanas and prunes, and 24 pickled cherries. Just before serving, melt 25 g (1 oz, 1 square) plain (semisweet) chocolate with the minimum of water and add it to the sauce, together with 15 g (½ oz, 1 tablespoon) beurre manié.

WINE A drink made from the juice of the grape, the sugar in the fruit being converted into alcohol by the action of yeasts in the process of fermentation.

According to the definition of the Wine & Spirit Association of Great Britain, wine is: 'The alcoholic beverage obtained from the juice of freshly gathered grapes, the fermentation of which has been carried through in the district of its origin and according to local tradition and practice.' This means that drinks made from fruits other than grapes are not, strictly speaking, 'wines'. Nor can alcoholic drinks made from dried grapes, imported grape concentrate and grape and fruit extracts be described as 'wine' – they are categorized in Europe as 'made wines', and in Britain as 'British wines' or 'British . . . style wine'. But it is important to recognize the distinction between 'British wine' (as defined above) and 'English wine', which is made from grapes grown in England.

Red, rosé or white, still or sparkling, wine is enjoyed by millions of people and plays an important role in all kinds of celebrations. Its history is as old as that of civilization. The vine grew wild in Europe and the East, and the idea of obtaining a drink from it goes back probably to the remote past.

At Ur, Mesopotamia, a panel has been discovered representing a drink-offering scene. The Egyptians were including wine in their funeral ceremonies some 3000 years before Christ. The Bible makes numerous allusions to the Hebrews as being great lovers of wine.

The art of cultivating the vine and making wine was, according to mythology, taught to the Greeks by Dionysus. In fact, it was undoubtedly the Egyptians who spread this art throughout the Mediterranean, particularly in Sicily and southern Italy. The Romans inherited it, and their immense empire derived the benefits. The Gauls were familiar with

the vine well before the Roman conquest (1st century BC), but the quality of Roman wines and new methods introduced by the conquerors gave considerable impetus to viticulture. The Gauls became excellent vine growers and may have invented the cask, which took the place of the amphorae, which had been used until that time for the storing and transportation of wine. In AD 92 the high quality of Gallic production led the Roman Emperor Domitian, on the pretext of encouraging wheat growing but in reality to protect Roman vine growers from formidable competition, to order that half the Gallic vines should be pulled up.

In the Middle Ages viticulture was linked to the propagation of Christianity, each monastery producing its own wine for the Mass and medicinal use and working hard at improving the quality. Many famous wines of France, notably in Burgundy, are still grown around what were formerly monasteries.

French wines were exported to England and Scotland, the Scandinavian countries and as far away as the Near East (in spite of the Islamic ban, which at one time obliged some Bordeaux exporters to label as 'mineral water' the casks of wine sent to Turkey). In this way they acquired a reputation that continued to grow until the 18th century. The use of bottles for maturing wines became general in the 18th century. The French Revolution resulted in the parcelling out among innumerable small landowners of the vineyards that had belonged to the nobility and the religious communities. In 1867 phylloxera, a plant bug that spread to Europe from North America, destroyed the vines in the majority of European vineyards. Built up again later with vines grafted on to American rootstocks, which are resistant to phylloxera, European vineyards now extend over an enormous and increasing area, and wine is of major importance in the European economy.

The Institut National des Appellations d'Origine des Vins et Eaux-de-Vie (INAO) has classified French wines as follows:

• VINS DE TABLE Wines for daily consumption. Their labels must indicate the alcoholic strength and the capacity of the bottle. *Vin de Table Français* is a blend of French wines; *Vin de Différents Pays de la Communauté Européenne* is a blend from several EEC countries; *Vin de la CEE* is one made in a different country from that producing the grapes.

• VINS DE PAYS Wines made from specified grape varieties and produced in a particular region. They must reach a minimum alcohol level, be produced in limited quantities and satisfy a tasting panel.

• VINS DÉLIMITÉS DE QUALITÉ SUPÉRIEURE (VDQS) Wines that comply with conditions relating to the exact area of production, varieties of vines and cultivation and production methods; these are also subject to tasting panels. (This category is soon to be phased out.)

• APPELLATION D'ORIGINE CONTRÔLÉE (AOC) Wines representing the finest of France, whose production is strictly controlled at each stage. However, it should be borne in mind that a wine made wholly in compliance with all the strictest regulations may somehow, through natural chance or human error, fail to attain the highest standards of quality. The local syndicates within each region determine the conditions governing the area's AOCs. Essentially, the AOC determines: the exact area within which the vines are grown; the varieties of vines; the way they are grown and pruned; the permitted yield per hectare; and the alcoholic strength in the finished wine. The only great French wine that does not have to state its AOC on its label is champagne. The EU has adopted the French appellation system for categorizing wines so that AOC is equivalent to DOC (Spain), DOC (Portugal) and DOC (Italy).

■ **Wine production** Normally harvested when they are fully ripe, the grapes are treated differently according to whether they are to make red, white or rosé wine. In making red wine, the first stage is the crushing, the aim of this being to make the grapes discharge their juice without squashing the seeds or splitting the stalks and stems. This crushing was formerly done with bare feet but is now carried out mechanically in various ways. Stalks are sometimes removed by a destalking machine prior to crushing. The crushed grapes are then usually placed in a vat, formerly of wood, today sometimes of cement but increasingly of stainless steel. Here the must (grape juice) undergoes fermentation by the action of yeast bacteria, which transform it into wine. The colour of red wine is produced by leaving the skins of black grapes in the must so that the pigments tint it. The yeasts convert the natural sugar in the juice into ethyl alcohol and carbonic gas. The length of the fermentation varies – on average it is from eight to ten days although it can go on for much longer. The fermented must (now wine) is then drawn off and goes either into another vat or tank or into casks. The marc (the solid residue of the grapes) is then pressed, and this *vin de presse* may be mixed with the main wine.

White wine is made in two main ways. Either it comes solely from white grapes (and is called *blanc de blancs*) or it is made from a mixture of black and white grapes, the skins of the black grapes being removed before the pigments in them can impart colour to the must.

For rosé wine, the skins of black grapes remain in contact with the must for long enough to impart colour.

When the first stage of fermentation has been completed, the wine – either in cask or vat – may be subjected to certain forms of treatment. One of these is a type of clarification known as 'fining', in which one of various substances (egg white is a well-known fining agent) is introduced into the cask, attracts particles in suspension in the wine and causes them to cling to it and gradually sink to the bottom of the vessel. In addition, wine in cask is 'racked off' – that is, it is pumped off any deposit that may have been formed in the cask. Finally, before bottling, wine will usually be filtered to ensure that it is 'star bright' as customers prefer.

■ **The cellar** The best storage place for wine is the cellar, but sadly this is becoming a rarity in modern houses. The first requirement for a wine cellar is a constant temperature, preferably fairly cool: the ideal temperature is about 12°C (54°F). The ageing of the wine may be slowed down below this temperature and accelerated slightly above it; sudden changes of temperature are particularly harmful. The cellar must also be aerated and have a reasonable degree of humidity so that the corks do not dry out, but a very damp atmosphere, although good for the long-lasting wines, can damage labels. A strong light can cause white wines to turn brown, particularly if it comes from fluorescent tubes. More difficult to eliminate in towns is traffic vibration, which can cause wine to age prematurely. Finally, products giving off a strong smell, such as paraffin or paint, should not be stored in the cellar, neither should fruit, which could ferment. Delicate wines easily take on flavours through their corks, even when these are covered with a metal or plastic capsule.

Bottles of wine are stored horizontally in wooden or metal racks and arranged by region and year, preferably with their labels visible. A cellar book, which lists all the wines by name with their vintage, price, supplier, date of receipt, date of consumption and any tasting notes, is an invaluable asset.

Once or twice a year it is a good idea to examine every bottle to ensure that each is well corked and filled; the cork must remain in contact with the liquid if it is to function properly and prevent air from getting into the wine. Wine must be stored lying down, so that the cork remains wet and swollen. Spirits, however, must stand up, as the cork or stopper may rot if it is in contact with the spirit.

If no true cellar is available, a dark quiet place, of constant temperature, can be fitted with wine bins and, if necessary, with a humidifier.

There are now on sale portable cellars (*caves d'appartement*), which have constant temperature and atmospheric humidity and are mounted on shock absorbers to absorb vibrations. These are obviously of a limited capacity but can be placed anywhere.

In general, white wines do not last as long as reds, but this depends on the quality of the wine, the grape variety, the maker and the vintage; some great white Burgundies and Rieslings, for example, can last a surprisingly long time. Most champagne and sparkling wines are sold when they are ready to drink. Many dry white wines are probably most enjoyable when consumed within 12–18 months of their vintage; the very finest, including some great white Burgundies and the finest Alsace wines, may have much longer lives. The luscious sweet wines, such as the Sauternes, Barsacs and Riesling Trocken-beerenausleses, will certainly not decline in quality for many years. Rosé wines do not usually have long lives. Red wines, however, vary enormously – the lighter ones may well be at their most enjoyable when young and fresh, whereas the great clarets and red Burgundies can have very long lives in certain vintages.

■ **Serving and tasting** Whether it is coming out of a home cellar or from the wine merchant, fine wine should ideally rest for several hours, standing up, before being drunk, so that any deposit sinks to the bottom of the bottle. Decanting is the careful transferring of the wine into a carafe, allowing the sediment to be eliminated and aerating the wine, which usually improves it. Bordeaux wines are decanted when they are considered to be a little 'closed' or have thrown a heavy deposit, so that they may open out on contact with the air (see *decant*).

White wines, both dry and fuller bodied, should be drunk between 5 and 8°C (41–46°F), rosé wines between 8 and 10°C (46–50°F), and light red wines between 10 and 12°C (50–54°F); full-bodied red wines are served chambré – that is, between 15 and 18°C (59–64°F). A fine red Burgundy is usually served between 15 and 17°C (59–63°F), a great Bordeaux around 18°C (64°F). The bringing of a wine to the correct temperature must always be gradual; white wine must not be cooled by putting it in the freezer, nor should a red wine be warmed by placing it near the fire or over the stove.

When opening a bottle, first wipe the capsule, then, after removing this, wipe the cork. Once this is drawn, the inside of the neck of the bottle is also wiped with a clean cloth. The wine is poured as steadily as possible, avoiding any shaking, preferably into a colourless glass, with a sufficiently long stem to enable it to be held without the hand heating its contents.

When a meal includes several wines, they are served in a certain order. According to Brillat-Savarin: 'The order of the drinks goes from the most moderate to the headiest and the most fragrant.' As a rule, dry whites are served before sweet whites, white wines before reds, young wines before old ones. The wine should also go with the dish it accompanies. For example, serving a great sweet white wine with game or red meat should be avoided, as should serving a great red wine with fish or shellfish. But all this is often a matter of personal taste and opportunity. Here are some suggestions by Dr Paul Ramain, a French expert in oenology, about possible food and wine combinations.

• *Dry white wines* Hors d'oeuvre, white fish, shellfish soups, shellfish, veal.
• *Fuller bodied white wines* Melon, oily fish, spiced shellfish, foie gras, chicken *à la crème*.
• *Sweet white wines* Foie gras without truffles, desserts and sweet dishes.
• *Dry champagne* May be drunk throughout the meal.
• *Sweet champagne* Desserts.
• *Vins gris and light rosés* Charcuterie, hors d'oeuvre, cold meats, veal, quail.
• *Full-bodied rosés* Crayfish, caviar, fish soup, *brandade* (salt cod), poultry.
• *Light red wines* Poultry, white meats, lamb, quail, cold meats, charcuterie, meat pies, cheese.
• *Full-bodied red wines* Red meats, game, cheese.

■ **Wine vocabulary** Professional tasters and well-informed wine enthusiasts sometimes use technical jargon when discussing wine, of which the following are among the most commonly used terms.

acerbe (bitter) Rough and acid.
ambré (amber-coloured) Describing an old white wine that has acquired a golden colour like that of amber, due to the oxidation of its colouring matter; this colour is a defect in a young wine.
arôme (aroma) The specific smell imparted by each variety of grape to the wine that is made from it.
astringent Having excessive tannin; this characteristic can disappear with age.
bouchonné (corked) Having a mouldy, musty smell or taste; this defect is harmless but makes the wine smell and taste unpleasant.
bouquet The sum of the olfactory qualities acquired by the wine in the course of its fermentation and ageing.
brillant Perfectly clear.
brut (extra-dry) Very dry (describing champagne).
caractère (character) Describing a wine whose qualities are very marked and easily recognizable.
charnu (fleshy) Having body; giving the impression of filling the mouth.
charpenté (constructed) Full-bodied and *charnu*.
corsé (full-bodied) Seemingly rich, well-coloured and of marked character.
coulant (flowing) Fresh, pleasant to drink.
court (short) Not leaving a lasting impression on the palate.
croûté (crusty) Said of an old red wine whose sediment has stuck to the inside of the bottle and that needs to be decanted.
délicat (delicate) Rather light, fine and elegant.
distingué (distinguished) Of high class.
doux (sweet) Some wines are naturally sweet because of the sugar in the grape juice; they are quite different from wines that are sweetened. Sugar not converted into alcohol is referred to as 'residual sugar'.
dur (hard) Lacking charm, through excessive tannin or acidity; this defect sometimes disappears as the wine matures.
élégant Fine and high-class.
enveloppé (wrapped) Mellow and velvety.
épanoui (opening out) Describing a bouquet that fills the mouth.
équilibré (balanced) Describing a wine whose characteristics are neither too weak nor too marked.
éventé (flat) Oxidized, generally because of aeration during bottling or because it is too old.
faible (weak) Low, usually in alcohol and bouquet.
fin (fine) Distinguished; most AOC wines should be *fin*.
frais (fresh) Describing a young wine that is fruity and not excessively acid. (However, the instruction *servir frais* means 'serve cool'.)
franc (clean) Healthy; straightforward.
fruité (fruity) Having a flavour of fruit; few wines either smell or taste of grapes, but the fruity character should be evident.
généreux (generous) Full-bodied; rich in alcohol.
gouleyant (mouth-filling) Easily drunk; 'moreish': sometimes describes a light wine that is served chilled.
gras (fat) *Charnu*, mellow and supple.

jeune (young) Describing a wine that has not reached maturity; a wine that has to age or a wine made to be drunk young and fresh.

léger (light) Low in alcohol.

liquoreux (liqueur-like) Sweet, usually in relation to white wine.

louche (dubious) Cloudy.

lourd (heavy) Dull; undistinguished.

madérisé (browning) Oxidized; when used of a white wine, the colour and smell are said to be reminiscent of Madeira.

maigre (lean) Insufficiently fruity; lacking agreeable character.

moelleux (mellow) Sweetish: usually describing white wines.

nerveux (nervous) Vigorous, sinewy; describing a wine of definite character and style.

nouveau (new) Young; the term is often used nowadays for wines made to be drinkable without ageing.

onctueux (smooth) Full-bodied; fat.

perlant (forming minute bubbles) Giving off a very slight amount of carbonic acid gas, which creates a sensation of tingling in the mouth.

pétillant (slightly sparkling) Less than fully sparkling but more so than *perlant*.

piqué (tart) Having a 'pricked' taste, an indication that it may shortly turn to vinegar.

plat (flat) Describing a sparkling wine that is no longer sparkling; describing a still wine that is uninteresting.

plein (full) Rounded; ample.

racé (distinguished) Implies breeding.

robe (appearance) Indicates the colour.

robuste (robust) Full-bodied and assertive.

rond (rounded) Well-balanced; harmonious.

sain (healthy) Clean-tasting; in good condition.

sec (dry) Used mainly to describe dry still white wines. A champagne described as *sec* is actually slightly sweet.

séché (dried) Describing a wine that has lost its freshness and fruit.

souple (supple) On the smooth side.

suave (pleasant) Agreeable; possibly sweetish.

taché (stained) Describing a white wine that has become slightly pink, either because it has been in a cask that has contained red wine or because it has been allowed to take on colour from the skins of black grapes.

tendre (tender) Young, fresh, agreeable and easy to drink.

terne (dull) Lacking character.

tranquille (still) Not sparkling.

tuilé (tile-coloured) Describing a red wine that has taken on a tawny tone because it is getting old.

usé (worn out) Describing a wine that has lost its qualities.

velouté (velvety) Mellow; smooth.

vert (green) Coming from insufficiently ripe grapes; high in acidity.

vif (lively) Young, fresh and attractive.

vineux (vinous) Somewhat alcoholic and without lingering fragrance.

■ **Cooking with wine** The custom of using wine in the preparation of food goes back to ancient times. White, red, and rosé wines, as well as champagne, figure in numerous recipes; local wines are used in regional dishes.

There are certain general rules on the use of wine in cooking. Whatever its colour, the wine must be clean and without a harsh, aggressive taste. Very cheap table wine sometimes does not react well in cooking, and it is better to use something slightly superior in quality, although this does not have to be a great wine. Red wine, which should be fairly full bodied, is indispensable for coq au vin, daubes, game ragoûts, beef bourguignon, fish stews and marinades. Accompanied by garlic, onion and, often, mushrooms, it is also used in numerous thickened sauces. Red wine may be used to cook certain vegetables, such as red kidney beans, and it also features in some desserts, being used to macerate strawberries or cook pears. White wines suitable for cooking are usually dry and rather acid, such as Muscadet and Aligoté. Their natural acidity is even increased by the addition of lemon juice when deglazing the pan used for frying meats; for long slow cooking, on the other hand, it is sometimes necessary to reduce this acidity by boiling the wine, uncovered, for about ten minutes. White wine is included as an ingredient of a courtbouillon used for cooking fish or shellfish. It goes well with chicken and white meats cooked in fricassées.

WINE CELLAR A cellar is the best place to store wines, being (ideally) dark, airy and quiet, with a constant temperature and protected from unpleasant smells. It should not be subject to seasonal temperature changes and should also be slightly damp and draught-free. If conditions are too damp, moulds may grow on the outside of the corks and the labels may deteriorate, although this does not affect the wine. See *wine*.

WING Either of the front limbs of a bird, including the muscles that operate it. The latter form the delicate white meat of the breast. When cooked whole, both the wing and breast of young and tender birds (especially chicken or young turkey) is called a suprême; on older birds it is called (incorrectly) a 'poultry cutlet'.

WINKLE A small marine snail harvested from coastal waters. It is recognized by its brown or black shell with its pointed spine; the hard operculum must be removed before eating.

Winkles are eaten cold with bread and butter, after poaching for five minutes in salted water (it should be possible to remove them whole from their shells with a pin; if they are cooked for too long, they become brittle). They are also eaten in salads.

WINTERTHUR A dish of langouste prepared like lobster cardinal but filled with shrimps and a salpicon of langouste. It is named after a Swiss town in the canton of Zurich.

WOK A large pan with a rounded base. Traditionally made of cast iron, the wok is designed for cooking over a brazier or gas burner. It is widely used in Chinese cooking, mainly to prepare stir-fried dishes, but also for roasts, sautés, steamed dishes and even soups. Similar pans are used in other South-East Asian countries, and a smaller, shallow, rounded pan (*tawa*) also features in Indian equipment. The wok's advantage for stir-frying is that it allows food to be tossed and stirred constantly while cooking; in this way it can be cooked rapidly over a high heat. The wok has become popular all over the world.

WOOD BLEWIT The generic name given to a range of plump-gilled mushrooms, with cap or stem, or both, of a violet-amethyst or lilac blue colour. Wood blewits are very late, and they are found in woods, at the edge of forests or in cool, damp fields. Three species are of particular gastronomic interest: the wood blewit, naked tricholoma (*tricholome nu*), the most sought-after, is violet-blue all over, with a delicate floral aroma; the sinister tricholoma (*tricholome sinistre*) or amethyst foot, is very pretty, with a fine, intense violet colour on the stem only; the squalid tricholoma (*tricholoma sordide*), or squalid blue foot, is often of modest size, with a very intense amethyst colour. After cooking, the tender flesh of this blewit has a smooth flavour, which is an excellent accompaniment for white meats and dishes of fish served with sauce.

WOODCOCK A migratory bird with a wingspan of 60 cm (24 in), a long bill and short legs. In France woodcock are hunted in March and April and October and November (they are fatter and more tender in the autumn); in Britain they are classified as game birds and can be shot only between September and January. The bird is fairly rare and difficult to find because it is well-camouflaged – its plumage is the colour of dead leaves. It has long been regarded as a delicacy. In classic cuisine, it is hung for 4–8 days (until the skin on the belly is shiny, the feathers and tail come away easily, and the beak can be broken with the fingers) and then used to make salmis, pâtés and mousses. Modern recipes, however, prefer it not to be hung, and it is usually roasted undrawn, except for the gizzard, and often served on a toast base.

The parts of the bird most esteemed by such French authors on gastronomy as Godard d'Aucour are the entrails. These should be collected from cooked birds, seasoned with spices and lemon juice, then mixed with chopped fatty bacon or foie gras, laced with brandy and eaten spread on fried bread or toast.

RECIPES

preparation of woodcock
Unlike poultry and other game, woodcock is not trussed with string; it trusses itself. The long pointed beak goes through the thighs and the legs are raised and held together. It is customary to remove the eyes of the woodcock, but not the intestines (except for the gizzard). After cooking, the intestines are spread on toast.

casserole of woodcock
Truss the woodcock and bard with thin bacon. Brown in some butter, season, then place in an ovenproof dish and roast in a preheated oven at 240°C (475°F, gas 9) for 15–18 minutes, basting frequently, until the bird is cooked. Drain the bird, remove the bacon and keep warm. Pour a dash of brandy into the dish and, if possible, a few tablespoons of game stock. Remove the intestines and chop with an equal quantity of fresh bacon. Add salt and pepper, a pinch of grated nutmeg and a dash of Cognac, Armagnac or Calvados. Fry a slice of bread (white or brown), spread it with the intestines and then put it in a very hot oven for a few minutes to cook the bacon. Serve the woodcock on the toast canapé and moisten with the cooking juices.

casserole of woodcock à la crème
Prepare and cook a woodcock as in the recipe for casserole of woodcock. Add to the casserole a dash of Cognac, Armagnac, or Calvados and a few tablespoons of crème fraîche. Return to the oven to warm through.

cold timbale of woodcock
Line a raised pie dish with lining pastry (see *short pastry*) and then with thin slices of bacon. Cover the bottom and sides of the lined dish with a game forcemeat flavoured with diced truffle. Bone 2 woodcocks, stuff with foie gras studded with truffle, roll into ballotines and seal by frying in butter. Place the woodcock in the dish and fill the gaps between with the fine forcemeat mixed with foie gras and the chopped intestines, well seasoned and flavoured with a dash of Cognac. Spread a layer of game forcemeat over the whole, shaping it into a dome, then top with thin rashers (slices) of fat bacon. Cover with hot-water crust shaped to fit the top of the pie. Seal the edges to form a crimped ridge and garnish the top of the pie with pastry shapes. Make a small hole in the pastry lid to allow steam to escape. Bake in a preheated oven at 180°C (350°F, gas 4) for 1¼ hours. Allow to cool thoroughly before turning out of the mould. Serve on a dish covered with a napkin.

cold woodcock à la Diane
Roast the woodcock until rare and slice the meat. Pound the intestines with a knob of foie gras, a knob of butter, nutmeg and brandy. Sieve and season well. Reshape the sliced flesh around the intestine mixture, arranging it on large slices of raw truffle marinated in brandy to resemble a woodcock, and coat with a firm game aspic. Chill well in the refrigerator before serving.

hot woodcock pâté à la périgourdine

Bone 2 woodcocks, spread out the birds on a table, and fill with stuffing as in the recipe for woodcock casserole *à la périgourdine*. Roll the woodcocks into ballotines and wrap each one separately in muslin (cheesecloth). Poach for 12 minutes in a Madeira braising stock prepared with the carcass and trimmings. Drain and allow to cool. Unwrap when cold. Meanwhile, prepare a fine forcemeat composed of two-thirds game forcemeat and one-third veal forcemeat. Line the bottom and sides of an oval pâté mould with a thin layer of shortcrust pastry (basic pie dough) and spread the forcemeat over this. Place the ballotines side by side in the mould. Cover with 10 slices of foie gras fried in butter and 20 slices of truffle. Cover with the remaining forcemeat. Cover the pâté with a layer of pastry and seal and trim the edges. Make a hole in the pastry lid for the steam to escape. Garnish with shaped pastry trimmings and brush with egg. Place the pâté on a baking sheet and bake in a preheated oven at 180°C (350°F, gas 4) for 1¼ hours. Just before serving, pour a few tablespoons of Périgueux sauce into the pâté through the hole in the lid.

roast woodcock on toast

Truss the woodcock, bard, tie up with string and roast on a spit or in a preheated oven about 240°C (475°F, gas 9) for 18–20 minutes. Prepare a toast canapé as for casserole of woodcock and serve the woodcock on top of the canapé. The dish may be garnished with large peeled grapes.

sautéed woodcock in Armagnac

Cut the woodcock into pieces. Use the carcass and the trimmings to prepare a fumet and add rich demi-glace. Put the pieces of woodcock in a sauté pan just big enough to hold them and brown briskly in butter. Cover the pan and simmer for 8 minutes. Drain the pieces, arrange in a timbale or in a shallow dish and keep hot. Dilute the pan juices with 2 tablespoons Armagnac, add the strained concentrated woodcock fumet and boil for a few moments. Thicken this sauce with the chopped intestines, season with a small pinch of cayenne and add 1 teaspoon butter and a dash of lemon juice. Strain the sauce and pour it over the woodcock while it is piping hot.

truffled roast woodcock

Mix together chicken forcemeat and finely diced truffles tossed in butter and use this to stuff the woodcock. Also insert a few slices of truffle between the skin and the flesh of the bird. Truss and leave in a cool place for 48 hours. Wrap the woodcock in buttered greaseproof (wax) paper and tie up with string. Cook in a preheated oven at about 240°C (475°F, gas 9) for 18–20 minutes.

Meanwhile, prepare the toast canapé as for casserole of woodcock. Serve the truffled woodcock on the toast. Deglaze the cooking pan with a dash of Cognac or Armagnac and pour over the bird.

woodcock casserole à la périgourdine

Fill the woodcock with a stuffing made from the chopped intestines, diced foie gras, truffle, allspice and a dash of Armagnac. Truss the bird, brown in butter in a flameproof casserole, season, add 2 tablespoons Armagnac, cover and cook in a preheated oven at 240°C (475°F, gas 9) for 15–18 minutes. Remove the woodcock from the casserole and deglaze the dish with a little game or chicken stock. Reheat and serve the woodcock in the casserole. Very small peeled truffles may be cooked with this dish.

other recipes See *pâté, Riche, salmis, Souvarov.*

WOOD PIGEON A species of pigeon that is prepared in the same way as ordinary pigeon, although its flesh is more delicate and flavoursome. In the Bordeaux region it is enjoyed in a salmi or roasted; in the Basque country it is eaten lightly grilled (broiled) or as a confit.

In south-western France, where it is known as *palombe*, the wood pigeon is traditionally hunted with nets (*palombières*) during its annual migration over the Pyrenees.

WOODRUFF Also known as sweet woodruff, *Galium odoratum* is a herb with a flavour described as similar to new-mown hay, honey and vanilla. In Germany where it is known as *waldemeister*, literally 'master of the forest', and Eastern European countries, woodruff is used to flavour sausages. It is also steeped in Rhine wine to make an aromatic wine drink, *Maibowle* or *Maitrunk*, traditionally consumed on May Day.

WORCESTERSHIRE SAUCE An English condiment whose recipe was apparently discovered in the East Indies by Sir Marcus Sandys, a native of Worcestershire. On returning home, he asked the English grocers Lea & Perrins to make up a sauce that resembled his favourite condiment. It was launched commercially in 1838. The present-day 'Original and Genuine Worcestershire sauce', which still bears the names of its inventors, is made of malt vinegar, molasses, sugar, onions, garlic, tamarind, anchovies and other secret flavourings and spices. It is used to season ragoûts, soups, stuffings, vinaigrette, devilled or tomato sauces, steak tartare and exotic dishes; it also flavours various cocktails and tomato juice.

WORK To incorporate one or more ingredients into another using a spatula, mixing spoon or a small palette knife, until they are thoroughly mixed. This operation is particularly used in making beurre manié (see *butter*).

WRASSE A fish of the *Labridae* family, which is fished on coasts from Norway to Senegal and also in the Mediterranean. The wrasse, also called labre, is about 40 cm (16 in) long and can live for 20 years.

Its habitat is among seaweed, where it feeds off small crustaceans and molluscs. The superb colours of its body, with green or red predominating, are flecked with gold lights, but its soft and rather insipid flesh is riddled with bones. The pearly or ballan wrasse, the best and most common variety, which is found in the English Channel and the Atlantic, is usually baked. In Brittany it is cooked in the oven on a bed of onions. The green wrasse, which is elongated in shape, and the more thickset *merle* are smaller Mediterranean fish used in making bouillabaisse; the *coquette*, found on rocky sea beds, is also used in fish soups.

RECIPE

wrasse with potatoes

Blanch 250 g (9 oz) thick, streaky, lightly salted bacon in water and cut into small strips. Peel and slice 150 g (5 oz, generous 1 cup) shallots. Peel 1 kg (2¼ lb) potatoes, cut into thin slices, wash and wipe dry. Grease an ovenproof dish with lard and arrange the strips of bacon and potatoes in it in alternate layers, sprinkled with shallots. Season with salt and pepper. Moisten with 500 ml (17 fl oz, 2 cups) white wine. Place in a preheated oven at 200°C (400°F, gas 6) for 30 minutes.

Meanwhile, scale, clean and wash 4 wrasse, each weighing about 400 g (14 oz), and rub them outside and inside with salt and pepper. Place them on the potatoes, sprinkle with small pieces of lard and return to the oven for 10 minutes. Turn the fish over and continue cooking for a further 5 minutes. Serve very hot in the baking dish.

WUCHTELN An Austrian dessert consisting of squares of yeast dough folded over a plum jam filling, put in a warm place to rise, then baked and served hot, dusted with icing (confectioner's) sugar and accompanied with a compote of prunes.

XYZ

XAVIER A cream soup or consommé thickened with arrowroot or rice flour and garnished with diced plain or chicken royale. It may also be flavoured with Madeira, garnished with small savoury pancakes or served with *oeufs filés* (threads of egg white cooked in the soup).

RECIPE

Xavier soup
Prepare 1.5 litres (2¾ pints, 6½ cups) chicken consommé*. Thicken it with 3 tablespoons *crème de riz* (rice flour) or cornflour (corn starch) slaked with milk or water. Away from the heat, add 3 egg yolks mixed with 100 ml (4 fl oz, 7 tablespoons) double (heavy) cream. Stir in 50 g (2 oz, ¼ cup) butter. Garnish with diced chicken royale and serve in cups.

XIMENIA A small tropical shrub with edible, though rather sour, fruit.

YAK A long-haired, domesticated ruminant that lives on mountainous pastures of central Asia. It is used as a pack animal and also provides meat and milk. Yak meat (*gyak* in Tibetan) is cooked mainly as thin slices fried quickly in butter or grilled (broiled) on bamboo sticks; larger joints are boiled, after marinating if the animal is old. Dried complete with the bones, the meat is sometimes reduced to a coarse powder used as a basis for soups and porridges made with yak's milk. The Tibetans use yak's milk also to make small very hard, cube-shaped cheeses and butter, which is eaten when rancid.

YAKITORI A Japanese dish of chicken kebabs cooked over charcoal embers. They usually include pieces of chicken meat, skin, gizzard and liver. Balls of minced (ground) chicken mixed with spring onions (scallions), mushrooms and sometimes quail's eggs, peppers or ginkgo nuts can be used. Other birds are also used for *yakitori*. The ingredients are threaded on to thin bamboo skewers, then grilled for 4–5 minutes. *Yakitori* are served with drinks as snacks rather than as part of a main meal. In Japan restaurants specialize in *yakitori*, offering a whole range of these kebabs. They are also sold in the streets.

YA-LANE A tree originally from China whose buds are cooked before flowering and preserved in vinegar to make an excellent condiment. The dried flowers are used to spice rice dishes.

YAM The round or elongated edible tuber of a tropical climbing plant of the *Dioscorea* genus, of which several species are cultivated in Africa, Asia and America. The flesh is white, yellow or pink, and the skin may be rough or smooth and white, pink, yellow or blackish-brown in colour, depending on the species. The tubers vary in size from small examples resembling large potatoes to giants of 20 kg (45 lb) or up to three times that size. The typical yam in the Western supermarket has rough, thick, brown skin, white flesh and is about twice the size of a potato.

In the United States the name 'yam' is used for the sweet potato, the tuber of *Ipomoea batatas*, a plant in the *Convolvulaceae* family, commonly known as the 'morning glory' family of plants.

Yams can be used in the same way as potatoes or sweet potatoes. They can be boiled, peeled or in their skins, or baked, or used in a wide variety of dishes, including soups, ragoûts, purées, soufflés, croquettes, fritters, gratins, chips and so on, as well as in various sweet dishes. The flesh tastes similar to that of potato and its texture is floury. A starch extract from yams, called Guyana arrowroot, is widely used in cookery and confectionery.

YASSA A Senegalese dish consisting of pieces of grilled (broiled) mutton, chicken or fish (originally monkey), which have been marinated in lime juice and highly seasoned condiments. It is served with rice or millet, and the marinade is used as a sauce.

RECIPE

chicken yassa
The day before the meal (or at least 2 hours in advance) cut up a chicken into 4 or 6 pieces; marinate them in the juice of 3 limes with half a chilli pepper, finely chopped, 1 tablespoon groundnut (peanut) oil, 3 large onions (sliced), salt and pepper. Remove the chicken pieces and grill them, preferably over hot embers, browning them well all over. Remove the onions from the marinade and brown them with a little oil in a sauté pan, then moisten with the marinade and 2 tablespoons water. Add the chicken pieces, cover the pan and simmer for about 25 minutes. Serve the chicken very hot coated with the sauce, in the centre of a ring of rice *à la créole*.

YEAST A microscopic fungus that multiplies rapidly in suitable conditions and is used as a raising (leavening) agent in various kinds of dough. In the right conditions, when yeast is mixed with flour and liquid to make dough, it ferments and converts sugar and starch into ethanol (ethyl alcohol) and carbon dioxide. This gas causes the dough to rise. The use of brewer's yeast in baking dates from 1665, when a baker had the idea of adding some to his leaven: Empress Maria Theresa of Austria was so delighted with the bread produced in this way that the loaf was called a 'queen loaf'.

■ **Types of yeast** Yeast for cooking is available fresh or dried; brewer's yeast is not used. The same results can be achieved using fresh or dried yeast, but the techniques by which they are incorporated with the main ingredients differ. When dried yeasts are used always check the manufacturer's instructions for the correct method of incorporating the product and for the optimum temperature of liquids to promote fermentation.

• FRESH (COMPRESSED) YEAST This is beige in colour, firm but moist and easily flaked or crumbled. It should smell fresh; yeast that is dark or dried in places or that smells acidic or unpleasant should be discarded. Fresh yeast will keep for several days in the refrigerator; it also freezes well.

Fresh yeast should be mixed to a thin, smooth paste with lukewarm water and a pinch of sugar. The water must not be too hot as this kills the yeast. The yeast mixture is then combined with a little

extra liquid and covered, or it may be poured into a well in the flour mixture for a dough and the surface sprinkled with a little flour, then left in a warm place until active and frothy. Once the yeast liquid is fermenting vigorously, it is combined with the remaining ingredients. Mixtures leavened with fresh yeast are allowed to rise, knocked back (punched down) and shaped, then risen a second time into their finished form before baking.

• DRIED YEAST Standard dried yeast is reconstituted in lukewarm water, usually with a little sugar added, then left to ferment in the same way as fresh yeast before being combined with the remaining ingredients. The yeasted mixture is allow to rise twice, as for fresh yeast.

• EASY-BLEND DRIED YEAST This takes the form of fine granules, which are thoroughly mixed with the dry ingredients. Then the liquid is added to make the dough (or other mixture, such as batter). Ideally, the liquid used for this type of yeast should be slightly hotter – hand hot rather than lukewarm – to encourage fermentation. The mixture is allowed to rise twice, as when fresh or ordinary dried yeast is used.

• FAST-ACTION EASY-BLEND DRIED YEAST Taking the form of fine granules, this type of dried yeast is mixed with the dry ingredients in the same way as easy-blend dried yeast. It has ingredients such as ascorbic acid and flour improvers added, and these influence the result, making a lighter dough. This type of yeast does not require two rising stages, but the mixture can be shaped or placed in the tin (pan) in which it is to be baked once it has been kneaded or beaten according to type. After one rising it is ready for baking or cooking.

YOGURT Also known as yoghurt and by various other spellings. A fermented milk product with a slightly sour taste, obtained by the combined action of two species of bacteria, *Streptococcus thermophilus* and *Thermobacterium bulgaricum*; these were discovered in the early 20th century by the Russian biologist Ilya Metchnikoff.

Made for centuries in the Balkans, Turkey and Asia, yogurt appeared briefly in France during the reign of François I: a Jewish doctor from Constantinople treated the king's intestinal trouble with yogurt, but later returned to the East with the secret of its preparation. The product really caught on only after World War I, when Greek and Georgian immigrants started serving it in their restaurants or producing it on a small scale for local dairymen. Marcel Aymé, in *Maison basse* (1935), still considered it necessary to explain the term: 'One morning, he was putting away some pots of yogurt, a kind of curdled milk which was rather popular, but whose spelling was uncertain.'

Yogurt (both the product and the word) is of Turkish origin, although many French dictionaries give the French *yaourt* as derived from the Bulgarian *jaurt*. However, the product is also traditional in India, Arabic countries, central Asia and countries of the former Ottoman Empire, whose peoples attribute to it their health and longevity. Authentic Turkish yogurt is quite different from the factory product that dominates supermarket shelves. The milk of the cow, ewe or buffalo (the latter, according to connoisseurs, gives a denser and better tasting product) is boiled until reduced by about one-third, then poured into a leather bottle or terracotta jar and left to ferment naturally.

■ **Yogurt products** There is a wide choice of plain yogurts, with various fat contents and textures. Set yogurt has a light, slightly jellied texture. Strained yogurt is thick and creamy. Yogurt made from full-fat milk is creamy. Some yogurt products are thickened with starch or set with gelling agents. Fruit and nuts are popular flavouring ingredients; many flavoured commercial yogurts have a very high sugar content. Yogurt drinks, dressings, dips and frozen yogurt are all available.

■ **Use** There is a host of traditional uses for yogurt. Apart from an iced drink, prepared by beating yogurt with water, it is used as a medium in which to cook meat and vegetables, as a topping for baked dishes, to dress salads, in soups and in sauces. Yogurt is popular as a snack, dessert or for breakfast; plain yogurt is often sweetened with sugar, honey, jam, or fresh or dried fruit. It is widely used in contemporary Western cooking in savoury dishes, dressings, sauces, refreshing drinks and desserts.

RECIPES

cucumber salad with yogurt
Peel a large cucumber, split lengthways, and remove the seeds. Cut the flesh into very thin half-slices, dust with 1 teaspoon fine salt and leave for 30 minutes in a colander for the cucumber to lose some of its water. Rinse under the cold tap, wipe well and mix with 3 tablespoons yogurt sauce.

yogurt cocktail
Reduce to a purée 1 small peeled banana and 2 slices canned pineapple, using a blender or processor. Blend in 2 pots of natural yogurt and 1 tablespoon pineapple syrup. Add sugar to taste.

This cocktail may also be made with banana and strawberries, pear and peach, or mango and lemon.

yogurt sauce
Mix 1 small pot of natural yogurt with 1 teaspoon paprika; season with salt and pepper, then add 1 teaspoon lemon juice and the same quantity of chopped chervil and chopped chives.

Use to dress a salad of cucumber, tomatoes, courgettes (zucchini), sweet (bell) peppers, cauliflower, green beans or potatoes.

YORKAISE, À LA
A term used for egg dishes containing York ham. Cold eggs *à la yorkaise* are poached, arranged on small, round, thick slices of ham, garnished with chervil and tarragon, then coated with Madeira jelly. Fried eggs *à la yorkaise* are made with hard-boiled (hard-cooked) eggs: these are cut in half and the yolks sieved and mixed with a salpicon of ham bound with béchamel sauce; the eggs are then reassembled, breaded, fried and served with tomato sauce.

YORKSHIRE PUDDING
A British speciality from the north of England, Yorkshire pudding is made of a batter of eggs, flour and milk, which is traditionally baked in the fat of roast beef, for which it is the classic accompaniment. Fat from the cooked roast is poured into a shallow ovenproof dish and the pudding batter then added; it is cooked in the oven until well-risen, crisp and brown and served with the roast, together with gravy, roast potatoes, a green vegetable, mustard and horseradish sauce.

RECIPE

Yorkshire pudding
Whisk 2 eggs until frothy with 2 teaspoons salt; mix in 150 g (5 oz, 1¼ cups) plain (all-purpose) flour, whisking constantly. Add 250 ml (8 fl oz, 1 cup) milk in a thin stream and beat until the mixture is smooth. Put in a cool place for 1 hour. In an ovenproof dish heat 2 tablespoons roast beef fat (or, failing this, lard) until it sizzles; beat the batter once more, adding 3–4 tablespoons cold water, and pour into the dish. Bake in the top of a preheated oven at 220°C (425°F, gas 7) for 15 minutes, then lower the temperature to 200°C (400°F, gas 6) and bake for about a further 15 minutes; the pudding should be well-risen, crisp and brown. Serve very hot.

ZABAGLIONE
A light, foamy dessert of Italian origin, made by whisking egg yolks, wine and sugar together over a gentle heat. Zabaglione is served barely warm in cups or glasses (like those of the Café Greco, in Rome, of which it is a speciality); it can also be poured over a dessert, poached fruit, a pastry or ice cream. The word is derived from the Neapolitan dialect word *zapillare*, meaning 'to foam'.

Zabaglione can be made with dry white wine (Asti or champagne), sweet white wine (Sauternes), Marsala, fortified wine (Frontignan, Málaga, Banyuls), port or else a mixture of white wine and a liqueur (Chartreuse, Kümmel) or white wine and a spirit (brandy, whisky, rum, kirsch). It can also be flavoured with lemon or vanilla. Its preparation requires some skill, as the yolks must thicken without coagulating and the end result must be very frothy. Sometimes whisked egg whites are added to zabaglione after it has been beaten, just before serving.

The term 'sabayon' is also applied to a sort of mousseline sauce, usually made with champagne, which is served with fish or shellfish.

RECIPES

zabaglione

Put 5 egg yolks into a basin and add the grated zest of half a lemon, a pinch of powdered vanilla or a few drops of vanilla essence (extract) and 180 g (6½ oz, ¾ cup) granulated sugar. Whisk until the mixture is thick and pale, then place the basin in a bain marie and continue whisking, adding 200 ml (7 fl oz, ¾ cup) white wine and 100 ml (4 fl oz, 7 tablespoons) Marsala, a little at a time. When the zabaglione is thick and frothy, take the basin out of the bain marie. Frost the rim of 6–8 sundae dishes with lemon juice and granulated sugar. Divide the zabaglione among these dishes and serve with plain petits fours.

rum zabaglione with marrons glacés

Beat 10 egg yolks and 200 g (7 oz, 1 cup) granulated sugar with a whisk in a bain marie, until the mixture becomes pale and thick. Mix in 3 wine glasses white wine and 3 tablespoons white rum, beating all the time, until the mixture becomes thick and frothy. Flavour lightly with a few drops of vanilla essence (extract). Arrange some marrons glacés in sundae dishes, cover with zabaglione and chill in the refrigerator until required.

strawberry gratin with lemon zabaglione

Cut 24 large strawberries in half and arrange them on the bottom of a gratin dish, with the cut side down. Make a lemon zabaglione: put 4 whole eggs, the grated zest and juice of 4 lemons, 100 g (4 oz, ½ cup) granulated sugar and 100 g (4 oz, ½ cup) butter into a saucepan (preferably copper-bottomed). Beat the mixture with a whisk, in a bain marie, until it becomes very frothy. Cover the strawberries with this mixture and brown quickly under the grill (broiler).

ZAKUSKI In Russian cooking an assortment of small hot or cold savouries served before a meal, with vodka, as hors d'oeuvre. In former times the zakuski constituted part of the meal, although they were served in a room adjacent to the dining room. The extent and variety of the zakuski reflected the prosperity of the host and the status accorded to the guest. The array of dishes was often such that diners would over-indulge before starting the main meal. A full zakuski table, which is similar to the Scandinavian smörgasbord, may consist of: caviare and smoked fish eggs on buttered black bread canapés; rye bread croûtons, hollowed out and filled with sauerkraut and slices of smoked goose; piroshki (little dumplings or filled pastries) with different fillings; soused or smoked fish (salmon, eel, sturgeon); meatballs; herring pâté; stuffed eggs; fish or chicken salads; beetroot (red beet) and potatoes dressed with herbs; sweet-and-sour gherkins; and pickled beetroot, quetsch plums and mushrooms. These are accompanied by different sorts of bread, mainly rye bread flavoured with cumin, onion or poppy seed.

Zakuski are arranged on a sideboard or on trays for guests to help themselves. If intended simply as cocktail snacks with the vodka, zakuski are often restricted to filled canapés and piroshki.

ZAMPONE An Italian speciality from Modena, consisting of a boned and stuffed pig's trotter (foot), sold ready to cook or precooked and served hot or cold. It is stuffed with a forcemeat of pork, green (unsmoked) bacon, truffles and seasoning, and then cured, smoked, boiled and often served with lentils.

The word comes from zampa (paw): a large trotter is called a zampone; a small one a zampino.

RECIPE

zampone

Soak a ready-to-cook zampone in cold water for 3 hours; scrape the skin well and prick it all over with a barding needle. Wrap it in a thin cloth, tie at each end and in the centre, then put it into a flameproof casserole and cover with cold water. Bring to the boil and poach for 3 hours. Serve either hot, with mashed potatoes or lentil purée and braised spinach or cabbage; or cold, sliced like a sausage, with parsley.

ZANDER Alternative name for a pike-perch. See pike-perch.

ZARZUELA A Catalan speciality consisting of a fish and seafood ragoût. Zarzuela (the name literally means 'operetta') combines many kinds of seafood (mariscos), such as clams, mussels, squills, squid, shrimps and scampi, as well as various rock fish, cut into sections; lobster, langouste (crawfish) or scallops may also be added. The ingredients are cooked with onions and peppers browned in olive oil and garlic, together with sliced smoked ham, chopped tomatoes, ground almonds, bay leaf, saffron, parsley and pepper, all moistened with white wine and lemon juice.

Zarzuela is served in the casserole in which it is cooked, with small croûtons fried in oil; it is sometimes seasoned with a few drops of absinthe.

ZEBU A domesticated ox, originally from India and widespread also in Malaysia, Africa and, especially, Madagascar. The zebu is distinguished by its humped back. It is used as a draught animal and for its meat.

ZEPHYR The name (meaning literally 'a light wind') given to various savoury or sweet dishes, served hot or cold, characterized by a light and frothy consistency.

A zephyr is often a soufflé. The name is also given to quenelles, mousses or small savoury puddings made in dariole moulds and consisting of pounded lean veal, chicken meat or fish mixed with butter, egg yolks, and either crème fraîche or stiffly whisked egg whites.

In the West Indies zephyrs are balls of vanilla and rum ice cream surrounded by meringue shells and accompanied by a chocolate zabaglione, served as a dessert. Zephyrs may also be small light cakes made of layers of sweet pastry or meringue covered with praline- or coffee-flavoured buttercream, sandwiched together, then iced (frosted) with fondant.

RECIPE

seafood zephyr
Wash 2 litres (3½ pints, 2 quarts) mussels and open them; shell 300 g (11 oz) shrimps. Reserve 6 mussels and 12 shrimps and finely chop the remainder together.

Now prepare a soufflé: mix together over a low heat 50 g (2 oz, ¼ cup) butter and 65 g (2½ oz, ⅔ cup) plain (all-purpose) flour, then mix in 500 ml (17 fl oz, 2 cups) cold milk and bring to the boil. Add 5 egg yolks, then the chopped seafood. Whisk the 5 egg whites to stiff peaks and fold them lightly into the mixture. Butter a 20 cm (8 in) soufflé dish and empty the mixture into it, three-quarters filling it. Level the surface by shaking the dish. Cook in a preheated oven at 190°C (375°F, gas 5) for about 20 minutes.

Meanwhile, dip the reserved mussels and shrimps in a mixture of half an egg yolk and 25 g (1 oz, ¼ cup) grated Gruyère cheese. When the soufflé is almost cooked (after about 20 minutes), scatter these mussels and shrimps over the top, together with a little grated cheese (this must be done extremely rapidly so that the soufflé does not collapse). Brown in a very hot oven for about 5 minutes and serve immediately.

ZEST The coloured and perfumed outer rind of an orange, lemon or other citrus fruit. The zest is separated from the whitish part of the skin by using a special knife (called a zester) or a potato peeler. Cut into fine strips or small pieces, the zest is used to flavour creams, cake mixtures and desserts. It may also be candied, pickled in vinegar, grated or rubbed on to lump sugar. Candied orange zest, sometimes chocolate coated, is called *écorces d'orange* or *orangettes*.

RECIPE

lemon zest preserved in vinegar
Remove the zest from 3 lemons and cut into fine strips, making a julienne. Put this into a small saucepan of boiling water and boil gently for 10–15 minutes. Remove and drain the julienne, clean the saucepan, then replace the julienne along with 1 tablespoon sugar and 1 wine glass vinegar. Cook very gently until all the liquid has evaporated, then thoroughly mix the julienne with the caramel that has formed.

Zests prepared in this way are used particularly to flavour chicken terrines and can also be used as a condiment, like chutney.

ZEWELEWAI An onion tart made in Alsace, traditionally served as a hot entrée. A tart plate lined with shortcrust pastry (basic pie dough) is filled with a mixture of sliced onions, lightly cooked until soft in butter or lard, cream, beaten eggs, salt, pepper and nutmeg. Before baking, a few lardons of blanched and browned smoked streaky (slab) bacon may be placed on top.

ZINFANDEL A black grape variety, very widespread in the United States, particularly in California. Zinfandel makes light, elegant, blush wines, ranging from dry to sweet, as well as fragrant rosés and reds, which can be light and fruity to concentrated and full-bodied with excellent structure. It is thought to be related to the Italian Primitivo grape variety.

ZINGARA A sauce or garnish containing paprika and tomato (*zingara* means 'gypsy' in Italian). Zingara sauce is a mixture of demi-glace and tomato sauce mixed with ham, pickled tongue and mushrooms (truffle is an optional extra) and seasoned with paprika. It is served with small cuts of meat, poultry and soft-boiled (soft-cooked) or poached eggs. The garnish consists of the same ingredients and goes with veal escalopes or sautéed chicken, dusted with paprika and served with a sauce made by deglazing the pan juices with tomato sauce and Madeira.

RECIPES

sautéed chicken à la zingara
Season a 1.25 kg (2¾ lb) chicken with salt and pepper, cut it into 4 pieces and dust with paprika. Brown the pieces in oil in a flameproof casserole, reduce the heat, cover and continue cooking. After 30 minutes add 4 tablespoons strips of ham and the same quantity of pickled tongue and mushrooms; add a little truffle and a small sprig of tarragon. When the chicken is cooked, arrange it on a serving dish, together with its garnish (without the tarragon), and keep hot.

Deglaze the casserole with 60 ml (2 fl oz, ¼ cup) Madeira and 2 tablespoons tomato fondue*. Reduce until almost dry, then add 150 ml (¼ pint, ⅔ cup) demi-glace* sauce and heat through. Toast 4 slices of sandwich bread; quickly fry in butter 4 small round slices of ham; place the ham on the pieces of toast and arrange alongside the chicken. Coat the chicken with the sauce and sprinkle with chopped parsley. Serve very hot.

soft-boiled (or poached) eggs à la zingara
Brown some slices of stale sandwich bread in butter and cover with strips of unsmoked ham with the fat removed. Arrange a soft-boiled (soft-cooked) or poached egg on each of these croûtons, coat with zingara sauce and serve very hot.

zingara sauce
Prepare 250 ml (8 fl oz, 1 cup) demi-glace* sauce, 2 tablespoons sieved tomato* sauce and a julienne

consisting of 1 tablespoon each of cooked ham, pickled tongue and mushrooms cooked gently in butter for about 5 minutes, until their liquor has evaporated, plus a little truffle. Add the julienne to the demi-glace sauce and mix in the tomato sauce. Add a dash of paprika and taste the sauce for seasoning, then keep hot in a bain marie until ready to serve.

ZOLA, ÉMILE French novelist (born Paris, 1840; died Paris, 1902). His Italian ancestry (on his father's side) and his childhood spent at Aix-en-Provence gave Zola an abiding taste for Mediterranean, Provençal and Piedmontese dishes. Escoffier, whom he met in London, relates that he 'worshipped stuffed cabbage *à la mode de Grasse*'; he also liked grilled (broiled) sardines sprinkled with olive oil, as well as blanquette of milk lamb *à la provençale*. Zola himself admitted: 'What will be the death of me are bouillabaisses, food spiced with pimiento, shellfish, and a load of exquisite rubbish which I eat in disproportionate quantities.'

His contemporaries described him as more of a gourmand than a refined gourmet. Zola regarded luxury food as a status symbol, and for this reason was sometimes regarded as a parvenu; indeed, the dinners he gave were often ostentatious.

Was his aim, as in his novels, to denounce 'the pleasure-seeking tastes of the bourgeoisie'? Whatever his motives, his works offer us a panorama of contemporary Parisian cuisine.

ZUCCHINI See *courgette*.

ZUPPA INGLESE A dessert invented by Neapolitan pastrycooks and ice-cream makers who settled in the big cities of Europe during the 19th century. Inspired by the English puddings that were fashionable at the time, *zuppa inglese* (literally 'English soup') usually consists of a sponge soaked with kirsch, filled with confectioner's custard (pastry cream) and crystallized (candied) fruits macerated in kirsch or Maraschino, then covered with Italian meringue and browned in the oven. In another version, alternate layers of slices of brioche loaf browned in the oven and crystallized fruits macerated in rum are placed in a gratin dish and soaked in boiling milk mixed with beaten eggs and sugar; after cooking, the dessert is covered with Italian meringue and browned in the oven.

GENERAL INDEX

RECIPE INDEX

Picture Acknowledgements

PHOTOGRAPHS

Amiard H. – *Top*: p. 107;
Barde J.-L. – *Scope*: pp. 487,
546, 674, 873, 1001; **Bloch-
Lainé J.-L.** : p. 373, 1286;
Cabanne P. et Ryman C. –
Coll. Larousse: pp. 14, 63, 83,
121, 171, 233, 305, 333, 338,
339, 393, 409, 421, 435, 479,
481, 499, 523, 689, 695, 769,
785, 789, 889, 895, 973, 1013,
1137, 1143, 1169, 1089;
Coataner H. – *Scope*: p. 515;
C.T.I.F.L. : p. 864, poire Guyot;
CZAP – *Coll. Larousse*: p. 953;
Daniel de Nève – *Top*: p. 49;
De Wilde P. – *Hoa-Qui*:
p. 157; **Doug A.** – *Fotogram-
Stone*: p. 318; **Eshraghi I.** –
Scope: p. 287; **Freeman M.** –
ANA: p. 629; **Gérard J.-C.** –
Diaf: pp. 343, 882; **Gotin M.** –
Scope: p. 1226; **Guillard J.** –
Scope: pp. 13, 25, 182, 184,
244, 674, 799, 1060, 1043;
Guillard M. – *Scope*: pp. 135,
342, 546, 1226; **Gyssels H.** –
Diaf: p. 882; **Kiefer H.** –
Madame Figaro: p. 985;
Magis J.-J. – *Coll. Larousse*:
pp. 279, 649, 659, 893, 929,
1021, 1023, 1057, 1107, 1111,
1117, 1167, 1199, 1241, 1265,
1283; **Magis J.-J.** – *La
Photothèque culinaire*:
pp. 215, 251, 639, 673, 747,
763, 773, 817, 827, 881, 1029,
1064, 1245; **Mazin R.**: pp. 12,
59, 159, 799, 821, 940, 1211;
Mendel G. – *Rapho*: p. 711;
Miller G. – *Coll. Larousse*: pp.
213, 1097, 1187, 129; **Neele D.**
– *Fotogram-Stone*: p. 413
Overseas – *La Photothèque
culinaire*: p. 1209; **Pratt-Pries**
– *Diaf*: pp. 515, 872;
Quéméré E. – *Diaf*: p. 173;
Richer – *Hoa-Qui*: p. 765;
Rivière-Lecoeur A. – *Top*:
p. 182; **Sappa C.** – *Rapho*
p. 1131; **Senechal C.** – *Diaf*:
p. 1176; **Sierpinski J.**:
p. 1060; **Sioen G.** – *Rapho*:
pp. 119, 623; **Studiaphot** –
Coll. Larousse: pp. 31, 35, 43,
47, 53, 89, 174, 191, 208–a,
226, 237, 281, 351, 383, 403,
489–491, 530, 531, 575, 604,
669, 683, 685, 735, 812, 815,
864, 869, 963, 1073, 1080,
1082–1083, 1217, 1266, 1269;
Studio Vézelay – *Coll.
Larousse*: pp. 44, 54, 92, 110,
124, 131, 141, 208–b, 216, 217,
273, 290, 309, 311, 403, 440,
451, 492, 493, 498, 563, 556,
576, 607, 617, 635, 643, 666,
688, 694, 737, 778, 796, 837,
858, 897, 946, 955, 1063, 1092,
1087, 1011, 1127, 1038, 1113,
1152, 1160, 1161, 1238, 1259,
1247, 1235, 1239; **Sudres J.-D.**
– *Coll. Larousse*: pp. 33, 211,
291, 359, 557, 571, 655, 739,
756, 841, 847, 863, 971, 1191;
Sudres J.-D. – *Diaf*: pp. 134,
244 ; **Sudres J.-D.**: pp. 618,
619, 702, 1001; **Tessier Y.** –
Reflexion: p. 207 ; **Travert Y.**
– *Diaf*: pp. 455, 583; **Tulane
M.** – *Rapho*: p. 925; **Valentin
E.** – *Hoa-Qui*: p. 940; **Weyl L.**
– *Ask Images*: p. 1277;
Wheeler N. – *Diaf*: p. 743

MAPS

p. 14; 57; 94; 136; 183; 245;
553; 627; 1129; 1175; 1255:
European Map Graphics,
Palimpseste, Marie-Thérèse
Ménager.

ILLUSTRATIONS

p. 96–98; 664–665; 91; 1262:
Nicole Ho-Laigret.